D1510407

MODERN CRIMINAL PROCEDURE

CASES, COMMENTS AND QUESTIONS

Tenth Edition

By

Yale Kamisar

Clarence Darrow Distinguished University Professor of Law
University of Michigan
Professor of Law
University of San Diego

Wayne R. LaFave

Professor Emeritus in the College of Law
and Center for Advanced Study,
University of Illinois

Jerold H. Israel

Ed Rood Eminent Scholar in Trial Advocacy and Procedure,
University of Florida, College of Law
Alene and Allan F. Smith Professor of Law Emeritus,
University of Michigan

Nancy J. King

Professor of Law and Associate Dean,
Vanderbilt University School of Law

AMERICAN CASEBOOK SERIES®

WEST GROUP

A THOMSON COMPANY

Mat #40043220

American Casebook Series, and the West Group symbol
are registered trademarks used herein under license.

COPYRIGHT © 1965, 1966, 1969, 1974, 1994 WEST PUBLISHING CO.
COPYRIGHT © 1980, 1986, 1990 YALE KAMISAR
                        WAYNE R. LaFAVE
                        JEROLD H. ISRAEL
COPYRIGHT © 1999 By WEST GROUP
COPYRIGHT © 2002 By WEST GROUP
                        610 Opperman Drive
                        P.O. Box 64526
                        St. Paul, MN 55164–0526
                        1–800–328–9352

All rights reserved
Printed in the United States of America

ISBN 0–314–26373–X

 TEXT IS PRINTED ON 10% POST CONSUMER RECYCLED PAPER

To the memory of

Joseph D. Grano

*the criminal procedure professor
who educated us all.*

*

UNITED STATES SUPREME COURT
SINCE 1940

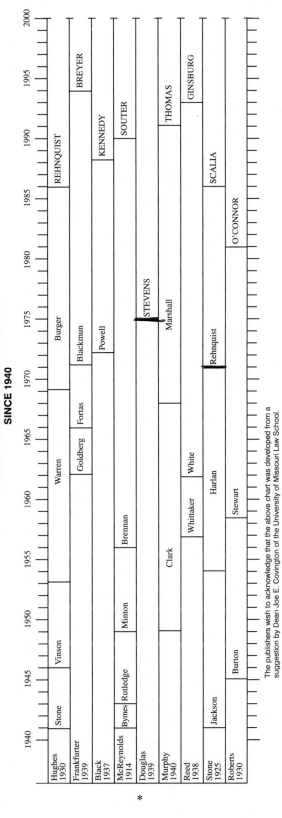

The publishers wish to acknowledge that the above chart was developed from a suggestion by Dean Joe E. Covington of the University of Missouri Law School.

*

Preface to the Tenth Edition

Several eventful Supreme Court Terms, numerous legislative changes and lower court rulings, and much significant law review commentary has occurred since the cut-off date for the ninth edition. Because of the need to integrate all of this new material, strenuous efforts were made to compress some of the older material. This produced a volume almost 30 pages shorter than the ninth edition, but this is still (and we have "probable cause" to believe always will be) a big book.

This is so because we have taken pains to set forth the views of *all* the Justices in the leading cases; because we believe that often the student should see the subsequently overruled or distinguished opinion "in the original" rather than rely on the overruling and distinguishing case's version of the earlier opinion; because we have retained older cases which contribute significantly to an understanding of new trends and developments; because we have covered significant non-constitutional issues, as well as traditional constitutional matters; because, in treating non-constitutional issues, we have looked to state law (with its frequent variations) as well as federal law; and because, at many places, we have sought to enrich the case materials with authors' Notes and Questions or extracts from illuminating and stimulating books, reports, articles, model codes and proposed standards.

The size of this book—the result of striving both for breadth of coverage and depth of treatment—indicates clearly enough that our purpose is not to provide a volume to be taught from cover to cover in a single one semester course on the subject. Rather it is to present materials that afford a teacher maximum freedom to shape his or her own course—in light of a particular teacher's own sense of priorities and interests and other related courses available at that teacher's school. In many schools, two criminal procedure courses are offered—one on the "investigatory process" and the other on the "adversary process." These materials divide quite naturally for such courses, with Chapters 1-11 covering the investigatory process and 12-29 (possibly supplemented by Chapter 1) covering the adversary process. In other schools, a single course is given surveying various aspects of the process. Here, the opening sections of the chapters on such subjects as prosecutorial discretion, grand jury review, preliminary hearings, and discovery can be used for an abbreviated coverage of those subjects. Finally, for a single course that focuses on constitutional limitations as they run throughout the process, the relevant materials can readily be pulled together from different chapters. For self-incrimination, for example, the subject can be thoroughly covered by combining materials from Chapter 2, § 2 (e.g., *Schmerber*); Chapter 8 (e.g., *Miranda*); Chapter 10, §§ 2 & 3 (e.g., *Boyd, Fisher, Hubbell,* and *Doe II*); Chapter 11, §§ 3 & 4 (e.g., *Harris* and *Elstad*); Chapter 21, § 3 (e.g., *Williams*) and Chapter 25, § 4 (e.g., *Griffin v. California*). Our extensive index includes headings that should help in pulling together the various materials that relate to any particular right or privilege. The index also has proven especially helpful to students (along with the cross-references in the Notes and Questions) in increasing their understanding of the interrelationship of various aspects of the process.

In the main, we have followed a chronological approach in ordering the materials which appear in this book. Following the introductory materials, which include an overview of the criminal justice system and a general consideration of due process, the system is examined from arrest and search to post-conviction review. We have occasionally departed from the chronological scheme when it seemed appropriate to do so. For example, the initial chapter on the right to counsel (Ch. 3) is included in the introductory part of the book as background for the confessions and lineups materials. This chapter is also included in the introductory part on the assumption that a student should get some understanding of how and when an attorney becomes involved in a criminal case before examining the procedural issues that will confront the attorney. Wiretapping and other surveillance activities are discussed after search and seizure on the ground that the student must first grasp the basic Fourth Amendment doctrines that have developed in the latter area, while the entrapment material is presented following the surveillance chapter because of the relationship between entrapment and other uses of secret agents.

This volume includes significant developments up to January 1, 2002. Important developments thereafter will appear in annual supplements, which will also contain relevant federal court rules and statutory materials. The supplement accompanying this book and published simultaneously with it will contain all notable cases handed down by the Supreme Court during the 2001-2002 Term. It will also include the Federal Rules of Criminal Procedure and various statutes.

Case citations in the text and the footnotes of judicial opinions and in the writings of commentators have been omitted without so specifying. Numbered footnotes are from the original materials; lettered footnotes are ours.[1] Omissions from the text of the original are indicated by asterisks and brackets.

One or more of the authors has been fortunate enough to participate actively in four major criminal procedure projects: The American Bar Association's project on *Standards for Criminal Justice*; The American Law Institute's *Model Code of Pre-Arraignment Procedure*; The National Conference of Commissioners on Uniform State Laws' *Uniform Rules of Criminal Procedure*; and the ongoing revision of the *Federal Rules of Criminal Procedure*. We are indebted to the members of the various committees with whom we have worked for providing us with many leads and insights. We are also indebted to the many users of this book who have offered helpful suggestions on content as to this edition and previous editions. That list, like the list of our student research assistants over the years, has now grown far too long to mention each person individually.

---

1. Standard abbreviations are used throughout. On occasion, a book or article is used so frequently in a chapter as to call for a shorter citation form. Here we have given the full citation to the book or article in the first footnote of the chapter and indicated there the shorter citation form. For our own books, we simply have used the shorter citation form throughout the book. These are:

LaFave, *Search and Seizure: A Treatise on the Fourth Amendment* (3d ed. 1996), available on Westlaw under the database SEARCHSZR and cited as SEARCHSZR §__.

LaFave, Israel, and King, *Criminal Procedure Treatise* (2d ed. 1999), available on Westlaw under the database CRIMPROC and cited as CRIMPROC §__.

Articles collected in Kamisar, *Police Interrogation and Confessions: Essays in Law and Policy* (1980) are usually cited as Kamisar essays.

We are especially appreciative of the able secretarial assistance provided on this tenth edition, too often under great stress, by Rosemary Getty, Carol Haley, Mary Lebert, Carolyn Lloyd, Janis Stewart, and Cindy Zimmerman.

YALE KAMISAR
WAYNE R. LaFAVE
JEROLD H. ISRAEL
NANCY J. KING

June, 2002

*

Acknowledgments

Excerpts from the following books and articles appear with the kind permission of the copyright holders.

Arenella, Peter, Foreword: O.J. Lessons, 69 S.Cal. 1233 (1996). Copyright © 1996 by the University of Southern California. Reprinted by permission.

Beale, Sara Sun, Reconsidering Supervisory Power in Criminal Cases: Constitutional and Statutory Limits on the Authority of the Federal Courts, 84 Colum.L.Rev. 1433 (1984). Copyright © 1984 by the Columbia Law Review Association. Reprinted by permission.

Bloom, Robert M., Inevitable Discovery: An Exception beyond the Fruits, 20 Am.J.Crim.law 79 (1992). Copyright © 1992 by the American Journal of Criminal Law. Reprinted by permission.

Bradley, Craig M., Two Models of the Fourth Amendment, 83 Mich.L.Rev. 1468 (1985). Copyright © 1985 by the Michigan Law Review. Reprinted by permission.

Caplan, Gerald M., Questioning *Miranda*, 38 Vand.L.Rev. 1417 (1985). Copyright © 1985 by the Vanderbilt Law Review. Reprinted by permission.

Cassell, Paul G., *Miranda*'s Social Costs: An Empirical Assessment, 90 Nw.U.L.Rev. 387 (1996). Copyright © 1996 by the Northwestern University Law Review. Reprinted by special permission of Northwestern University School of Law, *Law Review*, vol. 90, issue 2, 1996.

_____, The Paths Not Taken: The Supreme Court's Failures in *Dickerson*, 99 Mich.L.Rev. 898 (2001). Copyright © 2001 by the Michigan Law Review Association. Reprinted by permission.

Cloud, Morgan; Shepherd, George B.; Barkoff, Alison Nodwin; and Shur, Justin V., Words Without Meaning: The Constitution, Confessions, and Mentally Retarded Suspects, 69 U.Chi.L.Rev. 495 (2002). Copyright © 2002 by the University of Chicago Law Review. Reprinted by permission.

Colb, Sherry F., Why the Supreme Court Should Overrule the *Massiah* Doctrine and Permit *Miranda* Alone to Govern Interrogations, Findlaw's Writ at <http://writ.news.findlaw.com/colb/20010509.html> (May 9, 2001). Copyright © 2001 by Findlaw's Writ. Reprinted by permission.

Dressler, Joshua, Understanding Criminal Procedure (2d ed. 1997). Copyright © 1997 by Matthew Bender & Co. Inc. Reprinted by permission.

Dripps, Donald A., Constitutional Theory for Criminal Procedure: *Miranda, Dickerson*, and the Continuing Quest for Broad-But-Shallow, 43 Wm. & Mary L. Rev. 1 (2001). Copyright © 2001 by the William and Mary Law Review. Reprinted by permission.

Goldsmith, Michael, The Supreme Court and Title III: Rewriting the Law of Electronic Surveillance, 74 J.Crim.L. & Criminology 1 (1983). Copyright © 1983 by the Northwestern University School of Law. Reprinted by permission.

Goldwasser, Katherine, After Abscam: An Examination of Congressional Proposals to Limit Targeting Discretion in Federal Undercover Investigations, 36 Emory L.J. 75 (1987). Copyright © 1987 by the Emory University School of Law. Reprinted by permission.

Skolnick, Jerome and Fyfe, James, Above the Law: Police and the Excessive Use of Force (1993). The Free Press. Copyright © 1993 by Jerome H. Skolnick and James F. Fyfe. Reprinted by permission.

Stuntz, William J., The Uneasy Relationship Between Criminal Procedure and Criminal Justice, 107 Yale L.J. (1997). Copyright © 1997 by the Yale Law Journal Co., Inc. Reprinted by permission of the Yale Law Journal Company and William S. Hein Company from *The Yale Law Journal*, Vol. 107, pages 1-76.

_____, Waiving Rights in Criminal Procedure, 75 Va.L.Rev. 761 (1989). Copyright © 1989 by the Virginia Law Review. Reprinted by permission.

_____, Warrants, and Fourth Amendment Remedies, 77 Va.L.Rev. 881 (1991). Copyright © 1991 by the Virginia Law Review. Reprinted by permission.

_____, *Miranda*'s Mistake, 99 Mich.L.Rev. 975 (2001). Copyright © 2001 by the Michigan Law Review Association. Reprinted by permission.

Taylor, Stuart, Jr., Politically Incorrect Profiling: A Matter of Life or Death, Nov. 3, 2001, p. 3406. Copyright © 2001 by the National Journal. Reprinted by permission.

Thomas, George C. III, Plain Talk about the *Miranda* Empirical Debate: A "Steady-State" Theory of Confessions, 43 U.C.L.A.L.Rev. 933 (1966). Copyright © 1996 by the U.C.L.A. Law Review. Reprinted by permission.

_____, Separated at Birth but Siblings Nonetheless: *Miranda* and the Due Process Notice Cases, 99 Mich.L.Rev. 1081 (2001). Copyright © 2001 by the Michigan Law Review Association. Reprinted by permission.

Weisselberg, Charles, Saving *Miranda*, 84 Cornell L.Rev. 109 (1998). Copyright © 1998 by the Cornell Law Review. Reprinted by permission.

White, Welsh S., What Is an Involuntary Confession Now?, 50 Rutgers L.Rev. 2001 (1998). Copyright © 1998 by the Rutgers Law Review. Reprinted by permission.

_____, *Miranda*'s Waning Protections (2001). Copyright © 2001 by the University of Michigan. Reprinted by permission.

Whitebread, Charles, and Slobogin, Christopher, Criminal Procedure (4th ed. 2000). Copyright © 2000 by The Foundation Press, Inc. Reprinted by permission.

Wollin, David, Policing the Police: Should *Miranda* Violations Bear Fruit?, 53 Ohio State L.J. 805 (1992). Copyright © 1992 by the Ohio State Law Journal. Reprinted by permission.

*

Summary of Contents

PART FOUR.   THE ADVERSARY SYSTEM AND THE DETERMINATION OF GUILT OR INNOCENCE

PART FIVE.   APPEALS, POST–CONVICTION REVIEW

Table of Contents

PART ONE

INTRODUCTION

PART THREE

THE COMMENCEMENT OF FORMAL PROCEEDINGS

PART FOUR

THE ADVERSARY SYSTEM AND THE DETERMINATION OF GUILT OR INNOCENCE

PART FIVE

APPEALS, POST-CONVICTION REVIEW

*

Table of Cases

The principal cases are in bold type. Cases cited or discussed in the text are roman type. References are to pages. For Commonwealth v. _____, People v. _____, State v. _____, United States v. _____, see the name of the other party. For Ex parte _____, In re _____, In the Matter of _____, see the name of the party. For People ex rel. _____, State ex rel. _____, United States ex rel. _____, see the name of the first party. Where a case is discussed in another case, reference is made only to the first page at which it is cited. No reference is made to discussion of a principal case in the Notes and Questions that follow that case.

*

Table of Articles, Books, Proposed Standards and Reports

Bold type indicates major extracts

*

MODERN CRIMINAL PROCEDURE

CASES, COMMENTS AND QUESTIONS

Tenth Edition

*

Part One

INTRODUCTION

Chapter 1

AN OVERVIEW OF THE CRIMINAL JUSTICE PROCESS[aa]

This chapter provides an introduction for three different books–*Modern Criminal Procedure*, *Basic Criminal Procedure* (containing chapters 1–11 of *Modern*), and *Advanced Criminal Procedure* (containing chapters 1 and 12–29 of *Modern*). All three books are designed for use in courses on the "criminal justice process"—that is, the process through which the substantive criminal law is enforced. That process starts with the investigation of possible criminality and the apprehension of the suspected criminal, the primary subjects considered in *Basic Criminal Procedure* and in the first half of *Modern Criminal Procedure*. The process then proceeds through the charging decision, a variety of pre-adjudication proceedings, the adjudication of the charge, the imposition of sentence upon persons found guilty, and any subsequent challenges to the conviction and sentence. These subjects are considered in *Advanced Criminal Procedure* and in the second half of *Modern Criminal Procedure*.

Single courses on the criminal justice process typically concentrate on only a portion of the process. Thus, a course may cover the investigative stages (as in a "police practices" course) or concentrate on the post-investigative stages of the process (as in the course commonly described as the "adversary process" or "bail to jail" course), or it may treat selective parts of both the investigative and subsequent stages of the process (as in the courses that concentrate on the various constitutional provisions regulating the process). A single semester simply is too short to explore *all* of the stages of the process. Yet, a general understanding of the totality of the process is critical to placing in context any portion of the process. The primary objective of this chapter is to provide that understanding through the overview of the process set forth in section three of the chapter. Hopefully, this overview will provide the student with a useful backdrop for considering the selected aspects of the process that are explored in greater detail in the particular course.

Overviews of the American criminal justice process almost invariably start by noting that there is no single American criminal justice system, but multiple systems that differ substantially from state to state and from locality to locality within a single state. That process diversity is the product of a divergence from

---

aa. For a more detailed examination of the topics considered in this chapter, see 1 Wayne R. LaFave, Jerold H. Israel, & Nancy J. King, Criminal Procedure, ch.1 (2d ed. 1999). This treatise is available on Westlaw under the database "CRIMPROC" and is hereafter cited as CRIMPROC.

one lawmaking jurisdiction to another in the laws governing the process and divergence from one community to another even in the administration of those laws. Section one of this chapter explores the diversity in legal regulation, and section two explores the diversity in administration.

SECTION 1. DIVERSITY IN LEGAL REGULATION

1. *Fifty-two separate legal structures.* Under the American version of federalism, both the federal (i.e., national) government and each of the fifty states has independent authority to enact its own criminal code. Each also has the authority to enforce its criminal laws through its own criminal justice system— that is through its own criminal justice agencies and its own laws regulating enforcement procedures. The state exercises this authority pursuant to the state's police powers, which allows the state to act to promote the general welfare. The federal government, in contrast, can enact criminal laws, and establish enforcement agencies and procedures, only where necessary and proper to the implementation of those specific areas of regulatory authority granted to the national government by the Constitution. Utilizing its general legislative authority over the District of Columbia, Congress has enacted a criminal code and enforcement process for the District of Columbia, creating what is very similar to a state criminal justice system, applicable to crimes committed in whole or in part within the District. Utilizing other aspects of the federal regulatory authority (e.g., the regulation of interstate commerce and the protection of federal agencies), Congress has created a federal criminal code applicable throughout the nation, which is enforced by federal agencies through prosecutions brought in the federal district courts. Thus, we have in this country fifty-two separate criminal justice jurisdictions—fifty-one "state" systems (counting the District of Columbia system as, in effect, a state system) and the national "federal system."

In other fields in which the federal government and the states share regulatory authority, the federal system dominates and its regulatory impact far outstrips that of all of the states combined. That certainly has not occurred in the criminal justice field. Of the roughly 1.75 million felony cases prosecuted in this country each year, only about 3% are brought in the federal system. Of the more than 13 million prosecutions for minor offenses, less than 1% are brought in the federal system. Of course, the federal system has far greater influence than its small proportion of the total caseload might suggest. Due to its concentration upon certain types of crimes (e.g., white collar offenses) that often attract public attention, and due to the number of states that look to it in modeling their own criminal process laws, the federal system is often characterized as the "most important" of the fifty-two criminal justice jurisdictions. Nonetheless, it remains no more than a leader among the fifty-two, not the actor that dwarfs all others.

2. *Divergence.* Because of the practical significance of the state systems, one cannot begin to understand the character of the laws governing criminal procedure in this country without examining the laws that govern the state systems as well as the laws that govern the federal system. However, various elements in criminal justice lawmaking naturally promote divergence in the approaches of the fifty-two jurisdictions, leading to considerable diversity in their laws. Of the various factors pointing toward different states adopting different standards in their regulation of criminal procedure, four factors, in particular, appear to be most influential: (1) criminal procedure is not one of those areas of lawmaking in which a need for reciprocity or the interaction of transactions forces the states to seek uniformity; a lack of uniformity in the criminal justice processes of adjoining states is not likely to be a deterrent to the free flow of goods, services, or persons between the states or to restrain economic development within the state; (2) the criminal justice process must be shaped in light of the state's administrative environment, including the demography of the population, the resources available to the process, and the structure of the institutions responsible for the administration of the process (particularly police, prosecutor, and judiciary); states vary considerably as to that administrative environment, particularly as to states that are largely urban and largely rural and as to different regions of the country; (3) criminal process issues tend to be issues of high visibility and, often, high emotional content, leading to lawmaking decisions (at least legislative lawmaking decisions[a]) that are influenced more by symbolic politics (which tend to vary with the ideological assumptions of the local constituency) than the views of those with presumed technical expertise; and (4) the integrated character of the criminal justice means that a divergence between states in their law governing one part of the process most likely will necessitate further differences at other stages of the process.

In many respects, the factors pointing toward divergence are even stronger as they relate to the potential for differences between the laws governing the federal criminal justice system and the laws governing state criminal justice systems. In particular, the institutional setting for federal system enforcement is quite different from that found in any state system. The crimes investigated and prosecuted in the federal system have a somewhat different character (with greater emphasis on white collar crime and less emphasis on street crime); federal enforcement officers have different qualifications, different training, and different responsibilities (which do not include the general peacekeeping, traffic control, and social service functions of local police departments); federal prosecutors exercise considerably more control over the investigative process, are not elected officials, and are subject to a central authority (the Attorney General); and federal trial judges are totally insulated from the electorate and have a criminal caseload which is substantial, but still considerably lighter than that carried by state trial judges of urban courts.

Notwithstanding the factors pointing toward divergence, the laws regulating the criminal justice processes of all fifty-two jurisdictions are very similar in many of their basic elements. Also, where substantial differences do exist, the majority of the fifty-two jurisdictions usually can be characterized as following one or the other of two or three basic alternative approaches. Such commonality in the laws of the fifty-two jurisdictions largely is the product of the features discussed in the notes that follow—a significant common source of regulation (the federal constitution), a common heritage (the English common law), and certain highly influential models that have shaped state lawmaking.

3. *The United States Constitution.* The Bill of Rights of the federal constitution includes 16 guarantees that are applicable to the criminal justice process—all of the guarantees of the Fourth, Sixth, and Eighth Amendments, and all but one of the guarantees (the just compensation guarantee) of the Fifth Amendment. Prior to the adoption of the Fourteenth Amendment in 1868, those

---

a. Legislative lawmaking plays a critical role in the field of criminal procedure as many states have detailed statutory codes of criminal procedure. Judicial lawmaking through the common law development of procedural requirements, once the most common form of judicial lawmaking, is now fairly rare. See CRIMPROC § 1.6(h). Judicial lawmaking occurs primarily in the adoption of court rules, although in several states (as in the federal system), court rules go into effect only if accepted by the legislature. Id. at § 1.6(f). Courts also may be viewed as engaged in lawmaking in their interpretations of constitutions, statutes, and court rules.

While commentators generally agree that symbolic politics drives legislative lawmaking in the criminal justice field, most would not extend that characterization to judicial lawmaking. Many would, however, point to the value judgments of the judges as driving judicial lawmaking and that factor would similarly produce divergence in shaping the law.

guarantees had no bearing on the state criminal justice systems, as they applied only to the federal government (in both the federal criminal justice system and the systems created for the District of Columbia and for the federal territories that later became states). The Fourteenth Amendment added several general guarantees directed at state governments, including its due process clause. The Supreme Court initially held that the due process clause of the Fourteenth Amendment required the state criminal justice systems to adhere to certain fundamental standards which might also be found in certain Bill of Rights' guarantees, but then, in the 1960s, concluded that the due process clause actually incorporated and made applicable to the states almost all of the criminal justice guarantees of the Bill of Rights. Thus, those "incorporated" guarantees came to operate as a common source of regulation for all fifty-two jurisdictions.

The constitutional guarantees and their interpretation by the Supreme Court accordingly constitute the starting point for understanding the law applicable to all fifty-two criminal justice systems. The federal system and each of the state systems must, at a minimum, meet the requirements of those guarantees. However, each jurisdiction remains free to insist on safeguards more rigorous than those imposed by the constitutional guarantee. Each jurisdiction also is free to adopt its own standards as to those aspects of the criminal justice process that simply are not regulated by the federal constitutional guarantees.

The significance of federal constitutional regulation varies with the different stages of the criminal justice process. Three models provide a rough picture of that variation. First, as to some procedures (e.g., the preliminary hearing), the Constitution says very little. Here, legal regulation comes primarily from the laws of the individual jurisdiction. Second, as to other procedures, such as searches, the constitutional regulation is so comprehensive as to rival the Internal Revenue Code in its detail and complexity. Here, constitutional standards tend to dominate. Some jurisdictions may add more rigorous standards, and many may add their own requirements as to minor aspects of administration, but the constitutional standards constitute the critical legal standards for most of the country as to the basic regulation of the particular procedure. Finally, for still other elements of the process, such as the jury trial, the federal constitution provides a substantial, though not comprehensive, set of regulations. Here, it is not uncommon for a fairly large group of states to impose more rigorous standards under state law, and almost all will look to state law to cover important features that are not treated by the constitutional standards.

Our discussion of a particular step in the process will always start with a consideration of the applicable federal constitutional requirements (if any). When our coverage concentrates entirely on the constitutional standards as set forth by the Supreme Court, it can be assumed that the first model prevails, i.e., the number of jurisdictions that add substantial requirements of their own is fairly small, and for the vast majority of the fifty-two jurisdictions, the federal constitutional standards provide the basic legal regulation. Where the constitution provides very little direction, or many jurisdictions establish standards more rigorous than the constitutional standard, our discussion will go beyond the constitutional standards and consider the general patterns of regulation under the laws of the fifty-two jurisdictions (as discussed in note 5 infra).[b]

---

b. While federal statutes regulating criminal procedure generally apply only to the federal system, Congress in a few instances has utilized its regulatory authority (e.g., its authority over interstate commerce) to prescribe criminal process standards that govern in both the federal and state systems. The prime example is the federal law governing wiretapping and other forms of electronic surveillance. Where such a statute is applicable, our discussion focuses on that federal statute rather than the laws of the states.

4. *The common law heritage.* The English common law provided a common starting point for the law of the states and the federal government, and while many of its aspects have been discarded or modified, it continues to provide an element of commonality in the regulation of several aspects of the process. The American colonies operated under the English legal system, which was sometimes modified to suit conditions in the particular colony. In large part, the guiding legal principles were those set forth by Blackstone in his description of the English common law. After the Revolution, the newly independent states included in their constitutions safeguards responsive to the numerous grievances that had been advanced against the Crown's administration of the colonial criminal justice processes. However, apart from these safeguards, designed to hedge governmental authority in the application of the common law processes, the colonial version of the English common law largely survived and provided a common core of principles applicable throughout the country.

Over the nineteenth century, those common law principles had to be adjusted to accommodate new developments in the administrative structure of the process, such as the creation of police departments, the granting to public prosecutors of a virtual monopoly over the decision to prosecute (replacing private prosecution), and the shift to sentences of incarceration (with the creation of the penitentiary). So too, adjustments were needed to accommodate major changes in the process itself, such as allowing the defendant to offer sworn testimony at trial and providing for regularized appellate review of convictions. In the course of making adjustments, different jurisdictions often took different approaches, resulting in greater divergence in the process from one state to another. The codification movement also took hold in the field of criminal procedure, and while the codes incorporated much of the common law, some states viewed the codification quest for "rationality" in the law as requiring the elimination or reform of various "archaic" common law concepts.

Notwithstanding the legislative and judicial movement in different directions in the modification of many common law concepts, other common law concepts have survived largely intact as a part of the law in the vast majority of our fifty-two jurisdictions. Those common law concepts of continuing vitality will be the focus of our discussion in several chapters, since they provide a useful vehicle for understanding prevailing legal standards. It should be kept in mind, however, that the laws shaped by such concepts may well differ in administrative detail from one jurisdiction to another. Also, at least a few jurisdictions are likely to have rejected or substantially altered each such concept, producing standards quite unlike those found elsewhere.

5. *Models.* The laws of the fifty-two jurisdictions are most likely to vary where (1) federal constitutional regulation is not detailed and comprehensive and (2) the particular procedure either was unknown at common law or was substantially modified as a result of institutional and process changes not anticipated by the common law. Nonetheless, certain general patterns often can be found in the laws of most of the jurisdictions even as to such aspects of the process. Those patterns are a product of a tendency of lawmakers to consider, and often emulate, what has been done in other jurisdictions. In particular, legal standards adopted in a few key jurisdictions may become models for many other jurisdictions. The end result is that the law in a substantial majority of the fifty-two jurisdictions will be quite similar in its basic components or will be divided among two or three distinctive approaches advanced by conflicting models. Thus, an examination of no more than a few critical models provides a fairly representative view of the primary legal standards applicable to the particular procedure in all but a handful of the fifty-two jurisdictions.

Key models, emulated by other jurisdictions, are not a new development. When the early nineteenth century codes, in particular the Field Code of New York, offered modifications of the common law, many states included those modifications in the codes they subsequently adopted. Some of those modifications remain in current law. During the last decades of the nineteenth century and the first decades of the twentieth century, the Progressive Movement produced a series of legislative reforms that also have a continuing significance in a large number of states. Most significant, however, are two later models that bear particularly upon the post-charge stages of the process—the "federal model" and the American Bar Association Standards. Both of these models have found favor in numerous states in the past, and both are likely to continue to do so in their future revisions.

The federal law of criminal procedure is undoubtedly the single most influential model in shaping the nonconstitutional law of the states. Notwithstanding the significant distinctions in the role and institutions of the federal and state systems (see note 2 supra), as to almost every aspect of the criminal justice process, a grouping of states, ranging from a handful to a majority, have adopted the basic features of the nonconstitutional law of the federal system. Thus, the discussion of that federal law in later chapters is presented not only to describe the law of the federal system, but also the law of a fair number of states.

The Federal Rules of Criminal Procedure provide the most prominent illustration of the influence of the "federal model." Roughly half of the states have court rules or statutory codes that borrow heavily from the Federal Rules (set forth in Appendix C of the Supplement to this book). Admittedly, only a handful of these states have adopted fairly complete replications of the Federal Rules, but all largely follow the basic structure of the Federal Rules in their court rules or code, and all have accepted at least a majority of the legal standards contained in the Federal Rules. Similarly, prominent federal legislative reforms, such as the Bail Reform Acts of 1966 and 1984 and the Speedy Trial Act of 1968 (set full in Appendix B) have served as models for various states (although the state versions typically will depart from one or more of the provisions of such federal statutes).

In many other fields in which state law plays a major regulatory role, distinguished groups within the legal profession have proposed models for state enactments that have been quite successful in achieving uniformity in state law. Those same groups have also been at work in the field of criminal procedure, but with much more limited impact. The American Law Institute put forth a Code of Criminal Procedure in 1931 and a Model Code of Pre–Arraignment Procedure in 1975. The National Conference of Commissioners on Uniform State Laws in 1952 adopted its first version of the Uniform Rules of Criminal Procedure, and in 1987 adopted a redraft of the 1974 Rules that produced the current version of the Uniform Rules. The American Bar Association completed its original version of the ABA's Standards for Criminal Justice in 1973, issued a revised second edition in 1978–79, and has recently introduced parts of its third edition. Although not offering nearly as comprehensive coverage, various national commissions, dating back to the Wickersham Commission of 1929–31, have advanced models for reform on particular aspects of the process. The influence of these models has varied. All included proposals that were adopted in at least a few states, and most advanced at least one proposal that gained the support of a substantial body of states. Only the ABA Standards, however, have had a widespread influence on numerous aspects of the criminal justice process.

The ABA Standards have been cited thousands of times by appellate courts and have been utilized by numerous states in formulating their court rules or statutes. Unlike the Federal Rules, however, the Standards have been incorporated into state law on a piecemeal basis, with the state reforms typically looking either to an individual standard or a grouping of standards dealing with a particular aspect of the process (e.g., pretrial discovery). Still, the majority of the Standards have been incorporated into state law in at least a few states, and many reflect the governing law in most states. Many of the Standards receiving the broadest support simply duplicate the Federal Rules, but where the Standards differ, they will be cited as indicative of the position taken by at least some of the states not following the federal model.

SECTION 2. DIVERSITY IN ADMINISTRATION

1. *The significance of discretion.* The American criminal justice system commonly is pictured as presenting a tremendous chasm between its day-to-day practice and its legal doctrine. That chasm is often attributed to deviance by the professional participants in the process—that is, the failure of police, prosecutors, magistrates, trial judges, and defense counsel to follow the dictates of the law in the performance of their roles. Indeed, some would contend that, for the police, deviance is a pervasive feature of administrative practice due to various influences that encourage police to disregard certain legal limits placed upon the investigative portion of the process.[a] Even if that contention is accepted, however, it clearly is discretion, rather than deviance, that explains by far the largest part of what is characterized as the "gap" between the "law in the books" and the "law in action."

The law grants those responsible for the administration of the process the authority to institute certain procedures under specified conditions, but typically also gives the administrator the discretion not to exercise the authority even where those conditions exist. So too, the law grants to the individuals that are subjected to such authority the right to insist that it is exercised within the limits set forth in the law, but at the same time, it often gives them the discretion not to exercise that right. The end result is that the discretionary decisionmaking of the participants can produce a practice that looks quite different from what one might expect from a reading of constitutional provisions, statutes, court rules or judicial decisions. Those sources set forth process standards which may appear on their face to be mandated requirements, but are often rendered no more than possible options as a result of the discretion also allowed under the law. They speak of rights and powers, but discretion may produce a system in which those rights and powers are not exercised in many or most instances. Thus, a reading of the statutes may suggest that arrested persons are always searched, because the statutes give that authority to the police, but the practice of the police may be not to exercise that authority where persons are arrested for minor offenses. So too, many trials may not be to a jury (although the law provides for a trial by jury) because defendants are willing to waive that right, and the reciprocal disclosure of witnesses' prior recorded statements may come well before trial, even though disclosure at trial is the time frame mandated by law, because the parties regularly find it more convenient to make that exchange at a much earlier point in the process.

The discretion granted to public administrators (i.e., the police, prosecutor, magistrate, and trial judge) also opens the door to diversity in the application of

a. See CRIMPROC § 1.8(b) and Chapter Four of *Modern Criminal Procedure* and *Basic Criminal Procedure*. While the literature tends to focus on police deviance, studies have cited deviance by all of the professional participants—e.g., prosecutors who charge as a means of "punishing" though lacking a legal grounding for charging, magistrates who deny bail so as to facilitate guilty plea offers of time already served, judges who regularly engage in ex parte communications with prosecutors or defense counsel, and defense counsel who "trade" the interests of one client for another in plea negotiations.

the process within a single jurisdiction. Wherever there exists a legal normlessness or a legal norm so broad as to allow reference to personal values,[b] different administrators may adopt different standards in the exercise of their discretion, producing diversity in the administration of the process. This applies not only to the decision to proceed or not proceed, but also as to how one proceeds. For example, the law of a particular jurisdiction may provide that, once a police officer has a sufficient grounding to arrest a person for shoplifting, and decides to proceed, the officer has discretion to either take that person into custody or release him on the issuance of a summons, and if the person is taken into custody, the officer has discretion to conduct a full search of the person, to frisk the person, or to do neither. Thus, discretion may result in a diverse administration of the law as to five identically situated persons subject to a shoplifting arrest, with one person simply "let off" with a warning, another person proceeded against but released on a summons, another taken into custody without a search or frisk, another taken into custody and frisked, and another taken into custody and searched. The notes that follow examine some of the factors that produce diversity in the exercise of discretion, focusing particularly on how those factors produce differences in the administration of the law from one community to another.

2. *Localism.* To some extent, diversity in the exercise of discretion is an inevitable byproduct of the number of different actors making discretionary decisions, as it can hardly be expected that all actors performing the same role will uniformly share the same values in exercising their discretion. However, the more significant influence is the institutional framework that shapes the decisions of the individual actor. Though differences in the perceptions, values, and abilities of individual administrators are undoubtedly reflected in the exercise of discretion, to a considerable extent those qualities are a product of, and subordinate to, the influence of both the agencies and groups of which the administrators are a part and the local community in which they operate. Initially, the agencies (in the case of appointed officials, such as police officers) and the community (in the case of elected officials, such as prosecutors) commonly play a substantial role in determining the type of people who will be placed in the various roles of criminal justice administrators. Even more significantly, they combine to shape the administrative environment that heavily influences the individual official in her or his choice of action. Indeed, in some settings, the agency will seek through administrative regulation formally to confine or guide various aspects of discretionary decisionmaking. Formal regulations are not necessary, however, as control over training, promotion, assignments, and socialization give agencies ample tools for influencing the exercise of discretion. Of course, considerable room will always remain for administrative decisionmaking based upon the idiosyncratic values of the individual, but as to the administrative practice as a whole, numerous studies

b. Discretionary decisions are not necessarily decisions totally unregulated by the law, but decisions to which the law grants the actor sufficient leeway to look to personal value judgments. The leeway granted to the administrator tends to be broadest where the decision is not to exercise governmental power adversely to the individual (sometimes described as "ameliorative discretion"). Yet, even here, there usually are some legal limits. A prosecutor has great latitude, for example, in deciding not to prosecute, but that decision cannot be based on a bribe. Where the official exercises governmental power and the choice is between alternative procedures (e.g., the police officer's choice between taking a detained misdemeanant into custody or releasing him on issuance of a summons), the governing law tends to offer somewhat less discretionary latitude. Here the law typically will specify some general prerequisites for taking action, but then give the administrator a choice, based upon an open-ended standard, between different alternatives. Open-ended standards, such as that requiring that an action be consistent with "the interests of justice," commonly are seen as allowing for basically "discretionary" decisionmaking, though subject to judicial review.

suggest that the dominant influence in the long run is the administrative environment shaped by agency bureaucracy and the local community.

A critical feature of that administrative environment is that it is the product of localism. From the very outset, the primary responsibility for the administration of state criminal justice processes was assigned to officials of local governments. The prosecutor, sheriff, magistrate, and trial judge were all officials of local government units, and when police departments were created, they too were established as local agencies. Today, state police agencies and state attorneys general often have some enforcement responsibilities, but the primary police and prosecutorial agencies remain local agencies.[c] Trial judges are now part of a statewide system, but in over three-fourths of the states, they must stand for local election (even if only a retention election under the Missouri Plan). So too, magistrates typically are either themselves elected or appointed by local elected officials.

Localism produces an administrative environment that varies from community to community. Indeed, insofar as police agencies shape that environment, a single community may present several distinctive environments. Within a single county, there will be one sheriff's office and a number of different municipal police departments, each fostering its own administrative culture. In a major metropolitan area, consisting of several counties, one is likely to find from 50 to over 100 police agencies enforcing the state law, separate prosecutors' offices for each county, a variety of magistrate courts,[d] and separate trial courts for each county (each court being subject to statewide administrative control, but also having local rulemaking discretion that fosters its own administrative style).

Where the exercise of discretion plays a major rule in the application of a particular step in the criminal justice process, our discussion usually will offer illustrations of some alternative modes of exercising that discretion. Those illustrations come from studies which focus on the exercise of discretion in particular localities. Ordinarily, it can be assumed that something close to the same administrative environment can be found in certain other communities and the same style of discretionary decisionmaking probably prevails there. But it also is clear that the illustrations hardly cover the full range of possibilities, and that there are many communities in which a quite different use of discretion will be found. The potential for such variation is evidenced by the character of the factors that studies have shown to be particularly influential in shaping the use of discretion. Those factors are briefly surveyed in the notes that follow.

3. *Organizational variations.* Various studies establish that police and prosecutors tend to be heavily influenced in their exercise of discretion by the "administrative ethos" of the organizations of which they are a part.[e] Those

c. See CRIMPROC § 1.9 (also noting that three states are exceptions as to prosecutorial authority, as those states (Alaska, Delaware, and Rhode Island) vest that authority entirely in the attorney general).

d. Magistrate courts, as discussed in section 3, typically handle preliminary matters in felony cases and have trial jurisdiction in misdemeanor cases. Approximately half of the states have magistrate courts of basically uniform jurisdiction. The other half have more than one type of magistrate court, with each type having a somewhat different trial jurisdiction (and each often following somewhat different procedural rules). In many of those states, one type of magistrate court allows for nonlaw-

yer judges, and in rural areas, magistrates in those courts, quite often are not lawyers. See CRIMPROC § 1.7(f).

e. Because defense counsel's responsibility to the individual client extends to the exercise of discretion, defense counsel are not commonly characterized as acting as members of an organization, even when defense counsel are employed by a public defender agency. Yet, public defender offices have been known to promote a particular style of lawyering, primarily through selection process, division of responsibility, and socialization. Privately retained and court appointed counsel also are, in a sense, members of an "organization." Most counsel will be part of a particular segment of

studies also suggest that a wide range of factors contribute to the manner and direction of each organization's approach to the exercise of discretion. To some extent, that approach will be shaped by the character of the local community and the leadership of the organization. However, other factors, more structural in nature, often play a most important role in setting the administrative culture of the organization.

The studies cite a wide range of differences in various aspects of police and prosecutorial agencies. They suggest further that most of those differences will contribute, in varying degrees, to the character of the administrative ethos of the individual agency. The most frequently cited differences relate to the following factors: (1) the range of responsibilities of the organization (e.g., whether a police agency is a specialized agency, charged only with a criminal investigatory function, as in the case of the F.B.I., or a general agency that has such additional responsibilities as traffic control, providing basic social services, and maintenance of the public order, as in the case of a municipal police department[f]); (2) the size of the organization (with the most striking differences found among local police agencies, where over one-fourth of all departments have less than five officers, while departments of medium-sized cities have several hundred officers, and departments of large cities have several thousand); (3) standards for selecting personnel (e.g., educational qualifications for police departments, and the choice between non-partisan, merit oriented or highly political hiring standards for prosecutors' offices); (4) allocation of responsibilities within the organization [e.g., in a prosecutor's office, whether the general assignment system is "horizontal," with different assistants assigned to each major stage in the process (e.g., intake, preliminary hearing, and trial), or "vertical," with the assistant starting with the case at intake and carrying it through to final disposition, and whether all cases come within the general assignment system or specialized units are charged with prosecuting certain types of crimes (e.g., sexual assaults) or selected offenders (e.g., "career" criminals)]; and (5) caseload pressures (which vary considerably, with prosecutors' offices in smaller communities often having caseloads per prosecutor only half of that found in larger communities). Quite obviously, with the great potential for variation as to such factors individually and in combination, criminal justice organizations can be expected to develop a broad range of differing perspectives as the exercise of most elements of their discretionary authority.

4. *Variations in administrative interactions.* As the commentators also have noted, analysis of administrative decisionmaking in the criminal justice process cannot be restricted to a "one-party" focus. Each participant in the

the bar, and especially as to the segment sometimes characterized as "courthouse regulars" (primarily solo practitioners dealing with heavy caseloads of garden variety charges against clients of a lower economic status), a particular style of representation, bearing particularly upon discretionary decisionmaking, is encouraged through socialization. See CRIMPROC § 1.9(d).

Studies of judicial decisionmaking suggest that, both as to trial judges and magistrates, organizational influences also play a critical role in shaping discretionary decisionmaking. Thus, the combination of resource limitations, the special expertise of certain courthouse personnel, and a shared perspective as to the role of the particular multijudge court will strongly influence the individual judge's exercise of discretionary authority, prevailing over what otherwise might be the judge's personal preference. Judges act independently in making legal judgments, but remain a part of a bureaucracy in utilizing other elements of their authority. CRIMPROC § 1.9(d).

f. Indeed, municipal police departments often tend to promote different policing styles as to the same function for officers that are a part of units having different primary responsibilities. Thus, officers who are members of units concerned primarily with criminal investigation (e.g., detectives or tactical squads) may be encouraged to utilize their arrest authority and authority to interrogate quite differently than patrol officers, who typically spend only a small portion of their time in investigative activities (many patrol officers will not have made a felony arrest in over a year). See CRIMPROC §§ 1.3(d), 1.3(g), and 1.9(d).

process, whether police officer, prosecutor, defense counsel, or judge, is influenced not only by the institutional concerns of the organization of which he is a part, but also by concerns that flow from the necessity of interacting with representatives of those other organizations that share in the administration of the process. The criminal justice system is a blend of interdependent parts, thereby creating a functional interlocking among its key administrators. As a result, each unit must take account of the responses of the others in shaping its administrative decisions. In many instances, those decisions will be made in settings that require explicit interchange between different participants, as in the many courtroom actions that require participation of the judge, prosecutor, and defense counsel. In others, though the administrative action may appear to be taken unilaterally (as in the case of the police officer's exercise of arrest authority), the underlying decision nonetheless entails predictions of, and reactions to, the administrative decisions of subsequent participants. Thus, though a local prosecutor has no direct regulatory authority over the local police departments within the prosecutorial district, a prosecutorial charging policy which downgrades a particular offense (perhaps even refusing to prosecute under certain circumstances) may readily convince the local police departments that, even though they disagree with that policy, a wise use of their resources points to exercising their discretion not to arrest for that offense. Of course, the discretionary outputs of an earlier participant similarly shape the discretionary decisions of a later participant (and may even preclude any decision by the later participant by ending the case before it reaches that participant).

A commonplace consequence of recurring interactions of persons with interdependent administrative responsibility is the development of informal workgroups with their own distinctive norms, values, and social relationships, and the criminal justice process is no exception in this regard. Indeed, some commentators have suggested that the workgroup relationships developed through recurring interactions of criminal justice administrators may become more influential than any other element in the administrative setting, including the personal values of individual administrators, the administrative ethos of the "sponsoring organizations" of the workgroup members, and the character of the local community. Not surprisingly, the studies suggest that the workgroup influence tends to be at its highest where the group of interacting participants is small, stable, and homogeneous. Those qualities are most often found in courthouse workgroups in small communities, where there is likely to be only one or two judges, a prosecutor's office with no more than a few attorneys, a defense bar that is only slightly larger, and a social setting that produces ties beyond the courtroom. However, stability and smallness, if not homogeneity, can also be found even in courts of the largest cities. Under fairly common assignment systems that give trial judges long term assignments to the criminal division and prosecutors and public defenders fairly long term assignments to the courtroom of a particular judge, the same handful of persons will be interacting with each other on a daily basis month after month.

5.   _Community variations._ Many elements of the administrative structure of the criminal justice process clearly are aimed at ensuring that the local community has a substantial input in shaping the enforcement of the criminal law to suit its needs and values. Primary administrative responsibility is placed in units of local government, and with respect to the police, fragmentation is carried to the point where even the smallest local governmental units have their own police agency. The key administrative officials are either themselves elected (as in the case of sheriffs, judges, and prosecutors) or appointed by local elected officials (as in the case of the local police departments). Although the local officials are bound to follow state law, broad grants of discretionary authority provide substantial leeway for administrative variations that reflect the differences in local communities.

The success of such structural arrangements in ensuring responsiveness to the local community is a matter of ongoing debate. Some commentators contend that the bearing of community values on discretionary decisionmaking is insubstantial, as compared to the influence of the internal values of agency bureaucracies and interacting workgroups. They acknowledge that in small insular communities, the dominant community values are likely to have a bearing upon discretionary decisionmaking at every stage in the process. However, in the larger communities, with a more divergent population, they see community values as having a significant impact only for those exceptional cases that touch a special nerve in the community as a whole or in a particular segment of the community that is politically potent. In the everyday administration of justice, a combination of developments—including, most notably, the removal of politics from the selection process for various officials, an increased tendency of the public to defer to claims of "professional expertise," and the decrease in the visibility of performance to the general public—are said to have largely insulated administrators from the will of the community. Other commentators contend that community values continue to exercise considerable influence over criminal justice administration even in mid-sized and large communities. They argue that responsiveness to the community is not keyed to political vulnerability, and that administrators, even when shielded by the low visibility of their actions and the protection of civil service, will nonetheless feel constrained to act in accord with the dominant values of the local community. Moreover, they conclude that those values will differ in many specifics even when the communities share the same general attitudes on crime control, and that those differences will be reflected in distinctive styles of administration that vary from one community to another.

SECTION 3. THE STEPS IN THE PROCESS

This section presents an overview of the procedural steps that carry the process from start to finish in an individual case. The basic objectives of the overview are to position each step within the typical progression of the process, to introduce the relevant terminology, and to briefly describe what occurs at each step. This information should provide a useful backdrop for the discussion in later chapters. An additional objective is to provide the reader with a general indication of the significance of each step as measured by its quantitative impact.[a] Though lawyers typically approach an issue from the perspective of its bearing upon the individual case, they also must keep in mind the systemic implications of the issue as it relates to the administration of the process in general, and those implications clearly include a quantitative element.[b]

Our overview is limited in scope. First, it focuses on the processing only of

a. For each stage in the process, our overview relies upon such statistics as are available regarding the use and outcome of the procedures applied at that stage. For citations to the sources of these statistics, see CRIMPROC § 1.3. Criminal justice statistics usually are collected by for a particular unit of government (e.g., city, county, or state) or a special grouping of units (e.g., 75 largest counties) and rarely are parallel statistics available for all units throughout the nation. Accordingly, the statistics cited should not be viewed as representative of the practice throughout the nation, but only as rough generalization for the type of unit that provides the statistics (typically, large urban counties).

b. As many commentators have noted, the overall quantitative "shape" of the process is that of a funnel. More crimes are reported than investigated, more investigated than arrests made, more persons arrested than charged, more charged than convicted, and more convicted than sentenced to incarceration. An extreme example of this "funnel effect," as to felonies, is illustrated by one author's analysis of the "statistics for New York City" in 1988. These statistics started with 550,000 felonies reported to police (evidencing, perhaps, one million felonies committed), 124,000 arrests on felony charges, 35,000 felony indictments, 27,800 felony convictions, and 16,755 persons "sent to jail or prison".

felony offenses, excluding the far more common misdemeanor offenses.[c] At almost every stage of the process, both the law and practice produce significant distinctions in the processing of persons as to misdemeanor and felony charges.[d] Second, as to felonies, distinctions are often drawn between capital and non-capital felonies, but the overview considers only the non-capital felony.

Third, the overview does not take account of many possible variations in chronology. It provides a single chronology as representative of that followed in the majority of felony cases in most jurisdictions. Thus, prosecutorial screening is placed after the arrest, although certain types of cases commonly lead to the prosecutor setting the charge before the police make an arrest. So too, the very division of the process into separate steps suggests a separation in timing which does not always exist. While some steps have definite starting and ending points, others may be continuing and often overlap later steps. Investigatory procedures, for example, do not always stop with the filing of charges, but may continue through to the initiation (and sometimes the end) of the trial.

Step 1: The Reported Crime. Descriptions of the sequence of events in the criminal justice process commonly start with the commission of a crime. Our focus, however, is on the major steps taken in the *administration* of the process. From that perspective, the starting point ordinarily is the event that brings to the attention of the police the possible commission of a crime, for it is that event which commonly triggers the enforcement process. Police may learn about possible crimes from reports of citizens (usually victims), discovery in the field (usually observation on patrol), or from investigative and intelligence work. Where the police conclude that a crime may well have been committed, it will be recorded as a "reported crime" or "known offense." This record-keeping function has no legal significance with respect to further police action; police are not required to investigate further because a crime is recorded as a "known offense" and they are

c. The federal system and roughly half of the states classify as felonies all crimes punishable by a maximum term of imprisonment of more than one year; crimes punishable by imprisonment for one year or less are then misdemeanors. Most of the remaining jurisdictions look to the location of the possible imprisonment: if the crime is potentially punishable by incarceration in a penitentiary, it is a felony; if punishable only by a jail term, it is a misdemeanor. As a matter of practice, both dividing lines produce the same result since the corrections codes in the latter jurisdictions commonly tie possible imprisonment in a penitentiary to a maximum incarceration term exceeding one year.

The ratio of misdemeanors to felonies varies with the stage of the process, but apart from the federal system, all jurisdictions report misdemeanors vastly outnumbering felonies in arrests, prosecutions, and convictions. Thus, in a typical state system, roughly 60–80% of all arrests will be for misdemeanors, with more arrests for the misdemeanor of driving-under-the-influence than for any other offense. The percentage of all prosecutions that are for misdemeanors tends to be even higher, as does the percentage of all convictions that are for misdemeanors.

d. At the investigative stage, many jurisdictions draw a distinction in arrest authority between felonies and misdemeanors, and the release of the individual upon issuance of a summons or citation, as the alternative to an arrest, is far more common for misdemeanors. At the pretrial stage, differences in processing misdemeanors include: utilizing the complaint as the charging instrument; not requiring the screening of either a grand jury or a magistrate at a preliminary hearing; far more common pretrial release on personal recognizance; and separate (and often narrower) standards governing such defense rights as pretrial discovery and appointment of counsel to assist the indigent. At the trial stage, differences commonly include: trial before a magistrate court; a smaller (6–person) jury; and where the magistrate court is not of record, a trial without a jury followed by a right of a convicted defendant to a de novo jury trial in a court of general jurisdiction.

In some states, misdemeanors carrying more significant penalties (e.g., 6 months imprisonment or more) are lumped together with felonies and the pretrial and trial distinctions noted above apply primarily to lower-level misdemeanors. Municipal ordinances violations which carry misdemeanor penalties (common where ordinances duplicate misdemeanor offenses) are treated as misdemeanors in many states, but other states treat ordinance violations as quasi-criminal, resulting in further procedural distinctions.

not prevented from seeking to obtain information where they do not have knowledge of an offense. The long standing tradition of police departments, however, is to devote the vast bulk of their investigative efforts to solving "known offenses."

Step 2: Prearrest Investigation. Various distinctions are used in grouping prearrest investigatory procedures, but the most common are the agency involved (distinguishing primarily between the investigative activities of the police and the prosecutor) and the focus of the procedure (distinguishing primarily between activities aimed at solving known crimes and activities aimed at anticipated crimes). Those distinctions create three basic groups of prearrest investigative procedures: (1) police procedures that are aimed at solving specific past crimes known to the police (commonly described as "reactive" investigative procedures), (2) police procedures that are aimed at anticipated ongoing and future criminal activity (commonly described as "proactive" procedures), and (3) prosecutorial and other non-police investigations conducted primarily through the use of subpoena authority. Each of these groups is discussed below, but initially note should be taken of the large number of arrests made by police with little or no prearrest investigation.

"On–Scene Arrests." A substantial percentage of arrests for a wide range of crimes are of the "on-scene" variety. These are arrests made during the course of the crime or immediately thereafter, either at the place where the crime occurred or in its immediate vicinity. Ordinarily, on-scene arrests will be based on the officer's own observation (leading to the alternative description of such arrests as "on-view"), although they will sometimes be based on the direction of a witness who has just viewed the crime. For some offenses, on-scene arrests typically are the product of proactive investigative activities designed to place the police in a position where the officer will be able to view the crime as it is committed. That usually is the case, for example, with so-called "victimless" crimes (i.e., crimes which do not involve an interaction with a victim, such as possession of a weapon, and crimes which ordinarily involve willing participants, such as vice crimes or narcotics-transfer offenses).

For most felony offenses, on-scene arrests typically come about with basically no investigative activity beyond the immediate response to the event that calls the commission of the crime to the officer's attention. Thus, a prompt response to a victim's call for assistance or a burglar alarm may place the officer in a position to make an arrest while the crime is in progress or immediately following its completion. So too, the officer may simply come across a crime, open to view, in the course of regular patrol activities. For felonies that are not readily solved through the subsequent investigation of a reported crime, such on-scene arrests can constitute a substantial portion of all arrests. Thus, one study indicated that 42% of all arrests for nonviolent property crimes (basically theft and burglary) were made within 5 minutes of the commission of the offense. Indeed, even as to robberies and other violent crimes involving interaction with a victim, where there is a better chance of later solving the offense because the victim has seen the offender (and may be able to provide a useful description), as many as a quarter of all arrests may be made within 5 minutes of the commission of the offense.

Reactive Investigations. Where the police learn of the previous commission of a crime, but are not in the position to make an "on-scene" arrest, their responsibility then is to "solve" that crime. This involves (1) determining whether there actually was a crime committed, (2) if so, determining who committed the crime, (3) collecting evidence of that person's guilt, and (4) locating the offender so that he can be taken into custody. Investigations directed at performing these crime-solving functions commonly are described as "reactive" or "retrospective" in nature because they focus on past criminal (or presumably criminal) activity. They reflect what is characterized as an "incident-driven" or "complaint-responsive" style of policing, which has long dominated the deployment of police investigative resources.

A wide variety of investigative activities may be utilized prearrest in the course of a reactive investigation. These include: (1) the interviewing of victims; (2) the interviewing of witnesses at the crime scene; (3) canvassing the neighborhood for (and interviewing) other witnesses; (4) the interviewing of suspects, which may require a physical stopping of the suspect on the street and a frisking of the suspect (i.e., pat-down of the outer clothing) for possible weapons; (5) the examination of the crime scene and the collection of physical evidence found there; (6) checking departmental records and computer files; (7) seeking information from informants; (8) searching for physical evidence of the crime (e.g., stolen property or weapons) in places accessible to the suspect (e.g., his home or automobile) and seizing any evidence found there; (9) surveillance of a suspect (including electronic surveillance) aimed at obtaining leads to evidence or accomplices; and (10) using undercover operatives to gain information from the suspect. As to some of these techniques, the law imposes certain prerequisites (e.g., probable cause for a search) and as to the search of a home (and electronic eavesdropping), it commonly requires prior authorization by a court (in the form of a search warrant, typically issued by a magistrate). As to other techniques, such as canvassing the neighborhood and checking records, the police are free to utilize the technique whenever they choose to do so.

A variety of factors will determine which of the investigative practices noted above will be used in a particular investigation. One of the most important is the investigative direction suggested by those "traces" of the crime that are immediately available to the police. In some instances, the limitations of available traces foreclose the use of a particular investigative practice. Any attempt to interview suspects depends upon the presence of some trace (e.g., a witness who can describe the criminal or a unique modus operandi) that allows for the designation of a manageable group of persons who might be considered possible suspects. A search for physical evidence only makes sense if the traces indicate that the criminal activity was of a type which might produce such evidence. In other instances, though the available traces will not absolutely rule out the use of a particular investigative practice, they suggest that the likelihood of gaining useful information will be so remote that the time, energy, and financial costs involved simply do not make use of that practice worthwhile. There is almost always some possibility, for example, that canvassing the neighborhood will produce a witness who saw the offender, but police frequently will not canvass for witnesses unless there is a fairly substantial likelihood that such a person might be found.

In general, the strength and nature of the available leads will determine the scope of the investigation, but other factors may alter that natural correlation. A more serious offense may lead police to utilize a technique that would be rejected as to a less serious crime because it is not sufficiently likely to be successful. A technique less likely to be successful may be chosen over one more likely to be successful because the latter simply is not available under the law without stronger leads and the former presents no legal difficulties. In such a situation, the second-choice procedure hopefully will produce additional information that will enable the police legally to use their first choice, but that strategy may not be successful and the investigation may end without the police ever using the preferred procedure.

Where the traces of the crime are very weak and the offense is not of an especially serious nature, the police are likely to terminate their investigation after having done little more than interview the victim and any other witnesses available at the scene. Police are aware that, for most crimes, the odds of arresting the offender are slim unless there are witnesses at the scene who can provide information that either specifically identifies the offender or makes that identification readily determinable. While the absence of such information from witnesses will not necessarily lead to an immediate termination of the investigation, it will certainly work against a substantial extension of the investigation (unless further steps are especially fruitful). The end result is that for a great many crimes, including even offenses as serious as burglary, very little is done besides interviewing the person reporting the crime.

While the variation among investigations is far too great to characterize any single combination of investigative procedures as "typical," even for a particular type of offense, it is clear that prearrest investigations rarely take on the characteristics of popularized depictions of the crime solving process. In general, investigations do not involve the use of scientific methods of investigation, confrontations with crafty criminals, or reliance upon informants. A study of robbery and burglary investigations found, for example, that the interviewing of the victim and the examination of the crime scene were by far the most common steps in the prearrest process. Aside from the canvassing for and interviewing of additional witnesses, no other procedure was used in as many as a third of all cases. In burglary cases, two of the departments surveyed reported that evidence was collected at the scene of the crime only in roughly 15% of all investigations. The frequency of interviews of suspects varied considerably among the different departments, but even as to robberies (where victims were more likely to identify a specific suspect), such interviews occurred in less than 25% of all cases. Interviews of informants occurred in less than 5% of all investigations. Other sources, bearing upon all types of investigations, indicate that prearrest searches of premises are even rarer. The most complete data on the use of an investigative procedure is for non-consensual electronic eavesdropping (primarily telephone wiretapping). That procedure is used in less than a thousand instances annually throughout the United States.

Proactive Investigations. General purpose police agencies, who employ over 85% of all full-time police officers in this country, devote the vast majority of their investigative efforts to the solving of known crimes. However, those agencies also have a long tradition of engaging as well in proactive investigations, and in recent years, many local police agencies have sought to make greater use of proactive investigative procedures. Also, many special-function police agencies (such as the federal Drug Enforcement Administration) traditionally have devoted a substantial portion of their resources to proactive investigations.

Proactive investigations are aimed at uncovering criminal activity that is not specifically known to the police. The investigation may be aimed at placing the police in a position where they can observe ongoing criminal activity that otherwise would both be hidden from public view and not reported (as typically is the case with the continuing possession of contraband). It may be aimed at inducing persons who have committed crimes of a certain type, including many unknown to the police, to reveal themselves (as in a "fencing sting"). Proactive investigations also often are aimed at anticipating future criminality and placing police in a position to intercept when the crime is attempted. Here, the investigative technique may be designed simply to gain information that will permit the police to predict when and where a crime is likely to be committed, or it may be designed to "instigate" or "induce" the criminal attempt at a particular time and place by creating a setting likely to spur into action those prone to criminality.

A variety of different procedures may be used in a proactive investigation, with the choice of procedure largely tied to the specific objective of the investigation. Deception is a common element of many proactive procedures. In traditional undercover operations, the police assume a false identity and present themselves as willing to participate in criminal activities (as where undercover agents "set up" fencing operations or narcotics transactions). So too, deception is the key to a "decoy tactic" of providing what appears to be an easy target for victimization (e.g., a drunk with an exposed wallet or a business of the type that is readily subject to extortion). Where police utilize as informants persons whose activities expose them to a criminal milieu, they are counting on the criminals associating with those persons believing that they will be discrete (usually because the persons are themselves engaged in criminal activity, gain their livelihood in part from criminals, or have social ties to the criminals). Surveillance through stake-outs, covert patrols, and electronic monitoring also rests on deception by hiding the surveillance.

Other proactive techniques rely on intrusive confrontations designed to place police in a position where they can observe what otherwise would be hidden or to elicit nervous or unthinking incriminatory responses that will provide a legal grounding for taking further investigative action (e.g., an arrest or stop). Thus, police following an aggressive motorized patrol strategy will fully utilize traffic laws to maximize stops of motorists, thereby gaining greater opportunity to peer into car windows, to ask questions, and to request consent to a search of the vehicle. Similarly, under a practice of heavy field interrogation, police will frequently approach pedestrians and initiate questions to determine who they are and what they are doing. Such intrusive confrontations are most often used on a selective basis, with police concentrating their efforts on those characteristics of the social environment that suggest to them possible criminality (e.g., high-crime neighborhood, suspicious class of persons, unusual behavior).[e] In general, proactive procedures are more resource intensive, more intrusive, arguably more likely to foster community opposition, and clearly pose more legal problems than typical reactive procedures.

Prosecutorial Investigations. Not all prearrest investigations are conducted by police. For certain types of crimes, and for certain types of traces of crime, the best investigatory tool is the subpoena—a court order directing a person to appear in a particular proceeding for the purpose of testifying and presenting specified physical evidence (e.g., documents) within his possession. The subpoena authority generally is available for the investigation of crime only through the grand jury, although other agencies may be able to use it to investigate specific types of crimes in particular jurisdictions. The grand jury, though it tends to be known more for its screening function in reviewing the prosecution's decision to charge (see step 11), also has authority to conduct investigations into the possible commission of crimes within the judicial district in which it sits. In carrying out this function, the grand jurors, being a group of laypersons with no special expertise in investigation, quite naturally rely heavily on the direction provided by their legal advisor, who is the prosecutor. Thus, grand jury investigations become, for all practical purposes, investigations by the prosecutor.

Compared to police investigations, grand jury investigations are expensive, time consuming, and logistically cumbersome. Accordingly, they usually are reserved for special settings where a grand jury investigation has a distinctive advantage over a police investigation. Typically, those settings involving crimes of public corruption (e.g., bribery), misuse of economic power (e.g., price-fixing), and widespread distribution of illegal services or goods (e.g., organized crime operations). With the exception of the federal system, those offenses provide only a

e. Thus, a national driver survey indicates that the percentage of driver stops leading to a search of the car or person is less than 7% (with roughly a third of those searches based on driver consent), although that produces roughly 1.3 million searches out of roughly 19.3 million driver stops.

minute portion of all reported offenses or prosecutions, suggesting that grand jury investigations are used in a fraction of 1% of all criminal investigations.

Step 3: Arrest. Once a police officer has obtained sufficient information to justify arresting a suspect (i.e., probable cause to believe that person has committed a crime), the arrest ordinarily becomes the next step in the criminal justice process. The term "arrest" is defined differently for different purposes. We refer here only to the act of taking a person into custody for the purpose of charging that person with a crime (the standard commonly used in the reporting of arrest statistics). This involves the detention of the suspect (by force if necessary) for the purpose of first transporting him to a police facility and then requesting that charges be filed against him. Where there is no immediate need to arrest a suspect, an officer may seek to obtain an arrest warrant (a court order, typically issued by a magistrate, authorizing the arrest) prior to taking the person into custody. To obtain a warrant, the police must make a showing of probable cause, either by affidavits or live testimony of either the investigating officer or a witness (usually the victim). Arrests also can be made without a warrant, and that is the dominant practice for felony arrests in the state systems (with some variation from community to community, but typically with warrants used for less than 10% of all felony arrests).

Step 4: Booking. Immediately after making an arrest, the arresting officer usually will search the arrestee's person and remove any weapons, contraband, or evidence relating to a crime. If the arrested person was driving a vehicle, the officer may also search the passenger compartment of the vehicle for the same items. The arrestee will then be taken, either by the arresting officer or other officers called to the scene, to the police station, a centrally located jail, or some similar "holding" facility. It is at this facility that the arrestee will be taken through a process known as "booking." Initially, the arrestee's name, the time of his arrival, and the offense for which he was arrested are noted in the police "blotter" or "log." This is strictly a clerical procedure, and it does not control whether the arrestee will be charged or what charge might be brought. As part of the booking process, the arrestee also will be photographed and fingerprinted.[f]

Following booking, a person arrested on a low-level felony offense may be able to gain his release upon posting a cash security deposit ("stationhouse bail") with the police. Persons arrested for more serious offenses, and those eligible for stationhouse bail but lacking the resources, will remain at the holding facility until presented before a magistrate (see step 9). Ordinarily they will be placed in a "lockup," which usually is some kind of cell. Before entering the lockup, they will be subjected to another search, more thorough than that conducted at the point of arrest. This search is designed primarily to inventory the arrestee's personal belongs and to prevent the introduction of contraband into the lockup.

Step 5: Post–Arrest Investigation. The initial post-arrest investigation by the police consists of the search of the person (and possibly the interior of the automobile) as discussed above. The extent of any further post-arrest investigation will vary with the fact situation. In some cases, such as where the arrestee was caught "red-handed," there will be little left to be done. In others, police will utilize many of the same kinds of investigative procedures as are used before arrest (e.g., interviewing witnesses, searching the suspect's home, and viewing the

---

f. A substantial percentage of all felony arrestees (e.g., 10–15%) will be subject to the juvenile justice system, with that percentage varying considerably with the offense. Ordinarily, juvenile arrestees will be separated from adult arrestees shortly after they are taken into custody, and will be processed through the juvenile justice system. However, where the juvenile court may waive its jurisdiction, a small percentage of the juveniles (e.g., 5%) will later be returned to the regular criminal justice process and be prosecuted as adults. From this point onward, we assume that the juveniles have been removed from the process.

scene of the crime). Post-arrest investigation does offer one important investigative source, however, that ordinarily is not available prior to the arrest—the person of the arrestee. Thus, the police may seek to obtain an eyewitness identification of the arrestee by placing him in a lineup, having the witness view him individually (a "showup"), or taking his picture and showing it to the witness (usually with the photographs of several other persons in a "photographic lineup"). They may also require the arrestee to provide handwriting or hair samples that can be compared with evidence the police have found at the scene of the crime. The arrest similarly facilitates questioning the arrestee at length about either the crime for which he was arrested or other crimes thought to be related (although warnings must be given prior to the custodial interrogation).

Although we do not have precise data on the use of these post-arrest procedures involving the arrestee, the best available estimates indicate they are not utilized in the vast majority of cases. In most communities, they are used almost exclusively in the investigation of felony cases and even then their use is tied to need and likely success. Eyewitness identification, for example, is not sought where there were no eyewitnesses, where an eyewitness was well acquainted with the arrestee, or where the officer observed the crime and immediately thereafter made the arrest. Police more frequently seek to engage felony arrestees in sustained interrogation, but in many police departments, a substantial portion of all felony arrestees (in some departments, even a majority) are either never questioned or simply given warnings and asked if they desire to make a statement.

Step 6: The Decision to Charge. The initial decision to charge a suspect with the commission of a crime ordinarily comes with the decision of a police officer to arrest the suspect. That decision will subsequently be reviewed, first by the police and then by the prosecutor. As discussed in step 9, the arrestee must be brought before a magistrate within a relatively short period (typically 24 or 48 hours), and prior to that point, the charges against the arrestee must be filed with the magistrate. It is during this period that the police will review the arresting officer's initial decision to charge. The prosecutor's review of the decision to charge often occurs during this same period, but prosecutorial review is, in any event, an ongoing process. Whether or not the charges were initially reviewed before being filed, they remain subject to review (and possible rejection) by the prosecutor up to and through the trial. Thus, the decision to charge a person with a crime may be seen as having four components: (1) the decision of the investigating officer to arrest and charge; (2) the police review of that decision prior to filing charges; (3) possible prosecutorial review prior to filing; and (4) ongoing prosecutorial review after the filing. The first component has already been noted in step (3) (the arrest), and we consider here the remaining three.

Pre–Filing Police Screening. Sometime between the booking of the arrestee and the point at which the arrestee is to be taken before the magistrate, there will be an internal police review of a warrantless arrest. Ordinarily that occurs shortly after the booking, when the arresting officer prepares an arrest report to be given to his or her supervisor. The supervisor may approve the bringing of charges at the level recommended in the police report, raise or reduce the level of the recommended charges, or decide against bringing charges. A decision not to bring charges ordinarily will be based on the supervisor's conclusion either that the evidence is insufficient to charge or that the offense can more appropriately be handled by a "stationhouse adjustment."[g] If the supervising officer decides

---

g. In some instances, the arresting officer's primary purpose in making the arrest may not have been prosecution, but an objective such as terminating a potentially inflammatory situation through the removal of the arrestee, placing pressure on the arrestee to furnish information relating to some other investigation, or simply providing a "warning" to a person suspected of low-level participation in ongoing criminality. The stationhouse adjustment is

against prosecution, the arrestee will be released from the lockup on that officer's direction (though some departments follow the practice of seeking prosecutor approval before releasing any felony arrestees). Studies that track the attrition of felony arrests indicate that police are likely to decide against proceeding in the range 4–10% of those arrests.

Pre–Filing Prosecutor Screening. Prosecutors' offices vary substantially in their approach to pre-filing review of the decision to charge. Typically, prosecutors will screen the vast majority of the felony charges, but there are jurisdictions in which prosecutors review only the most serious felony charges before they are filed. In these jurisdictions, the primary prosecutorial screening of felony charges ordinarily occurs sometime between the first appearance and the preliminary hearing or grand jury review (see steps 9 and 10 infra). Prosecutors' offices also vary as to the information that typically will be considered in pre-filing screening. Some will utilize only the police officer's arrest report. Others will regularly interview the arresting officer and some will also insist upon interviewing the victim in certain types of felony cases. The screening prosecutor may accept the charge recommended by the police, raise or reduce that charge, request that the police obtain further evidence (which may require releasing the arrestee at this point and then rearresting him when and if that evidence is obtained), decide against prosecution if the arrestee will participate in a diversion program, or simply decide against prosecution without condition.

A prosecutorial decision not to proceed commonly is described as a "rejection," "declination" or "no-paper" decision. The leading statistical studies on pre-charge prosecutor review have sorted out 6 major grounds for that decision. These are: (1) insufficient evidence; (2) witness difficulties; (3) due process problems (e.g., critical evidence was obtained illegally and will not be admissible at trial); (4) adequate disposition will be provided by other criminal proceedings (e.g., prosecution by another jurisdiction, probation revocation, or prosecution for another offense); (5) the "interests of justice" (a determination that prosecution is not appropriate even though proof of guilt is not troublesome); and (6) anticipated use of a diversion program.[h] The first two grounds are the most frequently cited.

As one might expect from the differences among prosecutors' offices in the proportion of arrests reviewed pre-filing, the differences in the depth of such review, and the subjective nature of many of the grounds for declining prosecution, studies reveal considerable variation from one community to another in the impact of pre-filing prosecutorial screening. Thus, a study of 13 urban prosecutorial districts found that the percentage of felony arrests that did not result in charges ranged from a low of 0% (in a jurisdiction which apparently did no pre-filing screening) to a high of 38%. The most comprehensive study, covering six states, reported a pre-filing rejection rate of 11%.

Once the prosecutor decides to charge, a series of other decisions must be made. First, the prosecutor must determine whether the appropriate level of the charge is that recommended by the police. Prosecutors most often reduce the recommended charge because they believe that the evidence only supports a lower

likely to be tied to that objective and therefore can consist of no more than an admonishment and release, or an agreement not to proceed in exchange for information.

h. A diversion program offers the arrestee the opportunity to avoid conviction if he or she is willing to perform prescribed "rehabilitative steps" (e.g., making restitution to the victim, undertaking a treatment program). The diversion agreement operates, in effect, to place the arrestee on a probationary status without con-viction. Diversion tends to be used far more sparingly for felonies than misdemeanors. A study of 13 urban prosecutorial districts found that all but two of the districts placed on diversion no more than 6% of their felony arrestees. Typically, the felony arrestees placed on diversion are first-offenders charged with non-violent offenses (resulting in a higher percentage of felony diversions where offenses such as passing worthless checks are felonies).

charge, but reductions also may be based on the prosecutor's determination that the penalty for the higher charge is too severe for the nature of the crime or that the additional process costs involved in proceeding on a felony charge (rather than a misdemeanor charge) are not justified. In some offices, certain felony offenses are viewed as so clearly overgraded legislatively as to necessitate almost automatic reductions on arrests for that offense (e.g., where shoplifting is a felony and all first offender cases are reduced to misdemeanor petty larceny charges). Second, where the offender is subject to multiple charges, the prosecution must determine whether each charge should be brought separately or the multiple charges should be combined (and subsequently tried together). In some instances, the law may require that charges arising from the same criminal episode be brought together, but the prosecution often has discretion to treat separately each charge. Where multiple parties were involved, the prosecutor also often has the discretion to either charge the accomplices together (typically leading to a single trial) or to charge them separately (typically leading to separate trials). Finally, as to offenses committed in more than one place, the prosecution may be able to choose between different judicial districts as the site for filing the charge.

Post–Filing Prosecutor Screening. Post-filing prosecutorial review of the charging decision is inherent in the many post-filing procedures that require the prosecutor to review the facts of the case. If the prosecutor should determine that the charge is not justified, a dismissal can be obtained through a *nolle prosequi* motion (noting the prosecutor's desire to relinquish prosecution), which ordinarily will be granted in a perfunctory fashion by the court. Similarly, if the prosecutor considers the charge to be too high, a motion can be entered to reduce the charges. In deciding whether to make such motions, the prosecutor will look to basically the same grounds that might justify a pre-filing rejection or reduction of the charge recommended by the police. Even where a charge was carefully screened and approved prior to filing, post-filing review can readily lead to a contrary conclusion as circumstances change (e.g., evidence becomes unavailable) or the prosecutor learns more about the facts of the case. Of course, where the charge was not previously screened or was screened only on a skimpy arrest report, post-filing review is even more likely to lead to a decision to drop or reduce the charges.

Available statistics make it difficult to measure the precise impact of post-filing prosecutorial screening. Dismissal rates for a particular jurisdiction commonly will include both dismissals based on a prosecutor's decision that the case does not merit prosecution and dismissals that are a part of a negotiated plea. The same is also true of statistics on charge reductions made on motion of the prosecution. Studies on the attrition of felony arrests do indicate, however, that the combination of pre-filing review and post-filing review is likely to produce a total rejection rate in the neighborhood of 30–45% for a "typical" urban jurisdiction. As would be expected, a higher rate of rejection by *nolle* motions is likely to be found where there is only limited pre-filing screening. Thus a jurisdiction which screens out less than 10% of its felony arrests prior to charging is likely to have a dismissal rate (exclusive of plea-bargaining dismissals) that approximates 30%. A similar pattern is indicated for charge reductions, as jurisdictions with limited pre-filing screening tend to have a somewhat higher percentage of post-filing reductions of felonies to misdemeanors.

Step 7: Filing the Complaint. Assuming that the pre-filing screening results in a decision to prosecute, the next step is the filing of charges with the magistrate court. Typically, the initial charging instrument will be called a "complaint." The complaint serves to set forth the charges only before the magistrate court; for a felony, an information or indictment will replace the complaint as the charging instrument when the case reaches the general trial court.

For most offenses, the complaint will be a fairly brief document. Its basic function is to set forth concisely the allegation that the accused, at a particular time and place, committed specified acts constituting a violation of a particular criminal statute. The complaint will be signed by a "complainant," a person who swears under oath that he or she believes the factual allegations of the complaint to be true. The complainant usually will be either the victim or the investigating officer. When an officer-complainant did not observe the offense being committed, but relied on information received from the victim or other witnesses, the officer ordinarily will note that the allegations in the complaint are based on "information and belief." With the filing of the complaint, the person accused in the complaint will have become a "defendant" in a criminal proceeding.

Step 8: Magistrate Review of the Arrest. Following the filing of the complaint and prior to or at the start of the first appearance (see step 9), the magistrate must undertake what is often described as the "*Gerstein* review." As prescribed by the Supreme Court's decision in *Gerstein v. Pugh* (see § 3.5(a) infra), if a person was arrested without a warrant and remains in custody, the magistrate must determine that there exists probable cause for that person's continued detention. This ordinarily is an *ex parte* determination, similar to that made in the issuance of an arrest warrant and relying on the same sources of information. Where the arrest was made pursuant to a warrant, the judicial probable cause determination has already been made and a *Gerstein* review is not required. If the magistrate finds that probable cause has not been established, he will direct the prosecution to promptly produce more information or release the arrested person. Such instances are exceedingly rare, however.

Step 9: The First Appearance. Once the complaint is filed, the case is before the magistrate court, and the accused must appear before the court within a specified period. This appearance of the accused is usually described as the "first appearance," although the terminology varies, with jurisdictions also using "preliminary appearance," "initial presentment," "preliminary arraignment," "arraignment on the warrant," and "arraignment on the complaint." Where the accused was arrested and kept in custody (typically the case for the felony arrestee), he must be brought before the magistrate court "without unnecessary delay." Ordinarily, the time consumed in booking, transportation, limited post-arrest investigation, reviewing the decision to charge, and preparing and filing the complaint makes it unlikely that an arrestee will be presented before the magistrate until at least several hours after his arrest. Accordingly, if the magistrate court does not have an evening session, a person arrested in the afternoon or evening will not be presented before the magistrate until the next day. Many jurisdictions do not allow any longer detention than this, as they require that the first appearance be within 24 hours of the arrest. Others allow up to 48 hours for the first appearance, although that type of delay typically occurs only on weekends.

The first appearance often is a quite brief proceeding. Initially, the magistrate will make certain that the person before the court is the person named in the complaint. The magistrate then will inform the defendant of the charge in the complaint and will note various rights that the defendant may have in further proceedings. Commonly, the magistrate also will inform the defendant of his right to remain silent and warn him that anything he says in court or to the police may be used against him at trial. The magistrate also will advise the felony defendant of the next step in the process, the preliminary hearing, and will set a date for that hearing unless the defendant desires to waive it.

At least where the defendant is not accompanied by counsel, the magistrate will inform the defendant of his right to be represented by retained counsel, and, if indigent, his right to court appointed counsel. A sampling of felony defendants in the 75 largest counties indicated that approximately 80% receive court appointed attorneys. Three basic systems are used to provide counsel for indigent defendants: (1) representation by a state or county public defender agency; (2) the "assigned counsel" system under which the court selects a private attorney who is then compensated by the state according to a set fee schedule, with the selection (automatized in some judicial districts and ad hoc in others) coming from a list of attorneys who have expressed a willingness to accept appointments (and in some districts, also have met certain qualifications as to experience); and (3) a "contract system" under which a private law firm or a nonprofit organization (such as a bar association) contracts to provide representation for the bulk of the indigent defendants. The public defender system is dominant in metropolitan judicial districts; the assignment system dominant in less urbanized areas (although it also is used widely as a backup to the public defender system for cases in which a conflict prevents representation by a public defender); and the least favored contract system is used as the primary provider in a considerably smaller group of districts.

One of the most important first-appearance functions of the magistrate is to set bail (i.e., the conditions under which the defendant can obtain his release from custody pending the final disposition of the charges against him). At one time, bail was limited almost entirely to the posting of cash or a secured bond purchased from a professional bondsman. Today, those are only two of several alternatives available to the magistrate. Others are: (1) release upon a promise to appear (release on "personal recognizance"); (2) release on making a personal promise to forfeit a specified dollar amount upon a failure to appear (an "unsecured" personal bond); (3) release upon the imposition of one or more nonfinancial conditions (e.g., restrictions on defendant's associations or travel); and (4) the posting with the court of a percentage of the bail forfeiture amount (commonly 10%), which will be returned to the defendant if he appears as scheduled. In general, the magistrate is directed to impose such bail conditions as appear reasonably needed to assure that the defendant will make court appearances as scheduled throughout the proceedings.

If the accused is unable to meet the condition deemed needed to assure his appearance (e.g., is unable to meet required financial conditions), he will not be released. Roughly half of the fifty-two jurisdictions also allow for preventive detention—a procedure under which the magistrate orders that the accused be detained because no bail condition will provide satisfactory assurance against his commission of an offense posing danger to the community. A study of the nation's 75 largest counties found that 37% of all felony defendants were detained until the final disposition of their charges, and that percentage rose to 50% or above for those charged with murder, rape, or robbery. As for the felony defendants who were released, more were released on nonfinancial then on financial conditions alone. However, the persons released did not necessarily remain free, as a non-appearance rate of roughly 22% and a rearrest rate (for new offenses) of 16% led to revocation of bail for a significant number. Also, at the end of the year, 6% of those released were unapprehended fugitives.

Step 10: Preliminary Hearing. Following the first appearance, the next scheduled step in a felony case ordinarily is the preliminary hearing (sometimes called a preliminary "examination"). For various reasons, however, a preliminary hearing may not be held. Initially, in many jurisdictions, a substantial portion of the felony caseload will be disposed of during the period (usually one or two weeks) between the first appearance and the scheduled preliminary examination. Particularly, where the primary screening by the prosecutor occurs after the complaint is filed, a substantial number of felony charges are likely to be dismissed or reduced to a misdemeanor during this period. For those felony charges that remain, a substantial percentage of defendants (e.g., 30–50%) will waive their right to a preliminary hearing, usually because they intend to plead guilty. Finally, even though the defendant desires a preliminary hearing, state law commonly allows the prosecutor to bypass the hearing by immediately obtaining a grand jury indictment, and in some localities, prosecutors use that bypass authority with great frequency (see fn. i infra).

Where the preliminary hearing is held, it will provide, like grand jury review, a screening of the decision to charge by a neutral body. In the preliminary hearing, that neutral body is the magistrate, who must determine whether, on the evidence presented, there is probable cause to believe that defendant committed the crime charged. Ordinarily, the magistrate will already have determined that probable cause exists as part of the *ex parte* screening of the complaint (see step 8). The preliminary hearing, however, provides screening in an adversary proceeding in which both sides are represented by counsel. Jurisdictions vary in the evidentiary rules applicable to the preliminary hearing, but most require that the parties rely primarily on live witnesses rather than affidavits. Typically, the prosecution will present its key witnesses and the defense will limit its response to the cross-examination of those witnesses. The defendant has the right to present his own evidence at the hearing, but conventional defense strategy advises against possibly helping the prosecution prepare for trial by presenting its witnesses and subjecting them to cross-examination at this pretrial stage.

If the magistrate concludes that the evidence presented establishes probable cause, she will "bind the case over" to the next stage in the proceedings. In an indictment jurisdiction (see step 11), the case is boundover to the grand jury, and in an "information jurisdiction" (see step 12), the case is boundover directly to the general trial court. If the magistrate finds that the probable cause supports only a misdemeanor charge, she will reject the felony charge and allow the prosecutor to substitute the lower charge, which will then be set for trial in the magistrate court. If the magistrate finds that the prosecution's evidence does not support any charge, she will order that the defendant be released. The rate of dismissals at the preliminary hearing quite naturally varies with the degree of previous screening exercised by the prosecutor. In a jurisdiction with fairly extensive screening, the percentage of dismissals is likely to fall in the range of 5–10% of the hearings held. However, in jurisdictions in which the hearings are more sparingly utilized, the dismissal rules can readily be in the range of 20–30%.

Step 11: Grand Jury Review. Although almost all American jurisdictions have provisions authorizing grand jury screening of felony charges, such screening is mandatory only in those jurisdictions requiring felony prosecutions to be instituted by an indictment, a charging instrument issued by the grand jury. Eighteen states, the federal system, and the District of Columbia currently require grand jury indictments for all felony prosecutions (unless waived by the defendant). Four additional states require prosecution by indictment only for felonies subject to the most severe punishment (life imprisonment and capital punishment). In the remaining states, the prosecution is allowed to proceed at its option either by indictment or by information, a charging instrument issued on the authority of the prosecutor. Because prosecutors here most often choose to proceed by information, these states are commonly described as "information states," while the jurisdictions mandating indictments are described as "indictment jurisdictions."

The grand jury is a group of private citizens, typically selected randomly from the same pool as petit jurors, but serving a longer term (typically, at least several months). Although the grand jury also participates in investigations directed by the prosecutor (see step 2 supra), its primary function in indictment jurisdictions is to review cases presented by the prosecutor and decide whether there is sufficient evidence to justify a trial on the charge sought by the prosecutor. This screening function is similar to that performed by the magistrate at a preliminary hearing,[i] but the grand jury's screening process is quite different from preliminary hearing screening. The grand jury meets in a closed session and hears only the evidence presented by the prosecution. The defendant has no right to offer his own evidence or to be present during grand jury proceedings. If a majority of the grand jurors conclude that the prosecution's evidence is sufficient, the grand jury will issue the indictment requested by the prosecutor. If the grand jury majority refuses to approve a proposed indictment, the charges against the defendant will be dismissed. In most indictment jurisdictions, grand juries refuse to indict in only a small percentage (e.g., 3 to 5%) of the cases presented before them.

    Step 12: The Filing of the Indictment or Information. If the prosecution was presented to the grand jury and an indictment was issued, it will be filed with the general trial court and will replace the complaint as the accusatory instrument in the case. If the prosecution is permitted by information (either because a grand jury indictment is not required or the defendant waived), that instrument will be filed with the trial court. In most "information states," the charge in the information must be supported by a preliminary hearing bindover (unless the preliminary hearing was waived), but several information states allow for "direct filing" by the prosecutor without either a bindover or a waiver.

    Step 13: Arraignment on the Information or Indictment. After the indictment or information has been filed, the felony defendant is arraigned—i.e., he is brought before the trial court, informed of the charges against him, and asked to enter a plea of guilty, not guilty, or, as is permitted under some circumstances, *nolo contendere*. In the end, most of those felony defendants whose cases reach the trial court will plead guilty. At the arraignment, however, they are likely to enter a plea of not guilty. Where there has not been a preliminary hearing, defense counsel probably will not be fully apprised of the strength of the prosecution's case at this point in the proceedings. Also, guilty pleas in felony cases commonly are the product of plea negotiations with the prosecution, and in many places, that process does not start until after the arraignment. When the defendant enters a plea of not guilty at the arraignment, the judge will set a trial date, but the usual expectation is that the trial will not be held.

    Between the arraignment and the scheduled trial date, four procedural actions will result in the termination of the vast majority of cases without trial. First, although there will have been extensive prosecutorial screening by this point, changed circumstances and new information typically will lead to dismissals on a prosecutor's *nolle prosequi* motion in roughly 5–15% of the cases. Second, a smaller percentage of the informations or indictments will be dismissed on the motion of the defense, as discussed in step 14. Third, a small percentage of cases will be dismissed on the court's own motion (or on the prosecutor's motion) to clear the docket of cases in which the defendant is unavailable for trial (e.g., is dead, has fled the jurisdiction, or is incarcerated elsewhere and cannot be

---

    i. The grand jury and the preliminary hearing are not necessarily alternative screening devices. In most information states, where the prosecution chooses the option of seeking a grand jury indictment, that selection is made to avoid a preliminary hearing. Thus, defendants in information states will have either a preliminary hearing (the usual situation) or a grand jury review (the unusual). Similarly, in some indictment jurisdictions, prosecution policy is almost always to proceed directly to the grand jury, thereby cutting off the preliminary hearing, and leaving the accused with only grand jury screening. However, in other indictment states, felony cases usually are presented first to a magistrate at a preliminary hearing (unless the defendant waives) and then to the grand jury, so defendants will receive the benefit of both screenings. The grand jury is in no way bound by any prior ruling at the preliminary hearing. It may indict even though the magistrate dismissed the charge at the preliminary hearing and may refuse to indict even though the magistrate found probable cause.

obtained). Finally, there will be guilty pleas, which account for the vast majority of all trial court dispositions without trial.

Guilty pleas in felony cases commonly will be entered in response to a plea agreement under which the prosecution offers certain concessions in return for the defendant's entry of the plea. Those concessions may take the form of a reduction of the charges (sometimes to a misdemeanor and sometimes to a lesser felony charge), a dismissal of related charges where the defendant faces multiple charges, a recommendation on sentence, or a specific sentence (when agreed to by the trial court). Plea bargaining varies considerably from one prosecutorial district to another. Prosecutors' offices differ as to the types of the concessions they will offer and their willingness to bargain over concessions (as opposed to presenting a take-it-or-leave-it offer). They also differ as to the types of cases in which they will offer concessions, with some generally refusing to do so on the most serious charges. Indeed, there are districts in which prosecutors will not plea bargain, although defendants here may still find an inducement to plead guilty in a general policy of trial judges to give favorable weight in sentencing to the defendant's willingness to plead guilty.

Although it is a rare prosecutorial district in which guilty pleas do not account for a majority of the trial court dispositions, the dominance of the guilty plea varies considerably from one prosecutorial district to another. In urban settings, the range of 60–85% guilty pleas covers most (but certainly not all) districts. Of course, when trial court dispositions by *nolle prosequi* motions and judicial dismissals are excluded, and only guilty pleas and trials are compared, the rate of guilty pleas will be much higher.[j] Thus, a leading study of 14 communities found a median ratio of 11 pleas for every trial, with one jurisdiction having as many as 37 pleas for each trial.

Step 14: Pretrial Motions. In most jurisdictions, a broad range of objections must be raised by a pretrial motion. Those motions include challenges to the institution of the prosecution (e.g., claims regarding the grand jury indictment process), challenges to the sufficiency of the charging instrument, challenges to the scope of the prosecution (joinder of charges and parties), challenges to the location and timing of the prosecution, claims that the government has violated discovery rules by failing to disclose evidence within its possession, and requests for the suppression of evidence allegedly acquired by the government through a constitutional violation. While some pretrial motions are made only by defendants who intend to go to trial, other motions (e.g., for further discovery) may benefit as well defendants who expect in the end to plead guilty. Nevertheless, pretrial motions are likely to be made in only a small portion of all felony cases before the trial court. Their use does vary considerably, however, with the nature of the case. In narcotics cases, for example, motions to suppress are quite common. In the typical forgery case, on the other hand, pretrial motions of any type are quite rare.

j. On the other hand, as discussed in the paragraph infra reviewing the disposition of all felony arrests (see step 15), guilty plea dispositions are considerably less dominant when one looks at the totality of dispositions, including those that occur without reaching the trial court. Since the dispositions that preclude cases reaching the trial court consist primarily of dismissals and refusals to proceed, a 85% rate of guilty pleas before the trial court hardly suggests an overall 85% guilty plea conviction rate as to all persons arrested on felony charges, or even as to all felony complaints filed.

In some districts, however, a significant portion of the dispositions before the magistrate do add to the number of guilty plea convictions. Here, plea bargaining begins while the case is before the magistrate and felony charges are often reduced to misdemeanor charges in return for a guilty plea entered before the magistrate (in contrast to the more common practice in which bargaining and entry of a plea to a reduced charge occurs before the trial court).

As a group, pretrial motions are likely to result in the dismissal of not more than 5% of all of the felony cases coming before the trial judge.

Step 15: The Trial. Assuming that there has not been a dismissal and the defendant has not entered a guilty plea (or a *nolle contendere* plea), the next step in the criminal process is the trial. In most respects, the criminal trial resembles the civil trial. There are, however, several distinguishing features that are either unique to criminal trials or of special importance in such trials. These include: (1) the presumption of defendant's innocence; (2) the requirement of proof beyond a reasonable doubt; (3) the right of the defendant not to take the stand; (4) the exclusion of evidence obtained by the state in an illegal manner; and (5) the more frequent use of incriminating statements of defendants.

As noted previously, a trial clearly is the exception rather than the general rule in the disposition of felony charges. Quite commonly, only 5–15% of the felony cases before the trial court actually will go to trial. The median time frame from the arrest of the defendant to the start of the trial will vary substantially from one community to another, but in congested urban districts, it is likely to fall within the range of 5–10 months. While most jurisdictions have speedy trials requirements that impose time limits of 6 months or less, there are various excludable time periods (for factors such as witness unavailability and the processing of motions) which commonly extend the time limit by at least a few months.

The trial itself tends to be relatively short. Most felony jury trials in state courts will be completed within 2–3 days. One variable will be the local practice governing *voir dire* (the questioning of prospective jurors, either by judge or counsel), as some jurisdictions tend to spend considerably more time on jury selection than others. Another will be the type of case, as certain types of offenses (e.g., complex white collar offenses and capital homicide cases) produce trials substantially longer than the typical felony. In general, trials to the bench are considerably shorter, and unlikely to last more than a day.

While the felony defendant universally has a right to a jury trial (typically before a 12–person jury), that right can be waived. The waiver percentage varies from one community to another, but the national average for bench trials in felony cases is roughly 30%. Whether a criminal case is tried to the bench or the jury, the odds favor conviction over acquittal. A fairly typical ratio for felony trials will be 3 convictions for every acquittal. That ratio may vary significantly, however, with the nature of the offense. In some jurisdictions, the rate of conviction at trial tends to be substantially lower (though still well above 50%) for some crimes (e.g., rape and murder) than for others (e.g., drug trafficking). In all but a few jurisdictions, the jury verdict, whether for acquittal or conviction, must be unanimous. Where the jurors cannot agree, no verdict is entered and the case may be retried. Such "hung juries" occur in only a very small percentage of the cases tried to a jury (e.g., 3–6%).

With the end of the trial stage, the criminal justice process will have produced a disposition as to all persons who originally entered the process through a felony arrest. Only one out of a hundred is likely to have had the case against him carried through to a trial that resulted in an acquittal. A much larger portion of the felony arrestees, roughly between 30–50% for most urban districts, also will not have been convicted, but the dispositions in their favor will have been produced without a trial—at the very outset, through pre-filing police and prosecutor screening, during subsequent magistrate or trial court proceedings, through *nolle prosequi* motions or judicial dismissals, or at grand jury screening. Of the 50–70% of the felony arrestees who will have been convicted, many will not have been convicted of felonies. Depending upon the plea negotiation practices followed in the particular jurisdiction, anywhere from 10–30% of those felony arrestees eventually convicted are likely to have been convicted of misdemeanors.

Step 16: Sentencing. Following conviction, the next step in the process is the determination of the sentence. In all but a few jurisdictions (which allow for jury sentencing, even apart from capital punishment), the sentence determination is the function of the court. Basically three different types of sentences may be used: (1) financial sanctions (e.g., fines, restitution orders); (2) some form of release into the community (e.g., probation, unsupervised release, house arrest); and (3) incarceration in a jail (for lesser sentences) or prison (for longer sentences). The process applied in determining the sentence is shaped in considerable part by the sentencing options made available to the court by the legislature. For a particular offense, the court may have no choice. The legislature may have prescribed that conviction automatically carries with it a certain sentence and there is nothing left for the court to do except impose that sentence. Most frequently, however, legislative narrowing of options on a particular offense does not go beyond eliminating the community release option (by requiring incarceration) and setting some limits on the use of those sanctions that remain available.

The sentence of incarceration for a felony offense probably presents the widest diversity of approach to judicial sentencing authority. The sentence may be indeterminate (setting a maximum and minimum term of imprisonment, with the parole board determining the actual release date within the span set by those two terms) or determinate (a set term, with the defendant required to serve a high percentage of that term, less credits for good behavior). In some jurisdictions, the court has complete discretion in setting the term or terms within its control. In others, however, sentencing guidelines direct the judge in exercising her authority, although departures from the guidelines are allowed upon a judicial finding of specific justification.

The process utilized in felony sentencing varies to some extent according to whether judicial discretion is broad or is channeled or limited by guideline or legislative reference to specific sentencing circumstances. In all jurisdictions, the process is designed to obtain for the court information beyond that which will have come to its attention in the course of trial or in the acceptance of a guilty plea. The primary vehicle here is the presentence report prepared by the probation department, although the prosecution and defense commonly will be allowed to present additional information and to challenge the information contained in the presentence report. The presentation of this information is not subject to the rules governing the presentation of information at trial. The rules of evidence do not apply, and neither side is given an automatic right to call witnesses or to cross-examine the sources of adverse information presented in the presentence report or in any additional documentation presented by the opposing side. However, where the sentencing authority of the judge is restricted by guidelines or legislative mandates that require findings of fact as to specific factors, the sentencing process tends to be more formal. Here, the court often will find it necessary to hold an evidentiary hearing and utilize trial-type procedures if the presence of a critical factor is controverted.

Although individual sentences quite naturally vary (with courts considering such case-specific factors as aggravating and mitigating circumstances, past criminal convictions, criminal behavior that did not result in a conviction, and the defendant's acceptance of responsibility), and sentencing patterns vary from one jurisdiction to another, studies of state sentences in felony cases suggest an overall pattern tied to the gravity of the crime for which the sentence is imposed. Felony arrestees convicted of lower-level felonies and plea-reduced misdemeanors commonly receive a limited sentence of incarceration (often to a short jail term), although a substantial proportion of such offenders (e.g., 30–40%) are likely to be sentenced only to probation (or another sentence not involving incarceration). Convictions for higher-level felonies typically produce sentences of incarceration in prison. For offenses such as burglary and drug trafficking, the proportion of offenders sentenced to prison is likely to approach or exceed 50%, with the remainder equally divided between jail sentences (often combined with probation) and straight probation. Serious violent crimes such as rape and robbery have the highest rate of prison sentences, ranging as high as 80%. While the terms will vary by offense and sentence structure, illustrative mean sentences for the offenses of robbery and rape, measured by time actually served, would be in the neighborhood of 29–41 months for robbery and 33–48 months for rape. Substantially longer terms will be imposed, however, where the defendant is proceeded against as a recidivist.

Step 17: Appeals. For criminal cases disposed of in the general trial court, the initial appeal is to the intermediate appellate court. If the state has no intermediate appellate court, then the initial and final appeal within the state system is to the state's court of last resort. Although all convicted defendants are entitled to appeal their convictions, appeals are taken predominantly by convicted defendants who were sentenced to imprisonment. In most jurisdictions, appeals challenging the conviction itself (rather than just the sentence) come primarily from imprisoned defendants who were convicted at trial (as opposed to those convicted on a guilty plea). In some jurisdictions, as many as 90% of the defendants who were convicted after trial and sentenced to prison will appeal their convictions. Even with almost automatic appeal by this group, however, the total number of appeals to the intermediate appeals court is likely to amount to less than 10% of all convictions entered by the state's general trial court. Where the jurisdiction provides for extensive appellate review of sentencing, that percentage is likely to be somewhat higher.

Defense success on appeal varies with the particular appellate court. State intermediate appellate courts commonly have a reversal rate on defense appeals of right in the 5–10% range, although some have higher rates when reversals in-part are included. Courts of last resort with discretionary jurisdiction are most likely to limit their review to close cases and therefore, may have a substantially higher rate of reversals.

Step 18: Postconviction Remedies. After the appellate process is exhausted, imprisoned defendants may be able to use postconviction remedies to challenge their convictions on limited grounds. In particular, federal postconviction remedies are available to state as well as federal prisoners to challenge their convictions in the federal courts on most constitutional grounds. In the year 2000, federal district courts received roughly 21,000 state-prisoner postconviction applications. Relief is granted on less than 3% of these petitions, however, and the relief often is limited to requiring a further hearing. In the state system, annual postconviction challenges typically fall below 5% of all felony filings.

Chapter 2

THE NATURE AND SCOPE OF FOUR-TEENTH AMENDMENT DUE PROCESS; RETROACTIVITY; THE FEDERAL "SUPERVISORY POWER"; STATE RIGHTS PROTECTIONS

SECTION 1. THE "ORDERED LIBERTY"—"FUNDAMENTAL FAIRNESS," "TOTAL INCORPORATION" AND "SELECTIVE INCORPORATION" THEORIES

In *Twining v. New Jersey*, 211 U.S. 78, 29 S.Ct. 14, 53 L.Ed. 97 (1908); *Palko v. Connecticut*, 302 U.S. 319, 58 S.Ct. 149, 82 L.Ed. 288 (1937); and *Adamson v. California*, 332 U.S. 46, 67 S.Ct. 1672, 91 L.Ed. 1903 (1947), the Court rejected the "total incorporation" view of the history of the Fourteenth Amendment, the view—which has never commanded a majority—that the Fourteenth Amendment made all of the provisions of the federal Bill of Rights fully applicable to the states.[a] But *Twining* recognized that "it is possible that some of the personal rights safeguarded by the first eight Amendments against National action may also be safeguarded against state action, because a denial of them would be a denial of due process of law." And the Court early found among the procedural requirements of Fourteenth Amendment due process certain rules paralleling provisions of the first eight amendments. For example, it held in *Powell v.*

---

a. *Palko*, which held that the Fourteenth Amendment did not encompass at least certain aspects of double jeopardy prohibition of the Fifth Amendment, was later overruled in *Benton v. Maryland*, 395 U.S. 784, 89 S.Ct. 2056, 23 L.Ed.2d 707 (1969). The position taken in *Twining* and *Adamson*—that the Fifth Amendment privilege against self-incrimination was not incorporated in the Fourteenth—was rejected in *Malloy v. Hogan* (1964), discussed below. *Griffin v. California*, Ch. 25, § 3, subsequently applied *Malloy* to overrule the specific holdings of *Twining* and *Adamson*, which had permitted comment on a state defendant's failure to take the stand. These later decisions, while overruling *Palko*, *Twining* and *Adamson*, were still consistent with the rejection of the "total incorporation" interpretation.

The total incorporation position had received its strongest support in the *Adamson* dissents. In the principal dissent, Justice Black, joined by Douglas, J., maintained that the history of the Fourteenth Amendment suggested its pur-

pose was to totally incorporate the federal Bill of Rights. Dissenting separately in *Adamson*, Justice Murphy, joined by Rutledge, J., "agree[d] that the specific guarantees of the Bill of Rights should be carried over intact into [the Fourteenth but was] not prepared to say that the latter is entirely and necessarily limited by the Bill of Rights. Occasions may arise where a proceeding falls so far short of conforming to fundamental standards of procedure as to warrant constitutional condemnation in terms of a lack of due process despite the absence of a specific provision of the Bill of Rights."

Responding to the dissents, Justice Frankfurter's concurring opinion in *Adamson* stressed the "independent potency" of the Fourteenth Amendment Due Process Clause, maintaining that that Amendment "neither comprehends the specific provisions by which the founders deemed it appropriate to restrict the federal government nor is confined to them."

30

Alabama (1932) (discussed at pp. 61, 65) that defendants in a capital case were denied due process when a state refused them the aid of counsel. "The logically critical thing, however," pointed out Justice Harlan years later, "was not that the rights had been found in the Bill of Rights, but that they were deemed [to] be fundamental." *Duncan v. Louisiana,* Ch. 23, § 1. (dissenting opinion joined by Stewart, J.).

Particular procedural safeguards included in the Bill of Rights were said to be applicable to the states if they were "implicit in the concept of ordered liberty," Cardozo J., in *Palko;* "of the very essence of a scheme of ordered liberty," ibid.; "a fair and enlightened system of justice would be impossible without them," ibid.; required by "the 'immutable principles of justice' as conceived by a civilized society," Frankfurter, J., concurring in *Adamson;* or "fundamental to the American scheme of justice," White, J., in *Duncan v. Louisiana.*

As Justice WHITE noted (fn. 14) for the Court in DUNCAN v. LOUISIANA, 391 U.S. 145, 88 S.Ct. 1444, 20 L.Ed.2d 491 (1968) (holding the Sixth Amendment right to jury trial applicable to the states via the Fourteenth), the different phraseology is not without significance:

"Earlier the Court can be seen as having asked, when inquiring into whether some particular procedural safeguard was required of a State, if a civilized system could be imagined that would not accord the particular protection [quoting from *Palko*]. The recent cases, on the other hand, have proceeded upon the valid assumption that state criminal processes are not imaginary and theoretical schemes but actual systems bearing virtually every characteristic of the common-law system that has been developing contemporaneously in England and this country. The question thus is whether given this kind of system a particular procedure is fundamental—whether, that is, a procedure is necessary to an Anglo-American regime of ordered liberty. It is this sort of inquiry that can justify the conclusions that state courts must exclude evidence seized in violation of the Fourth Amendment, *Mapp v. Ohio* [p. 110] [and] that state prosecutors may not comment on a defendant's failure to testify, *Griffin v. California* [Ch. 24, § 4]. [Of] each of these determinations that a constitutional provision originally written to bind the Federal Government should bind the States as well it might be said that the limitation in question is not necessarily fundamental to fairness in every criminal system that might be imagined but is fundamental in the context of the criminal processes maintained by the American States.

"When the inquiry is approached in this way the question whether the States can impose criminal punishment without granting a jury trial appears quite different from the way it appeared in the older cases opining that States might abolish jury trial. A criminal process which was fair and equitable but used no juries is easy to imagine. It would make use of alternative guarantees and protections which would serve the purposes that the jury serves in the English and American systems. Yet no American State has undertaken to construct such a system. Instead, every American State, including Louisiana, uses the jury extensively, and imposes very serious punishments only after a trial at which the defendant has a right to a jury's verdict. In every State, including Louisiana, the structure and style of the criminal process—the supporting framework and the subsidiary procedures—are of the sort that naturally complement jury trial, and have developed in connection with and in reliance upon jury trial."[b]

b. See also Justice Powell, concurring in the companion 1972 "jury unanimity" cases of *Johnson v. Louisiana* and *Apodaca v. Oregon* (discussed below) (fn. 9):

"I agree with Mr. Justice White's analysis in *Duncan* that the departure from earlier decisions was, in large measure, a product of a change in focus in the Court's approach to due process. No longer are questions regarding the

Although the Court has remained unwilling to accept the total incorporationists' reading of the Fourteenth Amendment, in the 1960's it "selectively" "incorporated" or "absorbed" more and more of the specifics of the Bill of Rights into the Fourteenth Amendment. As Justice White observed in *Duncan:*

"In resolving conflicting claims concerning the meaning of this spacious [Fourteenth Amendment] language, the Court has looked increasingly to the Bill of Rights for guidance; many of the rights guaranteed by the first eight Amendments to the Constitution have been held to be protected against state action by the Due Process Clause of the Fourteenth Amendment. That clause now protects [the] Fourth Amendment rights to be free from unreasonable searches and seizures and to have excluded from criminal trials any evidence illegally seized; the right guaranteed by the Fifth Amendment to be free of compelled self-incrimination; and the Sixth Amendment rights to counsel, to a speedy and public trial [*Klopfer v. North Carolina,* p. 1072], to confrontation of opposing witnesses [see generally Ch. 25] and to compulsory process for obtaining witnesses [*Washington v. Texas,* p. 1226]."ᶜ

Moreover, the Court seemed to be "incorporating" not only the basic notion or general concept of the "selected" provision of the Bill of Rights, but applying the provision to the states *to the same extent* it applied to the federal government. As some Justices, especially Harlan, protested, the federal guarantees were being incorporated into the Fourteenth "freighted with their entire accompanying body of federal doctrine" (Harlan, J., joined by Clark, J., dissenting in *Malloy v. Hogan,* discussed below); "jot-for-jot and case-for-case" (Harlan, J., joined by Stewart, J., dissenting in *Duncan*); "bag and baggage, however securely or insecurely affixed they may be by law and precedent to federal proceedings" (Fortas, J., concurring in *Duncan*).

Thus, Justice Brennan observed for a majority of the Court in *Malloy v. Hogan,* 378 U.S. 1, 84 S.Ct. 1489, 12 L.Ed.2d 653 (1964):

"We hold that the Fourteenth Amendment guaranteed the petitioner the protection of the Fifth Amendment's privilege against self-incrimination, and that *under the applicable federal standard,* the [state court] erred in holding that the privilege was not properly invoked. [The State urges] that the availability of the federal privilege to a witness in a state inquiry is to be determined according to a less stringent safeguard than is applicable in a federal proceeding. We disagree.

constitutionality of particular criminal procedures resolved by focusing alone on the element in question and ascertaining whether a system of criminal justice might be imagined in which a fair trial could be afforded in the absence of that particular element. Rather, the focus is, as it should be, on the fundamentality of that element viewed in the context of the basic Anglo-American jurisprudential system common to the States. That approach to due process readily accounts both for the conclusion that jury trial *is* fundamental and that unanimity *is not.*"

c. See also Justice Black, joined by Douglas, J., concurring in *Duncan:* "[I] believe as strongly as ever that the Fourteenth Amendment was intended to make the Bill of Rights applicable to the States. I have been willing to support the selective incorporation doctrine, however, as an alternative, although perhaps less historically supportable than complete incorporation [because it] keeps judges from

roaming at will in their own notions of what policies outside the Bill of Rights are desirable and what are not. And, most importantly for me, the selective incorporation process has the virtue of having already worked to make most of the Bill of Rights' protections applicable to the States."

In the area of criminal procedure, the Court has indeed come very close to incorporation of all of the relevant Bill of Rights guarantees. In addition to the provisions noted above, the double jeopardy prohibition has also been made applicable to the states in *Benton,* fn. a supra. The Court has refused, however, to apply to the states the Fifth Amendment requirement that prosecution be initiated by grand jury indictment. See Ch. 15. On the application of the prohibition against excessive bail, see Ch. 12. See also Israel, *Selective Incorporation Revisited,* 71 Geo. L.J. 253 (1982), for an overview of the development and application of the selective incorporation doctrine.

We have held that the guarantees of the First Amendment, the prohibition of unreasonable searches and seizures of the Fourth Amendment, and the right to counsel guaranteed by the Sixth Amendment, *Gideon v. Wainwright* [p. 64], are all to be enforced against the States under the Fourteenth Amendment *according to the same standards that protect those personal rights against federal encroachment.* [The] Court thus has rejected the notion that the Fourteenth Amendment applies to the States only a 'watered-down, subjective version of the individual guarantees of the Bill of Rights.' " (Emphasis added.)

And Justice White put it for a majority of the Court in *Duncan:* "Because we believe that trial by jury in criminal cases is fundamental to the American scheme of justice, we hold that the Fourteenth Amendment guarantees a right of jury trial in all criminal cases which—*were they to be tried in a federal court*—would come within the Sixth Amendment's guarantee." (Emphasis added.)

Justice Harlan repeatedly voiced his opposition to the *Malloy-Duncan* approach to Fourteenth Amendment Due Process. "The consequence," he protested in his *Malloy* dissent, "is inevitably disregard of all relevant differences which may exist between state and federal criminal law and its enforcement. The ultimate result is compelled uniformity, which is inconsistent with the purpose of our federal system and which is achieved either by encroachment on the State's sovereign powers or by dilution in federal law enforcement of the specific protections found in the Bill of Rights." See also Justice Harlan's concurring opinion in *Pointer v. Texas*, 380 U.S. 400, 85 S.Ct. 1065, 13 L.Ed.2d 923 (1965) (holding that an accused's Sixth Amendment right to confront the witnesses against him applies in its entirety to the states via the Fourteenth Amendment) and his dissenting opinion in *Benton v. Maryland*, fn. a supra.

In the 1970's matters were brought to a head by the "right to jury trial" cases:[d] BALDWIN v. NEW YORK, 399 U.S. 117, 90 S.Ct. 1914, 26 L.Ed.2d 446 (1970) (no offense can be deemed "petty," thus dispensing with the Fourteenth and Sixth Amendment rights to jury trial, where more than six months incarceration is authorized); WILLIAMS v. FLORIDA, 399 U.S. 78, 90 S.Ct. 1893, 26 L.Ed.2d 446 (1970) ("that jury at common law was composed of precisely 12 is an historical accident, unnecessary to effect the purposes of the jury system"; thus 6-person jury in criminal cases does not violate Sixth Amendment, as applied to the states via Fourteenth);[e] and the 1972 *Apodaca* and *Johnson* cases, discussed below, dealing with whether unanimous jury verdicts are required in criminal cases.

Dissenting in *Baldwin* and concurring in *Williams*, Justice HARLAN maintained:

"[*Williams*] evinces [a] recognition that the 'incorporationist' view of the Due Process Clause of the Fourteenth Amendment, which underlay *Duncan* and is now carried forward into *Baldwin*, must be tempered to allow the States more elbow room in ordering their own criminal systems. With that much I agree. But to accomplish this by diluting constitutional protections within the federal system itself is something to which I cannot possibly subscribe. Tempering the rigor of *Duncan* should be done forthrightly, by facing up to the fact that at least in this area the 'incorporation' doctrine does not fit well with our federal structure, and by the same token that *Duncan* was wrongly decided.

d. For a fuller discussion of these cases, see Ch. 23, § 1.

e. But the Court subsequently held, in *Ballew v. Georgia*, 435 U.S. 223, 98 S.Ct. 1029, 55 L.Ed.2d 234 (1978), that a state trial in a non-petty criminal case to a jury of only five persons did deprive a defendant of the right to trial by jury guaranteed him by the Sixth and Fourteenth Amendments.

[handwritten margin notes: "① 6 or 12 member jury ② unanimous jury decision — are they required?"]

"[Rather] than bind the States by the hitherto undeviating and unquestioned federal practice of 12–member juries, the Court holds, based on a poll of state practice, that a six-man jury satisfies the guarantee of a trial by jury in a federal criminal system and consequently carries over to the States. This is a constitutional *renvoi*. With all respect, I consider that before today it would have been unthinkable to suggest that the Sixth Amendment's right to a trial by jury is satisfied by a jury of six, or less, as is left open by the Court's opinion in *Williams,* or by less than a unanimous verdict, a question also reserved in today's decision.[f]

[handwritten margin notes: "due process approach ✓ selective incorporation"]

"[These] decisions demonstrate that the difference between a 'due process' approach, that considers each particular case on its own bottom to see whether the right alleged is one 'implicit in the concept of ordered liberty,' and 'selective incorporation' is not an abstract one whereby different verbal formulae achieve the same results. The internal logic of the selective incorporation doctrine cannot be respected if the Court is both committed to interpreting faithfully the meaning of the federal Bill of Rights and recognizing the governmental diversity that exists in this country. The 'backlash' in *Williams* exposes the malaise, for there the Court dilutes a federal guarantee in order to reconcile the logic of 'incorporation,' the 'jot-for-jot and case-for-case' application of the federal right to the States, with the reality of federalism. Can one doubt that had Congress tried to undermine the common law right to trial by jury before *Duncan* came on the books the history today recited would have barred such action? Can we expect repeat performances when this Court is called upon to give definition and meaning to other federal guarantees that have been 'incorporated'? * * *

" 'Incorporation' in *Duncan* closed the door on debate, irrespective of local circumstances, such as the backlogs in urban courts like those of New York City, and has, without justification, clouded with uncertainty the constitutionality of these differing states modes of proceeding pending approval by this Court; it now promises to dilute in other ways the settled meaning of the federal right to a trial by jury. Flexibility for experimentation in the administration of justice should be returned to the States here and in other areas that now have swept into the rigid mold of 'incorporation.'

"[It] is time, I submit, for this Court to face up to the reality implicit in today's holdings and reconsider the 'incorporation' doctrine before its leveling tendencies further retard development in the field of criminal procedure by stifling flexibility in the States and by discarding the possibility of federal leadership by example."

[handwritten margin notes: "Justice Powell believes that BOR does not have to be applied in the same way to State & Fed cts."]

In the companion cases of *Apodaca v. Oregon,* 406 U.S. 404, 92 S.Ct. 1628, 32 L.Ed.2d 184 (1972) and *Johnson v. Louisiana,* 406 U.S. 356, 92 S.Ct. 1620, 32 L.Ed.2d 152 (1972), upholding the constitutionality of less-than-unanimous jury verdicts in state criminal cases, eight Justices adhered to the *Duncan* position that each element of the Sixth Amendment right to jury trial applies to the states to the same extent it applies to the federal government, but split 4–4 over whether the federal guarantee *did require* jury unanimity in criminal cases. State convictions by less than unanimous votes were sustained only because the ninth member of the Court, newly appointed Justice Powell read the Sixth Amendment as requiring jury unanimity, but—taking a Harlan-type approach—concluded that *this feature* of the federal right is not "so fundamental to the essentials of jury

---

f. Cf. Frankfurter, J., for the Court in *Rochin v. California* (1952) (discussed in the next section): "Words being symbols do not speak without a gloss. [T]he gloss may be the deposit of history, whereby a term gains technical content. Thus the requirements of the Sixth and Seventh Amendments for trial by jury in the federal courts have a rigid meaning. No changes or chances can alter the content of the verbal symbol of 'jury'—a body of twelve men who must reach a unanimous conclusion if the verdict is to go against the defendant."

trial" as to require unanimity in state criminal cases as a matter of Fourteenth Amendment Due Process.[g]

Observed Powell: "[I]n holding that the Fourteenth Amendment has incorporated 'jot-for-jot and case-for-case' every element of the Sixth Amendment, the Court derogates principles of federalism that are basic to our system. In the name of uniform application of high standards of due process, the Court has embarked upon a course of constitutional interpretation that deprives the States of freedom to experiment with adjudicatory processes different from the federal model. At the same time, the Court's understandable unwillingness to impose requirements that it finds unnecessarily rigid (e.g., *Williams*), has culminated in the dilution of federal rights that were, until these decisions, never seriously questioned. The doubly undesirable consequence of this reasoning process, labeled by Mr. Justice Harlan as 'constitutional schizophrenia,' may well be detrimental both to the state and federal criminal justice systems. Although it is perhaps late in the day for an expression of my views, I [believe] that, at least in defining the elements of the right to jury trial, there is no sound basis for interpreting the Fourteenth Amendment to require blind adherence by the States to all details of the federal Sixth Amendment standards."[h]

Dissenting Justice Brennan, joined by Marshall, J., observed: "Readers of today's opinions may be understandably puzzled why convictions by 11–1 and 10–2 jury votes are affirmed [when] a majority of the Court agrees that the Sixth Amendment requires a unanimous verdict in federal criminal jury trials, and a majority also agrees that the right to jury trial guaranteed by the Sixth Amendment is to be enforced against the States according to the same standards that protect that right against federal encroachment. The reason is that while my Brother Powell agrees that a unanimous verdict is required in federal criminal trials, he does not agree that the Sixth Amendment right to a jury trial is to be applied in the same way to State and Federal Governments. In that circumstance, it is arguable that the affirmance of the convictions * * * is not inconsistent with a view that today's decision is a holding that only a unanimous verdict will afford the accused in a state criminal prosecution the jury trial guaranteed him by the Sixth Amendment. In any event, the affirmance must not obscure that the majority of the Court remains of the view that, as in the case of every specific of the Bill of Rights that extends to the States, the Sixth Amendment's jury trial guarantee, however it is to be construed, has identical application against both State and Federal Governments."[i]

SECTION 2. THE PROBLEM OF BODILY EXTRACTIONS: ANOTHER LOOK AT THE "DUE PROCESS" AND "SELECTIVE INCORPORATION" APPROACHES

g. But the Court subsequently held, in *Burch v. Louisiana*, Ch. 22, § 1, per Rehnquist, J. (without a dissent on this issue), that conviction by a nonunanimous *six-person* jury in a state criminal trial for a non-petty offense did violate the Sixth and Fourteenth Amendment rights to trial by jury.

h. In his continued resistance to "jot-for-jot" or "bag and baggage" incorporation of a "selected" provision of the Bill of Rights, Justice Powell soon gained two allies. See Powell, J., joined by the Chief Justice and Rehnquist, J., dissenting in *Crist v. Bretz*, Ch. 26, § 1. In *Ballew*, fn. e supra, although he concurred in

the judgment, Justice Powell, again joined by the Chief Justice and Rehnquist, J., did not join Justice Blackmun's opinion because it "assumes full incorporation of the Sixth Amendment, contrary to my view in *Apodaca*."

i. In a separate dissent, Stewart, J., joined by Brennan Marshall, J.J., protested that "unless *Duncan* is to be overruled," "the only relevant question here is whether the Sixth Amendment [guarantees] that the verdict of the jury must be unanimous. The answer to that question is clearly 'yes,' as my Brother Powell has cogently demonstrated * * *."

As noted in the previous section, dissenting in *Baldwin* and concurring in *Williams,* Justice Harlan maintained that "the difference between a 'due process' approach [and] 'selective incorporation' is not an abstract one whereby different formulae achieve the same results." But he made this observation in the context of the applicability to the states of the Sixth Amendment right to trial by jury, which had, or was thought to have, a relatively rigid meaning. Most language in the Bill of Rights, however, is rather vague and general, at least when specific problems arise under a particular phrase. In such cases, does dwelling on the literal language simply *shift the focus of broad judicial inquiry* from "due process" to, e.g., "freedom of speech," "establishment of religion," "unreasonable searches and seizures," "excessive bail," "cruel and unusual punishments," and "the assistance of counsel"? See Donald A. Dripps, *At the Borders of the Fourth Amendment: Why A Real Due Process Test Should Replace the Outrageous Government Conduct Defense,* 1993 U.Ill.L.Rev. 261 (defending, "as both more faithful to conventional sources of constitutional law and more consonant with the political values of a free society, a revitalized due process test"); John E. Nowak, *Due Process Methodology in the Postincorporation World,* 70 J. Crim. L. & C. 397, 400–01 (1979) (arguing that decisions based on specific guarantees tend to rely on definitional analysis and fail to explore the interest at stake). Consider too, Note 1, p. 39. See also Henry J. Friendly, *The Bill of Rights as a Code of Criminal Procedure,* 53 Calif.L.Rev. 929, 937 (1965); Sanford H. Kadish, *Methodology and Criteria in Due Process Adjudication—A Survey and Criticism,* 66 Yale L.J. 319, (1957).

In considering whether the right to counsel "begins" at the time of arrest, preliminary hearing, arraignment, or not until the trial itself, or includes probation and parole revocation hearings or applies to juvenile delinquency proceedings, deportation hearings or civil commitments, or, where the defendant is indigent, includes the right to *assigned* counsel or an assigned psychiatrist at state expense, how helpful is the Sixth Amendment language entitling an accused to "the assistance of counsel for his defense"? Is the specificity or direction of this language significantly greater than the "due process" clause?

To turn to another cluster of problems—which form the basis for this section—in considering whether, and under what conditions, the police may direct the "pumping" of a person's stomach to uncover incriminating evidence, or the taking of a blood sample from him, without his consent, do the "specific guarantees" in the Bill of Rights against "unreasonable searches and seizures" and against compelling a person to be "a witness against himself" free the Court from the demands of appraising and judging involved in answering these questions by interpreting the "due process" clause?

ROCHIN v. CALIFORNIA, 342 U.S. 165, 72 S.Ct. 205, 96 L.Ed. 183 (1952), arose as follows: Having "some information" that Rochin was selling narcotics, three deputy sheriffs "forced open the door of [his] room and found him sitting partly dressed on the side of the bed, upon which his wife was lying. On a 'night stand' beside the bed the deputies spied two capsules. When asked 'Whose stuff is this?' Rochin seized the capsules and put them in his mouth. A struggle ensued in the course of which the three officers 'jumped upon him' and [unsuccessfully] attempted to extract the capsules. [Rochin] was handcuffed and taken to a hospital. At the direction of one of the officers, a doctor forced an emetic solution through a tube into Rochin's stomach against his will. This 'stomach pumping' produced vomiting. In the vomited matter were found two capsules which proved to contain morphine. [Rochin was convicted of possessing morphine] and sentenced to sixty days' imprisonment. The chief evidence against him was the two capsules."

The Court, per FRANKFURTER, J., concluded that the police conduct violated fourteenth amendment due process: "This is conduct that shocks the conscience. Illegally breaking into the privacy of the petitioner, the struggle to open his mouth and remove what was there, the forcible extraction of his stomach's contents—this course of proceeding by agents of government to obtain evidence is bound to offend even hardened sensibilities. They are methods too close to the rack and the screw to permit of constitutional differentiation.

"It has long since ceased to be true that due process of law is heedless of the means by which otherwise relevant and credible evidence is obtained. [The confession] decisions [are] only instances of the general requirement that States in their prosecutions respect certain decencies of civilized conduct. Due process of law, as a historic and generative principle, precludes defining, and thereby confining, these standards of conduct more precisely than to say that convictions cannot be brought about by methods that offend 'a sense of justice.' It would be a stultification of the responsibility which the course of constitutional history has cast upon this Court to hold that in order to convict a man the police cannot extract by force what is in his mind but can extract what is in his stomach.

"[E]ven though statements contained in them may be independently established as true, [c]oerced confessions offend the community's sense of fair play and decency. So here, to sanction the brutal conduct which naturally enough was condemned by the court whose judgment is before us, would be to afford brutality the cloak of law. Nothing would be more calculated to discredit law and thereby to brutalize the temper of a society."

Concurring Justice BLACK reasoned that the Fifth Amendment's protection against compelled self-incrimination applied to the states and that "a person is compelled to be a witness against himself not only when he is compelled to testify, but also when as here, incriminating evidence is forcibly taken from him by a contrivance of modern science." He maintained that "faithful adherence to the specific guarantees in the Bill of Rights insures a more permanent protection of individual liberty than that which can be afforded by the nebulous [Fourteenth Amendment due process] standards stated by the majority."

In a separate concurring opinion, Justice DOUGLAS also criticized the majority's approach. He contended that the privilege against self-incrimination applied to the states as well as the federal government and because of the privilege "words taken from [an accused's] lips, capsules taken from his stomach, blood taken from his veins are all inadmissible provided they are taken from him without his consent. [This] is an unequivocal, definite and workable rule of evidence for state and federal courts. But we cannot in fairness free the state courts from the [restraints of the Fifth Amendment privilege against self-incrimination] and yet excoriate them for flouting the 'decencies of civilized conduct' when they admit the evidence. This is to make the rule turn not on the Constitution but on the idiosyncracies of the judges who sit here."

Irvine v. California, 347 U.S. 128, 74 S.Ct. 381, 98 L.Ed. 561 (1954), limited *Rochin* to situations involving coercion, violence or brutality to the person.[a]

a. In *Irvine* the police made repeated illegal entries into petitioner's home, first to install a secret microphone and then to move it to the bedroom, in order to listen to the conversations of the occupants—for over a month.

Jackson, J., who announced the judgment of the Court and wrote the principal opinion, recognized that "few police measures have come to our attention that more flagrantly, deliberately, and persistently violated the fun-

damental principle declared by the Fourth Amendment as a restriction on the Federal Government," but adhered to the holding in *Wolf v. Colorado* (1949), p. 108, that the exclusionary rule in federal search and seizure cases is not binding on the states. (*Wolf* was overruled in *Mapp v. Ohio* (1961), p. 110.) Nor did Justice Jackson deem *Rochin* applicable: "However obnoxious are the facts in the case before us, they do not involve coercion, vio-

BREITHAUPT v. ABRAM, 352 U.S. 432, 77 S.Ct. 408, 1 L.Ed.2d 448 (1957), illustrated that under the *Rochin* test state police had considerable leeway even when the body of the accused was "invaded." In *Breithaupt,* the police took a blood sample from an unconscious person who had been involved in a fatal automobile collision. A majority, per CLARK, J., affirmed a manslaughter conviction based on the blood sample (which showed intoxication), stressing that the sample was "taken under the protective eye of a physician" and that "the blood test procedure has become routine in our everyday life." "[T]he interests of society in the scientific determination of intoxication, one of the great causes of the mortal hazards of the road," outweighed "so slight an intrusion" of a person's body.

Dissenting Chief Justice WARREN, joined by Black and Douglas, JJ., deemed *Rochin* controlling and argued that police efforts to curb the narcotics traffic, involved in *Rochin,* "is surely a state interest of at least as great magnitude as the interest in highway law enforcement. * * * Only personal reaction to the stomach pump and the blood test can distinguish the [two cases]."

Justice DOUGLAS, joined by Black, J., also wrote a separate dissent, maintaining that "if the decencies of a civilized state are the test, it is repulsive to me for the police to insert needles into an unconscious person in order to get the evidence necessary to convict him, whether they find the person unconscious, give him a pill which puts him to sleep, or use force to subdue him."

Nine years later, even though in the meantime the Court had held in *Mapp* that the federal exclusionary rule in search and seizure cases was binding on the states and in *Malloy v. Hogan,* supra, that the Fifth Amendment's protection against compelled self-incrimination was likewise applicable to the states, the Court still upheld the taking by a physician, at police direction, of a blood sample from an injured person, over his objection. SCHMERBER v. CALIFORNIA, 384 U.S. 757, 86 S.Ct. 1826, 16 L.Ed.2d 908 (1966).[b] In affirming the conviction for operating a vehicle while under the influence of intoxicating liquor, a 5–4 majority, per BRENNAN, J., ruled: (1) that the extraction of blood from petitioner under the aforementioned circumstances "did not offend 'that "sense of justice"'" of which we spoke in *Rochin,*" thus reaffirming *Breithaupt;* (2) that the privilege against self-incrimination, now binding on the states, "protects an accused only from being compelled to testify against himself, or otherwise provide the State with evidence of a testimonial or communicative nature and that the withdrawal of blood and use of the analysis in question did not involve compulsion to these ends";[c] and (3) that the protection against unreasonable search and seizure, now

---

lence or brutality to the person [as did *Rochin*], but rather a trespass to property, plus eavesdropping."

Because of the "aggravating" and "repulsive" police misconduct in *Irvine,* Frankfurter, J., joined by Burton, J., dissented, maintaining that *Rochin* was controlling, not *Wolf.* (He had written the majority opinions in both cases.) Black, J., joined by Douglas, J., dissented separately, arguing that petitioner had been convicted on the basis of evidence "extorted" from him in violation of the Fifth Amendment's privilege against compelled self-incrimination, which he considered applicable to the states. Douglas, J., dissenting separately, protested against the use in state prosecutions of evidence seized in violation of the Fourth Amendment.

Speaking for himself and Chief Justice Warren, Justice Jackson suggested that copies of the Court's opinion and the record in the case be sent to the U.S. Attorney General for possible federal prosecution. The FBI did conduct an investigation which revealed that the officers who placed the microphone in Irvine's home were acting under orders of the Chief of Police and with the full knowledge of the local prosecutor. Thus, concluded the Department of Justice, "it would be both useless and inadvisable to present [the] matter to the Federal grand jury." See Comment, 7 Stan.L.Rev. 76, 94, fn. 75 (1954).

b. For other aspects of *Schmerber,* see p. 235.

c. In fn. 7 to its opinion, the Court compared "Wigmore's view, 'that the privilege is limited to testimonial disclosure. It was direct-

binding on the states, was satisfied because (a) "there was plainly probable cause" to arrest and charge petitioner and to suggest "the required relevance and likely success of a test of petitioner's blood for alcohol"; (b) the officer "might reasonably have believed that he was confronted with an emergency, in which the delay necessary to obtain a warrant, under the circumstances, threatened 'the destruction of evidence' "; and (c) "the test chosen to measure petitioner's blood-alcohol level was a reasonable one * * * performed in a reasonable manner."

Dissenting Justice BLACK, joined by Justice Douglas, expressed amazement at the majority's "conclusion that compelling a person to give his blood to help the State to convict him is not equivalent to compelling him to be a witness against himself." "It is a strange hierarchy of values that allows the State to extract a human being's blood to convict him of a crime because of the blood's content but proscribes compelled production of his lifeless papers."[d]

Notes and Questions

1. In light of *Rochin, Breithaupt* and *Schmerber,* when courts decide constitutional questions by "looking to" the Bill of Rights, to what extent do they proceed, as Justice Black expressed it in *Adamson,* "within clearly marked constitutional boundaries"? To what extent does resort to these "particular standards" enable courts to avoid substituting their "own concepts of decency and fundamental justice" for the language of the Constitution?

2. Did *Mapp* and *Malloy,* decided in the interim between *Breithaupt* and *Schmerber,* affect any Justice's vote? Did the applicability of the "particular standards" of the Fourth and Fifth Amendments inhibit Justices Black, Douglas or Brennan from employing their own concepts of "decency" and "justice" in *Schmerber?* After *Schmerber,* how much force is there in Justice Black's view, concurring in *Rochin,* that "faithful adherence to the specific guarantees in the Bill of Rights assures a more permanent protection of individual liberty than that which can be afforded by the nebulous standards stated by the majority"?

3. Applying the "shocks-the-conscience" test first articulated in the *Rochin* case, COUNTY OF SACRAMENTO v. LEWIS, 523 U.S. 833, 118 S.Ct. 1708, 140 L.Ed.2d 1043 (1998) (also discussed at p. 304), held, per SOUTER, J., that a police officer did not violate substantive due process by causing death through "reckless indifference" to, or "reckless disregard" for, a person's life in a high-speed automobile chase of a speeding motorcyclist. (The chase resulted in the death of the motorcyclist's passenger when the police car skidded into the passenger after the cycle had tipped over). In such circumstances, concluded the Court, "only a purpose to cause harm unrelated to the legitimate object of arrest will satisfy the element of arbitrary conduct shocking to the conscience, necessary for a due process violation [and for police liability under 42 U.S.C. § 1983]."

The Court recalled that it had held in *Graham v. Connor,* 490 U.S. 386, 109 S.Ct. 1865, 104 L.Ed.2d 443 (1989), that "where a particular amendment provides an explicit textual source of constitutional protection against a particular sort of government behavior, that Amendment, not the more generalized notion of

ed at the employment of legal process *to extract from the person's own lips* an admission of guilt, which would thus take the place of other evidence.' 8 Wigmore, *Evidence* § 2263 (McNaughton rev. 1961)." "Our holding today," noted the Court, "is not to be understood as adopting the Wigmore formulation." But see *United States v. Wade,* p. 618.

d. Warren, C.J., and Douglas, J., dissented in separate opinions,, each adhering to his dis-

senting views in *Breithaupt.* In a third dissenting opinion, Fortas, J., maintained that "petitioner's privilege against self-incrimination applies" and, moreover, "under the Due Process Clause, the State, in its role as prosecutor, has no right to extract blood from an accused or anyone else, over his protest."

substantive due process, must be the guide for analyzing [claims of substantive due process violations]." But the "more-specific-provision" rule of *Graham* did not bar respondents' lawsuit because neither the high-speed chase of the motorcycle nor the accidental killing of the motorcycle passenger constituted a Fourth Amendment "seizure." The Court then addressed respondents' substantive due process claim:

"Our cases dealing with abusive executive action have repeatedly emphasized that only the most egregious official conduct can be said to be 'arbitrary in the constitutional sense.' [For] half a century now we have spoken of the cognizable level of executive abuse of power as that which shocks the conscience. We first put the test this way in *Rochin* [and] we have repeatedly adhered to *Rochin*'s benchmark."

The Court emphasized that much turns on the particular context in which the executive misconduct arises. Thus, in a prison custodial situation, when the state has rendered an individual unable to care for himself, and at the same time fails to provide for his basic needs, "the point of the conscience-shocking is reached" when injuries are produced by reckless or grossly negligent executive conduct. On the other hand, "deliberate indifference does not suffice for constitutional liability (albeit under the Eighth Amendment) even in prison circumstances when a prisoner's claim arises not from normal custody but from response to a violent disturbance." Continued the Court:

"[A] police officer deciding whether to give chase must balance on one hand the need to stop a suspect and show that flight from the law is no way to freedom, and, on the other, the high-speed threat to everyone within stopping range, be they suspects, their passengers, other drivers, or bystanders. To recognize a substantive due process violation in these circumstances when only mid-level fault has been shown [i.e., something more than simple negligence, but something less than intentional misconduct] would be to forget that liability for deliberate indifference to inmate welfare rests upon the luxury enjoyed by prison officials of having time to make unhurried judgments, upon the chance for repeated reflection, largely uncomplicated by the pulls of competing obligations. When such extended opportunities to do better are teamed with protracted failure even to care, indifference is truly shocking. But when unforeseen circumstances demand an officer's instant judgment, even precipitate recklessness fails to inch close enough to harmful purpose to spark the shock that implicates 'the large concerns of the governors and the governed.' Just as a purpose to cause harm is needed for Eighth Amendment liability in a riot case, so it ought to be needed for Due Process liability in a pursuit case. Accordingly, we hold that high-speed chases with no intent to harm suspects physically or to worsen their legal plight do not give rise to liability under the Fourteenth Amendment, redressible by an action under § 1983. [Regardless of whether the officer's] behavior offended the reasonableness held up by tort law or the balance struck in law enforcement's own codes of sound practice, it does not shock the conscience * * *."[a]

---

a. Concurring in the judgment, Scalia, J., joined by Thomas J. would not have decided the case by applying the "shocks-the-conscience" test but "on the ground that respondents offer no textual or historical support for their alleged due process right." The concurring Justices maintained that in *Washington v. Glucksberg*, 521 U.S. 702, 117 S.Ct. 2258, 138 L.Ed.2d 772 (1997) (upholding a criminal prohibition against physician-assisted suicide), "the Court specifically rejected the method of substantive-due-process analysis employed by Justice Souter in that case, which is the very same method employed by Justice Souter in his opinion for the Court today."

Justice Kennedy, joined by O'Connor, J. joined the opinion of the Court, but also wrote separately. They "share[d] Justice Scalia's concerns about using the phrase 'shocks the conscience' in a manner suggesting that it is a self-defining test." The phrase, they observed, "has the unfortunate connotation of a standard laden with subjective assessments. In that

4. Continued application of "free-standing" due process. As indicated in *County of Sacramento,* the Court in the "post-incorporation era" has continued to apply the independent content of due process that exists apart from the selectively incorporated guarantees (also described as "free-standing" due process). The applicable standard for cases presenting issues of procedural due process (in contrast to substantive due process) has been whether the state practice "offends some principle of justice so rooted in the traditions and conscience of our people to be ranked as fundamental." *Medina v. California,* 505 U.S. 437, 112 S.Ct. 2572, 120 L.Ed.2d 353 (1992). Jerold Israel, *Free-Standing Due Process and Criminal Procedure: The Supreme Court's Search for Interpretive Guidelines,* 45 St. Louis U.L.J. 303 (2001), reviews the Court's application of that standard in the post-incorporation decades. The article concludes that while the Court has set forth various guidelines for determining the independent content of due process, it has not been consistent in applying those guidelines. The Court has noted that "beyond the specific guarantees enumerated in the Bill of Rights, the Due Process Clause has limited operation" and will be "construed very narrowly." *Dowling v. United States,* 493 U.S. 342, 110 S.Ct. 668, 107 L.Ed.2d 708 (1990). This position rests on the ground that, since the "Bill of Rights speaks in explicit terms to many aspects of criminal procedure," the expansion of constitutional regulation under the "open-ended rubric of the Due Process Clause * * * invite[s] undue interference with both considered legislative judgments and the careful balance that the constitution strikes between liberty and order." *Medina v. California,* supra. Notwithstanding such statements, free-standing due process has emerged as: (1) the dominant source of constitutional regulation of the pre-trial and post-trial stages of the process (most notable as to guilty pleas and sentencing); (2) a major source of constitutional regulation of the trial; (3) a lesser, but still significant source of regulation of police practices (see e.g., ch. 9, § 3). So too, while the Court has repeatedly stressed that the historical acceptance of a practice is a strong indicator that the practice does not offend fundamental fairness, it has on various occasions relied on deductive reasoning (often tied to the character of a "fair hearing") to hold unconstitutional practices that were entirely consistent with the common law (typically without discussing historical acceptance). Most often, the Court has described free-standing due process as looking to the circumstances of the particular case and resting, at least in part, on fact-sensitive determinations (particularly as to a likelihood of prejudicial impact), but in several areas, the Court has relied on free-standing due process to formulate per se prohibitions and automatically presume prejudice. The Court at times has advance a procedural due process counterpart of *Graham v. Connor,* but at other times has turned to free-standing due process without first considering the possible application of a specific guarantee (indeed, even announcing a preference for relying on free-standing due process in *Pennsylvania v. Ritchie*).

SECTION 3. THE RETROACTIVE EFFECT OF A HOLDING OF UNCONSTITUTIONALITY[a]

Rejecting what it called the Blackstonian theory that a new ruling merely sets forth the law as it always existed, *Linkletter v. Walker,* 381 U.S. 618, 85 S.Ct. 1731, 14 L.Ed.2d 601 (1965), declined to apply *Mapp v. Ohio* (p. 110) (overruling *Wolf v. Colorado,* and imposing the Fourth Amendment exclusionary rule on the states as a matter of Fourteenth Amendment Due Process) to cases which had

respect, it must be viewed with considerable skepticism."

a. This cluster of problems has generated a vast literature, starting in the 1960's. For a helpful discussion, see Richard H. Fallon & Daniel J. Meltzer, *New Law, Non–Retroactivity, and Constitutional Remedies,* 104 Harv. L.Rev. 1733 (1991).

become final (i.e., direct appellate review had been exhausted) prior to the overturning of *Wolf*. The *Linkletter* Court maintained that the retroactivity of *Mapp* should be determined by examining the purpose of the exclusionary rule, the reliance of the states on prior law, and the effect on the administration of justice of a retroactive application of the exclusionary rule.

The prime purpose of *Mapp*, emphasized the Court, was to deter future police misconduct and the purpose would not be advanced by applying the rule to "finalized" cases. The Court recognized that it had given full retroactive effect to some recent law-changing decisions—*Gideon* (p. 64), *Griffin v. Illinois* (p. 74), and the coerced confession cases—but, unlike *Mapp*, the principles established in those cases "went to the fairness of the trial—the very integrity of the fact-finding process. [Here] the fairness of the trial is not under attack."

Relying upon the *Linkletter* analysis, *Stovall v. Denno*, 388 U.S. 293, 87 S.Ct. 1967, 18 L.Ed.2d 1199 (1967), set forth a framework for determining whether a new ruling should be given retroactive effect. The "criteria guiding the resolution of the question," observed *Stovall*, "implicate (a) the purpose to be served by the new standards, (b) the extent of the reliance by law enforcement authorities on the old standards, (c) the effect on the administration of justice of a retroactive application of the new standards." These three criteria were later described as the "*Linkletter* standard," "the *Stovall* standard," or the "*Linkletter–Stovall*" standard.

Prior to *Linkletter*, the *Mapp* case had already been applied to cases still pending on direct appeal, so the only issue considered by the *Linkletter* Court was whether *Mapp* should be applied to a collateral attack upon a conviction (there, habeas corpus challenge). In applying the *Linkletter* standard, however, *Stovall* and subsequent cases did not draw a distinction between final convictions attacked collaterally and convictions challenged at various stages of trial and direct review.

Moreover, in limiting the retroactive effect of new rulings, cases applying the *Linkletter* standard selected different "starting points." Because *Escobedo* (p. 450) and *Miranda* (p. 462) were not primarily designed to protect the innocent from wrongful conviction, *Johnson v. New Jersey*, 384 U.S. 719, 86 S.Ct. 1772, 16 L.Ed.2d 882 (1966) held that those landmark confession rulings affected only cases in which *the trial began* after the date of those decisions. Because the use of unfair lineups could still be challenged on due process grounds even if the law-changing decisions on lineups were not applied retroactively, *Stovall v. Denno*, supra, declined to give retroactive effect to *Wade* and *Gilbert* (p. 618), the 1967 cases establishing the right to counsel at certain pretrial lineups. But this time the Court selected a different starting point for application of the nonretroactive rulings: *Wade* and *Gilbert* "affect only those cases [involving] *confrontations for identification purposes* conducted in the absence of counsel *after* [the date of these decisions]." (Emphasis added).[b]

Selection of the date of the challenged *police conduct* as the starting point, rather than the date of the trial or some other point in the criminal process, indicated that *police reliance* on the overturned rule was a major factor in

---

b. Although "at first glance the prospectivity rule appears to be an act of judicial self-abnegation," "in reality," observes Francis Allen, *The Judicial Quest for Penal Justice: The Warren Court and the Criminal Cases*, 1975 U.Ill.L.F. 518, 530, such a rule "encourages the making of new law by reducing some of the social costs." See also James Haddad, *Retroactivity Should be Rethought: A Call for the End*

of the Linkletter Doctrine, 60 J.Crim.L.C. & P.S. 417, 439 (1969): "The alternative to the prospective-only technique is a more conservative approach to constitutional criminal procedure. * * * Detailed federal standards such as those laid down in *Miranda* would no longer be possible. Adoption of safeguards, such as the right to counsel at lineups, which not a single state anticipated, would also be impossible."

retroactivity disputes. In this respect, *Desist v. United States*, 394 U.S. 244, 89 S.Ct. 1030, 22 L.Ed.2d 248 (1969), followed *Johnson v. New Jersey*. The *Desist* Court held that *Katz v. United States* (p. 138) (overruling *Olmstead*, p. 348, and holding that electronic surveillance is subject to Fourth Amendment restraints) should be given what the Court called "wholly prospective application," i.e., applied only to *police activity* occurring *after* the date of the *Katz* decision.[c]

The *Desist* Court saw no significant distinction for retroactivity purposes between direct review and collateral attack: All of the reasons for making *Katz* prospective only "also undercut any distinction between final convictions and those still pending on review. Both the deterrent purpose of the exclusionary rule and the reliance of law enforcement officers focus upon *the time of the search*, not any subsequent point in the prosecution as the relevant date." (Emphasis added.)

Twenty years later, Justice Harlan's dissent in *Desist* seems a good deal more significant than the opinion of the Court in that case. Unable to accept a rationale that "permits this Court to apply a 'new' constitutional rule entirely prospectively, while making an exception only for the particular litigant whose case was chosen as the vehicle for establishing that rule," dissenting Justice Harlan maintained:

"[A]ll 'new' rules of constitutional law must, at a minimum, be applied to all those cases which are still subject to direct review by this Court at the time the 'new' decision is handed down.

"[We release a prisoner] only because the Government has offended constitutional principle in the conduct of his case. And when another similarly situated defendant comes before us, we must grant the same relief or give a principled reason for acting differently. We depart from this basic judicial tradition when we simply pick and choose from among similarly situated defendants those who alone will receive the benefit of a 'new' rule of constitutional law.

" * * * If a 'new' constitutional doctrine is truly right, we should not reverse lower courts which have accepted it; nor should we affirm those which have rejected the very arguments we have embraced. Anything else would belie the truism that it is the task of this Court, like that of any other, to do justice to each litigant on the merits of his own case. It is only if each of our decisions can be justified in terms of this fundamental premise that they may properly be considered the legitimate products of a court of law, rather than the commands of a super-legislature."

RETHINKING RETROACTIVITY: HARLAN'S VIEWS COME TO THE FORE

More than a decade after the *Desist* Court had found no valid distinction for retroactivity purposes between final convictions and those still pending on direct review, the Court, relying heavily on Harlan, J.'s dissent in *Desist,* deemed such a distinction persuasive and applied it in *United States v. Johnson*, 457 U.S. 537, 102 S.Ct. 2579, 73 L.Ed.2d 202 (1982) (per Blackmun, J.). *Johnson* applied *Payton v. New York* (1980) (p. 251) (holding that police must obtain an arrest warrant when entering a suspect's home to make a routine felony arrest) to cases still pending on direct appeal at the time *Payton* was handed down. The Court pointed

c. The Court recognized that "[o]f course, Katz himself benefitted from the new principle announced on [the date of the *Katz* decision], and [to] that extent the decision has not technically been given wholly prospective application. But [this] is an 'unavoidable consequence of the necessity that constitutional adjudications not stand as mere dictum.' Whatever inequity may arguably result from applying the new rule to those 'chance beneficiaries' is 'an insignificant cost for adherence to sound principles of decision-making.'"

out that "*Payton* overturned no long-standing practice approved by a near-unanimous body of lower court authority [and thus] does not fall into that narrow class of decisions whose nonretroactivity is effectively preordained because they unmistakably signal 'a clean break with the past.' "

The *Johnson* Court "express[ed] no view on the retroactive application of decisions construing any constitutional provision other than the Fourth Amendment," but as *Shea v. Louisiana,* immediately below, soon made clear, the *Johnson* approach was not to be confined to the Fourth Amendment setting.

SHEA v. LOUISIANA, 470 U.S. 51, 105 S.Ct. 1065, 84 L.Ed.2d 38 (1985) arose as follows: Upon being read his *Miranda* rights, petitioner asserted his right to counsel and the interview was then terminated. But the next day, before petitioner had communicated with a lawyer and without any indication from him that he was willing to be questioned, the police again read petitioner the *Miranda* warnings. Petitioner agreed to talk and confessed. The confession was admitted into evidence and petitioner was convicted. While his appeal was pending, the U.S. Supreme Court ruled in *Edwards v. Arizona,* p. 522, that a suspect's rights were violated by the use of his confession obtained by police-instigated interrogation—without counsel present—after he had requested a lawyer. The state supreme court held *Edwards* inapplicable to a case pending on direct appeal at the time *Edwards* was decided. The Court, per BLACKMUN, J., disagreed:

"The primary difference between *United States v. Johnson,* on the one hand, and *Solem v. Stumes,* 465 U.S. 638, 104 S.Ct. 1338, 79 L.Ed.2d 579 (1984) [holding that *Edwards* does not apply retroactively to a state-court conviction finally affirmed by the state supreme court *before Edwards* was decided], on the other, is the difference between a pending and undecided direct review of a judgment of conviction and a federal collateral attack upon a state conviction which has become final. We must acknowledge [that] *Johnson* does not directly control the disposition of the present case.[a] [But] [w]e now conclude [that there] is nothing about a Fourth Amendment rule that suggests that in this context it should be given greater retroactive effect than a Fifth Amendment rule. Indeed, a Fifth Amendment violation may be more likely to affect the truthfinding process than a Fourth Amendment violation. And Justice Harlan's reasoning—that principled decisionmaking and fairness to similarly situated petitioners requires application of a new rule to all cases pending on direct review—is applicable with equal force to the situation presently before us.

"[It is argued] that drawing a distinction between a case pending on direct review and a case on collateral attack produces inequities and injustices that are not any different from those that *Johnson* purported to cure. The argument is that the litigant whose *Edwards* claim will not be considered because it is presented on collateral review will be just as unfairly treated as the direct-review litigant whose claim would be by-passed were *Edwards* not the law. The distinction, however, properly rests on considerations of finality in the judicial process. The one litigant already has taken his case through the primary system. The other has not. For the latter, the curtain of finality has not been drawn. Somewhere, the closing must come."

WHITE, J., joined by the Chief Justice, and Rehnquist and O'Connor, JJ., dissented:

a. The Court noted that *Johnson* specifically declined to address the implications of its approach to non-Fourth Amendment cases and "also declined to address situations clearly controlled by existing retroactivity precedents, such as where the new rule of law is so clean a break with the past that it has been considered nonretroactive almost automatically. Whatever the merits of a different retroactivity rule for cases of that kind may be, [*Stumes*] recognized that *Edwards* was 'not the kind of clean break with the past that is automatically nonretroactive.' "

"We concluded [in *Stumes*] that the prophylactic purpose of the *Edwards* rule, the justifiable failure of police and prosecutors to foresee the Court's decision in *Edwards*, and the substantial disruption of the criminal justice system that retroactive application of *Edwards* would entail all indicated the wisdom of holding *Edwards* nonretroactive. Today, however, the majority concludes that notwithstanding the substantial reasons for restricting the application of *Edwards* to cases involving interrogations that postdate the Court's opinion in [that case], the *Edwards* rule must be applied retroactively to all cases in which the process of direct appeal had not yet been completed when *Edwards* was decided.

"[The] futility of this latest attempt to use retroactivity doctrine to avoid the super-legislature difficulty is highlighted by the majority's unwillingness to commit itself to the logic of its position. For even as it maintains that retroactivity is essential to the judicial function, today's majority, like the majority in *Johnson*, continues to hold out the possibility that a 'really' new rule—one that marks a clear break with the past—may not have to be applied retroactively even to cases pending on direct review at the time the new decision is handed down. Of course, if the majority were truly concerned with the super-legislature problem it would be 'clear break' decisions that would trouble it the most. Indeed, one might expect that a Court as disturbed about the problem as the majority purports to be would swear off such decisions altogether, not reserve the power both to issue them and to decline to apply them retroactively. In leaving open the possibility of an exception for 'clear break' decisions, the majority demonstrates the emptiness of its proposed solution to the super-legislature problem.

"[The] majority recognizes that the distinction between direct review and habeas is problematic, but justifies its differential treatment by appealing to the need to draw 'the curtain of finality' on those who were unfortunate enough to have exhausted their last direct appeal at the time *Edwards* was decided. Yet the majority offers no reasons for its conclusion that finality should be the decisive factor. When a conviction is overturned on direct appeal on the basis of an *Edwards* violation, the remedy offered the defendant is a new trial at which any inculpatory statements obtained in violation of *Edwards* will be excluded. It is not clear to me why the majority finds such a burdensome remedy more acceptable when it is imposed on the state on direct review than when it is the result of a collateral attack. The disruption attendant upon the remedy does not vary depending on whether it is imposed on direct review or habeas; accordingly, if the remedy must be granted to defendants on direct appeal, there is no strong reason to deny it to prisoners attacking their convictions collaterally. Conversely, if it serves no worthwhile purpose to grant the remedy to a defendant whose conviction was final before *Edwards*, it is hard to see why the remedy should be available on direct review.

"[The] principles of retroactivity set forth in *Linkletter* and most recently applied in *Stumes* provide a rational framework for thinking about the question whether retroactive application of any particular decision makes sense—that is, whether the benefits of retroactivity outweigh its costs. Because the Court has already determined that the relevant considerations set forth in *Linkletter* (the purpose of the new rule, the extent of law enforcement officials' justifiable reliance on the prior rule, and the effects on the criminal justice system of retroactivity) dictate nonretroactive application of the rule in *Edwards*, I cannot join in the majority's conclusion that that rule should be applied retroactively to cases pending on direct review at the time of our decision in *Edwards*."

Notes and Questions

1. Rejection of the "clear break" exception. Answering a question left open in the *Johnson* and *Shea* cases, *Griffith v. Kentucky,* 479 U.S. 314, 107 S.Ct. 708, 93 L.Ed.2d 649 (1987), applied *Batson v. Kentucky* (Ch. 23, § 2) (defendant may establish prima facie case of racial discrimination in selection of petit jury on basis of prosecution's use of peremptory challenges at defendant's trial) to all convictions not final at the time of the ruling even though *Batson* was "an explicit and substantial break with prior precedent." Observed a 6–3 majority, per Blackmun, J.: "[T]he 'clear break' exception * * * reintroduces precisely the type of case-specific analysis that Justice Harlan rejected as inappropriate for cases pending on direct review [and] creates the same problem of not treating similarly situated defendants the same. [The] fact that the new rule may constitute a clear break with the past has no bearing on the 'actual inequity that results' when only one of many similarly situated defendants receives the benefit of the new rule."

2. Adoption of the other part of Harlan's approach to retroactivity. Justice Harlan believed that new rulings should always be applied retroactively to cases on *direct* review (a view adopted in *Shea*), but that generally new rulings should not be applied retroactively to cases on *collateral* review. In TEAGUE v. LANE, 489 U.S. 288, 109 S.Ct. 1060, 103 L.Ed.2d 334 (1989) (set forth in Ch. 29, § 4), seven Justices adopted Harlan's basic position with respect to retroactivity on collateral review. There was, however, no clear majority as to what the exceptions to this general approach should be.

A four-Justice plurality, per O'CONNOR, J. (joined by Rehnquist, C.J., and Scalia and Kennedy, JJ.), identified two exceptions: A new ruling should be applied retroactively to cases on collateral review only (1) if it "places 'certain kinds of primary, private individual conduct beyond the power of the criminal law-making authority to proscribe'" or (2) if it mandates "new procedures without which the likelihood of an accurate conviction is seriously diminished." The latter exception is "'best illustrated by recalling the classic grounds for the issuance of a writ of habeas corpus—that the proceeding was dominated by mob violence; that the prosecutor knowingly made use of perjured testimony; or that the conviction was based on a confession extorted from the defendant by brutal methods.'"

A fifth member of the Court, concurring Justice White, characterized the plurality's view as "an acceptable application in collateral proceedings of the theories embraced by the Court in dealing with direct review." Two other members of the Court, concurring Justice STEVENS, joined by Blackmun, J., agreed that "the Court should adopt Justice Harlan's analysis of retroactivity for habeas corpus cases as well as for cases still on direct review," but disagreed with the plurality about the exceptions to such a general approach.

3. What constitutes a "new rule"? The *Teague* plurality, per O'Connor, J., observed that "a case announces a new rule when it breaks new ground or imposes a new obligation on [the government]. To put it differently, a case announces a new rule if the result was not *dictated* by precedent existing at the time the defendant's conviction became final."

Consider *Butler v. McKellar* (1990), discussed more extensively in Ch. 28, § 1. At issue in *Butler* was the retroactive application on habeas of *Arizona v. Roberson* (1988) (p. 523). *Roberson* held that *Edwards v. Arizona* (1981), which prohibits the police from initiating further interrogation once a suspect has asserted his right to counsel, applies even when (unlike the facts in *Edwards*) the further interrogation relates to a different crime. Although the *Roberson* Court had characterized its ruling as "controlled" by *Edwards*, the *Butler* Court held that

Roberson had announced a "new rule" under the *Teague* standard: Although the *Roberson* Court had said that its decision was within the "logical compass" of *Edwards*, "the outcome in *Roberson* was susceptible to debate among reasonable minds"—"it would not have been an illogical or even a grudging application of *Edwards* to decide that it did not extend to the facts of *Roberson*."

Is *Teague*'s definition of the claims that will be deemed to rest on new law—and thus barred from relitigation on habeas, unless they fall within an exception—far too expansive? Don't most cases, as Justice Brennan argued in his *Teague* dissent, "involve a question of law that is at least debatable, permitting a rational judge to resolve the case in more than one way"? By disabling federal habeas corpus from granting relief whenever reasonable disagreement is possible about the scope or application of an existing rule, does *Teague* "reduce the incentives for state courts, and state law enforcement officials, to take account of the evolving direction of the law"? Should a "new rule" be defined more narrowly, "to exclude rules and decisions that are clearly foreshadowed, not just those that are 'dictated by precedents' "? See Richard H. Fallon & Daniel J. Meltzer, *New Law, Non-Retroactivity, and Constitutional Remedies,* 104 Harv.L.Rev. 1731, 1816–17 (1991).

start prob pg 55

SECTION 4. THE FEDERAL COURTS' "SUPERVISORY POWER" OVER THE ADMINISTRATION OF FEDERAL CRIMINAL JUSTICE

As the Court, per FRANKFURTER, J., observed in McNABB v. UNITED STATES (1943) (more extensively discussed at p. 446), "while the power of this Court to undo convictions in *state* courts is limited to the enforcement of those 'fundamental principles of liberty and justice' secured by [fourteenth amendment due process]" (emphasis added), the standards of *federal* criminal justice "are not satisfied merely by observance of those minimal historic safeguards." Rather, "[i]n the exercise of its supervisory authority over the administration of criminal justice in the federal courts, [this Court has] formulated rules of evidence to be applied in federal criminal prosecutions." Thus, in *McNabb,* the Court held incriminating statements obtained during prolonged and hence unlawful detention (i.e., while the suspect was held in violation of federal statutory requirements that he be promptly taken before a committing magistrate) inadmissible in federal courts "[q]uite apart from the Constitution."

For a long, hard look at *McNabb* itself and the federal "supervisory power" generally, see Sara Sun Beale, *Reconsidering Supervisory Power in Criminal Cases: Constitutional and Statutory Limits on the Authority of the Federal Courts,* 84 Colum.L.Rev. 1433 (1984). Professor Beale maintains, inter alia, that "the supervisory power has blurred the constitutional and statutory limitations on the authority of the federal courts [and] fostered the erroneous view that the federal courts exercise general supervision over federal prosecutors and investigators"; and that "there is no statutory or constitutional source of authority broad enough to encompass all of the supervisory power decisions." Id. at 1434–35.

"In cases not involving questions of judicial procedure or a statutory violation," concludes Beale, id. at 1521–22, the federal courts lack the authority "to exclude evidence or to dismiss a prosecution unless the government's conduct violated the Constitution. This analysis requires the federal courts to decide some constitutional issues they are now able to avoid—or at least defer—by grounding their rulings on supervisory power. [Requiring the federal courts to ground decisions on a constitutional basis] would be likely to result in eliminating some restrictions on federal investigators and prosecutors that have been grounded solely on supervisory power. This is as it should be.

"But this approach need not straitjacket the courts. Where there has been a legislative grant of authority, such as the rules enabling legislation, the power of the courts is extensive. Amendments to the Federal Rules of Criminal Procedure may properly regulate some matters that have been the subject of highly questionable supervisory power rulings. * * * But the concept of separation of powers dictates that federal prosecutors and investigators, like their state counterparts, should perform their duties subject only to the requirements imposed by the federal Constitution and statutes, not subject to the federal judiciary's preference for particular policies and practices."

In *United States v. Russell (1973)* (discussed at p. 391), in the course of rejecting respondent's argument that he had been "entrapped" because there had been an intolerable degree of government involvement in the criminal enterprise, the Court, per Rehnquist, J., observed:

"[Several lower federal court decisions] have undoubtedly gone beyond this Court's [precedents] in order to bar prosecutions because of what they [considered] 'overzealous law enforcement.' But the [entrapment defense] was not intended to give the federal judiciary a 'chancellor's foot' veto over law enforcement practices of which it does not disapprove. The execution of the federal laws under our Constitution is confined primarily to the Executive Branch of the Government, subject to applicable constitutional and statutory limitations and to judicially fashioned rules to enforce those limitations."

When a three-justice plurality (Rehnquist, J., joined by the Chief Justice and White, J.,) quoted the "chancellor's foot" passage with approval in *Hampton v. United States* (1976) (discussed at p. 402), concurring Justice Powell, joined by Blackmun, J., observed:

"The plurality's use of the 'chancellor's foot' passage from *Russell* may suggest that it also would foreclose reliance on our supervisory power to bar conviction of [a defendant predisposed to commit the crime] because of outrageous police conduct. * * * I do not understand *Russell* to have gone so far. There we indicated only that we should be extremely reluctant to invoke the supervisory power in cases of this kind because that power does not give the 'federal judiciary a "chancellor's foot" veto over law enforcement practices of which it [does] not approve.' * * * I therefore am unwilling to join the plurality in concluding that, no matter what the circumstances, neither due process principles nor our supervisory power could support a bar to conviction in any case where the Government is able to prove predisposition [to commit the crime]."[a]

Whatever the implications of the "chancellor's foot" passage, both in *Payner,* infra, and in *Hasting,* infra, the Court left no doubt that it took a dim view of the federal courts' exercise of their "supervisory power."

UNITED STATES v. PAYNER, 447 U.S. 727, 100 S.Ct. 2439, 65 L.Ed.2d 468 (1980), arose as follows: An IRS investigation into the financial activities of American citizens in the Bahamas focused on a certain Bahamian bank. When an official of that bank visited the United States, IRS agents stole his briefcase for a time, removed hundreds of documents from the briefcase and photographed them. As a result of this "briefcase caper," defendant Payner was convicted of federal income tax violations. Because Payner lacked "standing" to challenge the "briefcase caper" under the Court's Fourth Amendment precedents (see Ch. 11, § 1), the federal district court invoked its supervisory power to exclude the tainted

---

a. Dissenting Justice Brennan, joined by Stewart and Marshall, JJ., agreed with Justices Powell and Blackmun that "*Russell* does not foreclose imposition of a bar to conviction—based upon our supervisory power or due process principles—where the conduct of law enforcement authorities is sufficiently offensive, even though the individuals entitled to invoke such a defense might be 'predisposed.'"

evidence. The district court found, and these findings were undisturbed by the higher courts, that "the Government counsels its agents that the Fourth Amendment standing limitation permits them to purposefully conduct an unconstitutional search and seizure of one individual in order to obtain evidence against third parties who are the real targets of the government intrusion" and that IRS agents "transacted the 'briefcase caper' with a purposeful, bad faith hostility toward the Fourth Amendment rights of [the bank official] in order to obtain evidence against persons like Payner." But a 6–3 majority, per POWELL, J., held that the supervisory power "does not authorize a federal court" to exclude evidence that did not violate the defendant's Fourth Amendment rights:

"[T]he interest in deterring illegal searches does not justify the exclusion of tainted evidence at the instance of a party who was not the victim of the challenged practices. The values assigned to the competing interests do not change because a court has elected to analyze the question under the supervisory power instead of the Fourth Amendment. In either case, the need to deter the underlying conduct and the detrimental impact of excluding the evidence remain precisely the same." [The] district court's reasoning, which the [Sixth Circuit] affirmed, amounts to a substitution of individual judgment for the controlling decisions of this Court. Were we to accept this use of the supervisory power, we would confer on the judiciary discretionary power to disregard the considered limitations of the law it is charged with enforcing."

Dissenting Justice MARSHALL, joined by Brennan and Blackmun, JJ., maintained that the Court's holding "effectively turns the standing rules created by this Court for assertions of Fourth Amendment violations into a sword to be used by the Government to permit it deliberately to invade one person's Fourth Amendment rights in order to obtain evidence against another person. Unlike the Court, I do not believe that the federal courts are unable to protect the integrity of the judicial system from such gross government misconduct." Continued the dissent:

"The Court's decision to engraft the standing limitations of the Fourth Amendment onto the exercise of supervisory powers is puzzling not only because it runs contrary to the major purpose behind the exercise of the supervisory powers—to protect the integrity of the court—but also because it appears to render the supervisory powers superfluous. In order to establish that suppression of evidence under the supervisory powers would be proper, the Court would also require Payner to establish a violation of his Fourth or Fifth Amendment rights, in which case suppression would flow directly from the Constitution. This approach is totally unfaithful to our prior supervisory power cases, which, contrary to the Court's suggestion, are not constitutional cases in disguise."

UNITED STATES v. HASTING, 461 U.S. 499, 103 S.Ct. 1974, 76 L.Ed.2d 96 (1983), arose as follows: Five defendants were convicted of kidnapping and transporting women across state lines for immoral purposes. Concluding that the prosecutor had violated *Griffin v. California* (p. 30, fn. a) by, in effect, commenting on the failure of any defendant to take the stand in his own defense, the U.S. Court of Appeals for the Seventh Circuit reversed. The Seventh Circuit was motivated at least in part by what it perceived to be continuing violations of *Griffin* by the prosecutors within its jurisdiction. Although impermissible comment on a defendant's failure to take the stand is subject to a "harmless error" doctrine (See Ch. 28, § 5), the Seventh Circuit declined to apply that doctrine, stating that its application "would impermissibly compromise the clear constitutional violation of the defendants' Fifth Amendment rights." The Court, per BURGER, C.J., reversed:

"[W]e proceed on the assumption that, without so stating, the court was exercising its supervisory powers to discipline the prosecutors of its jurisdiction. * * * We hold that the [harmless error doctrine] may not be avoided by an assertion of supervisory power, simply to justify a reversal of these criminal convictions.

"[I]n the exercise of supervisory powers, federal courts may, within limits, formulate procedural rules not specifically required by the Constitution or the Congress. The purposes underlying use of the supervisory powers are threefold: to implement a remedy for violation of recognized rights; to preserve judicial integrity by ensuring that a conviction rests on appropriate considerations validly before the jury; and finally, as a remedy designed to deter illegal conduct.

"[These goals] are not, however, significant in the context of this case if, as the Court of Appeals plainly implied, the errors alleged are harmless. Supervisory power to reverse a conviction is not needed as a remedy when the error to which it is addressed is harmless since by definition, the conviction would have been obtained notwithstanding the asserted error. Further, in this context, the integrity of the process carries less weight, for it is the essence of the harmless error doctrine that a judgment may stand only when there is no 'reasonable possibility that the [practice] complained of might have contributed to the conviction.' Finally, deterrence is an inappropriate basis for reversal where, as here, the prosecutor's remark is at most an attenuated violation of *Griffin* and where means more narrowly tailored to deter objectionable prosecutorial conduct are available.[5]

"To the extent that the values protected by supervisory authority are at issue here, these powers may not be exercised in a vacuum. Rather, reversals of convictions under the court's supervisory power must be approached 'with some caution,' *Payner,* and with a view toward balancing the interests involved. [T]he Court of Appeals failed in this case to give appropriate—if, indeed, any—weight to these relevant interests. It did not consider the trauma the victims of these particularly heinous crimes would experience in a new trial [or] the practical problems of retrying these sensitive issues more than four years after the events. The conclusion is inescapable that the Court of Appeals focused exclusively on its concern that the prosecutors within its jurisdiction were indifferent to the frequent admonitions of the court. The court appears to have decided to deter future similar comments by the drastic step of reversal of these convictions. But the interests preserved by the doctrine of harmless error cannot be so lightly and casually ignored in order to chastise what the court viewed as prosecutorial overreaching."[b]

Justice BRENNAN, joined by Marshall, J., concurred in part and dissented in part, observing:

"[Various cases] indicate that the policy considerations supporting the harmless error rule and those supporting the existence of an appellate court's supervisory powers are not in irreconcilable conflict. Both the harmless error rule and the

---

5. Here, for example, the court could have dealt with the offending argument by directing the District Court to order the prosecutor to show cause why he should not be disciplined, or by asking the Department of Justice to initiate a disciplinary proceeding against him. The Government informs us that in the last three years, the Department of Justice's Office of Professional Responsibility has investigated 28 complaints of unethical conduct and that one assistant United States attorney resigned in the face of an investigation that he made improper arguments to a grand jury. The Court also could have publicly chastised the prosecutor by identifying him in its opinion.

b. Stevens, J., concurred in the judgment, deeming the prosecutor's comments "free of constitutional error." Blackmun, J., would vacate the judgment and remand the case for consideration of whether the Fifth Amendment violation it perceived was "harmless."

exercise of supervisory powers advance the important judicial and public interest in the orderly and efficient administration of justice. [If] Government prosecutors have engaged in a pattern and practice of intentionally violating defendants' constitutional rights, a court of appeals certainly might be justified in reversing a conviction, even if the error at issue is harmless, in an effort to deter future violations. If effective as a deterrent, the reversal could avert further damage to judicial integrity. [It] is certainly arguable that the public's interests in preserving judicial integrity and in insuring that Government prosecutors, as its agents, refrain from intentionally violating defendants' rights are stronger than its interest in upholding the conviction of a particular criminal defendant. Convictions are important, but they should not be protected at any cost."

[handwritten margin notes: "not allowing sup powers could taint gov't's own integrity"; "Sup Power Acts as a deterrent"]

Notes and Questions

1. Under the *Massiah* doctrine (p. 448), an indicted defendant has a Sixth Amendment right to counsel as well as his *Miranda* safeguards. Stressing that the "strict standard" governing waiver of counsel at trial should apply to an alleged waiver of the *Massiah* right to counsel as well, in *United States v. Mohabir,* 624 F.2d 1140 (2d Cir.1980), the court invoked its federal supervisory power to hold that a "valid waiver of the Sixth Amendment right to have counsel present during post-indictment interrogation must be preceded by a federal judicial officer's explanation of the content and significance of this right." However, in *Patterson v. Illinois* (1988) (p. 602), the Supreme Court specifically rejected *Mohabir*'s holding that warnings in addition to the *Miranda* warnings are required to effectuate a waiver of the *Massiah* right (see fn. 8 in *Patterson*), without mentioning that *Mohabir* was an exercise of the Second Circuit's federal supervisory power.

2. The *Hasting* Court noted that, within limits, federal courts may exercise their "supervisory power [to] formulate procedural rules not specifically required by the Constitution or the Congress." After *Payner* and *Hasting, what* procedural rules? Consider Note 4, p. 662 (exercise of federal supervisory power over grand juries). After *Payner* and *Hasting,* may the federal courts still *exclude evidence* or reverse a conviction based in part on inadmissible evidence if such exclusion or reversal is not required by the Constitution or the Congress? Cf. *Bank of Nova Scotia v. United States*, 487 U.S. 250, 108 S.Ct. 2369, 101 L.Ed.2d 228 (1988) (set forth in Ch. 15, § 4).

[handwritten margin note: "May cts still exclude evidence if such exclusion or reversal is not required by Const. or Congress?"]

3. Why has the effort to impose "extraconstitutional" standards on federal law enforcement officials, best illustrated by *McNabb* and its progeny, fared so badly in recent decades? Consider Bennett Gershman, *The New Prosecutors*, 53 U.Pitt.L.Rev. 393, 432 (1992): "First, [the supervisory power] required judges to impose on government officials their own notions of 'good policy.' The judiciary has resisted this invitation. Second, supervisory power increasingly has been viewed as an unwarranted judicial intrusion into the exclusive domain of a coordinate branch of the government. Finally, once supervisory power became subservient to the harmless error rule, it became largely irrelevant."

SECTION 5. TRENDS AND COUNTERTRENDS: THE "NEW FEDERALISM IN CRIMINAL PROCEDURE" AND NEW LIMITATIONS ON STATE RIGHTS PROTECTIONS[a]

When the Warren Court's "criminal procedure revolution" came to a halt, a number of state courts "greeted the Burger Court's retreat from activism not with

---

a. The phrase "new federalism in criminal procedure" was coined by Professor Donald E. Wilkes, Jr., in his 1974 article, *The New Feder-* *alism in Criminal Procedure: State Court Evasion of the Burger Court*, 62 Ky.L.J. 421.

submission, but with a stubborn independence that displays a determination to keep alive the Warren Court's philosophical commitment to protection of the criminal suspect." Donald E. Wilkes, *More on the New Federalism in Criminal Procedure,* 63 Ky.L.J. 873 (1975). The most influential article on the subject of state constitutional rights is Justice William Brennan's *State Constitutions and the Protection of Individual Rights,* 90 Harv.L.Rev. 489 (1977), one of the most frequently cited law review articles of modern times. See, too, Justice Brennan's updated views in *The Bill of Rights and the States: The Revival of State Constitutions as Guardians of Individual Rights,* 61 N.Y.U.L.Rev. 535 (1986). See also e.g., Barry Latzer, *State Constitutional Criminal Procedure* (1995); Robert F. Williams, *State Constitutional Law: Cases & Materials* (2d ed. 1993) (especially Ch.3); Ronald Collins, Foreword: *The Once "New Judicial Federalism" and Its Critics,* 64 Wash.L.Rev. 5 (1989); Hans Linde, *First Things First: Rediscovering the States' Bill of Rights,* 9 U.Balt.L.Rev. 379 (1980).

A state supreme court bent on providing the accused with greater protection than that said to be required by the federal constitution may insulate its decision from U.S. Supreme Court review if, to quote the High Court in *Michigan v. Long* (p. 54), the state court "indicates clearly and expressly" that its decision rests on "adequate and independent state grounds." Typically, the state court construes a state constitutional provision more expansively than the U.S. Supreme Court has interpreted a *textually identical or parallel* provision of the Federal Bill of Rights. But sometimes, as in *People v. Jackson,* 391 Mich. 323, 217 N.W.2d 22 (1974) (rejecting the position taken by the U.S. Supreme Court in two pretrial identification cases, *Kirby v. Illinois* (p. 631), and *United States v. Ash* (p. 636), the state court may rest its decision on its authority to establish rules of evidence for its own courts.

Justice Brennan and Marshall, who often found themselves in a dissenting role in the 1970's, frequently pointed to—and approved and encouraged—the practice of some state courts (a distinct minority) to interpret state procedural rights more expansively than does the current U.S. Supreme Court. See especially Justice Brennan's dissenting opinion in *Michigan v. Mosley* (p. 521). Justice Brennan also forcefully stated his views on this matter in his 1977 law review article, supra, emphasizing that "the decisions of the [U.S. Supreme] Court are not, and should not be, dispositive of questions regarding rights guaranteed by counterpart provisions of state law. [A]lthough in the past it might have been safe for counsel to raise only federal constitutional issues in state courts, plainly it would be most unwise these days not also to raise the state constitutional questions."

Justice Brennan's advice has not gone unheeded. A dozen years after Brennan wrote his first article on state constitutional rights, Washington Supreme Court Justice Robert Utter, *State Constitutional Law, the United States Supreme Court, and Democratic Accountability,* 64 Wash.L.Rev. 19, 27 (1989), reported that "more than 450 published state court opinions [had interpreted] state constitutions as going beyond federal constitutional guarantees."

For example, a number of state courts have declined to adopt the U.S. Supreme Court's position in *United States v. Leon,* p. 114 (establishing a so-called "good faith" exception to the fourth amendment exclusionary rule at least in search warrant cases); *Illinois v. Gates* (p. 169) (establishing a new approach to "probable cause"); *Harris v. New York* (permitting use of statements obtained in violation of *Miranda* for impeachment purposes); and *Moran v. Burbine* (p. 538) (police need not inform a suspect that a lawyer retained by relatives or friends is trying to reach him). See generally Charles H. Whitebread & Christopher Slogbogin, *Criminal Procedure* § 34.02 (c) (4th ed. 2000).

—————

The New Federalism has not escaped strong criticism. Some judges and commentators, for example, have charged that it generates uncertainty and confusion among state officials and that "state activism" not based on local factors is a result-oriented response to U.S. Supreme Court decisions and therefore unprincipled. See Whitebread & Slobogin, supra, at 1035–42 and cases and authorities discussed therein.

Although the "new federalism in criminal procedure" became apparent in the early 1970's, "recent constitutional and statutory changes in state law * * * have imposed new restrictions on the new federalism." Donald E. Wilkes, *The New Federalism in Criminal Procedure in 1984: Death of the Phoenix?*, in Developments in State Constitutional Law 166, 169 (B. McGraw ed. 1985) (hereinafter referred to as "Wilkes").

"Many of the best and brightest of the new federalism decisions have come from the California Supreme Court," Wilkes at 171, but The California Victims' Bill of Rights, often called Proposition 8, an initiative approved by the voters in 1982, "represents a major victory for the opponents of the new federalism in California, who have become increasingly vocal in their attacks since the early 1970s." Id. Proposition 8 added a new Section 28 to Article I of the California Bill of Rights. A so-called "right to truth-in-evidence" provision of the new section reads: "Except as provided by statute hereafter enacted by a two thirds vote of the membership in each house of the Legislature, relevant evidence shall not be excluded in any criminal proceeding * * *." *In re Lance W.*, 694 P.2d 744 (Cal.1985), held that this provision abrogated the vicarious exclusionary rule that was established in *People v. Martin* (1955) (p. 749) and applied to both Fourth Amendment and state constitutional violations.

The New Federalism also suffered a setback in Florida. When the state supreme court held that the state guarantee against unreasonable search and seizure, Art. 1, § 12 of the Florida Constitution, furnished more protection against governmental intrusion than did the Fourth Amendment to the U.S. Constitution, Florida voters amended the state guarantee so that it now provides that "[t]his right shall be construed in conformity with the 4th Amendment to the United States Constitution, as interpreted by the United States Supreme Court." Unlike the California Amendment, which only affects the exclusionary remedy, the Florida amendment eliminates the power of its state courts to develop their own substantive law of search and seizure. See generally Christopher Slobogin, *State Adoption of Federal Law: Exploring the Limits of Florida's "Forced Linkage" Amendment*, 39 U.Fla.L.Rev. 653 (1987).

—————

As might be expected, the state courts' interpretation of state constitutional provisions so that they provide greater protection than that required by the present Supreme Court's interpretation of analogous provisions of the Bill of Rights has received a chilly reception in some U.S. Supreme Court Justices' chambers. Thus, concurring in the dismissal of the writ of certiorari as improvidently granted in *Florida v. Casal*, 462 U.S. 637, 103 S.Ct. 3100, 77 L.Ed.2d 277 (1983), Chief Justice Burger expressed satisfaction with the 1982 amendment to the Florida Constitution. "As amended," he noted, Art. 1, § 12 "ensures that Florida courts will no longer be able to rely on the State Constitution to suppress evidence that would be admissible under the decisions of the Supreme Court of the United States. [W]hen state courts interpret state law to require *more* than the Federal Constitution requires, the citizens of the state must be aware that they have the power to amend state law to ensure rational law enforcement."

In MICHIGAN v. LONG, 463 U.S. 1032, 103 S.Ct. 3469, 77 L.Ed.2d 1201 (1983) (also discussed at p. 322), rejecting the argument that "the Michigan courts have provided greater protection from searches and seizures under the state constitution than is afforded under the Fourth Amendment, and the [state supreme court's] references to the state constitution therefore establishes an adequate and independent ground for the decision below," the Court, per O'CON-NOR, J., took the occasion to "reexamine our treatment of [the] jurisdictional issue in order to achieve the consistency that is necessary" when various forms of references to state law are said to constitute adequate and independent state grounds:

"[W]hen, as in this case, a state court decision fairly appears to rest primarily on federal law, or to be interwoven with the federal law, and when the adequacy and independence of any possible state law ground is not clear from the face of the opinion, we will accept as the most reasonable explanation that the state court decided the case the way it did because it believed that federal law required it to do so. If a state court chooses merely to rely on federal precedents as it would on the precedents of all other jurisdictions, then it need only make clear by a plain statement [that] the federal cases are being used only for the purpose of guidance, and do not themselves compel the result that the court has reached. In this way, both justice and judicial administration will be greatly improved. If the state court decision indicates clearly and expressly that it is alternatively based on bona fide separate, adequate, and independent grounds, we, of course, will not undertake to review the decision.

"The principle that we will not review judgments of state courts that rest on adequate and independent state grounds is based, in part, on 'the limitations of our own jurisdiction.' The jurisdictional concern is that we not 'render an advisory opinion, and if the same judgment would be rendered by the state court after we corrected its views of federal laws, our review could amount to nothing more than an advisory opinion.' Our requirement of a 'plain statement' that a decision rests upon adequate and independent state grounds does not in any way authorize the rendering of advisory opinions. Rather, in determining, as we must, whether we have jurisdiction to review a case that is alleged to rest on adequate and independent state grounds, we merely assume that there are no such grounds when it is not clear from the opinion itself that the state court relied upon an adequate and independent state ground and when it fairly appears that the state court rested its decision primarily on federal law."[a]

Dissenting Justice STEVENS could not accept the Court's decision "to presume that adequate state grounds are intended to be dependent on federal law unless the record plainly shows otherwise." He continued:

"I am confident that all members of this Court agree that there is a vital interest in the sound management of scarce federal judicial resources. All of those policies counsel against the exercise of federal jurisdiction. They are fortified by my belief that a policy of judicial restraint—one that allows other decisional bodies to have the last word in legal interpretation until it is truly necessary for this

a. The Court then reviewed the decision below under this framework and came away "unconvinced that it rests upon an independent state ground."

Court to intervene—enables this Court to make its most effective contribution to our federal system of government.

"The nature of the case before us hardly compels a departure from tradition. These are not cases in which an American citizen has been deprived of a right secured by the United States Constitution or a federal statute. Rather, they are cases in which a state court has upheld a citizen's assertion of a right, finding the citizen to be protected under both federal and state law. The complaining party is an officer of the state itself, who asks us to rule that the state court interpreted federal rights too broadly and 'over-protected' the citizen. Such cases should not be of inherent concern to this Court. * * *

"In this case the State of Michigan has arrested one of its citizens and the Michigan Supreme Court has decided to turn him loose. The respondent is a United States citizen as well as a Michigan citizen, but since there is no claim that he has been mistreated by the State of Michigan, the final outcome of the state processes offended no federal interest whatever. Michigan simply provided greater protection to one of its citizens than some other State might provide or, indeed, than this Court might require throughout the country.

"[Until] recently we had virtually no interest in cases of this type. Some time during the past decade, * * * our priorities shifted. The result is a docket swollen with requests by states to reverse judgments that their courts have rendered in favor of their citizens. I am confident that a future Court will recognize the error of this allocation of resources. When that day comes, I think it likely that the Court will also reconsider the propriety of today's expansion of our jurisdiction."[b]

See also *Florida v. Meyers,* 466 U.S. 380, 104 S.Ct. 1852, 80 L.Ed.2d 381 (1984) (per curiam), summarily reversing a state intermediate appellate court because it "either misunderstood or ignored our prior rulings with respect to the constitutionality of the warrantless search of an impounded automobile." (The state supreme court had denied discretionary review.) Respondent argued that the Court should not review the search and seizure issue because the state court had reversed the conviction on two independent grounds, one of which (restricted cross-examination) the state did not contest. But the Court found no "clear indication that the cross-examination ruling provided an independent and adequate basis for reversal of the conviction. See *Michigan v. Long.*"

Dissenting Justice Stevens, joined by Brennan and Marshall, JJ., who saw "no reason why we cannot leave to the Florida Supreme Court the task of managing its own discretionary docket," took issue with the Court's reliance on *Long.* And he noted: "Since the beginning of the October 1981 Term, the Court has decided in summary fashion 19 cases, including this one, concerning the constitutional rights of persons accused or convicted of crimes. All 19 were decided on the petition of the warden or prosecutor, and in all he was successful in obtaining reversal of a decision upholding a claim of constitutional right. [T]his pattern of results, and in particular the fact that in its last two and one-half Terms the Court has been unwilling in even a single criminal case to employ its discretionary power of summary disposition in order to uphold a claim of constitutional right, is quite striking."

b. Although he was satisfied that the Court had jurisdiction in this particular case, concurring Justice Blackmun did not join the part of the Court's opinion "fashioning a new presumption of jurisdiction over cases coming here from state courts." Brennan, J., joined by Marshall, J., agreed that the Court had jurisdiction to decide the case, but dissented on the merits of the search and seizure issue. (See p. 322).

Chapter 3

THE RIGHT TO COUNSEL, TRANSCRIPTS AND OTHER AIDS; POVERTY, EQUALITY AND THE ADVERSARY SYSTEM

REPORT OF THE ATTORNEY GENERAL'S COMMITTEE ON POVERTY AND THE ADMINISTRATION OF FEDERAL CRIMINAL JUSTICE 5–11 (1963)[a]

POVERTY AND CRIMINAL JUSTICE: THE NATURE OF GOVERNMENT'S OBLIGATION * * *

a. *The Concept of "Poverty."* [The] concept proved an elusive one and the difficulties of definition substantial.[b] It is apparent that a total absence in the accused of all means and resources cannot be adequate for these purposes. Even the constitutional rights to the appointment of counsel are not conditioned on a showing of total destitution. Rather, the criterion appears to be a lack of financial resources adequate to permit the accused to hire his own lawyer.[c] Reflection led the Committee to the conclusion that the poverty must be viewed as a relative concept with the consequence that the poverty of accused must be measured in each case by reference to the particular need or service under consideration.

Thus in the criminal process a problem of poverty may arise at each stage of the proceedings. There is a problem of poverty if the defendant is unable to obtain pre-trial release by reason of financial inability to meet the bail requirements or to retain a lawyer to represent him at the trial. There is also a problem of poverty if the accused is unable to finance a pretrial investigation of the case or to obtain the services of expert witnesses when such investigation or testimony is essential to an adequate defense.[d] So, too, in the appellate process, there is a problem of poverty if through lack of means the accused is inhibited or prevented from presenting grounds of reversal to the appellate court or from making adequate presentation.

a. The Report is often called *The Allen Report*, after the Chairman of the Committee, Professor Francis A. Allen.

b. "[F]ew statutory standards are available to guide the [trial court] in its determination of indigency sufficient to warrant court-appointed counsel; as a result, the courts have utilized various criteria for determining eligibility. While some courts have limited the scope of inquiry, for example, to whether the accused is working and has money to hire a lawyer, other courts have considered the accused's assets, debts, employment, ability to post bail, and responsibility for dependents. The confusion and lack of consistency that exist in federal indigency standards are mirrored in the state courts." Note, 12 U.S.F.L.Rev. 717, 720–21 (1978).

c. Should the test of eligibility for court-appointed counsel be whether a private attorney would be interested in representing the defendant in his present economic circumstances? Can this standard be applied with any uniformity?

d. On the indigent's right to investigatory, expert and other assistance in addition to counsel, see *Ake v. Oklahoma* (p. 83) and accompanying Notes.

It follows that concern with poverty and the administration of criminal justice requires attention to be extended beyond those who are unable at the outset of the proceedings to obtain release on bail or to hire counsel.[e] It requires consideration, also, of those who, although possessing means to obtain some elements of an adequate defense (such as hiring a lawyer), lack means to secure other essential elements.[f] Indeed, it requires attention be given to the plight of the accused with substantial means rendered indigent by the levy of a jeopardy assessment and thus unable to hire the services of an accountant in defense of a net-worth tax prosecution.

[In] summary, the Committee believes that, for the purposes at hand, poverty must be conceived as a relative concept. An impoverished accused is not necessarily one totally devoid of means. A problem of poverty arises for the system of criminal justice when at any stage of the proceedings lack of means in the accused substantially inhibits or prevents the proper assertion of a right or a claim of right.

b. *The Obligation of "Equal Justice."*

[It] should be understood that governmental obligation to deal effectively with problems of poverty in the administration of criminal justice does not rest or depend upon some hypothetical obligation of government to indulge in acts of public charity. It does not presuppose a general commitment on the part of the federal government to relieve impoverished persons of the consequences of limited means, whenever or however manifested. It does not even presuppose that government is always required to take into account the means of the citizen when dealing directly with its citizens.

[The] obligation of government in the criminal cases rests on wholly different considerations and reflects principles of much more limited application. The essential point is that the problems of poverty with which this Report is concerned arise in a process *initiated* by government for the achievement of basic governmental purposes. It is, moreover, a process that has as one of its consequences the imposition of severe disabilities on the persons proceeded against. Duties arise from action. When a course of conduct, however legitimate, entails the possibility of serious injury to persons, a duty on the actor to avoid the reasonably avoidable injuries is ordinarily recognized. When government chooses to exert its powers in the criminal area, its obligation is surely no less than that of taking reasonable measures to eliminate those factors that are irrelevant to just administration of the law but which, nevertheless, may occasionally affect determinations of the accused's liability or penalty. While government may not be required to relieve the accused of his poverty, it may properly be required to minimize the influence of poverty on its administration of justice.

The Committee, therefore, conceives the obligation of government less as an undertaking to eliminate "discrimination" against a class of accused persons and more as a broad commitment by government to rid its processes of all influences that tend to defeat the ends a system of justice is intended to serve. Such a concept of "equal justice" does not confuse equality of treatment with identity of treatment. We assume that government must be conceded flexibility in devising its measures and that reasonable classifications are permitted. The crucial question is, has government done all that can reasonably be required of it to eliminate

e. *A.B.A. Standards* § 5–6.1 provides that assigned counsel "should not be denied merely because friends or relatives have resources adequate to retain counsel or because bond has been or can be posted."

f. *A.B.A. Standards* § 5–6.1 provides: "Supporting services necessary to an adequate defense should be available to all persons eligible for representation *and to the clients of retained counsel* who are financially unable to afford necessary supporting services." (Emphasis added.)

those factors that inhibit the proper and effective assertion of grounds relevant to the criminal liability of the accused or to the imposition of sanctions and disabilities on the accused at all stages of the criminal process?

c. *Poverty and the Adversary System.*

[The] essence of the adversary system is challenge. The survival of our system of criminal justice and the values which it advances depend upon a constant, searching, and creative questioning of official decisions and assertions of authority at all stages of the process. The proper performance of the defense function is thus as vital to the health of the system as the performance of the prosecuting and adjudicatory functions. It follows that insofar as the financial status of the accused impedes vigorous and proper challenges, it constitutes a threat to the viability of the adversary system. We believe that the system is imperiled by the large numbers of accused persons unable to employ counsel or to meet even modest bail requirements and by the large, but indeterminate, numbers of persons, able to pay some part of the costs of defense, but unable to finance a full and proper defense.[g] Persons suffering such disabilities are incapable of providing the challenges that are indispensable to satisfactory operation of the system. The loss to the interests of accused individuals, occasioned by these failures, are great and apparent. It is also clear that a situation in which persons are required to contest a serious accusation but are denied access to the tools of contest is offensive to fairness and equity. Beyond these considerations, however, is the fact that the conditions produced by the financial incapacity of the accused are detrimental to the proper functioning of the system of justice and that the loss in vitality of the adversary system, thereby occasioned, significantly endangers the basic interests of a free community.

Notes and Questions

1. *The indigent defendant's "obligation" to repay the government for defense costs; reimbursement as a condition of probation.* Rinaldi v. Yeager, 384 U.S. 305, 86 S.Ct. 1497, 16 L.Ed.2d 577 (1966), invalidated a New Jersey statute which required only those indigent defendants who were sentenced to prison to reimburse the state for the cost of a transcript on appeal, finding an "invidious discrimination" between those convicted defendants and others sentenced only to pay fines or subject only to a suspended sentence or to probation. *James v. Strange,* 407 U.S. 128, 92 S.Ct. 2027, 32 L.Ed.2d 600 (1972), held that a Kansas recoupment statute (which applied whether or not the indigent defendant was convicted) violated equal protection because the indigent defendant could not avail himself of restrictions on wage garnishments and other protective exemptions afforded to other civil judgment debtors.

Fuller v. Oregon, 417 U.S. 40, 94 S.Ct. 2116, 40 L.Ed.2d 642 (1974), however, upheld an Oregon recoupment statute which, under certain circumstances, authorized repayment to the state of the costs of a free legal defense as a condition of probation. A 7–2 majority, per Stewart, J., stressed that "the recoupment statute is quite clearly directed only at those convicted defendants who are indigent at the time of the criminal proceedings against them but who subsequently gain the ability to pay the expenses of legal representation. Defendants with no likelihood of having the means to repay are not put under even a conditional obligation to do so, and those upon whom a conditional obligation is imposed are not subjected to

---

g. The percentage of state felony cases in which defendants were given appointed counsel rose from just under 50% in the late 1970s to about 80% by 1992. See William J. Stuntz, *The Uneasy Relationship Between Criminal Procedure and Criminal Justice,* 107 Yale L.J. 1, 9 (1997).

collection procedures until their indigency has ended and no 'manifest hardship' [to defendant or his immediate family] will result."

Distinguishing *James* and *Rinaldi,* the Court rejected petitioner's equal protection challenge. It pointed out that Oregon had not denied exemptions from execution afforded to other judgment debtors. Unlike the classification struck down in *Rinaldi,* it deemed a distinction between defendants who are convicted, on the one hand, and those acquitted or whose convictions are reversed, on the other hand, "wholly noninvidious": "Oregon could surely decide with objective rationality that when a defendant has been forced to submit to a criminal prosecution that does not end in conviction, he will be freed of any potential liability to reimburse the state for the costs of his defense."

Nor was the Court impressed with the argument that a defendant's knowledge that he may be obligated to reimburse the state for expenses incurred in providing him a legal defense might lead him to reject the services of appointed counsel and thus "chill" his constitutional right to counsel: "The fact that an indigent who accepts [appointed counsel] knows that he might someday be required to repay the costs of these services in no way affects his eligibility to obtain counsel. The Oregon statute is carefully designed to insure that only those who actually become capable of repaying the State will ever be obliged to do so."

Dissenting Justice Marshall, joined by Brennan, J., protested that "the important fact which the majority ignores" is that because the repayment of the indigent defendant's debt to the state can be made a condition of his probation, as it was in this case, "[p]etitioner's failure to pay his debt can result in his being sent to prison. In this respect the indigent defendant in Oregon, like [his counterpart in *James*], is treated quite differently from other civil judgment debtors."

2. Notwithstanding the *Fuller* case, *A.B.A. Standards* § 5–6.2 (commentary) "recommends that defendants be ordered to [make reimbursement] for their defense only in instances where they have made fraudulent representations for purposes of being found eligible for counsel. [The] offer of free legal assistance is rendered hollow if defendants are required to make payments for counsel for several years following conviction. Reimbursement requirements also may serve to discourage defendants from exercising their right to counsel * * *."

SECTION 1. THE RIGHT TO APPOINTED COUNSEL AND RELATED PROBLEMS

A. THE RIGHT TO APPOINTED COUNSEL IN CRIMINAL PROCEEDINGS

Introduction

A look at early English law reveals that the right to counsel had "surprisingly modest beginnings." James Tomkovicz, *The Right to the Assistance of Counsel* ___ (2002) (forthcoming). Originally only those accused of minor offenses could be represented by counsel. (Evidently the monarch believed that permitting representation by defense counsel generally would prevent the successful prosecution of serious cases.) However, against a background of a decade of false treason charges against the Whigs, the Treason Act of 1695 provided that those prosecuted for high treason should be allowed to defend themselves by "counsel learned in the law." Thus, at the time of the adoption of the U.S. Constitution, England recognized a right to *retain* counsel to argue matters of fact only for those accused of misdemeanors or high treason. See id.[a]

From the earliest times, the general practice in serious criminal cases in the American colonies was self-representation, not representation by counsel. But by the time the nation was about to ratify the Constitution, most states had granted criminal defendants the right to be represented by a lawyer. No state, however, guaranteed the right to *appointed* counsel. As Professor Tomkovicz has observed, "[i]t seems highly probable that the Sixth Amendment was designed to grant a legal representative of one's own choosing [thereby rejecting the restricted British approach], but no right to have counsel provided by the government." See id.

One hundred and fifty-one years after the ratification of the Sixth Amendment and some sixty years after the adoption of the Fourteenth, the Supreme Court handed down its first significant opinion concerning the right to counsel—*Powell v. Alabama* (1932) (discussed infra). Although the *Powell* opinion contains sweeping, much-quoted language (such as "the right to be heard would be in many cases of little avail if it did not comprehend the right to be heard by counsel") the Court dwelt on the special circumstances—"above all that [the defendants] stood in peril of their lives." In a case *such as this* the Court told us, "the failure of the trial court to give [the defendants] reasonable time and opportunity to secure counsel was a clear denial of due process." *And in a case with these facts*, "the right to have counsel appointed [is] *a logical corollary of the constitutional right to be heard by counsel.*" (Emphasis added.)

Powell, of course, was a state case. Six years later, in *Johnson v. Zerbst* (1938) (discussed infra), the Court held, without discussing the likely intent of the Sixth Amendment, that the Amendment guaranteed indigent *federal* defendants (at least all felony defendants) a right to *appointed* counsel. But it would take another twenty-five years before the Court would conclude that the Constitution guaranteed *state* defendants the same unqualified right.

BETTS v. BRADY
316 U.S. 455, 62 S.Ct. 1252, 86 L.Ed. 1595 (1942).

Justice ROBERTS delivered the opinion of the Court.

Petitioner, an indigent, was indicted for robbery. His request for counsel was denied because local practice permitted appointment only in rape and murder prosecutions. Petitioner then pled not guilty and elected to be tried without a jury. At the trial he chose not to take the stand. He was convicted and sentenced to eight years imprisonment.

[The] due process clause of the Fourteenth Amendment does not incorporate, as such, the specific guarantees found in the Sixth Amendment although a denial by a state of rights or privileges specifically embodied in that and others of the first eight amendments may, in certain circumstances, * * * deprive a litigant of due process of law in violation of the Fourteenth. [Due process] formulates a concept less rigid and more fluid than those envisaged in other specific and particular provisions of the Bill of Rights. Its application is less a matter of rule. Asserted denial is to be tested by an appraisal of the totality of facts in a given case.

---

a. At some point in the development of the right to counsel in England, retained counsel could appear on behalf of a felony defendant to argue, but only to argue, matters of law. "When it came to presenting evidence and arguing as to the strength of the evidence, the felony defendant was on his own." 1 Wayne R. LaFave, Jerold H. Israel & Nancy J. King, *Criminal Procedure* § 1.5(b) (2d ed. 1999). However, the distinction between matters of fact and matters of law was hazy and by the middle of the nineteenth century "questions of law" seem to have been extended to include both direct examination and cross-examination. See id.

[Petitioner] says the rule to be deduced from our former decisions is that, in every case, whatever the circumstances, one charged with crime, who is unable to obtain counsel, must be furnished counsel by the state. Expressions in the opinions of this court lend color to the argument, but, as the petitioner admits, none of our decisions squarely adjudicates the question now presented.

In *Powell v. Alabama,* 287 U.S. 45, 53 S.Ct. 55, 77 L.Ed. 158 [1932], ignorant and friendless negro youths, strangers in the community, without friends or means to obtain counsel, were hurried to trial for a capital offense without effective appointment of counsel on whom the burden of preparation and trial would rest, and without adequate opportunity to consult even the counsel casually appointed to represent them. [This] court held the resulting convictions were without due process of law. It said that, in the light of all the facts, the failure of the trial court to afford the defendants reasonable time and opportunity to secure counsel was a clear denial of due process. The court stated further that "under the circumstances [the] necessity of counsel was so vital and imperative that the failure of the trial court to make an effective appointment of counsel was likewise a denial of due process," but added: "whether this would be so in other criminal prosecutions, or under other circumstances, we need not determine. All that it is necessary now to decide, as we do decide, is that in a capital case, where the defendant is unable to employ counsel, and is incapable adequately of making his own defense because of ignorance, feeblemindedness, illiteracy, or the like, it is the duty of the court, whether requested or not, to assign counsel for him as a necessary requisite of due process of law * * *."

* * * We have construed the [Sixth Amendment] to require appointment of counsel in all [federal] cases where a defendant is unable to procure the services of an attorney, and where the right has not been intentionally and competently waived. [*Johnson v. Zerbst,* 304 U.S. 458, 58 S.Ct. 1019, 82 L.Ed. 1461 (1938)].[a] Though [the] amendment lays down no rule for the conduct of the states, the question recurs whether the constraint laid by the amendment upon the national courts expresses a rule so fundamental and essential to a fair trial, and so, to due process of law, that it is made obligatory upon the states by the Fourteenth Amendment. Relevant data on the subject are afforded by constitutional and statutory provisions subsisting in the colonies and the states prior to the inclusion of the Bill of Rights in the national Constitution, and in the constitutional, legislative, and judicial history of the states to the present date.

[I]n the great majority of the states, it has been the considered judgment of the people, their representatives and their courts that appointment of counsel is not a fundamental right, essential to a fair trial. On the contrary, the matter has generally been deemed one of legislative policy. In the light of this evidence we are unable to say that the concept of due process incorporated in the Fourteenth Amendment obligates the states, whatever may be their own views, to furnish counsel in every such case. Every court has power, if it deems proper, to appoint counsel where that course seems to be required in the interest of fairness.

The practice of the courts of Maryland gives point to the principle that the states should not be straight-jacketed in this respect, by a construction of the

---

a. In holding that the Sixth Amendment required appointment of counsel, the Court, per Black, J., had reasoned: "The Sixth Amendment stands as a constant admonition that if the constitutional safeguards it provides be lost, justice will not 'still be done.' Cf. *Palko.* It embodies a realistic recognition of the obvious truth that the average defendant does not have the professional legal skill to protect himself when brought before a tribunal with power to take his life or liberty, wherein the prosecution is presented by experienced and learned counsel. [The] Sixth Amendment withholds from federal courts, in all criminal proceedings, the power and authority to deprive an accused of his life or liberty unless he has or waives the assistance of counsel."

Fourteenth Amendment. Judge Bond's opinion states, and counsel at the bar confirmed the fact, that in Maryland the usual practice is for the defendant to waive a trial by jury. This the petitioner did in the present case. Such trials, as Judge Bond remarks, are much more informal than jury trials and it is obvious that the judge can much better control the course of the trial and is in a better position to see impartial justice done than when the formalities of a jury trial are involved.

In this case there was no question of the commission of a robbery. The State's case consisted of evidence identifying the petitioner as the perpetrator. The defense was an alibi. Petitioner called and examined witnesses to prove that he was at another place at the time of the commission of the offense. The simple issue was the veracity of the testimony for the State and that for the defendant. As Judge Bond says, the accused was not helpless, but was a man forty-three years old, of ordinary intelligence and ability to take care of his own interests on the trial of that narrow issue. He had once before been in a criminal court, pleaded guilty to larceny and served a sentence and was not wholly unfamiliar with criminal procedure. It is quite clear that in Maryland, if the situation had been otherwise and it had appeared that the petitioner was, for any reason, at a serious disadvantage by reason of the lack of counsel, a refusal to appoint would have resulted in the reversal of a judgment of conviction.

[To] deduce from the due process clause a rule binding upon the states in this matter would be to impose upon them, as Judge Bond points out, a requirement without distinction between criminal charges of different magnitude or in respect of courts of varying jurisdiction. As he says: "Charges of small crimes tried before justices of the peace and capital charges tried in the higher courts would equally require the appointment of counsel. Presumably it would be argued that trials in the Traffic Court would require it." * * *

[While] want of counsel in a particular case may result in a conviction lacking [in] such fundamental fairness, we cannot say that the [Fourteenth Amendment] embodies an inexorable command that no trial for any offense, or in any court, can be fairly conducted and justice accorded a defendant who is not represented by counsel.

The judgment is affirmed.

Justice BLACK, dissenting, with whom Justice DOUGLAS and Justice MURPHY concur.

To hold that the petitioner had a constitutional right to counsel in this case does not require us to say that "no trial for any offense, or in any court, can be fairly conducted and justice accorded a defendant who is not represented by counsel." This case can be determined by resolution of a narrower question: whether in view of the nature of the offense and the circumstances of his trial and conviction, this petitioner was denied the procedural protection which is his right under the federal constitution. I think he was.

The petitioner [was] a farm hand, out of a job and on relief. [The] court below found that [he] had "at least an ordinary amount of intelligence." It is clear from his examination of witnesses that he was a man of little education.

If this case had come to us from a federal court, it is clear we should have to reverse it, because the Sixth Amendment makes the right to counsel in criminal cases inviolable by the federal government. I believe that the Fourteenth Amendment made the sixth applicable to the states. But this view [has] never been accepted by a majority of this Court and is not accepted today. * * * I believe, however, that under the prevailing view of due process, as reflected in the opinion just announced, a view which gives this Court such vast supervisory powers that I am not prepared to accept it without grave doubts, the judgment below should be reversed.

[The] right to counsel in a criminal proceeding is "fundamental." *Powell v. Alabama.* [A] practice cannot be reconciled with "common and fundamental ideas of fairness and right" which subjects innocent men to increased dangers of conviction merely because of their poverty. Whether a man is innocent cannot be determined from a trial in which as here, denial of counsel has made it impossible to conclude, with any satisfactory degree of certainty, that the defendant's case was adequately presented.[b] * * *

Denial to the poor of the request for counsel in proceedings based on charges of serious crime has long been regarded as shocking to the "universal sense of justice" throughout this country. In 1854, for example, the Supreme Court of Indiana said: "It is not to be thought of, in a civilized community, for a moment, that any citizen put in jeopardy of life or liberty should be debarred of counsel because he was too poor to employ such aid * * *" *Webb v. Baird,* 6 Ind. 13, 18. And most of the other states have shown their agreement by constitutional provisions, statutes, or established practice judicially approved which assure that no man shall be deprived of counsel merely because of his poverty. Any other practice seems to me to defeat the promise of our democratic society to provide equal justice under the law.

THE AFTERMATH OF BETTS v. BRADY— NOTES AND QUESTIONS

1. *Was Betts "prejudiced"?* When the Court reviewed Betts' case, he had appellate counsel, but his lawyer was confident—too confident—that the Court would apply the full measure of the Sixth Amendment right to counsel to the states. Thus he did not make any analysis of the trial and present any specific examples of how Betts might have been prejudiced by the absence of counsel. For the view that a number of such examples could have been shown and that competent trial counsel could have raised many more issues than "the simple issue [of] the veracity of the testimony for the State and that for the defendant," see Kamisar, *The Right to Counsel and the Fourteenth Amendment,* 30 U.Chi. L.Rev. 1, 42–56 (1962).

2. *The "flat" requirement of counsel in capital cases.* In *Bute v. Illinois,* 333 U.S. 640, 676, 68 S.Ct. 763, 781, 92 L.Ed. 986, 1006 (1948), and subsequent noncapital cases, the Court suggested that there was a "flat" requirement of counsel in capital cases. In *Hamilton v. Alabama,* 368 U.S. 52, 55, 82 S.Ct. 157, 159, 7 L.Ed.2d 114, 117 (1961), holding that arraignment is so critical a stage in Alabama procedure that denial of counsel at that stage in a capital case violates due process, a unanimous Court declared, per Douglas, J., that "when one pleads to a capital charge without benefit of counsel, we do not stop to determine whether prejudice resulted. [T]he degree of prejudice can never be known." For an explanation and criticism of the Court's distinction between capital and noncapital cases, see Francis A. Allen, *The Supreme Court, Federalism, and State Systems of Criminal Justice,* 8 DePaul L.Rev. 213, 230–31 (1959).

b. Consider William Beaney, *The Right to Counsel in American Courts* 163, 185 (1955): "Surely the [*Betts*] majority, in adopting [Judge] Bond's position that counsel could have done little or nothing for the defendant was pursuing a line of reasoning which would inevitably destroy all rights. Rights are agreed upon in order to insure that justice will be done prospectively, in the ordinary run of affairs. To hold that an individual can be deprived of rights except in those cases where a retrospective view of events reveals a shocking situation is to defeat the whole rationale of the rule of law." See also Note 1 infra.

3. *The absolute right to retained counsel.* During the *Betts* reign, the Court made it clear that denying a defendant the assistance of *his own lawyer* on *any* issue in the trial of *any* case, constituted a per se violation of "fundamental fairness." Thus, in *Chandler v. Fretag,* 348 U.S. 3, 75 S.Ct. 1, 99 L.Ed. 4 (1954), the Court stamped the right of petitioner "to be heard through his own counsel" as "unqualified." And *Ferguson v. Georgia,* 365 U.S. 570, 81 S.Ct. 756, 5 L.Ed.2d 783 (1961), held, in effect, that a state may not deny a criminal defendant the right to have his own counsel guide him on direct examination. Could these cases be reconciled with *Betts?* See Israel, *Gideon v. Wainwright: The "Art" of Overruling,* 1963 Sup.Ct.Rev. 211, 243; Kamisar, *Betts v. Brady Twenty Years Later,* 61 Mich.L.Rev. 219, 227?28, 256–60 (1962).

GIDEON v. WAINWRIGHT
372 U.S. 335, 83 S.Ct. 792, 9 L.Ed.2d 799 (1963).

Justice BLACK delivered the opinion of the Court.

Petitioner was charged in a Florida state court with having broken and entered a poolroom with intent to commit a misdemeanor. This offense is a felony under Florida law. Appearing in court without funds and without a lawyer, petitioner asked the court to appoint counsel for him, whereupon the following colloquy took place:

"The Court: Mr. Gideon, I am sorry, but I cannot appoint Counsel to represent you in this case. Under the laws of the State of Florida, the only time the Court can appoint Counsel to represent a Defendant is when that person is charged with a capital offense. * * *

"The Defendant: The United States Supreme Court says I am entitled to be represented by Counsel."

Put to trial before a jury, Gideon conducted his defense about as well as could be expected from a layman. He made an opening statement to the jury, cross-examined the State's witnesses, presented witnesses in his own defense, declined to testify himself, and made a short argument "emphasizing his innocence to the charge contained in the Information filed in this case." The jury returned a verdict of guilty, and petitioner was sentenced to serve five years in the state prison. Later, petitioner [unsuccessfully attacked his conviction and sentence in the state supreme court on the ground that the trial court's refusal to appoint counsel for him violated his constitutional rights]. Since 1942, when *Betts v. Brady* was decided by a divided Court, the problem of a defendant's federal constitutional right to counsel in a state court has been a continuing source of controversy and litigation in both state and federal courts. To give this problem another review here, we granted certiorari [and] appointed counsel to represent [petitioner].

We accept *Betts's* assumption, based as it was on our prior cases, that a provision of the Bill of Rights which is "fundamental and essential to a fair trial" is made obligatory upon the States by the Fourteenth Amendment. We think the Court in *Betts* was wrong, however, in concluding that the Sixth Amendment's guarantee of counsel is not one of these fundamental rights. Ten years before *Betts,* this Court, after full consideration of all the historical data examined in *Betts,* had unequivocally declared that "the right to the aid of counsel is of this fundamental character." *Powell.* While the Court at the close of its *Powell* opinion did by its language, as this Court frequently does, limit its holding to the particular facts and circumstances of that case, its conclusions about the fundamental nature of the right to counsel are unmistakable. [The] fact is that in deciding as it did—that "appointment of counsel is not a fundamental right, essential to a fair trial"—the [*Betts* Court] made an abrupt break with its own well-considered precedents. In returning to these old precedents, sounder we believe than the new, we but restore constitutional principles established to achieve a fair system of justice. Not only these precedents but also reason and reflection require us to recognize that in our adversary system of criminal justice, any person haled into court, who is too poor to hire a lawyer, cannot be assured a fair trial unless counsel is provided for him. This seems to us to be an obvious truth. Governments, both state and federal, quite properly spend vast sums of money to establish machinery to try defendants accused of crime. Lawyers to prosecute are everywhere deemed essential to protect the public's interest in an orderly society. Similarly, there are few defendants charged with crime, few indeed, who fail to hire the best lawyers they can get to prepare and present their defenses. That government hires lawyers to prosecute and defendants who have the money hire lawyers to defend are the strongest indications of the widespread belief that lawyers in criminal courts are necessities, not luxuries. The right of one charged with crime to counsel may not be deemed fundamental and essential to fair trials in some countries, but it is in ours. From the very beginning, our state and national constitutions and laws have laid great emphasis on procedural and substantive safeguards designed to assure fair trials before impartial tribunals in which every defendant stands equal before the law. This noble ideal cannot be realized if the poor man charged with crime has to face his accusers without a lawyer to assist him. * * *

The Court in *Betts* departed from the sound wisdom upon which the Court's holding in *Powell* rested. Florida, supported by two other States, has asked that *Betts v. Brady* be left intact. Twenty-two States, as friends of the Court, argue that *Betts* was "an anachronism when handed down" and that it should now be overruled. We agree. * * *

Reversed.[a]

Justice CLARK, concurring in the result.

[T]he Constitution makes no distinction between capital and noncapital cases. The Fourteenth Amendment requires due process of law for the deprival of "liberty" just as for deprival of "life," and there cannot constitutionally be a difference in the quality of the process based merely upon a supposed difference in the sanction involved. How can the Fourteenth Amendment tolerate a procedure which it condemns in capital cases on the ground that deprival of liberty may be less onerous than deprival of life—a value judgment not universally accepted—or that only the latter deprival is irrevocable? * * *

Justice HARLAN, concurring.

I agree that *Betts* should be overruled, but consider it entitled to a more respectful burial than has been accorded, at least on the part of those of us who were not on the Court when that case was decided. I cannot subscribe to the view that *Betts* represented "an abrupt break with its own well-considered precedents." [In *Powell*] this Court declared that under the particular facts there presented— "the ignorance and illiteracy of the defendants, their youth, the circumstances of public hostility [and] above all that they stood in deadly peril of their lives"—the state court had a duty to assign counsel for the trial as a necessary requisite of due process of law. It is evident that these limiting facts were not added to the opinion as an afterthought; they were repeatedly emphasized [and] were clearly regarded as important to the result.

a. Gideon was retried, this time with appointed counsel, and acquitted. See Anthony Lewis, *Gideon's Trumpet* 223–38 (1964).

Thus when this Court, a decade later, decided *Betts,* it did no more than to admit of the possible existence of special circumstances in noncapital as well as capital trials, while at the same time to insist that such circumstances be shown in order to establish a denial of due process. The right to appointed counsel had been recognized as being considerably broader in federal prosecutions, see *Johnson v. Zerbst,* but to have imposed these requirements on the States would indeed have been "an abrupt break" with the almost immediate past. The declaration that the right to appointed counsel in state prosecutions, as established in *Powell,* was not limited to capital cases was in truth not a departure from, but an extension of, existing precedent.

The principles declared in *Powell* and in *Betts,* however, had a troubled journey throughout the years that have followed first the one case and then the other.

[In] noncapital cases, the "special circumstances" rule has continued to exist in form while its substance has been substantially and steadily eroded. In the first decade after *Betts,* there were cases in which the Court found special circumstances to be lacking, but usually by a sharply divided vote. However, no such decision has been cited to us, and I have found none, [after] 1950. At the same time, there have been not a few cases in which special circumstances were found in little or nothing more than the "complexity" of the legal questions presented, although those questions were often of only routine difficulty. The Court has come to recognize, in other words, that the mere existence of a serious criminal charge constituted in itself special circumstances requiring the services of counsel at trial. In truth the *Betts* rule is no longer a reality.

This evolution, however, appears not to have been fully recognized by many state courts, in this instance charged with the front-line responsibility for the enforcement of constitutional rights. To continue a rule which is honored by this Court only with lip service is not a healthy thing and in the long run will do disservice to the federal system.

The special circumstances rule has been formally abandoned in capital cases, and the time has now come when it should be similarly abandoned in noncapital cases, at least as to offenses which, as the one involved here, carry the possibility of a substantial prison sentence. (Whether the rule should extend to all criminal cases need not now be decided.) * * *

Notes and Questions

1. *The significance of Powell v. Alabama and Johnson v. Zerbst.* Did the Court in *Betts* make, as Justice Black asserts in *Gideon,* "an abrupt break with its own well-considered precedents"? Did *Powell* furnish a steppingstone to either a *Betts* or a *Gideon,* depending on how far and fast the Supreme Court was willing to use the opinion's potential for expansion? Did the *Palko* doctrine constitute a clear warning that the Court would not impose the same requirements for appointed counsel upon the states as it had upon the federal government in *Johnson v. Zerbst?* See Israel, *Gideon v. Wainwright: The "Art" of Overruling,* 1963 Supreme Court Rev. 211, 234–38, 240–41.

2. *Alternative techniques of overruling available in Gideon.* Among the traditional arts of overruling are the arguments that (a) the old precedent has not withstood the "lessons of experience" and (b) that its rejection is required by later "inconsistent precedents." See e.g., *Mapp v. Ohio,* p. 110. Were these arguments available in *Gideon?* As to (b) reconsider, for example, the *Chandler* and *Ferguson* cases, establishing the unqualified right to the assistance of counsel *one can hire;* and the post-*Betts* development of the "automatic right" to appoint-

ed counsel in capital cases and its implicit admission of the unsoundness of the "fair trial" rule. As to (a), consider how, in the two decades since *Betts,* the assumption that a lawyerless defendant would usually be able to defend himself had fared in light of the constant expansion of the "special circumstances" concept; and how the assumption that a "special circumstances" test was more consistent with the "obligations of federalism" than an "absolute rule" had stood up in the face of the proliferation of federal habeas corpus cases produced by the *Betts* rule and the resulting friction between state and federal courts. See generally Israel, supra at 242–69.

3. ***Why did the Gideon opinion take the route it did?*** If the foregoing techniques of overruling were available in *Gideon,* why did Justice Black fail to utilize them? Would it have been most desirable to emphasize that the overruling of *Betts* was not attributable to recent changes in personnel, but that it constituted the product of a long line of Justices who, over two decades, participated in various decisions undermining *Betts?* See Israel, supra at 225, 269. Is the failure to employ the usual overruling "arts" in *Gideon* attributable to Justice Black's personal interest in vindicating his own dissenting opinion in *Betts?* Or his reluctance to admit even the *original validity* of a decision that exemplifies the evils (to him) of the "fundamental rights" interpretation of the fourteenth amendment? See id. at 270–72.

4. ***The unrealized dream of Gideon.*** For the view, spelled out at considerable length, that more than thirty years after *Gideon,* the dream of that landmark case—the dream of a country "in which every person charged with a crime will be capably defended, no matter what his economic circumstances"—remains largely unrealized, see Stephen B. Bright, *Counsel for the Poor: the Death Sentence not for the Worst Crime but for the Worst Lawyer,* 103 Yale L.J. 1835 (1994). According to Bright, id. at 1870, "a properly working adversary system will never be achieved unless defender organizations are established and properly funded to employ lawyers at wages and benefits equal to what is spent on the prosecution, to retain expert and investigative assistance, to assign lawyers to capital cases, to recruit and support local lawyers and to supervise the performance of counsel defending capital cases. Judges are not equipped to do this. Management of the defense is not a proper judicial function."

5. ***Our double standards of criminal defense.*** Consider the comments on the O.J. Simpson case by Professors Arenella and Rhodes at pp. 93–94.

In ARGERSINGER v. HAMLIN, 407 U.S. 25, 92 S.Ct. 2006, 32 L.Ed.2d 530 (1972), the Court, per DOUGLAS, J., struck down a Florida rule (following the line marked out in the jury trial cases) requiring that counsel be appointed only "for nonpetty offenses punishable by more than six months imprisonment," and held that "absent a knowing and intelligent waiver, no person may be *imprisoned* for any offense, whether classified as petty, misdemeanor, or felony unless he was represented by counsel" (emphasis added):

"While there is historical support for limiting the [right] to trial by jury [to] 'serious criminal cases,' there is no such support for a similar limitation on the right to assistance of counsel. [Thus,] we reject [the] premise that since prosecutions for crimes punishable by imprisonment for less than six months may be tried without a jury, they may always be tried without a lawyer. [The] requirement of counsel may well be necessary for a fair trial even in a petty offense prosecution. We are by no means convinced that legal and constitutional questions involved in a case that actually leads to imprisonment even for a brief period are any less complex than when a person can be sent off for six months or more. * * *

"Beyond the problem of trials and appeals is that of the guilty plea, a problem which looms large in misdemeanor as well as in felony cases. Counsel is needed so that the accused may know precisely what he is doing, so that he is fully aware of the prospect of going to jail or prison, and so that he is treated fairly by the prosecution.

"In addition, the volume of misdemeanor cases, far greater in number than felony prosecutions, may create an obsession for speedy dispositions, regardless of the fairness of the result. * * *

"We must conclude, therefore, that the problems associated with misdemeanor and petty offenses often require the presence of counsel to insure the accused a fair trial. [In his concurring opinion,] Mr. Justice Powell suggests that these problems are raised even in situations where there is no prospect of imprisonment. We need not consider the requirements of the Sixth Amendment as regards the right to counsel where loss of liberty is not involved, however, for here, petitioner was in fact sentenced to jail * * *.

"Under the rule we announce today, every judge will know when the trial of a misdemeanor starts that no imprisonment may be imposed, even though local law permits it, unless the accused is represented by counsel. He will have a measure of the seriousness and gravity of the offense and therefore know when to name a lawyer to represent the accused before the trial starts."[a]

Analyzing the problem in terms of general due process rather than the sixth amendment right to counsel, concurring Justice POWELL, joined by Rehnquist, J., concluded that "there is a middle course, between the extremes of Florida's six month rule and the Court's rule, which comports with the requirements of the Fourteenth Amendment"—"fundamental fairness" requires that a defendant have the assistance of counsel in petty cases when, but only when, "necessary to assure a fair trial":

"Due process, perhaps the most fundamental concept in our law, embodies principles of fairness rather than immutable line-drawing as to every aspect of a criminal trial. While counsel is often essential to a fair trial, this is by no means a universal fact. Some petty offense cases are complex; others are exceedingly simple. [The] government often does not hire lawyers to prosecute petty offenses; instead the arresting police officer presents the case. Nor does every defendant who can afford to do so hire lawyers to defend petty charges. Where the possibility of a jail sentence is remote and the probable fine seems small, or where the evidence of guilt is overwhelming, the costs of assistance of counsel may exceed the benefits. It is anomalous that the Court's opinion today will extend the right of appointed counsel to indigent defendants in cases where the right to counsel would rarely be exercised by nonindigent defendants.

"Indeed, one of the effects of this ruling will be to favor defendants classified as indigents over those not so classified yet who are in low income groups where engaging counsel in a minor petty offense case would be a luxury the family could not afford. The line between indigency and assumed capacity to pay for counsel is necessarily somewhat arbitrary, drawn differently from State to State and often resulting in serious inequities to accused persons. The Court's new rule will accent the disadvantage of being barely self-sufficient economically.

a. Burger, C.J., concurred in the result. Brennan, J., joined by Douglas and Stewart, JJ., joined the Court's opinion and, in a brief concurring opinion, added the observation that "law students as well as practicing attorneys may provide an important source of legal representation for the indigent. [M]ore than 125 of the country's 147 accredited law schools have established clinical programs in which faculty-supervised students aid clients in a variety of civil and criminal matters."

"[The] rule adopted today [is] limited to petty offense cases in which the sentence is some imprisonment. The thrust of the Court's position indicates, however, that when the decision must be made, the rule will be extended to all petty offense cases except perhaps the most minor traffic violations. If the Court rejects on constitutional grounds, as it has today, the exercise of any judicial discretion as to need for counsel if a jail sentence is imposed, one must assume a similar rejection of discretion in other petty offense cases. * * *

"I would hold that the right to counsel in petty offense cases is not absolute but is one to be determined by the trial courts exercising a judicial discretion on a case-by-case basis. * * * [T]hree general factors should be weighed. First, the court should consider the complexity of the offense charged. Second, the court should consider the probable sentence that will follow if a conviction is obtained. The more serious the likely consequences, the greater is the probability that a lawyer should be appointed. Third, the court should consider the individual factors peculiar to each case. These, of course, would be the most difficult to anticipate. One relevant factor would be the competency of the individual defendant to present his own case. The attitude of the community toward a particular defendant or particular incident would be another consideration. * * *

"Such a rule is similar in certain respects to the special circumstances rule applied to felony cases in *Betts,* which this Court overruled in *Gideon.* One of the reasons for seeking a more definitive standard in felony cases was the failure of many state courts to live up to their responsibilities in determining on a case-by-case basis whether counsel should be appointed. But this Court should not assume that the past insensitivity of some state courts to the rights of defendants will continue. Certainly if the Court follows the course of reading rigid rules into the Constitution, so that the state courts will be unable to exercise judicial discretion within the limits of fundamental fairness, there is little reason to think that insensitivity will abate."

Petitioner, an indigent, was charged with shoplifting merchandise valued at less than $150, punishable by as much as a $500 fine, or one year in jail, or both. He was not provided counsel. After a bench trial he was convicted of the offense and fined $50. The Supreme Court of Illinois declined to "extend *Argersinger*" to a case where one is charged with an offense for which imprisonment upon conviction is authorized but not actually imposed. A 5–4 majority of the Supreme Court, per REHNQUIST, J., agreed, SCOTT v. ILLINOIS, 440 U.S. 367, 99 S.Ct. 1158, 59 L.Ed.2d 383 (1979):

"[W]e believe that the central premise of *Argersinger*—that actual imprisonment is a penalty different in kind from fines or the mere threat of imprisonment—is eminently sound and warrants adoption of actual imprisonment as the line defining the constitutional right to appointment of counsel. * * * We therefore hold that the Sixth and Fourteenth Amendments [require] only that no indigent criminal defendant be sentenced to a term of imprisonment unless the State has afforded him the right to assistance of appointed counsel in his defense."

Concurring Justice POWELL noted that "the drawing of a line based on whether there is imprisonment (even for overnight) can have the practical effect of precluding provision of counsel in other types of cases in which conviction can have more serious consequences." He also thought that an "actual imprisonment" rule "tends to impair the proper functioning of the criminal justice system in that trial judges, in advance of hearing any evidence and before knowing anything about the case except the charge, all too often will be compelled to forego the legislatively granted option to impose a sentence of imprisonment upon conviction." Nevertheless, Justice Powell joined the opinion of the Court because "[i]t is important that this Court provide clear guidance to the hundreds of courts across the country that confront this problem daily." He hoped, however, "that in due time a majority will recognize that a more flexible rule is consistent with due process and will better serve the cause of justice."

Justice BRENNAN, joined by Marshall and Stevens, JJ., dissented:

2 dimensional test

"[*Argersinger*] established a 'two dimensional' test for the right to counsel: the right attaches to any 'non-petty' offense punishable by more than six months in jail and in addition to any offense where actual incarceration is likely regardless of the maximum authorized penalty. See Steven B. Duke, *The Right to Appointed Counsel: Argersinger and Beyond,* 12 Am.Crim.L.Rev. 601 (1975).

"The offense of 'theft' with which Scott was charged is certainly not a 'petty' one. It is punishable by a sentence of up to one year in jail. Unlike many traffic or other 'regulatory' offenses, it carries the moral stigma associated with common-law crimes traditionally recognized as indicative of moral depravity. The State indicated at oral argument that the services of a professional prosecutor were considered essential to the prosecution of this offense. Likewise, nonindigent defendants charged with this offense would be well advised to hire the 'best lawyers they can get.' Scott's right to the assistance of appointed counsel is thus plainly mandated by the logic of the Court's prior cases, including *Argersinger* itself.

"Perhaps the strongest refutation of respondent's alarmist prophecies that an authorized imprisonment standard would wreak havoc on the States is that the standard has not produced that result in the substantial number of States that already provide counsel in all cases where imprisonment is authorized—States that include a large majority of the country's population and a great diversity of urban and rural environments. * * * It may well be that adoption by this Court of an authorized imprisonment standard would lead state and local governments to re-examine their criminal statutes. A state legislature or local government might determine that it no longer desired to authorize incarceration for certain minor offenses in light of the expense of meeting the requirements of the Constitution. In my view this re-examination is long overdue. In any event, the Courts actual imprisonment standard must inevitably lead the courts to make this re-examination, which plainly should more properly be a legislative responsibility."

In a separate dissent, Justice Blackmun maintained that the right to counsel "extends at least as far as the right to jury trial" and thus that "an indigent defendant in a state criminal case must be afforded appointed counsel whenever the defendant is prosecuted for a nonpetty criminal offense, that is, one punishable by more than six months' imprisonment, *or* whenever the defendant is actually subjected to a term of imprisonment."

Notes and Questions

1. Were Justice Powell's reasons for switching from his position in *Argersinger* to the "actual confinement" approach in *Scott*—to "provide clear guidance" to lower courts and to reach a result consistent with *Argersinger*—persuasive? Did Justice Powell explain why the "actual confinement" test provides clearer guidance than the alternative to it? Did he explain why he declined to join Justice Blackmun's dissenting opinion? Of all the opinions in *Scott*, does the Blackmun opinion diverge least from the views Powell expressed in *Argersinger*? See Lawrence Herman & Charles A. Thompson, *Scott v. Illinois and the Right to Counsel: A Decision in Search of a Doctrine?* 17 Am.Crim.L.Rev. 71, 94 (1979).

2. Are unrepresented defendants likely to waive their right to a jury trial, hoping that a judge who sits as factfinder will be able to provide assistance? If so, how in a *non-jury* case, can a judge *properly* make an intelligent pre-trial determination as to whether the sentence is likely to include incarceration, at least where he will hear the case? Isn't a considerable amount of potentially prejudicial information likely to be injected into the factfinding process? If an indigent defendant charged with an offense usually punished only by a fine is appointed counsel, would a *different* judge hearing the case assume that a colleague had found that the defendant had a "bad record" or had committed the minor offense in an egregious manner? See Commentary to Unif.R.Crim.P. 321(b); Note, 1979 U.Ill.L.F. 739, 752.

3. May the problems raised in Note 2 never be reached because of judicial reluctance to conduct pretrial inquiries about the likely sentence? Consider Note, 93 Harv.L.Rev. 82, 87 (1979): "It seems far more likely that, due to the sheer volume of misdemeanor cases, judges simply will not appoint counsel, thereby relinquishing their discretion to impose the penalty of imprisonment." If so, would this constitute improper judicial interference with the legislature's judgment concerning the appropriate range of penalties? See id.

4. *Gideon revisited—and criticized.* Although he recognizes that "probably no decision in the field of constitutional criminal procedure enjoys anything like the unqualified and unanimous approval" that *Gideon* has received, Professor Dripps criticizes the case for focusing on the language of the Sixth Amendment rather than taking a more general due process approach. Donald A. Dripps, *Criminal Procedure as Constitutional Law* ___ (2002) (Ch. 5) (forthcoming):

"[*Gideon*] took a Procrustean approach to the Sixth Amendment. Where the amendment says the defendant may appear through counsel, *Gideon* stretches the amendment to cover subsidizing counsel for the poor. Where the amendment says ['in *all* criminal prosecutions'], *Gideon* reduces the amendment to covering [felony cases and only those misdemeanor cases leading to incarceration]. Would the Court now or ever uphold a federal statute that forbade a misdemeanor defendant from appearing through privately-retained counsel? If not, how can 'all' mean 'all' when the issue is prohibiting appearance through counsel, but mean 'some' when the issue is providing indigent defense? * * * [By] relying on the Sixth Amendment (albeit in a distorted fashion) the Warren Court deflected attention from instrumental reliability in favor of a formalistic focus on the textually-referenced 'assistance of counsel.' The incorporation approach necessarily failed to describe Gideon's constitutional right with appropriate generality. There is nothing *intristically* valuable about lawyers; that is why subsequent cases have developed the idea, if not the reality, that defense counsel's assistance must be *effective.* * * * Gideon's right was not be a lawyer, but to a trial that ran no more than some practically irreducible risk of falsely convicting him."

5. *Can an uncounseled misdemeanor conviction still lead to incarceration or be used to enhance a prison sentence?* If a defendant is not afforded counsel, can he be given a suspended sentence or placed on probation? It "seem[ed] obvious" to the court in *United States v. Reilley*, 948 F.2d 648 (10th Cir.1991), that since a defendant not furnished counsel "cannot be ordered to serve a term of imprisonment, [a] conditional sentence of imprisonment is equally invalid. [The] court's conditional threat to imprison [a defendant] itself is hollow and should be considered a nullity." But cf. *United States v. Ortega*, 94 F.3d 764 (2d Cir.1996).

Can a prior uncounseled conviction be used to enhance a defendant's prison sentence when, after being given counsel, he is convicted of a second crime? Overruling an earlier decision (*Baldasar v. Illinois*, 446 U.S. 222, 100 S.Ct. 1585,

64 L.Ed.2d 169 (1980)), the Court, per REHNQUIST, C.J., held in NICHOLS v. UNITED STATES, 511 U.S. 738, 114 S.Ct. 1921, 128 L.Ed.2d 745 (1994), that a "logical consequence" of *Scott* is that "an uncounseled conviction valid under *Scott* [because no prison term was imposed] may be relied upon to enhance the sentence for a subsequent offense, even though that sentence entails imprisonment. Enhancement statutes, whether in the nature of criminal history provisions such as those contained in the Sentencing Guidelines, or recidivist statutes that are commonplace in state criminal laws, do not change the penalty imposed for the earlier conviction." (Seven years earlier, when not represented by counsel, Nichols had pled *nolo contendere* to a state misdemeanor (DUI) and paid a $250 fine. This misdemeanor conviction was used to enhance his sentence when he was subsequently convicted of a federal drug offense.)

The Chief Justice pointed out: "Sentencing courts have not only taken into consideration a defendant's prior convictions, but have also considered a defendant's past criminal behavior, even if no conviction resulted from that behavior. We have upheld the constitutionality of considering such previous conduct * * *. [Thus, Nichols] could have been sentenced more severely based simply on evidence of the underlying conduct that gave rise to the previous DUI offense. And the state need prove such conduct only by a preponderance of the evidence. Surely, then, it must be constitutionally permissible to consider a prior uncounseled conviction based on the same conduct where that conduct must be proved beyond a reasonable doubt."[a]

BLACKMUN, J., joined by Stevens and Ginsburg, JJ., dissented: "It is more logical, and more consistent with the reasoning in *Scott*, to hold that a conviction that is invalid for imposing a sentence for the offense remains invalid for increasing the term of imprisonment imposed for a subsequent conviction. [We] consistently have read the Sixth Amendment to require that courts decrease the risk of unreliability, through the provision of counsel, where a conviction results in imprisonment. That the sentence in *Scott* was imposed in the first instance and the sentence here was the result of an enhancement statute is a distinction without a constitutional difference. [Moreover,] as a practical matter, introduction of a record of conviction generally causes greater weight than other evidence of pure conduct. * * * Realistically, then, the conclusion that a state may prove prior conduct in a sentencing proceeding [in a subsequent case] does not support, much less compel a conclusion that the state may, in lieu of proving directly the prior conduct, rely on a conviction obtained against an uncounseled defendant."[b]

B. THE "BEGINNINGS" OF THE RIGHT TO COUNSEL: HEREIN OF "CRIMINAL PROSECUTIONS" AND "CRITICAL STAGES"

The point at which the right to the assistance of counsel "begins" or first "attaches" is a question that arises in a number of different contexts and one that

a. The Court also rejected the argument that due process requires a misdemeanor defendant to be warned that his conviction might be used for enhancement purposes should he later be convicted of another crime: "[A] large number of misdemeanor convictions take place in police or justice courts which are not courts of record"; therefore, "there would be no way to memorialize any such warning." "Nor is it at all clear how expansive the warning would have to be. [And] a warning at the completely general level—that if he is brought back into court on another criminal charge [he] will be treated more harshly—would merely tell him what he must surely already know."

b. Souter, J. concurred only in the judgment, concluding that the enhanced sentence was permissible because the Sentencing Guidelines do not provide for "automatic enhancement" based on prior uncounseled convictions. Therefore, "a defendant has the chance to convince the sentencing court of the unreliability of any prior valid but uncounseled convictions in reflecting the seriousness of his past criminal conduct or predicting the likelihood of recidivism."

is considered at various parts of the book. See, e.g., *Miranda* (p. 462) ("custodial interrogation"); *United States v. Wade* (p. 618) (pretrial lineups); *Coleman v. Alabama* (Ch. 14, § 2) (preliminary hearing).

Compelled self-incrimination considerations aside, a defendant is not entitled to the assistance of counsel unless (a) adversary judicial proceedings have commenced (the Sixth Amendment right to counsel is guaranteed only "in all criminal prosecutions")[a] *and* (b) the encounter is a "critical stage" of the criminal proceeding. Two pretrial identifications make the point. In *Kirby v. Illinois* (1967) (p. 631), the Court held that defendant was not entitled to a lawyer at his lineup, because the lineup had been held *prior* to his indictment. In *United States v. Ash* (1973) (p. 636), in a successful effort to identify the defendant as the culprit, the prosecutor showed photographs of defendant and others to witnesses *after* adversary criminal proceedings had begun. Nevertheless, the Court held that defendant was still not entitled to the presence of counsel at the identification because, unlike a corporeal identification, a photographic display was not a "critical stage" of the prosecution.[b]

Although at one time the *Escobedo* case (p. 450) indicated otherwise, it is now clear that the right to counsel does not come into play simply because a person is or becomes the "prime suspect" or "focal point," or even when he is arrested (absent "interrogation" or its equivalent). "[A] person is entitled to the help of a lawyer"—assuming the stage of the "prosecution" is a "critical" one—"at or after the time that judicial proceedings have been initiated against him—'whether by way of formal charge, preliminary hearing, indictment, information, or arraignment [presumably as early as the first appearance before a judicial officer].' " *Brewer v. Williams* (p. 594) (the Court, per Stewart, J.).

As indicated by the cases dealing with the use of informants and other secret government agents to obtain incriminating statements (see, e.g., *Hoffa, Osborn* and *White,* all discussed in Ch. 6, § 4), when judicial proceedings have not been initiated against a person, the privilege against self-incrimination as interpreted in *Miranda*—and *Miranda* alone—strikes the appropriate balance. If and when the conditions surrounding or inherent in a "preformal charge" confrontation are sufficiently coercive, "interrogation" or its equivalent may bring the "*Miranda* right to counsel" into play. But the right to counsel as such, what might be called the "pure" right to counsel, is not brought into play. At the "pre-charge" stage, at least when the suspect neither has nor has expressed a desire for counsel, the

a. As Justice Stewart observed, concurring in a pretrial identification case, *United States v. Ash* (p. 636), "the requirement that there be a 'prosecution' means that [the] 'right to counsel attaches only at or after the time that the adversary proceedings have been initiated against [an accused].' 'It is this point [that] marks the commencement of the "criminal prosecution" to which alone the explicit guarantees of the Sixth Amendment are applicable.' "

b. The Court, per Blackmun, J., observed that the right to counsel has always been limited to "trial-like confrontations" between prosecuting authorities and the accused where the lawyer acts as "a spokesman for, or advisor to the accused." Concurring Justice Stewart emphasized that "a photographic identification is quite different from a lineup, for there are substantially fewer possibilities of impermissi-

ble suggestion when photographs are used, and those unfair influences can be readily constructed at trial."

Dissenting Justice Brennan, joined by Douglas and Marshall, JJ., insisted that, regardless of whether the accused is physically present, "a 'stage' of the prosecution must be deemed 'critical' for the purpose of the Sixth Amendment if it is one at which the presence of counsel is necessary 'to protect the fairness of *the trial itself.*' " Responding to Justice Stewart's argument, the dissenters maintained that "the risks [of misidentification] are obviously as great at a photographic display as at a lineup." In fact, " 'because of the inherent limitations of photography, . . . [a] photographic identification, even when properly obtained, is clearly inferior to a properly obtained corporeal identification.' "

right to counsel is triggered by, and dependent on, forces that "jeopardize" the privilege against compelled self-incrimination; it has no life it can call its own.

The importance of the commencement of adversary criminal proceedings for right to counsel purposes is underscored in UNITED STATES v. GOUVEIA, 467 U.S. 180, 104 S.Ct. 2292, 81 L.Ed.2d 146 (1984). During the investigation of murders of fellow inmates in a federal prison, defendants were isolated in administrative detention for periods ranging from eight to nineteen months until their indictment on federal criminal charges. The Ninth Circuit reasoned that the administrative detention of prison inmates for more than 90 days because of a pending felony investigation constitutes an "accusation" for right to counsel purposes and required that the prisoners either be provided counsel or released back into the prison population. The Supreme Court, per REHNQUIST, J., disagreed:

"[O]ur cases have long recognized that the right to counsel attaches only at or after the initiation of adversary proceedings against the defendant [referring to *Kirby v. Illinois* and subsequent cases]. Although we have extended an accused's right to counsel to certain 'critical' pre-trial proceedings, we have done so recognizing that at those proceedings, 'the accused [is] confronted, just as at trial, by the procedural system, or by his expert adversary, or by both,' in a situation where the results of the confrontation 'might well settle the accused's fate and reduces the trial itself to a mere formality.' [But] our cases have never suggested that the purpose of the right to counsel is to provide a defendant with a pre-indictment private investigator, and we see no reason to adopt that novel interpretation of the right to counsel in this case."[a]

SECTION 2. THE *GRIFFIN-DOUGLAS* "EQUALITY" PRINCIPLE

GRIFFIN v. ILLINOIS: "THERE CAN BE NO EQUAL JUSTICE WHERE THE KIND OF TRIAL A MAN GETS DEPENDS ON THE MONEY HE HAS"

Prior to GRIFFIN v. ILLINOIS, 351 U.S. 12, 76 S.Ct. 585, 100 L.Ed. 891 (1956), full direct appellate review could only be had in Illinois by furnishing the appellate court with a bill of exceptions or report of the trial proceedings, certified by the trial judge. Preparation of these documents was sometimes impossible without a stenographic transcript of the trial proceedings, but such a transcript was furnished free only to indigent defendants sentenced to death. *Griffin* upheld by a 5–4 vote the contention that the due process and equal protection clauses of the fourteenth amendment require that *all* indigent defendants be furnished a transcript, at least where allegations that manifest errors occurred at the trial are not denied. See generally Francis A. Allen, *Griffin v. Illinois: Antecedents and Aftermath,* 25 U.Chi.L.Rev. 151, 152 (1957).

a. Stevens, J., joined by Brennan, J., concurred in the result on the ground that under the circumstances defendants' administrative detention "did not serve an accusatorial function," but a concern for the welfare of other inmates or defendants themselves. Marshall, J. dissented.

In *United States v. Moody*, 206 F.3d 609 (6th Cir.2000), the Sixth Circuit relied on *Gouveia* to hold that the Sixth Amendment right to counsel does not "attach" during preindictment plea bargaining. Thus, defendant could not be given the benefit of the plea bargain he rejected due to the ineffective assistance of counsel.

There was no opinion of the Court in *Griffin*. Justice Black announced the Court's judgment in a four-justice opinion; Justice Frankfurter concurred specially. In the course of his opinion, Justice BLACK observed: "In criminal trials a State can no more discriminate on account of poverty than on account of religion, race, or color. Plainly the ability to pay costs in advance bears no rational relationship to a defendant's guilt or innocence and could not be used as an excuse to deprive a defendant of a fair trial. [It] is true that a State is not required by the federal constitution to provide appellate courts or a right to appellate review at all. [But] that is not to say that a State that does grant appellate review can do so in a way that discriminates against some convicted defendants on account of their poverty. * * *

"All of the States now provide some method of appeal from criminal convictions, recognizing the importance of appellate review to a correct adjudication of guilt or innocence. Statistics show that a substantial proportion of criminal convictions are reversed by state appellate courts. Thus to deny adequate review to the poor means that many of them may lose their life, liberty or property because of unjust convictions which appellate courts would set aside. Many States have recognized this and provided aid for convicted defendants who have a right to appeal and need a transcript but are unable to pay for it. A few have not. Such a denial is a misfit in a country dedicated to affording equal justice to all and special privileges to none in the administration of its criminal law. There can be no equal justice where the kind of trial a man gets depends on the amount of money he has. Destitute defendants must be afforded as adequate appellate review as defendants who have money enough to buy transcripts."

A. APPLICATION (OR EXTENSION) OF *GRIFFIN*

In the decade and a half following *Griffin*, its underlying principle was broadly applied. See *Burns v. Ohio*, 360 U.S. 252, 79 S.Ct. 1164, 3 L.Ed.2d 1209 (1959) (state cannot require indigent defendant to pay filing fee before permitting him to appeal); *Smith v. Bennett*, 365 U.S. 708, 81 S.Ct. 895, 6 L.Ed.2d 39 (1961) (extending ban on filing fees to state post-conviction proceedings); *Long v. District Court of Iowa*, 385 U.S. 192, 87 S.Ct. 362, 17 L.Ed.2d 290 (1966) (indigent must be furnished a free transcript of a state habeas corpus hearing for use on appeal from a denial of habeas corpus, although availability of transcript not a sine qua non to access to the appellate court); *Gardner v. California*, 393 U.S. 367, 89 S.Ct. 580, 21 L.Ed.2d 601 (1969) (indigent prisoner entitled to free transcript of lower court habeas proceeding for use in filing application for a new habeas proceeding before a higher state court, even though that application need contain only a "brief statement" of prior proceedings and need not assign errors or refer to testimony in the prior proceeding); *Roberts v. LaVallee*, 389 U.S. 40, 88 S.Ct. 194, 19 L.Ed.2d 41 (1967) (indigent defendant entitled to free transcript of preliminary hearing for use at trial, even though both defendant and his counsel attended preliminary hearing and no indication of use to which preliminary hearing transcript could be put—points stressed by dissenting Justice Harlan); *Williams v. Illinois*, 399 U.S. 235, 90 S.Ct. 2018, 26 L.Ed.2d 586 (1970) (defendant unable to pay fine could not be incarcerated beyond maximum term fixed by statute; equal protection requires that "statutory ceiling" on imprisonment be same for all "irrespective of their economic status"); *Tate v. Short*, 401 U.S. 395, 91 S.Ct. 668, 28 L.Ed.2d 130 (1971) (indigent convicted of offenses punishable by fine only cannot be incarcerated a sufficient time to satisfy fines);[a] *Britt v. North Carolina*, 404 U.S. 226, 92

---

a. A decade later, the Court relied on *Williams* and *Tate* to hold that a sentencing court cannot "automatically revoke" probation because a defendant cannot pay his fine without determining that the defendant "had not made sufficient bona fide efforts to pay or that

S.Ct. 431, 30 L.Ed.2d 400 (1971) (recognition that under ordinary circumstances indigent would be entitled to free transcript of previous trial ending with a hung jury because such a transcript would be "valuable to the defendant" as a discovery device and "as a tool at the [second] trial itself for the impeachment of prosecution witnesses").

In MAYER v. CHICAGO, 404 U.S. 189, 92 S.Ct. 410, 30 L.Ed.2d 372 (1971), a unanimous Court, per BRENNAN, J., carried the *Griffin* principle further than it ever has the *Gideon* principle by holding that an indigent appellant "cannot be denied a 'record of sufficient completeness' to permit proper consideration of his claims" because he was convicted of ordinance violations punishable by fine only. "The size of the defendant's pocketbook bears no more relationship to his guilt or innocence in a non-felony than in a felony case." Nor was the Court impressed with the argument that appellant's interest in a transcript in a case where he is not subject to imprisonment is outweighed by the State's fiscal and other interests in not burdening the appellate process:

"*Griffin* does not represent a balance between the needs of the accused and the interests of society; its principle is a flat prohibition against pricing indigent defendants out of as effective an appeal as would be available to others able to pay their own way. The invidiousness of the discrimination that exists when criminal procedures are made available only to those who can pay is not erased by any differences in the sentences that may be imposed. The State's fiscal interest is, therefore, irrelevant.

"We add that even approaching the problem in the terms the city suggests hardly yields the answer the city tenders. The practical effects of conviction of even petty offenses of the kind involved here are not to be minimized. A fine may bear as heavily on an indigent accused as forced confinement.[b] The collateral consequences of conviction may be even more serious, as when (as was apparently a possibility in this case) the impecunious medical student finds himself barred from the practice of medicine because of a conviction he is unable to appeal for lack of funds."[c]

B. The Impact of the "Equality" Principle on Those Who Cannot Afford Counsel or Other Forms of Assistance

Prior to *Gideon*, the *Griffin* case posed a challenge to *Betts:* How could the *Betts* line of cases be reconciled with the language, if not the holding, of *Griffin?* Since there was an unqualified right to have one's own paid counsel of his choosing at state trial, capital or not, did *Griffin* not imply that an indigent also has this unqualified right? By requiring *special circumstances* to exist before the indigent was entitled to appointed counsel in non-capital state cases, was the indigent not denied equal protection of the law? When the Supreme Court finally overruled the *Betts* case, somewhat surprisingly, it did not rely on *Griffin* at all, but *Douglas v. California,* infra, decided the same day, is another story.

DOUGLAS v. CALIFORNIA, 372 U.S. 353, 83 S.Ct. 814, 9 L.Ed.2d 811 (1963), arose as follows: Indigent defendants requested, and were denied, the assistance of counsel on appeal. In accordance with a California rule of criminal procedure, the California District Court of Appeals stated that it had "gone

adequate alternative forms of punishment did not exist." *Bearden v. Georgia,* 461 U.S. 660, 103 S.Ct. 2064, 76 L.Ed.2d 221 (1983).

b. But cf. *Argersinger v. Hamlin,* p. 67; *Scott v. Illinois,* p. 69.

c. Chief Justice Burger joined the Court's opinion, but in a separate opinion emphasized that "there are alternatives in the majority of cases to a full verbatim transcript of an entire trial."

through" the record and had come to the conclusion that "no good whatever could be served by appointment of counsel." Under the California procedure, appellate courts had to appoint counsel only if in their opinion it would be helpful to the defendant or the court. A 6–3 majority, per DOUGLAS, viewed the denial of counsel on appeal to an indigent under these circumstances "a discrimination at least as invidious as that condemned in [*Griffin*]:

"[Whether the issue is a transcript on appeal or the assistance of counsel on appeal] the evil is the same: discrimination against the indigent. For there can be no equal justice where the kind of an appeal a man enjoys 'depends on the amount of money he has.' * * *

"When an indigent is forced to run this gantlet of a preliminary showing of merit, the right to appeal does not comport with fair procedure. [T]he discrimination is not between 'possibly good and obviously bad cases,' but between cases where the rich man can require the court to listen to argument of counsel before deciding on the merits, but a poor man cannot. There is lacking that equality demanded by the Fourteenth Amendment where the rich man, who appeals as of right, enjoys the benefit of counsel's examination into the record, research of the law, and marshalling of arguments on his behalf, while the indigent, already burdened by a preliminary determination that his case is without merit, is forced to shift for himself. The indigent, where the record is unclear or the errors are hidden, has only the right to a meaningless ritual, while the rich man has a meaningful appeal."[a]

Justice HARLAN, whom Stewart, J. joined, dissented,[b] maintaining that "the Equal Protection Clause is not apposite, and its application to cases like the present one can lead only to mischievous results." He thought the case "should be judged solely under the Due Process Clause" and that the California procedure did not violate that provision. In rejecting the equal protection argument, Harlan observed:

"Every financial exaction which the State imposes on a uniform basis is more easily satisfied by the well-to-do than by the indigent. Yet I take it that no one would dispute the constitutional power of the State to levy a uniform sales tax, to charge tuition at a state university, to fix rates for the purchase of water from a municipal corporation, to impose a standard fine for criminal violations, or to establish minimum bail for various categories of offenses. Nor could it be contended that the State may not classify as crimes acts which the poor are more likely to commit than are the rich. * * *

"Laws such as these do not deny equal protection to the less fortunate for one essential reason: the Equal Protection Clause does not impose on the States 'an affirmative duty to lift the handicaps flowing from differences in economic circumstances.' To so construe it would be to read into the Constitution a philosophy of leveling that would be foreign to many of our basic concepts of the proper relations between government and society. The State may have a moral obligation to eliminate the evils of poverty, but it is not required by the Equal Protection Clause to give to some whatever others can afford.

"[I]t should be noted that if the present problem may be viewed as one of equal protection, so may the question of the right to appointed counsel at trial, and the Court's analysis of that right in *Gideon* [is] wholly unnecessary. The short way to dispose of *Gideon*, in other words, would be simply to say that the State

---

a. The Court pointed out it was dealing "only with the first appeal, granted as a matter of right," not deciding whether a state had to provide counsel for an indigent seeking discretionary review.

b. Justice Clark wrote a separate dissenting opinion.

deprives the indigent of equal protection whenever it fails to furnish him with legal services, and perhaps with other services as well, equivalent to those that the affluent defendant can obtain."[c]

ROSS v. MOFFITT

417 U.S. 600, 94 S.Ct. 2437, 41 L.Ed.2d 341 (1974).

Justice REHNQUIST delivered the opinion of the Court.

[Like many other states, the North Carolina appellate system is multitiered, providing for both an intermediate Court of Appeals and a Supreme Court. North Carolina authorizes appointment of counsel for a convicted defendant appealing to the intermediate court of appeals, but not for a defendant who seeks either discretionary review in the state supreme court or a writ of certiorari in the U.S. Supreme Court. In one case, the Mecklenburg County forgery conviction, respondent sought appointed counsel for discretionary review in the state supreme court. In another case, the Guilford County forgery conviction, respondent was represented by the public defender in the state supreme court, but sought court-appointed counsel to prepare a writ of certiorari to the U.S. Supreme Court. On federal habeas corpus, a unanimous panel of the U.S. Court of Appeals for the Fourth Circuit, per Haynsworth, C.J., held that the *Douglas* rationale required appointment of counsel in both instances.]

[In *Griffin,* the Court struck down] an Illinois rule allowing a convicted criminal defendant to present claims of trial error to the [state supreme court] only if he procured a transcript of the testimony adduced at his trial. No exception was made for the indigent defendant, and thus one who was unable to pay the cost of obtaining such a transcript was precluded from obtaining appellate review of asserted trial error.

[*Griffin* and succeeding cases, such as *Burns v. Ohio* and *Smith v. Bennett* (the filing fee cases summarized at p. 75),] stand for the proposition that a State cannot arbitrarily cut off appeal rights for indigents while leaving open avenues of appeal for more affluent persons. In *Douglas,* however, [the] Court departed somewhat from the limited doctrine of [these] cases and undertook an examination of whether an indigent's access to the appellate system was adequate. [The *Douglas* Court] concluded that a State does not fulfill its responsibility toward indigent defendants merely by waiving its own requirements that a convicted defendant procure a transcript or pay a fee in order to appeal, and held that the State must go further and provide counsel for the indigent on his first appeal as of right. It is this decision we are asked to extend today.

[The] precise rationale for the *Griffin* and *Douglas* lines of cases has never been explicitly stated, some support being derived from the Equal Protection Clause of the Fourteenth Amendment, and some from the Due Process Clause of that Amendment. Neither clause by itself provides an entirely satisfactory basis for the result reached, each depending on a different inquiry which emphasizes different factors. "Due process" emphasizes fairness between the State and the individual dealing with the State, regardless of how other individuals in the same situation may be treated. "Equal protection," on the other hand, emphasizes disparity in treatment by a State between classes of individuals whose situations

---

c. One may ask, too, why the Court failed even to discuss the applicability of the *Griffin-Douglas* "equality" principle to the issue raised in *Scott v. Illinois* p. 69. Since it is plain that one charged with an offense *punishable* by incarceration may *retain* counsel for his de- fense, does not the "equality" principle suggest that the "actual imprisonment" standard, even if it defensibly defines the Sixth Amendment right to appointed counsel, is unsatisfactory under the equal protection clause?

are arguably indistinguishable. We will address these issues separately in the succeeding sections.

Recognition of the due process rationale in *Douglas* is found both in the Court's opinion and in the dissenting opinion of Mr. Justice Harlan. The Court in *Douglas* stated that "[w]hen an individual is forced to run this gauntlet of a preliminary showing of merit, the right to appeal does not comport with fair procedure." Mr. Justice Harlan thought that the due process issue in *Douglas* was the only one worthy of extended consideration. * * *

We do not believe that the Due Process Clause requires North Carolina to provide respondent with counsel on his discretionary appeal to the State Supreme Court. At the trial stage of a criminal proceeding, the right of an indigent defendant to counsel [is] fundamental and binding upon the States by virtue of the Sixth and Fourteenth Amendments. But there are significant differences between the trial and appellate stages of a criminal proceeding. The purpose of the trial stage from the State's point of view is to convert a criminal defendant from a person presumed innocent to one found guilty beyond a reasonable doubt. To accomplish this purpose, the State employs a prosecuting attorney who presents evidence to the court, challenges any witnesses offered by the defendant, argues rulings of the court, and makes direct arguments to the court or jury seeking to persuade them of the defendant's guilt. Under these circumstances " * * * reason and reflection require us to recognize that in our adversary system of criminal justice, any person haled into court, who is too poor to hire a lawyer, cannot be assured a fair trial unless counsel is provided for him." *Gideon.*

By contrast, it is ordinarily the defendant, rather than the State, who initiates the appellate process, seeking not to fend off the efforts of the State's prosecutor but rather to overturn a finding of guilt made by a judge or jury below. The defendant needs an attorney on appeal not as a shield to protect him against being "haled into court" by the State and stripped of his presumption of innocence, but rather as a sword to upset the prior determination of guilt. This difference is significant for, while no one would agree that the State may simply dispense with the trial stage of proceedings without a criminal defendant's consent, it is clear that the State need not provide any appeal at all. *McKane v. Durston.* The fact that an appeal *has* been provided does not automatically mean that a State then acts unfairly by refusing to provide counsel to indigent defendants at every stage of the way. Unfairness results only if indigents are singled out by the State and denied meaningful access to that system because of their poverty. That question is more profitably considered under an equal protection analysis.

Language invoking equal protection notions is prominent both in *Douglas* and in other cases treating the rights of indigents on appeal. * * * Despite the tendency of all rights "to declare themselves absolute to their logical extreme," there are obviously limits beyond which the equal protection analysis may not be pressed without doing violence to principles recognized in other decisions of this Court. The Fourteenth Amendment "does not require absolute equality or precisely equal advantages," nor does it require the State to "equalize economic conditions." *Griffin* (Frankfurter, J., concurring). It does require [that] indigents have an adequate opportunity to present their claims fairly within the adversarial system. The State cannot adopt procedures which leave an indigent defendant "entirely cut off from any appeal at all," by virtue of his indigency, *Lane,* or extend to such indigent defendants merely a "meaningless ritual" while others in better economic circumstances have a "meaningful appeal." *Douglas.* The question is not one of absolutes, but one of degrees. In this case we do not believe that the Equal Protection Clause when interpreted in the context of these cases, requires North Carolina to provide free counsel for indigent defendants seeking to take discretionary appeals to the North Carolina Supreme Court, or to file petitions for certiorari in this Court.

[The] facts show that respondent, in connection with his Mecklenburg County conviction, received the benefit of counsel in examining the record of his trial and in preparing an appellate brief on his behalf for the state Court of Appeals. Thus, prior to his seeking discretionary review in the State Supreme Court, his claims "had once been presented by a lawyer and passed upon by an appellate court." *Douglas.* We do not believe that it can be said, therefore, that a defendant in respondent's circumstances is denied meaningful access to the North Carolina Supreme Court simply because the State does not appoint counsel to aid him in seeking review in that court. At that stage he will have, at the very least, a transcript or other record of trial proceedings, a brief on his behalf in the Court of Appeals setting forth his claims of error, and in many cases an opinion by the Court of Appeals disposing of his case. These materials, supplemented by whatever submission respondent may make *pro se,* would appear to provide the Supreme Court of North Carolina with an adequate basis on which to base its decision to grant or deny review.

We are fortified in this conclusion by our understanding of the function served by discretionary review in the North Carolina Supreme Court. The critical issue in that court, as we perceive it, is not whether there has been "a correct adjudication of guilt" in every individual case, but rather whether "the subject matter of the appeal has significant public interest," whether "the cause involves legal principles of major significance to the jurisprudence of the state," or whether the decision below is in probable conflict with a decision of the Supreme Court. The Supreme Court may deny certiorari even though it believes that the decision of the Court of Appeals was incorrect, since a decision which appears incorrect may nevertheless fail to satisfy any of the criteria discussed above. Once a defendant's claims of error are organized and presented in a lawyer-like fashion to the Court of Appeals, the justices of the Supreme Court of North Carolina who make the decision to grant or deny discretionary review should be able to ascertain whether his case satisfies the standards established by the legislature for such review.

This is not to say, of course, that a skilled lawyer, particularly one trained in the somewhat arcane art of preparing petitions for discretionary review, would not prove helpful to any litigant able to employ him. An indigent defendant seeking review in the Supreme Court of North Carolina is therefore somewhat handicapped in comparison with a wealthy defendant who has counsel assisting him in every conceivable manner at every stage in the proceeding. But both the opportunity to have counsel prepare an initial brief in the Court of Appeals and the nature of discretionary review in the Supreme Court of North Carolina make this relative handicap far less than the handicap borne by the indigent defendant denied counsel on his initial appeal as of right in *Douglas.* And the fact that a particular service might be of benefit to an indigent defendant does not mean that the service is constitutionally required. The duty of the State under our cases is not to duplicate the legal arsenal that may be privately retained by a criminal defendant in a continuing effort to reverse his conviction, but only to assure the indigent defendant an adequate opportunity to present his claims fairly in the context of the State's appellate process. We think respondent was given that opportunity under the existing North Carolina system.

Much of the discussion in the preceding section is equally relevant to the question of whether a State must provide counsel for a defendant seeking review of his conviction in this Court. North Carolina will have provided counsel for a convicted defendant's only appeal as of right, and the brief prepared by that counsel together with one and perhaps two North Carolina appellate opinions will be available to this Court in order that it may decide whether or not to grant certiorari. This Court's review, much like that of the Supreme Court of North Carolina, is discretionary and depends on numerous factors other than the perceived correctness of the judgment we are asked to review.

There is also a significant difference between the source of the right to seek discretionary review in the Supreme Court of North Carolina and the source of the right to seek discretionary review in this Court. The former is conferred by the statutes of the State of North Carolina, but the latter is granted by statutes enacted by Congress. Thus the argument relied upon in the *Griffin* and *Douglas* cases, that the State having once created a right of appeal must give all persons an equal opportunity to enjoy the right, is by its terms inapplicable. The right to seek certiorari in this Court is not granted by any State, and exists by virtue of federal statute with or without the consent of the State whose judgment is sought to be reviewed.

The suggestion that a State is responsible for providing counsel to one petitioning this Court simply because it initiated the prosecution which led to the judgment sought to be reviewed is unsupported by either reason or authority. It would be quite as logical under the rationale of *Douglas* and *Griffin,* and indeed perhaps more so, to require that the Federal Government or this Court furnish and compensate counsel for petitioners who seek certiorari here to review state judgments of conviction. Yet this Court has followed a consistent policy of denying applications for appointment of counsel by persons seeking to file jurisdictional statements or petitions for certiorari in this Court. In the light of these authorities, it would be odd, indeed, to read the Fourteenth Amendment to impose such a requirement on the States, and we decline to do so.

We do not mean by this opinion to in any way discourage those States which have, as a matter of legislative choice, made counsel available to convicted defendants at all stages of judicial review. Some States which might well choose to do so as a matter of legislative policy may conceivably find that other claims for public funds within or without the criminal justice system preclude the implementation of such a policy at the present time. [T]he Fourteenth Amendment leaves these choices to the State * * *.

Reversed.

Justice DOUGLAS, with whom Justice BRENNAN and Justice MARSHALL concur, dissenting.

[In his opinion below] Chief Judge Haynsworth could find "no logical basis for differentiation between appeals of right and permissive review procedures in the context of the Constitution and the right to counsel." More familiar with the functioning of the North Carolina criminal justice system than are we, he concluded that "in the context of constitutional questions arising in criminal prosecutions, permissive review in the state's highest court may be predictably the most meaningful review the conviction will receive." The North Carolina Court of Appeals, for example, will be constrained in diverging from an earlier opinion of the State Supreme Court, even if subsequent developments have rendered the earlier Supreme Court decision suspect. "[T]he state's highest court remains the ultimate arbiter of the rights of its citizens."

Chief Judge Haynsworth also correctly observed that the indigent defendant proceeding without counsel is at a substantial disadvantage relative to wealthy defendants represented by counsel when he is forced to fend for himself in seeking discretionary review from the State Supreme Court or from this Court. It may well not be enough to allege error in the courts below in layman's terms; a more sophisticated approach may be demanded:

"An indigent defendant is as much in need of the assistance of a lawyer in preparing and filing a petition for certiorari as he is in the handling of an appeal as of right. In many appeals, an articulate defendant could file an effective brief by telling his story in simple language without legalisms, but the technical requirement for applications for writs of certiorari are hazards which one untrained in the law could hardly be expected to negotiate. * * * "

[The] right to discretionary review is a substantial one, and one where a lawyer can be of significant assistance to an indigent defendant. It was correctly perceived below that the "same concepts of fairness and equality which require counsel in a first appeal of right, require counsel in other and subsequent discretionary appeals."

ON THE MEANING OF *ROSS v. MOFFITT*

1. Is *Mayer v. Chicago* (p. 76) "good law" after *Ross?* Are *Long v. District Court, Gardner v. California, Roberts v. LaVallee,* and *Britt v. North Carolina* (all summarized at pp. 75–76) "good law" after *Ross?* Does the *Long-Gardner* line of cases (never mentioned by the *Ross* Court) constitute a significant "departure" from what the *Ross* Court calls the "limited doctrine" of *Griffin* and succeeding cases?

2. Consider Laurence H. Tribe, *American Constitutional Law* 1647 (2d ed.1988): "[The *Ross* Court] disengaged *Griffin* from *Douglas,* deftly rewove the *Griffin* transcript and filing fee decisions together as minimal access cases rather than equal protection cases, and neatly severed *Douglas* from this newly created body of law." See also Yale Kamisar, *Poverty, Equality, and Criminal Procedure,* in National College of District Attorneys, *Constitutional Law Deskbook* 1–97 to 1–100 (1977).

3. Does the *Ross* opinion's "equal protection analysis" closely resemble a "due process analysis"? Indeed, now that *Ross* is on the books, does the "equality" principle *add anything* to what the indigent defendant or prisoner already has in his arsenal? Consider Kamisar, supra, at 1–101 to 1–108:

"[The *Ross* 'equal protection analysis'] seems to put to one side the admitted fact that an indigent seeking discretionary review is 'somewhat handicapped in comparison with a wealthy defendant who has counsel assisting him' and focuses instead on whether an indigent seeking discretionary review without counsel has a *'meaningful* opportunity' (emphasis added) to present his claims in the state supreme court—to provide the court 'with an *adequate* basis for its decision to grant or deny review' (emphasis added)—*regardless* of whether a wealthy defendant who has counsel at this stage has a *significantly better* opportunity to present his claims.

"[What *Ross*] really seems to be asking, and deciding, is whether an indigent in respondent's circumstances has a *fair chance,* a *fighting chance* (or the requisite *minimum* chance), to get the attention of the state supreme court. [This] is 'due process,' not 'equal protection' reasoning. * * *

"So long as the indigent defendant's 'brand of justice' satisfies certain minimal standards—passes government inspection, one might say—[*Ross* tells us that] *it need not be* the same brand of justice or the same 'choice' or 'prime' grade of justice as the wealthy man's. [In some phases of the criminal process an indigent will not have 'meaningful access' to the hearing body or an 'adequate opportunity' to present his claim], but in [such] cases 'fundamental fairness'— 'due process'—will require the state to furnish counsel. In those cases where due process *does not* impose a duty on the state to provide counsel, *neither,* it seems, *will 'equal protection.'* "

4. What light, if any, is shed on the meaning of *Ross* by *United States v. MacCollom*, 426 U.S. 317, 96 S.Ct. 2086, 48 L.Ed.2d 666 (1976)? *MacCollom* upheld the constitutionality of 28 U.S.C. § 753 (f), which provides for a free transcript for indigent prisoners seeking relief under 28 U.S.C. § 2255 (the statutory counterpart to habeas corpus for federal prisoners) *only if* the trial judge certifies that (a) the claim is "not frivolous" and (b) the transcript is needed to decide the issues presented." The principal opinion was written by Rehnquist, J., joined by Burger, C.J., and Stewart and Powell, JJ.

Concurring Justice Blackmun, who provided the fifth vote for the Court's judgment, thought it clear that "there is no constitutional requirement that the [government] provide an indigent with a transcript when that transcript is not necessary in order for him to prove his claim, or when his claim is frivolous on its face. Nor does the Constitution require that an indigent be furnished every possible legal tool, no matter how devoid of assistance it may be, merely because a person of unlimited means might choose to waste his resources in a quest of that kind."

Dissenting Justice Brennan, joined by Marshall, J., maintained, that the government's refusal to furnish a free transcript in a § 2255 proceeding "upon merely a showing of indigency" violated the "equal protection" element of fifth amendment due process: "The *Griffin* principle of equality was not limited to transcripts for purposes of direct appellate review [discussing, e.g., *Lane v. Brown, Long v. District Court, Gardner v. California*]."[a]

5. What light, if any, is shed on the meaning of *Ross* by *Ake v. Oklahoma*, immediately below.

C. THE INDIGENT DEFENDANT'S RIGHT TO EXPERT SERVICES IN ADDITION TO COUNSEL

In AKE v. OKLAHOMA, 470 U.S. 68, 105 S.Ct. 1087, 84 L.Ed.2d 53 (1985), the Court broke its thirty-year silence on the issue of an indigent defendant's right to a psychiatrist and other expert assistance and held that (1) at least when a defendant has made a preliminary showing that his sanity at the time of the offense is likely to be a significant factor at trial, the state must provide access to "the psychiatric examination and assistance necessary to prepare an effective defense based on [the defendant's] mental condition" and (2) when, at a capital sentencing proceeding, the state presents psychiatric evidence of the defendant's future dangerousness, due process requires access to psychiatric assistance.

The case arose as follows: Ake, an indigent, was charged with first-degree murder. At his arraignment, Ake's behavior was so bizarre that the trial judge ordered him to be examined by a psychiatrist. The examining psychiatrist found Ake incompetent to stand trial. Six weeks after being committed to the state mental hospital, Ake was found to be competent to stand trial on the condition that he continue to be sedated with an antipsychotic drug. Petitioner's attorney informed the court that he would raise an insanity defense, but his motion for a psychiatric evaluation at state expense was denied. The jury rejected the insanity defense and petitioner was convicted of first-degree murder. At the capital sentencing proceeding, the state asked for the death penalty, relying on the examining psychiatrist's testimony to establish the likelihood of petitioner's

---

a. In a separate dissent, Stevens, J., joined by Brennan, White and Marshall, JJ., maintained that § 753(f) should be construed to make free transcripts available as a matter of course to § 2255 petitioners, as well as to convicted defendants pursuing direct appeals. The plurality's response was that Justice Stevens' construction of § 753(f) "would do violence to the intent of Congress."

future dangerousness. Petitioner had no expert witness to rebut this testimony or to give evidence in mitigation of his punishment, and he was sentenced to death. In reversing, the Court observed, per MARSHALL, J:

"This Court has long recognized that when a State brings its judicial power to bear on an indigent defendant in a criminal proceeding, it must take steps to assure that the defendant has a fair opportunity to present his defense. This elementary principle, grounded in significant part on the Fourteenth Amendment's due process guarantee of fundamental fairness, derives from the belief that justice cannot be equal where, simply as a result of his poverty, a defendant is denied the opportunity to participate meaningfully in a judicial proceeding in which his liberty is at stake. [Thus,] this Court held almost 30 years ago that once a State offers to criminal defendants the opportunity to appeal their cases, it must provide a trial transcript to an indigent defendant if the transcript is necessary to a decision on the merits of the appeal. *Griffin v. Illinois.* Indeed, in *Little v. Streater,* 452 U.S. 1, 101 S.Ct. 2202, 68 L.Ed.2d 627 (1981), we extended this principle of meaningful participation to a 'quasi-criminal' proceeding and held that, in a paternity action, the State cannot deny the putative father blood grouping tests, if he cannot otherwise afford them.

"Meaningful access to justice has been the consistent theme of these cases. [A] criminal trial is fundamentally unfair if the State proceeds against an individual defendant without making certain that he has access to the raw materials integral to the building of an effective defense. Thus, while the Court has not held that a State must purchase for the indigent defendant all the assistance that his wealthier counterpart might buy, see *Ross v. Moffitt,* it has often reaffirmed that fundamental fairness entitles indigent defendants to 'an adequate opportunity to present their claims fairly within the adversary system,' id. To implement this principle, we have focused on identifying the 'basic tools of an adequate defense or appeal,' and we have required that such tools be provided to those defendants who cannot afford to pay for them.

"[W]ithout the assistance of a psychiatrist to conduct a professional examination on issues relevant to the defense, to help determine whether the insanity defense is viable to present testimony, and to assist in preparing the cross-examination of a State's psychiatric witnesses, the risk of an inaccurate resolution of sanity issues is extremely high. With such assistance, the defendant is fairly able to present at least enough information to the jury, in a meaningful manner, as to permit it to make a sensible determination.

"A defendant's mental condition is not necessarily at issue in every criminal proceeding, however, and it is unlikely that psychiatric assistance of the kind we have described would be of probable value in cases where it is not. The risk of error from denial of such assistance, as well as its probable value, are most predictably at their height when the defendant's mental condition is seriously in question. When the defendant is able to make an ex parte threshold showing to the trial court that his sanity is likely to be a significant factor in his defense, the need for the assistance of a psychiatrist is readily apparent. It is in such cases that a defense may be devastated by the absence of a psychiatric examination and testimony; with such assistance, the defendant might have a reasonable chance of success. In such a circumstance, where the potential accuracy of the jury's determination is so dramatically enhanced, and where the interests of the individual and the State in an accurate proceeding are substantial, the State's interest in its fisc must yield.

"We therefore hold that when a defendant demonstrates [that] his sanity at the time of the offense is to be a significant factor at trial, the State must, at a minimum, assure the defendant access to a competent psychiatrist who will conduct an appropriate examination and assist in evaluation, preparation, and presentation of the defense. This is not to say, of course, that the indigent defendant has a constitutional right to choose a psychiatrist of his personal liking or to receive funds to hire his own. Our concern is that the indigent defendant have access to a competent psychiatrist for the purpose we have discussed, and as in the case of provision of counsel we leave to the State the decision on how to implement this right.

"Ake also was denied the means of presenting evidence to rebut the State's evidence of his future dangerousness. The foregoing discussion compels a similar conclusion in the context of a capital sentencing proceeding, when the State presents psychiatric evidence of the defendants future dangerousness. * * *

"This Court has upheld the practice [in state capital sentencing proceedings] of placing before the jury psychiatric testimony on the question of future dangerousness, at least where the defendant has had access to an expert of his own. * * * Without a psychiatrist's assistance, the defendant cannot offer a well-informed expert's opposing view, and thereby loses a significant opportunity to raise in the jurors' minds questions about the State's proof of an aggravating factor. In such a circumstance, where the consequence of error is so great, the relevance of responsive psychiatric testimony so evident, and the burden on the State so slim, due process requires access to a psychiatric examination on relevant issues, to the testimony of the psychiatrist, and to assistance in preparation at the sentencing phase."[a]

Notes and Questions

1. **The Sixth Amendment vs. Fourteenth Amendment due process.** Although one might maintain that a right to a court-appointed psychiatrist under certain circumstances is implicit in the right to counsel or implements or effectuates that right, *Ake* is not written that way. It is a free-standing procedural due process decision; one that applies "the Fourteenth Amendment's due process guarantee of fundamental fairness." Consider Donald A. Dripps, *Criminal Procedure as Constituional Law* ___ (2002) (Ch.6) (forthcoming): "The *Ake* Court described the appropriate inquiry as whether the defense had access to 'the basic tools' of an effective defense. This test has not been generously interpreted by the lower courts. Nonetheless, it is an illuminating comment on the power of doctrine that even a conservative majority could be moved to order the expenditure of public funds when faced with the prospect that a criminal trial ran a gratuitous risk of error, despite compliance with every specific safeguard in the Bill of Rights."

2. **Ake's impact on the equality principle.** How much of an exaggeration, if any, is it to say, as one commentator has, that "*Ake* represents the final and complete collapse of the equality principle into due process analysis" and "the full ascendancy of Justice Harlan's position in *Griffin* and *Douglas*"? See David Harris, *The Constitution and Truth Seeking: A New Theory on Expert Services for Indigent Defendants,* 83 J.Crim.L. & C. 469, 482, 488 (1992).

a. Burger, C.J. concurred in the judgment, maintaining: "The facts of this case and the question presented confine the actual holding of the Court. In capital cases the finality of the sentence imposed warrants protections that may or may not be required in other cases. Nothing in the Court's opinion reaches non-capital cases." Can (should) the Court's opinion be limited to capital cases? See Note, 84 Mich.L.Rev. 1326 (1986).

Rehnquist, J., dissented. He did not believe that "the facts of this case warrant" the establishment of the constitutional rule announced by the Court and, in any event, he thought the rule "far too broad." He would limit it to capital cases and "make clear that the entitlement is to an independent psychiatric evaluation, not to a defense consultant." Is it clear that the entitlement *is* to a "defense consultant?"

3. *The breadth of the supporting services that may be needed.* "Quality legal representation," emphasizes *A.B.A. Standards* § 5–1.4 (commentary), "cannot be rendered either by defenders or by assigned counsel unless the lawyers have available for their use adequate supporting services. These [include] expert witnesses * * *, personnel skilled in social work and related disciplines to provide assistance at pretrial release hearings and at sentencing, and trained investigators to interview witnesses and to assemble demonstrative evidence. The quality of representation at trial, for example, may be excellent and yet valueless to the defendant if the defense requires the assistance of a psychiatrist or handwriting expert and no such services are available. If the defense attorney must personally conduct factual investigations, the financial cost to the justice system is likely to be greater. Moreover, when an attorney personally interviews witnesses, [he] may be placed in the untenable position of either taking the stand to challenge their credibility if their testimony conflicts with statements previously given or withdrawing from the case."

4. *The meaning of "basic tools."* Under *Ake*, how basic does a tool have to be before a state is required to supply it to an indigent defendant? Consider Harris, Note 1 supra, at 486–87:

"As lower courts have struggled to define 'basic tools,' they have asked whether the particular resource requested by an indigent defendant is a 'virtual necessity' for the defense. Is the resource so important that the defense simply cannot do without it? Thus, 'basic tool' has come to mean not just something fundamental to a defendant's legal arsenal, but a resource without which the defense fails. Under this interpretation, most expert services remain luxuries for indigent defendants because the tasks experts perform and the issues with which they deal are not usually outcome determinative by themselves. Rather, the service any one expert or investigator provides is typically germane only to one or a few elements of the crime. If any one of the links in the evidentiary chain weakens, an acquittal may result, but this usually does not depend on the testimony of a single expert, such as the psychiatrist in *Ake*. Since lower courts have interpreted *Ake* to mean that the defense receives assistance only when the accused's case will fail without it, the basic tools standard does very little for most indigent defendants."

5. *A new approach.* Instead of trying to make indigent defendants "equal" or giving them "basic tools," Professor David Harris suggests, id. at 491–92, that courts use a theory that "targets the implications of economic disparity in criminal justice by focusing on whether the defendant's poverty could prevent the jury from hearing all of the relevant evidence on contested issues. Based on the Sixth Amendment, this theory would have judges ask two questions in deciding whether to grant a request for expert services. First, is the issue to which the requested resource pertains in dispute? Second, is the information that could be brought to trial as a result of granting the defendant's request for expert services helpful to the factfinder's decision? In other words, could this information, either by itself or in combination with other information, be the basis for a finding of reasonable doubt?"

6. *The resource imbalance—a problem the Simpson case illustrated in reverse.* Reconsider Professor Arenella's comments, set forth at p. 93, as to how, usually, the "resource factor" greatly favors the prosecution.

SECTION 3. THE RIGHT TO APPOINTED COUNSEL IN PROCEEDINGS OTHER THAN CRIMINAL PROSECUTIONS: THE CONTINUED VITALITY OF THE *BETTS V. BRADY* APPROACH

A. PROBATION AND PAROLE REVOCATION HEARINGS: JUVENILE COURT PROCEEDINGS; PARENTAL STATUS TERMINATION PROCEEDINGS

GAGNON v. SCARPELLI, 411 U.S. 778, 93 S.Ct. 1756, 36 L.Ed.2d 656 (1973), arose as follows: After pleading guilty to armed robbery, Scarpelli was sentenced to 15 years imprisonment. However, his sentence was suspended and he was placed on probation. A month later, he and a "known criminal" were apprehended while burglarizing a house. Probation was revoked without a hearing on the stated grounds that (a) Scarpelli had associated with known criminals in violation of probation conditions and (b) while associating with a known criminal he had been involved in a burglary. The Court held, per POWELL, J., that an indigent probationer or parolee has no unqualified due process right to be represented by counsel at revocation hearings:[a]

"In *Mempa v. Rhay*,[b] the Court held a probationer is entitled to be represented by appointed counsel at a combined revocation and sentencing hearing. Reasoning that counsel is required 'at every stage of a criminal proceeding where substantial rights of a criminal accused may be affected,' and that sentencing is one such stage, the Court concluded that counsel must be provided an indigent at sentencing even when it is accomplished as part of a subsequent, probation revocation proceeding. But this line of reasoning does not require a hearing or counsel at the time of probation revocation in a case such as the present one, where the probationer was sentenced at the time of that trial.[c]

"[The] introduction of counsel into a revocation proceeding will alter significantly the nature of the proceeding. If counsel is provided for the probationer or parolee, the State in turn will normally provide its own counsel; lawyers, by training and disposition, are advocates and bound by professional duty to present all available evidence and arguments in support of their clients' positions and to contest with vigor all adverse evidence and views. The role of the hearing body itself, aptly described in *Morrissey* as being 'predictive and discretionary' as well as fact-finding, may become more akin to that of a judge at a trial, and less attuned to the rehabilitative needs of the individual probationer or parolee. In the

---

a. Since Scarpelli did not attempt to *retain* counsel, the Court reserved judgment on "whether a probationer or parolee has a right to be represented at a revocation hearing by retained counsel in situations other than those where the State would be obliged to furnish counsel for an indigent."

b. In *Mempa*, 389 U.S. 128, 88 S.Ct. 254, 19 L.Ed.2d 336 (1967), petitioners' sentencing was deferred subject to probation. The prosecutor subsequently moved to have their probation revoked on the ground that petitioners had committed other crimes. At these hearings neither petitioner was represented by counsel or offered counsel. As a result of these hearings, each petitioner's probation was revoked and he was sentenced to a term of imprisonment. A unanimous Court, per Marshall, J.,

held that "a lawyer must be afforded at this [deferred sentencing] procedure whether it be labeled a revocation of probation or a deferred sentencing."

c. But see Fred Cohen, *Sentencing, Probation, and the Rehabilitative Ideal*, 47 Texas L.Rev. 1, 2–6 (1968), viewing *Mempa* as "the beginning of judicial activity in the sentencing-to-final discharge area of law, and not as a rear guard mopping-up operation in the natural evolution of right-to-counsel decisions," and stressing that "[t]here is no other area of law, except perhaps the civil commitment of the mentally ill, where the lives of so many people are so drastically affected by officials who exercise a virtually absolute, unreviewed discretion."

greater self-consciousness of its quasi-judicial role, the hearing body may be less tolerant of marginal deviant behavior and feel more pressure to reincarcerate rather than continue nonpunitive rehabilitation. Certainly, the decision-making process will be prolonged, and the financial cost to the State—for appointed counsel, counsel for the State, a longer record, and the possibility of judicial review—will not be insubstantial.

"In some cases, these modifications in the nature of the revocation hearing must be endured and the costs borne because [the] probationer's or parolee's version of a disputed issue can fairly be represented only by a trained advocate. But due process is not so rigid as to require that the significant interests in informality, flexibility, and economy must always be sacrificed.

"In so concluding, we are of course aware that the case-by-case approach to the right to counsel in felony prosecutions adopted in *Betts* [was] later rejected in favor of a *per se* rule. [But we do not] draw from *Gideon* and *Argersinger* the conclusion that a case-by-case approach to furnishing counsel is necessarily inadequate to protect constitutional rights asserted in varying types of proceedings: there are critical differences between criminal trials and probation or parole revocation hearings, and both society and the probationer or parolee have stakes in preserving these differences.

"In a criminal trial, the State is represented by a prosecutor; formal rules of evidence are in force; a defendant enjoys a number of procedural rights which may be lost if not timely raised; and, in a jury trial, a defendant must make a presentation understandable to untrained jurors. In short, a criminal trial under our system is an adversary proceeding with its own unique characteristics. In a revocation hearing, on the other hand, the State is represented not by a prosecutor but by a parole officer with the orientation described above; formal procedures and rules of evidence are not employed; and the members of the hearing body are familiar with the problems and practice of probation or parole. The need for counsel at revocation hearings derives not from the invariable attributes of those hearings but rather from the peculiarities of particular cases. * * *

"We [find] no justification for a new inflexible constitutional rule with respect to the requirement of counsel. We think, rather, that the decision as to the need for counsel must be made on a case-by-case basis in the exercise of a sound discretion by the state authority charged with responsibility for administering the probation and parole system. * * * Presumptively, it may be said that counsel should be provided in cases where, after being informed of his right to request counsel, the probationer or parolee makes such a request, based on a timely and colorable claim (i) that he has not committed the alleged violation of the conditions upon which he is at liberty; or (ii) [that] there are substantial reasons which justified or mitigated the violation and make revocation inappropriate and that the reasons are complex or otherwise difficult to develop or present. In passing on a request for the appointment of counsel, the responsible agency also should consider, especially in doubtful cases, whether the probationer appears to be capable of speaking effectively for himself. * * *

"We return to the facts of the present case. Because respondent was not afforded either a preliminary hearing or a final hearing, the revocation of his probation did not meet the standards of due process prescribed in *Morrissey*.[d] [Accordingly,] respondent was entitled to a writ of habeas corpus. [Because of

---

d. *Morrissey v. Brewer*, 408 U.S. 471, 92 S.Ct. 2593, 33 L.Ed.2d 484 (1972), held that even though the revocation of parole is not a part of the criminal prosecution, the loss of liberty involved is a serious deprivation requir-

ing that the parolee be accorded due process. That means a preliminary and a final revocation hearing under the conditions specified in *Morrissey*.

respondent's assertions regarding his confession to the crime] we conclude that the failure [to] provide[him] with the assistance of counsel should be reexamined in light of this opinion."[e]

Notes and Questions

1. *Betts, Gideon and Gagnon compared.* How likely is it that a probationer or parolee will be able to convince a court, *without* the benefit of counsel, on the basis of a record made *without* the assistance of counsel, that there are "substantial reasons which justified or mitigated the violation" or that "the reasons are complex or otherwise difficult to develop or present"? How many probationers or parolees will know *what* to point to or look for and *why?* How intelligent a decision can be made as to whether "the probationer appears to be capable of speaking effectively for himself" without knowing what justifications or mitigations a competent lawyer might have raised or developed? Can *Gagnon* escape the criticism of *Betts?* Consider, *ABA Standards* § 18–7.5 (commentary; Kamisar, *The Right to Counsel and the Fourteenth Amendment: A Dialogue on "the Most Pervasive Right" of an Accused,* 30 U.Chi.L.Rev. 53, 65 (1962).

2. *Juvenile court proceedings.* The *Gagnon* Court talked about "the rehabilitative needs of the individual probationer or parolee" and viewed the probation or parole officer's function "not so much to compel conformance to a strict code of behavior as to supervise a course of rehabilitation." But compare *In re Gault,* 387 U.S. 1, 87 S.Ct. 1428, 18 L.Ed.2d 527 (1967), holding that, in respect to juvenile delinquency proceedings that may result in loss of the juvenile's freedom, fourteenth amendment due process requires that "the child and his parent [be] notified of the child's right to be represented by [retained counsel] or, if they are unable to afford counsel that counsel will be appointed to represent the child." The Court stressed the need for counsel to assure a fair hearing in a proceeding "comparable in seriousness to a felony prosecution." It rejected the state's suggestion that the probation officers, parents, and judge might be relied on to "represent the child," finding "no material difference in this respect between adult and juvenile proceedings of the sort involved here."

Gault was hailed as demonstrating the Court's reluctance to be "hemmed in by such artificial labels as 'criminal,' 'civil', or 'quasi-administrative,'" and for taking the position that "a desire to help—the rehabilitation ideal—no longer will serve as the incantation before which procedural safeguards must succumb." Fred Cohen, *Sentencing, Probation, and the Rehabilitative Ideal,* 47 Texas L.Rev. 1, 2 (1968).

3. *Summary courts-martial; loss of liberty does not trigger the Sixth Amendment right to counsel.* In *Middendorf v. Henry,* 425 U.S. 25, 96 S.Ct. 1281, 47 L.Ed.2d 556 (1976), a 7–2 majority held there is no right to appointed counsel at summary courts-martial, even though the officer conducting these proceedings can impose a maximum punishment of 30 days confinement at hard labor. In rejecting even the view that counsel must be provided in "special circumstances," the Court, per Rehnquist J., observed:

"[E]ven were the Sixth Amendment to be held applicable to court-martial proceedings, the summary court-martial provided for in these cases was not a 'criminal prosecution' within the meaning of that Amendment. [T]he fact that the outcome of a proceeding may result in loss of liberty does not by itself, even in civilian life, mean that the Sixth Amendment's guarantee of counsel is applicable.

---

e. Dissenting in part, Justice Douglas maintained that "due process requires the appointment of counsel in this case because of the claim that respondent's confession of the burglary was made under coercion."

In *Gagnon,* the respondent faced the prospect of being sent to prison as a result of the revocation of his probation, but we held that the revocation proceeding was nonetheless not a 'criminal proceeding.' [In *Gault*] the juvenile faced possible initial confinement as a result of the proceeding in question, but the Court nevertheless based its conclusion that counsel was required on [Fourteenth Amendment due process], rather than on any determination that the hearing was a 'criminal prosecution' within the meaning of the Sixth Amendment."

4. *Parental status termination proceedings; is potential loss of liberty a necessary, if not a sufficient, requirement, for the automatic right to appointed counsel?* Over the dissenters' protest that "the unique importance of a parent's interest in the care and custody of his or her child cannot constitutionally be extinguished through formal judicial proceedings without the benefit of counsel" and the dissenters' charge that the Court was "reviv[ing] an ad hoc approach thoroughly discredited nearly 20 years ago in *Gideon,*" in *Lassiter v. Department of Social Services,* 452 U.S. 18, 101 S.Ct. 2153, 68 L.Ed.2d 640 (1981), a 5–4 majority, per Stewart, J., rejected the view that due process requires the appointment of counsel in every parental status termination proceeding involving indigent parents. Thus, the Court left the appointment of counsel in such proceedings to be determined by the state courts on a case-by-case basis.

"The pre-eminent generalization that emerges from the Court's precedents on an indigent's right to appointed counsel," observed the Court, "is that such a right has been recognized to exist only where the litigant may lose his physical liberty if he loses the litigation. * * * Significantly, as a litigant's interest in personal liberty diminishes, so does his right to appointed counsel. [Thus, *Gagnon*] declined to hold that indigent probationers have, *per se,* a right to counsel at revocation hearings, and instead left the decision whether counsel should be appointed to be made on a case-by-case basis."

The Court then examined the termination hearing and found it to be fundamentally fair. "In light of the unpursued avenues of defense, and of the experiences petitioner underwent at this hearing," the dissenters found the Court's conclusion "virtually incredible." Consider Laurence Tribe, *American Constitutional Law* 1651–52 (2d ed. 1988): "[The *Lassiter* majority's conclusion]— after reading a cold record that had been compiled without the aid of counsel— that the case before the Court 'presented no specially troublesome points of law, either procedural or substantive' * * * parallels the infamous rule of *Betts v. Brady,* which the Court had denounced two decades earlier."

5. *Where to draw the line.* Was the *Lassiter* Court's greatest concern where to draw the line? If the state must provide indigents counsel in parental termination proceedings, why not in a child custody fight growing out of a divorce action when one parent is indigent? Why not in an eviction proceeding, when an indigent is about to lose his place of residence? Is there a stronger case for providing counsel in parental termination proceedings than in these other proceedings? Why (not)? See Kamisar, *Gideon v. Wainwright A Quarter–Century Later,* 10 Pace L.Rev. 343, 357–59 (1990).

B. COLLATERAL ATTACK PROCEEDINGS

[As is discussed more extensively elsewhere in this book (see Ch. 29, § 1), an indigent prisoner has no federal constitutional right to assigned counsel in postconviction proceedings. See *Pennsylvania v. Finley* (1987) (p. 1587). A 5–4 majority held in *Murray v. Giarratano* (1989) (p. 1586) that this rules applies no differently in capital cases than in noncapital cases.]

Part Two

POLICE PRACTICES

Chapter 4

SOME GENERAL REFLECTIONS ON LAW ENFORCEMENT OFFICIALS, THE LEGISLATURES, THE COURTS AND THE CRIMINAL PROCESS*

MICHAEL J. KLARMAN—THE RACIAL ORIGINS OF MODERN CRIMINAL PROCEDURE

99 Mich.L.Rev. 48, 52, 82–83, 93–94 (2000).

[*Moore v. Dempsey*, 261 U.S. 86 (1923), overturning a conviction obtained through a mob-dominated trial; the related cases of *Powell v. Alabama*, 287 U.S. 45 (1932) (holding that, under the circumstances of this capital case, due process

* In addition to the articles extracted in this chapter, see Francis A. Allen, *The Judicial Quest for Penal Justice: The Warren Court and the Criminal Cases*, 1975 U.Ill.L.F. 518; Albert Alschuler, *Failed Pragmatism: Reflections on the Burger Court*, 100 Harv.L.Rev. 1436 (1987); Akhil Reed Amar, *The Constitution and Criminal Procedure: First Principles* (1997); Anthony Amsterdam, *The Supreme Court and the Rights of Suspects in Criminal Cases*, 45 N.Y.U.L.Rev. 785 (1970); Peter Arenella, *Rethinking the Functions of Criminal Procedure: The Warren and Burger Courts' Competing Ideologies*, 72 Geo.L.J. 185 (1983); Susan Bandes, *"We the People" and Our Enduring Values*, 96 Mich.L.Rev. 1376 (1998) (Book Review); Craig Bradley, *The Failure of the Criminal Procedure Revolution* (1993); Donald Dripps, *Akhil Amar on Criminal Procedure and Constitutional Law: "Here I Go Down the Wrong Road Again,"* 74 N.C.L.Rev. 1559 (1996); Jerold Israel, *Criminal Procedure, the Burger Court, and the Legacy of the Warren Court*, 75 Mich.L.Rev. 1319 (1977); Yale Kamisar, *The Warren Court and Criminal Justice*, in The Warren Court: A Retrospective 116

(Bernard Schwartz ed. 1996); Herbert Packer, *The Courts, the Police and the Rest of Us*, 57 J.Crim.L.C. & P.S. (1966); William Pizzi, *Punishment and Procedure: A Different View of the American Criminal Justice System*, 13 Const. Comm. 55 (1996); Stephen Saltzburg, *Foreword: The Flow and Ebb of Constitutional Criminal Procedure in the Warren and Burger Courts*, 69 Geo.L.J. 1512 (1980); Stephen Schulhofer, *The Constitution and the Police: Individual Rights and Law Enforcement*, 66 Wash.U.L.Q. 11 (1988); Louis Michael Seidman, *Criminal Procedure as the Servant of Politics*, 12 Const.Comm. 207 (1995); Carol Steiker, *Counter-Revolution in Constitutional Criminal Procedure? Two Audiences, Two Answers*, 94 Mich.L.Rev. 2466 (1996); George Thomas III, *Remapping the Criminal Procedure Universe*, 83 Va.L.Rev. 1819 (1997) (Book Review); Robert Weisberg, *Criminal Procedure Doctrine: Some Versions of the Skeptical*, 76 J.Crim.L. & C. 832 (1985); Charles Whitebread, *The Burger Court's Counter–Revolution in Criminal Procedure*, 24 Washburn L.J. 471 (1985).

required the appointed of counsel) and *Norris v. Alabama*, 294 U.S. 587 (1935) (reversing a conviction under the Equal Protection Clause where blacks had been intentionally excluded from the jury); and *Brown v. Mississippi*, 297 U.S. 278 (1936), marking the first time the Supreme Court overturned a state conviction based on coerced confessions] arose out of three quite similar episodes. Southern black defendants were charged with serious crimes against whites—either rape or murder. All three sets of defendants nearly were lynched before their cases could be brought to trial. * * * Lynchings were avoided only through the presence of state militiamen armed with machine guns surrounding the courthouse. There was a serious doubt—not just with the aid of historical hindsight, but at the time of the trial—as to whether any of the defendants were in fact guilty of the crime charged. * * * Trials took place quickly after the alleged crimes in order to avoid a lynching. [The] trials were completed within a matter of hours [and] the jurors, from which blacks were intentionally excluded * * *, deliberated for only a matter of minutes before imposing death sentences. * * *

It is impossible to measure the amount of physical coercion employed by southern sheriffs to extract confessions from black suspects, and thus one cannot say for sure what effect *Brown v. Mississippi* had on this practice. Supreme Court cases from the 1940s, however, make it clear that beating blacks into confessing remained a common practice in the South after *Brown*. For a variety of reasons, *Brown* had, at most, a limited impact on southern police practices. First, it must be recalled that the deputy sheriff who had administered the beatings in *Brown* made no effort to hide his behavior. The likeliest effect of the Supreme Court's decision, then, was to reduce the candor of state law enforcement officials. * * * Tortured confessions, if detected, might eventually be reversed by the Supreme Court or even by a state appellate court, but the vast majority of criminal cases never made it that far in the system. Thus, most convictions based on coerced confessions were unlikely to be overturned. Moreover, the narrow construction provided to federal civil rights statutes at this time made it very difficult to prosecute law enforcement officials who used physical violence against black suspects. Even in those unusual cases where a federal violation could be established, convincing all-white southern jurors to indict and convict law enforcement officials who had mistreated black defendants proved virtually impossible. * * *

[The rulings in *Moore, Powell, Norris* and *Brown*] support the claim made by several recent commentators that the Supreme Court's constitutional interventions tend to be less countermajoritarian than is commonly supposed. [The four rulings] almost certainly were consonant with dominant national opinion at the time. Even within the South, significant support existed for the results in these cases. [These] rulings only bound the southern states to abstract norms of behavior that they generally had embraced on their own. In the North, meanwhile, although blacks suffered oppressive discrimination in housing, employment, and public accommodations, the criminal justice system approached somewhat nearer to the ideal of colorblindness. Thus, it is erroneous to conceive of these landmark criminal procedure cases as instances of judicial protection of minority rights from majoritarian oppression. Rather, they better exemplify the paradigm of judicial imposition of a national consensus on resistant state outliers (with the qualification that even the southern states generally accepted these norms in the abstract).

Relatedly, these criminal procedure decisions raise the interesting possibility that during the interwar period the Supreme Court reflected national opinion on racial issues better than did Congress. These rulings imposed constitutional constraints on southern lynch law at almost precisely the same time that the national legislature was debating the imposition of statutory constraints on lynching. The House of Representatives approved anti-lynching bills three times, in 1922, 1937, and 1940. But these measures never survived in the Senate, mainly because that institution's antimajoritarian filibuster rules enabled intensely committed southern Senators (with the aid of some largely indifferent westerners) to block passage. Similarly, the House approved anti-poll tax bills five times in the 1940s, but they never passed the Senate, while the Supreme Court that same decade struck a momentous blow for black suffrage by invalidating the white primary.

DONALD A. DRIPPS—CONSTITUTIONAL THEORY FOR CRIMINAL PROCEDURE: *DICKERSON, MIRANDA*, AND THE CONTINUING QUEST FOR BROAD—BUT—SHALLOW
43 Wm. & Mary L.Rev. 1, 45–46 (2001).

American legislatures consistently have failed to address defects in the criminal process, even when they rise to crisis-level proportions. For example, when the *Miranda* Court invited Congress and the states to experiment with alternatives to traditional backroom police interrogation, Congress responded by adopting Title II,[a] which stubbornly insisted on the traditional practice. To this day only two American jurisdictions, Alaska and Minnesota, require taping interrogations. In both instances the state courts, rather than the state legislature, were the sources of reform.

Legislatures across the United States have found billions of dollars for prisons, but the support for indigent defense is shamefully inadequate. No legislature has adopted reforms of police identification procedures, even though we have known since the 1930s that mistaken identification is the leading cause of false convictions. Legislatures have not filled the voids created by contemporary pro-government criminal procedure rulings. They have not, for instance, adopted statutory regulations of undercover operations, even though the Court has left such operations unregulated by the Fourth Amendment. They have not adopted statutory requirements for judicial warrants, or the preservation of exculpatory evidence, or plugged holes in the exclusionary rule, let alone delivered the effective tort remedy exclusionary rule critics have advocated for decades.

The record is not an accident, but the product of rational political incentives. Almost everyone has an interest in controlling crime. Only young men, disproportionately black, are at significant risk of erroneous prosecution for garden-variety felonies. Abuses of police search and seizure or interrogation powers rarely fall upon middle-aged, middle-class citizens. When powerful interest groups are subject to the exercise of police powers that pale in comparison to what is visited on young black men luckless enough to reside in a "high crime area," things are different. [But] so long as the vast bulk of police and prosecutorial power targets the relatively powerless (and when will that ever be otherwise?), criminal procedure rules that limit public power will come from the courts or they will come from nowhere.

PETER ARENELLA—FOREWORD: O. J. LESSONS
69 S.Cal.L.Rev. 1233, 1234–35 (1996).

Lawyers control adversarial trials. They decide what evidence to present and how to massage it into a story of guilt, innocence, or reasonable doubt. In such a lawyer-dominated system, the trial's outcome may hinge on which side has the

---

a. The relevant provision of Title II (which purported to "overrule" *Miranda* and reinstate the old due process-voluntariness test) is set forth at p. 559. The provision was struck down in *Dickerson v. United States* (2000), set forth at p. 561.

superior resources to pay for the best investigators, experts, and counsel. Money can have a greater impact on the verdict than the "facts" because it dictates how those "facts" are transformed into legally admissible and persuasive evidence.

This resource factor usually favors the state because most criminal defendants are poor. The prosecutor can use law enforcement agencies, state and private forensic laboratories, and experts on the public payroll to develop, shape, and present her evidence. Crime victims and witnesses usually cooperate with the prosecution. If they do not, the prosecutor can command their appearance before a grand jury and compel their testimony.

In contrast, a skilled and experienced public defender is lucky if she gets an investigator to spend a few hours investigating the "facts." Crime victims and civilian witnesses frequently refuse to answer the investigator's questions. If the public defender needs expert assistance, she must petition the court for funds to pay for the expert's time. The one or two state-funded experts she may obtain won't be [the caliber of O. J. Simpson's experts] and they will rarely spend hundreds of hours looking for flaws in the state's case.

This resource imbalance is particularly egregious in death penalty prosecutions. Given the horrific nature of these crimes, the defendant's life often depends on the defense's ability and capacity to make the client's humanity apparent to the jury deciding his fate at the sentencing phase of the trial.[4] Far too often, underpaid defense lawyers in capital cases spend less time and effort on death penalty cases than the Simpson defense team expended prepping for his preliminary hearing.

The "trial of the century" illustrated this resource imbalance problem in reverse. One of [O. J. Simpson's defense lawyer's] wisest decisions was to hire some of this country's leading medical, forensic, and legal experts before Simpson was even arrested. With the aid of [these experts], the defense's forensic attorney team * * * transformed incriminating hair, blood, DNA, and fiber data into evidence of police and criminalist incompetence and corruption. While defense counsel for the indigent can read the Simpson trial transcripts and learn new ways to attack forensic evidence, they lack the resources to buy the experts whose prestige and skills made the "garbage in-garbage out" strategy so effective.[a]

WILLIAM J. STUNTZ—THE UNEASY RELATIONSHIP BETWEEN CRIMINAL PROCEDURE AND CRIMINAL JUSTICE
107 Yale L.J. 1, 3–12, 72–76 (1997).

Most talk about the law of criminal procedure treats that law as a self-contained universe. The picture looks something like this: The Supreme Court

---

4. This is no easy task. Explaining how one's client became a killer will not work unless the defendant's life story includes factors that trigger the jury's compassion. Constructing such a story requires extensive investigation into the offender's past, documentation of whatever factors "victimized" the offender at an early age, evidence of how the "system" failed to address these factors, and expert testimony explaining why these factors diminished the offender's capacity to control his anti-social impulses. Accounts of the offender's early victimizations may well fall on deaf ears unless the defense can also make some showing of why the offender is not beyond redemption.

a. See also Deborah L. Rhodes, *Simpson Sound Bites: What Is and Isn't News About Domestic Violence*, in Postmortem: The O. J. Simpson Case 83, 84 (Jeffrey Abramson ed. 1996). After observing that a single public defender often handles hundreds of cases per year and usually lacks adequate time or resources for investigation and expert testimony, Professor Rhode continues: "By contrast, in the Simpson case, [the] complete defense bill, including legal fees, may have reached $10 million. That figure exceeds what some states spend on appointed counsel for thousands of indigent defendants."

says that suspects and defendants have a right to be free from certain types of police or prosecutorial behavior. Police and prosecutors, for the most part, then do as they're told. When they don't, and when the misconduct is tied to criminal convictions, the courts reverse the convictions, thereby sending a message to misbehaving officials. Within the bounds of this picture there is room for a lot of debate about the wisdom or constitutional pedigree of particular doctrines, and the literature is filled with debate of that sort. There is also room for theorizing about the optimal specificity of the rules the Supreme Court creates; the literature contains some of that, though less than it should. Finally, there is room for arguing about remedies—about whether reversing criminal convictions is an appropriate means of getting the police, prosecutors, and trial judges to do what the law says they ought to do. At least in the sphere of Fourth and Fifth Amendment law, a lively debate along those lines exists. But for all their variety, these debates take for granted the same basic picture of the process, a process whose only variables are the rules themselves and the remedies for their violation.

The picture is, of course, wrong. Criminal procedure's rules and remedies are embedded in a larger system, a system that can adjust to those rules in ways other than obeying them. And the rules can in turn respond to the system in a variety of ways, not all of them pleasant. The more one focuses on that dynamic, the more problematic the law of criminal procedure seems.

The heart of the problem is the system's structure. The criminal justice system is dominated by a trio of forces: crime rates, the definition of crime (which of course partly determines crime rates), and funding decisions—how much money to spend on police, prosecutors, defense attorneys, judges, and prisons. These forces determine the ratio of crimes to prosecutors and the ratio of prosecutions to public defenders, and those ratios in turn go far toward determining what the system does and how the system does it. But the law that defines what the criminal process looks like, the law that defines defendants' rights, is made by judges and Justices who have little information about crime rates and funding decisions, and whose incentives to take account of those factors may be perverse. High crime rates make it easy for prosecutors to substitute cases without strong procedural claims for cases with such claims. Underfunding of criminal defense counsel limits the number of procedural claims that can be pressed. Both phenomena make criminal procedure doctrines seem inexpensive to the appellate judges who define those doctrines. Unsurprisingly, given that regulating the criminal justice system has seemed cheap, the courts have done a lot of regulating—more, one suspects, than they would have done in a world where defendants could afford to litigate more often and more aggressively, or where prosecutors could not so easily substitute some cases for others. Criminal procedure is thus distorted by forces its authors probably do not understand.

The distortion runs both ways. As courts have raised the cost of criminal investigation and prosecution, legislatures have sought out devices to reduce those costs. Severe limits on defense funding are the most obvious example, but not the only one. Expanded criminal liability makes it easier for the government to induce guilty pleas, as do high mandatory sentences that serve as useful threats against recalcitrant defendants. And guilty pleas avoid most of the potentially costly requirements that criminal procedure imposes. These strategies would no doubt be politically attractive anyway, but the law of criminal procedure makes them more so. Predictably, underfunding, overcriminalization, and oversentencing have increased as criminal procedure has expanded.

Nor are the law's perverse effects limited to courts and legislatures. Constitutional criminal procedure raises the cost of prosecuting wealthier defendants by giving those defendants more issues to litigate. The result, at the margin, is to steer prosecutors away from such defendants and toward poorer ones. By giving defendants other, cheaper claims to raise, constitutional criminal procedure also raises the cost to defense counsel of investigating and litigating factual claims, claims that bear directly on their clients' innocence or guilt. The result is to steer defense counsel, again at the margin, away from those sorts of claims and toward constitutional issues. More Fourth, Fifth, and Sixth Amendment claims probably mean fewer self-defense claims and mens rea arguments. This turns the standard conservative criticism of the law of criminal procedure on its head. Ever since the 1960s, the right has argued that criminal procedure frees too many of the guilty. The better criticism may be that it helps to imprison too many of the innocent.

It also does little about the concern that, more than anything else, prompted its creation. The post–1960 constitutionalization of criminal procedure arose, in large part, out of the sense that the system was treating black suspects and defendants much worse than white ones. Warren-era constitutional criminal procedure began as a kind of antidiscrimination law. But the criminal justice system is characterized by extraordinary discretion—over the definition of crimes (legislatures can criminalize as much as they wish), over enforcement (police and prosecutors can arrest and charge whom they wish), and over funding (legislatures can allocate resources as they wish). In a system so dominated by discretionary decisions, discrimination is easy, and constitutional law has surprisingly little to say about it. * * *

Interestingly, judicial intervention in other aspects of the criminal justice system—the definition of crimes and the funding of criminal defense—does not seem likely to have these sorts of perverse effects. Constitutionalizing procedure, in a world where substantive law and funding are the province of legislatures, may tend to encourage bad substantive law and underfunding. But constitutionalizing some aspects of substantive criminal law and defense funding would not tend to encourage bad procedure, or bad anything else. Yet substance and funding are the areas where courts have most deferred to legislatures, where passivity rather than activism has been the judicial norm. It may be that the broad structure of constitutional regulation of criminal justice has it backward, that courts have been not too activist, but activist in the wrong places. * * *

Broader substantive criminal law allows the state to end-run much of criminal procedure. In a world where trivial crimes stay on the books, or one where routine traffic offenses count as crimes, the requirement of probable cause to arrest may mean almost nothing. Officers can arrest for a minor offense—everyone violates the traffic rules—in order to search or question a suspect on a major one.[6] This allows arrests and searches of suspected drug dealers without any ex ante support for the suspicion, the very thing the probable cause standard is supposed to forbid. In a world where sodomy laws remain valid long after their enforcement has ceased, prosecutors can induce guilty pleas in some problematic sexual assault cases—the need to prove nonconsent disappears, and with it (again, in some cases) the ability to mount a plausible defense. This amounts to convicting defendants of sexual assault without proving the crime, by pointing to another crime that serves as the excuse for punishment, but not the reason.

[Legislatures] fund the system. Legislatures decide how many police officers, prosecutors, and judges to have, and how much to pay them. They also decide how generously to fund criminal defense counsel in those cases (the majority) in which the court appoints counsel. * * *

Over the course of the past couple of decades, legislatures have exercised this funding power to expand substantially the resources devoted to law enforcement,

---

6. See *Whren v. United States* (1996) [p. 226] (holding that police can detain motorists where there is a probable cause to believe that they have violated traffic laws, regardless of whether the stop is pretextual).

though the budget increases appear less substantial in light of parallel increases in crime. * * * [N]otwithstanding nominal budget increases, spending on indigent defendants in constant dollars per case appears to have declined significantly between the late 1970s and the early 1990s.

The predictable result is public defenders' offices with very large ratios of cases to lawyers. One recent study found a jurisdiction in which some public defenders represented over four hundred felony defendants in an eight-month span, and the average representation was more than half that number. [Those familiar with the system agree:] Public defenders are terribly overburdened. The story is essentially the same in jurisdictions that use separately appointed defense counsel rather than public defenders. * * * [A] typical appointed defense lawyer faces something like the following pay scale: $30 or $40 an hour for the first twenty to thirty hours, and zero thereafter. * * *

[There] are a great many constitutional rules, most of which are highly contestable. The rules are produced by a court system that acts quite independently of legislative preference, at least in this area. (*Mapp v. Ohio* and *Miranda v. Arizona* were hardly examples of majoritarian lawmaking.) Perhaps more so than anywhere else in constitutional law, in criminal procedure the broad exercise of judicial power tends to be justified precisely by legislators' unwillingness to protect constitutional interests. Yet these judge-made rules are enforced through the efforts of criminal defense counsel who, in most cases, are paid by the state—the same state whose preferences the rules purport to trump. By buying less criminal defense, the state can buy less enforcement of constitutional criminal procedure. It can, to some degree, trump the trump. Of course, if it does so it necessarily also buys less of whatever else criminal defense counsel do. * * *

* * * Why has constitutional law focused so heavily on criminal procedure, and why has it so strenuously avoided anything to do with substantive criminal law and the funding of defense counsel? * * *

The real difficulty with regulating substantive criminal law and funding decisions may be [that there] is no nonarbitrary way to arrive at the proper legal rules, no way to get to sensible bottom lines by something that looks and feels like legal analysis. Whether proportionality review is lodged in appellate or trial courts, the only way to do it is to do it, to decide that this sentence is too great but not that one. There is no metric for determining right answers, no set of analytic tools that defines what a given sentence ought to be. That, after all, was the problem with discretionary sentencing regimes, the problem that produced the current infatuation with guidelines. Similarly, heightened mens rea requirements for overbroad crimes beg the question of which crimes are overbroad.

[The] only way to set funding floors is to set them—to say, states must spend this much on criminal defense, but need not spend more. There is no analytic structure that allows one to specify the right dollar amount. [A] good deal of constitutional law may consist of judicial policy preferences with a thin legal veneer, but here the veneer seems transparent.

That simple point may be the source of much of constitutional law's troubled relationship with criminal justice. Constitutional law has focused relentlessly on the sorts of issues that are susceptible to legal analysis—how to select juries, when to require warrants, which mistrials permit retrial and which ones mean the defendant must go free. These are classic lawyers' issues; they give rise to classic lawyers' arguments. But courts' decisions on those issues are embedded in a system shaped by more open-ended—and more flagrantly political—judgments: How bad should something be before we call it a crime? How much money should we spend on criminal defense? Perhaps courts would do a sufficiently poor job of making these open-ended political judgments that we are better off leaving them to other actors. That is the system's current premise, and the premise is entirely plausible. But if that premise is right, those other actors—chiefly legislators and prosecutors—are able to defeat courts' work on courts' own turf: All those judge-made procedural rules are likely not to work the way they are supposed to. In the criminal justice system's three-legged stool—procedure, substance, and money—procedure is the least stable leg, the one that most depends on the others for support.

So criminal procedure may be no more than an instance of courts properly recognizing the need to intervene in a system that imposes terrible costs on large numbers of people, and then doing what comes naturally, regulating the kinds of things courts are used to regulating. That includes avoiding a kind of decision-making that, for courts, seems unnatural. All of which might be fine if the judicially regulated sphere could be isolated from the rest of the system. Sadly, it cannot. * * *

[The law of criminal procedure prevents some serious wrongs and produces other benefits, some of which are quite familiar.] Yet there are substantial tradeoffs, and the tradeoffs are not so familiar. The criminal process is much harder to control than courts suppose; it is driven by forces the courts do not, and perhaps cannot, direct. When courts do act, their actions are shaped by those forces in ways the courts themselves may not understand, ways that are at best ambiguous and at worst bad. Some part of what the Fourth, Fifth, and Sixth Amendments protect has probably come at the cost of a criminal justice system that is less focused on the merits and hence more likely to convict innocents, a system that disproportionately targets the poor, and a system that convicts for "crimes" that cover vastly more than anyone would wish to punish. The merits of this bargain are at least open to question. * * *

[For] the past thirty-five years, the legal system's discussion of criminal defendants' rights has suffered from an air of unreality, a sense that all goals can be satisfied and all values honored—that we can, for example, have the jury selection process we want at no cost to anything else we might want. A sense of rank ordering, of assigning priority to some constitutional norms rather than treating all as equally deserving of regulatory attention, is absent.

That should change. It is time to acknowledge the tradeoffs, to take seriously the nature of the system the law of criminal procedure regulates and the ways in which that system can evade or undermine the regulation. In a regime like ours, countermajoritarian restraints on the criminal process can succeed only at a cost, the cost is probably substantial, and it is disproportionately imposed on those who least deserve to bear it. Leaving more of the process to majoritarian institutions might be better, not least for some of the defendants the process is designed to protect.

That need not mean leaving defendants to the mercies of state legislatures and local prosecutors. If constitutional law's response to criminal justice has failed, it has failed not just from too much intervention but from too little as well. Making *Gideon* a formal right only, without any ancillary funding requirements, has produced a criminal process that is, for poor defendants, a scandal. Courts' reluctance to police legislatures' criminalization and sentencing decisions—coupled with the way those legislative decisions can be used in a system that gives prosecutors blanket authority to choose whom to go after and for what—has produced its own scandals. Defendants' interests might best be protected by less procedure, coupled with a much more activist judicial posture toward funding, the definition of crime, and sentencing—all areas where judges have been loath to take dramatic stands.

This judicial reticence seems to have been motivated by a desire not to trench on the prerogatives of the politicians, a desire to stick to the more law-like and presumably less contentious ground of process. That the 1960s produced a revolution in criminal *procedure* may testify to the underrated conservatism of Warren Court constitutional thought, to that radical Court's willingness to confine its intervention to conventional categories. If so, in this area these conservative instincts may have been misplaced—as, perhaps, was the Court's reformist (procedural) zeal. The system might be better off today had Warren and his colleagues worried less about criminal procedure, and more about criminal justice.

JEROME H. SKOLNICK & JAMES J. FYFE—ABOVE THE LAW: POLICE AND THE EXCESSIVE USE OF FORCE*
115–16, 119–20, 131–33, 194–95 (1993).

[The] view of police officers as soldiers engaged in a war on crime not only diverts attention from more effective strategies for crime control but also is a major cause of police violence and the violation of citizens' rights. Those who hold and urge this view wrongly presume—or worse, *pretend*—that grand strategies devised by police chiefs, no-nonsense prosecutors, drug czars, law-and-order politicians, and other would-be generals can banish crime, disorder, and the scourge of drugs. They have urged a *war model* of policing that aggrandizes these top cops, hardnosed prosecutors, and other assorted tough guys in suits, most of whom have never made a drug buy, never made an arrest, never faced physical danger, and never come face to face with a criminal on a dark street. Less obviously, it reduces the role of the cop on the street to that of unquestioning grunt in the trenches.
* * *

* * * Every day, out of their supervisors' sight, police officers at the lowest levels of their departments make what law scholar Joseph Goldstein called "low visibility decisions" that have great effects on the lives and liberties of individual members of the public. At any moment, for example, police officers throughout the United States are deciding whether to ticket or merely to warn this motorist; whether or not to destroy the marijuana cigarette that kid was found holding and send him on his way without marking his life history with a record of arrest; whether or not to arrest this abusive husband; whether to back off a bit or stand firm and shoot the oncoming emotionally disturbed person wielding the knife.

These are momentous decisions that can be reviewed only after the fact and, often, only after their consequences have been realized. Before there is any opportunity to determine whether the officer has acted appropriately, the ticket has been issued, the arrest or release has occurred, the shot has struck flesh. Further, absent videotaping or other reasonably objective recording, reviews usually must rely solely upon the accounts of the officers and citizens involved. When citizens benefit from officers' exercise of discretion, as when they are given what police call *scares* rather than tickets, any opportunity officially to review the appropriateness of officers' decisions disappears with them as they leave the scenes of their encounters with police. When the wisdom or reasonableness of officers' actions is challenged, review frequently consists of trying to *eff the ineffable*—attempting to resolve irresolvable swearing contests between citizens and police officers. Conversely, whenever police chiefs make decisions, their discretion is recorded and subject to comment by myriad critics, both before and

* For a thoughtful exploration of whether "community policing" offers a promising means of preventing the abuses discussed in *Above the Law*, see Debra Ann Livingston, *Brutality in Blue: Community, Authority, and the Elusive Promise of Police Reform*, 92 Mich. L.Rev. 1556 (1994). For a critical view of community policing, see Bernard E. Harcourt, *Illusion of Order: The False Promise of Broken-Windows Policing* (2001).

after the fact. As an old saw has it, police chiefs' decisions are put on paper in the form of orders and policy statements and are there for everybody to see; but cops' decisions quickly disappear into the ozone, where there is nobody to criticize the cops' version of what occurred. It is hard to think of any hierarchical organization in which the lowest-level employees routinely exercise such great discretion with such little opportunity for objective review. * * *

Over time [the] analogy between local police and the FBI has proved no more apt than that between the military and the police. Hoover was successful because the enemy in his war was not so much crime as a few sensational public enemies—the John Dillingers and Baby Face Nelsons—who were relatively easy to catch. This, we began to discover during the mid–1960s, is not the crime problem facing our local police.

Today the police work in inner cities, where poverty, unemployment, teenage pregnancy, and drug use have achieved nearly institutional status and where young men are steered by their peers to commit crimes before they have reached puberty. In such circumstances, cops' wars on crime are unwinnable. Police detectives—or FBI agents—can track down a few *individual criminals*. They do so with some success, considerable prestige, and the resulting sense of a job well done. But in the grand picture, all police administrators know that their investigators' best efforts and most spectacular arrests will never solve the *problem* of inner-city violence.

* * * Day after day, patrol officers—trained and socialized to think of themselves as soldiers—see around them the evidence that their enforcement efforts are in vain. One of us (Skolnick) was riding with an NYPD cop in Washington Heights, the main marketplace of New York City's drug scene. Youthful drug sellers were standing in threes and fours on virtually every corner.

Our police companion, an experienced narcotics officer, was asked, "How effective are the police in controlling the drug trade?" "We are," he answered, "like a gnat biting on a horse's ass." * * *

[The] widespread belief that the Supreme Court's best-known decisions on search, seizure, and interrogation somehow have *handcuffed* the police or otherwise have made citizens less safe is not supported by any objective evidence. * * * Most offenders are caught redhanded in circumstances so rich in incriminating evidence that the police simply do not need to ask them for anything but their names and addresses. When police *buy* narcotics on the street and *bust* the seller, or search a crack house and seize the drugs, attempts to obtain confessions serve only to gild the lily of already invulnerable prosecution cases. * * *

Popular overestimation or exaggeration of the court's effects on police effectiveness is a matter of more than academic interest. Like the view of *cops-as-soldiers,* the charges that due process protections foil the war on crime not only distract us from more promising strategies of crime control but also increase the likelihood of police violence and violation of citizens' rights. Cops who feel that *their enemy* has been given unreasonable advantages by people who have not themselves experienced the battle may come to disrespect all the rules and to administer "street justice"—as in the case of Rodney King—to ensure that offenders are appropriately and severely punished. * * *

TRACEY MACLIN—"BLACK AND BLUE ENCOUNTERS"— SOME PRELIMINARY THOUGHTS ABOUT FOURTH AMENDMENT SEIZURES: SHOULD RACE MATTER?*
26 Valparaiso U.L.Rev. 243, 250, 252–61, 265–70 (1991).

* See also Elizabeth A. Gaynes, *The Urban Criminal Justice System: Where Young +* *Black + Male = Probable Cause,* 20 Ford.Urb. L.J. 621 (1993); David A. Harris, *Factors for*

* * * I submit that the dynamics surrounding an encounter between a police officer and a black male are quite different from those that surround an encounter between an officer and the so-called average, reasonable person. My tentative proposal is that the Court should disregard the notion that there is an average, hypothetical, reasonable person out there by which to judge the constitutionality of police encounters. When assessing the coercive nature of an encounter, the Court should consider the race of the person confronted by the police, and how that person's race might have influenced his attitude toward the encounter.

* * * [The] Supreme Court has said over and over that *all citizens*—not just rich, white men from the suburbs—are free to ignore a police officer who accosts them. In *Florida v. Royer,* Justice White explained that: "The person approached . . . need not answer any question put to him; indeed, he may decline to listen to the questions at all and may go on his way. He may not be detained even momentarily without reasonable, objective grounds for doing so; and his refusal to listen or answer does not, without more, furnish those grounds."[43]

This is what the law is supposed to be; black men, however, know that a different "law" exists on the street. Black men know they are liable to be stopped at anytime, and that when they question the authority of the police, the response from the cops is often swift and violent. This applies to black men of all economic strata, regardless of their level of education, and whatever their job status or place in the community.

If the stories of black men in Boston are not convincing, consider what happened to Don Jackson, a former police officer from southern California. Mr. Jackson was trying to document that the police in Long Beach, California were discriminating against and harassing minority citizens who lived and visited Long Beach. [When he asked the officers why they had stopped him while driving] an officer pushed Mr. Jackson through a plate glass store window. Unknown to the officers, an NBC camera crew filmed the entire incident.

In a *New York Times* op-ed article entitled, *Police Embody Racism To My People,* Mr. Jackson wrote: "Operating free of constitutional limitations, the police have long been the greatest nemesis of blacks, irrespective of whether we are complying with the law or not. We have learned that there are cars we are not supposed to drive, streets we are not supposed to walk. We may still be stopped and asked 'Where are you going, boy?' Whether we're in a Mercedes or a Volkswagen."

Mr. Jackson's remarks demonstrate the illusory quality of the Court's view that police encounters are not deserving of Fourth Amendment scrutiny because citizens will feel free to leave and *know* of their right to ignore a police officer who has accosted them. The Court's approach, as it is applied in the case of black men, is flawed not because black males have not been informed, as a technical matter, of their legal rights. I have spoken with a number of black lawyers and law students who know their constitutional rights but never feel free to ignore the police. The Court's view is wrong because it is out of touch with the reality on the

Reasonable Suspicion: When Black and Poor Means Stopped and Frisked, 69 Ind.L.J. 659 (1994); David A. Harris, *Driving While Black and All Other Traffic Offenses: The Supreme Court and Pretextual Traffic Stops,* 87 J.Crim.L. & C. 554 (1997); Sheri Lynn Johnson, *Race and the Decision to Detain a Suspect,* 93 Yale L.J. 214 (1983); Sheri Lynn Johnson, *Unconscious Racism and the Criminal Law,* 73 Cornell L.Rev. 1016 (1988); Randall Kennedy, *The State, Criminal Law, and Racial Discrimination: A Comment,* 107 Harv.L.Rev. 1255 (1994); *Developments in the Law—Race and the Criminal Process,* 101 Harv.L.Rev. 1472 (1988).

43. Florida v. Royer [p. 313], (1983) (plurality opinion) * * *.

streets of America. Most black men simply do not trust police officers to respect their rights.

* * * Black males learn at an early age that confrontations with the police should be avoided; black teenagers are advised never to challenge a police officer, even when the officer is wrong. Even if a police officer has arguable grounds for stopping a black male, such an encounter often engenders distinct feelings for the black man. Those feelings are fear of possible violence or humiliation.

To be sure, when whites are stopped by the police, they too feel uneasy and often experience fear. [But] I wonder whether the average white person worries that an otherwise routine police encounter may lead to a violent confrontation. When they are stopped by the police, do whites contemplate the possibility that they will be physically abused for questioning why an officer has stopped them? White teenagers who walk the streets or hang-out in the local mall, do they worry about being strip-searched by the police? Does the average white person ever see himself experiencing what Rodney King or Don Jackson went through during their encounters with the police?

Police officers have shown [that] they will not hesitate to "teach a lesson" to any black male who, even in the slightest way challenges his authority. For example, in Los Angeles, even before [the Rodney King beating], blacks knew not to argue with the police unless they wanted to risk death in a police choke-hold that seemed to be applied more frequently in the case of black males than other citizens.[56]

In addition to fear, distrust is another component that swirls around encounters between black males and the police. Over the years, black males have learned that police officers have little regard for their Fourth Amendment rights. Two years ago in Boston, for instance, a city learned what can happen when a police department is encouraged to ignore the constitutional rights of a targeted class of individuals—black males. In the aftermath of a tragic shooting of a white couple and the declaration of a "war" against teenage gangs and their associates, black males were subjected to what one state judge called "martial law"[57] tactics by a police department that offered no apologies for its disregard of constitutional liberties.[58] * * *

* * * [B]eing black constitutes a "double-brand" in the mind of the police. Black men are associated with "crimes against the person, with bodily harm to police officers, and with a general lack of support for the police."[67] Also, because of their race, black males "are bound to appear discordant to policemen in most of the environment of a middle-class white society. For this reason, black males doubly draw the attention of police officers."[68] In essence, the police officer "identif[ies] the black man with danger."[69]

56. See City of Los Angeles v. Lyons, 461 U.S. 95, 116 n. 3 (1983) (Marshall, J., dissenting) ("[S]ince 1975 no less than sixteen persons have died following use of a chokehold by an LAPD police officer. Twelve have been Negro males. [Thus] in a city where Negro males constitute nine per cent of the population, they have accounted for seventy-five per cent of the deaths resulting from the use of chokehold."). * * *

57. Commonwealth v. Phillips and Woody, No. 080275–6, Memorandum and Order, at 3 (Suffolk Sup.Ct. Sept. 17, 1989) (Judge Cortland Mathers found that a police order that all known gang members and their associates would be searched on sight was "a proclamation of martial law in Roxbury for a narrow class of people, young blacks, suspected of membership in a gang or perceived by the police to be in the company of someone thought to be a member."). * * *

58. Boston Police Deputy Superintendent William Celester had been quoted as saying: " 'People are going to say we're violating their [gang members'] constitutional rights, but we're not too concerned about that.... If we have to violate their rights, if that's what it takes, then that's what we're going to do." * * *

67. D. Bagley & H. Mendelsohn, *Minorities and the Police* 107 (1969).

68. Id.

From the perspective of the black man, however, these police attitudes only reinforce the view that " '[t]he police system is a dictatorship toward the black people.' "[70]* * * Black men are considered suspicious and targeted for questioning not because of any objective or empirical evidence that they are involved in criminality, but because of police bias and societal indifference to the plight of black males who are on the receiving-end of aggressive police tactics. In effect, black men are accorded "sub-citizen" status for Fourth Amendment purposes. * * *

* * * Currently, the Court assesses the coercive nature of a police encounter by considering the *totality of the circumstances* surrounding the confrontation. All I want the Court to do is to consider the role race might play, along with the other factors it considers, when judging the constitutionality of the encounter.

Some will no doubt object to the explicit use of race in deciding constitutional questions. Understandably, some will ask: If we really wish to live in a future non-racial society, shouldn't we be moving away from procedures and decisions in which people are classified by their race?

I too would like to see a future in which decision-makers will not have to consider the race of individuals in deciding important legal and constitutional questions. But in *today's* world, where the anger and distrust between black males and the police is rising, not decreasing, we must recall Justice Blackmun's familiar stance in the affirmative action debate. "In order to get beyond racism, we must first take account of race. There is no other way."[108]

RANDALL L. KENNEDY—RACE, CRIME, AND THE LAW
158–60 (1997).

When a Mexican–American motorist is selected for questioning in part on the basis of his perceived ancestry, he is undoubtedly being burdened more heavily at that moment on account of his race than his white Anglo counterpart. He is being made to pay a type of racial tax for the campaign against illegal immigration that whites, blacks, and Asians escape. Similarly, a young black man selected for questioning by police as he alights from an airplane or drives a car is being made to pay a type of racial tax for the war against drugs that whites and other groups escape. That tax is the cost of being subjected to greater scrutiny than others. But is that tax illegitimate?

One defense of it is that, under the circumstances, people of other races are simply not in a position to pay the tax effectively. In contrast to apparent Mexican ancestry, neither apparent white nor black nor Asian ancestry appreciably raises the risk that a person near the Mexican border is illegally resident in the United States. Similarly, the argument would run that in contrast to the young black man, the young white man is not as likely to be a courier of illicit drugs. The defense could go on to say that, in this context, race is *not* being used invidiously. It is not being used as a marker to identify people to harm through enslavement, or exclusion, or segregation. Rather, race is being used merely as a signal that facilitates efficient law enforcement. In this context, apparent Mexican ancestry or blackness is being used for unobjectionable ends in the same way that whiteness is used in the affirmative action context: as a marker that has the effect, though not

69. J. Skolnick, *Justice Without Trial* 49 (1966).

70. B. Blauner, *Black Lives, White Lives* 110 (1989).

108. Regents of Univ. of Cal. v. Bakke, 438 U.S. 265, 407, 438 U.S. 265, 407 (1978) (Blackmun, J., dissenting).* * *

the purpose, of burdening a given racial group. Whereas whites are make to pay a racial tax for the purpose of opening up opportunities for people of color in education and employment, Mexican–Americans and blacks are made to pay a racial tax for the purpose of more efficient law enforcement.

We need to pause here to consider the tremendous controversy that has surrounded affirmative action policies aimed at helping racial minorities. Many of the same arguments against race-based affirmative action are applicable as well in the context of race-based police stops. With affirmative action, many whites claim that they are victims of racial discrimination. With race-based police stops, many people of color complain that they are victims of racial discrimination. With affirmative action, many adversely affected whites claim that they are *innocent* victims of a policy that penalizes them for the misconduct of others who also happened to have been white. With race-based police stops, many adversely affected people of color maintain that they are *innocent* victims of a policy that penalizes them for the misconduct of others who also happen to be colored. Many whites claim that a major drawback of affirmative action which makes it more costly than valuable is the fact of their intense resentment against such programs. Many people of color claim that one of the drawbacks of race-based police stops that makes it more costly than valuable is their resentment against such policies.

There, exist, however, a remarkable difference in reactions to these racial policies, both of which involve race-dependent decisionmaking. While affirmative action is under tremendous pressure politically and legally, racial policing is not.[a]

* * *

STUART TAYLOR JR.—POLITICALLY INCORRECT PROFILING: A MATTER OF LIFE OR DEATH
National Journal, Nov. 3, 2001, p. 3406

What would happen if another 19 well-trained al Qaeda terrorists, this time with 19 bombs in their bags, tried to board 19 airliners over the next 19 months? Many would probably succeed, blowing up lots of planes and thousands of people, if the forces of head-in-the-sand political correctness prevail—as they did before Sept. 11—in blocking use of national origin as a factor in deciding which passengers' bags to search with extra care.

But a well-designed profiling system might well catch all 19. Such a system would not be race-based; indeed, most Arab–Americans would not fit the profile. It would factor in suspicious behavior, along with national origin, gender, and age. It could spread the burden by selecting at least one white (or black, or Asian) passenger to be searched for every Middle Easterner so selected. And it should be done politely and respectfully.

We have no good alternative. For the foreseeable future, the shortage of high-tech bomb-detection machines and the long delays required to search luggage by hand will make it impossible to effectively screen more than a small percentage of checked bags. The only real protection is to make national origin a key factor in choosing those bags. Otherwise, federalizing airport security and confiscating toenail clippers will be futile gestures.

I revisit this issue in part because research since my Sept. 24 column reinforces my conviction that national-origin profiling may be the only way (in the short term) to avoid hundreds or thousands of deaths.[a] At the same time, critics

---

a. Consider, too, Randall L. Kennedy, *Suspect Policy: Racial profiling by the police isn't necessarily motivated by bigotry. In fact, it's quite rational. But whatever benefits it may produce in the war against crime are out-* weighed by the damage it does to the very legitimacy of law enforcement, New Republic, Sept. 13 & 20, 1999, pp. 30, 33–34.

a. In his September 22nd column, *The Case for Racial Profiling at Airports*, National Jour-

have persuaded me that the "racial" profiling of "Arab-looking" people that I previously advocated would be less effective than profiling based on apparent origin in any of the nations known to be exporters of anti-American terrorism— not only nations in the Arab world, but also most, or all, of the nations in the Muslim world. Millions of Arab–Americans would not fit the profile because their American roots would be apparent—from their accents and speech patterns—to trained security screeners.

We have heard a great deal about the dismay of Middle Eastern passengers who have been searched and (in some cases) rudely treated on flights or unjustifiably ejected from airliners. We have heard far less about the dangers of not searching. The reason is that "large and important parts of the American news media practice a virulent form of political correctness that is indistinguishable from censorship," in the words of Richard Cohen, the mostly liberal *Washington Post* columnist.

Opponents of national-origin profiling claim it would be more effective to focus solely on suspicious behavior. They are wrong. Competent terrorists know how to avoid the suspicious-behavior trap. They are not likely to buy one-way tickets the next time. Or to pay in cash. Or to fly from Afghanistan to Pakistan to New York. Or to hang around airport security checkpoints with video cameras. These people are not stupid.

The hardest thing to hide if you are an Islamic terrorist is your Islamic-world origin, as evinced by speech patterns, facial characteristics, skin color, or (to a lesser extent) dress and travel documents. Sure, there is always the risk that the next attack will come from another homegrown Timothy McVeigh, or a Swedish Girl Scout, or (more likely) a mush-headed leftist French coed recruited by al Qaeda. But there are a lot more Islamic terrorists than there are Timothy McVeighs. And not many people from outside the Islamic world appear eager to volunteer for suicide missions. Many Arab–Americans—if not their purported leaders—now seem to understand this. In a *Detroit Free Press* poll of 527 local Arab–Americans, 61 percent supported extra scrutiny of people with Middle Eastern features or accents.

nal, p. 2877, Mr. Taylor contrasted racial profiling of people boarding airlines with the racial profiling that occurs when highway police pull over African–Americans in hugely disproportionate numbers to search for drugs. He thought racial profiling of that kind "should be deemed unconstitutional even where there is a statistically valid basis for believing that it will help catch more drug dealers or violent criminals." Taylor continued:

"Such racial profiling is hard to distinguish from—and sometimes involves—plain old racist harassment. It subjects thousands of innocent people to the kind of humiliation that characterizes police states. It hurts law enforcement by fomenting fear and distrust among potential witnesses, tipsters, and jurors. It is rarely justified by any risk of imminent violence. And it makes a mockery of conservative preachings that the Constitution is colorblind.

"Stopping hijacking is different. First, preventing mass murder is infinitely more important than finding illegal drugs or guns. Second, 100 percent of the people who have hijacked airplanes to mass-murder Americans have been Arab men. Third, a virulent perversion of Islam is the only mass movement in the world so committed to mass-murdering Americans that its fanatics are willing to kill themselves in the process. Fourth, this movement includes people who have lived legally in America for years—some of whom may be citizens—so the risk of weapons being smuggled onto airplanes cannot be eliminated by giving special scrutiny only to foreign nationals.

"In short, the mathematical probability that a randomly chosen Arab passenger might attempt a mass-murder-suicide hijacking—while tiny—is considerably higher than the probability that a randomly chosen white, black, Hispanic, or Asian passenger might. In constitutional law parlance, while racial profiling may be presumptively unconstitutional, that presumption is overcome in the case of airline passengers, because the government has a compelling interest in preventing mass-murder-suicide hijackings, and because close scrutiny of Arab-looking people is narrowly tailored to protect that interest."

Political pressure from Arab–American and liberal groups spurred the Clinton and Bush administrations to bar use of national origin as a profiling component before Sept. 11. * * * Accordingly, the Federal Aviation Administration, in unveiling its Computer–Assisted Passenger Screening program, stressed that the Justice Department's Civil Rights Division—an ultraliberal bastion—had certified that the CAPS criteria "do not consider passengers' race, color, national or ethnic origin, religion, or gender," or even "names or modes of dress." That left few criteria for flagging possible terrorists other than reservation histories—as any competent terrorist would have known.

The FAA bent even further to avoid offending hypersensitive passengers by restricting CAPS to the checked baggage—not the carry-ons or persons—of passengers whose papers the computers flagged as suspicious. European nations and Israel, by contrast, have long subjected those who fit their profiles to questioning and manual searches. And Israel's El Al has shut out terrorists since 1968.

The politically correct approach to profiling achieved its goal of minimizing complaints * * *. It did not work so well at preventing mass murder. On Sept. 11, the CAPS system flagged only six of the 19 Middle Eastern hijackers for extra scrutiny, which was apparently confined to the bags of the two who checked luggage. None of the 19 men or their carry-ons appear to have been individually searched. And the FAA's 1999 decision to seal CAPS off from all law enforcement databases—after complaints from liberal groups that criminal records were error-prone—may help explain why the FBI had not told the FAA that two of the 19 were on its watch list of suspected terrorists.

It's unclear whether national-origin profiling would have prevented the hijackings, in part because FAA rules did not bar small knives—although some airlines have suggested that they would have confiscated any box cutters they detected. But politically correct profiling virtually guaranteed that the hijackers' weapons would go undetected.

The Bush administration's profiling policy, if any, is cloaked in politically cowardly and dangerous ambiguity. The FAA and Attorney General John Ashcroft have implied opposition to national-origin profiling, even as Ashcroft's subordinates have detained with minimal explanation more than 1,000 people, most Middle–Easterners against whom there appears to be scant evidence of terrorist activity. The administration should have the courage to preach what it practices.

Some arguments repeatedly advanced by opponents of national-origin illustrate the weakness of their logic:

• *You are suggesting that all Middle Easterners are terrorists.* Nonsense. Obviously, only a minuscule number are terrorists. But any passenger might be a terrorist. That's why we all go through security screening. The logic of profiling is to identify for more-careful screening those small groups who, based on historical experience, seem much more likely than others to include suicide bombers (or just bombers). History tells us that all 19 of the Sept. 11 suicide bombers, and most or all other terrorists known to have murdered planeloads of people, have been Middle Eastern men. Million of others clamor to join this jihad.

• *What about all the white male American terrorists?* The list is not long: Timothy McVeigh, Ted Kaczynski, a handful of anti-abortion extremists, a few others. In all, they have killed fewer than 200 people—less than 5 percent of the number killed on Sept. 11 alone, not to mention the more than 600 Americans and thousands of others previously killed (mostly overseas) by Middle Eastern terrorists.

• *Profiling will foster racist hysteria.* The opposite is more likely. The disgraceful ejections of Middle Easterners from airliners since Sept. 11 were spurred less by racism than by well-founded fears of the ease with which weapons could be smuggled aboard. The best way to prevent such episodes is to give crews and passengers confidence that any would-be terrorists have been carefully searched.

• *Once you start profiling, there's no stopping point.* Yes, there is. The police's stopping of people for "driving while black," for example, has rightly been discredited because the costs—both to those searched and to the long-term interests of law enforcement—far exceed any benefits. Stopping people for "driving while Arab" would be similarly unwarranted. Flying while Middle Eastern poses a dramatically different cost-benefit calculus.

If considered unblinkingly, this is not a close call. It has nothing to do with prejudice. It is a matter of life or death.

Chapter 5

ARREST, SEARCH AND SEIZURE[a]

SECTION 1. THE EXCLUSIONARY RULE[b]

WOLF v. COLORADO

338 U.S. 25, 69 S.Ct. 1359, 93 L.Ed. 1782 (1949).

Justice FRANKFURTER delivered the opinion of the Court.

The precise question for consideration is this: Does a conviction by a State court for a State offense deny the "due process of law" required by the Fourteenth Amendment, solely because evidence that was admitted at the trial was obtained under circumstances which would have rendered it inadmissible in a prosecution for violation of a federal law in a court of the United States because there deemed to be an infraction of the Fourth Amendment as applied in *Weeks v. United States*, 232 U.S. 383, 34 S.Ct. 341, 58 L.Ed. 652 [1914]? * * *

The security of one's privacy against arbitrary intrusion by the police—which is at the core of the Fourth Amendment—is basic to a free society. It is therefore implicit in "the concept of ordered liberty" and as such enforceable against the States through the Due Process Clause. * * *

Accordingly, we have no hesitation in saying that were a State affirmatively to sanction such police incursion into privacy it would run counter to the guaranty of the Fourteenth Amendment. But the ways of enforcing such a basic right raise questions of a different order. How such arbitrary conduct should be checked, what remedies against it should be afforded, the means by which the right should be made effective, are all questions that are not to be so dogmatically answered as to preclude the varying solutions which spring from an allowable range of judgment on issues not susceptible of quantitative solution.

In *Weeks v. United States,* this Court held that in a federal prosecution the Fourth Amendment barred the use of evidence secured through an illegal search and seizure. This ruling * * * was not derived from the explicit requirements of the Fourth Amendment; it was not based on legislation expressing Congressional policy in the enforcement of the Constitution. The decision was a matter of judicial implication. Since then it has been frequently applied and we stoutly

---

a. For detailed treatment of this subject and reference to other secondary sources, consult Wayne R. LaFave, *Search and Seizure: A Treatise on the Fourth Amendment* (5 vols., 3d ed.1996) [cited herein by its Westlaw database name SEARCHSZR].

b. The concern herein is with the exclusion of evidence obtained in violation of the Fourth Amendment. An arrest or search which passes Fourth Amendment muster may nonetheless violate state law, and the exclusionary sanction is also used when state constitutional provisions similar to the Fourth Amendment have been violated, though if a state chooses not to do so this does not violate federal due process. *California v. Greenwood*, p. 142. As for violations of statutes, court rules and administrative regulations, it is customary to require exclusion if the violation significantly affected the defendant's substantial rights.

adhere to it. But the immediate question is whether the basic right to protection against arbitrary intrusion by the police demands the exclusion of logically relevant evidence obtained by an unreasonable search and seizure because, in a federal prosecution for a federal crime, it would be excluded. As a matter of inherent reason, one would suppose this to be an issue as to which men with complete devotion to the protection of the right of privacy might give different answers. When we find that in fact most of the English-speaking world does not regard as vital to such protection the exclusion of evidence thus obtained, we must hesitate to treat this remedy as an essential ingredient of the right. The contrariety of views of the States is particularly impressive in view of the careful reconsideration which they have given the problem in the light of the *Weeks* decision.

* * * As of today 30 States reject the *Weeks* doctrine, 17 States are in agreement with it. * * * Of 10 jurisdictions within the United Kingdom and the British Commonwealth of Nations which have passed on the question, none has held evidence obtained by illegal search and seizure inadmissible. * * *

The jurisdictions which have rejected the *Weeks* doctrine have not left the right to privacy without other means of protection. Indeed, the exclusion of evidence is a remedy which directly serves only to protect those upon whose person or premises something incriminating has been found. We cannot, therefore, regard it as a departure from basic standards to remand such persons, together with those who emerge scatheless from a search, to the remedies of private action and such protection as the internal discipline of the police, under the eyes of an alert public opinion, may afford. Granting that in practice the exclusion of evidence may be an effective way of deterring unreasonable searches, it is not for this Court to condemn as falling below the minimal standards assured by the Due Process Clause a State's reliance upon other methods which, if consistently enforced, would be equally effective. * * * There are, moreover, reasons for excluding evidence unreasonably obtained by the federal police which are less compelling in the case of police under State or local authority. The public opinion of a community can far more effectively be exerted against oppressive conduct on the part of police directly responsible to the community itself than can local opinion, sporadically aroused, be brought to bear upon remote authority pervasively exerted throughout the country.

We hold, therefore, that in a prosecution in a State court for a State crime the Fourteenth Amendment does not forbid the admission of evidence obtained by an unreasonable search and seizure. * * *

Justice BLACK, concurring.

* * * I agree with what appears to be a plain implication of the Court's opinion that the federal exclusionary rule is not a command of the Fourth Amendment but is a judicially created rule of evidence which Congress might negate. * * *

Justice MURPHY, with whom Justice RUTLEDGE joins, dissenting.

[T]here is but one alternative to the rule of exclusion. That is no sanction at all.

* * * Little need be said concerning the possibilities of criminal prosecution. Self-scrutiny is a lofty ideal, but its exaltation reaches new heights if we expect a District Attorney to prosecute himself or his associates for well-meaning violations of the search and seizure clause during a raid the District Attorney or his associates have ordered. But there is an appealing ring in another alternative. A trespass action for damages is a venerable means of securing reparation for unauthorized invasion of the home. Why not put the old writ to a new use? When the Court cites cases permitting the action, the remedy seems complete.

But what an illusory remedy this is, if by "remedy" we mean a positive deterrent to police and prosecutors tempted to violate the Fourth Amendment. The appealing ring softens when we recall that in a trespass action the measure of damages is simply the extent of the injury to physical property. If the officer searches with care, he can avoid all but nominal damages—a penny, or a dollar. Are punitive damages possible? Perhaps. But a few states permit none, whatever the circumstances. In those that do, the plaintiff must show the real ill will or malice of the defendant, and surely it is not unreasonable to assume that one in honest pursuit of crime bears no malice toward the search victim. If that burden is carried, recovery may yet be defeated by the rule that there must be physical damages before punitive damages may be awarded. In addition, some states limit punitive damages to the actual expenses of litigation. * * * Even assuming the ill will of the officer, his reasonable grounds for belief that the home he searched harbored evidence of crime is admissible in mitigation of punitive damages. * * * The bad reputation of the plaintiff is likewise admissible. * * * If the evidence seized was actually used at a trial, that fact has been held a complete justification of the search, and a defense against the trespass action. * * * And even if the plaintiff hurdles all these obstacles, and gains a substantial verdict, the individual officer's finances may well make the judgment useless—for the municipality, of course, is not liable without its consent. Is it surprising that there is so little in the books concerning trespass actions for violation of the search and seizure clause? * * *

Justice DOUGLAS, dissenting.

* * * I agree with Justice Murphy that * * * in absence of [an exclusionary] rule of evidence the Amendment would have no effective sanction. * * *

MAPP v. OHIO
367 U.S. 643, 81 S.Ct. 1684, 6 L.Ed.2d 1081 (1961).

Justice CLARK delivered the opinion of the Court. * * *

On May 23, 1957, three Cleveland police officers arrived at appellant's residence in that city pursuant to information that "a person [was] hiding out in the home who was wanted for questioning in connection with a recent bombing, and that there was a large amount of policy paraphernalia being hidden in the home." Miss Mapp and her daughter by a former marriage lived on the top floor of the two-family dwelling. Upon their arrival at that house, the officers knocked on the door and demanded entrance but appellant, after telephoning her attorney, refused to admit them without a search warrant. * * *

The officers again sought entrance some three hours later when four or more additional officers arrived on the scene. When Miss Mapp did not come to the door immediately, at least one of the several doors to the house was forcibly opened and the policemen gained admittance. Meanwhile Miss Mapp's attorney arrived, but the officers, having secured their own entry, and continuing in their defiance of the law, would permit him neither to see Miss Mapp nor to enter the house. [When the officers broke into the hall, Miss Mapp] demanded to see the search warrant. A paper, claimed to be a warrant, was held up by one of the officers. She grabbed the "warrant" and placed it in her bosom. A struggle ensued in which the officers recovered the piece of paper and as a result of which they handcuffed appellant because she had been "belligerent" in resisting their official rescue of the "warrant" from her person. * * * Appellant, in handcuffs, was then forcibly taken upstairs to her bedroom where the officers searched a dresser, a chest of drawers, a closet and some suitcases. * * * The search spread to the rest of the second floor * * *. The basement of the building and a trunk found therein were also searched. The obscene materials for possession of which she was ultimately convicted were discovered in the course of that widespread search.

At the trial no search warrant was produced by the prosecution, nor was the failure to produce one explained or accounted for. At best [as the Ohio Supreme Court, which affirmed the conviction, expressed it], "there is, in the record, considerable doubt as to whether there ever was any warrant for the search of defendant's home." * * *

The State says that even if the search were made without authority, or otherwise unreasonably, it is not prevented from using the unconstitutionally seized evidence at trial, citing *Wolf v. Colorado,* * * *. On this appeal, * * * it is urged once again that we review that holding. * * *

The Court in *Wolf* first stated that "[t]he contrariety of views of the States" on the adoption of the exclusionary rule of *Weeks* was "particularly impressive" * * * While in 1949, prior to the *Wolf* case, almost two-thirds of the States were opposed to the use of the exclusionary rule, now, despite the *Wolf* case, more than half of those since passing upon it, by their own legislative or judicial decision, have wholly or partly adopted or adhered to the *Weeks* rule. * * * Significantly, among those now following the rule is California which, according to its highest court, was "compelled to reach that conclusion because other remedies have completely failed to secure compliance with the constitutional provisions * * *." In connection with this California case, we note that the second basis elaborated in *Wolf* in support of its failure to enforce the exclusionary doctrine against the States was that "other means of protection" have been afforded "the right to privacy." The experience of California that such other remedies have been worthless and futile is buttressed by the experience of other States. * * *

It, therefore, plainly appears that the factual considerations supporting the failure of the *Wolf* Court to include the *Weeks* exclusionary rule when it recognized the enforceability of the right to privacy against the States in 1949, while not basically relevant to the constitutional consideration, could not, in any analysis, now be deemed controlling.

* * * Today we once again examine *Wolf's* constitutional documentation of the right to privacy free from unreasonable state intrusion, and, after its dozen years on our books, are led by it to close the only courtroom door remaining open to evidence secured by official lawlessness in flagrant abuse of that basic right, reserved to all persons as a specific guarantee against that very same unlawful conduct. We hold that all evidence obtained by searches and seizures in violation of the Constitution is, by that same authority, inadmissible in a state court.

Since the Fourth Amendment's right of privacy has been declared enforceable against the States through the Due Process Clause of the Fourteenth, it is enforceable against them by the same sanction of exclusion as is used against the Federal Government. Were it otherwise then just as without the *Weeks* rule the assurance against unreasonable federal searches and seizures would be "a form of words," valueless and undeserving of mention in a perpetual charter of inestimable human liberties, so too, without that rule the freedom from state invasions of privacy would be so ephemeral and so neatly severed from its conceptual nexus with the freedom from all brutish means of coercing evidence as not to merit this Court's high regard as a freedom "implicit in 'the concept of ordered liberty.'"

* * * [I]n extending the substantive protections of due process to all constitutionally unreasonable searches—state or federal—it was logically and constitutionally necessary that the exclusion doctrine—an essential part of the right to privacy—be also insisted upon as an essential ingredient of the right newly

recognized by the *Wolf* case. In short, the admission of the new constitutional right by *Wolf* could not consistently tolerate denial of its most important constitutional privilege, namely, the exclusion of the evidence which an accused had been forced to give by reason of the unlawful seizure. To hold otherwise is to grant the right but in reality to withhold its privilege and enjoyment. Only last year the Court itself recognized that the purpose of the exclusionary rule "is to deter—to compel respect for the constitutional guaranty in the only effectively available way—by removing the incentive to disregard it."

Indeed, we are aware of no restraint, similar to that rejected today, conditioning the enforcement of any other basic constitutional right. The right to privacy, no less important than any other right carefully and particularly reserved to the people, would stand in marked contrast to all other rights declared as "basic to a free society." * * * [N]othing could be more certain than that when a coerced confession is involved, "the relevant rules of evidence" are overridden without regard to "the incidence of such conduct by the police," slight or frequent. Why should not the same rule apply to what is tantamount to coerced testimony by way of unconstitutional seizure of goods, papers, effects, documents, etc.? We find that, as to the Federal Government the Fourth and Fifth Amendments and, as to the States, the freedom from unconscionable invasions of privacy and the freedom from convictions based upon coerced confessions do enjoy an "intimate relation" in their perpetuation of "principles of humanity and civil liberty * * *." They express "supplementing phases of the same constitutional purpose—to maintain inviolate large areas of personal privacy." The philosophy of each Amendment and of each freedom is complementary to, although not dependent upon, that of the other in its sphere of influence—the very least that together they assure in either sphere is that no man is to be convicted on unconstitutional evidence.

Moreover, our holding * * * is not only the logical dictate of prior cases, but it also makes very good sense. There is no war between the Constitution and common sense. Presently, a federal prosecutor may make no use of evidence illegally seized, but a State's attorney across the street may, although he supposedly is operating under the enforceable prohibitions of the same Amendment. Thus the State, by admitting evidence unlawfully seized, serves to encourage disobedience to the Federal Constitution which it is bound to uphold. * * *

There are those who say, as did Justice (then Judge) Cardozo, that under our constitutional exclusionary doctrine "[t]he criminal is to go free because the constable has blundered." *People v. Defore*, 150 N.E. 585 (N.Y.1926). In some cases this will undoubtedly be the result. But, "there is another consideration—the imperative of judicial integrity." The criminal goes free, if he must, but it is the law that sets him free. Nothing can destroy a government more quickly than its failure to observe its own laws, or worse, its disregard of the charter of its own existence. As Justice Brandeis, dissenting, said in *Olmstead v. United States* [p. 348]: "Our government is the potent, the omnipresent teacher. For good or for ill, it teaches the whole people by its example. * * * If the government becomes a lawbreaker, it breeds contempt for law; it invites every man to become a law unto himself; it invites anarchy." Nor can it lightly be assumed that, as a practical matter, adoption of the exclusionary rule fetters law enforcement. Only last year this Court expressly considered that contention and found that "pragmatic evidence of a sort" to the contrary was not wanting. *Elkins v. United States*, 364 U.S. 206, 80 S.Ct. 1437, 4 L.Ed.2d 1669 (1960). * * * The Court noted that:

"The federal courts themselves have operated under the exclusionary rule of *Weeks* for almost half a century; yet it has not been suggested either that the Federal Bureau of Investigation has thereby been rendered ineffective, or that the administration of criminal justice in the federal courts has thereby been disrupted.

Moreover, the experience of the states is impressive * * *. The movement toward the rule of exclusion has been halting but seemingly inexorable.''

The ignoble shortcut to conviction left open to the State tends to destroy the entire system of constitutional restraints on which the liberties of the people rest. Having once recognized that the right to privacy embodied in the Fourth Amendment is enforceable against the States, and that the right to be secure against rude invasions of privacy by state officers is, therefore, constitutional in origin, we can no longer permit that right to remain an empty promise. Because it is enforceable in the same manner and to like effect as other basic rights secured by the Due Process Clause, we can no longer permit it to be revocable at the whim of any police officer who, in the name of law enforcement itself, chooses to suspend its enjoyment. Our decision, founded on reason and truth, gives to the individual no more than that which the Constitution guarantees him, to the police officer no less than that to which honest law enforcement is entitled, and, to the courts, that judicial integrity so necessary in the true administration of justice. * * *

Reversed and remanded.[a]

Justice HARLAN, whom Justice FRANKFURTER and Justice WHITTAKER join, dissenting. * * *

I would not impose upon the States this federal exclusionary remedy. The reasons given by the majority for now suddenly turning its back on *Wolf* seem to me notably unconvincing.

First, it is said that ''the factual grounds upon which *Wolf* was based'' have since changed, in that more States now follow the *Weeks* exclusionary rule than was so at the time *Wolf* was decided. While that is true, a recent survey indicates that at present one half of the States still adhere to the common-law non-exclusionary rule, and one, Maryland, retains the rule as to felonies. * * * But in any case surely all this is beside the point, as the majority itself indeed seems to recognize. Our concern here, as it was in *Wolf*, is not with the desirability of that rule but only with the question whether the States are Constitutionally free to follow it or not as they may themselves determine, and the relevance of the disparity of views among the States on this point lies simply in the fact that the judgment involved is a debatable one. Moreover, the very fact on which the majority relies, instead of lending support to what is now being done, points away from the need of replacing voluntary state action with federal compulsion.

The preservation of a proper balance between state and federal responsibility in the administration of criminal justice demands patience on the part of those who might like to see things move faster among the States in this respect. Problems of criminal law enforcement vary widely from State to State. One State, in considering the totality of its legal picture, may conclude that the need for embracing the *Weeks* rule is pressing because other remedies are unavailable or inadequate to secure compliance with the substantive Constitutional principle involved. Another, though equally solicitous of Constitutional rights, may choose to pursue one purpose at a time, allowing all evidence relevant to guilt to be brought into a criminal trial, and dealing with Constitutional infractions by other means. Still another may consider the exclusionary rule too rough and ready a remedy, in that it reaches only unconstitutional intrusions which eventuate in criminal prosecution of the victims. Further, a State after experimenting with the *Weeks* rule for a time may, because of unsatisfactory experience with it, decide to revert to a non-exclusionary rule. And so on. * * * For us the question remains, as it has always been, one of state power, not one of passing judgment on the

---

a. Concurring opinions by Black and Douglas, JJ., and a memorandum by Stewart, J., are   omitted.

wisdom of one state course or another. In my view this Court should continue to forbear from fettering the States with an adamant rule which may embarrass them in coping with their own peculiar problems in criminal law enforcement. * * *

* * * Our role in promulgating the *Weeks* rule and its extensions * * * was quite a different one than it is here. There, in implementing the Fourth Amendment, we occupied the position of a tribunal having the ultimate responsibility for developing the standards and procedures of judicial administration within the judicial system over which it presides. Here we review State procedures whose measure is to be taken not against the specific substantive commands of the Fourth Amendment but under the flexible contours of the Due Process Clause. I do not believe that the Fourteenth Amendment empowers this Court to mould state remedies effectuating the right to freedom from "arbitrary intrusion by the police" to suit its own notions of how things should be done * * *.

Finally, it is said that the overruling of *Wolf* is supported by the established doctrine that the admission in evidence of an involuntary confession renders a state conviction constitutionally invalid. Since such a confession may often be entirely reliable, and therefore of the greatest relevance to the issue of the trial, the argument continues, this doctrine is ample warrant in precedent that the way evidence was obtained and not just its relevance, is constitutionally significant to the fairness of a trial. I believe this analogy is not a true one. The "coerced confession" rule is certainly not a rule that any illegally obtained statements may not be used in evidence. I would suppose that a statement which is procured during a period of illegal detention is, as much as unlawfully seized evidence, illegally obtained, but this Court has consistently refused to reverse state convictions resting on the use of such statements. * * *

The point, then, must be that in requiring exclusion of an involuntary statement of an accused, we are concerned not with an appropriate remedy for what the police have done, but with something which is regarded as going to the heart of our concepts of fairness in judicial procedure. The operative assumption of our procedural system is that "ours is the accusatorial as opposed to the inquisitorial system. * * *." * * * The pressures brought to bear against an accused leading to a confession, unlike an unconstitutional violation of privacy, do not, apart from the use of the confession at trial, necessarily involve independent Constitutional violations. What is crucial is that the trial defense to which an accused is entitled should not be rendered an empty formality by reason of statements wrung from him, for then "a prisoner * * * [has been] made the deluded instrument of his own conviction." That this is a *procedural right,* and that its violation occurs at the time his improperly obtained statement is admitted at trial, is manifest. * * *

This, and not the disciplining of the police, as with illegally seized evidence, is surely the true basis for excluding a statement of the accused which was unconstitutionally obtained. In sum, I think the coerced confession analogy works strongly *against* what the Court does today. * * *

UNITED STATES v. LEON
468 U.S. 897, 104 S.Ct. 3405, 82 L.Ed.2d 677 (1984).

Justice WHITE delivered the opinion of the Court. * * *

This case presents the question whether the Fourth Amendment exclusionary rule should be modified so as not to bar the use in the prosecution's case-in-chief of evidence obtained by officers acting in reasonable reliance on a search warrant issued by a detached and neutral magistrate but ultimately found to be unsupported by probable cause. * * *

The Fourth Amendment contains no provision expressly precluding the use of evidence obtained in violation of its commands, and an examination of its origin and purposes makes clear that the use of fruits of a past unlawful search or seizure "work[s] no new Fourth Amendment wrong." The wrong condemned by the Amendment is "fully accomplished" by the unlawful search or seizure itself, and the exclusionary rule is neither intended nor able to "cure the invasion of the defendant's rights which he has already suffered." The rule thus operates as "a judicially created remedy designed to safeguard Fourth Amendment rights generally through its deterrent effect, rather than a personal constitutional right of the person aggrieved."

Whether the exclusionary sanction is appropriately imposed in a particular case, our decisions make clear, is "an issue separate from the question whether the Fourth Amendment rights of the party seeking to invoke the rule were violated by police conduct." Only the former question is currently before us,[a] and it must be resolved by weighing the costs and benefits of preventing the use in the prosecution's case-in-chief of inherently trustworthy tangible evidence obtained in reliance on a search warrant issued by a detached and neutral magistrate that ultimately is found to be defective.

The substantial social costs exacted by the exclusionary rule for the vindication of Fourth Amendment rights have long been a source of concern. "Our cases have consistently recognized that unbending application of the exclusionary sanction to enforce ideals of governmental rectitude would impede unacceptably the truth-finding functions of judge and jury." An objectionable collateral consequence of this interference with the criminal justice system's truth-finding function is that some guilty defendants may go free or receive reduced sentences as a result of favorable plea bargains.[6] Particularly when law enforcement officers have acted in objective good faith or their transgressions have been minor, the magnitude of the benefit conferred on such guilty defendants offends basic concepts of the criminal justice system. Indiscriminate application of the exclusionary rule, therefore, may well "generat[e] disrespect for the law and the administration of justice." Accordingly, "[a]s with any remedial device, the application of the rule has been restricted to those areas where its remedial objectives are thought most efficaciously served."

a. A large quantities of drugs were suppressed on the ground the warrant had not issued on probable cause, in that the affidavit reported only the allegations of an untested informant and limited corroboration by police surveillance of events themselves "as consistent with innocence as * * * with guilt." The Court earlier noted that whether this warrant would pass muster under the intervening and less demanding test of *Illinois v. Gates,* p. 169, "has not been briefed or argued," and thus chose "to take the case as it comes to us."

6. Researchers have only recently begun to study extensively the effects of the exclusionary rule on the disposition of felony arrests. One study suggests that the rule results in the nonprosecution or nonconviction of between 0.6% and 2.35% of individuals arrested for felonies. Davies, *A Hard Look at What We Know (and Still Need to Learn) About the "Costs" of the Exclusionary Rule: The NIJ Study and Other Studies of "Lost" Arrests,* 1983 A.B.F.Res.J. 611, 621. The estimates are higher for particular crimes the prosecution of which depends heavily on physical evidence.

Thus, the cumulative loss due to nonprosecution or nonconviction of individuals arrested on felony drug charges is probably in the range of 2.8% to 7.1%. Davies' analysis of California data suggests that screening by police and prosecutors results in the release because of illegal searches or seizures of as many as 1.4% of all felony arrestees, id., at 650, that 0.9% of felony arrestees are released because of illegal searches or seizures at the preliminary hearing or after trial, *id.,* at 653, and that roughly 0.5% of all felony arrestees benefit from reversals on appeal because of illegal searches. * * *

Many of these researchers have concluded that the impact of the exclusionary rule is insubstantial, but the small percentages with which they deal mask a large absolute number of felons who are released because the cases against them were based in part on illegal searches or seizures. * * * Because we find that the rule can have no substantial deterrent effect in the sorts of situations under consideration in this case, we conclude that it cannot pay its way in those situations.

Close attention to those remedial objectives has characterized our recent decisions concerning the scope of the Fourth Amendment exclusionary rule. The Court has, to be sure, not seriously questioned, "in the absence of a more efficacious sanction, the continued application of the rule to suppress evidence from the [prosecution's] case where a Fourth Amendment violation has been substantial and deliberate * * *." Nevertheless, the balancing approach that has evolved in various contexts—including criminal trials—"forcefully suggest[s] that the exclusionary rule be more generally modified to permit the introduction of evidence obtained in the reasonable good-faith belief that a search or seizure was in accord with the Fourth Amendment."

In *Stone v. Powell,* 428 U.S. 465, 96 S.Ct. 3037, 49 L.Ed.2d 1067 (1976), the Court emphasized the costs of the exclusionary rule, expressed its view that limiting the circumstances under which Fourth Amendment claims could be raised in federal habeas corpus proceedings would not reduce the rule's deterrent effect, and held that a state prisoner who has been afforded a full and fair opportunity to litigate a Fourth Amendment claim may not obtain federal habeas relief on the ground that unlawfully obtained evidence had been introduced at his trial. Proposed extensions of the exclusionary rule to proceedings other than the criminal trial itself have been evaluated and rejected under the same analytic approach[, as in *United States v. Calandra,* p. 131, and *United States v. Janis,* p. 134.]

[C]ases considering the use of unlawfully obtained evidence in criminal trials themselves [also] make clear [that] it does not follow from the emphasis on the exclusionary rule's deterrent value that "anything which deters illegal searches is thereby commanded by the Fourth Amendment." *Alderman v. United States* [p. 750]. * * * Standing to invoke the rule has thus been limited to cases in which the prosecution seeks to use the fruits of an illegal search or seizure against the victim of police misconduct. *Rakas v. Illinois* [p. 754]. Even defendants with standing to challenge the introduction in their criminal trials of unlawfully obtained evidence cannot prevent every conceivable use of such evidence. Evidence obtained in violation of the Fourth Amendment and inadmissible in the prosecution's case in chief may be used to impeach a defendant's direct testimony. *Walder v. United States* [p. 788]. * * *

When considering the use of evidence obtained in violation of the Fourth Amendment in the prosecution's case in chief, moreover, we have declined to adopt a *per se* or "but for" rule that would render inadmissible any evidence that came to light through a chain of causation that began with an illegal arrest. *Brown v. Illinois* [p. 766]; *Wong Sun v. United States* [p. 765]. We also have held that a witness' testimony may be admitted even when his identity was discovered in an unconstitutional search. *United States v. Ceccolini* [p. 774]. The perception underlying these decisions—that the connection between police misconduct and evidence of crime may be sufficiently attenuated to permit the use of that evidence at trial—is a product of considerations relating to the exclusionary rule and the constitutional principles it is designed to protect. * * * Not surprisingly in view of this purpose, an assessment of the flagrancy of the police misconduct constitutes an important step in the calculus. *Brown v. Illinois,* supra. * * *

As yet, we have not recognized any form of good-faith exception to the Fourth Amendment exclusionary rule. But the balancing approach that has evolved during the years of experience with the rule provides strong support for the modification currently urged upon us. As we discuss below, our evaluation of the costs and benefits of suppressing reliable physical evidence seized by officers reasonably relying on a warrant issued by a detached and neutral magistrate leads to the conclusion that such evidence should be admissible in the prosecution's case in chief. * * *

Only [when a warrant is grounded upon an affidavit knowingly or recklessly false] has the Court set forth a rationale for suppressing evidence obtained pursuant to a search warrant;[b] in the other areas, it has simply excluded such evidence without considering whether Fourth Amendment interests will be advanced. To the extent that proponents of exclusion rely on its behavioral effects on judges and magistrates in these areas, their reliance is misplaced. First, the exclusionary rule is designed to deter police misconduct rather than to punish the errors of judges and magistrates. Second, there exists no evidence suggesting that judges and magistrates are inclined to ignore or subvert the Fourth Amendment or that lawlessness among these actors requires application of the extreme sanction of exclusion.[14]

Third, and most important, we discern no basis, and are offered none, for believing that exclusion of evidence seized pursuant to a warrant will have a significant deterrent effect on the issuing judge or magistrate. Many of the factors that indicate that the exclusionary rule cannot provide an effective "special" or "general" deterrent for individual offending law enforcement officers apply as well to judges or magistrates. And, to the extent that the rule is thought to operate as a "systemic" deterrent on a wider audience, it clearly can have no such effect on individuals empowered to issue warrants. Judges and magistrates are not adjuncts to the law enforcement team; as neutral judicial officers, they have no stake in the outcome of particular criminal prosecutions. The threat of exclusion thus cannot be expected significantly to deter them. Imposition of the exclusionary sanction is not necessary meaningfully to inform judicial officers of their errors, and we cannot conclude that admitting evidence obtained pursuant to a warrant while at the same time declaring that the warrant was somehow defective will in any way reduce judicial officers' professional incentives to comply with the Fourth Amendment, encourage them to repeat their mistakes, or lead to the granting of all colorable warrant requests.[18]

If exclusion of evidence obtained pursuant to a subsequently invalidated warrant is to have any deterrent effect, therefore, it must alter the behavior of individual law enforcement officers or the policies of their departments. One could argue that applying the exclusionary rule in cases where the police failed to demonstrate probable cause in the warrant application deters future inadequate presentations or "magistrate shopping" and thus promotes the ends of the Fourth Amendment. Suppressing evidence obtained pursuant to a technically defective warrant supported by probable cause also might encourage officers to scrutinize more closely the form of the warrant and to point out suspected judicial errors. We find such arguments speculative and conclude that suppression of evidence obtained pursuant to a warrant should be ordered only on a case-by-case basis and

b. The reference is to the *Franks* case, p. 185, where the Court declared "it would be an unthinkable imposition upon [the magistrate's] authority if a warrant affidavit, revealed after the fact to contain a deliberately or recklessly false statement, were to stand beyond impeachment."

14. Although there are assertions that some magistrates become rubber stamps for the police and others may be unable effectively to screen police conduct, we are not convinced that this is a problem of major proportions.

18. Limiting the application of the exclusionary sanction may well increase the care with which magistrates scrutinize warrant applications. We doubt that magistrates are more desirous of avoiding the exclusion of evidence obtained pursuant to warrants they have issued than of avoiding invasions of privacy.

Federal magistrates, moreover, are subject to the direct supervision of district courts. They may be removed for "incompetency, misconduct, neglect of duty, or physical or mental disability." 28 U.S.C. § 631(i). If a magistrate serves merely as a "rubber stamp" for the police or is unable to exercise mature judgment, closer supervision or removal provides a more effective remedy than the exclusionary rule.

only in those unusual cases in which exclusion will further the purposes of the exclusionary rule.[19]

We have frequently questioned whether the exclusionary rule can have any deterrent effect when the offending officers acted in the objectively reasonable belief that their conduct did not violate the Fourth Amendment. "No empirical researcher, proponent or opponent of the rule, has yet been able to establish with any assurance whether the rule has a deterrent effect * * *." But even assuming that the rule effectively deters some police misconduct and provides incentives for the law enforcement profession as a whole to conduct itself in accord with the Fourth Amendment, it cannot be expected, and should not be applied, to deter objectively reasonable law enforcement activity. * * *[20]

This is particularly true, we believe, when an officer acting with objective good faith has obtained a search warrant from a judge or magistrate and acted within its scope. In most such cases, there is no police illegality and thus nothing to deter. It is the magistrate's responsibility to determine whether the officer's allegations establish probable cause and, if so, to issue a warrant comporting in form with the requirements of the Fourth Amendment. In the ordinary case, an officer cannot be expected to question the magistrate's probable-cause determination or his judgment that the form of the warrant is technically sufficient. "[O]nce the warrant issues, there is literally nothing more the policeman can do in seeking to comply with the law." Penalizing the officer for the magistrate's error, rather than his own, cannot logically contribute to the deterrence of Fourth Amendment violations.[22]

We conclude that the marginal or nonexistent benefits produced by suppressing evidence obtained in objectively reasonable reliance on a subsequently invalidated search warrant cannot justify the substantial costs of exclusion. We do not suggest, however, that exclusion is always inappropriate in cases where an officer has obtained a warrant and abided by its terms. [T]he officer's reliance on the magistrate's probable-cause determination and on the technical sufficiency of the

19. Our discussion of the deterrent effect of excluding evidence obtained in reasonable reliance on a subsequently invalidated warrant assumes, of course, that the officers properly executed the warrant and searched only those places and for those objects that it was reasonable to believe were covered by the warrant. * * *

20. We emphasize that the standard of reasonableness we adopt is an objective one. Many objections to a good-faith exception assume that the exception will turn on the subjective good faith of individual officers. "Grounding the modification in objective reasonableness, however, retains the value of the exclusionary rule as an incentive for the law enforcement profession as a whole to conduct themselves in accord with the Fourth Amendment." The objective standard we adopt, moreover, requires officers to have a reasonable knowledge of what the law prohibits. As Professor Jerold Israel has observed:

"The key to the [exclusionary] rule's effectiveness as a deterrent lies, I believe, in the impetus it has provided to police training programs that make officers aware of the limits imposed by the fourth amendment and emphasize the need to operate within those limits.

[An objective good-faith exception] * * * is not likely to result in the elimination of such programs, which are now viewed as an important aspect of police professionalism. Neither is it likely to alter the tenor of those programs; the possibility that illegally obtained evidence may be admitted in borderline cases is unlikely to encourage police instructors to pay less attention to fourth amendment limitations. Finally, [it] * * * should not encourage officers to pay less attention to what they are taught, as the requirement that the officer act in 'good faith' is inconsistent with closing one's mind to the possibility of illegality."

22. * * * Our cases establish that the question whether the use of illegally obtained evidence in judicial proceedings represents judicial participation in a Fourth Amendment violation and offends the integrity of the courts "is essentially the same as the inquiry into whether exclusion would serve a deterrent purpose." * * * Absent unusual circumstances, when a Fourth Amendment violation has occurred because the police have reasonably relied on a warrant issued by a detached and neutral magistrate but ultimately found to be defective, "the integrity of the courts is not implicated."

warrant he issues must be objectively reasonable,[23] and it is clear that in some circumstances the officer[24] will have no reasonable grounds for believing that the warrant was properly issued.

Suppression therefore remains an appropriate remedy if the magistrate or judge in issuing a warrant was misled by information in an affidavit that the affiant knew was false or would have known was false except for his reckless disregard of the truth. The exception we recognize today will also not apply in cases where the issuing magistrate wholly abandoned his judicial role in the manner condemned in *Lo-Ji Sales, Inc. v. New York,* [p. 191][c], in such circumstances, no reasonably well-trained officer should rely on the warrant. Nor would an officer manifest objective good faith in relying on a warrant based on an affidavit "so lacking in indicia of probable cause as to render official belief in its existence entirely unreasonable." Finally, depending on the circumstances of the particular case, a warrant may be so facially deficient—i.e., in failing to particularize the place to be searched or the things to be seized—that the executing officers cannot reasonably presume it to be valid.

* * * The good-faith exception for searches conducted pursuant to warrants is not intended to signal our unwillingness strictly to enforce the requirements of the Fourth Amendment, and we do not believe that it will have this effect. As we have already suggested, the good-faith exception, turning as it does on objective reasonableness, should not be difficult to apply in practice. When officers have acted pursuant to a warrant, the prosecution should ordinarily be able to establish objective good faith without a substantial expenditure of judicial time.

Nor are we persuaded that application of a good-faith exception to searches conducted pursuant to warrants will preclude review of the constitutionality of the search or seizure, deny needed guidance from the courts, or freeze Fourth Amendment law in its present state.[25] There is no need for courts to adopt the inflexible practice of always deciding whether the officers' conduct manifested objective good faith before turning to the question whether the Fourth Amendment has been violated. Defendants seeking suppression of the fruits of allegedly unconstitutional searches or seizures undoubtedly raise live controversies which Article III empowers federal courts to adjudicate. * * *

If the resolution of a particular Fourth Amendment question is necessary to guide future action by law enforcement officers and magistrates, nothing will

23. [O]ur good-faith inquiry is confined to the objectively ascertainable question whether a reasonably well-trained officer would have known that the search was illegal despite the magistrate's authorization. In making this determination, all of the circumstances—including whether the warrant application had previously been rejected by a different magistrate—may be considered.

24. References to "officer" throughout this opinion should not be read too narrowly. It is necessary to consider the objective reasonableness, not only of the officers who eventually executed a warrant, but also of the officers who originally obtained it or who provided information material to the probable-cause determination. Nothing in our opinion suggests, for example, that an officer could obtain a warrant on the basis of a "bare bones" affidavit and then rely on colleagues who are ignorant of the circumstances under which the warrant was obtained to conduct the search.

c. There the magistrate was held not to have "manifest[ed] that neutrality and detachment demanded of a judicial officer when presented with a warrant application," where he went to the scene and made judgments there about what should be seized as obscene, as he "allowed himself to become a member, if not the leader of the search party which was essentially a police operation."

25. The argument that defendants will lose their incentive to litigate meritorious Fourth Amendment claims as a result of the good-faith exception we adopt today is unpersuasive. Although the exception might discourage presentation of insubstantial suppression motions, the magnitude of the benefit conferred on defendants by a successful motion makes it unlikely that litigation of colorable claims will be substantially diminished.

prevent reviewing courts from deciding that question before turning to the good-faith issue.[26] Indeed, it frequently will be difficult to determine whether the officers acted reasonably without resolving the Fourth Amendment issue. Even if the Fourth Amendment question is not one of broad import, reviewing courts could decide in particular cases that magistrates under their supervision need to be informed of their errors and so evaluate the officers' good faith only after finding a violation. In other circumstances, those courts could reject suppression motions posing no important Fourth Amendment questions by turning immediately to a consideration of the officers' good faith. We have no reason to believe that our Fourth Amendment jurisprudence would suffer by allowing reviewing courts to exercise an informed discretion in making this choice. * * *

In the absence of an allegation that the magistrate abandoned his detached and neutral role, suppression is appropriate only if the officers were dishonest or reckless in preparing their affidavit or could not have harbored an objectively reasonable belief in the existence of probable cause. Only respondent Leon has contended that no reasonably well-trained police officer could have believed that there existed probable cause to search his house; significantly, the other respondents advance no comparable argument. Officer Rombach's application for a warrant clearly was supported by much more than a "bare bones" affidavit. The affidavit related the results of an extensive investigation and, as the opinions of the divided panel of the Court of Appeals make clear, provided evidence sufficient to create disagreement among thoughtful and competent judges as to the existence of probable cause. Under these circumstances, the officers' reliance on the magistrate's determination of probable cause was objectively reasonable, and application of the extreme sanction of exclusion is inappropriate.

Accordingly, the judgment of the Court of Appeals is *reversed.*

Justice BLACKMUN, concurring. * * *

What must be stressed * * * is that any empirical judgment about the effect of the exclusionary rule in a particular class of cases necessarily is a provisional one. * * * If it should emerge from experience that, contrary to our expectations, the good faith exception to the exclusionary rule results in a material change in police compliance with the Fourth Amendment, we shall have to reconsider what we have undertaken here. The logic of a decision that rests on untested predictions about police conduct demands no less. * * *

Justice BRENNAN, with whom Justice MARSHALL joins, dissenting. * * *

[The majority's reading of the Fourth Amendment] appears plausible, because, as critics of the exclusionary rule never tire of repeating, the Fourth Amendment makes no express provision for the exclusion of evidence secured in violation of its commands. A short answer to this claim, of course, is that many of the Constitution's most vital imperatives are stated in general terms and the task of giving meaning to these precepts is therefore left to subsequent judicial decision-making in the context of concrete cases. * * *

* * * Because seizures are executed principally to secure evidence, and because such evidence generally has utility in our legal system only in the context of a trial supervised by a judge, it is apparent that the admission of illegally obtained evidence implicates the same constitutional concerns as the initial seizure of that evidence. Indeed, by admitting unlawfully seized evidence, the judiciary becomes a part of what is in fact a single governmental action prohibited

26. It has been suggested, in fact, that "the recognition of a 'penumbral zone,' within which an inadvertent mistake would not call for exclusion, * * * will make it less tempting for judges to bend fourth amendment standards to avoid releasing a possibly dangerous criminal because of a minor and unintentional miscalculation by the police."

by the terms of the Amendment. Once that connection between the evidence-gathering role of the police and the evidence-admitting function of the courts is acknowledged, the plausibility of the Court's interpretation becomes more suspect. Certainly nothing in the language or history of the Fourth Amendment suggests that a recognition of this evidentiary link between the police and the courts was meant to be foreclosed. It is difficult to give any meaning at all to the limitations imposed by the Amendment if they are read to proscribe only certain conduct by the police but to allow other agents of the same government to take advantage of evidence secured by the police in violation of its requirements. The Amendment therefore must be read to condemn not only the initial unconstitutional invasion of privacy—which is done, after all, for the purpose of securing evidence—but also the subsequent use of any evidence so obtained. * * *

[T]he question whether the exclusion of evidence would deter future police misconduct was never considered a relevant concern in the early cases from *Weeks* to *Olmstead*. In those formative decisions, the Court plainly understood that the exclusion of illegally obtained evidence was compelled not by judicially fashioned remedial purposes, but rather by a direct constitutional command. * * *

* * * Indeed, no other explanation suffices to account for the Court's holding in *Mapp*, since the only possible predicate for the Court's conclusion that the States were bound by the Fourteenth Amendment to honor the *Weeks* doctrine is that the exclusionary rule was "part and parcel of the Fourth Amendment's limitation upon [governmental] encroachment of individual privacy."

Despite this clear pronouncement, however, the Court * * * has gradually pressed the deterrence rationale for the rule back to center stage. The various arguments advanced by the Court in this campaign have only strengthened my conviction that the deterrence theory is both misguided and unworkable. First, the Court has frequently bewailed the "cost" of excluding reliable evidence. In large part, this criticism rests upon a refusal to acknowledge the function of the Fourth Amendment itself. If nothing else, the Amendment plainly operates to disable the government from gathering information and securing evidence in certain ways. In practical terms, of course, this restriction of official power means that some incriminating evidence inevitably will go undetected if the government obeys these constitutional restraints. It is the loss of that evidence that is the "price" our society pays for enjoying the freedom and privacy safeguarded by the Fourth Amendment. Thus, some criminals will go free *not*, in Justice (then Judge) Cardozo's misleading epigram, "because the constable has blundered," but rather because official compliance with Fourth Amendment requirements makes it more difficult to catch criminals. Understood in this way, the Amendment directly contemplates that some reliable and incriminating evidence will be lost to the government; therefore, it is not the exclusionary rule, but the Amendment itself that has imposed this cost.

In addition, the Court's decisions over the past decade have made plain that the entire enterprise of attempting to assess the benefits and costs of the exclusionary rule in various contexts is a virtually impossible task for the judiciary to perform honestly or accurately. Although the Court's language in those cases suggests that some specific empirical basis may support its analyses, the reality is that the Court's opinions represent inherently unstable compounds of intuition, hunches, and occasional pieces of partial and often inconclusive data. * * * To the extent empirical data is available regarding the general costs and benefits of the exclusionary rule, it has shown, on the one hand, as the Court acknowledges today, that the costs are not as substantial as critics have asserted in the past, and, on the other hand, that while the exclusionary rule may well have certain deterrent effects, it is extremely difficult to determine with any degree of precision whether the incidence of unlawful conduct by police is now lower than it was prior to *Mapp*. The Court has sought to turn this uncertainty to its advantage by casting the burden of proof upon proponents of the rule. "Obviously," however, "the assignment of the burden of proof on an issue where evidence does not exist and cannot be obtained is outcome determinative. [The] assignment of the burden is merely a way of announcing a predetermined conclusion."

By remaining within its redoubt of empiricism and by basing the rule solely on the deterrence rationale, the Court has robbed the rule of legitimacy. A doctrine that is explained as if it were an empirical proposition but for which there is only limited empirical support is both inherently unstable and an easy mark for critics. The extent of this Court's fidelity to Fourth Amendment requirements, however, should not turn on such statistical uncertainties. * * *

Even if I were to accept the Court's general approach to the exclusionary rule, I could not agree with today's result. * * *

At the outset, the Court suggests that society has been asked to pay a high price—in terms either of setting guilty persons free or of impeding the proper functioning of trials—as a result of excluding relevant physical evidence in cases where the police, in conducting searches and seizing evidence, have made only an "objectively reasonable" mistake concerning the constitutionality of their actions. But what evidence is there to support such a claim?

Significantly, the Court points to none, and, indeed, as the Court acknowledges, recent studies have demonstrated that the "costs" of the exclusionary rule—calculated in terms of dropped prosecutions and lost convictions—are quite low. Contrary to the claims of the rule's critics that exclusion leads to "the release of countless guilty criminals," these studies have demonstrated that federal and state prosecutors very rarely drop cases because of potential search and seizure problems. For example, a 1979 study prepared at the request of Congress by the General Accounting Office reported that only 0.4% of all cases actually declined for prosecution by federal prosecutors were declined primarily because of illegal search problems. If the GAO data are restated as a percentage of *all* arrests, the study shows that only 0.2% of all felony arrests are declined for prosecution because of potential exclusionary rule problems.[11] Of course, these data describe only the costs attributable to the exclusion of evidence in all cases; the costs due to the exclusion of evidence in the narrower category of cases where police have made objectively reasonable mistakes must necessarily be even smaller. The Court, however, ignores this distinction and mistakenly weighs the aggregated costs of exclusion in *all* cases, irrespective of the circumstances that led to

11. In a series of recent studies, researchers have attempted to quantify the actual costs of the rule. A recent National Institute of Justice study based on data for the four year period 1976–1979 gathered by the California Bureau of Criminal Statistics showed that 4.8% of all cases that were declined for prosecution by California prosecutors were rejected because of illegally seized evidence. However, if these data are calculated as a percentage of all arrests that were declined for prosecution, they show that only 0.8% of all arrests were rejected for prosecution because of illegally seized evidence.

In another measure of the rule's impact—the number of prosecutions that are dismissed or result in acquittals in cases where evidence has been excluded—the available data again show that the Court's past assessment of the rule's costs has generally been exaggerated. For example, a study based on data from 9 mid-sized counties in Illinois, Michigan and Pennsylvania reveals that motions to suppress physical evidence were filed in approximately 5% of the 7,500 cases studied, but that such motions were successful in only 0.7% of all these cases. The study also shows that only 0.6% of all cases resulted in acquittals because evidence had been excluded. In the GAO study, suppression motions were filed in 10.5% of all federal criminal cases surveyed, but of the motions filed, approximately 80–90% were denied. Evidence was actually excluded in only 1.3% of the cases studied, and only 0.7% of all cases resulted in acquittals or dismissals after evidence was excluded. And in another study based on data from cases during 1978 and 1979 in San Diego and Jacksonville, it was shown that only 1% of all cases resulting in nonconviction were caused by illegal searches.

exclusion, against the potential benefits associated with only those cases in which evidence is excluded because police reasonably but mistakenly believe that their conduct does not violate the Fourth Amendment. When such faulty scales are used, it is little wonder that the balance tips in favor of restricting the application of the rule.

What then supports the Court's insistence that this evidence be admitted? Apparently, the Court's only answer is that even though the costs of exclusion are not very substantial, the potential deterrent effect in these circumstances is so marginal that exclusion cannot be justified. The key to the Court's conclusion in this respect is its belief that the prospective deterrent effect of the exclusionary rule operates only in those situations in which police officers, when deciding whether to go forward with some particular search, have reason to know that their planned conduct will violate the requirements of the Fourth Amendment.

* * * But what the Court overlooks is that the deterrence rationale for the rule is not designed to be, nor should it be thought of as, a form of "punishment" of individual police officers for their failures to obey the restraints imposed by the Fourth Amendment. Instead, the chief deterrent function of the rule is its tendency to promote institutional compliance with Fourth Amendment requirements on the part of law enforcement agencies generally. Thus, as the Court has previously recognized, "over the long term, [the] demonstration [provided by the exclusionary rule] that our society attaches serious consequences to violation of constitutional rights is thought to encourage those who formulate law enforcement policies, and the officers who implement them, to incorporate Fourth Amendment ideals into their value system." It is only through such an institution-wide mechanism that information concerning Fourth Amendment standards can be effectively communicated to rank and file officers.[13]

If the overall educational effect of the exclusionary rule is considered, application of the rule to even those situations in which individual police officers have acted on the basis of a reasonable but mistaken belief that their conduct was authorized can still be expected to have a considerable long-term deterrent effect. If evidence is consistently excluded in these circumstances, police departments will surely be prompted to instruct their officers to devote greater care and attention to providing sufficient information to establish probable cause when applying for a warrant, and to review with some attention the form of the warrant that they have been issued, rather than automatically assuming that whatever document the magistrate has signed will necessarily comport with Fourth Amendment requirements.

After today's decision, however, that institutional incentive will be lost. Indeed, the Court's "reasonable mistake" exception to the exclusionary rule will tend to put a premium on police ignorance of the law. Armed with the assurance provided by today's decision that evidence will always be admissible whenever an officer has "reasonably" relied upon a warrant, police departments will be encouraged to train officers that if a warrant has simply been signed, it is reasonable, without more, to rely on it. Since in close cases there will no longer be any incentive to err on the side of constitutional behavior, police would have every reason to adopt a "let's-wait-until-its-decided" approach in situations in which there is a question about a warrant's validity or the basis for its issuance.[14]

---

13. * * * A former United States Attorney and now Attorney General of Maryland, Stephen Sachs, has described the impact of the rule on police practices in similar terms: "I have watched the rule deter, routinely, throughout my years as a prosecutor * * *. [P]olice-prosecutor consultation is customary in all our cases when Fourth Amendment concerns arise * * *. In at least three Maryland jurisdictions, for example, prosecutors are on twenty-four hour call to field search and seizure questions presented by police officers."

14. The authors of a recent study of the warrant process in seven cities concluded that

Although the Court brushes these concerns aside, a host of grave consequences can be expected to result from its decision to carve this new exception out of the exclusionary rule. A chief consequence of today's decision will be to convey a clear and unambiguous message to magistrates that their decisions to issue warrants are now insulated from subsequent judicial review. Creation of this new exception for good faith reliance upon a warrant implicitly tells magistrates that they need not take much care in reviewing warrant applications, since their mistakes will from now on have virtually no consequence: If their decision to issue a warrant was correct, the evidence will be admitted; if their decision was incorrect but the police relied in good faith on the warrant, the evidence will also be admitted. Inevitably, the care and attention devoted to such an inconsequential chore will dwindle. Although the Court is correct to note that magistrates do not share the same stake in the outcome of a criminal case as the police, they nevertheless need to appreciate that their role is of some moment in order to continue performing the important task of carefully reviewing warrant applications. Today's decision effectively removes that incentive.

Moreover, the good faith exception will encourage police to provide only the bare minimum of information in future warrant applications. The police will now know that if they can secure a warrant, so long as the circumstances of its issuance are not "entirely unreasonable," all police conduct pursuant to that warrant will be protected from further judicial review. The clear incentive that operated in the past to establish probable cause adequately because reviewing courts would examine the magistrate's judgment carefully, has now been so completely vitiated that the police need only show that it was not "entirely unreasonable" under the circumstances of a particular case for them to believe that the warrant they were issued was valid. The long-run effect unquestionably will be to undermine the integrity of the warrant process.

Finally, even if one were to believe, as the Court apparently does, that police are hobbled by inflexible and hypertechnical warrant procedures, today's decision cannot be justified. This is because, given the relaxed standard for assessing probable cause established just last Term in *Illinois v. Gates*, the Court's newly fashioned good faith exception, when applied in the warrant context, will rarely, if ever, offer any greater flexibility for police than the *Gates* standard already supplies.[d] In *Gates*, the Court held that "the task of an issuing magistrate is simply to make a practical, common-sense decision whether, given all the circumstances set forth in the affidavit before him, * * * there is a fair probability that contraband or evidence of a crime will be found in a particular place." The task of a reviewing court is confined to determining whether "the magistrate had a 'substantial basis' for concluding that probable cause existed." Given such a relaxed standard, it is virtually inconceivable that a reviewing court, when faced with a defendant's motion to suppress, could first find that a warrant was invalid under the new *Gates* standard, but then, at the same time, find that a police officer's reliance on such an invalid warrant was nevertheless "objectively reasonable" under the test announced today. * * *

application of a good faith exception where an officer relies upon a warrant "would further encourage police officers to seek out the less inquisitive magistrates and to rely on boiler-plate formulae, thereby lessening the value of search warrants overall. * * *"

d. Thus STEVENS, J., dissenting, objected: "It is probable, though admittedly not certain, that the Court of Appeals would now conclude that the warrant in *Leon* satisfied the Fourth Amendment if it were given the opportunity to reconsider the issue in the light of *Gates*. Adherence to our normal practice following the announcement of a new rule would therefore postpone, and probably obviate, the need for the promulgation of the broad new rule the Court announces today."

Notes and Questions

1. Must (should) the Fourth Amendment be read, as dissenting Justice Brennan maintains, "to condemn not only the initial unconstitutional invasion of privacy" but "also the subsequent use of any evidence so obtained"? Consider Arnold H. Loewy, *Police-Obtained Evidence and the Constitution: Distinguishing Unconstitutionally Obtained Evidence from Unconstitutionally Used Evidence*, 87 Mich.L.Rev. 907, 909–11, 939 (1989):

"[F]reedom from unreasonable searches and seizures is a substantive protection available to all inhabitants of the United States, whether or not charged with crime. The right thus differs from protections under most of the fifth amendment and all of the sixth amendment, which refers to persons charged with crime or the 'accused.' * * * [Because] the fourth amendment, in language and origin, is clearly substantive [the] Court was correct in holding the exclusionary rule to be simply a remedial device designed to make the substantive right more meaningful, rather than an independent procedural right.

" * * * Procedural rights are supposed to exclude evidence. Substantive rights need not. Consequently, fourth amendment rights should be deemed different from, but not less important than, the procedural rights protected by the fifth, sixth and fourteenth amendments. By way of comparison, first and third amendment rights are substantive, but nobody would deem them second class. * * *

"Whether evidence is unconstitutionally obtained or unconstitutionally used makes a difference. If the only constitutional wrong inheres in using the evidence, the Court has no business considering concepts of deterrence. The Court should prohibit use of such evidence. Conversely, when obtaining evidence is the constitutional wrong, exclusion should be subjected to a cost/benefit analysis."

2. Which of the Supreme Court's express or implicit assumptions in *Mapp* and *Leon* regarding the behavior of police and judges are correct? Consider Myron W. Orfield, *Deterrence, Perjury, and the Heater Factor: An Exclusionary Rule in the Chicago Criminal Courts*, 63 U.Colo.L.Rev. 75, 82–83 (1992), summarizing the views of interviewed actors in the Chicago criminal justice system:

"Respondents in the Courts Study[e] report the same perceptions of the deterrent effect of the rule as the officers in the Police Study.[f] First, respondents uniformly believe that officers care about convictions and experience adverse personal reactions when they lose evidence. Respondents report that police change their behavior in response to the suppression of evidence. They also believe that suppression effectively educates officers in the law of search and seizure and that the law is not too complicated for police officers to do their jobs effectively.

"The Courts Study respondents believe even more strongly than the Police Study respondents that the exclusionary rule's deterrent effect is greater when officers are working on big or important cases. They also believe the exclusionary rule has a greater deterrent effect on officers in specialized units like the Narcotics Section.

"Respondents also stated that the exclusionary rule fosters a closer working relationship between prosecutors and police. They note that prosecutors help police officers conduct proper searches and understand why evidence is suppressed. * * *

---

e. 14 public defenders, 14 prosecutors and 13 judges, all assigned to the felony trial courtrooms in the Criminal Division of the Circuit Court of Cook County.

f. 26 police officers in the Narcotics Section of the Organized Crime Division, Chicago Police Department.

"Significantly, the Courts respondents outlined a pattern of pervasive police perjury intended to avoid the requirements of the Fourth Amendment. Dishonesty occurs in both the investigative process and the courtroom. The respondents report systematic fabrications in case reports and affidavits for search warrants, creating artificial probable cause which forms the basis of later testimony. Moreover, police keep dual sets of investigatory files; official files and 'street files.' Exculpatory material in the street files may be edited from the official record. Respondents, including prosecutors, estimate that police commit perjury between 20 and 50% of the time they testify on Fourth Amendment issues. This perjury may be tolerated, or even encouraged, by prosecutors at each step in the process in both direct and indirect ways.

"The Courts respondents, including judges, also believe that judges may purposefully ignore the law to prevent evidence from being suppressed, and even more often, knowingly accept police perjury as truthful. When the crime is serious, this judicial 'cheating' is more likely to occur due to three primary reasons; first, the judge's sense that it is unjust to suppress the evidence under the circumstances of a particular case, second, the judge's fear of adverse publicity, and third, the fear that the suppression will hurt their chances in judicial elections. In addition, serious cases in Chicago are diverted to judges who are more likely to convict the defendant.

"However, even in the face of persistent police perjury and judicial abdication of function, the Courts respondents, like the police respondents, believe that the exclusionary rule, although imperfect and often avoided, clearly leads to increased police professionalism and greater observance of the law of the Fourth Amendment. They do not believe that the rule causes significant harm to police work. Although the Courts respondents acknowledge that the rule can sometimes be unjust to crime victims, they believe that the rule's benefits to society equal or exceed its costs. Respondents report that there is no more effective remedy for Fourth Amendment violations, and that a tort remedy would be less effective. Finally, they believe the rule should be retained."

3. Does (should) *Leon* mean that "when the Court speaks of the good faith of the police, it is talking about their good faith *before going* to the magistrate and not about their good faith *after* they have received the warrant"? Craig M. Bradley, *The "Good Faith" Exception Cases: Reasonable Exercises in Futility*, 60 Ind.L.J. 287, 297 (1985). Consider *Malley v. Briggs*, p. 128, fn. h, which the majority explained involved application of "the same standard of objective reasonableness that we applied in the context of a suppression hearing in *Leon*."

4. Will (should) *Leon* be extended to warrantless arrests and searches? In *Lopez-Mendoza*, p. 134, involving a warrantless arrest, White, J., dissenting, asserted *Leon* was applicable, so that "if the agents neither knew nor should have known that they were acting contrary to the dictates of the Fourth Amendment, evidence will not be suppressed even if it is held that their conduct was illegal." If that is wrong, then does it follow, as concluded in *United States v. O'Neal*, 17 F.3d 239 (8th Cir.1994), that *Leon* cannot save a search warrant where it now appears that some of the facts essential to the probable cause showing in the affidavit were acquired in a prior illegal warrantless search?

5. In the companion case of MASSACHUSETTS v. SHEPPARD, 468 U.S. 981, 104 S.Ct. 3424, 82 L.Ed.2d 737 (1984), a detective prepared an affidavit for a search warrant to search for specified evidence of a homicide but, because it was Sunday, could only find a warrant form for controlled substances. He presented his affidavit and that form to a judge and pointed out the problem to him, and the judge, unable to locate a more suitable form, told the detective that he would make the necessary changes to make it a proper warrant. He made some changes, but failed to change that part of the warrant which authorized a search only for controlled substances and related paraphernalia. The detective took the two documents and he and other officers then executed the warrant, seizing evidence of the homicide. That evidence was suppressed in the state court because the warrant failed to particularly describe the items to be seized, as required by the Fourth Amendment. The Supreme Court, per WHITE, J., held this situation fell within *Leon* because "there was an objectively reasonable basis for the officers' mistaken belief" that "the warrant authorized the search that they conducted." As for defendant's objection that the detective knew when he went to the judge that the warrant was defective, the Court stated: "Whatever an officer may be required to do when he executes a warrant without knowing beforehand what items are to be seized,[6] we refuse to rule that an officer is required to disbelieve a judge who has just advised him, by word and by action, that the warrant he possesses authorizes him to conduct the search he has requested."

What if the detective who obtained the warrant had simply turned it over to another officer for execution and that officer, after a careful reading of the warrant, had made a search for and found drugs within an envelope, a place he would not have been entitled to look had he been aware that the warrant should have described certain larger items which could not be concealed in the envelope?

6. What result under *Leon* and *Sheppard* on the following facts, essentially those in *People v. Deitchman,* 695 P.2d 1146 (Colo.1985)? Four teenage girls were sexually assaulted in the same area over a 10–day span, and they gave a similar general description of their assailant. One said he wore distinctively marked shoes; one said he had a red bandana; and two said his car license was CN–4714. Those facts were put into a search warrant affidavit, along with a statement that investigation "revealed that CN–4714 lists to Jerry M. Deitchman of 1755 South Pecos Street." The affidavit asserted, without explanation, that there was "reason to believe" that the shoes and bandana were at 3300 West Ohio Avenue; the magistrate issued a warrant to search that location for the shoes and bandana, which were found there in execution of the warrant. Police had earlier been unable to locate Deitchman until his employer said he had moved to 3300 West Ohio, and police arrested him there prior to obtaining the warrant, but those facts were not reported to the magistrate.

7. Are there other "limitations" which might well be imposed upon the exclusionary rule? Consider the two proposals made in John Kaplan, *The Limits of the Exclusionary Rule,* 26 Stan.L.Rev. 1027 (1974) (1) that "the rule not apply in the most serious cases—treason, espionage, murder, armed robbery, and kidnapping by organized groups" (where exclusion would occur only under the Rochin, p. 36, test), because "the political costs of the rule, the possibility of releasing serious and dangerous offenders into the community, and the disproportion between the magnitude of the policeman's constitutional violation and the crime in which the evidence is to be suppressed are sufficient reasons to modify the rule"; and (2) "to hold the exclusionary rule inapplicable to cases where the police department in question has taken seriously its responsibility to adhere to the fourth amendment," as reflected by "a set of published regulations giving guidance to police officers as to proper behavior in situations such as the one under litigation, a

---

6. Normally, when an officer who has not been involved in the application stage receives a warrant, he will read it in order to determine the object of the search. In this case, Detective O'Malley, the officer who directed the search, knew what items were listed in the affidavit presented to the judge, and he had good reason to believe that the warrant authorized the seizure of those items. Whether an officer who is less familiar with the warrant application or who has unalleviated concerns about the proper scope of the search would be justified in failing to notice a defect like the one in the warrant in this case is an issue we need not decide. We hold only that it was not unreasonable for the police in this case to rely on the judge's assurances that the warrant authorized the search they had requested.

training program calculated to make violations of the fourth amendment rights isolated occurrences, and, perhaps most importantly, a history of taking disciplinary action where such violations are brought to its attention."[g]

8. Should the Court instead abolish the exclusionary rule entirely on the ground that the deterrence function stressed in *Leon* is more generally not served by exclusion? Consider Burger, C.J., dissenting in *Bivens v. Six Unknown Named Agents,* p. 128 n. h, asserting a lack of deterrent efficacy because: (i) "The rule does not apply any direct sanction to the individual official whose illegal conduct results in the exclusion of evidence in a criminal trial." (ii) Police "have no * * * stake in successful prosecutions," and "the prosecutor who loses his case because of police misconduct is not an official in the police department; he can rarely set in motion any corrective action or administrative penalties." (iii) "Policemen do not have the time, inclination, or training to read and grasp the nuances of the appellate opinions that ultimately define the standards of conduct they are to follow." (iv) "[T]here are large areas of police activity which do not result in criminal prosecutions—hence the rule has virtually no applicability and no effect in such situations." Would such abolition be more palatable if, as the Chief Justice also suggested in *Bivens,* Congress were to "develop an administrative or quasi-judicial remedy against the government itself to afford compensation and restitution for persons whose Fourth Amendment rights have been violated"?[h] Consider also Richard A. Posner, *Excessive Sanctions for Governmental Misconduct in*

g. For strong criticism of Professor Kaplan's proposal that the exclusionary rule not apply in the most serious cases and of a similar proposal by James D. Cameron & Richard Lustiger, *The Exclusionary Rule: A Cost–Benefit Analysis,* 101 F.R.D. 109 (1984) that the rule apply neither in the most serious cases nor in any case where the reprehensibility of the defendant's crime is greater than the gravity of the officer's illegality, see Yale Kamisar, *"Comparative Reprehensibility" and the Fourth Amendment Exclusionary Rule,* 86 Mich.L.Rev. 1 (1987).

h. As for existing federal remedies, 42 U.S.C. § 1983 provides: "Every person who, under color of any statute, ordinance, regulation, custom, or usage, of any State or Territory, subjects, or causes to be subjected, any citizen of the United States or other person within the jurisdiction thereof to the deprivation of any rights, privileges, or immunities secured by the Constitution and laws, shall be liable to the party injured in an action at law, suit in equity, or other proper proceeding for redress." State and local police officers thus may be sued for damages for violation of Fourth Amendment rights, but the officers have an objective good faith defense. This is so even with respect to a police officer's action in applying for an arrest warrant; notwithstanding the magistrate's issuance of the warrant, the question "is whether a reasonably well-trained officer in petitioner's position would have known that his affidavit failed to establish probable cause and that he should not have applied for the warrant." *Malley v. Briggs,* 475 U.S. 335, 106 S.Ct. 1092, 89 L.Ed.2d 271 (1986). *Monell v. New York City Dep't of Social Services,* 436 U.S. 658, 98 S.Ct. 2018, 56 L.Ed.2d 611 (1978), cautioned that the statute did not "impose liability vicariously

on governing bodies solely on the basis of the existence of an employer-employee relationship with a tortfeasor," and thus concluded "that a local government may not be sued for an injury inflicted solely by its employees or agents. Instead, it is when execution of a government's policy or custom, whether made by its lawmakers or by those whose edicts or acts may fairly be said to represent official policy, inflicts the injury that the government as an entity is responsible under § 1983."

Section 1983 applies only to persons acting under color of state law, thus excluding federal officers acting under color of their authority. In *Bivens v. Six Unknown Named Agents,* 403 U.S. 388, 91 S.Ct. 1999, 29 L.Ed.2d 619 (1971), the Court held that, although Congress had not provided a tort remedy under such circumstances, a complaint alleging that the Fourth Amendment had been violated by federal agents acting under color of their authority gives rise to a federal cause of action for damages. Here as well, there is personal liability only in the absence of "objective legal reasonableness.". *Anderson v. Creighton,* 483 U.S. 635, 107 S.Ct. 3034, 97 L.Ed.2d 523 (1987). As for liability of the federal government, the Court in *Bivens* stated this issue was better left to Congress because "the federal purse was involved." In 1974 Congress amended the Federal Tort Claims Act to make it applicable "to acts or omissions of investigative or law enforcement officers of the United States Government" on any subsequent claim arising "out of assault, battery, false imprisonment, false arrest, abuse of process, or malicious prosecution. For the purpose of this subsection, 'investigative or law enforcement officer' means any officer of the United States who is empowered by law to execute searches, to seize evidence,

Criminal Cases, 57 Wash.L.Rev. 635 (1982), applying an economic analysis to the problem and concluding it should suffice if the government were required to compensate the victim of an illegal search for his "cleanup costs."

Compare Donald Dripps, *The Case for the Contingent Exclusionary Rule,* 38 Am.Crim.L.Rev.1, 2–4 (2001), proposing "that courts should begin to experiment with suppression orders that are contingent on the failure of the police department to pay damages set by the court [in an amount] equal to the expected governmental gain from the violation. * * * Properly set, the damages should leave the government indifferent between exclusion and damages in the ordinary case, yet still free to pay the damages when the illegality turns up an exceptionally culpable or dangerous crime." The "contingent suppression remedy," Dripps explains, "would encourage honest fact-finding and fair interpretations of the Constitution," as "the suppression hearing judge * * * can reject improbable police testimony without freeing the guilty. The police department will be responsible for the escape of the guilty, for only on a refusal to pay damages set high enough to deter would the criminal go free." But George C. Thomas III, *Judges are Not Economists and Other Reasons to be Skeptical of Contingent Suppression Orders: A Response to Professor Dripps,* 38 Am.Crim.L.Rev. 47, 48–49 (2001), argues that judges "are not likely to be institutionally capable of crafting the discerning solution that Dripps envisions," and proposes "an alternative model * * * requir[ing] legislative adoption," whereby "a screening jury would decide whether to suppress the evidence or fine the officer who violated the Fourth Amendment."

9. In *Michigan v. DeFillippo,* 443 U.S. 31, 99 S.Ct. 2627, 61 L.Ed.2d 343 (1979), the Court reaffirmed its earlier holdings "that the exclusionary rule required suppression of evidence obtained in searches carried out pursuant to statutes" subsequently held unconstitutional when the statutes, "by their own terms, authorized searches under circumstances which did not satisfy the traditional warrant and probable cause requirements of the Fourth Amendment." But after *Leon* the Court concluded otherwise in the 5–4 decision in ILLINOIS v. KRULL, 480 U.S. 340, 107 S.Ct. 1160, 94 L.Ed.2d 364 (1987), concerning an unconstitutional search made pursuant to a statute authorizing warrantless inspection of the records of licensed motor vehicle and vehicular parts sellers. The Court, per BLACKMUN, J., reasoned:

"The approach used in *Leon* is equally applicable to the present case. The application of the exclusionary rule to suppress evidence obtained by an officer acting in objectively reasonable reliance on a statute would have as little deterrent effect on the officer's actions as would the exclusion of evidence when an officer acts in objectively reasonable reliance on a warrant. Unless a statute is clearly unconstitutional, an officer cannot be expected to question the judgment of the legislature that passed the law. * * *

"Any difference between our holding in *Leon* and our holding in the instant case, therefore, must rest on a difference between the effect of the exclusion of evidence on judicial officers and the effect of the exclusion of evidence on legislators. Although these two groups clearly serve different functions in the criminal justice system, those differences are not controlling for purposes of this case. We noted in *Leon* as an initial matter that the exclusionary rule was aimed at deterring police misconduct. Thus, legislators, like judicial officers, are not the focus of the rule. Moreover, to the extent we consider the rule's effect on legislators, our initial inquiry, as set out in *Leon,* is whether there is evidence to

or to make arrests for violations of Federal law." 28 U.S.C. § 2680(h).

suggest that legislators 'are inclined to ignore or subvert the Fourth Amendment.' * * *

"There is no evidence suggesting that Congress or state legislatures have enacted a significant number of statutes permitting warrantless administrative searches violative of the Fourth Amendment. * * * Thus, we are given no basis for believing that legislators are inclined to subvert their oaths and the Fourth Amendment and that 'lawlessness among these actors requires application of the extreme sanction of exclusion.' *United States v. Leon.*

"Even if we were to conclude that legislators are different in certain relevant respects from magistrates, because legislators are not officers of the judicial system, the next inquiry necessitated by *Leon* is whether exclusion of evidence seized pursuant to a statute subsequently declared unconstitutional will 'have a significant deterrent effect' on legislators enacting such statutes. Respondents have offered us no reason to believe that applying the exclusionary rule will have such an effect. Legislators enact statutes for broad, programmatic purposes, not for the purpose of procuring evidence in particular criminal investigations. Thus, it is logical to assume that the greatest deterrent to the enactment of unconstitutional statutes by a legislature is the power of the courts to invalidate such statutes. Invalidating a statute informs the legislature of its constitutional error, affects the admissibility of all evidence obtained subsequent to the constitutional ruling, and often results in the legislature's enacting a modified and constitutional version of the statute, as happened in this very case. There is nothing to indicate that applying the exclusionary rule to evidence seized pursuant to the statute prior to the declaration of its invalidity will act as a significant, additional deterrent."

O'CONNOR, J., for the dissenters, emphasized: (1) "[B]oth the history of the Fourth Amendment and this Court's later interpretations of it, support application of the exclusionary rule to evidence gathered under the 20th century equivalent of the act authorizing the writ of assistance." (2) "The distinction drawn between the legislator and the judicial officer is sound" because "a legislature's unreasonable authorization of searches may affect thousands or millions" and thus "poses a greater threat to liberty." (3) "[L]egislators by virtue of their political role are more often subjected to the political pressures that may threaten Fourth Amendment values than are judicial officers." (4) "Providing legislatures a grace period during which the police may freely perform unreasonable searches in order to convict those who might have otherwise escaped creates a positive incentive to promulgate unconstitutional laws." (5) "The scope of the Court's good-faith exception is unclear," as "it is not apparent how much constitutional law the reasonable officer is expected to know. In contrast, *Leon* simply instructs courts that police officers may rely upon a facially valid search warrant. Each case is a fact-specific self-terminating episode. Courts need not inquire into the officer's probable understanding of the state of the law except in the extreme instance of a search warrant upon which no reasonable officer would rely. Under the decision today, however, courts are expected to determine at what point a reasonable officer should be held to know that a statute has, under evolving legal rules, become 'clearly' unconstitutional."

10. What if a police officer at the time of his search or seizure had relied upon law then authorizing such action, but that law was not in a statute (as in *Krull*) but rather in an appellate court decision since disapproved by a Supreme Court case which, per the Court's current retroactivity doctrine (see Ch. 2, § 3), relates back to the time of the officer's conduct? Such was the situation in *State v. Ward*, 604 N.W.2d 517 (Wis.2000), where the court concluded that because the officer's Fourth Amendment violation was "not due to negligence, a mistake of law, or willful or malicious misconduct," but rather because of reliance upon the case law then existing, such "good faith reliance upon the pronouncements of this court" is on a par with the "good faith reliance upon an apparently valid statute" in *Krull*, meaning that here as there "excluding the evidence seized by the police [would not] serve any remedial objective."

11. Should the fruits of constitutional but yet illegal arrests and searches be excluded? Reconsider fn. b, p. 108, and consider UNITED STATES v. CACERES, 440 U.S. 741, 99 S.Ct. 1465, 59 L.Ed.2d 733 (1979), holding that the failure of an IRS agent to follow IRS electronic surveillance regulations did not require suppression. STEVENS, J., for the majority, could not "ignore the possibility that a rigid application of an exclusionary rule to every regulatory violation could have a serious deterrent impact on the formulation of additional standards to govern prosecutorial and police procedures. Here, the Executive itself has provided for internal sanctions in cases of knowing violations of the electronic surveillance regulations. To go beyond that, and require exclusion in every case, would take away from the Executive Department the primary responsibility for fashioning the appropriate remedy for the violation of its regulations. But since the content, and indeed the existence, of the regulations would remain within the Executive's sole authority, the result might well be fewer and less protective regulations. In the long run, it is far better to have rules like those contained in the IRS Manual, and to tolerate occasional erroneous administration of the kind displayed by this record, than either to have no rules except those mandated by statute, or to have them framed in a mere precatory form."

12. Although an illegal arrest or other unreasonable seizure of the person is itself a violation of the Fourth and Fourteenth Amendments, the exclusionary sanction comes into play only when the police have obtained evidence as a result of the unconstitutional seizure. It is no defense to a state or federal criminal prosecution that the defendant was illegally arrested or forcibly brought within the jurisdiction of the court. The trial of such a defendant violates neither Fifth nor Fourteenth Amendment Due Process nor any federal legislation. *Frisbie v. Collins,* 342 U.S. 519, 72 S.Ct. 509, 96 L.Ed. 541 (1952); *Ker v. Illinois,* 119 U.S. 436, 7 S.Ct. 225, 30 L.Ed. 421 (1886).[i] In *Gerstein v. Pugh,* p. 211, the Court declined to "retreat from the established rule that illegal arrest or detention does not void a subsequent conviction." See also *United States v. Crews,* p. 769, holding an illegally arrested defendant "is not himself a suppressible 'fruit' and the illegality of his detention cannot deprive the Government of the opportunity to prove his guilt through the introduction of evidence wholly untainted by the police misconduct."

NOTES ON THE "DIMENSIONS" OF
THE EXCLUSIONARY RULE

1. *Evidence obtained by government agents, used as basis for questions to grand jury witness.* In UNITED STATES v. CALANDRA, 414 U.S. 338, 94 S.Ct. 613, 38 L.Ed.2d 561 (1974), the Court, per POWELL, J., held that a grand jury witness may not refuse to answer questions on the ground that they are based on evidence obtained from him in an earlier unlawful search. After observing that a contrary holding would unduly interfere with the effective and expeditious discharge of the grand jury's duties [see p. 679], the Court asserted:

i. In *United States v. Alvarez–Machain,* 504 U.S. 655, 112 S.Ct. 2188, 119 L.Ed.2d 441 (1992), the Court held that *Ker,* involving forcible abduction from a foreign country, was "fully applicable to this case" despite the fact that here the abduction was from Mexico, with whom the U.S. has an extradition treaty. "The Treaty says nothing about the obligations of the [parties] to refrain from forcible abductions of people from the territory of the other nation, or the consequences under the Treaty if such an abduction occurs."

"Whatever deterrence of police misconduct may result from the exclusion of illegally-seized evidence from criminal trials, it is unrealistic to assume that application of the rule to grand jury proceedings would significantly further that goal. Such an extension would deter only police investigation consciously directed toward the discovery of evidence solely for use in a grand jury investigation. The incentive to disregard the requirement of the Fourth Amendment solely to obtain an indictment from a grand jury is substantially negated by the inadmissibility of the illegally-seized evidence in a subsequent criminal prosecution of the search victim. For the most part, a prosecutor would be unlikely to request an indictment where a conviction could not be obtained. We therefore decline to embrace a view that would achieve a speculative and undoubtedly minimal advance in the deterrence of police misconduct at the expense of substantially impeding the role of the grand jury."

BRENNAN, J., joined by Douglas and Marshall, JJ., dissenting, quoted from *Weeks* to show that "the twin goals of enabling the judiciary to avoid the taint of partnerships in official lawlessness and of assuring the people * * * that the government would not profit from its lawless behavior, * * * not the rule's possible deterrent effect, were uppermost in the minds of the framers of the rule," and then argued: "It is no answer, as the Court suggests, that the grand jury witnesses' Fourth Amendment rights will be sufficiently protected 'by the inadmissibility of the illegally-seized evidence in a subsequent criminal prosecution of the search victim.' This, of course, is no alternative for Calandra, since he was granted transactional immunity and cannot be criminally prosecuted. But the fundamental flaw of the alternative is that to compel Calandra to testify in the first place under penalty of contempt necessarily 'thwarts' his Fourth Amendment protection and 'entangle the courts in the illegal acts of Government agents' * * *."

2. **Evidence obtained by government agents, used in criminal case after conviction.** Should illegally seized evidence be admissible after conviction for consideration by the judge in determining the sentence to be imposed? *Verdugo v. United States,* 402 F.2d 599 (9th Cir.1968), holding no, was distinguished in *United States v. Schipani,* 315 F.Supp. 253 (E.D.N.Y.1970), aff'd, 435 F.2d 26 (2d Cir.1970), in that the decision in *Verdugo* was "predicated upon the fact that the search which had produced the improper evidence was conducted outside the course of the regular criminal investigation. It was undertaken, not to obtain evidence to support an indictment and conviction, but to recover contraband and thus to enhance the possibility of a heavier sentence after the basic investigation had been completed. [Under these circumstances,] law enforcement officials would have little to lose, but much to gain, in violating the Fourth Amendment." That situation was not present in *Schipani,* and thus the court concluded that "no appreciable increment in deterrence would result from applying a second exclusion at sentencing after the rule has been applied at the trial itself."

In PENNSYLVANIA BOARD OF PROBATION AND PAROLE v. SCOTT, 514 U.S. 357, 118 S.Ct. 2014, 141 L.Ed.2d 344 (1998), parole officers made an illegal search of parolee Scott's residence and found weapons there, which were later admitted at his parole revocation hearing, resulting in Scott being recommitted to serve 36 months. Thereafter, the state supreme court, although following the prevailing general rule against application of the exclusionary rule at parole revocation hearings, carved out an exception for cases in which the officer who conducted the search was aware of the person's parole status. The Supreme Court, in a 5–4 decision, disagreed. THOMAS, J., for the majority, relying upon *Calandra,* supra, and *Janis* and *Lopez-Mendoza,* infra, declined "to extend the operation of the exclusionary rule beyond the criminal trial context" because "application of the exclusionary rule would both hinder the functioning of state parole systems and alter the traditionally flexible, administrative nature of parole revocation proceedings," but at the same time "would provide only minimal deterrence benefits in this context." On the matter of deterrence, the majority declared it would be "minimal" even in the special situation which concerned the state court, for if the searcher was a police officer he would be deterred by the risk of exclusion of evidence at a criminal trial and would be unaffected by what happened at the parole proceeding, which, in the words of *Janis*, "falls outside the offending officer's zone of primary interest." If the searcher was a parole officer, he will likewise be deterred by the risk of evidence exclusion at a criminal trial, and, in any event, is not "engaged in the often competitive enterprise of ferreting out crime" and thus can be sufficiently deterred by "departmental training and discipline and the threat of damages actions."

The dissenters, per SOUTER, J., noted "the police very likely do know a parolee's status when they go after him," which is significant because (1) police officers with such knowledge, "especially those employed by the same sovereign that runs the parole system, * * * have every incentive not to jeopardize a recommitment by rendering evidence inadmissible," and thus could be deterred by the threat of exclusion at a parole hearing; (2) "the actual likelihood of trial is often far less than the probability of a petition for parole revocation" because, as the Court itself noted on an earlier occasion, parole revocation "is often preferred to a new prosecution because of the procedural ease of recommitting the individual on the basis of a lesser showing by the State," and this means there will be "nothing 'marginal' about the deterrence provided by an exclusionary rule operating" in the parole revocation context, and (3) "the cooperation between parole and police officers * * * casts serious doubt upon the aptness of treating police officers differently from parole officers," who themselves "are considered police officers with respect to the offenders under their jurisdiction" and who, consequently, can no more than other police be thought to be adequately deterred by the risk of departmental discipline or the threat of damages actions.

3. *Evidence obtained by government agents, used in "quasi-criminal" or civil case.* In ONE 1958 PLYMOUTH SEDAN v. PENNSYLVANIA, 380 U.S. 693, 85 S.Ct. 1246, 14 L.Ed.2d 170 (1965), a unanimous Court held that the *Weeks-Mapp* exclusionary rule applies to forfeiture proceedings. *Boyd v. United States*, "the leading case on the subject of search and seizure * * * itself was not a criminal case," pointed out the majority, "but was a proceeding by the United States to forfeit 35 cases of plate glass which had allegedly been imported without payment of the customs duty * * *. [As] pointed out in *Boyd*, a forfeiture proceeding is quasi-criminal in character. Its object, like a criminal proceeding, is to penalize for the commission of an offense against the law. In this case * * * the driver and owner of the automobile was arrested and charged with a criminal offense against the Pennsylvania liquor laws. * * * In this forfeiture proceeding he was subject to the loss of his automobile, which at the time involved had an estimated value of approximately $1,000, a higher amount than the maximum fine in the criminal proceeding. It would be anomalous indeed, under these circumstances, to hold that in the criminal proceeding the illegally seized evidence is excludable, while in the forfeiture proceeding, requiring the determination that the criminal law has been violated, the same evidence would be admissible."

Los Angeles police seized wagering records and $4,940 in cash pursuant to a search warrant, and then notified the IRS, which made an assessment against Janis for wagering taxes and levied upon the seized cash in partial satisfaction. After Janis' motion to suppress was granted in the state criminal proceedings, he sued for refund of the money and to quash the assessment because it was based upon illegally seized evidence. The federal district court ruled for Janis, and the court of appeals affirmed. In UNITED STATES v. JANIS, 428 U.S. 433, 96 S.Ct. 3021, 49 L.Ed.2d 1046 (1976), the Court, per BLACKMUN, J., reversed: "Working, as we must, with the absence of convincing empirical data, common sense dictates that the deterrent effect of the exclusion of relevant evidence is highly attenuated when the 'punishment' imposed upon the offending criminal enforcement officer is the removal of that evidence from a civil suit by or against a different sovereign. In *Elkins* [p. 112] the Court indicated that the assumed interest of criminal law enforcement officers in the criminal proceedings of another sovereign counterbalanced this attenuation sufficiently to justify an exclusionary rule. Here, however, the attenuation is further augmented by the fact that the proceeding is one to enforce only the civil law of the other sovereign.

"This attenuation coupled with the existing deterrence effected by the denial of use of the evidence by either sovereign in the criminal trials with which the searching officer is concerned, creates a situation in which the imposition of the exclusionary rule sought in this case is unlikely to provide significant much less substantial, additional deterrence. It falls outside the offending officer's zone of primary interest."

BRENNAN and Marshall, JJ., dissented on the basis of their *Calandra* dissent. STEWART, J., dissenting, argued that the majority's deterrence theory compelled the opposite result in light of the fact that "federal and local law enforcement personnel regularly provide federal tax officials with information, obtained in criminal investigations, indicating liability under the wagering tax. The pattern is one of mutual cooperation and coordination, with the federal wagering tax provisions buttressing state and federal criminal sanctions." He noted that it was admitted by the local police officer in the instant case that he notified the IRS whenever he uncovered a gambling operation involving a substantial amount of cash.

Utilizing the *Janis* cost-benefit approach, the Court held 5–4 in I.N.S. v. LOPEZ–MENDOZA, 468 U.S. 1032, 104 S.Ct. 3479, 82 L.Ed.2d 778 (1984), that the exclusionary rule is inapplicable in a civil deportation hearing. O'CONNOR, J., explained that the deterrent value of the exclusionary rule in this context was reduced because (i) "deportation will still be possible when evidence not derived directly from the arrest is sufficient to support deportation," (ii) INS agents know "that it is highly unlikely that any particular arrestee will end up challenging the lawfulness of his arrest," (iii) "the INS has its own comprehensive scheme for deterring Fourth Amendment violations" by training and discipline, and (iv) "alternative remedies" including the "possibility of declaratory relief" are available for institutional practices violating the Fourth Amendment. On the cost side, the Court continued, are these factors: (i) that application of the exclusionary rule "in proceedings that are intended not to punish past transgressions but to prevent their continuance or renewal would require courts to close their eyes to ongoing violations of the law," (ii) that invocation of the exclusionary rule at deportation hearings, where "neither the hearing officers nor the attorneys * * * are likely to be well versed in the intricacies of Fourth Amendment law," "might significantly change and complicate the character of these proceedings," and (iii) that because many INS arrests "occur in crowded and confused circumstances," application of the exclusionary rule "might well result in the suppression of large amounts of information that had been obtained entirely lawfully." WHITE, J., dissenting, objected that "unlike the situation in *Janis,* the conduct challenged here falls within 'the offending officer's zone of primary interest,'" and concluded that "the costs and benefits of applying the exclusionary rule in civil deportation proceedings do not differ in any significant way from the costs and benefits of applying the rule in ordinary criminal proceedings."

4. *Evidence obtained by private persons, used in criminal proceedings.* In *Burdeau v. McDowell*, 256 U.S. 465, 41 S.Ct. 574, 65 L.Ed. 1048 (1921), the exclusionary rule was characterized "as a restraint upon the activities of sovereign authority and * * * not * * * a limitation upon other than governmental agencies," and on this basis courts have declined to exclude evidence in criminal cases when obtained by private persons. However, the Fourth Amendment *is* applicable "to private individuals who are acting as instruments or agents of the government. * * * Whether a private individual is an agent of the government is determined by a totality-of-the-circumstances test. Circumstances to be considered in this test include the motive of the private actor; any compensation or other benefit the private actor receives from the government; and the advice, direction, and level of participation given by the government. Using this test, if it is found that the private actor was sufficiently influenced and supported by the state, the exclusionary rule will apply to any evidence obtained by the private actor." Comment, 65 U.Cin.L.Rev. 665, 672 (1997).

One issue which frequently arises with respect to private person searches is whether, if that person then summons the police, police activity with respect to the same object is a separate "search" subject to Fourth Amendment constraints. For example, in UNITED STATES v. JACOBSEN, 466 U.S. 109, 104 S.Ct. 1652, 80 L.Ed.2d 85 (1984), Federal Express employees opened a damaged box and found newspapers covering a tube which, when cut open, was found to contain plastic bags of white powder. Federal drug agents were summoned, but before their arrival the bags had been put back into the tube and the tube and newspapers back into the box, which was left open. A federal agent reopened the packaging to the extent necessary to expose the powder, which he field tested and found to be cocaine. The Court, per STEVENS, J., concluded the agent's actions were not a significant expansion of the earlier private search and that consequently no warrant was required. "Respondents could have no privacy interest in the contents of the package, since it remained unsealed and since the Federal Express employees had just examined the package and had, of their own accord, invited the federal agent to their offices for the express purpose of viewing its contents. The agent's viewing of what a private party had freely made available for his inspection did not violate the Fourth Amendment.

"Similarly, the removal of the plastic bags from the tube and the agent's visual inspection of their contents enabled the agent to learn nothing that had not previously been learned during the private search. It infringed no legitimate expectation of privacy and hence was not a 'search' within the meaning of the Fourth Amendment."[a]

Three members of the Court rejected that reasoning. WHITE, J., objected: "The majority opinion is particularly troubling when one considers its logical implications. I would be hard-pressed to distinguish this case, which involves a private search, from (1) one in which the private party's knowledge, later communicated to the government, that a particular container concealed contraband and nothing else arose from his presence at the time the container was sealed; (2) one in which the private party learned that a container concealed contraband and nothing else when it was previously opened in his presence; or (3) one in which the private party knew to a certainty that a container concealed contraband and nothing else as a result of conversations with its owner. In each of these cases, the approach adopted by the Court today would seem to suggest that the owner of the container has no legitimate expectation of privacy in its contents and that government agents opening that container without a warrant on the

---

a. As for the field test, see p. 154.

strength of information provided by the private party would not violate the Fourth Amendment.''

5. *Evidence obtained by virtue of conduct of nonpolice government employee, used in criminal proceedings.* The *Burdeau* rule, grounded in the proposition that the Fourth Amendment is entirely inapplicable where there is no governmental action, must be distinguished from that recognized in ARIZONA v. EVANS, 514 U.S. 1, 115 S.Ct. 1185, 131 L.Ed.2d 34 (1995): that some government searches covered by the Fourth Amendment are nonetheless inappropriate occasions for use of the exclusionary rule, considering the kind of government official who was at fault. After Evans was stopped for a traffic violation, the patrol car's computer indicated he had an outstanding arrest warrant, so Evans was arrested; incident thereto, the officer found marijuana. It was later learned that this warrant (issued because of Evans' nonappearance on several traffic violations) had been quashed upon Evans' voluntary appearance in court a few weeks earlier, but that apparently the court clerk had not thereafter followed the usual procedure of notifying the sheriff's department so that the warrant could be removed from the computer records. The state supreme court held this amounted to a violation of the Fourth Amendment and that consequently the evidence must be suppressed, but the Supreme Court, per REHNQUIST, C.J., considering only the latter point, disagreed:

"This holding is contrary to the reasoning of *Leon*, [p. 114]; *Massachusetts v. Sheppard* [p. 126]; and *Krull* [p. 129]. If court employees were responsible for the erroneous computer record, the exclusion of evidence at trial would not sufficiently deter future errors so as to warrant such a severe sanction. First, as we noted in *Leon*, the exclusionary rule was historically designed as a means of deterring police misconduct, not mistakes by court employees. Second, respondent offers no evidence that court employees are inclined to ignore or subvert the Fourth Amendment or that lawlessness among these actors requires application of the extreme sanction of exclusion. To the contrary, the Chief Clerk of the Justice Court testified at the suppression hearing that this type of error occurred once every three or four years.

"Finally, and most important, there is no basis for believing that application of the exclusionary rule in these circumstances will have a significant effect on court employees responsible for informing the police that a warrant has been quashed. Because court clerks are not adjuncts to the law enforcement team engaged in the often competitive enterprise of ferreting out crime, they have no stake in the outcome of particular criminal prosecutions. The threat of exclusion of evidence could not be expected to deter such individuals from failing to inform police officials that a warrant had been quashed.

"If it were indeed a court clerk who was responsible for the erroneous entry on the police computer, application of the exclusionary rule also could not be expected to alter the behavior of the arresting officer. * * * There is no indication that the arresting officer was not acting objectively reasonably when he relied upon the police computer record. Application of the *Leon* framework supports a categorical exception to the exclusionary rule for clerical errors of court employees.[5]"

---

5. The Solicitor General, as amicus curiae, argues that an analysis similar to that we apply here to court personnel also would apply in order to determine whether the evidence should be suppressed if police personnel were responsible for the error. As the State has not made any such argument here, we agree that "[t]he record in this case ... does not adequately present that issue for the Court's consideration." Accordingly, we decline to address that question.

O'CONNOR, J., joined by Souter and Bryer, concurring, cautioned: "Surely it would not be reasonable for the police to rely, say, on a recordkeeping system, their own or some other agency's, that has no mechanism to ensure its accuracy over time and that routinely leads to false arrests, even years after the probable cause for any such arrest has ceased to exist (if it ever existed)."

STEVENS, J., dissenting, objected: "Taken on its own terms, *Leon*'s logic does not extend to the time after the warrant has issued; nor does it extend to court clerks and functionaries, some of whom work in the same building with police officers and may have more regular and direct contact with police than with judges or magistrates."

GINSBURG, J., joined by Stevens, while mainly disagreeing with the majority's invocation of "the *Long* presumption" [see p. 54] to assert jurisdiction, made these comments on the merits: "In the Court's view, exclusion of evidence, even if capable of deterring police officer errors, cannot deter the carelessness of other governmental actors.[5] Whatever federal precedents may indicate—an issue on which I voice no opinion—the Court's conclusion is not the lesson inevitably to be drawn from logic or experience.

"In this electronic age, particularly with respect to recordkeeping, court personnel and police officers are not neatly compartmentalized actors. Instead, they serve together to carry out the State's information-gathering objectives. Whether particular records are maintained by the police or the courts should not be dispositive where a single computer database can answer all calls. Not only is it artificial to distinguish between court clerk and police clerk slips; in practice, it may be difficult to pinpoint whether one official, e.g., a court employee, or another, e.g., a police officer, caused the error to exist or to persist."

In *New Jersey v. T.L.O.*, p. 329, involving search of a student by a high school administrator, the Court reaffirmed that "the Fourth Amendment [is] applicable to the activities of civil as well as criminal authorities." However, because the search was found to be reasonable, the Court avoided expressing any opinion about the question which prompted the original grant of certiorari: whether the exclusionary rule is also applicable to searches by school authorities. In light of *Evans*, what is the answer to that question?

6. *Evidence obtained by foreign officials, used in domestic criminal proceedings.* Would any purpose be served by applying the exclusionary rule in such circumstances? What if American authorities requested or participated in the actions of the foreign police?

Even if there has been direct U.S. involvement in the foreign search, the Fourth Amendment may be inapplicable for yet another reason. In *United States v. Verdugo–Urquidez*, 494 U.S. 259, 110 S.Ct. 1056, 108 L.Ed.2d 222 (1990), the opinion of the Court, per Rehnquist, C.J., declared that the phrase "the people" in the Fourth Amendment (and the First, Second, Ninth and Tenth Amendments) "refers to a class of persons who are part of a national community or who have otherwise developed sufficient connection with this community to be considered

---

5. It has been suggested that an exclusionary rule cannot deter carelessness, but can affect only intentional or reckless misconduct. This suggestion runs counter to a premise underlying all of negligence law—that imposing liability for negligence, i.e., lack of due care, creates an incentive to act with greater care. That the mistake may have been made by a clerical worker does not alter the conclusion that application of the exclusionary rule has deterrent value. Just as the risk of respondeat superior liability encourages employers to supervise more closely their employees' conduct, so the risk of exclusion of evidence encourages policymakers and systems managers to monitor the performance of the systems they install and the personnel employed to operate those systems. In the words of the trial court, the mistake in Evans' case was "perhaps the negligence of the Justice Court, or the negligence of the Sheriff's office. But it is still the negligence of the State."

part of that community." The defendant in the instant case was deemed not to be such a person; he was a Mexican citizen and resident who, to be sure, just two days before the search of his residence in Mexico had been turned over to U.S. authorities by Mexican police, but "this sort of presence—lawful but involuntary—is not the sort to indicate any substantial connection with our country." (The Court added it was an open question whether even the illegal aliens in *Lopez–Mendoza,* p. 134, were such persons, though their situation was different from the defendant's here because they "were in the United States voluntarily and presumably had accepted some societal obligations.") The three dissenters agreed, as Blackmun, J., put it, "that when a foreign national is held accountable for purported violations of United States criminal laws, he has effectively been treated as one of 'the governed' and therefore is entitled to Fourth Amendment protections." Because the two concurring Justices placed great emphasis upon the inapplicability of the Fourth Amendment's warrant clause to the search in the instant case (Kennedy, J., stressing this was not a case in which "the full protections of the Fourth Amendment would apply" because of the "absence of local judges or magistrates available to issue warrants"; Stevens, J., that "American magistrates have no power to authorize such searches"), the application of *Verdugo–Urquidez* to a foreign search of an alien's property made even without probable cause is not entirely clear.

SECTION 2. PROTECTED AREAS AND INTERESTS

KATZ v. UNITED STATES
389 U.S. 347, 88 S.Ct. 507, 19 L.Ed.2d 576 (1967).

Justice STEWART delivered the opinion of the Court.

The petitioner was convicted [of] transmitting wagering information by telephone from Los Angeles to Miami and Boston in violation of a federal statute. At trial the Government was permitted, over the petitioner's objection, to introduce evidence of the petitioner's end of telephone conversations, overheard by FBI agents who had attached an electronic listening and recording device to the outside of the public telephone booth from which he had placed his calls. In affirming his conviction, the Court of Appeals rejected the contention that the recordings had been obtained in violation of the Fourth Amendment, because "[t]here was no physical entrance into the area occupied by [the petitioner]." We granted certiorari in order to consider the constitutional questions thus presented.

The petitioner has phrased those questions as follows:

"A. Whether a public telephone booth is a constitutionally protected area so that evidence obtained by attaching an electronic listening recording device to the top of such a booth is obtained in violation of the right to privacy of the user of the booth.

"B. Whether physical penetration of a constitutionally protected area is necessary before a search and seizure can be said to be violative of the Fourth Amendment to the United States Constitution."

We decline to adopt this formulation of the issues. In the first place the correct solution of Fourth Amendment problems is not necessarily promoted by incantation of the phrase "constitutionally protected area." Secondly, the Fourth Amendment cannot be translated into a general constitutional "right to privacy." That Amendment protects individual privacy against certain kinds of governmental intrusion, but its protections go further, and often have nothing to do with privacy at all. Other provisions of the Constitution protect personal privacy from other forms of governmental invasion. But the protection of a person's *general* right to privacy—his right to be let alone by other people—is, like the protection of his property and of his very life, left largely to the law of the individual States.

Because of the misleading way the issues have been formulated, the parties have attached great significance to the characterization of the telephone booth from which the petitioner placed his calls. The petitioner has strenuously argued that the booth was a "constitutionally protected area." The Government has maintained with equal vigor that it was not. But this effort to decide whether or not a given "area," viewed in the abstract, is "constitutionally protected" deflects attention from the problem presented by this case. For the Fourth Amendment protects people, not places. What a person knowingly exposes to the public, even in his own home or office, is not a subject of Fourth Amendment protection. * * * But what he seeks to preserve as private, even in an area accessible to the public, may be constitutionally protected. * * *

The Government stresses the fact that the telephone booth from which the petitioner made his calls was constructed partly of glass, so that he was as visible after he entered it as he would have been if he had remained outside. But what he sought to exclude when he entered the booth was not the intruding eye—it was the uninvited ear. He did not shed his right to do so simply because he made his calls from a place where he might be seen. No less than an individual in a business office, in a friend's apartment, or in a taxicab, a person in a telephone booth may rely upon the protection of the Fourth Amendment. One who occupies it, shuts the door behind him, and pays the toll that permits him to place a call, is surely entitled to assume that the words he utters into the mouthpiece will not be broadcast to the world. To read the Constitution more narrowly is to ignore the vital role that the public telephone has come to play in private communication.

The Government contends, however, that the activities of its agents in this case should not be tested by Fourth Amendment requirements, for the surveillance technique they employed involved no physical penetration of the telephone booth from which the petitioner placed his calls.

* * * [A]lthough a closely divided Court supposed in Olmstead [p. 348] that surveillance without any trespass and without the seizure of any material object fell outside the ambit of the Constitution, we have since departed from the narrow view on which that decision rested. Indeed, we have expressly held that the Fourth Amendment governs not only the seizure of tangible items, but extends as well to the recording of oral statements overheard without any "technical trespass under * * * local property law." Silverman v. United States. Once this much is acknowledged, and once it is recognized that the Fourth Amendment protects people—and not simply "areas"—against unreasonable searches and seizures it becomes clear that the reach of that Amendment cannot turn upon the presence or absence of a physical intrusion into any given enclosure.

We conclude that the underpinnings of Olmstead and Goldman [p. 352] have been so eroded by our subsequent decisions that the "trespass" doctrine there enunciated can no longer be regarded as controlling. The Government's activities in electronically listening to and recording the petitioner's words violated the privacy upon which he justifiably relied while using the telephone booth and thus constituted a "search and seizure" within the meaning of the Fourth Amendment. The fact that the electronic device employed to achieve that end did not happen to penetrate the wall of the booth can have no constitutional significance.

The question remaining for decision, then, is whether the search and seizure conducted in this case complied with constitutional standards. In that regard, the Government's position is that its agents acted in an entirely defensible manner: They did not begin their electronic surveillance until investigation of the petitioner's activities had established a strong probability that he was using the telephone in question to transmit gambling information to persons in other States, in violation of federal law. Moreover, the surveillance was limited, both in scope and in duration to the specific purpose of establishing the contents of the petitioner's unlawful telephonic communications. The agents confined their surveillance to the brief periods during which he used the telephone booth, and they took great care to overhear only the conversations of the petitioner himself.

Accepting this account of the Government's actions as accurate, it is clear that this surveillance was so narrowly circumscribed that a duly authorized magistrate, properly notified of the need for such investigation, specifically informed of the basis on which it was to proceed, and clearly apprised of the precise intrusion it would entail, could constitutionally have authorized, with appropriate safeguards, the very limited search and seizure that the Government asserts in fact took place. * * *

The Government * * * urges the creation of a new exception to cover this case. It argues that surveillance of a telephone booth should be exempted from the usual requirement of advance authorization by a magistrate upon a showing of probable cause. We cannot agree. Omission of such authorization "bypasses the safeguards provided by an objective predetermination of probable cause, and substitutes instead the far less reliable procedure of an after-the-event justification for the * * * search, too likely to be subtly influenced by the familiar shortcomings of hindsight judgment." And bypassing a neutral predetermination of the *scope* of a search leaves individuals secure from Fourth Amendment violations "only in the discretion of the police."

These considerations do not vanish when the search in question is transferred from the setting of a home, an office, or a hotel room, to that of a telephone booth. Wherever a man may be, he is entitled to know that he will remain free from unreasonable searches and seizures. The government agents here ignored "the procedure of antecedent justification * * * that is central to the Fourth Amendment," procedure that we hold to be a constitutional precondition of the kind of electronic surveillance involved in this case. * * *

Judgment reversed.[a]

Justice HARLAN, concurring. * * *

As the Court's opinion states, "The Fourth Amendment protects people, not places." The question, however, is what protection it affords to those people. Generally, as here, the answer to that question requires reference to a "place." My understanding of the rule that has emerged from prior decisions is that there is a twofold requirement, first that a person have exhibited an actual (subjective) expectation of privacy and, second, that the expectation be one that society is prepared to recognize as "reasonable."[b] Thus a man's home is, for most purposes, a place where he expects privacy, but objects, activities, or statements that he exposes to the "plain view" of outsiders are not "protected" because no intention to keep them to himself has been exhibited. On the other hand, conversations in

---

a. Justice Marshall took no part in the case. Concurring opinions by Douglas, J., joined by Brennan, J., and by White, J., are omitted.

b. Consider Anthony Amsterdam, *Perspectives on the Fourth Amendment*, 58 Minn. L.Rev. 349, 384 (1974): "But Justice Harlan himself [dissenting in *United States v. White*, p. 382] later expressed second thoughts about this conception, and rightly so. An actual, subjective expectation of privacy obviously has no place in a statement of what *Katz* held or in a theory of what the fourth amendment protects. It can neither add to, nor can its absence detract from, an individual's claim to fourth amendment protection. If it could, the government could diminish each person's subjective expectation of privacy merely by announcing half-hourly on television * * * that we were all forthwith being placed under comprehensive electronic surveillance."

the open would not be protected against being overheard, for the expectation of privacy under the circumstances would be unreasonable. * * *

The critical fact in this case is that "[o]ne who occupies it, [a telephone booth] shuts the door behind him, and pays the toll that permits him to place a call, is surely entitled to assume" that his conversation is not being intercepted. The point is not that the booth is "accessible to the public" at other times, but that it is a temporarily private place whose momentary occupants' expectations of freedom from intrusion are recognized as reasonable. * * *

Justice BLACK, dissenting. * * *

Tapping telephone wires, of course, was an unknown possibility at the time the Fourth Amendment was adopted. But eavesdropping (and wiretapping is nothing more than eavesdropping by telephone) was * * * "an ancient practice which at common law was condemned as a nuisance. In those days the eavesdropper listened by naked ear under the eaves of houses or their windows, or beyond their walls seeking out private discourse." There can be no doubt that the Framers were aware of this practice, and if they had desired to outlaw or restrict the use of evidence obtained by eavesdropping, I believe that they would have used the appropriate language to do so in the Fourth Amendment. They certainly would not have left such a task to the ingenuity of language-stretching judges. * * *

* * * By clever word juggling the Court finds it plausible to argue that language aimed specifically at searches and seizures of things that can be searched and seized may, to protect privacy, be applied to eavesdropped evidence of conversations that can neither be searched nor seized. Few things happen to an individual that do not affect his privacy in one way or another. Thus, by arbitrarily substituting the Court's language, designed to protect privacy, for the Constitution's language, designed to protect against unreasonable searches and seizures, the Court has made the Fourth Amendment its vehicle for holding all laws violative of the Constitution which offend the Court's broadest concept of privacy. * * *

Notes and Questions

1. **Fourth Amendment interests.** In *Katz,* the Court held that the police conduct "constituted a 'search and seizure' within the meaning of the Fourth Amendment" because of the intrusion upon the defendant's privacy interest. But this does not mean that privacy is the *only* interest protected by the Fourth Amendment. The Fourth Amendment also protects the interests in possession of property and liberty of person, as in *United States v. Place,* p. 154 (detention of traveler's luggage 90 minutes was an unreasonable seizure in two respects, as it constituted a deprivation of defendant's "possessory interest in his luggage" and his "liberty interest in proceeding with his itinerary").

In *Soldal v. Cook County,* 506 U.S. 56, 113 S.Ct. 538, 121 L.Ed.2d 450 (1992), a § 1983 action was commenced against sheriff's deputies who knowingly participated in an unlawful eviction which involved disconnecting the plaintiff's trailer home from its utilities and hauling it off the landlord's property, in the process of which the trailer was badly damaged. The court of appeals affirmed the officers' motion for summary judgment on the ground that the Fourth Amendment offered no protection where, as here, the intrusion upon a possessory interest was unaccompanied by an intrusion upon a privacy interest or, for that matter, upon a liberty interest. A unanimous Supreme Court reversed, holding "that seizures of property are subject to Fourth Amendment scrutiny even though no search within the meaning of the Amendment has taken place."

2. Garbage. In CALIFORNIA v. GREENWOOD, 486 U.S. 35, 108 S.Ct. 1625, 100 L.Ed.2d 30 (1988), police on two occasions had the neighborhood garbage collector pick up opaque plastic bags of garbage, which Greenwood had left at his curb for pick-up, and turn them over without mixing their contents with other garbage collected. On each occasion evidence of narcotics use was found, and each discovery served as the basis for a search warrant to search Greenwood's home which, upon execution, led to the discovery of narcotics. In reversing the state court's holding that these actions violated the Fourth Amendment, the Court, per WHITE, J., reasoned:

"It may well be that respondents did not expect that the contents of their garbage bags would become known to the police or other members of the public. An expectation of privacy does not give rise to Fourth Amendment protection, however, unless society is prepared to accept that expectation as objectively reasonable.[c]

"Here, we conclude that respondents exposed their garbage to the public sufficiently to defeat their claim to Fourth Amendment protection. It is common knowledge that plastic garbage bags left on or at the side of a public street are readily accessible to animals, children, scavengers, snoops, and other members of the public. Moreover, respondents placed their refuse at the curb for the express purpose of conveying it to a third party, the trash collector, who might himself have sorted through respondents' trash or permitted others, such as the police, to do so. Accordingly, having deposited their garbage 'in an area particularly suited for public inspection and, in a manner of speaking, public consumption, for the express purpose of having strangers take it,' respondents could have had no reasonable expectation of privacy in the inculpatory items that they discarded.

"Furthermore, as we have held, the police cannot reasonably be expected to avert their eyes from evidence of criminal activity that could have been observed by any member of the public. Hence, '[w]hat a person knowingly exposes to the public, even in his own home or office, is not a subject of Fourth Amendment protection.' *Katz.* We held in *Smith v. Maryland,* 442 U.S. 735, 99 S.Ct. 2577, 61 L.Ed.2d 220 (1979), for example, that the police did not violate the Fourth Amendment by causing a pen register to be installed at the telephone company's offices to record the telephone numbers dialed by a criminal suspect. An individual has no legitimate expectation of privacy in the numbers dialed on his telephone, we reasoned, because he voluntarily conveys those numbers to the telephone company when he uses the telephone. Again, we observed that 'a person has no legitimate expectation of privacy in information he voluntarily turns over to third parties.'

"Similarly, we held in *California v. Ciraolo,* 476 U.S. 207, 106 S.Ct. 1809, 90 L.Ed.2d 210 (1986) that the police were not required by the Fourth Amendment to obtain a warrant before conducting surveillance of the respondent's fenced back-yard from a private plane flying at an altitude of 1,000 feet. We concluded that the respondent's expectation that his yard was protected from such surveillance was unreasonable because '[a]ny member of the public flying in this airspace who glanced down could have seen everything that these officers observed.'[d]"

c. As for the respondents' reliance upon their right to privacy in garbage recognized by California law, the Court later stated: "Respondent's argument is no less than a suggestion that concepts of privacy under the laws of each State are to determine the reach of the Fourth Amendment. We do not accept this submission."

d. *Ciraolo* was a 5–4 decision. The dissenters objected that "the actual risk to privacy from commercial or pleasure aircraft is virtually nonexistent. Travelers on commercial flights, as well as private planes used for business or personal reasons, normally obtain at most a fleeting, anonymous, and nondiscriminating glimpse of the landscape and buildings over which they pass. The risk that a passen-

Dissent

BRENNAN, J., for the two dissenters, objected that a "trash bag, like any of the above-mentioned containers, 'is a common repository for one's personal effects' and, even more than many of them, is 'therefore ... inevitably associated with the expectation of privacy.' A single bag of trash testifies eloquently to the eating, reading, and recreational habits of the person who produced it. A search of trash, like a search of the bedroom, can relate intimate details about sexual practices, health, and personal hygiene. Like rifling through desk drawers or intercepting phone calls, rummaging through trash can divulge the target's financial and professional status, political affiliations and inclinations, private thoughts, personal relationships, and romantic interests. It cannot be doubted that a sealed trash bag harbors telling evidence of the 'intimate activity associated with the "sanctity of a man's home and the privacies of life," which the Fourth Amendment is designed to protect. * * *

"Nor is it dispositive that 'respondents placed their refuse at the curb for the express purpose of conveying it to a third party, ... who might himself have sorted through respondents' trash or permitted others, such as police, to do so.' In the first place, Greenwood can hardly be faulted for leaving trash on his curb when a county ordinance commanded him to do so, and prohibited him from disposing of it in any other way. More importantly, even the voluntary relinquishment of possession or control over an effect does not necessarily amount to a relinquishment of a privacy expectation in it. Were it otherwise, a letter or package would lose all Fourth Amendment protection when placed in a mail box or other depository with the 'express purpose' of entrusting it to the postal officer or a private carrier; those bailees are just as likely as trash collectors (and certainly have greater incentive) to 'sor[t] through' the personal effects entrusted to them, 'or permi[t] others, such as police to do so.' Yet, it has been clear for at least 110 years that the possibility of such an intrusion does not justify a warrantless search by police in the first instance. See *Ex parte Jackson,* 96 U.S. (6 Otto) 727, 24 L.Ed. 877 (1878)."

Compares to Letter or Package

Should *Greenwood* apply even when the defendant has resorted to rather extraordinary means to ensure that the incriminating character of his garbage is not perceived by others? Yes is the answer given in *United States v. Scott,* 975 F.2d 927 (1st Cir.1992), where IRS agents painstakingly reassembled documents which defendant shredded into $\frac{5}{32}$—inch strips before putting them in the garbage later placed outside his curtilage. The court offered this analogy: "A person who prepares incriminating documents in a secret code (or for that matter in some obscure foreign language), and thereafter blithely discards them as trash, relying on the premise or hope that they will not be deciphered [or translated] by the authorities could well be in for an unpleasant surprise if his code is 'broken' by the police [or a translator is found for the abstruse language], but he cannot make a valid claim that his subjective expectation in keeping the contents private by use of the secret code [or language] was reasonable in a constitutional sense."

shredded documents in trash

3. *"Curtilage" vs. "open fields."* After *Greenwood,* what result as to garbage left for pickup in a can well within the curtilage, if (i) the police merely enter and take the garbage, or (ii) the police have the garbage collector pick up and segregate the garbage from that can? More generally, what lands are protected by the Fourth Amendment from what kinds of police intrusions? Consider:

(a) In OLIVER v. UNITED STATES, 466 U.S. 170, 104 S.Ct. 1735, 80 L.Ed.2d 214 (1984), the Court, per POWELL, J., held that the "open fields" doctrine of *Hester v. United States,* 265 U.S. 57, 44 S.Ct. 445, 68 L.Ed. 898 (1924), by which police entry and examination of a field is free of any Fourth Amendment

ger on such a plane might observe private activities, and might connect those activities with particular people, is simply too trivial to protect against."

restraints, had not been implicitly overruled by *Katz*. This was because the *Hester* rule "was founded upon the explicit language of the Fourth Amendment. That Amendment indicates with some precision the places and things encompassed by its protections. As Justice Holmes explained for the Court in his characteristically laconic style: '[T]he special protection accorded by the Fourth Amendment to the people in their "persons, houses, papers, and effects," is not extended to the open fields. The distinction between the latter and the house is as old as the common law.' "

The Court in *Oliver* reasoned that this interpretation of the Amendment was consistent with *Katz,* as "open fields do not provide the setting for those intimate activities that the Amendment is intended to shelter from government interference or surveillance. There is no societal interest in protecting the privacy of those activities, such as the cultivation of crops, that occur in open fields. Moreover, as a practical matter these lands usually are accessible to the public and the police in ways that a home, an office or commercial structure would not be. It is not generally true that fences or no trespassing signs effectively bar the public from viewing open fields in rural areas. And both petitioner Oliver and respondent Thornton concede that the public and police lawfully may survey lands from the air. For these reasons, the asserted expectation of privacy in open fields is not an expectation that 'society recognizes as reasonable.'

"The historical underpinnings of the 'open fields' doctrine also demonstrate that the doctrine is consistent with respect for 'reasonable expectations of privacy.' As Justice Holmes, writing for the Court, observed in *Hester,* the common law distinguished 'open fields' from the 'curtilage,' the land immediately surrounding and associated with the home. The distinction implies that only the curtilage, not the neighboring open fields, warrants the Fourth Amendment protections that attach to the home. At common law, the curtilage is the area to which extends the intimate activity associated with the 'sanctity of a man's home and the privacies of life,' and therefore has been considered part of home itself for Fourth Amendment purposes. Thus, courts have extended Fourth Amendment protection to the curtilage; and they have defined the curtilage, as did the common law, by reference to the factors that determine whether an individual reasonably may expect that an area immediately adjacent to the home will remain private.[e] Conversely, the common law implies, as we reaffirm today, that no expectation of privacy legitimately attaches to open fields."

As for the contention of Oliver and Thornton that the circumstances may sometimes show the existence of a reasonable expectation of privacy, the Court said it was answered by the "language of the Fourth Amendment," but added that such a case-by-case approach would in any event be unworkable because "police officers would have to guess before every search whether landowners had erected fences sufficiently high, posted a sufficient number of warning signs, or located contraband in an area sufficiently secluded to establish a right of privacy." The *Oliver* majority also asserted that it rejected "the suggestion that steps taken to

e. As the Court explained in *United States v. Dunn*, 480 U.S. 294, 107 S.Ct. 1134, 94 L.Ed.2d 326 (1987), "curtilage questions should be resolved with particular reference to four factors: the proximity of the area claimed to be curtilage to the home, whether the area is included within an enclosure surrounding the home, the nature of the uses to which the area is put, and the steps taken by the resident to protect the area from observation by people passing by." Applying these factors, the Court then concluded the barn into which the police looked was not within the curtilage, as it was 60 yards from the house, was outside the area surrounding the house enclosed by a fence, did not appear to the police to be "used for intimate activities of the home," and the fences outside the barn were not of a kind "to prevent persons from observing what lay inside the enclosed area." The Court added that even assuming the barn was protected business premises, it still was no search to look into the open barn from an open fields vantage point.

protect privacy establish that expectations of privacy in an open field are legitimate. It is true, of course, that petitioner Oliver and respondent Thornton, in order to conceal their criminal activities, planted the marijuana upon secluded land and erected fences and no trespassing signs around the property. And it may be that because of such precautions, few members of the public stumbled upon the marijuana crops seized by the police. Neither of these suppositions demonstrates, however, that the expectation of privacy was *legitimate* in the sense required by the Fourth Amendment. The test of legitimacy is not whether the individual chooses to conceal assertedly 'private' activity. Rather, the correct inquiry is whether the government's intrusion infringes upon the personal and societal values protected by the Fourth Amendment. As we have explained, we find no basis for concluding that a police inspection of open fields accomplishes such an infringement."

MARSHALL, J., for the three dissenters, argued (1) that the Court's first ground could not be squared with earlier decisions, including *Katz* itself, for "neither a public telephone booth nor a conversation conducted therein can fairly be described as a person, house, paper, or effect"; and (2) that society *is* prepared to recognize as reasonable the expectations of Oliver and Thornton, which were supported by the law of criminal trespass, the private uses to which privately owned lands could be put, and the precautions which they had taken to manifest their privacy interest to others. From this the dissenters posited this "clear, easily administrable rule": "Private land marked in a fashion sufficient to render entry thereon a criminal trespass under the law of the state in which the land lies is protected by the Fourth Amendment's proscription of unreasonable searches and seizures."[f]

(c) FLORIDA v. RILEY, 488 U.S. 445, 109 S.Ct. 693, 102 L.Ed.2d 835 (1989), presented the question: "Whether surveillance of the interior of a partially covered greenhouse in a residential backyard from the vantage point of a helicopter located 400 feet above the greenhouse constitutes a 'search' for which a warrant is required under the Fourth Amendment." WHITE, J., for the 4-Justice plurality, concluded it did not "make a difference for Fourth Amendment purposes that the helicopter was flying at 400 feet when the officer saw what was growing in the greenhouse through the partially open roof and sides of the structure. We would have a different case if flying at that altitude had been contrary to law or regulation. But helicopters are not bound by the lower limits of the navigable airspace allowed to other aircraft. Any member of the public could legally have been flying over Riley's property in a helicopter at the altitude of 400 feet and could have observed Riley's greenhouse. The police officer did no more. This is not to say that an inspection of the curtilage of a house from an aircraft will always pass muster under the Fourth Amendment simply because the plane is within the navigable airspace specified by law. But it is of obvious importance that the helicopter in this case was *not* violating the law, and there is nothing in the record or before us to suggest that helicopters flying at 400 feet are sufficiently rare in this country to lend substance to respondent's claim that he reasonably anticipated that his greenhouse would not be subject to observation from that altitude. Neither is there any intimation here that the helicopter interfered with respondent's normal use of the greenhouse or of other parts of the curtilage. As far as this record reveals, no intimate details connected with the use of the home or curtilage were observed, and there was no undue noise, no wind, dust, or threat of injury. In these circumstances, there was no violation of the Fourth Amendment."

f. See Stephen A. Saltzburg, *Another Victim of Illegal Narcotics: The Fourth Amendment (As Illustrated by the Open Fields Doctrine)*, 48 U.Pitt.L.Rev. 1 (1986).

O'CONNOR, J., concurring only in the judgment because "the plurality's approach rests the scope of Fourth Amendment protection too heavily on compliance with FAA regulations whose purpose is to promote air safety not to protect" Fourth Amendment rights, concluded: "Because there is reason to believe that there is considerable public use of airspace at altitudes of 400 feet and above, and because Riley introduced no evidence to the contrary before the Florida courts, I conclude that Riley's expectation that his curtilage was protected from naked-eye aerial observation from that altitude was not a reasonable one. However, public use of altitudes lower than that—particularly public observations from helicopters circling over the curtilage of a home—may be sufficiently rare that police surveillance from such altitudes would violate reasonable expectations of privacy, despite compliance with FAA air safety regulations."

BRENNAN, J., joined by Marshall and Stevens, JJ., dissenting, objected: "Under the plurality's exceedingly grudging Fourth Amendment theory, the expectation of privacy is defeated if a single member of the public could conceivably position herself to see into the area in question without doing anything illegal. It is defeated whatever the difficulty a person would have in so positioning herself, and however infrequently anyone would in fact do so. In taking this view the plurality ignores the very essence of *Katz*. * * * Finding determinative the fact that the officer was where he had a right to be, at bottom, an attempt to analogize surveillance from a helicopter to surveillance by a police officer standing on a public road and viewing evidence of crime through an open window or a gap in a fence. In such a situation, the occupant of the home may be said to lack any reasonable expectation of privacy in what can be seen from that road—even if, in fact, people rarely pass that way.

"The police officer positioned 400 feet above Riley's backyard was not, however, standing on a public road. The vantage point he enjoyed was not one any citizen could readily share. His ability to see over Riley's fence depended on his use of a very expensive and sophisticated piece of machinery to which few ordinary citizens have access. In such circumstances it makes no more sense to rely on the legality of the officer's position in the skies than it would to judge the constitutionality of the wiretap in *Katz* by the legality of the officer's position outside the telephone booth. The simply inquiry whether the police officer had the legal right to be in the position from which he made his observations cannot suffice, for we cannot assume that Riley's curtilage was so open to the observations of passersby in the skies that he retained little privacy or personal security to be lost to police surveillance. The question before us must be not whether the police were where they had a right to be, but whether public observation of Riley's curtilage was so commonplace that Riley's expectation of privacy in his backyard could not be considered reasonable."

BLACKMUN, J., dissenting, first concluded that "a majority of this Court" (himself, the other three dissenters and O'Connor, J.) agreed "that the reasonableness of Riley's expectation depends, in large measure, on the frequency of nonpolice helicopter flights at an altitude of 400 feet." As for how this factual issue should be decided, he noted Brennan "suggests that we may resolve it ourselves without any evidence in the record on this point," while O'Connor "would impose the burden of proof on Riley" but would not now "allow Riley an opportunity to meet this burden." Blackmun, on the other hand, would impose upon the prosecution the burden of proving those "facts necessary to show that Riley lacked a reasonable expectation of privacy" and, "because our prior cases gave the parties little guidance on the burden of proof issue," would "remand this case to allow the prosecution an opportunity to meet this burden."

4. *Other premises.* (a) *Business and commercial premises* are covered by the Fourth Amendment. As stated in *See v. City of Seattle,* 387 U.S. 541, 87 S.Ct.

1737, 18 L.Ed.2d 943 (1967), "[t]he businessman, like the occupant of a residence, has a constitutional right to go about his business free from unreasonable official entries upon his private commercial property."

(b) *Private areas in public places.* What if a police officer, positioned at an overhead vent above a rest room, looks down into an individual closed stall and observes criminal conduct? See *State v. Bryant,* 177 N.W.2d 800 (Minn.1970) (is a search). What, however, if the stalls had no doors?

(c) *Detention facilities.* In *Hudson v. Palmer,* 468 U.S. 517, 104 S.Ct. 3194, 82 L.Ed.2d 393 (1984), involving a § 1983 action brought by a state prison inmate who alleged a prison guard had conducted a "shakedown" search of his cell and had destroyed his noncontraband property for purposes of harassment, the Court held, 5–4, "that the Fourth Amendment has no applicability to a prison cell." The Chief Justice reasoned: "A right of privacy in traditional Fourth Amendment terms is fundamentally incompatible with the close and continual surveillance of inmates and their cells required to ensure institutional security and internal order. We are satisfied that society would insist that the prisoner's expectation of privacy always yield to what must be considered the paramount interest in institutional security. We believe that it is accepted by our society that '[l]oss of freedom of choice and privacy are inherent incidents of confinement.'" The Court added that for "the same reasons" the seizure and destruction of a prisoner's effects did not fall within the protections of the Fourth Amendment. It is unclear whether *Hudson* applies to the search of the person of a prisoner[g] or, in any event, to a pretrial detention facility.[h]

5. Vehicles. (a) In *Cardwell v. Lewis,* 417 U.S. 583, 94 S.Ct. 2464, 41 L.Ed.2d 325 (1974), police seized a car from a public parking lot and later took a small paint sample off the car and matched the tire tread with tracks at a crime scene. The Court divided on the propriety of the seizure of the car, but the plurality opinion seemed to view the later activity as no search: "With the 'search' limited to the examination of the tire on the wheel and the taking of paint scraping from the exterior of the vehicle left in the public parking lot, we fail to comprehend what expectation of privacy was infringed."

(b) In *New York v. Class,* 475 U.S. 106, 106 S.Ct. 960, 89 L.Ed.2d 81 (1986), an officer stopped a car for traffic violations and then, after the driver exited the car, opened the door and reached in to move papers obscuring the dashboard Vehicle Identification Number, at which time he saw a gun inside the car. Noting that "federal law requires that the VIN be placed in the plain view of someone *outside* the automobile," the Court concluded "there was no reasonable expectation of privacy in the VIN," so that the "mere viewing of the formerly obscured VIN was not" a search. But the Court then concluded that because "a car's interior [is] subject to Fourth Amendment protection," the officer's action in reaching inside the car "constituted a 'search'" (albeit a reasonable one in the circumstances).[i]

---

g. As the dissenters noted, the majority "appears to limit its holding to a prisoner's 'papers and effects' located in his cell" and apparently "believes that at least a prisoner's 'person' is secure from unreasonable search and seizure." In *Bell v. Wolfish,* 441 U.S. 520, 99 S.Ct. 1861, 60 L.Ed.2d 447 (1979), where the Court declared that at best prisoners have a "reasonable expectation of privacy * * * of a diminished scope," it was held that neither strip searches nor body cavity inspections of pretrial detainees after contact visits with outsiders were unreasonable.

h. Much, but certainly not all, of the Court's analysis in *Hudson* has to do with circumstances existing in facilities housing those convicted of crime. But O'Connor, J., concurring, stated the broader proposition that the "fact of arrest and incarceration abates all legitimate Fourth Amendment privacy and possessory interests in personal effects."

i. See Tracey Maclin, *New York v. Class: A Little-Noticed Case With Disturbing Implications,* 78 J.Crim.L. & C. 1 (1987).

6. *Effects*. During a lawful stop of a Greyhound bus, federal agents walked through the bus and squeezed the soft luggage passengers had placed in the overhead storage spaces. An agent noticed thereby that one bag contained a brick-like object; passenger Downs admitted the bag was his and allowed the agent to open it, revealing a brick of methamphetamine. In BOND v. UNITED STATES, 529 U.S. 334, 120 S.Ct. 1462, 146 L.Ed.2d 365 (2000), the Court, per REHN-QUIST, C.J., preliminarily noted: (1) that a "traveler's personal luggage is clearly an 'effect' protected by the Fourth Amendment"; (2) that the government's reliance on such cases as *Riley* was misplaced because "[p]hysical invasive inspection is simply more intrusive than purely visual inspection"; and (3) that while Bond's "bag was not part of his person," "travelers are particularly concerned about their carry-on luggage; they generally use it to transport personal items that, for whatever reason, they prefer to keep close at hand." The Court then concluded: "When a bus passenger places a bag in an overhead bin, he expects that other passengers or bus employees may move it for one reason or another. Thus, a bus passenger clearly expects that his bag may be handled. He does not expect that other passengers or bus employees will, as a matter of course, feel the bag in an exploratory manner. But this is exactly what the agent did here. We therefore hold that the agent's physical manipulation of petitioner's bag violated the Fourth Amendment."

BREYER and Scalia, JJ., dissenting, objected: (1) that the squeezing did not "differ from the treatment that overhead luggage is likely to receive from strangers in a world of travel that is somewhat less gentle than it used to be"; (2) that whether "tactile manipulation * * * is more intrusive or less intrusive than visual observation * * * necessarily depends on the particular circumstances"; and (3) that "the decision will lead to a constitutional jurisprudence of 'squeezes,' thereby complicating further already complex Fourth Amendment law."

What is the significance of *Bond* with respect to tactile examination of the carry-on luggage of train and airplane passengers, and of the checked luggage of passengers on various forms of public transportation?

7. *Enhancing the senses*. Generally speaking, it is fair to say that it is not a search for an officer, lawfully present at a certain place, to detect something by one of his natural senses. *United States v. Mankani*, 738 F.2d 538 (2d Cir.1984) (no search where conversations in adjoining motel room "were overheard by the naked human ear"). The result ordinarily is the same when common means of enhancing the senses, such as a flashlight or binoculars, are used.[j] As for use of more sophisticated or less common means, consider the following material.

KYLLO v. UNITED STATES
533 U.S. 27, 121 S.Ct. 2038, 150 L.Ed.2d 94 (2001).

Justice SCALIA delivered the opinion of the Court. * * *

In 1991 Agent William Elliott of the United States Department of the Interior came to suspect that marijuana was being grown in the home belonging to petitioner Danny Kyllo, part of a triplex on Rhododendron Drive in Florence, Oregon. Indoor marijuana growth typically requires high-intensity lamps. In order

---

j. But consider *Raettig v. State*, 406 So.2d 1273 (Fla.App.1981) (use of flashlight to look into camper through half-inch wide crack a search, as "a minute crack on the surface of such area can hardly be regarded as an implied invitation to any curious passerby to take a look"); *State v. Ward*, 617 P.2d 568 (Hawaii 1980) (use of binoculars to see crap game in 7th story apartment from closest vantage point an eighth of a mile away a search, as "the constitution does not require that in all cases a person, in order to protect his privacy, must shut himself off from fresh air, sunlight and scenery").

to determine whether an amount of heat was emanating from petitioner's home consistent with the use of such lamps, at 3:20 a.m. on January 16, 1992, Agent Elliott and Dan Haas used an Agema Thermovision 210 thermal imager[a] to scan the triplex. Thermal imagers detect infrared radiation, which virtually all objects emit but which is not visible to the naked eye. The imager converts radiation into images based on relative warmth—black is cool, white is hot, shades of gray connote relative differences; in that respect, it operates somewhat like a video camera showing heat images. The scan of Kyllo's home took only a few minutes and was performed from the passenger seat of Agent Elliott's vehicle across the street from the front of the house and also from the street in back of the house. The scan showed that the roof over the garage and a side wall of petitioner's home were relatively hot compared to the rest of the home and substantially warmer than neighboring homes in the triplex. Agent Elliott concluded that petitioner was using halide lights to grow marijuana in his house, which indeed he was. Based on tips from informants, utility bills, and the thermal imaging, a Federal Magistrate Judge issued a warrant authorizing a search of petitioner's home, and the agents found an indoor growing operation involving more than 100 plants. Petitioner was indicted on one count of manufacturing marijuana, in violation of 21 U. S. C. § 841(a)(1). He unsuccessfully moved to suppress the evidence seized from his home and then entered a conditional guilty plea[, and the court of appeals affirmed]. * * *

It would be foolish to contend that the degree of privacy secured to citizens by the Fourth Amendment has been entirely unaffected by the advance of technology. For example, * * * the technology enabling human flight has exposed to public view (and hence, we have said, to official observation) uncovered portions of the house and its curtilage that once were private. See *Ciraolo*, [p. 142]. The question we confront today is what limits there are upon this power of technology to shrink the realm of guaranteed privacy.

The *Katz* test—whether the individual has an expectation of privacy that society is prepared to recognize as reasonable—has often been criticized as circular, and hence subjective and unpredictable. While it may be difficult to refine *Katz* when the search of areas such as telephone booths, automobiles, or even the curtilage and uncovered portions of residences are at issue, in the case of the search of the interior of homes—the prototypical and hence most commonly litigated area of protected privacy—there is a ready criterion, with roots deep in the common law, of the minimal expectation of privacy that exists, and that is acknowledged to be reasonable. To withdraw protection of this minimum expectation would be to permit police technology to erode the privacy guaranteed by the Fourth Amendment. We think that obtaining by sense-enhancing technology any information regarding the interior of the home that could not otherwise have been obtained without physical "intrusion into a constitutionally protected area" constitutes a search—at least where (as here) the technology in question is not in general public use. This assures preservation of that degree of privacy against government that existed when the Fourth Amendment was adopted. On the basis of this criterion, the information obtained by the thermal imager in this case was the product of a search.[2]

a. As the Court later elaborated, "the District Court found that the Agema 210 'is a nonintrusive device which emits no rays or beams and shows a crude visual image of the heat being radiated from the outside of the house'; it 'did not show any people or activity within the walls of the structure'; '[t]he device used cannot penetrate walls or windows to reveal conversations or human activities'; and '[n]o intimate details of the home were observed.' "

2. The dissent's repeated assertion that the thermal imaging did not obtain information regarding the interior of the home is simply inaccurate. A thermal imager reveals the relative heat of various rooms in the home. The dissent may not find that information particu-

The Government maintains, however, that the thermal imaging must be upheld because it detected "only heat radiating from the external surface of the house." The dissent makes this its leading point, contending that there is a fundamental difference between what it calls "off-the-wall" observations and "through-the-wall surveillance." But just as a thermal imager captures only heat emanating from a house, so also a powerful directional microphone picks up only sound emanating from a house—and a satellite capable of scanning from many miles away would pick up only visible light emanating from a house. We rejected such a mechanical interpretation of the Fourth Amendment in *Katz*, where the eavesdropping device picked up only sound waves that reached the exterior of the phone booth. Reversing that approach would leave the homeowner at the mercy of advancing technology—including imaging technology that could discern all human activity in the home. While the technology used in the present case was relatively crude, the rule we adopt must take account of more sophisticated systems that are already in use or in development.[3] * * *

The Government also contends that the thermal imaging was constitutional because it did not "detect private activities occurring in private areas." * * * The Fourth Amendment's protection of the home has never been tied to measurement of the quality or quantity of information obtained. * * * In the home, our cases show, all details are intimate details, because the entire area is held safe from prying government eyes. Thus, in *Karo,* [p. 156], the only thing detected was a can of ether in the home; and in *Arizona v. Hicks,* [p. 224], the only thing detected by a physical search that went beyond what officers lawfully present could observe in "plain view" was the registration number of a phonograph turntable. These were intimate details because they were details of the home, just as was the detail of how warm—or even how relatively warm—Kyllo was heating his residence.

Limiting the prohibition of thermal imaging to "intimate details" would not only be wrong in principle; it would be impractical in application, failing to provide "a workable accommodation between the needs of law enforcement and the interests protected by the Fourth Amendment." To begin with, there is no necessary connection between the sophistication of the surveillance equipment and the "intimacy" of the details that it observes—which means that one cannot say (and the police cannot be assured) that use of the relatively crude equipment at issue here will always be lawful. * * * We * * * would have to develop a jurisprudence specifying which home activities are "intimate" and which are not. And even when (if ever) that jurisprudence were fully developed, no police officer would be able to know in advance whether his through-the-wall surveillance picks

larly private or important, but there is no basis for saying it is not information regarding the interior of the home. The dissent's comparison of the thermal imaging to various circumstances in which outside observers might be able to perceive, without technology, the heat of the home—for example, by observing snow-melt on the roof—is quite irrelevant. The fact that equivalent information could sometimes be obtained by other means does not make lawful the use of means that violate the Fourth Amendment. The police might, for example, learn how many people are in a particular house by setting up year-round surveillance; but that does not make breaking and entering to find out the same information lawful. In any event, on the night of January 16, 1992, no outside observer could have discerned the relative heat of Kyllo's home without thermal imaging.

3. The ability to "see" through walls and other opaque barriers is a clear, and scientifically feasible, goal of law enforcement research and development. The National Law Enforcement and Corrections Technology Center, a program within the United States Department of Justice, features on its Internet Website projects that include a "Radar–Based Through-the-Wall Surveillance System," "Handheld Ultrasound Through the Wall Surveillance," and a "Radar Flashlight" that "will enable law officers to detect individuals through interior building walls." www.nlectc.org/techproj/ (visited May 3, 2001). Some devices may emit low levels of radiation that travel "through-the-wall," but others, such as more sophisticated thermal imaging devices, are entirely passive, or "off-the-wall" as the dissent puts it.

up "intimate" details—and thus would be unable to know in advance whether it is constitutional.

The dissent's proposed standard—whether the technology offers the "functional equivalent of actual presence in the area being searched"—would seem quite similar to our own at first blush. The dissent concludes that *Katz* was such a case, but then inexplicably asserts that if the same listening device only revealed the volume of the conversation, the surveillance would be permissible. Yet if, without technology, the police could not discern volume without being actually present in the phone booth, Justice STEVENS should conclude a search has occurred.* * * The same should hold for the interior heat of the home if only a person present in the home could discern the heat. Thus the driving force of the dissent, despite its recitation of the above standard, appears to be a distinction among different types of information—whether the "homeowner would even care if anybody noticed." The dissent offers no practical guidance for the application of this standard, and for reasons already discussed, we believe there can be none. The people in their houses, as well as the police, deserve more precision.[6]

We have said that the Fourth Amendment draws "a firm line at the entrance to the house." That line, we think, must be not only firm but also bright—which requires clear specification of those methods of surveillance that require a warrant. While it is certainly possible to conclude from the videotape of the thermal imaging that occurred in this case that no "significant" compromise of the homeowner's privacy has occurred, we must take the long view, from the original meaning of the Fourth Amendment forward. * * *

Since we hold the Thermovision imaging to have been an unlawful search, it will remain for the District Court to determine whether, without the evidence it provided, the search warrant issued in this case was supported by probable cause—and if not, whether there is any other basis for supporting admission of the evidence that the search pursuant to the warrant produced. * * *

Justice STEVENS, with whom THE CHIEF JUSTICE, Justice, Justice O'CONNOR, and Justice KENNEDY join, dissenting. * * *

While the Court "take[s] the long view" and decides this case based largely on the potential of yet-to-be-developed technology that might allow "through-the-wall surveillance," this case involves nothing more than off-the-wall surveillance by law enforcement officers to gather information exposed to the general public from the outside of petitioner's home. All that the infrared camera did in this case was passively measure heat emitted from the exterior surfaces of petitioner's home; all that those measurements showed were relative differences in emission levels, vaguely indicating that some areas of the roof and outside walls were warmer than others. As still images from the infrared scans show, no details regarding the interior of petitioner's home were revealed. Unlike an x-ray scan, or other possible "through-the-wall" techniques, the detection of infrared radiation emanating from the home did not accomplish "an unauthorized physical penetration into the premises," nor did it "obtain information that it could not have obtained by observation from outside the curtilage of the house."

---

6. The dissent argues that we have injected potential uncertainty into the constitutional analysis by noting that whether or not the technology is in general public use may be a factor. That quarrel, however, is not with us but with this Court's precedent. See *Ciraolo* ("In an age where private and commercial flight in the public airways is routine, it is unreasonable for respondent to expect that his marijuana plants were constitutionally protected from being observed with the naked eye from an altitude of 1,000 feet"). Given that we can quite confidently say that thermal imaging is not "routine," we decline in this case to reexamine that factor.

Indeed, the ordinary use of the senses might enable a neighbor or passerby to notice the heat emanating from a building, particularly if it is vented, as was the case here. Additionally, any member of the public might notice that one part of a house is warmer than another part or a nearby building if, for example, rainwater evaporates or snow melts at different rates across its surfaces. Such use of the senses would not convert into an unreasonable search if, instead, an adjoining neighbor allowed an officer onto her property to verify her perceptions with a sensitive thermometer. Nor, in my view, does such observation become an unreasonable search if made from a distance with the aid of a device that merely discloses that the exterior of one house, or one area of the house, is much warmer than another. Nothing more occurred in this case. * * *

Notwithstanding the implications of today's decision, there is a strong public interest in avoiding constitutional litigation over the monitoring of emissions from homes, and over the inferences drawn from such monitoring. Just as "the police cannot reasonably be expected to avert their eyes from evidence of criminal activity that could have been observed by any member of the public," *Greenwood*, [p. 142], so too public officials should not have to avert their senses or their equipment from detecting emissions in the public domain such as excessive heat, traces of smoke, suspicious odors, odorless gases, airborne particulates, or radioactive emissions, any of which could identify hazards to the community. In my judgment, monitoring such emissions with "sense-enhancing technology," and drawing useful conclusions from such monitoring, is an entirely reasonable public service.

On the other hand, the countervailing privacy interest is at best trivial. After all, homes generally are insulated to keep heat in, rather than to prevent the detection of heat going out, and it does not seem to me that society will suffer from a rule requiring the rare homeowner who both intends to engage in uncommon activities that produce extraordinary amounts of heat, and wishes to conceal that production from outsiders, to make sure that the surrounding area is well insulated. * * *

Despite the Court's attempt to draw a line that is "not only firm but also bright," the contours of its new rule are uncertain because its protection apparently dissipates as soon as the relevant technology is "in general public use." Yet how much use is general public use is not even hinted at by the Court's opinion, which makes the somewhat doubtful assumption that the thermal imager used in this case does not satisfy that criterion.[5] In any event, putting aside its lack of clarity, this criterion is somewhat perverse because it seems likely that the threat to privacy will grow, rather than recede, as the use of intrusive equipment becomes more readily available.

It is clear, however, that the category of "sense-enhancing technology" covered by the new rule is far too broad. It would, for example, embrace potential mechanical substitutes for dogs trained to react when they sniff narcotics. But in *United States v. Place*, [p. 154], we held that a dog sniff that "discloses only the presence or absence of narcotics" does "not constitute a 'search' within the meaning of the Fourth Amendment," and it must follow that sense-enhancing equipment that identifies nothing but illegal activity is not a search either.

---

5. The record describes a device that numbers close to a thousand manufactured units; that has a predecessor numbering in the neighborhood of 4,000 to 5,000 units; that competes with a similar product numbering from 5,000 to 6,000 units; and that is "readily available to the public" for commercial, personal, or law enforcement purposes, and is just an 800–number away from being rented from "half a dozen national companies" by anyone who wants one. Since, by virtue of the Court's new rule, the issue is one of first impression, perhaps it should order an evidentiary hearing to determine whether these facts suffice to establish "general public use."

Nevertheless, the use of such a device would be unconstitutional under the Court's rule, as would the use of other new devices that might detect the odor of deadly bacteria or chemicals for making a new type of high explosive * * *.

Because the new rule applies to information regarding the "interior" of the home, it is too narrow as well as too broad. Clearly, a rule that is designed to protect individuals from the overly intrusive use of sense-enhancing equipment should not be limited to a home. If such equipment did provide its user with the functional equivalent of access to a private place—such as, for example, the telephone booth involved in *Katz*, or an office building—then the rule should apply to such an area as well as to a home. * * *

The two reasons advanced by the Court as justifications for the adoption of its new rule are both unpersuasive. First, the Court suggests that its rule is compelled by our holding in *Katz*, because in that case, as in this, the surveillance consisted of nothing more than the monitoring of waves emanating from a private area into the public domain. Yet there are critical differences between the cases. In *Katz*, the electronic listening device attached to the outside of the phone booth allowed the officers to pick up the content of the conversation inside the booth, making them the functional equivalent of intruders because they gathered information that was otherwise available only to someone inside the private area; it would be as if, in this case, the thermal imager presented a view of the heat-generating activity inside petitioner's home. By contrast, the thermal imager here disclosed only the relative amounts of heat radiating from the house; it would be as if, in *Katz*, the listening device disclosed only the relative volume of sound leaving the booth, which presumably was discernible in the public domain. * * *

Second, the Court argues that the permissibility of "through-the-wall surveillance" cannot depend on a distinction between observing "intimate details" such as "the lady of the house [taking] her daily sauna and bath," and noticing only "the nonintimate rug on the vestibule floor" or "objects no smaller than 36 by 36 inches." This entire argument assumes, of course, that the thermal imager in this case could or did perform "through-the-wall surveillance" that could identify any detail "that would previously have been unknowable without physical intrusion." In fact, the device could not and did not enable its user to identify either the lady of the house, the rug on the vestibule floor, or anything else inside the house, whether smaller or larger than 36 by 36 inches. * * *

Although the Court is properly and commendably concerned about the threats to privacy that may flow from advances in the technology available to the law enforcement profession, it has unfortunately failed to heed the tried and true counsel of judicial restraint. Instead of concentrating on the rather mundane issue that is actually presented by the case before it, the Court has endeavored to craft an all-encompassing rule for the future. It would be far wiser to give legislators an unimpeded opportunity to grapple with these emerging issues rather than to shackle them with prematurely devised constitutional constraints. * * *

Notes and Questions

1. Katz vs. Kyllo. Is it a fair conclusion, as stated in Richard H. Seamon, *Kyllo v. United States and the Partial Ascendance of Justice Scalia's Fourth Amendment*, 79 Wash.U.L.Q. 1013, 1022 (2001), that "the *Kyllo* majority did not apply the *Katz* test to the case before it"? If so, has Justice Scalia thereby avoided the faults he attributed to that test in *Minnesota v. Carter*, namely that it "has no plausible foundation in the text of the Fourth Amendment," is "notoriously unhelpful" in identifying what government conduct constitutes a search, and is "self-indulgent" because it allows judges to decide what privacy expectations are "reasonable"?

dog sniff
ok no vio
of 4th

limited
disclosure

2. *The canine nose.* In UNITED STATES v. PLACE, dealing with a temporary seizure of luggage at an airport so that it could be brought into contact with a drug detection dog, the majority declared "that a person possesses a privacy interest in the contents of personal luggage that is protected by the Fourth Amendment. A 'canine sniff' by a well-trained narcotics detection dog, however, does not require opening the luggage. It does not expose noncontraband items that otherwise would remain hidden from public view, as does, for example, an officer's rummaging through the contents of the luggage. Thus, the manner in which information is obtained through this investigative technique is much less intrusive than a typical search. Moreover, the sniff discloses only the presence or absence of narcotics, a contraband item. Thus, despite the fact that the sniff tells the authorities something about the contents of the luggage, the information obtained is limited. This limited disclosure also ensures that the owner of the property is not subjected to the embarrassment and inconvenience entailed in less discriminate and more intrusive investigative methods.

"In these respects, the canine sniff is *sui generis.* We are aware of no other investigative procedure that is so limited both in the manner in which the information is obtained and in the content of the information revealed by the procedure. Therefore, we conclude that the particular course of investigation that the agents intended to pursue here—exposure of respondent's luggage, which was located in a public place, to a trained canine—did not constitute a 'search' within the meaning of the Fourth Amendment."[a]

Is the notion that "the fourth amendment exists to protect the innocent and may normally be invoked by the guilty only when necessary to protect the innocent," so that "if a device could be invented that accurately detected weapons and did not disrupt the normal movement of people, there could be no fourth amendment objection to its use"? Arnold H. Loewy, *The Fourth Amendment as a Device for Protecting the Innocent,* 81 Mich.L.Rev. 1229, 1246, 1248 (1983). Is the use of these dogs nonetheless objectionable because people have a right to be free of unwanted suspicion, Martin R. Gardner, *Sniffing for Drugs in the Classroom,* 74 Nw.U.L.Rev. 803, 844–47 (1980), or is the answer that the innocent are benefited by "the dog that freed them from the unwarranted suspicion which otherwise would have continued"? Loewy, supra, at 1247. What then of other concerns about the use of such dogs: "To the extent that the dog is less than perfectly accurate, innocent people run the risk of being searched. Additionally, the very act of being subjected to a body sniff by a German Shepherd may be offensive at best or harrowing at worst to the innocent sniffee." Id. at 1246–47.

Place was relied upon in *United States v. Jacobsen,* p. 135, holding that where police lawfully came upon a white powder in a package originally opened by private parties, an on-the-spot chemical test of a trace of the powder which would reveal only whether or not it was cocaine was not a search. "Here, as in *Place,* the likelihood that official conduct of the kind disclosed by the record will actually compromise any legitimate interest in privacy seems much too remote to characterize the testing as a search subject to the Fourth Amendment." Brennan and Marshall, JJ., dissenting, objected that "under the Court's analysis in these cases, law enforcement officers could release a trained cocaine-sensitive dog * * * to roam the streets at random, alerting the officers to people carrying cocaine. Or, if

a. Brennan and Marshall, JJ., concurring in the result, objected that this issue, neither reached by the court of appeals nor briefed and argued in the Supreme Court, should not be decided in "a discussion unnecessary to the judgment." Blackmun, J., concurring separately, expressed the same concern and added: "While the Court has adopted one plausible analysis of the issue, there are others. For example, a dog sniff may be a search, but a minimally intrusive one that could be justified in this situation under *Terry* upon mere reasonable suspicion."

a device were developed that, when aimed at a person, would detect instantaneously whether the person is carrying cocaine, there would be no Fourth Amendment bar, under the Court's approach, to the police setting up such a device on a street corner and scanning all passersby. In fact, the Court's analysis is so unbounded that if a device were developed that could detect, from the outside of a building, the presence of cocaine inside, there would be no constitutional obstacle to the police cruising through a residential neighborhood and using the device to identify all homes in which the drug is present.''[b]

3. *Weapons detector.* The device imagined by Prof. Loewy back in 1983 may now be a reality. As a result of Department of Justice funding, several organizations are developing concealed weapons detection technology in order to produce a commercially and technologically viable device that can do an "electronic frisk" of a suspect from a distance of ten to twenty feet. Two of the detectors use magnetic fields, albeit in quite different ways. Raytheon's device illuminates the subject with a low intensity electromagnetic pulse and then measures the time decay of the radiated energy from metal objects carried by the person. The device detects only metal objects, but produces no images. Rather, by measurement of the intensity and the time decay of the secondary radiation, there are produced "signatures" which can be identified as indicating whether the detected metal object is or is not a gun. By comparison, the INEL system uses magnetic gradiometers to measure fluctuations produced when anything made of ferromagnetic material moves through the earth's magnetic field. No electronic energy is directed at the subject, as these instruments merely measure what certain objects do to the earth's magnetic field. By use of target recognition software, the readings are compared with known "signatures" of weapons of similar mass, shape and density to determine the likelihood that the device has focused upon a weapon. The third device, the Millitech system, uses passive millimeter wave imaging technology. The amplitude of radiation at which the waves are emitted varies with the object's temperature and other properties, and thus the Millitech detector scans the waves emitted by the human body and any objects concealed on the person and produces a small image on the back of the device in which the outlines of concealed objects, usually dark, are clearly visible against the much brighter image of the body.

Would the use of any or all of these systems constitute a Fourth Amendment search? Would the answer be the same in those twenty-five jurisdictions which have enacted some variety of a concealed weapon permit statute? See David Harris, *Superman's X–Ray Vision and the Fourth Amendment: The New Gun Detection Technology*, 69 Temple L.Rev. 1 (1996).

4. *Electronic tracking.* With the consent of a chemical company, police installed a "beeper," a battery operated radio transmitter, into a container of chloroform, a chemical used to manufacture illicit drugs, prior to its purchase. By a combination of visual surveillance and monitoring of the beeper signal the police tracked the container as it was carried in Petschen's automobile to Knotts' cabin in a rural area. On that evidence and other information, a search warrant for the cabin was issued, and an illicit drug lab was discovered within. In *United States v. Knotts,* 460 U.S. 276, 103 S.Ct. 1081, 75 L.Ed.2d 55 (1983), the Court held that the use of the "beeper" did not constitute a Fourth Amendment search:

---

b. What if a dog were utilized for this purpose? Compare *United States v. Thomas,* 757 F.2d 1359 (2d Cir.1985) (reading *Place* with *United States v. Karo,* p. 156, and concluding such use of those dogs is a search); with *United States v. Colyer,* 878 F.2d 469 (D.C.Cir.1989) (questioning and distinguishing *Thomas* in holding there was no search where a drug dog in the public corridor of a train "alerted" to a particular sleeper compartment). Is *Kyllo* irrelevant on this issue because, as asserted in *State v. Bergmann,* 633 N.W.2d 328 (Iowa 2001), "a drug sniffing dog is not 'technology' of the type addressed in *Kyllo.*"

"Visual surveillance from public places along Petschen's route or adjoining Knotts' premises would have sufficed to reveal all of these facts to the police. The fact that the officers in this case relied not only on visual surveillance, but on the use of the beeper to signal the presence of Petschen's automobile to the police receiver, does not alter the situation. Nothing in the Fourth Amendment prohibited the police from augmenting the sensory faculties bestowed upon them at birth with such enhancement as science and technology afforded them in this case." To Knotts' objection that under such a view "twenty-four hour surveillance of any citizen of this country will be possible, without judicial knowledge or supervision," the Court responded that "if such dragnet type law enforcement practices as respondent envisions should eventually occur, there will be time enough then to determine whether different constitutional principles may be applicable."

In UNITED STATES v. KARO, 468 U.S. 705, 104 S.Ct. 3296, 82 L.Ed.2d 530 (1984), the Court was "called upon to address two questions left unresolved in *Knotts*: (1) whether installation of a beeper in a container of chemicals with the consent of the original owner constitutes a search or seizure within the meaning of the Fourth Amendment when the container is delivered to a buyer having no knowledge of the presence of the beeper, and (2) whether monitoring of a beeper falls within the ambit of the Fourth Amendment when it reveals information that could not have been obtained through visual surveillance." The Court, per WHITE, J., answered the first question in the negative, reasoning that the mere transfer of the can containing an unmonitored beeper "infringed no privacy interest" because it "conveyed no information that [the recipient] wished to keep private, for it conveyed no information at all," and thus was no search, and that "it cannot be said that anyone's possessory interest was interfered with in a meaningful way," and thus there was no seizure. (STEVENS, Brennan and Marshall, JJ., dissenting on this branch of the case, argued that by "attaching the beeper and using the container to conceal it, the Government in the most fundamental sense was asserting 'dominion and control' over the property," which "is a 'seizure' in the most basic sense of the term.")

The Court answered the second question in the affirmative, first noting that unquestionably it would be an unreasonable search to surreptitiously enter a residence without a warrant to verify that the container was there. "For purpose of the Amendment, the result is the same where, without a warrant, the Government surreptitiously employs an electronic device to obtain information that it could not have obtained by observation from outside the curtilage of the house. The beeper tells the agent that a particular article is actually located at a particular time in the private residence and is in the possession of the person or persons whose residence is being surveilled. Even if visual surveillance has revealed that the article to which the beeper is attached has entered the house, the later monitoring not only verifies the officers' observations but also establishes that the article remains on the premises." The Court next concluded that absent "truly exigent circumstances" such use of the beeper was governed by "the general rule that a search of a house should be conducted pursuant to a warrant."[c] Such monitoring was characterized by the Court as "less intrusive than a full-scale search," but the Court did not have occasion to decide whether as a consequence such a warrant could issue upon reasonable suspicion rather than probable cause.[d]

c. In response to the government's claim that a warrant should not be required because of the difficulty in satisfying the particularity requirement of the Fourth Amendment, in that it is usually not known in advance to what place the container with the beeper in it will be taken, the Court concluded that it would suffice if the warrant were "to describe the object into which the beeper is to be placed, the circumstances that led agents to wish to install the beeper, and the length of time for which beeper surveillance is requested."

d. See Clifford Fishman, *Electronic Tracking Devices and the Fourth Amendment:*

5. *Cellular phone tracking.* An FCC rule requires cellular telephone companies to have the capability of determining the location from which a cellular phone call originates to within 125 meters. "The cellular telephone call location technology now mandated by the FCC will turn each of the more than fifty million cell phones in the United States into a tracking device. It will enable police not just to pinpoint the location of cell phone calls to 911 operators, but to track the location of all cellular phone users, no matter who they are calling, both as they are actually making calls and after the fact through phone company computer records. Moreover, because cellular telephones send out signals to the cellular system every few minutes to keep the system informed of their location, police will be able to remotely track any individual with a cellular telephone that is turned on, whether or not they are actually placing a call. Cellular telephone location technology thus will provide law enforcement with an extraordinarily powerful new tool for monitoring the movement of individuals."[e] In light of *Smith v. Maryland*, p. 142, and *Karo*, p. 156, is law enforcement use of this technology a search?

6. *Photographic magnification.* In DOW CHEMICAL CO. v. UNITED STATES, 476 U.S. 227, 106 S.Ct. 1819, 90 L.Ed.2d 226 (1986), the Court, per BURGER, C.J., held that aerial photography of a chemical company's industrial complex was not a Fourth Amendment "search": "It may well be, as the Government concedes, that surveillance of private property by using highly sophisticated surveillance equipment not generally available to the public, such as satellite technology, might be constitutionally proscribed absent a warrant. But the photographs here are not so revealing of intimate details as to raise constitutional concerns. Although they undoubtedly give EPA more detailed information than naked-eye views, they remain limited to an outline of the facility's buildings and equipment. The mere fact that human vision is enhanced somewhat, at least to the degree here, does not give rise to constitutional problems.[6] An electronic device to penetrate walls or windows so as to hear and record confidential discussions of chemical formulae or other trade secrets would raise very different and far more serious questions; other protections such as trade secret laws are available to protect commercial activities from private surveillance by competitors.

"We conclude that the open areas of an industrial plant complex with numerous plant structures spread over an area of 2,000 acres are not analogous to the 'curtilage' of a dwelling for purposes of aerial surveillance; such an industrial complex is more comparable to an open field and as such it is open to the view and observation of persons in aircraft lawfully in the public airspace immediately above or sufficiently near the area for the reach of cameras."

POWELL, J., for the dissenters, objected that "Dow has taken every feasible step to protect information claimed to constitute trade secrets from the public and particularly from its competitors," and accordingly "has a reasonable expectation of privacy in its commercial facility in the sense required by the Fourth Amend-

---

Knotts, Karo, and the Questions Still Unanswered, 34 Cath.U.L.Rev. 277 (1985).

e. Note, 10 Stan.L. & Pol'y Rev. 103, 104 (1998).

6. The partial dissent emphasizes Dow's claim that under magnification power lines as small as ½-inch diameter can be observed. But a glance at the photographs in issue shows that those power lines are observable only because of their stark contrast with the snow-white background. No objects as small as ½—inch diameter such as a class ring, for example, are

recognizable, nor are there any identifiable human faces or secret documents captured in such a fashion as to implicate more serious privacy concerns. Fourth Amendment cases must be decided on the facts of each case, not by extravagant generalizations. "[W]e have never held that potential, as opposed to actual, invasions of privacy constitute searches for purposes of the Fourth Amendment." *United States v. Karo*, [p. 156]. On these facts, nothing in these photographs suggests that any reasonable expectations of privacy have been infringed.

ment." Moreover, the rationale of *Ciraolo*, [p. 142], is inapplicable here, for "the camera used in this case was highly sophisticated in terms of its capability to reveal minute details of Dow's confidential technology and equipment. The District Court found that the photographs revealed details as 'small as ½ inch in diameter.' Satellite photography hardly could have been more informative about Dow's technology. Nor are 'members of the public' likely to purchase $22,000.00 cameras."

7. *Enclosed space detection system.* "The ESDS, or heartbeat detector, is a surveillance tool designed to detect the presence of people 'hiding in enclosed spaces of vehicles' by identifying the presence of a 'human ballistocardiogram.' With each beat of the human heart, a ballistocardiogram or a small mechanical shock wave propagates through the body. This shock wave, in turn, causes the entire vehicle holding the person to vibrate 'at a frequency dissimilar from any other source.'

"The heart's ability to move an entire vehicle, even a big truck, provides law enforcement with a previously unavailable window through which to view the contents of vehicles passing at various checkpoints. Officers can merely require known occupants to turn off the engine and exit the vehicle. Then, such officers temporarily can place 'sensitive seismic geophones' on the 'roof, bumper, or other flat surface' of the vehicle. When a heartbeat's vibrations move a weight suspended in an electromagnetic field of a geophone, the reaction generates an electrical signal. This signal then transmits to a computer that determines whether a beating heart concealed within the vehicle caused the small vibrations." George M. Dery, *The Loss of Privacy is Just a Heartbeat Away: An Exploration of Government Heartbeat Detection Technology and Its Impact on Fourth Amendment Protections*, 7 Wm. & Mary Bill Rts. J. 401, 403–04 (1999). Does detection of a person in this way sometimes/always not constitute a search because, as stated id. at 424, "the heartbeat detector is as limited as a canine sniff both in manner of obtaining facts and in the content of the information it reveals."

8. *CRT Microspy.* "Due to the electromagnetic nature of computer equipment it is possible to monitor computer activity from a location as remote as five hundred feet with specialized electronic surveillance equipment. Computers, monitors, keyboards, and printers leak electronic signals in all directions in the form of radio frequency energy. A receiver specifically designed for the task can pick up these radio waves and display the captured images on a monitor screen. * * * Computers can be shielded from remote surveillance, but such protection is quite expensive [and thus] it seems unlikely that ordinary computer users would take this precaution, making their computer activity vulnerable to microspy scanning. * * * Computers and their peripherals broadcast radio signals in all directions, just like waves emanating from a stone dropped in water. Also, computer monitors bear an FCC warning alerting users to the fact that they are unintentional radiators."[f] Does the presence of those two factors, similar to those relied upon in denying Fourth Amendment protection to the earlier, unsophisticated cordless telephones, e.g., *State v. Smith*, 438 N.W.2d 571 (Wis.1989), mean that law enforcement use of CRT Microspy to obtain copies of images a person displays on his office or home computer does not constitute a search?

9. *Digital Contraband Detector.* Another "special technique for acquiring otherwise-private computer data * * * is unique because it discovers only 'digital contraband' (that is, 'any computer file that, outside of very specific authorized exceptions, cannot be legally possessed,' such as 'digital videos of child pornography' or 'a "cracked" copy of a commercial program—one that has been illegally modified to remove licensing protection'). Apparently a computer program

---

f. Note, 60 U.M.K.C.L.Rev. 139, 143, 164 (1991).

can be designed to search through any hard drive connected to the Internet for a file matching one already in possession of the person making such a search. Indeed, it even may be possible to run such a search program on a large number of networked hard drives simultaneously. And thus a law enforcement officer who had come into possession of one specific piece of digital contraband might then run a Net-wide search for that very contraband. In doing so, he might 'identify dozens, hundreds, or even thousands of individuals who did have a copy on their computer and for whom he would then have probable cause to request a search warrant.' Such a search, to be sure, 'presents a novel set of characteristics: As part of a dragnet search, individuals' hard drives are searched without their permission and without any particularized cause to believe them guilty, and the search scans through a vast amount of very personal information located within people's offices and homes. At the same time, however, the search has a minimal impact on property, produces no false positives, need not be noticeable, and reveals nothing to officials beyond the identity of some individuals who possess this particular piece of digital contraband.' "[g] Would use of such a computer program constitute a search?

    10. *Facial Character Recognition.* "Although few spectators at last Sunday's Super Bowl were aware of it, surveillance cameras photographed their faces as they filed into Raymond James Stadium. Those images were then relayed instantly by cable to computers that scanned and compared them with images in a police database of criminals and criminal suspects. A Tampa Bay police spokesman described the system as a potentially 'priceless' tool for detecting dangerous individuals and preventing terrorist acts. * * * Citizens do accept surveillance cameras at, say, automated teller machines to help deter robbery and provide a sense of safety. But the Super Bowl snooping represented random surveillance of a huge public event, exploiting not one but two potentially invasive technologies. One is video surveillance, which has become increasingly common throughout American society. The other is what is known as facial character recognition, a technology that allows computers to create and compare digital images using 128 facial characteristics."[h] Is such use of this technology a search, or, as a Tampa councilman said when the police placed three dozen cameras with face-recognition software in a downtown district popular with locals and tourists. is it "no different than having a cop walking around with a mug shot"[i]? What then of what might be called "vehicle character recognition," a digital license plate reader[j] which can read a license plate from 250 feet away and thus identify a vehicle as being at a certain place (e.g., an airport parking lot) at a particular time or as being involved in a videotaped offense (e.g., running a red light)?

    11. *Gas Chromatography* involves using an extremely sensitive filtering machine to break down a gas sample or a liquid mixture into its molecular subcomponents. The sample to be tested is forced through a column, which is a glass tube filled with special filtration material, and a detector attached at the outgoing end of the column records the quantity and concentration of each particular molecular compound contained in the sample. Government-funded product development in recent years has turned GC from simply "a scientific laboratory technique" to one that is also used "on the streets." A law enforcement

    g. SEARCHSZR § 2.6, quoting Note, 105 Yale L.J. 1093 (1996).

    h. *Super Bowl Snooping*, N.Y.Times, Feb. 4, 2001, at § 4, p. 16. There has also been discussion of using such equipment at airport checkins, with the cameras linked to a database of potential terrorists. Barnaby J. Feder, *Exploring Technology to Protect Passengers* *With Fingerprint or Retina Scans*, N.Y. Times, Sept. 19, 2001, at B3.

    i. Dana Canedy, *TV Cameras Seek Criminals in Tampa's Crowds*, N.Y.Times, July 4, 2001, at A1.

    j. See Catherine Greenman, *Zeroing In on the Suspicious Number Above the State Motto*, N.Y.Times, Oct. 25, 2001, at D11.

agent can use an eight-pound sampling unit, which resembles a large flashlight and works like a vacuum, to suck in vapors and particles from the immediate vicinity of a suspected container or individual. The analytical unit, also at the scene, then takes this sample and produces a chemical sketch of it, which is then compared to the make-up of known explosives (under one version of the equipment) or drugs (under another). The assumption is that a positive GC report establishes the presence of explosives or drugs, as the case may be, upon the object person or within the object container. Is such use of a portable unit, sometimes characterized as an "electronic canine," governed by the *Place* decision, p. 154? See Bober, *The "Chemical Signature" of the Fourth Amendment: Gas Chromatography/Mass Spectometry and the War on Drugs*, 8 Seton Hall Const.L.J. 75 (1997).

In *Gouled v. United States,* 255 U.S. 298, 41 S.Ct. 261, 65 L.Ed. 647 (1921), the Court held that search warrants "may not be used as a means of gaining access to a man's house or office and papers solely for the purpose of making search to secure evidence to be used against him in a criminal or penal proceeding." The Court derived from *Boyd v. United States,* p. 663, the proposition that warrants may be resorted to "only when a primary right to such search and seizure may be found in the interest which the public or the complainant may have in the property to be seized, or in the right to the possession of it, or when a valid exercise of the police power renders possession of the property by the accused unlawful and provides that it may be taken," that is, when the property is an instrumentality or fruit of crime or contraband. This "mere evidence" rule, as it came to be called, was finally repudiated in *Warden v. Hayden,* 387 U.S. 294, 87 S.Ct. 1642, 18 L.Ed.2d 782 (1967). Stressing that "the principal object of the Fourth Amendment is the protection of privacy rather than property," the Court noted that "privacy 'would be just as well served by a restriction on search to the even-numbered days of the month. * * * And it would have the extra advantage of avoiding hair-splitting questions.' " The government need not have a property interest in the property to be seized, as "government has an interest in solving crime," and that interest and the protection of privacy are best accommodated, the Court reasoned, by merely requiring probable cause that "the evidence sought will aid in a particular apprehension or conviction." But the Court cautioned:

"The items of clothing involved in this case are not 'testimonial' or communicative' in nature, and their introduction therefore did not compel respondent to become a witness against himself in violation of the Fifth Amendment. This case thus does not require that we consider whether there are items of evidential value whose very nature precludes them from being the object of a reasonable search and seizure."

ANDRESEN v. MARYLAND
427 U.S. 463, 96 S.Ct. 2737, 49 L.Ed.2d 627 (1976).

Justice BLACKMUN delivered the opinion of the Court.

[State authorities obtained search warrants to search petitioner's law office and also corporate offices for specified documents pertaining to a fraudulent sale of land. The papers found in the execution of the warrants were admitted against the petitioner at his trial, and he was convicted.]

The Fifth Amendment * * * provides that "[n]o person * * * shall be compelled in any criminal case to be a witness against himself." * * * The "historic function" of the privilege has been to protect a " 'natural individual from compulsory incrimination through his own testimony or personal records.' " There is no question that the records seized from petitioner's offices and introduced against him were incriminating. Moreover, it is undisputed that some of these business records contain statements made by petitioner. The question, therefore, is whether the seizure of these business records, and their admission into evidence at his trial, compelled petitioner to testify against himself in violation of the Fifth Amendment. This question may be said to have been reserved in *Warden v. Hayden*.

Petitioner contends that "the Fifth Amendment prohibition against compulsory self-incrimination applies as well to personal business papers seized from his offices as it does to the same papers being required to be produced under a subpoena." He bases his argument, naturally, on dicta in a number of cases which imply, or state, that the search for and seizure of a person's private papers violate the privilege against self-incrimination. Thus, in *Boyd v. United States* the Court said: "[W]e have been unable to perceive that the seizure of a man's private books and papers to be used in evidence against him is substantially different from compelling him to be a witness against himself." And in *Hale v. Henkel* [p. 669], it was observed that "the substance of the offense is the compulsory production of private papers, whether under a search warrant or a *subpoena duces tecum*, against which the person * * * is entitled to protection."

We do not agree, however, that these broad statements compel suppression of this petitioner's business records as a violation of the Fifth Amendment. In the very recent case of *Fisher v. United States* [p. 706], the Court held that an attorney's production, pursuant to a lawful summons, of his client's tax records in his hands did not violate the Fifth Amendment privilege of the taxpayer "because enforcement against a taxpayer's lawyer would not 'compel' the taxpayer to do anything—and certainly would not compel him to be a 'witness' against himself." We recognized that the continued validity of the broad statements contained in some of the Court's earlier cases had been discredited by later opinions. In those earlier cases, the legal predicate for the inadmissibility of the evidence seized was a violation of the Fourth Amendment; the unlawfulness of the search and seizure was thought to supply the compulsion of the accused necessary to invoke the Fifth Amendment. Compulsion of the accused was also absent in *Couch v. United States*, 409 U.S. 322, 93 S.Ct. 611, 34 L.Ed.2d 548 (1973), where the Court held that a summons served on a taxpayer's accountant requiring him to produce the taxpayer's personal business records in his possession did not violate the taxpayer's Fifth Amendment rights.

Similarly, in this case, petitioner was not asked to say or to do anything. The records seized contained statements that petitioner had voluntarily committed to writing. The search for and seizure of these records were conducted by law enforcement personnel. Finally, when these records were introduced at trial, they were authenticated by a handwriting expert, not by petitioner. Any compulsion of petitioner to speak, other than the inherent psychological pressure to respond at trial to unfavorable evidence, was not present.

This case thus falls within the principle stated by Mr. Justice Holmes: "A party is privileged from producing the evidence but not from its production." * * * Thus, although the Fifth Amendment may protect an individual from complying with a subpoena for the production of his personal records in his possession because the very act of production may constitute a compulsory authentication of incriminating information, a seizure of the same materials by law enforcement officers differs in a crucial respect—the individual against whom the search is directed is not required to aid in the discovery, production, or authentication of incriminating evidence.

A contrary determination that the seizure of a person's business records and their introduction into evidence at a criminal trial violates the Fifth Amendment, would undermine the principles announced in earlier cases. * * * These cases recognize a general rule: "There is no special sanctity in papers, as distinguished from other forms of property, to render them immune from search and seizure, if only they fall within the scope of the principles of the cases in which other property may be seized, and if they be adequately described in the affidavit and warrant."

Moreover, a contrary determination would prohibit the admission of evidence traditionally used in criminal cases and traditionally admissible despite the Fifth Amendment. For example, it would bar the admission of an accused's gambling records in a prosecution for gambling; a note given temporarily to a bank teller during a robbery and subsequently seized in the accused's automobile or home in a prosecution for bank robbery; and incriminating notes prepared, but not sent, by an accused in a kidnapping or blackmail prosecution. * * *

Finally we do not believe that permitting the introduction into evidence of a person's business records seized during an otherwise lawful search would offend or undermine any of the policies undergirding the privilege.

In this case, petitioner, at the time he recorded his communication, at the time of the search, and at the time the records were admitted at trial, was not subjected to "the cruel trilemma of self-accusation, perjury or contempt." Indeed, he was never required to say or to do anything under penalty of sanction. Similarly, permitting the admission of the records in question does not convert our accusatorial system of justice into an inquisitorial system. * * * Further, the search for and seizure of business records pose no danger greater than that inherent in every search that evidence will be "elicited by inhumane treatment and abuses." In this case, the statements seized were voluntarily committed to paper before the police arrived to search for them, and petitioner was not treated discourteously during the search. Also, the "good cause" to "disturb," petitioner was independently determined by the judge who issued the warrants; and the State bore the burden of executing them. Finally, there is no chance in this case, of petitioner's statements being self-deprecatory and untrustworthy because they were extracted from him—they were already in existence and had been made voluntarily. * * *

Justice BRENNAN, dissenting. * * *

The matter cannot be resolved on any simplistic notion of compulsion. Search and seizure is as rife with elements of compulsion as subpoena. The intrusion occurs under the lawful process of the State. The individual is not free to resist that authority. * * *

Until today, no decision by this Court had held that the seizure of testimonial evidence by legal process did not violate the Fifth Amendment. Indeed, with few exceptions, the indications were strongly to the contrary. * * * These cases all reflect the root understanding of *Boyd v. United States:* "It is not the breaking of his doors, and the rummaging of his drawers, that constitutes the essence of the offence [to the Fifth Amendment]; but it is the invasion of his indefeasible right of personal security, personal liberty and private property. * * * [A]ny forcible and compulsory extortion of a man's own testimony or his private papers to be used as evidence to convict him of crime * * *, is within the condemnation of [the Amendment]. In this regard the fourth and fifth amendments run almost into each other."[a]

---

a. Marshall, J., dissented on other grounds and thus found it unnecessary to reach the   Fifth Amendment issue.

Notes and Questions

1. If the item to be seized was a diary instead of the business records in *Andresen,* would there be a stronger Fourth Amendment[b] or Fifth Amendment[c] argument against permitting the seizure? Consider *Model Pre–Arraignment Code* § SS 210.3(2): "With the exception of handwriting samples, and other writings or recordings of evidentiary value for reasons other than their testimonial content, things subject to seizure * * * shall not include personal diaries, letters, or other writings or recordings, made solely for private use or communication to an individual occupying a family, personal, or other confidential relation, other than a relation in criminal enterprise, unless such things have served or are serving a substantial purpose in furtherance of a criminal enterprise."

2. In ZURCHER v. STANFORD DAILY, 436 U.S. 547, 98 S.Ct. 1970, 56 L.Ed.2d 525 (1978), police obtained and executed a warrant to search the offices of the Stanford Daily for negatives, film and pictures relevant to identification of those who had injured nine policemen during a campus demonstration. The Daily later brought a civil action in federal district court, where declaratory relief was granted. That court held (i) that the Fourth Amendment forbade the issuance of a warrant to search for materials in the possession of one not suspected of crime except upon a showing of probable cause a subpoena *duces tecum* would be impracticable; and (ii) that the First Amendment bars search of newspaper offices except upon a clear showing that important materials would otherwise be destroyed or removed and that a restraining order would be futile.

The Supreme Court, per WHITE, J., concluded that "it is untenable to conclude that property may not be searched unless its occupant is reasonably suspected of crime and is subject to arrest. * * * The Fourth Amendment has itself struck the balance between privacy and public need, and there is no occasion or justification for a court to revise the Amendment and strike a new balance by denying the search warrant in the circumstances present here and by insisting that the investigation proceed by subpoena *duces tecum,* whether on the theory that the latter is a less intrusive alternative, or otherwise. * * *

"In any event, the reasons presented by the District Court and adopted by the Court of Appeals for arriving at its remarkable conclusion do not withstand analysis. First, as we have said, it is apparent that whether the third-party occupant is suspect or not, the State's interest in enforcing the criminal law and recovering the evidence remains the same; and it is the seeming innocence of the property owner that the District Court relied on to foreclose the warrant to search. But as respondents themselves now concede, if the third party knows that contraband or other illegal materials are on his property, he is sufficiently culpable to justify the issuance of a search warrant. Similarly, if his ethical stance is the determining factor, it seems to us that whether or not he knows that the sought-after articles are secreted on his property and whether or not he knows that the articles are in fact the fruits, instrumentalities, or evidence of crime, he will be so informed when the search warrant is served, and it is doubtful that he should then be permitted to object to the search, to withhold, if it is there, the

---

b. In *Fisher,* relied upon in *Andresen,* the Court, after stating that the taxpayers "have not raised arguments of a Fourth Amendment nature * * * and could not be successful if they had," cautioned that the "[s]pecial problems of privacy which might be presented by subpoena of a personal diary * * * are not involved here." See also n. 7 on p. 707.

c. "[I]t has been thought that a diary in which its author has recited his criminal conduct, seized in an otherwise lawful search, should not be used against him, just as any other kind of involuntary confession is unusable under the Fifth Amendment." *United States v. Boyette,* 299 F.2d 92 (4th Cir.1962).

evidence of crime reasonably believed to be possessed by him or secreted on his property, and to forbid the search and insist that the officers serve him with a subpoena *duces tecum.*

"Second, we are unpersuaded that the District Court's new rule denying search warrants against third parties and insisting on subpoenas would substantially further privacy interests without seriously undermining law enforcement efforts. As the District Court understands it, denying third-party search warrants would not have substantial adverse effects on criminal investigations because the nonsuspect third party, once served with a subpoena, will preserve the evidence and ultimately, lawfully respond. The difficulty with this assumption is that search warrants are often employed early in an investigation, perhaps before the identity of any likely criminal and certainly before all the perpetrators are or could be known. The seemingly blameless third party in possession of the fruits or evidence may not be innocent at all; and if he is, he may nevertheless be so related to or so sympathetic with the culpable that he cannot be relied upon to retain and preserve the articles that may implicate his friends, or at least not to notify those who would be damaged by the evidence that the authorities are aware of its location. In any event, it is likely that the real culprits will have access to the property, and the delay involved in employing the subpoena *duces tecum,* offering as it does the opportunity to litigate its validity, could easily result in the disappearance of the evidence, whatever the good faith of the third party. * * *[8]

"We are also not convinced that the net gain to privacy interests by the District Court's new rule would be worth the candle.[9] In the normal course of events, search warrants are more difficult to obtain than subpoenas, since the latter do not involve the judiciary and do not require proof of probable cause. Where, in the real world, subpoenas would suffice, it can be expected that they will be employed by the rational prosecutor. On the other hand, when choice is available under local law and the prosecutor chooses to use the search warrant, it is unlikely that he has needlessly selected the more difficult course. His choice is more likely to be based on the solid belief, arrived at through experience but difficult, if not impossible, to sustain a specific case, that the warranted search is necessary to secure and to avoid the destruction of evidence.

"[The Framers] did not forbid warrants where the press was involved, did not require special showings that subpoenas would be impractical, and did not insist that the owner of the place to be searched, if connected with the press, must be

---

8. It is also far from clear, even apart from the dangers of destruction and removal, whether the use of the subpoena *duces tecum* under circumstances where there is probable cause to believe that a crime has been committed and that the materials sought constitute evidence of its commission will result in the production of evidence with sufficient regularity to satisfy the public interest in law enforcement. Unlike the individual whose privacy is invaded by a search, the recipient of a subpoena may assert the Fifth Amendment privilege against self-incrimination in response to a summons to produce evidence or give testimony. See *Maness v. Meyers,* 419 U.S. 449, 95 S.Ct. 584, 42 L.Ed.2d 574 (1975). This privilege is not restricted to suspects. We have construed it broadly as covering any individual who might be incriminated by the evidence in connection with which the privilege is asserted. *Hoffman v. United States,* 341 U.S. 479, 71 S.Ct. 814, 95 L.Ed. 1118 (1951). The burden of overcoming an assertion of the Fifth Amendment privilege,

even if prompted by a desire not to cooperate rather than any real fear of self-incrimination, is one which prosecutors would rarely be able to meet in the early stages of an investigation despite the fact they did not regard the witness as a suspect. Even time spent litigating such matters could seriously impede criminal investigations.

9. We reject totally the reasoning of the District Court that additional protections are required to assure that the Fourth Amendment rights of third parties are not violated because of the unavailability of the exclusionary rule as a deterrent to improper searches of premises in the control of nonsuspects. * * * It is probably seldom that police during the investigatory stage when most searches occur will be so convinced that no potential defendant will have standing to exclude evidence on Fourth Amendment grounds that they will feel free to ignore constitutional restraints. * * *

shown to be implicated in the offense being investigated. Further, the prior cases do no more than insist that the courts apply the warrant requirements with particular exactitude when First Amendment interests would be endangered by the search.[d] As we see it, no more than this is required where the warrant requested is for the seizure of criminal evidence reasonably believed to be on the premises occupied by a newspaper. Properly administered, the pre-conditions for a warrant—probable cause, specificity with respect to the place to be searched and the things to be seized, and overall reasonableness—should afford sufficient protection against the harms that are assertedly threatened by warrants for searching newspaper offices."

Justices STEWART and Marshall, dissenting, raised a First Amendment objection because of the "serious burden on a free press imposed by an unannounced police search of a newspaper office: the possibility of disclosure of information received from confidential sources, or of the identity of the sources themselves. Protection of those sources is necessary to ensure that the press can fulfill its constitutionally designated function of informing the public, because important information can often be obtained only by an assurance that the source will not be revealed.

Justice STEVENS, dissenting, raised a Fourth Amendment objection, namely, that a "showing of probable cause that was adequate to justify the issuance of a warrant to search for stolen goods in the 18th century does not automatically satisfy the new dimensions of the Fourth Amendment in the post-*Hayden* era. * * * The only conceivable justification for an unannounced search of an innocent citizen is the fear that, if notice were given, he would conceal or destroy the object of the search. Probable cause to believe that the custodian is a criminal, or that he holds a criminal's weapons, spoils, or the like, justifies that fear, and therefore such a showing complies with the Clause. But if nothing said under oath in the warrant application demonstrates the need for an unannounced search by force, the probable cause requirement is not satisfied. In the absence of some other showing of reasonableness, the ensuing search violates the Fourth Amendment."

3. Compare *O'Connor v. Johnson*, 287 N.W.2d 400 (Minn.1979), involving a warrant issued for an attorney's office to search for and seize a certain client's business records: "Even the most particular warrant cannot adequately safeguard client confidentiality, the attorney-client privilege, the attorney's work product, and the criminal defendant's constitutional right to counsel of all of the attorney's clients. It is unreasonable, in any case, to permit law enforcement officers to peruse miscellaneous documents in an attorney's office while attempting to locate documents listed in a search warrant. Even if it were possible to meet the particularity requirement regarding the place to be searched, the file would still contain some confidential information that is immune from seizure under the attorney-client privilege or the work product doctrine. Once that information is

---

d. This does *not* mean, the Court later held in *New York v. P.J. Video, Inc.*, 475 U.S. 868, 106 S.Ct. 1610, 89 L.Ed.2d 871 (1986), that a higher probable cause standard applies in such cases. The Court deemed sufficient "the long-standing special protections" established in its earlier cases, namely: (a) "that the police may not rely on the 'exigency' exception to the Fourth Amendment's warrant requirement in conducting a seizure of allegedly obscene materials, under circumstances where such a seizure would effectively constitute a 'prior restraint' "; (b) "that the large-scale seizure of books or films constituting a 'prior restraint'

must be preceded by an adversary hearing on the question of obscenity"; (c) "that, even where a seizure of allegedly obscene materials would not constitute a 'prior restraint,' but instead would merely preserve evidence for trial, the seizure must be made pursuant to a warrant and there must be an opportunity for a prompt post-seizure judicial determination of obscenity"; and (d) "that a warrant authorizing the seizure of materials presumptively protected by the First Amendment may not issue based solely on the conclusory allegations of a police officer that the sought-after materials are obscene."

revealed to the police, the privileges are lost, and the information cannot be erased from the minds of the police. * * *

"It will not unreasonably burden prosecutors' offices and effective law enforcement to require officers to proceed by subpoena duces tecum in seeking documents held by an attorney. Attorneys are required by statute, the Code of Professional Responsibility, and the oath of admission to the bar to preserve and protect the judicial process. Thus, attorneys must respond faithfully and promptly, while still being allowed the opportunity to assert applicable privileges by a motion to quash."

4. It is noted in 67 A.B.A.J. 33 (1981) "that California's legislative response to the problem of surprise searches of offices of 'privilege-holders' may serve as a model for other states. The law calls for appointment of a special master to spearhead the search. * * *

"The California solution hasn't satisfied everyone, however. John Cleary, head of the federal public defender office in San Diego, said the law is 'unhealthy. There is an illusion of protection.' Robert Philibosian, chief assistant California attorney general, said: 'We vigorously opposed [the law].' He said it impairs law enforcement, especially in the white-collar crime area: 'We have to jump through hoops [to obtain evidence].' "[e]

5. Compare *Model Pre–Arraignment Code* §§ 220.5(2) & (3) providing that if the documents to be seized "cannot be searched for or identified without examining the contents of other documents, or if they constitute items or entries in account books, diaries, or other documents containing matter not specified in the warrant, the executing officer shall not examine the documents but shall either impound them under appropriate protection where found, or seal and remove them for safekeeping pending further proceedings." At a later adversary judicial hearing, a motion may be made for return of the documents or for "specification of such conditions and limitations on the further search for the documents to be seized as may be appropriate to prevent unnecessary or unreasonable invasion of privacy." If return is not ordered, "the search shall proceed under such conditions and limitations as the order shall prescribe."

SECTION 3. "PROBABLE CAUSE"

SPINELLI v. UNITED STATES
393 U.S. 410, 89 S.Ct. 584, 21 L.Ed.2d 637 (1969).

Justice HARLAN delivered the opinion of the Court.

William Spinelli was convicted * * of traveling to St. Louis, Missouri, from a nearby Illinois suburb with the intention of conducting gambling activities proscribed by Missouri law. At every appropriate stage in the proceedings in the lower courts, the petitioner challenged the constitutionality of the warrant which authorized the FBI search that uncovered the evidence necessary for his conviction. * * * Believing it desirable that the principles of [*Aguilar v. Texas*, 378 U.S. 108, 84 S.Ct. 1509, 12 L.Ed.2d 723 (1964)] should be further explicated, we granted certiorari * * *.

In *Aguilar,* a search warrant had issued upon an affidavit of police officers who swore only that they had "received reliable information from a credible person and do believe" that narcotics were being illegally stored on the described

e. See Ronald Goldstock & Steven Chananie, *"Criminal" Lawyers: The Use of Electronic Surveillance and Search Warrants in the Investigation and Prosecution of Attorneys Suspected of Criminal Wrongdoing,* 136 U.Pa.L.Rev. 1855 (1988).

premises. While recognizing that the constitutional requirement of probable cause can be satisfied by hearsay information, this Court held the affidavit inadequate for two reasons. First, the application failed to set forth any of the "underlying circumstances" necessary to enable the magistrate independently to judge of the validity of the informant's conclusion that the narcotics were where he said they were. Second, the affiant-officers did not attempt to support their claim that their informant was " 'credible' or his information 'reliable.' " The Government is, however, quite right in saying that the FBI affidavit in the present case is more ample than that in *Aguilar*. Not only does it contain a report from an anonymous informant, but it also contains a report of an independent FBI investigation which is said to corroborate the informant's tip. We are, then, required to delineate the manner in which *Aguilar's* two-pronged test should be applied in these circumstances.

In essence, the affidavit * * * contained the following allegations:

1. The FBI had kept track of Spinelli's movements on five days during the month of August 1965. On four of these occasions, Spinelli was seen crossing one of two bridges leading from Illinois into St. Louis, Missouri, between 11 a.m. and 12:15 p.m. On four of the five days, Spinelli was also seen parking his car in a lot used by residents of an apartment house at 1108 Indian Circle Drive in St. Louis, between 3:30 p.m. and 4:45 p.m. On one day, Spinelli was followed further and seen to enter a particular apartment in the building.

2. An FBI check with the telephone company revealed that this apartment contained two telephones listed under the name of Grace P. Hagen, and carrying the numbers WYdown 4–0029 and WYdown 4–0136.

3. The application stated that "William Spinelli is known to this affiant and to federal law enforcement agents and local law enforcement agents as a bookmaker, an associate of bookmakers, a gambler, and an associate of gamblers."

4. Finally, it was stated that the FBI "has been informed by a confidential reliable informant that William Spinelli is operating a handbook and accepting wagers and disseminating wagering information by means of the telephones which have been assigned the numbers WYdown 4–0029 and WYdown 4–0136."

There can be no question that the last item mentioned, detailing the informant's tip, has a fundamental place in this warrant application. Without it, probable cause could not be established. The first two items reflect only innocent-seeming activity and data. Spinelli's travels to and from the apartment building and his entry into a particular apartment on one occasion could hardly be taken as bespeaking gambling activity; and there is surely nothing unusual about an apartment containing two separate telephones. Many a householder indulges himself in this petty luxury. Finally, the allegation that Spinelli was "known" to the affiant and to other federal and local law enforcement officers as a gambler and an associate of gamblers is but a bald and unilluminating assertion of suspicion that is entitled to no weight in appraising the magistrate's decision. *Nathanson v. United States*, 290 U.S. 41, 46, 54 S.Ct. 11, 12, 78 L.Ed. 159 (1933).

So much indeed the Government does not deny. Rather, following the reasoning of the Court of Appeals, the Government claims that the informant's tip gives a suspicious color to the FBI's reports detailing Spinelli's innocent-seeming conduct and that, conversely, the FBI's surveillance corroborates the informant's tip, thereby entitling it to more weight. * * * We believe, however, that the "totality of circumstances" approach taken by the Court of Appeals paints with too broad a brush. Where, as here, the informer's tip is a necessary element in a finding of probable cause, its proper weight must be determined by a more precise analysis.

The informer's report must first be measured against *Aguilar's* standards so that its probative value can be assessed. If the tip is found inadequate under *Aguilar,* the other allegations which corroborate the information contained in the hearsay report should then be considered. At this stage as well, however, the standards enunciated in *Aguilar* must inform the magistrate's decision. He must ask: Can it fairly be said that the tip, even when certain parts of it have been corroborated by independent sources, is as trustworthy as a tip which would pass *Aguilar's* tests without independent corroboration? * * *

I

Applying these principles to the present case, we first consider the weight to be given the informer's tip when it is considered apart from the rest of the affidavit. It is clear that a Commissioner could not credit it without abdicating his constitutional function. Though the affiant swore that his confidant was "reliable," he offered the magistrate no reason in support of this conclusion. Perhaps even more important is the fact that *Aguilar's* other test has not been satisfied. The tip does not contain a sufficient statement of the underlying circumstances from which the informer concluded that Spinelli was running a bookmaking operation. We are not told how the FBI's source received his information—it is not alleged that the informant personally observed Spinelli at work or that he had ever placed a bet with him. Moreover, if the informant came by the information indirectly, he did not explain why his sources were reliable. In the absence of a statement detailing the manner in which the information was gathered, it is especially important that the tip describe the accused's criminal activity in sufficient detail so that the magistrate may know that he is relying on something more substantial than a casual rumor circulating in the underworld or an accusation based merely on an individual's general reputation.

tip needs to be detailed

The detail provided by the informant in *Draper v. United States,* 358 U.S. 307, 79 S.Ct. 329, 3 L.Ed.2d 327 (1959), provides a suitable benchmark. While Hereford, the FBI's informer in that case, did not state the way in which he had obtained his information, he reported that Draper had gone to Chicago the day before by train and that he would return to Denver by train with three ounces of heroin on one of two specified mornings. Moreover, Hereford went on to describe, with minute particularity, the clothes that Draper would be wearing upon his arrival at the Denver station. A magistrate, when confronted with such detail, could reasonably infer that the informant had gained his information in a reliable way. Such an inference cannot be made in the present case. Here, the only facts supplied were that Spinelli was using two specified telephones and that these phones were being used in gambling operations. This meager report could easily have been obtained from an off-hand remark heard at a neighborhood bar.

Compare to Draper

Draper tip much more detailed

Nor do we believe that the patent doubts *Aguilar* raises as to the report's reliability are adequately resolved by a consideration of the allegations detailing the FBI's independent investigative efforts. At most, these allegations indicated that Spinelli could have used the telephones specified by the informant for some purpose. This cannot by itself be said to support both the inference that the informer was generally trustworthy and that he had made his charge against Spinelli on the basis of information obtained in a reliable way. Once again, *Draper* provides a relevant comparison. Independent police work in that case corroborated much more than one small detail that had been provided by the informant. There, the police, upon greeting the inbound Denver train on the second morning specified by informer Hereford, saw a man whose dress corresponded precisely to Hereford's detailed description. It was then apparent that the informant had not been fabricating his report out of whole cloth; since the report was of the sort which in common experience may be recognized as having been obtained in a reliable way, it was perfectly clear that probable cause had been established.

the phones from tip could have been used for some other purpose

We conclude, then, that in the present case the informant's tip—even when corroborated to the extent indicated—was not sufficient to provide the basis for a finding of probable cause. * * *

The judgment of the Court of Appeals is reversed * * *.

Justice WHITE, concurring. * * *

The tension between *Draper* and the *Nathanson-Aguilar* line of cases is evident from the course followed by the majority opinion. * * * Since [the informant's] specific information about Spinelli using two phones with particular numbers had been verified, did not his allegation about gambling thereby become sufficiently more believable if the *Draper* principle is to be given any scope at all? I would think so, particularly since the information from the informant which was verified was not neutral, irrelevant information but was material to proving the gambling allegation: two phones with different numbers in an apartment used away from home indicates a business use in an operation, like bookmaking, where multiple phones are needed. The *Draper* approach would reasonably justify the issuance of a warrant in this case, particularly since the police had some awareness of Spinelli's past activities. The majority, however, while seemingly embracing *Draper*, confines that case to its own facts. Pending full scale reconsideration of that case, on the one hand, or of the *Nathanson-Aguilar* cases on the other, I join the opinion of the Court and the judgment of reversal especially since a vote to affirm would produce an equally divided Court.[a]

ILLINOIS v. GATES

462 U.S. 213, 103 S.Ct. 2317, 76 L.Ed.2d 527 (1983).

Justice REHNQUIST delivered the opinion of the Court.

* * * A chronological statement of events usefully introduces the issues at stake. Bloomingdale, Ill., is a suburb of Chicago located in DuPage County. On May 3, 1978, the Bloomingdale Police Department received by mail an anonymous handwritten letter which read as follows:

> "This letter is to inform you that you have a couple in your town who strictly make their living on selling drugs. They are Sue and Lance Gates, they live on Greenway, off Bloomingdale Rd. in the condominiums. Most of their buys are done in Florida. Sue his wife drives their car to Florida, where she leaves it to be loaded up with drugs, then Lance flys down and drives it back. Sue flys back after she drops the car off in Florida. May 3 she is driving down there again and Lance will be flying down in a few days to drive it back. At the time Lance drives the car back he has the trunk loaded with over $100,000.00 in drugs. Presently they have over $100,000.00 worth of drugs in their basement.

> "They brag about the fact they never have to work, and make their entire living on pushers.

> "I guarantee if you watch them carefully you will make a big catch. They are friends with some big drugs dealers, who visit their house often. * * * "

The letter was referred by the Chief of Police of the Bloomingdale Police Department to Detective Mader, who decided to pursue the tip. Mader learned, from the office of the Illinois Secretary of State, that an Illinois driver's license had been issued to one Lance Gates, residing at a stated address in Bloomingdale.

a. Black, Fortas, and Stewart, JJ., dissent-   case.
ed separately; Marshall, J., took no part in the

He contacted a confidential informant, whose examination of certain financial records revealed a more recent address for the Gates, and he also learned from a police officer assigned to O'Hare Airport that "L. Gates" had made a reservation on Eastern Airlines flight 245 to West Palm Beach, Fla., scheduled to depart from Chicago on May 5 at 4:15 p.m.

Mader then made arrangements with an agent of the Drug Enforcement Administration for surveillance of the May 5 Eastern Airlines flight. The agent later reported to Mader that Gates had boarded the flight, and that federal agents in Florida had observed him arrive in West Palm Beach and take a taxi to the nearby Holiday Inn. They also reported that Gates went to a room registered to one Susan Gates and that, at 7:00 a.m. the next morning, Gates and an unidentified woman left the motel in a Mercury bearing Illinois license plates and drove northbound on an interstate frequently used by travelers to the Chicago area. In addition, the DEA agent informed Mader that the license plate number on the Mercury registered to a Hornet station wagon owned by Gates. The agent also advised Mader that the driving time between West Palm Beach and Bloomingdale was approximately 22 to 24 hours.

Mader signed an affidavit setting forth the foregoing facts, and submitted it to a judge of the Circuit Court of DuPage County, together with a copy of the anonymous letter. The judge of that court thereupon issued a search warrant for the Gates' residence and for their automobile. The judge, in deciding to issue the warrant, could have determined that the *modus operandi* of the Gates had been substantially corroborated. As the anonymous letter predicted, Lance Gates had flown from Chicago to West Palm Beach late in the afternoon of May 5th, had checked into a hotel room registered in the name of his wife, and, at 7:00 a.m. the following morning, had headed north, accompanied by an unidentified woman, out of West Palm Beach on an interstate highway used by travelers from South Florida to Chicago in an automobile bearing a license plate issued to him.

At 5:15 a.m. on May 7th, only 36 hours after he had flown out of Chicago, Lance Gates, and his wife, returned to their home in Bloomingdale, driving the car in which they had left West Palm Beach some 22 hours earlier. The Bloomingdale police were awaiting them, searched the trunk of the Mercury, and uncovered approximately 350 pounds of marijuana. A search of the Gates' home revealed marijuana, weapons, and other contraband. The Illinois Circuit Court ordered suppression of all these items, on the ground that the affidavit submitted to the Circuit Judge failed to support the necessary determination of probable cause to believe that the Gates' automobile and home contained the contraband in question. This decision was affirmed in turn by the Illinois Appellate Court and by a divided vote of the Supreme Court of Illinois.

The Illinois Supreme Court concluded—and we are inclined to agree—that, standing alone, the anonymous letter sent to the Bloomingdale Police Department would not provide the basis for a magistrate's determination that there was probable cause to believe contraband would be found in the Gates' car and home. The letter provides virtually nothing from which one might conclude that its author is either honest or his information reliable; likewise, the letter gives absolutely no indication of the basis for the writer's predictions regarding the Gates' criminal activities. Something more was required, then, before a magistrate could conclude that there was probable cause to believe that contraband would be found in the Gates' home and car.

The Illinois Supreme Court also properly recognized that Detective Mader's affidavit might be capable of supplementing the anonymous letter with information sufficient to permit a determination of probable cause. In holding that the affidavit in fact did not contain sufficient additional information to sustain a

Ch. 5 GATES 171

determination of probable cause, the Illinois court applied a "two-pronged test," derived from our decision in *Spinelli v. United States.* The Illinois Supreme Court, like some others, apparently understood *Spinelli* as requiring that the anonymous letter satisfy each of two independent requirements before it could be relied on. According to this view, the letter, as supplemented by Mader's affidavit, first had to adequately reveal the "basis of knowledge" of the letter writer—the particular means by which he came by the information given in his report. Second, it had to provide facts sufficiently establishing either the "veracity" of the affiant's informant, or, alternatively, the "reliability" of the informant's report in this particular case.

The Illinois court, alluding to an elaborate set of legal rules that have developed among various lower courts to enforce the "two-pronged test,"[4] found that the test had not been satisfied. First, the "veracity" prong was not satisfied because, "there was simply no basis [for] * * * conclud[ing] that the anonymous person [who wrote the letter to the Bloomingdale Police Department] was credible." The court indicated that corroboration by police of details contained in the letter might never satisfy the "veracity" prong, and in any event, could not do so if, as in the present case, only "innocent" details are corroborated. In addition, the letter gave no indication of the basis of its writer's knowledge of the Gates' activities. The Illinois court understood *Spinelli* as permitting the detail contained in a tip to be used to infer that the informant had a reliable basis for his statements, but it thought that the anonymous letter failed to provide sufficient detail to permit such an inference. Thus, it concluded that no showing of probable cause had been made.

We agree with the Illinois Supreme Court that an informant's "veracity," "reliability" and "basis of knowledge" are all highly relevant in determining the value of his report. We do not agree, however, that these elements should be understood as entirely separate and independent requirements to be rigidly exacted in every case, which the opinion of the Supreme Court of Illinois would imply. Rather, as detailed below, they should be understood simply as closely intertwined issues that may usefully illuminate the common sense, practical question whether there is "probable cause" to believe that contraband or evidence is located in a particular place.

This totality of the circumstances approach is far more consistent with our prior treatment of probable cause than is any rigid demand that specific "tests" be satisfied by every informant's tip. Perhaps the central teaching of our decisions bearing on the probable cause standard is that it is a "practical, nontechnical conception." *Brinegar v. United States,* 338 U.S. 160, 69 S.Ct. 1302, 93 L.Ed. 1879 (1949). "In dealing with probable cause, * * * as the very name implies, we deal with probabilities. These are not technical; they are the factual and practical considerations of everyday life on which reasonable and prudent men, not legal technicians, act." Our observation in *United States v. Cortez,* [p. 306], regarding "particularized suspicion," is also applicable to the probable cause standard:

> The process does not deal with hard certainties, but with probabilities. Long before the law of probabilities was articulated as such, practical people

4. In summary, these rules posit that the "veracity" prong of the *Spinelli* test has two "spurs"—the informant's "credibility" and the "reliability" of his information. Various interpretations are advanced for the meaning of the "reliability" spur of the "veracity" prong. Both the "basis of knowledge" prong and the "veracity" prong are treated as entirely separate requirements, which must be independently satisfied in every case in order to sustain a determination of probable cause. Some ancillary doctrines are relied on to satisfy certain of the foregoing requirements. For example, the "self-verifying detail" of a tip may satisfy the "basis of knowledge" requirement, although not the "credibility" spur of the "veracity" prong. Conversely, corroboration would seem not capable of supporting the "basis of knowledge" prong, but only the "veracity" prong. * * *

formulated certain common-sense conclusions about human behavior; jurors as factfinders are permitted to do the same—and so are law enforcement officers. Finally, the evidence thus collected must be seen and weighed not in terms of library analysis by scholars, but as understood by those versed in the field of law enforcement.

As these comments illustrate, probable cause is a fluid concept—turning on the assessment of probabilities in particular factual contexts—not readily, or even usefully, reduced to a neat set of legal rules. Informants' tips doubtless come in many shapes and sizes from many different types of persons. * * * Rigid legal rules are ill-suited to an area of such diversity. "One simple rule will not cover every situation."[7]

Moreover, the "two-pronged test" directs analysis into two largely independent channels—the informant's "veracity" or "reliability" and his "basis of knowledge." There are persuasive arguments against according these two elements such independent status. Instead, they are better understood as relevant considerations in the totality of circumstances analysis that traditionally has guided probable cause determinations: a deficiency in one may be compensated for, in determining the overall reliability of a tip, by a strong showing as to the other, or by some other indicia of reliability.

If, for example, a particular informant is known for the unusual reliability of his predictions of certain types of criminal activities in a locality, his failure, in a particular case, to thoroughly set forth the basis of his knowledge surely should not serve as an absolute bar to a finding of probable cause based on his tip. Likewise, if an unquestionably honest citizen comes forward with a report of criminal activity—which if fabricated would subject him to criminal liability—we have found rigorous scrutiny of the basis of his knowledge unnecessary. Conversely, even if we entertain some doubt as to an informant's motives, his explicit and detailed description of alleged wrongdoing, along with a statement that the event

---

7. The diversity of informants' tips, as well as the usefulness of the totality of the circumstances approach to probable cause, is reflected in our prior decisions on the subject. In *Jones v. United States,* 362 U.S. 257, 80 S.Ct. 725, 4 L.Ed.2d 697 (1960), we held that probable cause to search petitioners' apartment was established by an affidavit based principally on an informant's tip. The unnamed informant claimed to have purchased narcotics from petitioners at their apartment; the affiant stated that he had been given correct information from the informant on a prior occasion. This, and the fact that petitioners had admitted to police officers on another occasion that they were narcotics users, sufficed to support the magistrate's determination of probable cause.

Likewise, in *Rugendorf v. United States,* 376 U.S. 528, 84 S.Ct. 825, 11 L.Ed.2d 887 (1964), the Court upheld a magistrate's determination that there was probable cause to believe that certain stolen property would be found in petitioner's apartment. The affidavit submitted to the magistrate stated that certain furs had been stolen, and that a confidential informant, who previously had furnished confidential information, said that he saw the furs in petitioner's home. Moreover, another confidential informant, also claimed to be reliable, stated that one Schweihs had stolen the furs. Police

reports indicated that petitioner had been seen in Schweihs' company and a third informant stated that petitioner was a fence for Schweihs.

Finally, in *Ker v. California,* 374 U.S. 23, 83 S.Ct. 1623, 10 L.Ed.2d 726 (1963), we held that information within the knowledge of officers who searched the Ker's apartment provided them with probable cause to believe drugs would be found there. The officers were aware that one Murphy had previously sold marijuana to a police officer; the transaction had occurred in an isolated area, to which Murphy had led the police. The night after this transaction, police observed Ker and Murphy meet in the same location. Murphy approached Ker's car, and, although police could see nothing change hands, Murphy's *modus operandi* was identical to what it had been the night before. Moreover, when police followed Ker from the scene of the meeting with Murphy he managed to lose them after performing an abrupt U-turn. Finally, the police had a statement from an informant who had provided reliable information previously, that Ker was engaged in selling marijuana, and that his source was Murphy. We concluded that "To say that this coincidence of information was sufficient to support a reasonable belief of the officers that Ker was illegally in possession of marijuana is to indulge in understatement."

was observed first-hand, entitles his tip to greater weight than might otherwise be the case. Unlike a totality of circumstances analysis, which permits a balanced assessment of the relative weights of all the various indicia of reliability (and unreliability) attending an informant's tip, the "two-pronged test" has encouraged an excessively technical dissection of informants' tips, with undue attention being focused on isolated issues that cannot sensibly be divorced from the other facts presented to the magistrate. * * *

We also have recognized that affidavits "are normally drafted by non-lawyers in the midst and haste of a criminal investigation. Technical requirements of elaborate specificity once exacted under common law pleading have no proper place in this area." Likewise, search and arrest warrants long have been issued by persons who are neither lawyers nor judges, and who certainly do not remain abreast of each judicial refinement of the nature of "probable cause." The rigorous inquiry into the *Spinelli* prongs and the complex superstructure of evidentiary and analytical rules that some have seen implicit in our *Spinelli* decision, cannot be reconciled with the fact that many warrants are—quite properly—issued on the basis of nontechnical, common-sense judgments of laymen applying a standard less demanding than those used in more formal legal proceedings. Likewise, given the informal, often hurried context in which it must be applied, the "built-in subtleties" of the "two-pronged test" are particularly unlikely to assist magistrates in determining probable cause.

Similarly, we have repeatedly said that after-the-fact scrutiny by courts of the sufficiency of an affidavit should not take the form of *de novo* review. A magistrate's "determination of probable cause should be paid great deference by reviewing courts." "A grudging or negative attitude by reviewing courts toward warrants" is inconsistent with the Fourth Amendment's strong preference for searches conducted pursuant to a warrants; "courts should not invalidate * * * warrant[s] by interpreting affidavit[s] in a hypertechnical, rather than a common-sense, manner."

If the affidavits submitted by police officers are subjected to the type of scrutiny some courts have deemed appropriate, police might well resort to warrantless searches, with the hope of relying on consent or some other exception to the warrant clause that might develop at the time of the search. In addition, the possession of a warrant by officers conducting an arrest or search greatly reduces the perception of unlawful or intrusive police conduct, by assuring "the individual whose property is searched or seized of the lawful authority of the executing officer, his need to search, and the limits of his power to search." Reflecting this preference for the warrant process, the traditional standard for review of an issuing magistrate's probable cause determination has been that so long as the magistrate had a "substantial basis for * * * conclud[ing]" that a search would uncover evidence of wrongdoing, the Fourth Amendment requires no more. We think reaffirmation of this standard better serves the purpose of encouraging recourse to the warrant procedure and is more consistent with our traditional deference to the probable cause determinations of magistrates than is the "two-pronged test."

Finally, the direction taken by decisions following *Spinelli* poorly serves "the most basic function of any government": "to provide for the security of the individual and of his property". The strictures that inevitably accompany the "two-pronged test" cannot avoid seriously impeding the task of law enforcement. If, as the Illinois Supreme Court apparently thought, that test must be rigorously applied in every case, [anonymous tips would be] of greatly diminished value in police work. Ordinary citizens, like ordinary witnesses, generally do not provide extensive recitations of the basis of their everyday observations. Likewise, as the Illinois Supreme Court observed in this case, the veracity of persons supplying anonymous tips is by hypothesis largely unknown, and unknowable. As a result, anonymous tips seldom could survive a rigorous application of either of the *Spinelli* prongs. Yet, such tips, particularly when supplemented by independent police investigation, frequently contribute to the solution of otherwise "perfect crimes." While a conscientious assessment of the basis for crediting such tips is required by the Fourth Amendment, a standard that leaves virtually no place for anonymous citizen informants is not.

For all these reasons, we conclude that it is wiser to abandon the "two-pronged test" established by our decisions in *Aguilar* and *Spinelli*.[11] In its place we reaffirm the totality of the circumstances analysis that traditionally has informed probable cause determinations. The task of the issuing magistrate is simply to make a practical, common-sense decision whether, given all the circumstances set forth in the affidavit before him, including the "veracity" and "basis of knowledge" of persons supplying hearsay information, there is a fair probability that contraband or evidence of a crime will be found in a particular place. And the duty of a reviewing court is simply to ensure that the magistrate had a "substantial basis for * * * conclud[ing]" that probable cause existed. We are convinced that this flexible, easily applied standard will better achieve the accommodation of public and private interests that the Fourth Amendment requires than does the approach that has developed from *Aguilar* and *Spinelli*.

Our earlier cases illustrate the limits beyond which a magistrate may not venture in issuing a warrant. A sworn statement of an affiant that "he has cause to suspect and does believe that" liquor illegally brought into the United States is located on certain premises will not do. *Nathanson v. United States*. An affidavit must provide the magistrate with a substantial basis for determining the existence of probable cause, and the wholly conclusory statement at issue in *Nathanson* failed to meet this requirement. An officer's statement that "affiants have received reliable information from a credible person and believe" that heroin is stored in a home, is likewise inadequate. *Aguilar v. Texas*. As in *Nathanson*, this is a mere conclusory statement that gives the magistrate virtually no basis at all for making a judgment regarding probable cause. Sufficient information must be presented to the magistrate to allow that official to determine probable cause; his action cannot be a mere ratification of the bare conclusions of others. In order to ensure that such an abdication of the magistrate's duty does not occur, courts must continue to conscientiously review the sufficiency of affidavits on which warrants are issued. But when we move beyond the "bare bones" affidavits present in cases such as *Nathanson* and *Aguilar*, this area simply does not lend itself to a prescribed set of rules, like that which had developed from *Spinelli*. Instead, the flexible, common-sense standard articulated in *Jones, Ventresca*, and *Brinegar* better served the purposes of the Fourth Amendment's probable cause requirement.

Justice Brennan's dissent suggests in several places that the approach we take today somehow downgrades the role of the neutral magistrate, because *Aguilar* and *Spinelli* "preserve the role of magistrates as independent arbiters of probable cause * * *." Quite the contrary, we believe, is the case. Nothing in our opinion in any way lessens the authority of the magistrate to draw such reasonable inferences as he will from the material supplied to him by applicants for a

---

11. * * * Whether the allegations submitted to the magistrate in *Spinelli* would, under the view we now take, have supported a finding of probable cause, we think it would not be profitable to decide. There are so many variables in the probable cause equation that one determination will seldom be a useful "prece-dent" for another. Suffice it to say that while we in no way abandon *Spinelli's* concern for the trustworthiness of informers and for the principle that it is the magistrate who must ultimately make a finding of probable cause, we reject the rigid categorization suggested by some of its language.

warrant; indeed, he is freer than under the regime of *Aguilar* and *Spinelli* to draw such inferences, or to refuse to draw them if he is so minded.

The real gist of Justice Brennan's criticism seems to be a second argument, somewhat at odds with the first, that magistrates should be restricted in their authority to make probable cause determinations by the standards laid down in *Aguilar* and *Spinelli* and that such findings "should not be authorized unless there is some assurance that the information on which they are based has been obtained in a reliable way by an honest or credible person." However, under our opinion magistrates remain perfectly free to exact such assurances as they deem necessary, as well as those required by this opinion, in making probable cause determinations. Justice Brennan would apparently prefer that magistrates be restricted in their findings of probable cause by the development of an elaborate body of case law dealing with the "veracity" prong of the *Spinelli* test, which in turn is broken down into two "spurs"—the informant's "credibility" and the "reliability" of his information, together with the "basis of knowledge" prong of the *Spinelli* test. That such a labyrinthine body of judicial refinement bears any relationship to familiar definitions of probable cause is hard to imagine. * * *

Justice Brennan's dissent also suggests that "words such as 'practical,' 'nontechnical,' and 'common sense,' as used in the Court's opinion, are but code words for an overly permissive attitude towards police practices in derogation of the rights secured by the Fourth Amendment." * * * "Fidelity" to the commands of the Constitution suggests balanced judgment rather than exhortation. The highest "fidelity" is achieved neither by the judge who instinctively goes furthest in upholding even the most bizarre claim of individual constitutional rights, any more than it is achieved by a judge who instinctively goes furthest in accepting the most restrictive claims of governmental authorities. The task of this Court, as of other courts, is to "hold the balance true," and we think we have done that in this case.

Our decisions applying the totality of circumstances analysis outlined above have consistently recognized the value of corroboration of details of an informant's tip by independent police work.

Our decision in *Draper v. United States*, however, is the classic case on the value of corroborative efforts of police officials. There, an informant named Hereford reported that Draper would arrive in Denver on a train from Chicago on one of two days, and that he would be carrying a quantity of heroin. The informant also supplied a fairly detailed physical description of Draper, and predicted that he would be wearing a light colored raincoat, brown slacks and black shoes, and would be walking "real fast." Hereford gave no indication of the basis for his information.[12]

On one of the stated dates police officers observed a man matching this description exit a train arriving from Chicago; his attire and luggage matched Hereford's report and he was walking rapidly. We explained in *Draper* that, by this point in his investigation, the arresting officer "had personally verified every facet of the information given him by Hereford except whether petitioner had accomplished his mission and had the three ounces of heroin on his person or in his bag. And surely with every other bit of Hereford's information being thus

---

12. The tip in *Draper* might well not have survived the rigid application of the "two-pronged test" that developed following *Spinelli*. The only reference to Hereford's reliability was that he had "been engaged as a 'special employee' of the Bureau of Narcotics at Denver for about six months, and from time to time gave information to [the police] for small sums of money, and that [the officer] had always found the information given by Hereford to be accurate and reliable." Likewise, the tip gave no indication of how Hereford came by his information. At most, the detailed and accurate predictions in the tip indicated that, however Hereford obtained his information, it was reliable.

personally verified, [the officer] had 'reasonable grounds' to believe that the remaining unverified bit of Hereford's information—that Draper would have the heroin with him—was likewise true."

The showing of probable cause in the present case was fully as compelling as that in *Draper*. Even standing alone, the facts obtained through the independent investigation of Mader and the DEA at least suggested that the Gates were involved in drug trafficking. In addition to being a popular vacation site, Florida is well-known as a source of narcotics and other illegal drugs. Lance Gates' flight to Palm Beach, his brief, overnight stay in a motel, and apparent immediate return north to Chicago in the family car, conveniently awaiting him in West Palm Beach, is as suggestive of a prearranged drug run, as it is of an ordinary vacation trip.

In addition, the magistrate could rely on the anonymous letter, which had been corroborated in major part by Mader's efforts—just as had occurred in *Draper*.[13] The Supreme Court of Illinois reasoned that *Draper* involved an informant who had given reliable information on previous occasions, while the honesty and reliability of the anonymous informant in this case were unknown to the Bloomingdale police. While this distinction might be an apt one at the time the police department received the anonymous letter, it became far less significant after Mader's independent investigative work occurred. The corroboration of the letter's predictions that the Gates' car would be in Florida, that Lance Gates would fly to Florida in the next day or so, and that he would drive the car north toward Bloomingdale all indicated, albeit not with certainty, that the informant's other assertions also were true. "Because an informant is right about some things, he is more probably right about other facts," *Spinelli, supra* (White, J., concurring)—including the claim regarding the Gates' illegal activity. This may well not be the type of "reliability" or "veracity" necessary to satisfy some view of the "veracity prong" of *Spinelli*, but we think it suffices for the practical, common-sense judgment called for in making a probable cause determination. It is enough, for purposes of assessing probable cause, that "corroboration through other sources of information reduced the chances of a reckless or prevaricating tale," thus providing "a substantial basis for crediting the hearsay."

Finally, the anonymous letter contained a range of details relating not just to easily obtained facts and conditions existing at the time of the tip, but to future actions of third parties ordinarily not easily predicted. The letter writer's accurate information as to the travel plans of each of the Gates was of a character likely obtained only from the Gates themselves, or from someone familiar with their not entirely ordinary travel plans. If the informant had access to accurate information of this type a magistrate could properly conclude that it was not unlikely that he

---

13. The Illinois Supreme Court thought that the verification of details contained in the anonymous letter in this case amounted only to "the corroboration of innocent activity," and that this was insufficient to support a finding of probable cause. We are inclined to agree, however, with the observation of Justice Moran in his dissenting opinion that "In this case, just as in *Draper*, seemingly innocent activity became suspicious in the light of the initial tip." And it bears noting that *all* of the corroborating detail established in *Draper, supra*, was of entirely innocent activity—a fact later pointed out by the Court in both *Jones v. United States, and Ker v. California*.

This is perfectly reasonable. As discussed previously, probable cause requires only a probability or substantial chance of criminal activity, not an actual showing of such activity. By hypothesis, therefore, innocent behavior frequently will provide the basis for a showing of probable cause; to require otherwise would be to *sub silentio* impose a drastically more rigorous definition of probable cause than the security of our citizens demands. We think the Illinois court attempted a too rigid classification of the types of conduct that may be relied upon in seeking to demonstrate probable cause. In making a determination of probable cause the relevant inquiry is not whether particular conduct is "innocent" or "guilty," but the degree of suspicion that attaches to particular types of non-criminal acts.

also had access to reliable information of the Gates' alleged illegal activities.[14] Of course, the Gates' travel plans might have been learned from a talkative neighbor or travel agent; under the "two-pronged test" developed from *Spinelli*, the character of the details in the anonymous letter might well not permit a sufficiently clear inference regarding the letter writer's "basis of knowledge." But, as discussed previously, probable cause does not demand the certainty we associate with formal trials. It is enough that there was a fair probability that the writer of the anonymous letter had obtained his entire story either from the Gates or someone they trusted. And corroboration of major portions of the letter's predictions provides just this probability. It is apparent, therefore, that the judge issuing the warrant had a "substantial basis for * * * conclud[ing]" that probable cause to search the Gates' home and car existed. The judgment of the Supreme Court of Illinois therefore must be

[handwritten: pc requires only probability not actual showing of crim activity]

    Reversed.   *[handwritten: → for police (π)]*

    Justice WHITE, concurring in the judgment.[a]

[handwritten: Concur but use Aguilar-Spinelli]

    * * * Although I agree that the warrant should be upheld, I reach this conclusion in accordance with the *Aguilar-Spinelli* framework.

    For present purposes, the *Aguilar-Spinelli* rules can be summed up as follows. First, an affidavit based on an informer's tip, standing alone, cannot provide probable cause for issuance of a warrant unless the tip includes information that apprises the magistrate of the informant's basis for concluding that the contraband is where he claims it is (the "basis of knowledge" prong), *and* the affiant informs the magistrate of his basis for believing that the informant is credible (the "veracity" prong).[20] Second, if a tip fails under either or both of the two prongs,

[handwritten: even if tip fails, PC can still be estab by invest work]

14. The dissent seizes on one inaccuracy in the anonymous informant's letter—its statement that Sue Gates would fly from Florida to Illinois, when in fact she drove—and argues that the probative value of the entire tip was undermined by this allegedly "material mistake." We have never required that informants used by the police be infallible, and can see no reason to impose such a requirement in this case. Probable cause, particularly when police have obtained a warrant, simply does not require the perfection the dissent finds necessary.

[handwritten: I mistake in letter]

    Likewise, there is no force to the dissent's argument that the Gates' action in leaving their home unguarded undercut the informant's claim that drugs were hidden there. Indeed, the line-by-line scrutiny that the dissent applies to the anonymous letter is akin to that we find inappropriate in reviewing magistrate's decisions. The dissent apparently attributes to the magistrate who issued the warrant in this case the rather implausible notion that persons dealing in drugs always stay at home, apparently out of fear that to leave might risk intrusion by criminals. If accurate, one could not help sympathizing with the self-imposed isolation of people so situated. In reality, however, it is scarcely likely that the magistrate ever thought that the anonymous tip "kept one spouse" at home, much less that he relied on the theory advanced by the dissent. The letter simply says that Sue would fly from Florida to Illinois, without indicating whether the Gates' made the bitter choice of leaving the drugs in

[handwritten: unguarded home]

their house, or those in their car, unguarded. The magistrate's determination that there might be drugs or evidence of criminal activity in the Gates' home was well-supported by the less speculative theory, noted in text, that if the informant could predict with considerable accuracy the somewhat unusual travel plans of the Gates, he probably also had a reliable basis for his statements that the Gates' kept a large quantity of drugs in their home and frequently were visited by other drug traffickers there.

a. In an omitted portion of his opinion, Justice White argued for adoption of a "good-faith" exception to the exclusionary rule.

20. The "veracity" prong is satisfied by a recitation in the affidavit that the informant previously supplied accurate information to the police, see *McCray v. Illinois,* [p. 186], or by proof that the informant gave his information against his penal interest, see *United States v. Harris,* 403 U.S. 573, 91 S.Ct. 2075, 29 L.Ed.2d 723 (1971) (plurality opinion). [Editor's Note: In *Harris,* the informant said that he had purchased illicit whiskey from defendant for two years, most recently within the past two weeks, and had often seen defendant get the whiskey for him and others from a certain building. The plurality opinion concluded that because "people do not lightly admit a crime and place critical evidence in the hands of the police in the form of their own admissions," such admissions "carry their own indicia of credibility—sufficient at least to support finding of probable cause to search" when, as here,

probable cause may yet be established by independent police investigatory work that corroborates the tip to such an extent that it supports "both the inference that the informer was generally trustworthy and that he made his charge on the basis of information obtained in a reliable way." In instances where the officers rely on corroboration, the ultimate question is whether the corroborated tip "is as trustworthy as a tip which would pass *Aguilar's* tests without independent corroboration."

In the present case, it is undisputed that the anonymous tip, by itself, did not furnish probable cause. The question is whether those portions of the affidavit describing the results of the police investigation of the respondents, when considered in light of the tip, "would permit the suspicions engendered by the informant's report to ripen into a judgment that a crime was probably being committed." * * *

In my view, the lower court's characterization of the Gates' activity here as totally "innocent" is dubious. In fact, the behavior was quite suspicious. I agree with the Court that Lance Gates' flight to Palm Beach, an area known to be a source of narcotics, the brief overnight stay in a motel, and apparent immediate return North, suggest a pattern that trained law-enforcement officers have recognized as indicative of illicit drug-dealing activity.

Even, however, had the corroboration related only to completely innocuous activities, this fact alone would not preclude the issuance of a valid warrant. The critical issue is not whether the activities observed by the police are innocent or suspicious. Instead, the proper focus should be on whether the actions of the suspects, whatever their nature, give rise to an inference that the informant is credible and that he obtained his information in a reliable manner.

Thus, in *Draper v. United States* an informant stated on Sept. 7 that Draper would be carrying narcotics when he arrived by train in Denver on the morning of Sept. 8 or Sept. 9. The informant also provided the police with a detailed physical description of the clothes Draper would be wearing when he alighted from the train. The police observed Draper leaving a train on the morning of Sept. 9, and he was wearing the precise clothing described by the informant. The Court held that the police had probable cause to arrest Draper at this point, even though the police had seen nothing more than the totally innocent act of a man getting off a train carrying a briefcase. As we later explained in *Spinelli,* the important point was that the corroboration showed both that the informant was credible, *i.e.* that he "had not been fabricating his report out of whole cloth," and that he had an adequate basis of knowledge for his allegations, "since the report was of the sort which in common experience may be recognized as having been obtained in a reliable way." The fact that the informer was able to predict, two days in advance, the exact clothing Draper would be wearing dispelled the possibility that his tip was just based on rumor or "an off-hand remark heard at a neighborhood bar." Probably Draper had planned in advance to wear these specific clothes so that an accomplice could identify him. A clear inference could therefore be drawn that the

the basis of knowledge is also indicated (as almost inevitably will be the case when there is such an admission). The four dissenters objected that "the effect of adopting such a rule would be to encourage the Government to prefer as informants participants in criminal enterprises rather than ordinary citizens, a goal the Government specifically eschews in its brief in this case upon the explicit premise that such persons are often less reliable than those who obey the law."] The "basis of knowledge" prong is satisfied by a statement from the informant that he personally observed the criminal activity, or, if he came by the information indirectly, by a satisfactory explanation of why his sources were reliable, or, in the absence of a statement detailing the manner in which the information was gathered, by a description of the accused's criminal activity in sufficient detail that the magistrate may infer that the informant is relying on something more substantial than casual rumor or an individual's general reputation. *Spinelli v. United States.*

informant was either involved in the criminal scheme himself or that he otherwise had access to reliable, inside information.[22]

As in *Draper,* the police investigation in the present case satisfactorily demonstrated that the informant's tip was as trustworthy as one that would alone satisfy the *Aguilar* tests. The tip predicted that Sue Gates would drive to Florida, that Lance Gates would fly there a few days after May 3, and that Lance would then drive the car back. After the police corroborated these facts, the magistrate could reasonably have inferred, as he apparently did, that the informant, who had specific knowledge of these unusual travel plans, did not make up his story and that he obtained his information in a reliable way. * * * I therefore conclude that the judgment of the Illinois Supreme Court invalidating the warrant must be reversed.

The Court agrees that the warrant was valid, but, in the process of reaching this conclusion, it overrules the *Aguilar-Spinelli* tests and replaces them with a "totality of the circumstances" standard. As shown above, it is not at all necessary to overrule *Aguilar-Spinelli* in order to reverse the judgment below. Therefore, because I am inclined to believe that, when applied properly, the *Aguilar-Spinelli* rules play an appropriate role in probable cause determinations, and because the Court's holding may foretell an evisceration of the probable cause standard, I do not join the Court's holding.

The Court reasons that the "veracity" and "basis of knowledge" tests are not independent, and that a deficiency as to one can be compensated for by a strong showing as to the other. Thus, a finding of probable cause may be based on a tip from an informant "known for the unusual reliability of his predictions" or from "an unquestionably honest citizen," even if the report fails thoroughly to set forth the basis upon which the information was obtained. If this is so, then it must follow *a fortiori* that "the affidavit of an officer, known by the magistrate to be honest and experienced, stating that [contraband] is located in a certain building" must be acceptable. It would be "quixotic" if a similar statement from an honest informant, but not one from an honest officer, could furnish probable cause. But we have repeatedly held that the unsupported assertion or belief of an officer does not satisfy the probable cause requirement. Thus, this portion of today's holding can be read as implicitly rejecting the teachings of these prior holdings.

The Court may not intend so drastic a result. Indeed, the Court expressly reaffirms the validity of cases such as *Nathanson* that have held that, no matter

---

22. Thus, as interpreted in *Spinelli,* the Court in *Draper* held that there was probable cause because "the kind of information related by the informant [was] not generally sent ahead of a person's arrival in a city except to those who are intimately connected with making careful arrangements for meeting him." *Spinelli* (White, J., concurring). As I said in *Spinelli,* the conclusion that *Draper* itself was based on this fact is far from inescapable. Prior to *Spinelli, Draper* was susceptible to the interpretation that it stood for the proposition that "the existence of the tenth and critical fact is made sufficiently probable to justify the issuance of a warrant by verifying nine other facts coming from the same source." *Spinelli* (White, J., concurring). But it now seems clear that the Court in *Spinelli* rejected this reading of *Draper.*

Justice Brennan erroneously interprets my *Spinelli* concurrence as espousing the view that "corroboration of certain details in a tip may be sufficient to satisfy the veracity, but not the basis of knowledge, prong of *Aguilar.*" I did not say that corroboration could *never* satisfy the basis of knowledge prong. My concern was, and still is, that the prong might be deemed satisfied on the basis of corroboration of information that does not in any way suggest that the informant had an adequate basis of knowledge for his report. If, however, as in *Draper,* the police corroborate information from which it can be inferred that the informant's tip was grounded on inside information, this corroboration is sufficient to satisfy the basis of knowledge prong. *Spinelli* (White, J., concurring). The rules would indeed be strange if, as Justice Brennan suggests, the basis of knowledge prong could be satisfied by detail in the tip alone, but not by independent police work.

how reliable the affiant-officer may be, a warrant should not be issued unless the affidavit discloses supporting facts and circumstances. The Court limits these cases to situations involving affidavits containing only "bare conclusions" and holds that, if an affidavit contains anything more, it should be left to the issuing magistrate to decide, based solely on "practical[ity]" and "common-sense," whether there is a fair probability that contraband will be found in a particular place.

Thus, as I read the majority opinion, it appears that the question whether the probable cause standard is to be diluted is left to the common-sense judgments of issuing magistrates. I am reluctant to approve any standard that does not expressly require, as a prerequisite to issuance of a warrant, some showing of facts from which an inference may be drawn that the informant is credible and that his information was obtained in a reliable way. * * * Hence, I do not join the Court's opinion rejecting the *Aguilar-Spinelli* rules.

Justice BRENNAN, with whom Justice MARSHALL joins, dissenting.

Although I join Justice Stevens' dissenting opinion and agree with him that the warrant is invalid even under the Court's newly announced "totality of the circumstances" test, I write separately to dissent from the Court's unjustified and ill-advised rejection of the two-prong test for evaluating the validity of a warrant based on hearsay announced in *Aguilar v. Texas,* and refined in *Spinelli v. United States.* * * *

The [*Spinelli*] Court held that the *Aguilar* test should be applied to the tip, and approved two additional ways of satisfying that test. First, the Court suggested that if the tip contained sufficient detail describing the accused's criminal activity it might satisfy *Aguilar's* basis of knowledge prong. Such detail might assure the magistrate that he is "relying on something more substantial than a casual rumor circulating in the underworld or an accusation based merely on an individual's general reputation." Although the tip in the case before it did not meet this standard, "[t]he detail provided by the informant in *Draper v. United States* provide[d] a suitable benchmark" because "[a] magistrate, when confronted with such detail, could reasonably infer that the informant had gained his information in a reliable way."

Second, the Court stated that police corroboration of the details of a tip could provide a basis for satisfying *Aguilar*. The Court's opinion is not a model of clarity on this issue since it appears to suggest that corroboration can satisfy both the basis of knowledge and veracity prongs of *Aguilar*. Justice White's concurring opinion, however, points the way to a proper reading of the Court's opinion. After reviewing the Court's decision in *Draper v. United States,* Justice White concluded that "[t]he thrust of *Draper* is not that the verified facts have independent significance with respect to proof of [another unverified fact]." In his view, "[t]he argument instead relates to the reliability of the source: because an informant is right about some things, he is more probably right about other facts, usually the critical, unverified facts." Justice White then pointed out that prior cases had rejected "the notion that the past reliability of an officer is sufficient reason for believing his current assertions." Justice White went on to state:

> "Nor would it suffice, I suppose, if a reliable informant states there is gambling equipment in Apartment 607 and then proceeds to describe in detail Apartment 201, a description which is verified before applying for the warrant. He was right about 201, but that hardly makes him more believable about the equipment in 607. But what if he states that there are narcotics locked in a safe in Apartment 300, which is described in detail, and the apartment manager verifies everything but the contents of the safe? I doubt that the report about the narcotics is made appreciably more believable by the verification. The informant could still have gotten his information concerning

the safe from others about whom nothing is known or could have inferred the presence of narcotics from circumstances which a magistrate would find unacceptable.''

I find this reasoning persuasive. Properly understood, therefore, *Spinelli* stands for the proposition that corroboration of certain details in a tip may be sufficient to satisfy the veracity, but not the basis of knowledge, prong of *Aguilar*. As noted, *Spinelli* also suggests that in some limited circumstances considerable detail in an informant's tip may be adequate to satisfy the basis of knowledge prong of *Aguilar*. * * *

[O]ne can concede that probable cause is a ''practical, nontechnical'' concept without betraying the values that *Aguilar* and *Spinelli* reflect. As noted, *Aguilar* and *Spinelli* require the police to provide magistrates with certain crucial information. They also provide structure for magistrates' probable cause inquiries. In so doing, *Aguilar* and *Spinelli* preserve the role of magistrates as independent arbiters of probable cause, insure greater accuracy in probable cause determinations, and advance the substantive value of precluding findings of probable cause, and attendant intrusions, based on anything less than information from an honest or credible person who has acquired his information in a reliable way. Neither the standards nor their effects are inconsistent with a ''practical, nontechnical'' conception of probable cause. Once a magistrate has determined that he has information before him that he can reasonably say has been obtained in a reliable way by a credible person, he has ample room to use his common sense and to apply a practical, nontechnical conception of probable cause. * * *

The Court also insists that the *Aguilar-Spinelli* standards must be abandoned because they are inconsistent with the fact that non-lawyers frequently serve as magistrates. To the contrary, the standards help to structure probable cause inquiries and, properly interpreted, may actually help a non-lawyer magistrate in making a probable cause determination. * * *

Justice STEVENS, with whom Justice BRENNAN joins, dissenting.

* * * The informant had indicated that ''Sue drives their car to Florida *where she leaves it to be loaded up with drugs * * *. Sue flies back after she drops the car off in Florida.*'' (emphasis added). Yet Detective Mader's affidavit reported that she ''left the West Palm Beach area driving the Mercury northbound.''

The discrepancy between the informant's predictions and the facts known to Detective Mader is significant for three reasons. First, it cast doubt on the informant's hypothesis that the Gates already had ''over $100,000 worth of drugs in their basement.'' The informant had predicted an itinerary that always kept one spouse in Bloomingdale, suggesting that the Gates did not want to leave their home unguarded because something valuable was hidden within. That inference obviously could not be drawn when it was known that the pair was actually together over a thousand miles from home.

Second, the discrepancy made the Gates' conduct seem substantially less unusual than the informant had predicted it would be. It would have been odd if, as predicted, Sue had driven down to Florida on Wednesday, left the car, and flown right back to Illinois. But the mere facts that Sue was in West Palm Beach with the car,[1] that she was joined by her husband at the Holiday Inn on Friday,[2]

---

1. The anonymous note suggested that she was going down on Wednesday, but for all the officers knew she had been in Florida for a month.

2. Lance does not appear to have behaved suspiciously in flying down to Florida. He made a reservation in his own name and gave an accurate home phone number to the airlines. And Detective Mader's affidavit does not report that he did any of the other things drug couriers are notorious for doing, such as paying for the ticket in cash, dressing casually, looking

and that the couple drove north together the next morning[3] are neither unusual nor probative of criminal activity.

Third, the fact that the anonymous letter contained a material mistake undermines the reasonableness of relying on it as a basis for making a forcible entry into a private home.

Of course, the activities in this case did not stop when the magistrate issued the warrant. The Gates drove all night to Bloomingdale, the officers searched the car and found 400 pounds of marijuana, and then they searched the house. However, none of these subsequent events may be considered in evaluating the warrant, and the search of the house was legal only if the warrant was valid. I cannot accept the Court's casual conclusion that, *before the Gates arrived in Bloomingdale*, there was probable cause to justify a valid entry and search of a private home. No one knows who the informant in this case was, or what motivated him or her to write the note. Given that the note's predictions were faulty in one significant respect, and were corroborated by nothing except ordinary innocent activity, I must surmise that the Court's evaluation of the warrant's validity has been colored by subsequent events. * * *[a]

Notes and Questions

1. In MASSACHUSETTS v. UPTON, 466 U.S. 727, 104 S.Ct. 2085, 80 L.Ed.2d 721 (1984), police Lt. Beland assisted in the execution of a search warrant for a motel room reserved by one Richard Kelleher, which produced several items of identification belonging to two persons whose homes had recently been burglarized. Other items taken in the burglaries, such as jewelry, silver and gold, were not found. A few hours later Beland received a call from an unidentified female who told him that there was "a motor home full of stolen stuff," including jewelry, silver and gold, at George Upton's premises. After verifying that a motor home was parked there, Beland prepared an application for a search warrant, to which he attached the police reports on the two prior burglaries, along with lists of the stolen property, and his affidavit with the above information and the following:

"She further stated that George Upton was going to move the motor home any time now because of the fact that Ricky Kelleher's motel room was raided and that George Upton had purchased these stolen items from Ricky Kelleher. This

pale and nervous, improperly filling out baggage tags, carrying American Tourister luggage, not carrying any luggage, or changing airlines en route.

3. Detective Mader's affidavit hinted darkly that the couple had set out upon "that interstate highway commonly used by travelers to the Chicago area." But the same highway is also commonly used by travelers to Disney World, Sea World, and Ringling Brothers and Barnum and Bailey Circus World. It is also the road to Cocoa Beach, Cape Canaveral, and Washington, D.C. I would venture that each year dozens of perfectly innocent people fly to Florida, meet a waiting spouse, and drive off together in the family car.

a. For criticism of *Gates*, see Yale Kamisar, *Gates, "Probable Cause," "Good Faith," and Beyond*, 69 Iowa L.Rev. 557 (1984); Wayne R. LaFave, *Fourth Amendment Vagaries (of Improbable Cause, Imperceptible Plain View, No-*

torious Privacy, and Balancing Askew), 74 J.Crim.L. & C. 1171, 1186–99 (1983); Arnold H. Loewy, *Protecting Citizens from Cops and Crooks: An Assessment of the Supreme Court's Interpretation of the Fourth Amendment During the 1982 Term*, 62 N.C.L.Rev. 329, 336–45 (1984) (criticizing the Court's handling of "probable cause," but not its abandonment of the "two-pronged test"); Silas J. Wasserstrom, *The Incredible Shrinking Fourth Amendment*, 21 Am.Crim.L.Rev. 257, 274–75, 329–40 (1984) (same). Cf. Charles A. Moylan, *Illinois v. Gates: What It Did and Did Not Do*, 20 Crim.L.Bull. 93 (1984) (criticizing the Court's "rhetoric," but maintaining that, on its facts, *Gates* is an exceedingly narrow holding). For a strong defense of *Gates*, see Joseph D. Grano, *Probable Cause and Common Sense: A Reply to the Critics of Illinois v. Gates*, 17 U.Mich.J.L.Ref. 465 (1984).

unidentified female stated that she had seen the stolen items but refused to identify herself because 'he'll kill me,' referring to George Upton. I then told this unidentified female that I knew who she was, giving her the name of Lynn Alberico, who I had met on May 16, 1980, at George Upton's repair shop off Summer St., in Yarmouthport. She was identified to me by George Upton as being his girlfriend, Lynn Alberico. The unidentified female admitted that she was the girl that I had named, stating that she was surprised that I knew who she was. She then told me that she'd broken up with George Upton and wanted to burn him. She also told me that she wouldn't give me her address or phone number but that she would contact me in the future, if need be."

[margin note: cop guessed informents name]

A magistrate issued the warrant, and a subsequent search of the motor home produced the described items. The Supreme Court, per curiam upheld the warrant:

[margin note: Ct upheld w]

"Examined in light of *Gates*, Lt. Beland's affidavit provides a substantial basis for the issuance of the warrant. No single piece of evidence in it is conclusive. But the pieces fit neatly together and, so viewed, support the magistrate's determination that there was 'a fair probability that contraband or evidence of crime' would be found in Upton's motor home. The informant claimed to have seen the stolen goods and gave a description of them which tallied with the items taken in recent burglaries. She knew of the raid on the motel room—which produced evidence connected to those burglaries—and that the room had been reserved by Kelleher. She explained the connection between Kelleher's motel room and the stolen goods in Upton's motor home. And she provided a motive both for her attempt at anonymity—fear of Upton's retaliation—and for furnishing the information—her recent breakup with Upton and her desire 'to burn him.' "[b]

[margin note: informant gave description / connection / motive]

2. While the Fourth Amendment expressly requires probable cause for a valid arrest warrant or search warrant, police are often permitted to make arrests and searches without first obtaining a warrant, in which case the Fourth Amendment's protection against "unreasonable searches and seizures" applies. But, because a "principal incentive" for the procurement of warrants would be destroyed if police needed less evidence when acting without a warrant, the requirements in such instances "surely cannot be less stringent" than when a warrant is obtained, *Wong Sun v. United States*, 371 U.S. 471, 83 S.Ct. 407, 9 L.Ed.2d 441 (1963), meaning probable cause is also required for warrantless arrests and searches.[c]

3. It is generally assumed that the same quantum of evidence is required whether one is concerned with probable cause to arrest or probable cause to search. However, probable cause for search requires a somewhat different kind of conclusion than probable cause for arrest. For arrest, there must be a substantial probability that a crime has been committed and that the person to be arrested committed it; for search, there must be a substantial probability that certain items are the fruits, instrumentalities or evidence of crime and that these items are presently to be found at a certain place.

Because the latter type of probable cause has to do with the *present* location of certain objects, it may be found to be lacking because the time of the facts relied upon is unknown or highly uncertain. Does this mean, as held in *Schmidt v. State*,

b. Brennan and Marshall, JJ., dissented from the summary disposition of the case and would have denied the petition for certiorari. After remand, *Commonwealth v. Upton*, 476 N.E.2d 548 (Mass.1985), held that *Aguilar* and *Spinelli* "provide a more appropriate structure for probable cause inquiries" under the *state* constitution, and concluded that the affidavit failed to establish probable cause.

c. However, as discussed in §§ 7, 8 of this chapter, certain kinds of searches and seizures, because they involve a lesser degree of intrusion or interference, are permitted upon less than the traditional amount of probable cause.

[margin note: depends on degree of intrusion]

659 S.W.2d 420 (Tex.Crim.App.1983), that there was no probable cause to search defendant's car for drugs when the affidavit said defendant, "presently under medical attention," had been found in that vehicle in need of medical attention and had said then that he "had been sniffing cocaine," in that the only reference to time is ambiguous because it is not clear whether defendant had been under medical attention "for a few hours or a few months"? When the time of the facts is given probable cause will sometimes be lacking because that information has become "stale."[d] See, e.g., *United States v. Steeves*, 525 F.2d 33 (8th Cir.1975) (warrant to search for clothing, ski mask, hand gun, money and money bag, all sought as evidence of bank robbery which occupant of premises participated in three months earlier; held, there was no probable cause the money or bag would still be there, but there was probable cause the other items would be there, as "a highly incriminating or consumable item of personal property is less likely to remain in one place as long as an item of property which is not consumable or which is innocuous in itself or not particularly incriminating"). Finally, even if no such problems are present, it must be remembered that to have probable cause to search there must be a sufficient connection of the items sought with a particular place. Thus, while a valid search warrant can sometimes issue even when the perpetrator of the crime is unknown, it does not necessarily follow that probable cause to arrest a person will likewise constitute probable cause to search that person's residence for evidence of that crime. See, e.g., *United States v. Lalor*, 996 F.2d 1578 (4th Cir.1993) (where informants gave information re defendant's drug sales at certain street corner, probable cause to search defendant's residence elsewhere lacking where affidavit does not "explain the geographic relationship between the area where the drug sales occurred" and defendant's residence).

4. Does "probable cause" always (or sometimes) mean more probable than not? Consider *State v. Thomas*, 421 S.E.2d 227 (W.Va.1992), where police, investigating a sexual assault-murder apparently committed by one person acting alone, obtained separate search warrants to search the homes and cars of Mosier and Thomas, each of whom was known to have had contact with the victim on the night of her death and to fit the FBI psychological profile of a possible perpetrator of such crimes. As the court recognized, such facts starkly present this issue: "If the same facts can be used to implicate more than one person in a crime that could have been committed by one of them, can probable cause be found to exist?" Relying on the *Gates* assertion that no "numerically precise degree of certainty" is required to show probable cause, the *Thomas* court answered in the affirmative and thus upheld the search warrant which resulted in discovery of a minute portion of the victim's type of blood in defendant's car.

Should the result be the same if it was known that a drug dealer sold a usable amount of marijuana to one person on a specific single occasion and that the only two people to have contact with the dealer in that time frame were Mosier and Thomas? Consider William J. Stuntz, *O.J. Simpson, Bill Clinton, and the Transubstantive Fourth Amendment*, 114 Harv.L.Rev. 842, 847, 852, 870 (2001), contending that while "the Fourth Amendment treats one crime just like another," that should not be so because a "large factor in government need * * * is the crime the government is investigating." Thus: "Probable cause in homicide cases should be enough to justify house searches, without the need for a warrant. Indeed, perhaps a standard lower than probable cause would be appropriate.

d. In contrast to the "stale" information problem, the question is sometimes raised whether the information is premature, in the sense that it only shows that certain goods are to be at a certain place at some future time. Most courts agree with *People v. Glen*, 282 N.E.2d 614 (N.Y.1972), noted in 19 Wayne L.Rev. 1339 (1973) (search warrant issued on information that package containing narcotics would arrive at designated premises on future date; held: "as long as the evidence creates substantial probability that the seizable property will be on the premises when searched, the warrant should be sustained").

Meanwhile, for less-than-serious drug cases—anything associated with marijuana would be a good example—probable cause and a warrant should perhaps not be enough."

5. When the police act without a warrant, they initially make the probable cause decision themselves, although it is subject to after-the-fact review by a judicial officer upon a motion to suppress evidence found because of the arrest or search. When the police act with a warrant, the probable cause decision is made by a magistrate in the first instance, but his decision may likewise be challenged in an adversary setting upon a motion to suppress (except insofar as the question is avoided entirely by reliance on *United States v. Leon,* p. 144). In a warrant case, the issue upon the motion to suppress is usually cast in terms of whether the facts set out in the complaint or affidavit upon which the warrant was issued establish probable cause.[e] However, the dissenters in *Aguilar* suggested that a defective affidavit might be cured by what the judge was told at the time the warrant was sought, and they would also resuscitate the affidavit on the basis of the officer's subsequent testimony on the motion to suppress.

As to the first possibility, consider *United States v. Clyburn,* 24 F.3d 613 (4th Cir.1994) (the "Fourth Amendment does not require that the basis for probable cause be established in a written affidavit," and thus "magistrates may consider sworn, unrecorded oral testimony in making probable cause determinations during warrant proceedings," even though "presentation of written affidavits or recorded testimony provides a preferable way of securing a search warrant"; Fed.R.Crim.P. 41(c)(1) requirement that all information showing probable cause be in affidavit not applicable here, as warrant at issue obtained by local police from local magistrate). As to the second possibility, consider *Whiteley v. Warden,* 401 U.S. 560, 91 S.Ct. 1031, 28 L.Ed.2d 306 (1971): "Under the cases of this Court, an otherwise insufficient affidavit cannot be rehabilitated by testimony concerning information possessed by the affiant when he sought the warrant but not disclosed to the issuing magistrate. * * * A contrary rule would, of course, render the warrant requirements of the Fourth Amendment meaningless."

6. Does it follow that the defendant may not challenge an affidavit which is sufficient on its face? No, the Court answered in FRANKS v. DELAWARE, 438 U.S. 154, 98 S.Ct. 2674, 57 L.Ed.2d 667 (1978). Reasoning that (i) "a flat ban on impeachment of veracity could denude the probable cause requirement of all real meaning," (ii) "the hearing before the magistrate not always will suffice to discourage lawless or reckless misconduct," (iii) "the alternative sanctions of a perjury prosecution, administrative discipline, contempt, or a civil suit are not likely to fill the gap," (iv) "allowing an evidentiary hearing, after a suitable preliminary proffer of material falsity, will not diminish the importance and solemnity of the warrant-issuing process," (v) "the claim that a post-search hearing will confuse the issue of the defendant's guilt with the issue of the State's possible misbehavior is footless," and (vi) allowing impeachment does not really extend the exclusionary rule "to a 'new' area," the Court, per BLACKMUN, J., held "that, where the defendant makes a substantial preliminary showing that a false statement knowingly and intentionally, or with reckless disregard for the truth, was included by the affiant in the warrant affidavit, and if the allegedly false statement is necessary to the finding of probable cause, the Fourth Amendment requires that a hearing be held at the defendant's request. In the event that at that hearing the allegation of perjury or reckless disregard is established by the defendant by a preponderance of the evidence, and, with the affidavit's false

---

e. But consider *United States v. Marin–Buitrago,* 734 F.2d 889 (2d Cir.1984), holding that police are required "to report [to the magistrate who issued the warrant] any mate-rial changes in the facts contained in a warrant affidavit that occur before the warrant is executed."

material set to one side, the affidavit's remaining content is insufficient to establish probable cause, the search warrant must be voided and the fruits of the search excluded to the same extent as if probable cause was lacking on the face of the affidavit."[f]

Shouldn't the same result obtain if the false statement was negligently made, as reasoned in *Theodor v. Superior Court*, 501 P.2d 234 (Cal.1972), given "the overriding principle of reasonableness which governs the application of the Fourth Amendment"? Shouldn't the same result follow even as to innocently made falsehoods, where "[a]n honestly-erring individual * * * has substituted his erroneous judgment for that of the magistrate," as argued in Comment, 19 U.C.L.A.L.Rev. 96, 140 (1971)? If there was a deliberate false statement, then why shouldn't this *always* invalidate the warrant because, as stated in *United States v. Carmichael*, 489 F.2d 983 (7th Cir.1973), "[t]he fullest deterrent sanctions of the exclusionary rule should be applied to such serious and deliberate government wrongdoing"?

Should *Franks* apply where defendant's objection is that the police left out of the affidavit some additional information which would have put into question the probable cause shown by the information included? If so, what constitutes a material omission for this purpose, and what is the applicable mental state regarding the affiant's failure to include that information?

NOTES ON THE INFORMER'S PRIVILEGE

1. In McCRAY v. ILLINOIS, 386 U.S. 300, 87 S.Ct. 1056, 18 L.Ed.2d 62 (1967), petitioner was arrested and found to have heroin on his person. At the suppression hearing, the arresting officers testified that an informant who had supplied reliable information in about 20 previous cases told them that he had observed McCray selling narcotics at a certain corner and then accompanied them to that corner and pointed him out. Both officers were asked for the name and address of the informant, but objections to these questions were sustained. Petitioner's motion was denied, and he was subsequently convicted. The Court, per STEWART, J., affirmed:

"When the issue is not guilt or innocence, but, as here, the question of probable cause for an arrest or search, the Illinois Supreme Court has held that police officers need not invariably be required to disclose an informant's identity if the trial judge is convinced, by evidence submitted in open court and subject to cross-examination, that the officers did rely in good faith upon credible information supplied by a reliable informant. This Illinois evidentiary rule is consistent with the law of many other States. * * *

"The reasoning of the Supreme Court of New Jersey in judicially adopting the same basic evidentiary rule was instructively expressed by Chief Justice Weintraub in *State v. Burnett*, 42 N.J. 377, 201 A.2d 39 [1964]:

" 'If a defendant may insist upon disclosure of the informant in order to test the truth of the officer's statement that there is an informant or as to what the informant related or as to the informant's reliability, we can be sure that every defendant will demand disclosure. He has nothing to lose and the prize may be the suppression of damaging evidence if the State cannot afford to reveal its source, as is so often the case. And since there is no way to test the good faith of a defendant who presses the demand, we must assume the routine demand would have to be

f. Rehnquist, J., joined by the Chief Justice, dissenting, argued: "If the function of the warrant requirement is to obtain the determination of a neutral magistrate as to whether sufficient grounds have been urged to support the issuance of a warrant, that function is fulfilled at the time the magistrate concludes that the requirement has been met."

routinely granted. The result would be that the State could use the informant's information only as a lead and could search only if it could gather adequate evidence of probable cause apart from the informant's data. Perhaps that approach would sharpen investigatorial techniques, but we doubt that there would be enough talent and time to cope with crime upon that basis. Rather we accept the premise that the informer is a vital part of society's defensive arsenal. The basic rule protecting his identity rests upon that belief. * * *

" 'We must remember also that we are not dealing with the trial of the criminal charge itself. There the need for a truthful verdict outweighs society's need for the informer privilege. Here, however, the accused seeks to avoid the truth. The very purpose of a motion to suppress is to escape the inculpatory thrust of evidence in hand, not because its probative force is diluted in the least by the mode of seizure, but rather as a sanction to compel enforcement officers to respect the constitutional security of all of us under the Fourth Amendment. * * * If the motion to suppress is denied, defendant will still be judged upon the untarnished truth. * * *

" 'The Fourth Amendment is served if a judicial mind passes upon the existence of probable cause. Where the issue is submitted upon an application for a warrant, the magistrate is trusted to evaluate the credibility of the affiant in an *ex parte* proceeding. As we have said, the magistrate is concerned, not with whether the informant lied, but with whether the affiant is truthful in his recitation of what he was told. If the magistrate doubts the credibility of the affiant, he may require that the informant be identified or even produced. It seems to us that the same approach is equally sufficient where the search was without a warrant, that is to say, that it should rest entirely with the judge who hears the motion to suppress to decide whether he needs such disclosure as to the informant in order to decide whether the officer is a believable witness.' * * *

"[W]e are now asked to hold that the Constitution somehow compels Illinois to abolish the informer's privilege from its law of evidence, and to require disclosure of the informer's identity in every such preliminary hearing where it appears that the officers made the arrest or search in reliance upon facts supplied by an informer they had reason to trust ... * * *

"Nothing in the Due Process Clause of the Fourteenth Amendment requires a state court judge in every such hearing to assume the arresting officers are committing perjury."

DOUGLAS, J., joined by The Chief Justice, and Justices Brennan and Fortas, dissented:

"There is no way to determine the reliability of Old Reliable, the informer, unless he is produced, at the trial and cross-examined. Unless he is produced, the Fourth Amendment is entrusted to the tender mercies of the police. What we do today is to encourage arrests and searches without warrants. The whole momentum of criminal law administration should be in precisely the opposite direction, if the Fourth Amendment is to remain a vital force. Except in rare and emergency cases, it requires magistrates to make the findings of 'probable cause.' We should be mindful of its command that a judicial mind should be interposed between the police and the citizen. We should also be mindful that 'disclosure, rather than suppression, of relevant materials ordinarily promotes the proper administration of criminal justice.' "

2. How valid is the following criticism of *McCray* by Irving Younger, a former federal prosecutor, in *The Perjury Routine*, The Nation, May 8, 1967, pp. 596–97:

"[The *McCray* majority] said that 'nothing in the Due Process Clause of the Fourteenth Amendment requires a state court judge in every such hearing to assume the arresting officers are committing perjury.' Why not? Every lawyer who practices in the criminal courts knows that police perjury is commonplace.

"The reason is not hard to find. Policemen see themselves as fighting a two-front war—against criminals in the street and against 'liberal' rules of law in court. All's fair in this war, including the use of perjury to subvert 'liberal' rules of law that might free those who 'ought' to be jailed. * * *

"Far from adopting a presumption of perjury, the *McCray* case almost guarantees wholesale police perjury. When his conduct is challenged as constituting an unreasonable search and seizure, all the policeman need say is that an unnamed 'reliable informant' told him that the defendant was committing a crime. Henceforth, every policeman will have a genie-like informer to legalize his master's arrests."

3. Appellate decisions reversing a trial judge's denial of disclosure are extremely rare, and typically involve a situation in which the court could have simply said that probable cause had not been shown. But a growing number of cases are to be found along the lines of *People v. Darden,* 313 N.E.2d 49 (N.Y.1974), concluding it is "fair and wise, in a case such as this, where there is insufficient evidence to establish probable cause apart from the testimony of the arresting officer as to communications received from an informer, when the issue of identity of the informer is raised at the suppression hearing, for the suppression judge then to conduct an in camera inquiry. The prosecution should be required to make the informer available for interrogation before the Judge. The prosecutor may be present but not the defendant or his counsel. Opportunity should be afforded counsel for defendant to submit in writing any questions which he may desire the Judge to put to the informer. The Judge should take testimony, with recognition of the special need for protection of the interests of the absent defendant, and make a summary report as to the existence of the informer and with respect to the communications made by the informer to the police to which the police testify. That report should be made available to the defendant and to the People and the transcript of testimony should be sealed to be available to the appellate courts if the occasion arises." Contra: *State v. Richardson,* 529 A.2d 1236 (Conn.1987): "Requiring an informant to attend an in camera hearing involves a substantial risk that his identity will be discovered."

NOTES ON OTHER SOURCES OF PROBABLE CAUSE

The probable cause decisions of the United States Supreme Court, almost exclusively concerned with when information from an informant, with or without some corroborating facts, is sufficient for arrest or search, are not fairly representative of the full range of probable cause issues confronted by the police. Consider these situations:

1. *Information from an alleged victim of, or witness to, a crime.* A major distinction between the victim-witness cases and the informant cases is that prior reliability need not be shown as to the former. As explained in *State v. Paszek,* 184 N.W.2d 836 (Wis.1971): "Information supplied to officers by the traditional police informer is not given in the spirit of a concerned citizen, but often is given in exchange for some concession, payment, or simply out of revenge against the subject. The nature of these persons and the information which they supply convey a certain impression of unreliability, and it is proper to demand that some evidence of their credibility and reliability be shown. * * *

"However, an ordinary citizen who reports a crime which has been committed in his presence, or that a crime is being or will be committed, stands on much different ground than a police informer. He is a witness to criminal activity who acts with an intent to aid the police in law enforcement because of his concern for society or for his own safety. He does not expect any gain or concession in exchange for his information. An informer of this type usually would not have more than one opportunity to supply information to the police, thereby precluding proof of his reliability by pointing to previous accurate information which he has supplied."

In the victim-witness cases, the critical question usually is whether the general description given by the victim or witness is sufficient to justify the arrest of any one person. For example, in *Brown v. United States,* 365 F.2d 976 (D.C.Cir.1966), the police received a radio report at 4:30 a.m. of a recent armed robbery, and were told to be on the lookout for a heavily built black male driving a maroon 1954 Ford. Shortly thereafter, 20 blocks from the robbery scene, the police saw what they thought to be such a car (actually, it was a 1952 Ford), and radioed for details about the robber. They were told that the robber was about five feet five inches, and that he was wearing a brown jacket and cream-colored straw hat. The suspect was about five feet eleven inches, was wearing blue, and had only a felt hat, but he was nonetheless arrested. Held: "These discrepancies, which can be the result of the victim's excitement or poor visibility or of the suspect's changing clothes, did not destroy the ascertainment made on the basis of the accurate portion of the identification, which was by itself enough to constitute probable cause."

2. *Direct observations by police.* Most troublesome, because the situations are so varied, are those cases in which the probable cause determination must be made solely upon suspicious conduct observed by police. For example, in *Brooks v. United States,* 159 A.2d 876 (D.C.Mun.App.1960), an officer observed two men, both known to have prior convictions for larceny, carrying a console-type record player in the commercial area at 6:30 p.m. The officer noted that the player was new and still bore store tags. Upon questioning, one of the suspects said the machine belonged to his mother and that he was taking it in to be repaired. When the officer pointed out the tags, the suspect changed his story and said that the machine had been given to him by an unknown person, whom he was unable to describe. The officer then placed the two men under arrest. The court, noting that "the probabilities must be measured by the standards of the reasonable, cautious and prudent peace officer as he sees them, and not those of the casual passerby," held that the officer had acted on probable cause.

What if the officer had not known of the suspects' past records? What if the suspects had refused to answer any questions? Or, what if the suspect had not changed his first story? If the officer had been aware of the fact that larcenies were common in that area, would this be relevant?[a] What if the suspects had taken flight upon being stopped? Cf. Note 7, p. 311. What if they had engaged in "furtive gestures" upon seeing the police? To what extent, if at all, should account

---

a. Consider *United States v. Davis,* 458 F.2d 819 (D.C.Cir.1972): "Although no presumption of guilt arises from the activities of inhabitants of an area in which the police know that narcotics offenses frequently occur, the syndrome of criminality in those areas cannot realistically go unnoticed by the judiciary. It too is a valid consideration when coupled with other reliable indicia or suspicious circumstances. We make this statement warily, for it is all too clear that few live in these areas by choice."

Compare Jerome H. Skolnick, *Justice Without Trial* 217–18 (1966): "If an honest citizen resides in a neighborhood heavily populated by criminals, just as the chances are high that he might be one, so too are the chances high that he might be mistaken for one. The probabilities, from the point of view of the individual, are always the same—either he is or is not culpable. Thus, behavior which seems 'reasonable' to the police because of the character of the neighborhood is seen by the honest citizen in it as irresponsible and unreasonable. About *him,* more errors will necessarily be made under a 'reasonableness' standard."

be taken of the expertise of the police in ascertaining what is probably criminal conduct?[b]

3. *Information and orders from official channels.* In *Whiteley v. Warden*, 401 U.S. 560, 91 S.Ct. 1031, 28 L.Ed.2d 306 (1971), Laramie, Wyoming police arrested two men fitting a description given in a police bulletin emanating from the office of the Carbon County Sheriff and transmitted over the state police radio network, indicating that the two described men were wanted for breaking and entering and that a warrant had been issued for their arrest. Although the warrant had not issued on probable cause, the state claimed that the arrests made by the Laramie officers were nonetheless legal because "they reasonably assumed that whoever authorized the bulletin had probable cause to direct Whiteley's and Daley's arrest." The Court, per Justice Harlan, disagreed: "We do not of course question that the Laramie police were entitled to act on the strength of the radio bulletin. Certainly police officers called upon to aid other officers in executing arrest warrants are entitled to assume that the officers requesting aid offered the magistrate the information requisite to support an independent judicial assessment of probable cause. Where, however, the contrary turns out to be true, an otherwise illegal arrest cannot be insulated from challenge by the decision of the instigating officer to rely on fellow officers to make the arrest."[c] What is the status of *Whiteley* after *Evans*, p. 136, where the Court distinguished *Whiteley*, relied upon by the defendant, because it mistakenly "treated identification of a Fourth Amendment violation as synonymous with application of the exclusionary rule to evidence secured incident to that violation"?

SECTION 4. SEARCH WARRANTS

A. ISSUANCE OF THE WARRANT

1. *The "neutral and detached magistrate" requirement.* In *Coolidge v. New Hampshire*, 403 U.S. 443, 91 S.Ct. 2022, 29 L.Ed.2d 564 (1971), the State Attorney General (authorized by state law to issue search warrants as a justice of the peace) issued a search warrant for the defendant's car in the course of a murder investigation of which he had taken personal charge and for which he later served as chief prosecutor at trial. The Court, per Stewart, J., held that this procedure "violated a fundamental premise of both the Fourth and Fourteenth Amendments" because "the state official who was the chief investigator and prosecutor in this case * * * was not the neutral and detached magistrate required by the Constitution," and summarily rejected "the proposition that the existence of probable cause renders noncompliance with the warrant procedure an irrelevance."

Compare *Shadwick v. City of Tampa*, 407 U.S. 345, 92 S.Ct. 2119, 32 L.Ed.2d 783 (1972), where a unanimous Court, per Powell, J., upheld a city charter provision authorizing municipal court clerks to issue *arrest* warrants for municipal ordinance violations. Rejecting the notion "that all warrant authority must reside exclusively in a lawyer or judge" (and noting that "even within the federal system

---

b. Compare *United States v. 1964 Ford Thunderbird*, 445 F.2d 1064 (3d Cir.1971) ("The standard is not what a police officer trained in a particular field would conclude, but rather it is what a reasonable prudent man would conclude"); with *United States v. Hoyos*, 892 F.2d 1387 (9th Cir.1989) (the "experience and expertise of the officers involved in the investigation and arrest may be considered in determining probable cause").

c. Compare *United States v. Webster*, 750 F.2d 307 (5th Cir.1984) (arrest illegal notwithstanding probable cause at the source of the request, as defendant was arrested in response to a request which merely asked that anyone discovered in the area of the crime be picked up).

warrants were until recently widely issued by nonlawyers"), the Court concluded that "an issuing magistrate must meet two tests. He must be neutral and detached, and he must be capable of determining whether probable cause exists for the requested arrest or search." The clerk possesses the requisite detachment, as he "is removed from prosecutor or police and works within the judicial branch subject to the supervision of the municipal court judge."[a] As to capacity: "We presume from the nature of the clerk's position that he would be able to deduce from the facts on an affidavit before him whether there was probable cause to believe a citizen guilty of impaired driving, breach of peace, drunkenness, trespass or the multiple other common offenses covered by a municipal code. There has been no showing that this is too difficult a task for a clerk to accomplish. Our legal system has long entrusted nonlawyers to evaluate more complex and significant factual data than that in the case at hand. Grand juries daily determine probable cause prior to rendering indictments, and trial juries assess whether guilt is proved beyond a reasonable doubt." On the basis of *Shadwick,* could court clerks be authorized to issue arrest warrants in all cases? To issue search warrants? If so, can *Shadwick* be reconciled with *Leon,* p. 114?

In *Connally v. Georgia,* 429 U.S. 245, 97 S.Ct. 546, 50 L.Ed.2d 444 (1977), a unanimous Court held that the search warrant had not been issued by a "neutral and detached magistrate" where the issuing justice of the peace was unsalaried and, so far as search warrants were concerned, was paid a fee of $5 if he issued a warrant but nothing if he denied the application.

In *Rooker v. Commonwealth,* 508 S.W.2d 570 (Ky.App.1974), the court, in ruling that evidence obtained in execution of a search warrant must be suppressed, held: "Where a judge issues a search warrant based upon an affidavit which he does not read, he makes no determination of probable cause but merely serves as a rubber stamp for the police. Such action is improper even though the affidavit actually shows probable cause for the issuance of the warrant."

United States v. Davis, 346 F.Supp. 435 (S.D.Ill.1972), involved these facts: A Treasury agent, accompanied by an assistant U.S. attorney, went to Magistrate Ghiglieri and presented an affidavit for a search warrant. The agent did not swear to the affidavit, but the magistrate dated and signed the affidavit and indicated that it was denied. The following day the agent, again accompanied by the assistant, went to Magistrate Giffin and presented the same affidavit. Giffin, after being apprised of the proceedings before Ghiglieri, issued a search warrant. The court found this procedure to be "highly improper" and concluded: "Magistrate Ghiglieri's decision was final and binding, and his denial of the application * * * equitably estopped Magistrate Giffin from issuing a search warrant on the exact same showing." Is this a desirable result, in that it limits magistrate-shopping? If the first magistrate was in error, what recourse should be open to the affiant-officer?

2. *Particular description of the place to be searched.* As for the Fourth Amendment requirement of particularity in the description of the place to be searched, it "is enough if the description is such that the officer with a search warrant can, with reasonable effort ascertain and identify the place intended." *Steele v. United States,* 267 U.S. 498, 45 S.Ct. 414, 69 L.Ed. 757 (1925). The common practice is to identify premises in an urban area by street address, which is sufficient. Less particularity is required for rural premises; for example,

a. Is the magistrate sufficiently detached from the police if it is his practice to assist the police in the preparation of search warrant affidavits? See *United States v. Steed,* 465 F.2d 1310 (9th Cir.1972); *Albitez v. Beto,* 465 F.2d 954 (5th Cir.1972). If he assists the police in execution of the warrant? See *Lo-Ji Sales, Inc. v. New York,* 442 U.S. 319, 99 S.Ct. 2319, 60 L.Ed.2d 920 (1979).

description of a farm by the name of the owner and general directions for reaching the farm is adequate.

Most of the problems which arise concerning the particularity of description occur not because the warrant description is facially vague, but rather because upon execution it proves to be not as certain as theretofore assumed. One possibility is that the description will turn out not to be sufficiently precise, as where the warrant refers to apartment 3 in a certain building but the officers find apartments with that number on each floor. In this kind of case, courts are receptive to a showing that the executing officers had other information (e.g., the occupant's name), via the affidavit or otherwise, which made it apparent which place was intended.

Another type of case is that in which the executing officers find that some but not all of the descriptive facts fit the same place. Illustrative is *State v. Blackburn*, 511 P.2d 381 (Or.1973), where the apartment in a particular building was said to be apartment number 2 with "the letters ECURB on the door," but the officer found one apartment with the numeral 2 on the door and another with no numeral but the letters ECURB on the door. In upholding the search of the latter apartment, the court held that "there could be no real doubt as to which of the premises was intended" because "[n]o one could have made a mistake or been confused about a word like ECURB, but anyone could easily have made a mistake about a numeral."

In the absence of a probable cause showing as to all the separate living units in a multiple-occupancy structure, the warrant for such a building must describe the particular unit to be searched. But, if the building in question from its outward appearance would be taken to be a single-occupancy structure and neither the affiant nor other investigating officers nor the executing officers knew or had reason to know otherwise until execution of the warrant was under way, then the warrant is not defective for failure to specify a unit within the building.

A similar situation, was involved in MARYLAND v. GARRISON, 480 U.S. 79, 107 S.Ct. 1013, 94 L.Ed.2d 72 (1987), where police obtained a search warrant to search the person of one McWebb and "the premises known as 2036 Park Avenue third floor apartment," but discovered only after uncovering contraband during execution that they were in respondent's separate apartment. The Court, per STEVENS, J., concluded: (i) that the search warrant authorized search of the entire third floor but yet "was valid when it issued," for such validity "must be assessed on the basis of the information that the officers disclosed, or had a duty to discover and to disclose, to the issuing magistrate"; (ii) that the execution of the search warrant was valid because "the officers' failure to realize the over-breadth of the warrant was objectively understandable and reasonable." BLACK-MUN, J., for the three dissenters, objected: (i) that the search warrant did not authorize search of the entire third floor, but only the apartment on that floor belonging to McWebb; and (ii) that the police knew the building was a multiple-occupancy structure and should have known before obtaining the search warrant and did know before executing it that there were seven apartments in the 3-story building, and thus unreasonably assumed the third floor was but one apartment.

3. Particular description of the things to be seized. The Fourth Amendment requirement of particularity in the description of the persons[b] or things to be seized is intended to prevent general searches, to prevent the seizure of objects on the mistaken assumption that they fall within the magistrate's authorization, and to prevent "the issuance of warrants on loose, vague or

---

b. Search warrants are usually issued to search for and seize evidence of crime, but are sometimes issued to seek a person who is to be arrested, see *Steagald v. United States*, p. 259, or "who is unlawfully restrained," Fed. R.Crim.P. 41(b).

doubtful bases of fact." *Go-Bart Importing Co. v. United States,* 282 U.S. 344, 51 S.Ct. 153, 75 L.Ed. 374 (1931). As noted in SEARCHSZR § 4.6:

"Consistent with these three purposes are certain general principles which may be distilled from the decided cases in this area. They are: (1) A greater degree of ambiguity will be tolerated when the police have done the best that could be expected under the circumstances, by acquiring all the descriptive facts which reasonable investigation of this type of crime could be expected to uncover and by ensuring that all of those facts were included in the warrant.[18] (2) A more general type of description will be sufficient when the nature of the objects to be seized are such that they could not be expected to have more specific characteristics.[19] (3) A less precise description is required of property which is, because of its particular character, contraband. (4) Failure to provide all of the available descriptive facts is not a basis for questioning the adequacy of the description when the omitted facts could not have been expected to be of assistance to the executing officer.[21] (5) An error in the statement of certain descriptive facts is not a basis for questioning the adequacy of the description if the executing officer was nonetheless able to determine, from the other facts provided, that the object seized was that intended by the description.[22] (6) Greater care in description is ordinarily called for when the type of property sought is generally in lawful use in substantial quantities.[23] (7) A more particular description than otherwise might be necessary is required when other objects of the same general classification are likely to be found at the particular place to be searched.[24] (8) The greatest care in description is required when the consequences of a seizure of innocent articles by mistake is most substantial, as when the objects to be seized are books or films or indicia of membership in an association, or where the place to be searched is an attorney's office. (9) The mere fact that some items were admittedly improperly seized in execution of the warrant 'does not mean that the warrant was not sufficiently particular.' "

4. *Neutrality, particularity, and "good faith."* Consider the impact of *United States v. Leon,* p. 114, and *Massachusetts v. Sheppard,* p. 126, in this context.

B. EXECUTION OF THE WARRANT

1. *Time of execution.* Statutes and court rules commonly provide that a search warrant must be executed within a certain time, such as 10 days. Execution within that time is proper, "provided that the probable cause recited in the affidavit continues until the time of execution, giving consideration to the intervening knowledge of the officers and the passage of time." *United States v. Nepstead,* 424 F.2d 269 (9th Cir.1970) (execution of warrant, for seizure of equipment used to manufacture LSD, 6 days after issuance timely, as premises

---

18. * * * Compare * * *United States v. Blakeney,* 942 F.2d 1001 (6th Cir.1991) ("jewelry" insufficient where inventory available of what taken in jewelry store robbery) * * *.

19. * * * *State v. Salsman,* 290 A.2d 618 (N.H.1972) (description of 42 sheets of plywood sufficient, "considering the nature of these items"). * * *

21. * * * *United States v. Scharfman,* 448 F.2d 1352 (2d Cir.1971) (any effort to describe more particularly which furs in fur stores were stolen "would have required a legion of fur experts" to execute the warrant).

22. *United States v. Rytman,* 475 F.2d 192 (5th Cir.1973) (compressor of described brand and with serial number approximating that stated in the warrant could be seized); * * *

23. * * * *People v. Prall,* 145 N.E. 610 (Ill.1924) (thus description of "certain automobile tires and tubes" insufficient); * * *

24. * * * *United States v. Cook,* 657 F.2d 730 (5th Cir.1981) ("cassettes onto which * * * copyrighted films * * * have been electronically transferred" insufficient as to place with many other cassettes). * * *

under daily surveillance and no activity noted until after first 5 days).[c] Compare *State v. Neely*, 862 P.2d 1109 (Mont.1993) (where probable cause for search warrant not stale when it issued, warrant may be lawfully executed any time within 10–day statutory period); and consider the somewhat reverse situation in *State v. Miller*, 429 N.W.2d 26 (S.D.1988) (where violation of statutory 10–day rule but probable cause had not dissipated, suppression not necessary, as "the letter, not the spirit, of the law was broken").

Also, in many jurisdictions a search warrant may be served only in the daytime unless it expressly states to the contrary, and a warrant so stating often can be obtained only by meeting special requirements—e.g., obtaining the concurrence of two magistrates, showing that the property is definitely in the place to be searched, or showing some need for prompt action. In GOODING v. UNITED STATES, 416 U.S. 430, 94 S.Ct. 1780, 40 L.Ed.2d 250 (1974), holding that the federal statute relating to searches for controlled substances required no special showing for a nighttime search other than that the contraband is likely to be on the property at that time, Justice MARSHALL, joined by Douglas and Brennan, JJ., noted in dissent that while the "constitutional question is not presented in this case and need not be resolved here," the principle that nighttime searches "involve a greater intrusion than ordinary searches and therefore require a greater justification * * * may well be a constitutional imperative. It is by now established Fourth Amendment doctrine that increasingly severe standards of probable cause are necessary to justify increasingly intrusive searches. In *Camara v. Municipal Court* [p. 326], after holding that search warrants were required to authorize administrative inspections, we held that the quantum of probable cause required for issuance of an inspection warrant must be determined in part by the reasonableness of the proposed search. As Justice White stated, 'there can be no ready test for determining reasonableness other than by balancing the need to search against the invasion which the search entails.' The Court in *Camara* thus approved the issuance of area inspection warrants in part because such searches 'involve a relatively limited invasion of the urban citizen's privacy.' I do not regard this principle as a one-way street, to be used only to water down the requirement of probable cause when necessary to authorize governmental intrusions. In some situations—and the search of a private home during nighttime would seem to be a paradigm example—this principle requires a showing of additional justification for a search over and above the ordinary showing of probable cause."

In *United States v. Gervato*, 474 F.2d 40 (3d Cir.1973), the court emphasized the various protections provided by Fed.R.Crim.P. 41 in rejecting the district court's holding "that a search warrant executed in the absence of the occupant constitutes an unreasonable search because there exists the possibility of a general search and 'pilferage by officers of the law.'" So-called "sneak-and-peak" search warrants, authorizing police to enter premises, look around (e.g., to determine the status of a clandestine drug lab) and then depart without leaving any notice of the search, are deliberately executed when it is known no one is present. Given the Fourth Amendment requirement of notice of a search absent "some showing of special facts," *Berger v. New York*, p. 352, courts have imposed two limitations on such warrants: (i) "the court should not allow the officers to dispense with advance or contemporaneous notice of the search unless they have made a showing of reasonable necessity for the delay"; and (ii) "the court should nonetheless require the officers to give the appropriate person notice of the search within a reasonable time of the covert entry." *United States v. Villegas*, 899 F.2d 1324 (2d Cir.1990). (When property is seized pursuant to a warrant, there is also a *due process* requirement that police "take reasonable steps to give notice that the

c. See also *United States v. Marin–Buitra-go*, fn. e at p. 185.

property has been taken so the owner can pursue available remedies for its return," which can be met when no one is present by leaving a "notice of service" with a list of the property seized attached. *City of West Covina v. Perkins*, 525 U.S. 234, 119 S.Ct. 678, 142 L.Ed.2d 636 (1999).) The 2001 antiterrorist legislation includes provision for a delayed notice search warrant.[d]

Gaining Entry

2. *Gaining entry.* In *Wilson v. Arkansas*, 514 U.S. 927, 115 S.Ct. 1914, 131 L.Ed.2d 976 (1995), a unanimous Court, per Thomas, J., proceeded "to resolve the conflict among the lower courts" by holding that the common law doctrine which "recognized a law enforcement officer's authority to break open the doors of a dwelling, but generally indicated that he first ought to announce his presence and authority," "forms a part of the reasonableness inquiry under the Fourth Amendment." The Court cautioned that the "Fourth Amendment's flexible requirement of reasonableness should not be read to mandate a rigid rule of announcement that ignores countervailing law enforcement interests," for "the common-law principle of announcement was never stated as an inflexible rule."

In RICHARDS v. WISCONSIN, 520 U.S. 385, 117 S.Ct. 1416, 137 L.Ed.2d 615 (1997), a unanimous Court, per STEVENS, J., rejected the state supreme court's holding that police officers are *never* required to knock and announce their presence when executing a search warrant in a felony drug investigation:

Knock + Announce

USSC yes cops are required to knock

"The Wisconsin court explained its blanket exception as necessitated by the special circumstances of today's drug culture, and the State asserted at oral argument that the blanket exception was reasonable in 'felony drug cases because of the convergence in a violent and dangerous form of commerce of weapons and the destruction of drugs.' But creating exceptions to the knock-and-announce rule based on the 'culture' surrounding a general category of criminal behavior presents at least two serious concerns.

here are due to circumstances

"First, the exception contains considerable overgeneralization. For example, while drug investigation frequently does pose special risks to officer safety and the preservation of evidence, not every drug investigation will pose these risks to a substantial degree. For example, a search could be conducted at a time when the only individuals present in a residence have no connection with the drug activity and thus will be unlikely to threaten officers or destroy evidence. Or the police could know that the drugs being searched for were of a type or in a location that made them impossible to destroy quickly. In those situations, the asserted governmental interests in preserving evidence and maintaining safety may not outweigh the individual privacy interests intruded upon by a no-knock entry. Wisconsin's blanket rule impermissibly insulates these cases from judicial review.

exception too generalized

"A second difficulty with permitting a criminal-category exception to the knock-and-announce requirement is that the reasons for creating an exception in one category can, relatively easily, be applied to others. Armed bank robbers, for example, are, by definition, likely to have weapons, and the fruits of their crime may be destroyed without too much difficulty. If a per se exception were allowed

d. 18 U.S.C. § 3103a(b) provides that, as to issuance of a search warrant "to search for and seize any property or material that constitutes evidence of a criminal offense in violation of the laws of the United States, any notice required, or that may be required, to be given may be delayed if (1) the court finds reasonable cause to believe that providing immediate notification of the execution of the warrant may have an adverse result [i.e., (A) endangering the life or physical safety of an individual; (B) flight from prosecution; (C) destruction of or tampering with evidence; (D) intimidation of potential witnesses; or (E) otherwise seriously jeopardizing an investigation or unduly delaying a trial]; (2) the warrant prohibits the seizure of any tangible property, any wire or electronic communication (as defined in section 2510), or, except as expressly provided in chapter 121, any stored wire or electronic information, except where the court finds reasonable necessity for the seizure; and (3) the warrant provides for the giving of such notice within a reasonable period of its execution, which period may thereafter be extended by the court for good cause shown."

for each category of criminal investigation that included a considerable—albeit hypothetical—risk of danger to officers or destruction of evidence, the knock-and-announce element of the Fourth Amendment's reasonableness requirement would be meaningless.

"Thus, the fact that felony drug investigations may frequently present circumstances warranting a no-knock entry cannot remove from the neutral scrutiny of a reviewing court the reasonableness of the police decision not to knock and announce in a particular case. Instead, in each case, it is the duty of a court confronted with the question to determine whether the facts and circumstances of the particular entry justified dispensing with the knock-and-announce requirement.

must justify 'no-knock'

"In order to justify a 'no-knock' entry, the police must have a reasonable suspicion that knocking and announcing their presence, under the particular circumstances, would be dangerous or futile, or that it would inhibit the effective investigation of the crime by, for example, allowing the destruction of evidence. This standard—as opposed to a probable cause requirement—strikes the appropriate balance between the legitimate law enforcement concerns at issue in the execution of search warrants and the individual privacy interests affected by no-knock entries. * * * This showing is not high, but the police should be required to make it whenever the reasonableness of a no-knock entry is challenged."

The Court concluded with two additional points: (1) The trial judge had correctly concluded that the police were excused from the knock-and-announce requirement because of the facts of the particular case. The officer who knocked at the door of defendant's hotel room claimed to be a maintenance man, defendant opened the door slightly and upon seeing a uniformed officer slammed the door, at which the police kicked the door in and entered. As the Court explained, once "the officers reasonably believed that Richards knew who they were * * * it was reasonable for them to force entry immediately given the disposable nature of the drugs." (2) The refusal of the magistrate issuing the search warrant to issue a no-knock warrant[e] did not alter this conclusion, as "a magistrate's decision not to authorize a no-knock entry should not be interpreted to remove the officers authority to exercise independent judgment concerning the wisdom of a no-knock entry at the time the warrant is being executed."

must knock unless special circ

In light of the test set out in *Richards* and the illustrations therein of what would *not* suffice, which of the following bits of information would justify an unannounced entry to execute a search warrant for drugs: (a) that the small amount of narcotics was always kept near a toilet; (b) that there was but a small amount of drugs; (c) that there was an unknown quantity of drugs; (d) that the person who planned to sell the drugs was present; (e) that the person who used the drugs was present; (f) that a person whose relationship to the drugs was unknown was present.

In UNITED STATES v. RAMIREZ, 523 U.S. 65, 118 S.Ct. 992, 140 L.Ed.2d 191 (1998), the Court, per REHNQUIST, C.J., unanimously held that whether the *Richards* reasonable suspicion test has been met "depends in no way on whether police must destroy property in order to enter." The Court then concluded that no

e. Wisconsin is among those few jurisdictions specifically authorizing magistrates to issue such search warrants, allowing entry without prior announcement, upon a sufficient showing to the magistrate of a need to do so. A "reverse twist" on the *Richards* view regarding a magistrate's *refusal* to issue such a warrant is the position, stated in *Parsley v. Superior Court*, 513 P.2d 611 (Cal.1973), that a magistrate's *issuance* of such a warrant is of no effect because "unannounced entry is excused only on the basis of exigent circumstances existing at the time an officer approached a site to make an arrest or execute a warrant," and thus "can be judged only in light of circumstances of which the officer is aware at the latter moment."

Fourth Amendment violation had occurred in the instant case, where police executing a search warrant authorizing entry to seize a wanted person broke a garage window in order to deter the occupants of the premises (who thereafter exited and surrendered) from entering the garage to obtain weapons thought to be stored there: "A reliable confidential informant had notified the police that Alan Shelby might be inside respondent's home, and an officer had confirmed this possibility. Shelby was a prison escapee with a violent past who reportedly had access to a large supply of weapons. He had vowed that he would 'not do federal time.' The police certainly had a 'reasonable suspicion' that knocking and announcing their presence might be dangerous to themselves or to others."

bJk 4

3. *Search of persons on the premises.* On the basis of information from an informant that he had frequently and recently observed tinfoil packets of heroin behind the bar and on the person of the bartender of a certain tavern and that the bartender told him he would that day have heroin for sale, a warrant authorizing search of the tavern and bartender for heroin was issued. The warrant was executed during the late afternoon by 7–8 officers, who proceeded to pat down each of the 9–13 customers then present. A cigarette package was located and retrieved from customer Ybarra's pocket, and tinfoil packets of heroin were found therein. State courts held the heroin admissible because found in a search authorized by a statute[f] deemed constitutional as applied in the instant case. In YBARRA v. ILLINOIS, 444 U.S. 85, 100 S.Ct. 338, 62 L.Ed.2d 238 (1979), the Court, in a 6–3 decision, reversed. STEWART, J., for the majority, stated:

"There is no reason to suppose that, when the search warrant was issued on March 1, 1976, the authorities had probable cause to believe that any person found on the premises of the Aurora Tap Tavern, aside from [bartender] 'Greg,' would be violating the law. The Complaint for Search Warrant did not allege that the bar was frequented by persons illegally purchasing drugs. It did not state that the informant had ever seen a patron of the tavern purchase drugs from 'Greg' or from any other person. Nowhere, in fact, did the complaint even mention the patrons of the Aurora Tap Tavern.

"Not only was probable cause to search Ybarra absent at the time the warrant was issued; it was still absent when the police executed the warrant. Upon entering the tavern, the police did not recognize Ybarra and had no reason to believe that he had committed, was committing or was about to commit any offense under state or federal law. Ybarra made no gestures indicative of criminal conduct, made no movements that might suggest an attempt to conceal contraband, and said nothing of a suspicious nature to the police officers. * * *

"It is true that the police possessed a warrant based on probable cause to search the tavern in which Ybarra happened to be at the time the warrant was executed. But, a person's mere propinquity to others independently suspected of criminal activity does not, without more, give rise to probable cause to search that person. * * *[7]"

frisk?

As for the state's claim "that the first patdown search of Ybarra constituted a reasonable frisk for weapons under the doctrine of *Terry v. Ohio*," p. 291, the Court responded that the frisk was "not supported by a reasonable belief that he was armed and presently dangerous, a belief which this Court has invariably held

---

f. This statute, Ill.Comp.Stat. ch. 725, § 5/108–9, reads: "In the execution of the warrant the person executing the same may reasonably detain to search any person in the place at the time: (a) To protect himself from attack, or (b) To prevent the disposal or concealment of any instruments, articles or things particularly described in the warrant."

7. [W]e need not consider situations where the warrant itself authorizes the search of unnamed persons in a place and is supported by probable cause to believe that persons who will be in the place at the time of the search will be in possession of illegal drugs.

must form the predicate to a patdown of a person for weapons. * * * Upon seeing Ybarra, [the police] neither recognized him as a person with a criminal history nor had any particular reason to believe that he might be inclined to assault them. Moreover, as police agent Johnson later testified, Ybarra, whose hands were empty, gave no indication of possessing a weapon, made no gestures or other actions indicative of an intent to commit an assault, and acted generally in a manner that was not threatening."

Emphasizing "the ease with which the evidence of narcotics possession may be concealed or moved around from person to person," the State next contended that the *Terry* standard "should be made applicable to aid the evidence-gathering function of the search warrant." The Court answered: "The 'long prevailing' constitutional standard of probable cause embodies "the best compromise that has been found for accommodating the [ ] often opposing interests" in "safeguard[ing] citizens from rash and unreasonable interferences with privacy" and in "seek[ing] to give fair leeway for enforcing the law in the community's protection.'"

REHNQUIST, J., for the dissenters, reasoned that the *Terry* individualized suspicion standard, "important in the case of an on-the-street stop, where the officer must articulate some reason for singling the person out of the general population," was of "less significance in the present situation" for two reasons: (i) "in place of the requirement of 'individualized suspicion' as a guard against arbitrary exercise of authority, we have here the determination of a neutral and detached magistrate that a search was necessary"; and (ii) "the task performed by the officers executing a search warrant is inherently more perilous than is a momentary encounter on the street."

4. *Detention of persons on the premises.* MICHIGAN v. SUMMERS, 452 U.S. 692, 101 S.Ct. 2587, 69 L.Ed.2d 340 (1981), involved these facts: "As Detroit police officers were about to execute a warrant to search a house for narcotics, they encountered respondent descending the front steps. They requested his assistance in gaining entry and detained him while they searched the premises. After finding narcotics in the basement and ascertaining that respondent owned the house, the police arrested him, searched his person, and found in his coat pocket an envelope containing 8.5 grams of heroin." The Court, per STEVENS, J., upheld the seizure on the basis of the principle derived from *Terry* and related cases, namely, that "some seizures * * * constitute such limited intrusions on the personal security of those detained and are justified by such substantial law enforcement interests that they may be made on less than probable cause, so long as police have an articulable basis for suspecting criminal activity":

"Of prime importance in assessing the intrusion is the fact that the police had obtained a warrant to search respondent's house for contraband. A neutral and detached magistrate had found probable cause to believe that the law was being violated in that house and had authorized a substantial invasion of the privacy of the persons who resided there. The detention of one of the residents while the premises were searched, although admittedly a significant restraint on his liberty, was surely less intrusive than the search itself. Indeed, we may safely assume that most citizens—unless they intend flight to avoid arrest—would elect to remain in order to observe the search of their possessions. Furthermore, the type of detention imposed here is not likely to be exploited by the officer or unduly prolonged in order to gain more information, because the information the officers seek normally will be obtained through the search and not through the detention. Moreover, because the detention in this case was in respondent's own residence, it could add only minimally to the public stigma associated with the search itself and would involve neither the inconvenience nor the indignity associated with a compelled visit to the police station. * * *

"In assessing the justification for the detention of an occupant of premises being searched for contraband pursuant to a valid warrant, both the law enforcement interest and the nature of the "articulable facts" supporting the detention are relevant. Most obvious is the legitimate law enforcement interest in preventing flight in the event that incriminating evidence is found. Less obvious, but sometimes of greater importance, is the interest in minimizing the risk of harm to the officers. Although no special danger to the police is suggested by the evidence in this record, the execution of a warrant to search for narcotics is the kind of transaction that may give rise to sudden violence or frantic efforts to conceal or destroy evidence. The risk of harm to both the police and the occupants is minimized if the officers routinely exercise unquestioned command of the situation. Finally, the orderly completion of the search may be facilitated if the occupants of the premises are present. Their self-interest may induce them to open locked doors or locked containers to avoid the use of force that is not only damaging to property but may also delay the completion of the task at hand.

"It is also appropriate to consider the nature of the articulable and individualized suspicion on which the police base the detention of the occupant of a home subject to a search warrant. We have already noted that the detention represents only an incremental intrusion on personal liberty when the search of a home has been authorized by a valid warrant. The existence of a search warrant, however, also provides an objective justification for the detention. A judicial officer has determined that police have probable cause to believe that someone in the home is committing a crime. Thus a neutral magistrate rather than an officer in the field has made the critical determination that the police should be given a special authorization to thrust themselves into the privacy of a home. The connection of an occupant to that home gives the police officer an easily identifiable and certain basis for determining that suspicion of criminal activity justifies a detention of that occupant."

STEWART, J., joined by Brennan and Marshall, JJ., dissenting, objected that *Terry* and related cases required "some governmental interest independent of the ordinary interest in investigating crime and apprehending suspects," which was not present here, and also that the majority's "view that the detention here is of the limited, unintrusive sort" required under *Terry* was in error, as "a detention 'while a proper search is being conducted' can mean a detention of several hours."

5. *Intensity and duration of the search.* Although a search under a search warrant may extend to all parts of the premises described in the warrant, it does not follow that the executing officers may look everywhere within the described premises; they may only look where the items described in the warrant might be concealed. For example, if a search warrant indicated that the items sought were stolen television sets, the officer would not be authorized to rummage through desk drawers and other places too small to hold these items. Once the items named in the search warrant have been found, the search must cease.

6. *Seizure of items not named in the search warrant.* In HORTON v. CALIFORNIA, 496 U.S. 128, 110 S.Ct. 2301, 110 L.Ed.2d 112 (1990), a police officer's affidavit established probable cause to search defendant's home for the proceeds of a robbery (including three specified rings) and for the weapons used in that robbery, but the magistrate issued a warrant only for the proceeds. They were not found in execution of the warrant, but the guns were; they were seized. The defendant claimed this seizure did not come within Justice Stewart's plurality decision in *Coolidge v. New Hampshire,* 403 U.S. 443, 91 S.Ct. 2022, 29 L.Ed.2d 564 (1971), that items found in "plain view" may be seized "where it is immediately apparent to the police that they have evidence before them," because he also required "that the discovery of evidence in plain view must be inadvertent." The Court in *Horton,* 7–2, disagreed. STEVENS, J., explained:

"Justice Stewart concluded that the inadvertence requirement was necessary to avoid a violation of the express constitutional requirement that a valid warrant must particularly describe the things to be seized. He explained:

'The rationale of the exception to the warrant requirement, as just stated, is that a plain-view seizure will not turn an initially valid (and therefore limited) search into a "general" one, while the inconvenience of procuring a warrant to cover an inadvertent discovery is great. But where the discovery is anticipated, where the police know in advance the location of the evidence and intend to seize it, the situation is altogether different. The requirement of a warrant to seize imposes no inconvenience whatever, or at least none which is constitutionally cognizable in a legal system that regards warrantless searches as *"per se* unreasonable" in the absence of "exigent circumstances."

'If the initial intrusion is bottomed upon a warrant that fails to mention a particular object, though the police know its location and intend to seize it, then there is a violation of the express constitutional requirement of "Warrants ... particularly describing ... [the] things to be seized." '

"We find two flaws in this reasoning. First, evenhanded law enforcement is best achieved by the application of objective standards of conduct, rather than standards that depend upon the subjective state of mind of the officer. The fact that an officer is interested in an item of evidence and fully expects to find it in the course of a search should not invalidate its seizure if the search is confined in area and duration by the terms of a warrant or a valid exception to the warrant requirement. If the officer has knowledge approaching certainty that the item will be found, we see no reason why he or she would deliberately omit a particular description of the item to be seized from the application for a search warrant. Specification of the additional item could only permit the officer to expand the scope of the search. On the other hand, if he or she has a valid warrant to search for one item and merely a suspicion concerning the second, whether or not it amounts to probable cause, we fail to see why that suspicion should immunize the second item from seizure if it is found during a lawful search for the first. The hypothetical case put by Justice White in his dissenting opinion in *Coolidge* is instructive:

'Let us suppose officers secure a warrant to search a house for a rifle. While staying well within the range of a rifle search, they discover two photographs of the murder victim, both in plain sight in the bedroom. Assume also that the discovery of the one photograph was inadvertent but finding the other was anticipated. The Court would permit the seizure of only one of the photographs. But in terms of the "minor" peril to Fourth Amendment values there is surely no difference between these two photographs: the interference with possession is the same in each case and the officers' appraisal of the photograph they expected to see is no less reliable than their judgment about the other. And in both situations the actual inconvenience and danger to evidence remain identical if the officers must depart and secure a warrant.'

"Second, the suggestion that the inadvertence requirement is necessary to prevent the police from conducting general searches, or from converting specific warrants into general warrants, is not persuasive because that interest is already served by the requirements that no warrant issue unless it 'particularly describ[es] the place to be searched and the persons or things to be seized,' and that a warrantless search be circumscribed by the exigencies which justify its initiation. Scrupulous adherence to these requirements serves the interests in limiting the area and duration of the search that the inadvertence requirement inadequately protects. Once those commands have been satisfied and the officer has a lawful right of access, however, no additional Fourth Amendment interest is furthered by requiring that the discovery of evidence be inadvertent. If the scope of the search exceeds that permitted by the terms of a validly issued warrant or the character of the relevant exception from the warrant requirement, the subsequent seizure is unconstitutional without more."

BRENNAN, J., joined by Marshall, J. dissenting, asserted: "When an officer with probable cause to seize an item fails to mention that item in his application for a search warrant—for whatever reason—and then seizes the item anyway, his conduct is *per se* unreasonable. * * *

"* * * It is true that the inadvertent discovery requirement furthers no privacy interests. The requirement in no way reduces the scope of a search or the number of places into which officers may look. But it does protect possessory interests. Cf. *Illinois v. Andreas,* [p. 277] ('The plain-view doctrine is grounded on the proposition that once police are lawfully in a position to observe an item first-hand, its owner's privacy interest in that item is lost; *the owner may retain the incidents of title and possession* but not privacy') (emphasis added). The inadvertent discovery requirement is essential if we are to take seriously the Fourth Amendment's protection of possessory interests as well as privacy interests. The Court today eliminates a rule designed to further possessory interests on the ground that it fails to further privacy interests. I cannot countenance such constitutional legerdemain."

In determining whether the discovered article is incriminating in nature, how carefully may the police examine it? See *Stanley v. Georgia,* 394 U.S. 557, 89 S.Ct. 1243, 22 L.Ed.2d 542 (1969) (obscene films suppressed where police found reels of film while searching for gambling paraphernalia and then viewed the film on a projector and screen found in another room); cf. *Arizona v. Hicks,* p. 244; and compare *State v. Ruscoe,* 563 A.2d 267 (Conn.1989) (where in executing warrant for silver "candlesticks, napkin holders and a silver mug" police moved a TV, 2 VCR's and a tape deck and noticed they without serial numbers, this a lawful discovery under *Hicks,* as "the police moved items in the course of searching for items listed in the warrant").

7. *Presence of third parties.* Police executing search warrants are sometimes accompanied by others. The most common situation was noted in *Wilson v. Layne,* 526 U.S. 603, 119 S.Ct. 1692, 143 L.Ed.2d 818 (1999): "Where the police enter a home under the authority of a warrant to search for stolen property, the presence of third parties for the purpose of identifying the stolen property has long been approved by this Court and our common-law tradition." But in *Wilson,* which involved execution of an *arrest* warrant within premises, the police were accompanied by a reporter and a photographer from the Washington Post. Citing such cases as *Summers,* p. 198, and *Horton,* p. 199, in support of the proposition that the Fourth Amendment requires "that police actions in execution of a warrant be related to the objectives of the authorized intrusion," a unanimous Court concluded the presence of members of the media was unconstitutional because it "was not in aid of the execution of the warrant." Had the media representatives been present during execution of a *search* warrant, would any evidence first discovered by them be inadmissible? Would all the evidence found by the police be inadmissible? In *Wilson,* which was a § 1983 case, the Court, speaking of the media presence, dropped this footnote: "Even though such actions might violate the Fourth Amendment, if the police are lawfully present, the violation of the Fourth Amendment is the presence of the media and not the presence of the police in the home. We have no occasion here to decide whether the exclusionary rule would apply to any evidence discovered or developed by the media representatives."

C. The "Preference" for Warrants

1. The Supreme Court has long expressed a strong preference for searches made pursuant to a search warrant, e.g., *United States v. Ventresca*, 380 U.S. 102, 85 S.Ct. 741, 13 L.Ed.2d 684 (1965), and on occasion has even asserted "that the police must, whenever practicable, obtain advance judicial approval of searches and seizures." *Terry v. Ohio*, p. 291. But this is far from being an accurate portrayal of current law or practice; the fact of the matter is that a great majority of police seizures and searches are made and upheld notwithstanding the absence of a warrant.

This is so because, as elaborated later in this Chapter, the Supreme Court has recognized a considerable variety of circumstances in which the police may lawfully make a search or a seizure without the prior approval of a magistrate. A warrant is excused in situations other than those in which there existed genuine exigent circumstances making it unfeasible for the police to utilize the often time-consuming warrant process. Sometimes this is explained by the Court on the ground that the police activity being permitted without a warrant intrudes only upon lesser Fourth Amendment values. Illustrative is *California v. Carney*, p. 260, allowing warrantless search of vehicles because of the "diminished expectation of privacy" in them. Sometimes warrant excusal is rationalized on the ground that the permitted police activity is merely "routine," as with the inventory allowed in *Colorado v. Bertine*, p. 283. On other occasions the Supreme Court has recognized an exception to the warrant requirement because of a purported need for "bright lines" in the rules governing police conduct. Illustrative is *United States v. Watson*, p. 203, holding a warrant is never needed to arrest in a public place because a contrary holding would "encumber criminal prosecutions with endless litigation with respect to the existence of exigent circumstances, whether it was practicable to get a warrant, whether the suspect was about to flee, and the like." The tension between these and other considerations has not always produced predictable or consistent results in the Court's decisions concerning what is permissible warrantless police action.

2. The preference for the warrant process is commonly explained on the ground that it, more so than the post-search suppression process, *prevents* illegal searches. Compare William S. Stuntz, *Warrants and Fourth Amendment Remedies*, 77 Va.L.Rev. 881, 893 (1991): "Unfortunately, given our existing system, warrants may not have the desired preventive effect. Police officers are not the only ones who can get the relevant legal standards wrong; other actors in the system make mistakes as well. And while requiring warrants does reduce the odds of police mistake in applying the relevant legal standards, it also creates additional opportunities for error by magistrates. This is no small problem. Magistrates (1) may do a bad job of applying the probable cause standard because of deficiencies in the warrant process (review is ex parte and cursory), and (2) nevertheless receive a great deal of deference by judges after the fact. Requiring warrants therefore may lead to many *more* bad searches than would a simple system of police decisionmaking followed by after-the-fact review.

"And even if warrants do prevent bad searches, so do after-the-fact sanctions. An ounce of prevention may indeed be worth a pound of cure, but the pound of cure—after-the-fact sanctions—is itself a preventive device, since the threat of ex post penalties affects behavior ex ante. This is a simple point, but an important one. Police officers, like other regulated actors, respond to legal signals and alter their behavior in order to avoid after-the-fact sanctions. In most other contexts, that is thought to be the cheapest means of achieving a given level of deterrence * * *. Thus, to defend warrants, one must point to some reason why after-the-fact deterrence will work unusually poorly in the search and seizure context—some argument that explains why search and seizure law should be treated *differently* than most other regulatory regimes."

Stuntz, id. at 884, suggests some other reasons—that "the exclusionary rule generates an additional pair of problems for fourth amendment law, problems that warrants might plausibly help solve. Exclusion * * * may bias judges' after-the-fact probable cause determinations by requiring that they be made in cases where the officer actually found incriminating evidence. Similarly, the lack of a credible opponent (the defendant has, after all, been found with incriminating evidence) invites the police to subvert the governing legal standard by testifying falsely at suppression hearings. Warrants can reduce both problems by forcing the necessary judicial decision to be made, and the police officer's account of the facts to be given, before the evidence is found."

3. Craig M. Bradley, *Two Models of the Fourth Amendment*, 83 Mich.L.Rev. 1468, 1471–72 (1985), after noting that extant Fourth Amendment doctrine on when a warrant is required is "mired in exceptions and modifications (with resultant confusion)," asserts that there "are two, and only two, ways of looking at the fourth amendment which will provide the police with reasonably coherent direction as to how they must proceed and the courts with a consistent basis for decision": (1) The "no lines" model, i.e., that a "search or seizure must be reasonable, considering all relevant factors on a case-by-case basis," considering such factors as "whether probable cause existed, whether a warrant was obtained, whether exigent circumstances existed, and the nature of the intrusion, the quantum of evidence possessed by the police, and the seriousness of the offense under investigation." This model, "by presenting an unabashedly *unclear* rule that provides no guidelines, will never have to be modified to suit an unusual fact situation," and thus will "work considerably better than the present system where the Court purports to set forth clear rules but does not actually do so." (2) The "bright line" model, i.e., that "a warrant is always required for every search and seizure when it is practicable to obtain one," but "the warrant need not be in writing but rather may be phoned or radioed into a magistrate * * * who will authorize or forbid the search orally." Under this model, "the police would know what is expected of them and would be able to conform their conduct to the requirement of the law, much as they have accommodated their behavior to the *Miranda* requirements."

SECTION 5. WARRANTLESS ARRESTS AND SEARCHES OF THE PERSON

UNITED STATES v. WATSON

423 U.S. 411, 96 S.Ct. 820, 46 L.Ed.2d 598 (1976).

Justice WHITE delivered the opinion of the Court.

[Reliable informant Khoury told a federal postal inspector that Watson had supplied him with a stolen credit card and had agreed to furnish additional cards at their next meeting, scheduled for a few days later. At that meeting, which occurred in a restaurant, Khoury signaled the inspector that Watson had the cards, at which point the inspector arrested Watson without a warrant, as he was authorized to do under 18 U.S.C. § 3061 and applicable postal regulations. The court of appeals held the arrest unconstitutional because the inspector had failed to secure an arrest warrant although he concededly had time to do so, and this was a significant factor in the court's additional holding that Watson's consent to a search of his car was not voluntary.]

Postal insp can arrest w/out w → as long as pc

* * * Section 3061 represents a judgment by Congress that it is not unreasonable under the Fourth Amendment for postal inspectors to arrest without a warrant provided they have probable cause to do so. This was not an isolated or quixotic judgment of the legislative branch. Other federal law enforcement officers have been expressly authorized by statute for many years to make felony arrests on probable cause but without a warrant. * * *

Because there is a "strong presumption of constitutionality due to an Act of Congress, especially when it turns on what is 'reasonable,' * * * [o]bviously the Court should be reluctant to decide that a search thus authorized by Congress was unreasonable and that the Act was therefore unconstitutional." Moreover, there is nothing in the Court's prior cases indicating that under the Fourth Amendment a warrant is required to make a valid arrest for a felony. Indeed, the relevant prior decisions are uniformly to the contrary. * * *[a]

The cases construing the Fourth Amendment thus reflect the ancient common-law rule that a peace officer was permitted to arrest without a warrant for a misdemeanor or felony committed in his presence as well as for a felony not committed in his presence if there was reasonable grounds for making the arrest. This has also been the prevailing rule under state constitutions and statutes. * * *

Because the common-law rule authorizing arrests without warrant generally prevailed in the States, it is important for present purposes to note that in 1792 Congress invested United States Marshals and their deputies with "the same powers in executing the laws of the United States, as sheriffs and their deputies in their several states have by law, in executing the laws of their respective states." The Second Congress thus saw no inconsistency between the Fourth Amendment and giving United States Marshals the same power as local peace officers to arrest for a felony without a warrant.[8] * * *

US Marshall can arrest w/out w)

The balance struck by the common law in generally authorizing felony arrests on probable cause, but without a warrant, has survived substantially intact. It appears in almost all of the States in the form of express statutory authorization. * * *

This is the rule Congress has long directed its principal law enforcement officers to follow. Congress has plainly decided against conditioning warrantless arrest power on proof of exigent circumstances. Law enforcement officers may find it wise to seek arrest warrants where practicable to do so, and their judgments about probable cause may be more readily accepted where backed by a warrant issued by a magistrate. But we decline to transform this judicial preference into a constitutional rule when the judgment of the Nation and Congress has for so long been to authorize warrantless public arrests on probable cause rather than to encumber criminal prosecutions with endless litigation with respect to the existence of exigent circumstances, whether it was practicable to get a warrant, whether the suspect was about to flee, and the like. * * *

USSC for π

Reversed.

Justice STEVENS took no part in the consideration or decision of this case.

Justice POWELL, concurring. * * *

a. The Court noted by way of footnote that because the arrest here was in a public place, it did not have to resolve the "still unsettled question" of whether a warrant is needed to enter private premises to make an arrest. This issue is considered at p. 251.

8. Of equal import is the rule recognized by this Court that even in the absence of a federal statute granting or restricting the authority of federal law enforcement officers, "the law of the state where an arrest without warrant takes place determines its validity." *United States v. Di Re,* 332 U.S. 581, 68 S.Ct. 222, 92 L.Ed. 210 (1948). * * *

On its face, our decision today creates a certain anomaly. There is no more basic constitutional rule in the Fourth Amendment area than that which makes a warrantless search unreasonable except in a few "jealously and carefully drawn" exceptional circumstances. * * * In short, the course of judicial development of the Fourth Amendment with respect to searches has remained true to the principles so well expressed by Justice Jackson:

> "Any assumption that evidence sufficient to support a magistrate's disinterested determination to issue a search warrant will justify the officers in making a search without a warrant would reduce the Amendment to a nullity and leave the people's homes secure only in the discretion of police officers. * * * When the right of privacy must reasonably yield to the right of search is, as a rule, to be decided by a judicial officer, not by a policeman or Government enforcement agent." *Johnson v. United States,* 333 U.S. 10, 14, 68 S.Ct. 367, 369, 92 L.Ed. 436 (1948).

Since the Fourth Amendment speaks equally to both searches and seizures, and since an arrest, the taking hold of one's person, is quintessentially a seizure, it would seem that the constitutional provision should impose the same limitations upon arrests that it does upon searches. Indeed, as an abstract matter an argument can be made that the restrictions upon arrest perhaps should be greater. A search may cause only annoyance and temporary inconvenience to the law-abiding citizen, assuming more serious dimension only when it turns up evidence of criminality. An arrest, however, is a serious personal intrusion regardless of whether the person seized is guilty or innocent. Although an arrestee cannot be held for a significant period without some neutral determination that there are grounds to do so, no decision that he should go free can come quickly enough to erase the invasion of his privacy that already will have occurred. Logic therefore would seem to dictate that arrests be subject to the warrant requirement at least to the same extent as searches.

[handwritten margin note: arrest more serious intrusion]

But logic sometimes must defer to history and experience. The Court's opinion emphasizes the historical sanction accorded warrantless felony arrests. * * *

Moreover, a constitutional rule permitting felony arrests only with a warrant or in exigent circumstances could severely hamper effective law enforcement. Good police practice often requires postponing an arrest, even after probable cause has been established, in order to place the suspect under surveillance or otherwise develop further evidence necessary to prove guilt to a jury. Under the holding of the Court of Appeals such additional investigative work could imperil the entire prosecution. Should the officers fail to obtain a warrant initially, and later be required by unforeseen circumstances to arrest immediately with no chance to procure a last-minute warrant, they would risk a court decision that the subsequent exigency did not excuse their failure to get a warrant in the interim since they first developed probable cause. If the officers attempted to meet such a contingency by procuring a warrant as soon as they had probable cause and then merely held it during their subsequent investigation, they would risk a court decision that the warrant had grown stale by the time it was used.[5] Law enforcement personnel caught in this squeeze could ensure validity of their arrests only by obtaining a warrant and arresting as soon as probable cause existed,

---

5. The probable cause to support issuance of an arrest warrant normally would not grow stale as easily as that which supports a warrant to search a particular place for particular objects. This is true because once there is probable cause to believe that someone is a felon the passage of time often will bring new supporting evidence. But in some cases the original grounds supporting the warrant could be disproved by subsequent investigation that at the same time turns up wholly new evidence supporting probable cause on a different theory. In those cases the warrant could be stale because based upon discredited information.

thereby foreclosing the possibility of gathering vital additional evidence from the suspect's continued actions. * * *

Justice STEWART, concurring in the result. * * *

Justice MARSHALL, with whom Justice BRENNAN joins, dissenting. * * *

The signal of the reliable informant that Watson was in possession of stolen credit cards gave the postal inspectors probable cause to make the arrest. * * * When law enforcement officers have probable cause to believe that an offense is taking place in their presence and that the suspect is at that moment in possession of the evidence, exigent circumstances exist. Delay could cause the escape of the suspect or the destruction of the evidence. Accordingly, Watson's warrantless arrest was valid under the recognized exigent circumstances exception to the warrant requirement, and the Court has no occasion to consider whether a warrant would otherwise be necessary. * * *

[T]he substance of the ancient common-law rule provides no support for the far-reaching modern rule that the Court fashions on its model. * * *

* * * Only the most serious crimes were felonies at common law, and many crimes now classified as felonies under federal or state law were treated as misdemeanors. * * * To make an arrest for any of these crimes at common law, the police officer was required to obtain a warrant, unless the crime was committed in his presence. Since many of these same crimes are commonly classified as felonies today however, under the Court's holding a warrant is no longer needed to make such arrests, a result in contravention of the common law.

[T]he only clear lesson of history is contrary to the one the Court draws: the common law considered the arrest warrant far more important than today's decision leaves it. * * *

[W]e must now consider (1) whether the privacy of our citizens will be better protected by ordinarily requiring a warrant to be issued before they may be arrested; and (2) whether a warrant requirement would unduly burden legitimate governmental interests.

The first question is easily answered. Of course the privacy of our citizens will be better protected by a warrant requirement. We have recognized that "the Fourth Amendment protects people, not places." Indeed, the privacy guaranteed by the Fourth Amendment is quintessentially personal. Thus a warrant is required in search situations not because of some high regard for property, but because of our regard for the individual, and *his* interest in his possessions and person. * * *

The Government's assertion that a warrant requirement would impose an intolerable burden stems, in large part, from the specious supposition that procurement of an arrest warrant would be necessary as soon as probable cause ripens. There is no requirement that a search warrant be obtained the moment police have probable cause to search. The rule is only that present probable cause be shown and a warrant obtained before a search is undertaken. The same rule should obtain for arrest warrants, where it may even make more sense. Certainly, there is less need for prompt procurement of a warrant in the arrest situation. Unlike probable cause to search, probable cause to arrest, once formed will continue to exist for the indefinite future, at least if no intervening exculpatory facts come to light.

This sensible approach obviates most of the difficulties that have been suggested with an arrest warrant rule. Police would not have to cut their investigation short the moment they obtain probable cause to arrest, nor would undercover agents be forced suddenly to terminate their work and forfeit their covers. Moreover, if in the course of the continued police investigation exigent circumstances develop that demand an immediate arrest, the arrest may be made without fear of unconstitutionality, so long as the exigency was unanticipated and not used to avoid the arrest warrant requirement. Likewise, if in the course of the continued investigation police uncover evidence tying the suspect to another crime, they may immediately arrest him for that crime if exigency demands it, and still be in full conformity with the warrant rule. This is why the arrest in this case was not improper.[15] Other than where police attempt to evade the warrant requirement, the rule would invalidate an arrest only in the obvious situation: where police, with probable cause but without exigent circumstances, set out to arrest a suspect. Such an arrest must be void, even if exigency develops in the course of the arrest that would ordinarily validate it; otherwise the warrant requirement would be reduced to a toothless prescription. * * *

It is suggested, however, that even if application of this rule does not require police to secure a warrant as soon as they obtain probable cause, the confused officer would nonetheless be prone to do so. If so, police "would risk a court decision that the warrant had grown stale by the time it was used." (Powell, J., concurring). This fear is groundless. First, as suggested above, the requirement that police procure a warrant before an arrest is made is rather simple of application. Thus, there is no need for the police to find themselves in this "squeeze." Second, the "squeeze" is nonexistent. Just as it is virtually impossible for probable cause for an arrest to grow stale between the time of formation and the time a warrant is procured, it is virtually impossible for probable cause to become stale between procurement and arrest. Delay by law enforcement officers in executing an arrest warrant does not ordinarily affect the legality of the arrest. * * *

Notes and Questions

1. Consider SEARCHSZR § 5.1: "A study conducted for the President's Commission on Law Enforcement and Administration of Justice indicated that, while nearly fifty percent of all arrests are made within two hours of the crime as a result of a 'hot' search of the crime scene or a 'warm' search of the general vicinity of the crime, very few additional arrests occur immediately thereafter. Rather, there is a delay while further investigation is conducted; about 45 percent of all arrests occur more than a day after the crime, and nearly 35 percent of all arrests are made after the passage of over a week. In these latter instances, * * * the risk is negligible that the defendant will suddenly flee between the time the police solve the case and the time which would be required to obtain and serve an arrest warrant. Indeed, in such cases the need to arrest before an arrest warrant can be obtained is likely to be considerably less apparent than the need to search before a search warrant can be acquired and executed; the defendant is unlikely suddenly to decide to flee or go into hiding at that point, but he well might have reached the stage where he is about to dispose of the fruits of his crime or destroy or abandon items of physical evidence which might link him with the crime."

2. As for the *Watson* dissenters' conclusion that "the privacy of our citizens will be better protected by ordinarily requiring a warrant to be issued before they may be arrested," consider Edward Barrett, *Criminal Justice: The Problem of Mass Production,* in The American Assembly, Columbia University, The Courts, the Public, and the Law Explosion 85, 117–18 (H.W. Jones ed. 1965): "How can a magistrate be more than a 'rubber stamp' in signing warrants unless he devotes

---

15. Although the postal inspectors here anticipated the occurrence of the second crime, they could not have obtained a warrant for Watson's arrest for that crime until probable cause formed, just moments before the arrest. A warrant based on anticipated facts is premature and void. *United States v. Roberts,* 333 F.Supp. 786 (E.D.Tenn.1971).

at least some minutes in each case to reading the affidavits submitted to him in support of the request for a warrant, and inquiring into the background of the conclusions stated therein? And where is the judicial time going to be found to make such inquiries in the generality of cases? The Los Angeles Municipal Court with annual filings of about 130,000 (excluding parking and traffic) *finds itself so pressed that in large areas of its caseload it averages but a minute per case in receiving pleas and imposing sentence.* How could it cope with the added burden that would be involved in the issuance of warrants to govern the approximately 200,000 arrests made per year in Los Angeles for offenses other than traffic"?

3. Is the "preference" for arrest warrants nonetheless justified on the ground that, at least the police must make a record before the event of the basis for their actions? Consider Jerome H. Skolnick, *Justice Without Trial* 214–15 (1966): "[T]he policeman perceives * * * the need to be able to reconstruct a set of complex happenings in such a way that, subsequent to the arrest, probable cause can be found according to appellate court standards. In this way, as one district attorney expressed it, 'the policeman fabricates probable cause.' By saying this, he did not mean to assert that the policeman is a liar, but rather that he finds it necessary to construct an *ex post facto* description of the preceding events so that these conform to legal arrest requirements, whether in fact the events actually did so or not at the time of the arrest. Thus, the policeman respects the necessity for 'complying' with the arrest laws. His 'compliance,' however, may take the form of *post hoc* manipulation of the facts rather than before-the-fact behavior."

4. Given the concern regarding "*post hoc* manipulation of the facts," should the arrest of a person booked for one offense be upheld on the ground that the police actually had sufficient evidence of a quite different offense? Compare Chief Justice Warren, dissenting from the dismissal of the writ of certiorari in *Wainwright v. New Orleans,* 392 U.S. 598, 88 S.Ct. 2243, 20 L.Ed.2d 1322 (1968) ("I see no more justification for permitting the State to disregard its own booking record than for permitting any other administrative body to disregard its own records. * * * If the police in this case really believed that petitioner was the murder suspect, and if they had probable cause to so believe, all they had to do was to arrest and book him for murder"); with *Hatcher v. State,* 410 N.E.2d 1187 (Ind.1980) ("public policy in detecting and prosecuting criminal offenders outweighs the value of having arresting officers choose and enunciate the correct legal theory for the arrest").

5. Some but by no means all relevant authorities have described the common law warrantless arrest power of police regarding misdemeanors as having two limitations: (i) that the offense have occurred in the officer's presence; and (ii) that the offense constitute a "breach of the peace." These authorities were relied upon by the plaintiff in the § 1983 case of ATWATER v. CITY OF LAGO VISTA, 532 U.S. 318, 121 S.Ct. 1536, 149 L.Ed.2d 549 (2001), involving these facts:

"In March 1997, Petitioner Gail Atwater was driving her pickup truck in Lago Vista, Texas, with her 3–year–old son and 5–year–old daughter in the front seat. None of them was wearing a seatbelt. Respondent Bart Turek, a Lago Vista police officer at the time, observed the seatbelt violations and pulled Atwater over. According to Atwater's complaint (the allegations of which we assume to be true for present purposes), Turek approached the truck and 'yell[ed]' something to the effect of '[w]e've met before' and '[y]ou're going to jail.'[1] He then called for backup

---

1. Turek had previously stopped Atwater for what he had thought was a seatbelt violation, but had realized that Atwater's son, although seated on the vehicle's armrest, was in fact belted in. Atwater acknowledged that her son's seating position was unsafe, and Turek issued a verbal warning.

and asked to see Atwater's driver's license and insurance documentation, which state law required her to carry. When Atwater told Turek that she did not have the papers because her purse had been stolen the day before, Turek said that he had 'heard that story two-hundred times.'

"Atwater asked to take her 'frightened, upset, and crying' children to a friend's house nearby, but Turek told her, '[y]ou're not going anywhere.' As it turned out, Atwater's friend learned what was going on and soon arrived to take charge of the children. Turek then handcuffed Atwater, placed her in his squad car, and drove her to the local police station, where booking officers had her remove her shoes, jewelry, and eyeglasses, and empty her pockets. Officers took Atwater's 'mug shot' and placed her, alone, in a jail cell for about one hour, after which she was taken before a magistrate and released on $310 bond.

"Atwater was charged with driving without her seatbelt fastened, failing to secure her children in seatbelts, driving without a license, and failing to provide proof of insurance. She ultimately pleaded no contest to the misdemeanor seatbelt offenses and paid a $50 fine; the other charges were dismissed."

Although Texas law at that time gave the officer total discretion to choose between a custodial arrest and issuance of a citation in such circumstances, Atwater claimed the arrest was contrary to common law and hence in violation of the Fourth Amendment. The Court, per SOUTER, J., agreed that the common law view was "obviously relevant, if not entirely dispositive," as to what the Fourth Amendment's framers thought was reasonable, but then concluded that her "historical argument * * * ultimately fails" because the English and American cases and commentators reached "divergent conclusions" regarding any breach-of-the-peace requirement. Moreover, the post-Amendment history "is of two centuries of uninterrupted (and largely unchallenged) state and federal practice permitting warrantless arrests for misdemeanors not amounting to or involving breach of the peace."[a]

6. *Atwater* is one of several recent cases in which the Supreme Court has made the principal criterion for identifying violations of the Fourth Amendment "whether a particular governmental action * * * was regarded as an unlawful search or seizure under the common law when the Amendment was framed," *Wyoming v. Houghton*, p. 273. This approach, which "departs dramatically from the largely ahistorical approach the Court has taken to the Fourth Amendment for most of the past thirty years," has been criticized as "find[ing] support neither in the constitutional text, nor in what we know of the intentions of the 'Framers,'" and as obscuring the fact "that the Fourth Amendment places on courts a burden of judgment, and that the burden cannot be relieved by the common law's sporadic, contradictory, and necessarily time-bound rules of search and seizure." David A. Sklansky, *The Fourth Amendment and Common Law*, 100 Colum.L.Rev. 1739, 1813–14 (2000). As for use of the technique in *Atwater*, a leading Fourth Amendment historian has concluded that Justice "Souter's claims bear little resemblance to authentic framing-era arrest doctrine," and "that his supposed historical analysis consisted almost entirely of rhetorical ploys and distortions of the historical sources. * * * A robust comparison of the analysis and holding in *Atwater* with the pertinent historical sources reveals that the Framers neither expected nor intended for officers to exercise the sort of unfettered arrest authority that *Atwater* permits." Thomas A. Davies, *The Fictional Character of Law-and-Order Originalism: A Case Study of the Distortions and Evasions of*

---

a. Four members of the Court dissented on another branch of the case, discussed at p. 221, but as to the above matter agreed "that warrantless misdemeanor arrests were not the subject of a clear and consistently applied rule at common law."

Framing–Era Arrest Doctrine in Atwater v. Lago Vista, 37 Wake Forest L.Rev. 239, 246–47 (2002).

7. The common law "in presence" requirement for a warrantless misdemeanor arrest has sometimes caused the courts difficulties. Consider *People v. Burdo,* 223 N.W.2d 358 (Mich.App.1974) (officer could not arrest for misdemeanor of driving under influence of liquor when he came on scene of auto accident and found defendant there, even though defendant obviously was intoxicated and admitted he had been driving); *People v. Dixon,* 222 N.W.2d 749 (Mich.1974) (after stopping noisy vehicle, officer could arrest driver for misdemeanor of driving without a license after being advised via police radio that defendant's license had been suspended).

8. Some states use the felony-arrest rule for *all* offenses, and when such provisions have been challenged as unconstitutional it has been held that the Fourth Amendment should not "be interpreted to prohibit warrantless arrests for misdemeanors committed outside an officer's presence." *Street v. Surdyka,* 492 F.2d 368 (4th Cir.1974). Is this so after *Atwater?* Consider that in *Atwater* the Court dropped this footnote: "We need not, and thus do not, speculate whether the Fourth Amendment entails an 'in the presence' requirement for purposes of misdemeanor arrests. Cf. *Welsh v. Wisconsin*, p. 256 (White, J., dissenting) ('[T]he requirement that a misdemeanor must have occurred in the officer's presence to justify a warrantless arrest is not grounded in the Fourth Amendment')."

9. Rejecting the contention that if the *Watson* probable cause "requirement is satisfied the Fourth Amendment has nothing to say about *how* that seizure is made," the Court in TENNESSEE v. GARNER, 471 U.S. 1, 105 S.Ct. 1694, 85 L.Ed.2d 1 (1985), held that the use of deadly force to arrest a fleeing felon is sometimes unreasonable under the Fourth Amendment. WHITE, J., stated for the majority:

"The use of deadly force to prevent the escape of all felony suspects, whatever the circumstances, is constitutionally unreasonable. It is not better that all felony suspects die than that they escape. Where the suspect poses no immediate threat to the officer and no threat to others, the harm resulting from failing to apprehend him does not justify the use of deadly force to do so. It is no doubt unfortunate when a suspect who is in sight escapes, but the fact that the police arrive a little late or are a little slower afoot does not always justify killing the suspect. A police officer may not seize an unarmed, nondangerous suspect by shooting him dead. The Tennessee statute is unconstitutional insofar as it authorizes the use of deadly force against such fleeing suspects.

"It is not, however, unconstitutional on its face. Where the officer has probable cause to believe that the suspect poses a threat of serious physical harm, either to the officer or to others, it is not constitutionally unreasonable to prevent escape by using deadly force. Thus, if the suspect threatens the officer with a weapon or there is probable cause to believe that he has committed a crime involving the infliction or threatened infliction of serious physical harm, deadly force may be used if necessary to prevent escape, and if, where feasible, some warning has been given. As applied in such circumstances, the Tennessee statute would pass constitutional muster."

O'CONNOR, J., joined by the Chief Justice and Rehnquist, J., dissenting, objected: "A proper balancing of the interests involved suggests that use of deadly force as a last resort to apprehend a criminal suspect fleeing from the scene of a nighttime burglary is not unreasonable within the meaning of the Fourth Amendment. Admittedly, the events giving rise to this case are in retrospect deeply regrettable. No one can view the death of an unarmed and apparently nonviolent 15-year old without sorrow, much less disapproval. Nonetheless, the reasonableness of Officer Hymon's conduct for purposes of the Fourth Amendment cannot be evaluated by what later appears to have been a preferable course of police action. The officer pursued a suspect in the darkened backyard of a house that from all indications had just been burglarized. The police officer was not certain whether the suspect was alone or unarmed; nor did he know what had transpired inside the house. He ordered the suspect to halt, and when the suspect refused to obey and attempted to flee into the night, the officer fired his weapon to prevent escape. The reasonableness of this action for purposes of the Fourth Amendment is not determined by the unfortunate nature of this particular case; instead, the question is whether it is constitutionally impermissible for police officers, as a last resort, to shoot a burglary suspect fleeing the scene of the crime."[b]

The Fourth Amendment reasonableness standard, the Court later declared in *Graham v. Connor*, 490 U.S. 386, 109 S.Ct. 1865, 104 L.Ed.2d 443 (1989), (1) applies to "*all* claims that law enforcement officers have used excessive force—deadly or not—in the course of an arrest, investigatory stop, or other 'seizure' of a free citizen";[c] (2) "requires careful attention to the facts and circumstances of each particular case, including the severity of the crime at issue, whether the suspect poses an immediate threat to the safety of the officers or others, and whether he is actively resisting arrest or attempting to evade arrest by flight"; (3) "must embody allowance for the fact that police officers are often forced to make split-second judgments—in circumstances that are tense, uncertain, and rapidly evolving—about the amount of force that is necessary in a particular situation"; and (4) asks "whether the officers' actions are 'objectively reasonable' in light of the facts and circumstances confronting them, without regard to their underlying intent or motivation."

What is the meaning of the term "deadly force" in *Garner*? In *Vera Cruz v. City of Escondido*, 139 F.3d 659 (9th Cir.1997), an officer acting solely to terminate a person's flight released his "K–9 companion," who bit the fleeing party on the arm and held him until the officer took away the arrestee's knife, resulting in wounds requiring surgery and eight days of hospitalization. In a § 1983 action, plaintiff argued for the Model Penal Code definition, "force that the actor uses with the purpose of causing or that he knows to create a substantial risk of causing death or serious bodily injury," but the court ruled that "deadly force is that force which is reasonably likely to cause death." Which is correct?

10. In GERSTEIN v. PUGH, 420 U.S. 103, 95 S.Ct. 854, 43 L.Ed.2d 54 (1975), the Court, per POWELL, J., held:

"[A] policeman's on-the-scene assessment of probable cause provides legal justification for arresting a person suspected of crime, and for a brief period of detention to take the administrative steps incident to arrest. Once the suspect is in custody, however, the reasons that justify dispensing with the magistrate's neutral judgment evaporate. There no longer is any danger that the suspect will escape or commit further crimes while the police submit their evidence to a magistrate. And, while the State's reasons for taking summary action subside, the suspect's need for a neutral determination of probable cause increases significantly. The consequences of prolonged detention may be more serious than the interference occasioned by arrest. Pretrial confinement may imperil the suspect's job, interrupt his source of income, and impair his family relationships. Even pretrial release may be accompanied by burdensome conditions that effect a

---

b. See H. Richard Uviller, *Seizure by Gunshot: The Riddle of the Fleeing Felon,* 14 N.Y.U.Rev.L. & Soc.Chg. 705 (1986).

c. If the police conduct causing death or bodily harm was not a search or seizure, then the Fourteenth Amendment due process shocks-the-conscience test, rather than the Fourth Amendment reasonableness test, applies. See *County of Sacramento v. Lewis,* p. 39.

significant restraint on liberty. When the stakes are this high, the detached judgment of a neutral magistrate is essential if the Fourth Amendment is to furnish meaningful protection from unfounded interference with liberty. Accordingly, we hold that the Fourth Amendment requires a judicial determination of probable cause as a prerequisite to extended restraint on liberty following arrest.[d]

"This result has historical support in the common law that has guided interpretation of the Fourth Amendment. At common law it was customary, if not obligatory, for an arrested person to be brought before a justice of the peace shortly after arrest. The justice of the peace would 'examine' the prisoner and the witnesses to determine whether there was reason to believe the prisoner had committed a crime. If there was, the suspect would be committed to jail or bailed pending trial. If not, he would be discharged from custody. The initial determination of probable cause also could be reviewed by higher courts on a writ of habeas corpus. This practice furnished the model for criminal procedure in America immediately following the adoption of the Fourth Amendment, and there are indications that the Framers of the Bill of Rights regarded it as a model for a 'reasonable' seizure."

The Court then concluded the Court of Appeals had erred in holding "that the determination of probable cause must be accompanied by the full panoply of adversary safeguards—counsel, confrontation, cross-examination, and compulsory process for witnesses." The Court of Appeals had required that the state provide, in effect, a "full preliminary hearing * * * modeled after the procedure used in many States to determine whether the evidence justifies going to trial under an information or presenting the case to a grand jury." The Fourth Amendment, the Court noted, did not require such an adversary proceeding:

"The sole issue is whether there is probable cause for detaining the arrested person pending further proceedings. This issue can be determined reliably without an adversary hearing. That standard—probable cause to believe the suspect has committed a crime—traditionally has been decided by a magistrate in a nonadversary proceeding on hearsay and written testimony, and the Court has approved these informal modes of proof. * * * The use of an informal procedure is justified not only by the lesser consequences of a probable cause determination but also by the nature of the determination itself. It does not require the fine resolution of conflicting evidence that a reasonable-doubt or even a preponderance standard demands, and credibility determinations are seldom crucial in deciding whether the evidence supports a reasonable belief in guilt. This is not to say that confrontation and cross-examination might not enhance the reliability of probable cause determinations in some cases. In most cases, however, their value would be too slight to justify holding, as a matter of constitutional principle, that these formalities and safeguards designed for trial must also be employed in making the Fourth Amendment determination of probable cause."[e]

---

d. In a subsequent footnote, the Court indicated that a grand jury determination to indict would provide such a "judicial determination." In distinguishing the prosecutor's determination that probable cause exists, the Court noted: "By contrast, the Court has held that an indictment, 'fair upon its face,' and returned by a 'properly constituted grand jury' conclusively determines the existence of probable cause and requires issuance of an arrest warrant without further inquiry. The willingness to let a grand jury judgment substitute for that of a neutral and detached magistrate is attributable to the grand jury's relationship to the courts and its historical role of protecting individuals from unjust prosecution."

e. Stewart, J., joined by Douglas, Brennan and Marshall, JJ., refused to join this portion of the Court's opinion. Justice Stewart noted: "I see no need in this case for the Court to say that the Constitution extends less procedural protection to an imprisoned human being than is required to test the propriety of garnishing a commercial bank account, *North Georgia Finishing, Inc. v. Di–Chem, Inc.*, 419 U.S. 601, 95 S.Ct. 719, 42 L.Ed.2d 751 [(1975)], the custody of a refrigerator, *Mitchell v. W. T. Grant Co.*, 416 U.S. 600, 94 S.Ct. 1895, 40 L.Ed.2d 406

" * * * There is no single preferred pretrial procedure, and the nature of the probable cause determination usually will be shaped to accord with a State's pretrial procedure viewed as a whole. * * * It may be found desirable, for example, to make the probable cause determination at the suspect's first appearance before a judicial officer,[24] the determination may be incorporated into the procedure for setting bail or fixing other conditions of pretrial release. * * * Whatever procedure a State may adopt, it must provide a fair and reliable determination of probable cause as a condition for any significant pretrial restraint on liberty,[26] and this determination must be made by a judicial officer either before or promptly after arrest.[27]"

11. In COUNTY OF RIVERSIDE v. McLAUGHLIN, 500 U.S. 44, 111 S.Ct. 1661, 114 L.Ed.2d 49 (1991), the Court confronted the question of "what is 'prompt' under *Gerstein*" and concluded, 5–4, per O'CONNOR, J., that "it is important to provide some degree of certainty so that States and counties may establish procedures with confidence that they fall within constitutional bounds. Taking into account the competing interests articulated in *Gerstein*, we believe that a jurisdiction that provides judicial determinations of probable cause within 48 hours of arrest will, as a general matter, comply with the promptness requirement of *Gerstein*.[f] For this reason, such jurisdictions will be immune from systemic challenges.

[(1974)], the temporary suspension of a public school student, *Goss v. Lopez*, 419 U.S. 565, 95 S.Ct. 729, 42 L.Ed.2d 725 [(1975)], or the suspension of a driver's license, *Bell v. Burson*, 402 U.S. 535, 91 S.Ct. 1586, 29 L.Ed.2d 90 [(1971)]. Although it may be true that the Fourth Amendment's 'balance between individual and public interests always has been thought to define the "process that is due" for seizures of person or property in criminal cases,' this case does not involve an initial arrest, but rather the continuing incarceration of a presumptively innocent person. Accordingly, I cannot join the Court's effort to foreclose any claim that the traditional requirements of constitutional due process are applicable in the context of pretrial detention."

24. Several States already authorize a determination of probable cause at this stage or immediately thereafter. This Court has interpreted the Federal Rules of Criminal Procedure to require a determination of probable cause at the first appearance.

26. Because the probable cause determination is not a constitutional prerequisite to the charging decision, it is required only for those suspects who suffer restraints on liberty other than the condition that they appear for trial. There are many kinds of pretrial release and many degrees of conditional liberty. We cannot define specifically those that would require a prior probable cause determination, but the key factor is significant restraint on liberty. [Editors' note: Consider *In re Walters*, 543 P.2d 607 (Cal.1975): "As the posting of bail may impose an unwarranted burden on an accused if probable cause to detain is lacking, the accused is entitled to have that determination made prior to electing to post or not to post bail."]

27. In his concurring opinion, Mr. Justice Stewart objects to the Court's choice of the Fourth Amendment as the rationale for decision and suggests that the Court offers less procedural protection to a person in jail than it requires in certain civil cases. Here we deal with the complex procedures of a criminal case and a threshold right guaranteed by the Fourth Amendment. The historical basis of the probable cause requirement is quite different from the relatively recent application of variable procedural due process in debtor-creditor disputes and termination of government-created benefits. The Fourth Amendment was tailored explicitly for the criminal justice system, and its balance between individual and public interests always has been thought to define the "process that is due" for seizures of person or property in criminal cases, including the detention of suspects pending trial. Moreover, the Fourth Amendment probable cause determination is in fact only the *first* stage of an elaborate system, unique in jurisprudence, designed to safeguard the rights of those accused of criminal conduct. The relatively simple civil procedures (e.g., prior interview with school principal before suspension) presented in the cases cited in the concurring opinion are inapposite and irrelevant in the wholly different context of the criminal justice system. * * *

f. SCALIA, J., dissenting, reasoned that "the only element bearing upon the reasonableness of delay was * * * the arresting officer's ability, once the prisoner had been secured, to reach a magistrate who could issue the needed warrant for further detention," and that consequently the time at which the presumption should shift ought to be only 24 hours.

"This is not to say that the probable cause determination in a particular case passes constitutional muster simply because it is provided within 48 hours. Such a hearing may nonetheless violate *Gerstein* if the arrested individual can prove that his or her probable cause determination was delayed unreasonably. Examples of unreasonable delay are delays for the purpose of gathering additional evidence to justify the arrest, a delay motivated by ill will against the arrested individual, or delay for delay's sake. In evaluating whether the delay in a particular case is unreasonable, however, courts must allow a substantial degree of flexibility. Courts cannot ignore the often unavoidable delays in transporting arrested persons from one facility to another, handling late-night bookings where no magistrate is readily available, obtaining the presence of an arresting officer who may be busy processing other suspects or securing the premises of an arrest, and other practical realities.

"Where an arrested individual does not receive a probable cause determination within 48 hours, the calculus changes. In such a case, the arrested individual does not bear the burden of proving an unreasonable delay. Rather, the burden shifts to the government to demonstrate the existence of a bona fide emergency or other extraordinary circumstance. The fact that in a particular case it may take longer than 48 hours to consolidate pretrial proceedings does not qualify as an extraordinary circumstance. Nor, for that matter, do intervening weekends. A jurisdiction that chooses to offer combined proceedings must do so as soon as is reasonably feasible, but in no event later than 48 hours after arrest."

12. Assuming a *Gerstein* violation, what bearing should it have if the individual is later prosecuted? In *Powell v. Nevada,* 511 U.S. 79, 114 S.Ct. 1280, 128 L.Ed.2d 1 (1994), holding *McLaughlin* retroactive to that case, the Court, per Ginsburg, J., noted: "It does not necessarily follow, however, that Powell must 'be set free' or gain other relief, for several questions remain open for decision on remand," including "the appropriate remedy for a delay in determining probable cause (an issue not resolved by *McLaughlin*)." In *Powell,* an untimely probable cause determination was made four days after defendant's arrest, shortly after he gave the police an incriminating statement. In declaring that "whether a suppression remedy applies in that setting remains an unresolved question," Justice Ginsburg took note of two arguably analogous rules pointing in opposite directions: (i) that an after-the-fact judicial determination of probable cause does not make admissible evidence obtained in a search in violation of the Fourth Amendment's search warrant requirement; and (ii) that under *Harris,* p. 769, suppression of a statement subsequently obtained elsewhere is not required because of defendant's warrantless arrest inside premises in violation of the Fourth Amendment.

13. The governor of Michigan issued an arrest warrant for Doran pursuant to a request for extradition from the governor of Arizona. Attached to the Arizona requisition were an arrest warrant for theft, two supporting affidavits, and the original complaint on which the charge was based. Relying upon *Gerstein* and language of the Uniform Criminal Extradition Act that the "indictment, information, or affidavit made before the magistrate must substantially charge the person demanded with having committed a crime," the state supreme court held that Doran could not be extradited because the "complaint and arrest warrant are both phrased in conclusory language" and "the two supporting affidavits fail to set out facts which could justify a Fourth Amendment finding of probable cause." But in *Michigan v. Doran,* 439 U.S. 282, 99 S.Ct. 530, 58 L.Ed.2d 521 (1978), the Court, per Burger, C.J., held "that once the governor of the asylum state has acted on a requisition for extradition based on the demanding state's judicial determination that probable cause existed, no further judicial inquiry may be had on that issue in the asylum state." Emphasizing that the Extradition Clause[g] "was intended to enable each state to bring offenders to trial as swiftly as possible in the state where the alleged offense was committed," the Court concluded that to "allow plenary review in the asylum state of issues that can be fully litigated in the charging state would defeat the plain purposes of the summary and mandatory procedure authorized by" the Clause.

Three concurring Justices, after noting the absence of any discussion in the majority opinion of the significance of the Fourth Amendment, reasoned that the "extradition process involves an 'extended restraint of liberty following arrest' even more severe than that accompanying detention within a single State. [T]herefore, the Amendment's language and the holding in *Gerstein* mean that, even in the extradition context, where the demanding State's 'charge' rests upon something less than an indictment, there must be a determination of probable cause by a detached and neutral magistrate, and that the asylum State need not grant extradition unless that determination has been made. The demanding State, of course, has the burden of so demonstrating." They then concluded that this burden had been met in the instant case because the Arizona arrest warrant declared that a probable cause finding had been made.

UNITED STATES v. ROBINSON
414 U.S. 218, 94 S.Ct. 467, 38 L.Ed.2d 427 (1973).

Justice REHNQUIST delivered the opinion of the Court. * * *

On April 23, 1968, at approximately 11 o'clock p.m., Officer Richard Jenks, a 15–year veteran of the District of Columbia Metropolitan Police Department, observed the respondent driving a 1965 Cadillac near the intersection of 8th and C Streets, Southeast, in the District of Columbia. Jenks, as a result of previous investigation following a check of respondent's operator's permit four days earlier, determined there was reason to believe that respondent was operating a motor vehicle after the revocation of his operator's permit. This is an offense defined by statute in the District of Columbia which carries a mandatory minimum jail term, a mandatory minimum fine, or both.

Jenks signaled respondent to stop the automobile, which respondent did, and all three of the occupants emerged from the car. At that point Jenks informed respondent that he was under arrest for "operating after revocation and obtaining a permit by misrepresentation." It was assumed by the majority of the Court of Appeals, and is conceded by the respondent here, that Jenks had probable cause to arrest respondent, and that he effected a full custody arrest.

In accordance with procedures prescribed in Police Department instructions,[2] Jenks then began to search respondent. He explained at a subsequent hearing

---

g. U.S. Const., Art. IV, § 2: "A Person charged in any State with Treason, Felony, or other Crime, who shall flee from Justice, and be found in another State, shall on Demand of the executive Authority of the State from which he fled, be delivered up, to be removed to the State having Jurisdiction of the Crime."

2. The government introduced testimony at the evidentiary hearing upon the original remand by the Court of Appeals as to certain standard operating procedures of the Metropolitan Police Department. Sergeant Dennis C. Donaldson, a Training Division Instructor, testified that when a police officer makes "a full

custody arrest" which he defined as where an officer "would arrest a subject and subsequently transport him to a police facility for booking," the officer is trained to make a full "field type search" * * *. Sergeant Donaldson testified that officers are instructed to examine the "contents of all of the pockets" of the arrestee in the course of the field search. * * * Those regulations also provide that in the case of some traffic offenses, including the crime of operating a motor vehicle after revocation of an operator's permit, the officer shall make a summary arrest of the violator and take the violator, in custody, to the stationhouse for booking. D.C.Metropolitan Police Department

that he was "face to face" with the respondent, and "placed [his] hands on [the respondent], my right hand to his left breast like this (demonstrating) and proceeded to pat him down thus (with the right hand)." During this patdown, Jenks felt an object in the left breast pocket of the heavy coat respondent was wearing, but testified that he "couldn't tell what it was" and also that he "couldn't actually tell the size of it." Jenks then reached into the pocket and pulled out the object, which turned out to be a "crumpled up cigarette package." Jenks testified that at this point he still did not know what was in the package: "As I felt the package I could feel objects in the package but I couldn't tell what they were. * * * I knew they weren't cigarettes."

The officer then opened the cigarette pack and found 14 gelatin capsules of white powder which he thought to be, and which later analysis proved to be, heroin. Jenks then continued his search of respondent to completion, feeling around his waist and trouser legs, and examining the remaining pockets. The heroin seized from the respondent was admitted into evidence at the trial which resulted in his conviction in the District Court[, which was reversed by the Court of Appeals].

It is well settled that a search incident to a lawful arrest is a traditional exception to the warrant requirement of the Fourth Amendment. This general exception has historically been formulated into two distinct propositions. The first is that a search may be made of the *person* of the arrestee by virtue of the lawful arrest. The second is that a search may be made of the area within the control of the arrestee.

Examination of this Court's decisions in the area show that these two propositions have been treated quite differently. The validity of the search of a person incident to a lawful arrest has been regarded as settled from its first enunciation, and has remained virtually unchallenged until the present case. The validity of the second proposition, while likewise conceded in principle, has been subject to differing interpretations as to the extent of the area which may be searched. * * *

Thus the broadly stated rule, and the reasons for it, have been repeatedly affirmed in the decisions of this Court since *Weeks v. United States* nearly 60 years ago. Since the statements in the cases speak not simply in terms of an exception to the warrant requirement, but in terms of an affirmative authority to search, they clearly imply that such searches also meet the Fourth Amendment's requirement of reasonableness. * * *

Virtually all of the statements of this Court affirming the existence of an unqualified authority to search incident to a lawful arrest are dicta. We would not therefore be foreclosed by principles of *stare decisis* from further examination into history and practice in order to see whether the sort of qualifications imposed by the Court of Appeals in this case were in fact intended by the Framers of the Fourth Amendment or recognized in cases decided prior to *Weeks*. Unfortunately such authorities as exist are sparse. * * *

While these earlier authorities are sketchy, they tend to support the broad statement of the authority to search incident to arrest found in the successive decisions of this Court, rather than the restrictive one which was applied by the Court of Appeals in this case. * * *

The Court of Appeals in effect determined that the *only* reason supporting the authority for a *full* search incident to lawful arrest was the possibility of discovery of evidence or fruits. Concluding that there could be no evidence or fruits in the

General Order No. 3, series 1959 (April 24, 1959). Such operating procedures are not, of course, determinative of the constitutional issues presented by this case.

case of an offense such as that with which respondent was charged, it held that any protective search would have to be limited by the conditions laid down in *Terry* [*v. Ohio*, p. 291] for a search upon less than probable cause to arrest. Quite apart from the fact that *Terry* clearly recognized the distinction between the two types of searches, and that a different rule governed one than governed the other, we find additional reason to disagree with the Court of Appeals.

The justification or reason for the authority to search incident to a lawful arrest rests quite as much on the need to disarm the suspect in order to take him into custody as it does on the need to preserve evidence on his person for later use at trial. The standards traditionally governing a search incident to lawful arrest are not, therefore, commuted to the stricter *Terry* standards by the absence of probable fruits or further evidence of the particular crime for which the arrest is made.

Nor are we inclined, on the basis of what seems to us to be a rather speculative judgment, to qualify the breadth of the general authority to search incident to a lawful custodial arrest on an assumption that persons arrested for the offense of driving while their license has been revoked are less likely to be possessed of dangerous weapons than are those arrested for other crimes.[5] It is scarcely open to doubt that the danger to an officer is far greater in the case of the extended exposure which follows the taking of a suspect into custody and transporting him to the police station than in the case of the relatively fleeting contact resulting from the typical *Terry*-type stop. This is an adequate basis for treating all custodial arrests alike for purposes of search justification.

But quite apart from these distinctions, our more fundamental disagreement with the Court of Appeals arises from its suggestion that there must be litigated in each case the issue of whether or not there was present one of the reasons supporting the authority for a search of the person incident to a lawful arrest. We do not think the long line of authorities of this Court dating back to *Weeks*, nor what we can glean from the history of practice in this country and in England, requires such a case by case adjudication. A police officer's determination as to how and where to search the person of a suspect whom he has arrested is necessarily a quick *ad hoc* judgment which the Fourth Amendment does not require to be broken down in each instance into an analysis of each step in the search. The authority to search the person incident to a lawful custodial arrest, while based upon the need to disarm and to discover evidence, does not depend on what a court may later decide was the probability in a particular arrest situation that weapons or evidence would in fact be found upon the person of the suspect. A custodial arrest of a suspect based on probable cause is a reasonable intrusion under the Fourth Amendment; that intrusion being lawful, a search incident to the arrest requires no additional justification. It is the fact of the lawful arrest which establishes the authority to search, and we hold that in the case of a lawful custodial arrest a full search of the person is not only an exception to the warrant requirement of the Fourth Amendment, but is also a "reasonable" search under that Amendment.

---

5. Such an assumption appears at least questionable in light of the available statistical data concerning assaults on police officers who are in the course of making arrests. The danger to the police officer flows from the fact of the arrest, and its attendant proximity, stress and uncertainty, and not from the grounds for arrest. One study concludes that approximately 30% of the shootings of police officers occur when the officer approaches a person seated in a car. Bristow, *Police Officer Shootings—A* *Tactical Evaluation*, 54 J.Crim.L.C. & P.S. 93 (1963). The Government in its brief notes that the Uniform Crime Reports, prepared by the Federal Bureau of Investigation, indicate that a significant percentage of murders of police officers occurs when the officers are making traffic stops. Brief for the United States, at 23. Those reports indicate that during January–March, 1973, 35 police officers were murdered; 11 of those officers were killed while engaged in traffic stops. Ibid.

The search of respondent's person conducted by Officer Jenks in this case and the seizure from him of the heroin, were permissible under established Fourth Amendment law. * * * Since it is the fact of custodial arrest which gives rise to the authority to search, it is of no moment that Jenks did not indicate any subjective fear of the respondent or that he did not himself suspect that respondent was armed.[7] Having in the course of a lawful search come upon the crumpled package of cigarettes, he was entitled to inspect it; and when his inspection revealed the heroin capsules, he was entitled to seize them as "fruits, instrumentalities, or contraband" probative of criminal conduct. The judgment of the Court of Appeals holding otherwise is reversed.

Reversed.

Justice MARSHALL, with whom Justice DOUGLAS and Justice BRENNAN join, dissenting. * * *

The majority's attempt to avoid case-by-case adjudication of Fourth Amendment issues is not only misguided as a matter of principle, but is also doomed to fail as a matter of practical application. As the majority itself is well aware, the powers granted the police in this case are strong ones, subject to potential abuse. Although, in this particular case, Officer Jenks was required by Police Department regulation to make an in-custody arrest rather than to issue a citation, in most jurisdictions and for most traffic offenses the determination of whether to issue a citation or effect a full arrest is discretionary with the officer. There is always the possibility that a police officer, lacking probable cause to obtain a search warrant, will use a traffic arrest as a pretext to conduct a search. I suggest this possibility not to impugn the integrity of our police, but merely to point out that case-by-case adjudication will always be necessary to determine whether a full arrest was effected for purely legitimate reasons or, rather, as a pretext for searching the arrestee.

The majority states that "A police officer's determination as to how and where to search the person of a suspect whom he has arrested is necessarily a quick *ad hoc* judgment which the Fourth Amendment does not require to be broken down in each instance into an analysis of each step in the search." No precedent is cited for this broad assertion—not surprisingly, since there is none. Indeed, we only recently rejected such "a rigid all-or-nothing model of justification and regulation under the Amendment, [for] it obscures the utility of limitations upon the scope, as well as the initiation, of police action as a means of constitutional regulation. This Court has held in the past that a search which is reasonable at its inception may violate the Fourth Amendment by virtue of its intolerable intensity and scope." *Terry v. Ohio*. As we there concluded, "in determining whether the seizure and search were 'unreasonable' our inquiry is a dual one—whether the officer's action was justified at its inception, and whether it was reasonably related in scope to the circumstances which justified the interference in the first place."

As I view the matter, the search in this case divides into three distinct phases: the patdown of respondent's coat pocket; the removal of the unknown object from the pocket; and the opening of the crumpled up cigarette package.

No question is raised here concerning the lawfulness of the patdown of respondent's coat pocket. The Court of Appeals unanimously affirmed the right of

---

7. The United States concedes that "in searching respondent, [Officer Jenks] was not motivated by a feeling of imminent danger and was not specifically looking for weapons." Brief for the United States. Officer Jenks testified, "I just searched him [Robinson]. I didn't think about what I was looking for. I just searched him." Officer Jenks also testified that upon removing the cigarette package from the respondent's custody, he was still unsure what was in the package, but that he knew it was not cigarettes.

a police officer to conduct a limited frisk for weapons when making an in-custody arrest, regardless of the nature of the crime for which the arrest was made. * * *

With respect to the removal of the unknown object from the coat pocket, * * * Officer Jenks had no reason to believe and did not in fact believe that the object in respondent's coat pocket was a weapon. He admitted later that the object did not feel like a gun. * * *

Since the removal of the object from the pocket cannot be justified as part of a limited *Terry* weapons frisk, the question arises whether it is reasonable for a police officer, when effecting an in-custody arrest of a traffic offender, to make a fuller search of the person than is permitted pursuant to *Terry.* * * *

The Government does not now contend that the search of respondent's pocket can be justified by any need to find and seize evidence in order to prevent its concealment or destruction, for as the Court of Appeals found, there are no evidence or fruits of the offense with which respondent was charged. The only rationale for a search in this case, then, is the removal of weapons which the arrestee might use to harm the officer and attempt an escape. This rationale, of course, is identical to the rationale of the search permitted in *Terry.* * * *

Since the underlying rationale of a *Terry* search and the search of a traffic violator are identical, the Court of Appeals held that the scope of the searches must be the same. * * *

The problem with this approach, however, is that it ignores several significant differences between the context in which a search incident to arrest for a traffic violation is made, and the situation presented in *Terry*. Some of these differences would appear to suggest permitting a more thorough search in this case than was permitted in *Terry;* other differences suggest a narrower, more limited right to search than was there recognized.

The most obvious difference between the two contexts relates to whether the officer has cause to believe that the individual he is dealing with possesses weapons which might be used against him. *Terry* did not permit an officer to conduct a weapons frisk of anyone he lawfully stopped on the street, but rather, only where "he has reason to believe that he is dealing with an armed and dangerous individual. * * *" While the policeman who arrests a suspected rapist or robber may well have reason to believe he is dealing with an armed and dangerous person, certainly this does not hold true with equal force with respect to persons arrested for motor vehicle violations of the sort involved in this case.

Nor was there any particular reason in this case to believe that respondent was dangerous. He had not attempted to evade arrest, but had quickly complied with the police both in bringing his car to a stop after being signalled to do so and in producing the documents Officer Jenks requested. In fact, Jenks admitted that he searched respondent face-to-face rather than in spread-eagle fashion because he had no reason to believe respondent would be violent.

While this difference between the situation presented in *Terry* and the context presented in this case would tend to suggest a lesser authority to search here than was permitted in *Terry,* other distinctions between the two contexts suggest just the opposite. As the Court of Appeals noted, a crucial feature distinguishing the in-custody arrest from the *Terry* context "is not the greater likelihood that a person taken into custody is armed, but rather the increased likelihood of danger to the officer *if* in fact the person is armed." A *Terry* stop involves a momentary encounter between officer and suspect, while an in-custody arrest places the two in close proximity for a much longer period of time. If the individual happens to have a weapon on his person, he will certainly have much more opportunity to use it against the officer in the in-custody situation. The prolonged proximity also makes it more likely that the individual will be able to extricate any small hidden weapon which might go undetected in a weapons frisk, such as a safety pin or razor blade. In addition, a suspect taken into custody may feel more threatened by the serious restraint on his liberty than a person who is simply stopped by an officer for questioning, and may therefore be more likely to resort to force.

Thus, in some senses there is less need for a weapons search in the in-custody traffic arrest situation than in a *Terry* context, while in other ways, there is a greater need. Balancing these competing considerations in order to determine what is a reasonable warrantless search in the traffic arrest context is a difficult process, one for which there may be no easy analytical guideposts. We are dealing in factors not easily quantified and, therefore, not easily weighed one against the other. And the competing interests we are protecting—the individual's interest in remaining free from unnecessarily intrusive invasions of privacy and society's interest that police officers not take unnecessary risks in the performance of their duties—are each deserving of our most serious attention and do not themselves tip the balance in any particular direction. * * *

The majority relies on statistics indicating that a significant percentage of police officer murders occur when the officers are making traffic stops. But these statistics only confirm what we recognized in *Terry*—that "American criminals have a long tradition of armed violence, and every year in this country many law enforcement officers are killed in the line of duty, and thousands more are wounded." As the very next sentence in *Terry* recognized, however, "Virtually all of these deaths and a substantial portion of the injuries are inflicted with guns and knives." The statistics relied on by the Government in this case support this observation. Virtually all of the killings are caused by guns and knives, the very type of weapons which will not go undetected in a properly conducted weapons frisk.[5] * * *

The majority opinion fails to recognize that the search conducted by Officer Jenks did not merely involve a search of respondent's person. It also included a separate search of effects found on his person. And even were we to assume, *arguendo,* that it was reasonable for Jenks to remove the object he felt in respondent's pocket, clearly there was no justification consistent with the Fourth Amendment which would authorize his opening the package and looking inside.

To begin with, after Jenks had the cigarette package in his hands, there is no indication that he had reason to believe or did in fact believe that the package contained a weapon. More importantly, even if the crumpled up cigarette package had in fact contained some sort of small weapon, it would have been impossible for respondent to have used it once the package was in the officer's hands. Opening the package therefore did not further the protective purpose of the search. * * *

It is suggested, however, that since the custodial arrest itself represents a significant intrusion into the privacy of the person, any additional intrusion by way of opening or examining effects found on the person is not worthy of constitutional protection. But such an approach was expressly rejected by the Court in *Chimel* [p. 238]. There it was suggested that since the police had lawfully entered petitioner's house to effect an arrest, the additional invasion of privacy stemming from an accompanying search of the entire house was inconsequential. The Court answered: "[W]e see no reason why, simply because some interference with an individual's privacy and freedom of movement has lawfully taken place,

---

5. The Uniform Crime Reports prepared by the Federal Bureau of Investigation which are relied on by the majority, see *ante,* at n. 5, indicate that 112 police officers were killed nationwide in 1972. Of these, 108 were killed by firearms. Two of the remaining four were killed with knives, and the last two cases involved a bomb and an automobile.

further intrusions should automatically be allowed despite the absence of a warrant that the Fourth Amendment would otherwise require." * * *

The Government argues that it is difficult to see what constitutionally protected "expectation of privacy" a prisoner has in the interior of a cigarette pack. One wonders if the result in this case would have been the same were respondent a businessman who was lawfully taken into custody for driving without a license and whose wallet was taken from him by the police. Would it be reasonable for the police officer, because of the possibility that a razor blade was hidden somewhere in the wallet, to open it, remove all the contents, and examine each item carefully? Or suppose a lawyer lawfully arrested for a traffic offense is found to have a sealed envelope on his person. Would it be permissible for the arresting officer to tear open the envelope in order to make sure that it did not contain a clandestine weapon—perhaps a pin or a razor blade? Would it not be more consonant with the purpose of the Fourth Amendment and the legitimate needs of the police to require the officer, if he has any question whatsoever about what the wallet or letter contains, to hold onto it until the arrestee is brought to the precinct station? * * *

NOTES AND QUESTIONS ON UNNECESSARY, PRETEXTUAL, AND ARBITRARY ARRESTS

1. In the companion case of *Gustafson v. Florida*, 414 U.S. 260, 94 S.Ct. 488, 38 L.Ed.2d 456 (1973), marijuana cigarettes were found on petitioner's person in a search incident to his custodial arrest for failure to have his operator's license with him while driving. Petitioner contended his case was different from *Robinson* in that (a) the offense for which he was arrested was "benign or trivial in nature," carrying with it no mandatory minimum sentence; and (b) there were no police regulations which required the officer to take petitioner into custody[a] or which required full scale body searches upon arrest in the field. The Court did "not find these differences determinative of the constitutional issue," and thus upheld the search on the basis of *Robinson*. Stewart, J., concurring, stated "that a persuasive claim might have been made in this case that the custodial arrest of the petitioner for a minor traffic offense violated his rights under the Fourth and Fourteenth Amendments," but since petitioner had "fully conceded the constitutional validity of his custodial arrest," the search of his person should be accepted as incidental to that arrest.

Nearly thirty years later, the issue noted by Justice Stewart was addressed in ATWATER v. CITY OF LAGO VISTA, p. 208, where the Court, per SOUTER, J., responded to plaintiff's second argument, "for a modern arrest rule, one not necessarily requiring violent breach of the peace, but nonetheless forbidding custodial arrest, even upon probable cause, when conviction could not ultimately carry any jail time and when the government shows no compelling need for immediate detention.

a. Note, in this regard, the variation in state law governing traffic "arrests." Some states require that persons halted for violations of misdemeanor traffic laws be released upon issuance of a citation unless they fall within certain exceptions. The exceptions usually are divided into two categories: (1) persons who must be arrested and taken before a magistrate—usually those violating several specified laws (e.g., driving with a suspended license, or driving under the influence of alcohol); and (2) person who may be released on citation or taken before a magistrate at the option of the police officer—e.g., those who have violated several other specified laws (e.g., reckless driving or failure to submit to vehicle inspection), who fail to have a license in their possession, or who fail to furnish satisfactory evidence of identification. Other states require that persons in certain categories be taken into custody, but grant the officer discretion as to whether to take other misdemeanor violators into custody or to release them upon issuance of a citation. Special requirements are often imposed for release of nonresident drivers.

"If we were to derive a rule exclusively to address the uncontested facts of this case, Atwater might well prevail. She was a known and established resident of Lago Vista with no place to hide and no incentive to flee, and common sense says she would almost certainly have buckled up as a condition of driving off with a citation. In her case, the physical incidents of arrest were merely gratuitous humiliations imposed by a police officer who was (at best) exercising extremely poor judgment. Atwater's claim to live free of pointless indignity and confinement clearly outweighs anything the City can raise against it specific to her case.

"But we have traditionally recognized that a responsible Fourth Amendment balance is not well served by standards requiring sensitive, case-by-case determinations of government need, lest every discretionary judgment in the field be converted into an occasion for constitutional review. See, e.g., *United States v. Robinson*, [p. 215]. Often enough, the Fourth Amendment has to be applied on the spur (and in the heat) of the moment, and the object in implementing its command of reasonableness is to draw standards sufficiently clear and simple to be applied with a fair prospect of surviving judicial second-guessing months and years after an arrest or search is made. Courts attempting to strike a reasonable Fourth Amendment balance thus credit the government's side with an essential interest in readily administrable rules.

"At first glance, Atwater's argument may seem to respect the values of clarity and simplicity, so far as she claims that the Fourth Amendment generally forbids warrantless arrests for minor crimes not accompanied by violence or some demonstrable threat of it (whether 'minor crime' be defined as a fine-only traffic offense, a fine-only offense more generally, or a misdemeanor). But the claim is not ultimately so simple, nor could it be, for complications arise the moment we begin to think about the possible applications of the several criteria Atwater proposes for drawing a line between minor crimes with limited arrest authority and others not so restricted.

"One line, she suggests, might be between 'jailable' and 'fine-only' offenses, between those for which conviction could result in commitment and those for which it could not. The trouble with this distinction, of course, is that an officer on the street might not be able to tell. It is not merely that we cannot expect every police officer to know the details of frequently complex penalty schemes, but that penalties for ostensibly identical conduct can vary on account of facts difficult (if not impossible) to know at the scene of an arrest. Is this the first offense or is the suspect a repeat offender? Is the weight of the marijuana a gram above or a gram below the fine-only line? Where conduct could implicate more than one criminal prohibition, which one will the district attorney ultimately decide to charge? And so on.

"But Atwater's refinements would not end there. She represents that if the line were drawn at nonjailable traffic offenses, her proposed limitation should be qualified by a proviso authorizing warrantless arrests where 'necessary for enforcement of the traffic laws or when [an] offense would otherwise continue and pose a danger to others on the road.' (Were the line drawn at misdemeanors generally, a comparable qualification would presumably apply.) The proviso only compounds the difficulties. Would, for instance, either exception apply to speeding? * * *

"There is no need for more examples to show that Atwater's general rule and limiting proviso promise very little in the way of administrability. It is no answer that the police routinely make judgments on grounds like risk of immediate repetition; they surely do and should. But there is a world of difference between making that judgment in choosing between the discretionary leniency of a summons in place of a clearly lawful arrest, and making the same judgment when the

question is the lawfulness of the warrantless arrest itself. It is the difference between no basis for legal action challenging the discretionary judgment, on the one hand, and the prospect of evidentiary exclusion or (as here) personal § 1983 liability for the misapplication of a constitutional standard, on the other. Atwater's rule therefore would not only place police in an almost impossible spot but would guarantee increased litigation over many of the arrests that would occur.
* * *

would This lead to increased litigation

"One may ask, of course, why these difficulties may not be answered by a simple tie breaker for the police to follow in the field: if in doubt, do not arrest. The first answer is that in practice the tie breaker would boil down to something akin to a least-restrictive-alternative limitation, which is itself one of those 'ifs, ands, and buts' rules, generally thought inappropriate in working out Fourth Amendment protection. Beyond that, whatever help the tie breaker might give would come at the price of a systematic disincentive to arrest in situations where even Atwater concedes that arresting would serve an important societal interest.
* * *

"Just how easily the costs could outweigh the benefits may be shown by asking, as one Member of this Court did at oral argument, 'how bad the problem is out there.' The very fact that the law has never jelled the way Atwater would have it leads one to wonder whether warrantless misdemeanor arrests need constitutional attention, and there is cause to think the answer is no. So far as such arrests might be thought to pose a threat to the probable-cause requirement, anyone arrested for a crime without formal process, whether for felony or misdemeanor, is entitled to a magistrate's review of probable cause within 48 hours, and there is no reason to think the procedure in this case atypical in giving the suspect a prompt opportunity to request release. Many jurisdictions, moreover, have chosen to impose more restrictive safeguards through statutes limiting warrantless arrests for minor offenses. It is of course easier to devise a minor-offense limitation by statute than to derive one through the Constitution, simply because the statute can let the arrest power turn on any sort of practical consideration without having to subsume it under a broader principle. It is, in fact, only natural that States should resort to this sort of legislative regulation, for * * * it is in the interest of the police to limit petty-offense arrests, which carry costs that are simply too great to incur without good reason. Finally, and significantly, under current doctrine the preference for categorical treatment of Fourth Amendment claims gives way to individualized review when a defendant makes a colorable argument that an arrest, with or without a warrant, was conducted in an extraordinary manner, unusually harmful to [his] privacy or even physical interests.' *Whren v. United States*, [p. 226].

"The upshot of all these influences, combined with the good sense (and, failing that, the political accountability) of most local lawmakers and law-enforcement officials, is a dearth of horribles demanding redress. Indeed, when Atwater's counsel was asked at oral argument for any indications of comparably foolish, warrantless misdemeanor arrests, he could offer only one. We are sure that there are others, but just as surely the country is not confronting anything like an epidemic of unnecessary minor-offense arrests. That fact caps the reasons for rejecting Atwater's request for the development of a new and distinct body of constitutional law."

DISSENT

O'CONNOR, J., for the four dissenters, responded: "A custodial arrest exacts an obvious toll on an individual's liberty and privacy, even when the period of custody is relatively brief. The arrestee is subject to a full search of her person and confiscation of her possessions. *United States v. Robinson*, supra. If the arrestee is the occupant of a car, the entire passenger compartment of the car, including packages therein, is subject to search as well. See *New York v. Belton*, [p. 278].

toll on indiv liberty privacy

[handwritten margin note: Arrestee can be held up to 48 hrs w/potentaly dangerous people]

The arrestee may be detained for up to 48 hours without having a magistrate determine whether there in fact was probable cause for the arrest. See *County of Riverside v. McLaughlin*, [p. 213]. Because people arrested for all types of violent and nonviolent offenses may be housed together awaiting such review, this detention period is potentially dangerous. And once the period of custody is over, the fact of the arrest is a permanent part of the public record.

"We have said that 'the penalty that may attach to any particular offense seems to provide the clearest and most consistent indication of the State's interest in arresting individuals suspected of committing that offense.' *Welsh v. Wisconsin*, [p. 256]. If the State has decided that a fine, and not imprisonment, is the appropriate punishment for an offense, the State's interest in taking a person suspected of committing that offense into custody is surely limited, at best. This is not to say that the State will never have such an interest. A full custodial arrest may on occasion vindicate legitimate state interests, even if the crime is punishable only by fine. Arrest is the surest way to abate criminal conduct. It may also allow the police to verify the offender's identity and, if the offender poses a flight risk, to ensure her appearance at trial. But when such considerations are not present, a citation or summons may serve the State's remaining law enforcement interests every bit as effectively as an arrest.

"Because a full custodial arrest is such a severe intrusion on an individual's liberty, its reasonableness hinges on 'the degree to which it is needed for the promotion of legitimate governmental interests.' In light of the availability of citations to promote a State's interests when a fine-only offense has been committed, I cannot concur in a rule which deems a full custodial arrest to be reasonable in every circumstance. Giving police officers constitutional carte blanche to effect an arrest whenever there is probable cause to believe a fine-only misdemeanor has been committed is irreconcilable with the Fourth Amendment's command that seizures be reasonable. Instead, I would require that when there is probable cause to believe that a fine-only offense has been committed, the police officer should issue a citation unless the officer is 'able to point to specific and articulable facts which, taken together with rational inferences from those facts, reasonably warrant [the additional] intrusion' of a full custodial arrest.

"The majority insists that a bright-line rule focused on probable cause is necessary to vindicate the State's interest in easily administrable law enforcement rules. Probable cause itself, however, is not a model of precision. * * * The rule I propose—which merely requires a legitimate reason for the decision to escalate the seizure into a full custodial arrest—thus does not undermine an otherwise 'clear and simple' rule.

"While clarity is certainly a value worthy of consideration in our Fourth Amendment jurisprudence, it by no means trumps the values of liberty and privacy at the heart of the Amendment's protections. * * *

"The Court's error, however, does not merely affect the disposition of this case. The per se rule that the Court creates has potentially serious consequences for the everyday lives of Americans. A broad range of conduct falls into the category of fine-only misdemeanors. * * *

"To be sure, such laws are valid and wise exercises of the States' power to protect the public health and welfare. My concern lies not with the decision to enact or enforce these laws, but rather with the manner in which they may be enforced. Under today's holding, when a police officer has probable cause to believe that a fine-only misdemeanor offense has occurred, that officer may stop the suspect, issue a citation, and let the person continue on her way. Or, if a traffic violation, the officer may stop the car, arrest the driver, search the driver, search the entire passenger compartment of the car including any purse or package inside, and impound the car and inventory all of its contents. Although the Fourth Amendment expressly requires that the latter course be a reasonable and proportional response to the circumstances of the offense, the majority gives officers unfettered discretion to choose that course without articulating a single reason why such action is appropriate.

"Such unbounded discretion carries with it grave potential for abuse. The majority takes comfort in the lack of evidence of 'an epidemic of unnecessary minor-offense arrests.' But the relatively small number of published cases dealing with such arrests proves little and should provide little solace. Indeed, as the recent debate over racial profiling demonstrates all too clearly, a relatively minor traffic infraction may often serve as an excuse for stopping and harassing an individual. After today, the arsenal available to any officer extends to a full arrest and the searches permissible concomitant to that arrest. An officer's subjective motivations for making a traffic stop are not relevant considerations in determining the reasonableness of the stop. See *Whren v. United States*, supra. But it is precisely because these motivations are beyond our purview that we must vigilantly ensure that officers' poststop actions—which are properly within our reach—comport with the Fourth Amendment's guarantee of reasonableness."

2. Would/should the result in *Atwater* be different had there been a state law proscribing custodial arrest in the case of seat belt violations? Consider *United States v. Mota*, 982 F.2d 1384 (9th Cir.1993), where state officers found counterfeit money in the search of two brothers incident to their custodial arrest for the municipal ordinance violation of operating a food cart without a license. Because a state statute required that such violators merely be given a citation, the court ruled the Fourth Amendment required suppression of their money. Is this because the *arrest* (not claimed to be pretextual) violated the Fourth Amendment? The *Mota* court seemed to think so, stating: "Given the state's expression of disinterest in allowing warrantless arrests for mere infractions, we conclude that a custodial arrest for such infractions is unreasonable, and thus unlawful under the Fourth Amendment." Given that there is considerable authority to the contrary,[b] should the court in *Mota* instead have said that it was the search and not the arrest which violated the Fourth Amendment because *Robinson* upholds a search on incident-to-arrest grounds only when the arrest is a "lawful custodial arrest," which must mean lawful as a matter of state law?

3. Compare with *Atwater* the situation regarding arrest of a person as a material witness (a tactic used with some frequency in the investigation immediately following the 9/11/01 attack). In *Bacon v. United States*, 449 F.2d 933 (9th Cir.1971), the court held that the power to arrest and detain a person as a material witness was "fairly inferable" from 18 U.S.C. § 3149, App. B, but then relied upon the Fourth Amendment in concluding that such arrest was permissible only upon a need-for-custody showing. *Bacon* thus concluded that a material witness arrest warrant must be based upon probable cause, which must be tested by two criteria: (1) "that the testimony of a person is material," and (2) "that it may become impracticable to secure his presence by subpoena." The court's added observation that the first of these could be met by "a mere statement by a responsible official, such as the United States Attorney," was later subjected to a Fourth Amendment challenge on the ground that it "permits a much lower standard than that required for the issuance of a standard arrest warrant," *United States v. Oliver*, 683 F.2d 224 (7th Cir.1982), to which the court responded: "We believe requiring a materiality representation by a responsible official of the United States Attorney's Office strikes a proper and adequate balance between

---

b. See, e.g., *Barry v. Fowler*, 902 F.2d 770 (9th Cir.1990), holding that in a § 1983 action claiming an unconstitutional arrest, the plaintiff cannot prevail if the arrest was made on probable cause but was in violation of state law.

protecting the secrecy of the grand jury's investigation and subjecting an individual to an unjustified arrest."[c]

4. As for the pretext arrest issue raised by the *Robinson* dissenters, it was finally addressed by the Supreme Court in WHREN v. UNITED STATES, 517 U.S. 806, 116 S.Ct. 1769, 135 L.Ed.2d 89 (1996). Justice SCALIA delivered the opinion of a unanimous Court:

"On the evening of June 10, 1993, plainclothes vice-squad officers of the District of Columbia Metropolitan Police Department were patrolling a 'high drug area' of the city in an unmarked car. Their suspicions were aroused when they passed a dark Pathfinder truck with temporary license plates and youthful occupants waiting at a stop sign, the driver looking down into the lap of the passenger at his right. The truck remained stopped at the intersection for what seemed an unusually long time—more than 20 seconds. When the police car executed a U-turn in order to head back toward the truck, the Pathfinder turned suddenly to its right, without signalling, and sped off at an 'unreasonable' speed. The policemen followed, and in a short while overtook the Pathfinder when it stopped behind other traffic at a red light. They pulled up alongside, and Officer Ephraim Soto stepped out and approached the driver's door, identifying himself as a police officer and directing the driver, petitioner Brown, to put the vehicle in park. When Soto drew up to the driver's window, he immediately observed two large plastic bags of what appeared to be crack cocaine in petitioner Whren's hands. Petitioners were arrested, and quantities of several types of illegal drugs were retrieved from the vehicle.

"Petitioners were charged in a four-count indictment with violating various federal drug laws. At a pretrial suppression hearing, they challenged the legality of the stop and the resulting seizure of the drugs. They argued that the stop had not been justified by probable cause to believe, or even reasonable suspicion, that petitioners were engaged in illegal drug-dealing activity; and that Officer Soto's asserted ground for approaching the vehicle—to give the driver a warning concerning traffic violations—was pretextual. The District Court denied the suppression motion * * *.

"Petitioners were convicted of the counts at issue here. The Court of Appeals affirmed the convictions, holding with respect to the suppression issue that, 'regardless of whether a police officer subjectively believes that the occupants of an automobile may be engaging in some other illegal behavior, a traffic stop is permissible as long as a reasonable officer in the same circumstances could have stopped the car for the suspected traffic violation.'

"The Fourth Amendment guarantees '[t]he right of the people to be secure in their persons, houses, papers, and effects, against unreasonable searches and seizures.' Temporary detention of individuals during the stop of an automobile by the police, even if only for a brief period and for a limited purpose, constitutes a 'seizure' of 'persons'" within the meaning of this provision. An automobile stop is thus subject to the constitutional imperative that it not be 'unreasonable' under the circumstances. As a general matter, the decision to stop an automobile is reasonable where the police have probable cause to believe that a traffic violation has occurred.

"Petitioners accept that Officer Soto had probable cause to believe that various provisions of the District of Columbia traffic code [regarding inattentive driving, speeding, and turning without signalling] had been violated. They argue,

c. On the constitutionality and wisdom of the statutes to be found in all jurisdictions permitting severe restrictions on the liberty of persons needed as witnesses in criminal proceedings, see Ronald L. Carlson & Mark S. Voepel, *Material Witness and Material Injustice*, 58 Wash.U.L.Q. 1 (1980).

[Handwritten margin notes: Traffic Stops; Pathfinder stopped 20 seconds at stop sign; cops stopped car at light; crack bags observed through window; Δ argues stop - no pc; ACt - for π; DCt - for π; Δ agrees with stop but disagrees → pc is not enough]

however, that 'in the unique context of civil traffic regulations' probable cause is not enough. Since, they contend, the use of automobiles is so heavily and minutely regulated that total compliance with traffic and safety rules is nearly impossible, a police officer will almost invariably be able to catch any given motorist in a technical violation. This creates the temptation to use traffic stops as a means of investigating other law violations, as to which no probable cause or even articulable suspicion exists. Petitioners, who are both black, further contend that police officers might decide which motorists to stop based on decidedly impermissible factors, such as the race of the car's occupants. To avoid this danger, they say, the Fourth Amendment test for traffic stops should be, not the normal one (applied by the Court of Appeals) of whether probable cause existed to justify the stop; but rather, whether a police officer, acting reasonably, would have made the stop for the reason given.

"Petitioners contend that the standard they propose is consistent with our past cases' disapproval of police attempts to use valid bases of action against citizens as pretexts for pursuing other investigatory agendas. We are reminded that in *Florida v. Wells*, [p. 290], we stated that 'an inventory search must not be used as a ruse for a general rummaging in order to discover incriminating evidence'; that in *Colorado v. Bertine*, [p. 283], in approving an inventory search, we apparently thought it significant that there had been 'no showing that the police, who were following standard procedures, acted in bad faith or for the sole purpose of investigation'; and that in *New York v. Burger*, [p. 327], we observed, in upholding the constitutionality of a warrantless administrative inspection, that the search did not appear to be 'a "pretext" for obtaining evidence of ... violation of ... penal laws.' But only an undiscerning reader would regard these cases as endorsing the principle that ulterior motives can invalidate police conduct that is justifiable on the basis of probable cause to believe that a violation of law has occurred. In each case we were addressing the validity of a search conducted in the absence of probable cause. Our quoted statements simply explain that the exemption from the need for probable cause (and warrant), which is accorded to searches made for the purpose of inventory or administrative regulation, is not accorded to searches that are not made for those purposes.

" * * * Not only have we never held, outside the context of inventory search or administrative inspection (discussed above), that an officer's motive invalidates objectively justifiable behavior under the Fourth Amendment; but we have repeatedly held and asserted the contrary. In *United States v. Villamonte–Marquez*, 462 U.S. 579, 584, n. 3, 103 S.Ct. 2573, 2577, n. 3, 77 L.Ed.2d 22 (1983), we held that an otherwise valid warrantless boarding of a vessel by customs officials was not rendered invalid 'because the customs officers were accompanied by a Louisiana state policeman, and were following an informant's tip that a vessel in the ship channel was thought to be carrying marihuana.' We flatly dismissed the idea that an ulterior motive might serve to strip the agents of their legal justification. In *United States v. Robinson*, [p. 215], we held that a traffic-violation arrest (of the sort here) would not be rendered invalid by the fact that it was 'a mere pretext for a narcotics search,' and that a lawful postarrest search of the person would not be rendered invalid by the fact that it was not motivated by the officer-safety concern that justifies such searches. And in *Scott v. United States*, [p. 362], in rejecting the contention that wiretap evidence was subject to exclusion because the agents conducting the tap had failed to make any effort to comply with the statutory requirement that unauthorized acquisitions be minimized, we said that '[s]ubjective intent alone ... does not make otherwise lawful conduct illegal or unconstitutional.' We described *Robinson* as having established that 'the fact that the officer does not have the state of mind which is hypothecated by the reasons which provide the legal justification for the officer's action does not invalidate the action taken as long as the circumstances, viewed objectively, justify that action.'

"We think these cases foreclose any argument that the constitutional reasonableness of traffic stops depends on the actual motivations of the individual officers involved. We of course agree with petitioners that the Constitution prohibits selective enforcement of the law based on considerations such as race. But the constitutional basis for objecting to intentionally discriminatory application of laws is the Equal Protection Clause, not the Fourth Amendment. Subjective intentions play no role in ordinary, probable-cause Fourth Amendment analysis.

"Recognizing that we have been unwilling to entertain Fourth Amendment challenges based on the actual motivations of individual officers, petitioners disavow any intention to make the individual officer's subjective good faith the touchstone of 'reasonableness.' They insist that the standard they have put forward—whether the officer's conduct deviated materially from usual police practices, so that a reasonable officer in the same circumstances would not have made the stop for the reasons given—is an 'objective' one.

"But although framed in empirical terms, this approach is plainly and indisputably driven by subjective considerations. Its whole purpose is to prevent the police from doing under the guise of enforcing the traffic code what they would like to do for different reasons. Petitioners' proposed standard may not use the word 'pretext,' but it is designed to combat nothing other than the perceived 'danger' of the pretextual stop, albeit only indirectly and over the run of cases. Instead of asking whether the individual officer had the proper state of mind, the petitioners would have us ask, in effect, whether (based on general police practices) it is plausible to believe that the officer had the proper state of mind.

"Why one would frame a test designed to combat pretext in such fashion that the court cannot take into account actual and admitted pretext is a curiosity that can only be explained by the fact that our cases have foreclosed the more sensible option. If those cases were based only upon the evidentiary difficulty of establishing subjective intent, petitioners' attempt to root out subjective vices through objective means might make sense. But they were not based only upon that, or indeed even principally upon that. Their principal basis—which applies equally to attempts to reach subjective intent through ostensibly objective means—is simply that the Fourth Amendment's concern with 'reasonableness' allows certain actions to be taken in certain circumstances, whatever the subjective intent. See, e.g., *Robinson,* supra ('Since it is the fact of custodial arrest which gives rise to the authority to search, it is of no moment that [the officer] did not indicate any subjective fear of the [arrestee] or that he did not himself suspect that [the arrestee] was armed'). But even if our concern had been only an evidentiary one, petitioners' proposal would by no means assuage it. Indeed, it seems to us somewhat easier to figure out the intent of an individual officer than to plumb the collective consciousness of law enforcement in order to determine whether a 'reasonable officer' would have been moved to act upon the traffic violation. While police manuals and standard procedures may sometimes provide objective assistance, ordinarily one would be reduced to speculating about the hypothetical reaction of a hypothetical constable—an exercise that might be called virtual subjectivity.

"Moreover, police enforcement practices, even if they could be practicably assessed by a judge, vary from place to place and from time to time. We cannot accept that the search and seizure protections of the Fourth Amendment are so variable, and can be made to turn upon such trivialities. The difficulty is illustrated by petitioners' arguments in this case. Their claim that a reasonable officer would not have made this stop is based largely on District of Columbia police regulations which permit plainclothes officers in unmarked vehicles to enforce traffic laws 'only in the case of a violation that is so grave as to pose an immediate threat to the safety of others.' This basis of invalidation would not apply in jurisdictions that had a different practice. And it would not have applied even in the District of Columbia, if Officer Soto had been wearing a uniform or patrolling in a marked police cruiser.

"Petitioners argue that our cases support insistence upon police adherence to standard practices as an objective means of rooting out pretext. They cite no holding to that effect, and dicta in only two cases. In *Abel v. United States,* 362 U.S. 217, 80 S.Ct. 683, 4 L.Ed.2d 668 (1960), the petitioner had been arrested by the Immigration and Naturalization Service (INS), on the basis of an administrative warrant that, he claimed, had been issued on pretextual grounds in order to enable the Federal Bureau of Investigation (FBI) to search his room after his arrest. We regarded this as an allegation of 'serious misconduct,' but rejected Abel's claims on the ground that '[a] finding of bad faith is ... not open to us on th[e] record' in light of the findings below, including the finding that ' "the proceedings taken by the [INS] differed in no respect from what would have been done in the case of an individual concerning whom [there was no pending FBI investigation]." ' But it is a long leap from the proposition that following regular procedures is some evidence of lack of pretext to the proposition that failure to follow regular procedures proves (or is an operational substitute for) pretext. *Abel,* moreover, did not involve the assertion that pretext could invalidate a search or seizure for which there was probable cause—and even what it said about pretext in other contexts is plainly inconsistent with the views we later stated in [the cases summarized above]. In the other case claimed to contain supportive dicta, *United States v. Robinson,* in approving a search incident to an arrest for driving without a license, we noted that the arrest was 'not a departure from established police department practice.' That was followed, however, by the statement that '[w]e leave for another day questions which would arise on facts different from these.' This is not even a dictum that purports to provide an answer, but merely one that leaves the question open.

"In what would appear to be an elaboration on the 'reasonable officer' test, petitioners argue that the balancing inherent in any Fourth Amendment inquiry requires us to weigh the governmental and individual interests implicated in a traffic stop such as we have here. That balancing, petitioners claim, does not support investigation of minor traffic infractions by plainclothes police in unmarked vehicles; such investigation only minimally advances the government's interest in traffic safety, and may indeed retard it by producing motorist confusion and alarm—a view said to be supported by the Metropolitan Police Department's own regulations generally prohibiting this practice. And as for the Fourth Amendment interests of the individuals concerned, petitioners point out that our cases acknowledge that even ordinary traffic stops entail 'a possibly unsettling show of authority'; that they at best 'interfere with freedom of movement, are inconvenient, and consume time' and at worst 'may create substantial anxiety.' That anxiety is likely to be even more pronounced when the stop is conducted by plainclothes officers in unmarked cars.

"It is of course true that in principle every Fourth Amendment case, since it turns upon a 'reasonableness' determination, involves a balancing of all relevant factors. With rare exceptions not applicable here, however, the result of that balancing is not in doubt where the search or seizure is based upon probable cause. That is why petitioners must rely upon cases like *Prouse* to provide examples of actual 'balancing' analysis. There, the police action in question was a random traffic stop for the purpose of checking a motorist's license and vehicle registration, a practice that—like the practices at issue in the inventory search and administrative inspection cases upon which petitioners rely in making their 'pretext' claim—involves police intrusion without the probable cause that is its traditional justification. Our opinion in *Prouse* expressly distinguished the case from a stop based on precisely what is at issue here: 'probable cause to believe that a driver is violating any one of the multitude of applicable traffic and equipment regulations.' It noted approvingly that '[t]he foremost method of enforcing traffic and vehicle safety regulations ... is acting upon observed violations,' which afford the '"quantum of individualized suspicion" 'necessary to ensure that police discretion is sufficiently constrained. What is true of *Prouse* is also true of other cases that engaged in detailed 'balancing' to decide the constitutionality of automobile stops: the detailed 'balancing' analysis was necessary because they involved seizures without probable cause.

"Where probable cause has existed, the only cases in which we have found it necessary actually to perform the 'balancing' analysis involved searches or seizures conducted in an extraordinary manner, unusually harmful to an individual's privacy or even physical interests—such as, for example, seizure by means of deadly force, see *Tennessee v. Garner,* [p. 210], unannounced entry into a home, see *Wilson v. Arkansas,* [p. 195], entry into a home without a warrant, see *Welsh v. Wisconsin,* [p. 256], or physical penetration of the body, see *Winston v. Lee,* [p. 235]. The making of a traffic stop out-of-uniform does not remotely qualify as such an extreme practice, and so is governed by the usual rule that probable cause to believe the law has been broken 'outbalances' private interest in avoiding police contact.

"Petitioners urge as an extraordinary factor in this case that the 'multitude of applicable traffic and equipment regulations' is so large and so difficult to obey perfectly that virtually everyone is guilty of violation, permitting the police to single out almost whomever they wish for a stop. But we are aware of no principle that would allow us to decide at what point a code of law becomes so expansive and so commonly violated that infraction itself can no longer be the ordinary measure of the lawfulness of enforcement. And even if we could identify such exorbitant codes, we do not know by what standard (or what right) we would decide, as petitioners would have us do, which particular provisions are sufficiently important to merit enforcement.

"For the run-of-the-mine case, which this surely is, we think there is no realistic alternative to the traditional common-law rule that probable cause justifies a search and seizure."

5. As the Supreme Court was advised in the briefs of the petitioners and amici, the tactic at issue in *Whren* is one which has been commonly employed by police in recent years in their "war against drugs." Both in urban areas and on the interstates, police are on the watch for "suspicious" travellers, and once one is spotted it is only a matter of time before some technical or trivial offense produces the necessary excuse for pulling him over. Perhaps because the offenses are so often insignificant, the driver is typically told at the outset that he will merely be given a warning. But then things often turn ugly. The driver and passengers are usually closely questioned about their identities, the reason for their travels, their intended destination, and the like. The subject of drugs comes up, and often the driver is induced to "consent" to a full search of the vehicle and all effects therein for drugs. If such consent is not forthcoming, another police vehicle with a drug-sniffing dog may appear on the scene. See, e.g., *United States v. Mesa,* 62 F.3d 159 (6th Cir.1995); *United States v. Roberson,* 6 F.3d 1088 (5th Cir.1993) (noting the trooper's "remarkable record" of turning traffic stops into drug arrests on 250 prior occasions); *State v. Dominguez–Martinez,* 895 P.2d 306 (Or.1995).[d]

6. Two illustrations from the many reported cases of this genre reveal how little it takes to supply grounds for a traffic stop acceptable to the courts. In one, a Texas state trooper passing a van noticed it had four black occupants, so the officer crested a hill, pulled onto the shoulder and doused his lights. When the van approached, the driver cautiously changed lanes to distance the van from the vehicle on the shoulder, but failed to signal—hardly surprising considering that the van was the only moving vehicle on that stretch of road. Yet the stop for an illegal lane change was upheld. *United States v. Roberson,* supra. In the other case, the stop occurred after a Utah deputy patrolling Interstate 70 saw an automobile driven by a black man straddle the center line for about one second before proceeding to the other lane of traffic. The stop was upheld on the grounds that the officer had sufficient suspicion the operator was driving while impaired. *United States v. Lee,* 73 F.3d 1034 (10th Cir.1996).

7. The dissent by Chief Judge Seymour in *United States v. Botero–Ospina,* 71 F.3d 783 (10th Cir.1995), a pre-*Whren* decision which squares with the *Whren* holding, provides an interesting contrast to the later Scalia opinion in *Whren.* That dissent states in part:

"In addition to producing the intrusion any individual experiences when subjected to a traffic stop, the majority's standard frees a police officer to target members of minority communities for the selective enforcement of otherwise unenforced statutes. The Supreme Court recognized in *Terry [v. Ohio,* p. 291] that the harassment of minority groups by certain elements of the police population does occur, and that 'the degree of community resentment aroused by particular practices is clearly relevant to an assessment of the quality of the intrusion upon reasonable expectations of personal security caused by those practices.' By refusing to examine either the arbitrariness with which a particular statute is enforced or the motivation underlying its enforcement in a particular case, the majority standard does nothing to curb the ugly reality that minority groups are sometimes targeted for selective enforcement.[e] As a result, the majority standard adds the onus of discrimination and resentment to the already significant burden imposed by traffic stops generally. * * *

"The Supreme Court held in *Terry* that to justify a particular intrusion, a 'police officer must be able to point to specific and articulable facts which, taken together with the rational inferences from those facts, reasonably warrant that intrusion.' It is difficult to justify a stop as reasonable, even if supported by an observed violation, if the undisputed facts indicate that the violation does not

---

d. A recent study estimates that in 1999 19.3 millions persons were subjected to a traffic stop; that in 1.3 million of these stops the police conducted a search (including, 80% of the time, a search of the vehicle); that about a third of the searches were with consent, while the rest were made without seeking consent or, occasionally, after consent had been denied; and that most drivers who consented to a search felt the police lacked a legitimate reason for the search. Patrick A. Langan et al., *Contacts between Police and the Public* (U.S. Dep't of Justice, 2001).

e. "As part of the settlement of a civil rights lawsuit, the Maryland State Police tracked the race of drivers stopped since January 1995.

"Statistics released last November showed that 73 percent of drivers who were stopped and searched on Interstate 95 between Baltimore and Delaware were African–American. A corresponding American Civil Liberties Union study concluded that only 14 percent of drivers on the highway were black.

"And in central Florida, black drivers on the Florida Turnpike were 6.5 times more likely to be searched than white drivers, according to an analysis by the *Orlando Sentinel*, which studied more than 3,800 traffic stops between January 1996 and April 1997." Michael Higgins, *Looking the Part,* 48 A.B.A.J. 48, 49 (Nov. 1997). See also David A. Harris, *"Driving While Black" and All Other Traffic Offenses: The Supreme Court and Pretextual Traffic Stops,* 87 J.Crim.L. & Criminology 544 (1997).

ordinarily result in a stop. Moreover, the Court in *Terry* described in detail the appropriate reasonableness inquiry in language that is utterly irreconcilable with the majority standard. The Court stated that in assessing the reasonableness of a particular stop 'it is imperative that the facts be judged against an objective standard: would the facts available to the officer at the moment of the seizure or the search "warrant a man of reasonable caution in the belief" that the action taken was appropriate?' It would hardly seem necessary to point out that the Court's mandate to determine what a reasonable officer would do in the circumstances cannot be fulfilled by merely ascertaining in a vacuum what a particular officer could do under state law.

"Given the 'multitude of applicable traffic and equipment regulations' in any jurisdiction, upholding a stop on the basis of a regulation seldom enforced opens the door to the arbitrary exercise of police discretion condemned in *Terry* and its progeny. 'Anything less [than the reasonable officer standard] would invite intrusions upon constitutionally guaranteed rights based on nothing more substantial than inarticulate hunches, a result this Court has consistently refused to sanction.' *Terry*."

8. Is Chief Judge Seymour's concern about harassment of minorities met by Justice Scalia's observation that selective enforcement based on race is barred by the Equal Protection Clause? How could the petitioners in *Whren* have proved such an equal protection violation? Does/should the "rigorous standard for discovery" against the government upon a defendant's claim of race-based selective prosecution, see *United States v. Armstrong*, Ch. 13, § 3, also apply in this setting? And even if the *Whren* petitioners *did* prove that the traffic stop was itself a violation of the Equal Protection Clause, would that bar prosecution on the *drug* charges? Would it require suppression of the drugs? Cf. *United States v. Jennings*, 985 F.2d 562 (6th Cir.1993) (dictum by majority that if defendant had proved he had been selected for a consensual encounter solely because of his race, then the evidence obtained in a consent search during that encounter ought to be excluded, as "evidence seized in violation of the Equal Protection Clause should be suppressed"; concurring opinion notes that the case cited in support by the majority, *Elkins v. United States*, p. 112, "provides absolutely no support for the majority's position").

9. Does Justice Scalia ever respond directly to the *Whren* petitioners' argument that probable cause is not enough "in the unique context of civil traffic regulations" because it is possible for a police officer to catch any given motorist in a technical violation? Is the proper response, as Scalia says at one point, that the matter of police purpose is relevant only in situations represented by *Wells*, *Bertine* and *Burger*, where the search is allowed without probable cause? Is the risk of pretext greater in those situations, where the police must show they complied with "standard procedures" or "reasonable legislative or administrative standards," than as to traffic stops?

Where does *Whren* end and *Bertine* begin? Consider *State v. Sullivan*, 16 S.W.3d 551 (Ark.2000), where the Court declined "to sanction conduct where a police officer can trail a targeted vehicle with a driver merely suspected of criminal activity, wait for the driver to exceed the speed limit by one mile per hour, arrest the driver for speeding, and conduct a full-blown inventory search of the vehicle with impunity." The Supreme Court summarily reversed because of the Arkansas court's erroneous claim that it could "interpret[] the U.S. Constitution more broadly than the United States Supreme Court," and added that *Whren*, itself a traffic stop case, also applied to custodial arrests. *Arkansas v. Sullivan*, 532 U.S. 769, 121 S.Ct. 1876, 149 L.Ed.2d 994 (2001). The four concurring Justices said the above quotation from the state court opinion manifested "a concern rooted in the Fourth Amendment," but then concluded that "such exercises of official discretion are unlimited by the Fourth Amendment" in light of *Whren*. Is that a correct reading of *Whren*?

NOTES AND QUESTIONS ON OTHER
SEARCHES OF THE PERSON

1. Full searches of an arrested person are more typically made when that person has been delivered to the place of his forthcoming detention. These searches are typically upheld on two bases: (1) as a delayed *Robinson* search incident to arrest; and (2) as an inventory incident to booking to safeguard the property of the accused and to ensure that weapons and contraband are not introduced into the jail. However, some jurisdictions have rejected the *Robinson* rule and have also limited the extent of permissible inventory. See, e.g., *State v. Kaluna,* 520 P.2d 51 (Hawaii 1974) (police matron subjected female arrested for armed robbery to strip search, resulting in discovery of packet of drugs in her bra; held, not a valid search incident to arrest because no reason to believe weapons or evidence of the crime there, and not valid inventory because the packet could have been inventoried without opening it). Also, in some jurisdictions a search at the station is deemed unlawful if the defendant was not afforded a sufficient opportunity to gain his release. See, e.g., *Zehrung v. State,* 569 P.2d 189 (Alaska 1977), on rehearing, 573 P.2d 858 (1978) ("when one is arrested and brought to a jail for a minor offense for which bail has already been set in a bail schedule, he should be allowed a reasonable opportunity to attempt to raise bail before being subjected to remand and booking procedures and the incidental inventory search"; but on rehearing court admits state may be correct in saying this impractical in smaller communities with no separate holding cells in unsecured area, and that there the search may be proper unless defendant presently has the bail money).

2. ILLINOIS v. LAFAYETTE, 462 U.S. 640, 103 S.Ct. 2605, 77 L.Ed.2d 65 (1983), concerned the admissibility of amphetamines found in respondent's shoulder bag during an at-the-station inventory of his effects following his arrest for disturbing the peace. The Court, per BURGER, C.J., concluded:

"The governmental interests underlying a stationhouse search of the arrestee's person and possessions may in some circumstances be even greater than those supporting a search immediately following arrest. Consequently, the scope of a stationhouse search will often vary from that made at the time of arrest. Police conduct that would be impractical or unreasonable—or embarrassingly intrusive—on the street can more readily—and privately—be performed at the station. For example, the interests supporting a search incident to arrest would hardly justify disrobing an arrestee on the street, but the practical necessities of routine jail administration may even justify taking a prisoner's clothes before confining him, although that step would be rare. This was made clear in *United States v. Edwards,* [p. 234].[2]

"At the stationhouse, it is entirely proper for police to remove and list or inventory property found on the person or in the possession of an arrested person who is to be jailed. A range of governmental interests support an inventory process. It is not unheard of for persons employed in police activities to steal property taken from arrested persons; similarly, arrested persons have been known to make false claims regarding what was taken from their possession at the stationhouse. A standardized procedure for making a list or inventory as soon as reasonable after reaching the stationhouse not only deters false claims but also inhibits theft or careless handling of articles taken from the arrested person.

2. We were not addressing in *Edwards,* and do not discuss here, the circumstances in which a strip search of an arrestee may or may not be appropriate.

Arrested persons have also been known to injure themselves—or others—with belts, knives, drugs or other items on their person while being detained. Dangerous instrumentalities—such as razor blades, bombs, or weapons—can be concealed in innocent-looking articles taken from the arrestee's possession. The bare recital of these mundane realities justifies reasonable measures by police to limit these risks—either while the items are in the police possession or at the time they are returned to the arrestee upon his release. Examining all the items removed from the arrestee's person or possession and listing or inventorying them is an entirely reasonable administrative procedure. It is immaterial whether the police actually fear any particular package or container; the need to protect against such risks arises independent of a particular officer's subjective concerns. Finally, inspection of an arrestee's personal property may assist the police in ascertaining or verifying his identity. In short, every consideration of orderly police administration benefiting both police and the public points toward the appropriateness of the examination of respondent's shoulder bag prior to his incarceration. * * *

"The Illinois court held that the search of respondent's shoulder bag was unreasonable because 'preservation of the defendant's property and protection of police from claims of lost or stolen property, "could have been achieved in a less intrusive manner." For example, * * * the defendant's shoulder bag could easily have been secured by sealing it within a plastic bag or box and placing it in a secured locker.' Perhaps so, but the real question is not what 'could have been achieved,' but whether the Fourth Amendment *requires* such steps; it is not our function to write a manual on administering routine, neutral procedures of the stationhouse. Our role is to assure against violations of the Constitution.

" * * * We are hardly in a position to second-guess police departments as to what practical administrative method will best deter theft by and false claims against its employees and preserve the security of the stationhouse. It is evident that a stationhouse search of every item carried on or by a person who has lawfully been taken into custody by the police will amply serve the important and legitimate governmental interests involved.

"Even if less intrusive means existed of protecting some particular types of property, it would be unreasonable to expect police officers in the everyday course of business to make fine and subtle distinctions in deciding which containers or items may be searched and which must be sealed as a unit. * * * "[3]

3. UNITED STATES v. EDWARDS, 415 U.S. 800, 94 S.Ct. 1234, 39 L.Ed.2d 771 (1974), concerned the admissibility of paint chips obtained from defendant's clothing, taken from him without a warrant while he was in jail about 10 hours after his arrest for attempted breaking and entering. The clothing was seized because investigation subsequent to the arrest showed that paint had been chipped from a window when entry was attempted with a pry bar. The Court, per WHITE, J., concluded "that once the defendant is lawfully arrested and is in custody, the effects in his possession at the place of detention that were subject to search at the time and place of his arrest may lawfully be searched and seized without a warrant even though a substantial period of time has elapsed between the arrest and subsequent administrative processing on the one hand and the taking of the property for use as evidence on the other. This is true where the clothing or effects are immediately seized upon arrival at the jail, held under the defendant's name in the 'property room' of the jail and at a later time searched and taken for use at the subsequent criminal trial. The result is the same where the property is not physically taken from the defendant until sometime after his

---

3. The record is unclear as to whether respondent was to have been incarcerated after being booked for disturbing the peace. That is an appropriate inquiry on remand.

incarceration."[a] The Court added it was not holding "that the warrant clause of the Fourth Amendment is never applicable to postarrest seizures of the effects of an arrestee," and by footnote to that caveat stated it was expressing no view "concerning those circumstances surrounding custodial searches incident to incarceration which might 'violate the dictates of reason either because of their number or their manner of perpetration.'"

STEWART, J., joined by Douglas, Brennan, and Marshall, JJ., dissented, arguing that they could "see no justification for dispensing with the warrant requirement here. The police had ample time to seek a warrant, and no exigent circumstances were present to excuse their failure to do so," as the government "has not even suggested that [the defendant] was aware of the presence of the paint chips on his clothing."

4.   After *Robinson, Lafayette* and *Edwards,* is a person in custody following a lawful arrest "fair game" for a search for evidence of crimes other than the crime for which the arrest was made? Compare *People v. Trudeau,* 187 N.W.2d 890 (Mich.1971) (defendant was under arrest for breaking and entering, in recent attempted burglary with similar modus operandi watchman was killed and heel print was left at scene, police subsequently took defendant's shoe and matched it with heel print; held, seizure illegal because police "had no probable cause to believe that the seized shoes were evidence linked to the crime").

5.   In SCHMERBER v. CALIFORNIA, [the facts and other aspects of which are discussed at p. 38], the Court per BRENNAN, J., observed:

"Although the facts which established probable cause to arrest in this case also suggested the required relevance and likely success of a test of petitioner's blood for alcohol, the question remains whether the arresting officer was permitted to draw these inferences himself, or was required instead to procure a warrant before proceeding with the test. Search warrants are ordinarily required for searches of dwellings, and, absent an emergency, no less could be required where intrusions into the human body are concerned. * * *

"The officer in the present case, however, might reasonably have believed that he was confronted with an emergency, in which the delay necessary to obtain a warrant, under the circumstances, threatened the destruction of evidence * * *. We are told that the percentage of alcohol in the blood begins to diminish shortly after drinking stops, as the body functions to eliminate it from the system. Particularly in a case such as this, where time had to be taken to bring the accused to a hospital and to investigate the scene of the accident, there was no time to seek out a magistrate and secure a warrant. Given these special facts, we conclude that the attempt to secure evidence of blood-alcohol content in this case was an appropriate incident to petitioner's arrest."[b]

6.   Applying the *Schmerber* balancing test, the Court in WINSTON v. LEE, 470 U.S. 753, 105 S.Ct. 1611, 84 L.Ed.2d 662 (1985), held that the proposed court-

---

a. A search incident to arrest made at the station is deemed unlawful if the grounds for the arrest have dissipated prior to the time of the search. See *United States v. Coughlin,* 338 F.Supp. 1328 (E.D.Mich.1972) (defendant arrested upon leaving house at which mailman had just delivered package containing narcotics; at the station, police put his hands under fluorescent light and determined that defendant had handled the narcotics which the police had previously dusted with fluorescent powder; held, search illegal because promptly after arrest police learned that defendant was

not the addressee of the package, so that there was not probable cause for further detention).

b. Is it essential that this be characterized as a search incident to arrest? What if the defendant had not been arrested and the blood sample was taken while he was in the emergency room of the hospital for treatment of injuries he received in an accident in which he was involved, because it reasonably appeared to the police investigating the accident that he was intoxicated? Is this issue resolved by *Cupp v. Murphy,* discussed in Note 9 infra?

ordered surgery on defendant, for the purpose of removing a bullet expected to show that defendant was the robber hit by the victim's gunfire, would constitute an unreasonable search. "The reasonableness of surgical intrusions beneath the skin," the Court stated per BRENNAN, J., "depends on a case-by-case approach, in which the individual's interests in privacy and security are weighed against society's interests in conducting the procedure." Taking into account medical evidence that the operation would require a general anesthetic, might last over two hours, and could require probing of muscle tissue which might cause injury to the muscle as well as to nerves, blood vessels and other tissue, the Court concluded the "operation sought will intrude substantially on respondent's protected interests." Such an intrusion would not be reasonable, the Court then decided, given the state's failure "to demonstrate a compelling need for it." No such need was deemed to be present, as the state had considerable other evidence connecting defendant with the robbery, including a prompt identification of him by the victim and his location near the robbery shortly after it occurred.[c]

7. In light of *Schmerber* and *Winston,* what about other scientific tests and intrusions into the body after arrest? Consider *United States ex rel. Guy v. McCauley,* 385 F.Supp. 193 (E.D.Wis.1974), concerning a stationhouse search of the vagina of an incarcerated female which resulted in the discovery of a packet of narcotics. The court held the search violated due process because not conducted "by skilled medical technicians." But what if it had been so conducted? In *Guy,* the defendant also objected that the search was not made upon probable cause, but the court, while noting that the search was apparently prompted by "vague information several years old that [she] was known to carry heroin in her vagina," asserted that this objection "missed the mark" in light of *Robinson* and *Edwards.* Is that so? What then of other warrantless searches of the body of an arrestee which have been upheld, including "the placing of the arrestee's hands under an ultraviolet lamp; examining the arrestee's arms to determine the age of burn marks; swabbing the arrestee's hands with a chemical substance; taking scrapings from under the arrestee's fingernails; taking a small sample of hair from the arrestee's head; obtaining a urine sample from the arrestee; giving the arrestee a breathalyzer examination; swabbing the arrestee's penis; taking dental impressions from the arrestee; or taking pubic hair combings from him." SEARCHSZR § 5.3(c).

8. In KNOWLES v. IOWA, 525 U.S. 113, 119 S.Ct. 484, 142 L.Ed.2d 492 (1998), a policeman stopped Knowles for speeding and then, pursuant to a statute authorizing (but not requiring) him to issue a citation in lieu of arrest for most bailable offenses, issued Knowles a citation. The officer then made a full search of Knowles car and found a bag of marijuana. That search was upheld by the state courts on the ground that because an Iowa statute declared that issuance of a citation in lieu of arrest "does not affect the officer's authority to conduct an otherwise lawful search," it sufficed here that the officer had probable cause to make a custodial arrest. A unanimous Supreme Court, per REHNQUIST, C.J., reversed. Looking at the two historical rationales for search incident to arrest discussed in *Robinson,* the Court reasoned: (i) The "threat to officer safety from issuing a traffic citation * * * is a good deal less than in the case of a custodial arrest," where (as it was put in *Robinson*) there is "the extended exposure which follows the taking of a suspect into custody and transporting him to the police station," and thus the "concern for officer safety" incident to a traffic stop is sufficiently met by the officer's authority to order the driver and passengers out of the car, to "perform a 'patdown' of a driver and any passengers upon reasonable

c. See Ronald J. Bacigal, *Dodging a Bullet, But Opening Old Wounds in Fourth Amendment Jurisprudence,* 16 Seton Hall L.Rev. 597 (1986).

d. In *Pennsylvania v. Mimms,* 434 U.S. 106, 98 S.Ct. 330, 54 L.Ed.2d 331 (1977), offi-

suspicion that they may be armed and dangerous,"[e] and to conduct a patdown "of the passenger compartment of a vehicle upon reasonable suspicion that an occupant is dangerous and may gain immediate control of a weapon."[f] (ii) The "need to discover and preserve evidence" does not exist here, as "no further evidence of excessive speed was going to be found either on the person of the offender or in the passenger compartment of the car," and any concern with destruction of evidence as to identity can be met by arresting the driver whenever the officer is not satisfied with his identification.

Considering that Knowles "did not argue * * * that the statute could never be lawfully applied" and that the Court only passed upon "the search at issue," are there circumstances in which a search made under this statute would be lawful? Consider *State v. Greenslit,* 559 A.2d 672 (Vt.1989) (upholding search of person incident to issuance of notice to appear for present use of marijuana). What if Iowa reformulated its statute to conform to language used in some other states, i.e., that if an officer makes an arrest, the lawfulness of a search incident thereto is not affected by a subsequent decision at the scene to issue a citation and release the arrestee? Or, even absent such reformulation, may Iowa police, given their broad statutory authority to elect either citation or arrest as they wish, merely delay that decision until after a search, and then justify productive searches under the principle of the *Rawlings* case, note g infra?

9. As for search of the person without any prior seizure, consider CUPP v. MURPHY, 412 U.S. 291, 93 S.Ct. 2000, 36 L.Ed.2d 900 (1973). The Court, per STEWART, J., held that where Murphy voluntarily appeared at the station for questioning concerning the strangulation of his wife, at which time the police noticed what appeared to be blood on his finger, and the police had probable cause to arrest him but did not formally place him under arrest,[g] the warrantless taking of scrapings from his fingernails "was constitutionally permissible." Noting that Murphy was aware of the police suspicion and tried to wipe his fingers clean, the Court concluded that "the rationale of *Chimel* [p. 238] justified the police in subjecting him to the very limited search necessary to preserve the highly evanescent evidence they found under his fingernails." But, because a person not under formal arrest "might well be less hostile to the police and less likely to take conspicuous, immediate steps to destroy incriminating evidence on his person," the Court emphasized it was *not* holding "that a full *Chimel* search would have been justified in this case without a formal arrest and without a warrant."

cers stopped a vehicle with an expired license plate for the purpose of issuing a traffic summons and then ordered the driver out of the car, which resulted in the observation of a large bulge under his pocket, and this prompted a frisk and discovery of a gun. Rejecting the state court's holding that the driver could be directed to get out of the car only upon a reasonable suspicion he "posed a threat to police safety," the Court reasoned that "this additional intrusion can only be described as de minimis" and was justified because it "reduces the likelihood that the officer will be the victim of an assault." In *Maryland v. Wilson,* 519 U.S. 408, 117 S.Ct. 882, 137 L.Ed.2d 41 (1997), the Court held "that an officer making a traffic stop may order passengers to get out of the car pending completion of the stop." The Court agreed that "there is not the same basis for ordering the passengers out of the car as there is for ordering the driver out," but yet deemed "the additional intrusion on the passenger" to be "minimal" and justified in light of the fact that "danger to an officer from a traffic stop is likely to be greater when there are passengers in addition to the driver in the stopped car."

e. As authorized by *Terry v. Ohio,* p. 291.

f. As authorized by *Michigan v. Long,* p. 322.

g. Murphy was not arrested until over a month later, and thus the case is unlike those in which the arrest followed the search by a matter of minutes. The prevailing view is that a search "incident" to arrest may actually come before the formal making of an arrest if the police had grounds to arrest at the time the search was made. As stated in *Rawlings v. Kentucky* (other aspects of which are discussed at p. 756): "Where the formal arrest followed quickly on the heels of the challenged search of petitioner's person, we do not believe it particularly important that the search preceded the arrest rather than vice versa."

MARSHALL, J., concurring, noted that the police could not have preserved the evidence by "close surveillance" and that detaining Murphy while a warrant was sought "would have been as much a seizure as detaining him while his fingernails were scraped." DOUGLAS, J., dissenting, argued: "There was time to get a warrant; Murphy could have been detained while one was sought; and that detention would have preserved the perishable evidence the police sought."

SECTION 6. WARRANTLESS ENTRIES AND SEARCHES OF PREMISES

CHIMEL v. CALIFORNIA

395 U.S. 752, 89 S.Ct. 2034, 23 L.Ed.2d 685 (1969).

Justice STEWART delivered the opinion of the Court. * * *

The relevant facts are essentially undisputed. Late in the afternoon of September 13, 1965, three police officers arrived at the Santa Ana, California, home of the petitioner with a warrant authorizing his arrest for the burglary of a coin shop. The officers knocked on the door, identified themselves to the petitioner's wife, and asked if they might come inside. She ushered them into the house, where they waited 10 or 15 minutes until the petitioner returned home from work. When the petitioner entered the house, one of the officers handed him the arrest warrant and asked for permission to "look around." The petitioner objected, but was advised that "on the basis of the lawful arrest," the officers would nonetheless conduct a search. No search warrant had been issued.

Accompanied by the petitioner's wife, the officers then looked through the entire three-bedroom house, including the attic, the garage, and a small workshop. In some rooms the search was relatively cursory. In the master bedroom and sewing room, however the officers directed the petitioner's wife to open drawers and "to physically move contents of the drawers from side to side so that [they] might view any items that would have come from [the] burglary." After completing the search, they seized numerous items—primarily coins, but also several medals, tokens, and a few other objects. The entire search took between 45 minutes and an hour.

At the petitioner's subsequent state trial on two charges of burglary, the items taken from his house were admitted into evidence against him, over his objection that they had been unconstitutionally seized. He was convicted, and the judgments * * * affirmed * * *.

Without deciding the question, we proceed on the hypothesis that the California courts were correct in holding that the arrest of the petitioner was valid under the Constitution. This brings us directly to the question whether the warrantless search of the petitioner's entire house can be constitutionally justified as incident to that arrest. The decisions of this Court bearing upon that question have been far from consistent, as even the most cursory review makes evident.[a]

---

a. In an omitted portion of the opinion, the Court described how dictum on search incident to arrest broadened from search of the "person," *Weeks v. United States*, 232 U.S. 383, 34 S.Ct. 341, 58 L.Ed. 652 (1914), to search for what is "upon his person or in his control," *Carroll v. United States*, 267 U.S. 132, 45 S.Ct. 280, 69 L.Ed. 543 (1925), to search of "persons lawfully arrested" and "the place where the arrest is made," *Agnello v. United States*, 269 U.S. 20, 46 S.Ct. 4, 70 L.Ed. 145 (1925). Then,

in *Marron v. United States*, 275 U.S. 192, 48 S.Ct. 74, 72 L.Ed. 231 (1927), concerning seizure of evidence at a place where illegal liquor sales were occurring, the Court held that because the police had made an arrest on the premises they "had a right without a warrant contemporaneously to search the place in order to find and seize the things used to carry on the criminal enterprise." But in *Go-Bart Importing Co. v. United States*, 282 U.S. 344, 51

In 1950 * * * came *United States v. Rabinowitz,* 339 U.S. 56, 70 S.Ct. 430, 94 L.Ed. 653 (1950), the decision upon which California primarily relies in the case now before us. In *Rabinowitz,* federal authorities had been informed that the defendant was dealing in stamps bearing forged overprints. On the basis of that information they secured a warrant for his arrest, which they executed at his one-room business office. At the time of the arrest, the officers "searched the desk, safe, and file cabinets in the office for about an hour and a half," and seized 573 stamps with forged overprints. The stamps were admitted into evidence at the defendant's trial, and this Court affirmed his conviction, rejecting the contention that the warrantless search had been unlawful. The Court held that the search in its entirety fell within the principle giving law enforcement authorities "[t]he right 'to search the place where the arrest is made in order to find and seize things connected with the crime * * *.' " * * * The test, said the Court, "is not whether it is reasonable to procure a search warrant, but whether the search was reasonable."

Rabinowitz has come to stand for the proposition, inter alia, that a warrantless search "incident to a lawful arrest" may generally extend to the area that is considered to be in the "possession" or under the "control" of the person arrested. And it was on the basis of that proposition that the California courts upheld the search of the petitioner's entire house in this case. That doctrine, however, at least in the broad sense in which it was applied by the California courts in this case, can withstand neither historical nor rational analysis.

Even limited to its own facts, the *Rabinowitz* decision was, as we have seen, hardly founded on an unimpeachable line of authority. * * *

Nor is the rationale by which the State seeks here to sustain the search of the petitioner's house supported by a reasoned view of the background and purpose of the Fourth Amendment. Justice Frankfurter wisely pointed out in his *Rabinowitz* dissent that the Amendment's proscription of "unreasonable searches and seizures" must be read in light of "the history that gave rise to the words"—a history of "abuses so deeply felt by the Colonies as to be one of the potent causes of the Revolution * * *." The Amendment was in large part a reaction to the general warrants and warrantless searches that had so alienated the colonists and had helped speed the movement for independence. In the scheme of the Amendment, therefore, the requirement that "no Warrants shall issue, but upon probable cause," plays a crucial part. * * * Even in the *Agnello* case the Court relied upon the rule that "[b]elief, however well founded, that an article sought is concealed in a dwelling house furnishes no justification for a search of that place without a warrant. And such searches are held unlawful notwithstanding facts unquestionably showing probable cause." Clearly, the general requirement that a search warrant be obtained is not lightly to be dispensed with, and "the burden is on those seeking [an] exemption [from the requirement] to show the need for it * * *."

* * * When an arrest is made, it is reasonable for the arresting officer to search the person arrested in order to remove any weapons that the latter might seek to use in order to resist arrest or effect his escape. Otherwise, the officer's

S.Ct. 153, 75 L.Ed. 374 (1931), *Marron* was limited to where the items seized "were visible and accessible and in the offender's immediate custody" and there "was no threat of force or general search or rummaging of the place." This limitation was reiterated in *United States v. Lefkowitz,* 285 U.S. 452, 52 S.Ct. 420, 76 L.Ed. 877 (1932), which, like *Go-Bart,* held unlawful a search of a desk despite the fact the search had accompanied a lawful arrest, but was abandoned in *Harris v. United States,* 331 U.S. 145, 67 S.Ct. 1098, 91 L.Ed. 1399 (1947), upholding the search of a four-room apartment as "incident to arrest." But *Harris* was not followed in *Trupiano v. United States,* 334 U.S. 699, 68 S.Ct. 1229, 92 L.Ed. 1663 (1948), declaring that "law enforcement agents must secure and use search warrants wherever reasonably practicable."

safety might well be endangered, and the arrest itself frustrated. In addition, it is entirely reasonable for the arresting officer to search for and seize any evidence on the arrestee's person in order to prevent its concealment or destruction. And the area into which an arrestee might reach in order to grab a weapon or evidentiary items must, of course, be governed by a like rule. A gun on a table or in a drawer in front of one who is arrested can be as dangerous to the arresting officer as one concealed in the clothing of the person arrested. There is ample justification, therefore, for a search of the arrestee's person and the area "within his immediate control"—construing that phrase to mean the area from within which he might gain possession of a weapon or destructible evidence.

There is no comparable justification, however, for routinely searching rooms other than that in which an arrest occurs—or, for that matter, for searching through all the desk drawers or other closed or concealed areas in that room itself. Such searches, in the absence of well-recognized exceptions, may be made only under the authority of a search warrant. The "adherence to judicial processes" mandated by the Fourth Amendment requires no less. * * *

It is argued in the present case that it is "reasonable" to search a man's house when he is arrested in it. But that argument is founded on little more than a subjective view regarding the acceptability of certain sorts of police conduct, and not on considerations relevant to Fourth Amendment interests. Under such an unconfined analysis, Fourth Amendment protection in this area would approach the evaporation point. It is not easy to explain why, for instance, it is less subjectively "reasonable" to search a man's house when he is arrested on his front lawn—or just down the street—than it is when he happens to be in the house at the time of arrest. * * *

It would be possible, of course, to draw a line between *Rabinowitz* and *Harris* on the one hand, and this case on the other. For *Rabinowitz* involved a single room, and *Harris* a four-room apartment, while in the case before us an entire house was searched. But such a distinction would be highly artificial. The rationale that allowed the searches and seizures in *Rabinowitz* and *Harris* would allow the searches and seizures in this case. No consideration relevant to the Fourth Amendment suggests any point of rational limitation, once the search is allowed to go beyond the area from which the person arrested might obtain weapons or evidentiary items. The only reasoned distinction is one between a search of the person arrested and the area within his reach on the one hand, and more extensive searches on the other.[12]

The petitioner correctly points out that one result of decisions such as *Rabinowitz* and *Harris* is to give law enforcement officials the opportunity to engage in searches not justified by probable cause, by the simple expedient of

---

12. It is argued in dissent that so long as there is probable cause to search the place where an arrest occurs, a search of that place would be permitted even though no search warrant has been obtained. This position seems to be based principally on two premises: first, that once an arrest has been made, the additional invasion of privacy stemming from the accompanying search is "relatively minor"; and second, that the victim of the search may "shortly thereafter" obtain a judicial determination of whether the search was justified by probable cause. With respect to the second premise, one may initially question whether all of the States in fact provide the speedy suppression procedures the dissent assumes. More fundamentally, however, we cannot accept the view that Fourth Amendment interests are vindicated so long as "the rights of the criminal" are "protect[ed] * * * against introduction of evidence seized without probable cause." The Amendment is designed to prevent, not simply to redress, unlawful police action. In any event, we cannot join in characterizing the invasion of privacy that results from a top-to-bottom search of a man's house as "minor." And we can see no reason why, simply because some interference with an individual's privacy and freedom of movement has lawfully taken place, further intrusions should automatically be allowed despite the absence of a warrant that the Fourth Amendment would otherwise require.

arranging to arrest suspects at home rather than elsewhere. We do not suggest that the petitioner is necessarily correct in his assertion that such a strategy was utilized here, but the fact remains that had he been arrested earlier in the day, at his place of employment rather than at home, no search of his house could have been made without a search warrant. * * *

Rabinowitz and *Harris* have been the subject of critical commentary for many years, and have been relied upon less and less in our own decisions. It is time, for the reasons we have stated, to hold that on their own facts, and insofar as the principles they stand for are inconsistent with those that we have endorsed today, they are no longer to be followed.

Application of sound Fourth Amendment principles to the facts of this case produces a clear result. The search here went far beyond the petitioner's person and the area from within which he might have obtained either a weapon or something that could have been used as evidence against him. There was no constitutional justification, in the absence of a search warrant, for extending the search beyond that area. The scope of the search was, therefore, "unreasonable" under the Fourth and Fourteenth Amendments, and the petitioner's conviction cannot stand.

Reversed.

Justice HARLAN, concurring. * * *

The only thing that has given me pause in voting to overrule *Harris* and *Rabinowitz* is that as a result of *Mapp v. Ohio,* every change in Fourth Amendment law must now be obeyed by state officials facing widely different problems of local law enforcement. We simply do not know the extent to which cities and towns across the Nation are prepared to administer the greatly expanded warrant system which will be required by today's decision; nor can we say with assurance that in each and every local situation, the warrant requirement plays an essential role in the protection of those fundamental liberties protected against state infringement by the Fourteenth Amendment. * * *

Justice WHITE, with whom Justice BLACK joins, dissenting.

* * * The Court has always held, and does not today deny, that when there is probable cause to search and it is "impracticable" for one reason or another to get a search warrant, then a warrantless search may be reasonable. This is the case whether an arrest was made at the time of the search or not. * * *

This case provides a good illustration of my point that it is unreasonable to require police to leave the scene of an arrest in order to obtain a search warrant when they already have probable cause to search and there is a clear danger that the items for which they may reasonably search will be removed before they return with a warrant. Petitioner was arrested in his home after an arrest whose validity will be explored below, but which I will now assume was valid. There was doubtless probable cause not only to arrest petitioner, but to search his house. He had obliquely admitted both to a neighbor, and to the owner of the burglarized store, that he had committed the burglary. In light of this, and the fact that the neighbor had seen other admittedly stolen property in petitioner's house, there was surely probable cause on which a warrant could have issued to search the house for the stolen coins. Moreover, had the police simply arrested petitioner, taken him off to the station house, and later returned with a warrant,[5] it seems

---

5. There were three officers at the scene of the arrest, one from the city where the coin burglary had occurred, and two from the city where the arrest was made. Assuming that one policeman from each city would be needed to bring the petitioner in and obtain a search warrant, one policeman could have been left to guard the house. However, if he not only could have remained in the house against petitioner's wife's will, but followed her about to as-

very likely that petitioner's wife, who in view of petitioner's generally garrulous nature must have known of the robbery, would have removed the coins. For the police to search the house while the evidence they had probable cause to search out and seize was still there cannot be considered unreasonable.

This line of analysis, supported by the precedents of this Court, hinges on two assumptions. One is that the arrest of petitioner without a valid warrant[7] was constitutional as the majority assumes;[b] the other is that the police were not required to obtain a search warrant in advance, even though they knew that the effect of the arrest might well be to alert petitioner's wife that the coins had better be removed soon.

* * * It must very often be the case that by the time probable cause to arrest a man is accumulated, the man is aware of police interest in him or for other good reasons is on the verge of flight. Moreover, it will likely be very difficult to determine the probability of his flight. Given this situation, it may be best in all cases simply to allow the arrest if there is probable cause, especially since that issue can be determined very shortly after the arrest. * * *

If circumstances so often require the warrantless arrest that the law generally permits it, the typical situation will find the arresting officers lawfully on the premises without arrest or search warrant. * * * [W]here as here the existence of probable cause is independently established and would justify a warrant for a broader search for evidence, I would follow past cases and permit such a search to be carried out without a warrant, since the fact of arrest supplies an exigent circumstance justifying police action before the evidence can be removed, and also alerts the suspect to the fact of the search so that he can immediately seek judicial determination of probable cause in an adversary proceeding, and appropriate redress. * * *

NOTES ON SEARCH OF PREMISES INCIDENT
TO AND AFTER ARREST THEREIN

1. Is the *Chimel* dissent strengthened or weakened by the Court's later decision in *Watson*, p. 203?

2. Some of the cases which have applied the *Chimel* "immediate control" test seem to assume that defendants maintain control over a considerable area even after they have been arrested. See, e.g., *People v. Perry*, 266 N.E.2d 330 (Ill.1971) (4 officers broke into a 10 by 12 foot motel room, saw defendant place something in a dresser drawer, handcuffed him, and took him out into the corridor; their immediately subsequent search of the partially open dresser drawer and a purse on the bed was within *Chimel* rule, "since it was within the area from which defendant could have obtained a weapon or something that could have been used as evidence against him"). Are such cases best explained on the ground that *Chimel* should be construed so as to give the police a "bright line" rule (cf. *New York v. Belton*, p. 278), one which, as concluded in *People v. Hufnagel*, 745 P.2d 242 (Colo.1987), makes it irrelevant whether "the arrestee was physically able to reach the exact place searched at the exact second it was searched"?

3. *Chimel* also requires attention to the question of when, if ever, officers may look into other areas of the defendant's home *after* the defendant has been placed under arrest there. Consider:

sure that no evidence was being tampered with, the invasion of her privacy would be almost as great as that accompanying an actual search. Moreover, had the wife summoned an accomplice, one officer could not have watched them both.

7. An arrest warrant was in fact issued, but it was issued on an inadequate supporting affi-

davit and was therefore invalid, so that the case must be considered as though no warrant had issued.

b. But see the later decision in *Payton v. New York*, p. 251.

(a) *When it is necessary for the arrestee to put on street clothes.* See, e.g., *Giacalone v. Lucas,* 445 F.2d 1238 (6th Cir.1971) (defendant arrested at front door went into bedroom to change into street clothes; held, police could look into dresser drawer defendant was about to open, and gun found therein admissible; dissent argues defendant initially told police he was ready to go immediately, thereby expressing "his desire to limit the officers' intrusion into the privacy of his home," and that he went to get dressed upon order of the police).

(b) *When the officers are acting for their own protection.* The question of when a "protective sweep" is permissible reached the Court in MARYLAND v. BUIE, 494 U.S. 325, 110 S.Ct. 1093, 108 L.Ed.2d 276 (1990), where the state court had required full probable cause of a dangerous situation. By analogy to *Terry v. Ohio,* p. 291, and *Michigan v. Long,* p. 322, the Court opted for a less demanding reasonable suspicion test. The state had argued for a "bright-line rule" to the effect that "police should be permitted to conduct a protective sweep whenever they make an in-home arrest for a violent crime"; the Court responded that *Terry* requires individualized suspicion, but then adopted a two-part sweep rule which included another kind of bright line. Specifically, the Court (7–2), per WHITE, J., concluded:

"We agree with the State, as did the court below, that a warrant was not required. We also hold that as an incident to the arrest the officers could, as a precautionary matter and without probable cause or reasonable suspicion, look in closets and other spaces immediately adjoining the place of arrest from which an attack could be immediately launched. Beyond that, however, we hold that there must be articulable facts which, taken together with the rational inferences from those facts, would warrant a reasonable prudent officer in believing that the area to be swept harbors an individual posing a danger to those on the arrest scene. * * *

"We should emphasize that such a protective sweep, aimed at protecting the arresting officers, if justified by the circumstances, is nevertheless not a full search of the premises, but may extend only to a cursory inspection of those spaces where a person may be found. The sweep lasts no longer than is necessary to dispel the reasonable suspicion of danger and in any event no longer than it takes to complete the arrest and depart the premises."

The Court remanded for application of this test. The facts, as stated in the Supreme Court opinions, are these: Two men (one wearing a red running suit) committed an armed robbery of a restaurant on Feb. 3; warrants for them (Buie and Allen) were issued that day, and Buie's home was immediately placed under surveillance. On Feb. 5, after a police department secretary called the residence and verified that Buie was there, 6 or 7 officers proceeded to the house and fanned out through the first and second floors. Officer Rozar said he would "freeze" the basement so that no one could come up; he drew his weapon and twice shouted into the basement for anyone there to come out, and Buie then emerged from the basement. He was arrested, searched and handcuffed by Rozar. Once Buie was outside the house, Officer Frolich entered the basement, noticed a red running suit in plain view and seized it. Rozar testified he was not worried about any possible danger when he arrested Buie; Frolich said he entered the basement "in case there was someone else" down there, though he "had no idea who lived there." What should the result be on remand?

(c) *When the officers are seeking other offenders.* See, e.g., *People v. Block,* 499 P.2d 961 (Cal.1971) (officers knocked on door to check out tip concerning narcotics suspect, when door was opened they detected smell of burning marijuana, five persons in living room and two in dining room with odor of marijuana on their breath were arrested, after which one of the officers went upstairs and looked into bedrooms, where he found marijuana; held, in view of "undetermined number of participants" and fact upstairs light was on, officers had "reasonable cause to believe" other participants might be present; dissent objects there was not probable cause here and distinguishes *Guevara v. Superior Court*, 86 Cal.Rptr. 657 (App.1970), where informant had told police confederates were probably present). If a "potential accomplice" is located, should the police then be allowed to search areas within *his* immediate control?

4. In some circumstances, the Court concluded in WASHINGTON v. CHRISMAN, 455 U.S. 1, 102 S.Ct. 812, 70 L.Ed.2d 778 (1982), a warrantless *entry* of premises will be permissible incident to and following an arrest elsewhere. There, a campus policeman arrested an apparently underage student as he left a campus dormitory carrying a half-gallon bottle of gin, accompanied the student back to his room so that he could obtain his identification, and there observed marijuana seeds and a marijuana pipe. The state court had held that the entry was unlawful, but the Supreme Court, per BURGER, C.J., disagreed:

"Every arrest must be presumed to present a risk of danger to the arresting officer. Cf. *United States v. Robinson*, [p. 215], n. 5. There is no way for an officer to predict reliably how a particular subject will react to arrest or the degree of the potential danger. Moreover, the possibility that an arrested person will attempt to escape if not properly supervised is obvious. Although the Supreme Court of Washington found little likelihood that Overdahl could escape from his dormitory room, an arresting officer's custodial authority over an arrested person does not depend upon a reviewing court's after-the-fact assessment of the particular arrest situation. Cf. *New York v. Belton* [p. 278].

"We hold, therefore, that it is not 'unreasonable' under the Fourth Amendment for a police officer, as a matter of routine, to monitor the movements of an arrested person, as his judgment dictates, following the arrest."[c]

NOTES ON WARRANTLESS SEIZURES WHILE IN PREMISES TO ARREST

1. If an officer is lawfully present within premises to make an arrest, he may observe certain items not within the "immediate control" of the arrestee which will nonetheless be subject to warrantless seizure under the so-called "plain view" doctrine. But, as cautioned in *Coolidge v. New Hampshire*, 403 U.S. 443, 91 S.Ct. 2022, 29 L.Ed.2d 564 (1971), such "extension of the original justification is legitimate only where it is immediately apparent[a] to the police that they have evidence before them; the 'plain view' doctrine may not be used to extend a general exploratory search from one object to another until something incriminating at last emerges."

2. In ARIZONA v. HICKS, 480 U.S. 321, 107 S.Ct. 1149, 94 L.Ed.2d 347 (1987), police lawfully entered premises from which a weapon was fired, and within one officer "noticed two sets of expensive stereo components, which seemed out of place in the squalid and otherwise ill-appointed four-room apartment. Suspecting that they were stolen, he read and recorded their serial numbers—

---

c. White, Brennan and Marshall, JJ., dissenting, could "perceive no justification for what is in effect a per se rule that an officer in Daugherty's circumstances could always enter the room and stay at the arrestee's elbow."

a. In *Texas v. Brown*, p. 276, the plurality opinion asserted that this phrase "was very likely an unhappy choice of words, since it can be taken to imply that an unduly high degree of certainty as to the incriminating character of evidence is necessary for an application of the 'plain view' doctrine," and then concluded it was intended to be merely a "statement of the rule * * * requiring probable cause for seizure in the ordinary case."

moving some of the components, including a Bang and Olufsen turntable, in order to do so—which he then reported by phone to his headquarters. On being advised that the turntable had been taken in an armed robbery, he seized it immediately. It was later determined that some of the other serial numbers matched those on other stereo equipment taken in the same armed robbery, and a warrant was obtained and executed to seize that equipment as well," SCALIA, J., for a 6–3 majority, concluded the moving of the equipment was an unreasonable search, while the dissenters relied on the fact that "the overwhelming majority of both state and federal courts have held that probable cause is not required for a minimal inspection of an item in plain view." The majority responded:

"Justice O'Connor's dissent suggests that we uphold the action here on the ground that it was a cursory inspection rather than a full-blown search, and could therefore be justified by reasonable suspicion instead of probable cause. As already noted, a truly cursory inspection—one that involves merely looking at what is already exposed to view, without disturbing it—is not a 'search' for Fourth Amendment purposes, and therefore does not even require reasonable suspicion. We are unwilling to send police and judges into a new thicket of Fourth Amendment law, to seek a creature of uncertain description that is neither a plain-view inspection nor yet a full-blown search. Nothing in the prior opinions of this Court supports such a distinction * * *.

"Justice Powell's dissent reasonably asks what it is we would have had Officer Nelson do in these circumstances. The answer depends, of course, upon whether he had probable cause to conduct a search, a question that was not preserved in this case. If he had, then he should have done precisely what he did. If not, then he should have followed up his suspicions, if possible, by means other than a search—just as he would have had to do if, while walking along the street, he had noticed the same suspicious stereo equipment sitting inside a house a few feet away from him, beneath an open window. It may well be that, in such circumstances, no effective means short of a search exist. But there is nothing new in the realization that the Constitution sometimes insulates the criminality of a few in order to protect the privacy of us all. Our disagreement with the dissenters pertains to where the proper balance should be struck; we choose to adhere to the textual and traditional standard of probable cause."

NOTES ON WARRANTLESS SEARCH OF PREMISES UNDER EXIGENT CIRCUMSTANCES

1. In VALE v. LOUISIANA, 399 U.S. 30, 90 S.Ct. 1969, 26 L.Ed.2d 409 (1970), officers possessing two warrants for Vale's arrest and having information that he was residing at a specified address set up a surveillance of the house in an unmarked car. After about 15 minutes they observed a car drive up and sound the horn twice. A man they recognized as Vale then came out of the house and walked up to the car, had a brief conversation with the driver, looked up and down the street and then returned to the house. A few minutes later he reappeared on the porch, looked cautiously up and down the street, and then proceeded to the car and leaned through the window. Convinced that a narcotics sale had just occurred, the officers approached. Vale retreated toward the house while the driver of the car began driving off. The police blocked the car and saw the driver, one Saucier, place something in his mouth. Vale was then arrested on his front steps and the police advised him they were going to search the house. An officer made a cursory inspection of the house to ascertain if anyone else was present, after which Vale's mother and brother entered the house and were told of the arrest and impending search. A quantity of narcotics were found in a rear bedroom. The Court, per STEWART, J., concluded (without deciding whether *Chimel* should be accorded

retroactive effect[a]) that "no precedent of this Court can sustain the constitutional validity of the search in the case before us":

"A search may be incident to an arrest 'only if it is substantially contemporaneous with the arrest and is confined to the *immediate* vicinity of the arrest.' If a search of a house is to be upheld as incident to an arrest, that arrest must take place *inside* the house, not somewhere outside—whether two blocks away, twenty feet away, or on the sidewalk near the front steps. 'Belief, however well founded, that an article sought is concealed in a dwelling house furnishes no justification for a search of that place without a warrant.' That basic rule 'has never been questioned in this Court.'

"The Louisiana Supreme Court thought the search independently supportable because it involved narcotics, which are easily removed, hidden, or destroyed. It would be unreasonable, the Louisiana court concluded, 'to require the officers under the facts of the case to first secure a search warrant before searching the premises, as time is of the essence inasmuch as the officers never know whether there is anyone on the premises to be searched who could very easily destroy the evidence.' Such a rationale could not apply to the present case, since by their own account the arresting officers satisfied themselves that no one else was in the house when they first entered the premises. But entirely apart from that point, our past decisions make clear that only in 'a few specifically established and well-delineated' situations, may a warrantless search of a dwelling withstand constitutional scrutiny, even though the authorities have probable cause to conduct it. The burden rests on the State to show the existence of such an exceptional situation. And the record before us discloses none. * * *

"The officers were able to procure two warrants for the appellant's arrest. They also had information that he was residing at the address where they found him. There is thus no reason, so far as anything before us appears, to suppose that it was impracticable for them to obtain a search warrant as well. We decline to hold that an arrest on the street can provide its own 'exigent circumstance' so as to justify a warrantless search of the arrestee's house."

Justice BLACK, joined by The Chief Justice, dissented:

"[When Vale and Saucier were arrested,] the police had probable cause to believe that Vale was engaged in a narcotics transfer, and that a supply of narcotics would be found in the house, to which Vale had returned after his first conversation, from which he had emerged furtively bearing what the police could readily deduce was a supply of narcotics, and toward which he hurried after seeing the police. But the police did not know then who else might be in the house. Vale's arrest took place near the house, and anyone observing from inside would surely have been alerted to destroy the stocks of contraband which the police believed Vale had left there. The police had already seen Saucier, the narcotics addict, apparently swallow what Vale had given him. Believing that some evidence had already been destroyed and that other evidence might well be, the police were faced with the choice of risking the immediate destruction of evidence or entering the house and conducting a search. I cannot say that their decision to search was unreasonable. Delay in order to obtain a warrant would have given an accomplice just the time he needed.

"That the arresting officers did, in fact, believe that others might be in the house is attested to by their actions upon entering the door left open by Vale. The police at once checked the small house to determine if anyone else was present. Just as they discovered the house was empty, however, Vale's mother and brother

---

a. *Chimel* was later held not to be retroactive in *Williams v. United States*, 401 U.S. 646, 91 S.Ct. 1148, 28 L.Ed.2d 388 (1971).

arrived. Now what had been a suspicion became a certainty: Vale's relatives were in possession and knew of his arrest. To have abandoned the search at this point, and left the house with Vale, would not have been the action of reasonable police officers. * * *

"Moreover, the circumstances here were sufficiently exceptional to justify a search, even if the search was not strictly 'incidental' to an arrest. The Court recognizes that searches to prevent the destruction or removal of evidence have long been held reasonable by this Court. Whether the 'exceptional circumstances' justifying such a search exist or not is a question which may be, as it is here, quite distinct from whether or not the search was incident to a valid arrest. It is thus unnecessary to determine whether the search was valid as incident to the arrest * * *.

"[T]he Court seems to argue that the search was unreasonable because the police officers had time to obtain a warrant. I agree that the opportunity to obtain a warrant is one of the factors to be weighed in determining reasonableness. But the record conclusively shows that there was no such opportunity here. As I noted above, once the officers had observed Vale's conduct in front of the house they had probable cause to believe that a felony had been committed and that immediate action was necessary. At no time after the events in front of Mrs. Vale's house would it have been prudent for the officers to leave the house in order to secure a warrant.

"The Court asserts, however, that because the police obtained two warrants for Vale's arrest there is 'no reason * * * to suppose that it was impracticable for them to obtain a search warrant as well.' The difficulty is that the two arrest warrants on which the Court seems to rely so heavily were not issued because of any present misconduct of Vale's; they were issued because the bond had been increased for an earlier narcotics charge then pending against Vale. When the police came to arrest Vale, they knew only that his bond had been increased. There is nothing in the record to indicate that, absent the increased bond, there would have been probable cause for an arrest, much less a search. Probable cause for the search arose for the first time when the police observed the activity of Vale and Saucier in and around the house."

2. What *should* the officers have done in *Vale?* Consider *United States v. Grummel,* 542 F.2d 789 (9th Cir.1976) (defendant picked up package known to contain heroin at post office; 10 minutes after taking the package into his home he was arrested there; because his mother was home, agent gave her the option of leaving the premises or remaining inside with him while another agent left to get a search warrant; held, it was proper on these facts to "secure the premises to the extent necessary to prevent destruction of the evidence until a warrant could be obtained"). Consider, in assessing the reasonableness of this alternative, the possibility of obtaining a warrant very promptly via telephone, as authorized in some jurisdictions (see, e.g., Fed.R.Crim.P. 41(c)(2)).

In SEGURA v. UNITED STATES, 468 U.S. 796, 104 S.Ct. 3380, 82 L.Ed.2d 599 (1984), the police, upon confirming that they had in fact observed a drug sale by Colon and Segura, went to their apartment building. Segura was arrested in the lobby, and when Colon answered a knock on the door she was also arrested. Police made a warrantless entry of the apartment and remained there until a search warrant was issued, which occurred some 19 hours later because of "administrative delay." The Court held "that where officers, having probable cause, enter premises, and with probable cause, arrest the occupants who have legitimate possessory interests in its contents and take them into custody and, for no more than the period here involved, secure the premises from within to preserve the status quo while others, in good faith, are in the process of obtaining a warrant, they do not violate the Fourth Amendment's proscription against unreasonable seizures." The Court also held that the evidence first discovered in execution of the warrant was not a fruit of the illegal entry. (See p. 772.) The first holding was explicated in a portion of an opinion by BURGER, C.J., in which only O'Connor, J., joined. Without deciding whether the petitioners were correct in characterizing the police action as a seizure of the entire contents of the apartment, they concluded any such seizure was not unreasonable. Noting that in other contexts the Court had approved warrantless seizures in circumstances where a warrantless search could not have been held (see the *Chadwick* and *Sanders* cases, discussed in *California v. Acevedo*, p. 266), they could see "no reason * * * why the same principle should not apply when a dwelling is involved." These two Justices continued:

"In this case, the agents entered and secured the apartment from within. Arguably, the wiser course would have been to depart immediately and secure the premises from the outside by a 'stakeout' once the security check revealed that no one other than those taken into custody were in the apartment. But the method actually employed does not require a different result under the Fourth Amendment, insofar as the *seizure* is concerned. As the Court of Appeals held, absent exigent circumstances, the entry may have constituted an illegal search, or interference with petitioners' privacy interests, requiring suppression of all evidence observed during the entry. Securing of the premises from within, however, was no more an interference with the petitioners' possessory interests in the contents of the apartment than a perimeter 'stakeout.' In other words, the initial entry—legal or not—does not affect the reasonableness of the seizure. Under either method—entry and securing from within or a perimeter stakeout—agents control the apartment pending arrival of the warrant; both an internal securing and a perimeter stakeout interfere to the same extent with the possessory interests of the owners. * * *

"Of course, a seizure reasonable at its inception because based upon probable cause may become unreasonable as a result of its duration or for other reasons. Here, because of the delay in securing the warrant, the occupation of the apartment continued throughout the night and into the next day. Such delay in securing a warrant in a large metropolitan center unfortunately is not uncommon; this is not, in itself, evidence of bad faith. And there is no suggestion that the officers, in bad faith, purposely delayed obtaining the warrant. The asserted explanation is that the officers focused first on the task of processing those whom they had arrested before turning to the task of securing the warrant. It is not unreasonable for officers to believe that the former should take priority, given, as was the case here, that the proprietors of the apartment were in the custody of the officers throughout the period in question.

"There is no evidence that the agents in any way exploited their presence in the apartment; they simply awaited issuance of the warrant. Moreover, more than half of the 19–hour delay was between 10 p.m. and 10 a.m. the following day, when it is reasonable to assume that judicial officers are not as readily available for consideration of warrant requests. Finally, and most important, we observed in *United States v. Place*, [p. 154], that '[t]he intrusion on possessory interests occasioned by a seizure * * * can vary both in its nature and extent. The seizure may be made after the owner has relinquished control of the property to a third party or * * * from the immediate custody and control of the owner.' Here, of course, Segura and Colon, whose possessory interests were interfered with by the occupation, were under arrest and in the custody of the police throughout the entire period the agents occupied the apartment. The actual interference with their possessory interests in the apartment and its contents was, thus, virtually nonexistent, We are not prepared to say under these limited circumstances that the seizure was unreasonable under the Fourth Amendment.''

The four dissenters, per STEVENS, J., argued that the occupation was an unreasonable search, infringing upon a reasonable expectation of privacy, and an unreasonable seizure, involving exercise of "complete dominion and control over the apartment and its contents"; that the Fourth Amendment protects possessory interests in a residence even when the occupants are in custody; and that "what is even more strange about the Chief Justice's conclusion is that it permits the authorities to benefit from the fact that they had unlawfully arrested" an occupant of the apartment.[b]

In ILLINOIS v. McARTHUR, 531 U.S. 326, 121 S.Ct. 946, 148 L.Ed.2d 838 (2001), two police officers stood by outside to keep the peace while defendant's wife removed her effects from the family residence, a trailer. Upon exiting, she told the officers her husband had hidden marijuana under the couch, so the officers sought his permission to search the premises. When he refused, one officer left to obtain a search warrant, while another officer remained on the porch with defendant, who was told he could not reenter unless he was accompanied by the officer. A warrant was obtained and executed two hours later, but in the interim defendant entered the trailer two or three times, and on each occasion the officer stood just inside the door and observe his actions. The Court, per BREYER, J., held:

"We conclude that the restriction at issue was reasonable, and hence lawful in light of the following circumstances, which we consider in combination. First, the police had probable cause to believe that McArthur's trailer home contained evidence of a crime and contraband, namely, unlawful drugs. The police had had an opportunity to speak with Tera McArthur and make at least a very rough assessment of her reliability. They knew she had had a firsthand opportunity to observe her husband's behavior, in particular with respect to the drugs at issue. And they thought, with good reason, that her report to them reflected that opportunity.

"Second, the police had good reason to fear that, unless restrained, McArthur would destroy the drugs before they could return with a warrant. They reasonably might have thought that McArthur realized that his wife knew about his marijuana stash; observed that she was angry or frightened enough to ask the police to accompany her; saw that after leaving the trailer she had spoken with the police; and noticed that she had walked off with one policeman while leaving the other outside to observe the trailer. They reasonably could have concluded that McArthur, consequently suspecting an imminent search, would, if given the chance, get rid of the drugs fast.

"Third, the police made reasonable efforts to reconcile their law enforcement needs with the demands of personal privacy. They neither searched the trailer nor arrested McArthur before obtaining a warrant. Rather, they imposed a significantly less restrictive restraint, preventing McArthur only from entering the trailer unaccompanied. They left his home and his belongings intact—until a neutral Magistrate, finding probable cause, issued a warrant.

"Fourth, the police imposed the restraint for a limited period of time, namely, two hours. As far as the record reveals, this time period was no longer than reasonably necessary for the police, acting with diligence, to obtain the warrant.

b. For criticism of *Segura*, see Joshua Dressler, *A Lesson in Incaution, Overwork, and Fatigue: The Judicial Miscraftsmanship of* *Segura v. United States,* 26 Wm. & Mary L.Rev. 375 (1985).

Given the nature of the intrusion and the law enforcement interest at stake, this brief seizure of the premises was permissible.[c]

3. Although in *Vale* the Court noted in passing that "the goods ultimately seized were not in the process of destruction," many lower courts have not taken that language too seriously in light of the Court's assumption that not even a threat of destruction was present.[d] In *United States v. Rubin*, 474 F.2d 262 (3d Cir.1973), the court upheld a warrantless search[e] pursuant to this test:

"When Government agents, however, have probable cause to believe contraband is present and, in addition, based on the surrounding circumstances or the information at hand, they reasonably conclude that the evidence will be destroyed or removed before they can secure a search warrant, a warrantless search is justified. The emergency circumstances will vary from case to case, and the inherent necessities of the situation at the time must be scrutinized. Circumstances which have seemed relevant to courts include (1) the degree of urgency involved and the amount of time necessary to obtain a warrant * * *, (2) reasonable belief that the contraband is about to be removed * * *; (3) the possibility of danger to police officers guarding the site of the contraband while a search warrant is sought * * *; (4) information indicating the possessors of the contraband are aware that the police are on their trail * * *; and (5) the ready destructibility of the contraband and the knowledge 'that efforts to dispose of narcotics and to escape are characteristic behavior of persons engaged in the narcotics traffic.' "

4. Assuming no such exigent circumstances, is it permissible for police to engage in a subterfuge which causes an occupant to remove the evidence to another place where warrantless search is permissible? See *State v. Hendrix*, 782 S.W.2d 833 (Tenn.1989) (proper for police to telephone residence with anonymous false "tip" that police were on their way there with search warrant, causing defendant to leave with drugs in car, which was then stopped and searched). What if the telephoning police had falsely reported a gas leak and likely explosion?

c. Justice Souter, concurring, reasoned that had defendant remained inside the trailer then the "probability of destruction" of the marijuana "in anticipation of a warrant * * * would have justified the police in entering McArthur's trailer promptly to make a lawful, warrantless search," that this risk "abated and so did the reasonableness of entry by the police" once he came outside, but that once he came outside it was reasonable for the police to keep him from reentering not because "the law officiously insists on safeguarding a suspect's privacy from search," but rather because of "the law's strong preference for warrants, which underlies the rule that a search with a warrant has a stronger claim to justification on later, judicial review than a search without one. * * * The law can hardly raise incentives to obtain a warrant without giving the police a fair chance to take their probable cause to a magistrate and get one."

As for defendant's reliance upon *Welsh v. Wisconsin*, p. 256, the *McArthur* majority distinguished *Welsh* because (a) the offense involved here was punishable by up to 30 days in jail, and (b) "the restriction at issue here is less serious." Justice Stevens dissented as to the applicability of the *Welsh* doctrine.

d. See Barbara Salken, *Balancing Exigency and Privacy in Warrantless Searches to Prevent Destruction of Evidence*, 39 Hastings L.J. 283 (1988).

e. The facts in *Rubin* were as follows: Customs agents received reliable information that a bronze statute containing a large shipment of illicit drugs would be shipped to a hospital in a certain area. Agents were posted at the airport and waterfront, and finally a crate answering the general description given by the informant arrived at the airport from abroad. It was inspected and found to contain narcotics. Agents observed one Agnes pick up the crate and take it to a certain address, where it was unloaded at about 5 p.m. After one agent was dispatched to secure a search warrant, Agnes left the premises in his car but without the crate. He was tailed for a short distance, but when his evasive actions led agents to believe he was aware of the tail, they arrested him. When he was placed under arrest about six blocks from the house in question, he yelled to spectators to call his brother. At this point the agents, fearing disposal of the narcotics if they waited for the search warrant, entered the house and searched for and seized the narcotics.

5. Although several courts had held that when the police are summoned to the scene of a homicide they may remain on those premises without a warrant (and, perhaps, return after a brief absence) to conduct a general investigation into the cause of the death, in *Mincey v. Arizona,* 437 U.S. 385, 98 S.Ct. 2408, 57 L.Ed.2d 290 (1978), the Court, confronted with a rather broad variation of the so-called homicide scene exception to the warrant requirement (the criminal nature and perpetrator of the homicide were known from the outset, no occupant of the premises had summoned the police, and the searches upheld by the lower court continued for four days), "decline[d] to hold that the seriousness of the offense under investigation itself creates exigent circumstances of the kind that under the Fourth Amendment justify a warrantless search." *Mincey* was later applied in *Thompson v. Louisiana,* 469 U.S. 17, 105 S.Ct. 409, 83 L.Ed.2d 246 (1984), to invalidate a two-hour general search of premises to which police were summoned because of defendant's attempt to get medical assistance after shooting her husband. The Court noted the authorities, "while they were in petitioner's house to offer her assistance," could have seized evidence in plain view and could also have made a limited search for a suspect or for other victims.

In *Flippo v. West Virginia,* 528 U.S. 11, 120 S.Ct. 7, 145 L.Ed.2d 16 (1999), after defendant's 911 call that he and his wife had been attacked at a cabin in a state park, police arrived at the scene and found defendant outside wounded and his wife inside dead. The contents of a briefcase near the body, found upon a warrantless police reentry and search several hours later, were held admissible by the trial judge because found "within the crime scene area," a position the Court unanimously concluded "squarely conflicts with *Mincey.*" As for the state's contention "that the trial court's ruling is supportable on the theory that petitioner's direction of the police to the scene of the attack implied consent to search as they did," the Court expressed no opinion because this "factual" issue had not been raised below.

6. When evidence of crime is fortuitously discovered by the police without a warrant while they are performing other functions, courts find it necessary to assess the reasonableness of the police conduct under the Fourth Amendment. Compare *Geimer v. State,* 591 N.E.2d 1016 (Ind.1992) (evidence admissible, as entry was on "a reasonable belief that a person within the premises is in need of aid" where one of missing person's sons said "it was unlike his father to leave town for a period of time without notifying anyone" and other son, who lived with father, "told various persons differing stories regarding the victim's sudden absence"); with *State v. Geisler,* 610 A.2d 1225 (Conn.1992) (evidence suppressed, as where car at accident scene suffered minor damage, key left in ignition, car door left open, and no response when officer rang bell and knocked at home of car owner, such "facts could not reasonably lead to the conclusion that the driver might have suffered the type of injury that would require emergency aid").

PAYTON v. NEW YORK
445 U.S. 573, 100 S.Ct. 1371, 63 L.Ed.2d 639 (1980).

Justice STEVENS delivered the opinion of the Court. * * *

On January 14, 1970, after two days of intensive investigation, New York detectives had assembled evidence sufficient to establish probable cause to believe that Theodore Payton had murdered the manager of a gas station two days earlier. At about 7:30 a.m. on January 15, six officers went to Payton's apartment in the Bronx, intending to arrest him. They had not obtained a warrant. Although light and music emanated from the apartment, there was no response to their knock on the metal door. They summoned emergency assistance and, about 30 minutes later, used crowbars to break open the door and enter the apartment. No one was there. In plain view, however, was a 30–caliber shell casing that was seized and later admitted into evidence at Payton's murder trial. * * *

On March 14, 1974, Obie Riddick was arrested for the commission of two armed robberies that had occurred in 1971. He had been identified by the victims in June of 1973 and in January 1974 the police had learned his address. They did not obtain a warrant for his arrest. At about noon on March 14, a detective, accompanied by three other officers, knocked on the door of the Queens house where Riddick was living. When his young son opened the door, they could see Riddick sitting in bed covered by a sheet. They entered the house and placed him under arrest. Before permitting him to dress, they opened a chest of drawers two feet from the bed in search of weapons and found narcotics and related paraphernalia. Riddick was subsequently indicted on narcotics charges. * * *

The New York Court of Appeals, in a single opinion, affirmed the convictions of both Payton and Riddick. * * *a

It is a "basic principle of Fourth Amendment law" that searches and seizures inside a home without a warrant are presumptively unreasonable. Yet it is also well-settled that objects such as weapons or contraband found in a public place may be seized by the police without a warrant. The seizure of property in plain view involves no invasion of privacy and is presumptively reasonable, assuming that there is probable cause to associate the property with criminal activity. * * *

As the late Judge Leventhal recognized, this distinction has equal force when the seizure of a person is involved. Writing on the constitutional issue now before us for the United States Court of Appeals for the District of Columbia Circuit sitting en banc, *Dorman v. United States*, 435 F.2d 385 (D.C.Cir.1970), Judge Leventhal first noted the settled rule that warrantless arrests in public places are valid. He immediately recognized, however, that

> "[a] greater burden is placed [ ] on officials who enter a home or dwelling without consent. Freedom from intrusion into the home or dwelling is the archetype of the privacy protection secured by the Fourth Amendment."

His analysis of this question then focused on the long-settled premise that, absent exigent circumstances, a warrantless entry to search for weapons or contraband is unconstitutional even when a felony has been committed and there is probable cause to believe that incriminating evidence will be found within. He reasoned that the constitutional protection afforded to the individual's interest in the privacy of his own home is equally applicable to a warrantless entry for the purpose of arresting a resident of the house; for it is inherent in such an entry that a search for the suspect may be required before he can be apprehended. Judge Leventhal concluded that an entry to arrest and an entry to search for and to seize property implicate the same interest in preserving the privacy and the sanctity of the home, and justify the same level of constitutional protection. * * * We find this reasoning to be persuasive and in accord with this Court's Fourth Amendment decisions.

The majority of the New York Court of Appeals, however, suggested that there is a substantial difference in the relative intrusiveness of an entry to search for property and an entry to search for a person. It is true that the area that may legally be searched is broader when executing a search warrant than when executing an arrest warrant in the home. See *Chimel v. California*, [p. 238]. This

a. At this point, the Court "put to one side other related problems that are *not* presented today": whether there were exigent circumstances justifying a warrantless entry; whether police can "enter a third party's home to arrest a suspect"; whether "the police lacked probable cause to believe that the suspect was at home when they entered"; and whether the entry was consented to.

difference may be more theoretical than real, however, because the police may need to check the entire premises for safety reasons, and sometimes they ignore the restrictions on searches incident to arrest.

But the critical point is that any differences in the intrusiveness of entries to search and entries to arrest are merely ones of degree rather than kind. The two intrusions share this fundamental characteristic: the breach of the entrance to an individual's home. * * * In terms that apply equally to seizures of property and to seizures of persons, the Fourth Amendment has drawn a firm line at the entrance to the house. Absent exigent circumstances, that threshold may not reasonably be crossed without a warrant. * * *[b]

The parties have argued at some length about the practical consequences of a warrant requirement as a precondition to a felony arrest in the home. In the absence of any evidence that effective law enforcement has suffered in those States that already have such a requirement, we are inclined to view such arguments with skepticism. More fundamentally, however, such arguments of policy must give way to a constitutional command that we consider to be unequivocal.

Finally, we note the State's suggestion that only a search warrant based on probable cause to believe the suspect is at home at a given time can adequately protect the privacy interests at stake, and since such a warrant requirement is manifestly impractical, there need be no warrant of any kind. We find this ingenious argument unpersuasive. It is true that an arrest warrant requirement may afford less protection than a search warrant requirement, but it will suffice to interpose the magistrate's determination of probable cause between the zealous officer and the citizen. If there is sufficient evidence of a citizen's participation in a felony to persuade a judicial officer that his arrest is justified, it is constitutionally reasonable to require him to open his doors to the officers of the law. Thus, for Fourth Amendment purposes, an arrest warrant founded on probable cause implicitly carries with it the limited authority to enter a dwelling in which the suspect lives when there is reason to believe the suspect is within.

Because no arrest warrant was obtained in either of these cases, the judgments must be reversed * * *.

Justice BLACKMUN, concurring. * * *

Justice WHITE, with whom THE CHIEF JUSTICE and Justice REHNQUIST join, dissenting. * * *

Today's decision ignores the carefully crafted restrictions on the common-law power of arrest entry and thereby overestimates the dangers inherent in that

b. At this point, Stevens, J., observed that New York argued that "the reasons supporting the *Watson* [p. 203] holding require a similar result here. In *Watson* the Court relied on (a) the well-settled common-law rule that a warrantless arrest in a public place is valid if the arresting officer had probable cause to believe the suspect is a felon; (b) the clear consensus among the States adhering to that well-settled common-law rule; and (c) the expression of the judgment of Congress that such an arrest is 'reasonable.' We consider each of these reasons as it applies to a warrantless entry into a home for the purpose of making a routine felony arrest."

In an extended analysis, the *Payton* majority concluded (a) that "the relevant common law does not provide the same guidance that was present in *Watson*," as there is "no direct authority supporting forcible entries into a home to make a routine arrest and the weight of the scholarly opinion is somewhat to the contrary"; (b) that presently 24 states permit such warrantless entries, 15 prohibit them, and 11 have taken no position, with "a significant decline during the last decade in the number of States permitting warrantless entries for arrest"; and (c) that "no congressional determination that warrantless entries into the home are 'reasonable' has been called to our attention." While the majority then concluded from this that "neither history nor this Nation's experience" lent support to the New York position, the *Payton* dissenters read essentially the same data as supporting their position.

practice. At common law, absent exigent circumstances, entries to arrest could be made only for felony. Even in cases of felony, the officers were required to announce their presence, demand admission, and be refused entry before they were entitled to break doors. Further, it seems generally accepted that entries could be made only during daylight hours. And, in my view, the officer entering to arrest must have reasonable grounds to believe, not only that the arrestee has committed a crime, but also that the person suspected is present in the house at the time of the entry.[13]

These four restrictions on home arrests—felony, knock and announce, daytime, and stringent probable cause—constitute powerful and complementary protections for the privacy interests associated with the home. The felony requirement guards against abusive or arbitrary enforcement and ensures that invasions of the home occur only in case of the most serious crimes. The knock and announce and daytime requirement protect individuals against the fear, humiliation and embarrassment of being aroused from the beds in states of partial or complete undress. And these requirements allow the arrestee to surrender at his front door, thereby maintaining his dignity and preventing the officers from entering other rooms of the dwelling. The stringent probable cause requirement would help ensure against the possibility that the police would enter when the suspect was not home, and, in searching for him, frighten members of the family or ransack parts of the house, seizing items in plain view. In short, these requirements, taken together, permit an individual suspected of a serious crime to surrender at the front door of his dwelling and thereby avoid most of the humiliation and indignity that the Court seems to believe necessarily accompany a house arrest entry. Such a front door arrest, in my view, is no more intrusive on personal privacy than the public warrantless arrests which we found to pass constitutional muster in *Watson*.[14]

All of these limitations on warrantless arrest entries are satisfied on the facts of the present cases. The arrests here were for serious felonies—murder and armed robbery—and both occurred during daylight hours. The authorizing statutes required that the police announce their business and demand entry; neither Payton nor Riddick makes any contention that these statutory requirements were not fulfilled. And it is not argued that the police had no probable cause to believe that both Payton and Riddick were in their dwellings at the time of the entries. Today's decision, therefore, sweeps away any possibility that warrantless home entries might be permitted in some limited situations other than those in which exigent circumstances are present. The Court substitutes, in one sweeping decision, a rigid constitutional rule in place of the common-law approach, evolved over hundreds of years, which achieved a flexible accommodation between the demands of personal privacy and the legitimate needs of law enforcement.

A rule permitting warrantless arrest entries would not pose a danger that officers would use their entry power as a pretext to justify an otherwise invalid warrantless search. A search pursuant to a warrantless arrest entry will rarely, if ever, be as complete as one under authority of a search warrant. If the suspect surrenders at the door, the officers may not enter other rooms. Of course, the

13. I do not necessarily disagree with the Court's discussion of the quantum of probable cause necessary to make a valid home arrest. The Court indicates that only an arrest warrant, and not a search warrant, is required. To obtain the warrant, therefore, the officers need only show probable cause that a crime has been committed and that the suspect committed it. However, under today's decision, the officers apparently need an extra increment of probable cause when executing the arrest warrant, namely grounds to believe that the suspect is within the dwelling.

14. If the suspect flees or hides, of course, the intrusiveness of the entry will be somewhat greater; but the policeman's hands should not be tied merely because of the possibility that the suspect will fail to cooperate with legitimate actions by law enforcement personnel.

suspect may flee or hide, or may not be at home, but the officers cannot anticipate the first two of these possibilities and the last is unlikely given the requirement of probable cause to believe that the suspect is at home. Even when officers are justified in searching other rooms, they may seize only items within the arrestee's position [sic] or immediate control or items in plain view discovered during the course of a search reasonably directed at discovering a hiding suspect. Hence a warrantless home entry is likely to uncover far less evidence than a search conducted under authority of a search warrant. Furthermore, an arrest entry will inevitably tip off the suspects and likely result in destruction or removal of evidence not uncovered during the arrest. I therefore cannot believe that the police would take the risk of losing valuable evidence through a pretextual arrest entry rather than applying to a magistrate for a search warrant.

While exaggerating the invasion of personal privacy involved in home arrests, the Court fails to account for the danger that its rule will "severely hamper effective law enforcement." The policeman on his beat must now make subtle discriminations that perplex even judges in their chambers. As Justice Powell noted, concurring in *United States v. Watson,* police will sometimes delay making an arrest, even after probable cause is established, in order to be sure that they have enough evidence to convict. Then, if they suddenly have to arrest, they run the risk that the subsequent exigency will not excuse their prior failure to obtain a warrant. This problem cannot effectively be cured by obtaining a warrant as soon as probable cause is established because of the chance that the warrant will go stale before the arrest is made.

Further, police officers will often face the difficult task of deciding whether the circumstances are sufficiently exigent to justify their entry to arrest without a warrant. This is a decision that must be made quickly in the most trying of circumstances. If the officers mistakenly decide that the circumstances are exigent, the arrest will be invalid and any evidence seized incident to the arrest or in plain view will be excluded at trial. On the other hand, if the officers mistakenly determine that exigent circumstances are lacking, they may refrain from making the arrest, thus creating the possibility that a dangerous criminal will escape into the community. The police could reduce the likelihood of escape by staking out all possible exits until the circumstances become clearly exigent or a warrant is obtained. But the costs of such a stakeout seem excessive in an era of rising crime and scarce police resources.

The uncertainty inherent in the exigent circumstances determination burdens the judicial system as well. In the case of searches, exigent circumstances are sufficiently unusual that this Court has determined that the benefits of a warrant outweigh the burdens imposed, including the burdens on the judicial system. In contrast, arrests recurringly involve exigent circumstances, and this Court has heretofore held that a warrant can be dispensed with without undue sacrifice in Fourth Amendment values. The situation should be no different with respect to arrests in the home. Under today's decision, whenever the police have made a warrantless home arrest there will be the possibility of "endless litigation with respect to the existence of exigent circumstances, whether it was practicable to get a warrant, whether the suspect was about to flee, and the like."

* * * It would be far preferable to adopt a clear and simple rule: after knocking and announcing their presence, police may enter the home to make a daytime arrest without a warrant when there is probable cause to believe that the person to be arrested committed a felony and is present in the house. * * *[c]

c. See Joseph D. Harbaugh & Nancy L. Faust, *"Knock on Any Door"—Home Arrests* *After Payton and Steagald,* 86 Dick.L.Rev. 191 (1982).

Notes and Questions

Hot Pursuit Rule

don't have to delay

One step in One step out

public place

1. The Supreme Court has approved of warrantless entries to arrest under some circumstances. In *Warden v. Hayden,* 387 U.S. 294, 87 S.Ct. 1642, 18 L.Ed.2d 782 (1967), where police were reliably informed that an armed robbery had taken place and that the perpetrator had entered a certain house five minutes earlier, the Court concluded they "acted reasonably when they entered the house and began to search for a man of the description they had been given and for weapons which he had used in the robbery or might use against them.[d] The Fourth Amendment does not require police officers to delay in the course of an investigation if to do so would gravely endanger their lives or the lives of others." And in *United States v. Santana,* 427 U.S. 38, 96 S.Ct. 2406, 49 L.Ed.2d 300 (1976), it was held that *United States v. Watson,* p. 203, permitted the police to attempt a warrantless arrest of the defendant when she was found "standing directly in the doorway—one step forward would have put her outside, one step backward would have put her in the vestibule of her residence." The Court reasoned that she "was in a public place," as she "was not merely visible to the public but was exposed to public view, speech, hearing and touch as if she had been standing completely outside her house." Thus, under the *Hayden* "hot pursuit" rule the police could pursue her without a warrant when she sought refuge within upon their approach.

What then if the person to be arrested answers a knock on the door by the police but does not step onto or over the threshold? What if he does because of a police request or subterfuge which conceals their purpose in being there? Or, what if the police use such tactics to gain entry into the premises?

2. In *Dorman,* relied upon in *Payton,* the court found that exceptional circumstances were present by assessing these considerations: (1) "that a grave offense is involved, particularly one that is a crime of violence"; (2) "that the suspect is reasonably believed to be armed"; (3) "that there exists not merely the minimum of probable cause, that is requisite even when a warrant has been issued, but beyond that a clear showing of probable cause, including 'reasonably trustworthy information,' to believe that the suspect committed the crime involved"; (4) "strong reason to believe that the suspect is in the premises being entered"; (5) "a likelihood that the suspect will escape if not swiftly apprehended"; (6) "the circumstance that the entry, though not consented, is made peaceably"; and (7) "time of entry—whether it is made at night," which however "works in more than one direction," as "the late hour may underscore the delay (and perhaps impracticability of) obtaining a warrant and hence serve to justify proceeding without one," while "the fact that an entry is made at night raises a particular concern over its reasonableness * * * and may elevate the degree of probable cause required, both as implicating the suspect, and as showing that he is in the place entered."

Δ witnessed driving erratically

Δ was arrested in home minutes later

3. The Supreme Court focused upon the first *Dorman* factor in WELSH v. WISCONSIN, 466 U.S. 740, 104 S.Ct. 2091, 80 L.Ed.2d 732 (1984), where Welsh was arrested within his own home minutes after a witness had seen him nearby driving erratically and then departing on foot in an apparently inebriated condition after driving off the road into a field. The Court, per BRENNAN, J., held "that an important factor to be considered when determining whether any exigency exists is the gravity of the underlying offense for which the arrest is being made. Moreover, although no exigency is created simply because there is

---

d. Thus, the Court held admissible clothing found in a washing machine, where an officer looked for weapons "prior to or immediately contemporaneous with Hayden's arrest."

probable cause to believe that a serious crime has been committed, see *Payton*, application of the exigent-circumstances exception in the context of a home entry should rarely be sanctioned when there is probable cause to believe that only a minor offense, such as the kind at issue in this case, has been committed.

"Application of this principle to the facts of the present case is relatively straightforward. The petitioner was arrested in the privacy of his own bedroom for a noncriminal, traffic offense. The State attempts to justify the arrest by relying on the hot-pursuit doctrine, on the threat to public safety, and on the need to preserve evidence of the petitioner's blood-alcohol level. On the facts of this case, however, the claim of hot pursuit is unconvincing because there was no immediate or continuous pursuit of the petitioner from the scene of a crime. Moreover, because the petitioner had already arrived home, and had abandoned his car at the scene of the accident, there was little remaining threat to the public safety. Hence, the only potential emergency claimed by the State was the need to ascertain the petitioner's blood-alcohol level.

"Even assuming, however, that the underlying facts would support a finding of this exigent circumstance, mere similarity to other cases involving the imminent destruction of evidence is not sufficient. The State of Wisconsin has chosen to classify the first offense for driving while intoxicated as a noncriminal, civil forfeiture offense for which no imprisonment is possible. This is the best indication of the state's interest in precipitating an arrest, and is one that can be easily identified both by the courts and by officers faced with a decision to arrest. Given this expression of the state's interest, a warrantless home arrest cannot be upheld simply because evidence of the petitioner's blood-alcohol level might have dissipated while the police obtained a warrant. To allow a warrantless home entry on these facts would be to approve unreasonable police behavior that the principles of the Fourth Amendment will not sanction."

WHITE, J., joined by Rehnquist, J., dissenting, agreed that the gravity of the offense is "a factor to be considered," but asserted that "if, under all the circumstances of a particular case, an officer has probable cause to believe that the delay involved in procuring an arrest warrant will gravely endanger the officer or other persons or will result in the suspect's escape, I perceive no reason to disregard those exigencies on the ground that the offense for which the suspect is sought is a 'minor' one." By like reasoning, they concluded that "nothing in our previous decisions suggests that the fact that a State has defined an offense as a misdemeanor for a variety of social, cultural, and political reasons necessarily requires the conclusion that warrantless in-home arrests designed to prevent the imminent destruction or removal of evidence of that offense are always impermissible. * * * A test under which the existence of exigent circumstances turns on the perceived gravity of the crime would significantly hamper law enforcement and burden courts with pointless litigation concerning the nature and gradation of various crimes."

Would the result in *Welsh* have been different if the police were in immediate hot pursuit? See *State v. Bolte*, 560 A.2d 644 (N.J.1989) (rejecting state's argument answer is yes because "citizens should not be encouraged to elude arrest by retreating into their homes").

4. MINNESOTA v. OLSON, 495 U.S. 91, 110 S.Ct. 1684, 109 L.Ed.2d 85 (1990) (also discussed at p. 759), another warrantless entry to arrest case, involved these facts: "Shortly before 6 a.m. on Saturday, July 18, 1987, a lone gunman robbed an Amoco gasoline station in Minneapolis, Minnesota, and fatally shot the station manager. A police officer heard the police dispatcher report and suspected Joseph Ecker. The officer and his partner drove immediately to Ecker's home, arriving at about the same time that an Oldsmobile arrived. The Oldsmobile took

evasive action, spun out of control, and came to a stop. Two men fled the car on foot. Ecker, who was later identified as the gunman, was captured shortly thereafter inside his home. The second man escaped.

"Inside the abandoned Oldsmobile, police found a sack of money and the murder weapon. They also found a title certificate with the name Rob Olson crossed out as a secured party, a letter addressed to a Roger R. Olson of 3151 Johnson Street, and a videotape rental receipt made out to Rob Olson and dated two days earlier. The police verified that a Robert Olson lived at 3151 Johnson Street.

"The next morning, Sunday, July 19, a woman identifying herself as Dianna Murphy called the police and said that a man by the name of Rob drove the car in which the gas-station killer left the scene and that Rob was planning to leave town by bus. About noon, the same woman called again, gave her address and phone number, and said that a man named Rob had told a Maria and two other women, Louanne and Julie, that he was the driver in the Amoco robbery. The caller stated that Louanne was Julie's mother and that the two women lived at 2406 Fillmore Northeast. The detective-in-charge who took the second phone call sent police officers to 2406 Fillmore to check out Louanne and Julie. When police arrived they determined that the dwelling was a duplex and that Louanne Bergstrom and her daughter Julie lived in the upper unit but were not home. Police spoke to Louanne's mother, Helen Niederhoffer, who lived in the lower unit. She confirmed that a Rob Olson had been staying upstairs but was not then in the unit. She promised to call the police when Olson returned. At 2 p.m., a pickup order, or 'probable cause arrest bulletin,' was issued for Olson's arrest. The police were instructed to stay away from the duplex.

"At approximately 2:45 p.m., Niederhoffer called police and said Olson had returned. The detective-in-charge instructed police officers to go to the house and surround it. He then telephoned Julie from headquarters and told her Rob should come out of the house. The detective heard a male voice say 'tell them I left.' Julie stated that Rob had left, whereupon at 3 p.m. the detective ordered the police to enter the house. Without seeking permission and with weapons drawn, the police entered the upper unit and found respondent hiding in a closet."

The Court, per WHITE, J., determined that "the Minnesota Supreme Court was correct in holding that there were no exigent circumstances that justified the warrantless entry into the house to make the arrest.

"The Minnesota Supreme Court applied essentially the correct standard in determining whether exigent circumstances existed. The court observed that 'a warrantless intrusion may be justified by hot pursuit of a fleeing felon, or imminent destruction of evidence, or the need to prevent a suspect's escape, or the risk of danger to the police or to other persons inside or outside the dwelling.' The court also apparently thought that in the absence of hot pursuit there must be at least probable cause to believe that one or more of the other factors justifying the entry were present and that in assessing the risk of danger, the gravity of the crime and likelihood that the suspect is armed should be considered. Applying this standard, the state court determined that exigent circumstances did not exist.

"We are not inclined to disagree with this fact-specific application of the proper legal standard. The court pointed out that although a grave crime was involved, respondent 'was known not to be the murderer but thought to be the driver of the getaway car,' and that the police had already recovered the murder weapon. 'The police knew that Louanne and Julie were with the suspect in the upstairs duplex with no suggestion of danger to them. Three or four Minneapolis police squads surrounded the house. The time was 3 p.m., Sunday.... It was evident the suspect was going nowhere. If he came out of the house he would have been promptly apprehended.' We do not disturb the state court's judgment that these facts do not add up to exigent circumstances."

5. In STEAGALD v. UNITED STATES, 451 U.S. 204, 101 S.Ct. 1642, 68 L.Ed.2d 38 (1981), police entered Steagald's home in an effort to find one Lyons, for whom they had an arrest warrant; they did not find Lyons but did find drugs in plain view, resulting in Steagald's prosecution and conviction. In reversing the conviction, the Court, per MARSHALL, J., reasoned that "whether the arrest warrant issued in this case adequately safeguarded the interests protected by the Fourth Amendment depends upon what the warrant authorized the agents to do. To be sure, the warrant embodied a judicial finding that there was probable cause to believe that Ricky Lyons had committed a felony, and the warrant therefore authorized the officers to seize Lyons. However, the agents sought to do more than use the warrant to arrest Lyons in a public place or in his home; instead, they relied on the warrant as legal authority to enter the home of a third person based on their belief that Ricky Lyons might be a guest there. Regardless of how reasonable this belief might have been, it was never subjected to the detached scrutiny of a judicial officer. Thus, while the warrant in this case may have protected Lyons from an unreasonable seizure, it did absolutely nothing to protect petitioner's privacy interest in being free from an unreasonable invasion and search of his home. Instead, petitioner's only protection from an illegal entry and search was the agent's personal determination of probable cause. In the absence of exigent circumstances, we have consistently held that such judicially untested determinations are not reliable enough to justify an entry into a person's home to arrest him without a warrant, or a search of a home for objects in the absence of a search warrant. We see no reason to depart from this settled course when the search of a home is for a person rather than an object.

"A contrary conclusion—that the police, acting alone and in the absence of exigent circumstances, may decide when there is sufficient justification for searching the home of a third party for the subject of an arrest warrant—would create a significant potential for abuse. Armed solely with an arrest warrant for a single person, the police could search all the homes of that individual's friends and acquaintances. See, e.g., *Lankford v. Gelston,* 364 F.2d 197 (C.A.4 1966) (enjoining police practice under which 300 homes searched pursuant to arrest warrants for two fugitives). Moreover, an arrest warrant may serve as the pretext for entering a home in which the police have a suspicion, but not probable cause to believe, that illegal activity is taking place."

Though the majority went on to conclude that this result was not contrary to common law precedent and "will not significantly impede effective law enforcement efforts," in that "the situations in which a search warrant will be necessary are few" and in those situations "the inconvenience incurred by the police is simply not that significant," REHNQUIST and White, JJ., dissenting, argued that "the common law as it existed at the time of the framing of the Fourth Amendment" did not support such a result, and concluded:

"The genuinely unfortunate aspect of today's ruling is not that fewer fugitives will be brought to book, or fewer criminals apprehended, though both of these consequences will undoubtedly occur; the greater misfortune is the increased uncertainty imposed on police officers in the field, committing magistrates, and trial judges, who must confront variations and permutations of this factual situation on a day-to-day basis. They will, in their various capacities, have to weigh the time during which a suspect for whom there is an outstanding arrest warrant has been in the building, whether the dwelling is the suspect's home, how long he has lived there, whether he is likely to leave immediately, and a number of related and equally imponderable questions. Certainty and repose, as Justice Holmes said, may not be the destiny of man, but one might have hoped for a higher degree of certainty in this one narrow but important area of the law than is offered by today's decision."

6. An unannounced entry of premises to make an arrest therein is subject to the Fourth Amendment limitations like those regarding unannounced entry to execute a search warrant, as set out in *Richards v. Wisconsin*, p. 195. See, e.g., *United States v. Fields*, 113 F.3d 313 (2d Cir.1997). State statutes declaring an officer may not enter to arrest unless he has been denied admittance after giving "notice of his office and purpose" have usually been interpreted as codifying the common law exception for "exigent circumstances" when there is a reasonable belief compliance "would increase his peril, frustrate an arrest, or permit the destruction of evidence." *People v. Rosales*, 437 P.2d 489 (Cal.1968).

SECTION 7. WARRANTLESS SEIZURES AND SEARCHES OF VEHICLES AND CONTAINERS

CALIFORNIA v. CARNEY

471 U.S. 386, 105 S.Ct. 2066, 85 L.Ed.2d 406 (1985).

Chief Justice BURGER delivered the opinion of the Court. * * *

On May 31, 1979, Drug Enforcement Agency Agent Robert Williams watched respondent, Charles Carney, approach a youth in downtown San Diego. The youth accompanied Carney to a Dodge Mini Motor Home parked in a nearby lot. Carney and the youth closed the window shades in the motor home, including one across the front window. Agent Williams had previously received uncorroborated information that the same motor home was used by another person who was exchanging marihuana for sex. Williams, with assistance from other agents, kept the motor home under surveillance for the entire one and one-quarter hours that Carney and the youth remained inside. When the youth left the motor home, the agents followed and stopped him. The youth told the agents that he had received marijuana in return for allowing Carney sexual contacts.

At the officers' request, the youth returned to the motor home and knocked on its door; Carney stepped out. The agents identified themselves as law enforcement officers. Without a warrant or consent, one agent entered the motor home and observed marihuana, plastic bags, and a scale of the kind used in weighing drugs on a table. Agent Williams took Carney into custody and took possession of the motor home. A subsequent search of the motor home at the police station revealed additional marihuana in the cupboards and refrigerator.

Respondent was charged with possession of marihuana for sale. At a preliminary hearing, he moved to suppress the evidence discovered in the motor home. The Magistrate denied the motion, [but later the state supreme court reversed the conviction, holding the search was unreasonable because no warrant was obtained.]

* * * There are, of course, exceptions to the general rule that a warrant must be secured before a search is undertaken; one is the so-called "automobile exception" at issue in this case. This exception to the warrant requirement was first set forth by the Court 60 years ago in *Carroll v. United States*, 267 U.S. 132, 45 S.Ct. 280, 69 L.Ed. 543 (1925). There, the Court recognized that the privacy interests in an automobile are constitutionally protected; however, it held that the ready mobility of the automobile justifies a lesser degree of protection of those interests. The Court rested this exception on a long-recognized distinction between stationary structures and vehicles:

"[T]he guaranty of freedom from unreasonable searches and seizures by the Fourth Amendment has been construed, practically since the beginning of Government, as recognizing a necessary difference between a search of a store, dwelling house or other structure in respect of which a proper official warrant readily may be obtained, and a search of a ship, motor boat, wagon or automobile, for contraband goods, where it is not practicable to secure a warrant because the vehicle can be *quickly moved* out of the locality or jurisdiction in which the warrant must be sought."

The capacity to be "quickly moved" was clearly the basis of the holding in *Carroll,* and our cases have consistently recognized ready mobility[a] as one of the principal bases of the automobile exception. * * *

However, although ready mobility alone was perhaps the original justification for the vehicle exception, our later cases have made clear that ready mobility is not the only basis for the exception. The reasons for the vehicle exception, we have said, are twofold. "Besides the element of mobility, less rigorous warrant requirements govern because the expectation of privacy with respect to one's automobile is significantly less than that relating to one's home or office."

Even in cases where an automobile was not immediately mobile, the lesser expectation of privacy resulting from its use as a readily mobile vehicle justified application of the vehicular exception. In some cases, the configuration of the vehicle contributed to the lower expectations of privacy; for example, we held in *Cardwell v. Lewis,* 417 U.S. [583], 94 S.Ct. [2464, 41 L.Ed.2d 325 (1974)], that, because the passenger compartment of a standard automobile is relatively open to plain view, there are lesser expectations of privacy. But even when enclosed "repository" areas have been involved, we have concluded that the lesser expectations of privacy warrant application of the exception. We have applied the exception in the context of a locked car trunk, *Cady v. Dombrowski,* 413 U.S. 433, 93 S.Ct. 2523, 37 L.Ed.2d 706 (1973), a sealed package in a car trunk, *United States v. Ross,* [p. 266], a closed compartment under the dashboard, *Chambers v. Maroney,* [p. 265], the interior of a vehicle's upholstery, *Carroll, supra,* or sealed packages inside a covered pickup truck, *United States v. Johns,* [p. 268].

These reduced expectations of privacy derive not from the fact that the area to be searched is in plain view, but from the pervasive regulation of vehicles capable of traveling on the public highways. As we explained in *South Dakota v. Opperman,* [p. 284], an inventory search case:

"Automobiles, unlike homes, are subjected to pervasive and continuing governmental regulation and controls, including periodic inspection and licensing

---

a. The Court's earlier cases make it clear that "ready mobility" does *not* refer to the actual likelihood that the vehicle would be moved if a search warrant were sought. *Chambers v. Maroney,* 399 U.S. 42, 90 S.Ct. 1975, 26 L.Ed.2d 419 (1970) (police stopped station wagon on probable cause occupants had just committed a robbery; occupants were arrested and car was driven to police station, where thorough search revealed a revolver under dashboard; search upheld over dissent's reasoning that there was no need for a warrantless search because the car could have been held in police custody until a warrant was obtained); *Colorado v. Bannister,* 449 U.S. 1, 101 S.Ct. 42, 66 L.Ed.2d 1 (1980) (unanimous Court concludes that where probable cause to search developed after car stopped for a traffic violation, "it would be especially unreasonable to require a detour to a magistrate before the unanticipated evidence could be lawfully seized"); *Michigan v. Thomas,* 458 U.S. 259, 102 S.Ct. 3079, 73 L.Ed.2d 750 (1982) ("the justification to conduct such a warrantless search does not vanish once the car has been immobilized; nor does it depend upon a reviewing court's assessment of the likelihood in each particular case that the car would have been driven away, or that its contents would have been tampered with, during the period required for the police to obtain a warrant"); *Florida v. Meyers,* 466 U.S. 380, 104 S.Ct. 1852, 80 L.Ed.2d 381 (1984) (lower court erred in concluding warrantless search of car improper where, as here, the car had been impounded eight hours earlier and was presently stored in a secure area).

requirements. As an everyday occurrence, police stop and examine vehicles when license plates or inspection stickers have expired, or if other violations, such as exhaust fumes or excessive noise, are noted, or if headlights or other safety equipment are not in proper working order."

The public is fully aware that it is accorded less privacy in its automobiles because of this compelling governmental need for regulation. Historically, "individuals always [have] been on notice that movable vessels may be stopped and searched on facts giving rise to probable cause that the vehicle contains contraband, without the protection afforded by a magistrate's prior evaluation of those facts." In short, the pervasive schemes of regulation, which necessarily lead to reduced expectations of privacy, and the exigencies attendant to ready mobility justify searches without prior recourse to the authority of a magistrate so long as the overriding standard of probable cause is met.

When a vehicle is being used on the highways, or if it is readily capable of such use and is found stationary in a place not regularly used for residential purposes—temporary or otherwise—the two justifications for the vehicle exception come into play. First, the vehicle is obviously readily mobile by the turn of a switch key, if not actually moving. Second, there is a reduced expectation of privacy stemming from its use as a licensed motor vehicle subject to a range of police regulation inapplicable to a fixed dwelling. At least in these circumstances, the overriding societal interests in effective law enforcement justify an immediate search before the vehicle and its occupants become unavailable.

While it is true that respondent's vehicle possessed some, if not many of the attributes of a home, it is equally clear that the vehicle falls clearly within the scope of the exception laid down in *Carroll* and applied in succeeding cases. Like the automobile in *Carroll*, respondent's motor home was readily mobile. Absent the prompt search and seizure, it could readily have been moved beyond the reach of the police. Furthermore, the vehicle was licensed to "operate on public streets; [was] serviced in public places; * * * and [was] subject to extensive regulation and inspection." And the vehicle was so situated that an objective observer would conclude that it was being used not as a residence, but as a vehicle.

Respondent urges us to distinguish his vehicle from other vehicles within the exception because it was *capable of functioning as a home.* In our increasingly mobile society, many vehicles used for transportation can be and are being used not only for transportation but for shelter, i.e., as a "home" or "residence." To distinguish between respondent's motor home and an ordinary sedan for purposes of the vehicle exception would require that we apply the exception depending upon the size of the vehicle and the quality of its appointments. Moreover, to fail to apply the exception to vehicles such as a motor home ignores the fact that a motor home lends itself easily to use as an instrument of illicit drug traffic and other illegal activity. In *United States v. Ross,* we declined to distinguish between "worthy" and "unworthy" containers, noting that "the central purpose of the Fourth Amendment forecloses such a distinction." We decline today to distinguish between "worthy" and "unworthy" vehicles which are either on the public roads and highways, or situated such that it is reasonable to conclude that the vehicle is not being used as a residence.

Our application of the vehicle exception has never turned on the other uses to which a vehicle might be put. The exception has historically turned on the ready mobility of the vehicle, (and) on the presence of the vehicle in a setting that objectively indicates that the vehicle is being used for transportation.[3] These two

---

3. We need not pass on the application of the vehicle exception to a motor home that is situated in a way or place that objectively indicates that it is being used as a residence.

requirements for application of the exception ensure that law enforcement officials are not unnecessarily hamstrung in their efforts to detect and prosecute criminal activity, and that the legitimate privacy interests of the public are protected. Applying the vehicle exception in these circumstances allows the essential purposes served by the exception to be fulfilled, while assuring that the exception will acknowledge legitimate privacy interests. * * *

This search was not unreasonable; it was plainly one that the magistrate could authorize if presented with these facts. * * *

The judgment of the California Supreme Court is reversed * * *.

Justice STEVENS, with whom Justice BRENNAN and Justice MARSHALL join, dissenting. * * *

As we explained in *Ross*, the automobile exception * * * has been developed to ameliorate the practical problems associated with the search of vehicles that have been stopped on the streets or public highways because there was probable cause to believe they were transporting contraband. Until today, however, the Court has never decided whether the practical justifications that apply to a vehicle that is stopped in transit on a public way apply with the same force to a vehicle parked in a lot near a court house where it could easily be detained while a warrant is issued.[15]

In this case, the motor home was parked in an off-the-street lot only a few blocks from the courthouse in downtown San Diego where dozens of magistrates were available to entertain a warrant application.[16] The officers clearly had the element of surprise with them, and with curtains covering the windshield, the motor home offered no indication of any imminent departure. The officers plainly had probable cause to arrest the petitioner and search the motor home, and on this record, it is inexplicable why they eschewed the safe harbor of a warrant.

In the absence of any evidence of exigency in the circumstances of this case, the Court relies on the inherent mobility of the motor home to create a conclusive presumption of exigency. This Court, however, has squarely held that mobility of the place to be searched is not a sufficient justification for abandoning the warrant requirement. In *United States v. Chadwick*, 433 U.S. 1, 97 S.Ct. 2476, 53

Among the factors that might be relevant in determining whether a warrant would be required in such a circumstance is its location, whether the vehicle is readily mobile or instead, for instance, elevated on blocks, whether the vehicle is licensed, whether it is connected to utilities, and whether it has convenient access to a public road.

15. In *Coolidge v. New Hampshire*, 403 U.S. 443, 91 S.Ct. 2022, 29 L.Ed.2d 564 (1971), a plurality refused to apply the automobile exception to an automobile that was seized while parked in the driveway of the suspect's house, towed to a secure police compound, and later searched:

"The word 'automobile' is not a talisman in whose presence the Fourth Amendment fades away and disappears. And surely there is nothing in this case to invoke the meaning and purpose of the rule of *Carroll v. United States*—no alerted criminal bent on flight, no fleeting opportunity on an open highway after a hazardous chase, no contraband or stolen goods or weapons, no confederates waiting to move the evidence, not even the inconvenience of a special police detail to guard the immobi-

lized automobile. In short, by no possible stretch of the legal imagination can this be made into a case where 'it is not practicable to secure a warrant,' and the 'automobile exception' despite its label, is simply irrelevant." (opinion of Stewart, J., joined by Douglas, Brennan and Marshall, JJ.).

In *Cardwell v. Lewis*, 417 U.S. 583, 94 S.Ct. 2464, 41 L.Ed.2d 325 (1974), a different plurality approved the seizure of an automobile from a public parking lot, and a later examination of its exterior. (opinion of Blackmun, J.). Here, of course, we are concerned with the reasonableness of the search, not the seizure. Even if the diminished expectations of privacy associated with an automobile justify the warrantless search of a parked automobile notwithstanding the diminished exigency, the heightened expectations of privacy in the interior of motor home require a different result.

16. In addition, a telephonic warrant was only 20 cents and the nearest phone booth away.

L.Ed.2d 538 (1977), the Court held that a warrantless search of a footlocker violated the Fourth Amendment even though there was ample probable cause to believe it contained contraband. The Government had argued that the rationale of the automobile exception applied to movable containers in general, and that the warrant requirement should be limited to searches of homes and other "core" areas of privacy. We categorically rejected the Government's argument observing that there are greater privacy interests associated with containers than with automobiles, and that there are less practical problems associated with the temporary detention of a container than with the detention of an automobile.

* * * It is perfectly obvious that the citizen has a much greater expectation of privacy concerning the interior of a mobile home than of a piece of luggage such as a footlocker. If "inherent mobility" does not justify warrantless searches of containers, it cannot rationally provide a sufficient justification for the search of a person's dwelling place.

Unlike a brick bungalow or a frame Victorian, a motor home seldom serves as a permanent lifetime abode. The motor home in this case, however, was designed to accommodate a breadth of ordinary everyday living. Photographs in the record indicate that its height, length and beam provided substantial living space inside: stuffed chairs surround a table; cupboards provide room for storage of personal effects; bunk-beds provide sleeping space; and a refrigerator provides ample space for food and beverages. Moreover, curtains and large opaque walls inhibit viewing the activities inside from the exterior of the vehicle. The interior configuration of the motor home establishes that the vehicle's size, shape, and mode of construction should have indicated to the officers that it was a vehicle containing mobile living quarters.

The State contends that officers in the field will have an impossible task determining whether or not other vehicles contain mobile living quarters. It is not necessary for the Court to resolve every unanswered question in this area in a single case, but common English usage suggests that we already distinguish between a "motor home" which is "equipped as a self-contained traveling home," a "camper" which is only equipped for "casual travel and camping," and an automobile which is "designed for passenger transportation." Surely the exteriors of these vehicles contain clues about their different functions which could alert officers in the field to the necessity of a warrant.[21] * * *

In my opinion, searches of places that regularly accommodate a wide range of private human activity are fundamentally different from searches of automobiles which primarily serve a public transportation function. Although it may not be a castle, a motor home is usually the functional equivalent of a hotel room, a vacation and retirement home, or a hunting and fishing cabin. These places may be as spartan as a humble cottage when compared to the most majestic mansion, but the highest and most legitimate expectations of privacy associated with these temporary abodes should command the respect of this Court. In my opinion, a warrantless search of living quarters in a motor home is "presumptively unreasonable absent exigent circumstances."

I respectfully dissent.

21. In refusing to extend the California Supreme Court's decision in *Carney* beyond its context, the California Courts of Appeals have had no difficulty in distinguishing the motor home involved there from a Ford van and a cab-high camper shell on the back of a pick-up truck. There is no reason to believe that trained officers could not make similar distinctions between different vehicles, especially when state vehicle laws already require them to do so.

Notes and Questions

1. In *Maryland v. Dyson*, 527 U.S. 465, 119 S.Ct. 2013, 144 L.Ed.2d 442 (1999), the Court, per curiam, summarily reversed a state court decision holding "that in order for the automobile exception to the warrant requirement to apply, there must not only be probable cause to believe that evidence of a crime is contained in the automobile, but also a separate finding of exigency precluding the police from obtaining a warrant." That holding, the Court declared, "rests upon an incorrect interpretation of the automobile exception to the Fourth Amendment's warrant requirement," which "does not have a separate exigency requirement."

2. In *Florida v. White*, 526 U.S. 559, 119 S.Ct. 1555, 143 L.Ed.2d 748 (1999), upholding the warrantless *seizure* of a car under the state forfeiture law on probable cause that the vehicle was contraband, the Court took note of "the special considerations recognized in the context of movable items" in the *Carroll-Carney* line of cases, and then concluded the need was "equally weighty when the *automobile*, as opposed to its contents, is the contraband that the police seek to secure." The Court also emphasized that "our Fourth Amendment jurisprudence has consistently accorded law enforcement officials greater latitude in exercising their duties in public places," and deemed the instant case "nearly indistinguishable" in this respect from *G.M. Leasing Corp. v. United States*, 429 U.S. 338, 97 S.Ct. 619, 50 L.Ed.2d 530 (1977), upholding the warrantless seizure from a public area of automobiles in partial satisfaction of income tax assessments. Two dissenting Justices in *White* objected (i) that an exigent circumstances rationale has no application "when the seizure is based upon a belief that the automobile may have been used at some time in the past to assist in illegal activity and the owner is already in custody," and (ii) that a warrant requirement "is bolstered by the inherent risks of hindsight at post-seizure hearings and law enforcement agencies' pecuniary interest in the seizure of such property."

3. In *Chambers v. Maroney*, 399 U.S. 42, 90 S.Ct. 1975, 26 L.Ed.2d 419 (1970), the Court stated that what is required, even if no warrant need first be obtained, is "probable cause to search a particular auto for particular articles." Consider the following cases, both holding that the facts stated justified a warrantless search of the car under *Chambers*: *United States v. Jones*, 452 F.2d 884 (8th Cir.1971) (defendant was stopped after he made illegal turn and ran red light while driving car without plates; as officer approached he saw defendant tear paper into small pieces and push them between seat and back cushions; defendant was arrested and placed in squad car after he displayed driver's license of another person; officer then retrieved the pieces of paper, which turned out to be stolen welfare check); *People v. Hering*, 327 N.E.2d 583 (Ill.App.1975) (trooper stopped car because one headlight out; as he was writing ticket defendant drove off and, when overtaken, could not explain why he did so, trooper then searched the car).

Compare *United States v. Coleman*, 322 F.Supp. 550 (E.D.Pa.1971) (officer checking out two suspicious persons obtained consent to look in trunk of car owned by one of them and found a gun, after which the two were arrested; later a detective came to scene of arrests and searched the car and seized a revolver, two ski masks and two shopping bags; held, evidence suppressed: "Knowing all this, we have no idea what [the detective] reasonably expected to find inside the car other than its interior").

4. The probable cause to search must also be assessed in order to ascertain whether an otherwise lawful warrantless search of a vehicle was properly limited in scope and intensity, as is illustrated by *Maldonado v. State*, 528 S.W.2d 234 (Tex.Crim.1975) (truck searched on probable cause it was stolen, officers pulled up flooring and found false compartment containing 650 packages of marijuana; held, that part of search illegal because it "could not reasonably be expected that evidence of theft might be uncovered by these means"); *Wimberly v. Superior Court,* 547 P.2d 417 (Cal.1976) (after vehicle stopped for traffic violation, officer saw pipe and 12 marijuana seeds on floor and smelled odor of marijuana, passenger compartment was searched and bag with very small amount of marijuana was found in jacket pocket, trunk of car then searched and several pounds of marijuana found there; held, latter search illegal, as police had probable cause occupants of car were occasional users rather than dealers, and thus "it was not reasonable to infer that petitioners had additional contraband hidden in the trunk"). Compare *United States v. Loucks,* 806 F.2d 208 (10th Cir.1986) (such user-dealer distinction is "illogical and unreasonable").

5. Assuming grounds to make a warrantless search of a car, but the absence of grounds to arrest some occupant of the car, may that occupant also be searched if the items sought are of such a nature that they could be concealed on his person? No, the Supreme Court held in *United States v. Di Re,* p. 204. However, *Model Pre–Arraignment Code* § SS 260.3 provides otherwise (except as to passengers in a common carrier) if the officer has not found the items sought in the vehicle and has "reason to suspect that one or more of the occupants of the vehicle may have the things subject to seizure so concealed." The Reporters argue that "it seems absurd to say that the occupants can take the narcotics out of the glove compartment and stuff them in their pockets, and drive happily away after the vehicle has been fruitlessly searched." Can that position be squared with *Ybarra v. Illinois,* p. 197?

CALIFORNIA v. ACEVEDO

500 U.S. 565, 111 S.Ct. 1982, 114 L.Ed.2d 619 (1991).

Justice BLACKMUN delivered the opinion of the Court.

[One Daza picked up from a Federal Express office a package the police knew contained marijuana and took it to his apartment. About two hours later, Acevedo entered that apartment and shortly thereafter left carrying a brown paper bag the size of one of the wrapped marijuana packages. He placed the bag in the trunk of his car and drove off; the police then stopped him, opened the trunk and bag, and found marijuana. The California Court of Appeal held the marijuana should have been suppressed, the state supreme court denied review, and the Supreme Court then granted certiorari.]

In *United States v. Ross,* 456 U.S. 798, 102 S.Ct. 2157, 72 L.Ed.2d 572, decided in 1982, we held that a warrantless search of an automobile under the *Carroll* doctrine could include a search of a container or package found inside the car when such a search was supported by probable cause. The warrantless search of Ross' car occurred after an informant told the police that he had seen Ross complete a drug transaction using drugs stored in the trunk of his car. The police stopped the car, searched it, and discovered in the trunk a brown paper bag containing drugs. We decided that the search of Ross' car was not unreasonable under the Fourth Amendment: "The scope of a warrantless search based on probable cause is no narrower—and no broader—than the scope of a search authorized by a warrant supported by probable cause." Thus, "[i]f probable cause justifies the search of a lawfully stopped vehicle, it justifies the search of every part of the vehicle and its contents that may conceal the object of the search." In *Ross,* therefore, we clarified the scope of the *Carroll* doctrine as properly including a "probing search" of compartments and containers within the automobile so long as the search is supported by probable cause.

In addition to this clarification, *Ross* distinguished the *Carroll* doctrine from the separate rule that governed the search of closed containers. The Court had announced this separate rule, unique to luggage and other closed packages, bags, and containers, in *United States v. Chadwick*, 433 U.S. 1, 97 S.Ct. 2476, 53 L.Ed.2d 538 (1977). In *Chadwick*, federal narcotics agents had probable cause to believe that a 200–pound double-locked footlocker contained marijuana. The agents tracked the locker as the defendants removed it from a train and carried it through the station to a waiting car. As soon as the defendants lifted the locker into the trunk of the car, the agents arrested them, seized the locker, and searched it. In this Court, the United States did not contend that the locker's brief contact with the automobile's trunk sufficed to make the *Carroll* doctrine applicable. Rather, the United States urged that the search of movable luggage could be considered analogous to the search of an automobile.

The Court rejected this argument because, it reasoned, a person expects more privacy in his luggage and personal effects than he does in his automobile. Moreover, it concluded that as "may often not be the case when automobiles are seized," secure storage facilities are usually available when the police seize luggage.

In *Arkansas v. Sanders*, 442 U.S. 753, 99 S.Ct. 2586, 61 L.Ed.2d 235 (1979), the Court extended *Chadwick*'s rule to apply to a suitcase actually being transported in the trunk of a car. In *Sanders*, the police had probable cause to believe a suitcase contained marijuana. They watched as the defendant placed the suitcase in the trunk of a taxi and was driven away. The police pursued the taxi for several blocks, stopped it, found the suitcase in the trunk, and searched it. Although the Court had applied the *Carroll* doctrine to searches of integral parts of the automobile itself, (indeed, in *Carroll*, contraband whiskey was in the upholstery of the seats), it did not extend the doctrine to the warrantless search of personal luggage "merely because it was located in an automobile lawfully stopped by the police." Again, the *Sanders* majority stressed the heightened privacy expectation in personal luggage and concluded that the presence of luggage in an automobile did not diminish the owner's expectation of privacy in his personal items.

In *Ross*, the Court endeavored to distinguish between *Carroll*, which governed the *Ross* automobile search, and *Chadwick*, which governed the *Sanders* automobile search. It held that the *Carroll* doctrine covered searches of automobiles when the police had probable cause to search an entire vehicle but that the *Chadwick* doctrine governed searches of luggage when the officers had probable cause to search only a container within the vehicle. Thus, in a *Ross* situation, the police could conduct a reasonable search under the Fourth Amendment without obtaining a warrant, whereas in a *Sanders* situation, the police had to obtain a warrant before they searched.

The dissent is correct, of course, that *Ross* involved the scope of an automobile search. *Ross* held that closed containers encountered by the police during a warrantless search of a car pursuant to the automobile exception could also be searched. Thus, this Court in *Ross* took the critical step of saying that closed containers in cars could be searched without a warrant because of their presence within the automobile. Despite the protection that *Sanders* purported to extend to closed containers, the privacy interest in those closed containers yielded to the broad scope of an automobile search. * * *

This Court in *Ross* rejected *Chadwick*'s distinction between containers and cars. It concluded that the expectation of privacy in one's vehicle is equal to one's expectation of privacy in the container, and noted that "the privacy interests in a car's trunk or glove compartment may be no less than those in a movable container." It also recognized that it was arguable that the same exigent circumstances that permit a warrantless search of an automobile would justify the warrantless search of a movable container. In deference to the rule of *Chadwick* and *Sanders,* however, the Court put that question to one side. It concluded that the time and expense of the warrant process would be misdirected if the police could search every cubic inch of an automobile until they discovered a paper sack, at which point the Fourth Amendment required them to take the sack to a magistrate for permission to look inside. We now must decide the question deferred in *Ross:* whether the Fourth Amendment requires the police to obtain a warrant to open the sack in a movable vehicle simply because they lack probable cause to search the entire car. We conclude that it does not.

Dissenters in *Ross* asked why the suitcase in *Sanders* was "more private, less difficult for police to seize and store, or in any other relevant respect more properly subject to the warrant requirement, than a container that police discover in a probable-cause search of an entire automobile?" We now agree that a container found after a general search of the automobile and a container found in a car after a limited search for the container are equally easy for the police to store and for the suspect to hide or destroy. In fact, we see no principled distinction in terms of either the privacy expectation or the exigent circumstances between the paper bag found by the police in *Ross* and the paper bag found by the police here. Furthermore, by attempting to distinguish between a container for which the police are specifically searching and a container which they come across in a car, we have provided only minimal protection for privacy and have impeded effective law enforcement.

The line between probable cause to search a vehicle and probable cause to search a package in that vehicle is not always clear, and separate rules that govern the two objects to be searched may enable the police to broaden their power to make warrantless searches and disserve privacy interests. * * * At the moment when officers stop an automobile, it may be less than clear whether they suspect with a high degree of certainty that the vehicle contains drugs in a bag or simply contains drugs. If the police know that they may open a bag only if they are actually searching the entire car, they may search more extensively than they otherwise would in order to establish the general probable cause required by *Ross.*

Such a situation is not far fetched. In *United States v. Johns,* 469 U.S. 478, 105 S.Ct. 881, 83 L.Ed.2d 890 (1985), customs agents saw two trucks drive to a private airstrip and approach two small planes. The agents drew near the trucks, smelled marijuana, and then saw in the backs of the trucks packages wrapped in a manner that marijuana smugglers customarily employed. The agents took the trucks to headquarters and searched the packages without a warrant. Relying on *Chadwick,* the defendants argued that the search was unlawful. The defendants contended that *Ross* was inapplicable because the agents lacked probable cause to search anything but the packages themselves and supported this contention by noting that a search of the entire vehicle never occurred. We rejected that argument and found *Chadwick* and *Sanders* inapposite because the agents had probable cause to search the entire body of each truck, although they had chosen not to do so.[a] We cannot see the benefit of a rule that requires law enforcement officers to conduct a more intrusive search in order to justify a less intrusive one.

---

a. However, "the central issue" in *Johns* was whether the warrantless search was permissible in light of the fact that the packages were not opened until three days after they had been removed from the trucks. The majority answered in the affirmative:

"We do not suggest that police officers may indefinitely retain possession of a vehicle and its contents before they complete a vehicle search. Nor do we foreclose the possibility that the owner of a vehicle or its contents might attempt to prove that delay in the completion of a vehicle search was unreasonable because it adversely affected a privacy or possessory interest. We note that in this case there was probable cause to believe that the trucks contained contraband and there is no plausible argument that the object of the search could not have been concealed in the packages. Respondents do not challenge the legitimacy of

To the extent that the *Chadwick–Sanders* rule protects privacy, its protection is minimal. Law enforcement officers may seize a container and hold it until they obtain a search warrant. "Since the police, by hypothesis, have probable cause to seize the property, we can assume that a warrant will be routinely forthcoming in the overwhelming majority of cases." And the police often will be able to search containers without a warrant, despite the *Chadwick–Sanders* rule, as a search incident to a lawful arrest [under] *Belton* [p. 278]. * * *

Finally, the search of a paper bag intrudes far less on individual privacy than does the incursion sanctioned long ago in *Carroll*. In that case, prohibition agents slashed the upholstery of the automobile. This Court nonetheless found their search to be reasonable under the Fourth Amendment. If destroying the interior of an automobile is not unreasonable, we cannot conclude that looking inside a closed container is. In light of the minimal protection to privacy afforded by the *Chadwick–Sanders* rule, and our serious doubt whether that rule substantially serves privacy interests, we now hold that the Fourth Amendment does not compel separate treatment for an automobile search that extends only to a container within the vehicle.

The *Chadwick–Sanders* rule not only has failed to protect privacy but it has also confused courts and police officers and impeded effective law enforcement. * * *

The discrepancy between the two rules has led to confusion for law enforcement officers. For example, when an officer, who has developed probable cause to believe that a vehicle contains drugs, begins to search the vehicle and immediately discovers a closed container, which rule applies? The defendant will argue that the fact that the officer first chose to search the container indicates that his probable cause extended only to the container and that *Chadwick* and *Sanders* therefore require a warrant. On the other hand, the fact that the officer first chose to search in the most obvious location should not restrict the propriety of the search. The *Chadwick* rule, as applied in *Sanders,* has developed into an anomaly such that the more likely the police are to discover drugs in a container, the less authority they have to search it. * * *

The interpretation of the *Carroll* doctrine set forth in *Ross* now applies to all searches of containers found in an automobile. In other words, the police may search without a warrant if their search is supported by probable cause. * * * In the case before us, the police had probable cause to believe that the paper bag in the automobile's trunk contained marijuana. That probable cause now allows a warrantless search of the paper bag. The facts in the record reveal that the police did not have probable cause to believe that contraband was hidden in any other part of the automobile and a search of the entire vehicle would have been without probable cause and unreasonable under the Fourth Amendment. * * *

Justice SCALIA, concurring in the judgment.

I agree with the dissent that it is anomalous for a briefcase to be protected by the "general requirement" of a prior warrant when it is being carried along the street, but for that same briefcase to become unprotected as soon as it is carried into an automobile. On the other hand, I agree with the Court that it would be anomalous for a locked compartment in an automobile to be unprotected by the "general requirement" of a prior warrant, but for an unlocked briefcase within the automobile to be protected. I join in the judgment of the Court because I think its holding is more faithful to the text and tradition of the Fourth Amendment,

the seizure of the trucks or the packages, and they never sought return of the property. Thus, respondents have not even alleged, much less proved, that the delay in the search of packages adversely affected legitimate interests protected by the Fourth Amendment."

and if these anomalies in our jurisprudence are ever to be eliminated that is the direction in which we should travel. * * *

Although the Fourth Amendment does not explicitly impose the requirement of a warrant, it is of course textually possible to consider that implicit within the requirement of reasonableness. For some years after the (still continuing) explosion in Fourth Amendment litigation that followed our announcement of the exclusionary rule in *Weeks v. United States,* [p. 108], our jurisprudence lurched back and forth between imposing a categorical warrant requirement and looking to reasonableness alone. * * *

In my view, the path out of this confusion should be sought by returning to the first principle that the "reasonableness" requirement of the Fourth Amendment affords the protection that the common law afforded. I have no difficulty with the proposition that that includes the requirement of a warrant, where the common law required a warrant; and it may even be that changes in the surrounding legal rules (for example, elimination of the common-law rule that reasonable, good-faith belief was no defense to absolute liability for trespass), may make a warrant indispensable to reasonableness where it once was not. But the supposed "general rule" that a warrant is always required does not appear to have any basis in the common law, and confuses rather than facilitates any attempt to develop rules of reasonableness in light of changed legal circumstances, as the anomaly eliminated and the anomaly created by today's holding both demonstrate.

And there are more anomalies still. Under our precedents (as at common law), a person may be arrested outside the home on the basis of probable cause, without an arrest warrant. *United States v. Watson* [p. 203]. Upon arrest, the person, as well as the area within his grasp, may be searched for evidence related to the crime. *Chimel v. California* [p. 238]. Under these principles, if a known drug dealer is carrying a briefcase reasonably believed to contain marijuana (the unauthorized possession of which is a crime), the police may arrest him and search his person on the basis of probable cause alone. And, under our precedents, upon arrival at the station house, the police may inventory his possessions, including the briefcase, even if there is no reason to suspect that they contain contraband. *Illinois v. Lafayette* [p. 233]. According to our current law, however, the police may not, on the basis of the same probable cause, take the less intrusive step of stopping the individual on the street and demanding to see the contents of his briefcase. That makes no sense *a priori,* and in the absence of any common-law tradition supporting such a distinction, I see no reason to continue it.

I would reverse the judgment in the present case, not because a closed container carried inside a car becomes subject to the "automobile" exception to the general warrant requirement, but because the search of a closed container, outside a privately owned building, with probable cause to believe that the container contains contraband, and when it in fact does contain contraband, is not one of those searches whose Fourth Amendment reasonableness depends upon a warrant. For that reason I concur in the judgment of the Court.

Justice WHITE, dissenting.

Agreeing as I do with most of Justice Stevens' opinion and with the result he reaches, I dissent and would affirm the judgment below.

Justice STEVENS, with whom Justice MARSHALL joins, dissenting.

At the end of its opinion, the Court pays lip service to the proposition that should provide the basis for a correct analysis of the legal question presented by this case: It is " 'a cardinal principle that "searches conducted outside the judicial process, without prior approval by judge or magistrate, are *per se* unreasonable under the Fourth Amendment—subject only to a few specifically established and well-delineated exceptions." ' * * * "

[The warrant] requirement * * * reflects the sound policy judgment that, absent exceptional circumstances, the decision to invade the privacy of an individual's personal effects should be made by a neutral magistrate rather than an agent of the Executive. * * *

In *Chadwick*, the Department of Justice had mounted a frontal attack on the warrant requirement. The Government's principal contention was that "the Fourth Amendment Warrant Clause protects only interests traditionally identified with the home." We categorically rejected that contention, relying on the history and text of the amendment, the policy underlying the warrant requirement, and a line of cases spanning over a century of our jurisprudence. We also rejected the Government's alternative argument that the rationale of our automobile search cases demonstrated the reasonableness of permitting warrantless searches of luggage.

We concluded that neither of the justifications for the automobile exception could support a similar exception for luggage. We first held that the privacy interest in luggage is "substantially greater than in an automobile." Unlike automobiles and their contents, we reasoned, "[l]uggage contents are not open to public view, except as a condition to a border entry or common carrier travel; nor is luggage subject to regular inspections and official scrutiny on a continuing basis." Indeed, luggage is specifically intended to safeguard the privacy of personal effects, unlike an automobile, "whose primary function is transportation."

We then held that the mobility of luggage did not justify creating an additional exception to the Warrant Clause. Unlike an automobile, luggage can easily be seized and detained pending judicial approval of a search. Once the police have luggage "under their exclusive control, there [i]s not the slightest danger that the [luggage] or its contents could [be] removed before a valid search warrant could be obtained. . . . With the [luggage] safely immobilized, it [i]s unreasonable to undertake the additional and greater intrusion of a search without a warrant" (footnote omitted). * * *

[W]e recognized in *Ross* that *Chadwick* and *Sanders* had not created a special rule for container searches, but rather had merely applied the cardinal principle that warrantless searches are per se unreasonable unless justified by an exception to the general rule. *Ross* dealt with the scope of the automobile exception; *Chadwick* and *Sanders* were cases in which the exception simply did not apply.

In its opinion today, the Court recognizes that the police did not have probable cause to search respondent's vehicle and that a search of anything but the paper bag that respondent had carried from Daza's apartment and placed in the trunk of his car would have been unconstitutional. Moreover, as I read the opinion, the Court assumes that the police could not have made a warrantless inspection of the bag before it was placed in the car. Finally, the Court also does not question the fact that, under our prior cases, it would have been lawful for the police to seize the container and detain it (and respondent) until they obtained a search warrant. Thus, all of the relevant facts that governed our decisions in *Chadwick* and *Sanders* are present here whereas the relevant fact that justified the vehicle search in *Ross* is not present.

The Court does not attempt to identify any exigent circumstances that would justify its refusal to apply the general rule against warrantless searches. Instead, it advances these three arguments: First, the rules identified in the foregoing cases are confusing and anomalous. Second, the rules do not protect any significant interest in privacy. And, third, the rules impede effective law enforcement. None of these arguments withstands scrutiny. * * *

The Court summarizes the alleged "anomaly" created by the coexistence of *Ross, Chadwick,* and *Sanders* with the statement that "the more likely the police are to discover drugs in a container, the less authority they have to search it." This juxtaposition is only anomalous, however, if one accepts the flawed premise that the degree to which the police are likely to discover contraband is correlated with their authority to search *without a warrant.* Yet, even proof beyond a reasonable doubt will not justify a warrantless search that is not supported by one of the exceptions to the warrant requirement. And, even when the police have a warrant or an exception applies, once the police possess probable cause, the extent to which they are more or less certain of the contents of a container has no bearing on their authority to search it.

To the extent there was any "anomaly" in our prior jurisprudence, the Court has "cured" it at the expense of creating a more serious paradox. For, surely it is anomalous to prohibit a search of a briefcase while the owner is carrying it exposed on a public street yet to permit a search once the owner has placed the briefcase in the locked trunk of his car. One's privacy interest in one's luggage can certainly not be diminished by one's removing it from a public thoroughfare and placing it—out of sight—in a privately owned vehicle. Nor is the danger that evidence will escape increased if the luggage is in a car rather than on the street. In either location, if the police have probable cause, they are authorized to seize the luggage and to detain it until they obtain judicial approval for a search. Any line demarking an exception to the warrant requirement will appear blurred at the edges, but the Court has certainly erred if it believes that, by erasing one line and drawing another, it has drawn a clearer boundary.

The Court's statement that *Chadwick* and *Sanders* provide only "minimal protection to privacy" is also unpersuasive. Every citizen clearly has an interest in the privacy of the contents of his or her luggage, briefcase, handbag or any other container that conceals private papers and effects from public scrutiny. That privacy interest has been recognized repeatedly in cases spanning more than a century.

Under the Court's holding today, the privacy interest that protects the contents of a suitcase or a briefcase from a warrantless search when it is in public view simply vanishes when its owner climbs into a taxicab. Unquestionably the rejection of the *Sanders* line of cases by today's decision will result in a significant loss of individual privacy.

To support its argument that today's holding works only a minimal intrusion on privacy, the Court suggests that "[i]f the police know that they may open a bag only if they are actually searching the entire car, they may search more extensively than they otherwise would in order to establish the general probable cause required by *Ross.*" As I have already noted, this fear is unexplained and inexplicable. Neither evidence uncovered in the course of a search nor the scope of the search conducted can be used to provide *post hoc* justification for a search unsupported by probable cause at its inception.

The Court also justifies its claim that its holding inflicts only minor damage by suggesting that, under *New York v. Belton,* the police could have arrested respondent and searched his bag if respondent had placed the bag in the passenger compartment of the automobile instead of the trunk. In *Belton,* however, the justification for stopping the car and arresting the driver had nothing to do with the subsequent search, which was based on the potential danger to the arresting officer. The holding in *Belton* was supportable under a straightforward application of the automobile exception. I would not extend *Belton's* holding to this case, in which the container—which was protected from a warrantless search before it was placed in the car—provided the only justification for the arrest. Even accepting *Belton's* application to a case like this one, however, the Court's logic extends its holding to a container placed in the *trunk* of a vehicle, rather than in the passenger compartment. And the Court makes this extension without any justification whatsoever other than convenience to law enforcement. * * *

Despite repeated claims that *Chadwick* and *Sanders* have "impeded effective law enforcement," the Court cites no authority for its contentions. * * *

Even if the warrant requirement does inconvenience the police to some extent, that fact does not distinguish this constitutional requirement from any other procedural protection secured by the Bill of Rights. It is merely a part of the price that our society must pay in order to preserve its freedom. * * *

Notes and Questions

[handwritten: Not the driver's purse]

1. After police stopped a vehicle for speeding, the driver admitted that he had used the syringe visible in his shirt pocket to take drugs. The police then ordered the two female passengers out of the car and searched the passenger compartment for contraband. On the back seat they found a purse that passenger Houghton claimed as hers; the police searched it and found drugs and drug paraphernalia. Houghton was convicted after her efforts to have the drugs suppressed failed, but the state supreme court overturned the conviction, reasoning that the search violated the Fourth Amendment because the officer "knew or should have known that the purse did not belong to the driver, but to one of the passengers," and because "there was no probable cause to search the passengers' personal effects and no reason to believe that contraband had been placed within the purse." But in WYOMING v. HOUGHTON, 526 U.S. 295, 119 S.Ct. 1297, 143 L.Ed.2d 408 (1999), the Supreme Court, per SCALIA, J., reversed, reasoning that "neither *Ross* itself nor the historical evidence it relied upon admits of a distinction among packages or containers based on ownership. When there is probable cause to search for contraband in a car, it is reasonable for police officers—like customs officials in the Founding era—to examine packages and containers without a showing of individualized probable cause for each one. A passenger's personal belongings, just like the driver's belongings or containers attached to the car like a glove compartment, are 'in' the car, and the officer has probable cause to search for contraband in the car.

"Even if the historical evidence, as described by *Ross*, were thought to be equivocal, we would find that the balancing of the relative interests weighs decidedly in favor of allowing searches of a passenger's belongings. Passengers, no less than drivers, possess a reduced expectation of privacy with regard to the property that they transport in cars, which 'trave[l] public thoroughfares,' 'seldom serv[e] as ... the repository of personal effects,' are subjected to police stop and examination to enforce 'pervasive' governmental controls '[a]s an everyday occurrence,' and, finally, are exposed to traffic accidents that may render all their contents open to public scrutiny.

"In this regard—the degree of intrusiveness upon personal privacy and indeed even personal dignity—the two cases the Wyoming Supreme Court found dispositive differ substantially from the package search at issue here. *United States v. Di Re*, [p. 207], held that probable cause to search a car did not justify a body search of a passenger. And *Ybarra v. Illinois*, [p. 197], held that a search warrant for a tavern and its bartender did not permit body searches of all the bar's patrons. These cases turned on the unique, significantly heightened protection afforded against searches of one's person. 'Even a limited search of the outer clothing ... constitutes a severe, though brief, intrusion upon cherished personal security, and it must surely be an annoying, frightening, and perhaps humiliating experience.'

Such traumatic consequences are not to be expected when the police examine an item of personal property found in a car.[34]

"Whereas the passenger's privacy expectations are, as we have described, considerably diminished, the governmental interests at stake are substantial. Effective law enforcement would be appreciably impaired without the ability to search a passenger's personal belongings when there is reason to believe contraband or evidence of criminal wrongdoing is hidden in the car. As in all car-search cases, the 'ready mobility' of an automobile creates a risk that the evidence or contraband will be permanently lost while a warrant is obtained. In addition, a car passenger—unlike the unwitting tavern patron in *Ybarra*—will often be engaged in a common enterprise with the driver, and have the same interest in concealing the fruits or the evidence of their wrongdoing. A criminal might be able to hide contraband in a passenger's belongings as readily as in other containers in the car—perhaps even surreptitiously, without the passenger's knowledge or permission. (This last possibility provided the basis for respondent's defense at trial; she testified that most of the seized contraband must have been placed in her purse by her traveling companions at one or another of various times, including the time she was 'half asleep' in the car.)

"To be sure, these factors favoring a search will not always be present, but the balancing of interests must be conducted with an eye to the generality of cases. To require that the investigating officer have positive reason to believe that the passenger and driver were engaged in a common enterprise, or positive reason to believe that the driver had time and occasion to conceal the item in the passenger's belongings, surreptitiously or with friendly permission, is to impose requirements so seldom met that a 'passenger's property' rule would dramatically reduce the ability to find and seize contraband and evidence of crime. Of course these requirements would not attach (under the Wyoming Supreme Court's rule) until the police officer knows or has reason to know that the container belongs to a passenger. But once a 'passenger's property' exception to car searches became widely known, one would expect passenger-confederates to claim everything as their own. And one would anticipate a bog of litigation—in the form of both civil lawsuits and motions to suppress in criminal trials—involving such questions as whether the officer should have believed a passenger's claim of ownership, whether he should have inferred ownership from various objective factors, whether he had probable cause to believe that the passenger was a confederate, or to

---

34. The dissent begins its analysis with an assertion that this case is governed by our decision in *United States v. Di Re*, which held, as the dissent describes it, that the automobile exception to the warrant requirement did not justify "searches of the passenger's pockets and the space between his shirt and underwear." It attributes that holding to "the settled distinction between drivers and passengers," rather than to a distinction between search of the person and search of property, which the dissent claims is "newly minted" by today's opinion—a "new rule that is based on a distinction between property contained in clothing worn by a passenger and property contained in a passenger's briefcase or purse."

In its peroration, however, the dissent quotes extensively from Justice Jackson's opinion in *Di Re*, which makes it very clear that it is precisely this distinction between search of the person and search of property that the case relied upon: "The Government says it would

not contend that, armed 'with a search warrant for a residence only, it could search all persons found in it. But an occupant of a house could be used to conceal this contraband on his person quite as readily as can an occupant of a car.'" Does the dissent really believe that Justice Jackson was saying that a house-search could not inspect property belonging to persons found in the house—say a large standing safe or violin case belonging to the owner's visiting godfather? Of course that is not what Justice Jackson meant at all. He was referring precisely to that "distinction between property contained in clothing worn by a passenger and property contained in a passenger's briefcase or purse" that the dissent disparages. This distinction between searches of the person and searches of property is assuredly not "newly minted." And if the dissent thinks "pockets" and "clothing" do not count as part of the person, it must believe that the only searches of the person are strip searches.

believe that the driver might have introduced the contraband into the package with or without the passenger's knowledge.[35] When balancing the competing interests, our determinations of "reasonableness" under the Fourth Amendment must take account of these practical realities. We think they militate in favor of the needs of law enforcement, and against a personal-privacy interest that is ordinarily weak.

"Finally, if we were to invent an exception from the historical practice that *Ross* accurately described and summarized, it is perplexing why that exception should protect only property belonging to a passenger, rather than (what seems much more logical) property belonging to anyone other than the driver. Surely Houghton's privacy would have been invaded to the same degree whether she was present or absent when her purse was searched. And surely her presence in the car with the driver provided more, rather than less, reason to believe that the two were in league. It may ordinarily be easier to identify the property as belonging to someone other than the driver when the purported owner is present to identify it—but in the many cases (like *Ross* itself) where the car is seized, that identification may occur later, at the station-house; and even at the site of the stop one can readily imagine a package clearly marked with the owner's name and phone number, by which the officer can confirm the driver's denial of ownership. The sensible rule (and the one supported by history and caselaw) is that such a package may be searched, whether or not its owner is present as a passenger or otherwise, because it may contain the contraband that the officer has reason to believe is in the car."

STEVENS, J., for the three dissenters, objected that in "all of our prior cases applying the automobile exception to the Fourth Amendment's warrant requirement, either the defendant was the operator of the vehicle and in custody of the object of the search, or no question was raised as to the defendant's ownership or custody. In the only automobile case confronting the search of a passenger defendant—*United States v. Di Re*—the Court held that the exception to the warrant requirement did not apply. In *Di Re*, as here, the information prompting the search directly implicated the driver, not the passenger. Today, instead of adhering to the settled distinction between drivers and passengers, the Court fashions a new rule that is based on a distinction between property contained in clothing worn by a passenger and property contained in a passenger's briefcase or purse. In cases on both sides of the Court's newly minted test, the property is in a 'container' (whether a pocket or a pouch) located in the vehicle. Moreover, unlike the Court, I think it quite plain that the search of a passenger's purse or briefcase involves an intrusion on privacy that may be just as serious as was the intrusion in *Di Re*. * * * [a]

35. The dissent is "confident in a police officer's ability to apply a rule requiring a warrant or individualized probable cause to search belongings that are ... obviously owned by and in the custody of a passenger." If this is the dissent's strange criterion for warrant protection ("obviously owned by and in the custody of") its preceding paean to the importance of preserving passengers' privacy rings a little hollow on rehearing. Should it not be enough if the passenger says he owns the briefcase, and the officer has no concrete reason to believe otherwise? Or would the dissent consider that an example of "obvious" ownership? On reflection, it seems not at all obvious precisely what constitutes obviousness—and so even the dissent's on-the-cheap protection of passengers' privacy interest in their property turns out to

be unclear, and hence unadministrable. But maybe the dissent does not mean to propose an obviously-owned-by-and-in-the-custody-of test after all, since a few sentences later it endorses, simpliciter, "a rule requiring a warrant or individualized probable cause to search passenger belongings." For the reasons described in text, that will not work.

a. Compare BREYER, concurring: "Purses are special containers. They are repositories of especially personal items that people generally like to keep with them at all times. So I am tempted to say that a search of a purse involves an intrusion so similar to a search of one's person that the same rule should govern both. However, given this Court's prior cases, I cannot argue that the fact that the container

"Nor am I persuaded that the mere spatial association between a passenger and a driver provides an acceptable basis for presuming that they are partners in crime or for ignoring privacy interests in a purse. Whether or not the Fourth Amendment required a warrant to search Houghton's purse, at the very least the trooper in this case had to have probable cause to believe that her purse contained contraband. The Wyoming Supreme Court concluded that he did not.

"Finally, in my view, the State's legitimate interest in effective law enforcement does not outweigh the privacy concerns at issue. I am as confident in a police officer's ability to apply a rule requiring a warrant or individualized probable cause to search belongings that are—as in this case—obviously owned by and in the custody of a passenger as is the Court in a 'passenger-confederate[']s' ability to circumvent the rule. Certainly the ostensible clarity of the Court's rule is attractive. But that virtue is insufficient justification for its adoption. Moreover, a rule requiring a warrant or individualized probable cause to search passenger belongings is every bit as simple as the Court's rule; it simply protects more privacy. * * * 2"

2. Reassess the law and facts of *Chadwick*, p. 267 in light of *Acevedo*. Absent true exigent circumstances, is a search warrant still required for a container having no connection with a vehicle? If so, is there actually a sufficient container-vehicle connection in *Chadwick* to make the *Acevedo* no-warrant rule applicable?

3. If there *is* a general rule that absent exigent circumstances search warrants are needed for the search of containers not sufficiently connected with vehicles, are there exceptions? Consider:

(a) Fn. 13 in *Sanders:* "Not all containers and packages found by police during the course of a search will deserve the full protection of the Fourth Amendment. Thus, some containers (for example a kit of burglar tools or a gun case) by their very nature cannot support any reasonable expectation of privacy because their contents can be inferred from their outward appearance. Similarly, in some cases the contents of a package will be open to 'plain view,' thereby obviating the need for a warrant."

(b) In *Texas v. Brown*, 460 U.S. 730, 103 S.Ct. 1535, 75 L.Ed.2d 502 (1983), involving a warrantless search of a knotted opaque party balloon found with several plastic vials, a quantity of loose white powder, and a bag of balloons, Stevens, J., for three members of the Court, after characterizing the plurality's explanation for why no search warrant was needed to search the balloon as "incomplete," speculated that the balloon "could be one of those rare single-purpose containers which 'by their very nature cannot support any reasonable expectation of privacy because their contents can be inferred from their outward appearance.' Whereas a suitcase or a paper bag may contain an almost infinite variety of items, a balloon of this kind might be used only to transport drugs. Viewing it where he did could have given the officer a degree of certainty that is equivalent to the plain view of the heroin itself. If that be true, I would conclude

---

was a purse automatically makes a legal difference, for the Court has warned against trying to make that kind of distinction. But I can say that it would matter if a woman's purse, like a man's billfold, were attached to her person. It might then amount to a kind of 'outer clothing' which under the Court's cases would properly receive increased protection. In this case, the purse was separate from the person, and no one has claimed that, under those circumstances, the type of container makes a difference. For that reason, I join the Court's opinion."

2. In response to this dissent the Court has crafted an imaginative footnote suggesting that the *Di Re* decision rested, not on Di Re's status as a mere occupant of the vehicle and the importance of individualized suspicion, but rather on the intrusive character of the search. That the search of a safe or violin case would be less intrusive than a strip search does not, however, persuade me that the *Di Re* case would have been decided differently if Di Re had been a woman and the gas coupons had been found in her purse. * * *

that the plain view doctrine supports the search as well as the seizure even though the contents of the balloon were not actually visible to the officer.

"This reasoning leads me to the conclusion that the Fourth Amendment would not require exclusion of the balloon's contents in this case if, but only if, there was probable cause to search the entire vehicle or there was virtual certainty that the balloon contained a controlled substance.[5]"

(c) After customs agents found marijuana inside a table shipped into the country, it was repackaged and delivered to defendant by police posing as delivery men. Surveilling police saw defendant pull the container into his apartment, and when he reemerged with it 30 to 45 minutes later he was arrested and the package searched without a warrant. The state court, relying upon *Sanders* and *Chadwick*, held the marijuana inadmissible, but the Supreme Court, in ILLINOIS v. ANDREAS, 463 U.S. 765, 103 S.Ct. 3319, 77 L.Ed.2d 1003 (1983), disagreed. The Court, per BURGER, C.J., first addressed the threshold question of "whether an individual has a legitimate expectation of privacy in the contents of a previously lawfully searched container. It is obvious that the privacy interest in the contents of a container diminishes with respect to a container that law enforcement authorities have already lawfully opened and found to contain illicit drugs. No protected privacy interest remains in contraband in a container once government officers lawfully have opened that container and identified its contents as illegal. The simple act of resealing the container to enable the police to make a controlled delivery does not operate to revive or restore the lawfully invaded privacy rights.

"This conclusion is supported by the reasoning underlying the 'plain view' doctrine. The plain view doctrine authorizes seizure of illegal or evidentiary items visible to a police officer whose access to the object has some prior Fourth Amendment justification and who has probable cause to suspect that the item is connected with criminal activity. The plain view doctrine is grounded on the proposition that once police are lawfully in a position to observe an item firsthand, its owner's privacy interest in that item is lost; the owner may retain the incidents of title and possession but not privacy. That rationale applies here; once a container has been found to a certainty to contain illicit drugs, the contraband becomes like objects physically within the plain view of the police, and the claim to privacy is lost. Consequently the subsequent opening is not a 'search' within the intendment of the Fourth Amendment."

The Court then noted that "perfect" controlled deliveries are often impossible, so that there may result "a gap in surveillance" during which "it is possible that the container will be put to other uses—for example, the contraband may be removed or other items may be placed inside." On the resulting question of "at what point after an interruption of control or surveillance, courts should recognize the individual's expectation of privacy in the container as a legitimate right protected by the Fourth Amendment," the Court adopted the "workable," "reasonable" and "objective" standard of "whether there is a substantial likelihood that the contents of the container have been changed during the gap in surveillance. We hold that absent a substantial likelihood that the contents have been changed, there is no legitimate expectation of privacy in the contents of a container previously opened under lawful authority." The Court then concluded there was no substantial likelihood in the instant case. "The unusual size of the

---

5. Sometimes there can be greater certainty about the identity of a substance within a container than about the identity of a substance that is actually visible. One might actually see a white powder without realizing that it is heroin, but be virtually certain a balloon contains such a substance in a particular context. It seems to me that in evaluating whether a person's privacy interests are infringed, "virtual certainty" is a more meaningful indicator than visibility.

container, its specialized purpose, and the relatively short break in surveillance, combine to make it substantially unlikely that the respondent removed the table or placed new items inside the container while it was in his apartment.''

BRENNAN and Marshall, JJ., dissenting, objected that while after the customs search "any reasonable expectation respondent may have had that the existence of the contraband would remain secret was lost, and could not be regained," he still had a Fourth Amendment right "to be 'let alone' " which "is, at the very least, the right not to have one's repose and possessions disturbed" without a warrant. Moreover, "if a person has no reasonable expectation of privacy in a package whose contents are already legally known to the authorities, a reasonable expectation of privacy should reattach if the person has unobserved access to the package and any opportunity to change its contents." STEVENS, J., dissenting separately, would remand for reconsideration under his "virtual certainty" test in *Texas v. Brown.*

NEW YORK v. BELTON

453 U.S. 454, 101 S.Ct. 2860, 69 L.Ed.2d 768 (1981).

Justice STEWART delivered the opinion of the Court. * * *

[After a state policeman was passed by another automobile travelling at an excessive rate of speed, he overtook the speeding vehicle and ordered its driver to pull it over. The officer asked to see the driver's license and automobile registration, and discovered that none of the four men in the car owned the vehicle or was related to its owner. Meanwhile, he had smelled burnt marihuana and had seen on the floor of the car an envelope marked "Supergold" that he associated with marihuana, so he directed the men to get out of the car and placed them under arrest for the unlawful possession of marihuana. He patted down each of the men and "split them up into four separate areas of the Thruway at this time so they would not be in physical touching area of each other." He then picked up the envelope marked "Supergold" and found that it contained marihuana, and then searched each one of them. He then searched the passenger compartment of the car. He unzipped one of the pockets of the jacket he found on the back seat and discovered cocaine. Placing the jacket in his automobile, he drove the four arrestees to a nearby police station. Passenger Belton, the owner of the jacket, was subsequently indicted for criminal possession of a controlled substance. He pleaded guilty to a lesser included offense, but preserved his claim that the cocaine had been illegally seized. The New York Court of Appeals reversed, holding that a "warrantless search of the zippered pockets of an unaccessible jacket may not be upheld as a search incident to a lawful arrest where there is no longer any danger that the arrestee or a confederate might gain access to the article."]

It is a first principle of Fourth Amendment jurisprudence that the police may not conduct a search unless they first convince a neutral magistrate that there is probable cause to do so. This Court has recognized, however, that "the exigencies of the situation" may sometimes make exemption from the warrant requirement "imperative." Specifically, the Court held in *Chimel v. California* [p. 238], that a lawful custodial arrest creates a situation which justifies the contemporaneous search without a warrant of the person arrested and of the immediately surrounding area. Such searches have long been considered valid because of the need "to remove any weapons that [the arrestee] might seek to use in order to resist arrest or effect his escape" and the need to prevent the concealment or destruction of evidence.

The Court's opinion in *Chimel* emphasized the principle that, "The scope of [a] search must be 'strictly tied to and justified by' the circumstances which rendered its initiation permissible." Thus while the Court in *Chimel* found "ample justification" for a search of "the area from within which [an arrestee] might gain possession of a weapon or destructible evidence," the Court found "no comparable justification * * * for routinely searching any room other than that in which an arrest occurs—or, for that matter, for searching through all the desk drawers or other closed or concealed areas in that room itself."

Although the principle that limits a search incident to a lawful custodial arrest may be stated clearly enough, courts have discovered the principle difficult to apply in specific cases. Yet, as one commentator has pointed out, the protection of the Fourth and Fourteenth Amendments "can only be realized if the police are acting under a set of rules which, in most instances, makes it possible to reach a correct determination beforehand as to whether an invasion of privacy is justified in the interest of law enforcement." LaFave, *"Case-by-Case Adjudication" versus "Standardized Procedures": The Robinson Dilemma*, 1974 Sup.Ct.Rev. 127, 142. This is because

> "Fourth Amendment doctrine, given force and effect by the exclusionary rule, is primarily intended to regulate the police in their day-to-day activities and thus ought to be expressed in terms that are readily applicable by the police in the context of the law enforcement activities in which they are necessarily engaged. A highly sophisticated set of rules, qualified by all sorts of ifs, ands, and buts and requiring the drawing of subtle nuances and hairline distinctions, may be the sort of heady stuff upon which the facile minds of lawyers and judges eagerly feed, but they may be 'literally impossible of application by the officer in the field.' " Id., at 141.

In short, "A single, familiar standard is essential to guide police officers, who have only limited time and expertise to reflect on and balance the social and individual interests involved in the specific circumstances they confront." *Dunaway v. New York* [p. 325].

So it was that, in *United States v. Robinson* [p. 215], the Court hewed to a straightforward rule, easily applied, and predictably enforced: "[I]n the case of a lawful custodial arrest a full search of the person is not only an exception to the warrant requirement, but it is also a 'reasonable' search under that amendment." In so holding, the Court rejected the suggestion "that there must be litigated in each case the issue of whether or not there was present one of the reasons supporting the authority for a search of the person incident to a lawful arrest."

But no straightforward rule has emerged from the litigated cases respecting the question involved here—the question of the proper scope of a search of the interior of an automobile incident to a lawful custodial arrest of its occupants. The difficulty courts have had is reflected in the conflicting views of the New York judges who dealt with the problem in the present case, and is confirmed by a look at even a small sample drawn from the narrow class of cases in which courts have decided whether, in the course of a search incident to the lawful custodial arrest of the occupants of an automobile, police may search inside the automobile after the arrestees are no longer in it. * * *

When a person cannot know how a court will apply a settled principle to a recurring factual situation, that person cannot know the scope of his constitutional protection, nor can a policeman know the scope of his authority. While the *Chimel* case established that a search incident to an arrest may not stray beyond the area within the immediate control of the arrestee, courts have found no workable definition of "the area within the immediate control of the arrestee" when that area arguably includes the interior of an automobile and the arrestee is its recent occupant. Our reading of the cases suggests the generalization that articles inside the relatively narrow compass of the passenger compartment of an automobile are in fact generally, even if not inevitably, within "the area into which an arrestee might reach in order to grab a weapon or evidentiary item." In order to establish the workable rule this category of cases requires, we read *Chimel*'s definition of the limits of the area that may be searched in light of that generalization. Accordingly, we hold that when a policeman has made a lawful custodial arrest of the occupant of an automobile, he may, as a contemporaneous incident of that arrest, search the passenger compartment of that automobile.[3]

It follows from this conclusion that the police may also examine the contents of any containers found within the passenger compartment, for if the passenger compartment is within reach of the arrestee, so also will containers in it be within his reach.[4] Such a container may, of course, be searched whether it is open or closed, since the justification for the search is not that the arrestee has no privacy interest in the container, but that the lawful custodial arrest justifies the infringement of any privacy interest the arrestee may have. Thus, while the Court in *Chimel* held that the police could not search all the drawers in an arrestee's house simply because the police had arrested him at home, the Court noted that drawers within an arrestee's reach could be searched because of the danger their contents might pose to the police.

It is true, of course, that these containers will sometimes be such that they could hold neither a weapon nor evidence of the criminal conduct for which the suspect was arrested. However, in *United States v. Robinson,* the Court rejected the argument that such a container—there a "crumpled up cigarette package"— located during a search of Robinson incident to his arrest could not be searched: "The authority to search the person incident to a lawful custodial arrest, while based upon the need to disarm and to discover evidence, does not depend on what a court may later decide was the probability in a particular arrest situation that weapons or evidence would in fact be found upon the person of the suspect. A custodial arrest of a suspect based on probable cause is a reasonable intrusion under the Fourth Amendment; that intrusion being lawful, a search incident to the arrest requires no additional justification." * * *

It is not questioned that the respondent was the subject of a lawful custodial arrest on a charge of possessing marihuana. The search of the respondent's jacket followed immediately upon that arrest. The jacket was located inside the passenger compartment of the car in which the respondent had been a passenger just before he was arrested. The jacket was thus within the area which we have concluded was "within the arrestee's immediate control" within the meaning of the *Chimel* case.[6] The search of the jacket, therefore, was a search incident to a lawful custodial arrest, and it did not violate the Fourth and Fourteenth Amendments. Accordingly, the judgment is reversed. * * *

Justice STEVENS, concurring in the judgment.

For the reasons stated in my dissenting opinion in *Robbins v. California,* I agree [that] this judgment should be reversed. [That opinion follows.—ed.]

3. Our holding today does no more than determine the meaning of *Chimel*'s principles in this particular and problematic content. It in no way alters the fundamental principles established in the *Chimel* case regarding the basic scope of searches incident to lawful custodial arrests.

4. "Container" here denotes any object capable of holding another object. It thus includes closed or open glove compartments, consoles, or other receptacles located anywhere within the passenger compartment, as well as luggage, boxes, bags, clothing, and the like. Our holding encompasses only the interior of the passenger compartment of an automobile and does not encompass the trunk.

6. Because of this disposition of the case, there is no need here to consider whether the search and seizure were permissible under the so-called "automobile exception."

The Court's careful and repeated use of the term "lawful custodial arrest" seems to imply that a significant distinction between custodial arrests and ordinary arrests exists. I am familiar with the distinction between a "stop," see, e.g., *Terry v. Ohio,* [p. 291], and an "arrest," but I am not familiar with any difference between custodial arrests and any other kind of arrest.[a] It is, of course, true that persons apprehended for traffic violations are frequently not required to accompany the arresting officer to the police station before they are permitted to leave on their own recognizance or by using their driver's licenses as a form of bond. It is also possible that state law or local regulations may in some cases forbid police officers from taking persons into custody for violation of minor traffic laws. As a matter of constitutional law, however, any person lawfully arrested for the pettiest misdemeanor may be temporarily placed in custody.[11] Indeed, as the Court has repeatedly held, every arrest is a seizure of the person within the meaning of the Fourth Amendment. The rule of constitutional law the Court fashions today therefore potentially applies to every arrest of every occupant of an automobile.[12]

After the vehicle in which respondent was riding was stopped, the officer smelled marihuana and thereby acquired probable cause to believe that the vehicle contained contraband. A thorough search of the car was therefore reasonable. But if there were no reason to believe that anything more than a traffic violation had occurred, I should think it palpably unreasonable to require the driver of a car to open his briefcase or his luggage for inspection by the officer. The driver so compelled, however, could make no constitutional objection to a decision by the officer to take the driver into custody and thereby obtain justification for a search of the entire interior of the vehicle. Indeed, under the Court's new rule, the arresting officer may find reason to follow that procedure whenever he sees an interesting looking briefcase or package in a vehicle that has been stopped for a traffic violation. That decision by a police officer will therefore provide the constitutional predicate for broader vehicle searches than any neutral magistrate could authorize by issuing a warrant. * * *

Justice BRENNAN, with whom Justice MARSHALL joins, dissenting. * * *

By approving the constitutionality of the warrantless search in this case, the Court carves out a dangerous precedent that is not justified by the concerns underlying *Chimel.* Disregarding the principle "that the scope of a warrantless

a. Consider in this regard the search-of-vehicle-incident-to-citation case of *Knowles v. Iowa,* p. 236.

11. Justice Stewart apparently believes that the Fourth and Fourteenth Amendments might provide some impediment to police taking a defendant into custody for violation of a "minor traffic offense." See *Gustafson v. Florida* (Stewart, J. concurring). Although I agree that a police officer's authority to restrain an individual's liberty should be limited in the context of stops for routine traffic violations, the Court has not directly considered the question whether "there are constitutional limits upon the use of 'custodial arrests' as the means for invoking the criminal process when relatively minor offenses are involved." See 2 W. LaFave, *Search and Seizure* § 5.2, p. 290 (1978); see also id. § 5.1, p. 256–260, § 5.2, p. 281–291. To the extent that the Court has considered the scope of an officer's authority in making routine traffic stops, the Court has not imposed constitutional restrictions on that au-

thority. Thus the Court may be assuming that its new rule will be limited by a constitutional restriction that does not exist.

12. After today, the driver of a vehicle stopped for a minor traffic violation must look to state law for protection from unreasonable searches. Such protection may come from two sources. Statutory law may provide some protection. Legislatures in some states permit officers to take traffic violators into custody only for certain violations. In some states, however, the police officer has the discretion to make a "custodial arrest" for violation of any motor vehicle law. Additionally, the failure to produce a satisfactory bond will often justify "detention and custodial arrest." Given the incomplete protection afforded by statutory law, drivers in many States will have to persuade state supreme courts to interpret their state constitution's equivalent to the Fourth Amendment to prohibit the unreasonable searches permitted by the Court here.

search must be commensurate with the rationale that excepts the search from the warrant requirement," the Court for the first time grants police officers authority to conduct a warrantless "area" search under circumstances where there is no chance that the arrestee "might gain possession of a weapon or destructible evidence." Under the approach taken today, the result would presumably be the same even if Officer Nicot had handcuffed Belton and his companions in the patrol car before placing them under arrest, and even if his search had extended to locked luggage or other inaccessible containers located in the back seat of the car. * * *

The Court seeks to justify its departure from the principles underlying *Chimel* by proclaiming the need for a new bright line rule to guide the officer in the field. As we pointed out in *Mincey v. Arizona,* [p. 251], however, "the mere fact that law enforcement may be made more efficient can never by itself justify disregard of the Fourth Amendment." Moreover, the Court's attempt to forge a "bright line" rule fails on its own terms. * * * The Court's new approach leaves open too many questions and, more important, it provides the police and the courts with too few tools with which to find the answers.

Thus, although the Court concludes that a warrantless search of a car may take place even though the suspect was arrested outside the car, it does not indicate how long after the suspect's arrest that search may validly be conducted. Would a warrantless search incident to arrest be valid if conducted five minutes after the suspect left his car? Thirty minutes? Three hours? Does it matter whether the suspect is standing in close proximity to the car when the search is conducted? Does it matter whether the police formed probable cause to arrest before or after the suspect left his car? And *why* is the rule announced today necessarily limited to searches of cars? What if a suspect is seen walking out of a house where the police, peering in from outside, had formed probable cause to believe a crime was being committed? Could the police then arrest that suspect and enter the house to conduct a search incident to arrest? Even assuming today's rule is limited to searches of the "interior" of cars—an assumption not demanded by logic—what is meant by "interior"? Does it include locked glove compartments, the interior of door panels, or the area under the floorboards? Are special rules necessary for station wagons and hatchbacks, where the luggage compartment may be reached through the interior, or taxicabs, where a glass panel might separate the driver's compartment from the rest of the car? Are the only containers that may be searched those that are large enough to be "capable of holding another object"? Or does the new rule apply to any container, even if it "could hold neither a weapon nor evidence of the criminal conduct for which the suspect was arrested"?

The Court does not give the police any "bright line" answers to these questions. More important, because the Court's new rule abandons the justifications underlying *Chimel, it offers no guidance to the police officer seeking to work out these answers for himself.* * * *

The standard announced in *Chimel* is not nearly as difficult to apply as the Court suggests. To the contrary, I continue to believe that *Chimel* provides a sound, workable rule for determining the constitutionality of a warrantless search incident to arrest. Under *Chimel,* searches incident to arrest may be conducted without a warrant only if limited to the person of the arrestee, or to the area within the arrestee's "immediate control." While it may be difficult in some cases to measure the exact scope of the arrestee's immediate control, relevant factors would surely include the relative number of police officers and arrestees, the manner of restraint placed on the arrestee, and the ability of the arrestee to gain access to a particular area or container.[5] Certainly there will be some close cases, but when in doubt the police can always turn to the rationale underlying *Chimel*—the need to prevent the arrestee from reaching weapons or contraband—before exercising their judgment. A rule based on that rationale should provide more guidance than the rule announced by the Court today. Moreover, unlike the Court's rule, it would be faithful to the Fourth Amendment.

Justice WHITE, with whom Justice MARSHALL joins, dissenting.

* * * The Court now holds that as incident to the arrest of the driver or any other person in an automobile, the interior of the car and any container found therein, whether locked or not, may not only be seized but also searched even absent probable cause to believe that contraband or evidence of crime will be found. As to luggage, briefcases or other containers, this seems to me an extreme extension of *Chimel* and one to which I cannot subscribe. * * *[b]

What does it take to make a person an "occupant" within the meaning of the *Belton* rule? One view is noted in *Florida v. Thomas*, 532 U.S. 774, 121 S.Ct. 1905, 150 L.Ed.2d 1 (2001), where, while officers were investigating marijuana sales and making arrests at a certain home, Thomas drove up, parked in the driveway and walked toward the back of his car, where one officer then met him and asked for identification. A check revealed an outstanding warrant, so the officer arrested Thomas, handcuffed him, and took him inside the home, and then searched the car and found drugs. The state court's conclusion in favor of Thomas, that "*Belton*'s bright-line rule is limited to situations where the law enforcement officer initiates contact with the defendant" while defendant remains in the car, was not ruled on by the Supreme Court; the Court decided it lacked jurisdiction because after so holding the state court had remanded for further factfinding and a determination of the outcome under *Chimel*.

COLORADO v. BERTINE
479 U.S. 367, 107 S.Ct. 738, 93 L.Ed.2d 739 (1987).

Chief Justice REHNQUIST delivered the opinion of the Court.

On February 10, 1984, a police officer in Boulder, Colorado arrested respondent Steven Lee Bertine for driving while under the influence of alcohol. After Bertine was taken into custody and before the arrival of a tow truck to take Bertine's van to an impoundment lot,[1] a ~~backup officer inventoried~~ the contents of

---

5. The Court sets up a straw man when it claims that under the "exclusive control" approach taken by the Court of Appeals, "no search or seizure incident to a lawful custodial arrest would ever be valid; by seizing an article even on the arrestee's person, an officer may be said to have reduced that article to his 'exclusive control.'"

If a police officer could obtain exclusive control of an article by simply holding it in his hand, I would certainly agree with the Court. But as we recognized in *United States v. Chadwick*, exclusive control means more than that. It means sufficient control such that there is no significant risk that the arrestee or his confederates "might gain possession of a weapon or destructible evidence." *Chimel v. Califor-*

nia. The issue of exclusive control presents a question of fact to be decided under the circumstances of each case, just as the New York Court of Appeals has decided it here.

b. For close analyses of *Belton*, see Joseph D. Grano, *Rethinking the Fourth Amendment Warrant Requirement*, 19 Am.Crim.L.Rev. 603 (1982); Lewis R. Katz, *Automobile Searches and Diminished Expectations in the Warrant Clause*, 19 Am.Crim.L.Rev. 557 (1982); David S. Rudstein, *The Search of an Automobile Incident to an Arrest: An Analysis of New York v. Belton*, 67 Marq.L.Rev. 205 (1984).

1. Section 7–7–2(a)(4) of the Boulder Revised Code authorizes police officers to impound vehicles when drivers are taken into custody. Section 7–7–2(a)(4) provides:

the van. The officer opened a closed backpack in which he found controlled substances, cocaine paraphernalia, and a large amount of cash. Bertine was subsequently charged with driving while under the influence of alcohol, unlawful possession of cocaine with intent to dispense, sell, and distribute, and unlawful possession of methaqualone. We are asked to decide whether the Fourth Amendment prohibits the State from proving these charges with the evidence discovered during the inventory of Bertine's van. We hold that it does not. * * *

After Bertine was charged with the offenses described above, he moved to suppress the evidence found during the inventory search on the ground, *inter alia,* that the search of the closed backpack and containers [therein] exceeded the permissible scope of such a search under the Fourth Amendment. The Colorado trial court * * * determined that the inventory search did not violate Bertine's rights under the Fourth Amendment of the United States Constitution. The court, nevertheless, granted Bertine's motion to suppress, holding that the inventory search violated the Colorado Constitution.

On the State's interlocutory appeal, the Supreme Court of Colorado affirmed. In contrast to the District Court, however, the Colorado Supreme Court premised its ruling on the United States Constitution. The court recognized that in *South Dakota v. Opperman,* 428 U.S. 364, 96 S.Ct. 3092, 49 L.Ed.2d 1000 (1976), we had held inventory searches of automobiles to be consistent with the Fourth Amendment, and that in *Illinois v. Lafayette,* [p. 233], we had held that the inventory search of personal effects of an arrestee at a police station was also permissible under that Amendment. The Supreme Court of Colorado felt, however, that our decisions in *Arkansas v. Sanders,* [p. 267], and *United States v. Chadwick,* [p. 267], holding searches of closed trunks and suitcases to violate the Fourth Amendment, meant that *Opperman* and *Lafayette* did not govern this case.

[I]nventory searches are now a well-defined exception to the warrant requirement of the Fourth Amendment. The policies behind the warrant requirement are not implicated in an inventory search, nor is the related concept of probable cause:

> "The standard of probable cause is peculiarly related to criminal investigations, not routine, noncriminal procedures.... The probable-cause approach is unhelpful when analysis centers upon the reasonableness of routine administrative caretaking functions, particularly when no claim is made that the protective procedures are a subterfuge for criminal investigations."

For these reasons, the Colorado Supreme Court's reliance on *Arkansas v. Sanders* and *United States v. Chadwick* was incorrect. Both of these cases concerned searches solely for the purpose of investigating criminal conduct, with the validity of the searches therefore dependent on the application of the probable cause and warrant requirements of the Fourth Amendment.

By contrast, an inventory search may be "reasonable" under the Fourth Amendment even though it is not conducted pursuant to warrant based upon probable cause. In *Opperman,* this Court assessed the reasonableness of an inventory search of the glove compartment in an abandoned automobile impounded by the police. We found that inventory procedures serve to protect an owner's property while it is in the custody of the police, to insure against claims of lost, stolen, or vandalized property, and to guard the police from danger. In light of these strong governmental interests and the diminished expectation of privacy in an automobile, we upheld the search. In reaching this decision, we observed that

"A peace officer is authorized to remove or cause to be removed a vehicle from any street, parking lot, or driveway when:

. . .

(4) The driver of a vehicle is taken into custody by the police department." Boulder Rev.Code § 7–7–2(a)(4) (1981).

our cases accorded deference to police caretaking procedures designed to secure and protect vehicles and their contents within police custody.

In our more recent decision, *Lafayette*, a police officer conducted an inventory search of the contents of a shoulder bag in the possession of an individual being taken into custody. In deciding whether this search was reasonable, we recognized that the search served legitimate governmental interests similar to those identified in *Opperman*. We determined that those interests outweighed the individual's Fourth Amendment interests and upheld the search.

In the present case, as in *Opperman* and *Lafayette*, there was no showing that the police, who were following standardized procedures, acted in bad faith or for the sole purpose of investigation. In addition, the governmental interests justifying the inventory searches in *Opperman* and *Lafayette* are nearly the same as those which obtain here. In each case, the police were potentially responsible for the property taken into their custody. By securing the property, the police protected the property from unauthorized interference. Knowledge of the precise nature of the property helped guard against claims of theft, vandalism, or negligence. Such knowledge also helped to avert any danger to police or others that may have been posed by the property.[5]

The Supreme Court of Colorado opined that *Lafayette* was not controlling here because there was no danger of introducing contraband or weapons into a jail facility. Our opinion in *Lafayette*, however, did not suggest that the station-house setting of the inventory search was critical to our holding in that case. Both in the present case and in *Lafayette*, the common governmental interests described above were served by the inventory searches.

The Supreme Court of Colorado also expressed the view that the search in this case was unreasonable because Bertine's van was towed to a secure, lighted facility and because Bertine himself could have been offered the opportunity to make other arrangements for the safekeeping of his property. But the security of the storage facility does not completely eliminate the need for inventorying; the police may still wish to protect themselves or the owners of the lot against false claims of theft or dangerous instrumentalities. And while giving Bertine an opportunity to make alternate arrangements would undoubtedly have been possible, we said in *Lafayette*:

> "[t]he real question is not what 'could have been achieved,' but whether the Fourth Amendment *requires* such steps ... The reasonableness of any particular governmental activity does not necessarily or invariably turn on the existence of alternative 'less intrusive' means."

We conclude that here, as in *Lafayette*, reasonable police regulations relating to inventory procedures administered in good faith satisfy the Fourth Amendment, even though courts might as a matter of hindsight be able to devise equally reasonable rules requiring a different procedure.[6]

5. In arguing that the latter two interests are not implicated here, the dissent overlooks the testimony of the back-up officer who conducted the inventory of Bertine's van. According to the officer, the vehicle inventory procedures of the Boulder Police Department are designed for the "[p]rotection of the police department" in the event that an individual later claims that "there was something of value taken from within the vehicle." The officer added that inventories are also conducted in order to check "[f]or any dangerous items such as explosives [or] weapons." The officer testified that he had found such items in vehicles.

6. We emphasize that, in this case, the trial court found that the police department's procedures mandated the opening of closed containers and the listing of their contents. Our decisions have always adhered to the requirement that inventories be conducted according to standardized criteria.

By quoting a portion of the Colorado Supreme Court's decision out of context, the dissent suggests that the inventory here was not

The Supreme Court of Colorado also thought it necessary to require that police, before inventorying a container, weigh the strength of the individual's privacy interest in the container against the possibility that the container might serve as a repository for dangerous or valuable items. We think that such a requirement is contrary to our decisions in *Opperman* and *Lafayette*:

> "Even if less intrusive means existed of protecting some particular types of property, it would be unreasonable to expect police officers in the everyday course of business to make fine and subtle distinctions in deciding which containers or items may be searched and which must be sealed as a unit." *Lafayette,* supra.

Bertine finally argues that the inventory search of his van was unconstitutional because departmental regulations gave the police officers discretion to choose between impounding his van and parking and locking it in a public parking place. The Supreme Court of Colorado did not rely on this argument in reaching its conclusion, and we reject it. Nothing in *Opperman* or *Lafayette* prohibits the exercise of police discretion so long as that discretion is exercised according to standard criteria and on the basis of something other than suspicion of evidence of criminal activity. Here, the discretion afforded the Boulder police was exercised in light of standardized criteria, related to the feasibility and appropriateness of parking and locking a vehicle rather than impounding it.[7] There was no showing that the police chose to impound Bertine's van in order to investigate suspected criminal activity. * * *

Reversed.

Justice BLACKMUN, with whom Justice POWELL and Justice O'CONNOR join, concurring. * * * I join the Court's opinion, but write separately to underscore [that] it is permissible for police officers to open closed containers in an inventory search only if they are following standard police procedures that mandate the opening of such containers in every impounded vehicle. * * *

Justice MARSHALL, with whom Justice BRENNAN joins, dissenting. * * *

As the Court acknowledges, inventory searches are reasonable only if conducted according to standardized procedures. In both *Opperman* and *Lafayette,* the Court relied on the absence of police discretion in determining that the inventory searches in question were reasonable. * * *

The Court today attempts to evade these clear prohibitions on unfettered police discretion by declaring that "the discretion afforded the Boulder police was exercised in light of standardized criteria, related to the feasibility and appropriateness of parking and locking a vehicle rather than impounding it." This vital assertion is flatly contradicted by the record in this case. The officer who conducted the inventory, Officer Reichenbach, testified at the suppression hearing that the decision not to "park and lock" respondent's vehicle was his "own individual discretionary decision." Indeed, application of these supposedly stan-

authorized by the standard procedures of the Boulder Police Department. Yet that court specifically stated that the procedure followed here was "officially authorized." In addition, the court did not disturb the trial court's finding that the police procedures for impounding vehicles required a detailed inventory of Bertine's van.

7. In arguing that the Boulder Police Department procedures set forth no standardized criteria guiding an officer's decision to impound a vehicle, the dissent selectively quotes from the police directive concerning the care

and security of vehicles taken into police custody. The dissent fails to mention that the directive establishes several conditions that must be met before an officer may pursue the park and lock alternative. For example, police may not park and lock the vehicle where there is reasonable risk of damage or vandalism to the vehicle or where the approval of the arrestee cannot be obtained. Not only do such conditions circumscribe the discretion of individual officers, but they also protect the vehicle and its contents and minimize claims of property loss.

dardized "criteria" upon which the Court so heavily relies would have yielded a different result in this case. Since there was ample public parking adjacent to the intersection where respondent was stopped, consideration of "feasibility" would certainly have militated in favor of the "park and lock" option, not against it. I do not comprehend how consideration of "appropriateness" serves to channel a field officer's discretion; nonetheless, the "park and lock" option would seem particularly appropriate in this case, where respondent was stopped for a traffic offense and was not likely to be in custody for a significant length of time.

Indeed, the record indicates that no standardized criteria limit a Boulder police officer's discretion. According to a departmental directive,[1] after placing a driver under arrest, an officer has three options for disposing of the vehicle. First, he can allow a third party to take custody. Second, the officer or the driver (depending on the nature of the arrest) may take the car to the nearest public parking facility, lock it, and take the keys.[3] Finally, the officer can do what was done in this case: impound the vehicle, and search and inventory its contents, including closed containers.[4]

Under the first option, the police have no occasion to search the automobile. Under the "park and lock" option, "[c]losed containers that give no indication of containing either valuables or a weapon *may not be opened and the contents searched* (i.e., inventoried)." Only if the police choose the third option are they entitled to search closed containers in the vehicle. Where the vehicle is not itself evidence of a crime, as in this case, the police apparently have totally unbridled discretion as to which procedure to use. Consistent with this conclusion, Officer Reichenbach testified that such decisions were left to the discretion of the officer on the scene.

Once a Boulder police officer has made this initial completely discretionary decision to impound a vehicle, he is given little guidance as to which areas to search and what sort of items to inventory. The arresting officer, Officer Toporek,

1. Subsections 7–7–2(a)(1) and 7–7–2(a)(4) of the Boulder Revised Code authorize police to impound a vehicle if the driver is taken into custody or if the vehicle obstructs traffic. A departmental directive authorizes inventory searches of impounded vehicles. See General Procedure issued from the office of the Chief of Police, Boulder Police Department, concerning Motor Vehicle Impounds, effective September 7, 1977.

3. If the vehicle and its contents are not evidence of a crime and the owner consents, § III of the General Procedure provides, in relevant part:

"A. Upon placing the operator of a motor vehicle in custody, Officers *may* take the following steps in securing the arrestee's vehicle and property . . . :

. . .

"4. The Officer shall drive the vehicle off the roadway and legally park the vehicle in the nearest PUBLIC parking area. The date, time, and location where the vehicle is parked shall be indicated on the IMPOUND FORM.

"5. The Officer shall remove the ignition keys, and lock all doors of the vehicle.

"6. During the booking process, the arrestee shall be given a continuation form for his

signature which indicates the location of his vehicle. One copy of the continuation form is to be retained in the case file." (emphasis added).

4. Section II(A) of the General Procedure establishes the following impoundment procedures:

"1. If the vehicle or its contents have been used in the commission of a crime or are themselves the fruit of a crime, the Officer shall conduct a detailed vehicle inspection and inventory and record it upon the VEHICLE IMPOUND FORM.

"2. Personal items of value should be removed from the vehicle and subsequently placed into Property for safekeeping.

"3. The Officer shall request a Tow Truck, and upon its arrival have the Tow Truck operatory sign the IMPOUND FORM, keeping one copy in his possession, before the Officer releases the vehicle for impoundment in the City of Boulder impoundment facility."

Subsection (B) of the directive provides that this procedure is also to be followed when a vehicle involved in a traffic accident is to be held for evidentiary purposes.

testified at the suppression hearing as to what items would be inventoried: "That would I think be very individualistic as far as what an officer may or may not go into. I think whatever arouses his suspicious [*sic*] as far as what may be contained in any type of article in the car." In application, these so-called procedures left the breadth of the "inventory" to the whim of the individual officer. Clearly, "[t]he practical effect of this system is to leave the [owner] subject to the discretion of the official in the field."

Inventory searches are not subject to the warrant requirement because they are conducted by the government as part of "community caretaking" function, "totally divorced from the detection, investigation, or acquisition of evidence relating to the violation of a criminal statute." Standardized procedures are necessary to ensure that this narrow exception is not improperly used to justify, after the fact, a warrantless investigative foray. Accordingly, to invalidate a search that is conducted without established procedures, it is not necessary to establish that the police actually acted in bad faith, or that the inventory was in fact a "pretext." By allowing the police unfettered discretion, Boulder's discretionary scheme is unreasonable because of the " 'grave danger' of abuse of discretion."

In *South Dakota v. Opperman,* and *Illinois v. Lafayette,* both of which involved inventories conducted pursuant to standardized procedures, we balanced the individual's expectation of privacy against the government's interests to determine whether the search was reasonable. Even if the search in this case did constitute a legitimate inventory, it would nonetheless be unreasonable under this analysis.

The Court greatly overstates the justifications for the inventory exception to the Fourth Amendment. Chief Justice Burger, writing for a plurality in *Opperman,* relied on three governmental interests to justify the inventory search of an unlocked glove compartment in an automobile impounded for overtime parking: (i) "the protection of the owner's property while it remains in police custody"; (ii) "the protection of the police against claims or disputes over lost or stolen property"; and (iii) "the protection of the police from potential danger." The majority finds that "nearly the same" interests obtain in this case. As Justice Powell's concurring opinion in *Opperman* reveals, however, only the first of these interests is actually served by an automobile inventory search.

The protection-against-claims interest did not justify the inventory search either in *Opperman* or in this case. As the majority apparently concedes, the use of secure impoundment facilities effectively eliminates this concern.[6] As to false claims, "inventories are [not] a completely effective means of discouraging false claims, since there remains the possibility of accompanying such claims with an assertion that an item was stolen prior to the inventory or was intentionally omitted from the police records."

Officer Reichenbach's inventory in this case would not have protected the police against claims lodged by respondent, false or otherwise. Indeed, the trial court's characterization of the inventory as "slip-shod" is the height of understatement. For example, Officer Reichenbach failed to list $150 in cash found in respondent's wallet or the contents of a sealed envelope marked "rent," $210, in the relevant section of the property form. His reports make no reference to other items of value, including respondent's credit cards, and a converter, a hydraulic jack, and a set of tire chains, worth a total of $125. The $700 in cash found in respondent's backpack, along with the contraband, appeared only on a property form completed later by someone other than Officer Reichenbach. The interior of

---

6. The impoundment lot in *South Dakota v. Opperman* was "the old county highway yard. It ha[d] a wooden fence partially around part of it, and kind of a dilapidated wire fence, a makeshift fence."

the vehicle was left in disarray, and the officer "inadvertently" retained respondent's keys—including his house keys—for two days following his arrest.

The third interest—protecting the police from potential danger—failed to receive the endorsement of a majority of the Court in *Opperman.* After noting that "there is little danger associated with impounding unsearched vehicles," Justice Powell recognized that "there does not appear to be any effective way of identifying in advance those circumstances or classes of automobile impoundments which represent a greater risk." As with the charge of overtime parking in *Opperman,* there is nothing in the nature of the offense for which respondent was arrested that suggests he was likely to be carrying weapons, explosives, or other dangerous items.

Thus, only the government's interest in protecting the owner's property actually justifies an inventory search of an impounded vehicle. While I continue to believe that preservation of property does not outweigh the privacy and security interests protected by the Fourth Amendment, I fail to see how preservation can even be asserted as a justification for the search in this case. In *Opperman,* the owner of the impounded car was not available to safeguard his possessions, and it could plausibly be argued that, in his absence, the police were entitled to act for his presumed benefit. When the police conducted the inventory in *Opperman,* they could not predict how long the car would be left in their possession. In this case, however, the owner was "present to make other arrangements for the safekeeping of his belongings," yet the police made no attempt to ascertain whether in fact he wanted them to "safeguard" his property. Furthermore, since respondent was charged with a traffic offense, he was unlikely to remain in custody for more than a few hours. He might well have been willing to leave his valuables unattended in the locked van for such a short period of time.

Thus, the government's interests in this case are weaker than in *Opperman,* but the search here is much more intrusive. *Opperman* did not involve a search of closed containers or other items that " 'touch upon intimate areas of an individual's personal affairs' "; nor can the Court's opinion be read to authorize the inspection of "containers which might themselves be sealed, removed and secured without further intrusion." To expand the *Opperman* rationale to include containers in which the owner clearly has a reasonable expectation of privacy, the Court relies on *Illinois v. Lafayette.* Such reliance is fundamentally misplaced, however; the inventory in *Lafayette* was justified by considerations which are totally absent in this context.

In *Lafayette,* we upheld a station house inventory search of an arrestee's shoulder bag. Notwithstanding the Court's assertions to the contrary, the inventory in that case *was* justified primarily by compelling governmental interests unique to the station house, preincarceration context. There is a powerful interest in preventing the introduction of contraband or weapons into a jail.

Notes and Questions

1. A narrower view is taken in some jurisdictions. For example, the South Dakota Supreme Court held on remand in *Opperman* that the inventory search violated the search and seizure guarantee of the South Dakota Constitution, the language of which "is almost identical to that found in the Fourth Amendment." *State v. Opperman,* 247 N.W.2d 673 (S.D.1976). Under the state constitutional provision, warrantless inventory searches of automobiles "must be restricted to safeguarding those articles which are within plain view of the officer's vision."

2. Consider the dissent of Ely, J., in *United States v. Mitchell,* 458 F.2d 960 (9th Cir.1972), suggesting that an "effective compromise" would be "to permit

extensive inventory searches of seized vehicles, so as fully to protect the police, but to forbid, over the objection of one having standing, the use of any item seized in the search as evidence against the objector.''

3. Evidence found in an otherwise lawful inventory must be suppressed if the prior impoundment of the vehicle was not justified. See, e.g., *Dyke v. Taylor Implement Mfg. Co.*, 391 U.S. 216, 88 S.Ct. 1472, 20 L.Ed.2d 538 (1968) (search of car outside courthouse while driver, arrested for reckless driving, inside to post bond was improper, as ''there is no indication that the police had purported to impound or to hold the car [or] that they were authorized by any state law to do so''); *State v. Simpson,* 622 P.2d 1199 (Wash.1980) (where defendant arrested at home, impoundment of his truck lawfully parked in front of house illegal).

4. In *Florida v. Wells,* 495 U.S. 1, 110 S.Ct. 1632, 109 L.Ed.2d 1 (1990), all members of the Court agreed that the inventory of a locked suitcase found in an impounded vehicle was unlawful under *Bertine* because ''the Florida Highway Patrol had no policy whatever with respect to the opening of closed containers encountered during an inventory search.'' The Chief Justice, for five members of the Court, went on to say that the state court erred in saying *Bertine* requires a policy either mandating or barring inventory of all containers:

''But in forbidding uncanalized discretion to police officers conducting inventory searches, there is no reason to insist that they be conducted in a totally mechanical 'all or nothing' fashion. * * * A police officer may be allowed sufficient latitude to determine whether a particular container should or should not be opened in light of the nature of the search and characteristics of the container itself. Thus, while policies of opening all containers or of opening no containers are unquestionably permissible, it would be equally permissible, for example, to allow the opening of closed containers whose contents officers determine they are unable to ascertain from examining the containers' exteriors. The allowance of the exercise of judgment based on concerns related to the purposes of an inventory search does not violate the Fourth Amendment.''

Brennan and Marshall, JJ., concurring, declined to join the majority opinion because, in ''pure dictum given the disposition of the case,'' it ''goes on to suggest that a State may adopt an inventory policy that vests individual police officers with *some* discretion to decide whether to open such containers.'' Blackmun, J., concurring, agreed that the Fourth Amendment did not impose an ''all or nothing'' requirement, so that a state ''probably could adopt a policy which requires the opening of all containers that are not locked, or a policy which requires the opening of all containers over or under a certain size, even though these policies do not call for the opening of all or no containers,'' but objected it was ''an entirely different matter, however, to say, as this majority does, that an individual policeman may be afforded discretion in conducting an inventory search.'' Stevens, J., concurring separately, agreed with the Blackmun opinion.

5. If the inventory cannot be upheld when the department has no policy (as in *Wells*) or when the only standard practice identified is that of the individual officer (as in *United States v. Kordosky,* 909 F.2d 219 (7th Cir.1990)), then what if (unlike *Bertine*) the purported department policy followed was not in writing but was merely testified to by the inventorying officer? Most courts, e.g., *United States v. Ford,* 986 F.2d 57 (4th Cir.1993), have held that is sufficient, but this result has been questioned: ''A primary concern, of course, is the possibility of undetected arbitrariness, a risk which takes on much greater proportions when the supposed 'standardized procedures' are established only by the self-serving and perhaps inaccurate oral statements of a police officer, and are not memorialized in the department's previous written instructions to its officers. Another * * * is that what is represented as department policy may constitute nothing more than a custom, hardly deserving the deference which an actual policy receives." Wayne R. LaFave, *Controlling Discretion by Administrative Regulations: The Use, Misuse, and Nonuse of Police Rules and Policies in Fourth Amendment Adjudication*, 89 Mich.L.Rev. 442, 456–57 (1990).

6. Consider *Ex parte Boyd*, 542 So.2d 1276 (Ala.1989): "We are unaware of any case, federal or state, that presents the issue of whether a search can be valid as an inventory notwithstanding a four-day lapse of time between the impoundment and the inventory. We are of the opinion that the Fourth Amendment requires that, without a demonstrable justification based upon exigent circumstances other than the mere nature of automobiles, the inventory be conducted either contemporaneously with the impoundment or as soon thereafter as would be safe, practical, *and* satisfactory in light of the objectives for which this exception to the Fourth Amendment warrant requirement was created. In other words, to be valid, there must be a sufficient temporal proximity between the impoundment and the inventory. * * * The justifications for the intrusion— protecting the owner's property, protecting the police from false claims or disputes, and protecting the police from danger—are simply not served, however, when the inventory is inexcusably postponed; in that circumstance, the inventory becomes unreasonable."

SECTION 8. STOP AND FRISK

TERRY v. OHIO

392 U.S. 1, 88 S.Ct. 1868, 20 L.Ed.2d 889 (1968).

Chief Justice WARREN delivered the opinion of the court.

[Officer McFadden, a Cleveland plainclothes detective, became suspicious of two men standing on a street corner in the downtown area at about 2:30 in the afternoon. One of the suspects walked up the street, peered into a store, walked on, started back, looked into the same store, and then joined and conferred with his companion. The other suspect repeated this ritual, and between them the two men went through this performance about a dozen times. They also talked with a third man, and then followed him up the street about ten minutes after his departure. The officer, thinking that the suspects were "casing" a stickup and might be armed, followed and confronted the three men as they were again conversing. He identified himself and asked the suspects for their names. The men only mumbled something, and the officer spun Terry around and patted his breast pocket. He felt a pistol, which he removed. A frisk of Terry's companion also uncovered a pistol; a frisk of the third man did not disclose that he was armed, and he was not searched further. Terry was charged with carrying a concealed weapon, and he moved to suppress the weapon as evidence. The motion was denied by the trial judge, who upheld the officer's actions on a stop-and-frisk theory. The Ohio court of appeals affirmed, and the state supreme court dismissed Terry's appeal.]

* * * The question is whether in all the circumstances of this on-the-street encounter, [Terry's] right to personal security was violated by an unreasonable search and seizure.

We would be less than candid if we did not acknowledge that this question thrusts to the fore difficult and troublesome issues regarding a sensitive area of police activity—issues which have never before been squarely presented to this Court. * * *

On the one hand, it is frequently argued that in dealing with the rapidly unfolding and often dangerous situations on city streets the police are in need of an escalating set of flexible responses, graduated in relation to the amount of information they possess. For this purpose it is urged that distinctions should be made between a "stop" and an "arrest" (or a "seizure" of a person), and between a "frisk" and a "search." Thus, it is argued, the police should be allowed to "stop" a person and detain him briefly for questioning upon suspicion that he may be connected with criminal activity. Upon suspicion that the person may be armed, the police should have the power to "frisk" him for weapons. If the "stop" and the "frisk" give rise to probable cause to believe that the suspect has committed a crime, then the police should be empowered to make a formal "arrest," and a full incident "search" of the person. This scheme is justified in part upon the notion that a "stop" and a "frisk" amount to a mere "minor inconvenience and petty indignity," which can properly be imposed upon the citizen in the interest of effective law enforcement on the basis of a police officer's suspicion.

On the other side the argument is made that the authority of the police must be strictly circumscribed by the law of arrest and search as it has developed to date in the traditional jurisprudence of the Fourth Amendment. It is contended with some force that there is not—and cannot be—a variety of police activity which does not depend solely upon the voluntary cooperation of the citizen and yet which stops short of an arrest based upon probable cause to make such an arrest. The heart of the Fourth Amendment, the argument runs, is a severe requirement of specific justification for any intrusion upon protected personal security, coupled with a highly developed system of judicial controls to enforce upon the agents of the State the commands of the Constitution. * * *

* * * The State has characterized the issue here as "the right of a police officer * * * to make an on-the-street stop, interrogate and pat down for weapons (known in the street vernacular as 'stop and frisk')." But this is only partly accurate. For the issue is not the abstract propriety of the police conduct, but the admissibility against petitioner of the evidence uncovered by the search and seizure. * * * [I]n our system evidentiary rulings provide the context in which the judicial process of inclusion and exclusion approves some conduct as comporting with constitutional guarantees and disapproves other actions by state agents. A ruling admitting evidence in a criminal trial, we recognize, has the necessary effect of legitimizing the conduct which produced the evidence, while an application of the exclusionary rule withholds the constitutional imprimatur.

The exclusionary rule has its limitations, however, as a tool of judicial control. It cannot properly be invoked to exclude the products of legitimate police investigative techniques on the ground that much conduct which is closely similar involves unwarranted intrusions upon constitutional protections. Moreover, in some contexts the rule is ineffective as a deterrent. Street encounters between citizens and police officers are incredibly rich in diversity. They range from wholly friendly exchanges of pleasantries or mutually useful information to hostile confrontations of armed men involving arrests, or injuries, or loss of life. Moreover, hostile confrontations are not all of a piece. Some of them begin in a friendly enough manner, only to take a different turn upon the injection of some unexpected element into the conversation. Encounters are initiated by the police for a wide variety of purposes, some of which are wholly unrelated to a desire to prosecute for crime. Doubtless some police "field interrogation" conduct violates the Fourth Amendment. But a stern refusal by this Court to condone such activity does not necessarily render it responsive to the exclusionary rule. Regardless of how effective the rule may be where obtaining convictions is an important objective of the police, it is powerless to deter invasions of constitutionally guaranteed rights where the police either have no interest in prosecuting or are willing to forego successful prosecution in the interest of serving some other goal.

Proper adjudication of cases in which the exclusionary rule is invoked demands a constant awareness of these limitations. The wholesale harassment by certain elements of the police community, of which minority groups, particularly Negroes, frequently complain, will not be stopped by the exclusion of any evidence from any criminal trial. Yet a rigid and unthinking application of the exclusionary rule, in futile protest against practices which it can never be used effectively to control, may exact a high toll in human injury and frustration of efforts to prevent crime. No judicial opinion can comprehend the protean variety of the street encounter, and we can only judge the facts of the case before us. * * *

[W]e turn our attention to the quite narrow question posed by the facts before us: whether it is always unreasonable for a policeman to seize a person and subject him to a limited search for weapons unless there is probable cause for an arrest.

* * * It is quite plain that the Fourth Amendment governs "seizures" of the person which do not eventuate in a trip to the station house and prosecution for crime—"arrests" in traditional terminology. It must be recognized that whenever a police officer accosts an individual and restrains his freedom to walk away, he has "seized" that person. And it is nothing less than sheer torture of the English language to suggest that a careful exploration of the outer surfaces of a person's clothing all over his or her body in an attempt to find weapons is not a "search." Moreover, it is simply fantastic to urge that such a procedure performed in public by a policeman while the citizen stands helpless, perhaps facing a wall with his hands raised, is a "petty indignity."[13] It is a serious intrusion upon the sanctity of the person, which may inflict great indignity and arouse strong resentment, and it is not to be undertaken lightly.

* * * We therefore reject the notions that the Fourth Amendment does not come into play at all as a limitation upon police conduct if the officers stop short of something called a "technical arrest" or a "full-blown search."

In this case there can be no question, then, that Officer McFadden "seized" petitioner and subjected him to a "search" when he took hold of him and patted down the outer surfaces of his clothing. We must decide whether at that point it was reasonable for Officer McFadden to have interfered with petitioner's personal security as he did.[16] And in determining whether the seizure and search were "unreasonable" our inquiry is a dual one—whether the officer's action was justified at its inception, and whether it was reasonably related in scope to the circumstances which justified the interference in the first place.

If this case involved police conduct subject to the Warrant Clause of the Fourth Amendment, we would have to ascertain whether "probable cause" existed to justify the search and seizure which took place. However, that is not the case. We do not retreat from our holdings that the police must, whenever practicable, obtain advance judicial approval of searches and seizures through the warrant

---

13. Consider the following apt description: "[T]he officer must feel with sensitive fingers every portion of the prisoner's body. A thorough search must be made of the prisoner's arms and armpits, waistline and back, the groin and area about the testicles, and entire surface of the legs down to the feet." Priar & Martin, *Searching and Disarming Criminals*, 45 J.Crim.L.C. & P.S. 481 (1954).

16. We thus decide nothing today concerning the constitutional propriety of an investigative "seizure" upon less than probable cause for purposes of "detention" and/or interroga-

tion. Obviously, not all personal intercourse between policemen and citizens involves "seizures" of persons. Only when the officer, by means of physical force or show of authority, has in some way restrained the liberty of a citizen may we conclude that a "seizure" has occurred. We cannot tell with any certainty upon this record whether any such "seizure" took place here prior to Officer McFadden's initiation of physical contact for purposes of searching Terry for weapons, and we thus may assume that up to that point no intrusion upon constitutionally protected rights had occurred.

procedure, * * * or that in most instances failure to comply with the warrant requirement can only be excused by exigent circumstances. * * * But we deal here with an entire rubric of police conduct—necessarily swift action predicated upon the on-the-spot observations of the officer on the beat—which historically has not been, and as a practical matter could not be, subjected to the warrant procedure. Instead, the conduct involved in this case must be tested by the Fourth Amendment's general proscription against unreasonable searches and seizures.

Nonetheless, the notions which underlie both the warrant procedure and the requirement of probable cause remain fully relevant in this context. In order to assess the reasonableness of Officer McFadden's conduct as a general proposition, it is necessary "first to focus upon the governmental interest which allegedly justifies official intrusion upon the constitutionally protected interests of the private citizen," for there is "no ready test for determining reasonableness other than by balancing the need to search [or seize] against the invasion which the search [or seizure] entails." *Camara v. Municipal Court* [p. 326]. And in justifying the particular intrusion the police officer must be able to point to specific and articulable facts which, taken together with rational inferences from those facts, reasonably warrant that intrusion. The scheme of the Fourth Amendment becomes meaningful only when it is assured that at some point the conduct of those charged with enforcing the laws can be subjected to the more detached, neutral scrutiny of a judge who must evaluate the reasonableness of a particular search or seizure in light of the particular circumstances. And in making that assessment it is imperative that the facts be judged against an objective standard: would the facts available to the officer at the moment of the seizure or the search "warrant a man of reasonable caution in the belief" that the action taken was appropriate? * * * Anything less would invite intrusions upon constitutionally guaranteed rights based on nothing more substantial than inarticulate hunches, a result this Court has consistently refused to sanction. * * *

Applying these principles to this case, we consider first the nature and extent of the governmental interests involved. One general interest is of course that of effective crime prevention and detection; it is this interest which underlies the recognition that a police officer may in appropriate circumstances and in an appropriate manner approach a person for purposes of investigating possibly criminal behavior even though there is no probable cause to make an arrest. It was this legitimate investigative function Officer McFadden was discharging when he decided to approach petitioner and his companions. He had observed Terry, Chilton, and Katz go through a series of acts, each of them perhaps innocent in itself, but which taken together warranted further investigation. There is nothing unusual in two men standing together on a street corner, perhaps waiting for someone. Nor is there anything suspicious about people in such circumstances strolling up and down the street, singly or in pairs. Store windows, moreover, are made to be looked in. But the story is quite different where, as here, two men hover about a street corner for an extended period of time, at the end of which it becomes apparent that they are not waiting for anyone or anything; where these men pace alternately along an identical route, pausing to stare in the same store window roughly 24 times; where each completion of this route is followed immediately by a conference between the two men on the corner; where they are joined in one of these conferences by a third man who leaves swiftly; and where the two men finally follow the third and rejoin him a couple of blocks away. It would have been poor police work indeed for an officer of 30 years' experience in the detection of thievery from stores in this same neighborhood to have failed to investigate this behavior further.

The crux of this case, however, is not the propriety of Officer McFadden's taking steps to investigate petitioner's suspicious behavior, but rather, whether there was justification for McFadden's invasion of Terry's personal security by searching him for weapons in the course of that investigation. We are now concerned with more than the governmental interest in investigating crime; in addition, there is the more immediate interest of the police officer in taking steps to assure himself that the person with whom he is dealing is not armed with a weapon that could unexpectedly and fatally be used against him. Certainly it would be unreasonable to require that police officers take unnecessary risks in the performance of their duties. American criminals have a long tradition of armed violence, and every year in this country many law enforcement officers are killed in the line of duty, and thousands more are wounded. Virtually all of these deaths and a substantial portion of the injuries are inflicted with guns and knives.

In view of these facts, we cannot blind ourselves to the need for law enforcement officers to protect themselves and other prospective victims of violence in situations where they may lack probable cause for an arrest. When an officer is justified in believing that the individual whose suspicious behavior he is investigating at close range is armed and presently dangerous to the officer or to others, it would appear to be clearly unreasonable to deny the officer the power to take necessary measures to determine whether the person is in fact carrying a weapon and to neutralize the threat of physical harm. * * *

Petitioner * * * does not say that an officer is always unjustified in searching a suspect to discover weapons. Rather, he says it is unreasonable for the policeman to take that step until such time as the situation evolves to a point where there is probable cause to make an arrest. * * *

There are two weaknesses in this line of reasoning however. First, it fails to take account of traditional limitations upon the scope of searches, and thus recognizes no distinction in purpose, character, and extent between a search incident to an arrest and a limited search for weapons. The former, although justified in part by the acknowledged necessity to protect the arresting officer from assault with a concealed weapon, is also justified on other grounds, and can therefore involve a relatively extensive exploration of the person. A search for weapons in the absence of probable cause to arrest, however, must, like any other search, be strictly circumscribed by the exigencies which justify its initiation. Thus it must be limited to that which is necessary for the discovery of weapons which might be used to harm the officer or others nearby, and may realistically be characterized as something less than a "full" search, even though it remains a serious intrusion.

A second, and related, objection to petitioner's argument is that it assumes that the law of arrest has already worked out the balance between the particular interests involved here—the neutralization of danger to the policeman in the investigative circumstance and the sanctity of the individual. But this is not so. An arrest is a wholly different kind of intrusion upon individual freedom from a limited search for weapons, and the interests each is designed to serve are likewise quite different. An arrest is the initial stage of a criminal prosecution. It is intended to vindicate society's interest in having its laws obeyed, and it is inevitably accompanied by future interference with the individual's freedom of movement, whether or not trial or conviction ultimately follows. The protective search for weapons, on the other hand, constitutes a brief, though far from inconsiderable intrusion upon the sanctity of the person. It does not follow that because an officer may lawfully arrest a person only when he is apprised of facts sufficient to warrant a belief that the person has committed or is committing a crime, the officer is equally unjustified, absent that kind of evidence, in making any intrusions short of an arrest. Moreover, a perfectly reasonable apprehension of danger may arise long before the officer is possessed of adequate information to justify taking a person into custody for the purpose of prosecuting him for a crime. * * *

Our evaluation of the proper balance that has to be struck in this type of case leads us to conclude that there must be a narrowly drawn authority to permit a reasonable search for weapons for the protection of the police officer, where he has reason to believe that he is dealing with an armed and dangerous individual, regardless of whether he has probable cause to arrest the individual for a crime. The officer need not be absolutely certain that the individual is armed; the issue is whether a reasonably prudent man in the circumstances would be warranted in the belief that his safety or that of others was in danger. * * * And in determining whether the officer acted reasonably in such circumstances, due weight must be given, not to his inchoate and unparticularized suspicion or "hunch", but to the specific reasonable inferences which he is entitled to draw from the facts in light of his experience.

We must now examine the conduct of Officer McFadden in this case to determine whether his search and seizure of petitioner were reasonable, both at their inception and as conducted. He had observed Terry, together with Chilton and another man, acting in a manner he took to be preface to a "stick-up." We think on the facts and circumstances Officer McFadden detailed before the trial judge a reasonably prudent man would have been warranted in believing petitioner was armed and thus presented a threat to the officer's safety while he was investigating his suspicious behavior. The actions of Terry and Chilton were consistent with McFadden's hypothesis that these men were contemplating a daylight robbery—which, it is reasonable to assume, would be likely to involve the use of weapons—and nothing in their conduct from the time he first noticed them until the time he confronted them and identified himself as a police officer gave him sufficient reason to negate that hypothesis. Although the trio had departed the original scene, there was nothing to indicate abandonment of an intent to commit a robbery at some point. Thus, when Officer McFadden approached the three men gathered before the display window at Zucker's store he had observed enough to make it quite reasonable to fear that they were armed; and nothing in their response to his hailing them, identifying himself as a police officer, and asking their names served to dispel that reasonable belief. We cannot say his decision at that point to seize Terry and pat his clothing for weapons was the product of a volatile or inventive imagination, or was undertaken simply as an act of harassment; the record evidences the tempered act of a policeman who in the course of an investigation had to make a quick decision as to how to protect himself and others from possible danger, and took limited steps to do so.

The manner in which the seizure and search were conducted is, of course, as vital a part of the inquiry as whether they were warranted at all. The Fourth Amendment proceeds as much by limitations upon the scope of governmental action as by imposing preconditions upon its initiation. The entire deterrent purpose of the rule excluding evidence seized in violation of the Fourth Amendment rests on the assumption that "limitations upon the fruit to be gathered tend to limit the quest itself." * * * Thus, evidence may not be introduced if it was discovered by means of a seizure and search which were not reasonably related in scope to the justification for their initiation.

[A protective search for weapons,] unlike a search without a warrant incident to a lawful arrest, is not justified by any need to prevent the disappearance or destruction of evidence of crime. The sole justification of the search in the present situation is the protection of the police officer and others nearby, and it must therefore be confined in scope to an intrusion reasonably designed to discover guns, knives, clubs, or other hidden instruments for the assault of the police officer.

The scope of the search in this case presents no serious problem in light of these standards. Officer McFadden patted down the outer clothing of petitioner and his two companions. He did not place his hands in their pockets or under the outer surface of their garments until he had felt weapons, and then he merely reached for and removed the guns. He never did invade Katz's person beyond the outer surfaces of his clothes, since he discovered nothing in his pat down which might have been a weapon. Officer McFadden confined his search strictly to what was minimally necessary to learn whether the men were armed and to disarm them once he discovered the weapons. He did not conduct a general exploratory search for whatever evidence of criminal activity he might find.

We conclude that the revolver seized from Terry was properly admitted in evidence against him. At the time he seized petitioner and searched him for weapons, Officer McFadden had reasonable grounds to believe that petitioner was armed and dangerous, and it was necessary for the protection of himself and others to take swift measures to discover the true facts and neutralize the threat of harm if it materialized. The policeman carefully restricted his search to what was appropriate to the discovery of the particular items which he sought. Each case of this sort will, of course, have to be decided on its own facts. We merely hold today that where a police officer observes unusual conduct which leads him reasonably to conclude in light of his experience that criminal activity may be afoot and that the persons with whom he is dealing may be armed and presently dangerous; where in the course of investigating this behavior he identifies himself as a policeman and makes reasonable inquiries; and where nothing in the initial stages of the encounter serves to dispel his reasonable fear for his own or others' safety, he is entitled for the protection of himself and others in the area to conduct a carefully limited search of the outer clothing of such persons in an attempt to discover weapons which might be used to assault him. Such a search is a reasonable search under the Fourth Amendment, and any weapons seized may properly be introduced in evidence against the person from whom they were taken.

Affirmed. *For π -officer*

Justice HARLAN, concurring.

* * * The holding has * * * two logical corollaries that I do not think the Court has fully expressed.

In the first place, if the frisk is justified in order to protect the officer during an encounter with a citizen, the officer must first have constitutional grounds to insist on an encounter, to make a *forcible* stop. Any person, including a policeman, is at liberty to avoid a person he considers dangerous. If and when a policeman has a right instead to disarm such a person for his own protection, he must first have a right not to avoid him but to be in his presence. That right must be more than the liberty (again, possessed by every citizen) to address questions to other persons, for ordinarily the person addressed has an equal right to ignore his interrogator and walk away; he certainly need not submit to a frisk for the questioner's protection. I would make it perfectly clear that the right to frisk in this case depends upon the reasonableness of a forcible stop to investigate a suspected crime.

Where such a stop is reasonable, however, the right to frisk must be immediate and automatic if the reason for the stop is, as here, an articulable suspicion of a crime of violence. Just as a full search incident to a lawful arrest requires no additional justification, a limited frisk incident to a lawful stop must often be rapid and routine. There is no reason why an officer, rightfully but forcibly confronting a person suspected of a serious crime, should have to ask one question and take the risk that the answer might be a bullet. * * *

Justice WHITE, concurring.

* * * I think an additional word is in order concerning the matter of interrogation during an investigative stop. There is nothing in the Constitution which prevents a policeman from addressing questions to anyone on the streets. Absent special circumstances, the person approached may not be detained or frisked but may refuse to cooperate and go on his way. However, given the proper circumstances, such as those in this case, it seems to me the person may be briefly detained against his will while pertinent questions are directed to him. Of course, the person stopped is not obliged to answer, answers may not be compelled, and refusal to answer furnishes no basis for an arrest, although it may alert the officer to the need for continued observation. * * *

Justice DOUGLAS, dissenting.

* * * Had a warrant been sought, a magistrate would * * * have been unauthorized to issue one, for he can act only if there is a showing of "probable cause." We hold today that the police have greater authority to make a "seizure" and conduct a "search" than a judge has to authorize such action. We have said precisely the opposite over and over again. * * *

THE SIGNIFICANCE OF THE STOP–AND–FRISK CASES[a]

A.   The Utility of the Balancing Test

1.   What qualifies a particular police practice for assessment under the *Terry* balancing test?[b] In *Michigan v. Summers,* p. 198, Stewart, J., joined by Brennan and Marshall, JJ., dissenting, objected to the majority's use of the balancing test in holding that a warrant to search premises for contraband authorizes police to detain the occupants while the warrant is executed. They reasoned "that before a court can uphold a detention on less than probable cause on the ground that it is 'reasonable' in the light of the competing interests, the government must demonstrate an important purpose beyond the normal goals of criminal investigation,[c] or must demonstrate an extraordinary obstacle to such investigation," which they believed had not been done in the instant case.

2.   Should the balancing test also be used to keep the evidentiary requirements for a given police practice "flexible," so that, for example, less evidence would be required when the crime being investigated is a serious one? Consider Justice Jackson, dissenting in *Brinegar v. United States,* 338 U.S. 160, 69 S.Ct. 1302, 93 L.Ed. 1879 (1949): "If we assume, for example, that a child is kidnapped and the officers throw a roadblock about the neighborhood and search every outgoing car, it would be a drastic and undiscriminating use of the search. The officers might be unable to show probable cause for searching any particular car. However, I should candidly strive hard to sustain such an action, executed fairly and in good faith, because it might be reasonable to subject travelers to that indignity if it was the only way to save a threatened life and detect a vicious crime. But I should not strain to sustain such a roadblock and universal search to salvage a few bottles of bourbon and catch a bootlegger."[d]

a. For an exhaustive assessment of *Terry* by over 30 analysts, reflecting an interesting variety of viewpoints, see Symposium, *Terry v. Ohio 30 Years Later,* 72 St.John's L.Rev. 721–1524 (1998). Especially intriguing is John Q. Barrett, *Deciding the Stop and Frisk Cases: A Look Inside the Supreme Court's Conference,* id. at 749, which uses the available papers of former Justices to illuminate the role of indi-vidual members of the Court in resolving these cases.

b. See Scott E. Sundby, *A Return to Fourth Amendment Basics: Undoing the Mischief of Camara and Terry,* 72 Minn.L.Rev. 383 (1988).

c. See § 9 of this Chapter.

d. Compare *Dunaway v. New York,* p. 325.

B. POLICE ACTION SHORT OF A SEIZURE

1. FLORIDA v. BOSTICK, 501 U.S. 429, 111 S.Ct. 2382, 115 L.Ed.2d 389 (1991), involved these facts, as stated by the state supreme court: "Two officers, complete with badges, insignia and one of them holding a recognizable zipper pouch, containing a pistol, boarded a bus bound from Miami to Atlanta during a stopover in Fort Lauderdale. Eyeing the passengers, the officers admittedly without articulable suspicion, picked out the defendant passenger and asked to inspect his ticket and identification. The ticket, from Miami to Atlanta, matched the defendant's identification and both were immediately returned to him as unremarkable. However, the two police officers persisted and explained their presence as narcotics agents on the lookout for illegal drugs. In pursuit of that aim, they then requested the defendant's consent to search his luggage. Needless to say, there is a conflict in the evidence about whether the defendant consented to the search of the second bag in which the contraband was found and as to whether he was informed of his right to refuse consent. However, any conflict must be resolved in favor of the state, it being a question of fact decided by the trial judge." That court ruled that "an impermissible seizure result[s] when police mount a drug search on buses during scheduled stops and question boarded passengers without articulable reasons for doing so, thereby obtaining consent to search the passengers' luggage." The Supreme Court reversed; O'CONNOR, J., for the majority, stated:

"Our cases make it clear that a seizure does not occur simply because a police officer approaches an individual and asks a few questions. So long as a reasonable person would feel free 'to disregard the police and go about his business,' the encounter is consensual and no reasonable suspicion is required. The encounter will not trigger Fourth Amendment scrutiny unless it loses its consensual nature. * * *

"There is no doubt that if this same encounter had taken place before Bostick boarded the bus or in the lobby of the bus terminal, it would not rise to the level of a seizure. The Court has dealt with similar encounters in airports and has found them to be 'the sort of consensual encounter[s] that implicat[e] no Fourth Amendment interest.' We have stated that even when officers have no basis for suspecting a particular individual, they may generally ask questions of that individual, ask to examine the individual's identification, and request consent to search his or her luggage—as long as the police do not convey a message that compliance with their requests is required.

"Bostick insists that this case is different because it took place in the cramped confines of a bus. A police encounter is much more intimidating in this setting, he argues, because police tower over a seated passenger and there is little room to move around. Bostick claims to find support in cases indicating that a seizure occurs when a reasonable person would believe that he or she is not 'free to leave.' Bostick maintains that a reasonable bus passenger would not have felt free to leave under the circumstances of this case because there is nowhere to go on a

---

On the use of roadblocks, consider *Model Pre–Arraignment Code* § 110.2, providing in part:

"(2) *Stopping of Vehicles at Roadblock.* A law enforcement officer may, if

"(a) he has reasonable cause to believe that a felony has been committed; and

"(b) stopping all or most vehicles moving in a particular direction or directions is reason-

ably necessary to permit a search for the perpetrator or victim of such felony in view of the seriousness and special circumstances of such felony,

order the drivers of such vehicles to stop, and may search such vehicles to the extent necessary to accomplish such purpose. Such action shall be accomplished as promptly as possible under the circumstances."

bus. Also, the bus was about to depart. Had Bostick disembarked, he would have risked being stranded and losing whatever baggage he had locked away in the luggage compartment.

"The Florida Supreme Court found this argument persuasive, so much so that it adopted a *per se* rule prohibiting the police from randomly boarding buses as a means of drug interdiction. The state court erred, however, in focusing on whether Bostick was 'free to leave', rather than on the principle that those words were intended to capture. When police attempt to question a person who is walking down the street or through an airport lobby, it makes sense to inquire whether a reasonable person would feel free to continue walking. But when the person is seated on a bus and has no desire to leave, the degree to which a reasonable person would feel that he or she could leave is not an accurate measure of the coercive effect of the encounter.

"Here, for example, the mere fact that Bostick did not feel free to leave the bus does not mean that the police seized him. Bostick was a passenger on a bus that was scheduled to depart. He would not have felt free to leave the bus even if the police had not been present. Bostick's movements were 'confined' in a sense, but this was the natural result of his decision to take the bus; it says nothing about whether or not the police conduct at issue was coercive.

"In this respect, the Court's decision in *INS v. Delgado,* [466 U.S. 210, 104 S.Ct. 1758, 80 L.Ed.2d 247 (1984)] is dispositive. At issue there was the INS' practice of visiting factories at random and questioning employees to determine whether any were illegal aliens. Several INS agents would stand near the building's exits, while other agents walked through the factory questioning workers. The Court acknowledged that the workers may not have been free to leave their worksite, but explained that this was not the result of police activity: 'Ordinarily, when people are at work their freedom to move about has been meaningfully restricted, not by the actions of law enforcement officials, but by the workers' voluntary obligations to their employers.' We concluded that there was no seizure because, even though the workers were not free to leave the building without being questioned, the agents' conduct should have given employees 'no reason to believe that they would be detained if they gave truthful answers to the questions put to them or if they simply refused to answer.'

"The present case is analytically indistinguishable from *Delgado*. Like the workers in that case, Bostick's freedom of movement was restricted by a factor independent of police conduct—*i.e.*, by his being a passenger on a bus. Accordingly, the 'free to leave' analysis on which Bostick relies is inapplicable. In such a situation, the appropriate inquiry is whether a reasonable person would feel free to decline the officers' requests or otherwise terminate the encounter. This formulation follows logically from prior cases and breaks no new ground. We have said before that the crucial test is whether, taking into account all of the circumstances surrounding the encounter, the police conduct would 'have communicated to a reasonable person that he was not at liberty to ignore the police presence and go about his business.' Where the encounter takes place is one factor, but it is not the only one. And, as the Solicitor General correctly observes, an individual may decline an officer's request without fearing prosecution. We have consistently held that a refusal to cooperate, without more, does not furnish the minimal level of objective justification needed for a detention or seizure.

"The facts of this case, as described by the Florida Supreme Court, leave some doubt whether a seizure occurred. Two officers walked up to Bostick on the bus, asked him a few questions, and asked if they could search his bags. As we have explained, no seizure occurs when police ask questions of an individual, ask to examine the individual's identification, and request consent to search his or her luggage—so long as the officers do not convey a message that compliance with their requests is required. Here, the facts recited by the Florida Supreme Court indicate that the officers did not point guns at Bostick or otherwise threaten him and that they specifically advised Bostick that he could refuse consent.

"Nevertheless, we refrain from deciding whether or not a seizure occurred in this case. The trial court made no express findings of fact, and the Florida Supreme Court rested its decision on a single fact—that the encounter took place on a bus—rather than on the totality of the circumstances. We remand so that the Florida courts may evaluate the seizure question under the correct legal standard. We do reject, however, Bostick's argument that he must have been seized because no reasonable person would freely consent to a search of luggage that he or she knows contains drugs. This argument cannot prevail because the 'reasonable person' test presupposes an *innocent* person. * *, *

"The dissent also attempts to characterize our decision as applying a lesser degree of constitutional protection to those individuals who travel by bus, rather than by other forms of transportation. This, too, is an erroneous characterization. Our Fourth Amendment inquiry in this case—whether a reasonable person would have felt free to decline the officers' requests or otherwise terminate the encounter—applies equally to police encounters that take place on trains, planes, and city streets. It is the dissent that would single out this particular mode of travel for differential treatment by adopting a *per se* rule that random bus searches are unconstitutional."

MARSHALL, J., for the three dissenters, interpreted the state court holding as not a "*per se* rule" but rather as a decision based on all the facts, but then added that in any event the Supreme Court could determine the "question of law" of whether *all* the facts set forth in the state court opinion add up to a Fourth Amendment seizure. Accepting the majority's "free to decline" test, Marshall continued:

"Unlike the majority, I have no doubt that the answer to this question is no. Apart from trying to accommodate the officers, respondent had only two options. First, he could have remained seated while obstinately refusing to respond to the officers' questioning. But in light of the intimidating show of authority that the officers made upon boarding the bus, respondent reasonably could have believed that such behavior would only arouse the officers' suspicions and intensify their interrogation. Indeed, officers who carry out bus sweeps like the one at issue here frequently admit that this is the effect of a passenger's refusal to cooperate. The majority's observation that a mere refusal to answer questions, 'without more,' does not give rise to a reasonable basis for seizing a passenger, is utterly beside the point, because a passenger unadvised of his rights and otherwise unversed in constitutional law *has no reason to know* that the police cannot hold his refusal to cooperate against him.

"Second, respondent could have tried to escape the officers' presence by leaving the bus altogether. But because doing so would have required respondent to squeeze past the gun-wielding inquisitor who was blocking the aisle of the bus, this hardly seems like a course that respondent reasonably would have viewed as available to him. The majority lamely protests that nothing in the stipulated facts shows that the questioning officer '*point[ed]* [his] gu[n] at [respondent]' or otherwise *threatened* him' with the weapon. Our decisions recognize the obvious point, however, that the choice of the police to 'display' their weapons during an encounter exerts significant coercive pressure on the confronted citizen. We have never suggested that the police must go so far as to put a citizen in immediate apprehension of *being shot* before a court can take account of the intimidating effect of being questioned by an officer with weapon in hand.

"Even if respondent had perceived that the officers would *let* him leave the bus, moreover, he could not reasonably have been expected to resort to this means of evading their intrusive questioning. For so far as respondent knew, the bus' departure from the terminal was imminent. Unlike a person approached by the police on the street or at a bus or airport terminal after reaching his destination, a passenger approached by the police at an intermediate point in a long bus journey cannot simply leave the scene and repair to a safe haven to avoid unwanted probing by law-enforcement officials. The vulnerability that an intrastate or interstate traveler experiences when confronted by the police outside of his 'own familiar territory' surely aggravates the coercive quality of such an encounter.

"The case on which the majority primarily relies, *INS v. Delgado,* is distinguishable in every relevant respect. In *Delgado,* this Court held that workers approached by law-enforcement officials inside of a factory were not 'seized' for purposes of the Fourth Amendment. The Court was careful to point out, however, that the presence of the agents did not furnish the workers with a reasonable basis for believing that they were not free to leave the factory, as at least some of them did. Unlike passengers confronted by law-enforcement officials on a bus stopped temporarily at an intermediate point in its journey, workers approached by law-enforcement officials at their workplace need not abandon personal belongings and venture into unfamiliar environs in order to avoid unwanted questioning. Moreover, the workers who did not leave the building in *Delgado* remained free to move about the entire factory, a considerably less confining environment than a bus. Finally, contrary to the officer who confronted respondent, the law-enforcement officials in *Delgado* did not conduct their interviews with guns in hand.

"Rather than requiring the police to justify the coercive tactics employed here, the majority blames respondent for his own sensation of constraint. The majority concedes that respondent 'did not feel free to leave the bus' as a means of breaking off the interrogation by the Broward County officers. But this experience of confinement, the majority explains, 'was the natural result of *his* decision to take the bus.' Thus, in the majority's view, because respondent's 'freedom of movement was restricted by a factor independent of police conduct—*i.e.,* by his being a passenger on a bus,' respondent was not seized for purposes of the Fourth Amendment.

"This reasoning borders on sophism and trivializes the values that underlie the Fourth Amendment. Obviously, a person's 'voluntary decision' to place himself in a room with only one exit does not authorize the police to force an encounter upon him by placing themselves in front of the exit. It is no more acceptable for the police to force an encounter on a person by exploiting his 'voluntary decision' to expose himself to perfectly legitimate personal or social constraints. By consciously deciding to single out persons who have undertaken interstate or intrastate travel, officers who conduct suspicionless, dragnet-style sweeps put passengers to the choice of cooperating or of exiting their buses and possibly being stranded in unfamiliar locations. It is exactly because this 'choice' is no 'choice' at all that police engage this technique.''

2. In CALIFORNIA v. HODARI D., 499 U.S. 621, 111 S.Ct. 1547, 113 L.Ed.2d 690 (1991), Hodari fled upon seeing an approaching police car, only to be pursued on foot by Officer Pertoso, after which Hodari tossed away what appeared to be a small rock but which when retrieved by the police proved to be crack cocaine. The state court suppressed the cocaine as the fruit of a seizure made without reasonable suspicion, but the Supreme Court, per SCALIA, J., reversed:

"To say [as the common law authorities do] that an arrest is effected by the slightest application of physical force, despite the arrestee's escape, is not to say that for Fourth Amendment purposes there is a *continuing* arrest during the period of fugitivity. If, for example, Pertoso had laid his hands upon Hodari to arrest him, but Hodari had broken away and had *then* cast away the cocaine, it would hardly be realistic to say that that disclosure had been made during the course of an arrest. Cf. *Thompson v. Whitman,* 18 Wall. 457, 471 (1874) ('A seizure is a single act, and not a continuous fact'). The present case, however, is even one step further removed. It does not involve the application of any physical force; Hodari was untouched by Officer Pertoso at the time he discarded the cocaine. His defense relies instead upon the proposition that a seizure occurs 'when the officer, by means of physical force *or show of authority,* has in some way restrained the liberty of a citizen.' *Terry v. Ohio,* [p. 291]. Hodari contends (and we accept as true for purposes of this decision) that Pertoso's pursuit qualified as a 'show of authority' calling upon Hodari to halt. The narrow question before us is whether, with respect to a show of authority as with respect to application of physical force, a seizure occurs even though the subject does not yield. We hold that it does not.

"The language of the Fourth Amendment, of course, cannot sustain respondent's contention. The word 'seizure' readily bears the meaning of a laying on of hands or application of physical force to restrain movement, even when it is ultimately unsuccessful. ('She seized the purse-snatcher, but he broke out of her grasp.') It does not remotely apply, however, to the prospect of a policeman yelling 'Stop, in the name of the law!' at a fleeing form that continues to flee. That is no seizure. Nor can the result respondent wishes to achieve be produced—indirectly, as it were—by suggesting that Pertoso's uncomplied-with show of authority was a common-law arrest, and then appealing to the principle that all common-law arrests are seizures. An arrest requires *either* physical force (as described above) *or,* where that is absent, *submission* to the assertion of authority. * * *

"We do not think it desirable, even as a policy matter, to stretch the Fourth Amendment beyond its words and beyond the meaning of arrest, as respondent urges. Street pursuits always place the public at some risk, and compliance with police orders to stop should therefore be encouraged. Only a few of those orders, we must presume, will be without adequate basis, and since the addressee has no ready means of identifying the deficient ones it almost invariably is the responsible course to comply. Unlawful orders will not be deterred, moreover, by sanctioning through the exclusionary rule those of them that are *not* obeyed. Since policemen do not command 'Stop!' expecting to be ignored, or give chase hoping to be outrun, it fully suffices to apply the deterrent to their genuine, successful seizures."

STEVENS, J., for the two dissenters, objected: "The deterrent purposes of the exclusionary rule focus on the conduct of law enforcement officers, and on discouraging improper behavior on their part, and not on the reaction of the citizen to the show of force. In the present case, if Officer Pertoso had succeeded in tackling respondent before he dropped the rock of cocaine, the rock unquestionably would have been excluded as the fruit of the officer's unlawful seizure. Instead, under the Court's logic-chopping analysis, the exclusionary rule has no application because an attempt to make an unconstitutional seizure is beyond the coverage of the Fourth Amendment, no matter how outrageous or unreasonable the officer's conduct may be.

"It is too early to know the consequences of the Court's holding. If carried to its logical conclusion, it will encourage unlawful displays of force that will frighten countless innocent citizens into surrendering whatever privacy rights they may still have. It is not too soon, however, to note the irony in the fact that the Court's own justification for its result is its analysis of the rules of the common law of arrest that antedated our decisions in *Katz* [p. 138] and *Terry.* Yet, even in those days the common law provided the citizen with protection against an attempt to make an unlawful arrest. The central message of *Katz* and *Terry* was that the protection the Fourth Amendment provides to the average citizen is not rigidly confined by ancient common-law precept. The message that today's literal-minded majority conveys is that the common law, rather than our understanding of the Fourth Amendment as it has developed over the last quarter of a century, defines, and limits, the scope of a seizure. The Court today defines a seizure as commencing, not with egregious police conduct, but rather, with submission by the citizen. Thus, it both delays the point at which 'the Fourth Amendment becomes relevant' to an encounter and limits the range of encounters that will come under the heading of 'seizure.' Today's qualification of the Fourth Amendment means that innocent citizens may remain 'secure in their persons ... against unreasonable searches and seizures' only at the discretion of the police."[e]

3. After citing *Hodari D.* to support the conclusion "that a police pursuit in attempting to seize a person does not amount to a 'seizure' within the meaning of the Fourth Amendment," the Court in *County of Sacramento v. Lewis,* p. 39, also concluded "that no Fourth Amendment seizure would take place where a 'pursuing police car sought to stop the suspect only by the show of authority represented by flashing lights and continuing pursuit,' but accidentally stopped the suspect by crashing into him." This is because for a Fourth Amendment seizure there must be "a governmental termination of freedom of movement *through means intentionally applied.*"

4. What result would the Court have reached if, before Hodari threw away the cocaine, Officer Pertoso had (a) fired his pistol at Hodari, barely missing him; (b) fired his pistol at Hodari, causing a wound which slowed down but did not stop him; (c) cornered Hodari in a dead-end alley; or (d) grabbed the collar of Hodari's jacket, only to have him slip out of the garment? Compare *United States v. Lender,* 985 F.2d 151 (4th Cir.1993) (officer called defendant to stop, defendant responded "you don't want me" and continued walking, officer again called defendant to stop and defendant did stop, at which loaded pistol fell to the ground, which officer prevented defendant from picking up; no prior seizure of defendant, as court refuses "to characterize as capitulation conduct that is fully consistent with preparation to whirl and shoot the officers"); with *United States v. Wood,* 981 F.2d 536 (D.C.Cir.1992) (when officer ordered defendant to stop, defendant "froze in his tracks and immediately dropped the [theretofore unobserved] weapon between his feet," there was a prior seizure; court "cannot imagine a more submissive response"). Compare *Tom v. Voida,* 963 F.2d 952 (7th Cir.1992) (where flight and pursuit and, when suspect fell on ice, officer kneeled on him but suspect violently resisted and broke away, seizure occurred when officer "overtook him on the ice and physically touched him"); with *United States v. Holloway,* 962 F.2d 451 (5th Cir.1992) (where after defendant's car boxed in by police cars defendant accelerated into police car behind him, no prior seizure, as no "touching" of defendant and no submission given that he then "decided to flee").

5. What result under *Bostick* and *Hodari D.* if, when an intercity bus has stopped for an equipment change, necessitating that all passengers leave the bus with their luggage, the police board the bus and announce that they have a narcotics canine outside the bus and that the dog will "alert" to anyone carrying narcotics? Does it depend upon whether "the tenor and tone of [the] announcement was informative rather than confrontational"? On whether the passengers are told to exit "in a normal fashion with your carry-on," or instead to disembark "with all their carry-on luggage in their right hand so that the luggage would pass by the dog"? Compare *United States v. Jones,* 914 F.Supp. 421 (D.Colo.1996); with *United States v. Brumfield,* 910 F.Supp. 1528 (D.Colo.1996).

e. For criticism of *Bostick* and *Hodari D.,* see Wayne R. LaFave, *Pinguitudinous Police,* *Pachydermatous Prey: Whence Fourth Amendment "Seizures"?,* 1991 U.Ill.L.Rev. 729.

6. In *United States v. Wilson*, 953 F.2d 116 (4th Cir.1991), involving an airport encounter between a DEA agent and a drug courier suspect, Wilson granted the agent's request to speak with him and submitted to questioning, produced identification upon request, and allowed the agent and an associate to search his bag and his person. But when the agent asked to search the two coats Wilson was carrying, Wilson angrily refused and walked away. The agent stayed with him, repeatedly requesting that Wilson consent to search of the coats and repeatedly asking Wilson to explain why he would not allow the search. Wilson continued walking through the terminal and then outside on the sidewalk, objecting the entire time to the harassment, but he finally consented to the search, which uncovered a bag of cocaine. If Wilson claims his consent to the search was the fruit of an illegal seizure, what result under *Bostick* and *Hodari D.?*

7. In *Bostick* and *Hodari D.* the defendants were black. Is that relevant? Consider Tracey Maclin, *"Black and Blue Encounters"—Some Preliminary Thoughts About Fourth Amendment Seizures: Should Race Matter?*, 26 Val. U.L.Rev. 243, 250 (1991): "I submit that the dynamics surrounding an encounter between a police officer and a black male are quite different from those that surround an encounter between an officer and the so-called average, reasonable person. My tentative proposal is that the Court should disregard the notion that there is an average, hypothetical, reasonable person out there by which to judge the constitutionality of police encounters. When assessing the coercive nature of an encounter, the Court should consider the race of the person confronted by the police, and how that person's race might have influenced his attitude toward the encounter."

Cf. *In re J.M.*, 619 A.2d 497 (D.C.App.1992) (majority, applying *Bostick* objective standard, concludes 14–year–old bus passenger had not been seized during his on-bus interrogation which culminated in the youth's supposed consent to a search of his bag and pat-down of his person; two concurring judges argue it "consistent with the teaching of the Supreme Court opinions that specific, objectively observable characteristics of the person who is the object of police conduct be considered by a court in determining whether a seizure has occurred," so that issue here is "whether a reasonable person who is a child would have thought that he or she was free to leave under the circumstances"; another judge "would factor into the totality of the circumstances the relevant characteristics of age and race," and suggests "that no reasonable innocent black male (with any knowledge of American history) would feel free to ignore or walk away from a drug interdicting team").

8. Is the fact the encountered suspect is black relevant in another sense? Reconsider Note 8, p. 232; and consider *Brown v. City of Oneonta*, 221 F.3d 329 (2d Cir.2000). Oneonta has about 10,000 full-time residents plus some 7,500 students who attend the local branch of the state university; fewer than 300 blacks live in the town, and 2% of the students are black. A 77–year-old woman attacked in her home at 2 a.m. told police her assailant was black and young and had cut himself on the hand with his knife. A police canine unit tracked the assailant's scent from the scene of the crime toward the campus, but lost the trail after several hundred yards. Police obtained from the university a list of its black male students and then attempted to locate and question each of them. When that endeavor produced no suspects, over the next several days police conducted a "sweep" of Oneonta, approaching and questioning non-white persons on the streets and inspecting their hands for cuts. More than two hundred persons were questioned during that period, but no suspect was apprehended. Some of those affected then brought a § 1983 action based upon both the Fourth Amendment and the Equal Protection Clause. The court of appeals concluded that under the

Bostick test no seizures had occurred and then dismissed the equal protection claims on the pleadings, distinguishing the *Oneonta* investigation from racial profiling and concluding that the plaintiffs' pleadings failed to identify "any law or policy that contains an express racial classification." See R. Richard Banks, *Race-Based Suspect Selection and Colorblind Equal Protection Doctrine and Discourse*, 48 UCLA L.Rev. 1075 (2001), critiquing *Oneonta* and concluding that "law enforcement use of race-based suspect description is as much of a racial classification as is racial profiling."

C. GROUNDS FOR TEMPORARY SEIZURE FOR INVESTIGATION

1. Under *Terry,* what grounds are needed for a stop, and how do they differ from those needed for a full-fledged arrest? Shortly after *Terry,* one commentator suggested that for arrest it must be "more probable than not that the person is the offender," while for a *Terry* stop "it should be sufficient that there is a substantial possibility that a crime has been or is about to be committed and that the suspect is the person who committed or is planning the offense."[f] Compare the Court's later elaboration in UNITED STATES v. CORTEZ, 449 U.S. 411, 101 S.Ct. 690, 66 L.Ed.2d 621 (1981):

"Courts have used a variety of terms to capture the elusive concept of what cause is sufficient to authorize police to stop a person. Terms like 'articulable reasons' and 'founded suspicion' are not self-defining; they fall short of providing clear guidance dispositive of the myriad factual situations that arise. But the essence of all that has been written is that the totality of the circumstances—the whole picture—must be taken into account. Based upon that whole picture the detaining officers must have a particularized and objective basis for suspecting the particular person stopped of criminal activity.

"The idea that an assessment of the whole picture must yield a particularized suspicion contains two elements, each of which must be present before a stop is permissible. First, the assessment must be based upon all the circumstances. The analysis proceeds with various objective observations, information from police reports, if such are available, and consideration of the modes or patterns of operation of certain kinds of lawbreakers. From these data, a trained officer draws inferences and makes deductions—inferences and deductions that might well elude an untrained person.

"The process does not deal with hard certainties, but with probabilities. Long before the law of probabilities was articulated as such, practical people formulated certain common sense conclusions about human behavior; jurors as factfinders are permitted to do the same—and so are law enforcement officers. Finally, the evidence thus collected must be seen and weighed not in terms of library analysis by scholars, but as understood by those versed in the field of law enforcement.

"The second element contained in the idea that an assessment of the whole picture must yield a particularized suspicion is the concept that the process just described must raise a suspicion that the particular individual being stopped is engaged in wrongdoing."

f. Wayne R. LaFave, *"Street Encounters" and the Constitution: Terry, Sibron, Peters and Beyond,* 67 Mich.L.Rev. 40, 73–75 (1968). An excellent illustration is provided by *Luckett v. State,* 284 N.E.2d 738 (Ind.1972), where an officer stopped for investigation a green car bearing a license plate prefix 82J upon information that such a car had been used by persons fleeing from a burglary earlier in the evening. The court concluded that the officer had "probable cause to stop the automobile" even though it was "readily apparent" that he "did not have probable cause to stop every green automobile with an 82J license prefix and formally arrest its occupants."

2. In SIBRON v. NEW YORK, 392 U.S. 40, 88 S.Ct. 1889, 20 L.Ed.2d 917 (1968), a companion case to *Terry,* the facts as stated by the Court were as follows: "At the hearing on the motion to suppress, Officer Martin testified that while he was patrolling his beat in uniform on March 9, 1965, he observed Sibron 'continually from the hours of 4:00 P.M. to 12:00, midnight * * * in the vicinity of 742 Broadway.' He stated that during this period of time he saw Sibron in conversation with six or eight persons whom he (Patrolman Martin) knew from past experience to be narcotics addicts. The officer testified that he did not overhear any of these conversations, and that he did not see anything pass between Sibron and any of the others. Late in the evening Sibron entered a restaurant. Patrolman Martin saw Sibron speak with three more known addicts inside the restaurant. Once again, nothing was overheard and nothing was seen to pass between Sibron and the addicts. Sibron sat down and ordered pie and coffee, and as he was eating, Patrolman Martin approached him and told him to come outside. Once outside, the officer said to Sibron, 'You know what I am after.' According to the officer, Sibron 'mumbled something and reached into his pocket.' Simultaneously, Patrolman Martin thrust his hand into the same pocket, discovering several glassine envelopes, which, it turned out, contained heroin."

Though the Court, per WARREN, C.J., focused primarily upon the lack of grounds for and the improper manner of the frisk (see Notes 1 and 3, pp. 320–21, it was intimated that there were not even grounds for a stop because "Patrolman Martin was completely ignorant regarding the content of these conversations, and * * * he saw nothing pass between Sibron and the addicts. So far as he knew, they might indeed 'have been talking about the World Series.' The inference that persons who talk to narcotics addicts are engaged in the criminal traffic in narcotics is simply not the sort of reasonable inference required to support an intrusion by the police upon an individual's personal security."

Do you believe that Officer Martin was less certain of what Sibron was up to than Officer McFadden was as to what Terry and his companions were up to? Are there other considerations at play here? HARLAN, J., concurring in *Sibron,* observed that "in *Terry,* the police officer judged that his suspect was about to commit a violent crime and that he had to assert himself in order to prevent it. Here there was no reason for Officer Martin to think that an incipient crime, or flight, or the destruction of evidence would occur if he stayed his hand; indeed, there was no more reason for him to intrude upon Sibron at the moment when he did than there had been four hours earlier, and no reason to think the situation would have changed four hours hence. While no hard-and-fast rule can be drawn, I would suggest that one important factor, missing here, that should be taken into account in determining whether there are reasonable grounds for a forcible intrusion is whether there is any need for immediate action."

3. In FLORIDA v. J.L., 529 U.S. 266, 120 S.Ct. 1375, 146 L.Ed.2d 254 (2000), an anonymous caller reported to police than a young black male standing at a particular bus stop and wearing a plaid shirt was carrying a gun; officers went there and saw such a person but did not see a firearm or any unusual movements, and had no reason to suspect him apart from the tip. A frisk of the suspect, which produced a firearm, was held by the Court, per GINSBURG, J., to be unreasonable: "Unlike a tip from a known informant whose reputation can be assessed and who can be held responsible if her allegations turn out to be fabricated, 'an anonymous tip alone seldom demonstrates the informant's basis of knowledge or veracity,' *Alabama v. White,* [496 U.S. 325, 110 S.Ct. 2412, 110 L.Ed.2d 301 (1990)]. As we have recognized, however, there are situations in which an anonymous tip, suitably corroborated, exhibits 'sufficient indicia of reliability to provide reasonable suspicion to make the investigatory stop.' The question we here confront is whether the tip pointing to J.L. had those indicia of reliability.

White case

↓

need more than anon tip alone

"In *White*, the police received an anonymous tip asserting that a woman was carrying cocaine and predicting that she would leave an apartment building at a specified time, get into a car matching a particular description, and drive to a named motel. Standing alone, the tip would not have justified a *Terry* stop. Only after police observation showed that the informant had accurately predicted the woman's movements, we explained, did it become reasonable to think the tipster had inside knowledge about the suspect and therefore to credit his assertion about the cocaine. Although the Court held that the suspicion in *White* became reasonable after police surveillance, we regarded the case as borderline. Knowledge about a person's future movements indicates some familiarity with that person's affairs, but having such knowledge does not necessarily imply that the informant knows, in particular, whether that person is carrying hidden contraband. We accordingly classified *White* as a 'close case.'

tip here left no means to test credibility or reliability

"The tip in the instant case lacked the moderate indicia of reliability present in *White* and essential to the Court's decision in that case. The anonymous call concerning J.L. provided no predictive information and therefore left the police without means to test the informant's knowledge or credibility. That the allegation about the gun turned out to be correct does not suggest that the officers, prior to the frisks, had a reasonable basis for suspecting J.L. of engaging in unlawful conduct: The reasonableness of official suspicion must be measured by what the officers knew before they conducted their search. All the police had to go on in this case was the bare report of an unknown, unaccountable informant who neither explained how he knew about the gun nor supplied any basis for believing he had inside information about J.L. If *White* was a close case on the reliability of anonymous tips, this one surely falls on the other side of the line. * * *

"An accurate description of a subject's readily observable location and appearance is of course reliable in this limited sense: It will help the police correctly identify the person whom the tipster means to accuse. Such a tip, however, does not show that the tipster has knowledge of concealed criminal activity. The reasonable suspicion here at issue requires that a tip be reliable in its assertion of illegality, not just in its tendency to identify a determinate person. * * *

Terry

↓

still need RS

"Firearms are dangerous, and extraordinary dangers sometimes justify unusual precautions. Our decisions recognize the serious threat that armed criminals pose to public safety; *Terry*'s rule, which permits protective police searches on the basis of reasonable suspicion rather than demanding that officers meet the higher standard of probable cause, responds to this very concern. But an automatic firearm exception to our established reliability analysis [advanced by Florida and the United States as *amicus*] would rove too far. Such an exception would enable any person seeking to harass another to set in motion an intrusive, embarrassing police search of the targeted person simply by placing an anonymous call falsely reporting the target's unlawful carriage of a gun. Nor could one securely confine such an exception to allegations involving firearms. Several Courts of Appeals have held it per se foreseeable for people carrying significant amounts of illegal drugs to be carrying guns as well. If police officers may properly conduct *Terry* frisks on the basis of bare-boned tips about guns, it would be reasonable to maintain under the above-cited decisions that the police should similarly have discretion to frisk based on bare-boned tips about narcotics. * * *

exception here would stretch bounds

"The facts of this case do not require us to speculate about the circumstances under which the danger alleged in an anonymous tip might be so great as to justify a search even without a showing of reliability. We do not say, for example, that a report of a person carrying a bomb need bear the indicia of reliability we demand for a report of a person carrying a firearm before the police can constitutionally conduct a frisk. Nor do we hold that public safety officials in quarters where the reasonable expectation of Fourth Amendment privacy is

in school or airport

less 4th am requirements so could do search here on an anon tip diminished, such as airports and schools, cannot conduct protective searches on the basis of information insufficient to justify searches elsewhere.

"Finally, the requirement that an anonymous tip bear standard indicia of reliability in order to justify a stop in no way diminishes a police officer's prerogative, in accord with *Terry*, to conduct a protective search of a person who has already been legitimately stopped. We speak in today's decision only of cases in which the officer's authority to make the initial stop is at issue. In that context, we hold that an anonymous tip lacking indicia of reliability of the kind contemplated in *Adams* [p. 320] and *White* does not justify a stop and frisk whenever and however it alleges the illegal possession of a firearm.'"

Justice KENNEDY, joined by The Chief Justice, concurring., added: "It seems appropriate to observe that a tip might be anonymous in some sense yet have certain other features, either supporting reliability or narrowing the likely class of informants, so that the tip does provide the lawful basis for some police action. One such feature, as the Court recognizes, is that the tip predicts future conduct of the alleged criminal. There may be others. For example, if an unnamed caller with a voice which sounds the same each time tells police on two successive nights about criminal activity which in fact occurs each night, a similar call on the third night ought not to be treated automatically like the tip in the case now before us. In the instance supposed, there would be a plausible argument that experience cures some of the uncertainty surrounding the anonymity, justifying a proportionate police response. In today's case, however, the State provides us with no data about the reliability of anonymous tips. Nor do we know whether the dispatcher or arresting officer had any objective reason to believe that this tip had some particular indicia of reliability.

"If an informant places his anonymity at risk, a court can consider this factor in weighing the reliability of the tip. An instance where a tip might be considered anonymous but nevertheless sufficiently reliable to justify a proportionate police response may be when an unnamed person driving a car the police officer later describes stops for a moment and, face to face, informs the police that criminal activity is occurring. This too seems to be different from the tip in the present case.

"Instant caller identification is widely available to police, and, if anonymous tips are proving unreliable and distracting to police, squad cars can be sent within seconds to the location of the telephone used by the informant. Voice recording of telephone tips might, in appropriate cases, be used by police to locate the caller. It is unlawful to make false reports to the police, and the ability of the police to trace the identity of anonymous telephone informants may be a factor which lends reliability to what, years earlier, might have been considered unreliable anonymous tips.'"

4. In UNITED STATES v. SOKOLOW, 490 U.S. 1, 109 S.Ct. 1581, 104 L.Ed.2d 1 (1989), the defendant was stopped at the Honolulu airport by agents who knew "that (1) he paid $2,100 for two airplane tickets from a roll of $20 bills; (2) he traveled under a name that did not match the name under which his telephone number was listed; (3) his original destination was Miami, a source city for illicit drugs; (4) he stayed in Miami for only 48 hours, even though a round-trip flight from Honolulu to Miami takes 20 hours; (5) he appeared nervous during his trip; and (6) he checked none of his luggage." The Court, per REHNQUIST, C.J., held this amounted to reasonable suspicion (said to be a level of suspicion "considerably less than proof of wrongdoing by a preponderance of the evidence") defendant was a drug courier:

"We do not agree with respondent that our analysis is somehow changed by the agents' belief that his behavior was consistent with one of the DEA's 'drug courier profiles.' A court sitting to determine the existence of reasonable suspicion must require the agent to articulate the factors leading to that conclusion, but the fact that these factors may be set forth in a 'profile' does not somehow detract from their evidentiary significance as seen by a trained agent.''

MARSHALL, J., joined by Brennan, J., dissenting, objected: "It is highly significant that the DEA agents stopped Sokolow because he matched one of the DEA's 'profiles' of a paradigmatic drug courier. In my view, a law enforcement officer's mechanistic application of a formula of personal and behavioral traits in deciding whom to detain can only dull the officer's ability and determination to make sensitive and fact-specific inferences 'in light of his experience,' *Terry*, particularly in ambiguous or borderline cases. Reflexive reliance on a profile of drug courier characteristics runs a far greater risk than does ordinary, case-by-case police work, of subjecting innocent individuals to unwarranted police harassment and detention. This risk is enhanced by the profile's 'chameleon-like way of adapting to any particular set of observations.' ''

5. Should either the seriousness of the suspected crime or the time of its apparent commission have any bearing on whether a *Terry* stop is permissible? In UNITED STATES v. HENSLEY, 469 U.S. 221, 105 S.Ct. 675, 83 L.Ed.2d 604 (1985), the Court, per O'CONNOR, J., held by analogy to *Whiteley v. Warden*, p. 190, "that, if a flyer or bulletin has been issued on the basis of articulable facts supporting a reasonable suspicion that the wanted person has committed an offense, then reliance on that flyer or bulletin justifies a stop to check identification, to pose questions to the person, or to detain the person briefly while attempting to obtain further information." But the Court first rejected the lower court's position that *Terry* is limited to ongoing criminal activity:

" * * * The precise limits on investigatory stops to investigate past criminal activity are more difficult to define. The proper way to identify the limits is to apply the same test already used to identify the proper bounds of intrusions that further investigations of imminent or ongoing crimes. That test, which is grounded in the standard of reasonableness embodied in the Fourth Amendment, balances the nature and quality of the intrusion on personal security against the importance of the governmental interests alleged to justify the intrusion. When this balancing test is applied to stops to investigate past crimes, we think that probable cause to arrest need not always be required.

"The factors in the balance may be somewhat different when a stop to investigate past criminal activity is involved rather than a stop to investigate ongoing criminal conduct. This is because the governmental interest and the nature of the intrusions involved in the two situations may differ. As we noted in *Terry*, one general interest present in the context of ongoing or imminent criminal activity is 'that of effective crime prevention and detection.' A stop to investigate an already completed crime does not necessarily promote the interest of crime prevention as directly as a stop to investigate suspected ongoing criminal activity. Similarly, the exigent circumstances which require a police officer to step in before a crime is committed or completed are not necessarily as pressing long afterwards. Public safety may be less threatened by a suspect in a past crime who now appears to be going about his lawful business than it is by a suspect who is currently in the process of violating the law. Finally, officers making a stop to investigate past crimes may have a wider range of opportunity to choose the time and circumstances of the stop.

"Despite these differences, where police have been unable to locate a person suspected of involvement in a past crime, the ability to briefly stop that person, ask questions, or check identification in the absence of probable cause promotes the strong government interest in solving crimes and bringing offenders to justice.

Restraining police action until after probable cause is obtained would not only hinder the investigation, but might also enable the suspect to flee in the interim and to remain at large. Particularly in the context of felonies or crimes involving a threat to public safety, it is in the public interest that the crime be solved and the suspect detained as promptly as possible. The law enforcement interests at stake in these circumstances outweigh the individual's interest to be free of a stop and detention that is no more extensive than permissible in the investigation of imminent or ongoing crimes.

"We need not and do not decide today whether *Terry* stops to investigate all past crimes, however serious, are permitted. It is enough to say that, if police have a reasonable suspicion, grounded in specific and articulable facts, that a person they encounter was involved in or is wanted in connection with a completed felony, then a *Terry* stop may be made to investigate that suspicion."[g]

[margin note: Can use Terry stop for completed]

6. Are there grounds for the stops made on the following facts, essentially those in *United States v. Feliciano,* 45 F.3d 1070 (7th Cir.1995)? An officer on patrol near a train station at midnight saw *F* and *M* walking in an area of a parking lot where there were no cars and which led to the river embankment. *M* then approached *K,* who was standing near the tracks with a suitcase, spoke with him for a while, and then left, rejoined *F,* and departed the scene in a direction opposite of that *K* then headed. The officer approached *K,* who told the officer that *M* had tried to lure him to the embankment to help an injured friend, but that *K* had refused. *K* explained that he had also seen *F* earlier and thus knew he was not injured; *K* surmised that the two had been planning to mug him. The officer asked his backup officer to stop *F* and *M.* The backup officer, who recognized *F* as a gang member recently released from prison, where *F* had served time for robbery, then stopped *F* and *M* as they walked toward their homes through the apparently deserted downtown area.

7. In ILLINOIS v. WARDLOW, 528 U.S. 119, 120 S.Ct. 673, 145 L.Ed.2d 570 (2000), a Chicago police officer in the last car of a 4–car caravan, which was converging on an area known for heavy narcotics trafficking in order to investigate drug transactions, saw defendant look in the direction of the officers and then run away; defendant was stopped and frisked and found to be carrying a handgun. The Court, per REHNQUIST, C.J., held "that the officer's stop did not violate the Fourth Amendment," reasoning: "An individual's presence in an area of expected criminal activity, standing alone, is not enough to support a reasonable, particularized suspicion that the person is committing a crime. But officers are not required to ignore the relevant characteristics of a location in determining whether the circumstances are sufficiently suspicious to warrant further investigation. Accordingly, we have previously noted the fact that the stop occurred in a 'high crime area' among the relevant contextual considerations in a *Terry* analysis.

[margin note: flight + fleeing from cops unprovoked; indiv presence in high crime area]

"In this case, moreover, it was not merely respondent's presence in an area of heavy narcotics trafficking that aroused the officers' suspicion but his unprovoked flight upon noticing the police. Our cases have also recognized that nervous, evasive behavior is a pertinent factor in determining reasonable suspicion. Headlong flight—wherever it occurs—is the consummate act of evasion; it is not necessarily indicative of wrongdoing, but it is certainly suggestive of such." The

---

g. But, what if the stop is made other than at a crime scene because the individual is thought to have information about the criminal activity of others? A stop for such a purpose was involved in *United States v. Ward,* 488 F.2d 162 (9th Cir.1973), where FBI agents used their siren to stop a person driving a car, after which he displayed a false draft card. The court held that the seizure was improper because there was no emergency requiring the interview of that person at that particular time, and went on to note that *Terry* "cannot be stretched so far as to allow detentive stops for generalized criminal inquiries."

Court emphasized in addition that while it had previously held that "refusal to cooperate, without more, does not furnish the minimal level of objective justification needed for a detention or seizure," "unprovoked flight is simply not a mere refusal to cooperate"; and that while it "is undoubtedly true" that "there are innocent reasons for flight from police," *Terry* "recognized that the officers could detain the individuals to resolve the ambiguity."

STEVENS, J., for the four Justices concurring in part and dissenting in part, first noted the majority had "wisely" not endorsed either the state's per se rule that flight at the sight of police is always grounds for a stop or the defendant's rule that such flight is never grounds for a stop, for the "inference we can reasonably draw about the motivation for a person's flight * * * will depend on a number of different circumstances. Factors such as the time of day, the number of people in the area, the character of the neighborhood, whether the officer was in uniform, the way the runner was dressed, the direction and speed of flight, and whether the person's behavior was otherwise unusual might be relevant in specific cases." (As for the State's claim "for a *per se* rule regarding 'unprovoked flight upon seeing a clearly identifiable police officer,' the four Justices responded that even this 'described a category of activity too broad and varied to permit a *per se* reasonable inference regarding the motivation for the activity.' ") Noting that instead "the totality of the circumstances, as always, must dictate the result," the dissenters found the record as a whole failed to establish reasonable suspicion, considering that it did not show whether any vehicles in the caravan were marked, whether any other officers in the group were in uniform, where the intended destination of the officers was in relation to where defendant was seen, whether the caravan had passed before defendant ran, etc., and then concluded:

"The State, along with the majority of the Court, relies as well on the assumption that this flight occurred in a high crime area. Even if that assumption is accurate, it is insufficient because even in a high crime neighborhood unprovoked flight does not invariably lead to reasonable suspicion. On the contrary, because many factors providing innocent motivations for unprovoked flight are concentrated in high crime area, the character of the neighborhood arguably makes an inference of guilt less appropriate, rather than more so.[h] Like unprovoked flight itself, presence in a high crime neighborhood is a fact too generic and susceptible to innocent explanation to satisfy the reasonable suspicion inquiry."

Regarding the scope of the majority opinion: What kind of movement away from the police, short of what the majority calls "headlong flight" in *Wardlow*, will qualify as "flight"? What police conduct would make the flight other than "unprovoked"? Does only flight "upon noticing the police" count, and if so what evidence is needed to establish that element? If the flight must coexist with presence in a "high crime area," what if anything needs to be shown about the nature of the crime problem in the area and where the area is vis-a-vis the suspect's location?

Considering the kinds of things the dissenters listed as shortcomings in the record, how would they have come out if the record had shown that the vehicles were marked, the officers were uniformed, the destination was nearby, and the

h. As the dissenters elsewhere stated: "Among some citizens, particularly minorities and those residing in high crime areas, there is also the possibility that the fleeing person is entirely innocent, but, with or without justification, believes that contact with the police can itself be dangerous, apart from any criminal activity associated with the officer's sudden presence. For such a person, unprovoked flight is neither 'aberrant' nor 'abnormal.' Moreover, these concerns and fears are known to the police officers themselves, and are validated by law enforcement investigations into their own practices. Accordingly the evidence supporting the reasonableness of these beliefs is too pervasive to be dismissed as random or rare, and too persuasive to be disparaged as inconclusive or insufficient."

caravan had not passed yet when defendant ran? In what way do the other "factors" listed by the dissenters (e.g., "time of day") manifest the likely presence or absence of an innocent motivation?

Consider Tracey L. Meares & Bernard E. Harcourt, *Transparent Adjudication and Social Science Research in Constitutional Criminal Procedure*, 90 J.Crim.L. & Criminology 733, 786–92 (2000), concluding that a "pathbreaking study of street stops in New York City released on December 1, 1999, about six weeks before *Wardlow* was published, provides critical insight to the central question in *Wardlow*." The overall ratio of stops to arrests was 9:1 (i.e., there were 9 stops for every 1 eventual arrest), but the stop/arrest ratio for blacks was twice as high as for whites, "suggest[ing] that minority individuals have a relationship with the police that makes interpretation of flight extremely difficult." The stop/arrest ratio for all cases where the stop was undertaken because of the suspect's flight was 26:1, but as to stops in the more discrete category of flight to elude the police the ratio was 15.8:1, but if that category was narrowed down further by considering only such stops in a high crime area the ratio was 45:1, which "is suggestive that in high-crime urban communities where the population is disproportionately minority, flight from an identifiable police officer is a very poor indicator that crime is afoot."

[margin note: stop/arrest ratio]

8. *Terry* relied upon the *Camara* case, p. 326, allowing safety inspections of buildings without such individualized suspicion when pursuant to an established scheme or plan. And in *Brown v. Texas*, 443 U.S. 47, 99 S.Ct. 2637, 61 L.Ed.2d 357 (1979), a unanimous Court declared that the Fourth Amendment requires that a brief detention for investigation "be based on specific, objective facts indicating that society's legitimate interests require the seizure of the particular individual, or that the seizure must be carried out pursuant to a plan embodying explicit, neutral limitations on the conduct of individual officers." Does this mean that such a plan is a sufficient substitute for individualized suspicion? How might such a plan be drafted?

[margin note: to pg 3/5]

D. Permissible Extent of Temporary Seizure

1. Assuming that the police only have grounds to make a temporary seizure on the street for purposes of investigation, what limits must be observed by them to prevent the seizure from becoming illegal? What if the officer approaches with a drawn gun and orders the suspect to raise his hands? What if the officer asserts that the suspect is under arrest? And what of the length of detention? Compare *United States v. Jennings*, 468 F.2d 111 (9th Cir.1972) (25 minutes too long where suspect cooperated fully and no greater suspicion developed); with *United States v. Richards*, 500 F.2d 1025 (9th Cir.1974) (1 hour not too long where suspects gave implausible responses to questions, thereby adding to initial suspicion, and police diligently pursued the most plausible means of clarifying the situation). What if the suspect was transported to a nearby crime scene for possible identification as the perpetrator, held impermissible in *People v. Harris*, 540 P.2d 632 (Cal.1975), whenever the witnesses could be transported to the detention scene?[i] As for detention at the police station, see pp. 323–26.

[margin note: wk 3]

2. In FLORIDA v. ROYER, 460 U.S. 491, 103 S.Ct. 1319, 75 L.Ed.2d 229 (1983), detectives questioned Royer on an airport concourse and then asked him to accompany them to a small room about 40 feet away. His luggage was retrieved

---

i. Compare *People v. Bloyd*, 331 N.W.2d 447 (Mich.1982), concluding that because transportation of a suspect even a short distance is more intrusive than a mere stop, it "should be dependent upon knowledge that a crime has been committed" and impermissible when the defendant's conduct was suspicious but "there has not been any report of a crime" recently in the vicinity.

from the airline and brought to that room, and Royer was then asked to consent to a search of the suitcases, which he did. About 15 minutes had elapsed since the initial encounter. The *Royer* plurality[j] first commented:

"The predicate permitting seizures on suspicion short of probable cause is that law enforcement interests warrant a limited intrusion on the personal security of the suspect. The scope of the intrusion permitted will vary to some extent with the particular facts and circumstances of each case. This much, however, is clear: an investigative detention must be temporary and last no longer than is necessary to effectuate the purpose of the stop. Similarly, the investigative methods employed should be the least intrusive means reasonably available to verify or dispel the officer's suspicion in a short period of time. It is the State's burden to demonstrate that the seizure it seeks to justify on the basis of a reasonable suspicion was sufficiently limited in scope and duration to satisfy the conditions of an investigative seizure."

The plurality then concluded "that at the time Royer produced the key to his suitcase, the detention to which he was then subjected was a more serious intrusion on his personal liberty than is allowable on mere suspicion of criminal activity." They stressed: (i) that the situation "had escalated into an investigatory procedure in a police interrogation room," so that "[a]s a practical matter, Royer was under arrest"; and (ii) that "the officers' conduct was more intrusive than necessary to effectuate an investigative detention otherwise authorized by the *Terry* line of cases," as while "there are undoubtedly reasons of safety and security that would justify moving a suspect from one location to another during an investigatory detention, such as from an airport concourse to a more private area," there was "no indication in this case that such reasons prompted the officers to transfer the site of the encounter from the concourse to the interrogation room. It appears, rather, that the primary interest of the officers was not in having an extended conversation with Royer but in the contents of his luggage, a matter which the officers did not pursue orally with Royer until after the encounter was relocated to the police room. The record does not reflect any facts which would support a finding that the legitimate law enforcement purposes which justified the detention in the first instance were furthered by removing Royer to the police room prior to the officer's attempt to gain his consent to a search of his luggage. As we have noted, had Royer consented to a search on the spot, the search could have been conducted with Royer present in the area where the bags were retrieved by Officer Johnson and any evidence recovered would have been admissible against him. If the search proved negative, Royer would have been free to go much earlier and with less likelihood of missing his flight, which in itself can be a very serious matter in a variety of circumstances.

"Third, the State has not touched on the question whether it would have been feasible to investigate the contents of Royer's bags in a more expeditious way. The courts are not strangers to the use of trained dogs to detect the presence of controlled substances in luggage. There is no indication here that this means was not feasible and available. If it had been used, Royer and his luggage could have been momentarily detained while this investigative procedure was carried out. Indeed, it may be that no detention at all would have been necessary. A negative result would have freed Royer in short order; a positive result would have resulted in his justifiable arrest on probable cause."[k]

---

j. White, J., joined by Marshall, Powell and Stevens, JJ.

k. The plurality then concluded "that probable cause to arrest Royer did not exist at the time he consented to the search of his lug-

gage," so that the consent was the fruit of an illegal arrest. The dissenters, believing the detention in the room was permissible under *Terry,* found it unnecessary to address the probable cause issue.

BRENNAN, J., concurring, addressed this point in a footnote: "I interpret the plurality's requirement that the investigative methods employed pursuant to a *Terry* stop be 'the least intrusive means reasonably available to verify or dispel the officer's suspicion in a short period of time,' to mean that the availability of a less intrusive means may make an otherwise reasonable stop unreasonable. I do not interpret it to mean that the absence of a less intrusive means can make an otherwise unreasonable stop reasonable."

BLACKMUN, J., dissenting because he believed Royer consented to go to the room, added that he could not "accept the 'least intrusive' alternative analysis the plurality would impose on the law of the Fourth Amendment." REHNQUIST, J., joined by the Chief Justice and O'Connor, J., dissenting, also found no support in prior cases for the plurality's "least intrusive means" principle and concluded that the plurality's analysis "adds up to little more than saying that if my aunt were a man, she would be my uncle. The officers might have taken different steps than they did to investigate Royer, but the same may be said of virtually every investigative encounter that has more than one step to it. The question we must decide is what was *unreasonable* about the steps which *these officers* took with respect to *this* suspect in the Miami Airport on this particular day."

3. What limits, if any, does *Royer* place upon *Terry* stops? Does the case justify the conclusion (i) that such a stop may not extend as long as 15 minutes? (ii) that the person detained may never be moved to another location? (iii) that the person detained may not be moved from a public area to a private one? (iv) that the police must opt for the most expeditious means of investigation? Consider UNITED STATES v. SHARPE, 470 U.S. 675, 105 S.Ct. 1568, 84 L.Ed.2d 605 (1985). There, a federal drug agent, patrolling in an unmarked car in a highway area under surveillance for drug trafficking, saw an apparently overloaded camper truck traveling in tandem with a Pontiac. He radioed for assistance, and when a highway patrolman responded they attempted to stop the two vehicles. The Pontiac pulled over, but the truck continued on, pursued by the patrolman. Once the drug agent obtained identification from the driver of the Pontiac, he sought without success to reach the patrolman by radio. He then radioed for more assistance, and when local police appeared he left them with the Pontiac and drove ahead to where the patrolman had stopped the truck. After smelling the odor of marijuana coming from the vehicle, he opened it and saw bales of marijuana and then arrested the driver of the truck, one Savage. The Court of Appeals held that the 20–minute detention of Savage "failed to meet the [Fourth Amendment's] requirement of brevity," but the Supreme Court, per BURGER, C.J., disagreed:

"* * * Obviously, if an investigative stop continues indefinitely, at some point it can no longer be justified as an investigative stop. But our cases impose no rigid time limitation on *Terry* stops. * * * Much as a 'bright line' rule would be desirable, in evaluating whether an investigative detention is unreasonable, common sense and ordinary human experience must govern over rigid criteria.[l]

"In assessing whether a detention is too long in duration to be justified as an investigative stop, we consider it appropriate to examine whether the police diligently pursued a means of investigation that was likely to confirm or dispel their suspicions quickly, during which time it was necessary to detain the defendant. A court making this assessment should take care to consider whether the police are acting in a swiftly developing situation, and in such cases the court should not indulge in unrealistic second-guessing. A creative judge engaged in *post*

---

l. Compare *Model Code of Pre–Arraignment Procedure* § 110.2(1), recommending a maximum of 20 minutes for a *Terry* stop.

hoc evaluation of police conduct can almost always imagine some alternative means by which the objectives of the police might have been accomplished. But '[t]he fact that the protection of the public might, in the abstract, have been accomplished by "less intrusive" means does not, in itself, render the search unreasonable.' The question is not simply whether some other alternative was available, but whether the police acted unreasonably in failing to recognize or to pursue it."

Stressing that the "delay in this case was attributable almost entirely to the evasive actions of Savage," that most of the 20 minutes was consumed by the agent trying to reach the patrolman and to obtain additional assistance, and that when the agent reached Savage "he proceeded expeditiously," the majority in *Sharpe* concluded the delay was not unreasonable. MARSHALL, J., though concurring because the "prolonged encounter" was attributable to "the evasive actions" of Savage, argued that "fidelity to the rationales that justify *Terry* stops require that the intrusiveness of the stop be measured independently of law enforcement needs. A stop must first be found not unduly intrusive, particularly in its length, before it is proper to consider whether law enforcement aims warrant limited investigation." BRENNAN, J., dissenting, objected that record did not clearly show that Savage had tried to elude the police, and that the government had not met its burden under *Royer* to "show at a minimum that the 'least intrusive means reasonably available' were used in carrying out the stop."

4. Will the most common investigative technique, interrogation, ordinarily be the most expeditious? Does that depend upon the significance which can be attached to noncooperation? Cf. KOLENDER v. LAWSON, 461 U.S. 352, 103 S.Ct. 1855, 75 L.Ed.2d 903 (1983), where the Court overturned on void for vagueness grounds a statute which, as construed, made it a criminal offense for a person lawfully stopped under *Terry* to fail to provide "credible and reliable" identification and to account for his presence, as the statute "contains no standard for determining what a suspect has to do in order to satisfy the requirement to provide a 'credible and reliable' identification." The majority thus found it unnecessary to address other issues, but BRENNAN, J., concurring, asserted that "under the Fourth Amendment, police officers with reasonable suspicion that an individual has committed or is about to commit a crime may detain that individual, using some force if necessary, for the purpose of asking investigative questions. They may ask their questions in a way calculated to obtain an answer. But they may not *compel* an answer, and they must allow the person to leave after a reasonably brief period of time unless the information they have acquired during the encounter has given them probable cause sufficient to justify an arrest.[4]"

5. Reconsider the pretext traffic stop tactic discussed in Notes 5–8, pp. 230–32. To what extent does the *Terry* requirement that the seizure be "reasonably related in scope to the circumstances which justified the interference in the first place" provide meaningful limits upon the opportunity for the police to conduct a narcotics investigation during a traffic stop? For example, on the following facts, taken from *United States v. Ramos,* 20 F.3d 348 (8th Cir.1994), on reh. 42 F.3d 1160 (8th Cir.1994), at what point, if at all, did the officer cross the line?

At 7 a.m. the trooper stopped a pickup on Interstate 80 when he saw the passenger was not wearing a seat belt. The trooper asked the passenger for identification, and the passenger produced his driver's license. The trooper then

---

4. * * * In some circumstances it is even conceivable that the mere fact that a suspect refuses to answer questions once detained, viewed in the context of the facts that gave rise to reasonable suspicion in the first place, would be enough to provide probable cause. A court confronted with such a claim, however, would have to evaluate it carefully to make certain that the person arrested was not being penalized for the exercise of his right to refuse to answer.

asked the driver for his license as well, which was also produced. (The trooper later testified he needed only the passenger's identification to prepare a citation.) The trooper then asked the driver to accompany him to the patrol car, where the trooper radioed for a computer check on the two men and the truck. While awaiting a response, the trooper questioned the driver about various matters, including his precise destination, the purpose of his trip, and his employment. When a negative response was received from the computer inquiry, the trooper returned the driver's license and then asked him to stay in the patrol car while he gave the warning ticket to the passenger. The trooper gave the warning ticket, which bore the time 7:40 a.m., to the passenger and then asked him about his destination and whether there were any drugs in the truck. The trooper then went back to his patrol car and questioned the driver again about where he was from and his destination, and asked if there were drugs in the truck. The trooper then asked the driver to consent to a search of the truck, and the driver signed a consent form which also bore the time 7:40 a.m. The trooper then called for a second officer, who arrived at the scene 10 minutes later, and then the searched commenced.

6. The cases analyzing such traffic stops usually take the view that if the officer who made the stop has checked out the driver's license and vehicle registration and has written up the traffic citation or warning, then any *extension* of the stop thereafter for the purpose of questioning about drugs or seeking consent to search for drugs is illegal. See, e.g., *United States v. Fernandez,* 18 F.3d 874 (10th Cir.1994); *People v. Banks,* 650 N.E.2d 833 (N.Y.1995). Dictum in some cases, e.g., *United States v. Cummins,* 920 F.2d 498 (8th Cir.1990), suggests that *all* of the officer's investigative activity must be limited to the offense for which the stop was made unless reasonable suspicion develops as to other criminality, e.g., drug possession. However, courts often deem questioning on unrelated matters absent such suspicion as unobjectionable *provided* it is accomplished within the permissible time span of the traffic stop. See, e.g., *United States v. Crain,* 33 F.3d 480 (5th Cir.1994).

It is thus sometimes necessary to determine whether a traffic stop was extended or instead terminated at a certain point. Even if it is apparent to the defendant that the officer has completed writing up the ticket or warning, that does not terminate the stop if the officer continues to hold the defendant's license, vehicle registration, or other credentials. *United States v. Fernandez,* supra. But if, on the other hand, the officer *has* returned those credentials, does this mean that the seizure has terminated even if the officer then uses the Lt. Colombo gambit ("Oh, one more thing, . . .") in order to question the defendant about drugs? See *United States v. Werking,* 915 F.2d 1404 (10th Cir.1990) (return of his papers manifested to the driver that he "was free to leave the scene," so that when he instead remained and responded to the questions he "chose to engage in a consensual encounter").

7. OHIO v. ROBINETTE, 519 U.S. 33, 117 S.Ct. 417, 136 L.Ed.2d 347 (1996), involved these facts: a sheriff's deputy on "drug interdiction patrol" stopped defendant for speeding. The deputy examined defendant's license, ran a computer check indicating no previous violations, issued a verbal warning and returned defendant's license, and then immediately asked defendant if he had drugs in the car; when defendant answered in the negative, the deputy asked to search the car and defendant consented, resulting in a search which uncovered a small amount of marijuana and a single pill which was a controlled substance. The state supreme court concluded the evidence must be suppressed, reasoning that the "right to be secure in one's person and property requires that citizens stopped for traffic offenses be clearly informed by the detaining officer when they are free to go after a valid detention, before an officer attempts to engage in a consensual

[handwritten marginalia: When are you free to leave?]

[handwritten marginalia: ?'s on unrelated Matters]

[handwritten marginalia: SEE SUPP Pg 43]

[handwritten marginalia: traffic stop]

[handwritten marginalia: When are you free to go]

[handwritten marginalia: should the officer told A that he was free to leave before next ?'s]

interrogation." The Supreme Court, per REHNQUIST, C.J., focused on the issue stated in the certiorari petition, whether such a warning is a prerequisite to a voluntary consent, and answered in the negative. The state court's per se rule was deemed inconsistent with the approach to Fourth Amendment issues by the Supreme Court, which has "consistently eschewed bright-line rules, instead emphasizing the fact-specific nature of the reasonableness inquiry." Moreover, the Court reasoned in *Robinette,* requiring such warnings would be just as impractical as the right-to-refuse-consent warnings held unnecessary by the Court in *Schneckloth v. Bustamonte* [p. 332].

Only Justice STEVENS, dissenting, fully considered an alternative characterization of the state court's holding, namely, that (i) the officer's failure to tell defendant he was free to leave meant that a reasonable person would continue to believe he was not free to leave, so that the seizure had not yet ended at the time the consent was obtained; (ii) the seizure by that time was illegal, as it had exceeded its lawful purpose, the giving of a warning about the traffic offense; and (iii) consequently the evidence obtained via the voluntary consent was a suppressible fruit of that poisonous tree. He concluded that the evidence in the case (including the fact that this deputy had used this tactic to make 786 consent searches in one year) supported that conclusion, so that the suppression of evidence by the state court was justified.

The *Robinette* majority was not totally silent regarding this theory. The defendant argued the Court could not reach the voluntariness issue because the state court decision set out a valid alternative ground in the following language: "When the motivation behind a police officer's continued detention of a person stopped for a traffic violation is not related to the purpose of the original, constitutional stop, and when that continued detention is not based on articulable facts giving rise to a suspicion of some separate illegal activity justifying an extension of the detention, the continued detention constitutes an illegal seizure." Relying on the *Whren* case, p. 226, the Chief Justice declared that the state court was in error because "the subjective intentions of the officer did not make the continued detention of respondent illegal under the Fourth Amendment." Is this a proper application of *Whren?* Does it mean that in applying the *Terry* scope limitation, the fact the officer decided only to give a warning instead of a ticket is irrelevant? Or, is Justice Stevens correct in concluding that the irrelevant subjective motivation was drug interdiction, but that the subjective purpose of giving a warning bears on the justification for the continued detention, so that by the time the consent was obtained "the lawful traffic stop had come to an end" because the defendant "had been given his warning"?

E. TEMPORARY SEIZURE OF EFFECTS

1. In *United States v. Van Leeuwen,* 397 U.S. 249, 90 S.Ct. 1029, 25 L.Ed.2d 282 (1970) a postal clerk in Mt. Vernon, Washington, advised a policeman that he was suspicious of two packages of coins just mailed. The policeman immediately noted that the return address was fictitious and that the individual who mailed the packages had Canadian license plates, and later investigation disclosed that the addressees (one in California, the other in Tennessee) were under investigation for trafficking in illegal coins. Upon this basis a search warrant for both packages was obtained, but not until the packages had been held for slightly more than a day. A unanimous Court, although acknowledging that "detention of mail could at some point become an unreasonable seizure of 'papers' or 'effects' within the meaning of the Fourth Amendment," cited *Terry* in upholding this "detention, without a warrant, while an investigation was made." The Court emphasized that the investigation was conducted promptly and that most of the delay was attributable to the fact that because of the time differential the Tennessee authorities could not be reached until the following day.

2. In UNITED STATES v. PLACE, 462 U.S. 696, 103 S.Ct. 2637, 77 L.Ed.2d 110 (1983), federal agents stopped respondent, a suspected drug courier, at LaGuardia Airport, seized his luggage for the purported purpose of taking it to a judge while a warrant was sought, and then allowed respondent to go his way. They took the bags to Kennedy Airport, where a trained narcotics dog reacted positively to one of them and ambiguously to the other, but because it was late Friday afternoon held the bags until Monday morning, when a warrant was obtained for the first bag and cocaine was found in execution of the warrant. The Court, per O'CONNOR, J., first recognized "the reasonableness under the Fourth Amendment of warrantless seizures of personal luggage from the custody of the owner on the basis of less than probable cause for the purpose of pursuing a limited course of investigation, short of opening the luggage, that would quickly confirm or dispel the authorities' suspicion." Applying the *Terry* balancing of interests approach, the Court concluded that "the governmental interest in seizing the luggage briefly to pursue further investigation is substantial," and that because "seizures of property can vary in intrusiveness, some brief detentions of personal effects may be so minimally intrusive of Fourth Amendment interests that strong countervailing governmental interests will justify a seizure based only on specific articulable facts that the property contains contraband or evidence of a crime.

" * * * Particularly in the case of detention of luggage within the traveler's immediate possession, the police conduct intrudes on both the suspect's possessory interest in his luggage as well as his liberty interest in proceeding with his itinerary. The person whose luggage is detained is technically still free to continue his travels or carry out other personal activities pending release of the luggage. Moreover, he is not subjected to the coercive atmosphere of a custodial confinement or to the public indignity of being personally detained. Nevertheless, such a seizure can effectively restrain the person since he is subjected to the possible disruption of his travel plans in order to remain with his luggage or to arrange for its return.[8] Therefore, when the police seize luggage from the suspect's custody, we think the limitations applicable to investigative detentions of the person should define the permissible scope of an investigative detention of the person's luggage on less than probable cause. Under this standard, it is clear that the police conduct here exceeded the permissible limits of a *Terry*-type investigative stop.

"The length of the detention of respondent's luggage alone precludes the conclusion that the seizure was reasonable in the absence of probable cause. Although we have recognized the reasonableness of seizures longer than the momentary ones involved in *Terry,* the brevity of the invasion of the individual's Fourth Amendment interests is an important factor in determining whether the seizure is so minimally intrusive as to be justifiable on reasonable suspicion. Moreover, in assessing the effect of the length of the detention, we take into account whether the police diligently pursue their investigation. We note that here the New York agents knew the time of Place's scheduled arrival at LaGuardia, had ample time to arrange for their additional investigation at that location, and thereby could have minimized the intrusion on respondent's Fourth Amendment interests. Thus, although we decline to adopt any outside time limitation for a permissible *Terry* stop, we have never approved a seizure of the person for the

8. "At least when the authorities do not make it absolutely clear how they plan to reunite the suspect and his possessions at some future time and place, seizure of the object is tantamount to seizure of the person. This is because that person must either remain on the scene or else seemingly surrender his effects permanently to the police." 3 W. LaFave, *Search and Seizure* § 9.6, p. 61 (1982 Supp.).

prolonged 90–minute period involved here and cannot do so on the facts presented by this case.

"Although the 90–minute detention of respondent's luggage is sufficient to render the seizure unreasonable, the violation was exacerbated by the failure of the agents to accurately inform respondent of the place to which they were transporting his luggage, of the length of time he might be dispossessed, and of what arrangements would be made for return of the luggage if the investigation dispelled the suspicion."

BRENNAN, J., joined by Marshall, J., concurring in the result, objected that the majority's approval of brief detention of luggage was "unnecessary to the Court's judgment" and "finds no support in *Terry* or its progeny and significantly dilutes the Fourth Amendment's protections against government interference with personal property." They contended that when the officers "did not develop probable cause to arrest respondent during their encounter with him," "they had to let him go" and could not then subject him "to an independent dispossession of his personal effects based simply on reasonable suspicion." They argued that the *Terry* "balancing inquiries should not be conducted except in the most limited circumstances," while BLACKMUN, J., concurring separately, similarly expressed concern "with what appears to me to be an emerging tendency on the part of the Court to convert the *Terry* decision into a general statement that the Fourth Amendment requires only that any seizure be reasonable."

F. PROTECTIVE SEARCH

1. After *Terry*, what is the test for determining whether an officer may conduct a "frisk"? Consider *Sibron*, p. 307, where the Court stated: "In the case of the self-protective search for weapons, [the officer] must be able to point to particular facts from which he reasonably inferred that the individual was armed and dangerous. Patrolman Martin's testimony reveals no such facts. The suspect's mere act of talking with a number of known narcotics addicts over an eight-hour period no more gives rise to reasonable fear of life or limb on the part of the police officer than it justifies an arrest for committing a crime. Nor did Patrolman Martin urge that when Sibron put his hand in his pocket, he feared that he was going for a weapon and acted in self-defense. His opening statement to Sibron—'You know what I am after'—made it abundantly clear that he sought narcotics, and his testimony at the hearing left no doubt that he thought there were narcotics in Sibron's pocket."

Compare *Adams v. Williams*, 407 U.S. 143, 92 S.Ct. 1921, 32 L.Ed.2d 612 (1972), where the majority concluded the officer "had ample reason to fear for his own safety"[m] upon being told by an informant that defendant, seated in a nearby car, was carrying narcotics and had a gun at his waist. Marshall, J., joined by Douglas, J., dissenting, objected: "The fact remains that Connecticut specifically authorizes persons to carry guns so long as they have a permit. Thus, there was no reason for the officer to infer from anything that the informant said that the respondent was dangerous."

Is the quantum and reliability of information needed to support a frisk the same or less than that needed to support a stop? For example, what if the stop

---

m. The Court footnoted that statement with the following:

"Figures reported by the Federal Bureau of Investigation indicate that 125 policemen were murdered in 1971, with all but five of them having been killed by gunshot wounds. Federal Bureau of Investigation *Law En-* *forcement Bulletin*, February 1972, p. 33. According to one study, approximately 30% of police shootings occurred when a police officer approached a suspect seated in an automobile. Bristow, *Police Officer Shootings—A Tactical Evaluation*, 54 J.Crim.L.C. & P.S. 93 (1963)."

was made on a reliable informant's information the suspect possessed illegal gambling paraphernalia, and the officer had also received a report from an anonymous informant that this same person regularly carries a gun? Reconsider the final paragraph of Justice Ginsburg's opinion in *J. L.*, note 3 supra.

2. Consider David A. Harris, *Frisking Every Suspect: The Withering of Terry*, 28 U.C. Davis L.Rev. 1, 5, 43–44 (1994): "Perhaps as a result of the high-visibility use of frisks as a contemporary crime control device, or because of general public antipathy to crime, lower courts have stretched the law governing frisks to the point that the Supreme Court might find it unrecognizable. Lower courts have consistently expanded the *types of offenses* always considered violent regardless of the individual circumstances. At the same time, lower courts have also found that certain *types of persons and situations* always pose a danger of armed violence to police [e.g., those present in a high-crime or drug-involved location who engage in allegedly evasive behavior toward the police]. When confronted with these offenses, persons, or situations, police may *automatically* frisk, whether or not any individualized circumstances point to danger. * * *

" * * * African–Americans and Hispanic–Americans pay a higher personal price for [these] contemporary stop and frisk practices than whites do."

3. As for the requisite search procedure, the Court in *Sibron* stated: "The search for weapons approved in *Terry* consisted solely of a limited patting of the outer clothing of the suspect for concealed objects which might be used as instruments of assault. Only when he discovered such objects did the officer in *Terry* place his hands in the pockets of the men he searched. In this case, with no attempt at an initial limited exploration for arms, Patrolman Martin thrust his hand into Sibron's pocket and took from him envelopes of heroin. His testimony shows that he was looking for narcotics, and he found them. The search was not reasonably limited in scope to the accomplishment of the only goal which might conceivably have justified its inception—the protection of the officer by disarming a potentially dangerous man."

Compare *Adams v. Williams*, where the officer immediately reached into the car and removed a theretofore concealed gun from defendant's waistband. The Court stated: "When Williams rolled down his window, rather than complying with the policeman's request to step out of the car so that his movements could more easily be seen, the revolver allegedly at Williams' waist became an even greater threat. Under these circumstances the policeman's action in reaching to the spot where the gun was thought to be hidden constituted a limited intrusion designed to insure his safety, and we conclude that it was reasonable."

4. Assuming that there are grounds for a protective search, how extensive a "patting down" of the suspect is permissible? Consider the description quoted in note 13 of *Terry*. Is the right to make a protective search limited to the person of the suspect? What if the suspect is carrying an attache case, a shopping bag, a purse, or similar object?

In *Minnesota v. Dickerson*, 508 U.S. 366, 113 S.Ct. 2130, 124 L.Ed.2d 334 (1993), the frisking officer felt a small lump in the suspect's front pocket and then, upon further tactile examination, concluded the lump was crack cocaine in a plastic or cellophane bag, which the officer removed from the suspect's pocket. Noting the state court's findings that the officer "determined that the lump was contraband only after 'squeezing, sliding and otherwise manipulating the outside of the defendant's pocket' after the officer knew it contained no weapon, the Supreme Court held the state court "was correct in holding that the police officer in this case overstepped the bounds of the 'strictly circumscribed' search for weapons allowed under *Terry*."

5. In MICHIGAN v. LONG, 463 U.S. 1032, 103 S.Ct. 3469, 77 L.Ed.2d 1201 (1983), two deputies saw a car swerve into a ditch and stopped to investigate. Long, the only occupant of the car, met the deputies at the rear of the car, supplied his driver's license upon demand, and started back toward the open door when asked for his vehicle registration. The officers saw a large hunting knife on the floorboard, so Long was frisked and one officer then entered the vehicle and found an open pouch of marijuana under an armrest. The Supreme Court, per O'CONNOR, J., held:

"Our past cases indicate then that protection of police and others can justify protective searches when police have a reasonable belief that the suspect poses a danger, that roadside encounters between police and suspects are especially hazardous, and that danger may arise from the possible presence of weapons in the area surrounding a suspect. These principles compel our conclusion that the search of the passenger compartment of an automobile, limited to those areas in which a weapon may be placed or hidden, is permissible if the police officer possesses a reasonable belief based on 'specific and articulable facts which, taken together with the rational inferences from those facts, reasonably warrant' the officers in believing that the suspect is dangerous and the suspect may gain immediate control of weapons. * * *

"The circumstances of this case clearly justified Deputies Howell and Lewis in their reasonable belief that Long posed a danger if he were permitted to reenter his vehicle. The hour was late and the area rural. Long was driving his automobile at excessive speed, and his car swerved into a ditch. The officers had to repeat their questions to Long, who appeared to be 'under the influence' of some intoxicant. Long was not frisked until the officers observed that there was a large knife in the interior of the car into which Long was about to reenter. The subsequent search of the car was restricted to those areas to which Long would generally have immediate control, and that could contain a weapon. The trial court determined that the leather pouch containing marijuana could have contained a weapon. It is clear that the intrusion was 'strictly circumscribed by the exigencies which justifi[ed] its initiation.' * * *

"The Michigan Supreme Court appeared to believe that it was not reasonable for the officers to fear that Long could injure them, because he was effectively under their control during the investigative stop and could not get access to any weapons that might have been located in the automobile. This reasoning is mistaken in several respects. During any investigative detention, the suspect is 'in the control' of the officers in the sense that he 'may be briefly detained against his will * * *.' Just as a *Terry* suspect on the street may, despite being under the brief control of a police officer, reach into his clothing and retrieve a weapon, so might a *Terry* suspect in Long's position break away from police control and retrieve a weapon from his automobile. In addition, if the suspect is not placed under arrest, he will be permitted to reenter his automobile, and he will then have access to any weapons inside. Or, as here, the suspect may be permitted to reenter the vehicle before the *Terry* investigation is over, and again, may have access to weapons. In any event, we stress that a *Terry* investigation, such as the one that occurred here, involves a police investigation 'at close range,' when the officer remains particularly vulnerable in part *because* a full custodial arrest has not been effected, and the officer must make a 'quick decision as to how to protect himself and others from possible danger * * *.' In such circumstances, we have not required that officers adopt alternate means to ensure their safety in order to avoid the intrusion involved in a *Terry* encounter."

BRENNAN and Marshall, JJ., dissenting, objected: "Putting aside the fact that the search at issue here involved a far more serious intrusion than that 'involved in a *Terry* encounter,' and as such might suggest the need for resort to 'alternate means,' the Court's reasoning is perverse. The Court's argument in essence is that the *absence* of probable cause to arrest compels the conclusion that a broad search, traditionally associated in scope with a search incident to arrest, must be permitted based on reasonable suspicion. But *United States v. Robinson, supra,* stated: 'It is scarcely open to doubt that the danger to an officer is far greater in the case of the extended exposure which follows the taking of a suspect into custody and transporting him to the police station than in the case of the relatively fleeting contact resulting from the typical *Terry*-type stop.' In light of *Robinson*'s observation, today's holding leaves in grave doubt the question of whether the Court's assessment of the relative dangers posed by given confrontations is based on any principled standard."

6. Can a limited search for any other reason ever be undertaken incident to a lawful stop? In *State v. Flynn,* 285 N.W.2d 710 (Wis.1979), one of two suspects lawfully stopped for investigation of a just-completed burglary admitted he had identification in his wallet but refused to identify himself, so the officer removed the wallet and examined it to the extent necessary to find the suspect's name and then arrested the suspect when a radio check revealed he was wanted for an earlier crime. Reasoning that "unless the officer is entitled to at least ascertain the identity of the suspect, the right to stop him can serve no useful purpose at all," that the search was a very limited one, and "that defendant could himself have substantially avoided the intrusion simply by producing the identification himself as his companion did," the court held the officer's actions reasonable under the *Terry* balancing test. Compare *People v. Williams,* 234 N.W.2d 541 (Mich.App.1975) (even though officer had good reason to believe lawfully stopped suspect was lying when he said he had no identification, looking in his wallet at driver's license violated the Fourth Amendment). Cf. *Arizona v. Hicks,* p. 244; and *Ybarra v. Illinois,* p. 197.

What then of on-the-scene fingerprinting? In *Hayes v. Florida,* 470 U.S. 811, 105 S.Ct. 1643, 84 L.Ed.2d 705 (1985), the majority in dictum opined this would be permissible "if there is reasonable suspicion that the suspect has committed a criminal act, if there is a reasonable basis for believing that fingerprinting will establish or negate the suspect's connection with that crime, and if the procedure is carried out with dispatch." Brennan and Marshall, JJ., concurring, responded "that on-site fingerprinting (apparently undertaken in full view of any passerby) would involve a singular intrusion on the suspect's privacy, an intrusion that would not be justifiable (as was the patdown in *Terry*) as necessary for the officer's protection."

G. OTHER BRIEF DETENTION FOR INVESTIGATION

1. In DAVIS v. MISSISSIPPI, 394 U.S. 721, 89 S.Ct. 1394, 22 L.Ed.2d 676 (1969), petitioner and 24 other black youths were detained for questioning and fingerprinting in connection with a rape for which the only leads were a general description given by the victim and a set of fingerprints around the window through which the assailant entered. Petitioner's prints were found to match those at the scene of the crime, and this evidence was admitted at his trial. The Court, per BRENNAN, J., held that the prints should have been excluded as the fruits of a seizure of petitioner in violation of the Fourth Amendment, but intimated that a detention for such a purpose might sometimes be permissible on evidence insufficient for arrest:

"Detentions for the sole purpose of obtaining fingerprints are no less subject to the constraints of the Fourth Amendment. It is arguable, however, that because of the unique nature of the fingerprinting process, such detentions might, under narrowly defined circumstances, be found to comply with the Fourth Amendment even though there is no probable cause in the traditional sense. Detention for fingerprinting may constitute a much less serious intrusion upon personal security than other types of police searches and detentions. Fingerprinting involves none of the probing into an individual's private life and thoughts which marks an interrogation or search. Nor can fingerprint detention be employed repeatedly to harass any individual, since the police need only one set of each person's prints. Furthermore, fingerprinting is an inherently more reliable and effective crime-solving tool than eyewitness identifications or confessions and is not subject to such abuses as the improper line-up[n] and the 'third degree.' Finally, because there is no danger of destruction of fingerprints, the limited detention need not come unexpectedly or at an inconvenient time. For this same reason, the general requirement that the authorization of a judicial officer be obtained in advance of detention would seem not to admit of any exception in the fingerprinting context.

"We have no occasion in this case, however, to determine whether the requirements of the Fourth Amendment could be met by narrowly circumscribed procedures for obtaining, during the course of a criminal investigation, the fingerprints of individuals for whom there is no probable cause to arrest. For it is clear that no attempt was made here to employ procedures which might comply with the requirements of the Fourth Amendment: the detention at police head-quarters of petitioner and the other young Negroes was not authorized by a judicial officer; petitioner was unnecessarily required to undergo two fingerprint-ing sessions; and petitioner was not merely fingerprinted during the December 3 detention but also subjected to interrogation.'"[o]

2. *United States v. Dionisio*, p. 673, holds that the Fourth Amendment was not violated by subpoenaing witnesses to appear before a grand jury to give voice exemplars. No preliminary showing of "probable cause" or "reasonableness" is required in such a case, as: (a) "a subpoena to appear before a grand jury is not a 'seizure' in the Fourth Amendment sense," and thus "*Davis* is plainly inappo-site"; and (b) the requirement that the witness give exemplars does not infringe upon Fourth Amendment rights, as "the physical characteristics of a person's voice, its tone and manner, as opposed to the content of a specific conversation, are constantly exposed to the public," so that "no person can have a reasonable expectation that others will not know the sound of his voice." *United States v. Mara*, p. 676, reached the same result as to the subpoenaing of a witness to give handwriting exemplars.

3. A few jurisdictions have adopted statutes or rules of court which autho-rize brief detention at the station (usually pursuant to court order), on less than the grounds needed to arrest, for the purpose of conducting certain identification procedures. Such provisions have been upheld by the courts, and some other cases have upheld similar procedures even absent such a provision. For example, in *In re Fingerprinting of M.B.*, 309 A.2d 3 (N.J.Super.1973), the court affirmed an order requiring all 22 male members of the eighth grade class of a particular school to submit to fingerprinting. A ring of that elementary school's graduating class was found near the body of a homicide victim, and later the victim's car was located. Fingerprints other than those of the victim were found both inside and outside the vehicle. Upon request of the prosecutor, the court ordered all male

n. In *Wise v. Murphy*, 275 A.2d 205 (D.C.App.1971), the court noted the negative reference in *Davis* was only to an "improper line-up" and thus concluded that upon a prop-er showing, lacking in the instant case, a court could order a person to appear in a lineup even if grounds for arrest were lacking, at least for investigation of "serious felonies involving grave personal injuries."

o. *Davis* was reaffirmed in *Hayes v. Flori-da*, p. 323, where the Court again suggested "the Fourth Amendment might permit the ju-diciary to authorize the seizure of a person on less than probable cause and his removal to the police station for the purpose of fingerprint-ing."

members of that graduating class to submit to fingerprinting; the order permitted the pupils to be accompanied by a parent, guardian or attorney, directed that the prints be used only in the investigation of the homicide, and specified further that upon completion of the investigation the prints should be destroyed. The appellate court, in affirming commented:

"[T]here [is] a substantial basis to suspect that a member of the school class in question may have had some implication in or material knowledge of the homicide such that fingerprinting of all the male members of the class was reasonable, having in mind the protective provision of the order for destruction of the prints after completion of the investigation. Under all the circumstances extant and the terms of the order below we find the existence of such 'narrowly circumscribed procedures' as render the order reasonable within the view of the Fourth Amendment adumbrated in *Davis*."

4. In DUNAWAY v. NEW YORK, 442 U.S. 200, 99 S.Ct. 2248, 60 L.Ed.2d 824 (1979), the police, lacking grounds to arrest petitioner but suspecting he was implicated in an attempted robbery and homicide, had him "picked up" for questioning. He was placed in an interrogation room at police headquarters, where he was questioned by officers after being given the *Miranda* warnings. Petitioner waived counsel and within an hour gave incriminating statements. His conviction following a trial at which those statements were admitted was affirmed by the state court on the ground that officers "may detain an individual upon reasonable suspicion for questioning for a reasonable and brief period of time under carefully controlled conditions which are ample to protect the individual's Fifth and Sixth Amendment Rights." The Supreme Court, per BRENNAN, J., reversed:

"In contrast to the brief and narrowly circumscribed intrusions involved in [*Terry* and its progeny], the detention of petitioner was in important respects indistinguishable from a traditional arrest. Petitioner was not questioned briefly where he was found. Instead, he was taken from a neighbor's home to a police car, transported to a police station, and placed in an interrogation room. He was never informed that he was 'free to go'; indeed, he would have been physically restrained if he had refused to accompany the officers or had tried to escape their custody. The application of the Fourth Amendment's requirement of probable cause does not depend on whether an intrusion of this magnitude is termed an 'arrest' under state law. The mere facts that petitioner was not told he was under arrest, was not 'booked,' and would not have had an arrest record if the interrogation had proved fruitless, * * * obviously do not make petitioner's seizure even roughly analogous to the narrowly defined intrusions involved in *Terry* and its progeny. Indeed, any 'exception' that could cover a seizure as intrusive as that in this case would threaten to swallow the general rule that Fourth Amendment seizures are 'reasonable' only if based on probable cause. * * *

"In effect, respondents urge us to adopt a multifactor balancing test of 'reasonable police conduct under the circumstances' to cover all seizures that do not amount to technical arrests. But the protections intended by the Framers could all too easily disappear in the consideration and balancing of the multifarious circumstances presented by different cases, especially when that balancing may be done in the first instance by police officers engaged in the 'often competitive enterprise of ferreting out crime.' A single, familiar standard is essential to guide police officers, who have only limited time and expertise to reflect on and balance the social and individual interests involved in the specific circumstances they confront. Indeed, our recognition of these dangers, and our consequent reluctance to depart from the proven protections afforded by the general rule, is reflected in the narrow limitations emphasized in the cases employing the balancing test. For all but those narrowly defined intrusions, the requisite 'balancing' has been performed in centuries of precedent and is embodied in the principle that seizures are 'reasonable' only if supported by probable cause."

Justice Brennan then concluded "that the treatment of petitioner, whether or not it is technically characterized as an arrest, must be supported by probable cause" because "detention for custodial interrogation—regardless of its label—intrudes so severely on interests protected by the Fourth Amendment as necessarily to trigger the traditional safeguards against illegal arrest."

WHITE, J., concurring, cautioned that the majority opinion should not be read to mean that *Terry* "is an almost unique exception to a hard-and-fast standard of probable cause," and added that it was "enough, for me, that the police conduct here is similar enough to an arrest that the normal level of probable cause is necessary before the interests of privacy and personal security must give way." REHNQUIST, J., joined by the Chief Justice in dissent, indicated he "would have little difficulty joining" the opinion of the Court but for his conclusion that no Fourth Amendment seizure had occurred: "After learning that the person who answered the door was petitioner, the officer asked him if he would accompany the officers to police headquarters for questioning, and petitioner responded that he would. Petitioner was not told that he was under arrest or in custody and was not warned not to resist or flee. No weapons were displayed and petitioner was not handcuffed. Each officer testified that petitioner was not touched or held during the trip downtown; his freedom of action was not in any way restrained by the police. In short, the police behavior in this case was entirely free of 'physical force or show of authority.'"

SECTION 9. ADMINISTRATIVE INSPECTIONS AND REGULATORY SEARCHES: MORE ON BALANCING THE NEED AGAINST THE INVASION OF PRIVACY

The Supreme Court has upheld a rather broad range of searches and seizures even when conducted without the traditional quantum of probable cause. These decisions manifest further application of the *Camara* balancing test, also used by the Court in *Terry*, p. 291, to assay the discrete police practice of stop-and-frisk. But *Camara* itself was an administrative inspection type of case, and thus it is not surprising that this balancing process has since been utilized most often regarding various other administrative inspections and regulatory searches, where the Court typically has emphasized certain "special needs" beyond those present in the more typical law enforcement context.

Collectively, the cases briefly summarized below reflect two kinds of departures from the traditional probable cause requirement. One, as in *Terry*, is to require individualized suspicion (typically referred to as reasonable suspicion) less compelling than is need for the usual arrest or search. (In contrast to the rule in a regular law enforcement context, see *Ybarra*, p. 197, and *Hicks*, p. 244, such reasonable suspicion sometimes suffices even to search for incriminating evidence.) Another kind of departure is to require no individualized suspicion whatsoever, but instead to require that the seizure or search be conducted pursuant to some neutral criteria which guard against arbitrary selection of those subjected to such procedures (similar to the impoundment-inventory process approved in *Bertine*, p. 283).

1. **Safety inspections.** In *Camara v. Municipal Court,* 387 U.S. 523, 87 S.Ct. 1727, 18 L.Ed.2d 930 (1967), dealing with fire, health, and housing code inspection programs directed at dwellings, the Court concluded that if an occupant

did not consent to an inspection the authorities would ordinarily have to get a warrant,[a] but "that 'probable cause' to issue a warrant to inspect must exist if reasonable legislative or administrative standards for conducting an area inspection are satisfied with respect to a particular dwelling. Such standards, which will vary with the municipal program being enforced, may be based upon the passage of time, the nature of the building (e.g., a multi-family apartment house), or the condition of the entire area, but they will not necessarily depend upon specific knowledge of the condition of the particular dwelling." Among the "persuasive factors" identified by the Court "to support the reasonableness of area code-enforcement inspections" were (i) doubt "that any other canvassing technique would achieve acceptable results," and (ii) that the contemplated inspections "involve a relatively limited invasion of the urban citizen's privacy" as compared to execution of the more traditional search warrant.[b]

A *Camara*-type warrant "showing that a specific business has been chosen * * * on the basis of a general administrative plan * * * derived from neutral sources" also suffices for inspection of business premises. *Marshall v. Barlow's, Inc.,* 436 U.S. 307, 98 S.Ct. 1816, 56 L.Ed.2d 305 (1978). But the Court has often upheld warrantless business inspections by emphasizing the "closely regulated" nature of the business and that the inspection permitted by statute or regulations is "carefully limited in time, place, and scope," as in *New York v. Burger,* 482 U.S. 691, 107 S.Ct. 2636, 96 L.Ed.2d 601 (1987). In *Burger,* the Court upheld such warrantless inspections of junkyards even though the administrative scheme concerned a social problem (stolen property) also addressed in the penal law, police officers were allowed to make the inspections, and the inspections would often uncover evidence of crime. (But see Note 7.)

2. *Border searches*. In *United States v. Ramsey,* 431 U.S. 606, 97 S.Ct. 1972, 52 L.Ed.2d 617 (1977), upholding a customs inspection of mail entering the United States (which, by regulation, could not extend to reading of correspondence), the Court stressed (i) that the search was constitutional under the longstanding rule generally applicable to border searches, namely, that such searches are "considered to be 'reasonable' by the single fact that the person or item in question had entered into our country from outside"; and (ii) that the lower court was wrong in concluding a warrant would be needed as to mail, for "the 'border search' exception is not based on the doctrine of 'exigent circumstances' at all."

---

a. Three dissenters objected: "This boxcar warrant will be identical as to every dwelling in the area, save the street number itself. I daresay they will be printed up in pads of a thousand or more—with space for the street number to be inserted—and issued by magistrates in broadcast fashion as a matter of course."

b. Another type of safety inspection is that conducted after a fire. In *Michigan v. Clifford,* 464 U.S. 287, 104 S.Ct. 641, 78 L.Ed.2d 477 (1984), four Justices concluded that a burning building creates exigent circumstances justifying authorities to enter to fight the blaze and to remain a reasonable time to investigate the cause of the fire, but that later entries without consent require a warrant—an administrative warrant "to determine the cause and origin of a recent fire" on the showing "that a fire of undetermined origin has occurred on the prem-

ises, that the scope of the proposed search is reasonable and will not intrude unnecessarily on the fire victim's privacy, and that the search will be executed at a reasonable and convenient time"; or a conventional search warrant on probable cause if the "primary objective of the search is to gather evidence of criminal activity." A fifth Justice, concurring, opined that a "traditional criminal search warrant" should be required for any later entry without advance notice to the owner. The four dissenters agreed that a conventional warrant was required to search the balance of the home, but declared that a warrantless inspection of the fire scene was permissible because "the utility of requiring a magistrate to evaluate the grounds for a search following a fire is so limited that the incidental protection of an individual's privacy interests simply does not justify imposing a warrant requirement."

As for nonroutine border inspections, lower courts have generally held that "a real suspicion" is needed for a strip search, and the "clear indication" of *Schmerber,* p. 38, for a body cavity search. See, e.g., *Henderson v. United States,* 390 F.2d 805 (9th Cir.1967). In *United States v. Montoya de Hernandez,* 473 U.S. 531, 105 S.Ct. 3304, 87 L.Ed.2d 381 (1985), the Court held that when customs agents "reasonably suspect that the traveler is smuggling contraband in her alimentary canal" she may be detained so long as is "necessary to either verify or dispel the suspicion" (i.e., if the suspect declines to submit to an x-ray, until a bowel movement occurs).

3. *Vehicle checkpoints.* In a series of cases dealing with the stopping of vehicles away from the border to see if they were occupied by illegal aliens, the Court held that while roving patrols could stop and search vehicles for illegal aliens only on probable cause, *Almeida–Sanchez v. United States,* 413 U.S. 266, 93 S.Ct. 2535, 37 L.Ed.2d 596 (1973), only *Terry*-type reasonable suspicion was needed for such patrols to engage in the more "modest" interference with Fourth Amendment interests which attends the stopping of motorists and inquiring briefly as to their residential status. Even at a permanent checkpoint away from the border, search of a vehicle for aliens is not permissible absent probable cause, *United States v. Ortiz,* 422 U.S. 891, 95 S.Ct. 2585, 45 L.Ed.2d 623 (1975), but the brief questioning of vehicle occupants at such checkpoints is permissible without any individualized suspicion whatsoever. *United States v. Martinez–Fuerte,* 428 U.S. 543, 96 S.Ct. 3074, 49 L.Ed.2d 1116 (1976). As to the latter practice, the Court emphasized (i) that "the potential interference with legitimate traffic is minimal"; and (ii) that such checkpoint operations "involve less discretionary enforcement activity," as "the officer may stop only those cars passing the checkpoint," which "is not chosen by officers in the field, but by officials responsible for making overall decisions as to the most effective allocation of limited enforcement resources."[c] The Court in *Martinez–Fuerte* also concluded that if more than the briefest inquiry was needed in a particular instance the vehicle could be referred to a secondary inspection area "on the basis of criteria that would not sustain a roving-patrol stop."

Consistent with those cases, the Court held in *Delaware v. Prouse,* 440 U.S. 648, 99 S.Ct. 1391, 59 L.Ed.2d 660 (1979), that absent reasonable suspicion the police may not stop individual vehicles for the purpose of checking the driver's license and the registration of the automobile. But the Court stressed it was not precluding states "from developing methods for spot checks that involve less intrusion or that do not involve the unconstrained exercise of discretion," and gave as "one possible alternative" the "questioning of all oncoming traffic at roadblock-type stops."

Then came *Michigan Dep't of State Police v. Sitz,* 496 U.S. 444, 110 S.Ct. 2481, 110 L.Ed.2d 412 (1990), upholding the sobriety checkpoint program there at issue. Important ingredients in that conclusion were: (i) the intrusion upon motorists is "slight"; (ii) the program sufficiently limited officers' discretion, as "checkpoints are selected pursuant to [established] guidelines, and uniformed police officers stop every approaching vehicle"; (iii) the program addressed the very serious "drunken driving problem"; and (iv) there was support in the record for the law enforcement judgment that such checkpoints were among the "reasonable alternatives" available for dealing with that problem. The Court emphasized it was addressing "only the initial stop of each motorist passing through a

c. The Court also rejected the argument "that routine stops at a checkpoint are permissible only if a warrant has given judicial authorization to the particular checkpoint location." As for defendant's reliance on *Camara* in this connection, the Court answered that there but not here a warrant was necessary to provide assurance to the individual involved that the government agent was acting under proper authorization.

checkpoint and the associated preliminary questioning and observation by checkpoint officers," and cautioned that "detention of particular motorists for more extensive field sobriety testing may require satisfaction of an individualized suspicion standard."

4. Search of students. Utilizing the *Camara* balancing test, the Court in *New Jersey v. T.L.O.*, 469 U.S. 325, 105 S.Ct. 733, 83 L.Ed.2d 720 (1985), struck "the balance between the school child's legitimate expectations of privacy and the school's equally legitimate needs to maintain an environment in which learning can take place" by holding: (i) "that school officials need not obtain a warrant before searching a student who is under their authority"; (ii) that ordinarily "a search of a student by a teacher or other school official will be 'justified at its inception' when there are reasonable grounds for suspecting that the search will turn up evidence that the student has violated or is violating either the law or the rules of the school"; and (iii) that such a search "will be permissible in its scope when the measures adopted are reasonably related to the objectives of the search and not excessively intrusive in light of the age and sex of the student and the nature of the infraction."

5. Supervision of parolees and probationers. In *Griffin v. Wisconsin*, 483 U.S. 868, 107 S.Ct. 3164, 97 L.Ed.2d 709 (1987), the Court concluded that a "State's operation of a probation system * * * likewise presents 'special needs' beyond normal law enforcement that may justify departures from the usual warrant and probable cause requirements." No warrant was required for search of the probationer's home, for it would not only "make it more difficult for probation officials to respond quickly to evidence of misconduct," but also would interfere with the probation officer's judgment as to "how close a supervision the probationer requires." Moreover, full probable cause was not required either, as such a requirement would also "reduce the deterrent effect of the supervisory arrangement" and would be "both unrealistic and destructive of the * * * continuing probation relationship."

6. Drug testing. While lower courts have approved government-mandated drug testing of government or private employees upon individualized reasonable suspicion, two programs not requiring such suspicion have been upheld by the Supreme Court. In *National Treasury Employees Union v. Von Raab*, 489 U.S. 656, 109 S.Ct. 1384, 103 L.Ed.2d 685 (1989), the Court held "that the suspicionless testing of employees who apply for promotion to positions directly involving the interdiction of illegal drugs, or to positions which require the incumbent to carry a firearm, is reasonable." The Court reasoned that because the testing program at issue "is not designed to serve the ordinary needs of law enforcement," a balancing process was proper, in which the "Government's compelling interests in preventing the promotion of drug users to positions where they might endanger the integrity of our Nation's borders or the life of the citizenry" outweighed the "diminished expectation of privacy" of "those who seek promotion to these positions."[d]

By similar balancing, the Court in *Skinner v. Railway Labor Executives' Ass'n*, 489 U.S. 602, 109 S.Ct. 1402, 103 L.Ed.2d 639 (1989), upheld blood and urine testing of railroad employees following major train accidents or incidents and the breath and urine testing of railroad employees who violate certain safety rules. In allowing such testing even "in the absence of * * * reasonable suspicion that any particular employee may be impaired," the Court emphasized (i) the special danger presented by the performance of "certain sensitive tasks while

d. Two Justices who joined the Court's decision in *Skinner* because of "the demonstrated frequency of drug and alcohol use by the targeted class of employees, and the demonstrated connection between such use and grave harm," dissented in *Von Raab* because the government was unable to cite "even a single instance" of such use or connection to harm.

under the influence"; (ii) the "diminished expectation of privacy that attaches to information pertaining to the fitness of covered employees"; and (iii) "the limited discretion" railroad employers had regarding who and when to test.

In *Vernonia School District 47J v. Acton,* 515 U.S. 646, 115 S.Ct. 2386, 132 L.Ed.2d 564 (1995), the Court upheld the district's policy under which each week 10% of the students then participating in school athletics were randomly selected for urinalysis. In reaching this conclusion, the Court emphasized (i) that "the schools' custodial and tutelary responsibility for children" means "students within the school environment have a lesser expectation of privacy than members of the population generally," especially as to medical examinations and procedures; (ii) that "legitimate privacy expectations are even less with regard to student athletes," who by going out for a team "voluntarily subject themselves to a degree of regulation even higher than that imposed on students generally"; (iii) that the "privacy-invasive aspect of urinalysis" was kept at a minimum; (iv) that the district court's findings that a large segment of the student body was "in a state of rebellion * * * fueled by alcohol and drug abuse" manifested "an immediate crisis of greater proportions than existed" in *Skinner* or *Von Raab*; and (v) "that a drug problem largely fueled by the 'role model' effect of athletes' drug use, and of particular danger to athletes, is effectively addressed by making sure that athletes do not use drugs." But the Court in *Acton* then "caution[ed] against the assumption that suspicionless drug testing will readily pass constitutional muster in other contexts."[e]

7. *"Special needs" vs. ordinary law enforcement.* Whenever departure from the usual warrant and/or probable cause requirements is claimed to be justified on the basis of some "special need," it is necessary that this need be sufficiently different from and divorced from the state's general law enforcement interest, as is highlighted in two recent cases: *City of Indianapolis v. Edmond,* 531 U.S. 32, 121 S.Ct. 447, 148 L.Ed.2d 333 (2000); and *Ferguson v. City of Charleston,* 532 U.S. 67, 121 S.Ct. 1281, 149 L.Ed.2d 205 (2001).

In *Edmond,* the Court held that city-operated vehicle checkpoints, complete with drug dogs, undertaken to interdict unlawful drugs, contravened the Fourth Amendment. As for the city's reliance on *Martinez-Fuerte, Prouse* and *Sitz,* the *Edmond* majority, per O'Connor, J., distinguished those cases because in none of them "did we indicate approval of a checkpoint program whose primary purpose was to detect evidence of ordinary criminal wrongdoing."[f] As for the city's response that securing the border and apprehending drunk drivers "are * * * law enforcement activities, and law enforcement officers employ arrests and criminal prosecutions in pursuit of these goals," the Court responded that analysis at that "high level of generality" would mean there "would be little check on the ability

---

e. Compare *Chandler v. Miller,* 520 U.S. 305, 117 S.Ct. 1295, 137 L.Ed.2d 513 (1997), invalidating a Georgia statute requiring each candidate for public office to submit to drug testing, where the Court stated: "Georgia asserts no evidence of a drug problem among the State's elected officials, those officials typically do not perform high-risk, safety-sensitive tasks, and the required certification immediately aids no interdiction effort. The need revealed, in short, is symbolic, not 'special,' as that term draws meaning from our case law." As for the state's reliance on *Von Raab,* the Court noted that there the affected employees and their work product were not amenable to "day-to-day scrutiny," and then concluded:

"Candidates for public office, in contrast, are subject to relentless scrutiny—by their peers, the public, and the press. Their day-to-day conduct attracts attention notable beyond the norm in ordinary work environments."

f. But the Court did add: "Of, course, there are circumstances that may justify a law enforcement checkpoint where the primary purpose would otherwise, but for some emergency, relate to ordinary crime control. For example, * * * the Fourth Amendment would almost certainly permit an appropriately tailored roadblock set up to thwart an imminent terrorist attack or to catch a dangerous criminal who is likely to flee by way of a particular route."

of the authorities to construct roadblocks for almost any conceivable law enforcement purpose."[g]

In *Ferguson*, a task force made up of representatives of the Charleston public hospital, police and other public officials developed a policy for identifying and testing pregnant patients suspected of drug use and then turning the results over to law enforcement agents without the knowledge or consent of the patients. This policy, which also contained procedures for arresting patients and for prosecuting them for drug offenses and/or child neglect, was challenged by a group of obstetrical patients at that hospital who had been arrested after testing positive for cocaine. The question, as the Court, per Stevens, J., put it, was "whether the interest in using the threat of criminal sanctions to deter pregnant women from using cocaine can justify a departure from the general rule that an official nonconsensual search is unconstitutional if not authorized by a valid warrant." The majority noted that the instant case was different from *Acton* and the Court's other prior drug testing cases in several material respects: for one, in the previous cases "there was no misunderstanding about the purpose of the test or the potential use of the test results, and there were protections against the dissemination of the results to third parties." But the "critical difference" between the earlier cases and the instant one, the Court emphasized, "lies in the nature of the 'special need' asserted as justification for the warrantless searches," for in all the earlier cases the "special need" advanced was "one divorced from the State's general interest in law enforcement," while here "the central and indispensable feature of the policy from its inception was the use of law enforcement to coerce the patients into substance abuse treatment." As for the respondents' argument that their ultimate purpose of protecting both the mother and child was "a beneficent one," the majority responded that the policy itself "plainly reveals" that the purpose actually served "is ultimately indistinguishable from the general interest in crime control," for "an initial and continuing focus of the policy was on the arrest and prosecution of drug-abusing mothers," and local "prosecutors and police were extensively involved in the day-to-day administration of the policy." And it made no difference that the "threat of law enforcement" may have been "a means to an end," for if that did make a difference then "virtually any nonconsensual suspicionless search could be immunized under the special needs doctrine by defining the search solely in terms of its ultimate, rather than immediate purpose."[h]

SECTION 10. CONSENT SEARCHES

Consent searches are frequently relied upon by the police because they involve no time-consuming paper work and offer an opportunity to search even when probable cause is lacking. Thus, the constitutional protection against unreasonable search and seizure widens or narrows, depending on the difficulty or

g. Rehnquist, C.J., for the three dissenters, argued that the checkpoints at issue shared the critical characteristics of those previously approved by the Court: they "effectively serve the State's legitimate interests; they are executed in a regularized and neutral manner, and they only minimally intrude upon the privacy of the motorists."

h. Kennedy, J., concurring, questioned the latter point and would have rested the decision solely on the fact that none of the Court's "special needs precedents has sanctioned the routine inclusion of law enforcement, both in the design of the policy and in using arrests, either threatened or real, to implement the system designed for the special needs objectives." Scalia, J., for the three dissenters, objected that it was not so that "the addition of a law-enforcement related purpose to a legitimate medical purpose destroys applicability of the 'special-needs' doctrine," "since the special-needs doctrine was developed, and is ordinarily employed, precisely to enable searches by law enforcement officials who, of course, ordinarily have a law enforcement objective," as illustrated by *Griffin*.

ease with which the prosecution can establish that the defendant (or some other authorized person) has "consented" to what would otherwise be an unconstitutional invasion of his privacy.

A. THE NATURE OF "CONSENT"

SCHNECKLOTH v. BUSTAMONTE

412 U.S. 218, 93 S.Ct. 2041, 36 L.Ed.2d 854 (1973).

Justice STEWART delivered the opinion of the Court. * * *

[A police officer stopped a car containing six men when he observed that one headlight and the license plate light were burned out. After the driver could not produce a license, the officer asked a passenger who claimed he was the vehicle owner's brother if he could search the car, and the passenger replied, "Sure, go ahead." The driver "helped in the search of the car, by opening the trunk and glove compartment." Stolen checks were found under a seat, leading to charges against passenger Bustamonte, whose motion to suppress was denied. His conviction was affirmed on appeal; the federal district court denied his petition for a writ of habeas corpus, but the 9th Circuit court of appeals set aside the district court's order.]

The precise question in this case, then, is what must the state prove to demonstrate that a consent was "voluntarily" given. * * *

The most extensive judicial exposition of the meaning of "voluntariness" has been developed in those cases in which the Court has had to determine the "voluntariness" of a defendant's confession for purposes of the Fourteenth Amendment. * * * It is to that body of case law to which we turn for initial guidance on the meaning of "voluntariness" in the present context. * * *

The significant fact about all of these decisions is that none of them turned on the presence or absence of a single controlling criterion; each reflected a careful scrutiny of all the surrounding circumstances. In none of them did the Court rule that the Due Process Clause required the prosecution to prove as part of its initial burden that the defendant knew he had a right to refuse to answer the questions that were put. While the state of the accused's mind, and the failure of the police to advise the accused of his rights, were certainly factors to be evaluated in assessing the "voluntariness" of an accused's responses, they were not in and of themselves determinative.

Similar considerations lead us to agree with the courts of California that the question whether a consent to a search was in fact "voluntary" or was the product of duress or coercion, express or implied, is a question of fact to be determined from the totality of all the circumstances. While knowledge of the right to refuse consent is one factor to be taken into account, the government need not establish such knowledge as the *sine qua non* of an effective consent. As with police questioning, two competing concerns must be accommodated in determining the meaning of a "voluntary" consent—the legitimate need for such searches and the equally important requirement of assuring the absence of coercion.

In situations where the police have some evidence of illicit activity, but lack probable cause to arrest or search, a search authorized by a valid consent may be the only means of obtaining important and reliable evidence. In the present case for example, while the police had reason to stop the car for traffic violations, the State does not contend that there was probable cause to search the vehicle or that the search was incident to a valid arrest of any of the occupants. Yet, the search yielded tangible evidence that served as a basis for a prosecution, and provided some assurance that others, wholly innocent of the crime, were not mistakenly brought to trial. And in those cases where there is probable cause to arrest or search, but where the police lack a warrant, a consent search may still be valuable. If the search is conducted and proves fruitless, that in itself may convince the police that an arrest with its possible stigma and embarrassment is unnecessary, or that a far more extensive search pursuant to a warrant is not justified. In short a search pursuant to consent may result in considerably less inconvenience for the subject of the search, and, properly conducted, is a constitutionally permissible and wholly legitimate aspect of effective police activity.

But the Fourth and Fourteenth Amendments require that a consent not be coerced, by explicit or implicit means, by implied threat or covert force. For, no matter how subtly the coercion were applied, the resulting "consent" would be no more than a pretext for the unjustified police intrusion against which the Fourth Amendment is directed. * * *

The problem of reconciling the recognized legitimacy of consent searches with the requirement that they be free from any aspect of official coercion cannot be resolved by an infallible touchstone. To approve such searches without the most careful scrutiny would sanction the possibility of official coercion; to place artificial restrictions upon such searches would jeopardize their basic validity. Just as was true with confessions, the requirement of a "voluntary" consent reflects a fair accommodation of the constitutional requirements involved. In examining all the surrounding circumstances to determine if in fact the consent to search was coerced, account must be taken of subtly coercive police questions, as well as the possibly vulnerable subjective state of the person who consents. Those searches that are the product of police coercion can thus be filtered out without undermining the continuing validity of consent searches. In sum, there is no reason for us to depart in the area of consent searches, from the traditional definition of "voluntariness."

The approach of the Court of Appeals for the Ninth Circuit finds no support in any of our decisions that have attempted to define the meaning of "voluntariness." Its ruling, that the State must affirmatively prove that the subject of the search knew that he had a right to refuse consent, would, in practice, create serious doubt whether consent searches could continue to be conducted. There might be rare cases where it could be proved from the record that a person in fact affirmatively knew of his right to refuse—such as a case where he announced to the police that if he didn't sign the consent form, "you [police] are going to get a search warrant;" or a case where by prior experience and training a person had clearly and convincingly demonstrated such knowledge. But more commonly where there was no evidence of any coercion, explicit or implicit, the prosecution would nevertheless be unable to demonstrate that the subject of the search in fact had known of his right to refuse consent.

The very object of the inquiry—the nature of a person's subjective understanding—underlines the difficulty of the prosecution's burden under the rule applied by the Court of Appeals in this case. Any defendant who was the subject of a search authorized solely by his consent could effectively frustrate the introduction into evidence of the fruits of that search by simply failing to testify that he in fact knew he could refuse to consent. And the near impossibility of meeting this prosecutorial burden suggests why this Court has never accepted any such litmus-paper test of voluntariness. * * *

One alternative that would go far towards proving that the subject of a search did know he had a right to refuse consent would be to advise him of that right before eliciting his consent. That, however, is a suggestion that has been almost universally repudiated by both federal and state courts, and, we think, rightly so. For it would be thoroughly impractical to impose on the normal consent search the detailed requirements of an effective warning.[a] Consent searches are part of the standard investigatory techniques of law enforcement agencies. They normally occur on the highway, or in a person's home or office, and under informal and unstructured conditions. The circumstances that prompt the initial request to search may develop quickly or be a logical extension of investigative police questioning. The police may seek to investigate further suspicious circumstances or to follow up leads developed in questioning persons at the scene of a crime. These situations are a far cry from the structured atmosphere of a trial where, assisted by counsel if he chooses, a defendant is informed of his trial rights. And, while surely a closer question, these situations are still immeasurably far removed from "custodial interrogation" where, in *Miranda v. Arizona* [p. 462], we found that the Constitution required certain now familiar warnings as a prerequisite to police interrogation. * * *

It is said, however, that a "consent" is a "waiver" of a person's rights under the Fourth and Fourteenth Amendments. The argument is that by allowing the police to conduct a search, a person "waives" whatever right he had to prevent the police from searching. It is argued that under the doctrine of *Johnson v. Zerbst*, 304 U.S. 458, 58 S.Ct. 1019, 82 L.Ed. 1461 (1938), to establish such a "waiver" the state must demonstrate "an intentional relinquishment or abandonment of a known right or privilege." * * *

Almost without exception the requirement of a knowing and intelligent waiver has been applied only to those rights which the Constitution guarantees to a criminal defendant in order to preserve a fair trial. Hence, and hardly surprisingly in view of the facts of *Johnson* itself, the standard of a knowing and intelligent waiver has most often been applied to test the validity of a waiver of counsel, either at trial, or upon a guilty plea. And the Court has also applied the *Johnson* criteria to assess the effectiveness of a waiver of other trial rights such as the right to confrontation, to a jury trial, and to a speedy trial, and the right to be free from twice being placed in jeopardy. Guilty pleas have been carefully scrutinized to determine whether the accused knew and understood all the rights to which he would be entitled at trial, and that he had intentionally chosen to forgo them. And the Court has evaluated the knowing and intelligent nature of the waiver of trial rights in trial-type situations, such as the waiver of the privilege against compulsory self-incrimination before an administrative agency or a congressional committee, or the waiver of counsel in a juvenile proceeding.

The guarantees afforded a criminal defendant at trial also protect him at certain stages before the actual trial, and any alleged waiver must meet the strict standard of an intentional relinquishment of a "known" right. But the "trial" guarantees that have been applied to the "pretrial" stage of the criminal process are similarly designed to protect the fairness of the trial itself. * * *[b]

The standards of *Johnson* were, therefore, found to be a necessary prerequisite to a finding of a valid waiver.[29] * * *

---

a. Relying upon this language, the Court later held in *Ohio v. Robinette*, 519 U.S. 33, 117 S.Ct. 417, 136 L.Ed.2d 347 (1996), that if a person has been lawfully seized, for example, because of commission of a traffic violation, and following the point at which the detainee would be free to go he consents to a search, that consent is not involuntary because the officer failed to specifically advise the detainee that he was free to go, as a requirement of such warnings would be equally "unrealistic."

b. At this point, the Court noted that "the standard of a knowing and intelligent waiver" applies to waiver of counsel at a lineup under *United States v. Wade*, p. 618, and *Gilbert v. California*, p. 618, because counsel is provided to protect the right of cross-examination at trial; and that the same standard applies to waiver of counsel at custodial interrogation under *Miranda v. Arizona*, p. 462, because counsel is provided to ensure that the safeguards concerning the giving of testimony at trial do not "become empty formalities."

29. As we have already noted, *Miranda* itself involved interrogation of a suspect detained in custody and did not concern the

A strict standard of waiver has been applied to those rights guaranteed to a criminal defendant to insure that he will be accorded the greatest possible opportunity to utilize every facet of the constitutional model of a fair criminal trial. Any trial conducted in derogation of that model leaves open the possibility that the trial reached an unfair result precisely because all the protections specified in the Constitution were not provided. A prime example is the right to counsel. For without that right, a wholly innocent accused faces the real and substantial danger that simply because of his lack of legal expertise he may be convicted. * * *

The protections of the Fourth Amendment are of a wholly different order, and have nothing whatever to do with promoting the fair ascertainment of truth at a criminal trial. Rather, as Justice Frankfurter's opinion for the Court put it in *Wolf v. Colorado* [p. 108], the Fourth Amendment protects the "security of one's privacy against arbitrary intrusion by the police. . . . " * * *

Nor can it even be said that a search, as opposed to an eventual trial, is somehow "unfair" if a person consents to a search. While the Fourth and Fourteenth Amendments limit the circumstances under which the police can conduct a search, there is nothing constitutionally suspect in a person voluntarily allowing a search. The actual conduct of the search may be precisely the same as if the police had obtained a warrant. And, unlike those constitutional guarantees that protect a defendant at trial, it cannot be said every reasonable presumption ought to be indulged against voluntary relinquishment. We have only recently stated: "[I]t is no part of the policy underlying the Fourth and Fourteenth Amendments to discourage citizens from aiding to the utmost of their ability in the apprehension of criminals." *Coolidge v. New Hampshire,* [p. 190]. Rather the community has a real interest in encouraging consent, for the resulting search may yield necessary evidence for the solution and prosecution of crime, evidence that may insure that a wholly innocent person is not wrongly charged with a criminal offense.

Those cases that have dealt with the application of the *Johnson v. Zerbst* rule make clear that it would be next to impossible to apply to a consent search the standard of "an intentional relinquishment or abandonment of a known right or privilege." To be true to *Johnson* and its progeny, there must be examination into the knowing and understanding nature of the waiver, an examination that was designed for a trial judge in the structured atmosphere of a courtroom. * * * It would be unrealistic to expect that in the informal, unstructured context of a consent search, a policeman, upon pain of tainting the evidence obtained, could make the detailed type of examination demanded by *Johnson.* And, if for this reason a diluted form of "waiver" were found acceptable, that would itself be ample recognition of the fact that there is no universal standard that must be applied in every situation where a person forgoes a constitutional right.[33]

investigatory procedures of the police in general on-the-scene questioning. By the same token, the present case does not require a determination of the proper standard to be applied in assessing the validity of a search authorized solely by an alleged consent that is obtained from a person after he has been placed in custody. We do note, however, that other courts have been particularly sensitive to the heightened possibilities for coercion when the "consent" to a search was given by a person in custody.

33. It seems clear that even a limited view of the demands of "an intentional relinquish-ment or abandonment of a known right or privilege" standard would inevitably lead to a requirement of detailed warnings before any consent search—a requirement all but universally rejected to date. As the Court stated in *Miranda* with respect to the privilege against compulsory self-incrimination: "[W]e will not pause to inquire in individual cases whether the defendant was aware of his rights without a warning being given. Assessments of the knowledge the defendant possessed, based on information as to his age, education, intelligence, or prior contact with authorities, can never be more than speculation; a warning is a clearcut fact."

Similarly, a "waiver" approach to consent searches would be thoroughly inconsistent with our decisions that have approved "third party consents." In *Coolidge v. New Hampshire,* where a wife surrendered to the police guns and clothing belonging to her husband, we found nothing constitutionally impermissible in the admission of that evidence at trial since the wife had not been coerced. *Frazier v. Cupp,* [p. 346], held that evidence seized from the defendant's duffel bag in a search authorized by his cousin's consent was admissible at trial. We found that the defendant had assumed the risk that his cousin with whom he shared the bag would allow the police to search it. And in *Hill v. California,* 401 U.S. 797, 91 S.Ct. 1106, 28 L.Ed.2d 484 (1971), we held that the police had validly seized evidence from the petitioner's apartment incident to the arrest of a third party, since the police had probable cause to arrest the petitioner and reasonably though mistakenly believed the man they had arrested was he. Yet it is inconceivable that the Constitution could countenance the waiver of a defendant's right to counsel by a third party, or that a waiver could be found because a trial judge reasonably though mistakenly believed a defendant had waived his right to plead not guilty.
* * *

Much of what has already been said disposes of the argument that the Court's decision in the *Miranda* case requires the conclusion that knowledge of a right to refuse is an indispensable element of a valid consent. The considerations that informed the Court's holding in *Miranda* are simply inapplicable in the present case. In *Miranda* the Court found that the techniques of police questioning and the nature of custodial surroundings produce an inherently coercive situation. The Court concluded that "[u]nless adequate protective devices are employed to dispel the compulsion inherent in custodial surroundings, no statement obtained from the defendant can truly be the product of his free choice." And at another point the Court noted that "without proper safeguards the process of in-custody interrogation of persons suspected or accused of crime contains inherently compelling pressures which work to undermine the individual's will to resist and to compel him to speak where he would not otherwise do so freely."

In this case there is no evidence of any inherently coercive tactics—either from the nature of the police questioning or the environment in which it took place. Indeed, since consent searches will normally occur on a person's own familiar territory, the spectre of incommunicado police interrogation in some remote station house is simply inapposite. There is no reason to believe, under circumstances such as are present here, that the response to a policeman's question is presumptively coerced; and there is, therefore, no reason to reject the traditional test for determining the voluntariness of a person's response. *Miranda,* of course, did not reach investigative questioning of a person not in custody, which is most directly analogous to the situation of a consent search, and it assuredly did not indicate that such questioning ought to be deemed inherently coercive.

It is also argued that the failure to require the Government to establish knowledge as a prerequisite to a valid consent, will relegate the Fourth Amendment to the special province of "the sophisticated, the knowledgeable, and the privileged." We cannot agree. The traditional definition of voluntariness we accept today has always taken into account evidence of minimal schooling, low intelligence, and the lack of any effective warnings to a person of his rights; and the voluntariness of any statement taken under those conditions has been carefully scrutinized to determine whether it was in fact voluntarily given.

Our decision today is a narrow one. We hold only that when the subject of a search is not in custody and the State attempts to justify a search on the basis of his consent, the Fourth and Fourteenth Amendments require that it demonstrate that the consent was in fact voluntarily given, and not the result of duress or coercion, express or implied. Voluntariness is a question of fact to be determined from all the circumstances, and while the subject's knowledge of a right to refuse is a factor to be taken into account, the prosecution is not required to demonstrate such knowledge as a prerequisite to establishing a voluntary consent.[c]

Justice MARSHALL, dissenting. * * *

The Fifth Amendment, in terms, provides that no person "shall be compelled in any criminal case to be a witness against himself." Nor is the interest protected by the Due Process Clause of the Fourteenth Amendment any different. The inquiry in a case where a confession is challenged as having been elicited in an unconstitutional manner is, therefore, whether the behavior of the police amounted to compulsion of the defendant. * * *

In contrast, this case deals not with "coercion," but with "consent," a subtly different concept to which different standards have been applied in the past. Freedom from coercion is a substantive right, guaranteed by the Fifth and Fourteenth Amendments. Consent, however, is a mechanism by which substantive requirements, otherwise applicable, are avoided. * * * Thus, consent searches are permitted not because such an exception to the requirements of probable cause and warrant is essential to proper law enforcement, but because we permit our citizens to choose whether or not they wish to exercise their constitutional rights. Our prior decisions simply do not support the view that a meaningful choice has been made solely because no coercion was brought to bear on the subject. * * *

If consent to search means that a person has chosen to forego his right to exclude the police from the place they seek to search, it follows that his consent cannot be considered a meaningful choice unless he knew that he could in fact exclude the police. * * * I would therefore hold, at a minimum, that the prosecution may not rely on a purported consent to search if the subject of the search did not know that he could refuse to give consent. Where the police claim authority to search yet in fact lack such authority, the subject does not know that he may permissibly refuse them entry, and it is this lack of knowledge that invalidates the consent. * * *

The burden on the prosecutor would disappear, of course, if the police, at the time they requested consent to search, also told the subject that he had a right to refuse consent and thus his decision to refuse would be respected. The Court's assertions to the contrary notwithstanding, there is nothing impractical about this method of satisfying the prosecution's burden of proof. * * *

The Court contends that if an officer paused to inform the subject of his rights, the informality of the exchange would be destroyed. I doubt that a simple statement by an officer of an individual's right to refuse consent would do much to alter the informality of the exchange, except to alert the subject to a fact that he surely is entitled to know. It is not without significance that for many years the agents of the Federal Bureau of Investigation have routinely informed subjects of their right to refuse consent, when they request consent to search. The reported cases in which the police have informed subject of their right to refuse consent show, also, that the information can be given without disrupting the casual flow of events. What evidence there is, then, rather strongly suggests that nothing disastrous would happen if the police, before requesting consent, informed the

c. Powell, J., joined by the Chief Justice and Rehnquist, J., concurred on the ground "that federal collateral review of a state prisoner's Fourth Amendment claims—claims which rarely bear on innocence—should be confined solely to the question of whether the petitioner was provided a fair opportunity to raise and have adjudicated the question in state courts." Blackmun, J., concurred to ex-

press substantial agreement with the Powell opinion. Douglas, J., dissenting, would have remanded for a determination of whether Alcala knew he had the right to refuse. Brennan, J., dissenting, declared: "It wholly escapes me how our citizens can meaningfully be said to have waived something as precious as a constitutional guarantee without ever being aware of its existence."

subject that he had a right to refuse consent and that his refusal would be respected.[12]

I must conclude, with some reluctance, that when the Court speaks of practicality, what it really is talking of is the continued ability of the police to capitalize on the ignorance of citizens so as to accomplish by subterfuge what they could not achieve by relying only on the knowing relinquishment of constitutional rights. * * *

NOTES ON THE RELEVANT FACTORS IN DETERMINING THE VALIDITY OF A CONSENT

1. *What is the issue?* Some courts, as did the court of appeals in *Busta-monte,* 448 F.2d 699 (9th Cir.1971), characterize a consent to search as "a waiver of a constitutional right" and thus focus upon the state of mind of the person allegedly giving the consent. Some other courts look instead to the state of mind of the officer seeking the consent; the question is said to be whether "the officers, as reasonable men, could conclude that defendant's consent was given," e.g., *People v. Henderson,* 210 N.E.2d 483 (Ill.1965). Does *Bustamonte* clearly indicate a choice of either of these theories? Cf. *Florida v. Jimeno,* p. 340, and *Illinois v. Rodriguez,* p. 341. An illustration of how the choice of one of these theories over the other might affect the outcome is provided by *United States v. Elrod,* 441 F.2d 353 (5th Cir.1971), holding: "No matter how genuine the belief of the officers is that the consenter is apparently of sound mind and deliberately acting, the search depending upon his consent fails if it is judicially determined that he lacked mental capacity. It is not that the actions of the officers were imprudent or unfounded. It is that the key to validity—consent—is lacking for want of mental capacity, no matter how much concealed."

2. *Claim or show of authority.* In *Bumper v. North Carolina,* 391 U.S. 543, 88 S.Ct. 1788, 20 L.Ed.2d 797 (1968), defendant's grandmother allowed the police to search her house after one of them announced, "I have a search warrant to search your house." At the hearing on the motion to suppress the rifle found therein, the prosecutor did not rely upon a warrant to justify the search. The Supreme Court was advised that the officers did have a warrant, but none was ever returned and nothing was known about the conditions under which it was issued. The Court held, 7–2, per Stewart, J., that a search cannot be justified on the basis of consent "when that 'consent' has been given only after the official conducting the search has asserted that he possesses a warrant," as when "a law enforcement officer claims authority to search a home under a warrant, he announces in effect that the occupant has no right to resist the search. The situation is instinct with coercion—albeit colorably lawful coercion. Where there is coercion there cannot be consent."

What if the grandmother had responded to the police, "You don't need a search warrant, go ahead"? What if the officer in *Bumper* had merely threatened to obtain a search warrant? Consider *United States v. Boukater,* 409 F.2d 537 (5th Cir.1969) (coercive unless the officer actually had grounds to obtain a warrant or he merely said he would seek a search warrant). The "claim of lawful authority"

---

12. The Court's suggestion that it would be "unrealistic" to require the officers to make "the detailed type of examination" involved when a court considers whether a defendant has waived a trial right, deserves little comment. The question before us relates to the inquiry to be made in court when the prosecution seeks to establish that consent was given.

I therefore do not address the Court's strained argument that one may waive constitutional rights without making a knowing and intentional choice so long as the rights do not relate to the fairness of a criminal trial. I would suggest, however, that that argument is fundamentally inconsistent with the law of unconstitutional conditions.

referred to in *Bumper* need not involve mention of a search warrant; a flat assertion by the police that they have come to search will suffice. *Amos v. United States,* 255 U.S. 313, 41 S.Ct. 266, 65 L.Ed. 654 (1921).

3. *Prior illegal police action.* Under the "fruit of the poisonous tree" doctrine of *Wong Sun,* p. 765, a consent may be held ineffective because obtained in exploitation of a prior illegal arrest.

4. *Mental or emotional state of the person.* Compare *United States v. Elrod,* Note 1 supra; and *Commonwealth v. Angivoni,* 417 N.E.2d 422 (Mass.1981) (voluntary consent of defendant in hospital emergency room with dislocated hip not established, as "defendant's understanding and ability to reason reflectively may have been impaired by intoxication or as a result of his injuries or an emotional trauma attendant to his just having been in an accident"); with the Supreme Court's more recent application of the voluntariness test in *Colorado v. Connelly,* p. 588.

5. *Denial of guilt.* Doesn't the ready discovery of incriminating evidence pursuant to the "consent" of a person who has denied his guilt manifest that the consent must have been involuntary? Yes, concluded the court in *Higgins v. United States,* 209 F.2d 819 (D.C.Cir.1954): "No sane man who denies his guilt would actually be willing that policemen search his room for contraband which is certain to be discovered." But in *Florida v. Bostick,* p. 299, in response to the defendant's contention that "no reasonable person would freely consent to a search of luggage that he or she knows contains drugs," the Court responded that such an "argument cannot prevail because the 'reasonable person' test presupposes an *innocent* person."

6. *Custody; Warning of Fourth Amendment rights.* In *United States v. Watson,* p. 203, the majority concluded that the failure to give the defendant Fourth Amendment warnings "is not to be given controlling significance" where, as there, the defendant "had been arrested and was in custody, but his consent was given while on a public street, not in the confines of the police station." Marshall and Brennan, JJ., dissenting, objected that the case should be remanded for reconsideration of the consent issue by the court of appeals in light of the fact that the "lack of custody was of decisional importance in *Schneckloth,* which repeatedly distinguished the case before it from one involving a suspect in custody."

In *Gentile v. United States,* 419 U.S. 979, 95 S.Ct. 241, 42 L.Ed.2d 191 (1974), where consent was obtained from the defendant during stationhouse custodial interrogation after the giving of the *Miranda* warnings but without Fourth Amendment warnings, Douglas and Marshall, JJ., dissenting from the denial of certiorari, noted: "When a suspect is in custody the situation is in control of the police. The pace of events will not somehow deny them an opportunity to give a warning, as the [*Schneckloth*] Court apparently feared would happen in noncustodial settings. Moreover, the custodial setting will permit easy documentation of both the giving of a warning and the arrestee's response."

7. *Warning of Fifth Amendment rights.* It has sometimes been held that a valid consent to search, given by a person in custody, must be preceded by *Miranda* warnings because "the request to search is a request that defendant be a witness against himself which he is privileged to refuse under the Fifth Amendment." *State v. Williams,* 432 P.2d 679 (Or.1967). But the prevailing view, as stated in *United States v. LaGrone,* 43 F.3d 332 (7th Cir.1994), is that "because requesting consent to search is not likely to elicit an incriminating statement, such questioning is not interrogation, and thus *Miranda* warnings are not required."

8. *Right to counsel*. In *Tidwell v. Superior Court,* 95 Cal.Rptr. 213 (App. 1971), the police asked petitioner, who was in jail, if they could search his car, which had been impounded. Petitioner allegedly replied, "Go ahead and search." The court held that petitioner's consent was ineffective since at the time he had been arraigned on a burglary charge and counsel had been appointed, yet the police had asked him to consent to the search without notifying his lawyer. Rejecting the argument that *Massiah* [p. 448] should apply only to "statements elicited and not to consents given," the court observed: "This distinction is very thin considering the incriminating effect a consent to search may have. The reasoning of [the cases protecting] defendants' right to effective aid of counsel applies equally to a consent given at the instigation of the police."

9. *"Consent" by deception*. In contrast to the type of deception allegedly used in *Bumper,* Note 3 supra, the police sometimes obtain evidence of criminal activity by acting in an undercover capacity and obtaining a "consent" which the defendant would not have given had he known the officer's true identity; see *Lewis v. United States,* p. 376, upholding this practice upon the facts presented. A third situation is that in which the officer's true identity is known but he misleads the suspect as to his intentions. Compare *Graves v. Beto,* 424 F.2d 524 (5th Cir.1970) (rape defendant's consent to blood test which resulted in matching his blood with that at crime scene not freely and intelligently given where his acquiescence was obtained by intimating that test was to be taken simply to determine whether he had a sufficient quantity of alcohol in his blood stream to be detained on a charge of public drunkenness); with *United States v. Andrews,* 746 F.2d 247 (5th Cir.1984) (federal agents asked to see shotgun on ruse they were trying to connect it with robberies, actual purpose was to establish defendant's crime of illegal possession of firearm by convicted felon; consent voluntary, *Graves* distinguished because "there is no evidence indicating that Andrews was assured his production of the guns would only be used to investigate the robberies").

10. *Scope of consent*. The standard for measuring the scope of a suspect's consent, the Court concluded in *Florida v. Jimeno,* 500 U.S. 248, 111 S.Ct. 1801, 114 L.Ed.2d 297 (1991), is neither the suspect's intent nor the officer's perception thereof but rather "that of 'objective' reasonableness—what would the typical reasonable person have understood by the exchange between the officer and the suspect?" Given the officer's statement in *Jimeno* that he would be looking for narcotics, "it was objectively reasonable for the police to conclude that the general consent to search respondent's car included consent to search containers within that car which might bear drugs." But, the nature of the container is also relevant. "It is very unreasonable to think that a suspect, by consenting to the search of his trunk, has agreed to the breaking open of a locked briefcase within the trunk, but it is otherwise with respect to a closed paper bag."

Does the *Jimeno* principle, that "the scope of the search is generally defined by its expressed object," suffice as to consent searches of the person? Consider *United States v. Rodney,* 956 F.2d 295 (D.C.Cir.1992) (sweeping motion over crotch area during consent search for drugs lawful, as it no more intrusive than a *Terry* frisk; court distinguishes *United States v. Blake,* 888 F.2d 795 (11th Cir.1989), suppressing drugs found on person, as that case involved "a direct 'frontal touching' of the defendant's private parts").

Does a consent, voluntary when given, justify a second search of the same place at a later time after a fruitless first search? Compare *People v. Nawrocki,* 148 N.W.2d 211 (Mich.App.1967) (defendant's consent to search his car construed as "permission to search the car at any time," thus justifying second search hours later after the car was impounded and the defendant was in jail); with *State v. Brochu,* 237 A.2d 418 (Me.1967) (contra where passage of time was greater, second search involved re-entry of defendant's home, and defendant's status had changed from suspect to accused in interim).

B. THIRD PARTY CONSENT[a]

ILLINOIS v. RODRIGUEZ

497 U.S. 177, 110 S.Ct. 2793, 111 L.Ed.2d 148 (1990).

Justice SCALIA delivered the opinion of the Court. * * *

[Gail Fischer, who showed signs of a severe beating, told police that she had been assaulted by Rodriguez earlier that day in an apartment on South California. Fischer stated that Rodriguez was then asleep in the apartment, and she consented to travel there with the police in order to unlock the door with her key so that the officers could enter and arrest him. During this conversation, Fischer several times referred to the apartment on South California as "our" apartment, and said that she had clothes and furniture there. The police drove to the apartment accompanied by Fischer, who unlocked the door with her key and gave the officers permission to enter. Inside they observed in plain view drug paraphernalia and containers filled with cocaine. The officers arrested Rodriguez and seized the drugs and related paraphernalia. Rodriguez, charged with possession of a controlled substance with intent to deliver, moved to suppress all evidence seized at the time of his arrest. The court granted the motion, holding that at the time she consented to the entry Fischer did not have common authority over the apartment.]

The Fourth Amendment generally prohibits the warrantless entry of a person's home, whether to make an arrest or to search for specific objects. The prohibition does not apply, however, to situations in which voluntary consent has been obtained, either from the individual whose property is searched, or from a third party who possesses common authority over the premises, see *United States v. Matlock,* [415 U.S. 164, 94 S.Ct. 988, 39 L.Ed.2d 242 (1974)]. The State of Illinois contends that that exception applies in the present case.

As we stated in *Matlock,* "[c]ommon authority" rests "on mutual use of the property by persons generally having joint access or control for most purposes."[b] The burden of establishing that common authority rests upon the State. On the basis of this record, it is clear that burden was not sustained. The evidence showed that although Fischer, with her two small children, had lived with Rodriguez beginning in December 1984, she had moved out on July 1, 1985, almost a month before the search at issue here, and had gone to live with her mother. She took her and her children's clothing with her, though leaving behind some furniture and household effects. During the period after July 1 she sometimes spent the night at Rodriguez's apartment, but never invited her friends there, and never went there herself when he was not home. Her name was not on the lease nor did she contribute to the rent. She had a key to the apartment, which she said at trial she had taken without Rodriguez's knowledge (though she testified at the preliminary hearing that Rodriguez had given her the key). On these facts the State has not established that, with respect to the South California apartment, Fischer had "joint access or control for most purposes." To the

---

a. See Mary I. Coombs, *Shared Privacy and the Fourth Amendment, or the Right of Relationships,* 75 Calif.L.Rev. 1593 (1987).

b. Where there is such "common authority," the Court went on to say in *Matlock,* "it is reasonable to recognize that any of the co-inhabitants has the right to permit the inspection in his own right and that the others have assumed the risk that one of their number might permit the common area to be searched."

contrary, the Appellate Court's determination of no common authority over the apartment was obviously correct.

[R]espondent asserts that permitting a reasonable belief of common authority to validate an entry would cause a defendant's Fourth Amendment rights to be "vicariously waived." We disagree.

We have been unyielding in our insistence that a defendant's waiver of his trial rights cannot be given effect unless it is "knowing" and "intelligent." We would assuredly not permit, therefore, evidence seized in violation of the Fourth Amendment to be introduced on the basis of a trial court's mere "reasonable belief"—derived from statements by unauthorized persons—that the defendant has waived his objection. But one must make a distinction between, on the one hand, trial rights that *derive* from the violation of constitutional guarantees and, on the other hand, the nature of those constitutional guarantees themselves. * * *

What Rodriguez is assured by the trial right of the exclusionary rule, where it applies, is that no evidence seized in violation of the Fourth Amendment will be introduced at his trial unless he consents. What he is assured by the Fourth Amendment itself, however, is not that no government search of his house will occur unless he consents; but that no such search will occur that is "unreasonable." There are various elements, of course, that can make a search of a person's house "reasonable"—one of which is the consent of the person or his cotenant. The essence of respondent's argument is that we should impose upon this element a requirement that we have not imposed upon other elements that regularly compel government officers to exercise judgment regarding the facts: namely, the requirement that their judgment be not only responsible but correct.[c]

[I]n order to satisfy the "reasonableness" requirement of the Fourth Amendment, what is generally demanded of the many factual determinations that must regularly be made by agents of the government—whether the magistrate issuing a warrant, the police officer executing a warrant, or the police officer conducting a search or seizure under one of the exceptions to the warrant requirement—is not that they always be correct, but that they always be reasonable. As we put it in *Brinegar v. United States,* [p. 298]:

> "Because many situations which confront officers in the course of executing their duties are more or less ambiguous, room must be allowed for some mistakes on their part. But the mistakes must be those of reasonable men, acting on facts leading sensibly to their conclusions of probability."

We see no reason to depart from this general rule with respect to facts bearing upon the authority to consent to a search. Whether the basis for such authority exists is the sort of recurring factual question to which law enforcement officials must be expected to apply their judgment; and all the Fourth Amendment requires is that they answer it reasonably. The Constitution is no more violated when officers enter without a warrant because they reasonably (though erroneously) believe that the person who has consented to their entry is a resident of the premises, than it is violated when they enter without a warrant because they reasonably (though erroneously) believe they are in pursuit of a violent felon who is about to escape.

Stoner v. California, [p. 345] is in our view not to the contrary. There, in holding that police had improperly entered the defendant's hotel room based on

---

c. In an omitted portion of the opinion, illustrations were given: (i) the probable cause requirement for a warrant, as to which the magistrate may act on "seemingly reliable but factually inaccurate information"; (ii) the warrant requirement, as to which the officer may be reasonably mistaken as to the warrant's scope, *Maryland v. Garrison,* p. 192; and (iii) the search incident to arrest doctrine, where the officer may be reasonably mistaken as to the person to be arrested, *Hill v. California,* p. 336.

the consent of a hotel clerk, we stated that "the rights protected by the Fourth Amendment are not to be eroded ... by unrealistic doctrines of 'apparent authority.'" It is ambiguous, of course, whether the word "unrealistic" is descriptive or limiting—that is, whether we were condemning as unrealistic all reliance upon apparent authority, or whether we were condemning only such reliance upon apparent authority as is unrealistic. Similarly ambiguous is the opinion's earlier statement that "there [is no] substance to the claim that the search was reasonable because the police, relying upon the night clerk's expressions of consent, had a reasonable basis for the belief that the clerk had authority to consent to the search." Was there no substance to it because it failed as a matter of law, or because the facts could not possibly support it? At one point the opinion does seem to speak clearly:

> "It is important to bear in mind that it was the petitioner's constitutional right which was at stake here, and not the night clerk's nor the hotel's. It was a right, therefore, which only the petitioner could waive by word or deed, either directly or through an agent."

But as we have discussed, what is at issue when a claim of apparent consent is raised is not whether the right to be free of searches has been *waived*, but whether the right to be free of *unreasonable* searches has been *violated*. Even if one does not think the *Stoner* opinion had this subtlety in mind, the supposed clarity of its foregoing statement is immediately compromised, as follows:

> "It is true that the night clerk clearly and unambiguously consented to the search. But there is nothing in the record to indicate that *the police had any basis whatsoever to believe that* the night clerk had been authorized by the petitioner to permit the police to search the petitioner's room."

The italicized language should have been deleted, of course, if the statement two sentences earlier meant that an appearance of authority could never validate a search. In the last analysis, one must admit that the rationale of *Stoner* was ambiguous—and perhaps deliberately so. It is at least a reasonable reading of the case, and perhaps a preferable one, that the police could not rely upon the obtained consent because they knew it came from a hotel clerk, knew that the room was rented and exclusively occupied by the defendant, and could not reasonably have believed that the former had general access to or control over the latter. * * *

As *Stoner* demonstrates, what we hold today does not suggest that law enforcement officers may always accept a person's invitation to enter premises. Even when the invitation is accompanied by an explicit assertion that the person lives there, the surrounding circumstances could conceivably be such that a reasonable person would doubt its truth and not act upon it without further inquiry. As with other factual determinations bearing upon search and seizure, determination of consent to enter must "be judged against an objective standard: would the facts available to the officer at the moment ... 'warrant a man of reasonable caution in the belief'" that the consenting party had authority over the premises? If not, then warrantless entry without further inquiry is unlawful unless authority actually exists. But if so, the search is valid.

In the present case, the Appellate Court found it unnecessary to determine whether the officers reasonably believed that Fischer had the authority to consent, because it ruled as a matter of law that a reasonable belief could not validate the entry. Since we find that ruling to be in error, we remand for consideration of that question. * * *

Justice MARSHALL, with whom Justice BRENNAN and Justice STEVENS join, dissenting. * * *

Unlike searches conducted pursuant to the recognized exceptions to the warrant requirement, third-party consent searches are not based on an exigency and therefore serve no compelling social goal. Police officers, when faced with the choice of relying on consent by a third party or securing a warrant, should secure a warrant, and must therefore accept the risk of error should they instead choose to rely on consent. * * *

Acknowledging that the third party in this case lacked authority to consent, the majority seeks to rely on cases suggesting that reasonable but mistaken factual judgments by police will not invalidate otherwise reasonable searches. The majority reads these cases as establishing a "general rule" that "what is generally demanded of the many factual determinations that must regularly be made by agents of the government—whether the magistrate issuing a warrant, the police officer executing a warrant, or the police officer conducting a search or seizure under one of the exceptions to the warrant requirement—is not that they always be correct, but that they always be reasonable."

The majority's assertion, however, is premised on the erroneous assumption that third-party consent searches are generally reasonable. The cases the majority cites thus provide no support for its holding. In *Brinegar v. United States*, for example, the Court confirmed the unremarkable proposition that police need only probable cause, not absolute certainty, to justify the arrest of a suspect on a highway. As *Brinegar* makes clear, the possibility of factual error is built into the probable cause standard, and such a standard, by its very definition, will in some cases result in the arrest of a suspect who has not actually committed a crime. Because probable cause defines the reasonableness of searches and seizures outside of the home, a search is reasonable under the Fourth Amendment whenever that standard is met, notwithstanding the possibility of "mistakes" on the part of police. In contrast, our cases have already struck the balance against warrantless home intrusions in the absence of an exigency. Because reasonable factual errors by law enforcement officers will not validate unreasonable searches, the reasonableness of the officer's mistaken belief that the third party had authority to consent is irrelevant. * * *[d]

NOTES ON WHO MAY CONSENT

1. **Husband-wife.** In *United States v. Duran*, 957 F.2d 499 (7th Cir.1992), holding defendant's wife could consent to search of a separate building on their farm which he used as a gym, the court concluded the requisite access was established by the wife's testimony that she could have entered that building at any time, though the wife had not theretofore done so and had none of her personal effects there. This is not to say, the court cautioned, that there is "a per se rule that common spousal authority extends to every square inch of property upon which a couple's residence is built"; such an approach "presumes that spouses, in forging a marital bond, remove any and all boundaries between them," which "does not reflect reality, either in practice or in the eyes of the law." The *Duran* court thus opted for this position: "In the context of a more intimate marital relationship [as compared to other co-occupants], the burden upon the government should be lighter. We hold that a spouse presumptively has authority to consent to a search of all areas of the homestead; the nonconsenting spouse may rebut this presumption only by showing that the consenting spouse was

---

d. As for the other illustrations given by the majority, the dissenters explained that "*Hill* should be understood no less than *Brinegar* as simply a gloss on the meaning of 'probable cause,'" while *Garrison* "was premised on the [fact that] searches based on warrants are generally reasonable," and "like *Brinegar*, thus tells us nothing about the reasonableness under the Fourth Amendment of a warrantless arrest."

denied access to the particular area searched." Query, what is the effect of the rebuttal in light of *Rodriguez?*

2. *Parent-child.* If a child is living at the home of his parents, the courts are in agreement that the head of the household may give consent to a search of the child's living quarters. A contrary result is sometimes reached if the "child" living with his parents has reached adulthood. A child may not give consent to a full search of the parent's house. However, where it is not unusual or unauthorized for the child to admit visitors into the home, the mere entry of police on the premises with the consent of the child is not improper.

3. *Landlord-tenant; co-tenants.* A landlord may not consent to a search of his tenant's premises (as compared to areas of common usage), and this is so even though the landlord may have some right of entry for purposes of inspecting or cleaning the premises. *Chapman v. United States,* 365 U.S. 610, 81 S.Ct. 776, 5 L.Ed.2d 828 (1961). Hotel employees may not consent to the search of a particular room during the period in which it has been rented by a guest. *Stoner v. California,* 376 U.S. 483, 84 S.Ct. 889, 11 L.Ed.2d 856 (1964). But "where two or more persons occupy a dwelling place jointly, the general rule is that a joint tenant can consent to police entry and search of the entire house or apartment, even though they occupy separate bedrooms." *State v. Thibodeau,* 317 A.2d 172 (Me.1974).

4. *Employer-employee.* As to consent by defendant's employer, compare *Gillard v. Schmidt,* 579 F.2d 825 (3d Cir.1978) (consent invalid as to search of defendant's desk; protection of the Fourth Amendment "does not turn on the nature of the property interest in the searched premises, but on the reasonableness of the person's privacy expectation," and defendant had a high expectation concerning his desk because he worked "in an office secured by a locked door and a desk containing psychological profiles and other confidential student records"); with *Commonwealth v. Glover,* 405 A.2d 945 (Pa.Super.1979) (factory owner could consent to search of items on top of work bench, as it not an area assigned to defendant or used exclusively by him).

Whether an employee can give a valid consent to a search of his employer's premises depends upon the scope of his authority. Generally, the courts have been of the view that the average employee, such as a clerk, janitor, driver, or other person temporarily in charge, may not give consent. However, if the employee is a manager or other person of considerable authority who is left in complete charge for a substantial period of time, then the prevailing view is that such a person can waive his employer's rights.

5. *Bailor-bailee.* If a person leaves his car at a garage for repairs, does he assume the risk that the repairman might permit police to look inside the car to determine whether it is stolen, as held in *State v. Baker,* 310 S.E.2d 101 (N.C.App.1983)? If so, is a different result called for if the repairman turns the vehicle over to the police so that they can inspect it more closely at another location, as in *State v. Farrell,* 443 A.2d 438 (R.I.1982)?

NOTES ON LIMITS ON THIRD-PARTY CONSENT

Even if the consent was given by a third party who, at least in some circumstances, could give effective consent, it may still be questioned whether other circumstances of the particular case made that person's consent ineffective vis-a-vis the defendant. Consider:

1. *Antagonism.* What if, for example, a wife calls the police into the house and points out incriminating evidence because she is angry at her husband?

Compare *State v. Gonzalez–Valle,* 385 So.2d 681 (Fla.App.1980) (where "the motive of the defendant's wife in consenting to the search was clearly one of spite," she "had no right to waive her husband's protection against unreasonable searches and seizures"); with *Commonwealth v. Martin,* 264 N.E.2d 366 (Mass. 1970) ("while they are both living in the premises the equal authority does not lapse and revive with the lapse and revival of amicable relations between the spouses").

2.　*Defendant's instructions.* If the defendant had previously instructed the third party not to allow a search, should those instructions be controlling? In *People v. Fry,* 76 Cal.Rptr. 718 (App.1969), the court held: "When the officers solicited consent of the wife to enter for the purpose of seizing property they knew her husband had instructed her not to consent and, under these circumstances, were not entitled to rely upon her consent as justification for their conduct" in searching the family home. *Fry* was distinguished in *People v. Reynolds,* 127 Cal.Rptr. 561 (App.1976), because in the later case the police were unaware of the husband's instructions to his wife. Is the *Matlock* test relevant on this issue?

3.　*Defendant's refusal or failure to consent.* In *Matter of Welfare of D.A.G.,* 484 N.W.2d 787 (Minn.1992), the court concluded: "The 'waiver' and 'assumption of risk' rationales, however, are not compelling in a case such as this, where the person against whom the search is directed is present and the consenting joint occupant is not. First, an absent third-party's consent should not be used to 'waive' another individual's constitutional rights when that individual is present at the search to give or withhold consent in his or her own right. Similarly, the risk that one co-inhabitant might permit the common area of a jointly occupied premises to be searched in the absence of another is qualitatively different from the risk that a warrantless search will be conducted over the objection of a present joint occupant: A present, objecting joint occupant cannot be said to have assumed the risk that an absent third party will vicariously waive his or her constitutional rights. We agree that 'the risk assumed by joint occupancy is merely an inability to control access to the premises during one's absence.' * * * We do not, however, decide what the result would be where both consenting and non-consenting joint occupants are present when the police request permission to search a premises."

4.　*Exclusive control by defendant of effects or areas within shared premises or objects.* In *State v. Evans,* 372 P.2d 365 (Hawaii 1962), the court held the wife could not consent to a search of personal items found in a cuff link case located in her husband's dresser drawer. Is this holding consistent with the *Matlock* test? Consider also the relevance of *Frazier v. Cupp,* 394 U.S. 731, 89 S.Ct. 1420, 22 L.Ed.2d 684 (1969), where the Court concluded that one of petitioner's contentions, namely, that the police illegally searched and seized clothing from his duffel bag, could "be dismissed rather quickly":

"This duffel bag was being used jointly by petitioner and his cousin Rawls and it had been left in Rawls' home. The police, while arresting Rawls, asked him if they could have his clothing. They were directed to the duffel bag and both Rawls and his mother consented to its search. During this search, the officers came upon petitioner's clothing and it was seized as well. Since Rawls was a joint user of the bag, he clearly had authority to consent to its search. The officers therefore found evidence against petitioner while in the course of an otherwise lawful search. * * * Petitioner argues that Rawls only had actual permission to use one compartment of the bag and that he had no authority to consent to a search of the other compartments. We will not, however, engage in such metaphysical subleties in judging the efficacy of Rawls' consent. Petitioner, in allowing Rawls to use the bag and in leaving it in his house, must be taken to have assumed the risk that Rawls would allow someone else to look inside."

5. *Seizure vs. search.* "Up to now, [the third-party consent] principle has found expression only in the context of consent to the search of property—but there is no sound reason to restrict the principle rigidly to that milieu," as "the logic of third-party consent can be adapted to seizures in some instances." *United States v. Woodrum*, 202 F.3d 1 (1st Cir.2000) (relying on third-party consent in upholding a program whereby police may stop to check on the safety of drivers of those cabs bearing a decal indicating the owner is voluntarily participating in a program contemplating such stops, reasoning that "these decals symbolized both the owner's and the driver's consent to future stops," that "the driver's command of the taxi allows him to maintain control over the vehicle's speed and route of travel," and that "the driver has the authority to consent to a stop in his own right, and that the passenger, by entering the cab, assumes the risk that the driver may exercise his right to stop briefly along the way").

Chapter 6

WIRETAPPING, ELECTRONIC EAVES-DROPPING, THE USE OF SECRET AGENTS TO OBTAIN INCRIMINA-TING STATEMENTS, AND THE FOURTH AMENDMENT[a]

SECTION 1. HISTORICAL BACKGROUND

A. CONSTITUTIONAL PERMISSION

OLMSTEAD v. UNITED STATES, 277 U.S. 438, 48 S.Ct. 564, 72 L.Ed. 944 (1928), held (5–4), per Chief Justice TAFT, that wiretapping did not amount to a search and seizure for reasons that have since been rejected by the Court. The Fourth Amendment itself, observed Taft, "shows that the search is to be of material things—the person, the house, his papers or his effects. The description of the warrant necessary to make the proceeding lawful, is that it must specify the place to be searched and the person or *things* to be seized." Moreover, not only did the police fail to violate the amendment by tapping, as such, but neither did they do so at any point along the way, in the course of gaining access to the wiretap evidence: "The evidence was secured by the use of the sense of hearing and that only. There was no entry of the houses or offices of the defendants."

Although the evidence which led to the conviction for conspiracy to violate the National Prohibition Act was obtained by federal prohibition agents in violation of a statute of the state of Washington, which made it a misdemeanor to "intercept" telegraphic or telephonic messages, the Chief Justice pointed out that "this statute does not declare that evidence obtained by such interception shall be inadmissible, and by the common law [it] would not be." Moreover, "clearly a [state statute] cannot affect the rules of evidence applicable in courts of the United States."[b]

In an exhaustive dissenting opinion, Justice BRANDEIS observed:

a. This chapter does not attempt to cover in detail Title III of the Crime Control Act of 1968, as amended by the Electronic Communication Privacy Act of 1986, and the extensive litigation these statutes have generated. For more comprehensive treatment, see James Carr, *The Law of Electronic Surveillance* (1977); Clifford S. Fishman, *Wiretapping and Eavesdropping* (1978); Michael Goldsmith, *The Supreme Court and Title III: Rewriting the Law of Electronic Surveillance*, 74 J.Crim.L. & C. 1 (1983). For a fairly brief but very helpful examination of various aspects of Title III, and of electronic surveillance generally, see Chap-

ter 14 of Charles H. Whitebread & Christopher Slobogin, *Criminal Procedure* (4th ed. 2000).

b. "Taft did not challenge the fourth amendment exclusionary rule; he *confined* it. Rejecting the argument that 'unethically,' as well as unconstitutionally, secured evidence should be barred, he concluded that 'the exclusion of evidence should be confined to cases where *rights under the Constitution* would be violated by *admitting* it'" (emphasis added.) Kamisar, *Does (Did) (Should) the Exclusionary Rule Rest on a "Principled Basis" Rather than an "Empirical Proposition"?*, 16 Creighton L.Rev. 565, 603 (1983).

"The progress of science in furnishing the government with means of espionage is not likely to stop with wire tapping. Ways may some day be developed by which the government, without removing papers from secret drawers, can reproduce them in court, and by which it will be enabled to expose to a jury the most intimate occurrences of the home. Advances in the psychic and related sciences may bring means of exploring unexpressed beliefs, thoughts and emotions. * * * Can it be that the Constitution affords no protection against such invasions of individual security?

"[In] *Ex parte Jackson,* 96 U.S. 727, 24 L.Ed. 877 [1877], it was held that a sealed letter intrusted to the mail is protected by the amendments. The mail is a public service furnished by the government. The telephone is a public service furnished by its authority. There is, in essence, no difference between the sealed letter and the private telephone message.

"[The] evil incident to invasion of the privacy of the telephone is far greater than that involved in tampering with the mails. Whenever a telephone line is tapped, the privacy of the persons at both ends of the line is invaded, and all conversations between them upon any subject, and although proper, confidential, and privileged, may be overheard. Moreover, the tapping of one man's telephone line involves the tapping of the telephone of every other person whom he may call, or who may call him. As a means of espionage, writs of assistance and general warrants are but puny instruments of tyranny and oppression when compared with wire tapping.

"Time and again this court, in giving effect to the principle underlying the Fourth Amendment, has refused to place an unduly literal construction upon it. * * * No court which looked at the words of the amendment rather than at its underlying purpose would hold, as this court did in *Ex parte Jackson,* that its protection extended to letters in the mails.

"[The] makers of our Constitution * * * conferred, as against the government, the right to be let alone—the most comprehensive of rights and the right most valued by civilized men. To protect that right, every unjustifiable intrusion by the government upon the privacy of the individual, whatever the means employed, must be deemed a violation of the Fourth Amendment. And the use, as evidence in a criminal proceeding, of facts ascertained by such intrusion must be deemed a violation of the Fifth. * * *

"Independently of the constitutional question, I am of opinion that the judgment should be reversed. By the laws of Washington, wire tapping is a crime. To prove its case, the government was obliged to lay bare the crimes committed by its officers on its behalf. A federal court should not permit such a prosecution to continue. * * *

"Decency, security, and liberty alike demand that government officials shall be subjected to the same rules of conduct that are commands to the citizen. In a government of laws, existence of the government will be imperiled if it fails to observe the law scrupulously. Our government is the potent, the omnipresent teacher. For good or for ill, it teaches the whole people by its example. Crime is contagious. If the government becomes a lawbreaker, it breeds contempt for law; it invites every man to become a law unto himself; it invites anarchy. To declare that in the administration of the criminal law the end justifies the means—to declare that the government may commit crimes in order to secure the conviction of a private criminal—would bring terrible retribution. Against that pernicious doctrine this court should resolutely set its face."

In a brief separate dissent, Justice HOLMES commented:

"While I do not deny it I am not prepared to say that the penumbra of the Fourth and Fifth Amendments covers the defendants, although I fully agree that courts are apt to err by sticking too closely to the words of a law where these words import a policy that goes beyond them. [But] I think, as Justice Brandeis says, that apart from the Constitution the government ought not to use evidence obtained and only obtainable by a criminal act. * * * It is desirable that criminals should be detected, and to that end that all available evidence should be used. It also is desirable that the government should not itself foster and pay for other crimes, when they are the means by which the evidence is to be obtained. * * * We have to choose, and for my part I think it is a less evil that some criminals should escape than that the government should play an ignoble part.

"For those who agree with me no distinction can be taken between the government as prosecutor and the government as judge. If the existing code does not permit district attorneys to have a hand in such dirty business it does not permit the judge to allow such iniquities to succeed. [And] if all that I have said so far be accepted it makes no difference that in this case wire tapping is made a crime by the law of the state, not by the law of the United States. * * * I am aware of the often-repeated statement that in a criminal proceeding the court will not take notice of the manner in which papers offered in evidence have been obtained. But that somewhat rudimentary mode of disposing of the question has been overthrown by *Weeks*. [T]he reason for excluding evidence obtained by violating the Constitution seems to me logically to lead to excluding evidence obtained by a crime of the officers of the law."

Notes and Questions

1. **Different views of constitutional interpretation.** For a close study of the opinions of Chief Justice Taft and Justice Brandeis in the *Olmstead* case and an insightful discussion of the two Justices' different views of constitutional interpretation, see James Boyd White, *Judicial Criticism*, 20 Ga.L.Rev. 835, 847–70 (1986).

2. **Shedding light on the original bases of the exclusionary rule.** Although often quoted by proponents of the fourth amendment exclusionary rule, the most famous passages in the Holmes–Brandeis dissents are arguments for extending the exclusionary rule to situations where the federal government has not violated the Constitution, or even federal law, but only a state anti-wiretapping law. "Nevertheless," observes Kamisar, fn. b, p. 348, "these famous dissents shed light on the original bases and purposes of the exclusionary rule. [They] underscore that the exclusionary rule is [or at least was thought to be] based on principle—one might also say that it has an important symbolic quality—not on estimates of how substantially the exclusion of evidence affects police behavior."

B. Statutory Prohibition: § 605 of the 1934 Federal Communications Act[a]

Chief Justice Taft noted in his *Olmstead* opinion that "Congress may of course protect the secrecy of telephone messages by making them when intercepted, inadmissible in evidence in federal criminal trials, by direct legislation, and thus depart from the common law of evidence." Such a development occurred with the passage of the Federal Communications Act of 1934. Section 605 of the Act

---

a. Section 605 of the 1934 Act was "amended" by Title III of the Crime Control Act of 1968, permitting court-approved wiretapping and electronic eavesdropping by federal and state law enforcement officials in the investigation of many listed offenses.

read in part: "[N]o person not being authorized by the sender shall intercept any communication and divulge or publish the existence, contents, substance, purport, effect, or meaning of such intercepted communication to any person * * *." This wording was held to cover wiretapping by state or federal officers as well as by private persons, *Nardone v. United States,* 302 U.S. 379, 58 S.Ct. 275, 82 L.Ed. 314 (1937), 308 U.S. 338, 60 S.Ct. 266, 84 L.Ed. 307 (1939); *Benanti v. United States,* 355 U.S. 96, 78 S.Ct. 155, 2 L.Ed.2d 126 (1957); and to apply to intrastate as well as interstate communications, *Weiss v. United States,* 308 U.S. 321, 60 S.Ct. 269, 84 L.Ed. 298 (1939).

The Department of Justice and the FBI took the position that Section 605 did not prohibit wiretapping *alone,* only tapping *followed by* "divulgence," and, further, that it was not a "divulgence" when one member of the government communicated to another, but only when he communicated outside the government, e.g., sought to introduce the wiretap information into evidence. See e.g., William P. Rogers, *The Case for Wire Tapping,* 63 Yale L.J. 792, 793 (1954). For sharp criticism of this view see, e.g., Edward Bennett Williams, *The Wiretapping–Eavesdropping Problem; A Defense Counsel's View,* 44 Minn.L.Rev. 855, 860 (1960).

C.   Wiretapping, § 605 and Federal–State Relations

Since it involved the use of state-gathered wiretap evidence in a state prosecution, *Schwartz v. Texas,* 344 U.S. 199, 73 S.Ct. 232, 97 L.Ed. 231 (1952), posed the wiretapping counterpart of *Wolf v. Colorado.* Although the Court recognized that "the problem under '605 is somewhat different [than *Wolf*] because the introduction of the intercepted communication would itself be a violation of the statute," i.e., a prohibited "divulgence," it nevertheless relied on *Wolf* to hold the evidence admissible. Only Douglas, J., dissented.

More weight was given to the Federal Communication Act's "built-in" exclusionary rule in *Benanti v. United States,* supra, which barred state-gathered wiretap evidence proffered in a *federal* prosecution, even though at the time the great weight of authority (later overruled in *Elkins,* pp. 112, 134) allowed federal prosecutors to use evidence obtained by illegal state searches so long as there was no "collusion" between the two "sovereignties."

Two days before the electronic surveillance provisions of the Crime Control Act of 1968 were signed into law, *Schwartz* was overruled by *Lee v. Florida,* 392 U.S. 378, 88 S.Ct. 2096, 20 L.Ed.2d 1166 (1968): "*Schwartz* cannot survive the demise of *Wolf.* [*Mapp*] imposed a judicially devised exclusionary rule. [In] the present case the federal law itself explicitly protects intercepted communications from divulgence, in a court or any other place."

D.   Non–Telephonic Electronic Eavesdropping

1. *Brandeis' fears become a reality.* Several studies in the 1950s and 60s, e.g., Samuel Dash, Robert Knowlton & Richard Schwartz, *The Eavesdroppers* 339–79 (1959); Allan F. Westin, *Privacy and Freedom* 69–89 (1967); indicated that modern developments in electronic eavesdropping had made the prophetic fears voiced by Justice Brandeis in his *Olmstead* dissent a reality. According to these studies: Tiny microphones can be secreted behind a picture or built into a coat button. Highly directive microphones known as "parabolic microphones" are capable of eavesdropping on a conversation taking place in an office on the *opposite side of a busy street* or on a park bench or outdoor restaurant terrace hundreds of feet away. Laser beams can pick sound waves off closed windows. A small, continuous-

ly operating transmitter can be placed beneath the fender of an automobile and its signal picked up by a receiver in another car or in a fixed plant. A special gun developed for American military authorities can shoot a small dart containing a wireless radio microphone into a tree, window pane, awning or any other object near the subject of investigation.

However, while electronic eavesdropping appeared to be "the ultimate invasion of privacy," Williams, supra, at 866, for decades the law furnished much less protection against this danger than it did against wiretapping. The Federal Communications Act applied only when telephone, telegraph, or radiotelegraph conversations were overheard and until the 1960's the constitutional protection against unreasonable search and seizure applied only when electronic snooping was accomplished by a physical invasion or "trespass". No such "trespass" occurred in *Olmstead* (the taps from house lines were made in the streets near the house) or in *Goldman v. United States,* 316 U.S. 129, 62 S.Ct. 993, 86 L.Ed. 1322 (1942) (where federal officers placed a detectaphone *against the wall* of a private office) or in *On Lee v. United States* (1952) (Sec. 3, infra) (where incriminating statements were picked up via a "wired for sound" former acquaintance of petitioner).

That the Constitution does furnish *some* protection against the electronic seizure of conversations as well as the seizure of "papers and effects" was made plain by *Silverman v. United States,* 365 U.S. 505, 81 S.Ct. 679, 5 L.Ed.2d 734 (1961). There, a unanimous Court, per Stewart, J., held that listening to incriminating conversations within a house by inserting an electronic device (a so-called "spike mike") into a party wall and making contact with a heating duct serving the house occupied by petitioners, "thus converting their entire heating system into a conductor of sound," amounted to an illegal search and seizure.

Justice Douglas concurred, maintaining: "The depth of the penetration of the electronic device—even the degree of its remoteness from the inside of the house—is not measure of the injury. * * * Our concern should not be with the trivialities of the local law of trespass, as the opinion of the Court indicates. But neither should the command of the Fourth Amendment be limited by nice distinctions turning on the kind of electronic equipment employed. Rather our sole concern should be with whether the privacy of the home was invaded."

Silverman not only established that conversations could be "seized" within the meaning of the Fourth Amendment, but suggested that a Fourth Amendment "search" for them might occur without any trespass. This seemed even more certain when three years later, in *Clinton v. Virginia,* 377 U.S. 158, 84 S.Ct. 1186, 12 L.Ed.2d 213 (1964) (per curiam), the Court summarily rejected the state court's holding that *Silverman* did not apply where the spike mike "was not driven into the wall but was 'stuck in' it." Any lingering doubts were dispelled by *Katz v. United States* (p. 138).

SECTION 2. *BERGER, KATZ* AND TITLE III OF THE CRIME CONTROL ACT

A. THE IMPLICATIONS OF *BERGER* AND *KATZ*

BERGER v. NEW YORK, 388 U.S. 41, 87 S.Ct. 1873, 18 L.Ed.2d 1040 (1967),[a] left the dissenting Justices (and many others) wondering whether *any* wiretapping

---

a. The case grew out of a state investigation of alleged bribery of state liquor authority officials. Pursuant to the challenged New York statute, a court order was obtained permitting the installation of a recording device in a lawyer's office for up to 60 days. On the basis of

or electronic eavesdropping statute could pass constitutional muster. The Court, per CLARK, J., struck down a New York electronic surveillance statute, calling it a "blanket grant of permission to eavesdrop * * * without adequate supervision or protective procedures."

The statute, observed Justice Clark, (1) permitted a court order to issue merely on reasonable grounds to believe that evidence of crime may be obtained, without specifying what crime has been or is being committed and without describing what conversations are to be overheard—thus failing to "particularly [describe] the place to be searched, and the person or things to be seized," as required by the Fourth Amendment[b]—(2) permitted installation and operation of surveillance equipment for 60 days—"the equivalent of a series of intrusions, searches and seizures pursuant to a single showing of probable cause"—(3) permitted renewal of the order on the basis of the original grounds on which the initial order was issued—"this we believe insufficient without a showing of present probable cause for continuance of the eavesdrop"—(4) placed no termination on the eavesdrop once the conversation sought is seized—"this is left entirely to the discretion of the officer"—and (5) did not provide for a return on the warrant—"thereby leaving full discretion in the officer as to the use of seized conversations of innocent as well as guilty parties."

The Court contrasted the New York statute's "broadside authorization" of electronic surveillance with the "precise and discriminate" procedures followed in *Osborn v. United States*, 385 U.S. 323, 87 S.Ct. 429, 17 L.Ed.2d 394 (1966), where, on the basis of a detailed affidavit alleging that an attorney was attempting to bribe a juror, two federal judges authorized a tape recorder to be concealed on the person of the attorney's "employee" (actually a secret government agent) for a specific meeting with the attorney.[c] Because *Osborn* involved such a rare fact situation, one atypical of police electronic surveillance, the Court's reference to this case raised further doubts about the constitutionality of most electronic surveillance.[d]

DOUGLAS, J., concurred in the result, maintaining that electronic surveillance is "a search for 'mere evidence,'" which is a violation of the Fourth and Fifth Amendments regardless of "the nicety and precision with which a warrant may be drawn."[e] "If a statute were to authorize placing a policeman in every home or office where it was shown that there was probable cause to believe that

---

information gathered from this eavesdrop, a second order was obtained, authorizing the installation of a recording device in another person's office. As a result of evidence obtained from the second eavesdrop, petitioner was indicted for, and convicted of, conspiracy to bribe the chairman of the state liquor authority.

b. The statute did require the naming of "the person or persons whose communications, conversations or discussions are to be overheard or recorded," but, said the Court, "this does no more than identify the person whose constitutionally protected area is to be invaded rather than 'particularly describing' the communications, conversations, or discussions to be seized. As with general warrants, this leaves too much to the discretion of the officer executing the order."

c. Is there a "certain irony" in the *Berger* Court's approval of *Osborn?* If the *Osborn* order was properly issued without any statutory authorization, why didn't the *Berger* Court consider the particularity of the order issued in

this case without regard to the constitutionality of the New York statute? See Kent Greenawalt, *The Consent Problem in Wiretapping and Eavesdropping*, 68 Colum.L.Rev. 189, 201–02 (1968).

d. See Samuel Dash, *Katz—Variations on a Theme by Berger*, 17 Cath.L.Rev. 296, 311–13 (1968).

e. Since *Berger* was briefed and argued prior to *Warden v. Hayden* (p. 160), petitioner argued at some length that the New York statute authorized "general searches" for "mere evidence." But the Court, per Clark, J., rejected the contention in a brisk footnote (fn. 2), stating that it had been "disposed of in *Hayden* adversely to petitioner's assertion here." For the view that it had not, that *Hayden* had been careful to leave open the possibility of some "testimonial limit" on the permissible objects of seizure, see Telford Taylor, *Two Studies in Constitutional Interpretation* 68–71, 101–03 (1969).

evidence would be obtained," he observed, "there is little doubt that it would be struck down as a bald invasion of privacy, far worse than the general warrants prohibited by the Fourth Amendment. I can see no difference between such a statute and one authorizing electronic surveillance, which, in effect, places an invisible policeman in the home. If anything, the latter is more offensive because the homeowner is completely unaware of the invasion of privacy."[f]

STEWART, J., concurred in the result. He fully agreed with the dissenters that the challenged New York law was constitutional, but he concluded that "the affidavits on which the judicial order issued in this case did not constitute a showing of probable cause adequate to justify the authorizing order." The standard of reasonableness embodied in the Fourth Amendment, "he observed," demands that the showing of justification match the degree of intrusion. "The affidavits" "might be enough to satisfy the standards of the Fourth Amendment for a conventional search or arrest," but not "an intrusion of the scope and duration that was permitted in this case."

Responding to the contentions that court-ordered electronic surveillance fails to specify with adequate particularity the conversations to be seized and allows a general and indiscriminate search and seizure, Justice HARLAN observed: "Just as some exercise of dominion, beyond mere perception, is necessary for the seizure of tangibles, so some use of the conversation beyond the initial listening process is required for the seizure of the spoken word."

Similarly, dissenting Justice WHITE maintained that an electronic surveillance that is continued over a span of time is no more a "general search" barred by the Fourth Amendment than the typical execution of a search warrant over a described area: "Petitioner suggests that the search is inherently overbroad because the eavesdropper will overhear conversations which do not relate to criminal activity. But the same is true of almost all searches of private property which the Fourth Amendment permits. In searching for seizable matters, the police must necessarily see or hear, and comprehend, items which do not relate to the purpose of the search. That this occurs, however, does not render the search invalid, so long as it is authorized by a suitable search warrant and so long as the police, in executing that warrant, limit themselves to searching for items which may constitutionally be seized."

———

A short time after *Berger*, the Court, per STEWART, J., made plain in KATZ v. UNITED STATES (p. 138) that the "trespass" doctrine enunciated in *Olmstead* and *Goldman* was no longer viable and that the "penetration" of the governmental intrusion "can have no constitutional significance." But the *Katz* Court thought it "clear that [the surveillance involved in this case] was so narrowly circumscribed that a duly authorized magistrate, properly notified of the need for such investigation, specifically informed of the basis on which it was to proceed, and clearly apprised of the precise intrusion it would entail, could constitutionally have authorized, with appropriate safeguards, the very limited search and seizure that the Government asserts in fact took place."[a]

f. How can this argument be met? Could a police officer lawfully hide in the closet of a suspect's home for 30 days? Ten? Twenty-four hours? Does it matter whether the officer looks through the keyhole as well as listens? As you limit the area of the search, may the time be increased? May a tap be distinguished from a bug on the ground that the former is a "search" of a much narrower "area"?

a. FBI agents had attached an electronic listening and recording device to the outside of the public phone booth from which petitioner had placed his calls. The agents "did not begin their electronic surveillance until investigation had established a strong possibility that he was

The Court likened the "discriminate circumstances" of the electronic surveillance in *Katz* to those in *Osborn* where, the *Berger* Court had said, the court order "afforded similar protections to those [of] conventional warrants authorizing the seizure of tangible evidence." "Here, too," observed the *Katz* Court, "a similar judicial order could have accommodated 'the legitimate needs of law enforcement' by authorizing the carefully limited use of electronic surveillance."

Although he dissented in *Katz*, Justice BLACK was encouraged: "[T]oday's opinion differs sharply from *Berger*, [which] set up what appeared to be insuperable obstacles to the valid passage [of] wiretapping laws. [The] Court's opinion [in] this case [removes] the doubts about state power in this field and abates to a large extent the confusion and near paralyzing effect of the *Berger* holding."

―――――――

The basis for Justice Black's view that the *Katz* opinion "differs sharply from *Berger*" is unclear. *Both opinions* referred to *Osborn* with approval. And the surveillance in *Katz* itself, as well as in *Osborn*, was very narrowly circumscribed. But the Congress seemed to read *Katz* the same way Justice Black did. Within seven months of *Katz*, in Title III of the Omnibus Crime Control and Safe Streets Act of 1968 (commonly referred to as Title III), discussed immediately below, Congress adopted legislation granting law enforcement officials extensive powers to conduct wiretapping and electronic surveillance.

B. TITLE III: AN OVERVIEW

The relevant provisions of Title III are set forth in App. B of the Annual Supplement to this casebook. For useful summaries of Title III, on which the following brief discussion heavily relies, see Wayne R. LaFave, Jerold H. Israel & Nancy J. King, *Criminal Procedure Treatise*, Ch. 4 (2d ed. 1999) (hereafter cited as CRIMPROC), Charles H. Whitebread & Christopher Slobogin, *Criminal Procedure* Ch. 14 (4th ed. 2000) (hereafter Whitebread & Slobogin); Michael Goldsmith, *The Supreme Court and Title III: Rewriting the Law of Electronic Surveillance*, 74 J.Crim.L. & Criminology 1, (1983) (hereafter Goldsmith).

1. *The scope of Title III.* As amended in 1986, Title III prohibits the "interception" of "wire, oral or electronic communications" unless such interception is authorized by the statute.[a] The prohibition covers electronic mail, computer-to-computer communications and cellular telephones among other modern communication techniques. Protected, too, are electronic storage and processing of information. (As pointed out by Whitebread & Slobogin 331, "to the extent such storage or processing is under the auspices of a third party computer operator, the [1986 amendments] provide protection the Fourth Amendment may not, since the Fourth Amendment is not implicated when information is sought from a party to whom it has voluntarily been surrendered."[b]

using the telephone in question to transmit gambling information [in] violation of federal law. Moreover, the surveillance was limited, both in scope and in duration, to the specific purpose of establishing the contents of the petitioner's unlawful telephone communications. The agents confined their surveillance to the brief periods during which he used the telephone booth, and they took great care to overhear only the conversations of the petitioner himself."

a. 28 U.S.C. § 2510(4).

b. "However, the core Title III protection extends only to the 'interception' of the aural transfer, which occurs as the voice mail transfer is made and placed in storage. To gain access to completed voice mail messages already held in storage, law enforcement officers only need comply with [18 U.S.C. §§ 2701–2711], which is not enforced by an exclusionary remedy." CRIMPROC § 4.3(a).

An "oral" communication is one "uttered by a person exhibiting an expectation that such communication is not subject to interception under circumstances justifying such expectation, but such term does not include any electronic communication" (§ 2510(2)). The mode of communication here is "sound waves" as opposed to an "electronic medium." As noted in CRIMPROC § 4.3(a), "the critical element of [the] definition is its limitation to persons having a justifiable expectation that their conversations would not be intercepted. The legislative history indicates that this limitation was intended 'to reflect existing law' and it follows the Fourth Amendment 'reasonable expectation of privacy standard' as set forth in *Katz v. United States*."

2.   *The definition of "interception"; herein of "pen registers," "trap and trace" devices and silent video surveillance.* As amended in 1986, Title III defines "intercept" as meaning the *aural* or other acquisition of the *contents* of any * * * *communication* through the use of any electronic, mechanical or other device." § 2510(4) (emphasis added).

Thus, "pen registers" (which do not record phone conversations, but only the numbers dialed from a given phone and the times the number was dialed) are not covered by Title III. As the Court observed in *United States v. New York Telephone Co.*, 434 U.S. 159, 98 S.Ct. 364, 54 L.Ed.2d 376 (1977), these devices "do not acquire the 'contents' of communications" as that term is used in Title III and, because they do not hear sound, they "do not accomplish the 'aural acquisition' of anything."[a] Nor does Title III govern "trap and trace" devices, which capture impulses identifying the originating number of an instrument or device from which a wire or electronic communication was transmitted.[b]

Moreover, although it may well be the most invasive type of technological surveillance of all, surreptitious video surveillance is not covered by Title III. As pointed out in *United States v. Torres* (p. 368), a person televised while silently making a bomb "is not engaged in any form of communication"; nor is a visual observation in any sense "an 'aural acquisition.'" However, some courts have applied Title III's provisions by analogy.[c]

3.   *Nonconsensual electronic surveillance.* Title III only regulates "nonconsensual" electronic surveillance (i.e., electronic surveillance where *none* of the parties overheard have consented to the interception).[a] Thus, as pointed out in CRIMPROC, § 4.3(c), "law enforcement authorities are free to make consensual

---

a. The Court subsequently held, *Smith v. Maryland* (1979) (p. 142) that the use of a pen register did not constitute a "search" within the meaning of the Fourth Amendment either.

b. In 1986, Congress enacted special legislation prohibiting use of pen registers and trap and trace devices without a court order. (See 18 U.S.C. § 3127.) To obtain such an order, however, a government attorney need only certify that the information sought is "relevant" to an ongoing criminal investigation and identify the possible relevant offenses. The court's function is to determine the completeness of the application; it need not make an independent investigation of the facts.

c. See pp. 368–69.

a. §§ 2511(2)(c) & (d) provide that "it shall not be unlawful under this chapter for a person [to] intercept a wire, oral or electronic communication where such person is a party to the communication or *one of the parties* to the

communication has given prior consent to such interception." (Emphasis added.) Consensual electronic surveillance is not restricted by the Fourth Amendment. See *Lopez v. United States* (1963) (p. 374); *United States v. White* (1971) (p. 382).

The National Wiretap Commission, *Majority Report* (1976) found that consensual electronic surveillance "is especially vital for the investigation of certain criminal activities, particularly official corruption, extortion, and loansharking," and that "it also serves to protect police officers, informants, and complainants, or whoever is the consenting participant to the conversation." The Majority Report deemed court authorization for such surveillance "unnecessary for the protection of privacy because it is not a 'search' within the meaning of the Fourth Amendment" and because "it serves not to intercept conversations, but merely to corroborate them, improving the accuracy of evidence for use in court."

interceptions in a variety of ways: (1) by having the consenting party wear or carry a tape recorder with which he records his face-to-face conversations with another; (2) by having the consenting party wear a transmitter which broadcasts his conversations to agents equipped with a receiver; or (3) by having the consenting party to a telephone conversation record it or permit another to listen in on an extension."

4. _Title III's "exclusionary rule."_ Title III has a general exclusion provision, § 2515, which applies to private, as well as government, interceptions. Section 2515 also states that no part of the contents of any communication intercepted in violation of the statute "may be received in evidence in any trial, hearing or other proceeding in or before any court, grand jury, * * * agency, regulatory body, legislative committee" or any federal or state authority. Thus, Title III's exclusionary rule has been called one that "transcends its constitutional counterpart by being applicable to all governmental, judicial, quasi-judicial, and administrative proceedings." Goldsmith 40.[a] As the Supreme Court has construed Title III, however, exclusion of the evidence is not the consequence of _every_ failure to comply with the statute's provisions. Exclusion is required only when the particular statutory provision violated "was intended to play a central role in the statutory scheme." Compare _United States v. Giordano,_ 416 U.S. 505, 94 S.Ct. 1820, 40 L.Ed.2d 341 (1974) with _United States v. Chavez,_ 416 U.S. 562, 94 S.Ct. 1849, 40 L.Ed.2d 380 (1974).

5. _Applications for court orders._ Federal applications may be authorized only by the Attorney General or a specially designated Assistant Attorney General, see § 2516(1), a requirement designed to ensure that discretion is exercised by a senior and politically accountable executive official before a court is asked to pass on an application. (When authorized by state law, the "principal prosecuting attorney of any state or political subdivision thereof" may apply to a state judge for an electronic surveillance order. The state provisions are thus less centralized, but this was deemed necessitated by realities of state law enforcement systems.) Only federal district and appellate judges and their state counterparts may issue surveillance orders. See § 2510(9).

Except for "emergencies"—§ 2518(7) permits warrantless electronic surveillance when "an emergency situation exists" involving "conspiratorial activities threatening the national security interest" or "conspiratorial activities characteristic of organized crime" or (pursuant to a 1984 amendment) "immediate danger of death or serious physical injury to any person"[a]—no electronic surveillance is permitted without a properly authorized application. See § 2518(1).

Each application must be in writing and under oath; disclose the identity of the officer making the application and the officer authorizing it (see _United States v. Chavez,_ supra); and include a "full and complete" statement of the circumstances justifying the belief that an order should be issued, including (i) details as to the particular offense, (ii) a particular description of the communication facility,

---

a. _Calandra_ (1974) (p. 131), it will be recalled, refused to allow a grand jury witness to invoke the Fourth Amendment exclusionary rule. In _Gelbard v. United States,_ 408 U.S. 41, 92 S.Ct. 2357, 33 L.Ed.2d 179 (1972), however, a 5–4 majority, per Brennan, J., held that grand jury witnesses may refuse to testify where their testimony is sought on the basis of illegal electronic surveillance.

a. There must be "grounds upon which an order could be entered under this chapter to authorize such interception"; the situation must require an interception before a court order "can with due diligence be obtained"; and, within 48 hours after the interception has begun to occur, an application must be filed seeking retroactive approval for such interception.

See generally Clifford Fishman, _Interception of Communications in Exigent Circumstances,_ 22 Ga.L.Rev. 1, 35–48 (1987). The "emergency surveillance" provision "has been invoked only rarely, and there has been virtually no judicial discussion or interpretation of it." Id. at 35.

(iii) a particular description of "the type of communication" sought to be intercepted, and (iv) "the identity of the person, if known, committing the offense, and whose conversation is to be intercepted."[b] "In other words," comments Goldsmith at 42, "there must be probable cause to believe that a particular person involved in a designated crime will have discussion pertinent to that crime using a particular phone (or at a particular place) during a specified time period."

Moreover, to discourage routine use of tapping or electronic eavesdropping, the application must include "full and complete" statements as to "whether or not other investigative procedures have been tried or failed or why they reasonably appear to be unlikely to succeed if tried or to be too dangerous"[c] and of the facts concerning all previous applications "involving any of the same persons, facilities or places specified in the application, and the action taken by the judge on each such application." See § 2518(1)(c), (e).

6. *Entering an order.* The judge may enter an order as requested or as modified upon determining, on the basis of the facts submitted, that "normal investigative procedures" are not a viable alternative and that there is probable cause for believing three things: an individual has committed or is about to commit a particular offense enumerated in the statute; "particular communications concerning that offense will be obtained through such interception"; and the facilities or place where the communications are to be intercepted are being, or about to be, used in connection with the offense or "are leased to, listed in the name of, or commonly used by such person." See § 2518(3).

The court order must designate the personnel authorized to conduct the surveillance, identify both the person (if known) and the facilities or place targeted for interception, specify the period of surveillance, and furnish a "particular description of the type of communication sought to be intercepted, and a statement of the particular offense to which it relates."[a] See § 2518(4). In addition, each order must provide, § 2518(5), that the authorization to intercept "shall be executed as soon as practicable, shall be conducted in such a way as to *minimize the interception of communications not otherwise subject to interception*" (emphasis added),[b] and "must terminate upon attainment of the authorized objective, or in any event in thirty days."

7. *"National security" surveillance and the FISA.* When Title III was originally enacted, it contained a provision, § 2511(3), stating that nothing in the statute "shall limit the constitutional power of the President to take such measures as he deems necessary to protect the Nation against actual or potential attack or other hostile acts or a foreign power, to obtain foreign intelligence deemed essential to the security of the United States, or to protect national security information against foreign intelligence activities." In addition, the provision stated that nothing in the statute "shall [be] deemed to limit the

---

b. On the obligation of the government to discover and name the person to be heard, see *United States v. Kahn*, 415 U.S. 143, 94 S.Ct. 977, 39 L.Ed.2d 225 (1974). For the consequences of noncompliance with this provision, see *United States v. Donovan*, 429 U.S. 413, 97 S.Ct. 658, 50 L.Ed.2d 652 (1977).

c. In practice, maintains James Carr, *The Law of Electronic Surveillance* 179 (1977), this requirement has been watered down to "one of investigatory utility, rather than necessity."

a. What was intended by "type of communication" is unclear. It now "appears to be generally accepted that [this requirement] can be fulfilled by indicating the offense under

investigation, without further details about the anticipated conversations," Carr, fn. i supra, at 173.

b. But see *Scott v. United States* (1978) (p. 362), rejecting the contention that the failure of the surveilling officers to make any effort to comply with a minimization requirement was alone a basis for suppression. The Court took the position that "subjective intent alone does not make otherwise lawful conduct illegal," meaning that the officers' presumed failure to make even a good-faith effort to comply with the requirement was not itself a reason for excluding the evidence obtained.

constitutional power of the President to take such measures as he deems necessary to protect the United States against the overthrow of the Government [by] unlawful means or against any other clear and present danger to the structure or existence of the Government." In *United States v. United States District Court*, 407 U.S. 297, 92 S.Ct. 2125, 32 L.Ed.2d 752 (1972) (sometimes called *Keith*, after then District Judge Damon Keith), the government contended that this provision allowed it to conduct a warrantless surveillance of a purely domestic radical group engaged in a conspiracy to destroy federal government property. But, without a dissent, the Court, per Powell, J., held that the circumstances did not "justify departure [from] the customary Fourth Amendment requirement of judicial approval prior to initiation of a search or surveillance." The Court emphasized that the warrantless surveillance had been directed at a "domestic organization," i.e., one "composed of citizens of the United states and which has no significant connection with a foreign power, its agents or agencies." (However, the Court saw no occasion to spell out what kind of connection with a foreign power would suffice to distinguish the instant case.)

The matter is now dealt with by another statute, the Foreign Intelligence Surveillance Act of 1978 (FISA).[a] This Act provides that the Chief Justice of the United States is to designate (a) seven federal district judges who shall have jurisdiction to act on applications for orders approving electronic surveillance anywhere within the United States and (b) three other federal judges who shall "comprise a court of review," one which shall review the denial of any application made under this law.

Upon a proper application, a judge of this court is to enter an ex parte order approving electronic surveillance for 90 days (or until its purpose is achieved, whichever is less) on finding "probable cause to believe" that "the target" of the electronic surveillance is "a foreign power or an agent of a foreign power" and that each of the places at which the electronic surveillance is directed is being used, or is about to be used by "a foreign power or an agent of a foreign power."[b] The judge *need not* find probable cause to believe that the requested surveillance will in fact lead to the gathering of foreign intelligence information. Nevertheless, the Act has been upheld against a variety of challenges by the lower federal courts.

What about electronic surveillance *without* a court order? The FISA provides that "the President, through the Attorney General," may authorize *warrantless* surveillance "to acquire foreign intelligence information for periods of up to one year" if, inter alia, the Attorney General certifies that the surveillance is "solely to be directed at" the acquisition of the contents of communications "transmitted by means of communications used exclusively between or among foreign power" and that no "substantial likelihood" exists that "the surveillance will acquire the contents of any communication to which a United States person is a party."[c]

---

a. 50 U.S.C. §§ 1801–1811. See generally CRIMPROC, § 4.3(d); Senate Select Committee on Intelligence, *The Foreign Surveillance Act of 1978: The First Five Years*, S.Doc. No.660, 98th Cong., 2d Sess. 3 (1984); William Webster, *Sophisticated Surveillance–Intolerable Intrusion or Prudent Protection?*, 63 Wash. U.L.Q. 351 (1985); Note 71 Mich.L.Rev. 1116 (1980).

The provision of Title III at issue in *United States District Court* was repealed upon enactment of the FISA.

b. The FISA further provides that no "United States person may be considered a foreign power or an agent of a foreign power

solely upon the basis of activities protected by the First Amendment."

c. The FISA was amended in a number of respects by the USA PATRIOT Act of 2001, the anti-terrorism law enacted in response to the destruction of the World Trade Center. For example, an FISA requirement that a senior official certify that the collection of foreign intelligence is "*the* purpose" (emphasis added) of the FISA search or surveillance has been changed so that obtaining foreign intelligence information need only be "*a significant purpose*" (emphasis added).

"As a result of this change," observes the Task Force on Technology and Law Enforce-

C. CAN TITLE III BE RECONCILED WITH THE FOURTH AMENDMENT?

Title III does meet at least some of the objections voiced by the *Berger* Court when it invalidated the state law involved in that case. The federal statute requires that surveillance cease once "the objective of the authorization" is achieved, § 2815(5), and it permits electronic surveillance extensions only upon a new showing of probable cause and only by resort to the procedures required in obtaining the initial order. (See id.) But Title III does allow continued electronic surveillance for up to 30 days on the basis of a single showing of probable cause, id., and it permits an unlimited number of 30 day extensions, albeit on renewed showings of probable cause. See id.

"Allowing such lengthy surveillance, possibly for years," argues a leading critic of police electronic eavesdropping, HERMAN SCHWARTZ, *The Legitimation of Electronic Eavesdropping*: *The Politics of "Law and Order,"* 67 Mich.L.Rev. 455, 461 (1969), "conflicts sharply with *Berger's* clear disapproval of the two-month authorization permitted by the New York statute. Moreover, sections 2518(1)(d) and 4(e) of the Act do not limit the eavesdropping to specific points in time, unlike the [situation] in *Katz* and the cases approvingly cited in *Berger,* but rather allow uninterrupted eavesdropping over a 'period of time.' Under such a provision, officers may install a tap or a bug which will be in *continuous* operation throughout the days or months for which the interception is authorized. This would seem to pose a rather clear conflict with the Supreme Court's holding in *Berger,* which disapproved the uninterrupted interception as allowing 'indiscriminate' seizure and approved the *Osborn* interception because 'the order authorized one limited intrusion rather [than] a continuous surveillance'."[a]

Shortly after Title III became law, Professor Schwartz expressed the belief that it "will turn out to be either a provision of relatively little value in the struggle against organized crime or a verbal smoke screen for continuing illegality" (id. at 468–69, 471–72):

"According to its proponents, the special advantage of electronic surveillance is that it is a valuable tool for gathering strategic intelligence about organized crime and that it thus enables law enforcement officials to obtain 'a look at the overall picture' for 'prevention' purposes. The techniques of fighting organized crime differ from those used in ordinary criminal investigation. The former involves accumulating a great deal of superficially irrelevant information which is then collated. Furthermore, in investigating organized crime the police do not work from a known crime to an unknown or suspected criminal, but 'backwards' from a 'known criminal' to a hoped-for discovery of an as-yet-unknown crime.

"[The] fact is that searches for strategic intelligence, without a specific crime as the objective, cannot be squared with *Berger, Katz,* and *Osborn.* Judging by the language used by the Court, the facts at issue in those cases, and the kinds of

ment, *ABA Electronic Standards on Electronic Surveillance* (3d ed. 2001) (Introduction), "court-ordered FISA surveillance is permissible when it is undertaken both for purposes of gathering foreign intelligence information and for use in a criminal prosecution, so long as the former purpose is 'a significant one.'" However, the change is "less dramatic than might appear from simply comparing the language of the statute before and after its amendment, since a number of courts have interpreted the requirement that 'the purpose' of the surveil-

lance be to obtain foreign intelligence to mean that it be 'the *primary* purpose' of the surveillance, thus permitting an FISA order to be obtained even when a criminal prosecution was a purpose, but not the primary one, of the surveillance." Id.

The USA PATRIOT Act also amends the FISA to allow issuance of "roving" wiretaps on the same basis that it is permitted under Title III. See p. 366.

a. But see *United States v. Cafero,* p. 361.

permissible electronic surveillance cited in the various opinions, it would seem that gathering tactical intelligence is the only kind of surveillance that is justifiable under present theories of the fourth amendment. And in this respect, [Title III] is verbally consistent with the cases in limiting eavesdropping to such tactical intelligence purposes.

"[This] is surely an odd result, for if the war against organized crime—the justification for Title III—really requires strategic intelligence, how will that war be advanced by legislation which seems to permit the acquisition of only tactical intelligence? And if the Act does not grant law enforcement officers the power to obtain allegedly crucial strategic information, will we not again experience the same kind of widespread flouting of clear legal limitations that has recently come to light? In sum, even the very loose Title III is too restrictive to accomplish the purposes advanced by its proponents, and this raises serious questions about the reasons for their support of the legislation, and about how meaningful they expect its ostensible limitations to be."[b]

But see National Wiretap Commission, *Majority Report* (1976),[c] "vigorously reaffirm[ing] the findings and statements of policy made by Congress in 1968 that organized criminals make extensive use of wire and oral communications in their criminal activities" and that "the interception of such communications to obtain evidence of the commission of crimes or to prevent their commission is an indispensable aid to law enforcement and the administration of justice."

Surprisingly, the Supreme Court has never explicitly considered the facial validity of Title III. But there is no hint in the Court's many decisions interpreting various provisions of Title III that the statute is facially invalid. And the lower federal courts have consistently upheld the statute against constitutional challenge.

Lower court decisions reconciling continuing electronic surveillance up to 30 days, permitted by Title III, with the Fourth Amendment, "rely upon the analysis of Justices Harlan and White, [both of whom] dissented in *Berger.* [See p. 354]. Their contention was that an electronic surveillance which is continued over a span of time is no more a general search than the typical execution of a search warrant over a described area." CRIMPROC § 4.2(b). Illustrative of the lower federal courts' rejection of constitutional challenges to Title III is UNITED STATES v. CAFERO, 473 F.2d 489 (3d Cir.1973), (ALDISERT, J.):

As for the contention that the statute is unconstitutional because it permits as much as 30 days of surveillance: "[W]e interpret § 2518(5) as requiring automatic termination upon attainment of the objective of the authorization irrespective of whether a statement to this effect has been included by the authorizing judge." As for the argument that Title III is fatally defective because it fails to require prompt notice to those people whose conversations have been intercepted after authorized surveillance has been completed: "We find it difficult to accept the proposition that a search may be deemed reasonable, and therefore constitutional, during the various stages of application for authorization, execu-

---

b. Professor Goldsmith maintains, however, Goldsmith at 52 n. 322, that Professor Schwartz's contention that Title III's limitation on surveillance for purely strategic intelligence is inconsistent with its drafters' goal of providing a means to combat organized crime on a long term basis "overlooks [that] strategic intelligence is often legitimately overheard during the course of actual surveillance."

c. Title III was enacted as a compromise of various conflicting views of the form any legislation regulating electronic surveillance should

take. The National Commission for the Review of Federal and State Laws Relating to Wiretapping and Electronic Surveillance (National Wiretap Commission) was created, as part of the compromise, to, among other duties, conduct a comprehensive study and review of the operation of Title III in the first six years after its enactment. The majority and minority reports issued in 1976 were the result of two years of work by the Commission.

tion, supervision of the interception, and termination, only to be invalidated *ab initio* because of the operation of some condition subsequent, to wit, a failure to give notice of the items seized." As for the complaint that the inventory procedure set forth in § 2518(8)(d) lacks the degree of promptness required by the Constitution: "[The] constitutional standard for searches and seizures relating to both tangible objects and communications is the reasonableness of the governmental action. [A] statute which requires an inventory to be filed within 'a reasonable time' cannot, without more, be said to offend this test. If, in a given case there is undue delay, that contention may be pressed in an appropriate averment alleging non-compliance with the statute."

It will be recalled that, concurring in the result in *Berger,* Justice Stewart concluded that although the evidence might have been adequate "for a conventional search or arrest," it was "constitutionally insufficient to constitute probable cause to justify an intrusion of the scope and duration that was permitted in this case." (See p. 354.) This argument, however, has not prevailed. Illustrative is *United States v. Falcone,* 505 F.2d 478 (3d Cir.1974): "Probable cause is not a matter of degree. Although *Berger* and *Katz* call for extra vigilance in the supervision of electronic eavesdropping, neither case separates probable cause into degrees. Moreover, no special probable cause requirement can be found in the statutory scheme."[a]

SECTION 3. SOME APPLICATIONS OF TITLE III

After considerable discussion, Professor Michael Goldsmith concludes that Title III is constitutional on its face, Goldsmith at 55, but he quickly adds: "The real question today * * * is not Title III's facial validity, but the manner in which it has been applied. Congress intended that the statute be strictly enforced under careful judicial supervision. Indeed, given the many questions raised about its facial validity, the law's ultimate constitutionality was said by some to depend upon such enforcement. Yet, ironically, the Supreme Court, which originally took the initiative in advising Congress as to the drafting of electronic surveillance legislation, has since failed to enforce Title III in a consistently scrupulous manner." Consider the following:

A. "MINIMIZ[ING] THE INTERCEPTION OF COMMUNICATIONS NOT OTHERWISE SUBJECT TO INTERCEPTION"; WHAT WEIGHT, IF ANY, SHOULD BE GIVEN TO THE OFFICER'S UNDERLYING INTENT OR MOTIVATION?

One of the limiting provisions of Title III is found in § 2518(5), requiring every order to contain a provision that the authorization to intercept "be conducted in such a way as to minimize the interception of communications not otherwise subject to interception." In SCOTT v. UNITED STATES, 436 U.S. 128, 98 S.Ct. 1717, 56 L.Ed.2d 168 (1978), pursuant to a court wiretap order requiring "minimization," government agents intercepted for a one-month period virtually all conversations over a particular telephone suspected of being used in furtherance

---

a. But consider Posner, J., in *United States v. Torres,* p. 368; Whitebread & Slobogin, p. 369.

of a conspiracy to import and distribute narcotics. Only forty percent of the conversations were shown to be narcotics related and the Special Agent who conducted the wiretap testified that "he and the agents working under him knew of the minimization requirement but made no attempt to comply therewith." Rejecting petitioners' argument that the failure to make good-faith efforts to comply with the minimization requirement is itself a violation of § 2518(5), a 7–2 majority per REHNQUIST, J., agreed with the Court of Appeals that an evaluation of compliance with the minimization requirement, like evaluation of all alleged violations of the Fourth Amendment, should "be based on the reasonableness of the actual interceptions and not on whether the agents subjectively intended to minimize their interceptions." Observed the Court:

"The Government [contends] that petitioners' argument fails to properly distinguish between what is necessary to establish a statutory or constitutional violation and what is necessary to support a suppression remedy once a violation has been established. In view of the deterrent purposes of the exclusionary rule, consideration of official motives may play some part in determining whether application of the exclusionary rule is appropriate *after* a statutory or constitutional violation has been established. But the existence *vel non* of such a violation turns on an objective assessment of the officer's actions in light of the facts and circumstances confronting him at the time. Subjective intent alone, the Government contends, does not make otherwise lawful conduct illegal or unconstitutional.

"[The Government's position] embodies the proper approach for evaluating compliance with the minimization requirement. [A]lmost without exception in evaluating alleged violations of the Fourth Amendment the Court has first undertaken an objective assessment of an officer's actions in light of the facts and circumstances then known to him. The language of the Amendment itself proscribes only 'unreasonable' searches and seizures.

"[In] the very section in which it directs minimization, Congress, by its use of the word 'conducted,' made it clear that the focus was to be on the agents' actions, not their motives. Any lingering doubt is dispelled by the legislative history [which declares that] § 2515 was not 'intended generally to press the scope of the suppression role beyond present search and seizure law.' "[m]

Analyzing the reasonableness of the agents' conduct, the Court observed: "[B]lind reliance on the percentage of nonpertinent calls intercepted is not a sure guide to the correct answer. Such percentages may provide assistance, but there are surely cases, such as the one at bar, where the percentage of nonpertinent calls is relatively high and yet their interception was still reasonable. The reasons for this may be many. Many of the nonpertinent calls may have been very short. Others may have been one-time only calls. Still others may have been ambiguous in nature or involve guarded or coded language. In all these circumstances agents can hardly be expected to know that their calls are not pertinent prior to their termination.

"[We] find nothing to persuade us that the Court of Appeals was wrong in its rejection of [the minimization] claims. Forty percent of the calls were clearly narcotics related * * *. Many of the remaining calls were very short, such as wrong number calls [and] calls to persons who were not available to come to the phone. [In] a case such as this, involving a wide-ranging conspiracy with a large

m. This is not to say, of course, that the question of motive plays absolutely no part in the suppression inquiry. On occasion, the motive with which the officer conducts an illegal search may have some relevance in determining the propriety of applying the exclusionary rule. [This] focus on intent, however, becomes relevant only after it has been determined that the Constitution was in fact violated. * * *

number of participants, even a seasoned listener would have been hard pressed to determine with any precision the relevancy of many of the calls before they were completed. A large number were ambiguous in nature, making characterization virtually impossible until the completion of these calls. * * *

"We are thus left with the seven calls between [petitioner] Jenkins and her mother. [After pointing out that most of the calls were intercepted at the beginning of the surveillance and that several indicated that the mother may have known of the conspiracy, the Court concluded that] [a]lthough none of these conversations turned out to be material to the investigation at hand, we cannot say that the Court of Appeals was incorrect in concluding that the agents did not act unreasonably at the time they made these interceptions."

Dissenting Justice BRENNAN, joined by Marshall, J., maintained that the Court's reasoning "is thrice flawed":

"First, and perhaps most significant, it totally disregards the explicit congressional command that the wiretap be *conducted* so as to minimize interception of communications not subject to interception. Second, it blinks reality by accepting as a substitute for the good-faith exercise of judgment as to which calls should not be intercepted by the agent most familiar with the investigation, the *post hoc* conjectures of the Government as to how the agent would have acted had he exercised his judgment. [In] the nature of things it is impossible to know how many fewer interceptions would have occurred had a good-faith judgment been exercised, and it is therefore totally unacceptable to permit the failure to exercise the congressionally imposed duty to be excused by the difficulty in predicting what might have occurred had the duty been exercised. Finally, the Court's holding permits government agents deliberately to flout the duty imposed upon them by Congress. In a linguistic *tour de force* the Court converts the mandatory language that the interception shall be conducted to a precatory suggestion."

Notes and Questions

1. **Commentary on Scott.** For criticism of *Scott*, see John Burkoff, *The Court that Devoured the Fourth Amendment: The Triumph of an Inconsistent Exclusionary Doctrine*, 58 Or.L.Rev. 151, 187–88 (1979) ("[i]ronically, the *Scott* Court's use of one test for determining the existence of a fourth amendment violation and a second test for application of an exclusionary remedy appears to have as its casuistic end the exclusion of deterrence from the first test although deterrence is the key element of the second test"); Goldsmith at 108–09 ("[g]iven the greater intrusion occasioned by electronic surveillance, [the] fourth amendment's reasonableness clause would seem to require such searches to be undertaken in good faith"). But see LaFave, Israel & King, § 3.1(d), maintaining that *Scott* properly rejected the contention that "lack of good faith efforts" required suppression even if no minimization would have been feasible in this case.

2. **Should the minimization provision be amended?** Consider Clifford Fishman, *The "Minimization" Requirement in Electronic Surveillance: Title III, the Fourth Amendment and the Dread Scott Decision*, 28 Am.U.L.Rev. 315, 354–55 (1979):

"[A] purely objective analysis of reasonableness may be adequate to decide whether an officer was justified in making an isolated arrest, stop, frisk, search or seizure, [but]is wholly inadequate when several weeks of continuous, surreptitious interceptions of otherwise private conversations are at issue. Particularly in complex investigations, where the government, with superficial plausibility can retroactively defend total interception, it is unlikely that any minimization will be achieved unless a good-faith effort is made to do so. [The] minimization provision should be amended to read: 'Every order and extension thereof shall contain a provision that the [interception] shall be conducted in a *good faith and reasonable manner in order to* minimize the interception of communications not otherwise subject to interception under this chapter.''

B. ELECTRONIC SURVEILLANCE WHICH INVOLVES COVERT ENTRY INTO PRIVATE PREMISES TO INSTALL EQUIPMENT; HAS THE COURT'S STATUTORY PERSPECTIVE UNDERGONE A FUNDAMENTAL CHANGE?

DALIA v. UNITED STATES, 441 U.S. 238, 99 S.Ct. 1682, 60 L.Ed.2d 177 (1979), arose as follows: Finding reasonable cause to believe that petitioner was conspiring to steal goods being shipped in interstate commerce and that his business office was being used by petitioner and others in connection with the alleged conspiracy, a federal district court authorized the interception of all oral communications concerning the conspiracy at petitioner's office. Although the court order did not explicitly authorize entry into petitioner's office, FBI agents secretly entered the office one midnight by prying open a window and spent three hours in the building installing a listening device in the ceiling. All electronic surveillance of petitioner ended some six weeks later, at which time the agents secretly re-entered petitioner's office and removed the bug. Partly on the basis of conversations intercepted pursuant to this order, petitioner was convicted of receiving stolen goods and related charges. The Court, per POWELL, J., upheld the electronic surveillance:

First, "[t]he Fourth Amendment does not prohibit *per se* a covert entry performed for the purpose of installing otherwise legal electronic bugging equipment." *Second,* the Court rejected the contention [that] Congress had not given the courts statutory authority to approve covert entries for electronic surveillance purposes: "Those considering the surveillance legislation understood that, by authorizing electronic interception of oral communications in addition to wire communications, they were necessarily authorizing surreptitious entries."

Third, the Court rejected the contention that, because the authorizing court did not explicitly set forth its approval of covert entries, the entry violated petitioner's Fourth Amendment privacy rights: The Warrant Clause of the Fourth Amendment requires only that warrants be issued by "neutral, disinterested magistrates"; that they be based on probable cause [and] that they "particularly describe" the things to be seized as well as the place to be searched. Nothing in [the] Fourth Amendment or the Court's decisions "suggests that, in addition to [these three requirements], search warrants also must include a specification of the precise manner in which they are to be executed."

Dissenting Justice STEVENS, joined by Brennan and Marshall, JJ., maintained: "Only one relevant conclusion can be drawn from a review of the entire legislative history of Title III. The legislators never even considered the possibility that they were passing a statute that would authorize federal agents to break into private premises without any finding of necessity by a neutral and detached magistrate. * * * Without a legislative mandate that is both explicit and specific, I would presume that this flagrant invasion of the citizen's privacy is prohibited."

In a separate opinion, concurring in part and dissenting in part, Justice BRENNAN, joined by Stewart, J., maintained that "even reading Title III to authorize covert entries, the Justice Department's present practice of securing specific authorization for covert entries is not only preferable, but also constitutionally required": "Breaking and entering into private premises for the purpose of planting a bug cannot be characterized as a mere mode of warrant execution to be left to the discretion of the executing officer. The practice entails an invasion of privacy of constitutional significance distinct from that which attends nontrespassory surveillance; indeed, it is tantamount to an independent search and seizure."

Notes and Questions

1. Consider, Comment, 70 J.Crim.L. & C. 510, 526–27 (1979): "[The *Dalia* majority's approach] is inconsistent with the overall emphasis of Title III—an emphasis upon minimizing the intrusiveness of an intercept order. [By] construing the statutory language—or the absence thereof—so as to require that breaking and entering be employed only when alternative means have been tried and have failed or else reasonably appear too unlikely to succeed if tried, the Supreme Court would merely have been extending the express requirement of sections 2518(1)(c) and 2518(3)(c)."

2. "In all likelihood," observes Goldsmith at 116–18, "the [*Dalia*] majority's pragmatic analysis more closely reflected congressional intent; [it] is inconceivable that, after years of debate, Congress would have failed to realize that most bugs necessitate covert entries. * * * Nevertheless, as enacted the statute contained a potential defect which had to be remedied. Ultimately, in *Dalia,* judicial process was used to rectify this legislative interstice. Hence, the true significance of *Dalia* lay not in the Court's holding that Title III conferred authority to effect covert entries, but in the manner in which this decision was made. * * * *Dalia* abandoned the mode of analysis adopted in *District Court* [p. 359] to remedy what Congress might otherwise have made explicit. In the process, the Court's statutory perspective seems to have undergone a fundamental change; although Title III had been designed to constitute a blanket prohibition against electronic surveillance, subject to narrowly tailored statutory exceptions, Justice Powell's analysis now suggested that the law conferred a general grant of authority subject to narrowly tailored prohibitions. Thus, analytically and perhaps philosophically, *Dalia* symbolized the extent to which the Supreme Court had changed direction since 1968 when Title III was enacted."

[handwritten margin note: Symboled how USSC changed direction]

C. "Roving" Surveillance

A "roving" wiretap permits electronic surveillance of an individual rather than a specific telephone, cell phone or computer terminal. Prior to the 1986 amendments, Title III required that all eavesdropping warrants specify the facility or place of the anticipated communication. As amended in 1986, however, Title III orders need not designate the surveillance site—

(a) if in the case of an application with respect to the interception of an *oral* communication "the application contains a full and complete statement as to why such specification is *not practical*" and the judge finds such specification "*not practical,*" § 2518(11)(a) (emphasis added); and

(b) if "in the case of an application with respect to a *wire* or *electronic* communication, [the] applicant makes a showing that there is probable cause to believe that the person's actions *could have the effect of thwarting interception* from a specified facility and the judge finds that such showing has been adequately made," § 2518(11)(b) (emphasis added).

Michael Goldsmith, *Eavesdropping Reform: The Legality of Roving Surveillance,* 1987 U.Ill.L.Rev. 401, 413 (hereinafter Goldsmith), notes that "[t]he legislative history's only attempt to illustrate [the meaning of the 'not practical'] concept involves 'a suspect who moves from room to room in a hotel to avoid a bug and who sets up a meeting with another suspect for a beach or field. [This] observation is undoubtedly accurate, but fails to provide guidance in other situations."

Why did the 1986 amendment impose more stringent requirements on roving *wiretapping* interceptions than on roving *oral* interceptions? According to Clifford Fishman, *Interception of Communications in Exigent Circumstances*, 22 Ga.L.Rev. 1, 55–56 (1987) (hereinafter Fishman), it was "because of concerns expressed by lobbyists for the nation's telephone companies, [who] wanted statutory protection for their clients, who might suddenly be told to 'wire up' large numbers of pay telephones on short notice." Goldsmith 414 regards the "thwarting interception" requirement unduly restrictive and voices concern that "courts may interpret the 'thwart' restriction for wiretaps as evincing congressional intent to construe the term 'not practical' [the term governing roving oral interceptions] narrowly as well."

At the time of the 1986 Amendments, questions were raised about the constitutionality of roving surveillance. See Fishman, supra, at 66–69; Goldsmith, supra, at 416–28. These questions were raised again when § 206 of the USA PATRIOT Act of 2001 modified the FISA to allow "roving" wiretaps on the same showing that they are obtainable under Title III.

Tracey Maclin, *Amending the Fourth: Another Grave Threat to Liberty*, National L. J., Nov. 12, 2001, maintains that "a wiretap that follows a person instead of a phone is at odds with the text and history of the Fourth Amendment"[a] and that "the requirement that a search warrant particularly describe the place to be searched was designed to bar multiple-specific search warrants that identified the target or object of a search or arrest, but authorized many places to be searched."[b] He continues (referring to *Steagald v. United States*, p. 259): "The Supreme Court has already recognized that particularizing the target of a government search or seizure violates the privacy rights of third parties who are subjected to unreasonable governmental intrusion while officers look for their target or evidence of criminal conduct."

See also David Markus, *Fourth Amendment Forum*, The Champion (publication of the National Association of Criminal Defense Lawyers), Dec. 2001, pp. 36, 40: The power to conduct electronic surveillance for an individual rather than a specific telephone means that "government officials [would] be listening not only to [suspect] A, but to the hundreds of other very innocent people who use [his phone lines] as well. The government would be permitted to listen [to] A's family, who uses the home phone lines, and to his co-workers who use the work lines. Moreover, anyone who sends e-mail from A's computers, including his family and co-workers, would be watched. And because A uses pay phones, police would be listening to random conversations in the airport."

But see Milton Hirsch, *Fourth Amendment Forum*, The Champion, pp. 37–38: "*Even without* [Attorney General Ashcroft's proposed amendments to the FISA,] all the lines [mentioned in Markus's hypothetical] can be tapped; it just requires more paperwork, prepared by more federal agents and submitted to more federal judges. The Ashcroft proposal reflects the facts of modern life reflected in [Markus's] example: nowadays, more people spend more time sending and receiving more information over more phones and phone lines. Changes in technology

a. As Professor Maclin notes, the second clause of the Fourth Amendment states: "no Warrants shall issue, but upon probable cause, * * * and particularly describing the place to be searched and the persons or things to be seized." Adds Maclin: "The warrant clause requires greater precision for a search than for a seizure."

b. "The Framers," observes Professor Maclin, "were well aware of the danger associated with multiple-specific search warrants. In 1706, for example, colonial officials used such warrants to search every home in New Hampshire."

have inevitably necessitated judicial and legislative responses. We do not live in the world of horse-drawn carriages, and we do not apply the Constitution as if we did."

SECTION 4. OTHER FORMS OF TECHNOLOGICAL SURVEILLANCE*

A. VIDEO SURVEILLANCE

Secret Video Surveillance of Private Areas

Title III does not cover video surveillance (and various attempts to legislate such surveillance have failed). Yet "[n]othing more dramatically conjures up the image of an 'Orwellian society' than a surreptitiously planted government 'eye' in one's living room." Whitebread & Slobogin 352.

Consider UNITED STATES v. TORRES, 751 F.2d 875 (7th Cir.1984), which arose as follows: The FBI obtained judicial authorization to install cameras in "safehouses" being used by members of FALN, a Puerto Rico separatist group suspected of making explosives for terrorist purposes. (The government had not invoked the Foreign Intelligence Surveillance Act.) The videotapes had no sound-tracks, but at the same time that the FBI was televising the interior of the house (in some respects more like a business than a home) it was recording the sounds on different equipment. (The admissibility of the sound tapes was not an issue in this appeal.) As Judge Posner, author of the Seventh Circuit majority opinion in the case, explained, "the FBI wanted to see as well as hear because it had reason to believe that the [suspects], concerned that they might be bugged, would play the radio loudly when they were speaking to each other and also would speak in code and that the actual assembly of the bombs would be carried out in silence." The district court held that Title III did not authorize such surveillance and in the absence of any statutory basis for the authorizing order, the videotaping had violated the Fourth Amendment.

The Seventh Circuit reversed. A majority of the court, per POSNER, J., agreed that there was no statutory authorization for the court order to install the cameras, but held that the district court nevertheless had the authority—under both Fed.R.Crim.P. 41(b) and its inherent judicial power to issue warrants—to issue a warrant authorizing the television surveillance. Although the court concluded that Title III neither authorized nor prohibited silent video surveillance, it made clear that, "because television surveillance is potentially so menacing to personal privacy," a warrant that failed to satisfy (as the government *did* satisfy in this case) the provisions of Title III would violate the Fourth Amendment.

"The usual way in which judges interpreting the Fourth Amendment take account of the fact that searches vary in the degree to which they invade personal privacy," observed Judge Posner, "is by requiring a higher degree of probable cause (to believe that the search will yield incriminating evidence), and by being more insistent that a warrant be obtained if at all feasible, the more intrusive the search is. But maybe in dealing with so intrusive a technique as television surveillance, other methods of control as well, such as banning the technique outright from use in the home in connection with minor crimes, will be required in order to strike a proper balance between public safety and personal privacy. That question is not before us, but we mention it to make clear that in declining to hold televison surveillance unconstitutional *per se* we do not suggest that the Constitution must be interpreted to allow it to be used as generally as less

---

* See also *Kyllo v. United States*, p. 148, and Notes 3 to 11 following *Kyllo*.

intrusive techniques can be. * * * [A] search could be unreasonable, though conducted pursuant to an otherwise valid warrant, by intruding on personal privacy to an extent disproportionate to the likely benefits from obtaining fuller compliance with the law. '[T]here can be no ready test for determining reasonableness other than by balancing the need to search against the invasion which the search entails.' *Camara v. Municipal Court* [p. 326]."

Professors Whitebread and Slobogin believe (supra at 353) that, considering "its heightened level of intrusiveness," video surveillance "ought to be subject to *greater* restriction than electronic eavesdropping":

"First, because minimization is particularly difficult to enforce where cameras are involved, a stringent prohibition [against] bad faith viewing of activities which are innocent or which do not involve the suspects is appropriate. * * * One appropriate minimization method [is] prohibition of video surveillance until audio surveillance indicates criminal activity is taking place.

"Indeed, one can argue that a warrant for video surveillance should not be issued unless no other method, including eavesdropping, can accomplish the investigative objective. In *Torres*, for instance, there may have been probable cause sufficient to obtain a search warrant authorizing entry of the safehouses while the bombs were being made. This alternative may not have produced as much evidence as video surveillance but may still have been preferable to it. In *People v. Teicher*,[133] on the other hand, there probably was no alternative to installing a camera focused on the dental chair of a dentist suspected of sexually abusing his patients. [Furthermore,] stated the court, 'the use of a police decoy without the protection of visual surveillance would not have produced the needed evidence in this case, since the decoy, of necessity, would have been heavily sedated and might not have been able to relate what transpired.' * * *

"[S]hortening the duration of video surveillance under each warrant is also a worthwhile idea. Given the intrusiveness of video surveillance, if evidence of criminal activity sufficient to make a case is not obtained within a very short time, police should have to justify further surveillance."

Video Surveillance in Public Places; Biometric Technology

Is video surveillance in public places a good idea? Americans have different views, as illustrated by their different reactions to the news that the government plans to install a closed-circuit television system at the Washington Monument and the Lincoln, Jefferson, Franklin D. Roosevelt, Vietnam and Korean War Memorials. See Peter T. Kilborn, *For Security, Tourists To Be on Other Side of Cameras*, N.Y. Times, Mar. 23, 2002, p. A12.[a]

When told of the news, one visitor to Washington, D.C. responded: "With all the crime we have in our nation, I think it's a real good idea." A second person said: "That watchful eye is protecting me. I feel more protected when someone is watching over my shoulder." But other visitors disagreed. One said: "Where do we cross the line? When do we become a police state? [With the eye of a camera watching me strolling on the lawn,] I'll feel like I felt in Tiananmen Square." *Id.*

---

133.   422 N.E.2d 506 (N.Y.1981).

a. The article also pointed out that "[n]ationwide, surveillance cameras have become commonplace in airports, highway toll booths, parking garages, stores, malls, banks, A.T.M.'s, the Statue of Liberty and at the Golden Gate Bridge." Under this technique, "police officers monitor the CCTV screens and can dispatch assistance immediately when anything unusual appears on the screen. The officer on monitoring duty can adjust the camera for a better viewing angle and focus on suspected criminal activity. The most sophisticated aspect of the system, however, is a technological breakthrough known as light amplification ability. This feature permits the system to be used at night, thus giving constant twenty-four hour surveillance." Note, 13 U.Mich.J.L.Ref. 571, 573 (1980).

Does the Fourth Amendment prohibit (or at least impose some limits on) this type of surveillance, or is the Fourth Amendment irrelevant in this context because, as Kilborn notes, a government official told Congress that these cameras watch areas "where there is no expectation of privacy"? Compare *State v. Abislaiman*, 437 So.2d 181 (Fla.App. 1983) (leaving open question of whether other use of such equipment a search, court holds that nocturnal operation and monitoring of camera with zoom lens as security measure in hospital parking lot did not infringe upon defendant's rights, as "a hospital's emergency room parking lot is one of the few places where one would expect a certain amount of traffic even at 2:30 a.m."); with *State v. Solis*, 214 Mont. 310, 693 P.2d 518 (Mont. 1984) (warrantless videotaping of transactions in pawn shop operated undercover by police illegal under state constitution, as "there is a reasonable expectation that hidden monitoring is not taking place"). Consider Jennifer M. Granholm, *Video Surveillance of Public Streets: The Constitutionality of Invisible Citizen Searches*, 64 U.Det.L.Rev. 687 (1987) (arguing public has a justified expectation of privacy of a limited nature, so that reasonable suspicion should be required for such surveillance).

Whether or not grounded in the Fourth Amendment are certain limits upon extended video surveillance in public places needed? Consider *A.B.A. Standards* § 2–6.3(b) (3d ed. 1998): "Overt video surveillance for a protracted period * * * is permissible when:

"(i) A politically accountable law enforcement official or the relevant politically accountable governmental authority concludes that it will (A) Not view a private activity or condition; and (B) Will be reasonably likely to achieve a legitimate law enforcement objective; and

"(ii) In cases where deterrence rather than investigation is the primary objective, the public to be affected by the surveillance: (A) Is notified of the intended location and general capability of the camera; and (B) Has the opportunity, both prior to the initiation of the surveillance and periodically during it, to express its views of the surveillance and propose changes in its execution, through a hearing or some other appropriate means."

An official of the U.S. Park Police (which will monitor the cameras) told Congress that there was no plan to use face-recognition technology, "which compares faces in crowds with those of fugitives in [government] files." *Id.* But consider Jeffrey Rosen, *A Watchful State*, N.Y. Times Magazine, Oct. 7, 2001, pp. 38, 40:

"[Visionics] is an industry leader in the fledgling science of biometrics, a method of identifying people by scanning and quantifying their unique physical characteristics—their facial structures, for example, or their retinal patterns. Visionics manufactures a face-recognition technology called Faceit, which creates identification codes for individuals based on 80 unique aspects of their facial structures, like the width of the nose and the location of the temples. Faceit can instantly compare an image of any individual's face with a database of the faces of suspected terrorists, or anyone else.[a]

"[The head of Visionics] proposes to wire up Reagan National Airport in Washington and other vulnerable airports throughout the country with more than 300 cameras each. Cameras would scan the faces of passengers standing in line,

---

a. "When biometrics is more fully developed," observes Amitai Etzioni, *The Limits of Privacy* 115 (1999), "an individual doing something for which he or she needs to be identified (e.g., buying a gun, applying for a job, or receiving government aid) would place a hand on a machine or stand with his or her eyes near a retinal scanner that would verify whether the hand or retina matches the record in a database. If voice recognition is employed, the individual would be asked to speak."

and biometric technology would be used to analyze their faces and make sure they are not on an international terrorist 'watch list.' " * * * In the wake of the Sept. 11 attacks, Howard Safir, the former New York police commissioner, recommended the installation of 100 biometric surveillance cameras in Time Square to scan the faces of pedestrians and compare them with a database of suspected terrorists. [Since] the attacks [Visionics] has been approached by local and federal authorities from across the country about the possibility of installing biometric surveillance cameras in stadiums and subway systems and near national monuments."

"[Before] Sept. 11, the idea that Americans would voluntarily agree to live their lives under the gaze of a network of biometric surveillance cameras peering at them in government buildings, shopping malls, subways and stadiums would have seemed unthinkable * * *. But in fact, over the past decade, this precise state of affairs has materialized, not in the United States but in the United Kingdom."

Does the Fourth Amendment prohibit, or at least impose limits on, this type of surveillance? Or is the Court likely to say, quoting *United States v. Knotts* (the "beeper" case discussed at p. 155), that "[n]othing in the Fourth Amendment prohibit[s] the police from augmenting the sensory faculties bestowed upon them at birth with such enhancement as science and technology afford them"? May limitations be imposed on such surveillance, as Whitebread and Slobogin suggest, at 354, "under the Fourth Amendment's Reasonableness Clause"? If cameras are installed, should the public be notified of their presence, in order (a) to ensure that people who frequent the area will know that their activities are being monitored and (b) to promote the deterrent effect of the surveillance? See id.

B. "CARNIVORE" (A.K.A. DCS–1000)

Once a court order is obtained under Title III, "Carnivore," an Internet-surveillance program developed by the FBI, is used to filter through Internet communications, including e-mail messages, to select the relevant ones. "A computer loaded with Carnivore can be plugged into an Internet-service provider's network, allowing the software to monitor the routing information for billions of distinct Internet communications such as e-mails and to make copies of full messages sent by or received from [a] suspect." Ted Bridis, *Congressional Panel Debates Carnivore as FBI Moves to Mollify Privacy Worries*, Wall St. J., July 25, 2000, at A24. Carnivore does its work without altering data or preventing messages from continuing to their intended destination. Moreover, "the FBI maintains that no record is kept of any unrelated messages sent by innocent customers of the same Internet provider." Bridis, supra.

Carnivore has generated much fear and controversy. According to the FBI, however, in the first 18 months since the software's inception in April, 1999, it has only been used about 25 times to collect any electronic information. See Wall St. J., Nov. 21, 2000, at A4.

In meetings with lawmakers, the FBI has emphasized and sought to demonstrate, how the system could tailor its search so as to capture only the e-mails moving into and out of one particular account. See Ted Bridis & Neil King Jr., *Carnivore E–Mail Tool Won't Eat Up Privacy, Says FBI*, Wall St. J., July 20, 2000, at A28. The FBI claims that "Carnivore is smart enough to capture a suspect's e-mails while leaving untouched messages sent by his or her spouse or children." Id. If a judge so instructs the government, "Carnivore can be set to merely trace Internet communications to and from a suspect, called a 'pen register' or 'trap and trace.' Carnivore records the Internet addresses of passing traffic, but not, for example, the contents or even the subject line of an e-mail." Id.[a]

Carnivore's critics complain that since the FBI adamantly opposes disclosing the "blueprints" for how its software works—even to Congress—there is no way of knowing how broad the FBI "snooping" really is. See id. A spokesperson for the ACLU testified that the Carnivore system is "roughly the equivalent to a wiretap capable of accessing the contents of all of the phone company's customers with the assurance that the FBI will record only conversations of the specific target." Moreover, added Cong. Jerold Nadler, even if civilian experts could look at Carnivore's blueprints, they would only be looking at something that is continually being upgraded and modified. "It could change at any time," observed the Congressman. "You can't trust a police agency forever." Id.

A review of the "Carnivore" system by a panel chaired by Henry Perritt Jr., dean of the Chicago—Kent College of Law expressed confidence overall in the FBI's use of the software. See Wall St. J., Nov. 21, 2000 at A4. But a group of five prominent computer-security experts concluded that, so far, the FBI has failed to ease personal-privacy concerns raised by the program. See Wall St. J., Dec. 5, 2000, at B6. One of the experts disclosed that the five-person group had come upon "a relatively common scenario in which Carnivore could miss collecting important evidence." According to the expert, the glitch is quite serious "because it could cause the FBI to miss e-mails that might suggest a person's innocence in a crime or allow agents to collect Internet traffic from innocent citizens unrelated to their investigation." Id.

The FBI has never liked the name "Carnivore." "In an apparent attempt to remove associations of bloodthirstiness and improve the sniffer's image," reports David Wilson, *Sniffing Out the Unsavory on the Internet*, South China Morning Post, Dec. 5, 2001, at 7, the FBI recently renamed the program DCS–1000. "But the change has only aroused more suspicion—as one commentator said, even if Carnivore had been renamed Bambi, the fears would remain."

C. SHOULD LAW ENFORCEMENT AUTHORITIES BE PERMITTED TO UNSCRAMBLE AN ENCRYPTED COMMUNICATION BACK INTO READABLE FORM?

As pointed out in Orin S. Kerr, *The Fourth Amendment in Cyberspace: Can Encryption Create A "Reasonable Expectation of Privacy?,"* 33 Conn. L.Rev. 503 (2001), when a computer file is encrypted using software such as P.G.P. (for Pretty Good Privacy), the file is scrambled into an unreadable form (known at "ciphertext"). At this point, without the encryption key, it becomes virtually impossible for anyone (including law enforcement authorities) to convert the message back into readable form (known as "plaintext").

Speculation that those who attacked the World Trade Center and the Pentagon may have used encryption to cloak their communications have led some lawmakers to seek legislation requiring encryption companies to include a "back door" that would allow law enforcement agencies access when a suspected terrorist may have used encryption. See John Schwartz, *Disputes on Electronic*

---

a. It is "widely rumored," however, that the "Echelon" surveillance network operated overseas by the National Security Agency does have this capability, See Bridis & King, supra. Echelon "is an international network of sniffers and other snooping technologies run by the intelligence organizations of the U.S., Great Britain, Canada, Australia and New Zea-land. "Created nearly 40 years ago to keep tabs on the Soviet Union, its focus has switched from espionage to surveillance of terrorists, organized crime, sensitive diplomatic negotiations [and] domestic political groups thought to be a threat." David Wilson, *Sniffing Out the Unsavory on the Internet*, South China Morning Post, Dec. 5, 2001, at 7.

Message Encryption Take on New Urgency, N.Y. Times, Sept. 25, 2001, at C1.[a] Proposals for such access systems are known as "key escrow" because a key that unlocks encrypted messages would be stored and made available to law enforcement. These proposals were the subject of a bitter debate in the mid–1990s when the Clinton Administration proposed a back-door access technology, popularly known as the "Clipper Chip." See id.

"The privacy implications of encryption," notes Kerr, supra, "have led many Internet law scholars to declare encryption regulation constitutionally off-limits" on the ground that "encrypting an electronic communication creates a 'reasonable expectation of privacy' in the communication's content, triggering Fourth Amendment protection." Some commentators, adds Professor Kerr, have analogized encryption to a lock and key: just as locking a box with a key creates a reasonable expectation of privacy in its contents, locking a communication by encrypting it with an encryption key does the same."

Professor Kerr disagrees strongly with those who believe that the Fourth Amendment protects encryption. He maintains that the Fourth Amendment provides no protection because the Amendment "regulates government access to communications, not the cognitive understanding of communications already obtained. Once ciphertext is in plain view, the communication itself is in plain view for Fourth Amendment purposes. Although the government must unscramble the communication to understand it, the Fourth Amendment cannot regulate the cognitive process by which the government attempts to extract meaning from an encrypted communication in its possession." How persuasive do you find this argument?[b]

D. A FINAL WORD ON THREATS OF TERRORISM, THREATS TO PRIVACY, AND THE PUBLIC'S RESPONSE

Among the proposed high-technology responses to the threat of terrorism sure to be on the agenda in the year 2002, reports John Schwartz, *Technology: Cybersecurity; Threat of Terrorism on U.S. Infrastructure*, N.Y. Times, Dec. 11, 2001, at C3, "are renewed calls for a natural identification card and extended wiretapping and Internet monitoring authority for law enforcement agents. A

a. Amitai Etzioni, *The Limits of Privacy*, 78 (1999), points out that "Aldrich Ames, a CIA official who spied on the United States for the Soviet Union, encrypted files on his personal computer. Members of the Aum Shinri Kyo (Supreme Truth) cult, which launched a deadly nerve gas attack on the Tokyo subway in 1995, encrypted computer files that contained details about their plans to inflict mass destruction in the United States. [After] the bombing of the U.S. embassies in Kenya and Tanzania in 1998 it was revealed that the CIA had foiled three other attacks in 1997 by using electronic interceptions. These would not have been possible if the terrorists had used strong encryption."

b. Although the Task Force on Technology and Law Enforcement, *ABA Standards on Electronic Surveillance* (3d ed. 2001), does not directly address encryption, because "no consensus emerged within the Task Force on this issue," it notes (Introduction, fn. 14):

"In the absence of legal authority for requiring an electronic communication service provider to provide a law enforcement officer with an encryption key when a court orders that encrypted communications may be intercepted, law enforcement continues its search for other means to decrypt communications. Inevitably, some of those means will be subject to legal challenge. See *F.B.I. Use of New Technology to Gather Evidence Challenged*, New York Times, July 30, 2001, p. C7, describing a challenge by [a defendant] to 'evidence gathered by a controversial new law enforcement technology: a system that recorded every keystroke typed on a computer, including the password that investigators used to unscramble [the defendant's] files.' The defendant claims, inter alia, that the use of this 'key logger' system required an electronic surveillance order. Invoking the Classified Information Procedure Act, the Justice Department has resisted publicly revealing how the system works. *U.S. Refuses to Disclose PC Tracking*, New York Times, August 25, 2001, p. C1."

controversial system installed on a criminal suspect's computer by the government to capture the encryption passwords of a criminal suspect is nearing its second phase; the F.B.I. has acknowledged that it is developing a similar monitoring system, called 'Magic Lantern,' that could be installed remotely."

One need not peer into the future. As Lisa Guernsey, *Living Under an Electronic Eye*, N.Y. Times, Sept. 27, 2001, p. G1, observes: "A wealth of new electronic information is already available to law enforcement agencies. With a court order, agents can retrieve records of credit-card purchases, peruse the logs kept by automated toll booths to determine which cars drove through., listen to voice mail left in databases, gather lists of library books checked out by patrons, watch videos recorded by public surveillance cameras and find out which television shows a subscriber has ordered on pay-per-view services."

What has the public's response been to law enforcement's use of the new electronic information? What is the response likely to be to new threats to privacy? Consider Guernsey, supra:

"It is an open question [whether] people view digital surveillance as intrusive, especially given their new fears about terrorism. By reviewing some of those seemingly mundane electronic records, investigators have been able to retrace the movements of terrorists who carried out the attacks on Sept. 11. Agents have searched computers at a public library and a Kinko's shop in Florida that appear to have been used by the hijackers to buy airline tickets. Videotape of automobile traffic at Logan Airport in Boston revealed that one of them, Mohamed Atta, drove through the area at least five times before the attacks, perhaps making dry runs.

"A year ago, during the presidential election campaign, political pollsters were finding that voters seemed increasingly wary of privacy invasions by companies or by the government. Today, concerns about security are trumping such wariness. In a poll conducted on Sept. 13 and 14 by The New York Times and CBS News, respondents were asked whether they believed that Americans would have to 'give up some personal freedoms in order to make the country safe from terrorist attacks.' 'Yes' was the response of 74 percent. A week later that number rose to 79 percent.

"The same poll showed a strengthening of support for governmental monitoring of e-mail and phone conversations of ordinary Americans on a regular basis. About 45 percent said they would be willing to allow such monitoring, up from 39 percent the week before; 56 percent of people also favored the idea of national electronic ID cards."

SECTION 5. THE USE OF SECRET AGENTS (WITH AND WITHOUT ELECTRONIC DEVICES) TO OBTAIN INCRIMINATING STATEMENTS

In LOPEZ v. UNITED STATES, 373 U.S. 427, 83 S.Ct. 1381, 10 L.Ed.2d 462 (1963), petitioner made an unsolicited bribe offer to Davis, an IRS agent, who, following his superiors' instructions to "pretend to play along with the scheme," met petitioner in the latter's office and recorded his subsequent bribe offers by means of a concealed wire recorder. Relying heavily on *On Lee v. United States*[c]

---

    c. In *On Lee,* 343 U.S. 747, 72 S.Ct. 967, 96 L.Ed. 1270 (1952), Chin Poy, an old acquaintance and former employee of defendant, entered the latter's laundry and engaged him in conversation, in the course of which defendant made incriminating statements. Unknown to defendant, Chin Poy was a "wired for sound" secret government agent, and the microphone concealed on his person transmitted all sounds to a narcotics agent stationed outside. Chin

and *Rathbun v. United States,*[d] the Court, per HARLAN, J., rejected the argument that considering the agent's falsification of his mission, he gained access to Lopez's office by misrepresentation and consequently illegally "seized" Lopez's words:

"[T]his case involves no 'eavesdropping' whatever in any proper sense of that term. The Government did not use an electronic device to listen in on conversations it could not otherwise have heard. Instead, the device was used only to obtain the most reliable evidence possible of a conversation in which the Government's own agent was a participant and which that agent was fully entitled to disclose. And the device was not planted by means of an unlawful physical invasion of petitioner's premises under circumstances which would violate the Fourth Amendment. It was carried in and out by an agent who was there with petitioner's assent, and it neither saw nor heard more than the agent himself. * * *

"Stripped to its essentials, petitioner's argument amounts to saying that he has a constitutional right to rely on possible flaws in the agent's memory, or to challenge the agent's credibility without being beset by corroborating evidence that is not susceptible of impeachment. For no other argument can justify excluding an accurate version of a conversation that the agent could testify to from memory. We think the risk that petitioner took in offering a bribe to Davis fairly included the risk that the offer would be accurately reproduced in court, whether by faultless memory or mechanical recording."

Chief Justice WARREN concurred separately, agreeing with the *Lopez* dissenters that *On Lee* was wrongly decided, but finding *On Lee* and the instant case "quite dissimilar constitutionally":

"The only purpose the recording served [in the instant case] was to protect the credibility of [Agent] Davis against that of a man who wished to corrupt a public servant in the performance of his public trust. I find nothing unfair in this procedure. [The] use and purpose of the transmitter in *On Lee* was substantially different from the use of the recorder here. Its advantage was not to corroborate the testimony of Chin Poy, but rather, to obviate the need to put him on the stand. [Had] Chin Poy been available for cross-examination, [the defense could have explored] the possibility of entrapments, police pressure brought to bear to persuade Chin Poy to turn informer, and Chin Poy's own recollection of the contents of the conversation. His testimony might not only have seriously discredited the prosecution, but might also have raised questions of constitutional proportions."

Poy was not called to testify about defendant's incriminating statements—probably because "the very defects of character and blemishes of record which [led defendant to confide in him] would make a jury distrust his testimony"— but the narcotics agent was allowed to relate the conversations he overheard. A 5–4 majority, per Jackson, J., rejected the claim that Chin Poy had committed a trespass because consent to enter defendant's laundry was obtained by fraud. And the Court dismissed as "verging on the frivolous" the further contention that the agent stationed outside the laundry was "a trespasser" because, by virtue of the microphone concealed on Chin Poy, he overheard what went on inside. "It would be a dubious service to the genuine liberties protected by the Fourth Amendment," observed the Court, "to make them bedfellows with spurious liber-

ties improvised by farfetched analogies which would liken eavesdropping on a conversation, with the connivance of one of the parties, to an unreasonable search and seizure."

d. In *Rathbun,* 355 U.S. 107, 78 S.Ct. 161, 2 L.Ed.2d 134 (1957), the Court held, per Warren, C.J., that the overhearing of a conversation on a regularly used telephone extension with the consent of one party to the conversation was not a violation of § 605 of the Federal Communications Act: "Each party to a telephone conversation takes the risk that the other party may have an extension telephone and may allow another to overhear the conversation. When such takes place there has been no violation of any privacy of which the parties may complain. Consequently, one element of Section 605, *interception,* has not occurred."

Justice BRENNAN, joined by Douglas and Goldberg, JJ., dissented, finding *On Lee* indistinguishable from the instant case and maintaining that the evidence should have been excluded in both cases:

"[Not] all communications are privileged. On Lee assumed the risk that his acquaintance would divulge their conversation; Lopez assumed the same risk *vis-à-vis* Davis. The risk inheres in all communications which are not in the sight of the law privileged. [But] the risk which both *On Lee* and today's decision impose is of a different order. It is the risk that third parties, whether mechanical auditors like the Minifon or human transcribers of mechanical transmissions as in *On Lee*—third parties who cannot be shut out of a conversation as conventional eavesdroppers can be, merely by a lowering of voices, or withdrawing to a private place—may give independent evidence of any conversation. There is only one way to guard against such a risk, and that is to keep one's mouth shut on all occasions.

"[There] is a qualitative difference between electronic surveillance [and] conventional police stratagems such as eavesdropping and disguise. The latter do not so seriously intrude upon the right of privacy. The risk of being overheard by an eavesdropper or betrayed by an informer or deceived as to the identity of one with whom one deals is probably inherent in the conditions of human society. It is the kind of risk we necessarily assume whenever we speak. But as soon as electronic surveillance comes into play, the risk changes crucially. There is no security from that kind of eavesdropping, no way of mitigating the risk, and so not even a residuum of true privacy."

Notes and Questions

1. If conversations are within the protection of the Fourth Amendment, why should it matter whether the conversation was "seized" by an electronic device? Was the police practice involved in *On Lee* any dirtier business than it would have been had the defendant's old acquaintance simply elicited the incriminating admissions and then testified? Why does the fact that On Lee would have been better able to attack the acquaintance's credibility than he was to challenge that of the narcotics bureau agent make the original deceit more moral? See Kent Greenawalt, *The Consent Problem in Wiretapping and Eavesdropping*, 68 Colum.L.Rev. 189, 193 (1968); Edmund W. Kitch, *Katz v. United States: The Limits of the Fourth Amendment*, 1968 Supreme Court Rev. 133, 141–42.

2. Is the issue not whether secret agents and informers can be monitored, but whether a warrant is necessary for such monitoring? To what extent is Justice Brennan's position based on the premise that "the warrant procedure can be adapted to electronic surveillance of specific persons at specific places for a limited period of time," but—inasmuch as informers and secret agents "must be developed or placed over a long period of time and the objectives of their 'search' will almost always be broad and impossible to delineate with any precision in advance"?the Fourth Amendment warrant requirement would "prevent altogether the use of informers and secret agents"? See Kitch, supra, at 142.

———

In LEWIS v. UNITED STATES, 385 U.S. 206, 87 S.Ct. 424, 17 L.Ed.2d 312 (1966), decided the same day as *Hoffa*, infra, a federal narcotics agent, by misrepresenting his identity as "Jimmy the Pollack [sic]" and expressing a willingness to purchase narcotics, was invited into petitioner's home where an unlawful narcotics transaction took place. At petitioner's trial, the agent testified as to what occurred in petitioner's home and the narcotics were introduced.

Petitioner relied on *Gouled v. United States,* 255 U.S. 298, 41 S.Ct. 261, 65 L.Ed. 647 (1921) (other aspects of which are discussed at p. 160), which excluded incriminating documents obtained when, acting under federal officers' orders, a business acquaintance of defendant obtained entry into defendant's office by pretending that he intended only to pay a social visit, but in defendant's absence searched the office. The *Gouled* Court held that "whether entrance to the home or office of a [suspect] be obtained by a [government agent] by stealth or through social acquaintance, or in the guise of a business call, and whether the owner be present or not when he enters, any search and seizure subsequently and secretly made in his absence falls within the scope of the prohibition of the Fourth Amendment * * * "

Distinguishing *Gouled,* the Court, per WARREN, C.J., stressed that "in the instant case [the] petitioner invited the undercover agent to his home for the specific purpose of executing a felonious sale of narcotics. [During] neither of his visits to petitioner's home did the agent see, hear, or take anything that was not contemplated and in fact intended by petitioner as a necessary part of his illegal business. Were we to hold the deceptions of the agent in this case constitutionally prohibited, we would come near to a rule that the use of undercover agents in any manner is virtually unconstitutional per se.[a] [W]hen, as here, the home is converted into a commercial center to which outsiders are invited for purposes of transacting unlawful business, that business is entitled to no greater sanctity than if it were carried on in a store, a garage, a car or on the street. [This case has been well summarized by the Government as follows:] '[T]he only statements repeated were those that were willingly made to the agent and the only things taken were the packets of marihuana voluntarily transferred to him. The pretense resulted in no breach of privacy; it merely encouraged the suspect to say things which he was willing and anxious to say to anyone who would be interested in purchasing marihuana.' "[b]

Why didn't the *Lewis* Court dismiss petitioner's argument out of hand with a citation to *Lopez?* Why instead, in a case in which no electronic device was used, did the Court assume that the use of a secret agent raised a serious Fourth Amendment problem. See Kitch, supra, at 141–43.

———

a. Consider Daniel Rotenberg, *The Police Detection Practice of Encouragement: Lewis v. United States and Beyond,* 4 Houston L.Rev. 609, 614 (1967): "To say that public encouragement [the author defines 'encouragement' as the activity of police or their agents acting in the capacity of 'victims' and communicating this feigned willingness to be a victim to the suspect] is proper, but private encouragement is not, is to tell narcotics sellers to 'move indoors.' [Where] the *modus operandi* of the criminal includes both public and private places, the encouraging officer, if he is to complete the encouragement detection, has no choice except to enter the defendant's private quarters. Observations of the practices of prostitutes show that some of them operate out of hotel rooms or private residences using the telephone to make appointments. If a policeman is to detect the prostitute's commission of a solicitation he must, playing the role of a client, enter her private room or residence and encourage her. It follows that, if the narcotics

seller were, in effect, told to 'move indoors,' he would. Copying the homosexual [in a jurisdiction where only public solicitation by a homosexual is criminal] and prostitute, he would use the telephone to set up sales, or would roam the streets locating buyers and then retreat into privacy before making the outlawed sale. The [*Lewis*] Court obviously appreciated the inseparable relationship of public and private encouragement."

As Professor Rotenberg has observed, id. at 612, "the practice [of police encouragement], although not the label," was before the Court in *Lewis,* but what significance, if any, the case has for police encouragement and the defense of entrapment is unclear for, as the Court noted, "petitioner does not argue that he was entrapped, as he could not on the facts of this case." See generally Ch. 7, infra.

b. Only Justice Douglas dissented. See p. 379.

James Hoffa was convicted for endeavoring to bribe members of a jury, during the so-called Test Fleet trial, which ended in a hung jury. A substantial element in the government's proof was the testimony of one Partin, a local union official. After being released from jail where he had been held pending state and federal charges, Partin had made frequent visits to the Hoffa hotel suite, on which occasions he was continually in the company of Hoffa and his associates. Proceeding upon the premise that Partin was a "governmental informer" from the time he first arrived on the scene in the Test Fleet and that the government had compensated him for his services as such, the Court nevertheless affirmed the conviction, HOFFA v. UNITED STATES, 385 U.S. 293, 87 S.Ct. 408, 17 L.Ed.2d 374 (1966),[a] in an opinion by Justice STEWART:

"The argument is that Partin's failure to disclose his role as a government informer vitiated the consent that the petitioner gave to Partin's repeated entries into [Hoffa's hotel] suite, and that by listening to the petitioner's statements Partin conducted an illegal 'search' for verbal evidence. [Where] the argument falls is in its misapprehension of the fundamental nature and scope of Fourth Amendment protection. What the Fourth Amendment protects is the security a man relies upon when he places himself or his property within a constitutionally protected area, be it his home or his office, his hotel room or his automobile.[b]

"[In] the present case, however, it is evident that no interest legitimately protected by the Fourth Amendment is involved. [Partin] was in the suite by invitation, and every conversation which he heard was either directed to him or knowingly carried on in his presence. The petitioner, in a word, was not relying on the security of the hotel room; he was relying upon his misplaced confidence that Partin would not reveal his wrongdoing. * * * Neither this Court nor any member of it has ever expressed the view that the Fourth Amendment protects a wrongdoer's misplaced belief that a person to whom he voluntarily confides his wrongdoing will not reveal it. Indeed, the Court unanimously rejected that very contention less than four years ago in *Lopez*. [The] Court was divided [on the admissibility of the surreptitious recording]. But there was no dissent from the view that testimony about the conversation by Davis himself was clearly admissible. [In] the words of the dissenting opinion in *Lopez*, 'the risk of being overheard by an eavesdropper or betrayed by an informer or deceived to the identity of one with whom one deals is probably inherent in the conditions of human society. It is the kind of risk we necessarily assume whenever we speak.' "[c]

Chief Justice WARREN dissented, deeming it unnecessary to reach any constitutional questions "for the affront to the quality and fairness of federal law which this case presents is sufficient to require an exercise of our supervisory powers":

"Here, Edward Partin, a jailbird languishing in a Louisiana jail under indictments for such state and federal crimes as embezzlement, kidnapping, and manslaughter (and soon to be charged with perjury and assault), contacted federal authorities and told them he was willing to become, and would be useful as, an informer against Hoffa who was then about to be tried in the Test Fleet case. A motive for his doing this is immediately apparent—namely, his strong desire to

a. *Hoffa* was decided the same day as *Lewis* and *Osborn* (p. 353), where, on the basis of a tape recorded meeting between defendant and his "employee" (a secret government agent), one of Hoffa's lawyers was convicted of attempting to bribe a juror.

b. But compare the same Justice's analysis for the Court a year later in *Katz*, p. 138.

c. Note well that at the time the meetings at which Partin was present occurred Hoffa had not been indicted for bribing a juror nor had judicial proceedings otherwise commenced against him with respect to this crime. If they had, Hoffa would have had the benefit of the *Massiah* doctrine. See generally Ch. 8, § 5.

work his way out of jail and out of his various legal entanglements with the State and Federal Governments. And it is interesting to note that, if this was his motive, he has been uniquely successful in satisfying it. In the four years since he first volunteered to be an informer against Hoffa he has not been prosecuted on any of the serious federal charges for which he was at that time jailed, and the state charges have apparently vanished into thin air. This type of informer and the uses to which he was put in this case evidence a serious potential for undermining the integrity of the truth-finding process in the federal courts. Given the incentives and background of Partin, no conviction should be allowed to stand when based heavily on his testimony. And that is exactly the quicksand upon which these convictions rest.

"[In] performing its duty to prosecute crime the Government must take the witnesses as it finds them. [But here] the Government reaches into the jailhouse to employ a man who was himself facing indictments far more serious (and later including one for perjury) than the one confronting the man against whom he offered to inform. It employed him not for the purpose of testifying to something that had already happened, but rather for the purpose of infiltration to see if crimes would in the future be committed. * * * Certainly if a criminal defendant insinuated his informer into the prosecution's camp in this manner he would be guilty of obstructing justice. * * *"

Justice Clark, joined by Justice Douglas, would have dismissed the writs of certiorari as improvidently granted for the reason that the district court's finding that the government did *not* "place" Partin in the defendant's midst could not be regarded "clearly erroneous." However, in the companion case of *Osborn,* fn. a, p. 378, Justice DOUGLAS, the lone dissenter in that case, made it plain that if he had been satisfied in *Hoffa* that the government had "placed" Partin in Hoffa's councils he would have voted to reverse the conviction: "[A] person may take the risk that a friend will turn on him and report to the police. But that is far different from the Government's 'planting' a friend in a person's entourage so that he can secure incriminating evidence. In the one case the Government has merely been the willing recipient of information supplied by a fickle friend. In the other, the Government has actively encouraged and participated in a breach of privacy by sending in an undercover agent. [T]he Government unlawfully enters a man's home when its agent crawls through a window, breaks down a door, enters surreptitiously, or, as alleged here, gets in by trickery and fraud."[d]

Notes and Questions

1. Had Hoffa opened his hotel suite for the conduct of any business? Did any specificity of purpose or duration limit Partin's presence there? Why "while so carefully limiting its holding in *Lewis,*" did the Court "at the same time approve the extensive intrusion in *Hoffa* without even acknowledging the substantial differences in the breadth of the searches involved in the two cases"? See *The Supreme Court, 1966 Term,* 81 Harv.L.Rev. 69, 192–93 (1967).

2. Was Hoffa, as the majority put it, "relying upon his misplaced confidence that Partin would not reveal his wrongdoing" or also on the assumption that the government would not attempt to spy on him in the privacy of his hotel room? Was Partin a friend who later "revealed wrongdoing" or was he working for the government at the very time Hoffa spoke? Must people take the risk that their "friends" or associates are "government agents," i.e., have been "planted" by the government or have already promised to report whatever they see or hear to the government? See Kitch, supra, at 151–52; Note, 76 Yale L.J. 994, 1009–13 (1967).

d. Justices Fortas and White took no part in the case.

If so, then why does one using the phone not "assume the risk" that the police will be tapping the wire? And why does one using the mails not assume that the police will be reading his letters? Are these other risks small only because the Court has made them so? Should the inquiry be not whether a person has "assumed the risk," but what risks of governmental intrusion citizens of a free society *should have to assume?* Is the view that one "assumes the risk" that the friend in whom he confides is a "government agent" anything more than a conclusion that the probability of accomplishing some social good by such a tactic outweighs the invasion of privacy and therefore the risk is tolerable in a free society? Consider Harlan, J., dissenting in *United States v. White,* p. 382.

3. Consider Note, 76 Yale L.J. 994, 1010 (1967):

"Though rejected by the Court in Lopez, Brennan's dichotomy between bugging and secret agents became in *Hoffa* the basis of the Court's decision that secret agents do not threaten privacy enough to merit Fourth Amendment limitation. But it is difficult to accept, at least without explanation, [this reasoning]. Consider, for example, the likely reactions of the citizenry if asked to rank the offensiveness of three practices:

"(1) the police will be allowed to search your home, without force during daylight hours;

"(2) the police will be allowed to offer your friends very strong inducements to report to them any illegal activities on your part;

"(3) the police will be allowed to employ agents, who may be strangers, business associates or friends, to invite or encourage you to take part in a criminal venture.

"The clear state of the constitutional law after *Hoffa* and its companion cases is that (1) represents an invasion of privacy abhorrent to the American way of life, but (2) and (3) are quite proper. The average citizen would hardly agree."

Does an undercover agent's participation in a pretrial meeting between defendant and his lawyer constitute a *per se* violation of defendant's right to the effective assistance of counsel with respect to the pending criminal action? If not, under what circumstances does such governmental activity fatally taint the trial? Consider WEATHERFORD v. BURSEY, 429 U.S. 545, 97 S.Ct. 837, 51 L.Ed.2d 30 (1977): Bursey and Weatherford (a state undercover agent) vandalized a selective service office. Weatherford reported the incident to the police, but in order to maintain his undercover status and his usefulness on other current matters in that capacity, he was arrested and charged along with Bursey. Both were released on bond and retained separate attorneys. Then, at the request of Bursey's attorney, who sought Weatherford's presence in order to discuss his client's defense, Weatherford attended two pretrial meetings with Bursey and his attorney. Weatherford had no discussions either with his superiors or the prosecution concerning anything said at the attorney-client meetings. Although Weatherford had not expected to be a witness at the trial, and had so told Bursey, on the day of the trial (because Weatherford had been seen in the company of police officers shortly before and his effectiveness as an undercover agent thus impaired), the prosecution decided to call him as a witness.[a] Weatherford's testimony related only to events prior to the meetings with Bursey and his lawyer and did not refer

a. Bursey's contention that the government was constitutionally forbidden to conceal Weatherford's identity from him during his trial preparation and to permit Weatherford to "deny" that he would testify against him is treated in Ch. 22, § 5.

to anything said at these meetings. Nor was there any evidence that any of Weatherford's testimony was the product of anything said at these meetings. Bursey was convicted. After he had served his sentence, he brought an action against Weatherford under 42 U.S.C. § 1983, alleging that the latter's participation in the pretrial meetings had deprived him of the effective assistance of counsel as well as his right to a fair trial. The Court, per WHITE, J., held that Bursey's constitutional rights were not violated and that the right to counsel establishes no *per se* rule forbidding an undercover agent to meet with a defendant's counsel:

"[As] long as the information possessed by Weatherford remained uncommunicated, he posed no substantial threat to Bursey's Sixth Amendment rights. Nor do we believe [that] prosecutors will be so prone to lie or the difficulties of proof so great that we must always assume not only that an informant communicates what he learns from an encounter with the defendant and his counsel but also that what he communicates has the potential for detriment or benefit to the prosecutor's case.

"[That a *per se* rule] would operate prophylactically and effectively is very likely true; but it would require the informant to refuse to participate in attorney-client meetings, even though invited, and thus for all practical purposes to unmask himself. Our cases, however, have recognized the unfortunate necessity of undercover work and the value it often is to effective law enforcement.

"[There] being no tainted evidence in this case, no communication of defense strategy to the prosecution, and no purposeful intrusion by Weatherford, there was no violation of the [right to counsel]."

Justice MARSHALL, joined by Brennan, J., dissented, unable to "join in providing even the narrowest of openings to the practice of spying upon attorney-client communications":

"[E]ven if I could agree that unintended and undisclosed interceptions by government witness-employers [violate no constitutional rights], I still could not join in upholding the practice. For [the] precious constitutional rights at stake here, like other constitutional rights, need 'breathing space to survive' and a prophylactic prohibition on all intrusions of this sort is therefore essential. A rule that offers defendants relief only when they can prove 'intent' or 'disclosure' is, I fear, little better than no rule at all. Establishing [an intent or desire to spy] will seldom be possible * * *. Proving that an informer reported to the prosecution on defense strategy will be equally difficult * * *."

Is a Justice Department Order Permitting the Monitoring of Communications Between Federal Prisoners and Their Lawyers Supported by Weatherford v. Bursey?

A new Justice Department rule, effective October 30, 2001, amending Bureau of Prison regulations (28 C.F.R. 500–501), allows federal authorities to monitor mail and conversations between federal prisoners and their attorneys (or their attorneys' agents) where the Attorney General has certified that "reasonable suspicion" exists to believe that inmates may use communications with their attorneys (or their attorneys' agents) to facilitate acts of violence or terrorism. In the analysis he issued along with the order, Attorney General Ashcroft observed:

"The monitoring is not surreptitious; on the contrary, the defendant and his or her attorney are required to be given notice of the government's listening activities. The rule requires that privileged information not be retained by the government monitors and that, apart from disclosures necessary to thwart an imminent act of violence or terrorism, any disclosures to investigators or prosecutors must be approved by a federal judge.

"In following these procedures, it is intended that the use of a taint team and the building of a firewall will ensure that the communications which fit under the protection of the attorney-client privilege will never be revealed to prosecutors and investigators."

Some defense lawyers doubted that the "firewall" constructed between teams monitoring attorney-client conversations and government lawyers prosecuting the monitored defendants would prove very substantial. They ridiculed the notion that the "taint team" would not share information with the prosecutors. See David Rovella, *Ashcroft Rule Puts Defenders in a Bind*, Nat'l L.J., Dec. 3, 2001, p. 1. But the Attorney General relied specifically on *Weatherford v. Bursey*, where, as he put it, the Supreme Court held that "when the government possesses a legitimate law enforcement interest in monitoring [conversations between a defendant and his attorney] no Sixth Amendment violation occurs so long as privileged communications are protected from disclosure and no information recovered through monitoring is used by the government in a way that deprives the defendant of a fair trial."

Consider, however, David Moran, *Ashcroft's Monitoring Violates Attorney–Client Rights*, Detroit News, Nov. 28, 2001, p. 13A: "It is true [that] the Supreme Court once held that the Sixth Amendment was not necessarily violated when a defendant unwittingly brought along an undercover informant to a meeting with his lawyer. But that case * * * is a far cry from an order requiring the attorney and client to meet under the government's watchful eyes and listening ears."[a]

UNITED STATES v. WHITE
401 U.S. 745, 91 S.Ct. 1122, 28 L.Ed.2d 453 (1971).

Justice WHITE announced the judgment of the Court and an opinion in which The Chief Justice, Justice STEWART, and Justice BLACKMUN join.

[On numerous occasions a government informer, carrying a concealed radio transmitter, engaged defendant in conversations which were electronically overheard by federal narcotics agents. The conversations in a restaurant, defendant's home and in the informer's car were overheard by the use of radio equipment. A number of conversations in the informer's home were not only electronically overheard by an agent stationed outside the house but by another agent who, with the informer's consent, concealed himself in the latter's kitchen closet.[a] At no time did the agents obtain a warrant or court order. The informer was not produced at the trial, but the testimony of the "eavesdropping" agents was admitted and led to defendant's conviction of narcotics violations. The U.S. Court of Appeals for the Seventh Circuit read *Katz* as overruling *On Lee* and interpreted the Fourth Amendment as prohibiting testimony about the electronically overheard statements.]

[The *Hoffa* case], left undisturbed by *Katz,* held that however strongly a defendant may trust an apparent colleague, his expectations in this respect are not protected by the Fourth Amendment when it turns out that the colleague is a government agent regularly communicating with the authorities. * * *

Conceding that *Hoffa, Lewis,* and *Lopez* remained unaffected by *Katz,* the Court of Appeals nevertheless read both *Katz* and the Fourth Amendment to require a different result if the agent not only records his conversations with the

---

a. For a discussion of the Justice Department order in the context of the right to effective counsel, see p. 1141.

a. No testimony by this agent was offered at trial. See Note 4 following this case.

defendant but instantaneously transmits them electronically to other agents equipped with radio receivers.

[To] reach this result it was necessary for the Court of Appeals to hold that *On Lee* was no longer good law. In that case, [the] Court first rejected claims of a Fourth Amendment violation because the informer had not trespassed when he entered the defendant's premises and conversed with him. To this extent the Court's rationale cannot survive *Katz*. But the Court announced a second and independent ground for its decision; for it went on to say that overruling *Olmstead* and *Goldman* [which the Court subsequently did in *Katz*] would be of no aid to On Lee since he "was talking confidentially and indiscreetly with one he trusted, and he was overheard. * * * " We see no indication in *Katz* that the Court meant to disturb that understanding of the Fourth Amendment or to disturb the result reached in the *On Lee* case, nor are we now inclined to overturn this view of the Fourth Amendment.

Concededly a police agent who conceals his police connections may write down for official use his conversations with a defendant and testify concerning them, without a warrant authorizing his encounters with the defendant and without otherwise violating the latter's Fourth Amendment rights. *Hoffa*. For constitutional purposes, no different result is required if the agent instead of immediately reporting and transcribing his conversations with defendant, either (1) simultaneously records them with electronic equipment which he is carrying on his person, *Lopez;* (2) or carries radio equipment which simultaneously transmits the conversations either to recording equipment located elsewhere or to other agents monitoring the transmitting frequency. *On Lee.* If the conduct and revelations of an agent operating without electronic equipment do not invade the defendant's constitutionally justifiable expectations of privacy, neither does a simultaneous recording of the same conversations made by the agent or by others from transmissions received from the agent to whom the defendant is talking and whose trustworthiness the defendant necessarily risks.

Our problem is not what the privacy expectations of particular defendants in particular situations may be or the extent to which they may in fact have relied on the discretion of their companions. Very probably, individual defendants neither know nor suspect that their colleagues have gone or will go to the police or are carrying recorders or transmitters. Otherwise, conversation would cease and our problem with these encounters would be nonexistent or far different from those now before us. Our problem, in terms of the principles announced in *Katz*, is what expectations of privacy are constitutionally "justifiable"—what expectations the Fourth Amendment will protect in the absence of a warrant. So far, the law permits the frustration of actual expectations of privacy by permitting authorities to use the testimony of those associates who for one reason or another have determined to turn to the police, as well as by authorizing the use of informants in the manner exemplified by *Hoffa* and *Lewis*. If the law gives no protection to the wrongdoer whose trusted accomplice is or becomes a police agent, neither should it protect him when that same agent has recorded or transmitted the conversations which are later offered in evidence to prove the State's case.

Inescapably, one contemplating illegal activities must realize and risk that his companions may be reporting to the police. If he sufficiently doubts their trustworthiness, the association will very probably end or never materialize. But if he has no doubts, or allays them, or risks what doubt he has, the risk is his. In terms of what his course will be, what he will or will not do or say, we are unpersuaded that he would distinguish between probable informers on the one hand and probable informers with transmitters on the other.

[It is] untenable to consider the activities and reports of the police agent himself, though acting without a warrant, to be a "reasonable" investigative effort and lawful under the Fourth Amendment but to view the same agent with a recorder or transmitter as conducting an "unreasonable" and unconstitutional search and seizure. * * * No different result should obtain where, as in *On Lee* and the instant case, the informer disappears and is unavailable at trial; for the issue of whether specified events on a certain day violate the Fourth Amendment should not be determined by what later happens to the informer. [R]eversed.[b]

Justice DOUGLAS, dissenting. * * *

On Lee and *Lopez* are of a vintage opposed to *Berger* and *Katz*. However they may be explained, they are products of the old common-law notions of trespass. *Katz,* on the other hand, emphasized that with few exceptions "searches conducted outside the judicial process, without prior approval by judge or magistrate, are *per se* unreasonable under the Fourth Amendment. * * * "

Monitoring, if prevalent, certainly kills free discourse and spontaneous utterances. Free discourse—a First Amendment value—may be frivolous or serious, humble or defiant, reactionary or revolutionary, profane or in good taste; but it is not free if there is surveillance. Free discourse liberates the spirit, though it may produce only froth. The individual must keep some facts concerning his thoughts within a small zone of people. At the same time he must be free to pour out his woes or inspirations or dreams to others. He remains the sole judge as to what must be said and what must remain unspoken. This is the essence of the idea of privacy implicit in the First and Fifth Amendments as well as in the Fourth. * * *

Justice HARLAN, dissenting.

[The] plurality opinion seeks to erase the crucial distinction between the facts before us and [the holdings in *Lopez, Lewis* and *Hoffa*] by the following reasoning: if A can relay verbally what is revealed to him by B (as in *Lewis* and *Hoffa*), or record and later divulge it (as in *Lopez*), what difference does it make if A conspires with another to betray B by contemporaneously transmitting to the other all that is said? The contention is, in essence, an argument that the distinction between third-party monitoring and *other* undercover techniques is one of form and not substance. The force of the contention depends on the evaluation of two separable but intertwined assumptions: first, that there is no greater invasion of privacy in the third-party situation, and, second, that uncontrolled consensual surveillance in an electronic age is a tolerable technique of law enforcement, given the values and goals of our political system.

The first of these assumptions takes as a point of departure the so-called "risk analysis" approach of *Lewis,* and *Lopez,* and to a lesser extent *On Lee,* or the expectations approach of *Katz.* While these formulations represent an advance over the unsophisticated trespass analysis of the common law, they too have their limitations and can, ultimately, lead to the substitution of words for analysis. The analysis must, in my view, transcend the search for subjective expectations or legal attribution of assumptions of risk. Our expectations, and the risks we assume, are in large part reflections of laws that translate into rules the customs and values of the past and present.

b. The plurality opinion also upheld the admissibility of the evidence of defendant's incriminating statements on another ground: the events in question took place long prior to *Katz* and *Desist,* p. 43, had held that *Katz* applied only to those electronic surveillances which occurred subsequent to the date of that decision. Justice Brennan, whose concurring opinion is summarized infra, concurred in the result, agreeing that *Desist* required affirmance, but differing on the issue of the continued viability of *On Lee.* Justice Black concurred in the result for the reasons set forth in his *Katz* dissent, but adhered to his view that *Katz* should be applied retroactively. Dissenting Justices Douglas, Harlan and Marshall would apply *Katz* retroactively and viewed it as overruling *On Lee.*

Since it is the task of the law to form and project, as well as mirror and reflect, we should not, as judges, merely recite the expectations and risks without examining the desirability of saddling them upon society. The critical question, therefore, is whether under our system of government, as reflected in the Constitution, we should impose on our citizens the risks of the electronic listener or observer without at least the protection of a warrant requirement.

[The] impact of the practice of third-party bugging, must, I think, be considered such as to undermine that confidence and sense of security in dealing with one another that is characteristic of individual relationships between citizens in a free society. It goes beyond the impact on privacy occasioned by the ordinary type of "informer" investigation upheld in *Lewis* and *Hoffa*. The argument of the plurality opinion, to the effect that it is irrelevant whether secrets are revealed by the mere tattletale or the transistor, ignores the differences occasioned by third-party monitoring and recording which insures full and accurate disclosure of all that is said, free of the possibility of error and oversight that inheres in human reporting.

[I]t is too easy to forget—and, hence, too often forgotten—that the issue here is whether to interpose a search warrant procedure between law enforcement agencies engaging in electronic eavesdropping and the public generally. By casting its "risk analysis" solely in terms of the expectations and risks that "wrongdoers" or "one contemplating illegal activities" ought to bear, the plurality opinion, I think, misses the mark entirely. *On Lee* does not simply mandate that criminals must daily run the risk of unknown eavesdroppers prying into their private affairs; it subjects each and every law-abiding member of society to that risk. * * * Abolition of *On Lee* would not end electronic eavesdropping. It would prevent public officials from engaging in that practice unless they first had probable cause to suspect an individual of involvement in illegal activities and had tested their version of the facts before a detached judicial officer. The interest *On Lee* fails to protect is the expectation of the ordinary citizen, who has never engaged in illegal conduct in his life, that he may carry on his private discourse freely, openly, and spontaneously without measuring his every word against the connotations it might carry when instantaneously heard by others unknown to him and unfamiliar with his situation or analyzed in a cold, formal record played days, months, or years after the conversation. Interposition of a warrant requirement is designed not to shield "wrongdoers," but to secure a measure of privacy and a sense of personal security throughout our society. * * *

Justice MARSHALL, dissenting.

I am convinced that the correct view of the Fourth Amendment in the area of electronic surveillance is one that brings the safeguards of the warrant requirement to bear on the investigatory activity involved in this case. In this regard I agree with the dissents of Justice Douglas and Justice Harlan. In short, I believe that *On Lee* cannot be considered viable in light of the constitutional principles articulated in *Katz* and other cases. * * *

[Justice BRENNAN concurred in the result, agreeing that *Katz* should not be applied retroactively but emphasizing that on the issue of the viability of *On Lee,* neither the dissenters' views nor Justice White's "commands the support of a majority of the Court."[c] He would "go further" than the dissenters; their

c. Aren't there "five votes" in *White* sustaining *On Lee?* Recall that the "fifth Justice," Black, concurred in the *White* result for the reasons advanced in his *Katz* dissent, where he viewed Fourth Amendment protection of privacy as extending only to "unreasonable searches and seizures of 'persons, houses, papers and effects.'" Recall, too, Justice Black's *Berger* dissent, where he could not read the Fourth Amendment as applying to "the spoken word" as well as "tangible things."

reasoning "compels the conclusion" that *Lopez,* as well as *On Lee,* is "no longer sound law. [C]urrent Fourth Amendment jurisprudence interposes a warrant requirement not only in cases of third-party electronic monitoring (the situation in *On Lee* and in this case) but also in cases of electronic recording by a government agent of a face-to-face conversation with a criminal suspect, which was the situation in *Lopez.*" As he viewed it, *Katz* had adopted the "doctrinal basis" of his *Lopez* dissent and that meant that both *On Lee* and *Lopez,* which presented "rationally indistinguishable" situations,[d] should now be regarded as overruled.[e]]

Notes and Questions

1. After *White,* what, if anything, is left of anyone's "justifiable reliance" on the privacy of his conversation (*Katz*)? Did *Katz* mean that a citizen must adjust his expectations of privacy to new laws and electronic techniques or that these new laws and techniques should conform to present expectations? Did *Katz* mean, or should it be read as meaning, that the individual only "assumes the risk" that he objectively perceives and no more? That *reasonable* reliance on the privacy of one's conversation suffices to invoke the protection of the Fourth Amendment? See Note, 52 B.U.L.Rev. 831, 838–44 (1972).

Didn't defendant White take reasonable steps to protect against governmental intrusion by choosing the locations he did for his private conversations? Didn't federal agents employ an informer and conceal a radio transmitter on his person for the very reason that they anticipated defendant White would make reasonable efforts to avoid being overheard? Does the *White* plurality opinion mean the privacy of one's conversation is unprotected if one can anticipate *any* risk that his words might be disclosed to third parties? If so, how does the Fourth Amendment protect the privacy of one's conversations unless one *completely stops* communicating to others? See Note, 85 Harv.L.Rev. 250, 254 (1971). See also Hufstedler, J., dissenting in *Holmes v. Burr,* 486 F.2d 55, 61, 71–76 (9th Cir.1973).

2. Did the *White* plurality opinion refuse to recognize normal expectations of privacy because to do so would restrict a "normal" police stratagem? Is the "reasonableness" of privacy expectations to be measured by how the average person views a given situation or by whether affording Fourth Amendment protection would "unreasonably" impede the police? See 52 B.U.L.Rev. at 838; Note, Harv.L.Rev. 63, 192–93 (1968).

3. The *White* plurality opinion observes that "the law gives no protection to the wrongdoer whose trusted accomplice [*unequipped* with an electronic device] *is* or *becomes* a police agent." (Emphasis added.) Should the law distinguish between (1) a "trusted accomplice" who, absent prior arrangements with the police, *subsequently* supplies them with evidence; and (2) a "trusted accomplice" who was a "police agent" all along, who was "planted" by the government to secure incriminating evidence? Reconsider Chief Justice Warren's dissenting opinion in *Hoffa,* p. 378; and Justice Douglas' dissenting opinion in *Osborn* and *Lewis,* p. 379.

Might the *White* dissenters have read *Katz* more broadly than they did? Might they have argued, alternatively, that if, as the *White* plurality opinion maintains, "the difference between the electronically equipped [governmental 'plant'] and the unequipped [governmental 'plant'] is [not] substantial enough to require discrete

---

Justice Black did dissent in *On Lee*—solely on the ground that the Court should reject the evidence in the exercise of its supervisory authority over federal criminal justice. Why didn't he make that argument in *White?*

d. Did they?

e. As to whether the government has a constitutional obligation to retain tapes of conversations for the defendant's possible use, see Ch. 25, § 3.

constitutional recognition," then *Katz* should be read as overruling *Hoffa* as well as *On Lee?* May it be said of the *Hoffa* case—using the language in *Katz*—that the government's use of defendant's trusted friend to obtain evidence against him "violated the privacy upon which [defendant] justifiably relied" and thus constituted a "search" or "seizure"?

4. Both the Seventh Circuit and Supreme Court opinions in *White* dealt only with the use of *electronically* overheard conversations because only such evidence was offered at trial. If the *White* dissenters had prevailed, would their reasoning also have led to the exclusion of the testimony of the narcotics agent (not equipped with an electronic device) who had overheard defendant's conversations from his hiding place in the informer's kitchen closet? Why (not)?

5. *Renewed doubts about the validity of White.* In *Marshall v. Barlow's* (p. 327), the government maintained that the pervasiveness of state and national safety regulations refuted the view that an employer can have a "realistic privacy interest" in employee work areas. Rejecting this argument, the Court, per White, J., observed: "Employees are not prohibited from reporting OSHA violations. What they observe in their daily functions is undoubtedly beyond the employer's reasonable expectation of privacy. The Government inspector, however, is not an employee. Without a warrant he stands in no better position than a member of the public. [That] an employee is free to report, and the Government is free to use, any evidence of noncompliance with OSHA that the employee observes furnishes no justification for federal agents to enter a place of business from which the public is restricted and to conduct their own warrantless search."

Does *Barlow's* raise serious questions and renewed doubts about the validity of *White* and other cases dealing with participant monitoring? By talking to a confidant, did the defendant in *White* consent to government information-gathering any more than the defendant in *Barlow's* did, by permitting employees to observe his premises? See Joseph D. Grano, *Perplexing Questions About Three Basic Fourth Amendment Issues,* 69 J.Crim.L. & C. 425, 435–38 (1978).

Chapter 7

POLICE "ENCOURAGEMENT"
AND THE DEFENSE OF
ENTRAPMENT

"The mode adopted [to] bring to light the malfeasance of the defendant, had no necessary connection with his violation of law. He exercised his own volition * * *. Even if inducements to commit crime could be assumed to exist in this case, the allegation of the defendant would be but the repetition of the plea as ancient as the world, and first interposed in Paradise: 'The serpent beguiled me and I did eat.' That defense was overruled by the great Lawgiver, and whatever estimate we may form, or whatever judgment pass upon the character or conduct of the tempter, this plea has never since availed to shield crime or give indemnity to the culprit, and it is safe to say that under any code of civilized, not to say christian ethics, it never will."

—Bacon, J., in *Board of Commissioners v. Backus*, 29 How.Pr. 33, 42 (N.Y.Sup.Ct.1864).

"[T]wo deeply seated and widely shared intuitive judgments [explain the creation and survival of the entrapment defense]. The first is that a person is somewhat less culpable if tempted into crime by certain kinds of inducements. The second is that it is extremely dangerous to allow government the power to stress test the morality of ordinary citizens by dangling substantial inducements before them. [But] where do [these] intuitions come from?"

—Louis Michael Seidman, *The Supreme Court, Entrapment, and Our Criminal Justice Dilemma*, 1981 Sup.Ct.Rev. 111, 146.

" 'Encouragement' is descriptive of an intentional technique of police agencies used in the detection of a certain class of crimes. [It] denotes activity of the police or their agent: (1) acting in the capacity of a victim, (2) intending by his actions to suggest his willingness to be a victim, (3) actually communicating this feigned willingness to the suspect, and (4) thereby having some influence upon his commission of the crime. It is not necessarily a single act; it usually consists of a series of acts by the officer which are part of the normal interplay between victim and suspect in the specific crime. It is utilized as a device in dealing with certain crimes having the common element of vice—prostitution, homosexuality, liquor sales, narcotics, and gambling. The reason that the same technique is adapted to all these crimes is suggested by the 'vice' label applicable to all of them, that these offenses are committed privately with a willing victim who will not complain, making normal detection virtually impossible. 'Encouragement,' to state it more succinctly, is a process of persuasion. * * *

"[It] is by no means a wholesome police practice. It is founded upon deception. Not only must the participating officer deliberately deceive, but he must often say and do things that are vulgar, profane and indecent. However, to condemn the characteristics is to condemn the practice, because deception, vulgarity, profanity, and indecency are often essential to the simulation of reality which encouragement attempts to achieve. When to these characteristics is added the unfortunate fact that on occasion encouragement induces persons to commit crime who ordinarily would not, it is understandable that the practice is roundly criticized. But if there is no way to protect society effectively from certain criminal harms except through detection by encouragement, then it is as idle to criticize the practice continually as it would be to criticize surgery for its efforts to eliminate disease because the surgical method, of necessity, cuts and hurts the body. The fact should not be overlooked that the fault lies more with the social harm and the human hurt and their causes than with the methods of eradication."

> —Daniel Rotenberg, *The Police Detection Practice of Encouragement,* 49 Va.L.Rev. 871, 874 (1963).

———

"Manifestly, [the function of law enforcement] does not include the manufacturing of crime. Criminal activity is such that stealth and strategy are necessary weapons in the arsenal of the police officer. However, 'A different question is presented when the criminal design originates with the officials of the government, and they implant in the mind of an innocent person the disposition to commit the alleged offense and induce its commission in order that they may prosecute.' Then stealth and strategy become as objectionable police methods as the coerced confession and the unlawful search. * * * To determine whether entrapment has been established a line must be drawn between the trap for the unwary innocent and the trap for the unwary criminal."

> —Warren, C.J., for the Court in *Sherman v. United States,* 356 U.S. 369, 372, 78 S.Ct. 819, 2 L.Ed.2d 848 (1958).

———

"The purpose of the entrapment defense * * * must be to prohibit unlawful governmental activity in instigating crime. [If] so, then whether the particular defendant was 'predisposed' or 'otherwise innocent' is irrelevant; and the important question becomes whether the Government's conduct in inducing the crime was beyond judicial toleration."

> —Stewart, J., dissenting in *United States v. Russell,* 411 U.S. 423, 442, 93 S.Ct. 1637, 36 L.Ed.2d 366 (1973).

———

"If the police entice someone to commit a crime who would not have done so without their blandishments, and then arrest him and he is prosecuted, convicted, and punished, law enforcement resources are squandered in the following sense: resources that could and should have been used in an effort to reduce the nation's unacceptably high crime rate are used instead in the entirely sterile activity of first inciting and then punishing a crime. However, if the police are just inducing someone to commit sooner a crime he would have committed eventually, but to do so in controlled circumstances where the costs to the criminal justice system of apprehension and conviction are minimized, the police are economizing on resources. It is particularly difficult to catch arsonists, so if all the police were doing here was making it easier to catch an arsonist—not inducing someone to become an arsonist—they were using law enforcement resources properly and there is no occasion for judicial intervention. * * *

"Thus in my view 'entrapment' is merely the name we give to a particularly unproductive use of law enforcement resources, which our system properly condemns. If this is right, the implementing concept of 'predisposition to crime' calls less for psychological conjecture than for a common-sense assessment of whether it is likely that the defendant would have committed the crime anyway—without the blandishments the police used on him—but at a time and place where it would have been more difficult for them to apprehend him and the state to convict him, or whether the police used threats or promises so powerful that a law-abiding individual was induced to commit a crime. If the latter is the case, the police tactics do not merely affect the timing and location of a crime; they cause crime."

—Posner, J., concurring in *United States v. Kaminski,* 703 F.2d 1004, 1010 (7th Cir.1983).

"If the investigators were too creative or squandered their limited resources, this is a political problem. Congress can hold oversight hearings or pass a law; we shouldn't apply a chancellor's foot veto. Dissipating law enforcement resources injures persons who become victims of crime when the deterrent force of the law declines. Reversing convictions of the guilty cannot apply balm to these wounds. Those who protest that social interests would have been served by prosecuting someone else (or some additional, similarly situated persons) routinely lose. We deem it enough to support punishment that this person committed this offense, leaving to other institutions the redirection of investigative or prosecutorial resources. So it should be here."

—Easterbrook, J., concurring in *United States v. Miller,* 891 F.2d 1265, 1271–72 (7th Cir.1989).

"Our national integrity has been on a downhill slide for seven years; we really don't need the FBI to grease the skids with Operation ABSCAM.[a] Where no crime has been contemplated, the FBI has, through entrapment, induced to crime men

a. "Abscam" is an acronym combining the first two letters of Abdul Enterprises, a fictitious Middle Eastern corporation, and "scam," a slang term for swindle or confidence game. Abscam began as a standard "sting" operation, i.e., an FBI undercover scheme to recover stolen securities and paintings. In 1978, the operation shifted to political corruption in the New Jersey area. A year later, it had turned its attention to the "Asylum Scenario"; unsuspecting "middlemen" (private persons unaware that they were part of a government undercover operation) passed the word to various Congressmen, or to their aides and acquaintances, that wealthy Arabs were willing to bribe members of Congress in order to ensure that they would introduce private immigration bills on the Arabs' behalf if and when necessary. In early 1980, shortly before shutting down, the operation shifted to political corruption in Philadelphia.

As a result of Abscam, a U.S. Senator, six U.S. Representatives and a number of other public officials and lawyers were convicted of various corrupt acts. Although many of the defendants (and many critics of the operation both in and out of Congress) charged that the FBI's methods constituted entrapment and/or violated the due process rights of the individuals caught in the operation, not a single Abscam defendant prevailed in the courts. See, e.g., *United States v. Kelly* (D.C.Cir.1983), p. 407, which discusses one phase of the Abscam operation at considerable length.

who were previously involved in no wrongdoing. Aren't there enough naturally encouraging crimes to keep the FBI busy? Must they spend astronomical sums creating crime?"

—Letter to the Editor, Newsweek, Mar. 1, 1980, p. 5.

———

"House Speaker Thomas P. (Tip) O'Neill may have thundered that '[Operation ABSCAM] was a setup, a goddam setup,' but a crook is a crook is a crook. Whether set up or not, honest people do not take bribes."

—Letter to the Editor, Newsweek Mar. 1, 1980, p. 5.

———

"We assume that there are a few people who would not commit any criminal acts no matter what the provocation or enticement. We will not refer further to such saintly or misguided individuals. Everyone else, we assume has a price. [If] this assumption is true, then everyone except saints is predisposed to commit crimes. But that in turn means that 'predisposition' cannot usefully distinguish anyone from anyone else. The only salient question is whether a person's price has been met, not whether he has one, since by hypothesis everyone but the saintly does. * * * [T]he person who does not take the bait almost surely would take a higher, even if greatly higher, bait. The failure to take this one is evidence of his price, but not of predisposition."

—Ronald J. Allen, Melissa Luttrell & Anne Kreeger, *Clarifying Entrapment,* 89 J. Crim. L. & Criminology 407, 413 (1999).

———

SECTION 1. THE TESTS FOR ENTRAPMENT[a]

UNITED STATES v. RUSSELL
411 U.S. 423, 93 S.Ct. 1637, 36 L.Ed.2d 366 (1973).

Justice REHNQUIST delivered the opinion of the Court.

[After] a jury trial in the District Court, in which his sole defense was entrapment, respondent was convicted [of] having unlawfully manufactured and processed methamphetamine ("speed") and of having unlawfully sold and delivered that drug. [On] appeal, the United States Court of Appeals for the Ninth Circuit [reversed] the conviction solely for the reason that an undercover agent supplied an essential chemical for manufacturing the methamphetamine which formed the basis of respondent's conviction. * * *

There is little dispute concerning the essential facts in this case. On December 7, 1969, Joe Shapiro, an undercover agent for the Federal Bureau of Narcotics

---

a. "Entrapment" is sometimes confused with, but should be distinguished from, "estoppel," which occurs when defendants rely on the assurances of government authorities that their contemplated conduct is lawful only to be prosecuted for such conduct. See *Cox v. Louisiana*, 379 U.S. 559, 85 S.Ct. 476, 13 L.Ed.2d 487 (1965) (to sustain appellant's conviction "for demonstrating where [public officials] told him he could 'would be to sanction an indefensible sort of entrapment by the State * * * '"); *Raley v. Ohio*, 360 U.S. 423, 79 S.Ct. 1257, 3 L.Ed.2d 1344 (1959); *People v. Donovan*, 279 N.Y.S.2d 404 (Ct.Spec.Sess. 1967), 81 Harv. L.Rev. 895 (1968).

and Dangerous Drugs, went to respondent's home [where] he met with respondent and his two codefendants, John and Patrick Connolly. Shapiro's assignment was to locate a laboratory where it was believed that methamphetamine was being manufactured illicitly. He told the respondent and the Connollys that he represented an organization [that] was interested in controlling the manufacture and distribution of methamphetamine. He then made an offer to supply the defendants with the chemical phenyl-2-propanone, an essential ingredient in the manufacture of methamphetamine, in return for one-half of the drug produced. This offer was made on the condition that Agent Shapiro be shown a sample of the drug which they were making and the laboratory where it was being produced.

During the conversation, Patrick Connolly revealed that he had been making the drug since May 1969 and since then had produced three pounds of it. John Connolly gave the agent a bag containing a quality of methamphetamine that he represented as being from "the last batch that we made." Shortly thereafter, Shapiro and Patrick Connolly left respondent's house to view the laboratory which was located in the Connolly house on Whidbey Island. At the house, Shapiro observed an empty bottle bearing the chemical label phenyl-2-propanone.

By prearrangement, Shapiro returned to the Connolly house on December 9, 1969, to supply 100 grams of propanone and observe the manufacturing process. When he arrived he observed Patrick Connolly and the respondent cutting up pieces of aluminum foil and placing them in a large flask. There was testimony that some of the foil pieces accidentally fell on the floor and were picked up by the respondent and Shapiro and put into the flask. Thereafter, Patrick Connolly added all of the necessary chemicals, including the propanone brought by Shapiro, to make two batches of methamphetamine. The manufacturing process having been completed the following morning, Shapiro was given one-half of the drug and respondent kept the remainder. Shapiro offered to buy, and the respondent agreed to sell, part of the remainder for $60.

About a month later, Shapiro returned to the Connolly house and met with Patrick Connolly to ask if he was still interested in their "business arrangement." Connolly replied that he was interested but that he had recently obtained two additional bottles of phenyl-2-propanone and would not be finished with them for a couple of days. He provided some additional methamphetamine to Shapiro at that time. Three days later Shapiro returned to the Connolly house with a search warrant and, among other items, seized an empty 500-gram bottle of propanone and a 100-gram bottle, not the one he had provided, that was partially filled with the chemical.

There was testimony at the trial of respondent and Patrick Connolly that phenyl-2-propanone was generally difficult to obtain. At the request of the Bureau of Narcotics and Dangerous Drugs, some chemical supply firms had voluntarily ceased selling the chemical.

At the close of the evidence, and after receiving the District Judge's standard entrapment instruction,[4] the jury found the respondent guilty on all counts charged. On appeal, the respondent conceded that the jury could have found him predisposed to commit the offenses, but argued that on the facts presented there was entrapment as a matter of law. The Court of Appeals agreed, although it did not find the District Court had misconstrued or misapplied the traditional

---

4. The District Judge stated the governing law on entrapment as follows: "Where a person already has the willingness and the readiness to break the law, the mere fact that the government agent provides what appears to be a favorable opportunity is not entrapment." He then instructed the jury to acquit respon-

dent if it had a "reasonable doubt whether the defendant had the previous intent or purpose to commit the offense * * * and did so only because he was induced or persuaded by some officer or agent of the government." No exception was taken by respondent to this instruction.

standards governing the entrapment defense. Rather, the court in effect expanded the traditional notion of entrapment, which focuses on the predisposition of the defendant, to mandate dismissal of a criminal prosecution whenever the court determines that there has been "an intolerable degree of governmental participation in the criminal enterprise." In this case the court decided that the conduct of the agent in supplying a scarce ingredient essential for the manufacture of a controlled substance established that defense.

This new defense was held to rest on either of two alternative theories. One theory is based on two lower court decisions which have found entrapment, regardless of predisposition, whenever the government supplies contraband to the defendants. The second theory, a non-entrapment rationale, is based on a recent Ninth Circuit decision that reversed a conviction because a government investigator was so enmeshed in the criminal activity that the prosecution of the defendants was held to be repugnant to the American criminal justice system. The court below held that these two rationales constitute the same defense, and that only the label distinguishes them. In any event, it held that "[b]oth theories are premised on fundamental concepts of due process and evince the reluctance of the judiciary to countenance 'overzealous law enforcement.' "

This Court first recognized and applied the entrapment defense in *Sorrells v. United States,* 287 U.S. 435, 53 S.Ct. 210, 77 L.Ed. 413 (1932), [where] a federal prohibition agent visited the defendant while posing as a tourist and engaged him in conversation about their common war experiences. After gaining the defendant's confidence, the agent asked for some liquor, was twice refused, but upon asking a third time the defendant finally capitulated, and was subsequently prosecuted for violating the National Prohibition Act.

Chief Justice Hughes, speaking for the Court, held that as a matter of statutory construction the defense of entrapment should have been available to the defendant. Under the theory propounded by the Chief Justice, the entrapment defense prohibits law enforcement officers from instigating a criminal act by persons "otherwise innocent in order to lure them to its commission and to punish them." Thus, the thrust of the entrapment defense was held to focus on the intent or predisposition of the defendant to commit the crime. "[I]f the defendant seeks acquittal by reason of entrapment he cannot complain of an appropriate and searching inquiry into his own conduct and predisposition as bearing upon that issue."

Justice Roberts concurred but was of the view "that courts must be closed to the trial of a crime instigated by the government's own agents." The difference in the view of the majority and the concurring opinions is that in the former the inquiry focuses on the predisposition of the defendant, whereas in the latter the inquiry focuses on whether the government "instigated the crime."

In *Sherman v. United States,* 356 U.S. 369, 78 S.Ct. 819, 2 L.Ed.2d 848 (1958) the Court again considered the theory underlying the entrapment defense and expressly reaffirmed the view expressed by the *Sorrells* majority. In *Sherman* the defendant was convicted of selling narcotics to a Government informer. As in *Sorrells,* it appears that the Government agent gained the confidence of the defendant and, despite initial reluctance, the defendant finally acceded to the repeated importunings of the agent to commit the criminal act. On the basis of *Sorrells,* this Court [overturned the] conviction.

In affirming the theory underlying *Sorrells,* [the Court, per Chief Justice Warren] held that "[t]o determine whether entrapment has been established, a line must be drawn between the trap for the unwary innocent and the trap for the unwary criminal." Justice Frankfurter [maintained in a concurring opinion that] Justice Roberts had the better view in *Sorrells* and [thus] would have framed the question to be asked in an entrapment defense in terms of "whether the police conduct revealed in the particular case falls below standards [for] the proper use of governmental power."

In the instant case, [respondent] argues that the level of Shapiro's involvement in the manufacture of the methamphetamine was so high that a criminal prosecution for the drug's manufacture violates the fundamental principles of due process. [He] contends that the same factors that led this Court to apply the exclusionary rule to illegal searches and seizures [and] confessions should be considered here. But he would have the Court go further in deterring undesirable official conduct by requiring that any prosecution be barred absolutely because of the police involvement in criminal activity. The analogy is imperfect in any event, for the principal reason behind the adoption of the exclusionary rule was the Government's "failure to observe its own laws." [Here, however, the government's conduct] violated no independent constitutional right of the respondent. Nor did Shapiro violate any federal statute or rule or commit any crime in infiltrating the respondent's drug enterprise.

Respondent would overcome this basic weakness in his analogy to the exclusionary rule cases by having the Court adopt a rigid constitutional rule that would preclude any prosecution when it is shown that the criminal conduct would not have been possible had not an undercover agent "supplied an indispensable means to the commission of the crime that could not have been obtained otherwise, through legal or illegal channels." Even if we were to surmount the difficulties attending the notion that due process of law can be embodied in fixed rules, and those attending respondent's particular formulation, the rule he proposes would not appear to be of significant benefit to him. For, on the record presented, it appears that he cannot fit within the terms of the very rule he proposes.

[The] defendants admitted making the drug both before and after those batches made with the propanone supplied by Shapiro. [Thus, the record amply demonstrates] that the propanone used in the illicit manufacture of methamphetamine not only *could* have been obtained without the intervention of Shapiro but was in fact obtained by these defendants.

While we may some day be presented with a situation in which the conduct of law enforcement agents is so outrageous that due process principles would absolutely bar the government from invoking judicial processes to obtain a conviction, the instant case is distinctly not of that breed. Shapiro's contribution of propanone to the criminal enterprise already in process was scarcely objectionable. The chemical is by itself a harmless substance and its possession is legal. While the Government may have been seeking to make it more difficult for drug rings, such as that of which respondent was a member, to obtain the chemical, the evidence described above shows that it nonetheless was obtainable. The law enforcement conduct here stops far short of violating that "fundamental fairness, shocking to the universal sense of justice," mandated by the Due Process Clause of the Fifth Amendment.

The illicit manufacture of drugs is not a sporadic, isolated criminal incident, but a continuing, though illegal, business enterprise. In order to obtain convictions for illegally manufacturing drugs, the gathering of evidence of past unlawful conduct frequently proves to be an all but impossible task. Thus in drug-related offenses law enforcement personnel have turned to one of the only practicable means of detection: the infiltration of drug rings and a limited participation in their unlawful present practices. Such infiltration is a recognized and permissible means of investigation; if that be so, then the supply of some item of value that the drug ring requires must, as a general rule, also be permissible. For an agent will not be taken into the confidence of the illegal entrepreneurs unless he has something of value to offer them. Law enforcement tactics such as this can hardly be said to violate "fundamental fairness" or "shocking to the universal sense of justice."

[This] Court's opinions in *Sorrells* and *Sherman* held that the principal element in the defense of entrapment was the defendant's predisposition to commit the crime. Respondent conceded [that] "he may have harbored a predisposition to commit the charged offenses." Yet he argues that the jury's refusal to find entrapment under the charge submitted to it by the trial court should be overturned and the views of Justices Roberts and Frankfurter, in *Sorrells* and *Sherman*, respectively, which make the essential element of the defense turn on the type and degree of governmental conduct, be adopted as the law. We decline to overrule these cases. [Since] the defense is not of a constitutional dimension, Congress may address itself to the question and adopt any substantive definition of the defense that it may find desirable.

Critics of the rule laid down in *Sorrells* and *Sherman* have suggested that its basis in the implied intent of Congress is largely fictitious, and have pointed to what they conceive to be the anomalous difference between the treatment of a defendant who is solicited by a private individual and one who is entrapped by a government agent. Questions have been likewise raised as to whether "predisposition" can be factually established with the requisite degree of certainty. [Such arguments] have been twice previously made to this Court, and twice rejected by it, first in *Sorrells* and then in *Sherman*.

We believe that at least equally cogent criticism has been made of the concurring views in these cases. Commenting in *Sherman* on Mr. Justice Roberts' position in *Sorrells* that "although the defendant could claim that the Government had induced him to commit the crime, the Government could not reply by showing that the defendant's criminal conduct was due to his own readiness and not to the persuasion of government agents," Mr. Chief Justice Warren quoted the observation of Judge Learned Hand in an earlier stage of that proceeding:

> " 'Indeed, it would seem probable that, if there were no reply [to the claim of inducement], it would be impossible ever to secure convictions of any offences which consist of transactions that are carried on in secret.' "

Nor does it seem particularly desirable for the law to grant complete immunity from prosecution to one who himself planned to commit a crime, and then committed it, simply because government undercover agents subjected him to inducements which might have seduced a hypothetical individual who was not so predisposed.

[Several lower federal court decisions] have undoubtedly gone beyond this Court's opinions in *Sorrells* and *Sherman* in order to bar prosecutions because of what they thought to be, for want of a better term, "overzealous law enforcement." But the defense of entrapment enunciated in those opinions was not intended to give the federal judiciary a "chancellor's foot" veto over law enforcement practices of which it did not approve. The execution of the federal laws under our Constitution is confided primarily to the Executive Branch of the Government, subject to applicable constitutional and statutory limitations and to judicially fashioned rules to enforce those limitations. We think that the decision of the Court of Appeals in this case quite unnecessarily introduces an unmanageably subjective standard which is contrary to the holdings of this Court in *Sorrells* and *Sherman*.

[In light of *Sorrells* and *Sherman*, respondent's concession] that the jury finding as to predisposition was supported by the evidence [is], therefore, fatal to his claim of entrapment. He was an active participant in an illegal drug manufacturing enterprise which began before the Government agent appeared on the

scene, and continued after the Government agent had left the scene. He was, in the words of *Sherman,* not an "unwary innocent" but an "unwary criminal."
* * *

Reversed.

Justice STEWART, with whom Justice BRENNAN and Justice MARSHALL join, dissenting.

[In] *Sorrells* and *Sherman* the Court took what might be called a "subjective" approach to the defense of entrapment. [This] approach focuses on the conduct and propensities of the particular defendant in each individual case: if he is "otherwise innocent," he may avail himself of the defense; but if he had the "predisposition" to commit the crime, or if the "criminal design" originated with him, then—regardless of the nature and extent of the Government's participation—there has been no entrapment. And, in the absence of a conclusive showing one way or the other, the question of the defendant's "predisposition" to the crime is a question of fact for the jury. The Court today adheres to this approach.

The concurring opinion of Justice Roberts, joined by Justices Brandeis and Stone, in the *Sorrells* case, and that of Justice Frankfurter, joined by Justices Douglas, Harlan, and Brennan, in the *Sherman* case, took a different view of the entrapment defense. In their concept, the defense is [grounded] on the belief that "the methods employed on behalf of the Government to bring about conviction cannot be countenanced." Thus, the focus of this approach is not on the propensities and predisposition of a specific defendant, but on "whether the police conduct revealed in the particular case falls below standards, to which common feelings respond, for the proper use of governmental power." Phrased another way, the question is whether—regardless of the predisposition to crime of the particular defendant involved—the governmental agents have acted in such a way as is likely to instigate or create a criminal offense. Under this approach, the determination of the lawfulness of the Government's conduct must be made—as it is on all questions involving the legality of law enforcement methods—by the trial judge, not the jury.

In my view, this objective approach to entrapment [is] the only one truly consistent with the underlying rationale of the defense.[1] * * * I find it impossible to believe that the purpose of the defense is to effectuate some unexpressed congressional intent to exclude from its criminal statutes persons who committed a prohibited act, but would not have done so except for the Government's inducements.

[Furthermore,] to say that such a defendant is "otherwise innocent" or not "predisposed" to commit the crime is misleading, at best. The very fact that he has committed an act that Congress has determined to be illegal demonstrates conclusively that he is not innocent of the offense. He may not have originated the precise plan or the precise details, but he was "predisposed" in the sense that he has proved to be quite capable of committing the crime. That he was induced, provoked, or tempted to do so by government agents does not make him any more innocent or any less predisposed than he would be if he had been induced, provoked, or tempted by a private person—which, of course, would not entitle him to cry "entrapment." Since the only difference between these situations is the identity of the tempter, it follows that the significant focus must be on the conduct of the government agents, and not on the predisposition of the defendant.

---

1. Both the Proposed New Federal Criminal Code (1971), Final Report of the National Commission on Reform of Federal Criminal Laws § 702, and the American Law Institute's Model Penal Code § 2.13 (Proposed Official Draft, 1962), adopt this objective approach.

[Moreover,] a test that makes the entrapment defense depend on whether the defendant had the requisite predisposition permits the introduction into evidence of all kinds of hearsay, suspicion, and rumor—all of which would be inadmissible in any other context—in order to prove the defendant's predisposition. It allows the prosecution, in offering such proof, to rely on the defendant's bad reputation or past criminal activities, including even rumored activities of which the prosecution may have insufficient evidence to obtain an indictment, and to present the agent's suspicions as to why they chose to tempt this defendant. This sort of evidence is not only unreliable, as the hearsay rule recognizes; but it is also highly prejudicial, especially if the matter is submitted to the jury, for, despite instructions to the contrary, the jury may well consider such evidence as probative not simply of the defendant's predisposition, but of his guilt of the offense with which he stands charged.

More fundamentally, focusing on the defendant's innocence or predisposition has the direct effect of making what is permissible or impermissible police conduct depend upon the past record and propensities of the particular defendant involved. Stated another way, this subjective test means that the Government is permitted to entrap a person with a criminal record or bad reputation, and then to prosecute him for the manufactured crime, confident that his record or reputation itself will be enough to show that he was predisposed to commit the offense anyway. [In] my view, a person's alleged "predisposition" to crime should not expose him to government participation in the criminal transaction that would be otherwise unlawful.

* * * [G]overnment agents may engage in conduct that is likely, when objectively considered, to afford a person ready and willing to commit the crime an opportunity to do so. But when the agents' involvement in criminal activities goes beyond the mere offering of such an opportunity, and when their conduct is of a kind that could induce or instigate the commission of a crime by one not ready and willing to commit it, then—regardless of the character or propensities of the particular person induced—I think entrapment has occurred. For in that situation, the Government has engaged in the impermissible manufacturing of crime, and the federal courts should bar the prosecution in order to preserve the institutional integrity of the system of federal criminal justice.

[What] the agent did here was to meet with a group of suspected producers of methamphetamine, including the respondent; to request the drug; to offer to supply the chemical phenyl–2–propanone in exchange for one-half of the methamphetamine to be manufactured therewith; and, when that offer was accepted, to provide the needed chemical ingredient, and to purchase some of the drug from the respondent. [Although] the Court of Appeals found that the phenyl–2–propanone could not have been obtained without the agent's intervention—that "there could not have been the manufacture, delivery, or sale of the illicit drug had it not been for the Government's supply of one of the essential ingredients"— the Court today rejects this finding as contradicted by the facts revealed at trial. The record, as the Court states, discloses that one of the respondent's accomplices, though not the respondent himself, had obtained phenyl–2–propanone from independent sources both before and after receiving the agent's supply, and had used it in the production of methamphetamine. This demonstrates, it is said, that the chemical was obtainable other than through the government agent; and hence the agent's furnishing it for the production of the methamphetamine involved in this prosecution did no more than afford an opportunity for its production to one ready and willing to produce it. Thus, the argument seems to be, there was no entrapment here, any more than there would have been if the agent had furnished common table salt, had that been necessary to the drug's production.

It cannot be doubted that if phenyl–2–propanone had been wholly unobtainable from other sources, the agent's undercover offer to supply it to the respondent in return for part of the illicit methamphetamine produced therewith—an offer initiated and carried out by the agent for the purpose of prosecuting the respondent for producing methamphetamine—would be precisely the type of governmental conduct that constitutes entrapment under any definition. For the agent's conduct in that situation would make possible the commission of an otherwise totally impossible crime, and, I should suppose, would thus be a textbook example of instigating the commission of a criminal offense in order to prosecute someone for committing it.[a]

[The] chemical ingredient was available only to licensed persons, and the Government itself had requested suppliers not to sell that ingredient even to people with a license. Yet the Government agent readily offered, and supplied, that ingredient to an unlicensed person and asked him to make a certain illegal drug with it. The Government then prosecuted that person for making the drug produced *with the very ingredient* which its agent had so helpfully supplied. This strikes me as the very pattern of conduct that should be held to constitute entrapment as a matter of law. * * *[b]

COMMENTARY ON THE "SUBJECTIVE" AND "OBJECTIVE" TESTS

1. *Support for the "hypothetical person" or "objective" test.* As pointed out in 2 Wayne R. LaFave, Jerold H. Israel, Nancy J. King, *Criminal Procedure Treatise* § 5.2(b)(2d ed. 1999) (hereafter CRIMPROC), "the objective test is favored by most commentators, and is reflected in the formulation of the entrapment defense appearing in the *Model Penal Code* § 2.13. Its first authoritative acceptance came by judicial decision in *Grossman v. State,* 457 P.2d 226 (Alaska 1969), and now a dozen other states have adopted it either by statute or case law. See Piccaretta & Keenan, *Entrapment Targets and Tactics: Jacobson v. United States,* 29 Crim.L.Bull. 241, 252 (1993).

See, e.g., *People v. Barraza,* 591 P.2d 947 (Cal.1979), per Mosk, J., holding that the proper test of entrapment in California is: "was the [police conduct] likely to induce a normally law-abiding person to commit the offense?" Observed the court:

"[W]e presume that [a normally law-abiding] person would resist the temptation to commit a crime presented by the simple opportunity to act unlawfully. [But] it is impermissible for the police or their agents to pressure the suspect by overbearing conduct such as badgering, cajoling, importuning, or other affirmative acts likely to induce a normally law-abiding person to commit the crime."

"[G]uidance will generally be found in the application of one or both of two principles. First, if the [police conduct] would generate in a normally law-abiding person a motive for the crime other than ordinary criminal intent, entrapment will be established. An example of such conduct would be an appeal by the police that would induce such a person to commit the act because of friendship or sympathy, instead of a desire for personal gain or other typical criminal purpose. Second, affirmative police conduct that would make commission of the crime

---

a. But see *Hampton v. United States,* p. 402.

b. In a separate dissent, Justice Douglas, joined by Brennan, J., maintained that "[f]ederal agents play a debased role when they become the instigators of the crime, or part-ners in its commission, or the creative brain behind the illegal scheme. That is what the federal agent did here when he furnished the accused with one of the chemical ingredients needed to manufacture the unlawful drug."

unusually attractive to a normally law-abiding person will likewise constitute entrapment. Such conduct would include, for example, a guarantee that the act is not illegal or the offense will go undetected, an offer of exorbitant consideration, or any similar enticement."[a]

2. *Doubts about the efficacy of the "objective" test.* Roger Park, *The Entrapment Controversy,* 60 Minn.L.Rev. 163, 270–71 (1976), voices doubts that the "hypothetical person" test could control the conduct of police and informers: "Standardized procedures cannot govern the sundry and unpredictable events that occur during encounters between target and tempter. Moreover, even if such procedures could be formulated and somehow taught to the army of addicts and criminals used by police to set up controlled offenses, it is doubtful that they would be followed—particularly since the rules would inevitably become known to targets as well as police agents.

" * * * Because many targets are professional criminals, judges will be reluctant to rule that entrapment has occurred simply because an agent found it necessary to appeal to friendship, make multiple requests, or offer a substantial profit. Yet approval of such conduct would lead to unfair results in cases where the target was law-abiding but ductile. For example, conviction of someone who has been solicited by a friend may be fair enough in the general run of cases, but unfair if the target was a nondisposed person who would not have committed the type of crime charged but for a request from that particular friend.

"The danger of acquitting wolves and convicting lambs would be ameliorated if courts following the hypothetical-person test allow predisposition evidence to be introduced for its bearing on the propriety of the agent's inducement. The degree of persistence permitted would then depend upon whether the agent had sound reasons to believe that his target was already engaged in criminal enterprise. However, this approach would create even greater uncertainty about the boundaries of permissible inducement and further limit the defense's utility as a guide to police conduct.

"[The federal defense] attempts to distinguish between persons who are blameworthy and persons who are not. In the absence of extraordinary circumstances, that should be the goal of our law of crimes."

3. *Should the "subjective" test be retained, but stripped of its indiscriminate attitude toward "predisposition" evidence?* The "subjective" test, protested Stewart, J., dissenting in *United States v. Russell,* permits the use of otherwise inadmissible "hearsay, suspicion and rumor" to prove defendant's predisposition.[b] The defendant, in effect, is "put on trial for his past offenses and character." *Grossman v. State,* 457 P.2d 226, 229 (Alaska 1969) (adopting the objective test).

But, maintains Park, supra, at 272, "the indiscriminate attitude toward predisposition evidence"—"the greatest fault" of the subjective test—"is by no means a necessary feature of the subjective test. If the accused was already engaged in a course of criminal conduct, the prosecution should be able to develop an arsenal of reliable predisposition evidence. If it cannot, the danger of wrongful acquittal is outweighed by the danger of convicting a person whose only real vice is a bad reputation. Reputation and other hearsay evidence should not become admissible merely because the accused has raised the defense of entrapment. If

a. Under this test, emphasized the court, "the character of the suspect, his predisposition to commit the offense, and his subjective intent are irrelevant." On this point, see Note 3 infra.

b. Not only prior convictions, but prior arrests, acts of prior misconduct, "reputation testimony" and "suspicious conduct" have been admitted on this issue. See CRIMPROC § 5.2(c).

construed to exclude such testimony, the subjective defense should present more reliable evidence to the fact-finder than the hypothetical-person defense. The latter focuses upon the nature of the inducement offered; consequently, trials are likely to be reduced to a swearing match between unreliable witnesses about words said in private."

4. *Is the distinction between the objective and subjective approaches overstated?* Consider Louis Michael Seidman, *The Supreme Court, Entrapment, and Our Criminal Justice Dilemma*, 1981 Sup.Ct.Rev. 111, 118–20:

"The [subjective test] is premised on the notion that it is possible to isolate the class of 'unwary criminals' who are 'ready and willing' to engage in crime apart from the inducements offered by the government. But whether a person is 'ready and willing' to break the law depends on what the person expects to get in return—that is, on the level of inducement. Like the rest of us, criminals do not generally work for free. Their willingness to take the risks of crime varies with the incentive which is provided. To be sure, the less cynical among us may believe that there is still a class of people who 'have no price.' [But] even if one concedes that such people can be found somewhere, they are, by definition, not among the ranks of entrapped defendants, since such defendants must have succumbed to some inducement in order to be entrapped.

"Consequently, so long as one equates 'predisposition' with a readiness to commit crime, no definition of 'predisposition' can be complete without an articulation of the level of inducement to which a 'predisposed' defendant would respond. Furthermore, the 'predisposed' cannot be distinguished from the 'nondisposed' without focusing on the propriety of the government's conduct—the very factor that the subjective approach professes to ignore. This is true because a defendant who responds favorably to a 'proper' inducement has thereby conclusively demonstrated that he is disposed to crime when such an inducement is offered.[c] It would seem, then, that so long as government agents restrict themselves to 'proper' inducements, they run no risk of violating the entrapment rules. The entrapment test is 'subjective' only in the sense that even if the government offers an 'excessive' inducement, the defendant may nonetheless be convicted under such a test if he would have responded favorably to a proper one."[d]

5. *Was the distinction between the subjective and objective tests smudged in the DeLorean case?* Because John DeLorean was prosecuted for drug violations in federal court, the judge instructed the jury to consider the entrapment claim in accordance with the subjective test. However, points out Maura Whelan, *Lead Us Not Into (Unwarranted) Temptation: A Proposal to Replace the Entrapment Defense with a Reasonable Suspicion Requirement*, 133 U.Pa.L.Rev. 1193, 1199–1200 (1985), "it seems from the jurors' remarks" after the acquittal that "they followed the objective approach instead. Those jurors who discussed the entrapment issue with reporters emphasized the impropriety of the operation, not DeLorean's character. One juror expressed the view that the FBI went after DeLorean only because he was an influential person. There were several indications that the agents viewed DeLorean as a highly desirable arrest. [It] was undoubtedly the spirit of the hunt that led [one agent] to report to FBI

c. In the Abscam cases, observes Bennett Gershman, *Abscam, the Judiciary, and the Ethics of Entrapment*, 91 Yale L.J. 1565, 1581 (1982), "the jury was allowed to infer predisposition simply from the defendant's affirmative response to the government's inducements. For instance, that [two defendants] readily accepted cash payments was found to constitute sufficient evidence that they had a *preexisting* intention to take a bribe. In other words, the defendant is said to be predisposed because he committed the act, and then is held responsible for the act because he was predisposed. The pernicious circularity of this approach is obvious."

d. Reconsider the extract from the Allen–Luttrell–Kreeger article at p. 391.

headquarters that DeLorean was 'involved in large scale narcotics transactions, in addition to the laundering [of] large amounts of illegally received income,' although he knew it wasn't true. His explanation for this message? 'I thought it sounded pretty good.' "[e]

OTHER ISSUES RAISED BY THE ENTRAPMENT DEFENSE[a]

1. *Contingent fee arrangements.* In *Williamson v. United States*, 311 F.2d 441 (5th Cir.1962), the informer had been promised $200 and $100, respectively, for producing legally admissible evidence that two specified persons were engaged in illicit liquor dealings. Using its supervisory powers over the administration of federal criminal justice,[b] the court held that absent a special justification for its use in a particular case, a conviction is invalid if it rests on evidence of informants hired on such a basis. *Williamson* "could have been construed to limit the widespread practice of offering leniency to arrested persons who agree to incriminate others by making purchases of contraband," but the case "has had virtually no impact. Courts faced with a defense based on it have almost invariably found a way to distinguish it." Park, supra, at 175.

Williamson was, in effect, disapproved in *United States v. Grimes*, 438 F.2d 391 (6th Cir.1971), reasoning that a contingent fee informer is "no more likely to [lie and manufacture crimes] than witnesses acting for other, more common reasons," such as a codefendant hoping for leniency or an informant who feels that his future employment may depend upon success on this occasion. But are not contingent fee informers likely to be more desperate then informers generally? Are they not likely to have a stronger incentive for overreaching and falsification? See CRIMPROC, § 5.4(a).

2. *"Inconsistent" defenses.* The traditional view had been that the defense of entrapment is not available to one who denies commission of the criminal act with which he is charged, for the reason that the denial is inconsistent with the assertion of such a defense. But *Mathews v. United States*, 485 U.S. 58, 108 S.Ct. 883, 99 L.Ed.2d 54 (1988) holds that "even if the defendant denies one or more

---

e. According to newspaper accounts of the DeLorean trial, summarized in Whelan, supra, at 1197–99, by 1980 DeLorean desperately needed ten million dollars to save his automobile company. About this time, he was invited to participate in a major cocaine transaction by FBI informant James Hoffman, a former neighbor of DeLorean and an admitted perjurer and occasional drug dealer. The FBI had no reason to believe that DeLorean was involved in drugs in any way until Hoffman came forward with his allegation that DeLorean wanted to make money quickly in a big narcotics deal and hoped that Hoffman could arrange something.

According to the original scenario, DeLorean would invest two million dollars toward the purchase of the cocaine and make as much as sixty million dollars. When DeLorean reported that he would have to withdraw from the operation because of his inability to raise the money, either Hoffman or an FBI agent proposed an alternative: simply put up two million dollars of collateral, which included various property. DeLorean also signed over the entire vot-

ing stock of his company to the federal agents who were posing as drug dealers. An FBI agent recommended that DeLorean "launder" any profits from the operation through one of his companies.

The jury's acquittal of DeLorean was based both on disapproval of the FBI's methods and the conclusion that the government had failed to prove that DeLorean had committed a crime.

a. Because three issues—(1) when a private person should be considered a "government agent" for purposes of the entrapment defense; (2) whether a government agent should be allowed to solicit an offense absent "probable cause" or at least "reasonable suspicion" that his target is engaged in criminal activity; and (3) whether judicial authorization should be required for an undercover operation—received prominent attention as a result of the Abscam cases, treatment of these issues is postponed until the Notes and Questions following *United States v. Kelly*, p. 407.

b. See generally pp. 47–51.

elements of the crime, he is entitled to an entrapment instruction whenever there is sufficient evidence from which a reasonable jury could find entrapment."

3. *Triable by court or jury.* Recall that *Sorrells* rejected, and *Sherman* declined to reconsider, the argument that the issue of entrapment should be tried separately to the court without a jury. Although most commentators favor a judicial determination of the issue, the defense has traditionally been regarded as a matter for the jury, except in those unusual cases where entrapment is established as a matter of law. It has been argued, in support of this position, that a jury has special, or at least traditional, competence to judge matters of credibility and motivation and to assess the subjective response to the stimulus of police encouragement. Moreover, if the matter is placed in the hands of the jury, there is an opportunity for "jury nullification" if the police conduct evokes "moral revulsion." See generally CRIMPROC § 5.3(b).

On the other hand, it has been said that where the subjective test prevails "the most urgent considerations" support judicial determination of the issue—to avoid the great impact on the jury of prior convictions, prior arrests and "reputation testimony"—but that in those jurisdictions that follow the objective approach "the case for separate trial to the court is more evenly balanced." See Comment to *Model Penal Code* § 2.10(2) (Tent. Draft No. 9, 1959). It has been argued, however, that here, too, the case for having the matter decided by the court is a strong one: It is the function of the court to preserve its own purity; to the extent that the objective approach is based on a deterrence-of-police rationale, this is the function of the court, just as it is when the court rules on suppression motions; and, as Frankfurter, J., maintained in *Sherman,* only the court can provide government agents with the necessary guidance. See CRIMPROC, supra.

4. *Burden of proof.* In those jurisdictions following the subjective approach, it is generally agreed that the defendant must establish the fact of inducement by a government agent. Once the defendant satisfies this threshold requirement (and it is unclear whether he need only produce "some evidence" of inducement or sustain a burden of persuasion by a preponderance of the evidence), the burden is then on the government to negate the defense by establishing the defendant's "predisposition" beyond a reasonable doubt. See CRIMPROC, § 5.3(d).

In states where the objective test prevails, entrapment is viewed as an "affirmative defense" rather than something that negates the existence of an element of the crime charged, and the entire burden of production and persuasion is on the defendant. The defendant must establish the defense by a preponderance of the evidence. The *Model Penal Code* § 2.13(2) also takes this position. For criticism of this approach, see Park, supra, at 265–67, suggesting that the real basis for placing the burden of persuasion on the defendant is that entrapment is a disfavored defense.

SECTION 2. MORE ON THE DUE PROCESS DEFENSE TO GOVERNMENT "OVERINVOLVEMENT" IN A CRIMINAL ENTERPRISE[a]

HAMPTON v. UNITED STATES, 425 U.S. 484, 96 S.Ct. 1646, 48 L.Ed.2d 113 (1976), grew out of the following facts: Petitioner was convicted of distributing heroin in violation of federal law. The district court refused to give petitioner's

a. Although the claim that the government has unduly "dominated" or become impermissibly "overinvolved" in the criminal activity has often been viewed as a species of the objective test entrapment, it seems preferable to view it as the basis for a separate test for entrapment or as a due process defense independent of general entrapment theory.

requested instruction that if it were found, as he claimed, that the narcotics he sold to government agents (posing as narcotics buyers) had been supplied to him by a government informant[b] he must be acquitted as a matter of law regardless of his predisposition to commit the offense charged. On appeal, petitioner conceded that he was "predisposed." A majority of the Court rejected petitioner's contention, but there was no opinion of the Court. Justice REHNQUIST, who announced the judgment of the Court in an opinion in which Burger, C.J., and White, J., joined, observed:

"In *Russell* [we] ruled out the possibility that the defense of entrapment could ever be based upon governmental misconduct in a case, such as this one, where the predisposition of the defendant to commit the crime was established. [In] view of [*Sorrells, Sherman* and *Russell*], petitioner correctly recognizes that his case does not qualify as one involving 'entrapment' at all, [but] relies on the language in *Russell* that 'we may some day be presented with a situation in which the conduct of law enforcement agents is so outrageous that due process principle would absolutely bar the government from invoking judicial processes to obtain a conviction.'

"[In] urging that this [is such a case], petitioner misapprehends the meaning of the quoted language in *Russell*. Admittedly petitioner's case is different from Russell's but the difference is one of degree, not of kind. In *Russell* the ingredient supplied by the government agent was a legal drug which the defendants demonstrably could have obtained from other sources besides the Government. Here the drug which the government informant allegedly supplied [was] both illegal and constituted the *corpus delicti* for the sale of which the petitioner was convicted. The Government obviously played a more significant role in enabling petitioner to sell contraband in this case than it did in *Russell*.

"But in each case the government agents were acting in concert with the defendant, and in each case either the jury found or the defendant conceded that he was predisposed to commit the crime for which he was convicted. The remedy of the criminal defendant with respect to the acts of government agents, which, far from being resisted, are encouraged by him, lies solely in the defense of entrapment. But, as noted, petitioner's conceded predisposition rendered this defense unavailable to him.

"To sustain petitioner's contention here would run directly contrary to our statement in *Russell* that the defense of entrapment is not intended 'to give the federal judiciary a "chancellor's foot" veto over law enforcement practices of which it did not approve. * * * ' " [The limitations of the Due Process Clause of the Fifth Amendment come into play only when the Government activity in question violates some protected right of the defendant. [If] the police engage in illegal activity in concert with a defendant beyond the scope of their duties the remedy lies, not in freeing the equally culpable defendant, but in prosecuting the police under the applicable provisions of state or federal law. But the police

b. According to petitioner's version of the events, the informant not only supplied the narcotics but was the first to propose the criminal enterprise. Petitioner alleged that when he stated that he was short of cash, the informant responded by proposing they sell drugs that he could get from a pharmacist friend. Evidently, petitioner did not deem this particular aspect of his version of the facts significant. Evidently, too, a majority of the Court considered it irrelevant so long as petitioner was "predisposed" to commit the offense and the governmental activity had not "implant[ed] in the mind of an *innocent* person the disposition to commit the alleged offense." (Emphasis added.) No member of the majority disputed dissenting Justice Brennan's characterization of the case as one where "the two sales for which petitioner was convicted were allegedly instigated by Government agents." See also Judge Adams's dissent in *United States v. Twigg* (p. 405, fn. a infra) (describing *Hampton* as a case where the government "suggested the operation"). But see the majority opinion in *Twigg* and Note, 67 Geo.L.J. 1455, 1464 & fn. 73, 1466 (1979).

conduct here no more deprived defendant of any right secured to him by the United States Constitution than did the police conduct in *Russell* deprive Russell of any rights."

Concurring Justice POWELL, joined by Blackmun, J., agreed that "this case is controlled completely by *Russell*," but was "unwilling to join the plurality in concluding that, no matter what the circumstances, neither due process principles nor our supervisory power could support a bar to conviction in any case where the Government is able to prove disposition": "[Disposition of the claims in *Russell* and earlier cases] did not require the Court to consider whether overinvolvement of government agents in contraband offenses could ever reach such proportions as to bar conviction of a predisposed defendant as a matter of due process. Nor have we had occasion yet to confront Government overinvolvement in areas outside the realm of contraband offenses. In these circumstances, I am unwilling to conclude that an analysis other than one limited to predisposition would never be appropriate under due process principles."[c]

Justice BRENNAN, joined by Stewart and Marshall, JJ., dissented, urging that conviction be "barred as a matter of law where the subject of the criminal charge is the sale of contraband provided to the defendant by a Government agent."[d] The dissenters reiterated their support for the "objective" approach to entrapment, under which, they maintained, petitioner's claims "would plainly be held to constitute entrapment as a matter of law," but considered reversal compelled even "for those who follow the 'subjective' approach." Where the Government's agent "deliberately sets up the accused by supplying him with contraband and then bringing him to another agent as a potential purchaser," protested the dissent, "the Government's role has passed the point of toleration. The Government is doing nothing less than buying contraband from itself through an intermediary and jailing the intermediary."[e]

Notes and Questions

1. "The depth of our confusion concerning the proper limits on government power in this area," observes Louis Michael Seidman, *The Supreme Court, Entrapment, and Our Criminal Justice Dilemma,* 1981 Sup.Ct.Rev. 111, 116 n. 20, "is illustrated by comparing the intuitions of Justice Powell with those of the authors of the Model Penal Code. Justice Powell hints that his objective, due process test would be violated if the government induced beatings or armed robberies. [See fn. c to his concurring opinion in *Hampton*.] Yet the Model Penal Code [§ 2.13(3)] makes an entrapment defense unavailable in precisely those cases where the defendant causes or threatens bodily injury."

2. Leslie Abramson & Lisa Lindeman, *Entrapment and Due Process in the Federal Courts,* 8 Am.J.Crim.Law 139, 180–82 (1980), concludes, inter alia: "Many courts treat the constitutional due process defense as an illegitimate offspring of entrapment, and recognize the issue reluctantly when it is presented in the pleadings. It is then granted only cursory review. The better approach, therefore, is to plead the defense independently of the general entrapment defense, with

c. At this point Justice Powell quotes from Judge Friendly's view in *United States v. Archer,* 486 F.2d 670, 676 (2d Cir.1973), that "it would be unthinkable, for example, to permit government agents to instigate robberies and beatings merely to gather evidence to convict other members of a gang of hoodlums."

d. The dissent deemed it sufficient "for present purposes" to adopt this rule "under our supervisory power and leave to another day whether it ought to be made applicable to the States under the Due Process Clause." For a general discussion of the federal courts' supervisory power over criminal justice, see pp. 47–51.

e. Stevens, J., took no part in the consideration or decision of the case.

police misconduct as the exclusive basis. In that case, the due process defense cannot later be dismissed by a finding of predisposition, because a defendant can prove police misconduct and overreaching without having to disprove his own predisposition. The trial court can then decide the due process question as a matter of law." [The] due process defense requires a stricter scrutiny of government conduct than the traditional entrapment defense. Possibly, as in *United States v. Twigg*,[a] lower courts will soon accept the need for a constitutional due process defense independent of the general entrapment theory. To protect the constitutional rights of an individual does not necessarily require application of a 'chancellor's foot.' "

3. *Is the due process defense in entrapment cases so unruly and so subjective that it should no longer be considered?* As a strong proponent of the due process defense in entrapment cases, Paul Marcus, recognizes, *The Due Process Defense in Entrapment Cases: The Journey Back*, 27 Am.Crim.L.Rev. 457, 458 (1990): "It will take a great deal to persuade courts that entrapment-like schemes violate due process. Some courts have announced that they have *never* overturned convictions on this basis."

See, e.g., *United States v. Simpson*, 813 F.2d 1462 (9th Cir.1987), holding that (1) the FBI's "manipulation" of a prostitute (Helen Miller), who was a heroin user

a. 588 F.2d 373 (3d Cir.1978). In *Twigg*, apparently the only post-*Hampton* federal court of appeals decision to invalidate a conviction on the basis of the due process defense, the informant contacted an old acquaintance, defendant Neville, and proposed that they set up a "speed" laboratory. Neville assumed responsibility for raising the capital and arranging for distribution of the product. The informant assumed responsibility for acquiring the necessary equipment, raw materials, and a production site. The DEA assisted the informant in carrying out his part of the operation by providing two and one-half gallons of the essential and hard to obtain ingredient, propanone; some glassware; and a rented farmhouse for the laboratory site. Defendant Twigg joined the operation, at the invitation of Neville. The laboratory operated for one week, producing about six pounds of speed. The informant alone had the expertise to manufacture the drug and thus was completely in charge of the laboratory.

Neville and Twigg were convicted of conspiracy to manufacture speed. On appeal, a 2–1 majority, per Rosenn, J., reversed. Distinguishing *Russell* as a case in which the defendant was an active participant before the government agent arrived on the scene, and *Hampton* as concerned with the sale of an illegal drug—"a much more fleeting and elusive crime to detect than the operation of an illicit drug laboratory"—the *Twigg* majority concluded that the government involvement was so "overreaching," "egregious" and "outrageous" as to bar prosecution as a matter of due process. The court emphasized (a) that the "illicit plan did not originate with the criminal defendants"; (b) that the informant's expertise was "an indispensable requisite to this criminal enterprise"; and (c) that Neville was "lawfully

and peacefully minding his own affairs" until approached by the defendant.

As dissenting Judge Adams read the relevant Supreme Court cases, due process analysis "was not intended simply to reestablish the objective approach to entrapment under a new name." He dissented because he did not believe that "this situation presents the intolerable set of circumstances necessary to warrant resort to the due process clause." He thought the facts less persuasive for reversal than were those in *Hampton* because none of the chemicals, equipment or skill provided by the government "was itself contraband." The government, through its agent, did suggest the operation, "but that is the situation in many undercover operations, and was the case in *Hampton*."

Twigg suggests that the oft-proposed but rarely applied "reasonable suspicion" requirement (see p. 411) "may on occasion emerge as an aspect of the due process limits upon encouragement activity. The point seems to be that overinvolvement by the government to the extent reflected in *Twigg* is permissible, if at all, only against a person who is 'reasonably suspected of criminal conduct or design.' " CRIMPROC § 5.4(c). See also Note, 67 Geo. L.J. 1455, 1461, 1467 (1979).

Another important principle recognized in *Twigg* is that "the practicalities of combatting" a certain type of criminal activity must be considered in determining whether "more extreme methods of investigation" are constitutionally permissible. But *Twigg* may have misapplied this principle. Consider Note, 67 Geo.L.J. at 1463: "[A] drug laboratory, which by nature is sophisticated and covert, arguably is *more* difficult to detect than the sale of drugs."

and a fugitive from drug charges, into becoming an informant; (2) the fact that Ms. Miller continued to use heroin and engage in acts of prostitution during the investigation of defendant; (3) Ms. Miller's "use of sex" to deceive defendant into believing she was "an intimate friend" so that she could "lure him into selling heroin to undercover FBI agents"; and (4) the FBI's continued use of Ms. Miller as an informant even after learning of her sexual involvement with defendant was "not so shocking as to violate the due process clause." Although Simpson "may have suffered severe emotional trauma and felt stripped of his dignity upon learning that [Ms. Miller's] apparent affection for him was contrived," his treatment by her "falls short of the brutality and coercion underlying previous successful outrageous conduct challenges."

See also *United States v. Miller* 891 F.2d 1265 (7th Cir.1989), where the undercover agent had a contingent fee arrangement with the government, had been a cocaine addict both before and during her employment and had earlier been sexually intimate with the defendant. But these factors "neither separately or combined" amounted to " 'truly outrageous' government conduct." Concurring Judge Easterbrook would have gone farther. He argued that there should not even be a due process defense in entrapment cases:

" 'Outrageousness' " as a defense * * * creates serious problems of consistency. [How] much is 'too much'? The nature of the question exposes it as (a) unanswerable, and (b) political. What, if anything, could separate stirring up of crime in unpalatable ways here [from] Operation Greylord [or] the 'creative' endeavors in Abscam? From any of the 'sting' operations? [Any] line we draw would be unprincipled and therefore not judicial in nature. More likely there would be no line; judges would vote their lower intestines. Such a meandering, personal approach is the antithesis of justice under law, and we ought not indulge it. Inability to describe in general terms just what makes tactics too outrageous to tolerate suggests that there is no definition?—and 'I know it when I see it' is not a rule of any kind, let alone a command of the Due Process Clause.

"The kinds of prosecution that trouble me most are not those like Operation Greylord or offers of sex in exchange for cocaine, but those that impose costs on the innocent. Take for example a sting in which the FBI sets up a fence and buys stolen goods. The money the government pumps into the business must lead people to steal things to sell to the FBI—with misery for the victims of the burglary and potential violence in the process. Stings have been upheld consistently, however * * *. Methods such as those used to ensnare [the defendant in this case] do not trouble me. Other judges are offended by immorality (such as sponsoring an informant's use of sexual favors as currency) or by acts that endanger informants (such as supplying them with drugs for personal use) but not by a traditional sting. This shows the subjective basis of the concern—all the more reason not to have such a doctrine in our law."[b]

But consider Marcus, supra, at 465: "[The due process defense in entrapment cases] is important because it creates outer limits on appropriate law enforcement techniques and because it clearly demonstrates to the legal and law enforcement communities, and to society at large, that courts are indeed willing to draw some lines that cannot be crossed even in pursuit of criminals. [As for Judge Easterbrook's argument that the inability of reasonable people to agree on the application of the defense indicates that it is not a rule of any kind,] it is not factually accurate. There will be fact situations where reasonable people could agree that the law enforcement behavior was utterly outrageous. Certainly, Judge Friendly's

---

b. Some courts have followed Judge Easterbrook's lead in rejecting or greatly restricting the "outrageous governmental conduct" defense. See *United States v. Gaviria*, 116 F.3d 1498 (D.C.Cir.1997); *United States v. Tucker*, 28 F.3d 1420 (6th Cir.1994).

hypothetical problem of government agents beating some members of a gang in order to get to other members of a gang is just such a case."

UNITED STATES v. KELLY
707 F.2d 1460 (D.C.Cir.1983).

[The phase of the Abscam operation that resulted in the indictment of Kelly and other Congressmen was conceived by convicted confidence man Weinberg and approved by the FBI. It was to spread the word that wealthy Arabs were willing to bribe members of Congress to ensure that they would introduce private immigration legislation on the Arabs' behalf if and when necessary.

[Among those to whom the word was passed was codefendant Ciuzio, an acquaintance of Congressman Kelly. At a November, 1979 meeting, Ciuzio told Kelly that he had some Arab clients with immigration difficulties and asked Kelly if he could help them. Kelly indicated that he would be glad to do so, particularly since Ciuzio indicated the Arabs might invest in his district. Ciuzio told Kelly that he—Ciuzio—would receive a large fee if Kelly helped the Arabs. Kelly replied that the fee would cause no difficulties. Ciuzio then told codefendant Weisz, who was a business associate of Rosenberg (who was helping Weinberg locate politicians willing to assist the latter's "Arab-employers"), that Kelly would be happy to help the Arabs. The word was passed via the Abscam "middlemen" to Weinberg that a "candidate" was available who would assist with the Arabs' immigration problems and that he wanted $250,000. Weinberg suggested that the Congressman be paid $25,000 down, with the balance paid when legislation was required.

[At a December 19 meeting among Ciuzio, Weinberg and FBI agent Amoroso (Weinberg's immediate supervisor), Ciuzio was told what assistance would be expected of the Congressman. Ciuzio indicated that the Congressman was Kelly and intimated that he and Kelly had had previous dealings of a similar nature. Ciuzio suggested that he had told Kelly of the offer and claimed that Kelly had left the arrangements to him. But Ciuzio opposed direct payment to Kelly and suggested that the money instead be escrowed through Weisz.

[A January 8, 1980 meeting was arranged between Kelly and the "Arabs' representatives" at the FBI's townhouse in Washington, D.C. Soon after his arrival, Ciuzio, in a private meeting with Weinberg and Amoroso, sought to dissuade them from attempting to bribe Kelly directly. It was ultimately agreed that Kelly would acknowledge that the money was in exchange for his agreement to assist the Arabs, but that Ciuzio would actually take the money from the meeting.

[Finally, later that evening, Congressman Kelly met with Amoroso alone. When Amoroso proposed a payoff, Kelly told him that he was interested in the investment in his district, that he didn't "know anything about" Amoroso's arrangement with Ciuzio and others—"I'm not involved with it"—but that Amoroso's arrangement with Ciuzio and others was "fine."

[After Amoroso received a phone call from an Assistant United States Attorney who was monitoring the meeting and who told Amoroso that Kelly was "being cute," Amoroso sought to clarify Kelly's position. Kelly maintained that he wanted the money given to Ciuzio. Amoroso indicated that all of the money was supposed to go to Kelly, that Ciuzio would be compensated separately, and that giving the money directly to Kelly would avoid witnesses, thus protecting Kelly. The Congressman then agreed that that was "the best way of doing it." Amoroso then gave Kelly $25,000 in packets of $100 bills and Kelly stuffed the money in the pockets of his suit.]

PER CURIAM: Judge MacKinnon files an opinion in Parts I, II, III(A), and IV of which Chief Judge Robinson concurs.[a] Judge Ginsburg files an opinion in which Chief Judge Robinson concurs. Thus Parts I, II, III(A) and IV of Judge Mac-Kinnon's opinion together with Judge Ginsburg's opinion constitute the opinion of the court. * * *

MacKINNON, Circuit Judge. [On] January 8, 1980, Congressman Richard Kelly accepted $25,000 from an agent of the FBI who was posing as a representative of two wealthy Arabs as part of the FBI's elaborate Abscam investigation. In return, Kelly agreed to use his position in Congress to assist the Arabs to become permanent residents of the United States. Unbeknownst to Kelly, the FBI recorded the entire illegal transaction on video tape.

On the basis of this and other evidence, Kelly and [Ciuzio and Weisz] were charged with [bribery and other federal offenses]. A jury found each defendant guilty on all counts. However, the district court granted Kelly's motion to dismiss the indictment, entering a judgment of acquittal in his favor, because it concluded that the FBI's actions in furtherance of Abscam were so outrageous that prosecution of Kelly was barred by principles of due process. * * *

III. ANALYSIS

A. *The Due Process Defense*

"[Our task] is to assess whether the FBI's conduct in Abscam reached a "demonstrable level of outrageousness" [Powell, J., concurring in *Hampton*], while keeping in mind the difficulties inherent in detecting corrupt public officials. Measured against this standard, the FBI's conduct did not violate due process.

B. *Abscam*

[S]tripped of [its] trappings of wealth, Abscam was no more than an "opportunity for the commission of crime by those willing to do so." *United States v. Myers,* 692 F.2d 823, 837 (2d Cir.1982). Amoroso and Weinberg let it be known that they would pay substantial sums of money to congressmen willing to promise to assist the wealthy Arabs with their immigration difficulties. Thereafter, the FBI operatives simply waited for the grapevine to work and to see who appeared to take bribes. No congressmen were targeted for investigation; rather, Abscam pursued all who were brought to the operation by the grapevine.[50] In essence, then, Abscam was *not* significantly different from an undercover drug or fencing operation offering to buy from all who appear at its door.[51] Instead of buying

---

a. Part I, a detailed discussion of the facts, and Part II, a discussion of the district court opinion dismissing the indictment, are omitted.

50. However, not all officials brought to Abscam were offered bribes. The Abscam operatives recognized that they had no control over the representations made by intermediaries such as Ciuzio, Rosenberg, and Weisz. Accordingly, the FBI *always* discussed the asylum scenario with the officials prior to the offer of a bribe. That was certainly the case with Kelly; Amoroso carefully discussed the details of the asylum scenario with Kelly *before* any bribe money was paid. See discussion infra. In one instance, where this discussion revealed that the official was unaware of the corrupt nature of the proposal, the FBI terminated the meeting.

51. The district court concluded that Abscam was unlike ordinary, "passive" undercov-

er operations because it used "recruiting agents" to spread the word that bribes were available. I disagree. I seriously doubt that the government would establish an undercover drug or fencing operation without spreading the word, through informants and criminal elements (labeled "recruiting agents" by the district court), that its services were available. The Abscam investigators did no more.

My colleagues term Abscam an extraordinary operation. It was extraordinary only in the positions of some of the individuals involved and in the intangible nature of the "commodity" purchased. Otherwise, it is strikingly similar to ordinary undercover operations. * * *

My colleagues also criticize the failure of the FBI to closely supervise the Abscam operation. To the extent that this criticism extends to the non-FBI middlemen, such as Ciuzio, Rosenberg

stolen goods or contraband drugs, Abscam bought corrupt official influence in Congress. Such government involvement in crime does not violate principles of due process.

We need not determine the exact limits on government involvement in crime imposed by the due process clause for it is clear that the FBI's involvement in Abscam was less than that government involvement found unobjectionable by the Supreme Court.[52]

[In *Russell* and *Hampton*] the government not only provided an *opportunity* to commit a crime, but also provided the *means* to commit that crime. Nevertheless, in each case the Supreme Court concluded that the government's conduct did not violate due process. Where, as in Abscam, the government simply provides the opportunity to commit a crime, prosecution of a defendant does not violate principles of due process. This conclusion is in accord with decisions of the Second and Third Circuits upholding Abscam convictions challenged on due process grounds. *United States v. Williams,* 705 F.2d 603 (2d Cir.1983); *Myers,* supra; *United States v. Alexandro,* 675 F.2d 34 (2d Cir.); *United States v. Jannotti,* 673 F.2d 578 (3d Cir.) (en banc).[53]

C. *Specific Claims*

1. *Reasonable Suspicion*[b]

Nor do any of the specifically challenged FBI actions in furtherance of Abscam reach that "demonstrable level of outrageousness" which would bar Kelly's prosecution. The district court stressed that Abscam's asylum scenario was not triggered by any suspicion of corruption in government. [But] prior to the January 8 meeting with Kelly, the Abscam operatives had evidence from which they could conclude that Kelly was, in fact, corrupt. [Thus,] the FBI had [the requisite reasonable suspicion] to justify pursuing the asylum scenario and Kelly, if such suspicion was necessary.[58] * * *

2. *Utilization of Weinberg*

[The] argument that the FBI violated due process by utilizing the services of an admitted confidence man, Melvin Weinberg, in Abscam should likewise be rejected. Successful creation of an "elaborate hoax" such as Abscam may well *require* employment of "experts" such as Weinberg to give the operation an aura of "credibility" and "contacts" with criminal elements. The employment of a convicted confidence man in Abscam is analogous to the entirely proper employment of a convicted seller of drugs to purchase drugs from a suspected distributor. * * *

and Weisz, involved in Abscam, their activities could hardly be "supervised" because they did not know Abscam was an undercover investigation. The FBI took considerable precautions to compensate for its inability to control the representations of the middlemen. See note 50 supra. * * *

52. For this reason, we need not decide the validity of the due process test formulated by the district court—whether the temptation offered is "one which the individual is likely to encounter in the ordinary course." It is suggested, however, that criminal conduct being as highly varied as it is that such test is unduly speculative.

53. The Third Circuit's decision in *Jannotti* is particularly significant because it held that *Twigg,* the only post-*Hampton* case to uphold a due process challenge to prosecution because of excessive government involvement, did not control its consideration of Abscam. Thus Kelly's reliance on *Twigg* is misplaced.

b. See Notes 1–3 following this case.

58. Although we need not decide the question, both the Second and Third Circuits have rejected the argument that the government must have reasonable suspicion of wrongdoing before proceeding with an undercover operation such as Abscam.

4. Multiple Bribe Offers

Finally, Kelly contends that the FBI operatives violated due process when they persisted in offering a bribe after what he characterizes as his initial rejection. *Kelly asserts that he rejected the bribe at his meeting with Ciuzio on December 23, that Ciuzio informed Amoroso and Weinberg of that fact at the townhouse on January 8, and that he rejected the bribe several times in his meeting with Amoroso.* Kelly argues, and the district court agreed, that under these circumstances Amoroso's several bribe offers to Kelly were outrageous and violated due process. I cannot agree.

The evidence in this case clearly demonstrates that at no time did Kelly reject Abscam's corrupt immigration proposal. On both December 23 and January 8, Kelly agreed to assure the wealthy Arabs that he would help them with their immigration problems as a favor to Ciuzio, despite the fact that Kelly knew that in return the Arabs would pay substantial sums to Ciuzio [and others]. It is also clear that Kelly understood that part of the arrangement was that the Arabs would make substantial investments in his district. Such agreements, which would benefit Kelly indirectly, constitute violations of the bribery statute. Furthermore, the discussions between Ciuzio, Kelly, and the Abscam operatives at the townhouse of January 8 focused on the *manner* in which the bribe would be paid, not on whether it would be paid. Ciuzio told Weinberg not to bribe Kelly directly, but agreed that he would take the money for Kelly. After agreeing that Amoroso was going to give him some money at the meeting, Kelly asked Amoroso to pay the bribe to Ciuzio—to "deal with [Ciuzio] about it." In my view, Congressman Kelly "did not reject a bribe, he [initially] rejected its payment under circumstances he feared would be incriminating." *Myers.*

I likewise reject Kelly's characterization of his conversation with Amoroso on January 8 as a *series* of bribe offers. Although the terms of the corrupt Abscam proposal were mentioned several times during that conversation, Amoroso's discussion reflects the evasive and circumspect negotiation to be expected of a person seeking to corrupt a public official. In my view, Amoroso's conversation with Kelly on January 8 can be fairly characterized only as a *single offer* of a corrupt proposal to Kelly. For these reasons I reject Kelly's contention that he initially rejected a bribe, that the Abscam agents persisted in offering him a bribe, and that they thus violated due process.

IV. Conclusion

[The] Supreme Court has made it clear that "a successful due process defense must be predicated on *intolerable government conduct* which goes beyond that necessary to sustain an entrapment defense." *Jannotti* (emphasis added). Considering the genuine need to detect corrupt public officials, as well as the difficulties inherent in doing so, we conclude that the FBI's conduct in furtherance of its Abscam operation, insofar as it involved Kelly, simply did not reach intolerable levels. * * *

RUTH BADER GINSBURG, Circuit Judge: ["Abscam"] was an extraordinary operation. The investigation was steered in large part by a convicted swindler; it relied upon con men to identify and attract targets, to whom legitimate as well as illegitimate inducements were offered; it proceeded without close supervision by responsible officials.[1]

---

1. * * * We do not share Judge MacKinnon's view that, apart from "trappings of wealth," Abscam "was *not* significantly different from" run-of-the-mill "passive" undercover operations. As the District Court's opinion sets out in painstaking detail, the Abscam actors did a good deal more than simply "spread the word." Nor can we agree with Judge MacKinnon that the FBI "had ample suspicion of corruption to justify pursuing * * * Kelly."

[The] District Court stated and attempted to apply an objective test to determine when government investigation exceeds tolerable limits: Was the crime-inducing conduct in which the government engaged, the temptation presented to the target, modeled on reality? This test, the District Court indicated, should apply when the government had no knowledge of prior wrongdoing by the target and no reason to believe the target was about to commit a crime; it would serve as a check against government creation (rather than apprehension) of criminals by offers or importuning that would never occur in the real world.

The real-world test, as applied by the District Court, is speculative. The District Judge assumed that a person who offers a bribe would retreat upon encountering an initial rejection and would not "have the audacity" to press on "for fear of being reported." But the first overture renders the party offering the bribe vulnerable to prosecution. "In for a calf," such a person might press on if he perceives any chance of ultimate success.[9] Nonetheless, were the slate clean, we might be attracted to an approach similar to the District Court's, and would perhaps ask whether, in real-world circumstances, the person snared would ever encounter bait as alluring as the offer the government tendered.

However, our slate contains references that lower courts are not positioned to erase. We may not alter the contours of the entrapment defense under a due process cloak,[11] and we lack authority, where no *specific* constitutional right of the defendant has been violated, to dismiss indictments as an exercise of supervisory power over the conduct of federal law enforcement agents. *See United States v. Payner* [p. 48]. Precedent dictates that we refrain from applying the general due process constraint to bar a conviction except in the rare instance of "[p]olice overinvolvement in crime" that reaches "a demonstrable level of outrageousness." *Hampton* (Powell, J., concurring) * * *; *Russell*. The requisite level of outrageousness, the Supreme Court has indicated, is not established [unless there is] "coercion, violence or brutality to the person."[c]

The importuning of Congressman Kelly and the offers made to him, extraordinary and in excess of real-world opportunities as they appear to have been, did not involve the infliction of pain or physical or psychological coercion. We are therefore constrained to reverse, although we share the District Court's grave concern that the Abscam drama, both in its general tenor, and in "the [particular] manner in which Kelly was handled," unfolded as "an unwholesome spectacle."

Notes and Questions

1. *The "reasonable suspicion" requirement.* A number of commentators have maintained that the government should not be permitted to solicit an offense absent "probable cause" or at least "reasonable suspicion" that the target is engaged in criminal activity, but current lower federal court authority "overwhelmingly holds that no 'reasonable cause' requirement exits." Note, 67 Geo.L.J. 1455, 1467 (1979). Moreover, *"Russell* seems to have sapped [this theory] of any

That suspicion, as Judge MacKinnon recites, was based on Ciuzio's report to Amoroso and Weinberg that "Kelly was, in fact, corrupt." But as the District Court observed:

"Ciuzio went to great lengths to make it appear that he had virtual control over the Congressman, indicating at the time that Kelly was dishonest and was already taking money and had various other weaknesses. He indicated that he had known and cultivated Kelly for

about 2 1/2 years. None of this was true. No attempt was made to verify it; and there is no indication that Weinberg and Amoroso believed it."

9. As the government points out, parties to real-world transactions could readily adjust to a one-refusal rule: the bribe taker would always resist the first overture.

11. See *Twigg* (Adams, J., dissenting).

c. See Note 3, p. 405.

remaining vitality by indicating that the entrapment defense is intended to protect nondisposed defendants rather than to control police conduct." Roger Park, *The Entrapment Controversy,* 60 Minn.L.Rev. 163, 197 (1976).[a]

Operation Abscam, however, has prompted renewed interest in this issue, for there a convicted swindler and other "middlemen," themselves under investigation, decided which politicians would be offered bribes. Congressman Don Edwards, a former FBI agent, voiced concern about "free-floating surveyors, middlemen, who work with the FBI and are the ones who finger people," and his colleague, Representative John Seiberling, balked at "the idea of giving some people of dubious ethical standards free rein to entice anyone they can entice to commit a crime." See N.Y. Times, Feb. 17, 1980, pp. 1, 20. Indeed, Professor Paul Chevigny maintains that "Abscam shows [that the] central evil of entrapment is discriminatory law enforcement, whether the police zero in on a 'politician' or a 'drug dealer.' " *A Rejoinder,* The Nation, Feb. 23, 1980, p. 205[b]. Consider, too, Bennett Gershman, *Abscam, the Judiciary, and the Ethics of Entrapment,* 91 Yale L.J. 1565, 1584–85 (1982), who emphasizes that, although Operation Abscam intruded on people's privacy and autonomy to a much greater degree than the typical search and seizure, the operation was not restricted by procedural safeguards such as the requirement of a warrant: "Government agents secretly monitored the Abscam defendants for many months, recorded their intimate conversations and surreptitiously videotaped meetings they attended. No judge authorized such procedures; indeed it is unlikely that any judge would have authorized this type of surveillance absent prior suspicion."

Professor Gershman proposes a federal entrapment statute that, inter alia, requires government agents to offer inducements "only to individuals currently engaged in, or reasonably suspected of engaging in, criminal activity." Id. at 1588. Such a requirement would allow courts "to dispense with the predisposition inquiry and to use instead the concept of 'reasonable suspicion' to test whether an individual is 'nondisposed.' " Id.

2. Are official corruption investigations different? Katherine Goldwasser, *After Abscam: An Examination of Congressional Proposals to Limit Targeting Discretion in Federal Undercover Investigations,* 36 Emory L.J. 75, 124–25 (1987); balks at imposing a probable cause or reasonable suspicion requirement for undercover targeting: "[D]eterrence is not the only societal benefit to be derived from targeting [public officials] without a factual basis. Such targeting—integrity testing—usually provides no other societal benefit because the integrity of most potential undercover targets is not particularly important to society. But integrity testing of public officials is different. Public officials routinely are confronted with tests of their corruptibility because of the official power they wield. Those who 'fail' cause considerable harm to society. In short, [the] testing of public officials does serve significant societal ends. [Such testing] without a factual basis would provide a strong deterrent against corruption, but would pose little risk to the personal privacy of public officials and would generate no generalized atmosphere of suspicion and mistrust throughout society."

a. It should be noted, however, that in *United States v. Luttrell,* 889 F.2d 806 (9th Cir.1989), a panel opinion by Judge Dorothy Nelson of the Ninth Circuit took the position that government agents violate due process when, lacking "reasoned grounds" for believing their targets are involved in crime, they approach them and provide them with a specific opportunity to engage in criminal conduct. But the Ninth Circuit, sitting en banc, vacated the portion of the panel opinion discussing a "reasoned grounds" or "reasonable suspicion" requirement, noting that a number of other circuits had explicitly rejected such a requirement. See 923 F.2d 764 (9th Cir.1991).

b. But compare the views of Chevigny's colleague, Professor Stephen Gillers, *In Defense of Abscam: Entrapment, Where is Thy Sting?,* The Nation, Feb. 23, 1980, p. 203.

    3. *When is a private person a "government agent" for entrapment purposes? The use of "unwitting agents."* Defending Operation Abscam, then Assistant Attorney General Phillip Heymann emphasized: "No one associated with the United States ever picked any politician for the investigation. The middlemen did all that." N.Y. Times, Mar. 5, 1980 p. 18. But this raises another problem. Many of the people involved in Abscam were "unsuspecting middlemen," i.e., private persons who were unaware that they were working with, or for, government agents. But because entrapment is ultimately concerned with government conduct, it offers no defense to those who succumb to the inducements of private individuals acting alone. For entrapment purposes, should "unsuspecting middlemen," such as those utilized in Abscam, be regarded as agents of the government, albeit "unwitting agents"?

    When government agents have persuaded a "middleman" to induce *a particular target selected by the agents* to commit a crime, the courts generally extend the entrapment defense to the ultimate targets. See, e.g., *People v. McIntire,* 591 P.2d 527 (Cal.1979), where a narcotics agent, posing as a high school student, importuned a classmate, the brother of the defendant, to obtain marijuana from his sister. Rejecting the prosecution's argument that entrapment cannot be effected through an "unwitting agent" (in this case, the defendant's brother), the court, per Mosk, J., observed: "The purposes of the entrapment defense can be fulfilled only if it is understood that one can act as a [government agent] without realizing the identity of his principal; the unwitting agent, though he may not appreciate the true nature of his role, is nonetheless being manipulated as the officer's tool in a plan to foster a crime and entrap its perpetrator."

    However, when investigations are not aimed at a specific target, even though there is "substantial certainty that the person solicited by the police for the commission of a crime will seek the participation of another," such as when the agent requests the middleman to seek unidentified public officials who will accept bribes, the federal courts have "sharply disagreed" on how to apply the law of entrapment. See Note, 95 Harv.L.Rev. 1122, 1126–27 (1982). "Whenever it is reasonable to expect that the investigation will result in a secondary target's committing an offense," maintains the Harvard Note, "whether the secondary target was selected by [a government agent] or [the unsuspecting middleman], the additional offense must be considered 'the creature of [the agent's] purpose' unless the government can prove that the defendant was predisposed to commit a similar crime." Id. at 1128.

    Moreover, "even when the government has no reason to expect that [the initial target] of an investigation will induce a nonessential [third party] to join in criminal activity, the third party should still be able to plead entrapment if it is found that the initial target was himself entrapped. If the original target was entrapped, the government has by definition created the actions that the initial target took in pursuing the illegal activity." Id. at 1129.

SECTION 3. CONTINUING CONTROVERSY OVER THE ENTRAPMENT DEFENSE

JACOBSON v. UNITED STATES
503 U.S. 540, 112 S.Ct. 1535, 118 L.Ed.2d 174 (1992).

Justice WHITE delivered the opinion of the Court.

    On September 24, 1987, [petitioner] was indicted for violating a provision of the Child Protection Act of 1984, which criminalizes the knowing receipt through the mails of a "visual depiction [that] involves the use of a minor engaging in sexually explicit conduct. . . ." Petitioner defended on the ground that the Government entrapped him into committing the crime through a series of communications from undercover agents that spanned the 26 months preceding his arrest. [He was found guilty after a jury trial. The Eighth Circuit, sitting en banc, affirmed, concluding that "Jacobson was not entrapped as a matter of law."]

Because the Government overstepped the line between setting a trap for the "unwary innocent" and the "unwary criminal," and as a matter of law failed to establish that petitioner was independently predisposed to commit the crime for which he was arrested, we reverse * * *.

[In] February 1984, petitioner, a 56–year-old veteran-turned-farmer who supported his elderly father in Nebraska, ordered two magazines and a brochure from a California adult bookstore. The magazines, entitled *Bare Boys I* and *Bare Boys II,* contained photographs of nude preteen and teenage boys. The contents of the magazines startled petitioner, who testified that he had expected to receive photographs of "young men 18 years or older." [The] young men depicted in the magazines were not engaged in sexual activity, and petitioner's receipt of the magazines was legal under both federal and Nebraska law. Within three months, the law with respect to child pornography changed; Congress passed the Act illegalizing the receipt through the mails of sexually explicit depictions of children. In the very month that the new provision became law, postal inspectors found petitioner's name on the mailing list of the California bookstore that had mailed him *Bare Boys I* and *II.* There followed over the next 2½ years, repeated efforts by two Government agencies, through five fictitious organizations and a bogus pen pal, to explore petitioner's willingness to break the new law by ordering sexually explicit photographs of children through the mail.

The Government began its efforts in January 1985 when a postal inspector sent petitioner a letter supposedly from the American Hedonist Society, which in fact was a fictitious organization. The letter included a membership application and stated the Society's doctrine: that members had the "right to read what we desire, the right to discuss similar interests with those who share our philosophy, and finally that we have the right to seek pleasure without restrictions being placed on us by outdated puritan morality." Petitioner enrolled in the organization and returned a sexual attitude questionnaire that asked him to rank on a scale of one to four his enjoyment of various sexual materials, with one being "really enjoy," two being "enjoy," three being "somewhat enjoy," and four being "do not enjoy." Petitioner ranked the entry "[p]re-teen sex" as a two, but indicated that he was opposed to pedophilia.

For a time, the Government left petitioner alone. But then a new "prohibited mail specialist" in the Postal Service found petitioner's name in a file and in May 1986 petitioner received a solicitation from a second fictitious consumer research company, "Midlands Data Research," seeking a response from those who "believe in the joys of sex and the complete awareness of those lusty and youthful lads and lasses of the neophite *[sic]* age." The letter never explained whether "neophite" referred to minors or young adults. Petitioner responded: "Please feel free to send me more information, I am interested in teenage sexuality. Please keep my name confidential."

Petitioner then heard from yet another Government creation, "Heartland Institute for a New Tomorrow" (HINT), which proclaimed that it was "an organization founded to protect and promote sexual freedom and freedom of choice. We believe that arbitrarily imposed legislative sanctions restricting your sexual freedom should be rescinded through the legislative process." The letter also enclosed a second survey. Petitioner indicated that his interest in "[p]reteen sex-homosexual" material was above average, but not high. In response to another question, petitioner wrote: "Not only sexual expression but freedom of the press is under attack. We must be ever vigilant to counter attack right wing fundamentalists who are determined to curtail our freedoms."

"HINT" replied, portraying itself as a lobbying organization seeking to repeal "all statutes which regulate sexual activities, except those laws which deal with violent behavior, such as rape. HINT is also lobbying to eliminate any legal definition of 'the age of consent'." These lobbying efforts were to be funded by sales from a catalog to be published in the future "offering the sale of various items which we believe you will find to be both interesting and stimulating." HINT also provided computer matching of group members with similar survey responses; and, although petitioner was supplied with a list of potential "pen pals," he did not initiate any correspondence.

Nevertheless, the Government's "prohibited mail specialist" began writing to petitioner, using the pseudonym "Carl Long." The letters employed a tactic known as "mirroring," which the inspector described as "reflect[ing] whatever the interests are of the person we are writing to." Petitioner responded at first, indicating that his interest was primarily in "male-male items." Inspector "Long" wrote back:

"My interests too are primarily male-male items. Are you satisfied with the type of VCR tapes available? Personally, I like the amateur stuff better if its [sic] well produced as it can get more kinky and also seems more real. I think the actors enjoy it more."

Petitioner responded:

"As far as my likes are concerned, I like good looking young guys (in their late teens and early 20's) doing their thing together."

Petitioner's letters to "Long" made no reference to child pornography. After writing two letters, petitioner discontinued the correspondence.

By March 1987, 34 months had passed since the Government obtained petitioner's name from the mailing list of the California bookstore, and 26 months had passed since the Postal Service had commenced its mailings to petitioner. Although petitioner had responded to surveys and letters, the Government had no evidence that petitioner had ever intentionally possessed or been exposed to child pornography. The Postal Service had not checked petitioner's mail to determine whether he was receiving questionable mailings from persons—other than the Government—involved in the child pornography industry.

At this point, a second Government agency, the Customs Service, included petitioner in its own child pornography sting, "Operation Borderline," after receiving his name on lists submitted by the Postal Service. Using the name of a fictitious Canadian company called "Produit Outaouais," the Customs Service mailed petitioner a brochure advertising photographs of young boys engaging in sex. Petitioner placed an order that was never filled.

The Postal Service also continued its efforts in the Jacobson case, writing to petitioner as the "Far Eastern Trading Company Ltd." The letter began:

"As many of you know, much hysterical nonsense has appeared in the American media concerning 'pornography' and what must be done to stop it from coming across your borders. This brief letter does not allow us to give much comments; however, why is your government spending millions of dollars to exercise international censorship while tons of drugs, which makes yours the world's most crime ridden country are passed through easily."

The letter went on to say:

"[W]e have devised a method of getting these to you without prying eyes of U.S. Customs seizing your mail.... After consultations with American solicitors, we have been advised that once we have posted our material through your system, it cannot be opened for any inspection without authorization of a judge."

The letter invited petitioner to send for more information. [He] responded. A catalogue was sent and petitioner ordered *Boys Who Love Boys,* a pornographic magazine depicting young boys engaged in various sexual activities. Petitioner was arrested after a controlled delivery of a photocopy of the magazine.

When petitioner was asked at trial why he placed such an order, he explained that the Government had succeeded in piquing his curiosity:

"Well, the statement was made of all the trouble and the hysteria over pornography and I wanted to see what the material was. * * * I didn't know for sure what kind of sexual action they were referring to in the Canadian letter...."

In petitioner's home, the Government found the *Bare Boys* magazines and materials that the Government had sent to him in the course of its protracted investigation, but no other materials that would indicate that petitioner collected or was actively interested in child pornography. * * *

The trial court instructed the jury on [the] entrapment defense,[1] petitioner was convicted, and [the] Eighth Circuit affirmed * * *.

[In] their zeal to enforce the law [the Government] may not originate a criminal design, implant in an innocent person's mind the disposition to commit a criminal act, and then induce commission of the crime so that the Government may prosecute. Where the Government has induced an individual to break the law and the defense of entrapment is at issue, as it was in this case, the prosecution must prove beyond reasonable doubt that the defendant was disposed to commit the criminal act prior to first being approached by Government agents.[2]

1. The jury was instructed:

"As mentioned, one of the issues in this case is whether the defendant was entrapped. If the defendant was entrapped he must be found not guilty. The government has the burden of proving beyond a reasonable doubt that the defendant was not entrapped.

"If the defendant before contact with law-enforcement officers or their agents did not have any intent or disposition to commit the crime charged and was induced or persuaded by law-enforcement officers o[r] their agents to commit that crime, then he was entrapped. On the other hand, if the defendant before contact with law-enforcement officers or their agents did have an intent or disposition to commit the crime charged, then he was not entrapped even though law-enforcement officers or their agents provided a favorable opportunity to commit the crime or made committing the crime easier or even participated in acts essential to the crime."

2. Inducement is not at issue in this case. The Government does not dispute that it induced petitioner to commit the crime. The sole issue is whether the Government carried its burden of proving that petitioner was predisposed to violate the law *before* the Government

intervened. The dissent is mistaken in claiming that this is an innovation in entrapment law and in suggesting that the Government's conduct prior to the moment of solicitation is irrelevant. * * * Indeed, the proposition that the accused must be predisposed prior to contact with law enforcement officers is so firmly established that the Government conceded the point at oral argument, submitting that the evidence it developed during the course of its investigation was probative because it indicated petitioner's state of mind *prior* to the commencement of the Government's investigation.

This long-established standard in no way encroaches upon Government investigatory activities. Indeed, the Government's internal guidelines for undercover operations provide that an inducement to commit a crime should not be offered unless:

"(a) there is a reasonable indication, based on information developed through informants or other means, that the subject is engaging, has engaged, or is likely to engage in illegal activity of a similar type; *or*

"(b) The opportunity for illegal activity has been structured so that there is reason for believing that persons drawn to the opportu-

Thus, an agent deployed to stop the traffic in illegal drugs may offer the opportunity to buy or sell drugs, and, if the offer is accepted, make an arrest on the spot or later. In such a typical case, or in a more elaborate "sting" operation involving government-sponsored fencing where the defendant is simply provided with the opportunity to commit a crime, the entrapment defense is of little use because the ready commission of the criminal act amply demonstrates the defendant's predisposition. Had the agents in this case simply offered petitioner the opportunity to order child pornography through the mails, and petitioner—who must be presumed to know the law—had promptly availed himself of this criminal opportunity, it is unlikely that his entrapment defense would have warranted a jury instruction.

But that is not what happened here. By the time petitioner finally placed his order, he had already been the target of 26 months of repeated mailings and communications from Government agents and fictitious organizations. Therefore, although he had become predisposed to break the law by May 1987, it is our view that the Government did not prove that this predisposition was independent and not the product of the attention that the Government had directed at petitioner since January 1985.

The prosecution's evidence of predisposition falls into two categories: evidence developed prior to the Postal Service's mail campaign, and that developed during the course of the investigation. The sole piece of preinvestigation evidence is petitioner's 1984 order and receipt of the Bare Boys magazines. But this is scant if any proof of petitioner's predisposition to commit an illegal act, the criminal character of which a defendant is presumed to know. It may indicate a predisposition to view sexually-oriented photographs that are responsive to his sexual tastes; but evidence that merely indicates a generic inclination to act within a broad range, not all of which is criminal, is of little probative value in establishing predisposition.

Furthermore, petitioner was acting within the law at the time he received these magazines. * * * Evidence of predisposition to do what once was lawful is not, by itself, sufficient to show predisposition to do what is now illegal, for there is a common understanding that most people obey the law even when they disapprove of it. [Hence,] the fact that petitioner legally ordered and received the Bare Boys magazines does little to further the Government's burden of proving that petitioner was predisposed to commit a criminal act. This is particularly true given petitioner's unchallenged testimony was that he did not know until they arrived that the magazines would depict minors.

The prosecution's evidence gathered during the investigation also fails to carry the Government's burden. Petitioner's responses to the many communications prior to the ultimate criminal act were at most indicative of certain personal inclinations, including a predisposition to view photographs of preteen sex and a willingness to promote a given agenda by supporting lobbying organizations. Even so, petitioner's responses hardly support an inference that he would commit the crime of receiving child pornography through the mails.[3]

[On] the other hand, the strong arguable inference is that, by waving the banner of individual rights and disparaging the legitimacy and constitutionality of

---

nity, or brought to it, are predisposed to engage in the contemplated illegal activity." *Attorney General's Guidelines on FBI Undercover Operations* (Dec. 31, 1980).

3. We do not hold, as the dissent suggests, that the Government was required to prove that petitioner knowingly violated the law. We

simply conclude that proof that petitioner engaged in legal conduct and possessed certain generalized personal inclinations is not sufficient evidence to prove beyond a reasonable doubt that he would have been predisposed to commit the crime charged independent of the Government's coaxing.

efforts to restrict the availability of sexually explicit materials, the Government not only excited petitioner's interest in sexually explicit materials banned by law but also exerted substantial pressure on petitioner to obtain and read such material as part of a fight against censorship and the infringement of individual rights. * * *

Petitioner's ready response to these solicitations cannot be enough to establish beyond reasonable doubt that he was predisposed, prior to the Government acts intended to create predisposition, to commit the crime of receiving child pornography through the mails. The evidence that petitioner was ready and willing to commit the offense came only after the Government had devoted 2½ years to convincing him that he had or should have the right to engage in the very behavior proscribed by law. Rational jurors could not say beyond a reasonable doubt that petitioner possessed the requisite predisposition prior to the Government's investigation and that it existed independent of the Government's many and varied approaches to petitioner. As was explained in *Sherman,* where entrapment was found as a matter of law, "the Government [may not] pla[y] on the weaknesses of an innocent party and beguil[e] him into committing crimes which he otherwise would not have attempted."

Law enforcement officials go too far when they "implant in the mind of an innocent person the *disposition* to commit the alleged offense and induce its commission in order that they may prosecute." *Sorrells* (emphasis added). [When] the Government's quest for convictions leads to the apprehension of an otherwise law-abiding citizen who, if left to his own devices, likely would have never run afoul of the law, the courts should intervene. * * *

Justice O'CONNOR, with whom The Chief Justice and Justice KENNEDY join, and with whom Justice SCALIA joins except as to Part II, dissenting.

Keith Jacobson was offered only two opportunities to buy child pornography through the mail. Both times, he ordered. Both times, he asked for opportunities to buy more. He needed no Government agent to coax, threaten, or persuade him; no one played on his sympathies, friendship, or suggested that his committing the crime would further a greater good. In fact, no Government agent even contacted him face-to-face. The Government contends that from the enthusiasm with which Mr. Jacobson responded to the chance to commit a crime, a reasonable jury could permissibly infer beyond a reasonable doubt that he was predisposed to commit the crime. I agree.

[The] first time the Government sent Mr. Jacobson a catalog of illegal materials, he ordered a set of photographs advertised as picturing "young boys in sex action fun." He enclosed the following note with his order: "I received your brochure and decided to place an order. If I like your product, I will order more later." For reasons undisclosed in the record, Mr. Jacobson's order was never delivered.

The second time the Government sent a catalog of illegal materials, Mr. Jacobson ordered a magazine called "Boys Who Love Boys," described as: "11 year old and 14 year old boys get it on in every way possible. Oral, anal sex and heavy masturbation. If you love boys, you will be delighted with this." Along with his order, Mr. Jacobson sent the following note: "Will order other items later. I want to be discreet in order to protect you and me."

Government agents admittedly did not offer Mr. Jacobson the chance to buy child pornography right away. Instead, they first sent questionnaires in order to make sure that he was generally interested in the subject matter. Indeed, a "cold call" in such a business would not only risk rebuff and suspicion, but might also shock and offend the uninitiated, or expose minors to suggestive materials. Mr.

Jacobson's responses to the questionnaires gave the investigators reason to think he would be interested in photographs depicting preteen sex.

The Court, however, concludes that a reasonable jury could not have found Mr. Jacobson to be predisposed beyond a reasonable doubt on the basis of his responses to the Government's catalogs, even though it admits that, by that time, he was predisposed to commit the crime. The Government, the Court holds, failed to provide evidence that Mr. Jacobson's obvious predisposition at the time of the crime "was independent and not the product of the attention that the Government had directed at petitioner." In so holding, I believe the Court fails to acknowledge the reasonableness of the jury's inference from the evidence, redefines "predisposition," and introduces a new requirement that Government sting operations have a reasonable suspicion of illegal activity before contacting a suspect.

This Court has held previously that a defendant's predisposition is to be assessed as of the time the Government agent first suggested the crime, not when the Government agent first became involved. * * * [Even] in *Sherman,* [where entrapment was found] as a matter of law, the Government agent had repeatedly and unsuccessfully coaxed the defendant to buy drugs, ultimately succeeding only by playing on the defendant's sympathy. The Court found lack of predisposition based on the Government's numerous unsuccessful attempts to induce the crime, not on the basis of preliminary contacts with the defendant.

Today, the Court holds that Government conduct may be considered to create a predisposition to commit a crime, even before any Government action to induce the commission of the crime. In my view, this holding changes entrapment doctrine. Generally, the inquiry is whether a suspect is predisposed before the Government induces the commission of the crime, not before the Government makes initial contact with him. There is no dispute here that the Government's questionnaires and letters were not sufficient to establish inducement; they did not even suggest that Mr. Jacobson should engage in any illegal activity. If all the Government had done was to send these materials, Mr. Jacobson's entrapment defense would fail. Yet the Court holds that the Government must prove not only that a suspect was predisposed to commit the crime before the opportunity to commit it arose, but also before the Government came on the scene.

The rule that preliminary Government contact can create a predisposition has the potential to be misread by lower courts as well as criminal investigators as requiring that the Government must have sufficient evidence of a defendant's predisposition *before it ever seeks to contact him.* Surely the Court cannot intend to impose such a requirement, for it would mean that the Government must have a reasonable suspicion of criminal activity before it begins an investigation, a condition that we have never before imposed. The Court denies that its new rule will affect run-of-the-mill sting operations and one hopes that it means what it says. Nonetheless, after this case, every defendant will claim that something the Government agent did before soliciting the crime "created" a predisposition that was not there before. For example, a bribe taker will claim that the description of the amount of money available was so enticing that it implanted a disposition to accept the bribe later offered. A drug buyer will claim that the description of the drug's purity and effects was so tempting that it created the urge to try it for the first time. In short, the Court's opinion could be read to prohibit the Government from advertising the seductions of criminal activity as part of its sting operation, for fear of creating a predisposition in its suspects. That limitation would be especially likely to hamper sting operations such as this one, which mimic the advertising done by genuine purveyors of pornography. No doubt the Court would protest that its opinion does not stand for so broad a proposition, but the apparent lack of a principled basis for distinguishing these scenarios exposes a flaw in the more limited rule the Court today adopts.

The Court's rule is all the more troubling because it does not distinguish between Government conduct that merely highlights the temptation of the crime itself, and Government conduct that threatens, coerces, or leads a suspect to commit a crime in order to fulfill some other obligation. For example, in *Sorrells,* the Government agent repeatedly asked for illegal liquor, coaxing the defendant to accede on the ground that "one former war buddy would get liquor for another." In *Sherman,* the Government agent played on the defendant's sympathies, pretending to be going through drug withdrawal and begging the defendant to relieve his distress by helping him buy drugs.

The Government conduct in this case is not comparable. While the Court states that the Government "exerted substantial pressure on petitioner to obtain and read such material as part of a fight against censorship and the infringement of individual rights," one looks at the record in vain for evidence of such "substantial pressure." The most one finds is letters advocating legislative action to liberalize obscenity laws, letters which could easily be ignored or thrown away. * * * Nowhere did the Government suggest that the proceeds of the sale of the illegal materials would be used to support legislative reforms. * * * Mr. Jacobson's curiosity to see what " 'all the trouble and the hysteria' " was about is certainly susceptible of more than one interpretation. And it is the jury that is charged with the obligation of interpreting it. In sum, the Court fails to construe the evidence in the light most favorable to the Government, and fails to draw all reasonable inferences in the Government's favor. It was surely reasonable for the jury to infer that Mr. Jacobson was predisposed beyond a reasonable doubt, even if other inferences from the evidence were also possible.

The second puzzling thing about the Court's opinion is its redefinition of predisposition. The Court acknowledges that "[p]etitioner's responses to the many communications prior to the ultimate criminal act [were] indicative of certain personal inclinations, including a predisposition to view photographs of preteen sex...." If true, this should have settled the matter; Mr. Jacobson was predisposed to engage in the illegal conduct. Yet, the Court concludes, "petitioner's responses hardly support an inference that he would commit the crime of receiving child pornography through the mails."

The Court seems to add something new to the burden of proving predisposition. Not only must the Government show that a defendant was predisposed to engage in the illegal conduct, here, receiving photographs of minors engaged in sex, but also that the defendant was predisposed to break the law knowingly in order to do so. The statute violated here, however, does not require proof of specific intent to break the law; it requires only knowing receipt of visual depictions produced by using minors engaged in sexually explicit conduct. Under the Court's analysis, however, the Government must prove *more* to show predisposition than it need prove in order to convict.

[The] crux of the Court's concern in this case is that the Government went too far and "abused" the "processes of detection and enforcement" by luring an innocent person to violate the law. Consequently, the Court holds that the Government failed to prove beyond a reasonable doubt that Mr. Jacobson was predisposed to commit the crime. It was, however, the jury's task, as the conscience of the community, to decide whether or not Mr. Jacobson was a willing participant in the criminal activity here or an innocent dupe. [There] is no dispute that the jury in this case was fully and accurately instructed on the law of entrapment, and nonetheless found Mr. Jacobson guilty. Because I believe there was sufficient evidence to uphold the jury's verdict, I respectfully dissent.

Notes and Questions

1. *Is behavior in an artificial world largely uninformative of behavior in this one?* To what extent does the following commentary by Ronald J. Allen, Melissa Luttrell & Anne Kreeger, *Clarifying Entrapment*, 89 J. Crim. L. & Criminology 407, 415–16 (1999), reflect the view of the *Jacobson* majority: "None of [the primary relevant objectives of the criminal law] is likely to be accomplished by the punishment of an individual who accepted an extra-market inducement to act. The concern of deterrence surely is to reduce the occurrence of criminal acts in the world we actually inhabit, not some hypothetically different one. That a person responds to extra-market prices [including both financial and emotional markets] is uninformative of how he will respond to market prices, and thus is uninformative on the justification for incapacitation. A person who accepts extra-market prices provides evidence that indeed virtually everybody has a price, but not that this person is in need of rehabilitation, given the world we actually inhabit. The point generalized is that criminal acts occur in the real world, not an artificial one, and behavior in an artificial world is largely uninformative of behavior in this one."

2. *Unproductive use of law enforcement resources.* Consider Note, 61 U.Cin.L.Rev. 1067, 1090–91 (1993): "To allow law enforcement officials to go on 'fishing expeditions' based on only the most generalized suspicion is to allow a tremendous waste of resources and to risk the targeting of unpopular groups, such as gay men. Judge Posner has indicated that entrapment is, at its most basic, a label given to the unproductive use of law enforcement resources. [*United States v. Kaminski*, 703 F.2d 1004, 1010 (7th Cir.1983) (concurring opinion.)][a] [The] *Jacobson* case exemplifies this inefficient use of law enforcement resources, in that an individual with no apparent history of dealing in child pornography became the focus of an investigation lasting two and one-half years, culminating in his arrest and conviction for receiving a single magazine that was supplied by the government. The government's stated purpose in investigations of this sort is to eliminate child pornography, yet the only child pornography present in this case was that manufactured and distributed by the government."

Should second-guessing the government's use of its law enforcement resources be the business of the courts? See Adams, J., dissenting in *United States v. Twigg*, 588 F.2d 373 (3d Cir.1978). If government investigators squander their limited resources, should this be regarded as a political problem to be addressed by oversight hearings? See Easterbrook, J., concurring in *United States v. Miller*, 891 F.2d 1265, 1271–72 (7th Cir.1989).[b]

3. *"Reasonable suspicion" that the target was predisposed to commit the crime.* Is *Jacobson* likely, as Justice O'Connor suggests, to be interpreted by lower courts and criminal investigators "as requiring that the Government must have sufficient evidence of a defendant's predisposition *before it ever seeks to contact him*"? The majority observes that when Jacobson was arrested the government found no evidence—aside from the *Bare Boys* magazines and the material the government had sent him—indicating that he "collected or was actively interested in child pornography." Suppose government agents *had* found other material establishing that Jacobson collected child pornography *even though they were unaware* that such evidence existed before they arrested him? Wouldn't the prosecution have been able to defeat Jacobson's entrapment claim by estab-

---

a. For an extract from Judge Posner's opinion see p. 390.

b. For an extract from Judge Easterbrook's opinion see p. 390.

lishing that his predisposition was independent and not the product of the government's many and varied approaches to him?

Note, too, the majority points out that if, absent any prior dealings between the government and Jacobson, federal agents had simply offered him the opportunity to order child pornography through the mails and he had promptly agreed, Jacobson's entrapment defense would have failed. For in such a case "the ready commission of the criminal act amply demonstrates the defendant's predisposition." But wouldn't this be so *regardless* of whether government agents had any indication of Jacobson's predisposition before they offered him the opportunity to obtain child pornography?

4. What must the government prove before it "comes on the scene"? Does *Jacobson* hold, as the dissenters maintain, that "the Government must prove not only that a suspect was predisposed to commit the crime before the opportunity to [do so] arose, but also before the Government came on the scene"?

If an undercover agent gradually became a close friend of a target but never brought up the subject of drugs in the first ten months of their acquaintanceship (during which time the agent simply socialized with, and gained the confidence of, the target), would it matter whether there was any evidence that the target was predisposed to commit a drug offense when the government agent initiated contact with the target or first "came on the scene"? Is *Jacobson* a different case because when a fictitious organization first sent Jacobson a mailing, the government had not *merely* initiated contact with him or arrived on the scene but (as far as a majority of the Court was concerned) had begun "working on" Jacobson?

5. Did the Jacobson Court blend the "subjective" and "objective" entrapment tests? As noted by Michael L. Piccarreta & Jefferson Keenan, *Entrapment Targets and Tactics: Jacobson v. United States*, 29 Crim.L.Bull. 241, 249 (1993), *Jacobson* "is the first Supreme Court opinion concerning entrapment in which none of the Justices even adverted to the 'objective' theory of entrapment." However, although the *Jacobson* majority purported to be applying the "subjective" test of entrapment, it also seemed quite offended by the tactics used by the government to induce Jacobson to order pornographic material. As the majority described it, some of the literature sent to Jacobson by the fictitious organizations created by the government disparaged the legitimacy of efforts to restrict the availability of sexually explicit material and came close to *challenging* Jacobson to assert his right to obtain and read such material. Does this feature of the case fit more easily within the framework of the "objective" test? Might it even constitute reprehensible or offensive conduct under that test?

But consider Note, 68 Wash.L.Rev. 185, 198–99 (1993): "Although the fictitious organizations did decry the criminalization of some forms of pornography, that very message signaled the illegality of the material. That Jacobson was aware that he was committing an unlawful act was not disputed. As the [Court's] opinion states, 'there is a common understanding that most people obey the law even when they disapprove of it.' If we analogize this fact pattern to a bribery sting, it is fantastic to suggest that a defendant could support an entrapment claim by avowing that the undercover agent avouched, 'Bribery is illegal—but it really shouldn't be.' "

6. In "reverse sting" cases, should the objective and subjective approaches be combined? Unlike the traditional "sting" (where undercover agents pose as buyers of illicit goods or services), in "reverse sting" cases, such as *Jacobson*, government agents act as sellers. According to Damon D. Camp, *Out of the Quagmire after Jacobson v. United States: Toward a More Balanced Entrapment Standard*, 83 J.Crim.L. & C. 1055, 1056 (1993), the subjective entrapment test works reasonably well in traditional sting cases. In such cases proclivity to engage in criminal conduct is difficult to deny because the defendant actually provides contraband to a government agent. In reverse stings, however, "the notion of predisposition becomes a significant issue, and the role of enforcement officers in securing cooperation becomes critical." In such cases, maintains Professor Camp, the key question should be whether predisposition to commit the crime or the government's conduct was a more important influence on the defendant's participation in crime.

HOW ARE THE FEDERAL COURTS INTERPRETING *JACOBSON*?

In UNITED STATES v. GENDRON, 18 F.3d 955 (1st Cir.1994), in the course of holding that defendant was not entrapped into receiving child pornography, Chief Judge (now Supreme Court Justice) BREYER observed:

"As the Supreme Court has recently stated: 'When the Government's quest for conviction leads to the apprehension of an *otherwise law-abiding citizen* who, *if left to his own devices*, likely would never have been afoul of the law, the courts should intervene.' *Jacobson v. United States* (emphasis added). Since the Court has repeatedly expressed concern about *both* government 'abuse' of its enforcement powers (or the like) *and* the 'otherwise law-abiding citizen' (or the like), it is not surprising that the defense has two parts, one that focuses upon government 'inducement' and the other upon the defendant's 'predisposition.'

"[The Supreme Court] saw in the entrapment defense not so much a sanction used to control police conduct, but rather a protection of the ordinary law-abiding citizen against government overreaching. Consequently, it saw no need to permit a defendant to take advantage of that defense unless he himself was such a citizen. The upshot is that we must find out just who that 'innocent person' is. Who is the '*otherwise* law-abiding citizen' who would not 'otherwise' have committed the crime?

"[The] right way to ask the question, it seems to us, is to abstract from—to assume away—the present circumstances *insofar as they reveal government overreaching*. That is to say, we should ask how the defendant likely would have reacted to an *ordinary* opportunity to commit the crime. *See Jacobson*, n. 2. By using the word 'ordinary,' we mean an opportunity that lacked those special features of the government's conduct that made of it an 'inducement,' or an 'overreaching.' Was the defendant 'predisposed' to respond affirmatively to a *proper*, not to an *improper*, lure? * * *

"We turn now to *Jacobson* * * *. In three respects [government agents] did more than provide an ordinary opportunity to buy child pornography: First, the solicitations reflected a psychologically 'graduated' set of responses to Jacobson's own noncriminal responses, beginning with innocent lures and progressing to frank offers. [Second,] the government's soliciting letters sometimes depicted their senders as 'free speech' lobbying organizations and fighters for the 'right to read what we desire'; they asked Jacobson to 'fight against censorship and the infringement of individual rights.' Third, the government's effort to provide an 'opportunity' to buy child pornography stretched out over two and a half years. Taken together, one might find in these three sets of circumstances—the graduated response, the long time period, the appeal to a proper (free speech) motive—a substantial risk of inducing an ordinary law-abiding person to commit the crime. Indeed, the government conceded in *Jacobson*, that its methods amounted, for entrapment purposes, to an improper 'inducement.' Id. at n. 2.

"*Jacobson's* importance, however, concerns the 'predisposition' part of the entrapment defense. The Court held that the evidence, as a matter of law, required acquittal because a reasonable jury would have had to doubt Jacobson's predisposition. [The government] failed to show 'predisposition' (beyond a reasonable doubt). That means (as we understand it) that the government's evidence did not show how Jacobson would have acted had he been faced with an ordinary 'opportunity' to commit the crime rather than a special 'inducement.'

"[The evidence in this case,] taken together, reveals a defendant who met an initial opportunity to buy child pornography with enthusiasm, who responded to each further government initiative with a purchase order, and who, unlike Jacobson, showed no particular interest in an anti-censorship campaign. [This evidence] permits a jury to find (beyond a reasonable doubt) that Gendron would have responded affirmatively to the most ordinary of opportunities, and hence, was 'predisposed' to commit the crime. We therefore find the jury's entrapment decision lawful."

Compare UNITED STATES v. HOLLINGSWORTH, 27 F.3d 1196 (7th Cir. 1994) (en banc). In the course of holding that the defendants, Pickard (an orthodontist) and Hollingsworth (a farmer), had been entrapped as a matter of law into engaging in a money laundering scheme, a 6–5 majority, per POSNER, C.J., observed:

"[Had] the Court in *Jacobson* believed that the legal concept of predisposition is exhausted in the demonstrated willingness of the defendant to commit the crime without threats or promises by the government, then Jacobson was predisposed, in which event the Court's reversal of his conviction would be difficult to explain. The government did not offer Jacobson any inducements to buy pornographic magazines or threaten him with harm if he failed to buy them. It was not as if the government had had to badger Jacobson for 26 months in order to overcome his resistance to committing a crime. He *never* resisted.

" * * * [W]e are naturally reluctant to suppose that [*Jacobson*] is limited to the precise facts before the Court, or to ignore the Court's definition of entrapment, which concludes the analysis portion of the opinion and is not found in previous opinions, as 'the apprehension of an otherwise law-abiding citizen who, if left to his own devices, likely would have never run afoul of the law.' That was Jacobson. However impure his thoughts, he was law abiding. A farmer in Nebraska, his access to child pornography was limited. As far as the government was aware, over the period of more than two years in which it was playing cat and mouse with him, he did not receive any other solicitations to buy pornography. So, had he been 'left to his own devices,' in all likelihood he would 'have never run afoul of the law.' If the same can be said of [the defendants in this case,] Pickard and Hollingsworth, they too are entitled to be acquitted. * * *

"Recently the First Circuit, struggling as are we to understand the scope of *Jacobson*, suggested that all it stands for is that the government may not, in trying to induce the target of a sting to commit a crime, confront him with circumstances that are different from the ordinary or typical circumstances of a private inducement. *Gendron*. The [First Circuit] thought that the government's attempt to persuade Jacobson that he had a First Amendment right to consume child pornography had departed from typicality. We are not so sure. Just as the gun industry likes to wrap itself in the mantle of the Second Amendment, so the pornography industry likes to wrap itself in the mantle of the First Amendment. But however that may be, the government made no effort in *this* case to show that a real customer for money laundering would have responded to an advertisement to sell a Grenadan bank * * *.

"We put the following hypothetical case to the government's lawyer at the reargument. Suppose the government went to someone and asked him whether he would like to make money as a counterfeiter, and the reply was, 'Sure, but I don't know anything about counterfeiting.' Suppose the government then bought him a printer, paper, and ink, showed him how to make the counterfeit money, hired a staff for him, and got everything set up so that all he had to do was press a button to print the money; and then offered him $10,000 for some quantity of counterfeit bills. The government's lawyer acknowledged that the counterfeiter would have a strong case that he had been entrapped, even though he was perfectly willing to commit the crime once the government planted the suggestion and showed him how and the government neither threatened him nor offered him an overwhelming inducement.[a]

"We do not suggest that *Jacobson* adds a new element to the entrapment defense—'readiness' or 'ability' or 'dangerousness' on top of inducement and, most important, predisposition. Predisposition is not a purely mental state, the state of being willing to swallow the government's bait. It has positional as well as dispositional force. [The] defendant must be so situated by reason of previous training or experience or occupation or acquaintances that it is likely that if the government had not induced him to commit the crime some criminal would have done so; only then does a sting or other arranged crime take a dangerous person out of circulation. A public official is in a position to take bribes; a drug addict to deal drugs; a gun dealer to engage in illegal gun sales. For these and other traditional targets of stings all that must be shown to establish the predisposition and thus defeat the defense of entrapment is willingness to violate the law without extraordinary inducements; ability can be presumed. It is different when the defendant is not in a position without the government's help to become involved in illegal activity. * * *

"There is no evidence that before 'Hinch' began his campaign to inveigle them into a money-laundering scheme either Pickard or Hollingsworth had contemplated engaging in such behavior. [When] the opportunity to become *crooked* international financiers beckoned, they were willing enough, though less willing than Jacobson had been to violate the federal law against purchasing child pornography through the mails—Jacobson never evinced reluctance, even though he had received no financial inducements. Pickard and Hollingsworth had no prayer of becoming money launderers without the government's aid.

"[The] point is not that Pickard and Hollingsworth were *incapable* of engaging in the act of money laundering. Obviously they were capable of the act. [But] to get into the international money-laundering business you need underworld contacts, financial acumen or assets, access to foreign banks or bankers, or other assets. Pickard and Hollingsworth had none. [They] were objectively harmless.

"We do not wish to be understood as holding that lack of *present* means to commit a crime is alone enough to establish entrapment if the government supplies the means. [Suppose] that before Hinch chanced on the scene (for *Jacobson* makes clear [that] a predisposition *created* by the government cannot be used to defeat a defense of entrapment), Pickard had decided to smuggle arms to Cuba but didn't know where to buy a suitable boat. On a hunch, a government agent sidles up to Pickard and gives him the address of a boat dealer; and Pickard is arrested after taking possession of the boat and setting sail, and is charged with attempted smuggling. That would be a case in which the defendant had the idea for the crime all worked out and lacked merely the present means to commit it, and if the government had not supplied them someone else very well might have. It would be a case in which the government had merely furnished the opportunity to commit the crime to someone already predisposed to commit it. * * *

"Our two would-be international financiers were at the end of their tether, making it highly unlikely that if Hinch had not providentially appeared someone

a. Did the government's lawyer concede too much?

else would have guided them into money laundering. No real criminal would do business with such tyros. Or so it appears * * *."**b**

Consider, too, UNITED STATES v. KNOX, 112 F.3d 802 (5th Cir.1997), which arose as follows: Defendant Brace was the pastor of a church that was heavily in debt. In an effort to raise $10 million to pay the church's creditors, Brace hired a financial advisor, who in turn contacted other people. At the same time, undercover federal agents were conducting a sting operation designed to catch money launderers. Brace's financial advisor and the advisor's contacts told the undercover agents that they knew of a minister who would be interested in laundering drug money. Finally, the undercover agents met with Brace himself and told him that he was being asked to launder money that came from the sale of cocaine. Brace replied that he had no trouble with that. The jury rejected the entrapment defense and convicted Brace of laundering drug proceeds. "Because the government failed to prove that the preacher was likely to engage in money laundering absent the government's conduct," the Fifth Circuit, per DeMOSS, J., held that Brace was entrapped "as a matter of law":

"The en banc Seventh Circuit recently wrestled with the meaning of *Jacobson* [in the *Hollingsworth* case]. Writing for the majority, Chief Judge Posner stated that in examining predisposition, we must ask ourselves what the defendant would have done had the government not been involved. To properly answer the question, we must look to more than the defendant's mental state; we must also consider the defendant's skills, background and contacts. * * *

"We recognize that the Seventh Circuit's reading of *Jacobson* has not been universally embraced. The Ninth Circuit has rejected the Seventh Circuit's positional predisposition requirement and the First Circuit has adopted a different test. In *Gendron,* then Chief Judge (now Justice) Breyer held that *Jacobson* stands for the proposition that in trying to induce the target of a sting to commit a crime, the government may not confront him with circumstances that are different from the ordinary circumstances a real criminal would use in inducing one to engage in wrongdoing. [Thus,] the Government must show that a defendant would have committed the crime when 'faced with an ordinary "opportunity" to commit the crime rather than a special "inducement.' "

"Nonetheless, we are persuaded that the Seventh Circuit's Hollingsworth decision is correct. See Paul Marcus, *Presenting Back From the [Almost] Dead, the Entrapment Defense*, 47 Fla.L.Rev. 205, 233–34 (1995) (arguing *Hollingsworth* is proper approach to entrapment law). The Supreme Court instructs that in determining predisposition we are to ask what the defendant would have done absent government involvement. To give effect to that command, we must look not only to the defendant's mental state (his 'disposition'), but also to whether the defendant was able and likely, based on experience, training, and contacts, to actually commit the crime (his 'position').**c**

"[We] are called upon to determine whether the government proved beyond a reasonable doubt that Brace was predisposed to launder money. Following *Hollingsworth,* we look to Brace's position, as well as his mental disposition. [The]

---

b. In three separate dissents, Judges Coffey, Easterbrook and Ripple voiced strong disagreement with the majority's interpretation of *Jacobson.*

c. The court noted that "in this case the result would not differ under the First Circuit's *Gendron* test. The government failed to

prove that real drug dealers would provide the same, or even similar, terms to a launderer as the undercover agents offered Brace. Thus, the government failed to offer any evidence that Brace would accept an 'ordinary opportunity' to launder money."

government failed to prove that Brace, absent government involvement, was in a position to launder money. Therefore, the evidence is insufficient to prove that Brace was predisposed to launder money.

"[When] we ask the question of what Brace would have done if he had never met the undercover agents, we cannot answer 'launder money for real drug dealers.' In all likelihood, Brace never would have laundered money * * *."

Chapter 8

POLICE INTERROGATION
AND CONFESSIONS

SECTION 1. SOME DIFFERENT PERSPECTIVES

FRED E. INBAU: POLICE INTERROGATION—
A PRACTICAL NECESSITY

52 J.Crim.L.C. & P.S. 16 (1961), reprinted in Police Power
and Individual Freedom 147 (Sowle ed. 1962).

One completely false assumption accounts for most of the legal restrictions on police interrogations. It is this, and the fallacy is certainly perpetuated to a very considerable extent by mystery writers, the movies, and TV: whenever a crime is committed, if the police will only look carefully at the crime scene they will almost always find some clue that will lead them to the offender and at the same time establish his guilt; and once the offender is located, he will readily confess or disclose his guilt by trying to shoot his way out of the trap. But this is pure fiction; in actuality the situation is quite different. As a matter of fact, the art of criminal investigation has not developed to a point where the search for and the examination of physical evidence will always, or even in most cases, reveal a clue to the identity of the perpetrator or provide the necessary proof of his guilt. In criminal investigations, even of the most efficient type, there are many, many instances where physical clues are entirely absent, and the only approach to a possible solution of the crime is the interrogation of the criminal suspect himself, as well as others who may possess significant information. Moreover, in most instances these interrogations, particularly of the suspect himself, must be conducted under conditions of privacy and for a reasonable period of time; and they frequently require the use of psychological tactics and techniques that could well be classified as "unethical," if we are to evaluate them in terms of ordinary, everyday social behavior.

To protect myself from being misunderstood, I want to make it unmistakably clear that I am not an advocate of the so-called "third degree," for I am unalterably opposed to the use of any interrogation tactic or technique that is apt to make an innocent person confess. I am opposed, therefore, to the use of force, threats, or promises of leniency—all of which might well induce *an innocent person* to confess; but I do approve of such psychological tactics and techniques as trickery and deceit that are not only helpful but frequently necessary in order to secure incriminating information from the guilty, or investigate leads from otherwise uncooperative witnesses or informants.

My position, then, is this, and it may be presented in the form of three separate points, each accompanied by case illustrations:

1. *Many criminal cases, even when investigated by the best qualified police departments, are capable of solution only by means of an admission or confession*

from the guilty individual or upon the basis of information obtained from the questioning of other criminal suspects.

As to the validity of this statement, I suggest that consideration be given to the situation presented by cases such as these. A man is hit on the head while walking home late at night. He did not see his assailant, nor did anyone else. A careful and thorough search of the crime scene reveals no physical clues. Then take the case of a woman who is grabbed on the street at night and dragged into an alley and raped. Here, too, the assailant was unaccommodating enough to avoid leaving his hat or other means of identification at the crime scene; and there are no other physical clues. All the police have to work on is the description of the assailant given by the victim herself. She described him as about six feet tall, white, and wearing a dark suit. Or consider this case, an actual recent one in Illinois. Three women are vacationing in a wooded resort area. Their bodies were found dead alongside a foot trail, the result of physical violence, and no physical clues are present.

In cases of this kind—and they all typify the difficult investigation problem that the police frequently encounter—how else can they be solved, if at all, except by means of the interrogation of suspects or of others who may possess significant information?

There are times, too, when a police interrogation may result not only in the apprehension and conviction of the guilty, but also in the release of the innocent from well-warranted suspicion. Here is one such actual case within my own professional experience.

The dead body of a woman was found in her home. Her skull had been crushed, apparently with some blunt instrument. A careful police investigation of the premises did not reveal any clues to the identity of the killer. No fingerprints or other significant evidence were located; not even the lethal instrument itself could be found. None of the neighbors could give any helpful information. Although there was some evidence of a slight struggle in the room where the body lay, there were no indications of a forcible entry into the home. The deceased's young daughter was the only other resident of the home and she had been away in school at the time of the crime. The daughter could not give the police any idea of what, if any, money or property had disappeared from the home.

For several reasons the police considered the victim's husband a likely suspect. He was being sued for divorce; he knew his wife had planned on leaving the state and taking their daughter with her; and the neighbors reported that the couple had been having heated arguments, and that the husband was of a violent temper. He also lived conveniently near—in a garage adjoining the home. The police interrogated him and although his alibi was not conclusive his general behavior and the manner in which he answered the interrogator's questions satisfied the police of his innocence. Further investigation then revealed that the deceased's brother-in-law had been financially indebted to the deceased; that he was a frequent gambler; that at a number of social gatherings which he had attended money disappeared from some of the women's purses; that at his place of employment there had been a series of purse thefts; and that on the day of the killing he was absent from work. The police apprehended and questioned him. As the result of a few hours of competent interrogation—unattended by any abusive methods, but yet conducted during a period of delay in presenting the suspect before a committing magistrate as required by state statute—the suspect confessed to the murder. * * *

Without an opportunity for interrogation the police could not have solved this case. The perpetrator of the offense would have remained at liberty, perhaps to repeat his criminal conduct.

2. *Criminal offenders, except, of course, those caught in the commission of their crimes, ordinarily will not admit their guilt unless questioned under conditions of privacy, and for a period of perhaps several hours.*

* * * Self-condemnation and self-destruction not being normal behavior characteristics, human beings ordinarily do not utter unsolicited, spontaneous confessions. They must first be questioned regarding the offense. In some instances, a little bit of information inadvertently given to a competent interrogator by the suspect may suffice to start a line of investigation which might ultimately establish guilt. Upon other occasions, a full confession, with a revelation of details regarding a body, the loot, or the instruments used in the crime, may be required to prove the case. But whatever the possible consequences may be, it is impractical to expect any but a very few confessions to result from a guilty conscience unprovoked by an interrogation. It is also impractical to expect admissions or confessions to be obtained under circumstances other than privacy. Here again recourse to our everyday experience will support the basic validity of this requirement. For instance, in asking a personal friend to divulge a secret, or embarrassing information, we carefully avoid making the request in the presence of other persons, and seek a time and place when the matter can be discussed in private. The very same psychological factors are involved in a criminal interrogation, and even to a greater extent. For related psychological considerations, if an interrogation is to be had at all, it must be one based upon an unhurried interview, the necessary length of which will in many instances extend to several hours, depending upon various factors such as the nature of the case situation and the personality of the suspect. * * *

If the right to counsel arises only at the time of trial, or even when the judicial process begins, as at a preliminary hearing or at the time of indictment, the police have at least some opportunity for an interrogation. On the other hand, if the right is considered to exist immediately upon arrest, the interrogation opportunity, for all practical purposes, is gone—because of the prevailing concept that the role of defense counsel is to advise his client, "keep your mouth shut; don't say anything to anybody." * * *

In my judgment the right to counsel at the time of trial, or even at the very start of the judicial process, should be accorded *and provided* to all indigent defendants, insofar as practicable, regardless of whether the case involves a capital or non-capital offense, or even if it amounts only to a misdemeanor. What I do object to is an extension of the right to arrestees, indigent or non-indigent, prior to the start of the judicial process. It is not constitutionally required, and practical considerations will not tolerate such an extension, and particularly so if the extension is supplemented by a rule of court that would nullify, as a violation of due process, a confession obtained during a period of police detention before the start of the judicial process. Moreover, sometime in the near future we will have to come to grips with this interrogation problem and consider the passage of legislation, by all the states as well as the federal government, which will specifically provide for a reasonable period of police detention for the interrogation of suspects who are not otherwise unwilling to talk. * * *

Regarding the routine advice of counsel to an arrestee to remain silent and refuse to answer questions put to him by the police, it is my suggestion that the legal profession give serious consideration to the adoption of an alternative practice, which would require counsel to say to his client, the arrestee: "Although you do not have to say anything, my advice to you is that you discuss this matter with the police and that you tell them the truth; I'll stand by to protect you from any harm or abuse." With the advent of such a change in the ethical concept of the role of counsel, we might then be able to say that all arrestees should be entitled to counsel from the time of their arrest. As matters now stand, however, public protection and safety require that we adhere to the present viewpoint that there is no right to counsel during the investigative, non-judicial stage of the case.

3. *In dealing with criminal offenders, and consequently also with criminal suspects who may actually be innocent, the interrogator must of necessity employ less refined methods than are considered appropriate for the transaction of ordinary, everyday affairs by and between law-abiding citizens.*

To illustrate this point, permit me to revert to the previously discussed case of the woman who was murdered by her brother-in-law. His confession was obtained largely as a result of the interrogator adopting a friendly attitude in questioning the suspect, when concededly no such genuine feeling existed; by pretending to sympathize with the suspect because of his difficult financial situation; by suggesting that perhaps the victim had done or said something which aroused his anger and which would have aroused the anger of anyone else similarly situated to such an extent as to provoke a violent reaction; and by resorting to other similar expressions, or even overtures of friendliness and sympathy such as a pat on the suspect's shoulder or knee. In all of this, of course, the interrogation was "unethical" according to the standards usually set for professional, business and social conduct. But the pertinent issue in this case was no ordinary, lawful, professional, business or social matter. It involved the taking of a human life by one who abided by no code of fair play toward his fellow human beings. The killer would not have been moved one bit toward a confession by subjecting him to a reading or lecture regarding the morality of his conduct. It would have been futile merely to give him a pencil and paper and trust that his conscience would impel him to confess. Something more was required—something which was in its essence an "unethical" practice on the part of the interrogator. But, under the circumstances involved in this case, how else would the murderer's guilt have been established? Moreover, let us bear this thought in mind. From the criminal's point of view, *any* interrogation of him is objectionable. To *him* it may be a "dirty trick" to be talked into a confession, for surely it was not done for his benefit. Consequently, any interrogation of him might be labeled as deceitful or unethical.

Of necessity, criminal interrogators must deal with criminal offenders on a somewhat lower moral plane than that upon which ethical, law-abiding citizens are expected to conduct their everyday affairs. That plane, in the interest of innocent suspects need only be subject to the following restriction: Although both "fair" and "unfair" interrogation practices are permissible, nothing shall be done or said to the subject that will be apt to make an innocent person confess.

If all this be so, why then the withholding of this essential interrogation opportunity from the police? And we do, insofar as the stated law is concerned. It comes in the form of statutes or rules that require the prompt delivery of an arrested person before a magistrate for a preliminary hearing or arraignment. Moreover, the United States Supreme Court has decreed that in federal cases no confession is to be received in evidence, regardless of its voluntariness or trustworthiness, if it was obtained during a period of unnecessary delay in delivering the arrestee to a federal commissioner or judge for arraignment. In the federal jurisdiction of Washington, D.C., which must cope with a variety of criminal offenses and problems similar to any other city of comparable size, this federal court rule has had a very crippling effect on police investigations.[6]

---

6. In addition, some concern should be exhibited over the risk involved in freeing obviously guilty offenders as a result of the courts' efforts to discipline the police. For instance, following the Supreme Court's reversal of his rape conviction, and his release from custody, the defendant in *Mallory* [p. 446] committed two other offenses against female victims. For the latest one he was found guilty and sentenced to the penitentiary by a Pennsylvania Court. * * *

One incongruity of the prompt arraignment rule is this. It is lawful for the police to arrest upon *reasonable belief* that the arrestee has committed the offense, following which they must take him before a magistrate, without unnecessary delay, and charge him with the crime; but for legal proof of the charge, his guilt at the time of trial must be established *beyond reasonable doubt*. Moreover, when the accused gets into the hands of a magistrate for the preliminary hearing, the opportunity for an effective interrogation is ended, many times because of the advice he receives from his attorney to keep his mouth shut.

If we view this whole problem realistically, we must come to the conclusion that an interrogation opportunity is necessary and that legislative provision ought to be made for a privately conducted police interrogation, covering a reasonable period of time, of suspects who are not unwilling to be interviewed, and that the only tactics or techniques that are to be forbidden are those which are apt to make an innocent person confess. * * *

The only real, practically attainable protection we can set up for ourselves against police interrogation abuses (just as with respect to arrest and detention abuses) is to see to it that our police are selected and promoted on a merit basis, that they are properly trained, adequately compensated, and that they are permitted to remain substantially free from politically inspired interference. In the hands of men of this competence there will be a minimum degree of abusive practices. And once again I suggest that the real interest that should be exhibited by the legislatures and the courts is with reference to the protection of the innocent from the hazards of tactics and techniques that are apt to produce confessions of guilt or other false information. Individual civil liberties can survive in such an atmosphere, alongside the protective security of the public.[a]

YALE KAMISAR—EQUAL JUSTICE IN THE GATEHOUSES AND MANSIONS OF AMERICAN CRIMINAL PROCEDURE

In Kamisar, Inbau & Arnold, Criminal Justice in Our Time 19–36 (Howard ed. 1965).

THE SHOW IN THE "GATEHOUSE" VS. THE SHOW IN THE "MANSION" * * *

The courtroom is a splendid place where defense attorneys bellow and strut and prosecuting attorneys are hemmed in at many turns. But what happens before an accused reaches the safety and enjoys the comfort of this veritable mansion? Ah, there's the rub. Typically he must first pass through a much less pretentious edifice, a police station with bare back rooms and locked doors.

In this "gatehouse" of American criminal procedure—through which most defendants journey and beyond which many never get—the enemy of the state is a depersonalized "subject" to be "sized up" and subjected to "interrogation tactics and techniques most appropriate for the occasion";[55] he is "game" to be stalked and cornered.[56] Here, ideals are checked at the door, "realities" faced, and the

---

a. See also Inbau, Reid & Buckley, Criminal Interrogation and Confessions xiii (3d ed. 1986) (introduction); Grano, *Selling the Idea to Tell the Truth: The Professional Interrogator and Modern Confessions Law,* 84 Mich.L.Rev. 662 (1986) (essay review of Inbau, Reid & Buckley, supra) (new edition of Inbau book is "a manual for successful interrogation that a free, civilized, and just society can and should endorse without apology").

55. Inbau & Reid, *Criminal Interrogation and Confessions* 20 (1962).

56. "[T]he interrogator's task is somewhat akin to that of a hunter stalking his game. Each must patiently maneuver himself into a position from which the desired objective may be attained; and in the same manner that the hunter may lose his game by a noisy dash through the bush, can the interrogator fail by not exercising the proper degree of patience." Inbau & Reid, *Lie Detection and Criminal Interrogation* 185 (3d ed. 1953). The authors have dropped this graphic language from their later work.

prestige of law enforcement vindicated. Once he leaves the "gatehouse" and enters the "mansion"—if he ever gets there—the enemy of the state is repersonalized, even dignified, the public invited, and a stirring ceremony in honor of individual freedom from law enforcement celebrated.

I suspect it is not so much that society knows and approves of the show in the gatehouse, but that society does not know or care. "[S]ociety, by its insouciance, has divested itself of a moral responsibility and unloaded it on to the police. Society doesn't want to know about criminals, but it does want them put away, and it is incurious how this can be done provided it is done. Thus society, in giving the policeman power and wishing to ignore what his techniques must be, has made over to him part of its own conscience."[57]

True, the man in the street would have considerable difficulty explaining why the Constitution requires so much in the courtroom and means so little in the police station, but that is not his affair. "The task of keeping the two shows going at the same time without losing the patronage or the support of the Constitution for either," as Thurman Arnold once observed, is "left to the legal scholar."[58] Perhaps this is only fitting and proper, for as Thomas Reed Powell used to say, if you can think about something that is related to something else without thinking about the thing to which it is related, then you have the legal mind.

That the legal mind passes by or shuts out the *de facto* inquisitorial system which has characterized our criminal procedure for so long is bad enough. What is worse is that such an attitude leads many—perhaps requires many—to recoil with horror and dismay at any proposal which recognizes the grim facts of the criminal process and seeks to do something about them.

[At this point, the author discusses suggestions in the late 1920's that (rather than a police officer) a magistrate, or a prosecutor in the presence of a magistrate, do the interrogation, and a proposal in the early 1940's that in federal cases a commissioner do the interrogation at preliminary hearings, but only after advising the suspect of his right to counsel and his right to remain silent. Both proposals were "beaten down to the accompaniment of cries" that they were "opposed to our traditions of fair play," "contrary to the basic traditions of Anglo–American procedure" and violative of the constitutional guarantee against self-incrimination.]

Evidently, so long as neither the proceedings nor the presiding officer is "judicial," basic traditions are honored and self-incrimination problems avoided. * * *

Four score years ago, Sir James Fitzjames Stephen noted with pride that the fact that "the prisoner is absolutely protected against all judicial questioning before or at the trial * * * contributes greatly to the dignity and apparent humanity of a criminal trial. It effectually avoids the appearance of harshness, not to say cruelty, which often shocks an English spectator in a French court of justice." Whatever the case then, one would have to underscore the "apparent" and "the appearance" in that statement today. Stephen also told us that "the fact that the prisoner cannot be questioned stimulates the search for independent evidence." Whatever the case then, one cannot but wonder today how often the only thing "stimulated" by the inability of judicial officers to question a prisoner is questioning by police officers. One cannot but wonder how often the availability of the privilege (or, perhaps more aptly, the inability of the State to undermine the privilege), once the accused reaches the safety and comfort of the mansion,

---

57. MacInnes, *The Criminal Society,* in The Police and the Public 101 (Rolph ed. 1962).

58. Arnold, *The Symbols of Government* 156 (Harbinger ed. 1962).

only furnishes the State with an *additional incentive* for proving the charge against him out of his own mouth before he leaves the gatehouse.

Is the Privilege Checked at the "Gatehouse" Door?

[O]ne who would apply the privilege to the police station may select from the vast conglomerate of determinants which form its history the fact that the maxim "no man shall be compelled to accuse himself" first meant (and until the seventeenth century probably only meant) that no man shall be compelled to make the *first charge* against himself, to submit to a "fishing" interrogation about his crimes, to furnish his own indictment from his own lips. Until the 1600's all parties concerned seemed to have operated on the premise that *after* pleading to the indictment, the accused could be compelled to incriminate himself. * * * When we apply the privilege to "arrests for investigation" or "routine pickups," do we disguise a revolutionary idea in the garb of the past or do we restore the privilege to its primordial state?

Nor should it be forgotten that for many centuries there were simply no "police interrogators" to whom the privilege could be applied. Although what Dean Wigmore calls "the first part" of the history of the privilege, the opposition to the ex officio oath of the ecclesiastical courts, began in the 1200's "criminal investigation by the police, with its concomitant of police interrogation, is a product of the late nineteenth century";[82] in eighteenth-century America as in eighteenth-century England "there were no police [in the modern sense] and, though some states seem to have had prosecutors, private prosecution was the rule rather than the exception."[83] In fact as well as in theory, observes Professor Edmond M. Morgan, "there can be little question that the modern American police have taken over the functions performed originally by the English committing magistrates [and at least by some colonial magistrates]; they are in a real sense administrative officers and their questioning of the person under arrest is an investigative proceeding in which testimony is taken." If modern police are permitted to interrogate under the coercive influence of arrest and secret detention, then, insists Professor Albert R. Beisel, "they are doing the very same acts which historically the judiciary was doing in the seventeenth century but which the privilege against self-incrimination abolished."

I do not contend that "the implications of a tangled and obscure history" dictate that the privilege apply to the police station, only that they permit it. I do not claim that this long and involved history displaces judgment, only that it liberates it. I do not say that the distinct origins of the confession and self-incrimination rules are irrelevant, only that it is more important (if we share Dean Charles T. McCormick's views) that "the kinship of the two rules is too apparent for denial" and that "such policy as modern writers are able to discover as a basis for the self-incrimination privilege * * * pales to a flicker beside the flaming demands of justice and humanity for protection against extorted confessions."

Those who applaud the show in the mansion without hissing the show in the gatehouse may also:

Find refuge in the notion that compulsion to testify means *legal* compulsion. Since he is threatened neither with perjury for testifying falsely nor contempt for refusing to testify at all, it cannot be said, runs the argument, that the man in the back room of the police station is being "compelled" to be a "witness against

---

82. Note, *An Historical Argument for the Right to Counsel During Police Interrogation,* 73 Yale L.J. 1000, 1034 (1964).

83. Id. at 1041. See also Barrett, *Police Practices and the Law—From Arrest to Release or Charge,* 50 Calif.L.Rev. 11, 16–19 (1962). * * *

himself" within the meaning of the privilege. Since the police have no legal right to make him answer, "there is no legal obligation to which a privilege in the technical sense can apply."[91]

Can we accept this analysis without forgetting as lawyers and judges what we know as men? Without permitting logic to triumph over life? So long as "what on their face are merely words of request take on color from the officer's badge, gun and demeanor";[94] so long as his interrogators neither advise him of his rights nor permit him to consult with a lawyer who will; can there be any doubt that many a "subject" will *assume* that the police have a legal right to an answer? That many an incriminating statement will be extracted under "color" of law? So long as the interrogator is instructed to "get the idea across [that he] has 'all the time in the world'"; so long as "the power [legal or otherwise] to extract answers begets a forgetfulness of the just limitations of the power" and "the simple and peaceful process of questioning breeds a readiness to resort to bullying and to physical force"; can there be any doubt that many a subject will assume that there is an *illegal* sanction for contumacy?

If these inferences are unfair, if very few "subjects" are misled to believe that there is either a legal obligation to talk or unlimited time and illegal means available to make them do so—if, in short, they know they can "shut up"—why are the police so bent on preventing counsel from telling them what they already know? Why, at least, don't the officers themselves tell their "subjects" plainly and emphatically that they need not and cannot be made to answer? That they will be permitted to consult with counsel, or be brought before a magistrate in short order? And why is the "subject" questioned in *secret?* Why does the modest proposal that a suspect be interrogated by or before an impartial functionary immediately after arrest "meet with scant favor in police circles, even from the most high-minded and highly respected elements in those circles"?[99]

Finally, those who have learned to live with the widespread practices in the gatehouse may take the "waiver" tack. They may:

Concede that the privilege against self-incrimination exists in the police station, but maintain that when (instead of exercising his right to remain silent or to make only self-serving remarks) a suspect "volunteers" damaging statements he has *waived* his rights. This is not much of a concession for "if the privilege is easily waived, there is really no privilege at all."[100] However, if "when the state is putting questions, the answers to which will disclose criminal activities by the witness, there is likely to be an especially high insistence checked by an especially high reluctance," then there is likely to be an especially low incidence of valid waiving of the privilege.

So long as "the classic definition of waiver enumerated in *Johnson v. Zerbst—* 'an intelligent relinquishment or abandonment of a known right or privilege'— furnishes the controlling standard,"[102] so long as the courts "indulge every reasonable presumption against [such] waiver," it is difficult to see how the contention that an unadvised suspect waives the privilege simply by talking even presents a substantial question. "The Fourteenth Amendment," announced the Supreme Court only a year ago, "secures against state invasion the same privilege that the Fifth Amendment guarantees against federal infringement—the right of a

---

91. See Mayers, *Shall We Amend the Fifth Amendment?* 82–83, 223–33 (1959); 8 Wigmore, *Evidence* 329 n. 27 (McNaughton rev. 1961). But both authors are quick to marshal the contrary arguments.

94. Foote, *The Fourth Amendment: Obstacle or Necessity in the Law of Arrest?* in Police Power and Individual Freedom 29, 30 (Sowle ed. 1962).

99. Mayers 90.

100. Note, 5 Stan.L.Rev. 459, 477 (1953).

102. *Fay v. Noia* [Ch. 28, § 2].

person to remain silent unless he chooses to speak in the unfettered exercise of his own will."[104] Can it seriously be said of the routine police interrogation that the suspect so speaks? Again, only a year ago, the Court pointed out that "no system of criminal justice can, or should, survive if it comes to depend for its continued effectiveness on the citizens' abdication through unawareness of their constitutional rights."[105] On what else does the existing system depend?

[The] trouble with both the "waiver" and "no legal compulsion" rationalizations of the existing *de facto* inquisitorial system is this: when we expect the police dutifully to notify a suspect of the very means he may utilize to frustrate them— when we rely on them to advise a suspect unbegrudgingly and unequivocally of the very rights he is being counted on *not* to assert—we demand too much of even our best officers. As Dean Edward L. Barrett has asked: "[I]s it the duty of the police to persuade the suspect to talk or persuade him not to talk? They cannot be expected to do both."[110]

Suspects there are who feel in a "pleading guilty" mood, for some of the many reasons most defendants do plead guilty. Suspects there are who would intentionally relinquish their rights for some hoped-for favor from the state. I do not deny this. I do deny that such suspects do not need a lawyer.

Surely the man who, in effect, is pleading guilty in the gatehouse needs a lawyer no less than one who arrives at the same decision only after surviving the perilous journey through that structure.[a]

JOSEPH D. GRANO—CONFESSIONS, TRUTH, AND THE LAW
129–36 (1993).

[Professor Laurence Benner] correctly noted that English judges in the nineteenth century came to regard it as their duty to advise suspects at the pretrial examination that they need not respond to questions, a requirement ultimately codified in 1848.[90] Because these developments occurred after the Fifth Amendment's adoption, however, they do not shed much light on the principle that the framers thought they were constitutionalizing. Moreover, judicial questioning of the accused at the preliminary examination persisted in some American states, such as New York, until the middle of the nineteenth century. At least one commentator has speculated that the privilege came to be viewed as a bar to judicial questioning at the pretrial examination only after the examination court ceased to perform an investigatory function and assumed more of an ordinary judicial role. This thesis finds support in the observation of a British Home Office working group that the nineteenth-century development of organized police forces made possible the separation of the investigative and judicial functions that had previously been combined in the pretrial examination court.

[It] should not be surprising [that] the mid-nineteenth-century statutory restrictions on judicial questioning of the accused created in some quarters "a

---

104. *Malloy v. Hogan* [p. 456].

105. *Escobedo v. Illinois* [p. 450].

110. Brief Amicus Curiae, p. 9, *People v. Dorado*, 398 P.2d 361 (1965) (on rehearing).

a. Compare Stephen A. Saltzburg, *Miranda v. Arizona Revisited: Constitutional Law or Judicial Fiat*, 26 Washburn L.J. 1, 14 (1986) (drafters of self-incrimination clause could not have intended to prohibit any magistrate or judge from compelling a person to answer questions, but to permit other officials to do so in secret sessions and without any judicial pro-

tection against the nature and manner of questioning) with Joseph D. Grano, *Selling the Idea to Tell the Truth: The Professional Interrogator and Modern Confessions Law*, 84 Mich.L.Rev. 662, 683–84, 686 (1986) (in an historical sense, no "compulsion" within meaning of self-incrimination clause is present in the stationhouse; moreover, "mere questioning by itself" is hardly equivalent to compulsion).

90. Benner, *Requiem for Miranda: The Rehnquist Court's Voluntariness Doctrine in Historical Perspective*, 67 Wash. U.L.Q. 59, 81–82.

sense of resistance to police interrogation"; in Professor Mark Berger's words, "[h]aving given up the role of interrogator, the justices of the peace were uncertain whether police could be allowed to perform that function."[99] As already seen, however, the development of organized police forces and the concomitant ban on judicial questioning, at least at the pretrial examination, did not take hold either in Britain or in this country until well after the Fifth Amendment was adopted. In any event, uncertainty about the propriety of police interrogation and a ban on police interrogation are two different matters, and the former never evolved into the latter. On the contrary, as Professor George Dix has documented, nineteenth-century voluntariness law in England tolerated confessions induced by trickery and made exceptions to the rule excluding confessions induced by promises, while American courts displayed even "less enthusiasm" for the common-law rules.[100]

[Thus, the *Miranda* Court] erred, at least from a historical perspective, in perceiving an "intimate connection"[a] between the privilege, which prohibited compulsory oaths and mandatory judicial questioning of the accused, and the issues pertaining to the admissibility of extrajudicial confessions. [Although] the common law had developed a voluntariness requirement for confessions prior to the adoption of the Fifth Amendment, neither the voluntariness rule nor its underlying trustworthiness rationale referred to the protection against compulsory self-incrimination. Concededly, some voices did question how police interrogation could be deemed consistent with the mid-nineteenth-century ban on mandatory judicial questioning of the accused at the pretrial examination, but in neither Great Britain nor the United States did the voluntariness rule or the privilege evolve to the point of prohibiting police interrogation. Indeed, not even [the *Miranda* case] went that far. * * *

Some may contend that the privilege, if applied to the police station, should make police-initiated interrogation unlawful. This would make the privilege in the police station coextensive with the privilege at trial, where both the prosecutor and judge are forbidden from questioning an accused who does not "waive" Fifth Amendment rights by taking the stand in his own defense. If this is the privilege to be applied, however, the "kinship" between it and the common-law voluntariness rule, far from being "too apparent for denial," is difficult to fathom, for the common-law voluntariness rule, as the previous section indicated, never condemned police interrogation as such.

Still, some may find it incongruous to bar interrogation at trial but to permit police questioning before trial. [Some 30 years ago] Bernard Weisberg complained in an influential article that we "would be hard put to explain to visitors from a legal Mars how ... secret questioning in a police station fits into a system of criminal law which recognizes the privilege against self-incrimination," and he specifically contrasted the scope of an accused's protections at trial with the absence of corresponding protections in the police station.[106] Building on this theme, Professor Kamisar similarly contrasted in colorful, metaphoric prose the "show in the gatehouse," where "ideals are checked at the door and 'realities'

---

99. Berger, *Legislating Confession Law in Great Britain: A Statutory Approach to Police Interrogations,* 24 U.Mich.J.L.Ref. 1, 10 n. 34 (1990).

100. Dix, *Mistake, Ignorance, Expectation of Benefit, and the Modern Law of Confessions,* 1975 Wash.U.L.Q. 275, 282–84.

a. After quoting extensively from several police interrogation manuals which recommended and spelled out various methods of

obtaining incriminating statements from a suspect taken into custody, the *Miranda* Court commented (384 U.S. at 458, 86 S.Ct. at 1619): "From the foregoing, we can readily perceive an intimate connection between the privilege against self-incrimination and police custodial questioning."

106. Weisberg, *Police Interrogation of Arrested Persons: A Skeptical View,* 52 J.Crim.L. & P.S. 21 (1961).

faced," and the "show in the mansion," where "the defendant is 'even dignified, the public invited, and a stirring ceremony in honor of individual freedom from law enforcement celebrated.'"

[The] answer to the charge of incongruity is rooted both in history and in the "realities" that Professor Kamisar disparagingly referred to. Despite the questions that were raised, nineteenth-century courts in both Great Britain and this country refused to prohibit police interrogation or to render it ineffective by onerous restrictions. Although debate has never abated, courts in both countries, particularly in recent years, have continued to recognize the importance of police interrogation. Indeed, [the] transformation of the judicial role that occurred in the nineteenth century was probably made possible by the development of police forces that assumed the investigative function previously performed by the pretrial examination court.

[The] division of the investigative and adjudicative functions makes sense from a separation of powers perspective. Moreover, reflecting their own perceptions of fairness, American criminal justice systems in particular have deemed it important to separate the prosecutorial and the judicial roles. Whatever a system's structure or underlying ideology, however, the investigative authority must be lodged somewhere for the system to be viable. Because successful investigation often depends on the questioning of reluctant witnesses and suspects, and on other intrusive strategies as well, the investigative stage, as a practical matter, cannot be subject to the same restraints that govern the adjudicative stage. The operative rules will be different because the institutions that dominate the successive stages of the process have dissimilar functions and responsibilities. Simply put, an investigation is not, and cannot be, a trial. * * *

One might still object [that] an argument invoking history and practical considerations does not provide a principled response to the gatehouse-mansion dichotomy. After all, the fact remains that the accused is not subject to interrogation at trial unless he elects to testify, and on principle the institution of police interrogation seems inconsistent with this limitation. The answer to this is that the alleged inconsistency is not nearly as obvious as it seems. Rather than referring to a single rule, the "privilege ... embraces several distinct rules of law, each having an independent development." Nonetheless, in most situations, the "privilege is merely an *option of refusal,* not a prohibition of inquiry."

Thus, * * * a grand jury may subpoena even a target of its investigation, and the targeted individual has the burden of invoking the privilege on a question-by-question basis. Similarly, even under *Miranda,* targets of police interrogation who are not in custody are not entitled to warnings and have the burden of affirmatively invoking the privilege when questioned.

[If] the privilege cannot plausibly be viewed as a ban on police-initiated questioning, what can it mean in the context of police interrogation, and what establishes its "kinship" to the voluntariness rule for confessions? [O]ne might concede that the privilege would prohibit any attempt formally to require suspects, in custody or not, to answer questions. Such a prohibition would be vacuous, however, if governmental officials could force suspects to answer questions by the use of physical or psychological coercion. Not surprisingly, therefore, although the privilege did not play a significant role in the abolition of torture to secure statements in English procedure, various individuals on both sides of the Atlantic came to regard torture as inconsistent with the privilege. Viewed in this light, an obvious kinship exists between the privilege and the voluntariness requirement; indeed, had a voluntariness requirement not independently developed, one might early have been inferred as a logical imperative of the privilege. All this leads, however, to the unremarkable conclusion that the Fifth Amendment, if properly applied to police interrogation at all, prohibits coerced or involuntary confessions. That is, in the context of police interrogation, to "compel" a suspect to become a witness against himself can only mean to "coerce" a suspect to become a witness against himself.

This conclusion, however, is bothersome for *Miranda*'s supporters. For example, Professors Irene and Yale Rosenberg have asserted that "it seems unlikely that the long struggle culminating in the incorporation of the Fifth Amendment prohibition against compelled testimony could have been simply an heroic effort to provide an official synonym for involuntariness."[128] Likewise, regarding it as almost self-evident that the privilege was "more than the 'voluntary' test masquerading under a different label," Professor Kamisar has declared that it takes "real dexterity" to purport to apply the Fifth Amendment to the police station and "yet conclude that [this] does not change things very much." But, to repeat, unless the Fifth Amendment is read as a prohibition on all police questioning, custodial and noncustodial, it can be read in the context of police interrogation only as providing protection against involuntariness or coercion. Indeed, the *Miranda* Court read the Fifth Amendment this way, for it found the Fifth Amendment applicable to the "informal compulsion" exerted by the police, concluded that "custodial" interrogation was "inherently compelling," and distinguished on-the-scene questioning, which it exempted from its holding, on the ground that "the compelling atmosphere inherent in the process of in-custody interrogation is not necessarily present."

The possibility remains, of course, that *coercion* for Fifth Amendment purposes should be a less demanding concept than *coercion* for due process purposes and that, accordingly, *involuntariness* should have different meanings under the two amendments. The Court in *Miranda* took such an approach, for none of its previous due process voluntariness cases had sought to protect the suspect merely from the inherent pressures of custodial questioning. Indeed, the Court candidly admitted, even if it understated the point, that it "might not find the defendants' statements to have been involuntary in traditional terms." The question that *Miranda* did not answer, however, is why the concepts of coercion and involuntariness should have different meanings in the Fifth Amendment and due process contexts.

SECTION 2. HISTORICAL BACKGROUND[a]

[handwritten: Voluntariness Cases]

A. The Interests Protected by the Due Process "Voluntariness" Test for Admitting Confessions

The first rules governing the admissibility of confessions were laid down in the eighteenth and nineteenth centuries, a time when illegal police methods were relevant only insofar as they affected the trustworthiness of the evidence. Whatever the meaning of the elusive terms "involuntary" and "coerced" confessions

---

128. Rosenberg & Rosenberg, *A Modest Proposal for the Abolition of Custodial Confessions*, 68 N.C.L.Rev. 69, 108–9 (1989).

a. For a much more detailed treatment of the subject matter of this Note, see Mark Berger, *Taking the Fifth* 99–124 (1980); Joseph D. Grano, *Confessions, Truth, and the Law* 59–172 (1993); Otis Stephens, *The Supreme Court and Confessions of Guilt* 17–119 (1973); 3 Wigmore, *Evidence* §§ 817–26 (Chadbourn rev. 1970); Anthony G. Amsterdam, *The Supreme Court and the Rights of Suspects in Criminal Cases*, 45 N.Y.U. L.Rev. 785, 803–10 (1970);

Laurence A. Benner, *Requiem for Miranda: The Rehnquist's Court's Voluntariness Doctrine in Historical Perspective*, 67 Wash. U.L.Q. 59 (1989); Gerald M. Caplan, *Questioning Miranda*, 38 Vand.L.Rev. 1417, 1427–43 (1985); Catherine Hancock, *Due Process before Miranda*, 70 Tul.L.Rev. 2195 (1996); Yale Kamisar, *What is an "Involuntary" Confession?*, 17 Rutgers L.Rev. 728 (1963); Welsh S. White, *What is an Involuntary Confession Now?*, 50 Rutgers L.Rev. 2001 (1998).

since 1940, for centuries the rule that a confession was admissible so long as it was "voluntary" was more or less an alternative statement of the rule that a confession was admissible so long as it was free of influence which made it untrustworthy or "probably untrue." See generally Charles T. McCormick, *Evidence* 226 (1954); 3 John Henry Wigmore, *Evidence* § 822 (3d ed. 1940).

Indeed, Dean Wigmore condemned the use of the "voluntary" terminology for the reason that "there is nothing in the mere circumstance of compulsion to speak in general * * * which create any risk of untruth." 3 Wigmore, § 843. But the courts' continued reference to the term "voluntariness" in enunciating the requisites for the admissibility of a confession under the due process clause was defended by Dean McCormick, who suggested that it might be prompted "not only by a liking for its convenient brevity, but also by a recognition that there is an interest here to be protected closely akin to the interest of a witness or of an accused person which is protected by the privilege against compulsory self-incrimination." McCormick, *The Scope of Privilege in the Law of Evidence,* 16 Texas L.Rev. 447, 453 (1938).

At least in its advanced stage (the early 1960s), the "due process" or "involuntariness" test appeared to have *three* underlying values or goals. It barred the use of confessions (a) which were of doubtful reliability because of the police methods used to obtain them;[b] (b) which were produced by offensive methods even though the reliability of the confession was not in question; and (c) which were involuntary *in fact* (e.g., obtained from a drugged person) even though the confession was entirely trustworthy and not the product of any conscious police wrongdoing.[c]

At the outset, however, the primary (and perhaps the exclusive) basis for excluding confessions under the due process "voluntariness" test was the "untrustworthiness" rationale, the view that the confession rule was designed merely to protect the integrity of the fact-finding process. This rationale sufficed to explain the exclusion of the confession in *Brown v. Mississippi,* 297 U.S. 278, 56 S.Ct. 461, 80 L.Ed. 682 (1936), the first fourteenth amendment due process confession case (where the deputy who had presided over the beating of the defendants conceded that one prisoner had been whipped but "not too much for a Negro; not as much as I would have done if it were left to me"), and the cases which immediately followed for they, too, were pervaded by threats of, or outright, physical violence. "But when cases involving the more subtle 'psychological' pressures began to appear—usually instances of prolonged interrogation [it] was no longer possible easily to assume that the confessions exacted were unreliable as evidence of guilt. [In *Ashcraft v. Tennessee,* 322 U.S. 143, 64 S.Ct. 921, 88 L.Ed. 1192 (1944)] a conviction was reversed where a confession had been obtained after some thirty-six hours of continuous interrogation of the defendant by the police. In effect, the Court ruled that the extended questioning raised a conclusive presumption of 'coercion.' Considering the facts as revealed in the record of the *Ashcraft* case, it is fair to suggest that the result reached by the Court reflected

b. But see *Colorado v. Connelly* (1986) (p. 588), viewing the unreliability of a confession as "a matter to be governed by the evidentiary laws of the forum and not by the Due Process Clause."

c. As for the third underlying value, see *Townsend v. Sain,* 372 U.S. 293, 83 S.Ct. 745, 9 L.Ed.2d 770 (1963), excluding a confession obtained from one given a drug with the properties of a truth serum, even though the police were unaware of the drug's effect and had engaged in no conscious wrongdoing (although they may have been negligent), and even though the confession was apparently reliable. "Any questioning by police officers which *in fact* produces a confession which is not the product of free intellect," observed the Court, "renders the confession inadmissible."

However, in *Colorado v. Connelly* (1986) (p. 588), the Court looked back at *Townsend* as a case that "presented [an] instance of police wrongdoing."

less a concern with the reliability of the confession as evidence of guilt in the particular case than disapproval of police methods which a majority of the Court conceived as generally dangerous and subject to serious abuse." Francis Allen, *The Supreme Court, Federalism, and State Systems of Criminal Justice,* 8 DePaul L.Rev. 213, 235 (1959). See also Monrad Paulsen, *The Fourteenth Amendment and the Third Degree,* 6 Stan.L.Rev. 411, 418–19 (1954).

As Professor Catherine Hancock has recently observed, *Due Process Before Miranda,* 70 Tul. 2195, 2226 (1996), "*Ashcraft* was a milestone because it prefigured *Miranda*'s recognition of the coercion inherent in all custodial interrogations. [In] a prophetic dictum, [dissenting Justice Jackson] declared that 'even one hour' of interrogation would be inherently coercive, and so there could be no stopping point to the *Ashcraft* doctrine. However, more than twenty years elapsed before this prophecy came to pass in the form of *Miranda*'s presumption that even a few moments of custodial interrogation are inherently coercive."

In *Watts v. Indiana,* 338 U.S. 49, 69 S.Ct. 1347, 93 L.Ed. 1801 (1949) and the companion cases of *Harris v. South Carolina,* 338 U.S. 68, 69 S.Ct. 1354, 93 L.Ed. 1815 (1949) and *Turner v. Pennsylvania,* 338 U.S. 62, 69 S.Ct. 1352, 93 L.Ed. 1810 (1949), the Court reversed three convictions resting on coerced confessions without disputing the accuracy of Justice Jackson's observation (concurring in *Watts* and dissenting in the other cases) that "checked with external evidence they [the confessions in each case] are inherently believable and were not shaken as to truth by anything that occurred at the trial."

The majority, per Frankfurter, J., commented: "In holding that the Due Process Clause *bars police procedure* which violates the basic notions of our accusatorial mode of prosecuting crime and vitiates a conviction based on the fruits of such procedure, we apply the Due Process Clause to its historic function of *assuring appropriate procedure* before liberty is curtailed or life is taken." (Emphasis added.) And three years later, in the famous "stomach-pumping" case of *Rochin v. California,* p. 36, the Court, again speaking through Justice Frankfurter, viewed the coerced confession cases as "only instances of the general requirement that States in their prosecutions respect certain decencies of civilized conduct," pointing out: "Use of involuntary verbal confessions in State criminal trials is constitutionally obnoxious not only because of their unreliability. They are inadmissible under the Due Process Clause even though statements contained in them may be independently established as true. Coerced confessions offend the community's sense of fair play and decency."

That the Court was applying a "police methods"—as well as a "trustworthiness"—test was made clear by *Spano v. New York,* 360 U.S. 315, 79 S.Ct. 1202, 3 L.Ed.2d 1265 (1959); *Blackburn v. Alabama,* 361 U.S. 199, 80 S.Ct. 274, 4 L.Ed.2d 242 (1960) and *Rogers v. Richmond,* 365 U.S. 534, 81 S.Ct. 735, 5 L.Ed.2d 760 (1961). Thus, the Court, per Warren, C.J., pointed out in *Spano* that the ban against "involuntary" confessions turns not only on their reliability but on the notion that "the police must obey the law while enforcing the law." And the Court, again speaking through the Chief Justice, acknowledged in *Blackburn* that "a *complex of values* underlies the strictures against use by the state of confessions which, by way of *convenient shorthand,* this Court terms involuntary." (Emphasis added.)

Perhaps the most emphatic statement of the point that the untrustworthiness of a confession was not (or no longer) the principal reason for excluding it appears in one of Justice Frankfurter's last opinions on the subject. Writing for the Court in *Rogers,* he observed: "Our decisions under [the Fourteenth Amendment] have made clear that convictions following the admission into evidence of [involuntary confessions] cannot stand * * * not so much because such confessions are unlikely to be true but because the methods used to extract them offend an underlying principle in the enforcement of our criminal law: that ours is an accusatorial and not an inquisitorial system. * * * Indeed, in many of the cases [reversing] state convictions involving the use of confessions obtained by impermissible methods, independent corroborating evidence left little doubt of the truth of what the defendant had confessed."[d]

Although, theoretically, the "police methods" and "trustworthiness" standards for admitting confessions are to be applied independently of each other, in practice they often overlap. Even though it might be conclusively demonstrated that "offensive" police interrogation methods did not produce an "untrustworthy" confession *in the particular case* before the Court, the continued use of such methods is likely to create a substantial risk that other suspects subjected to similar tactics would falsely confess. See Kamisar, *What is an "Involuntary" Confession?*, 17 Rutgers L.Rev. 728, 754–55 (1963), reprinted in Kamisar, Police Interrogation and Confessions 1, 20–22 (1980) (hereinafter referred to as Kamisar Essays).

What *are* the objectionable police methods which render a resulting confession "involuntary"? In the advanced stages of the test, at least, the use or threatened use of physical violence or the kind of protracted relay interrogation that occurred in *Ashcraft*, supra, rendered any resulting confession inadmissible *per se*. In the main, however, it is difficult to isolate any particular interrogation tactic and say that, standing alone, it is so "coercive" or so "offensive" that it requires the exclusion of any resulting confession. For the significant fact about the great bulk of the "involuntary confessions" cases is that "none of them turned on the presence or absence of a single controlling criterion; each reflected a careful scrutiny of all the surrounding circumstances" *Schneckloth v. Bustamonte* (p. 332) at 226, 93 S.Ct. at 2047. And the totality of the surrounding circumstances included "both the characteristics of the accused [many of whom were uneducated, of low mentality or emotionally unstable] and the details of the interrogation." Ibid.

Nevertheless, the pre-*Escobedo*, pre-*Miranda* cases reveal numerous police practices which, if not impermissible *per se*, certainly militate heavily against the "voluntariness" of any resulting confession: stripping off defendant's clothes and keeping him naked for several hours, *Malinski v. New York*, 324 U.S. 401, 65 S.Ct. 781, 89 L.Ed. 1029 (1945); informing defendant that state financial aid for her infant children would be cut off, and her children taken from her, if she failed to "cooperate" with police, *Lynumn v. Illinois*, 372 U.S. 528, 83 S.Ct. 917, 9 L.Ed.2d 922 (1963); after defendant persisted in his denial of guilt, pretending to "bring in" defendant's wife (who suffered from arthritis) for questioning, *Rogers v. Richmond*, supra; repeatedly rejecting defendant's requests to phone his wife and repeatedly informing him that he would not be able to call her or anyone else unless and until he gave the police a statement, *Haynes v. Washington*, 373 U.S. 503, 83 S.Ct. 1336, 10 L.Ed.2d 513 (1963); removing defendant from jail to a distant place in order to thwart the efforts of his friends or relatives to secure his release, or at least to contact him, *Ward v. Texas*, 316 U.S. 547, 62 S.Ct. 1139, 86 L.Ed. 1663 (1942); utilization of a state-employed psychiatrist, with considerable knowledge of hypnosis, who posed as a "general practitioner" who would provide

---

d. In admitting the confession, the *Rogers* trial court had found that the interrogation tactics "had no tendency to produce a confession that was not in accord with the truth." The Supreme Court did not consider the finding *unwarranted*, but *irrelevant*. The admissibility of the confession had been decided "by reference to a legal standard which took into account the circumstance of probable truth or falsity"—"and this is not a permissible standard under the Due Process Clause." See Stephen J. Schulhofer, *Confessions and the Court*, 79 Mich.L.Rev. 865, 867 (1981).

defendant with the medical relief he needed and succeeded in obtaining a confession from defendant by skillful and suggestive questioning, *Leyra v. Denno,* 347 U.S. 556, 74 S.Ct. 716, 98 L.Ed. 948 (1954); utilization of defendant's "childhood friend," then a fledgling police officer, who, pursuant to his superiors' instructions, pretended that defendant's phone call had gotten his "friend" "in a lot of trouble," so much so that his "friend's" job was in jeopardy, and loss of his job would prove disastrous to his "friend's" wife and children, *Spano,* supra.

Consider Albert Alschuler, *Constraint and Confessions,* 74 Denv.U.L.Rev. 957 (1997): "The Court should define the term coerced confession to mean a confession caused by offensive governmental conduct, period. * * * Shifting their attention almost entirely from the minds of suspects to the conduct of government officers, courts should abandon the search for 'overborne wills' and attempts to assess the quality of individual choices."

B. The Shortcomings of the "Voluntariness" Test

Although the Supreme Court customarily used the terms "voluntariness" and "involuntariness" in explaining and applying the due process test for the admissibility of confessions, the "voluntariness" concept seems to be at once too wide and too narrow. In one sense, in the sense of wanting to confess, or doing so in a completely spontaneous manner, "in the sense of a confession to a priest merely to rid one's soul of a sense of guilt" (Jackson, J., dissenting in *Ashcraft v. Tennessee*), few criminal confessions reviewed by the courts, if any, had been "voluntary." On the other hand, in the sense that the situation always presents a "choice" between two alternatives, either one disagreeable, to be sure, *all* confessions are "voluntary." See 3 Wigmore, § 824.

Moreover, as the rationales for the Court's coerced confession cases evolved, it became increasingly doubtful that terms such as "voluntariness," "coercion," and "breaking the will" were very helpful in resolving the issue. For such terms do not focus directly on either the risk of untrue confessions or the offensiveness of police interrogation methods employed in eliciting the confession. See Paulsen, supra, at 429–30.

As the Court, per O'Connor, J., observed in *Miller v. Fenton,* 474 U.S. 104, 106 S.Ct. 445, 88 L.Ed.2d 405 (1985) (holding that the "voluntariness" of a confession is not a "factual issue" but "a legal question meriting independent consideration in a federal habeas corpus proceeding"): "[T]he admissibility of a confession turns as much on whether the techniques for extracting the statements, as applied to *this* suspect, are compatible with a system that presumes innocence and assures that a conviction will not be secured by inquisitorial means as on whether the defendant's will was in fact overborne. [The] hybrid quality of the voluntariness inquiry, subsuming, as it does, a 'complex of values,' *Blackburn,* itself militates against treating the question as one of simple historical fact." As the *Miller* Court also noted, "[t]he voluntariness rubric has been variously condemned as 'useless,' 'perplexing,' and 'legal "double-talk." ' "

Nor was "the elusive, measureless standard of psychological coercion heretofore developed in this Court by accretion on almost an ad hoc, case-by-case basis," as Justice Clark described it, dissenting in *Reck v. Pate,* 367 U.S. 433, 81 S.Ct. 1541, 6 L.Ed.2d 948 (1961); a test which seemed to permit constitutionally permissible police interrogation to vary widely according to how dull or alert or soft or tough the particular suspect, see e.g., Maguire, *Evidence of Guilt* 134 fn. 5 (1959); likely to guide or to shape police conduct very much, if at all.

Moreover, as pointed out in Schulhofer, fn. d supra, at 869–70, because of its ambiguity and "its subtle mixture of factual and legal elements," the "voluntariness" test "virtually invited [trial judges] to give weight to their subjective preferences" and "discouraged review even by the most conscientious appellate judges." See also Kamisar Essays at 12–25, 69–76; LaFave & Israel, § 6.2(d); Herman, *The Supreme Court, the Attorney General, and the Good Old Days of Police Interrogation*, 48 Ohio St.L.J. 733, 745–55 (1987); Stone, *The Miranda Doctrine in the Burger Court*, 1977 Sup.Ct.Rev. 99, 102–03; W. White, *Defending Miranda: A Reply to Professor Caplan*, 39 Vand.L.Rev. 1, 7–9, 11–16 (1986).[a]

As police interrogators made greater use of "psychological" techniques over the years, the always difficult problems of proof confronting the alleged victims of improper interrogation practices became increasingly arduous. Disputes over whether physical violence occurred are not always easy to resolve, but evidence of "mental" or "psychological" coercion is especially elusive. Frequently, the defendant was inarticulate, which aggravated the difficulties of recreating the tenor and atmosphere of the police questioning or the *manner* in which the appropriate advice about the suspect's rights might have been given or, if properly given, subsequently undermined.

Moreover, the local courts almost always resolved the almost inevitable "swearing contest" over what happened behind the closed doors in favor of the police, perhaps for the reasons suggested by Walter Schaefer, *Federalism and State Criminal Procedure*, 70 Harv.L.Rev. 1, 7 (1956): "In the field of criminal procedure [a] strong local interest competes only against an ideal. Local interest is concerned with the particular case and with the guilt or innocence of the particular individual. * * * While it is hard indeed for any judge to set apart the question of the guilt or innocence of a particular defendant and focus solely upon the procedural aspect of the case, it becomes easier [in] a reviewing court where the impact of the evidence is diluted. The more remote the court, the easier it is to consider the case in terms of a hypothetical defendant accused of crime, instead of a particular man whose guilt has been established."[b]

---

a. But consider Gerald Caplan, *Questioning Miranda*, 38 Vand.L.Rev. 1417, 1433–34 (1985): "[The voluntariness test] allowed the Court to move carefully, to feel its way, and to make its judgments without fear of prematurely constitutionalizing interrogation practices. [The] Court's failure to state the basis for a particular decision or its blurring of a holding in the veiled attire of the 'totality of the circumstances' can be seen as shrewd and responsible pragmatism. Pragmatism may have been preferable to principles at a time when there was little general agreement on the principles to be applied. [If] the development of the voluntariness test had not come to a near end with the advent of *Miranda*, perhaps the test would have continued to achieve definition and improved serviceability."

b. This may help to explain the strikingly different reactions of the state courts and the U.S. Supreme Court to the situation in *Mincey v. Arizona*, 437 U.S. 385, 98 S.Ct. 2408, 57 L.Ed.2d 290 (1978) (other aspects of which are discussed at pp. 2310–32, 777). Just a few hours before the interrogation occurred, Mincey had been seriously wounded during a narcotics raid which resulted in the death of a police officer. According to the attending physician, Mincey had arrived at the hospital "depressed almost to the point of coma." At the time Detective Hust questioned him, Mincey's

condition was still sufficiently serious that he was in the intensive care unit. Lying on his back on a hospital bed, encumbered by tubes, needles and breathing apparatus, Mincey (according to the Supreme Court) clearly and repeatedly expressed his wish not to be interrogated, but Hust continued to question him. Unable to speak because of the tube in his mouth, Mincey responded to Hust's questions by writing answers on pieces of paper provided by the hospital, at one point writing: "This is all I can say without a lawyer." (In a written report dated about a week later, Hust transcribed Mincey's answers and added the questions he believed he had asked.)

Under these circumstances, the trial court found "with unmistakable clarity" that Mincey's statements were "voluntary" and thus, despite being obtained in violation of *Miranda*, admissible for impeachment purposes. (On this point, see Ch. 11, § 4 infra). The state supreme court unanimously affirmed. On the basis of its independent evaluation of the record, the Court, per Stewart, J., reversed. It noted, inter alia, that "the reliability of Hust's report [reconstructing the interrogation] is uncertain." It concluded that "the undisputed evidence makes clear that Mincey wanted *not* to answer Detective Hust" but that—"weakened by pain and shock, isolated from family, friends and

Under the old case-by-case approach, however, the defendant could not often avail himself of the "remoteness" of the U.S. Supreme Court. In the thirty years since *Brown v. Mississippi,* the Court had taken an average of about one state confession case per year and *two-thirds of these* had been "death penalty" cases. Indeed, the Court's workload was so great that it even denied a hearing in most "death penalty" cases. See Kamisar Essays 75. Almost no garden-variety criminal defendant who cried "coerced confession" but lost the "swearing contest" below was likely to survive the winnowing process above. Not surprisingly, Justice Black remarked in the course of the oral arguments in *Miranda:* "[I]f you are going to determine [the admissibility of the confession] each time on the circumstances, [if] this Court will take them one by one [it] is more than we are capable of doing."

Although the 1964 *Massiah* and *Escobedo* cases and the 1966 *Miranda* case (all discussed infra) were to catch heavy criticism, "[g]iven the Court's inability to articulate a clear and predictable definition of 'voluntariness,' the apparent persistence of state courts in utilizing the ambiguity of the concept to validate confessions of doubtful constitutionality, and the resultant burden on its own workload, it seemed inevitable that the Court would seek 'some automatic device by which the potential evils of incommunicado interrogation [could] be controlled.'" Geoffrey R. Stone, *The Miranda Doctrine in the Burger Court,* 1977 Sup.Ct.Rev. 102–03 (quoting from Schaefer, *The Suspect and Society* 10 (1967)).[c]

C. The *McNabb-Mallory* Rule: Supervisory Authority Over Federal Criminal Justice vs. Fourteenth Amendment due Process

As Justice FRANKFURTER pointed out for the majority in the famous case of McNABB v. UNITED STATES, 318 U.S. 332, 63 S.Ct. 608, 87 L.Ed. 819 (1943), while the power of the Court to upset *state* convictions is limited to the enforcement of fourteenth amendment due process, the standards of *federal* criminal

legal counsel, and barely conscious"—Mincey's "will was simply overborne."

Rehnquist, J., dissented from the holding that Mincey's statements were involuntary and—as was true of so many of the older "involuntariness" cases—disputed the Court's reading of the record: "[The Court] ignores entirely some evidence of voluntariness and distinguishes away yet other testimony. * * * Despite the contrary impression given by the Court, [the state supreme court's] opinion casts no doubt on the testimony or report of Detective Hust. The Court is thus left solely with its own conclusions as to the reliability of various witnesses based on a re-examination of the record on appeal. * * * I believe that the trial court was entitled to conclude that, notwithstanding Mincey's medical condition, his statements in the intensive care unit were admissible. [T]hat the same court might have been equally entitled to reach the opposite conclusion does not justify this Court's adopting the opposite conclusion."

c. *The continued vitality of the pre-Miranda voluntariness test.* Since the landmark *Miranda* case, the police must give a suspect the now familiar warnings and obtain a waiver of his rights before subjecting him to "custodial interrogation." However, the "old" due process-voluntariness test is still important in a

number of situations, e.g., when the police question a suspect not in "custody"; when the police question a suspect who waives his rights and agrees to talk, but denies any involvement in the crime. See generally this Ch., § 4. Moreover, the distinction between an "involuntary" confession and one obtained only in violation of *Miranda* is important in a number of procedural contexts, e.g., use of the confession for impeachment purposes. See generally Ch. 11, § 4.

Thus, "[c]areful attention to the voluntariness issue remains an imperative, though sometimes overlooked, obligation of court and counsel," Schulhofer, supra, at 878. To illustrate his point, Professor Schulhofer refers to *United States v. Mesa,* discussed at pp. 495, 514. The *Mesa* court's rejection of a *Miranda* challenge, observes Schulhofer, id. at 878 n. 58, was "based on particularities of *Miranda's* rationale and would by no means preclude a voluntariness claim. Yet the defense never argued, and so the [Third Circuit] never considered, whether the statements made by this psychologically distraught suspect, on the verge of suicide, [who had barricaded himself in a motel room and threatened that he would not surrender peacefully], in the course of a three-and-one-half-hour conversation [with an FBI crisis negotiator] under highly charged circumstances, were admissible under the due process test."

justice "are not satisfied merely by observance of those minimal historic safeguards." Rather, the Court can, and has, formulated rules of evidence in the exercise of its "supervisory authority" over the administration of federal criminal justice which go well beyond due process requirements.[a] A good example was the significance given to the fact that incriminating statements were obtained during illegal detention, i.e., while the suspect was held in violation of federal statutory requirements that he be promptly taken before a committing magistrate to ascertain whether good cause exists to hold him for trial. Although, during this period, an otherwise voluntary confession was not rendered inadmissible in a *state* prosecution solely because it was elicited during prolonged and hence illegal precommitment detention (this was only *one* of many factors in determining whether a confession was voluntary), the 1943 *McNabb* case, although hardly free from ambiguity, seemed to hold that such a confession had to be excluded from *federal* prosecutions.

The *McNabb* rule was heavily criticized by law enforcement spokesmen and many members of Congress and begrudgingly interpreted by most lower federal courts. See generally James E. Hogan & Joseph M. Snee, *The McNabb–Mallory Rule: Its Rise, Rationale and Rescue,* 47 Geo.L.J. 1 (1958). However, it was emphatically reaffirmed in MALLORY v. UNITED STATES, 354 U.S. 449, 77 S.Ct. 1356, 1 L.Ed.2d 1479 (1957), where, speaking for a unanimous Court, Justice FRANKFURTER observed:

"We cannot sanction this extended delay [some seven hours], resulting in confession, without subordinating [Fed.R.Crim.P. 5(a), requiring that an arrestee be taken 'without unnecessary delay' to the nearest available committing officer] to the discretion of arresting officers in finding exceptional circumstances for its disregard. [There is no escape] from the constraint laid upon the police by that Rule in that two other suspects were involved for the same crime. Presumably, whomever the police arrest they must arrest on 'probable cause.' It is not the function of the police to arrest, as it were, at large and to use an interrogating process at police headquarters in order to determine whom they should charge before a committing magistrate on 'probable cause.' "

Only a handful of states adopted the *McNabb-Mallory* rule or its equivalent on their own initiative.[b] But many hoped (and many others feared) that some day

---

a. For a long, hard look at the federal courts' exercise of "supervisory powers" over the administration of federal criminal justice generally and a look back at *McNabb,* regarded by many as the first supervisory power decision, see Sara Sun Beale, *Reconsidering Supervisory Power in Criminal Cases: Constitutional and Statutory Limits on the Authority of the Federal Courts,* 84 Colum.L.Rev. 1433 (1984). Extracts from Professor Beale's article appear at p. 47.

b. It was not until 1960 that the states' unanimity in refusing to follow the Supreme Court's lead in the *McNabb-Mallory* line of cases was broken. See *People v. Hamilton,* 102 N.W.2d 738, 741–43 (Mich.1960); Rothblatt & Rothblatt, *Police Interrogation: The Right to Counsel and to Prompt Arraignment,* 27 Brooklyn L.Rev. 24, 40–44 (1960). On the eve of *Miranda,* two more states adopted an equivalent of the rule, Delaware, see *Webster v. State,* 213 A.2d 298, 301 (Del.1965); and Connecticut, by legislation, see *State v. Vollhardt,* 244 A.2d 601, 607 (Conn.1968) (subsequent case construing statute). In recent years at least three more state courts—Maryland, Montana, and Pennsylvania—adopted some equivalent of the rule. See *Johnson v. State,* 384 A.2d 709, 714–18 (Md.1978); *State v. Benbo,* 570 P.2d 894, 899–900 (Mont.1977); *Commonwealth v. Davenport,* 370 A.2d 301, 306 (Pa.1977); *Commonwealth v. Futch,* 290 A.2d 417, 418–19 (Pa. 1972).

The life of Maryland's version of the *McNabb-Mallory* rule, adopted in the 1978 *Johnson* case, "was short and unhappy." Donald E. Wilkes, *The New Federalism in Criminal Procedure in 1984: Death of the Phoenix?,* in Developments in State Constitutional Law 166, 170 (B. McGraw ed. 1985). The *Johnson* rule was usually interpreted begrudgingly and—in a "legislative blow to the new federalism"—repealed by statute in 1981. See id. at 169–171.

For a close examination and strong criticism of the "state court revival" *McNabb-Mallory* rule, see Note, 72 J.Crim.L. & C. 204 (1981).

the Court would apply the rule to the states as a matter of fourteenth amendment due process. The Court never did. Instead, in the years since the 1957 *Mallory* decision, the last of the *McNabb* line of cases, the Court closed in on the state confession problem by making increasing resort to the right to counsel and the privilege against self-incrimination. By such means the state confession rules were eventually to *go beyond* the *McNabb-Mallory* doctrine in a number of respects.[c]

D. THE RIGHT TO COUNSEL AND THE ANALOGY
TO THE ACCUSATORIAL, ADVERSARY TRIAL

CROOKER v. CALIFORNIA, 357 U.S. 433, 78 S.Ct. 1287, 2 L.Ed.2d 1448 (1958), involved a petitioner who attended one year of law school, during which time he studied criminal law, and who indicated in his dealings with the police that he was fully aware of his right to remain silent. On the basis of a challenged confession, he was convicted of murder of his paramour and sentenced to death. He contended that by persisting in interrogating him after denying his specific request to contact his lawyer the police violated his due process right to legal representation and advice and that therefore use of any confession obtained from him under these circumstances should be barred even though "freely" and "voluntarily" made under traditional standards. Such a rule retorted the Court, per CLARK, J., "would have [a] devastating effect on enforcement of criminal law, for it would effectively preclude police questioning—*fair as well as unfair*—until the accused was afforded opportunity to call his attorney. Due process, a concept 'less rigid and more fluid than those envisaged in other specific and particular provisions of the Bill of Rights,' *Betts v. Brady,* demands no such rule."

In his dissenting opinion, Justice DOUGLAS, with whom Warren, C.J., and Black and Brennan, JJ., joined, insisted: "The right to have counsel at the pretrial stage is often necessary to give meaning and protection to the right to be heard at the trial itself. It may also be necessary as a restraint on the coercive power of the police. [The] demands of our civilization expressed in the Due Process Clause require that the accused who wants a counsel should have one at any time after the moment of arrest."

In the companion case of CICENIA v. LA GAY, 357 U.S. 504, 78 S.Ct. 1297, 2 L.Ed.2d 1523 (1958), not only did petitioner unsuccessfully ask to see his lawyer while he was being questioned by the police, but his lawyer, who arrived at the police station while petitioner was being interrogated, repeatedly (and unsuccessfully) asked to see his client. Moreover, petitioner was not well educated as was Crooker. Nevertheless, the Court affirmed the murder conviction (which led to a life sentence), disposing of petitioner's contention that he had a constitutional right to confer with counsel on the authority of *Crooker.* With the exception of Justice Brennan, who took no part in the case, the Court split along the same lines it had in *Crooker.*

The following year, however, by virtue of SPANO v. NEW YORK, it appeared that the Court had reached the view that once a person was *formally charged* by indictment or information his constitutional right to counsel had "begun"—at least his right to the assistance of counsel he himself had retained. Four concurring Justices took this position in *Spano:* Justices Black, Douglas and Brennan, all

The Note maintains, id. at 241, that "current constitutional law addresses many of the original concerns underlying delay statutes, obviating the need for reliance on a doctrine of implied statutory exclusion."

c. Title II of the Omnibus Crime Control and Safe Streets Act of 1968 purports to repeal (among other judicial doctrines) the *McNabb-Mallory* rule. Because the possible constitutional vulnerability of this 1968 provision turns in part on an appraisal of *Miranda,* treatment of this point is postponed until p. 560.

of whom had dissented in *Crooker;* and newly appointed Justice Stewart, who had replaced Justice Burton.

In separate concurring opinions both Justice Douglas (joined by Black and Brennan, JJ.) and Justice Stewart (joined by Douglas and Brennan, JJ.) stressed that *Spano* was not a case where the police were questioning a suspect in the course of investigating an unsolved crime but one where the subject of interrogation was already under indictment for murder when he surrendered to the authorities. Both concurring opinions also measured the proceedings in the "interrogation" room against the standard of a public trial and formal judicial proceedings. Thus Justice STEWART observed: "Under our system of justice an indictment is supposed to be followed by an arraignment and a trial. * * * What followed the petitioner's surrender in this case was not arraignment in a court of law, but an all-night inquisition in a prosecutor's office, a police station, and an automobile. * * * Our Constitution guarantees the assistance of counsel to a man on trial for his life in an orderly courtroom, presided over by a judge, open to the public, and protected by all the procedural safeguards of the law. Surely a Constitution which promises that much can vouchsafe no less to the same man under midnight inquisition in the squad room of a police station."

As we have already seen, a majority of the *Spano* Court did not go off on "right to counsel" grounds, finding the confession inadmissible on straight "coerced confession" grounds, but the Chief Justice, who wrote the majority opinion, had taken the position, a year earlier in *Crooker,* that the right to counsel should "begin" even earlier than at the point of indictment. Thus, counting heads, it appeared that by 1959 the view of the concurring Justices in *Spano* commanded a majority of the Court.

E. *MASSIAH AND ESCOBEDO*: THE COURT CLOSES IN ON THE "CONFESSION PROBLEM"

"There is a case in the Supreme Court now from Illinois, *People v. Escobedo,* that involves this very issue [of when the right to counsel begins] and I am scared that the Court is going to hold that this right exists from the time of arrest—if a person asks for counsel and he is not given counsel, anything you get from him after that has to be excluded."

—Fred E. Inbau, *A Forum on the Interrogation of the Accused,* 49 Corn.L.Q. 382, 401 (January 31, 1964).

Five years after *Spano,* in MASSIAH v. UNITED STATES, 377 U.S. 201, 84 S.Ct. 1199, 12 L.Ed.2d 246 (1964), a 6–3 majority (consisting of the four concurring Justices in *Spano,* Chief Justice Warren, and newly appointed Justice Goldberg) adopted the view advanced in the *Spano* concurring opinions. *Massiah* arose as follows: After he had been indicted for federal narcotics violations, Massiah retained a lawyer, pled not guilty, and was released on bail. A codefendant, Colson, invited him to discuss the pending case in Colson's car, parked on a city street. Unknown to Massiah, Colson had decided to cooperate with federal agents in their continuing investigation of the case. A radio transmitter was installed under the front seat of Colson's car, enabling a nearby agent (Murphy), who was equipped with a recording device, to overhear the Massiah–Colson conversation. As expected, Massiah made several damaging admissions.

It is hardly surprising that the *Massiah* dissenters considered the facts of the case a "peculiarly inappropriate" setting for a major breakthrough on the "police interrogation"-"confession" front. Even if the *Spano* concurring opinions had come to represent the majority view, argued then Solicitor General Archibald Cox, Massiah's statements should still be admissible because at the time he made them he was neither in "custody"—not even in the loosest sense—nor undergoing "police interrogation." He was under no "official pressure" to answer questions or even to engage in conversation; his conversation "was not affected by even that degree of constraint which may result from a suspect's knowledge that he is talking to a law enforcement officer."[a] Moreover, Colson, a layman unskilled in the art of interrogation, did not and probably could not utilize any of the standard techniques to induce Massiah to incriminate himself.[b]

Nevertheless, as the *Massiah* majority, per STEWART, J., saw it, the decisive feature of the case was that after he had been indicted—"and therefore at a time when he was clearly entitled to a lawyer's help" and at a time when he was awaiting trial "in an orderly courtroom, presided over by a judge, open to the public, and protected by all the procedural safeguards of the law"—Massiah had been subjected to a "completely extrajudicial" police-orchestrated proceeding designed to obtain incriminating statements from him. Besides, if in one respect—the lack of an inherently or potentially "coercive atmosphere"—Massiah had been less seriously imposed upon than the average "confession" defendant, he was more seriously imposed upon in another respect—he did not, and could not be expected to, keep his guard up because he was not even aware that he was dealing with a government agent[c]: "We hold that the petitioner was denied the basic protections of [the right to counsel] when there was used against him at his trial evidence of his own incriminating words, which federal agents had deliberately elicited from him after he had been indicted and in the absence of his counsel. It is true that in the *Spano* case the defendant was interrogated in a police station, while here the damaging testimony was elicited from [him] without his knowledge while he was free on bail. But, as Judge Hays pointed out in his dissent in the [Second Circuit], 'if such a rule is to have any efficacy it must apply to indirect and surreptitious interrogations as well as those conducted in the jailhouse. In this case, Massiah was more seriously imposed upon * * * because he did not even know that he was under interrogation by a government agent.' * * *

"We do not question that in this case, as in many cases, it was entirely proper to continue an investigation of the suspected criminal activities of the defendant and his alleged confederates, even though the defendant had already been indicted. All that we hold is that the defendant's own incriminating statements, obtained by federal agents under the circumstances here disclosed, could not constitutionally be used by the prosecution as evidence against *him* at his trial."

Dissenting Justice WHITE, joined by Clark and Harlan, JJ., protested: "[H]ere there was no substitution of brutality for brains, no inherent danger of police coercion justifying the prophylactic effect of another exclusionary rule. Massiah was not being interrogated in a police station, was not surrounded by numerous officers or questioned in relays, and was not forbidden access to others.

---

a. Extensive extracts from the Government's brief and oral argument in *Massiah* appear in Kamisar Essays 171–73.

b. The Massiah–Colson conversation was not only broadcast to a nearby federal agent, but secretly tape-recorded by Colson. In the district court, however, Massiah successfully objected to the admission of these tapes on the ground that they implicated other defendants and contained privileged matters. The Government maintained that the recording confirmed the testimony of Agent Murphy that Colson did not coerce Massiah into making any incriminating statements or even induce him by appeals to talk in the guise of friendship and filed the recording with the clerk of the Court. Colson did not testify himself. Massiah did not testify either or otherwise contradict Murphy's testimony about the meeting. See Kamisar Essays at 278 fn. 202.

c. Massiah's unawareness that he was, in effect, talking to the police, and thus his inability to protect himself, "was a nice point (or counterpoint), but it was hardly the decisive one." Kamisar Essays 174. Any doubts that the *Massiah* doctrine also applies when the suspect realizes he is in the presence of the police were removed in *Brewer v. Williams* (1977), p. 594.

Law enforcement may have the elements of a contest about it, but it is not a game."

The dissenters were "unable to see how this case presents an unconstitutional interference with Massiah's right to counsel. Massiah was not prevented from consulting with counsel as often as he wished. No meetings with counsel were disturbed or spied upon. Preparation for trial was in no way obstructed. It is only a sterile syllogism—an unsound one besides—to say that because Massiah had a right to counsel's aid before and during the trial, his out-of-court conversations and admissions must be excluded if obtained without counsel's consent or presence."

"This case," maintained the dissenters, "cannot be analogized to [Canon 9 of the ABA's Canons of Professional Ethics] forbidding an attorney to talk to the opposing party litigant outside the presence of his counsel.[d] Aside from the fact that [the canons] are not of constitutional dimensions, [Canon 9] deals with the conduct of lawyers and not with the conduct of investigators.[e] Lawyers are forbidden to interview the opposing party because of the supposed imbalance of legal skill and acumen between the lawyer and the party litigant; the reason for the rule does not apply to nonlawyers and certainly not to Colson, Massiah's codefendant."

Were the *Massiah* dissenters right when they observed that "the reason given for the result here—the admissions were obtained in the absence of counsel—would seem equally pertinent to statements obtained at any time after the right to counsel attaches, whether there has been an indictment or not"? Does a suspect who has not yet been indicted need "a lawyer's help" every bit as much as one who has been formally charged? By drawing the line at the initiation of formal judicial proceedings, had Justice Stewart (author of *Massiah,* but a dissenter in *Escobedo,* infra) "painted himself into a corner [from] which he could extricate himself only by a highly formalistic reading of the Sixth Amendment"? See Lawrence Herman, *The Supreme Court and Restrictions on Police Interrogation,* 25 Ohio St.L.J. 449, 491 (1964).

As made plain a short five weeks later in the same Term, ESCOBEDO v. ILLINOIS, 378 U.S. 478, 84 S.Ct. 1758, 12 L.Ed.2d 977 (1964), a majority of the Court was not about to give the Sixth Amendment a formalistic reading. Escobedo's interrogation had occurred before "judicial" or "adversary" proceedings had commenced against him, but, as dissenting Justice Stewart characterized the *Escobedo* majority's reasoning, "[t]he Court disregards this basic difference between the present case and Massiah's, with the bland assertion that 'that fact should make no difference.'"

Escobedo arose as follows: On the night of January 19, petitioner's brother-in-law was fatally shot. A few hours later petitioner was taken into custody for questioning, but he made no statement and was released the following afternoon pursuant to a writ of habeas corpus obtained by his retained counsel. On January 30, one Di Gerlando, who was then in police custody and who was later indicted for the murder along with petitioner, stated that petitioner had fired the shots which killed his brother-in-law. That evening petitioner was again arrested and

---

d. Does (should) this ethical rule apply to criminal proceedings? See Note 4, p. 605.

e. But consider Breitel, C.J., in *People v. Hobson,* 348 N.E.2d 894, 898 (N.Y.1976): "[I]t would not be rational, logical, moral or realistic to make any distinction between a lawyer acting for the State who [by seeking a waiver of the right to counsel from a suspect in the absence of, and without notification to, his lawyer] violates [the Code of Professional Responsibility] directly and one who indirectly uses the admissions improperly obtained by a police officer, who is the badged and uniformed representative of the State." See also *United States v. Springer,* 460 F.2d 1344, 1354–55 (7th Cir.1972) (Judge (now Justice) Stevens, dissenting).

taken to police headquarters. En route to the police station he was told that Di Gerlando had named him as the one who fired the fatal shots and that he might as well admit it, but petitioner replied (probably because his attorney had obtained his release from police custody only 11 days earlier or because he had consulted with his attorney in the meantime): "I am sorry but I would like to have advice from my lawyer." Shortly after petitioner reached police headquarters, his retained lawyer arrived and spent the next several hours trying unsuccessfully to speak to his client. He talked to every officer he could find, but was repeatedly told that he could not see his client and that he would have to get a writ of habeas corpus. In the meantime, petitioner repeatedly but unsuccessfully asked to speak to his lawyer. Instead, the police arranged a confrontation between petitioner and Di Gerlando. Petitioner denied that he had fired the fatal shots, claiming that Di Gerlando had done so, but thereby implicated himself in the murder plot. Petitioner's subsequent statement, to an assistant prosecutor who asked carefully framed questions, was admitted into evidence and he was convicted of murder. The Supreme Court of Illinois affirmed.

When certiorari was granted, the lawyers involved realized, as did close students of the problem, that *Escobedo* might be a momentous case. Bernard Weisberg, author of an important article on police interrogation, *Police Interrogation of Arrested Persons: A Skeptical View*, 52 J.Crim.L. & P.S. 21 (1961), argued the case for the ACLU, as *amicus curiae*. Because he thought it "playing Hamlet without the ghost to discuss police questioning without knowing what such questioning is really like," in his article Weisberg had made very extensive use of the interrogation manuals. He did the same in his *Escobedo* brief, maintaining that these books "are invaluable because they vividly describe the kind of interrogation practices which are accepted as lawful and proper under the best current standards of professional police work." What these manuals reveal, argued Weisberg, "is that 'fair and reasonable' and 'effective interrogation' is basically unfair and inherently coercive."[f]

Former Northwestern University law professor James Thompson (who later became Governor of Illinois) argued the *Escobedo* case for the state. He warned the U.S. Supreme Court: "[A decision that the right to counsel begins at the moment of arrest] means the end of confessions as a tool of law enforcement. [For] once this petitioner's claim with Illinois is settled, the inevitable progression of the law must follow:

"*First,* if the right to counsel attaches at the moment of arrest [as the dissent in *Crooker* maintained], then it can hardly be denied that this right must be available to the poor as well as to the rich. * * *

"*Second,* if indigent criminal defendants are entitled to counsel from the moment of arrest, then already established law makes it clear that such a right does not depend upon a request. [N]ot only must the state furnish counsel to the indigent defendant at this stage of the criminal proceeding, it must make sure that he does not waive the right through ignorance of its existence. * * * "[g]

---

f. Weisberg's article on confessions, apparently the first to make extensive use of the interrogation manuals, and his *Escobedo* brief set the fashion for civil libertarians. The ACLU brief in *Miranda,* primarily the work of Professors Anthony Amsterdam and Paul Mishkin, reprinted a full chapter from one interrogation manual. In turn, Chief Justice Warren's opinion for the Court in *Miranda,* infra, devoted six full pages to extracts from various police manuals and texts "document[ing] procedures employed with success in the past, [and] recom-

mend[ing] various other effective tactics." Many of the examples selected by the *Miranda* Court in 1966 were the same ones Weisberg used in his 1961 article and his 1964 *Escobedo* brief.

g. Thompson's discussion of "the inevitable progression of the law" was, of course, the statement of an advocate; Illinois deemed it advantageous to underscore the extent to which the rule espoused by its adversaries would "cripple" law enforcement. But Escobe-

Added Thompson: "Criminal defendants, rich as well as poor, enjoy more protection from unjust conviction today than at any time in our history. 'The terrible engine' of the criminal law has been repeatedly braked by this Court, by state courts and legislatures and by fair and honest administration of the law by prosecutors and police. We need to guard against its derailment. * * * "

A 5–4 majority of the Court, per GOLDBERG, J., struck down Escobedo's confession, but, until *Miranda* moved *Escobedo* off center stage two years later, the scope and meaning of the decision was a matter of strong and widespread disagreement. In large part this was due to the accordion-like quality of the *Escobedo* opinion. At some places the opinion launched so broad an attack on the use of confessions in general and rejected the arguments for an "effective interrogation opportunity" so forcefully that it threatened (or promised) to eliminate virtually all police interrogation. At other places, however, the language of the opinion was so narrow and confining that it arguably limited the case to its special facts:

"The interrogation here was conducted before petitioner was formally indicted. But in the context of this case, that fact should make no difference. When petitioner requested, and was denied, an opportunity to consult with his lawyer, the investigation had ceased to be a general investigation of 'an unsolved crime.' Petitioner had become the accused, and the purpose of the interrogation was to 'get him' to confess his guilt despite his constitutional right not to do so. At the time of his arrest and throughout the course of the interrogation, the police told petitioner that they had convincing evidence that he had fired the fatal shots. Without informing him of his absolute right to remain silent in the face of this accusation, the police urged him to make a statement. * * *

"Petitioner, a layman, was undoubtedly unaware that under Illinois law an admission of 'mere' complicity in the murder plot was legally as damaging as an admission of firing of the fatal shots. The 'guiding hand of counsel' was essential to advise petitioner of his rights in this delicate situation. This was the 'stage when legal aid and advice' were most critical to petitioner. *Massiah.* * * *

"[It] is argued that if the right to counsel is afforded prior to indictment, the number of confessions obtained by the police will diminish significantly, because most confessions are obtained during the period between arrest and indictment, and 'any lawyer worth his salt will tell the suspect in no uncertain terms to make no statement to police under any circumstances.' This argument, of course, cuts two ways. The fact that many confessions are obtained during this period points up its critical nature as a 'stage when legal aid and advice' are surely needed. *Massiah.* The right to counsel would indeed be hollow if it began at a period when few confessions were obtained. * * *

"We have learned the lesson of history, ancient and modern, that a system of criminal law enforcement which comes to depend on the 'confession' will, in the long run, be less reliable and more subject to abuses than a system which depends on extrinsic evidence independently secured through skillful investigation. * * *

"We have also learned the companion lesson of history that no system of criminal justice can, or should, survive if it comes to depend for its continued effectiveness on the citizens' abdication through unawareness of their constitutional rights. No system worth preserving should have to *fear* that if an accused is

do's lawyers were advocates, too, and they could not, or at least did not try to, minimize the impact of the rule they sought. Neither the ACLU brief nor the brief filed by Escobedo's own lawyers ever cited *Gideon, Douglas, Griffin,* or *Carnley.*

Moreover, shortly after *Escobedo* was decided, Thompson continued to view the case essentially the same way, now not as an advocate, but as assistant director of the Northwestern University Law School's Criminal Law Program. See fn. i infra.

permitted to consult with a lawyer, he will become aware of, and exercise, these rights. If the exercise of constitutional rights will thwart the effectiveness of a system of law enforcement, then there is something very wrong with that system.[h]

"We hold, therefore, that where, as here, the investigation is no longer a general inquiry into an unsolved crime but has begun to focus on a particular suspect, the suspect has been taken into police custody, the police carry out a process of interrogations that lends itself to eliciting incriminating statements, the suspect has requested and been denied an opportunity to consult with his lawyer, and the police have not effectively warned him of his absolute constitutional right to remain silent, the accused has been denied 'the Assistance of Counsel' in violation of the Sixth Amendment to the Constitution as 'made obligatory upon the States by the Fourteenth Amendment,' *Gideon,* and that no statement elicited by the police during the interrogation may be used against him at a criminal trial. * * *

"Nothing we have said today affects the power of the police to investigate 'an unsolved crime' by gathering information from witnesses and by other 'proper investigative efforts.' We hold only that when the process shifts from investigatory to accusatory—when its focus is on the accused and its purpose is to elicit a confession—our adversary system begins to operate, and, under the circumstances here, the accused must be permitted to consult with his lawyer."[i]

Dissenting Justice STEWART protested:

"*Massiah* is not in point here. * * * Putting to one side the fact that the case now before us is not a federal case, the vital fact remains that this case does not involve the deliberate interrogation of a defendant after the initiation of judicial proceedings against him. The Court disregards this basic difference between the present case and Massiah's, with the bland assertion that "that fact should make no difference."

"It is 'that fact,' I submit, which makes all the difference. Under our system of criminal justice the institution of formal, meaningful judicial proceedings, by way of indictment, information, or arraignment, marks the point at which a criminal investigation has ended and adversary litigative proceedings have commenced. It is at this point that the constitutional guarantees attach which pertain to a criminal trial."

---

h. But consider Gerald Caplan, *Questioning Miranda,* 38 Vand.L.Rev. 1417, 1440 (1985): "This statement is misleading because the right that the Court was defending, far from being of long standing, was newly discovered, indeed created, in this very opinion. What may have been 'very wrong' was not the extant 'system,' but the right the Court just announced."

i. As to whether *Escobedo* extended the constitutional role of counsel to the preindictment stage "when the process shifts from investigatory to accusatory—when its focus is on the accused and its purpose is to elicit a confession"—or when the process so shifts *and* one or some combination or all of the limiting facts in *Escobedo* are also present, see the summary of the wide disagreement over the probable meaning of the case in Kamisar Essays at 161 fn. 26.

Although many lower courts construed *Escobedo* quite narrowly, James Thompson, who had the distinction of making the losing argument in the case, read it quite broadly. He told a group of prosecuting attorneys attending a criminal law program that "in all cases where the police desire to obtain a confession from a suspect under circumstances like those in *Escobedo* [and] the suspect does not have retained counsel and does not request counsel, the police should, before interrogation, (a) inform him of his right not to say anything; and (b) inform him that anything he does say might be used against him." He also observed: [I]n dealing with [a suspect who, unlike Danny Escobedo,] has not expressly indicated that he is aware of his right to counsel, absolute compliance with the *Escobedo* rule may well require a warning of the right to counsel along with the warning of the privilege against self-incrimination." See the extensive extracts from Thompson's analysis of *Escobedo* in Kamisar Essays, at 66–68.

In a separate dissent, Justice WHITE, joined by Stewart and Clark, JJ., observed:

"[*Massiah*] held that as of the date of the indictment the prosecution is disentitled to secure admissions from the accused. The Court now moves that date back to the time when the prosecution begins to 'focus' on the accused. Although the opinion purports to be limited to the facts of this case, it would be naive to think that the new constitutional right announced will depend upon whether the accused has retained his own counsel, or has asked to consult with counsel in the course of interrogation. At the very least the Court holds that once the accused becomes a suspect and, presumably, is arrested, any admission made to the police thereafter is inadmissible in evidence unless the accused has waived his right to counsel. * * *

"It is incongruous to assume that the provision for counsel in the Sixth Amendment was meant to amend or supersede the self-incrimination provision of the Fifth Amendment, which is now applicable to the States. That amendment addresses itself to the very issue of incriminating admissions of an accused and resolves it by proscribing only compelled statements.

"[The] Court chooses [to] rely on the virtues and morality of a system of criminal law enforcement which does not depend on the 'confession.' No such judgment is to be found in the Constitution. The only 'inquisitions' the Constitution forbids are those which compel incrimination. Escobedo's statements were not compelled and the Court does not hold that they were. * * *

"[The] Court may be concerned with a narrower matter: the unknowing defendant who responds to police questioning because he mistakenly believes that he must and that his admissions will not be used against him. But this worry hardly calls for the broadside the Court has now fired. [If] an accused is told he must answer and did not know better, it would be very doubtful that the resulting admissions could be used against him. When the accused has not been informed of his rights at all the Court characteristically and properly looks very closely at the surrounding circumstances. I would continue to do so. But, in this case Danny Escobedo knew full well that he need not answer and knew full well that his lawyer had advised him not to answer."[j]

ON THE MEANING OF *ESCOBEDO*

1. **What right comes into play?** Once the investigation has ceased to be "a general inquiry of an unsolved crime but has begun to focus on a particular suspect," what right comes into play? The right of the suspect to consult with his lawyer before resuming the interrogation or the right to enjoy his attorney's *continued presence* and *constant advice* from that point on, as a protection in the face of any further police interrogation? Cf. *Massiah*.

2. **The role of counsel.** Consider Gerald Caplan, *Questioning Miranda*, 38 Vand.L.Rev. 1417, 1440–41 (1985): "Danny Escobedo's lawyer had advised him not to say anything to the police. If the homicide detectives had granted Escobedo's request to see his attorney again, there would have been nothing additional for his attorney to communicate. Escobedo had already been given all the assistance his counsel could provide without actually being present to assist his client on a question-by-question basis. Was Escobedo's attorney seeking the right to be present during the interrogation? Probably not. His intent in seeking entry to the homicide bureau was most likely to bring the interrogation to a close. Given

---

j. In a brief separate dissent, Justice Harlan agreed with Justice White that "the rule announced today is most ill-conceived and that it seriously and unjustifiably fetters perfectly legitimate methods of criminal law enforcement."

that a defense attorney's usual objective is to stop the interrogation, it is hard to understand why the Court was so certain that 'no system worth preserving should have to fear that if an accused person is permitted to consult with a lawyer, he will become aware of, and exercise [his] rights,' unless the Court simply believed that there was no social utility in police interrogation. The *Escobedo* opinion contains no hint of anxiety that harm may accrue from a right to counsel: that there may be fewer confessions, and more crime."

3. The "right to remain silent." As we have seen, *Escobedo* refers to a suspect's "absolute constitutional right to remain silent." Where does this right come from? Does the privilege against self-incrimination confer (or was it intended to confer) a right to remain silent or a right to refuse to respond to incriminating questions or only the right to be free of compulsion? See Albert W. Alschuler, *A Peculiar Privilege in Historical Perspective: The Right to Remain Silent*, 94 Mich.L.Rev. 2625, 2630–32 (1996); Joseph D. Grano, *Confessions, Truth, and the Law* 141–43 (1993).

Does the Court simply mean that since the police lack legislative authorization to compel answers, a suspect is not required to provide any? Does the Court mean more—that the Constitution would prevent a legislature from investing police with the power to compel non-incriminating answers? Or does the Court mean that since a layperson cannot be expected to know what statements may be incriminating, if *in the absence of counsel,* she chooses not to incriminate herself, the only practical way she can assure that she will not do so is to remain completely silent?

F.   A Late Arrival on the Scene: The Privilege Against Self-Incrimination

"[Despite] a great deal of emotional writing which elevates the privilege against self-incrimination to 'one of the great landmarks in man's struggle to make himself civilized,' [the] most abundant proof [that it does not prohibit pretrial interrogation] is to be found in the United States. There the privilege is in the Federal Constitution and in [forty-eight state constitutions]. But in none of the forty-nine jurisdictions does it apply to what happens in the police station. The police interrogate freely, sometimes for seven to eight hours on end. The statements thus extracted are given in evidence. [O]nly statements made voluntarily may be given in evidence, but that seems to be interpreted rather liberally, judged by our standards."

—Judge V.G. Hiemstra of the Supreme Court of South Africa, *Abolition of the Right Not to be Questioned,* 80 South African L.J. 187, 194–95 (1963).

As long ago as 1931, Ernest Hopkins, a member of the Wickersham Commission staff, forcefully argued that the "third degree"-indeed, all secret police interrogation as typically practiced-was fundamentally in violation of the privilege against self-incrimination. Ernest Hopkins, *Our Lawless Police* 193–95 (1931). As we have seen, however, the concurring justice in *Spano* and the majorities in *Massiah* and *Escobedo* relied primarily on the right to counsel, not the privilege against self-incrimination-the other essential mainstay of the accusatorial, adversary system. But the "prime suspect"-"focal point"-"accusatory state" test(s) of *Escobedo* threatened the admissibility of even "volunteered" statements. There was reason to think that the Court might be in the process of shaping "a novel right not to confess except knowingly and with the tactical assistance of counsel," Arnold Enker & Sheldon Elsen, *Counsel for the Suspect: Massiah v. United States and Escobedo v. Illinois,* 49 Minn.L.Rev. 47, 60–61, 69, 83 (1964). Thus *critics of Escobedo* turned to the privilege against self-incrimination as a less restrictive alternative. Dissenting in *Escobedo,* Justice White, joined by Clark and Stewart, JJ., observed:

"It is incongruous to assume that the provision for counsel in the Sixth Amendment was meant to amend or supersede the self-incrimination provision of the Fifth Amendment which is now applicable to the States. [*Malloy v. Hogan,* infra.] That amendment addresses itself to the very issue of incriminating admissions and resolves it by proscribing only compelled statements. [That amendment provides no support] for the idea that an accused has an absolute constitutional right not to answer even in the absence of compulsion, [no support for the view that he has] the constitutional right not to incriminate himself by making voluntary disclosures."

Even as Justice White spoke, there was reason to think that, at long last, the privilege against self-incrimination was knocking on the door of the interrogation room. Only a few months before *Escobedo* had been decided, the Court, in MALLOY v. HOGAN, 378 U.S. 1, 84 S.Ct. 1489, 12 L.Ed.2d 653 (1964) (per Brennan, J.), had performed "what might have seemed to some a shotgun wedding of the privilege [against self-incrimination] to the confession rule," Lawrence Herman, *The Supreme Court and Restrictions on Police Interrogation,* 25 Ohio St.L.J. 449, 465 (1965), by declaring that "today the admissibility of a confession in a state criminal prosecution is tested by the same standard applied in federal prosecutions since 1897, when in *Bram v. United States,* 168 U.S. 532, 18 S.Ct. 183, 42 L.Ed. 568, the Court held that '[i]n criminal trials, in the courts of the United States, wherever a question arises whether a confession is incompetent because not voluntary, the issue is controlled by [the self-incrimination] portion of the Fifth Amendment.' "[a]

Whether or not this approach to police interrogation and confessions makes good sense it constitutes very questionable history—at least since *Brown v. Mississippi* (1936). The old *Bram* case might well have furnished a steppingstone to the standard advanced in *Malloy,* but until *Escobedo,* at any rate, it only seemed to amount to an early excursion from the prevailing multifactor or "totality of circumstances" approach. In none of the dozens of federal *or* state confession cases decided by the Court in the 1930's, 1940's and 1950's had the privilege against self-incrimination, certainly not as it applied to judicial proceedings, been the basis for judgment (although it had occasionally been mentioned in an opinion). If the privilege against self-incrimination had been the way to resolve the confession problem, then all the state courts and lower federal courts that had admitted confessions would have been reversed *per curiam.* For it was plain that law enforcement officers could, and without hesitation did, resort to methods they would never consider utilizing at the trial, that they had much greater power over a suspect or defendant away from the restraining influence of a public trial in an open courtroom.

Although certain factors, such as the length of pre-arraignment detention, had been taking on increasing significance, as Justice Frankfurter described the situation in *Culombe v. Connecticut* (1961), neither the privilege against self-incrimination nor any other "single litmus-paper test for constitutionally impermissible interrogation [had] been evolved: neither extensive cross-questioning-deprecated by the English judges; nor undue delay in arraignment-proscribed by *McNabb;* nor failure to caution a prisoner-enjoined by the [English] Judges' Rules;

a. Until the 1960's *Bram* had become a largely forgotten case, but in recent years it has been the subject of close analysis and spirited debate. Compare Lawrence A. Benner, *Requiem for Miranda: The Rehnquist Court's Voluntariness Doctrine in Historical Perspective,* 67 Wash.U.L.Q. 59, 107–11 (1989) and Stephen A. Saltzburg, *Miranda v. Arizona Revisited: Constitutional Law or Judicial Fiat,* 26 Washburn L.J. 1, 4–14 (1986) with Joseph D. Grano, *Confessions, Truth, and the Law* 123–31 (1993).

nor refusal to permit communication with friends and legal counsel at stages in the proceedings when the prisoner is still only a suspect-prohibited by several state statutes." That was why, as Justice Goldberg put it for a majority in *Haynes v. Washington*, 373 U.S. 503, 83 S.Ct. 1336, 10 L.Ed.2d 513 (1963) (only a year before he wrote the opinion of the Court in *Escobedo*), "the line between proper and permissible police conduct and techniques and methods offensive to due process is, at best, a difficult one to draw, particularly in cases such as this where it is necessary to make fine judgments as to the effect of psychologically coercive pressures and inducements on the mind and will of an accused."

Why had the privilege against self-incrimination been excluded from the stationhouse all these years? The legal reasoning was that compulsion to testify meant *legal* compulsion. Since he is threatened neither with perjury for testifying falsely nor contempt for refusing to testify at all, it cannot be said, ran the argument, that the subject of police interrogation is being "compelled" to be "a witness against himself" within the meaning of the privilege-even though he may assume or be led to believe that there *are* legal (or extralegal) sanctions for contumacy. Since the police have no *legal right* to make a suspect answer, there is no legal obligation to answer to which a privilege in the technical sense can apply. For an appraisal of this argument, see Lewis Mayers, *Shall We Amend the Fifth Amendment?*, 82–83, 223–33 (1959); Walter Schaefer, *The Suspect and Society* 16–18 (1967); 8 John Henry Wigmore, *Evidence* 329 fn. 27 (McNaughton rev. 1961). Consider, too, Note 2, p. 691, and Note 5, p. 694.

It has been suggested that the reasoning above "had a great deal more to commend it than merely the inherent force of its 'logic' or the self-restraint and tenderness of the exempted class of interrogators," Kamisar Essays 59–60; and that among the forces at work were *"necessity"*—the conviction that police interrogation without advising the suspect of his rights was "indispensable" in law enforcement—and the *invisibility* of the process, which made it easy for society to be complacent about what was really going on and to readily accept police-prosecution "sanitized" versions of what was going on. Id. at 60–63.

How the *Malloy* opinion looked back, however, was not as important as how it looked forward. Whatever one thought of the manner in which *Malloy* had recorded the recent past, one could not treat lightly the way it anticipated the near future.

SECTION 3. THE *MIRANDA* "REVOLUTION"

ORAL ARGUMENTS IN *MIRANDA* AND COMPANION CASES[a]

* * *

MR. DUANE R. NEDRUD, on behalf of the National District Attorneys Association, *Amicus Curiae.* * * *

THE CHIEF JUSTICE: May I ask you this, please, Mr. Nedrud: if you agree on the facts that *Escobedo* should not be overruled, what would you say as to the man who did not have a lawyer, but who said he wanted a lawyer before he talked?

MR. NEDRUD: If he asked for a lawyer, and he does not waive his right to counsel, I think that he should have a lawyer. [I] would go so far as to say that I

---

a. These extracts from the oral arguments are not taken from an "official transcript"—no such transcript is available–but from a transcript the Institute of Criminal Law and Procedure of the Georgetown University Law Center and several private parties, including the edi-

tors of this book, arranged to have made. Substantial extracts from the oral arguments also appear in Richard J. Medalie, *From Escobedo to Miranda: The Anatomy of a Supreme Court Decision* (1966) (Inst. of Crim.L & P., Geo.U.).

think the state should appoint a lawyer if he asks for a lawyer. I do not think, however, that we should in effect encourage him to have a lawyer.

THE CHIEF JUSTICE: Why do you say we should not encourage him to have a lawyer? Are lawyers a menace? * * *

MR. NEDRUD: I think [a lawyer] is not a menace at the trial level. He is not a menace, per se, but he is, in doing his duty, going to prevent a confession from being obtained. * * *

JUSTICE DOUGLAS: * * * [A lawyer] needs time to prepare for the trial, so the appointment must be at some point anterior to the trial. Our question here is how far anterior. * * *

MR. NEDRUD: The question comes down I think, Mr. Justice Douglas, to whether or not we are going to allow the trial court to determine guilt or innocence or the defense counsel. If the defense counsel comes in at the arrest stage, he will, as he should, prevent the defendant from confessing to his crime, and you will have fewer convictions. If this is what is wanted, this is what will occur.

JUSTICE BLACK: I guess there is no doubt, is there, as to the effect of the provision which provides for protection against compelling him to give testimony. Is it not fewer convictions?

MR. NEDRUD: [I believe] there is a point of diminishing returns and at some stage the police must be in a position to protect us.

JUSTICE BLACK: * * * Can you think of any time when [a person] needs a lawyer more than [at] the point of detention?

MR. NEDRUD: Mr. Justice Black, again, the question is are we interested in convicting the defendant, or are we interested in protecting or acquitting him? This is the only point that I can, in effect, make, if you say that this defendant needs counsel at this time.

For example, if I may use this illustration, I worked when I was a professor of law, which I was prior to taking this position, I worked on the defense project for the American Bar Association. In the questionnaire there was a statement, "When is the ideal time for counsel to be appointed for the defendant?"

Actually, the question is, "When is the ideal time for whom, the people or the defendant?" If it is for the defendant, then it is the earliest possible opportunity; if it is for the people, it should not be until a critical stage. * * *

JUSTICE BLACK: I have found out over many years a very critical stage is when a person is taken to the police headquarters. * * *

A person is taken to police headquarters and placed under arrest or detention. He can't leave, if he wants to, unless they let him. Would you call that voluntary for him, then, for [the police] to have him there in that situation and probe him about probable conviction of crime? Would you think of that as voluntary?

MR. NEDRUD: As being voluntarily in the police station, no. * * *

MR. VICTOR M. EARLE, III on behalf of the petitioner in VIGNERA v. NEW YORK. * * *

JUSTICE FORTAS: [Are you saying] that when the point of time comes where it appears that the police have enough information to satisfy themselves that the fellow really did the act, then the right to arrange for counsel or to give the warning attaches?

MR. EARLE: I think that is correct, although we don't have to look into the mind of the police necessarily to be able to determine that. * * * If in doubt, push it out on the other side of the warning. That is why I don't see that it should pose so much of a problem. I think the FBI Agents give warnings on this proceeding.

JUSTICE STEWART: What should this warning contain? What should this warning be?

MR. EARLE: The Chief of Police in the District of Columbia last August promulgated a warning which, I understand, is now being given by all police officials in the District. It goes something like this: You have been placed under arrest. You are not required to say anything to us any time or to answer any questions. Anything you say may be used as evidence in court. You may call a lawyer or a relative or a friend. Your lawyer may be present here, and you may talk with him. If you cannot obtain a lawyer, one will be appointed for you when your case first goes to court.

I might have a little quibble with that third point, because it suggests a little bit that you might not be able to get a lawyer now.

JUSTICE FORTAS: Much more than a little bit of quibble on the basis of what you have argued so far—that he has an absolute right for a lawyer to be appointed for him at that point, unless he waives it.

MR. EARLE: Yes, sir, unless he waives it. The question might come up of how do the police, or what do the police do when the fellow says, "Thanks. I would like a lawyer now that you mention it, but I don't happen to have any money." They have a choice. They can give him ten cents and the number of a legal aid society.

They have another alternative—just stop interrogating. That alternative was never mentioned. * * *

JUSTICE WHITE: They give him the warning, and he nods his head, yes. (laughter)

JUSTICE WHITE: What happens?

MR. EARLE: It takes a conscious relinquishing of his known rights, those rights I have been telling you about, Justice White.

JUSTICE WHITE: I thought that is what you would say. What happens then if the fellow just nods his head and just looks at him?

MR. EARLE: If we can believe he nodded his head, it is possible that he waives it. I would be very reluctant to come to that conclusion on [that] hypothesis.

JUSTICE WHITE: What else besides giving a warning and right to counsel?

MR. EARLE: I think if he writes down in his own handwriting, "I have been warned, I understand that I have a right to a lawyer now, to talk to him this minute, if I want to, or the right to say nothing if I want to. I understand that. I would like to go ahead and cooperate with the police. Signed: Michael Vignera." That would be enough.

JUSTICE WHITE: That is just barely the first stage.

MR. EARLE: That is what the police have to say.

JUSTICE WHITE: Sure, but if they want to rely on a waiver at any time, is this the only ground that you would accept for a lawyer not being present, a written waiver? Isn't that right?

MR. EARLE: I think that is right. It should be definitely recorded.

JUSTICE WHITE: It should be a written waiver?

MR. EARLE: Absolutely. It shouldn't be something he is conned into giving. * * *

JUSTICE WHITE: What if he doesn't waive? He says, "I do want counsel," and the state says, "Fine. Here is a dime, and there is the legal aid number," and the fellow calls him. He talks to the lawyer, and he comes back and sits down, and you ask him some questions, and he answers them.

MR. EARLE: Without his lawyer being present, for example?

JUSTICE WHITE: Yes.

MR. EARLE: I take it that would be a decision made by his lawyer, and the lawyer can waive rights for his client.

JUSTICE WHITE: Is that a waiver in your book? What is it, a waiver of the right to consult counsel or a waiver of the right to have counsel present?

MR. EARLE: I think it is a waiver to have a counsel in all the ways it is meant. The lawyer can make the determination of whether he should be present or not. Lawyers have waived many rights, like not filing the 30th day and the notice of appeal and the like * * *

JUSTICE WHITE: My question is really going to what you think the scope of the right is. You think the scope of the right is to have counsel present and that you must waive not only the right to consult counsel, but the right to have counsel present?

MR. EARLE: I think that is right, Mr. Justice White. I want to elaborate on it, if I might. In a deposition in a civil case, for example, customarily, the plaintiff and the defendant can have counsel present. I can certainly conceive that one lawyer will not be present. The client, through him, would, therefore, waive that right. It would seem that the only way we could distinguish this case from *Escobedo* is the fact that Vignera did not make a request. What we have been talking about is doing that.

Obviously, it wasn't the request of the individual that made the right attach. The significance of the request, I think, in *Escobedo* was that it was a subjective piece of evidence to show that a stage had been reached. * * *

JUSTICE STEWART: How can there be a waiver, if these are Constitutional rights and are important? How can anybody waive them without the consent of counsel or without the advice of counsel? Doesn't he need a lawyer before he can waive them, if you are right?

MR. EARLE: You are entitled to waive in other situations. It is true in court when they want to plead guilty, for example, the judge will decline assignment of counsel, and the judge will, typically, interrogate him to some length to realize the significance of his act, and that is a lot more advisable a situation than—and more conducive to our being receptive to the idea of a waiver than the police station. I agree that is the worst place for waiver. The party alleging waiver has control of the party alleged to have waived.

JUSTICE STEWART: It seems to follow that he needs a lawyer before he can waive his right to a lawyer.

MR. EARLE: I wouldn't be unhappy to have lawyers in the police station.

JUSTICE STEWART: It follows naturally.

MR. EARLE: It doesn't follow naturally, because a majority of the court in *Escobedo* said these rights can be waived. I think we do have to recognize some of the realities of law enforcement. They do have to investigate. They do have the public duty of—if crimes are being committed by the minute, they do have to operate out of the police station. * * *

JUSTICE HARLAN: Is there a claim that the confession was coerced?

MR. EARLE: In no sense. I don't think it was coerced at all. Mr. Justice White asked yesterday a question about compelling someone to give up his Fifth Amendment privilege. I think there is a substantial difference between that and coercing a confession. I mean, it wasn't until 1964 that the Fifth Amendment privilege applied to the states, and so * * * all through until the 1960's, really, state convictions were overturned only by looking to the generality of the totality of the circumstances under the due process clause.

Now, we have specific Constitutional guarantees that are applied in branch to the states, of both the Fifth and Sixth Amendment rights. It is true that the word "compel" is used in the Fifth Amendment with respect to the privilege, but it is quite different to say that the privilege is cut down and impaired by detention and to say a man's will has been so overborne a confession is forced from him. * * *

I hate to sound cynical, but if we go back to the totality of circumstances, that means this Court will sit all by itself as it has so many years to overturn the few confessions it can take, necessarily, by the bulk of the work. The lower courts won't do their job. We need some specific guidelines as *Escobedo* to help them along the way. * * *

MR. WILLIAM I. SIEGEL, on behalf of the respondent in VIGNERA v. NEW YORK. * * *

JUSTICE FORTAS: Mr. Siegel, [the problem presented by these cases] really affects the basic relationship of the individual and the state. It really goes beyond the administration of justice, and that has been the history of mankind. * * *

MR. SIEGEL: [T]here is an immediate objective, also, and the immediate objective is to protect society; because, if society isn't protected, it, in one degree or another, lapses into anarchy because of crime and then the opportunity to reach this beautiful ideal is gone. It is the function of the police—.

JUSTICE FORTAS: (Interrupting) * * * The problem is to reconcile a good many objectives that are not totally consonant.

I am a little troubled, I must say, when I sit here and hear so much reference to this problem as if it were merely a pragmatic problem of convicting people who did a crime, because there are many more dimensions, I suggest, to the problem than just that simple statement.

MR. SIEGEL: * * * The problem that is before this Court, it seems to me, is just how to keep the balance between the ultimate necessity of the civilized, peaceful society and the constitutional rights of a specific defendant.

JUSTICE BLACK: Don't you think that the Bill of Rights has something to do with making that balance?

MR. SIEGEL: Yes, sir.

JUSTICE BLACK: There is not any doubt, is there, that no person should be convicted on evidence he has been compelled to give? Why do we have to get into a discussion of society or the beauties of the ideal civilization when that is the issue before us?

MR. SIEGEL: Because the Bill of Rights only says that [one] shall not be compelled, but the word "compelled" is not self-defining. We, for many, many years, were told [by] a great majority of Your Honors' predecessors, that compelled meant that which couldn't make a man talk by the exercise of process.

JUSTICE BLACK: By what?

MR. SIEGEL: By the exercise of process. You couldn't subpoena him into a court and, under pain of punishment, make him talk. * * *

SOLICITOR GENERAL THURGOOD MARSHALL, on behalf of the government in WESTOVER v. UNITED STATES. * * *

JUSTICE BLACK: [As] I understand you to say, of course, any person that has a lawyer or has the money to get a lawyer could get one immediately. This man has no lawyer and has no money to get one. The only reason he doesn't have a lawyer is for that reason. Does that raise any principles as to what an indigent is entitled to? He is certainly not getting treated like a man who has the money to get a lawyer.

MR. MARSHALL: He is not being denied anything. The state is not affirmatively denying anything. The state is just not furnishing him anything. * * *

JUSTICE BLACK: I understood you to say if he had the money he would have the right to have the lawyer but the man that has no money has no chance to. That is the situation that we had in *Griffin.*

MR. MARSHALL: *Griffin* was a different point. You can't equalize the whole thing. I don't believe that we can. * * *

"I was introduced for my accomplishments primarily as being of counsel in *Miranda,* and consistently I must disabuse everyone of the accomplishment * * *. When certiorari was granted and we were asked by the ACLU to prepare and file the brief, we had a meeting in our law office in which we agreed that the briefs should be written with the entire focus on the Sixth Amendment [right to counsel] because that is where the Court was headed after *Escobedo,* and, as you are all aware, in the very first paragraph [of the *Miranda* opinion] Chief Justice Warren said, 'It is the Fifth Amendment to the Constitution that is at issue today.' That was Miranda's effective use of counsel."

—John J. Flynn, *Panel Discussion on the Exclusionary Rule,* 61 F.R.D. 259, 278 (1972).

MIRANDA v. ARIZONA (NO. 759)*
384 U.S. 436, 86 S.Ct. 1602, 16 L.Ed.2d 694 (1966).

Chief Justice WARREN delivered the opinion of the Court.

The cases before us raise questions which go to the roots of American criminal jurisprudence: the restraints society must observe [in] prosecuting individuals for crime. More specifically, we deal with the admissibility of statements obtained from an individual who is subjected to custodial police interrogation and the necessity for procedures which assure that the individual is accorded his privilege under the Fifth Amendment to the Constitution not to be compelled to incriminate himself. * * *

We start here, as we did in *Escobedo* with the premise that our holding is not an innovation in our jurisprudence, but is an application of principles long recognized and applied in other settings. We have undertaken a thorough reexamination of the *Escobedo* decision and the principles it announced, and we reaffirm it. That case was but an explication of basic rights that are enshrined in

---

* Together with No. 760, *Vignera v. New*   [and] No. 584, *California v. Stewart* * * *.
York [and] No. 761, *Westover v. United States*

our Constitution—that "No person * * * shall be compelled in any criminal case to be a witness against himself," and that "the accused [shall] have the Assistance of Counsel"—rights which were put in jeopardy in that case through official overbearing. * * *

Our holding will be spelled out with some specificity in the pages which follow but briefly stated it is this: the prosecution may not use statements, whether exculpatory or inculpatory, stemming from custodial interrogation of the defendant unless it demonstrates the use of procedural safeguards effective to secure the privilege against self-incrimination. By custodial interrogation, we mean questioning initiated by law enforcement officers after a person has been taken into custody or otherwise deprived of his freedom of action in any significant way.[4] As for the procedural safeguards to be employed, unless other fully effective means are devised to inform accused persons of their right of silence and to assure a continuous opportunity to exercise it, the following measures are required. Prior to any questioning, the person must be warned that he has a right to remain silent, that any statement he does make may be used as evidence against him, and that he has a right to the presence of an attorney, either retained or appointed. The defendant may waive effectuation of these rights, provided the waiver is made voluntarily, knowingly and intelligently. If, however, he indicates in any manner and at any stage of the process that he wishes to consult with an attorney before speaking there can be no questioning. Likewise, if the individual is alone and indicates in any manner that he does not wish to be interrogated, the police may not question him. The mere fact that he may have answered some questions or volunteered some statements on his own does not deprive him of the right to refrain from answering any further inquiries until he has consulted with an attorney and thereafter consents to be questioned.

The constitutional issue we decide in each of these cases is the admissibility of statements obtained from a defendant questioned while in custody and deprived of his freedom of action in any significant way. In each, the defendant was questioned by police officers, detectives, or a prosecuting attorney in a room in which he was cut off from the outside world. In none of these cases was the defendant given a full and effective warning of his rights at the outset of the interrogation process. In all the cases, the questioning elicited oral admissions, and in three of them, signed statements as well which were admitted at their trials. They all thus share salient features—incommunicado interrogation of individuals in a police-dominated atmosphere, resulting in self-incriminating statements without full warnings of constitutional rights. * * *

Again we stress that the modern practice of in-custody interrogation is psychologically rather than physically oriented. * * * Interrogation still takes place in privacy. Privacy results in secrecy and this in turn results in a gap in our knowledge as to what in fact goes on in the interrogation rooms. A valuable source of information about present police practices, however, may be found in various police manuals and texts which document procedures employed with success in the past, and which recommend various other effective tactics. These texts are used by law enforcement agencies themselves as guides.[9] It should be noted that

---

4. This is what we meant in *Escobedo* when we spoke of an investigation which had focused on an accused.

9. The methods described in Inbau and Reid, *Criminal Interrogation and Confessions* (1962), are a revision and enlargement of material presented in three prior editions of a predecessor text, *Lie Detection and Criminal Interrogation* (3d ed. 1953). The authors and their associates are officers of the Chicago Police Scientific Crime–Detection Laboratory and have had extensive experience in writing, lecturing and speaking to law enforcement authorities over a 20–year period. They say that the techniques portrayed in their manuals reflect their experiences and are the most effective psychological stratagems to employ during interrogations. Similarly, the techniques described in O'Hara, *Fundamentals of Criminal Investigation* (1959), were gleaned from long

these texts professedly present the most enlightened and effective means presently used to obtain statements through custodial interrogation. By considering these texts and other data, it is possible to describe procedures observed and noted around the country. * * *

To highlight the isolation and unfamiliar surroundings, the manuals instruct the police to display an air of confidence in the suspect's guilt and from outward appearance to maintain only an interest in confirming certain details. The guilt of the subject is to be posited as a fact. The interrogator should direct his comments toward the reasons why the subject committed the act, rather than court failure by asking the subject whether he did it. Like other men, perhaps the subject has had a bad family life, had an unhappy childhood, had too much to drink, had an unrequited desire for women. The officers are instructed to minimize the moral seriousness of the offense, to cast blame on the victim or on society. These tactics are designed to put the subject in a psychological state where his story is but an elaboration of what the police purport to know already—that he is guilty. Explanations to the contrary are dismissed and discouraged.

The texts thus stress that the major qualities an interrogator should possess are patience and perseverance. * * *

[When other techniques] prove unavailing, the texts recommend they be alternated with a show of some hostility. One ploy often used has been termed the "friendly-unfriendly" or the "Mutt and Jeff" act:

> "[In] this technique, two agents are employed. Mutt, the relentless investigator, who knows the subject is guilty and is not going to waste any time. He's sent a dozen men away for this crime and he's going to send the subject away for the full term. Jeff, on the other hand, is obviously a kindhearted man. He has a family himself. He has a brother who was involved in a little scrape like this. He disapproves of Mutt and his tactics and will arrange to get him off the case if the subject will cooperate. He can't hold Mutt off for very long. The subject would be wise to make a quick decision. The technique is applied by having both investigators present while Mutt acts out his role. Jeff may stand by quietly and demur at some of Mutt's tactics. When Jeff makes his plea for cooperation, Mutt is not present in the room."

The interrogators sometimes are instructed to induce a confession out of trickery. The technique here is quite effective in crimes which require identification or which run in series. In the identification situation, the interrogator may take a break in his questioning to place the subject among a group of men in a line-up. "The witness or complainant (previously coached, if necessary) studies the line-up and confidently points out the subject as the guilty party." Then the questioning resumes "as though there were now no doubt about the guilt of the subject." A variation on this technique is called the "reverse line-up":

> "The accused is placed in a line-up, but this time he is identified by several fictitious witnesses or victims who associated him with different offenses. It is expected that the subject will become desperate and confess to the offense under investigation in order to escape from the false accusations."

The manuals also contain instructions for police on how to handle the individual who refuses to discuss the matter entirely, or who asks for an attorney or relatives. The examiner is to concede him the right to remain silent. "This usually has a very undermining effect. First of all, he is disappointed in his expectation of an unfavorable reaction on the part of the interrogator. Secondly, a

service as observer, lecturer in police science, and work as a federal criminal investigator. All these texts have had rather extensive use among law enforcement agencies and among students of police science, with total sales and circulation of over 44,000.

concession of this right to remain silent impresses the subject with the apparent fairness of his interrogator." After this psychological conditioning, however, the officer is told to point out the incriminating significance of the suspect's refusal to talk:

> "Joe, you have a right to remain silent. That's your privilege and I'm the last person in the world who'll try to take it away from you. If that's the way you want to leave this, O.K. But let me ask you this. Suppose you were in my shoes and I were in yours and you called me in to ask me about this and I told you, 'I don't want to answer any of your questions.' You'd think I had something to hide, and you'd probably be right in thinking that. That's exactly what I'll have to think about you, and so will everybody else. So let's sit here and talk this whole thing over."

Few will persist in their initial refusal to talk, it is said, if this monologue is employed correctly.

In the event that the subject wishes to speak to a relative or an attorney, the following advice is tendered:

> "[T]he interrogator should respond by suggesting that the subject first tell the truth to the interrogator himself rather than get anyone else involved in the matter. If the request is for an attorney, the interrogator may suggest that the subject save himself or his family the expense of any such professional service, particularly if he is innocent of the offense under investigation. The interrogator may also add, 'Joe, I'm only looking for the truth, and if you're telling the truth, that's it. You can handle this by yourself.'"

From these representative samples of interrogation techniques, the setting prescribed by the manuals and observed in practice becomes clear. In essence, it is this: To be alone with the subject is essential to prevent distraction and to deprive him of any outside support. The aura of confidence in his guilt undermines his will to resist. He merely confirms the preconceived story the police seek to have him describe. Patience and persistence, at times relentless questioning, are employed. To obtain a confession, the interrogator must "patiently maneuver himself or his quarry into a position from which the desired object may be obtained." When normal procedures fail to produce the needed result, the police may resort to deceptive stratagems such as giving false legal advice. It is important to keep the subject off balance, for example, by trading on his insecurity about himself or his surroundings. The police then persuade, trick, or cajole him out of exercising his constitutional rights.

Even without employing brutality, the "third degree" or the specific stratagems described above, the very fact of custodial interrogation exacts a heavy toll on individual liberty and trades on the weakness of individuals.

In the cases before us today, given this background, we concern ourselves primarily with this interrogation atmosphere and the evils it can bring. In *Miranda v. Arizona,* the police arrested the defendant and took him to a special interrogation room where they secured a confession. In *Vignera v. New York,* the defendant made oral admissions to the police after interrogation in the afternoon, and then signed an inculpatory statement upon being questioned by an assistant district attorney later the same evening. In *Westover v. United States,* the defendant was handed over to the Federal Bureau of Investigation by local authorities after they had detained and interrogated him for a lengthy period, both at night and the following morning. After some two hours of questioning, the federal officers had obtained signed statements from the defendant. Lastly, in *California v. Stewart,* the local police held the defendant five days in the station and interrogated him on nine separate occasions before they secured his inculpatory statement.

In these cases, we might not find the defendants' statements to have been involuntary in traditional terms. Our concern for adequate safeguards to protect precious Fifth Amendment rights is, of course, not lessened in the slightest. In each of the cases, the defendant was thrust into an unfamiliar atmosphere and run through menacing police interrogation procedures. The potentiality for compulsion is forcefully apparent, for example, in *Miranda,* where the indigent Mexican defendant was a seriously disturbed individual with pronounced sexual fantasies, and in *Stewart,* in which the defendant was an indigent Los Angeles Negro who had dropped out of school in the sixth grade. To be sure, the records do not evince overt physical coercion or patented psychological ploys. The fact remains that in none of these cases did the officers undertake to afford appropriate safeguards at the outset of the interrogation to insure that the statements were truly the product of free choice.

It is obvious that such an interrogation environment is created for no purpose other than to subjugate the individual to the will of his examiner. This atmosphere carries its own badge of intimidation. To be sure, this is not physical intimidation, but it is equally destructive of human dignity. The current practice of incommunicado interrogation is at odds with one of our Nation's most cherished principles—that the individual may not be compelled to incriminate himself. Unless adequate protective devices are employed to dispel the compulsion inherent in custodial surroundings, no statement obtained from the defendant can truly be the product of his free choice.

From the foregoing, we can readily perceive an intimate connection between the privilege against self-incrimination and police custodial questioning. It is fitting to turn to history and precedent underlying the Self–Incrimination Clause to determine its applicability in this situation.

We sometimes forget how long it has taken to establish the privilege against self-incrimination, the sources from which it came and the fervor with which it was defended. Its roots go back into ancient times.[27] * * *

[W]e may view the historical development of the privilege as one which groped for the proper scope of governmental power over the citizen. As a "noble principle often transcends its origins," the privilege has come rightfully to be recognized in part as an individual's substantive right, a "right to a private enclave where he may lead a private life. That right is the hallmark of our democracy." We have recently noted that the privilege against self-incrimination—the essential mainstay of our adversary system—is founded on a complex of values. *Murphy v. Waterfront Comm'n* [p. 692]. All these policies point to one overriding thought: the constitutional foundation underlying the privilege is the respect a government—state or federal—must accord to the dignity and integrity of its citizens. To maintain a "fair state-individual balance," to require the government "to shoulder the entire load," 8 Wigmore, *Evidence* (McNaughton rev., 1961), to respect the inviolability of the human personality, our accusatory system of criminal justice demands that the government seeking to punish an individual produce the evidence against him by its own independent labors, rather than by the cruel, simple expedient of compelling it from his own mouth. In sum, the privilege is fulfilled only when the person is guaranteed the right "to remain silent unless he chooses to speak in the unfettered exercise of his own will." *Malloy v. Hogan* [p. 456].

---

27. Thirteenth century commentators found an analogue to the privilege grounded in the Bible. * * * [See generally Irene Rosenberg & Yale Rosenberg, *In the Beginning: The Tal-* *mudic Rule Against Self–Incrimination,* 63 N.Y.U.L.Rev. 955 (1988) and the authorities discussed therein].

* * * We are satisfied that all the principles embodied in the privilege apply to informal compulsion exerted by law-enforcement officers during in-custody questioning. An individual swept from familiar surroundings into police custody, surrounded by antagonistic forces, and subjected to the techniques of persuasion described above cannot be otherwise than under compulsion to speak. As a practical matter, the compulsion to speak in the isolated setting of the police station may well be greater than in courts or other official investigations, where there are often impartial observers to guard against intimidation or trickery.

This question in fact could have been taken as settled in federal courts almost seventy years ago [by] *Bram v. United States* (1897) [discussed at pp. 456, 579]. Because of the adoption by Congress of Rule 5(a) of the Federal Rules of Criminal Procedure, and this Court's effectuation of that Rule in *McNabb* and *Mallory,* we have had little occasion in the past quarter century to reach the constitutional issues in dealing with federal interrogations. These supervisory rules, requiring production of an arrested person before a commissioner "without unnecessary delay" and excluding evidence obtained in default of that statutory obligation, were nonetheless responsive to the same considerations of Fifth Amendment policy that unavoidably face us now as to the States. In [the *McNabb* and *Mallory* cases] we recognized both the dangers of interrogation and the appropriateness of prophylaxis stemming from the very fact of interrogation itself.[32]

Our decision in *Malloy v. Hogan* necessitates an examination of the scope of the privilege in state cases as well. In *Malloy,* we squarely held the privilege applicable to the States, and held that the substantive standards underlying the privilege applied with full force to state court proceedings. The implications [of *Malloy*] were elaborated in our decision in *Escobedo,* decided one week after *Malloy* applied the privilege to the States.

[In *Escobedo*], as in the cases today, we sought a protective device to dispel the compelling atmosphere of the interrogation. In *Escobedo,* however, the police did not relieve the defendant of the anxieties which they had created in the interrogation rooms. Rather, they denied his request for the assistance of counsel.[35] This heightened his dilemma, and made his later statements the product of this compulsion. [The] denial of the defendant's request for his attorney thus undermined his ability to exercise the privilege—to remain silent if he chose or to speak without any intimidation, blatant or subtle. The presence of counsel, in all the cases before us today, would be the adequate protective device necessary to make the process of police interrogation conform to the dictates of the privilege. His presence would insure that statements made in the government-established atmosphere are not the product of compulsion.

* * * Without the protections flowing from adequate warnings and the rights of counsel, "all the careful safeguards erected around the giving of testimony, whether by an accused or any other witness, would become empty formalities in a procedure where the most compelling possible evidence of guilt, a confession, would have already been obtained at the unsupervised pleasure of the police." *Mapp v. Ohio* (Harlan, J., dissenting).

Today, then, there can be no doubt that the Fifth Amendment privilege is available outside of criminal court proceedings and serves to protect persons in all

---

32. Our decision today does not indicate in any manner, of course, that these rules can be disregarded. When federal officials arrest an individual, they must as always comply with the dictates of the congressional legislation and cases thereunder. * * *

35. The police also prevented the attorney from consulting with his client. Independent of any other constitutional proscription, this action constitutes a violation of the Sixth Amendment right to the assistance of counsel and excludes any statement obtained in its wake. See *People v. Donovan,* 13 N.Y.2d 148, 243 N.Y.S.2d 841, 193 N.E.2d 628 (N.Y.1963) (Fuld, J.).

settings in which their freedom of action is curtailed from being compelled to incriminate themselves. We have concluded that without proper safeguards the process of in-custody interrogation of persons suspected or accused of crime contains inherently compelling pressures which work to undermine the individual's will to resist and to compel him to speak where he would not otherwise do so freely. In order to combat these pressures and to permit a full opportunity to exercise the privilege against self-incrimination, the accused must be adequately and effectively apprised of his rights and the exercise of those rights must be fully honored.

It is impossible for us to foresee the potential alternatives for protecting the privilege which might be devised by Congress or the States in the exercise of their creative rule-making capacities. Therefore we cannot say that the Constitution necessarily requires adherence to any particular solution for the inherent compulsions of the interrogation process as it is presently conducted. Our decision in no way creates a constitutional straitjacket which will handicap sound efforts at reform, nor is it intended to have this effect. We encourage Congress and the States to continue their laudable search for increasingly effective ways of protecting the rights of the individual while promoting efficient enforcement of our criminal laws. However, unless we are shown other procedures which are at least as effective in apprising accused persons of their right of silence and in assuring a continuous opportunity to exercise it, the following safeguards must be observed.[a]

At the outset, if a person in custody is to be subjected to interrogation, he must first be informed in clear and unequivocal terms that he has the right to remain silent. For those unaware of the privilege, the warning is needed simply to make them aware of it—the threshold requirement for an intelligent decision as to its exercise. More important, such a warning is an absolute prerequisite in overcoming the inherent pressures of the interrogation atmosphere. It is not just the subnormal or woefully ignorant who succumb to an interrogator's imprecations, whether implied or expressly stated, that the interrogation will continue until a confession is obtained or that silence in the face of accusation is itself damning and will bode ill when presented to a jury.[37] Further, the warning will show the individual that his interrogators are prepared to recognize his privilege should he choose to exercise it.

The Fifth Amendment privilege is so fundamental to our system of constitutional rule and the expedient of giving an adequate warning as to the availability of the privilege so simple, we will not pause to inquire in individual cases whether the defendant was aware of his rights without a warning being given. Assessments of the knowledge the defendant possessed, based on information as to his age, education, intelligence, or prior contact with authorities, can never be more than

---

a. Ed. Note—Chief Justice Warren inserted the language in this paragraph at the suggestion of Justice Brennan, who wrote a lengthy memorandum to Warren, commenting on an early draft of the *Miranda* opinion. Brennan "agree[d] that, largely for the reasons you have stated, all four cases must be reversed for lack of any safeguards against denial of the right [against self-incrimination]. [But] should we not leave Congress and the States latitude to devise other means (if they can) which might also create an interrogation climate which has the similar effect of the fettering of a person's own will?" Ironically, the language that Chief Justice Warren used at Brennan's suggestion was seized upon by Justice Rehnquist in *Michigan v. Tucker* (1974) (p. 487) as evidence that *Miranda* was not a constitutional decision.

For a discussion of, and substantial extracts from, Justice Brennan's memorandum to Chief Justice Warren, see Charles D. Weisselberg, *Saving Miranda*, 84 Cornell L.Rev. 109, 123–25 (1998).

37. [In] accord with this decision, it is impermissible to penalize an individual for exercising his Fifth Amendment privilege when he is under police custodial interrogation. The prosecution may not, therefore, use at trial the fact that he stood mute or claimed his privilege in the face of accusation.

speculation;[38] a warning is a clearcut fact. More important, whatever the background of the person interrogated, a warning at the time of the interrogation is indispensable to overcome its pressures and to insure that the individual knows he is free to exercise the privilege at that point in time.

The warning of the right to remain silent must be accompanied by the explanation that anything said can and will be used against the individual in court. This warning is needed in order to make him aware not only of the privilege, but also of the consequences of forgoing it. It is only through an awareness of these consequences that there can be any assurance of real understanding and intelligent exercise of the privilege. Moreover, this warning may serve to make the individual more acutely aware that he is faced with a phase of the adversary system—that he is not in the presence of persons acting solely in his interest.

The circumstances surrounding in-custody interrogation can operate very quickly to overbear the will of one merely made aware of his privilege by his interrogators. Therefore, the right to have counsel present at the interrogation is indispensable to the protection of the Fifth Amendment privilege under the system we delineate today. Our aim is to assure that the individual's right to choose between silence and speech remains unfettered throughout the interrogation process. A once-stated warning, delivered by those who will conduct the interrogation, cannot itself suffice to that end among those who most require knowledge of their rights. A mere warning given by the interrogators is not alone sufficient to accomplish that end. Prosecutors themselves claim that the admonishment of the right to remain silent without more "will benefit only the recidivist and the professional." Brief for the National District Attorneys Association as *amicus curiae.* Even preliminary advice given to the accused by his own attorney can be swiftly overcome by the secret interrogation process. Thus, the need for counsel to protect the Fifth Amendment privilege comprehends not merely a right to consult with counsel prior to questioning but also to have counsel present during any questioning if the defendant so desires.

The presence of counsel at the interrogation may serve several significant subsidiary functions as well. If the accused decides to talk to his interrogators, the assistance of counsel can mitigate the dangers of untrustworthiness. With a lawyer present the likelihood that the police will practice coercion is reduced, and if coercion is nevertheless exercised the lawyer can testify to it in court. The presence of a lawyer can also help to guarantee that the accused gives a fully accurate statement to the police and that the statement is rightly reported by the prosecution at trial.

An individual need not make a preinterrogation request for a lawyer. While such request affirmatively secures his right to have one, his failure to ask for a lawyer does not constitute a waiver. No effective waiver of the right to counsel during interrogation can be recognized unless specifically made after the warnings we here delineate have been given. The accused who does not know his rights and therefore does not make a request may be the person who most needs counsel. * * *

Accordingly we hold that an individual held for interrogation must be clearly informed that he has the right to consult with a lawyer and to have the lawyer with him during interrogation under the system for protecting the privilege we delineate today. As with the warnings of the right to remain silent and that anything stated can be used in evidence against him, this warning is an absolute

38. Cf. *Betts v. Brady,* and the recurrent inquiry into special circumstances it necessitated. * * *

prerequisite to interrogation. No amount of circumstantial evidence that the person may have been aware of this right will suffice to stand in its stead. Only through such a warning is there ascertainable assurance that the accused was aware of this right.

If an individual indicates that he wishes the assistance of counsel before any interrogation occurs, the authorities cannot rationally ignore or deny his request on the basis that the individual does not have or cannot afford a retained attorney. The financial ability of the individual has no relationship to the scope of the rights involved here. The privilege against self-incrimination secured by the Constitution applies to all individuals. The need for counsel in order to protect the privilege exists for the indigent as well as the affluent. In fact, were we to limit these constitutional rights to those who can retain an attorney, our decisions today would be of little significance. The cases before us as well as the vast majority of confession cases with which we have dealt in the past involve those unable to retain counsel. While authorities are not required to relieve the accused of his poverty, they have the obligation not to take advantage of indigence in the administration of justice.[41] Denial of counsel to the indigent at the time of interrogation while allowing an attorney to those who can afford one would be no more supportable by reason or logic than the similar situation at trial and on appeal struck down in *Gideon* and *Douglas v. California.*

In order fully to apprise a person interrogated of the extent of his rights under this system then, it is necessary to warn him not only that he has the right to consult with an attorney, but also that if he is indigent a lawyer will be appointed to represent him. Without this additional warning, the admonition of the right to consult with counsel would often be understood as meaning only that he can consult with a lawyer if he has one or has the funds to obtain one. The warning of a right to counsel would be hollow if not couched in terms that would convey to the indigent—the person most often subjected to interrogation—the knowledge that he too has a right to have counsel present. As with the warnings of the right to remain silent and of the general right to counsel, only by effective and express explanation to the indigent of this right can there be assurance that he was truly in a position to exercise it.[43]

Once warnings have been given, the subsequent procedure is clear. If the individual indicates in any manner, at any time prior to or during questioning, that he wishes to remain silent, the interrogation must cease.[44] At this point he has shown that he intends to exercise his Fifth Amendment privilege; any statement taken after the person invokes his privilege cannot be other than the product of compulsion, subtle or otherwise. Without the right to cut off questioning, the setting of in-custody interrogation operates on the individual to overcome free choice in producing a statement after the privilege has been once invoked. If the individual states that he wants an attorney, the interrogation must cease until an attorney is present. At that time, the individual must have an opportunity to

41. See Kamisar, *Equal Justice in the Gatehouses and Mansions of American Criminal Procedure,* in Criminal Justice in Our Time (1965), 64–81; * * * Report of the Attorney General's Committee on *Poverty and the Administration of Federal Criminal Justice* (1963), p. 9 * * *.

43. While a warning that the indigent may have counsel appointed need not be given to the person who is known to have an attorney or is known to have ample funds to secure one, the expedient of giving a warning is too simple and the rights involved too important to engage in *ex post facto* inquiries into financial ability when there is any doubt at all on that score.

44. If an individual indicates his desire to remain silent, but has an attorney present, there may be some circumstances in which further questioning would be permissible. In the absence of evidence of overbearing, statements then made in the presence of counsel might be free of the compelling influence of the interrogation process and might fairly be construed as a waiver of the privilege for purposes of these statements.

confer with the attorney and to have him present during any subsequent questioning. If the individual cannot obtain an attorney and he indicates that he wants one before speaking to police, they must respect his decision to remain silent.

This does not mean, as some have suggested, that each police station must have a "station house lawyer" present at all times to advise prisoners. It does mean, however, that if police propose to interrogate a person they must make known to him that he is entitled to a lawyer and that if he cannot afford one, a lawyer will be provided for him prior to any interrogation. If authorities conclude that they will not provide counsel during a reasonable period of time in which investigation in the field is carried out, they may do so without violating the person's Fifth Amendment privilege so long as they do not question him during that time.

If the interrogation continues without the presence of an attorney and a statement is taken, a heavy burden rests on the Government to demonstrate that the defendant knowingly and intelligently waived his privilege against self-incrimination and his right to retained or appointed counsel. This Court has always set high standards of proof for the waiver of constitutional rights, *Johnson v. Zerbst,* and we reassert these standards as applied to in-custody interrogation. Since the State is responsible for establishing the isolated circumstances under which the interrogation takes place and has the only means of making available corroborated evidence of warnings given during incommunicado interrogation, the burden is rightly on its shoulders.

An express statement that the individual is willing to make a statement and does not want an attorney followed closely by a statement could constitute a waiver. But a valid waiver will not be presumed simply from the silence of the accused after warnings are given or simply from the fact that a confession was in fact eventually obtained [referring to *Carnley v. Cochran,* 369 U.S. 506, 82 S.Ct. 884, 8 L.Ed.2d 70 (1962)].

* * * Moreover, where in-custody interrogation is involved, there is no room for the contention that the privilege is waived if the individual answers some questions or gives some information on his own prior to invoking his right to remain silent when interrogated.[45]

Whatever the testimony of the authorities as to waiver of rights by an accused, the fact of lengthy interrogation or incommunicado incarceration before a statement is made is strong evidence that the accused did not validly waive his rights. In these circumstances the fact that the individual eventually made a statement is consistent with the conclusion that the compelling influence of the interrogation finally forced him to do so. It is inconsistent with any notion of a voluntary relinquishment of the privilege. Moreover, any evidence that the accused was threatened, tricked, or cajoled into a waiver will, of course, show that the defendant did not voluntarily waive his privilege. The requirement of warnings and waiver of rights is a fundamental with respect to the Fifth Amendment privilege and not simply a preliminary ritual to existing methods of interrogation.

The warnings required and the waiver necessary in accordance with our opinion today are, in the absence of a fully effective equivalent, prerequisites to the admissibility of any statement made by a defendant. No distinction can be

---

45. Although this Court held in *Rogers v. United States,* [discussed in Note 4, p. 694] over strong dissent, that a witness before a grand jury may not in certain circumstances decide to answer some questions and then refuse to answer others that decision has no application to the interrogation situation we deal with today. No legislative or judicial fact-finding authority is involved here, nor is there a possibility that the individual might make self-serving statements of which he could make use at trial while refusing to answer incriminating statements.

drawn between statements which are direct confessions and statements which amount to "admissions" of part or all of an offense. The privilege against self-incrimination protects the individual from being compelled to incriminate himself in any manner; it does not distinguish degrees of incrimination. Similarly, for precisely the same reason, no distinction may be drawn between inculpatory statements and statements alleged to be merely "exculpatory." If a statement made were in fact truly exculpatory it would, of course, never be used by the prosecution. In fact, statements merely intended to be exculpatory by the defendant are often used to impeach his testimony at trial or to demonstrate untruths in the statement given under interrogation and thus to prove guilt by implication. These statements are incriminating in any meaningful sense of the word and may not be used without the full warnings and effective waiver required for any other statement. In *Escobedo* itself, the defendant fully intended his accusation of another as the slayer to be exculpatory as to himself.

The principles announced today deal with the protection which must be given to the privilege against self-incrimination when the individual is first subjected to police interrogation while in custody at the station or otherwise deprived of his freedom of action in any significant way. It is at this point that our adversary system of criminal proceedings commences, distinguishing itself at the outset from the inquisitorial system recognized in some countries. Under the system of warnings we delineate today or under any other system which may be devised and found effective, the safeguards to be erected about the privilege must come into play at this point.

Our decision is not intended to hamper the traditional function of police officers in investigating crime. When an individual is in custody on probable cause, the police may, of course, seek out evidence in the field to be used at trial against him. Such investigation may include inquiry of persons not under restraint. General on-the-scene questioning as to facts surrounding a crime or other general questioning of citizens in the fact-finding process is not affected by our holding. It is an act of responsible citizenship for individuals to give whatever information they may have to aid in law enforcement. In such situations the compelling atmosphere inherent in the process of in-custody interrogation is not necessarily present.[46]

In dealing with statements obtained through interrogation, we do not purport to find all confessions inadmissible. Confessions remain a proper element in law enforcement. Any statement given freely and voluntarily without any compelling influences is, of course, admissible in evidence. The fundamental import of the privilege while an individual is in custody is not whether he is allowed to talk to the police without the benefit of warnings and counsel, but whether he can be interrogated. There is no requirement that police stop a person who enters a police station and states that he wishes to confess to a crime, or a person who calls the police to offer a confession or any other statement he desires to make. Volunteered statements of any kind are not barred by the Fifth Amendment and their admissibility is not affected by our holding today.

To summarize, we hold that when an individual is taken into custody or otherwise deprived of his freedom by the authorities in any significant way and is subjected to questioning, the privilege against self-incrimination is jeopardized. Procedural safeguards must be employed to protect the privilege, and unless other

46. The distinction and its significance has been aptly described in the opinion of a Scottish court:

"In former times such questioning, if undertaken, would be conducted by police officers visiting the house or place of business of the suspect and there questioning him, probably in the presence of a relation or friend. However convenient the modern practice may be, it must normally create a situation very unfavorable to the suspect." *Chalmers v. H.M. Advocate*, [1954] Sess.Cas. 66, 78 (J.C.).

fully effective means are adopted to notify the person of his right of silence and to assure that the exercise of the right will be scrupulously honored, the following measures are required. He must be warned prior to any questioning that he has the right to remain silent, that anything he says can be used against him in a court of law, that he has the right to the presence of an attorney, and that if he cannot afford an attorney one will be appointed for him prior to any questioning if he so desires. Opportunity to exercise these rights must be afforded to him throughout the interrogation. After such warnings have been given, and such opportunity afforded him, the individual may knowingly and intelligently waive these rights and agree to answer questions or make a statement. But unless and until such warnings and waiver are demonstrated by the prosecution at trial, no evidence obtained as a result of interrogation can be used against him. * * *

If the individual desires to exercise his privilege, he has the right to do so. This is not for the authorities to decide. An attorney may advise his client not to talk to police until he has had an opportunity to investigate the case, or he may wish to be present with his client during any police questioning. In doing so an attorney is merely exercising the good professional judgment he has been taught. This is not cause for considering the attorney a menace to law enforcement. He is merely carrying out what he is sworn to do under his oath—to protect to the extent of his ability the rights of his client. In fulfilling this responsibility the attorney plays a vital role in the administration of criminal justice under our Constitution.

In announcing these principles, we are not unmindful of the burdens which law enforcement officials must bear, often under trying circumstances. * * * This Court, while protecting individual rights, has always given ample latitude to law enforcement agencies in the legitimate exercise of their duties. The limits we have placed on the interrogation process should not constitute an undue interference with a proper system of law enforcement. [Although] confessions may play an important role in some convictions, the cases before us present graphic examples of the overstatement of the "need" for confessions. In each case authorities conducted interrogations ranging up to five days in duration despite the presence, through standard investigating practices, of considerable evidence against each defendant.[51] Further examples are chronicled in our prior cases.

It is also urged that an unfettered right to detention for interrogation should be allowed because it will often redound to the benefit of the person questioned. When police inquiry determines that there is no reason to believe that the person has committed any crime, it is said, he will be released without need for further formal procedures. The person who has committed no offense, however, will be better able to clear himself after warnings, with counsel present than without. It can be assumed that in such circumstances a lawyer would advise his client to talk freely to police in order to clear himself.

Custodial interrogation, by contrast, does not necessarily afford the innocent an opportunity to clear themselves. A serious consequence of the present practice of the interrogation alleged to be beneficial for the innocent is that many arrests "for investigation" subject large numbers of innocent persons to detention and interrogation. In one of the cases before us, *California v. Stewart,* police held four persons, who were in the defendant's house at the time of the arrest, in jail for five days until defendant confessed. At that time they were finally released. Police stated that there was "no evidence to connect them with any crime." Available

---

51. Miranda, Vignera, and Westover were identified by eyewitnesses. Marked bills from the bank robbed were found in Westover's car. Articles stolen from the victim as well as from several other robbery victims were found in Stewart's home at the outset of the investigation.

statistics on the extent of this practice where it is condoned indicate that these four are far from alone in being subjected to arrest, prolonged detention, and interrogation without the requisite probable cause.

[The] experience in some other countries * * * suggests that the danger to law enforcement in curbs on interrogation is overplayed. The English procedure since 1912 under the Judges' Rules is significant. As recently strengthened, the Rules require that a cautionary warning be given an accused by a police officer as soon as he has evidence that affords reasonable grounds for suspicion; they also require that any statement made be given by the accused without questioning by police.[57] The right of the individual to consult with an attorney during this period is expressly recognized. * * *

57. [1964] Crim.L.Rev. 166–170. These Rules provide in part:

"II. As soon as a police officer has evidence which would afford reasonable grounds for suspecting that a person has committed an offence, he shall caution that person or cause him to be cautioned before putting to him any questions, or further questions, relating to that offence.

"The caution shall be in the following terms:

" 'You are not obliged to say anything unless you wish to do so but what you say may be put into writing and given in evidence.'

"When after being cautioned a person is being questioned, or elects to make a statement, a record shall be kept of the time and place at which any such questioning or statement began and ended and of the persons present.

* * *

"(b) It is only in exceptional cases that questions relating to the offence should be put to the accused person after he has been charged or informed that he may be prosecuted.

* * *

"IV. All written statements made after caution shall be taken in the following manner:

"(a) If a person says that he wants to make a statement he shall be told that it is intended to make a written record of what he says.

"He shall always be asked whether he wishes to write down himself what he wants to say; if he says that he cannot write or that he would like someone to write it for him, a police officer may offer to write the statement for him. * * *

"(b) Any person writing his own statement shall be allowed to do so without any prompting as distinct from indicating to him what matters are material.

* * *

"(d) Whenever a police officer writes the statement, he shall take down the exact words spoken by the person making the statement, without putting any questions other than such as may be needed to make the statement coherent, intelligible and relevant to the material matters: he shall not prompt him." * * *

Ed. Note—*England curtails the right to silence.* In the fall of 1994, the British Parliament adopted various restrictions on the right to silence, effective March 1, 1995. These restrictions were similar to those Parliament had imposed on Northern Ireland in 1988. The new law permits judges and jurors to draw adverse inferences when, during interrogation, suspects do not tell the police any fact subsequently relied upon in their defense at trial, if under the circumstances, the suspects would have "been "reasonably expected" to mention that fact to the police. (This section corresponds to a provision of the Northern Ireland Order, which, according to the government, was designed to end terrorists' use of the "ambush defense," whereby terrorists would remain silent during interrogation and thus prevent the prosecution from preparing a rebuttal to subsequent defense claims.)

[The new law also permits judges and jurors to draw adverse inferences when suspects fail to respond to police questions about any suspicious objects, substances, or marks which are found on their persons or clothing or when suspects do not explain to the police why they were present at a place at or about the time of the crime for which they were arrested. Finally, if the defendant fails to testify at trial, the new law permits the jury to draw such adverse inferences "as appear proper"—including the "common sense" inference that there is no explanation for the evidence produced against the defendant and that the defendant is guilty. See generally, Mark Berger, *Of Policy, Politics, and Parliament: The Legislative Rewriting of the British Right to Silence,* 22 Am.J.Crim.L. 391 (1995); Gregory W. O'Reilly, *England Limits the Right to Silence and Moves Toward an Inquisitional System of Justice,* 85 J.Crim.L. & C. 402 (1994).

[For the view that silence during police interrogation does not cause police to drop charges or prosecutors to dismiss cases or courts to acquit defendants; that using adverse inferences will not induce suspects to talk to the police or to reveal their defenses; that there is no indication that in the past a defendant's right to silence has been frequently invoked at trial; and that adverse inferences about a defendant's failure to testify at trial

Because of the nature of the problem and because of its recurrent significance in numerous cases, we have to this point discussed the relationship of the Fifth Amendment privilege to police interrogation without specific concentration on the facts of the cases before us. We turn now to these facts to consider the application to these cases of the constitutional principles discussed above. In each instance, we have concluded that statements were obtained from the defendant under circumstances that did not meet constitutional standards for protection of the privilege.

No. 759. *Miranda v. Arizona.*

On March 13, 1963, petitioner, Ernesto Miranda, was arrested at his home and taken in custody to a Phoenix police station. He was there identified by the complaining witness. The police then took him to "Interrogation Room No. 2" of the detective bureau. There he was questioned by two police officers. The officers admitted at trial that Miranda was not advised that he had a right to have an attorney present. Two hours later, the officers emerged from the interrogation room with a written confession signed by Miranda. At the top of the statement was a typed paragraph stating that the confession was made voluntarily, without threats or promises of immunity and "with full knowledge of my legal rights, understanding any statement I make may be used against me."[67]

[Miranda] was found guilty of kidnapping and rape. [On] appeal, the Supreme Court of Arizona held that Miranda's constitutional rights were not violated in obtaining the confession and affirmed the conviction. In reaching its decision, the court emphasized heavily the fact that Miranda did not specifically request counsel.

We reverse. From the testimony of the officers and by the admission of respondent, it is clear that Miranda was not in any way apprised of his right to consult with an attorney and to have one present during the interrogation, nor was his right not to be compelled to incriminate himself effectively protected in any other manner. Without these warnings the statements were inadmissible. The mere fact that he signed a statement which contained a typed-in clause stating that he had "full knowledge" of his legal rights does not approach the knowing and intelligent waiver required to relinquish constitutional rights. * * *

No. 760. *Vignera v. New York.*

Petitioner, Michael Vignera, was picked up by New York police on October 14, 1960, in connection with the robbery three days earlier of a Brooklyn dress shop. They took him to the 17th Detective Squad headquarters in Manhattan. Sometime thereafter he was taken to the 66th Detective Squad. There a detective questioned Vignera with respect to the robbery. Vignera orally admitted the robbery to the detective. [T]he defense was precluded from making any showing that warnings had not been given. While at the 66th Detective Squad, Vignera was identified by the store owner and a saleslady as the man who robbed the dress shop. At about 3:00 p.m. he was formally arrested. The police then transported him to still another station, the 70th Precinct in Brooklyn, "for detention". At 11:00 p.m. Vignera was questioned by an assistant district attorney in the presence of a hearing reporter who transcribed the questions and Vignera's answers. This verbatim account of these proceedings contains no statement of any warnings given by the assistant district attorney. * * *

will not foster testimony by defendants, see O'Reilly, supra, at 431–42.]

67. One of the officers testified that he read this paragraph to Miranda. Apparently, however, he did not do so until after Miranda had confessed orally.

Vignera was [convicted of first degree robbery]. We reverse. The foregoing indicates that Vignera was not warned of any of his rights before the questioning by the detective and by the assistant district attorney. No other steps were taken to protect these rights. Thus he was not effectively apprised of his Fifth Amendment privilege or of his right to have counsel present and his statements are inadmissible.

No. 761. *Westover v. United States.*

At approximately 9:45 p.m. on March 20, 1963, petitioner, Carl Calvin Westover, was arrested by local police in Kansas City as a suspect in two Kansas City robberies. A report was also received from the FBI that he was wanted on a felony charge in California. * * * Kansas City police interrogated Westover on the night of his arrest. He denied any knowledge of criminal activities. The next day local officers interrogated him again throughout the morning. Shortly before noon they informed the FBI that they were through interrogating Westover and that the FBI could proceed to interrogate him. There is nothing in the record to indicate that Westover was ever given any warning as to his rights by local police. At noon, three special agents of the FBI continued the interrogation in a private interview room of the Kansas City Police Department, this time with respect to the robbery of a savings and loan association and a bank in Sacramento, California. After two or two and one-half hours, Westover signed separate confessions to each of these two robberies which had been prepared by one of the agents during the interrogation. At trial one of the agents testified, and a paragraph on each of the statements states, that the agents advised Westover that he did not have to make a statement, that any statement he made could be used against him, and that he had the right to see an attorney.

[We reverse Westover's federal conviction of the California robberies.] On the facts of this case we cannot find that Westover knowingly and intelligently waived his right to remain silent and his right to consult with counsel prior to the time he made the statement. At the time the FBI agents began questioning Westover, he had been in custody for over 14 hours and had been interrogated at length during that period. The FBI interrogation began immediately upon the conclusion of the interrogation by Kansas City police and was conducted in local police headquarters. Although the two law enforcement authorities are legally distinct and the crimes for which they interrogated Westover were different, the impact on him was that of a continuous period of questioning. There is no evidence of any warning given prior to the FBI interrogation nor is there any evidence of an articulated waiver of rights after the FBI commenced their interrogation. The record simply shows that the defendant did in fact confess a short time after being turned over to the FBI following interrogation by local police. Despite the fact that the FBI agents gave warnings at the outset of their interview, from Westover's point of view the warnings came at the end of the interrogation process. In these circumstances an intelligent waiver of constitutional rights cannot be assumed.

We do not suggest that law enforcement authorities are precluded from questioning any individual who has been held for a period of time by other authorities and interrogated by them without appropriate warnings. A different case would be presented if an accused were taken into custody by the second authority, removed both in time and place from his original surroundings, and then adequately advised of his rights and given an opportunity to exercise them. But here the FBI interrogation was conducted immediately following the state interrogation in the same police station—in the same compelling surroundings. Thus, in obtaining a confession from Westover the federal authorities were the beneficiaries of the pressure applied by the local in-custody interrogation. In these circumstances the giving of warnings alone was not sufficient to protect the privilege.

No. 584. *California v. Stewart.*

In the course of investigating a series of purse-snatch robberies in which one of the victims had died of injuries inflicted by her assailant, respondent, Roy Allen Stewart, was pointed out to Los Angeles police as the endorser of dividend checks taken in one of the robberies. At about 7:15 p.m., January 31, 1963, police officers went to Stewart's house and arrested him. One of the officers asked Stewart if they could search the house, to which he replied, "Go ahead." The search turned up various items taken from the five robbery victims. At the time of Stewart's arrest, police also arrested Stewart's wife and three other persons who were visiting him. These four were jailed along with Stewart and were interrogated. Stewart was taken to the University Station of the Los Angeles Police Department where he was placed in a cell. During the next five days, police interrogated Stewart on nine different occasions. Except during the first interrogation session, when he was confronted with an accusing witness, Stewart was isolated with his interrogators.

During the ninth interrogation session, Stewart admitted that he had robbed the deceased and stated that he had not meant to hurt her. Police then brought Stewart before a magistrate for the first time. Since there was no evidence to connect them with any crime, the police then released the other four persons arrested with him.

Nothing in the record specifically indicates whether Stewart was or was not advised of his right to remain silent or his right to counsel. In a number of instances, however, the interrogating officers were asked to recount everything that was said during the interrogations. None indicated that Stewart was ever advised of his rights.

[The] jury found Stewart guilty of robbery and first degree murder and fixed the penalty as death. On appeal, the Supreme Court of California reversed. It held that under this Court's decision in *Escobedo,* Stewart should have been advised of his right to remain silent and of his right to counsel and that it would not presume in the face of a silent record that the police advised Stewart of his rights.

We affirm. In dealing with custodial interrogation, we will not presume that a defendant has been effectively apprised of his rights and that his privilege against self-incrimination has been adequately safeguarded on a record that does not show that any warnings have been given or that any effective alternative has been employed. Nor can a knowing and intelligent waiver of these rights be assumed on a silent record. Furthermore, Stewart's steadfast denial of the alleged offenses through eight of the nine interrogations over a period of five days is subject to no other construction than that he was compelled by persistent interrogation to forgo his Fifth Amendment privilege.

Therefore, in accordance with the foregoing, [*Miranda*,[1] *Vignera,* and *Westover* are reversed and *Stewart* is affirmed].[2]

Justice CLARK, dissenting in [*Miranda, Vignera,* and *Westover,* and concurring in the result in *Stewart.*]

[I cannot] agree with the Court's characterization of the present practices of police and investigatory agencies as to custodial interrogation. The materials referred to as "police manuals" are not shown by the record here to be the official

---

1. On retrial, *Miranda* was again convicted of kidnapping and rape. The conviction was affirmed in *State v. Miranda,* 450 P.2d 364 (Ariz.1969). For a rich narrative of *Miranda* from arrest to reconviction, see L. Baker, *Miranda: Crime, Law & Politics* (1983).

2. A week later, the Court ruled that *Escobedo* and *Miranda* applied only to trials begun after the decisions were announced.

manuals of any police department, much less in universal use in crime detection. Moreover, the examples of police brutality mentioned by the Court are rare exceptions to the thousands of cases that appear every year in the law reports. * * *

[The Court's] strict constitutional specific inserted at the nerve center of crime detection may well kill the patient. Since there is at this time a paucity of information and an almost total lack of empirical knowledge on the practical operation of requirements truly comparable to those announced by the majority, I would be more restrained lest we go too far too fast. * * *

Rather than employing the arbitrary Fifth Amendment rule which the Court lays down I would follow the more pliable dictates of Due Process Clauses of the Fifth and Fourteenth Amendments which we are accustomed to administering and which we know from our cases are effective instruments in protecting persons in police custody. In this way we would not be acting in the dark nor in one full sweep changing the traditional rules of custodial interrogation which this Court has for so long recognized as a justifiable and proper tool in balancing individual rights against the rights of society. It will be soon enough to go further when we are able to appraise with somewhat better accuracy the effect of such a holding. * * *

Justice HARLAN, whom Justice STEWART and Justice WHITE join, dissenting. * * *

While the fine points of [the Court's new constitutional code of rules for confessions] are far less clear than the Court admits, the tenor is quite apparent. The new rules are not designed to guard against police brutality or other unmistakably banned forms of coercion. Those who use third-degree tactics and deny them in court are equally able and destined to lie as skillfully about warnings and waivers. Rather, the thrust of the new rules is to negate all pressures, to reinforce the nervous or ignorant suspect, and ultimately to discourage any confession at all. The aim in short is toward "voluntariness" in a utopian sense, or to view it from a different angle, voluntariness with a vengeance.

To incorporate this notion into the Constitution requires a strained reading of history and precedent and a disregard of the very pragmatic concerns that alone may on occasion justify such strains. I believe that reasoned examination will show that the Due Process Clauses provide an adequate tool for coping with confessions and that, even if the Fifth Amendment privilege against self-incrimination be invoked, its precedents taken as a whole do not sustain the present rules. Viewed as a choice based on pure policy, these new rules prove to be a highly debatable if not one-sided appraisal of the competing interests, imposed over wide-spread objection, at the very time when judicial restraint is most called for by the circumstances. * * *

[The] Court's asserted reliance on the Fifth Amendment [is] an approach which I frankly regard as a *trompe l'oeil*. The Court's opinion in my view reveals no adequate basis for extending the Fifth Amendment's privilege against self-incrimination to the police station. Far more important, it fails to show that the Court's new rules are well supported, let alone compelled, by Fifth Amendment precedents. Instead, the new rules actually derive from quotation and analogy drawn from precedents under the Sixth Amendment, which should properly have no bearing on police interrogation. * * *

Having decided that the Fifth Amendment privilege does apply in the police station, the Court reveals that the privilege imposes more exacting restrictions than does the Fourteenth Amendment's voluntariness test. It then emerges from a discussion of *Escobedo* that the Fifth Amendment requires for an admissible confession that it be given by one distinctly aware of his right not to speak and shielded from "the compelling atmosphere" of interrogation. From these key premises, the Court finally develops the safeguards of warning, counsel, and so forth. I do not believe these premises are sustained by precedents under the Fifth Amendment.[9]

The more important premise is that pressure on the suspect must be eliminated though it be only the subtle influence of the atmosphere and surroundings. The Fifth Amendment, however, has never been thought to forbid *all* pressure to incriminate one's self in the situations covered by it. * * *

A closing word must be said about the Assistance of Counsel Clause of the Sixth Amendment, which is never expressly relied on by the Court but whose judicial precedents turn out to be linchpins of the confession rules announced today.

[The] only attempt in this Court to carry the right to counsel into the station house occurred in *Escobedo*, the Court repeating several times that that stage was no less "critical" than trial itself. * * * This is hardly persuasive when we consider that a grand jury inquiry, the filing of a certiorari petition, and certainly the purchase of narcotics by an undercover agent from a prospective defendant may all be equally "critical" yet provision of counsel and advice on that score have never been thought compelled by the Constitution in such cases. The sound reason why this right is so freely extended for a criminal trial is the severe injustice risked by confronting an untrained defendant with a range of technical points of law, evidence, and tactics familiar to the prosecutor but not to himself. This danger shrinks markedly in the police station where indeed the lawyer in fulfilling his professional responsibilities of necessity may become an obstacle to truthfinding. See infra, n. 12.

[The] Court's new rules aim to offset [the] minor pressures and disadvantages intrinsic to any kind of police interrogation. The rules do not serve due process interests in preventing blatant coercion since, as I noted earlier, they do nothing to contain the policeman who is prepared to lie from the start. The rules work for reliability in confessions almost only in the Pickwickian sense that they can prevent some from being given at all.[12] * * *

What the Court largely ignores is that its rules impair, if they will not eventually serve wholly to frustrate, an instrument of law enforcement that has long and quite reasonably been thought worth the price paid for it. There can be little doubt that the Court's new code would markedly decrease the number of confessions. To warn the suspect that he may remain silent and remind him that his confession may be used in court are minor obstructions. To require also an express waiver by the suspect and an end to questioning whenever he demurs must heavily handicap questioning. And to suggest or provide counsel for the suspect simply invites the end of the interrogation. See supra, n. 12. * * *

While passing over the costs and risks of its experiment, the Court portrays the evils of normal police questioning in terms which I think are exaggerated. Albeit stringently confined by the due process standards interrogation is no doubt often inconvenient and unpleasant for the suspect. However, it is no less so for a man to be arrested and jailed, to have his house searched, or to stand trial in

---

9. I lay aside *Escobedo* itself; it contains no reasoning or even general conclusions addressed to the Fifth Amendment and indeed its citation in this regard seems surprising in view of *Escobedo's* primary reliance on the Sixth Amendment.

12. The Court's vision of a lawyer "mitigat[ing] the dangers of untrustworthiness" by witnessing coercion and assisting accuracy in the confession is largely a fancy; for if counsel arrives, there is rarely going to be a police station confession. *Watts v. Indiana* (separate opinion of Jackson, J.): "[A]ny lawyer worth his salt will tell the suspect in no uncertain terms to make no statement to police under any circumstances."

court, yet all this may properly happen to the most innocent given probable cause, a warrant, or an indictment. Society has always paid a stiff price for law and order, and peaceful interrogation is not one of the dark moments of the law.

This brief statement of the competing considerations seems to me ample proof that the Court's preference is highly debatable at best and therefore not to be read into the Constitution. However, it may make the analysis more graphic to consider the actual facts of one of the four cases reversed by the Court. *Miranda* serves best, being neither the hardest nor easiest of the four under the Court's standards.[15]

On March 3, 1963, an 18–year-old girl was kidnapped and forcibly raped near Phoenix, Arizona. Ten days later, on the morning of March 13, petitioner Miranda was arrested and taken to the police station. At this time Miranda was 23 years old, indigent, and educated to the extent of completing half the ninth grade. He had "an emotional illness" of the schizophrenic type, according to the doctor who eventually examined him; the doctor's report also stated that Miranda was "alert and oriented as to time, place, and person", intelligent within normal limits, competent to stand trial, and sane within the legal definition. At the police station, the victim picked Miranda out of a lineup, and two officers then took him into a separate room to interrogate him, starting about 11:30 a.m. Though at first denying his guilt, within a short time Miranda gave a detailed oral confession and then wrote out in his own hand and signed a brief statement admitting and describing the crime. All this was accomplished in two hours or less without any force, threats or promises and—I will assume this though the record is uncertain * * *—without any effective warnings at all.

Miranda's oral and written confessions are now held inadmissible under the Court's new rules. One is entitled to feel astonished that the Constitution can be read to produce this result. These confessions were obtained during brief, daytime questioning conducted by two officers and unmarked by any of the traditional indicia of coercion. They assured a conviction for a brutal and unsettling crime, for which the police had and quite possibly could obtain little evidence other than the victim's identifications, evidence which is frequently unreliable. There was, in sum, a legitimate purpose, no perceptible unfairness, and certainly little risk of injustice in the interrogation. Yet the resulting confessions, and the responsible course of police practice they represent, are to be sacrificed to the Court's own finespun conception of fairness which I seriously doubt is shared by many thinking citizens in this country.

[It is] instructive to compare the attitude in this case of those responsible for law enforcement with the official views that existed when the Court undertook three major revisions of prosecutorial practice prior to this case, *Johnson v. Zerbst, Mapp,* and *Gideon.* In *Johnson,* which established that appointed counsel must be offered the indigent in federal criminal trials, the Federal Government all but conceded the basic issue, which had in fact been recently fixed as Department of Justice policy. In *Mapp,* which imposed the exclusionary rule on the States for Fourth Amendment violations, more than half of the States had themselves already adopted some such rule. In *Gideon,* which extended *Johnson v. Zerbst* to the States, an *amicus* brief was filed by 22 States and Commonwealths urging that course; only two States beside the respondent came forward to protest. By contrast, in this case new restrictions on police questioning have been opposed by the United States and in an *amicus* brief signed by 27 States and Common-

---

15. In *Westover,* a seasoned criminal was practically given the Court's full complement of warnings and did not heed them. The *Stewart* case, on the other hand, involves long de- tention and successive questioning. In *Vignera,* the facts are complicated and the record somewhat incomplete.

wealths, not including the three other States who are parties. No State in the country has urged this Court to impose the newly announced rules, nor has any State chosen to go nearly so far on its own.

[The] law of the foreign countries described by the [majority] reflects a more moderate conception of the rights of the accused as against those of society when other data is considered. Concededly, the English experience is most relevant. In that country, a caution as to silence but not counsel has long been mandated by the "Judges' Rules," which also place other somewhat imprecise limits on police cross-examination of suspects. However, in the court's discretion confessions can be and apparently quite frequently are admitted in evidence despite disregard of the Judges' Rules, so long as they are found voluntary under the common-law test. Moreover, the check that exists on the use of pretrial statements is counter-balanced by the evident admissibility of fruits of an illegal confession and by the judge's often-used authority to comment adversely on the defendant's failure to testify. * * *

[S]ome reference must be made to [the] ironic untimeliness [of these confession rules]. There is now in progress in this country a massive re-examination of criminal law enforcement procedures on a scale never before witnessed. Participants in this undertaking include a Special Committee of the American Bar Association, under the chairmanship of Chief Judge Lumbard of the Court of Appeals for the Second Circuit; a distinguished study group of the American Law Institute, headed by Professor Vorenberg of the Harvard Law School; and the President's Commission on Law Enforcement and Administration of Justice, under the leadership of the Attorney General of the United States. Studies are also being conducted by [other groups] equipped to do practical research.

[It] is no secret that concern has been expressed lest long-range and lasting reforms be frustrated by this Court's too rapid departure from existing constitutional standards. Despite the Court's disclaimer, the practical effect of the decision made today must inevitably be to handicap seriously sound efforts at reform, not least by removing options necessary to a just compromise of competing interests. [T]he legislative reforms when they came would have the vast advantage of empirical data and comprehensive study, they would allow experimentation and use of solutions not open to the courts, and they would restore the initiative in criminal law reform to those forums where it truly belongs. * * *

Justice WHITE, with whom Justice HARLAN and Justice STEWART join, dissenting.

The proposition that the privilege against self-incrimination forbids in-custody interrogation without the warnings specified in the majority opinion and without a clear waiver of counsel has no significant support in the history of the privilege or in the language of the Fifth Amendment. As for the English authorities and the common-law history, the privilege, firmly established in the second half of the seventeenth century, was never applied except to prohibit compelled judicial interrogations. The rule excluding coerced confessions matured about 100 years later, "[b]ut there is nothing in the reports to suggest that the theory has its roots in the privilege against self-incrimination. And so far as the cases reveal, the privilege, as such, seems to have been given effect only in judicial proceedings, including the preliminary examinations by authorized magistrates." Morgan, *The Privilege Against Self–Incrimination,* 34 Minn.L.Rev. 1, 18 (1949).

[That] the Court's holding today is neither compelled nor even strongly suggested by the language of the Fifth Amendment, is at odds with American and English legal history, and involves a departure from a long line of precedent does not prove either that the Court has exceeded its powers or that the Court is wrong or unwise in its present reinterpretation of the Fifth Amendment. It does, however, underscore the obvious—that the Court has not discovered or found the law in making today's decision, nor has it derived it from some irrefutable sources; what it has done is to make new law and new public policy in much the same way that it has in the course of interpreting other great clauses of the Constitution. This is what the Court historically has done. Indeed, it is what it must do and will continue to do until and unless there is some fundamental change in the constitutional distribution of governmental powers.

But if the Court is here and now to announce new and fundamental policy to govern certain aspects of our affairs, it is wholly legitimate to examine the mode of this or any other constitutional decision in this Court and to inquire into the advisability of its end product in terms of the long-range interest of the country. At the very least the Court's text and reasoning should withstand analysis and be a fair exposition of the constitutional provision which its opinion interprets. Decisions like these cannot rest alone on syllogism, metaphysics or some ill-defined notions of natural justice, although each will perhaps play its part.

[The Court] extrapolates a picture of what it conceives to be the norm from police investigatorial manuals, published in 1959 and 1962 or earlier, without any attempt to allow for adjustments in police practices that may have occurred in the wake of more recent decisions of state appellate tribunals or this Court. But even if the relentless application of the described procedures could lead to involuntary confessions, it most assuredly does not follow that each and every case will disclose this kind of interrogation or this kind of consequence.[2] Insofar as it appears from the Court's opinion, it has not examined a single transcript of any police interrogation, let alone the interrogation that took place in any one of these cases which it decides today. Judged by any of the standards for empirical investigation utilized in the social sciences the factual basis for the Court's premises is patently inadequate.

Although in the Court's view in-custody interrogation is inherently coercive, it says that the spontaneous product of the coercion of arrest and detention is still to be deemed voluntary. An accused, arrested on probable cause, may blurt out a confession which will be admissible despite the fact that he is alone and in custody, without any showing that he had any notion of his right to remain silent or of the consequences of his admission. Yet, under the Court's rule, if the police ask him a single question such as "Do you have anything to say?" or "Did you kill your wife?" his response, if there is one, has somehow been compelled, even if the accused has been clearly warned of his right to remain silent. Common sense informs us to the contrary. While one may say that the response was "involuntary" in the sense the question provoked or was the occasion for the response and thus the defendant was induced to speak out when he might have remained silent if not arrested and not questioned, it is patently unsound to say the response is compelled.

[If] the rule announced today were truly based on a conclusion that all confessions resulting from custodial interrogation are coerced, then it would simply have no rational foundation. * * * Even if one were to postulate that the Court's concern is not that all confessions induced by police interrogation are

---

2. In fact, the type of sustained interrogation described by the Court appears to be the exception rather than the rule. A survey of 399 cases in one city found that in almost half of the cases the interrogation lasted less than 30 minutes. Barrett, *Police Practices and the Law—From Arrest to Release or Charge,* 50 Calif.L.Rev. 11, 41–45 (1962). Questioning tends to be confused and sporadic and is usual- ly concentrated on confrontations with witnesses or new items of evidence, as these are obtained by officers conducting the investigation. See generally LaFave, *Arrest: The Decision to Take a Suspect into Custody* 386 (1965); ALI, *Model Pre–Arraignment Procedure Code,* Commentary § 5.01, at 170, n. 4 (Tent.Draft No. 1, 1966).

coerced but rather that some such confessions are coerced and present judicial procedures are believed to be inadequate to identify the confessions that are coerced and those that are not, it would still not be essential to impose the rule that the Court has now fashioned. Transcripts or observers could be required, specific time limits, tailored to fit the cause, could be imposed, or other devices could be utilized to reduce the chances that otherwise indiscernible coercion will produce an inadmissible confession.

On the other hand, even if one assumed that there was an adequate factual basis for the conclusion that all confessions obtained during in-custody interrogation are the product of compulsion, the rule propounded by the Court would still be irrational, for, apparently, it is only if the accused is also warned of his right to counsel and waives both that right and the right against self-incrimination that the inherent compulsiveness of interrogation disappears. But if the defendant may not answer without a warning a question such as "Where were you last night?" without having his answer be a compelled one, how can the court ever accept his negative answer to the question of whether he wants to consult his retained counsel or counsel whom the court will appoint? And why if counsel is present and the accused nevertheless confesses, or counsel tells the accused to tell the truth, and that is what the accused does, is the situation any less coercive insofar as the accused is concerned? The court apparently realizes its dilemma of foreclosing questioning without the necessary warnings but at the same time permitting the accused, sitting in the same chair in front of the same policemen, to waive his right to consult an attorney. It expects, however, that not too many will waive the right; and if it is claimed that he has, the State faces a severe, if not impossible burden of proof.

All of this makes very little sense in terms of the compulsion which the Fifth Amendment proscribes. That amendment deals with compelling the accused himself. It is his free will that is involved. Confessions and incriminating admissions, as such, are not forbidden evidence; only those which are compelled are banned. I doubt that the Court observes these distinctions today. By considering any answers to any interrogation to be compelled regardless of the content and course of examination and by escalating the requirements to prove waiver, the Court not only prevents the use of compelled confessions but for all practical purposes forbids interrogation except in the presence of counsel. That is, instead of confining itself to protection of the right against compelled self-incrimination the Court has created a limited Fifth Amendment right to counsel—or, as the Court expresses it, a "right to counsel to protect the Fifth Amendment privilege * * *." The focus then is not on the will of the accused but on the will of counsel and how much influence he can have on the accused. Obviously there is no warrant in the Fifth Amendment for thus installing counsel as the arbiter of the privilege.

In sum, for all the Court's expounding on the menacing atmosphere of police interrogation procedures it has failed to supply any foundation for the conclusions it draws or the measures it adopts.

Criticism of the Court's opinion, however, cannot stop at a demonstration that the factual and textual bases for the rule it propounds are, at best, less than compelling. Equally relevant is an assessment of the rule's consequences measured against community values. The Court's duty to assess the consequences of its action is not satisfied by the utterance of the truth that a value of our system of criminal justice is "to respect the inviolability of the human personality" and to require government to produce the evidence against the accused by its own independent labors. More than the human dignity of the accused is involved; the human personality of others in the society must also be preserved. Thus the values reflected by the privilege are not the sole desideratum; society's interest in the general security is of equal weight.

The obvious underpinning of the Court's decision is a deep-seated distrust of all confessions. As the Court declares that the accused may not be interrogated without counsel present, absent a waiver of the right to counsel, and as the Court all but admonishes the lawyer to advise the accused to remain silent, the result adds up to a judicial judgment that evidence from the accused should not be used against him in any way, whether compelled or not. This is the not so subtle overtone of the opinion?that it is inherently wrong for the police to gather evidence from the accused himself. And this is precisely the nub of this dissent. I see nothing wrong or immoral, and certainly nothing unconstitutional, with the police asking a suspect whom they have reasonable cause to arrest whether or not he killed his wife or with confronting him with the evidence on which the arrest was based, at least where he has been plainly advised that he may remain completely silent. * * * Particularly when corroborated, as where the police have confirmed the accused's disclosure of the hiding place of implements or fruits of the crime, such confessions have the highest reliability and significantly contribute to the certitude with which we may believe the accused is guilty.

[The] rule announced today [is] a deliberate calculus to prevent interrogations, to reduce the incidence of confessions and pleas of guilty and to increase the number of trials. [Under] the present law, the prosecution fails to prove its case in about 30% of the criminal cases actually tried in the federal courts. But it is something else again to remove from the ordinary criminal case all those confessions which heretofore have been held to be free and voluntary acts of the accused and to thus establish a new constitutional barrier to the ascertainment of truth by the judicial process. There is, in my view, every reason to believe that a good many criminal defendants, who otherwise would have been convicted on what this Court has previously thought to be the most satisfactory kind of evidence, will now, under this new version of the Fifth Amendment, either not be tried at all or acquitted if the State's evidence, minus the confession, is put to the test of litigation.

I have no desire whatsoever to share the responsibility for any such impact on the present criminal process. * * *

There is another aspect to the effect of the Court's rule on the person whom the police have arrested on probable cause. The fact is that he may not be guilty at all and may be able to extricate himself quickly and simply if he were told the circumstances of his arrest and were asked to explain. This effort, and his release, must now await the hiring of a lawyer or his appointment by the court, consultation with counsel and then a session with the police or the prosecutor. Similarly, where probable cause exists to arrest several suspects as where the body of the victim is discovered in a house having several residents, it will often be true that a suspect may be cleared only through the results of interrogation of other suspects. Here too the release of the innocent may be delayed by the Court's rule.

Much of the trouble with the Court's new rule is that it will operate indiscriminately in all criminal cases, regardless of the severity of the crime or the circumstances involved. It applies to every defendant whether the professional criminal or one committing a crime of momentary passion who is not part and parcel of organized crime. It will slow down the investigation and the apprehension of confederates in those cases where time is of the essence, such as kidnapping, [those] involving the national security, [and] some organized crime situations. In the latter context the lawyer who arrives may also be the lawyer for the defendants' colleagues and can be relied upon to insure that no breach of the organization's security takes place even though the accused may feel that the best thing he can do is to cooperate.

At the same time, the Court's *per se* approach may not be justified on the ground that it provides a "bright line" permitting the authorities to judge in advance whether interrogation may safely be pursued without jeopardizing the admissibility of any information obtained as a consequence. Nor can it be claimed that judicial time and effort, assuming that is a relevant consideration, will be conserved because of the ease of application of the new rule. Today's decision leaves open such questions as whether the accused was in custody, whether his statements were spontaneous or the product of interrogation, whether the accused has effectively waived his rights, and whether nontestimonial evidence introduced at trial is the fruit of statements made during a prohibited interrogation, all of which are certain to prove productive of uncertainty during investigation and litigation during prosecution. For all these reasons, if further restrictions on police interrogation are desirable at this time, a more flexible approach makes much more sense than the Court's constitutional strait-jacket which forecloses more discriminating treatment by legislative or rule-making pronouncements.

Justice Kennedy's Question About Miranda's *Constitutional Status*

During the oral arguments in *Dickerson v. United States* (p. 561), which took place 34 years after *Miranda*, U.S. Solicitor General Seth Waxman maintained that a 1968 federal statutory provision (discussed immediately below), which purported to replace *Miranda* with the pre-*Miranda* "voluntariness" test, was unconstitutional. He told the Court that Congress lacked the authority to "overrule" *Miranda* because *Miranda* was a constitutional rule. When reminded by Justice O'Connor that in the past the Department of Justice had taken the position that the *Miranda* warnings are not constitutionally required, Mr. Waxman agreed they are not. At this point Justice Kennedy interrupted: "You say the warnings are not constitutionally required, but the *Miranda* rule is constitutional.... I don't understand that."

How would you respond to Justice Kennedy?

CAN (DID) CONGRESS "REPEAL" *MIRANDA*? (and why treatment of this issue should be postponed)

A provision of Title II of the Omnibus Crime Control and Safe Streets Act of 1968, a provision usually called § 3501 (because of its designation under Title 18 of the U.S. Code), purports, in effect, to "repeal" or "overrule" *Miranda* and to reinstate the old "totality of circumstances"-"voluntariness" test.[a] At various places, the *Miranda* Court appears to say that it is interpreting the Fifth Amendment. At one point, for example, the *Miranda* Court states that application of "the constitutional principles" discussed in its opinion to the four cases before it leads to the conclusion that in each instance "the statements were obtained under circumstances that did not meet constitutional standards for protection of the privilege." (See p. 475.) Thus, it seems highly likely that the Court would have upheld § 3501 if it had considered its validity shortly after it was enacted.[b] But

---

a. The text of § 3501 is set forth at p. 559.

b. Indeed, in *Orozco v. Texas* (1969) (p. 495), the Court, per Black, J., told us that it was holding a confession inadmissible because

obtaining it "in the absence of the required warnings was a flat violation of the Self-Incrimination Clause of the Fifth Amendment as construed in *Miranda*."

the Court did not do so. Indeed, it did not decide the fate of § 3501 until it handed down *Dickerson v. United States*–in the year 2000.[c]

In the thirty-four years between *Miranda* and *Dickerson* the Burger and Rehnquist Court's characterization of and comments about *Miranda* furnished good reason to believe that the Court's thinking about that famous case had changed dramatically since it was first decided—and therefore that § 3501's attempt to overturn *Miranda* might well succeed.

Although it was not an easy call, the editors of this book concluded that since a number of the post-*Miranda* cases seemed to downgrade and to "deconstitutionalize" that landmark decision, e.g., by referring to the *Miranda* warnings as "prophylactic" and "not themselves rights protected by the Constitution," it would be preferable to postpone discussion of § 3501 and *Dickerson* until the students had read and thought about (a) the many cases applying and explaining *Miranda* from 1966–2000 and (b) what various Justices had to say, in all that time, about the desirability, efficacy and legitimacy of *Miranda*.

Here as elsewhere, of course, reasonable people may differ. Those instructors who would rather discuss the constitutionality of § 3501 at this point in the course, not later, need only turn to pp. 559 to 571 to do so.

THREE AND A HALF DECADES WITH *MIRANDA:* AN OVERVIEW

Because *Miranda* was the centerpiece of the Warren Court's "revolution in American criminal procedure" and the prime target of those who thought the courts were "soft" on criminals, almost everyone expected the so-called Burger Court to treat *Miranda* unkindly. And it did—at first. But it must also be said that the post-Warren Court interpreted *Miranda* fairly generously in some important respects.

The first blows the Burger Court dealt *Miranda* were the impeachment cases, *Harris v. New York* (1971) (Ch. 11, § 4) and *Oregon v. Hass* (1975) (Ch. 11, § 4). *Harris* held that statements preceded by defective warnings, and thus inadmissible to establish the prosecution's case-in-chief, could nevertheless be used to impeach the defendant's credibility if he chose to take the stand in his own defense. The Court noted, but seemed unperturbed by the fact, that some language in the *Miranda* opinion could be read as barring the use of statements obtained in violation of *Miranda* for *any* purpose.

The Court went a step beyond *Harris* in the *Hass* case. In this case, after being advised of his rights, the defendant asserted them. Nevertheless, the police refused to honor the defendant's request for a lawyer and continued to question him. The Court ruled that here, too, the resulting incriminating statements could be used for impeachment purposes. Since many suspects make incriminating statements even after the receipt of complete *Miranda* warnings, *Harris* might have been explained—and contained—on the ground that permitting impeachment use of statements acquired without complete warnings would not greatly encourage the police to violate *Miranda*. But now that *Hass* is on the books, when

---

c. *Dickerson* is set forth at p. 561.

a suspect asserts his rights, it seems the police have virtually nothing to lose and everything to gain by continuing to question him.[a]

Although language in *Miranda* could be read as establishing a *per se* rule against any further questioning of one who has asserted his "right to silence" (as opposed to his *right to counsel,* discussed below), *Michigan v. Mosley* (1975) (p. 521) held that under certain circumstances (and what they are is unclear), if they cease questioning on the spot, the police may "try again," and succeed at a later interrogation session. At the very least, it seems, the police must promptly terminate the original interrogation, resume questioning after the passage of a significant period of time, and give the suspect a fresh set of warnings at the outset of the second session. Whether *Mosley* requires more is a matter of dispute.

The Court has read "custody" or "*custodial* interrogation" rather narrowly. *Oregon v. Mathiason* (1977) (p. 496) and *California v. Beheler* (1983) (p. 496) illustrate that even *police station* questioning designed to produce incriminating statements is not necessarily "custodial interrogation." The result in *Mathiason* is more easily defensible because the suspect went down to the station house on his own after an officer had requested that he meet him there at a convenient time and he had agreed to do so. In *Beheler,* however, the suspect went to the station house in the company of the police. (He was said to have "voluntarily agreed" to accompany the police.)

In *Brown v. Illinois* (1975) (Ch. 11, § 3), the Court declined an invitation to do serious damage to the Fourth Amendment by making the *Miranda* warnings, in effect, a "cure-all." The Court rejected the contention that the giving of the warnings should purge the taint of any preceding illegal arrest—a view that would have permitted the admissibility at trial of any resulting incriminating statements to be considered without regard to the illegal arrest and thus would have encouraged such arrests.[b]

In the early 1980's *Miranda* seemed to enjoy a "second honeymoon." Considering the alternatives (e.g., a mechanical approach to "interrogation," one limited to situations where the police directly address a suspect), the Court gave the key term "interrogation" a fairly generous reading in *Rhode Island v. Innis* (1980) (p. 497). Although the *Innis* case itself involved police "speech," the Court's definition of "interrogation" embraces interrogation techniques that do not. The following year, in *Edwards v. Arizona* (1981) (p. 522), the Court reinvigorated *Miranda* in an important respect. In effect, it added a "bright line" test to the "bright line" *Miranda* rules. Sharply distinguishing *Mosley,* the *Edwards* Court held that when a suspect asserts his right to counsel (as opposed to his right to remain silent), the police *cannot* "try again." Under these circumstances, a suspect cannot be questioned anew "*until* counsel has been made available to him, *unless* [he] himself *initiates* further communication, exchanges or conversations with the police" (emphasis added).[c]

But then language in Supreme Court opinions which seemed to "deconstitutionalize" *Miranda*, language which first appeared in MICHIGAN v. TUCKER, 417 U.S. 433, 94 S.Ct. 2357, 41 L.Ed.2d 182 (1974), began to reappear. Although

---

a. More recently, the Court held that a defendant's prior silence could be used to impeach him when he testified in his own defense, *Jenkins v. Anderson* (1980) (Ch. 11, § 4), and that even a defendant's *post*arrest silence (so long as he was not given the *Miranda* warnings) could be used for impeachment purposes, *Fletcher v. Weir* (1982) (Ch. 11, § 4). Both *Jenkins* and *Weir* distinguished *Doyle v. Ohio* (1976) (Ch. 11, § 4), which deemed it a violation of due process to use a

defendant's silence for impeachment purposes when the defendant remained silent *after* being given *Miranda* warnings.

b. *Brown* was reaffirmed and fortified in *Dunaway v. New York* (1979) and *Taylor v. Alabama* (1982), both discussed in Ch. 11, § 3.

c. In recent years the Court has read *Edwards* expansively. See *Arizona v. Roberson* (1988) (p. 523) and *Minnick v. Mississippi* (1990) (p. 524). But see *Oregon v. Bradshaw* (1983) (p. 529).

supporters of *Miranda* were troubled by the "impeachment cases" and by decisions giving "custody" and "custodial interrogation" a narrow reading, they were troubled still more by the way the post-Warren Court characterized *Miranda* and the *Miranda* warnings.

Michigan v. Tucker was a very attractive case from the prosecutor's point of view. First of all, the police questioning occurred before *Miranda* was decided, although the defendant's trial took place afterward. Thus *Miranda* was barely applicable.[a] Second, *Tucker* dealt with the admissibility not of the defendant's own statements—they had been excluded—but only with the testimony of a witness whose identity had been discovered *as a result of* questioning the suspect without giving him a complete set of warnings.

Justice REHNQUIST's opinion for the Court in *Tucker*, holding the witness's testimony admissible, can be read very narrowly. But the opinion contains a considerable amount of broad language. The opinion seems to equate the "compulsion" barred by the privilege against self-incrimination with "coercion" or "involuntariness" under the pre-*Miranda* "totality of circumstances"-"involuntariness" test. By lumping together self-incrimination "compulsion" and pre-*Miranda* "involuntariness" and then declaring that a *Miranda* violation is not necessarily a violation of the self-incrimination clause—it only is if the confession was "involuntary" under traditional standards—the *Tucker* majority seemed to reject the core premise of *Miranda*. See Geoffrey R. Stone, *The Miranda Doctrine in the Burger Court*, 1977 Sup.Ct.Rev. 99, 118–19. If *Tucker*'s view of *Miranda* were correct, it is hard to see what that landmark case would have accomplished by applying the privilege against self-incrimination to the proceedings in the police station.

Miranda supporters were troubled by other language in *Tucker* as well. The *Tucker* majority stated that the *Miranda* Court itself had "recognized that [the *Miranda* rules] were not themselves right protected by the Constitution," but only "measures to insure that the right against compulsory self-incrimination was protected," only procedures that "provid[ed] practical reinforcement for the right against compulsory self-incrimination."

A decade after *Tucker* was decided, the Court reiterated *Tucker*'s way of looking at, and thinking about, *Miranda*, in two cases: *New York v. Quarles* (1984) (p. 509) (which recognized a "public safety" exception and thus held admissible both the suspect's statement, "the gun is over there" and the gun found as a result of the statement) and *Oregon v. Elstad* (1985) (p. 781), ruling that the fact that the police had earlier obtained a statement from defendant in violation of his *Miranda* rights (when they questioned him in his home) did not bar the admissibility of a subsequent statement (obtained at the police station) when, this time, the police complied with *Miranda*.[a] In both *Quarles* and *Elstad* the Court underscored the distinction between *actual* coercion by physical violence or threats of violence (the pre-*Miranda* "voluntariness" test) and *inherent* or *irrebuttably presumed* coercion (the basis for the *Miranda* rules) or statements

---

a. The Court held, a week after *Miranda*, that *Miranda* affected only those cases in which *the trial* began after that decision. *Johnson v. New Jersey* (1966) (p. 42). The Court probably should have held that *Miranda* affected only *those confessions obtained* after the date of the decision.

a. In declining to apply the "fruit of the poisonous tree" doctrine to the second statement, the *Elstad* majority per O'Connor, J., observed: "If errors are made by law enforce-

ment officers in administering the prophylactic *Miranda* procedures, they should not breed the same irremediable consequences as police infringement of the Fifth Amendment itself. [There] is a vast difference between the direct consequences from coercion of a confession by physical violence or other deliberate means [and] the uncertain consequences of disclosure of a 'guilty secret' freely given in response to an unwarned but noncoercive question, as is this case."

obtained *merely* in violation of *Miranda*'s "procedural safeguards" or "prophylactic rules."[b]

The *Tucker-Quarles—Elstad* way of thinking about *Miranda* left defenders of that famous case somewhat in disarray. They braced themselves for the day when the Court would overturn *Miranda,* doing so either on its own initiative or by upholding § 3501, the federal statutory provision that purported, basically, to "repeal" *Miranda* and to turn the clock back to the days when the "totality of circumstances"-"voluntariness" test was the only test for the admissibility of confessions. (As it turned out, however, that day never came.)

WK 9

APPLYING AND EXPLAINING *MIRANDA*

1. *"Exploiting a criminal's ignorance or stupidity"; "intelligent" waivers vs. "wise" ones.* Consider STATE v. McKNIGHT, 243 A.2d 240 (N.J. 1968), per WEINTRAUB, C.J.:

"The Constitution is not at all offended when a guilty man stubs his toe. On the contrary, it is decent to hope that he will. [T]he Fifth Amendment does not say that a man shall not be permitted to incriminate himself, or that he shall not be persuaded to do so. It says no more than that a man shall not be 'compelled' to give evidence against himself. [It] is consonant with good morals, and the Constitution, to exploit a criminal's ignorance or stupidity in the detectional process. This must be so if Government is to succeed in its primary mission to live free from criminal attack.

" * * * Nowhere does *Miranda* suggest that the waiver of counsel at the detectional stage would not be 'knowing' or 'intelligent' if the suspect did not understand the law relating to the crime, the possible defenses, and the hazards of talking without the aid of counsel, or if the suspect was not able to protect his interests without such aid, [or] if it was not 'wise' of the prisoner to forego counsel or the right to silence. * * * However relevant to 'waiver' of the right to counsel at trial or in connection with a plea of guilty, those factors are foreign to the investigational scene where the detection of crime is the legitimate aim.

"Hence if a defendant has been given the *Miranda* warnings, if the coercion of custodial interrogation was thus dissipated, his 'waiver' was no less 'voluntary' and 'knowing' and 'intelligent' because he misconceived the inculpatory thrust of the facts he admitted, or because he thought that what he said could not be used because it was only oral or because he had his fingers crossed, or because he could well have used a lawyer. A man need not have the understanding of a lawyer to waive one. Such matters, irrelevant when the defendant volunteers his confession to a friend or to a policeman passing on his beat, are equally irrelevant when the confession is made in custody after the coercion of custodial interrogation has been dispelled by the *Miranda* warnings. With such warnings, the essential fact remains that defendant understood he had the right to remain silent and thereby to avoid the risk of self-incrimination. That is what the Fifth Amendment privilege is about."

See also *Collins v. Brierly,* 492 F.2d 735 (3d Cir.1974) (en banc): "*Miranda* speaks of 'intelligent' waiver [in the sense] that the individual must know of his

---

b. Dissenting in *Elstad,* Justice Stevens attacked "the Court's attempt to fashion a distinction between actual coercion [and] irrebuttably presumed coercion." He maintained that the presumption of coercion "is only legitimate if it is assumed that there is always a coercive aspect to custodial interrogation that is not preceded by adequate advice of the constitu-

tional right to remain silent. [If] the presumption arises whenever the accused has been taken into custody, [it] will surely be futile to try to develop subcategories of custodial interrogation. Indeed, a major purpose of treating the presumption of coercion as irrebuttable is to avoid the kind of fact-bound inquiry that today's decision will surely engender."

available options before deciding what he thinks best suits his particular situation. In this context intelligence is not equated with wisdom." Consider, too, James J. Tomkovicz, *Standards for Invocation and Waiver of Counsel in Confession Contexts,* 71 Iowa L.Rev. 975, 1049 (1986): "The policies of the fifth amendment privilege do not demand rationality, intelligence, or knowledge, but only a voluntary choice not to remain silent." Is this (ought this be) so?

2. *Adequacy of warnings.* Consider DUCKWORTH v. EAGAN, 492 U.S. 195, 109 S.Ct. 2875, 106 L.Ed.2d 166 (1989), which arose as follows: Respondent Eagan, suspected of murdering a woman, denied any involvement in the crime. He agreed to go to police headquarters for further questioning. At the stationhouse an officer read him a waiver form which provided, inter alia:

> "You have a right to talk to a lawyer for advice before we ask you any questions, and to have him with you during questioning. You have the right to the advice and presence of a lawyer even if you cannot afford to hire one. *We have no way of giving you a lawyer, but one will be appointed for you, if you wish, if and when you go to court.* If you wish to answer questions now without a lawyer present, you have the right to stop answering questions at any time. You also have the right to stop answering at any time until you've talked to a lawyer." (Emphasis added.)

Eagan signed the waiver form, but again denied any involvement in the crime. He was then placed in the "lock up" at police headquarters. Some 29 hours later, the police met with Eagan again. Before questioning him, an officer read from a differently worded waiver form. Eagan signed it and then confessed to stabbing the woman. A 5–4 majority, per REHNQUIST, C.J., concluded that the initial warnings given to Eagan at police headquarters "touched all of the bases required by *Miranda*":

> "*Miranda* has not been limited to station-house questioning, and the officer in the field may not always have access to printed *Miranda* warnings, or he may inadvertently depart from routine practice, particularly if a suspect requests an elaboration of the warnings. The prophylactic *Miranda* warnings are 'not themselves rights protected by the Constitution but [are] instead measures to insure that the right against compulsory self-incrimination [is] protected.' *Michigan v. Tucker.* Reviewing courts therefore need not examine *Miranda* warnings as if construing a will or defining the terms of an easement. The inquiry is simply whether the warnings reasonably 'convey] to [a suspect] his rights as required by *Miranda*.' *California v. Prysock,* 453 U.S. 355, 101 S.Ct. 2806, 69 L.Ed.2d 696 (1981) (per curiam) [where, in the course of upholding the challenged warnings, the Supreme Court observed: "This Court has never indicated that the 'rigidity' of *Miranda* extends to the precise formulation of the warnings given a criminal defendant."]

> "[On federal habeas corpus, the U.S. Court of Appeals for the Seventh Circuit thought that the] 'if and when you go to court' language suggested that 'only those accused who can afford an attorney have the right to have one present before answering any questions,' and 'implie[d] that if the accused does not 'go to court,' i.e., the government does not file charges, the accused is not entitled to [counsel] at all.'

> "In our view, the Court of Appeals misapprehended the effect of the inclusion of 'if and when you go to court' language * * *. First, this instruction accurately described the procedure for the appointment of counsel in Indiana, [where] counsel is appointed at the defendant's initial appearance in court and formal charges must be filed at or before that hearing. We think it must be relatively commonplace for a suspect, after receiving *Miranda* warnings, to ask *when* he will obtain counsel. The 'if and when you go to court' advice simply anticipates that

question. Second, *Miranda* does not require that attorneys be producible on call, but only that the suspect be informed, as here, that he has the right to an attorney before and during questioning, and that an attorney would be appointed for him if he could not afford one. The Court in *Miranda* emphasized that it was not suggesting that 'each police station must have a "station house lawyer" present at all times to advise prisoners.' If the police cannot provide appointed counsel, *Miranda* requires only that the police not question a suspect unless he waives his right to counsel. Here, respondent did just that. * * *."

Dissenting Justice MARSHALL, joined by Brennan, Blackmun and Stevens, JJ., maintained:

"Under *Miranda,* a police warning must *'clearly infor[m]'* a suspect taken into custody 'that if he cannot afford an attorney one will be appointed for him *prior to any questioning* if he so desires.' (Emphasis added.) A warning qualified by an 'if and when you go to court' caveat does nothing of the kind; instead, it leads the suspect to believe that a lawyer will not be provided until some indeterminate time in the future *after questioning.* I refuse to acquiesce in the continuing debasement of this historic precedent * * *.

"Even if the typical suspect could draw the inference [from the initial warning that] the majority does—that questioning will not commence until a lawyer is provided at a later court appearance—a warning qualified by an 'if and when' caveat still fails to give a suspect any indication of *when* he will be taken to court. Upon hearing the warnings given in this case, a suspect would likely conclude that no lawyer would be provided until trial. In common parlance, 'going to court' is synonymous with 'going to trial.' Furthermore, the negative implication of the caveat is that, if the suspect is never taken to court, he 'is not entitled to an attorney at all.' An unwitting suspect harboring uncertainty on this score is precisely the sort of person who may feel compelled to talk 'voluntarily' to the police, without the presence of counsel, in an effort to extricate himself from his predicament * * *."

Notes and Questions

(a) *Access to a Miranda card.* An officer "in the field," notes the Court, "may not always have access to printed *Miranda* warnings" or may "inadvertently depart from routine practice, particularly if a suspect requests an elaboration of the warnings." What bearing should this have on a case like *Duckworth v. Eagan,* where the suspect was questioned at police headquarters and never asked for an elaboration of the warnings? Moreover, would it be burdensome or unreasonable to require police officers always to carry a standard *Miranda* card?

(b) *Anticipating a suspect's questions.* Should it be the business of the police to "anticipate" a suspect's questions? Does this confuse the role of the police officer with that of the defense lawyer? "Anticipating" a question by Eagan, the police informed him that if he could not afford a lawyer "we have no way of giving you a lawyer" before or during questioning. What impact could that information have other than to make it *less likely* that Eagan would assert his right to appointed counsel? Should the police have "anticipated" *another* question: "If you cannot give me a lawyer now, what happens if I ask for one now?" Under *Edwards v. Arizona* (1981) (p. 522), would the truthful answer to that question have been: "Then, we would be very restricted as to how we could proceed. We would have to cease questioning on the spot. And we could not resume questioning at a later time. We could not talk to you any more about this case unless and until you yourself initiated further communication with us." What would the impact of that information be other than to make it *more likely* that Eagan would assert his right to appointed counsel?

Are the police likely to "anticipate" this question by a suspect: "What happens if I ask for a lawyer right now?" Are the police likely to "anticipate" *any* questions the answers to which further the suspect's interests, not theirs? Are the police (should the police be) free to "anticipate" those questions they would like to answer and free *not* to "anticipate" those questions they would rather not answer? Does *Duckworth* give them that freedom? See Kamisar, *Duckworth v. Eagan: A Little–Noticed Miranda Case that May Cause Much Mischief,* 25 Crim. L.Bull. 550 (1989).

(c) *Complying with Miranda.* According to *Miranda,* "if police propose to interrogate a person they must make known to him that he is entitled to a lawyer and that if he cannot afford one, a lawyer will be provided for him prior to any interrogation." Was Eagan told, in effect, that if he could not afford a lawyer, one would *not* be—and *could not* be—provided for him prior to (or during) any questioning?

(d) *"For or against you."* Suppose, instead of giving the second *Miranda* warning the way it is usually given, an officer advised a suspect: "Anything you say *can be used for or* against you." Isn't it true that sometimes something a suspect tells the police *might be* used *for* him? In light of *Duckworth v. Eagan,* would this version of the second warning constitute compliance with *Miranda*?

(e) *"In court."* Does a warning that fails to inform a suspect that anything he says can be used against him *in court* satisfy *Miranda*? Compare *United States v. Tillman,* 963 F.2d 137 (6th Cir.1992) with *United States v. Frankson,* 83 F.3d 79 (4th Cir.1996).

3. *Need for police admonitions in addition to the four Miranda warnings.*

(a) *The consequences of silence.* If, as *Miranda* points out, many suspects will assume that "silence in the face of accusation is itself damning and will bode ill when presented to a jury" (text at fn. 37), should the suspect be explicitly advised not only that any statement he makes may be used against him but that his silence may *not* be used against him? Isn't a suspect likely to ask himself most urgently: "How do I get out of this mess and avoid looking guilty?" Absent assurance on this point, are many suspects likely to stand by their *Miranda* rights? An interrogator can truthfully tell a suspect that once the police advise him of his right to remain silent the prosecution may not comment at trial on his reliance on that right, but can he truthfully tell him that his silence will not be used against him *in any way*? For example, won't the suspect's silence affect the decision to prosecute? See Sheldon Elsen & Arthur Rosett, *Protections for the Suspect under Miranda v. Arizona,* 67 Colum.L.Rev. 645, 654–55 (1967).

(b) *The right to be made aware of the subject matter of the questioning.*

In COLORADO v. SPRING, 479 U.S. 564, 107 S.Ct. 851, 93 L.Ed.2d 954 (1987), a 7–2 majority, per POWELL, J., held that "a suspect's awareness of all the possible subjects of questioning in advance of interrogation is not relevant to determining whether the suspect voluntarily, knowingly, and intelligently waived his Fifth Amendment privilege." The case arose as follows:

An informant told agents of the Bureau of Alcohol, Tobacco and Firearms (ATF) that Spring (a) was engaged in the interstate shipment of stolen firearms and (b) had been involved in a Colorado killing. The ATF agents set up an undercover operation to purchase firearms from Spring. On March 30, ATF agents arrested Spring in Missouri during the undercover purchase. Spring was advised of his *Miranda* rights and signed a written waiver form.

The agents first questioned Spring about the firearms transactions that led to his arrest. They then asked him if he had ever shot anyone. Spring admitted that he had "shot [a] guy once." On May 26, Colorado officers visited Spring in jail and advised him of his *Miranda* rights. He again signed a written waiver form. The officers then informed Spring that they wanted to question him about the Colorado homicide. Spring confessed to the crime and was convicted of murder.

Spring contended that his waiver of *Miranda* rights before the March 30 statement was invalid because the ATF agents had not informed him that he would be questioned about the Colorado murder and that the May 26 confession was the illegal "fruit" of the March 30 admission. The Colorado Supreme Court agreed, but the U.S. Supreme Court reversed:

"[There] is no doubt that Spring's [March 30 waiver] was knowingly and intelligently made: that is, that Spring understood that he had the right to remain silent and that anything he said could be used as evidence against him. The Constitution does not require that a criminal suspect know and understand every possible consequence of a waiver of the Fifth Amendment privilege." Nor, held that Court, does the failure to inform a suspect of the potential subjects of interrogation constitute the police trickery and deception condemned in *Miranda:*

"This Court has never held that mere silence by law enforcement officials as to the subject matter of an interrogation is 'trickery' sufficient to invalidate a suspect's waiver of *Miranda* rights, and we expressly decline so to hold today. Once *Miranda* warnings are given, it is difficult to see how official silence could cause a suspect to misunderstand the nature of his constitutional right? 'his right to refuse to answer any question which might incriminate him.' '[W]e have never read the Constitution to require that the police supply a suspect with a flow of information to help him calibrate his self-interest in deciding whether to speak or stand by his rights.' *Moran v. Burbine* [p. 538]. Here, the additional information could affect only the wisdom of a *Miranda* waiver, not its essentially voluntary and knowing nature. Accordingly, the failure [to] inform Spring of the subject matter of the interrogation could not affect [his] decision to waive his Fifth Amendment privilege in a constitutionally significant manner."

MARSHALL, joined by Brennan, J., dissented:

"The interrogation tactics utilized in this case demonstrate the relevance of the information Spring did not receive. The [ATF] agents evidently hoped to obtain from Spring a valid confession to the federal firearms charge for which he was arrested and then parlay this admission into an additional confession of first degree murder. Spring could not have expected questions about the latter, separate offense when he agreed to waive his rights, as it occurred in a different state and was a violation of state law outside the normal investigative focus of federal [ATF] agents.

"[The] coercive aspects of the psychological ploy intended in this case, when combined with an element of surprise which may far too easily rise to a level of deception, cannot be justified in light of *Miranda*'s strict requirements that the suspect's waiver and confession be voluntary, knowing, and intelligent. If a suspect has signed a waiver form with the intention of making a statement regarding a specifically alleged crime, the Court today would hold this waiver valid with respect to questioning about any other crime, regardless of its relation to the charges the suspect believes he will be asked to address. Yet once this waiver is given and the intended statement made, the protections afforded by *Miranda* against the 'inherently compelling pressures' of the custodial interrogation have effectively dissipated. Additional questioning about entirely separate and more serious suspicions of criminal activity can take unfair advantage of the suspect's psychological state, as the unexpected questions cause the compulsive pressures suddenly to reappear. Given this technique of interrogation, a suspect's understanding of the topics planned for questioning is, therefore, at the very least 'relevant' to assessing whether his decision to talk to the officers was voluntarily, knowingly, and intelligently made.''

Notes and Questions

(i) Should the *Spring* Court have given weight to the fact that the ATF agents had deprived defendant of information regarding the *more serious charge?* Since the agents had arrested Spring in the act of selling illegal firearms, is it likely that Spring decided to talk to the agents because he felt he had nothing more to lose? See Note, 30 Ariz.L.Rev. 551, 564 (1988).

(ii) Would the Court have reached the same result if Spring had asked the ATF agents what crimes they planned to question him about and the agents (a) had remained silent or (b) had replied that the firearms transactions were the only crimes under investigation? If so, why? If not, is it sound "to fashion a confession law doctrine which turns on the fortuity of a suspect asking the right questions"? See id. at 560–61.

4. "Custody" vs. "focus." After defining "custodial interrogation" in the text, the *Miranda* Court, as one commentator put it, Kenneth W. Graham, *What Is "Custodial Interrogation"?*, 14 U.C.L.A.Rev. 59, 114 (1966), dropped an "obfuscating footnote [4]": "This is what we meant in *Escobedo* when we spoke of an investigation which has focused on an accused." This footnote led some to think that "custody" and "focus" were alternative grounds for requiring the warnings, but these are different events and they have very different consequences.[a] The likely explanation for footnote 4 was the *Miranda* Court's understandable effort to maintain some continuity with a recent precedent. Despite that footnote, however, *Miranda* actually marked a fresh start in describing the circumstances under which constitutional protections first come into play.

The "focus" test, as it had generally been understood at the time of *Escobedo* was expressly rejected in BECKWITH v. UNITED STATES, 425 U.S. 341, 96 S.Ct. 1612, 48 L.Ed.2d 1 (1976). Agents of the Intelligence Division of the IRS did not arrest petitioner, but met with him in a private home where he occasionally stayed. Petitioner argued that the "interview," which produced incriminating statements, should have been preceded by full *Miranda* warnings (instead of the modified *Miranda* warning which petitioner received) because the taxpayer is clearly the "focus" of a criminal investigation when a case is assigned to the Intelligence Division and such a confrontation "places the taxpayer under 'psychological restraints' which are the functional, and therefore, the legal equivalent of custody." The Court per BURGER, C.J., was "not impressed with this argument in the abstract nor as applied to the particular facts of [petitioner's] interrogation":

"[Although] the 'focus' of an investigation may indeed have been on [petitioner] at the time of the interview in the sense that it was his tax liability which was under scrutiny, he hardly found himself in the custodial situation described by the *Miranda* Court as the basis for its holding. *Miranda* specifically defined 'focus,' for its purposes, as 'questioning initiated by law enforcement officers after a person has been taken into custody or otherwise deprived of his freedom of action in any significant way.' "[b]

---

a. *Hoffa v. United States*, p. 378, emphasized, albeit not in a *Miranda* context, that "there is no constitutional right to be arrested" and that the police "are under no constitutional duty to call a halt to a criminal investigation the moment they have the minimum evidence to establish probable cause."

b. See also Chief Justice Burger's plurality opinion in *United States v. Mandujano*, p. 696, rejecting the argument that a "putative" or "virtual" defendant called before the grand jury is entitled to full *Miranda* warnings and stressing that the *Miranda* warnings "were aimed at the evils seen by the Court as endem-

In *Stansbury v. California*, 511 U.S. 318, 114 S.Ct. 1526, 128 L.Ed.2d 293 (1994) (per curiam), the Court held, "not for the first time, that an officer's subjective and undisclosed view concerning whether the person being interrogated is a suspect is irrelevant to the assessment whether the person is in custody." Unless they are communicated to the person being questioned, emphasized the Court, "an officer's evolving but unarticulated suspicions do not affect the objective circumstances of an interrogation or interview, and thus cannot affect the *Miranda* custody inquiry."

5. *What constitutes "custody" or "custodial interrogation"?* According to Israel, *Criminal Procedure, the Burger Court and the Legacy of the Warren Court*, 75 Mich.L.Rev. 1320, 1383–84 (1977), "difficulties [with *Miranda*] have arisen primarily in situations involving questioning 'on the street.' [P]olice can easily identify what constitutes 'custodial interrogation' where that concept is limited to questioning at the police station or a similar setting." In the main, the concept has been so limited.

Most courts have concluded that absent special circumstances (such as arresting a suspect at gunpoint or forcibly subduing him),[a] police questioning "on

ic to police interrogation of a person in custody. [*Miranda*] recognized that many official investigations, such as grand jury questioning, take place in a setting wholly different from custodial police interrogation. [To] extend [*Miranda*] concepts to questioning before a grand jury inquiring into criminal activity under the guidance of a judge is an extravagant expansion [of that case]." But see Justice Brennan's concurring opinion in *Mandujano*.

a. See *Orozco v. Texas*, 394 U.S. 324, 89 S.Ct. 1095, 22 L.Ed.2d 311 (1969) (applying *Miranda* to a situation where defendant was questioned in his bedroom by four police officers at 4:00 a.m., circumstances that produced a "potentiality for compulsion" equivalent to police station interrogation); *New York v. Quarles* (1984) (p. 509) (defendant in "custody" when questioned in a supermarket minutes after arrested at gunpoint, surrounded by four officers, "frisked" and handcuffed, but "public safety" exception to *Miranda* applied).

The "custodial interrogation" issue arose in a unique setting in *United States v. Mesa*, 638 F.2d 582 (3d Cir.1980). After shooting and wounding both his wife and daughter, Mesa barricaded himself in a motel room. FBI agents cleared the area and repeatedly called to him, through a bullhorn, to surrender. Mesa did not respond. Believing that Mesa was armed (he was) and not knowing whether he had hostages (he did not), the FBI brought in a "hostage negotiator." Mesa agreed to take a mobile phone into his room. Before Mesa finally surrendered peacefully, the negotiator and Mesa conversed over the mobile phone for three and a half hours. The conversation consisted mainly of long narrative monologues by Mesa, but in the course of his exchange of remarks with the negotiator Mesa did make some incriminating statements about the shootings. At no

time was he given the *Miranda* warnings. A 2–1 majority of the Third Circuit held that Mesa's statements were admissible, but because one judge decided the case solely on the ground that the exchange between Mesa and the negotiator did not constitute "interrogation," there was no majority opinion on the "custody" issue.

Maintaining that *Miranda's* description of the custodial setting "demonstrates that, at a minimum, the police must have immediate control over the suspect," Chief Judge Seitz concluded that Mesa had not been subjected to *custodial* interrogation: "Mesa successfully had barricaded himself [in] such a way that he prevented [the police] from exercising immediate control over his actions. [*Miranda*] should not be expanded to encompass the present situation where the giving of warnings could have disastrous effects on the suspect and perhaps on others in the vicinity."

Dissenting Judge Weiner appraised the situation quite differently: "Mesa was isolated in his room and in communication only with law enforcement officers. [In] a very real sense, therefore, he was under the direct and immediate control of the authorities and was effectively being restrained by them in his freedom of movement. [Although] a person barricaded in a motel room with a gun retains some ability to 'call the shots,' the overall 'balance of power' was with the authorities surrounding the motel, who were clearly in command of the situation."

Did the judges who addressed the "custody" issue in *Mesa* make the "logical error" of assuming that exclusion of the incriminating statements would somehow *require* the police to give *Miranda* warnings in such situations? Is the best resolution of "standoff situations" for the police "simply [to] decide, as they prob-

the street," in a public place or in a person's home or office is not "custodial." Cf. *Schneckloth v. Bustamonte* (p. 332) (warning requirement need not be imposed on "normal consent searches" because they occur on highways, homes or offices and "under informal and unstructured conditions" "immeasurably far removed from 'custodial interrogations.'")[b]

Indeed, *Oregon v. Mathiason*, 429 U.S. 492, 97 S.Ct. 711, 50 L.Ed.2d 714 (1977) (per curiam), makes it plain that *Miranda* may not apply even when police questioning *does* take place in the station house. Mathiason, a suspect in a burglary, agreed over the phone to meet with a police officer at a convenient time and place (the state patrol office, only two blocks from the suspect's apartment). Mathiason went to the patrol office on his own. When he arrived the officer told him he was not under arrest. The officer then said he wanted to talk to the suspect about a burglary. When Mathiason confessed a few moments later he was not, held the Court, being subjected to "custodial interrogation."

There was some reason to think that *Mathiason* might be limited to situations where suspects go to the station house *unaccompanied* by police officers. But *California v. Beheler*, 463 U.S. 1121, 103 S.Ct. 3517, 77 L.Ed.2d 1275 (1983) (per curiam), made it plain that *Mathiason* could not be read that narrowly. Some hours after the murder weapon (which defendant claimed others had hidden) was found in his backyard, Beheler, as the Court described it, "voluntarily agreed to accompany police to the station house, although the police specifically told [him] that he was not under arrest." At the station house, Beheler agreed to talk about the murder, but the police did not advise him of his *Miranda* rights. The incriminating statements made at the police station, ruled the Court, were not the product of "custodial interrogation."

Illustrative of the current approach to what constitutes "custody" or "custodial interrogation" is BERKEMER v. McCARTY, 468 U.S. 420, 104 S.Ct. 3138, 82 L.Ed.2d 317 (1984), where the Court, per MARSHALL, J., one of *Miranda*'s strongest defenders, held that "the roadside questioning of a motorist detained pursuant to a routine traffic stop" does not amount to "custodial interrogation":

"Two features of an ordinary traffic stop mitigate the danger that a person questioned will be induced 'to speak where he would not otherwise do so freely,' *Miranda*. First, detention of a motorist pursuant to a traffic stop is presumptively temporary and brief. The vast majority of roadside detentions last only a few

---

ably did here, that it [is] better to withhold the *Miranda* warnings and do without the evidence obtained during the conversation"? See Gibbons, J., dissenting from the denial of a petition for rehearing en banc in *Mesa*. See also Note, 91 Yale L.J. 344 (1981).

How would *Miranda* and a "hostage situation" be resolved if it arose today? See Note (a), p. 514.

b. Consider *Minnesota v. Murphy*, 465 U.S. 420, 104 S.Ct. 1136, 79 L.Ed.2d 409 (1984). Murphy, a probationer, arranged to meet with his probation officer in her office as she had requested. He then admitted, in response to her questioning, that he had committed a rape and a murder a number of years earlier. Although the terms of his probation required Murphy to report to his probation officer periodically and to respond truthfully to all her questions, and although the officer had substantial reason to believe that Murphy's answers to her questions were likely to be incriminating, a 6–3 majority, per White,

J., concluded that Murphy could not claim the "in custody" exception to the general rule that the privilege against self-incrimination is not self-executing:

"Custodial arrest is said to convey to the suspect a message that he has no choice but to submit to the officers' will and to confess. It is unlikely that a probation interview, arranged by appointment at a mutually convenient time, would give rise to a similar impression. [Murphy's] regular meetings with his probation officer should have served to familiarize him with her and her office and to insulate him from psychological intimidation that might overbear his desire to claim the privilege. Finally, [since] Murphy was not physically restrained and could have left the office, any compulsion he might have felt from the possibility that terminating the meeting would have led to revocation of probation was not comparable to the pressure on a suspect who is painfully aware that he literally cannot escape a persistent custodial interrogator."

minutes. A motorist's expectations, when he sees a policeman's light flashing behind him, are that he will be obliged to spend a short period of time answering questions and waiting while the officer checks his license and registration, that he may then be given a citation, but that in the end he most likely will be allowed to continue on his way. In this respect, questioning incident to an ordinary traffic stop is quite different from stationhouse interrogation * * *.

"Second, circumstances associated with the typical traffic stop are not such that the motorist feels completely at the mercy of the police. * * * Perhaps most importantly, the typical traffic stop is public, at least to some degree. [This] exposure to public view both reduces the ability of an unscrupulous policeman to use illegitimate means to elicit self-incriminating statements and diminishes the motorist's fear that, if he does not cooperate, he will be subjected to abuse. [In] short, the atmosphere surrounding an ordinary traffic stop is substantially less 'police dominated' than that surrounding the kinds of interrogation at issue in *Miranda* itself and in the subsequent cases in which we have applied *Miranda*.

"In both of these respects, the usual traffic stop is more analogous to a so-called '*Terry* stop' than to a formal arrest. [Typically, an officer who makes a *Terry* stop] may ask the detainee a moderate number of questions to determine his identity and to try to obtain information confirming or dispelling the officer's suspicions. But the detainee is not obliged to respond. And, unless the detainee's answers provide the officer with probable cause to arrest him, he must then be released. The comparatively nonthreatening character of detentions of this sort explains the absence of any suggestion in our opinions that *Terry* stops are subject to the dictates of *Miranda*. * * * "[a]

When an officer stops a motorist, must all of the officer's activity be limited to the offense for which the stop was made? Unless reasonable suspicion develops as to other criminality, is it improper for the police to question a motorist about matters unrelated to the offense for which he was stopped? See Note 7, p. 317.

6. *What constitutes interrogation within the meaning of Miranda?*

RHODE ISLAND v. INNIS

446 U.S. 291, 100 S.Ct. 1682, 64 L.Ed.2d 297 (1980).

Justice STEWART delivered the opinion of the Court.

[*Miranda*] held that, once a defendant in custody asks to speak with a lawyer, all interrogation must cease until a lawyer is present. The issue in this case is whether the respondent was "interrogated" in violation [of *Miranda*].[a]

[At approximately 4:30 a.m., a patrolman arrested respondent, suspected of robbing a taxicab driver and murdering him with a shotgun blast to the back of the head. Respondent was unarmed. He was advised of his rights. Within minutes

---

a. The Court rejected the argument that *Miranda* does not apply to misdemeanor traffic offenses and held that one subjected to custodial interrogation is entitled to the *Miranda* warnings "regardless of the nature or severity of the offense of which he is suspected or for which he was arrested." Thus, since it was clear that McCarty was "in custody" when he was formally placed under arrest and ordered into the police car, and he had not been informed of his rights at that point, his subsequent admission should not have been used against him.

a. Why is *this* the issue? Since respondent asserted his right to counsel, why isn't the issue whether the police "scrupulously honored" the exercise of that right? Cf. *Michigan v. Mosley* (p. 521). Or why isn't the issue (a) whether the police impermissibly "prompted" respondent to change his mind after he invoked his right to counsel or (b) whether respondent "*himself initiate[d]* further communication, exchanges or conversations with the police," *Edwards v. Arizona* (p. 522) (emphasis added), after initially invoking his right to counsel?

a sergeant (who advised respondent of his rights) and then a captain arrived at the scene of the arrest. The captain also gave respondent the *Miranda* warnings, whereupon respondent asked to speak with a lawyer. The captain then directed that respondent be placed in a police vehicle with a wire screen mesh between the front and rear seats and be driven to the police station. Three officers were assigned to accompany the arrestee. Although the record is somewhat unclear, it appears that Patrolman Williams was in the back seat with respondent and that Patrolmen Gleckman and McKenna were in front.]

While enroute to the central station, Patrolman Gleckman initiated a conversation with Patrolman McKenna concerning the missing shotgun.[1] As Patrolman Gleckman later testified:

> "A. At this point, I was talking back and forth with Patrolman McKenna stating that I frequent this area while on patrol and [that because a school for handicapped children is located nearby,] there's a lot of handicapped children running around in this area, and God forbid one of them might find a weapon with shells and they might hurt themselves."

Patrolman McKenna apparently shared his fellow officer's concern:

> "A. I more or less concurred with him [Gleckman] that it was a safety factor and that we should, you know, continue to search for the weapon and try to find it."

[Respondent then interrupted the conversation, stating that he would show the officers where the gun was located. He told the police that he understood his rights, but "wanted to get the gun out of the way because of the kids in the area in the school." He then led the police to a nearby field, where he pointed out the shotgun under some rocks.]

[Respondent was convicted of murder. The trial judge admitted the shotgun and testimony related to its discovery. On appeal, the Rhode Island Supreme Court concluded that the police had "interrogated" respondent without a valid waiver of his right to counsel; the conversation in the police vehicle had constituted "subtle coercion" that was the equivalent of *Miranda* "interrogation."]

[In determining whether respondent had been "interrogated" in violation of *Miranda*] we first define the term "interrogation" under *Miranda* before turning to a consideration of the facts of this case. [The] concern of the Court in *Miranda* was that the "interrogation environment" created by the interplay of interrogation and custody would "subjugate the individual to the will of his examiner" and thereby undermine the privilege against compulsory self-incrimination. The police practices that evoked this concern included several that did not involve express questioning [such as] the so-called "reverse lineup" in which a defendant would be identified by coached witnesses as the perpetrator of a fictitious crime, [to induce] him to confess to the actual crime of which he was suspected in order to escape the false prosecution. [It] is clear that these techniques of persuasion, no less than express questioning, were thought, in a custodial setting, to amount to interrogation.[3]

This is not to say, however, that all statements obtained by the police after a person has been taken into custody are to be considered the product of interrogation. [The *Miranda* warnings] are required not where a suspect is simply taken

---

1. Although there was conflicting testimony about the exact seating arrangements, it is clear that everyone in the vehicle heard the conversation.

3. To limit the ambit of *Miranda* to express questioning would "place a premium on the ingenuity of the police to devise methods of indirect interrogation, rather than to implement the plain mandate of *Miranda*." *Commonwealth v. Hamilton*, 445 Pa. 292, 297, 285 A.2d 172, 175 [(1971)].

into custody, but rather where a suspect in custody is subjected to interrogation. "Interrogation," as conceptualized [in *Miranda*], must reflect a measure of compulsion above and beyond that inherent in custody itself.[4]

We conclude that the *Miranda* safeguards come into play whenever a person in custody is subjected to either express questioning or its functional equivalent. That is to say, the term "interrogation" under *Miranda* refers not only to express questioning, but also to any words or actions on the part of the police (other than those normally attendant to arrest and custody)[a] that the police should know are reasonably likely to elicit an incriminating response from the suspect. The latter portion of this definition focuses primarily upon the perceptions of the suspect, rather than the intent of the police. This focus reflects the fact that the *Miranda* safeguards were designed to vest a suspect in custody with an added measure of protection against coercive police practices, without regard to objective proof of the underlying intent of the police. A practice that the police should know is reasonably likely to evoke an incriminating response from a suspect thus amounts to interrogation.[7] But, since the police surely cannot be held accountable for the unforeseeable results of their words or actions, the definition of interrogation can extend only to words or actions on the part of police officers that they *should have known* were reasonably likely to elicit an incriminating response.[8]

Turning to the facts of the present case, we conclude that the respondent was not "interrogated" within the meaning of *Miranda*. It is undisputed that the first prong of the definition of "interrogation" was not satisfied, for the [Gleckman–McKenna conversation] included no express questioning of the respondent. [Moreover,] it cannot be fairly concluded that the respondent was subjected to the

---

4. There is language in the opinion of the Rhode Island Supreme Court in this case suggesting that the definition of "interrogation" under *Miranda* is informed by this Court's decision in *Brewer v. Williams*, [p. 594, reaffirming and expansively interpreting the *Massiah* doctrine]. This suggestion is erroneous. Our decision in *Brewer* rested solely on the Sixth and Fourteenth Amendment right to counsel. That right, as we held in *Massiah*, prohibits law enforcement officers from "deliberately elicit[ing]" incriminating information from a defendant in the absence of counsel after a formal charge against the defendant has been filed. Custody in such a case is not controlling; indeed, the petitioner in *Massiah* was not in custody. By contrast, the right to counsel at issue in the present case is based not on the Sixth and Fourteenth Amendments, but rather on the Fifth and Fourteenth Amendments as interpreted in the *Miranda* opinion. The definitions of "interrogation" under the Fifth and Sixth Amendments, if indeed the term "interrogation" is even apt in the Sixth Amendment context, are not necessarily interchangeable, since the policies underlying the two constitutional protections are quite distinct. See Kamisar, *Brewer v. Williams, Massiah and Miranda: What is "Interrogation"? When Does it Matter?*, 67 Geo.L.J. 1, 41–55 (1978).

a. In *South Dakota v. Neville*, 459 U.S. 553, 103 S.Ct. 916, 74 L.Ed.2d 748 (1983), the Court noted (fn. 15) that "in the context of an arrest for driving while intoxicated, a police inquiry of whether the suspect will take a blood-alcohol test is not an interrogation within the meaning of *Miranda*." Recalling that *Innis* had excluded "police words or actions 'normally attendant to arrest and custody'" from the definition of "interrogation," the *Neville* Court added: "The police inquiry here is highly regulated by state law, and is presented in virtually the same words to all suspects. It is similar to a police request to submit to fingerprinting or photography. Respondent's choice of refusal thus enjoys no prophylactic *Miranda* protection outside the basic Fifth Amendment protection. See generally Peter Arenella, *Schmerber and the Privilege Against Self-Incrimination: A Reappraisal*, 20 Am.Crim. L.Rev. 31, 56–58 (1982)."

7. This is not to say that the intent of the police is irrelevant, for it may well have a bearing on whether the police should have known that their words or actions were reasonably likely to evoke an incriminating response. In particular, where a police practice is designed to elicit an incriminating response from the accused, it is unlikely that the practice will not also be one which the police should have known was reasonably likely to have that effect.

8. Any knowledge the police may have had concerning the unusual susceptibility of a defendant to a particular form of persuasion might be an important factor in determining whether the police should have known that their words or actions were reasonably likely to elicit an incriminating response from the suspect.

"functional equivalent" of questioning. It cannot be said [that the officers] should have known that their conversation was reasonably likely to elicit an incriminating response from the respondent. There is nothing in the record to suggest that the officers were aware that the respondent was peculiarly susceptible to an appeal to his conscience concerning the safety of handicapped children [or that] the police knew that the respondent was unusually disoriented or upset at the time of his arrest.[9]

[The] Rhode Island Supreme Court erred, in short, in equating "subtle compulsion" with interrogation. That the officers' comments struck a responsive cord is readily apparent. Thus, it may be said, as the Rhode Island Supreme Court did say, that the respondent was subjected to "subtle compulsion." But that is not the end of the inquiry. It must also be established that a suspect's incriminating response was the product of words or actions on the part of the police that they should have known were reasonably likely to elicit an incriminating response.[10] This was not established in the present case. * * *

Chief Justice BURGER, concurring in the judgment.

Since the result is not inconsistent with *Miranda*, I concur in the judgment. The meaning of *Miranda* has become reasonably clear and law enforcement practices have adjusted to its strictures; I would neither overrule *Miranda*, disparage it, nor extend it at this late date. I fear, however, that [the Court's opinion] may introduce new elements of uncertainty; under the Court's test, a police officer, in the brief time available, apparently must evaluate the suggestibility and susceptibility of an accused. * * *

Justice MARSHALL, with whom Justice BRENNAN joins, dissenting.

I am substantially in agreement with the Court's definition of "interrogation" within the meaning of *Miranda*. In my view, the *Miranda* safeguards apply whenever police conduct is intended or likely to produce a response from a suspect in custody. As I read the Court's opinion, its definition of "interrogation" for *Miranda* purposes is equivalent, for practical purposes, to my formulation. [The] Court requires an objective inquiry into the likely effect of police conduct on a typical individual, taking into account any special susceptibility of the suspect to certain kinds of pressure of which the police know or have reason to know. I am utterly at a loss, however, to understand how this objective standard as applied to the facts before us can rationally lead to the conclusion that there was no interrogation. * * *

One can scarcely imagine a stronger appeal to the conscience of a suspect—*any* suspect—than the assertion that if the weapon is not found an innocent person will be hurt or killed. And not just any innocent person, but an innocent child—a little girl—a helpless, handicapped little girl on her way to school. [As] a matter of fact, the appeal to a suspect to confess for the sake of others, to "display some evidence of decency and honor," is a classic interrogation technique.

Gleckman's remarks would obviously have constituted interrogation if they had been explicitly directed to petitioner, and the result should not be different

---

9. The record in no way suggests that the officers' remarks were *designed* to elicit a response. It is significant that the trial judge, after hearing the officers' testimony, concluded that it was "entirely understandable that [the officers] would voice their concern [for the safety of the handicapped children] to each other."

10. By way of example, if the police had done no more than to drive past the site of the concealed weapon while taking the most direct route to the police station, and if the respondent, upon noticing for the first time the proximity of the school for handicapped children, had blurted out that he would show the officers where the gun was located, it could not seriously be argued that this "subtle compulsion" would have constituted "interrogation" within the meaning of the *Miranda* opinion.

because they were nominally addressed to McKenna. [The officers] knew petitioner would hear and attend to their conversation, and they are chargeable with knowledge of and responsibility for the pressures to speak which they created.

I firmly believe that this case is simply an aberration, and that in future cases the Court will apply the standard adopted today in accordance with its plain meaning.

Justice STEVENS, dissenting.

[In] my view any statement that would normally be understood by the average listener as calling for a response is the functional equivalent of a direct question, whether or not it is punctuated by a question mark. The Court, however, takes a much narrower view. It holds that police conduct is not the "functional equivalent" of direct questioning unless the police should have known that what they were saying or doing was likely to elicit an incriminating response from the suspect. This holding represents a plain departure from the principles set forth in *Miranda*.

[In] order to give full protection to a suspect's right to be free from any interrogation at all, the definition of "interrogation" must include any police statement or conduct that has the same purpose or effect as a direct question. Statements that appear to call for a response from the suspect, as well as those that are designed to do so, should be considered interrogation. By prohibiting only those relatively few statements or actions that a police officer should know are likely to elicit an incriminating response, the Court today accords a suspect considerably less protection. Indeed, since I suppose most suspects are unlikely to incriminate themselves even when questioned directly, this new definition will almost certainly exclude every statement that is not punctuated with a question mark from the concept of "interrogation."

The difference between the approach required by a faithful adherence to *Miranda* and the stinted test applied by the Court today can be illustrated by comparing three different ways in which Officer Gleckman could have communicated his fears about the possible dangers posed by the shotgun to handicapped children. He could have:

(1) directly asked Innis:

Will you please tell me where the shotgun is so we can protect handicapped schoolchildren from danger?

(2) announced to the other officers in the wagon:

If the man sitting in the back seat with me should decide to tell us where the gun is, we can protect handicapped children from danger.

or (3) stated to the other officers:

It would be too bad if a little handicapped girl would pick up the gun that this man left in the area and maybe kill herself.

In my opinion, all three of these statements should be considered interrogation because all three appear to be designed to elicit a response from anyone who in fact knew where the gun was located.[12] Under the Court's test, on the other hand, the form of the statements would be critical. The third statement would not be interrogation because in the Court's view there was no reason for Officer Gleckman to believe that Innis was susceptible to this type of an implied appeal; therefore, the statement would not be reasonably likely to elicit an incriminating

---

12. See Welsh White, *Rhode Island v. Innis: The Significance of a Suspect's Assertion of His Right to Counsel,* 17 Amer.Crim.L.Rev. 53, 68 (1979), where the author proposes the same test and applies it to the facts of this case * * *.

response. Assuming that this is true, then it seems to me that the first two statements, which would be just as unlikely to elicit such a response, should also not be considered interrogation. But, because the first statement is clearly an express question, it *would* be considered interrogation under the Court's test. The second statement, although just as clearly a deliberate appeal to Innis to reveal the location of the gun, would presumably not be interrogation because (a) it was not in form a direct question and (b) it does not fit within the "reasonably likely to elicit an incriminating response" category that applies to indirect interrogation.

As this example illustrates, the Court's test creates an incentive for police to ignore a suspect's invocation of his rights in order to make continued attempts to extract information from him. If a suspect does not appear to be susceptible to a particular type of psychological pressure, the police are apparently free to exert that pressure on him despite his request for counsel, so long as they are careful not to punctuate their statements with question marks. And if, contrary to all reasonable expectations, the suspect makes an incriminating statement, that statement can be used against him at trial. The Court thus turns *Miranda's* unequivocal rule against any interrogation at all into a trap in which unwary suspects may be caught by police deception.

* * * I think the Court is clearly wrong in holding, as a matter of law, that Officer Gleckman should not have realized that his statement was likely to elicit an incriminating response. [Moreover,] there is evidence in the record to support the view that Officer Gleckman's statement was intended to elicit a response from Innis. Officer Gleckman, who was not regularly assigned to the caged wagon, was directed by a police captain to ride with respondent to the police station. [The] record does not explain why, notwithstanding the fact that respondent was handcuffed, unarmed, and had offered no resistance when arrested by an officer acting alone, the captain ordered Officer Gleckman to ride with respondent. It is not inconceivable that two professionally trained police officers concluded that a few well-chosen remarks might induce respondent to disclose the whereabouts of the shotgun. This conclusion becomes even more plausible in light of the emotionally charged words chosen by Officer Gleckman ("God forbid" that a "little girl" should find the gun and hurt herself).[19] * * *

Notes and Questions

(a) If Officer Gleckman's remarks had been explicitly directed to Innis, would they have constituted "interrogation" regardless of whether they were reasonably likely—or at all likely—to elicit an incriminating response? If so, why should words or actions that are the "functional equivalent" of express questioning have to satisfy a "reasonable likelihood" or "apparent probability" of success standard? Why isn't it sufficient that the police speech or conduct—unlike "administrative questioning" (routine questions asked of all arrestees "booked" or otherwise processed) and unlike casual conversation in no way related to the case—would normally be understood as *calling for* a response about the merits of the case or be *likely to be viewed* as *having the same force and effect* as a question about the merits of the case? See Welsh White, *Interrogation without Questions,* 78 Mich. L.Rev. 1209, 1227–36 (1980); Jesse H. Choper, Yale Kamisar & Laurence H. Tribe, *The Supreme Court: Trends and Developments, 1979–80* at 88–89, 92–95 (1981) (remarks of Professor Kamisar).

19. In his article [fn. 12,] Professor White also points out that the officers were probably aware that the chances of a handicapped child finding the weapon at a time when police were not present were relatively slim. Thus, he con- cluded that it was unlikely that the true purpose of the conversation was to voice a genuine concern over the children's welfare. [See also Note (d), following this case].

(b) If Gleckman *had admitted* that his remarks to McKenna were *designed* to get Innis to make incriminating statements, would (should) they have constituted "interrogation" regardless of Gleckman's apparent likelihood of success? Why (not)? Reconsider fns. 7 & 9 to the majority opinion. But see fn. 6 to *New York v. Quarles,* p. 509. Did it (should it) matter whether the "Christian burial speech" delivered in *Brewer v. Williams,* p. 594, was reasonably likely to elicit an incriminating response from Williams? Why (not)?

(c) In ARIZONA v. MAURO, 481 U.S. 520, 107 S.Ct. 1931, 95 L.Ed.2d 458 (1987), a 5–4 majority, per POWELL, J., held that it was not "custodial interrogation" within the meaning of *Miranda* for the police to accede to the request of defendant's wife, also a suspect in the murder of their son, to speak with defendant (being held in a room at the station house) in the presence of a police officer (Detective Manson), who placed a tape recorder in plain sight on a desk. (Defendant had been given the *Miranda* warnings and had asserted his right to counsel.) Observed the Court:

"There is no evidence that the officers sent Mrs. Mauro in to see her husband for the purpose of eliciting incriminating statements. [T]he officers tried to discourage her from talking to her husband, but finally 'yielded to her insistent demands.' Nor was Detective Manson's presence improper. [There were] a number of legitimate reasons—not related to securing incriminating statements—for having a police officer present. Finally, the weakness of Mauro's claim that he was interrogated is underscored by examining the situation from his perspective. * * * We doubt that a suspect, told by officers that his wife will be allowed to speak to him, would feel that he was being coerced to incriminate himself in any way.

"[The state supreme court] was correct to note that there was a 'possibility' that Mauro would incriminate himself while talking to his wife [and] that the officers were aware of that possibility. [But] the actions in this case were far less questionable than the 'subtle compulsion' [held] *not* to be interrogation in *Innis*. Officers do not interrogate a suspect simply by hoping that he will incriminate himself. * * *

"[In] deciding whether particular police conduct is interrogation, we must remember the purpose behind [*Miranda*]: preventing government officials from using the coercive nature of confinement to extract confessions that would not be given in an unrestrained environment. The government actions in this case do not implicate the purpose in any way."

Dissenting Justice STEVENS, joined by Brennan, Marshall and Blackmun, JJ., maintained:

"[The] facts compel the conclusion that the police took advantage of Mrs. Mauro's request to visit her husband, setting up a confrontation between them at a time when he manifestly desired to remain silent. Because they allowed [Mauro's] conversation with his wife to commence at a time when they knew it was reasonably likely to produce an incriminating statement, the police interrogated him.

"[The] intent of the detectives is clear from their own testimony. They both knew that if the conversation took place, incriminating statements were likely to be made. With that in mind, they decided to take in a tape recorder, sit near [Mauro] and his wife and allow the conversation to commence. * * *

"It is undisputed that a police decision to place two suspects in the same room and then to listen to or record their conversation may constitute a form of interrogation even if no questions are asked by any police officers.[a] That is exactly

a. Does Justice Stevens mean that this situation may constitute a form of interrogation within the meaning of *Miranda* even if the suspects are *unaware* that the police are listen-

what happened here. [The Mauros] were both suspects in the murder of their son. Each of them had been interrogated separately before the officers decided to allow them to converse, an act that surely did not require a tape recorder or the presence of a police officer within hearing range. Under the circumstances, the police knew or should have known that [this encounter] was reasonably likely to produce an incriminating statement. * * *

"[Under] the circumstances, the mere fact that [Mrs. Mauro] made the initial request leading to the conversation does not alter [the fact that the police violated *Miranda*]. [They] exercised exclusive control over whether and when the suspects spoke with each other; the police knew that whatever Mauro wished to convey to his wife at that moment, he would have to say under the conditions unilaterally imposed by the officers. In brief, the police exploited the custodial situation and the understandable desire of Mrs. Mauro to speak with [her husband] to conduct an interrogation."

Notes and Questions

(i) *Likelihood of incrimination.* According to the *Mauro* majority, the meeting between Mauro and his wife did not "present a sufficient likelihood of incrimination" to satisfy the *Innis* standard [fn. 6]. What if it did? What if, as the dissenters maintained, the police did know or should have known that the meeting between Mauro and his wife was likely to produce an incriminating statement. Should this be decisive in a case like *Mauro*?

Should the *Innis* language defining police interrogation or its functional equivalent be taken literally? Did the *Innis* Court assume a basic factual setting—police conduct equivalent to direct police questioning in terms of its compulsion or pressure? Did the *Innis* Court have in mind conduct *by the police* and in *the presence of the suspect*, such as confronting the suspect with a report indicating that he "flunked" a lie detector exam or confronting him with the confession of an accomplice or bringing an effusive and accusing accomplice into the same room with the police and the suspect?[b]

(ii) *"Police blue" compulsion.* If a spouse or parent or friend meets with someone in custody, does that add significantly to the *official* compulsion, the *"police blue"* compulsion? If not, why should this conduct be considered the equivalent of "custodial *police* interrogation"?

(iii) *The purpose of the police.* The *Mauro* majority emphasizes the lack of any evidence that the police sent Mrs. Mauro to see her husband "for the purpose of eliciting incriminating statements." What if the detectives had asked Mrs. Mauro to try to get her husband to confess and she had agreed to do so? Would she have become an "agent" of the police? Why does this matter for *Miranda* purposes? If defendant *were unaware* of his wife's or the detectives' purpose, how would that purpose render defendant's environment more "compelling" or make him more likely to feel that he was being "coerced" to incriminate himself? How would the

ing to, or recording, their conversation? If so, why? Where is the "compulsion"? See the discussion following this case and the discussion in Note 8.

b. Although the *Innis* case involved police "speech," the Court's definition of "interrogation" embraces police tactics that do not. Thus, the Court seems to have repudiated the position taken by a number of courts prior to *Innis*

that *confronting* a suspect with physical or documentary evidence (e.g., a ballistics report or a bank surveillance photograph) or *arranging a meeting in the presence of the police* between an arrestee and an accomplice who has already confessed is not "interrogation" because it does not involve verbal conduct on the part of the police. For criticism of these pre-*Innis* cases, see Kamisar Essays at 156–58 n. 21.

undisclosed purpose of the police alter the situation *from the defendant's perspective?*

(iv) *The suspect's awareness that the police are present.* Is the key factor in a case like *Mauro* not the intent of the police but the suspect's awareness that the police are present, or listening, when he meets with a spouse or friend? If Detective Manson had not been physically present, but the police had *secretly recorded* defendant's meeting with his wife, would *Mauro* have been a much easier case? Why (not)? See next Note.

7. *The "jail plant" situation; "surreptitious interrogation."* Suppose a secret government agent, posing as a fellow-prisoner, is placed in the same cell or cellblock with an incarcerated suspect and induces him to discuss the crime for which he has been arrested. Does this constitute "custodial interrogation"? No, answered the Court in ILLINOIS v. PERKINS, 496 U.S. 292, 110 S.Ct. 2394, 110 L.Ed.2d 243 (1990); "*Miranda* warnings are not required when the suspect is unaware that he is speaking to a law enforcement officer and gives a voluntary statement."

The case arose as follows: Respondent Perkins, who was suspected of committing the Stephenson murder, was incarcerated on charges unrelated to the murder. The police placed Charlton (who had been a fellow inmate of Perkins in another prison) and Parisi (an undercover officer) in the same cellblock with Perkins. The secret government agents were instructed to engage Perkins in casual conversation and to report anything he said about the Stephenson murder. The cellblock consisted of 12 separate cells that opened onto a common room. When Charlton met Perkins in the prison he introduced Parisi by his alias. Parisi suggested that the three of them escape. There was further conversation. Parisi asked Perkins if he had ever "done" anybody. Perkins replied that he had and proceeded to describe his involvement in the Stephenson murder in detail.

In an opinion joined by six other Justices, KENNEDY, J., explained why Perkins' statements were not barred by *Miranda:*

"The essential ingredients of a 'police-dominated atmosphere' and compulsion are not present when an incarcerated person speaks freely to someone that he believes to be a fellow inmate. Coercion is determined from the perspective of the suspect. [When] a suspect considers himself in the company of cellmates and not officers, the coercive atmosphere is lacking.

"[It] is the premise of *Miranda* that the danger of coercion results from the interaction of custody and official interrogation. We reject the argument that *Miranda* warnings are required whenever a suspect is in custody in a technical sense and converses with someone who happens to be a government agent. [When] the suspect has no reason to think that the listeners have official power over him, it should not be assumed that his words are motivated by the reaction he expects from his listeners. '[W]hen the agent carries neither badge nor gun and wears not "police blue," but the same prison gray' as the suspect, there is no '*interplay* between police interrogation and police custody.' Kamisar, *Brewer v. Williams, Massiah and Miranda: What is 'Interrogation?' When Does it Matter?,* 67 Geo.L.J. 1, 67, 63 (1978). [The] only difference between this case and *Hoffa* is that the suspect here was incarcerated, but detention, whether or not for the crime in question, does not warrant a presumption that the use of an undercover agent to speak with an incarcerated suspect makes any confession thus obtained involuntary. * * *

"[This] Court's Sixth Amendment decisions in [the *Massiah* line of cases] also do not avail respondent. [No] charges had been filed [against him] on the subject of the interrogation, and our Sixth Amendment precedents are not applicable.''[a]

Only MARSHALL, J., dissented, maintaining that "[t]he conditions that require the police to apprise a defendant of his constitutional rights—custodial interrogation conducted by an agent of the police—were present in this case. Because [respondent] received no *Miranda* warnings before he was subjected to custodial interrogation, his confession was not admissible." Continued Justice Marshall:

"Because Perkins was interrogated by police while he was in custody, *Miranda* required that the officer inform him of his rights. In rejecting that conclusion, the Court finds that 'conversations' between undercover agents and suspects are devoid of the coercion inherent in stationhouse interrogations conducted by law enforcement officials who openly represent the State. *Miranda* was not, however, concerned solely with police *coercion*. It dealt with *any* police tactics that may operate to compel a suspect in custody to make incriminating statements without full awareness of his constitutional rights. [Thus,] when a law enforcement agent structures a custodial interrogation so that a suspect feels compelled to reveal incriminating information, he must inform the suspect of his constitutional rights and give him an opportunity to decide whether or not to talk. * * *

"[The] psychological pressures inherent in confinement increase the suspect's anxiety, making him likely to seek relief by talking with others. [The] inmate is thus more susceptible to efforts by undercover agents to elicit information from him. Similarly, where the suspect is incarcerated, the constant threat of physical danger peculiar to the prison environment may make him demonstrate his toughness to other inmates by recounting or inventing past violent acts. [In] this case, the police deceptively took advantage of Perkins' psychological vulnerability by including him in a sham escape plot, a situation in which he would feel compelled to demonstrate his willingness to shoot a prison guard by revealing his past involvement in a murder.

"[Thus,] the pressures unique to custody allow the police to use deceptive interrogation tactics to compel a suspect to make an incriminating statement. The compulsion is not eliminated by the suspect's ignorance of his interrogator's true identity. The Court therefore need not inquire past the bare facts of custody and interrogation to determine whether *Miranda* warnings are required. * * *''

Notes and Questions

(a) Is *Perkins* a case where, as dissenting Justice Marshall maintains, "a law enforcement agent structures a custodial interrogation so that a suspect feels compelled to reveal incriminating information" or is it a case where a law enforcement agent structures a situation so that a suspect feels free to reveal incriminating information?

(b) Consider Fred Cohen, *Miranda and Police Deception in Interrogation,* 26 Crim.L.Bull. 534, 543–44 (1990): "Can it be that the *Miranda* rule was intended to be responsive only to force while leaving in place and indeed encouraging the

---

a. Brennan, J., concurred in the judgment of the Court, "agree[ing] that when a suspect does not know that his questioner is a police agent, such questioning does not amount to 'interrogation' in an 'inherently coercive' environment so as to require application of *Miranda*"—"the only issue raised at this stage of the litigation." But he went on to say that "the deception and manipulation practiced on re-

spondent raise a substantial claim that the confession was obtained in violation of the Due Process Clause." For "the deliberate use of deception and manipulation by the police appears to be incompatible 'with a system that presumes innocence and assures that a conviction will not be secured by inquisitional means' and raises serious concerns that respondent's will was overborne."

refinement of other methods for achieving an *uninformed* confession? The word *uninformed* is emphasized because I believe strongly that *Miranda* was intended to achieve some form of rough informational equivalency between the state and the accused during the interrogative phase of the investigatory stage in a criminal proceeding. [If] *Miranda* was fashioned solely to ameliorate the inherent coercion associated with a police-dominated environment, then *Perkins* was correctly decided. If *Miranda* was concerned also with informational equivalency and with giving suspects an opportunity to obtain counsel and, in effect, barter information, instead of making an uninformed gift, then *Perkins* was wrongly decided."

8. More on "custodial interrogation" and the "booking question exception" to Miranda. Consider PENNSYLVANIA v. MUNIZ, 496 U.S. 582, 110 S.Ct. 2638, 110 L.Ed.2d 528 (1990). The case arose as follows:

Respondent Muniz was arrested for driving while intoxicated. Without advising him of his *Miranda* rights, Officer Hosterman asked Muniz to perform three standard field sobriety tests. Muniz performed poorly and then admitted that he had been drinking. Muniz was taken to a Booking Center. Following its routine practice for receiving persons suspected of driving under the influence, the Booking Center videotaped the ensuing proceedings. Muniz was told that his action and voice were being recorded, but again he was not advised of his *Miranda* rights. Officer Hosterman first asked Muniz his name, address, height, weight, eye color, date of birth, and current age (the "first seven questions" or the seven "booking" questions). Both the delivery and content of his answers were incriminating. Next the officer asked Muniz what the Court called "the sixth birthday question": "Do you know what the date was of your sixth birthday?" Muniz responded, "No, I don't."

The officer then requested Muniz to perform the same sobriety tests that he had been asked to do earlier during the initial roadside stop. While performing the tests, Muniz made several audible and incriminating statements. Finally, Muniz was asked to submit to a breathalyzer test. He refused. At this point, for the first time, Muniz was advised of his *Miranda* rights. Both the video and audio portions of the videotape were admitted into evidence, along with the arresting officer's testimony that Muniz failed the roadside sobriety tests and made incriminating statements at the time. Muniz was convicted of driving while intoxicated.

The Court excluded only Muniz's response to the "sixth birthday question" (by a 5–4 vote). BRENNAN, J., wrote the opinion of the Court, except as to the grounds for admitting Muniz's answers to the first seven questions or "booking" questions.

Some of the issues raised by the case were relatively easy. Muniz's answers to direct questions were not barred by *Miranda* "merely because the slurred nature of his speech was incriminating." Under *Schmerber v. California* (discussed at pp. 38, 235) and its progeny, "any slurring of speech and other evidence of lack of muscular coordination revealed by Muniz's responses * * * constitute nontestimonial components of those responses." Muniz's incriminating utterances during the physical sobriety tests were also admissible because "not prompted by an interrogation within the meaning of *Miranda*." Officer Hosterman's conversation with Muniz concerning the tests "consisted primarily of carefully scripted instructions as to how the tests were to be performed," instructions "not likely to be perceived as calling for any verbal response" and thus "not 'words or actions' constituting custodial interrogation."[a]

a. "Similarly," added the Court, "*Miranda* does not require suppression of the statements Muniz made when asked to submit to a breathalyzer examination." The officer who requested Muniz to take the breathalyzer test "carefully limited her role to providing Muniz with relevant information about [the] test and the implied consent law. She questioned Muniz

More difficult issues were whether Muniz's response to the sixth birthday question should be allowed into evidence and whether Muniz's answers to the first seven questions asked him at the Booking Center (the seven "booking" questions) were admissible—and if not, *why* not.

In contrast to a number of other questions Muniz was asked, the sixth birthday question, observed the Court, per Brennan, J., "required a testimonial response. When Officer Hosterman asked Muniz if he knew the date of his sixth birthday and Muniz, for whatever reason, could not remember or calculate that date, he was [placed in a predicament the self-incrimination clause was designed to prevent]. By hypothesis, the inherently coercive environment created by the custodial interrogation precluded the option of remaining silent. Muniz was left with the choice of incriminating himself by admitting that he did not then know the date of his sixth birthday, or answering untruthfully by reporting a date that he did not then believe to be accurate (an incorrect guess would be incriminating as well as truthful). [The] incriminating inference of impaired mental facilities stemmed, not just from the fact that Muniz slurred his response, but also from a testimonial aspect of that response."

REHNQUIST, C.J., joined by White, Blackmun and Stevens, JJ., disagreed:

"The sixth birthday question here was an effort on the part of the police to check how well Muniz was able to do a simple mathematical exercise. Indeed, had the question related only to the date of his birthday, it presumably would have come under the 'booking exception' to *Miranda* to which the Court refers elsewhere in its opinion. [See discussion below.] [If] the police may require Muniz to use his body in order to demonstrate the level of his physical coordination, there is no reason why they should not be able to require him to speak or write in order to determine his mental coordination. That was all that was sought here. Since it was permissible for the police to extract and examine a sample of Schmerber's blood to determine how much that part of his system had been affected by alcohol, I see no reason why they may not examine the functioning of Muniz's mental processes for the same purpose."

Eight members of the Court agreed that the answers to the "booking" questions were admissible, but they differed as to the reason. Four Justices (Rehnquist, C.J., joined by White, Blackmun and Stevens, JJ.) did not consider the questions "testimonial." Thus, they did not address the issue whether, even if the questions were "testimonial," they came under a "booking exception" to *Miranda*. The other four Justices (Brennan, J., joined by O'Connor, Scalia and Kennedy, JJ.,) believed the first seven questions were "testimonial" and did amount to "custodial interrogation" within the meaning of *Miranda*. Nonetheless, they concluded that Muniz's answers were admissible because of a "routine booking question" exception to *Miranda*—one that permits questions "to secure the 'biographical data necessary to complete booking or pretrial services.' " The state court had found that the first seven questions were "requested for record-keeping purposes only"; thus, "the questions appear reasonably related to the police's administrative concerns."

Only MARSHALL, J., would have kept out the answers to the first seven questions. He rejected both the Brennan group's and the Rehnquist group's rationales for admitting Muniz's answers to these questions:

only as to whether he understood her instructions and wished to submit to the test. These limited and focused inquiries were necessarily 'attendant to' the legitimate police procedure [and] not likely to be perceived as calling for any incriminating response."

The Court noted that "Muniz does not and cannot challenge the introduction into evidence of his refusal to submit to the breathalyzer test." See *South Dakota v. Neville* (p. 499).

"[The questions] sought 'testimonial' responses for the same reason the sixth birthday question did: because the content of the answers would indicate Muniz's state of mind. The booking questions, like the sixth birthday question, required Muniz to (1) answer correctly, indicating lucidity, (2) answer incorrectly, implying that his mental facilities were impaired, or (3) state that he did not know the answer, also indicating impairment. Muniz's initial incorrect response to the question about his age and his inability to give his address without looking at his license, like his inability to answer the sixth birthday question, in fact gave rise to the incriminating inference that his mental facilities were impaired."

As for the Brennan group's rationale for admitting Muniz's answers—the questions fell within a "routine booking question" exception to *Miranda*—even if such an exception was appropriate in some instances, responded Marshall, J., the exception "should not extend to booking questions [asked in circumstances, such as the instant case, which] the police should know are reasonably likely to elicit incriminating responses." More generally, Justice Marshall balked at creating "yet another exception" to *Miranda* because "[s]uch exceptions undermine *Miranda's* fundamental principle that the doctrine should be clear so that it can be easily applied by both police and courts."

9. *Questioning prompted by concern for "public safety."*

NEW YORK v. QUARLES
467 U.S. 649, 104 S.Ct. 2626, 81 L.Ed.2d 550 (1984).

Justice REHNQUIST delivered the opinion of the Court.

[At approximately 12:30 a.m., police apprehended respondent in the rear of a supermarket. He matched the description of the man who had just raped a woman. The woman had told the police that the rapist had just entered the supermarket and that he was carrying a gun. Apparently upon seeing Officer Kraft enter the store, respondent turned and ran toward the rear. Officer Kraft pursued him with a drawn gun and, upon regaining sight of him, ordered him to stop and put his hands over his head. Although several other officers had arrived at the scene by then, Kraft was the first to reach respondent. He frisked him and discovered he was wearing an empty shoulder holster. After handcuffing him, the officer asked where the gun was. Respondent nodded in the direction of some empty cartons and responded, "the gun is over there." At that time, emphasized the New York Court of Appeals, respondent was surrounded by four officers whose guns had been returned to their holsters because, as one testified, the situation was under control.

[The gun was not visible, but Officer Kraft reached into one of the cartons and retrieved a loaded revolver. Respondent was then formally placed under arrest and advised of his *Miranda* rights. Respondent waived his rights. In response to questions, he then stated that he owned the revolver and had purchased it in Miami.

[In the subsequent prosecution of respondent for criminal possession of a weapon (the record does not reveal why the state failed to pursue the rape charge), the New York courts suppressed the statement "the gun is over there" as well as the gun itself because they had been obtained in violation of respondent's *Miranda* rights. Respondent's statements about his ownership of the gun and the place of purchase were also excluded as having been fatally tainted by the seizure of the gun and the prewarning response as to its location.]

* * * We conclude that under the circumstances involved in this case, overriding considerations of public safety justify the officer's failure to provide

Miranda warnings before he asked questions devoted to locating the abandoned weapon.

[In] this case we have before us no claim that respondent's statements were actually compelled by police conduct which overcame his will to resist. Thus the only issue before us is whether Officer Kraft was justified in failing to make available to respondent the procedural safeguards associated with the privilege against compulsory self-incrimination since *Miranda*.[5]

The New York Court of Appeals was undoubtedly correct in deciding that the facts of this case come within the ambit of the *Miranda* decision as we have subsequently interpreted it. [The] New York Court of Appeals' majority declined to express an opinion as to whether there might be an exception to the *Miranda* rule if the police had been acting to protect the public, because the lower courts in New York had made no factual determination that the police had acted with that motive.

We hold that on these facts there is a "public safety" exception to the requirement that *Miranda* warnings be given before a suspect's answers may be admitted into evidence, and that the availability of that exception does not depend upon the motivation of the individual officers involved. In a kaleidoscopic situation such as the one confronting these officers, where spontaneity rather than adherence to a police manual is necessarily the order of the day, the application of the exception which we recognize today should not be made to depend on *post hoc* findings at a suppression hearing concerning the subjective motivation of the arresting officer.[6] Undoubtedly most police officers, if placed in Officer Kraft's position, would act out of a host of different, instinctive, and largely unverifiable motives—their own safety, the safety of others, and perhaps as well the desire to obtain incriminating evidence from the suspect.

Whatever the motivation of individual officers in such a situation, we do not believe that the doctrinal underpinnings of *Miranda* require that it be applied in all its rigor to a situation in which police officers ask questions reasonably prompted by a concern for the public safety.

[The] police in this case, in the very act of apprehending a suspect, were confronted with the immediate necessity of ascertaining the whereabouts of a gun which they had every reason to believe the suspect had just removed from his empty holster and discarded in the supermarket. So long as the gun was concealed somewhere in the supermarket, with its actual whereabouts unknown, it obviously posed more than one danger to the public safety: an accomplice might make use of it, a customer or employee might later come upon it.

In such a situation, if the police are required to recite the familiar *Miranda* warnings before asking the whereabouts of the gun, suspects in Quarles' position might well be deterred from responding. Procedural safeguards which deter a suspect from responding were deemed acceptable in *Miranda* in order to protect

---

5. The dissent curiously takes us to task for "endors[ing] the introduction of coerced self-incriminating statements in criminal prosecutions." [Of] course our decision today does nothing of the kind. [R]espondent is certainly free on remand to argue that his statement was coerced under traditional due process standards. Today we merely reject the only argument that respondent has raised to support the exclusion of his statement, that the statement must be *presumed* compelled because of Officer Kraft's failure to read him his *Miranda* warnings.

6. Similar approaches have been rejected in other contexts. See *Innis* (officer's subjective intent to incriminate not determinative of whether "interrogation" occurred); *Mendenhall* (opinion of Stewart, J.) (officer's subjective intent to detain not determinative of whether a "seizure" occurred within the meaning of the Fourth Amendment); *Robinson* (officer's subjective fear not determinative of necessity for "search incident to arrest" exception to the Fourth Amendment warrant requirement).

the Fifth Amendment privilege; when the primary social cost of those added protections is the possibility of fewer convictions, the *Miranda* majority was willing to bear that cost. Here, had *Miranda* warnings deterred Quarles from responding to Officer Kraft's question about the whereabouts of the gun, the cost would have been something more than merely the failure to obtain evidence useful in convicting Quarles. Officer Kraft needed an answer to his question not simply to make his case against Quarles but to insure that further danger to the public did not result from the concealment of the gun in a public area.

We conclude that the need for answers to questions in a situation posing a threat to the public safety outweighs the need for the prophylactic rule protecting the Fifth Amendment's privilege against self-incrimination. We decline to place officers such as Officer Kraft in the untenable position of having to consider, often in a matter of seconds, whether it best serves society for them to ask the necessary questions without the *Miranda* warnings and render whatever probative evidence they uncover inadmissible, or for them to give the warnings in order to preserve the admissibility of evidence they might uncover but possibly damage or destroy their ability to obtain that evidence and neutralize the volatile situation confronting them.[7]

[This exception] will not be difficult for police officers to apply because in each case it will be circumscribed by the exigency which justifies it. We think police officers can and will distinguish almost instinctively between questions necessary to secure their own safety or the safety of the public and questions designed solely to elicit testimonial evidence from a suspect.

The facts of this case clearly demonstrate that distinction and an officer's ability to recognize it. Officer Kraft asked only the question necessary to locate the missing gun before advising respondent of his rights. It was only after securing the loaded revolver and giving the warnings that he continued with investigatory questions about the ownership and place of purchase of the gun. The exception which we recognize today, far from complicating the thought processes and the on-the-scene judgments of police officers, will simply free them to follow their legitimate instincts when confronting situations presenting a danger to the public safety.[8]

We hold that the [court below] erred in excluding the statement, "the gun is over there," and the gun because of the officer's failure to read respondent his *Miranda* rights before attempting to locate the weapon. Accordingly [it] also erred in excluding the subsequent statements as illegal fruits of a *Miranda* violation.[9]
* * *

7. The dissent argues that a public safety exception to *Miranda* is unnecessary because in every case an officer can simply ask the necessary questions to protect himself or the public, and then the prosecution can decline to introduce any incriminating responses at a subsequent trial. But absent actual coercion by the officer, there is no constitutional imperative requiring the exclusion of the evidence that results from police inquiry of this kind; and we do not believe that the doctrinal underpinnings of *Miranda* require us to exclude the evidence, thus penalizing officers for asking the very questions which are the most crucial to their efforts to protect themselves and the public.

8. Although it involves police questions in part relating to the whereabouts of a gun, *Orozco v. Texas* [p. 495, fn. a] is in no sense

inconsistent with our disposition of this case. [In *Orozco*,] the questions about the gun were clearly investigatory; they did not in any way relate to an objectively reasonable need to protect the police or the public from any immediate danger associated with the weapon. In short there was no exigency requiring immediate action by the officers beyond the normal need expeditiously to solve a serious crime.

Innis also involved the whereabouts of a missing weapon, but our holding in that case depended entirely on our conclusion that no police interrogation took place so as to require consideration of the applicability of the *Miranda* prophylactic.

9. Because we hold that there is no violation of *Miranda* in this case, we have no occasion to [decide whether] the gun is admissible either because it is nontestimonial or because

Justice O'CONNOR, concurring in part in the judgment and dissenting in part. * * *

[Justice O'Connor would suppress the respondent's initial statement, "the gun is over there"—but not the gun itself because "nothing in *Miranda* or the privilege itself requires exclusion of nontestimonial evidence derived from informal custodial interrogation." Justice O'Connor's views on why *Miranda* requires that respondent's initial statement be suppressed are set forth below. Her views on the admissibility of the gun itself and her thoughts about the statements elicited after the *Miranda* warnings were given are set forth at p. 781. See also Justice O'Connor's discussion of the application (or nonapplication) of the "fruit of the poisonous tree" doctrine in her opinion for the Court in *Oregon v. Elstad*, p. 781.]

In my view, a "public safety" exception unnecessarily blurs the edges of the clear line heretofore established and makes *Miranda's* requirements more difficult to understand. In some cases, police will benefit because a reviewing court will find that an exigency excused their failure to administer the required warnings. But in other cases, police will suffer because, though they thought an exigency excused their noncompliance, a reviewing court will view the "objective" circumstances differently and require exclusion of admissions thereby obtained. The end result will be a finespun new doctrine on public safety exigencies incident to custodial interrogation, complete with the hair-splitting distinctions that currently plague our Fourth Amendment jurisprudence.

[*Miranda*] has never been read to prohibit the police from asking questions to secure the public safety. Rather, the critical question *Miranda* addresses is who shall bear the cost of securing the public safety when such questions are asked and answered: the defendant or the State. *Miranda*, for better or worse, found the resolution of that question implicit in the prohibition against compulsory self-incrimination and placed the burden on the State. When police ask custodial questions without administering the required warnings, *Miranda* quite clearly requires that the answers received be presumed compelled and that they be excluded from evidence at trial. * * *

Justice MARSHALL, with whom Justice BRENNAN and Justice STEVENS join, dissenting * * *.

The majority's entire analysis rests on the factual assumption that the public was at risk during Quarles' interrogation. This assumption is completely in conflict with the facts as found by New York's highest court. * * * Contrary to the majority's speculations, Quarles was not believed to have, nor did he in fact have, an accomplice to come to his rescue. When the questioning began, the arresting officers were sufficiently confident of their safety to put away their guns.

[The] New York court's conclusion that neither Quarles nor his missing gun posed a threat to the public's safety is amply supported by the evidence presented at the suppression hearing. [Although] the supermarket was open to the public, Quarles' arrest took place during the middle of the night when the store was apparently deserted except for the clerks at the checkout counter. The police could easily have cordoned off the store and searched for the missing gun. Had they done so, they would have found the gun forthwith. [As] the State acknowledged

the police would inevitably have discovered it absent their questioning.

[A year earlier, in *Nix v. Williams* (*Williams II*), p. 775, the Court had held that the "fruit of the poisonous tree" doctrine did not bar the use of evidence derived from a constitutional violation if such evidence would "ultimately" or "inevitably" have been discovered even if the police had acted lawfully. The "fruits" doctrine, formulated initially in applying the Fourth Amendment exclusionary rule, prohibits the use of evidence derived from, and thus "tainted" by, a constitutional violation.]

Dissent

before the New York Court of Appeals: "After Officer Kraft had handcuffed and frisked the defendant in the supermarket, *he knew with a high degree of certainty that the defendant's gun was within the immediate vicinity of the encounter.* He undoubtedly would have searched for it in the carton a few feet away without the defendant having looked in that direction and saying that it was there." (Emphasis added.)

[This] case is illustrative of the chaos the "public-safety" exception will unleash. The circumstances of Quarles' arrest have never been in dispute. [T]he New York Court of Appeals concluded that there was "no evidence in the record before us that there were exigent circumstances posing a risk to the public safety." Upon reviewing the same facts and hearing the same arguments, a majority of this Court has come to precisely the opposite conclusion * * *.[4]

Though unfortunate, the difficulty of administering the "public-safety" exception is not the most profound flaw in the majority's decision. The majority has lost sight of the fact that *Miranda* and our earlier custodial-interrogation cases all implemented a constitutional privilege against self-incrimination. The rules established in these cases were designed to protect criminal defendants against prosecutions based on coerced self-incriminating statements. The majority today turns its back on these constitutional considerations, and invites the government to prosecute through the use of what necessarily are coerced statements.

[Whether] society would be better off if the police warned suspects of their rights before beginning an interrogation or whether the advantages of giving such warnings would outweigh their costs did not inform the *Miranda* decision. On the contrary, the *Miranda* Court was concerned with the proscriptions of the Fifth Amendment, and, in particular, whether the Self–Incrimination Clause permits the government to prosecute individuals based on statements made in the course of custodial interrogations.

[In] fashioning its "public-safety" exception to *Miranda,* the majority makes no attempt to deal with the constitutional presumption established by that case. [The] majority's only contention is that police officers could more easily protect the public if *Miranda* did not apply to custodial interrogations concerning the public's safety. But *Miranda* was not a decision about public safety; it was a decision about coerced confessions. Without establishing that interrogations concerning the public's safety are less likely to be coercive than other interrogations, the majority cannot endorse the "public-safety" exception and remain faithful to the logic of *Miranda*.

[The] irony of the majority's decision is that the public's safety can be perfectly well protected without abridging the Fifth Amendment. If a bomb is about to explode or the public is otherwise imminently imperiled, the police are free to interrogate suspects without advising them of their constitutional rights. [If] trickery is necessary to protect the public, then the police may trick a suspect into confessing. While the Fourteenth Amendment sets limits on such behavior, nothing in the Fifth Amendment or our decision in *Miranda* proscribes this sort of emergency questioning. All the Fifth Amendment forbids is the introduction of coerced statements at trial. * * *[b]

---

4. One of the peculiarities of the majority's decision is its suggestion that police officers can "distinguish almost instinctively" questions tied to public safety and questions designed to elicit testimonial evidence. Obviously, these distinctions are extraordinarily difficult to draw. In many cases—like this one—custodial questioning may serve both purposes. It is therefore wishful thinking for the majority to suggest that the intuitions of police officers will render its decision self-executing.

b. For the portion of Justice Marshall's dissenting opinion dealing with the admissibility of the gun discovered as a result of Quarles' statement, see p. 781.

Notes and Questions

(a) If a case like *Innis* or *Mesa* (the "hostage negotiator" case) arose today, would the courts quickly dispose of it by invoking the "public safety" exception to *Miranda*? For a case that does just that, see *State v. Finch*, 975 P.2d 967 (Wash.1999).

(b) *Quarles* and *Miranda*. The *Quarles* case, observes Charles Weisselberg, *Saving Miranda*, 84 Cornell L.Rev. 109, 129 (1998), "struck at the Court's original version of *Miranda* in several respects": It "reinforced the notion that the warning requirement was divorced from the Fifth Amendment"; the majority's cost-benefit analysis "represents a wholly different view of the value of the Fifth Amendment than was expressed in *Miranda*"; and "[t]hird, by creating a vague and ill-defined exception to the warning requirement, the Court reduced the efficacy of *Miranda*'s bright-line rules." However, adds Professor Weisselberg, *Quarles* "did not—as it turns out—open the door to other large exceptions to the *Miranda* rule. In the fourteen years since *Quarles* was decided, the Supreme Court has not approved any other instances of custodial interrogations in which warnings need not be given."

(c) Is the *Quarles* Court's attempt to distinguish *Orozco* (see fn. 8) convincing? In *Orozco,* the police entered a sleeping defendant's room and questioned him about a gun used in a murder several hours earlier. They had ample cause to believe that defendant was the murderer and, as it turned out, the murder weapon *was* hidden in his room. There was no need to protect *the public* from immediate danger, but why wasn't there a need to protect *the police?* Does the Court's treatment of *Orozco* mean that, at least where there is no threat to members of the public, *Quarles* only permits the police to ask about the location of a gun when they come upon the scene in "hot pursuit?"

(d) *The "rescue doctrine."* Somewhat similar to the "public safety" exception is the "rescue doctrine." Should statements obtained in violation of *Miranda* be admissible if police interrogation of a suspected kidnapper is motivated primarily by a desire to save the victim's life? Yes, answer *People v. Dean*, 114 Cal.Rptr. 555 (Cal.App.1974) and *People v. Krom*, 461 N.E.2d 276 (N.Y.1984). See generally William T. Pizzi, *The Privilege Against Self–Incrimination in a Rescue Situation*, 76 J.Crim.L. & C. (1985). It is unsound, maintains Professor Pizzi, id. at 595–603, to approach the scope of the privilege against self-incrimination "solely from the defendant's point of view while totally ignoring the threat to the lives of others and the purpose and function of the police conduct"; the privilege and its attendant rules should not control "where the police are functioning in a situation which is primarily noninvestigative and where life is at stake."

Are there (should there be) any limits on what a police officer may do to a suspected kidnapper in order to get him to reveal the location of a kidnap victim? Cf. *Leon v. State*, 410 So.2d 201 (Fla.App.1982), holding, over a forceful dissent, that the use of police threats and physical violence at the scene of arrest in order to ascertain the kidnap victim's whereabouts "did not constitutionally infect the later confessions." Consider Pizzi, supra, at 606: "[T]here are [due process] limits on the conduct of the police in their treatment of suspects even in an emergency situation where life is at stake," but "[i]n determining those limits [the] traditional scope of police conduct permitted in a purely investigative context is only a starting point."

10. *Meeting the "heavy burden" of demonstrating waiver: should tape recordings of the warnings and police questioning be required?* Five years *before* the *Miranda* case, one close student of the problem, Bernard Weis-

Reorder
Military

berg, *Police Interrogation of Arrested Persons: A Skeptical View*, 52 J. Crim.L. &
P.S. 21, 48 (1961), attacked the secrecy surrounding police interrogation: "No
other case comes to mind in which an administrative official is permitted the
broad discretionary power assumed by the police interrogator, together with the
power to prevent objective recordation of the facts. The absence of a record makes
disputes inevitable about the conduct of the police and, sometimes, about what the
prisoner has actually said. It is secrecy, not privacy, which accounts for the
absence of a reliable record of interrogation proceedings in a police station. If the
need for some pre-judicial questioning is assumed, privacy may be defended on
grounds of necessity; secrecy cannot be defended on this or any other ground."

Recall, too, that before turning to the police manuals for valuable information
about current police practices, the *Miranda* Court noted that the secrecy surrounding police questioning "results in a gap in our knowledge as to what in fact
goes on in the interrogation rooms." (See p. 463.) However, as pointed out by
Richard A. Leo, *Inside the Interrogation Room*, 86 J. Crim.L. & Criminology 266
(1996), three decades after *Miranda*, we know "scant more" about actual police
interrogation practices than we did at the time that famous case was decided.

At one point, the *Miranda* opinion (see p. 471) came to the very edge of
requiring law enforcement officers to tape, where feasible, the warning, waiver
and subsequent questioning and statements made in response: "If the interrogation continues without the presence of an attorney and a statement is taken, a
heavy burden rests on the Government to demonstrate that the defendant
knowingly and intelligently waived his [rights]. Since the State is responsible for
establishing the isolated circumstances under which the interrogation takes place
and *has the only means of making available corroborated evidence* of warnings
given during incommunicado interrogation, the burden is rightly on its shoulders." (Emphasis added.) However, the *Miranda* Court fell short of imposing a
tape recording requirement on police interrogators—perhaps because it was well
aware that such a requirement would add much fuel to the criticism that it was
exercising undue control over police practices—that it was "legislating."

Despite the references to "heavy burden" and "corroborated evidence" in the
Miranda opinion and the strong support for video, or at least audio, taping in the
literature, all but two state courts have held that—even when taping the proceedings in the interrogation room is feasible—the uncorroborated testimony of an
officer that he gave complete *Miranda* warnings and obtained a waiver is sufficient. The two exceptions are *Stephan v. State*, 711 P.2d 1156 (Alaska 1985) and
State v. Scales, 518 N.W.2d 587 (Minn.1994).

PAUL G. CASSELL, *Miranda's Social Costs: An Empirical Assessment*, 90
Nw. U.L.Rev. 387, 486–97 (1996), has forcefully argued that a recording requirement should be viewed as an *alternative* to *Miranda*:

"Videotaping interrogations would certainly be as effective as *Miranda* in
preventing police coercion and probably more so. The *Miranda* regime appears to
have had little effect on the police misconduct that does exist. In contrast,
videotaping, when used, has often reduced claims of police coercion and probably
real coercion as well. To be sure, police conceivably could alter tapes or deploy
force off-camera. But if you were facing a police officer with a rubber hose, would
you prefer a world in which he was required to mumble the *Miranda* warnings
and have you waive your rights, all as reported by him in later testimony? Or a
world in which the interrogation is videorecorded and the burden is on law
enforcement to explain if it is not; where date and time are recorded on the
videotape; where your physical appearance and demeanor during the interrogation
are permanently recorded?[a]

a. "Recent and substantial experience with   tian," notes Cassell, "suggests that such a re-
a mandatory recording requirement in Bri-   quirement would not significantly harm police

A[In] light of the benefits of videotaping and the costly features of *Miranda*, what might a replacement for *Miranda* look like? Suspects could continue to be advised of their rights as follows:

(1) You do not have to say anything.

(2) Anything you do say may be used as evidence.

(3) You have the right to be represented by a lawyer when we bring you before a judge.

(4) If you cannot afford a lawyer, the judge will appoint one for you without charge.

(5) We are required to bring you before a judge without unnecessary delay.

"While adding a new, fifth warning that is not required by *Miranda*, the modified warnings would dispense with the *Miranda* offer of counsel, identified as a particularly harmful aspect of *Miranda* and, in any event, a right that has proven to be purely theoretical since police always terminate questioning rather than finding a lawyer. Also, the alternative would dispense with the requirement that police obtain an affirmative waiver of rights from suspects, another particularly harmful feature of *Miranda*. However, police could continue to ask suspects whether they understood the rights communicated to them, since nothing in the empirical literature identifies this aspect of *Miranda* as being particularly harmful. Also eliminated would be the requirement that police immediately terminate an interview whenever the suspect requests an end to the interview or an opportunity to meet with counsel. These features have been identified as harming the confession rate.[634]

"[Since] police are still required to give modified warnings and since they will be videotaped while conducting interrogations, police will not gain the mistaken impression that any judicial supervision of the interrogation process has ended.[b]

efforts to obtain confessions." In 1988, a Code of Practice went into effect that generally required the police to tape record interviews with suspects. A review of this requirement five years later by the Royal Commission on Criminal Justice reported that tape recording in the stationhouse had "proved to be a strikingly successful innovation providing better safeguards for the suspect and the police officer alike." According to one survey, some 90 percent of police officers approval of the practice, with two-thirds reporting "very favorable" news about it.

Consider, too, William A. Geller, *Videotaping Interrogations and Confessions* (1990), in Miranda: Law, Justice and Policing 303 (Richard A. Leo & George C. Thomas eds. 1998). In 1990, reports Geller, approximately one-third of all police and sheriffs departments in town or cities of 50,000 or more were doing some videotaping of police interrogation. According to Geller, the great majority of the agencies who have used videotaping had positive things to say about it.

If procedures relating to tape recordings are established, should the police inform the suspect that what he says is being recorded?

Would such a requirement inhibit too many from talking? On the other hand, would such a requirement bring home to suspects the seriousness of their situations? See Kamisar Essays at 133 n. 22.

634. Continued persistence to convince a suspect to change his mind will, at some point, render a confession involuntary and thus inadmissible under Fifth Amendment principles.
* * *

b. See also Richard A. Leo, *The Impact of Miranda Revisited*, 86 J. Crim. L. & Criminology 621, 680–82 (1996). Although he believes *Miranda* should neither be overruled nor strengthened doctrinally, Professor Leo maintains that substantive due process requires the electronic recording of custodial interrogations in all felony cases and that such a requirement constitutes the most adequate solution to the problems *Miranda* failed to resolve, such as "the problems of adjudicating the 'swearing contest' between officer and suspect in court; the problem of false allegations of police improprieties; the problem of police perjury; the problem of false confessions; and most notably, the problem of determining the voluntariness of a confession."

Professor Cassell's article evoked a response from STEPHEN J. SCHULHOF-ER, *Miranda's Practical Effect: Substantial Benefits and Vanishingly Small Social Costs*, 90 Nw. U.L.Rev. 556–60 (1996). Professor Schulhofer agreed that videotaping is an extremely valuable tool—for both the police interrogator and the suspect—but rejected the notion that videotaping could be *a* substitute for *Miranda*. He maintained that Cassell's proposed replacement for *Miranda* would expose suspects to violations of their constitutional rights:

"No doubt a videotaped record would often prevent police abuse and manipulation of the 'swearing contest.' But without clear substantive requirements against which to test the police behavior that the videotape will reveal, the objective record will lack any specific legal implications.

"The heart of the Cassell proposals is his recommendation to strip arrested suspects of their right to consult counsel during pre-arraignment interrogation, to eliminate the requirement that interrogation be preceded by an explicit waiver of rights, and to eliminate *Miranda*'s requirement that interrogation cease if a suspect makes a clear request to break off questioning or to consult with counsel. The requirements he would eliminate are not only central to the *Miranda* safeguards but have now become entrenched in the interrogation procedures of many countries around the world.[242]

"[Under Cassell's proposal,] [s]uspects would have no right to consult with counsel prior to formal arraignment. They would be told they have a right to remain silent, but the protective effect of that warning would be immediately negated by police actions. Instead of "scrupulously honoring" a suspect's decision to remain silent, as *Miranda* requires, police would be authorized to ignore the suspect's decision and press forward with the interrogation. Will suspects treated this way really have (or think they have) the right to remain silent? All they will have (mixed messages notwithstanding) is the legally sanctioned obligation to submit to an unwanted custodial interrogation.

"[The Cassell proposal would bring about a] return to the vague due process test [one that] would compel hundreds of thousands of unwilling suspects (roughly half a million suspects per year) to submit to involuntary questioning, and it would leave police (and courts) without any predictable framework for judging how long such an involuntary interrogation could last and what kinds of tactics could be used. * * *

11. *Implied waiver.* Although a waiver is not established merely by showing that a defendant was given complete *Miranda* warnings and thereafter made an incriminating statement, *Tague v. Louisiana*, 444 U.S. 469, 100 S.Ct. 652, 62 L.Ed.2d 622 (1980), this does not mean that a waiver of *Miranda* rights will never be recognized unless "specifically made" after the warnings are given. As the Court, per STEWART, J., observed in NORTH CAROLINA v. BUTLER, 441 U.S. 369, 99 S.Ct. 1755, 60 L.Ed.2d 286 (1979):

"The question is not one of form, but rather whether the defendant knowingly and voluntarily waived [his *Miranda* rights]. [Although] mere silence is not enough [that] does not mean that the defendant's silence, coupled with an

---

242. See Craig M. Bradley, *The Emerging International Consensus as to Criminal Procedure Rules*, 14 Mich.J.Int'l L. 171, 185 (1993) ("England's interrogation rules are *more stringent* than *Miranda*.") (emphasis added); id. at 197–98 (noting that in Canada, a suspect must be informed upon arrest of his right to counsel, and that police "must refrain from attempting to elicit evidence from the detainee until he has a reasonable opportunity to retain and instruct counsel") (quoting Martin's Annual Criminal Code CH–21 (1991); id. at 214–15 (Germany requires warning of rights to silence and right "*at all times, even before his examination,* to consult with defense counsel of his choice") (emphasis added) (quoting German Code of Criminal Procedure § 136); id. at 217–18 (noting that Italian interrogation rules prohibit use of statements made in the absence of counsel).

understanding of his rights and a course of conduct indicating waiver, may never support a conclusion that a defendant has waived his rights. The courts must presume that a defendant did not waive his rights; the prosecution's burden is great; but in at least some cases waiver can be clearly inferred from the actions and words of the person interrogated."[1]

Dissenting Justice BRENNAN, joined by Marshall and Stevens, JJ., protested: "[The Court] shrouds in half-light the question of waiver, allowing courts to construct inferences from ambiguous word and gestures. But the very premise of *Miranda* requires that ambiguity be interpreted against the interrogator. [Under the conditions inherent in custodial interrogation], only the most explicit waiver of rights can be considered knowingly and freely given. [S]ince the Court agrees that *Miranda* requires the police to obtain some kind of waiver—whether express or implied—the requirement of an express waiver would impose no burden on the police not imposed by the Court's interpretation. It would merely make that burden explicit. Had [the agent] simply elicited a clear answer to the question, 'Do you waive your right to a lawyer?' this journey through three courts would not have been necessary."

Notes and Questions

(a) *The "intelligent and knowing" test in practice.* Consider Mark Berger, *Compromise and Continuity: Miranda Waivers, Confession Admissibility, and the Retention of Interrogation Protections,* 49 U.Pitt.L.Rev. 1007, 1063 (1988): "Current indications are that [the requirement that *Miranda* waivers meet an intelligent and knowing test] extends no further than a general awareness by the suspect that he has the right to remain silent and have the assistance of counsel, and that anything he says can be used against him. Of course, these are the elements contained in the *Miranda* warning itself, and there is no sign that the Supreme Court is likely to require anything more to meet the knowing test. In practice, it appears that as long as the warnings are given and the suspect exhibits no overt signs of a lack of capacity to understand them, his waiver will be upheld."

(b) *Should the Johnson v. Zerbst standard apply to Miranda waivers?* Under *Johnson v. Zerbst* (1938) (quoted at p. 61), the prosecution must demonstrate "an intentional relinquishment or abandonment of a known right" in order to establish a waiver of counsel *at trial.* The *Miranda* Court (p. 471) cited *Zerbst* for the proposition that "this Court has always set high standards of proof for the waiver of constitutional rights." As noted in Berger, supra, at 1031, however, the *Miranda* Court "did not specifically adopt the *Zerbst* criteria." But in the same paragraph citing *Zerbst* the Court stated that "a heavy burden rests on the Government to demonstrate that the defendant knowingly and intelligently waived" his *Miranda* rights. Was *this* an adoption of the *Zerbst* "intentional relinquishment" standard? If so, did the *Miranda* Court too hurriedly lump together *Miranda* rights and the right to counsel at trial? Should the *Zerbst* criteria and "waiver" terminology be expelled from *Miranda* law? Yes, maintains

---

1. After reading the FBI's "Advice of Rights" form, defendant was asked whether he understood his rights. He replied that he did, but refused to sign the waiver at the bottom of the form. He was then told that he need neither speak nor sign the form, but that the agents would like him to talk to them. He replied, "I will talk to you but I am not signing any form." He then made incriminating statements. Because defendant had said nothing when advised of his right to counsel, and because the state supreme court read *Miranda* as requiring a specific waiver of each right, it concluded that defendant had not waived his right to counsel. The U.S. Supreme Court disagreed: "By creating an inflexible rule that no implicit waiver [of *Miranda* rights] can ever suffice, the [state court] has gone beyond the requirements of federal organic law."

James Tomkovicz, *Standards for Invocation and Waiver of Counsel in Confession Contexts,* 71 Iowa L.Rev. 975, 1050–53 (1986):

"Elimination of the *Zerbst* formula [is] preferable not only because *Zerbst* does not accurately capture fifth amendment decisions in the abstract, but also because actual applications in fifth amendment cases prove that the formula does not describe the waivers that have been acceptable. Furthermore, those interpretations threaten to dilute the demands of the 'voluntary and knowing' standard and thereby to undermine its ability to shelter other constitutional rights for which it is appropriate. A weakened *Zerbst* waiver standard for *Miranda*'s fifth amendment counsel, for example, is easily borrowed for sixth amendment counsel waiver determinations. The vigor of that guarantee, however, depends on more stringent protection against surrender than the *Butler* dilution of *Zerbst* affords."

12. *"Qualified" waiver.* As *North Carolina v. Butler* itself illustrates (see fn. a supra), a suspect may refuse to sign a waiver but nonetheless indicate that he is willing to talk.[1] Or he may object to any notetaking by an officer but agree to talk about the case or indicate that he will talk only if a tape recorder is turned off. Are oral waivers effective in the face of such objections? A number of courts have held that they are. See, e.g., *United States v. Frazier,* 476 F.2d 891 (D.C.Cir.1973) (en banc) *(Frazier II).* But see LaFave & Israel, § 6.9(f) (in these situations defendant probably acted as he did "because of a mistaken impression that an oral confession which was not contemporaneously recorded could not be used against him"; therefore, police should be required to "clear up misunderstandings of this nature which are apparent to any reasonable observer").[2]

The Court addressed this general problem in CONNECTICUT v. BARRETT, 479 U.S. 523, 107 S.Ct. 828, 93 L.Ed.2d 920 (1987). While in custody, respondent, a suspect in a sexual assault case, was thrice advised of his *Miranda* rights. On each occasion, after signing an acknowledgment that he had been informed of his rights, respondent indicated that he would not make a written statement, but that he was willing to talk about the incident that led to his arrest. On the second and third such occasions, respondent added that he would not make a written statement outside the presence of counsel, and then orally admitted his involvement in the crime. An officer reduced to writing his recollection of respondent's last such statement, and the confession was admitted into evidence at respondent's trial. The Court, per REHNQUIST, C.J., rejected the contention that respondent's expressed desire for counsel before making a written statement served as an invocation of the right for all purposes:

"[W]e know of no constitutional objective that would be served by suppression in this case. It is undisputed that Barrett desired the presence of counsel before making a written statement. [His] limited requests for counsel, however, were accompanied by affirmative announcements of his willingness to speak with the authorities. The fact that officials took [this opportunity] to obtain an oral confession is quite consistent with the Fifth Amendment. *Miranda* gives the defendant a right to choose between speech and silence, and Barrett chose to speak.

" * * * Barrett made clear his intentions and they were honored. [To] conclude that [he] invoked his right to counsel for all purposes requires not a

---

1. The *Butler* Court did not hold that this constituted a valid waiver, but only rejected the state court's view that nothing short of an express waiver would satisfy *Miranda.*

2. One study indicates that 45 percent of post-*Miranda* defendants mistakenly believed that oral statements could not be used against them. See Lawrence S. Leiken, *Police Interro-* gation in Colorado: The Implementation of Miranda, 47 Denver L.J. 1, 15–16, 33 (1970). If so many people do not realize the significance of an oral statement, should the warning take this form: "You have a right to remain silent and anything you say, *orally or* in writing, may (will) be used against you"? *Unif.R.Crim.P.* 212(b) and 243 so provide.

broad interpretation of an ambiguous statement, but disregard of the ordinary meaning of respondent's statement. [The] fact that some might find Barrett's decision illogical is irrelevant, for we have never 'embraced the theory that a defendant's ignorance of the full consequences of his decisions vitiates their voluntariness.' "

BRENNAN, J., concurred in the judgment. Although "Barrett's contemporaneous waiver of his right to silence and limited invocation of his right to counsel (for the purpose of making a written statement) suggested that he did not understand that anything he *said* could be used against him," he testified that "he understood his *Miranda* rights, i.e., he knew that he need not talk to the police without a lawyer and that anything he said could be used against him. Under these circumstances, the waiver of the right to silence and the limited invocation of the right to counsel were valid."

Had the prosecution been without Barrett's trial testimony, Brennan would have dissented: "As a general matter, I believe that this odd juxtaposition (a willingness to talk and an unwillingness to have anything preserved) militates against finding a knowing or intelligent waiver of the right to silence. [But] the State has carried its 'heavy burden' of demonstrating waiver. It has shown that Barrett received the *Miranda* warnings, that he had the capacity to understand them and *in fact* understood them, and that he expressly waived his right to silence. [In] my view, each of these findings was essential to the conclusion that a voluntary, knowing, and intelligent waiver of the *Miranda* rights occurred."[1]

13. What constitutes an invocation of Miranda rights? In FARE v. MICHAEL C., 442 U.S. 707, 99 S.Ct. 2560, 61 L.Ed.2d 197 (1979), after being fully advised of his *Miranda* rights, a juvenile, who had been taken into custody on suspicion of murder, asked, "Can I have my probation officer here?" The police officer replied that he was "not going to call [the probation officer] right now," then continued: "If you want to talk to us without an attorney present, you can. If you don't want to, you don't have to." The juvenile then agreed to talk to the police without an attorney being present and made incriminating statements. The Court, per BLACKMUN, J., held the statements admissible, deeming the request to see a probation officer not a *per se* invocation of *Miranda* rights—not the equivalent of asking for a lawyer. The admissibility of the statements on the basis of waiver turned on "the totality of the circumstance surrounding the interrogation" (e.g., evaluation of the juvenile's age, experience, background and intelligence).

"The *per se* aspect of *Miranda*," emphasized the Court, was "based on the unique role the lawyer plays in the adversarial system of criminal justice in this country. [A] probation officer is not in the same posture with regard to either the accused or the system of justice as a whole. * * * Moreover, [he] is the employee of the State which seeks to prosecute the alleged offender. He is a peace officer, and as such is allied, to a greater or lesser extent, with his fellow peace officers. [It is the] pivotal role of legal counsel [in the administration of criminal justice] that justifies the *per se* rule established in *Miranda* and that distinguishes the request for counsel from the request for a probation officer, a clergyman, or a close friend."

Justice MARSHALL, joined by Brennan and Stevens, JJ., dissented. Noting that the California Supreme Court had "determined that probation officers have a statutory duty to represent minors' interests and, indeed, are 'trusted guardian figure[s]' to whom a juvenile would likely turn for assistance," the dissenters maintained that "*Miranda* requires that interrogation cease whenever a juvenile

1. Stevens, J., joined by Marshall, J., dissented, deeming respondent's request for the   assistance of counsel indistinguishable from the request in *Edwards.*

requests an adult who is obligated to represent his interests." Such request "constitutes both an attempt to obtain advice and a general invocation of the right to silence. For, as the California Supreme Court recognized, 'it is fatuous to assume that a minor in custody will be in a position to call an attorney for assistance,' or that he will trust the police to obtain an attorney for him. A juvenile in these circumstances will likely turn to his parents, or another adult responsible for his welfare, as the only means of securing legal counsel. Moreover, a request for such adult assistance is surely inconsistent with a present desire to speak freely."[1]

Does *Fare v. Michael C.* stand for the broad proposition that a request by any suspect (with the possible exception of a young, inexperienced juvenile; Michael C. was an "experienced" 16½ year old) to see anyone *other than an attorney,* whether it be a parent, spouse or best friend, does not *per se* constitute an assertion or invocation of *Miranda* rights? If so, is this because neither parent, spouse or best friend has the "unique ability to protect the Fifth Amendment rights" of a suspect undergoing custodial interrogation? How much weight, if any, should be given to the fact that the mother, father or husband requested by the suspect plays a "unique role" in the life of the particular suspect?

14. ***The scope of "second-level" Miranda safeguards—the procedures that must be followed when suspects do assert their rights—and the distinction between invoking the right to remain silent and the right to counsel.*** In most *Miranda* cases, the issue is the need for the *Miranda* warnings or the adequacy of the warnings given or the suspect's alleged waiver in response to the warnings. But different issues arise when the suspect *asserts* his rights— thereby triggering what have been called "second level" *Miranda* safeguards. Although this development may have surprised the *Miranda* Court, it turns out that the procedures that must be followed when a suspect invokes his rights depends on whether he asserted the right to remain silent or the right to counsel.

The Court first addressed this issue in **MICHIGAN v. MOSLEY**, 423 U.S. 96, 96 S.Ct. 321, 46 L.Ed.2d 313 (1975). Mosley was arrested in connection with certain robberies. After being given *Miranda* warnings by a robbery detective, Mosley declined to talk about the robberies (but he did not request a lawyer). The detective promptly ceased questioning and made no effort to persuade Mosley to reconsider his position. Mosley was then taken to a cell block in the building. After a two-hour interval, a homicide detective brought Mosley from the cell block to the homicide bureau for questioning about "an unrelated holdup murder." Mosley was again advised of his rights. This time he waived them and made an incriminating statement. A 7–2 majority, per STEWART, J., held the statement admissible.

After studying the *Miranda* opinion, the Court concluded that "the admissibility of statements obtained after the person in custody has decided to remain silent depends [on] whether his 'right to cut off questioning' was 'scrupulously honored.'" After examining the facts, the Court concluded that Mosley's right had been honored. The questioning by the homicide detective, emphasized the Court, had "focused exclusively on [a] crime different in nature and in time and place by occurrence from the robberies for which Mosley had been arrested and interrogated by [the robbery detective]" and the subsequent questioning by another detective about an unrelated homicide was "quite consistent with a reasonable interpretation of Mosley's earlier refusal to answer any questions about the robberies." Therefore, "this is not a case [where] the police failed to honor a

---

1. Justice Powell wrote a separate dissent, "not satisfied that this particular 16–year-old boy, in this particular situation was subjected to a fair interrogation free from inherently coercive circumstances."

decision [to] cut off questioning, either by refusing to discontinue the interrogation upon request or by persisting in repeated efforts to wear down [the suspect's] resistance and make him change his mind. [The] police here immediately ceased the interrogation, resumed questioning only after the passage of a significant period of time and the provision of a fresh set of warnings, and restricted the second interrogation to a crime that had not been a subject of the earlier interrogation."

Concurring Justice WHITE foreshadowed his opinion for the Court six years later in *Edwards v. Arizona,* below, by observing: "[The *Miranda* Court showed in its opinion] that when it wanted to create a *per se* rule against further interrogation after assertion of a right, it knew how to do so. The Court there said 'if the individual states that he wants an attorney, the interrogation must cease *until an attorney is present.*' [Emphasis added by White, J.]"

———

Three factors seem to be *minimal requirements* for the resumption of questioning once a suspect asserts his right to remain silent: (1) immediately ceasing the interrogation; (2) suspending questioning entirely for a significant period; (3) giving a fresh set of *Miranda* warnings at the outset of the second interrogation. May these three circumstances also be *the only* critical factors? May *Mosley* mean that these three circumstances suffice without more to eliminate the coercion inherent in the continuing custody and the renewed questioning? How significant is it that a different officer resumed the questioning? That the second interrogation occurred at another location? That the second interrogation was limited to a separate and "unrelated" crime? Compare Geoffrey Stone, *The Miranda Doctrine in the Burger Court,* 1977 Sup.Ct.Rev. 99, 134 (last factor "seems critical") with Kamisar, *The Warren Court (Was It Really So Defense–Minded?), the Burger Court (Is It Really So Prosecution–Oriented?) and Police Investigatory Practices,* in The Burger Court: The Counter–Revolution That Wasn't 62, 83 & n. 133 (V. Blasi ed. 1983) (not at all clear that *Mosley* was meant to be or will be so limited).

———

Distinguishing the *Mosley* case, EDWARDS v. ARIZONA, 451 U.S. 477, 101 S.Ct. 1880, 68 L.Ed.2d 378 (1981), held that once a suspect has invoked his right to counsel he may not be "subject[ed] to further interrogation [until] counsel has been made available to him unless [he] himself initiates further communication, exchanges or conversations with the police."

Edwards was arrested for burglary, robbery and murder and taken to the police station. He waived his rights and agreed to talk about these crimes. But some time later he asserted his right to counsel. At this point, questioning ceased and Edwards was taken to jail. The next morning, two detectives, colleagues of the officer who had questioned Edwards the previous day, came to the jail, met with Edwards and again informed him of his rights.[1] This time Edwards agreed to talk about the same crimes. He then made incriminating statements which led to his conviction for these crimes. The state supreme court held that although Edwards had asserted his right to counsel the day before, he waived this right the following day when he agreed to talk after again being given his *Miranda* warnings. The Court, per WHITE, J., disagreed:

1. When a guard informed Edwards that two detectives wanted to talk to him, Edwards replied that he did not want to talk to anyone. But the guard told him "he had" to talk to the detectives and then took him to meet with them. The opinion of the Court, however, seems to be written without regard to these particular facts.

"[H]owever sound the conclusion of the state courts as to the voluntariness of Edwards' admission may be, [neither court] undertook to focus on whether Edwards understood his right to counsel and intelligently and knowingly relinquished it. It is thus apparent that the decision below misunderstood the requirement for finding a valid waiver of the right to counsel, once invoked.

"[A]dditional safeguards [for waiver] are necessary when the accused asks for counsel; and we now hold that when an [in-custody suspect does assert this right a valid waiver of it] cannot be established by showing only that he responded to further police-initiated custodial interrogation even if he has been advised of his rights. [An] accused, such as Edwards, having expressed his desire to deal with the police only through counsel, is not subject to further interrogation by the authorities until counsel has been made available to him, unless the accused himself initiates further communication, exchanges or conversations with the police."[2]

15. *Clarification (and extension?) of the Edwards rule.* In ARIZONA v. ROBERSON, 486 U.S. 675, 108 S.Ct. 2093, 100 L.Ed.2d 704 (1988), a 6–2 majority, per STEVENS, J., held that once a suspect effectively asserts his *Miranda-Edwards* right to counsel, the police cannot even initiate interrogation about crimes *other than* the one for which the suspect has invoked his right to counsel:

not over other than crime

"[The] presumption raised by a suspect's request for counsel—that he considers himself unable to deal with the pressure of custodial interrogation without legal assistance—does not disappear simply because the police have approached the suspect, still in custody, still without counsel, about a separate investigation. [We] also disagree with [the] contention that fresh sets of *Miranda* warnings will 'reassure' a suspect who has been denied the counsel he has clearly requested that his rights have remained untrammeled. Especially in a case such as this, in which a period of three days elapsed between the unsatisfied request for counsel and the interrogation about a second offense, there is a serious risk that the mere repetition of the *Miranda* warnings would not overcome the presumption of coercion that is created by prolonged police custody."[1]

Newly appointed Justice KENNEDY, joined by Chief Justice Rehnquist, dissented, emphasizing that "*Edwards* is our rule, not a constitutional command; and it is our obligation to justify its expansion." According to Justice Kennedy the majority's approach was not "consistent with the practical realities of suspects' rights and police investigations":

"It is a frequent occurrence that [a custodial suspect] is wanted for questioning with respect to crimes unrelated to the one for which he has been apprehended. The rule announced today will bar law enforcement officials, even those from [some] other jurisdiction, from questioning a suspect about an unrelated matter if he is in custody and has requested counsel to assist in answering questions put to him about the crime for which he was arrested.

"[Having] observed that his earlier invocation of rights was effective in terminating questioning and having been advised that further questioning may not relate to that crime, [the suspect] would understand that he may invoke his rights again with respect to the new investigation, and so terminate questioning

2. Chief Justice Burger and Justices Powell and Rehnquist concurred in the result.

1. The Court "attach[ed] no significance to the fact that the officer who conducted the second interrogation did not know that respondent had made a request for counsel. In addition to the fact that *Edwards* focuses on the state of mind of the suspect and not of the police, custodial interrogation must be conducted pursuant to established procedures, and those procedures in turn must enable an officer who proposes to initiate an interrogation to determine whether the suspect has previously requested counsel."

regarding that investigation as well. Indeed, the new warnings and explanations will reinforce his comprehension of a suspect's rights."[2]

* * *

When, two years later, the Court read the *Edwards* rule still more expansively in *Minnick,* set forth below, many Court watchers were surprised to learn that Justice Kennedy, the forceful dissenter in *Roberson,* had written the opinion of the Court.

MINNICK v. MISSISSIPPI
498 U.S. 146, 111 S.Ct. 486, 112 L.Ed.2d 489 (1990).

Justice KENNEDY delivered the opinion of the Court.

* * * The issue in the case before us is whether *Edwards'* protection ceases once the suspect has consulted with an attorney.

[Petitioner Minnick and fellow prisoner Dykes escaped from a Mississippi jail and broke into a trailer in search of weapons. In the course of the burglary, they killed two people. Minnick and Dykes fled to Mexico, where they fought, and Minnick then proceeded alone to California where, some four months after the murders, he was arrested by local police and placed in a San Diego jail. The day following his arrest, Saturday, two FBI agents came to the jail to interview him. After being advised of his rights and acknowledging that he understood them, Minnick refused to sign a rights waiver form, but agreed to answer some questions. He maintained that Dykes had killed one victim and forced him to shoot the other, but otherwise he hesitated to discuss what happened at the trailer.]

[At this point] the [FBI] agents reminded him he did not have to answer questions without a lawyer present. According to the [FBI] report, "Minnick stated that he would make a more complete statement then with his lawyer present." The FBI interview ended.

After the FBI interview, an appointed attorney met with petitioner. [He] spoke with the lawyer on two or three occasions, though it is not clear from the record whether all of these conferences were in person.

On Monday [Denham, a Mississippi deputy sheriff,] came to the San Diego jail to question Minnick. Minnick testified that his jailers * * * told him he would "have to talk" to Denham and that he "could not refuse." Denham advised petitioner of his rights, and petitioner again declined to sign a rights waiver form. [However, Minnick agreed to answer some questions and made a number of incriminating statements].

Minnick was tried for murder in Mississippi. He moved to suppress all statements given to the FBI or other police officers, including Denham. The trial court denied the motion with respect to petitioner's statements to Denham, but suppressed his other statements. Petitioner was convicted on two counts of capital murder and sentenced to death. [The state supreme court affirmed.]

[The *Edwards* rule] ensures that any statement made in subsequent interrogation is not the result of coercive pressures. *Edwards* conserves judicial resources which would otherwise be expended in making difficult determinations of voluntariness, and implements the protections of *Miranda* in practical and straightforward terms. [*Edwards'* merit] lies in the clarity of its command and the certainty

---

2. O'Connor, J., took no part in the consideration or decision of the case.

of its application. [The] rule provides " 'clear and unequivocal' guidelines to the law enforcement profession."

[A] fair reading of *Edwards* and subsequent cases demonstrates that we have interpreted the rule to bar police-initiated interrogation unless the accused has counsel with him at the time of questioning. Whatever the ambiguities of our earlier cases on this point, we now hold that when counsel is requested, interrogation must cease, and officials may not reinitiate interrogation without counsel present, whether or not the accused has consulted with his attorney.

We consider our ruling to be an appropriate and necessary application of the *Edwards* rule. A single consultation with an attorney does not remove the suspect from persistent attempts by officials to persuade him to waive his rights, or from the coercive pressures that accompany custody and that may increase as custody is prolonged. The case before us well illustrates the pressures, and abuses, that may be concomitants of custody. Petitioner testified that though he resisted, he was required to submit to both the FBI and the Denham interviews. In the latter instance, the compulsion to submit to interrogation followed petitioner's unequivocal request during the FBI interview that questioning cease until counsel was present. The case illustrates also that consultation is not always effective in instructing the suspect of his rights. One plausible interpretation of the record is that petitioner thought he could keep his admissions out of evidence by refusing to sign a formal waiver of rights. If the authorities had complied with Minnick's request to have counsel present during interrogation, the attorney could have corrected Minnick's misunderstanding, or indeed counseled him that he need not make a statement at all. We decline to remove protection from police-initiated questioning based on isolated consultations with counsel who is absent when the interrogation resumes.

The exception to *Edwards* here proposed [would] undermine the advantages flowing from *Edwards'* "clear and unequivocal" character. Respondent concedes that even after consultation with counsel, a second request for counsel should reinstate the *Edwards* protection. We are invited by this formulation to adopt a regime in which *Edwards'* protection could pass in and out of existence multiple times prior to arraignment, at which point the same protection might reattach by virtue of our Sixth Amendment jurisprudence, see *Michigan v. Jackson* [p. 535]. Vagaries of this sort spread confusion through the justice system and lead to a consequent loss of respect for the underlying constitutional principle.

In addition, adopting the rule proposed would leave far from certain the sort of consultation required to displace *Edwards*. Consultation is not a precise concept, for it may encompass variations from a telephone call to say that the attorney is in route, to a hurried interchange between the attorney and client in a detention facility corridor, to a lengthy in-person conference in which the attorney gives full and adequate advice respecting all matters that might be covered in further interrogations. * * *

Justice SCALIA, with whom The Chief Justice joins, dissenting.

The Court today establishes an irrebuttable presumption that a criminal suspect, after invoking his *Miranda* right to counsel, can *never* validly waive that right during any police-initiated encounter, even after the suspect has been provided multiple *Miranda* warnings and has actually consulted his attorney. This holding builds on foundations already established in *Edwards*, but "the rule of *Edwards* is our rule, not a constitutional command; and it is our obligation to justify its expansion." *Arizona v. Roberson* (Kennedy, J., dissenting). Because I see no justification for applying the *Edwards* irrebuttable presumption when a criminal suspect has actually consulted with his attorney, I respectfully dissent.
* * *

Notwithstanding our acknowledgment that *Miranda* rights are "not themselves rights protected by the Constitution [but] measures to insure that the right against compulsory self-incrimination [is] protected," *Michigan v. Tucker,* we have adhered to the principle that nothing less than the *Johnson v. Zerbst* standard for the waiver of constitutional rights [see p. 471] applies to the waiver of *Miranda* rights. Until *Edwards,* however, we refrained from imposing on the States a *higher* standard for the waiver of *Miranda* rights. For example, in *Michigan v. Mosley,* we rejected a proposed irrebuttable presumption that a criminal suspect, after invoking the *Miranda* right to remain silent, could not validly waive the right during any subsequent questioning by the police. * * *

Edwards, however, broke with this approach. [The] case stands as a solitary exception to our waiver jurisprudence. [In] the narrow context in which it applies, [it] " 'prevent[s] police from badgering a defendant' "; it "conserves judicial resources which would otherwise be expended in making difficult determinations of voluntariness"; and it provides' " "clear and unequivocal" guidelines to the law enforcement profession.' " But so would a rule that simply excludes all confessions by all persons in police custody. The value of any prophylactic rule (assuming the authority to adopt a prophylactic rule) must be assessed not only on the basis of what is gained, but also on the basis of what is lost. In all other contexts we have thought the above-described consequences of abandoning *Zerbst* outweighed by " 'the need for police questioning as a tool for effective enforcement of criminal laws,' " *Moran v. Burbine* [p. 538].

[The *Edwards* rule] should not, in my view, extend beyond the circumstances present in *Edwards* itself—where the suspect in custody asked to consult an attorney, and was interrogated before that attorney had ever been provided. In those circumstances, the *Edwards* rule rests upon an assumption similar to that of *Miranda* itself: that when a suspect in police custody is first questioned he is likely to be ignorant of his rights and to feel isolated in a hostile environment. This likelihood is thought to justify special protection against unknowing or coerced waiver of rights. After a suspect has seen his request for an attorney honored, however, and has actually spoken with that attorney, the probabilities change. The suspect then knows that he has an advocate on his side, and that the police will permit him to consult that advocate. He almost certainly also has a heightened awareness (above what the *Miranda* warning itself will provide) of his right to remain silent—since at the earliest opportunity "any lawyer worth his salt will tell the suspect in no uncertain terms to make no statement to the police under any circumstances."

* * * Clear and simple rules are desirable, but only in pursuance of authority that we possess. We are authorized by the Fifth Amendment to exclude confessions that are "compelled," which we have interpreted to include confessions that the police obtain from a suspect in custody without a knowing and voluntary waiver of his right to remain silent. Undoubtedly some bright-line rules can be adopted to implement that principle, marking out the situations in which knowledge or voluntariness cannot possibly be established—for example, a rule excluding confessions obtained after five hours of continuous interrogation. But a rule excluding all confessions that follow upon even the slightest police inquiry cannot conceivably be justified on this basis. It does not rest upon a reasonable prediction that all such confessions, or even most such confessions, will be unaccompanied by a knowing and voluntary waiver.

It can be argued that the same is true of the category of confessions excluded by the *Edwards* rule itself. I think that is so, [but] the presumption of involuntariness is at least more plausible for that category. [Drawing] a distinction between police-initiated inquiry before consultation with counsel and police-initiated inquiry after consultation with counsel is assuredly more reasonable than other distinctions *Edwards* has already led us into—such as the distinction between police-initiated inquiry after assertion of the *Miranda* right to remain silent, and police-initiated inquiry after assertion of the *Miranda* right to counsel, see Kamisar, The *Edwards* and *Bradshaw* Cases: The Court Giveth and the Court Taketh Away, in 5 The Supreme Court: Trends and Developments 157 (J. Choper, Y. Kamisar, & L. Tribe eds. 1984) ("[E]ither *Mosley* was wrongly decided or *Edwards* was"); or the distinction between what is needed to prove waiver of the *Miranda* right to have counsel present and what is needed to prove waiver of rights found in the Constitution. * * *

Today's extension of the *Edwards* prohibition is the latest stage of prophylaxis built upon prophylaxis, producing a veritable fairyland castle of imagined constitutional restriction upon law enforcement. This newest tower, according to the Court, is needed to avoid "inconsisten[cy] with [the] purpose" of *Edwards'* prophylactic rule, which was needed to protect *Miranda*'s prophylactic right to have counsel present, which was needed to protect the right against *compelled self-incrimination* found (at last!) in the Constitution.

[Both *Edwards* and today's decision] are explicable, in my view, only as an effort to protect suspects against what is regarded as their own folly. The sharp-witted criminal would know better than to confess; why should the dull-witted suffer for his lack of mental endowment? Providing him an attorney at every stage where he might be induced or persuaded (though not coerced) to incriminate himself will even the odds. Apart from the fact that this protective enterprise is beyond our authority under the Fifth Amendment or any other provision of the Constitution, it is unwise. [That] some clever criminals may employ those protections to their advantage is poor reason to allow criminals who have not done so to escape justice.

Thus, even if I were to concede that an honest confession is a foolish mistake, I would welcome rather than reject it; a rule that foolish mistakes do not count would leave most offenders not only unconvicted but undetected. More fundamentally, however, it is wrong, and subtly corrosive of our criminal justice system, to regard an honest confession as a "mistake." [Not] only for society, but for the wrongdoer himself, "admissio[n] of guilt [if] not coerced, [is] inherently desirable," because it advances the goals of both "justice *and* rehabilitation." *Michigan v. Tucker* (emphasis added). [We should] rejoice at an honest confession, rather than pity the "poor fool" who has made it; and we should regret the attempted retraction of that good act, rather than seek to facilitate and encourage it. To design our laws on premises contrary to these is to abandon belief in either personal responsibility or the moral claim of just government to obedience. Cf. Caplan, Questioning *Miranda*, 38 Vand.L.Rev. 1417, 1471–1473 (1985). * * *

Notes and Questions

(a) *Do the opinions in Minnick reflect the attitudes of the majority opinion and the Harlan and White dissenting opinions in Miranda?* Consider Note, 82 J.Crim.L. & C. 878, 893–94 (1992): "The [*Minnick*] majority recognized that police have a duty to try to make suspects talk. [The majority,] therefore, views the realities of interrogation beyond the stationhouse door with due skepticism. [In] contrast, Justice Scalia based his dissent [on] an underlying belief that police conduct during custodial [interrogation] is not as harsh and abusive as the Court contended. [He] also apparently believed that feelings of guilt motivate confessions more than custodial interrogation by the police. The opinions in *Minnick* thus reflect the attitudes of the majority and [dissenting opinions] in *Miranda* in the way the Justices differ on the realities of custodial interrogation."

(b) *The need to prevent the police from "badgering" a suspect who has previously asserted his rights.* The *Minnick* majority reiterates that the *Edwards* rule is "designed to prevent police from badgering a defendant into waiving his previously asserted" *right to counsel* and to "ensure that any statement made in subsequent interrogation is not the result of coercive pressures." But why isn't there a comparable need for a rule designed to prevent the police from badgering or pressuring a suspect into waiving his previously asserted *right to remain silent?*

16. When does the "question-proof status" of a person who has asserted his right to counsel come to an end? Does a sentenced prisoner who has settled into the routine of his new life in the prison population need the extra protection of Edwards? Consider UNITED STATES v. GREEN, 592 A.2d 985 (D.C.App.1991), *cert. granted,* 504 U.S. 908, 112 S.Ct. 1935, 118 L.Ed.2d 542 *vacated and cert. dismissed,* 507 U.S. 545, 113 S.Ct. 1835, 123 L.Ed.2d 260 (1993). When arrested on a drug charge on July 18, 1989, defendant refused to answer any questions without having a lawyer present. The next day an attorney was appointed to represent him. Defendant remained incarcerated. On September 27, he pled guilty to a lesser included offense. He was then moved to a juvenile facility while a presentence report was being prepared (On Feb. 26, 1990, he was sentenced on the drug charge.) On January 4, 1990, the police obtained an arrest warrant charging defendant with an unrelated murder that had occurred six months before he had been arrested on the drug charge. The next day, January 5th, defendant was taken to the homicide division. After being advised of his rights he agreed to talk to a detective about the murder and admitted his involvement in that crime. He was then indicted for first degree murder.

Defendant contended that his confession to the murder had been obtained in violation of *Edwards* in view of his original refusal at the time of his arrest on the drug charge to answer questions without counsel being present—an event that occurred more than five months before he had been advised of his rights in connection with the murder and had agreed to talk about his involvement in that crime. The trial judge initially denied the motion to suppress. Three days after the court's initial ruling, however, the Supreme Court handed down *Minnick.* The trial judge then reversed his earlier ruling and suppressed the confession.

A 2–1 majority of the District of Columbia Court of Appeals, per FARRELL, J., affirmed. True, defendant had confessed to the murder more than three months after he had pled guilty in the drug case, the case in which he had requested, and obtained, counsel. But his plea in the drug case was "consistent with his election to communicate with the police only through counsel." Thus his guilty plea in the drug case "cannot be the pivotal break in events that *Edwards* demands before a waiver can be regarded as an initial election by the accused to deal with the authorities on his own." True, too, between the time the defendant asserted his right to counsel in the drug case and the time he agreed to talk about the unrelated murder, more than five months had elapsed. But assigning decisive weight to the passage of time between an invocation of the right to counsel and a subsequent confession would blur a rule that the Supreme Court had insisted should be kept "clear and unequivocal."

When defendant died in March of 1993, the Supreme Court vacated the order granting certiorari—but not before oral arguments had been heard in the case. See 52 Crim.L.Rep. 3096. The government maintained that "a dramatic change of circumstances that changes the position of the suspect * * * makes it unreasonable to continue application of *Edwards'* irrebuttable presumption of coercion." Thus, when the suspect pleads guilty to the charge which prompted him to assert his right to counsel or a substantial period of time has elapsed between his initial invocation of rights and the second interrogation or there has been "a break in the custody of the suspect," the police may approach the suspect, in counsel's absence, to ask questions about unrelated offenses. Do you agree?

If so, does a person experience a "break in custody" when he starts serving a prison term? Yes, answers Laurie Magid, *Questioning the Question–Proof Inmate: Defining Miranda Custody for Incarcerated Suspects*, 58 Ohio State L.J. 883, 892 (1997) (one who "has settled into the routine of prison life is [no longer] in *Miranda* custody, and will return to custody for *Miranda* purposes only when he is subjected to some additional restraint beyond those of his normal life as an inmate.")

17. *What constitutes "initiating" further communication with the police?* The *Edwards* rule was deemed inapplicable in OREGON v. BRADSHAW, 462 U.S. 1039, 103 S.Ct. 2830, 77 L.Ed.2d 405 (1983). Bradshaw, suspected of causing the death of Reynolds, a minor, by drunken driving, was arrested for furnishing liquor to Reynolds. Bradshaw agreed to talk to an officer about the fatal crash, but when the officer suggested that Bradshaw had been behind the wheel of the truck when Reynolds died, Bradshaw denied his involvement and expressed a desire to talk to a lawyer. The officers immediately terminated the conversation.

A few minutes later, either while still at the police station or enroute to the jail, Bradshaw asked the officer: "Well, what is going to happen to me now?" In response, the officer said that Bradshaw didn't have to talk to him and, because he had requested a lawyer, he didn't want Bradshaw to talk to him unless he decided to do so as a matter of his "own free will." Bradshaw said he understood. General conversation followed, in the course of which there was a discussion about where Bradshaw was being taken and the crime(s) for which he would be charged. The officer reiterated his own theory of how Bradshaw had caused Reynolds' death and then suggested that Bradshaw take a lie detector test to "clean the matter up." Bradshaw agreed.[a]

a. Should Bradshaw have been advised of his rights and a valid waiver obtained at this point (not the next day, just before Bradshaw took the lie-detector test)? Does the critical moment occur when a suspect *agrees* to take a lie detector test (or agrees to submit to further interrogation) regardless of whether the test is given (or further interrogation takes place) then or later? Compare *Bradshaw* with *Wyrick v. Fields*, 459 U.S. 42, 103 S.Ct. 394, 74 L.Ed.2d 214 (1982) (per curiam), which arose as follows: After discussing the matter with his private counsel and with a military attorney, Fields, a soldier charged with rape, requested a polygraph examination. Prior to undergoing the examination, Fields signed a waiver-of-rights form. He was also told: "If you are now going to discuss the offense under investigation, which is rape, with or without a lawyer present, you have a right to stop answering questions at any time or speak to a lawyer before answering further, even if you sign a waiver certificate. Do you want a lawyer at this time?" Fields answered: "No."

At the conclusion of the polygraph examination, which took less than two hours, a CID agent told Fields that there had been some deceit and asked him if he could explain why his answers were bothering him. Fields then made some incriminating statements. On fed-

eral habeas corpus, the Eighth Circuit found that the State had failed to satisfy its burden of proving that Fields knowingly and intelligently waived his right to have counsel present at the *post*-test interrogation. The Supreme Court disagreed:

"The only plausible explanation for the [Eighth Circuit's] holding is that, encouraged by what it regarded as a *per se* rule established in *Edwards,* it fashioned another rule of its own: that, notwithstanding a voluntary, knowing, and intelligent waiver of the right to have counsel present at a polygraph examination, and notwithstanding clear evidence that the suspect understood that right and was aware of his power to stop questioning at any time or to speak to an attorney at any time, the police again must advise the suspect of his rights before questioning him at the same interrogation about the results of the polygraph. [This approach] certainly finds no support in *Edwards,* which emphasizes that the totality of the circumstances, including the fact that the suspect initiated the questioning, is controlling. Nor is the rule logical; the questions put to Fields after the examination would not have caused him to forget the rights of which he had been advised and which he had understood moments before. The rule is simply an unjusti-

The next day, just before he took the lie detector test, Bradshaw was given another set of *Miranda* warnings and he signed a written waiver of his rights. At the conclusion of the test, the polygraph examiner told Bradshaw that he had not been truthful in response to certain questions. Bradshaw then admitted that he had been driving the vehicle in which Reynolds was killed and that he had consumed a considerable amount of alcohol before passing out at the wheel.

The Supreme Court held that under the circumstances Bradshaw could not avail himself of the *Edwards* rule, but there was no opinion of the Court. Justice REHNQUIST, joined by Burger, C.J., and White and O'Connor, JJ., observed:

"There are some inquiries, such as a request for a drink of water or a request to use a telephone that are so routine that they cannot be fairly said to represent a desire on the part of an accused to open up a more generalized discussion relating directly or indirectly to the investigation. Such inquiries or statements, by either an accused or a police officer, relating to routine incidents of the custodial relationship, will not generally 'initiate' a conversation in the sense in which that word was used in *Edwards*.

"Although ambiguous, the respondent's question in this case as to what was going to happen to him evinced a willingness and a desire for a generalized discussion about the investigation; it was not merely a necessary inquiry arising out of the incidents of the custodial relationship. It could reasonably have been interpreted by the officer as relating generally to the investigation. That the police officer so understood it is apparent from the fact that he immediately reminded the accused that 'you do not have to talk to me,' and only after the accused told him that he 'understood' did they have a generalized conversation. On these facts we believe that there was not a violation of the *Edwards* rule.

"[The next inquiry, therefore] was 'whether a valid waiver of [Bradshaw's rights] had occurred, that is, whether the purported waiver was knowing and intelligent and found to be so under the totality of the circumstances, including the necessary fact that the accused, not the police, reopened the dialogue with the authorities.' *Edwards*.

"[The] state trial court [found that a valid waiver of defendant's rights did occur and] we have no reason to dispute these conclusions * * *."

Concurring Justice POWELL, whose vote was decisive, agreed that Bradshaw had knowingly and intelligently waived his right to counsel, but saw no need for a two-step analysis—whether the suspect "initiated" a conversation with the police, and if so, whether under the "totality of circumstances" a valid waiver of rights followed. According to Powell, J.: "Fragmenting the standard into a novel two-step analysis—if followed literally—often would frustrate justice as well as common sense. Courts should engage in more substantive inquiries than 'who said what first.' [The *Edwards* rule] cannot in my view fairly be reduced to this."

MARSHALL, J., joined by Brennan, Blackmun and Stevens, JJ., dissented, "agree[ing] with the plurality that, in order to constitute 'interrogation' under *Edwards,* an accused's inquiry must demonstrate a desire to discuss the subject matter of the criminal investigation," but expressing "baffle[ment] [at] the plurality's application of that standard to the facts of this case":

fiable restriction on reasonable police questioning."

Dissenting Justice Marshall underscored the distinction between "an agreement to submit to a polygraph examination" and "the initiation of an ordinary conversation with the authorities": "[A] polygraph examination is a discrete test. It has a readily identifiable begin-

ning and end. An individual who submits to such an examination does not necessarily have any reason whatsoever to expect that he will be subjected to a post-examination interrogation." In any event, Justice Marshall did "not believe that this substantial constitutional question should be disposed of summarily."

"The plurality asserts that respondent's question, 'What is going to happen to me now?', evinced both 'a willingness and a desire for a generalized discussion about the investigation.' If respondent's question had been posed by Jean–Paul Sartre before a class of philosophy students, it might well have evinced a desire for a 'generalized' discussion. But under the circumstances of this case, it is plain that respondent's only 'desire' was to find out where the police were going to take him. As the Oregon Court of Appeals stated, respondent's query came only minutes after his invocation of the right to counsel and was simply 'a normal reaction to being taken from the police station and placed in a police car, obviously for transport to some destination.'

"[To] hold that respondent's question in this case opened a dialogue with the authorities flies in the face of the basic purpose of the *Miranda* safeguards. When someone in custody asks, 'What is going to happen to me now?', he is surely responding to his custodial surroundings. The very essence of custody is the loss of control over one's freedom of movement. [To] allow the authorities to recommence an interrogation based on such a question is to permit them to capitalize on the custodial setting. Yet *Miranda's* procedural protections were adopted precisely in order 'to dispel the compulsion inherent in custodial surroundings.' "

Notes and Questions

(i) *Is the Edwards–Bradshaw test for "initiating" further communication with the police a satisfactory one?* Consider James Tomkovicz, *Standards for Invocation and Waiver of Counsel in Confession Contexts,* 74 Iowa L.Rev. 975, 1033–34 (1986), maintaining that the *Edwards-Bradshaw* test, "which at most demands evidence of a generalized desire or willingness to discuss the investigation" is too broad and too spongy because "it allows officers to recommence interrogation in many situations in which suspects may not have changed their minds [about desiring counsel]." According to Professor Tomkovicz, a definition of suspect initiation of further communication with the police "must describe conduct by the individual that revokes the earlier claim [of counsel] and conveys the message that the added support of counsel is not desired."

(ii) *The suspect's counterpart to "administrative questioning."* Should a "natural response" to arrest or transportation to a jail or police station be viewed as the suspect's counterpart to "administrative questioning"? Consider the remarks of Professor Kamisar in Choper, Kamisar & Tribe, *The Supreme Court: Trends and Developments 1982–83* (1984) at 165–66:

"When the [*Innis* Court defined 'police interrogation'] it excluded police words or actions 'normally attendant to arrest and custody' and properly so. Such statements, often called 'administrative questioning,' e.g., the routine questions asked of all persons 'booked' or otherwise processed, do not enhance the pressures and anxiety generated by arrest and detention. Thus, any incriminating statements in response to administrative questioning is, and should be, viewed as a 'volunteered' statement.

"The suspect's counterpart to 'administrative questioning' [is] an expression of fear, anxiety or confusion *normally attendant* to arrest, removal from the scene of arrest, or transportation to the stationhouse or jail. These expressions, such as, Where am I being taken? When can I call my lawyer? and, yes, What's going to happen to me? should not count as "initiation of dialogue" for *Edwards* purposes.

"Of course, if the officer *answers* one of the arrestee's questions about what's going to happen to him by *telling him* where he is being taken [or] when he will be able to meet with an attorney that should not count either. But when the officer's response to the suspect's expression of concern or confusion clearly goes beyond the scope of the suspect's question—when the officer exploits the situation, as he did in [*Bradshaw*]—that *should* count as 'police interrogation.' [Under] such circumstances, the suspect did not 'invite' or 'initiate' conversation about the merits of the case—the officer 'initiated' a *new* conversation.''

18. *How direct, assertive and unambiguous must a suspect be in order to invoke the right to counsel?* A year before the decision in *Davis v. United States*, set forth immediately below, Professor Janet Ainsworth pointed out that sociolinguistic research indicates that certain discrete segments of the population (women and a majority of minority racial and ethnic groups) are far more likely than other groups to avoid strong, assertive means of expression and to use indirect and hedged speech patterns that give the impression of uncertainty or equivocality. See Janet E. Ainsworth, *In a Different Register: The Pragmatics of Powerlessness in Police Interrogation*, 103 Yale L.J. 259 (1993). However, observed Ainsworth, in determining whether a suspect had effectively invoked his or her right to counsel, a majority of the lower courts assumed that "direct and assertive speech—a mode of expression more characteristic of men than women—is or should be, the norm." This assumption not only manifests a "kind of gender bias"; it "does not serve the interests of the many speech communities whose discourse patterns deviate from the implicit norms in standard, 'male register' English."

Moreover, since the custodial police interrogation setting involves an imbalance of power between the suspect and his or her interrogator(s), such a setting increases the likelihood that a suspect will adopt an indirect or hedged—and thus ambiguous—means of expression. Even within speech communities whose members do not ordinarily use indirect modes of expression, one who is situationally powerless, that is, aware of the dominant power of the person he or she is addressing (and it is hard to think of a better example than a custodial suspect confronting one or more police interrogators), may also adopt a hedging or otherwise deferential speech register. According to Professor Ainsworth, only a *per se* invocation standard, a rule requiring all police questioning to cease upon any request for or reference to counsel, however equivocal or ambiguous, would provide "both assertive and deferential suspects with equivalent protection" and furnish "the powerless [the] same constitutional protections as the powerful."

However, in DAVIS v. UNITED STATES, 512 U.S. 452, 114 S.Ct. 2350, 129 L.Ed.2d 362 (1994), Justice O'CONNOR, speaking for five members of the Court rejected the view that (a) the courts should not place a premium on suspects making direct, assertive unqualified invocations of the right to counsel and (b) all arguable references to counsel should be treated as valid invocations of the right. The *Davis* case arose as follows:

Davis, a member of the U.S. Navy, was suspected of murdering another sailor. When interviewed by agents of the Naval Investigative Service (NIS) at the NIS office, he initially waived his *Miranda* rights. About an hour and a half into the interview, he said: "Maybe I should talk to a lawyer." At this point, according to the uncontradicted testimony of one of the agents, "we made it very clear [that] we weren't going to pursue the matter unless we have it clarified is he asking for a lawyer or is he just making a comment about a lawyer" and Davis replied, "No, I'm not asking for a lawyer" and then said, "No, I don't want a lawyer."

After a short break, the agents then reminded Davis of his *Miranda* rights and the interview continued for another hour—until Davis said, "I think I want a lawyer before I say anything." At this point, questioning ceased. A military judge admitted Davis's statements and he was convicted of murder. The U.S. Court of Appeals affirmed the conviction—as did the U.S. Supreme Court:

"[To invoke the *Edwards* rule] the suspect must unambiguously request counsel. As we have observed, 'a statement either is such an assertion of the right to counsel or it is not.' *Smith v. Illinois*, 469 U.S. 91, 105 S.Ct. 490, 83 L.Ed.2d 488 (1984). [Although] a suspect need not 'speak with the discrimination of an Oxford don' (Souter, J., concurring in judgment), he must articulate his desire to have counsel present sufficiently clearly that a reasonable police officer in the circumstances would understand the statement to be a request for an attorney. If the statement fails to meet the requisite level of clarity, *Edwards* does not require that the officers stop questioning the suspect. * * *

"We decline petitioner's invitation to extend *Edwards* and require law enforcement officers to cease questioning immediately upon the making of an ambiguous or equivocal reference to an attorney. [When] the officers conducting the questioning reasonably do not know whether or not the suspect wants a lawyer, a rule requiring the immediate cessation of questioning 'would transform the *Miranda* safeguards into wholly irrational obstacles to legitimate police investigative activity,' because it would needlessly prevent the police from questioning a suspect in the absence of counsel even if the suspect did not wish to have a lawyer present. * * *

"We recognize that requiring a clear assertion of the right to counsel might disadvantage some suspects who—because of fear, intimidation, lack of linguistic skills, or a variety of other reasons—will not clearly articulate their right to counsel although they actually want to have a lawyer present. But the primary protection afforded suspects subject to custodial interrogation is the *Miranda* warnings themselves. [A] suspect who knowingly and voluntarily waives his right to counsel after having that right explained to him has indicated his willingness to deal with the police unassisted. Although *Edwards* provides an additional protection—if a suspect subsequently requests an attorney, questioning must cease—it is one that must be affirmatively invoked by the suspect.

"[If] we were to require questioning to cease if a suspect makes a statement that *might* be a request for an attorney, [the *Edwards* Rule's] clarity and ease of application would be lost. Police officers would be forced to make difficult judgment calls about whether the suspect in fact wants a lawyer even though he hasn't said so, with the threat of suppression if they guess wrong. We therefore hold that, after a knowing and voluntary waiver of the *Miranda* rights, law enforcement officers may continue questioning until and unless the suspect clearly requests an attorney.

"[To] recapitulate: We held in *Miranda* that a suspect is entitled to the assistance of counsel during custodial interrogation even though the Constitution does not provide for such assistance. We held in *Edwards* that if the suspect invokes the right to counsel at any time, the police must immediately cease questioning him until an attorney is present. But we are unwilling to create a third layer of prophylaxis to prevent police questioning when the suspect *might* want a lawyer. Unless the suspect actually requests an attorney, questioning may continue."

Justice SOUTER, joined by Blackmun, Stevens and Ginsburg, JJ., wrote a separate opinion. Although he concurred in the judgment affirming Davis's conviction, "resting partly on evidence of statements given after agents ascertained that he did not wish to deal with them through counsel," Justice Souter could not join the majority's "further conclusion that if the investigators here had been so inclined, they were at liberty to disregard Davis's reference to a lawyer entirely, in accordance with a general rule that interrogators have no legal obligation to discover what a custodial subject meant by an ambiguous statement that could reasonably be understood to express a desire to consult a lawyer":

"[For nearly three decades], two precepts have commanded broad assent: that the *Miranda* safeguards exist 'to assure that *the individual's right to choose* between speech and silence remains unfettered throughout the interrogation process,' and that the justification for *Miranda* rules, intended to operate in the real world, 'must be consistent [with] practical realities.' *Arizona v. Roberson* (Kennedy, J., dissenting). A rule barring government agents from further interrogation until they determine whether a suspect's ambiguous statement was meant as a request for counsel fulfills both ambitions. It assures that a suspect's choice whether or not to deal with police through counsel will be 'scrupulously honored' and it faces both the real-world reasons why misunderstandings arise between suspect and interrogator and the real-world limitations on the capacity of police and trial courts to apply fine distinctions and intricate rules.

"Tested against the same two principles, the approach the Court adopts does not fare so well. First, as the majority expressly acknowledges, criminal suspects who may (in *Miranda*'s words) be 'thrust into an unfamiliar atmosphere and run through menacing police interrogation procedures,' would seem an odd group to single out for the Court's demand of heightened linguistic care. A substantial percentage of them lack anything like a confident command of the English language, many are 'woefully ignorant,' and many more will be sufficiently intimidated by the interrogation process or overwhelmed by the uncertainty of their predicament that the ability to speak assertively will abandon them.[4] Indeed, the awareness of just these realities has, in the past, dissuaded the Court from placing any burden of clarity upon individuals in custody, but has led it instead to require that requests for counsel be 'give[n] a broad, rather than a narrow, interpretation' and that courts 'indulge every reasonable presumption,' *Johnson v. Zerbst,* that a suspect has not waived his right to counsel under *Miranda*.

"[Nor] may the standard governing waivers as expressed in these statements be deflected away by drawing a distinction between initial waivers of *Miranda* rights and subsequent decisions to reinvoke them, on the theory that so long as the burden to demonstrate waiver rests on the government, it is only fair to make the suspect shoulder a burden of showing a clear subsequent assertion. *Miranda* itself discredited the legitimacy of any such distinction. The opinion described the object of the warning as being to assure 'a continuous opportunity to exercise [the right of silence].' '[C]ontinuous opportunity' suggests an unvarying one, governed by a common standard of effectiveness.

"[It] is easy, amidst the discussion of layers of protection, to lose sight of a real risk in the majority's approach, going close to the core of what the Court has held that the Fifth Amendment provides. [When] a suspect understands his (expressed) wishes to have been ignored (and by hypothesis, he has said something that an objective listener could 'reasonably,' although not necessarily, take to be a request), in contravention of the 'rights' just read to him by his interrogator, he may well see further objection as futile and confession (true or not) as the only way to end his interrogation. * * *

"Our cases are best respected by a rule that when a suspect under custodial interrogation makes an ambiguous statement that might reasonably be under-

---

4. Social science confirms what common sense would suggest, that individuals who feel intimidated or powerless are more likely to speak in equivocal or nonstandard terms when no ambiguity or equivocation is meant. Suspects in police interrogation are strong candidates for these effects. Even while resort by the police to the 'third degree' has abated since *Miranda*, the basic forms of psychological pressure applied by police appear to have changed less. * * *

stood as expressing a wish that a lawyer be summoned (and questioning cease), interrogators' questions should be confined to verifying whether the individual meant to ask for a lawyer. While there is reason to expect that trial courts will apply today's ruling sensibly (without requiring criminal suspects to speak with the discrimination of an Oxford don) and that interrogators will continue to follow what the Court rightly calls 'good police practice' (compelled up to now by a substantial body of state and Circuit law), I believe that the case law under *Miranda* does not allow them to do otherwise."

Ascertaining the suspect's choice vs. influencing that choice. Sometimes a police officer will respond to a suspect's ambiguous reference to a lawyer *not* by asking questions designed to clarify the suspect's wishes, but by making statements designed to *convey the message* that the suspect has no need for a lawyer or that obtaining a lawyer will not be in the suspect's best interest. See, e.g., *Mueller v. Commonwealth*, 422 S.E.2d 380 (Va.1992). Mueller waived his *Miranda* rights and agreed to talk to a detective. Two hours into the interrogation, Mueller asked the detective: "Do you think I need an attorney here?" The detective responded by shaking his head slightly, holding his arms out and his palms up in a shrug-like manner, and replying: "You're just talking to us." Several moments later, Mueller confessed to the crime (rape-murder) for which he was later sentenced to death.

The Supreme Court of Virginia held that (a) Mueller's question did not constitute the unambiguous request for counsel needed to invoke the *Edwards* rule and (b) the detective's response did not violate Mueller's *Miranda* rights. But in the brief it filed in the *Davis* case, the United States specifically disapproved of the *Mueller* ruling because the detective's response to Mueller's question conveyed the message that he did not really need a lawyer. Once a suspect has made an ambiguous reference to counsel, observed the United States, the officer's questions "must be objectively neutral and limited to ascertaining, not influencing, the choice that the suspect is entitled to make freely under *Miranda* and *Edwards*." See also *Collazo v. Estelle*, 940 F.2d 411 (9th Cir.1991) (en banc), where a 7–4 majority per Trott, J., emphasized that the police cannot attempt to discourage a suspect from speaking to a lawyer, cannot lead him to think that he can "reap some legal benefit" by excluding a defense lawyer from the process or suggest that somehow he will be "penalized" if he invokes his right to a lawyer.

19. ***The Miranda–Edwards–Roberson rule and the Sixth Amendment right to counsel compared and contrasted.*** In *Michigan v. Jackson*, 475 U.S. 625, 106 S.Ct. 1404, 89 L.Ed.2d 631 (1986), defendants had waived their rights and agreed to talk to the police without counsel before their "arraignments" (in the setting of the *Jackson* case, this proceeding is often called the "first appearance"). When brought before the magistrate, however, defendants requested that counsel be appointed for them because they were indigent. After the "arraignment" and before defendants had an opportunity to consult with counsel, the police again advised them of their rights, obtained written waivers, questioned them and obtained confessions. The Court, per Stevens, J., agreed with the state supreme court that "the *Edwards* rule 'applies by analogy to those situations where an accused requests counsel before the arraigning magistrate * * *.' [The] reasons for prohibiting the interrogation of an uncounseled prisoner who has asked for the help of a lawyer are even stronger after he has been formally charged with an offense than before." Thus, because the police initiated the questioning, the post-arraignment waivers of Sixth Amendment rights were invalid.

The Court rejected the argument that defendants' requests for appointed counsel may have encompassed only representation at trial and in other formal legal proceedings, not during further questioning by the police: "[The State] has the burden of establishing a valid waiver. Doubts must be resolved in favor of protecting the constitutional claim. This settled approach to questions of waiver requires us to give a broad, rather than a narrow, interpretation to a defendant's request for counsel—we presume that the defendant requests the lawyer's services at every critical stage of the prosecution."[a]

However, in McNEIL v. WISCONSIN, 501 U.S. 171, 111 S.Ct. 2204, 115 L.Ed.2d 158 (1991) (where a suspect asserted his Sixth Amendment right to counsel by his appearance with counsel at a bail hearing concerning an offense with which he had been charged), a 6–3 majority, per SCALIA, J., made it clear that the Sixth Amendment right to counsel provides less protection than does the *Miranda-Edwards–Roberson* rule. Unlike the latter rule, which, when invoked, protects one from police-initiated interrogation with respect to *any* crime, the Sixth Amendment right is "offense-specific." Thus, even though a defendant invokes this right, the police can initiate questioning about crimes *other than* the one with which he was charged.

The case arose as follows: After his arrest for armed robbery McNeil was represented by a public defender at a bail hearing. A short time later, a deputy sheriff visited McNeil in jail. After McNeil waived his *Miranda* rights, the deputy questioned him about a murder and attempted murder *factually unrelated* to the armed robbery with which he had been charged.[a] McNeil's statements were admitted into evidence and he was convicted of murder and attempted murder. The Court, per Scalia, J., rejected his contention that his appearance at the bail hearing for the armed robbery constituted an invocation of the *Miranda-Edwards–Roberson* right to counsel:

"[To] invoke the Sixth Amendment interest is, as a matter of *fact, not* to invoke the *Miranda-Edwards* interest. One might be quite willing to speak to the police without counsel present concerning many matters, but not the matter under prosecution. It can be said, perhaps, that it is *likely* that one who has asked for counsel's assistance in defending against a prosecution would want counsel present for all custodial interrogation, even interrogation unrelated to the charge. [But] even if [that] were true, the *likelihood* that a suspect would wish counsel to be present is not the test for applicability of *Edwards*. [That rule] requires, at a minimum, some statement that can reasonably be construed to be expression of a desire for the assistance of an attorney *in dealing with custodial interrogation by the police.* Requesting the assistance of an attorney at a bail hearing does not bear that construction.

"[Petitioner's] proposed rule [would] seriously impede effective law enforcement. The Sixth Amendment right to counsel attaches at the first formal proceeding against an accused, and in most States, at least with respect to serious offenses, free counsel is made available at that time and ordinarily requested. Thus, if we were to adopt petitioner's rule, most persons in pretrial custody for

---

a. Dissenting Justice Rehnquist, joined by Powell and O'Connor, JJ., maintained that "the prophylactic rule set forth in *Edwards* makes no sense at all except when linked to the Fifth Amendment's prohibition against compelled self-incrimination." Chief Justice Burger concurred in the judgment, observing that although "stare decisis calls for my following the rule of *Edwards* in the context," "plainly the subject calls for reexamination."

For forceful criticism of *Jackson,* see H. Richard Uviller, *Evidence from the Mind of the Criminal Suspect,* 87 Colum.L.Rev. 1137, 1190 (1987).

a. Once the right to counsel attaches to the offense charged, does (should) it also attach to any other offense "closely related to" or "inextricably intertwined with" the particular offense charged? See *Texas v. Cobb,* p. 611.

serious offenses would be *unapproachable* by police officers suspecting them of involvement in other crimes, *even though they have never expressed any unwillingness to be questioned.* Since the ready ability to obtain uncoerced confessions is not an evil but an unmitigated good, society would be the loser."

20.   *"Anticipatorily" invoking the Miranda–Edwards–Roberson right to counsel.*

Dissenting in *McNeil* (joined by Marshall and Blackmun, J.J.), Justice Stevens (author of *Michigan v. Jackson*) maintained that *McNeil* "demeans the importance of the right to counsel." But he took comfort in the fact that *McNeil* "probably will have only a slight impact on current custodial interrogation procedures":

"[If] petitioner in this case had made [a] statement indicating that he was invoking his Fifth Amendment right to counsel as well as his Sixth Amendment right to counsel, the entire offense-specific house of cards that the Court has erected today would collapse, pursuant to our holding in *Roberson,* that a defendant who invokes the right to counsel for interrogation on one offense may not be reapproached regarding any offense unless counsel is present. In future preliminary hearings, competent counsel can be expected to make sure that they, or their clients, make a statement on the record that will obviate the consequences of today's holding. That is why I think this decision will have little, if any, practical effect on police practices."

But Justice Scalia replied:

"We have in fact never held that a person can invoke his *Miranda* rights anticipatorily, in a context other than 'custodial interrogation' which a preliminary hearing will not always or even usually involve. [If] the *Miranda* right to counsel can be invoked at a preliminary hearing, it could be argued, there is no logical reason why it could not be invoked by a letter prior to arrest, or indeed even prior to identification as a suspect. Most rights must be asserted when the government seeks to take the action they protect against. The fact that we have allowed the *Miranda* right to counsel, once asserted, to be effective with respect to future custodial interrogation does not necessarily mean that we will allow it to be asserted initially outside the context of custodial interrogation, with similar future effect."

Is Justice Scalia correct? Is even a person taken in to police custody *unable* to assert his *Miranda-Edwards–Roberson* right "in a context other than 'custodial interrogation' "? (Emphasis added.) Consider the following *alternative* hypothetical situations:

(1) A murder suspect is arrested in his apartment and told he is being taken to police headquarters where he will be questioned by the lieutenant in charge of the case. He tells the arresting officers: "Before I leave my apartment and go with you, I want to make one thing perfectly clear. When I get to the police station, I'm not talking to the lieutenant or anybody else unless my lawyer is present."

(2) Same facts as above except that the suspect says nothing until he arrives at the police station and is ushered into the office of the lieutenant in charge of the case. At this point, the suspect tells the lieutenant: "Before you ask me anything, I want you to know that I am well aware that I have a right to a lawyer and I want one at my side before I answer any questions."

(3) Same facts as above except that when the suspect enters the lieutenant's office, the lieutenant tells him: "I'm in charge of this case. I want you to know that I am going to treat you fairly and squarely. As soon as you take off your coat and sit down in that chair next to my desk I am going to advise you fully of your rights." The suspect, who has said nothing to any officer up to this point, remains

standing and replies: "Don't bother to read me my rights. I know my rights and I want a lawyer right now. I'm not going to answer a single question without a lawyer being present."

Assume further that in each of these alternative hypothetical situations the lieutenant proceeds to give the suspect the *Miranda* warnings and in each instance the suspect *agrees* to talk to the police about his involvement in the murder when he is advised of his rights. In which instance, if any, has the suspect effectively invoked his *Miranda-Edwards* right to counsel?

The position taken by the lower courts. Relying heavily on footnote 3 to Justice Scalia's opinion in *McNeil*, most courts that have addressed the issue have balked at the notion that *Miranda-Edwards* protections can be triggered anticipatorily. However, they have left open the possibility that a suspect might be able to invoke the *Miranda-Edwards* right to counsel if custodial interrogation is about to begin or is "imminent." See *Alston v. Redman*, 34 F.3d 1237 (3d Cir.1994); *United States v. LaGrone*, 43 F.3d 332 (7th Cir.1994); *United States v. Wright*, 962 F.2d 953 (9th Cir.1992); *Sapp v. State*, 690 So.2d 581 (Fla.1997).[a]

21. If a suspect has not requested a lawyer but, unbeknownst to him, somebody else has retained one for him, does the failure to inform the suspect that a lawyer is trying to see him vitiate the waiver of his Miranda rights? If the police mislead the attorney about whether her client will be questioned or otherwise deceive an inquiring attorney, should the confession be excluded?

MORAN v. BURBINE
475 U.S. 412, 106 S.Ct. 1135, 89 L.Ed.2d 410 (1986).

Justice O'CONNOR delivered the opinion of the Court.

After being informed of his rights pursuant to *Miranda* and after executing a series of written waivers, respondent confessed to the murder of a young woman. At no point during the course of the interrogation, which occurred prior to arraignment, did he request an attorney. While he was in police custody, his sister attempted to retain a lawyer to represent him. The attorney telephoned the police station and received assurances that respondent would not be questioned further until the next day. In fact, the interrogation session that yielded the inculpatory statements began later that evening. The question presented is whether either the

a. But cf. *United States v. Goodson*, 18 M.J. 243 (Ct.Mil.App.1984), vac'd and remanded for further consideration in light of *Smith v. Illinois* (p. 533). Goodson was one of nine soldiers arrested for drug violations and taken to a military police station for interrogation by Military Police Investigator Allinder. While waiting his turn to be interrogated (Allinder didn't get around to him until nine hours later), Goodson asked a sergeant whether he could contact a lawyer. But when his turn came to be questioned and he was advised of his rights by Allinder, Goodson signed a waiver-of-rights form. He then made an incriminating statement. Goodson never indicated to Allinder that he wanted, or had previously requested, counsel. And Allinder did not recall anyone telling him that Goodson had requested counsel.

In upholding the admissibility of Goodson's statement, a 2–1 majority, per Cook, J., distinguished *Edwards* on the ground that "Goodson made all of his requests for counsel *before* he was advised of his rights and while the case was still in the investigatory state. [T]he right to appointed counsel does not arise until in-custody interrogation has begun. The corollary is that a waiver of the *Miranda* rights cannot occur unless there has been a full advisement of rights."

Dissenting Chief Judge Everett maintained that "even if a waiver of *Miranda* rights cannot proceed without full advisement of those rights," it does not follow "that a request for counsel which precedes this advice can be ignored, as was done here." Moreover, the Court's approach "is an invitation to hairsplitting." By vacating the judgment and remanding the case for further consideration in light of *Smith v. Illinois,* did the Supreme Court indicate support for dissenting Chief Judge Everett's views?

conduct of the police or respondent's ignorance of the attorney's efforts to reach him taints the validity of the waivers and therefore requires exclusion of the confessions.

On the morning of March 3, 1977, Mary Jo Hickey was found unconscious in a factory parking lot in Providence, Rhode Island. Suffering from injuries to her skull apparently inflicted by a metal pipe found at the scene, she was rushed to a nearby hospital. Three weeks later she died from her wounds.

Several months after her death, the Cranston, Rhode Island police arrested respondent and two others in connection with a local burglary. Shortly before the arrest, Detective Ferranti of the Cranston police force had learned from a confidential informant that the man responsible for Ms. Hickey's death lived at a certain address and went by the name of "Butch." Upon discovering that respondent lived at that address and was known by that name, Detective Ferranti informed respondent of his *Miranda* rights. When respondent refused to execute a written waiver, Detective Ferranti spoke separately with the two other suspects arrested on the breaking and entering charge and obtained statements further implicating respondent in Ms. Hickey's murder. At approximately 6:00 p.m., Detective Ferranti telephoned the police in Providence to convey the information he had uncovered. An hour later, three officers from that department arrived at the Cranston headquarters for the purpose of questioning respondent about the murder.

That same evening, at about 7:45 p.m., respondent's sister telephoned the Public Defender's Office to obtain legal assistance for her brother. Her sole concern was the breaking and entering charge, as she was unaware that respondent was then under suspicion for murder. [She tried to contact the attorney who was to represent her brother on the breaking and entering charge, but when unable to do so, wound up talking to another Assistant Public Defender (Ms. Munson) about her brother's situation. At 8:15 p.m. Ms. Munson phoned the Cranston police station, asked that her call be transferred to the detective division, and stated that she would act as Burbine's counsel in the event the police intended to put him in a lineup or question him. An unidentified person told her that neither act would occur and that the police were "through" with Burbine "for the night." Ms. Munson was told neither that the Providence police were at the stationhouse nor that Burbine was a suspect in Mary's murder.]

At all relevant times, respondent was unaware of his sister's efforts to retain counsel and of the fact and contents of Ms. Munson's telephone conversation.

Less than an hour later, the police brought respondent to an interrogation room and conducted the first of a series of interviews concerning the murder. Prior to each session, respondent was informed of his *Miranda* rights, and on three separate occasions he signed a written form acknowledging that he understood his right to the presence of an attorney and explicitly indicating that he "[did] not want an attorney called or appointed for [him]" before he gave a statement. Uncontradicted evidence at the suppression hearing indicated that at least twice during the course of the evening, respondent was left in a room where he had access to a telephone, which he apparently declined to use. Eventually, respondent signed three written statements fully admitting to the murder.

[The trial judge denied respondent's motion to suppress the statements. The jury found respondent guilty of first degree murder. On federal habeas corpus, the First Circuit held that the police conduct had fatally tainted respondent's "otherwise valid" waiver.]

We granted certiorari to decide whether a pre-arraignment confession preceded by an otherwise valid waiver must be suppressed either because the police misinformed an inquiring attorney about their plans concerning the suspect or because they failed to inform the suspect of the attorney's efforts to reach him. We now reverse. * * *

Echoing the standard first articulated in *Johnson v. Zerbst*, *Miranda* holds that "[t]he defendant may waive effectuation" of the rights conveyed in the warnings "provided the waiver is made voluntarily, knowingly and intelligently." The inquiry has two distinct dimensions. First the relinquishment of the right must have been voluntary in the sense that it was the product of a free and deliberate choice rather than intimidation, coercion or deception. Second, the waiver must have been made with a full awareness both of the nature of the right being abandoned and the consequences of the decision to abandon it.

[Under] this standard, we have no doubt that respondent validly waived his right to remain silent and to the presence of counsel. [Nonetheless, on federal habeas corpus, the First Circuit] believed that the "[d]eliberate or reckless" conduct of the police, in particular their failure to inform respondent of the telephone call, fatally undermined the validity of the otherwise proper waiver. We find this conclusion untenable as a matter of both logic and precedent.

Events occurring outside of the presence of the suspect and entirely unknown to him surely can have no bearing on the capacity to comprehend and knowingly relinquish a constitutional right. Under the analysis of the Court of Appeals, the same defendant, armed with the same information and confronted with precisely the same police conduct, would have knowingly waived his *Miranda* rights had a lawyer not telephoned the police station to inquire about his status. Nothing in any of our waiver decisions or in our understanding of the essential components of a valid waiver requires so incongruous a result. No doubt the additional information would have been useful to respondent; perhaps even it might have affected his decision to confess. But we have never read the Constitution to require that the police supply a suspect with a flow of information to help him calibrate his self interest in deciding whether to speak or stand by his rights. Once it is determined that a suspect's decision not to rely on his rights was uncoerced, that he at all times knew he could stand mute and request a lawyer, and that he was aware of the state's intention to use his statements to secure a conviction, the analysis is complete and the waiver is valid as a matter of law.[1] The Court of Appeals' conclusion to the contrary was in error.

Nor do we believe that the level of the police's culpability in failing to inform respondent of the telephone call has any bearing on the validity of the waiver. [W]hether intentional or inadvertent, the state of mind of the police is irrelevant to the question of the intelligence and voluntariness of respondent's election to abandon his rights. Although highly inappropriate, even deliberate deception of an attorney could not possibly affect a suspect's decision to waive his *Miranda* rights unless he were at least aware of the incident. Compare *Escobedo* (excluding confession where police incorrectly told the *suspect* that his lawyer " 'didn't want to see' him"). Nor was the failure to inform respondent of the telephone call the kind of "trick[ery]" that can vitiate the validity of a waiver. *Miranda*. [Because] respondent's voluntary decision to speak was made with full awareness and comprehension of all the information *Miranda* requires the police to convey, the waivers were valid.

---

1. The dissent incorrectly reads our analysis of the components of a valid waiver to be inconsistent [with] *Edwards*. [But the] dissent never comes to grips with the crucial distinguishing feature of this case—that Burbine at no point requested the presence of counsel, as was his right under *Miranda* to do. [We reject] the dissent's entirely undefended suggestion that the Fifth Amendment "right to counsel" requires anything more than that the police inform the suspect of his right to representation and honor his request that the interrogation cease until his attorney is present.

* * * Regardless of any issue of waiver, [contends respondent], the Fifth Amendment requires the reversal of a conviction if the police are less than forthright in their dealings with an attorney or if they fail to tell a suspect of a lawyer's unilateral efforts to contact him. Because the proposed modification ignores the underlying purposes of the *Miranda* rules and because we think that the decision as written strikes the proper balance between society's legitimate law enforcement interests and the protection of the defendant's Fifth Amendment rights, we decline the invitation to further extend *Miranda*'s reach.

At the outset, while we share respondent's distaste for the deliberate misleading of an officer of the court, reading *Miranda* to forbid police deception of an *attorney* "would cut [the decision] completely loose from its own explicitly stated rationale."

[The] purpose of the *Miranda* warnings * * * is to dissipate the compulsion inherent in custodial interrogation and, in so doing, guard against abridgement of the suspect's Fifth Amendment rights. Clearly, a rule that focuses on how the police treat an attorney—conduct that has no relevance at all to the degree of compulsion experienced by the defendant during interrogation—would ignore both *Miranda*'s mission and its only source of legitimacy.

Nor are we prepared to adopt a rule requiring that the police inform a suspect of an attorney's efforts to reach him. While such a rule might add marginally to *Miranda*'s goal of dispelling the compulsion inherent in custodial interrogation, overriding practical considerations counsel against its adoption. As we have stressed on numerous occasions, "[o]ne of the principal advantages" of *Miranda* is the ease and clarity of its application. We have little doubt that the approach urged by respondent and endorsed by the Court of Appeals would have the inevitable consequence of muddying *Miranda*'s otherwise relatively clear waters. The legal questions it would spawn are legion: To what extent should the police be held accountable for knowing that the accused has counsel? Is it enough that someone in the station house knows, or must the interrogating officer himself know of counsel's efforts to contact the suspect? Do counsel's efforts to talk to the suspect concerning one criminal investigation trigger the obligation to inform the defendant before interrogation may proceed on a wholly separate matter? We are unwilling to modify *Miranda* in a manner that would so clearly undermine the decision's central "virtue of informing police and prosecutors with specificity [what] they may do in conducting [a] custodial interrogation, and of informing courts under what circumstances statements obtained during such interrogation are not admissible." *Fare v. Michael C.*

[Moreover,] reading *Miranda* to require the police in each instance to inform a suspect of an attorney's efforts to reach him would work a substantial and, we think, inappropriate shift in the subtle balance struck in that decision. Custodial interrogations implicate two competing concerns. On the one hand, "the need for police questioning as a tool for effective enforcement of criminal laws" cannot be doubted. [On] the other hand, the Court has recognized that the interrogation process is "inherently coercive" and that, as a consequence, there exists a substantial risk that the police will inadvertently traverse the fine line between legitimate efforts to elicit admissions and constitutionally impermissible compulsion. *Miranda* attempted to reconcile these opposing concerns by giving the *defendant* the power to exert some control over the course of the interrogation. Declining to adopt the more extreme position that the actual presence of a lawyer was necessary to dispel the coercion inherent in custodial interrogation, the Court found that the suspect's Fifth Amendment rights could be adequately protected by less intrusive means. Police questioning, often an essential part of the investigatory process, could continue in its traditional form, the Court held, but only if the suspect clearly understood that, at any time, he could bring the proceeding to a halt or, short of that, call in an attorney to give advice and monitor the conduct of his interrogators.

The position urged by respondent would upset this carefully drawn approach in a manner that is both unnecessary for the protection of the Fifth Amendment privilege and injurious to legitimate law enforcement. Because, as *Miranda* holds, full comprehension of the rights to remain silent and request an attorney are sufficient to dispel whatever coercion is inherent in the interrogation process, a rule requiring the police to inform the suspect of an attorney's efforts to contact him would contribute to the protection of the Fifth Amendment privilege only incidentally, if at all. This minimal benefit, however, would come at a substantial cost to society's legitimate and substantial interest in securing admissions of guilt.

[Respondent] also contends that the Sixth Amendment requires exclusion of his three confessions. [The] difficulty for respondent is that the interrogation sessions that yielded the inculpatory statements took place *before* the initiation of "adversary judicial proceedings." He contends, however, that this circumstance is not fatal to his Sixth Amendment claim. [The] right to noninterference with an attorney's dealings with a criminal suspect, he asserts, arises the moment that the relationship is formed, or, at the very least, once the defendant is placed in custodial interrogation.

We are not persuaded. At the outset, subsequent decisions foreclose any reliance on *Escobedo* and *Miranda* for the proposition that the Sixth Amendment right, in any of its manifestations, applies prior to the initiation of adversary judicial proceedings. Although *Escobedo* was originally decided as a Sixth Amendment case, "the Court in retrospect perceived that the 'prime purpose' of *Escobedo* was not to vindicate the constitutional right to counsel as such, but, like *Miranda,* 'to guarantee full effectuation of the privilege against self-incrimination....'" *Kirby v. Illinois* [p. 631]. Clearly then, *Escobedo* provides no support for respondent's argument. Nor, of course, does *Miranda,* the holding of which rested exclusively on the Fifth Amendment.

[Precedent aside,] we find respondent's understanding of the Sixth Amendment both practically and theoretically unsound. As a practical matter, it makes little sense to say that the Sixth Amendment right to counsel attaches at different times depending on the fortuity of whether the suspect or his family happens to have retained counsel prior to interrogation. More importantly, the suggestion that the existence of an attorney-client relationship itself triggers the protections of the Sixth Amendment misconceives the underlying purposes of the right to counsel. The Sixth Amendment's intended function is not to wrap a protective cloak around the attorney-client relationship for its own sake any more than it is to protect a suspect from the consequences of his own candor. [By] its very terms, [the Sixth Amendment] becomes applicable only when the government's role shifts from investigation to accusation. * * *

Finally, respondent contends that the [police treatment of Assistant Public Defender Munson] was so offensive as to deprive him of the fundamental fairness guaranteed by [due process]. We do not question that on facts more egregious than those presented here police deception might rise to a level of a due process violation. Accordingly, Justice Stevens' apocalyptic suggestion that we have approved any and all forms of police misconduct is demonstrably incorrect.[4] We hold

---

4. Among its other failings, the dissent declines to follow *Oregon v. Elstad* [p. 781], a decision that categorically forecloses Justice Stevens' major premise—that *Miranda* requires the police to inform a suspect of any and all information that would be useful to a deci-sion whether to remain silent or speak with the police. The dissent also launches a novel "agency" theory of the Fifth Amendment under which any perceived deception of a lawyer is automatically treated as deception of his or her client. This argument entirely disregards

only that, on these facts, the challenged conduct falls short of the kind of misbehavior that so shocks the sensibilities of civilized society as to warrant a federal intrusion into the criminal processes of the States. * * *

Justice STEVENS, with whom Justice BRENNAN and Justice MARSHALL join, dissenting.

[Until] today, incommunicado questioning has been viewed with the strictest scrutiny by this Court; today, incommunicado questioning is embraced as a societal goal of the highest order that justifies police deception of the shabbiest kind. * * * Police interference with communications between an attorney and his client is a recurrent problem. [The] near-consensus of state courts and the [ABA Standards of Criminal Justice] about this recurrent problem lends powerful support to the conclusion that police may not interfere with communications between an attorney and the client whom they are questioning. Indeed, at least two opinions from this Court seemed to express precisely that view.[20] The Court today flatly rejects that widely held view and [adopts] the most restrictive interpretation of the federal constitutional restraints on police deception, misinformation, and interference in attorney-client communications. * * *

Well-settled principles of law lead inexorably to the conclusion that the failure to inform Burbine of the call from his attorney makes the subsequent waiver of his constitutional rights invalid. Analysis should begin with an acknowledgment that the burden of proving the validity of a waiver of constitutional rights is always on the *government*. When such a waiver occurs in a custodial setting, that burden is an especially heavy one because custodial interrogation is inherently coercive, because disinterested witnesses are seldom available to describe what actually happened, and because history has taught us that the danger of overreaching during incommunicado interrogation is so real. * * *

[*Miranda*] clearly condemns threats or trickery that cause a suspect to make an unwise waiver of his rights even though he fully understands those rights. In my opinion there can be no constitutional distinction—as the Court appears to draw—between a deceptive misstatement and the concealment by the police of the critical fact that an attorney retained by the accused or his family has offered assistance, either by telephone or in person.

the elemental and established proposition that the privilege against compulsory self-incrimination is, by hypothesis, a personal one that can only be invoked by the individual whose testimony is being compelled.

Most importantly, the dissent's misreading of *Miranda* itself is breathtaking in its scope. For example, it reads *Miranda* as creating an undifferentiated right to the presence of an attorney that is triggered automatically by the initiation of the interrogation itself. [The] dissent condemns us for embracing "incommunicado questioning [as] a societal goal of the highest order that justifies police deception of the shabbiest kind." We, of course, do nothing of the kind. As any reading of *Miranda* reveals, the decision, rather than proceeding from the premise that the rights and needs of the defendant are paramount to all others, embodies a carefully crafted balance designed to fully protect *both* the defendant's and society's interests. The dissent may not share our view that the Fifth Amendment rights of the defendant are amply protected by application of *Miranda as written*. But the dissent is "simply wrong"

in suggesting that exclusion of Burbine's three confessions follows perfunctorily from *Miranda*'s mandate. Y. Kamisar, *Police Interrogation and Confessions* 217–218, n. 94 (1980).

Quite understandably, the dissent is outraged by the very idea of police deception of a lawyer. Significantly less understandable is its willingness to misconstrue this Court's constitutional holdings in order to implement its subjective notions of sound policy.

20. See *Miranda* at n. 35 (in *Escobedo*, "[t]he police also prevented the attorney from consulting with his client. Independent of any other constitutional proscription, this action constitutes a violation of the Sixth Amendment right to the assistance of counsel and excludes any statement obtained in its wake"); *Escobedo* ("[I]t 'would be highly incongruous if our system of justice permitted the district attorney, the lawyer representing the State, to extract a confession from the accused while his own lawyer, seeking to speak with him, was kept from him by the police' ").

[If,] as the Court asserts, "the analysis is at an end" as soon as the suspect is provided with enough information to have the *capacity* to understand and exercise his rights, I see no reason why the police should not be permitted to make the same kind of misstatements to the suspect that they are apparently allowed to make to his lawyer. *Miranda,* however, clearly establishes that both kinds of deception vitiate the suspect's waiver of his right to counsel.

[In] short, settled principles about construing waivers of constitutional rights and about the need for strict presumptions in custodial interrogations, as well as a plain reading of the *Miranda* opinion itself, overwhelmingly support the conclusion reached by almost every state court that has considered the matter—a suspect's waiver of his right to counsel is invalid if police refuse to inform the suspect of his counsel's communications.

The Court makes the alternative argument that requiring police to inform a suspect of his attorney's communications to and about him is not required because it would upset the careful "balance" of *Miranda.* [The] Court's balancing approach is profoundly misguided. The cost of suppressing evidence of guilt will always make the value of a procedural safeguard appear "minimal," "marginal," or "incremental." Indeed, the value of any trial at all seems like a "procedural technicality" when balanced against the interest in administering prompt justice to a murderer or a rapist caught redhanded. The individual interest in procedural safeguards that minimize the risk of error is easily discounted when the fact of guilt appears certain beyond doubt.

What is the cost of requiring the police to inform a suspect of his attorney's call? It would decrease the likelihood that custodial interrogation will enable the police to obtain a confession. This is certainly a real cost, but it is the same cost that this Court has repeatedly found necessary to preserve the character of our free society and our rejection of an inquisitorial system. [At] the time attorney Munson made her call to the Cranston Police Station, she was acting as Burbine's attorney. Under ordinary principles of agency law the deliberate deception of Munson was tantamount to deliberate deception of her client. [The] majority brushes aside the police deception involved in the misinformation of attorney Munson. It is irrelevant to the Fifth Amendment analysis, concludes the majority, because that right is personal; it is irrelevant to the Sixth Amendment analysis, continues the majority, because the Sixth Amendment does not apply until formal adversary proceedings have begun.

In my view, as a matter of law, the police deception of Munson was tantamount to deception of Burbine himself. It constituted a violation of Burbine's right to have an attorney present during the questioning that began shortly thereafter. The existence of that right is undisputed. Whether the source of that right is the Sixth Amendment, the Fifth Amendment, or a combination of the two is of no special importance, for I do not understand the Court to deny the existence of the right.

[The] possible reach of the Court's opinion is stunning. For the majority seems to suggest that police may deny counsel all access to a client who is being held. At least since *Escobedo,* it has been widely accepted that police may not simply deny attorneys access to their clients who are in custody. This view has survived the recasting of *Escobedo* from a Sixth Amendment to a Fifth Amendment case that the majority finds so critically important. That this prevailing view is shared *by the police* can be seen in the state court opinions detailing various forms of police deception of attorneys. For, if there were no obligation to give attorneys access, there would be no need to take elaborate steps to avoid access, such as shuttling the suspect to a different location, or taking the lawyer to different locations; police could simply refuse to allow the attorneys to see the suspects. But the law enforcement profession has apparently believed, quite rightly in my view, that denying lawyers access to their clients is impermissible. The Court today seems to assume that this view was error?that, from the federal constitutional perspective, the lawyer's access is, as a question from the Court put it in oral argument, merely "a matter of prosecutorial grace." Certainly, nothing in the Court's Fifth and Sixth Amendments analysis acknowledges that there is *any* federal constitutional bar to an absolute denial of lawyer access to a suspect who is in police custody.

[In] my judgment, police interference in the attorney-client relationship is the type of governmental misconduct on a matter of central importance to the administration of justice that the Due Process Clause prohibits. Just as the police cannot impliedly promise a suspect that his silence will not be used against him and then proceed to break that promise, so too police cannot tell a suspect's attorney that they will not question the suspect and then proceed to question him. Just as the government cannot conceal from a suspect material and exculpatory evidence, so too the government cannot conceal from a suspect the material fact of his attorney's communication.

[This] case turns on a proper appraisal of the role of the lawyer in our society. If a lawyer is seen as a nettlesome obstacle to the pursuit of wrongdoers—as in an inquisitorial society—then the Court's decision today makes a good deal of sense. If a lawyer is seen as an aid to the understanding and protection of constitutional rights—as in an accusatorial society—then today's decision makes no sense at all.
* * *

Notes and Questions

(a) *"Incommunicado questioning."* Consider Note, 100 Harv.L.Rev. 125, 126 (1986): "*Burbine* betrays the spirit of *Miranda* by placing a judicial seal of approval on official deception, thereby encouraging incommunicado interrogation and suggesting that police may deny counsel all access to a detained client." Do you agree? May the police tell a suspect no attorney has called, when in fact one has? If a suspect has not requested a lawyer, but someone else has retained a lawyer for him, how long may the police deny that lawyer access to the suspect? What exactly is meant by "incommunicado" or "incommunicado questioning" (terms used frequently by dissenting Justice Stevens)? These terms may mean either (1) preventing a prisoner from communicating with or meeting with counsel; or (2) not informing the outside world of the prisoner's whereabouts; or (3) denying a prisoner's friends, relatives or lawyers access to him. In which sense, if any, was Burbine held "incommunicado"?

(b) *The Miranda warnings and the need for a lawyer's advice.* Consider the Harvard Note, supra, at 133: "[T]o the extent that the population at large is unaware of its fifth and sixth amendment rights, the role of the lawyer—possibly the only one capable of safeguarding these rights—must be protected." Is *a suspect advised of his rights* (as opposed to "the population at large") unaware of his rights? If a lawyer is "the only one capable of safeguarding these rights," did the *Miranda* Court commit grievous error by not requiring that a suspect first consult with a lawyer or actually have a lawyer present in order for his waiver of rights to be effective?

(c) *The Burbine dissent's reliance on fn. 35 to Miranda.* In fn. 20 to his dissenting opinion, Justice Stevens maintains that the majority opinion cannot be reconciled with fn. 35 to *Miranda*, which, discussing *Escobedo*, states that "prevent[ing] [an] attorney from consulting with his client" violates the Sixth Amendment "independent of any other constitutional proscription." Should this statement be read in light of *Escobedo*'s particular facts? Consider Kamisar, Essays 217 n. 94 (1980):

"It is hard to believe that in the course of writing a 60–page opinion *based on the premise* that police-issued warnings can adequately protect a suspect's rights the [*Miranda*] Court would say in the next breath that such warnings are insufficient when, but only when, a suspect's lawyer is not allowed to consult with him—that even though a suspect has been emphatically and unequivocally advised of his rights and insists on talking, what he says is inadmissible [when] a lawyer *whose services he has not requested* has, *unbeknown to him,* entered the picture.

"Although the police did not advise Escobedo of any of his rights, 'he repeatedly asked to speak to his lawyer.' * * * Indeed, [the *Escobedo*] opinion begins: 'The critical issue in this case is whether [the] refusal by the police to honor petitioner's request to consult with his lawyer during the course of an interrogation constitutes a denial of "the Assistance of Counsel." '[If the refusal of the police to let Escobedo's lawyer meet with him] has any relevance, it is only because Escobedo became *aware of the fact* that the police were preventing his lawyer from talking to him, and this realization may well have underscored the police domination of the situation and the gravity of his plight."

(d) *Does the Burbine case dramatize "the Court's changed vision of Miranda"?* According to William Stuntz, *Self-Incrimination and Excuse,* 88 Colum.L.Rev. 1227, 1268 n. 141 (1988) the *Burbine* case "offers a striking example of the Court's changed vision of *Miranda.* Justice Steven's dissent in that case argues forcefully that *Miranda* is designed to prevent police from obtaining confessions by taking advantage of suspects' ignorance or bad judgment, and thereby to ensure that waivers of the right to remain silent result only from rational, self-interested choices by suspects. [This] reasoning is quite consistent with the reasoning of [the *Miranda* majority opinion]. On the other hand, Justice O'Connor's majority opinion in *Burbine* argues that station house confessions are essential to the proper enforcement of the criminal law [and] that the Constitution in no way protects suspects against unwise decisions to confess. [This] line of argument tracks not Warren's *Miranda* majority, but rather Justice White's *Miranda* dissent. *Burbine* thus exemplifies a (perhaps *the*) central truth about modern *Miranda* doctrine: while the holding of *Miranda* remains intact, it has been shaped to serve very different ends than those its original authors had in mind." See also Joshua Dressler, *Understanding Criminal Procedure,* 418–19 (2d ed. 1997) (*Burbine* case demonstrates the considerable distance the Court has traveled since the days of *Escobedo* and *Miranda*).

(e) *Should Burbine dishearten or encourage Miranda's defenders?* Consider Kamisar, *The "Police Practice" Phases of the Criminal Process and the Three Phases of the Burger Court,* in The Burger Years (Herman Schwartz ed. 1987) at 143, 150: "[The *Burbine* Court's view of *Miranda* as not 'proceeding from the premise that the rights and needs of the defendant are paramount to all others, [but as a case that] embodies a carefully crafted balance designed to fully protect *both* the defendant's and society's interests'] [see fn. 4 to the Court's opinion] is the way *Miranda*'s defenders—not its critics—have talked about the case for the past twenty years. [The *Burbine* Court's view of *Miranda* as a serious effort to strike a proper 'balance,' between, or to 'reconcile,' competing interests may turn out to be more important than its specific ruling." See also Kamisar, *Remembering the "Old World" of Criminal Procedure: A Reply to Professor Grano,* 23 U.Mich.J.L.Ref. 537, 575–84 (1990).

(f) *What result if, before being taken away by the police, a suspect asks a relative to contact a lawyer?* Would the result in *Burbine* have been different if, before being taken to the police station (a) the defendant had asked his sister to contact the Public Defender's Office and get somebody in the office to represent him; (b) his sister had done so; (c) the assistant public defender who had agreed to represent defendant had told the police she wanted to meet with her client immediately; but (d) the police had failed to inform defendant of this development? Why (not)? Cf. *People v. Griggs*, 604 N.E.2d 257 (Ill. 1992).

(g) *Reaction of the state courts.* Can a person fully comprehend the nature of his right to counsel and the consequences of a decision to waive this right without being informed that a lawyer, who could explain the consequences of a waiver, has been retained to represent him and is immediately able to consult with him? Relying on independent state grounds, a number of state courts have answered in the negative, thereby rejecting the U.S. Supreme Court's reasoning in *Burbine*. See *State v. Stoddard*, 537 A.2d 446 (Conn.1988); *Haliburton v. State*, 514 So.2d 1088 (Fla.1987); *People v. McCauley*, 645 N.E.2d 923 (Ill. 1994); *People v. Bender*, 551 N.W.2d 71 (1996); *People v. McCauley*, 645 N.E.2d 923 (Ill.1994).

21. *Use of a pretrial psychiatric examination at a capital sentencing proceeding.* ESTELLE v. SMITH, 451 U.S. 454, 101 S.Ct. 1866, 68 L.Ed.2d 359 (1981), arose as follows: Respondent was indicted for murder in Texas. The state announced its intention to seek the death penalty. Thereafter, although defense counsel had not put into issue his client's competency to stand trial or his sanity at the time of the offense, a judge informally ordered the prosecution to arrange a psychiatric examination of respondent by Dr. Grigson to determine respondent's capacity to stand trial. After respondent was convicted of murder, the doctor also testified—on the basis of his pretrial examination of respondent—as to respondent's "future dangerousness," one of the critical issues to be resolved by a Texas jury at the capital sentencing proceeding. The jury answered the "future dangerousness" question and other requisite questions in the affirmative and, thus, under Texas law, the death penalty for respondent was mandatory.

Although respondent had not been warned before the pretrial psychiatric examination that anything he said during the examination could be used against him at the sentencing proceeding, the state argued that the privilege against self-incrimination was inapplicable because (a) Dr. Grigson's testimony was used only to determine punishment after conviction, not to establish guilt; and (b) respondent's communications to Dr. Grigson were "nontestimonial" in nature. Rejecting these contentions, the Court held, per BURGER, C.J., that both respondent's Fifth and Sixth Amendment rights were violated by the use of Dr. Grigson's testimony at the penalty phase of the case:

"Just as the Fifth Amendment prevents a criminal defendant from being made 'the deluded instrument of his own conviction,' it protects him as well from being made the 'deluded instrument' of his own execution." As for the argument that respondent's communications to the examining psychiatrist were "nontestimonial" in nature, "Dr. Grigson's prognosis as to future dangerousness rested on statements respondent made and remarks he omitted in reciting the details of the crime. [Thus,] the State used as evidence against respondent the substance of his disclosures during the pretrial psychiatric examination."[a]

a. Because respondent had been indicted and assigned counsel before Dr. Grigson examined him and the examination had taken place without notice to respondent's counsel, Stewart, J., joined by Powell, J., concurred in the judgment on *Massiah* grounds without reaching the *Miranda* issue. Although he dissented, in effect, on the *Miranda* issue, Rehnquist, J., also concurred in the result of *Massiah*

grounds. Thus, the Court's judgment that respondent's Sixth Amendment right to counsel had been violated was unanimous.

See also *Powell v. Texas*, 492 U.S. 680, 109 S.Ct. 3146, 106 L.Ed.2d 551 (1989) (that defendant raised insanity defense "no basis for concluding" he waived Sixth Amendment right to counsel set out in *Estelle*).

22. *Use of psychiatric examinations in proceedings to commit individuals found to be "sexually dangerous persons."* Allen v. Illinois, 478 U.S. 364, 106 S.Ct. 2988, 92 L.Ed.2d 296 (1986), arose as follows: The state sought to declare Allen "sexually dangerous" under the Illinois Sexually Dangerous Persons Act and to commit him. Pursuant to the Act, Allen had to submit to a psychiatric examination. Partly on the basis of the psychiatrists' testimony, Allen was found to be a sexually dangerous person under the Act. Although proceedings under the Act are accompanied by procedural safeguards usually found in criminal trials, a 5–4 majority, per Rehnquist, J., concluded that the proceedings were not "criminal" within the meaning of the Fifth Amendment privilege against compelled self-incrimination. The Court emphasized that the State "had indicated quite clearly its intent that these commitment proceedings be civil in nature."

Dissenting Justice Stevens, joined by Brennan, Marshall and Blackmun, JJ., protested: "In many respects, [this] proceeding is virtually identical to Illinois' proceeding for prosecution of sex-related crimes. When the criminal law casts so long a shadow on a putatively civil proceeding, I think it clear that the procedure must be deemed a 'criminal case' within the meaning of the Fifth Amendment."

See also *Kansas v. Hendricks*, 521 U.S. 346, 117 S.Ct. 2072, 138 L.Ed.2d 501 (1997) (state statute providing for involuntary civil commitment of sexual predators "does not establish criminal proceedings" and "involuntary confinement pursuant to the Act is not punitive").

23. *Miranda and mentally retarded suspects: The Cloud–Shepherd–Barkoff–Shur study.* The results of an empirical study, Morgan Cloud, George B. Shepherd, Alison Nodwin Barkoff and Justin V. Shur, *Words Without Meaning: The Constitution, Confessions, and Mentally Retarded Suspects*, 69 U. Chi. L.Rev. 495 (2002) (hereinafter called the Cloud study) "indicate that mentally retarded people simply do not understand the *Miranda* warnings. Virtually all of the disabled subjects failed to understand the context in which the interrogation occurs, the legal consequences embedded in the rules or the significance of confessing, the meaning of the sentences that comprise the warnings, or even the individual operative words used to construct the warnings.[a] In contrast, comparably large percentages of the non-disabled control group did understand the individual words, the complete warnings, and their legal significance."

The results of the Cloud study support two additional conclusions about the validity of confessions obtained from mentally retarded suspects:

First, "the number of people to whom the *Miranda* warnings are meaningless [appears to be] much larger than previously acknowledged within the criminal justice system. [The warnings] also are incomprehensible to people whose mental retardation is classified as mild, as well as some people whose 'intelligence quotient' (IQ) scores exceed 70, the number typically used to demarcate mental retardation."

Second, the study raises "disquieting questions" about the capacity of current doctrine to "accommodate the special problems accompanying police interrogation of mentally retarded suspects": "When confronted with challenges to the validity of a mentally retarded suspect's waiver of the *Miranda* 'rights,' courts typically revert to a 'totality of the circumstances' analysis to determine whether the suspect was capable of understanding the *Miranda* warnings." But the results of

a. According to the authors of the study, "the best available data suggests that at least forty–five thousand, and perhaps more than two hundred thousand mentally retarded peo- ple currently are imprisoned in the United States. Undoubtedly, these people have been arrested. Many, probably most, have been "Mirandized" and interrogated while in custo-

the study "suggest that the 'totalities' analysis ... is incapable of identifying suspects competent to understand the *Miranda* warnings.... Multiple regression analysis demonstrates that variations in age, education and experience with the criminal justice system or the *Miranda* warnings do not compensate for a mentally retarded person's inability to comprehend the *Miranda* warnings. If mental retardation is present, then the disabled person will not understand the warnings, regardless of the presence of the other factors."

Another serious problem posed by mentally retarded persons' confessions is that it now seems indisputable that "mentally retarded suspects are likely to confess falsely, that is confess to crimes they did not commit, far more frequently than do suspects of average and above average intelligence. Similarly, interrogation tactics generally believed to be acceptable with most suspects are more likely to produce false confessions from mentally retarded suspects."[b]

What is the solution? Should the courts take the position that *any* confession from a mentally retarded suspect is inadmissible in a criminal case? Should law enforcement officers be required to administer simplified warnings? Are the mentally retarded likely to understand warnings containing simplified synonyms for difficult words in the *Miranda* warnings much better than they do the original vocabulary of the warnings? See Part V. of the Cloud study.

24. *Comparing and contrasting Miranda with (a) the prohibition against the use of involuntary or compelled statements and (b) the Fourth Amendment exclusionary rule.*

WITHROW v. WILLIAMS

507 U.S. 680, 113 S.Ct. 1745, 123 L.Ed.2d 407 (1993).

Justice SOUTER delivered the opinion of the Court.

In *Stone v. Powell* [p. 116], we held that when a State has given a full and fair chance to litigate a Fourth Amendment claim, federal habeas review is not available to a state prisoner alleging that his conviction rests on evidence obtained through an unconstitutional search or seizure. Today we hold [that *Stone*] does not extend to a state prisoner's claim that his conviction rests on statements obtained in violation [of] *Miranda*.

[Although respondent Williams, a murder suspect, was not advised of his *Miranda* rights until the police had taken him into custody and questioned him for some 40 minutes, during which time he made incriminating statements, a Michigan court declined to suppress any of these statements. He was then convicted on two counts of murder. After these convictions were affirmed, Williams turned to the federal courts. A federal district court found that his *Miranda* rights had been violated. The court also concluded, although neither party had addressed the issue, that Williams' statements, after receiving the *Miranda* warnings, were involuntary and thus likewise subject to suppression.[a] The U.S. Court of Appeals for the Sixth Circuit affirmed], summarily rejecting the argument that [*Stone*] should apply to bar habeas review of Williams' *Miranda* claim. We granted certiorari to review the significant issue thus presented.

dy. Some have waived their rights and made statements to investigators."

b. "By some estimates," points out the study, "as many as 20 percent of the people on death row are mentally retarded, and death penalty opponents contend that at least three dozen mentally retarded people have been executed in the quarter century since the death penalty was reinstated."

The authors of the study ask: Should the Constitution permit a retarded person to be convicted on the basis of his confession?

a. The Court later noted, in a portion of the opinion that has been deleted, that the district court acted incorrectly in reaching this issue without giving the state an opportunity to address it.

We have made it clear that *Stone*'s limitations on federal habeas relief was not jurisdictional in nature, but rested on prudential concerns counseling against the application of the Fourth Amendment exclusionary rule on collateral review. * * * We simply concluded in *Stone* that the costs of applying the exclusionary rule on collateral review outweighed any potential advantage to be gained by applying it there. * * *

Over the years, we have repeatedly declined to extend the rule in *Stone* beyond its original bounds. In *Jackson v. Virginia* [Ch. 28, § 2], for example, we denied a request to apply *Stone* to bar habeas consideration of a Fourteenth Amendment due process claim of insufficient evidence to support a state conviction. We stressed that the issue was "central to the basic question of guilt or innocence," unlike a claim that a state court had received evidence in violation of the Fourth Amendment exclusionary rule, and we found that to review such a claim on habeas imposed no great burdens on the federal courts.

After a like analysis, in *Rose v. Mitchell* [Ch. 28, § 2], we decided against extending *Stone* to foreclose habeas review of an equal protection claim of racial discrimination in selecting a state grand-jury foreman. A charge that state adjudication had violated the direct command of the Fourteenth Amendment implicated the integrity of the judicial process, we reasoned, and failed to raise the "federalism concerns" that had driven the Court in *Stone.*

[In] a third instance, in *Jackson v. Virginia* [Ch. 28, § 2], we again declined to extend *Stone,* in that case to bar habeas review of certain claims of ineffective assistance of counsel under the Sixth Amendment. We explained that unlike the Fourth Amendment, which confers no "trial right," the Sixth confers a "fundamental right" on criminal defendants, one that "assures the fairness, and thus the legitimacy, of our adversary process." [In] this case, the argument for extending *Stone* again falls short.

[The *Miranda* Court] acknowledged that, in barring introduction of a statement obtained without the required warnings, *Miranda* might exclude a confession that we would not condemn as "involuntary in traditional terms," and for this reason we have sometimes called the *Miranda* safeguards "prophylactic" in nature. * * * Calling the *Miranda* safeguards "prophylactic," however, is a far cry from putting *Miranda* on all fours with *Mapp,* or from rendering *Miranda* subject to *Stone.*

As we explained in *Stone,* the *Mapp* rule "is not a personal constitutional right," but serves to deter future constitutional violations; although it mitigates the juridical consequences of invading the defendant's privacy, the exclusion of evidence at trial can do nothing to remedy the completed and wholly extrajudicial Fourth Amendment violation. Nor can the *Mapp* rule be thought to enhance the soundness of the criminal process by improving the reliability of evidence introduced at trial.

Miranda differs from *Mapp* in both respects. "Prophylactic" though it may be, in protecting a defendant's Fifth Amendment privilege against self-incrimination *Miranda* safeguards "a fundamental *trial* right." [The privilege] reflects "many of our fundamental values and most noble aspirations" [quoting *Murphy v. Waterfront Comm'n,* pp. 692, 702].

Nor does the Fifth Amendment "trial right" protected by *Miranda* serve some value necessarily divorced from the correct ascertainment of guilt. [By] bracing against "the possibility of unreliable statements in every instance of in-custody interrogation," *Miranda* serves to guard against "the use of unreliable statements at trial."

Finally, and most importantly, eliminating review of *Miranda* claims would not significantly benefit the federal courts in their exercise of habeas jurisdiction, or advance the cause of federalism in any substantial way. [For it] would not prevent a state prisoner from simply converting his barred *Miranda* claim into a due process claim that his conviction rested on an involuntary confession.

If that is so, the federal courts would certainly not have heard the last of *Miranda* on collateral review. Under the due process approach, [courts] look to the totality of circumstances to determine whether a confession was voluntary. Those potential circumstances include [the] failure of police to advise the defendant of his rights to remain silent and to have counsel present during custodial interrogation. * * * We could lock the front door against *Miranda,* but not the back.

We thus fail to see how abdicating *Miranda*'s bright-line (or, at least, brighter-line) rules in favor of an exhaustive totality-of-circumstances approach on habeas would do much of anything to lighten the burdens placed on busy federal courts. * * * We likewise fail to see how purporting to eliminate *Miranda* issues from federal habeas would go very far to relieve such tensions as *Miranda* may now raise between the two judicial systems. Relegation of habeas petitioners to straight involuntariness claims would not likely reduce the amount of litigation, and each such claim would in any event present a legal question requiring an "independent federal determination" on habeas. * * *

Justice O'CONNOR, with whom The Chief Justice joins, concurring in part and dissenting in part.

[Because] the principles that inform our habeas jurisprudence—finality, federalism, and fairness—counsel decisively against the result the Court reaches, I respectfully dissent * * *. Like the suppression of the fruits of an illegal search or seizure, the exclusion of statements obtained in violation of *Miranda* is not constitutionally required. This Court repeatedly has held that *Miranda*'s warning requirement is not a dictate of the Fifth Amendment itself, but a prophylactic rule. [Unlike] involuntary or compelled statements—which are of dubious reliability and are therefore inadmissible for any purpose—confessions obtained in violation of *Miranda* are not necessarily untrustworthy. In fact, because *voluntary* statements are "trustworthy" even when obtained without proper warnings, their suppression actually *impairs* the pursuit of truth by concealing probative information from the trier of fact.

[When] the case is on direct review, that damage to the truth-seeking function is deemed an acceptable sacrifice for the deterrence and respect for constitutional values that the *Miranda* rule brings. But once a case is on collateral review, the balance between the costs and benefits shifts; the interests of federalism, finality, and fairness compel *Miranda*'s exclusion from habeas. The benefit of enforcing *Miranda* through habeas is marginal at best. * * *

Excluding *Miranda* claims from habeas * * * denies collateral relief only in those cases in which the prisoner's statement was neither compelled nor involuntary but merely obtained without the benefit of *Miranda*'s prophylactic warnings. The availability of a suppression remedy in such cases cannot be labeled a "fundamental trial right," for there is no constitutional right to the suppression of *voluntary* statements. [If] the principles of federalism, finality, and fairness ever counsel in favor of withholding relief on habeas, surely they do so where there is no constitutional harm to remedy.

Similarly unpersuasive is the Court's related argument, that the Fifth Amendment trial right is not "necessarily divorced" from the interest of reliability. Whatever the Fifth Amendment's relationship to reliability, *Miranda*'s prophylactic rule is not merely "divorced" from the quest for truth but at war with it as well. The absence of *Miranda* warnings does not by some mysterious alchemy convert a voluntary and trustworthy statement into an involuntary and unreliable one. To suggest otherwise is both unrealistic and contrary to precedent.

[The] consideration the Court identifies as being "most importan[t]" of all, is an entirely pragmatic one. Specifically, the Court "project[s] that excluding *Miranda* questions from habeas will not significantly promote efficiency or federalism because some *Miranda* issues are relevant to a statement's voluntariness. It is true that barring *Miranda* claims from habeas poses no barrier to the adjudication of voluntariness questions. But that does not make it "reasonable to suppose that virtually all *Miranda* claims [will] simply be recast" and litigated as voluntariness claims. [A] *Miranda* claim [requires] no evidence of police overreaching whatsoever; it is enough that law enforcement officers commit a technical error. Even the forgetful failure to issue warnings to the most wary, knowledgeable, and seasoned of criminals will do. [If, as the Court maintains,] the police have truly grown in "constitutional * * * sophistication," then certainly it is reasonable to suppose that most technical errors in the administration of *Miranda*'s warnings are just that.

In any event, I see no need to resort to supposition. The published decisions of the lower federal courts show that what the Court assumes to be true demonstrably is not. In case after case, the courts are asked on habeas to decide purely technical *Miranda* questions that contain not even a hint of police overreaching. [Whether] the suspect was in "custody," whether or not there was "interrogation," whether warnings were given or were adequate, whether the defendant's equivocal statement constituted an invocation of rights, whether waiver was knowing and intelligent—this is the stuff that *Miranda* claims are made of.

[Even] assuming that many *Miranda* claims could "simply be recast" as voluntariness claims, it does not follow that barring *Miranda*'s prophylactic rule from habeas would unduly complicate their resolution. * * * *Miranda* creates as many close questions as it resolves. The task of determining whether a defendant is in "custody" has proved to be "a slippery one." And the supposedly "bright" lines that separate interrogation from spontaneous declaration, the exercise of a right from waiver, and the adequate warning from the inadequate, likewise have turned out to be rather dim and ill-defined. [Yet] *Miranda* requires those lines to be drawn with precision in each case.

The totality-of-the-circumstances approach, on the other hand, permits each fact to be taken into account without resort to formal and dispositive labels. [Thus,] it is true that the existence of warnings is still a consideration under the totality-of-the-circumstances approach, but it is unnecessary to determine conclusively whether "custody" existed and triggered the warning requirement, or whether the warnings given were sufficient. It is enough that the habeas court look to the warnings or their absence, along with all other factors, and consider them in deciding what is, after all, the ultimate question: whether the confession was compelled and involuntary or the product of a free and unimpaired will.

[As] the Court emphasizes today, *Miranda*'s prophylactic rule is now 26 years old; the police and the state courts have indeed grown accustomed to it. But it is precisely because the rule is well accepted that there is little further benefit to enforcing it on habeas. We can depend on law enforcement officials to administer warnings in the first instance and the state courts to provide a remedy when law enforcement officers err. * * *

Justice SCALIA, with whom Justice THOMAS joins, concurring in part and dissenting in part.

The issue in this case—whether the extraordinary remedy of federal habeas corpus should routinely be available for claimed violations of *Miranda* rights—involves not *jurisdiction* to issue the writ, but the *equity* of doing so. In my view, both the Court and Justice O'Connor disregard the most powerful equitable consideration: that Williams has already had full and fair opportunity to litigate this claim. [The] question at this stage is whether [a] federal habeas court should now reopen the issue and adjudicate the *Miranda* claim anew. The answer seems to me obvious: it should not. That would be the course followed by a federal habeas court reviewing a *federal* conviction; it mocks our federal system to accord state convictions less respect.

[The] question before us is not whether a holding unique to Fourth Amendment claims (and resting upon nothing more principled than our estimation that Fourth Amendment exclusion claims are not very important) should be expanded to some other arbitrary category beyond that; but rather, whether the general principle that is the only valid justification for *Stone* should for some reason *not* be applied to *Miranda* claims. I think the answer to that question is clear: Prior opportunity to litigate an issue should be an important equitable consideration in *any* habeas case, and should ordinarily preclude the court from reaching the merits of a claim, unless it goes to the fairness of the trial process or to the accuracy of the ultimate result.

Our case law since *Stone* is entirely consistent with this view. As the Court notes, we have held that the rule in *Stone* does not apply in three cases. *Kimmelman v. Morrison* involved alleged denial of the Sixth Amendment right to counsel, which unquestionably goes to the fairness of the trial process. *Rose v. Mitchell* involved alleged discrimination by the trial court in violation of the Fourteenth Amendment. [And] *Jackson v. Virginia* involved a claim that "no rational trier of fact could have found proof of guilt beyond a reasonable doubt," which is obviously a direct challenge to the accuracy of the ultimate result. * * *

Notes and Questions

(a) *Does Withrow affirm that the Miranda rule contains a constitutional command?* "If the Court had viewed *Miranda* as truly non-constitutional," comments Charles D. Weisselberg, *Saving Miranda*, 84 Cornell L.Rev. 109, 130–31 (1998), "then it had little reason to refuse *Withrow*'s invitation to take mere *Miranda* violations out of federal habeas corpus. The Court in *Withrow* thus kept the universe of *Miranda* claims within the Constitution."

(b) *Do Fifth Amendment violations occur only at trial? Withrow* talks about "the Fifth Amendment 'trial right' " and about "*Miranda* safeguard[ing] 'a fundamental *trial* right.' " However, Weisselberg, supra at 180, observes that "a number of cases have found Fifth Amendment violations in circumstances in which witnesses suffered penalties for asserting the privilege against self-incrimination, even though they faced no criminal charges and had no criminal trial." [He refers to such cases as *Lefkowitz v. Cunningham*, 431 U.S. 801, 97 S.Ct. 2132, 53 L.Ed.2d 1 (1977), holding that a grand jury witness cannot be divested of political office as a penalty for exercising his Fifth Amendment privilege; and *Gardner v. Broderick*, 392 U.S. 273, 88 S.Ct. 1913, 20 L.Ed.2d 1082 (1968), holding that a police officer cannot lose his job for asserting the privilege before a grand jury.] These cases are impossible to square with the notion that Fifth Amendment violations occur only at trial."

According to Professor Weisselberg, if police question a suspect at the police station in violation of *Miranda* "the best view" may be that "the violation occurs at the station house, but continues or recurs at trial. The values that underlie the Fifth Amendment include preserving autonomy, maintaining our adversarial system, curtailing inhumane treatment and police misconduct, avoiding false confessions, and complying with our sense of fair play. Custodial interrogation can undermine most of these values in the station house at the time that the questioning occurs."

25. Other Miranda problems discussed elsewhere in the book. Is *Miranda*'s prohibition against police trickery and deception confined to their use in obtaining a waiver of rights or does it also bar such tactics *after* a person has validly waived his rights? See the next section.

If a defendant takes the stand in his own defense, may the prosecution impeach him by using statements obtained from him in violation of *Miranda*? See Ch. 11, § 4, infra. May a defendant's *prior silence,* even his *post* arrest silence, be used to impeach his credibility when he chooses to testify at his trial? See id.

Suppose, after a suspect is illegally arrested, he is advised of his rights, waives them, and confesses? Do the *Miranda* warnings "cure" the illegality of the arrest? See Ch. 11, § 3, infra.

Suppose, a couple of hours after the police obtain an incriminating statement from a suspect in violation of *Miranda,* they give him the complete warnings and the suspect waives his rights and confesses? Is the "second confession" admissible or is it "the fruit" of the first inadmissible statement? See Ch. 11, § 3, infra. Suppose, as the result of a statement obtained in violation of *Miranda,* the police find the murder weapon or locate an important witness. Is the testimony of the witness or the murder weapon admissible? Or is it the "fruit of the poisonous tree"? See id.

THE IMPACT OF *MIRANDA* IN PRACTICE

In 1988, a special committee of the ABA's Criminal Justice Section—Special Committee on Criminal Justice in a Free Society, *Criminal Justice in Crisis* 28 (1988)—reported that "a very strong majority of those surveyed—prosecutors, judges, and police officers—agree that compliance with *Miranda* does not present serious problems for law enforcement." This report, taken together with many earlier empirical studies indicating that *Miranda* posed no significant barrier to effective law enforcement, appeared to be, as the ABA Special Committee put it, "a strong repudiation of the claim that law enforcement would be greatly improved if *Miranda* were repealed or overruled."

However, in *Miranda's Social Costs: An Empirical Reassessment,* 90 Nw. U.L.Rev. 387 (1996), Professor Paul G. Cassell attacked the general consensus, contending that despite the "conventional academic wisdom" to the contrary, "*Miranda* has significantly harmed law enforcement efforts in this country." Stephen J. Schulhofer, *Miranda's Practical Effect: Substantial Benefits and Vanishingly Small Social Costs,* 90 N.W.U.L.Rev. 500 (1996), sharply disputed Professor Cassell's statistics and emphasized that "even if we can assume that the studies [Cassell relies on] give a reliable picture of *Miranda*'s costs thirty years ago, there is strong reason to believe that such costs were transitory and that confession rates have since rebounded from any temporary decline."[a]

In his rejoinder, *All Benefits, No Costs: The Grand Illusion of Miranda's Defenders,* 90 Nw.U.L.Rev. 1084 (1996), Professor Cassell maintained that both clearance rate data and confession rate data demonstrate that "over the long haul,

---

a. Professor Cassell's article and Professor Schulhofer's response, as well as other articles on *Miranda*'s impact in the police station by Richard A. Leo, George C. Thomas III, and Cassell and Bret S. Hayman are reprinted in large part in Richard A. Leo & George C. Thomas III, *The Miranda Debate* (1998).

law enforcement never recovered from the blow inflicted by *Miranda*." Cassell relied, inter alia, on a 1994 study of police interrogation in Salt Lake City that he co-authored, Cassell & Bret Hayman, *Police Interrogation in the 1990s: An Empirical Study of the Effects of Miranda*, 43 UCLA L.Rev. 839 (1996). According to Schulhofer, supra, however the Salt Lake County study's low confession rate *includes* non-custodial interrogations (although the best reading of the pre-*Miranda* studies is that they involved only custodial interrogation) and *excludes* cases in which the suspect gave "denials with explanation" although a substantial number of such "denials" probably should have been classified as incriminating statements.

George C. Thomas III, *Plain Talk about the Miranda Empirical Debate: A "Steady–State" Theory of Confessions*, 43 U.C.L.A. L.Rev. 933 (1996), criticized the Cassell–Hayman study on grounds similar to Schulhofer's. Moreover, observed Professor Thomas: "Cassell and Hayman conclude that 12.1% of felony suspects 'who were questioned invoked their rights before police were successful in interrogation.' [If] the *Miranda* dissenters and the police in 1966 had been told that the effect of *Miranda* would be limited to 12.1% of felony suspects, they would have cheered in relief. Thus, while significant, 12.1% is hardly crippling to the law-enforcement enterprise."

Continued Thomas: "[The] available data [seems] to demonstrate that more suspects invoke their [rights] and the rate of confessions is roughly the same. This divergence supports my steady-state theory: *Miranda* encourages some suspects not to talk and encourages other to talk too much. It is possible that, in the pre-*Miranda* era, fewer suspects refused to talk but more suspects gave terse answers. Perhaps more suspects refuse to talk today, but those who do talk have a *Miranda*-created incentive to tell a fuller story."

In 1997, the Cassell–Schulhofer debate continued in the pages of another law journal. As evidence of Miranda's harmful effects, Professor Cassell noted that in 1965 the clearance rate for violent crime [stood] at nearly 60 percent—only to plunge more than twelve percentage points in the next three years. See Paul G. Cassell, *Miranda's "Negligible" Effect on Law Enforcement: Some Skeptical Observations*, 20 Harv.J.L.Pub.Pol'y 327, 333–35 (1997). Professor Schulhofer responded that clearance capacity (the number of officers and dollars available to investigate each reported crime) collapsed in the late 1960s as crime rose sharply and that the dramatic reduction in clearance *capacity* provides "the most likely explanation" for the significant decline in the clearance *rates* that occurred at the same time. See Schulhofer, *Bashing Miranda is Unjustified—and Harmful*, 20 Harv.J.L.Pub.Pol'y 347, 357–62 (1997).

At this point, another law professor joined the debate, Peter Arenella, *Miranda Stories*, 20 Harv.J.L.Pub.Pol'y 375 (1997), observing: "Neither the 'conservative' nor the 'liberal' tale provides a fully plausible account of *Miranda*'s impact on our criminal justice system because both stories commit the same fundamental error: exaggerating either *Miranda*'s costs (Cassell) or benefits (Schulhofer). Moreover, each story generates an obvious question that neither author answers persuasively. If Cassell's account is accurate, why have the police and a conservative Supreme Court shown no interest in eliminating the *Miranda* regime? Conversely, if Schulhofer is right (and I believe he is) that the *Miranda* regime has not impaired law enforcement's ability to secure incriminating admissions, how exactly does *Miranda*'s negligible impact demonstrate its success in eliminating the 'inherent coerciveness' of police interrogation?"

In 1998, a new critic of Cassell's work, Professor John J. Donohue III entered the fray. He took issue with a new empirical study co-authored by Cassell and Richard Fowles, *Handcuffing the Cops? A Thirty–Year Perspective on Miranda's*

Harmful Effects on Law Enforcement, 50 Stan.L.Rev. 1055 (1998), a study maintaining that *Miranda* has had a significantly adverse and long-term effect on clearance rates for both violent and property crimes. According to Donohue, *Did Miranda Diminish Police Effectiveness?*, 50 Stan.L.Rev. 1147 (1998), the Cassell–Fowles study showed no significant relationship between *Miranda* and the clearance rate for murder—the most accurately reported crime. Donohue suggests that *Miranda*'s only real impact upon clearance rates may be that it prevents the police from obtaining information from custodial suspects about crimes other than the one(s) for which the suspects have been arrested.

Finally, consider Charles D. Weisselberg, *Saving Miranda*, 84 Cornell L.Rev. 109, 172–77 (1998). Although he called Cassell's writings "the most detailed and determined empirical effort to measure *Miranda*'s costs," Weisselberg maintained that no methodology can assess *Miranda*'s "benefits." Indeed, he continues, "in arguing that *Miranda* costs too much to maintain, [Cassell] largely avoids any analysis of *Miranda*'s virtues." "The *Miranda* debate," concluded Weisselberg, "can have no empirical resolution. That *Miranda* has an impact may mean nothing more than it works as the Court intended."

HOW TO GET PEOPLE TO CONFESS IN THE POST-*MIRANDA* WORLD: HAVE MODERN POLICE INTERROGATORS "ADAPTED" TO *MIRANDA* OR ARE THEY VIOLATING IT?

In 1988, after persuading the Baltimore police department to grant him unlimited access to the city's homicide unit for a full year, David Simon, a *Baltimore Sun* reporter, took a leave of absence from the *Sun* and followed one shift of detectives as they traveled from interrogations to autopsies and from crime scenes to hospital emergency rooms. Simon's 1991 book, *Homicide: A Year on the Killing Streets*, was the result. In an author's note, Simon tells us that *Homicide* is a "work of journalism" and that the events he has written about "occurred in the manner described."

How, despite the seemingly formidable obstacle of *Miranda*, do the Baltimore police manage to get so many suspects to incriminate themselves? According to Simon (see pp. 194–207 of his book), the following, or something close to it, occurs:

(1) The detective produces an "Explanation of Rights" sheet, reads the warnings one at a time and when the suspect responds that he understands them, gets the suspect to initial each warning.

(2) Next, the detective gets the suspect to sign his name just below a sentence that reads: "I have read the explanation of my rights and fully understand it."

(3) At this point—and before the suspect is asked whether he wants to waive his rights and talk about the case—the detective assures the suspect that he will honor his rights if he invokes them, but in the next breath warns him that asserting his rights would make matters worse for him. For it would prevent his friend, the detective, from writing up the case as manslaughter or perhaps even self-defense, rather than first degree murder. The detective emphasizes that he is affording the suspect the opportunity to tell his side of the story (Did the man you stabbed come at you? Was it self-defense?), "but once you up and call for that lawyer, son, we can't do a damn thing for you ... Now's the time to speak up ... because once I walk out of this room any chance you have of telling your side of the story is gone."

(4) In a typical case, the detective also tells the suspect (falsely) that the evidence against him is overwhelming, and the only reason he is interested in hearing the suspect's version of what happened is "to make sure that there ain't nothing you can say for yourself before I write it all up" (as murder in the first degree).

(5) The suspect cautiously indicates a willingness to talk about the case or at least to consider talking about it. The suspect also indicates that he likes the suggestion that the slain man had "come at him." The detective smiles inwardly. He has given the suspect "the Out" and the suspect has taken it.

(6) The suspect is now eager to tell his story, but the detective cuts him off. Before proceeding any further, there is some "paperwork" to be completed—to do this the right way the suspect must first sign a form stating that he is willing to answer police questions without having a lawyer present and that his decision to do so has been "free and voluntary" on his part.

(7) The suspect signs the form and the detective encourages him to resume telling his story. At the same time, the detective tells himself: "End of the road, pal. It's over. It's history."

Recent articles indicate that the Baltimore detectives' tactics described by Simon are utilized by detectives in many other police departments as well. See Richard A. Leo, *Miranda's Revenge: Police Interrogation as a Confidence Game*, 30 Law & Society Rev. 259 (1996) (based on 500 hours of participant observation in three police departments); Richard A. Leo & Welsh S. White, *Adapting to Miranda: Modern Interrogators' Strategies for Dealing with the Obstacles Posed by Miranda*, 84 Minn.L.Rec. 397 (1999); Peter Carlson, *You Have the Right to Remain Silent . . .* , Washington Post Magazine, Sept. 13, 1998, pp. 6–11, 19–24 (based largely on interviews with police interrogators from Washington, D.C., and surrounding Maryland and Virginia suburbs).[a]

There is reason to believe that Mr. Simon (and many members of the Baltimore homicide unit) think that the aforementioned interrogation techniques are permitted by *Miranda*. At one point, for example, Simon observes that, forced to deal with *Miranda*, a detective "follows the requirements of the law to the letter—or close enough so as not to jeopardize his case. Just as carefully, he ignores the law's spirit and intent. He becomes a salesman, a huckster as thieving and silver-tongued as any man who ever moved used cars or aluminum siding * * *." But consider the following:

YALE KAMISAR—KILLING *MIRANDA* IN BALTIMORE: REFLECTIONS ON DAVID SIMON'S *HOMICIDE*
JURIST: Books-on-Law, Feb. 1999, vol.2, no.2 (*http://jurist.law.pitt.edu/lawbooks/*) (archived).

"[I]f the admissibility of a statement obtained as a result of the methods described [by Mr. Simon] were challenged by a defense lawyer, a Baltimore

a. Thus, Professors White and Leo observe that "[o]ne of the most powerful [*Miranda*] de-emphasizing strategies involves focusing the suspect's attention on the importance of telling his story to the interrogator. The interrogators communicate to the suspect that they want to hear his 'side of the story' but they will not be able to do so until the suspect waives his *Miranda* rights." Still another common way to de-emphasize *Miranda*, report Leo and White, "is to create the appearance of a non-adver-sarial relationship between the interrogator and a suspect. An interrogator employing this strategy portrays himself as the suspect's friend, confidant or guardian, whose goal is not to obtain incriminating statements but rather to help the suspect improve his situation." This strategy, continue Leo and White, "not only de-emphasizes the *Miranda* warnings but also suggest to the suspect that waiving his *Miranda* warnings will be to his advantage."

prosecutor would be in a strong position. For she would be armed with a signed waiver of rights form (and a signed explanation of rights form as well). But she would be in a strong position only if—as would hardly be surprising—the detective(s) involved in the case lied about, or conveniently failed to remember, how the suspect was induced to sign the waiver of rights form. If all the facts were known—if, for example, the entire transaction had been tape recorded—no court could or would admit the statement unless it was prepared to overrule *Miranda* itself.

Despite Mr. Simon's comments to the contrary, the Baltimore police do not follow the requirements of *Miranda* closely enough to avoid jeopardizing their cases, nor do they merely ignore *Miranda*'s spirit. Indeed, it would be more accurate to say they flout the substance of that famous case.

One of the principal purposes of the warning is, to quote from the *Miranda* opinion, "to make the individual more acutely aware that he is faced with a phase of the adversary system—that he is not in the presence of persons acting solely in his interest." But the Baltimore detectives seriously undermine this purpose by leading the suspect to believe that it is in his best interest to waive his rights and to talk to "your friends in the city homicide unit" about the case, and by pretending to be not only the suspect's friend but his protector (or at least a buffer) against the detectives' heartless superiors and the zealous prosecutor waiting outside the door, a prosecutor who has no compunctions about charging the suspect with first degree murder without bothering to hear his "side of the story."

[At one point in *Miranda*, the Court observed:] "[A]ny evidence that the accused was threatened, tricked, or cajoled into a waiver will, of course, show that the defendant did not voluntarily waive his privilege. The requirement of warnings and waiver of rights is a fundamental [and] not simply a preliminary ritual to existing methods of interrogation." Unfortunately, the very police conduct that *Miranda* tried to forbid seems to be occurring in Baltimore police stations. The police *are* threatening the suspect: they are telling him that unless he talks to them about the homicide, they will write it up as first degree murder and turn him over to a [heartless] assistant state's attorney. They *are* tricking the suspect: they are leading him to believe that it is in his best interest to tell them his side of the story; indeed, they are pretending that this is the suspect's only chance to get the homicide charge reduced (or perhaps even dismissed).

[To] quote the *Miranda* opinion again, transforming its requirements of warnings and waiver of rights into "simply a preliminary ritual to existing methods of interrogation" is also a pretty good description of what is taking place in Baltimore police stations. Indeed, to put it somewhat differently, although the police are not supposed to subject a custodial suspect to interrogation *unless and until* they obtain a waiver of his rights, what they are really doing in Baltimore (and who knows how many other places) is subjecting individuals to "interrogation" *before* they waive their rights.

At one point, Mr. Simon notes that "[t]he fraud that claims it is somehow in a suspect's interest to talk with police will forever be the catalyst in any criminal interrogation." Exactly right. This is why the methods used by the Baltimore police to get a suspect to waive his rights—methods that simultaneously manipulate him into talking about the case and, eventually, incriminating himself—should be classified as "interrogation." Whatever deception, seduction and trickery a police interrogator may be able to utilize *after* the suspect effectively waives his rights and agrees to talk (and, more than 30 years after *Miranda*, what the interrogator may do at this stage is still far from clear), the police cannot resort to any of these techniques *before* the suspect waives his rights, and they cannot use any of these techniques to *get him* to waive his rights.

Once the police have taken a suspect into custody, there is no such thing (at least there is no lawful basis for any such thing) as a "pre-interview' or 'pre-waiver" interrogation. The waiver of rights transaction is supposed to take place as soon as the curtain goes up, not postponed until the second or third act.

Mr. Simon's graphic description of how the Baltimore Homicide Unit (and who knows how many other police departments?) goes about getting custodial suspects to make incriminating statements underscores the need to record on video or audio tape the entire proceedings in the police station—the reading of rights, the waiver transactions and any subsequent interrogation. Perhaps because it feared that requiring electronic recording of police questioning, whenever feasible, would have added fuel to the criticism that it was "legislating," the *Miranda* Court permitted the police to obtain waivers of a person's constitutional rights without the presence of any disinterested observer and without any objective recording of the proceedings.

[The] only startling thing about [the tape-recording] issue is that, after all these years, American law enforcement officials are still able to prevent objective recordation of all the facts of police "interviews" or "conversations" with a suspect and, of course, how the warnings are delivered and how the waiver of rights is obtained. But if you were a member of the Baltimore homicide unit (or a member of other police departments employing the same interrogation methods), would you favor tape-recording (and making available for public inspection) what really happens in the interrogation room?

David Simon describes how Baltimore interrogators manage to get custodial suspects to sign waivers of their *Miranda* rights, but what happens if a suspect *invokes* his right to remain silent or her right to counsel? There is reason to think that some detectives in some police departments continue to question the suspects in order (a) to obtain incriminating statements which will enable the prosecution to impeach the suspect if he subsequently takes the stand in his own defense or (b) to obtain evidence *derived from* statements made in violation of *Miranda*, derivative evidence such as the existence of an eyewitness or the location of the murder weapon. Discussion of these police tactics is postponed until Chapter 11, which contains materials on the "fruit of the poisonous tree" and the use of illegally obtained evidence for impeachment purposes. See pp. 801–03.

CAN (DID) CONGRESS "REPEAL" *MIRANDA*?

Consider *Title II of the Omnibus Crime Control and Safe Streets Act of 1968*,[a] which provides in relevant part:

"§ 3501. Admissibility of confessions

"(a) In any criminal prosecution brought by the United States or by the District of Columbia, a confession, as defined in subsection (e) hereof, shall be

a. For the legislative history of Title II of the Crime Control Act, see Adam C. Breckenridge, *Congress Against the Court* (1970); Fred P. Graham, *The Self-Inflicted Wound* 305–32 (1970); Richard Harris, *The Fear of Crime* (1969); Yale Kamisar, *Can (Did) Congress* *"Overrule" Miranda?*, 85 Cornell L.Rev. 883, 887–906 (2000); Michael Edmund O'Neill, *Undoing Miranda*, 2000 BYU L.Rev. 185; Otis H. Stephens, Jr., *The Supreme Court and Confessions of Guilt*, 139–45, 163–66 (1973).

admissible in evidence if it is voluntarily given. Before such confession is received in evidence, the trial judge shall, out of the presence of the jury, determine any issue as to voluntariness. If the trial judge determines that the confession was voluntarily made it shall be admitted in evidence and the trial judge shall permit the jury to hear relevant evidence on the issue of voluntariness and shall instruct the jury to give such weight to the confession as the jury feels it deserves under all the circumstances.

"(b) The trial judge in determining the issue of voluntariness shall take into consideration all the circumstances surrounding the giving of the confession, including (1) the time elapsing between arrest and arraignment of the defendant making the confession, if it was made after arrest and before arraignment, (2) whether such defendant knew the nature of the offense with which he was charged or of which he was suspected at the time of making the confession, (3) whether or not such defendant was advised or knew that he was not required to make any statement and that any such statement could be used against him, (4) whether or not such defendant had been advised prior to questioning of his right to the assistance of counsel; and (5) whether or not such defendant was without the assistance of counsel when questioned and when giving such confession.

"The presence or absence of any of the above-mentioned factors to be taken into consideration by the judge need not be conclusive on the issue of voluntariness of the confession. * * *

"(d) Nothing contained in this section shall bar the admission in evidence of any confession made or given voluntarily by any person to any other person without interrogation by anyone, or at any time at which the person who made or gave such confession was not under arrest or other detention.

"(e) As used in this section, the term 'confession' means any confession of guilt of any criminal offense or any self-incriminating statement made or given orally or in writing."[b]

Some thirty years after § 3501 became law, *United States v. Dickerson*, 166 F.3d 667 (4th Cir.1999), held, against the express wishes of the Department of Justice, that the pre-*Miranda* due process-voluntariness test set forth in § 3501, rather than *Miranda*, governed the admissibility of confessions in the federal courts. Thus, concluded the Fourth Circuit, the district court had erred when it

---

b. Another provision of § 3501, Part (c), is aimed squarely at a rule that law-enforcement officials strongly disliked, the *McNabb-Mallory* rule (p. 445). Part (c) provides that in any federal criminal prosecution a confession by a person under arrest or other detention "shall not be inadmissible solely because of delay in bringing such person before a commissioner * * * if such confession is found by the trial judge to have been voluntarily made [and] if such confession was made [within] six hours immediately following [the person's] arrest or other detention." Moreover, the six-hour time limitation does not apply where the delay in bringing such person before a commissioner beyond the six-hour period "is found by the trial judge to be reasonable considering the means of transportation and the distance to be traveled to the nearest available commissioner."

Since the *McNabb-Mallory* rule was fashioned "quite apart from the Constitution," *McNabb*, and in the exercise of the Supreme Court's "supervisory authority over the administration of [federal] criminal justice," id., it *is* subject to repeal by Congress. However, it is unclear whether Congress has only seriously weakened the *McNabb-Mallory* rule or whether it has completely abolished it. In *United States v. Alvarez–Sanchez*, 511 U.S. 350, 114 S.Ct. 1599, 128 L.Ed.2d 319 (1994), the government argued that § 3501 repudiated the *McNabb-Mallory* rule in its entirety and that the admissibility of a confession obtained beyond the six-hour limit is controlled by § 3501 (a), which provides that a confession is admissible so long as "it is voluntarily given." But the Court saw no need to decide the question because "the terms of § 3501 (c) were never triggered in this case."

had excluded a voluntary confession simply because it was obtained in violation of *Miranda*. In upholding the constitutionality of § 3501, the Fourth Circuit relied heavily on the fact that the Burger and Rehnquist Courts had "consistently referred to the *Miranda* warnings as 'prophylactic'" and "not themselves rights protected by the Constitution."

When the Supreme Court granted certiorari, most experts thought the vote would be close. Most thought that Justices Stevens, Souter, Ginsburg and Breyer were almost certain to invalidate § 3501 and that the Chief Justice and Justices Scalia and Thomas were almost certain to uphold it. Most considered Justice O'Connor and Kennedy the "swing votes." But a number of *Miranda* supporters feared that, on the basis of her majority opinion in *Oregon v. Elstad* and her strong dissent in *Withrow v. Williams*, Justice O'Connor would vote to uphold § 3501. As it turned out, most experts were wide of the mark.

DICKERSON v. UNITED STATES

530 U.S. 428, 120 S.Ct. 2326, 147 L.Ed.2d 405 (2000).

Chief Justice REHNQUIST delivered the opinion of the Court.

[In] the wake of [*Miranda*], Congress enacted 18 U.S.C. § 3501, which in essence laid down a rule that the admissibility of [a custodial suspect's] statements should turn only on whether or not they were voluntarily made. We hold that *Miranda*, being a constitutional decision of this Court, may not be in effect overruled by an Act of Congress, and we decline to overrule *Miranda* ourselves. We therefore hold that *Miranda* and its progeny in this Court govern the admissibility of statements made during custodial interrogation in both state and federal courts.

Petitioner Dickerson was indicted for bank robbery [and] conspiracy to commit bank robbery. [Before] trial, [he] moved to suppress a statement he had made at [an FBI] field office, on the grounds that he had not received "*Miranda* warnings" before being interrogated. The District Court granted his motion to suppress, and the Government took an interlocutory appeal to the United States Court of Appeals for the Fourth Circuit. That court [reversed.] It agreed [that] petitioner had not received *Miranda* warnings before making his statement. But it went on to hold that § 3501, which in effect makes the admissibility of statements such as Dickerson's turn solely on whether they were made voluntarily, was satisfied in this case. It then concluded that our decision in *Miranda* was not a constitutional holding, and that therefore Congress could by statute have the final say on the question of admissibility.

* * * Prior to *Miranda*, we evaluated the admissibility of a suspect's confession under a voluntariness test. [Over] time, our cases recognized two constitutional bases for the requirement that a confession be voluntary to be admitted into evidence: the Fifth Amendment right against self-incrimination and the Due Process Clause of the Fourteenth Amendment. See, *e.g., Bram v. United States* (1897) (stating that the voluntariness test "is controlled by that portion of the Fifth Amendment ... commanding that no person 'shall be compelled in any criminal case to be a witness against himself'"); *Brown v. Mississippi* (1936) (reversing a criminal conviction under the Due Process Clause because it was based on a confession obtained by physical coercion).

While *Bram* was decided before *Brown* and its progeny, for the middle third of the 20th century our cases based the rule against admitting coerced confessions primarily, if not exclusively, on notions of due process. We applied the due process voluntariness test in "some 30 different cases decided during the era that intervened between *Brown* and *Escobedo v. Illinois.*" Those cases refined the test into an inquiry that examines "whether a defendant's will was overborne" by the circumstances surrounding the giving of a confession. The due process test takes into consideration "the totality of all the surrounding circumstances—both the characteristics of the accused and the details of the interrogation." * * *

We have never abandoned this due process jurisprudence, and thus continue to exclude confessions that were obtained involuntarily. But our decisions in *Malloy* and *Miranda* changed the focus of much of the inquiry in determining the admissibility of suspects' incriminating statements. In *Malloy*, we held that the Fifth Amendment's Self–Incrimination Clause is incorporated in the Due Process Clause of the Fourteenth Amendment and thus applies to the States. We decided *Miranda* on the heels of *Malloy*.

In *Miranda*, we noted that the advent of modern custodial police interrogation brought with it an increased concern about confessions obtained by coercion. Because custodial police interrogation, by its very nature, isolates and pressures the individual, we stated that "even without employing brutality, the 'third degree' or [other] specific stratagems, . . . custodial interrogation exacts a heavy toll on individual liberty and trades on the weakness of individuals." We concluded that the coercion inherent in custodial interrogation blurs the line between voluntary and involuntary statements, and thus heightens the risk that an individual will not be "accorded his privilege under the Fifth Amendment . . . not to be compelled to incriminate himself." Accordingly, we laid down "concrete constitutional guidelines for law enforcement agencies and courts to follow."

Two years after *Miranda* was decided, Congress enacted § 3501. * * *

Given § 3501's express designation of voluntariness as the touchstone of admissibility, its omission of any warning requirement, and the instruction for trial courts to consider a nonexclusive list of factors relevant to the circumstances of a confession, we agree with the Court of Appeals that Congress intended by its enactment to overrule *Miranda*. Because of the obvious conflict between our decision in *Miranda* and § 3501, we must address whether Congress has constitutional authority to thus supersede *Miranda*. If Congress has such authority, § 3501's totality-of-the-circumstances approach must prevail over *Miranda*'s requirement of warnings; if not, that section must yield to *Miranda*'s more specific requirements.

The law in this area is clear. This Court has supervisory authority over the federal courts, and we may use that authority to prescribe rules of evidence and procedure that are binding in those tribunals. However, the power to judicially create and enforce nonconstitutional "rules of procedure and evidence for the federal courts exists only in the absence of a relevant Act of Congress." Congress retains the ultimate authority to modify or set aside any judicially created rules of evidence and procedure that are not required by the Constitution.

But Congress may not legislatively supersede our decisions interpreting and applying the Constitution. See, *e.g.*, *Boerne v. Flores*, 521 U.S. 507, 117 S.Ct. 2157, 138 L.Ed.2d 624 (1997). This case therefore turns on whether the *Miranda* Court announced a constitutional rule or merely exercised its supervisory authority to regulate evidence in the absence of congressional direction. [Relying] on the fact that we have created several exceptions to *Miranda*'s warnings requirement and that we have repeatedly referred to the *Miranda* warnings as "prophylactic," *Quarles*, and "not themselves rights protected by the Constitution," *Tucker*, the Court of Appeals concluded that the protections announced in *Miranda* are not constitutionally required.

We disagree * * *, although we concede that there is language in some of our opinions that supports the view taken by that court. But first and foremost of the factors on the other side—that *Miranda* is a constitutional decision—is that both *Miranda* and two of its companion cases applied the rule to proceedings in state courts—to wit, Arizona, California, and New York. Since that time, we have consistently applied *Miranda*'s rule to prosecutions arising in state courts. It is beyond dispute that we do not hold a supervisory power over the courts of the several States. With respect to proceedings in state courts, our "authority is limited to enforcing the commands of the United States Constitution."[1]

The *Miranda* opinion itself begins by stating that the Court granted certiorari "to explore some facets of the problems [of] applying the privilege against self-incrimination to in-custody interrogation, *and to give concrete constitutional guidelines for law enforcement agencies and courts to follow*." (emphasis added). In fact, the majority opinion is replete with statements indicating that the majority thought it was announcing a constitutional rule. Indeed, the Court's ultimate conclusion was that the unwarned confessions obtained in the four cases before the Court in *Miranda* "were obtained from the defendant under circumstances that did not meet constitutional standards for protection of the privilege."[5]

Additional support for our conclusion that *Miranda* is constitutionally based is found in the *Miranda* Court's invitation for legislative action to protect the constitutional right against coerced self-incrimination. [The] Court emphasized that it could not foresee "the potential alternatives for protecting the privilege which might be devised by Congress or the States," and it accordingly opined that the Constitution would not preclude legislative solutions that differed from the prescribed *Miranda* warnings but which were "at least as effective in apprising accused persons of their right of silence and in assuring a continuous opportunity to exercise it."[6]

The Court of Appeals also relied on the fact that we have, after our *Miranda* decision, made exceptions from its rule in cases such as *Quarles* and *Harris v. New York* [p. 789]. But we have also broadened the application of the *Miranda* doctrine in cases such as *Doyle v. Ohio*, [p. 799] and *Arizona v. Roberson* [p. 523]. These decisions illustrate the principle—not that *Miranda* is not a constitutional rule—but that no constitutional rule is immutable. No court laying down a general rule can possibly foresee the various circumstances in which counsel will seek to apply it, and the sort of modifications represented by these cases are as much a normal part of constitutional law as the original decision.

---

1. Our conclusion regarding *Miranda*'s constitutional basis is further buttressed by the fact that we have allowed prisoners to bring alleged *Miranda* violations before the federal courts in habeas corpus proceedings. * * * Habeas corpus proceedings are available only for claims that a person "is in custody in violation of the Constitution or laws or treaties of the United States." 28 U.S.C. § 2254(a). Since the *Miranda* rule is clearly not based on federal laws or treaties, our decision allowing habeas review for *Miranda* claims obviously assumes that *Miranda* is of constitutional origin.

5. Many of our subsequent cases have also referred to *Miranda*'s constitutional underpinnings. See, *e.g.*, *Withrow v. Williams* [p. 549] ("'Prophylactic' though it may be, in protecting a defendant's Fifth Amendment privilege against self-incrimination, *Miranda* safeguards

a 'fundamental trial right' ''); *Illinois v. Perkins*, [p. 505] (describing *Miranda*'s warning requirement as resting on "the Fifth Amendment privilege against self-incrimination"); * * * *Michigan v. Jackson* [p. 535] ("The Fifth Amendment protection against compelled self-incrimination provides the right to counsel at custodial interrogations") * * *.

6. The Court of Appeals relied in part on our statement that the *Miranda* decision in no way "creates a 'constitutional straightjacket.' " However, a review of our opinion in *Miranda* clarifies that this disclaimer was intended to indicate that the Constitution does not require police to administer the particular *Miranda* warnings, not that the Constitution does not require a procedure that is effective in securing Fifth Amendment rights.

The Court of Appeals also noted that in *Elstad, we* stated that " 'the *Miranda* exclusionary rule ... serves the Fifth Amendment and sweeps more broadly than the Fifth Amendment itself.' " Our decision in that case—refusing to apply the traditional "fruits" doctrine developed in Fourth Amendment cases—does not prove that *Miranda* is a nonconstitutional decision, but simply recognizes the fact that unreasonable searches under the Fourth Amendment are different from unwarned interrogation under the Fifth Amendment.

As an alternative argument for sustaining the Court of Appeals' decision, the court-invited *amicus curiae*[7] contends that the section complies with the requirement that a legislative alternative to *Miranda* be equally as effective in preventing coerced confessions. We agree with the *amicus'* contention that there are more remedies available for abusive police conduct than there were at the time *Miranda* was decided. But we do not agree that these additional measures supplement § 3501's protections sufficiently to meet the constitutional minimum. *Miranda* requires procedures that will warn a suspect in custody of his right to remain silent and which will assure the suspect that the exercise of that right will be honored. As discussed above, § 3501 explicitly eschews a requirement of pre-interrogation warnings in favor of an approach that looks to the administration of such warnings as only one factor in determining the voluntariness of a suspect's confession. The additional remedies cited by *amicus* do not, in our view, render them, together with § 3501 an adequate substitute for the warnings required by *Miranda*.

The dissent argues that it is judicial overreaching for this Court to hold § 3501 unconstitutional unless we hold that the *Miranda* warnings are required by the Constitution, in the sense that nothing else will suffice to satisfy constitutional requirements. But we need not go farther than *Miranda* to decide this case. In *Miranda*, the Court noted that reliance on the traditional totality-of-the-circumstances test raised a risk of overlooking an involuntary custodial confession, a risk that the Court found unacceptably great when the confession is offered in the case in chief to prove guilt. The Court therefore concluded that something more than the totality test was necessary. Section 3501 reinstates the totality test as sufficient. [The statute] therefore cannot be sustained if *Miranda* is to remain the law.

Whether or not we would agree with *Miranda*'s reasoning and its resulting rule, were we addressing the issue in the first instance, the principles of *stare decisis* weigh heavily against overruling it now.

* * * *Miranda* has become embedded in routine police practice to the point where the warnings have become part of our national culture. [While] we have overruled our precedents when subsequent cases have undermined their doctrinal underpinnings, we do not believe that this has happened to the *Miranda* decision. If anything, our subsequent cases have reduced the impact of the *Miranda* rule on legitimate law enforcement while reaffirming the decision's core ruling that unwarned statements may not be used as evidence in the prosecution's case in chief.

The disadvantage of the *Miranda* rule is that statements which may be by no means involuntary, made by a defendant who is aware of his "rights," may nonetheless be excluded and a guilty defendant go free as a result. But experience suggests that the totality-of-the-circumstances test which § 3501 seeks to revive is more difficult than *Miranda* for law enforcement officers to conform to, and for courts to apply in a consistent manner. The requirement that *Miranda* warnings

---

7. Because no party to the underlying litigation argued in favor of § 3501's constitutionality in this Court, we invited Professor Paul Cassell to assist our deliberations by arguing in support of the judgment below.

be given does not, of course, dispense with the voluntariness inquiry. But * * * "[c]ases in which a defendant can make a colorable argument that a self-incriminating statement was 'compelled' despite the fact that the law enforcement authorities adhered to the dictates of *Miranda* are rare."

In sum, we conclude that *Miranda* announced a constitutional rule that Congress may not supersede legislatively. Following the rule of *stare decisis*, we decline to overrule *Miranda* ourselves. * * *

Justice SCALIA, with whom Justice THOMAS joins, dissenting.

Those to whom judicial decisions are an unconnected series of judgments that produce either favored or disfavored results will doubtless greet today's decision as a paragon of moderation, since it declines to overrule *Miranda*. Those who understand the judicial process will appreciate that today's decision is not a reaffirmation of *Miranda*, but a radical revision of the most significant element of *Miranda* (as of all cases): the rationale that gives it a permanent place in our jurisprudence.

Marbury v. Madison held that an Act of Congress will not be enforced by the courts if what it prescribes violates the Constitution of the United States. That was the basis on which *Miranda* was decided. One will search today's opinion in vain, however, for a statement (surely simple enough to make) that what § 3501 prescribes—the use at trial of a voluntary confession, even when a *Miranda* warning or its equivalent has failed to be given—violates the Constitution. The reason the statement does not appear is not only (and perhaps not so much) that it would be absurd, inasmuch as § 3501 excludes from trial precisely what the Constitution excludes from trial, viz., compelled confessions; but also that Justices whose votes are needed to compose today's majority are on record as believing that a violation of *Miranda* is *not* a violation of the Constitution. And so, to justify today's agreed-upon result, the Court must adopt a significant *new*, if not entirely comprehensible, principle of constitutional law. As the Court chooses to describe that principle, statutes of Congress can be disregarded, not only when what they prescribe violates the Constitution, but when what they prescribe contradicts a decision of this Court that "announced a constitutional rule." As I shall discuss in some detail, the only thing that can possibly mean in the context of this case is that this Court has the power, not merely to apply the Constitution but to expand it, imposing what it regards as useful "prophylactic" restrictions upon Congress and the States. That is an immense and frightening antidemocratic power, and it does not exist.

It takes only a small step to bring today's opinion out of the realm of power-judging and into the mainstream of legal reasoning: The Court need only go beyond its carefully couched iterations that "*Miranda* is a constitutional decision," that "*Miranda* is constitutionally based," that *Miranda* has "constitutional underpinnings," and come out and say quite clearly: "We reaffirm today that custodial interrogation that is not preceded by *Miranda* warnings or their equivalent violates the Constitution of the United States." It cannot say that, because a majority of the Court does not believe it. The Court therefore acts in plain violation of the Constitution when it denies effect to this Act of Congress.

* * * The power we recognized in *Marbury* [will] permit us, indeed require us, to "disregard" § 3501, a duly enacted statute governing the admissibility of evidence in the federal courts, only if it "be in opposition to the Constitution"—here, assertedly, the dictates of the Fifth Amendment.

It was once possible to characterize the so-called *Miranda* rule as resting (however implausibly) upon the proposition that what the statute here before us permits—the admission at trial of un-*Mirandized* confessions—violates the Constitution. That is the fairest reading of the *Miranda* case itself. [Having] extended the privilege into the confines of the station house, the Court liberally sprinkled throughout its sprawling 60–page opinion suggestions that, because of the compulsion inherent in custodial interrogation, the privilege was violated by any statement thus obtained that did not conform to the rules set forth in *Miranda*, or some functional equivalent.

[The] dissenters, for their part, also understood *Miranda*'s holding to be based on the "premise [that] pressure on the suspect must be eliminated though it be only the subtle influence of the atmosphere and surroundings." (Harlan, J., dissenting). [And] at least one case decided shortly after *Miranda* explicitly confirmed the view. See *Orozco v. Texas* [p. 495] ("The use of these admissions obtained in the absence of the required warnings was a flat violation of the Self–Incrimination Clause of the Fifth Amendment as construed in *Miranda*").

So understood, *Miranda* was objectionable for innumerable reasons, not least the fact that cases spanning more than 70 years had rejected its core premise that, absent the warnings and an effective waiver of the right to remain silent and of the (thitherto unknown) right to have an attorney present, a statement obtained pursuant to custodial interrogation was necessarily the product of compulsion. See *Crooker v. California.* * * * Moreover, history and precedent aside, the decision in *Miranda*, if read as an explication of what the Constitution *requires*, is preposterous. There is, for example, simply no basis in reason for concluding that a response to the very first question asked, by a suspect who already *knows* all of the rights described in the *Miranda* warning, is anything other than a volitional act. And even if one assumes that the elimination of compulsion absolutely requires informing even the most knowledgeable suspect of his right to remain silent, it cannot conceivably require the right to have *counsel* present. There is a world of difference, which the Court recognized under the traditional voluntariness test but ignored in *Miranda*, between compelling a suspect to incriminate himself and preventing him from foolishly doing so of his own accord. Only the latter (which is *not* required by the Constitution) could explain the Court's inclusion of a right to counsel and the requirement that it, too, be knowingly and intelligently waived. Counsel's presence is not required to tell the suspect that he *need* not speak; the interrogators can do that. The only good reason for having counsel there is that he can be counted on to advise the suspect that he *should* not speak. * * *

Preventing foolish (rather than compelled) confessions is likewise the only conceivable basis for the rules (suggested in *Miranda*) that courts must exclude any confession elicited by questioning conducted, without interruption, after the suspect has indicated a desire to stand on his right to remain silent, or initiated by police after the suspect has expressed a desire to have counsel present. Nonthreatening attempts to persuade the suspect to reconsider that initial decision are not, without more, enough to render a change of heart the product of anything other than the suspect's free will. Thus, what is most remarkable about the *Miranda* decision—and what made it unacceptable as a matter of straightforward constitutional interpretation in the *Marbury* tradition—is its palpable hostility toward the act of confession *per se*, rather than toward what the Constitution abhors, *compelled* confession.

[For] these reasons, and others more than adequately developed in the *Miranda* dissents and in the subsequent works of the decision's many critics, any conclusion that a violation of the *Miranda* rules *necessarily* amounts to a violation of the privilege against compelled self-incrimination can claim no support in history, precedent, or common sense, and as a result would at least presumptively be worth reconsidering even at this late date. But that is unnecessary, since the Court has (thankfully) long since abandoned the notion that failure to comply with *Miranda*'s rules is itself a violation of the Constitution.

As the Court today acknowledges, since *Miranda* we have explicitly, and repeatedly, interpreted that decision as having announced, not the circumstances in which custodial interrogation runs afoul of the Fifth or Fourteenth Amendment, but rather only "prophylactic" rules that go beyond the right against compelled self-incrimination. Of course the seeds of this "prophylactic" interpretation of *Miranda* were present in the decision itself. [In] subsequent cases, the seeds have sprouted and borne fruit: The Court has squarely concluded that it is possible—indeed not uncommon—for the police to violate *Miranda* without also violating the Constitution.

Michigan v. Tucker, an opinion for the Court written by then-Justice Rehnquist, rejected the true-to-*Marbury,* failure-to-warn-as-constitutional-violation interpretation of *Miranda.* It held that exclusion of the "fruits" of a *Miranda* violation—the statement of a witness whose identity the defendant had revealed while in custody—was not required. The opinion explained that the question whether the "police conduct complained of directly infringed upon respondent's right against compulsory self-incrimination" was a "separate question" from "whether it instead violated only the prophylactic rules developed to protect that right." The "procedural safeguards" adopted in *Miranda,* the Court said, "were not themselves rights protected by the Constitution but were instead measures to insure that the right against compulsory self-incrimination was protected," and to "provide practical reinforcement for the right." [It] is clear from our cases, of course, that if the statement in *Tucker had* been obtained in violation of the Fifth Amendment, the statement and its fruits would have been excluded. See *Nix v. Williams* [p. 775].

The next year, in *Oregon v. Hass* [p. 790], the Court held that a defendant's statement taken in violation of *Miranda* that was nonetheless *voluntary* could be used at trial for impeachment purposes. This holding turned upon the recognition that violation of *Miranda* is not unconstitutional compulsion * * *.

Nearly a decade later, in *Quarles,* the Court relied upon the fact that "the prophylactic *Miranda* warnings [are] 'not themselves rights protected by the Constitution,'" (quoting *Tucker*), to create a "public safety" exception. [The Court] explicitly acknowledged that if the *Miranda* warnings were an imperative of the Fifth Amendment itself, such an exigency exception would be impossible, since the Fifth Amendment's bar on compelled self-incrimination is absolute, and its "'strictures, unlike the Fourth's, are not removed by showing reasonableness.'"

[The] next year, the Court again declined to apply the "fruit of the poisonous tree" doctrine to a *Miranda* violation, this time allowing the admission of a suspect's properly warned statement even though it had been preceded (and, arguably, induced) by an earlier inculpatory statement taken in violation of *Miranda, Elstad.* "Errors [that] are made by law enforcement officers in administering the prophylactic *Miranda* procedures"[, the Court told us,] "should not breed the same irremediable consequences as police infringement of the Fifth Amendment itself."

In light of these cases, and our statements to the same effect in others, it is simply no longer possible for the Court to conclude, even if it wanted to, that a violation of *Miranda's* rules is a violation of the Constitution. [What] makes a decision "constitutional" in the only sense relevant here—in the sense that renders it impervious to supersession by congressional legislation such as § 3501—is the determination that the Constitution *requires* the result that the decision announces and the statute ignores. By disregarding congressional action that concededly does not violate the Constitution, the Court flagrantly offends

fundamental principles of separation of powers, and arrogates to itself prerogatives reserved to the representatives of the people.

The Court seeks to avoid this conclusion in two ways: First, by misdescribing
these post-*Miranda* cases as mere dicta. [But it] is not a matter of *language*; it is a
matter of *holdings*. The proposition that failure to comply with *Miranda*'s rules
does not establish a constitutional violation was central to the *holdings* of *Tucker,
Hass, Quarles,* and *Elstad.*

The second way the Court seeks to avoid the impact of these cases is simply to
disclaim responsibility for reasoned decisionmaking. It says:

"These decisions illustrate the principle—not that *Miranda* is not a constitutional rule—but that no constitutional rule is immutable." * * *

[The] issue, however, is not whether court rules are "mutable"; they assuredly are. It is not whether, in the light of "various circumstances," they can be
"modified"; they assuredly can. The issue is whether, *as mutated and modified*,
they must *make sense*. The requirement that they do so is the only thing that
prevents this Court from being some sort of nine-headed Caesar, giving thumbs-
up or thumbs-down to whatever outcome, case by case, suits or offends its
collective fancy. And if confessions procured in violation of *Miranda* are confessions "compelled" in violation of the Constitution, the post-*Miranda* decisions I
have discussed do not make sense. The only reasoned basis for their outcome was
that a violation of *Miranda* is *not* a violation of the Constitution. [To] say simply
that "unreasonable searches under the Fourth Amendment are different from
unwarned interrogation under the Fifth Amendment" is true but supremely
unhelpful.

Finally, the Court asserts that *Miranda* must be a "constitutional decision"
announcing a "constitutional rule," and thus immune to congressional modification, because we have since its inception applied it to the States. If this argument
is meant as an invocation of *stare decisis*, it fails because, though it is true that
our cases applying *Miranda* against the States must be reconsidered if *Miranda* is
not required by the Constitution, it is likewise true that our cases (discussed
above) based on the principle that *Miranda* is *not* required by the Constitution
will have to be reconsidered if it *is*. So the *stare decisis* argument is a wash. [In]
my view, our continued application of the *Miranda* code to the States despite our
consistent statements that running afoul of its dictates does not necessarily—or
even usually—result in an actual constitutional violation, represents not the
source of *Miranda*'s salvation but rather evidence of its ultimate illegitimacy. See
generally Joseph Grano, *Confessions, Truth, and the Law* 173–198 (1993); Joseph
Grano, *Prophylactic Rules in Criminal Procedure: A Question of Article III
Legitimacy*, 80 Nw. U. L. Rev. 100 (1985). * * *

There was available to the Court a means of reconciling the established
proposition that a violation of *Miranda* does not itself offend the Fifth Amendment with the Court's assertion of a right to ignore the present statute. That
means of reconciliation was argued strenuously by both petitioner and the United
States, who were evidently more concerned than the Court is with maintaining
the coherence of our jurisprudence. It is not mentioned in the Court's opinion
because, I assume, a majority of the Justices intent on reversing believes that
incoherence is the lesser evil. They may be right.

Petitioner and the United States contend that there is nothing at all exceptional, much less unconstitutional, about the Court's adopting prophylactic rules
to buttress constitutional rights, and enforcing them against Congress and the
States. Indeed, the United States argues that "prophylactic rules are now and
have been for many years a feature of this Court's constitutional adjudication."
That statement is not wholly inaccurate, if by "many years" one means since the

mid–1960's. However, in their zeal to validate what is in my view a lawless practice, the United States and petitioner greatly overstate the frequency with which we have engaged in it. * * *

Petitioner and the United States are right on target [in] characterizing the Court's actions in a case decided within a few years of *Miranda, North Carolina v. Pearce* [p. 1535]. There, the Court concluded that due process would be offended were a judge vindictively to resentence with added severity a defendant who had successfully appealed his original conviction. Rather than simply announce that vindictive sentencing violates the Due Process Clause, the Court went on to hold that "in order to assure the absence of such a [vindictive] motivation, [the] reasons for [imposing the increased sentence] must affirmatively appear" and must "be based upon objective information concerning identifiable conduct on the part of the defendant occurring after the time of the original sentencing proceeding." The Court later explicitly acknowledged *Pearce*'s prophylactic character, see *Michigan v. Payne* [p. 1538]. It is true, therefore, that the case exhibits the same fundamental flaw as does *Miranda* when deprived (as it has been) of its original (implausible) pretension to announcement of what the Constitution itself required. That is, although the Due Process Clause may well prohibit punishment based on judicial vindictiveness, the Constitution by no means vests in the courts "any general power to prescribe particular devices 'in order to assure the absence of such a motivation' " (Black, J., dissenting). Justice Black surely had the right idea when he derided the Court's requirement as "pure legislation if there ever was legislation," although in truth *Pearce*'s rule pales as a legislative achievement when compared to the detailed code promulgated in *Miranda*.

The foregoing demonstrates that, petitioner's and the United States' suggestions to the contrary notwithstanding, what the Court did in *Miranda* (assuming, as later cases hold, that *Miranda* went beyond what the Constitution actually requires) is in fact extraordinary. That the Court has, on rare and recent occasion, repeated the mistake does not transform error into truth, but illustrates the potential for future mischief that the error entails. [The] power with which the Court would endow itself under a "prophylactic" justification for *Miranda* goes far beyond what it has permitted Congress to do under authority of [U.S. Const., Amdt. 14, § 5]. Whereas we have insisted that congressional action under § 5 of the Fourteenth Amendment must be "congruent" with, and "proportional" to, a *constitutional violation*, see *Boerne v. Flores*, the *Miranda* nontextual power to embellish confers authority to prescribe preventive measures against not only constitutionally prohibited compelled confessions, but also (as discussed earlier) foolhardy ones.

I applaud, therefore, the refusal of the Justices in the majority to enunciate this boundless doctrine of judicial empowerment as a means of rendering today's decision rational. In nonetheless joining the Court's judgment, however, they overlook two truisms: that actions speak louder than silence, and that (in judge-made law at least) logic will out. Since there is in fact no other principle that can reconcile today's judgment with the post-*Miranda* cases that the Court refuses to abandon, what today's decision will stand for, whether the Justices can bring themselves to say it or not, is the power of the Supreme Court to write a prophylactic, extraconstitutional Constitution, binding on Congress and the States.

Thus, while I agree with the Court that § 3501 cannot be upheld without also concluding that *Miranda* represents an illegitimate exercise of our authority to review state-court judgments, I do not share the Court's hesitation in reaching that conclusion. For while the Court is also correct that the doctrine of *stare decisis* demands some "special justification" for a departure from longstanding precedent—even precedent of the constitutional variety—that criterion is more than met here.

* * *

Neither am I persuaded by the argument for retaining *Miranda* that touts its supposed workability as compared with the totality-of-the-circumstances test it purported to replace. *Miranda*'s proponents cite *ad nauseam* the fact that the Court was called upon to make difficult and subtle distinctions in applying the "voluntariness" test in some 30–odd due process "coerced confessions" cases in the 30 years between *Brown* and *Miranda*. It is not immediately apparent, however, that the judicial burden has been eased by the "bright-line" rules adopted in *Miranda*. In fact, in the 34 years since *Miranda* was decided, this Court has been called upon to decide nearly 60 cases involving a host of *Miranda* issues * * * .

Moreover, it is not clear why the Court thinks that the "totality-of-the-circumstances test [is] more difficult than *Miranda* for law enforcement officers to conform to, and for courts to apply in a consistent manner." Indeed, I find myself persuaded by Justice O'Connor's rejection of this same argument in her opinion in *Withrow v. Williams* [p. 551] (O'Connor, J., joined by Rehnquist, C.J., concurring in part and dissenting in part) * * *.

But even were I to agree that the old totality-of-the-circumstances test was more cumbersome, it is simply not true that *Miranda* has banished it from the law and replaced it with a new test. Under the current regime, which the Court today retains in its entirety, courts are frequently called upon to undertake *both* inquiries. That is [because] voluntariness remains the *constitutional* standard, and as such continues to govern the admissibility for impeachment purposes of statements taken in violation of *Miranda*, the admissibility of the "fruits" of such statements, and the admissibility of statements challenged as unconstitutionally obtained *despite* the interrogator's compliance with *Miranda*.

Finally, I am not convinced by petitioner's argument that *Miranda* should be preserved because the decision occupies a special place in the "public's consciousness." As far as I am aware, the public is not under the illusion that we are infallible. I see little harm in admitting that we made a mistake in taking away from the people the ability to decide for themselves what protections (beyond those required by the Constitution) are reasonably affordable in the criminal investigatory process. And I see much to be gained by reaffirming for the people the wonderful reality that they govern themselves—which means that "the powers not delegated to the United States by the Constitution" that the people adopted, "nor prohibited ... to the States" by that Constitution, "are reserved to the States respectively, or to the people," U.S. Const., Amdt. 10.

* * *

Today's judgment converts *Miranda* from a milestone of judicial overreaching into the very Cheops' Pyramid (or perhaps the Sphinx would be a better analogue) of judicial arrogance. In imposing its Court-made code upon the States, the original opinion at least *asserted* that it was demanded by the Constitution. Today's decision does not pretend that it is—and yet *still* asserts the right to impose it against the will of the people's representatives in Congress. Far from believing that *stare decisis* compels this result, I believe we cannot allow to remain on the books even a celebrated decision—*especially* a celebrated decision—that has come to stand for the proposition that the Supreme Court has power to impose extraconstitutional constraints upon Congress and the States. This is not the system that was established by the Framers, or that would be established by any sane supporter of government by the people.

I dissent from today's decision, and, until § 3501 is repealed, will continue to apply it in all cases where there has been a sustainable finding that the defendant's confession was voluntary.

Notes and Questions

1. Reconciling the prophylactic-rule cases with Miranda. Consider Donald A. Dripps, *Constitutional Theory for Criminal Procedure: Miranda, Dickerson, and the Continuing Quest for Broad–But–Shallow*, 43 Wm. & Mary L.Rev. 1, 33 (2001): "Once the court granted [certiorari in *Dickerson*] court-watchers knew the hour had come. At long last the Court would have to either repudiate *Miranda*, repudiate the prophylactic-rule cases [the cases viewing *Miranda*'s requirements as not rights protected by the Constitution, but merely "prophylactic rules"] or offer some ingenious reconciliation of the two lines of precedent. The Supreme Court of the United States, however, doesn't 'have to' do anything as the decision in *Dickerson* again reminds us."

2. Original rationale. According to the Chief Justice's opinion in *Dickerson*, the *Miranda* Court "noted that reliance on the traditional totality-of-the-circumstances test raised a risk of overlooking an involuntary custodial confession, a risk that the Court found unacceptably great." Was that the original rationale of Miranda?

3. Foolish confessions. Does Miranda, as Justice Scalia maintains in his Dickerson dissent, prevent suspects from foolishly deciding to talk to the police? Don't most custodial suspects waive their Miranda rights? Are not almost all decisions by suspects to talk to the police about their cases before meeting with a lawyer foolish decisions?

4. Why did Chief Justice Rehnquist come to the rescue of Miranda? Did the Chief Justice decide to vote with the majority so that he could assign the opinion to himself rather than let it go to someone like Justice John Paul Stevens? Did the Chief Justice conclude that the best resolution of *Dickerson* would be a compromise, one that "reaffirmed" *Miranda*'s constitutional status, but preserved all the qualifications and exceptions the much-criticized case had acquired over three and a half decades? Did the Chief Justice regard *Dickerson* as an occasion for the court to maintain its power against Congress?[a] Did he consider § 3501 "a slap at the Court"?[b] Was the Chief Justice interested in assuming an increasingly large leadership rule, as opposed to his more partisan days as Associate Justice?[c]

Was the Chief Justice concerned that the "overruling" of *Miranda* by legislation would have wiped out some 35 years of jurisprudence—nearly 60 cases? Why pay the price when, whatever their initial experience with *Miranda*, the police now seem to be living comfortably with it?[d] Did the Chief Justice know that the police obtain waiver of rights in the "overwhelming majority" of cases and that

a. Consider Craig Bradley, *Behind the Dickerson Decision*, TRIAL, Oct. 2000, at 80.

b. Whether or not the Chief Justice did, some commentators did. See Michael C. Dorf & Barry Freedman, *Shared Constitutional Interpretation*, 2001 Sup.Ct.Rev. 61, 72: "[Section 3501] was a slap at the Court and if any Court was likely to slap back it was this one." See also Susan R. Klein, *Identifying and (Re)Formulating Prophylactic Rules, Safe Harbors, and Incidental Rights in Constitutional Criminal Procedure*, 99 Mich.L.Rev. 1030, 1057

(2001), calling § 3501 "an angry, disrespectful, and disingenuous attempt" to "overrule a decision [Congress] loathed."

c. Bradley, supra note a.

d. Richard A. Leo, *Questioning the Relevance of Miranda in the Twenty–First Century*, 99 Mich.L.Rev. 975, 1027 (2001), sums up the current situation as follows: "Once feared to be the equivalent of sand in the machinery of criminal justice, *Miranda* has now become a standard part of the machine."

once they do "*Miranda* offers very little, if any, meaningful protection"?[e] Was the Chief Justice aware that once the police have complied with *Miranda* and a suspect has waived his rights (as suspects usually do) "it is very difficult for a defendant to establish" that any resulting confession was "involuntary" in the pre-*Miranda* due process voluntariness sense?[f]

Would overturning *Miranda* after all this time have caused much confusion? Would it have been easy to figure out what combination of circumstances satisfied the ever-changing voluntariness test in the twenty-first century? Would it have been easy to know exactly how the police should respond when persons *not warned* of their "rights" *asserted* what they thought were their rights on their own initiative or *asked the police* whether they had a right to a lawyer or a right to remain silent?[g]

5. Does Dickerson leave Miranda incoherent? Consider Paul G. Cassell, *The Paths Not Taken: The Supreme Court's Failures in Dickerson*, 99 Mich.L.Rev. 898, 901–04 (2001):

"[The] issue of the Court's 'deconstitutionalization' of *Miranda* lies at the heart of the question presented in *Dickerson*. Yet, by my count, the majority opinion devotes only three substantive sentences to explaining why the Court's own, repeated statements should not be taken at face value. [The] majority's cursory treatment of this central issue leaves *Miranda* doctrine incoherent. [T]here is no rationale for numerous results over the last twenty-five years. Why can the 'fruits' of *Miranda* violations be used against a defendant? The traditional rule excludes fruits of, for example, unconstitutional searches. In *Oregon v. Elstad*, the Court said very specifically that the reason for not following the Fourth Amendment rule in the *Miranda* context was that 'a simple failure to administer *Miranda* warnings is not in itself a violation of the Fifth Amendment.' * * * Similarly in *New York v. Quarles* the Court carved out a 'public safety' exception to *Miranda*. The Fifth Amendment admits of no such public safety exception; the police cannot coerce an involuntary statement from a suspect and use it against him even if there are strong public safety reasons for doing so. The rationale *Quarles* gave, however, was that the *Miranda* rules were nonconstitutional rules subject to modification by the Court. [As] Akhil Amar has written, *Dickerson* reads like little more than the pronouncement: 'The Great and Powerful Oz Has Spoken!'[23] * * * My thesis is that *Dickerson* could have been written coherently—that the Court could have crafted other resolutions that would have allowed it to harmonize its doctrine far more effectively than the skimpy, jerry-built opinion the Court announced. * * *

"Perhaps the simplest way for the Court to reconcile its various pronouncements was to treat *Miranda* as a form of 'constitutional common law,' to use the phrase made famous [by Henry Monaghan].[26] Under this view, the *Miranda* rules are interim remedies not required by the Constitution, but designed in the absence of legislation to assist in protecting constitutional rights. [For] present purposes, the salient feature of constitutional common law is that it is subject to

---

e. Id. To be sure, suspects who agree to talk to the police may still cut off questioning or invoke their right to have counsel—but they "almost never" do. William J. Stuntz, *Miranda's Mistake*, 99 Mich.L.Rev. 975, 977 (2001).

f. See Welsh S. White, *Miranda's Failure to Restrain Pernicious Interrogation Practices*, 99 Mich.L.Rev. 1211, 1219 (2001). See also Louis Michael Seidman, *Brown and Miranda*, 80 Calif.L.Rev. 673, 743–47 (1992).

g. See Yale Kamisar, *Miranda Thirty–Five Years Later: A Close Look at the Majority and Dissenting Opinions in Dickerson*, 33 Ariz.St. L.J. 387, 388–90 (2001).

23. Akhil Reed Amar, *Foreword: The Document and the Doctrine*, 114 Harv.L.Rev. 26, 89 n.212 (2000).

26. Henry P. Monaghan, *Foreword: Constitutional Common Law*, 89 Harv.L.Rev. 1, 42 (1975).

change—change by the Court and, in appropriate cases, by Congress. [The] touchstone for assessing the constitutionality of Congress's remedial regime [is] not whether it matched in every respect the judicially-devised regime for which it substituted. Rather, the touchstone [is] whether the congressional regime provided 'meaningful' protection for the constitutional right at issue. If it did, then its strength compared to the judicially-devised scheme was irrelevant."

6. *How will pre-Dickerson cases grudgingly interpreting Miranda be affected by Dickerson?* As pointed out by Professor Cassell in Note 5, several pre-*Dickerson* cases, such as *Quarles* and *Elstad*, seem to be based on the premise that *Miranda* is not a constitutional decision. Does it follow that such cases will (should) now be overruled? Or will defense lawyers discover (to borrow a line from Professor Laurie Magid) that the *Dickerson* Court reaffirmed *Miranda* with all its qualifications and exceptions "frozen in time"? Will defense lawyers be reminded by the Court, to quote *Dickerson*, that "no constitutional rule is immutable" and that "the sort of modifications" represented by the cases interpreting and applying *Miranda* narrowly "are as much a normal part of constitutional law as the original decision itself"? Will defense lawyers also be reminded, to quote *Dickerson* again, that cases giving *Miranda* a begrudging reading "have reduced the impact of the *Miranda* rule on legitimate law enforcement while reaffirming the decision's core ruling that unwarned statements [as opposed to evidence brought to light as a result of these improperly obtained statements] may not be used as evidence in the prosecutor's case-in-chief [as opposed to its use on cross-examination if the defendant has the audacity to take the stand in his own defense]"?

7. *Is a "due process" explanation of Miranda and its progeny a better fit than the traditional explanations of Miranda?* Consider George C. Thomas III, *Separated at Birth but Siblings Nonetheless: Miranda and the Due Process Notice Cases*, 99 Mich.L.Rev. 1081, 1083, 1098–1102 (2001): "[A]lmost everyone thinks fairness requires telling suspects that they do not have to answer police questions, but courts find waiver of the right not to answer on any evidence that the suspect understood the warnings. Is this really an application of the venerable privilege not to be compelled to take the witness stand at trial? More is going on here than meets the eye. * * * Whatever the *Miranda* majority contemplated, my thesis is that later, and somewhat hostile, Courts have transformed *Miranda* from a case about the Fifth Amendment privilege against self incrimination to one about due process.

" * * * One reason to prefer a due process understanding [is] that *Miranda* waiver looks very different from waiving the privilege at trial. The *Miranda* opinion hints that the Court expected a high percentage of suspects to invoke the right to remain silent and the right to counsel. Had that occurred, one could argue that the *Miranda* protection of the privilege was sturdy enough, in an informal way, for rough parity with the formal courtroom application of the privilege. If most suspects say nothing that could be used against them later, or if they request counsel to advise them about answering police questions, there would be little practical difference, in the total universe of cases, between the *Miranda* protection and that of the 'real' Fifth Amendment privilege. But that is not the reality of how *Miranda* operates. Roughly eighty percent of all suspects waive *Miranda*, and the vast majority of those suspects incriminate themselves. This is not parity with the courtroom application and its waiver standard.

* * *

"[For] eighty percent of suspects, the law that applies is not in fact *Miranda* but the law that *Miranda* sought to change. It seems odd, at best, to say that the Fifth Amendment requires suspects to be warned that they have a privilege not to answer police questions, but that once they agree to answer, they are in the due process soup where police can lie and cheat to get a confession. This view of the Fifth Amendment impoverishes it. [This] evidence suggests that *Miranda* is not really about the Fifth Amendment privilege. No, my students had it right all along—*Miranda* is about fair notice that suspects have no duty to answer police questions. Once the police give that notice, the basic rationale of *Miranda* is satisfied and everyone is happy. The suspect gets the notice he deserves, the police get a statement, the prosecutor gets a conviction, and the appellate court will affirm (as long as the suspect understands the language in which the warnings are given).''

8. Why does the "right" seek to do away with Miranda's restrictions on police questioning? Why does the "left" (or center) seek to maintain them? Does Dickerson represent an opportunity missed? Consider William J. Stuntz, *Miranda's Mistake*, 99 Mich.L.Rev. 975, 976–77 (2001):

"*Miranda* imposes only the slightest of costs on the police, and its existence may well forestall more serious, and more successful, regulation of police questioning. The right should therefore be either indifferent to *Miranda* or supportive of it. Meanwhile, *Miranda* does nothing to protect suspects against abusive police tactics. The left should therefore be its enemy, and should rejoice at the prospect of seeing it fall, since anything that took its place would likely be an improvement. Another, better answer is that *Miranda* should attract support from neither right nor left. Its effects are probably small, perhaps vanishingly so. But what effects it has are probably perverse * * *. *Dickerson* represents not a bullet dodged but an opportunity missed. As things stand now, from almost any plausible set of premises, police interrogation is badly regulated. Because of *Dickerson*, it will continue to be badly regulated for a long time to come.

"The reason has to do with *Miranda*'s regulatory strategy. The essence of that strategy was to shift, from courts to suspects, the burden of separating good police interrogation from bad. Instead of courts deciding based on all the circumstances (or at least all the circumstances disclosed during the suppression hearing) whether the suspect's confession was voluntary, *Miranda* left it for suspects to decide, by either agreeing to talk or by calling a halt to questioning and/or calling for the help of a lawyer, whether the police were behaving too coercively. A growing literature on the empirics of police questioning shows why that strategy has failed. Suspects do not, in fact, separate good questioning from bad; once suspects agree to talk to police, they almost never call a halt to questioning or invoke their right to have the assistance of counsel. Instead, suspects separate *themselves*, not the police, into two categories: talkative and quiet. The sorting says nothing at all about the police, because it happens before police questioning has begun, hence before any police coercion has begun. Rather, the sorting is a signal of the suspect's savvy and experience. Because of *Miranda*, sophisticated suspects have a right to be free from questioning altogether—not simply free from coercive questioning—while unsophisticated suspects have very nearly no protection at all. The first group receives more than it deserves, while the second receives less than it needs."

9. Is Congress still free to replace Miranda warnings with other procedures? Is it likely to do so? Consider Yale Kamisar, *Miranda Thirty–Five Years Later: A Close Look at the Majority and Dissenting Opinions in Dickerson*, 33 Ariz.St.L.J. 387, 425 (2001): "*Miranda* left the door open for Congress to replace the warnings with other safeguards that perform the same function. Unfortunately, Congress did not walk in the door. But the door remains open.

"The alternative often mentioned is a system of audiotaping or videotaping police questioning *and* a modified set of warnings.[a] I think such a system would

---

a. See Note 10, p. ___. Consider, too **judicial or judicially supervised questioning,** another frequently mentioned alternative to police interrogation. Paul Kauper, *Judicial Ex*

and should pass constitutional muster. (It seems clear, however, that, no matter how fool-proof, a tape recording system that dispensed with all warnings would not be upheld.[212])

"If such a system replaced the four-fold *Miranda* warnings it would make clear that 'a decision may be *both* an interpretation of the Constitution *and* a principle that Congress may modify.'[213] However, I doubt that any legislature will enact any audiotaping or videotaping system that contains some warnings of rights or any other *effective* alternative to the *Miranda* regime. For any alternative that *is* equally effective is likely to be 'politically unacceptable for precisely the reason that saves it from being constitutionally unacceptable—it would be at least as protective of the suspect (and therefore at least as burdensome to investigators) as *Miranda* itself.'[214]

"I believe Stephen Schulhofer is quite right—'politically attractive alternatives to *Miranda* can't pass constitutional muster, and constitutional alternatives cannot attract political support.'[215] That is why the *Miranda* warnings will probably be with us for a long time."

   10. *Unrepentant dissenters.* Recall that, dissenting in *Dickerson*, Justice Scalia vowed that, until § 3501 was repealed by Congress, he would "continue to apply it in all cases where there had been a sustainable finding that the defendant's confession was voluntray." Is this position defensible? Consider Donald A. Dripps, Note 1, supra, at 65–66:

amination of the Accused—A Remedy for the Third Degree, 30 Mich.L.Rev. 1224 (1932), seems to be the first commentator to spell out the desirability of, and historical support, for judicial questioning. In the wake of *Miranda*, two eminent judges returned to the Kauper model and built upon it. See Walter Schaeper, *The Suspect and Society*, 76–81 (1967); Henry Friendly, *The Fifth Amendment Tomorrow: The Case for Constitutional Change*, 37 U.Cin.L.Rev. 671, 713–16 (1968). Under the "Kauper–Schaefer–Friendly" model, discussed at length in Kamisar, *Kauper's Judicial Examination of the Accused" Forty Years Later—Some Comments on a Remarkable Article*, 73 Mich.L.Rev. 15 (1974), a suspect questioned either by or before a judicial officer would have the assistance of counsel and be informed that she need not answer any questions. But she would also be told that if subsequently prosecuted her refusal to answer questions at the earlier proceeding would be disclosed at trial.

   Does *Griffin v. California* (1965) (set forth in Ch. 25, § 4), which forbids comment on a defendant's failure to testify at trial, stand in the way of this proposal? As have many other commentators, both Judges Friendly and Schaefer assumed that their proposal could not be effectuated without a constitutional amendment. But Albert W. Alschuler, *A Peculiar Privilege in Historical Perspective: The Right to Remain Silent*, 94 Mich.L.Rev. 2625, 2670–72 (1996), and Marvin Frankel, *From Private Rights to Public Justice*, 51 N.Y.U.L.Rev. 516, 531 (1976), have forcefully argued to the contrary. They have maintained that such an alternative would probably promote accurate

fact-finding (both when it would help the suspect and when it would hurt him) and sharply reduce the amount of truly compelled self-incrimination in our society.

   Recently, Akhil Reed Amar & Renée B. Lettow, *Fifth Amendment First Principles: The Self–Incrimination Clause*, 93 Mich.L.Rev. 857, 858, 898, 908 (1995), revisited and revised the "Kauper–Schaefer–Friendly" proposal. Under the Amar–Lettow version, the suspect at a judicially supervised pretrial hearing who failed to answer truthfully would be held in contempt. If he did answer, he would only be entitled to "testimonial immunity," i.e., his compelled *words* could not be introduced in a criminal trial, but the evidence derived from those words—such as the whereabouts of damaging physical evidence or a potential witness for the prosecution—would be admissible. For strong criticism of the Amar–Lettow proposal see Kamisar, *On the "Fruits of Miranda Violations, Coerced Confessions, and Compelled Testimony*, 93 Mich.L.Rev. 929, 932–33 (1995).

   212. As the *Dickerson* Court told us, referring to very similar language in the *Miranda* opinion, "*Miranda* requires procedures that will warn a suspect in custody of his right to remain silent and which will assure the suspect that the exercise of that right will be honored."

   213. David A. Strauss, *Miranda, The Constitution and Congress*, 99 Mich.L.Rev. 958, 960 (2001).

   214. Stephen J. Schulhofer, *Miranda, Dickerson and the Puzzling Persistence of Fifth Amendment Exceptionalism*, 99 Mich.L.Rev. 941, 955 (2001).

   215. Id.

"Whatever the theory on which the doctrine of judicial supremacy rests, no justice can consistently maintain judicial supremacy while regarding herself as unobligated by decisions of the Court. This is not to say that civil disobedience is never justified. * * * Judicial civil disobedience, however, is especially hard to defend. Judges, unlike ordinary citizens, swear an oath to uphold the law. Unlike ordinary citizens, they claim the obedience of others to their decisions on the basis of a general obligation to obey the law."

SECTION 4. THE "DUE PROCESS"— "VOLUNTARINESS" TEST REVISITED

Although one might say (and many commentators have) that *Miranda* displaced the due process-totality of circumstances-voluntariness test, in a number of important situations "the primary criterion of [confession] admissibility under current law is [still] the 'old' due process voluntariness test." Stephen J. Schulhofer, *Confessions and the Court*, 79 Mich.L.Rev. 865, 877 (1981). For one thing, empirical studies indicate that most suspects waive their rights and submit to police questioning. "Because the admissibility of statements given after a valid waiver of Miranda rights must be determined on the basis of the voluntariness test, that test remains vitally important." Welsh S. White, *What is an Involuntary Confession Now?*, 50 Rutgers L.Rev. 2001, 2004 (1998). Moreover, as Schulhofer, supra, points out, the voluntariness test is important when suspects not in custody are questioned by the police; when suspects in a custody-like situation are questioned (or threatened) by private citizens (e.g. *Commonwealth v. Mahnke*, 335 N.E.2d 660 (Mass.1975)); or when the prosecution seeks to use a confession to impeach a defendant's testimony at trial or to use the "fruits" of the confession (e.g., the murder weapon), but not the confession itself. As discussed in Ch. 11, §§ 2,3, although statements obtained in violation of *Miranda* may be used for impeachment purposes, "coerced" or "involuntary" statements may not. Moreover, although the distinctions have not yet been fully developed, the Court has left little doubt that it is much more likely to permit the use of evidence derived from a *Miranda* violation than the "fruits" of an "involuntary" confession.

A. *Miller v. Fenton*: What Kinds of Trickery or Deception, If Any, May the Police Employ *After* a Suspect Has Waived His Rights?

Is *Miranda's* prohibition against police deception and trickery limited to their use in obtaining a waiver of *Miranda* rights or does it also bar such police techniques after a person has validly waived his rights? Suppose a suspect waives his rights and expresses a willingness to talk, but denies any involvement in the case. May the police then display apparent sympathy? Turn the suspect over to a friendly, gentle interrogator and then to a hostile, short-tempered one (the "Mutt and Jeff" routine)? Although such techniques seemed to have vented Chief Justice Warren's judicial ire in *Miranda*, that landmark case "did not condemn any specific techniques as such or hold that evidence obtained by use of them would be inadmissible. Reliance was placed on warning and counsel to protect the suspect." Sheldon Elsen & Arthur Rosett, *Protections for the Suspect under Miranda v. Arizona*, 67 Colum.L.Rev. 645, 667 (1967). More than three decades after *Miranda*, the issue has yet to be clearly resolved.[a]

a. Cf. *Frazier v. Cupp*, 394 U.S. 731, 89 S.Ct. 1420, 22 L.Ed.2d 684 (1969) (admitting a confession in a pre-*Miranda* case although the police had falsely told the defendant that another had confessed and had also "sympathetically" suggested that the victim's homosexual

A year after *Miranda*, Professor Fred Inbau and Mr. John Reid published a new edition of their leading interrogation manual and maintained that "all but a very few of the interrogation techniques presented in our earlier [pre-Escobedo, pre-Miranda] publication are still valid if used after the recently prescribed warnings have been given to the suspect under interrogation, and after he has waived his self-incriminating privilege and his right to counsel." See *Criminal Interrogation and Confessions*, (2d ed. 1967). See also Inbau, Reid & Buckley, *Criminal Interrogation and Confessions* 216 (3d ed. 1986), maintaining that, although the Court did not explicitly address the issue in *Frazier v. Cupp*, fn. a supra, that case "implicitly recognized" the essentiality of interrogation practices involving trickery or deceit, and approved of them. [Moreover,] there are many appellate court cases holding that a confession is admissible even when it was obtained by trickery and deceit, [provided that the trickery does not] 'shock the conscience' [or is not] apt to induce a false confession."[b]

Welsh S. White, *Police Trickery in Inducing Confessions*, 127 U.Pa.L.Rev. 581–90, 599–600, 628–29 (1979), takes a very different view of police use of trickery in the post-Miranda era, maintaining that, because they are likely to render a resulting confession involuntary or because they distort the meaning or vitiate the effect of the *Miranda* warnings or because they "undermine [a] suspect's independent right to an attorney," "several widely employed interrogation tactics * * * should be absolutely prohibited." Among the techniques Professor White considers "impermissible per se" are deception that distorts the seriousness of the matter under investigation (e.g., falsely informing a murder suspect that the victim is still alive), the "assumption of non-adversary roles" by interrogating officers (e.g., assuming the role of a father figure or religious counselor), repeated assurances that the suspect is known to be guilty, and the "Mutt and Jeff" routine. See also Note, 40 Stan.L.Rev. 1593, 1612–15 (1988).

But police deception and trickery did not prevent the admissibility of the resulting confession in *Miller v. Fenton*, below. Miller is a dramatic illustration that the problems raised by the old "totality of the circumstances"—"due process"—"voluntariness" test have not disappeared in the post-Miranda era.

When he accompanied the police to a state police barracks, Miller, the prime suspect in the brutal murder of Ms. Margolin, was advised of his rights and signed "a Miranda card," waiving his rights.[a] Thus, the issue in MILLER v. FENTON, 796 F.2d 598 (3d Cir.1986), was the "voluntariness" of the defendant's murder

---

advances may have started the fight). See also *Oregon v. Mathiason* (p. 496) (interrogator's false statement to defendant that his fingerprints were found at scene may have bearing on other issues in case, but "has nothing to do with whether [defendant] was in custody for [*Miranda*] purposes").

b. Although agreeing that a goodly number of lower courts have interpreted *Frazier* as "definitively ruling that police trickery is a mere factor to be included in a court's assessment of a confession's involuntariness under a totality of the circumstances analysis," Note, 40 Stan.L.Rev. 1593, 1607–08 (1988), maintains that "several factors make *Frazier* a particularly bad case for a definitive ruling on police trickery":

"First, the opinion does not recognize as trickery the detective's feigned sympathy in his suggestion that a homosexual advance was a reason for the fight. Also, Frazier was tried

and decided before the *Miranda* decision, and so the Court's indictment of police misconduct in *Miranda* did not apply. * * * Third, apart from the one recognized and one unrecognized instances of police trickery, the interrogators' behavior was exemplary. The police gave coercive conduct a wide berth, questioning Frazier for only forty-five minutes immediately after he was brought to the police station. In addition, the interrogation was tape-recorded and the tape played for the trial judge, who subsequently concluded that the confession was voluntary. Last and most important, the police lie that [another person] had confessed, the only trickery recognized by the Court, does *not* seem to have induced Frazier's confession."

a. Several hours earlier, Miller had been questioned by the police for about 45 minutes at his place of employment, but had denied any involvement in the murder.

confession.[b] A 2–1 majority, per BECKER, J. (joined by Seitz, J.), framed the issue in terms of whether the tactics of Detective Boyce during the 53–minute interrogation "were sufficiently manipulative to overbear the will of a person with [defendant's] characteristics" and viewed the limits of permissible interrogation as turning on "a weighing of the circumstances of pressure [applied by the police] against the power of resistance of the person confessing." After listening to Detective Boyce's questions and defendant Miller's responses (the police had taped the interrogation), the majority concluded that "under the totality of circumstances of this case" Miller's confession was "voluntarily given":

"It is clear that Boyce made no threats and engaged in no physical coercion of Miller. To the contrary, throughout the interview, Detective Boyce assumed a friendly, understanding manner and spoke in a soft tone of voice. He repeatedly assured Miller that he was sympathetic to him and wanted to help him unburden his mind. [The detective's] statements of sympathy at times approached the maudlin. [E.g., 'This hurts me more than it hurts you because I love people * * * I'm on your side, Frank * * * I'm your brother, you and I are brothers, Frank [and] I want to help my brother.']

"Boyce also gave Miller certain factual information, some of which was untrue. At the beginning of the interrogation, for example, Boyce informed Miller that the victim was still alive; this was false. During the interview, Boyce told Miller that Ms. Margolin had just died, although in fact she had been found dead several hours earlier.

"Detective Boyce's major theme throughout the interrogation was that whoever had committed such a heinous crime had mental problems and was desperately in need of psychological treatment. [The] Detective stated several times that Miller was not a criminal who should be punished, but a sick individual who should receive help. * * *

"Boyce also appealed to Miller's conscience and described the importance of Miller's purging himself of the memories that must be haunting him. [E.g., 'First thing we have to do is let it all come out. Don't fight it because it's worse * * * It's hurting me because I feel it. I feel it wanting to come out, but it's hurting me, Frank. * * * I know how you feel inside, Frank, it's eating you up, am I right? * * * You've got to come forward. You've got to do it for yourself, for your family, for your father, this is what's important, the truth, Frank.']

"When Miller at last confessed [almost an hour after the interrogation session began], he collapsed in a state of shock. He slid off his chair and onto the floor with a blank stare on his face. The police officers sent for a first aid squad that took him to the hospital. * * *

"[Psychological] ploys may play a part in the suspect's decision to confess, but as long as that decision is a product of the suspect's own balancing of competing considerations, the confession is voluntary. The question we must answer [is] whether [the detective's] statements were so manipulative or coercive that they deprived Miller of his ability to make an unconstrained autonomous decision to confess. To that inquiry we now turn. * * *

b. The case has a long procedural history. After a New Jersey trial court admitted his confession, Miller was convicted of murder. A three-judge panel of an intermediate state appellate court reversed, holding Miller's confession "involuntary." But a 4–3 majority of the New Jersey Supreme Court reinstated the conviction, deeming the confession "voluntary." On federal habeas corpus, the Third Circuit, deferring to the state court's finding of "voluntariness," upheld the admissibility of the confession. The U.S. Supreme Court reversed (see p. 443), holding that on federal habeas corpus the "voluntariness" of a confession is a matter for independent federal court determination, and remanding the case for a fuller analysis under the correct standard.

"Miller is a mature adult, thirty-two years of age [and] has some high school education. Such a person is more resistant to interrogation than a person who is very young, uneducated or weak-minded. [Moreover,] Miller [had] served a jail sentence. Thus, he was aware of the consequences of confessing. [He had also] received Miranda warnings. Detective Boyce's interrogation of Miller lasted less than an hour. [I]t is thus distinguishable from the lengthy interrogations during incommunicado detention that have been held to result in involuntary confessions. * * *

"Boyce's supportive, encouraging manner was an interrogation tactic aimed at winning Miller's trust and making him feel comfortable about confessing. Excessive friendliness on the part of an interrogator can be deceptive. In some instances, in combination with other tactics, it might create an atmosphere in which a suspect forgets that his questioner is in an adversarial role, and thereby prompt admissions that the suspect would ordinarily make only to a friend, not to the police. [But] the 'good guy' approach is recognized as a permissible interrogation tactic. * * *

"[While an officer's] lie [about] an important aspect of the case may affect the voluntariness of the confession, the effect of the lie must be analyzed in the context of all the circumstances of the interrogation. See, e.g., *Frazier v. Cupp* * * *. We do not believe that the lie about the time of Ms. Margolin's death, by itself, constituted sufficient trickery to overcome Miller's will. [The] drama of the announcement of the victims death [during the interrogation] might have prompted particularly acute feelings in Miller, which could have helped to induce his confession. However, the record suggests that this emotional reaction did not occur, for it appears that Miller was not affected at all by the news of the death. Indeed, he remained quite impassive. * * *

"Detective Boyce's statements that Miller was not a criminal, but rather a mentally ill individual not responsible for his actions, and Boyce's promises to help Miller raise a more serious question about the voluntariness of Miller's confession. By telling Miller that he was not responsible for anything he might have done, Boyce may have been understood to be making an implied promise to Miller that [he] would not be prosecuted, or that if he were prosecuted Boyce would aid him in presenting the insanity defense. Similarly, the promises of psychiatric help might have suggested to Miller that he would be treated, rather than prosecuted. If these promises, implicit and explicit, tricked Miller into confessing, his confession may have been involuntary. To determine whether Boyce's promises affected the voluntariness of Miller's confession, we must consider how manipulative these tactics in fact were.

"In *Bram v. United States*, (1897) [p. 456] [the Court] endorsed the view that to be voluntary a confession must not have been 'extracted by any sort of threats or violence, nor obtained by any direct or implied promises, however slight.' [Emphasis added.] Although the *Bram* test has been reaffirmed [it] has not been interpreted as a per se proscription against promises made during interrogation.[c] Nor does the Supreme Court even use a but-for test when promises have been made during an interrogation.

c. But cf. CRIMPROC § 6.2(c): "[L]ower courts have rather consistently held that a confession is involuntary if made in response to a promise that the result will be nonprosecution, the dropping of some charges, or a certain reduction in the punishment defendant may receive. But the cases go both ways on the question of what the result should be when a confession has been obtained in response to a police assertion that cooperation would facilitate prompt release on bail or would mean that the defendant would fare better in subsequent proceedings. Especially as to the latter situation, '[m]uch of the difficulty arises from failure to reconcile the voluntariness requirement with the plea bargaining process and especially the role of the police in that practice.' "

"[At] no time did Detective Boyce state that Miller would not be prosecuted or that he could successfully avail himself of the insanity defense. [While] innuendo might rise to the level of trickery, it is not so likely to break down resistance as is a promise that is spelled out. Indeed, Boyce's statements that Miller was 'not a criminal' need not be understood as assurances of leniency at all. Since [Boyce's] strategy was to present himself as a friend to whom Miller could unburden himself, he of course attempted throughout the interview to persuade Miller to trust him and confide in him. The statement at issue can be viewed as a means of convincing Miller that Boyce was sympathetic, no matter what the state's reaction might be. 'You are not responsible' and 'You are not a criminal' thus would mean 'In my eyes, you are not responsible or a criminal and therefore you should relieve your conscience by talking to me, who understands you.'

"While such a statement might have made Miller feel more comfortable about speaking to Boyce, it would not render his confession the product of a mistaken belief that the state would grant him leniency. Detective Boyce never stated that anyone but he thought that Miller was 'not a criminal' nor did he state that he had any authority to affect the charges brought against Miller. Miller's confession may have been made in the hope of leniency, but that does not mean that it was made in response to a promise of leniency.

"[While] Boyce's promises of psychiatric help and statements that Miller was 'not a criminal,' in combination with his friendly manner, may have been a form of psychological trickery, we do not believe that these elements of the interrogation affected the voluntariness of the confession. Miller's personal characteristics support a conclusion that the confession was voluntary, for Miller does not seem to be the type of person whose will would be easily overborne by Boyce's remarks. Miller's age, intelligence and experience rendered him resistant to the level of persuasiveness that Boyce employed.

"Moreover, throughout the interview, Miller made remarks that indicate that he knew that this was an ordinary police interrogation rather than an encounter with a compassionate friend, and that he was aware that a confession would result in criminal prosecution and possibly in conviction and sentence. Throughout the session, he appears to have retained a suspicious, guarded attitude. * * *

"[In light of some statements by Miller indicating that his] prior experience with the law had made him wary of policemen [it] is difficult for us to believe that [he] was tricked into confessing. Rather, it seems that Miller made an uncoerced decision to unburden his inner tensions and to acknowledge his guilt. Indeed, from the tape of the interrogation, it clearly appears that the precipitating cause of Miller's confession was a desire to make a clean breast of it, rather than a reliance on any promise of leniency or psychiatric help. * * *

"We have little doubt that Detective Boyce's encouraging words, perhaps in contribution with the sad announcement that the victim had just died, helped Miller to reach his decision to unburden himself. However, the test for voluntariness is not a but-for test, but a question of whether the confession was a product of free choice. * * * Many criminals experience an urge during interrogation to own up to their crimes. * * * Boyce's manner and his statements may have stirred this urge in Miller, but, in our view, they did not produce psychological pressure strong enough to overbear the will of a mature, experienced man, who was suffering from no mental or physical illness and was interrogated for less than an hour at a police station close to his home.

"Detective Boyce's method of interrogation might have overborne the will of another detainee, for example, a young, inexperienced person of lower intelligence than Miller, or a person suffering from a painful physical ailment. It might have overcome the will of Miller himself if the interrogation had been longer or if Miller had been refused food, sleep, or contact with a person he wished to see. Moreover, if Miller had made remarks that indicated that he truly believed that the state would treat him leniently because he was 'not responsible' for what he had done or that he believed that he would receive psychiatric help rather than punishment, we might not find the confession voluntary. We hold simply that, under the totality of the circumstances of this case, the confession was voluntarily given.''

Dissenting Judge GIBBONS protested:

"[B]y endorsing a thoroughly bad piece of police work, the majority sends a signal to the police community * * * likely to have the harmful consequence of encouraging coercion of defendants in place of acceptable methods of investigation. [T]he police did not need to conduct an interrogation directed at investigating the murder; [they had acquired so much information pointing to Miller that the case] was already solved so far as they were concerned. [They] conducted an interrogation directed at obtaining a confession from the sole suspect, and that investigation was designed to assure Miller's prosecution for felony murder rather than a lesser offense.

"For me, although obviously not for the majority, the most significant circumstance in this case supporting the conclusion that Miller's admission was obtained in a manner inconsistent with the Constitution is the complete absence of any legitimate investigative purpose for the interrogation. The circumstances of this case provide a classic illustration of the once common practice of obtaining guilty pleas in the back rooms of police stations rather than in open court. Moreover, the evidence of the method of interrogation must be examined in light of Officer Boyce's sole purpose—the obtaining of admissions of guilt, not the solution of a crime which Boyce believed to be solved already. * * *

"The majority stresses that Boyce 'repeatedly assured Miller that he was sympathetic to him and wanted to help him unburden his mind.' Admittedly, Boyce did feign sympathy for Miller, but clearly unburdening Miller's mind was not Boyce's purpose. The repeated assurances, the friendly, understanding manner, and the soft tone of voice to which the majority makes reference were all directed to a single purpose—making an unwilling defendant admit his guilt. Referring to the detective's statement of sympathy as 'maudlin' is deceptive. Every word, every nuance of expression, every change in tone of voice, was calculated toward one end, and one end only—obtaining an admission of guilt. From the tone of the majority opinion one might believe that its author actually credits these deceptive expressions of sympathy. But as the majority well knows the state police are not in the business of acting as religious or psychiatric counselors. Boyce was not sympathetic. He was no more interested in helping Miller 'unburden his inner tensions' than he was in any other aspect of Miller's health. Instead Boyce was determined and ultimately successful in obtaining from an unwilling defendant the one thing that was his purpose—a confession. * * *

"The majority, acknowledging that the police had previously lied to Miller that Ms. Margolin had survived and that Boyce repeated the lie about the time of her death, attempts to put the deliberate trickery in a positive light, observing,

'We do not believe that the lie about the time of Ms. Margolin's death, by itself, constituted sufficient trickery to overcome Miller's will. Because Boyce never suggested that the time of Ms. Margolin's death might be relevant in linking Miller to the crime, the only possible effect of Boyce's initial statement that she was alive, followed by his report that she had just died, would be an emotional response in Miller.'

"There are several glaring deficiencies in this attempted justification. First, it ignores the plain fact that, by initially suggesting to Miller that Ms. Margolin survived, the police intended to leave him with the impression that she would eventually identify him. When that ploy proved to be unsuccessful in breaking down his will, Boyce shifted to a different tactic, by announcing, falsely, that she had just died. Boyce hoped, as the majority concedes, to evoke an emotional response in Miller. Admitting that this was an attempt at psychological coercion, the majority explains it away with the preposterous statement, 'However, the record suggests that this emotional reaction did not occur, for it appears that Miller was not affected at all by the news of the death.' What the record actually discloses is that the interrogation continued as follows:

BOYCE: Are you, do you feel what I feel right now?

MILLER: I feel pretty bad.

BOYCE: Do you want to talk to me about it?

MILLER: There's nothing I can tell . . .

BOYCE: About how you feel?

MILLER: . . . there's nothing I can talk, I mean I feel sorry for this girl, I mean, uh, this is something that, you know

. . .

BOYCE: That what?

MILLER: Well, it's a shame, uh . . .

* * *

BOYCE: Frank, you're very, very nervous. Now, I, I don't, you know, you, you're, you understand what I'm saying?

MILLER: Yeah, I know what you're saying.

BOYCE: Now, there's a reason for that, isn't there?

MILLER: Yes.

BOYCE: Do you want to tell me about it?

MILLER: Being involved in something like this is . . .

BOYCE: Is what, does it, does it, does it visibly shake you physically?

MILLER: Yes, it does, * * *.

"At this point, twenty-seven minutes into the second interrogation, it was briefly interrupted while the recording cassette was turned over. Boyce had by then spent seven minutes attempting to capitalize on the emotional response he attempted to elicit by his staged phone call about Ms. Margolin's recent death. I leave it to the reader to judge whether this colloquy establishes that, in the words of the majority opinion, Miller 'remained quite impassive.' Having listened to the tape recording on several occasions, I represent that Miller sounds, at this point of the interrogation, increasingly tense and emotional. So emotional, indeed, that the interrogator, Boyce, stated, 'Frank, you're very, very nervous.'

"The colloquy above, occurring immediately following Boyce's lie about the time of death, is not mentioned by the majority in connection with the police lies because the majority, bent on a result, has chosen to judge the police conduct not in light of the totality of the circumstances, but by subdividing each instance of police misconduct and discussing it in isolation. Thus, it chooses to treat the colloquy that immediately followed Boyce's lies under the heading of Boyce's promises. These are dismissed with the observation, 'While such a statement might have made Miller feel more comfortable about speaking to Boyce, it would not render his confession the product of a mistaken belief that the state would grant him leniency.' The total unfairness of that cavalier dismissal of the intended effect upon Miller's will may best be judged in light of the colloquy that continued as soon as the tape recorder was turned on:

BOYCE: Now listen to me Frank. This hurts me more than it hurts you, because I love people.

MILLER: It can't hurt you anymore than it hurts me. * * *

BOYCE: Okay, listen Frank. If I promise to, you know, do all I can with the psychiatrist and everything, and we get the proper help for you, and get the proper help for you, will you talk to me about it?

MILLER: I can't talk to you about something I'm not . . .

BOYCE: Alright, listen Frank, alright, honest. I know, I know what's going on inside you, Frank. I want to help you, you know, between us right now. I know what going on inside you, Frank, you've got to come forward and tell me that you want to help yourself. You've got to talk to me about it. This is the only way we'll be able to work it out. I mean, you know, listen, I want to help you, because you are in my mind, you are not responsible. You are not responsible, Frank. Frank, what's the matter?

MILLER: I feel bad.

BOYCE: Frank, listen to me, honest to God, I'm I'm telling you, Frank (inaudible). I know, it's going to bother you, Frank, it's going to bother you. It's there, it's not going to go away, it's there. It's right in front of you, Frank. Am I right or wrong?

MILLER: Yeah.

BOYCE: You can see it Frank, you can feel it, you can feel it, but you are not responsible. This is what I'm trying to tell you, but you've got to come forward and tell me. Don't, don't, don't let it eat you up, don't, don't fight it. You've got to rectify it, Frank. We've got to get together on this thing, or I, I mean really, you need help, you need proper help and you know it, my God, you know, in God's name you, you, you know it. You are not a criminal, you are not a criminal.

MILLER: Alright. Yes, I was over there and I talked to her about the cow and left. I left in my car and I stopped up on the road where, you know, where the cow had been and she followed me in her car . . .

"Thus, approximately thirty minutes into the second interrogation, Miller made his first incriminating statement. By far the largest part of that thirty minutes is comprised of lies and promises by Boyce. The majority's suggestion that these lies and promises had no effect upon Miller's will is utter speculation. The lies and promises were directed to the sole purpose of obtaining a confession. There is nothing in the record from which it can be inferred that Miller's abandonment of his self-interested denials of involvement in the homicide was the product of any other influence. The majority opinion describes Boyce's conduct as if he were a confessor, offering solace under the seal of the confessional, or a psychiatrist offering relief from anxiety under the shelter of a physician-patient privilege, rather than what he was—a wily interrogator determined to break down Miller's resistance by lies and false promises. The majority's treatment of the police tactics leading to Miller's collapse is about as fair as those tactics. Confession may be good for the soul, but it was Miller's freedom, not his soul, that was at stake, and it was his freedom, not his soul, that interested Boyce. * * *

"The reason why the state had to preserve and make use of the tape-recorded interrogation appears in Boyce's testimony at the suppression hearing:

Q. I gather that [a] statement was never taken, is that right?

A. It was not.

Q. Why was that, Officer?

A. Momentarily after terminating this particular interview Mr. Miller went into as I can best define it a state of shock.

Q. What do you mean by that, sir?

A. He was sitting on a chair? . . . Mr. Miller had been sitting on a chair, had slid off the chair on the floor maintaining a blank stare on his face, staring straight ahead and we were unable to get any type of verbal response from him.
* * *

"Incredibly, the only reference in the majority's opinion to Miller's collapse is the cryptic sentence [that] 'One hour into the interrogation, Miller confessed to the murder of Deborah Margolin, then passed out.' The majority does not even recognize Miller's collapse into a catatonic state and his transportation to a hospital as relevant circumstances in its totality of the circumstances analysis! This most telling of all indications as to the effect on Miller of Boyce's tactics is simply ignored. Instead the majority opinion perversely reasons that Boyce's manner and statements may have stirred in Miller the urge to confess, 'but, in our view, they did not produce psychological pressure strong enough to overbear the will of a mature, experienced man, who was suffering from no mental or physical illness. . . .' The reasoning is perverse because it ignores the fact that at the end of the interrogation Miller collapsed and was taken to a hospital. How can it be honestly represented that he was suffering from no mental or physical illness? And, unless the majority identifies some other reason for Miller's abrupt abandonment of his self-interested denials of guilt than the psychological coercion exercised by Boyce, what other cause is left? * * *

"It has long been established that confessions obtained by virtue of even implied promises of leniency are deemed to be inadmissible. See *Bram v. United States* (1897). The majority attempts to undercut the authority of the *Bram* rule by suggesting that it is no longer interpreted as a per se proscription against promises made during interrogations. [But the] Supreme Court has never retreated from the *Bram* holding. Indeed, other federal circuit courts of appeals have consistently cited the *Bram* test as the standard by which voluntariness will be evaluated. [Thus,] when promises, however slight, are made in the interrogation room rather than in the presence of counsel, those promises render the resulting confession inadmissible.

"Boyce's second interrogation cannot be read in pieces. Its effect was cumulative, as it was intended to be. From the moment he began it, Boyce put relentless psychological pressure on Miller. Boyce repeatedly assured Miller that he only wanted to help Miller, that Miller was not a criminal, that Miller was not responsible for his actions, and that Miller would not be punished. In addition to these express promises, Boyce confused Miller by lying to him about the time of Ms. Margolin's death and the strength of the evidence against Miller.

"The majority emphasizes that the key issue is whether, in the totality of the circumstances, Miller's will was overborne. While I agree with the majority's general focus, I disagree with the majority's method of analysis. In ascertaining the effects of Boyce's interrogation tactics on Miller, the majority attempts to place itself in Miller's position and thereby evaluate the impact of Boyce's promises and lies. Unfortunately, we cannot know what effects those promises and lies had on Miller's will. Instead what we can know is that when, as in this case, the record reveals a series of repeated promises of psychological help and assurances that the suspect will not be punished, *Bram* requires as a matter of law that we hold the resulting confession to be coerced. Any other rule leads to the kind of subjective speculation that the majority engages in. Thus applying the Bram rule within the totality of the circumstances of Miller's interrogation, the confession used to commit Miller must be declared inadmissible as a violation of Miller's fifth amendment right to remain silent."

Notes and Questions

1. *Should "police trickery" in obtaining confessions be barred? What is "trickery" in the confession context?* Consider Note, 40 Stan.L.Rev. 1593, 1594–95 (1988): "The courts have not clearly defined the term 'trickery' and 'trickery' has been used interchangeably with 'misrepresentation,' 'artifice,' 'deception,' 'fraud,' and 'subterfuge.' This note argues that the term trickery, when used in the confessions context, should be defined as police elicitation of a confession by deliberate distortion of material fact, by failure to disclose to the defendant a material fact, or by playing on a defendant's emotions or scruples. Police trickery should be viewed as a type of fraud, the use of which as an interrogation tool is inconsistent with our adversarial system of criminal justice because it allows the prosecution an unfair, indeed an unconstitutional, advantage at trial."

2. *The relationship between Miller and Detective Boyce.* At one point the Miller majority observes that Boyce's statements to Miller that he is "not a criminal" who should be punished, and "not responsible" for anything he might have done "need not be understood as assurances of leniency" but could be viewed as the expression of sympathy by "a friend"—"a means of convincing Miller that Boyce [personally] was sympathetic, no matter what the state's reaction might be." At another point, however, the majority opinion observes that Miller's responses indicated "he knew that this was an ordinary police interrogation, rather than an encounter with a compassionate friend." Which is it?

To avoid the prohibition against obtaining confessions by promises of leniency, one might say, as the majority does at one point, that Boyce's "interrogation strategy was to present himself as a friend to whom Miller would unburden," and that, as the majority suggests at several places, the detective's strategy succeeded. If so, however, doesn't this raise another problem? If Boyce led Miller to believe he was a sympathetic friend didn't Boyce cause Miller to forget that his questioner was in an adversarial role and thus negate the effect of the Miranda warnings?

3. *Drawing a line between expressions of sympathy and implied promises of leniency.* Compare the Stanford Note with Phillip Johnson, *A Statutory Replacement for the Miranda Doctrine*, 24 Am.Crim.L.Rev. 303, 305 (1987), proposing that the police be forbidden to make "any statement which is intended to imply or may reasonably be understood as implying that the suspect will not be prosecuted or punished," but approving police expressions of sympathy and compassion, whether real or feigned; police appeals to the suspect's conscience, religious or otherwise; and police appeals to the suspect's sympathy for the victim or other affected persons.

Observes Professor Johnson, id. at 310–11: "Offers of leniency can be made later in the plea bargaining process, where the accused is represented by counsel and can properly evaluate what is being offered. Promises of leniency from the police during interrogation are too likely to be deceptive, and too likely to give even an innocent suspect the impression that confession is the only way to escape conviction or mitigate the punishment. [However, police expressions of sympathy and compassion should be permitted because] a pose of sympathy is not overbearing or coercive, nor is it likely by itself to encourage an innocent person to provide a confession. A difficulty in this area is that the difference between expressions of compassionate understanding on the one hand, and implied promises of leniency on the other, is at the margin sometimes a matter of emphasis and nuance." Did Detective Boyce cross the line in the Miller case? See id. at 311.

4. *How should the law respond to empirical data indicating that the interrogation tactics of threatening harsh punishment if the suspect does not confess and/or significant leniency if he does are likely to induce false confessions?* According to studies of the interrogation process and of sixty known and probable false confession cases by Professors Richard J. Ofshe and Richard A. Leo, see *The Consequences of False Confessions*, 88 J.Crim.L. & C. 429 (1998) and *The Social Psychology of Police Interrogation*, 16 Studies in Law, Politics & Society 189 (1997), threatening a suspect with harsh punishment if he does not confess and/or promising him leniency if he does are "coercive" police interrogation tactics likely to induce false confessions. What follows from this? See Welsh S. White, *What Is a Voluntary Confession* Now?, 50 Rutgers L.Rev. 2001, 2052–53 (1998). After discussing *Leyra v. Denno* (1954) (p. 443) and *Lynumn v. Illinois* (1963) (p. 442), two pre-Miranda "voluntariness" cases "which suggest that interrogation tactics that threaten the suspect with harsh punishments if she does not confess or offer express or implied promises of significant sentencing advantages if she does may exert such unfair pressure on the suspect as to render the resulting confession involuntary," Profess White comments: "[T]he Court could establish the rule that interrogation tactics that threaten harsh consequences if the suspect does not confess or suggest that she will receive significant leniency in terms of disposition [citing Miller v. Fenton] or sentence if she does will generally be sufficient to render a resulting confession involuntary."

5. *Distinguishing among different kinds of trickery.* The Ofshe–Leo studies, supra Note 4, indicate that in certain situations the tactic of misrepresenting evidence of the suspect's guilt is likely to produce an untrustworthy confession and that "false evidence ploys based on scientific procedures" are more likely to produce a false confession than similar ploys based on eyewitness reports. Professor White, supra Note 4, at 2055, believes that the Leo–Ofshe data "provide a clear basis for distinguishing among different kinds of trickery. Based on [this data], a court applying the Due Process test could properly hold that certain types of misrepresentation should be strongly condemned and perhaps sufficient in themselves to render a resulting confession involuntary. Specifically, misrepresentations designed to convince the suspect that his guilt has been established by either forensic evidence or his failure to pass a lie detector test should be prohibited, or at least viewed as likely to render a resulting confession involuntary."

6. *More on false verbal assertions by the police vs. the fabrication of scientific evidence.* Interestingly, long before the Leo–Ofshe empirical studies had been published, one lower court drew a line between police deception generally (which does not render a confession involuntary per se) and the "manufacturing" of false documents or scientific evidence by the police (which "has no place in our criminal justice system"). *State v. Cayward*, 552 So.2d 971 (Fla.App.1989). The case arose as follows: The police suspected defendant of sexually assaulting and killing his five-year-old niece. They intentionally fabricated laboratory reports indicating that a scientific test established that the semen stains on the victim's underwear came from defendant and showed the reports to him. He confessed soon after. In upholding the trial court's suppression of the confession, the District Court of Appeal of Florida observed:

"We think [that] both the suspect's and the public's expectations concerning the built-in adversariness of police interrogations do not encompass the notion that the police will knowingly fabricate tangible documentation or physical evidence against an individual. [The] manufacturing of false documents by police officials offends our traditional notions of due process. [Moreover,] manufactured documents have the potential of indefinite life and the facial appearance of authenticity." Thus, they "might be disclosed to the media as a result of the public records law" or find their way into the courtroom.

Is there, as the Florida court believed, an "intrinsic" or "qualitative" difference between police lying, e.g., the false assertion that the suspect's fingerprints were found at the scene of the crime, and manufactured evidence? If, as the Florida court maintained, sanctioning police fabrication of documents "would greatly lessen the respect the public has for the criminal justice system and for those sworn to uphold and enforce the law," doesn't this concern apply to false verbal assertions by police interrogators as well? See Jerome H. Skolnick and Richard A. Leo, *The Ethics of Deceptive Interrogation*, Crim.Justice Ethics, Winter/Spring 1992, pp. 3, 7–9.

    7. *Offering to protect a prisoner from physical harm at the hands of other inmates.* Consider ARIZONA v. FULMINANTE, 499 U.S. 279, 111 S.Ct. 1246, 113 L.Ed.2d 302 (1991) (other aspects of which are discussed in Ch. 27). The case arose as follows: After defendant Fulminante's 11–year-old stepdaughter, Jeneane, was murdered, he was convicted of an unrelated federal crime and incarcerated in a federal prison. There he was befriended by another inmate, Sarivola, who was a paid informant for the FBI masquerading as an organized crime figure. Upon hearing a rumor that defendant had killed his stepdaughter, Sarivola brought up the subject several times, but defendant repeatedly denied any involvement in the murder. Then Sarivola told defendant that he knew he was "starting to get some tough treatment" from other inmates because of the rumor that he had killed his stepdaughter but that he, Sarivola, would protect defendant from his fellow inmates if he told him the truth about the murder. Defendant then confessed to Sarivola that he had sexually molested and killed Jeneane. The confession was admitted at defendant's trial and he was convicted of murder and sentenced to death. On appeal, the state supreme court held that the confession was coerced. Although it considered the question "a close one," a 5–4 majority of the Supreme Court, per WHITE, J., agreed with the state supreme court:

    "In applying the totality of the circumstances test to determine that the confession to Sarivola was coerced, the Arizona Supreme Court focused on a number of relevant facts. First, the court noted that 'because [Fulminante] was an alleged child murderer, he was in physical harm at the hands of other inmates.' In addition, Sarivola was aware that Fulminante was receiving 'rough treatment from the guys.' Using his knowledge of these threats, Sarivola offered to protect Fulminante in exchange for a confession to Jeneane's murder and 'in response to Sarivola's offer of protection [Fulminante] confessed.' Agreeing with Fulminante that 'Sarivola's promise was "extremely coercive,"' the Arizona Court declared: '[T]he confession was obtained as a direct result of extreme coercion and was tendered in the belief that the defendant's life was in jeopardy if he did not confess. * * *'

    "We normally give great deference to the factual findings of the state court. Nevertheless, 'the ultimate issue of "voluntariness" is a legal question requiring independent federal determination.' Although the question is a close one, we agree [that] Fulminante's confession was coerced. The Arizona Supreme Court found a credible threat of physical violence unless Fulminante confessed. [A] finding of coercion need not depend upon actual violence by a government agent; a credible threat is sufficient. [As] in *Payne v. Arkansas*, 356 U.S. 560, 78 S.Ct. 844, 2 L.Ed.2d 975 (1958)], where the Court found that a confession was coerced because the interrogating police officer had promised that if the accused confessed, the officer would protect the accused from an angry mob outside the jailhouse door, so too here, the Arizona Supreme Court found that it was fear of physical violence, absent protection from his friend (and Government agent) Sarivola, which motivated Fulminante to confess. Accepting the Arizona court's finding, permissible on this record, that there was a credible threat of physical violence, we agree that Fulminante's will was overborne in such a way as to render his confession the product of coercion."

Dissenting on this issue, REHNQUIST, C.J., joined by O'Connor, Kennedy and Souter, JJ., was "at a loss to see how the Supreme Court of Arizona reached the conclusion that it did":

"Fulminante offered no evidence that he believed his life was in danger or that he in fact confessed to Sarivola in order to obtain the proffered protection. Indeed, he had stipulated that '[a]t no time did the defendant indicate he was in fear of other inmates nor did he ever seek Mr. Sarivola's "protection." ' Sarivola's testimony that he told Fulminante that 'if [he] would tell the truth, he could be protected,' adds little if anything to the substance of the parties' stipulation. The decision of the Supreme Court of Arizona rests on an assumption that is squarely contrary to this stipulation, and one that is not supported by any testimony of Fulminante.

"The facts of record in the present case are quite different from those present in cases where we have found confessions to be coerced and involuntary. Since Fulminante was unaware that Sarivola was an FBI informant, there existed none of 'the danger of coercion result[ing] from the interaction of custody and official interrogation.' *Illinois v. Perkins* [p. 505]. [The] conversations between Sarivola and Fulminante were not lengthy, and the defendant was free at all times to leave Sarivola's company. Sarivola at no time threatened him or demanded that he confess; he simply requested that he speak the truth about the matter. Fulminante was an experienced habitue of prisons, and presumably able to fend for himself. In concluding on these facts that Fulminante's confession was involuntary, the Court today embraces a more expansive definition of that term than is warranted by any of our decided cases."

B. Colorado v. Connelly: Did the Court Decline to Expand the "Voluntariness" Test or Did it Revise the Test Significantly?

In COLORADO v. CONNELLY, 479 U.S. 157, 107 S.Ct. 515, 93 L.Ed.2d 473 (1986) (also discussed at p. 440, fns. b and c), the Court held, per REHNQUIST, C.J., that "coercive police activity is a necessary predicate to the finding that a confession is not 'voluntary' within the meaning of the Due Process Clause"; "[a]bsent police conduct causally related to the confession, there is simply no basis for concluding that any state action has deprived a criminal defendant of due process of law." The case arose as follows:

Respondent, a mentally ill person flew from Boston to Denver, approached a uniformed police officer on a downtown Denver street and, without any prompting, told the officer that "he had killed someone" and wanted to talk to the officer about it. Respondent was then handcuffed and informed of his Miranda rights. After stating that he understood his rights, respondent elaborated further on the initial statement. A homicide detective soon arrived on the scene. He readvised respondent of his rights, and asked him "what he had on his mind." Respondent then stated that he had come all the way from Boston because he wanted to confess to murdering a young girl, a crime he had committed in Denver nine months earlier. He then gave the detective the name of the victim. Next, respondent was taken to police headquarters, where records revealed that an unidentified female body had been discovered in the area respondent described. Connelly then made more incriminating statements and took the police to the place where he said the murder had occurred.

Respondent was initially found incompetent to stand trial. But he achieved competency after six months of hospitalization and treatment with antipsychotic and sedative medication. A psychiatrist, previously appointed to conduct a competency examination of respondent, testified for the defense that Connelly's statements to the police had resulted from "command auditory hallucinations," a symptom of his mental disorder. The "voice of God" had told Connelly to return to Denver to confess his crime. When he returned, the same voice became stronger and told him either to confess to the killing or to commit suicide. At that point, reluctantly following the voice's command, Connelly approached the first officer he could find and confessed. Because people suffering from command hallucinations feel they must do whatever the voice tells them, the psychiatrist was of the opinion that Connelly was unable to make a free and intelligent decision about whether to speak with, and to confess to, the police.

The trial court suppressed Connelly's statements because they were "involuntary"; respondent had not exercised "free will" in choosing to speak to the police, but had been "compelled" by his illness to confess. In upholding the trial court on this issue, the Colorado Supreme Court observed that "[o]ne's capacity for rational judgment and free choice may be overborne as much by certain forms of severe illness as by external pressure." The U.S. Supreme Court reversed:

"[The confession cases] considered by this Court over the 50 years since Brown v. Mississippi have focused upon the crucial element of police overreaching. [A]ll have contained a substantial element of coercive police conduct. Absent police conduct causally related to the confession, there is simply no basis for concluding that any state actor has deprived a criminal defendant of due process of law. * * *

"Respondent relies on *Blackburn v. Alabama*, 361 U.S. 199, 80 S.Ct. 274, 4 L.Ed.2d 242 (1960), and *Townsend v. Sain* [discussed briefly at p. 440, fn. c, a case some commentators had read as barring the use of confessions obtained from a person whose volitional power is seriously impaired, whatever the reason]. But respondent's reading of *Blackburn* and *Townsend* ignores the integral element of police overreaching present in both cases. In Blackburn, the Court found that [defendant] was probably insane at the time of his confession and the police learned during the interrogation that he had a history of mental problems.

"The police exploited this weakness with coercive tactics [and these] tactics supported a finding that the confession was involuntary. * * * Townsend presented a similar instance of police wrongdoing. In that case, a police physician had given Townsend a drug with truth-serum properties. The subsequent confession, obtained by officers who knew that Townsend had been given drugs, was held involuntary. These two cases demonstrate that while mental condition is surely relevant to an individual's susceptibility to police coercion, mere examination of the confessant's state of mind can never conclude the due process inquiry.

"[The] difficulty with the approach of the Supreme Court of Colorado is that it fails to recognize the essential link between coercive activity of the State, on the one hand, and a resulting confession by a defendant, on the other. The flaw in respondent's constitutional argument is that it would expand our previous line of 'voluntariness' cases into a far-ranging requirement that courts must divine a defendant's motivation for speaking or acting as he did even though there be no claim that governmental conduct coerced his decision.

"The most outrageous behavior by a private party seeking to secure evidence against a defendant does not make that evidence inadmissible under the Due

Process Clause. * * * [S]uppressing respondent's statements would serve absolutely no purpose in enforcing constitutional guarantees. The purpose of excluding confessions seized in violation of the Constitution is to substantially deter future violations of the Constitution. Only if we were to establish a brand new constitutional right—the right of a criminal defendant to confess to his crime only when totally rational and properly motivated—could respondent's present claim be sustained.

"We have previously cautioned against expanding 'currently applicable exclusionary rules by erecting additional barriers to placing truthful and probative evidence before state juries * * *.' *Lego v. Twomey* (1972) [p. 809]. We abide by that counsel now. [Respondent] would now have us require sweeping inquiries into the state of mind of a criminal defendant who has confessed, inquiries quite divorced from any coercion brought to bear on the defendant by the State. We think the Constitution rightly leaves this sort of inquiry to be resolved by state laws governing the admission of evidence and erects no standard of its own in this area. A statement rendered by one in the condition of respondent might be proved to be quite unreliable, but this is a matter to be governed by the evidentiary laws of the forum and not by the Due Process Clause * * *."

Dissenting Justice BRENNAN, joined by Marshall, J., recalled that the Blackburn Court had observed: "Surely in the present stage of our civilization a most basic sense of justice is affronted by the spectacle of incarcerating a human being upon the basis of a statement he made while insane * * *." "[T]he use of a mentally ill person's involuntary confession," maintained Justice Brennan, "is antithetical to the notion of fundamental fairness embodied in the Due Process Clause." He argued that "[the] holding that involuntary confessions are only those procured through police misconduct [is] inconsistent with the Court's historical insistence that only confessions reflecting an exercise of free will be admitted into evidence" and that "[u]ntil today, we have never upheld the admission of a confession that does not reflect the exercise of free will."[a] He continued:

"Since the Court redefines voluntary confessions to include confessions by mentally ill individuals, the reliability of these confessions becomes a central concern. A concern for reliability is inherent in our criminal justice system, which relies upon accusatorial rather than inquisitorial practices. * * *

"Because the admission of a confession so strongly tips the balance against the defendant in the adversarial process, we must be especially careful about a confession's reliability. We have to date not required a finding of reliability for involuntary confessions only because all such confessions have been excluded upon a finding of involuntariness, regardless of reliability. The Court's adoption today of a restrictive definition of an 'involuntary' confession will require heightened scrutiny of a confessions' reliability.

"The instant case starkly highlights the danger of admitting a confession by a person with a severe mental illness. The trial court made no findings concerning

---

a. The dissenters took sharp exception to the majority's reading of *Townsend* : "[Although the majority maintains that the confession in that case was obtained by officers who knew that a police doctor had given defendant a drug with truth-serum properties], in fact [as the *Townsend* Court pointed out], 'the police * * * did not know what [medications] the doctor had given [the defendant].' And the *Townsend* Court expressly states that police wrongdoing was not an essential factor:

" 'It is not significant that the drug may have been administered and the questions asked by persons unfamiliar with [the drug's] properties as a" truth serum," if these properties exist. Any questioning by police officers which *in fact* produces a confession which is not the product of a free intellect renders that confession inadmissible. The Court has usually so stated the test.' (Emphasis in original.)"

the reliability of Mr. Connelly's involuntary confession, since it believed that the confession was excludable on the basis of involuntariness. However, the overwhelming evidence in the record points to the unreliability of Mr. Connelly's delusional mind. * * *

"Moreover, the record is barren of any corroboration of the mentally ill defendant's confession. No physical evidence links the defendant to the alleged crime. Police did not identify the alleged victim's body as the woman named by the defendant. Mr. Connelly identified the alleged scene of the crime, but it has not been verified that the unidentified body was found there or that a crime actually occurred there. There is not a shred of competent evidence in this record linking the defendant to the charged homicide. There is only Mr. Connelly's confession.

"Minimum standards of due process should require that the trial court find substantial indicia of reliability, on the basis of evidence extrinsic to the confession itself, before admitting the confession of a mentally ill person into evidence. I would require the trial court to make such a finding on remand. To hold otherwise allows the State to imprison and possibly to execute a mentally ill defendant based solely upon an inherently unreliable confession."

Notes and Questions

1. ***Is "the (exclusionary) tail wagging the (due process) dog"?*** Consider Laurence Benner, *Requiem for Miranda: The Rehnquist Court's Voluntariness Doctrine in Historical Perspective*, 67 Wash.U.L.Q. 59, 136–37 (1989):

"[The *Connelly* Court] concluded that in the absence of coercive police misconduct 'suppressing [Connelly's] statements would serve absolutely no purpose in enforcing constitutional guarantees.' From this narrow premise, the Court then leaped to the broad conclusion that the use of Connelly's deranged statements as evidence against him did not violate the due process clause.

"But surely this is the (exclusionary) tail wagging the (due process) dog, for the upshot of the Court's position is that unless exclusion will deter someone in an official capacity, there can be no due process violation no matter how unjust the result. By allowing the deterrence rationale for the exclusionary rule to control the nature of the due process inquiry, the Court thus permits the logic of deterrence to shape the actual content of due process itself. Under this formula any concern for justice is excluded from the equation. Indeed, any attempt to develop a coherent theory of justice under the due process clause is precluded."

2. ***Confessions vs. guilty pleas.*** The *Connelly* Court balked at requiring "sweeping inquiries into the state of mind of a criminal defendant who has confessed, inquiries quite divorced from any [police] coercion brought to bear on the defendant." Would such inquiries be any more burdensome than constitutionally required inquiries into a defendant's competency to stand trial, to waive her right to counsel, or to be executed? See Benner, supra, at 137. Connelly, recalls Professor Benner, "was found incompetent to stand trial immediately following the making of his custodial confession. Does it not therefore appear incongruous that Connelly could not have pled guilty in open court, on the same day he sealed his fate with a confession obtained within the precincts of the Denver police headquarters?"

3. ***Should the admissibility of a confession turn on whether*** **in fact it** ***is the product of a "free will" or whether in fact it is voluntary?*** What is the Connelly dissenters' argument? That a confession by a mentally ill (or drugged) person is inherently unreliable or at least highly suspect? Or that the use of a mentally ill (or drugged) person's confession violates due process regardless of how impressively corroborated or otherwise reliable the confession turns out to be? Or both? If a confession is not the product of police overreaching and doubts about its reliability have been dispelled, why should it matter whether it was in fact involuntarily made?

(a) *Changing the facts of the Townsend case.* In *Townsend*, the defendant was suffering from severe heroin withdrawal symptoms. A police doctor was called in to treat this condition and injected the suspect with a drug that, unknown to the doctor or the police who subsequently questioned him (according to the record), had the properties of a "truth serum." About an hour later, defendant confessed.

Suppose that Townsend's sister had visited him in his cell and given him pills to relieve his suffering and that, unknown to her, these pills had the properties of a "truth serum." Suppose further that after taking these pills Townsend had told a guard that he wanted to confess and then had proceeded to do so. Would (should) such a confession be excluded? Why (not)?

Is the confession in the hypothetical *Townsend* case any more an exercise of "free will" or any less involuntary in fact than the confession in the actual Townsend case? If there is a distinction, is it that in the actual case the police doctor or the police who subsequently questioned Townsend were negligent? That even if the "truth serum" were not the result of police wrongdoing, it was still the result of their doing?

(b) *Changing the facts of the Connelly case.* Suppose that Connelly had never returned to Denver, but had phoned a Denver police officer from Boston and—with the "voice of God" ringing in his ears—had made a detailed confession over the phone. Or suppose Connelly had stayed in Boston and—with the "voice of God" doing the dictation—had written out a detailed confession and mailed it to the Denver police department. Would (should) such confessions be admissible? What would Justices Brennan and Marshall say? How, if at all, are the confessions in the hypotheticals different from the statements Connelly made in the actual case?

(c) A court should care whether a confession is the product of police wrongdoing or whether it is reliable, but why should it care whether it is voluntary or involuntary in fact? If a confession is neither the product of impermissible police methods nor untrustworthy (i.e. if doubts about its reliability have been removed), why should the confession's voluntariness be a relevant constitutional question?

(d) Was the question presented in *Connelly* whether the Court should adopt a new rule or whether it should rid itself of the terminology of the old one? Would *Connelly* have been an appropriate occasion to scrap the "voluntariness" terminology altogether and to consider directly the "complex of values" underlying, but long masked by, the rhetoric? See Albert W. Alschuler, *Constraint and Confession*, 74 Denv.U.L.Rev. 957, 959 (1997).

4. *Does the Connelly case mark the decline and fall of the "reliability" element?* As we have seen (pp. 439–43), the reliability of a confession does not necessarily make it admissible. But should the unreliability of a confession (or the absence of substantial indicia of reliability) render a confession inadmissible as a matter of federal constitutional law? Compare George Dix, *Federal Constitutional Confession Law: The 1986 and 1987 Supreme Court Terms*, 67 Tex.L.Rev. 231, 272–76 (1988) with Albert Alschuler, Note 3 (d) supra, at 959–60.

Professor Dix finds "the rejection of reliability as a relevant consideration in federal constitutional law" "the most surprising aspect" of *Connelly*. The opinion, comments Dix, "misleadingly represents that the Court's prior decisions definitively settled the matter, when in fact, until *Connelly*, reliability played an important role in traditional confession law analysis." Dix concludes that "at least in the absence of more thorough consideration than *Connelly* demonstrates, a total deconstitutionalization of traditionally important reliability issues is unjustified."

"Just as the Constitution does not mandate the exclusion of unreliable eyewitness testimony," maintains Professor Alschuler, "it does not mandate the exclusion of unreliable confessions. [The] Constitution requires the exclusion of unreliable eyewitness testimony only when improper governmental conduct—for example, an impermissibly suggestive police line-up—has produced it. The rule should be no different for unreliable confessions. Unless improper governmental conduct has generated a confession, the Constitution should give the defendant only a right to present evidence of the confession's unreliability to the jury."

5. *Confessions given by mentally handicapped suspects:* Consider Welsh S. White, *Miranda's Waning Protections* 202–03 (2001):

"In determining whether interrogation methods employed by the police exerted unfair or coercive pressure on the suspect, the voluntariness test should take into account the suspect's special vulnerabilities, weighing the extent to which these vulnerabilities might make the suspect prone to respond to interrogation methods by providing statements sought by the interrogator regardless of his or her initial belief in the truth of those statements. In applying this approach, moreover, weight should be given to the empirical evidence indicating that for mentally handicapped suspects, 'even the average level of stress built into an interrogation can be excessive and overbearing.'

"This approach is admittedly inconsistent with *Connelly*'s dictum intimating that an interrogated suspect's mental problems are constitutionally irrelevant unless the interrogating officer is or should be aware of them. [But] *Connelly*'s dictum is inconsistent with the Court's approach in pre-*Miranda* due process cases. Moreover, determining the legitimacy of an interrogation method on the basis of what an officer knew or should have known about the suspect's mental weaknesses is not administratively feasible. Interrogating officers could often plausibly assert that they were not in fact aware and had no reason to be aware of a suspect's particular weakness, such as mental retardation. Reviving the pre-*Miranda* due process test's approach of considering the individual characteristics of suspects subjected to interrogation is thus the only viable means of providing mentally handicapped suspects with protection from interrogation methods substantially likely to produce untrustworthy confessions."[a]

SECTION 5. *MASSIAH* REVISITED; *MASSIAH* AND *MIRANDA* COMPARED AND CONTRASTED

A. The Revivification of *Massiah*

"Until the Christian burial speech case [Brewer v. Williams, set forth below] * * * lasting fame had eluded *Massiah v. United States* [p. 448]. It was apparently lost in the shuffle of fast-moving events that reshaped constitutional-criminal procedure in the 1960s. [In] constitutional-criminal procedure circles, 1964 was the year of *Escobedo v. Illinois* [p. 450], and *Massiah* was understandably neglected in the hue and cry raised over the Illinois case. To the extent that *Massiah* was remembered at all, it was [only as a] stepping stone to *Escobedo* * * *.

"*Escobedo* may have seized the spotlight from *Massiah*, but *Esobedo* was soon shoved offstage by that blockbuster, *Miranda*, [a case that] '[did] not [enlarge]

a. Consider, too, the extracts from the Cloud empirical study, Note 23, p. 548.

Escobedo as much as [it] displaced it.' Assuming that *Escobedo* had not already done so, did *Miranda* also displace *Massiah*? After *Miranda*, was the institution of judicial proceedings, by way of indictment or otherwise, no more constitutionally relevant than whether the investigation had 'begun to focus on a particular suspect?' [If] one searches the *Miranda* opinion for answers to these questions, [one] discovers that *Massiah* is never mentioned—not once in Chief Justice Warren's sixty-page opinion for the Court, nor in any of the three dissenting opinions, which total another forty-six pages. Yet very little else even remotely bearing on the general subject is left out."

—Kamisar, *Police Interrogation and Confessions* 160–64 (1980).

———————

BREWER v. WILLIAMS (WILLIAMS I)
430 U.S. 387, 97 S.Ct. 1232, 51 L.Ed.2d 424 (1977).

Justice STEWART delivered the opinion of the Court. * * *

On the afternoon of December 24, 1968, a 10–year-old girl named Pamela Powers went with her family to the YMCA in Des Moines, Iowa. [When] she failed to return from a trip to the washroom, a search for her began. The search was unsuccessful.

Robert Williams, who had recently escaped from a mental hospital, was a resident of the YMCA. Soon after the girl's disappearance Williams was seen in the YMCA lobby carrying some clothing and a large bundle wrapped in a blanket. He obtained help from a 14–year-old boy in opening the street door of the YMCA and the door to his automobile parked outside. When Williams placed the bundle in the front seat of his car the boy "saw two legs in it and they were skinny and white." Before anyone could see what was in the bundle Williams drove away. His abandoned car was found the following day in Davenport, Iowa, roughly 160 miles east of Des Moines. A warrant was then issued in Des Moines for his arrest on a charge of abduction.

On the morning of December 26, a Des Moines lawyer named Henry McKnight went to the Des Moines police station and informed the officers present that he had just received a long distance call from Williams, and that he had advised Williams to turn himself in to the Davenport police. Williams did surrender that morning to the police in Davenport, and they booked him on the charge specified in the arrest warrant and gave him the [Miranda warnings]. The Davenport police then telephoned their counterparts in Des Moines to inform them that Williams had surrendered. McKnight, the lawyer, was still at the Des Moines police headquarters, and Williams conversed with McKnight on the telephone. In the presence of the Des Moines Chief of Police and a Police Detective named Leaming [a captain and 20–year veteran of the Des Moines police department], McKnight advised Williams that Des Moines police officers would be driving to Davenport to pick him up, that the officers would not interrogate him or mistreat him, and that Williams was not to talk to the officers about Pamela Powers until after consulting with McKnight upon his return to Des Moines. As a result of these conversations, it was agreed between McKnight and the Des Moines police officials that Detective Leaming and a fellow officer would drive to Davenport to pick up Williams, that they would bring him directly back to Des Moines, and that they would not question him during the trip.

In the meantime Williams was arraigned before a judge in Davenport on the outstanding arrest warrant.[a] The judge advised him of his Miranda rights and committed him to jail. Before leaving the courtroom, Williams conferred with a lawyer named Kelly, who advised him not to make any statements until consulting with McKnight back in Des Moines.

Detective Leaming and his fellow officer arrived in Davenport about noon to pick up Williams and return him to Des Moines. Soon after their arrival they met with Williams and Kelly, who, they understood, was acting as Williams' lawyer. Detective Leaming repeated the Miranda warnings, and told Williams:

"* * * we both know that you're being represented here by Mr. Kelly and you're being represented by Mr. McKnight in Des Moines, [and] I want you to remember this because we'll be visiting between here and Des Moines."

Williams then conferred again with Kelly alone, and after this conference Kelly reiterated to Detective Leaming that Williams was not to be questioned about the disappearance of Pamela Powers until after he had consulted with McKnight back in Des Moines. When Leaming expressed some reservations, Kelly firmly stated that the agreement with McKnight was to be carried out—that there was to be no interrogation of Williams during the automobile journey to Des Moines. Kelly was denied permission to ride in the police car back to Des Moines with Williams and the two officers.

The two Detectives, with Williams in their charge, then set out on the 160–mile drive. At no time during the trip did Williams express a willingness to be interrogated in the absence of an attorney. Instead, he stated several times that "[w]hen I get to Des Moines and see Mr. McKnight, I am going to tell you the whole story." Detective Leaming knew that Williams was a former mental patient, and knew also that he was deeply religious.

The Detective and his prisoner soon embarked on a wide-ranging conversation covering a variety of topics, including the subject of religion. Then, not long after leaving Davenport and reaching the interstate highway, Detective Leaming delivered what has been referred to [as] the "Christian burial speech." Addressing Williams as "Reverend," the Detective said:

"I want to give you something to think about while we're traveling down the road. * * * Number one, I want you to observe the weather conditions, it's raining, it's sleeting, it's freezing, driving is very treacherous, visibility is poor, it's going to be dark early this evening. They are predicting several inches of snow for tonight, and I feel that you yourself are the only person that knows where this little girl's body is, that you yourself have only been there once, and if you get a snow on top of it you yourself may be unable to find it. And, since we will be going right past the area on the way into Des Moines, I feel that we could stop and locate the body, that the parents of this little girl should be entitled to a Christian burial for the little girl who was snatched away from them on Christmas Eve and murdered. And I feel we should stop and locate it on the way in rather than waiting until morning and trying to come back out after a snow storm and possibly not being able to find it at all."[b]

---

a. At the time *Williams* was decided, it did not seem to matter that the defendant was arraigned on the charge of abduction, not the charge of murder that grew out of the abduction. Evidently the Court assumed that when the Sixth Amendment right to counsel attached to the abduction charge it attached to the factually related crime of murder as well. But see *Texas v. Cobb*, p. 611.

b. Although no member of the Supreme Court discussed, or even noted, this point, Cap-

tain Leaming offered two different versions of the "Christian burial speech." The captain's first version was given at a pretrial hearing to suppress evidence; his second version, the only one quoted and discussed by the Supreme Court and lower federal courts, was given four weeks later at the trial. See Kamisar, *Foreword: Brewer v. Williams—A Hard Look at a Discomfiting Record*, 66 Geo.L.J. 209, 215–18 (1977). For the view that these two versions are significantly different, see id. at 218–33.

Williams asked Detective Leaming why he thought their route to Des Moines would be taking them past the girl's body, and Leaming responded that he knew the body [was near] Mitchellville—a town they would be passing on the way to Des Moines.[1] Leaming then stated: "I do not want you to answer me. I don't want to discuss it further. Just think about it as we're riding down the road."

As the car approached Grinell, a town approximately 100 miles west of Davenport, Williams asked whether the police had found the victim's shoes. When Detective Leaming replied that he was unsure, Williams directed the officers to a service station where he said he had left the shoes; a search for them proved unsuccessful. As they continued towards Des Moines, Williams asked whether the police had found the blanket, and directed the officers to a rest area where he said he had disposed of the blanket. Nothing was found. The car continued towards Des Moines, and as it approached Mitchellville, Williams said that he would show the officers where the body was. He then directed the police to the body of Pamela Powers.

[The trial judge admitted all evidence relating to or resulting from statements Williams made in the car ride. He found that "an agreement" had been made between defense counsel and the police that Williams would not be questioned on the return trip to Des Moines, but ruled that Williams had waived his rights before giving such information. Williams was convicted of murder. The Iowa Supreme Court affirmed. On federal habeas, the District Court concluded that] the evidence in question had been wrongly admitted at Williams' trial. This conclusion was based on three alternative and independent grounds: (1) that Williams had been denied his constitutional right to the assistance of counsel; (2) that he had been denied [his Miranda rights]; and (3) that in any event, [his] statements [had] been involuntarily made. [The] Court of Appeals appears to have affirmed the judgment on [the first two] grounds. We have concluded that only one of them need be considered here.

Specifically, there is no need to review the [*Miranda* doctrine] [or the] ruling [that] Williams' self-incriminating statements [were] involuntarily made. For it is clear that the judgment before us must in any event be affirmed upon the ground that Williams was deprived of a different constitutional right—the right to the assistance of counsel. * * * Whatever else it may mean, the right to counsel * * * means at least that a person is entitled to the help of a lawyer at or after the time that judicial proceedings have been initiated against him—"whether by way of formal charge, preliminary hearing, indictment, information, or arraignment." *Kirby v. Illinois* [p. 631].

There can be no doubt in the present case that judicial proceedings had been initiated against Williams before the start of the automobile ride from Davenport to Des Moines. A warrant had been issued for his arrest, he had been arraigned on that warrant before a judge in a Davenport courtroom, and he had been committed by the court to confinement in jail. The State does not contend otherwise.

There can be no serious doubt, either, that Detective Leaming deliberately and designedly set out to elicit information from Williams just as surely as—and

Justice Stewart notes that the captain addressed Williams as "Reverend," and then gives the captain's *second* version of the speech and related testimony *in its entirety*. But Captain Leaming did not testify that he addressed Williams as "Reverend" in the second version, only in the first. Justice Stewart may have called attention to the "Reverend" address because the Attorney General of Iowa was suffi-

ciently troubled by it to go outside the record to explain in his brief why Captain Leaming employed it. See Kamisar, supra, at 223. For a discussion of the significance of the "'Reverend' ploy," see id. at 221–23.

1. The fact of the matter, of course, was that Detective Leaming possessed no such knowledge.

perhaps more effectively than—if he had formally interrogated him. Detective Leaming was fully aware before departing for Des Moines that Williams was being represented in Davenport by Kelly and in Des Moines by McKnight. Yet he purposely sought during Williams' isolation from his lawyers to obtain as much incriminating information as possible. Indeed, Detective Leaming conceded as much when he testified at Williams' trial:

> "Q. In fact, Captain, whether he was a mental patient or not, you were trying to get all the information you could before he got to his lawyer, weren't you?

> "A. I was sure hoping to find out where that little girl was, yes, sir.

> "Q. Well, I'll put it this way: You [were] hoping to get all the information you could before Williams got back to McKnight, weren't you?

> "A. Yes, sir."[6]

The state courts clearly proceeded upon the hypothesis that Detective Leaming's "Christian burial speech" had been tantamount to interrogation. Both courts recognized that Williams had been entitled to the assistance of counsel at the time he made the incriminating statements. Yet no such constitutional protection would have come into play if there had been no interrogation.

The circumstances of this case are thus constitutionally indistinguishable from those presented in *Massiah*. [That] the incriminating statements were elicited surreptitiously in [*Massiah*], and otherwise here, is constitutionally irrelevant. Rather, the clear rule of *Massiah* is that once adversary proceedings have commenced against an individual, he has a right to legal representation when the government interrogates him.[c] It thus requires no wooden or technical application of the *Massiah* doctrine to conclude that Williams was entitled to the assistance of counsel guaranteed to him by the Sixth and Fourteenth Amendments.

The Iowa courts recognized that Williams had been denied the constitutional right to the assistance of counsel. They held, however, that he had waived that right during the course of the automobile trip from Davenport to Des Moines.

[It] was incumbent upon the State to prove "an intentional relinquishment or abandonment of a known right or privilege." *Johnson v. Zerbst*. [That] strict standard applies equally to an alleged waiver of the right to counsel whether at trial or at a critical stage of pretrial proceedings. [Judged by that standard,] the record in this case falls far short of sustaining the State's burden. It is true that Williams had been informed of and appeared to understand his right to counsel. But waiver requires not merely comprehension but relinquishment, and Williams' consistent reliance upon the advice of counsel in dealing with the authorities refutes any suggestion that he waived that right. [His] statements while in the car that he would tell the whole story after seeing McKnight in Des Moines were the clearest expressions [that] he desired the presence of an attorney before any interrogation took place. But even before making these statements, Williams had effectively asserted his right to counsel by having secured attorneys at both ends of the automobile trip, both of whom, acting as his agents, had made clear to the police that no interrogation was to occur during the journey. Williams knew of

---

6. Counsel for the State, in the course of oral argument in this Court, acknowledged that the "Christian burial speech" was tantamount to interrogation * * *.

c. Isn't the clear rule of *Massiah* that once adversary proceedings have commenced against an individual, he has a right to counsel when the government *deliberately elicits* incriminating information from him (whether or not the government's efforts to obtain information constitute "interrogation" within the meaning of *Miranda*'s Fifth Amendment rights)? Did Justice Stewart, in effect, correct himself three years later in fn. 4 to his opinion in *Rhode Island v. Innis* (p. 497)?

that agreement and, particularly in view of his consistent reliance on counsel, there is no basis for concluding that he disavowed it.

Despite Williams' express and implicit assertions of his right to counsel, Detective Leaming proceeded to elicit incriminating statements from Williams. Leaming did not preface this effort by telling Williams that he had a right to the presence of a lawyer, and made no effort at all to ascertain whether Williams wished to relinquish that right. The circumstances of record in this case thus provide no reasonable basis for finding that Williams waived his right to the assistance of counsel.

The Court of Appeals did not hold, nor do we, that under the circumstances of this case Williams could not, without notice to counsel, have waived his rights under the Sixth and Fourteenth Amendments. It only held, as do we, that he did not.

* * * Although we do not lightly affirm the issuance of a writ of habeas corpus in this case, so clear a violation of the Sixth and Fourteenth Amendments as here occurred cannot be condoned.

[The] judgment of the Court of Appeals is affirmed.[12]

Justice MARSHALL, concurring.

I concur wholeheartedly in my Brother Stewart's opinion for the Court, but add these words in light of the dissenting opinions filed today. The dissenters have, I believe, lost sight of the fundamental constitutional backbone of our criminal law. They seem to think that Detective Leaming's actions were perfectly proper, indeed laudable, examples of "good police work." In my view, good police work is something far different from catching the criminal at any price. It is equally important that the police, as guardians of the law, fulfill their responsibility to obey its commands scrupulously.

[In] this case, there can be no doubt that Detective Leaming consciously and knowingly set out to violate Williams' Sixth Amendment right to counsel and his Fifth Amendment privilege against self-incrimination, as Leaming himself understood those rights. * * * Leaming surely understood, because he had overheard McKnight tell Williams as much, that the location of the body would be revealed to police. Undoubtedly Leaming realized the way in which that information would be conveyed to the police: McKnight would learn it from his client and then he would lead police to the body. Williams would thereby be protected by the attorney-client privilege from incriminating himself by directly demonstrating his knowledge of the body's location, and the unfortunate Powers child could be given a "Christian burial."

[If] Williams is to go free—and given the ingenuity of Iowa prosecutors on retrial or in a civil commitment proceeding, I doubt very much that there is any chance a dangerous criminal will be loosed on the streets, the blood-curdling cries

---

12. The District Court stated that its decision "does not touch upon the issue of what evidence, if any, beyond the incriminating statements themselves must be excluded as 'fruit of the poisonous tree.' " We too have no occasion to address this issue, and in the present posture of the case there is no basis for the view of our dissenting Brethren [that] any attempt to retry the respondent would probably be futile. While neither Williams' incriminating statements themselves nor any testimony describing his having led the police to the victim's body can constitutionally be admitted into evidence, evidence of where the body was found and of its condition might well be admissible on the theory that the body would have been discovered in any event, even had incriminating statements not been elicited from Williams. In the event that a retrial is instituted, it will be for the state courts in the first instance to determine whether particular items of evidence may be admitted.

[On retrial, the state court ruled that the body of Pamela Powers "would have been found in any event" and Williams was again convicted of murder. The U.S. Supreme Court upheld the state court's use of the "inevitable discovery" exception. See *Williams II*, p. 775.]

of the dissents notwithstanding—it will hardly be because he deserves it. It will be because [Leaming] intentionally denied Williams the right of every American under the Sixth Amendment to have the protective shield of a lawyer between himself and the awesome power of the State. * * *

Justice POWELL, concurring. * * *

[The] dissent of the Chief Justice concludes that prior to [making his incriminating statements], Williams had "made a valid waiver" of his right to have counsel present. This view disregards the record evidence clearly indicating that the police engaged in interrogation of Williams. [The Chief Justice also maintains] that the Court's holding today "conclusively presumes a suspect is legally incompetent to change his mind and tell the truth until an attorney is present." I find no justification for this view. On the contrary, the opinion of the Court is explicitly clear that the right to assistance of counsel may be waived, after it has attached, without notice to or consultation with counsel. We would have such a case here if the State had proved that the police officers refrained from coercion and interrogation, as they had agreed, and that Williams freely on his own initiative had confessed the crime. * * *[d]

Chief Justice BURGER, dissenting.   _Dissent_

The result in this case ought to be intolerable in any society which purports to call itself an organized society. It continues the Court—by the narrowest margin—on the much-criticized course of punishing the public for the mistakes and misdeeds of law enforcement officers, instead of punishing the officer directly, if in fact he is guilty of wrongdoing. It mechanically and blindly keeps reliable evidence from juries whether the claimed constitutional violation involves gross police misconduct or honest human error.

Williams is guilty of the savage murder of a small child; no member of the Court contends he is not. While in custody, and after no fewer than five warnings [_had_] of his rights to silence and to counsel, he led police to the concealed body of his victim. The Court concedes Williams was not threatened or coerced and that he [_5 warnings_] spoke and acted voluntarily and with full awareness of his constitutional rights. In the face of all this, the Court now holds that because Williams was prompted by the detective's statement—not interrogation but a statement—the jury must not be told how the police found the body.

[The] evidence is uncontradicted that Williams had abundant knowledge of his right to have counsel present and of his right to silence. Since the Court does not question his mental competence, it boggles the mind to suggest that Williams could not understand that leading police to the child's body would have other than the most serious consequences. * * *

One plausible but unarticulated basis for the result reached is that once a suspect has asserted his right not to talk without the presence of an attorney, it becomes legally impossible for him to waive that right until he has seen an attorney. But constitutional rights are personal, and an otherwise valid waiver should not be brushed aside by judges simply because an attorney was not present.

[Even] if there was no waiver, and assuming a technical violation occurred, the Court errs gravely in mechanically applying the exclusionary rule without considering whether that draconian judicial doctrine should be invoked in these

d. Stevens, J., joined the opinion of the Court, but also added a brief comment concluding: "If, in the long run, we are seriously concerned about the individual's effective representation by counsel, the State cannot be permitted to dishonor its promise to this lawyer."

circumstances, or indeed whether any of its conceivable goals will be furthered by its application here.

* * * Today's holding interrupts what has been a more rational perception of the constitutional and social utility of excluding reliable evidence from the truth-seeking process. In its Fourth Amendment context, we have now recognized that the exclusionary rule is in no sense a personal constitutional right, but a judicially conceived remedial device designed to safeguard and effectuate guaranteed legal rights generally [referring to *Stone v. Powell*, p. 116; *United States v. Janis*, p. 134; and *United States v. Calandra*, p. 131]. We have repeatedly emphasized that deterrence of unconstitutional or otherwise unlawful police conduct is the only valid justification for excluding reliable and probative evidence from the criminal factfinding process.

Accordingly, unlawfully obtained evidence is not automatically excluded from the factfinding process in all circumstances. In a variety of contexts we inquire whether application of the rule will promote its objectives sufficiently to justify the enormous cost it imposes on society. * * *

Against this background, it is striking that the Court fails even to consider whether the benefits secured by application of the exclusionary rule in this case outweigh its obvious social costs. Perhaps the failure is due to the fact that this case arises not under the Fourth Amendment, but under *Miranda*, and the Sixth Amendment right to counsel. The Court apparently perceives the function of the exclusionary rule to be so different in these varying contexts that it must be mechanically and uncritically applied in all cases arising outside the Fourth Amendment. * * *

Justice WHITE, with whom Justice BLACKMUN and Justice REHNQUIST join, dissenting.

[The] issue in this case is whether respondent—who was entitled not to make any statements to the police without consultation with and/or presence of counsel[1] —validly waived those rights.

[I disagree with the majority's finding that no waiver was proved in this case.] That respondent knew of his right not to say anything to the officers without advice and presence of counsel is established on this record to a moral certainty. He was advised of the right by three officials of the State—telling at least one that he understood the right—and by two lawyers.[4] Finally, he further demonstrated his knowledge of the right by informing the police that he would tell them the story in the presence of McKnight when they arrived in Des Moines. The issue in this case, then, is whether respondent relinquished that right intentionally.

Respondent relinquished his right not to talk to the police about his crime when the car approached the place where he had hidden the victim's clothes. Men usually intend to do what they do and there is nothing in the record to support the proposition that respondent's decision to talk was anything but an exercise of his own free will. Apparently, without any prodding from the officers, respondent—who had earlier said that he would tell the whole story when he arrived in Des Moines—spontaneously changed his mind about the timing of his disclosures when the car approached the places where he had hidden the evidence. However, even if his statements were influenced by Detective Leaming's above-quoted

---

1. It does not matter whether the right not to make statements in the absence of counsel stems from *Massiah*, or *Miranda*. In either case the question is one of waiver. Waiver was not addressed in *Massiah* because there the statements were being made to an informant and the defendant had no way of knowing that

he had a right not to talk to him without counsel.

4. Moreover, he in fact received advice of counsel on at least two occasions on the question whether he should talk to the police on the trip to Des Moines.

statement, respondent's decision to talk in the absence of counsel can hardly be viewed as the product of an overborne will. The statement by Leaming was not coercive; it was accompanied by a request that respondent not respond to it; and it was delivered hours before respondent decided to make any statement. Respondent's waiver was thus knowing and intentional.

[A] conceivable basis for the majority's holding is the implicit suggestion that the right involved in *Massiah*, as distinguished from the right involved in *Miranda*, is a right not to be asked any questions in counsel's absence rather than a right not to answer any questions in counsel's absence, and that the right not to be asked questions must be waived before the questions are asked. Such wafer thin distinctions cannot determine whether a guilty murderer should go free.[e] The only conceivable purpose for the presence of counsel during questioning is to protect an accused from making incriminating answers. Questions, unanswered, have no significance at all. Absent coercion—no matter how the right involved is defined—an accused is amply protected by a rule requiring waiver before or simultaneously with the giving by him of an answer or the making by him of a statement.

* * *

Justice BLACKMUN, with whom Justice WHITE and Justice REHNQUIST join, dissenting. * * *

The Court rules that the Sixth Amendment was violated because Detective Leaming "purposely sought during Williams' isolation from his lawyers to obtain as much incriminating information as possible." I cannot regard that as unconstitutional per se.

First, the police did not deliberately seek to isolate Williams from his lawyers so as to deprive him of the assistance of counsel. Cf. *Escobedo*. The isolation in this case was a necessary incident of transporting Williams to the county where the crime was committed.

Second, Leaming's purpose was not solely to obtain incriminating evidence. The victim had been missing for only two days, and the police could not be certain that she was dead. Leaming, of course, and in accord with his duty, was "hoping to find out where that little girl was," but such motivation does not equate with an intention to evade the Sixth Amendment.[f] * * *

Third, not every attempt to elicit information should be regarded as "tantamount to interrogation." I am not persuaded that Leaming's observations and comments, made as the police car traversed the snowy and slippery miles between Davenport and Des Moines that winter afternoon, were an interrogation, direct or subtle, of Williams. Williams, after all, was counseled by lawyers, and warned by

e. But see Joseph D. Grano, *Rhode Island v. Innis: A Need to Reconsider the Constitutional Premises Underlying the Law of Confessions*, 17 Am.Crim.L.Rev. 1, 34 (1979): "Justice White could not be more wrong in his criticism. The whole point of *Massiah* is the prevention of the state from taking advantage of an uncounseled defendant once Sixth Amendment rights attach. The Christian burial speech case was an attempt to take advantage of Williams. The attempt itself is what *Massiah* prohibits. The attempt itself violates the constitutional mandate that the system proceed, after some point, only in an accusatorial manner."

f. But see Kamisar, *Police Interrogation and Confessions* 146–47 (1980), maintaining that although at one point Leaming did testify that he was "hoping to find out where that little *girl* was," in light of the entire record he apparently meant the girl's *body*. Leaming testified that he heard Williams' lawyer say to him over the phone that he would have to tell the police "where *the body* is" when he got back. Leaming also testified that before he drove to Davenport to pick up Williams, Williams' lawyer told him that the girl "was dead when [Williams] left the YMCA with her."

the arraigning judge in Davenport and by the police, and yet it was he who started the travel conversations and brought up the subject of the criminal investigation.

[In] summary, it seems to me that the Court is holding that *Massiah* is violated whenever police engage in any conduct, in the absence of counsel, with the subjective desire to obtain information from a suspect after arraignment. Such a rule is far too broad. Persons in custody frequently volunteer statements in response to stimuli other than interrogation. * * *

Notes and Questions

1.   Was it constitutionally irrelevant whether the "Christian burial speech" constituted "interrogation"? Did the Court deem it necessary (or at least important) to classify Leaming's speech as a "form of interrogation" or "tantamount to interrogation"? If so, why? Once the Court chose the "Sixth Amendment–*Massiah*" route over a "Fifth Amendment–Miranda" approach, did the question whether Leaming engaged in "interrogation" become, or should it have become, constitutionally irrelevant? Did the secret government agent engage in "interrogation" in *Massiah*?

2.   Even if Brewer v. Williams were deemed a "Miranda case," would whether Leaming engaged in "interrogation" still be the wrong question? Since Williams had asserted both his right to remain silent and his right to counsel several times before he was driven back to Des Moines, should the relevant question have been whether Leaming "fully respected" or "scrupulously honored" Williams' *Miranda* rights? Cf. *Michigan v. Mosley*, p. 521. How could it be said that Leaming did, when he "deliberately and designedly set out to elicit information" from Williams?

Brewer v. Williams was decided four years before *Edwards v. Arizona*, p. 522. Looking back at Williams in light of Edwards, if Williams were a "*Miranda* case," should the relevant question have been whether, after expressing his unwillingness to talk to the police without his lawyer, Williams changed his mind on his own initiative or whether Leaming "persuaded" or "prompted" him to change his mind?

3.   What constitutes a valid waiver of the "Sixth Amendment–Massiah" right? PATTERSON v. ILLINOIS, 487 U.S. 285, 108 S.Ct. 2389, 101 L.Ed.2d 261 (1988), per WHITE, J., rejected "petitioner's argument, which has some acceptance from courts and commentators, that since 'the sixth amendment right [to counsel] is far superior to that of the fifth amendment right' and since '[t]he greater the right the greater the loss from a waiver of that right,' waiver of an accused's Sixth Amendment right to counsel should be 'more difficult' to effectuate than waiver of a suspect's Fifth Amendment rights." The Court ruled instead that "[a]s a general matter [an] accused who is [given the *Miranda* warnings] has been sufficiently apprised of the nature of the Sixth Amendment rights, and of the consequences of abandoning those rights, so that his waiver on this basis will be considered a knowing and intelligent one."

The case arose as follows: Patterson and other members of a street gang were arrested in the course of investigating the murder of Jackson. Patterson was advised of his *Miranda* rights and agreed to answer questions, but denied knowing anything about Jackson's death. He was held in custody while the investigation continued. Two days later, Patterson and two other gang members were indicted for the murder of Jackson. The same officer who had questioned him earlier told him that because he had been indicted he was being transferred from the lockup, where he was being held, to the county jail. Patterson asked the officer which of the gang members had been indicted for Jackson's murder, and upon learning that one particular gang member had not been indicted, responded: "[W]hy wasn't he indicted, he did everything."

Patterson then began to explain that a witness would support his account of the crime. At this point, the officer handed Patterson a *Miranda* waiver form and read the warnings aloud. Patterson initialed each of the warnings, signed the form and made a lengthy incriminating statement. He subsequently made additional statements. He was found guilty of murder, but maintained that the warnings he received, although they protected his *Miranda* rights, did not adequately inform him of his Sixth Amendment right to counsel during postindictment questioning. A 5–4 majority disagreed:

"[The] key inquiry in a case such as this one must be: Was the accused, who waived his Sixth Amendment rights during postindictment questioning, made sufficiently aware of his right to have counsel present during the questioning, and of the possible consequences of a decision to forgo the aid of counsel? In this case, we are convinced that by admonishing petitioner with the *Miranda* warnings, [the State] has met this burden and that petitioner's waiver of his right to counsel at questioning was valid. * * *

"Our conclusion is supported by petitioner's inability, in the proceedings before this Court, to articulate with precision what additional information should have been provided to him before he would have been competent to waive his right to counsel. * * *[8]" As a general matter, then, an accused who is admonished with the [*Miranda* warnings] has been sufficiently apprised of the nature of his Sixth Amendment rights, and of the consequences of abandoning these rights, so that his waiver on this basis will be considered a knowing and intelligent one.[9]

"[While] our cases have recognized a 'difference' between the Fifth Amendment and Sixth Amendment rights to counsel, and the 'policies' behind these Constitutional guarantees, we have never suggested that one right is 'superior' or 'greater' than the other, nor is there any support in our cases for the notion that because a Sixth Amendment right may be involved, it is more difficult to waive than the Fifth Amendment counterpart.

"[W]e require a more searching or formal inquiry before permitting an accused to waive his right to counsel at trial than we require for a Sixth

---

8. [Some courts have suggested] that, in addition to the *Miranda* warnings, an accused should be informed that he has been indicted before a postindictment waiver is sought. Because, in this case, petitioner concedes that he was so informed, we do not address [this issue].

Beyond this, only one Court of Appeals—the Second Circuit—has adopted substantive or procedural requirements (in addition to *Miranda*) that must be completed before a Sixth Amendment waiver can be effectuated for postindictment questioning. See *United States v. Mohabir*, 624 F.2d 1140 (1980). [Stressing that the "strict standard" governing waiver of counsel at trial should apply to an alleged waiver of the *Massiah* right to counsel as well, the *Mohabir* court exercised its supervisory power over federal criminal justice to hold that a valid waiver of the "Sixth Amendment—*Massiah*" right "must be preceded by a federal judicial officer's explanation of the content and significance of this right."] As have a majority of the Court of Appeals, we reject *Mohabir's* holding that some "additional" warnings or discussions with an accused are required in

this situation or that any waiver in this context can only properly be made before a "neutral * * * judicial officer."

9. This does not mean, of course, that all Sixth Amendment challenges to the conduct of postindictment questioning will fail whenever the challenged practice would pass constitutional muster under *Miranda*. For example, we have permitted a *Miranda* waiver to stand where a suspect was not told that his lawyer was trying to reach him during questioning; in the Sixth Amendment context, this waiver would not be valid. See *Moran v. Burbine* * * *.

Thus, because the Sixth Amendment's protection of the attorney-client relationship— "the right to rely on counsel as a 'medium' between [the accused] and the State"—extends beyond *Miranda's* protection of the Fifth Amendment right to counsel, there will be cases where a waiver which would be valid under *Miranda* will not suffice for Sixth Amendment purposes.

Amendment waiver during postindictment questioning—not because postindictment questioning is 'less important' than a trial [but] because the full 'dangers and disadvantages of self-representation,' *Faretta*, during questioning are less substantial and more obvious to an accused than they are at trial. Because the role of counsel at questioning is relatively simple and limited, we see no problem in having a waiver procedure at that stage which is likewise simple and limited."

Justice STEVENS, joined by Brennan and Marshall, JJ., dissented:

"The Court should not condone unethical forms of trial preparation by prosecutors or their investigators. In civil litigation it is improper for a lawyer to communicate with his or her adversary's client without either notice to opposing counsel or the permission of the court [referring to Disciplinary Rule 7–104 of the *ABA Model Code of Professional Responsibility* (1982)]. An attempt to obtain evidence for use at trial by going behind the back of one's adversary would be not only a serious breach of professional ethics but also a manifestly unfair form of trial practice. In the criminal context, the same ethical rules apply and, in my opinion, notions of fairness that are at least as demanding should also be enforced.

" * * * Given the significance of the initiation of formal proceedings and the concomitant shift in the relationship between the state and the accused, I think it quite wrong to suggest that *Miranda* warnings—or for that matter, any warnings offered by an adverse party—provide a sufficient basis for permitting the undoubtedly prejudicial—and, in my view, unfair—practice of permitting trained law enforcement personnel and prosecuting attorneys to communicate with as-of-yet unrepresented criminal defendants.

"[The] majority premises its conclusions that *Miranda* warnings lay a sufficient basis for accepting a waiver of the right to counsel on the assumption that those warnings make clear to an accused 'what a lawyer could "do for him" during the postindictment questioning: namely, advise [him] to refrain from making any [incriminating] statements.' Yet, this is surely a gross understatement of the disadvantage of proceeding without a lawyer and an understatement of what a defendant must understand to make a knowing waiver. The *Miranda* warnings do not, for example, inform the accused that a lawyer might examine the indictment for legal sufficiency before submitting his or her client to interrogation or that a lawyer is likely to be considerably more skillful at negotiating a plea bargain and that such negotiations may be most fruitful if initiated prior to any interrogation. Rather, the warnings do not even go so far as to explain to the accused the nature of the charges pending against him—advice that a court would insist upon before allowing a defendant to enter a guilty plea with or without the presence of an attorney."[a]

Notes and Questions

(a) In addition to his principal contention, Patterson also argued (unsuccessfully) that someone in his situation should be equated with a preindictment suspect who asserts his right to counsel, thereby triggering *Edwards*. Even if this is so, didn't Patterson, when being transferred to the county jail, "initiate" further communication with the police within the meaning of *Edwards*?

(b) Reconsider fn. 9 to the majority opinion in *Patterson*. Is the Court saying that even if a postindictment interrogatee were unaware that a friend or relative had retained a lawyer on his behalf, a waiver of his Sixth Amendment right to

a. Blackmun, J., wrote a separate dissent, "agree[ing] with most of what Justice Stevens said." He would equate someone in Patterson's situation with a suspect who asserted his Fifth Amendment right to counsel, thus invoking the protection of *Edwards*.

counsel would not be valid unless the police informed him that he had a lawyer and that that lawyer was trying to reach him? If so, why? Does this view make the Sixth Amendment right to counsel "superior" to the Fifth when somebody happens to retain a lawyer for the defendant, but not when the defendant is too unlucky or friendless for this to occur? Should the test for waiver of the Sixth Amendment right to counsel vary at different times "depending on the fortuity of whether [the suspect's family] happens to have retained counsel [for him] prior to interrogation"? Cf. *Moran v. Burbine.*

4. *The "no-contact" rule: Should prosecutors be bound by the ethical rule prohibiting a lawyer from communicating with an opposing party represented by counsel without the consent of the other lawyer?* The "no-contact" or "anti-contact" ethical rule discussed by Justice Stevens in his Patterson dissent has a long history in legal ethics: The rule is designed to protect laypersons from overreaching by those who have superior legal skills and knowledge and to protect the attorney-client relationship. The most common version of the ethical rule is Rule 4.2 of the *ABA Model Rules of Professional Conduct*, which provides: "In representing a client, a lawyer shall not communicate about the subject of the representation with a party the lawyer knows to be represented by another lawyer in the matter, unless the lawyer has the consent of the other lawyer or is authorized by law to do so." Disciplinary Rule 7–104 (A) (1) of the *Model Code of Professional Responsibility* is a virtually identical provision. Every state and the District of Columbia has adopted a version of the Model Code or Model Rules to govern the conduct of lawyers admitted to practice in that jurisdiction.

Should this rule apply in criminal, as well as civil, proceedings or should communications between a prosecutor and a suspect or defendant be judged by the special body of law developed by *Massiah* and its progeny? Do disciplinary rules such as Rule 4.2 take into account the full range of interests governing the balance between effective law enforcement and defendants' rights? Are the interests protected by Rule 4.2 adequately protected in the criminal context by the Sixth Amendment and the Federal Rules of Criminal Procedure? See Roger Cramton & Lisa Udel, *State Ethics Rules and Federal Prosecutors*, 53 U.Pitt.L.Rev. 291, 332–33 (1992); F. Dennis Saylor & J. Douglas Wilson, *Putting a Square Peg in a Round Hole: The Application of Model Rule 4.2 to Federal Prosecutors*, 53 U.Pitt.L.Rev. 459, 464–65 (1992).

Vindicating the views of the American Bar Association and state ethics authorities who have long maintained that federal prosecutors should be held to the same standards as other lawyers, the Citizens Protection Act, 28 U.S.C. § 530B, went into effect on April 19, 1999. The Act requires federal prosecutors to comply with state laws and rules, as well as local federal court rules, that govern lawyer conduct in the states where the federal prosecutors work.

The Act went into effect over the strong objections of Sen. Orrin Hatch, who argued that it "would cripple the ability of the Department of Justice to enforce federal law and cede authority to regulate the conduct of federal criminal investigations and prosecutors to more than 50 state bar associations," 64 Crim.L.Rep. 319, 337–38 (Feb. 3, 1999). Moreover, at a March 24 hearing before the U.S. Senate Judiciary Committee's Subcommittee on Criminal Justice Oversight, current and former prosecutors warned that the ability of federal prosecutors to supervise multistate investigations would be seriously hindered by state ethics rules restricting lawyers' direct contacts with persons represented by counsel. However, other witnesses testified that federal government lawyers should be governed by the same rules of ethics that apply to lawyers generally and maintained that the Department of Justice (DOJ) had not substantiated its claim that it needed an exemption from these rules. See 65 Crim.L.Rep. 1, 19 (April 7, 1999).

The same day the Citizens' Protection Act went into effect, the DOJ issued an interim final regulation implementing the new statute. The interim rule, *Ethical Standards for Attorneys for the Government*, 28 CFR 77.1–77.5 (set forth in full in 65 Crim.L.Rep. 77, 110 (April 28, 1999)), requires DOJ attorneys and lawyers acting pursuant to DOJ authorization to comply only with state rules of ethical conduct, such as codes of professional responsibility—not with state evidentiary and procedural rules or substantive state law.

The DOJ's interim rule supersedes the much-criticized 1994 Justice regulation, 28 CFR 77.10(a), which purported to exempt federal government lawyers from state ethical rules prohibiting ex parte communications with persons represented by counsel if the communication occurred prior to the initiation of formal proceedings against the person. As indicated by the discussion in 9th ed. at 632–33, the 1994 regulation received a rocky reception in the federal courts.

United States v. Lowery, 166 F.3d 1119 (11th Cir.1999) held, per Carnes, J., that even though the Citizens Protection Act requires federal prosecutors to comply with state or local rules of professional conduct, it does not follow that evidence obtained in violation of such rules has to be excluded:

"Assuming for present purposes that the [Florida Bar Rules of Professional Conduct are] violated when a prosecutor promises a witness some consideration regarding charges or sentencing in return for testimony, a state rule of professional conduct cannot provide an adequate basis for a federal court to suppress evidence that is otherwise admissible. [When] it comes to the admissibility of evidence in federal court, the federal interest in enforcement of federal law, including federal evidentiary rules, is paramount. [The] question is whether Congress' recent statutory directive * * * is aimed at admission of evidence in federal court. In other words, did Congress intend by the enactment to turn over to state supreme courts in every state—and state legislatures, too, assuming they can also enact codes of professional conduct for attorneys—the authority to decide that otherwise admissible evidence cannot be used in federal court? We think not."

5. *If the government obtains incriminating statements from a defendant after her right to counsel has attached, but the government does so for legitimate reasons unrelated to the gathering of evidence concerning charges to which the right to counsel has attached (e.g. to investigate a report that defendant plans to harm a witness), are the statements admissible at the trial of the crimes for which formal charges had already been filed?* No, answered the Court, per BRENNAN, J., in MAINE v. MOULTON, 474 U.S. 159, 106 S.Ct. 477, 88 L.Ed.2d 481 (1985):

"In *Massiah*, the Government also contended that incriminating statements obtained as a result of its deliberate efforts should not be excluded because law enforcement agents had 'the right, if not indeed the duty, to continue their investigation of [*Massiah*] and his alleged criminal associates.' [We] rejected this argument, and held:

" 'We do not question [that] it was entirely proper to continue an investigation of the suspected criminal activities of the defendant and his alleged confederates, even though the defendant had already been indicted. [But] the defendant's own incriminating statements, obtained by federal agents under the circumstances here disclosed, could not constitutionally be used by the prosecution as evidence against him at his trial.' (Emphasis omitted.)

"We reaffirm this holding, which states a sensible solution to a difficult problem. The police have an interest in the thorough investigation of crimes for which formal charges have already been filed. They also have an interest in investigating new or additional crimes. Investigations of either type of crime may require surveillance of individuals already under indictment. Moreover, law enforcement officials investigating an individual suspected of committing one crime and formally charged with having committed another crime obviously seek to discover evidence useful at a trial of either crime. In seeking evidence pertaining to pending charges, however, the Government's investigative powers are limited by the Sixth Amendment rights of the accused. To allow the admission of evidence obtained from the accused in violation of his Sixth Amendment rights whenever the police assert an alternative, legitimate reason for their surveillance [in this case, to insure the safety of their secret agent and to gather information concerning a report that defendant was planning to kill a witness] invites abuse by law enforcement personnel in the form of fabricated investigations and risks the evisceration of the Sixth Amendment right recognized in *Massiah*. On the other hand, to exclude evidence pertaining to charges as to which the Sixth Amendment right to counsel had not attached at the time the evidence was obtained, simply because other charges were pending at that time, would unnecessarily frustrate the public's interest in the investigation of criminal activities. Consequently, incriminating statements pertaining to pending charges are inadmissible at the trial of those charges, notwithstanding the fact that the police were also investigating other crimes, if, in obtaining this evidence, the State violated the Sixth Amendment by knowingly circumventing the accused's right to the assistance of counsel."

Chief Justice BURGER, joined by White, Rehnquist and O'Connor, JJ., dissented, maintaining that "application of the exclusionary rule here makes little sense."

"We have explained, [that] 'the deterrent purpose of the exclusionary rule necessarily assumes that the police have engaged in willful, or at the very least negligent, conduct which has deprived the defendant of some right.' Here the trial court found that the State obtained statements from respondent 'for legitimate purposes not related to the gathering of evidence concerning the crime for which [respondent] had been indicted.' Since the State was not trying to build its theft case against respondent in obtaining the evidence, excluding the evidence from the theft trial will not affect police behavior at all. The exclusion of evidence 'cannot be expected, and should not be applied, to deter objectively reasonable law enforcement activity.' *Leon*. Indeed, [it] is impossible to identify any police 'misconduct' to deter in this case. In fact, if anything, actions by the police of the type at issue here should be encouraged. The diligent investigation of the police in this case may have saved the lives of several potential witnesses and certainly led to the prosecution and conviction of respondent for additional serious crimes."

B. "PASSIVE" VS. "ACTIVE" SECRET AGENTS

The *Massiah* doctrine probably reached its high point in UNITED STATES v. HENRY, 447 U.S. 264, 100 S.Ct. 2183, 65 L.Ed.2d 115 (1980), which applied the doctrine to a situation where the FBI had instructed its paid government informant, ostensibly defendant's "cellmate," not to question defendant about the crime, and there had been no showing that he had. Nevertheless, a 6–3 majority, per BURGER, C.J., rejected the argument that the incriminating statements were not the result of any "affirmative conduct" on the part of the government agent to solicit evidence. The informant "was not a passive listener; rather he had 'some conversations with Mr. Henry' while he was in jail and Henry's incriminating statements were 'the product of this conversation.'" Moreover, and more generally—

"[Even if we accept the FBI agent's statement that] he did not intend that [the informant] would take affirmative steps to secure incriminating information, he must have known that such propinquity likely would lead to that result. [By] intentionally creating a situation likely to induce Henry to make incriminating statements without the assistance of counsel [after Henry had been indicted and counsel had been appointed for him], the government violated [his] Sixth Amendment right to counsel."

This broad language would seem to prohibit the government from "planting" even a completely "passive" secret agent in a person's cell once adversary proceedings have commenced against him. But the Henry Court cautioned that it was not "called upon to pass on the situation where an informant is placed in [close] proximity [to a prisoner] but makes no effort to stimulate conversations about the crime charged."

Moreover, concurring Justice POWELL made it plain that he could not join the majority opinion if it held that "the mere presence or incidental conversation of an informant in a jail cell would violate *Massiah*." The *Massiah* doctrine, emphasized Powell, "does not prohibit the introduction of spontaneous statements that are not elicited by governmental action. Thus, the Sixth Amendment is not violated when a passive listening device collects, but does not induce, incriminating comments."[a]

As the most recent "jail plant" case, *Kuhlmann v. Wilson* (discussed below), well illustrates, the line between "active" and "passive" secret agents—between "stimulating" conversations with a defendant in order to "elicit" incriminating statements and taking no action "beyond merely listening"—is an exceedingly difficult one to draw.

KUHLMANN v. WILSON, 477 U.S. 436, 106 S.Ct. 2616, 91 L.Ed.2d 364 (1986), arose as follows: Respondent Wilson and two confederates robbed a garage and fatally shot a dispatcher. He admitted that he had witnessed the robbery and murder, but denied any involvement in the crimes and denied knowing who the robbers were. After his arraignment for robbery and murder, Wilson was placed in a cell with a prisoner (Lee) who was a secret police informant. According to his arrangement with the police, Lee was not to ask any questions, but simply to "keep his ears open." Without any prompting, Wilson told Lee the same story he had told the police. Lee advised Wilson that his story "didn't sound too good" and that "things didn't look too good for him," but Wilson did not alter his story at that time. However, several days later, after a visit from his brother, who mentioned that members of the family were upset because they believed he had killed the dispatcher, Wilson changed his story. He admitted to Lee that he and two other men had planned and carried out the robbery and killed the dispatcher. Lee reported these incriminating statements to the police.

The trial court denied Wilson's motion to suppress his statements. Wilson was convicted of murder. The conviction was affirmed and he was denied federal habeas relief. However, following the decision in *Henry*, Wilson relitigated his claim. This time the Court of Appeals for the Second Circuit granted federal habeas relief, viewing the circumstances of his case indistinguishable from the facts of *Henry*. The Supreme Court, per POWELL, J., reversed:

"[Since]" the Sixth Amendment is not violated whenever—by luck or happenstance—the State obtains incriminating statements from the accused after the right to counsel has attached, *Moulton*, a defendant does not make out a violation of that right simply by showing that an informant, [reported] his incriminating statements to the police. Rather, the defendant must demonstrate that the police and their informant took some action, beyond merely listening, that was designed deliberately to elicit incriminating remarks. It is thus apparent that the Court of Appeals erred in concluding that respondent's right to counsel was violated under the circumstances of this case. [It failed] to accord to the state trial court's factual findings the presumption of correctness expressly required by 28 U.S.C. § 2254(d).

"The state court found that, [following police instructions, Lee] 'at no time asked any questions' of respondent concerning the pending charges, and that he 'only listened' to respondent's 'spontaneous' and 'unsolicited' statements. The only remark made by Lee that has any support in this record was his comment that respondent's initial version of his participation in the crimes 'didn't sound too good.' [The] Court of Appeals focused on that one remark and gave a description of Lee's interaction with respondent that is completely at odds with the facts found by the trial court. [After] thus revising some of the trial court's findings, and ignoring other more relevant findings, the Court of Appeals concluded that the police 'deliberately elicited' respondent's incriminating statements. This conclusion conflicts with the decision of every other state and federal judge who reviewed this record, and is clear error in light of the provisions and intent of § 2254(d)."[b]

Dissenting Justice BRENNAN, joined by Marshall, J., maintained that "the state trial court simply found that Lee did not ask respondent any direct questions about the crime for which respondent was incarcerated. [The] Court of Appeals did not disregard the state court's finding that Lee asked respondent no direct questions regarding the crime. Rather, [it] expressly accepted that finding, but concluded that, as a matter of law, the deliberate elicitation standard of *Henry* and *Massiah*, encompasses other, more subtle forms of stimulating incriminating admissions than overt questioning. [The court] observed that, while Lee asked respondent no questions, Lee nonetheless stimulated conversation concerning respondents' role in [the] robbery and murder by remarking that respondent's exculpatory story did not 'sound too good' and that he had better come up with a better one. Thus,[it] concluded that the respondent's case [was] virtually indistinguishable from *Henry*.

"[Like the police informant in *Henry*,] Lee encouraged respondent to talk about his crime by conversing with him on the subject over the course of several days and by telling respondent that his exculpatory story would not convince anyone without more work. However, unlike the situation in *Henry*, a disturbing visit from respondent's brother, rather than a conversation with the informant, seems to have been the immediate catalyst for respondent's confession to Lee. While it might appear from this sequence of events that Lee's comment regarding respondent's story and his general willingness to converse with respondent about the crime were not the immediate causes of respondent's admission, I think that the deliberate elicitation standard requires consideration of the entire course of government behavior.

b. Chief Justice Burger, the author of *Henry*, joined the opinion of the Court, but also wrote a brief concurring opinion noting "a vast difference between placing an 'ear' in the suspect's cell and placing a voice in the cell to encourage conversation for the 'ear' to record."

"The State intentionally created a situation in which it was foreseeable that respondent would make incriminating statements without the assistance of counsel. The informant, while avoiding direct questions, nonetheless developed a relationship of cellmate camaraderie with respondent and encouraged him to talk about his crime. While the coup de grace was delivered by respondent's brother, the groundwork for respondent's confession was laid by the State. Clearly the State's actions had a sufficient nexus with respondent's admission of guilt to constitute deliberate elicitation within the meaning of *Henry*."[c]

Notes and Questions

1. The distinction between placing an "ear" in the defendant's cell and placing a "voice" there to encourage conversations. As a practical matter, is there any difference, let alone "a vast difference" (see fn. b, supra), between placing an "ear" in the cell and placing a "voice" there? Doesn't the "voice" go with the "ear"?

Is a defendant likely to make incriminating statements to a "cellmate" unless the latter has developed a relationship of trust and confidence with the defendant? Doesn't a police informant have to exchange remarks with the defendant if only to avoid "alerting" the defendant that something is amiss? If two people share the same cell for days or even weeks, don't they both talk—and talk back and forth? How likely is it that the flow of conversation and the progression of various conversations can be accurately reconstructed? How much incentive does the informant have to do so? Once formal proceedings have been initiated, is the only effective way to prevent police interference with the attorney-client relationship to prohibit any government agent from approaching a defendant in the absence of counsel? See the remarks of Professor Kamisar in Choper, Kamisar & Tribe, *The Supreme Court: Trends and Development*, 1979–80 (1981) at 107–08.

2. Are the courts asking the wrong questions in cases like Henry and Wilson? Is the true issue in these cases "privacy"? Yes, maintains H. Richard Uviller, *Evidence from the Mind of the Criminal Suspect*, 87 Colum.L.Rev. 1137, 1191, 1195 (1987):

"The fourth amendment is the guardian of privacy and the questions the courts should be asking are: Did the defendant enjoy a protected expectation of privacy in the circumstances, and if so did the state have a properly predicated warrant to encroach, or some good basis for the lack of it? * * *

"[W]hile a defendant may be required to bear the risk of ordinary disloyalty among trusted associates, it does not follow that he must also bear the risk that the government is engaging in surreptitious invasions. The fact that informers are commonplace in the councils of criminals does not deprive the criminals of reasonable expectations of privacy for fourth amendment purposes any more than the frequency of wiretaps in Mafia investigations excuses the government from the duty to take its case to a judge for advance authorization of an electronic surveillance. [The *Hoffa* Court, see p. 378] should have regarded Partin as the human bug he was and treated his intrusion as a search and seizure (unless, of course, the government was right in the claim that they had not 'placed' him in Hoffa's company).

"Thus, Stewart [, who wrote the opinion of the Court in both *Hoffa* and *Massiah*,] unnaturally distorted the sixth amendment's promise of a skilled advocate in order to narrow the interval in which the suspect's mind could be

c. Stevens, J., filed a separate dissent, agreeing with Justice Brennan's analysis of the merits of respondent's habeas petition.

probed and unwisely shortened the reach of the fourth amendment's guarantee of security by permitting the government deliberately to insert a human spy into the suspect's private space to report on declarations and behavior that might betray a guilty mind."

3. But consider James Tomkovicz, *An Adversary System Defense of the Right to Counsel Against Informants: Truth, Fair Play, and the Massiah Doctrine*, 22 U.C.Davis L.Rev. 1, 36–38 (1988):

"[If the fourth amendment] were the real basis for protection against government informants, the resulting doctrine would have to be considerably different than the current *Massiah* doctrine. For example, fourth amendment protection would not depend either on the initiation of adversarial proceedings or on active elicitation.

"More important, *Massiah's* substantive sixth amendment protection is radically different than the substance of prospective fourth amendment shelter. The prohibition against 'unreasonable' searches would provide a limited safeguard against the informant surveillance itself. The *Massiah* right, on the other hand, raises an absolute barrier not to the surveillance, but to the use of its products at trial. Consequently, one cannot rationalize the current *Massiah* entitlement upon a fourth amendment foundation. Both the doctrine and the right belie any fourth amendment roots.[175]"

4. *Private citizens vs. state agents.* As pointed out in Tomkovicz, supra, at 72 n. 283, "lower courts have struggled to discern standards for determining when private citizens become state agents for *Massiah* purposes," relying upon several interrelated criteria: the existence of an explicit agreement or prearrangement between law enforcement and an informant; the source of an informant's motivation; the benefits accruing to the informant; and the governmental involvement in placing the informant near the defendant. Should the *Massiah* doctrine govern an informant's conduct "if a reasonable person would conclude that the informant has secured and reported inculpatory remarks at least in part because of affirmative governmental encouragement"? See id. at 74.

ONCE THE SIXTH AMENDMENT RIGHT TO COUNSEL ARISES, DOES IT ATTACH TO ALL OTHER OFFENSES CLOSELY RELATED TO THE PARTICULAR OFFENSE CHARGED?

TEXAS v. COBB
532 U.S. 162, 121 S.Ct. 1335, 149 L.Ed.2d 321 (2001).

Chief Justice REHNQUIST delivered the opinion of the Court.

[Respondent confessed to the burglary of a home, but denied knowing anything about the disappearance of a woman and child from the home. He was indicted for the burglary and counsel was appointed to represent him. While in

175. This statement is not meant to imply that the Court's unease with its repeated refusals to accord any fourth amendment protection against informant surveillance [has] not contributed to the birth and perpetuation of the *Massiah* doctrine. Although not a principled basis, the Court's discomfort cannot be

discounted entirely as an actual influence upon the law in this area.

In addition, the textual discussion is not meant to imply that the fourth amendment should not have a role in informant contexts. [Rather,] the point [is] that the *Massiah* doctrine is not fourth amendment law in disguise.

police custody, he waived his *Miranda* rights and confessed to the murders of the woman and child who had disappeared from the home. (After the woman had confronted him during the burglary, he had killed her and buried her and her baby.) He was convicted of capital murder and sentenced to death. The Texas Court of Appeals reversed respondent's conviction, concluding that his Sixth Amendment right to counsel had attached on the capital murder charge even though he had not yet been charged with that offense: "Once the right to counsel attaches to the offense charged, it also attaches to any other offense that is very closely related factually to the offense charged." But the U.S. Supreme Court disagreed.]

In *McNeil v. Wisconsin* [p. 536], we explained [that when the Sixth Amendment right to counsel] arises "[it] is offense specific. It cannot be invoked once for all future prosecutions, for it does not attach until a prosecution is commenced * * *." Accordingly, we held that a defendant's statements regarding offenses for which he had not been charged were admissible notwithstanding the attachment of the Sixth Amendment right to counsel on other charged offenses.

Some [lower courts], however, have read into *McNeil's* offense-specific definition an exception for crimes that are "factually related" to a charged offense. * * * We decline to do so.

[Respondent] predicts that the offense-specific rule will prove "disastrous" to suspects' constitutional rights and will "permit law enforcement officers almost complete and total license to conduct unwanted and uncounseled interrogations." Besides offering no evidence that such a parade of horribles has occurred in those jurisdictions that have not enlarged upon *McNeil,* he fails to appreciate the significance of two critical considerations. First, there can be no doubt that a suspect must be apprised of his rights against compulsory self-incrimination and to consult with an attorney before authorities may conduct custodial interrogation. In the present case, police scrupulously followed *Miranda's* dictates when questioning respondent.[2] Second, it is critical to recognize that the Constitution does not negate society's interest in the ability of police to talk to witnesses and suspects, even those who have been charged with other offenses. "Since the ready ability to obtain uncoerced confessions is not an evil but an unmitigated good, [if the government could not use statements resulting from valid *Miranda* waivers.] society would be the loser. * * * " *McNeil* (quoting *Moran v. Burbine*).

[Although] it is clear that the Sixth Amendment right to counsel attaches only to charged offenses, we have recognized in other contexts that the definition of an "offense" is not necessarily limited to the four corners of a charging instrument. In *Blockburger v. United States*, [discussed in *United States v. Dixon*, p. 1033], we explained that "where the same act or transaction constitutes a violation of two distinct statutory provisions, the test to be applied to determine whether there are two offenses or only one, is whether each provision requires proof of a fact which the other does not." We have since applied the *Blockburger* test to delineate the scope of the Fifth Amendment's Double Jeopardy Clause, which prevents multiple or successive prosecutions for the "same offence." We see no constitutional difference between the meaning of the term "offense" in the contexts of double

---

2. Curiously, while predicting disastrous consequences for the core values underlying the Sixth Amendment, the dissenters give short shrift to the Fifth Amendment's role (as expressed in *Miranda* and *Dickerson*) in protecting a defendant's right to consult with counsel before talking to police. Even though the Sixth Amendment right to counsel has not attached to uncharged offenses, defendants re-

tain the ability under *Miranda* to refuse any police questioning, and, indeed, charged defendants presumably have met with counsel and have had the opportunity to discuss whether it is advisable to invoke those Fifth Amendment rights. Thus, in all but the rarest of cases, the Court's decision today will have no impact whatsoever upon a defendant's ability to protect his Sixth Amendment right. * * *

jeopardy and of the right to counsel. Accordingly, we hold that when the Sixth Amendment right to counsel attaches, it does encompass offenses that, even if not formally charged, would be considered the same offense under the *Blockburger* test.[3]

While simultaneously conceding that its own test "lacks the precision for which police officers may hope," the dissent suggests that adopting *Blockburger's* definition of "offense" will prove difficult to administer. But it is the dissent's vague iterations of the " 'closely related to' " or " 'inextricably intertwined with' " test that would defy simple application. The dissent seems to presuppose that officers will possess complete knowledge of the circumstances surrounding an incident, such that the officers will be able to tailor their investigation to avoid addressing factually related offenses. Such an assumption, however, ignores the reality that police often are not yet aware of the exact sequence and scope of events they are investigating—indeed, that is why police must investigate in the first place. Deterred by the possibility of violating the Sixth Amendment, police likely would refrain from questioning certain defendants altogether.

It remains only to apply these principles to the facts at hand. [As] defined by Texas law, burglary and capital murder are not the same offense under *Blockburger*. [Accordingly,] the Sixth Amendment right to counsel did not bar police from interrogating respondent regarding the murders, and respondent's confession was therefore admissible. * * *

Justice KENNEDY, with whom Justice SCALIA and Justice THOMAS join, concurring. * * *

As the facts of the instant case well illustrate, it is difficult to understand the utility of a Sixth Amendment rule that operates to invalidate a confession given by the free choice of suspects who have received proper advice of their *Miranda* rights but waived them nonetheless. The *Miranda* rule, and the related preventative rule of *Edwards v. Arizona,* serve to protect a suspect's voluntary choice not to speak outside his lawyer's presence. The parallel rule announced in *Jackson,* however, supersedes the suspect's voluntary choice to speak with investigators. [While] the *Edwards* rule operates to preserve the free choice of a suspect to remain silent, if *Jackson* were to apply it would override that choice. [The] Sixth Amendment right to counsel attaches quite without reference to the suspect's choice to speak with investigators after a *Miranda* warning. It is the commencement of a formal prosecution, indicated by the initiation of adversary judicial proceedings, that marks the beginning of the Sixth Amendment right. These events may be quite independent of the suspect's election to remain silent, the interest which the *Edwards* rule serves to protect with respect to *Miranda* and the Fifth Amendment, and it thus makes little sense for a protective rule to attach absent such an election by the suspect. We ought to question the wisdom of a judge-made preventative rule to protect a suspect's desire not to speak when it cannot be shown that he had that intent.

Even if *Jackson* is to remain good law, its protections should apply only where a suspect has made a clear and unambiguous assertion of the right not to speak outside the presence of counsel, the same clear election required under *Edwards.* Cobb made no such assertion here, yet Justice Breyer's dissent rests upon the assumption that the *Jackson* rule should operate to exclude the confession no matter. * * *

3. In this sense, we could just as easily describe the Sixth Amendment as "prosecution specific," insofar as it prevents discussion of charged offenses as well as offenses that, under *Blockburger,* could not be the subject of a later prosecution. And, indeed, the text of the Sixth Amendment confines its scope to "all criminal *prosecutions.*"

Justice Breyer defends *Jackson* by arguing that, once a suspect has accepted counsel at the commencement of adversarial proceedings, he should not be forced to confront the police during interrogation without the assistance of counsel. But the acceptance of counsel at an arraignment or similar proceeding only begs the question: acceptance of counsel for what? It is quite unremarkable that a suspect might want the assistance of an expert in the law to guide him through hearings and trial, and the attendant complex legal matters that might arise, but nonetheless might choose to give on his own a forthright account of the events that occurred. A court-made rule that prevents a suspect from even making this choice serves little purpose, especially given the regime of *Miranda* and *Edwards*.

Justice BREYER, with whom Justice STEVENS, Justice SOUTER, and Justice GINSBURG join, dissenting. * * *

This case focuses [upon] the meaning of the words "offense specific." These words appear in this Court's Sixth Amendment case law, not in the Sixth Amendment's text. See U.S. Const., Amdt. 6 (guaranteeing right to counsel "[i]n all criminal prosecutions"). The definition of these words is not self-evident. Sometimes the term "offense" may refer to words that are written in a criminal statute; sometimes it may refer generally to a course of conduct in the world, aspects of which constitute the elements of one or more crimes; and sometimes it may refer, narrowly and technically, just to the conceptually severable aspects of the latter. This case requires us to determine whether an "offense"—for Sixth Amendment purposes—includes factually related aspects of a single course of conduct other than those few acts that make up the essential elements of the crime charged.

We should answer this question in light of the Sixth Amendment's basic objectives as set forth in this Court's case law. At the very least, we should answer it in a way that does not undermine those objectives. But the Court today decides that "offense" means the crime set forth within "the four corners of a charging instrument," along with other crimes that "would be considered the same offense" under the test established by *Blockburger*. In my view, this unnecessarily technical definition undermines Sixth Amendment protections while doing nothing to further effective law enforcement.

For one thing, the majority's rule, while leaving the Fifth Amendment's protections in place, threatens to diminish severely the additional protection that, under this Court's rulings, the Sixth Amendment provides when it grants the right to counsel to defendants who have been charged with a crime and insists that law enforcement officers thereafter communicate with them through that counsel.

Justice Kennedy, Justice Scalia, and Justice Thomas, if not the majority, apparently believe these protections constitutionally unimportant, for, in their view, "the underlying theory of *Jackson* seems questionable." (Kennedy, J., concurring). Both the majority and concurring opinions suggest that a suspect's ability to invoke his Fifth Amendment right and "refuse any police questioning" offers that suspect adequate constitutional protection. [But] that is not so.

Jackson focuses upon a suspect—perhaps a frightened or uneducated suspect—who, hesitant to rely upon his own unaided judgment in his dealings with the police, has invoked his constitutional right to legal assistance in such matters. * * * *Jackson* says that, once such a request has been made, the police may not simply throw that suspect—who does not trust his own unaided judgment—back upon his own devices by requiring him to rely for protection upon that same unaided judgment that he previously rejected as inadequate. In a word, the police may not force a suspect who has asked for legal counsel to make a critical legal choice without the legal assistance that he has requested and that the Constitution guarantees. [The] Constitution does not take away with one hand what it gives with the other. * * *

Justice Kennedy [criticizes] *Jackson* on the ground that it prevents a suspect "[from] making th[e] choice" to "give [a] forthright account of the events that occurred." But that is not so. A suspect may initiate communication with the police, thereby avoiding the risk that the police induced him to make, unaided, the kind of critical legal decision best made with the help of counsel, whom he has requested.

Unlike Justice Kennedy, the majority does not call *Jackson* itself into question. But the majority would undermine that case by significantly diminishing the Sixth Amendment protections that the case provides. That is because criminal codes are lengthy and highly detailed, often proliferating "overlapping and related statutory offenses" to the point where prosecutors can easily "spin out a startlingly numerous series of offenses from a single * * * criminal transaction." Thus, an armed robber who reaches across a store counter, grabs the cashier, and demands "your money or your life," may through that single instance of conduct have committed several "offenses," in the majority's sense of the term, including armed robbery, assault, battery, trespass, use of a firearm to commit a felony, and perhaps possession of a firearm by a felon, as well. A person who is using and selling drugs on a single occasion might be guilty of possessing various drugs, conspiring to sell drugs, being under the influence of illegal drugs, possessing drug paraphernalia, possessing a gun in relation to the drug sale, and, depending upon circumstances, violating various gun laws as well. A protester blocking an entrance to a federal building might also be trespassing, failing to disperse, unlawfully assembling, and obstructing Government administration all at one and the same time.

The majority's rule permits law enforcement officials to question those charged with a crime without first approaching counsel, through the simple device of asking questions about any other related crime not actually charged in the indictment. Thus, the police could ask the individual charged with robbery about, say, the assault of the cashier not yet charged, or about any other uncharged offense (unless under *Blockburger's* definition it counts as the "same crime"), all *without notifying counsel.* Indeed, the majority's rule would permit law enforcement officials to question anyone charged with any crime in any one of the examples just given about his or her conduct on the single relevant occasion without notifying counsel unless the prosecutor has charged every possible crime arising out of that same brief course of conduct. What Sixth Amendment sense— what common sense—does such a rule make? The majority's approach [will] undermine the lawyer's role as " 'medium' " between the defendant and the government. And it will, on a random basis, remove a significant portion of the protection that this Court has found inherent in the Sixth Amendment.

[In] *Brewer v. Williams,* the effect of the majority's rule would have been even more dramatic. Because first-degree murder and child abduction each required proof of a fact not required by the other, and because at the time of the impermissible interrogation Williams had been charged only with abduction of a child, Williams' murder conviction should have remained undisturbed.[a] [This] is

a. But see Craig M. Bradley, *Seas, Bogs and Police Interrogation,* Trial, Oct. 2001, pp. 71, 73: "It is true that under *Cobb,* the fact that Williams had a right to counsel as to the kidnapping charge would not protect him from interrogation on the murder charge. But there are several reasons why *Williams* would still come out the same way even after *Cobb.* The first is that, unlike Cobb, Williams was not given his *Miranda* warnings before the interrogation in the police car. Second, Williams had been given *Miranda* warnings earlier and had indicated that he didn't want to speak to the police without counsel. Thus, although Williams might not have a *Sixth* Amendment right to counsel, his *Fifth* Amendment rights

not to suggest that this Court has previously addressed and decided the question presented by this case. Rather, it is to point out that the Court's conception of the Sixth Amendment right at the time [that] *Brewer* [was] decided naturally presumed that it extended to factually related but uncharged offenses.

At the same time, the majority's rule threatens the legal clarity necessary for effective law enforcement. That is because the majority, aware that the word "offense" ought to encompass something beyond "the four corners of the charging instrument," imports into Sixth Amendment law the definition of "offense" set forth in *Blockburger*, a case interpreting the Double Jeopardy Clause of the Fifth Amendment, which Clause uses the word "offence" but otherwise has no relevance here. Whatever Fifth Amendment virtues *Blockburger* may have, to import it into this Sixth Amendment context will work havoc.

[The] simple-sounding *Blockburger* test has proved extraordinarily difficult to administer in practice. Judges, lawyers, and law professors often disagree about how to apply it. [The] test has emerged as a tool in an area of our jurisprudence that The Chief Justice has described as "a veritable Sargasso Sea which could not fail to challenge the most intrepid judicial navigator." Yet the Court now asks, not the lawyers and judges who ordinarily work with double jeopardy law, but police officers in the field, to navigate *Blockburger* when they question suspects. Some will apply the test successfully; some will not. Legal challenges are inevitable. The result, I believe, will resemble not so much the Sargasso Sea as the criminal law equivalent of Milton's "Serbonian Bog ... Where Armies whole have sunk."

There is, of course, an alternative. We can, and should, define "offense" in terms of the conduct that constitutes the crime that the offender committed on a particular occasion, including criminal acts that are "closely related to" or "inextricably intertwined with" the particular crime set forth in the charging instrument. This alternative is not perfect. The language used lacks the precision for which police officers may hope; and it requires lower courts to specify its meaning further as they apply it in individual cases. Yet virtually every lower court in the United States to consider the issue has defined "offense" in the Sixth Amendment context to encompass such closely related acts. * * *

One cannot say in favor of this commonly followed approach that it is perfectly clear—only that, because it comports with common sense, it is far easier to apply than that of the majority. One might add that, unlike the majority's test, it is consistent with this Court's assumptions in previous cases [citing *Maine v. Moulton* and *Brewer v. Williams*]. And, most importantly, the "closely related" test furthers, rather than undermines, the Sixth Amendment's "right to counsel," a right so necessary to the realization in practice of that most "noble ideal," a fair trial.

The Texas Court of Criminal Appeals, following this commonly accepted approach, found that the charged burglary and the uncharged murders were "closely related." All occurred during a short period of time on the same day in the same basic location. The victims of the murders were also victims of the burglary. Cobb committed one of the murders in furtherance of the [burglary,] the other to cover up the crimes. The police, when questioning Cobb, knew that he already had a lawyer representing him on the burglary charges and had demonstrated their belief that this lawyer also represented Cobb in respect to the murders by asking his permission to question Cobb about the murders on previous occasions. The relatedness of the crimes is well illustrated by the impossibility of questioning Cobb about the murders without eliciting admissions about the

would still have been violated. Third, the police had promised counsel that they would not interrogate him during the car trip, so they may have violated William's due process rights when they broke that promise."

burglary. [Nor,] in my view, did Cobb waive his right to counsel. These considerations are sufficient. The police officers ought to have spoken to Cobb's counsel before questioning Cobb. * * *

SHOULD *MASSIAH* BE OVERRULED?

Should the *Cobb* Court have abolished *Massiah* altogether? Consider SHERRY F. COLB, *Why the Supreme Court Should Overrule the Massiah Doctrine and Permit Miranda Alone to Govern Interrogations*, <http://writ.news.find-law.com/colb/20010509.html> (May 9, 2001):

"[When the Court handed down its decision in *Miranda*], [m]any of us expected *Massiah* eventually to disappear. After all, once *Miranda* was decided, it seemed no longer necessary and even counterproductive to apply different legal standards to interrogations, depending on whether a suspect had been indicted.

"[In] defense of *Massiah*'s 'indictment' distinction, the Court has claimed that indictment is 'a critical stage' in prosecuting a defendant, for then the defendant can harm himself irreparably by statements he makes before a lawyer arrives on the scene, before the trial even begins. Fair enough. But that argument simply suggests that *Massiah* rights should be triggered long before trial—without explaining why they should not be triggered long before indictment, too.

"There is nothing to stop a pre-indictment suspect from doing exactly the same self-inflicted harm as his post-indictment counterpart. Indeed, a suspect may do even greater harm prior to indictment, since an indictment can serve to put a suspect on notice that a prosecutor has made the decision to target him in particular and that he therefore ought to exercise discretion.

"*Massiah* rights will thus often come into being too late to be of any use to the defendant. The fortuity of when the prosecution decides to charge him with a particular crime, a matter over which the defendant has no control, can therefore be decisive.

"The *Cobb* Court could—and should—have gotten rid of *Massiah*'s distinction, and let *Miranda* alone protect suspects. But it did not.

"[The] *Cobb* dissenters argued [that] *Miranda* does not sufficiently protect suspects from interrogation they feel ill-equipped to handle on their own. The dissenters may be right. [But] whether one agrees with the majority or with the dissent, it should be *Miranda*—not *Massiah*—that is at issue.

"The dissent's arguments are really arguments for expanding *Miranda*, either by defining *Miranda* 'interrogation' more broadly, by extending its protections beyond the custodial setting, or by making a waiver of *Miranda* rights more difficult. These arguments are not, however, arguments for preserving *Massiah*'s groundless distinction between those who have, and those who have not, been indicted.

"The Court should abandon the separate *Massiah* doctrine, and conduct the important debate that is waiting in the wings, about the scope of *Miranda*. That debate will probably turn largely on the perceived desirability of obtaining voluntary (but ill-advised) confessions from criminal suspects. The Court could have hashed out that debate more fully in *Cobb*; let us hope that it will take the chance to do so in the next *Massiah* case it hears."

Chapter 9

LINEUPS, SHOWUPS AND OTHER PRE–TRIAL IDENTIFICATION PROCEDURES

"[N]umerous analyses over several decades have consistently shown that mistaken eyewitness identification is the single largest source of wrongful convictions. [A 1988] review of 205 cases of proven wrongful conviction, for example, showed that 52% were associated with mistaken eyewitness identification."

—Gary L. Wells & Eric P. Seelau, *Eyewitness Identification and Legal Policy on Lineups*, 1 Psychology, Pub. Pol'y. & L. 765 (1995).

"Who hasn't seen the sensational news reports of cases in which DNA evidence has been used to exonerate individuals previously convicted of crimes? What evidence, then, was used to obtain these convictions in the first place? And how could justice have repeatedly gone so awry?

"When researchers and criminal justice practitioners began to ask these and corollary questions, they uncovered some startling results. Of the first 60 wrongful convictions revealed by DNA technology, 53 had relied to some extent on confident, but mistaken, eyewitnesses."

—James M. Doyle, Mark R. Larson, & Caterina M. DiTraglia, *The Eyes Have It–Or Do They?*, Criminal Justice (ABA Criminal Justice Section), Fall, 2001, p. 12.

SECTION 1. *WADE* AND *GILBERT*: CONSTITUTIONAL CONCERN ABOUT THE DANGERS INVOLVED IN EYEWITNESS IDENTIFICATIONS

UNITED STATES v. WADE*
388 U.S. 218, 87 S.Ct. 1926, 18 L.Ed.2d 1149 (1967).

Justice BRENNAN delivered the opinion of the Court.

The question here is whether courtroom identifications of an accused at trial are to be excluded from evidence because the accused was exhibited to the witnesses before trial at a post-indictment lineup conducted for identification purposes without notice to and in the absence of the accused's appointed counsel.

---

* The Court decided two other pretrial identification cases the same day: *Gilbert v. California*, 388 U.S. 263, 87 S.Ct. 1951, 18 L.Ed.2d 1178 (1967) and *Stovall v. Denno*, 388 U.S. 293, 87 S.Ct. 1967, 18 L.Ed.2d 1199 (1967), both discussed infra.

The federally insured bank in Eustace, Texas, was robbed on September 21, 1964. A man with a small strip of tape on each side of his face entered the bank, pointed a pistol at the female cashier and the vice president, the only persons in the bank at the time, and forced them to fill a pillowcase with the bank's money. The man then drove away with an accomplice who had been waiting in a stolen car outside the bank. On March 23, 1965, an indictment was returned against respondent, Wade, and two others for conspiring to rob the bank, and against Wade and the accomplice for the robbery itself. Wade was arrested on April 2, and counsel was appointed to represent him on April 26. Fifteen days later [after counsel was appointed] an FBI agent, without notice to Wade's lawyer, arranged to have the two bank employees observe a lineup made up of Wade and five or six other prisoners and conducted in a courtroom of the local county courthouse. Each person in the line wore strips of tape such as allegedly worn by the robber and upon direction each said something like "put the money in the bag," the words allegedly uttered by the robber. Both bank employees identified Wade in the lineup as the bank robber.

At trial the two employees, when asked on direct examination if the robber was in the courtroom, pointed to Wade. The prior lineup identification was then elicited from both employees on cross-examination.

[The] fact that the lineup involved no violation of Wade's privilege against self-incrimination[a] does not [dispose] of his contention that the courtroom identifications should have been excluded because the lineup was conducted without notice to and in the absence of his counsel. [In] this case it is urged that the assistance of counsel at the lineup was indispensable to protect Wade's most basic right as a criminal defendant—his right to a fair trial at which the witnesses against him might be meaningfully cross-examined.

[T]he principle of *Powell v. Alabama* and succeeding cases requires that we scrutinize any pretrial confrontation of the accused to determine whether the presence of his counsel is necessary to preserve the defendant's basic right to a fair trial as affected by his right meaningfully to cross-examine the witnesses against him and to have effective assistance of counsel at the trial itself. It calls upon us to analyze whether potential substantial prejudice to defendant's rights inheres in the particular confrontation and the ability of counsel to help avoid that prejudice.

The Government characterizes the lineup as a mere preparatory step in the gathering of the prosecution's evidence, not different—for Sixth Amendment purposes—from various other preparatory steps, such as systematized or scientific analyzing of the accused's fingerprints, blood sample, clothing, hair, and the like. We think there are differences which preclude such stages being characterized as critical stages at which the accused has the right to the presence of his counsel. Knowledge of the techniques of science and technology is sufficiently available, and the variables in techniques few enough, that the accused has the opportunity for a meaningful confrontation of the Government's case at trial through the ordinary processes of cross-examination of the Government's expert witnesses and the presentation of the evidence of his own experts. The denial of a right to have

---

a. On this issue, relying on *Schmerber v. California* (p. 38), a 5–4 majority ruled that neither requiring a person to appear in a lineup and to speak for identification (*Wade*) nor requiring a person to provide handwriting exemplars (*Gilbert*) violated the privilege. *Schmerber*, which involved the taking of a blood sample, over his objection, from a person arrested for drunken driving, rejected the contention that the defendant had been "com-pelled [to] be a witness against himself" in violation of the Fifth Amendment. The self-incrimination clause, observed the Court, "protects an accused only from being compelled to testify against himself, or otherwise provide the State with evidence of a testimonial or communicative nature." See also the discussion of these rulings in *Doe v. United States*, p. 738, and Note 6, p. 747.

his counsel present at such analyses does not therefore violate the Sixth Amendment; they are not critical stages since there is minimal risk that his counsel's absence at such stages might derogate from his right to a fair trial.[b]

But the confrontation compelled by the State between the accused and the victim or witnesses to a crime to elicit identification evidence is peculiarly riddled with innumerable dangers and variable factors which might seriously, even crucially, derogate from a fair trial. The vagaries of eyewitness identification are well-known; the annals of criminal law are rife with instances of mistaken identification. [A] major factor contributing to the high incidence of miscarriage of justice from mistaken identification has been the degree of suggestion inherent in the manner in which the prosecution presents the suspect to witnesses for pretrial identification. A commentator has observed that "[t]he influence of improper suggestion upon identifying witnesses probably accounts for more miscarriages of justice than any other single factor—perhaps it is responsible for more such errors than all other factors combined." Wall, *Eye-Witness Identification in Criminal Cases* 26 [1965]. Suggestion can be created intentionally or unintentionally in many subtle ways. And the dangers for the suspect are particularly grave when the witness' opportunity for observation was insubstantial, and thus his susceptibility to suggestion the greatest.

Moreover, "[i]t is a matter of common experience that, once a witness has picked out the accused at the line-up, he is not likely to go back on his word later on, so that in practice the issue of identity may (in the absence of other relevant evidence) for all practical purposes be determined there and then, before the trial."

The pretrial confrontation for purpose of identification may take the form of a lineup, also known as an "identification parade" or "showup," as in the present case, or presentation of the suspect alone to the witness, as in *Stovall v. Denno*.[c] It is obvious that risks of suggestion attend either form of confrontation and increase the dangers inhering in eyewitness identification. But as is the case with secret interrogations, there is serious difficulty in depicting what transpires at lineups and other forms of identification confrontations. [The] defense can seldom reconstruct the manner and mode of lineup identification for judge or jury at trial. [The] impediments to an objective observation are increased when the victim is the witness. Lineups are prevalent in rape and robbery prosecutions and present a particular hazard that a victim's understandable outrage may excite vengeful or spiteful motives. In any event, neither witnesses nor lineup participants are apt to be alert for conditions prejudicial to the suspect. And if they were, it would likely be of scant benefit to the suspect since neither witnesses nor lineup participants are likely to be schooled in the detection of suggestive influences.[13] Improper influences may go undetected by a suspect, guilty or not, who experiences the emotional tension which we might expect in one being confronted with potential accusers. Even when he does observe abuse, if he has a criminal record he may be reluctant to take the stand and open up the admission of prior convictions.

---

b. Consider, too, the companion case of *Gilbert*, where the Court held, 5–4 on this issue, that the taking of handwriting exemplars from petitioner "was not a 'critical' stage of the criminal proceedings entitling petitioner to the assistance of counsel" for "there is minimal risk that the absence of counsel might derogate from his right to a fair trial. [If,] for some reason, an unrepresentative exemplar is taken, this can be brought out and corrected through the adversary process at trial since the accused can make an unlimited number of additional

exemplars for analysis and comparison by government and defense handwriting experts."

c. See pp. 630 and 640.

13. An additional impediment to the detection of such influences by participants, including the suspect, is the physical conditions often surrounding the conduct of the lineup. In many, lights shine on the stage in such a way that the suspect cannot see the witness. [In] some a one-way mirror is used and what is said on the witness' side cannot be heard. * * *

Moreover any protestations by the suspect of the fairness of the lineup made at trial are likely to be in vain; the jury's choice is between the accused's unsupported version and that of the police officers present. In short, the accused's inability effectively to reconstruct at trial any unfairness that occurred at the lineup may deprive him of his only opportunity meaningfully to attack the credibility of the witness' courtroom identification.

[The] potential for improper influence is illustrated by the circumstances, insofar as they appear, surrounding the prior identifications in the three cases we decide today. In the present case, the testimony of the identifying witnesses elicited on cross-examination revealed that those witnesses were taken to the courthouse and seated in the courtroom to await assembly of the lineup. The courtroom faced on a hallway observable to the witnesses through an open door. The cashier testified that she saw Wade "standing in the hall" within sight of an FBI agent. Five or six other prisoners later appeared in the hall. The vice president testified that he saw a person in the hall in the custody of the agent who "resembled the person that we identified as the one that had entered the bank."

The lineup in *Gilbert* was conducted in an auditorium in which some 100 witnesses to several alleged state and federal robberies charged to Gilbert made wholesale identifications of Gilbert as the robber in each other's presence, a procedure said to be fraught with dangers of suggestion. And the vice of suggestion created by the identification in *Stovall* was the presentation to the witness of the suspect alone handcuffed to police officers. It is hard to imagine a situation more clearly conveying the suggestion to the witness that the one presented is believed guilty by the police.

The few cases that have surfaced therefore reveal the existence of a process attended with hazards of serious unfairness to the criminal accused and strongly suggest the plight of the more numerous defendants who are unable to ferret out suggestive influences in the secrecy of the confrontation. We do not assume that these risks are the result of police procedures intentionally designed to prejudice an accused. Rather we assume they derive from the dangers inherent in eyewitness identification and the suggestibility inherent in the context of the pretrial identification. Williams & Hammelmann, in one of the most comprehensive studies of such forms of identification, said, "[T]he fact that the police themselves have, in a given case, little or no doubt that the man put up for identification has committed the offense, and that their chief pre-occupation is with the problem of getting sufficient proof, because he has not 'come clean,' involves a danger that this persuasion may communicate itself even in a doubtful case to the witness in some way * * *." *Identification Parades, Part I,* [1963] Crim.L.Rev. 479, 483.

Insofar as the accused's conviction may rest on a courtroom identification in fact the fruit of a suspect pretrial identification which the accused is helpless to subject to effective scrutiny at trial, the accused is deprived of that right of cross-examination which is an essential safeguard to his right to confront the witnesses against him. And even though cross-examination is a precious safeguard to a fair trial, it cannot be viewed as an absolute assurance of accuracy and reliability. Thus in the present context, where so many variables and pitfalls exist, the first line of defense must be the prevention of unfairness and the lessening of the hazards of eyewitness identification at the lineup itself. The trial which might determine the accused's fate may well not be that in the courtroom but that at the pretrial confrontation, with the State aligned against the accused, the witness the sole jury, and the accused unprotected against the overreaching, intentional or unintentional, and with little or no effective appeal from the judgment there rendered by the witness—"that's the man."

Since it appears that there is grave potential for prejudice, intentional or not, in the pretrial lineup, which may not be capable of reconstruction at trial, and since presence of counsel itself can often avert prejudice and assure a meaningful confrontation at trial,[d] there can be little doubt that for Wade the post-indictment lineup was a critical stage of the prosecution at which he was "as much entitled to such aid [of counsel as] at the trial itself." *Powell v. Alabama.* Thus both Wade and his counsel should have been notified of the impending lineup, and counsel's presence should have been a requisite to conduct of the lineup, absent an "intelligent waiver." No substantial countervailing policy considerations have been advanced against the requirement of the presence of counsel. Concern is expressed that the requirement will forestall prompt identifications and result in obstruction of the confrontations. As for the first, we note that in the two cases in which the right to counsel is today held to apply, counsel had already been appointed and no argument is made in either case that notice to counsel would have prejudicially delayed the confrontations. Moreover, we leave open the question whether the presence of substitute counsel might not suffice where notification and presence of the suspect's own counsel would result in prejudicial delay.[27] And to refuse to recognize the right to counsel for fear that counsel will obstruct the course of justice is contrary to the basic assumptions upon which this Court has operated in Sixth Amendment cases. We rejected similar logic in *Miranda,* concerning presence of counsel during custodial interrogation.

[In] our view counsel can hardly impede legitimate law enforcement; on the contrary, for the reasons expressed, law enforcement may be assisted by preventing the infiltration of taint in the prosecution's identification evidence. That result cannot help the guilty avoid conviction but can only help assure that the right man has been brought to justice.[29]

Legislative or other regulations, such as those of local police departments, which eliminate the risks of abuse and unintentional suggestion at lineup proceedings and the impediments to meaningful confrontation at trial may also remove the basis for regarding the stage as "critical." But neither Congress nor the federal authorities have seen fit to provide a solution. What we hold today "in no way creates a constitutional strait-jacket which will handicap sound efforts at reform, nor is it intended to have this effect." *Miranda.*

We come now to the question whether the denial of Wade's motion to strike the courtroom identification by the bank witnesses at trial because of the absence of his counsel at the lineup required, as the Court of Appeals held, the grant of a new trial at which such evidence is to be excluded. We do not think this disposition can be justified without first giving the Government the opportunity to establish by clear and convincing evidence that the in-court identifications were based upon observations of the suspect other than the lineup identification. * * * Where, as here, the admissibility of evidence of the lineup identification itself is

---

d. At this point, the Court refers to and describes a model statute proposed in Daniel E. Murray, *The Criminal Lineup at Home and Abroad,* 1966 Utah L.Rev. 610, 627–28, a statute providing not only for counsel, but other safeguards as well.

27. Although the right to counsel usually means a right to the suspect's own counsel, provision for substitute counsel may be justified on the ground that the substitute counsel's presence may eliminate the hazards which render the lineup a critical stage for the presence of the suspect's *own* counsel.

29. Many other nations surround the lineup with safeguards against prejudice to the suspect. In England the suspect must be allowed the presence of his solicitor or a friend; Germany requires the presence of retained counsel; France forbids the confrontation of the suspect in the absence of his counsel; Spain, Mexico, and Italy provide detailed procedures prescribing the conditions under which confrontation must occur under the supervision of a judicial officer who sees to it that the proceedings are officially recorded to assure adequate scrutiny at trial. Murray, [fn. d supra, at 621–27].

not involved, a *per se* rule of exclusion of courtroom identification would be unjustified.[e] [A] rule limited solely to the exclusion of testimony concerning identification at the lineup itself, without regard to admissibility of the courtroom identification, would render the right to counsel an empty one. The lineup is most often used, as in the present case, to crystallize the witnesses' identification of the defendant for future reference. We have already noted that the lineup identification will have that effect. The State may then rest upon the witnesses' unequivocal courtroom identification, and not mention the pretrial identification as part of the State's case at trial. Counsel is then in the predicament in which Wade's counsel found himself—realizing that possible unfairness at the lineup may be the sole means of attack upon the unequivocal courtroom identification, and having to probe in the dark in an attempt to discover and reveal unfairness, while bolstering the government witness' courtroom identification by bringing out and dwelling upon his prior identification. Since counsel's presence at the lineup would equip him to attack not only the lineup identification but the courtroom identification as well, limiting the impact of violation of the right to counsel to exclusion of evidence only of identification at the lineup itself disregards a critical element of that right.

We think it follows that the proper test to be applied in these situations is that quoted in *Wong Sun v. United States* [p. 765], " '[W]hether, granting establishment of the primary illegality the evidence to which instant objection is made has been come at by exploitation of that illegality or instead by means sufficiently distinguishable to be purged of the primary taint.' Maguire, *Evidence of Guilt* 221 (1959)." Application of this test in the present context requires consideration of various factors; for example, the prior opportunity to observe the alleged criminal act, the existence of any discrepancy between any pre-lineup description and the defendant's actual description, any identification prior to lineup of another person, the identification by picture of the defendant prior to the lineup, failure to identify the defendant on a prior occasion, and the lapse of time between the alleged act and the lineup identification. It is also relevant to consider those facts which, despite the absence of counsel, are disclosed concerning the conduct of the lineup.[33]

On the record now before us we cannot make the determination whether the in-court identifications had an independent origin. [T]he appropriate procedure to be followed is to vacate the conviction pending a hearing to determine whether the in-court identifications had an independent source, or whether, in any event, the introduction of the evidence was harmless error, *Chapman v. California* [Ch. 27, § 5], and for the District Court to reinstate the conviction or order a new trial, as may be proper.[f] * * *

---

e. In *Gilbert*, however, the Court did apply a *per se* exclusionary rule to the testimony of various prosecution witnesses that they had also identified petitioner at a pretrial lineup. See fn. f infra.

33. Thus it is not the case that "[i]t matters not how well the witness knows the suspect, whether the witness is the suspect's mother, brother, or long-time associate, and no matter how long or well the witness observed the perpetrator at the scene of the crime" [quoting from Justice White's opinion in *Wade*]. Such factors will have an important bearing upon the true basis of the witness' in-court identification. * * *

f. Compare *Gilbert*, where various witnesses who identified petitioner in the court-

room also testified, on direct examination by the prosecution, that they had identified petitioner at a prior lineup. "That [pretrial lineup] testimony," ruled the Court, "is the direct result of the illegal lineup 'come at by exploitation of [the primary] illegality.' *Wong Sun*. The State is therefore not entitled to an opportunity to show that that testimony had an independent source. Only a *per se* exclusionary rule as to such testimony can be an effective sanction to assure that law enforcement authorities will respect the accused's constitutional right to the presence of his counsel at the critical lineup. [That] conclusion is buttressed by the consideration that the witness' testimony of his lineup identification will enhance the impact of his in-court identification on the jury and seriously

Dis/con

Almost impossible too early FOP?

Dissent

Justice BLACK, dissenting in part and concurring in part. * * *

I would reverse Wade's conviction without further ado had the prosecution at trial made use of his lineup identification either in place of courtroom identification or [as it did in *Gilbert*] to bolster in a harmful manner crucial courtroom identification. But the prosecution here did neither of these things. After prosecution witnesses under oath identified Wade in the courtroom, it was the defense, and not the prosecution, which brought out the prior lineup identification. While stating that "a *per se* rule of exclusion of courtroom identification would be unjustified," the Court, nevertheless remands this case for "a hearing to determine whether the in-court identifications had an independent source," or were the tainted fruits of the invalidly conducted lineup. From this holding I dissent.

In the first place, even if this Court has power to establish such a rule of evidence, I think the rule fashioned by the Court is unsound. The "tainted fruit" determination required by the Court involves more than considerable difficulty. I think it is practically impossible. How is a witness capable of probing the recesses of his mind to draw a sharp line between a courtroom identification due exclusively to an earlier lineup and a courtroom identification due to memory not based on the lineup? [In] my view, the Fifth and Sixth Amendments are satisfied if the prosecution is precluded from using lineup identification as either an alternative to or corroboration of courtroom identification. If the prosecution does neither and its witnesses under oath identify the defendant in the courtroom, then I can find no justification for stopping the trial in midstream to hold a lengthy "tainted fruit" hearing. * * *

Justice WHITE whom Justice HARLAN and Justice STEWART join, dissenting in part and concurring in part.

The Court has again propounded a broad constitutional rule barring the use of a wide spectrum of relevant and probative evidence, solely because a step in its ascertainment or discovery occurs outside the presence of defense counsel.

[The] Court's opinion is far-reaching. It proceeds first by creating a new *per se* rule of constitutional law: a criminal suspect cannot be subjected to a pretrial identification process in the absence of his counsel without violating the Sixth Amendment. If he is, the State may not buttress a later courtroom identification of the witness by any reference to the previous identification. Furthermore, the courtroom identification is not admissible at all unless the State can establish by clear and convincing proof that the testimony is not the fruit of the earlier identification made in the absence of defendant's counsel—admittedly a heavy burden for the State and probably an impossible one. To all intents and purposes, courtroom identifications are barred if pretrial identifications have occurred without counsel being present.

The rule applies to any lineup, to any other techniques employed to produce an identification and *a fortiori* to a face-to-face encounter between the witness and the suspect alone, regardless of when the identification occurs, in time or place, and whether before or after indictment or information. It matters not how well the witness knows the suspect, whether the witness is the suspect's mother, brother, or long-time associate, and no matter how long or well the witness observed the perpetrator at the scene of the crime. The kidnap victim who has lived for days with his abductor is in the same category as the witness who has had only a fleeting glimpse of the criminal. Neither may identify the suspect without defendant's counsel being present. The same strictures apply regardless of the number of other witnesses who positively identify the defendant and

aggravate whatever derogation exists of the accused's right to a fair trial. Therefore, unless the [state supreme court] is 'able to declare a belief that it was harmless beyond a reasonable doubt,' *Chapman*, Gilbert will be entitled on remand to a new trial * * *."

regardless of the corroborative evidence showing that it was the defendant who had committed the crime.

[The] Court apparently believes that improper police procedures are so widespread that a broad prophylactic rule must be laid down, requiring the presence of counsel at all pretrial identifications, in order to detect recurring instances of police misconduct.[1] I do not share this pervasive distrust of all official investigations. None of the materials the Court relies upon supports it. Certainly, I would bow to solid fact, but the Court quite obviously does not have before it any reliable, comprehensive survey of current police practices on which to base its new rule. Until it does, the Court should avoid excluding relevant evidence from state criminal trials.

[There] are several striking aspects to the Court's holding. First, the rule does not bar courtroom identifications where there have been no previous identifications in the presence of the police, although when identified in the courtroom, the defendant is known to be in custody and charged with the commission of a crime.[g] Second, the Court seems to say that if suitable legislative standards were adopted for the conduct of pretrial identifications, thereby lessening the hazards in such confrontations, it would not insist on the presence of counsel. But if this is true, why does not the Court simply fashion what it deems to be constitutionally acceptable procedures for the authorities to follow? Certainly the Court is correct in suggesting that the new rule will be wholly inapplicable where police departments themselves have established suitable safeguards.

Third, courtroom identification may be barred, absent counsel at a prior identification, regardless of the extent of counsel's information concerning the circumstances of the previous confrontation between witness and defendant—apparently even if there were recordings or sound-movies of the events as they occurred. But if the rule is premised on the defendant's right to have his counsel know, there seems little basis for not accepting other means to inform. A disinterested observer, recordings, photographs—any one of them would seem adequate to furnish the basis for a meaningful cross-examination of the eyewitness who identifies the defendant in the courtroom. * * *

I would not extend [the adversary] system, at least as it presently operates, to police investigations and would not require counsel's presence at pretrial identification procedures. Counsel's interest is in not having his client placed at the scene of the crime, regardless of his whereabouts. Some counsel may advise their clients to refuse to make any movements or to speak any words in a lineup or even to appear in one. [Others] will hover over witnesses and begin their cross-examination then, menacing truthful factfinding as thoroughly as the Court fears the police now do. Certainly there is an implicit invitation to counsel to suggest rules for the lineup and to manage and produce it as best he can.[h] I therefore doubt that the Court's new rule, at least absent some clearly defined limits on counsel's

1. Yet in *Stovall v. Denno* [p. 630] the Court recognizes that improper police conduct in the identification process has not been so widespread as to justify full retroactivity for its new rule.

g. Consider Joseph D. Grano, *Kirby, Biggers, and Ash: Do Any Constitutional Safeguards Remain Against the Danger of Convicting the Innocent?*, 72 Mich.L.Rev. 717, 785 (1974): "[A]n identification more unreliable than the witness's familiar selection of the conspicuous defendant, frequently after scan-

ning the courtroom for dramatic effect, is difficult to imagine. In effect, [these identifications are] one-man showups, albeit in the courtroom." Consider, too, H. Richard Uviller, *The Role of the Defense Lawyer at a Lineup in Light of the Wade, Gilbert and Stovall Decisions*, 4 Crim.L.Bull. 273, 284 (1968).

How can defense counsel avoid or minimize the impact of a suggestive confrontation between a witness and defendant in the courtroom? See Note 6 following this case.

h. But see Note 2 following this case.

role, will measurably contribute to more reliable pretrial identifications. My fears are that it will have precisely the opposite result. * * *

ON THE MEANING OF THE LINEUP DECISIONS

1. *Waiver.* If *Wade* seeks to protect the reliability of the identification process and to make available testimony about the conditions under which such process is carried out, why should the right to counsel at the lineup be subject to waiver? Permitting waiver of *Miranda* rights may be defended on the ground that an important, legitimate object is served by permitting suspects to bear witness to the truth under conditions which safeguard the exercise of responsible choice, but what comparable value is served by allowing suspects to waive counsel at the identification process?

2. *The role of counsel.* What is the role of defense counsel at the lineup? Consider Commentary to the *Model Pre–Arraignment Code* at 429–33:

"The two extreme positions might be stated thus:

"(1) Counsel is to be present merely as an observer to assure against abuse and bad faith by law enforcement officers, and to provide the basis for any attack he might wish to make on the identification at trial.

"(2) The lineup procedure is to be a fully adversary proceeding in which the counsel for the suspect may make objections and proposals, which if they are proper or even reasonable must be respected.

"The cases and commentaries, as well as the practice since *Wade* would indicate that the first interpretation of the counsel's role comes closer to describing the general interpretation of the constitutional requirement and to describing the practice under it. The major difficulty with this interpretation is that by forcing counsel into the role of a merely passive observer it gives him a job which at best can be accomplished in a large variety of ways including video recording and at worst is uncomfortable or demeaning.

"[On] the other hand, any attempt to give counsel at identification a more active role is fraught with difficulties not only for the police but for counsel himself. For the police the difficulty is that a procedure which is often under the supervision not of lawyers but of police officers will be subject to manipulation and objection by a trained legal counsel for one side only.

"[The] assigning of a more active role to counsel has perils for counsel as well. If he is entitled to make objections at the lineup procedure, will he be held to have waived these objections if he does not make them at the procedure and he wishes later to question the fairness or accuracy of the identification at trial? If such a possibility of waiver exists will he not almost be under an obligation to raise every conceivable objection? Moreover, this hard choice would be imposed on a lawyer at a very early stage of his contact with the case. Indeed the lawyer who did this work is often likely to be a junior member of the public defender's staff assigned on rotation to do 'lineup work,' and thus would not likely be the lawyer to handle the case at trial.

"[Thus, where] a lawyer is present he should not be obliged to make his objections or be deemed to have waived them. Similarly, there does not appear to be any reason to require the police to abide by any objections or suggestions that the lawyer makes. All the Code would require is that any objections that the lawyer might have be made part of the record of the identification procedure. In this way if something has taken place to which defense counsel objects and which the record might not otherwise clearly show, the fact of the lawyer's objection will make this issue prominently available for use at the trial. At the same time, the police in hearing the objection would have the opportunity to remedy the situation if they chose. To be sure, the absence of any objection might possibly carry some factual implication that the defendant and his counsel acquiesced in an identification procedure to which they then find themselves subsequently objecting at trial. This possibility may be thought to provide just the right degree of incentive for defense counsel to make reasonable objections which the police might heed, rather than sitting back and hoping to trap the police in error."

3. ***Refusals to cooperate; obstructionist efforts.*** Since the lineup or the taking of exemplars is not protected by the privilege against self-incrimination, the prosecution may comment on the suspect's refusal to cooperate. The refusal is considered circumstantial evidence of consciousness of guilt. On occasion, courts have utilized civil or criminal contempt to coerce or punish the suspect who refuses to comply with a court order to participate in some identification proceeding. Still another possibility is for the police to proceed to conduct the identification proceeding over the suspect's objection. See LaFave & Israel, § 7.2(c).

What may be done in response to a suspect's drastic alteration of his appearance between the time of arrest (or the occurrence of the crime) and his appearance in a lineup?[a] One possibility is to bring this alteration to the attention of the jury for consideration as evidence of defendant's consciousness of guilt. Another possibility is to conduct the identification procedure in such a way as to simulate the defendant's prior appearance. See LaFave & Israel, § 7.2(d).

4. ***Invalid pre-trial identification procedures and the "independent origin" of in-court identifications.*** Reconsider Justice Black's complaint in *Wade* about the difficulties involved in determining whether or not an in-court identification is the "tainted fruit" of an improperly conducted lineup. Does it follow, as Justice Black maintained, that therefore *every* courtroom identification made subsequent to an illegal police lineup (so long as not supplemented or corroborated by the earlier lineup) should be admitted? Or do the very reasons advanced by Justice Black—the great difficulties, if not impossibility of ascertaining the "taint" or lack of it—suggest that *no* courtroom identification preceded by an illegal police lineup should be allowed?[b]

Is the requirement that the prosecution establish by clear and convincing proof that the courtroom testimony is untainted by the earlier illegal identification a "heavy" and "probably an impossible" burden, as Justice White maintained in *Wade*? If pre-trial identifications are held in violation of the suspect's right to counsel, does the *Wade-Gilbert* rule, as Justice White claimed, bar all courtroom identifications "to all intents and purposes"? Consider the remarks of A.J. Davis, *The Role of the Defense Lawyer at a Lineup in Light of the Wade, Gilbert and Stovall Decisions*, 4 Crim.L.Bull. 273, 294–95 (1968) (panel discussion), a year after the lineup cases were decided:

a. What ethical questions, if any, are raised by a defense lawyer who encourages his client to "disguise himself" prior to a lineup?

b. The difficulties of determining whether there is an "independent source" for in-court identifications following invalid pre-trial lineups are illustrated by *Clemons v. United States*, 408 F.2d 1230 (D.C.Cir.1968) and explored in Robert Pitler, *"The Fruit of the Poisonous Tree" Revisited and Shepardized*, 56 Calif.L.Rev. 579, 636–41 (1968); Note 45 Wash.L.Rev. 202 (1970). See generally Felice J. Levine & June L. Tapp, *The Psychology of Criminal Identifications: The Gap from Wade to Kirby*, 121 U.Pa.L.Rev. 1079 (1973). The

difficulties are compounded when a courtroom identification is preceded by a corporeal identification which, in turn, is preceded by a photographic identification. For the corporeal identification "may be based not upon the witness's recollection of the features of the guilty party, but upon his recollection of the photograph. Thus, although a witness who is asked to attempt a corporeal identification of a person whose photograph he has previously identified may say, 'That's the man that did it,' what he may actually mean is, 'That's the man whose photograph I identified.'" Patrick E. Wall, *Eye-Witness Identification in Criminal Cases* 68 (1965).

"How [is the defense lawyer] going to prove that the in-court identification that the victim is about to make is the fruit of [the invalid police lineup]? The Supreme Court may say the burden of proof is on the prosecution, but you know and I know that the attitude of the trial judge is going to be that the burden of proof is on [the defense lawyer] as a practical matter to convince that judge. He is not going to be terribly sympathetic to these cases.

"What is the prosecution going to do? The prosecution is going to put the victim on the stand and the victim is going to say, 'When this robber came to me and put that gun in my face, I looked at him and I formed a mental picture. [Then,] I had this lineup and I compared this portrait in my mind with the people in the lineup and I picked out that defendant. Now I am in court and what am I doing? I am not paying any attention to the lineup. I am again conjuring up that [mental picture] which I evolved in my mind at the time of the robbery, and I am taking that [picture] and putting it next to this defendant at the counsel table and I am saying that they are precisely the same,' and the judge is going to say, 'Whoopie, there's an independent origin,' and you can attempt to prove from today to tomorrow that the pre-trial identification was unfair, but the trial court has a finding of fact to make here, and nine times out of ten, unless you have a very exceptional trial court, he is going to find against you on this issue."

Mr. Davis has turned out to be a better prognosticator than Justice White. The cases support the conclusions of commentators that when confronted with invalid pre-trial identifications the lower courts have "easily found an 'independent source' for an in-court identification," Note, 55 Minn.L.Rev. 779, 818 (1971), and have "readily avoided reversing convictions by stretching, often beyond reason and logic, the doctrines of independent source and harmless error," Grano, p. 625, fn. g, at 722.

5. Defendant's right to a lineup or other identification procedure. Reconsider fn. g, p. 625. Should a defendant be allowed to sit among spectators or with nonsuspects at counsel table? Should he be entitled to an in-court lineup, or a pretrial lineup, before being required to confront witnesses in the courtroom?

Consider *Moore v. Illinois,* 434 U.S. 220, 98 S.Ct. 458, 54 L.Ed.2d 424 (1977) (also discussed at p. 634). In rejecting the contention that because the corporeal identification occurred "in the course of a judicial proceeding" (a preliminary hearing to determine whether petitioner should be bound over to the grand jury and to set bail) petitioner had no *Wade-Gilbert* right to counsel at the identification procedure, the Court, per Powell, J., pointed out that the identification, "a one-on-one confrontation," had been made under highly suggestive circumstances and that "[h]ad petitioner been represented by counsel, some or all of this suggestiveness could have been avoided." It then noted:

"For example, counsel could have requested that the hearing be postponed until a lineup could be arranged at which the victim would view petitioner in a less suggestive setting. Short of that, counsel could have asked that the victim be excused from the courtroom while the charges were read and the evidence against petitioner was recited, and that petitioner be seated with other people in the audience when the victim attempted an identification. * * * Because it is in the prosecution's interest as well as the accused's that witnesses' identifications remain untainted, we cannot assume that such requests would have been in vain. Such requests are usually addressed to the sound discretion of the court; we express no opinion as to whether the preliminary hearing court would have been required to grant any such requests."

Although such requests are occasionally granted, trial judges, in their discretion, often deny them. See generally Wayne R. LaFave, Jerold H. Israel, & Nancy J. King, *Criminal Procedure Treatise* § 7.4(f) (2d ed. 1999) (hereafter CRIM-

PROC). A leading case on this point is *Evans v. Superior Court,* 522 P.2d 681 (Cal.1974), holding that due process requires that in an appropriate case defendant should be afforded a pretrial lineup, but that such a right arises "only when eyewitness identification is shown to be in material issue and there exists a reasonable likelihood of a mistaken identification which a lineup would tend to resolve." See also *United States v. Archibald,* 734 F.2d 938 (2d Cir.1984), per Oakes, J., pointing out that defendant's request that he be seated away from the defense table and that other black men be seated in the courtroom "should not have been dismissed so quickly or so absolutely by the trial court. [While] it was not necessary for the court to conduct a true *Wade*-type lineup, these relatively minor steps were required to ensure that the identification was not unfair. The in-court identification procedure utilized here was so clearly suggestive as to be impermissible, however traditional it may be."[c]

Model Pre–Arraignment Code § 170.2 permits a person "arrested for or charged with an offense or a person who shows a reasonable basis for believing he may be so charged" to request a nontestimonial identification order requiring persons *other than himself* to appear (presumably to "clear" himself by shifting suspicion to another) or to request an identification procedure involving himself.[d]

6. *On the use of cautionary instructions.* Edith Greene, *Eyewitness Testimony and the Use of Cautionary Instructions,* 8 U.Bridgeport L.Rev. 15 (1987), casts serious doubt about the effectiveness of the most widely used cautionary instruction on eyewitness testimony. Jurors given this instruction seem to be no better informed about the governing legal standards and the factors that affect the reliability of eyewitness testimony than jurors who received no cautionary instruction. Thus, concludes Greene, the many judges who refuse to admit expert testimony about the factors that influence witness reliability because they believe a cautionary instruction will be effective at conveying the information to jurors are acting on an unwarranted assumption. This is not surprising, since other research shows that most jurors fail to understand most of the instructions they receive. See R. Charrow & V. Charrow, *Making Legal Language Understandable: A Psycholinguistic Study of Jury Instructions,* 79 Colum.L.Rev. 1306 (1979).

7. *The use of expert psychological testimony.* Increasingly, defendants are attempting to use experts to explain to the jury the frailty and fallibility of eyewitness testimony. But the admissibility of expert testimony is largely a matter of trial court discretion. And in the main the judicial response to such defense efforts has been very cool. For a discussion—and strong criticism—of the arguments against the use of expert testimony on eyewitness identification, see James Murphy, *An Evaluation of the Arguments Against the Use of Expert Testimony on Eyewitness Identification,* 8 U.Bridgeport L.Rev. 21 (1987). Professor Murphy maintains that "eyewitness testimony, not sufficiently understood by the jury is dangerous evidence which may easily result in miscarriages of justice," and that trial court discretion "is not a license for a court to shut its eyes to advancements

c. On petition for rehearing, 756 F.2d 223 (2d Cir.1984), *Archibald* was modified to make it clear that special in-court identification procedures are necessary "only when (1) identification is a contested issue; (2) the defendant has moved in a timely manner prior to trial for a lineup; and (3) despite that defense request, the witness has not had an opportunity to view a fair out-of-court lineup prior to his trial testimony."

d. Perhaps because trial judges frequently deny requests, to hold an in-court lineup or to seat the defendant in the courtroom audience before and during the testimony of the prosecution's identification witnesses, defense attorneys have sometimes resorted to "self-help," i.e., substituted another person for the defendant at counsel table without the court's permission or knowledge. This "has been viewed as a violation of ethical standards and an obstruction of justice punishable by criminal contempt." CRIMPROC, § 7.5(g).

in knowledge in other fields." See also Michael R. Leippe, *The Case for Expert Testimony About Eyewitness Testimony*, 1 Psychology, Pub. Pol'y & L. 909 (1995).

8. *Despite its unreliability, is eyewitness identification the source of only a relatively small number of wrongful convictions?* Yes, suggests Samuel Gross, *Loss of Innocence: Eyewitness Identification and Proof of Guilt*, 16 J.Legal Studies 395 (1987). "[W]hile convictions based on eyewitness errors may be more frequent than are other types of erroneous convictions," observes Professor Gross, id. at 396, "in absolute terms they are rare. And that presents a paradox: eyewitness identification is (1) a notoriously unreliable type of evidence, (2) the basis of numerous guilty verdicts, and yet (3) the source of only a small number of wrongful convictions. Why?"

According to Gross, "eyewitness testimony is frequently less important to the determination of the identity of a criminal than it appears to be because the eyewitness evidence is corroborated by other information that is often undervalued or inadmissible at trial." Gross examines an extensive set of criminal prosecutions ultimately proven to have been based on misidentifications. He "focuses on the informal mechanisms that are used to sort criminal cases before trial," id., in particular the various types of information that lead the police to suspect the defendant in the first place, and the process by which the prosecutor decides to dismiss some charges and press others.

"If [juries] return few erroneous convictions," maintains Gross, "it is because they are given few opportunities to judge innocent defendants." Id. at 432. Therefore, the best way to reduce the number of convictions based on misidentifications "is to improve the quality of pretrial determination of identity and to tighten the standards for prosecution in cases in which identity is in dispute. Some reforms in trial procedure might be useful, but primarily those designed to force the police and prosecutors to improve their investigations rather than those armed at improving the accuracy of courtroom judgments. The major impetus for change, however, must come from the law enforcement community itself." Id. at 448.

THE DUE PROCESS "BACK-UP" TEST

STOVALL v. DENNO, 388 U.S. 293, 87 S.Ct. 1967, 18 L.Ed.2d 1199 (1967) (a federal habeas corpus proceeding collaterally attacking a state criminal conviction) (discussed more extensively in § 3, infra), held that the newly announced *Wade-Gilbert* principles would not be applied retroactively but would affect only those identification procedures conducted in the absence of counsel after the date the *Wade* and *Gilbert* decisions were handed down.[a] The court did consider, however, whether "the confrontation conducted in this case was so unnecessarily suggestive and conducive to irreparable mistaken identification" that petitioner was denied due process of law—"a recognized ground of attack upon a conviction independent of any right to counsel claim," but one that must be evaluated in light of the totality of surrounding circumstances. Since the record revealed that the showing of petitioner to a victim of the assault "in an immediate hospital confrontation was imperative," the due process claim was denied. As *Stovall* illustrates, and as the Court later articulated the due process test when it applied it to a pretrial identification by photograph, the question is whether the identification procedure "was so *impermissibly* suggestive as to give rise to a very substantial likelihood of irreparable misidentification." *Simmons v. United States*, 390 U.S. 377, 88 S.Ct. 967, 19 L.Ed.2d 1247 (1968). (Emphasis added.)

a. For a general discussion of the retroactive effect of a new constitutional decision in the criminal procedure field, see pp. 41–47.

THE EYE–WITNESS TESTIMONY PROVISIONS
OF THE 1968 CRIME CONTROL ACT

Consider the constitutionality of Title II of the Omnibus Crime Control and Safe Streets Act of 1968, 18 U.S.C. § 3502, designed to "repeal" the *Wade-Gilbert* rule in federal prosecutions: "The testimony of a witness that he saw the accused commit or participate in the commission of the crime for which the accused is being tried shall be admissible in evidence in a criminal prosecution in any trial court ordained and established under article III of the Constitution of the United States."

Consider Judge Carl McGowan, *Constitutional Interpretation and Criminal Identification,* 12 Wm. & Mary L.Rev. 235, 249–50 (1970): "As a practical matter, the Congressional [response to *Wade-Gilbert–Stovall*] has proved to be meaningless. The inferior federal courts have considered themselves bound by the Supreme Court's reading of the Constitution rather than that of the Congress and have appeared to ignore the new statute. [Congress] appeared to overlook completely the threat to the conviction rate inherent in the impatience of juries with prosecution cases limited to in-court identification. It showed no awareness of the values that may reside, for the prosecution as well as the defense, in tightening up pretrial identification procedures so that impressively credible identification evidence can be adduced." See also Commentary to *Model Pre–Arraignment Code* at 427 & n. 15.

In light of its sparse legislative history, may § 3502 be read as excepting from its language lineups conducted in violation of due process, which *Stovall* recognized as a basis for attacking identification testimony independent of any right to counsel claim?

SECTION 2. THE COURT RETREATS:
KIRBY AND *ASH*

KIRBY v. ILLINOIS

406 U.S. 682, 92 S.Ct. 1877, 32 L.Ed.2d 411 (1972).

Justice STEWART announced the judgment of the Court in an opinion in which The Chief Justice, Justice BLACKMUN, and Justice REHNQUIST join.

[In] the present case we are asked to extend the *Wade-Gilbert* per se exclusionary rule to identification testimony based upon a police station show-up that took place *before* the defendant had been indicted or otherwise formally charged with any criminal offense.

On February 21, 1968, [one] Willie Shard reported to the Chicago police that the previous day two men had robbed him on a Chicago street of a wallet containing, among other things, travellers checks and a Social Security card. On February 22, two police officers [investigating an unrelated crime] stopped petitioner and a companion, [Bean], [on a Chicago street]. When asked for identification, the petitioner produced a wallet that contained three travellers checks and a Social Security card, all bearing the name of Willie Shard. * * *

Only after arriving at the police station, and checking the records there, did the arresting officers learn of the Shard robbery. [The police] picked up Shard and brought him to the police station. Immediately upon entering the room [where petitioner and Bean were seated], Shard positively identified them as [his robbers].[a] No lawyer was present [and neither suspect had asked for] or been advised of any right to the presence of counsel. [At the trial Shard] described his identification of the two men at the police station [and] identified them again in the courtroom as the men who had robbed him.

[In] a line of constitutional cases in this Court stemming back to the Court's landmark opinion in *Powell v. Alabama,* it has been firmly established that a person's Sixth and Fourteenth Amendment right to counsel attaches only at or after the time that adversary judicial proceedings have been initiated against him.

This is not to say that a defendant in a criminal case has a constitutional right to counsel only at the trial itself. [But] the point is [that] *all* of [the right to counsel cases] have involved points of time at or after the initiation of adversary judicial criminal proceedings—whether by way of formal charge, preliminary hearing, indictment, information, or arraignment.

The only seeming deviation from this long line of constitutional decisions was *Escobedo* [which] is not apposite here for two distinct reasons. First, the Court in retrospect perceived that the "prime purpose" of *Escobedo* was not to vindicate the constitutional right to counsel as such, but, like *Miranda,* "to guarantee full effectuation of the privilege against self-incrimination. * * * " *Johnson v. New Jersey* [p. 42]. Secondly, and perhaps even more important for purely practical purposes, the Court has limited the holding of *Escobedo* to its own facts, and those facts are not remotely akin to the facts of the case before us.

The initiation of judicial criminal proceedings is far from a mere formalism. It is the starting point of our whole system of adversary criminal justice. For it is only then that the Government has committed itself to prosecute, and only then that the adverse positions of Government and defendant have solidified. It is then that a defendant finds himself faced with the prosecutorial forces of organized society, and immersed in the intricacies of substantive and procedural criminal law. It is this point, therefore, that marks the commencement of the "criminal prosecutions" to which alone the explicit guarantees of the Sixth Amendment are applicable.

In this case we are asked to import into a routine police investigation an absolute constitutional guarantee historically and rationally applicable only after the onset of formal prosecutorial proceedings. We decline to do so. We decline to [impose] a *per se* exclusionary rule upon testimony concerning an identification that took place long before the commencement of any prosecution whatever.

What has been said is not to suggest that there may not be occasions during the course of a criminal investigation when the police do abuse identification procedures. Such abuses are not beyond the reach of the Constitution. [The] Due Process Clause of the Fifth and Fourteenth Amendments forbids a lineup that is unnecessarily suggestive and conducive to irreparable mistaken identification.[8] When a person has not been formally charged with a criminal offense, *Stovall* strikes the appropriate constitutional balance between the right of a suspect to be protected from prejudicial procedures and the interest of society in the prompt and purposeful investigation of an unsolved crime.

a. According to dissenting Justice Brennan, Shard testified that he identified petitioner and Bean only after the officers who brought him to the room asked him if they were the robbers.

8. In view of our limited grant of certiorari, we do not consider whether there might have been a deprivation of due process in the particularized circumstances of this case. That ques-

tion remains open for inquiry in a federal habeas corpus proceeding.

[Following the U.S. Supreme Court's decision, the denial of Kirby's petition for federal habeas corpus relief was affirmed by the Seventh Circuit in *United States ex rel. Kirby v. Sturges,* 510 F.2d 397 (1975).]

The judgment is affirmed.[b]

Justice BRENNAN, with whom Justice DOUGLAS and Justice MARSHALL join, dissenting. * * *

While it should go without saying, it appears necessary, in view of the plurality opinion today, to re-emphasize that *Wade* did not require the presence of counsel at pretrial confrontations for identification purposes simply on the basis of an abstract consideration of the words "criminal prosecutions" in the Sixth Amendment, [but] in order to safeguard the accused's constitutional rights to confrontation and the effective assistance of counsel at his trial.

In view of *Wade,* it is plain, and the plurality today does not attempt to dispute it, that there inhere in a confrontation for identification conducted after arrest[5] the identical hazards to a fair trial that inhere in such a confrontation conducted "after the onset of formal prosecutorial proceedings." [The] plurality offers no reason, and I can think of none, for concluding that a post-arrest confrontation for identification, unlike a post-charge confrontation, is not among those "critical confrontations of the accused by the prosecution at pretrial proceedings where the results might well settle the accused's fate and reduce the trial itself to a mere formality."

The highly suggestive form of confrontation employed in this case underscores the point. This showup was particularly fraught with the peril of mistaken identification. In the setting of a police station squad room where all present except petitioner and Bean were police officers, the danger was quite real that Shard's understandable resentment might lead him too readily to agree with the police that the pair under arrest, and the only persons exhibited to him, were indeed the robbers. [On] direct examination, Shard identified petitioner and Bean not as the alleged robbers on trial in the courtroom, but as the pair he saw at the police station. * * *

Wade and *Gilbert,* of course, happened to involve post-indictment confrontations. Yet even a cursory perusal of the opinions in those cases reveals that nothing at all turned upon that particular circumstance." * * *

Justice WHITE, dissenting.

Wade and *Gilbert* govern this case and compel reversal of the judgment below.

Notes and Questions

1. **Wade and Escobedo.** Does the "reinterpretation" of *Escobedo* (as designed not to vindicate the right to counsel as such but to effectuate the privilege against self-incrimination) support Justice Stewart's holding in *Kirby?* Consider Grano at 728: "*Wade,* like *Escobedo* in its new guise, did not vindicate the right to counsel as such, but rather vindicated the rights of cross-examination, confrontation, and fair trial. *Escobedo* still suggests that counsel must be provided at *any* pretrial stage when necessary to protect other constitutional rights."

2. **Wade and Powell.** Did the early right to counsel precedents, as Justice Stewart indicates, mandate the result in *Kirby?* Consider Grano at 727: "*Powell v. Alabama* [and its pre-*Gideon* progeny] relied on the fourteenth amendment due process clause rather than on the sixth amendment. Since the protections under the fourteenth amendment are not limited to any particular stage of a criminal

---

b. As he "would not extend the *Wade-Gilbert* exclusionary rule," Powell, J., concurred in the result.

5. This case does not require me to consider confrontations that take place before custo-

dy, nor accidental confrontations not arranged by the police, nor on-the-scene encounters shortly after the crime.

proceeding, the fact that the defendants in these cases had already been charged is irrelevant."

3. *"Custody" vs. "the initiation of adversary judicial criminal proceedings."* Is it sound to view (as does Justice Stewart for the plurality in *Kirby*) the "initiation of judicial criminal proceedings [as] the starting point of our whole system of adversary criminal justice"? Is it realistic to say, (as Justice Stewart does for the *Kirby* plurality) that "it is only then [that] the adverse positions of Government and defendant have solidified"? Is the postcustody police attitude supposed to be "neutral" or merely "investigative" rather than "accusatory"? Didn't the Court explicitly recognize in *Miranda* that the accusatory function begins very soon after the defendant is taken into custody? Again, see Grano at 726–27. Recall the statement in *Escobedo*—over Justice Stewart's strong dissent— that "it would exalt form over substance to make the right to counsel, under these circumstances, depend on whether at the time of the interrogation the authorities had secured a formal indictment. Petitioner had, for all practical purposes, already been charged * * *."

But consider Israel, *Criminal Procedure, the Burger Court, and the Legacy of the Warren Court,* 75 Mich.L.Rev. 1320, 1368 n. 224 (1977): "[A]ccepting the premise that the need for counsel is often equivalent in the post-indictment and pre-indictment lineup, it does not necessarily follow that appointment of counsel is constitutionally required in both situations. The sixth amendment, it can be argued, does not provide for counsel at every stage in which counsel's assistance is helpful. Rather, by its history, language, and function, the amendment sought to draw a starting point after which counsel's assistance is generally required as an element of our adversary system. That point, Justice Stewart argues, is the initiation of judicial criminal proceedings. Before that point, counsel may be constitutionally required only if essential to the protection of some other constitutional right, as in *Miranda*. *Kirby* obviously concluded that it was not so essential as to be required to implement the right of confronting the eyewitness at trial."

4. *Alley confrontations.* To what extent did *Kirby* reject the "custody" approach because such an approach would pose a serious threat to the common police practice of conducting "alley confrontations," i.e., prompt confrontations with the victim or an eyewitness at the scene of the crime? See Grano at 731. Prior to *Kirby* most courts exempted these identifications from the right to counsel requirement. See, e.g., *Russell v. United States*, 408 F.2d 1280 (D.C.Cir. 1969) (Bazelon, C.J.).

For the view that all the psychological assumptions on which *Russell* and similar cases are premised—(a) the victim or witness to a crime can be counted on to form an accurate mental image of the offender; (b) this image will be more accurate on the scene immediately after the crime than at the police station some hours later; and (c) the suggestion inherent in one-man confrontations is insignificant in light of the other factors—are speculative and questionable, see Grano at 734–38.

5. *When are adversary judicial criminal proceedings "initiated"?* In MOORE v. ILLINOIS, 434 U.S. 220, 98 S.Ct. 458, 54 L.Ed.2d 424 (1977), a police officer accompanied the victim to a courtroom where petitioner, a rape suspect, was to appear for his preliminary hearing to determine whether he should be bound over to the grand jury and to set bail. Petitioner was not represented by counsel at this hearing, nor offered appointed counsel. After petitioner's name was called and he was led before the bench, and after the prosecutor had recited evidence believed to implicate petitioner, the victim was asked by the prosecutor where she saw her assailant in the courtroom and she pointed at petitioner. At trial, the victim testified on direct that she had identified petitioner at the

preliminary hearing. In reversing the judgment of the federal court of appeals denying habeas corpus relief, the Court, per POWELL, J., rejected, inter alia, the contention that evidence of a corporeal identification conducted in the absence of defense counsel must be excluded only if the identification is made after the defendant is indicted:

"The prosecution in this case was commenced under Illinois law when the victim's complaint was filed in court. The purpose of the preliminary hearing was to determine whether there was probable cause to bind petitioner over to the grand jury and to set bail. Petitioner had the right to oppose the prosecution at that hearing by moving to dismiss the charges and to suppress the evidence against him. He faced counsel for the State * * *. It is plain that '[t]he government ha[d] committed itself to prosecute,' and that petitioner found 'himself faced with the prosecutorial forces of organized society, and immersed in the intricacies of substantive and procedural criminal law.' *Kirby*. The State candidly concedes that the preliminary hearing marked the 'initiation of adversary judicial criminal proceedings' against petitioner, and it hardly could contend otherwise."[a]

Section 160.3(2) of the *Model Code* "codifies" *Kirby* by granting a suspect a right to counsel at corporeal identification procedures "if a complaint has been filed charging a person with crime, or a person has been indicted for crime." Rule 403 of the *Model Rules* reads *Kirby* as giving a suspect "the right to a lawyer for any lineup connected with an arrest for which he was arrested or charged—and to have a lawyer appointed for this purpose if he cannot afford one—if the lineup is held following the start of criminal proceedings against him" (emphasis in the original) and provides further: "Criminal proceedings may be begun by any one of the following: a formal charge (sworn complaint); a preliminary hearing; an indictment; an arraignment; an initial appearance for a magistrate." See also Grano at 788–89.

Consider Israel, Note 3 supra, at 1368–69 n. 226: "Most defendants are arrested without warrants and are placed in lineups prior to their appearance before a magistrate—i.e., before a formal charge or a complaint has been filed against them. Where the individual has been arrested pursuant to a warrant, the complaint will have been filed before his arrest, but the lineup still is likely to be held prior to his first appearance before a magistrate. Arguably, *Wade* also would not apply in that situation. Even though a complaint has been filed in the process of obtaining a warrant, adversary judicial criminal proceedings may be viewed as being initiated only after the accused is brought before a magistrate on that complaint. [This] starting point would make sense from an administrative standpoint because counsel for the indigent ordinarily would not be appointed until the defendant has appeared before the magistrate."[b]

---

a. The Court also rejected the view that petitioner had no right to counsel at this identification procedure because "it was conducted in the course of a judicial proceeding": "The reasons supporting *Wade's* holding that a corporeal identification is a critical stage of a criminal prosecution for Sixth Amendment purposes apply with equal force to this identification. It is difficult to imagine a more suggestive manner in which to present a suspect to a witness for their critical first confrontation than was employed in this case. * * * Had petitioner been represented by counsel, some or all of this suggestiveness could have been avoided."

b. Professor Israel adds: "The English apparently use a similar starting point with re-

spect to counsel at lineups. The Parade Rules provide that the 'suspect should be informed that if he so desires he may have his solicitor or friend present at the identification parade.' *Home Office Circular on Identification Parades* ¶ 10, reprinted in Report to the Secretary of State for the Home Department of the Departmental Committee on Evidence of Identification in Criminal Cases 158, 159 (1976) [hereinafter cited as the Devlin Report (for the committee chairman, Lord Devlin)]. [The] Devlin Report states, however, that, for the overwhelming majority of suspects, the solicitor has to be provided by legal aid, and if the 'parade' is arranged 'before a suspect is brought before the magistrates,' legal aid assistance most often is unavailable. Devlin Re-

6. Do adversary judicial proceedings commence at the same time for Massiah and Kirby purposes? Consider Kamisar, *Brewer v. Williams, Massiah, and Miranda: What is "Interrogation"? When Does it Matter?*, 67 Geo.L.J., 86 n. 503 (1978): "Although the Supreme Court and courts generally seem to have treated the question of when judicial proceedings commence within the meaning of (1) *Massiah* and (2) *Kirby* as the same question, the different procedural contexts may have at least a strong subliminal impact on some courts. As a policy matter, it seems considerably more difficult to resist the presence of counsel at a lineup than in the interrogation room. When he can do so, a defense lawyer will usually prevent all police questioning, but he is unlikely—indeed, not empowered—to disrupt pretrial identification proceedings. Moreover, unlike the Warren Court 'confession' cases, which arguably 'furthered societal values not usually related to guilt or innocence,' the Warren Court pretrial identification cases 'explicitly sought to protect the innocent from wrongful conviction.' (Grano at 722.)"

UNITED STATES v. ASH

413 U.S. 300, 93 S.Ct. 2568, 37 L.Ed.2d 619 (1973).

Justice BLACKMUN delivered the opinion of the Court.

[Shortly before trial, almost three years after the crime, and long after defendant had been incarcerated and appointed counsel, the government conducted a photographic display without notifying counsel. The prosecutor showed five color photographs to four witnesses who previously had tentatively identified the black-and-white photograph of defendant. Three witnesses selected defendant's photo, but one was unable to make any selection. The U.S. Court of Appeals for the D.C. Circuit ruled that defendant's right to counsel had been violated when his attorney was not afforded the opportunity to be present at the photographic display. The Supreme Court reversed.]

[Although the right to counsel guarantee has been expanded beyond the formal trial itself], the function of the lawyer has remained essentially the same as his function at trial. In all cases considered by the Court, counsel has continued to act as a spokesman for, or advisor to, the accused. The accused's right to the "Assistance of Counsel" has meant just that, namely, the right of the accused to have counsel acting as his assistant. [In] *Massiah* counsel could have advised his client on the benefits of the Fifth Amendment and could have sheltered him from the overreaching of the prosecution.

[The] function of counsel in rendering "Assistance" continued at the lineup under consideration in *Wade* and its companion cases. Although the accused was not confronted there with legal questions, the lineup offered opportunities for prosecuting authorities to take advantage of the accused.

[A] substantial departure from the historical test would be necessary if the Sixth Amendment were interpreted to give Ash a right to counsel at the photographic identification in this case. Since the accused himself is not present at the time of the photographic display, and asserts no right to be present, no possibility arises that the accused might be misled by his lack of familiarity with the law or overpowered by his professional adversary. Similarly, the counsel guarantee would not be used to produce equality in a trial-like adversary confrontation. Rather, the guarantee was used by the Court of Appeals to produce confrontation at an event that previously was not analogous to an adversary trial.

port at ¶ 5.39. Accordingly, solicitors are not provided for many lineups conducted before the defendant's first appearance, notwithstanding the Parade Rules. The Devlin Report considered but rejected requiring counsel in all such cases."

Even if we were willing to view the counsel guarantee in broad terms as a generalized protection of the adversary process, we would be unwilling to go so far as to extend the right to a portion of the prosecutor's trial-preparation interviews with witnesses. Although photography is relatively new, the interviewing of witnesses before trial is a procedure that predates the Sixth Amendment. [The] traditional counterbalance in the American adversary system for these interviews arises from the equal ability of defense counsel to seek and interview witnesses himself.

That adversary mechanism remains as effective for a photographic display as for other parts of pretrial interviews. No greater limitations are placed on defense counsel in constructing displays, seeking witnesses, and conducting photographic identifications than those applicable to the prosecution. Selection of the picture of a person other than the accused, or the inability of a witness to make any selection, will be useful to the defense in precisely the same manner that the selection of a picture of the defendant would be useful to the prosecution.

[Pretrial] photographic identifications, [are] hardly unique in offering possibilities for the actions of the prosecutor unfairly to prejudice the accused. Evidence favorable to the accused may be withheld; testimony of witnesses may be manipulated; the results of laboratory tests may be contrived. In many ways the prosecutor, by accident or by design, may improperly subvert the trial. The primary safeguard against abuses of this kind is the ethical responsibility of the prosecutor, who, as so often has been said, may "strike hard blows" but not "foul ones." If that safeguard fails, review remains available under due process standards. These same safeguards apply to misuse of photographs. * * *

We are not persuaded that the risks inherent in the use of photographic displays are so pernicious that an extraordinary system of safeguards is required. * * *

Reversed and remanded.

Justice STEWART, concurring in the judgment. * * *

[The *Wade* Court held] that counsel was required at a lineup, primarily as an observer, to ensure that defense counsel could effectively confront the prosecution's evidence at trial. Attuned to the possibilities of suggestive influences, a lawyer could see any unfairness at a lineup, question the witnesses about it at trial, and effectively reconstruct what had gone on for the benefit of the jury or trial judge.*

A photographic identification is quite different from a lineup, for there are substantially fewer possibilities of impermissible suggestion when photographs are used, and those unfair influences can be readily reconstructed at trial. It is true that the defendant's photograph may be markedly different from the others displayed, but this unfairness can be demonstrated at trial from an actual comparison of the photographs used or from the witness' description of the display. Similarly, it is possible that the photographs could be arranged in a suggestive manner, or that by comment or gesture the prosecuting authorities might single out the defendant's picture. But these are the kinds of overt influence that a witness can easily recount and that would serve to impeach the identification testimony. In short, there are few possibilities for unfair suggestiveness—and those rather blatant and easily reconstructed. Accordingly, an accused

---

* I do not read *Wade* as requiring counsel because a lineup is a "trial-type" situation, nor do I understand that the Court required the presence of an attorney because of the advice or assistance he could give to his client at the lineup itself. Rather, I had thought the reasoning of *Wade* was that the right to counsel is essentially a protection for the defendant at trial, and that counsel is necessary at a lineup in order to ensure a meaningful confrontation and the effective assistance of counsel at trial.

would not be foreclosed from an effective cross-examination of an identification witness simply because his counsel was not present at the photographic display. For this reason, a photographic display cannot fairly be considered a "critical stage" of the prosecution.[a] * * *

Justice BRENNAN, with whom Justice DOUGLAS and Justice MARSHALL join, dissenting.

DISSENT

[T]oday's decision marks simply another step towards the complete evisceration of the fundamental constitutional principles established by this Court, only six years ago, in *Wade, Gilbert* and *Stovall.*

[To] the extent that misidentification may be attributable to a witness' faulty memory or perception, or inadequate opportunity for detailed observation during the crime, the risks are obviously as great at a photographic display as at a lineup. But "[b]ecause of the inherent limitations of photography, which presents its subject in two dimensions rather than the three dimensions of reality, [a] photographic identification, even when properly obtained, is clearly inferior to a properly obtained corporeal identification." P. Wall, *Eye-Witness Identification in Criminal Cases* 70 (1965). * * *

Moreover, as in the lineup situation, the possibilities for impermissible suggestion in the context of a photographic display are manifold.

[A]s with lineups, the defense can "seldom reconstruct" at trial the mode and manner of photographic identification. It is true, of course, that the photographs used at the pretrial display might be preserved for examination at trial. But "it may also be said that a photograph can preserve the record of a lineup; yet this does not justify a lineup without counsel."[b] Indeed, in reality, preservation of the photographs affords little protection to the unrepresented accused. [For] retention of the photographs [cannot] in any sense reveal to defense counsel the more subtle, and therefore more dangerous, suggestiveness that might derive from the manner in which the photographs were displayed or any accompanying comments or gestures.

[The] fundamental premise underlying *all* of this Court's decisions holding the right to counsel applicable at "critical" pretrial proceedings, is that a "stage" of the prosecution must be deemed "critical" for the purposes of the Sixth Amendment if it is one at which the presence of counsel is necessary "to protect the fairness of *the trial itself.*" *Schneckloth v. Bustamonte* (emphasis added). [This] established conception of the Sixth Amendment guarantee is, of course, in no sense dependent upon the physical "presence of the accused," at a "trial-like confrontation" with the Government, at which the accused requires the "guiding hand of counsel." * * *

[C]ontrary to the suggestion of the Court, the conclusion in *Wade* that a pretrial lineup is a "critical stage" of the prosecution did not in any sense turn on

a. Is a post-indictment corporeal lineup recorded on video tape and played for the trial court at the suppression hearing a "critical stage" within the meaning of *Wade?*

b. Doesn't it, at least after *Ash?* Suppose defense counsel was not notified of or in attendance at either a post-indictment lineup viewed by witness A or at the subsequent exhibition of a photograph of the lineup viewed by witness B. Would *Wade* prevent witness A from testifying that he had identified the accused at the uncounselled lineup or would the fact that the lineup was photographed and thus "preserved" for the trial court mean that

it was not a "critical stage"? Assuming arguendo that *Wade* would bar witness A from testifying that he had identified the accused at the uncounselled lineup, wouldn't *Ash* allow witness B to testify that he had identified the accused at the subsequent showing of the photograph of the lineup?

See *United States v. Barker*, 988 F.2d 77 (9th Cir.1993) holding that when the defendant is identified in a photograph of a lineup *Ash* applies, not *Wade* because, inter alia, the defendant's absence at the time the photo of the lineup is shown means that he cannot be "misled" or "overpowered."

the fact that a lineup involves the physical "presence of the accused" at a "trial-like confrontation" with the Government. And that conclusion most certainly did not turn on the notion that presence of counsel was necessary so that counsel could offer legal advice or "guidance" to the accused at the lineup. On the contrary, *Wade* envisioned counsel's function at the lineup to be primarily that of a trained observer, able to detect the existence of any suggestive influences and capable of understanding the legal implications of the events that transpire. Having witnessed the proceedings, counsel would then be in a position effectively to reconstruct at trial any unfairness that occurred at the lineup, thereby preserving the accused's fundamental right to a fair trial on the issue of identification.

There is something ironic about the Court's conclusion today that a pretrial lineup identification is a "critical stage" of the prosecution because counsel's presence can help to compensate for the accused's deficiencies as an observer, but that a pretrial photographic identification is not a "critical stage" of the prosecution because the accused is not able to observe at all. * * *

Notes and Questions

1. *Wade, Kirby and Ash.* The *Ash* majority, per Blackmun, J., looks back on *Wade* as concluding that "the lineup constituted a trial-like confrontation" requiring counsel in order "to render 'Assistance' [to a suspect] in counterbalancing any 'overreaching' by the prosecution," implying that counsel is to be an active adversary at this stage. Was the *Ash* majority compelled to so interpret *Wade* because its historical analysis led it to the conclusion that the lawyer's assistance is limited to the *immediate* aid he can give his client? See Note, 64 J.Crim.L.C. & P.S. 428 (1973). Does concurring Justice Stewart disclaim this reading of *Wade?* If so, which interpretation is more consistent with the cases, commentaries and practice since *Wade?* Reconsider Note 2, p. 626. Consider, too, 64 J.Crim.L.C. & P.S. at 433 & n. 40.

2. *Massiah and Ash.* According to the *Ash* majority, "in *Massiah* counsel could have advised his client on the benefits of the Fifth Amendment and could have sheltered him from the overreaching of the prosecution." Was the defendant in *Massiah* entitled to Fifth Amendment protection? Was he compelled to speak? How would the presence of counsel in *Massiah* have provided "assistance" at the "confrontation" unless counsel were aware the meeting was a confrontation? And if counsel were so aware, wouldn't he have *prevented* the confrontation from occurring? See Grano at 762 & n. 285.

3. *The significance of defendant's right to be personally present.* As noted by the Court, the defendant in *Ash* did not claim the right to be personally present at the photographic display. But does the right to counsel *only* exist when the defendant is entitled to be personally present? Voluntary absence or contumacious conduct (see *Illinois v. Allen,* Ch. 25, § 3) may cause a defendant to lose his right to be present at trial, but does it follow that he also loses his right to counsel? Defendants on appeal have the right to counsel, but do they have the right to be personally present? See generally Grano at 764–67.

4. *Justice Stewart's concurring opinion.* All of the distinctions Justice Stewart made between photographic displays and lineups—photographic displays are less vulnerable to improper suggestion, are easier to reconstruct at trial and are less indelible in their effect upon a witness—are sharply challenged in Grano at 767–70.

5. *Photographic displays and other pretrial interviews of prospective witnesses.* Both the majority and concurring opinions in *Ash* indicated concern that granting a right to counsel at photographic displays might lead to the extension of the right to counsel to all pretrial interviews of prospective witnesses. But consider Note, 26 Stan.L.Rev. 399, 416–17 (1974): "[The] basis for extending the right to counsel to the identification context was that identifications by eyewitnesses—like confessions—are such damning evidence that they may completely decide the guilt or innocence of the accused. Photographic identifications can be just as critical to the future outcome of a trial as can corporeal identifications. Routine interviews between the prosecutor and his witnesses, on the other hand, do not have the potential for such damaging results, at least assuming good faith on the part of the prosecutor."

SECTION 3. DUE PROCESS AND OTHER LIMITATIONS

As already pointed out, see p. 630 supra, one unable to make a *Wade-Gilbert* right to counsel argument may still establish that the identification procedure conducted in his case "was so unnecessarily suggestive and conducive to irreparable mistaken identification that he was denied due process of law." STOVALL v. DENNO, 388 U.S. 293, 87 S.Ct. 1967, 18 L.Ed.2d 1199 (1967). In this case, the stabbing victim (Mrs. Behrendt), was hospitalized for major surgery. Without affording petitioner time to retain counsel (an arraignment had been promptly held but then postponed until petitioner could retain counsel), the police, with the cooperation of the victim's surgeon, arranged a confrontation between petitioner and the victim in her hospital room. Petitioner was handcuffed to one of the seven law enforcement officials who brought him to the hospital room. He was the only black person in the room. After being asked by an officer whether petitioner "was the man," the victim identified him from her hospital bed. Both Mrs. Behrendt and the police then testified at the trial to her identification in the hospital. Despite the suggestiveness of the confrontation, the Court, per BRENNAN, J., affirmed the Second Circuit's denial of federal habeas corpus relief, observing:

"The practice of showing suspects singly to persons for the purpose of identification, and not as part of a lineup has been widely condemned. However, a claimed violation of due process of law in the conduct of a confrontation depends on the totality of the circumstances surrounding it, and the record in the present case reveals that the showing of Stovall to Mrs. Behrendt in an immediate hospital confrontation was imperative. The Court of Appeals en banc, stated [355 F.2d 731, 735 (2d Cir.1966) (per Moore, J.)]:

" 'Here was the only person in the world who could possibly exonerate Stovall. Her words, and only her words, "He is not the man" could have resulted in freedom for Stovall. The hospital was not far distant from the courthouse and jail. No one knew how long Mrs. Behrendt might live. Faced with the responsibility of identifying the attacker, with the need for immediate action and with the knowledge that Mrs. Behrendt could not visit the jail, the police followed the only feasible procedure and took Stovall to the hospital room. Under these circumstances, the usual police station line-up, which Stovall now argues he should have had, was out of the question.' "[a]

---

a. But consider Judge Friendly, joined by Waterman, J., dissenting below, 355 F.2d at 744–45:

"[The argument that law enforcement officials were confronted with an emergency] ignores the huge amount of circumstantial identification the excellent police investigation had produced; moreover, if the state officials were

motivated [by] solicitude [for Stovall], the natural course would have been to ask Stovall whether he wanted to go. The emergency argument fails both on the facts and on the law. [If] Mrs. Behrendt's condition had been as serious as my brothers suppose, nothing prevented the prosecutor from informing the state district judge at the preliminary hearing that Stovall

MANSON v. BRATHWAITE

432 U.S. 98, 97 S.Ct. 2243, 53 L.Ed.2d 140 (1977).

Justice BLACKMUN delivered the opinion of the Court. * * *

[Several minutes before sunset, Glover, a black undercover police officer, purchased heroin from a seller through the open doorway of an apartment while standing for two or three minutes within two feet of the seller in a hallway illuminated by natural light. A few minutes later, Glover described the seller to a back-up officer, D'Onofrio, as being "a colored man, approximately five feet eleven inches tall, dark complexion, black hair, short Afro style, and having high cheekbones, and of heavy build. He was wearing at the time blue pants and a plaid shirt."

[On the basis of the description, D'Onofrio thought that respondent might be the heroin seller. He obtained a single photograph of respondent from police files and left it at Glover's office. Two days later, while alone, Glover viewed the photograph and identified it as that of the seller. At respondent's trial, Glover testified that there was "no doubt whatsoever" that the person shown in the photograph was respondent. Glover also made a positive in-court identification. No explanation was offered by the prosecution for the failure to utilize a photographic array or to conduct a lineup.

[After the Connecticut Supreme Court affirmed respondent's conviction, he sought federal habeas corpus relief. The Second Circuit, per Friendly, J., held that because the showing of the single photograph was "suggestive" and concededly "unnecessarily so," evidence pertaining to it was subject to a *per se* rule of exclusion.]

Neil v. Biggers, 409 U.S. 188, 93 S.Ct. 375, 34 L.Ed.2d 401 (1972), concerned a respondent who had been convicted [of] rape, on evidence consisting in part of the victim's visual and voice identification of Biggers at a [one-person] station-house showup seven months after the crime. [The] Court expressed concern about the lapse of seven months between the crime and the confrontation, [but pointed out that the] "central question" [was] "whether under the 'totality of the circumstances' the identification was reliable even though the confrontation procedure was suggestive." Applying that test, the Court found "no substantial likelihood of misidentification. The evidence was properly allowed to go to the jury."[a]

---

had to be taken immediately before her, and suggesting that counsel be assigned forthwith for the limited purpose of advising him in that regard—rather than standing silent when Stovall told the judge of his desire to have counsel and then carting him off to a confrontation by the victim which counsel might have done something to mitigate."

Lower courts have not only followed *Stovall* in similar cases of serious injury to the victim or a witness but have applied it to situations where the *suspect* is seriously injured. See Commentary to § 160.5 of the *Model Pre-Arraignment Code* at 451–52. Is a "showup" in such cases necessary? Could a photographic array be utilized? If the suspect is hospitalized for an extended period, could the witness be

taken to several hospital rooms? See *Model Code* at 452.

a. The *Biggers* Court, per Powell, J., observed:

"The victim spent a considerable period of time with her assailant, up to half an hour. She was with him under adequate artificial light in her house and under a full moon outdoors, and at least twice, once in the house and later in the woods, faced him directly and intimately. [Her] description to the police, which included the assailant's approximate age, height, weight, complexion, skin texture, build, and voice [was] more than ordinarily thorough. She had 'no doubt' that respondent was the person who raped her. [The] victim here, a practical nurse by profession, had an

Biggers well might be seen to provide an unambiguous answer to the question before us: The admission of testimony concerning a suggestive and unnecessary identification procedure does not violate due process so long as the identification possesses sufficient aspects of reliability.[9] In one passage, however, the Court observed that the challenged procedure occurred pre-*Stovall* and that a strict rule would make little sense with regard to a confrontation that preceded the Court's first indication that a suggestive procedure might lead to the exclusion of evidence. One perhaps might argue that, by implication, the Court suggested that a different rule could apply post-*Stovall*. The question before us, then, is simply whether the *Biggers* analysis applies to post-*Stovall* confrontations as well to those pre-*Stovall*. * * *

Petitioner at the outset acknowledges that "the procedure in the instant case was suggestive [because only one photograph was used] and unnecessary" [because there was no emergency or exigent circumstance]. The respondent, in agreement with the Court of Appeals, proposes a *per se* rule of exclusion that he claims is dictated by the demands of the Fourteenth Amendment's guarantee of due process. He rightly observes that this is the first case in which this Court has had occasion to rule upon strictly post-*Stovall* out-of-court identification evidence of the challenged kind.

Since the decision in *Biggers*, the Courts of Appeals appear to have developed at least two approaches to such evidence. See Pulaski, *Neil v. Biggers: The Supreme Court Dismantles the Wade Trilogy's Due Process Protection*, 26 Stan. L.Rev. 1097, 1111–1114 (1974). The first, or *per se* approach, employed by the Second Circuit in the present case, focuses on the procedures employed and requires exclusion of the out-of-court identification evidence, without regard to reliability, whenever it has been obtained through unnecessarily suggested confrontation procedures.[10] The justifications advanced are the elimination of evidence of uncertain reliability, deterrence of the police and prosecutors, and the stated "fair assurance against the awful risks of misidentification."

unusual opportunity to observe and identify her assailant. She testified at the habeas corpus hearing that there was something about his face 'I don't think I could ever forget.'

"There was, to be sure, a lapse of seven months between the rape and the confrontation. This would be a seriously negative factor in most cases. Here, however, the testimony is undisputed that the victim made no previous identification at any of the showups, lineups, or photographic showings. Her record for reliability was thus a good one, as she had previously resisted whatever suggestiveness inheres in a showup. Weighing all the factors, we find no substantial likelihood of misidentification."

9. Justice Marshall argues in dissent that our cases have "established two different due process tests for two very different situations." Pretrial identifications are to be covered by *Stovall*, which is said to require exclusion of evidence concerning unnecessarily suggestive pretrial identifications without regard to reliability. In-court identifications, on the other hand, are to be governed by *Simmons [v. United States*, 390 U.S. 377, 88 S.Ct. 967, 19 L.Ed.2d 1247 (1968)] and admissibility turns on reliability. The Court's cases are sorted into one category or the other. *Biggers*, which clearly adopts the reliability of the identification as

the guiding factor in the admissibility of both pre-trial and in-court identifications, is condemned for mixing the two lines and for adopting a uniform rule.

[Our cases] hardly suggest the formal structure the dissent would impose on them. If our cases truly established two different rules, one might expect at some point at least passing reference to the fact. There is none. And if *Biggers* departed so grievously from the past cases, it is surprising that there was not at least some mention of the point in Justice Brennan's dissent. * * * *Biggers* is not properly seen as a departure from the past cases, but as a synthesis of them.

10. Although the *per se* approach demands the exclusion of testimony concerning unnecessarily suggestive identifications, it does permit the admission of testimony concerning a subsequent identification, including an in-court identification, if the subsequent identification is determined to be reliable. The totality approach, in contrast, is simpler: if the challenged identification is reliable, then testimony as to it and any identification in its wake is admissible.

The second, or more lenient, approach is one that continues to rely on the totality of the circumstances. It permits the admission of the confrontation evidence if, despite the suggestive aspect, the out-of-court identification possesses certain features of reliability. This second approach, in contrast to the other, is ad hoc and serves to limit the societal costs imposed by a sanction that excludes relevant evidence from consideration and evaluation by the trier of fact. * * *

There are, of course, several interests to be considered and taken into account. The driving force behind [*Wade, Gilbert* and *Stovall*] was the Court's concern with the problems of eyewitness identification. Usually the witness must testify about an encounter with a total stranger under circumstances of emergency or emotional stress. The witness' recollection of the stranger can be distorted easily by the circumstances or by later actions of the police. Thus, *Wade* and its companion cases reflect the concern that the jury not hear eyewitness testimony unless that evidence has aspects of reliability. It must be observed that both approaches before us are responsive to this concern. The *per se* rule, however, goes too far since its application automatically and peremptorily, and without consideration of alleviating factors, keeps evidence from the jury that is reliable and relevant.

The second factor is deterrence. Although the *per se* approach has the more significant deterrent effect, the totality approach also has an influence on police behavior. The police will guard against unnecessarily suggestive procedures under the totality rule, as well as the *per se* one, for fear that their actions will lead to the exclusion of identifications as unreliable.

The third factor is the effect on the administration of justice. Here the *per se* approach suffers serious drawbacks. Since it denies the trier reliable evidence, it may result, on occasion, in the guilty going free. Also, because of its rigidity, the *per se* approach may make error by the trial judge more likely than the totality approach. And in those cases in which the admission of identification evidence is error under the *per se* approach but not under the totality approach—cases in which the identification is reliable despite an unnecessarily suggestive identification procedure—reversal is a Draconian sanction. Certainly, inflexible rules of exclusion that may frustrate rather than promote justice have not been viewed recently by this Court with unlimited enthusiasm. * * *

We therefore conclude that reliability is the linchpin in determining the admissibility of identification testimony for both pre-and post-*Stovall* confrontations. The factors to be considered are set out in *Biggers*. These include the opportunity of the witness to view the criminal at the time of the crime, the witness' degree of attention, the accuracy of his prior description of the criminal, the level of certainty demonstrated at the confrontation, and the time between the crime and the confrontation. Against these factors is to be weighed the corrupting effect of the suggestive identification itself.

We turn, then, to the facts of this case and apply the analysis:

1. *The opportunity to view.* Glover testified that for two to three minutes he stood at the apartment door, within two feet of the respondent. The door opened twice, and each time the man stood at the door. * * * Natural light from outside entered the hallway through a window. There was natural light, as well, from inside the apartment.

2. *The degree of attention.* Glover was not a casual or passing observer, [but] a trained police officer on duty—and specialized and dangerous duty—when he [made the heroin purchase]. Glover himself was a Negro and unlikely to perceive only general features of [black males].

3. *The accuracy of the description.* Glover's description was given to D'Onofrio within minutes after the transaction. It included the vendor's race, his height, his build, the color and style of his hair, and the high cheekbone facial feature. It also included clothing the vendor wore. No claim has been made that respondent did not possess the physical characteristics so described. * * *

4. *The witness' level of certainty.* There is no dispute that the photograph in question was that of respondent. Glover, in response to a question whether the photograph was that of the person from whom he made the purchase, testified: "There is no question whatsoever." This positive assurance was repeated.

5. *The time between the crime and the confrontation.* Glover's description of his vendor was given to D'Onofrio within minutes of the crime. The photographic identification took place only two days later. We do not have here the passage of weeks or months between the crime and the viewing of the photograph.

These indicators of Glover's ability to make an accurate identification are hardly outweighed by the corrupting effect of the challenged identification itself. Although identifications arising from single-photograph displays may be viewed in general with suspicion, we find in the instant case little pressure on the witness to acquiesce in the suggestion that such a display entails. D'Onofrio had left the photograph at Glover's office and was not present when Glover first viewed it two days after the event. There thus was little urgency and Glover could view the photograph at his leisure. And since Glover examined the photograph alone, there was no coercive pressure to make an identification arising from the presence of another. The identification was made in circumstances allowing care and reflection. * * *

Surely, we cannot say that under all the circumstances of this case there is "a very substantial likelihood of irreparable misidentification." Short of that point, such evidence is for the jury to weigh. We are content to rely upon the good sense and judgment of American juries, for evidence with some element of untrustworthiness is customary grist for the jury mill. Juries are not so susceptible that they cannot measure intelligently the weight of identification testimony that has some questionable feature. * * *

We conclude that the criteria laid down in *Biggers* are to be applied in determining the admissibility of evidence offered by the prosecution concerning a post-*Stovall* identification, and that those criteria are satisfactorily met and complied with here.

[Reversed].[b]

Justice MARSHALL, with whom Justice BRENNAN joins, dissenting.

Today's decision can come as no surprise to those who have been watching the Court dismantle the protections against mistaken eyewitness testimony erected a decade ago in [*Wade, Gilbert* and *Stovall*]. But it is still distressing to see the Court virtually ignore the teaching of experience embodied in those decisions and blindly uphold the conviction of a defendant who may well be innocent.

[In] determining the admissibility of the *post-Stovall* identification in this case, the Court considers two alternatives, a *per se* exclusionary rule and a totality-of-the-circumstances approach. The Court weighs three factors in deciding

b. Stevens, J., concurring, joined the Court's opinion, but emphasized that although "the arguments in favor of fashioning new rules to minimize the danger of convicting the innocent on the basis of unreliable eyewitness testimony carry substantial force, [this] rule-making function can be performed 'more effectively by the legislative process than by somewhat clumsy judicial fiat,' and that the Federal Constitution does not foreclose experimentation by the States in the development of such rules."

that the totality approach, which is essentially the test used in *Biggers,* should be applied. In my view, the Court wrongly evaluates the impact of these factors.

First, the Court acknowledges that one of the factors, deterrence of police use of unnecessarily suggestive identification procedures, favors the *per se* rule. Indeed, it does so heavily, for such a rule would make it unquestionably clear to the police they must never use a suggestive procedure when a fairer alternative is available. I have no doubt that conduct would quickly conform to the rule.

Second, the Court gives passing consideration to the dangers of eyewitness identification recognized in the *Wade* trilogy. It concludes, however, that the grave risk of error does not justify adoption of the *per se* approach because that would too often result in exclusion of relevant evidence. In my view, this conclusion totally ignores the lessons of *Wade.* The dangers of mistaken identification are, as *Stovall* held, simply too great to permit unnecessarily suggestive identifications. * * *

Finally, the Court errs in its assessment of the relative impact of the two approaches on the administration of justice. The Court relies most heavily on this factor * * *.

First, the *per se* rule here is not "inflexible." Where evidence is suppressed, for example, as the fruit of an unlawful search, it may well be forever lost to the prosecution. Identification evidence, however, can by its very nature be readily and effectively reproduced. The in-court identification, permitted under *Wade* [if] it has a source independent of an uncounseled or suggestive procedure, is one example. Similarly, when a prosecuting attorney learns that there has been a suggestive confrontation, he can easily arrange another lineup conducted under scrupulously fair conditions. * * *

Second, other exclusionary rules have been criticized for preventing jury consideration of relevant and usually reliable evidence in order to serve interest unrelated to guilt or innocence, such as discouraging illegal searches or denial of counsel. Suggestively obtained eyewitness testimony is excluded, in contrast, precisely because of its unreliability and concomitant irrelevance. Its exclusion both protects the integrity of the truth-seeking function of the trial and discourages police use of needlessly inaccurate and ineffective investigatory methods.

[For] these reasons, I conclude that adoption of the *per se* rule would enhance, rather than detract from, the effective administration of justice. In my view, the Court's totality test will allow seriously unreliable and misleading evidence to be put before juries. * * *

Even more disturbing than the Court's reliance on the totality test, however, is the analysis it uses. [The] decision suggests that due process violations in identification procedures may not be measured by whether the government employed procedures violating standards of fundamental fairness. By relying on the probable accuracy of a challenged identification, instead of the necessity for its use, the Court seems to be ascertaining whether the defendant was probably guilty. * * *

Despite my strong disagreement with the Court over the proper standards to be applied in this case, I am pleased that its application of the totality test does recognize the continuing vitality of *Stovall.* In assessing the reliability of the identification, the Court mandates weighing "the corrupting effect of the suggestive identification itself" against the "indicators of [a witness'] ability to make an accurate identification." The Court holds, as *Biggers* failed to, that a due process identification inquiry must take account of the suggestiveness of a confrontation and the likelihood that it led to mis-identification, as recognized in *Stovall* and *Wade.* Thus, even if a witness did have an otherwise adequate opportunity to view a criminal, the later use of a highly suggestive identification procedure can render his testimony inadmissible. Indeed, it is my view that, assuming applicability of the totality test enunciated by the Court, the facts of the present case require that result.

I consider first the opportunity that Officer Glover had to view the suspect. Careful review of the record shows that he could see the heroin seller only for the time it took to speak three sentences of four or five short words, to hand over some money, and later after the door reopened, to receive the drugs in return. The entire face-to-face transaction could have taken as little as 15 or 20 seconds. But during this time, Glover's attention was not focused exclusively on the seller's face. He observed that the door was opened 12 to 18 inches, that there was a window in the room behind the door, and, most importantly, that there was a woman standing behind the man. Glover was, of course, also concentrating on the details of the transaction—he must have looked away from the seller's face to hand him the money and receive the drugs. The observation during the conversation thus may have been as brief as 5 or 10 seconds.

As the Court notes, Glover was a police officer trained in and attentive to the need for making accurate identifications. [But] the mere fact that he has been so trained is no guarantee that he is correct in a specific case. * * * Moreover, "identifications made by policemen in highly competitive activities, such as undercover narcotic [work], should be scrutinized with special care." P. Wall, *Eye-Witness Identification in Criminal Cases* 14 (1965). Yet it is just such a searching inquiry that the Court fails to make here.

Another factor on which the Court relies—the witness' degree of certainty in making the identification—is worthless as an indicator that he is correct.[10] Even if Glover had been unsure initially about his identification of respondent's picture, by the time he was called at trial to present a key piece of evidence for the State that paid his salary, it is impossible to imagine his responding negatively to such questions as "is there any doubt in your mind whatsoever" that the identification was correct. * * *

Next, the Court finds that because the identification procedure took place two days after the crime, its reliability is enhanced. While such temporal proximity makes the identification more reliable than one occurring months later, the fact is that the greatest memory loss occurs within hours after an event. After that, the dropoff continues much more slowly.[11] * * *

Finally, the Court makes much of the fact that Glover gave a description of the seller to D'Onofrio shortly after the incident. [But the description was only] a general summary of the seller's appearance. We may discount entirely the seller's clothing, for that was of no significance later in the proceeding. Indeed, to the extent that Glover noticed clothes, his attention was diverted from the seller's face. * * * Conspicuously absent is any indication that the seller was a native of the West Indies, certainly something which a member of the black community could immediately recognize from both appearance and accent.[12]

From all of this, I must conclude that the evidence of Glover's ability to make an accurate identification is far weaker than the Court finds it. In contrast, the procedure used to identify respondent was both extraordinarily suggestive and

10. See, e.g., P. Wall, supra, at 15–16 * * *.

11. See, e.g., Felice Levine & June Tapp, *The Psychology of Criminal Identification: The Gap From Wade to Kirby,* 121 U.Pa.L.Rev. 1079, 1100–01 (1973) * * *.

12. Brathwaite had come to the United States from his native Barbados as an adult. It is also noteworthy that the informant who witnessed the transaction and was described by Glover as "trustworthy," disagreed with Glover's recollection of the event. The informant testified that it was a woman in the apartment who took the money from Glover and gave him the drugs in return.

strongly conducive to error. [By] displaying a single photograph of respondent to the witness Glover under the circumstances in this record almost everything that could have been done wrong was done wrong.

In this case, [the] pressure [to identify respondent] was not limited to that inherent in the display of a single photograph. Glover, the identifying witness, was a state police officer on special assignment. He knew that D'Onofrio, an [experienced] narcotics detective, presumably familiar with local drug operations, believed respondent to be the seller. There was at work, then, both loyalty to another police officer and deference to a better-informed colleague. * * *

I must conclude that this record presents compelling evidence that there was "a very substantial likelihood of misidentification" of respondent Brathwaite. The suggestive display of respondent's photograph to the witness Glover likely erased any independent memory that Glover had retained of the seller from his barely adequate opportunity to observe the criminal. * * *

Notes and Questions

1. Deterrence. Will the *Manson* approach significantly deter the use of suggestive identification procedures? Consider Randolph Jonakait, *Reliable Identification: Could the Supreme Court Tell in Manson v. Brathwaite?*, 52 U.Colo. L.Rev. 511, 515 n. 15 (1981): "[R]egardless of how specifically opinions define what is unnecessarily suggestive, a police officer can never know whether he is violating a suspect's constitutional rights when he is conducting an identification procedure. That can be determined only when the indicia of reliability are examined. These factors may not be known to the officer and certainly cannot be controlled by him. The Court's approach leaves the officer without any firm rules as to what conduct violates the Constitution. If the officer has no way of knowing what actions are forbidden, he can hardly be deterred from those actions."

See also Steven Grossman, *Suggestive Identifications: The Supreme Court's Due Process Test Fails to Meet Its Own Criteria*, 11 Balt.L.Rev. 53, 59–60 (1981) (rather than deterring show-ups and the showing of single photographs, "the effect of *Biggers* and *Manson* has been to provide the police with a fairly clear signal that absent extremely aggravating circumstances, the one-on-one presentation of suspects to witnesses will result in no suppression"); Wallace Sherwood, *The Erosion of Constitutional Safeguards in the Area of Eyewitness Identification*, 30 How.L.J. 731, 770 (1987) (the "totality of circumstances" test, "which places a premium on the probable guilt of the accused, will not serve as a deterrent to police use of suggestive procedures but will have the opposite result").

2. *"The other side of the scale": suggestiveness.* Although the *Manson* Court offered guidelines to determine reliability, "it failed," comments Grossman, supra, at 80, 96–97, "to articulate such criteria in evaluating the other side of the scale, suggestiveness. Police and lower courts were not given examples of what types of identification procedures were objectionable and, perhaps more important in a weighing process, what forms of suggestive behavior were more likely than others to result in an unreliable identification. [As] a result, many courts have come to regard suggestion as a monolithic concept devoid of gradations or merely as a prerequisite to be met prior to analyzing the [*Biggers-Manson*] reliability factors. * * * [The] Supreme Court can [provide guidance] by indicating what types of suggestive conduct are more likely to result in unreliable identification testimony. As to these extreme forms of suggestive procedures [e.g., informing a witness that the suspect has confessed, having several witnesses view a display at the same time, presenting the suspect with a distinguishing trait or item also possessed by the perpetrator], a higher degree of reliability need be shown than that necessary to overcome nominal or less severe types of suggestive practices."

3. *Do the assumptions of the Manson majority find support in psychological research?* Drawing upon studies by Elizabeth Loftus and others, Jonakait, Note 1 supra, at 519–22, maintains that many of the assumptions made by the *Manson* majority are unwarranted. E.g., "studies do not support the idea that police make more reliable witnesses than civilians or that their training in any way improves their ability to make identifications"; dangerous police work generates great stress and, although the Court may think that danger heightens awareness, "psychologists have known for some time that stress does not aid perception and learning, but inhibits them"; research indicates no relationship between the expressed confidence of an eyewitness and the accuracy of his or her identification. See also Grossman, supra, at 72–79.

How to Increase the Accuracy of Eyewitness Identifications: Gary Wells' Writings and the NIJ's Eyewitness Evidence: A Guide for Law Enforcement

Maintaining that there is a need to articulate some simple and effective minimal requirements for lineups and photospreads in the average case, Gary L. Wells & Eric P. Seelau, *Eyewitness Identification: Psychological Research and Legal Policy on Lineups*, 1 Psychology, Pub. Pol'y. & L. 765 (1995), propose four rules to increase the accuracy of eyewitness identifications. They do so for three reasons: (1) there is little evidence to support the idea that jurors can understand and appreciate the influence of suggestive identification procedures; (2) many of the suggestive influences that can be handled by rules are *hidden* influences, such as nonverbal suggestions by the officer conducting the lineup or photospread not known to the jurors; and (3) rules serve to prevent the risky practices whereas the Supreme Court's current approach is try to assess or to diagnose the risky practices. Professors Wells and Seelau propose the following rules:

1. *The person conducting the lineup or photospread should not be aware of which member of the lineup or photospread is the suspect.* (It is current common practice for a police officer involved closely in the case, who knows where the suspect is placed, to conduct the lineup or to administer the photospread.)[a]

2. *Eyewitnesses should be told explicitly that the suspected offender might not be in the lineup or photospread, and, therefore that they should not feel they have to make an identification.* (The danger of false identification arises from a tendency for eyewitnesses to identify the person who most closely resembles the offender relative to the other in the lineup.)[b]

---

a. Administering the lineup "blind"—i.e., using the technique of assigning the lineup procedure to an officer who does not know which lineup member is the suspect—has been adopted in the New Jersey Attorney General's *Guidelines for Preparing and Conducting Photo and Lineup Identification Procedures*, the first set of state eyewitness evidence procedures based on the recommendations in National Institute of Justice: *A Guide for Law Enforcement* (1999).

b. Cf. Randolph N. Jonakait, *Reliable Identificaion; Could the Supreme Court Tell in Manson v. Brathwaite?*, 52 U.Colo.L.Rev. 511, 525 (1981); Gerald Lefcourt, *The Blank Lineup: An Aid to the Defense*, 14 Crim.L.Bull. 428 (1978), advocating the use of "blank" lineups. This entails the viewing of two separate lineups. The witness should be told the suspect may or may not be in the first lineup. Thereafter, the suspect is presented in the second lineup.

Consider, too, one of the techniques discussed in the *Guide for Law Enforcement*, fn. a supra, displaying people in a lineup one at a time—sequentially—rather than in a line at the same time, thereby reducing the chance that the witness will simply pick the person who looks most like the perpetrator of the crime.

3. *The suspect should not stand out in the lineup or photospread as being different from the distractors on the basis of the witness's previous description of the offender or other factors that would draw special attention to the suspect.* E.g., the suspect should not be the only one dressed in the type of clothes the victim said was worn by the offender or the suspect's photo should not be taken from a different angle than the other photos.

4. *At the time the identification is made, and prior to any feedback, a clear statement should be taken from the eyewitness regarding his degree of confidence that the person identified is the actual offender.* Confidence statements from eyewitnesses can be greatly affected by postidentification events that have nothing to do with the witness's memory. E.g., an eyewitness might learn, after his identification, that another witness has identified the same person or that the person he has identified has a prior record for offenses of the same type.

Professor Gary Wells has been a prolific writer, maintaining that research findings indicate that many common methods used in constructing and conducting lineups and photospreads contribute to false witness identification. The many articles he and various co-authors have written greatly influenced the law enforcement, legal, and research professionals convened by the National Institute of Justice (NIJ) in 1998. This group produced *Eyewitness Evidence: A Guide for Law Enforcement (1999)*, a compilation of refined investigative techniques that can be used by various jurisdictions in handling eyewitness evidence. James M. Doyle, Mark R. Larson & Caterina M. D. Traglia, *The Eyes Have It—or Do They?*, Criminal Justice (ABA Criminal Justice Section), Fall 2001, pp. 12, 19, report:

"The New Jersey Office of the Attorney General has integrated many of the *Guide*'s findings—as well as additional findings not embodied in the *Guide*—into that state's practice. Ideas and training are currently being exchanged freely, with none of the acrimony that often pervades the debate surrounding cases headed for court. [The] NIJ has remained involved and developed training materials for law enforcement based on the *Guide*. These are expected to be distributed shortly to every police department in the country."

Detention for Identification Procedures in the Absence of Probable Cause

In *Davis v. Mississippi* (1969) (p. 323), petitioner and 24 other black youths were detained for questioning and fingerprinting in connection with a rape for which the only leads were a general description given by the victim and a set of fingerprints around the window through which the assailant entered. Petitioner's prints were found to match those at the scene of the crime, and this evidence was admitted at his trial. The Court, per Brennan, J., held that the prints should have been excluded as the fruits of a seizure of petitioner in violation of the Fourth Amendment, but intimated that a detention for such a purpose might sometimes be permissible on evidence falling short of the traditional probable cause needed for an arrest.

See also *Hayes v. Florida*, 470 U.S. 811, 105 S.Ct. 1643, 84 L.Ed.2d 705 (1985). Although the Court, per White, J., held that *transporting a suspect to the police station* without probable cause or prior judicial authorization violated his Fourth Amendment right, it reserved the possibility, as it had in *Davis*, that "a brief detention *in the field* for the purpose of fingerprinting, where there is only reasonable suspicion not amounting to probable cause" (emphasis added), might pass constitutional muster. *Hayes* also left open the possibility that "under circumscribed procedures, the Fourth Amendment might permit *the judiciary to authorize* the seizure of a person on less than probable cause and his removal to the police station for the purpose of fingerprinting." (Emphasis added.)

As noted in Charles H. Whitebread & Christopher Slobogin, *Criminal Procedure* 482 (4th ed. 2000), "the reasoning of the dictum in *Hayes* would also justify seizures from the home for the purpose of a lineup or showup, based solely on a judicial finding of reasonable suspicion. Further, again assuming reasonable suspicion, *Hayes* would allow police to act on their own in arranging on-the-scene lineups or showups. On the other hand, suspicionless or random seizures of a person for such identification procedures would be impermissible."

On the basis of the *Davis* dictum, Art. 170 of the *Model Pre–Arraignment Code* delineates a court order procedure for detaining persons for nontestimonial identification purposes on less than "probable cause" and a number of states have passed similar legislation. See Commentary to Art. 170 at 475–77; LaFave, § 9.7(b); Note, 45 Fordham L.Rev. (1976) (hereafter referred to as "Fordham Note"). The Model Code article covers many "identification procedures," e.g., procedures to obtain identification by fingerprints, footprints, dental impressions, specimens or samples of blood, urine or hair, and procedures to obtain witness identification through lineups and handwriting exemplars. To what extent should the requisite basis for the detention vary with the kind of identification involved? For example, since eyewitness identifications are a less reliable form of evidence than fingerprints, should Fourth Amendment requirements for detentions for lineup purposes be significantly more stringent? Or should the basis for detention for lineup purposes be the same, but the suspect afforded the right to counsel at the lineup? See Fordham Note at 128–29.

Although the most serious Fourth Amendment question would seem to be whether, when the police lack "probable cause" to arrest a person *for any offense*, they may detain him for identification purposes (with or without a court order), Fourth Amendment problems also arise in other contexts. Courts have generally found no Fourth Amendment violation when a person *lawfully in custody for one crime* is ordered into a lineup for other crimes for which there is no probable cause to arrest him. But some courts have indicated that even under these circumstances there must be a "reasonable suspicion" that the person committed the crimes. See generally Fordham Note at 125–32. However, why should *the viewing* of suspects by witnesses—as opposed to *the basis for detaining* them in order to permit the viewing—raise any Fourth Amendment problems? Cf. *United States v. Dionisio* (1973) (p. 673).

When a defendant has been released on bail, he is generally subject to the control of the court, which is empowered to order his appearance. A number of courts have exercised this power to order defendants to appear in a lineup for an unrelated crime, but again it is unclear whether this may be done indiscriminately or only when there is at least "reasonable suspicion" that the defendant has committed the unrelated crime under investigation. See Fordham Note at 127.

Chapter 10

GRAND JURY INVESTIGATIONS

SECTION 1. THE ROLE OF THE INVESTIGATIVE GRAND JURY[aa]

A. THE INVESTIGATIVE AUTHORITY OF THE GRAND JURY

1. *Dual functions.* The grand jury is often described as constituting both "the shield" and "the sword" of the criminal justice process. It is said to provide a "shield" against mistaken and vindictive prosecutions in deciding whether or not to issue an indictment. In making that determination, the grand jury's role is to "screen" the prosecution's decision to charge, issuing indictments only where the available evidence is sufficient to justify a prosecution. On the other side, the grand jury is said to act as a "sword," combating crime, in the use of its investigative authority. Here, the grand jury's role is to uncover evidence not previously available to the government and thereby secure convictions that might otherwise not be obtained. The shielding function of the grand jury will be discussed in Chapter Fifteen.[a] In this Chapter we will concentrate upon the operation of the grand jury in its investigatory role. It should be kept in mind, however, that the two functions of the grand jury commonly are performed by the same grand jury. In particular, once a grand jury investigation is complete, the same group of grand jurors ordinarily will then be called upon to determine whether the evidence produced is sufficient to issue an indictment.

2. *Historical development.* The English origins of the grand jury are traced to the Assize of Clarendon, created in 1166 during the reign of Henry II. The Assize established juries of 12 persons, selected from each community, who were directed to accuse those persons in the community believed to have committed crimes. It was assumed initially that the jurors would accuse based on their own knowledge, but they soon sought out information from others. The Assize was designed not to protect against improper prosecutions by the Crown, but rather to lend assistance to government officials in the apprehension of criminals. The jurors were familiar with the local scene and could present charges that otherwise might not be known by the Crown's representatives. Any hesitancy the

---

aa. For citations to relevant source materials, as well as a more detailed discussion of the subject, see Sara Sun Beale, William C. Bryson, James E. Felman, & Michael J. Elston, *Grand Jury Law and Practice* (2d Ed. 1998) (hereafter cited as Beale et al.); Susan W. Brenner & Gregory G. Lockhart, *Federal Grand Jury* (1996) (hereafter cited as Brenner & Lockhart); Wayne R. LaFave, Jerold H. Israel, & Nancy J. King, *Criminal Procedure Treatise*, ch. 8 (2d ed. 1999) (available on Westlaw under the database CRIMPROC and hereafter cited as CRIMPROC).

a. Various aspects of the grand jury's procedure and structure relate both to its screening and investigatory functions. Those aspects that have a major impact upon its investigatory performance (e.g., grand jury secrecy) are discussed in this Chapter. Others that have a less significant bearing on investigations are discussed in Chapter 15. The composition of the grand jury, because it arguably has a greater impact on the screening function, is discussed in Chapter 15. See also Ch. 1, § 3, step (11).

jurors might have in bringing accusations against their neighbors would be overcome by the substantial fines the jurors faced for failing to bring forward any known offense.

By the end of the fourteenth century the English had turned to trial by jury rather than by ordeal and the original jury had been divided into two separate juries. The trial of guilt was before a 12 person petit jury, and the accusatory jury was expanded to a 23 person group, chosen from the entire county, which became known as "*le graunde inquest.*" At this point, the grand jury remained essentially a body designed to assist the Crown in ferreting out criminals. Accusations were either initiated by the jurors themselves, acting on the basis of community knowledge, or were initiated by a representative of the Crown, typically a justice of the peace, who produced witnesses to testify before the grand jury in support of a particular charge. When the accusation was initiated by the jury itself, its formal charge was described as a "presentment." When the accusation stemmed from a case placed before the jury by the Crown's representative, the grand jury's charging document was described as an "indictment."

Over the next few centuries, the grand jury began to assume a significant degree of independence, as evidenced by its occasional refusal to issue indictments sought by the Crown's representative. In the late seventeenth century, it established its reputation as a "bulwark against the oppression and despotism of the Crown" when it refused to indict various supporters of the Protestant cause (including, most notably, Stephen Colledge and the Earl of Shaftesbury). During the same period, the grand jury also achieved some prominence in fighting governmental corruption, as various presentments were issued based upon grand jury inquiries into the misconduct of minor officials in matters of local administration.

In this country, the colonial grand juries expanded upon the use of grand jury inquiries and issued not only presentments but also reports criticizing actions of local officials that fell short of criminal misconduct. The colonial grand juries achieved even greater prestige, however, when they refused to issue indictments requested by Crown officials. Thus, the infamous prosecution of John Peter Zenger for seditious libel was brought by a prosecutor's information because colonial grand juries twice refused to issue requested indictments. In light of such actions, it was not surprising that the constitutions of the original states generally required that all felony prosecutions be brought by grand jury indictment or presentment, and once it was decided to add a Bill of Rights to the federal constitution, the inclusion of a similar provision in the Fifth Amendment was accepted without controversy.

During the period before the Civil War, grand juries, particularly in the western states, actively reviewed a wide range of grievances presented by citizens, and often conducted "searching investigations into corruption in government or widespread evasion of the laws." While grand juries thus achieved a considerable reputation as a "public watchdog," the value and cost of grand jury screening of cases developed by local prosecutors came under sharp attack. In 1859, Michigan became the first state to grant prosecutors the option of proceeding either by grand jury indictment or by a prosecutor's information. It is noteworthy that neither Michigan nor the many other states that adopted similar option provisions abolished the grand jury, as the English eventually did. The grand jury was still viewed as a valuable instrument for occasional cases requiring the use of its investigatory authority.

Over the period between the Civil War and the mid–1900s, a majority of the states moved to allow prosecution by information. At the same time, however, grand juries remained active in both those "information" states and in the remaining "indictment" states in the investigation of corruption in local government. In several instances, the resulting indictments were so widespread as to unseat entire municipal administrations. As might be expected, local prosecutors were sometimes less than enthusiastic in cooperating with such investigations. Grand juries responded by seeking outside help (usually through court appointment of a special prosecutor) or by simply pushing forward against the wishes of a reluctant prosecutor. The most famous of these "runaway" grand jury investigations was the mid–1930s New York investigation of "racketeering" offenses, which led to the appointment of special prosecutor Thomas E. Dewey. The exploits of Dewey and his "racket busters" inspired a series of runaway grand jury investigations throughout the country and established the reputation of the grand jury as the nation's "number one instrument of discovery against organized crime."

3. *Current status.* While it was the shielding function that was responsible for the constitutional recognition of the grand jury in the indictment clause of the Fifth Amendment and in similar provisions in the early state constitutions, the grand jury's investigatory role has proven to have the greater staying power in the approximately two-thirds of our states which no longer require prosecution by indictment. The practice in these states is to bring the vast majority of prosecutions by information rather than indictment. Grand juries are still used, however, to conduct investigations where the police investigatory authority is thought to be less helpful, and that use explains most of those cases in the information states that are prosecuted by indictment. In the states that still require prosecution by indictment, the vast majority of grand juries are engaged simply in screening cases that the prosecution presents to the grand jury as fully investigated and ready for indictment. However, in a small percentage of the cases presented to grand juries in indictment states, extensive use is made of the grand jury's investigatory authority. The federal system, because of the nature of the crimes it prosecutes, makes the most extensive use of the grand jury's investigatory authority. But as in other indictment jurisdictions, the vast majority of the cases presented to federal grand juries require only screening.

The grand jury's investigative authority continues to be recognized as a major tool in uncovering organized crime and government corruption. Over the last few decades, federal grand jury investigations of white collar crime have added further luster to the grand jury's reputation as an investigative force. On the other hand, the grand jury's reputation has been sullied, at least in some quarters, by investigations that might suggest that its investigative authority was there used for partisan political ends. Some highly publicized investigations of public figures have produced damaging accusations that were clearly lacking in evidentiary support at trial, and federal investigations of the alleged criminal activities of "radical" groups (primarily during the Nixon administration) seemed to some observers to be directed more toward harassment than producing supportable indictments. Notwithstanding various legislative proposals aimed at restricting the investigative authority of federal grand juries and expanding the rights of grand jury witnesses (see e.g., A.B.A. Grand Jury Policy (1982); Report of the Commission to Reform the Federal Grand Jury, reprinted in *The Champion*, July 2000 issue), Congress has largely left regulation of federal grand juries to the federal courts and the internal regulations of the Department of Justice. Various states, on the other hand, have adopted legislation that expands the rights of grand jury witnesses and imposes additional prerequisites for use of the grand jury's investigative authority. See Note 10, p. 700; CRIMPROC § 8.2(c).

B.   Investigative Advantages

Compared to police investigations, grand jury investigations are expensive, time consuming, and logistically cumbersome. Accordingly, the grand jury ordinarily is used to investigate only when it has a distinct investigative advantage over the police. It usually has such an advantage where investigators must unravel a complex criminal structure, deal with victims reluctant to cooperate, obtain information contained in extensive business records, or keep a continuing investigative effort from the public gaze. Criminal activities presenting such investigative problems include public corruption (e.g., bribery), misuse of economic power (e.g., price-fixing), and widespread distribution of illegal services and goods (e.g., gambling or narcotics distribution), and most grand jury investigations are directed at such activities. The grand jury's advantages in investigating this type of criminal activity stem primarily from five elements of its investigatory processes—(1) the use of subpoena authority, (2) the psychological pressure imposed by the grand jury setting, (3) the use of immunity grants, (4) grand jury secrecy requirements, and (5) public confidence attributable to lay participation.

1. *Subpoena authority.* The basic investigative advantage of the grand jury stems from its ability to use the subpoena authority of the court that impaneled it. The grand jury may utilize the subpoena duces tecum to obtain tangible evidence and the subpoena ad testificandum to obtain testimony. Both subpoenas are supported by the court's authority to hold in contempt any person who willfully refuses, without legal justification, to comply with a subpoena's directive.[b]

The contempt sanction makes the grand jury subpoena particularly useful in obtaining statements from persons who will not voluntarily furnish information to the police. While those persons have the right to refuse to cooperate with the police, their refusal to comply with a grand jury subpoena invokes the threat of a possible jail sentence. Faced with that threat, a recalcitrant witness often will have a change of heart and will give to the grand jury information that he previously refused to give to the police. Of course, if the information sought could be incriminating, the witness (unless granted immunity) may still refuse to cooperate by relying on his privilege against self-incrimination. However, many persons unwilling to furnish information to the police, will willingly testify before the grand jury without regard to whether the self-incrimination privilege might offer an avenue for refusing to do so. Thus, the victim of a fraudulent gambling operation or a loansharking operation may be either too embarrassed or too fearful to voluntarily furnish information to the police, yet be willing to furnish that information to the grand jury when faced with the threat of contempt. Similarly, an employee may wish to avoid the appearance of voluntarily assisting officials investigating his employer, yet testify freely under the compulsion of a subpoena.

The grand jury subpoena ad testificandum also has the advantage of requiring witnesses to testify under oath. If a witness fails to tell the truth, he may be

---

b. The contemnor may be held in either civil or criminal contempt. Civil contempt is used to coerce the contemnor into complying with the subpoena. The contemnor is sentenced to imprisonment or to a fine (which may increase daily), but he may purge himself of the sentence by complying with the subpoena. As courts have frequently noted, he "carries the keys to the prison in his pocket." The civil contemnor who refuses to purge himself will remain under sentence until the grand jury completes its term and is discharged. Moreover, if the information the contemnor possesses is still needed, he may be subpoenaed by a successor grand jury and held in contempt again if he continues to refuse to supply that information.

prosecuted for perjury. Generally, a person who gives false information to a police officer will not have committed a crime (though there is such a crime as to federal officials). Accordingly, where a witness might be willing to talk to the police, but also is likely to "shade his story," requiring him to testify before a grand jury may produce more complete and truthful statements. Even where a witness is willing to give an entirely truthful statement to the police, there may be value in requiring him to testify before the grand jury. Arguably, a person who has testified under oath before the grand jury will be somewhat more hesitant to "change his story" when he testifies at trial. Also, if the witness does change his story and his prior statement is used to impeach him, the petit jurors may give greater weight to his prior grand jury testimony than they would to a prior statement he made to the police.

Finally, the grand jury subpoena duces tecum offers certain advantages over the primary device available to the police for obtaining records and physical evidence—the search pursuant to a warrant. Unlike the search warrant, the subpoena duces tecum can issue without a showing of probable cause. See § 2 infra. Moreover, even where probable cause could be established, there are times when the subpoena will be more appropriate. For example, there may be a need to seize so many records from various locations that a search would be impractical. At other times, there may be a need to obtain records from uninvolved third parties (e.g., a bank) and a subpoena will be preferred because it is far less disruptive to the third party's operations. Cf. *Zurcher v. Stanford Daily*, p. 163.

2. *Psychological pressure.* In addition to the compulsion of the subpoena, the psychological pressure of grand jury interrogation also is cited as a factor that frequently enables the grand jury to obtain statements from witnesses unwilling to cooperate with the police. Proponents of grand jury investigations claim that this pressure stems from the moral force exerted by the grand jury. Thus, two prosecuting attorneys note:

> "Most witnesses before grand juries feel a moral compulsion to be honest and forthright in discharging their duties as citizens, because their peers, the members of the grand jury, have also been taken away from their jobs, businesses, and private pursuits, and have accepted the inconvenience of becoming involved. The grand jurors manifest a serious purpose and are persons with whom witnesses can identify. Thus, even though their associates may be determined not to cooperate, certain witnesses may be ashamed to engage or persist in deceitful or obstreperous conduct to deny the grand jury the information it needs." John Keeney & Paul Walsh, *The American Bar Association's Grand Jury Principles: A Critique From A Federal Criminal Justice Perspective,* 14 Idaho L.Rev. 545, 579 (1978).

On the other side, critics of grand jury investigations claim that the psychological pressure stems primarily from what they describe as the "star chamber setting" of grand jury interrogation. "In all of the United States legal system," they note, "no person stands more alone than a witness before a grand jury; in a secret hearing he faces an often hostile prosecutor and 23 strangers with no judge present to guard his rights, no lawyer present to counsel him, and sometimes no indication of why he is being questioned."

3. *Immunity grants.* An immunity grant is a court order granting a witness sufficient immunity from future prosecution to supplant the witness' self-incrimination privilege. Once the recalcitrant witness has been granted immunity, he may no longer rely upon the privilege. Since immunity grants are tied to the exercise of the privilege by a person under a legal obligation to testify, they are not available to persons who simply refuse to give a statement to the police. At the investigatory stage, almost the only way the prosecution can make use of an immunity grant is in conjunction with a subpoena directing the uncooperative witness to testify before the grand jury. The immunity grant may be needed to gain information from various types of recalcitrant witnesses. For example, immunity quite frequently is given to a lower-level participant in organized crime in order to obtain testimony against higher-level participants. It also often is used to force testimony from witnesses who are not themselves involved in criminal activities, but desire not to give testimony that may hurt others. Although the privilege is not available simply to protect others (see Note 4, p. 694), witnesses who do not actually fear personal incrimination have been known to falsely claim that they do in order to avoid testifying against their friends. Since such claims are difficult to dispute, the prosecutor may simply prefer to grant the witness immunity.

4. Secrecy. Grand jury secrecy requirements vary somewhat from one jurisdiction to another, but even the weakest of secrecy requirements is thought to add to the grand jury's effectiveness as an investigative agency. All jurisdictions prohibit the prosecutor, the prosecutor's staff (including investigative agents), the grand jurors, and the grand jury stenographer from disclosing grand jury testimony and other information relating directly to grand jury proceedings (e.g., what persons have been subpoenaed), unless such disclosure is authorized by the court upon a special showing of need. Although several jurisdictions extend this obligation of secrecy to grand jury witnesses (who thereby are prohibited from disclosing their participation and their testimony to persons other than counsel until the grand jury investigation is completed), the vast majority (including the federal system) do not attempt to hold a witness to a secrecy obligation. Here, witnesses are free to disclose publicly or privately both their own testimony and whatever information was revealed to them in the course of giving that testimony.

In *United States v. Procter & Gamble Co.*, 356 U.S. 677, 78 S.Ct. 983, 2 L.Ed.2d 1077 (1958), the Supreme Court noted five objectives of grand jury secrecy requirements imposed in the federal system:

> "(1) to prevent the escape of those whose indictment may be contemplated; (2) to insure the utmost freedom to the grand jury in its deliberations, and to prevent persons subject to indictment or their friends from importuning the grand jurors; (3) to prevent subornation of perjury or tampering with the witnesses who may testify before grand jury and later appear at the trial of those indicted by it; (4) to encourage free and untrammeled disclosures by persons who have information with respect to the commission of crimes; (5) to protect the innocent accused who is exonerated from disclosure of the fact that he has been under investigation, and from the expense of standing trial where there was no probability of guilt."

While the second objective cited by the Court relates primarily to the screening function of the grand jury, the remaining four promote the grand jury's effectiveness as an investigative agency. The first objective—preventing the flight of the person being investigated—depends, of course, upon the cooperation of the grand jury witnesses. Since they are not sworn to secrecy, they may lawfully warn the target of the investigation. However, if the witnesses cooperate, grand jury secrecy requirements generally should deter the leaks that accompany most other types of investigation. If the target is kept unaware of the investigation until after the indictment is issued, the third objective cited by the Court also is served. When the witnesses against him have already testified, it is too late for the target to try to influence their grand jury testimony and it will be more difficult for him to successfully influence their trial testimony.

The fourth objective noted in *Procter & Gamble* probably is the most significant for investigatory success. Witnesses often are much more willing to testify if they know that their identity will be kept from the target of the investigation. While not sworn to secrecy themselves, if they decide not to reveal their participation and testimony, the obligation of secrecy imposed on the grand jurors, prosecution personnel, and grand jury personnel provides assurance that others will not reveal that information. Of course, if an indictment is issued and the grand jury witness is called as a trial witness (indeed, in some jurisdictions, if the prosecution simply anticipates possibly calling him as a trial witness), his participation (and his grand jury testimony) will become known to the defendant.[c] However, even if an indictment is issued, the grand jury witness may not be needed as a prospective trial witness (the witness' testimony may be unnecessary in light of leads he and others provide to more incriminating evidence) or a trial may not occur (e.g., the defendant may plead guilty). Moreover, if the grand jury witness can be assured that his identity will be revealed only in connection with the issuance of an indictment,[d] he may have fewer qualms about testifying fully and truthfully. He may be less wary of being criticized as an "informer" if he knows that his role will be revealed only after a grand jury has supported his judgment and veracity by issuing an indictment.

The fifth objective noted in *Procter & Gamble* serves, in part, to justify the sweeping investigative power granted to the grand jury. Where an investigation can be based on "tips" and "rumors" (see *Dionisio*, p. 675), there is special need to protect the reputation of the target of the investigation (who may well be innocent). That protection is provided by secrecy requirements that prohibit those involved in the grand jury investigation from disclosing to the media and others the identity of those under investigation. This shield of secrecy is thought to be especially important in the investigation of public figures, and, indeed, needed to overcome a natural hesitancy to pursue investigations of such persons in the absence of strong evidence of criminality.[e] Critics contend, however, that grand jury secrecy requirements are practically worthless in such investigations. They note that, in the vast majority of jurisdictions, the secrecy requirements are inapplicable to grand jury witnesses, and a witness hostile to the target may be

---

c. Where a witness testifies at trial, all jurisdictions will make his prior grand jury testimony available for impeachment purposes. See CRIMPROC § 24.3(c). In many jurisdictions, the prosecution must disclose in pretrial discovery the names of its intended witnesses and their prior recorded statements (which includes grand jury testimony). In others, including the federal system, pretrial disclosure of the names of prospective witnesses is not required. See CRIMPROC § 8.5(f), 20.3(i).

d. Whether or not an indictment is issued, disclosure is still a possibility should a court permit disclosure of grand jury testimony to participants in a civil litigation involving the same subject matter. However, courts considering requests that they order such disclosure give great weight to the grand jury witness' interest in keeping his testimony secret. Consider, e.g., *Douglas Oil Co. of California v. Petrol Stops Northwest*, 441 U.S. 211, 99 S.Ct. 1667, 60 L.Ed.2d 156 (1979), where the Supreme Court (in discussing the "particularized need" standard that must be met by the civil litigant to gain disclosure) noted: "[I]n considering the effects of disclosure on grand jury proceedings, the courts must consider not only the immediate effects upon a particular grand jury, but also the possible effect upon the functioning of future grand juries. Persons called upon to testify will consider the likelihood that their testimony may one day be disclosed to outside parties. Fear of future retribution or social stigma may act as powerful deterrents to those who would come forward and aid the grand jury in the performance of its duties. Concern as to the future consequences of frank and full testimony is heightened where the witness is an employee of a company under investigation. Thus, the interests in grand jury secrecy, although reduced, are not eliminated merely because the grand jury has ended its activities."

e. The argument here is that, because public awareness of the investigation could permanently stain the reputation of a public figure even though the investigation in the end reveals no basis for prosecuting, a prosecutor might hesitate to undertake such an investigation, where it would become public, unless fairly certain that it will produce sufficient evidence for a prosecution. Grand jury secrecy requirements are said to offset that hesitancy by providing reasonable assurance that the investigation will not be disclosed to the public if it does not, in fact, result in a prosecution.

eager to inform a curious media of questioning relating to the target. In many jurisdictions, those secrecy requirements also do not bar a prosecutor from releasing to the media a carefully worded description of the investigation and its targets that simply avoids reference to the activities of the grand jury itself.[f] More importantly, the critics argue, the potential sanctions for violating grand jury secrecy through improper leaking of grand jury testimony lose their effectiveness as a deterrent where targets are public figures; in such a case, the person leaking that information generally can do so through a reporter who will not only publish the information but also protect the identity of his source (even if that means risking a contempt sanction for refusing to provide that information, generally not privileged, in a subsequent judicial inquiry regarding the leak).

5. *Maintaining public confidence.* Where the subject to be investigated is a matter of public knowledge (as in the case of investigations into matters already given considerable media coverage), grand jury participation often helps in maintaining community confidence in the integrity of the investigatory process. This is especially important where the person under investigation is a public official. The community tends to be suspicious of partisan influences in such investigations, especially where the investigation results in a decision not to prosecute. As one court noted: "Where corruption is charged, it is desirable to have someone outside the administration [i.e., the grand jury] act, so that the image, as well as the fact of impartiality in the investigation can be preserved and allegations of cover-up or white-wash can be avoided." *Losavio v. Kikel,* 529 P.2d 306 (Colo.1974). The prosecutor may also look to the grand jury to help allay other public concerns, as in cases in which investigated parties are almost certain to claim police and prosecutor harassment.

6. *Grand jury reports.* Another potential investigative advantage, also relating to maintaining public confidence, lies in the grand jury's authority to issue reports in those situations in which an investigation reveals transactions that are of questionable propriety, though not criminal. A substantial number of jurisdictions permit a grand jury to issue a report summarizing the evidence found on non-indictable activities thought to merit public attention. Where such reports

---

f. Many state provisions are not nearly as broad in their coverage as Federal Rule 6(e), see CRIMPROC § 8.5, but even Rule 6(e) arguably permits certain statements of this character. Rule 6(e), which prohibits disclosure of "matter occurring before the grand jury," has been described by federal lower courts as "encompass[ing] not only the direct revelation of grand jury transcripts, but also the disclosure of information which would reveal the identities of witnesses * * *, the substance of testimony, the strategy or direction of the investigation, the deliberations or questions of the jurors, and the like." Ibid. However, the D.C. Circuit, which initially offered this broad description of Rule 6(e)'s coverage, latter added that it did not go so far as to preclude public discussion of activities of investigators or prosecutors, even though such discussions might suggest what would eventually come before the grand jury. See *In re Sealed Case No. 99-3091,* 192 F.3d 995 (D.C.Cir.1999) (Rule 6(e) was not violated when Office of Independent Counsel revealed that some of its prosecutors were debating whether to seek criminal charges against President Clinton based on his testimony before a grand jury; that the president had

been a witness before the grand jury was a matter of widespread public knowledge "that he had himself revealed," and the prosecutors descriptions of their "own internal deliberations" did not reveal what had been before the grand jury, as they did not suggest that their deliberations were based on other information that had been presented to the grand jury, and did not state that an "indictment has been sought or will be sought").

As to the lack of any statutory prohibition similar to Rule 6(e) of public disclosures by law enforcement officials regarding their own ongoing investigations, see Daniel C. Richman, *Grand Jury Secrecy: Plugging the Leaks in an Empty Bucket,* 36 Am.Crim.L.Rev. 399 (1999) (noting that several of the reasons underlying grand jury secrecy requirements would seem to apply to public disclosures regarding ongoing investigations in general, and asking whether the grand jury setting justifies the current secrecy distinction between grand jury investigations and other investigations); Barrett, *The Leak and the Craft: A Hard Line Proposal to Stop Unaccountable Disclosures of Law Enforcement Information,* 68 Fordham L.Rev. 613 (1999).

are critical of specific individuals, the law authorizing reports commonly will include certain procedural safeguards for those individuals (e.g., judicial review to ensure that the report's claims have evidentiary support, and a right of the individual to include a response). See Barry Stern, *Revealing Misconduct by Public Officials Through Grand Jury Reports,* 136 U.Pa.L.Rev. 73 (1987). Though obviously of less significance to the prosecutor than those grand jury powers that facilitate development of a successful prosecution, the alternative of issuing a report, if a crime is not found, may be helpful in maintaining the image of the prosecutor's office as an effective "public watchdog."

7. *Alternative investigative agencies.* A small number of states have adopted statutes providing for criminal investigations through the use of the subpoena power by an authority other than the grand jury. The object of these provisions is to grant to the particular authority at least some of the investigative advantages of the grand jury through a process that is "less cumbersome" than a grand jury investigation. These investigative alternatives include the "one-man grand jury" (a judge acting, in effect, as a grand jury, assisted by a specially appointed prosecutor), the "John Doe" proceeding (a prosecutorial inquiry into the commission of specified criminal activity, conducted before a judge), and the direct grant of subpoena power to the prosecutor (in some jurisdictions only with the prior approval of the court). Many elements of the law governing these proceedings are identical to those governing grand jury proceedings. Thus, most of the issues discussed in section three of this chapter with respect to the privilege against self-incrimination are also presented in these alternative investigative proceedings. However, certain witness challenges and witness rights typically not recognized in the grand jury setting (e.g., relevancy objections, and the presence of counsel) are commonly available in such proceedings.

C. Judicial Regulation: Some Differing Perspectives

1. *CRIMPROC § 8.2(c)*: "The grand jury investigation is frequently described as introducing an 'inquisitorial element' into a criminal justice system that is basically accusatorial. Critics argue that the grand jury's investigative authority should therefore be viewed as an anomaly and kept within narrow confines by close judicial supervision. They recognize that this position faces difficulties if history reveals that the grand jury inquest was accepted from the outset as an institution that coexisted with the accusatorial elements of the Anglo–American criminal justice process. The critics argue, however, that a careful reading of the history of the grand jury reveals no such accommodation. First, they note, the early grand juries did not frequently exercise the basic element of its modern investigative authority—its power to compel testimony—but instead relied primarily upon information known to the jurors or the voluntary testimony of aggrieved persons. Secondly, they argue, the investigative role of the grand jury was not critical to its initial acceptance in this country. It was the shielding role of the grand jury that earned it a place in the Bill of Rights and the early state constitutions. The grand jury's investigatory role was then viewed as entirely secondary and not necessarily distinct from its screening role. Today, it is argued, the significance of the two roles has been reversed.

"Supporters of the grand jury respond that the early history of the grand jury clearly establishes the legitimacy of its extensive investigative authority. The power of the grand jury to compel testimony was recognized well before the adoption of the Constitution and was used in some of the most notable grand jury inquests. At the time of the Constitution's adoption, the grand jury was a revered institution not simply because it served as a buffer between the state and the individual, but equally for its service as a watchdog against public corruption and its capacity to ferret out criminal activity that local officials either chose to ignore or were unable to investigate. The importance of this investigative authority was implicitly recognized, it is argued, in constitutional and statutory provisions authorizing the institution of prosecution by presentment as well as indictment.

"With few exceptions, American courts have accepted the position that the history of the grand jury provides a solid foundation for its broad investigative authority. The Supreme Court's discussion of that authority in *Blair v. United States* [see Note 2 infra] is typical. The Court there noted that the grand jury's authority to resort to compulsory process had been recognized in England as early as 1612, and the inquisitorial function of the grand jury was well established at the time of the Constitution's adoption. Both the Fifth Amendment and the earliest federal statutes recognized an investigative authority of the grand jury that included the 'same powers that pertained to its British prototype.' The Supreme Court would not view that authority with suspicion and subject it to new limitations. * * *

"Critics of the grand jury also contend that even if a broad investigative authority is sanctioned by history, the same historical sources also indicate that authority was tied to an assumption of substantial grand jury independence. * * * Today, the critics argue, the sweeping powers of the grand jury are exercised in reality by the prosecutor alone. Working with the police, the prosecutor determines what witnesses will be called and when they will appear. He examines the witnesses and advises the grand jury on the validity of any legal objections the witnesses might present. If a witness refuses to comply with a subpoena, it is the prosecutor who seeks a contempt citation. If a witness refuses to testify on grounds of self-incrimination, it is the prosecutor who determines whether an immunity grant will be obtained. The grand jury must, almost of necessity, rely upon the prosecutor's leadership. Few investigations can succeed without the investigative work, skillful interrogation, legal advice, and even the secretarial assistance, provided by the prosecutor and his staff. So too, grand jurors are neophytes in the field of criminal investigation and are participating only on a part-time basis; it is only natural that they are disposed to rely upon the prosecutor—the 'professional' who commands the expertise necessary to their venture.

"Critics argue that this change in the nature of the investigative grand jury, which [they say] has converted it into the 'prosecutor's puppet,' requires a corresponding change in judicial attitudes. The courts should not, they argue, feel bound by precedent that was developed during an era when grand juries were independent bodies. Instead, they should 'pull back the veil of history and view the investigating grand jury as one would view any other investigatory instrument of government.' The power of the grand jury should be subject to the same kinds of limitations as are imposed upon other weapons in the prosecutor's investigative arsenal.

"Supporters of the grand jury readily acknowledge that the prosecutor plays a substantial role in directing today's grand jury investigations. They suggest that this is a beneficial development that makes the investigatory authority more effective and helps to ensure that it is not misused. Moreover, it is noted, this development dates back over one hundred years, preceding many of the decisions that speak most eloquently of the necessary breadth of the grand jury's investigative authority. The key to the historical grant of that authority, they argue, was a legal structure that rendered the government's use of the grand jury's investigative powers subject to the veto of the jurors, who sat as community representatives. That structure has not been substantially altered, and its very presence, the argument continues, serves to hold the prosecutor in check and to distinguish grand jury investigations from investigatory tools granted directly to the prosecutor or the police.[g] The fact that the grand jury only occasionally exercises its power to override the prosecutor does not detract from the significance of that power. The prosecutor must respect the existence of that power and act in a way that he knows, from past experience, will be acceptable to the jurors."

2. BLAIR v. UNITED STATES, 250 U.S. 273, 39 S.Ct. 468, 63 L.Ed. 979 (1919). Responding to a grand jury witness' challenge to a subpoena on the ground that the federal government lacked constitutional authority to regulate, and the federal grand jury therefore lacked jurisdiction to investigate, the campaign practices of a candidate in a state primary election for U.S. Senator, PITNEY, J., speaking for a unanimous Court, noted:

"[T]he giving of testimony and the attendance upon court or grand jury in order to testify are public duties which every person within the jurisdiction of the Government is bound to perform upon being properly summoned, and for performance of which he is entitled to no further compensation than that which the statutes provide. The personal sacrifice involved is a part of the necessary contribution of the individual to the welfare of the public. The duty, so onerous at times, yet so necessary to the administration of justice according to the forms and modes established in our system of government is subject to mitigation in exceptional circumstances; there is a constitutional exemption from being compelled in any criminal case to be a witness against oneself, entitling the witness to be excused from answering anything that will tend to incriminate him; some confidential matters are shielded from considerations of policy, and perhaps in other cases for special reasons a witness may be excused from telling all that he knows.

"But, aside from exceptions and qualifications—and none such is asserted in the present case—the witness is bound not only to attend but to tell what he knows in answer to questions framed for the purpose of bringing out the truth of the matter under inquiry. He is not entitled to urge objections of incompetency or irrelevancy, such as a party might raise, for this is no concern of his. On familiar principles, he is not entitled to challenge the authority of the court or of the grand jury, provided they have a *de facto* existence and organization. He is not entitled to set limits to the investigation that the grand jury may conduct. * * * It is a grand inquest, a body with powers of investigation and inquisition, the scope of whose inquiries is not to be limited narrowly by questions of propriety or forecasts of the probable result of the investigation, or by doubts whether any particular individual will be found properly subject to an accusation of crime."

3. IN RE GRAND JURY PROCEEDINGS (SCHOFIELD I), 486 F.2d 85 (3d Cir.1973). Rejecting the government's claim that a grand jury witness should be held in contempt for failing to respond to a grand jury subpoena with no more showing as to the grounding of the subpoena than "what appears on the face of the subpoena", the Third Circuit (per GIBBONS, J.) noted:

g. See e.g., Justice Black's oft-quoted dissent in *In re Groban*, 352 U.S. 330, 77 S.Ct. 510, 1 L.Ed.2d 376 (1957). Commenting on the distinction between a grand jury proceeding (where Justice Black agreed that "a witness cannot insist, as a matter of constitutional right, on being represented by counsel") and a fire marshall's closed inquiry (where Justice Black, disagreeing with the *Groban* majority, argued that the witness had a constitutional right to be accompanied by counsel), Justice Black emphasized the special role of the grand jurors: "They bring into the grand jury room the experience, knowledge and viewpoint of all sections of the community. They have no axes to grind and are not charged personally with the administration of the law. No one of them is a prosecuting attorney or law-enforcement officer ferreting out crime. It would be very difficult for officers of the state seriously to abuse or deceive a witness in the presence of the grand jury. Similarly the presence of the jurors offers a substantial safeguard against the officers' misrepresentation, unintentional or otherwise, of the witness statements and conduct before the grand jury."

"[I]t is well to start with some fundamental propositions. First, although federal grand juries are called into existence by order of the district court, Fed.R.Crim.P. 6(a), they are 'basically ... a law enforcement agency.' They are for all practical purposes an investigative and prosecutorial arm of the executive branch of government. Second, although like all federal court subpoenas grand jury subpoenas are issued in the name of the district court over the signature of the clerk, they are issued pro forma and in blank to anyone requesting them. Fed.R.Crim.P. 17(a). The court exercises no prior control whatsoever upon their use. Third, although grand jury subpoenas are occasionally discussed as if they were the instrumentalities of the grand jury, they are in fact almost universally instrumentalities of the United States Attorney's office or of some other investigative or prosecutorial department of the executive branch. Grand jury subpoenas then, when they are brought before the federal courts for enforcement, for all practical purposes are exactly analogous to subpoenas issued by a federal administrative agency on the authority of a statute * * *. [A] court's determination under 28 U.S.C. § 1826(a) [the civil contempt enforcement provision] of the existence or nonexistence of just cause for refusing to obey a subpoena entails the same full judicial consideration as in the administrative subpoena cases."

4. UNITED STATES v. WILLIAMS, 504 U.S. 36, 112 S.Ct. 1735, 118 L.Ed.2d 352 (1992). The *Williams* majority opinion held that a federal court could not on its own initiative impose a duty on the government to present to the grand jury material exculpatory evidence within its possession, and the court accordingly could not dismiss an indictment because the prosecutor failed to present such evidence, even when the grand jury otherwise might not have approved the indictment. Explaining the limited authority of federal courts to mandate grand jury procedures beyond those "specifically required by the Constitution or Congress," SCALIA, J., noted:

" '[R]ooted in long centuries of Anglo–American history,' the grand jury is mentioned in the Bill of Rights, but not in the body of the Constitution. It has not been textually assigned, therefore, to any of the branches described in the first three Articles. It 'is a constitutional fixture in its own right.' In fact the whole theory of its function is that it belongs to no branch of the institutional government, serving as a kind of buffer or referee between the Government and the people. * * * Although the grand jury normally operates, of course, in the courthouse and under judicial auspices, its institutional relationship with the judicial branch has traditionally been, so to speak, at arm's length. Judges' direct involvement in the functioning of the grand jury has generally been confined to the constitutive one of calling the grand jurors together and administering their oaths of office. * * * The grand jury requires no authorization from its constituting court to initiate an investigation, nor does the prosecutor require leave of court to seek a grand jury indictment. And in its day-to-day functioning, the grand jury generally operates without the interference of a presiding judge. It swears in its own witnesses, Fed.Rule 6(c), and deliberates in total secrecy.

"True, the grand jury cannot compel the appearance of witnesses and the production of evidence, and must appeal to the court when such compulsion is required. And the court will refuse to lend its assistance when the compulsion the grand jury seeks would override rights accorded by the Constitution * * *. Even in this setting, however, we have insisted that the grand jury remain 'free to pursue its investigations unhindered by external influence or supervision so long as it does not trench upon the legitimate rights of any witness called before it.' *United States v. Dionisio* [p. 676]. Recognizing this tradition of independence, we have said that the Fifth Amendment's 'constitutional guarantee *presupposes* an investigative body "acting independently of either prosecuting attorney *or* judge"....' *Dionisio*.

"Given the grand jury's operational separateness from its constituting court, it should come as no surprise that we have been reluctant to invoke the judicial supervisory power as a basis for prescribing modes of grand jury procedure. Over the years, we have received many requests to exercise supervision over the grand jury's evidence-taking process, but we have refused them all, including some more appealing than the one presented today. [Citing *Calandra*, Note 4, p. 679]. * * * These authorities suggest that any power federal courts may have to fashion, on their own initiative, rules of grand jury procedure is a very limited one, not remotely comparable to the power they maintain over their own proceedings."

SECTION 2. FOURTH AMENDMENT CHALLENGES TO THE INVESTIGATION

A. The Initial Approach

BOYD v. UNITED STATES

116 U.S. 616, 6 S.Ct. 524, 29 L.Ed. 746 (1886).

[Customs officials seized 35 cases of glass, imported by the partnership of Boyd and Sons, and instituted a forfeiture proceeding. That proceeding was brought under a statute providing that any importer who defrauded the government and thereby avoided payment of customs revenue was subject to fine, incarceration, and forfeiture of the imported merchandise. Utilizing an 1874 statute, the government's attorney obtained a court "notice" directing Boyd to produce an invoice covering 29 of the cases of glass. That statute authorized the trial judge, on motion of the prosecutor describing a particular document and indicating what it might prove, to issue a notice directing the importer to produce the document. The importer could refuse to produce without being held in contempt (which distinguished the "notice" from a subpoena), but the consequence of a failure to produce was that the allegation of the prosecutor as to what the document stated was "taken as confessed." The defendants produced the invoice in compliance with the notice, but objected to the validity of the court's order, and objected again when the invoice was offered as evidence. The jury subsequently found for the United States, and a judgment of forfeiture against the 35 cases was granted.]

BRADLEY, J.

The clauses of the Constitution, to which it is contended that these laws are repugnant, are the Fourth and Fifth Amendments. * * * [I]n regard to Fourth Amendment, it is contended that * * * [the Act of 1874], under which the order in the present case was made, is free from constitutional objection, because it does not authorize the search and seizure of books and papers, but only requires the defendant or claimant to produce them. That is so; but it declares that if he does not produce them, the allegations which it is affirmed they will prove shall be taken as confessed. This is tantamount to compelling their production; for the prosecuting attorney will always be sure to state the evidence expected to be derived from them as strongly as the case will admit of. It is true that certain aggravating incidents of actual search and seizure, such as forcible entry into a man's house and searching amongst his papers, are wanting, and to this extent the proceeding under the act of 1874 is a mitigation of that which was authorized by the former acts; but it accomplishes the substantial object of those acts in forcing from a party evidence against himself. It is our opinion, therefore, that a compulsory production of a man's private papers to establish a criminal charge against him, or to forfeit his property, is within the scope of the Fourth Amendment to the Constitution, in all cases in which a search and seizure would be;

because it is a material ingredient, and effects the sole object and purpose of search and seizure.

The principal question, however, remains to be considered. Is a search and seizure, or, what is equivalent thereto, a compulsory production of a man's private papers, to be used in evidence against him in a proceeding to forfeit his property for alleged fraud against the revenue laws—is such a proceeding for such a purpose an "*unreasonable* search and seizure" within the meaning of the Fourth Amendment of the Constitution? or, is it a legitimate proceeding? * * *

As before stated, the [predecessor] act of 1863 was the first act in this country, and, we might say, either in this country or in England, so far as we have been able to ascertain, which authorized the search and seizure of a man's private papers, or the compulsory production of them, for the purpose of using them in evidence against him in a criminal case, or in a proceeding to enforce the forfeiture of his property. Even the act under which the obnoxious writs of assistance were issued did not go as far as this, but only authorized the examination of ships and vessels, and persons found therein, for the purpose of finding goods prohibited to be imported or exported, or on which the duties were not paid, and to enter into and search any suspected vaults, cellars, or warehouses for such goods. The search for and seizure of stolen or forfeited goods, or goods liable to duties and concealed to avoid the payment thereof, are totally different things from a search for and seizure of a man's private books and papers for the purpose of obtaining information therein contained, or of using them as evidence against him. The two things differ *toto coelo*. In the one case, the government is entitled to the possession of the property; in the other it is not. * * *

In order to ascertain the nature of the proceedings intended by the Fourth Amendment to the Constitution under the terms "unreasonable searches and seizures," it is only necessary to recall the contemporary or then recent history of the controversies on the subject, both in this country and in England. * * * Prominent and principal among these was the practice of issuing general warrants by the Secretary of State, for searching private houses for the discovery and seizure of books and papers that might be used to convict their owner of the charge of libel. * * * The case [which] will always be celebrated as being the occasion of Lord Camden's memorable discussion of the subject, was that of *Entick v. Carrington and Three Other King's Messengers,* reported at length in 19 Howell's State Trials, 1029. The action was trespass for entering the plaintiff's dwelling-house in November, 1762, and breaking open his desks, boxes, & c., and searching and examining his papers. The jury rendered a special verdict, and the case was twice solemnly argued at the bar. Lord Camden pronounced the judgment of the court in Michaelmas Term, 1765, and the law as expounded by him has been regarded as settled from that time to this, and his great judgment on that occasion is considered as one of the landmarks of English liberty. It was welcomed and applauded by the lovers of liberty in the colonies as well as in the mother country. It is regarded as one of the permanent monuments of the British Constitution, and is quoted as such by the English authorities on that subject down to the present time. As every American statesmen, during our revolutionary and formative period as a nation, was undoubtedly familiar with this monument of English freedom, and considered it as the true and ultimate expression of constitutional law, it may be confidently asserted that its propositions were in the minds of those who framed the Fourth Amendment to the Constitution, and were considered as sufficiently explanatory of what was meant by unreasonable searches and seizures. * * *

After describing the power claimed by the Secretary of State for issuing general search warrants, and the manner in which they were executed, Lord Camden says [in *Entick*]:

* * * Papers are the owner's goods and chattels; they are his dearest property; and are so far from enduring a seizure, that they will hardly bear an inspection; and though the eye cannot by the laws of England be guilty of a trespass, yet where private papers are removed and carried away the secret nature of those goods will be an aggravation of the trespass, and demand more considerable damages in that respect. Where is the written law that gives any magistrate such a power? I can safely answer, there is none; and therefore, it is too much for us, without such authority, to pronounce a practice legal which would be subversive of all the comforts of society. * * *

Lastly, it is urged as an argument of utility, that such a search is a means of detecting offenders by discovering evidence. I wish some cases had been shown, where the law forceth evidence out of the owner's custody by process. There is no process against papers in civil causes. It has been often tried, but never prevailed. Nay, where the adversary has by force or fraud got possession of your own proper evidence, there is no way to get it back but by action. In the criminal law such a proceeding was never heard of; and yet there are some crimes, such, for instance, as murder, rape, robbery, and house-breaking, to say nothing of forgery and perjury, that are more atrocious than libeling. But our law has provided no paper-search in these cases to help forward the conviction. Whether this proceedeth from the gentleness of the law towards criminals, or from a consideration that such a power would be more pernicious to the innocent than useful to the public, I will not say. It is very certain that the law obligeth no man to accuse himself; because the necessary means of compelling self-accusation, falling upon the innocent as well as the guilty, would be both cruel and unjust; and it would seem, that search for evidence is disallowed upon the same principle. Then, too, the innocent would be confounded with the guilty.

* * * The principles laid down in this opinion affect the very essence of constitutional liberty and security. They reach farther than the concrete form of the case then before the court, with its adventitious circumstances; they apply to all invasions on the part of the government and its employees of the sanctity of a man's home and the privacies of life. It is not the breaking of his doors, and the rummaging of his drawers, that constitutes the essence of the offence; but it is the invasion of his indefeasible right of personal security, personal liberty and private property, where that right has never been forfeited by his conviction of some public offence,—it is the invasion of this sacred right which underlies and constitutes the essence of Lord Camden's judgment. Breaking into a house and opening boxes and drawers are circumstances of aggravation; but any forcible and compulsory extortion of a man's own testimony or of his private papers to be used as evidence to convict him of crime or to forfeit his goods, is within the condemnation of that judgment. In this regard the Fourth and Fifth Amendments run almost into each other. * * *

Reverting then to the peculiar phraseology of this act, and to the information in the present case, which is founded on it, we have to deal with an act which expressly excludes criminal proceedings from its operation (though embracing civil suits for penalties and forfeitures), and with an information not technically a criminal proceeding, and neither, therefore, within the literal terms of the Fifth Amendment to the Constitution any more than it is within the literal terms of the Fourth. Does this relieve the proceedings or the law from being obnoxious to the prohibitions of either? We think not; we think they are within the spirit of both.

We have already noticed the intimate relation between the two amendments. They throw great light on each other. For the "unreasonable searches and seizures" condemned in the Fourth Amendment are almost always made for the purpose of compelling a man to give evidence against himself, which in criminal cases is condemned in the Fifth Amendment; and compelling a man "in a criminal case to be a witness against himself," which is condemned in the Fifth Amendment, throws light on the question as to what is an "unreasonable search and seizure" within the meaning of the Fourth Amendment. And we have been unable to perceive that the seizure of a man's private books and papers to be used in evidence against him is substantially different from compelling him to be a witness against himself. * * * We are also clearly of opinion that proceedings instituted for the purpose of declaring the forfeiture of a man's property by reason of offences committed by him, though they may be civil in form, are in their nature criminal. In this very case, the ground of forfeiture * * * consists of certain acts of fraud committed against the public revenue in relation to imported merchandise, which are made criminal by the statute * * *. As, therefore, suits for penalties and forfeitures incurred by the commission of offences against the law, are of this quasi-criminal nature, we think that they are within the reason of criminal proceedings for all the purposes of the Fourth Amendment of the Constitution, and of that portion of the Fifth Amendment which declares that no person shall be compelled in any criminal case to be a witness against himself; and we are further of opinion that a compulsory production of the private books and papers of the owner of goods sought to be forfeited in such a suit is compelling him to be a witness against himself, within the meaning of the Fifth Amendment to the Constitution, and is the equivalent of a search and seizure—and an unreasonable search and seizure—within the meaning of the Fourth Amendment.

Though the proceeding in question is divested of many of the aggravating incidents of actual search and seizure, yet, as before said, it contains their substance and essence, and effects their substantial purpose. It may be that it is the obnoxious thing in its mildest and least repulsive form; but illegitimate and unconstitutional practices get their first footing in that way, namely, by silent approaches and slight deviations from legal modes of procedure. This can only be obviated by adhering to the rule that constitutional provisions for the security of person and property should be liberally construed. A close and literal construction deprives them of half their efficacy, and leads to gradual depreciation of the right, as if it consisted more in sound than in substance. It is the duty of courts to be watchful for the constitutional rights of the citizen, and against any stealthy encroachments thereon. Their motto should be *obsta principiis*. * * *

Justice MILLER, with whom was The Chief Justice concurring:

I concur in the judgment of the court * * * and in so much of the opinion of this court as holds the 5th section of the act of 1874 void as applicable to the present case. * * * The order of the court under the statute is in effect a subpoena duces tecum, and, though the penalty for the witness's failure to appear in court with the criminating papers is not fine and imprisonment, it is one which may be made more severe, namely, to have charges against him of a criminal nature, taken for confessed, and made the foundation of the judgment of the court. That this is within the protection which the Constitution intended against compelling a person to be a witness against himself, is, I think, quite clear.

But this being so, there is no reason why this court should assume that the action of the court below, in requiring a party to produce certain papers as evidence on the trial, authorizes an unreasonable search or seizure of the house, papers, or effects of that party. There is in fact no search and no seizure authorized by the statute. No order can be made by the court under it which requires or permits anything more than service of notice on a party to the suit. * * *

Nothing in the nature of a search is here hinted at. Nor is there any seizure, because the party is not required at any time to part with the custody of the papers. They are to be produced in court, and, when produced, the United States attorney is permitted, under the direction of the court, to make examination in presence of the claimant, and may offer in evidence such entries in the books, invoices, or papers as relate to the issue. The act is careful to say that "the owner of said books and papers, his agent or attorney, shall have, subject to the order of the court, the custody of them, except pending their examination in court as aforesaid." ...

The things ... forbidden [by the Fourth Amendment] are two—search and seizure. * * * But what search does this statute authorize? If the mere service of a notice to produce a paper to be used as evidence, which the party can obey or not as he chooses is a search, then a change has taken place in the meaning of words, which has not come within my reading, and which I think was unknown at the time the Constitution was made. The searches meant by the Constitution were such as led to seizure when the search was successful. But the statute in this case uses language carefully framed to forbid any seizure under it, as I have already pointed out. * * *

Notes and Questions

1. **A civil liberties icon.** *Boyd* has been praised by commentators and courts as a landmark civil liberties case. Dissenting in *Olmstead v. United States*, 277 U.S. 438, 474, 48 S.Ct. 564, 72 L.Ed. 944 (1928), Justice Brandeis noted: "*Boyd v. United States* [is] a case that will be remembered as long as civil liberty lives in the United States." See also William J. Stuntz, *Privacy's Problem and the Law of Criminal Procedure*, 93 Mich.L.Rev. 1016 (1995) ("*Boyd* is conventionally seen as the *Miranda* of its day, a criminal procedure case that courageously protected the rights (particularly the privacy rights) of individuals against the government. Its passing—essentially nothing in *Boyd's* holding is good law anymore—is mourned as a sign of citizens' diminished protection against an overly aggressive criminal justice system").

What made *Boyd* a civil liberties icon? Was it the statement in last paragraph of the majority's opinion on the need for liberal construction of constitutional safeguards—a statement quoted with approval in numerous Supreme Court opinions? Was it the Court's attempt to bring together the Fourth and Fifth Amendment guarantees—its linking of the constitutional protection of "the privacies of life" not only to the restrictions on search and seizure but also to the privilege against self-incrimination? See Stuntz, supra. Was it the Court's focus on consequence rather than procedural form—its treatment of the court order to produce as a functional equivalent of a search and the production of an incriminating document through a search as the functional equivalent of being compelled to testify as to the incriminating contents of that document?[a]

2. Commentators have suggested that many aspects of the reasoning of *Boyd* do not "ring true" for a civil liberties icon. Thus, *Boyd* has been described as a product of "nineteenth century legal formalism" that was founded "on the view

---

a. This was the reading of *Boyd* provided in later cases—as a ruling limited to linking the production of documents to being compelled to provide the testimonial contents of these documents. See e.g., *United States v. White*, 322 U.S. 694, 64 S.Ct. 1248, 88 L.Ed. 1542 (1944). But compare Richard A. Nagareta, *Compulsion "To Be a Witness" and the Resurrection of Boyd*, 74 N.Y.U.L.Rev. 1575 (1999), arguing that: (1) the text of the Fifth Amendment, the content of related constitutional guarantees,

and the history of the privilege against self incrimination point to a privilege that is not tied to compelling testimony, but to compelling a person "to give evidence against himself," which includes the compelled production of physical evidence; and (2) *Boyd* adopted this interpretation of the Amendment, and its reasoning therefore was not limited to the production of papers. Consider also Justice Thomas' reading of *Boyd* in his dissent in *United States v. Hubbell*, set forth at p. 723.

that adjudication proceeds by deduction from virtually absolute principles rooted in natural law and enshrined in both the common law and the Constitution." Note, 90 Harv.L.Rev. 943 (1977). See also William J. Stuntz, *The Substantive Origins of Criminal Procedure*, 105 Yale L.J. 393 (1995) (comparing *Boyd* to the Supreme Court's pre–1930's substantive due process cases). Also, *Boyd* is characterized as a ruling grounded more on the protection of private property than the protection of privacy. See e.g., Stanton D. Krauss, *The Life and Times of Boyd v. United States (1886–1976)*, 76 Mich.L.Rev. 184 (1977) ("[C]onfidentiality was not the interest the Court sought to protect. Whether the Boyds had kept the invoice a secret to the world or whether they had made its contents a matter of public knowledge was irrelevant; either way the government's action was illegal").

Boyd, unlike most other civil liberties icons in the criminal procedure field, dealt with investigative techniques "far removed from ordinary criminal law." Stuntz, supra. As noted in Stuntz, Note 1 supra: "In the decades following the Court's decision, few ordinary criminal investigations led to *Boyd*-type claims, either in the form of challenges to subpoenas or as trespass actions against officers. On the other hand, regulatory cases were common. On a number of bankruptcy cases, the debtor sought to avoid certain kinds of compelled disclosure. Antitrust cases began to crop up following the Sherman Act in 1890, with defendants raising Fifth Amendment objections to subpoenas or questioning. Railroad regulation disputes were especially numerous and especially high-profile, with corporate officials striving to avoid testifying or producing documents in ICC proceedings." Indeed, it was concern for the barriers *Boyd* posed to economic regulation that led to the first step in the dismantling of *Boyd* in *Hale v. Henkel* (Note 2, p. 699).

3. ***The dismantling of Boyd.*** *Boyd* and its reasoning survived intact for less than two decades. Yet its dismantling took almost a century, and some would argue that at least a small remnant of the *Boyd* analysis has current vitality. See Note 2, p. 713. But see *Krause*, Note 2 supra ("*Boyd* is dead"). Initially, the Court in *Hale* (p. 699) separated *Boyd's* Fifth Amendment and Fourth Amendment analyses, concluded that corporations had no self-incrimination privilege, and announcing a separated (and more lenient) Fourth Amendment standard for the subpoena of documents. In later cases dealing with *Boyd's* commentary on the Fourth Amendment and searches, the Court first held that a search and seizure could extend to private property that constituted the instrumentality of the crime, *Marron v. United States*, 275 U.S. 192, 48 S.Ct. 74, 72 L.Ed. 231 (1927), then in 1967 rejected the reading of *Boyd* as prohibiting a search for property that constituted no more than "mere evidence" of a crime, *Warden v. Hayden* (p. 160), and finally in 1976 held that Fourth Amendment did not prohibit a search for documents, *Andresen v. Maryland* (p. 160).

The major developments in the Court's dismantling of *Boyd's* Fifth Amendment analysis and ruling are discussed in pts. C, D, and E of section 4 of this chapter. They included: (1) the recognition of an entity exception to the self-incrimination privilege, rendering that privilege unavailable where a subpoena seeks entity documents (including partnerships documents, which thereby overturned *Boyd* on its facts), as discussed in *Braswell v. United States* (p. 726); (2) the holding in *Shapiro v. United States* (Note 7, p. 735) that the privilege does not apply to business records that the government legitimately requires a business to keep and make open to inspection; (3) the *Fisher v. United States* (p. 706) reexamination of *Boyd* as applied to subpoenas directing individuals to produce their preexisting personal documents, resulting in the privilege being restricted to situations in which the act of producing the documents in compliance with the subpoena is itself both "testimonial" and "potentially incriminating"; and (4) the

Doe v. United States (p. 736) holding that even requiring a person to author a document may not be testimonial (in which case the privilege does not apply).

B. The Overbreadth Doctrine

1. *Hale v. Henkel (the introduction of the overbreadth doctrine).* In HALE v. HENKEL, 201 U.S. 43, 26 S.Ct. 370, 50 L.Ed. 652 (1906), the Court had before it a challenge to a subpoena directing the petitioner to produce before a grand jury (which was conducting an investigation into possible violations of the antitrust laws) various corporate documents. Petitioner's challenge was based on the combined impact of the Fourth and Fifth Amendments, but the Court initially separated those claims. Cases subsequent to *Boyd*, it noted, had "treated the Fourth and Fifth Amendments as quite distinct, having different histories, and performing separate functions." Turning first to the petitioner's self-incrimination claim, the Court found that claim clearly unsupportable since the statute authorizing the subpoena granted petitioner immunity from prosecution (see pt. B, p. 701) and the corporation itself had no self-incrimination privilege (see p. 727). The petitioner's Fourth Amendment claim did have merit, but for reasons other than what might have been assumed from *Boyd*. Speaking for the Court, BROWN, J., noted:

"Although * * * we are of the opinion that an officer of a corporation * * * cannot refuse to produce the books and papers of such corporation, we do not wish to be understood as holding that a corporation is not entitled to immunity, under the Fourth Amendment, against *unreasonable* searches and seizures. A corporation is, after all, but an association of individuals under an assumed name and with a distinct legal entity. In organizing itself as a collective body it waives no constitutional immunities appropriate to such body. * * * We are also of opinion that an order for the production of books and papers may constitute an unreasonable search and seizure within the Fourth Amendment. While a search ordinarily implies a quest by an officer of the law, and a seizure contemplates a forcible dispossession of the owner, still, as was held in the *Boyd* case, the substance of the offense is the compulsory production of private papers, whether under a search warrant or a subpoena duces tecum, against which the person, be he individual or corporation, is entitled to protection. Applying the test of reasonableness to the present case, we think the subpoena duces tecum is far too sweeping in its terms to be regarded as reasonable. It does not require the production of a single contract, or of contracts with a particular corporation, or a limited number of documents, but all understandings, contracts, or correspondence between the MacAndrews & Forbes Company, and no less than six different companies, as well as all reports made, and accounts rendered by such companies from the date of the organization of the MacAndrews & Forbes Company, as well as all letters received by that company since its organization from more than a dozen different companies, situated in seven different States in the Union.

"If the writ had required the production of all the books, papers and documents found in the office of the MacAndrews & Forbes Company, it would scarcely be more universal in its operation, or more completely put a stop to the business of that company. Indeed, it is difficult to say how its business could be carried on after it had been denuded of this mass of material, which is not shown to be necessary in the prosecution of this case, and is clearly in violation of the general principle of law with regard to the particularity required in the description of documents necessary to a search warrant or subpoena. Doubtless many, if not all, of these documents may ultimately be required, but some necessity should be shown, either from an examination of the witnesses orally, or from the known transactions of these companies with the other companies implicated, or some evidence of their materiality produced, to justify an order for the production of such a mass of papers. A general subpoena of this description is equally indefensible as a search warrant would be if couched in similar terms."

McKENNA, J., concurring separately in *Hale,* questioned the Court's Fourth Amendment analysis: "It is said 'a search implies a quest by an officer of the law; a seizure contemplates a forcible dispossession of the owner.' Nothing can be more direct and plain; nothing more expressive to distinguish a subpoena from a search warrant. Can a subpoena lose this essential distinction from a search warrant by the generality or speciality of its terms? I think not. The distinction is based upon what is authorized or directed to be done—not upon the form of words by which the authority or command is given. 'The quest of an officer' acts upon the things themselves—may be secret, intrusive, accompanied by force. The service of a subpoena is but the delivery of a paper to a party—is open and aboveboard. There is no element of trespass or force in it. It does not disturb the possession of property. It cannot be finally enforced except after challenge, and a judgment of the court upon the challenge. This is a safeguard against abuse the same as it is of other processes of the law, and it is all that can be allowed without serious embarrassment to the administration of justice."

2. Explaining the overbreadth doctrine. As Judge Friendly noted in *In re Horowitz,* 482 F.2d 72 (2d Cir.1973), "the Fourth Amendment portion of the *Boyd* decision was surely not based on the overbreadth of the Government's demand; the Government [there] sought only a single invoice of unquestionable relevance." Although relying on *Boyd, Hale v. Henkel*

> left the applicability of the Fourth Amendment to subpoena duces tecum in a most confusing state. None of the Justices seemed to think that such a subpoena could be issued only "upon probable cause, supported by oath or affirmation," as would be required for a search warrant. Nevertheless, except for Mr. Justice McKenna, all were of the view that an overbroad subpoena duces tecum against an individual would be an unreasonable search and seizure.

Judge Friendly suggested in *Horowitz* that the overbreadth doctrine of *Hale* might find firmer support in the due process clause than in the Fourth Amendment. Although a due process grounding for the doctrine is suggested in *Oklahoma Press Publishing Co. v. Walling,* 327 U.S. 186, 66 S.Ct. 494, 90 L.Ed. 614 (1946) (a leading case on the application of the overbreadth doctrine to an administrative agency subpoena[a]), more recent cases have referred to the doctrine as based on the Fourth Amendment.

a. Speaking to petitioner's claim that enforcement of the subpoena duces tecum would violate rights secured by the Fourth Amendment, Justice Rutledge noted that the "short answer" to this contention was that "these cases present no question of actual search and seizure" as they involved no attempt by government officials "to enter petitioners' premises against their will, to search them, or to seize or examine their books." He later added: "The primary source of misconception concerning the Fourth Amendment's function lies perhaps in the identification of cases involving so-called 'figurative' or 'constructive' search with cases of actual search and seizure. Only in this analogical sense can any question related to search and seizure be thought to arise in situations which, like the present ones, involve only the validity of authorized judicial orders."

Oklahoma Press set forth three prerequisites for administrative agency subpoenas: (1) the investigation must be for a "lawfully authorized purpose within the power of Congress"; (2) the documents sought must be "relevant to the inquiry"; (3) the element of "particularity" must be satisfied by a "specification of the documents to be produced adequate, but not excessive for the purpose of reasonable inquiry." Lower courts have described this standard as lenient, but not as lenient as "the lowest standard [which] is reserved for federal grand jury subpoenas." *Oman v. State,* 737 N.E.2d 1131 (Ind. 2000).

Accepting the Court's premise that the Fourth Amendment does apply to the subpoena duces tecum, why should the overbreadth doctrine be the sole Fourth Amendment limitation as to the subpoena duces tecum? One explanation is that the requirements of the Fourth Amendment's warrant clause are inapplicable in light of (1) the long history of subpoenas issued without regard to probable cause (particularly in the trial context, see Fed.R.Crim.P. 17), and (2) the lesser intrusion upon privacy resulting from a subpoena (as compared to the traditional search). This leaves applicable only the Fourth Amendment's general mandate of "reasonableness," which is reflected in the overbreadth doctrine. See Wayne R. LaFave, *Search and Seizure* § 4.13(e) (3d ed. 1996). This explanation makes *Hale* the forerunner of the Supreme Court's later line of cases which looked to similar factors in concluding that the Fourth Amendment permits administrative searches (e.g., health inspections) without a case-specific showing akin to probable cause or reasonable suspicion. See Ch. 5, § 9. But consider CRIMPROC § 8.7(a), responding that this explanation would seem to call for a standard of reasonableness that is more rigorous where there is a greater invasion of privacy due to the heightened confidentiality of the particular document (distinguishing for example between the subpoena of business documents and diaries), a position not suggested in *Hale*. "Also, such an analysis does not lead to protection conditioned on the subpoena compelling production of a substantial body of documents (as *Hale* seemed to suggest) and would not test overbreadth by reference to the economic burden imposed upon the individual or entity by being forced to relinquish those documents (as *Hale* clearly did)." Ibid.

A second explanation of *Hale* builds upon Justice McKenna's suggestion that the *Hale* majority found the Fourth Amendment applicable only when the subpoena was overly broad. The theory here is that the subpoena is not comparable to search, except where it potentially is too sweeping. Calling for a mass of documents without regard to what is relevant, necessarily requires a sifting through those documents to identify those that are relevant. Whether that sifting takes place on the premises of the owner or in the offices of the prosecutor assisting the grand jury, it would constitute a search, and therefore the Fourth prohibits a subpoena where it clearly is so sweeping as to include the relevant and the irrelevant. This explanation, although it arguably fits the subpoena in the *Hale* case, does not explain the emphasis in *Hale* upon the burden that the subpoena imposed upon the MacAndrew & Forbes Co.

A third explanation, stresses the different investigative focus of searches and grand jury subpoenas. The underlying premise of this explanation is that a Fourth Amendment that looks to the invasion of privacy would not on that ground draw a distinction between searches and subpoenas to produce documents.[b] Rather, the key to that distinction is "substantive necessity," as reflected in the character of the crime typically investigated by documentary subpoena as opposed to the

---

b. See William J. Stuntz, *Privacy's Problem and the Law of Criminal Procedure*, 93 Mich. L.Rev. 1016 (1995): "When the police search a car, they see anything that happens to be in the car, not just guns or drugs. A subpoena, on the other hand, asks only for the evidence being sought; nothing else need be disclosed. This difference could suggest that searches by their very nature invade privacy more than subpoenas do * * * [but] the line is incoherent in privacy terms. * * * The relevant privacy interest is the interest in keeping secret whatever the government is examining. The problem with a typical search is that the government's agent is examining whatever happens to be there, not just guns or cocaine. There may be no legitimate interest in keeping the guns or cocaine secret, but the officer sees innocent (albeit potentially embarrassing) things as well. Hence the overbreadth concern. But subpoenas do not do away with this problem unless they seek only guilty information—which they don't. Subpoenas for financial records or correspondence are common, and these documents can include a great deal of legitimately private information. Just as the police officer must search the whole car to find the hidden cocaine, the subpoena must demand a great deal of innocent-but-private material in order to turn up the smoking gun document."

crimes typically investigated through physical searches. See William J. Stuntz, *O.J. Simpson, Bill Clinton, and the Transsubstantive Fourth Amendment*, 114 Harv.L.Rev. 842 (2001): "[I]f the government is to regulate business and political affairs—the usual stuff of white-collar criminal law—it must have the power to subpoena witnesses and documents before it knows whether those witnesses and documents will yield incriminating evidence." Though *Hale* did not point to this reality in explaining its "lax" Fourth Amendment standard, the Court did so in another portion of the opinion, where it rejected *Hale's* Fifth Amendment argument "in a pair of dismissive sentences," noting: "[T]he privilege claimed would practically nullify the whole [Sherman Act]. Of what use would it be for the legislature to declare these combinations unlawful if the judicial power may close the door of access to every available source of information upon the subject?" [see fn. a, p. 727]. Here, it is argued, "[t]he Court did not deny that subpoenas infringe privacy, nor did it scoff at the degree of the infringement. Instead, the Court said that regardless of how serious it was, the infringement had to be tolerated: we need antitrust regulation, and we need a broad subpoena power in order to have antitrust regulation." Stuntz, supra.[c]

5. *Applying the overbreadth doctrine.* Lower courts applying the overbreadth doctrine in the grand jury setting frequently note that the doctrine requires a fact-specific judgment, with each ruling tied to the circumstances of the individual case. At the same time, they have sought to develop some general criteria to guide that judgment. Initially, the subpoena carries with it a presumption of regularity that will be called into question only if the subpoena has "sufficient breadth to suggest either that compliance will be burdensome or that the subpoena's scope may not have been shaped to the purposes of the inquiry." CRIMPROC § 8.7(c). If the subpoena has such breadth, the courts will then examine its scope in light of three criteria: (1) whether it "commands only the production of documents relevant to the investigation being pursued"; (2) whether the specification of the documents is made with "reasonable particularity" (measured by reference to both the subpoenaed party's ability to identify what "he is being asked to produce" and any "unreasonable business detriment" flowing from collecting and relinquishing the quantity and range of the documents requested); and (3) whether the documents to be produced cover "only a reasonable period of time." Ibid. Applying these criteria, courts have upheld subpoenas requiring production of as much as 50 tons of documents, see *Petition of Borden*, 75 F.Supp. 857 (N.D.Ill.1948); yet they also have rejected requests for records that presumably would have occupied no more than a single filing cabinet, see *In re Certain Chinese Family Benevolent Ass'n*, 19 F.R.D. 97 (N.D.Cal.1956) (rejecting subpoenas requiring various Chinese family associations to produce available membership lists, income records, and membership photographs, dating back to the association's origin, for use in an investigation of immigration fraud). Much depends upon the nature of the investigation, as courts recognize that certain types of investigations, such as antitrust, necessarily demand a broader range of documents since the violation may be reflected in many aspects of a company's business. See also *In re Corrado Brothers*, 367 F.Supp. 1126 (D.Del.1973) (where

c. Does it follow from this explanation that Court could have (and should have) insisted on a taking into account the need for such sweeping subpoena power in the individual case. Consider Stuntz, supra, describing "the road not yet taken in the law governing subpoenas"; "Courts could decide that the Fourth Amendment requires attention to substance, to the seriousness of the crime being investigated rather than to the odds that a particular subpoena will uncover evidence. When the subject of the investigation is the Oklahoma City bombing, an intrusive and drawn-out investigation is reasonable. When the subject is the truthfulness of deposition testimony about the details of an affair, it isn't. Just as the threshold for police entry into someone's home should be different in murder cases than in marijuana cases, the leeway prosecutors have to use the grand jury to haul in witnesses and documents should differ for more and less serious crimes."

the grand jury was investigating a kickback scheme involving the government highway department, all financial records were relevant since "cash for kickbacks can be readily generated by padding the * * * accounting records relating to a totally unrelated party"). Courts recognize also that "some exploration or fishing necessarily is inherent" since the grand jury will not ordinarily have a "catalogue of what books or papers exist nor any basis for knowing what their character or contents immediately are." *Schwimmer v. United States,* 232 F.2d 855 (8th Cir.1956). Although the overbreadth doctrine is a separate ground for challenging a subpoena duces tecum, as to the federal courts, it may largely overlap with the Rule 17(c) objection discussed in *R. Enterprises* (p. 680).

C.   COMPELLING TESTIMONY (AND IDENTIFICATION EXEMPLARS)

UNITED STATES v. DIONISIO
410 U.S. 1, 93 S.Ct. 764, 35 L.Ed.2d 67 (1973).

Justice STEWART delivered the opinion of the Court.

A special grand jury was convened in the Northern District of Illinois in February 1971, to investigate possible violations of federal criminal statutes relating to gambling. In the course of its investigation the grand jury received in evidence certain voice recordings that had been obtained pursuant to court orders. The grand jury subpoenaed approximately 20 persons, including the respondent Dionisio, seeking to obtain from them voice exemplars for comparison with the recorded conversations that had been received in evidence. Each witness was advised that he was a potential defendant in a criminal prosecution. Each was asked to examine a transcript of an intercepted conversation, and to go to a nearby office of the United States Attorney to read the transcript into a recording device. The witnesses were advised that they would be allowed to have their attorneys present when they read the transcripts. Dionisio and other witnesses refused to furnish the voice exemplars, asserting that these disclosures would violate their rights under the Fourth [Amendment]. * * * Following a hearing, the district judge rejected the witnesses' constitutional arguments and ordered them to comply with the grand jury's request. * * * When Dionisio persisted in his refusal to respond to the grand jury's directive, the District Court adjudged him in civil contempt and ordered him committed to custody. * * *

The Court of Appeals for the Seventh Circuit reversed. * * * The court found that the Fourth Amendment applied to the grand jury process * * *. Equating the procedures followed by the grand jury in the present case to the fingerprint detentions in *Davis v. Mississippi* [p. 323], the Court of Appeals reasoned that "[t]he dragnet effect here, where approximately 30 persons were subpoenaed for purposes of identification, has the same invidious effect on fourth amendment rights as the practice condemned in *Davis*."[a] The Court of Appeals held that the Fourth Amendment required a preliminary showing of reasonableness before a grand jury witness could be compelled to furnish a voice exemplar, and that in this case the proposed "seizures" of the voice exemplars would be unreasonable because of the large number of witnesses summoned by the grand jury and directed to produce such exemplars. We disagree. * * *

---

a. In *Davis*, petitioner and 24 other black youths were taken into custody, and questioned and fingerprinted, in connection with a rape for which the only leads were the victim's general description of the assailant and fingerprints around a window. The Supreme Court subsequently held that petitioner's prints should have been excluded from trial because they were obtained in violation of the Fourth Amendment. The Court left open the possibility that a court order directing that a person be detained briefly only for the purpose of obtaining his fingerprints could be sustained under the Fourth Amendment even though the individualized suspicion fell short of "probable cause in the traditional sense."

As [this] Court made clear in *Schmerber v. California* [p. 38], the obtaining of physical evidence from a person involves a potential Fourth Amendment violation at two different levels—the "seizure" of the "person" necessary to bring him into contact with government agents, see *Davis v. Mississippi*, and the subsequent search for and seizure of the evidence. * * * The constitutionality of the compulsory production of exemplars from a grand jury witness necessarily turns on the same dual inquiry—whether either the initial compulsion of the person to appear before the grand jury, or the subsequent directive to make a voice recording is an unreasonable "seizure" within the meaning of the Fourth Amendment.

It is clear that a subpoena to appear before a grand jury is not a "seizure" in the Fourth Amendment sense, even though that summons may be inconvenient or burdensome. Last Term we again acknowledged what has long been recognized, that "[c]itizens generally are not constitutionally immune from grand jury subpoenas...." *Branzburg v. Hayes* [Note 4, p. 686]. * * * [*Branzburg* and other decisions] are recent reaffirmations of the historically grounded obligations of every person to appear and give his evidence before the grand jury. "The personal sacrifice involved is a part of the necessary contribution of the individual to the welfare of the public." *Blair v. United States* [Note 2, p. 661].

The compulsion exerted by a grand jury subpoena differs from the seizure effected by an arrest or even an investigative "stop" in more than civic obligation. For, as Judge Friendly wrote for the Court of Appeals for the Second Circuit:

> "The latter is abrupt, is effected with force or the threat of it and often in demeaning circumstances, and, in the case of arrest, results in a record involving social stigma. A subpoena is served in the same manner as other legal process; it involves no stigma whatever; if the time for appearance is inconvenient, this can generally be altered; and it remains at all times under the control and supervision of a court."

Thus, the Court of Appeals for the Seventh Circuit correctly recognized in a case subsequent to the one now before us, that a "grand jury subpoena to testify is not that kind of governmental intrusion on privacy against which the Fourth Amendment affords protection, once the Fifth Amendment is satisfied." * * *

This case is thus quite different from *Davis v. Mississippi*, on which the Court of Appeals primarily relied. For in *Davis* it was the initial seizure—the lawless dragnet detention—that violated the Fourth and Fourteenth Amendments—not the taking of the fingerprints. * * * *Davis* is plainly inapposite to a case where the initial restraint does not itself infringe the Fourth Amendment.

This is not to say that a grand jury subpoena is some talisman that dissolves all constitutional protections. The grand jury cannot require a witness to testify against himself. It cannot require the production by a person of private books and records that would incriminate him. See *Boyd v. United States*. The Fourth Amendment provides protection against a grand jury subpoena *duces tecum* too sweeping in its terms "to be regarded as reasonable." *Hale v. Henkel*. And last Term, in the context of a First Amendment claim, we indicated that the Constitution could not tolerate the transformation of the grand jury into an instrument of oppression: "Official harassment of the press undertaken not for purposes of law enforcement but to disrupt a reporter's relationship with his news sources would have no justification. Grand juries are subject to judicial control and subpoenas to motions to quash. We do not expect courts will forget that grand juries must operate within the limits of the First Amendment as well as the Fifth." *Branzburg v. Hayes*.

But we are here faced with no such constitutional infirmities in the subpoena to appear before the grand jury or in the order to make the voice recordings.

There is * * * no valid Fifth Amendment claim. There was no order to produce private books and papers, and no sweeping subpoena *duces tecum*. And even if *Branzburg* be extended beyond its First Amendment moorings and tied to a more generalized due process concept, there is still no indication in this case of the kind of harassment that was of concern there.

The Court of Appeals found critical significance in the fact that the grand jury had summoned approximately 20 witnesses to furnish voice exemplars. We think that fact is basically irrelevant to the constitutional issues here. The grand jury may have been attempting to identify a number of voices on the tapes in evidence, or it might have summoned the 20 witnesses in an effort to identify one voice. But whatever the case, "[a] grand jury's investigation is not fully carried out until every available clue has been run down and all witnesses examined in every proper way to find if a crime has been committed." * * * The grand jury may well find it desirable to call numerous witnesses in the course of an investigation. It does not follow that each witness may resist a subpoena on the ground that too many witnesses have been called. Neither the order to Dionisio to appear, nor the order to make a voice recording was rendered unreasonable by the fact that many others were subjected to the same compulsion.

But the conclusion that Dionisio's compulsory appearance before the grand jury was not an unreasonable "seizure" is the answer to only the first part of the Fourth Amendment inquiry here. Dionisio argues that the grand jury's subsequent directive to make the voice recording was itself an infringement of his rights under the Fourth Amendment. We cannot accept that argument. In *Katz v. United States* [p. 138], we said that the Fourth Amendment provides no protection for what "a person knowingly exposes to the public, even in his home or office. . . ." The physical characteristics of a person's voice, its tone and manner, as opposed to the content of a specific conversation, are constantly exposed to the public. Like a man's facial characteristics, or handwriting, his voice is repeatedly produced for others to hear. No person can have a reasonable expectation that others will not know the sound of his voice, any more than he can reasonably expect that his face will be a mystery to the world. * * *

Since neither the summons to appear before the grand jury, nor its directive to make a voice recording infringed upon any interest protected by the Fourth Amendment, there was no justification for requiring the grand jury to satisfy even the minimal requirement of "reasonableness" imposed by the Court of Appeals. A grand jury has broad investigative powers to determine whether a crime has been committed and who has committed it. The jurors may act on tips, rumors, evidence offered by the prosecutor, or their own personal knowledge. *Branzburg v. Hayes.* No grand jury witness is "entitled to set limits to the investigation that the grand jury may conduct." *Blair v. United States.* And a sufficient basis for an indictment may only emerge at the end of the investigation when all the evidence has been received. * * * Since Dionisio raised no valid Fourth Amendment claim, there is no more reason to require a preliminary showing of reasonableness here than there would be in the case of any witness who, despite the lack of any constitutional or statutory privilege, declined to answer a question or comply with a grand jury request. Neither the Constitution nor our prior cases justify any such interference with grand jury proceedings.[14]

---

14. Mr. Justice Marshall in dissent suggests that a preliminary showing of "reasonableness" is required where the grand jury subpoenas a witness to appear and produce handwriting or voice exemplars, but not when it subpoenas him to appear and testify. Such a distinction finds no support in the Constitu- tion. The dissent argues that there is a potential Fourth Amendment violation in the case of a subpoenaed grand jury witness because of the asserted intrusiveness of the initial subpoena to appear—the possible stigma from a grand jury appearance and the inconvenience of the official restraint. But the initial directive to

The Fifth Amendment guarantees that no civilian may be brought to trial for an infamous crime "unless on a presentment or indictment of a Grand Jury." This constitutional guarantee presupposes an investigative body "acting independently of either prosecuting attorney or judge," whose mission is to clear the innocent, no less than to bring to trial those who may be guilty. Any holding that would saddle a grand jury with minitrials and preliminary showing would assuredly impede its investigation and frustrate the public's interest in the fair and expeditious administration of the criminal laws. The grand jury may not always serve its historic role as a protective bulwark standing solidly between the ordinary citizen and an overzealous prosecutor, but if it is even to approach the proper performance of its constitutional mission, it must be free to pursue its investigations unhindered by external influence or supervision so long as it does not trench upon the legitimate rights of any witness called before it. * * *

Justice MARSHALL, dissenting.[b]

* * * There can be no question that investigatory seizures effected by the police are subject to the constraints of the Fourth and Fourteenth Amendments. *Davis v. Mississippi.* * * * Like *Davis,* the present cases involve official investigatory seizures which interfere with personal liberty. The Court considers dispositive, however, the fact that the seizures were effected by the grand jury, rather than the police. I cannot agree. * * * [I]n *Hale v. Henkel,* the Court held that a subpoena *duces tecum* ordering "the production of books and papers [before a grand jury] may constitute an unreasonable search and seizure within the Fourth Amendment," and on the particular facts of the case, it concluded that the subpoena was "far too sweeping in its terms to be regarded as reasonable." Considered alone, *Hale* would certainly seem to carry a strong implication that a subpoena compelling an individual's personal appearance before a grand jury, like a subpoena ordering the production of private papers, is subject to the Fourth Amendment standard of reasonableness. The protection of the Fourth Amendment is not, after all, limited to personal "papers," but extends also to "persons," "houses," and "effects." It would seem a strange hierarchy of constitutional values that would afford papers more protection from arbitrary governmental intrusion than people.

The Court, however, offers two interrelated justifications for excepting grand jury subpoenas directed at "persons," rather than "papers," from the constraints of the Fourth Amendment. These are an "historically grounded obligation of every person to appear and give his evidence before the grand jury" [p. 674], and the relative unintrusiveness of the grand jury subpoena on an individual's liberty.

In my view, the Court makes more of history than is justified. The Court treats the "historically grounded obligation" which it now discerns as extending to all "evidence," whatever its character. Yet, so far as I am aware, the obligation "to appear and give evidence" has heretofore been applied by this Court only in the context of testimonial evidence, either oral or documentary. * * * In the present case, * * * it was not testimony that the grand jury sought from respondents, but physical evidence. * * *

appear is as intrusive if the witness is called simply to testify as it is if he is summoned to produce physical evidence.

b. In the companion case of *United States v. Mara,* 410 U.S. 19, 93 S.Ct. 774, 35 L.Ed.2d 99 (1973), the Court applied *Dionisio* to reject a lower court ruling that a preliminary showing of reasonableness was needed to justify a grand jury subpoena directing a witness to produce handwriting exemplars for the purpose of determining whether he was the author of certain writings. Justice Marshall's dissent was to both rulings. The separate dissents of Justices Douglas and Brennan are omitted. Justice Douglas' dissent proceeded from the premise, stated to now be "common knowledge," that "the grand jury, having been conceived as a bulwark between the citizen and the Government, is now a tool of the Executive."

The Court seems to reason that the exception to the Fourth Amendment for grand jury subpoenas directed at persons is justified by the relative unintrusiveness of the grand jury process on an individual's liberty. * * * It may be that service of a grand jury subpoena does not involve the same potential for momentary embarrassment as does an arrest or investigatory "stop." But this difference seems inconsequential in comparison to the substantial stigma which—contrary to the Court's assertion—may result from a grand jury appearance as well as from an arrest or investigatory seizure. Public knowledge that a man has been summoned by a federal grand jury investigating, for instance, organized criminal activity can mean loss of friends, irreparable injury to business, and tremendous pressures on one's family life. Whatever nice legal distinctions may be drawn between police and prosecutor, on the one hand, and the grand jury, on the other, the public often treats an appearance before a grand jury as tantamount to a visit to the station house. Indeed, the former is frequently more damaging than the latter, for a grand jury appearance has an air of far greater gravity than a brief visit "downtown" for a "talk." The Fourth Amendment was placed in our Bill of Rights to protect the individual citizen from such potentially disruptive governmental intrusion into his private life unless conducted reasonably and with sufficient cause.

Nor do I believe that the constitutional problems inherent in such governmental interference with an individual's person are substantially alleviated because one may seek to appear at a "convenient time." In *Davis v. Mississippi*, it was recognized that an investigatory detention effected by the police "need not come unexpectedly or at an inconvenient time." But this fact did not suggest to the Court that the Fourth Amendment was inapplicable * * *. No matter how considerate a grand jury may be in arranging for an individual's appearance, the basic fact remains that his liberty has been officially restrained for some period of time. In terms of its effect on the individual, this restraint does not differ meaningfully from the restraint imposed on a suspect compelled to visit the police station house. Thus, the nature of the intrusion on personal liberty caused by a grand jury subpoena cannot, without more, be considered sufficient basis for denying respondents the protection of the Fourth Amendment. * * *

Whatever the present day validity of the historical assumption of neutrality which underlies the grand jury process, it must at least be recognized that if a grand jury is deprived of the independence essential to the assumption of neutrality—if it effectively surrenders that independence to a prosecutor—the dangers of excessive and unreasonable official interference with personal liberty are exactly those which the Fourth Amendment was intended to prevent. So long as the grand jury carries on its investigatory activities only through the mechanism of testimonial inquiries, the danger of such official usurpation of the grand jury process may not be unreasonably great. Individuals called to testify before the grand jury will have available their Fifth Amendment privilege against self-incrimination. Thus, at least insofar as incriminating information is sought directly from a particular criminal suspect, the grand jury process would not appear to offer law enforcement officials a substantial advantage over ordinary investigative techniques.

But when we move beyond the realm of grand jury investigations limited to testimonial inquiries, as the Court does today, the danger increases that law enforcement officials may seek to usurp the grand jury process for the purpose of securing incriminating evidence from a particular suspect through the simple expedient of a subpoena. * * * Thus, if the grand jury may summon criminal suspects [to obtain handwriting and voice exemplars] without complying with the Fourth Amendment, it will obviously present an attractive investigative tool to prosecutor and police. For what law enforcement officers could not accomplish directly themselves after our decision in *Davis v. Mississippi,* they may now accomplish indirectly through the grand jury process.

Thus, the Court's decisions today can serve only to encourage prosecutorial exploitation of the grand jury process, at the expense of both individual liberty and the traditional neutrality of the grand jury. * * * [B]y holding that the grand jury's power to subpoena these respondents for the purpose of obtaining exemplars is completely outside the purview of the Fourth Amendment, the Court fails to appreciate the essential difference between real and testimonial evidence in the context of these cases, and thereby hastens the reduction of the grand jury into simply another investigative device of law enforcement officials. By contrast, the Court of Appeals, in proper recognition of these dangers, imposed narrow limitations on the subpoena power of the grand jury which are necessary to guard against unreasonable official interference with individual liberty but which would not impair significantly the traditional investigatory powers of that body. * * *

Notes and Questions

1. *Subpoenas and "seizures."* Are there any circumstances under which a grand jury subpoena might be viewed as producing "a 'seizure' in the Fourth Amendment sense" (see *Dionisio* at p. 674)? What if the subpoena calls for "forthwith" compliance, i.e., the immediate production of evidence for presentation to the grand jury or the immediate appearance of the witness before the grand jury? See CRIMPROC § 8.7(e) ("federal courts have refused to hold forthwith subpoenas per se invalid by concluding that the forthwith subpoena cannot be used like a search or arrest warrant" to allow agents to engage in an immediate search or seizure [of the person] over the opposition of a subpoenaed party who desires to contest the subpoena in court; but they also have "rejected the contention that * * * [immediate] compliance [by the party subpoenaed] is so suspect as to assume an involuntary relinquishment of rights," looking instead to "the circumstances of the case"). See also Brenner & Lockhart, § 14.5: "Because of the potential for abuse and the unfairness that can result from requiring an immediate response from a witness, a Department of Justice internal policy limits the use of forthwith subpoenas. The policy requires prosecutors to consider the following in deciding if a forthwith subpoena is warranted: (i) the risk of flight; (ii) the risk that evidence will be destroyed or fabricated; (iii) the need for the orderly presentation of evidence to the grand jury; and (iv) the degree of inconvenience to the witness. A forthwith subpoena must be approved in advance by the U.S. Attorney. Like other Department of Justice policies, this policy does not create any rights that can be enforced against the government."

2. *Other subpoena authority.* Where a subpoena to testify is used in a criminal investigation, but the grand jury plays no role, does it still follow that Fourth Amendment plays no role in regulating the issuance of such a subpoena? Although some of the states granting the prosecutor investigative subpoena authority (see Note 7, p. 659) condition that authority on a showing that the person is likely to have relevant information, others require no such showing. CRIMPROC § 8.1(c). They view requiring testimony pursuant to such a subpoena as not substantially different from requiring a person to give testimony in a discovery deposition (in both instances the witness may be accompanied by counsel and testifies outside the presence of the judge), and parties to a litigation need make no showing in their selection of persons to be deposed. Documentary subpoenas, on the other hand, are subjected to roughly the same Fourth Amendment standards as applied to administrative agency documentary subpoenas. See fn. a, p. 670.

3. *Other identification procedures.* Does the reasoning of *Dionisio* extend to a grand jury subpoena directing the subpoenaed party to appear in a lineup? Several courts have held that it does, although some (to preclude the use of such orders simply to assist a police investigation, see Note 1, p. 678) have required that such a subpoena be approved by the grand jury itself. See *In re Melvin,* 546 F.2d 1 (1st Cir.1976). Considering, however, *In re Kelley,* 433 A.2d 704 (D.C.App.1981) (en banc). The court there had earlier held that police could obtain a court order directing a non-arrested suspect to appear in a lineup upon a showing of reasonable suspicion (p. 649). However, the government here "candidly acknowledged" that it had put that procedure "in mothballs," and relying on *Dionisio,* had utilized a "grand jury pass-through"—i.e., the "government now passes such police requests through the grand jury and thereby obtains grand jury lineup directives." The *Kelley* court initially rejected the government's reliance on *Dionisio,* noting that *Dionisio*'s Fourth Amendment ruling dealt only with a summons to present evidence such as a voice sample or handwriting exemplar. A lineup, it noted, was a substantially different process: "A lineup appearance is not simply showing one's face to the public. It involves considerable social stigma and personal risk. It entails the humiliation of standing on a stage under floodlights, removed from counsel, subject to being compelled to speak certain words and perform actions directed by the police, all at considerably more risk of mistake and misidentification that the more scientifically grounded fingerprinting and, to some extent, voiceprinting techniques involved in *Dionisio* and *Mara.*"

The *Kelley* court concluded, however, that there was no need to decide whether *Dionisio*'s rejection of a Fourth Amendment restraint should apply as well to lineups. This was an appropriate setting for use of its supervisory power to avoid "the appearance of, or potential for, abuse of the grand jury system" inherent in the government's pass-through procedure. Accordingly, in the exercise of that power, it would hold that "a prosecutor seeking judicial enforcement of a grand jury directive to appear in a lineup must, by affidavit of law enforcement officer or * * * [prosecutor], make a minimal factual showing sufficient to permit the judge to conclude that there is a reason for the lineup which is consistent with the legitimate function of the grand jury." Consider also, *In re May 1991 Will County Grand Jury,* 604 N.E.2d 929 (Ill.1992) (with state constitutional counterpart of Fourth Amendment providing "greater protection than *Dionisio,*" grand jury subpoena for physical evidence of a "noninvasive nature, such as in-person appearance in a lineup or fingerprinting," will require some showing of individualized suspicion as well as relevance to the investigation; *Dionisio* must be read in light of cases like *Winston v. Lee* (p. 235) and *Schmerber* (pp. 38, 235), so a grand jury subpoena for pubic hair samples will require a showing of probable cause under both Fourth Amendment and state constitution). Courts have divided as to the showing needed for a grand jury subpoena for a blood sample. See *Woolverton v. Multi–County Grand Jury,* 859 P.2d 1112(Okla.Cr.App.1993) (probable cause required, as in *Schmerber*); *Henry v. Ryan,* 775 F.Supp. 247 (N.D.Ill.1991) ("individualized suspicion" sufficient, since grand jury subpoena affords an opportunity to challenge prior to taking the blood).

4. *Underlying Fourth Amendment violations.* In UNITED STATES v. CALANDRA, 414 U.S. 338, 94 S.Ct. 613, 38 L.Ed.2d 561 (1974), grand jury witness Calandra was asked questions about certain records (evidencing "loan-sharking" activities) that had been seized by federal agents in connection with a search of Calandra's office. Calandra initially invoked his privilege against self-incrimination, but subsequently was granted immunity. He then requested and received a postponement of the grand jury proceedings so that he could present a pre-charge motion for return and suppression of the seized evidence under Federal

Rule 41(e). The district court granted the motion, holding that the search had been unconstitutional. The district court also held that "Calandra need not answer any of the grand jury's questions based on suppressed evidence," since such questions constituted the fruit of the poisonous tree. A divided Supreme Court (6–3), per POWELL, J., reversed.

"In deciding whether to extend the exclusionary rule to grand jury proceedings, we must weigh the potential injury to the historic role and functions of the grand jury against the potential benefits of the rule as applied in this context. It is evident that this extension of the exclusionary rule would seriously impede the grand jury. Because the grand jury does not finally adjudicate guilt or innocence, it has traditionally been allowed to pursue its investigative and accusatorial functions unimpeded by the evidentiary and procedural restrictions applicable to a criminal trial. Permitting witnesses to invoke the exclusionary rule before a grand jury would precipitate adjudication of issues hitherto reserved for the trial on the merits and would delay and disrupt grand jury proceedings. Suppression hearings would halt the orderly progress of an investigation and might necessitate extended litigation of issues only tangentially related to the grand jury's primary objective. The probable result would be 'protracted interruptions of grand jury proceedings,' effectively transforming them into preliminary trials on the merits. In some cases the delay might be fatal to the enforcement of the criminal law. Just last Term we reaffirmed our disinclination to allow litigious interference with grand jury proceedings. *United States v. Dionisio.*

"Against this potential damage to the role and functions of the grand jury, we must weigh the benefits to be derived from this proposed extension of the exclusionary rule. * * * [The Court here considered the "incremental deterrent effect which might be achieved by extending the exclusionary rule to grand jury proceedings," and for reasons discussed in Note 1, p. 131, found "unrealistic" the assumption that such an extension would significantly further deterrence of illegal searches.] We decline to embrace a view that would achieve a speculative and undoubtedly minimal advance in the deterrence of police misconduct at the expense of substantially impeding the role of the grand jury."[c]

SECTION 3. OTHER OBJECTIONS TO THE INVESTIGATION

UNITED STATES v. R. ENTERPRISES, INC.
498 U.S. 292, 111 S.Ct. 722, 112 L.Ed.2d 795 (1991).

Justice O'CONNOR delivered the opinion of the Court.

This case requires the Court to decide what standards apply when a party seeks to avoid compliance with a subpoena *duces tecum* issued in connection with a grand jury investigation.

Since 1986, a federal grand jury sitting in the Eastern District of Virginia has been investigating allegations of interstate transportation of obscene materials. In early 1988, the grand jury issued a series of subpoenas to three companies—Model Magazine Distributors, Inc. (Model), R. Enterprises, Inc., and MFR Court Street Books, Inc. (MFR). Model is a New York distributor of sexually oriented paperback books, magazines, and videotapes. R. Enterprises, which distributes adult

---

c. In *Gelbard v. United States,* 408 U.S. 41, 92 S.Ct. 2357, 33 L.Ed.2d 179 (1972), the Court held that the broad exclusionary remedy of the Omnibus Crime Control Act (see fn. a, p. 357) gave grand jury witnesses the right to object to the grand jury's use of information derived from illegal electronic surveillance.

materials, and MFR, which sells books, magazines, and videotapes, are also based in New York. All three companies are wholly owned by Martin Rothstein. The grand jury subpoenas sought a variety of corporate books and records and, in Model's case, copies of 193 videotapes that Model had shipped to retailers in the Eastern District of Virginia. All three companies moved to quash the subpoenas, arguing that the subpoenas called for production of materials irrelevant to the grand jury's investigation and that the enforcement of the subpoenas would likely infringe their First Amendment rights.

The District Court, after extensive hearings, denied the motions to quash. As to Model, the court found that the subpoenas for business records were sufficiently specific and that production of the videotapes would not constitute a prior restraint. As to R. Enterprises, the court found a "sufficient connection with Virginia for further investigation by the grand jury." The court relied in large part on the statement attributed to Rothstein that the three companies were "all the same thing, I'm president of all three." Additionally, the court explained in denying MFR's motion to quash that it was "inclined to agree" with "the majority of the jurisdictions," which do not require the Government to make a "threshold showing" before a grand jury subpoena will be enforced. Even assuming that a preliminary showing of relevance was required, the court determined that the Government had made such a showing. It found sufficient evidence that the companies were "related entities," at least one of which "certainly did ship sexually explicit material into the Commonwealth of Virginia." * * * Notwithstanding these findings, the companies refused to comply with the subpoenas. The District Court found each in contempt and fined them $500 per day, but stayed imposition of the fine pending appeal.

The Court of Appeals for the Fourth Circuit upheld the business records subpoenas issued to Model, but remanded the motion to quash the subpoena for Model's videotapes. Of particular relevance here, the Court of Appeals quashed the business records subpoenas issued to R. Enterprises and MFR. In doing so, it applied the standards set out by this Court in *United States v. Nixon*, 418 U.S. 683, 94 S.Ct. 3090, 41 L.Ed.2d 1039 (1974). The court recognized that *Nixon* dealt with a trial subpoena, not a grand jury subpoena, but determined that the rule was "equally applicable" in the grand jury context. Accordingly, it required the Government to clear the three hurdles that *Nixon* established in the trial context—relevancy, admissibility, and specificity—in order to enforce the grand jury subpoenas. The court concluded that the challenged subpoenas did not satisfy the *Nixon* standards, finding no evidence in the record that either company had ever shipped materials into, or otherwise conducted business in, the Eastern District of Virginia. The Court of Appeals specifically criticized the District Court for drawing an inference that, because Rothstein owned all three businesses and one of them had undoubtedly shipped sexually explicit materials into the Eastern District of Virginia, there might be some link between the Eastern District of Virginia and R. Enterprises or MFR. It then noted that "any evidence concerning Mr. Rothstein's alleged business activities outside of Virginia, or his ownership of companies which distribute allegedly obscene materials outside of Virginia, would most likely be inadmissible on relevancy grounds at any trial that might occur," and that the subpoenas therefore failed "to meet the requirements [*sic*] that any documents subpoenaed under [Federal] Rule [of Criminal Procedure] 17(c) must be admissible as evidence at trial," citing *Nixon*. * * * We granted certiorari to determine whether the Court of Appeals applied the proper standard in evaluating the grand jury subpoenas issued to respondents. We now reverse.

The grand jury occupies a unique role in our criminal justice system. * * * [It] "can investigate merely on suspicion that the law is being violated, or even just because it wants assurance that it is not." * * * As a necessary consequence of its investigatory function, the grand jury paints with a broad brush. * * * A grand jury subpoena is thus much different from a subpoena issued in the context of a prospective criminal trial, where a specific offense has been identified and a particular defendant charged. * * *

This Court has emphasized on numerous occasions that many of the rules and restrictions that apply at a trial do not apply in grand jury proceedings. This is especially true of evidentiary restrictions. The same rules that, in an adversary hearing on the merits may increase the likelihood of accurate determinations of guilt or innocence do not necessarily advance the mission of a grand jury, whose task is to conduct an *ex parte* investigation to determine whether or not there is probable cause to prosecute a particular defendant. * * * The teaching of the Court's decisions is clear: A grand jury "may compel the production of evidence or the testimony of witnesses as it considers appropriate, and its operation generally is unrestrained by the technical procedural and evidentiary rules governing the conduct of criminal trials." *United States v. Calandra.*

This guiding principle renders suspect the Court of Appeals' holding that the standards announced in *Nixon* as to subpoenas issued in anticipation of trial apply equally in the grand jury context. The multifactor test announced in *Nixon* would invite procedural delays and detours while courts evaluate the relevancy and admissibility of documents sought by a particular subpoena. We have expressly stated that grand jury proceedings should be free of such delays. * * * *United States v. Dionisio.* Additionally, application of the *Nixon* test in this context ignores that grand jury proceedings are subject to strict secrecy requirements. See Fed.Rule Crim.Proc. 6(e). Requiring the Government to explain in too much detail the particular reasons underlying a subpoena threatens to compromise "the indispensable secrecy of grand jury proceedings." Broad disclosure also affords the targets of investigation far more information about the grand jury's internal workings than the Federal Rules of Criminal Procedure appear to contemplate.

The investigatory powers of the grand jury are nevertheless not unlimited. Grand juries are not licensed to engage in arbitrary fishing expeditions, nor may they select targets of investigation out of malice or an intent to harass. In this case, the focus of our inquiry is the limit imposed on a grand jury by Federal Rule of Criminal Procedure 17(c), which governs the issuance of subpoenas *duces tecum* in federal criminal proceedings. The Rule provides that "the court on motion made promptly may quash or modify the subpoena if compliance would be unreasonable or oppressive." * * * This standard is not self-explanatory. As we have observed, "what is reasonable depends on the context." In *Nixon,* this Court defined what is reasonable in the context of a jury trial. * * * But, for the reasons we have explained above, the *Nixon* standard does not apply in the context of grand jury proceedings. In the grand jury context, the decision as to what offense will be charged is routinely not made until after the grand jury has concluded its investigation. One simply cannot know in advance whether information sought during the investigation will be relevant and admissible in a prosecution for a particular offense.

To the extent that Rule 17(c) imposes some reasonableness limitation on grand jury subpoenas, however, our task is to define it. In doing so, we recognize that a party to whom a grand jury subpoena is issued faces a difficult situation. As a rule, grand juries do not announce publicly the subjects of their investigations. A party who desires to challenge a grand jury subpoena thus may have no conception of the Government's purpose in seeking production of the requested information. Indeed, the party will often not know whether he or she is a primary target of the investigation or merely a peripheral witness. Absent even minimal information, the subpoena recipient is likely to find it exceedingly difficult to persuade a court that "compliance would be unreasonable." As one pair of commentators has summarized it, the challenging party's "unenviable task is to seek to persuade the court that the subpoena that has been served on [him or her] could not possibly serve any investigative purpose that the grand jury could legitimately be pursuing." S. Beale & W. Bryson, *Grand Jury Law and Practice* § 6:28 (1986).

Our task is to fashion an appropriate standard of reasonableness, one that gives due weight to the difficult position of subpoena recipients but does not impair the strong governmental interests in affording grand juries wide latitude, avoiding minitrials on peripheral matters, and preserving a necessary level of secrecy. We begin by reiterating that the law presumes, absent a strong showing to the contrary, that a grand jury acts within the legitimate scope of its authority. * * * Consequently, a grand jury subpoena issued through normal channels is presumed to be reasonable, and the burden of showing unreasonableness must be on the recipient who seeks to avoid compliance. Indeed, this result is indicated by the language of Rule 17(c), which permits a subpoena to be quashed only "on motion" and "if *compliance* would be unreasonable" (emphasis added). To the extent that the Court of Appeals placed an initial burden on the Government, it committed error. Drawing on the principles articulated above, we conclude that where, as here, a subpoena is challenged on relevancy grounds, the motion to quash must be denied unless the district court determines that there is no reasonable possibility that the category of materials the Government seeks will produce information relevant to the general subject of the grand jury's investigation. Respondents did not challenge the subpoenas as being too indefinite nor did they claim that compliance would be overly burdensome. The Court of Appeals accordingly did not consider these aspects of the subpoenas, nor do we.

It seems unlikely, of course, that a challenging party who does not know the general subject matter of the grand jury's investigation, no matter how valid that party's claim, will be able to make the necessary showing that compliance would be unreasonable. After all, a subpoena recipient "cannot put his whole life before the court in order to show that there is no crime to be investigated." Consequently, a court may be justified in a case where unreasonableness is alleged in requiring the Government to reveal the general subject of the grand jury's investigation before requiring the challenging party to carry its burden of persuasion.[a] We need not resolve this question in the present case, however, as there is no doubt that respondents knew the subject of the grand jury investigation pursuant to which the business records subpoenas were issued. In cases where the recipient of the subpoena does not know the nature of the investigation, we are confident that district courts will be able to craft appropriate procedures that balance the interests of the subpoena recipient against the strong governmental interests in maintaining secrecy, preserving investigatory flexibility, and avoiding procedural delays. For example, to ensure that subpoenas are not routinely challenged as a form of discovery, a district court may require that the Government reveal the subject of the investigation to the trial court *in camera,* so that the court may determine whether the motion to quash has a reasonable prospect for success before it discloses the subject matter to the challenging party.[b]

Applying these principles in this case demonstrates that the District Court correctly denied respondents' motions to quash. It is undisputed that all three companies—Model, R. Enterprises, and MFR—are owned by the same person, that all do business in the same area, and that one of the three, Model, has shipped

---

a. The United States Attorneys' Manual directs that subpoenas contain an "advice of rights" statement (see Note 6, p. 698), which includes the following: "The grand jury is conducting an investigation of possible violations of federal criminal laws involving: (State here the general subject matter of inquiry, e.g., the conducting of an illegal gambling business in violation of 18 U.S.C. § 1955)." U.S.A.M. 9–11.150.

b. Justice Scalia did not join this paragraph of the Court's opinion.

sexually explicit materials into the Eastern District of Virginia. The District Court could have concluded from these facts that there was a reasonable possibility that the business records of R. Enterprises and MFR would produce information relevant to the grand jury's investigation into the interstate transportation of obscene materials. Respondents' blanket denial of any connection to Virginia did not suffice to render the District Court's conclusion invalid. A grand jury need not accept on faith the self-serving assertions of those who may have committed criminal acts. Rather, it is entitled to determine for itself whether a crime has been committed.

Both in the District Court and in the Court of Appeals, respondents contended that these subpoenas sought records relating to First Amendment activities, and that this required the Government to demonstrate that the records were particularly relevant to its investigation. The Court of Appeals determined that the subpoenas did not satisfy Rule 17(c) and thus did not pass on the First Amendment issue. We express no view on this issue and leave it to be resolved by the Court of Appeals. * * *

Justice STEVENS, with whom Justices MARSHALL and BLACKMUN join, concurring in part and concurring in the judgment.

Federal Rule of Criminal Procedure 17(c) * * * requires the district court to balance the burden of compliance, on the one hand, against the governmental interest in obtaining the documents on the other. A more burdensome subpoena should be justified by a somewhat higher degree of probable relevance than a subpoena that imposes a minimal or nonexistent burden. Against the procedural history of this case, the Court has attempted to define the term "reasonable" in the abstract, looking only at the relevance side of the balance. Because I believe that this truncated approach to the Rule will neither provide adequate guidance to the district court nor place any meaningful constraint on the overzealous prosecutor, I add these comments. * * *

The moving party has the initial task of demonstrating to the Court that he has some valid objection to compliance. This showing might be made in various ways. Depending on the volume and location of the requested materials, the mere cost in terms of time, money, and effort of responding to a dragnet subpoena could satisfy the initial hurdle. Similarly, if a witness showed that compliance with the subpoena would intrude significantly on his privacy interests, or call for the disclosure of trade secrets or other confidential information, further inquiry would be required. Or, as in this case, the movant might demonstrate that compliance would have First Amendment implications.

The trial court need inquire into the relevance of subpoenaed materials only after the moving party has made this initial showing. And, as is true in the parallel context of pretrial civil discovery, a matter also committed to the sound discretion of the trial judge, the degree of need sufficient to justify denial of the motion to quash will vary to some extent with the burden of producing the requested information. For the reasons stated by the Court, in the grand jury context the law enforcement interest will almost always prevail, and the documents must be produced. I stress, however, that the Court's opinion should not be read to suggest that the deferential relevance standard the Court has formulated will govern decision in every case, no matter how intrusive or burdensome the request. * * *

Notes and Questions

1. **The Schofield Approach.** In IN RE GRAND JURY PROCEEDINGS (*Schofield*), 486 F.2d 85 (3d Cir.1973), a pre-*R. Enterprises* ruling, the Third

Circuit adopted an approach to relevancy objections that was distinctive among the federal circuits. The petitioner there had refused to comply with a subpoena directing her to provide handwriting samples, photographs, and fingerprints to the grand jury, and the government had sought to have her held in civil contempt. The Third Circuit concluded that the petitioner could not be found in contempt since the government had failed to show that the items sought were "relevant to the grand jury's investigation of an offense falling within its jurisdiction." The Court (per GIBBONS, J.) reasoned:

"In view of the fact that information which would justify obtaining the handwriting exemplars, fingerprints, and a mug shot, is in the Government's sole possession, we think it reasonable that the Government be required to make some preliminary showing by affidavit that each item is at least relevant to an investigation being conducted by the grand jury and properly within its jurisdiction, and is not sought primarily for another purpose. We impose this requirement both pursuant to the federal courts' supervisory power over grand juries and pursuant to our supervisory power over civil [contempt] proceedings brought in the district court pursuant to 28 U.S.C. § 1826(a). We do not rule out the possibility that the Government's affidavit may be presented to the court *in camera*, but we do hold that Rule 6(e) does not require *in camera* presentation. * * * [U]nless extraordinary circumstances appear, the nature of which we cannot anticipate, the Government's supporting affidavit should be disclosed to the witness in the enforcement proceeding. If after such disclosure the witness makes application to the district court for additional discovery in the enforcement proceeding, the court must in deciding that request weigh the quite limited scope of an inquiry into abuse of the subpoena process, and the potential for delay, against any need for additional information which might cast doubt upon the accuracy of the Government's representations."

As noted in Beale et al., § 6.21, the Third Circuit has "generally deferred to the district courts' judgments about the sufficiency of particular '*Schofield* affidavits' in the circumstances of each case," and it accordingly has affirmed rulings holding "adequate even 'scanty' affidavits which describe the relevance of the subpoenaed material and the purpose of the grand jury investigation in only general terms." See e.g., *In re Grand Jury, Schmidt,* 619 F.2d 1022 (3d Cir.1980) (affidavit identified particular manufacturing practice under investigation, noted possible statutes violated, and identified witnesses as employees likely to be familiar with the practice and the whereabouts of relevant records). Even so interpreted, is the *Schofield* requirement consistent with the discussion in *R. Enterprises* of the applicable standard of reasonableness and the district court's authority in crafting appropriate procedures for relevancy challenges?

2. *Schofield* was subsequently applied to witness refusals to testify as well as refusals to comply with a subpoena *duces tecum.* However, where the witness cited for contempt had refused to give testimony, *Schofield*'s relevancy element was held to require a showing of relevancy only as to the general subject matter of the total group of questions rather than as to specific questions. See *In re Grand Jury Investigation (Bruno),* 545 F.2d 385 (3d Cir.1976). Since *R. Enterprises* was based on Rule 17(c), which refers only to a subpoena *duces tecum,* does it allow for application of a similar standard of relevancy (either as to a general group of questions or as to specific questions) with respect to witness testimony? Consider also the statement of *Blair,* Note 2, p. 661, as to witness objections to relevancy. Compare *Ex parte Jennings,* 240 S.W. 942 (Tex.Cr.App.1922) (to establish contempt, prosecutor must establish compliance with the statutory requirement that he first announced the "subject matter under investigation" and then asked "pertinent questions relative to the transaction in general terms").

3. Balancing. Would the balancing approach discussed in Justice Stevens dissent in *R. Enterprises* permit consideration of such factors as (1) the seriousness of the crime being investigated (see fn. c, p. 672), (2) the likelihood that the evidence subpoenaed would only duplicate evidence previously received (e.g., where the grand jury has previously received from a bank an individual's checking account records and now subpoenas those records from the individual) or (3) the breadth of information likely to be disclosed by compliance (e.g., where the subpoena requires a computer hard disk drive)? Lower courts have not read the *R. Enterprises* opinions as authorizing a general case-by-case balancing in applying Rule 17(c) to subpoenas duces tecum, but they have been open to requiring something more than *R. Enterprises* standard of relevance under special circumstances, as illustrated by Notes 4, 5, and 6 below.

4. "Chilling effect": First Amendment objections. Lower courts have divided as to the standard to be applied where the subpoenaed party claims that compliance would have a chilling impact upon the exercise of a First Amendment right. In *Branzburg v. Hayes*, 408 U.S. 665, 92 S.Ct. 2646, 33 L.Ed.2d 626 (1972), the Supreme Court rejected the contention that the First Amendment prohibited a subpoena compelling reporters to testify before the grand jury as to information received in confidence (including the identity of their confidential sources) absent a government showing of "compelling need." The Court concluded that even if requiring reporters to appear and testify might have a negative impact upon news gathering by deterring future confidential sources, that impact did not outweigh the interest of the public in the grand jury's investigation of crime. The majority noted (and Justice Powell's concurring opinion stressed in particular) that judicial control of the grand jury process was always available to provide an appropriate remedy if the grand jury process was used to "harass the press."

Relying on *Branzburg*, the Fourth Circuit, on remand in *R. Enterprises*, rejected the First Amendment claim that had not been considered by the Supreme Court. See *In re Grand Jury 87–3 Subpoena Duces Tecum*, 955 F.2d 229 (4th Cir.1992). The Fourth Circuit found unpersuasive the reasoning of the Ninth Circuit in *Bursey v. United States*, 466 F.2d 1059 (9th Cir.1972). *Bursey* had distinguished *Branzburg* as a case involving only a peripheral First Amendment concern. It had insisted upon the government showing a "substantial connection" between the information sought by the grand jury and an overriding government interest in the subject matter under investigation where disclosure of that information would bear directly on the exercise of First Amendment rights (applicable there, where the grand jury sought information relating to the activities of the Black Panthers and their publication of a newspaper, which had reported a threat against the president). The Fourth Circuit read *Branzburg* as having rejected requiring such a special showing of need, and having instead relied upon the district court's capacity to prevent the "bad faith" use of the subpoena authority to "harass" as "striking a proper balance" between the "obligation of all citizens to give relevant testimony with respect to criminal conduct" and the possible chilling impact on the exercise of First Amendment rights.

Other courts have also refused to require a special showing of need, but some have been divided in doing so. See *In re Grand Jury Matter (Gronowicz)*, 764 F.2d 983 (3d Cir.1985) (en banc) (where grand jury was investigating author's possible fraud in representing to the publisher that the book was based on interviews with high church officials, and it subpoenaed materials concerning the alleged interviews, no special First Amendment limitations would be imposed even though grand jury inquiry necessarily would be examining the truthfulness of the book's description of those interviews; two dissenters argued that the government lacked a sufficiently compelling interest for such an investigation, which would undermine First Amendment values, and it therefore could not justify the subpoena); *In re Grand Jury Subpoenas for Locals 17, 135, 257 and 608,* 528 N.E.2d 1195 (N.Y.1988) (where grand jury was investigating union corruption, possibly extending to rank and file members as well as officials, subpoena requesting names, addresses, telephone numbers and social security numbers of all 10,000 members is supported by a "legitimate and compelling" need as it will enable the grand jury to locate and identify potential witnesses "without unduly burdening or delaying the search and without having to proceed through the traditional channels of first notifying the union leaders and exposing witnesses to possible intimidation"; dissent concluded that disclosure would infringe "on associational and privacy rights by chilling members' participation in the full range of union activities," particularly with fear of newspaper leaks regarding the investigation, and the grand jury therefore should be required to show the inadequacy of seemingly viable alternatives, such as disclosure of a percentage of the membership, or protecting against the union learning of the key target groups by having it deliver the complete list to a neutral third party, with the government then obtaining from that custodian the needed information as to those groups).

5. *"Chilling effect": Attorney subpoenas.* Assume that a grand jury subpoenas the attorney representing one of several targets in an organized crime investigation and asks that attorney for information of possible relevancy to the investigation that is not protected by the attorney-client privilege (e.g., whether that target arranged for the legal representation of certain persons thought to be a member of the same organized crime "family"). Should a special showing of need, similar to that imposed in *Bursey,* Note 4 supra, be required to overcome the "chilling impact" that such questioning may have upon the lawyer-client relationship?[c] The several circuit courts considering the issue have all refused to impose such a requirement as a general rule (although some dissenting judges would have done so). See CRIMPROC § 8.8. They have noted that: (1) the target has no constitutional right to counsel with respect to the grand jury proceeding (see Note 8, p. 698); (2) the attorney-client privilege provides adequate protection of the attorney-client relationship; (3) it is at most a "speculative" and "abstract possibility" that the attorney's testimony before the grand jury will lead to his or her disqualification as defense counsel should the target eventually be indicted; (4) the target is asking, in effect, for the "same kind of preliminary showing which the Supreme Court had disapproved [in *Dionisio* and *Branzburg*] as causing indeterminate delays in grand jury investigations." At the same time, the district court has been held to have authority to quash such a subpoena under "compelling circumstances". See *In re Grand Jury Matters,* 751 F.2d 13 (1st Cir.1984) (attorneys were currently representing same client in a state criminal proceeding).

In 1990, the ABA amended Rule 3.8 of the Model Rules of Professional Responsibility to deal specifically with attorney subpoenas. Subsection (f) provided that a "prosecutor in a criminal case * * * shall not subpoena a lawyer in a grand jury or other criminal proceeding to present evidence about a past or current client unless (1) the prosecutor reasonably believes: (i) the information sought is not protected from disclosure by any applicable privilege; (ii) the evidence sought

c. As a matter of internal policy, the Department of Justice does impose special prerequisites for subpoenaing an attorney to furnish information regarding a past or current client. U.S. Attorneys' Manual 9–2.161(a) authorizes use of attorney subpoenas (upon approval of an Assistant Attorney General) where (i) there exists "reasonable grounds to believe that a crime has been or is being committed and that the information sought is reasonably needed for the successful completion of the investigation or prosecution," (ii) "all reasonable attempts to obtain the information from alternative sources shall have proved to be unsuccessful," (iii) the information is not "protected by a valid claim of privilege," and is not "peripheral or speculative," and (iv) the "reasonable need for the information * * * outweigh[s] the potential adverse effects upon the attorney-client relationship" (in particular, "the risk that the attorney will be disqualified from representation of the client as a result of having to testify against the client").

is essential to the successful completion of an ongoing investigation or prosecution; (iii) there is no other feasible alternative to obtain the information; and (2) the prosecutor obtains prior judicial approval after an opportunity for an adversarial proceeding." In 1995, the subparagraph (2) requirement of prior judicial approval was deleted from Rule 3.8(f). However several states had already adopted Rule 3.8 with that provision. When federal district courts sought to make those ethical rules applicable to United States Attorneys, two circuits divided on whether they had the authority to do so. See *United States v. Colorado Supreme Court*, 87 F.3d 1161 (10th Cir.1996) (collecting citations and also recognizing the standing of the U.S. Attorney to challenge the state high court's application of those rules to lawyers in that office).

In 1998, Congress adopted the Citizen Protection Act, 28 U.S.C.A § 530B, which provides that an "attorney for 'the Government' shall be subject to State laws and rules and local Federal court rules governing attorneys * * * to the same extent and in the same manner as other attorneys in that State." Where states have adopted the original version of Rule 3.8(f), does the Citizens Protection Act create federal district court jurisdiction to review under the standards of Rule 3.8(f) federal grand jury subpoenas directed to attorneys? In *Stern v. United States District Court*, 214 F.3d 4 (1st Cir.2000), the First Circuit held that the CPA did not encompass the 1991 version of ABA Model Rule 3.8, because the CPA extended only to "ethical standards," and Rule 3.8, though "doubtless motivated by ethical concerns," is "more than an ethical standard"; "it adds a novel procedural step—the opportunity for a pre-service adversarial hearing—and to compound the matter, ordains that the hearing be conducted with new substantive standards in mind."

United States v. Colorado Supreme Court, 189 F.3d 1281 (10th Cir.1999), considered the application in a non-grand jury setting of a state rule incorporating the amended ABA Rule 3.8. The Tenth Circuit concluded that the CPA did encompass such a rule, but the remedy for violation could only be a disciplinary proceeding, not quashing the subpoena, as there was no indication that Congress intended through the CPA to alter Federal Rule 17(c) and the substantive standards for issuing subpoenas developed under that rule. Does limiting the remedy for violating the CPA to disciplinary proceedings provide a sufficient implementation of Congress' presumed decision not to grant to the states authority to modify federal "substantive law." See Peter J. Henning, *Prosecutorial Misconduct in Grand Jury Investigations*, 51 S.Car.L.Rev. (1999) ("It would be odd to have the ethical rules of the profession become the vehicle for granting rights that are not mandated by the Constitution or adopted by the legislature; that federal officers would have [their] rules created by fifty-one different jurisdictions is perhaps odder still. * * * The filing of a complaint with the disciplinary authority is very serious business, and the potential for abuse is enough to raise a question whether the wholesale approach of the McDade Act is the best method of addressing prosecutorial misconduct. Unfortunately, Congress did not pause to consider these issues, adopting the provision without the benefit of much, if any, reflection.").

6. *Oppressive burdens.* Rule 17(c) and similar state provisions authorize quashing subpoenas where compliance would be "unreasonable or oppressive." Does oppressiveness constitute an alternative and distinct ground for quashing a grand jury subpoena? Consider in *In re Grand Jury Proceedings (Danbom)*, 827 F.2d 301 (8th Cir.1987). The Eighth Circuit acknowledged that a subpoena seeking records of all wire transfers of $1,000 or more over a 2 year period from Western Union's major Kansas City office met relevancy requirements for a grand jury investigating drug trafficking, but concluded that, under Rule 17(c), consideration could be given to Western Union's concern that the publicity resulting from its production of the records of many innocent persons would lead such persons to stop transmitting funds through Western Union.

7. *Subject matter challenges.* After commenting generally upon the scope of the grand jury's investigative authority and the corresponding obligations and rights of grand jury witnesses [see Note 2, p. 661], the Court in *Blair v. United States,* 250 U.S. 273, 39 S.Ct. 468, 63 L.Ed. 979 (1919), quickly disposed of the petitioners' claim that their refusal to testify was justified because the subject under investigation (possible violations of the Federal Corrupt Practices Act in the course of a primary election) was beyond the regulatory authority of the federal government. Justice Pitney noted for the Court: "And for the same reasons, witnesses are not entitled to take exception to the jurisdiction of the grand jury or the court over the particular subject-matter that is under investigation. In truth it is in the ordinary case no concern of one summoned as a witness whether the offense is within the jurisdiction of the court or not. At least, the court and grand jury have authority and jurisdiction to investigate the facts in order to determine the question whether the facts show a case within their jurisdiction. The present cases are not exceptional, and for the reasons that have been outlined we are of opinion that appellants were not entitled to raise any question about the constitutionality of the statutes under which the grand jury's investigation was conducted."

Prior to *R. Enterprises,* lower courts had divided as to whether *Blair* precluded consideration of a witness' objection that a grand jury inquiry concerns alleged criminal activity having no bearing upon the district in which the grand jury sits (and therefore activity for which the grand jury may not indict). Does *R. Enterprises* now make that a cognizable objection (albeit one difficult to sustain)? What of the challenge raised in *In re Sealed Case,* 827 F.2d 776 (D.C.Cir.1987)— that the grand jury subpoena was issued upon application of the office Independent Counsel and "that office violated constitutional principles of separation of powers"? In *Morrison v. Olson,* 487 U.S. 654, 108 S.Ct. 2597, 101 L.Ed.2d 569 (1988), the Court reached the merits of that claim (and rejected it), but noted that the Independent Counsel had failed to object in the district court to consideration of the merits of the challenge to her office, and such an objection, "is not 'jurisdictional' in the sense that it cannot be waived by failing to raise it at the proper time and place." As discussed in the notes below, federal courts have long held cognizable challenges to alleged prosecutorial misuse of grand jury subpoenas.

NOTES ON MISUSE OBJECTIONS

1. Both federal and state courts traditionally have recognized witness objections to alleged prosecutorial misuse of the grand jury process for purposes other than furthering the grand jury's investigation. Such instances of misuse include: (1) employment of the grand jury process "primarily" to elicit evidence for use in a pending or future civil action; (2) employment of the grand jury process "for the sole or dominating purpose of preparing an already pending indictment for trial"; (3) employment of the grand jury process to further independent investigations by police or prosecutor rather than to produce evidence for grand jury use; and (4) calling a witness for the purpose of "harassment," with "harassment" described as encompassing various objectives other than producing relevant evidence, such as burdening the witness with repeated appearances or seeking to punish the witness by forcing him into a situation where he will refuse to answer (or lie) and be held for contempt (or perjury). See CRIMPROC § 8.8. While misuse objections commonly are raised by witnesses, courts have recognized the right of other persons who are the targets of the misuse to seek a protective order restricting the grand jury investigation. See e.g., *United States v. Doe (Ellsberg)*, 455 F.2d 1270 (1st Cir.1972) (indicted defendant could seek protective order to bar the prosecution's use of grand jury to further prepare its case against him). Consider also Anne Bowen Poulin, *Supervising the Grand Jury*, 68 Wash.U.L.Q. 885 (1990) (in light of limitations placed upon challenges to indictments based upon alleged prosecutorial misconduct before the grand jury, courts should be more willing to consider target requests for judicial intervention to stop ongoing grand jury abuse).

2. As noted in CRIMPROC § 8.8, a common thread running through the judicial treatment of misuse objections is that "a presumption of regularity" attaches to the grand jury proceeding and the objecting party bears a substantial burden in seeking to overcome that presumption. It clearly is not sufficient simply to show that the use of the process has (or will) benefit the government with respect to civil discovery, criminal discovery on a pending indictment, or some other alleged improper purpose. Courts have stressed that misuse exists only if the "sole or dominant" prosecutorial purpose is improper, and that the prosecutor will not be enjoined from carrying forward a legitimate grand jury investigation simply because one byproduct may be the production of evidence useful in other proceedings in which the government has some interest. To gain an evidentiary hearing on a claim of alleged misuse, the objecting party ordinarily must at least point to surrounding circumstances "highly suggestive" of improper purpose.

What should constitute such a showing? Where a grand jury investigation was instituted shortly after the target's legal challenges stymied the government's civil investigation, does that suggest misuse notwithstanding a substantial overlap in the applicable civil and criminal law governing the activities in question? Cf. *In re Grand Jury Subpoenas, April, 1978*, 581 F.2d 1103 (4th Cir.1978). Where a grand jury is investigating the same basic activities that led to indictment of the objecting party, and that party alleges that some of the witnesses to be called before that grand jury may be defense witnesses, does that establish a sufficient grounding for an evidentiary hearing notwithstanding a government response that the grand jury investigation is aimed at determining whether others had also been involved in the offense? Cf. *United States v. Doe (Ellsberg)*, supra.

3. Even where the surrounding circumstances strongly suggest improper use to obtain civil discovery or discovery on a pending criminal indictment, courts have expressed a reluctance to judge the dominant purpose of the investigation while it is still ongoing. The objecting party, it is noted, should not be allowed to "break up the play before it was started and then claim the government was offsides." *United States v. Doe (Ellsberg)*, supra. A preferable remedy, courts note, is to allow the investigation to continue to its completion and then judge its purpose if the government should attempt to utilize the fruits of its alleged misuse in another proceeding. Where the alleged improper purpose is the development of evidence for a civil proceeding, the Rule 6(e) motion needed to disclose the grand jury material to civil attorneys (see fn. d, p. 657) ordinarily will provide the objecting party with an opportunity to challenge the purpose of the investigation after it has been completed. See *In re Grand Jury Subpoenas, April, 1978*, Note 2 supra. Where the alleged improper purpose is gaining additional information for use in the trial on a pending indictment, the judge presiding at that trial can determine whether to require an inquiry into the dominant purpose of the post-indictment grand jury investigation when (and if) the government makes use in its prosecution of the fruits of that allegedly tainted investigation. See *United States v. Doe (Ellsberg)*.

4. Claims that the grand jury process was used to further independent police investigations commonly are presented where the individual subpoenaed to appear before the grand jury was offered the opportunity to avoid the grand jury appearance by giving a statement to the police or prosecutor. Although noting that it is improper to use the grand jury subpoena "as a ploy to secure the attendance of a witness at the prosecutor's office," courts have held that offering the witness the option of presenting information informally is not misuse where the prosecutor intends (after screening) to present that information to the grand jury. CRIMPROC § 8.8. So too, where the witness was first approached by the police and refused to provide information, the prosecutor may convert the investigation into a grand jury inquiry and seek the same information by subpoena. Ibid.

SECTION 4. APPLICATION OF THE PRIVILEGE AGAINST SELF–INCRIMINATION

A.   GRAND JURY TESTIMONY[a]

1. *Application of the privilege.* *Counselman v. Hitchcock,* 142 U.S. 547, 12 S.Ct. 195, 35 L.Ed. 1110 (1892), put to rest any doubts as to whether the privilege against self-incrimination was available to a grand jury witness. The Court there rejected the contention that the privilege did not apply because the grand jury witness was not being compelled to incriminate himself "in a criminal case." The reference in the Fifth Amendment to compelled testimony "in a criminal case," the Court noted, was to the eventual use of testimony and not to the nature of the proceeding in which the testimony was compelled. The Fifth Amendment, it concluded, applies to a witness "in any proceeding" who is being compelled to give testimony that might be incriminating in a subsequent criminal prosecution. In support of this interpretation, the Court noted that "the privilege must have a broad construction in favor of the right it was intended to secure," and that its objective was to "insure that a person should not be compelled, when acting as a witness in any investigation, to give testimony which might tend to show that he himself had committed a crime." Does this reasoning, as the *Counselman* Court suggested, find "support" in "the ruling of [the] Court in *Boyd v. United States*"? Does it "miss the boat" in recognizing a witness self-incrimination right to refuse to testify in the grand jury proceeding, rather than simply a right to preclude use of that testimony in any subsequent criminal trial in which he might be a defendant? Consider fn. a at p. 702.

2. *The nature of "incriminating" testimony.* As *Counselman* noted, the privilege only applies to testimony which is "incriminating"—i.e., to testimony which may "tend to show" that the witness himself "had committed a crime." What standard is applied in determining whether particular testimony has that tendency and who makes that determination? The leading case on both questions is HOFFMAN v. UNITED STATES, 341 U.S. 479, 71 S.Ct. 814, 95 L.Ed. 1118 (1951). In that case, a witness subpoenaed before a federal grand jury relied on the privilege in refusing to answer questions as to his current occupation and his contacts with a fugitive witness. The district court found that there was "no real and substantial danger of incrimination" and the privilege therefore was inapplicable. When the witness persisted in his claim, he was held in contempt. In reversing that conviction, the Supreme Court (per CLARK, J.) set forth the following guidelines for the district courts:

a. The grand jury witness may also utilize any other testimonial privilege recognized in the particular jurisdiction. Thus, the privileges applicable before federal grand juries are those generally recognized in federal courts. See Fed. R.Evid. 1101(d)(2), 501. We have focused here on the privilege against self-incrimination because it provides "what is undoubtedly [the witness'] most significant safeguard in responding to a subpoena ad testificandum." CRIMPROC § 8.10(a).

"The privilege afforded not only extends to answers that would in themselves support a conviction under a federal criminal statute but likewise embraces those which would furnish a link in the chain of evidence needed to prosecute the claimant for a federal crime. But this protection must be confined to instances where the witness has reasonable cause to apprehend danger from a direct answer. The witness is not exonerated from answering merely because he declares that in so doing he would incriminate himself—his say-so does not of itself establish the hazard of incrimination. It is for the court to say whether his silence is justified, and to require him to answer if 'it clearly appears to the court that he is mistaken.' However, if the witness, upon interposing his claim, were required to prove the hazard in the sense in which a claim is usually required to be established in court, he would be compelled to surrender the very protection which the privilege is designed to guarantee. To sustain the privilege, it need only be evident from the implications of the question, in the setting in which it is asked, that a responsive answer to the question or an explanation of why it cannot be answered might be dangerous because injurious disclosure could result."

It has been suggested that under the *Hoffman* guidelines, it will be a "rare case" in which a court can reject a witness' assertion of the privilege. See CRIMPROC § 8.10(a). Consider in this connection the *Hoffman* case itself, where the Court had no difficulty in concluding that the district court erred in denying petitioner's claim of the privilege. The Court reasoned that, since the district court was aware that the grand jury was investigating racketeering, it should have recognized that questions concerning Hoffman's current occupation might require answers relating to violations of federal gambling laws. It also should have recognized that information concerning Hoffman's contacts with the fugitive witness might tie him to efforts to hide that witness. See also *Ohio v. Reiner.* 532 U.S. 17, 121 S.Ct. 1252, 149 L.Ed.2d 158 (2001) (state court erred in holding that privilege would not have been available to babysitter who later testified, under an immunity grant, that she had never shaken deceased infant or his twin brother and "she was unaware of and had nothing to do with the * * * injuries" to the two infants, as her testimony also acknowledged that she "spent extended periods of time alone with the children in the weeks immediately preceding discovery of their injuries" and "was with [the deceased infant] within the potential timeframe of [his] fatal trauma"; the standard of "reasonable cause to apprehend danger" by providing a "link in the chain of evidence" recognizes that "truthful responses of an innocent witness, as well as those of a wrongdoer may provide the government with incriminating evidence").

3. *Incrimination under the laws of another sovereign.* For many years, American courts took the position that the privilege protected only against incrimination under the laws of the sovereign which was attempting to compel the incriminating testimony. However, in *Murphy v. Waterfront Comm.*, 378 U.S. 52, 84 S.Ct. 1594, 12 L.Ed.2d 678 (1964), the Supreme Court rejected this "separate sovereign" limitation as applied to state and federal inquiries. Noting that a "separate sovereign" limitation would permit a witness to be "whipsawed into incriminating himself under both state and federal law," the Court concluded that the "policies and purposes" of the Fifth Amendment required that the privilege protect "a state witness against incrimination under federal as well as state law and a federal witness against incrimination under state as well as federal law." Does it follow from *Murphy* that the privilege should be available where the witness' testimony would be incriminating only in a foreign country?

In UNITED STATES v. BALSYS, 524 U.S. 666, 118 S.Ct. 2218, 141 L.Ed.2d 575 (1998), the Court majority (7–2) held that the separate sovereign doctrine continued to apply as to incrimination under the laws of a foreign country. Thus, respondent Balsys, a resident alien subpoenaed to testify about his possible participation in Nazi persecution during World War II, could not utilize the privilege to refuse to provide answers which could subject him to a "real and substantial danger of prosecution of Lithuania and Israel." (The only consequence of his testimony in this country was deportation, long established as having a 'civil character'). The Court majority (per SOUTER, J.) acknowledged that *Murphy* included reasoning that supported a complete rejection of the separate sovereign limitation. Thus, the two dissenting justices (Ginsberg, J. and Breyer, J.), relied in part on *Murphy's* reading of the legal history of the privilege (including the English common law), and on *Murphy's* analysis of the purposes of the privilege as inconsistent with a separate sovereign limitation. As to legal history, the *Balsys* majority rejected *Murphy's* conclusion that pre-*Murphy* Supreme Court precedent had misread the English common law precedent as to its recognition of a separate sovereign limitation. As to policy,[b] the Court noted that, while *Murphy* catalogued multiple "aspirations" of the self-incrimination clause (see p. 738), some of which might support the privilege's extension to the fear of foreign prosecution, *Murphy* had failed "to weigh the host of competing policy concerns that would be raised in a legitimate reconsideration of the Clause's scope." Those costs included the loss of evidence in domestic law enforcement, due to the government's inability to grant immunity that would extend to foreign prosecution.

The *Balsys* majority concluded that *Murphy* is better read as resting on an "alternative rationale," which tied its rejection of the separate sovereign limitation to the applicability of the self-incrimination privilege to both the federal and state governments. The Court explained:

"[M]urphy was undoubtedly correct, given the decision rendered that very same day in *Malloy v. Hogan* [fn. a., p. 30], which applied the doctrine of Fourteenth Amendment due process incorporation to the Self–Incrimination Clause, so as to bind the States as well as the National Government to recognize the privilege. * * * As the Court immediately thereafter said in *Murphy, Malloy* 'necessitate[d] a reconsideration' of the unqualified *Murdock* rule that a witness subject to testimonial compulsion in one jurisdiction, state or federal, could not plead fear of prosecution in the other. After *Malloy*, the Fifth Amendment limitation could no longer be seen as framed for one jurisdiction alone, each jurisdiction having instead become subject to the same claim of privilege flowing from the one limitation. Since fear of prosecution in the one jurisdiction bound by the Clause now implicated the very privilege binding upon the other, the *Murphy* opinion sensibly recognized that if a witness could not assert the privilege in such circumstances, the witness could be 'whipsawed into incriminating himself under both state and federal law even though the constitutional privilege against self-incrimination is applicable to each.' The whipsawing was possible owing to a feature unique to the guarantee against self-incrimination among the several Fifth Amendment privileges. In the absence of waiver, the other such guarantees are purely and simply binding on the government. But under the Self–Incrimination Clause, the government has an option to exchange the stated privilege for an immunity to prosecutorial use of any compelled inculpatory testimony. *Kastigar v. United States* [p. 703]. The only condition on the government when it decides to offer immunity in place of the privilege to stay silent is the requirement to provide an immunity as broad as the privilege itself. After *Malloy* had held the privilege binding on the state jurisdictions as well as the National Government, it would therefore have been intolerable to allow a prosecutor in one or the other jurisdiction to eliminate the privilege by offering immunity less complete than the privilege's dual jurisdictional reach. *Murphy* accordingly held that a federal court

---

b.　Justices Scalia and Thomas did not join Part IV of the opinion for the Court, which considered relevant both *Murphy's* discussion of self-incrimination policies and competing policy concerns not presented in *Murphy*.

could not receive testimony compelled by a State in the absence of a statute effectively providing for federal immunity, and it did this by imposing an exclusionary rule prohibiting the National Government 'from making any such use of compelled testimony and its fruits.' "

4. *Waiver.* Once a grand jury witness begins to provide incriminating information on a particular subject, does that action bar raising the privilege as to subsequent questions dealing with the same subject? If the answer might be incriminating as to a different offense, the privilege clearly is available, but that may not be the case where the only potential for incrimination is to the same offense suggested by the earlier testimony. Here the applicable standard is that set forth in *Rogers v. United States,* 340 U.S. 367, 71 S.Ct. 438, 95 L.Ed. 344 (1951). The Court there noted that "disclosure of [an incriminating] fact waives the privilege as to details" as the further disclosure does not then present "a reasonable danger of further incrimination in light of all the circumstances, including [the] previous disclosures." To allow a claim of the privilege as to details "would [only] open the way to distortion of facts by permitting a witness to select any stopping point in the testimony."

Application of the *Rogers* standard is not always easy, as the division of the Court in *Rogers* itself suggests. In that case, a grand jury was seeking various records of the Communist Party branch in Denver. The witness Rogers admitted that she had been treasurer of the branch, but stated that she had turned the records over to another person. When asked to name that person, she initially refused to do so on the ground that she would not subject other persons to "the same thing that I'm going through." After consulting with counsel, she shifted to reliance on her privilege against self-incrimination. A divided Supreme Court (5–3) rejected that claim (described by the Court majority as a "pure afterthought"). The majority noted that the privilege was "purely personal" and could not be utilized to protect others. Rogers had already incriminated herself by admitting her party membership and her prior possession and transfer of the records; the "mere disclosure of the name of the recipient of the books" presented no more than an "imaginary possibility" of "increasing the danger of her prosecution" for a possible conspiracy to violate the Smith Act. While it was true that "at least two persons are required to constitute a conspiracy, * * * the identity of the other members [is] not needed inasmuch as one person can be convicted of conspiring with persons whose names are unknown." The dissenters saw the matter quite differently. There was a clear potential for additional incrimination, they noted, since petitioner's conviction could well "depend on testimony of the witnesses she was * * * asked to identify." The Court's analysis, they contended, made the "protection [of the privilege] dependent on timing that was so refined that lawyers, let alone laymen, will have difficulty in knowing when to claim it."

5. *Exercise of the privilege by the target.* The self-incrimination privilege has long been held to prohibit the prosecution from forcing a defendant to appear as a witness at his own trial. Should the prosecutor similarly be prohibited from forcing the target of an investigation who desires to exercise the privilege to appear before the grand jury, or is the Fifth Amendment satisfied by simply allowing the target-witness, like any other witness, to refuse to respond to individual questions where his answer might be incriminating? A few state courts have argued that the target of an investigation is, in effect, a "putative" or "de facto" defendant, and he therefore should be allowed to exercise his privilege in much the same manner as a "de jure defendant" at trial. They suggest that, unless the target expressly waives his self-incrimination privilege, the prosecution cannot use the grand jury's subpoena authority to force him to appear. See CRIMPROC § 8.10(c). Consider also Justice Brennan's opinion in *United States v. Mandujano,* discussed in Note 6 infra. On the other side, the federal courts and most state courts have taken the position that the Fifth Amendment, as to the target as well as any other grand jury witness, presents only an "option of refusal and not a prohibition of inquiry." *O'Connell v. United States,* 40 F.2d 201 (2d Cir.1930).[c] The "obligation to appear," the Supreme Court noted in *Dionisio,* is "no different for a person who may himself be the subject of the grand jury inquiry." See p. 696.

What justifies the different treatment of the trial defendant and the grand jury target, even when that target is so close to indictment that a court will refer to him as a "putative" defendant? Consider the following arguments: (1) the defendant's right of silence grew out of the early common law rule on the incompetency of parties to testify, which had a bearing only on the trial; (2) the defendant's right not to take the stand at trial is aimed, in part, at protecting the defendant from being placed in a position where he may be forced to refuse to answer questions on self-incrimination grounds in the presence of the jury (who may conclude that he therefore has something to hide), but that protective feature has less significance in the grand jury setting since that body simply decides whether to charge and its proceedings therefore need not be conducted "with the assiduous regard for the preservation of procedural safeguards which normally attends the ultimate trial of the issues"; (3) the grand jury, having an obligation to "run down every clue," cannot ignore the possibility that the target's testimony may lead to the identification of others who also participated in the criminal enterprise; (4) the grand jury, having an obligation to "shield the innocent," must be able to seek the target's own testimony to determine whether it might not "explain away" the evidence against him; and (5) determining whether a witness is a "target" is not easy under any standard for establishing that status, so that a prohibition against compelling a target to appear invariably would lead to after-the-fact disputes as to whether a later-indicted witness actually had been a target.[d]

c. Internal Justice Department guidelines provide that, to avoid the possible "appearance of unfairness," where the testimony of a grand jury "target" (see fn. d infra) might be helpful, an effort should first be made to secure the voluntary appearance of the target. However, the grand jury and U.S. Attorney may jointly agree to subpoena the target in exceptional cases. In making that determination, the grand jury and U.S. Attorney are directed to give "careful attention" to the importance of the testimony sought from the target, whether the substance of that testimony could be provided by other witnesses, and whether the "questions the prosecutor and the grand jurors intend to ask * * * would be protected by a valid claim of the privilege." U.S. Attorneys' Manual 9–11.150. Should the subpoenaed "target and his or her attorney state in writing, signed by both, that the 'target' will refuse to testify on Fifth Amendment grounds, the witness ordinarily should be excused," but the "grand jury and United States Attorney [may] agree to insist on appearance" based on the considerations "which justified the subpoena in the first place." U.S.A.M. 9–11.154.

d. The United States Attorneys' Manual, in connection with its provisions on target subpoenas (see fn. c supra) and target notification (see Note 7 infra), uses the following definition of a target: "[A] person as to whom the prose-

cutor or the grand jury has substantial evidence linking him/her to the commission of a crime and who, in the judgment of the prosecutor, is a putative defendant." The target is distinguished from a "subject of an investigation," who is "a person whose conduct is within the scope of the grand jury's investigation." U.S.A.M. 9–11.151. Compare Ind.Code § 35–34–2–1 (target is a person "who is a subject of a grand jury investigation"). Concurring in *United States v. Mandujano,* discussed in Note 6 infra, Justice Brennan described the "target" as "one against whom [the government] has probable cause–as measured by an objective standard." Justice Brennan noted that "others have argued for a rule which would combine objective elements with the prosecutor's subjective intent subsequently to charge the individual by indictment * * * but this subjective intent requirement may pose grave administrative difficulties." But compare Arnold Enker and Sheldon Elson, *Counsel for the Suspect,* 49 Minn.L.Rev. 47, 74 (1964) (critical of a solely objective standard that asks only whether probable cause existed, as prosecutors, "having not yet analyzed the complete record of the investigation, or hav[ing] done so only tentatively or hastily, or hav[ing] made an error—as happens in any large human enterprise—may not realize that probable cause exists" as to witnesses they do not view as targets). As

6. Self-incrimination warnings. To what extent if any does the Fifth Amendment require that grand jury witnesses be advised prior to testifying of their right to exercise the privilege against self-incrimination? In UNITED STATES v. MANDUJANO, 425 U.S. 564, 96 S.Ct. 1768, 48 L.Ed.2d 212 (1976), there was considerable discussion bearing on that question although the Court found it unnecessary to resolve the issue. The defendant Mandujano, known by the prosecutor to be a narcotics user, was called before the grand jury in the hope that he would furnish information about significant dealers. Instead, he steadfastly denied any involvement in the sale of narcotics and specifically disclaimed having sought within the year to make a purchase for a third-party for $650.00. The latter statement was a lie since (as the prosecutor already knew) Mandujano had recently tried to make such a purchase for a person who was actually an undercover agent. Subsequently prosecuted for perjury, Mandujano moved to suppress the grand jury testimony that was the basis of the charge. The trial court granted the motion on the ground that Mandujano had not been given full *Miranda* warnings prior to testifying. He had been informed of his privilege against self-incrimination and had been advised that he could have a retained lawyer located outside the grand jury room for the purpose of consultation. However, when Mandujano responded that he could not afford a lawyer, the prosecutor did not state that an indigent could obtain appointed counsel (the last portion of the *Miranda* warnings).

The Supreme Court unanimously concluded that even if adequate warnings had not been provided, that would not constitute a defense to a perjury charge. The Court had previously held that sanctions could be imposed for perjury "even in instances where the perjuror complained the Government exceeded its constitutional powers in making the inquiry." Six of the justices also went on to speak to the adequacy of the warnings.

Speaking for four justices, CHIEF JUSTICE BURGER'S plurality opinion concluded that the warnings here were clearly adequate, as *Miranda* certainly did not apply to the grand jury witness. The *Miranda* Court itself, in distinguishing custodial interrogation in a police station from interrogation "in courts or other official investigations where there are often impartial observers to guard against intimidation or trickery," had recognized that investigations "such as grand jury questioning take place in a setting wholly different from custodial interrogation." "Indeed," it was noted, "the Court's opinion in *Miranda* reveals a focus on what was seen by the Court as police coercion derived from 'factual studies [relating to] police violence and the third degree * * *—beating, hanging, whipping—and to sustained and protracted questioning incommunicado in order to extort confessions.* * * 'To extend these concepts to questioning before a grand jury inquiring into criminal activity under the guidance of a judge is an extravagant expansion never remotely contemplated by this Court in *Miranda*; the dynamics of constitutional interpretation do not compel constant extension of every doctrine announced by the Court."

Chief Justice Burger added in a footnote that, since "warnings were provided in this case to advise respondent of his Fifth Amendment privilege," it was "unnecessary to consider whether any warning is required." However, in discussing the availability of the privilege, the Chief Justice suggested that grand jury witnesses, like witnesses in trial and administrative proceedings, were not constitutionally entitled to a warning even where the question posed had obvious potential for incrimination. The plurality opinion noted: "The very availability of the Fifth Amendment privilege to grand jury witnesses suggests that occasions

noted in Beale et al., § 6.23, "most of the court decisions and statutes addressing grand jury procedures do not address [the definitional] issue, but simply use terms such as 'suspect,' 'target,' 'subject' and 'prospective defendant' interchangeably."

will often arise when potentially incriminating questions will be asked in the ordinary course of the jury's investigation. * * * [T]he witness can, of course, stand on the privilege, assured that its protection 'is as broad as the mischief against which it seeks to guard.' *Counselman v. Hitchcock* [Note 1 supra]. The witness must invoke the privilege however, as the 'Constitution does not forbid the asking of criminative questions.' *United States v. Monia*, 317 U.S., at 433, 63 S.Ct., at 413, 87 L.Ed., at 383 [1943] (Frankfurter, J., dissenting):

> The [Fifth] Amendment speaks of compulsion. It does not preclude a witness from testifying voluntarily in matters which may incriminate him. If, therefore, he desires the protection of the privilege, he must claim it or he will not be considered to have been "compelled" within the meaning of the Amendment.

Absent a claim of the privilege, the duty to give testimony remains absolute."

BRENNAN, J., joined by Marshall, J., responded to what he viewed as a "denigration of the privilege against self-incrimination" in the Chief Justice's opinion. Justice Brennan did not challenge the Chief Justice's efforts to distinguish *Miranda*, but criticized instead the Chief Justice's "mechanical" reliance upon *United States v. Monia*. Justice Brennan argued *Monia* involved a deportation proceeding, and the Court had noted that the tribunal there had no notice of the likely incriminating quality of the witness' answer unless that potential was brought to its attention by the witness. But where the government is "acutely aware of the potentially incriminating nature of the disclosures sought," a knowing and completely voluntary waiver should be required. Just as grand jury could not call an indicted defendant before it and interrogate him concerning the subject matter of the charged crime, absent an intelligent and voluntary waiver, the same should be true of a *de facto* defendant. Accordingly, Justice Brennan noted: "I would hold that, in the absence of an intentional and intelligent waiver by the individual of his known right to be free from compulsory self-incrimination, the Government may not call before a grand jury one whom it has probable cause—as measured by an objective standard—to suspect committed a crime and by use of judicial compulsion compel him to testify with regard to that crime. In the absence of such a waiver, the Fifth Amendment requires that any testimony obtained in this fashion be unavailable to the Government for use at trial. Such a waiver could readily be demonstrated by proof that the individual was warned prior to questioning that he is currently subject to possible criminal prosecution for the commission of a stated crime, that he has a constitutional right to refuse to answer any and all questions that may tend to incriminate him, and by record evidence that the individual understood the nature of his situation and privilege prior to giving testimony."

Relying on the *Mandujano* plurality opinion, the lower federal courts generally have assumed that self-incrimination "warnings" are not constitutionally mandated even as to targets.[e] Several state courts, however, viewing the target grand jury witness as distinct from witnesses in other proceedings, have held that self-incrimination warnings for target witnesses are constitutionally required. See CRIMPROC § 8.10(d). In the federal system, internal prosecutorial guidelines

---

e. In *Minnesota v. Murphy*, fn. b, p. 496, the Supreme Court drew an analogy to the grand jury setting in holding that a probationer questioned by his probation officer was not entitled to *Miranda* warnings. The interview setting in *Murphy*, the Court noted, subjected the probationer to "less intimidating pressure than is imposed upon a grand jury witness." Accordingly, since the Court had "never held that [warnings] must be given to the grand jury witness," it would "decline to require them here." Federal lower courts have viewed *Murphy* as reaffirming the strong suggestion of *Mandujano* that the Constitution does not demand any warning, but the lower court cases have not squarely presented the issue, as they have involved target/witnesses who received some form of notification of the self-incrimination privilege. See e.g., *United States v. Gillespie*, 974 F.2d 796 (7th Cir.1992).

require that both subpoenaed "targets" and "subjects" (see fn. d supra) be informed of the self-incrimination privilege, both by an "advice of rights" statement appended to the subpoena and a statement of the prosecutor on record when the witness appears before the grand jury. The prescribed statement includes notification to the subpoenaed witness that "you may refuse to answer any question if a truthful answer to the question would tend to incriminate you" and that "anything that you do say may be used against you by the grand jury or in a subsequent legal proceeding." United States Attorneys' Manual 9–11.151. Warnings on the record also are common in state practice, at least as to targets, and are required by statute in roughly 10 jurisdictions. See Beale et al., § 6.24.

   7. Target warnings. In UNITED STATES v. WASHINGTON, 431 U.S. 181, 97 S.Ct. 1814, 52 L.Ed.2d 238 (1977), the Court answered one of the issues left open in *Mandujano:* a witness need not be warned that he is a target of the grand jury investigation. Noted the Court (per BURGER, C.J.):

   "After being sworn, respondent was explicitly advised that he had a right to remain silent and that any statements he did make could be used to convict him of crime. It is inconceivable that such a warning would fail to alert him to his right to refuse to answer any questions which might incriminate him. * * * Even in the presumed psychologically coercive atmosphere of police custodial interrogation, *Miranda* does not require that any additional warnings be given simply because the suspect is a potential defendant; indeed, such suspects are potential defendants more often than not. Respondent points out that unlike one subject to custodial interrogation, whose arrest should inform him only too clearly that he is a potential criminal defendant, a grand jury witness may well be unaware that he is targeted for possible prosecution. While this may be so in some situations, it is an overdrawn generalization. In any case, events here [which included prior questioning by the prosecutor] clearly put respondent on notice that he was a suspect in the motorcycle theft. * * * However, all of this is largely irrelevant, since we do not understand what constitutional disadvantage a failure to give potential defendant warnings could possibly inflict on a grand jury witness, whether or not he has received other warnings. * * * Because target witness status neither enlarges nor diminishes the constitutional protection against compelled self-incrimination, potential defendant warnings add nothing of value to protection of Fifth Amendment rights."

   Justice Brennan, joined by Justice Marshall, dissented, relying in substantial part on his discussion of the need for warnings in *Mandujano.* Several state courts, relying on a state statute or state constitutional provision, have held that target witnesses must be warned of their target status. United States Attorneys' Manual 9–11.151 states that the prosecutor should "advise witnesses who are known 'targets' that their conduct is being investigated for possible violation of federal criminal law." As to targets who are not witnesses, prosecutors are encouraged to provide notification of target status in "appropriate cases" (not the "ordinary clear case" or the case presenting a potential for flight or evidence tampering) in order to permit that person to request the opportunity to testify voluntarily. U.S.A.M. 9–11. 153

   8. Constitutional right to counsel. In UNITED STATES v. MANDUJA-NO (described in Note 6 supra), CHIEF JUSTICE BURGER'S plurality opinion also spoke to the grand jury witness' right to counsel. Initially, in rejecting the lower court's extension of *Miranda*, the plurality opinion also rejected the contention that the *"Miranda* right to counsel, fashioned to secure the suspect's Fifth Amendment privilege," should apply to grand jury questioning. Turning to other possible sources of a constitutional right to counsel, the plurality added: "Respondent was also informed that if he desired he could have the assistance of counsel, but that counsel could not be inside the grand jury room. That statement was plainly a correct recital of the law. No criminal proceedings had been instituted against respondent, hence the Sixth Amendment right to counsel had not come into play. *Kirby v. Illinois* [p. 631]. A witness 'before a grand jury cannot insist, as a matter of constitutional right, on being represented by his counsel. . . .' *In re Groban*, 352 U.S. 330, 77 S.Ct. 510, 1 L.Ed.2d 376 (1957). Under settled principles the witness may not insist upon the presence of his attorney in the grand jury room. Fed. Rule Crim. Proc. 6(d)."

Justice BRENNAN's separate opinion in *Mandujano* also challenged this portion of the plurality opinion. The statement from *Groban* quoted by the plurality was dictum that should be reexamined in light of *Miranda* and *Escobedo v. Illinois* [p. 460] and their "recognit[ion] of the 'substantive affinity' and therefore the 'coextensiveness' in certain circumstance of the right to counsel and the privilege against self-incrimination," and their rejection of the regime of "squalid discrimination" that distinguished between those "wealthy enough to hire a lawyer" and the indigent. Similarly, relying on *Kirby* was inappropriate because the line drawn there as to when "criminal proceedings had been instituted" (the "initiation of adversary judicial proceedings") assumed that the self-incrimination privilege was not "implicated." Where "the putative defendant is called and interrogated before the grand jury," as in the case of a person subjected to adversary judicial proceedings, he was "faced with the prosecutorial forces of organized society and immersed in the intricacies of substantive and procedural law."

Justice Brennan argued that, at a minimum, the putative defendant was entitled constitutionally to be told "that he has a right to consult with an attorney prior to questioning, that if he cannot afford an attorney one will be appointed for him, that during the questioning he may have that attorney wait outside the grand jury room, and that he may at any and all times during questioning consult with the attorney prior to answering any question posed." Justice Brennan also opened the door to a possibly broader constitutional protection: he noted that several commentators had argued that "the presence of counsel inside the grand jury room is required," and added that there "certainly * * * is no viable argument that allowing counsel to be present in the grand jury room for the purposes of consultation regarding testimonial privileges would subvert the nature or functioning of the grand jury proceeding."

The *Mandujano* plurality opinion generally is viewed as having put to rest any possible Sixth Amendment grounding for a constitutional right to counsel. See also Pt. B, p. 72. Several lower courts, however, following an analysis similar to that advanced by Justice Brennan, have suggested a Fifth Amendment grounding for the right to counsel. Beale, et al. § 6.26, suggest that this grounding has "broad implications that some courts may be hesitant to accept"—such as applicability to witnesses in other settings (e.g., administrative and civil proceedings relating to transactions that could conceivably involve criminality), recognizing a right to appointed counsel as well as a right to retained counsel, and creating a right to the effective assistance of counsel (at least as to advice relating to the exercise of the privilege).

A due process grounding for a right to counsel has also been suggested. Here, the right would flow from a general liberty interest of the individual to expend his resources to seek counsel's assistance whenever that assistance would not disrupt or alter the basic character of the proceeding involved. See Beale et al., § 6.26 (noting the statement in *Powell v. Alabama*, p. 61, that an "arbitrary" denial of a right to be represented by retained counsel even in a civil case would be viewed as a "denial of a hearing" and therefore a due process violation). Cf. Note 3, p. 64; fn. a at p. 87. In treating the issues discussed in Notes 9 and 10 below, several courts appear to have assumed the existence of such a due process right to retain and consult with counsel.

9. *Availability of counsel.* Pursuant to internal guidelines, all federal grand jury witnesses are advised that they may retain counsel (who may be located in the anteroom) and "that the grand jury will permit you a reasonable opportunity to step outside the grand jury room to consult with counsel if you so desire." U.S. Attorney's Manual, § 9–11.151. Where the witness requests the assistance of counsel, but notes that he is indigent, that request is often conveyed to the federal district judge, who may then request that the federal defender or private counsel (in districts without defenders) assume representation. However, the Criminal Justice Act does not provide for appointment of counsel for grand jury witnesses. See 18 U.S.C. § 3006A(a)(1).

Lawyers representing federal grand jury witnesses commonly urge their clients to take full advantage of the opportunity to leave the grand jury room and consult with counsel. Indeed, some lawyers insist that their clients consult after each question, which allows the lawyer to construct a complete record of the questions asked. Although federal prosecutors contend that this practice demands more than a "reasonable opportunity" to consult, it usually has not been contested. A few federal courts have stated that, at least where the witness has been granted immunity (and therefore does not need self-incrimination advice), the witness can be limited to consultations on a less regular basis (e.g., after every few questions). See National Lawyer's Guild, *Representation of Witnesses Before Federal Grand Juries* § 6.5(c) (3d ed. 1985).

Most states follow a practice similar to the federal practice as to notification of the right to consult with retained counsel and providing through an informal arrangement public defender assistance for the indigent witness who requests counsel (although several states provide by statute for the appointment of counsel for indigent witnesses). State courts may be somewhat less liberal, however, in allowing the witness to leave the grand jury for consultations. Those states that are less liberal commonly justify that position on two grounds—avoidance of "undue delay" and restricting counsel to his proper role. If witnesses are allowed to consult after each question, no matter what its nature, they may, it is argued, simply "wear down the grand jury." Moreover, if the attorney's advice properly is limited to counseling the witnesses on the exercise of testimonial privileges, there simply is no reason to allow consultation when the question clearly poses no such difficulty. See e.g., *People v. Ianniello,* 235 N.E.2d 439 (N.Y.1968) (where witness had been immunized and had previous opportunity to consult with counsel on the same line of questioning, grand jury appropriately refused to allow him to leave for the obvious purpose of obtaining "strategic advice" rather than counseling as to any legal right that would allow him to refuse to answer).

10. *The location of counsel.* Twenty states now have statutes permitting at least certain witnesses to be assisted by counsel located within the grand jury room. See Beale et al., § 6.27. Most of these provisions apply to all witnesses, but several are limited to targets or to witnesses who have not been immunized. The statutes commonly contain provisions limiting the role of counsel while before the grand jury. Several state that the lawyer may "advise the witness," but "may not otherwise take any part in the proceeding." One jurisdiction also allows counsel to "interpose objections on behalf of the witness." See Kan.Stat.Ann. § 22–3009 (2).

Proponents of such statutes argue that they are needed to adequately protect the rights of the grand jury witness. They contend that even the most liberal right to leave the grand jury room to consult with counsel imposes substantial burdens upon the client's access to counsel and counsel's ability to advise the client. Those opposing the presence of counsel in the grand jury room acknowledge that the location of counsel outside the grand jury room poses certain difficulties for the witness and counsel, but claim that those difficulties are not so great as to undermine the witness' ability to exercise his rights, particularly as to the privilege against self-incrimination. They see any additional protection of witness rights as clearly outweighed by the detrimental effect that counsel's presence would have upon the grand jury's capacity to conduct effective investigations. They argue that, notwithstanding statutory prohibitions, counsel accompanying witnesses would find techniques, such as stage whispers and objections presented through the witness, for challenging the prosecutor's questions, and conveying their arguments to the jurors. With no judge present to put an immediate stop to such tactics, the end result would be disruption and delay of the investigation. They further argue that with counsel at the witness' side, more witnesses will reply to questions by merely parroting responses formulated by counsel—responses that too often furnish as little information as possible or are purposely ambiguous so as to avoid potential perjury charges. The critics draw an analogy to the trial, where the defendant, once taking the stand, is not allowed to interrupt his testimony for further discussions with counsel. Finally, it is noted that, in some instances, the witness may not be entirely trustful of counsel and therefore prefer not to have counsel present. The witness may be forced to accept counsel provided by others (e.g., his employer) and fear retaliation if the full scope of his testimony is carried back to such persons. Once the law permits counsel to be present, the witness will be under pressure to allow counsel to accompany him, and will lose the capacity to be selective in the disclosure of his testimony to counsel.

B. IMMUNITY GRANTS

1. *Constitutionality.* The use of an immunity grant to preclude reliance upon the self-incrimination privilege dates back to the English practice known as providing "indemnity" against prosecution. See *Kastigar v. United States,* Note 2 infra (also noting the use of immunity grants in the American Colonies). Immunity grants were first upheld under the federal constitution in *Brown v. Walker,* 161 U.S. 591, 16 S.Ct. 644, 40 L.Ed. 819 (1896). A divided Court there concluded that the Fifth Amendment could not be "construed literally as authorizing the witness to refuse to disclose any fact which might tend to incriminate, disgrace, or expose him to unfavorable comments." The history of the Amendment, the majority noted, indicated that its object was only to "secure the witness against criminal prosecution." Thus, the self-incrimination privilege had been held inapplicable where the witness' compelled testimony would relate only to an offense as to which he had been pardoned or as to which the statute of limitations had run. So too, the privilege did not apply where the witness' response might tend to "disgrace him or bring him into disrepute" but would furnish no information relating to a criminal offense. The majority reasoned that, once it is accepted that the object of the privilege is limited to protecting the witness against criminal prosecution, the constitutionality of the immunity grant necessarily follows. Since the grant removes the danger against which the privilege protects, the witness can no longer rely upon the privilege.

2. *Scope of the Immunity.* *Counselman v. Hitchcock,* 142 U.S. 547, 12 S.Ct. 195, 35 L.Ed. 1110 (1892), struck down a federal immunity statute that granted the witness protection only against the use of his immunized testimony as evidence in any subsequent prosecution. The Supreme Court concluded that such limited protection immunity was not sufficient to replace the Fifth Amendment privilege. The Court stressed that there was no protection against derivative use of the witness' testimony. Thus, the statute "could not, and would not, prevent the use of his testimony to search out other testimony to be used in evidence against him.''[a] At the conclusion of its opinion, however, the Court spoke in terms of even broader protection. "To be valid," it noted, an immunity grant "must afford absolute immunity against future prosecution for the offense to which the question relates." This statement was read as indicating that the immunity grant must absolutely bar prosecution for any transaction noted in the witness' testimony. Accordingly, Congress adopted a new immunity statute providing for "transactional immunity." It provided that a witness directed to testify or produce documentary evidence pursuant to an immunity order could not be prosecuted "for or on account of any transaction, matter, or thing concerning which he may testify or produce evidence." The constitutionality of this provision was upheld in *Brown v. Walker,* supra, and subsequent state and federal immunity statutes were largely patterned upon the *Brown* statute.

Subsequent decisions—and the language of later statutes—recognized two limitations on the scope of transactional immunity. First, transactional immunity does not preclude a prosecution for perjury based on the immunized testimony. Second, transactional immunity does not extend to an event described in an answer totally unresponsive to the question asked. Thus, the witness cannot gain immunity from prosecution for all previous criminal acts by simply including a reference to those acts in his testimony without regard to the subject on which he was asked to testify.

In *Murphy v. Waterfront Commission,* Note 3, p. 692, the Court first upheld immunity that was not as broad in scope as the traditional transactional immunity. After rejecting the separate sovereign doctrine as a limitation on the privilege's availability in either federal or state proceedings, *Murphy* turned to the scope of the immunity that must be granted to supplant the privilege as it related to prosecution in another jurisdiction. It concluded that the immunity granted in one jurisdiction (federal or state) need not absolutely bar prosecution in the other; it was sufficient to bar both use and derivative use of the witness' testimony in the other jurisdiction.

Following *Murphy,* Congress adopted a general immunity provision that granted federal witnesses protection only against use and derivative use as to federal as well as state prosecutions. The statute provided that "no testimony or

a. Akhil Amar and Renee Letow, *Fifth Amendment First Principles: The Self–Incrimination Clause,* 93 Mich. L. Rev. 857 (1995), argue that *Counselman* erred in allowing a person to refuse to testify on self-incrimination grounds in a grand jury proceeding (or other proceeding outside of the person's criminal trial) and in insisting that immunity extend to evidentiary fruits. The privilege should have been read simply to prohibit later prosecution use at the criminal trial of the testimony compelled at the grand jury. The authors note: "The textual argument [for this position] is remarkably clean. A defendant cannot be forced to be a 'witness against himself'—to testify with his own words introduced against him—at trial *in* [his own] *criminal case. Witness* here is used in its natural sense, meaning someone whose testimony, or utterances, are introduced at trial. Witnesses are those who take the stand and testify, or whose out-of-court depositions or affidavits are introduced at trial in front of the jury. Indeed, this is exactly how the word *witness* seems to be used in the companion Sixth Amendment and in the Treason Clause of Article III. Physical evidence, on the other hand, can be introduced at trial whatever its source—even if that source is a compelled pretrial utterance. A witness testifies but physical evidence does not. A thing is not a witness. Although our suspect has indeed been forced to testify pretrial, that testimony occurred outside his own criminal case, beyond the earshot of the jury. Unless these words are introduced at trial, a suspect is not a *witness* against himself in a criminal case.

"This clean reading makes sense of all the words of the Self–Incrimination Clause and shows how they fit together (and with kindred words of the Sixth Amendment), but it also does much more than that. It flushes out the heretofore elusive rationale of the Self–Incrimination Clause, as best read: reliability. Compelled testimony may be partly or wholly misleading and unreliable; even an innocent person may say seemingly inculpatory things under pressure and suspicion and when flustered by trained inquisitors. But physical fruit is far more sturdy and reliable evidence, so it should be brought before the jury."

other information compelled under the [immunity] order (or any information directly or indirectly derived from such testimony or other information) may be used against the witness in any criminal case, except a prosecution for perjury, giving a false statement, or otherwise failing to comply with the order." 18 U.S.C. § 6002. In KASTIGAR v. UNITED STATES, 406 U.S. 441, 92 S.Ct. 1653, 32 L.Ed.2d 212 (1972), a divided Court (5–2) upheld the new federal provision.

Justice POWELL's opinion for the *Kastigar* majority discounted the "broad language in *Counselman*," which suggested the need for transactional immunity, as inconsistent with the "conceptual basis" of the *Counselman* ruling. The crucial question, as *Counselman* noted, was whether the immunity granted was "coextensive with the scope of the privilege against self-incrimination." Both *Murphy* and the cases applying the exclusionary rule to confessions obtained through Fifth Amendment violations indicated that the constitutional privilege required no more than a prohibition against use and derivative use. The new federal statute clearly met that standard: "The statute provides a sweeping proscription of any use, direct or indirect, of the compelled testimony and any information derived therefrom. This total prohibition on use provides a comprehensive safeguard, barring the use of compelled testimony as an 'investigatory lead,' and also barring the use of any evidence obtained by focusing investigation on a witness as a result of his compelled disclosures."

The *Kastigar* majority rejected the argument, relied on by the dissenters, that the bar against derivative use could not be enforced effectively. Appropriate procedures for "taint hearings" could ensure that derivative use was not made of immunized testimony. Those procedural safeguards were described as follows: "As stated in *Murphy*: 'Once a defendant demonstrates that he has testified, under a state grant of immunity to matters related to the federal prosecution, the federal authorities have the burden of showing that their evidence is not tainted by establishing that they had an independent, legitimate source for the disputed evidence.' This burden of proof, which we reaffirm as appropriate, is not limited to a negation of taint; rather, it imposes on the prosecution the affirmative duty to prove that the evidence it proposes to use is derived from a legitimate source wholly independent of the compelled testimony. This is very substantial protection, commensurate with that resulting from invoking the privilege itself. * * * [Indeed], a defendant against whom incriminating evidence has been obtained through a grant of immunity may be in a stronger position at trial than a defendant who asserts a Fifth Amendment coerced-confession claim. One raising a claim under this statute need only show that he testified under a grant of immunity in order to shift to the government the heavy burden of proving that all of the evidence it proposes to use was derived from legitimate independent sources. On the other hand, a defendant raising a coerced-confession claim under the Fifth Amendment must first prevail in a voluntariness hearing before his confession and evidence derived from it become inadmissible."

3. In a companion case to *Kastigar*, *Zicarelli v. New Jersey State Comm. of Investigation*, 406 U.S. 472, 92 S.Ct. 1670, 32 L.Ed.2d 234 (1972), the Court upheld a state counterpart of 18 U.S.C. § 6002, providing for use/derivative-use immunity in state proceedings. Since *Zicarelli* was decided, a substantial number of states have moved from transactional to use/derivative-use immunity. The A.B.A. and N.C.C.U.S.L. have urged retention of transactional immunity, however, and roughly twenty states continue to provide the broader immunity, see Beale et al., § 7.8. Those opposing a shift to use/derivative use immunity have argued that the opportunity it offers to prosecute based on independently obtained evidence is too insignificant as a practical matter to offset the risk that derivative use will not be detected by a taint hearing. Those supporting use/derivative use immunity contend that taint hearings are effective and that instances allowing permissible prosecutions of immunized witnesses, though small in number, should not be cut off where that is not constitutionally required. They also argue that use/derivative use immunity affords substantial advantages apart from the possibility of a subsequent prosecution. They maintain that such immunity encourages the immunized witness to provide as much detail as possible so as to make it more difficult for the government to survive a taint hearing should it subsequently decide to prosecute. They also contend that the absence of an absolute protection against subsequent prosecution makes the immunized witness' testimony more credible to the jury.

4. Subsequent prosecutions and the problem of taint. While use/derivative use immunity leaves open the possibility of prosecuting an immunized witness, the prosecution must meet the prerequisite of establishing that its evidence is independently derived, as described in *Kastigar*. Lower courts have read *Kastigar* to be satisfied by application of a preponderance of the evidence standard to this burden. See CRIMPROC § 8.11. Also, some courts have been willing to hold the *Kastigar* taint hearing after trial, thereby allowing the government to proceed to trial without providing the broad pretrial disclosure that is inherent in a pretrial taint hearing. Ibid. Nonetheless, prosecuting an immunized witness is not lightly undertaken, and commonly requires advance planning at the time the witness gives the immunized testimony.

The *Kastigar* burden is most likely to be met when the prosecution has completed or substantially completed its investigation before the witness is immunized. Thus, a prosecutor can readily meet the *Kastigar* burden where immunity was granted to force the testimony of a defendant who had already been convicted, but who had claimed the privilege because his appeal was still pending, and the prosecutor now seeks to reprosecute after an appellate reversal of that earlier conviction; the prosecution here can simply restrict itself to the evidence introduced at the earlier trial, which came before the grant of immunity. The *Kastigar* burden can also be met, although not as easily, in cases in which the prosecution had sufficient evidence to prosecute, and had intended to prosecute, but had an immediate need for use of the witness' testimony in a prosecution against another participant in the same general criminal enterprise. A similar possibility is presented where the prosecution was well on its way to obtaining an indictment when another governmental agency (a prosecutor in another jurisdiction or a legislative body) granted immunity. The preferred practice in such cases is for the prosecutor to make a record of all of the evidence collected prior to the grant of immunity, to file that record with the court, and then at the taint hearing, note its intent to utilize only that previously acquired evidence and further evidence directly acquired from that evidence. See Beale et al., § 7.20. That procedure may not be foolproof, however.

In *United States v. North*, 910 F.2d 843 (D.C.Cir.1990), the Independent Counsel conducting a grand jury investigation of the Iran–Contra affair followed such a procedure when Congress proceeded to hold public hearings and grant witness immunity to the target. Although the government's criminal prosecution rested on the testimony of witnesses who had testified before the grand jury before giving immunized testimony to Congress, and Independent Counsel had established a "Chinese Wall" to ensure that its staff was not exposed to that immunized testimony, that was held insufficient to met the *Kastigar* burden. The district court had found that the "witnesses had their memories refreshed with immunized testimony by 'hearing the testimony, reading about it, being questioned about aspects of it before the Select Committees and, to some extent, by exposure to it in the course of responding to inquiries within their respective agencies.'" Insofar as the testimony of the witnesses was shaped by their memories having been refreshed, the government was making "use" of the immunized testimony contrary to *Kastigar*. Accordingly the case was remanded for further proceedings to see if "it is possible * * * to separate the wheat of the witness' unspoiled memory from the chaff of North's immunized testimony."[b]

Assuming the prosecution can establish that the evidence it will use at trial is independently derived, some courts have found that mere prosecutorial familiarity with the immunized testimony poses difficulties because of the possibility of "nonevidentiary use." Indeed, *United States v. McDaniel*, 482 F.2d 305 (8th Cir.1973), characterized as "insurmountable" the government's burden in such a case, as the court could not "escape the conclusion that the testimony could not be wholly obliterated from the prosecutor's mind in his preparation and trial of the case." The *McDaniel* court reasoned that "if the immunity protection is to be coextensive with the Fifth Amendment privilege, as it must to be constitutionally sufficient, then it must forbid all prosecutorial use of the testimony, not merely that which results in the presentation of evidence before the jury." Other courts have disagreed, arguing that the Fifth Amendment privilege is concerned only with direct and indirect use of evidence and not such matters as "deciding to initiate prosecution, refusing to plea bargain, interpreting evidence, planning cross-examination, and otherwise generally planning trial strategy." *United States v. Serrano*, 870 F.2d 1 (1st Cir.1989).

5. *Prosecutorial discretion*. Although immunity statutes commonly require that the immunity order be issued by the court, the judge's role in ruling on a request for such an order often is limited to ensuring that the procedural requirements of the statute are met (e.g., under the federal statute, that the application was approved by one of the statutorily designated higher echelon Justice Department officials and that the order properly states the scope of the immunity[c]). Under such provisions, the judge may not refuse to grant the order because it disagrees with the prosecutor's judgment that a grant of immunity is in the public interest. United States Attorneys' Manual 9–23.21 directs the appropriate Justice Department official, in making that judgment, to consider a wide range of factors, including the following: (1) the importance of the investigation; (2) the value of the person's testimony; (3) the likelihood of prompt and full compliance, and the effectiveness of available sanctions if there is no compliance; (4) the person's relative culpability; (5) the possibility of successfully prosecuting the person prior to compelling testimony through immunization; and (6) the likelihood of adverse collateral consequences to the person if compelled to testify.

b. The lower court was directed to engage in a "line-by-line" inquiry into "the content as well as the sources" of each witness' testimony. On the denial of an application for rehearing, the Court of Appeals rejected the Independent Counsel's argument that *Kastigar* did not apply because its own activities were free from taint. The Court noted: "*Kastigar* is * * * violated whenever the prosecution puts on a witness whose testimony is shaped, directly or indirectly, by compelled testimony, regardless of *how or by whom* he was exposed to that compelled testimony." 920 F.2d 940 (D.C.Cir. 1990). The government subsequently was unable to meet its burden, the target's conviction was reversed and the charges against him dismissed.

c. Does it follow from the legislative authorization of immunity grants under specific procedures that the prosecutor should not be allowed to employ informal grants of immunity

(i.e., an agreement not to exercise prosecutorial authority in exchange for the witness' testimony)? Very often, the informal grants not only will bypass the statutory procedures for immunity grants, but also will contain prosecutorial promises that are substantially narrower than the immunity provided by statute. While such informal grants are dependent upon witness acceptance (i.e., the court will not force a witness to testify in response to such a nonstatutory promise), if the witness does accept and does testify, the court will require the prosecution to live up to its promise. See Hughes, *Agreements for Cooperation in Criminal Cases*, 45 Vand.L.Rev. 1 (1992). Federal prosecutors regularly utilize such informal grants as simply another exercise of the prosecutor's discretion over the decision to charge. See United States Attorneys' Manual 9–27.00, Beale et al., § 7.12.

C. THE COMPELLED PRODUCTION OF DOCUMENTS

FISHER v. UNITED STATES
425 U.S. 391, 96 S.Ct. 1569, 48 L.Ed.2d 39 (1976).

Justice WHITE delivered the opinion of the Court.

In these two cases we are called upon to decide whether a summons directing an attorney to produce documents delivered to him by his client in connection with the attorney-client relationship is enforceable over claims that the documents were constitutionally immune from summons in the hands of the client and retained that immunity in the hands of the attorney. In each case, an Internal Revenue agent visited the taxpayer or taxpayers and interviewed them in connection with an investigation of possible civil or criminal liability under the federal income tax laws. Shortly after the interviews * * *, the taxpayers obtained from their respective accountants certain documents relating to the preparation by the accountant of their tax returns. Shortly after obtaining the documents * * *, the taxpayers transferred the documents to their lawyers—each of whom was retained to assist the taxpayer in connection with the investigation. Upon learning of the whereabouts of the documents, the Internal Revenue Service served summonses on the attorneys directing them to produce documents listed therein. [Those documents were accountants' work sheets, retained copies of income tax returns, and the accountants' copies of correspondence between the accounting firm and the taxpayer]. * * * In each case, the lawyer declined to comply with the summons directing production of the documents, and enforcement actions were commenced by the Government. * * *

All of the parties in these cases and the Court of Appeals have concurred in the proposition that if the Fifth Amendment would have excused a *taxpayer* from turning over the accountant's papers had he possessed them, the *attorney* to whom they are delivered for the purpose of obtaining legal advice should also be immune from subpoena. Although we agree with this proposition for the reasons set forth * * * infra, we are convinced that, under our decision in *Couch v. United States,* 409 U.S. 322, 93 S.Ct. 611, 34 L.Ed.2d 548 (1973), it is not the taxpayer's Fifth Amendment privilege that would excuse the *attorney* from production.

The relevant part of that Amendment provides:

> "No person ... shall be *compelled* in any criminal case to be a *witness against himself.*" (Emphasis added.)

The taxpayer's privilege under this Amendment is not violated by enforcement of the summonses involved in these cases because enforcement against a taxpayer's lawyer would not "compel" the taxpayer to do anything—and certainly would not compel him to be a "witness" against himself. The Court has held repeatedly that the Fifth Amendment is limited to prohibiting the use of "physical or moral compulsion" exerted on the person asserting the privilege. In *Couch v. United States,* supra, we recently ruled that the Fifth Amendment rights of a taxpayer were not violated by the enforcement of a documentary summons directed to her accountant and requiring production of the taxpayer's own records in the possession of the accountant. We did so on the ground that in such a case "the ingredient of personal compulsion against an accused is lacking." Here, the taxpayers are compelled to do no more than was the taxpayer in *Couch.* The taxpayers' Fifth Amendment privilege is therefore not violated by enforcement of the summonses directed toward their attorneys. This is true whether or not the Amendment would have barred a subpoena directing the taxpayer to produce the documents while they were in his hands.

The fact that the attorneys are agents of the taxpayers does not change this result. *Couch* held as much, since the accountant there was also the taxpayer's agent, and in this respect reflected a longstanding view. * * * "It is extortion of information from the accused which offends our sense of justice." *Couch v. United States.* Agent or no, the lawyer is not the taxpayer. The taxpayer is the "accused," and nothing is being extorted from him. Nor is this one of those situations, which *Couch* suggested might exist, where constructive possession is so clear or relinquishment of possession so temporary and insignificant as to leave the personal compulsion upon the taxpayer substantially intact. * * *

The Court of Appeals suggested that because legally and ethically the attorney was required to respect the confidences of his client, the latter had a reasonable expectation of privacy for the records in the hands of the attorney and therefore did not forfeit his Fifth Amendment privilege with respect to the records by transferring them in order to obtain legal advice. It is true that the Court has often stated that one of the several purposes served by the constitutional privilege against compelled testimonial self-incrimination is that of protecting personal privacy. See e.g., *Murphy v. Waterfront Comm'n* [p. 692]. But the Court has never suggested that every invasion of privacy violates the privilege. Within the limits imposed by the language of the Fifth Amendment, which we necessarily observe, the privilege truly serves privacy interests; but the Court has never on any ground, personal privacy included, applied the Fifth Amendment to prevent the otherwise proper acquisition or use of evidence which, in the Court's view, did not involve compelled testimonial self-incrimination of some sort.

The proposition that the Fifth Amendment protects private information obtained without compelling self-incriminating testimony is contrary to the clear statements of this Court that under appropriate safeguards private incriminating statements of an accused may be overheard and used in evidence, if they are not compelled at the time they were uttered, *Katz v. United States* [p. 138], and that disclosure of private information may be compelled if immunity removes the risk of incrimination. *Kastigar v. United States* [p. 703]. If the Fifth Amendment protected generally against the obtaining of private information from a man's mouth or pen or house, its protections would presumably not be lifted by probable cause and a warrant or by immunity. The privacy invasion is not mitigated by immunity; and the Fifth Amendment's strictures, unlike the Fourth's are not removed by showing reasonableness. The Framers addressed the subject of personal privacy directly in the Fourth Amendment. * * * They did not seek in still another Amendment—the Fifth—to achieve a general protection of privacy but to deal with the more specific issue of compelled self-incrimination.

We cannot cut the Fifth Amendment completely loose from the moorings of its language, and make it serve as a general protector of privacy—a word not mentioned in its text and a concept directly addressed in the Fourth Amendment. We adhere to the view that the Fifth Amendment protects against "compelled self-incrimination, not [the disclosure of] private information." * * * Insofar as private information not obtained through compelled self-incriminating testimony is legally protected, its protection stems from other sources—the Fourth Amendment's protection against seizures without warrant or probable cause and against subpoenas which suffer from "too much indefiniteness or breadth in the things required to be 'particularly described,' " the First Amendment, or evidentiary privileges such as the attorney-client privilege.[7]

---

7. The taxpayers and their attorneys have not raised arguments of a Fourth Amendment nature before this Court and could not be successful if they had. The summonses are narrowly drawn and seek only documents of unquestionable relevance to the tax investigation. Special problems of privacy which might be presented by subpoena of a personal diary, *United States v. Bennett,* 409 F.2d 888, 897 (C.A.2 1969) (Friendly, J.), are not involved

* * * [While the] taxpayers have erroneously relied on the Fifth Amendment without urging the attorney-client privilege in so many words, they have nevertheless invoked the relevant body of law and policies that govern the attorney-client privilege. In this posture of the case, we feel obliged to inquire whether the attorney-client privilege applies to documents in the hands of an attorney which would have been privileged in the hands of the client by reason of the Fifth Amendment. * * * This Court and the lower courts have * * * uniformly held that pre-existing documents which could have been obtained by court process from the client when he was in possession may also be obtained from the attorney by similar process following transfer by the client in order to obtain more informed legal advice. * * * It is otherwise if the documents are not obtainable by subpoena duces tecum or summons while in the exclusive possession of the client, for the client will then be reluctant to transfer possession to the lawyer unless the documents are also privileged in the latter's hands. Where the transfer is made for the purpose of obtaining legal advice, the purposes of the attorney-client privilege would be defeated unless the privilege is applicable. * * *

Since each taxpayer [here] transferred possession of the documents in question from himself to his attorney in order to obtain legal assistance in the tax investigations in question, the papers, if unobtainable by summons from the client, are unobtainable by summons directed to the attorney by reason of the attorney-client privilege. We accordingly proceed to the question whether the documents could have been obtained by summons addressed to the taxpayer while the documents were in his possession. The only bar to enforcement of such summons asserted by the parties or the courts below is the Fifth Amendment's privilege against self-incrimination. * * *

The proposition that the Fifth Amendment prevents compelled production of documents over objection that such production might incriminate stems from *Boyd v. United States* * * *. Several of *Boyd's* express or implicit declarations have not stood the test of time. The application of the Fourth Amendment to subpoenas was limited by *Hale v. Henkel* [p. 699] and more recent cases. Purely evidentiary (but "nontestimonial") materials, as well as contraband and fruits and instrumentalities of crime, may now be searched for and seized under proper circumstances, *Warden v. Hayden* [p. 160]. Also, any notion that "testimonial" evidence may never be seized and used in evidence is inconsistent with [various cases] approving the seizure under appropriate circumstances of conversations of a person suspected of crime. See *Katz v. United States* [p. 138]. It is also clear that the Fifth Amendment does not independently proscribe the compelled production of every sort of incriminating evidence but applies only when the accused is compelled to make a *testimonial* communication that is incriminating. See *Schmerber v. California* [fn. a, p. 619]. * * * Furthermore, despite *Boyd,* neither a partnership nor the individual partners are shielded from compelled production of partnership records on self-incrimination grounds. *Bellis v. United States* [p. 728]. It would appear that under that case the precise claim sustained in *Boyd* would now be rejected for reasons not there considered.

The pronouncement in *Boyd* that a person may not be forced to produce his private papers has nonetheless often appeared as dictum in later opinions of this Court. * * * To the extent, however, that the rule against compelling production of private papers rested on the proposition that seizures of or subpoenas for "mere evidence," including documents, violated the Fourth Amendment and therefore also transgressed the Fifth, the foundations for the rule have been washed away. In consequence, the prohibition against forcing the production of private papers has long been a rule searching for a rationale consistent with the proscriptions of

here. First Amendment values are also plainly
not implicated in these cases.

the Fifth Amendment against compelling a person to give "testimony" that incriminates him. Accordingly, we turn to the question of what, if any, incriminating testimony within the Fifth Amendment's protection, is compelled by a documentary summons.

A subpoena served on a taxpayer requiring him to produce an accountant's workpapers in his possession without doubt involves substantial compulsion. But it does not compel oral testimony; nor would it ordinarily compel the taxpayer to restate, repeat, or affirm the truth of the contents of the documents sought. Therefore, the Fifth Amendment would not be violated by the fact alone that the papers on their face might incriminate the taxpayer, for the privilege protects a person only against being incriminated by his own compelled testimonial communications. *Schmerber v. California,* supra. The accountant's workpapers are not the taxpayer's. They were not prepared by the taxpayer, and they contain no testimonial declarations by him. Furthermore, as far as this record demonstrates, the preparation of all of the papers sought in these cases was wholly voluntary, and they cannot be said to contain compelled testimonial evidence, either of the taxpayers or of anyone else.[11] The taxpayer cannot avoid compliance with the subpoena merely by asserting that the item of evidence which he is required to produce contains incriminating writing, whether his own or that of someone else.

The act of producing evidence in response to a subpoena nevertheless has communicative aspects of its own, wholly aside from the contents of the papers produced. Compliance with the subpoena tacitly concedes the existence of the papers demanded and their possession or control by the taxpayer. It also would indicate the taxpayer's belief that the papers are those described in the subpoena. The elements of compulsion are clearly present, but the more difficult issues are whether the tacit averments of the taxpayer are both "testimonial" and "incriminating" for purposes of applying the Fifth Amendment. These questions perhaps do not lend themselves to categorical answers; their resolution may instead depend on the facts and circumstances of particular cases or classes thereof. In light of the records now before us, we are confident that however incriminating the contents of the accountant's workpapers might be, the act of producing them—the only thing which the taxpayer is compelled to do—would not itself involve testimonial self-incrimination.

It is doubtful that implicitly admitting the existence and possession of the papers rises to the level of testimony within the protection of the Fifth Amendment. The papers belong to the accountant, were prepared by him, and are the kind usually prepared by an accountant working on the tax returns of his client. Surely the Government is in no way relying on the "truthtelling" of the taxpayer to prove the existence of or his access to the documents. The existence and location of the papers are a foregone conclusion and the taxpayer adds little or nothing to the sum total of the Government's information by conceding that he in fact has the papers. Under these circumstances by enforcement of the summons "no constitutional rights are touched. The question is not of testimony but of surrender."

11. The fact that the documents may have been written by the person asserting the privilege is insufficient to trigger the privilege. *Wilson v. United States* [p. 727]. And, unless the government has compelled the subpoena person to write the document, cf. *Grosso v. United States* [p. 736], the fact that it was written by him is not controlling with respect to the Fifth Amendment. Conversations may be seized and introduced in evidence under proper safeguards * * * if not compelled. In the case of a documentary subpoena the only thing compelled is the act of producing the document and the compelled act is the same as one performed when a chattel or document not authored by the producer is demanded. [As to compelling a person to write a document, see Note 7, p. 735, and *Doe v. United States,* p. 736.]

When an accused is required to submit a handwriting exemplar he admits his ability to write and impliedly asserts that the exemplar is his writing. But in common experience, the first would be a near truism and the latter self-evident. In any event, although the exemplar may be incriminating to the accused and although he is compelled to furnish it, his Fifth Amendment privilege is not violated because nothing he has said or done is deemed to be sufficiently testimonial for purposes of the privilege. This Court has also time and again allowed subpoenas against the custodian of corporate documents or those belonging to other collective entities such as unions and partnerships and those of bankrupt businesses over claims that the documents will incriminate the custodian despite the fact that producing the documents tacitly admits their existence and their location in the hands of their possessor. The existence and possession or control of the subpoenaed documents being no more in issue here than in the above cases, the summons is equally enforceable.

Moreover, assuming that these aspects of producing the accountant's papers have some minimal testimonial significance, surely it is not illegal to seek accounting help in connection with one's tax returns or for the accountant to prepare workpapers and deliver them to the taxpayer. At this juncture, we are quite unprepared to hold that either the fact of existence of the papers or of their possession by the taxpayer poses any realistic threat of incrimination to the taxpayer.

As for the possibility that responding to the subpoena would authenticate the workpapers, production would express nothing more than the taxpayer's belief that the papers are those described in the subpoena. The taxpayer would be no more competent to authenticate the accountant's workpapers or reports by producing them than he would be to authenticate them if testifying orally. The taxpayer did not prepare the papers and could not vouch for their accuracy. The documents would not be admissible in evidence against the taxpayer without authenticating testimony. Without more, responding to the subpoena in the circumstances before us would not appear to represent a substantial threat of self-incrimination. * * *

Whether the Fifth Amendment would shield the taxpayer from producing his own tax records in his possession is a question not involved here; for the papers demanded here are not his "private papers," see *Boyd v. United States,* supra. We do hold that compliance with a summons directing the taxpayer to produce the accountant's documents involved in this case would involve no incriminating testimony within the protection of the Fifth Amendment.

Justice STEVENS took no part in the consideration or disposition of these cases.

Justice BRENNAN, concurring in the judgment.

Given the prior access by accountants retained by the taxpayers to the papers involved in these cases and the wholly business rather than personal nature of the papers, I agree that the privilege against compelled self-incrimination did not in either of these cases protect the papers from production in response to the summonses. See *Couch v. United States.* I do not join the Court's opinion, however, because of the portent of much of what is said of a serious crippling of the protection secured by the privilege against compelled production of one's private books and papers. * * * [I]t is but another step in the denigration of privacy principles settled nearly 100 years ago in *Boyd v. United States.* * * *

Expressions are legion in opinions of this Court that the protection of personal privacy is a central purpose of the privilege against compelled self-incrimination. * * * The Court pays lip-service to this bedrock premise of privacy in the statement that "[w]ithin the limits imposed by the language of the Fifth

Amendment, which we necessarily observe, the privilege truly serves privacy interests." But this only makes explicit what elsewhere highlights the opinion, namely, the view that protection of personal privacy is merely a byproduct and not, as our precedents and history teach, a factor controlling in part the determination of the scope of the privilege. This cart-before-the-horse approach is fundamentally at odds with the settled principle that the scope of the privilege is not constrained by the limits of the wording of the Fifth Amendment but has the reach necessary to protect the cherished value of privacy which it safeguards. * * * History and principle, not the mechanical application of its wording, have been the life of the amendment. * * *

History and principle teach that the privacy protected by the Fifth Amendment extends not just to the individual's immediate declarations, oral or written, but also to his testimonial materials in the form of books and papers. * * * The common-law and constitutional extension of the privilege to testimonial materials, such as books and papers, was inevitable. An individual's books and papers are generally little more than an extension of his person. They reveal no less than he could reveal upon being questioned directly. Many of the matters within an individual's knowledge may as easily be retained within his head as set down on a scrap of paper. I perceive no principle which does not permit compelling one to disclose the contents of one's mind but does permit compelling the disclosure of the contents of that scrap of paper by compelling its production. Under a contrary view, the constitutional protection would turn on fortuity, and persons would, at their peril, record their thoughts and the events of their lives. The ability to think private thoughts, facilitated as it is by pen and paper, and the ability to preserve intimate memories would be curtailed through fear that those thoughts or the events of those memories would become the subjects of criminal sanctions however invalidly imposed. Indeed, it was the very reality of those fears that helped provide the historical impetus for the privilege. * * *

The Court's treatment of the privilege falls far short of giving it the scope required by history and our precedents.[a] * * * [The Court's] analysis is patently incomplete: the threshold inquiry is whether the taxpayer is compelled to produce incriminating papers. That inquiry is not answered in favor of production merely because the subpoena requires neither oral testimony from nor affirmation of the papers' contents by the taxpayer. To be sure, the Court correctly observes that "[t]he taxpayer cannot avoid compliance with the subpoena *merely* by asserting that the item of evidence which he is required to produce contains incriminating writing, whether his own or that of someone else." For it is not enough that the production of a writing, or books and papers, is compelled. Unless those materials are such as to come within the zone of privacy recognized by the Amendment, the privilege against compulsory self-incrimination does not protect against their production.

We are not without guideposts for determining what books, papers, and writings come within the zone of privacy recognized by the Amendment. * * * *Couch v. United States* expressly held that the Fifth Amendment protected against

---

a. Justice Brennan's opinion also questioned whether the Court's reasoning was consistent with its own analysis: "I also question the Court's treatment of the question whether the act of producing evidence is 'testimonial.' I agree that the act of production implicitly admits the existence of the evidence requested and possession or control of that evidence by the party producing it. It also implicitly authenticates the evidence as that identified in the order to compel. I disagree, however, that implicit admission of the existence and possession or control of the papers in this case is not 'testimonial' merely because the Government could readily have otherwise proved existence and possession or control in these cases. I know of no Fifth Amendment principle which makes the testimonial nature of evidence and, therefore, one's protection against incriminating himself, turn on the strength of the Government's case against him."

the compelled production of testimonial evidence only if the individual resisting production had a reasonable expectation of privacy with respect to the evidence. * * * A precise cataloguing of private papers within the ambit of the privacy protected by the privilege is probably impossible. Some papers, however, do lend themselves to classification. Production of documentary materials created or authenticated by a State or the Federal Government, such as automobile registrations or property deeds, would seem ordinarily to fall outside the protection of the privilege. They hardly reflect an extension of the person. Economic and business records may present difficulty in particular cases. The records of business entities generally fall without the scope of the privilege. But, as noted, the Court has recognized that the privilege extends to the business records of the sole proprietor or practitioner. Such records are at least an extension of an aspect of a person's activities, though concededly not the more intimate aspects of one's life. Where the privilege would have protected one's mental notes of his business affairs in a less complicated day and age, it would seem that that protection should not fall away because the complexities of another time compel one to keep business records.

Nonbusiness economic records in the possession of an individual, such as canceled checks or tax records, would also seem to be protected. They may provide clear insights into a person's total lifestyle. They are, however, like business records and the papers involved in these cases, frequently, though not always, disclosed to other parties; and disclosure, in proper cases, may foreclose reliance upon the privilege. Personal letters constitute an integral aspect of a person's private enclave. And while letters, being necessarily interpersonal, are not wholly private, their peculiarly private nature and the generally narrow extent of their disclosure would seem to render them within the scope of the privilege. Papers in the nature of a personal diary are *a fortiori* protected under the privilege. * * *

Justice MARSHALL, concurring in the judgment.

* * * I would have preferred it had the Court found some room in its theory for recognition of the import of the contents of the documents themselves. * * * Nonetheless, I am hopeful that the Court's new theory, properly understood and applied, will provide substantially the same protection as our prior focus on the contents of the documents. * * * Indeed, there would appear to be a precise inverse relationship between the private nature of the document and the permissibility of assuming its existence. Therefore, under the Court's theory, the admission through production that one's diary, letters, prior tax returns, personally maintained financial records, or canceled checks exist would ordinarily provide substantial testimony. The incriminating nature of such an admission is clear, for while it may not be criminal to keep a diary, or write letters or checks, the admission that one does and that those documents are still available may quickly—or simultaneously—lead to incriminating evidence. If there is a "real danger" of such a result, that is enough under our cases to make such testimony subject to the claim of privilege. Thus, in practice, the Court's approach should still focus upon the private nature of the papers subpoenaed and protect those about which *Boyd* and its progeny were most concerned.

The Court's theory will also limit the prosecution's ability to use documents secured through a grant of immunity. If authentication that the document produced is the document demanded were the only testimony inherent in production, immunity would be a useful tool for obtaining written evidence. So long as a document obtained under an immunity grant could be authenticated through other sources, as would often be possible, reliance on the immunized testimony— the authentication—and its fruits would not be necessary, and the document could be introduced. The Court's recognition that the act of production also involves testimony about the existence and possession of the subpoenaed documents mandates a different result. Under the Court's theory, if the document is to be obtained the immunity grant must extend to the testimony that the document is presently in existence. Such a grant will effectively shield the contents of the document, for the contents are a direct fruit of the immunized testimony—that the document exists—and cannot usually be obtained without reliance on that testimony. Accordingly, the Court's theory offers substantially the same protection against procurement of documents under grant of immunity that our prior cases afford.* * *

Notes and Questions

1. **The role of privacy.** Looking back to *Boyd*, can the ruling there be viewed (as suggested by Justices Brennan and Marshall) as resting upon a privacy rationale of the Fifth Amendment? The *Fisher* majority apparently subscribed to the view (held by most commentators) that the *Boyd* ruling rested on a subsequently discarded "property rights" rationale. *Boyd*, under this view, simply utilized the privilege to characterize as "unreasonable" all "searches" (which included required production) aimed at obtaining a person's personal property for possible use against him in a "criminal case" (which included a forfeiture proceeding). See Robert Heidt, *The Fifth Amendment Privilege and Documents— Cutting Fisher's Tangled Line*, 49 Mo.L.Rev. 440 (1984). See also Note 2, p. 668. Yet, *Boyd*, particularly because of its reliance on *Entick v. Carrington* and the characterization there of the individual's papers as his "dearest property" (see p. 665), has also been viewed as suggesting a broad personal privacy grounding for the self-incrimination privilege. *Entick*, it is suggested, regards a person as being "embodied" in his papers and *Boyd* recognized that it was therefore a violation of the privilege to make his papers "speak" against him. *Entick*, however, had in mind the individual's personal political writings, while *Boyd* had before it an invoice written by another firm. See Robert Gerstein, *The Demise of Boyd: Self-Incrimination and Private Papers in the Burger Court*, 27 U.C.L.A. L. Rev. 343 (1979). Still another view is that *Boyd*, in merging Fourth and Fifth Amendment protections, advanced a much larger privacy protection, linked to property rights, but extending to all documents in recognition that "papers are among one's most private possessions." See William J. Stuntz, *Privacy's Problem and the Law of Criminal Procedure*, 93 Mich.L.Rev. 1016 (1995) (also arguing that *Boyd* went beyond what was feasible in a regulatory state by providing "absolute protection" for a "substantial class of private information," and even before *Fisher*, the Court had "abandoned all pretense of protecting privacy" where such absolute protection "would lead most directly to substantive restraint," as reflected by *Hale's* recognition of an entity exception (see Pt. D infra) and *Shapiro's* exception for "required records" (see Note 7, p. 735); "*Fisher* merely finished the job that *Hale* and *Shapiro* started.").

2. **Remnants of Boyd.** In UNITED STATES v. DOE, 465 U.S. 605, 104 S.Ct. 1237, 79 L.Ed.2d 552 (1984) (commonly described as *Doe I*, to distinguish it from *Doe II*, *Doe v. United States*, p. 736), the subpoena at issue directed a sole proprietor to produce for grand jury use a broad range of records, including billings, ledgers, canceled checks, telephone records, contracts and paid bills. The district court sustained the proprietor's claim of privilege. It concluded that compliance with the subpoena would require the proprietor to "admit that the records exist, that they are in his possession, and that they are authentic" and that each of these testimonial elements of production was potentially incriminatory. The Third Circuit agreed with this reasoning, but also added that the privilege applied because compelled disclosure of the contents of the documents violated the Fifth Amendment. Relying upon a privacy analysis of *Boyd*, it reasoned that the contents of personal records were privileged under the Fifth

Amendment and that "business records of a sole proprietorship are no different from the individual's personal records." Justice Powell's opinion for the Court in *Doe I* affirmed the rulings below insofar as they relied on the act-of-production doctrine of *Fisher*, but rejected the Third's Circuit conclusion that self-incrimination privilege also applied because it protected the contents of the papers.

Justice Powell initially acknowledged that the Court in *Fisher* had "declined to reach the question whether the Fifth Amendment privilege protects the contents of an individual's tax records in his possession" (see p. 710). The "rationale" underlying *Fisher's* holding, however, was equally persuasive as to such records and the records here. *Fisher* had emphasized that "the Fifth Amendment protects the person asserting the privilege only from compelled self-incrimination." That a record was prepared by a subpoenaed party and is in his possession is "irrelevant to the determination of whether its creation * * * was compelled." The business records here, like the accountant's workpapers in *Fisher*, had been prepared voluntarily, and therefore only their production, and not their creation, was compelled. The contention that the Fifth Amendment created a "zone of privacy" that protected the content of such papers had been rejected in *Fisher* and that rejection had been reinforced by the *Andresen v. Maryland* (p. 160) sustaining a search for personal business records. The respondent could not avoid compliance with a subpoena "merely by asserting that the item of evidence which he is required to produce contains incriminating writing, whether his own or that of someone else."

Although *Doe I* dealt with business records, the opinion did not suggest any opening for separate treatment of diaries (see fn. 7 of *Fisher*) or other documents of a more intimate nature. Justice O'Connor, in a separate concurring opinion, sought to shut the door on any such exception. She noted: "I write separately * * * to make explicit what is implicit in the analysis of [Justice Powell's] opinion: that the Fifth Amendment provides absolutely no protection for the contents of private papers of any kind. The notion that the Fifth Amendment protects the privacy of papers originated in *Boyd v. United States*, but our decision in *Fisher v. United States*, sounded the death-knell for *Boyd*. 'Several of *Boyd's* express or implicit declarations [had] not stood the test of time * * * and its privacy of papers concept ha[d] long been a rule searching for a rationale.' *Fisher*. Today's decision puts a long overdue end to that fruitless search."

Justice O'Connor's opinion brought forth a response from Justice Marshall, joined by Justice Brennan. "This case," Justice Marshall noted, "presented nothing remotely close to the question that Justice O'Connor eagerly poses and answers." The documents in question here were business records, "which implicate a lesser degree of concern for privacy interests than, for example, personal diaries." It accordingly could not be said that the Court had "reconsidered the question of whether the Fifth Amendment provides protection for the content of 'private papers of any kind.' "

As to the post *Doe I* lower court treatment of this issue, see CRIMPROC § 8.12(f): "In the years since *Doe I*, lower courts usually have found it unnecessary to decide whether anything remains of *Boyd*. 'If the contents of papers are protected at all,' they note, 'it is only in rare situations, where compelled disclosure would break the heart of our sense of privacy.' That might be the case as to subpoena compelling production of 'intimate papers such as private diaries and drafts of letters or essays,' but it certainly would not cover the business and other financial records that typically are in issue. * * * A growing number of courts, however, have come to the conclusion that the rationale of *Doe* and *Fisher* precludes self-incrimination protection of the contents of a voluntarily prepared document, no matter how personal the document. Thus, courts have held that the act-of-production doctrine provides the only protection for such personal records as diaries and pocket calendars. In all of those cases, however, once the concept of a *Boyd*-based content protection was rejected, the government was able to overcome an act-of-production objection because the documents had been shared with others and their existence, possession, and authentication were established as foregone conclusions. Ordinarily such documents are kept more privately and the individual required to produce them would implicitly be giving testimony as to those elements and therefore be entitled to the protection of the privilege."

Consider also Heidt, Note 1, supra (arguing that the protection of the most private documents from forced disclosure is more appropriately considered as a First Amendment issue, as procedural requirements applicable to Fifth Amendment claims, as prescribed in *Hoffman*, Note 2, p. 691, would restrict judicial inquiry into elements relevant to a privacy claim, such as whether the party actually authored the subpoenaed documents).

3. ***Third-party production.*** As noted in *Fisher*, (p. 707), *Couch* recognized that there may be situations in which "constructive possession is so clear or relinquishment of possession so temporary and insignificant as to leave the personal compulsion * * * [upon the owner of the subpoenaed record] substantially intact." Does that situation arise where a subpoena for records of a sole proprietor is directed to an office employee as custodian of the records and the sole proprietor seeks to assert the self-incrimination privilege? See *In re Grand Jury (Kent)*, 646 F.2d 963 (5th Cir.1981) (yes, where proprietor actively participated in management of small office where records were held and employee was "never delegated the exclusive responsibility for the preparation and custody of the subpoenaed records"); *In re Grand Jury Investigation (Heller)*, 921 F.2d 1184 (11th Cir.1991) (no, where legal secretary had intimate involvement in preparation and maintenance of subpoenaed trust account records of the attorney, although the attorney also was actively involved with records in his practice and maintained "a degree of control over them").

4. ***The foregone conclusion doctrine.*** *Fisher's* reasoning as to why the implicit admission of the existence and possession of accountant's workpapers did "not rise to the level of testimony under the protection of the Fifth Amendment" (p. 709) came to be known as the "foregone conclusion" doctrine. In *Doe I*, the Court described that doctrine as extending also to implicit admissions of authentication. The lower courts there had sustained Doe's claim that the act of producing the documents subpoenaed would "tacitly admit their existence and his possession" and would "reliev[e] the government of the need for authentication" under Fed. R. Evid. 901.[a] The Supreme Court, in turn, also accepted that claim based upon its traditional "reluctan[ce] to disturb findings of fact in which two courts below concurred." The Court also concluded that those findings were "sufficient to establish a valid claim of the privilege against self-incrimination," but it then added: "This is not to say that the government was foreclosed from rebutting respondents claim by producing evidence that possession existence, and authentication were a 'foregone conclusion.' *Fisher*. In this case, however, the Government failed to make such a showing." 465 U.S. at 614, fn. 13.

a. Fed. R. Evid. 901 provides that authentication "is satisfied by evidence sufficient to support a finding that the matter in question is what its proponent claims." Subdivisions (1)–(10) of Fed. R. Evid. 901 offer illustrations of evidence that may support such a finding, including testimony of a witness with knowledge (subdivision 1), expert and nonexpert testimony as to the genuineness of handwriting (subdivisions 2 and 3), and distinctive characteristics of the document as contained in its "appearance, contents, substance, internal patterns, or other distinctive characteristics, taken in conjunction with circumstances" (subdivision 4). Doe's claim apparently was that his act of production would have provided authentication under subdivision (1). Some of the documents may have been capable of authentication under subdivision (4), without reliance on Doe having produced the documents, but there was no discussion of this possibility.

As Justice Brennan notes in *Fisher* (see fn. a, p. 711), in determining whether a witness' testimony might be viewed as incriminatory under the *Hoffman* standard (see Note 2, p. 691), courts do not look to whether the facts conveyed in the witness' testimony might be established by the government through other sources. Does the *Fisher* ruling that the privilege does not apply when "possession, existence and authentication" are a "foregone conclusion" require precisely that inquiry in determining the communicative aspects of the act of production? If so, why this special treatment for that act? Consider in this connection, Robert Mosteller, *Simplifying Subpoena Law: Taking the Fifth Amendment Seriously,* 73 Va.L.Rev. 1, 32–33 (1987):

"More plausibly, the Court is suggesting [in its 'foregone conclusion' analysis] that when an implicit as opposed to an explicit communication is involved, it is necessary to consider whether the government is really asking a 'question' through the subpoena. Granted, the defendant's response to a documentary subpoena always reveals that the item does or does not exist; the government cannot eliminate the implicit question about the document's existence no matter how it phrases the subpoena's demand. But if the government already knows the answer to that question and is truly uninterested in the implicit answer provided by production, the witness' gratuitous communication of it should not violate the fifth amendment. In short, the *Fisher* decision suggests that constitutional rights are not violated by implicit communications that are inherent in a response to a documentary subpoena where those communications are unwanted because, though technically admissible, they are not substantially relevant to the prosecution's case given its other evidence."

5. *Establishing a foregone conclusion. Fisher* left lower courts uncertain as to what was required to establish existence and possession as a foregone conclusion. In that case, to raise the attorney-client privilege (and through it the protection coextensive with the client's incrimination privilege), the attorneys had to acknowledge that the papers existed and had been given to them by their clients. However, the Court spoke only of the "sum total of the Government's information" (p. 709), and that reference could well have included information from other sources (e.g., the accountants who prepared the workpapers).

In *Doe I,* the Court simply noted that the government had failed to make a "foregone conclusion" showing, but did not explain what that would have been required to make that showing. The Court did note that "respondent did not conceed in the District Court that the records listed in the subpoena actually existed or were in his possession." It also quoted from a portion of the lower court's opinion stating that the "most plausible inference to be drawn from the broad-sweeping subpoenas is that the Government, unable to prove that the subpoenaed documents exist—or that the appellee even is somehow connected to the business entities under investigation—is attempting to compensate for its lack of knowledge by requiring the appellee to become, in effect, the primary informant against himself." 465 U.S. at 614, fn. 12.

6. *Potential incrimination.* Assuming that the government does not establish that possession, authentication, and existence are a foregone conclusion, under what circumstances will the privilege nonetheless not be applicable because the likelihood of incrimination is not "substantial and real" (see *Doe I,* 465 U.S. at 614, fn. 13)? Note in this regard *Fisher's* comments on the incriminatory aspects of producing records that were authored by another and clearly could be lawfully possessed. What did the Court mean when it said that, "at this juncture," it was unwilling to hold that either the existence of the papers or their possession posed a realistic threat of incrimination (see p. 710)? Are the contents of the papers irrelevant to that determination? Assuming that the contents were incriminatory, wouldn't possession suggest knowledge of that content and thereby pose a realistic threat? Is the answer that the Court in *Fisher* may not have been willing to conclude, on the record before it, that a realistic threat existed that the contents were incriminatory? See CRIMPROC § 8.13(b).

In *Doe I*, the Court returned to the issue of incrimination in a footnote that responded to the government's contention that, even if the act of production there did have "testimonial aspects," any incrimination would be "so trivial" that the Fifth Amendment would not be implicated. The risk of incrimination here was "substantial and real," meeting the *Hoffman* standard (Note 2, p. 691), since the act of production established the existence and possession of the business records in question (points "not conceded" by Doe) and relieved the government of the need to otherwise establish authenticity under Fed. R. Evid. 901. 465 U.S. at 614, fn. 13. No reference was made to the general character of the documents, although, as in *Fisher*, they certainly were documents that could be "lawfully possessed," and in some instances, may have been authored by others.

7. *Act of production immunity.* The government in *Doe I* maintained that, accepting arguendo the lower court's finding of testimonial self-incrimination, the district court should nevertheless have enforced the subpoena and granted to Doe immunity as to his act of production. The government argued that it had, in effect, offered such immunity by telling the district court that it would not use the act of production against Doe. The Court responded that the government, if it wanted to grant act-of-production immunity, must make a proper application pursuant to the immunity statute. (See Note 5, p. 705). It did, however, reject Doe's contention that the immunity granted under the statute must extend to the contents of the documents subpoenaed. The Court reasoned: "Respondent argues that any grant of use immunity must cover the contents of the documents as well as the act of production. We find this contention unfounded. To satisfy the requirements of the Fifth Amendment, a grant of immunity need be only as broad as the privilege against self-incrimination. *Murphy v. Waterfront Commission* [p. 702]. As discussed above, the privilege in this case extends only to the act of production. Therefore, any grant of use immunity need only protect respondent from the self-incrimination that might accompany the act of producing his business records." 465 at 617, fn. 17.

In *Fisher*, Justice Marshall had suggested that where act-of-production immunity was needed because the government could not establish existence as a foregone conclusion, that grant of immunity would "effectively shield the contents of documents" from governmental use (see p. 713). Did the *Doe I* description of the act-of-production immunity necessarily undercut Justice Marshall's position?

8. *Hubbell.* The Court's latest ruling applying the act-of-production doctrine, *United States v. Hubbell*, set forth below, addressed several of the issues noted above.

UNITED STATES v. HUBBELL
530 U.S. 27, 120 S.Ct. 2037, 147 L.Ed.2d 24 (2000).

Justice STEVENS delivered the opinion of the Court. The two questions presented concern the scope of a witness' protection against compelled self-incrimination: (1) whether the Fifth Amendment privilege protects a witness from being compelled to disclose the existence of incriminating documents that the Government is unable to describe with reasonable particularity; and (3) if the witness produces such documents pursuant to a grant of immunity, whether 18 U.S.C. § 6002 prevents the Government from using them to prepare criminal charges against him.

This proceeding arises out of the second prosecution of respondent, Webster Hubbell, commenced by the Independent Counsel appointed in August 1994 to investigate possible violations of federal law relating to the Whitewater Development Corporation. The first prosecution was terminated pursuant to a plea bargain. In December 1994, respondent pleaded guilty to charges of mail fraud and tax evasion arising out of his billing practices as a member of an Arkansas law firm from 1989 to 1992, and was sentenced to 21 months in prison. In the plea agreement, respondent promised to provide the Independent Counsel with "full, complete, accurate, and truthful information" about matters relating to the Whitewater investigation.

The second prosecution resulted from the Independent Counsel's attempt to determine whether respondent had violated that promise. In October 1996, while respondent was incarcerated, the Independent Counsel served him with a subpoena duces tecum calling for the production of 11 categories of documents before a grand jury sitting in Little Rock, Arkansas. See Appendix, infra.[a] On November 19, he appeared before the grand jury and invoked his Fifth Amendment privilege against self-incrimination. In response to questioning by the prosecutor, respondent initially refused "to state whether there are documents within my possession, custody, or control responsive to the Subpoena." Thereafter, the prosecutor produced an order, which had previously been obtained from the District Court pursuant to 18 U.S.C. § 6003(a), directing him to respond to the subpoena and granting him immunity "to the extent allowed by law." Respondent then produced 13,120 pages of documents and records and responded to a series of questions that established that those were all of the documents in his custody or control that were responsive to the commands in the subpoena, with the exception of a few documents he claimed were shielded by the attorney-client and attorney work-product privileges.

The contents of the documents produced by respondent provided the Independent Counsel with the information that led to this second prosecution. On April

---

a. The Appendix to Justice Stevens' opinion set forth verbatim the "subpoena rider," which identified the 11 categories of documents in paragraphs (A)-(K). In essence, the 11 categories (each subject to a time frame limit of "January 1, 1993 to the present") were: (1) all documents "reflecting, referring, or relating to any direct or indirect sources of money or other things of value received by Webster Hubbell, his wife or children [collectively, the 'Hubbell family'] * * *, 'including but not limited to the identity of employers or clients of legal or any other type of work'; (3) all documents 'reflecting, referring, or related to' any 'direct or indirect sources of money or other things of value' received by the Hubbell family, including 'billing memoranda, draft statements, bills, final statements and/or bills for work performed or time billed'; (3) copies of all bank records of the Hubbell family, including 'statements, registers, ledgers, canceled checks, deposit items and wire transfers'; (4) all documents reflecting, referring, or related to 'time worked or billed by Webster Hubbell,' including 'original time sheets, books, notes, papers, and/or computer records'; (5) all documents reflecting 'expenses incurred by and/or disbursements of money by Webster Hubbell for work performed or to be performed'; (6) all documents 'reflecting, referring, or relating to Webster Hubbell's schedule of activities,' including 'all calendars, daytimers, time books, appointment books, diaries, records of reverse

telephone toll charges, credit card calls, telephone message slips, logs, other telephone records, minutes databases, electronic mail messages, travel records, itineraries, tickets for transportation of any kind, payments, bills, expense backup documentation, schedules, and/or any other document or database that would disclose Webster Hubbell's activities'; (7) all documents 'reflecting, referring, or relating to any retainer agreements or contracts for employment' of the Hubbell family; (8) all 'tax returns, tax return information, including but not limited to all W-2s, form 1099s, schedules, draft returns, work papers, and backup documents filed, created or held by or on behalf of [the Hubbell family], and/or any business in which [the Hubbell family] holds or has held an interest'; (9) all documents 'reflecting, referring, or relating to work performed or to be performed for the City of Los Angeles, the Los Angeles Department of Airports or any other Los Angeles municipal or governmental entity, Mary Leslie, and/or Alan Arkatov'; (10) all documents 'reflecting, referring, or related to work performed by [the Hubbell family] on the recommendation, counsel, or other influence of Mary Leslie and/or Alan Arkatov'; and (11) all documents related to work performed for or on behalf of specified entities (e.g., Lippo Ltd.) and specified individuals (e.g., James Riady) 'or any affiliate, subsidiary, or corporation owned or controlled by or related to the aforementioned entities or individuals.' "

30, 1998, a grand jury in the District of Columbia returned a 10–count indictment charging respondent with various tax-related crimes and mail and wire fraud. The District Court dismissed the indictment relying, in part, on the ground that the Independent Counsel's use of the subpoenaed documents violated § 6002 because all of the evidence he would offer against respondent at trial derived either directly or indirectly from the testimonial aspects of respondent's immunized act of producing those documents. Noting that the Independent Counsel had admitted that he was not investigating tax-related issues when he issued the subpoena, and that he had "learned about the unreported income and other crimes from studying the records' contents," the District Court characterized the subpoena as "the quintessential fishing expedition." * * *

The Court of Appeals vacated the judgment and remanded for further proceedings. The majority concluded that the District Court had incorrectly relied on the fact that the Independent Counsel did not have prior knowledge of the contents of the subpoenaed documents. The question the District Court should have addressed was the extent of the Government's independent knowledge of the documents' existence and authenticity, and of respondent's possession or control of them. It explained: "On remand, the district court should hold a hearing in which it seeks to establish the extent and detail of the [G]overnment's knowledge of Hubbell's financial affairs (or of the paperwork documenting it) on the day the subpoena issued. It is only then that the court will be in a position to assess the testimonial value of Hubbell's response to the subpoena. Should the Independent Counsel prove capable of demonstrating with reasonable particularity a prior awareness that the exhaustive litany of documents sought in the subpoena existed and were in Hubbell's possession, then the wide distance evidently traveled from the subpoena to the substantive allegations contained in the indictment would be based upon legitimate intermediate steps. To the extent that the information conveyed through Hubbell's compelled act of production provides the necessary linkage, however, the indictment deriving therefrom is tainted."

In the opinion of the dissenting judge, the majority failed to give full effect to the distinction between the contents of the documents and the limited testimonial significance of the act of producing them. In his view, as long as the prosecutor could make use of information contained in the documents or derived therefrom without any reference to the fact that respondent had produced them in response to a subpoena, there would be no improper use of the testimonial aspect of the immunized act of production. In other words, the constitutional privilege and the statute conferring use immunity would only shield the witness from the use of any information resulting from his subpoena response "beyond what the prosecutor would receive if the documents appeared in the grand jury room or in his office unsolicited and unmarked, like manna from heaven."

On remand, the Independent Counsel acknowledged that he could not satisfy the "reasonable particularity" standard prescribed by the Court of Appeals and entered into a conditional plea agreement with respondent. In essence, the agreement provides for the dismissal of the charges unless this Court's disposition of the case makes it reasonably likely that respondent's "act of production immunity" would not pose a significant bar to his prosecution. The case is not moot, however, because the agreement also provides for the entry of a guilty plea and a sentence that will not include incarceration if we should reverse and issue an opinion that is sufficiently favorable to the Government to satisfy that condition. Despite that agreement, we granted the Independent Counsel's petition for a writ of certiorari in order to determine the precise scope of a grant of immunity with respect to the production of documents in response to a subpoena. We now affirm.

It is useful to preface our analysis of the constitutional issue with a restatement of certain propositions that are not in dispute. The term "privilege against self-incrimination" is not an entirely accurate description of a person's constitutional protection against being "compelled in any criminal case to be a witness against himself." The word "witness" in the constitutional text limits the relevant category of compelled incriminating communications to those that are "testimonial" in character.[8] As Justice Holmes observed, there is a significant difference between the use of compulsion to extort communications from a defendant and compelling a person to engage in conduct that may be incriminating. Thus, even though the act may provide incriminating evidence, a criminal suspect may be compelled to put on a shirt, to provide a blood sample or handwriting exemplar, or to make a recording of his voice. The act of exhibiting such physical characteristics is not the same as a sworn communication by a witness that relates either express or implied assertions of fact or belief. * * *

More relevant to this case is the settled proposition that a person may be required to produce specific documents even though they contain incriminating assertions of fact or belief because the creation of those documents was not "compelled" within the meaning of the privilege. [*Fisher v. United States*]. * * * It is clear, therefore, that respondent Hubbell could not avoid compliance with the subpoena served on him merely because the demanded documents contained incriminating evidence, whether written by others or voluntarily prepared by himself. * * * On the other hand, we have also made it clear that the act of producing documents in response to a subpoena may have a compelled testimonial aspect. We have held that "the act of production" itself may implicitly communicate "statements of fact" [*Doe II*]. By "producing documents in compliance with a subpoena, the witness would admit that the papers existed, were in his possession or control, and were authentic." Moreover, as was true in this case, when the custodian of documents responds to a subpoena, he may be compelled to take the witness stand and answer questions designed to determine whether he has produced everything demanded by the subpoena. The answers to those questions, as well as the act of production itself, may certainly communicate information about the existence, custody, and authenticity of the documents. Whether the constitutional privilege protects the answers to such questions, or protects the act of production itself, is a question that is distinct from the question whether the unprotected contents of the documents themselves are incriminating.

Finally, the phrase "in any criminal case" in the text of the Fifth Amendment might have been read to limit its coverage to compelled testimony that is used against the defendant in the trial itself. It has, however, long been settled that its protection encompasses compelled statements that lead to the discovery of incriminating evidence even though the statements themselves are not incriminating and are not introduced into evidence. * * * Compelled testimony that communicates information that may "lead to incriminating evidence" is privileged even if the information itself is not inculpatory. * * * It is the Fifth Amendment's protection against the prosecutor's use of incriminating information derived directly or indirectly from the compelled testimony of the respondent that is of primary relevance in this case.

8. "It is consistent with the history of and the policies underlying the Self–Incrimination Clause to hold that the privilege may be asserted only to resist compelled explicit or implicit disclosures of incriminating information. Historically, the privilege was intended to prevent the use of legal compulsion to extract from the accused a sworn communication of facts which would incriminate him. Such was the process of the ecclesiastical courts and the Star Chamber—the inquisitorial method of putting the accused upon his oath and compelling him to answer questions designed to uncover uncharged offenses, without evidence from another source. * * * "*Doe v. United States* [p. 736, cited as *Doe II*].

Acting pursuant to 18 U.S.C. § 6002, the District Court entered an order compelling respondent to produce "any and all documents" described in the grand jury subpoena and granting him "immunity to the extent allowed by law." In *Kastigar v. United States* [p. 703], we upheld the constitutionality of § 6002 because the scope of the "use and derivative-use" immunity that it provides is coextensive with the scope of the constitutional privilege against self-incrimination. * * * We particularly emphasized the critical importance of protection against a future prosecution" 'based on knowledge and sources of information obtained from the compelled testimony.' " * * * [W]e held that the statute imposes an affirmative duty on the prosecution, not merely to show that its evidence is not tainted by the prior testimony, but "to prove that the evidence it proposes to use is derived from a legitimate source wholly independent of the compelled testimony." * * * The "compelled testimony" that is relevant in this case is not to be found in the contents of the documents produced in response to the subpoena. It is, rather, the testimony inherent in the act of producing those documents. The disagreement between the parties focuses entirely on the significance of that testimonial aspect.

The Government correctly emphasizes that the testimonial aspect of a response to a subpoena duces tecum does nothing more than establish the existence, authenticity, and custody of items that are produced. We assume that the Government is also entirely correct in its submission that it would not have to advert to respondent's act of production in order to prove the existence, authenticity, or custody of any documents that it might offer in evidence at a criminal trial; indeed, the Government disclaims any need to introduce any of the documents produced by respondent into evidence in order to prove the charges against him. It follows, according to the Government, that it has no intention of making improper "use" of respondent's compelled testimony. The question, however, is not whether the response to the subpoena may be introduced into evidence at his criminal trial. That would surely be a prohibited "use" of the immunized act of production. But the fact that the Government intends no such use of the act of production leaves open the separate question whether it has already made "derivative use" of the testimonial aspect of that act in obtaining the indictment against respondent and in preparing its case for trial. It clearly has.

It is apparent from the text of the subpoena itself that the prosecutor needed respondent's assistance both to identify potential sources of information and to produce those sources. See Appendix [fn. a supra]. Given the breadth of the description of the 11 categories of documents called for by the subpoena, the collection and production of the materials demanded was tantamount to answering a series of interrogatories asking a witness to disclose the existence and location of particular documents fitting certain broad descriptions. The assembly of literally hundreds of pages of material in response to a request for "any and all documents reflecting, referring, or relating to any direct or indirect sources of money or other things of value received by or provided to" an individual or members of his family during a 3-year period, is the functional equivalent of the preparation of an answer to either a detailed written interrogatory or a series of oral questions at a discovery deposition. Entirely apart from the contents of the 13,120 pages of materials that respondent produced in this case, it is undeniable that providing a catalog of existing documents fitting within any of the 11 broadly worded subpoena categories could provide a prosecutor with a "lead to incriminating evidence," or "a link in the chain of evidence needed to prosecute."

Indeed, the record makes it clear that that is what happened in this case. The documents were produced before a grand jury sitting in the Eastern District of Arkansas in aid of the Independent Counsel's attempt to determine whether respondent had violated a commitment in his first plea agreement. The use of those sources of information eventually led to the return of an indictment by a grand jury sitting in the District of Columbia for offenses that apparently are unrelated to that plea agreement. What the District Court characterized as a "fishing expedition" did produce a fish, but not the one that the Independent Counsel expected to hook. It is abundantly clear that the testimonial aspect of respondent's act of producing subpoenaed documents was the first step in a chain of evidence that led to this prosecution. The documents did not magically appear in the prosecutor's office like "manna from heaven." They arrived there only after respondent asserted his constitutional privilege, received a grant of immunity, and—under the compulsion of the District Court's order—took the mental and physical steps necessary to provide the prosecutor with an accurate inventory of the many sources of potentially incriminating evidence sought by the subpoena. It was only through respondent's truthful reply to the subpoena that the Government received the incriminating documents of which it made "substantial use ... in the investigation that led to the indictment." Brief for United States 3.

For these reasons, we cannot accept the Government's submission that respondent's immunity did not preclude its derivative use of the produced documents because its "possession of the documents [was] the fruit only of a simple physical act—the act of producing the documents." Brief, at 29. It was unquestionably necessary for respondent to make extensive use of "the contents of his own mind" in identifying the hundreds of documents responsive to the requests in the subpoena. The assembly of those documents was like telling an inquisitor the combination to a wall safe, not like being forced to surrender the key to a strongbox. *Doe II*, at n. 9 [p. 738]. The Government's anemic view of respondent's act of production as a mere physical act that is principally non-testimonial in character and can be entirely divorced from its "implicit" testimonial aspect so as to constitute a "legitimate, wholly independent source" (as required by *Kastigar*) for the documents produced simply fails to account for these realities.

In sum, we have no doubt that the constitutional privilege against self-incrimination protects the target of a grand jury investigation from being compelled to answer questions designed to elicit information about the existence of sources of potentially incriminating evidence. That constitutional privilege has the same application to the testimonial aspect of a response to a subpoena seeking discovery of those sources. Before the District Court, the Government arguably conceded that respondent's act of production in this case had a testimonial aspect that entitled him to respond to the subpoena by asserting his privilege against self-incrimination. * * * On appeal and again before this Court, however, the Government has argued that the communicative aspect of respondent's act of producing ordinary business records is insufficiently "testimonial" to support a claim of privilege because the existence and possession of such records by any businessman is a "foregone conclusion" under our decision in *Fisher v. United States*. This argument both misreads *Fisher* and ignores our subsequent decision in *Doe I*. * * * Whatever the scope of this "foregone conclusion" rationale, the facts of this case plainly fall outside of it. While in *Fisher* the Government already knew that the documents were in the attorneys' possession and could independently confirm their existence and authenticity through the accountants who created them, here the Government has not shown that it had any prior knowledge of either the existence or the whereabouts of the 13,120 pages of documents ultimately produced by respondent. The Government cannot cure this deficiency through the overbroad argument that a businessman such as respondent will always possess general business and tax records that fall within the broad categories described in this subpoena. The *Doe I* subpoenas also sought several broad categories of general business records, yet we upheld the District Court's finding that the act of producing those records would involve testimonial self-incrimination.

Given our conclusion that respondent's act of production had a testimonial aspect, at least with respect to the existence and location of the documents sought by the Government's subpoena, respondent could not be compelled to produce those documents without first receiving a grant of immunity under § 6003. As we construed § 6002 in *Kastigar*, such immunity is co-extensive with the constitutional privilege. *Kastigar* requires that respondent's motion to dismiss the indictment on immunity grounds be granted unless the Government proves that the evidence it used in obtaining the indictment and proposed to use at trial was derived from legitimate sources "wholly independent" of the testimonial aspect of respondent's immunized conduct in assembling and producing the documents described in the subpoena. The Government, however, does not claim that it could make such a showing. Rather, it contends that its prosecution of respondent must be considered proper unless someone—presumably respondent—shows that "there is some substantial relation between the compelled testimonial communications implicit in the act of production (as opposed to the act of production standing alone) and some aspect of the information used in the investigation or the evidence presented at trial." Brief for United States 9. We could not accept this submission without repudiating the basis for our conclusion in *Kastigar* that the statutory guarantee of use and derivative-use immunity is as broad as the constitutional privilege itself. This we are not prepared to do. Accordingly, the indictment against respondent must be dismissed. The judgment of the Court of Appeals is affirmed. * * *

Chief Justice REHNQUIST dissents and would reverse the judgment of the Court of Appeals in part, for the reasons given by Judge Williams in his dissenting opinion in that court, 167 F.3d 552, 597 (C.A.D.C.1999).[b]

Justice THOMAS, with whom Justice SCALIA joins, concurring.

Our decision today involves the application of the act-of-production doctrine, which provides that persons compelled to turn over incriminating papers or other physical evidence pursuant to a subpoena duces tecum or a summons may invoke the Fifth Amendment privilege against self-incrimination as a bar to production only where the act of producing the evidence would contain "testimonial" features. I join the opinion of the Court because it properly applies this doctrine, but I write separately to note that this doctrine may be inconsistent with the original meaning of the Fifth Amendment's Self–Incrimination Clause. A substantial body of evidence suggests that the Fifth Amendment privilege protects against the compelled production not just of incriminating testimony, but of any incriminating evidence. In a future case, I would be willing to reconsider the scope and meaning of the Self–Incrimination Clause.

---

b. Judge Williams reasoned that, since the prosecution had "relied on the documents only for the information they contained," it had not made use of any testimonial elements of the act of production with respect to Hubbell's possession or authentication. As to "existence," the *Fisher* reasoning should appropriately limit the testimonial element of the act of production to the act's acknowledging "responsiveness of the documents to the subpoena." That would prohibit the government from "referring back to the subpoena to identify the documents and to clarify relationships that were not clear on their face." But it would not extend to "existence in a quite different sense—the fact that these particular pieces of paper are in being," for that "is quite easily confirmed by these papers own physical existence." Whether or not the government could previously establish that physical existence as a foregone conclusion, the act of production was not testimonial in establishing that existence, just as the act of providing a blood sample or a handwriting exemplar is not testimonial in establishing what third persons observe—that blood or handwriting come from the particular person. Thus, just as the prosecutor could make use of data drawn from the blood and handwriting (blood type, DNA, or handwriting idiosyncracies), the prosecutor could use the contents of the documents.

The Fifth Amendment provides that "[n]o person ... shall be compelled in any criminal case to be a witness against himself." The key word at issue in this case is "witness." The Court's opinion, relying on prior cases, essentially defines "witness" as a person who provides testimony, and thus restricts the Fifth Amendment's ban to only those communications "that are 'testimonial' in character." None of this Court's cases, however, has undertaken an analysis of the meaning of the term at the time of the founding. A review of that period reveals substantial support for the view that the term "witness" meant a person who gives or furnishes evidence, a broader meaning than that which our case law currently ascribes to the term.[c] If this is so, a person who responds to a subpoena duces tecum would be just as much a "witness" as a person who responds to a subpoena ad testificandum.[1] * * *

This Court has not always taken the approach to the Fifth Amendment that we follow today. The first case interpreting the Self–Incrimination Clause—*Boyd v. United States*—was decided, though not explicitly, in accordance with the understanding that "witness" means one who gives evidence. * * * But this Court's decision in *Fisher v. United States*, rejected this understanding, permitting the Government to force a person to furnish incriminating physical evidence and protecting only the "testimonial" aspects of that transfer. In so doing, *Fisher* not only failed to examine the historical backdrop to the Fifth Amendment, it also required—as illustrated by extended discussion in the opinions below in this case—a difficult parsing of the act of responding to a subpoena duces tecum. None of the parties in this case has asked us to depart from *Fisher*, but in light of the historical evidence that the Self–Incrimination Clause may have a broader reach than *Fisher* holds, I remain open to a reconsideration of that decision and its progeny in a proper case.

Notes and Questions

1. Reasonable particularity. Does the *Hubbell* Court, in effect, sustain the lower court ruling that the government could utilize the contents of the documents to seek other evidence only if it could demonstrate with "reasonable particularity" prior awareness of the document? See CRIMPROC § 8.13(a) (2002 pocket part), arguing that *Hubbell* adopts such a standard as to establishing existence and possession as a foregone conclusion, and raising the question of "how precisely the government must identify the documents by reference to its prior knowledge * * *. Must it, for example identify a specific document as one known to be in the subpoenaed party's possession (e.g., an airline ticket for a known trip on a particular day) or may it refer to a somewhat broader grouping of documents upon showing that the party engaged in a particular type of activity

c. Justice Thomas cited the following sources from that period: (1) dictionary definitions of the term "witness"; (3) state constitutional provisions that granted a right against compulsion "to give evidence" or to "furnish evidence"; (3) the use of similar wording by the four states that proposed inclusion of a self-incrimination provision in the Bill of Rights, and the lack of any indication that Madison's "unique phrasing" in the proposal he offered to Congress was designed to narrow those state proposals; and (4) the Sixth Amendment's compulsory process clause, which the Court had long held to encompass the right to secure papers as well as testimony. For a more extensive review of this historical material, see Richard A. Nagareda, *Compulsion "To Be A Witness" and the Resurrection of Boyd*, 74 N.Y.U.L.Rev. 1575 (1999), also cited by Justice Thomas.

1. Even if the term "witness" in the Fifth Amendment referred to someone who provides testimony, as this Court's recent cases suggest without historical analysis, it may well be that at the time of the founding a person who turned over documents would be described as providing testimony. See Amey v. Long, 9 East. 472, 484, 103 Eng. Rep. 653, 658 (K.B.1808) (referring to documents requested by subpoenas duces tecum as "written ... testimony"). * * *

which involved receipt of such documents (e.g., airline tickets from a specific airline which the subpoenaed party regularly used)?"

2. Does *Hubbell's* reference to the subpoena requiring "respondent to make extensive use of the 'contents of his own mind'" (p. 722) in responding to the subpoena further require, to avoid a successful self-incrimination claim, that the subpoena use a description of the requested documents that would allow the subpoenaed party to identify the documents without reference "to his or her special knowledge of historical fact"–that is, identify the documents "by reference to such features as letterhead, signature, or location?" CRIMPROC § 8.13(a) (2002 pocket part) (questioning whether such particularity in identification is required where the foregone conclusion standard is met as to the particular class of document).

3. Would the combination of requiring "reasonable particularity" in the government's prior awareness of the subpoenaed party's possession of the document and "reasonable particularity" in the subpoena's description of the document be equivalent to requiring the probable cause needed to obtain a search warrant. See William J. Stuntz, *O.J. Simpson, Bill Clinton, and the Transsubstantive Fourth Amendment*, 114 Harv. L. Rev. 842 (2001): "Last Term, in *United States v. Hubbell*, the Supreme Court appeared to conclude that unless the government knows—really knows—of a particular document's existence, a subpoena's target is free to refuse to turn the document over, because the act of producing the document would testify to the fact that it does indeed exist. Of course, if the government really does know that the document exists, and hence knows what is in it (knowledge of content tends to track knowledge of existence), the government can probably get a warrant to search for and seize the document." Compare CRIMPROC § 8.13(a) (2001 pocket part), noting that the *Hubbell*, in distinguishing *Fisher*, did not necessarily indicate that a foregone conclusion showing must be as strong as that in *Fisher*, and even such a showing is hardly the equivalent of probable cause: "For example, the government may learn from an employee that a particular document exists and that it is the most likely of all documents to contain information relating to a particular criminal activity (e.g., price-fixing), but have only a mere suspicion that the crime was actually committed—and thus be short of probable cause, but have a proper basis for a grand jury investigation."

4. *Incrimination.* *Hubbell* notes, consistent with *Fisher* and *Doe I*, that whether the privilege protects the answers as to "existence, custody, and authenticity" provided by the act of production is a "question distinct from the question whether the unprotected contents of the documents are incriminating" (p. 720). But once it is determined that those answers are testimonial, does *Hubbell* now clearly establish that the potential incriminating character of the "unprotected contents of the document" is relevant in determining whether those answers suggest a sufficient likelihood of incrimination to be protected by the privilege? See Note 6, p. 716. Is *Hubbell* a case of limited value on the "potential-incrimination" issue because the Court there was examining the issue after the documents had been produced and the government had used the combination of those answers and the contents of the documents in obtaining derivative evidence, as compared to the usual setting of a challenge prior to the production of the documents (as in *Fisher* and *Doe I*)?

5. *Act-of-production immunity.* Does *Hubbell* confirm Justice Marshall's view of the consequences of providing act-of-production immunity? See Note 7, p. 717. Would the government be prohibited from making use of the contents of documents obtained through act-of-production immunity if the subpoenaed party, in identifying the documents, did not thereby furnish information as to the relationship of the documents to the transactions under investigation? For example, if the government, in a grand jury investigation of possible antitrust violations by a sole proprietor, give the sole proprietor act-of-production immunity for the production of a particular type of employment record that would identify those ex-employees who had been discharged over that time frame, would it then be prohibited from using information it gained from interviewing those ex-employees (possibly disgruntled and therefore a ripe source of information)?

6. *Compelled-to-give-evidence.* Does the position for which Justice Thomas urges reconsideration find support in any aspect of *Boyd* other than its precise holding? See fn. a, p. 667. Would the replacement of *Fisher* with a "compelled-to-give-evidence" standard also require reconsideration of the Court's modification of other aspect of *Boyd's* analysis (e.g., the recognition of a "collective entity exception," see Pt. D infra)? Would adoption of that standard require that the Court also reject the line of identification-procedure cases cited in *Hubbell* as illustrating the limitation of the privilege to "compelled incriminating communications" that are "testimonial in character" (p. 720)? *Nagareda*, fn. c, p. 724, notes that, while the concept of "giving evidence" is hardly limited to documentary evidence, in the identification-procedure cases, a distinction can be drawn where the government is not requiring the affirmative act of production, but simply is "taking the evidence" from the body of the person. See also fn. 9, p. 619.

D. THE ENTITY EXCEPTION

BRASWELL V. UNITED STATES
487 U.S. 99, 108 S.Ct. 2284, 101 L.Ed.2d 98 (1988).

Chief Justice REHNQUIST delivered the opinion of the Court.

This case presents the question whether the custodian of corporate records may resist a subpoena for such records on the ground that the act of production would incriminate him in violation of the Fifth Amendment. We conclude that he may not. * * *

[A federal grand jury issued a subpoena to petitioner Braswell, as the president of two corporations, requiring him to produce the books and records of the two corporations, Worldwide Machinery, Inc. and Worldwide Purchasing, Inc. Petitioner had funded Worldwide Purchasing with his 100 percent interest in Worldwide Machinery and was the sole shareholder of Worldwide Purchasing. While both corporations had three directors, petitioner, his wife, and his mother, only petitioner had authority over the business affairs of the corporations. The grand jury subpoena provided that petitioner could deliver the records to the grand jury agent serving the subpoena and did not require petitioner to testify. Petitioner moved to quash the subpoena, arguing that the act or producing the records would continue a violation of his Fifth Amendment privilege against self-incrimination. The district court denied the motion and the Fifth Circuit affirmed.]

There is no question but that the contents of the subpoenaed business records are not privileged. See *United States v. Doe* [p. 713, *Doe I*]; *Fisher v. United States*. Similarly, petitioner asserts no self-incrimination claim on behalf of the corporations; it is well established that such artificial entities are not protected by the Fifth Amendment. *Bellis v. United States*, 417 U.S. 85, 94 S.Ct. 2179, 40 L.Ed.2d 678 (1974). Petitioner instead relies solely upon the argument that his act of producing the documents has independent testimonial significance, which would incriminate him individually, and that the Fifth Amendment prohibits government compulsion of that act. The bases for this argument are extrapolated from the decisions of this Court in *Fisher* and *Doe*. * * *

Had petitioner conducted his business as a sole proprietorship, *Doe* would require that he be provided the opportunity to show that his act of production would entail testimonial self-incrimination. But petitioner has operated his business through the corporate form, and we have long recognized that for purposes of the Fifth Amendment, corporations and other collective entities are treated differently from individuals. This doctrine—known as the collective entity rule—has a lengthy and distinguished pedigree.

The rule was first articulated by the Court in the case of *Hale v. Henkel,* 201 U.S. 43, 26 S.Ct. 370, 50 L.Ed. 652 (1906). Hale, a corporate officer, had been served with a subpoena ordering him to produce corporate records and to testify concerning certain corporate transactions. Although Hale was protected by personal immunity, he sought to resist the demand for the records by interposing a Fifth Amendment privilege on behalf of the corporation. The Court rejected that argument: "[W]e are of the opinion that there is a clear distinction * * * between an individual and a corporation, and * * * the latter has no right to refuse to submit its books and papers for an examination at the suit of the State." The Court explained that the corporation "is a creature of the State," with powers limited by the State. As such, the State may, in the exercise of its right to oversee the corporation, demand the production of corporate records. * * * * a

Although *Hale* settled that a corporation has no Fifth Amendment privilege, the Court did not address whether a corporate officer could resist a subpoena for corporate records by invoking his personal privilege—Hale had been protected by immunity. In *Wilson v. United States,* 221 U.S. 361, 31 S.Ct. 538, 55 L.Ed. 771 (1911), the Court answered that question in the negative. * * * Wilson refused to produce [subpoenaed corporate] books, arguing that the Fifth Amendment prohibited compulsory production of personally incriminating books that he held and controlled. The Court rejected this argument, observing * * *: "[Wilson] held the corporate books subject to the corporate duty. If the corporation were guilty of misconduct, he could not withhold its books to save it; and if he were implicated in the violations of law, he could not withhold the books to protect himself from the effect of their disclosures. The [State's] reserved power of visitation would seriously be embarrassed, if not wholly defeated in its effective exercise, if guilty officers could refuse inspection of the records and papers of the corporation. No personal privilege to which they are entitled requires such a conclusion. * * * "

In a companion case, *Dreier v. United States,* 221 U.S. 394, 31 S.Ct. 550, 55 L.Ed. 784 (1911), the Court applied the holding in *Wilson* to a Fifth Amendment attack on a subpoena addressed to the corporate custodian. Although the subpoena in *Wilson* had been addressed to the corporation, the Court found the distinction irrelevant: "Dreier was not entitled to refuse the production of the corporate records. By virtue of the fact that they were the documents of the corporation in his custody, and not his private papers, he was under the obligation to produce them when called for by proper process."

The next significant step in the development of the collective entity rule occurred in *United States v. White,* 322 U.S. 694, 64 S.Ct. 1248, 88 L.Ed. 1542 (1944), in which the Court held that a labor union is a collective entity unprotected by the Fifth Amendment. * * * [We reasoned] that the Fifth Amendment privilege applies only to natural individuals and protects only private papers. Representatives of a "collective group" act as agents "[a]nd the official records and documents of the organization that are held by them in a representative rather than in a personal capacity cannot be the subject of the personal privilege

---

a. The Court also noted: "[T]he privilege claimed would practically nullify the whole Act of Congress [the Sherman Act]. Of what use would it be for the legislature to declare these combinations [in restraint of trade] unlawful if the judicial power may close the door of access to every available source of information upon the subject."

against self-incrimination, even though production of the papers might tend to incriminate them personally." With this principle in mind, the Court turned to whether a union is a collective group:

> "The test * * * is whether one can fairly say under all the circumstances that a particular type of organization has a character so impersonal in the scope of its membership and activities that it cannot be said to embody or represent the purely private or personal interests of its constituents, but rather to embody their common or group interests only. If so, the privilege cannot be invoked on behalf of the organization or its representatives in their official capacity. Labor unions—national or local, incorporated or unincorporated— clearly meet that test."

In applying the collective entity rule to unincorporated associations such as unions, the Court jettisoned reliance on the visitatorial powers of the State over corporations owing their existence to the State—one of the bases for earlier decisions.

The frontiers of the collective entity rule were expanded even further in *Bellis v. United States,* 417 U.S. 85, 94 S.Ct. 2179, 40 L.Ed.2d 678 (1974), in which the Court ruled that a partner in a small partnership could not properly refuse to produce partnership records. * * * After rehearsing prior precedent involving corporations and unincorporated associations, the Court examined the partnership form and observed that is had many of the incidents found relevant in prior collective entity decisions. The Court suggested that the test articulated in *White* for determining the applicability of the Fifth Amendment to organizations was "not particularly helpful in the broad range of cases." The Court rejected the notion that the "formulation in *White* can be reduced to a simple proposition based solely upon the size of the organization. It is well settled that no privilege can be claimed by the custodian of corporate records, regardless of how small the corporation may be." *Bellis* held the partnership's financial records in a "representative capacity" and therefore "his personal privilege against compulsory self-incrimination is inapplicable." Ibid.

The plain mandate of these decisions is that without regard to whether the subpoena is addressed to the corporation, or as here, to the individual in his capacity as a custodian, see *Dreier; Bellis,* a corporate custodian such as petitioner may not resist a subpoena for corporate records on Fifth Amendment grounds. Petitioner argues, however, that this rule falls in the wake of *Fisher* and *Doe.* In essence, petitioner's argument is as follows: In response to *Boyd v. United States,* with its privacy rationale shielding personal books and records, the Court developed the collective entity rule, which declares simply that corporate records are not private and therefore are not protected by the Fifth Amendment. The collective entity decisions were concerned with the contents of the documents subpoenaed, however, and not with the act of production. In *Fisher* and *Doe,* the Court moved away from the privacy based collective entity rule, replacing it with a compelled testimony standard under which the contents of business documents are never privileged but the act of producing the documents may be. Under this new regime, the act of production privilege is available without regard to the entity whose records are being sought. * * *

To be sure, the holding in *Fisher*—later reaffirmed in *Doe*—embarked upon a new course of Fifth Amendment analysis. We cannot agree, however, that it rendered the collective entity rule obsolete. The agency rationale undergirding the collective entity decisions, in which custodians asserted that production of entity records would incriminate them personally, survives. From *Wilson* forward, the Court has consistently recognized that the custodian of corporate or entity records holds those documents in a representative rather than a personal capacity.

Artificial entities such as corporations may act only through their agents, and, a custodian's assumption of his representative capacity leads to certain obligations, including the duty to produce corporate records on proper demand by the Government. Under those circumstances, the custodian's act of production is not deemed a personal act, but rather an act of the corporation. Any claim of Fifth Amendment privilege asserted by the agent would be tantamount to a claim of privilege by the corporation—which of course possesses no such privilege. * * *

Indeed, the opinion in *Fisher*—upon which petitioner places primary reliance—indicates that the custodian of corporate records may not interpose a Fifth Amendment objection to the compelled production of corporate records, even though the act of production may prove personally incriminating. The *Fisher* court cited the collective entity decisions with approval and offered those decisions to support the conclusion that the production of the accountant's workpapers would "not * * * involve testimonial self-incrimination." * * * In a footnote, the Court explained: "In these cases compliance with the subpoena is required even though the books have been kept by the person subpoenaed and his producing them would itself be sufficient authentication to permit their introduction against him." n. 14. The Court thus reaffirmed the obligation of a corporate custodian to comply with a subpoena addressed to him.

That point was reiterated by Justice Brennan in his concurrence in *Fisher*. Although Justice Brennan disagreed with the majority as to its use of the collective entity cases to support the proposition that the act of production is not testimonial, he nonetheless acknowledged that a custodian may not resist a subpoena on the ground that the act of production would be incriminating. * * * [For] "one in control of the records of an artificial organization undertakes an obligation with respect to those records foreclosing any exercise of his privilege." Thus, whether one concludes—as did the Court—that a custodian's production of corporate records is deemed not to constitute testimonial self-incrimination, or instead that a custodian waives the right to exercise the privilege, the lesson of *Fisher* is clear: A custodian may not resist a subpoena for corporate records on Fifth Amendment grounds.

Petitioner also attempts to extract support for his contention from *Curcio v. United States*, 354 U.S. 118, 77 S.Ct. 1145, 1 L.Ed.2d 1225 (1957). But rather than bolstering petitioner's argument, we think *Curcio* substantiates the Government's position. Curcio had been served with two subpoenas addressed to him in his capacity as secretary treasurer of a local union. One subpoena required that he produce union records, the other that he testify. Curcio appeared before the grand jury, stated that the books were not in his possession, and refused to answer any questions as to their whereabouts.

The *Curcio* Court made clear that with respect to a custodian of a collective entity's records, the line drawn was between oral testimony and other forms of incrimination. "A custodian, by assuming the duties of his office, undertakes the obligation to produce the books of which he is custodian in response to a rightful exercise of the State's visitorial [*sic*] powers. But he cannot lawfully be compelled, in the absence of a grant of adequate immunity from prosecution, to condemn himself by his own *oral testimony*. (Emphasis added). In distinguishing those cases in which a corporate officer was required to produce corporate records and merely identify them by oral testimony, the Court showed that it understood the testimonial nature of the act of production: "The custodian's act of producing books or records in response to a subpoena *duces tecum* is itself a representation that the documents produced are those demanded by the subpoena. Requiring the custodian to identify or authenticate the documents for admission in evidence merely makes explicit what is implicit in the production itself." In the face of this recognition, the Court nonetheless noted: "In this case petitioner might have been proceeded against for his failure to produce the records demanded by the subpoena *duces tecum.*"

We note further that recognizing a Fifth Amendment privilege on behalf of the records custodians of collective entities would have a detrimental impact on the Government's efforts to prosecute "white-collar crime," one of the most serious problems confronting law enforcement authorities. "The greater portion of evidence of wrongdoing by an organization or its representatives is usually found in the official records and documents of that organization. Were the cloak of the privilege to be thrown around these impersonal records and documents, effective enforcement of many federal and state laws would be impossible." *White.* If custodians could assert a privilege, authorities would be stymied not only in their enforcement efforts against those individuals but also in their prosecutions or organizations. In *Bellis*, the Court observed: "In view of the inescapable fact that an artificial entity can only act to produce its records through its individual officers or agents recognition of the individual's claim of privilege with respect to the financial records of the organization would substantially undermine the unchallenged rule that the organization itself is not entitled to claim any Fifth Amendment privilege, and largely frustrate legitimate governmental regulation of such organizations."

Petitioner suggests, however, that these concerns can be minimized by the simple expedient of either granting the custodian statutory immunity as to the act of production, 18 U.S.C. §§ 6002–6003, or addressing the subpoena to the corporation and allowing it to choose an agent to produce the records who can do so without incriminating himself. We think neither proposal satisfactorily addresses these concerns. Taking the last first, it is no doubt true that if a subpoena is addressed to a corporation, the corporation "must find some means by which to comply because no Fifth Amendment defense is available to it." The means most commonly used to comply is the appointment of an alternate custodian. But petitioner insists he cannot be required to aid the appointed custodian in his search for the demanded records, for any statement to the surrogate would itself be testimonial and incriminating. If this is correct, then petitioner's "solution" is a chimera. In situations such as this—where the corporate custodian is likely the only person with knowledge about the demanded documents—the appointment of a surrogate will simply not ensure that the documents sought will ever reach the grand jury room; the appointed custodian will essentially be sent on an unguided search.

This problem is eliminated if the Government grants the subpoenaed custodian statutory immunity for the testimonial aspects of his act of production. But that "solution" also entails a significant drawback. All of the evidence obtained under a grant of immunity to the custodian may of course be used freely against the corporation, but if the Government has any thought of prosecuting the custodian, a grant of act of production immunity can have serious consequences. Testimony obtained pursuant to a grant of statutory use immunity may be used neither directly nor derivatively. 18 U.S.C. § 6002. And "[o]ne raising a claim under [the federal immunity] statute need only show that he testified under a grant of immunity in order to shift to the government the heavy burden of proving that all of the evidence it proposes to use was derived from legitimate independent sources." *Kastigar* [p. 703]. Even in cases where the Government does not employ the immunized testimony for any purpose—direct or derivative— against the witness, the Government's inability to meet the "heavy burden" it bears may result in the preclusion of crucial evidence that was obtained legitimately.[10]

10. The dissent asserts that recognition of an act of production privilege on behalf of   corporate custodians will not seriously undermine law enforcement efforts directed against

Although a corporate custodian is not entitled to resist a subpoena on the ground that his act of production will be personally incriminating, we do think certain consequences flow from the fact that the custodian's act of production is one in his representative rather than personal capacity. Because the custodian acts as a representative, the act is deemed one of the corporation and not the individual. Therefore, the Government concedes, as it must, that it may make no evidentiary use of the "individual act" against the individual. For example, in a criminal prosecution against the custodian, the Government may not introduce into evidence before the jury the fact that the subpoena was served upon and the corporation's documents were delivered by one particular individual, the custodian. The Government has the right, however, to use the corporation's act of production against the custodian. The Government may offer testimony—for example, from the process server who delivered the subpoena and from the individual who received the records—establishing that the corporation produced the records subpoenaed. The jury may draw from the corporation's act of production the conclusion that the records in question are authentic corporate records, which the corporation possessed, and which it produced in response to the subpoena. And if the defendant held a prominent position within the corporation that produced the records, the jury may, just as it would had someone else produced the documents, reasonably infer that he had possession of the documents or knowledge of their contents. Because the jury is not told that the defendant produced the records, any nexus between the defendant and the documents results solely from the corporation's act of production and other evidence in the case.[11]

Consistent with our precedent, the United States Court of Appeals for the Fifth Circuit ruled that petitioner could not resist the subpoena for corporate documents on the ground that the act of production might tend to incriminate him. The judgment is therefore affirmed.

Justice KENNEDY, with whom Justice BRENNAN, Justice MARSHALL, and Justice SCALIA join, dissenting.

* * * The majority's apparent reasoning is that collective entities have no privilege and so their employees must have none either. The Court holds that a corporate agent must incriminate himself even when he is named in the subpoena and is a target of the investigation, and even when it is conceded that compliance requires compelled, personal, testimonial, incriminating assertions. I disagree with that conclusion; find no precedent for it; maintain that if there is a likelihood of personal self-incrimination the narrow use immunity permitted by statute can be granted without frustrating the investigation of collective entities; and submit that basic Fifth Amendment principles should not be avoided and manipulated, which is the necessary effect of this decision.

* * * The majority does not challenge the assumption that compliance with the subpoena here would require acts of testimonial self-incrimination from

those custodians because only the custodian's act of production need be immunized. But the burden of proving an independent source that a grant of immunity places on the Government could, in our view, have just such a deleterious effect on law enforcement efforts.

11. We reject the suggestion that the limitation on the evidentiary use of the custodian's act of production is the equivalent of constructive use immunity barred under our decision in *Doe* [see Note 7, p. 717]. Rather, the limitation is a necessary concomitant of the notion that a corporate custodian acts as an agent and not an individual when he produces corporate records in response to a subpoena addressed to him in his representative capacity.

We leave open the question whether the agency rationale supports compelling a custodian to produce corporate records when the custodian is able to establish, by showing for example that he is the sole employee and officer of the corporation, that the jury would inevitably conclude that he produced the records.

Braswell; indeed, the Government itself made this assumption in submitting its argument. The question presented, therefore, is whether an individual may be compelled, simply by virtue of his status as a corporate custodian, to perform a testimonial act which will incriminate him personally. The majority relies entirely on the collective entity rule in holding that such compulsion is constitutional.

* * * *Fisher* put to rest the notion that a privilege may be claimed with respect to the contents of business records that were voluntarily prepared. The act of producing documents stands on an altogether different footing. While a custodian has no necessary relation to the contents of documents within his control, the act of production is inescapably his own. Production is the precise act compelled by the subpoena, and obedience, in some cases, will require the custodian's own testimonial assertions. That was the basis of our recognition of the privilege in *United States v. Doe (Doe I)*. The entity processing the documents in *Doe* was, as the majority points out, a sole proprietorship, not a corporation, partnership, or labor union. But the potential for self-incrimination inheres in the act demanded of the individual, and as a consequence the nature of the entity is irrelevant to determining whether there is ground for the privilege.

* * * Recognition of the privilege here would * * * avoid adoption of the majority's metaphysical progression, which, I respectfully submit, is flawed. Beginning from ordinary principles of agency, the majority proceeds to the conclusion that when a corporate employee, or an employee of a labor union or partnership, complies with a subpoena for production of documents, his act is necessarily and solely the act of the entity. * * * [But] the heart of the matter, as everyone knows, is that the Government does not see Braswell as a mere agent at all; and the majority's theory is difficult to square with what will often be the Government's actual practice. The subpoena in this case was not directed to Worldwide Machinery Sales, Inc., or Worldwide Purchasing, Inc. It was directed to "Randy Braswell, President, Worldwide Machinery Sales, Inc., Worldwide Purchasing, Inc." and informed him that "[y]ou are hereby commanded" to provide the specified documents. The Government explained at oral argument that it often chooses to designate an individual recipient, rather than the corporation generally, when it serves a subpoena because "[we] want the right to make that individual comply with the subpoena." This is not the language of agency. By issuing a subpoena which the Government insists is "directed to petitioner personally," it has forfeited any claim that it is simply making a demand on a corporation that, in turn, will have to find a physical agent to perform its duty. What the Government seeks instead is the right to choose any corporate agent as a target of its subpoena and compel that individual to disclose certain information by his own actions.

The majority gives the corporate agent fiction a weight it simply cannot bear. In a peculiar attempt to mitigate the force of its own holdings, it impinges upon its own analysis by concluding that, while the Government may compel a named individual to produce records, in any later proceeding against the person it cannot divulge that he performed the act. But if that is so, it is because the Fifth Amendment protects the person without regard to his status as a corporate employee; and once this be admitted, the necessary support for the majority's case has collapsed. * * *

The majority's abiding concern is that if a corporate officer who is the target of a subpoena is allowed to assert the privilege, it will impede the Government's power to investigate corporations, unions, and partnerships, to uncover and prosecute white collar crimes, and otherwise to enforce its visitatorial powers. There are at least two answers to this. The first, and most fundamental, is that the text of the Fifth Amendment does not authorize exceptions premised on such rationales. Second, even if it were proper to invent such exceptions, the dangers prophesied by the majority are overstated.

Recognition of the right to assert a privilege does not mean it will exist in many cases. In many instances, the production of documents may implicate no testimonial assertions at all. * * * Further, to the extent testimonial assertions are being compelled, use immunity can be granted without impeding the investigation. Where the privilege is applicable, immunity will be needed for only one individual, and solely with respect to evidence derived from the act of production itself. The Government would not be denied access to the records it seeks, it would be free to use the contents of the records against everyone, and it would be free to use any testimonial act implicit in production against all but the custodian it selects. In appropriate cases the Government will be able to establish authenticity, possession, and control by means other than compelling assertions about them from a suspect.

In one sense the case before us may not be a particularly sympathetic one. Braswell was the sole stockholder of the corporation and ran it himself. Perhaps that is why the Court suggests he waived his Fifth Amendment self-incrimination rights by using the corporate form. One does not always, however, have the choice of his or her employer, much less the choice of the business enterprise through which the employer conducts its business. Though the Court here hints at a waiver, nothing in Fifth Amendment jurisprudence indicates that the acceptance of employment should be deemed a waiver of a specific protection that is as basic a part of our constitutional heritage as is the privilege against self-incrimination.

The law is not captive to its own fictions. Yet, in the matter before us the Court employs the fiction that personal incrimination of the employee is neither sought by the Government nor cognizable by the law. That is a regrettable holding, for the conclusion is factually unsound, unnecessary for legitimate regulation, and a violation of the Self–Incrimination Clause of the Fifth Amendment of the Constitution. For these reasons, I dissent.

Notes and Questions

1. *The collective entity rule.* Although neither the majority nor dissent in *Braswell* question the collective entity doctrine itself (as distinguished from its bearing on the availability of the privilege to the custodian), that doctrine has been questioned by commentators. See e.g., Mosteller, Note 4, p. 716; Gerstein, Note 6, p. 748; Stuntz, Note 1, p. 667. First, it is noted that several of the values traditionally cited as supporting the privilege (see p. 738) (e.g., a privacy interest) are clearly applicable to the prosecution of entities as well as individuals.[a] Second, it is suggested that the difficulties that application of the privilege would present

a. See e.g., Stuntz, Note 1, p. 667: "Even if harm to privacy is defined in purely dignitary terms, privacy is something that individuals possess within institutions not just outside of them." Moreover, the author notes, the "privacy interest in corporate documents was at least as plausible as Boyd's privacy interest in his invoices." The self-incrimination privilege has also been tied to various values (e.g., an accusatory system of justice, see Note 3, p. 743) that have long been extended to entities. In *Hale*, the dissent of Justices Brewer and Fuller argued that corporations had already been held to be "persons" under the due process clause, and therefore should be persons under the self-incrimination clause. Consider also the avail-

ability (and unavailability) to the collective entity of other constitutional rights, such as Fourth Amendment protection against unreasonable searches (applicable), Fifth Amendment protection against being placed twice in jeopardy (assumed to apply), the Fifth Amendment right to prosecution by grand jury indictment (not applicable, according to the Ninth Circuit, Since potential punishment, lacking imprisonment, is not "infamous"), the Sixth Amendment right to a jury trial (applicable). See Peter Henning, *The Conundrum of Corporate Criminal Liability: Seeking A Consistent Approach to the Constitutional Rights of Corporations in Criminal Prosecutions,* 63 Tenn.L. Rev. 793, (1996).

to "legitimate government regulation" (see p. 730) are also likely to be presented where a business is a sole proprietorship. Thus, the required records doctrine (see Note 5 infra), which also finds support in the state's regulatory authority, draws no distinction between collective entities and sole proprietors.[b] Finally, the point is made that the doctrine has been justified as not involving especially private records, as entity records are assumed to be accessible to various persons associated with the entity, but in some instances, the entity will be so small or particular records treated as so secretive as to limit accessibility to a single person.

2. Pragmatic consequences. Starting with *Hale* (see fn. a, p. 727) and continuing through *White, Bellis,* and *Braswell* (see p. 730), the Supreme Court has stressed the practical ramifications of allowing entities or their agents to claim the privilege against subpoenas to produce documents. Justice Kennedy responds that "the text of the Fifth Amendment does not authorize exceptions premised on such rationales" (pp. 732–33), but does that mean such concerns are irrelevant to resolving ambiguities in coverage? Cf. Stuntz, fn. c, p. 672 (arguing for greater recognition of the differences among crimes in the Fourth Amendment regulation of criminal investigation); Stuntz, Note 2, p. 668 (noting that early establishment of Fourth and Fifth Amendment limitations arose out of efforts to make more difficult the prosecution of a narrow range of objectional offenses, such as seditious libel).

3. Scope of the entity agent's obligation. In *Curcio v. United States,* discussed in *Braswell* (p. 729), the Court held that the obligation of the entity agent did not extend to explaining the whereabouts of records no longer in his possession. *Curcio* noted that lower court rulings had held that "a corporate officer who has been required by subpoena to produce corporate records may also be required, by oral testimony, to identify them," but those cases were "distinguishable" and the Court had no need "to pass on their validity." Does *Braswell* necessarily affirm those rulings? See *In re Custodian of Records of Variety Distributing,* 927 F.2d 244 (6th Cir.1991). Looking to *Braswell*'s discussion of *Curcio,* the *Variety Distributing* court concluded that the custodian can be required to authenticate the documents for admission in evidence, as that "merely makes explicit what is implicit in the production itself (*Curcio*)." This duty exists even though the necessary statements (e.g., that the custodian is familiar with the company's recordkeeping and knows the company has kept these records in the course of regular business activity) may be personally incriminating in some situations. However, "because the custodian of corporate records is acting in a representative rather than a personal capacity, he is protected against the future evidentiary use of the testimony." But see, Peter Henning, *Finding What Was Lost: Sorting Out the Custodian's Privilege Against Self–Incrimination From the Compelled Production of Records,* 77 Neb. L.Rev. 34 (1998) (*Variety Distributing* erred in reading *Curcio* as going beyond simply requiring the custodian "to testify before a grand jury only to make explicit to the grand jurors what was implicit in the production of records", and "compelling evidentiary testimony related solely to the trial phase").

---

b. Consider also Peter Henning, *Testing the Limits of Investigation and Prosecuting White Collar Crime,* 54 U. Pitt L.Rev. 406 (1992): "After *Braswell,* the production of the exact same types of records, such as invoices or ledgers, depends on whether the owner of the enterprise chose to incorporate the business, or maintain a sole proprietorship or small partnership arrangement. That decision can have momentous consequences, because if the business is not incorporated, the owner may be able to shield the records through the assertion of the Fifth Amendment privilege. It is even possible under *Braswell* for a person to own two businesses, one a corporation and the other a sole proprietorship, and be able to assert the privilege to resist production of one set of records yet be forced to produce the records for the other business. It is odd that the seemingly inconsequential choice of what organizational form to use for a business, which may have little if any effect of its operations, can determine the applicability of a constitutional right."

4. *The prohibition against evidentiary use of the custodian's act of production.* What is the grounding of the evidentiary-use prohibition imposed by *Braswell*? See Henning, supra Note 3, asking whether the Court here has established a "quasi-constitutional" prohibition or a standard based upon its "supervisory power." The prohibition of evidentiary use of the act of production does not bar use of the contents of the documents against the custodian. Justice Kennedy argues that the same would be true under statutory act-of-production immunity, which would protect the custodian only against the "testimonial act implicit in production" (p. 733). In light of the Court's subsequent decision in *Hubbell*, would the contents now be viewed as derived from that "testimonial act" (and therefore precluded from use by an immunity grant), assuming the government could not previously have established existence as a foregone conclusion? See Note 5, p. 725.

5. *Production by the "single-person" corporation.* What is the significance of the second paragraph of footnote 11 of *Braswell* ? In *In re Grand Jury 89–4 Subpoena Duces Tecum*, 727 F.Supp. 265 (E.D.Va.1989), suggested that the issue left open in that footnote could bear upon not only a one-person corporation, but also a small family corporation in which one member (Doe) was the dominant actor. The court noted that a two step inquiry was required: "(1) would a jury, told that the corporation produced the documents, nonetheless inevitably conclude that it was Doe who had possession of the documents and produced them, and if so (2) would this give rise to any incriminating inferences concerning a documents (i) existence, (ii) authenticity, or (iii) custody." Finding that an insufficient showing had been made as to the second step, the court found it unnecessary to consider the consequences if both inquiries produced affirmative responses. Would the court then hold the privilege applicable (and quash the subpoena), or could it simply require the corporation to make production through a specially appointed agent, with the jury informed that it was the agent who produced the documents on behalf of the corporation? If the latter approach is sufficient, would that agent be barred from testifying to conversations with the dominant actor that enabled him to identify the records (and to provide authentication, where needed)?

6. *Personal documents.* Where the document subpoenaed is a desk calendar, pocket diary, or similar item, the claim is oftener made that, through kept by a corporate employee, it constitutes a "personal record" and therefore is not subject to the entity doctrine. In responding to such a claim, courts apply a "multifactor balancing approach" that attempts to identify "the essential nature" of the document "in light of the entire context of [its] ownership preparation, and use." *In re Grand Jury Proceedings*, 55 F.3d 1012 (5th Cir.1995) ("We agree with the Second Circuit that the following nonexhaustive list of criteria is relevant in the inquiry: who prepared the document; the nature of its contents; its purpose or use; who possessed it; who had access to it; whether the corporation required its preparation; and whether its existence was necessary to or in furtherance of corporate business").

7. *"Required records."* *Shapiro v. United States*, 335 U.S. 1, 68 S.Ct. 1375, 92 L.Ed. 1787 (1948), expanding upon some dictum in *Wilson*, held that the self-incrimination clause is not violated by requiring a person to keep records of certain business activities and to make those records available for government inspection. Accordingly, a grand jury subpoena requiring the production of required records may not be successfully challenged on self-incrimination grounds even though the records are those of a business conducted as an individual proprietorship rather than an entity. See *Grand Jury Subpoena Duces Tecum (Underhill)*, 781 F.2d 64 (1986) (although act of production may be incriminating, *Fisher–Doe* do not apply to required records, as nothing in these opinions casts doubt as the "continuing validity of * * * *Shapiro* and its progeny"). Business records will not be classified as required records under *Shapiro* unless three prerequisites are met: (1) the governmental requirement that records be kept must be "essentially regulatory" in nature; (3) the records must be "of a kind which the regulated party has customarily kept," and (3) the records "must have assumed some 'public aspects' which render them at least analogous to public documents." *Grosso v. United States*, 390 U.S. 62, 88 S.Ct. 709, 19 L.Ed.2d 906 (1968). See also Stephen Saltzburg, *The Required Records Doctrine: Its Lessons for the Privilege Against Self–Incrimination*, 53 U.Chi.L.Rev. 6 (1986).[c]

8. The implications of the several doctrines discussed in this section were brought together in an unusual setting in *Baltimore City Department of Social Services v. Bouknight*, 493 U.S. 549, 110 S.Ct. 900, 107 L.Ed.2d 992 (1990). The Supreme Court there rejected a self-incrimination objection to a subpoena directing respondent Bouknight to produce her infant son, an abused child who had previously been declared a ward of the court. The Court noted that the respondent could not claim the privilege based upon "anything an examination of the [child] might reveal," as that would be a claim based upon "the contents or nature of the thing demanded." However, the mother could conceivably claim the privilege because "the act of production would amount to testimony regarding her control over and possession of [the child]." While the state could "readily introduce [other] evidence of Bouknight's continuing control over the child" (including the court order giving her limited custody and her previous statements reflecting control), her "implicit communication of control over [the child] at the moment of production might aid the state in prosecuting Bouknight [for child abuse]." The Court had no need to decide, however, whether "this limited testimonial assertion is sufficiently incriminating and sufficiently testimonial for purposes of the privilege." In receiving conditional custody from the juvenile court, the mother had "assumed custodial duties related to production" (analogous to that of an entity agent) and had done so as part of noncriminal regulatory scheme which included a production component (analogous to regulations sustained under the required records doctrine). The Court added that it had no need in the case before it "to define the precise limitations that may exist upon the State's ability to use the testimonial aspects of Bouknight's act of production in subsequent criminal proceedings," but the "imposition of such limitations," as done in *Braswell*, was not "foreclosed."

E.   FIFTH AMENDMENT VALUES: THE CASE OF COMPELLED WRITINGS

DOE v. UNITED STATES
487 U.S. 201, 108 S.Ct. 2341, 101 L.Ed.2d 184 (1988).

Justice BLACKMUN delivered the opinion of the Court.

This case presents the question whether a court order compelling a target of a grand jury investigation to authorize foreign banks to disclose records of his accounts, without identifying those documents or acknowledging their existence, violates the target's Fifth Amendment privilege against self-incrimination. * * *

---

c. The Court has also upheld other statutes requiring disclosure of information in a regulatory setting notwithstanding that such information "could well be 'a link in the chain' of evidence leading to prosecution." *California v. Byers*, 402 U.S. 424, 91 S.Ct. 1535, 29 L.Ed.2d 9 (1971). *Byers* sustained a state "hit and run" statute which required the driver of a motor vehicle involved in an accident to stop at the scene and give his name and address. The Court noted that such statutes were regulatory measures, "not intended to facilitate criminal convictions," and were directed to all persons who drove automobiles. Also, there was no disclosure of inherently illegal activity as "most automobile accidents occur without creating criminal liability."

[Petitioner, John Doe, was the target of a federal grand jury investigation of suspected fraudulent manipulation of oil cargoes and receipt of unreported income. Appearing before the grand jury pursuant to subpoena directing him to produce records of transactions in accounts at three named banks in the Cayman Islands and Bermuda, petitioner produced some of the records and testified that no additional records were within his possession. When questioned about the existence of additional records, he invoked the Fifth Amendment privilege against self-incrimination. Grand jury subpoenas then were issued to United States branches of each of the banks, but the banks refused to comply because their governments' laws prohibited disclosure of account records without the customer's consent. The prosecution then filed a motion with the district court requesting that petitioner be ordered to sign forms stating that he was "directing any bank * * * at which I may have a bank account of any kind or at which a corporation has a bank account of any kind upon which I am authorized to draw" to deliver records of those accounts to the grand jury. The form specifically noted that petitioner's directive was being made pursuant to court order, and that the directive was intended to provide compliance with the bank secrecy laws of the Cayman Islands and Bermuda. Petitioner refused to sign the consent directive on self-incrimination grounds, and after being held in contempt, sought appellate review. The Court of Appeals affirmed the contempt order.]

* * * Petitioner's sole claim is that his execution of the consent forms directing the banks to release records as to which the banks believe he has the right of withdrawal has independent testimonial significance that will incriminate him, and that the Fifth Amendment prohibits governmental compulsion of that act. * * * The execution of the consent directive at issue in this case obviously would be compelled, and we may assume that its execution would have an incriminating effect. The question on which this case turns is whether the act of executing the form is a "testimonial communication." The parties disagree about both the meaning of "testimonial" and whether the consent directive fits the proposed definitions.

Petitioner contends that a compelled statement is testimonial if the Government could use the content of the speech or writing, as opposed to its physical characteristics, to further a criminal investigation of the witness. The second half of petitioner's "testimonial" test is that the statement must be incriminating, which is, of course, already a separate requirement for invoking the privilege. Thus, Doe contends, in essence, that every written and oral statement significant for its content is necessarily testimonial for purposes of the Fifth Amendment. Under this view, the consent directive is testimonial because it is a declarative statement of consent made by Doe to the foreign banks, a statement that the Government will use to persuade the banks to produce potentially incriminating account records that would otherwise be unavailable to the grand jury.

The Government, on the other hand, suggests that a compelled statement is not testimonial for purposes of the privilege, unless it implicitly or explicitly relates a factual assertion or otherwise conveys information to the Government. It argues that, under this view, the consent directive is not testimonial because neither the directive itself nor Doe's execution of the form discloses or communicates facts or information. Petitioner disagrees.

The Government's view of the privilege * * * is derived largely from this Court's decisions in *Fisher* [p. 706] and *Doe I* [p. 713]. The issue presented in those cases was whether the act of producing subpoenaed documents, not itself the making of a statement, might nonetheless have some protected testimonial aspects. The Court concluded that the act of production could constitute protected testimonial communication because it might entail implicit statements of fact: by producing documents in compliance with a subpoena, the witness would admit that the papers existed, were in his possession or control, and were authentic. Thus, the Court made clear that the Fifth Amendment privilege against self-incrimination applies to acts that imply assertions of fact.

We reject petitioner's argument that this test does not control the determination as to when the privilege applies to oral or written statements. While the Court in *Fisher* and *Doe* did not purport to announce a universal test for determining the scope of the privilege, it also did not purport to establish a more narrow boundary applicable to acts alone. To the contrary, the Court applied basic Fifth Amendment principles. An examination of the Court's application of these principles in other cases indicates the Court's recognition that, in order to be testimonial, an accused's communication must itself, explicitly or implicitly, relate a factual assertion or disclose information.[9] Only then is a person compelled to be a "witness" against himself.

This understanding is perhaps most clearly revealed in those cases in which the Court has held that certain acts, though incriminating, are not within the privilege. Thus, a suspect may be compelled to furnish a blood sample, to provide a handwriting exemplar or a voice exemplar, to stand in a lineup, and to wear particular clothing. * * * These decisions are grounded on the proposition that "the privilege protects an accused only from being compelled to testify against himself, or otherwise provide the State with evidence of a testimonial or communicative nature." *Schmerber v. California* [p. 38]. * * * It is the "extortion of information from the accused," the attempt to force him "to disclose the contents of his own mind," that implicates the Self–Incrimination Clause. * * * "Unless some attempt is made to secure a communication—written, oral or otherwise—upon which reliance is to be placed as involving [the accused's] consciousness of the facts and the operations of his mind in expressing it, the demand made upon him is not a testimonial one." 8 J. Wigmore, Evidence § 2265 (McNaughton rev. 1961).

It is consistent with the history of and the policies underlying the Self–Incrimination Clause to hold that the privilege may be asserted only to resist compelled explicit or implicit disclosures of incriminating information. Historically, the privilege was intended to prevent the use of legal compulsion to extract from the accused a sworn communication of facts which would incriminate him. Such was the process of the ecclesiastical courts and the Star Chamber—the inquisitorial method of putting the accused upon his oath and compelling him to answer questions designed to uncover uncharged offenses, without evidence from another source. The major thrust of the policies undergirding the privilege is to prevent such compulsion. * * * The Court in *Murphy v. Waterfront Comm'n* [Note 3, p. 642] explained that the privilege is founded on

> "[1] our unwillingness to subject those suspected of crime to the cruel trilemma of self-accusation, perjury or contempt; [2] our preference for an accusatorial rather than an inquisitorial system of criminal justice; [3] our fear that self-incriminating statements will be elicited by inhumane treatment and abuses; [4] our sense of fair play which dictates 'a fair state-individual balance by requiring the government to leave the individual alone until good cause is shown for disturbing him and by requiring the government in its contest with the individual to shoulder the entire load,' . . . ; [5] our respect

---

9. We do not disagree with the dissent that "[t]he expression of the contents of an individual's mind" is testimonial communication for purposes of the Fifth Amendment. We simply disagree with the dissent's conclusion that the execution of the consent directive at issue here forced petitioner to express the contents of his mind. In our view, such compulsion is more like "be[ing] forced to surrender a key to a strong box containing incriminating documents," than it is like "be[ing] compelled to reveal the combination to [petitioner's] wall safe."

for the inviolability of the human personality and of the right of each individual 'to a private enclave where he may lead a private life,' ... ; [6] our distrust of self-deprecatory statements; and [7] our realization that the privilege, while sometimes 'a shelter to the guilty,' is often 'a protection to the innocent.' "

These policies are served when the privilege is asserted to spare the accused from having to reveal, directly or indirectly, his knowledge of facts relating him to the offense or from having to share his thoughts and beliefs with the Government.[11]

We are not persuaded by petitioner's arguments that our articulation of the privilege fundamentally alters the power of the Government to compel an accused to assist in his prosecution. There are very few instances in which a verbal statement, either oral or written, will not convey information or assert facts. The vast majority of verbal statements thus will be testimonial and, to that extent at least, will fall within the privilege. Furthermore, it should be remembered that there are many restrictions on the Government's prosecutorial practices in addition to the Self–Incrimination Clause. Indeed, there are other protections against governmental efforts to compel an unwilling suspect to cooperate in an investigation, including efforts to obtain information from him.[13] We are confident that these provisions, together with the Self–Incrimination Clause, will continue to prevent abusive investigative techniques.

* * * We turn, then, to consider whether Doe's execution of the consent directive at issue here would have testimonial significance. We agree with the Court of Appeals that it would not, because neither the form, nor its execution, communicates any factual assertions, implicit or explicit, or conveys any information to the Government.

The consent directive itself is not "testimonial." It is carefully drafted not to make reference to a specific account, but only to speak in the hypothetical. Thus, the form does not acknowledge that an account in a foreign financial institution is in existence or that it is controlled by petitioner. Nor does the form indicate whether documents or any other information relating to petitioner are present at the foreign bank, assuming that such an account does exist. The form does not even identify the relevant bank. Although the executed form allows the Govern-

---

11. Petitioner argues that at least some of these policies would be undermined unless the Government is required to obtain evidence against an accused from sources other than his compelled statements, whether or not the statements make a factual assertion or convey information. Petitioner accordingly maintains that the policy of striking an appropriate balance between the power of the Government and the sovereignty of the individual precludes the Government from compelling an individual to utter or write words that lead to incriminating evidence. Even if some of the policies underlying the privilege might support petitioner's interpretation of the privilege, "it is clear that the scope of the privilege does not coincide with the complex of values it helps to protect. Despite the impact upon the inviolability of the human personality, and upon our belief in an adversary system of criminal justice in which the Government must produce the evidence against an accused through its own independent labors, the prosecution is allowed to obtain and use ... evidence which although compelled is generally speaking not

'testimonial,' *Schmerber v. California.*" *Grosso v. United States,* 390 U.S. 62, 88 S.Ct. 709, 19 L.Ed.2d 906 (1968) (Brennan, J., concurring). If the societal interests in privacy, fairness, and restraint of governmental power are not unconstitutionally offended by compelling the accused to have his body serve as evidence that leads to the development of highly incriminating testimony, as *Schmerber* and its progeny make clear, it is difficult to understand how compelling a suspect to make a nonfactual statement that facilitates the production of evidence by someone else offends the privilege.

13. For example, the Fourth Amendment generally prevents the Government from compelling a suspect to consent to a search of his home; the attorney-client privilege prevents the Government from compelling a suspect to direct his attorney to disclose confidential communications; and the Due Process Clause imposes limitations on the Government's ability to coerce individuals into participating in criminal prosecutions, see generally *Rochin v. California* [p. 36].

ment access to a potential source of evidence, the directive itself does not point the Government toward hidden accounts or otherwise provide information that will assist the prosecution in uncovering evidence. The Government must locate that evidence "by the independent labor of its officers." As in *Fisher,* the Government is not relying upon the " 'truthtelling' " of Doe's directive to show the existence of, or his control over, foreign bank account records.

Given the consent directive's phraseology, petitioner's compelled act of executing the form has no testimonial significance either. By signing the form, Doe makes no statement, explicit or implicit, regarding the existence of a foreign bank account or his control over any such account. Nor would his execution of the form admit the authenticity of any records produced by the bank. Not only does the directive express no view on the issue, but because petitioner did not prepare the document, any statement by Doe to the effect that it is authentic would not establish that the records are genuine. Authentication evidence would have to be provided by bank officials.

Finally, we cannot agree with petitioner's contention that his execution of the directive admits or asserts Doe's consent. The form does not state that Doe "consents" to the release of bank records. Instead, it states that the directive "shall be construed as consent" with respect to Cayman Islands and Bermuda bank-secrecy laws. Because the directive explicitly indicates that it was signed pursuant to a court order, Doe's compelled execution of the form sheds no light on his actual intent or state of mind. The form does "direct" the bank to disclose account information and release any records that "may" exist and for which Doe "may" be a relevant principal. But directing the recipient of a communication to do something is not an assertion of fact or, at least in this context, a disclosure of information. In its testimonial significance, the execution of such a directive is analogous to the production of a handwriting sample or voice exemplar: it is a nontestimonial act. In neither case is the suspect's action compelled to obtain "any knowledge he might have."

We read the directive as equivalent to a statement by Doe that, although he expresses no opinion about the existence of, or his control over, any such account, he is authorizing the bank to disclose information relating to accounts over which, in the bank's opinion, Doe can exercise the right of withdrawal. * * * When forwarded to the bank along with a subpoena, the executed directive, if effective under local law, will simply make it possible for the recipient bank to comply with the Government's request to produce such records. As a result, if the Government obtains bank records after Doe signs the directive, the only factual statement made by anyone will be the *bank's* implicit declaration, by its act of production in response to the subpoena, that *it* believes the accounts to be petitioner's. Cf. *Fisher.* The fact that the bank's customer has directed the disclosure of his records "would say nothing about the correctness of the bank's representations." Brief for United States. Indeed, the Second and Eleventh Circuits have concluded that consent directives virtually identical to the one here are inadmissible as an admission by the signator of either control or existence. * * *

Justice STEVENS, dissenting.

A defendant can be compelled to produce material evidence that is incriminating. Fingerprints, blood samples, voice exemplars, handwriting specimens or other items of physical evidence may be extracted from a defendant against his will. But can he be compelled to use his mind to assist the prosecution in convicting him of a crime? I think not. He may in some cases be forced to surrender a key to a strong box containing incriminating documents, but I do not believe he can be compelled to reveal the combination to his wall safe—by word or deed.

The document the Government seeks to extract from John Doe purports to order third parties to take action that will lead to the discovery of incriminating evidence. The directive itself may not betray any knowledge petitioner may have about the circumstances of the offenses being investigated by the Grand Jury, but it nevertheless purports to evidence a reasoned decision by Doe to authorize action by others. The forced execution of this document differs from the forced production of physical evidence just as human beings differ from other animals.

If John Doe can be compelled to use his mind to assist the Government in developing its case, I think he will be forced "to be a witness against himself." The fundamental purpose of the Fifth Amendment was to mark the line between the kind of inquisition conducted by the Star Chamber and what we proudly describe as our accusatorial system of justice. It reflects "our respect for the inviolability of the human personality," *Murphy v. Waterfront Comm'n.* * * * In my opinion that protection gives John Doe the right to refuse to sign the directive authorizing access to the records of any bank account that he may control. Accordingly, I respectfully dissent.

Notes and Questions

1. **"Values analysis."** The Supreme Court has considered self-incrimination issues in a variety of different contexts, including police interrogation of suspects, compelled arrestee participation in identification procedures, grand jury subpoenas, suppression procedures, court-ordered defense discovery to the prosecution, the defendant's exercise of the privilege (through silence) at his trial, sentencing procedures, claims in civil proceedings, claims in legislative investigations, and regulatory schemes requiring disclosures. It has considered issues such as who is protected, what constitutes "compulsion," what constitutes "incrimination," what kinds of compelled and incriminatory evidence may not be used against defendant, how far that prohibition against use extends, what governmentally imposed burdens so impair the exercise of the privilege as to be unconstitutional, and what should be required for waiver of the privilege. The end result has been a variety of different doctrinal standards, each shaped to fit both the particular issue and the particular context in which it is presented. A common thread in the reasoning that produced those standards has been a reference to the basic "values" that underlie the privilege. While not every major Fifth Amendment opinion has included such a reference, a substantial majority have done so. Thus, Fifth Amendment values have been cited at least as frequently as two of the three other commonly cited points of reference (the language of the Amendment and the common law history of the privilege[a]), although probably not as frequently as the third (relevant Supreme Court precedents). See CRIMPROC § 8.14(a).

In analyzing the values of the privilege, the Court over the last several decades has most frequently cited Justice Goldberg's exhaustive listing of Fifth Amendment values in *Murphy v. Waterfront Comm'n*, quoted in full in *Doe II* (p. 738).

2. **Limiting "values analysis."** Though *Doe II* looks to the *Murphy* listing of values, it acknowledges in footnote 11 that the case before it may present one of those instances where "the scope of the privilege does not coincide with the complex of values it helps to protect." What justifies adopting a more limited view of the privilege than a logical extension of those values might suggest, particularly

---

a. The adoption of the Fifth Amendment itself "provides no helpful legislative history," *United States v. Balsys*, Note 3, p. 692, so the Court focuses on the common law history of privilege "on the assumption that the Framers adopted the privilege as it then existed at common law." CRIMPROC § 8.14(a).

in light of the admonition of *Counselman v. Hitchcock* (Note 1, p. 692) that the privilege be construed "as broad as the mischief against which it seeks to guard"?

Does the language of the self-incrimination clause impose limits upon conclusions drawn strictly from a values analysis? Consider e.g., Justice White's response in *Fisher* to the taxpayer's reliance there upon a "privacy" analysis [p. 707]. Consider also the contention that the clause's "witness terminology" precluded acceptance of the policy arguments of the *Doe II* petitioner, as discussed in fn. 11 of *Doe II*. Should it be easier to adopt a broad or narrower reading of a Fifth Amendment term based upon historical support for that reading than upon a policy argument that looks to the "basic values" of the Amendment? Compare in this regard the position of Justices Thomas and Scalia in *Balsys*, see fn. b, p. 693, and in *Hubbell* (p. 723).

Does the history of the privilege impose sharp limits upon a values analysis? In discussing that history, the Court has most often cited the common law development of the privilege as a response to the *ex-officio* oath procedure utilized in both the ecclesiastical courts and the Star Chamber?[b] Commentators have suggested that a construction of the privilege tied to that history and to other pre-revolutionary common law developments would produce a privilege far narrower than what we have—in particular, a privilege applicable only to compelling formal testimony under oath.[c] However, while the Court has often expressed agreement with Justice Frankfurter's comment that the "privilege * * * is a specific provision of which it is particularly true that 'a page of history is worth a volume of logic,'" *Ullman v. United States*, 350 U.S. 422 (1956) (speaking to the constitutionality of immunity provisions), it also has noted that "'a noble principle often transcends its origins.'" See *Miranda* at p. 466 (quoting in part from an observation by Judge Frank: "The critics of the Supreme Court * * *, in their over-emphasis on the history of the Fifth Amendment privilege, overlook the fact that a noble privilege often transcends its origins, that creative misunderstandings account for some of our most cherished values and institutions").

Commentators have characterized the coverage distinction drawn in *Doe II* and the identification cases on which it relies—i.e., the distinction between compelled communicative and non-communicative writings and acts—as one that "cannot be reconciled with the purposes served by the right against self-incrimination," finding its justification, instead, in "pragmatic compromise." Charles Geyh, *The Testimonial Component of The Right Against Self–Incrimination*, 36

b. As to this seventeenth century development, and the subsequent eighteenth century development of the privilege, see the essays collected in R. H. Hemholz, Charles Gray, John Langbein, Eben Moglen, Henry Smith, and Albert Alschuler, *The Privilege Against Self-Incrimination. It's Origins and Developments* (1997); Leonard Levy, *The Origins of the Fifth Amendment: The Right Against Self-Incrimination* (2d ed. 1986); CRIMPROC § 8.14(b).

c. See CRIMPROC § 8.14(b) (citing arguments for viewing the opposition to compelling testimony under oath as the key ingredient in the seventeenth and eighteenth century development of the privilege): "Questioning under oath did not simply pose the choice between self-accusation, perjury (for lying), or contempt (for refusing to testify); it placed an individual under an obligation to God to tell the truth though the threat of criminal punishment posed great temptation to at least shade the truth. This explanation of the privilege, as

resting on the spiritual coercion of the oath, finds support in the willingness of the common law to have the magistrate question the unsworn accused, pushing hard for his explanation of events, while prohibiting the magistrate from placing the accused under oath. It is consistent also with a system that placed great pressure on the accused to make an unsworn statement at trial, but prohibited the court or prosecution from placing the accused under oath, with an obligation to testify. So too, it explains the extension of self-incrimination privilege to witnesses, including witnesses in civil actions. On the other hand, it rests on a premise and a distinction (between sworn and unsworn statements) that obviously has lost considerable force (at least as to threat of supernatural sanctions) in today's world." See also Albert Alschuler, *A Peculiar Privilege in Historical Perspective: The Right to Remain Silent*, 94 Mich. L. Rev. 2590 (1996).

Catholic U.LRev. 611 (1987) (characterizing that compromise as one that preserves "the individual right to resist more egregious forms of self-incrimination" by allowing the state to obtain "vital nontestimonial physical evidence"). The "collective entity" exception has also been characterized as a doctrine inconsistent with self-incrimination values but reflective of enforcement needs. See Note 2, p. 734. Are those characterizations misguided in their view of Fifth Amendment values, or do enforcement needs also play a role in limiting the logical extension of self-incrimination values? Cf. Harlan, J., dissenting in *Spevack v. Klein,* 385 U.S. 511, 87 S.Ct. 625, 17 L.Ed.2d 574 (1967) (the Court "has chiefly derived its [Fifth Amendment] standards from consideration of two factors: the history and purposes of the privilege and the character and urgency of the other public interests involved").

The "complex of values" underlying the Fifth Amendment has been the subject of extensive commentary, and the commentators are virtually unanimous in concluding that at least some of the values cited in *Murphy* simply do not assist in explaining the privilege. See David Dolinko, *Is There a Rationale for the Privilege Against Self–Incrimination?,* 33 U.C.L.A.L.Rev. 1063 (1986).[d] The commentators have noted that while the privilege may incidentally serve the various values cited in *Murphy,* certain of those values (and for some commentators, all of those values) fail to provide a logical conceptual foundation for the existence of the privilege. Whether the Court has gone so far as to flatly reject the relevancy to Fifth Amendment interpretations of any of the values cited in *Murphy* is open to debate. Consider e.g., the comments regarding a privacy justification in *Fisher,* p. 707, and *Balsys,* fn. j, p. 748. Nobody disputes however that the Court has at least reached the conclusion that "some Fifth Amendment purposes are more important than others." Peter Arenella, *Schmerber and the Privilege Against Self–Incrimination: A Reappraisal,* 20 Am. Crim. L. Rev. 31 (1982). Interestingly, that determination has been explained as a reflection of the fact that certain values are more in line with the language and history of the privilege than others, rather than as a reflection of particular values being more important than others in achieving a fair criminal justice process. See e.g., *Doe II, Fisher,* and *Balsys,* fn. j, p. 748.

3. *Systemic rationales.* Commentators have most frequently discounted those values listed in *Murphy* that provide a "systemic rationale" for the privilege—i.e., the values that see the privilege as designed to further distinct procedural objectives of the criminal justice process, rather than as an end in itself, directed at safeguarding "human dignity and individuality". See Dolinko, Note 2 supra. Among these, the values most frequently cited as failing to explain the privilege are the 3rd, 6th, and 7th values cited in *Murphy.*

Murphy's sixth listed value sees the privilege as a reflection of the concern that incriminatory admissions are inherently unreliable. Admittedly, that concern has a rough historical counterpart in the common law rule that excluded all testimony by parties to a case because their inherent self-interest might lead them to lie. But it certainly was not reflected, at least as an absolute prohibition, in other aspects of the common law viewed at the time as consistent with the self-incrimination privilege. Magistrates could sharply interrogate the unsworn accused and recount any incriminatory admissions in their testimony before the trial court; confessions could be admitted into evidence if corroborated by other

---

d. The questioning of the conceptual foundation of the privilege dates back at least to Jeremy Bentham's classic critique of the privilege in 1827. See Jeremy Bentham, *A Rationale of Judicial Evidence* (1827). It has continued with each new generation of commentary. Professor Dolinko's article is the most widely cited and thorough critique of the current generation. For an extensive collection of additional commentary, both critical and supportive of the privilege, see CRIMPROC § 8.14(c).

evidence; and convictions could be based solely on guilty pleas. Thus, not surprisingly, when arguments for applying the privilege have been based entirely on *Murphy's* sixth value, they have not been successful. The "privilege against self-incrimination," the Court has noted "is not designed to enhance the reliability of the fact-finding determination: it stands in the constitution for entirely independent reasons." *Allen v. Illinois*, 478 U.S. 364, 106 S.Ct. 2988, 92 L.Ed.2d 296 (1986) (self-incrimination was not a safeguard that had to be applied in a non-criminal proceeding as part of due process reliability concerns). More significantly, the Court has not shaped the privilege to focus primarily on reliability concerns, as it has, for example, held that the privilege bars the use of reliable physical evidence uncovered through the use of a compelled statement of the accused, and applied the privilege to the compelled production of documents. See Amar and Lettow, fn. a, p. 702 (arguing for a reliability focus and critical of such rulings).

Murphy's seventh value—protecting the innocent—is seen by many as primarily related to the previously mentioned concern as to the reliability of self-deprecatory statements.[e] Some commentators have suggested, however, that the privilege may also protect the innocent where an innocent accused, if forced to testify, would leave the jury with a false impression as to his guilt (due to poor demeanor on the stand or an extensive criminal record used by the prosecution to impeach his credibility).[f] But this would explain only one aspect of the privilege (the defendant's right to refuse to testify), not the privilege as a whole. Moreover, the Supreme Court itself has noted that "the basic purposes that lie behind the privilege against self-incrimination do not relate to protecting the innocent from conviction." *Tehan v. United States ex rel. Shott*, 382 U.S. 406, 86 S.Ct. 459, 15 L.Ed.2d 453 (1966), although it has also described its *Miranda* ruling as serving exactly that purpose, *Withrow v. Williams* [p. 550].

The second and fourth values cited in *Murphy* have garnered the most commentator support among the systemic justifications for the privilege, but they too have fallen short for many commentators. In part, these two values simply

e. Dean Wigmore, in particular, advanced a variation on the reliability argument that looked to protecting the innocent. His rationale, sometimes described as the "lazy prosecutor rationale," was that the self-incrimination privilege was adopted to discourage overreliance on obtaining incriminatory statements of the accused (as illustrated by the historical use of the ex officio oath) and to thereby encourage more thorough investigations that would protect the innocent by having a better chance of uncovering exculpatory evidence and ensuring that guilt was based on more reliable evidence than compelled admissions. John Henry Wigmore, *Evidence* § 2251 (3d ed. 1940). Commentators critical of this rationale have pointed to the same historical arguments that are advanced against *Murphy's* sixth value. See CRIMPROC § 8.14(d) (also noting that a major eighteenth century development of the privilege—its availability to witnesses in both civil and criminal cases—gave it an impact in proceedings that did not involve the government's gathering of evidence, and could work to preclude an innocent defendant from producing evidence in his favor). While the Court has suggested that the privilege was a product of the concerns expressed by the lazy prosecutor rationale, see e.g. *Couch v. United States*, 409 U.S. 322, 327, 93 S.Ct.

611, 34 L.Ed.2d 548 (1973), its interpretation of the privilege has been criticized as being inconsistent with encouraging the prosecutor to seek out more reliable evidence (as in the case of documents and derivative physical evidence). Consider also Donald Dripps, *Against Police Interrogation—And the Privilege Against Self–Incrimination*, 78 J. Crm. L. & Criminology 699 (1988) (privilege poses such barriers to acquiring reliable evidence, including open court interrogation under oath, that it has operated to create "tolerance and even encouragement" for reliance upon the less reliable vehicle of police interrogation).

f. See Stephen Schulhofer, *Some Kind Words for the Privilege Against Self–Incrimination*, 26 Val. U. L. Rev. 311 (1991). Consider also the quite different theory advanced in Seidman & Stein, *The Right to Silence Helps the Innocent: A Game–Theoretic Analysis f the Fifth Amendment Privilege*, 114 Harv. L. Rev. 430 (2000) (right to silence helps in distinguishing guilty from innocent by inducing an anti-pooling effect that enhances the credibility of innocent suspects by affording the guilty an alternative to "imitating an innocent suspect through lies").

state in different terms the same basic objective of the process. The second value notes a preference for an "accusatorial process," but as the Court has noted in several opinions, an accusatorial process is basically one in which the government "shoulders the entire load" (part of *Murphy*'s fourth value). The imposition of this "entire load" obligation upon the prosecution may be seen as an aspect of neutralizing certain basic resource advantages of the state so as to achieve a "fair state-individual balance" (disparaged by Bentham as the "fox hunters' reason," designed to give the defendant a "sporting chance"), or it may be viewed as simply an additional safeguard to ensure against the conviction of the innocent. The end requirement, however, remains the same—that the state bear the full responsibility for establishing guilt, as contrasted to a system in which the defendant must establish his innocence.

Although frequently cited by the Court (perhaps more than any other justification for the privilege), the requirement that the state "bear the full responsibility for establishing guilt" fails to fully explain the self-incrimination doctrine. It fails to explain, for example, the availability of the privilege to witnesses in contexts in which the government is not seeking evidence, such as civil suits brought by private parties. Yet even where the government is seeking to establish its criminal case, the accusatorial structure of the process falls short of justifying distinctions drawn in applying the privilege. While the accusatorial structure commonly is described as mandating that the prosecution establish its case through its "own independent labors," the Fourth Amendment makes clear that this does not preclude the use of defendant as a source of evidence. The questions therefore arise as to why compelling the defendant to disclose evidence is distinguished from "taking evidence" from the accused (through a search), and why even that direct compulsion is limited to testimonial evidence and thereby fails to encompass all compelled acts of the defendant that produce evidence for the prosecution (e.g., the acts compelled in *Doe II*). The answers apparently lie in the special qualities of testimonial compulsion, but what gives those qualities particular significance is not the procedural structure produced by a preference for an accusatorial over an inquisitorial process,[g] but values that exist independent of that structure. They apparently stem, as the Court has recognized, from dignitary values. Thus, *Schmerber* [p. 38] acknowledged that "the compulsion [through forced participation in an identification procedure] violates at least one meaning of the requirement that the State procure the evidence against an accused 'by its own independent labors,' but concluded that the "independent-labors" concept, taken in light of other privilege values, was basically limited to precluding the state from producing evidence through "the cruel, simple expedient of compelling

g. *Murphy*'s description of the accusatorial process as one contrasted with an "inquisitorial process" might also be seen as seeking primarily to distinguish the non-adversarial aspect of an inquisitorial process. Under this view, the privilege is characterized as a natural attribute of the adversarial element of criminal justice process. See Abe Fortas, *The Fifth Amendment: Nemo Tenetur Prodere Seipsum*, 25 Cleve.B.A.J. 95 (1954): "[T]he principle that man is not obliged to furnish the state with ammunition to use against him is basic to this conception. Equals meeting in battle, owe no duty to one another, regardless of the obligations they may be under prior to battle." Here too, however, critics have responded that, in light of the state's capacity to use the defendant as a source of evidence in other ways, the restriction imposed by the privilege can no more be said to flow from the basic tenets of an adversarial system than from the basic tenets of an accusatorial system. The adversary process does not have as its objective the structuring of a "battle between equally meritorious combatants to see which of two inconsistent but equally weighty goals" will prevail, but rather the achievement of "accurate determinations" that "clear the innocent and convict the guilty." Kent Greenawalt, *Silence as a Moral and Constitutional Right*, 23 Wm. & Mary L.Rev. 15, 38–39 (1981). Thus, as evidenced by the prosecutor's obligation to disclose exculpatory evidence, it is not inconsistent with an adversary process to impose upon the litigants an obligation to produce evidence that contributes to an accurate fact-finding determination (just as it is appropriate to bar litigant concealment or destruction of relevant evidence), though that obligation obviously is contrary to their interests as adversaries.

it through [defendant's] own mouth." So too, the entity cases implicitly recognize that the privilege rests on values that go beyond implementing an accusatorial process, since a collective entity, no less than an individual, is entitled to the safeguards traditionally found in an accusatory process (e.g., the presumption of innocence). See fn. a, p. 733.

Murphy's fourth listed value also refers to requiring the "government to leave the individual alone until good cause is shown for disturbing him." The privilege obviously assists in this regard by restricting what the state can expect to gain through a prosecution that is a mere fishing expedition. It cannot "charge first" and then hope to make its case by forcing the defendant to explain his actions. Also, while the privilege does not bar prosecutorial attempts to harass by subjecting targets to grand jury questioning without any substantial basis for believing they are guilty of wrongdoing, it places in the hands of those targets a means of limiting their disclosures in response to such questioning. However, the protection against fishing expeditions hardly explains the availability of the privilege at trial, after the prosecution has produced enough evidence to justify a charge. In an early stage of its evolution, the privilege arose out of efforts to protect against persons being forced to submit to the oath without any properly supported accusation (see fn. b supra), but the self-incrimination privilege adopted in the Fifth Amendment had long since been extended to proceedings (e.g., the trial) that followed a formal independent determination by the grand jury that there existed sufficient evidence to charge the individual. So too, it had been made available to witnesses in civil proceedings, including those in no way connected to criminal investigations.

4. *Dignitary values.* Commentary explaining the policies underlying the privilege have most frequently looked to one or more "dignitary values"—that is, values that recognize the privilege as a means of preserving human dignity and individuality. The first, third, and fifth values of the *Murphy* listing fall in this category. Of these, the third value—"the fear that self-incriminating statements will be elicited by inhumane treatment and abuses"—tends to be seen as presenting the greatest difficulties in justifying the privilege in its current and its original scope.

Concern about inhumane treatment was certainly expressed in the earliest commentary on the privilege. Though, it is sometimes suggested that the origins of the common law privilege were tied to prohibiting torture, the official use of torture had been discontinued long before the abolishment of the oath *ex officio*, which gave rise to the recognition of the privilege. However, the *ex officio* oath procedure clearly was viewed by its opponents as an inhumane procedure (indeed, it was characterized by some as a species of torture). This might suggest a general understanding that it was inhumane and abusive to use any governmental power to force a person to present evidence against himself, leading to a privilege designed to ensure that would not occur through some new device, replacing the oath *ex officio*. Cf. Erwin Griswold, *The Fifth Amendment Today* 7 (1955) (drawing a parallel between compelled self-incrimination and requiring a condemned murderer to "sign his own death warrant or dig his grave"). Of course, such a reading of the privilege brings into question some of the limitations placed upon the privilege—see e.g. *Doe II*, the line of identification-procedure cases, and the required records cases. But more significantly, it does not appear to explain the common law privilege as it stood at the time of the adoption of the Fifth Amendment. At that time, the privilege was not viewed as precluding magistrates from pressuring, and even browbeating, an accused into offering an explanation of his actions (often incriminating) in an unsworn statement, with that statement (or the failure to respond) duly noted at trial. See CRIMPROC § 8.14(b) (also noting that the defendant at trial typically was not represented by counsel and therefore "had almost no choice but to take advantage of his right to make an unsworn presentation of his side of the case and respond to any questions of judge or jury"). Moreover, the critical practical significance of the privilege at that point had nothing to do with threatening or bullying a defendant. It was the availability of the privilege to *witnesses* being examined in open court in criminal and civil cases (defendants in criminal cases could not be called to testify, apart from any ramifications of the privilege, because of the prohibitions against parties to the action giving sworn testimony).

    5. *The cruel trilemma.* Although many commentators quarrel with the underlying moral judgment, almost all acknowledge that the privilege arose originally from a belief that it was uniquely cruel and inhumane to subject a person to what *Murphy* described as the "the cruel trilemma of self-accusation, perjury, or contempt."[h] Under this view, the privilege is appropriately limited to testimonial communications because if the compulsion does not "convey information or assert facts," it does not present as one of the forced alternatives the possibility of lying under oath, an act considered historically to be an "unpardonable and cardinal sin * * * simply not an option for a religious man." Levy, fn. b, supra.

    The cruel trilemma rationale also explains why the privilege was extended to witnesses and denied collective entities (which have no soul to damn), although denial of privilege to the entity agent arguably becomes more troublesome (even with the *Braswell* safeguard), as does the required records doctrine. Of course, *Miranda* also presents difficulties since neither perjury nor damnation follow from lying to the police. On the other hand, tying the privilege to the oath and the potential for a perjury conviction appears highly ritualistic (and outdated) when one recognizes the wide range of pressures that can be placed upon an individual to force him to reveal the contents of his mind.[i]

    6. *Protection of privacy.* The fifth value cited in *Murphy*—"respect for the inviolability of the human personality" and the need for a "private enclave"—has commonly been characterized as the "privacy" justification for the privilege. Both critics and supporters of this rationale acknowledge that it remains unpersuasive unless there exists a satisfactory answer to a critical question—why the particular element of privacy that falls within the privilege is given absolute protection, as compared to the relative protection given other privacy interests under the Fourth and First Amendments. The answer usually offered is that the privilege protects the most significant element of individual privacy, the privacy "of the mind"; it "respects a private inner sanctum of individual feeling and thought." *Couch v. United States* (p. 706). But this response only raises the further question as to why the privilege, if it is designed to protect mental privacy from state intrusion, affords such protection only as to thoughts, feelings, and beliefs that would furnish a link in the chain of evidence needed to establish criminal liability. See

h. See fns. b and c supra. The assumption that forcing such a choice upon a defendant is uniquely cruel was challenged by Bentham, supra fn. c (who characterized it as the "old woman's reason" for the privilege) and modern critics have built upon his analysis. They argue that the choice imposed here is no more cruel than that imposed in other settings (e.g., where a parent is forced to testify against a child), that it assumes a moral justification in refusing to confess to criminality that is contrary to commonly accepted moral and social standards in most other settings, and that forcing that choice upon the individual is justified by a legitimate state objective (determining the truth) no less significant than other interests thought to justify requiring a person to act against his natural instinct of self-preservation.

i. Thus, *Miranda* noted that the policies cited in *Murphy* "point to one overriding thought"—that the government must respect "the dignity and integrity of its citizens." That respect was missing where the compulsion of custodial interrogation, which "may well be greater" than that imposed by judicial process, is used to force the individual to furnish incriminatory evidence "from his own mouth."

United States v. Balsys, Note 3, p. 692.[j] One explanation for this limitation is that privilege seeks to protect only a "particular corner of the private enclave" that is especially significant in the development of "moral autonomy"—the "integrity of conscience." See Robert Gerstein, *The Demise of Boyd: Self–Incrimination and Private Papers in the Burger Court*, 27 U.C.L.A.L.Rev. 343 (1979). The critical element of the privilege, from this perspective, is that it preserves to the individual alone the essential right of determining whether and when to acknowledge responsibility for his actions. See Fortas, fn. e supra ("*Mea culpa* belongs to a man and his God. It is a plea that cannot be extracted from free men by human authority.") Accepting this view, should the privilege be even narrower than suggested in *Doe II*? Is there a sufficient element of compulsory "self-condemnation" present to render the privilege applicable when a person is required to furnish only factual information, especially where that information is not incriminatory on its face (as in the compelled disclosure of the combination to one's safe, see fn. 9, p. 738)?

j. The *Balsys* majority sharply questioned *Murphy's* suggestion that the self-incrimination' clause reflects the "the inviolability of the human personality and the right of each individual to a private enclave where he may lead a private life". It noted initially that" 'inviolability' is, after all, an uncompromising term, and we know as well from Fourth Amendment law * * * that breaches of privacy are complete at the moment of illicit intrusion, whatever use may or may not later be made of such fruits." "Inviolability", it pointed out, hardly describes a regime which allows the government to compel testimony provided it was willing to pay the price of "use and derivative use immunity." The Court then added: "One might reply that the choice of the word 'inviolability' was just unfortunate; while testimonial integrity may not be inviolable, it is sufficiently served by requiring the Government to pay a price in the form of use (and derivative use) immunity before a refusal to testify will be overruled. But that answer overlooks the fact that when a witness's response will raise no fear of criminal penalty, there is no protection for testimonial privacy at all. Thus, what we find in practice is not the protection of personal testimonial inviolability, but a conditional protection of testimonial privacy subject to basic limits recognized before the framing and refined through immunity doctrine in the intervening years."

Chapter 11

THE SCOPE OF THE EXCLUSIONARY RULES*

SECTION 1. "STANDING" TO OBJECT TO THE ADMISSION OF EVIDENCE (OR "THE EXTENT OF A PARTICULAR DEFENDANT'S RIGHTS UNDER THE FOURTH AMENDMENT")**

A. HISTORICAL BACKGROUND AND OVERVIEW

1. *Must the person asserting a Fourth Amendment claim have been the victim of the challenged search or seizure?* Long before the Supreme Court authoritatively resolved the issue, the lower courts had developed the doctrine that a defendant lacked "standing" to challenge evidence seized in violation of a third party's constitutional rights. The early basis for this doctrine seems to have been "the joint foundation of the Fourth Amendment and the self-incrimination clause of the Fifth," Comment, 58 Yale L.J. 144, 156 (1948). The rule was also "based on the theory that the evidence is excluded to provide a remedy for a wrong done to the defendant, and that accordingly, if the defendant has not been wronged he is entitled to no remedy." *People v. Martin*, 290 P.2d 855, 857 (Cal.1955) (Traynor, J.).

Six years before *Mapp*, the California Supreme Court's emphasis on the deterrence rationale for the exclusionary rule led it to abolish the "standing" requirement. *People v. Martin*, supra. "Such a limitation," observed the California court, "virtually invites law enforcement officers to violate the rights of third parties and to trade the escape of a criminal whose rights are violated for the conviction of others by the use of the evidence illegally obtained against them." Id.[a]

---

* Harmless error is treated elsewhere; see Ch. 27, § 4.

** *Rakas v. Illinois* (1978) (discussed at p. 754).

a. *In re Lance W.*, 694 P.2d 744 (Cal.1985) (discussed at p. 53), held that Proposition 8, an initiative approved by California voters in 1982, had abolished *Martin's* "vicarious exclusionary rule."

The California Supreme Court had ruled earlier, *People v. Varnum*, 427 P.2d 772 (Cal. 1967), that *Martin* did not apply to *Escobedo-Miranda* violations. The majority, per Traynor, J., reasoned: "Noncoercive questioning is not in itself unlawful [and the rights] protected by *Escobedo* [and] *Miranda* are violated only

when evidence obtained without the required warnings and waiver is introduced against the person whose questioning produced the evidence. The basis for the [*Miranda* warnings] is the privilege against self-incrimination [which] is not violated when the information elicited from an unwarned suspect is not used against him. [Unlike unreasonable searches and seizures], there is nothing unlawful in questioning an unwarned suspect so long as the police refrain [from tactics] condemned by due process and do not use against the suspect any evidence obtained."

For criticism of *Varnum*, see Notes, 37 U.Cin.L.Rev. 234 (1968); 15 U.C.L.A.L.Rev. 1060 (1968).

749

Ct abolished "standing" req.

California's abolition of the "standing" requirement was "enthusiastically endorsed by most commentators." 5 Wayne R. LaFave, *Search and Seizure: A Treatise on the Fourth Amendment* § 11.3(j)(3d ed.1996) (herein SEARCHSZR) (citing thirteen commentators), and when, in *Linkletter v. Walker* (1965) (p. 41), the U.S. Supreme Court seemed to explain and to justify the Fourth Amendment exclusionary rule as "the only effective deterrent to lawless police action," there was reason to think that the High Court, too, might scrap the "standing" requirement. Thus, two years after *Linkletter* and two years before *Alderman* infra, one commentator pointed out that "a system of classification based on 'victimness' provides no deterrence" against "searches that turn up evidence against persons other than the victim" and concluded that "the standing requirement is inconsistent with the presently accepted general deterrence theory of the exclusionary rule." Note, 34 U.Chi.L.Rev. 342, 358 (1967).

However, in ALDERMAN v. UNITED STATES, 394 U.S. 165, 89 S.Ct. 961, 22 L.Ed.2d 176 (1969), the Court, per WHITE, J., reaffirmed "the established principle [that] suppression of the product of a Fourth Amendment violation can be successfully urged only by those whose rights were violated by the search itself, not by those who are aggrieved solely by the introduction of damaging evidence. Coconspirators and codefendants have been accorded no special standing."[b] The Court was unmoved by the ascendancy of the deterrence rationale: "[We] are not convinced that the additional benefits of extending the exclusionary rule to other defendants would justify further encroachment upon the public interest in prosecuting those accused of crime and having them acquitted or convicted on the basis of all the evidence which exposes the truth."

Concurring in part and dissenting in part, FORTAS, J., argued that there was much to be said for abolishing the "standing" requirement: "The Fourth Amendment, unlike the Fifth, is couched in terms of a guarantee that the Government will not engage in unreasonable searches and seizures. It is a general prohibition[,] * * * not merely a privilege accorded to him whose domain has been lawlessly invaded. [It] is an assurance to all that the Government will exercise its formidable powers to arrest and to investigate only subject to the rule of law."[c]

2. Does Alderman represent a genuine effort to strike a balance between the costs of exclusion and the need for deterrence? Daniel Meltzer, *Deterring Constitutional Violations by Law Enforcement Officials: Plaintiffs and Defendants as Private Attorneys General*, 88 Colum.L.Rev. 247, 275 (1988) finds it hard to so understand the Court's standing doctrine: "It is possible, of course, that an effort to strike a desirable balance would result in a standing doctrine limited to those whose rights were violated by the illegal search. But such a result would be extremely surprising, as there are factors more relevant to the need for and benefits of deterrent remedies. These include the seriousness of the harm caused by the search; the likelihood of detection; the perception of the sanction's

b. A quarter-century later, in *United States v. Padilla*, 508 U.S. 77, 113 S.Ct. 1936, 123 L.Ed.2d 635 (1993) (per curiam), a unanimous Court quoted this language from *Alderman* in rejecting a so-called "coconspirator exception" to the standing doctrine. Under this exception, developed by the U.S. Court of Appeals for the Ninth Circuit, a coconspirator obtained a legitimate expectation of privacy for Fourth Amendment purposes if she had either a supervisory role in the conspiracy or joint control over the place of property involved in the challenged search or seizure. Such an exception, observed the *Padilla* Court is "not only contrary to the holding of *Alderman,* but at odds with [the

expectation of privacy approach taken in *Rakas*, p. 754, that now] govern[s] the analysis of Fourth Amendment search and seizure claims. Participants in a criminal conspiracy may have [exceptions of privacy and property interests], but the conspiracy itself neither adds to or detracts from them."

c. Justice Fortas' view is supported in Donald Doernberg, *"The Right of the People": Reconciling Collective and Individual Interests under the Fourth Amendment*, 58 N.Y.U.L.Rev. 259 (1983); Richard B. Kuhns, *The Concept of Personal Aggrievement in Fourth Amendment Standing Cases*, 65 Iowa L.Rev. 493 (1980).

severity; whether the violation was obvious or intentional; how susceptible to deterrence the search is; and how easily the resulting rules can be administered. A truly deterrence-focused standing doctrine would at least consider such factors, rather than simply assume that the optimal result is reached when only those who were victims of the search are empowered to suppress evidence."

3. *The tension between the standing requirement and the exclusionary rule.* Consider Joshua Dressler, *Understanding Criminal Procedure* 303 (2d ed.1997): "Professor Anthony Amsterdam once noted that there are two competing perspectives on the Fourth Amendment. One view, the 'atomistic' perspective, is that the Fourth Amendment is 'a collection of protections of atomistic spheres of interest of individual citizens.' That is, the Fourth Amendment protects isolated individuals ('atoms'), in the sense that the amendment 'safeguard[s] *my* person and *your* house and *her* papers and *his* effects against unreasonable searches and seizures.'[12] The second view, the 'regulatory' perspective, is that the Fourth Amendment functions 'as a regulation of governmental conduct.' In other words, the amendment is intended to safeguard the collective 'people,' as in 'we, the people,' from governmental overreaching.

"As Fourth Amendment jurisprudence has developed, standing—based as it is on the premise that a person may raise a Fourth Amendment challenge only if he *personally* was a victim of unreasonable police activity—is based on the atomistic philosophy. In contrast, the exclusionary rule is regulatory in nature, in that its purpose is to deter police misconduct, in order to safeguard society as a whole.

"Understood in this way, the standing requirement and the exclusionary rule act, at least in part, in opposition to each other. This is because evidence seized in violation of the Fourth Amendment is excluded at trial in order to deter police misconduct; but, the requirement of standing to raise a Fourth Amendment claim often undercuts this deterrence goal, as it limits the number of people ('atoms') who can bring the misconduct to the attention of the courts so that the exclusionary rule can be applied."

As an example, Professor Dressler cites the *Payner* case, discussed in the next Note.

4. *The use of the federal courts' "supervisory power" to overcome the standing requirement.* If there has ever been a case that called for the exercise of the federal courts' supervisory power to break out of the standing restriction it was UNITED STATES v. PAYNER, 447 U.S. 727, 100 S.Ct. 2439, 65 L.Ed.2d 468 (1980) (also discussed at p. 48). Nevertheless, a 6–3 majority, per POWELL, J., was unmoved.

Payner arose as follows: An IRS investigation into the financial activities of American citizens in the Bahamas focused on a certain Bahamian bank. When an official of that bank visited the United States, IRS agents stole his briefcase for a time, removed hundreds of documents from the briefcase, and photographed them. As a result of this "briefcase caper," *Payner*—precisely the kind of offender the IRS agents were seeking when they violated the bank official's rights—was convicted of federal income tax violations. Hemmed in by the standing requirement, but outraged by the government's "purposefully" illegal tactics, the federal district court invoked its supervisory power to exclude the tainted evidence.

But the Supreme Court rejected the federal court's "substitution of individual judgment for the controlling decisions of this Court." "The values assigned to the competing interests do not change," pointed out Justice Powell, "because a court

12. Anthony G. Amsterdam, *Perspectives on the Fourth Amendment*, 58 Minn.L.Rev. 349, 367 (1974).

has elected to analyze the question under the supervisory power instead of the Fourth Amendment. In either case, the need to deter the underlying conduct and the detrimental impact of excluding the evidence remain precisely the same."[d]

The *Payner* Court cautioned that exclusion of evidence in every case of illegality must be "weighed against the considerable harm that would flow from *indiscriminate application* of an exclusionary rule" (emphasis added), and that "*unbending application* of the exclusionary sanction * * * would impede unacceptably the truthfinding functions of judge and jury" (emphasis added). But consider Kamisar, *Does (Did) (Should) the Exclusionary Rule Rest on a "Principled Basis" Rather than an "Empirical Proposition"*?, 16 Creighton L.Rev. 565, 638 (1983):

"The relevant question in *Payner* [was] not whether the exclusionary rule should *always* be applied when police illegality is somewhere in the picture, but whether it should *ever* be applied—taking into account the seriousness or flagrancy of the illegality—when the defendant lacks 'standing.' The question was not whether the exclusionary rule should be given 'unbending application,' but whether *the 'standing' requirement* should be. By deciding that even in a case like *Payner* a federal court is *unable* to exercise its supervisory powers to bar the evidence—by holding that 'judicial impotency is *compelled* in the face of such scandalous conduct' [LaFave, § 11.3(h)]—the Court gave us its answer.

"[The] *Payner* Court seemed content [to rely on] the balance it had struck in the early standing cases. But because it grew out of special and outrageous circumstances, the interests to be balanced in *Payner* were different. The question presented was[:] When the government has *intentionally manipulated* the standing requirement of the fourth amendment—when it has *deliberately and patently* violated the constitutional rights of a third party in order to obtain evidence against its real targets, and defendant is one of those targets—does the interest in discouraging (or reducing) the incentive to make *such* searches justify the exclusion of tainted evidence at the instance of a party who was not the [direct] victim of the challenged practice? The *Payner* Court never really spoke to this issue because it never really asked this question."

5. *"Automatic" standing.* In *Jones v. United States,* 362 U.S. 257, 80 S.Ct. 725, 4 L.Ed.2d 697 (1960), the defendant was charged with selling and distributing narcotics and facilitating the concealment and sale of the same narcotics, which permitted conviction largely on proof of unexplained possession of narcotics. The lower court denied standing because defendant had failed either to assert a sufficient interest in the apartment where the search occurred[e] or to allege ownership or possession of the narcotics, although doing so would have "forced" him to allege facts that would tend to convict him. The Supreme Court reversed: The "same element in this prosecution which has caused a dilemma, i.e., that possession both convicts and confers standing, eliminates any necessity for a preliminary showing of an interest in the premises searched or the property seized, which ordinarily is required when standing is challenged." To hold otherwise "would be to permit the Government to have the advantage of contradictory positions as a basis of conviction."

d. "The Court's decision to engraft the standing limitations of the Fourth Amendment onto the exercise of supervisory powers," protested dissenting Justice Marshall, joined by Brennan and Blackmun, JJ., "appears to render the supervisory powers superfluous. In order to establish that suppression of evidence under the supervisory powers would be proper, the Court would also require Payner to establish a violation of his [constitutional rights]. This approach is totally unfaithful to our prior supervisory power cases [see generally pp. 47–51], which, contrary to the Court's suggestion, are not constitutional cases in disguise."

e. For this aspect of *Jones,* see Note 6 infra.

However, the Court subsequently held, in *Simmons v. United States*, 390 U.S. 377, 88 S.Ct. 967, 19 L.Ed.2d 1247 (1968), that testimony given by a defendant in order to establish his "standing" "may not thereafter be used against him at trial on the issue of guilt." Were it otherwise, "a defendant who wishes to establish standing must do so at the risk that the words which he utters may later be used to incriminate him."

On the basis of *Simmons*, the Court subsequently abolished the *Jones* "automatic standing" rule and held that "defendants charged with crimes of possession may only claim the benefits of the exclusionary rule if their own Fourth Amendment rights have in fact been violated." UNITED STATES v. SALVUCCI, 448 U.S. 83, 100 S.Ct. 2547, 65 L.Ed.2d 619 (1980). Observed the Court, per REHNQUIST, J.: "The 'dilemma' identified in *Jones* * * * was eliminated [by] *Simmons*, [which] not only extends protection against [the] risk of self-incrimination in all of the cases covered by *Jones*, but also grants a form of 'use' immunity to those defendants charged with nonpossessory crimes."[f]

As for the vice of prosecutorial contradiction, the Court stated it need not decide whether that "could alone support a rule countenancing the exclusion of probative evidence on the grounds that someone other than the defendant was denied a Fourth Amendment right," for at least after *Rakas* [p. 754] it is clear that "a prosecutor may simultaneously maintain that a defendant criminally possessed the seized good, but was not subject to a Fourth Amendment deprivation, without legal contradiction." For a "person in legal possession of a good seized during an illegal search has not necessarily been subject to a Fourth Amendment deprivation. * * * We simply decline to use possession of a seized good as a substitute for a factual finding that the owner of the good has a legitimate expectation of privacy in the area searched."[g]

6. *Residential premises.* It has long been true, and is still so under the current expectation-of-privacy approach discussed in the next subsection, that one with a present possessory interest in the premises searched, e.g., a member of the family regularly residing in a home, may challenge that search even though not present when the search was conducted. As the *Alderman* Court explained: "If the police make an unwarranted search of a house and seize tangible property belonging to third parties [the] home owner may object to its use against him, not because he had any interest in the seized items [but] because they were the fruits

---

f. Dissenting Justice Marshall, joined by Brennan, J., disagreed that "*Simmons* provides complete protection against the 'self-incriminating dilemma,' " for "the prosecutor may still be permitted to use the defendant's testimony [at the suppression hearing] to impeach him at trial." The *Salvucci* majority managed to sidestep this argument, but somewhat misleadingly it asserted that "the Court has held that 'the protective shield of *Simmons* is not to be converted into a license for false representations,' " quoting from *United States v. Kahan*, 415 U.S. 239, 94 S.Ct. 1179, 39 L.Ed.2d 297 (1974). But *Kahan* involved the impeachment use of false testimony given at a pretrial hearing to establish defendant's eligibility for appointed counsel and the *Kahan* Court pointed out: "We are not dealing, as was the Court in *Simmons*, with what was 'believed' by the claimant to be a 'valid' constitutional claim. Respondent was not, therefore, faced with the type of intolerable choice *Simmons* sought to relieve. The protective shield of

Simmons is not to be converted into a license for false representations *on the issue of indigency* free from the risk that the claimant will be held accountable for his falsehood." (Emphasis added.)

Consider CRIMPROC § 9.2(a): "The best analogy [is] *New Jersey v. Portash* [440 U.S. 450, 99 S.Ct. 1292, 59 L.Ed.2d 501 (1979)], holding that testimony given before a grand jury following a grant of use testimony could not be used for impeachment purposes at the subsequent criminal trial. [It] would seem that defendant's testimony at a suppression hearing [is] 'compelled' in the *Portash* sense, for, as *Simmons* teaches, the defendant is confronted with the choice 'either to give up what he believed, with advice of counsel, to be a valid Fourth Amendment claim or, in effect, to waive his Fifth Amendment privilege against self-incrimination.' "

g. See also *Rawlings v. Kentucky*, p. 756.

of an unauthorized search of his house, which is itself expressly protected by the Fourth Amendment." The *Alderman* majority thus concluded that a person should have standing to challenge the legality of electronically overheard conversations in which he participated "or *conversations occurring on his premises,* whether or not he was present or participated in those conversations" (emphasis added).[h]

In *Jones v. United States,* Note 5, the Court held that "anyone legitimately on premises where a search occurs may challenge its legality." The defendant not only had permission to use the apartment of his friend, but had a key to the apartment with which he admitted himself on the day of the search. He also kept some possessions in the apartment. In the more recent *Rakas* case (below), the Court rejected the *Jones* "legitimately on premises" *formulation*—this phrase "creates too broad a gauge for measurement of Fourth Amendment rights"—but it did not question *the result* in that case. The *Jones* holding "can best be explained," observed the *Rakas* Court, "by the fact that Jones had a legitimate expectation of privacy in the premises he was using [even] though his 'interest' in those premises might not have been a recognized property interest at common law."

[handwritten margin note: rejected by Rakas]

Thirty years after *Jones* was decided, the Court held in *Minnesota v. Olson* (1990) (also discussed at p. 257), that defendant's "status as an overnight guest" showed that he had "an expectation of privacy in the home that society is prepared to recognize as reasonable." Thus he had a sufficient interest in the home to challenge the legality of the warrantless entry there.

7. Business premises. In *Mancusi v. DeForte,* 392 U.S. 364, 88 S.Ct. 2120, 20 L.Ed.2d 1154 (1968), where state police seized records belonging to a union local from an office defendant shared with several other union officials, the Court viewed the "crucial issue" as "whether the area was one in which there was a reasonable expectation of freedom from governmental intrusion." The Court answered in the affirmative. Even though defendant shared an office with others, he "still could reasonably have expected that only those persons and [their guests] would ever enter the office, and that records would not be touched except with their permission or that of union higherups."

"Consistent with *Mancusi,* courts have held that a corporate or individual defendant in possession of the business premises searched has standing, and that an officer or employee of the business enterprise has standing if 'there was a demonstrated nexus between the area searched and the work space of the defendant.' Exclusive use would seem clearly to establish standing, but (as *Mancusi* teaches) there can be a justified expectation of privacy even absent exclusivity." CRIMPROC § 9.1(c).

B.   THE CURRENT APPROACH

In RAKAS v. ILLINOIS, 439 U.S. 128, 99 S.Ct. 421, 58 L.Ed.2d 387 (1978), as Charles H. Whitebread & Christopher Slobogin, *Criminal Procedure* 123 (3d.ed. 1993), observe, "the Court explicitly recognized the connection between search and standing analysis. That is, the Court held that standing should depend on whether the police action sought to be challenged is a search (i.e., a violation of legitimate expectations of privacy) *with respect to the person challenging the intrusion.*"

[handwritten margin note: police stopped and searched a car]

[handwritten margin note: owned or occupied]

h. Justice Harlan, joined by Stewart, J., argued that this should not be so when the eavesdropped occurred without physical penetration, for then the absent householder's property interest has not been disturbed, and he can claim no privacy interest in conversations in which he did not participate.

In *Rakas*, in the course of affirming a ruling that when the police stopped and searched a car, which petitioners neither owned nor leased but were occupying as passengers, the police violated none of *their* rights,[a] REHNQUIST, J., speaking for a 5–4 majority, asked "whether it serves any useful analytical purpose to consider [the principle that Fourth Amendment rights are personal rights] a matter of standing, distinct from the merits of a defendant's Fourth Amendment claim." He answered that inquiry in the negative: "[W]e think the better analysis forthrightly focuses on the extent of a particular defendant's rights under the Fourth Amendment, rather than on any theoretically separate, but invariably intertwined concept of standing. * * * Analyzed in these terms, the question is whether the challenged search or seizure violated the Fourth Amendment rights of a criminal defendant who seeks to exclude the evidence obtained during it. That inquiry in turn requires a determination of whether the disputed search and seizure has infringed an interest of the defendant which the Fourth Amendment was designed to protect."

Is there still something to be said for treating "standing" and the issue whether a Fourth Amendment violation has occurred at all as distinct inquiries? Consider SEARCHSZR § 11.3 at 121: "[It] is important to keep in mind that the question traditionally labeled as standing (did the police intrude upon *this defendant's* justified expectation of privacy?) is not identical to, for example, the question of whether any Fourth Amendment search has occurred (did the police intrude upon *anyone's* justified expectation of privacy?), and that therefore the [issues traditionally called "standing" issues] are still rather discrete and deserving of separate attention, no matter what label is put on them."[b]

In *Rakas*, it should be noted, Justice Rehnquist could "think of no decided cases of this Court that would have come out differently had we concluded, as we do now, that [the standing requirement] is more properly subsumed under

---

a. Suspecting that the vehicle might have been the "getaway car" in a recent robbery, police stopped the car in which petitioners were riding. After the occupants of the car (petitioners and two female companions) were ordered out, the police searched the interior of the vehicle and discovered a sawed-off rifle under the front passenger seat and a box of rifle shells in the glove compartment (which had been locked). Because petitioners did not assert ownership of the rifle or the shells and because they conceded that they did not own the automobile, but were simply passengers (the owner of the vehicle had been driving it at the time of the search), the trial court ruled that they lacked "standing" to contest the search and seizure. Thus the judge denied their motions to suppress the evidence, without ever reaching the question whether the police conduct involved was lawful.

Applying its new approach to what had traditionally been called "standing" problems, the U.S. Supreme Court agreed that "petitioners' claims must fail": "They asserted neither a property nor a possessory interest in the automobile, nor an interest in the property seized. And [the] fact that they were "legitimately on [the] premises" in the sense that they were in the car with the permission of its owner is not determinative of whether they had a legitimate expectation of privacy in the particular areas of the automobile searched. It is unnecessary for us to decide here whether the same expectations of privacy are warranted in a car as would be justified in a dwelling place in analogous circumstances. [But] here petitioners' claim is one which would fail even in an analogous situation in a dwelling place, since they made no showing that they had any legitimate expectation of privacy in the glove compartment or area under the seat of the car in which they were merely passengers. Like the trunk of an automobile, these are areas in which a passenger *qua* passenger simply would not normally have a legitimate expectation of privacy.

"[*Jones v. United States* (1960)] involved significantly different factual circumstances. Jones not only had permission to use the apartment of his friend, but had a key to the apartment with which he admitted himself on the day of the search and kept possessions in the apartment. Except with respect to his friend, Jones had complete dominion and control over the apartment and could exclude others from it. [Jones] could legitimately expect privacy in the areas which were the subject of the search and seizure [he] sought to contest. No such showing was made by these petitioners with respect to those portions of the automobile which were searched and from which incriminating evidence was seized."

b. See also Joshua Dressler, *Understanding Criminal Procedure* 302–03 (2d ed. 1997).

substantive Fourth Amendment doctrine." He also told us that although he believed that the traditional standing requirement "belongs more properly under the heading of substantive Fourth Amendment doctrine," he was "under no illusion that by dispensing with the rubric of standing * * * we have rendered any simpler the determination of whether the proponent of a motion to suppress is entitled to contest the legality of a search and seizure."

In *Rakas*, as pointed out earlier, neither passenger asserted ownership in the items taken from the car. The Court seemed to imply that if the passengers had done so, they could have challenged the police conduct. But RAWLINGS v. KENTUCKY, 448 U.S. 98, 100 S.Ct. 2556, 65 L.Ed.2d 633 (1980), rejected the argument that one could challenge a search of an area (in this instance another person's purse) simply because he claimed ownership of the property seized during the search. The case arose as follows:

On the day of the challenged police conduct, petitioner and Ms. Cox, who had been his companion for several days, were visitors at the house of one Marquess. Shortly before six police officers arrived, armed with a warrant for the arrest of Marquess, petitioner, who had been carrying a large quantity of illegal drugs, dumped them into the purse of Ms. Cox. Although there was a dispute about their discussion, petitioner testified that he had asked Ms. Cox "if she would carry this for me, and she said 'yes.' " (Although unclear, one plausible inference is that petitioner had put the contraband in the purse because he had seen police approaching the house.)

While unsuccessfully searching for Marquess in his house, the police came upon evidence of drug violations. Two of the officers then left to obtain a warrant to search the house, while the remaining officers detained the occupants, including petitioner and Cox, allowing them to leave only if they consented to a body search. Upon returning with the search warrant some 45 minutes later, the officers ordered Cox to empty her purse onto a table. As she poured out the contents of her purse, Cox told petitioner "to take what was his" and petitioner immediately claimed ownership of the drugs. Considering the "totality of the circumstances," including petitioner's admission at the suppression hearing that he did not believe that Cox's purse would be free from governmental intrusion, the state supreme court concluded that petitioner had no "standing" because he had failed to make "a sufficient showing that his legitimate or reasonable expectations of privacy were violated by the search of the purse." A 7–2 majority, again per REHNQUIST, J., found no reason to overturn that conclusion:

"[1] At the time petitioner dumped thousands of dollars worth of illegal drugs into Cox's purse, he had known her only a few days. [2] According to Cox's uncontested testimony, petitioner had never sought or received access to her purse prior to that sudden bailment. [3] Nor did petitioner have any right to exclude other persons access to Cox's purse. [4] In fact, [a third person] a longtime acquaintance and frequent companion of Cox's had free access to her purse. [5] [Moreover,] even assuming that petitioner's version of the bailment is correct [,the] precipitous nature of the transaction hardly supports a reasonable inference that petitioner took normal precautions to maintain his privacy. [6] [Finally] the record also contains a frank admission by petitioner that he had no subjective expectation that Cox's purse would remain free from governmental intrusion * * * c

---

c. According to SEARCHSZR § 11.3(c) at 154, none of the points made by Justice Rehnquist "can withstand close scrutiny." He then responds to Justice Rehnquist's points as follows (id. At 154–58):

(1) The fact that Rawlings had only known Ms. Cox for a few days "hardly establishes the absence of a justified expectation of privacy."

(2) Rawlings' expectation of privacy was not diminished because this was the first time he

"Petitioner contends nevertheless that, because he claimed ownership of the drugs in Cox's purse, he should be entitled to challenge the search regardless of his expectation of privacy. We disagree. While petitioner's ownership of the drugs is undoubtedly one fact to be considered in this case, *Rakas* emphatically rejected the notion that 'arcane' concepts of property law ought to control the ability to claim the protections of the Fourth Amendment. Had petitioner placed his drugs in plain view, he would still have owned them, but he could not claim any legitimate expectation of privacy. Prior to *Rakas*, petitioner might have been given 'standing' in such a case to challenge a 'search' that netted those drugs but probably would have lost his claim on the merits. After *Rakas*, the two inquiries merge into one: whether governmental officials violated any legitimate expectation of privacy held by petitioner."

BLACKMUN, J., joined the Court's opinion, but also wrote separately. He agreed with the majority that determining (1) whether the defendant has a "legitimate expectation of privacy" that has been invaded by the police and (2) whether "applicable cause and warrant requirements have been properly observed" " 'merge into one' in the sense that both are to be addressed under the principles of Fourth Amendment analysis developed in *Katz* and its progeny." But he did not read *Rawlings*, or *Rakas*, "as holding that it is improper for lower courts to treat these inquiries as distinct components of a Fourth Amendment claim." "Indeed," he added, "I am convinced that it would invite confusion to hold otherwise. It remains possible for a defendant to prove that his legitimate interest of privacy was invaded, and yet fail to prove that the police acted illegally

had used Ms. Cox's purse. Otherwise, "we would be left with the curious notion that a first-time bailment [would] not carry with it a justified expectation that one's goods are secure in the hands of the bailee."

As for (3), "while a 'right to exclude' may be an easy way to establish the requisite legitimate expectation of privacy, it hardly follows that it is the *only* way * * *. Reliance on this 'right to exclude' factor is also inconsistent with the later [holding] of *Minnesota v. Olson*, (1990) [p. 754], [that] an overnight guest had [a legitimate expectation of privacy in the premises] without regard to whether the guest 'had complete dominion and control over the apartment and could exclude others from it.' "

(4) The fact that a third party had access to Ms Cox's purse should not matter. The issue was not whether Rawlings "reasonably believed he was free from intrusion by *anyone*," but " 'whether the area [searched] was one in which there was a reasonable expectation of privacy from *governmental* intrusion.' "

As for (5), the argument that Rawlings did not take adequate precautions to maintain his privacy, "a container does not have to be locked to give rise to that especially strong expectation of privacy which makes the warrant clause of the Fourth Amendment applicable and thus it can hardly be said that an unlocked container carries with it no justified privacy expectation at all." Furthermore, if it can be said that Rawlings did not take adequate precautions in putting his effects into a closed container with the owner's consent, "then surely Ms. Cox likewise had no justified expectation of privacy in the same purse be-

cause she did not better safeguard her effects in that purse."

(6) The "frank admission" by Rawlings that "he had no subjective expectation that Cox's purse would remain free from governmental intrusion" turns out to be a "No, sir" answer when asked at the suppression hearing whether he thought the purse would be free from police intrusion. Rawlings was being asked "what he thought was going to happen *after* the police were on the scene and *after* they told him and others that a warrant was being sought and they could leave prior to the warrant execution only by submitting to a personal search. [But] if one can be deprived of Fourth Amendment standing by being informed in advance by the police of the intrusion they intend to make, [then] Rawlings likewise had no standing with respect to his own person, which he also expected would be intruded upon by the police."

According to Professor LaFave, id., "*Rawlings* is best viewed as an unusual case in which the result is more attributable to certain undercurrents in the case than to the reasoning offered by the Court." LaFave notes at this point that although none of the lower courts specifically found that Ms. Cox had not consented to the bailment, "the trial court was somewhat 'skeptical about [Rawlings'] version of events' and seemed to think that [he] probably saw the police approaching the premises and then thrust the controlled substances onto Cox over her objection. The thrust of the majority opinion in *Rawlings* strongly suggests the Court was influenced by an assumption that this latter version was correct."

in doing so. And it is equally possible for a defendant to prove that the police acted illegally, and yet fail to prove that his own privacy interest was affected."

It is interesting to note that in the very recent case of *Minnesota v. Carter*, set forth immediately below, "the parties' briefs to the U.S. Supreme Court, as well as the state supreme court's opinion, analyze[d] the case in terms of the defendants' 'standing' to assert a Fourth Amendment violation." 64 Crim.L.Rep. 2033, 2037 (Oct. 14, 1998). At one point during the oral arguments before the U.S. Supreme Court, the lawyer for the state referred to the defendants' "standing" to raise a search and seizure claim. This led Justice Kennedy to point out that in *Rakas* the Court had "abandoned the idea of 'standing' in the Fourth Amendment context." Id. Nevertheless, "throughout the oral arguments, the idea of Fourth Amendment 'standing' continued to be employed by the parties and the justices to describe the concepts at issue." *Id*.

MINNESOTA v. CARTER
525 U.S. 83, 119 S.Ct. 469, 142 L.Ed.2d, 373 (1998).

Chief Justice REHNQUIST delivered the opinion of the Court.

[A confidential informant told a Minnesota police officer (Thielen) that he had walked by the window of a ground-floor apartment and had seen people putting a white powder into bags. After looking in the same window through a gap in the closed blind and observing three men engaged in the bagging operation (respondents Carter and Johns and the apartment's lessee, Ms. Thompson), the officer notified headquarters, which began preparing affidavits for a search warrant. When respondents left the building in a previously identified vehicle, they were stopped and arrested. A later police search of the vehicle turned up cocaine. After seizing the vehicle, the police returned to the apartment and arrested the occupant, Ms. Thompson. A search of the apartment pursuant to a warrant revealed more evidence of cocaine.

[The police later learned that Carter and Johns had never been in Thompson's apartment before and were only in it for 2 ½ hours, and that they had come to the apartment for the sole purpose of packaging the cocaine. In return for the use of the apartment, Carter and Johns had given Thompson one-eighth of an ounce of the cocaine.

[Respondents were convicted of state drug offenses. The trial court held that (a) since they were only temporary out-of-state visitors, respondents could not challenge the legality of the government intrusion into Ms. Thompson's apartment; (b) Officer Thielen's observations through a gap in the closed blind was not a "search" within the meaning of the Fourth Amendment. The state supreme court reversed, holding that respondents did have "standing" because they had a " 'legitimate expectation of privacy in the invaded place' " (quoting *Rakas*). Even though "society does not recognize as valuable the task of bagging cocaine," observed the court, "society does recognize as valuable the rights of property owners or leaseholders to invite persons into the privacy of their homes to conduct a common task, be it legal or illegal activity." The court went on to hold that the officer's observation constituted an unreasonable "search" of the apartment. The U.S. Supreme Court reversed without reaching the question whether the officer's observation was a "search."]

The Minnesota courts analyzed whether respondents had a legitimate expectation of privacy under the rubric of "standing" doctrine, an analysis which this

Court expressly rejected 20 years ago in *Rakas*. In that case, we held that automobile passengers could not assert the protection of the Fourth Amendment against the seizure of incriminating evidence from a vehicle where they owned neither the vehicle nor the evidence. Central to our analysis was the idea that in determining whether a defendant is able to show the violation of his (and not someone else's) Fourth Amendment rights, the "definition of those rights is more properly placed within the purview of substantive Fourth Amendment law than within that of standing." Thus, we held that in order to claim the protection of the Fourth Amendment, a defendant must demonstrate that he personally has an expectation of privacy in the place searched, and that his expectation is reasonable; *i.e.*, one which has a "source outside of the Fourth Amendment, either by reference to concepts of real or personal property law or to understandings that are recognized and permitted by society."

[The Fourth] Amendment protects persons against unreasonable searches of "their persons [and] houses" and thus indicates that the Fourth Amendment is a personal right that must be invoked by an individual. See *Katz*. ("[T]he Fourth Amendment protects people, not places"). But the extent to which the Fourth Amendment protects people may depend upon where those people are. We have held that "capacity to claim the protection of the Fourth Amendment depends [upon] whether the person who claims the protection of the Amendment has a legitimate expectation of privacy in the invaded place." *Rakas*.

The text of the Amendment suggests that its protections extend only to people in "their" houses. But we have held that in some circumstances a person may have a legitimate expectation of privacy in the house of someone else. In *Minnesota v. Olson* (1990), for example, we decided that an overnight guest in a house had the sort of expectation of privacy that the Fourth Amendment protects. We said:

> "To hold that an overnight guest has a legitimate expectation of privacy in his host's home merely recognizes the every day expectations of privacy that we all share. Staying overnight in another's home is a longstanding social custom that serves functions recognized as valuable by society. We stay in others' home when we travel to a strange city for business or pleasure, we visit our parents, children, or more distant relatives out of town, when we are in between jobs or homes, or when we house-sit for a friend.

> "[From] the overnight guest's perspective, he seeks shelter in another's home precisely because it provides him with privacy, a place where he and his possessions will not be disturbed by anyone but his host and those his host allows inside. * * * "

In *Jones v. United States* (1960), the defendant seeking to exclude evidence resulting from a search of an apartment had been given the use of the apartment by a friend. He had clothing in the apartment, had slept there "maybe a night," and at the time was the sole occupant of the apartment. But while the holding of *Jones*—that a search of the apartment violated the defendant's Fourth Amendment rights—is still valid, its statement that "anyone legitimately on the premises where a search occurs may challenge its legality" was expressly repudiated in *Rakas*. Thus an overnight guest in a home may claim the protection of the Fourth Amendment, but one who is merely present with the consent of the householder may not.

Respondents here were obviously not overnight guests, but were essentially present for a business transaction and were only in the home a matter of hours. There is no suggestion that they had a previous relationship with Thompson, or that there was any other purpose to their visit. Nor was there anything similar to the overnight guest relationship in *Olson* to suggest a degree of acceptance into the household.[1] * * *

Property used for commercial purposes is treated differently for Fourth Amendment purposes than residential property. [And] while it was a "home" in which respondents were present, it was not their home. Similarly, the Court has held that in some circumstances a worker can claim Fourth Amendment protection over his own workplace. See, *e.g.* *O'Connor v. Ortega,* 480 U.S. 709, 107 S.Ct. 1492, 94 L.Ed.2d 714 (1987). But there is no indication that respondents in this case had nearly as significant a connection to Thompson's apartment as the worker in *O'Connor* had to his own private office.

If we regard the overnight guest in *Minnesota v. Olson* as typifying those who may claim the protection of the Fourth Amendment in the home of another, and one merely "legitimately on the premises" as typifying those who may not do so, the present case is obviously somewhere in between. But the purely commercial nature of the transaction engaged in here, the relatively short period of time on the premises, and the lack of any previous connection between respondents and the householder, all lead us to conclude that respondents' situation is closer to that of one simply permitted on the premises. We therefore hold that any search which may have occurred did not violate their Fourth Amendment rights. [Thus] we need not decide whether the police officer's observation constituted a "search." * * *

JUSTICE SCALIA, with whom JUSTICE THOMAS joins, concurring.

I join the opinion of the Court because I believe it accurately applies our recent case law, including *Minnesota v. Olson.* I write separately to express my view that that case law—like the submissions of the parties in this case—gives short shrift to the text of the Fourth Amendment, and to the well and long understood meaning of that text. Specifically, it leaps to apply the fuzzy standard of "legitimate expectation of privacy"—a consideration that is often relevant to whether a search or seizure covered by the Fourth Amendment is "unreasonable"—to the threshold question whether a search or seizure covered by the Fourth Amendment *has occurred.* If that latter question is addressed first and analyzed under the text of the Constitution as traditionally understood, the present case is not remotely difficult.

The Fourth Amendment protects "[t]he right of the people to be secure in *their* persons, houses, papers, and effects, against unreasonable searches and seizures...." U.S. Const., Amdt. 4 (emphasis added). [The] obvious meaning of the provision is that *each* person has the right to be secure against unreasonable searches and seizures in *his own* person, house, papers, and effects.

The Founding-era materials that I have examined confirm that this was the understood meaning. [Justice Scalia then discusses various historical materials, including *Semayne's Case,* 77 Eng.Rep. 194 (K.B. 1604), the leading English case for the common-law maxim that "a man's home is *his* castle"; and the leading American case of *Oystead v. Shed,* 13 Mass. 520 (1816), which reasoned that the "inviolability of dwellinghouses" described by various leading commentators extends to "the occupier or any of his family" and to those "who have made the house *their* home," but not to one such as "a stranger, or perhaps a visitor."]

---

1. Justice Ginsburg's dissent would render the operative language in *Minnesota v. Olson* almost entirely superfluous. There, we explained the justification for extending Fourth Amendment protection to the overnight visitor: "Staying overnight in another's home is a longstanding social custom that serves functions recognized as valuable by society ... We are at our most vulnerable when we are asleep because we cannot monitor our own safety or the security of our belongings." If any short-term business visit by a stranger entitles the visitor to share the Fourth Amendment protection of the lease holder's home, the Court's explanation of its holding in *Olson* was quite unnecessary.

Thus, in deciding the question presented today we write upon a slate that is far from clean. The text of the Fourth Amendment, the common-law background against which it was adopted, and the understandings consistently displayed after its adoption make the answer clear. We were right to hold in *Chapman v. United States* [p. 345] that the Fourth Amendment protects an apartment tenant against an unreasonable search of his dwelling, even though he is only a leaseholder. And we were right to hold in *Bumper v. North Carolina* [p. 338] that an unreasonable search of a grandmother's house violated her resident grandson's Fourth Amendment rights because the area searched "was *his* home" (emphasis added). We went to the absolute limit of what text and tradition permit in *Minnesota v. Olson*, when we protected a mere overnight guest against an unreasonable search of his hosts' apartment. But whereas it is plausible to regard a person's overnight lodging as at least his "temporary" residence, it is entirely impossible to give that characterization to an apartment that he uses to package cocaine.

[The] dissent believes that "[o]ur obligation to produce coherent results" requires that we ignore this clear text and four-century-old tradition, and apply instead the notoriously unhelpful test adopted in a "benchmar[k]" decision that is 31 years old, citing *Katz*. In my view, the only thing the past three decades have established about the *Katz* test (which has come to mean the test enunciated by Justice Harlan's separate concurrence in *Katz*) is that, unsurprisingly, those "actual (subjective) expectation[s] of privacy" that society is prepared to recognize as 'reasonable' "bear an uncanny resemblance to those expectations of privacy that this Court considers reasonable. When that self-indulgent test is employed (as the dissent would employ it here) to determine whether a "search or seizure" within the meaning of the Constitution has *occurred* (as opposed to whether that "search or seizure" is an "unreasonable" one), it has no plausible foundation in the text of the Fourth Amendment. That provision did not guarantee some generalized "right of privacy" and leave it to this Court to determine which particular manifestations of the value of privacy "society is prepared to recognize as 'reasonable.'"

[The] dissent may be correct that a person invited into someone else's house to engage in a common business (even common monkey-business, so to speak) *ought* to be protected against government searches of the room in which that business is conducted; and that persons invited in to deliver milk or pizza (whom the dissent dismisses as "classroom hypotheticals," as opposed, presumably, to flesh-and-blood hypotheticals) ought *not* to be protected against government searches of the rooms that they occupy. I am not sure of the answer to those policy questions. But I am sure that the answer is not remotely contained in the Constitution, which means that it is left—as *many*, indeed *most*, important questions are left—to the judgment of state and federal legislators. * * *

JUSTICE KENNEDY, concurring.

I join the Court's opinion, for its reasoning is consistent with my view that almost all social guests have a legitimate expectation of privacy, and hence protection against unreasonable searches, in their host's home.

[The] homeowner's right to privacy is not an issue in this case. The Court does not reach the question whether the officer's unaided observations of Thompson's apartment constituted a search. If there was in fact a search, however, then Thompson had the right to object to the unlawful police surveillance of her apartment and the right to suppress any evidence disclosed by the search. [Our] cases establish, however, that respondents have no independent privacy right, the violation of which results in exclusion of evidence against them, unless they can establish a meaningful connection to Thompson's apartment.

[In] this case respondents have established nothing more than a fleeting and insubstantial connection with Thompson's home. For all that appears in the record, respondents used Thompson's house simply as a convenient processing station, their purpose involving nothing more than the mechanical act of chopping and packing a substance for distribution.

[If] respondents here had been visiting twenty homes, each for a minute or two, to drop off a bag of cocaine and were apprehended by a policeman wrongfully present in the nineteenth home; or if they had left the goods at a home where they were not staying and the police had seized the goods in their absence, we would have said that *Rakas* compels rejection of any privacy interest respondents might assert. So it does here, given that respondents have established no meaningful tie or connection to the owner, the owner's home, or the owner's expectation of privacy.

We cannot remain faithful to the underlying principle in *Rakas* without reversing in this case, and I am not persuaded that we need depart from it to protect the homeowner's own privacy interests. * * *

Dissent

JUSTICE GINSBURG, with whom JUSTICE STEVENS and JUSTICE SOUTER join, dissenting.

The Court's decision undermines not only the security of short-term guests, but also the security of the home resident herself. In my view, when a homeowner or lessor personally invites a guest into her home to share in a common endeavor, whether it be for conversation, to engage in leisure activities, or for business purposes licit or illicit, that guest should share his host's shelter against unreasonable searches and seizures.

I do not here propose restoration of the "legitimately on the premises" criterion stated in *Jones*, for the Court rejected that formulation in *Rakas* * * *. First, the disposition I would reach in this case responds to the unique importance of the home—the most essential bastion of privacy recognized by the law. See *United States v. Karo*, [p. 156] ("Our cases have not deviated from this basic Fourth Amendment principle."); *Payton v. New York* [p. 251] ("The Fourth Amendment protects the individual's right to privacy in a variety of settings. In none is the zone of privacy more clearly defined than when bounded by the unambiguous physical dimensions of an individual's home.") Second, even within the home itself, the position to which I would adhere would not permit "a casual visitor who has never seen, or been permitted to visit, the basement of another's house to object to a search of the basement if the visitor happened to be in the kitchen of the house at the time of the search." *Rakas*. Further, I would here decide only the case of the homeowner who chooses to share the privacy of her home and her company with a guest, and would not reach classroom hypotheticals like the milkman or pizza deliverer.

My concern centers on an individual's choice to share her home and her associations there with persons she selects. Our decisions indicate that people have a reasonable expectation of privacy in their homes in part because they have the prerogative to exclude others. [The] power to exclude implies the power to include. See, e.g., Mary Irene Coombs, *Shared Privacy and the Fourth Amendment, or the Rights of Relationships*, 75 Calif.L.Rev. 1593, 1618 (1987); Albert W. Alschuler, *Interpersonal Privacy and the Fourth Amendment* 4 N.Ill.U.L.Rev. 1, 13 (1983). Our Fourth Amendment decisions should reflect those complementary prerogatives.

A home dweller places her own privacy at risk, the Court's approach indicates, when she opens her home to others, uncertain whether the duration of their stay, their purpose, and their "acceptance into the household" will earn protection. * * * Human frailty suggests that today's decision will tempt police to pry into private dwellings without warrant, to find evidence incriminating guests who do not rest there through the night. See Eulis Simien, *The Interrelationship of the Scope of the Fourth Amendment and Standing to Object to Unreasonable Searches,* 41 Ark.L.Rev. 487, 539 (1988) ("[I]f the police have no probable cause, they have everything to gain and nothing to lose if they search under circumstances where they know that at least one of the potential defendants will not have standing."). *Rakas* tolerates that temptation with respect to automobile searches. See Gerald D. Ashdown, *The Fourth Amendment and the "Legitimate Expectation of Privacy,"* 34 Vand.L.Rev. 1289, 1321 (1981). * * * I see no impelling reason to extend this risk into the home.

[Through] the host's invitation, the guest gains a reasonable expectation of privacy in the home. *Minnesota v. Olson,* so held with respect to an overnight guest. The logic of that decision extends to shorter term guests as well. See SEARCHSZR § 11.3(b). [In] sum, when a homeowner chooses to share the privacy of her home and her company with a short-term guest, the twofold requirement "emerg[ing] from prior decisions" has been satisfied: Both host and guest "have exhibited an actual (subjective) expectation of privacy"; that "expectation [is] one [our] society is prepared to recognize as 'reasonable.' " *Katz* (Harlan, J., concurring).[2] * * *

Our leading decision in *Katz* is key to my view of this case. There, we ruled that the Government violated the petitioner's Fourth Amendment rights when it electronically recorded him transmitting wagering information while he was inside a public telephone booth. We were mindful that "the Fourth Amendment protects people, not places," and held that this electronic monitoring of a business call "violated the privacy upon which [the caller] justifiably relied while using the telephone booth." Our obligation to produce coherent results in this often visited area of the law requires us to inform our current expositions by benchmarks already established.

[The] Court's decision in this case veers sharply from the path marked in *Katz.* I do not agree that we have a more reasonable expectation of privacy when we place a business call to a person's home from a public telephone booth on the side of the street, see *Katz,* than when we actually enter that person's premises to engage in a common endeavor. * * *[a]

Consider Craig Bradley, *The Fourth Amendment's Iron Triangle: Standing,Consent and Searchability,* Trial, Aug. 1999, p. 75: "Who may be searched? Who may consent to a search? Who has standing to protest a search? These three, seemingly unrelated, questions frequently arise in criminal cases. But though these issues have always appeared to the Supreme Court to be unconnected,

---

2. In his concurring opinion, Justice Kennedy maintains that respondents here lacked "an expectation of privacy that society recognizes as reasonable" because they "established nothing more than a fleeting and insubstantial connection" with the host's home. As the Minnesota Supreme Court reported, however, the stipulated facts showed that respondents were inside the apartment with the host's permission, remained inside for at least 2 1/2 hours, and, during that time, engaged in concert with the host in a collaborative venture. These stipulated facts—which scarcely resemble a stop of a minute or two at the 19th of 20 homes to drop off a packet—securely demonstrate that the host intended to share her privacy with respondents, and that respondents, therefore, had entered into the home-

land of Fourth Amendment protection. While I agree with the Minnesota Supreme Court that, under the rule settled since *Katz,* the reasonableness of the expectation of privacy controls, not the visitor's status as social guest, invitee, licensee, or business partner, I think it noteworthy that five Members of the Court would place under the Fourth Amendment's shield, at least, "almost all social guests."

a. Although Justice Breyer concurred in the judgment because he did not believe that Officer Thielen's observation of the apartment, "made from a public area outside the curtilage," constituted an "unreasonable search," he "agree[d] with Justice Ginsburg that respondents can claim the Fourth Amendment's protection."

consideration of two recent cases, *Wyoming v. Houghton* [p. 273] and *Minnesota v. Carter*, has led me to the conclusion that these three questions hinge on exactly the same issue: *What is the subject's interest in or connection to the place to be searched?* Further, they should all have the same answer. That is, if a person has authority to consent to a search, he also has standing to protest it, and is searchable if found at the scene of the search, and vice versa. Recognition that the answer to these questions is the same means that once the Court has put one side of this equilateral triangle into position, the position of the other two sides has been resolved as well. Moreover, it may cause decision makers to think more carefully about finding no standing for passengers in a car, for example, if they realize that will lead to a reduction in authority of such passengers to consent to a search and their 'searchability' by virtue of their presence in that car."

SECTION 2. THE "FRUIT OF THE POISONOUS TREE"

A. HISTORICAL BACKGROUND AND OVERVIEW

"In the simplest of exclusionary rule cases," observes CRIMPROC, § 9.3(a), "the challenged evidence is quite clearly 'direct' or 'primary' in its relationship to the prior arrest, search, interrogation [or lineup] [e.g., a confession made in response to impermissible interrogation or physical evidence obtained by an illegal search]." Not infrequently, however, points out CRIMPROC, "challenged evidence is 'secondary' or 'derivative' in character. This occurs when, for example, a confession is obtained after an illegal arrest[a] [or] physical evidence is located after an illegally obtained confession.[b] [In] these situations, it is necessary to determine whether the derivative evidence is 'tainted' by the prior constitutional or other violation. To use the phrase coined by Justice Frankfurter, it must be decided whether that evidence is 'the fruit of the poisonous tree.'"[c]

1. *Genesis of the rule; the doctrine of "attenuation."* (a) The genesis of the "taint" or "fruit of the poisonous tree" doctrine, as it came to be called, appears in *Silverthorne Lumber Co. v. United States*, 251 U.S. 385, 40 S.Ct. 182, 64 L.Ed. 319 (1920), where, in holding that the government could not use information obtained during an illegal search to subpoena the very documents illegally viewed, the Court, per Holmes, J., pointed out: "The essence of a provision forbidding the acquisition of evidence in a certain way is that not merely evidence so acquired shall not be used before the Court but that it shall not be used at all. Of course this does not mean that the facts thus obtained become sacred and inaccessible. If knowledge of them is gained from an independent source they may be proved like any others, but the knowledge gained by the Government's own wrong cannot be used by it in the way proposed."

Did *Silverthorne* mean that illegally seized *evidence* may never be used by the government although the *facts* revealed by that evidence may be obtained from an independent source? See Robert M. Pitler, *"The Fruit of the Poisonous Tree" Revisited and Shepardized*, 56 Calif.L.Rev. 579, 589 (1968).

(b) In *Nardone v. United States*, 308 U.S. 338, 60 S.Ct. 266, 84 L.Ed. 307 (1939), which first used the phrase "fruit of the poisonous tree," the Court, per Frankfurter, J., refused to permit the prosecution to avoid an inquiry into its use of information gained by illegal wiretapping, observing that "to forbid the direct use of methods [but] to put no curb on their full indirect use would only invite the very methods deemed 'inconsistent with ethical standards and destructive of

---

a. See, e.g., *Brown v. Illinois*, p. 766.

b. See, e.g., *New York v. Quarles*, p. 509.

c. *Nardone v. United States*, Note 1(b).

personal liberty.' "[a] The case also established the "attenuation" doctrine, being the first to authoritatively recognize that even where the challenged evidence did not have an "independent source" it might still be admissible: "Sophisticated argument may prove a causal connection between information obtained through illicit wire-tapping and the Government's proof. As a matter of good sense, however, such connection may have become so attenuated as to dissipate the taint."

2. **Verbal evidence as the "fruit" of illegal search and seizure.** In WONG SUN v. UNITED STATES, 371 U.S. 471, 83 S.Ct. 407, 9 L.Ed.2d 441 (1963) (other aspects of which are discussed at pp. 116, 183), six federal narcotics agents illegally broke into Toy's laundry, chased him into the living quarters at the back of his shop, where Toy's wife and child were sleeping, and handcuffed him. Toy then told the agents that Yee had been selling narcotics. The agents immediately went to Yee, who surrendered heroin to them and implicated Toy and a third party, Wong Sun. A 5–4 majority, per BRENNAN, J., held that both Toy's declarations, upon being handcuffed in his bedroom, *and* "the narcotics taken from Yee, to which [Toy's] declarations led the police" had to be excluded as the "fruits" of the agents' unlawful entry into Toy's bedroom and the "bedroom arrest."

The Court recognized that "traditionally" the exclusionary rule had barred only "physical, tangible materials," but concluded that "verbal evidence which derives so immediately from an unlawful entry and an unauthorized arrest [as here] is no less the 'fruit' of official illegality than the more common tangible fruits of the unwarranted intrusion."[b] Not "all evidence is 'fruit of the poisonous tree' simply because it would not have come to light but for the illegal actions of the police. Rather, the more apt question in such a case is 'whether, granting establishment of the primary illegality [the evidence] has been come at by exploitation of that illegality or instead by means sufficiently distinguishable to be purged of the primary taint.' J. Maguire, *Evidence of Guilt* 221 (1959). We think it clear that the narcotics [taken from Yee] were 'come at by the exploitation of that illegality [the lawless search and seizure of Toy]' and hence that they may not be used against Toy."

On the other hand, although Wong Sun had also been unlawfully arrested, his confession was not the "fruit" of his illegal arrest. Since he had been released on his own recognizance after a lawful arraignment and had returned voluntarily several days later to make the statement, "the connection between [Wong Sun's] arrest and [his] statement had 'become so attenuated as to dissipate the taint.' "

Notes and Questions

(a) *The relevant question.* Does the *Wong Sun* Court's talk of "purging the primary taint" obfuscate the relevant question—whether the admission of the secondary evidence will significantly encourage police misconduct in the future? See Pitler, *supra*, at 588–89; Note, 115 U.Pa.L.Rev. 1136, 1147 (1967).

(b) *"Purging the taint" of Fourth Amendment violations.* Are there events short of release from custody (which occurred in *Wong Sun*) which operate to "purge the taint" of an illegal arrest or search? Can the mere passage of time

---

a. But cf. *United States v. Calandra*, p. 131, holding that a witness may not refuse to answer grand jury questions on the ground that they are based on evidence obtained from him in an earlier unlawful search.

b. The dissenters, Clark, J., joined by Harlan, Stewart and White, JJ., did not challenge the manner in which the Court applied the "fruits" doctrine, but maintained that Toy's arrest was lawful and thus provided "no 'poisonous tree' whose fruits we must evaluate."

suffice? Or would such a rule only "postpone the testing" of the fruit but "not diminish its temptation"? See *Collins v. Beto,* 348 F.2d 823, 828 (5th Cir.1965). Would *Miranda* warnings purge the taint of an illegal arrest? See *Brown v. Illinois,* below.

3. *"Independent source"; "inevitable discovery."* The *Wong Sun* Court quoted from *Silverthorne,* supra, the proposition that the exclusionary rule has no application when "the Government learned of the evidence 'from an independent source.'" This means that if not even a "but for" test can be satisfied, the challenged evidence is not a fruit of the prior violation—a violation of a person's rights should not put him beyond the law's reach if his guilt can be established by evidence unconnected with or "untainted" by the violation.

A variation of the "independent source" exception is the "inevitable discovery" or "hypothetical independent source" rule, a doctrine long utilized by many lower courts and recently accepted by the U.S. Supreme Court.[a] This doctrine differs from the "independent source" exception in that the question is not whether the police *actually* acquired certain evidence by reliance upon an untainted source, but whether evidence in fact obtained illegally would inevitably or eventually or probably have been discovered lawfully.

The doctrine is most palatable, and has been most frequently applied, when the police misconduct occurred "while an investigation was already in progress and resulted in the discovery of evidence that would have eventually have been obtained through routine police investigatory procedure. The illegalities in such cases, therefore, had the effect of simply accelerating the discovery." Note, 74 Colum.L.Rev. 88, 90 (1974).

Because mechanical application of the "inevitable discovery" doctrine would seem to encourage unconstitutional shortcuts, and one purpose of the exclusionary rule is to discourage such shortcuts, it has been argued that the doctrine should be permitted only when the police have not acted in "bad faith" to accelerate the discovery of the challenged evidence. See, e.g., SEARCHSZR § 11.4(a) at 382. But the Court rejected such a limitation in *Nix v. Williams,* p. 775.

4. *Confession as the "fruit" of an illegal arrest.* BROWN v. ILLINOIS, 422 U.S. 590, 95 S.Ct. 2254, 45 L.Ed.2d 416 (1975), arose as follows: Following his illegal arrest, petitioner, a murder suspect, was taken to a police station where, after being given the *Miranda* warnings and waiving his rights, he made incriminating statements within two hours of the arrest. The state supreme court affirmed the murder conviction, taking the view that "the *Miranda* warnings in and of themselves" purged the taint of the prior illegal arrest. The Court, per BLACKMUN, J., reversed:

"The exclusionary rule, [when] utilized to effectuate the Fourth Amendment, serves interests and policies that are distinct from those it serves under the Fifth. [E]xclusion of a confession made without *Miranda* warnings might be regarded as necessary to effectuate the Fifth Amendment, but it would not be sufficient fully to protect the Fourth. *Miranda* warnings, and the exclusion of a confession made without them, do not alone sufficiently deter a Fourth Amendment violation.

"[If] *Miranda* warnings, by themselves, were held to attenuate the taint of an unconstitutional arrest, regardless of how wanton and purposeful the Fourth Amendment violation, the effect of the exclusionary rule would be substantially diluted. [Illegal arrests] would be encouraged by the knowledge that evidence derived therefrom hopefully could be made admissible at trial by the simple expedient of giving *Miranda* warnings. Any incentive to avoid Fourth Amendment

a. See *Nix v. Williams,* p. 775.

violations would be eviscerated by making the warnings, in effect, a 'cure-all' * * *.''

Although the Court rejected the *per se* rule of the Illinois court whereunder the *Miranda* warnings were deemed to break the causal connection between the arrest and confession, it declined to adopt a *per se* or "but for" rule running in the other direction. It concluded instead that such taint issues "must be answered on the facts of each case. No single fact is dispositive. [The] *Miranda* warnings are an important factor, to be sure, in determining whether the confession is obtained by exploitation of an illegal arrest. But they are not the only factor to be considered. The temporal proximity of the arrest and the confession, the presence of intervening circumstances and, particularly, the purpose and flagrancy of the official misconduct, are all relevant. The voluntariness of the statement is a threshold requirement. And the burden of showing admissibility rests, of course, on the prosecution.''

The Court then concluded that the prosecution had failed to sustain its burden: "[Petitioner's] first statement was separated from his illegal arrest by less than two hours, and there was no intervening event of significance whatsoever. * * * We could hold [petitioner's] first statement admissible only if we overrule *Wong Sun.* We decline to do so. [The] illegality here, moreover, had a quality of purposefulness. The impropriety of the arrest was obvious. [The] detectives embarked upon this expedition for evidence in the hope that something might turn up.''

Justice WHITE expressed agreement with the Court insofar as it "holds (1) that despite *Miranda* warnings the Fourth and Fourteenth Amendments require the exclusion from evidence of statements obtained as the fruit of an arrest which the arresting officers *knew or should have known* was without probable cause and unconstitutional, and (2) that the statements obtained in this case were in this category" (emphasis added), and therefore concurred in the judgment.

Justice POWELL, joined by Rehnquist, J., joined the Court insofar as it rejected the Illinois courts' *per se* rule, but "would remand the case for reconsideration under the general standards articulated in the Court's opinion." In Justice Powell's view, "the flagrantly abusive violations of Fourth Amendment rights, on the one hand, and 'technical' Fourth Amendment violations, [on the other] call for significantly different judicial responses":

"I would require the clearest indication of attenuation in cases in which official conduct was flagrantly abusive of Fourth Amendment rights. [In such cases] I would consider the equalizing potential of *Miranda* warnings rarely sufficient to dissipate the taint. [At] the opposite end of the spectrum lie 'technical' violations of Fourth Amendment rights where, for example, officers in good faith arrest an individual in reliance on a warrant later invalidated or pursuant to a statute that subsequently is declared unconstitutional. [In such cases] the deterrence rationale of the exclusionary rule does not obtain, and I can see no legitimate justification for depriving the prosecution of reliable and probative evidence. Thus, with the exception of statements given in the immediate circumstances of the illegal arrest—a constraint I think is imposed by existing exclusionary rule law—I would not require more than proof that effective *Miranda* warnings were given and that the ensuing statement was voluntary in the Fifth Amendment sense.''

In *Dunaway v. New York,* other aspects of which are discussed at p. 325, the Court, per Brennan, J., reaffirmed the view that *Miranda* warnings, by themselves, are not necessarily sufficient to attenuate the taint of an unconstitutional arrest: "The situation in this case is virtually a replica of the situation in *Brown.* Petitioner was also admittedly seized without probable cause in the hope that something might turn up, and confessed without any intervening event of significance. [To] admit petitioner's confession in such a case would allow 'law enforcement officers to violate the Fourth Amendment with impunity, safe in the knowledge that they could wash their hands in the "procedural safeguards" of the Fifth' [Comment, 25 Emory L.J. 227, 238 (1976)]."

Justice Stevens joined the Court's opinion but added a comment on "the significance of two factors that may be considered when determining whether a confession has been obtained by exploitation of an illegal arrest":

"The temporal relationship between the arrest and the confession may be an ambiguous factor. If there are no relevant intervening circumstances, a prolonged detention may well be a more serious exploitation of an illegal arrest than a short one. Conversely, even an immediate confession may have been motivated by a prearrest event such as a visit with a minister. The flagrancy of the official misconduct is relevant, in my judgment, only insofar as it has a tendency to motivate the defendant. A midnight arrest with drawn guns will be equally frightening whether the police acted recklessly or in good faith. Conversely, a courteous command has the same effect on the arrestee whether the officer thinks he has probable cause or knows that he does not. In either event, if the Fourth Amendment is violated, the admissibility question will turn on the causal relationship between that violation and the defendant's subsequent confession."[a]

———

The *Brown-Dunaway* rule was applied (extended?) to a complicated set of facts in *Taylor v. Alabama,* 457 U.S. 687, 102 S.Ct. 2664, 73 L.Ed.2d 314 (1982). A 5–4 majority, per Marshall, J., held that petitioner's confession was the impermissible fruit of his illegal arrest even though (a) six hours had elapsed between the illegal arrest and the time petitioner confessed; (b) petitioner was advised of his rights three times; and (c) he was allowed to visit briefly with his girlfriend and his neighbor shortly before he confessed.

Dissenting Justice O'Connor joined by the Chief Justice, and Powell and Rehnquist, JJ., maintained that *Brown* and *Dunaway* required a contrary result. As the dissent saw it, "[t]he petitioner's confession was not proximately caused by his illegal arrest, but was the product of a decision based both on knowledge of his constitutional rights and on the discussion with his friends."

Compare the *Brown-Dunaway-Taylor* line of cases with *Rawlings v. Kentucky* (1980), discussed at p. 756. Petitioner argued that his admission of the ownership of drugs which had been found in Ms. Cox's purse (after the contents of the purse had been emptied, pursuant to a police order) was the fruit of an illegal detention. The Court, per Rehnquist, J., disagreed. Assuming that Rawlings and others were illegally detained in a house while the police obtained a search warrant for the premises, the Court noted, inter alia, that the detention was in a "congenial atmosphere"; that petitioner's admissions were "apparently spontaneous reactions to the discovery of his drugs in Cox's purse" and not the product of the initial illegality, and the police action "does not rise to the level of conscious or flagrant misconduct requiring prophylactic exclusion of petitioner's statements. Contrast *Brown*."[b]

---

a. Rehnquist, J., joined by Burger, C.J., dissented, maintaining that the police had acted in "good faith and not in a flagrant manner" and that in such cases "no more [should be required] than that proper *Miranda* warnings [be] given and that the statement be voluntary within the meaning of the Fifth Amendment."

b. Dissenting Justice Marshall, joined by Brennan, J., maintained that "petitioner's admissions were obviously the fruit of the illegal detention."

5. *Identification of a person as a "fruit" of an illegal arrest.* United States v. Crews, 445 U.S. 463, 100 S.Ct. 1244, 63 L.Ed.2d 537 (1980), arose as follows: Immediately after being assaulted and robbed in a public restroom, the victim gave the police a full description of her assailant. Crews, who matched the suspect's description, was illegally taken into custody, photographed, and then released. Thereafter, when shown an array of eight photographs, the victim selected Crews' photograph as that of the man who had robbed her. At a court-ordered lineup, Crews was again positively identified. Finally, Crews was identified at the trial. Crews was convicted of robbery, but the District of Columbia Court of Appeals held the victim's in-court identification inadmissible, viewing it as obtained by official "exploitation" of the "primary illegality"—Crews' unlawful arrest.[a] The Court, per Brennan, J., disagreed:

A victim's in-court identification has "three distinct elements": "[1], the victim is present at trial to testify as to what transpired between her and the offender, and to identify the defendant as the culprit. [2], the victim possesses knowledge of and the ability to reconstruct the prior [crime] and to identify the defendant from her observations of him at the time of the crime. And [3], the defendant is also physically present in the courtroom, so that the victim can observe him and compare his appearance to that of the offender. In the present case, none of these three elements 'has been come at by exploitation' of the defendant's Fourth Amendment rights."

As for (1), the victim's presence and cooperation were "surely not the product of any police misconduct"; as for (3), because an "illegal arrest, without more, has never been viewed as a bar to subsequent prosecution," the defendant was "not himself a suppressible 'fruit,' and the illegality of his detention cannot deprive the Government of the opportunity to prove his guilt through the introduction of evidence wholly untainted by the police misconduct."

As for (2): "Nor did the illegal arrest infect the victim's ability to give accurate identification testimony. Based upon her observations at the time of the robbery, [she] constructed a mental image of her assailant. At trial, she retrieved this mnemonic representation, compared it [to] defendant, and positively identified him as the robber. No part of this process was affected by [the] illegal arrest."

Because it was clear that prior to his illegal arrest, the police both knew defendant's identity and had some reason to believe he was involved in the robbery, Justice Brennan would have reserved judgment as to whether a defendant's face could ever be considered a suppressible "fruit" of an illegal arrest.[b] But a majority of the Court, in two separate concurring opinions, explicitly rejected this possibility.

6. *Confession as the "fruit" of a Payton violation.* Payton v. New York (p. 251) holds that the Fourth Amendment prohibits the police from effecting a warrantless entry into a suspect's home in order to make a routine felony arrest. In NEW YORK v. HARRIS, 495 U.S. 14, 110 S.Ct. 1640, 109 L.Ed.2d 13 (1990), a 5–4 majority, per WHITE, J., held that where the police have probable cause to arrest a suspect, the exclusionary rule does not bar the use of a statement made by the suspect *outside* his home even though the statement is obtained after an *in-house* arrest in violation of *Payton*.

---

a. The trial court had excluded both the photographic and lineup identifications as the "fruits" of Crews' illegal arrest and on appeal the government conceded that both were inadmissible. Why? Wasn't *the lineup identification* missible. Why? Wasn't *the lineup identification*

admissible for the same reasons the Supreme Court held that the in-court identification was?

b. As Justice Brennan noted, this part of his opinion was joined only by Stewart and Stevens, JJ.

The police had probable cause to believe Harris had killed a woman. They went to his apartment to take him into custody, but did not first obtain an arrest warrant. After being advised of his *Miranda* rights and waiving them, Harris reportedly admitted that he had committed the homicide. He was then taken to the station house, where, after again being advised of his rights and again waiving them, he signed a written inculpatory statement. Since the state did not challenge the trial court's suppression of Harris' statement to the police while still inside his home, the sole issue was the admissibility of the statement he made at the station house. The New York Court of Appeals ruled that it was the inadmissible fruit of the *Payton* violation, but the Supreme Court reversed:

advised M + waived

"[As] emphasized in earlier cases, 'we have declined to adopt a *"per se* or 'but for' rule'" that would make inadmissible any evidence, whether tangible or live-witness testimony, which somehow came to light through a chain of causation that begins with an illegal arrest.' *United States v. Ceccolini* [p. 774]. Rather, in this context, we have stated that '[t]he penalties visited upon the Government, and in turn upon the public, because its officers have violated the law must bear some relation to the purposes which the law is to serve.' Id. In light of these principles, we decline to apply the exclusionary rule in this context because *Payton* was designed to protect the physical integrity of the home, [not] grant criminal suspects, like Harris, protection for statements made outside their premises where the police have probable cause to arrest the suspect. * * *

"Nothing in the reasoning of [*Payton*] suggests that an arrest in a home without a warrant but with probable cause somehow renders unlawful continued custody of the suspect once he is removed from the house. [Because] the officers had probable cause to arrest Harris for a crime, Harris was not unlawfully in custody when he was removed to the station house. [For] Fourth Amendment purposes, the legal issue is the same as it would be had the police arrested Harris on his door step, illegally entered his home to search for evidence, and later interrogated Harris at the station house. Similarly, if the police had made a warrantless entry into Harris' home, not found him there, but arrested him on the street when he returned, a later statement made by him after proper warnings would no doubt be admissible.

"[In *Brown, Dunaway* and *Taylor*], evidence obtained from a criminal defendant following arrest was suppressed because the police lacked probable cause. [These] cases stand for the familiar proposition that the indirect fruits of an illegal search or arrest should be suppressed when they bear a sufficiently close relationship to the underlying illegality. [But] attenuation analysis is only appropriate where, as a threshold matter, courts determine that 'the challenged evidence is in some sense the product of illegal governmental activity.' *Crews.* * * *

"Harris's statement taken at the police station was not the product of being in unlawful custody. Neither was it the fruit of having been arrested in the home rather than someplace else. The case is analogous to *Crews.* In that case, we refused to suppress a victim's in-court identification despite the defendant's illegal arrest. The Court found that the evidence was not 'come at by exploitation [of] the defendant's Fourth Amendment rights,' and that it was not necessary to inquire whether the 'taint' of the Fourth Amendment violation was sufficiently attenuated to permit the introduction of the evidence. Here, likewise, the police had a justification to question Harris prior to his arrest; therefore, his subsequent statement was not an exploitation of the illegal entry into Harris's home. * * *

"[S]uppressing the statement taken outside the house would not serve the purpose of the rule that made Harris's in-house arrest illegal. The warrant requirement for an arrest in the home is imposed to protect the home, and anything incriminating the police gathered from arresting Harris in his home, rather than elsewhere, has been excluded, as it should have been; the purpose of the rule has thereby been vindicated. [The] principal incentive to obey *Payton* still obtains: the police know that a warrantless entry will lead to the suppression of any evidence found or statements taken inside the home. If we did suppress statements like Harris's, moreover, the incremental deterrent value would be minimal. Given that the police have probable cause to arrest a suspect in Harris's position, they need not violate *Payton* in order to interrogate the suspect. It is doubtful therefore that the desire to secure a statement from a criminal suspect would motivate the police to violate *Payton*. As a result, suppressing a station-house statement obtained after a *Payton* violation will have little effect on the officers' actions, one way or another.''

Dissenting Justice MARSHALL, joined by Brennan, Blackmun and Stevens, JJ., deemed *Brown v. Illinois* controlling:

"An application of the *Brown* factors to this case compels the conclusion that Harris' statement at the station house must be suppressed. About an hour elapsed between the illegal arrest and Harris' confession, without any intervening factor other than the warnings required by *Miranda*. This Court has held, however, that '*Miranda* warnings, *alone* and *per se*, ... cannot assure in every case that the Fourth Amendment violation has not been unduly exploited.' *Brown*. Indeed, in *Brown*, we held that a statement made almost *two* hours after an illegal arrest, and after *Miranda* warnings had been given, was not sufficiently removed from the violation so as to dissipate the taint.

"[The] officers decided, apparently consistent with a 'departmental policy,' to violate Harris' Fourth Amendment rights so they could get evidence that they could not otherwise obtain. As the trial court held, 'No more clear violation of [*Payton*], in my view, could be established.' Where, as here, there is a particularly flagrant constitutional violation and little in the way of elapsed time or intervening circumstances, the statement in the police station must be suppressed.

"[The] majority's *per se* rule in this case fails to take account of our repeated holdings that violations of privacy in the home are especially invasive. Rather, its rule is necessarily premised on the proposition that the effect of a *Payton* violation magically vanishes once the suspect is dragged from his home. But the concerns that make a warrantless home arrest a violation of the Fourth Amendment are nothing so evanescent. A person who is forcibly separated from his family and home in the dark of night after uniformed officers have broken down his door, handcuffed him, and forced him at gunpoint to accompany them to a police station does not suddenly breathe a sigh of relief at the moment he is dragged across his doorstep. Rather, the suspect is likely to be so frightened and rattled that he will say something incriminating. These effects, of course, extend far beyond the moment the physical occupation of the home ends. The entire focus of the *Brown* factors is to fix the point at which those effects are sufficiently dissipated that deterrence is not meaningfully advanced by suppression. The majority's assertion, as though the proposition were axiomatic, that the effects of such an intrusion *must* end when the violation ends is both undefended and indefensible. * * *

"Perhaps the most alarming aspect of the Court's ruling is its practical consequences for the deterrence of *Payton* violations. Imagine a police officer who has probable cause to arrest a suspect but lacks a warrant. [The] officer knows that if he breaks into the house without a warrant and drags the suspect outside, the suspect, shaken by the enormous invasion of privacy he has just undergone, may say something incriminating. Before today's decision, the government would only be able to use that evidence if the Court found that the taint of the arrest had been attenuated; after the decision, the evidence will be admissible regardless of whether it was the product of the unconstitutional arrest.[5] Thus, the officer envisions the following best-case scenario if he chooses to violate the Constitution: he avoids a major expenditure of time and effort, ensures that the suspect will not escape, and procures the most damaging evidence of all, a confession. His worst-case scenario is that he will avoid a major expenditure of effort, ensure that the suspect will not escape, and will see evidence in the house (which would have remained unknown absent the constitutional violation) that cannot be used in the prosecution's case-in-chief. The Court thus creates powerful incentives for police officers to violate the Fourth Amendment. In the context of our constitutional rights and the sanctity of our homes, we cannot afford to presume that officers will be entirely impervious to those incentives."

7.   *A warrant search as the fruit of an illegal entry and occupation of the premises.* SEGURA v. UNITED STATES (1984) (also discussed at p. 247) arose as follows: When Segura, a suspected narcotics violator, entered his apartment building one evening, he was immediately arrested and taken to his apartment. The agents entered the apartment without requesting or obtaining permission. Four other people were there. The agents told them that Segura was under arrest and that a search warrant for the premises was being obtained.

The agents then conducted a limited security check of the apartment, in the process observing drug paraphernalia. They then took Segura and the other occupants of the apartment to headquarters. Two agents remained in the apartment awaiting the warrant. Because of "administrative delay," the search warrant was not issued until some 19 hours after the initial entry. When the agents executed the warrant they discovered narcotics and records of narcotics transactions.

Since the government did not dispute the rulings below that the initial entry and security search were unlawful, "the only issue" before the Court was whether items "not observed during the illegal entry and first discovered by the agents the day after the entry, under an admittedly valid search warrant, should have been suppressed."[a] A 5–4 majority, per BURGER, C.J., answered in the negative. The legality of the initial entry had no bearing on the admissibility of the challenged evidence "because there was an independent source for the warrant under which that evidence was seized": "No information obtained during the initial entry or occupation of the apartment was needed or used by the agents to secure the warrant. [The] valid warrant search was a 'means sufficiently distinguishable' to purge the evidence of any 'taint' arising from the entry."

Dissenting Justice STEVENS, joined by Brennan, Marshall and Blackmun, JJ., maintained that "the controlling question" was "whether the deterrent purposes of the exclusionary rule would be served or undermined by the suppression of this evidence." He thought the deterrence rationale "plainly applicable": "The agents impounded the apartment precisely because they wished to avoid risking a loss of access to the evidence within it. Thus, the unlawful benefit they [obtained] was exactly the benefit [that] motivated [them] in the case to violate the Constitution."

5.   Indeed, if the officer, as here, works in New York State, the Court's assertion that "[i]t is doubtful therefore that the desire to secure a statement from a criminal suspect would motivate the police to violate *Payton*" takes on a singularly ironic cast. The court below found as a matter of fact that the officers in this case had intentionally violated *Payton* for *precisely* the reason the Court identifies as "doubtful."

a.   Such illegal entries, observed the Court, are sufficiently deterred by the officers' realization that "whatever evidence they discover as a direct result of the entry may be suppressed." The four dissenters found the suggested distinction a puzzling one: "If the execution of a valid warrant takes the poison out of the hidden fruit, I should think that it would also remove the taint from the fruit in plain view."

In MURRAY v. UNITED STATES, 487 U.S. 533, 108 S.Ct. 2529, 101 L.Ed.2d 472 (1988), the Court, by a 4–3 vote (Brennan and Kennedy, JJ., not participating), declined to read *Segura* narrowly and held that evidence observed by the police during an illegal entry of premises need not be excluded if such evidence is subsequently discovered during the execution of an otherwise valid search warrant sought and issued on the basis of information wholly unconnected to the prior entry. After receiving information that a warehouse was being used for illegal drug activities, federal agents forced their way into the warehouse and observed in plain view bales of marijuana. The agents then left without disturbing the bales and applied for a search warrant. In their application, they did not mention the prior entry or include any recitations of their observations during that entry. Upon issuance of the warrant, the agents reentered the warehouse and seized the bales and other evidence of crime. In upholding the admissibility of the evidence, the Court, per SCALIA, J., observed:

"Knowledge that the marijuana was in the warehouse was assuredly acquired at the time of the unlawful entry. But it was also acquired at the time of entry pursuant to the warrant, and if that later acquisition was not the result of the earlier entry there is no reason why the independent source doctrine should not apply. Invoking the exclusionary rule would put the police (and society) not in the same position they would have occupied if no violation occurred, but in a *worse* one. See *Nix v. Williams* [p. 775]. We think this is also true with respect to the tangible evidence, the bales of marijuana. [S]o long as a later, lawful seizure is genuinely independent of an earlier, tainted one (which may well be difficult to establish where the seized goods are kept in the police's possession) there is no reason why the independent source doctrine should not apply.

"The ultimate question, therefore, is whether the search pursuant to warrant was in fact a genuinely independent source of the information and tangible evidence at issue here. This would not have been the case if the agents' decision to seek the warrant was prompted by what they had seen during the initial entry, or if information obtained during that entry was presented to the Magistrate and affected his decision to issue the warrant. [The] District Court found that the agents did not reveal their warrantless entry to the Magistrate and that they did not include in their application for a warrant any recitation of their observations in the warehouse. It did not, however, explicitly find that the agents would have sought a warrant if they had not earlier entered the warehouse. [Thus], we vacate the judgments and remand these cases [for] determination whether the warrant-authorized search of the warehouse was an independent source of the challenged evidence in the sense we have described."

Dissenting Justice MARSHALL, joined by Stevens and O'Connor, JJ., maintained that "the Court's decision, by failing to provide sufficient guarantees that the subsequent search was, in fact, independent of the illegal search, emasculates the Warrant Clause and undermines the deterrence function of the exclusionary rule":

"[When], as here, the same team of investigators is involved in both the first and second search, there is a significant danger that the 'independence' of the source will in fact be illusory, and that the initial search will have affected the decision to obtain a warrant notwithstanding the officers' subsequent assertions to the contrary. It is therefore crucial that the factual premise of the exception—complete independence—be clearly established before the exception can [apply]. I believe the Court's reliance on the intent of the law enforcement officers who conducted the warrantless search provides insufficient guarantees that the subsequent legal search was unaffected by the prior illegal search. * * *

"Segura is readily distinguished from the present case. The admission of evidence first discovered during a legal search does not significantly lessen the deterrence facing the law enforcement officers contemplating an illegal entry *so long as* the evidence that is seen is excluded. This was clearly the view of [the *Segura* majority]. [E]xtending *Segura* to cover evidence discovered during an initial illegal search will eradicate this remaining deterrence to illegal entry. Moreover, there is less reason to believe that an initial illegal entry was prompted by a desire to determine whether to bother to get a warrant in the first place, and thus was not wholly independent of the second search, if officers understand that evidence they discover during the illegal search will be excluded even if they subsequently return with a warrant.

Consider Craig M. Bradley, *Murray v. United States: The Bell Tolls for the Search Warrant Requirement*, 64 Ind.L.J. 907, 920 (1989):

"While I agree with the dissent in *Murray* that the decision 'emasculates the Warrant Clause,' I don't necessarily disagree with the result. This is [because] nothing in the amendment itself or, apparently, in the minds of its framers, requires a warrant as a prerequisite for a reasonable search; it only requires probable cause as a prerequisite for a warrant. [I]nstead of claiming that there is a warrant requirement and then, as recently illustrated in *Murray*, repeatedly finding ways to ignore it, the Court ought to adopt one of two models of the fourth amendment * * *.

[Professor Bradley then discusses the 'no lines' or 'general reasonableness' model, under which obtaining a warrant is only one of a number of relevant factors; and the 'bright line' approach, under which a warrant is *always* required for *every* search and seizure when it is practicable to obtain one.] With *Murray*, the Court clearly shows its preference for [a] reasonableness approach to fourth amendment law. *Murray* reeks of 'reasonableness' analysis and cannot be reconciled with the proposition that a search warrant is, in any meaningful sense, required."

8. *The "tainted" witness.* UNITED STATES v. CECCOLINI, 435 U.S. 268, 98 S.Ct. 1054, 55 L.Ed.2d 268 (1978), grew out of the following facts: An officer in a flower shop on a social visit illegally picked up an envelope and found it to contain money and policy slips. He then learned from his friend, Ms. Hennessey, an employee of the shop (who did not notice his discovery), that the envelope belonged to the defendant, the owner of the shop. The information reached the FBI four months later. An agent questioned Hennessey about defendant, without specifically mentioning the illegally discovered policy slips. She said she was willing to help, and she testified against defendant both before the grand jury and at his trial for perjury.

A 6–2 majority of the Court (Blackmun, J., not participating) held Hennessey's testimony admissible. Although it declined to adopt a *per se* rule that the testimony of a live witness should always be admissible,[a] the Court, per REHNQUIST, J., pointed out that various factors indicate that "the exclusionary rule should be invoked with much greater reluctance where the claim is based on a causal relationship between a constitutional violation and the discovery of a live

---

a. While Stevens, J., joined Justice Marshall's dissent, he noted in a separate dissent that he "remain[ed] convinced that the *Segura* decision itself was unacceptable" because it provided government agents with an "affirmative incentive" to conduct illegal searches.

a. Concurring Chief Justice Burger would adopt such a rule.

witness than when a similar claim is advanced to support suppression of an inanimate object":

"The greater the willingness of the witness to freely testify, the greater the likelihood that he or she will be discovered by legal means and, concomitantly, the smaller the incentive to conduct an illegal search to discover the witness. Witnesses are not like guns or documents which remain hidden from view until one turns over a sofa or opens a filing cabinet. Witnesses can, and often do, come forward and offer evidence entirely of their own volition. And evaluated properly, the degree of free will necessary to dissipate the taint will very likely be found more often in the case of live-witness testimony than other kinds of evidence."

"Moreover, exclusion of testimony" would perpetually disable a witness from testifying about relevant and material facts, regardless of how unrelated such testimony might be to the purpose of the originally illegal search or the evidence discovered thereby. [S]ince the cost of excluding live-witness testimony often will be greater, a closer, more direct link between the illegality and that kind of testimony is required."

Dissenting Justice MARSHALL, joined by Brennan, J., did not see how "the same tree, having its roots in an unconstitutional search or seizure, can bear two different kinds of fruit, with one kind less susceptible than the other to exclusion on Fourth Amendment grounds." The dissent charged the majority with "judicial 'double counting' ": "The majority allows a court to consider whether the witness came forward and then, if he did not, to consider that generally (but not in this case) witnesses come forward." As for the majority's argument that often the exclusion of live-witness testimony will be very costly to society, "at least as often the exclusion of physical evidence [will be equally] costly * * *."

B. The "Inevitable Discovery" Doctrine:
The Sequel to *Brewer v. Williams*

NIX v. WILLIAMS (WILLIAMS II)
467 U.S. 431, 104 S.Ct. 2501, 81 L.Ed.2d 377 (1984).

Chief Justice BURGER delivered the opinion of the Court.

[At] Williams' second trial [the] prosecution did not offer Williams' statements into evidence, nor did it seek to show that Williams had directed the police to the child's body. However, evidence of the condition of her body as it was found, articles and photographs of her clothing, and the results of post mortem medical and chemical tests on the body were admitted. The trial court concluded that the State had proved by a preponderance of the evidence that, if the search had not been suspended and Williams had not led the police to the victim, her body would have been discovered *"within a short time"* in essentially the same condition as it was actually found. The trial court also ruled that if the police had not located the body, "the search would clearly have been taken up again where it left off, given the extreme circumstances of this case and the body would [have] been found *in short order*" (emphasis added).

In finding that the body would have been discovered in essentially the same condition as it was actually found, the court noted that freezing temperatures had prevailed and tissue deterioration would have been suspended. The challenged evidence was admitted and the jury again found Williams guilty of first-degree murder; he was sentenced to life in prison.

[Both the Supreme Court of Iowa, which affirmed the conviction, and the U.S. District Court, which denied habeas relief, adopted the "inevitable discovery" exception to the exclusionary rule and sustained the conviction on that basis. But the U.S. Court of Appeals for the Eighth Circuit reversed the District Court's denial of habeas relief because, assuming an inevitable discovery exception, such an exception requires proof that the police did not act in "bad faith" and the record could not support such a finding.]

[The] core rationale consistently advanced by this Court for extending the Exclusionary Rule to evidence that is the fruit of unlawful police conduct has been that this admittedly drastic and socially costly course is needed to deter police from violations of constitutional and statutory protections. [On] this rationale, the prosecution is not to be put in a better position than it would have been in if no illegality had transpired.

By contrast, the derivative evidence analysis ensures that the prosecution is not put in a *worse* position simply because of some earlier police error or misconduct. The independent source doctrine allows admission of evidence that has been discovered by means wholly independent of any constitutional violation. That doctrine, although closely related to the inevitable discovery doctrine, does not apply here; Williams' statements to Leaming indeed led police to the child's body, but that is not the whole story. The independent source doctrine teaches us that the interest of society in deterring unlawful police conduct and the public interest in having juries receive all probative evidence of a crime are properly balanced by putting the police in the same, not a *worse,* position than they would have been in if no police error or misconduct had occurred.[4] When the challenged evidence has an independent source, exclusion of such evidence would put the police in a worse position than they would have been in absent any error or violation. There is a functional similarity between these two doctrines in that exclusion of evidence that would inevitably have been discovered would also put the government in a worse position, because the police would have obtained that evidence if no misconduct had taken place. Thus, while the independent source exception would not justify admission of evidence in this case, its rationale is wholly consistent with and justifies our adoption of the ultimate or inevitable discovery exception to the Exclusionary Rule.

It is clear that the cases implementing the Exclusionary Rule "begin with the premise that the challenged evidence is *in some sense* the product of illegal governmental activity." *United States v. Crews* (emphasis added). Of course, this does not end the inquiry. If the prosecution can establish by a preponderance of the evidence that the information ultimately or inevitably would have been discovered by lawful means—here the volunteers' search—then the deterrence rationale has so little basis that the evidence should be received.[5] Anything less would reject logic, experience, and common sense.

---

4. The ultimate or inevitable discovery exception to the Exclusionary Rule is closely related in purpose to the harmless-error rule of *Chapman.* The harmless-constitutional-error rule "serve[s] a very useful purpose insofar as [it] block[s] setting aside convictions for small errors or defects that have little, if any, likelihood of having changed the result of the trial." The purpose of the inevitable discovery rule is to block setting aside convictions that would have been obtained without police misconduct.

5. As to the quantum of proof, we have already established some relevant guidelines. In *United States v. Matlock* (1974) [p. 341] (emphasis added), we stated that "the controlling burden of proof at suppression hearings should impose *no greater burden* than proof by a preponderance of the evidence." In *Lego v.*

Twomey (1972) [p. 809] we observed "from our experience [that] no substantial evidence has accumulated that federal rights have suffered from determining admissibility by a preponderance of the evidence" and held that the prosecution must prove by a preponderance of the evidence that a confession sought to be used at trial was voluntary. We are unwilling to impose added burdens on the already difficult task of proving guilt in criminal cases by enlarging the barrier to placing evidence of unquestioned truth before juries.

Williams argues that the preponderance-of-the-evidence standard used by the Iowa courts is inconsistent with *United States v. Wade* [p. 618]. In requiring clear and convincing evidence of an independent source for an in-court identification, the Court gave weight to the

The requirement that the prosecution must prove the absence of bad faith, [would] place courts in the position of withholding from juries relevant and undoubted truth that would have been available to police absent any unlawful police activity. Of course, that view would put the police in a *worse* position than they would have been in if no unlawful conduct had transpired. And, of equal importance, it wholly fails to take into account the enormous societal cost of excluding truth in the search for truth in the administration of justice. Nothing in this Court's prior holdings supports any such formalistic, pointless, and punitive approach.

The Court of Appeals concluded, without analysis, that if an absence of bad faith requirement were not imposed, "the temptation to risk deliberate violations of the Sixth Amendment would be too great, and the deterrent effect of the Exclusionary Rule reduced too far." We reject that view. A police officer who is faced with the opportunity to obtain evidence illegally will rarely, if ever, be in a position to calculate whether the evidence sought would inevitably be discovered.

[On] the other hand, when an officer is aware that the evidence will inevitably be discovered, he will try to avoid engaging in any questionable practice. In that situation, there will be little to gain from taking any dubious "shortcuts" to obtain the evidence. Significant disincentives to obtaining evidence illegally— including the possibility of departmental discipline and civil liability—also lessen the likelihood that the ultimate or inevitable discovery exception will promote police misconduct. In these circumstances, the societal costs of the Exclusionary Rule far outweigh any possible benefits to deterrence that a good-faith requirement might produce.

[The] Court of Appeals did not find it necessary to consider whether the record fairly supported the finding that the volunteer search party would ultimately or inevitably have discovered the victim's body. However, three courts independently reviewing the evidence have found that the body of the child inevitably would have been found by the searchers.

[When this finding was challenged] the prosecution offered the testimony of Agent Ruxlow, [who] had organized and directed some 200 volunteers who were searching for the child's body. The searchers were instructed "to check all the roads, the ditches, any culverts * * *." Ruxlow testified that he marked off highway maps of Poweshiek and Jasper Counties in grid fashion, divided the volunteers into teams of four to six persons, and assigned each team to search specific grid areas. Ruxlow also testified that, if the search had not been suspended because of Williams' promised cooperation, it would have continued into Polk County, using the same grid system. Although he had previously marked off into grids only the highway maps of Poweshiek and Jasper Counties, Ruxlow had obtained a map of Polk County, which he said he would have marked off in the same manner had it been necessary for the search to continue.

[The] search was not resumed once it was learned that Williams had led the police to the body, which was found two and one-half miles from where the search had stopped in what would have been the easternmost grid to be searched in Polk County. There was testimony that it would have taken an additional three to five hours to discover the body if the search had continued; the body was found near a

effect an uncounseled pre-trial identification has in "crystalliz[ing] the witnesses' identification of the defendant for the future reference." The Court noted as well that possible unfairness at the lineup "may be the sole means of attack upon the unequivocal courtroom identification," and recognized the difficulty of determining whether an in-court identification was based on independent recollection unaided by the lineup identification. By contrast, inevitable discovery involves no speculative elements but focuses on demonstrated historical facts capable of ready verification or impeachment and does not require a departure from the usual burden of proof at suppression hearings.

culvert, one of the kinds of places the teams had been specifically directed to search.

On this record it is clear that the search parties were approaching the actual location of the body and we are satisfied, along with three courts earlier, that the volunteer search teams would have resumed the search had Williams not earlier led the police to the body and the body inevitably would have been found. * * *

Justice WHITE, concurring.

I join fully in the opinion of the Court. I write separately only to point out that many of Justice Stevens' remarks are beside the point when it is recalled that *Brewer v. Williams* was a 5–4 decision and that four members of the Court, including myself, were of the view that Officer Leaming had done nothing wrong at all, let alone anything unconstitutional. * * *

Justice STEVENS, concurring in the judgment.

[It] was the majority in *Williams I* that recognized that "evidence of where the body was found and of its condition might well be admissible on the theory that the body would have been discovered in any event, even had incriminating statements not been elicited from Williams." It was the author of today's opinion of the Court who characterized this rule of law as a "remarkable" and "unlikely theory." (Burger, C.J., dissenting).

[The] majority is correct to insist that any rule of exclusion not provide the authorities with an incentive to commit violations of the Constitution. If the inevitable discovery rule provided such an incentive [it] would undermine the constitutional guarantee itself, and therefore be inconsistent with the deterrent purposes of the Exclusionary Rule. But when the burden of proof on the inevitable discovery question is placed on the prosecution, *it* must bear the risk of error in the determination made necessary by its constitutional violation. The uncertainty as to whether the body would have been discovered can be resolved in its favor here only because, as the Court explains, petitioner adduced evidence demonstrating that at the time of the constitutional violation an investigation was already under way which, in the natural and probable course of events, would have soon discovered the body. This is not a case in which the prosecution can escape responsibility for a constitutional violation through speculation; to the extent uncertainty was created by the constitutional violation the prosecution was required to resolve that uncertainty through proof.[8]

[The] majority refers to the "societal cost" of excluding probative evidence. In my view, the more relevant cost is that imposed on society by police officers who decide to take procedural shortcuts instead of complying with the law. What is the consequence of the shortcut that Detective Leaming took when he decided to question Williams in this case and not to wait an hour or so until he arrived in Des Moines?[9] [Instead] of having a 1969 conviction affirmed in routine fashion, the case is still alive 15 years later. Thanks to Detective Leaming, the State of Iowa has expended vast sums of money and countless hours of professional labor in his defense. That expenditure surely provides an adequate deterrent to similar

---

8. I agree with the majority's holding that the prosecution must prove that the evidence would have been inevitably discovered by a preponderance of the evidence rather than by clear and convincing evidence. An inevitable discovery finding is based on objective evidence concerning the scope of the ongoing investigation which can be objectively verified or impeached. Hence an extraordinary burden of proof is not needed in order to preserve the defendant's ability to subject the prosecution's

case to the meaningful adversarial testing required by the Sixth Amendment.

9. In this connection, it is worth noting, as Justice Marshall did in *Williams I*, that in light of the assistance that respondent's attorney had provided to the Des Moines police, it seems apparent that the lawyer intended to learn the location of the body from his client and then reveal it to the police. Thus, the need for a shortcut was practically nonexistent.

violations; the responsibility for that expenditure lies not with the Constitution, but rather with the constable. * * *

Justice BRENNAN, with whom Justice MARSHALL joins, dissenting. * * *

[T]he Court concludes that unconstitutionally obtained evidence may be admitted at trial if it inevitably would have been discovered in the same condition by an independent line of investigation that was already being pursued when the constitutional violation occurred. As has every federal Court of Appeals previously addressing this issue, I agree * * *.

The inevitable discovery exception necessarily implicates a hypothetical finding that differs in kind from the factual finding that precedes application of the independent source rule. To ensure that this hypothetical finding is narrowly confined to circumstances that are functionally equivalent to an independent source, and to protect fully the fundamental rights served by the exclusionary rule, I would require clear and convincing evidence before concluding that the government had met its burden of proof on this issue. * * *a

Notes and Questions

1. ***Must the independent line of investigation be underway?*** In his dissent, Justice Brennan describes the *Williams II* majority as "conclud[ing] that unconstitutionally obtained evidence may be admitted at trial if it inevitably would have been discovered in the same condition by an independent line of investigation *that was already being pursued* when the constitutional violation occurred." (Emphasis added.) Consider also concurring Justice Stevens' observation that "[t]he uncertainty as to whether the body would have been discovered can be resolved in [the prosecution's] favor here *only because* [the prosecution demonstrated] that at the time of the constitutional violation an investigation *was already under way which, in the natural and probable course of events, would have soon discovered the body.*" (Emphasis added.) Is *Williams II* limited along the lines indicated by Justices Brennan and Stevens? Should it be? See generally, Stephen E. Hessler, *Establishing Inevitability Without Active Pursuit: Defining the Inevitable Discovery Exception to the Fourth Amendment Exclusionary Rule*, 99 Mich.L.Rev. 238 (2002).

2. ***Primary evidence vs. secondary evidence.*** *Nix* applied the inevitable discovery exception to secondary or derivative evidence, but most federal courts of appeals have also applied the exception to primary evidence (evidence acquired during the course of the search itself). See Robert M. Bloom, *Inevitable Discovery: An Exception beyond the Fruits*, 20 Am.J.Crim.L. 79, 87 (1992). Should a distinction between primary and secondary evidence be drawn on the ground that application of the inevitable discovery rule to secondary evidence does not excuse the unlawful police action by admitting what was obtained as a direct result of the initial misconduct, but that application of the rule to primary evidence constitutes an after the fact purging of initial wrongful conduct? See id. at 87–94.

3. ***The significance of Murray v. United States.*** Recall that in *Murray*, an *independent source* case, bales of marijuana (primary evidence) were discovered as the result of an illegal entry. Nevertheless, the Court allowed for the introduction of the bales, provided that the subsequent lawful entry with a warrant was

---

a. For an in-depth analysis of the Supreme Court's opinion in *Williams II*, see Silas J. Wasserstrom & William J. Mertens, *The Exclusionary Rule on the Scaffold: But Was it a Fair Trial?* 22 Am.Crim.L.Rev. 85, 130–79 (1984). For an incisive treatment of the "fruit of the poisonous tree" problems raised by the second *Williams* case, or Williams II, in the main case set forth at 772, prior to the Supreme Court's decision in that case, see Phillip E. Johnson, *The Return of the "Christian Burial Speech" Case*, 32 Emory L.J. 349 (1983).

not based on information related to the initial illegal entry. Does *Murray* support the use of the *inevitable discovery exception* to avoid suppression of primary evidence? See Bloom, supra, at 92–94.

4. Inevitable discovery and the warrant requirement. If the police have probable cause to conduct a search, but do not bother to obtain a warrant, although they had plenty of time to do so, can (should) the inevitable discovery exception be used to avoid the need for a warrant?[a] Consider Bloom, supra, at 95:

"Because the *Nix* decision dealt with a Sixth Amendment violation, the Court probably was not focusing on the effect this exception would have on the Fourth Amendment warrant requirement. To the extent that the *Nix* Court concluded that there would be a limited deterrence effect by utilizing the inevitable discovery exception, its reasoning was flawed with regard to the warrant requirement.

"[The] existence of the inevitable discovery exception *will* provide the police with an incentive to avoid the warrant requirement. The police might seek the most expeditious method of obtaining the evidence without regard to its illegality, knowing that, as long as they could have obtained the evidence legally, their efforts will not result in its suppression. [For] example, if the police can demonstrate that they *could* have gotten a search warrant, what incentive will there be for them to go actively through the procedural hassle of actually obtaining one, since the effects of an illegal warrantless search could be nullified by the application of the inevitable discovery exception?"

See also *United States v. Griffin*, 502 F.2d 959 (6th Cir.1974): "[P]olice who believe they have probable cause to search cannot enter a house without a warrant merely because they plan subsequently to get one. The assertion by police (after an illegal entry and after finding evidence of crime) that the discovery was 'inevitable' because they planned to get a search warrant and had sent an officer on such a mission, would as a practical matter be beyond judicial review." See generally SEARCHSZR § 11.4(a) and cases discussed therein.

5. Inevitable discovery and knock-and-announce requirements.. In *Wilson v. Arkansas*, the knock-and-announce case discussed at p. 195, the Court declined to reach an argument the state advanced as an alternative ground for affirming the denial of defendant's motion to suppress. Analogizing to the "independent source" doctrine applied in *Segura* and the "inevitable discovery" rule adopted in *Nix v. Williams*, the state argued that "any evidence seized after an unreasonable, unannounced entry is causally disconnected from the constitutional violation and that exclusion goes beyond the goal of precluding any benefit to the government flowing from the constitutional violation." If the state's argument were to prevail, would it completely gut all knock-and-announce requirements? See SEARCHSZR § 11.4 (2002 pocket part).

C.   Is a Confession Obtained in Violation of *Miranda* a "Poisonous Tree"?

Because a majority of the Court held that there was no violation of *Miranda* in NEW YORK v. QUARLES, (1984), p. 509, it had no occasion to reach the question whether, even if Quarles' initial statement should have been suppressed, the gun was nevertheless admissible because it was "nontestimonial" evidence or because the police would inevitably have discovered it absent their questioning.

a. A similar question may be asked about illegal searches of vehicles which turn up items that would have been discovered through an inventory search. On this issue compare *United States v. Halls*, 40 F.3d 275 (8th Cir.1994) and *United States v. Mancera–Londono*, 912 F.2d 373 (9th Cir.1990) with *United States v. $639,558.00 in United States Currency*, 955 F.2d 712 (D.C.Cir.1992) and *United States v. Infante–Ruiz*, 13 F.3d 498 (1st Cir.1994).

But Justice O'CONNOR, concurring in part and dissenting in part, devoted much of her opinion to a discussion of why she believed that the gun itself was admissible even though the statement that led to its discovery was not:

"* * * Only the introduction of a defendant's own *testimony* is proscribed by the Fifth Amendment's mandate that no person 'shall be compelled in any criminal case to be a witness against himself.' That mandate does not protect an accused from being compelled to surrender *nontestimonial* evidence against himself. The distinction between testimonial and nontestimonial evidence was explored in some detail in *Schmerber v. California* [p. 38], a decision this Court handed down within a week of deciding *Miranda*. [The blood tests at issue in *Schmerber* were held] admissible because they were neither testimonial nor communicative in nature.

"[W]hatever case can be made for suppression evaporates when the statements themselves are not admitted, given the rationale of the *Schmerber* line of cases. Certainly interrogation which provides leads to other evidence does not offend the values underlying the Fifth Amendment privilege any more than the compulsory taking of blood samples, fingerprints, or voice exemplars, all of which may be compelled in an 'attempt to discover evidence that might be used to prosecute [a defendant] for a criminal offense.' *Schmerber.* Use of a suspect's answers 'merely to find other evidence establishing his connection with the crime [simply] differs only by a shade from the permitted use for that purpose of his body or his blood.' H. Friendly, *Benchmarks* 280 (1967). [When]the only evidence to be admitted is derivative evidence such as a gun—derived not from actual compulsion but from a statement taken in the absence of *Miranda* warnings—[the values underlying the privilege] simply cannot require suppression, at least no more so than they would for other such nontestimonial evidence.[4] * * *[a]

Dissenting Justice MARSHALL, joined by Brennan and Stevens, JJ., considered Justice O'Connor's treatment of derivative evidence "a much more radical departure from precedent than that opinion acknowledges." Continued Justice Marshall:

"The gun was the direct product of a coercive custodial interrogation. In *Silverthorne* and *Wong Sun* this Court held that the Government may not introduce incriminating evidence derived from an illegally obtained source. [When] they ruled on the issue, the New York courts were entirely correct in deciding that Quarles' gun was the tainted fruit of a nonconsensual interrogation and therefore was inadmissible under our precedents.

"However, since the New York Court of Appeals issued its opinion, [this Court, in *Nix v. Williams,* has accepted the 'inevitable discovery' doctrine.] [The State] has argued that the 'inevitable-discovery' rule, if applied to this case, would permit the admission of Quarles' gun. [Under the circumstances] I believe that the proper disposition of the matter is to vacate the state court order suppressing Quarles' gun and remand the matter [for] further consideration in light of *Nix v. Williams.*"

OREGON v. ELSTAD

470 U.S. 298, 105 S.Ct. 1285, 84 L.Ed.2d 222 (1985).

Justice O'CONNOR delivered the opinion of the Court.

4. In suggesting that *Wong Sun* requires exclusion of the gun, Justice Marshall fails to acknowledge this Court's holding in *Michigan v. Tucker* [p. 487]. In *Tucker,* the Court very clearly held that *Wong Sun* is inapplicable in cases involving mere departures from *Miranda. Wong Sun* and its "fruit of the poisonous tree" analysis lead to exclusion of derivative evidence only where the underlying police misconduct infringes a "core" constitutional right. Failure to administer *Miranda* warnings violates only a nonconstitutional prophylactic. * * *

a. Compare Justice O'Connor's opinion for the Court in *Oregon v. Elstad,* below.

This case requires us to decide whether an initial failure of law enforcement officers to administer the warnings required by *Miranda,* without more, "taints" subsequent admissions made after a suspect has been fully advised of and has waived his *Miranda* rights. [Respondent was convicted of burglary.] The Oregon Court of Appeals reversed, holding that respondent's signed confession, although voluntary, was rendered inadmissible by a prior remark made in response to questioning without benefit of *Miranda* warnings. [We] reverse.

[When the Gross home was burglarized, a witness contacted the sheriff's office, implicating respondent Elstad, an 18–year-old neighbor and friend of the Grosses' teenage son. Officers Burke and McAllister went to Elstad's home, with a warrant for his arrest for the aforementioned burglary. Elstad's mother led the officers to his room. The officers asked Elstad to get dressed and to accompany them to the living room. Officer Burke sat down with Elstad in the living room and, without telling him that the police had a warrant for his arrest, stated that he "felt" Elstad was involved in the Gross burglary. Elstad replied, "Yes, I was there."

[Elstad was then transported to sheriff headquarters and, approximately an hour later, Officer McAllister, in the presence of Officer Burke, advised Elstad of his *Miranda* rights for the first time. Elstad agreed to talk to the police and made a statement detailing his involvement in the burglary. The statement was typed, reviewed by Elstad, read back to him for correction and signed by him.

[The trial judge excluded the incriminating remark Elstad made in his living room, but admitted the statement made at the sheriff's office. Following his conviction of burglary, Elstad appealed. The state conceded that Elstad had been in custody when he replied, "Yes, I was there," and thus that this statement was obtained in violation of *Miranda,* but maintained that any conceivable "taint" had been dissipated prior to Elstad's written confession by Officer McAllister's careful administration of the *Miranda* warnings. The Oregon Court of Appeals disagreed.

[In reversing Elstad's conviction, the Oregon court identified the crucial constitutional inquiry as whether there was "a sufficient break in the stream of events" between the inadmissible statement in respondent's living room and the written confession in the sheriff's office "to insulate the latter statement from the effect of what went before." It concluded that, because of the brief period separating the two incidents, the "cat was sufficiently out of the bag to exert a coercive impact on [respondent's] later admissions."]

[The] Oregon court assumed and respondent here contends that a failure to administer *Miranda* warnings necessarily breeds the same consequences as police infringement of a constitutional right, so that evidence uncovered following an unwarned statement must be suppressed as "fruit of the poisonous tree." We believe this view misconstrues the nature of the protections afforded by *Miranda* warnings and therefore misreads the consequences of police failure to supply them.

[A]s we explained in *Quarles* and *Tucker,* a procedural *Miranda* violation differs in significant respects from violations of the Fourth Amendment, which have traditionally mandated a broad application of the "fruits" doctrine. The purpose of the Fourth Amendment exclusionary rule is to deter unreasonable searches, no matter how probative their fruits.

[The] *Miranda* exclusionary rule, however, serves the Fifth Amendment and sweeps more broadly than the Fifth Amendment itself. It may be triggered even in the absence of a Fifth Amendment violation.[1] The Fifth Amendment prohibits use by the prosecution in its case in chief only of *compelled* testimony. Failure to administer *Miranda* warnings creates a presumption of compulsion.

[But] the *Miranda* presumption, though irrebuttable for purposes of the prosecution's case in chief, does not require that the statements and their fruits be discarded as inherently tainted [discussing *Harris v. New York,* (p. 789) (permitting the use of statements obtained in violation of *Miranda* for impeachment purposes) and *Tucker*]. Where an unwarned statement is preserved for use in situations that fall outside the sweep of the *Miranda* presumption, "the primary criterion of admissibility [remains] the 'old' due process voluntariness test." Schulhofer, *Confessions and the Court,* 79 Mich.L.Rev. 865, 877 (1981).

[In] deciding "how sweeping the judicially imposed consequences" of a failure to administer *Miranda* warnings should be, the *Tucker* Court noted that neither the general goal of deterring improper police conduct nor the Fifth Amendment goal of assuring trustworthy evidence would be served by suppression of the witness' testimony. The unwarned confession must, of course, be suppressed, but the Court ruled that introduction of the third-party witness' testimony did not violate Tucker's Fifth Amendment rights.

We believe that this reasoning applies with equal force when the alleged "fruit" of a noncoercive *Miranda* violation is neither a witness nor an article of evidence but the accused's own voluntary testimony. As in *Tucker,* the absence of any coercion or improper tactics undercuts the twin rationales—trustworthiness and deterrence—for a broader rule. Once warned, the suspect is free to exercise his own volition in deciding whether or not to make a statement to the authorities.

[If] errors are made by law enforcement officers in administering the prophylactic *Miranda* procedures, they should not breed the same irremediable consequences as police infringement of the Fifth Amendment itself. It is an unwarranted extension of *Miranda* to hold that a simple failure to administer the warnings, unaccompanied by any actual coercion or other circumstances calculated to undermine the suspect's ability to exercise his free will so taints the investigatory process that a subsequent voluntary and informed waiver is ineffective for some indeterminate period. Though *Miranda* requires that the unwarned admission must be suppressed, the admissibility of any subsequent statement should turn in these circumstances solely on whether it is knowingly and voluntarily made.

[There] is a vast difference between the direct consequences flowing from coercion of a confession by physical violence or other deliberate means calculated to break the suspect's will and the uncertain consequences of disclosure of a "guilty secret" freely given in response to an unwarned but noncoercive question, as in this case. Justice Brennan's contention that it is impossible to perceive any causal distinction between this case and one involving a confession that is coerced by torture is wholly unpersuasive.[3] Certainly, in respondent's case, the causal

---

1. Justice Stevens expresses puzzlement at our statement that a simple failure to administer *Miranda* warnings is not in itself a violation of the Fifth Amendment. Yet the Court so held in *Quarles* and *Tucker.* The *Miranda* Court itself recognized this point when it disclaimed any intent to create a "constitutional straight-jacket" and invited Congress and the States to suggest "potential alternatives for protecting the privilege." A *Miranda* violation does not *constitute* coercion but rather affords a bright-line, legal presumption of coercion, requiring suppression of all unwarned statements. It has never been remotely suggested that any statement taken from Mr. Elstad without benefit of *Miranda* warnings would be admissible.

3. Most of the 50 cases cited by Justice Brennan in his discussion of consecutive confessions concern an initial unwarned statement obtained through overtly or inherently coercive methods which raise serious Fifth Amendment and Due Process concerns [discussing many cases].

connection between any psychological disadvantage created by his admission and his ultimate decision to cooperate is speculative and attenuated at best. It is difficult to tell with certainty what motivates a suspect to speak. * * * We must conclude that, absent deliberately coercive or improper tactics in obtaining the initial statement, the mere fact that a suspect has made an unwarned admission does not warrant a presumption of compulsion. A subsequent administration of *Miranda* warnings to a suspect who has given a voluntary but unwarned statement ordinarily should suffice to remove the conditions that precluded admission of the earlier statement. In such circumstances, the finder of fact may reasonably conclude that the suspect made a rational and intelligent choice whether to waive or invoke his rights.

Though belated, the reading of respondent's rights was undeniably complete. [There] is no question that respondent knowingly and voluntarily waived his right to remain silent before he described his participation in the burglary. It is also beyond dispute that respondent's earlier remark was voluntary, within the meaning of the Fifth Amendment. Neither the environment nor the manner of either "interrogation" was coercive. The initial conversation took place at midday, in the living room area of respondent's own home, with his mother in the kitchen area, a few steps away.

[The] state has conceded the issue of custody and thus we must assume that Burke breached *Miranda* procedures in failing to administer *Miranda* warnings before initiating the discussion in the living room. [But] the incident had none of the earmarks of coercion. Nor did the officers exploit the unwarned admission to pressure respondent into waiving his right to remain silent.

Respondent, however, has argued that he was unable to give a fully *informed* waiver of his rights because he was unaware that his prior statement could not be used against him. Respondent suggests that Deputy McAllister, to cure this deficiency, should have added an additional warning to those given him at the Sheriff's office. Such a requirement is neither practicable nor constitutionally necessary. In many cases, a breach of *Miranda* procedures may not be identified as such until long after full *Miranda* warnings are administered and a valid confession obtained. The standard *Miranda* warnings explicitly inform the suspect of his right to consult a lawyer before speaking. Police officers are ill equipped to pinch-hit for counsel, construing the murky and difficult questions of when "custody" begins or whether a given unwarned statement will ultimately be held admissible.

[Where] the suspect's initial inculpatory statement, though technically in violation of *Miranda,* was voluntary, [the] relevant inquiry is whether, in fact, the second statement was also voluntarily made. [The] fact that a suspect chooses to speak after being informed of his rights is, of course, highly probative. We find that the dictates of *Miranda* and the goals of the Fifth Amendment proscription against use of compelled testimony are fully satisfied in the circumstances of this case by barring use of the unwarned statement in the case in chief. No further purpose is served by imputing "taint" to subsequent statements obtained pursuant to a voluntary and knowing waiver. We hold today that a suspect who has once responded to unwarned yet uncoercive questioning is not thereby disabled from waiving his rights and confessing after he has been given the requisite *Miranda* warnings. * * *

Justice BRENNAN, with whom Justice MARSHALL joins, dissenting.

Justice Brennan cannot seriously mean to equate such situations with the case at bar. Likewise inapposite are the cases the dissent cites concerning suspects whose invocation of their rights to remain silent and to have counsel present were flatly ignored while police subjected them to continued interrogation. * * *

[Today's decision] delivers a potentially crippling blow to *Miranda* and the ability of courts to safeguard the rights of persons accused of crime. For at least with respect to successive confessions, the Court today appears to strip remedies for *Miranda* violations of the "fruit of the poisonous tree" doctrine prohibiting the use of evidence presumptively derived from official illegality.[2]

[The] threshold question is this: What effect should an admission or confession of guilt obtained in violation of an accused's *Miranda* rights be presumed to have upon the voluntariness of subsequent confessions that are preceded by *Miranda* warnings? [This] Court has had long experience with the problem of confessions obtained after an earlier confession has been illegally secured. Subsequent confessions in these circumstances are not *per se* inadmissible, but the prosecution must demonstrate facts "sufficient to insulate the [subsequent] statement from the effect of all that went before." * * *

Our precedents did not develop in a vacuum. They reflect an understanding of the realities of police interrogation * * *. Expert interrogators and experienced lower-court judges will be startled, to say the least, to learn that the connection between multiple confessions is "speculative" and that a subsequent rendition of *Miranda* warnings "ordinarily" enables the accused in these circumstances to exercise his "free will" and to make "a rational and intelligent choice whether to waive or invoke his rights."

[The] correct approach, administered for almost 20 years by most courts with no untoward results, is to presume that an admission or confession obtained in violation of *Miranda* taints a subsequent confession unless the prosecution can show that the taint is so attenuated as to justify admission of the subsequent confession. Although the Court warns against the "irremediable consequences" of this presumption, it is obvious that a subsequent confession, just like any other evidence that follows upon illegal action, does not become "sacred and inaccessible." As with any other evidence, the inquiry is whether the subsequent confession "has been come at by exploitation of [the] illegality or instead by means sufficiently distinguishable to be purged of the primary taint." *Wong Sun.*

Until today the Court has recognized that the dissipation inquiry requires the prosecution to demonstrate that the official illegality did not taint the challenged confession, and we have rejected the simplistic view that abstract notions of "free will" are alone sufficient to dissipate the challenged taint. Instead, we have instructed courts to consider carefully such factors as the strength of the causal connection between the illegal action and the challenged evidence, their proximity in time and place, the presence of intervening factors, and the "purpose and flagrancy of the official misconduct."

[Where] an accused believes that it is futile to resist because the authorities already have elicited an admission of guilt, the mere rendition of *Miranda* warnings does not convey the information most critical at that point to ensuring his informed and voluntary decision to speak again: that the earlier confession may not be admissible and thus that he need not speak out of any feeling that he already has sealed his fate. The Court therefore is flatly wrong in arguing, as it does repeatedly, that the mere provision of *Miranda* warnings prior to subsequent interrogation supplies the accused with "the relevant information" and ensures that a subsequent confession "ordinarily" will be the product of "a rational and intelligent choice" and "an act of free will."

---

2. The Court repeatedly casts its analysis in terms of the "fruits" of a *Miranda* violation, but its dicta nevertheless surely should not be read as necessarily foreclosing application of derivative-evidence rules where the *Miranda* violation produces evidence other than a subsequent confession by the accused. See n. 29, infra.

[The] foundation of the derivative-evidence doctrine has always been that, where the authorities have acted illegally, *they* must bear the "ultimate burden" of proving that their misconduct did not "taint" subsequently obtained evidence. That is precisely the point of the derivative-evidence presumption. By rejecting this presumption in *Miranda* cases, the Court today appears to adopt a "go ahead and try to prove it" posture toward citizens whose Fifth Amendment *Miranda* rights have been violated, an attitude that marks a sharp break from the Court's traditional approach to official lawlessness. * * *

[The] Court does not limit its analysis to successive confessions, but recurrently refers generally to the "fruits" of the illegal confession. Thus the potential impact of the Court's reasoning might extend far beyond the "cat out of the bag" context to include the discovery of physical evidence and other derivative fruits of *Miranda* violations as well.[29] * * *

[The] Court today refuses to apply the derivative-evidence rule even to the extent necessary to deter objectively unreasonable failures by the authorities to honor a suspect's *Miranda* rights. Incredibly, faced with an obvious violation of *Miranda,* the Court asserts that it will not countenance suppression of a subsequent confession in such circumstances where the authorities have acted "legitimate[ly]" and have not used "improper tactics." One can only respond: whither went *Miranda?*

* * * How can the Court possibly expect the authorities to obey *Miranda* when they have every incentive now to interrogate suspects without warnings or an effective waiver, knowing that the fruits of such interrogations "ordinarily" will be admitted, that an admissible subsequent confession "ordinarily" can be obtained simply by reciting the *Miranda* warnings shortly after the first has been procured and asking the accused to repeat himself, and that unless the accused can demonstrate otherwise his confession will be viewed as an "act of free will" in response to "legitimate law enforcement activity"? * * *

Justice STEVENS dissenting.

[In] my opinion, the Court's attempt to fashion a distinction between actual coercion "by physical violence or other deliberate means calculated to break the suspect's will" and irrebuttably presumed coercion cannot succeed. The presumption is only legitimate if it is assumed that there is always a coercive aspect to custodial interrogation that is not preceded by adequate advice of the constitutional right to remain silent. Although I would not support it, I could understand a rule that refused to apply the presumption unless the interrogation took place in an especially coercive setting—perhaps only in the police station itself—but if the presumption arises whenever the accused has been taken into custody or his freedom has been restrained in any significant way, it will surely be futile to try to develop subcategories of custodial interrogation. Indeed, a major purpose of treating the presumption of coercion as irrebuttable is to avoid the kind of fact-bound inquiry that today's decision will surely engender. * * *

[For] me, the most disturbing aspect of the Court's opinion is its somewhat opaque characterization of the police misconduct in this case. The Court appears ambivalent on the question whether there was any constitutional violation. This

---

29. Notwithstanding the sweep of the Court's language, today's opinion surely ought not be read as also foreclosing application of the traditional derivative-evidence presumption to physical evidence obtained as a proximate result of a *Miranda* violation. The Court relies heavily on individual "volition" as an insulating factor in successive-confession cases.

Although the Court's reliance on this factor is clearly misplaced, the factor is altogether missing in the context of inanimate evidence.

As they have in successive-confession cases, most courts considering the issue have recognized that physical evidence proximately derived from a *Miranda* violation is presumptively inadmissible. * * *

ambivalence is either disingenuous or completely lawless. This Court's power to require state courts to exclude probative self-incriminatory statements rests entirely on the premise that the use of such evidence violates the Federal Constitution.[15] The same constitutional analysis applies whether the custodial interrogation is actually coercive or irrebuttably presumed to be coercive. If the Court does not accept that premise, it must regard the holding in the *Miranda* case itself, as well as all of the Federal jurisprudence that has evolved from that decision, as nothing more than an illegitimate exercise of raw judicial power. * * *

Notes and Questions

1. *The role of the police officer vs. the role of the defense lawyer.* During the oral argument in *Elstad,* one Justice suggested that it would not be unduly burdensome for the police to tell a suspect that they had treated him improperly at an earlier session and that therefore the incriminating statement(s) obtained at the earlier session would not be used against him. Such a requirement, responded the Attorney General of Oregon, "might do a great deal of mischief because it confuses the role of the police officer with that of the criminal defense attorney." Does this argument come pretty late in the day? Doesn't *Miranda* itself "confuse the role of the police officer with that of the criminal defense lawyer"?

Should the police at least be able to tell whether there is a *substantial question* about the admissibility of an earlier statement? Should they at least be required to give a supplementary warning that the earlier statement is or *may be* inadmissible? Or that it is *unclear* whether the earlier statement is admissible and that the suspect is entitled to the advise of counsel on this point? If the police are "ill equipped" to do even this much, then when they obtain a statement from a person without advising him of his rights and want to question him again, instead of asking or expecting them to "pinch-hit" for counsel, should we require them to let defense counsel "bat for himself"?

2. *Physical evidence obtained as a result of a Miranda violation.* Would the Court deliver a "crippling blow" to *Miranda* if it permitted the prosecution to use the nontestimonial fruits of a *Miranda* violation? Consider David Wollin, *Policing the Police: Should Miranda Violations Bear Fruit?,* 53 Ohio St.L.J. 805, 845–46 (1992):

"[There] are many reported cases where the police have arrested suspects and interrogated them without the *Miranda* warnings in order to discover the existence or location of nontestimonial evidence. This should not come as a surprise to those knowledgeable about police practices. Expert interrogators have long recognized, and continue to instruct, that a confession is a primary source for determining the existence and whereabouts of the fruits of a crime, such as documents or weapons. * * *

"Suppression of a suspect's unwarned statements alone will not provide sufficient deterrence of police misconduct. Police officers seeking physical evidence are not likely to view the loss of an unwarned confession as particularly great when weighed against the opportunity to recover highly probative evidence, such as a murder weapon or narcotics. Recovery of such evidence might well convince a suspect to forego a trial and plead guilty, thereby preventing the *Miranda* issue from ever being raised."

---

15. At least that is my view. In response to this dissent, however, the Court has added a fn. 1, implying that whenever the Court commands exclusion of a presumptively coerced confession, it is standing—not on a constitutional predicate—but merely on its own shoulders.

3. *How broadly have the lower courts read Elstad?* Dissenting in
Elstad, Justice Brennan maintained that the language and reasoning of the
majority opinion should not be read as foreclosing application of the "fruit of the
poisonous tree" doctrine to *physical evidence* derived from a *Miranda* violation.
However, according to Wollin, Note 3 supra at 835–36, "[f]ollowing *Elstad,* federal
and state courts have almost uniformly ruled that the prosecution can introduce
nontestimonial fruits of a *Miranda* violation in a criminal trial. The poisonous
tree doctrine will be applicable only if there is evidence of actual coercion or other
circumstances designed to overbear the suspect's will."

For the view that *Elstad* applies even when the police deliberately decide to
forego *Miranda* warnings until after an interrogation which results in a confession, an even when less than 30 minutes elapsed between the end of the suspect's
initial statement and the subsequent post-*Miranda* statement, see *Davis v. United
States,* 724 A.2d 1163 (D.C. App.1998).

4. *Edwards violations vs. "mere" Miranda violations.* For purposes of
Elstad, should *Edwards* violations, i.e., violations of a suspect's invocation of her
right to counsel, be treated differently than "mere" *Miranda* violations? *Correll v.
Thompson,* 63 F.3d 1279, 1290 (4th Cir.1995), answers in the negative, observing
that an *Edwards* violation "is also a technical violation of *Miranda,* not a Fifth
Amendment violation." But see Note, 62 Ind.L.J. 1061, 1099–1100 (1987), maintaining that "the right to counsel, once invoked by suspect in a custodial
interrogation, [is] more than a procedural device," and that the poisonous tree
doctrine should apply with its full vigor to the fruits of its violation.

5. *The physical fruits of coerced confessions.* Should courts ever admit
physical evidence derived from "involuntary" or coerced confessions? Is this a
logical extension of the sharp distinction the Court drew in *Schmerber* (p. 38)
between testimonial evidence and physical evidence? Did Justice O'Connor point
the way in her *Quarles* concurring opinion? Could the same result be reached by
expanding the "inevitable discovery" exception, i.e., by simply presuming that the
fruits of a coerced confession could or would always have come to light anyway?
Compare Akhil Reed Amar & Renée B. Lettow, *Fifth Amendment First Principles:
The Self–Incrimination Clause,* 93 Mich.L.Rev. 857 (1995) (yes) *with* Kamisar, *On
the Fruits of Miranda Violations, Coerced Confessions and Compelled Testimony,*
93 Mich.L.Rev. 929 (1995) (no).

SECTION 3. USE OF ILLEGALLY OBTAINED
EVIDENCE FOR IMPEACHMENT
PURPOSES

A. The Expansion of a Once-Narrow Exception

1. In *Walder v. United States,* 347 U.S. 62, 74 S.Ct. 354, 98 L.Ed. 503 (1954),
defendant, charged with various illegal narcotics transactions, asserted early on
his direct examination that he had never possessed any narcotics or sold or given
any narcotics to anyone in his life. The Court held, per Frankfurter, J., that this
assertion "opened the door," for purposes of attacking the defendant's credibility,
to evidence of heroin seized from the defendant's home, in his presence, in an
earlier, unrelated case. "Of his own accord," observed the Court, "the defendant
went beyond a mere denial of complicity in the crimes of which he was charged
and made the sweeping claim that he had never dealt in or possessed any
narcotics. [A defendant] must be free to deny all the elements of the case against
him without thereby giving leave to the Government to introduce by way of
rebuttal evidence illegally secured by it, and thereby not available for its case in

chief. Beyond that, however, there is hardly justification for letting the defendant affirmatively resort to perjurious testimony in reliance on the Government's disability to challenge his credibility."

The instant situation, emphasized the *Walder* Court, is to be "sharply contrasted" with that presented by *Agnello v. United States*, 269 U.S. 20, 46 S.Ct. 4, 70 L.Ed. 145 (1925). There, the government sought to "smuggle in" the tainted evidence on cross-examination by asking the defendant whether he had ever seen narcotics before, and eliciting the expected denial. In *Agnello*, the defendant "did nothing" to waive his constitutional protection or to justify cross-examination with respect to the illegally seized evidence.

2. HARRIS v. NEW YORK, 401 U.S. 222, 91 S.Ct. 643, 28 L.Ed.2d 1 (1971), often called the first blow the Burger Court struck *Miranda*, arose as follows: Petitioner, charged with selling heroin to an undercover officer, took the stand in his own defense. He admitted knowing the officer, but denied making a sale of heroin. Statements made by petitioner immediately following his arrest which partially contradicted his direct trial testimony were used to impeach his credibility. According to the Court, petitioner made no claim that the statements were coerced or involuntary,[a] but they were preceded by defective *Miranda* warnings, and thus inadmissible to establish the prosecution's case in chief. A 5-4 majority, per BURGER, C.J., held that under the circumstances "petitioner's credibility was appropriately impeached by use of his earlier conflicting statements."

The Court noted that "[s]ome comments in the *Miranda* opinion can indeed be read as indicating a bar to use of [a statement obtained in violation of *Miranda*] for any purpose," but dismissed this discussion as "not at all necessary to the Court's holding" and not "controlling."[b] The Court noted, but also seemed untroubled by the fact, "that *Walder* was impeached as to collateral matters included in his direct examination, whereas petitioner here was impeached as to testimony bearing more directly on the crimes charged." The Court next observed:

"The impeachment process here undoubtedly provided valuable aid to the jury in assessing petitioner's credibility, and the benefits of this process should not be lost [because] of the speculative possibility that impermissible police conduct will be encouraged thereby. Assuming that the exclusionary rule has a deterrent effect * * * sufficient deterrence flows when the evidence in question is made unavailable to the prosecution in its case in chief.

"[The privilege to testify in one's defense] cannot be construed to include the right to commit perjury. [The] prosecution here did no more than utilize the traditional truth-testing devices of the adversary process. [The] shield provided by *Miranda* cannot be perverted into a license to use perjury by way of a defense, free from the risk of confrontation with prior inconsistent utterances."

Dissenting Justice BRENNAN, joined by Douglas and Marshall, JJ., criticized the majority for disregarding language in *Miranda* and for selectively quoting from *Walder*. The dissent emphasized that "*Walder* was not a case where tainted evidence was used to impeach an accused's direct testimony on matters directly

---

a. According to Alan Dershowitz & John Hart Ely, *Harris v. New York: Some Anxious Observations on the Candor and Logic of the Emerging Nixon Majority*, 80 Yale L.J. 1198, 1201 (1971), "the record is clear" that he did.

b. But consider Geoffrey Stone, *The Miranda Doctrine in the Burger Court*, 1977 Sup. Ct.Rev. 99, 107–08: "Rightly or wrongly, *Miranda* was deliberately structured to canvass a wide range of problems, many of which were

not directly raised by the cases before the Court. This approach was thought necessary in order to 'give concrete constitutional guidelines for law enforcement agencies and courts to follow.' Thus, a technical reading of *Miranda*, such as that employed in *Harris*, would enable the Court to label many critical aspects of the decision mere dictum and therefore not 'controlling.'"

related to the case against him," but only such testimony "on matters *collateral* to the crime charged." Continued the dissent:

"While *Walder* did not identify the constitutional specifics that guarantee 'a defendant the fullest opportunity to meet the accusation against him [and permit him to be free to deny all the elements of the case against him,' in my view *Miranda* identified the Fifth Amendment's privilege against self-incrimination as one of those specifics. [It] is fulfilled only when an accused is guaranteed the right 'to remain silent unless he chooses to speak in the *unfettered* exercise of his own will' (emphasis added). The choice of whether to testify in one's own defense must therefore be 'unfettered' * * *. [But] the accused is denied an 'unfettered' choice when the decision whether to take the stand is burdened by the risk that an illegally obtained prior statement may be introduced to impeach his direct testimony denying complicity in the crime charged against him."[c]

3. **The Fourth Amendment vs. the Fifth.** Should the Court have considered the significance of *Miranda's* Fifth Amendment underpinning before applying (or extending) the Fourth Amendment *Walder* case to *Harris?* Is impeachment by means of evidence obtained in violation of the Fourth Amendment more defensible than such use of evidence obtained in violation of the Self–Incrimination Clause of the Fifth because the Fourth's "exclusionary rule" is a court-created device designed to deter the police and as the link between police illegality and subsequent evidence becomes more attenuated it becomes less likely that exclusion would affect future police conduct? On the other hand, is the essence of the constitutional wrong under the Fifth the *use* against him of a defendant's compelled testimony, not the mere act of compelling him to speak (otherwise no immunity statute would be constitutional)? Doesn't the Self–Incrimination Clause by its own terms seem to prohibit the use of statements obtained in violation of its command? See Dershowitz & Ely, fn. a supra, at 1214–15; Stone, fn. b supra, at 110–111.

4. The Court went a step beyond *Harris* in *Oregon v. Hass,* 420 U.S. 714, 95 S.Ct. 1215, 43 L.Ed.2d 570 (1975). In *Hass,* after being advised of his rights, the defendant *asserted* them—he asked for a lawyer. But the police refused to honor his request and continued to question him. A 6–2 majority, per Blackmun, J., ruled that here, too, the resulting statements could be used for impeachment purposes. "One might concede," wrote the Court, "that when proper *Miranda* warnings have been given, and the officer then continues his interrogation after the suspect asks for an attorney, the officer may be said to have little to lose and perhaps something to gain by way of possibly uncovering impeachment material. This speculative possibility, however, is even greater where the warnings are defective and the defect is not known to the officers. In any event, the balance was struck in *Harris,* and we are not disposed to change it now."

But wasn't a *different* balance struck in *Hass?* Dissenting Justice Brennan, joined by Marshall, J., thought so: "Even after *Harris,* police had some incentive for following *Miranda* by warning an accused of his [rights]. If the warnings were given, the accused might still make a statement which could be used in the prosecution's case-in-chief. Under today's holding, however, once the warnings are given, police have almost no incentive for following *Miranda's* requirement that '[i]f the individual states that he wants an attorney, the interrogation must cease until an attorney is present.' If the requirement is followed there will almost surely be no statement since the attorney will advise the accused to remain silent. If, however, the requirement is disobeyed, the police may obtain a statement which can be used for impeachment if the accused has the temerity to testify in his own defense."

c. Black, J., also dissented, without opinion.

5. *Does the Harris–Hass exception apply even when a police officer deliberately fails to honor a suspect's request for counsel for the very purpose of obtaining evidence for impeachment purposes? Even when an officer fails to honor a suspect's request for counsel pursuant to a police department policy to violate Miranda in order to obtain evidence for impeachment purposes?* In PEOPLE v. PEEVY, 953 P.2d 1212 (1998), the California Supreme Court, per GEORGE, J., answered the first question in the affirmative. However, it did not reach the second question because the issue had not been timely raised below. As for the first question, the court rejected the defendant's argument that the *Harris-Hass* rule was based upon the assumption that a *purposeful or deliberate* violation of *Miranda* and *Edwards* would not occur:

"Language in *Hass* and subsequent cases [demonstrates the U.S. Supreme Court's belief] that the *Harris* rule sufficiently deters individual police misconduct, *whether the misconduct occurred as the result of negligence or design.* In *Hass,* there is some indication that the violation of the suspect's rights was deliberate. [In] *Michigan v. Harvey* [p. 797], it is even more apparent that the interrogating police officer's failure to honor the defendant's Sixth Amendment right to counsel was deliberate.

"[Moreover,] it would be anomalous to hold that the applicability of the *Harris* rule depends upon the subjective intent of the interrogating police officer, when other applications of the *Miranda* rule generally do not turn upon the individual officer's state of mind, but rather upon the accused's perception of his or her circumstances. [Evidence] of deliberation on the part of the police and—as apparent in this case—of a purpose to violate the suspect's rights in order to secure evidence [may] call into question the accuracy of the high court's conclusion in *Harris* that police misconduct will be deterred adequately by excluding improperly obtained evidence from the prosecution's case-in-chief, but such evidence does not render the *Harris* rule inapplicable."

Although concurring Justice MOSK concurred in the result, he made clear his belief that if a statement secured in violation of a suspect's right to counsel had been obtained by a member of a law enforcement agency pursuant to that agency's policy to violate *Miranda*[a] the statement could not be used for impeachment purposes:

"Any policy of a law enforcement agency to obtain statements from criminal suspects in violation of *Miranda* would strike through the suspect's 'prophylactic' rights towards his substantive Fifth Amendment privilege against self-incrimination itself. [Moreover,] any policy of a law enforcement agency to obtain statements from criminal suspects in violation of *Miranda* would necessarily constitute proof that 'sufficient deterrence' of [police misconduct] does not, in fact, 'flow from exclusion of such statements from the prosecution's case-in-chief' [quoting from *Harris*]. It would rather present itself as an actual fact.

"[It] may indeed be true, as stated in *Michigan v. Tucker*, that '[where] official action [is] pursued in complete good faith [the] deterrence rationale loses much of its force.' But if so, it must also be true that, where official action is pursued in utter bad faith, as in accordance with the type of policy in question, the deterrence rationale retains its force without any diminution whatsoever."

---

a. Recent litigation has uncovered California training materials teaching police officers that it is permissible to continue to question suspects who have invoked their right to counsel or their right to remain silent in order to obtain statements that may be used for impeachment purposes or to discover other evidence. The police commonly refer to this technique as questioning "outside *Miranda.*" See Charles D. Weisselberg, *Saving Miranda*, 84 Cornell L.Rev. 109, 132–62 (1998). For more extensive discussion of questioning "outside *Miranda*," see p. 802.

6. In UNITED STATES v. HAVENS, 446 U.S. 620, 100 S.Ct. 1912, 64 L.Ed.2d 559 (1980), what had "started out in *Walder* as a narrow and reasonable exception" to the exclusionary rule took on "awesome proportions," CRIMPROC § 9.6(a). On direct examination, defendant denied being involved with his codefendant in the transportation of cocaine and on cross-examination denied being involved in sewing a pocket (in which drugs were found) into his codefendant's clothing or having in his own suitcase cloth from which the swatch was cut to make the pocket. Defendant's testimony was impeached by admitting the illegally seized cloth, but the Fifth Circuit reversed, maintaining that illegally seized evidence could be used for impeachment only if it contradicts a defendant's direct testimony. A 5–4 majority, per WHITE, J., disagreed:

"[The] policies of the exclusionary rule no more bar impeachment here than they did in *Walder, Harris,* and *Hass.* [The] incremental furthering of [the ends of the exclusionary rules] by forbidding impeachment of the defendant who testifies was deemed insufficient to permit or require that false testimony go unchallenged, with the resulting impairment of the integrity of the fact-finding goals of the criminal trial. We reaffirm this assessment of the competing interests, and hold that a defendant's statements made in response to proper cross-examination reasonably suggested by the defendant's direct examination are subject to otherwise proper impeachment by the government, albeit by evidence that has been illegally obtained."

Dissenting Justice BRENNAN, joined by Stewart, Marshall and Stevens, JJ., on this point, protested: "The identical issue was confronted in *Agnello,* which determined—contrary to the instant decision—that it was constitutionally impermissible to admit evidence obtained in violation of the Fourth Amendment to rebut a defendant's response to a matter first raised during the Government's cross-examination. [The] exclusionary rule exception established by *Harris* and *Hass* may be fairly easily cabined by defense counsel's unwillingness to forego certain areas of questioning. But [today's holding] passes control of the exception to the Government, since the prosecutor can lay the predicate for admitting otherwise suppressible evidence with his own questioning."

Justice Brennan (joined only by Marshall, J., on this point) then voiced "a more fundamental difference with the Court's holding here, which culminates the approach taken in *Harris* and *Hass*":

"[T]he Court has undertaken to strike a 'balance' between the 'policies' it finds in the Bill of Rights and the 'competing interest' in accurate trial determinations. This balancing effort is completely freewheeling. Far from applying criteria intrinsic to the Fourth and Fifth Amendments, the Court resolves succeeding cases simply by declaring that so much exclusion is enough to deter police misconduct. That hardly conforms to the disciplined analytical method described as 'legal reasoning,' through which judges endeavor to formulate or derive principles of decision that can be applied consistently and predictably.[a] [More] disturbingly, by treating Fourth and Fifth Amendment privileges as mere incentive schemes, the Court denigrates their unique status as *constitutional* protections."

7. *The Court refuses to extend the impeachment exception to defense witnesses other than the defendant.* In JAMES v. ILLINOIS, 493 U.S. 307, 110 S.Ct. 648, 107 L.Ed.2d 676 (1990), the Court halted nearly forty years of the impeachment exception's expansion. A 5–4 majority, per BRENNAN, J., refused to expand the "impeachment exception" to the exclusionary rule to permit the prosecution to impeach the testimony of *all* defense witnesses with illegally

a. Support for this criticism may be found in James Kainen, *The Impeachment Exception* to the Exclusionary Rules: Policies, Principles and Politics, 44 Stan.L.Rev. 1301 (1992).

obtained evidence. According to the majority, expanding the impeachment exception to such an extent "would not further the truthseeking value with equal force but would appreciably undermine the deterrent effect of the exclusionary rule."

The case arose as follows: A day after a murder occurred, the police took James, a suspect, into custody. He was found at his mother's beauty salon sitting under a hair dryer; when he emerged, his hair was black and curly. When the police questioned James about his prior hair color, he told them it had been reddish-brown, long, and combed straight back. When questioned later at the police station, James stated that he had his hair dyed black and curled at the beauty parlor in order to change his appearance. Because the police lacked probable cause for James' arrest, both statements regarding his hair were suppressed.

At the trial, five eye witnesses testified that the person responsible for the murder had long, "reddish" hair, worn in a slicked-back style and that they had seen James several weeks earlier, at which time he had the aforementioned hair color and style. James did not testify in his own defense. He called as a witness Jewel Henderson, a family friend. She testified that on the day of the shooting James' hair had been black. The state then impeached Henderson's testimony by reporting James' prior admissions that he had reddish hair at the time of the shooting and had dyed and curled his hair the next day in order to change his appearance. James ultimately was convicted of murder. The Illinois Supreme Court concluded, that, in order to deter "perjury by proxy," the impeachment exception ought to allow the state to impeach the testimony of defense witnesses other than the defendant himself. The U.S. Supreme Court reversed:

"Expanding the class of impeachable witnesses from the defendant alone to all defense witnesses would create different incentives affecting the behavior of both defendants and law enforcement officers. As a result, this expansion would not promote the truthseeking function to the same extent as did creation of the original exception, and yet it would significantly undermine the deterrent effect of the general exclusionary rule. Hence, we believe that this proposed expansion would frustrate rather than further the purposes underlying the exclusionary rule.

"The previously recognized exception penalizes defendants for committing perjury by allowing the prosecution to expose their perjury through impeachment using illegally obtained evidence. [But] the exception leaves defendants free to testify truthfully on their own behalf; they can offer probative and exculpatory evidence to the jury without opening the door to impeachment by carefully avoiding any statements that directly contradict the suppressed evidence. The exception thus generally discourages perjured testimony without discouraging truthful testimony.

"In contrast, expanding the impeachment exception to encompass the testimony of all defense witnesses would not have the same beneficial effects. First, the mere threat of a subsequent criminal prosecution for perjury is far more likely to deter a witness from intentionally lying on a defendant's behalf than to deter a defendant, already facing conviction for the underlying offense, from lying on his own behalf. Hence the Illinois Supreme Court's underlying premise that a defendant frustrated by our previous impeachment exception can easily find a witness to engage in 'perjury by proxy' is suspect.

"More significantly, expanding the impeachment exception to encompass the testimony of all defense witnesses likely would chill some defendants from presenting their best defense—and sometimes any defense at all—through the testimony of others. Whenever police obtained evidence illegally, defendants would have to assess prior to trial the likelihood that the evidence would be admitted to impeach the otherwise favorable testimony of any witness they call. Defendants might reasonably fear that one or more of their witnesses, in a position to offer truthful and favorable testimony, would also make some statement in sufficient tension with the tainted evidence to allow the prosecutor to introduce that evidence for impeachment. [As] a result, an expanded impeachment exception likely would chill some defendants from calling witnesses who would otherwise offer probative evidence.[6]

"This realization alters the balance of values underlying the current impeachment exception governing defendants' testimony. * * * Given the potential chill created by expanding the impeachment exception, the conceded gains to the truthseeking process from discouraging or disclosing perjured testimony would be offset to some extent by the concomitant loss of probative witness testimony. Thus, the truthseeking rationale supporting the impeachment of defendants in *Walder* and its progeny does not apply to other witnesses with equal force.

"Moreover, the proposed expansion of the current impeachment exception would significantly weaken the exclusionary rule's deterrent effect on police misconduct. This Court has characterized as a mere 'speculative possibility,' *Harris v. New York*, the likelihood that permitting prosecutors to impeach defendants with illegally obtained evidence would encourage police misconduct. Law enforcement officers will think it unlikely that the defendant will first decide to testify at trial and will also open the door inadvertently to admission of any illegally obtained evidence. Hence, the officers' incentive to acquire evidence through illegal means is quite weak.

"In contrast, expanding the impeachment exception to *all* defense witnesses would significantly enhance the expected value to the prosecution of illegally obtained evidence. First, this expansion would vastly increase the number of occasions on which such evidence could be used. Defense witnesses easily outnumber testifying defendants, both because many defendants do not testify themselves and because many if not most defendants call multiple witnesses on their behalf. Moreover, due to the chilling effect identified above, illegally obtained evidence holds even greater value to the prosecution for each individual witness than for each defendant. The prosecutor's access to impeachment evidence would not just deter perjury; it would also deter defendants from calling witnesses in the first place, thereby keeping from the jury much probative exculpatory evidence. For both of these reasons, police officers and their superiors would recognize that obtaining evidence through illegal means stacks the deck heavily in the prosecution's favor. It is thus far more than a 'speculative possibility' that police misconduct will be encouraged by permitting such use of illegally obtained evidence.

"The United States argues that this result is constitutionally acceptable because excluding illegally obtained evidence solely from the prosecution's case in chief would still provide a quantum of deterrence sufficient to protect the privacy interests underlying the exclusionary rule. We disagree. [Much] if not most of the time, police officers confront opportunities to obtain evidence illegally after they have already legally obtained (or know that they have other means of legally obtaining) sufficient evidence to sustain a prima facie case. In these situations, a rule requiring exclusion of illegally obtained evidence from only the government's case in chief would leave officers with little to lose and much to gain by

6. * * * [The] dissent embraces the Illinois Supreme Court's suggestion that prosecutors could be allowed to impeach witnesses only when their testimony is in "direct conflict" with the illegally seized evidence. [But] the result of [an] inquiry distinguishing between "direct" and "indirect" evidentiary conflicts is far from predictable. [The] uncertainty whether a court might find a witness' testimony to pose a "direct" conflict and therefore trigger the impeachment exception likely will chill defendant's presentation of potential witnesses in many cases.

overstepping constitutional limits on evidence gathering.[8] Narrowing the exclusionary rule in this manner, therefore, would significantly undermine the rule's ability 'to compel respect for the constitutional guaranty in the only effectively available way—by removing the incentive to disregard it.' So long as we are committed to protecting the people from the disregard of their constitutional rights during the course of criminal investigations, inadmissibility of illegally obtained evidence must remain the rule, not the exception."[a]

Dissenting Justice KENNEDY, joined by Rehnquist, C.J., and O'Connor and Scalia, JJ., maintained that the majority had given the exclusionary rule excessive protection but had afforded the truth-seeking function of the criminal trial inadequate weight:

"[The] line drawn by today's opinion grants the defense side in a criminal case broad immunity to introduce whatever false testimony it can produce from the mouth of a friendly witness. [A] more cautious course is available, one that retains Fourth Amendment protections and yet safeguards the truth-seeking function of the criminal trial.

"[The] interest in protecting the truth-seeking function of the criminal trial is every bit as strong in this case as in our earlier cases that allowed rebuttal with evidence that was inadmissible as part of the prosecution's case in chief. [To] deprive the jurors of knowledge that statements of the defendant himself revealed the witness' testimony to be false would result in a decision by triers of fact who were not just kept in the dark as to excluded evidence, but positively misled. The potential for harm to the truth-seeking process resulting from the majority's new rule in fact will be greater than if the defendant himself had testified. It is natural for jurors to be skeptical of self-serving testimony by the defendant. Testimony by a witness said to be independent has the greater potential to deceive. And if a defense witness can present false testimony with impunity, the jurors may find the rest of the prosecution's case suspect, for ineffective and artificial cross-examination will be viewed as a real weakness in the State's case. Jurors will assume that if the prosecution had any proof the statement was false, it would make the proof known. The majority does more than deprive the prosecution of evidence. The State must also suffer the introduction of false testimony and appear to bolster the falsehood by its own silence.

"The majority's fear that allowing the jury to know the whole truth will chill defendants from putting on any defense seems to me far too speculative to justify the rule here announced. No restriction on the defense results if rebuttal of testimony by witnesses other than the defendant is confined to the introduction of excludable evidence that is in direct contradiction of the testimony. [In] this context rebuttal can and should be confined to [such] situations. * * *

"[The] suggestion that the threat of a perjury prosecution will provide sufficient deterrence to prevent false testimony is not realistic. A heightened proof requirement applies in Illinois and other States, making perjury convictions difficult to sustain. Where testimony presented on behalf of a friend or family member is involved, the threat that a future jury will convict the witness may be an idle one.

---

8. Indeed, the detectives who unlawfully detained James and elicited his incriminating statements already knew that there were several eyewitnesses to the shooting. Because the detectives likely believed that the exclusion of any statement they obtained from James probably would not have precluded the prosecution from making a prima facie case, an exclusionary rule applicable only to the prosecution's case in chief likely would have provided little deterrent effect in this case.

a. Stevens, J., who joined the opinion of the Court, also wrote a separate opinion.

"[The] majority's concerns may carry greater weight where contradicting testimony is elicited from a defense witness on cross-examination. In that situation there might be a concern that the prosecution would attempt to produce such testimony as the foundation to put excluded evidence before the jury. We have found that possibility insufficient to justify immunity for a defendant's own false testimony on cross-examination. *Havens.* As to cross-examination of other witnesses, perhaps a different rule could be justified. * * *

"It is unrealistic to say that the decision to make an illegal search turns on a precise calculation of the possibilities of rebuttal at some future trial. There is no reason to believe a police officer, unschooled in the law, will assess whether evidence already in his possession would suffice to survive a motion for acquittal following the case in chief. The officer may or may not even know the identity of the ultimate defendant.[3] He certainly will not know anything about potential defense witnesses, much less what the content of their testimony might be. What he will know for certain is that evidence from an illegal search or arrest (which may well be crucial to securing a conviction) will be lost to the case in chief.

"[Where] the jury is misled by false testimony, otherwise subject to flat contradiction by evidence illegally seized, the protection of the exclusionary rule is 'perverted into a license to use perjury by way of a defense, free from the risk of confrontation with prior inconsistent utterances.' *Havens.* The perversion is the same where the perjury is by proxy."

Notes and Questions

(a) *The "Pinocchio defense witness" (a defense witness other than the defendant who lies at trial to benefit the defendant).* Consider Note, 1990 U.Ill.L.F. 375, 473: "Although Pinocchio is deterred from lying by the threat of perjury prosecution, cases abound where defense witnesses nevertheless commit perjury. [Meanwhile, the defendant, Stromboli (in the Pinocchio story the puppeteer who caused Pinocchio to become a liar)], benefits from the lies by receiving an acquittal. To further the truthfinding function of the criminal justice system, the goal of judicial integrity, and the policy against perjury, Stromboli also must be deterred from resorting to Pinocchio's perjurious testimony. * * * If perjurious testimony is an affront to the legal system, it does not matter whether the perjury comes from the defendant's own lips or the lips of the Pinocchio defense witness."

(b) *The dissent's selective assumptions.* The *James* dissent, notes James Spira, *James v. Illinois: A Halt to the Expansion of the Impeachment Exception,* 15 So.Ill.U.L.J. 27, 51 (1990), "is willing to assume that a defense witness, unschooled and unfamiliar with the law, will be well versed in the quantum of proof necessary for a perjury conviction, but is unwilling to assume that police, who are in and out of court constantly, will not realize that the discovery of illegally obtained evidence will aid a conviction in light of an expanded impeachment exception."

(c) *Why should the impeachment of defense witnesses be restricted more severely than impeachment of defendants?* Consider James Kainen, *The Impeach-*

---

3. In this case, contrary to the impression conveyed by the majority, n. 8, the arresting officers knew almost nothing of the state of a future prosecution case. The officers did know there were several eyewitnesses to the shooting. But these eyewitnesses had made no identification of any suspect. The officers did not know petitioner's real name or his true appearance, but had sought him out at the beauty parlor on an anonymous tip. They could not know what physical evidence, such as the murder weapon, they might find on petitioner, or might lose, to the case in chief as a result of illegal conduct. The suggestion that the officers' calculated assessment of a future trial allowed them to ignore the exclusionary rule finds no support in the record and, in fact, is pure speculation.

ment Exception to the Exclusionary Rules: Policies, Principles, and Politics, 44 Stan.L.Rev. 1301, 1322–23 (1992):

"Although he argued that limitations on the impeachment of defense witnesses were necessary to confine the incentive to gather proof illegally to an acceptable level, Justice Kennedy was unable to explain why identical restrictions should not also be applied to the impeachment of defendants. Alternatively, if the impeachment of defendants should not be restricted, then such restrictions are similarly unnecessary to protect defense witnesses. As a result, Justice Kennedy could not demonstrate that extending the exception as he proposed would effect net gains, just as the majority could not demonstrate that its result would effect net losses when both truth-seeking and deterrence costs were tallied. * * *

"Justice Kennedy's truth-seeking analysis contended that contradiction of defense witness testimony is particularly important because juries are more likely to believe such testimony. [If so,] witness testimony should be more readily impeached than that of defendants."

(d) *Are the impeachment exception cases based on a faulty premise?* Do *James* and other cases dealing with the impeachment exception rest on the premise that it is possible to accommodate both rules of evidence and principles of constitutional criminal procedure within a neutral framework? Is this premise sound? Are the contradictory values reflected in constitutional criminal procedure principles and evidentiary concepts susceptible to neutral accommodation? Should any analysis of the scope of the exclusionary rules be recast exclusively as an issue of constitutional procedure, rather than as a compromise between those rules and the rules of evidence? See Kainen, supra, at 1304–05, 1326–27, 1362–72.

B.   WHAT KINDS OF CONSTITUTIONAL OR OTHER VIOLATIONS ARE ENCOMPASSED WITHIN THE IMPEACHMENT EXCEPTION?

1. *New Jersey v. Portash*, 440 U.S. 450, 99 S.Ct. 1292, 59 L.Ed.2d 501 (1979) held, per Stewart, J. that testimony given by a person in response to a grant of legislative immunity could not be used to impeach him at his subsequent trial for extortion and misconduct in office. "Central to the decisions" in *Harris* and *Hass*, emphasized the Court, was the fact that the defendant made no claim that the statements were coerced. But testimony before a grand jury in response to a grant of use immunity "is the essence of coerced testimony." Balancing of interests was thought to be necessary in *Harris* and *Hass* "when the attempt to deter unlawful police conduct collided with the need to prevent perjury. Here, by contrast, we deal with the constitutional privilege against compulsory self-incrimination in its most pristine form. Balancing, therefore, is not simply unnecessary. It is impermissible."

2. In *Mincey v. Arizona* (1978), p. 444, the Court also distinguished *Harris* and *Hass* and made clear that the use of an "involuntary" or "coerced" statement even for impeachment purposes would constitute "a denial of due process of law." But the Court's discussion seemed to overlook the possibility that an "involuntary" statement may be trustworthy in a particular case.

3.   *Use of statements obtained in violation of the Sixth Amendment Jackson rule.* In MICHIGAN v. HARVEY, 494 U.S. 344, 110 S.Ct. 1176, 108 L.Ed.2d 293 (1990), a 5–4 majority, per REHNQUIST, C.J., held that statements obtained in violation of the rule established in *Michigan v. Jackson* (p. 535), may be used to impeach a defendant's false or inconsistent testimony:

"*Michigan v. Jackson* is based on the Sixth Amendment, but its roots lie in this Court's decisions in *Miranda* and succeeding cases. [*Edwards*] added a second layer of protection [to] *Miranda*, [establishing a] prophylactic rule designed to prevent police from badgering a defendant into waiving his previously asserted *Miranda* rights.

"*Jackson* simply superimposed the Fifth Amendment analysis of *Edwards* onto the Sixth Amendment. Reasoning that 'the Sixth Amendment right to counsel at a postarraignment interrogation requires at least as much protection as the Fifth Amendment right to counsel at any custodial interrogation,' [the *Jackson* Court] concluded that the *Edwards* protections should apply when a suspect charged with a crime requests counsel outside the context of interrogation. This rule, like *Edwards,* is based on the supposition that suspects who assert their right to counsel are unlikely to waive that right voluntarily in subsequent interrogations.

"We have already decided [that] statements taken in violation [of] the prophylactic *Miranda* rules [are] admissible to impeach conflicting testimony by the defendant. *Harris v. New York; Oregon v. Hass.* [There] is no reason for a different result in a *Jackson* case, where the prophylactic rule is designed to ensure voluntary, knowing, and intelligent waivers of the Sixth Amendment right to counsel rather than the Fifth Amendment privilege against self-incrimination or 'right to counsel.' [We] have never prevented use by the prosecution of relevant voluntary statements by a defendant, particularly when the violations alleged by a defendant relate only to procedural safeguards that are 'not themselves rights protected by the Constitution.' [In] such cases, we have decided that the 'search for truth in a criminal case' outweighs the 'speculative possibility' that exclusion of evidence might deter future violations of rules not compelled directly by the Constitution in the first place. *Hass.* [The *Hass* case] was decided 15 years ago, and no new information has come to our attention which should lead us to think otherwise now."

Dissenting Justice STEVENS (author of the Court's opinion in *Jackson*), joined by Brennan, Marshall and Blackmun, JJ., maintained that the Court had made it clear that "the constitutional rule recognized in *Jackson* is based on the Sixth Amendment interest in preserving 'the integrity of an accused's choice to communicate with police only through counsel,'" and that "the Court should acknowledge as much and hold that the Sixth Amendment is violated when the fruits of the State's impermissible encounter with the represented defendant are used for impeachment just as it is when the fruits are used in the prosecutor's case in chief":

"[Unlike the situation when evidence is seized in violation of the Fourth Amendment or a statement is obtained in violation of *Miranda,* the] exclusion of statements made by a represented and indicted defendant outside the presence of counsel follows not as a remedy for a violation that has preceded trial but as a necessary incident of the constitutional right itself.[7] '[T]he Sixth Amendment right to counsel exists, and is needed, in order to protect the fundamental right to a fair trial.' It is not implicated, as a general matter, in the absence of some effect of the challenged conduct on the trial process itself. It is thus the use of the evidence for trial, not the method of its collection prior to trial, that is the gravamen of the Sixth Amendment claim."

---

7. As Professor Schulhofer has commented:

"[T]he *Massiah* 'exclusionary rule' is not merely a prophylactic device; it is not designed to reduce the *risk* of actual constitutional violations and is not intended to deter any pretrial behavior whatsoever. Rather, *Massiah* explicitly permits government efforts to obtain information from an indicted suspect, so long as that information is not used 'as evidence against *him* at his trial.' The failure to exclude evidence, therefore, cannot be considered *collateral* to some more fundamental violation. Instead, it is the admission at trial that in itself denies the constitutional right." Stephen Schulhofer, *Confessions and the Court,* 79 Mich.L.Rev. 865, 889 (1981). * * *

4. *Use of statements obtained in violation of the Massiah right to counsel.* In *Harvey* the Court left open the question whether statements obtained in violation of *Massiah*—sometimes called the "core" Sixth Amendment protection, other times called the "pure" right to counsel—may be used to impeach a defendant. When the Court does address the issue, how should it decide it? How significant is it that unlike the *Jackson* rule, which the Court characterized as "prophylactic" in nature because based on *Edwards v. Arizona*, the *Massiah* doctrine is a constitutional rule (or is it)? How significant is it that the great bulk of statements obtained in violation of *Massiah* are voluntary statements? How significant is it that in *Patterson v. Illinois* (p. 602), the Court rejected the view that the *Massiah* right is "superior" to or "greater" than the *Miranda* right?

C. USE OF DEFENDANT'S PRIOR SILENCE FOR IMPEACHMENT PURPOSES

1. After being arrested for selling marijuana to an informant, defendants were given the *Miranda* warnings and chose to remain silent. At trial, each defendant claimed that he had been "framed" by narcotics agents. In an effort to undercut their testimony, the prosecution was allowed to ask each defendant why he had not told this story to the arresting officer. In *Doyle v. Ohio*, 426 U.S. 610, 96 S.Ct. 2240, 49 L.Ed.2d 91 (1976), a 6–3 majority, per Powell, J., held such use of a defendant's post-arrest silence, after receiving the *Miranda* warnings, impermissible. Not only is "every post-arrest silence * * * insolubly ambiguous because of what the State is required to advise the person arrested," but use of the silence to impeach would be "fundamentally unfair" given the fact that the *Miranda* warnings contain the "implicit" "assurance" that "silence will carry no penalty."[a] But *Doyle* has been distinguished in three subsequent impeachment cases.

2. ***Impeachment by prior inconsistent statements after receiving Miranda warnings.*** After being arrested while driving a stolen car and given the *Miranda* warnings, defendant agreed to talk to the police. But he gave a different version of the auto theft than he subsequently did when he testified in his own defense. On cross-examination, he was asked why he gave a different story at the time of his arrest. *Anderson v. Charles*, 447 U.S. 404, 100 S.Ct. 2180, 65 L.Ed.2d 222 (1980) (per curiam), had little difficulty in permitting such cross-examination: "[*Doyle*] does not apply to cross-examination that merely inquires into prior inconsistent statements. Such questioning makes no unfair use of silence, because a defendant who voluntarily speaks after receiving *Miranda* warnings has not been induced to remain silent."

3. ***Use of defendant's prearrest silence for impeachment purposes.*** In *Jenkins v. Anderson*, 447 U.S. 231, 100 S.Ct. 2124, 65 L.Ed.2d 86 (1980), where at his murder trial petitioner claimed self-defense, the prosecutor was allowed to question him about the fact that he had not surrendered to the authorities until two weeks after the killing. In closing argument, the prosecutor again referred to petitioner's prearrest silence, noting that he had "waited" at least two weeks before "reporting" the stabbing to anyone, suggesting that he would have spoken out if he had truly killed in self-defense. The Court, per Powell, J., held (1), relying heavily on *Raffel v. United States*, 271 U.S. 494, 46 S.Ct. 566, 70 L.Ed.

a. But cf. *South Dakota v. Neville* (1983) (also discussed at p. 499, fn. a), upholding a statute permitting a person suspected of driving while intoxicated to refuse to submit to a blood-alcohol test, but authorizing revocation of the driver's license of a person so refusing the test and also allowing such refusal to be used against him at trial. Although the defendant in *Neville* had not been told of the latter possibility, the Court thought it "unrealistic to say that the warnings given here implicitly assure a suspect that no consequences other than those mentioned will occur. Importantly, the warning that he could lose his driver's license made it clear that refusing the test was not a 'safe harbor' free of adverse consequences."

1054 (1926), that the Self–Incrimination Clause is not violated by the use of prearrest silence to impeach a defendant's credibility;[a] and (2) *Doyle* presents no obstacle for "no governmental action induced petitioner to remain silent before arrest. The failure to speak occurred before petitioner was taken into custody and given *Miranda* warnings."[b]

Dissenting Justice Marshall, joined by Brennan, J., contended that the Court's holding "has three patent—and in my view, fatal—defects": (1) Considering the various possible explanations for silence (e.g., Jenkins' story would have implicated him in the homicide), "the mere fact of prearrest silence is so unlikely to be probative of the falsity of the defendant's trial strategy that its use for impeachment is contrary to [due process]." (2) "[T]he drawing of an adverse inference from the failure to volunteer incriminating statements impermissibly infringes the privilege against self-incrimination." (3) "[T]he availability of the inference for impeachment purposes impermissibly burdens the decision to exercise the constitutional right to testify in one's own defense."

4.   *Use of defendant's post-arrest silence for impeachment purposes.* When arrested, Weir, a murder suspect, said nothing, but the "significant difference" between this case and *Doyle* is that Weir did not receive any *Miranda* warnings during the period in which he remained silent immediately after his arrest. When Weir testified at his trial that he had acted in self-defense, the prosecutor cross-examined him as to why, when arrested, he had not offered this exculpatory explanation. *Fletcher v. Weir*, 455 U.S. 603, 102 S.Ct. 1309, 71 L.Ed.2d 490 (1982) (per curiam), held that "in the absence of the sort of affirmative assurances embodied in the *Miranda* warnings" a state may permit cross-examination about post-arrest silence when a defendant chooses to take the stand. The Court rejected the argument that an arrest, by itself, is "governmental action which implicitly induces a defendant to remain silent," deeming such "broadening of *Doyle* * * * unsupported by the reasoning of that case and contrary to our post-*Doyle* decisions."

Notes and Questions

(a) Suppose, when arrested, Weir had said, "I believe I have a perfectly valid defense, but I don't think I should talk to you until I first have a chance to talk to my lawyer." Could that statement and/or the subsequent post-arrest silence be used for impeachment purposes?

(b) Suppose, when being driven to the station house, a suspect asks the arresting officer, "Do I have a right to remain silent?" Or, "Do I have a right to discuss my situation with a lawyer before saying anything about it to a police officer?" How should the officer respond?

(c) Suppose, when being driven to the station house, a suspect asks the arresting officer whether he has a right to remain silent or whether his silence can be used against him at the trial and the officer meets such questions with a stony silence? What result if the suspect then says nothing during the rest of the drive?

a. For strong criticism of this portion of the opinion, see Stephen A. Saltzburg, *Foreword: The Flow and Ebb of Constitutional Criminal Procedure in the Warren and Burger Courts,* 69 Geo. L.J. 151, 204–05 (1980).

b. But see Craig M. Bradley, *Havens, Jenkins, and Salvucci, and the Defendant's "Right" to Testify,* 18 Am.Crim.L.Rev. 419, 434–35 (1981), maintaining that the silence in *Jenkins* was just as equivocal as that in *Doyle*

for "an individual's reluctance to hand himself over to the police and admit a stabbing, in self-defense or otherwise," is not probative of guilt. "Anyone who believes that volunteering information to police is 'natural' for a resident of Detroit's inner-city has an unusually optimistic view of human nature." See also Note, 94 Harv.L.Rev. 77, 84–85 (1980).

What result if the suspect then starts talking and makes incriminating statements?

D. Use of Post-Miranda Warnings Silence or Assertion of Rights to Rebut Defense of Insanity

May a defendant's post-Miranda warnings silence or request for counsel be offered not to impeach but as substantive evidence to rebut defendant's defense of insanity at the time of the offense? No, answers *Wainwright v. Greenfield*, 474 U.S. 284, 106 S.Ct. 634, 88 L.Ed.2d 623 (1986). On three occasions shortly after his arrest in Florida for sexual battery, Greenfield was given the Miranda warnings. Each time he exercised his right to remain silent and stated that he wished to speak with an attorney before answering any questions. Greenfield later pled guilty by reason of insanity. At his trial two police officers described the occasions on which Greenfield had exercised his right to remain silent and had expressed a desire to consult with counsel. In his closing argument, the prosecutor reviewed this police testimony and suggested that Greenfield's responses to the warnings demonstrated a degree of comprehension inconsistent with his claim of insanity. Greenfield was convicted and sentenced to life imprisonment. The Court, per Stevens, J., overturned his conviction, holding that Doyle applied to his case:

"The point of [Doyle] is that it is fundamentally unfair to promise an arrested person that his silence will not be used against him and thereafter to breach that promise by using the silence to impeach his trial testimony. It is equally unfair to breach that promise by using silence to overcome a defendant's plea of insanity. In both situations [the State] implicitly promises that any exercise of these rights will not be penalized."[a]

E. How Much Leeway Do the "Impeachment" Cases and "Fruit of the Poisonous Tree" Cases Give A "Bad Man of the Law"?

"Ten years ago, Albert Alschuler hypothesized about the advice that 'Justice Holmes " 'bad man of the law' " might offer in a [police] training manual.[134] Alschuler thought that a bad officer, one who cared only about the material consequences of and not the reason for his conduct, might author a manual advising police to continue to interrogate a suspect who asked for counsel or wished to remain silent. Alschuler's writing proved prescient. In deciding [such cases as *Harris, Hass, Tucker* and *Elstad*] the Court could not have intended to give police grounds to disobey this portion of *Miranda* deliberately, but this disregard is the natural consequence of these decisions. [These cases] provide an unfortunate opening for the quintessential 'bad man of the law.' "

—Charles D. Weisselberg, *Saving Miranda* 84 Cornell L.Rev. 109, 132 (1998).

---

a. Rehnquist, J., joined by the Chief Justice, concurred in the result because one of the prosecutor's remarks was "an improper comment on respondent's silence." But he maintained that "a request for a lawyer may be highly relevant where the plea is based on insanity"—"there is no 'insoluble ambiguity' in the request; it is a perfectly straightforward statement tending to show that an individual is able to understand his rights and is not incoherent or obviously confused or unbalanced"—

and he did not read the warnings "as containing any promise, express or implied, that the words used in responding to notice of the right to a lawyer will not be used by the State to rebut a claim of insanity."

134. Albert W. Alschuler, *Failed Pragmatism: Reflections on the Burger Court*, 100 Harv.L.Rev. 1436, 1442 (1987) (quoting O. W. Holmes, *The Path of the Law*, 10 Harv.L.Rev. 457, 459 (1897).

Pointing to police training materials uncovered in the course of litigation seeking to stop officers in two California police departments from questioning custodial suspects after they have asserted their *Miranda* rights, Professor Weisselberg, supra, reports that "[in] California and, to a certain extent in other states, police have developed the tactics of questioning 'outside *Miranda*,' meaning questioning over the direct and unambiguous assertion of Fifth Amendment rights." Set forth below are extracts from the remarks of Devallis Rutledge in a California police training videotape. Mr. Rutledge is an Orange County Deputy District Attorney and a member of the California Commission on Peace Officer Standards and Training. The full transcript of the videotape is reprinted in the Appendix to Weisselberg's article.

CALIFORNIA POLICE TRAINING VIDEOTAPE—
QUESTIONING "OUTSIDE *MIRANDA*"
(1990)

This has to do with questioning "outside *Miranda*." * * *

What if you've got a guy [in custody] that you've only got one shot at? This is it, it's now or never because you're gonna lose him—he's gonna bail out or a lawyer's on the way down there, or you're gonna have to take him over to some other officials—you're never gonna have another chance at this guy, this is it. And you Mirandize him and he invokes [his rights]. What you can do—legally do—in that instance in go "outside *Miranda*" and continue to talk to him because you've got other legitimate purposes in talking to him other than obtaining an admission of guilt that can be used in his trial. And that's what *Miranda* protects him against—you compelling him to make a statement that is later used in trial to convict him of the charge.

But you may want to go "outside *Miranda*" and get information to help you clear cases. [Or,] maybe it will help you recover a dead body or missing person. * * * You may be able to recover stolen property. He tells you where the property is ditched, his statement will not be admissible against him in trial if you go "outside *Miranda*," but you'll get the property back and the owner will get the property back. That's a legitimate function. Maybe his statement "outside *Miranda*" will reveal methods—his methods of operation. How he was able to obtain these credit cards and how he was able to pull of his scam or whatever. * * *

Or his statements might reveal the existence and the location of physical evidence. You've got him, but you'd kinda like to have the gun that he used or the knife that he used or whatever else it was. But he ditched it somewhere and you can't find it. And so you've arrested him, he's invoked *Miranda* and you say, "Well I'd still like to find the evidence in the case." So you go "outside *Miranda*," and if he talks "outside *Miranda*"—if the only thing that was shutting him up was the chance of it being used against him in court—and then you go "outside *Miranda*" and take a statement and then he tells you where the stuff is, we can go and get all that evidence.

And it forces the defendant to commit to a statement that will prevent him from pulling out some defense and using it at trial—that he's cooked up with some defense lawyer—that wasn't true. So if you get a statement "outside *Miranda*" and he tells you that he did it and how he did it or if he gives you a denial of some sort, he's tied to that, he is married to that, because the U.S. Supreme Court [and] the California Supreme Court [have] told us that we can use statements "outside *Miranda*" to impeach or to rebut. We can't use them for our case-in-chief. The D.A. can't trot them out to the jury before he says, "I rest," but if the defendant then gets up there and gets on the stand and lies and says something different, we can use his "outside *Miranda*" statements to impeach him. We can use it to rebut his case.

* * * The *Miranda* exclusionary rule is limited to the defendant's own statement out of his mouth. That is all that is excluded under *Miranda*. It doesn't have a fruits of the poisonous tree theory attached to it the way constitutional violations do. When you violate *Miranda*, you're not violating the Constitution. *Miranda* is not in the Constitution. It's a court-created decision that affects the admissibility of testimonial evidence and that's all it is. [There's] no law says you can't question people "outside *Miranda*." You don't violate the Constitution. The Constitution doesn't say you have to do that. It's a court decision. So all you're violating is a court decision controlling admissibility of evidence. So you're not doing anything unlawful, you're not doing anything illegal, you're not violating anybody's civil rights, you're not doing nothing improper. [When we question someone who has invoked his *Miranda* rights] [all] we lose is the statement taken in violation of *Miranda*. We do not lose physical evidence that resulted from that. We do not lose the testimony of other witnesses that we learned about only by violating his *Miranda* invocation.

Consider Weisselberg, supra, at 184–85, 188:

"If the Court's pronouncement in *Miranda* is to receive the respect of law enforcement, it needs a legitimate foundation. Until the Court restores *Miranda*'s link to the Fifth Amendment, *Miranda* cannot escape the attack and evasion of those who claim that it describes merely optional procedures. [In] addition to excluding *Miranda*-violative statements from the prosecution's case-in-chief, [the] Court must adopt a rule of exclusion that deters officers from deliberately breaching *Miranda*. * * *

"This rule of exclusion should prove relatively simple to administer. The standard is objective, not subjective. Courts have clarified *Miranda*'s parameters during the last thirty years, so that a suspect must unequivocally assert Fifth Amendment rights for protection during a custodial interrogation. Consequently, courts should not experience any difficulty determining when an officer has acted in objective good or bad faith. Thus, when a court finds a genuine dispute whether the suspect was truly in custody or whether an officer's conduct amounted to interrogation, the prosecution may use the statement for impeachment, and the court may admit its fruits. But if an officer continues to question a suspect over the unambiguous invocation of Fifth Amendment rights, the court should not admit the statement or its fruits for any purpose.

" * * * Although the Court in the past has considered it a 'speculative' possibility that officers might violate *Miranda* deliberately, the evidence now shows that many receive training to do just that. [If] the Court allows [the tactic of questioning 'outside *Miranda*' to continue], the practice signifies the end of *Miranda*, or at least the original version of *Miranda*. [When] courts are unwilling to act in the face of open and direct defiance of a principle of law, that principle cannot survive."[a]

a. See also Charles D. Weisselberg, *In the Stationhouse After Dickerson*, 99 Mich.L.Rev. 1121 (2001).

SECTION 4. ALLOCATION OF THE BURDENS OF PROOF

PEOPLE v. BERRIOS
270 N.E.2d 709 (N.Y.1971).

SCILEPPI, Judge.

In each of [these] appeals, the defendants have been charged with possession of heroin and arresting officers have testified that glassine envelopes containing narcotics were dropped on the ground as the defendants were approached by the police.[b] We have been called upon to decide whether, in these "dropsy" cases, or for that matter whenever a warrantless search is presented, it is the People who must bear the burden of proving the legality of the search and seizure. [In each of the cases before the court, an officer testified that as he made a movement toward the defendant—leaving his car in one case, instructing the defendant to stop in another—the defendant dropped a glassine envelope containing narcotics. The officer was undercover in one case and in uniform in another.]

Simply stated, [defendants] have contended that the police testimony in these cases is inherently untrustworthy and the product of fabrication; hence, the argument is advanced that we should require that the People bear the burden of proving admissibility and depart from our present rule which places the burden of showing inadmissibility on the defendant. No argument is proffered that this departure is required by either the State or Federal Constitutions; rather, it is asserted that the change in burden of proof is necessary to alleviate the possibility of perjured police testimony. It is noted by this court that the District Attorney of New York County has joined defense counsel in [one] case in suggesting the change in burden of proof. This concession does not, however, relieve us from the performance of our judicial function and does not require us to adopt the proposal urged upon us. [W]e are not persuaded that a change in burden of proof is indicated.

Thus far, we have made it clear that where a defendant challenges the admissibility of physical evidence or makes a motion to suppress, he bears the ultimate burden of proving that the evidence should not be used against him. Indeed the very words employed by the Legislature in fashioning the motion to suppress suggest no other rational conclusion. Section 813–c of the Code of Criminal Procedure provides that "[a] *person claiming to be aggrieved* by an unlawful search and seizure and having reasonable grounds to believe that the property * * * *claimed to have been unlawfully obtained* may be used as evidence against him [may] move for the return [or] suppression of its use as evidence." (Emphasis supplied). Since such a person makes the claim because he contends

---

b. In New York, as in most jurisdictions, challenges to the admissibility of evidence on the ground that it was illegally obtained must be presented by a pretrial motion to suppress. The motion must set forth the objection with sufficient particularity, which usually requires that the defense specify the nature of the alleged illegality in the acquisition of evidence (e.g., that a statement was obtained in violation of *Miranda,* or that the search in question was incident to an arrest not supported by probable cause). See LaFave and Israel, § 10.1(b). Assuming the form of the motion is correct, the trial judge will then hold a pretrial hearing at which both sides can offer its testimony regarding the acquisition of the evidence and cross-examine the other side's witnesses.

Denial of the pretrial motion does not allow an immediate appeal by the defense, but the prosecution often can appeal the granting of the motion. See Ch. 27, § 3.

In those jurisdictions that do not require a pretrial motion, an objection may be made at trial, contemporaneously with the introduction of the evidence. An objection at this point ordinarily requires the trial court to recess the trial in order to conduct a hearing on the suppression objection. Whether a state requires a pretrial motion or a contemporaneous objection, failure to make a timely objection can result in the procedural forfeiture of the objection. See *Wainwright v. Sykes,* Ch. 29, § 3; and CRIMPROC § 10.2(a).

that he is aggrieved and requests the court to give redress to an alleged wrong, it is most reasonable to require him to bear the burden of proof of that wrong. The People must, of course, always show that police conduct was reasonable. Thus, though a defendant who challenges the legality of a search and seizure has the burden of proving illegality, the People are nevertheless put to "the burden of *going forward* to show the legality of the police conduct in the first instance". *People v. Baldwin,* 250 N.E.2d 62 (N.Y.1969). These considerations require that the People show that the search was made pursuant to a valid warrant, consent, incident to a lawful arrest or, in cases such as those here, that no search at all occurred because the evidence was dropped by the defendant in the presence of the police officer.

* * * We have been told that with the advent of *Mapp v. Ohio,* there has been a great incidence of "dropsy" testimony by police officers. Hence, this court has been asked to infer that the police are systematically evading the mandate of *Mapp* by fabricating their testimony. We cannot embrace this *post hoc ergo propter hoc* reasoning for, as the then Judge Warren Burger observed in *Bush v. United States,* 375 F.2d 602, 604 (D.C.Cir.1967), "[i]t would be a dismal reflection on society to say that when the guardians of its security are called to testify in court under oath, their testimony must be viewed with suspicion." Thus, we reject this frontal attack on the integrity of our entire law enforcement system. * * * Some police officers, as well as some in other callings may be tempted to tamper with the truth. But there is no valid proof that all members of law enforcement agencies or that all other citizens who testify are perjurers. Therefore, all policemen should not be singled out as suspect as a matter of law.

The fact that some witnesses may lie does not require a change in the burden of proof for it is our view that the proposal made in this appeal is no more effective in preventing perjury than the present burden of proof. Under both the suggested change and the present system, the defendant must still refute the testimony of the police officer. Thus, even where the officer testifies that glassine envelopes were dropped by the defendant or to facts which would sustain a warrantless search, the court would still be faced with the same credibility question. Since a change in the burden of proof would be ineffective to combat the alleged evil about which the defendants herein complain, principles of *stare decisis* do not allow a departure from our present rule of burden of proof.

[Where] the Judge at the suppression hearing determines that the testimony of the police officer is unworthy of belief, he should conclude that the People have not met their burden of coming forward with sufficient evidence and grant the motion to suppress. Similarly, appellate courts by a careful exercise of their jurisdiction, in reviewing the evidence, can effectively curtail the alleged abuses.

Additionally, there are more appropriate methods of dealing with the abuses about which the defendants complain. For example, as the District Attorney of Bronx County has suggested, a possible solution to the problem of some police fabrication can be found within the several police departments of this State. They can effectively formulate internal procedures and policies within the department to eliminate any such abuses. This should at the very least take the form of training and official action to prevent fabrication. Lastly, the district attorneys of this State should evaluate the testimony of police officers, as they do the testimony of all witnesses, in determining what proof will be offered in the prosecution of a case. * * *

FULD, Chief Judge (dissenting).

[The] District Attorney of New York County informs us [that]: "For the last ten years participants in the system of justice—judges, prosecutors, defense attorneys and police officials—have privately and publicly expressed the belief that in some substantial but indeterminable percentage of dropsy cases, the testimony [that a defendant dropped narcotics or gambling slips to the ground as a police officer approached him] is tailored to meet the requirements of search-and-seizure rulings" and "it is very difficult in many [such] cases to distinguish between fact and fiction." When so able and dedicated a prosecutor as District Attorney Frank Hogan believes that there is basis for questioning the truthfulness of the testimony in a "substantial * * * percentage of dropsy cases," the conclusion seems to me inescapable [that] the integrity of the judicial process demands that there be a reallocation of the burden of proof. * * *

Underlying the Fourth and Fourteenth Amendments is the basic proposition that "no man is to be convicted on unconstitutional evidence." In light of the situation as it today exists, the present rule—which imposes upon the accused the burden of proving the illegality of a seizure on a motion to suppress—subverts this principle by making it possible for some defendants to be convicted on evidence obtained in violation of constitutional guarantees. This follows from the fact that a trial judge who is unsure whether the prosecution's account of the seizure is credible must, nevertheless, resolve his doubt in favor of the People and admit the evidence. To thus increase the likelihood of a conviction on proof of dubious constitutionality must be stamped as highly unreasonable and unfair. A change in the rule will help assure that a defendant's constitutional rights will not be violated since, by placing the burden on the People, the judge will be permitted to suppress evidence in cases where, for instance, he finds the testimony of each side evenly balanced on the scales of credibility and is unable to make up his mind as to who is telling the truth.

[It] is noteworthy that commentators and judges—in addition to the New York County District Attorney—have noted the existence of possible fabrication, and the studies which have been made, based on research into arrest files and interviews with law enforcement officials, persuasively negate the court's charge that this conclusion is based on "*post hoc ergo propter hoc* reasoning." Those who recognize the problem and favor a change in the burden of proof rule do not, contrary to the majority's assertion, intend an "attack on the integrity of our entire law enforcement system." Rather, their concern is solely to promote adherence to the principles articulated in *Mapp v. Ohio.*

[In] point of fact, the suggested modification of the rule is not without support in the decisions. Thus, Federal courts and the courts of California hold that the prosecution should bear the burden of justifying a warrantless seizure of evidence. And, indeed, our court has already engrafted one exception on the present rule; "[w]hen a search and seizure is based upon consent," we declared, "the burden of proof rests heavily upon the People to establish the voluntariness of that waiver of a constitutional right." *People v. Whitehurst;* see, to same effect, *Bumper v. North Carolina* [p. 338].

In short, reason and the imperative of judicial integrity, as well as substantial authority, dictate that the burden of proving the lawfulness of a search or seizure should be cast on the People in all narcotics and gambling cases when the search or seizure has been effected without a warrant. To do less, to shift the burden of proof to the People only in the classic dropsy situation, seems to me, as it does to the New York County District Attorney, "unrealistic." This is so, as he observes, not only because an "untruthful officer fearing rejection of tailored dropsy testimony could easily shift to the other scenarios which are familiar in narcotics and gambling cases in the lower courts" but also because "it is the experience of many prosecutors and judges that the problems of credibility and fact-finding raised [are] not limited to literal dropsy cases [but] appear in all types of possessory narcotics and gambling cases."

BURKE, JASEN and GIBSON, JJ., concur with SCILEPPI, J. FULD, C.J., dissents and votes to reverse in a separate opinion in which BERGAN and BREITEL, JJ., concur.

Notes and Questions

1. *How common is police "falsification"?* As pointed out in Gabriel J. Chin & Scott C. Wells, *"The Blue Wall of Silence" As Evidence of Bias and Motive to Lie: A New Approach to Police Perjury,* 59 U.Pitt.L.Rev. 233, 234 (1998), in 1994 the Mollen Commission, established to investigate police misconduct in New York, "reported that police 'falsification'—which includes 'testimonial perjury, * * * documentary perjury, [and] falsification of police records'—is one of the most common forms of police corruption facing the nation's criminal justice system. In fact, the Mollen Commission indicated that in New York, 'the practice of police falsification [is] so common in certain precincts that it has spawned its own word: "testilying." See also Morgan Cloud, *Judges, "Testilying," and the Constitution,* 69 S.Cal.L.Rev. 1341 (1996); Donald A. Dripps, *Police, Plus Perjury, Equals Polygraphy,* 86 J.Crim.L. & C. 693 (1996); Christopher Slobogin, *Testilying: Police Perjury and What to Do About It,* 67 U.Colo.L.Rev. 1037 (1996).

2. *Was there police perjury in the O.J. Simpson case?* Detective Mark Fuhrman tried to defend the warrantless search of Simpson's residential property shortly after the murder of his former wife by testifying that at the time of the search the police did not know "if we have a murder-suicide, a kidnapping, another victim" and "we had to find out if there's anybody in the residence that's injured, to save their life, to save other people's lives." Despite the incredulous public response to the claim, two judges denied Simpson's suppression motions. For a discussion of why the police testimony about the purpose of the search of Simpson's residence "raised the specter of perjury designed to shield the fruits of an illegal search," see Morgan Cloud, supra, at 1357–61.

3. *State variations.* Aside from the justification of a search on the basis of consent—where the burden universally is placed on the prosecution—states vary considerably in the allocation of both the burden of going forward and the ultimate burden of proof (the burden of persuasion) on Fourth Amendment claims. Ignoring minor variations, the state's position on these burdens usually will fall within one of four general categories:

(a) Under the New York approach, as noted in *Berrios,* the prosecution has the burden of going forward—i.e., introducing evidence that, if accepted, would establish the legality of the search. Thus, in a case involving a search incident to arrest, the prosecution would initially introduce the testimony of an officer showing that probable cause for the arrest existed and that the search was within the scope permitted incident to an arrest. The burden of persuasion would then be on the defendant to rebut this evidence and prove that the search was invalid.

(b) Several states place *both* burdens of proof on the defendant. This position has been justified on several grounds: "(a) the burden should be upon the moving party, (b) there is a presumption of regularity attending the actions of law enforcement officials, (c) relevant evidence is generally admissible and thus exceptions must be justified by those claiming the exception, and (d) [this allocation] will deter spurious allegations wasteful of court time." SEARCHSZR § 11.2(b).

(c) A majority of the states follow the pattern of allocation adopted in the federal courts—if the search was pursuant to a warrant, the defendant has the burden of proof, but if the police acted without a warrant, the burden is on the prosecution. The burden of going forward follows the burden of proof. Where there was a search without a warrant, the defendant must make a prima facie showing of that fact before the prosecution is put to its burdens. Very often, however, the parties will agree as to how the evidence was obtained and an allegation of seizure without a warrant will be sufficient.

As noted in SEARCHSZR § 11.2(b), the federal pattern's "warrant-no-warrant dichotomy is typically explained on the ground that when the police have acted with a warrant 'an independent determination on the issue of probable cause has already been made by a magistrate, thereby giving rise to a presumption of legality,' while when they have acted without a warrant 'the evidence comprising probable cause is particularly within the knowledge and control of the arresting agencies.' Moreover, it is said that '[w]ithout such a rule there would be little reason for law enforcement agencies to bother with the formality of a warrant.'"

(d) In some jurisdictions, the prosecution has both burdens of proof on all Fourth Amendment objections. The reason commonly given as noted in SEARCHSZR § 11.2(b), is that "the state is the party which seeks to use the evidence and thus ought to bear the burden of establishing that it was lawfully come by."

4. *Practical consequences of the allocation.* Of what practical significance is the allocation of the ultimate burden of proof on Fourth Amendment claims? Compare the views of the majority and dissent in *Berrios* on the relation of the burden of proof to judicial treatment of police testimony in "dropsy" cases. Assuming one shared the objective of the dissent, would a better solution have been a direction to the lower courts to subject such testimony to "close scrutiny," in much the same way that a jury is directed that testimony of an accomplice or paid informer should be "scrutinized and received with care"? See Comment, 60 Geo.L.J. 507, 519–20 (1971).

Comments of defense counsel suggest that the allocation of the burden of going forward, and even the specificity required in the motion to suppress, may be more significant than the allocation of the ultimate burden of proof. Thus, Anthony Amsterdam, *Trial Manual for the Defense of Criminal Cases* § 252 (5th ed.1988), notes that a basic tactical objective of the defense is to avoid first disclosing its factual theories, lest the police "conform their testimony" to evade those theories. If defendant is required to go forward with the evidence, he often must, as a practical matter, first take the stand to tell "his side of the story." Although the officers, as prospective witnesses, usually may be excluded from the courtroom while this testimony is given, the defendant still is not in as good a position to rebut their testimony as he would be if he testified last. The defense bearing the burden of production may seek to satisfy it without using the defendant's testimony by calling the officers as its own witnesses. However, this tactic may backfire if the court is unwilling to treat the officers as "adverse" witnesses subject to impeachment. Id. at § 253.

5. *Constitutional requirements.* Why was it that the defendants in *Berrios* failed to argue that the federal constitution required the prosecution to bear the burden of proof? *Bumper v. North Carolina*, p. 338, held, as a matter of constitutional law, that when a prosecutor relies upon consent "he has the burden of proving that the consent was, in fact, freely and voluntarily given." If the Fourth Amendment requires that the prosecution bear the burden on this issue, why not on others? The Supreme Court has stated in various opinions that the Fourth Amendment generally requires a search warrant, and "the burden is on those seeking [an] exemption from [that] requirement to show the need for it." See, e.g., *Chimel v. California*, p. 238. Do such statements imply that, where a search is conducted without a warrant, the prosecution must bear the burden of proving facts that justify the search under one of the recognized exceptions to the warrant requirement, or do the statements refer only to the state's burden in

appellate argument of justifying any request that the Supreme Court recognize a new or expanded exception to the warrant requirement? See SEARCHSZR § 11.2(b) (the former interpretation seems closer to the mark).

6. *Confessions. Miranda* clearly places the burden on the prosecution to respond to a *Miranda* objection by showing that the "defendant knowingly and intelligently waived his privilege against self-incrimination and his right to retained or appointed counsel" (p. 471). Most jurisdictions also place upon the prosecution the burdens of production and persuasion in responding to a claim that a confession was involuntary. A few states, however, place the burden of proving involuntariness on the defendant. *Lego v. Twomey,* discussed at Note 10, raises serious doubts as to the constitutionality of this practice. Though concerned primarily with the applicable standard of proof, *Lego* indicated that it was the constitutional obligation of the prosecution to meet that standard of proof.

7. *Identification testimony. United States v. Wade,* p. 618, indicates that, once the Sixth Amendment is shown to be applicable, the prosecution carries the burden of establishing that defendant intelligently waived his right to counsel at a lineup. But what is the proper allocation of the burden on an objection that a lineup or other identification procedure was so unfairly conducted as to violate due process? Several courts have assumed, without extensive discussion, that the defendant, as the moving party, bears the burden of establishing the due process violation. CRIMPROC § 10.4(d). But compare *People v. Young,* 176 N.W.2d 420 (Mich.App.1970), holding that the prosecution bears the burdens of production and persuasion whenever the identification procedure was conducted "out of the presence of defendant's attorney." Does *Young* constitute an open invitation to defense "fishing expeditions," that will be "automatically available in all lineup-cases"? See *State v. Bishop,* 183 N.W.2d 536 (Minn.1971).

8. *Entrapment.* Reconsider Note 4 at p. 402.

9. *Exclusionary rule limitations.* Once a constitutional violation is established, does the burden of proof necessarily lie with the prosecution to establish that its evidence is not the fruit of the poisonous tree? See e.g., *Wade,* p. 618 (as to proof that the in-court identification was not tainted by the unconstitutional lineup); *Nardone,* p. 764 (once illegal wiretap established, government must convince the trial court that its proof had an independent origin). Consider also *Nix v. Williams,* p. 775, as to the government's burden in establishing that the same evidence would have inevitably been discovered by lawful means.

10. *Standards of proof.* Assuming that the prosecution bears the burden of persuasion on a particular exclusionary rule objection, what standard of proof should apply? In LEGO v. TWOMEY, 404 U.S. 477, 92 S.Ct. 619, 30 L.Ed.2d 618 (1972), the Court rejected the contention that the voluntariness of a confession must be established by proof beyond a reasonable doubt and accepted a preponderance of the evidence standard. Justice WHITE's opinion for the Court reasoned that *In re Winship,* 397 U.S. 358, 90 S.Ct. 1068, 25 L.Ed.2d 368 (1970), requiring proof beyond a reasonable doubt at trial, was not controlling: "Since the purpose that a voluntariness hearing is designed to serve has nothing whatever to do with improving the reliability of jury verdicts, we cannot accept the charge that judging the admissibility of a confession by a preponderance of the evidence undermines the mandate of *In re Winship.* * * * *Winship* [only] confirm[ed] the fundamental right that protects 'the accused against conviction except upon proof beyond a reasonable doubt of every fact necessary to constitute the crime with which he is charged.' A high standard of proof is necessary, we said, to ensure against unjust convictions by giving substance to the presumption of innocence. A guilty verdict is not rendered less reliable or less consonant with *Winship* simply because the admissibility of a confession is determined by a less stringent standard."

Lego also rejected the contention that application of a reasonable doubt standard was necessary "to give adequate protection to those values that the exclusionary rules are designed to serve": "Evidence obtained in violation of the Fourth Amendment has been excluded from federal criminal trials for many years. The same is true of coerced confessions offered in either federal or state trials. [But] no substantial evidence has accumulated that federal rights have suffered from determining admissibility by a preponderance of the evidence. Petitioner offers nothing to suggest [otherwise]. Without good cause, we are unwilling to expand currently applicable exclusionary rules by erecting additional barriers to placing truthful and probative evidence before state juries and by revising the standards applicable in collateral proceedings. [The] exclusionary rules are very much aimed at deterring lawless conduct by police and prosecution and it is very doubtful that escalating the prosecution's burden of proof in Fourth and Fifth Amendment suppression hearings would be sufficiently productive in this respect to outweigh the public interest in placing probative evidence before juries for the purpose of arriving at truthful decisions about guilt or innocence."[a]

11.   Is Lego inconsistent with the philosophy underlying *Chapman v. California* (Ch. 28, § 5)? Cf. Note, 7 Harv.C.R.-C.L.L.Rev. 651 (1972), suggesting that the reasoning that led the Lego majority to conclude that implementation of a constitutional right did not require proof beyond a reasonable doubt could just as readily have led the Court in Chapman to conclude that there was no need to require the especially stringent harmless error standard imposed there. The dissent in Lego (see fn. a supra) also argued that the majority's position there was inconsistent with "the rule that automatically reverses a conviction when an involuntary confession was admitted at trial." Cf. Stephen A. Saltzburg, *Standards of Proof and Preliminary Questions of Fact*, 27 Stan.L.Rev. 271 (1975), arguing that a reasonable doubt standard should have been required in Lego because, inter alia, the test of involuntariness (as opposed to other exclusionary rule standards) is designed to exclude unreliable evidence and the admission of unreliable confessions is especially dangerous because juries give such evidence great weight.

12.   The Supreme Court noted in Lego that, while due process was satisfied by application of the preponderance standard, the states were always "free, pursuant to their own law, to adopt a higher standard." Several states have done exactly that. See CRIMPROC § 10.4. On the other hand, the states uniformly have held that the standard of proof applicable to Fourth Amendment claims, except on the issue of consent, will be the preponderance standard. Id. In a jurisdiction that has adopted the reasonable doubt standard for the determination of the voluntariness of confession, why shouldn't the same standard apply to search and seizure claims? See Saltzburg, supra.

13.   *Waiver of Miranda rights.* In COLORADO v. CONNELLY, 479 U.S. 157, 107 S.Ct. 515, 93 L.Ed.2d 473 (1986), also discussed at p. 588, the Court held that the state need only prove a waiver of Miranda rights by the preponderance of the evidence. The majority, per REHNQUIST, C.J., reasoned:

"[The state supreme court] held that the State must bear its burden of proving waiver [by] 'clear and convincing evidence.' Although we have stated in

a.   Powell and Rehnquist, JJ., did not participate in the *Lego* decision. Dissenting Justice Brennan, joined by Justice Douglas and Marshall, argued that "the preponderance standard does not provide sufficient protection against the danger that involuntary confessions will be employed at trial." The preponderance standard, noted the dissent, was accepted in civil cases on the assumption that it was no more serious an error to have an erroneous decision in favor of one party or another, but the same could not be said for errors relating to the admission of confessions."

passing that the State bears a 'heavy' burden in proving waiver Miranda,[b] we have never held that the 'clear and convincing evidence' standard is the appropriate one. [In] *Lego v. Twomey,* [we] upheld a procedure in which the State established the voluntariness of a confession by no more than a preponderance of the evidence [for] two reasons. First, the voluntariness determination has nothing to do with the reliability of jury verdicts; rather, it is designed to determine the presence of police coercion. [Second,] we rejected Lego's assertion that a high burden of proof was required to serve the values protected by the exclusionary rule.

"[If,] as we held in *Lego* [a case the Court reaffirmed in *Connelly*], the voluntariness of a confession need be established only by a preponderance of the evidence, then a waiver of the auxiliary protections established in *Miranda* should require no higher burden of proof. * * * "[c]

Does *Connelly* make *Miranda* "a much less prophylactic rule and a substantially more direct application of the fifth amendment compulsion standard"? Does *Connelly* "fuse" the fifth amendment compulsion standard with *Miranda?* See Mark Berger, *Compromise and Continuity: Miranda Waivers, Confession Admissibility, and the Retention of Interrogation Protections,* 49 U.Pitt.L.Rev. 1007, 1040–41 (1988). What follows from the fact that *Miranda* establishes special prophylactic rules governing custodial police interrogation? That special procedural requirements regulating the waiver process are also called for? Or that further protections governing the waiver process are unnecessary and undesirable, because likely to interfere unduly with appropriate police questioning? See id. at 1062.

14. *The trier of fact.* The factfinder on the constitutionality of a search has traditionally been the judge, but prior to *Jackson v. Denno,* 378 U.S. 368, 84 S.Ct. 1774, 12 L.Ed.2d 908 (1964), many states followed one of two procedures that give factfinding responsibility to the jury in judging the voluntariness of a confession. In states following the "Massachusetts rule," the trial court initially ruled on the admissibility of the confession. If the judge found the confession involuntary, that ruling was final. However, if the judge found the confession voluntary, it was then admitted subject to the jury's independent determination of voluntariness. In states following the "New York rule," the determination of voluntariness was left primarily to the jury. The judge would make an initial determination as to whether reasonable persons could differ on the issue of voluntariness. Unless there were "no circumstances" under which the confession could be voluntary, the issue went to the jury. The jury was instructed on the voluntariness standard and told to consider the confession only if it found it to be voluntary.

Jackson overruled an 11 year old precedent and held the New York procedure unconstitutional. The crux of *Jackson's* reasoning was subsequently summarized in *Lego:* "We concluded that the New York procedure was constitutionally defective because at no point along the way did a criminal defendant receive a clear-cut determination that the confession used against him was in fact volun-

---

b. In dissent, Justice Brennan, joined by Marshall, J. argued that the Court's ruling ignored both "the explicit command of *Miranda*" in describing the state's burden as "heavy" and the implications of *Wade,* which specifically referred to the "clear and convincing" standard in describing the prosecution's burden of establishing that an in-court-identification was not tainted by an unconstitutional identification.

c. In dissent, Justice Brennan argued that *Lego* was distinguishable because it involved a situation in which the defendant was not in custody. The special setting of custodial interrogation, because it poses an increased danger of police overriding, justified "plac[ing] a higher burden of proof on the government in establishing a waiver of *Miranda* rights."

tary. The trial judge was not entitled to exclude a confession merely because he himself would have found it involuntary, and, while we recognized that the jury was empowered to perform that function, we doubted it could do so reliably. Precisely because confessions of guilt, whether coerced or freely given, may be truthful and potent evidence, we did not believe a jury [could] ignore the probative value of a truthful but coerced confession; it was also likely, we thought, that in judging voluntariness itself the jury would be influenced by the reliability of a confession it considered an accurate account of the facts. * * * "

15. As the Court noted in *Lego,* Jackson "cast no doubt upon" the Massachusetts procedure,[d] and many states continue to use that procedure (although most follow the "orthodox" procedure of having voluntariness determined initially and finally by the judge). Why should a defendant be given a "second crack" at the voluntariness issue, before the jury, where no such opportunity is given as to Fourth Amendment or other constitutional violations?

Of course, even under the orthodox procedure, the defendant may bring to the jury's attention the circumstances surrounding the confession for the purpose of challenging its credibility. Indeed, in *Crane v. Kentucky,* 476 U.S. 683, 106 S.Ct. 2142, 90 L.Ed.2d 636 (1986), a unanimous Court held that a trial court's foreclosure of a defendant's attempt to introduce testimony about the "physical and psychological environment" in which the confession was obtained deprived defendant of his "fundamental constitutional right to a fair opportunity to present a defense." As the Court there noted, "The [*Jackson*] requirement that the [trial] court make a pretrial *voluntariness* determination does not undercut the defendant's traditional prerogative to challenge the confession's *reliability* during the course of the same trial."

16. Does it follow from *Lego* that it would be improper for a trial court to hear testimony on a constitutional challenge to the admissibility of evidence without first excluding the jury? Consider WATKINS v. SOWDERS, 449 U.S. 341, 101 S.Ct. 654, 66 L.Ed.2d 549 (1981). *Watkins* involved two state cases in which hearings on the admissibility of identification testimony were held in the presence of the jury. In each case, in challenging an in-court identification, the defense sought to establish that the identification was based on a pretrial identification procedure that was so suggestive as to violate due process. Over defense objection, the challenge was heard in the presence of the jury, and was rejected by the trial judge. The Supreme Court found no constitutional error. It recognized that various lower courts had emphasized the prudence of holding a suppression hearing outside the presence of the jury, but stressed that it was concerned only with whether that practice was constitutionally required. On this issue, STEWART, J., noted for the Court:

"The Court in *Jackson* did reject the usual presumption that a jury can be relied upon to determine issues according to the trial judge's instructions, [but only] because of the peculiar problems the issue of the voluntariness of a confession presents. [Where] identification evidence is at issue, however, no such special considerations [apply]. It is the reliability of identification evidence that primarily determines its admissibility. *Manson v. Brathwaite* [p. 641]. And the

---

d. In distinguishing the Massachusetts procedure, the Court stressed that the judge there "himself resolves evidentiary conflicts and gives his own answer to the coercion issue" and the jury therefore only considers those confessions the judge believes to be voluntary. The dissenters responded that the acceptance of the Massachusetts rule revealed the "hol-lowness" of the Court's holding. They argued that the distinction between the New York and Massachusetts rule was more theoretical than real. They suggested, in particular, that in "cases of doubt," a judge operating under the Massachusetts rule was likely to "resolve the doubt in favor of admissibility, relying on the final determination by the jury."

proper evaluation of evidence under the instructions of the trial judge is the very task our system must assume juries can perform.

"[The] petitioners argue, however, [that] the presence of the jury deterred their lawyers from cross-examining the witnesses vigorously and fully as to the possible improprieties of the pretrial identifications in these cases. [They] point to no specific instances [when] their counsel were thus deterred, and the record reveals that the cross-examination on the identity issues was, if not always effective, both active and extended. Nonetheless, the petitioners rely on a passage from *Wade* [p. 623], which referred to, 'the predicament in which Wade's counsel found himself—realizing that possible unfairness at the lineup may be the sole means of attack upon the unequivocal courtroom identification, and having to probe in the dark in an attempt to discover and reveal unfairness, while bolstering the government witness' courtroom identification by bringing out and dwelling upon his prior identification.' [But the] 'predicament' described in *Wade* was no more than part of the Court's demonstration that, if identification stemming from an improperly conducted lineup was to be excluded, a courtroom identification based on such a lineup logically had to be excluded as well. A 'predicament,' if one chooses to call it that, is always presented when a lawyer decides on cross-examination to ask a question that may produce an answer unfavorable to his client. * * * We decline [to] hold that [due process] inevitably requires the abandonment of the time-honored process of cross-examination as the device best suited to determine the trustworthiness of testimonial evidence.

"A judicial determination outside the presence of the jury of the admissibility of identification evidence may often be advisable. In some circumstances, not presented here, such a determination may be constitutionally necessary. But it does not follow that the Constitution requires a *per se* rule compelling such a procedure in every case."[e]

e. The dissenting justices (Brennan, J., joined by Marshall, J.) argued that "the powerful impact that such eyewitness identification evidence has on juries, regardless of its reliability, virtually mandates that, when such evidence is inadmissible, the jury should know nothing about the evidence."

Part Three

THE COMMENCEMENT OF FORMAL PROCEEDINGS

Chapter 12

PRETRIAL RELEASE

SECTION 1. THE RIGHT TO BAIL; PRETRIAL RELEASE PROCEDURES

**BRIAN A. REAVES & TIMOTHY C. HART,
FELONY DEFENDANTS IN LARGE
URBAN COUNTIES, 1996[a]**

Bureau of Justice Statistics, U.S. Department of Justice (Oct.1999).

Rates of release and detention

An estimated 63% of [state] felony defendants in the 75 largest counties were released prior to the final disposition of their case.[b] By general offense category, defendants charged with a violent offense (55%) were less likely to be released than those whose most serious arrest charge was a public-order (71%), drug (66%), or property (65%) offense.

Within the violent offense category, release rates varied greatly. Just 16% of murder defendants were released compared to 66% of those charged with assault. Fifty-one percent of rape defendants and 39% of robbery defendants were released before the court disposed of their case. Among defendants charged with a property offense, about half of those charged with burglary (47%) were released, compared

---

a. Every 2 years, as part of its State Court Processing Statistics (SCPS) program, the Bureau of Justice Statistics tracks a sample of felony cases filed during the month of May in 40 of the Nation's 75 largest counties. The most recent SCPS study analyzed cases filed during May 1996. The SCPS sample was designed and selected by the U.S. Bureau of the Census under BJS supervision. It is a 2–stage stratified sample, with 40 of the 75 most populous counties selected at the first stage and a systematic sample of State court felony filings (defendants) within each county selected at the second stage. The second-stage sampling (filings) was designed to represent all defendants who had felony cases filed with the court during the month of May 1996. The participating

jurisdictions provided data for every felony case filed on selected days during that month. Data on 15,474 sample felony cases were collected from the 40 sampled jurisdictions. This sample represented 54,579 weighted cases filed during the month of May 1996 in the 75 most populous counties.

b. By comparison, almost all misdemeanor defendants obtain their release, as is reflected by the fact that studies covering both felonies and misdemeanors report release rates of 85% or higher. M. Sorin, *Out on Bail* (Nat'l Inst. Just., Study Guide, 1989); M. Torborg, *Pretrial Release: A National Evaluation of Practices and Outcomes* 6–20 (Nat'l Inst.Just. 1981).

to two-thirds of theft (66%) defendants and about three-fourths (77%) of those charged with other property offenses.

Among drug defendants, those charged with drug trafficking (62%) were less likely to be released than those charged with other drug offenses (71%).[c] Among public-order defendants, those charged with a driving-related offense (78%) were the most likely to be released.

Among the 37% of defendants who were detained in jail until case disposition, about 5 in 6 had a bail amount set but did not post the money required to secure release. Detained murder defendants were the exception to this rule, as about three-fourths of them, 61% of all murder defendants overall, were ordered held without bail. Overall, 6% of felony defendants in the 75 largest counties were denied bail.

A majority of the defendants released prior to case disposition, 34% of defendants overall, were released under nonfinancial conditions that did not require the posting of bail * * *. Release on personal recognizance, granted to 24% of all defendants and 38% of released defendants, was the type of release used most often.

Other nonfinancial types of release included conditional release (6% of all defendants and 9% of released defendants), and release on unsecured bond (4% and 7%).

Twenty-nine percent of defendants secured release through financial terms that involved the posting of a financial bond in the form of money or property. The most common type of financial release was surety bond (18% of all defendants and 29% of released defendants), which involves the services of a commercial bail bond agent. Other types of financial release included deposit bond (7% of all defendants and 11% of released defendants), full cash bond (2% and 3%), and property bond (2% and 3%). These bonds are posted directly with the court without the use of a bail bond agent.

About 1% of defendants were released prior to case disposition as the result of an emergency release used to relieve jail crowding. Such releases did not involve the use of any of the types of release mentioned above.

Bail amounts

About 3 in 5 felony defendants had a bail amount set by the court, and were required to post all or part of that amount to secure release while their case was pending. The remainder were granted nonfinancial release (34%), ordered held without bail (6%), or were part of an emergency release (1%). About half of those with a bail amount had it set at $10,000 or more, including 25% who had it set at $25,000 or more.

Among defendants with a bail amount set, those charged with a violent offense (40%) were about twice as likely as other defendants to have it set at $25,000 or more. Three-fourths of murder defendants with a bail amount had it set at $25,000 or more, as did just over half of robbery defendants (57%) and nearly half of rape defendants (47%).

Among property defendants with a bail amount set, those charged with burglary (27%) were about twice as likely to have bail set at $25,000 or more as other property defendants. Among drug defendants, those charged with drug

---

c. In some localities, arrestees are subject to urinalysis drug tests, and the results are taken into account by the judge in determining the risks which would be involved in releasing the defendant. For description and evaluation of these practices, see Richard B. Abell, *Pre-* *trial Drug Testing: Expanding Rights and Protecting Public Safety,* 57 Geo.Wash.L.Rev. 943 (1989); Cathryn Jo Rosen & John S. Goldkamp, *The Constitutionality of Drug Testing at the Bail Stage,* 80 J.Crim.L. & C. 114 (1989).

trafficking (27%) were about twice as likely to have bail set at $25,000 or more as other drug defendants (13%).

Overall, defendants who were detained until case disposition had a median bail amount 3 times that of defendants who secured release ($15,000 versus $5,000). The mean bail amount for detained defendants ($50,000) was more than 5 times that of defendants who secured release ($9,300).

Detained murder defendants had the highest median ($100,000) and mean ($198,400) bail amounts. Overall, the median bail amount for murder defendants was $50,000 and the mean was $133,100. Robbery defendants had an overall median bail amount of $25,000 and an overall mean bail amount of $75,900.

Overall, just under half (47%) of defendants who were required to post bail to secure release did so. About 7 in 10 defendants with a bail set at under $5,000 posted the amount needed for release, as did about 6 in 10 defendants with a bail amount of $5,000 to $9,999. In contrast, about 1 in 8 of those with bail set at $50,000 or more, and a fourth of those with a bail amount of at least $25,000 but less than $50,000 were able to meet the financial conditions required for release.

Among defendants given financial release, the average bail amount was highest for those released on property bond (a median of $7,500 and a mean of $12,400), and lowest for those released on full cash bond (a median of $1,000 and a mean of $2,900).

Defendants released on surety and deposit bond both had a median bail amount of $5,000. The mean for both was just under $10,000.

Unlike those released on full cash bond, defendants released on deposit bond generally posted 10% of the full bail amount with the court to secure release. However, they remained liable to the court for the full bail amount if they violated the terms of release.

Those released on surety bond paid a similar fee to a bail bond agent, who assumed liability to the court for the full bail amount if the defendant violated the terms of release. * * * Defendants released on an unsecured bond had a median bail amount of $5,000 and a mean bail amount of $10,000. These defendants did not have to post any of this amount, but like those on financial release, they were liable for the full bail amount if they violated the terms of release.

Time from arrest to release

Among defendants who were released prior to case disposition, about half were released within 1 day (49%), and about four-fifths were released within 1 week (79%). Nearly all releases during the 1–year study occurred within a month of arrest (92%).

By general offense category, defendants charged with a violent (41%) or drug (45%) offense were less likely to be released within 1 day of arrest than those charged with a public-order (57%) or property (56%) offense.

More than half of the defendants released after being charged with a property offense other than burglary, or a public-order offense that was not weapons-related were released within 1 day of their arrest.

Defendants charged with murder typically waited the longest to be released. For example, after 1 month, 66% of all murder defendant releases had occurred, compared to more than 90% of the releases of other defendants.

When differences among types of offense are held constant, defendants released under financial terms generally took longer to secure their release than those who were released under nonfinancial conditions. Among defendants who were released under financial conditions, the amount of time from arrest to pretrial release tended to increase as the bail amount did.

Criminal history and probability of release

Court decisions about bail and pretrial release are primarily based on the judgment of whether a defendant will appear in court as scheduled and whether there is potential danger to the community from crimes that a defendant may commit if released. Many States have established specific criteria to be considered by the courts when setting release conditions.

The SCPS data illustrate how release rates vary with some of these factors. For example, 73% of the defendants without an active criminal justice status at the time of their arrest for the current offense were released prior to case disposition, compared to 47% of those with such a status. Defendants on parole (27%) at the time of arrest were the least likely to be released. This compared with 42% of those on probation and 66% of those released pending disposition of a prior case.

Eighty-one percent of the defendants with no prior arrests were released, compared to 57% of those who had been previously arrested. Among defendants with an arrest record, those who had never missed a court appearance (62%) had a higher probability of being released than those who had failed to appear at least once during a previous case (53%).

Eighty percent of defendants without a prior conviction were released prior to disposition of the current case, compared to 53% of those with a conviction record. Among defendants with a conviction record, release rates ranged from 66% for those with a single prior conviction to 43% for those with five or more.

Less than half of the defendants with one or more prior felony convictions (47%) were released prior to disposition of the current case, compared to nearly two-thirds of those whose prior convictions involved only misdemeanors (65%). Those with a prior conviction for a violent felony (47%) had the same release rate as those whose most serious prior conviction was for a nonviolent felony (47%).

Conduct of released defendants

Among defendants who were released prior to case disposition, nearly a third committed some type of misconduct while in a release status. This may have been in the form of a failure to appear in court, an arrest for a new offense, or some other violation of release conditions that resulted in the revocation of that release by the court.

By original offense category, the proportion of defendants charged with pretrial misconduct ranged from about two-fifths among drug defendants (39%), to about a fourth of defendants charged with a public-order (24%) or violent offense (23%). Twenty-nine percent of property defendants committed some type of pretrial misconduct. The widest range of misconduct rates was found within the violent offense category, ranging from 34% of robbery defendants to 12% of rape defendants.

Failure to appear in court

Nearly four-fifths of the defendants who were released prior to case disposition made all scheduled court appearances (78%). Bench warrants for failing to appear in court were issued for the remaining 22%.

A higher percentage of released drug defendants (29%) and property defendants (22%) failed to appear in court than defendants charged with violent (14%) or public-order (14%) offenses. Within the violent offense category, failure-to-appear rates were higher for defendants charged with robbery (20%) than for other defendants. About a fourth of the defendants who failed to appear in court,

6% of all defendants, were still fugitives at the end of the 1–year study period. The remainder were returned to the court (either voluntarily or not) before the end of the study.

Defendants released after being charged with a drug (8%) or property (6%) offense were about twice as likely to be a fugitive after 1 year as defendants released after being charged with other offenses. No released murder defendants were in a fugitive status at the end of the 1–year study period.

Rearrest for a new offense

Overall, 16% of released defendants were rearrested for a new offense allegedly committed while they awaited disposition of their original case. Sixty-two percent of these defendants, 10% of all released defendants, were charged with a new felony. Sixty-three percent of the new felony arrests were for the same type of offense as the original charge.

By original arrest offense category, released drug defendants (20%) had the highest rearrest rate. This included 23% of defendants released after being charged with drug trafficking. Robbery defendants (22%) also had a higher rearrest rate than the overall average. Defendants released after being charged with murder (6%) or rape (8%) were the least likely to be rearrested.

———

Under the Bail Reform Act of 1984, set out in Supp. App. B, "release of the person on his personal recognizance, or upon execution of an unsecured appearance bond in an amount specified by the court" is the preferred form of release, as it is to be utilized "unless the judicial officer determines that such release will not reasonably assure the appearance of the person as required."[d] Otherwise, the judicial officer may release the person "on a condition or combination of conditions," but he must select "the least restrictive * * * condition or combination of conditions, that he determines will reasonably assure the appearance of the person as required." The Act lists many possible conditions, including that the person "execute a bail bond" or that he do various things while on release (e.g., maintain employment, comply with a curfew, return to custody during evening hours). However, the judicial officer "may not impose a financial condition that results in the pretrial detention of the person."[e] A person may be detained pending trial in certain situations (e.g., where there is "a serious risk that the person will flee")

d. Another consideration is whether release "will endanger the safety of any other person or the community." This preventive detention aspect of the Act is considered in § 2 of this Chapter.

e. In *United States v. Szott,* 768 F.2d 159 (7th Cir.1985), declining to reduce defendant's $1 million cash bail on "his bare say-so that he cannot post the bail," the court noted: "The statute does not require that a defendant be able to post the bail 'readily.' The purpose of bail is not served unless losing the sum would be a deeply-felt hurt to the defendant and his family; the hurt must be so severe that defendant will return for trial rather than flee. This implies that a court must be able to induce a defendant to go to great lengths to raise the funds without violating the condition in § 3142(c) that bail may not be used to deny release altogether."

In *United States v. Mantecon–Zayas,* 949 F.2d 548 (1st Cir.1991), defendant, after posting a $200,000 bond on Florida drug charges, was charged with additional drug offenses in Puerto Rico, where bail was set at an additional $200,000, which the lower court declined to reduce after defendant complained that raising the prior bond had "left him close to financial exhaustion." On appeal, the court held that such action was proper if that financial condition was necessary to ensure defendant's appearance, but if defendant could not meet that financial condition it then would be necessary for the court to meet the statutory requirements for a detention order, including "written findings of fact and a written statement of the reasons for the detention."

when "no condition or combination of conditions will reasonably assure the appearance of the person as required."[f]

During 1996, 34% of the 56,982 defendants charged with a federal offense were ordered by the court to be detained pending adjudication of the charges. Of those defendants released pending trial, 59.7% were released on their own recognizance (21.7%) or on an unsecured bond (38%). About a quarter of those released were required to post bail to gain release; however, 61.2% were unable to post bail on the day they were eligible for release. Defendants charged with drug (35.5%) or immigration (55.6%) offenses were required to post bail more often than those charged with other offenses. Among those eligible for release, 55% of drug offenders and 92.3% of immigration offenders did not post bail on the day they were eligible for release. Defendants charged with violent (49.7%), immigration (47.9%), or drug trafficking (45.7%) offenses were detained by the court for the entire pretrial period at a greater rate than other offenders. Defendants with a criminal history were ordered detained at a greater rate than first-time arrestees: 38.4% of defendants with at least one prior arrest were ordered detained compared to 26.7% of first-time arrestees. Defendants without established ties to the community were generally more likely to be ordered detained than other defendants: 52.7% of noncitizens, 51/8% of transients, and 63.6% of the homeless were ordered detained. John Scalia, *Federal Pretrial Release and Detention, 1996*, Bureau of Justice Statistics Program Special Report (Feb. 1999).

CONSTITUTIONAL LIMITS ON THE PRETRIAL RELEASE PROCESS

1. In STACK v. BOYLE, 342 U.S. 1, 72 S.Ct. 1, 96 L.Ed. 3 (1951), indictments had been returned charging the 12 petitioners with conspiring to violate the Smith Act (which made it a crime to advocate the overthrow of the government by force or violence). Bail was fixed in the district court in the uniform amount of $50,000 for each petitioner. Petitioners then moved to reduce bail on the ground that the bail as fixed was excessive under the Eighth Amendment, and in support submitted statements as to their financial resources, family relationships, health, prior criminal records, and other information. The only evidence offered by the government was a certified record showing that four persons previously convicted under the Smith Act had forfeited bail. Though the petitioners' factual statements were uncontroverted at the hearing on the motion, the motion was denied. The same district court thereafter denied writs of habeas corpus applied for by the petitioners, and the court of appeals affirmed. The Supreme Court granted the petition for certiorari, and held that bail had "not been fixed by proper methods" and that "petitioners' remedy is by [a renewed] motion to reduce bail" in the district court. VINSON, C.J., stated for the Court:

"From the passage of the Judiciary Act of 1789, to the present * * *, federal law has unequivocally provided that a person arrested for a non-capital offense *shall* be admitted to bail. This traditional right to freedom before conviction permits the unhampered preparation of a defense, and serves to prevent the infliction of punishment prior to conviction. * * * Unless this right to bail before

---

f. In *United States v. Orta,* 760 F.2d 887 (8th Cir.1985), the court stated: "In this case, the district court erred in interpreting the 'reasonably assure' standard set forth in the statute as a requirement that release conditions 'guarantee' community safety and the defendant's appearance. Such an interpretation contradicts both the framework and the intent of the pretrial release and detention provisions of the 1984 Act. Congress envisioned the pretrial detention of only a fraction of accused individuals awaiting trial. The district court's interpretation, however, virtually mandates the detention of almost every pretrial defendant: no other safeguards can 'guarantee' the avoidance of the statutory concerns."

trial is preserved, the presumption of innocence, secured only after centuries of struggle, would lose its meaning.

"The right to release before trial is conditioned upon the accused's giving adequate assurance that he will stand trial and submit to sentence if found guilty. * * * Like the ancient practice of securing the oaths of responsible persons to stand as sureties for the accused, the modern practice of requiring a bail bond or the deposit of a sum of money subject to forfeiture serves as additional assurance of the presence of an accused. Bail set at a figure higher than an amount reasonably calculated to fulfill this purpose is 'excessive' under the Eighth Amendment.

"Since the function of bail is limited, the fixing of bail for any individual defendant must be based upon standards relevant to the purpose of assuring the presence of that defendant. The traditional standards as expressed in the Federal Rules of Criminal Procedure[a] are to be applied in each case to each defendant. In this case petitioners are charged with offenses under the Smith Act and, if found guilty, their convictions are subject to review with the scrupulous care demanded by our Constitution. * * * Upon final judgment of conviction, petitioners face imprisonment of not more than five years and a fine of not more than $10,000. It is not denied that bail for each petitioner has been fixed in a sum much higher than that usually imposed for offenses with like penalties and yet there has been no factual showing to justify such action in this case. The Government asks the courts to depart from the norm by assuming, without the introduction of evidence, that each petitioner is a pawn in a conspiracy and will, in obedience to a superior, flee the jurisdiction. To infer from the fact of indictment alone a need for bail in an unusually high amount is an arbitrary act. Such conduct would inject into our own system of government the very principles of totalitarianism which Congress was seeking to guard against in passing the statute under which petitioners have been indicted.

"If bail in an amount greater than that usually fixed for serious charges of crimes is required in the case of any of the petitioners, that is a matter to which evidence should be directed in a hearing so that the constitutional rights of each petitioner may be preserved. In the absence of such a showing, we are of the opinion that the fixing of bail before trial in these cases cannot be squared with the statutory and constitutional standards for admission to bail."

As the Supreme Court noted in *Schilb v. Kuebel,* p. 824, "the Eighth Amendment's proscription of excessive bail has been assumed to have application to the States through the Fourteenth Amendment."

2. Justice Jackson, in a separate opinion in *Stack v. Boyle,* declared it would not be correct to say "that every defendant is entitled to such bail as he can provide." Compare the observations of Justice Douglas in *Bandy v. United States,* 81 S.Ct. 197, 5 L.Ed.2d 218 (1960): "To continue to demand a substantial bond which the defendant is unable to secure raises considerable problems for the equal administration of the law. We have held that an indigent defendant is denied equal protection of the law if he is denied an appeal on equal terms with other defendants, solely because of his indigence. *Griffin v. Illinois* [p. 74]. Can an indigent be denied freedom, where a wealthy man would not, because he does not happen to have enough property to pledge for his freedom?[b]

a. The reference is to Rule 46(c), which then stated: "Amount. If the defendant is admitted to bail, the amount thereof shall be such as in the judgment of the commissioner or court or judge or justice will insure the presence of the defendant, having regard to the nature and circumstances of the offense charged, the weight of the evidence against him, the financial ability of the defendant to give bail and the character of the defendant."

b. Consider, in this regard, *Tate v. Short,* p. 75; and *Williams v. Illinois,* p. 75.

"It would be unconstitutional to fix excessive bail to assure that a defendant will not gain his freedom. *Stack v. Boyle.* Yet in the case of an indigent defendant, the fixing of bail in even a modest amount may have the practical effect of denying him release. * * * The wrong done by denying release is not limited to the denial of freedom alone. That denial may have other consequences. In case of reversal, he will have served all or part of a sentence under an erroneous judgment. Imprisoned, a man may have no opportunity to investigate his case, to cooperate with his counsel, to earn the money that is still necessary for the fullest use of his right to appeal."[c]

Under the Douglas approach, is it equally objectionable to *grant* a wealthy person freedom on conditions an indigent could not meet? Consider *United States v. Patriarca,* 948 F.2d 789 (1st Cir.1991) (concurring judge raises question of fairness to indigents with respect to upholding district court's innovative set of release conditions, including all-hours video surveillance of defendant's home at defendant's expense).

3. Under a traditional bail system relying exclusively upon financial conditions, what amount of bail would be permissible under *Stack v. Boyle* in the following situations? What should the disposition be in each instance if the 1984 federal Act were applicable?

(a) "Golding, with a previous narcotics conviction, is now indicted on four counts of narcotics law violations (and one count of passport law violation), upon which he faces a maximum exposure of imprisonment of not less than ten years to life imprisonment, forfeiture, plus fines in excess of $170,000. Golding had been a fugitive for approximately two years before his arrest, had received three passports under various aliases, was currently unemployed, and had infrequent family contacts (he had not seen his parents for over two years), and had no significant community ties. A drug enforcement agency officer testified as to a government showing that Golding had dealt in multi-hundred thousand dollar cocaine deals, and was known to have several hundred thousand dollars in banks around the country and in foreign accounts." *United States v. Golding,* 742 F.2d 840 (5th Cir.1984).

(b) "It was shown that appellant voluntarily surrendered to the police officers following the shooting and had 'cooperated' with them to the extent of confessing to the shooting of deceased, the confession being found in our record.

c. Are there yet other consequences? Consider *Bellamy v. Judges and Justices,* 342 N.Y.S.2d 137 (1973), in which the bail system was challenged on the basis of the results of a study of 857 closed cases by the Legal Aid Society in conjunction with the Columbia University Bureau of Applied Social Research. As noted in the Plaintiffs' Memorandum: "The study, explained at length in the text, shows in essence the following: Those people who must wait in jail for the disposition of the criminal charges against them because they do not have enough money to purchase their freedom are far more often convicted, far more often given a prison term, and far more often given a long prison term than those people who obtain their release during this time. This disparity in treatment between those detained and those released is not accounted for by any factor related to the merits of the cases, such as the seriousness and nature of the charges, the weight of the evidence and the presence or absence of aggravated circumstances, prior criminal record, family and community ties, or the amount of bail. For example, a first offender who is detained in lieu of bail is more than three times as likely to be convicted and almost twice as likely to get a prison sentence as a recidivist with more than ten prior arrests who is released. The differences in outcome between the two groups of people, the detained and the released, are accounted for only by the fact of pre-trial detention itself."

The court upheld the constitutionality of the bail system, reasoning: "It is not because bail is required that the defendant is later convicted. It is because he is likely to be convicted that bail may be required." Thus, the statistics indicating that "those denied bail are more likely to be convicted * * * shows the system is working."

"Appellant testified that he was a life-long resident of the City of Amarillo and had attended school there; that he had never been convicted of any offense other than traffic violations and had never received a probated sentence. He was nineteen years of age at the time of the hearing. His father had been employed in the sanitation department of the City of Amarillo for twenty-five years as a truck driver; his mother also worked but her occupation was not disclosed. He was a part-time dishwasher and hay hauler.

"Appellant also testified that he had no money, credit, property, assets or savings of his own; but, that his father had obtained $500 (the inference in our record being that he borrowed it from a credit union), but that was all the funds he had to procure a bond to secure his release." *Ex parte Walton,* 583 S.W.2d 786 (Tex.Crim.App.1979).

(c) Defendant was charged with five counts of delivery of a controlled substance, carrying maximum penalties totalling 220 years. A report of the pretrial release officer "showed that the defendant: 1. Resides at his present home with his wife and daughter, where he has lived for six and one-half years; 2. Has three children, two of whom are in college in Indiana, and one of whom is in high school in Elkhart; 3. Has been married for twenty-five years and is buying his home, mortgaged through a local bank; 4. Has been a resident of Elkhart for twelve and one-half years; 5. Holds a Masters Degree in Biophysics and has completed work toward a Ph.D.; 6. Is Chairman of the Board and fifty percent (50%) shareholder in Geocel Corporation, located in Elkhart; 7. Has no prior criminal history; and that he 8. Has no assets outside the Elkhart area. Those assets which are available to him include equity in a home worth approximately $160,000–$180,000, a third interest in a Piper Cub airplane being financed through a local bank, and stock in his corporation worth approximately $800,000 but which is subject to buy-sell agreements, in accordance with which the stock may not be encumbered or pledged." *Sherelis v. State,* 452 N.E.2d 411 (Ind.App.1983).

4. In PUGH v. RAINWATER, 557 F.2d 1189 (5th Cir.1977), involving a challenge to the Florida bail system, the court, per SIMPSON, J., first concluded that money bail is not necessary to promote the state's interest in assuring the accused's appearance, as in the event of nonappearance only the bondsman loses money, and the defendant loses the money he posts with the bondsman whether or not he appears. The court then continued:

"These valid criticisms of the professional bondsman system persuade us to the view that, in the case of indigents, money bail is irrelevant in promoting the state's interest in assuring appearance. The indigent cannot on his own pay the amount of bail upon which his release has been conditioned. Unless a friend or relative qualifies as surety * * * and is willing to post bond, the indigent must resort to the professional bondsman. Even if the bondsman deems him an acceptable risk, he is unable to pay the bondsman's fee. The incongruity of a bail system premised on the risk of forfeiting property is apparent: Those who can afford to pay a bondsman do so and thus avoid risking forfeiture of their property; indigents, who cannot afford to pay a bondsman, have no property to forfeit in the first place.

"The real assurance of appearance under the present system is the risk of forfeiture assumed by the bondsman. Because the bondsman does not want to lose money, he has a powerful incentive to make sure that the defendant for whom he is surety appears at trial. Thus, the bondsman has long enjoyed legal protection as a modern day bounty hunter, entitled to arrest his principal 'even under extreme circumstances.' In this sense, the accused pays the bondsman to perform a police function—apprehension of a person who has jumped bail. An indigent defendant released on his own recognizance would face similar consequences. Presumably, then, the deterrence factor is comparable regardless of whether money bail has been posted.

"Even though it is manifest to us that money bail is not always necessary to assure a defendant's appearance, it is necessary to consider whether other 'less drastic' alternatives are available to the State. The Supreme Court of Florida in amending its rule regarding pretrial release, has in effect conceded that many alternatives to money bail are available. It has adopted five additional forms of release,[d] none of which is conditioned on a defendant's ability to pay. * * *

"While the new Florida rule expands the options available for pretrial release, it does not provide that indigent defendants will be required to pay money bail only in the event that no other form of release will reasonably assure their appearance at trial. Because it gives the judge essentially unreviewable discretion to impose money bail, the rule retains the discriminatory vice of the former system: When a judge decides to set money bail, the indigent will be forced to remain in jail. We hold that equal protection standards are not satisfied unless the judge is required to consider less financially onerous forms of release before he imposes money bail. Requiring a presumption in favor of non-money bail accommodates the State's interest in assuring the defendant's appearance at trial as well as the defendant's right to be free pending trial, regardless of his financial status. * * *

"Our holding is not that money bail may never be imposed on an indigent defendant. The record before us does not justify our telling the State of Florida that in no case will money bail be necessary to assure a defendant's appearance. We hold only that equal protection standards require a presumption against money bail and in favor of those forms of release which do not condition pretrial freedom on an ability to pay."

Upon rehearing en banc, 572 F.2d 1053 (5th Cir.1978), the Court, per VANCE, J., expressed "no doubt that in the case of an indigent, whose appearance at trial could reasonably be assured by one of the alternative forms of release, pretrial confinement for inability to post money bail would constitute imposition of an excessive restraint." But the new Florida rule (because it mandates that "all relevant factors" be considered in determining "what form of release is necessary to assure the defendant's appearance") does not require such a result, and therefore is not unconstitutional on its face. "Further adjudication of the merits of a constitutional challenge addressed to it should await presentation of a proper record reflecting application by the courts of the State of Florida."[e]

CLARK, J., specially concurring, noted: "I voted for en banc reconsideration because I thought that the panel opinion approach had the inevitable effect of rendering monetary bail unconstitutional, and because I considered that analysis misfocused and wrong. I cannot read the Constitution to either prohibit monetary bail or require a hierarchy of assurances of appearance. The Constitution's only explicit limitation on the imposition of bail is the eighth amendment's command that it may not be excessive. This constitutional imperative does not prevent a state from continuing to maintain a system for pretrial release of all persons based on monetary bail alone. That a state may also permit persons incarcerated

d. Namely, (i) release on personal recognizance or unsecured bond, (ii) release into the custody of a designated person or organization, (iii) release with restrictions on travel, association or place of abode, (iv) release upon deposit of 10% of the amount specified in an appearance bond, or (v) release on some other condition, such as that defendant return to custody after specified hours.

e. Simpson, J., joined by three other members of the court, dissenting, saw no reason for abstention, arguing that the 1977 Florida rule "ensconced the practice which the [state officials], in 1971, swore they followed" and which was the basis of the panel decision.

pending trial to obtain their freedom through other means should not create a constitutional requirement that a priority order be developed among the means permitted."

5. KINNEY v. LENON, 425 F.2d 209 (9th Cir.1970), involved a 17–year-old detained in a juvenile detention home pending trial in juvenile court on charges arising out of a schoolyard fight. He alleged that there were many potential witnesses to the fight, that he could not identify them by name but would recognize them by sight, that his attorneys were white though he and the potential witnesses were black, that his attorneys would consequently have great practical difficulty in interviewing and lining up the witnesses, and that he was the sole person who could do so. The court concluded:

"We * * * are of the opinion that, in the peculiar circumstances of this case, failure to permit appellant's release for the purpose of aiding the preparation of his defense unconstitutionally interfered with his due-process right to a fair trial.

"The ability of an accused to prepare his defense by lining up witnesses is fundamental, in our adversary system, to his chances of obtaining a fair trial. Recognition of this fact of course underlies the bail system. But it is equally implicit in the requirements that trial occur near in time, and place (U.S.Const. Amend. VI) to the offense, and that the accused have compulsory process to obtain witnesses in his behalf. Indeed, compulsory process as a practical matter would be of little value without an opportunity to contact and screen potential witnesses before trial.

"This is not a case where release from detention is sought simply for the convenience of the appellant. There is here a strong showing that the appellant is the only person who can effectively prepare his own defense. We may take notice, as judges and lawyers, of the difficulties often encountered, even by able and conscientious counsel, in overcoming the apathy and reluctance of potential witnesses to testify. It would require blindness to social reality not to understand that these difficulties may be exacerbated by the barriers of age and race. Yet the alternative to some sort of release for appellant is to cast the entire burden of assembling witnesses onto his attorneys, with almost certain prejudice to appellant's case."

6. SCHILB v. KUEBEL, 404 U.S. 357, 92 S.Ct. 479, 30 L.Ed.2d 502 (1971), upheld against a due process and equal protection challenge an Illinois statute which provided for the pretrial release of an eligible accused by: (1) personal recognizance; (2) execution of a bail bond and deposit of cash equal to 10% of the bond, in which event 10% of the amount deposited (i.e., 1% of the amount of the bond) was retained by the state as "bail bond costs"; or (3) execution of bail bond and deposit of the full amount of the bail, in which event there is no charge or retention. Appellant Schilb had utilized the 10% provision, depositing $75 on a $750 bond, and his challenge was directed to the $7.50 that was retained by the state after he was subsequently acquitted on one charge and convicted on another. Justice BLACKMUN's opinion for the majority noted:

"Prior to 1964 the professional bail bondsman system with all its abuses was in full and odorous bloom in Illinois. Under that system the bail bondsman customarily collected the maximum fee (10% of the amount of the bond) permitted by statute, and retained that entire amount even though the accused fully satisfied the conditions of the bond. Payment of this substantial 'premium' was required of the good risk as well as of the bad. The results were that a heavy and irretrievable burden fell upon the accused, to the excellent profit of the bondsman, and that professional bondsmen, and not the courts, exercised significant control over the actual workings of the bail system. One of the stated purposes of the new bail provisions in the 1963 Code was to rectify this offensive situation. The purpose appears to have been accomplished. It is said that the bail bondsman abruptly disappeared in Illinois 'due primarily to the success of the ten percent bail deposit provision.'

"Bail, of course, is basic to our system of law, and the Eighth Amendment's proscription of excessive bail has been assumed to have application to the States through the Fourteenth Amendment. But we are not at all concerned here with any fundamental right to bail or with any Eighth Amendment—Fourteenth Amendment question of bail excessiveness. Our concern, instead, is with the 1% cost-retention provision. This smacks of administrative detail and of procedure and is hardly to be classified as a 'fundamental' right or as based upon any suspect criterion. The applicable measure, therefore, must be the traditional one: Is the distinction drawn by the statutes invidious and without rational basis?

"[Appellant argues] * * * that [the 1% charge] is imposed on the poor and nonaffluent and not on the rich and affluent * * *. But it is by no means certain, as the appellants suggest, that the 10% deposit provision under § 110–7 is a provision for the benefit of the poor and the less affluent and that the full-deposit provision of § 110–8 is one for the rich and the more affluent. It should be obvious that the poor man's real hope and avenue for relief is the personal recognizance provision of § 110–2. We do not presume to say, as the appellants in their brief intimate, that § 110–2 is not utilized by Illinois judges and made available for the poor and the less affluent. Neither is it assured, as the appellants also suggest, that the affluent will take advantage of the full-deposit provision of § 110–8 with no retention charge, and that the less affluent are relegated to the 10% deposit provision of § 110–7 and the 1% retention charge. The record is silent, but the flow indeed may be the other way. The affluent, more aware of and more experienced in the marketplace, may see the advantage, in these days of high interest rates, in retaining the use of 90% of the bail amount. A 5% or greater return on this 90% in a short period of time more than offsets the 1% retention charge. In other words, it is by no means clear that the route of § 110–8 is more attractive to the affluent defendant than the § 110–7 route. The situation, therefore, wholly apart from the fact that appellant Schilb himself has not pleaded indigency, is not one where we may assume that the Illinois plan works to deny relief to the poor man merely because of his poverty."[f]

7. *Ackies v. Purdy*, 322 F.Supp. 38 (S.D.Fla.1970), was a class action challenging the use of master bond schedules for the setting of bail. It was shown that the booking officer in the sheriff's department set bail pursuant to a schedule which only took account of the nature of the offense, and did not involve consideration of the defendant's background, community ties, or financial ability. A defendant who could not obtain release remained in jail from three days to three weeks before he was brought before a judge. The court held: (1) that "since procedural due process requires a hearing in various administrative proceedings [citing *Goldberg v. Kelly*, 397 U.S. 254, 90 S.Ct. 1011, 25 L.Ed.2d 287 (1970), holding an evidentiary hearing is required before welfare payments may be discontinued], a fortiori, it requires a hearing before depriving a person of his liberty for periods of days, weeks, or months"; and (2) that the procedure also violated the equal protection clause because it is based upon an irrelevant classification, as "a poor man with strong ties in the community may be more likely to appear than a man with some cash and no community involvement."

f. Justices Stewart and Brennan dissented on other grounds relating to the state's failure to impose a similar retention fee upon persons who utilized the full-deposit provision. Justice Douglas dissented on the ground that the fee actually amounted to the imposition of court costs upon persons subsequently acquitted.

8. Is a bail hearing a "critical stage" at which there is a constitutional right to counsel? Cf. *Coleman v. Alabama* at p. 919 (preliminary hearing is a critical stage because, inter alia, "counsel can also be influential * * * in making effective arguments for the accused on such matters as * * * bail"). Douglas L. Colbert, *Thirty-Five Years After Gideon: The Illusory Right to Counsel at Bail Proceedings*, 1998 U.Ill.L.Rev. 1, 7, reports that "most states and localities deny indigent defendants counsel at the initial bail hearing. * * * [I]t is the exceptional jurisdiction which guarantees counsel when bail is set. Moreover, significant delay in assigning court-appointed counsel thereafter exacerbates the due process concerns and seriousness of states' denying counsel at the initial appearance."

9. Who should have the burden of producing evidence and the burden of proof at the bail hearing? Consider *Van Atta v. Scott*, 613 P.2d 210 (Cal.1980), holding (1) that the burden of *producing evidence* to establish defendant's ties to the community is on the defendant, as he "is clearly the best source for this information and for names of individuals who could verify such information" and "has a substantial incentive to cooperate in providing this information"; (2) that the burden of *producing evidence* regarding defendant's prior appearances or flight and the severity of the sentence he faces is on the prosecution, as "this information should be relatively easy and inexpensive for the prosecution to secure"; and (3) that "due process requires the burden of *proof* concerning the detainee's likelihood of appearing for future court proceedings to be borne by the prosecution," as so placing the burden "helps to preserve the respect for the individual's liberty and for the presumption of innocence that lies at the foundation of our judicial system, to maintain the respect and confidence of the community in the uniform application of the law and to systematically correct certain biases inherent in the OR decision-making process." With respect to the uniformity point, the court noted that because "the decision being made is predictive in nature" it is "peculiarly subject to abuse." On the matter of inherent biases, the court reasoned that anti-defendant distortion can easily occur because defendant's "incarceration prevents him from effectively locating witnesses or gathering other evidence to establish his local contacts and personal reliability" and because the "not infrequent practice" of overcharging "gives an inaccurate picture to the trial court of the detainee's likelihood of fleeing the jurisdiction."

10. In *State v. Williams*, 343 A.2d 29 (N.H.1975), the court held: "Defendant's own testimony regarding the crime may be critical to a court's determination whether he should be set free pending trial. Since the 'law favors the release of defendants pending determination of guilt or innocence', a defendant should be encouraged to testify at a hearing on a motion to set bail without the fear that what he says may later be used to incriminate him."[g]

Compare *United States v. Dohm*, 618 F.2d 1169 (5th Cir.1980), holding that defendant's statements at his bail hearing were inadmissible at trial because "the magistrate failed to accurately advise Dohm of his *Miranda* rights." But, the court rejected the broader claim by Dohm that in any event "he was compelled to forfeit his fifth amendment right to remain silent, in order to safeguard his eighth amendment right to reasonable bail." The defendant's analogy to *Simmons v. United States*, p. 753, was rejected by the court because in *Simmons* the Supreme Court stressed that "at one time, a defendant who wished to assert a fourth amendment objection was required to show that he was the owner or possessor of the seized property or that he had a possessory interest in the searched premises,"

g. If the defendant makes incriminating statements to the bail agency interviewer, should these be admissible against the defendant at trial? See *State v. Winston*, 219 N.W.2d 617 (Minn.1974), holding such a statement inadmissible where the agency manual prohibits asking the defendant about "the offense with which he is charged," as it is "appropriate to require that the state honor such an agreement."

while by contrast "a defendant at a bail bond hearing need not divulge the facts in his case in order to receive the benefits of the eighth amendment right to bail." A dissent questioned the latter conclusion, noting that the constitutional guarantee was "not just the right to bail, but the right to non-excessive bail," and that in the instant case "the defendant not unreasonably concluded that the recommended amount of bail would be determined to be appropriate for him unless he rebutted the government testimony portraying him as a big-time drug dealer." See also Note, 94 Harv.L.Rev. 426, 437 (1980), concluding that *Dohm* represents a clearly impermissible compelled election."

11. In *Harris v. United States,* 404 U.S. 1232, 92 S.Ct. 10, 30 L.Ed.2d 25 (1971), Justice Douglas, acting as Circuit Justice on an application for bail pending appeal, noted: "While there is no automatic right to bail after convictions, 'The command of the Eighth Amendment that "Excessive bail shall not be required* * *" *at the very least* obligates judges passing on the right to bail to deny such relief only for the strongest of reasons.' "

Most state constitutions guarantee the right to bail in noncapital cases, but only "before conviction." Consequently, state statutes tend to limit the opportunities for release on appeal or, in some instances, deny bail entirely in certain specified circumstances. But once the state makes provision for release on bail during appeal, under the Eighth and Fourteenth Amendments it may not be arbitrarily denied.

The seemingly strict federal provision, 18 U.S.C. § 3143(b), in Supp. App. B, has not been applied literally. For example, *United States v. Powell,* 761 F.2d 1227 (8th Cir.1985), holds "that a defendant who wishes to be released on bail after the imposition of a sentence including a term of imprisonment must first show that the question presented by the appeal is substantial, in the sense that it is a close question or one that could go either way. It is not sufficient to show simply that reasonable judges could differ (presumably every judge who writes a dissenting opinion is still 'reasonable') or that the issue is fairly debatable and not frivolous. On the other hand, the defendant does not have to show that it is likely or probable that he or she will prevail on the issue on appeal. If this part of the test is satisfied, the defendant must then show that the substantial question he or she seeks to present is so integral to the merits of the conviction that it is more probable than not that reversal or a new trial will occur if the question is decided in the defendant's favor. In deciding whether this part of the burden has been satisfied, the court or judge to whom application for bail is made must assume that the substantial question presented will go the other way on appeal and then assess the impact of such assumed error on the conviction."

SECTION 2. PREVENTIVE DETENTION

The term "preventive detention" is ordinarily used to describe pretrial detention of a defendant to protect other persons or the community at large from criminal conduct by that defendant. Even in bail systems which in theory have the single legitimate function of assuring the defendant's appearance at trial, the preventive detention function is often served sub rosa. But in recent years the preventive detention concept has been more openly discussed, and in several jurisdictions some form of preventive detention is now expressly authorized by law.

Such is the case with the federal Bail Reform Act of 1984, set out in Supp. App. B. For one thing, in determining the manner and conditions of release (discussed on p. 818), the Act makes ensuring "the safety of any other person or the community" a relevant consideration. Moreover, a detention hearing is to be held, upon motion of the attorney for the government, where the case involves a crime of violence, an offense for which the maximum penalty is death or life imprisonment, certain serious drug offenses, or any felony by one with two or more convictions of the aforementioned type offenses. Also, such a hearing is to be held on motion of either the attorney for the government or the judicial officer asserting the case involves a serious risk that the person will flee or will obstruct or attempt to obstruct justice or interfere with a prospective witness or juror.[a] If at the hearing the judicial officer "finds that no condition or combination of conditions will reasonably assure the appearance of the person as required and the safety of any other person and the community," then detention is to be ordered. (A rebuttable presumption in support of such a finding exists in certain circumstances.) The Act also makes nonviolation of any federal, state or local crime a condition of any release under the Act, and upon violation of that condition revocation of the release is required upon a finding of probable cause that such a crime was committed while on release, if there is also a finding that the person is unlikely to abide by any conditions of release or that there is no combination of release conditions that will assure the person will not flee or pose a danger. A person ordered detained may obtain review of the order from the court with original jurisdiction over the offense charged, and may appeal from the detention order.

Dep't of Justice, Bureau of Justice Statistics, *Special Report* (Feb. 1988), compares 1983 and 1985 statistics to show the effect of the 1984 Act. Among the findings: (1) About 54% of all defendants were released without financial conditions both years. (2) In '83 about 2% of all defendants were held on pretrial detention and financial conditions were set for 44%, while the respective figures for '85 were 19% and 27%, which "suggests that pretrial detention has largely been substituted for bail as a means of detaining defendants." (3) In '83 about 24% of all defendants were held until trial (2% by pretrial detention, 22% who did not make bail), while in '85 about 29% were held until trial (19% by pretrial detention, 10% who did not make bail).

UNITED STATES v. SALERNO
481 U.S. 739, 107 S.Ct. 2095, 95 L.Ed.2d 697 (1987).

Chief Justice REHNQUIST delivered the opinion of the Court.

The Bail Reform Act of 1984 allows a federal court to detain an arrestee pending trial if the government demonstrates by clear and convincing evidence after an adversary hearing that no release conditions "will reasonably assure ... the safety of any other person and the community." The United States Court of Appeals for the Second Circuit struck down this provision of the Act as facially unconstitutional, because, in that court's words, this type of pretrial detention violates "substantive due process." We granted certiorari because of a conflict among the Courts of Appeals regarding the validity of the Act. We hold that, as against the facial attack mounted by these respondents, the Act fully comports with constitutional requirements. We therefore reverse.

Responding to "the alarming problem of crimes committed by persons on release," Congress formulated the Bail Reform Act of 1984, 18 U.S.C. § 3141 et

a. The Act states that this detention hearing, except upon a grant of a continuance, "shall be held immediately upon the person's first appearance before the judicial officer." "Nothing in § 3142(f) indicates that compliance with the first appearance requirement is a precondition to holding the hearing or that failure to comply with the requirement renders such a hearing a nullity," and thus "a failure to comply with the first appearance requirement does not defeat the Government's authority to seek detention of the person charged." *United States v. Montalvo–Murillo,* 495 U.S. 711, 110 S.Ct. 2072, 109 L.Ed.2d 720 (1990).

seq., as the solution to a bail crisis in the federal courts. The Act represents the National Legislature's considered response to numerous perceived deficiencies in the federal bail process. By providing for sweeping changes in both the way federal courts consider bail applications and the circumstances under which bail is granted, Congress hoped to "give the courts adequate authority to make release decisions that give appropriate recognition to the danger a person may pose to others if released."

To this end, § 3141(a) of the Act requires a judicial officer to determine whether an arrestee shall be detained. Section 3142(e) provides that "[i]f, after a hearing pursuant to the provisions of subsection (f), the judicial officer finds that no condition or combination of conditions will reasonably assure the appearance of the person as required and the safety of any other person and the community, he shall order the detention of the person prior to trial." Section 3142(f) provides the arrestee with a number of procedural safeguards. He may request the presence of counsel at the detention hearing, he may testify and present witnesses in his behalf, as well as proffer evidence, and he may cross-examine other witnesses appearing at the hearing. If the judicial officer finds that no conditions of pretrial release can reasonably assure the safety of other persons and the community, he must state his findings of fact in writing, § 3142(i), and support his conclusion with "clear and convincing evidence," § 3142(f).

The judicial officer is not given unbridled discretion in making the detention determination. Congress has specified the considerations relevant to that decision. These factors include the nature and seriousness of the charges, the substantiality of the government's evidence against the arrestee, the arrestee's background and characteristics, and the nature and seriousness of the danger posed by the suspect's release. § 3142(g). Should a judicial officer order detention, the detainee is entitled to expedited appellate review of the detention order. §§ 3145(b), (c).

Respondents Anthony Salerno and Vincent Cafaro were arrested on March 21, 1986, after being charged in a 29–count indictment alleging various Racketeer Influenced and Corrupt Organizations Act (RICO) violations, mail and wire fraud offenses, extortion, and various criminal gambling violations. The RICO counts alleged 35 acts of racketeering activity, including fraud, extortion, gambling, and conspiracy to commit murder. At respondents' arraignment, the Government moved to have Salerno and Cafaro detained pursuant to § 3142(e), on the ground that no condition of release would assure the safety of the community or any person. The District Court held a hearing at which the Government made a detailed proffer of evidence. The Government's case showed that Salerno was the "boss" of the Genovese Crime Family of La Cosa Nostra and that Cafaro was a "captain" in the Genovese Family. According to the Government's proffer, based in large part on conversations intercepted by a court-ordered wiretap, the two respondents had participated in wide-ranging conspiracies to aid their illegitimate enterprises through violent means. The Government also offered the testimony of two of its trial witnesses, who would assert that Salerno personally participated in two murder conspiracies. Salerno opposed the motion for detention, challenging the credibility of the Government's witnesses. He offered the testimony of several character witnesses as well as a letter from his doctor stating that he was suffering from a serious medical condition. Cafaro presented no evidence at the hearing, but instead characterized the wiretap conversations as merely "tough talk."

The District Court granted the Government's detention motion, concluding that the Government had established by clear and convincing evidence that no condition or combination of conditions of release would ensure the safety of the community or any person:

"The activities of a criminal organization such as the Genovese Family do not cease with the arrest of its principals and their release on even the most stringent of bail conditions. The illegal businesses, in place for many years, require constant attention and protection, or they will fail. Under these circumstances, this court recognizes a strong incentive on the part of its leadership to continue business as usual. When business as usual involves threats, beatings, and murder, the present danger such people pose in the community is self-evident."

Respondents appealed, contending that to the extent that the Bail Reform Act permits pretrial detention on the ground that the arrestee is likely to commit future crimes, it is unconstitutional on its face. Over a dissent, the United States Court of Appeals for the Second Circuit agreed. Although the court agreed that pretrial detention could be imposed if the defendants were likely to intimidate witnesses or otherwise jeopardize the trial process, it found "§ 3142(e)'s authorization of pretrial detention [on the ground of future dangerousness] repugnant to the concept of substantive due process, which we believe prohibits the total deprivation of liberty simply as a means of preventing future crimes." The court concluded that the Government could not, consistent with due process, detain persons who had not been accused of any crime merely because they were thought to present a danger to the community. It reasoned that our criminal law system holds persons accountable for past actions, not anticipated future actions. Although a court could detain an arrestee who threatened to flee before trial, such detention would be permissible because it would serve the basic objective of a criminal system—bringing the accused to trial. The court distinguished our decision in *Gerstein v. Pugh* [p. 211], in which we upheld police detention pursuant to arrest. The court construed *Gerstein* as limiting such detention to the " 'administrative steps incident to arrest.' " The Court of Appeals also found our decision in *Schall v. Martin,* 467 U.S. 253, 104 S.Ct. 2403, 81 L.Ed.2d 207 (1984), upholding postarrest pretrial detention of juveniles, inapposite because juveniles have a lesser interest in liberty than do adults. The dissenting judge concluded that on its face, the Bail Reform Act adequately balanced the Federal Government's compelling interests in public safety against the detainee's liberty interests.

A facial challenge to a legislative Act is, of course, the most difficult challenge to mount successfully, since the challenger must establish that no set of circumstances exists under which the Act would be valid. The fact that the Bail Reform Act might operate unconstitutionally under some conceivable set of circumstances is insufficient to render it wholly invalid, since we have not recognized an "overbreadth" doctrine outside the limited context of the First Amendment. We think respondents have failed to shoulder their heavy burden to demonstrate that the Act is "facially" unconstitutional.[3]

Respondents present two grounds for invalidating the Bail Reform Act's provisions permitting pretrial detention on the basis of future dangerousness. First, they rely upon the Court of Appeals' conclusion that the Act exceeds the

---

3. We intimate no view on the validity of any aspects of the Act that are not relevant to respondents' case. Nor have respondents claimed that the Act is unconstitutional because of the way it was applied to the particular facts of their case. [Editors' Note: This issue has often been litigated in the lower courts. Typical is *United States v. El–Hage,* 213 F.3d 74 (2d Cir.2000) (confinement expected to last 30–33 months not a violation of due process, considering that "prosecution appears to bear very little responsibility for the delay of trial" and defendant "charged with playing a vital role in a worldwide terrorist organization"). Consider Floralynn Einesman, *How Long is Too Long? When Pretrial Detention Violates Due Process,* 60 Tenn.L.Rev. 1, 2 (1979), concluding that "the due process tests used to determine whether the pretrial detention has become punitive * * * are deficient because they fail to effectively protect the liberty interest of the accused."]

limitations placed upon the Federal Government by the Due Process Clause of the Fifth Amendment. Second, they contend that the Act contravenes the Eighth Amendment's proscription against excessive bail. We treat these contentions in turn.

The Due Process Clause of the Fifth Amendment provides that "No person shall ... be deprived of life, liberty, or property, without due process of law...." This Court has held that the Due Process Clause protects individuals against two types of government action. So-called "substantive due process" prevents the government from engaging in conduct that "shocks the conscience," or interferes with rights "implicit in the concept of ordered liberty." When government action depriving a person of life, liberty, or property survives substantive due process scrutiny, it must still be implemented in a fair manner. This requirement has traditionally been referred to as "procedural" due process.

Respondents first argue that the Act violates substantive due process because the pretrial detention it authorizes constitutes impermissible punishment before trial. The Government, however, has never argued that pretrial detention could be upheld if it were "punishment." The Court of Appeals assumed that pretrial detention under the Bail Reform Act is regulatory, not penal, and we agree that it is.

As an initial matter, the mere fact that a person is detained does not inexorably lead to the conclusion that the government has imposed punishment. To determine whether a restriction on liberty constitutes impermissible punishment or permissible regulation, we first look to legislative intent. Unless Congress expressly intended to impose punitive restrictions, the punitive/regulatory distinction turns on " 'whether an alternative purpose to which [the restriction] may rationally be connected is assignable for it, and whether it appears excessive in relation to the alternative purpose assigned [to it].' "

We conclude that the detention imposed by the Act falls on the regulatory side of the dichotomy. The legislative history of the Bail Reform Act clearly indicates that Congress did not formulate the pretrial detention provisions as punishment for dangerous individuals. Congress instead perceived pretrial detention as a potential solution to a pressing societal problem. There is no doubt that preventing danger to the community is a legitimate regulatory goal.

Nor are the incidents of pretrial detention excessive in relation to the regulatory goal Congress sought to achieve. The Bail Reform Act carefully limits the circumstances under which detention may be sought to the most serious of crimes. See 18 U.S.C. § 3142(f) (detention hearings available if case involves crimes of violence, offenses for which the sentence is life imprisonment or death, serious drug offenses, or certain repeat offenders). The arrestee is entitled to a prompt detention hearing, *ibid.* and the maximum length of pretrial detention is limited by the stringent time limitations of the Speedy Trial Act.[4] See 18 U.S.C. § 3161 *et seq.* Moreover, as in *Schall v. Martin,* the conditions of confinement envisioned by the Act "appear to reflect the regulatory purposes relied upon by the" government. As in *Schall,* the statute at issue here requires that detainees be housed in a "facility separate, to the extent practicable, from persons awaiting or serving sentences or being held in custody pending appeal." 18 U.S.C. § 3142(i)(2). We conclude, therefore, that the pretrial detention contemplated by the Bail Reform Act is regulatory in nature, and does not constitute punishment before trial in violation of the Due Process Clause.

4. We intimate no view as to the point at which detention in a particular case might become excessively prolonged, and therefore punitive, in relation to Congress' regulatory goal.

The Court of Appeals nevertheless concluded that "the Due Process Clause prohibits pretrial detention on the ground of danger to the community as a regulatory measure, without regard to the duration of the detention." Respondents characterize the Due Process Clause as erecting an impenetrable "wall" in this area that "no governmental interest—rational, important, compelling or otherwise—may surmount."

We do not think the Clause lays down any such categorical imperative. We have repeatedly held that the government's regulatory interest in community safety can, in appropriate circumstances, outweigh an individual's liberty interest. For example, in times of war or insurrection, when society's interest is at its peak, the government may detain individuals whom the government believes to be dangerous. See *Ludecke v. Watkins,* 335 U.S. 160, 68 S.Ct. 1429, 92 L.Ed. 1881 (1948) (approving unreviewable Executive power to detain enemy aliens in time of war); *Moyer v. Peabody,* 212 U.S. 78, 29 S.Ct. 235, 53 L.Ed. 410 (1909) (rejecting due process claim of individual jailed without probable cause by Governor in time of insurrection). Even outside the exigencies of war, we have found that sufficiently compelling governmental interests can justify detention of dangerous persons. Thus, we have found no absolute constitutional barrier to detention of potentially dangerous resident aliens pending deportation proceedings. *Carlson v. Landon,* 342 U.S. 524, 72 S.Ct. 525, 96 L.Ed. 547 (1952); *Wong Wing v. United States,* 163 U.S. 228, 16 S.Ct. 977, 41 L.Ed. 140 (1896). We have also held that the government may detain mentally unstable individuals who present a danger to the public, *Addington v. Texas,* 441 U.S. 418, 99 S.Ct. 1804, 60 L.Ed.2d 323 (1979), and dangerous defendants who become incompetent to stand trial, *Jackson v. Indiana,* 406 U.S. 715, 92 S.Ct. 1845, 32 L.Ed.2d 435 (1972); *Greenwood v. United States,* 350 U.S. 366, 76 S.Ct. 410, 100 L.Ed. 412 (1956). We have approved of postarrest regulatory detention of juveniles when they present a continuing danger to the community. *Schall v. Martin.* Even competent adults may face substantial liberty restrictions as a result of the operation of our criminal justice system. If the police suspect an individual of a crime, they may arrest and hold him until a neutral magistrate determines whether probable cause exists. *Gerstein v. Pugh.* Finally, respondents concede and the Court of Appeals noted that an arrestee may be incarcerated until trial if he presents a risk of flight or a danger to witnesses.

Respondents characterize all of these cases as exceptions to the "general rule" of substantive due process that the government may not detain a person prior to a judgment of guilt in a criminal trial. Such a "general rule" may freely be conceded, but we think that these cases show a sufficient number of exceptions to the rule that the congressional action challenged here can hardly be characterized as totally novel. Given the well-established authority of the government, in special circumstances, to restrain individuals' liberty prior to or even without criminal trial and conviction, we think that the present statute providing for pretrial detention on the basis of dangerousness must be evaluated in precisely the same manner that we evaluated the laws in the cases discussed above.

The government's interest in preventing crime by arrestees is both legitimate and compelling. In *Schall,* we recognized the strength of the State's interest in preventing juvenile crime. This general concern with crime prevention is no less compelling when the suspects are adults. Indeed, "[t]he harm suffered by the victim of a crime is not dependent upon the age of the perpetrator." The Bail Reform Act of 1984 responds to an even more particularized governmental interest than the interest we sustained in *Schall.* The statute we upheld in *Schall* permitted pretrial detention of any juvenile arrested on any charge after a showing that the individual might commit some undefined further crimes. The Bail Reform Act, in contrast, narrowly focuses on a particularly acute problem in which the government interests are overwhelming. The Act operates only on individuals who have been arrested for a specific category of extremely serious offenses. 18 U.S.C. § 3142(f). Congress specifically found that these individuals are far more likely to be responsible for dangerous acts in the community after arrest. Nor is the Act by any means a scattershot attempt to incapacitate those who are merely suspected of these serious crimes. The government must first of all demonstrate probable cause to believe that the charged crime has been committed by the arrestee, but that is not enough. In a full-blown adversary hearing, the government must convince a neutral decisionmaker by clear and convincing evidence that no conditions of release can reasonably assure the safety of the community or any person. 18 U.S.C. § 3142(f). While the government's general interest in preventing crime is compelling, even this interest is heightened when the government musters convincing proof that the arrestee, already indicted or held to answer for a serious crime, presents a demonstrable danger to the community. Under these narrow circumstances, society's interest in crime prevention is at its greatest.

On the other side of the scale, of course, is the individual's strong interest in liberty. We do not minimize the importance and fundamental nature of this right. But, as our cases hold, this right may, in circumstances where the government's interest is sufficiently weighty, be subordinated to the greater needs of society. We think that Congress' careful delineation of the circumstances under which detention will be permitted satisfies this standard. When the government proves by clear and convincing evidence that an arrestee presents an identified and articulable threat to an individual or the community, we believe that, consistent with the Due Process Clause, a court may disable the arrestee from executing that threat. Under these circumstances, we cannot categorically state that pretrial detention "offends some principle of justice so rooted in the traditions and conscience of our people as to be ranked as fundamental."

Finally, we may dispose briefly of respondents' facial challenge to the procedures of the Bail Reform Act. To sustain them against such a challenge, we need only find them "adequate to authorize the pretrial detention of at least some [persons] charged with crimes," whether or not they might be insufficient in some particular circumstances. We think they pass that test. As we stated in *Schall*, "there is nothing inherently unattainable about a prediction of future criminal conduct."

Under the Bail Reform Act, the procedures by which a judicial officer evaluates the likelihood of future dangerousness are specifically designed to further the accuracy of that determination. Detainees have a right to counsel at the detention hearing. 18 U.S.C. § 3142(f). They may testify in their own behalf, present information by proffer or otherwise, and cross-examine witnesses who appear at the hearing.[a] *Ibid.* The judicial officer charged with the responsibility of determining the appropriateness of detention is guided by statutorily enumerated factors, which include the nature and the circumstances of the charges, the weight of the evidence, the history and characteristics of the putative offender, and the danger to the community. § 3142(g). The government must prove its case by clear and convincing evidence. § 3142(f). Finally, the judicial officer must include written findings of fact and a written statement of reasons for a decision to detain. § 3142(i). The Act's review provisions, § 3145(c), provide for immediate appellate review of the detention decision.

---

a. Compare *Aime v. Commonwealth*, 611 N.E.2d 204 (Mass.1993) (state preventive detention statute unconstitutional under *Saler-* *no*, as defendant without right to testify in own behalf or to cross-examine state's witnesses).

We think these extensive safeguards suffice to repel a facial challenge. The protections are more exacting than those we found sufficient in the juvenile context, see *Schall,* and they far exceed what we found necessary to effect limited postarrest detention in *Gerstein v. Pugh.* Given the legitimate and compelling regulatory purpose of the Act and the procedural protections it offers, we conclude that the Act is not facially invalid under the Due Process Clause of the Fifth Amendment.

Respondents also contend that the Bail Reform Act violates the Excessive Bail Clause of the Eighth Amendment. The Court of Appeals did not address this issue because it found that the Act violates the Due Process Clause. We think that the Act survives a challenge founded upon the Eighth Amendment.

The Eighth Amendment addresses pretrial release by providing merely that "Excessive bail shall not be required." This Clause, of course, says nothing about whether bail shall be available at all. Respondents nevertheless contend that this Clause grants them a right to bail calculated solely upon considerations of flight. They rely on *Stack v. Boyle* [p. 819], in which the Court stated that "Bail set at a figure higher than an amount reasonably calculated [to ensure the defendant's presence at trial] is 'excessive' under the Eighth Amendment." In respondents' view, since the Bail Reform Act allows a court essentially to set bail at an infinite amount for reasons not related to the risk of flight, it violates the Excessive Bail Clause. Respondents concede that the right to bail they have discovered in the Eighth Amendment is not absolute. A court may, for example, refuse bail in capital cases. And, as the Court of Appeals noted and respondents admit, a court may refuse bail when the defendant presents a threat to the judicial process by intimidating witnesses. Respondents characterize these exceptions as consistent with what they claim to be the sole purpose of bail—to ensure integrity of the judicial process.

While we agree that a primary function of bail is to safeguard the courts' role in adjudicating the guilt or innocence of defendants, we reject the proposition that the Eighth Amendment categorically prohibits the government from pursuing other admittedly compelling interests through regulation of pretrial release. The above-quoted *dicta* in *Stack v. Boyle* is far too slender a reed on which to rest this argument. The Court in *Stack* had no occasion to consider whether the Excessive Bail Clause requires courts to admit all defendants to bail, because the statute before the Court in that case in fact allowed the defendants to be bailed. Thus, the Court had to determine only whether bail, admittedly available in that case, was excessive if set at a sum greater than that necessary to ensure the arrestees' presence at trial.

The holding of *Stack* is illuminated by the Court's holding just four months later in *Carlson v. Landon.* In that case, remarkably similar to the present action, the detainees had been arrested and held without bail pending a determination of deportability. The Attorney General refused to release the individuals, "on the ground that there was reasonable cause to believe that [their] release would be prejudicial to the public interest and *would endanger the welfare and safety of the United States.*" (emphasis added). The detainees brought the same challenge that respondents bring to us today: the Eighth Amendment required them to be admitted to bail. The Court squarely rejected this proposition:

> "The bail clause was lifted with slight changes from the English Bill of Rights Act. In England that clause has never been thought to accord a right to bail in all cases, but merely to provide that bail shall not be excessive in those cases where it is proper to grant bail. When this clause was carried over into our Bill of Rights, nothing was said that indicated any different concept. The Eighth Amendment has not prevented Congress from defining the classes

of cases in which bail shall be allowed in this country. Thus, in criminal cases bail is not compulsory where the punishment may be death. Indeed, the very language of the Amendment fails to say all arrests must be bailable."

Carlson v. Landon was a civil case, and we need not decide today whether the Excessive Bail Clause speaks at all to Congress' power to define the classes of criminal arrestees who shall be admitted to bail. For even if we were to conclude that the Eighth Amendment imposes some substantive limitations on the National Legislature's powers in this area, we would still hold that the Bail Reform Act is valid. Nothing in the text of the Bail Clause limits permissible government considerations solely to questions of flight. The only arguable substantive limitation of the Bail Clause is that the government's proposed conditions of release or detention not be "excessive" in light of the perceived evil. Of course, to determine whether the government's response is excessive, we must compare that response against the interest the government seeks to protect by means of that response. Thus, when the government has admitted that its only interest is in preventing flight, bail must be set by a court at a sum designed to ensure that goal, and no more. We believe that when Congress has mandated detention on the basis of a compelling interest other than prevention of flight, as it has here, the Eighth Amendment does not require release on bail.

In our society liberty is the norm, and detention prior to trial or without trial is the carefully limited exception. We hold that the provisions for pretrial detention in the Bail Reform Act of 1984 fall within that carefully limited exception. The Act authorizes the detention prior to trial of arrestees charged with serious felonies who are found after an adversary hearing to pose a threat to the safety of individuals or to the community which no condition of release can dispel. The numerous procedural safeguards detailed above must attend this adversary hearing. We are unwilling to say that this congressional determination, based as it is upon that primary concern of every government—a concern for the safety and indeed the lives of its citizens—on its face violates either the Due Process Clause of the Fifth Amendment or the Excessive Bail Clause of the Eighth Amendment.

Justice MARSHALL, with whom Justice BRENNAN joins, dissenting.

This case brings before the Court for the first time a statute in which Congress declares that a person innocent of any crime may be jailed indefinitely, pending the trial of allegations which are legally presumed to be untrue, if the Government shows to the satisfaction of a judge that the accused is likely to commit crimes, unrelated to the pending charges, at any time in the future. Such statutes, consistent with the usages of tyranny and the excesses of what bitter experience teaches us to call the police state, have long been thought incompatible with the fundamental human rights protected by our Constitution. Today a majority of this Court holds otherwise. Its decision disregards basic principles of justice established centuries ago and enshrined beyond the reach of governmental interference in the Bill of Rights. * * *

The majority approaches respondents' challenge to the Act by dividing the discussion into two sections, one concerned with the substantive guarantees implicit in the Due Process Clause, and the other concerned with the protection afforded by the Excessive Bail Clause of the Eighth Amendment. This is a sterile formalism, which divides a unitary argument into two independent parts and then professes to demonstrate that the parts are individually inadequate.

On the due process side of this false dichotomy appears an argument concerning the distinction between regulatory and punitive legislation. The majority concludes that the Act is a regulatory rather than a punitive measure. The ease with which the conclusion is reached suggests the worthlessness of the achievement. The major premise is that "[u]nless Congress expressly intended to impose punitive restrictions, the punitive/regulatory distinction turns on ' "whether an alternative purpose to which [the restriction] may rationally be connected is assignable for it, and whether it appears excessive in relation to the alternative purpose assigned [to it]." ' " The majority finds that "Congress did not formulate the pretrial detention provisions as punishment for dangerous individuals," but instead was pursuing the "legitimate regulatory goal" of "preventing danger to the community."[4] Concluding that pretrial detention is not an excessive solution to the problem of preventing danger to the community, the majority thus finds that no substantive element of the guarantee of due process invalidates the statute.

This argument does not demonstrate the conclusion it purports to justify. Let us apply the majority's reasoning to a similar, hypothetical case. After investigation, Congress determines (not unrealistically) that a large proportion of violent crime is perpetrated by persons who are unemployed. It also determines, equally reasonably, that much violent crime is committed at night. From amongst the panoply of "potential solutions," Congress chooses a statute which permits, after judicial proceedings, the imposition of a dusk-to-dawn curfew on anyone who is unemployed. Since this is not a measure enacted for the purpose of punishing the unemployed, and since the majority finds that preventing danger to the community is a legitimate regulatory goal, the curfew statute would, according to the majority's analysis, be a mere "regulatory" detention statute, entirely compatible with the substantive components of the Due Process Clause.

The absurdity of this conclusion arises, of course, from the majority's cramped concept of substantive due process. The majority proceeds as though the only substantive right protected by the Due Process Clause is a right to be free from punishment before conviction. The majority's technique for infringing this right is simple: merely redefine any measure which is claimed to be punishment as "regulation," and, magically, the Constitution no longer prohibits its imposition. Because, as I discuss infra, the Due Process Clause protects other substantive rights which are infringed by this legislation, the majority's argument is merely an exercise in obfuscation.

The logic of the majority's Eighth Amendment analysis is equally unsatisfactory. The Eighth Amendment, as the majority notes, states that "[e]xcessive bail shall not be required." The majority then declares, as if it were undeniable, that: "[t]his Clause, of course, says nothing about whether bail shall be available at all." If excessive bail is imposed the defendant stays in jail. The same result is achieved if bail is denied altogether. Whether the magistrate sets bail at $1 billion or refuses to set bail at all, the consequences are indistinguishable. It would be mere sophistry to suggest that the Eighth Amendment protects against the former decision, and not the latter. Indeed, such a result would lead to the conclusion that there was no need for Congress to pass a preventive detention measure of any kind; every federal magistrate and district judge could simply refuse, despite the

---

4. Preventing danger to the community through the enactment and enforcement of criminal laws is indeed a legitimate goal, but in our system the achievement of that goal is left primarily to the States. The Constitution does not contain an explicit delegation to the Federal Government of the power to define and administer the general criminal law. The Bail Reform Act does not limit its definition of dangerousness to the likelihood that the defendant poses a danger to others through the commission of *federal* crimes. Federal preventive detention may thus be ordered under the Act when the danger asserted by the Government is the danger that the defendant will violate state law. The majority nowhere identifies the constitutional source of congressional power to authorize the federal detention of persons whose predicted future conduct would not violate any federal statute and could not be punished by a federal court. I can only conclude that the Court's frequently expressed concern with the principles of federalism vanishes when it threatens to interfere with the Court's attainment of the desired result.

absence of any evidence of risk of flight or danger to the community, to set bail. This would be entirely constitutional, since, according to the majority, the Eighth Amendment "says nothing about whether bail shall be available at all."

But perhaps, the majority says, this manifest absurdity can be avoided. Perhaps the Bail Clause is addressed only to the judiciary. "[W]e need not decide today," the majority says, "whether the Excessive Bail Clause speaks at all to Congress' power to define the classes of criminal arrestees who shall be admitted to bail." The majority is correct that this question need not be decided today; it was decided long ago. Federal and state statutes which purport to accomplish what the Eighth Amendment forbids, such as imposing cruel and unusual punishments, may not stand. The text of the Amendment, which provides simply that "[e]xcessive bail shall not be required, nor excessive fines imposed, nor cruel and unusual punishments inflicted," provides absolutely no support for the majority's speculation that both courts and Congress are forbidden to inflict cruel and unusual punishments, while only the courts are forbidden to require excessive bail.[5]

The majority's attempts to deny the relevance of the Bail Clause to this case are unavailing, but the majority is nonetheless correct that the prohibition of excessive bail means that in order "to determine whether the government's response is excessive, we must compare that response against the interest the government seeks to protect by means of that response." The majority concedes, as it must, that "when the government has admitted that its only interest is in preventing flight, bail must be set by a court at a sum designed to ensure that goal, and no more." But, the majority says, "when Congress has mandated detention on the basis of a compelling interest other than prevention of flight, as it has here, the Eighth Amendment does not require release on bail." This conclusion follows only if the "compelling" interest upon which Congress acted is an interest which the Constitution permits Congress to further through the denial of bail. The majority does not ask, as a result of its disingenuous division of the analysis, if there are any substantive limits contained in both the Eighth Amendment and the Due Process Clause which render this system of preventive detention unconstitutional. The majority does not ask because the answer is apparent and, to the majority, inconvenient.

The essence of this case may be found, ironically enough, in a provision of the Act to which the majority does not refer. Title 18 U.S.C. § 3142(j) provides that "[n]othing in this section shall be construed as modifying or limiting the presumption of innocence." But the very pith and purpose of this statute is an abhorrent limitation of the presumption of innocence. The majority's untenable conclusion that the present Act is constitutional arises from a specious denial of the role of the Bail Clause and the Due Process Clause in protecting the invaluable guarantee afforded by the presumption of innocence.

"The principle that there is a presumption of innocence in favor of the accused is the undoubted law, axiomatic and elementary, and its enforcement lies at the foundation of the administration of our criminal law." *Coffin v. United States,* 156 U.S. 432, 453, 15 S.Ct. 394, 403, 39 L.Ed. 481 (1895). Our society's

---

5. The majority refers to the statement in *Carlson v. Landon* that the Bail Clause was adopted by Congress from the English Bill of Rights Act of 1689, 1 Wm. & Mary, Sess. 2, ch. II, § I(10), and that "[i]n England that clause has never been thought to accord a right to bail in all cases, but merely to provide that bail shall not be excessive in those cases where it is proper to grant bail." A sufficient answer to this meagre argument was made at the time by Justice Black: "The Eighth Amendment is in the American Bill of Rights of 1789, not the English Bill of Rights of 1689." *Carlson v. Landon* (dissenting opinion). Our Bill of Rights is contained in a written Constitution one of whose purposes is to protect the rights of the people against infringement by the Legislature, and its provisions, whatever their origins, are interpreted in relation to those purposes.

belief, reinforced over the centuries, that all are innocent until the state has proven them to be guilty, like the companion principle that guilt must be proved beyond a reasonable doubt, is "implicit in the concept of ordered liberty," and is established beyond legislative contravention in the Due Process Clause.

The statute now before us declares that persons who have been indicted may be detained if a judicial officer finds clear and convincing evidence that they pose a danger to individuals or to the community. The statute does not authorize the government to imprison anyone it has evidence is dangerous; indictment is necessary. But let us suppose that a defendant is indicted and the government shows by clear and convincing evidence that he is dangerous and should be detained pending a trial, at which trial the defendant is acquitted. May the government continue to hold the defendant in detention based upon its showing that he is dangerous? The answer cannot be yes, for that would allow the government to imprison someone for uncommitted crimes based upon "proof" not beyond a reasonable doubt. The result must therefore be that once the indictment has failed, detention cannot continue. But our fundamental principles of justice declare that the defendant is as innocent on the day before his trial as he is on the morning after his acquittal. Under this statute an untried indictment somehow acts to permit a detention, based on other charges, which after an acquittal would be unconstitutional. The conclusion is inescapable that the indictment has been turned into evidence, if not that the defendant is guilty of the crime charged, then that left to his own devices he will soon be guilty of something else.

To be sure, an indictment is not without legal consequences. It establishes that there is probable cause to believe that an offense was committed, and that the defendant committed it. Upon probable cause a warrant for the defendant's arrest may issue; a period of administrative detention may occur before the evidence of probable cause is presented to a neutral magistrate. See *Gerstein v. Pugh.* Once a defendant has been committed for trial he may be detained in custody if the magistrate finds that no conditions of release will prevent him from becoming a fugitive. But in this connection the charging instrument is evidence of nothing more than the fact that there will be a trial, and

> "release before trial is conditioned upon the accused's giving adequate assurance that he will stand trial and submit to sentence if found guilty. Like the ancient practice of securing the oaths of responsible persons to stand as sureties for the accused, the modern practice of requiring a bail bond or the deposit of a sum of money subject to forfeiture serves as additional assurance of the presence of an accused." *Stack v. Boyle.*[6]

The finding of probable cause conveys power to try, and the power to try imports of necessity the power to assure that the processes of justice will not be evaded or obstructed.[7] "Pretrial detention to prevent future crimes against society at large,

---

6. The majority states that denial of bail in capital cases has traditionally been the rule rather than the exception. And this of course is so, for it has been the considered presumption of generations of judges that a defendant in danger of execution has an extremely strong incentive to flee. If in any particular case the presumed likelihood of flight should be made irrebuttable, it would in all probability violate the Due Process Clause. Thus what the majority perceives as an exception is nothing more than an example of the traditional operation of our system of bail.

7. It is also true, as the majority observes, that the government is entitled to assurance,

by incarceration if necessary, that a defendant will not obstruct justice through destruction of evidence, procuring the absence or intimidation of witnesses, or subornation of perjury. But in such cases the government benefits from no presumption that any particular defendant is likely to engage in activities inimical to the administration of justice, and the majority offers no authority for the proposition that bail has traditionally been denied *prospectively,* upon speculation that witnesses would be tampered with. Cf. *Carbo v. United States,* 82 S.Ct. 662, 7 L.Ed.2d 769 (1962) (Douglas, J., in chambers) (bail pending appeal denied when

however, is not justified by any concern for holding a trial on the charges for which a defendant has been arrested." The detention purportedly authorized by this statute bears no relation to the government's power to try charges supported by a finding of probable cause, and thus the interests it serves are outside the scope of interests which may be considered in weighing the excessiveness of bail under the Eighth Amendment.

It is not a novel proposition that the Bail Clause plays a vital role in protecting the presumption of innocence. Reviewing the application for bail pending appeal by members of the American Communist Party convicted under the Smith Act, 18 U.S.C. § 2385, Justice Jackson wrote:

> "Grave public danger is said to result from what [the defendants] may be expected to do, in addition to what they have done since their conviction. If I assume that defendants are disposed to commit every opportune disloyal act helpful to Communist countries, it is still difficult to reconcile with traditional American law the jailing of persons by the courts because of anticipated but as yet uncommitted crimes. Imprisonment to protect society from predicted but unconsummated offenses is ... unprecedented in this country and ... fraught with danger of excesses and injustice...." *Williamson v. United States,* 95 L.Ed. 1379, 1382 (1950) (Jackson, J., in chambers) (footnote omitted).

As Chief Justice Vinson wrote for the Court in *Stack v. Boyle, supra:* "Unless th[e] right to bail before trial is preserved, the presumption of innocence, secured only after centuries of struggle, would lose its meaning."

* * * Honoring the presumption of innocence is often difficult; sometimes we must pay substantial social costs as a result of our commitment to the values we espouse. But at the end of the day the presumption of innocence protects the innocent; the shortcuts we take with those whom we believe to be guilty injure only those wrongfully accused and, ultimately, ourselves.

Throughout the world today there are men, women, and children interned indefinitely, awaiting trials which may never come or which may be a mockery of the word, because their governments believe them to be "dangerous." Our Constitution, whose construction began two centuries ago, can shelter us forever from the evils of such unchecked power. Over two hundred years it has slowly, through our efforts, grown more durable, more expansive, and more just. But it cannot protect us if we lack the courage, and the self-restraint, to protect ourselves. Today a majority of the Court applies itself to an ominous exercise in demolition. Theirs is truly a decision which will go forth without authority, and come back without respect.

I dissent.

Justice STEVENS, dissenting.

There may be times when the government's interest in protecting the safety of the community will justify the brief detention of a person who has not committed any crime. To use Judge Feinberg's example, it is indeed difficult to accept the proposition that the government is without power to detain a person when it is a virtual certainty that he or she would otherwise kill a group of innocent people in the immediate future. Similarly, I am unwilling to decide today that the police may never impose a limited curfew during a time of crises. These questions are obviously not presented in this case, but they lurk in the background and preclude me from answering the question that is presented in as broad a manner as Justice Marshall has. Nonetheless, I firmly agree with Justice Marshall that the provision of the Bail Reform Act allowing pretrial detention on

more than 200 intimidating phone calls made   to witness, who was also severely beaten).

the basis of future dangerousness is unconstitutional. Whatever the answers are to the questions I have mentioned, it is clear to me that a pending indictment may not be given any weight in evaluating an individual's risk to the community or the need for immediate detention.

If the evidence of imminent danger is strong enough to warrant emergency detention, it should support that preventive measure regardless of whether the person has been charged, convicted, or acquitted of some other offense. In this case, for example, it is unrealistic to assume that the danger to the community that was present when respondents were at large did not justify their detention before they were indicted, but did require that measure the moment that the grand jury found probable cause to believe they had committed crimes in the past. It is equally unrealistic to assume that the danger will vanish if a jury happens to acquit them. Justice Marshall has demonstrated that the fact of indictment cannot, consistent with the presumption of innocence and the Eighth Amendment's Excessive Bail Clause, be used to create a special class the members of which are, alone, eligible for detention because of future dangerousness.* * *

NOTES ON PREVENTIVE DETENTION IN THE STATES

1. Preventive detention practice in the fifty states is quite diverse, largely because of the different state constitutional provisions on bail to be found:

(a) In 9 states, these provisions are essentially the same as the Eighth Amendment, and thus probably lack independent significance, as they are likely to be interpreted as not foreclosing any variety of preventive detention that would pass muster under *Salerno*. It is noteworthy that most of these states have adopted preventive detention statutes. Some of these statutes are of a more limited type, as where a detention-justifying danger to persons or the community may be found or is presumed when the defendant has been charged with a certain crime after conviction for an earlier crime of that type, while on bail, or while on probation or parole, or when the defendant has violated some condition of pretrial release. But others are among the most expansive preventive detention provisions to be found, declaring as to a rather broad range of offenses that denial of bail is permissible upon a finding of such danger or upon the defendant's failure to rebut a declared presumption of danger.

(b) In 24 states, the constitution declares a right to bail subject to very limited exceptions; 18 of them adhere to the traditional approach ("All prisoners shall, before conviction, be bailable by sufficient sureties, except for capital offenses, where the proof is evident and the presumption great"), while 6 others instead or in addition declare an exception where the punishment was once capital, where the punishment is life imprisonment, or where some specified very serious offenses (e.g., murder, treason, rape) are charged.

(c) In the remaining 17 states there is once again a constitutional declaration of a right to bail, typically with an exception for capital cases or some other limited exception as in (b) above, but significantly the constitutional provision then, by virtue of recent amendment, goes on to describe other situations in which a form of preventive detention may be utilized. These amendments vary by the kinds of preventive detention provision included therein (some include more than one kind): (i) 12 states authorize preventive detention whenever the charge is of a certain type and in addition there is a finding that the defendant, if released, would present a danger to another person or the community. (ii) Others require a certain type of charge plus only some condition precedent, either that the defendant at the time of the alleged crime was already on bail for another offense of a certain type (5 states), that he was then on probation or parole (3 states), or that at the time of the alleged crime the defendant had previously been convicted of one or (usually) more offenses of a certain type (4 states). (iii) The provisions in 3 states combine the features of the other two categories, so that the defendant may be detained pending trial only if there was a specified condition precedent and in addition a finding of dangerousness.

2. In the great majority of states where the applicable constitution provision declares a right to bail but then states that capital offenses (or life imprisonment offenses, or specified very serious crimes) are excepted, a variety of issues have arisen as to the meaning of the exception. There is, for example, the question of whether a capital case exception applies when the state's death penalty provisions have been declared unconstitutional; compare *People v. Anderson*, 493 P.2d 880 (Cal.1972) (yes, as the "underlying gravity of those offenses endures"); with *Commonwealth v. Truesdale*, 296 A.2d 829 (Pa.1972) (no, as the "strong flight urge because of the possibility of an accused forfeiting his life" is then removed). As for the proof-evident/presumption-great requirement, this requires a "fair likelihood" that defendant would be convicted of capital murder, which, under the Supreme Court's decisions on constitutionally-mandated sentencing procedures in capital cases, means the question is whether or not an aggravating factor exists which would allow the jury to impose the death penalty. *State v. Engel*, 493 A.2d 1217 (N.J.1985). But this leads to such questions as who has the burden of proof, compare *Steigler v. Superior Court*, 252 A.2d 300 (Del.1969) (burden on defendant in custody to show status quo should be changed), with *State v. Konigsberg*, 164 A.2d 740 (N.J.1960) ("burden should rest on the party relying on the exception," the prosecution); what rules of evidence apply at the hearing, compare *Engel*, supra ("a defendant does not have a right *per se* to insist upon the opportunity for cross-examination at a bail hearing, and thus no bar to consideration of co-defendant's confession not admissible at trial against defendant because of lack of opportunity for cross-examination"), with *State v. Obstein*, 247 A.2d 5 (N.J.1968) (affidavits and grand jury transcripts may not be considered over defendant's objection, as he has right to cross-examination); and what the consequences are of a determination that "the proof is evident, or the presumption great," compare *Harnish v. State*, 531 A.2d 1264 (Me.1987) (such showing of defendant's guilt of capital offense, "while defeating a capital defendant's constitutional right to bail, leaves intact the discretionary power of the court to admit any defendant to bail"), with *People v. District Court*, 529 P.2d 1335 (Colo.1974) (in such circumstances court without power to release defendant).

Assume that a constitutional provision of the kind discussed in the preceding paragraph is challenged on the federal due process grounds explored in *Salerno*. Does the outcome depend upon whether the provision adheres to the traditional capital offense exception or not, or perhaps upon how some of the issues mentioned in the previous paragraph are resolved? Consider *Hunt v. Roth*, 648 F.2d 1148 (8th Cir.1981), judgment vacated for mootness, 455 U.S. 478, 102 S.Ct. 1181, 71 L.Ed.2d 353 (constitutional exception in cases of "sexual offenses involving penetration by force or against the will of the victim * * * where the proof is evident or the presumption great" has a "fatal flaw" because "the state has created an irrebuttable presumption that every individual charged with this particular offense is incapable of assuring his appearance by conditioning it upon reasonable bail or is too dangerous to be granted release"); *State v. Blackmer*, 631 A.2d 1134 (Vt.1993) (constitutional exception for offenses punishable by life imprisonment; no *Hunt* defect because "the trial court's discretion is extremely broad," and no *Salerno* defect though dangerousness inquiry not focused as in the federal statute, for "most or all of the procedural protections of the federal law" were followed, and information on which judge acted sufficed to support a presumption of danger to the public and "was unrebutted by defendant").

3. Consider next the more expansive preventive detention provisions to be found in many states, either as a result of a constitutional amendment proclaiming the right of the state to so detain in specified circumstances, or as a result of legislation in a state lacking a "right to bail" constitutional guarantee. Here again, the question is whether, in light of the analysis in *Salerno*, these provisions violate federal due process. As for that variety of state preventive detention most resembling that utilized in the federal act, which contemplates (sometimes by reliance upon a rebuttal presumption) a showing of dangerousness on a case-by-case basis, it has been suggested that even here several of the state provisions are vulnerable because many of them lack a sufficiently narrow "serious crime" limitation, fail to "limit detention to situations where proof of probable cause and clear and convincing evidence of potential danger are shown," or "contain only some" of the "procedural protections" enumerated in *Salerno*. Note, 22 Ga.L.Rev. 805, 823, 828 (1988). As for the serious crime requirement, consider *Aime v. Commonwealth*, 611 N.E.2d 204 (Mass.1993) (state statute permitting denial of bail upon a finding of dangerousness, applicable as to all arrestees without regard to charge, unconstitutional); *Mendonza v. Commonwealth*, 673 N.E.2d 22 (Mass. 1996) (though state list "is more extensive" than in federal act, this only "reflects the different roles of State and Federal law enforcement," and thus offenses involving violence or threats of violence within the family, even including some misdemeanors, properly included, as such offenses "are peculiarly within the province of State concern.") As for the lack of sufficient procedural protections, some state courts have responded by engrafting onto their prevent detention provisions those protections emphasized in *Salerno*. See, e.g., *Brill v. Gurich*, 965 P.2d 404 (Okl.Cr.1998).

What then of those state preventive detention provisions which substitute some sort of condition precedent (one or more prior convictions, or release on bail or on parole or probation at time of offense charged) for a case-by-case dangerousness determination? Should all the *Salerno* requirements apply there as well? Note, supra, at 825–27, suggests the answer is no as to a defendant who has a prior conviction or is out of probation or parole from such conviction "because such individuals pose a statistically greater danger to the community upon release than do first-time offenders," but that this argument is weaker where defendant has been charged with a crime allegedly committed while he was released on bail from an earlier charge, as such a defendants differs from others only in that he "has been accused twice rather than once," so that in the latter situation "each of the *Salerno* substantive due process conditions" must be met. Is that so? What then of the statute upheld in *Rendel v. Mummert*, 474 P.2d 824 (Ariz.1970), providing that a felony defendant released on bail may have his bail revoked upon a showing that he has thereafter committed another felony?

4. Finally, there is the question of whether the very common "right to bail" provision in a state constitution provides a barrier to many (or all) preventive detention schemes which are not themselves specifically excepted in that constitution, but which would pass muster under *Salerno*. Unquestionably such a state constitutional guarantee forbids many varieties of such detention which do not necessary violate the federal constitution. Consider *Simms v. Oedekoven*, 839 P.2d 381 (Wyo.1992) (on issue "of first impression" as to which no precedent found "in any other jurisdiction," namely, whether state rule modeled after 18 U.S.C. § 3142, and allowing detention if "judicial officer finds that no condition or combination of conditions will reasonably assure the appearance of the defendant as required," violates statute constitutional right to bail, court concludes that right-to-bail provision in state constitution "does not permit denial of bail on the ground that the accused is considered to be a serious flight risk"); *Ex parte Colbert*, 717 So.2d 868 (Ala.Crim.1998) (trial judge's denial of bail for armed robbery defendant because of various facts tending to show he dangerous to others violated right-to-bail provision in state constitution).

This is not to suggest, however, that a state right-to-bail clause will bar preventive detention under any circumstances not encompassed within a declared exception thereto. Perhaps the easiest case is where the defendant, while on release pending trial, made an effort to obstruct the fair disposition of the charges against him, as in *In re Mason*, 688 N.E.2d 552 (Ohio App.1996) (upon defendant's efforts at witness intimidation, it proper for judge to respond "by revoking bail and detaining the person attempting to thwart the proper functioning of the criminal justice system"). Does it follow that a right-to-bail clause does not stand in the way of bail revocation in *any* case where there has been a showing of some sort of criminal conduct or violation of some sort of release condition? Consider the *Rendel* case, Note 3 supra, where the statute was deemed not to violate the right-to-bail provision in the state constitution.

Compare *State v. Sauve*, 621 A.2d 1296 (Vt.1993), where the court concluded that the "absolute right to bail" in the state constitution meant that "liberty must remain the norm" and that exceptions must thus be limited to " 'special circumstances' where the state's interest is 'legitimate and compelling.' " The defendant in *Sauve* was on pretrial release after being charged with burglary, unlawful mischief, and trespass for entering the residence of the complaining witness, who continued to carry on an intimate relationship with defendant thereafter. When defendant later was determined to have committed another trespass and to have consumed alcohol, each a violation of an express condition of his release, his release was revoked on the basis of a statutory provision permitting such action for "repeatedly violated conditions of release." But that language, the appellate court concluded, "does not rise to the level of a compelling interest," as even repeated violations do "not show that the judicial process is endangered." For example, those defendants who "violate conditions of release by continuing to use drugs or alcohol" may be "uncooperative" or even "potentially dangerous," but they "will not necessarily threaten justice." Likewise, repeated crimes "may show disrespect for the judicial system, but these violations do not necessarily threaten the integrity of the judicial system, in the constitutionally limited sense that they thwart the prosecution of the defendant." Revocation in the instant case thus violated the state constitution, for to "justify a compelling state interest * * * there must be a nexus between defendant's repeated violations and a disruption of the prosecution."

Chapter 13

THE DECISION WHETHER
TO PROSECUTE

SECTION 1. THE OFFICE OF PROSECUTOR
AND THE NATURE OF THE DECISION
WHETHER TO PROSECUTE

1. *Federal prosecutors.* There are 93 United States Attorneys, one for each of the federal judicial districts except two Pacific districts that share one. Those offices range in size from just a few assistants in the sparsely populated districts to 250 lawyers in the most populous district. The U.S. Attorney is a presidential appointee, confirmed by the Senate. In practice, the appointee is almost invariably a member of the President's political party and is appointed on the recommendation of the Senators or Representatives from the particular state who are members of that party. When a president of a different political party takes office, the U.S. Attorney usually is replaced (tradition dictates that the U.S. Attorney, though appointed to a four year term, resign upon presidential request). The assistants are hired by the U.S. Attorney, usually without reference to their political affiliation. When a new U.S. Attorney is appointed, even after a shift in political party, the assistants no longer are replaced en masse. Nevertheless, assistants do not view their jobs as career positions, and the vast majority stay no more than several years (usually leaving to return to private practice).

Although U.S. Attorneys are subject to the supervisory authority of the Attorney General, they are given considerable autonomy in their exercise of prosecutorial discretion. The Attorney General has set forth a series of departmental guidelines, contained in the United States Attorneys' Manual, but those guidelines allow for considerable flexibility both as to prosecution priorities and practices. However, the use of certain types of litigation and investigative practices (e.g., the use of electronic surveillance or the granting of immunity to witnesses) requires the approval of the Attorney General's designated representative in Washington. Such approval is also required in several substantive areas where a national enforcement policy is deemed essential (e.g., internal security violations).

In a typical year, the United States Attorneys' offices open matters for investigation against about 125,000 criminal suspects, about 60% of whom are ultimately prosecuted in the district courts while another 10% are disposed of by magistrates. But various divisions within the Justice Department also exercise prosecutorial authority as to particular types of offenses. Criminal antitrust prosecutions are developed and presented by the Antitrust Division, and the Civil Rights Division often brings prosecutions within its area of expertise. The Criminal Division itself initiates prosecutions in several fields (e.g., organized crime, public corruption, and narcotics distribution), acting through its special Strike Forces and regional offices located in 25 major cities.

2. *Local prosecutors: the rural and small suburban office.* There are about 2,350 prosecutors' offices handling felony cases in state trial courts, in addition to those municipal and county attorneys who primarily operate in courts of limited jurisdiction. Over 90% of these offices serve districts with populations of fewer than 250,000. In contrast to large urban or suburban offices, many prosecutors in the smaller districts operate without even one full time assistant. Indeed, 26% of all local prosecutor's offices do not have even one full-time assistant. In districts with an especially small population, the prosecutor is likely to be a part-time official, maintaining a private practice in addition to his public office.

The criminal caseload in small districts often is fairly light, particularly as to felonies. One recent survey found that half of all local prosecutor's offices process fewer than 250 felony cases per year. Of course, in most of these districts, the prosecutor's responsibility is not limited to criminal prosecution. The prosecutor also handles juvenile cases and often has extensive civil responsibilities.

Small prosecutor's offices have no need for a bureaucratic structure. The assistants, if any, work closely with the prosecutor and should fully understand his prosecutorial policies. Dealings with defense counsel, who are likely to be known socially as well as professionally, require no formal guidelines. There is neither the resources nor the need for highly structured programs dealing with matters such as diversion or the investigation and prosecution of complex fraud or narcotics offenses. The former can be handled through relatively informal arrangements, and the latter is often best handled by turning the matter over to the state attorney general or federal authorities.

3. *Local prosecutors: the urban and large suburban office.* Prosecuting attorneys in metropolitan districts not uncommonly have a larger legal staff than even the largest of the private law firms in the community. Los Angeles County, with the largest prosecutorial office in the nation, has over 1,000 assistant prosecutors. Full-time prosecutor's offices in the 34 jurisdictions with 1,000,000 or more population have a median total staff size of 414, with a median of 163 assistant prosecutors. Notwithstanding their size, these offices commonly have extraordinarily heavy caseloads per prosecutor, often four or five times that found in smaller offices. In a recent year, these 34 offices closed nearly 440,000 felony cases. To assist the local prosecutor in handling that caseload, some counties have relieved the prosecutor's office of most of its civil responsibilities, or provided a separate staff for civil cases.

In a large office, the assignment of prosecutors may have a substantial bearing on the operation of the office. The two most common assignment systems are the vertical or integrated system and the horizontal or process system. The vertical system is most commonly found in districts in which a complaint once filed will be assigned to a specified caseflow resulting in its eventual presentation in a particular courtroom or before a particular judge. A single assistant prosecutor or a team of assistants will then be assigned to all cases docketed for that courtroom or judge, with the assistant handling those cases from the point of filing through their final disposition. The horizontal assignment system, in contrast, revolves around each process step rather than the individual case. Thus, separate assistants may be assigned to intake, preliminary hearings, grand jury review, arraignments, trials, and appeals. As the case moves from one step to another, a new prosecutor will take over. Under this system, the newest assistants are commonly assigned to the preliminary steps or to misdemeanor trials, with the more seasoned prosecutors handling felony trials or supervising at one of the other stages.

Large offices also vary in the degree to which they seek to control the assistants in their exercise of discretion. Some assign experienced assistants to major areas of discretionary decisionmaking (e.g., charging and plea negotiation) and allow basically autonomous exercise of that authority by each assistant. Others utilize detailed guidelines, require assistants to justify their decision in writing by reference to those guidelines, and require all variations to be approved by one of a selected group of senior assistants. Spot checks and statistical analyses are run to ensure that all prosecutors are adhering basically to the same policies. Even here, however, individual prosecutors retain considerable flexibility, particularly in evaluating the factual elements of the case.

4. *The charging decision: in general.* "The decision whether to file formal charges is a vitally important stage in the criminal process. It provides an opportunity to screen out cases in which the accused is apparently innocent, and it is at this stage that the prosecutor must decide in cases of apparent guilt whether criminal sanctions are appropriate."[a] In making this decision, the prosecutor must decide: (1) whether there is sufficient evidence to support a prosecution; (2) if so, whether there are nonetheless reasons for not subjecting the defendant to the criminal process; (3) if so, whether nonprosecution should be conditioned upon the defendant's participation in a diversion program; and (4) if prosecution is to be undertaken, with what offense or offenses the defendant should be charged.

"[Most] cases come to the attention of the prosecutor only after the police have instituted the criminal process by arresting a suspect. * * * As a consequence, the police exercise a very important influence over the initial decision as to whether to invoke the criminal process. Where a decision is made to arrest, there are procedures for review by the prosecutor and, ultimately, the court. Where, however, the police decide not to invoke the criminal process, effective methods of review and control are largely lacking, and this issue of the proper scope and function of police discretion is of great, current importance and difficulty."[b]

"A prosecutor should have several kinds of information if he is to make sound charge decisions. He must evaluate the strength of his case. Police reports usually provide him with some facts about the offense, but often he needs more. Before a prosecutor decides whether to charge or dismiss in any case that is not elementary, he should review the case file to determine whether more evidence and witnesses are available than the police have uncovered. In addition, the prosecutor needs to know enough about the offender to determine whether he should be diverted from the criminal track. * * * Often the prosecutor needs to know whether there are facilities in the community for treating such medical or behavioral problems as the offender may have and whether those facilities will accept him. * * *

"Defense counsel has an important role to play at this stage, and he should be involved wherever an intrusive disposition or significant penalty is likely. Counsel can assist in gathering information and formulating a treatment program; he can help persuade the prosecutor of the appropriateness of a noncriminal disposition."[c]

---

a. *Task Force Report, The Courts* 5 (1967).

b. Frank W. Miller & Frank J. Remington, *Procedures Before Trial*, 339 Annals 111, 115 (1962).

c. *Task Force Report,* supra, at 7. Consider, in this regard, George Frampton, *Some Practical and Ethical Problems of Prosecuting Public Officials,* 36 Md.L.Rev. 5, 21 (1976): "If the Watergate prosecutors were inclined to recommend an indictment based on a reasonable certainty of obtaining a conviction, they invited the prospective defendant's lawyer to come (with his client, if he desired) into the office to present an oral argument against indictment. Permitting an accused to make a pre-indictment 'presentation' to the prosecutors is not unheard of in white collar cases, but the Special Prosecutor's Office carried the policy to unusual lengths, making it into the equivalent of an informal adversary hearing on the indictment decision itself. * * *

5. *Charging: evidence sufficiency.* It is not possible to state categorically how much evidence is required before the prosecutor is justified in charging a suspect with a crime, as the law does not expressly provide a distinct probability of guilt standard for the charging decision.[d] Although the prosecutor's decision to charge is reflected in the post-arrest issuance of a warrant in most jurisdictions, and though it is clear that an arrest warrant may issue only upon "probable cause," this phrase has been interpreted by courts only in cases where the warrant was challenged as a basis for arrest rather than as a basis for the decision to charge. If a lawful arrest has been made, it does not necessarily follow that charging would be proper on the same evidence, as the arrest may be based upon "the factual and practical considerations of everyday life on which reasonable and prudent men, not legal technicians, act." *Brinegar v. United States,* 338 U.S. 160, 69 S.Ct. 1302, 93 L.Ed. 1879 (1949).

The prosecutor, as a legal technician, will of course have to consider whether his decision to charge will withstand review at the preliminary hearing and before the grand jury, assuming such steps are required and are not waived by the defendant. See Chapters 14 and 15 of this Book. As a practical matter, the prosecutor is likely to require admissible evidence showing a high probability of guilt, that is, sufficient evidence to justify confidence in obtaining a conviction. This, however, may vary from case to case, based upon the prosecutor's experience with juries in that district. For example, one former federal prosecutor has reported that in his office it was the practice to require a higher quantum of proof in receipt of stolen goods cases, where the prosecution witnesses were usually admitted thieves and the defendant would usually come from the middle class and not have a prior criminal record. By comparison, less than the normal amount of proof was found to be adequate in narcotics cases, where jury acquittals were rare and defendants were usually persons of lower class.[e] Even in the latter category of cases, however, it was the practice to insist upon a higher quantum of evidence in order to continue the 100% conviction record for these offenses and thereby induce pleas of guilty. Thus, the prosecutor "developed a vested interest in the principle that a jury acquittal in a narcotics case was impossible and hence tended to avoid prosecuting cases where this might happen."[f]

6. *Charging: screening out cases.* "In some cases invocation of the criminal process against marginal offenders seems to do more harm than good. Labeling a person a criminal may set in motion a course of events which will increase the probability of his becoming or remaining one. The attachment of criminal status itself may be so prejudicial and irreversible as to ruin the future of a person who previously had successfully made his way in the community, and it may foreclose legitimate opportunities for offenders already suffering from social, vocational, and educational disadvantages. Yet a criminal code has no way of

---

"Certainly it is reasonable to suggest that every prosecutor ought to be under an affirmative ethical obligation to ensure that both he and the grand jury are exposed to both sides of a prospective criminal case, and whenever possible the defendant should also have some opportunity for input into the charging decision, even if the opportunity falls short of a full adversary hearing. However, present ethical standards do not even touch on this subject."

d. But consider *A.B.A. Code of Prof. Resp.* D.R. 7–103(A): "A public prosecutor or other government lawyer shall not institute or cause to be instituted criminal charges when he knows or it is obvious that the charges are not supported by probable cause."

e. John Kaplan, *The Prosecutorial Discretion—A Comment,* 60 Nw.U.L.Rev. 174, 184–85 (1965).

f. Id. at 185. See also Jerome H. Skolnick, *Social Control in the Adversary System,* 11 J. Conflict Resolution 52, 57–58 (1967), noting that the prosecutor cares "less about winning than about *not losing,*" as "not only does the prosecutor desire to maintain a respectable record, but more than that, he seeks to maintain, insofar as possible, a reputation for utter credibility, inevitable truth, almost of invincibility."

describing the difference between a petty thief who is on his way to becoming an armed robber and a petty thief who succumbs once to a momentary impulse. The same criminal conduct may be the deliberate act of a professional criminal or an isolated aberration in the behavior of a normally law abiding person. The criminal conduct describes the existence of a problem, but not its nature or source. The system depends on prosecutors to recognize these distinctions when bringing charges.

"Among the types of cases in which thoughtful prosecutors commonly appear disinclined to seek criminal penalties are domestic disturbances;[g] assaults and petty thefts in which victim and offender are in a family or social relationship; statutory rape when both boy and girl are young; first offense car thefts that involve teenager taking a car for a short joyride; checks that are drawn upon insufficient funds; shoplifting by first offenders, particularly when restitution is made; and criminal acts that involve offenders suffering from emotional disorders short of legal insanity."[h]

7. *Charging: diversion.* "One alternative available to prosecutors in the processing of a criminal complaint is that of diversion, 'the channeling of criminal defendants into programs that may not involve incarceration'. * * * Diversion commonly operates in the following manner:

"The pretrial diversion concept typically calls for stopping the prosecution clock on less serious or first felony complaints before or after arrest and prior to the arraignment stage, although there is no indication that more serious alleged offenders could not be successfully diverted. Those selected for the program are offered counseling, career development, education and supportive treatment services. If the participant responds for a measurable period (e.g. 3–6 months), either the court or the prosecutor or both, depending on the authorization of the project, are asked to approve dismissal of the case prior to trial and adjudication. If the participant fails to meet program obligations, prosecution is resumed on the referral criminal charge."[i]

"In most places there is little liaison between the prosecutor and community agencies which could assist an offender. The prosecutor, frequently overworked, has difficulty searching out noncriminal dispositions, and it is open to question whether he is the appropriate official to perform this searching function. He may have few professional qualifications to decide what treatment alternatives are appropriate for particular offenders. Consultative services to analyze the offender's medical, psychiatric, and social situation; to consider that situation in light of available community resources; and to make appropriate recommendations are at best limited and in many places are not available. But the basic problem is that in many communities the resources for dealing with offenders and their problems are totally inadequate. The development of such resources is clearly essential * * *."[j]

---

g. This was an accurate description of the practice when this *Report* was written in 1967, but today many prosecutors follow a "no-drop" policy or some variation thereof under which the victim's expressed wish for no prosecution is much less often followed. See Cheryl Hanna, *No Right to Choose: Mandated Victim Participation in Domestic Violence Prosecutions*, 109 Harv.L.Rev. 1849, 1860 (1996).

h. *Task Force Report,* supra, at 5.

i. *N.D.A.A. National Prosecution Standards,* 152 (1977). For more on diversion, see N.D.A.A., *Deferred Prosecution* (1976); Raymond T. Nimmer, *Diversion* (1974); Notes, 50 Ind.L.J. 783 (1975); 28 Rutgers L.Rev. 1203 (1975), and sources cited therein.

j. *Task Force Report,* supra at 7. Other criticisms have been voiced. Franklin E. Zimring, *Measuring the Impact of Pretrial Diversion from the Criminal Justice System*, 41 U.Chi. L.Rev. 224, 238 (1974), notes that most diversion projects have focused upon "defendants who will represent the lowest risk to the community," although "treatment cannot greatly improve this group," because of pressure on the projects to "look good" by "reducing re-arrests in the treated group to the bare minimum." Note, 83 Yale L.J. 827, 835 (1974),

8. *Charging: selection of the charge.* "Once the prosecutor is personally convinced of the guilt of the accused, he then must determine the charge. * * * There is seldom difficulty in the heinous murder or simple petty theft. But what of the case where the offense could be aggravated battery, aggravated assault, battery, or simple assault? Should a charge be burglary, felonious theft, or petty theft? Should a 16–year old boy be charged with a technical burglary or should he be handled as a juvenile before the family court?[k] These are the situations that pose a real test to prosecutorial discretion. Further, evidence may be insufficient, witnesses may be unavailable, the complaining witness may not wish to prosecute, the evidence may have been illegally seized, witnesses may lack credibility, or the case may appear too weak to justify prosecution on the major, technical, or primary offense under the statute. Perhaps the offender has no previous criminal record; perhaps the injuries were too slight; perhaps the offense was the result of mutual combat; perhaps it was a domestic squabble; perhaps there was a considerable delay by the prosecuting witness in reporting the crime; perhaps identification witnesses are weak and unsure of themselves; perhaps the witnesses themselves are convicted criminals and subject to impeachment. These are some of the factors which must be weighed and given proper consideration by the prosecutor * * *."[l]

"Very often, an offender's conduct violates more than one criminal statute. This may be the situation because: (1) the offender has committed a series of offenses prior to apprehension, as, for example, a number of burglaries; (2) the offender may, by a single course of criminal conduct, violate more than one criminal statute of the jurisdiction where his conduct occurred, as, for example, in a situation where conduct may constitute both forgery and theft; (3) the offender may violate both state and federal law, as, for example, where theft of an automobile may violate a state statute and a federal statute if the vehicle is driven across a state line. In these situations, prosecutors must decide whether the offender's conduct is to be subjected to a single prosecution for more than one offense or to more than one prosecution.

"There is variation in practice, and there is, therefore, risk of oversimplification in generalizing. There is adequate evidence to show that charging more than one offense is routine practice in many jurisdictions. This gives to the sentencing judge the power to impose consecutive sentences, which occurs frequently in some jurisdictions and rarely in others where, typically, sentences for all of the offenses are made to run concurrently. It is apparent that the processes of charging, convicting, and sentencing the multiple offender are so closely interrelated as to make it impossible to understand completely the one without understanding the other. Charging a single offense may be the practice where the sentencing range available to the judge is adequate to deal with the offender taking cognizance of the totality of his criminal conduct. Charging a number of offenses may be the

observes: "One of the often stated advantages of pretrial diversion is the reduction of court docket congestion. This goal seems more ideal than real. Pretrial diversion saves court time only if, in its absence, the accused would go to trial. But most pretrial diversion cases, given the nonserious nature of the charges, would have been disposed of by negotiation and plea rather than trial on the merits."

k. See Wallace J. Mlyniec, *Juvenile Delinquent or Adult Convict—The Prosecutor's Choice,* 14 Am.Crim.L.Rev. 29 (1976), discussing and criticizing the discretion given to prosecutors in 16 states to decide whether a juvenile goes to criminal court or juvenile court. In

Russell v. Parratt, 543 F.2d 1214 (8th Cir. 1976), the court rejected defendant's claim, on habeas corpus, "that since, under the law of Nebraska at the time of his trial, the County Attorney had 'unbridled' discretion to proceed against him either as an adult or a juvenile offender, he has been denied due process in that such decision was made upon the County Attorney's authority alone and without evidentiary hearing." The court held that this is a part of the prosecutor's discretion.

l. Richard Mills, *The Prosecutor: Charging and "Bargaining,"* 1966 U.Ill.L.F. 511, 514–15.

practice where the penalty for one offense is thought to be disproportionately low in relation to the conduct involved. Also, here, as in relation to the selection of charge, the willingness of the defendant to plead guilty may be reflected in the number of offenses for which he is prosecuted."[m]

SECTION 2. SOME VIEWS ON DISCRETION IN THE CRIMINAL PROCESS AND THE PROSE-CUTOR'S DISCRETION IN PARTICULAR

WAYNE R. LAFAVE—THE PROSECUTOR'S DISCRETION IN THE UNITED STATES

18 Am.J.Comp.L. 532, 533–39 (1970).

The American prosecutor has traditionally exercised considerable discretion in deciding whether or not to prosecute, that is, in determining whether prosecution is called for in a given case as a matter of enforcement policy. Insufficient attention has been given to the question of precisely why this is so, but the most common explanations are these:

(1) Because of legislative "overcriminalization." As one commentator has said, "The criminal code of any jurisdiction tends to make a crime of everything that people are against, without regard to enforceability, changing social concepts, etc. The result is that the criminal code becomes society's trash bin." Examination of the typical state code of criminal law supports this judgment. Included therein are likely to be crimes which are over-defined for administrative convenience (e.g., the gambling statute which bars *all* forms of gambling so as "to confront the professional gambler with a statutory facade that is wholly devoid of loopholes"); crimes which merely constitute "state-declared ideals" (e.g., the crime of adultery, which is "unenforced because we want to continue our conduct, and unrepealed because we want to preserve our morals"); and now outdated crimes which found their way into the law because of "the mood that dominated a tribunal or legislature at strategic moments in the past, a flurry of public excitement on some single matter."

(2) Because of limitations in available enforcement resources. No prosecutor has available sufficient resources to prosecute all of the offenses which come to his attention. To deny the authority to exercise discretion under these circumstances, it is said, is "like directing a general to attack the enemy on all fronts at once." Thus, so the argument goes, the prosecutor must remain free to exercise his judgment in determining what prosecutions will best serve the public interest.

(3) Because of a need to individualize justice. A criminal code can only deal in general categories of conduct. As Roscoe Pound observed:

"No lawmaker has been able to foresee more than the broad outlines of the clash of interests or more than the main lines of the courses of conduct to which the law even of his own time must be applied. Moreover, a legal system which seeks to cover everything by a special provision becomes cumbrous and unworkable."

Individualized treatment of offenders, based upon the circumstances of the particular case, has long been recognized in sentencing, and it is argued that such individualized treatment is equally appropriate at the charging stage so as to relieve deserving defendants of even the stigma of prosecution. Were it otherwise,

m. Frank W. Miller & Frank J. Remington, supra, at 118–20.

so that the prosecutor acted "in strict accordance with rules of law, precisely and narrowly laid down, the criminal law would be ordered but intolerable."

The current practice, as set forth in a recently-published empirical study of the charging decision, clearly reflects these three considerations. * * *

A full appreciation of the extent of the prosecutor's power, however, requires consideration of the fact that his discretion may be exercised in the other direction; a particular individual may be selected out for prosecution notwithstanding the fact that the case is one which ordinarily would not result in an affirmative charging decision. Sometimes the purpose is to benefit the offender in some way,[20] but usually it is not. Such selection may occur in response to press and public pressure for "law and order," to rid society of certain "bad actors" who are thought to have committed more serious crimes, and for similar reasons.

Should this aspect of the prosecutor's discretion be a matter of concern? Some would undoubtedly say no, on the ground that only acts of leniency are involved, but there are two answers to this. For one thing, not all leniency is consistent with the public interest in effective law enforcement. Moreover, as Professor Kenneth Davis has aptly pointed out:

"A fundamental fact about the discretionary power to be lenient is extremely simple and entirely clear and yet is usually overlooked: *The discretionary power to be lenient is an impossibility without a concomitant discretionary power not to be lenient, and injustice from the discretionary power not to be lenient is especially frequent; the power to be lenient is the power to discriminate.*"

The discretion of the American prosecutor to decide, as a matter of policy, when to prosecute and when not to prosecute is clearly recognized in the case law. It is said, for example, that the prosecutor must be allowed to consider whether "a prosecution will promote the ends of justice, instill a respect for law, and advance the cause of ordered liberty," and to take into account "the degree of criminality, the weight of the evidence, the credibility of witnesses, precedent, policy, the climate of public opinion, timing, and the relative gravity of the offense." Indeed, it would hardly make sense to contend that the prosecutor should have *no* discretion; full enforcement would be neither possible nor tolerable. The issue is not discretion versus no discretion, but rather how discretion should be confined, structured, and checked. As Davis notes: "Half the problem is to cut back *unnecessary* discretionary power. The other half is to find effective ways to control *necessary* discretionary power."

1. *Confining the prosecutor's discretion to decide when to prosecute.* A significant part of the discretion currently exercised by American prosecutors is "unnecessary," in the sense that adequate reform of the substantive criminal law would eliminate, as a matter of law, many cases now screened out only at the option of the prosecutor. Clearly, "one of the major consequences of the state of penal law today is that administration has so largely come to dominate the field without effective guidance from the law."

No one would seriously contend that the prosecutor's discretion could be eliminated by penal law reform. It is clear, however, from even the most casual inspection of the typical state criminal code, that some significant portion of that discretion would be unnecessary if many obsolete or largely unenforceable statutes were repealed and if other statutes were more narrowly drawn. The principal

20. See, e.g., Francis A. Allen, *The Borderland of Criminal Justice* 5–6 (1964), describing the practice of prosecution and conviction of prospective mothers for some offense relating to extramarital sexual relations when they are without the financial resources to pay for the medical expenses of childbirth or the subsequent care of their offspring.

benefit of such reform would be that it would eliminate that part of the prosecutor's discretion which carries with it the greatest potential for misuse:

"The worst abuses of discretion in enforcement occur in connection with those offenses that are just barely taken seriously, like most consensual sex offenses. Here, especially in the case of fornication and adultery, enforcement is so sporadic as to be just one step short of complete cessation. And it is here that the greatest danger exists of using enforcement discretion in an abusive way: to pay off a score, to provide a basis for extortion, to stigmatize an otherwise deviant or unpopular figure."

2. *Structuring the prosecutor's discretion to decide when to prosecute.* Nearly forty years ago, Thurman Arnold noted that "the idea that a prosecuting attorney should be permitted to use his discretion concerning the laws which he will enforce and those which he will disregard appears to the ordinary citizen to border on anarchy." This may be the reason why this particular aspect of the prosecutor's discretion has traditionally been exercised sub rosa and on an ad hoc basis, and has thus remained largely unstructured.

The President's Commission on Law Enforcement and Administration of Justice identified three basic needs which must be met before the prosecutor's charging discretion may become more structured and thus more rational. They are:

(a) The need for more information. More detailed background information about the offender is needed so that it may be determined whether he is a dangerous or only marginal offender. (In the absence of any information, or only the limited information provided by a brief police report, the temptation is great to resort to rule-of-thumb policies based only upon the nature of the crime.) In addition, most prosecutors lack sufficient information about alternative treatment facilities and programs in the community to be able to make a rational determination of whether there exists some better course than prosecution.

(b) The need for established standards. "Standards should pertain to such matters as the circumstances that properly can be considered mitigating or aggravating, or the kinds of offenses that should be most vigorously prosecuted in view of the community's law enforcement needs." In large offices, the absence of such standards often results in a lack of uniformity in decision-making by the several assistant prosecutors. But even in a one-man office, consistency would seem more likely if the prosecutor had beforehand attempted to articulate general enforcement standards.

(c) The need for established procedures. These procedures might include a "precharge conference" at which the prosecutor and defense counsel could discuss the appropriateness of a noncriminal disposition. At least in serious cases, a decision not to prosecute should be supported by a written statement of the underlying reasons, and this statement should become a public record.

3. *Checking the prosecutor's discretion to decide when to prosecute.* Although the American criminal justice system has reasonably effective controls to ensure that the prosecutor does not abuse his power by prosecuting upon less than sufficient evidence, there are—as a practical matter—no comparable checks upon his discretionary judgment of whether or not to prosecute one against whom sufficient evidence exists. * * *

While it may be apparent that this is an unfortunate state of affairs, it is not so apparent how the situation might be best remedied. A system of close administrative review, perhaps modeled after the practice in West Germany, would seem to require a hierarchical arrangement quite different from the present structure of most state governments. Whether such a significant change in structure would be an improvement is not readily apparent. As for judicial review, it is probably true that courts have exercised undue restraint in responding to challenges of prosecutorial discretion. Yet, there may be something to the contention that courts are ill-equipped to make enforcement policy. Finally, greater control by the electorate could readily be achieved by exposing the prosecutor's nonenforcement decisions to the public, but it is by no means clear that the soundest enforcement policies are those which would draw approval from the "silent majority."

THURMAN W. ARNOLD—LAW ENFORCEMENT— AN ATTEMPT AT SOCIAL DISSECTION

42 Yale L.J. 1, 7–8, 17–18 (1932).
Reprinted with permission of the publisher; copyright
© 1932 by the Yale Law Journal Company, Inc.

The fact that prosecuting attorneys are compelled to [use discretion] is generally ignored, or when attention is called to it, regarded as evidence of some kind of social degeneration which must be preached away in public speech and judicial utterance. * * * Disorder must be curbed by law enforcement. If laws are not enforced, disorder will be conclusively presumed. Therefore failure to enforce laws is disorder in itself. The idea is essentially a religious one, and we are acclimated to a wide conflict between practice and utterance in the realm of such notions. Even those who regard the ideal as impracticable so far as their own conduct is concerned consider it good for the public in general. * * *

[An] important effect of the creed of Law Enforcement on legal theory is found in the contradictions in which it is continually involving the judicial system. These are reflected constantly in the complicated distinctions and reconciliations of the Criminal Law with the "law in action" which proceed under that elaborately embroidered verbal cloak. It is impossible to understand the "principles" of the Criminal Law without analyzing these contradictions. A few of them may be stated as follows: * * * (2) *Assumption.* Criminal Law is a body of governing rules, protecting certain social interests which are generally known and guide the ordinary citizen in his conduct. *Contradiction.* Substantive criminal law for the most part consists, not in a set of rules to be enforced, but in an arsenal of weapons to be used against such persons as the police or prosecutor may deem to be a menace to public safety. The choice of weapons is sufficiently elastic that the prosecutor may select a large number of offenses with different penalties to cover any single course of conduct.[a] (3) *Assumption.* It is the duty of the prosecuting attorney to enforce all criminal laws regardless of his own judgment of public convenience or safety. Compromises and "bargain days" in criminal courts lead to disrespect for law because this process conflicts with enforcement of law. *Contradiction.* It is the duty of the prosecuting attorney to solve the problem of public

---

a. Compare Robert H. Jackson, *The Federal Prosecutor*, 31 J.Crim.L. & Criminology 3, 5 (1940): "If the prosecutor is obliged to choose his cases, it follows that he can choose his defendants. Therein is the most dangerous power of the prosecutor: that he will pick people that he thinks he should get, rather than pick cases that need to be prosecuted. With the law books filled with a great assortment of crimes, a prosecutor stands a fair chance of finding at least a technical violation of some act on the part of almost anyone. In such a case, it is not a question of discovering the commission of a crime and then looking for the man who has committed it, it is a question of picking the man and then searching the law books, or putting investigators to work, to pin some offense on him. It is in this realm—in which the prosecutor picks some person whom he dislikes or desires to embarrass, or selects some group of unpopular persons and then looks for an offense, that the greatest danger of abuse of prosecuting power lies. It is here that law enforcement becomes personal and the real crime becomes that of being unpopular with the predominant or governing group, being attached to the wrong political views, or being personally obnoxious to or in the way of the prosecutor himself."

order and safety using the criminal code as an instrument rather than as a set of commands. This makes it proper and necessary that some laws should be enforced, others occasionally enforced, and others ignored according to the best judgment of the enforcing agency. The criminal problem must be looked at as a war on dangerous individuals and not as a law enforcement problem, unless we want to escape from reality by taking refuge in an ideal world of false assumptions concerning both criminal codes and criminals.[b]

A.B.A. STANDARDS
3d ed., 1993.

3–2.5 Prosecutor's handbook; policy guidelines and procedures.

(a) Each prosecutor's office should develop a statement of (i) general policies to guide the exercise of prosecutorial discretion and (ii) procedures of the office. The objectives of these policies as to discretion and procedures should be to achieve a fair, efficient, and effective enforcement of the criminal law.

(b) In the interest of continuity and clarity, such statement of policies and procedures should be maintained in an office handbook. This handbook should be available to the public, except for subject matters declared "confidential," when it is reasonably believed that public access to their contents would adversely affect the prosecution function.[c]

3–3.8 Discretion as to noncriminal disposition.

(a) The prosecutor should consider in appropriate cases the availability of noncriminal disposition, formal or informal, in deciding whether to press criminal charges which would otherwise be supported by

b. Compare Herbert L. Packer, *The Limits of the Criminal Sanction* 290–91 (1968): "[T]o admit the need for discretion is not to make a virtue of it. And it is far from being a virtue in the enforcement of the criminal sanction. The basic trouble with discretion is simply that it is lawless, in the literal sense of that term. If police or prosecutors find themselves free (or compelled) to pick and choose among known or knowable instances of criminal conduct, they are making a judgment which in a society based on law should be made only by those to whom the making of law is entrusted. For the rough approximation of community values that emerges from the legislative process there is substituted the personal and often idiosyncratic values of the law enforcer."

c. Similarly, Norman Abrams, *Internal Policy: Guiding the Exercise of Prosecutorial Discretion*, 19 U.C.L.A.L.Rev. 1, 34 (1971), concludes that "policy should be regularly published in a medium readily available to the defense bar and other interested persons." What then of the arguments, noted in Abrams, that the publication of policy will (a) encourage litigation on issues not presently the subject of judicial scrutiny; (b) give defense counsel more leverage and issues to raise; (c) tend to freeze the policy in its then-existing form; (d) improperly modify the deterrent effect of the criminal law; (e) weaken the standards set by the criminal law; (f) make the appearance of impartiality difficult to achieve and breed disrespect for the law; and (g) result in prosecutors being hesitant to articulate policy, particularly as to controversial issues?

Under current practices, guidelines usually are contained primarily in manuals, such as the U.S. Attorney's Manual, that ordinarily are not made available to the public generally nor the bar. Leland E. Beck, *The Administrative Law of Criminal Prosecution: The Development of Prosecutorial Policy*, 27 Am.U.L.Rev. 310, 314 n. 10 (1978), points out that now the "nine-volume *Manual* is available under the disclosure requirements of the Freedom of Information Act." But a recent Justice Department survey established that 83 of the 94 U.S. Attorneys also have their own individual written guidelines under which they regularly decline to prosecute, and that the criteria "vary substantially from one prosecutor's office to another." The Department refused to release the text of or even excerpts from these guidelines on the ground "that the guidelines, if released, would provide a 'road map' showing where crimes could be committed with the least chance of being prosecuted." *N.Y. Times*, Jan. 7, 1980, at A1, col. 1.

probable cause; especially in the case of a first offender, the nature of the offense may warrant noncriminal disposition.

(b) Prosecutors should be familiar with the resources of social agencies which can assist in the evaluation of cases for diversion from the criminal process.

3–3.9 Discretion in the charging decision.

(a) A prosecutor should not institute, or cause to be instituted, or to permit the continued pendency of criminal charges when the prosecutor knows that the charges are not supported by probable cause. A prosecutor should not institute, cause to be instituted, or permit the continued pendency of criminal charges in the absence of sufficient admissible evidence to support a conviction.

(b) The prosecutor is not obliged to present all charges which the evidence might support. The prosecutor may in some circumstances and for good cause consistent with the public interest decline to prosecute, notwithstanding that sufficient evidence may exist which would support a conviction. Illustrative of the factors which the prosecutor may properly consider in exercising his or her discretion are:

(i) the prosecutor's reasonable doubt that the accused is in fact guilty;

(ii) the extent of the harm caused by the offense;

(iii) the disproportion of the authorized punishment in relation to the particular offense or the offender;

(iv) possible improper motives of a complainant;

(v) reluctance of the victim to testify;

(vi) cooperation of the accused in the apprehension or conviction of others; and

(vii) availability and likelihood of prosecution by another jurisdiction.

(c) A prosecutor should not be compelled by his or her supervisor to prosecute a case in which he or she has a reasonable doubt about the guilt of the accused.

(d) In making the decision to prosecute, the prosecutor should give no weight to the personal or political advantages or disadvantages which might be involved or to a desire to enhance his or her record of convictions.

(e) In cases which involve a serious threat to the community, the prosecutor should not be deterred from prosecution by the fact that in the jurisdiction juries have tended to acquit persons accused of the particular kind of criminal act in question.

(f) The prosecutor should not bring or seek charges greater in number or degree than can reasonably be supported with evidence at trial or than are necessary to fairly reflect the gravity of the offense.

(g) The prosecutor should not condition a dismissal of charges, nolle prosequi, or similar action on the accused's relinquishment of the right to seek civil redress unless the accused has agreed to the action knowingly and intelligently, freely and voluntarily, and where such waiver is approved by the court.

H. RICHARD UVILLER—THE VIRTUOUS PROSECUTOR IN QUEST OF AN ETHICAL STANDARD: GUIDANCE FROM THE A.B.A.

71 Mich.L.Rev. 1145, 1151–53 (1973).

[T]he standards fail to address the question that worries Professor Freedman:[d] When should the prosecutor pursue a selected target, seeking evidence for prosecution? * * * Perhaps it is enough for some jurisdictions to call upon the prosecutor to bend his investigative efforts to every case of suspected crime, regardless of the girth of the reed of suspicion or the nature of the crime or criminal to be pursued. But for others, surely, the decision to investigate—that is, to undertake the long, arduous task of building a case when no clear evidence pokes through the surface—must, by necessity, be selective, and it requires one of the more significant exercises of discretion in the prosecutor's arsenal. Do the framers of the standards agree with Professor Freedman that it is unethical for the prosecutor to decide to investigate a person because he suspects that the person is engaged in one of a variety of criminal activities, and to seek to make a case against him for any crime he can support with evidence? Do the ethics of the choice dictate a prior resolve to investigate certain activity, *qua* activity, to catch whoever might be involved in it? If the framers feel—as I do—that the distinction between these two is an artificial one, unwarranted by any rational policy, then how should the prosecutor select his target, be it crime or criminal? * * *

As a matter of ethics, the problem sounds to be in tones of motivation. It is less important to me that a prosecutor spends his efforts bringing to bar a notorious pimp, while doing nothing to discover evidence of police corruption, than why this election was made. If a plea to the reduced crime of manslaughter is accepted by the prosecutor from a defendant who murdered a clerk during a holdup, while in another case the prosecutor offers no lesser plea to a man who kills a cop who interrupted a robbery, the important question is why the prosecutor insists on the full measure of guilt for the cop-killer and not for the clerk-killer. The ethical objective, it seems to me, is to keep the exercise of this important discretionary power of the prosecutor free of improper motivation.

I recognize the significance of my disparagement of objective consequences. Unequal results are unequal regardless of the motivation of the official who achieved them. * * * The prosecutor who senses the outrage of his constituency against the aggressive and unsightly hordes of prostitutes infesting the streets may ethically respond by stricter application of valid laws against prostitution. More questionable, it seems to me, is the same campaign waged by the prosecutor as self-appointed custodian of community morality, impelled by personal distaste generated by his own values. I do not suggest that the honorable prosecutor be the slave of his electorate. Indeed, in many matters his duty clearly lies in the defiance of community pressures. But, within the confines of law, I would rather see his

---

d. The reference is to Monroe H. Freedman, *The Professional Responsibility of the Prosecuting Attorney*, 55 Geo.L.J. 1030, 1034–35 (1967): "If the government cannot successfully prosecute a notorious criminal for the numerous serious offenses he is suspected of having committed, some prosecutors consider it to be proper to subject him to prosecutions for a variety of other crimes, ranging from traffic offenses to tax evasion, for which he would not be investigated and charged were it not for his notoriety. In support of such prac- tices, it is argued that if the individual is in fact guilty of the crime with which he is charged, the motive of the prosecutor is imma- terial. This contention overlooks the fact that there are few of us who have led such unblemished lives as to prevent a determined prosecutor from finding some basis for an indictment or an information. Thus, to say that the prosecutor's motive is immaterial, is to justify making virtually every citizen the potential victim of arbitrary discretion."

discretion guided by an honest effort to discern public needs and community concerns than by personal pique or moralistic impertinence.

KENNETH CULP DAVIS—DISCRETIONARY JUSTICE
189–90, 224–25 (1969).

* * * Even if we assume that a prosecutor has to have a power of selective enforcement, why do we not require him to state publicly his general policies and require him to follow those policies in individual cases in order to protect evenhanded justice? Why not subject prosecutors' decisions to a simple and general requirement of open findings, open reasons, and open precedents, except when special reason for confidentiality exists? Why not strive to protect prosecutors' decisions from political or other ulterior influence in the same way we strive to protect judges' decisions? * * *

The seeming unanimity of American prosecutors that their discretionary power must be completely uncontrolled is conclusively contradicted by the experience of West Germany, where the discretionary power of prosecutors is so slight as to be almost nonexistent, and where almost all they do is closely supervised.[e]

I think we Americans should learn from other nations that the huge discretionary power of prosecutors need not be unconfined, unstructured, and unchecked. We should reexamine the assumptions to which our drifting has led us— that a prosecutor should have uncontrolled discretion to choose one out of six cases to prosecute, without any requirement that the one most deserving of prosecution be chosen, or to trade a lesser charge for a plea of guilty in one case but not in another, with no guiding rules or standards, without disclosing findings or reasons, without any requirement of consistency, without supervision or check, and without judicial review.

Prosecutors, in my opinion, should be required to make and to announce rules that will guide their choices, stating as far as practicable what will and what will

---

e. At pp. 194–95, Professor Davis contrasts the German and American systems:

"The most important difference between the German system and the American system is this: *Whenever the evidence that the defendant has committed a serious crime is reasonably clear and the law is not in doubt, the German prosecutor, unlike the American prosecutor, is without discretionary power to withhold prosecution. This means that selective enforcement, a major feature of the American system, is almost wholly absent from the German system.* * * *

"The German and American systems also differ when the evidence or the law or both seem to the prosecutor to be doubtful. When a doubt seems to require a discretionary choice, the German prosecutor does not resolve the doubt; he almost always presents a doubtful case to the judge, who determines the sufficiency of the evidence and the proper interpretation of the law. Of course, in America the prosecutor makes a discretionary determination in every doubtful case, either to prosecute or not to prosecute.

"Even when the prosecutor finds prosecution of a suspect clearly inappropriate, the German system, unlike the American system, provides protection against abuse of power.

When a crime is reported by the police or by a private party, a file is opened and registered; the file can be traced at any time. A German prosecutor can never simply forget about the case as his American counterpart may do. The file cannot be closed without a statement of written reasons, which in important cases must be approved by the prosecutor's superior, and which must be reported to any victim of the crime and to any suspect who was interrogated. Every prosecutor is supervised by a superior in a hierarchical system headed by the Minister of Justice, who is himself responsible to the cabinet. The supervision is real, not merely a threat; files are in fact often reviewed. Availability to victims of crimes of procedure to compel prosecution constitutes still another check."

The commentators are not in agreement as to the correctness of the Davis characterization of the German system. Compare Abraham S. Goldstein & Martin Marcus, *The Myth of Judicial Supervision in Three "Inquisitorial" Systems: France, Italy, and Germany,* 87 Yale L.J. 240, 275–76 (1977); with John H. Langbein & Lloyd L. Weinreb, *Continental Criminal Procedure: "Myth" and Reality,* 87 Yale L.J. 1549, 1564 (1978).

not be prosecuted, and they should be required otherwise to structure their discretion.

––––––

NOTES ON THE PROSECUTOR'S DISCRETION

1. Should the prosecutor have the sole responsibility for determining when, on policy grounds, an offender should not be subjected to the criminal process, or should the police also be expected to make such decisions, as they frequently do when they decide not to arrest an offender who is lawfully subject to arrest? "It has been traditional to give explicit recognition to the propriety of discretion on the part of the prosecutor and either to deny or, more commonly, to ignore the issue of police discretion.[a] [There is apparently an] assumption that the average municipal police agency lacks any special competence to make policy decisions * * *. For example, the United States Supreme Court held it proper for the Federal Trade Commission to follow a policy of proceeding criminally against only major violators because there were insufficient resources to proceed against all violators.[b] This kind of judgment was said to be within the expertness of the enforcement agency, which is familiar with the economic problems being dealt with. Under similar circumstances, a Philadelphia court held an identical policy of the Philadelphia Police Commissioner to be improper.[c] The Philadelphia court gave no indication that it believed that the police commissioner was particularly qualified to decide how best to allocate the limited enforcement resources made available to him."[d]

"Although the prosecutor is legally accorded a wider area of discretion than the policeman, the setting of the policeman's role offers greater opportunity to behave inconsistently with the rule of law. Police discretion is 'hidden' insofar as the policeman often makes decisions in direct interaction with the suspect. * * * By contrast, prosecutorial discretion frequently takes place at a later stage in the system, after the initial charge has been made public. The public character of the charge may restrict the prosecutor's discretion in practice more than the policeman's, even though the scope of the prosecutor's discretion is far wider in theory."[e]

a. This issue seldom surfaces in appellate cases. A noteworthy exception, indicating *some* police discretion is properly exercised, is *City of Cambridge v. Phillips,* 612 N.E.2d 638 (Mass. 1993), where the defendant, cited by a police officer for an illegal left turn, challenged a statute expressly declaring with respect to such minor traffic violations that "the police officer may direct that a written warning be issued or may cite the violator." After noting that the defendant had *not* claimed a denial of equal protection, the court commented: "Police have some discretion in their administration and enforcement of the law. The defendant advances no authority to indicate that nondiscriminatory, nonarbitrary exercise of discretion by a police officer is unlawful if no standard guides the decision-making process. Prosecutors have wide ranges of discretion in deciding whether to bring charges and which specific charges to bring. In the administration of the law concerning civil motor vehicle infractions, the police act as prosecutors as a practical matter in presenting such infractions to clerk-magistrates and to judges. In any event, in the absence of unfair discrimination or some other improper exercise of discretion, the judgment of the 'cop on the beat' is not subject to a valid constitutionally-based criticism where the range of clearly defined, available options is as narrow as it is in this case. This case does not involve the delegation of a basic policy matter to the police for resolution."

b. *Moog Industries, Inc. v. FTC,* 355 U.S. 411, 78 S.Ct. 377, 2 L.Ed.2d 370 (1958).

c. *Bargain City U.S.A., Inc. v. Dilworth,* 29 U.S.L. Week 2002 (Pa.C.P., June 10, 1960), aff'd, 407 Pa. 129, 179 A.2d 439 (1962).

d. Wayne R. LaFave, *Arrest: The Decision to Take a Suspect Into Custody* 72–73 (1965).

e. Jerome H. Skolnick, *Justice Without Trial* 233–34 (1966).

Does this mean "the police should operate in an atmosphere which exhorts and commands them to invoke impartially all criminal laws within the bounds of *full enforcement*," so that "[r]esponsibility for the enactment, amendment, and repeal of the criminal laws will not, then, be abandoned to the whim of each police officer or department, but retained where it belongs in a democracy—with elected representatives"?[f] Consider in this regard that in some locales with respect to certain offenses the police have been placed in essentially a "full enforcement" posture. "At least 15 states and the District of Columbia have enacted mandatory arrest laws for misdemeanor violence calls. * * * In these jurisdictions, officers must arrest the defendant when they have probable cause to believe that a domestic violence assault has occurred. * * * Although these policies have received mixed reviews,[g] the clear trend in police practice is to arrest the batterer at the scene, regardless of the victim's wishes."[h]

2. The prosecutor's decision not to prosecute is often based upon the expectation that the judge or jury would refuse to convict notwithstanding proof of guilt beyond a reasonable doubt. The jury in a criminal case has uncontrolled discretion to acquit the guilty. An empirical study has shown that juries acquit the guilty because: (a) they sympathize with the defendant as a person; (b) they apply personal attitudes as to when self-defense should be recognized; (c) they take into account the contributory fault of the victim; (d) they believe the offense is *de minimus;* (e) they take into account the fact that the statute violated is an unpopular law; (f) they feel the defendant has already been punished enough; (g) they feel the defendant was subjected to improper police or prosecution practices; (h) they refuse to apply strict liability statutes to inadvertent conduct; (i) they apply their own standards as to when mental illness or intoxication should be a defense; and (j) they believe the offense is accepted conduct in the subculture of the defendant and victim. See Harry Kalven & Hans Zeisel, *The American Jury* chs. 15–27 (1966).

3. Because there is not agreement on whether such discretionary action by a jury is a desirable safety valve in the criminal justice system or an unavoidable evil, it is a debatable point whether it is proper for the trial judge to act in a similar fashion when a case is tried before him without a jury. The *Model Penal Code* would give the trial judge discretion to acquit the guilty under certain circumstances,[i] and an empirical study has established that judges acquit guilty defendants for the same reasons that juries do. See Donald J.Newman, *Conviction:*

f. Joseph Goldstein, *Police Discretion Not to Invoke the Criminal Process,* 69 Yale L.J. 543, 586 (1960). For more on police discretion, see Symposium, 47 Law & Contemp.Prob. 1 (1984).

g. E.g., see Development in the Law, 106 Harv.L.Rev. 1498, 1537–40 (1993); and compare Comment, 43 DePaul L.Rev. 1133, 1133–34, 1156–64 (1994); Note, 2 Am.U.J.Gender & L. 171, 171–74, 187–95 (1994); with Joan Zorza, *The Criminal Law of Misdemeanor Domestic Violence, 1970–1990,* 83 J.Crim.L. & Crimin. 46, 65–72 (1992); Recent Development, 11 Harv.Womens' L.J. 213, 215–16 (1988).

h. Cheryl Hanna, *No Right to Choose: Mandated Victim Participation in Domestic Violence Prosecutions,* 109 Harv.L.Rev. 1849, 1860 (1996).

i. When "the defendant's conduct:

"(1) was within a customary license or tolerance, neither expressly negatived by the person whose interest was infringed nor inconsistent with the purpose of the law defining the offense; or

"(2) did not actually cause or threaten the harm or evil sought to be prevented by the law defining the offense or did so only to an extent too trivial to warrant the condemnation of conviction; or

"(3) presents such other extenuations that it cannot reasonably be regarded as envisaged by the legislature in forbidding the offense." *Model Penal Code* § 2.12.

Five states have adopted this provision; see, e.g., *State v. Kargar,* 679 A.2d 81 (Me.1996) (where defendant, an Afghani, charged with gross sexual assault for kissing his young son's penis, charge properly dismissed on finding conduct "is accepted practice in his culture" and there "is nothing sexual" about it).

The Determination of Guilt or Innocence Without Trial chs. 9–12, 14 (Frank J. Remington ed. 1966).[j]

Should the trial judge, even in a jury case, be recognized as possessing authority essentially the same as that of the prosecutor, so that he might dismiss or reduce charges? Consider *United States v. Weinstein,* 452 F.2d 704 (2d Cir.1971) (nothing in the federal rules "gives the judge an overriding power to terminate a criminal prosecution in which the Government's evidence has passed the test of legal sufficiency simply because he thinks that course would be most consonant with the interests of justice"); *State v. Williamson,* 853 P.2d 56 (Kan.1993) (court may not dismiss aggravated assault charge on ground civil treatment of mental illness would be better, as that choice up to prosecutor subject to possibility of acquittal via insanity defense). However, about a dozen states have statutes or court rules authorizing a trial judge to dismiss criminal charges sua sponte in furtherance of justice. See *State v. Sauve,* 666 A.2d 1164 (Vt.1995) (collecting and discussing these provisions).

4. The federal Victim and Witness Protection Act of 1982 provides that "the victim of a serious crime, or in the case of a minor child or a homicide, the family of the victim, shall be consulted by the attorney for the Government in order to obtain the views of the victim or family about the disposition of any Federal criminal case brought as a result of such crime, including the views of the victim or family about * * * dismissal [or referral to a] pretrial diversion program." Section 6(a)(5) of the Act, in note to 18 U.S.C. § 1512. The Act requires the Justice Department to develop guidelines on "consultation with the victim," and these guidelines require consultation also with respect to "the decision not to seek an indictment or otherwise commence prosecution." Some states have similar legislation.

One commentator concludes: "Congress and the victims' movement must not expect too much. In the end, the victim's views, even when he appears personally, will be only one element in a wide variety of interests which prosecutor and judge—each in his respective sphere—must take into account. The distinctive thing about the victim is that he (like the defendant) is strategically located and motivated to watch closely how the law is being applied in a particular case—and to call attention to inaccuracy, illegality, and inequality in the administration of criminal justice."[k]

Should the prosecutor's dismissal or diversion decision be subject to challenge by the victim because of the prosecutor's failure to engage in the consultation required by statute? And in any event, if the prosecutor decides not to prosecute contrary to the victim's expressed wishes, should the victim be able to "challenge" that decision? If so, in what forum and with what possible remedy? Consider Note, 97 Yale L.J. 488, 489 (1988), which "proposes a model statute that would allow a private person who is the victim of an alleged criminal act to * * * challenge [such a decision]. The statute would authorize a court, upon an appropriate finding, to issue a declaratory judgment that a prosecutor has abused his discretion not to prosecute. While this judgment would not require that a prosecution be com-

---

j. Under the traditional view, the double jeopardy clause bars retrial after such an acquittal, *Fong Foo v. United States,* 369 U.S. 141, 82 S.Ct. 671, 7 L.Ed.2d 629 (1962), but if the judge acknowledged he was acting on policy grounds it might be claimed there is no acquittal unless "the ruling of the judge, whatever its label, actually represents a resolution, correct or not, of some or all of the factual elements of the offense charged." *United States v. Martin Linen Supply,* p. 1475.

k. Abraham S. Goldstein, *The Victim and Prosecutorial Discretion: The Federal Victim and Witness Protection Act of 1982,* 47 Law & Contemp.Prob. 225, 247 (1984). See also Sarah N. Welling, *Victims in the Criminal Process: A Utilitarian Analysis of the Victim's Participation in the Charging Decision,* 30 Ariz. L.Rev. 85 (1988).

menced, it could be expected to create public pressure on the prosecutor, giving the plaintiff political leverage that he might not otherwise have. In addition, the statutory procedure would allow for a public airing of grievances and serve as a device for 'signalling' executive abuse of discretion."

5. What decision would you, as prosecuting attorney, reach in the following cases? What additional facts, if any, would you desire in each case prior to making a decision?

(a) A man lured several 14–year-old boys to a mountain cabin, bound them up, and sexually molested them. One of the lads managed to free himself and the others, found a rifle in the cabin, and then shot and killed their abductor upon his later return to the cabin. The juvenile court law of the state gives the criminal courts exclusive jurisdiction over juveniles when they are charged with murder. The law of self-defense in the jurisdiction only permits the use of deadly force "to prevent imminent death or great bodily harm to himself or another," which was not the case here. See Joseph Sax, *Civil Disobedience,* Saturday Review, Sept. 28, 1968, p. 22.

(b) A woman returned home from work a few hours late in a disheveled condition and told her husband that she had been kidnapped and raped. The husband called the police, and on the basis of the information given by the woman two suspects were arrested the next day. Upon questioning the woman in more detail the following day, the police discovered some discrepancies in her story, and she finally admitted that she was carrying on an affair with a man and that she had fabricated the story in order to explain her absence to her husband. Filing a false felony report is a criminal offense punishable by a fine of up to $500 and imprisonment up to six months. See Wayne R. LaFave, *Arrest: The Decision to Take a Suspect Into Custody* 140 (Frank J. Remington ed. 1965).

(c) A woman called police to her residence because of a domestic dispute. When the police arrived, they saw that she had swelling on her face and arms. After she told police she had dialed 911 because her boyfriend had beaten her, the officers arrested him. Two weeks later, the woman met with the prosecutor and said that, despite the fact she had suffered abuse throughout the relationship, she did not want to proceed with the case. "I have AIDS," she said, "and I'm sure that the stress of my illness caused him to beat me." She added that she did not want her family to discover that she had AIDS, and that she and her boyfriend were now "working things out." See Cheryl Hanna, supra note h, at 1873–74.

(d) A man called the prosecutor's office to ask that his next door neighbor be prosecuted for tearing down part of his fence, which ran between their properties. Investigation disclosed that the offense of criminal damage to property had in fact occurred, but also that this was merely the latest incident in a longstanding feud between the two men concerning the boundaries of their respective properties. See Wayne R. LaFave, supra, at 119.

(e) A man lawfully arrested concerning another matter, as to which he was subsequently cleared, was found to have a small amount of heroin in his apartment. At the suggestion of his counsel, he was permitted to take a lie detector test, which indicated that he was unaware that the heroin was there. The test also indicated that the man was not telling the truth when he denied being involved in the narcotics traffic. See John Kaplan, *The Prosecutorial Discretion—A Comment,* 60 Nw.U.L.Rev. 174, 179 (1965).

(f) A landlord was owed a debt of $240 by his former tenant, who had moved out of the city without paying his rent. The landlord, upon seeing a tax refund check arrive at his tenant's former address, signed his debtor's name to the check (for $180) and cashed the check. This is a violation of the federal statute on forgery of government obligations, 18 U.S.C. § 471, punishable by a fine of up to $5,000 and imprisonment up to fifteen years. See John Kaplan, supra, at 188–89.

(g) An applicant for temporary employment as a mail carrier during the Christmas season completed a government employment application form in which he falsely denied ever having been arrested. A subsequent investigation disclosed that he had a record of several arrests for such offenses as drunkenness and vagrancy. This, however, did not become known until the man had been hired and had completed his temporary service for the post office department. His false statements were in violation of 18 U.S.C. § 1001, and are punishable by a fine of not more than $10,000 and imprisonment for five years. See John Kaplan, supra, at 189–90.

SECTION 3. CHALLENGING THE PROSECUTOR'S DISCRETION

I. THE DECISION NOT TO PROSECUTE

In INMATES OF ATTICA CORRECTIONAL FACILITY v. ROCKEFELLER, 477 F.2d 375 (2d Cir.1973), the inmates and others brought a class action seeking to require federal and state officials to investigate and prosecute persons who allegedly had violated certain federal and state criminal statutes in connection with treatment of inmates during and following the Attica prison uprising. The district court dismissed the complaint, and the court of appeals, per MANSFIELD, J., affirmed:

"With respect to the defendant United States Attorney, plaintiffs seek mandamus to compel him to investigate and institute prosecutions against state officers, most of whom are not identified, for alleged violations of 18 U.S.C. §§ 241 and 242. Federal mandamus is, of course, available only 'to compel an officer or employee of the United States * * * to perform a duty owed to the plaintiff.' 28 U.S.C. § 1361. And the legislative history of § 1361 makes it clear that ordinarily the courts are 'not to direct or influence the exercise of discretion of the officer or agency in the making of the decision.' More particularly, federal courts have traditionally and, to our knowledge, uniformly refrained from overturning, at the instance of a private person, discretionary decisions of federal prosecuting authorities not to prosecute persons regarding whom a complaint of criminal conduct is made.

"This judicial reluctance to direct federal prosecutions at the instance of a private party asserting the failure of United States officials to prosecute alleged criminal violations has been applied even in cases such as the present one where, according to the allegations of the complaint, which we must accept as true for purposes of this appeal, serious questions are raised as to the protection of the civil rights and physical security of a definable class of victims of crime and as to the fair administration of the criminal justice system.

"The primary ground upon which this traditional judicial aversion to compelling prosecutions has been based is the separation of powers doctrine. * * *

"In the absence of statutorily defined standards governing reviewability, or regulatory or statutory policies of prosecution, the problems inherent in the task of supervising prosecutorial decisions do not lend themselves to resolution by the judiciary. The reviewing courts would be placed in the undesirable and injudicious posture of becoming 'superprosecutors.' In the normal case of review of executive acts of discretion, the administrative record is open, public and reviewable on the basis of what it contains. The decision not to prosecute, on the other hand, may be based upon the insufficiency of the available evidence, in which event the secrecy of the grand jury and of the prosecutor's file may serve to protect the accused's reputation from public damage based upon insufficient, improper, or even malicious charges. *In camera* review would not be meaningful without access by the complaining party to the evidence before the grand jury or U.S. Attorney. Such interference with the normal operations of criminal investigations, in turn, based solely upon allegations of criminal conduct, raises serious questions of potential abuse by persons seeking to have other persons prosecuted. Any person, merely by filing a complaint containing allegations in general terms (permitted by the Federal Rules) of unlawful failure to prosecute, could gain access to the prosecutor's file and the grand jury's minutes, notwithstanding the secrecy normally attaching to the latter by law. See Rule 6(e), F.R.Cr.P.

"Nor is it clear what the judiciary's role of supervision should be were it to undertake such a review. At what point would the prosecutor be entitled to call a halt to further investigation as unlikely to be productive? What evidentiary standard would be used to decide whether prosecution should be compelled? How much judgment would the United States Attorney be allowed? Would he be permitted to limit himself to a strong 'test' case rather than pursue weaker cases? What collateral factors would be permissible bases for a decision not to prosecute, e.g., the pendency of another criminal proceeding elsewhere against the same parties? What sort of review should be available in cases like the present one where the conduct complained of allegedly violates state as well as federal laws? With limited personnel and facilities at his disposal, what priority would the prosecutor be required to give to cases in which investigation or prosecution was directed by the court?

"These difficult questions engender serious doubts as to the judiciary's capacity to review and as to the problem of arbitrariness inherent in any judicial decision to order prosecution. On balance, we believe that substitution of a court's decision to compel prosecution for the U.S. Attorney's decision not to prosecute, even upon an abuse of discretion standard of review and even if limited to directing that a prosecution be undertaken in good faith, would be unwise.

"Plaintiffs urge, however, that Congress withdrew the normal prosecutorial discretion for the kind of conduct alleged here by providing in 42 U.S.C. § 1987 that the United States Attorneys are 'authorized *and required* * * * to institute prosecutions against all persons violating any of the provisions of [18 U.S.C. §§ 241, 242]' (emphasis supplied), and, therefore, that no barrier to a judicial directive to institute prosecutions remains. This contention must be rejected. The mandatory nature of the word 'required' as it appears in § 1987 is insufficient to evince a broad Congressional purpose to bar the exercise of executive discretion in the prosecution of federal civil rights crimes. * * *

"Such language has never been thought to preclude the exercise of prosecutorial discretion. Indeed the same contention made here was specifically rejected in *Moses v. Kennedy,* 219 F.Supp. 762, 765 (D.D.C.1963), aff'd 342 F.2d 931 (1965), where seven black residents and one white resident of Mississippi sought mandamus to compel the Attorney General of the United States and the Director of the F.B.I. to investigate, arrest, and prosecute certain individuals, including state and local law enforcement officers, for willfully depriving the plaintiffs of their civil rights. There the Court noted that 'considerations of judgment and discretion apply with special strength to the area of civil rights, where the Executive Department must be largely free to exercise its considered judgment on questions of whether to proceed by means of prosecution, injunction, varying forms of persuasion, or other types of action.' * * *

"With respect to the state defendants, plaintiffs also seek prosecution of named and unknown persons for the violation of state crimes. However, they have pointed to no statutory language even arguably creating any mandatory duty upon the state officials to bring such prosecutions. To the contrary, New York law reposes in its prosecutors a discretion to decide whether or not to prosecute in a given case, which is not subject to review in the state courts."[a]

UNITED STATES v. COX, 342 F.2d 167 (5th Cir.1965), concerned the refusal of a United States Attorney, upon instructions from the Acting Attorney General, to prepare or sign indictments for a federal grand jury in the Southern District of Mississippi charging with perjury two Negroes who had testified in a civil rights action brought by the United States against a county voting registrar. A federal judge held the United States Attorney in contempt and also ordered that the Acting Attorney General show cause why he should not also be adjudged guilty of contempt. Three members of the court took the view that the United States Attorney was not obligated to either prepare or sign the indictments, three others that he was obligated to do both, and the seventh (who determined the majority) that he must prepare but need not sign the indictments.

Judge JONES, in the first group, wrote: "The role of the grand jury is restricted to a finding as to whether or not there is probable cause to believe that an offense has been committed. The discretionary power of the attorney for the United States in determining whether a prosecution shall be commenced or maintained may well depend upon matters of policy wholly apart from any question of probable cause. Although as a member of the bar, the attorney for the United States is an officer of the court, he is nevertheless an executive official of the Government, and it is as an officer of the executive department that he exercises a discretion as to whether or not there shall be a prosecution in a particular case. It follows, as an incident of the constitutional separation of powers, that the courts are not to interfere with the free exercise of the discretionary powers of the attorneys of the United States in their control over criminal prosecutions. The provision of Rule 7, requiring the signing of the indictment by the attorney for the Government, is a recognition of the power of Government counsel to permit or not to permit the bringing of an indictment. * * * [S]ince the United States Attorney cannot be required to give validity to an indictment by affixing his signature, he should not be required to indulge in an exercise of futility by the preparation of the form of an indictment which he is unwilling to vitalize with his signature."

Judges RIVES, Gewin and Bell explained their vote to compel the United States Attorney to both prepare and sign the indictments in this way:

"The grand jury may be permitted to function in its traditional sphere, while at the same time enforcing the separation of powers doctrine as between the executive and judicial branches of the government. This can best be done, indeed, it is mandatory, by requiring the United States Attorney to assist the grand jury

---

a. Many comparable decisions are to be found concerning the discretion of state prosecutors. See, e.g., *Manning v. Municipal Court,* 361 N.E.2d 1274 (Mass.1977) (spectator at Fenway Park, allegedly struck by baseball thrown from visiting team's bullpen by Ross Grimsley, cannot compel prosecutor to undertake assault and battery prosecution).

Compare *State ex rel. Ginsberg v. Naum,* 318 S.E.2d 454 (W.Va.1984) (court grants mandamus, on petition of Dep't of Human Services, for prosecution of welfare fraud cases; court relies on statute declaring it to be duty of every prosecutor "when he has information of the violation *of any penal law* committed within such county" to "institute and prosecute all necessary and proper proceedings against the offender," which makes it a prosecutor's non-discretionary duty to institute proceedings against persons when he has information giving him probable cause to believe that *any* penal law has been violated, "even if the prosecutor has insufficient manpower").

in preparing indictments which they wish to consider or return, and by requiring the United States Attorney to sign any indictment that is to be returned. Then, once the indictment is returned, the Attorney General or the United States Attorney can refuse to go forward. That refusal will, of course, be in open court and not in the secret confines of the grand jury room. To permit the district court to compel the United States Attorney to proceed beyond this point would invest prosecutorial power in the judiciary, power which under the Constitution is reserved to the executive branch of the government. It may be that the court, in the interest of justice, may require a showing of good faith, and a statement of some rational basis for dismissal. In the unlikely event of bad faith or irrational action, not here present, it may be that the court could appoint counsel to prosecute the case. In brief, the court may have the same inherent power to administer justice to the government as it does to the defendant. That question is not now before us and may never arise. Except for a very limited discretion, however, the court's power to withhold leave to dismiss an indictment is solely for the protection of the defendant."

Judge BROWN noted that his conclusion that the United States Attorney must prepare but need not sign the indictments "lacks logical consistency," but thought there were sound reasons for both positions. Since the signature of the federal prosecutor, together with that of the jury's foreman, "is a formal, effective initiation of a prosecution," so that "what was previously an unfettered discretionary right on the part of the executive not to initiate prosecution has now been set in motion and can be stopped only on the executive taking affirmative action for dismissal with all of the uncertainties which F.R.Crim.P. 48(a) generates," the signature should not be required. However, he concluded, the grand jury should be entitled to the legal assistance of the U.S. Attorney in the preparation of the indictment so that the document, as drafted, "would clearly reflect the conscientious conclusion of the Grand Jury itself" and "reveal the difference of view as between the Grand Jury and the prosecuting attorney."

Notes and Questions

1. *The court as a check on the prosecutor's decision not to prosecute.* Although all jurisdictions recognize that the prosecutor has a substantial range of discretion in deciding whether or not to prosecute, many have placed some controls on his discretion after initial steps toward prosecution have been taken. There is a split of authority, for example, on the question whether a prosecutor may nol pros (from the Latin phrase *nolle prosequi*—an entry on the record by the prosecutor declaring that he will not prosecute) after the magistrate has sent the case to the grand jury but before the grand jury has had an opportunity to make a formal accusation. When the law permits the prosecutor to forego indictment and prosecute by information (a formal charge prepared by the prosecutor), almost all jurisdictions permit the prosecutor to nol pros after the preliminary hearing and before an information has been filed, although some states require that he file a statement of his reasons with the court. After formal accusation by indictment or information, a few states still recognize the power which the prosecutor possessed in the common law to nol pros on his own. Some other states, however, have now placed this authority entirely within the discretion of the court, while others require the court's approval for entry of a nol pros.[b] Which system is preferable?

b. But in these jurisdictions it is sometimes held that the uncontrolled power of the prosecutor revives following return of the verdict and continues until judgment is entered and sentence is imposed. Compare *State ex rel. Norwood v. Drumm,* 691 S.W.2d 238 (Mo.1985), requiring court approval on the ground the court should take into account the fact that "the verdict rendered reveals that the jury, after hearing the evidence, found it sufficient to support the charge the prosecutor now seeks to dismiss."

In *State ex rel. Unnamed Petitioners v. Connors,* 401 N.W.2d 782 (Wis.1987), two professional football players allegedly assaulted a female dancer in a dressing room of a Milwaukee night club. The prosecutor, after investigation, decided not to issue a criminal complaint, "not on the basis of a lack of probable cause but upon his perceived inability to prove guilt [beyond a reasonable doubt] at trial." Upon petition of the dancer the matter was then assigned to a circuit judge, and she directed that proceedings be commenced under a statute reading: "If a district attorney refuses or is unavailable to issue a complaint, a circuit judge may permit the filing of a complaint, if the judge finds there is probable cause to believe that the person to be charged has committed an offense after conducting a hearing." The football players then sought a writ of prohibition. In holding that the statute "violates the separation-of-powers principle of the Wisconsin Constitution that prohibits a substantial encroachment by one branch on a function that is within the delegated province of another branch," the court distinguished its holding in an earlier case that judicial approval is required for dismissal of a charge already filed:

"The right of a court to refuse to accept prosecutorial discretion as the final word where a case has commenced is vastly different from a situation where no crime has been charged. It is obviously factually different. In addition, it is jurisprudentially different. A prosecutor who dismisses an already initiated claim is free to reprosecute it later. To allow on-again, off-again prosecutions that cease before a defendant has been subjected to jeopardy would be to permit the court system to be used for harassment and would expose a defendant to some of the hazards of attachment of jeopardy, i.e., damage to reputation, expense, and threat of criminal sanctions, without the protection that the constitutional prohibition against double jeopardy affords. In addition, the 'public interest' and that of third parties is implicated by a pending prosecution—a situation not present where a prosecution has not been commenced."

If court approval is required for dismissal of a charge, as in Fed.R.Crim.P. 48(a), what standard should the court apply in assessing the prosecutor's request? See *United States v. Welborn,* 849 F.2d 980 (5th Cir.1988), holding that a district court may deny an uncontested request only "in extremely limited circumstances in extraordinary cases * * * when the prosecutor's actions clearly indicate a 'betrayal of the public interest.'"

2. *The grand jury as a check.* Most jurisdictions permit the grand jury to initiate prosecution by indictment even though the prosecutor opposes prosecution. Some require only that the foreman, acting on behalf of the grand jury, sign the indictment. Others have provisions similar to Rule 7 requiring the prosecutor's signature; some of them take the *Cox* position, while others hold the view that the signature requirement mandates essentially a "clerical act" by the prosecutor. It takes a most unusual case, however, for a grand jury to act as a "runaway" and indict notwithstanding the prosecutor's opposition. See pp. 653, 659–61, 935–39.

3. *The state attorney general as a check.* At common law, the attorney general exercised wide powers of supervision over all criminal prosecutions, and in states in which he retains these powers he may initiate and prosecute criminal cases and may, at his discretion, supersede and replace the local prosecutor. Also, many states by statute confer upon the attorney general the power to initiate prosecution in cases where the local prosecutor has failed to act. In practice, however, attorneys general have seldom exercised much control over local prosecuting attorneys.

Consider *Johnson v. Pataki*, 655 N.Y.S.2d 463, aff'd 691 N.E.2d 1002 (N.Y. 1997). Upon adoption by the legislature of new death penalty legislation which included a provision that a death sentence could not be given unless the prosecutor elected before trial to seek it, one prosecutor issued a public statement of his "present intention not to utilized the death penalty provision" and instead to seek life imprisonment terms in homicide cases. This prosecutor later did not seek the death penalty against a defendant who had killed five people. Still later, another person was charged in that county with murder of a police officer, at which point the governor directed the Attorney General to assume control of that prosecution. The prosecutor and county taxpayers then unsuccessfully sought to challenge the governor's order. On appeal, the court held: "In furtherance of his Constitutional mandate to see that the laws of New York are faithfully executed, the Governor's apparent objective was to assure that those laws are being applied in a uniform fashion throughout the State's 62 counties. The wide discretionary authority that any district attorney does retain in executing the heavy responsibilities of his office must be held subservient to that overriding interest. The Governor had the power to determine the scope of this prosecution, before what he perceived to be the legislative will could be locally frustrated. Within Constitutional limits, the exercise of discretionary authority by the chief executive of the State in enforcing statutes is not subject to judicial review."

4. *Private prosecution when the prosecutor does not act.* Noting that some foreign jurisdictions permit private criminal prosecution when the public prosecutor fails to act, Comment, 65 Yale L.J. 209, 233 (1955), recommends that state legislatures enact statutes providing: "A trial court may in its discretion, upon petition of any person, substitute an attorney hired by the petitioner to replace a public prosecutor for any criminal prosecution if (a) the public prosecutor fails or refuses to prosecute the defendant or proceeds improperly, and (b) the crime charged is open and notorious or the petitioner has a cause of action against the defendant in tort on the facts alleged."

Compare *People v. Municipal Court*, 103 Cal.Rptr. 645 (App.1972), holding that an individual cannot institute criminal proceedings without the prosecutor's approval because: (1) for a court to accept such a complaint is in violation of the separation of powers provision of the state constitution, as it "encroaches upon the executive power"; and (2) the due process clauses of the United States and state constitutions prohibit it, as "all persons should be protected from having to defend against frivolous prosecutions and * * * one major safeguard against such prosecutions is the function of the district attorney in screening criminal cases prior to instituting a prosecution."[c]

5. *Substitution of special prosecutor.* "There appear to be three areas where the need for the services of a special prosecutor arises: 1. Conflict: The prosecuting attorney is legally precluded from proceeding due to a conflict of interest; 2. Complexity: The prosecutor is faced with a difficult case beyond his investigative and legal abilities; 3. Public trust: There is corruption within the judicial/governmental system, and public confidence requires an 'uninvolved' outsider to investigate and prosecute." Lawrence Taylor, *A Needed Legal Specialty: The Special Prosecutor,* 61 Judicature 220, 221 (1977).

c. Private prosecution must be distinguished from the practice, permitted in several states, of having private counsel retained by the victim assist the prosecutor in a criminal trial. See Comment, 25 Am.U.L.Rev. 754, 755 (1976), asserting "that the practice is outdated, unnecessary, unethical, and perhaps unconstitutional"; *State v. Berg*, 694 P.2d 427 (Kan.1985) (notwithstanding statute allowing prosecution witness to provide at own expense attorney to assist the prosecutor, that private attorney may not prosecute over wishes of prosecutor; "the person representing the state in a criminal proceeding must be a law-trained, independent public prosecutor rather than a vengeful persecutor").

In *Venhaus v. Brown,* 691 S.W.2d 141 (Ark.1985), the trial court appointed a special prosecutor because the prosecutor had failed to charge an attorney with complicity in the murder of the attorney's wife notwithstanding statements by the sheriff that he had evidence sufficient for conviction. The sheriff asserted that the prosecutor was giving favorable treatment to another lawyer, while the prosecutor asserted he failed to file charges because he believed the attorney was innocent. The appointment was held invalid as an improper interference with the prosecutor's discretion.

In *Morrison v. Olson,* 487 U.S. 654, 108 S.Ct. 2597, 101 L.Ed.2d 569 (1988), the Court upheld, 7–1, a federal statute (which lapsed in 1999) requiring the Attorney General to conduct a preliminary investigation of allegations that enumerated high-ranking federal officials have committed a crime and, unless the allegations prove insubstantial, to ask a special three-judge panel to appoint an "independent counsel" to complete the investigation and conduct any prosecutions. The Court, per Rehnquist, C.J., held that the Act did not violate the separation of powers doctrine, reasoning that while "the Act reduces the amount of control or supervision that the Attorney General and, through him, the President exercises over the investigation and prosecution of a certain class of alleged criminal activity," it "does give the Attorney General several means of supervising or controlling the prosecutorial powers that may be wielded by an independent counsel," most importantly the power to remove for "good cause."

II. THE DECISION TO PROSECUTE

UNITED STATES v. ARMSTRONG
517 U.S. 456, 116 S.Ct. 1480, 134 L.Ed.2d 687 (1996).

Chief Justice REHNQUIST delivered the opinion of the Court. * * *

In April 1992, respondents were indicted in the United States District Court for the Central District of California on charges of conspiring to possess with intent to distribute more than 50 grams of cocaine base (crack) and conspiring to distribute the same, in violation of 21 U.S.C. §§ 841 and 846, and federal firearms offenses. For three months prior to the indictment, agents of the Federal Bureau of Alcohol, Tobacco, and Firearms and the Narcotics Division of the Inglewood, California, Police Department had infiltrated a suspected crack distribution ring by using three confidential informants. On seven separate occasions during this period, the informants had bought a total of 124.3 grams of crack from respondents and witnessed respondents carrying firearms during the sales. The agents searched the hotel room in which the sales were transacted, arrested respondents Armstrong and Hampton in the room, and found more crack and a loaded gun. The agents later arrested the other respondents as part of the ring.

In response to the indictment, respondents filed a motion for discovery or for dismissal of the indictment, alleging that they were selected for federal prosecution because they are black. In support of their motion, they offered only an affidavit by a "Paralegal Specialist," employed by the Office of the Federal Public Defender representing one of the respondents. The only allegation in the affidavit was that, in every one of the 24 §§ 841 or 846 cases closed by the office during 1991, the defendant was black. Accompanying the affidavit was a "study" listing the 24 defendants, their race, whether they were prosecuted for dealing cocaine as well as crack, and the status of each case.

The Government opposed the discovery motion, arguing, among other things, that there was no evidence or allegation "that the Government has acted unfairly or has prosecuted non-black defendants or failed to prosecute them." The District

Court granted the motion. It ordered the Government (1) to provide a list of all cases from the last three years in which the Government charged both cocaine and firearms offenses, (2) to identify the race of the defendants in those cases, (3) to identify what levels of law enforcement were involved in the investigations of those cases, and (4) to explain its criteria for deciding to prosecute those defendants for federal cocaine offenses.

The Government moved for reconsideration of the District Court's discovery order. With this motion it submitted affidavits and other evidence to explain why it had chosen to prosecute respondents and why respondents' study did not support the inference that the Government was singling out blacks for cocaine prosecution. The federal and local agents participating in the case alleged in affidavits that race played no role in their investigation. An Assistant United States Attorney explained in an affidavit that the decision to prosecute met the general criteria for prosecution, because "there was over 100 grams of cocaine base involved, over twice the threshold necessary for a ten year mandatory minimum sentence; there were multiple sales involving multiple defendants, thereby indicating a fairly substantial crack cocaine ring; . . . there were multiple federal firearms violations intertwined with the narcotics trafficking; the overall evidence in the case was extremely strong, including audio and videotapes of defendants; . . . and several of the defendants had criminal histories including narcotics and firearms violations." The Government also submitted sections of a published 1989 Drug Enforcement Administration report which concluded that "[l]arge-scale, interstate trafficking networks controlled by Jamaicans, Haitians and Black street gangs dominate the manufacture and distribution of crack."

In response, one of respondents' attorneys submitted an affidavit alleging that an intake coordinator at a drug treatment center had told her that there are "an equal number of caucasian users and dealers to minority users and dealers." Respondents also submitted an affidavit from a criminal defense attorney alleging that in his experience many nonblacks are prosecuted in state court for crack offenses, and a newspaper article reporting that Federal "crack criminals . . . are being punished far more severely than if they had been caught with powder cocaine, and almost every single one of them is black."

The District Court denied the motion for reconsideration. When the Government indicated it would not comply with the court's discovery order, the court dismissed the case.[2]

A divided three-judge panel of the Court of Appeals for the Ninth Circuit reversed, holding that, because of the proof requirements for a selective-prosecution claim, defendants must "provide a colorable basis for believing that 'others similarly situated have not been prosecuted'" to obtain discovery. The Court of Appeals voted to rehear the case en banc, and the en banc panel affirmed the District Court's order of dismissal, holding that "a defendant is not required to demonstrate that the government has failed to prosecute others who are similarly situated." We granted certiorari to determine the appropriate standard for discovery for a selective-prosecution claim. * * *[a]

2. We have never determined whether dismissal of the indictment, or some other sanction, is the proper remedy if a court determines that a defendant has been the victim of prosecution on the basis of his race. Here, "it was the government itself that suggested dismissal of the indictments to the district court so that an appeal might lie."

a. In an omitted portion of the opinion the Court considered the respondents' claim they

were entitled to discovery under Fed.R.Crim.P. 16(a)(1)(C). The Court concluded "that in the context of Rule 16 'the defendant's defense' means the defendant's response to the Government's case-in-chief." In support, two reasons were given: (1) "If 'defense' means an argument in response to the prosecution's case-in-chief, there is a perceptible symmetry between documents 'material to the preparation of the defendant's defense,' and, in the very next

A selective-prosecution claim is not a defense on the merits to the criminal charge itself, but an independent assertion that the prosecutor has brought the charge for reasons forbidden by the Constitution. Our cases delineating the necessary elements to prove a claim of selective prosecution have taken great pains to explain that the standard is a demanding one. These cases afford a "background presumption" that the showing necessary to obtain discovery should itself be a significant barrier to the litigation of insubstantial claims.

A selective-prosecution claim asks a court to exercise judicial power over a "special province" of the Executive. The Attorney General and United States Attorneys retain " 'broad discretion' " to enforce the Nation's criminal laws. They have this latitude because they are designated by statute as the President's delegates to help him discharge his constitutional responsibility to "take Care that the Laws be faithfully executed." U.S. Const., Art. II, § 3. As a result, "[t]he presumption of regularity supports" their prosecutorial decisions and "in the absence of clear evidence to the contrary, courts presume that they have properly discharged their official duties." In the ordinary case, "so long as the prosecutor has probable cause to believe that the accused committed an offense defined by statute, the decision whether or not to prosecute, and what charge to file or bring before a grand jury, generally rests entirely in his discretion."

Of course, a prosecutor's discretion is "subject to constitutional constraints." One of these constraints, imposed by the equal protection component of the Due Process Clause of the Fifth Amendment, is that the decision whether to prosecute may not be based on "an unjustifiable standard such as race, religion, or other arbitrary classification," *Oyler v. Boles*, 368 U.S. 448, 82 S.Ct. 501, 7 L.Ed.2d 446 (1962). A defendant may demonstrate that the administration of a criminal law is "directed so exclusively against a particular class of persons ... with a mind so unequal and oppressive" that the system of prosecution amounts to "a practical denial" of equal protection of the law. *Yick Wo v. Hopkins*, 118 U.S. 356, 6 S.Ct. 1064, 30 L.Ed. 220 (1886).

In order to dispel the presumption that a prosecutor has not violated equal protection, a criminal defendant must present "clear evidence to the contrary." We explained in *Wayte* [*v. United States*, 470 U.S. 598, 105 S.Ct. 1524, 84 L.Ed.2d 547 (1985)], why courts are "properly hesitant to examine the decision whether to prosecute." Judicial deference to the decisions of these executive officers rests in part on an assessment of the relative competence of prosecutors and courts. "Such factors as the strength of the case, the prosecution's general deterrence value, the Government's enforcement priorities, and the case's relationship to the Government's overall enforcement plan are not readily susceptible to the kind of analysis the courts are competent to undertake." It also stems from a concern not to unnecessarily impair the performance of a core executive constitutional function.

phrase, documents 'intended for use by the government as evidence in chief at the trial.' " (2) "Rule 16(a)(2), as relevant here, exempts from defense inspection 'reports, memoranda, or other internal government documents made by the attorney for the government or other government agents in connection with the investigation or prosecution of the case.' * * * Because respondents construction of 'defense' creates the anomaly of a defendant's being able to examine all Government work product except the most pertinent, we find their construction implausible."

Justice Souter, concurring, joined the Court's discussion of Rule 16 "only to the extent of its application to the issue in this case." Justice Ginsburg, concurring, emphasized that the "Court was not called upon to decide here whether Rule 16(a)(1)(C) applies in any other context, for example, to affirmative defenses unrelated to the merits." Justice Breyer, concurring in part and concurring in the judgment, though concluding that "neither the alleged 'symmetry' in the structure of Rule 16(a)(1)(C), nor the work product exception of Rule 16(a)(2), supports the majority's limitation of discovery under Rule 16(a)(1)(C) to documents related to the government's 'case-in-chief,' " concluded that the defendants' discovery request failed to satisfy the Rule's requirement that the discovery be "material to the preparation of the defendant's defense."

"Examining the basis of a prosecution delays the criminal proceeding, threatens to chill law enforcement by subjecting the prosecutor's motives and decisionmaking to outside inquiry, and may undermine prosecutorial effectiveness by revealing the Government's enforcement policy."

The requirements for a selective-prosecution claim draw on "ordinary equal protection standards." The claimant must demonstrate that the federal prosecutorial policy "had a discriminatory effect and that it was motivated by a discriminatory purpose." To establish a discriminatory effect in a race case, the claimant must show that similarly situated individuals of a different race were not prosecuted. This requirement has been established in our case law since *Ah Sin v. Wittman*, 198 U.S. 500, 25 S.Ct. 756, 49 L.Ed. 1142 (1905). Ah Sin, a subject of China, petitioned a California state court for a writ of habeas corpus, seeking discharge from imprisonment under a San Francisco county ordinance prohibiting persons from setting up gambling tables in rooms barricaded to stop police from entering. He alleged in his habeas petition "that the ordinance is enforced 'solely and exclusively against persons of the Chinese race and not otherwise.' " We rejected his contention that this averment made out a claim under the Equal Protection Clause, because it did not allege "that the conditions and practices to which the ordinance was directed did not exist exclusively among the Chinese, or that there were other offenders against the ordinance than the Chinese as to whom it was not enforced."

The similarly situated requirement does not make a selective-prosecution claim impossible to prove. Twenty years before *Ah Sin*, we invalidated an ordinance, also adopted by San Francisco, that prohibited the operation of laundries in wooden buildings. *Yick Wo*, supra. The plaintiff in error successfully demonstrated that the ordinance was applied against Chinese nationals but not against other laundry-shop operators. The authorities had denied the applications of 200 Chinese subjects for permits to operate shops in wooden buildings, but granted the applications of 80 individuals who were not Chinese subjects to operate laundries in wooden buildings "under similar conditions." We explained in *Ah Sin* why the similarly situated requirement is necessary: "No latitude of intention should be indulged in a case like this. There should be certainty to every intent. Plaintiff in error seeks to set aside a criminal law of the State, not on the ground that it is unconstitutional on its face, not that it is discriminatory in tendency and ultimate actual operation as the ordinance was which was passed on in the *Yick Wo* case, but that it was made so by the manner of its administration. This is a matter of proof, and no fact should be omitted to make it out completely, when the power of a Federal court is invoked to interfere with the course of criminal justice of a State." Although *Ah Sin* involved federal review of a state conviction, we think a similar rule applies where the power of a federal court is invoked to challenge an exercise of one of the core powers of the Executive Branch of the Federal Government, the power to prosecute. * * *

Having reviewed the requirements to prove a selective-prosecution claim, we turn to the showing necessary to obtain discovery in support of such a claim. If discovery is ordered, the Government must assemble from its own files documents which might corroborate or refute the defendant's claim. Discovery thus imposes many of the costs present when the Government must respond to a prima facie case of selective prosecution. It will divert prosecutors' resources and may disclose the Government's prosecutorial strategy. The justifications for a rigorous standard for the elements of a selective-prosecution claim thus require a correspondingly rigorous standard for discovery in aid of such a claim.

The parties, and the Courts of Appeals which have considered the requisite showing to establish entitlement to discovery, describe this showing with a variety of phrases, like "colorable basis," "substantial threshold showing," "substantial and concrete basis," or "reasonable likelihood." However, the many labels for this showing conceal the degree of consensus about the evidence necessary to meet it. The Courts of Appeals "require some evidence tending to show the existence of the essential elements of the defense," discriminatory effect and discriminatory intent.

In this case we consider what evidence constitutes "some evidence tending to show the existence" of the discriminatory effect element. The Court of Appeals held that a defendant may establish a colorable basis for discriminatory effect without evidence that the Government has failed to prosecute others who are similarly situated to the defendant. We think it was mistaken in this view. The vast majority of the Courts of Appeals require the defendant to produce some evidence that similarly situated defendants of other races could have been prosecuted, but were not, and this requirement is consistent with our equal protection case law. * * *[3]

The Court of Appeals reached its decision in part because it started "with the presumption that people of all races commit all types of crimes—not with the premise that any type of crime is the exclusive province of any particular racial or ethnic group." It cited no authority for this proposition, which seems contradicted by the most recent statistics of the United States Sentencing Commission. Those statistics show that: More than 90% of the persons sentenced in 1994 for crack cocaine trafficking were black; 93.4% of convicted LSD dealers were white; and 91% of those convicted for pornography or prostitution were white. Presumptions at war with presumably reliable statistics have no proper place in the analysis of this issue.

The Court of Appeals also expressed concern about the "evidentiary obstacles defendants face." But all of its sister Circuits that have confronted the issue have required that defendants produce some evidence of differential treatment of similarly situated members of other races or protected classes. In the present case, if the claim of selective prosecution were well founded, it should not have been an insuperable task to prove that persons of other races were being treated differently than respondents. For instance, respondents could have investigated whether similarly situated persons of other races were prosecuted by the State of California, were known to federal law enforcement officers, but were not prosecuted in federal court. We think the required threshold—a credible showing of different treatment of similarly situated persons—adequately balances the Government's interest in vigorous prosecution and the defendant's interest in avoiding selective prosecution.

In the case before us, respondents' "study" did not constitute "some evidence tending to show the existence of the essential elements of" a selective-prosecution claim. The study failed to identify individuals who were not black, could have been prosecuted for the offenses for which respondents were charged, but were not so prosecuted. This omission was not remedied by respondents' evidence in opposition to the Government's motion for reconsideration. The newspaper article, which discussed the discriminatory effect of federal drug sentencing laws, was not relevant to an allegation of discrimination in decisions to prosecute. Respondents' affidavits, which recounted one attorney's conversation with a drug treatment center employee and the experience of another attorney defending drug prosecutions in state court, recounted hearsay and reported personal conclusions based on anecdotal evidence. The judgment of the Court of Appeals is therefore reversed, and the case is remanded for proceedings consistent with this opinion.

3. We reserve the question whether a defendant must satisfy the similarly situated requirement in a case "involving direct admissions by [prosecutors] of discriminatory purpose."

It is so ordered.

Justice STEVENS, dissenting. * * *

The Court correctly concludes that in this case the facts presented to the District Court in support of respondents' claim that they had been singled out for prosecution because of their race were not sufficient to prove that defense. Moreover, I agree with the Court that their showing was not strong enough to give them a right to discovery, either under Rule 16 or under the District Court's inherent power to order discovery in appropriate circumstances. Like Chief Judge Wallace of the Court of Appeals, however, I am persuaded that the District Judge did not abuse her discretion when she concluded that the factual showing was sufficiently disturbing to require some response from the United States Attorney's Office. Perhaps the discovery order was broader than necessary, but I cannot agree with the Court's apparent conclusion that no inquiry was permissible.

The District Judge's order should be evaluated in light of three circumstances that underscore the need for judicial vigilance over certain types of drug prosecutions. First, the Anti–Drug Abuse Act of 1986 and subsequent legislation established a regime of extremely high penalties for the possession and distribution of so-called "crack" cocaine. * * * These penalties result in sentences for crack offenders that average three to eight times longer than sentences for comparable powder offenders.

Second, the disparity between the treatment of crack cocaine and powder cocaine is matched by the disparity between the severity of the punishment imposed by federal law and that imposed by state law for the same conduct. For a variety of reasons, often including the absence of mandatory minimums, the existence of parole, and lower baseline penalties, terms of imprisonment for drug offenses tend to be substantially lower in state systems than in the federal system. * * *

Finally, it is undisputed that the brunt of the elevated federal penalties falls heavily on blacks. While 65% of the persons who have used crack are white, in 1993 they represented only 4% of the federal offenders convicted of trafficking in crack. Eighty-eight percent of such defendants were black. * * * The Sentencing Commission acknowledges that the heightened crack penalties are a "primary cause of the growing disparity between sentences for Black and White federal defendants."

The extraordinary severity of the imposed penalties and the troubling racial patterns of enforcement give rise to a special concern about the fairness of charging practices for crack offenses. Evidence tending to prove that black defendants charged with distribution of crack in the Central District of California are prosecuted in federal court, whereas members of other races charged with similar offenses are prosecuted in state court, warrants close scrutiny by the federal judges in that District. In my view, the District Judge, who has sat on both the federal and the state benches in Los Angeles, acted well within her discretion to call for the development of facts that would demonstrate what standards, if any, governed the choice of forum where similarly situated offenders are prosecuted.

Respondents submitted a study showing that of all cases involving crack offenses that were closed by the Federal Public Defender's Office in 1991, 24 out of 24 involved black defendants. To supplement this evidence, they submitted affidavits from two of the attorneys in the defense team. * * *

The majority discounts the probative value of the affidavits, claiming that they recounted "hearsay" and reported "personal conclusions based on anecdotal evidence." But the Reed affidavit plainly contained more than mere hearsay; Reed offered information based on his own extensive experience in both federal and state courts. * * *

The criticism that the affidavits were based on "anecdotal evidence" is also unpersuasive. I thought it was agreed that defendants do not need to prepare sophisticated statistical studies in order to receive mere discovery in cases like this one. Certainly evidence based on a drug counselor's personal observations or on an attorney's practice in two sets of courts, state and federal, can "ten[d] to show the existence" of a selective prosecution.

Even if respondents failed to carry their burden of showing that there were individuals who were not black but who could have been prosecuted in federal court for the same offenses, it does not follow that the District Court abused its discretion in ordering discovery. There can be no doubt that such individuals exist, and indeed the Government has never denied the same. In those circumstances, I fail to see why the District Court was unable to take judicial notice of this obvious fact and demand information from the Government's files to support or refute respondents' evidence. The presumption that some whites are prosecuted in state court is not "contradicted" by the statistics the majority cites, which show only that high percentages of blacks are convicted of certain federal crimes, while high percentages of whites are convicted of other federal crimes. Those figures are entirely consistent with the allegation of selective prosecution. The relevant comparison, rather, would be with the percentages of blacks and whites who commit those crimes. But, as discussed above, in the case of crack far greater numbers of whites are believed guilty of using the substance. The District Court, therefore, was entitled to find the evidence before her significant and to require some explanation from the Government.[6] * * *

Notes and Questions

1. **Discriminatory purpose.** (a) *Armstrong* says the defendant must show not only that the prosecutorial policy had "a discriminatory effect," but also "that it was motivated by a discriminatory purpose." Compare Daniel I. Givelber, *The Application of Equal Protection Principles to Selective Enforcement of the Criminal Law,* 1973 U.Ill.L.F. 88, 106: "Rather than requiring a defendant to prove the prosecutor's knowledge and motivation in order to establish a denial of equal protection, a court should hold that the burden of going forward shifts to the state once the defendant proves that only a few of the knowable violators of a law have been prosecuted or that the group prosecuted for violating a law differs from the group not prosecuted in characteristics irrelevant to law enforcement purposes. Only after the state explains what has produced the unequal treatment can the court determine whether the selective enforcement results from the application of unjustifiable or arbitrary enforcement criteria."

(b) In *Wayte*, relied upon in *Armstrong*, petitioner sent letters to government officials stating he had not registered for the draft and did not intend to do so. The letters were added to a Selective Service file of men who had written similar letters or who had been reported by others as having failed to register. Later the

---

6. Also telling was the Government's response to respondents' evidentiary showing. It submitted a list of more than 3,500 defendants who had been charged with federal narcotics violations over the previous 3 years. It also offered the names of 11 nonblack defendants whom it had prosecuted for crack offenses. All 11, however, were members of other racial or ethnic minorities. The District Court was authorized to draw adverse inferences from the Government's inability to produce a single example of a white defendant, especially when the very purpose of its exercise was to allay the Court's concerns about the evidence of racially selective prosecutions. As another court has said: "Statistics are not, of course, the whole answer, but nothing is as emphatic as zero...."

Service adopted a policy of passive enforcement under which only nonregistration cases in the file were brought to prosecution, and only if the individual remained unregistered after having been warned that failure to register could result in prosecution and after repeated urgings by government authorities to register. When petitioner was then indicted, he claimed a denial of equal protection because of selective enforcement against "vocal" nonregistrants who were exercising their First Amendment Rights. But the Supreme Court did not agree:

" * * *All petitioner has shown here is that those eventually prosecuted, along with many not prosecuted, reported themselves as having violated the law. He has not shown that the enforcement policy selected nonregistrants for prosecution on the basis of their speech. Indeed, he could not have done so given the way the 'beg' policy was carried out. The Government did not prosecute those who reported themselves but later registered. Nor did it prosecute those who protested registration but did not report themselves or were not reported by others. In fact, the Government did not even investigate those who wrote letters to Selective Service criticizing registration unless their letters stated affirmatively that they had refused to comply with the law. The Government, on the other hand, did prosecute people who reported themselves or were reported by others but who did not publicly protest. These facts demonstrate that the Government treated all reported nonregistrants similarly. It did not subject vocal nonregistrants to any special burden. Indeed, those prosecuted in effect selected themselves for prosecution by refusing to register after being reported and warned by the Government.

"Even if the passive policy had a discriminatory effect, petitioner has not shown that the Government intended such a result. The evidence he presented demonstrated only that the Government was aware that the passive enforcement policy would result in prosecution of vocal objectors and that they would probably make selective prosecution claims. As we have noted, however, "'[d]iscriminatory purpose" * * * implies more than * * * intent as awareness of consequences. It implies that the decisionmaker * * * selected or reaffirmed a particular course of action at least in part "because of," not merely "in spite of," its adverse effects upon an identifiable group.' In the present case, petitioner has not shown that the Government prosecuted him *because of* his protest activities. Absent such a showing, his claim of selective prosecution fails."

(c) In McCLESKEY v. KEMP, 481 U.S. 279, 107 S.Ct. 1756, 95 L.Ed.2d 262 (1987), the black defendant, sentenced to death for murdering a white victim, claimed racial discrimination in violation of equal protection. He relied upon a statistical study of over 2,000 murder cases arising in Georgia during the 1970s which showed, inter alia, that prosecutors sought the death penalty in 70% of the cases involving black defendants and white victims; 32% of the cases involving white defendants and white victims; 15% of the cases involving black defendants and black victims; and 19% of the cases involving white defendants and black victims.

The Court, per WHITE, J., held such statistics insufficient, for "McCleskey must prove that the decision-makers in *his* case acted with discriminatory purpose." The Court asserted that while it had "accepted statistics as proof of intent to discriminate in certain limited contexts," such as jury selection, where "the statistics relate to fewer entities, and fewer variables are relevant to the challenged decisions," the same approach would not be appropriate here. For one thing, state-wide statistics would not support an inference as to the policy of the prosecutor in this county: "Since decisions whether to prosecute and what to charge necessarily are individualized and involve infinite factual variations, coordination among DA offices across a State would be relatively meaningless." Secondly, "the policy considerations behind a prosecutor's traditionally 'wide discretion' suggest the impropriety of requiring prosecutors to defend their decisions to seek death penalties, 'often years after they were made.' " Moreover, the Constitution does not bar the exercise of discretion by the prosecutor as to when to seek the death penalty, as "discretion in the criminal justice system offers substantial benefits to the criminal defendant," and "the capacity of prosecutorial discretion to provide individualized justice is 'firmly entrenched in American law.' "[b]

BLACKMUN, J., for the four dissenters, argued that the defendant had established a prima facie case under the *Castaneda* [p. 1326] three-factor standard (factors one and two were established by the study, and factor three by testimony assistant prosecutors in the county operated without any guidelines as to when to seek the death penalty); disagreed with the majority's assertion "that there are fewer variables relevant to the decisions of jury commissioners or prosecutors in their selection of jurors," or that such decisions "are 'made by fewer entities' "; and asserted that the "Court's refusal to require that the prosecutor provide an explanation for his actions * * * is completely inconsistent with this Court's longstanding precedents" and with the recent decision in *Batson v. Kentucky*, p. 1334.[c]

(d) Bass, charged with two intentional killings, received notice of the government's intent to seek the death penalty. (Since 1995, only the Attorney General can authorize seeking the death penalty; individual prosecutors retain discretion in only three areas: whether to bring federal charges or defer to state prosecutions, whether to charge defendants with a capital-eligible offense, and whether to enter into a plea agreement.) Relying upon a 2000 Department of Justice survey showing, e.g., a significant difference between the percentage of white and black prisoners in federal prisons (57% and 38%, respectively) and those charged with death-eligible crimes (20% and 48%, respectively), and upon public comments by the then-Attorney General and then-Deputy Attorney General expressing concern about this disparity, the defendant sought discovery under *Armstrong* of the government's charging practices. In affirming the district court's grant of discovery, the court of appeals concluded: "If the Department of Justice's official position is that these statistics, standing alone, show sufficient evidence of the possibility of racial animus to warrant further study, we cannot fairly deny Bass the same opportunity to investigate when he has introduced not only the Survey, but several other statistics showing that the grave racial disparities identified by the Survey are unique to the death penalty protocol." As for the government's contention that *McCleskey* precluded the court from drawing any inference of intentional race discrimination from such statistics, the court responded: "*McCleskey* will certainly preclude Bass's selective prosecution claim if, at the end of

b. The part of the statistical study purporting to show racial discrimination by *juries* in opting for the death penalty was similarly assessed by the Court. Thus, the Court stressed the difficulty in deducing a policy "by studying the combined effects of the decisions of hundreds of juries that are unique in their composition"; the fact this disparity could not be explained because " 'considerations of . . . public policy' dictate that jurors 'cannot be called . . . to testify to the motives and influences that led to their verdict' "; and that "it is the jury's function to make the difficult and uniquely human judgments that defy codification and that 'buil[d] discretion, equity, and flexibility into a legal system.' "

c. In *Armstrong*, respondents relied upon *Batson*, but the Court responded that *Batson* was different: "During jury selection, the entire res gestae take place in front of the trial judge. Because the judge has before him the entire venire, he is well situated to detect whether a challenge to the seating of one juror is part of a 'pattern' of singling out members of a single race for peremptory challenges. He is in a position to discern whether a challenge to a black juror has evidentiary significance; the significance may differ if the venire consists mostly of blacks or of whites. Similarly, if the defendant makes out a prima facie case, the prosecutor is called upon to justify only decisions made in the very case then before the court. The trial judge need not review prosecutorial conduct in relation to other venires in other cases."

discovery, he fails to show any additional evidence that the United States intentionally discriminates against blacks through the death penalty protocol. It does not, however, pose any bar to Bass at this preliminary stage." *United States v. Bass*, 266 F.3d 532 (6th Cir.2001).

2. *The "arbitrary classification" requirement.* (a) What is an arbitrary classification? Is the enforcement policy proper if the distinction being drawn in practice is one which the legislature could have drawn? See *Taylor v. City of Pine Bluff*, 289 S.W.2d 679 (Ark.1956), holding that enforcement of a Sunday blue law only against groceries was not a violation of equal protection because the legislature could have so limited the statute. Is this view incorrect, in that it is not the function of enforcement officials "to make the broad policy judgments that may require such classification"? Comment, 61 Colum.L.Rev. 1103, 1118 (1961). Or, does this position not go far enough, in that a prosecutor must be free "to choose whom to prosecute after weighing such factors as the likelihood of successful prosecution, the social value of obtaining a conviction as against the time and expense to the state, and his own sense of justice in the particular case," id. at 1119, which are factors which could not be expressed in legislation? See *Futernick v. Sumpter Township*, 78 F.3d 1051 (6th Cir.1996), so concluding.

(b) In *United States v. Ojala*, 544 F.2d 940 (8th Cir.1976), defendant, a state legislator, established that he was targeted for prosecution for his failure to file income tax returns (while many others were not) because he publicly announced his refusal to comply with the filing requirements in order to protest the Vietnam war. Said the court: "It is difficult to conceive of a more legitimate object of prosecution than one who exploits his own public office and reputation to urge a political position by announcing publicly that he had gone on strike against the tax laws of the nation." Is this so? What then of the IRS's "Project ACE," which gave "special priorities" to the prosecution of tax crimes by attorneys and accountants because of their "special obligation and responsibility to the tax laws"? See *United States v. Swanson*, 509 F.2d 1205 (8th Cir.1975).

(c) After more traditional efforts to curb vice in the Times Square area had failed, city officials obtained federal funding for the Midtown Enforcement Project. A task force of fire, safety and health inspectors made frequent inspections only of "sex related" businesses in that area. Defendants, operators of an adult book store, sought dismissal of the charges of health and building code violations brought against them. In *People v. Mantel*, 388 N.Y.S.2d 565 (1976), the court declared that the test is "whether a particular classification bears a rational relationship to the broad purposes of the criminal law and is reasonably related to law enforcement objectives," and then concluded: "It cannot be seriously doubted that this concentrated effort, even assuming it is aimed at sex related establishments, is rationally related to legitimate law enforcement objectives. Any area of activity that carries with it a high incidence of crime is an appropriate choice for strenuous law enforcement."

(d) Compare *People v. Kail*, 501 N.E.2d 979 (Ill.App.1986), involving an arrest for violation of an otherwise unenforced city ordinance requiring bicycles to be equipped with bells, made "under a police-department policy requiring strict enforcement of all laws against suspected prostitutes," where the court held: "The purpose of the ordinance requiring a bell on a bicycle clearly does not envision the eradication of prostitution. There is no conceivable set of facts which would establish a rational relationship between the class of suspected prostitutes and the State's legitimate interest in enforcing the ordinance requiring bells on bicycles. We can conceive of no such set of facts, and the State has failed to propound any. To suggest that the requirement of a bell on one's bicycle should be enforced only against suspected prostitutes because it helps combat prostitution is clearly so attenuated as to render the classification arbitrary or irrational."

(e) It is the prosecutor's policy to prosecute for violations of the Sunday closing law only upon receipt of a citizen complaint, but for many years he never received one. Then the business manager of the meatcutters' union filed complaints against all supermarkets in the county but not against any so-called "Mom and Pop" groceries. What result if the supermarkets defend on equal protection grounds? Are the private complainant's reasons (concern over union members working on Sunday) relevant, or are they irrelevant because the prosecutor proceeds on all complaints without regard to what motivated them? If they are relevant, is this "an unseemly state of affairs openly inviting discrimination and harassment of one group by another," or may it be said that the complaints were designed "to achieve exactly what the statute intends"? See *People v. Acme Markets, Inc.*, 334 N.E.2d 555 (N.Y.1975).

(f) If, as has been recommended,[d] the prosecutor has a handbook setting out guidelines for the exercise of his discretion, is any deviation from them a denial of equal protection? If not, should a deviation from published policies be a defense anyway? Consider *Nichols v. Reno*, 931 F.Supp. 748 (D.Colo.1996), aff'd 124 F.3d 1376 (10th Cir.1997) (where U.S. Attorneys' Manual contemplates that decision to seek death penalty be made by Attorney General after review by U.S. Attorney and Attorney General's committee and upon consideration of aggravating circumstances plus mitigating circumstances submitted by defense counsel, but promptly following Oklahoma City bombing Attorney General stated at press conference that death penalty would be sought for then unknown perpetrators, Nichols entitled to no relief, as Manual does not provide him with any judicially enforceable rights). Cf. *United States v. Caceres*, p. 131.

3. Discriminatory effect. Given the discriminatory effect requirement, said in *Armstrong* to necessitate a showing that others "similarly situated * * * were not prosecuted," can intentional or purposeful discrimination existing within a scheme of general or random enforcement ever constitute a violation of equal protection? (a) In PEOPLE v. WALKER, 200 N.E.2d 779 (N.Y.1964), where the defendant claimed a violation of equal protection when she was prosecuted for violations of the Multiple Dwelling Law closely following her exposure of corrupt practices in the Department of Buildings, the court ordered a retrial at which she could have "a fair opportunity to establish" such intentional discrimination. A dissenting judge objected:

"If the constitutional defense of unequal protection of the laws were maintainable solely upon a showing of bad motive on the part of those responsible for the placing of the violations of which appellant is admittedly guilty, then I would concur for reversal. This, however, is not the law; nor does the court say it is. Since the legislation under which appellant has been convicted is itself valid, and since appellant is admittedly guilty of the violations, the defense of unequal protection is established only upon a showing of both bad motive in the subject case and nonenforcement as to others similarly situated * * *. The violations, among which are the creation of an additional room by a partition, an additional class B room out of a vestibule, and the maintenance of a defective sprinkler valve, are, in my experience, commonly enforced in New York City. * * *

"[Appellant's] offers of proof went solely to the point of bad motive in her individual case. Sympathetic as we may be toward appellant's unfortunate position as the result of what she alleges were numerous bribe solicitations by Building Department officials, we have no license to play fast and loose with the elements of so volatile a doctrine as equal protection of the laws. If the statutory requirements to which appellant was held were generally enforced, then there was no infringement of her constitutional right when she was prosecuted for their

d. See *A.B.A. Standards*, p. 854, at § 3–2.5(b).

violation—no matter how contemptible may have been the motives of those who enforced the law. Were the law otherwise all enforcement proceedings could be turned into subjective expeditions into motive without the stabilizing, objectively verifiable, element of an unequal pattern of enforcement. No one has a constitutional right to random enforcement of the law. No one has a constitutional right to sincere enforcement of the law. The right is to equal enforcement of the law."[e]

(b) Consider Recent Case, 78 Harv.L.Rev. 884, 885–86 (1965): "Once it is recognized that the equal protection clause requires each state to enact and enforce its laws in an impartial manner, it follows that Miss Walker should be given the opportunity to prove that even though there was general or random enforcement of the statute in question she would not have been prosecuted but for the purposeful discrimination on the part of the borough superintendent. For example, assume that the superintendent has a list of 1,000 known violators and reasonably exercises his discretion to enforce the law selectively by prosecuting every other person on the list, namely, even numbers. If Miss Walker's name is 149th on the list and the superintendent admits deviating from his selective enforcement formula in order to vent his personal prejudice against her, she has been deprived of equal protection of the laws and should be permitted to quash the prosecution."

Compare Note, 50 Cornell L.Q. 309, 315 (1965): "While a prosecutor does have the obligation to act in good faith in performing his duty, he ought not to be obligated to forego prosecuting a violator whom he believes to be guilty, merely because of some personal feeling or antagonism he has toward that violator.[f] A contrary rule might in fact result in discrimination against other violators." Would such an extension of the equal protection guarantee "be anomalous to criminal law as it is known today, for regardless of the motives of the prosecutor, the policy reasons which led to the enactment of the penal statute are being carried out, since society is still being protected from forbidden conduct"? Recent Decision, 39 St. John's L.Rev. 145, 149 (1964). And what of the point that "even if it can be proved that the prosecution might have been improperly motivated, it will be exceedingly difficult to prove that the defendant would not have been selected for prosecution in the normal course of events"? Recent Decision, 51 Va.L.Rev. 499, 507 (1965).

(c) But if the defendant shows the prosecutor had a "bad motive," why shouldn't the defendant prevail on that basis alone, even if there is no equal protection violation? Consider *State v. Annala,* 484 N.W.2d 138 (Wis.1992): When he was 15 years old, defendant molested an 8–year–old child he was babysitting; no criminal charges were pursued because even the victim's parents agreed that the best disposition would be for defendant to seek counseling, which he did. Five

---

e. Defendant Walker finally prevailed, but the decision in her favor was in part based upon more traditional notions of equal protection, in that "the manner of prosecution was not the same as that used in the case of other property owners similarly situated" because "the time allowed to defendant for correction of alleged housing violations was so unreasonably short as to make correction an impossibility and criminal conviction a certainty." *People v. Walker,* 271 N.Y.S.2d 447 (1966).

Should Ms. Walker prevail even on these facts? Consider *Futernick v. Sumpter Township,* Note 2(a) supra: "We do not believe that choosing to enforce the law against a particular individual is a 'classification' as that term is normally understood. *Webster's Third New In-*

ternational Dictionary 417 (1986) (defining 'classify' as 'to group or segregate in classes that have systematic relations usually founded on common properties or characters; sort')."

f. In *United States v. Bourque,* 541 F.2d 290 (1st Cir.1976), where defendant alleged that his prosecution for wilful failure to file corporate income tax returns was brought about because of a dispute between him and the IRS District Director of Intelligence on a personal matter, the court held that even if this were so, defendant was entitled to no relief because he failed to show that "prosecutions are normally not instituted for the offenses with which he was charged."

years later the prosecutor charged defendant with the sexual assault, apparently because of a letter from the victim's therapist indicating such action would be in the best interests of the victim. In response to the defendant's claim "that abuse of discretion should be found because the prosecutor brought the charges based on an improper motive," the court stated: "When probable cause exists for prosecution, the court should not consider the subjective motivations of the district attorney in making his charging decision, except to determine whether a discriminatory basis was involved. * * * Political review through the electoral process is sufficient to ensure the proper application of prosecutorial discretion. If this court placed the nondiscriminatory subjective motivations of the district attorney under scrutiny with respect to the charging decision, it would likely create an enormous amount of litigation challenging prosecutorial discretion that had little or nothing to do with the defendant's guilt or innocence." Is it significant that the majority in *Annala* went on to conclude that the prosecutor's decision to prosecute in order to aid the victim's rehabilitation was not an abuse of discretion, while the dissent states it was "Shylockian retribution"?

(d) UNITED STATES v. AGUILAR, 883 F.2d 662 (9th Cir.1989), illustrates that when the statute is being selectively enforced, there may arise the critical question of just who is and is not "similarly situated." The defendants in *Aguilar*, members of the sanctuary movement (which operated a modern-day underground railroad that smuggled Central American natives into the U.S. and dispersed them to safehouses throughout the country), contended they were singled out for prosecution because of their "vocal opposition to U.S. refugee and asylum policy and to U.S. foreign policy in Central America." They acknowledged that government enforcement of the immigration laws was not limited to those opposing government policies, but they claimed they should nonetheless prevail because "growers and ranchers employing illegal aliens had not been prosecuted in the previous ten years." The court responded:

"Appellants' definition of similarly situated fails because it does not insure that all distinctions extraneous to the first amendment expression are removed. The government argues that appellants are similarly situated to 'well-organized and structured alien smuggling conspiracies that were smuggling high volumes of aliens.' Agent Rayburn testified that immigration authorities had never uncovered a similar conspiracy by Arizona farmers or growers to transport illegal aliens outside the State of Arizona. The United States Attorney testified that the office's focus was upon organized smuggling rings.

"Appellants' suggested definition of similarly situated excludes the one class of immigration law violators with whom they are most analogous: organized smugglers operating for financial gain. This group is unlikely to have a political motivation for their conduct and is consequently unlikely to be a vocal opponent of United States foreign policy. They represent the perfect control group because they present a similar threat to immigration policy in terms of the numbers of aliens they smuggle, but they do not engage in the expression that appellants' claim motivated this prosecution.

"Appellants do not contend that the government generally does not prosecute organized alien smugglers. Their suggested focus exclusively upon agricultural employers seeks to distract attention away from the fact that the government generally *does* prosecute organized alien smugglers, albeit organized smugglers following the dollar instead of the cross. We reject appellants' suggested definition of the similarly situated class and thus their selective prosecution claim."

4. Selective enforcement vs. selective nonenforcement. If a certain statute is generally enforced except as to a certain identifiable group, does a defendant not in that group have a valid equal protection claim? See *United States* *v. Robinson,* 311 F.Supp. 1063 (W.D.Mo.1969) (conviction of private detective for wiretapping in violation of federal law overturned upon a showing that federal agents were not prosecuted for similar violations), commented on as follows in 55 Minn.L.Rev. 1234, 1243 (1971): "Implicit in the *Robinson* decision is the belief that presence of an invidious motive for prosecution is not required for a finding of discriminatory enforcement. The absence of a proper justification for not fully enforcing the statute makes any partial enforcement discriminatory. Though this seems to expand *Yick Wo,* it is probably justified."

5. *Selective enforcement vs. full enforcement.* Is the prosecutor's *failure* to exercise any discretion objectionable? In *State v. Pettitt,* 609 P.2d 1364 (Wash. 1980), the defendant, after his conviction for taking a motor vehicle without permission, was charged under the habitual criminal statute pursuant to the prosecutor's "mandatory policy of filing habitual criminal complaints against all defendants with three or more prior felonies," as he had prior convictions for taking a motor vehicle without permission, second degree burglary, and unauthorized use of a vehicle. The defendant argued that "a policy which prevents the prosecutor from considering mitigating factors is a failure to exercise discretion, which may, as in this case, result in an unfair and arbitrary result." The court agreed:

"In the present case, the prosecutor (now former prosecutor) admitted that he relied on the record alone in deciding to file the habitual criminal information. He testified that he did not consider any mitigating circumstances in reaching his decision, and that he could imagine no situation which would provide for an exception to the mandatory policy.

"In our view, this fixed formula which requires a particular action *in every case* upon the happening of a specific series of events constitutes an abuse of the discretionary power lodged in the prosecuting attorney."

However, a dissenting judge objected:

"The statute makes it clear that every person who falls into the ambit of the statute *shall* be sentenced to life imprisonment. This statute is mandatory and requires that the prosecutor file a supplemental information charging each such person with being a habitual criminal. It does not say that certain persons may be charged and others may not, and it provides no standards for the exercise of prosecutorial discretion. Here the prosecutor followed the mandate of the statute."

6. *Selective enforcement vs. random enforcement.* Consider Steven D. Clymer, *Unequal Justice: The Federalization of Criminal Law,* 70 So.Cal.L.Rev. 643, 712–14 (1997): "Some observers contend that purely random selection is consistent with equal protection because all are equally likely to be selected. * * * Arguably, in situations in which the government must selectively prosecute, random selection is unrelated to any objective that the government seeks to further.

"[I]ntentional randomness is not necessarily unrelated to government objectives. * * * Indeed, some contend that the imposition of random harsh sentences is a rational means of maximizing the deterrent effect of limited law enforcement resources. If this is true, then federal prosecutors may achieve a similar deterrent effect by selecting offenders for harsher treatment in federal court in a random or unprincipled manner. * * *

"However, the interests at stake in the selective enforcement of duplicative federal statutes are sufficiently high [see Note 3, p. 891] that the Department of Justice should refrain from adopting the view that purely random or unprincipled selection is constitutional * * *. It is difficult to reconcile the guarantee of equal protection with the intentional use of a policy that randomly subjects one offender to a small fine and another who is similarly situated to the near certainty of a ten-year term of imprisonment."

   7. Selective reversal of prior nonenforcement decisions. In *Wayte*, the Court declared that "the decision to prosecute may not be ' "deliberately based upon an unjustifiable standard such as race, religion, or other arbitrary classification," ' including the exercise of protected statutory and constitutional rights." But when the exercise of those rights prompting prosecution comes *after* the prosecutor had decided not to prosecute, does it (should it) make any difference why the particular nonenforcement decision was made? Consider DIXON v. DISTRICT OF COLUMBIA, 394 F.2d 966 (D.C.Cir.1968), which involved a black defendant stopped by two white police officers for alleged traffic violations. He was neither charged nor ticketed at that time, and two days later the defendant—a retired detective sergeant—filed a complaint with the police department concerning the conduct of the officers. Shortly thereafter defendant and the Corporation Counsel's office entered into a tacit agreement: defendant would proceed no further with his complaint and the government would not prosecute the traffic charges. Later, defendant did file a formal complaint with the D.C. Council on Human Relations, and after he refused to withdraw the complaint he was charged and convicted for the two traffic offenses. The Court of Appeals reversed; Chief Judge BAZELON had this to say:

   "Of course prosecutors have broad discretion to press or drop charges. But there are limits. If, for example, the Government had legitimately determined not to prosecute appellant and had then reversed its position solely because he filed a complaint, this would clearly violate the first amendment. The Government may not prosecute for the purpose of deterring people from exercising their right to protest official misconduct and petition for redress of grievances. Moreover, a prosecution under such circumstances would be barred by the equal protection clause since the Government employs an impermissible classification when it punishes those who complain against police misconduct and excuses those who do not.

   "Appellant's case, however, is more complicated. The record indicates that the Government's initial decision not to prosecute was based on appellant's tentative agreement not to proceed with his complaint. It would therefore be naive to say that the Government made a legitimate decision not to prosecute and then reversed it solely because appellant decided to complain. On the contrary, it may be that the Government should have prosecuted Dixon and that its failure to do so stemmed from an illegitimate desire to protect the two police officers. And if the Government should have prosecuted Dixon in the first place, there is arguably no reason why it should be barred from prosecuting him now.

   "But I believe reason is to be found in the need to prevent the type of agreement which was attempted in this case. * * *

   "The major evil of these agreements is not that charges are sometimes dropped against people who probably should be prosecuted. Much more important, these agreements suppress complaints against police misconduct which should be thoroughly aired in a free society. And they tempt the prosecutor to trump up charges for use in bargaining for suppression of the complaint. The danger of concocted charges is particularly great because complaints against the police usually arise in connection with arrests for extremely vague offenses such as disorderly conduct or resisting arrest.

   "Courts may not become the 'enforcers' of these odious agreements. We must therefore bar prosecutions which are brought because the defendant refused to promise or reneged on a promise not to file a complaint against the police. Prosecutors will then have no incentive to offer or make such agreements."

Judge Bazelon, relying on the federal entrapment cases, based his decision on the supervisory power of federal courts to grant immunity from prosecution because of government misconduct. Could *Dixon* instead have been decided as it was on equal protections grounds? On the grounds that there had been a vindictive prosecution under the *Goodwin* case, Note 5, p. 893?

Was the earlier agreement between the prosecutor and the defendant in *Dixon* "odious"? Compare *MacDonald v. Musick*, 425 F.2d 373 (9th Cir.1970) (state prosecutor's offer not to prosecute defendant for driving while intoxicated if defendant stipulated his arrest was made on probable cause, thus foreclosing possibility of false arrest suit, deemed to constitute the crime of extortion and also ethical misconduct of misuse of the criminal process to gain advantage in a civil case); with *Town of Newton v. Rumery*, 480 U.S. 386, 107 S.Ct. 1187, 94 L.Ed.2d 405 (1987) ("a court properly may enforce an agreement in which a criminal defendant releases his right to file a § 1983 action in return for a prosecutor's dismissal of pending criminal charges," as while "a promise is unenforceable if the interest in its enforcement is outweighed in the circumstances by a public policy harmed by enforcement of the agreement," the court of appeals was incorrect in concluding "that all release-dismissal agreements offend public policy," for these agreements also "protect public officials from the burdens of defending * * * unjust claims," and in this case the prosecutor "had an independent, legitimate reason to make this agreement directly related to his prosecutorial responsibilities," namely, sparing a sexual assault victim the "public scrutiny and embarrassment she would have endured if she had to testify in either" the criminal or § 1983 trial).

8. *Desuetude*. (a) In UNITED STATES v. ELLIOTT, 266 F.Supp. 318 (S.D.N.Y.1967), the defendants were charged with violating 18 U.S.C. § 956, making it an offense to conspire to destroy property of a public utility or of a foreign government or political subdivision thereof, when the property was situated in a foreign country with which the United States is at peace. The defendants contended "that the apparent absence of any prosecution under the statute since its promulgation in 1917 renders it void because of desuetude," but the court did not agree:

"Desuetude is a civil law doctrine rendering a statute abrogated by reason of its long and continued non-use. It is not part of English jurisprudence, although it is recognized in the law of Scotland.

"Its status in American law is unclear. One commentator has concluded that there are no means under American law by which a validly enacted statute can be rendered ineffective by non-use. 1 Sutherland, *Statutory Construction* § 2034 (Horach Ed.1943). Recent commentators, however, have found some vitality to the doctrine. * * *

"We find little analytical aid in merely applying, or refusing to apply, the rubric of desuetude. The problem must be approached in terms of that fundamental fairness owed to the particular defendant that is the eart of due process. An analysis of the problems posed to this defendant by this allegedly desuetudinal statute demonstrates the statute's continued vitality.

"Defendant's contentions to the contrary, we are not faced here with the enforcement of either a basically obsolete or an empty law whose function has long since passed. We are not here concerned with a law forbidding the sale of candy cigarettes, or prohibiting kite flying, or banning the exhibition of films depicting a felony. The function of the statute before us—' * * * to punish acts of interference with the foreign relations * * * of the United States' (40 Stat. 217

(1917))—is as vibrantly vital today as when it was passed. Indisputably, defendant is not being punished by the letter of a rule whose reason has long since passed.

"In some situations a desuetudinal statute could prevent serious problems of fair notice. However, this statute does not penalize conduct which, through a long period of non-enforcement, has acquired the status of customary usage, nor has opprobrium for the act been suddenly revived. Conspiring to destroy a bridge is not, and never has been, permitted by community mores. Defendant would have to know his act was wrong and if consummated a crime in Zambia. His surprise at finding the conspiracy an offense against the United States is naive in the extreme and clearly affords no defense.

"A desuetudinal statute also contains the potential for abuse that rests in any overbroad administrative discretion; its selective enforcement raises equal protection problems analogous to the *Yick Wo* doctrine. However, defendant, as we have already noted, has adduced not a scintilla of evidence even indicating that the government singled him out, by applying an unconstitutional standard, for punishment. Defendant, in short, consequently must establish that mere non-use of a statute deprives it of life. In the absence of some specific objection (such as indicated above), we hold that non-use alone does not abrogate a statute."

(b) In *John R. Thompson Co. v. District of Columbia,* 203 F.2d 579 (D.C.Cir. 1953), the court, although holding a criminal statute on refusal to serve blacks unenforceable on other grounds, added: "But we think it appropriate to comment, in this connection, that the enactments having lain unenforced for 78 years, in the face of a custom of race disassociation in the District, the decision of the municipal authorities to enforce them now, by the prosecution of the instant case, was, in effect, a decision legislative in character. That is to say, it was a determination that the enactments reflect a social policy which is now correct, although it was not correct—else the enactments would have been enforced—heretofore. Such a decision were better left, we think, to the Congress." On review, in *District of Columbia v. John R. Thompson Co.,* 346 U.S. 100, 73 S.Ct. 1007, 97 L.Ed. 1480 (1953), the Supreme Court disagreed: "The repeal of laws is as much a legislative function as their enactment. * * * Cases of hardship are put where criminal laws so long in disuse as to be no longer known to exist are enforced against innocent parties. But that condition does not bear on the continuing validity of the law; it is only an ameliorating factor in enforcement."

(c) Compare Arthur E. Bonfield, *The Abrogation of Penal Statutes by Nonenforcement,* 49 Iowa L.Rev. 389, 415–16 (1964): "The depth of the American commitment to the abrogation of enacted law by desuetude is perhaps best revealed by analogy to the due-process fair-notice or fair-warning cases. Where both the community and its law-enforcement agencies have notoriously ignored an enactment for an unduly protracted period, it should be constitutionally impermissible to suddenly prosecute its violation because the act's proscriptions have disappeared from the legal consciousness of the body politic. The statute has neither been obeyed nor applied for such an extended period that ample justification as long existed for the public's feeling that the act has lost the force of binding law."

(d) Compare also the "estoppel" defense in *Cox v. Louisiana,* fn. a at p. 391, and the defense in *Model Penal Code* § 2.04 where a defendant believes "that conduct does not legally constitute an offense [and] acts in reasonable reliance upon an official statement of the law, afterward determined to be invalid or erroneous, contained in * * * an official interpretation of the public officer or body charged by law with responsibility for the interpretation, administration or enforcement of the law defining the offense." Should it make any difference whether the prosecutor says that the contemplated conduct is not covered by the law or that it is covered by the law but that it is not his policy to prosecute for such conduct?

III. THE DIVERSION DECISION[a]

1. In *Shade v. Pennsylvania Dep't of Transportation,* 394 F.Supp. 1237 (M.D.Pa.1975), the plaintiffs requested the court to declare unconstitutional the Accelerated Rehabilitation Disposition (ARD) program, a pretrial diversion program embodied in Pa.R.Crim.P. 175 through 185, because the rules granted to the prosecutor the discretion to refuse to ask for ARD and instead to insist on prosecution of any particular defendant. The court declined to do so, reasoning:

"In the instant case the ARD program leaves intact the traditional principle that the prosecuting attorney should have the discretion to choose which crimes he wishes to prosecute. Even in the absence of the ARD program, the district attorney in his discretion could always *nolle pros* a criminal charge or enter into a plea bargain with a defendant. Thus ARD is merely one of several discretionary methods for disposition of criminal charges. The criminal law is not a computerized system and discretion—e.g., whether or not to arrest, indict, release, prosecute, dismiss, plea bargain, or accept a plea of guilty in a given case—is a necessary and inherent part of the criminal justice system."[b]

2. If, as stated in *Shade,* diversion is an aspect of the prosecutor's discretion, then to what extent are the prosecutor's diversion decisions subject to court review? Consider the applicability in this context of the separation of powers doctrine invoked in *Inmates of Attica,* p. 862, and the equal protection challenge discussed in *Armstrong,* p. 868. Consider also:

(a) *State v. Leonardis,* 375 A.2d 607 (N.J.1977): Noting that pretrial diversion was adopted in the state by the supreme court pursuant to its rule-making power, conferred by the state constitution, the court concluded that the "authority to engage in rule-making also includes the power to interpret and enforce court rules." Thus, "our rule-making power must be held to include the power to order the diversion of a defendant * * * where either the prosecutor or the program director arbitrarily fails to follow the guidelines in refusing to consent to diversion. Conversely, where the program director or the prosecutor would subvert the goals of the program by approving diversion, meaningful judicial review must also be cognizable."[c]

(b) *United States v. Smith,* 354 A.2d 510 (D.C.App.1976): After defendant was charged with the misdemeanor of marijuana possession, he moved to dismiss on the ground that criminal penalties for such conduct constitutes cruel and unusual punishment. The trial judge granted the motion, but this motion was reversed on appeal. Defendant then sought diversion pursuant to the prosecutor's program

---

a. For further discussion of some of the legal issues which can arise in this context, see Daniel L. Skoler, *Protecting the Rights of Defendants in Pretrial Intervention Programs,* 10 Crim.L.Bull. 473 (1974). For a recommended statutory scheme for diversion, see *Model Pre-Arraignment Code* §§ 320.5–320.9.

b. What then if the program *does* limit the prosecutor's discretion? In *State v. Greenlee,* 620 P.2d 1132 (Kan.1980), where the program was adopted by legislation which listed diversion criteria for prosecutors to apply, the court concluded the resulting limitation on the prosecutor's discretion did not violate the separation of powers doctrine, as the statute "does not * * * destroy or unreasonably restrict" that discretion. The court added that if such a

statute had specifically provided the courts were to administer the program, or if the program had been adopted by rule of court, it would be clear that the setting of standards would not encroach on the executive power because then "a judicial function" would be involved.

c. Compare *Cleveland v. State,* 417 So.2d 653 (Fla.1982) (because statutory pretrial diversion program "requires consent of the administrator of the program, victim, judge, and state attorney, but fails to provide for *any* form of review," "the pretrial diversion decision of the state attorney is prosecutorial in nature and, thus, is not subject to judicial review").

whereunder young people without prior records accused of minor misdemeanors not involving force or violence were ordinarily diverted. The prosecutor declined because it was is policy to deny such treatment to defendants who had chosen to litigate any issues in their case. The trial court found this objectionable and therefore dismissed the charges. On appeal, the court first distinguished this diversion program from that in New Jersey because the former "owes its existence and operation solely to prosecutorial discretion," and then concluded:

"We have no quarrel with the trial court's ruling that a policy intended to deter defendants from exercising their legal rights cannot be tolerated in the name of prosecutorial discretion. We disagree, however, with the court's finding that the defendant has made an adequate showing that the policy questioned here has any such objective or effect. The record makes clear that if a defendant applies for, is accepted into the program, and successfully completes the requisite activities, charges are dropped without his having to go to court, and no conviction or criminal record results.

"The beneficiary of such a disposition of charges against him can scarcely be said to be deterred from exercising his right to defend himself, for, by dismissing such charges, the government has done away with any reason for him to do so. Should the prosecutor deny first offender treatment to a defendant, the latter is in no way barred from then invoking his legal rights and defenses in any manner he chooses. An accused is not prejudiced, therefore, by any official policy that no issues be litigated while his application for diversionary treatment is pending.

" * * * If it is permissible, in plea bargaining, to induce a defendant to plead guilty and waive his right to trial, *a fortiori* no substantial constitutional question is presented when a prosecutor offers to drop all charges provided the accused conforms to certain conditions, including, *inter alia,* foregoing the filing of any motions or pleas in defense."

(c) *Morse v. Municipal Court,* 529 P.2d 46 (Cal.1974): By statute, certain defendants charged with drug offenses could be diverted upon their consent. Defendant, charged with possession of marijuana, moved to suppress the evidence on Fourth Amendment grounds, and only after that motion was denied did he consent to diversion. In the course of rejecting the prosecutor's contention that the consent was untimely, the court commented: "As a practical matter, the People's insistence upon a deferral of suppression motions requires that a defendant choose between potential diversion and the possibility of an immediate dismissal of charges. His opportunity to test the strength of the evidence against him *at the outset* of the case is entirely lost if he elects diversion. Although no loss of constitutional rights thereby occurs in view of the defendant's ability to move to suppress at any later resumption of criminal proceedings by reason of a failure to complete successfully a drug treatment program, such a choice may tend to discourage defendants from consenting to consideration for diversion. As in the case of petitioner, defendants may be wont to try for even a remote chance of dismissal by virtue of the exclusionary rule in lieu of immediately committing themselves to the restrictions imposed by required participation in a rehabilitation program."

3. If the defendant and prosecutor agree to diversion, is the prosecutor free to renege for any reason? Consider:

(a) *United States v. Bethea,* 483 F.2d 1024 (4th Cir.1973): Defendant claimed that his prosecution for failure to report for induction breached an agreement with the United States attorney, who said he would seek dismissal of the case if defendant submitted himself for induction. Defendant did submit, but the Army refused to induct him upon moral grounds. As to defendant's reliance upon *Santobello v. New York,* p. 1260, the court responded: "The concern of *Santobello* was to protect a defendant who by pleading guilty has surrendered valuable constitutional rights in exchange for the prosecution's assurances. That concern has no application to the facts of this case. Appellant's submission for induction surrendered none of the rights protected by *Santobello*. In the context of this case, Bethea's conduct was at most only a factor to be considered by the prosecutor in deciding whether or not to prosecute, a decision not reviewable here."[d]

(b) *United States v. Garcia*, 519 F.2d 1343 (9th Cir.1975): Defendant, arrested for selling marijuana to undercover agents, entered into a "deferred prosecution" agreement that within 90 days he would "attempt" to present the agents with a dealer in drugs who might, "in the estimation of Agents of DEA," be "capable of making" a sale of such drugs. The government agreed that if defendant did so, no charges would be sought on the previous sale, and that otherwise the government could seek an indictment within 150 days. The defendant failed to produce a dealer, but the indictment was sought only after the 150 days had expired. The court deemed *Santobello* to be controlling, as "by entering into the deferred prosecution agreement, Garcia waived his valuable right to a speedy trial."[e]

4. If diversion status is to be terminated, what procedures should (or must) be followed? Consider *N.D.A.A. National Prosecution Standards* 153–54 (1977):

"The procedural safeguards required of a termination have not been firmly established, but would seem to be analogous to procedures required for parole and probation revocation hearings. The standards established for this in *Morrissey v. Brewer* [p. 88 supra] include:

"a.   written notice of violation;

"b.   disclosure of evidence against the offender;

"c.   opportunity to be heard and present opposing evidence;

"d.   right to confront and cross-examine witnesses;

"e.   'neutral and detached' hearing body;[f] and

"f.   a written statement by the factfinders as to the reasons for revocation."

---

d. Compare *People v. Reagan*, 235 N.W.2d 581 (Mich.1975). Defendant, charged with assault to do great bodily harm, entered into an agreement with the prosecutor that if he passed a state police polygraph exam his prosecution would be dismissed. He passed the test and the charge was dropped, but the prosecutor later doubted the results in view of the compelling circumstantial evidence of defendant's criminal involvement. He consulted with a psychiatrist who advised that with respect to such crimes a schizophrenic nature will sometimes distort polygraph results and that therefore truth serum should be used. The prosecutor then notified defendant that the agreement would be honored only if defendant submitted to serum testing. Defendant refused, the prosecutor refiled the charge, and defendant was convicted. On appeal, the court noted that defendant "had much to gain and relatively little to lose by subjecting himself to the polygraph," but, notwithstanding the people's contention "that the bargain offered defendant was a 'gift-type' bargain which lacked the consideration necessary to make it binding," concluded "the analogy to contract law is inappropriate. * * * It was within the power of the prosecution to enter into this agreement. We therefore reject the contention that the agreement per se is against public policy * * *. In our view, a pledge of public faith in this instance gave force to an unwise agreement which became binding."

e. Compare *United States v. Gogarty*, 533 F.2d 93 (2d Cir.1976): "The appellant failed to live up to his obligation and this agreement, unlike the agreement in *Garcia*, supra, contained no time limit on the government's right to re-prosecute the defendant in the event of noncompliance. One who fails to carry out his part of the bargain cannot invoke the agreement against the government."

f. "[T]he revocation function would presumably be exercised by the prosecutor's office or program personnel. A 'neutral' hearing officer is required. The program staff members who have gathered the facts upon which the decision to bring the termination proceeding is made, and have made the decision to apply for termination, would not meet the required impartiality standard. The Court has recognized that prior involvement in some aspect of a case will not necessarily bar a welfare official from acting as a decision-maker, but that official should not, however, have participated in making the determination under review. If the same guarantee could be made in a hearing conducted by the prosecutor's office or staff

IV. SELECTION OF THE CHARGE

UNITED STATES v. BATCHELDER

442 U.S. 114, 99 S.Ct. 2198, 60 L.Ed.2d 755 (1979).

Justice MARSHALL delivered the opinion of the Court.

At issue in this case are two overlapping provisions of the Omnibus Crime Control and Safe Streets Act of 1968 (the Omnibus Act). Both prohibit convicted felons from receiving firearms, but each authorizes different maximum penalties. We must determine whether a defendant convicted of the offense carrying the greater penalty may be sentenced only under the more lenient provision when his conduct violates both statutes.

Respondent, a previously convicted felon, was found guilty of receiving a firearm that had traveled in interstate commerce, in violation of 18 U.S.C. § 922(h).[2] The District Court sentenced him under 18 U.S.C. § 924(a) to five years' imprisonment, the maximum term authorized for violation of § 922(h).

The Court of Appeals affirmed the conviction but, by a divided vote, remanded for resentencing. The majority recognized that respondent had been indicted and convicted under § 922(h) and that § 924(a) permits five years' imprisonment for such violations. However, noting that the substantive elements of § 922(h) and 18 U.S.C.App. § 1202(a) are identical as applied to a convicted felon who unlawfully receives a firearm, the court interpreted the Omnibus Act to allow no more than the two-year maximum sentence provided by § 1202(a).[4] * * *

This Court has previously noted the partial redundancy of §§ 922(h) and 1202(a), both as to the conduct they proscribe and the individuals they reach. However, we find nothing in the language structure or legislative history of the Omnibus Act to suggest that because of this overlap, a defendant convicted under § 922(h) may be imprisoned for no more than the maximum term specified in § 1202(a). As we read the Act, each substantive statute, in conjunction with its own sentencing provision, operates independently of the other. * * *

personnel, then it would arguably meet existing due process standards." Harvey L. Perlman & Peter Jaszi, *Legal Issues in Addict Diversion* 123 (1975).

2. In pertinent part, 18 U.S.C. § 922(h) provides:

"It shall be unlawful for any person—

"(1) who is under indictment for, or who has been convicted in any court of, a crime punishable by imprisonment for a term exceeding one year;

"(2) who is a fugitive from justice;

"(3) who is an unlawful user of or addicted to marihuana or any depressant or stimulant drug * * * or narcotic drug * * *; or

"(4) who has been adjudicated as a mental defective or who has been committed to any mental institution;

"to receive any firearm or ammunition which has been shipped or transported in interstate or foreign commerce."

4. Section 1202(a) states:

"Any person who—

"(1) has been convicted by a court of the United States or of a State or any political subdivision thereof of a felony, or

"(2) has been discharged from the Armed Forces under dishonorable conditions, or

"(3) has been adjudged by a court of the United States or of a State or any political subdivision thereof of being mentally incompetent, or

"(4) having been a citizen of the United States has renounced his citizenship, or

"(5) being an alien is illegally or unlawfully in the United States,

"and who receives, possesses, or transports in commerce or affecting commerce, after the date of enactment of this Act, any firearm shall be fined not more than $10,000 or imprisoned for not more than two years, or both." 18 U.S.C.App. § 1202(a).

In resolving the statutory question, the majority below expressed "serious doubts about the constitutionality of two statutes that provide different penalties for identical conduct." Specifically, the court suggested that the statutes might (1) be void for vagueness, (2) implicate "due process and equal protection interest[s] in avoiding excessive prosecutorial discretion and in obtaining equal justice," and (3) constitute an impermissible delegation of congressional authority. We find no constitutional infirmities.

It is a fundamental tenet of due process that "[n]o one may be required at peril of life, liberty or property to speculate as to the meaning of penal statutes." A criminal statute is therefore invalid if it "fails to give a person of ordinary intelligence fair notice that his contemplated conduct is forbidden." So too, vague sentencing provisions may pose constitutional questions if they do not state with sufficient clarity the consequences of violating a given criminal statute.

The provisions in issue here, however, unambiguously specify the activity proscribed and the penalties available upon conviction. That this particular conduct may violate both Titles does not detract from the notice afforded by each. Although the statutes create uncertainty as to which crime may be charged and therefore what penalties may be imposed, they do so to no greater extent than would a single statute authorizing various alternative punishments. So long as overlapping criminal provisions clearly define the conduct prohibited and the punishment authorized, the notice requirements of the Due Process Clause are satisfied.

This Court has long recognized that when an act violates more than one criminal statute, the Government may prosecute under either so long as it does not discriminate against any class of defendants. Whether to prosecute and what charge to file or bring before a grand jury are decisions that generally rest in the prosecutor's discretion.

The Court of Appeals acknowledged this "settled rule" allowing prosecutorial choice. Nevertheless, relying on the dissenting opinion in *Berra v. United States,* 351 U.S. 131, 76 S.Ct. 685, 100 L.Ed. 1013 (1956),[8] the court distinguished overlapping statutes with identical standards of proof from provisions that vary in some particular. In the court's view, when two statutes prohibit "exactly the same conduct," the prosecutor's "selection of which of two penalties to apply" would be "unfettered." Because such prosecutorial discretion could produce "unequal justice," the court expressed doubt that this form of legislative redundancy was constitutional. We find this analysis factually and legally unsound.

Contrary to the Court of Appeals' assertions, a prosecutor's discretion to choose between §§ 922(h) and 1202(a) is not "unfettered." Selectivity in the enforcement of criminal laws is, of course, subject to constitutional constraints.[9] And a decision to proceed under § 922(h) does not empower the Government to predetermine ultimate criminal sanctions. Rather, it merely enables the sentencing judge to impose a longer prison sentence than § 1202(a) would permit and precludes him from imposing the greater fine authorized by § 1202(a). More

---

8. *Berra* involved two tax evasion statutes, which the Court interpreted as proscribing identical conduct. The defendant, who was charged and convicted under the felony provision, argued that the jury should have been instructed on the misdemeanor offense as well. The Court rejected this contention and refused to consider whether the defendant's sentence was invalid because in excess of the maximum authorized by the misdemeanor statute. The dissent urged that permitting the prosecutor to control whether a particular act would be punished as a misdemeanor or a felony raised "serious constitutional questions."

9. The Equal Protection Clause prohibits selective enforcement "based upon an unjustifiable standard such as race, religion, or other arbitrary classification." *Oyler v. Boles,* 368 U.S. 448, 456, 82 S.Ct. 501, 506, 7 L.Ed.2d 446 (1962). Respondent does not allege that his prosecution was motivated by improper considerations.

importantly, there is no appreciable difference between the discretion a prosecutor exercises when deciding whether to charge under one of two statutes with different elements and the discretion he exercises when choosing one of two statutes with identical elements. In the former situation, once he determines that the proof will support conviction under either statute, his decision is indistinguishable from the one he faces in the latter context. The prosecutor may be influenced by the penalties available upon conviction, but this fact standing alone does not give rise to a violation of the Equal Protection or Due Process Clauses. Just as a defendant has no constitutional right to elect which of two applicable federal statutes shall be the basis of his indictment and prosecution neither is he entitled to choose the penalty scheme under which he will be sentenced.

Approaching the problem of prosecutorial discretion from a slightly different perspective, the Court of Appeals postulated that the statutes might impermissibly delegate to the Executive Branch the legislature's responsibility to fix criminal penalties. We do not agree. The provisions at issue plainly demarcate the range of penalties that prosecutors and judges may seek and impose. In light of that specificity, the power that Congress has delegated to those officials is no broader than the authority they routinely exercise in enforcing the criminal laws. Having informed the courts, prosecutors and defendants of the permissible punishment alternatives available under each Title, Congress has fulfilled its duty.

Accordingly, the judgment of the Court of Appeals is reversed.

Notes and Questions

1. Similarly, in HUTCHERSON v. UNITED STATES, 345 F.2d 964 (D.C.Cir.1965), the court rejected defendant's contention that he had been denied due process because he was indicted and convicted under federal statutes (providing that a third-time narcotics offender is to receive a fine of up to $20,000 and imprisonment from 10 to 40 years, without possibility of probation or suspension of sentence) rather than identical D.C. statutes (providing multiple offenders are punishable by a fine of $500 to $5,000 and/or imprisonment up to 10 years, with suspension of sentence and probation possible). BAZELON, C.J., dissenting in part, objected:

"The choice between felony and misdemeanor in *Berra* did not have as serious consequences as the choice involved in the instant case. On conviction for the felony charge in *Berra*, the trial judge could have imposed the penalties provided by the misdemeanor statute if he was convinced that the prosecutor was mistaken in charging a felony. Here, however, prosecution under Federal rather than District narcotics law precluded any sentence less than ten years. No correction of a prosecutorial 'mistake' would be possible. When the prosecutor 'chooses' a mandatory minimum sentence, he makes a sentencing decision, without either sentencing information or expertise in sentencing. * * *

"Recent instructions from the Attorney General relating to prosecutorial decisions in narcotic cases suggest that the United States Attorney does have certain administrative guidelines for his choice. Thus Title 2, § 86.2–86.3 of the United States Attorneys' Manual provides:

" 'The principal object of enforcement is * * * to prosecute the importers, dealers and traffickers * * *. The emphasis should be on prosecutions of the sellers or purveyors, particularly those who deal with minors, *and not the mere addict possessors.* * * * [C]riminal prosecutions of [addicts] in some instances may be justified so as *to compel an addict to undergo complete [rehabilitative] treatment.* * * * [P]rosecutions for such minor offenses which are considered to be local in character may well be and often are left to the state or local authorities.*

Not falling within such minor category are cases against persons, whether addicts or not, who engage in the importation or transportation or are in possession of these drugs under circumstances reasonably indicating that the drugs were intended for use in the illegal traffic. * * *

" 'In prosecutions for *serious* offenses by *traffickers* * * * *two* counts may be charged, one under the internal revenue laws and the other under [21 U.S.C. § 174].' [Emphasis supplied.] * * *

"These instructions may provide a suitable framework for structuring prosecutorial choice. The reference in the first instructions above to 'minor offenses which are considered to be local in character' suggests use of the 'local' or District statute in the absence of special circumstances. * * *

"I think it would have been open to defendant to attempt to show abuse of prosecutorial discretion on a pretrial motion to dismiss the indictment."

2. Is Judge Bazelon suggesting that Hutcherson should prevail if he shows the charging decision was not in accordance with the guidelines in the United States Attorneys' Manual? Is it relevant that the Manual states: "This Manual provides only internal Department of Justice guidance. It is not intended to, does not, and may not be relied upon to create any rights, substantive or procedural, enforceable at law by any party in any matter civil or criminal. Nor are any limitations hereby placed on otherwise lawful litigative prerogatives of the Department of Justice."[a]

3. A federal vs. state prosecution decision, similar to that in *Hutcherson*, is of some moment to the defendant. "Although the substance of federal criminal law has come to duplicate much of state criminal law, the procedures that apply and the sentences that convicted defendants receive and serve in the federal criminal justice system are often far different than those encountered in state courts. [The] differences between federal and state law that favor federal prosecutions are most striking in cases involving frequently charged duplicative federal statutes, like drug and firearms prosecutions. [There are] five ways in which defendants receive less favorable treatment in federal court than state court[: 1] the Federal Bail Reform Act of 1984 is more likely to result in pretrial detention without bail than state law[; 2] federal law often gives defendants less access to pretrial discovery than does state law[; 3] federal law often provides defendant with fewer opportunities for suppression of evidence as a result of constitutional violations than does state law[; 4] several aspects of federal sentencing law make federal prosecutions less favorable to defendants[, such as] greater maximum sentences[; and 5] defendants frequently serve a greater portion of the sentences imposed in federal court." Steven D. Clymer, *Unequal Justice: The Federalization of Criminal Law*, 70 So.Cal.L.Rev. 643, 668–75 (1997), who thus concludes at 739 that "the Department of Justice should amend its 'Principles of Federal Prosecution' to require that federal prosecutors not only avoid bad reasons for making charging decisions, but that they have good ones for treating federally prosecuted offenders differently than those charged in state court." In addition, should the defendant have some input prior to such a charging decision? Consider *United States v. Jacobs*, 4 F.3d 603 (8th Cir.1993) (defendant's argument that decision between state and federal prosecution where, as here, significant difference in penalty, requires resort to a "formal procedure * * * to determine which sovereign will charge * * * borders on the frivolous").

4. A somewhat different situation is that in which the prosecutor "revises" his charge selection upward following the exercise of some right by the defendant,

a. Quoted in Leland E. Beck, *The Administrative Law of Criminal Prosecution: The De-* *velopment of Prosecutorial Policy*, 27 Am. U.L.Rev. 310, 314 n. 10 (1978).

as in BLACKLEDGE v. PERRY, 417 U.S. 21, 94 S.Ct. 2098, 40 L.Ed.2d 628 (1974). After Perry's conviction of misdemeanor assault in district court (for which he received a sentence of 6 months), e exercised his right under state law to obtain a trial de novo in the superior court. The applicable statute provided that in such a situation the slate is wiped clean, the prior conviction is annulled, and the prosecution and defense begin anew in the superior court. Prior to Perry's appearance in superior court, the prosecutor obtained an indictment, based on the same conduct for which Perry had been tried, charging him with the felony of assault with a deadly weapon with intent to kill. Perry pleaded guilty[b] to that charge and was sentenced to a term of 5–7 years. Relying upon *North Carolina v. Pearce,* p. 1535 (holding that due process prohibits a judge from imposing a more severe sentence for the purpose of discouraging defendants from exercising their statutory right to appeal), Perry later claimed that the felony charge deprived him of due process. The Court, per STEWART, J., agreed:

"The lesson that emerges from *Pearce* [and its progeny] is that the Due Process Clause is not offended by all possibilities of increased punishment upon retrial after appeal, but only by those that pose a realistic likelihood of 'vindictiveness.' Unlike the circumstances presented by those cases, however, in the situation here the central figure is not the judge or the jury, but the prosecutor. The question is whether the opportunities for vindictiveness in this situation are such as to impel the conclusion that due process of law requires a rule analogous to that of the *Pearce* case. We conclude that the answer must be in the affirmative.

"A prosecutor clearly has a considerable stake in discouraging convicted misdemeanants from appealing and thus obtaining a trial *de novo* in the Superior Court, since such an appeal will clearly require increased expenditures of prosecutorial resources before the defendant's conviction becomes final, and may even result in a formerly convicted defendant going free. And, if the prosecutor has the means readily at hand to discourage such appeals—by 'upping the ante' through a felony indictment whenever a convicted misdemeanant pursues his statutory appellate remedy—the State can insure that only the most hardy defendants will brave the hazards of a *de novo* trial.

"There is, of course, no evidence that the prosecutor in this case acted in bad faith or maliciously in seeking a felony indictment against Perry. The rationale of our judgment in the *Pearce* case, however, was not grounded upon the proposition that actual retaliatory motivation must inevitably exist. Rather, we emphasized that 'since the fear of such vindictiveness may unconstitutionally deter a defendant's exercise of the right to appeal his first conviction, due process also requires that a defendant be freed of apprehension of such a retaliatory motivation on the part of the sentencing judge.' We think it clear that the same considerations apply here. A person convicted of an offense is entitled to pursue his statutory right to a trial *de novo,* without apprehension that the State will retaliate by substituting a more serious charge for the original one thus subjecting him to a significantly increased potential period of incarceration.[c]

b. The Court held that the guilty plea did not bar Perry from later raising the due process claim. See p. 1308.

c. In *Thigpen v. Roberts,* 468 U.S. 27, 104 S.Ct. 2916, 82 L.Ed.2d 23 (1984), the relevant facts were essentially identical to those in *Blackledge* except that the first trial was the responsibility of the county prosecutor while the indictment and trial on the felony was the responsibility of the district attorney. The Court noted: "It might be argued that if two different prosecutors are involved, a presump-

tion of vindictiveness, which arises in part from assumptions about the individual's personal stake in the proceedings, is inappropriate. On the other hand, to the extent the presumption reflects 'institutional pressure that * * * might * * * subconsciously motivate a vindictive prosecutorial * * * response to a defendant's exercise of his right to obtain a retrial of a decided question,' it does not hinge on the continued involvement of a particular individual. A district attorney burdened with the retrial of an already-convicted defen-

"Due process of law requires that such a potential for vindictiveness must not enter into North Carolina's two-tiered appellate process. We old, therefore, that it was not constitutionally permissible for the State to respond to Perry's invocation of his statutory right to appeal by bringing a more serious charge against him at the trial *de novo.*⁷"

REHNQUIST, J., dissenting, objected: "The prosecutor here elected to proceed initially in the state district court where felony charges could not be prosecuted for reasons which may well have been unrelated to whether he believed respondent was guilty of and could be convicted of the felony with which he was later charged. Both prosecutor and defendant stand to benefit from an initial prosecution in the District Court, the prosecutor at least from its less burdensome procedures and the defendant from the opportunity for an initial acquittal and the limited penalties. With the countervailing reasons for proceeding only on the misdemeanor charge in the District Court no longer applicable once the defendant has invoked his statutory right to a trial *de novo,* a prosecutor need not be vindictive to seek to indict and convict a defendant of the more serious of the two crimes of which he believes him guilty."

5. Goodwin was charged with several misdemeanor and petty offenses, including assault, and his case was assigned to a Department of Justice attorney detailed temporarily to try such cases before a magistrate and who did not have authority to seek indictments or try felony cases. Goodwin indicated a desire for jury trial, not then available in a trial before a magistrate, so the case was transferred to the district court, where an assistant U.S. Attorney obtained a four-count indictment charging Goodwin with a felony count of forcibly assaulting a federal officer and three related counts. After his conviction of the felony count and one misdemeanor count, Goodwin sought to set aside the verdict on the ground of prosecutorial vindictiveness; the district court denied relief, but the court of appeals reversed on the ground that *Blackledge* entitled Goodwin to such relief even though "the prosecutor did not act with actual vindictiveness." In UNITED STATES v. GOODWIN, 457 U.S. 368, 102 S.Ct. 2485, 73 L.Ed.2d 74 (1982), the Court, per STEVENS, J., disagreed:

"There is good reason to be cautious before adopting an inflexible presumption of prosecutorial vindictiveness in a pretrial setting. In the course of preparing a case for trial, the prosecutor may uncover additional information that suggests a basis for further prosecution or he simply may come to realize that information possessed by the State has a broader significance. At this stage of the proceedings, the prosecutor's assessment of the proper extent of prosecution may not have crystallized. In contrast, once a trial begins—and certainly by the time a conviction as been obtained—it is much more likely that the State has discovered and assessed all of the information against an accused and has made a determination, on the basis of that information, of the extent to which he should be prosecuted. Thus, a change in the charging decision made after an initial trial is completed is much more likely to be improperly motivated than is a pretrial decision.

dant might be no less vindictive because he did not bring the initial prosecution." But the Court then found it unnecessary to "determine the correct rule when two independent prosecutors are involved," for here the county prosecutor participated fully in the later proceedings, as was his statutory duty, and thus "the addition of the district attorney to the prosecutorial team changes little."

7. This would clearly be a different case if the State had shown that it was impossible to proceed on the more serious charge at the outset, as in *Diaz v. United States,* 223 U.S.

442, 32 S.Ct. 250, 56 L.Ed. 500 (1912). In that case the defendant was originally tried and convicted for assault and battery. Subsequent to the original trial, the assault victim died, and the defendant was then tried and convicted for homicide. Obviously, it would not have been possible for the authorities in *Diaz* to have originally proceeded against the defendant on the more serious charge, since the crime of homicide was not complete until after the victim's death.

"In addition, a defendant before trial is expected to invoke procedural rights that inevitably impose some 'burden' on the prosecutor. Defense counsel routinely file pretrial motions to suppress evidence; to challenge the sufficiency and form of an indictment; to plead an affirmative defense; to request psychiatric services; to obtain access to Government files; to be tried by jury. It is unrealistic to assume that a prosecutor's probable response to such motions is to seek to penalize and to deter. The invocation of procedural rights is an integral part of the adversary process in which our criminal justice system operates.

"Thus, the timing of the prosecutor's action in this case suggests that a presumption of vindictiveness is not warranted. A prosecutor should remain free before trial to exercise the broad discretion entrusted to him to determine the extent of the societal interest in prosecution. An initial decision should not freeze future conduct. As we made clear in *Bordenkircher* [*v. Hayes,* p. 1244], the initial charges filed by a prosecutor may not reflect the extent to which an individual is legitimately subject to prosecution.

"The nature of the right asserted by the respondent confirms that a presumption of vindictiveness is not warranted in this case. After initially expressing an interest in plea negotiation, respondent decided not to plead guilty and requested a trial by jury in District Court. In doing so, he forced the Government to bear the burdens and uncertainty of a trial. This Court in *Bordenkircher* made clear that the mere fact that a defendant refuses to plead guilty and forces the Government to prove its case is insufficient to warrant a presumption that subsequent changes in the charging decision are unjustified. Respondent argues that such a presumption is warranted in this case, however, because he not only requested a trial—he requested a trial by jury.

"We cannot agree. The distinction between a bench trial and a jury trial does not compel a special presumption of prosecutorial vindictiveness whenever additional charges are brought after a jury is demanded. To be sure, a jury trial is more burdensome than a bench trial. The defendant may challenge the selection of the venire; the jury itself must be impaneled; witnesses and arguments must be prepared more carefully to avoid the danger of a mistrial. These matters are much less significant, however, than the facts that before either a jury or a judge the State must present its full case against the accused and the defendant is entitled to offer a full defense. As compared to the complete trial *de novo* at issue in *Blackledge* a jury trial—as opposed to a bench trial—does not require duplicative expenditures of prosecutorial resources before a final judgment may be obtained. Moreover, unlike the trial judge in *Pearce,* no party is asked 'to do over what it thought it had already done correctly.' A prosecutor has no 'personal stake' in a bench trial and thus no reason to engage in 'self-vindication' upon a defendant's request for a jury trial. Perhaps most importantly, the institutional bias against the retrial of a decided question that supported the decisions in *Pearce* and *Blackledge* simply has no counterpart in this case.

"There is an opportunity for vindictiveness, [but] a mere opportunity for vindictiveness is insufficient to justify the imposition of a prophylactic rule. As *Blackledge* makes clear, 'the Due Process Clause is not offended by all possibilities of increased punishment * * * but only by those that pose a realistic likelihood of "vindictiveness." 'The possibility that a prosecutor would respond to a defendant's pretrial demand for a jury trial by bringing charges not in the public interest that could be explained only as penalty imposed on the defendant is so *unlikely* that a presumption of vindictiveness certainly is not warranted.

"In declining to apply a presumption of vindictiveness, we of course do not foreclose the possibility that a defendant in an appropriate case might prove objectively that the prosecutor's charging decision was motivated by a desire to punish him for doing something that the law plainly allowed him to do."

BLACKMUN, J., concurring in the judgment, found "no support in our prior cases for any distinction between pretrial and post-trial vindictiveness," but concluded there had been a permissible adjustment of the charges "based on 'objective information concerning identifiable conduct on the part of the defendant occurring after the time of the original' charging decision."[d]

BRENNAN, J., joined by Marshall, J., dissenting, objected: "The Court suggests that the distinction between a bench trial and a jury trial is unimportant in this context. Such a suggestion is demonstrably fallacious. Experienced criminal practitioners, for both prosecution and defense, know that a jury trial entails far more prosecutorial work than a bench trial. Defense challenges to the potential-juror array, *voir dire* examination of potential jurors, and suppression hearings all take up a prosecutor's time before a jury trial, adding to his scheduling difficulties and caseload. More care in the preparation of his requested instructions, of is witnesses, and of his own remarks is necessary in order to avoid mistrial or reversible error. And there is always the specter of the 'irrational' acquittal by a jury that is unreviewable on appeal. Thus it is simply inconceivable that a criminal defendant's election to be tried by jury would be a matter of indifference to his prosecutor. On the contrary, the prosecutor would almost always prefer that the defendant waive such a 'troublesome' right. And if the defendant refuses to do so, the prosecutor's subsequent elevation of the charges against the defendant manifestly poses a realistic likelihood of vindictiveness."

6. In a situation where *Blackledge* does apply, may a prosecutor escalate the charge only in the particular situation described in footnote 7 of that case? Of what significance is it that the Court has more recently stated in *Goodwin* that the *Blackledge* presumption "could be overcome by objective evidence justifying the prosecutor's action"? That in *Texas v. McCullough,* p. 1539, the Court declared that if the *Pearce* presumption were applicable there it could be overcome "by objective information * * * justifying the increased sentence"?

7. Does *Blackledge* or *Goodwin* apply when the prosecutor escalates the charges following a mistrial granted on defendant's motion because of the jury's inability to agree on a verdict? Compare *United States v. Mays,* 738 F.2d 1188 (11th Cir.1984); with *Murphy v. State,* 453 N.E.2d 219 (Ind.1983).[e]

8. Sometimes the charges are not escalated, but yet are not reduced as the prosecutor earlier indicated would be done. Illustrative is *People v. Navarroli,* 521 N.E.2d 891 (Ill.1988), where, at a hearing on defendant's motion for specific performance, it was established (i) that after defendant was charged with three drug offenses the prosecutor promised a reduction in the charges if defendant would act as an informant in various drug investigations, and (ii) that defendant had fully performed his portion of the agreement. The lower court granted the motion, but on appeal it was decided that the prosecutor's "refusal to carry out

d. In support he referred to footnote 2 of the majority opinion, reading: "By affidavit, the Assistant United States Attorney later set forth his reasons for this action: (1) he considered respondent's conduct on the date in question to be a serious violation of law, (2) Goodwin had a lengthy history of violent crime, (3) the prosecutor considered respondent's conduct to be related to major narcotics transactions, (4) the prosecutor believed that respondent had committed perjury at his preliminary hearing, and (5) Goodwin had failed to appear for trial as originally scheduled. The Govern-

ment attorney stated that his decision to seek a felony indictment was not motivated in any way by Goodwin's request for a jury trial in District Court."

e. For discussion of the *Blackledge–Goodwin* doctrine, see C. Peter Erlinder & David C. Thomas, *Prohibiting Prosecutorial Vindictiveness While Protecting Prosecutorial Discretion: Toward a Principled Resolution of a Due Process Dilemma,* 76 J.Crim.L. & C. 341 (1985); Barbara A. Schwartz, *The Limits of Prosecutorial Vindictiveness,* 69 Iowa L.Rev. 127 (1983).

the claimed bargain did not deprive the defendant of due process, and that therefore, the defendant was not entitled to have the assumed agreement enforced." The court distinguished *Santobello v. New York,* p. 1260, as a case where "the prosecutor breached the plea agreement after the defendant entered a plea of guilty," and asserted that in the instant case "the defendant has not entered a plea of guilty in reliance on the proposed plea agreement. He cannot say he was deprived of liberty by virtue of the State's refusal to abide by the terms of the claimed plea agreement." As for defendant's assertion that "he performed is part of the bargain in reliance on the agreement, making restoration of the pre-plea-agreement status impossible," the court responded that because "the defendant still has the option of pleading not guilty and going to trial," it could not be said "that specific performance of the bargain is the only adequate remedy."

A dissent declared that from a contracts perspective the majority's position was in error because it ignored the fact that the defendant provided "actual consideration" when "he provided the State with new information," and that from a public policy perspective the majority's conclusion was unsound because now "a prosecutor's promise to reduce the charges for a defendant in exchange for the defendant's assistance will not be enforceable; few informed defendants will aid the prosecution in return for a promise when they know that it is not enforceable by a trial court."

Query, does the *Navarroli* majority or dissent have the better of the argument? Consider *People v. Boyt,* 488 N.E.2d 264 (Ill.1985) (defendant agreed to testify against her codefendant in exchange for the state's promise to reduce the charge against her, but before defendant could testify the codefendant pleaded guilty, so the state refused to reduce the charges; held, defendant has no right to enforce the agreement, as the state's repudiation deprived defendant of no constitutionally protected interest); and *People v. Starks,* 478 N.E.2d 350 (Ill.1985) (defendant submitted to polygraph examination in exchange for prosecutor's promise to dismiss charges against him if he passed the test; held, when defendant passed the test he was entitled to enforcement of the agreement, as he had surrendered his Fifth Amendment privilege against self incrimination as part of the agreement). The *Navarroli* majority found the instant case more like *Boyt* than *Starks,* while the dissent reached the exact opposite conclusion.

9. Some jurisdictions follow the approach of the *Navarroli* dissent, so that a prosecutor's promise to reduce (or even drop) charges in exchange for some consideration provided by the defendant, even if not involving surrender of a constitutional right, is enforceable if the defendant has kept his side of the bargain. Illustrative is *Bowers v. State,* 500 N.E.2d 203 (Ind.1986), where, following defendant's arrest for burglary, the prosecutor entered into an agreement with him to dismiss charges related to defendant's arrest if defendant would provide information sufficient to obtain a search warrant for the residence of another person, as he did. What if Bowers had struck that agreement with the *police*? Cf. *United States v. Flemmi,* 225 F.3d 78 (1st Cir.2000).

10. Consider now a case somewhat like *Boyt,* except that the defendant *is* going to testify pursuant to the agreement, but the codefendant now claims that such a promise of leniency in exchange for testimony is itself proscribed by the criminal law. In *United States v. Singleton,* 144 F.3d 1343 (10th Cir.1998), a panel of the Tenth Circuit agreed with that contention, holding that testimony offered as a consequence of such an agreement should be suppressed because the government had violated the so-called "anti-gratuity statute," 18 U.S.C.A. § 201(c)(2), which makes it a criminal offense to give or offer "anything of value to any person, for or because of the testimony under oath or affirmation given or to be given by such person as a witness upon a trial." But upon rehearing en banc, 165 F.3d 1297 (10th Cir.1999), the court rejected that conclusion and affirmed the conviction obtained by use of testimony prompted by such an agreement. The court reasoned: (i) that a prosecutor who has entered into such an agreement "is the alter ego of the United States exercising its sovereign power of prosecution"; (ii) that the word "whoever," used in the statute to describe those to whom the statute applies, by its normal meaning "connotes a being" while the "United States is an inanimate entity, not a being"; (iii) that given the "longstanding" and "ingrained" practice of granting leniency in exchange for testimony, reading the statute as restricting that power would be "a diminution of sovereignty not countenanced in our jurisprudence"; and (iv) that, "had Congress intended that [the statute] overturn this ingrained aspect of American legal culture, it would have done so in clear, unmistakable, and unarguable language."[f]

f. The court added: "Our conclusion in no way permits an agent of the government to step beyond the limits of his or her office to make an offer to a witness other than one traditionally exercised by the sovereign. A prosecutor who offers something other than a concession normally granted by the government in exchange for testimony is no longer the alter ego of the sovereign and is divested of the protective mantle of the government. Thus, fears our decision would permit improper use or abuse of prosecutorial authority simply have no foundation."

Those fears were expressed by two concurring judges, who rejected the majority's approach and instead relied upon "long-established principles of statutory construction" for the proposition that "where specific statutes overlap with a general statute, the latter must give way, insofar as it would prohibit that which the narrow statutes would allow." This would mean, they explained, that "the general prohibition of § 201(c)(2)" *would* apply to prosecutors, subject to "specific exceptions" derived from other actions of Congress. Thus, they concluded: "Prosecutors may offer only those incentives that Congress has approved, and may bargain and execute agreements only within the narrow, specific procedures that Congress and the courts have articulated."

Chapter 14

THE PRELIMINARY HEARING[aa]

SECTION 1. THE FUNCTION(S) OF THE PRELIMINARY HEARING

A. Screening

"The object or purpose of the preliminary [hearing] is to prevent hasty, malicious, improvident, and oppressive prosecutions, to protect the person charged from open and public accusations of crime, to avoid both for the defendant and the public the expense of a public trial, and to save the defendant from the humiliation and anxiety involved in public prosecution, and to discover whether or not there are substantial grounds upon which a prosecution may be based."

Rosenberry, J., in *Thies v. State,* 189 N.W. 539 (Wis.1922).

The "screening" objective described by Justice Rosenberry is universally recognized as the primary function of the preliminary hearing. Indeed, most courts recognize it as the sole purpose of the preliminary hearing, and treat the other functions discussed below (i.e., discovery, perpetuation of testimony, etc.) as merely incidental byproducts of the screening process. The aims of the screening objective are well stated in *Thies.* Today, courts also stress two other aims of effective preliminary hearing screening: (1) ensuring that the defendant who has been unjustifiably charged will be promptly released from custody or, if he made bail, from the conditions of that bail; and (2) requiring reduction of excessive charges and thereby serving as a check against the prosecutorial practice of "overcharging" in anticipation of plea negotiations.

aa. While "preliminary hearing" is the most common terminology, states also refer to the hearing described in this chapter as a "preliminary examination," "probable cause hearing" or "bindover hearing." See step 10 of Ch. 1 (p. 23). It should be distinguished from the ex parte magistrate determination of probable cause to arrest made at or before the first appearance and commonly described as the "*Gerstein* review." See step 8 of Ch. 1 (p. 22) and Note 1, p. 906. Leading studies of preliminary hearings, each focusing on the use of the hearing in a particular jurisdiction or group of jurisdictions, include: Deborah Day Emerson and Nancy Ames, *The Role of the Grand Jury and the Preliminary Hearing in Pretrial Screening* (1984); Roy Flemming, *Elements of the Defense Attorney's Craft: An Adaptive Expectations Model of the Preliminary Hearing Decision,* 8 Law & Policy 33 (1986); Janet Gilboy, *Prosecutor's Discretionary Use of the Grand Jury to Initiate and Reinitiate Prosecution,* 1984 A.B.F.Res.J. 2; Kenneth Graham Jr. and Leon Letwin, *The Preliminary Hearing in Los Angeles: Some Field Findings and Legal Policy Observations,* 18 U.C.L.A.L.Rev. 635, 916 (1971); Lewis Katz, et al., *Justice Is The Crime* (1972); Frank Miller, *Prosecution: The Decision to Charge a Suspect with a Crime* (1969); John Van Dam, *Preliminary Hearings in a Truckload,* 8 Crim.Just.J. 195 (1986). These studies are hereafter cited by reference to the author's name. For a more extensive review of the law governing preliminary hearings, see Wayne R. LaFave, Jerold H. Israel, & Nancy J. King, *Criminal Procedure Treatise* (2d ed. 1999) (available in Westlaw under the database CRIMPROC and hereafter cited as CRIMPROC).

The effectiveness of the preliminary hearing in performing its screening function is a matter of considerable dispute. As in the case of the grand jury (see p. 935), commentators and courts have offered arguments and statistics on both sides. Fruitful evaluation of their conclusions is made especially difficult, however, by substantial variations in the hearing's structure and operation from one jurisdiction to another (and sometimes, in its operation from one county to another in the same jurisdiction). Studies of the preliminary hearing in different jurisdictions (see fn. a supra) have produced, for example, quite disparate statistics on preliminary hearing dispositions. The percentage of dismissals to the total number of hearings has ranged from 2% to 30%, with a 5–10% rate commonly described as typical. See Ch. 1, step 10 (p. 23); CRIMPROC § 14.1(a).

What factors might contribute to such substantial variations in the percentages of preliminary hearing dismissals and reductions? Consider the following potential differences in legal standards or local practices, all of which have been cited as arguably having a bearing on the frequency of dismissals and reductions in a particular jurisdiction: (1) whether prosecutorial screening before the case reaches the preliminary hearing stage is extensive (as in jurisdictions where 30–50% of the cases presented by the police do not result in the filing of charges) or is superficial or not even utilized for all but exceptional cases; (2) whether prosecutors are assigned horizontally to cases (with different prosecutors responsible for initial screening, preliminary hearing presentation, and trial) or vertically (with the same prosecutor responsible for the case from initial presentation to final disposition); (3) whether the prosecutor most often bypasses the preliminary hearing by taking the case directly to the grand jury (so that preliminary hearings are used in only a small group of cases) or regularly utilizes the preliminary hearing (see Notes 4–5, p. 909); (4) whether the use of the bypass procedure is tied to the strength of the particular case (see Note 6 at p. 910); (5) the qualifications of the magistrates conducting the hearing (ranging from the lay justice of the peace to the full-time lawyer/judge); (6) the extent of the magistrate's caseload, which may range from 2–3 preliminary hearings per day to 10–20 hearings per day; (7) whether the caseload at the trial level necessarily precludes trial of all cases which could justifiably be boundover (thereby encouraging the magistrate to reduce charges in cases more appropriately disposed of at the misdemeanor level); (8) whether cases are settled by plea bargains prior to the preliminary hearing stage or plea bargaining begins and cases are settled largely after the case reaches the trial level court; (9) whether defense counsel regularly insist upon a preliminary hearing even in open and shut cases (largely to obtain discovery) or usually waive the hearing in such cases (see Note 1, p. 905); (10) whether the evidentiary standard governing the magistrate's decision to bindover is essentially the same probable cause standard applied on the issuance of an arrest warrant or a standard comparable to that imposed by a trial judge in determining whether there is sufficient evidence to send a case to the jury (see § 3 infra); (11) whether the prosecutor must meet the bindover standard through evidence that would be admissible at trial or may rely instead on hearsay and other evidence generally inadmissible at trial (see § 4 infra); (12) whether the magistrate has the same leeway as a trial court factfinder in judging credibility (see Note 7, p. 916); (13) whether the scope of defense presentations is limited—e.g., whether the defense may establish affirmative defenses, and whether the leeway granted the defense in cross-examining prosecution witnesses and presenting defense witnesses generally approximates, or is considerably narrower than, that granted at trial (see § 4 infra); (14) whether the prosecution, even though not required to do so in order to satisfy the bindover standard, follows the practice of presenting all of its key witnesses, or instead seeks to limit defense discovery and reduce the burden on its witnesses by introducing just enough evidence to meet the bindover standard (which in some jurisdictions allows it to rely entirely on the testimony of the investigating officer); (15) whether the practical impact of a magistrate's order of dismissal is to end the case or the prosecutor frequently reinitiates prosecution without additional evidence by either taking the case to the grand jury or refiling when another judge is sitting as preliminary hearing magistrate (see Note 8, p. 917).

B. Discovery

"Although the primary purpose served by the federal preliminary examination is to insure that there is 'probable cause,' * * * in practice this hearing may provide the defense with the most valuable discovery technique available to him." Weinstein, D.J. in *United States ex rel. Wheeler v. Flood*, 269 F.Supp. 194 (E.D.N.Y.1967).

In meeting the evidentiary standard for a bindover, the prosecutor will necessarily provide the defense with some discovery of the prosecution's case. The defendant may obtain even more discovery by cross-examining the prosecution's witnesses at the hearing and by subpoenaing other potential trial witnesses to testify as defense witnesses at the hearing. The extent of the discovery obtained in this manner will depend upon several factors, including the following: (1) whether the prosecution can rely entirely on hearsay reports and thereby sharply limit the number of witnesses it presents; (2) whether, even assuming hearsay cannot be used, the bindover standard may be satisfied by the presentation of a minimal amount of testimony on each element of the offense; (3) whether, notwithstanding the ease with which the standard is met, the prosecution still follows a general practice of presenting most of its case; (4) whether the defendant is limited, both in cross-examination and in the presentation of witnesses, to direct rebuttal of material presented by the prosecution; (5) whether the defendant is willing to bear the tactical costs that may be incurred in utilizing his subpoena and cross-examination authority for discovery purposes.[a]

The importance to the defense of the limited discovery available through the preliminary hearing will depend in large part on the availability of alternative discovery procedures. When the prior statements of prospective witnesses (including the arresting officer's report) is readily available under state discovery rules, the discovery potential of the preliminary hearing may be relatively unimportant. Where, on the other hand, state law and practice provide very little pretrial discovery, the preliminary hearing may serve as the primary discovery device under local practice. Also, even though state law provides extensive discovery, if that discovery is not available until after the critical time for plea settlements has passed, the preliminary hearing may still serve as the primary discovery vehicle for the substantial percentage of cases resolved by guilty pleas.

a. Consider in this connection, Anthony Amsterdam, *Trial Manual for the Defense of Criminal Cases* § 139 (5th ed. 1989): "Frequently, counsel may find that s/he is working at cross-purposes in seeking to discover and to lay a foundation for impeachment simultaneously. * * *. If counsel vigorously cross-examines the witness, in an effort to get a contradiction or concession on record, the witness will normally dig in and give a minimum of information in an effort to save his or her testimonial position; and more than likely s/he will be uncooperative if counsel thereafter attempts to interview the witness prior to trial. On the other hand, if counsel engages the witness in routine examination, amiable and ranging, counsel may be able to pick up many clues for investigation and for planning of his defense." There may be even greater costs in seeking discovery by subpoenaing a potential state witness not called by the prosecution. The magistrate may refuse to permit the defendant to treat the witness as adverse on direct examination and allow the prosecution to lead the witness on cross-examination. Also, the defendant runs the risk of preserving damaging testimony that might not otherwise be available at trial. See id. at § 141.

C. FUTURE IMPEACHMENT

"[T]he skilled interrogation of witnesses [at the preliminary examination] by an experienced lawyer can fashion a vital impeachment tool for use in cross-examination of the State's witnesses at the trial." Brennan, J., in *Coleman v. Alabama*, 399 U.S. 1, 90 S.Ct. 1999, 26 L.Ed.2d 387 (1970).

Extensive cross-examination of prosecution witnesses at the preliminary hearing may be of value to the defense even though there is little likelihood of successfully challenging the prosecution's showing of probable cause and little to be gained by way of discovery. As Justice Brennan suggests, the skillful extraction of statements from a witness at the preliminary hearing may provide a solid foundation for effective cross-examination of that witness at trial. In many instances, witnesses are more likely to make damaging admissions or contradictory statements at the preliminary hearing because they are less thoroughly briefed for that proceeding than they are for trial. Also, with respect to some witnesses, the more they say before trial, the more likely that there will be some inconsistency between their trial testimony and their previous statements. Arguably, such inconsistencies may have a more damaging impact upon the witness' credibility when the inconsistency is with preliminary hearing testimony, as opposed to unsworn statements given to the police during interviews. Of course, cross-examination designed to lay the foundation for future impeachment carries with it certain dangers for the defense. If the cross-examination focuses too much on potential weaknesses in the witness' testimony, it may educate the witness as to these weaknesses. The witness may then attempt to rehabilitate himself at trial by stating that he was confused at the hearing, this caused him to review the events, and he now has everything clear in his mind. If the witness is one who otherwise might "soften" his view of the facts as time passes and his emotional involvement lessens, extensive cross-examination at the preliminary hearing may only harden his position and make him less able to retreat to a more friendly position.[b] Finally, if the witness becomes unavailable at trial, the defense counsel may find that he has perpetuated testimony more damaging than that which would have existed without the cross-examination. See pt. D below.

D. THE "PERPETUATION OF TESTIMONY"

"The function of perpetuating testimony should be of substantial concern to the prosecutor * * * because of the ever present possibility that an important witness may prove unavailable to testify at trial." Graham and Letwin, 925.

1. *Practical significance.* Preliminary hearing testimony traditionally has been admitted at trial as substantive evidence, under the "prior testimony" exception to the hearsay rule, where the witness is currently unavailable to testify. Thus, the hearing perpetuates the testimony of witnesses, ensuring that it may be used even if the witness should die, disappear, or otherwise become unavailable to testify.[c] While the Supreme Court has stated that a major advantage of the hearing for the defense is its availability to "preserve testimony

---

b. If the witness should retreat to such a position, the prosecution may be able to use the more favorable preliminary hearing testimony to impeach its own witness. Moreover, in some jurisdictions, the inconsistent preliminary hearing testimony may be used as substantive evidence (i.e., not merely for impeachment), even though the witness testifies at trial and refutes his earlier testimony. See e.g., Fed.R.Evid. 801(d)(1).

c. See Fed.R.Evid. 804(a) setting forth the traditional grounds of unavailability: " 'Unavailability as a witness' includes situations in which the declarant: (1) is exempted by ruling of the court on the ground of privilege from testifying concerning the subject matter of the declarant's statement; or (2) persists in refusing to testify concerning the subject matter of the declarant's statement despite an order of

favorable to the accused of a witness who does not appear at the trial," *Coleman v. Alabama* (p. 919), the hearing is not commonly used by the defense for this purpose. For various reasons (see Note 1, p. 926), the defense rarely will have its own witnesses testify at the preliminary hearing. Accordingly, the perpetuation of testimony is of practical significance primarily as it relates to prosecution witnesses, and the possibility of perpetuation tends to be viewed by the defense as a negative feature of the hearing.[d]

   2. *Confrontation clause challenges.* The admission of the preliminary hearing testimony of a prosecution witness who is unavailable at trial (and therefore is not subject to trial cross-examination) must be reconciled with the defendant's Sixth Amendment right of confrontation. CALIFORNIA v. GREEN, 399 U.S. 149, 90 S.Ct. 1930, 26 L.Ed.2d 489 (1970), established the basic guidelines for admitting such testimony consistent with defendant's Sixth Amendment right. The Court there upheld the constitutionality of admitting preliminary hearing testimony over a defense objection that it should not be admissible where the prosecution witness was "unavailable" solely because of a loss of memory. The primary point of concern in *Green* was the treatment of the witness' loss of memory as a type of "unavailability," but both the majority and dissent commented as well on the application of the "prior testimony" exception to preliminary hearing testimony. The majority opinion, per WHITE, J., noted in this regard:

   "[The witness] Porter's statement at the preliminary hearing had already been given under circumstances closely approximating those that surround the typical trial. Porter was under oath; respondent was represented by counsel—the same counsel in fact who later represented him at the trial; respondent had every opportunity to cross-examine Porter as to his statement; and the proceedings were conducted before a judicial tribunal, equipped to provide a judicial record of the hearings. * * * This Court long ago held that admitting the prior testimony of any unavailable witness does not violate the Confrontation Clause. *Mattox v. United States,* 156 U.S. 237, 15 S.Ct. 337, 39 L.Ed. 409 (1895). That case involved testimony given at the defendant's first trial by a witness who had died by the time of the second trial, but we do not find the instant preliminary hearing significantly different from an actual trial to warrant distinguishing the two cases for purposes of the Confrontation Clause. * * * In the present case respondent's counsel does not appear to have been significantly limited in any way in the scope or nature of his cross-examination of the witness Porter at the preliminary hearing."

   Justice BRENNAN, dissenting, argued that the admission of a witness' preliminary hearing statement violates the accused's right of confrontation "where the witness is in court and either is unwilling or unable to testify regarding the pertinent events." The dissent argued that such "unavailability"

---

the court to do so; or (3) testifies to a lack of memory of the subject matter of the declarant's statement; or (4) is unable to be present or to testify at the hearing because of death or then existing physical or mental illness or infirmity; or (5) is absent from the hearing and the proponent of a statement has been unable to procure the declarant's attendance * * * by process or other reasonable means. * * * "It should be noted, in connection with the 5th ground, that persons located outside the trial jurisdiction will not necessarily be "unavailable." If his whereabouts are known, a witness located in another state ordinarily may be subjected to compulsory process under the

Uniform Act to Secure The Attendance of Witnesses From Without A State In Criminal Proceedings 11 U.L.A. 2 (1974).

   d. If the prosecution has good reason to believe that the witness will be unavailable at trial, the witness' testimony can be preserved by use of deposition. See Note 5, p. 1186. The preliminary hearing offers the advantage of perpetuating the testimony of witnesses who unexpectedly become unavailable, as well as eliminating the burden of establishing likely unavailability that ordinarily must be met to gain judicial authorization to use the deposition.

was particularly suspect, and in that context (in contrast to the situation where the witness is "physically unavailable"), cross-examination at a preliminary hearing could not provide sufficient countervailing indicia of reliability. On the latter point, the dissent noted:

"Cross-examination at the [preliminary] hearing pales beside that which takes place at trial. This is so for a number of reasons. First, as noted, the objective of the hearing is to establish the presence or absence of probable cause, not guilt or innocence proved beyond a reasonable doubt; thus, if evidence suffices to establish probable cause, defense counsel has little reason at the preliminary hearing to show that it does not conclusively establish guilt—or, at least, he had little reason before today's decision. Second, neither defense nor prosecution is eager before trial to disclose its case by extensive examination at the preliminary hearing; thorough questioning of a prosecution witness by defense counsel may easily amount to a grant of gratis discovery to the state. Third, the schedules of neither court nor counsel can easily accommodate lengthy preliminary hearings. Fourth, even were the judge and lawyers not concerned that the proceedings be brief, the defense and prosecution have generally had inadequate time before the hearing to prepare for extensive examination. * * * It appears, then, that in terms of the purposes of the Confrontation Clause, an equation of face-to-face encounter at the preliminary hearing with confrontation at trial must rest largely on the fact that the witness testified at the hearing under oath, subject to the penalty for perjury and in a courtroom atmosphere. These factors are not insignificant, but by themselves they fall far short of satisfying the demands of constitutional confrontation. Moreover, the atmosphere and stakes are different in the two proceedings. In the hurried, somewhat *pro forma* context of the average preliminary hearing, a witness may be more careless in his testimony than in the more measured and searching atmosphere of a trial. Similarly, a man willing to perjure himself when the consequences are simply that the accused will stand trial may be less willing to do so when his lies may condemn the defendant to loss of liberty. In short, it ignores reality to assume that the purposes of the Confrontation Clause are met during a preliminary hearing. * * * "

3. *Opportunity vs. actual cross-examination.* OHIO v. ROBERTS, 448 U.S. 56, 100 S.Ct. 2531, 65 L.Ed.2d 597 (1980), commented further upon the scope of *Green.* The Court there held that *Green* permitted admission of preliminary hearing testimony of an unavailable prosecution witness who had been called by the defense at the preliminary hearing, but had been examined, in effect, as a hostile witness. While defense counsel had not formally asked that the witness be declared hostile and that he be allowed to cross-examine her, his questioning had been the functional equivalent of cross-examination. The Court noted that counsel, in his "direct examination," had challenged the witness' perception of events and her veracity, and had not been limited "in any way" in this line of questioning. The end result was, as in *Green,* a "substantial compliance with the purposes behind the confrontation requirement." The Court added that, in light of the facts before it, there was no need to determine whether *Green* applied where a defense counsel had not actually engaged in extensive questioning of the witness. Referring to the discussion in *Green* quoted in Note 2 supra, the majority (per BLACKMUN, J.) noted:

"This passage and others in the *Green* opinion suggest that the opportunity to cross-examine at the preliminary hearing—even absent actual cross-examination—satisfies the Confrontation Clause. Yet the record showed, and the Court recognized, that defense counsel in fact had cross-examined Porter at the earlier proceeding. Thus, Mr. Justice Brennan, writing in dissent, could conclude only that '[p]erhaps' 'the mere opportunity for face-to-face encounter [is] sufficient.' We need not decide whether the Supreme Court of Ohio correctly dismissed statements in *Green* suggesting that the mere opportunity to cross-examine rendered the prior testimony admissible. See Westen, *The Future of Confrontation,* 77 Mich.L.Rev. 1185, 1211 (1979) (issue is 'truly difficult to resolve under conventional theories of confrontation'). Nor need we decide whether *de minimus* questioning is sufficient, for defense counsel in this case tested [the currently unavailable witness'] testimony with the equivalent of significant cross-examination."

"Post-*Roberts* lower court rulings have focused upon the adequacy of the opportunity that had been available to counsel to cross-examine the now unavailable witness, rather than whether counsel actually used that opportunity." CRIMPROC § 14.1(d). But courts have not been in complete agreement as to what limitations rendered that opportunity less than adequate. See e.g., *State v. Griffin,* 818 S.W.2d 278 (Mo.1991) (the absence of an opportunity for discovery prior to the hearing does not preclude trial use of unavailable witness' preliminary hearing testimony when later-discovered impeachment material could be brought out at trial); *People v. McCambry,* 578 N.E.2d 1224 (Ill.App.1991) (preliminary hearing testimony of now unavailable robbery victim inadmissible where counsel had not questioned the witness concerning the suggestiveness of the lineup at which the witness identified the defendant; counsel learned only through subsequent discovery that, unlike defendant, 2 of the 3 other lineup participants wore caps and that there was a photograph of the lineup). Consider also *Cardenas v. State,* 811 P.2d 989 (Wyo.1991) (evidence rule conditioning use of unavailable witness' testimony at a prior proceeding on a similarity of motive for cross-examination between the prior proceeding and the trial was met where cross-examination at preliminary hearing was aimed at "analyzing and discounting" assault victim's testimony; counsel may have been restrained in cross-examination by a tactical goal of not revealing the theory of the defense at that early stage in the case, but that does not alter basic similarity of motive).

E.   OTHER FUNCTIONS

In a particular jurisdiction the preliminary hearing may be utilized by defense to serve other incidental functions besides discovery, preparation for trial cross-examination, and the perpetuation of testimony. Thus, in some jurisdictions, the preliminary hearing is viewed as an important opportunity for gaining reduction of bail or other terms of pretrial release. This is particularly true where bail is set at the initial appearance largely on the basis of a schedule tied to the offense charged, and the preliminary hearing provides the magistrate with his first extensive examination of the facts of the individual case.

The preliminary hearing also may serve as an integral part of the plea bargaining process, particularly where negotiations have been undertaken prior to the hearing. The hearing may then operate as a valuable "educational process" for the defendant who is not persuaded by his counsel's opinion that the prosecution has such a strong case that a negotiated plea is in the defendant's best interest. Flemming, 43–44. In some jurisdictions, the hearing may also provide the initial point at which the constitutional validity of the acquisition of certain prosecution evidence may be challenged. See Note 3 at p. 922. Where that is the case, the preliminary hearing objection may offer sufficient advantages over relying solely upon a suppression motion before the trial court as to lead defense counsel to insist upon a preliminary examination for the purpose of making that objection, even though the prosecution has sufficient additional evidence to justify a bindover. The preliminary hearing also may be desired because it will reveal factors mitigating the seriousness of the crime that will be helpful in sentencing. See Van Dam, 211.

F.   WAIVER OF THE PRELIMINARY HEARING

1. *Defense waiver.* The potential values of the preliminary hearing to the defense might suggest that waiver of the hearing would be rare. In fact, waiver rates vary substantially among jurisdictions and sometimes exceed 50%, even in jurisdictions which provide quite extensive preliminary hearings. Katz, 46–47; Flemming, 37–44. Commentators have pointed to a variety of factors that may influence the waiver rate in a particular jurisdiction. Those factors include: (1) the expansiveness of the hearing; (2) the availability of alternative screening and discovery devices; (3) the inadequacy of the payment schedule of appointed counsel for representation at a preliminary hearing; (4) a prosecution practice of offering significant concessions to defendants who waive their preliminary hearings; (5) a prosecution practice of negotiating pleas prior to the preliminary hearing stage; and (6) the "habit, tradition, and conventional wisdom" of the local bar. See Graham and Letwin, 923.

Practice manuals generally urge defense counsel not to waive a preliminary hearing unless the hearing presents a substantial danger to the defense that outweighs its value. Amsterdam, fn. a supra, cites five circumstances in which such a danger may exist: (1) an essential prosecution witness is able to testify at the preliminary hearing but may well be unavailable at trial; (2) a complainant is likely to "mellow" with time if he is not required at this point to put his testimony "on the record"; (3) the preliminary hearing will be an open proceeding, accessible to the press (see *Press–Enterprise II,* p. 1379), and adverse publicity from press coverage may make it difficult to obtain a fair trial; (4) the preliminary hearing will call the prosecutor's attention to a curable defect in the prosecution's case that otherwise would not be noticed until trial, when it would be too late to correct it; and (5) the preliminary hearing will alert the prosecutor to the fact that the defendant is undercharged. Id. at § 137.

2. *Prosecution waiver.* In many jurisdictions, the prosecutor has a right to insist upon the preliminary hearing even though the defendant desires to waive the hearing. See e.g., Cal.Pen.Code, § 860. The prosecutor's right is based on the premise that the state has an interest, independent of the defendant, in "determining whether or not there is sufficient probable cause." *People v. Wilcox,* 6 N.W.2d 518 (Mich.1942). Some prosecutors regularly insist upon the hearing because of its value in preparing for trial. See Graham and Letwin, 647. More commonly, the prosecutor will oppose a defense waiver only under special circumstances, as where (1) there appears to be a need to perpetuate testimony because a particular witness is likely to become unavailable, or (2) a particular witness is "shaky" and there would be some value in placing him under oath at this point.

SECTION 2. THE DEFENDANT'S RIGHT TO A PRELIMINARY HEARING

1. *Independent screening and the federal constitution.* Hurtado v. California, discussed in Ch. 15 at p. 933, was the first in a series of cases considering the contention that the federal constitution requires a pretrial screening of the prosecution's proposed charge by a neutral agency to ensure that there is adequate evidentiary support for the charge. In *Hurtado,* the defendant argued that the Fourteenth Amendment due process clause required such screening by a grand jury through the incorporation of the Fifth Amendment requirement that felony prosecutions be instituted only by grand jury indictment. For reasons discussed at p. 933, the Court rejected defendant's contention. It held that the Fifth Amendment guarantee of prosecution by indictment was *not* a fundamental right applicable to the states through the due process clause of the Fourteenth Amendment.

The California procedure challenged in *Hurtado* provided for charging by prosecutor's information, rather than by indictment, but it also required a magistrate's initial determination that probable cause existed, made at what was essentially a preliminary hearing. It therefore was not clear from *Hurtado* whether due process permitted a state to dispense with all forms of independent screening or just screening by a grand jury. Although there traditionally had been no screening procedure for misdemeanor offenses, states commonly required either an indictment or a magistrate's preliminary hearing bindover for a felony prosecution. In *Lem Woon v. Oregon*, 229 U.S. 586, 33 S.Ct. 783, 57 L.Ed. 1340 (1913), the elimination of all screening procedures was squarely presented by an Oregon procedure permitting direct filing of an information without "any examination, or commitment by a magistrate * * * or any verification other than [the prosecutor's] official oath." A unanimous Court held that the Oregon procedure did not violate due process. Justice Pitney's opinion for the Court relied primarily upon the reasoning of *Hurtado*. It rejected as "untenable" an attempt to distinguish *Hurtado* on the ground that the California procedure upheld there required an initial finding of probable cause by the magistrate. The *Lem Woon* opinion noted: "[T]his court has * * * held [that] the 'due process of law' clause does not require the State to adopt the institution and procedure of a grand jury, [and] we are unable to see upon what theory it can be held that an examination or the opportunity for one, prior to the formal accusation by the district attorney, is obligatory upon the States."

In *Gerstein v. Pugh*, 420 U.S. 103, 95 S.Ct. 854, 43 L.Ed.2d 54 (1975), the Court also rejected the contention that a preliminary hearing was required by the Fourth Amendment. The Court there held that the Fourth Amendment "requires a judicial determination of probable cause as a prerequisite to extended restraint following arrest," but added that such determination may be made ex parte as where the judge issues an arrest warrant. Justice Stewart, in a concurring opinion, asked why the Constitution "extends less procedural protection" to an arrested person who might not gain his release prior to trial than to defendants in civil cases, held to be constitutionally entitled to a pretrial hearing on the plaintiff's temporary seizure of their property to secure any future judgment. Justice Powell, speaking for the Court, responded that the "historical basis of the probable cause requirement is quite different from the relatively recent application of variable procedural due process in debtor-creditor disputes," and that the Fourth Amendment had always been thought "to define the 'process that is due' for seizure of person or property in criminal cases."

The *Gerstein* Court specifically reaffirmed *Lem Woon*, noting that

> In holding that the prosecutor's assessment of probable cause is not sufficient alone to justify restraint on liberty pending trial, we do not imply that the accused is entitled to judicial oversight or review of the decision to prosecute. Instead, we adhere to the Court's prior holding that a judicial hearing is not prerequisite to prosecution by information. * * * *Lem Woon v. Oregon*.

Neither Justice Powell nor Justice Stewart thought it necessary to explain why procedural due process did not protect the criminal defendant from the significant burdens imposed upon him apart from the seizure of his person (i.e., the burdens of accusation and litigation), and therefore require some form of independent screening under due process, apart from any Fourth Amendment concerns. Cf. CRIMPROC § 1.6 ("minimizing the risk of erroneous accusation" constitutes one of the basic goals of the criminal justice process). Did the absence of any due process right to independent screening to protect against an unfounded imposition of those burdens rest, by analogy to *Gerstein*'s Fourth Amendment reasoning, on the premise that the Fifth and Sixth Amendment guarantees governing the trial process prescribe all the process that is due the defendant? *Gerstein* characterized those provisions as establishing "an elaborate system, unique in jurisprudence, designed to safeguard the rights of those accused of crime".

In *Albright v. Oliver*, 510 U.S. 266, 114 S.Ct. 807, 127 L.Ed.2d 114 (1994), the Court majority (7–2) rejected the contention that substantive due process affords protection against the initiation of a prosecution without probable cause. The former defendant, now bringing a civil rights action, had received a preliminary hearing, at which he was bound over for trial, but he claimed that the charges (later dismissed) had been based on the false testimony of a police officer (who was relying on information received from a clearly unreliable informant). Four justices (Rehnquist, C.J., and O'Connor, Scalia, and Ginsburg) concluded that defendant could not look to due process, as the Fourth Amendment (which defendant did not raise) provided the only source of relief for the deprivations accompanying the charging of a defendant without probable cause. They noted that *Gerstein* and *Lem Woon* had previously established that "the accused is not entitled oversight or review of the decision to prosecute." Two justices (Kennedy and Thomas) concluded that defendant's complaint focused on concerns that stood apart from Fourth Amendment protections, allowing him to turn to due process, but due process simply did not prescribe "a standard for the initiation of prosecution" One justice (Souter) held open the possibility that due process might be violated where a defendant prosecuted without probable cause suffered significant injuries that stood apart from the custodial deprivations governed by the Fourth Amendment, but that was not the case here. Two dissenting justices (Stevens and Blackmun) found such deprivations in the impact of the prosecution itself, and concluded that *Hurtado* and *Lem Woon* gave the states procedural flexibility on the assumption that the "substance of the probable cause requirement remains adequately protected." That protection might not be afforded, even with a preliminary hearing, if the state had knowingly relied on false testimony.

2. ***Independent screening alternatives.*** Although due process may not demand an independent screening of the prosecutor's decision to file felony charges, all American jurisdictions provide at least one procedural avenue for obtaining such a screening. The vast majority of jurisdictions provide for an independent review by requiring (unless waived by the defendant) either or both a grand jury indictment (with the grand jury providing the screening) or a preliminary hearing bindover (with the magistrate providing the screening). The Notes that follow discuss the law and practice that largely determine whether one or the other (or both) of these screenings will be used in a particular case. The comparative merits of the two procedures are explored further in Notes 1–2 at pp. 935–38.

It should be noted, however, that a small group of states have introduced a third procedure for providing independent screening. That procedure is commonly described as "direct filing." In some of the direct-filing states, that procedure has replaced the preliminary hearing, which is no longer available. In others, it is an alternative to the preliminary hearing, to be used at the option of the prosecutor, who simply files in advance of the scheduled preliminary hearing and thereby cuts off that hearing. All direct-filing systems provide an opportunity for judicial review of the decision to charge (typically by the felony trial court rather than the magistrate). Beyond that, however, there is considerable variation. In some direct-filing states, judicial screening is mandated prior to filing and consists basically of an *ex parte* judicial determination of whether probable cause exists. That determination is based upon a prosecutor's affidavit summarizing the available evidence, although the judge has authority to ask for a further presentation of evidence. In others, the screening is introduced at the option of the defendant when the defendant makes a motion to dismiss the information. That motion is presented after defendant has obtained complete discovery of the prosecution's evidence, allowing the motion to operate in a fashion roughly similar to the motion for summary judgment in civil cases. Having before it a complete picture of the evidence, the court determines whether, if the case should go to trial, the prosecution's evidence would survive a motion for directed verdict of acquittal. See *State v. Knapstad,* 729 P.2d 48 (Wash.1986); *State v. Rud,* 359 N.W.2d 573 (Minn.1984). Proponents of this procedure argue that it is preferable to the preliminary hearing because it: (1) concentrates on screening, and leaves the other functions associated with preliminary hearings (e.g., discovery) to procedures specifically designed to serve those functions; (2) is far less time consuming and less expensive, as motions are made only in the small percentage of cases where some question exists as to the sufficiency of the evidence to proceed (usually because of a total lack of evidence on a particular element of the crime); (3) comes at a time when the court can gain a better picture of the full case; and (4) avoids issues of credibility, which are appropriately for the jury to decide. Proponents of the preliminary hearing respond that such an alternative procedure fails to provide prompt relief for those improperly charged and loses the advantages of subjecting witnesses to cross-examination.

3. *Preliminary hearings in the federal system.* The basic federal statutory provision on the defendant's right to a preliminary hearing is contained in the Federal Magistrate's Act, 18 U.S.C. § 3060. See also Fed.R.Crim.P. 5(c) (largely duplicating that provision). Section 3060 and Rule 5(c) initially state that "a defendant is entitled to a preliminary examination, unless waived, when charged with any offense, other than a petty offense, which is to be tried by a judge of the district court." Both provisions then set the time periods for the hearing ("within a reasonable time but in any event not later than 10 days following the initial appearance if the defendant is in custody" and 20 days if not in custody). Finally, they both include a critical proviso, set forth in Rule 5(c) as follows:

> provided, however, that the preliminary hearing shall not be held if the defendant is indicted * * * before the date set for the preliminary examination.

The above proviso restates the position that federal courts had reached under earlier versions of the Federal Rule that made no reference to the impact of intervening indictments. In a long line of decisions, the federal courts had held that the issuance of an indictment rendered "moot" the defendant's statutory right to a preliminary hearing. As stated in *Sciortino v. Zampano,* 385 F.2d 132 (2d Cir.1967): "The return of an indictment, which establishes probable cause, eliminates the need for a preliminary examination. * * * A post-indictment preliminary examination would be an empty ritual, as the government's burden of showing probable cause would be met merely by offering the indictment. Even if the [magistrate] disagreed with the grand jury, he could not undermine the authority of its finding."

In many federal districts, the impact of the proviso has been to eliminate virtually all preliminary hearings. Where a grand jury sits daily and can promptly dispose of submitted cases, the U.S. Attorney may regularly bypass scheduled preliminary hearings by obtaining prior indictments. This practice was well established prior to the adoption of the Magistrate's Act and proponents of the preliminary hearing argued against it, but Congress rejected that position. The "reasonable time" limitation of § 3060 was designed to ensure, however, that prosecutors utilizing the practice obtain indictments promptly and not resort to delay of the preliminary hearing until an indictment can first be obtained. Accordingly, in those federal districts in which docket backlogs or infrequent meetings of the grand jury commonly make it difficult to obtain indictments within the prescribed time limits, preliminary hearings are mooted far less frequently.

4. *Indictment states.* Slightly more than one-third of the states have provisions, similar to the Fifth Amendment, requiring prosecutions by indictment for all felonies (see p. 933). All of these "indictment states" also have statutes or court rules granting the defendant a right to a preliminary hearing within a specified period after his arrest. A few of these states sharply restrict the prosecutor's capacity to moot that right by seeking a prior indictment. The remainder allow bypassing without restriction, provided it is accomplished within the statutorily prescribed time period (which may allow for extensions or may state only that the preliminary hearing be held within a "reasonable time"). See e.g., *State ex rel. Holmes v. Salinas,* 784 S.W.2d 421 (Tex.Cr.App.1990) (magistrate lacked authority, upon scheduling the hearing, to include an order enjoining the prosecutor from mooting).

In general, prosecutors in indictment states, even when the law is most liberal in allowing bypassing, use that practice less frequently than federal prosecutors. In many state judicial districts, regular mooting would not be feasible since the grand jury's caseload is too heavy to permit consideration of charges prior to scheduled preliminary hearings. In others, prompt grand jury review is feasible, but prosecutors nonetheless follow the general practice of obtaining a preliminary hearing bindover prior to submitting the case to the grand jury. That practice may be the product of a tradition dating back to a time when prompt grand jury review was not feasible or of a determination that the preliminary hearing commonly offers the prosecution various advantages that offset the extra expenditure of prosecution resources (e.g., the better preparation of witnesses and the facilitation of plea negotiations). In some of those districts in which the typical process includes both a preliminary hearing and grand jury review, mooting is rare. In others, mooting tends to be utilized regularly, but for a small portion of the docket, identified by reference to the factors cited in the second paragraph of Note 6 infra. On the other side, many prosecutors in indictment states follow a practice of regularly bypassing the preliminary hearing, but recognize exceptions for certain significant classes of cases based upon the factors cited in the first paragraph of Note 6 infra. Finally, some state prosecutors bypass as extensively as most federal prosecutors.

5. *Information states.* Almost two-thirds of the states permit felony prosecutions to be brought by either indictment or information (although several deny that option for capital or life-sentence felonies, where indictment is mandated). Because of the heavy use of the information alternative in these states, they commonly are described as "information states." Several of these information states, as discussed in Note 2 supra, allow for direct filing of the information. The great majority, however, require the information to be supported by a preliminary hearing bindover (or a defense waiver of the right to a preliminary hearing). Most of these states do not bar prosecution by indictment, so they leave open the possibility, as in the federal system and in indictment states, that the prosecutor may bypass the preliminary hearing by obtaining an indictment prior to the time specified for the hearing. In general, however, prosecutors in these information states make infrequent use of that procedure. In some districts, the preliminary hearing is never mooted and in others the percentage of cases taken to the grand jury rarely exceeds 5%. There are some districts in certain information states, however, where the prosecutor will prefer the indictment to the information and preliminary hearings will not be available in the vast majority of felony prosecutions. See Emerson and Ames.

6. *Prosecutorial choice.* In a district in which grand jury review is available without delay and felony cases commonly are taken directly to the grand

jury, bypassing the preliminary hearing, what factors might lead a prosecutor to delay the grand jury presentation so as to first have a preliminary hearing? Available studies indicate that prosecutors look to a variety of factors in making that decision. Those include: (1) the need to perpetuate testimony for possible use at trial; (2) putting the witness to the test of testifying in public where there is some doubt as to whether the witness is willing to testify; (3) promoting the victim's interest in pursuing the matter by presenting it in a public forum; (4) gaining the defense perspective as to the events involved (e.g., through defense cross-examination) where there is some uncertainty as to what actually happened; (5) gaining a further identification of the suspect by having the witness make that identification at the hearing; (6) promoting public confidence in a sensitive prosecutorial decision by having the evidence presented in a public forum and the decision to proceed ratified by a magistrate (or, if the case is likely to be dismissed, by showing that the dismissal stemmed from deficiencies in the testimony of witnesses rather than any favoritism on the part of the prosecutor). In some districts, prosecutors will look to these factors on a case-by-case basis. In others the prosecutor will classify certain types of cases as especially appropriate for preliminary hearing review. Thus, the prosecutor may follow a regular practice of not bypassing the preliminary hearing in all cases alleging police brutality (looking to the 6th factor noted above), all assault cases involving acquaintances (looking to the 3rd and 4th factors), or all cases involving transient witnesses (looking to the 1st factor).

In a district in which the common practice is to have a preliminary hearing followed by the filing of an information (in an information state) or an indictment (in an indictment state), what factors might lead a prosecutor to bypass the preliminary hearing by promptly obtaining an indictment? Critics of the bypass procedure, arguing that the grand jury is by far the "easier" screening procedure, suggest that a prosecutor is likely to bypass the preliminary hearing where the prosecution evidence is weak, but available studies do not support that contention. See e.g., Gilboy, 8–9, 31–34; Emerson and Ames, 67–72, 108–113, 146–149. The studies suggest that, particularly where the bypass is used in only a small percentage of cases, it is likely to be an incidental by-product of some other objective which requires that the case be taken to the grand jury (e.g., use of the grand jury's investigative authority or obtaining a charge against a defendant who cannot be located or is outside the jurisdiction). Where the bypass procedure is a more frequent exception to the general rule, the likelihood is that bypasses will be used to avoid a preliminary hearing, but often for grounds unrelated to the strength of the prosecutor's case. Those grounds include: (1) the desire to save time where the preliminary hearing would be protracted due to the number of exhibits or witnesses or the number of separate hearings that would have to be held for separate defendants (the grand jury could save time in such situations due to the absence of cross-examination, less stringent application of evidentiary rules, and its capacity to consider a series of related cases in a single presentation); (2) the desire to preclude the defense discovery inherent in a preliminary hearing, particularly where a key witness is an informer whose identity should be shielded until trial; and (3) the desire to limit the number of times that a particular complainant (e.g., a victim of a sex offense) will be required to give testimony in public.

7. Equal protection. Equal protection challenges to prosecutorial bypassing of the preliminary hearing generally have failed. In a unique ruling, subsequently overturned by a state constitutional amendment, the California Supreme Court held that the preliminary hearing afforded the defendant so much greater screening protection than the grand jury that prosecutorial bypassing by obtaining a prior indictment constituted a per se violation of the state constitution's equal protection clause, without regard to the prosecutor's purpose in bypassing in the particular case. *Hawkins v. Superior Court*, 586 P.2d 916 (Cal.1978). The Oregon Supreme Court refused to go that far, but held that "a constitutional claim for equal treatment is made out when the accused shows that preliminary hearings are offered or denied to individual defendants, or to social, geographic, or other classes of defendants * * * purely haphazardly or otherwise in terms that have no satisfactory explanation." *State v. Clark*, 630 P.2d 810 (Or.1981) (offering as an illustration of an acceptable discrimination, a coherent and systematic policy of bypassing preliminary hearings in all cases of a certain type (e.g., homicide case), and as an illustration of unacceptable discrimination, the "choice of indictment over preliminary hearing" based on "such day-by-day logistical circumstances as the readiness of the prosecutor or the coincidence of an empty courtroom or crowded hearing calendar"). The dominant view, however, is that selectivity in the exercise of the bypass tactic only violates equal protection where the defendant can show "discriminatory purpose," as required under the Supreme Court's leading selective enforcement rulings (e.g., *United States v. Armstrong*, p. 868). See e.g., *State v. Edmonson*, 743 P.2d 459 (Idaho 1987). This requires, in effect, that the discussion to bypass be motivated by race, religion, or some similar arbitrary classification.

SECTION 3. THE BINDOVER DETERMINATION

RIDEOUT v. SUPERIOR COURT
432 P.2d 197 (Cal.1967).

BURKE, Justice. * * *

Following a preliminary hearing on the charge [unlawful transportation of marijuana], the committing magistrate held petitioners to answer. The information was filed, and a motion to set it aside on the ground they were committed without probable cause (Pen.Code, § 995) was denied. Petitioners thereafter filed the instant petition for prohibition based on the same ground (Pen.Code, § 999a).

The sole witness for the People at the preliminary hearing was Police Officer Bernard Hazen, who testified to the following effect:

About 1 p.m. on January 5, 1967, Officer Hazen observed a car being driven with a defective license plate light. He flashed his red light to direct the car to stop and pulled over behind it. The driver emerged without being asked to do so, met the officer in front of the police car, and identified himself as George Oliver.

The officer walked over to the car Oliver had been driving to check its registration and to obtain identification from the passengers. One Lopez was sitting on the front seat, and *petitioners* were on the *back seat*. The officer ascertained that the car was registered to Oliver's father. While checking the registration, the officer noticed several speakers and stereo tapes inside the car. Since he had information that such items had been stolen, he asked permission to search the car and Oliver replied, "Go right ahead."[2]

On the floor in front of the back seat the officer observed a matchbook folded in "a circular formation." He recognized it as a "crutch," a device "used to hold the used end of marijuana cigarettes." There were no burn marks on the "crutch," but the officer presumed it had been used because matchbooks ordinarily are not folded in that manner. The officer looked into the "well" of the car

---

2. Oliver denied having given permission to search. The credibility of witnesses at the preliminary hearing is, of course, a question of   fact within the province of the committing magistrate to determine.

behind the back seat where a convertible top folds down and saw "in plain view" a Tareyton cigarette package, which appeared to contain marijuana. (It was stipulated that the substance was marijuana.) The officer asked Oliver whom the package belonged to, and Oliver "did not state." No marijuana odor was detected in the car.

Evidence that will justify a prosecution need not be sufficient to support a conviction. "Probable cause is shown if a man of ordinary caution or prudence would be led to believe and conscientiously entertain a strong suspicion of the guilt of the accused." *Jackson v. Superior Court*, 399 P.2d 374 (Cal.1965) * * * An information will not be set aside or a prosecution thereon prohibited if there is some rational ground for assuming the possibility that an offense has been committed and the accused is guilty of it. A reviewing court may not substitute its judgment as to the weight of the evidence for that of the magistrate, and, if there is some evidence to support the information, the court will not inquire into its sufficiency. Every legitimate inference that may be drawn from the evidence must be drawn in favor of the information.

A defendant who has joint or exclusive possession of narcotics in a moving vehicle may be found guilty of unlawful transportation of narcotics. Knowledge by the defendant of both the presence of the drug and its narcotic character is essential to establish unlawful transportation, sale, or possession of narcotics. * * * [But] such knowledge may be shown by circumstantial evidence. * * * [F]rom the recited evidence the magistrate could reasonably have inferred that petitioners had possession of the marijuana and knowledge of its presence since they were the ones in closest proximity to the place where it was found, the place apparently was accessible to them, and they had an opportunity to deposit the marijuana there when the police directed the car in which they were riding to pull over. Likewise an inference of their knowledge of the narcotic character of the marijuana is warranted by the evidence of the presence of the "crutch" on the floor in front of the back seat where petitioners were sitting and the secretion of the marijuana in an ordinary package of cigarettes.

Petitioners rely upon *People v. Redrick,* 359 P.2d 255 (Cal.1961), and *People v. Jackson,* 18 Cal.Rptr. 214 (App.1961), neither of which involved the question of probable cause. The cited cases, which affirmed judgments of conviction of possession of narcotics, state that "proof of opportunity of access to a place where narcotics are found, without more, will not support a finding of unlawful possession." In the present case, however, the question is not whether the evidence will support a finding but whether there is probable cause, and here petitioners not only had an opportunity of access to the place where the marijuana was found, but they were the ones in closest proximity to that place and the "crutch" was at their feet. * * * The * * * peremptory writ is denied.

TRAYNOR, C.J., and McCOMB and MOSK, JJ., concur.

PETERS, Justice (dissenting). * * *

The writ of prohibition should issue if at the preliminary no evidence is introduced sufficient to establish probable cause that the accused committed the charged crime. That means that there must be some evidence upon which men of ordinary caution and prudence might believe the accused to be guilty. * * * In essence, the test is was there " 'some evidence' which, if unexplained would warrant a conviction by a trial jury." *Dong Haw v. Superior Court,* 183 P.2d 724 (Cal.App.1947). This means that there must be some evidence in regard to each element of the crime, and in narcotic cases this refers primarily to the element of scienter. * * * The crime charged in the instant case * * * has two scienter elements: the accused must know he possessed the drug and know it was narcotic in nature. There is no evidence of either element in this case. * * *

It has been held that knowledge of possession may be inferred when the narcotic is found in the accused's shirt pocket or hidden in the mattress of his bed. Knowledge of the narcotic nature of a substance possessed can, of course, also be implied, as where police observe a suspect suspiciously throwing away a cigarette and the man denies he had a "joint" (a term only one experienced with marijuana would be expected to use). The owner of a car or a tenant of a room may be reasonably supposed to know what is in his car, or room, or on his person. Thus, it may be implied that such a person had control or possession of substances found in his car, room or on his person. Thus, in the instant case, there may be enough evidence to hold the driver of the car, Oliver, for trial, since he had dominion and control of the car where the marijuana was found.

But Oliver is not before us. Only the two passengers sitting in the back seat of the car are involved. As to them there is a complete lack of evidence from which knowledge that there was marijuana in the car could be implied. The majority seek to imply such knowledge from the fact that had they looked at the floorboard near their feet they would have seen a rolled up matchbook of a type sometimes used, according to the evidence, as a marijuana "crutch." This "crutch" was not burned nor did it contain any marijuana. Nor was there any smell of marijuana in the car. Nor was there any evidence petitioners knew it was there. It is doubtful if an average man would recognize such a matchbook as a marijuana "crutch," and there is no reason offered why petitioners should be charged with such knowledge. But even if they recognize the matchbook as a marijuana "crutch" it does not follow that they knew marijuana was in the car. We are told by the majority that petitioners were in close proximity to the marijuana. But of what significance is proximity if there is no evidence of knowledge? Moreover, if petitioners had turned around on the back seat of the car and looked into the "well" into which the convertible top folded, there in plain sight they would have seen what appeared to be an ordinary package of Tareyton cigarettes. There was absolutely nothing to indicate that the package contained marijuana, and there were no suspicious circumstances. * * *

TOBRINER and SULLIVAN, JJ., concur.

Notes and Questions

1. **The applicable standard.** To what extent does the disagreement between the majority and dissenting opinions in *Rideout* rest upon differences in the "probable cause" standard each applies? The majority opinion defines "probable cause" in much the same terms used by the courts in describing the Fourth Amendment test for an arrest. The dissent speaks of "probable cause," but states that standard refers, "in essence," to the standard applied by a trial court in determining whether to reject a motion for directed acquittal (whether there is " 'some evidence' which, if unexplained, would warrant a conviction by a trial jury"). That standard is commonly termed the "directed acquittal" or "prima facie case" test (although the latter term is occasionally used as well in describing a traditional probable cause standard). Commentators commonly view the prima facie case as requiring a higher degree of probability because it asks whether a trial juror could possibly find the case sufficient for conviction (i.e., establishing proof beyond a reasonable doubt). But see Cal.Op.Atty.Gen. 441, 457 (1978) (probable cause and prima facie case standards refer to the same degree of probability, but are phrased differently because the prima facie case standard comes out of grand jury screening, which is a non-adversary proceeding, and the probable cause standard is associated with preliminary hearing screening, which is adversary); *Cummiskey v. Superior Court*, 839 P.2d 1059 (Cal.1992) (reaching same conclusion based on legislative history).

2. Appellate courts are not always precise in their description of the applicable bindover standard, and not always consistent in their descriptions from one case to another, as illustrated by the Utah experience recounted in STATE v. CLARK, 20 P.3d 300 (2001). Interpreting a court rule that requires a showing of "probable cause" that "the crime charged has been committed and the defendant committed it," a unanimous court (per DURANT J.) noted:

"We turn to the question of what quantum of evidence is sufficient to support a finding of probable cause at the preliminary hearing stage of a prosecution. We have taken various approaches in articulating an answer to this question. In some cases we have described the State's burden of proof at a preliminary hearing by comparing it to the burdens applicable at other stages of a criminal prosecution. We have held that the quantum of evidence necessary * * * is 'more than is required to establish probable cause for arrest'. To issue an arrest warrant, the facts presented must be sufficient to establish that an offense has been committed and a *reasonable belief* the defendant committed it * * *. We have further held that the probable cause standard is also 'less than would prove the defendant guilty beyond a reasonable doubt'. Indeed, we recently stated: 'The probable cause standard is lower, even, than a preponderance of the evidence standard applicable to civil cases'. Thus, our case law to this point places the level of proof necessary to support a preliminary hearing bindover somewhere between the reasonable belief necessary to support a warrant and the preponderance of the evidence standard in the civil context. * * * [But] in a number of cases, we have equated the preliminary hearing probable cause standard with the motion for directed verdict, * * * [stating in one case that] 'the prosecution must establish a prima facie case against the defendant from which the trier of fact could conclude the defendant was guilty of the offence,' [and in another] equating the probable cause standard with the standard for a directed verdict in a civil case, i.e., 'unless the evidence is wholly lacking and incapable of reasonable inference to prove some issue which supports the prosecution's claim, the magistrate should bind the defendant over for trial.' * * *

"However, any conclusion that the preliminary hearing probable cause standard is the same as the directed verdict standard is weakened by our other descriptions of the preliminary hearing standard. * * * [Thus, as noted above], we held that the probable cause standard at a preliminary hearing is 'lower, even, than a preponderance of the evidence standard applicable to civil cases.' In retrospect, * * * [that] guidance was more confusing than helpful. * * * 'When faced with conflicting evidence, the magistrate may not sift or weigh the evidence * * *, but must leave those tasks to the fact finder at trial.' However, the preponderance of evidence standard can only be met by weighing evidence. * * * Thus, our comparison of the probable cause standard to the preponderance standard was essentially a comparison of apples and oranges. * * * [D]espite our recent efforts to clarify the exact meaning of the probable cause standard, it remains somewhat confusing. Therefore, we take this opportunity to elucidate the standard.

"We hold that to prevail at a preliminary hearing, the prosecution must still produce 'believable evidence of all the elements of the crime charged,' *State v. Emmett*, 839 P.2d 781, 784 (Utah 1992), just as it would have to do to survive a motion for a directed verdict. However, unlike a motion for a directed verdict, this evidence need not be capable of supporting a finding of guilt beyond a reasonable doubt. * * * Instead, we hold that the quantum of evidence necessary to support a bindover is less than that necessary to survive a directed verdict motion. Specifically, we see no principled basis for attempting to maintain a distinction between the arrest warrant probable cause standard and the preliminary hearing probable cause standard. Our efforts to articulate a standard that is more rigorous than the arrest warrant standard and is still lower than a preponderance of the evidence standard have only resulted in confusion. Therefore, at both the arrest warrant and the preliminary hearing stages, the prosecution must present sufficient evidence to support a reasonable belief that an offense has been committed and that the defendant committed it. This "reasonable belief" standard has the advantage of being more easily understood while still allowing magistrates to fulfill the primary purpose of the preliminary hearing, ferreting out ... groundless and improvident prosecutions.[3]"

3. *Clark* probably presents the dominant reading of the bindover standard insofar as it applies an arrest warrant standard. See CRIMPROC § 14.3. Critics note that the initial formulation of an arrest-warrant bindover standard came in most states long before the Supreme Court's ruling in *Gerstein v. Pugh*, Note 1, p. 906,—i.e., at a time when there was no assurance that the probable cause needed to sustain an arrest would otherwise be determined by a neutral magistrate. Now that *Gerstein* requires that such a determination be made either in the magistrate's issuance of an arrest warrant prior to the arrest, or on the magistrate's review of a warrantless arrest at the arrestee's first appearance, an arrest-warrant bindover standard, from their viewpoint, is largely "duplicative," notwithstanding the distinctions noted in fn. 3 of *Clark*.

4. Only a few jurisdictions appear to have moved to a true prima facie case bindover standard, asking whether there is evidence, taken in the light most favorable to the prosecution, from which a jury could find guilt beyond a reasonable doubt. See CRIMPROC § 14.3. One reason for this sparse support may be the timing requirements for the preliminary hearing. New York, which had formerly used the prima facie case standard, moved to a probable cause standard when it shortened the time period within which the preliminary hearing had to be held. See Staff Comments, Proposed New York Procedure Law § 90.60 (1969) (noting further that a prima facie standard "does not really benefit a defendant" as it "may cause an arrested person to be held for a considerable time" while the case is being further investigated to meet that standard). Utilizing a prima facie case standard also has been criticized as not in tune with the procedural limitations of the preliminary hearing. A screening standard resembling that imposed by the trial court, it is argued, is most appropriately applied where the hearing has the characteristics of a mini-trial—i.e., with the rules of evidence fully applicable and procedural rights (particularly confrontation and subpoena authority) basically parallel to that at trial. A substantial majority of the states do not provide for such a hearing. However, even among the minority that do provide for a mini-trial type hearing, many more use a probable cause standard than a prima facie case standard.

5. Where courts have utilized a "probable cause" bindover standard, but described that standard as "greater" or "more rigorous" than the arrest warrant standard, they typically have not suggested that such a standard requires the magistrate to weigh conflicting evidence (compare *Clark*, discussing its previous description of the standard as requiring proof "somewhere between" the arrest warrant stand and the preponderance of the evidence standard). Those courts apparently "have in mind differences in the type of evidence required at each

---

3. "In a pragmatic sense, however, the State still has a higher bar at the preliminary hearing stage than at the arrest warrant stage: Although the hearing is not a trial per se, it is not an ex parte proceeding nor [a] one-sided determination of probable cause, and the accused is granted a statutory right to cross-examine the witnesses against him, and the right to subpoena and present witnesses in his

defense. Thus, the preliminary examination is an adversarial proceeding in which certain procedural safeguards are recognized as necessary to guarantee the accused's substantive right to a fair hearing. However, this distinction has been somewhat reduced by the recent amendment to the Utah Constitution allowing for the admission of reliable hearsay evidence at preliminary examinations. * * * "

stage." CRIMPROC § 14.3. For example, "under the arrest standard, considerable uncertainty must be tolerated on occasion because of the need to allow the police to take affirmative action in ambiguous circumstances, but no comparable exigencies are presented as the charging decision is made. Thus, a police officer may make an arrest where the circumstances suggest that the property possessed by the suspect may have been stolen, but the prosecutor ordinarily has no justification for proceeding to charge without first determining that a theft actually did occur." Ibid. So too, for an arrest, circumstantial evidence need not pinpoint a single person's culpability among a group of similarly situated suspects, but for a charging decision, the circumstantial evidence arguably should make it more probable than not that the accused was in fact the offender. Thus, in the classic hypothetical where the evidence clearly indicates that one of two persons at the scene committed the crime, but it cannot distinguish between the two, the probable cause standard applied to arrest warrants might allow for the arrest of both, but the "more rigorous" probable cause bindover standard would not allow a bindover of either. Ibid.

6. Commentators have argued that an important component of the more rigorous bindover standard should be its "forward looking" perspective. While the arrest standard looks to probability based upon the information available at the time of arrest, the preliminary hearing bindover, in reviewing a decision to charge, should insist not only on somewhat greater degree of probability based on the information then available, but also the likelihood that the government will be able to develop further evidence to establish guilt at trial. See e.g., Graham and Letwin, 655–66 (citing this forward looking approach as the grounding for a California case in which bindover was denied on a narcotics possession charge where, inter alia, an informant told the arresting officer that the accused was involved in narcotics activities, the officer confronted the accused and saw in his mouth several multicolored balloons, the defendant was able to flee and apparently flush the balloons down the toilet before he could be arrested, and narcotics experts testified that persons transporting narcotics often placed narcotic-filled balloons in their mouth, but the balloons also occasionally were used in that fashion by persons selling "phony narcotics"). This view of probable cause "as encompassing consideration of the prosecution's likely future development of the case finds support in occasional language in appellate opinions and magistrate explanations of bindover rejections. * * * However, 'a forward looking' interpretation of probable cause has been rejected by the few courts speaking directly to the issue." CRIMPROC § 14.3(a). They note that the adoption of a probable cause standard carries with it inherent presumption (not subject to revision by the magistrate in the individual case) that the prosecution may be able to "strengthen its case on trial." *Kennedy v. State*, 839 P.2d 667 (Okla.Crim.App.1992).

7. *Weighing credibility.* As pointed out in fn. 2 of *Rideout,* California allows the magistrate to weigh the credibility of the witnesses. Similar statements are found in other jurisdictions. Consider, however, *Hunter v. District Court,* 543 P.2d 1265 (Colo.1975), arguing that cases recognizing the magistrate's authority to judge credibility commonly also indicate that such authority is rather limited. Thus, *Hunter* notes, one court restricted the inquiry into credibility to judging "the plausibility of the story and not general trustworthiness," another held that the magistrate can resolve conflicts in testimony "only where the evidence is overwhelming," and still another stressed that the magistrate must not usurp the role of the trial jury in determining the "weight to be accorded the testimony of witnesses." In *Hunter,* the court held that the magistrate could consider credibility "only when, as a matter of law, the testimony is implausible or incredible. When there is a mere conflict in the testimony, a question of fact exists for the jury, and the [magistrate] must draw the inference favorable to the prosecution."

The majority opinion in *Hunter,* supra, suggests that the degree of authority given to the magistrate to judge credibility follows in large part from other aspects of preliminary hearing procedure. In refusing to follow California decisions granting the magistrate extensive authority in judging credibility, the *Hunter* majority stressed the more limited role of the Colorado preliminary hearing:

"The preliminary hearing in Colorado under Crim.P. 7(h) is not a mini-trial, but rather is. limited to the purpose of determining whether there is probable cause to believe that a crime was committed and that the defendant committed it. * * * It focuses upon a probable cause determination, rather than a consideration of the probability of conviction at the ensuing trial. See Note, 83 Yale L.J. 771 (1974) [contrasting the prima facie case standard]. * * * In light of its limited purpose, evidentiary and procedural rules in the preliminary hearing in Colorado are relaxed [e.g., hearsay evidence may be used]. * * * The preliminary hearing in California is a 'mini-trial,' emphasizing the probability of conviction at trial on admissible evidence. In such a situation, California * * * properly allows the judge to act as a trier of fact. In Colorado, however, the preliminary hearing is not a 'mini-trial,' and the judge in such a role is not a trier of fact. Rather, his function is solely to determine the existence or absence of probable cause."[a]

8.   *Consequences of a dismissal.* The states are divided as to granting the prosecution an appeal of right to the next highest court (typically the trial court) to contest a dismissal at a preliminary hearing. Where such an appeal is not provided, review may still be obtained by application for an extraordinary writ (e.g., mandamus), but that remedy is available only if the magistrate's ruling constitutes a "gross abuse" of his authority. The prosecution is more likely to look, in any event, to two alternative strategies for obtaining a "reversal" of a dismissal ruling—obtaining an indictment from the grand jury or seeking a second run at a preliminary hearing.

Since the preliminary hearing dismissal is prior to the attachment of jeopardy (see Note 1, p. 1449), there is no constitutional bar against reinstituting proceedings, and state law commonly imposes few, if any, restrictions on starting over again following a dismissal. If a grand jury is readily available, the prosecutor may present the same case to the grand jury for indictment. The grand jury may indict notwithstanding the magistrate's refusal to bindover, and most often the prosecutor need not even inform the grand jury that the magistrate refused to bindover on the same evidence. See CRIMPROC § 14.3(c). A substantial majority of the states also allow the prosecutor to refile the charges and seek another preliminary hearing on the same evidence. Use of this authority, however, may be subject to powerful institutional restraints. In some smaller judicial districts, the prosecutor may not be able to avoid having the refiled charge come before the same magistrate. Even where the charge comes before a different magistrate, he or she may be hesitant to reach a result inconsistent with the first ruling and to thereby call attention to the importance of the differing perspectives of members of the same bench.

A minority group of states prohibit refiling on the same evidence. These states typically provide for prosecution appeal from a dismissal and consider that the

---

a. Studies suggest that magistrates hesitate to resolve conflicts in testimony even in jurisdictions, like California and Michigan, granting the magistrate extensive authority to weigh credibility. See e.g., Graham and Letwin, 702–12, noting that magistrates in Los Angeles were reluctant to exercise that authority, preferring to "leave the credibility of the witness * * * for the trial jury." Miller, 102–105, found, in a study of Detroit practice, that the two factors that most frequently led to dismissals were (1) uncertain identification by key eyewitnesses, and (2) the reluctance of the complaining witness in testifying against the accused. Could the same factors provide the basis for dismissals in the jurisdictions (e.g., Colorado) which place more substantial limits upon the magistrate's authority to weigh credibility?

only appropriate avenue for challenge. However, such jurisdictions do allow the prosecutor to refile and seek a new preliminary hearing when it has "new evidence." *Jones v. State,* 481 P.2d 169 (Okla.Cr.App.1971). One view of new evidence for this purpose limits such evidence to that which was not "known at the time of the first preliminary hearing and which could [not] easily have been acquired at that time." *Jones v. State,* supra. Others simply require that the evidence adds substantially to what was presented at the first hearing. They note that prosecutors have a natural reluctance to disclose all available evidence at the preliminary hearing, and that the prosecutor's misjudgment as to the evidence needed should not immunize the defendant from further prosecution. But compare *Harper v. District Court,* 484 P.2d 891 (Okla.Cr.App.1971) (suggesting that the proper approach for a prosecutor who misjudges the evidence is to simply seek a continuance for the purpose of presenting additional available evidence in the initial hearing).

9. *Consequences of a bindover.* In an indictment state, if the defendant does not waive the right to be prosecuted by indictment, the bindover only leads to the presentation of the case before the grand jury. In making its decision on indictment, the grand jury is in no way controlled by the bindover. It may refuse to indict despite the bindover or may indict for a higher or lesser offense. Once the grand jury indicts, the indictment serves as the basis for the continued detention of the defendant and all further proceedings.

In an information state, the bindover leads directly to the filing of charges by information. In most information states, the information may charge only the offense on which the magistrate boundover. In these jurisdictions, if the magistrate's bindover is on a lesser charge than that stated in the complaint and the prosecution feels the higher charge is justified, it may either (1) appeal the refusal to bindover on the higher charge (if the jurisdiction allows for appeals, see Note 8 supra), (2) drop the complaint, refile on the higher charge, and seek a second preliminary hearing, or (3) take the case to the grand jury (where available) and seek an indictment on the higher charge.

In a small group of information states, the prosecution is not limited to charging in the information the precise charge on which the magistrate boundover. Those states require only that the charge in the information be transactionally related and supported by evidence presented at the preliminary hearing, as independently reviewed by the trial court. Thus, if the prosecution believes that the magistrate erred in binding over only on a lesser charge, it may file the higher charge, which it will then have to justify in response to a defense motion challenging its evidentiary support at the preliminary hearing. One of the states adopting this position is California [see CRIMPROC § 14.3(d)], but California also is a state giving the magistrate extensive authority to judge credibility (see Note 7 supra). Are the two positions consistent?

In all information states, the defendant may challenge the bindover (or the sufficiency of the preliminary hearing evidence where a higher charge is filed) by a motion to dismiss or quash the information. This motion must be made prior to trial, and in some jurisdictions, before entering a plea to the information. Typically, the review standard gives deference to the magistrate as the person who heard the evidence. Accordingly, the "magistrate's decision (ordinarily not accompanied by opinion or findings of fact) is most likely to be reversed when a misinterpretation of substantive law (or perhaps oversight) resulted in a total absence of proof on a particular item. On occasion, however, bindover decisions also are rejected on the ground that, without attempting to reconcile conflicts or judge the credibility of witnesses, the inferences drawn from the evidence simply are not sufficient to support a probable cause finding." CRIMPROC § 14.3(d).

10. *Review after conviction.* Assume that a magistrate binds over on a record that clearly fails to establish probable cause, and the prosecution follows with an information based on that bindover. A timely challenge at the trial court level is rejected, and an interlocutory appeal is unavailable (see Ch. 28, § 2). The defendant then is tried and convicted. On appeal, the defendant again raises the improper bindover issue. Should the subsequent conviction, based upon ample evidence at trial, render this issue moot? In some jurisdictions, a proper bindover is viewed as a jurisdictional prerequisite to the filing of the information, and, accordingly, a new trial is required if the bindover was not supported by sufficient evidence. See e.g., *State v. Mitchell,* 512 A.2d 140 (Conn.1986) (in light of the "intent of the legislature to adopt the preliminary probable cause hearing as a constitutional safeguard [affording] greater protection to the accused than the [previous] grand jury system," the treatment of that probable cause determination as a "constitutional prerequisite to the court's subsequent jurisdiction to hear the trial," and the lack of any other remedy for an invalid finding of probable cause, sufficiency of the preliminary hearing evidence may be challenged on postconviction appellate review). Others hold that the magistrate's error in binding over and the trial court's error in failing to quash the information are "cured where sufficient evidence to convict is adduced at trial." *State v. Franklin,* 234 N.W.2d 610 (Neb.1975) (noting that this position may make the trial court's ruling upholding a bindover "essentially unreviewable," but is needed "to avoid the evils of delay, proliferation of litigation, and piecemeal review"). Consider also Note 3, p. 931.

SECTION 4. PRELIMINARY HEARING PROCEDURES

A. RIGHT TO COUNSEL

1. Though a state is not required constitutionally to grant defendant a preliminary hearing (see Note 1, p. 905), COLEMAN v. ALABAMA, 399 U.S. 1, 90 S.Ct. 1999, 26 L.Ed.2d 387 (1970), holds that, once a state provides such a hearing, the Sixth Amendment right to counsel applies to that hearing. In *Coleman,* a divided Court (6–2) held that the Sixth Amendment rights of an indigent defendant were violated by the state's failure to appoint counsel to assist him in a preliminary hearing provided under state law prior to indictment. Applying the traditional "critical stage" standard for identifying those pretrial, post-accusation proceedings at which the Sixth Amendment requires counsel, a plurality opinion by Justice BRENNAN concluded that the presence of counsel at the preliminary hearing was "necessary to preserve the defendant's basic right to a fair trial as affected by his right meaningfully to cross-examine the witnesses against him and to have effective assistance of counsel at the trial itself." Justice Brennan was not persuaded by the argument of the state (and the dissenters) that counsel was not needed because state law ensured that the absence of counsel at the preliminary hearing would not adversely affect the defendant at trial. Although the state law did prohibit the prosecution from using at trial "anything that occurred" at a hearing involving an unrepresented defendant, that did not respond to the lost opportunities through which counsel at a preliminary hearing could have sought "to protect the indigent accused against an erroneous or improper prosecution." Justice Brennan cited in this regard four valuable functions of the preliminary hearing:

"Plainly the guiding hand of counsel at the preliminary hearing is essential to protect the indigent accused against an erroneous or improper prosecution. First, the lawyer's skilled examination and cross-examination of witnesses may expose fatal weaknesses in the State's case that may lead the magistrate to refuse to bind the accused over. Second, in any event, the skilled interrogation of witnesses by an experienced lawyer can fashion a vital impeachment tool for use in cross-examination of the State's witnesses at the trial, or preserve testimony favorable to the accused of a witness who does not appear at the trial. Third, trained counsel can more effectively discover the case the State has against his client and make possible the preparation of a proper defense to meet that case at the trial. Fourth, counsel can also be influential at the preliminary hearing in making effective arguments for the accused on such matters as the necessity for an early psychiatric examination or bail. The inability of the indigent accused on his own to realize these advantages of a lawyer's assistance compels the conclusion that the Alabama preliminary hearing is a 'critical stage' of the State's criminal process at which the accused is 'as much entitled to such aid [of counsel] * * * as at the trial itself.' "

2. Does *Coleman,* in providing a constitutional grounding to the right to counsel at the preliminary hearing, also provide a constitutional grounding for challenges to the waiver of the preliminary hearing made by defendants without counsel? Consider *People v. Houston,* 529 N.E.2d 292 (Ill.App.1988) (where hearing is held, Sixth Amendment waiver standard applies as to assistance of counsel and defendant ordinarily must be explicitly informed of that right; waiver of the hearing itself may be distinguished, and court leaves open whether that waiver is valid without advising defendant of right to counsel).

3. The prosecution in *Coleman* argued that even if defendant's right to counsel had been denied, that constitutional violation had proven harmless in light of defendant's subsequent indictment and conviction. It stressed in this regard that no testimony given at the preliminary hearing had been used at trial, where defendant had been represented by counsel and guilt had been proven beyond a reasonable doubt. Speaking for a Court majority on this issue, Justice Brennan responded: "The trial transcript indicates that the prohibition against use by the State at trial of anything that occurred at the preliminary hearing was scrupulously observed. But on the record it cannot be said whether or not petitioners were otherwise prejudiced by the absence of counsel at the preliminary hearing. That inquiry in the first instance should more properly be made by the Alabama courts. The test to be applied is whether the denial of counsel at the preliminary hearing was harmless error under *Chapman v. California* [p. 1570]. We accordingly vacate the petitioners' convictions and remand the case to the Alabama courts for such proceedings not inconsistent with this opinion as they may deem appropriate to determine whether such denial of counsel was harmless error, and therefore whether the convictions should be reinstated or a new trial ordered."

Justices Harlan and White, each writing separate opinions, also commented on the appropriate relief. Justice Harlan noted: "I consider the scope of the Court's remand too broad and amorphous. I do not think that reversal of these convictions, for lack of counsel at the preliminary hearing, should follow unless petitioners are able to show on remand that they have been prejudiced in their defense at trial, in that favorable testimony that might otherwise have been preserved was irretrievably lost by virtue of not having counsel to help present an affirmative case at the preliminary hearing."

Justice White expressed a somewhat similar view: "I would expect the application of the harmless-error standard on remand to produce results approximating those contemplated by Mr. Justice Harlan's separately stated views. * * * [The assessment of harmless error] cannot ignore the fact that petitioner has been tried and found guilty by a jury. The possibility that counsel would have detected preclusive flaws in the State's probable cause showing is for all practical purposes mooted by the trial where the State produced evidence satisfying the jury of the petitioner's guilt beyond a reasonable doubt. Also, it would be wholly speculative in this case to assume either (1) that the State's witnesses at the trial testified inconsistently with what their testimony would have been if petitioner had counsel to cross-examine them at the preliminary hearing, or (2) that counsel, had he been present at the hearing, would have known so much more about the State's case than he actually did when he went to trial that the result of the trial might have been different. So too it seems extremely unlikely that matters related to bail * * * would ever raise reasonable doubts about the integrity of the trial. There remains the possibility, as Mr. Justice Harlan suggests, that important testimony of witnesses unavailable at the trial could have been preserved had counsel been present to cross-examine opposing witnesses or to examine witnesses for the defense."

Lower courts, in applying *Coleman,* have adopted the analysis suggested by Justice White. Violation of the right to counsel at the preliminary hearing has been held to constitute reversible error only where the defense is able to point to specific aspects of the trial where it was adversely impacted by the lack of counsel at the preliminary hearing. This approach stands in stark contrast to the denial of counsel at trial, which is treated as automatic reversible error. The Supreme Court has noted that the denial of counsel at trial will not be subjected to a harmless error analysis because it is a structural defect "inherently indeterminate" in its impact. See Note 4, p. 1573. Does the *Coleman* harmless error inquiry, particularly under Justice White's view of that inquiry, reflect the view that the impact of the lack of counsel at the preliminary hearing is less speculative, or is it that the preliminary hearing simply is less significant as it bears upon the ultimate outcome of the criminal proceedings? See *Cleek v. State,* 748 P.2d 39 (Okla.Cr.App.1987) (because the preliminary hearing is mandated by the state constitution, the "right to counsel is much more 'critical' * * * than it was in *Coleman*" and denial therefore should constitute automatic reversible error; the closer Supreme Court precedent is *Hamilton v. Alabama,* 368 U.S. 52, 82 S.Ct. 157, 7 L.Ed.2d 114 (1961), where the Supreme Court reversed without inquiry as to prejudice upon finding that counsel had been denied at an arraignment at which trial rights could be "preserved or lost").

B. APPLICATION OF THE RULES OF EVIDENCE

1. Variations in state law. While all jurisdictions require magistrates to recognize testimonial privileges, jurisdictions vary considerably in their application of the other rules of evidence at preliminary hearings. See CRIMPROC § 14.4(b). A handful of states require full application of the rules of evidence, i.e., the magistrate may receive only evidence normally admissible at trial. These jurisdictions will not reject a bindover, however, simply because the magistrate relied erroneously on incompetent evidence. If the reviewing court concludes that there was sufficient competent evidence before the magistrate to sustain a finding of probable cause, the bindover will be upheld notwithstanding the magistrate's error. But see Graham and Letwin, 747 (criticizing this standard of review as reflecting the "attitude that the magistrate's assessment of evidence counts for little in the charging process"). Cf. Note 4, p. 956.

A somewhat larger group of jurisdictions hold the rules of evidence to be "largely applicable" to the preliminary hearings, but allow the magistrate to consider certain types of inadmissible evidence. In most of these jurisdictions, the exceptions are recognized by statute or court rule and are fairly limited. See e.g., Tenn.R.Crim.P. 5.1(a) (excepting a limited class of hearsay). In others, the directive to the magistrate is to follow generally the rules of evidence, making exceptions only upon some general principle relating to need or the special character of the preliminary hearing. See Mo.Stat. § 544.280 (evidence standards "same as governs in the trial of criminal cases * * * as far as practicable").

A third group of jurisdictions, perhaps the largest, have provisions stating that the rules of evidence (apart from privileges) "do not apply" to the preliminary hearing. See e.g., Fed.R.Evid. 1101(d)(3). Magistrates here generally have discretion to follow or not follow evidentiary rules at their discretion, although that discretion may be limited by provisions requiring acceptance of a specific type of evidence that would not be admissible at trial (most frequently found with respect to hearsay, see Note 2 infra). Studies suggest that magistrates given such discretion typically insist on adherence to many of the rules of evidence. See Miller, 95–96.

2. *Hearsay.* Where magistrates are not held to a full application of the rules of evidence, the most common class of otherwise inadmissible evidence considered at the preliminary hearing is hearsay. In those jurisdictions that carve out exceptions to the "largely applicable" rules of evidence, hearsay is the most frequently mentioned exception. In those jurisdictions in which magistrates generally are granted discretion on evidentiary standards, hearsay is often the subject of a statutory directive mandating admissibility. The primary arguments advanced for allowing use of hearsay (primarily witness affidavits) in preliminary examinations are: (1) many witnesses will give evidence on matters not really in dispute (e.g., the scientific expert testifying on drug content, or the burglary victim who can testify only as to what was missing from his home), and it places an undue burden on those persons to make them testify at the preliminary hearing as well as the trial; (2) witnesses in general will be less likely to assist police if they believe that, as a general rule, they will be required to make court appearances both for the preliminary hearing and the trial; (3) the grand jury can consider hearsay in most jurisdictions (see Notes 1–2, pp. 955–56) and imposing a stricter standard at the preliminary hearing will simply encourage the prosecutor to bypass the preliminary hearing by obtaining a prior indictment; and (4) magistrates, even when laypersons, are sufficiently familiar with the limitations of hearsay evidence to appropriately judge its degree of reliability.

In some jurisdictions, no limit is placed on the prosecution's use of hearsay. Those jurisdictions have provisions similar to Federal Rule 5.1(a), which states that the "finding of probable cause may be based upon hearsay evidence in whole or in part." More common are provisions that hold admissible certain specific types of hearsay or all types of hearsay under specific conditions. In the former category are provisions declaring automatically admissible the "written reports of experts," the written statements of persons attesting to their ownership of stolen or damaged property, and the written statements of persons attesting to the authenticity of their signature on a document. In the latter category are provisions that declare hearsay admissible if it is "demonstrably inconvenient to summon witnesses able to testify to facts from personal knowledge" or "there is a substantial basis for believing the source of the hearsay is credible and for believing there is a factual basis for the information furnished."

3. *Unconstitutionally obtained evidence.* A substantial majority of the states, including many which require adherence to the rules of evidence, do not recognize exclusionary rule objections at the preliminary hearing. See e.g., *State v. Moats,* 457 N.W.2d 299 (Wis.1990) (rules of evidence do not in themselves bar unconstitutionally obtained evidence). On the other hand, several states either specifically require or permit magistrates to exclude unconstitutionally obtained evidence. In a few of these states, defendants are authorized to make a suppression motion at the preliminary hearing. In the others, the defendant may present an exclusionary rule objection only if the prosecutor seeks to use at the hearing evidence that appears to have been obtained in a manner that may have been unconstitutional. States recognizing preliminary hearing challenges to the government's acquisition of evidence typically treat the magistrate's ruling on such objections as binding only in the preliminary hearing—i.e., the exclusion or admission of the evidence at trial will depend upon the outcome of a suppression motion made to the trial court, rather than the magistrate's determination.

The basic argument advanced in favor of applying the exclusionary rule at the preliminary hearing is the same as that advanced in support of applying other evidentiary rules—that reliance upon evidence inadmissible at trial is inconsistent with the screening function of the preliminary hearing. Arguments advanced in response rest largely on what the Federal Rules Advisory Committee described as consideration of "administrative necessity and the efficient administration of justice." 48 F.R.D. at 572. Giving the defendant two opportunities for what is commonly a time-consuming motion is seen as a wasteful use of judicial resources. Also, while the magistrate's ruling in favor of suppression is not binding on the trial court, it can have that impact, in practical effect, where the magistrate excludes the evidence and finds insufficient additional evidence to bindover. On review of that dismissal, the trial court will ordinarily accept the magistrate's factual findings, and if the review is by prerogative writ, the trial court can reverse only if there has been an abuse of the magistrate's authority (see Note 8, p. 917). Finally, the briefing that almost surely will accompany such a motion is seen as inconsistent with the objective of obtaining a preliminary hearing ruling within a short time frame following the arrest.

C.   The Defendant's Right of Cross-Examination

1.   The Supreme Court has long held that the Sixth Amendment's confrontation clause is a trial right and does not apply to the preliminary hearing. See *Goldsby v. United States,* 160 U.S. 70, 16 S.Ct. 216, 40 L.Ed. 343 (1895). But compare *Commonwealth ex rel. Buchanan v. Verbonitz,* 581 A.2d 172 (Pa.1990) (finding support in cases such as *Coleman v. Alabama,* Note 1, p. 919, for characterizing the preliminary hearing as "an adversary proceeding which is a critical stage in a criminal prosecution," and therefore subject to state constitutional provision which, like the Sixth Amendment, refers to the right of the accused to confront witnesses "in all criminal prosecutions"). In all jurisdictions, however, local law (usually statute or court rule) grants to the accused a right to cross-examine "adverse witnesses" who testify at the preliminary hearing. See e.g., Fed.R.Crim.P. 5.1(a). In general, the right to cross-examine at the preliminary hearing is not quite as extensive as the right to cross-examine at trial. Fairly typical is the standard set forth in *People v. Horton,* 358 N.E.2d 1121 (Ill.1976): "It [cross-examination] may not extend beyond the scope of direct examination and such further interrogation as is directed to show interest, bias, prejudice or motive of the witness to the extent that these factors are relevant to the question of probable cause." In restricting cross-examination at the preliminary hearing, magistrates most commonly cite two grounds: (1) that the defendant is attempting improperly to use cross-examination as a pretrial discovery device, and (2) that further cross-examination is unnecessary since it would only raise issues of credibility more appropriately left to the trial jury. As indicated in the notes that follow, states vary considerably in their treatment of each of these grounds.

2.   *Discovery and cross-examination.* Almost all jurisdictions have recognized the magistrate's authority to cut off cross-examination which appears to be aimed primarily at obtaining discovery. They differ, however, in the leeway granted to the magistrate to determine whether cross-examination is being used primarily to obtain discovery rather than to refute the prosecution's showing of probable cause.[b] Consider, for example, the following cases:

(a) In *Wilson v. State,* 208 N.W.2d 134 (Wis.1973), the victim's wife identified the defendant at the preliminary hearing as the man who shot her husband. On cross-examination, she acknowledged that she had given a description of the assailant to the police. Defense counsel was not allowed to question her, however, as to the details of that description or her subsequent identification of the defendant at a lineup. In holding that the magistrate erred in treating those questions as aimed primarily at discovery, the Wisconsin court noted: "There is a point where attacks on credibility become discovery. That point is crossed when one delves into general trustworthiness of the witness, as opposed to plausibility of the story. Because all that need be established for a bindover is probable cause, all that is needed is a believable account of the defendant's commission of a felony. Applying this standard to the case now before this court, defense counsel should have been allowed to cross-examine the state's witness on her prior description of the man who shot her husband. * * * [T]he question propounded did not merely go to the witness's general trustworthiness, but also to the plausibility of her description of the defendant, upon which the finding of probable cause rested."

(b) In *People ex rel. Pierce v. Thomas,* 334 N.Y.S.2d 666 (Sup.Ct.1972), the complaining witness identified the defendants at the preliminary hearing as the persons who had robbed him while he was riding a subway train. On cross-examination, defense counsel elicited the complainant's acknowledgment that he had never seen the defendants prior to the three-minute long incident. Counsel was not allowed to ask, however, whether other persons had been present at the time or whether the complainant had ever recovered his possessions. In sustaining the magistrate's refusal to permit such questions, the trial court noted that the "hearing is not intended as a pre-trial discovery device nor is it a substitute for the trial itself." While defense counsel's questions would be permitted at trial, they were "beyond the scope of the hearing." See also *United States v. Hinkle,* 307 F.Supp. 117 (D.D.C.1969) (upholding the magistrate's rejection of cross-examination designed to obtain from a police officer the names of persons interviewed at the scene of an assault).

Of course, the magistrate may have the authority to curtail cross-examination, yet prefer not to exercise that power. Many magistrates regularly permit the type of questioning advanced in *Hinkle,* and *Pierce,* provided the cross-examination is fairly brief. Thus, even in jurisdictions which take the narrowest view of permissible cross-examination, many lawyers regularly use the cross-examination for obvious discovery purposes. Note, however, fn. a, p. 900, discussing the possible tactical costs of using the cross-examination for that purpose.

3. *Cross-examination and the magistrate's judgment of credibility.*
At what point may a magistrate appropriately refuse to allow cross-examination on the ground that the direct testimony clearly establishes probable cause and therefore "nothing that cross-examination might reveal is likely to change the result"? While magistrates in most jurisdictions commonly follow such a practice, it has not been subjected to extensive scrutiny by higher courts. See e.g., *People v. Bonner,* 229 N.E.2d 527 (Ill.1967) (simply noting, in dictum, that the magistrate "may terminate the proceedings once probable cause is established"). The few courts that have considered and upheld the practice have emphasized either that

b. Differing views of the relationship between discovery and effective cross-examination also are reflected in the rules governing defendant's access to prior recorded statements of preliminary hearing witnesses possessed by the prosecution. Several jurisdictions grant the defense access to those statements for possible use in impeaching the witnesses. See e.g. Fed. R. Crim. P. 26.2 (g) Others hold, however, that disclosure of those statements is part of the pretrial or trial discovery process and access will not be granted until the time provided for such discovery.

(1) the magistrate has only limited authority to judge credibility or (2) the magistrate, as the finder of fact, may conclude that cross-examination along a certain path would not influence his judgment.

MYERS v. COMMONWEALTH, 298 N.E.2d 819 (Mass.1973) is the leading ruling restricting the magistrate's authority to bar further cross-examination (and to limit the presentation of defense testimony, see Note 2, p. 926) in light of a state showing sufficient to justify a bindover. *Myers* involved a preliminary hearing on a rape charge, at which only the complainant testified for the prosecution. When defense counsel questioned the complainant about her alleged belief in witchcraft, the magistrate terminated the preliminary hearing, noting that he had "heard enough testimony to find probable cause." The magistrate rejected defense counsel's objection that he wished to complete the cross-examination and to introduce evidence, including a psychiatric evaluation of the complaining witness. On review prior to trial, the appellate court (per TAURO, C.J.) ordered that a new preliminary hearing be held:

"The Commonwealth argues that once a prima facie showing of probable cause has been made by prosecution testimony, the examining magistrate can end the hearing before the defendant's attorney has had an opportunity to make a complete cross-examination of the prosecution witness or to present an affirmative defense. We fail to see how such a limited procedure could possibly effectuate the hearing's primary function of screening out cases that should not go to trial.* * * The primary function of the probable cause hearing of screening out 'an erroneous or improper prosecution,' *Coleman v. Alabama* [p. 919], can only be effectuated by an adversary hearing where the defendant is given a meaningful opportunity to challenge the credibility of the prosecution's witnesses and to raise any affirmative defenses he may have. * * * The facts of the instant case provide an excellent illustration of this point. The only witness at the petitioner's probable cause hearing was the complaining witness who repeated her accusation that the petitioner had raped her. If the petitioner had been afforded his statutory rights, he would have introduced testimony challenging the complaining witness's credibility and supporting his defense of a consensual sexual relationship. The examining magistrate could not have possibly made an informed judgment on the question of whether there was sufficient credible evidence of the defendant's guilt to support a bindover until he had considered all of this evidence.

"In some cases, the evidence introduced in behalf of the defendant will do no more than raise a conflict which can best be resolved by a jury at the actual trial where the Commonwealth must prove the defendant's guilt beyond a reasonable doubt. But, in other cases, the evidence elicited by defense counsel on cross-examination or from the testimony of defense witnesses or from other evidence may lead the examining magistrate to disbelieve the prosecution's witnesses and discharge the defendant for lack of probable cause. * * * Regardless of whether the petitioner's evidence in the instant case would have been sufficient to overcome the prosecution's case for probable cause, he had a statutory right to have the judge consider it before making his decision."

Myers also held that the proper bindover standard was a prima facie case standard. See Note 4, p. 915. Would the reasoning of the court there be any less persuasive under a traditional probable cause standard?

4. *The perpetuation of testimony.* As noted in Pt. D, p. 901, the preliminary hearing testimony of a witness unavailable at trial may be admitted as substantive evidence at trial, but only if the defense had an adequate opportunity to cross-examine the witness at the preliminary hearing. When would the restriction of cross-examination on the grounds considered in Notes 1–3 supra deprive the defendant of that opportunity? Consider also in this regard, the restrictions imposed in *Altman,* Note 3, p. 927. Should a magistrate refuse to restrict cross-examination, notwithstanding a valid prosecution objection based on the grounds discussed in Notes 1–3, in order to ensure that the preliminary hearing testimony will be preserved for possible trial use? See *State v. Faafiti,* 513 P.2d 697 (Hawai'i 1973) (urging magistrates, in the light of *California v. Green,* p. 902, "to permit the counsel for the defendant to examine fully and thoroughly witnesses at all preliminary hearings").

D. DEFENDANT'S RIGHT TO PRESENT WITNESSES

1. *Use of defense witnesses.* Most jurisdictions recognize, specifically or by implication, a general defense right of subpoena authority to present witnesses at the preliminary hearing. See e.g., Fed.R.Crim.P. 5.1(a). In several states, however, defense witnesses (other than the defendant himself) may be called only with the permission of the magistrate. The conventional wisdom on the use of defense witnesses appears to be much the same in both types of jurisdictions. Defense counsel generally operate on the principle that defense witnesses should not be presented unless the case is quite exceptional.

In many hearings, defense counsel's primary objectives are to obtain discovery and to establish a basis for the impeachment of the prosecution's witnesses at trial. Presenting defense witnesses ordinarily will not help in achieving either of these objectives. See also fn. a, p. 900 (citing risks involved in the defense tactic of calling adverse witnesses who were not subpoenaed by the prosecution in order to gain discovery). In other instances, counsel also may seek to vigorously challenge the prosecution's showing of probable cause, but even then, the usual approach is to rely entirely on cross-examination of prosecution witnesses. Unless the credibility of prosecution witnesses has been shaken substantially on cross-examination, the contrary testimony of defense witnesses is likely to be treated by the magistrate as simply presenting a credibility conflict that should be resolved by the fact-finder at trial. Moreover, by presenting the defense witness at the preliminary hearing, the defendant runs the risk of making that witness' testimony less effective at trial. Just as the defense may use its cross-examination of prosecution witnesses to gain discovery and to prepare for future impeachment, the prosecution may use its cross-examination of the defense witnesses to achieve the same goals. Whatever value defense witnesses may have in responding to the prosecution's probable cause showing is generally thought to be outweighed by the tactical advantages given the prosecution if the case should go to trial. See Van Dam, 195, 231 (calling defense witness only likely to be sound strategy where case is "an absolute winner" at the preliminary examination, or there "is substantial danger that the witness will be unavailable at trial and counsel wants to preserve the testimony").

2. *Discovery and credibility limitations.* The defense right to present witnesses, like the defense right to cross-examine witnesses, is subject to the limitations discussed in Notes 2 and 3 at pp. 923–25. The subpoena authority cannot be used primarily to obtain discovery and the magistrate can refuse to allow testimony that will serve merely to create a conflict that should be decided by the jury. Although the underlying concerns are the same, application of these limitations arguably is more complex where the ruling must be made with respect to a witness being allowed to testify at all, rather than to respond to particular questions. Consider in this regard, the standards set forth in *Desper v. State,* 318 S.E.2d 437 (W.Va.1984). The sole prosecution witness was a grocery store clerk who described being robbed at the store, identified the defendant as the robber, noted that he had previously identified the defendant from police photographs, and acknowledged having made a written statement to the police. Defense then sought to call as a witness the detective in charge of the case, informing the magistrate that his testimony would be significant because: (1) there was a discrepancy between the arrest warrant (which indicated that money taken by the robber was the property of the clerk) and the clerk's testimony (stating that the money was taken from the store's cash register); (2) the officer was familiar with the photographic identification procedure; and (3) the officer was familiar with the written statement of the clerk. The prosecution objected to allowing the defense to call the officer as a witness, claiming that its purpose was simple discovery, and the magistrate sustained that objection. On appeal prior to trial, the West Virginia Supreme Court reversed that ruling.

The *Desper* court noted that a defendant at a preliminary hearing "is not entitled * * * to explore testimony solely for discovery purposes," and the magistrate accordingly "has discretion to limit * * * testimony to the probable cause issue." It accordingly was appropriate for the magistrate to "require the defendant to explain the relevance to probable cause of the testimony the defendant seeks to elicit." Here, however, the defense had made such a showing on all three grounds it offered for eliciting the officer's testimony. Accordingly, the magistrate should have permitted the defense to call the officer, with the prosecution then having the right to object to any portion of the testimony it deemed "irrelevant to the probable cause issue." The court further noted: "In so holding, we recognize that, at a preliminary examination, testimony relating to probable cause is often difficult, if not impossible, to distinguish from testimony elicited for discovery purposes. Witnesses should not be called at a preliminary examination solely for discovery purposes. Furthermore, the 'examinatorial entitlements' of a criminal defendant at a preliminary examination, in challenging probable cause, do not necessarily justify the defendant in seeking to require an unlimited number of witnesses to testify. The discretion of the magistrate in this area is crucial. A preliminary examination should not fall victim to an endless wrangle relating to the existence of probable cause."

Should the burden placed upon the witness be a relevant factor in determining whether the defense may call the witness? Consider *Rex v. Sullivan*, 575 P.2d 408 (Colo.1978). At the preliminary hearing on charges of attempted murder, kidnaping, and sexual assault of a seven-year-old child, the investigating officer was the sole prosecution witness. The defense was permitted to call various persons referred to in the investigating officer's testimony, "including a physician and a forensic specialist," but not the child. The magistrate noted that the prosecution's own evidence showed that the child's testimony would be "weak or nonexistent" on the "points raised by the defense" (identification of the defendant as the assailant and whether the assailant's touchings constituted sexual crimes). The magistrate's ruling was upheld as within the authority of the presiding judge to limit the scope of the hearing "consistent with the screening purpose." While the presiding judge "may not *completely* curtail inquiry into matters relevant to the determination of probable cause," here there had been only "minimal curtailment" in light of the defense's complete cross-examination of the investigating officer and its calling of other potential prosecution witnesses at trial. Compare the ruling by the same court in the same year in *McDonald v. District Court*, 576 P.2d 169 (Colo.1978) (where two investigating officers were the only prosecution witnesses at a preliminary hearing on an attempted kidnaping charge, and defense sought to call the victim for the purpose of "testing her identification of the defendant," it was "an abuse of discretion" for the magistrate to deny defense that opportunity).

3. *"Affirmative defenses."* The states are divided as to the defendant's right to present at the preliminary hearing what are commonly characterized as "affirmative defenses"—i.e., defenses which do not negate any element of the crime, but operate, in effect, as a confession and avoidance that relieves the actor of liability. Two cases reflecting the opposing viewpoints on this issue (and on cross-examination relating to affirmative defenses) are *State v. Altman,* 482 P.2d 460 (Ariz.1971) and *Jennings v. Superior Court,* 428 P.2d 304 (Cal.1967). Both involved an attempt by defense counsel to develop an entrapment defense through cross-examination of prosecution witnesses and direct examination of defense witnesses. *Altman* upheld the magistrate's refusal to permit the defendant to raise the entrapment defense. The court emphasized the limited function of the preliminary hearing: "[E]ntrapment is an affirmative defense to be resolved at trial. * * * A preliminary examination is not a substitute for trial. * * * The issue of innocence or guilt is not before the magistrate. * * * The full and complete exploration of all facets of the case is reserved for trial and is not the function of a preliminary examination."

In *Jennings,* the court also stressed the role of the preliminary hearing, but reached an opposite conclusion: "[T]he People share a misconception * * * that as long as the prosecution's evidence showed probable cause to hold petitioner to answer it was irrelevant at that [preliminary hearing] stage 'whether the man was, in fact, framed' (quoting the magistrate). If this view were correct, of course, any cross-examination or testimony on behalf of the defendant would become superfluous. To accept the People's argument would be in effect to erase [Penal Code] sections 865 and 866 [providing that defendant may cross-examine witnesses and present his own witnesses] from the books and reduce the preliminary hearing to an ex parte proceeding at which the defendant's presence would be a meaningless gesture. * * * 'The purpose of the preliminary hearing is to weed out groundless or unsupported charges of grave offenses, and to relieve the accused of the degradation and expense of a criminal trial.' * * * To effectuate this constitutional and statutory purpose the defendant must be permitted, if he chooses, to elicit testimony or introduce evidence tending to overcome the prosecution's case or establish an affirmative defense."

If the presentation of defenses is to be limited at the preliminary hearing, should that limitation extend to: (1) all defenses that are affirmative in the sense that they do not negate the basic elements of the offense; (2) those affirmative defenses as to which the defendant would bear the burden of proof at trial under state law, see *People v. Moore,* 446 N.W.2d 834 (Mich.App.1989) (explaining why preliminary hearing magistrate could not decide entrapment claim); (3) those affirmative defenses as to which state law requires pretrial notification of an intent to raise the defense (e.g., insanity, see Note 1, p. 1208); (4) those affirmative defenses relating to events and circumstances other than those which prosecution ordinarily would investigate in the course of preparing to establish its case at the preliminary hearing (e.g., duress by a person not present at the scene of the crime).

4. ***Exculpatory evidence.*** *State v. Mitchell,* 512 A.2d 140 (Conn.1986), holds that the prosecutor's constitutional duty under the *Brady* doctrine [Ch. 25, § 2], to disclose material exculpatory evidence within its control, extends to the preliminary hearing, as well as the trial. In light of the hearing's status in Connecticut as "an essential part of the defendant's criminal prosecution," disclosure at that point was consistent with the "unmistakable tone" of *Brady* "that the exculpatory evidence be disclosed at a time when it can be used." See Note 1, p. 1198. Compare *State v. Benson,* 661 P.2d 908 (Okl.Crim.App.1983) (*Brady* disclosure relates to the trial and trial preparation, and therefore is within the exclusive authority of the trial court).

E. CHALLENGING PROCEDURAL RULINGS

1. *Pretrial objections to the information.* Assume that a magistrate makes an improper procedural ruling at a preliminary hearing. The magistrate subsequently binds over, and the defendant moves to dismiss the ensuing information, arguing that the magistrate's procedural error rendered the bindover invalid. Should the trial court apply a harmless error analysis (see Pt. A, p. 1562) in deciding whether to grant that relief? Most courts do so, conditioning relief on the probability that the procedural error influenced the magistrate's decision to bindover. In some, a new preliminary hearing will be ordered only if there is some showing that, had the error not occurred, the evidence before the magistrate would have been insufficient to support a bindover. In others, the question asked is not whether the prosecution's case "merely would be sufficient for a bindover notwithstanding the added defense showing [precluded by the error], but whether it would be so overwhelming that the magistrate's bindover clearly would not have been influenced by that additional showing." CRIMPROC § 14.4(e).

Consider, in contrast to these approaches, *Jennings v. Superior Court,* Note 3, p. 927. The *Jennings* court held that automatic reversal of a bindover is required where a magistrate's erroneous ruling at the preliminary hearing deprives the defendant of a "substantial right." Finding denial of such a right in the magistrate's refusal to allow the defendant to present evidence on entrapment (in part, through restriction of cross-examination), the court found unpersuasive the prosecution's contention that error was not prejudicial because the state's case would have been sufficient to support a bindover even if the defense had not been restricted on the entrapment issue. The crucial issue, the court noted, was whether the defendant was denied a "fair hearing," for if that were so, he was entitled to a new preliminary hearing "without further showing." A fair hearing was denied when a substantial right was violated, and while not all improper curtailment of cross-examination would necessarily fit in that category, there clearly was a denial of a fair hearing when the cross-examination restricted went "directly to the matter at issue." The substantial rights analysis of *Jennings* was later applied to a series of other errors, including improperly closing the preliminary hearing, improperly holding an open hearing where the defendant had a right to a closed hearing, and conducting the hearing in the absence of counsel. See *People v. Pompa–Ortiz,* 612 P.2d 941 (Cal.1980). Can that analysis be squared with the standard, also applied in California, that the admission of incompetent evidence, contrary to the applicable rules of evidence, will not require a new preliminary hearing if there was sufficient competent evidence to support a bindover? See Note 1, p. 921.

2. *Subsequent indictment.* Assume that a magistrate improperly curtails cross-examination or improperly denies a request to present a defense witness, but an indictment is issued before the magistrate's ruling can be challenged in the trial court. Has the defendant lost his right to relief even though the magistrate's ruling clearly resulted in an erroneous bindover? The traditional rule—followed in all but a few jurisdictions—is that all "defects" in the preliminary hearing are "cured by the subsequent indictment." This rule is based on the rationale that "once an indictment [has] been approved, the preliminary proceedings are not subject to either direct or collateral attack because the defendant has been afforded an independent determination that a prima facie case exists." *Commonwealth v. Gordon,* 385 A.2d 1013 (Pa.Super.1978).

Compare, however, COLEMAN v. BURNETT, 477 F.2d 1187 (D.C.Cir.1973). At defendant Dancis' preliminary hearing on a drug charge, the prosecution's case was presented through the hearsay testimony of the supervisor of an undercover agent, relating what he was told by the agent, who had been the sole eyewitness to the drug transaction. Defendant requested, but was denied a subpoena requiring the undercover agent himself to testify. Following the bindover, the defendant sought through various procedural routes to gain review prior to the presentation of the case before the grand jury, but was unsuccessful. The case came before the Court of Appeals on writ of mandamus after the grand jury had indicted, but before trial. The Court of Appeals (per ROBINSON, J.) initially determined that the magistrate's ruling was contrary to former Rule 5(c), now Rule 5.1, permitting the accused to "introduce evidence on his own behalf." It suggested, moreover, that more than a violation of the Federal Rules was involved: "These provisions of the Rules * * * are now reinforced by the holding in *Coleman v. Alabama* [Notes 1–3, pp. 919–21] that the Sixth Amendment secures for the accused the assistance of counsel at a preliminary hearing * * *. Among counsel's potential contributions, the Supreme Court stated, is 'skilled examination ... of witnesses [which] may expose fatal weaknesses in the [prosecution's] case that may lead the magistrate to refuse to bind the accused over.' * * * If the accused's counsel is reduced to a state of impotence in the discharge of this responsibility, it is evident that the accused is deprived of the very benefit which the Sixth Amendment's boon of counsel was designed to confer. So, an accused is normally entitled to subpoenas compelling the attendance at his preliminary hearing of witnesses whose testimony promises appreciable assistance on the issue of probable cause."

The Court of Appeals then turned to the question as "how the [magistrate's] mistake should be corrected." It first considered "whether the indictment returned against Dancis forecloses rectification of the error." It noted that the indictment "itself establishes probable cause," and a long line of cases had held that a defendant therefore "is not entitled to a preliminary hearing where he is indicted before a hearing is held" (see Note 3, p. 908). Dancis' case, however, was "markedly different" because he was given a hearing at which he was denied his right to examine a witness on his own behalf. The nature of that violation, the court concluded, "keeps Dancis in court despite the post-hearing rendition of the accused," and entitles him to appropriate remedial action. *Coleman v. Alabama,* the court further reasoned, pointed the way to the definition of that remedy:

"In *Coleman,* the Court could not determine from the record whether the absence of counsel from the accused's preliminary hearing actually worked prejudice at his trial, so it vacated the conviction and remanded the case to the Alabama courts for an inquiry on that score. [*Coleman*] charts the route to be traveled when the error is judicially detected only after conviction. But that is not Dancis' situation, for while he has been indicted he has not yet been tried. * * * We think, [however], that the problem of remediation arising pretrial, no less than when it emerges after conviction, is one to be addressed by the [trial] court itself. [The] concern is that the accused may suffer prejudice at his forthcoming trial by the infringement of his rights at the hearing, and avoidance of prejudice is the function and duty of the judge himself. [The] judge who is to preside at Dancis' trial is amply equipped to dissipate whatever risk of prejudice was bred by Dancis' inability to call the undercover officer as a witness at his preliminary hearing. [The] indictment against Dancis named the undercover agent, and it may well be that he testified before the grand jury. If so, the trial judge might consider making the agent's grand jury testimony available to defense counsel. Alternatively, since after indictment the Government no longer has had an interest in keeping the agent's identity secret, and obviously will have to produce him as a witness at trial, a voluntary interview may be indicated. If need be, the judge might set appropriate bounds for an interview and arrange for the agent's participation herein. It may be that, by consent of the parties and approval of the judge, a deposition by written interrogatories to the agent would suffice as an expedient.

Without any effort to exhaust the possibilities, we make these observations simply as suggestions of procedures calculated to safeguard Dancis against prejudice consistently with an orderly and expeditious progression of the case to trial."

Contrary to *Coleman v. Burnett,* most courts have viewed *Coleman v. Alabama* as having no constitutional bearing upon required preliminary hearing procedures apart from the appointment of counsel. However, in *Desper v. State,* Note 2, p. 926, the court agreed that critical stage analysis of *Coleman v. Alabama* should have a bearing on the remedy fashioned for a violation of the state procedural right to call witnesses for the purpose of challenging the prosecution's showing of probable cause. It concluded that relief along the lines suggested in *Coleman v. Burnett* was in order, notwithstanding an interceding indictment.

3. *Review after conviction.* Assume that the magistrate erroneously restricts defendant's right to cross-examination or to present evidence at a preliminary hearing. The magistrate subsequently binds over and an information is filed. Defense challenges the information as based on a defective preliminary hearing, but the trial court erroneously finds that the magistrate's rulings were proper. Interlocutory review is not available, and defendant's next opportunity to raise the issue is on appeal following conviction. Should the conviction then be viewed as having rendered harmless the magistrate's error—at least in the absence of a showing by defense counsel of resulting actual prejudice at trial?

Most information states take that position. It is followed even in jurisdictions which grant automatic reversal on pretrial review. See *People v. Pompa–Ortiz,* Note 1 supra ("relief without any showing of prejudice is limited to pretrial challenges of irregularities"; postconviction relief requires a defense showing that it "was denied a fair trial or otherwise suffered prejudice"). Moreover, while some courts hold open the possibility of a defendant gaining a reversal upon a showing that a preliminary hearing error resulted in trial prejudice of the type recognized in *Coleman v. Alabama* (Note 3, p. 920), others suggest that postconviction relief simply is not available. See e.g., *State v. Webb,* 467 N.W.2d 108 (Wis.1991) ("[A] conviction resulting from a fair and errorless trial in effect cures any error at the preliminary hearing. Accordingly, a defendant who claims error occurred at his preliminary hearing may only obtain relief before trial").

As in the case of challenges to the sufficiency of the evidence supporting a bindover, see Note 10, p. 919, a minority position allows for relief even on review following a conviction on the ground that the procedural error produced a jurisdictional defect. See e.g., *Mascarenas v. State,* 458 P.2d 789 (N.M.1969) (improper restriction of cross-examination amounted, in effect, to a "denial of a preliminary examination"; accordingly, since state law required a preliminary hearing as a prerequisite to "holding any person on an information," the trial court was "without jurisdiction" and the subsequent conviction was invalid). But compare *People v. Pompa–Ortiz,* supra (error at preliminary hearing is not truly jurisdictional; if it were, such errors could be raised at any time, including for the first time on appeal, but it has long been held that preliminary hearing flaws are waived by failure to timely object).

Chapter 15

GRAND JURY REVIEW[aa]

SECTION 1. THE ROLE OF GRAND JURY REVIEW

A. Prosecution by Indictment: Federal and State Requirements

In Chapter 10, we discussed the investigative function of the grand jury. In this Chapter, we are concerned with another major function of the grand jury, commonly characterized as its "shielding," "buffer," or "screening" function. The most frequently cited judicial description of this function comes from *Wood v. Georgia*, 370 U.S. 375, 82 S.Ct. 1364, 8 L.Ed.2d 569 (1962):

> "Historically, this body [the grand jury] has been regarded as a primary security to the innocent against hasty, malicious and oppressive persecution; it serves the invaluable function in our society of standing between the accuser and the accused, whether the latter be an individual, minority group, or other, to determine whether a charge is founded upon reason or was dictated by an intimidating power or by malice and personal ill will."

As we noted in Chapter 10, the grand jury originally was established to assist the Crown in reporting crimes, but it was its eventual development as a shield against arbitrary prosecutions by the Crown that led to its recognition in the federal constitution. That was achieved in the Fifth Amendment, which provides that, except in certain military cases, "no person shall be held to answer for a capital, or otherwise infamous crime, unless on a presentment or indictment of a Grand Jury." The Fifth Amendment thus ensures that a federal charge for a felony offense will not be brought without granting the accused the protection of the review and acceptance of the charge by the grand jury (as expressed through its issuance of an indictment).[a]

---

aa. For citations to additional source materials, as well as a more detailed discussion of the material discussed in this chapter, see Sara Sun Beale, William Bryson, James Felman, & Michael Elston, *Grand Jury Law and Practice* (2d ed.1998) (hereafter cited as Beale et al.); Susan Brenner & Gary Lockhart, *Federal Grand Jury* (1996) (hereafter cited as Brenner & Lockhart); Wayne R. LaFave, Jerold H. Israel, & Nancy S. King, *Criminal Procedure Treatise*, ch. 15 (2d ed. 1999) (available on Westlaw under the database CRIMPROC and hereafter cited as CRIMPROC). Deborah Day Emerson & Nancy Ames, *The Role of the Grand Jury and the Preliminary Hearing in Pretrial Screening* (1984) (hereafter cited as Emerson & Ames) is the leading empirical study of recent vintage on grand jury review.

a. The Amendment's reference to "infamous crimes" has been held to encompass all felony offenses. See CRIMPROC § 15.1(a). In misdemeanor prosecutions, where the amendment does not apply, federal law permits the prosecutor to proceed either by indictment or information. See Fed.R.Crim.P. 7(a). Although the Fifth Amendment refers to prosecution by "presentment" as well as "indictment," federal law now provides only for use of the indictment. See Fed.R.Crim.P. 7. Historically, a presentment was a formal charge similar to an indictment except that it was prepared by the grand jury on its own initiative. See CRIMPROC §§ 15.1(a), 15.1(d) (also noting view of Federal Rules Advisory Committee that presentment was not itself a charging instrument, but was converted to an indictment before the accused was held to answer).

At the time of the adoption of the Fifth Amendment, all of the states also required that felony prosecutions be brought by indictment. Today, however, only eighteen states make a grand jury indictment mandatory for the prosecution of all felonies (although four additional states require an indictment for capital and/or life imprisonment offenses). The remaining states permit prosecution either by indictment or information at the option of the prosecutor. Given that choice, prosecutors in these "information states" regularly have chosen the information alternative for the vast majority of their prosecutions. See Note 5, p. 909. Indeed, two of these states have repealed their statutory provisions on indicting grand juries, thereby forcing all prosecutions to be by information. See CRIMPROC § 15.1 (d)-(g).

The movement away from compulsory prosecution by indictment began with Michigan's adoption of the information alternative in 1859, and several states (including California) soon followed Michigan's lead. As expected, such a revolutionary change in the processing of felony cases did not go unchallenged. Its constitutionality reached the Supreme Court in HURTADO v. CALIFORNIA, 110 U.S. 516, 4 S.Ct. 111, 28 L.Ed. 232 (1884). The Court there sustained a California first degree murder conviction in which prosecution had been initiated by information rather than indictment. *Hurtado* was one of the first rulings interpreting the Fourteenth Amendment due process clause, and Justice Matthews' opinion for the majority stressed the need for a flexible interpretation of the clause. Due process, Justice MATTHEWS noted, should impose on the states only those "fundamental principles of liberty and justice which lie at the base of all our civil political institutions" and should emphasize the "substance" of those principles rather than their "forms and modes of attainment." The opinion concluded:

"Tried by these principles, we are unable to say that the substitution for a presentment or indictment by a grand jury of the proceeding by information, after examination and commitment by a magistrate, certifying to the probable guilt of the defendant, with the right on his part to the aid of counsel, and to the cross-examination of the witnesses produced for the prosecution, is not due process of law. It is, as we have seen, an ancient proceeding at common law, which might include every case of an offence of less grade than a felony, except misprision of treason; and in every circumstance of its administration, as authorized by the statute of California, it carefully considers and guards the substantial interest of the prisoner. It is merely a preliminary proceeding and can result in no final judgment, except as the consequence of a regular judicial trial, conducted precisely as in cases of indictments."

Justice Harlan's dissenting opinion stressed the history of the grand jury in English and American law and the recognition of the grand jury in the federal constitution. The dissent also stressed the need for screening by representatives of the community rather than by a magistrate, who will "hold office at the will of the government or at the will of the voters." Although the Supreme Court in the 1960s adopted a "selective incorporation" interpretation of the Fourteenth Amendment, and overruled various earlier decisions refusing to find in due process particular guarantees specified in the Bill of Rights, it has continued to adhere to the *Hurtado* holding that states need not prosecute by indictment. Thus, the indictment guarantee is the only Bill of Rights guarantee relating to the criminal process that clearly will not be applied to the states. See CRIMPROC §§ 2.6(a)-(b), 15.1(c).

B. THE USE OF GRAND JURY INDICTMENTS

1. *Indictment jurisdictions: the use of waiver.* While the Fifth Amendment and the various state constitutional provisions requiring grand jury indictments do not mention specifically the possibility of waiver, courts have almost uniformly held that these provisions do not preclude acceptance of a defense waiver. Several courts have suggested, however, that since waiver of indictment was not permitted at common law, it should be accepted only if authorized by statute. Most indictment jurisdictions now have statutes or court rules allowing knowing and voluntary waivers. A few permit waiver in all cases; several, like Federal Rule 7(a), permit waiver in all but capital cases; and several restrict the availability of waivers to certain types of non-capital cases. The effect of the waiver, where permitted, is to allow the prosecution to charge by information (typically without a preliminary hearing). See e.g., Fed.R.Crim.P. 7(b), 5(c).

2. The rate of waivers varies substantially among indictment jurisdictions. At one time the waiver rate in federal courts was as low as 5%, but in recent years, it has been in the neighborhood 20%. Reported state waiver rates tend not to be as high as the recent federal rates, but some fall within the 10–15% range. Studies suggest that waivers are most frequently made where the defendant pleads guilty, and many waivers probably are part of a plea bargain arrangement. Where the defendant intends to go to trial, the conventional wisdom advises against waiver, although not because it is anticipated that the grand jury will refuse to indict. Prosecution by indictment may offer the defense a potential advantage since local law may make pleading defects in an indictment more difficult to cure by amendment than similar defects in an information. See Note 3, p. 1005. Also, if the jurisdiction precludes the use of hearsay before the grand jury, key witnesses will have to testify before the grand jury and that testimony ordinarily will be available for impeachment use at trial. See Note 4, p. 1184. On the other hand, the conventional wisdom also recognizes that there are some situations in which a defendant who intends to go to trial may prefer to waive. The defense may be concerned that the prosecutor will gain valuable preparation for trial in presenting the witnesses before the grand jury. A defendant also has an incentive to waive if he is in jail or would otherwise be inconvenienced by delay and his case cannot promptly be presented to the grand jury.

3. *Information jurisdictions.* Prosecutors in almost all information states retain the option to proceed by indictment, and the use of that alternative varies from state to state and from one prosecutor to another in the same state. In some information states, there are no sitting grand juries and no prosecutions by indictment, as prosecutors have found no need to use the grand jury process even for investigations. In many other information states, grand jury indictments are regularly used, but in only a small percentage of felony prosecutions (e.g., 1–5%). The regular practice is to proceed by information and the indictment alternative is utilized only where it offers some special advantage. Where the prosecutor has need for the grand jury's investigative authority, the charges coming out of that investigation will be brought by that grand jury's indictment. So too, an indictment may be utilized to facilitate extradition (an information being unobtainable without the accused's presence for a preliminary hearing) or where exceptional circumstances make it desirable to avoid a preliminary hearing. See Note 6, p. 909. Prosecutors in other information states tend to make somewhat heavier use of the indictment process, utilizing it for certain general classes of cases deemed especially suited to a closed screening process (e.g., sex offenses), but still relying on the information as the primary mode of prosecution. Finally, in several information states, one or more exceptional districts will follow a local tradition of presenting the large bulk of all felony cases to the grand jury. See e.g., Emerson & Ames (describing two districts in Arizona, an information state, with one using the indictment process in 12% of its cases, and the other in 74%).

C.　EVALUATING THE GRAND JURY'S PERFORMANCE

1. ***The debate.*** Are the indictment states merely "being stubborn" in refusing to offer their prosecutors the option of proceeding by information? Did the information states fail to go "far enough" when they retained an option of proceeding by indictment, rather than requiring that an information be used in all cases? Both questions are hotly debated today as they have been for over a century. While many of the arguments advanced are the same as those put forth by Bentham and other early critics of grand jury screening, others reflect subsequent changes in the criminal justice process, such as the emergence of the full-time, professional prosecutor, the heavy reliance on negotiated guilty pleas, and the general pressures of extremely heavy caseloads.

Current critics of the grand jury tend to fall into three groups. First, there are those who view grand jury review as essentially worthless. The grand jury, as they see it, is merely a "rubber stamp" for the prosecutor. Thus, the California Supreme Court noted in *Hawkins v. Superior Court* (described in Note 7, p. 910):

> "The grand jury is independent only in the sense that it is not formally attached to the prosecutor's office; though legally free to vote as they please, grand jurors virtually always assent to the recommendations of the prosecuting attorney, a fact borne out by available statistical and survey data. * * * The pervasive prosecutorial influence reflected in such statistics has led an impressive array of commentators to endorse the sentiment expressed by United States District Judge William Campbell, a former prosecutor: 'Today, the grand jury is the total captive of the prosecutor who, if he is candid, will concede that he can indict anybody, at any time, for almost anything before any grand jury.' "

Critics in this category view the grand jury as a totally ineffective screening device and see no hope for making it an even minimally effective source for independent review. The basic problem, as they see it, lies not in any particular aspects of grand jury practice (e.g., in the reliance on hearsay testimony), but in the basic structure of the grand jury process. A process which is non-adversary, which forces the jurors to rely on the prosecutor's investigative resources and legal advice, and which allows the prosecutor to establish a close rapport with the grand jury, will inevitably produce a screening agency that serves as no more than the "prosecutor's puppet."[b] Accordingly, critics in this group would go beyond the position currently taken in most information states. They might preserve the grand jury for investigative purposes, but the prosecutor would not have an option to proceed by indictment. In every case, the prosecution would be required to proceed by information, combined with the preliminary hearing or other screening

---

b. Consider in this connection, Andrew Liepold, *Why Grand Juries Do Not (And Cannot) Protect The Accused*, 80 Cornell L.Rev. 260 (1995) (arguing that, while this position usually rests on the contention that "grand juries cannot screen because the procedures for presenting cases blunts their ability to do so", the barriers to grand jury screening go beyond that, as the grand jurors "simply * * * are not qualified" to answer "the probable cause question" that is put to them): "Whether probable cause exists is ultimately a legal determination about the sufficiency of the evidence: whether the prosecutor put forth enough information to suppress the legal threshold established by the probable cause standard. In submitting a case to the grand jury we are asking nonlawyers with no experience in weighing evidence to decide whether a legal test is satisfied, and to do so after the only lawyer in the room, the prosecutor, has concluded that it has. Because jurors lack any experience or expertise in deciding whether probable cause exists, it becomes not only predictable but also logical that the jurors will return a true bill. This is not because they are a rubber stamp, but because they have no benchmark against which to weigh the evidence, and thus no rational basis for rejecting the prosecutor's recommendation to indict."

procedure that is attached to the information process. Only a few states have adopted such an approach.

A second group of critics of the grand jury favor the dominant practice in most information states. These critics view the grand jury as a minimally adequate screening agency, but contend that it usually is less effective and less efficient than the preliminary hearing. They reject the concept of having both a grand jury review and a preliminary hearing as requiring useless duplication. Accordingly, they argue that all states should give the prosecutor the option to proceed by information, and prosecutors then should regularly use that option, reserving the grand jury alternative for exceptional cases.

Critics in this second category maintain that the preliminary hearing, because it is an adversary proceeding, ordinarily will provide better protection against unwarranted prosecutions than a grand jury, even if one assumes the grand jury exercises its judgment independently of the prosecutor. These critics also stress the preliminary hearing's value as an open screening procedure, as opposed to the secret grand jury proceeding. This feature is particularly important today, they say, when so many cases are resolved by guilty plea rather than by trial. They also note that grand jury review often can add to delay in processing cases since grand juries, particularly in rural areas, are not as readily available as magistrates. Use of the grand jury process is only justified, they argue, where the grand jury must review the evidence in any event in the course of a lengthy investigation or the nature of the case makes lay participation in screening especially valuable.

A third group of critics contend that the grand jury can be a satisfactory screening alternative, but that it needs substantial reform to curb prosecutorial power and prevent unworthy prosecutions. They call primarily for the following reforms (already in place in at least some jurisdictions): (1) requiring the court to fully inform the grand jurors of their independent authority and to impress upon them their obligations to screen out unworthy prosecutions; (2) giving the target the right to testify before the grand jury; (3) requiring the prosecutor to present all available exculpatory evidence; (4) forbidding the prosecutor's use of evidence which would be constitutionally inadmissible at trial; (5) prohibiting the use of hearsay testimony to support an indictment, except under narrowly defined circumstances; and (6) providing for a post-indictment pretrial hearing at which a judge or magistrate will review the grand jury transcript to ensure that there were no significant procedural violations and that the indictment was supported by sufficient evidence.

Supporters of the grand jury maintain that it is an extremely effective screening agency as it currently exists.[c] They note that, in most indictment jurisdictions, only a very small percentage of indictments result in trial dismissals for lack of substantial evidence. Most cases result in guilty pleas and those cases that go to trial rarely fail to survive a motion to dismiss. See e.g., Sullivan & Nachman, fn. c supra (citing a federal conviction rate of 85–90%). Supporters also argue that the grand jury is a better screening agency than the preliminary hearing. First, it brings a layman's sense of reality to the evaluation of the circumstances surrounding the alleged offense.[d] Second, its strength lies exactly

c. Not all supporters take this position. See e.g., Thomas Sullivan & Robert Nachman, *If It Ain't Broke, Don't Fix It: Why the Grand Jury's Accusatory Function Should Not Be Changed,* 75 J.Crim.L. & Criminology 1047 (1984), acknowledging that the grand jury is dominated by the prosecutor, but contending that the federal system does not need a better screening agency. The authors conclude that

"the best safeguard against grand jury abuse" lies in the selection of able and fair prosecutors and internal controls within the prosecutor's office (e.g., the internal review process for indictment decisions employed in various U.S. Attorneys' offices).

d. Although critics contend that the grand jurors tend to "just sit there, like a bump on a log," a leading study found that jurors not

where screening is most needed—in those cases where special factors, e.g., the involvement of politics or racial animosity, are likely to result in unjust accusations. The magistrate, they note, is restricted in his judgment of credibility (see Note 7, p. 916), while the grand jury can act very much like a trial jury. Lay participation permits the grand jury to evaluate the prosecution's case in light of community notions of justice and fairness. Indeed, the grand jury has a recognized authority to disregard legally sufficient evidence and indict for a lesser offense or refuse to indict altogether. Only the grand jury, they argue, can act effectively to leaven the rigidity of the law. (Critics respond that instances of nullification are rare, and that many of the most famous cases of grand jury nullification may have involved little more than political favoritism.)

Although the movement from grand jury review to preliminary hearing review was originally supported, in part, as a cost saving measure, supporters of mandatory grand jury review today can claim that it is the far less costly process. Studies suggest that routine grand jury cases involve substantially less time than the routine preliminary hearing, and there is no parallel in the grand jury process to the extensive preliminary hearings in some celebrated cases that have lasted several weeks and cost the state over $100,000. While the grand jury proceeding must bear the cost of the jurors, the preliminary hearing imposes the cost of a magistrate and the defense counsel for the indigent defendant. So too, with defense counsel frequently seeking continuances, the preliminary hearing is likely to result in greater delay. Supporters contend that difficulties in scheduling a prompt grand jury review should arise only in rural areas, and appropriate provisions for waiver and release on bail should substantially alleviate the consequences of those delays.

Finally, supporters contend that grand jury review clearly comes out ahead when the symbolic impact of the information and indictment processes are compared. What the grand jury loses through a non-adversary, secret proceeding is more than offset by its inclusion of community representatives in the screening process. Participation of laymen contributes to public confidence in the system and thereby justifies grand jury review even in cases that are "open and shut." Supporters note that, in a system where most cases do not go to trial, it is especially important that "private citizens" are given an "active role" in the "front lines" of the criminal justice process.

2. Statistics. As suggested above, both proponents and critics of the grand jury often seek support for their positions in the available statistics relating to grand jury performance. See e.g., *Hawkins v. Superior Court*, supra. The statistic most commonly looked to is the percentage of cases in which the grand jury refuses to indict. However, this statistic is not regularly published in any of the indictment states, so the proponents and critics have had to rely largely on the limited data contained in sporadic studies of grand jury actions in a single jurisdiction (often a single county) for a single year. The federal system has provided somewhat more complete data, and it indicates that federal grand juries have returned "no-bills" in less than 1% of the cases brought before them.

infrequently asked questions of witnesses in the two districts surveyed. See Emerson & Ames, 100–06. Witnesses were questioned by grand jurors in 66% of the cases reviewed, although the median number of questions per witness was less than 3. The Emerson and Ames study involved districts in which the jurors put their questions directly to the witnesses. In other jurisdictions, prosecutors commonly request that they be allowed to screen the questions to ensure that they are appropriate. See Brenner & Lockhart, § 6.6.5 (D.O.J. manual advises prosecutor to "excuse the witness, collect questions from jurors," seek to discourage "irrelevant, harassing and/or prejudicial questions," but ask questions if the juror persists and the jury as a whole wants the question asked, noting for the record "the prejudicial effect of the question").

Reports on state grand juries indicate "no bill" rates as low as 2% and as high as 20%. See CRIMPROC § 15.3(a).

Critics point to the low rates, particularly in the federal system. Supporters respond that even that minuscule rate does not establish that the grand jury is ineffective in its screening. Anticipating grand jury review, federal prosecutors may carefully select and present before the grand jury only cases that will easily pass the probable cause standard. The better test of jury screening, supporters argue, is the disposition of the indictments issued by federal grand juries. Only a very small percentage resulted in directed acquittals for insufficient evidence, suggesting that the grand jury has indicted in very few, if any, weak cases. Critics respond that a substantial portion of federal indictments result in guilty pleas, often to lesser charges, which may (or may not) reflect overcharging that was not prevented by the grand jury. Also, close to ten percent of all federal indictments typically are dismissed on motion of the prosecutor, and an unknown portion of those dismissals presumably reflect a federal prosecutor's realization that an indictment was obtained in a weak case.

3. *Variations in screening structure.* Both supporters and critics commonly discuss grand jury screening as if the structure and processes of the grand jury were uniform throughout the country. In fact, though the fundamental elements of a non-adversarial, secret proceeding are universal, jurisdictions vary considerably in their treatment of other, less basic features of grand jury screening. These include variations in: (1) selection process—while most jurisdictions use a traditional random selection system, several use a key-man system designed to obtain jurors with higher educational levels and greater standing in the community, see Note 1, p. 939, and Claude Rowland, *The Relationship Between Grand Jury Composition and Performance,* 60 Soc.Sci.Q. 323 (1979); (2) grand jury term— while some jurisdictions utilize a term approximating that for petit jury service, most utilize a far more extensive term (e.g., a year) that leads to the more frequent excusal of prospective jurors on hardship grounds and a disproportionate concentration of jurors who are dependent spouses, retirees, or employees of companies that will continue their compensation during jury service; (3) size of the grand jury—while most jurisdictions utilize grand juries considerably larger than the petit jury (e.g., 16 to 23), others use juries of the same size or even smaller (e.g., 7); (4) vote required to indict—while most jurisdictions require a bare majority for indictment, several insist upon a higher percentage (e.g., 75%); (5) evidentiary standards—while several states limit the grand jury to consideration of evidence that would be admissible at trial, and several permit consideration of only certain types of inadmissible evidence, the majority allow the indictment to rest entirely on inadmissible evidence (see § 3 infra); (6) control over the evidence produced—while the grand jury traditionally has the discretionary authority to insist upon the subpoena of witnesses beyond those presented by the prosecutor, some jurisdictions impose upon the grand jury a statutory obligation to call for any additional evidence that it "has reason to believe will explain away the charge" (and some jurisdictions impose a corresponding obligation upon the prosecutor to present before the grand jury known, material "exculpatory" evidence, see Note 4, p. 970); (7) testimony by the prospective defendant—while grand juries in most jurisdictions have the discretion to grant or deny a request by a prospective defendant to be allowed to testify, several give the prospective defendant a right to testify and require that he be notified of that right prior to indictment, where feasible; (8) the court's charge to the grand jurors on their powers—while most jurisdictions leave the scope of the charge to the discretion of the judge who impanels the grand jury, others require that the grand jurors be informed of various aspects of their authority (e.g., their rights to have further questions put to witnesses, to subpoena additional witnesses, and to question the legal advice of the prosecutor by seeking further advice from the court); (9) the standard for indictment—while some jurisdictions use a "prima facie case" or "directed verdict" standard, others employ a probable cause standard (cf. Notes 1–4, pp. 913–15); (10) the capacity to indict without approval of the prosecutor—while the federal system and some states give the prosecutor the authority to reject a grand jury charge by refusing to sign the indictment (see *Cox*, p. 864), the majority allow the grand jury to issue indictments without the prosecutor's agreement (either not requiring the prosecutor's signature on the indictment or treating the act of signing as ministerial); and (11) the consequences of a refusal to indict—while most jurisdictions allow the prosecutor to resubmit the case to another grand jury without restriction, some allow resubmission only upon court approval, which requires a finding "that the prosecutor has discovered additional evidence." For a more detailed review of these variations, see CRIMPROC §§ 8.4, 15.2; Beale, et al., § ch. 3, 4.

SECTION 2. CHALLENGES TO GRAND JURY COMPOSITION

1. *Grand jury selection procedures.* The selection of the grand jury is in some respects quite similar to, and in some respects quite different from, the selection of the petit jury. Initially, the process utilized in selecting that body of persons who will be summoned as prospective jurors (commonly described as the "array" or "venire") ordinarily will be the same for both grand and petit jurors. Most jurisdictions use a random selection from one or more representative lists (e.g., voter registration), but a small group continue with some form of key-person system that starts with a pool nominated by a group of community leaders. See Ch. 23, § 2. A few states have moved to random selection for petit juries, while retaining the key person system for grand juries; the objective here apparently is to insure that persons serving on grand juries (particularly those serving on investigative juries) be more "accomplished" than the persons who might be selected under a random selection process. Under either the random selection or key-person system, prospective jurors must meet the basic qualifications for jury service (e.g., residency, citizenship) and will be excused under automatic exemption provisions (e.g., for military personnel), which ordinarily are the same for both petit and grand jurors.

Once an array of qualified and non-exempt jurors is established, the grand jury selection process begins to depart substantially from the process used for selecting petit jurors. Initially, because the grand jury sits for a longer term, a larger portion of the array is likely to be excused on hardship grounds. Secondly, there is no regularized procedure for participation of the defense counsel and the prosecutor in the selection process. Indeed, the defense counsel ordinarily does not enter the picture until after the grand jury has completed its work and charged counsel's client with a crime.[a] The selection process for grand jurors does not involve voir dire conducted by counsel or peremptory challenges, and its version of

---

a. It is for this reason that most jurisdictions allow all defendants to raise challenges to the grand jury selection procedure after the indictment has issued (albeit sometimes within a quite short period after indictment, see 28 U.S.C. § 1867(a), reprinted in App. A). Of course, if a person is first arrested and brought before the magistrate and "held to answer," he knows that his case is about to be presented to the grand jury and could well have a reasonable opportunity to object to the selection process before being indicted. A small group of jurisdictions make an exception for such persons and insist that they present their objections prior to indictment, rather than afterwards. The Supreme Court has held that stringent timing requirements for composition challenges comply with due process provided that, as applied, they do not deny the defendant a reasonable opportunity to raise a constitutionally based claim. See CRIMPROC § 15.4(b).

a challenge for cause tends to be narrower and utilized in a much different fashion.

In general, once prospective grand jurors pass the stage of hardship excuses, they are seated automatically and any challenges to their capacity to fairly judge a particular case will first be raised after indictment, as discussed in Notes 5 and 6 infra. There are, however, a few avenues that may lead to jurors being excused on that ground prior to their taking action on an indictment. In some jurisdictions, before impaneling the grand jury, the presiding judge will ask the prospective jurors general questions about their background as it relates to particular types of offenses (e.g., drug offenses) and will excuse those jurors who might have difficulties in fairly judging such cases. In many jurisdictions, the prosecutor, after briefly introducing a case, will ask the already impaneled jurors whether there is any reason that they should not participate (e.g., whether they know one of the subjects or witnesses), and jurors will occasionally be excused through this process. So too, on rare occasions, the court, on the recommendation of the prosecutor, will dismiss a juror for "cause shown," such as frequent dozing during past proceedings or excessive absences.

2. *Equal protection objections.* Supreme Court decisions in the latter part of the nineteenth century clearly established that, while the states were not required to use a grand jury in the charging process, if they did so, they could not engage in intentional racial discrimination in selecting the grand jury. In all of its judicial procedures, whether optional or due process mandated, the state remained subject to the command of the Fourteenth Amendment's equal protection clause. The Court's rulings also established that the basic elements of a defendant's equal protection challenge to selection procedures would be the same for both grand and petit juries. This position was reaffirmed in *Campbell v. Louisiana*, 523 U.S. 392, 118 S.Ct. 1419, 140 L.Ed.2d 551 (1998), where the Court held that the standing rule of *Powers v. Ohio* (Note 4, p. 1342) applies to grand jury selection as well as petit jury selection and therefore a "white criminal defendant had standing to object to discrimination against black persons in the selection of the grand jurors." The Court rejected the state's argument that the *Powers* doctrine should not be carried over to grand juries because it had been established in the context of peremptory challenges, an aspect of jury selection not applicable to grand jury selection.

While the equal protection prohibition reaches only purposeful discrimination in jury selection, a prima facie case of purposeful discrimination can be established, which shifts the burden to the state to show that the discriminatory impact was not purposeful. See Note 5, p. 1325. Equal protection challenges to grand jury selection typically have concentrated on the selection of the array, where that presumption is most commonly established through statistical analysis. Indeed, many of the leading cases involving such analysis (e.g., *Castaneda v. Partida,* p. 1326) have involved grand jury selection.

Equal protection claims as to petit jury selection also are directed at the removal of individual jurors from the array (usually by peremptory challenges) under the standards developed in *Batson v. Kentucky* and its progeny. See p. 1334. Removal challenges are far less common as to grand jury selection. However, they can arise, as in a case where the defendant challenged a practice of excusing jurors on the basis of race in order to achieve a grand jury that more accurately reflected the overall racial composition of the community. See *State v. Ramseur,* 524 A.2d 188 (N.J.1987) (*Batson* distinguished as it prohibits a prosecutor's use of peremptory challenges to reduce minority representation, whereas judge here excused minorities only when the jury already would have a substantial minority representation); *Ramseur v. Beyer,* 983 F.2d 1215 (3d Cir.1992) (en banc) (majority found no need to rule on the equal protection claim since the two minorities originally excused were later seated when vacancies occurred, but three judges, in dissent, concluded that the practice "of temporarily excluding qualified African–American grand jurors and allowing them to serve only on condition that whites were unavailable * * * does violence to the principle of equal protection," "undermines public confidence in the justice system," and "cannot be cured by the mere assertion of good intention or 'harmless error' ").

3. *Cross-section violations.* With respect to the petit jury, the Supreme Court has held that the Sixth Amendment, as applied to the states through the Fourteenth Amendment, requires that the jury be drawn from a "fair cross-section of the community." See pp. 1321–25. A fair cross-section violation differs in several respects from an equal protection violation. It does not require purposeful discrimination and arguably prohibits underrepresentation of "distinctive groups" who would not be "suspect classes" under equal protection analysis. See Notes 1–3, p. 1324. Accordingly, the fair cross-section requirement may prohibit selection procedures that would not be prohibited under an equal protection analysis. See *Ramseur v. Beyer,* Note 2 supra. However, whether such a constitutional requirement applies to grand jury selection remains uncertain.

Various lower federal courts have assumed that the fair cross-section requirement applies to the federal grand jury process as an attribute of the Fifth Amendment's grand jury provision. See CRIMPROC § 15.4(d). That assumption has been questioned, however, on the ground that the fair cross-section requirement has been explained by the Supreme Court as a device aimed at ensuring jury impartiality, see *Holland v. Illinois,* 493 U.S. 474, 110 S.Ct. 803, 107 L.Ed.2d 905 (1990), and the grand jury clause of the Fifth Amendment, unlike the petit jury clause of the Sixth Amendment, does not refer to an "impartial" jury. See also *United States v. Knowles,* Note 5 infra. Of course, even if a fair cross-section requirement is implicit in the Fifth Amendment's guarantee of prosecution by indictment, that would not carry the requirement over to the states. See *Hurtado,* p. 933. Accordingly, it has been argued that there is no federal constitutional right to a state grand jury drawn from a cross-section of the community. See Beale et al., § 3.12 (also noting that many states impose such a requirement under state law).

Occasional lower court opinions have assumed that a constitutionally mandated cross-section requirement does apply to state procedures for selecting the grand jury array. See e.g., *State v. Jenison,* 405 A.2d 3 (R.I.1979) (citing Supreme Court opinions noting that " 'the very idea of a jury,' whether it be grand or petit jury, is 'a body truly representative of the community' "). Support for this position is said to be found in *Hobby v. United States,* discussed in Note 4 infra. In the course of measuring the impact of discrimination in the selection of the grand jury foreman, the *Hobby* majority noted that there had been no impairment of "defendant's due process interest in assuring that grand jury includes persons with a range of experiences and perspectives." Quoting from *Peters v. Kiff,* also described in Note 4 infra, the Court further described this "due process concern" as ensuring that "no large and identifiable segment of the community be excluded from jury service." In *Campbell v. Louisiana,* Note 2 supra, the Court found it unnecessary to determine the exact content of that due process requirement. Upon finding that the defendant had standing to raise a "*Peters v. Kiff* due process claim" as to selection of a grand jury foreperson, it remanded the case to the lower court to consider the merits of that claim. The Court noted that, "as to the nature and full extent of due process in the context of grand jury selection," that "issue, to the extent it is still open based on our earlier precedents," would be determined by the lower court. However, the Court apparently viewed that due process requirement as distinct from a cross-section requirement for it also noted that defendant had presented a "fair-cross section claim," but that claim was not open for review because of a procedural default in the lower courts.

4. *Selection of the foreperson.* A jury composition problem unique to the grand jury is presented in the selection of the foreperson. Unlike the petit jury foreperson, the grand jury foreperson commonly is appointed by the court (rather than being selected by the jurors). In *Rose v. Mitchell,* Note 7 infra, the Supreme Court "assume[d] without deciding that discrimination with regard to the selection of only the foreman requires that a subsequent conviction be set aside, just as if the discrimination proved had tainted the selection of the entire grand jury venire." In HOBBY v. UNITED STATES, 468 U.S. 339, 104 S.Ct. 3093, 82 L.Ed.2d 260 (1984), the Court returned to the issue of discrimination in the selection of the foreman, and held that it did not demand dismissal of an indictment in the context presented there.

The defendant in *Hobby* claimed that the trial judge had discriminated against blacks and women in the selection of the grand jury foreman. Since defendant was a white male and equal protection claims were at that time thought to be available only to defendants who were members of the class discriminated against (a position later rejected, see *Campbell v. Louisiana,* Note 2 supra), he framed his claim as a due process objection, relying on the analysis of *Peters v. Kiff,* 407 U.S. 493, 92 S.Ct. 2163, 33 L.Ed.2d 83 (1972). In that case, Justice Marshall's opinion for three justices had sustained a white defendant's due process objection to racial discrimination against blacks in the selection of the grand jury. Justice Marshall had concluded that a "state cannot, consistent with due process, subject a defendant to indictment * * * by a jury that has been selected in an arbitrary and discriminatory manner, in violation of the Constitution." He reasoned that "the exclusion from jury service of a substantial and identifiable class of citizens has a potential impact that is too subtle and too pervasive" to assume it had an impact only upon the cases of defendants who were members of that group.

Chief Justice BURGER's opinion for the Court majority in *Hobby* acknowledged that "purposeful discrimination against Negroes or women in the selection of federal grand jury foremen is forbidden by the Fifth Amendment." Unlike the dissent, which argued that that was enough to justify dismissal of the indictment (in light of "injury done to public confidence in the judicial process"), the majority concluded that the discrimination did not require dismissal of the indictment unless it adversely affected the due process interests raised by the defendant. Here, there was no violation of the "representational due process values" recognized in *Peters* since the discriminatory selection of the foreman did not alter the composition "of the grand jury as a whole." Unlike the situation presented in *Rose,* where the foreperson was appointed from outside of the grand jury panel, the foreperson here was a member of the randomly selected jury. Thus, the persons voting on the indictment had been fairly selected, without discrimination.

Chief Justice Burger also rejected the contention that the discrimination in the selection of the foreman had "impugn[ed] the fundamental fairness of the [grand jury] process itself." Again in contrast to *Rose,* where the foreman had substantial powers that might be used in influencing the other jurors (e.g., the authority to issue subpoenas for witnesses), the foreman of a federal grand jury performed basically ministerial duties that would have no bearing upon the substantive decisions of the grand jury. Accordingly, it would have made no appreciable difference in the outcome whether one jury member or another had been appointed foreman.

Both of the factors noted above would limit the significance of the issue left undecided in *Rose* to a small group of states. Only a few states appoint forepersons from outside the regularly selected grand jury panel, and a substantial majority give the foreperson powers not significantly broader than those granted in the federal system. However, the *Hobby* majority also distinguished *Rose* on a third ground. Speaking to the distinctive nature of the equal protection claim presented in *Rose,* the Court noted: "As members of the class allegedly excluded from service as the grand jury foreman, the *Rose* defendants had suffered the injuries of stigmatization and prejudice associated with racial discrimination." Relying on this language, several lower courts have held that discrimination in the selection of the foreperson can still be raised as an equal protection claim even if the foreperson is selected from among the grand jury members and has only ministerial duties. See *Johnson v. Puckett,* 929 F.2d 1067 (5th Cir.1991); *Ramseur v. Beyer,* Note 2 supra. But compare *State v. Ramseur,* Note 2 supra. The Supreme Court had no need to consider this issue in *Campbell v. Louisiana,* 523 U.S. 392, 118 S.Ct. 1419, 140 L.Ed.2d 551 (1998), as the foreperson there was selected "from the grand jury venire before the remaining members of the grand jury ha[d] been chosen by lot." Thus, the alleged racial discrimination went to the composition of the grand jury (the foreperson having the full voting powers of a panel member), not simply to the exercise of the foreperson's duties, and it did not matter that the foreperson had only "ministerial duties," as in *Hobby.* The *Campbell* Court further noted, however, that a criminal defendant (of any race) is given standing to challenge racial discrimination in grand jury selection in order to permit him to vindicate the rights of persons excluded from the foreperson position on racial grounds—a grounding arguably applicable even where the excluded persons were already members of the panel and the foreperson had only ministerial duties.

   5. ***Pre-indictment publicity.*** Does the federal constitution prohibit indictment by a grand jury that may have been "prejudiced" against the defendant as a result of adverse pre-indictment publicity? Cf. Ch. 24, § 1 (discussing the impact of pretrial publicity on the selection of petit jurors). In *Beck v. Washington,* 369 U.S. 541, 82 S.Ct. 955, 8 L.Ed.2d 98 (1962), a divided Court found it unnecessary to determine whether a state violated due process in accepting an indictment issued by a grand jury allegedly prejudiced by adverse publicity. The petitioner in *Beck* "did not contend that any particular grand juror was prejudiced or biased," but argued "that the judge impaneling the grand jury had breached his duty to ascertain * * * whether any prospective [grand] juror had been influenced by the adverse publicity and that this error had been compounded by his failure to adequately instruct the grand jury concerning bias and prejudice." The plurality opinion rejected this claim. The presiding judge had informed the grand jury of the subject of the investigation (possible crimes committed by officers of the Teamsters Union) and had asked whether they were conscious of any prejudice in the matter. Three jurors who acknowledged possible prejudice were excused, as were three others who had been members of unions affiliated with the Teamsters Union. The judge did not admonish the grand jurors to disregard previous news reports, but "[t]aking the instructions as a whole, they made manifest that the jurors were to sift the charges by careful investigation, interrogation of witnesses, and examinations of records, not by newspaper stories." The plurality concluded: "[E]ven if due process would require a state to furnish an unbiased body once it resorted to grand jury procedure—a question upon which we do not remotely intimate any view—we have concluded that Washington, so far as is shown by the record, did so in this case."

   Most lower courts have assumed that the issue left open in *Beck* would be answered in the negative. Many take the position that prejudicial pre-indictment publicity cannot justify the dismissal of an indictment "since the lack of impartiality of a grand jury is not a ground for dismissal." *Jones v. State,* 385 N.E.2d 426 (Ind.1979). They rely basically on the rationale advanced in *United States v. Knowles,* 147 F.Supp. 19 (D.D.C.1957), a leading case in the line of lower court rulings rejecting all types of bias challenges to grand jurors (see also Note 6 infra): "The basic theory of the functions of a grand jury, does not require that grand jurors should be impartial and unbiased. In this respect, their position is entirely different from that of petit jurors. The Sixth Amendment to the Constitution of the United States expressly provides that the trial jury in a criminal case must be 'impartial.' No such requirement in respect to grand juries is found in the Fifth Amendment, which contains the guaranty against prosecutions for infamous crimes unless on a presentment or indictment of a grand jury. It is hardly necessary to be reminded that each of these Amendments was adopted at the same time as a part of the group consisting of the first ten Amendments. A grand jury does not pass on the guilt or innocence of the defendant, but merely determines whether he should be brought to trial. It is purely an accusatory body. This review can be demonstrated by the fact that a grand jury may undertake an investigation on its own initiative, or at the behest of one of its members. In such event, the grand juror who instigated the proceeding that may result in an indictment, obviously can hardly be deemed to be impartial, but he is not disqualified for that reason."

Other courts rejecting challenges based on pre-indictment publicity stress the administrative difficulties that would be presented by recognition of such a challenge. The impact of pretrial publicity on prospective petit jurors commonly is explored through defense voir dire of the jury panel, but such defense voir dire, it is noted, is not feasible in the non-adversary grand jury proceeding. A judicial inquiry into possible juror bias, such as that conducted in *Beck,* ordinarily also is not feasible; the impaneling court usually charges the grand jury only at the start of its term and is not familiar with all of the cases it will consider during the term. Although that court may occasionally be aware that the grand jury is considering a case that has received considerable publicity, it cannot be expected to alter its procedure based upon that happenstance. Consider also the argument advanced in *People ex rel. Sears v. Romiti,* 277 N.E.2d 705 (Ill.1971): "The adverse effect of prejudicial publicity upon the trial of a defendant can be eliminated or alleviated by transferring the case for trial in another county. This remedy is unavailable, however, in the case of pre-indictment publicity, for an indictment must be returned by a grand jury of the county in which the alleged offense occurred. To permit such an attack upon an indictment would tend to immunize persons involved in events upon which the news media concentrated their attention."

Accepting the premise that due process requires the state to furnish an unbiased grand jury, several federal courts, in contrast to the above decisions, have suggested that an indictment would be dismissed on the basis of prejudicial pretrial publicity in an appropriate case. However, those courts have also concluded that it is inappropriate in the grand jury setting to apply the concept of "inherently prejudicial publicity," which sometimes is used to presume petit juror bias. See Ch. 24, § 1. To support a dismissal, the defendant must show "actual bias" on the part of the seated juror—that is, that the prejudicial publicity resulted in a preconception of guilt that the juror could not put aside. How would a defendant make such a showing? Consider CRIMPROC § 15.4(h): "Since defendant has no right to voir dire the grand jurors and access to the grand jury transcript is both difficult to obtain and not very likely to reveal juror bias, this required showing has been aptly characterized as rendering preindictment publicity claims almost 'inevitably doomed as a matter of law' ".

6. Personal bias. In his dissent in *Beck v. Washington,* Note 5 supra, Justice Douglas asked: "Could we possibly sustain a conviction obtained in either a state or federal court where the grand jury that brought the charge was composed of the accused's political enemies?" Due process, Justice Douglas suggested, would surely require that the conviction be reversed on the basis of grand jury bias. Several federal courts, however, have held an indictment may not be challenged on the ground that a grand juror lacked impartiality due to some special interest or knowledge about the case. In adopting Federal Rule 6(b), the Supreme Court rejected a preliminary draft proposal to allow an objection to a grand juror "on the ground that * * * a state of mind exists on his part which may prevent him from acting impartially." 1943 Preliminary Draft, Rule 7(b)(1). Decisions rejecting bias objections often rely upon the rejection of that proposal as well as the rationale of *Knowles,* quoted in Note 5 supra.

A few federal courts have suggested that bias objections can be recognized under the Fed.R. 6(b) provision permitting a challenge to a legally "unqualified" juror. The requirement that grand jurors be unbiased, they note, follows from the language and reasoning of various Supreme Court decisions, particularly the equal protection decisions barring racial discrimination in the grand jury selection process (see Note 1 supra). As Justice Douglas noted in his *Beck* dissent, the "systematic exclusion of Negroes from grand jury service" was barred because it "infects the accusatory process * * * [with] unfairness" in much the same way as juror bias infects the process. See also *Costello v. United States,* p. 949, where the Court referred to the validity on its face of "an indictment returned by a legally constituted and *unbiased* grand jury" (emphasis added). But see *Hopkins v. State,* 329 A.2d 738 (Md.App.1974): "Mr. Justice Douglas' interpretation of [the racial discrimination cases] * * * overlooks the fact that it is the manner of selection— as opposed to the mental attitude of those selected—that violates the equal protection * * * [clause]. Exclusion of Negroes from panels is not indicative of the mental attitude of white persons actually selected * * *."

A substantial minority of the states recognize at least limited bias objections. In some, that objection is tied to a narrow statutory prohibition against specified persons (e.g., relatives of the victim) serving on the grand jury. In others, it is based on more broadly worded provisions (e.g., prohibiting the seating of a person "whose state of mind prevents him from acting impartially"). In still others, it is viewed by the courts as implicit in a statutory or constitutional right to an unbiased grand jury. See *State v. Murphy,* 538 A.2d 1235 (N.J.1988) (rejecting the reasoning of cases like *Knowles,* Note 5 supra, as "rooted more to history than in justice"; in "contemporary society," we no longer expect local jurors personally to know "the character of the parties and the witnesses," but seek instead to impanel jurors who have no knowledge of the case or its participants[b]). Even in jurisdictions adopting the broadest definition of bias in this context, the practice is to limit objections largely to the juror who has some special relationship to the victim, the target, or a key witness.

In jurisdictions recognizing bias objections, most objections relate to the failure of the court to excuse jurors where the supervising judge or prosecutor was aware of a witness' relationship to the case that provided a ground for challenge and failed to conduct an adequate inquiry as to whether the person could be impartial. See e.g., *State v. Murphy,* supra (prosecutor aware that jurors were employed by insurance companies that were victims of the crime, but failed to inform the judge). Once the indictment is issued, the defense will have great difficulty establishing that a particular juror had a challengeable bias, apart from the unusual situation in which a juror has a relationship to the case (e.g., relative

---

b. Note, however, that in at least one situation, the grand jurors themselves may be witnesses to the crime for which they indict. See *People v. Ward,* 323 N.Y.S.2d 316 (App.Div. 1971), rejecting the argument that due process precluded a grand jury from indicting a person for contempt committed before the same grand jury. Compare *In re Murchison,* 349 U.S. 133, 75 S.Ct. 623, 99 L.Ed. 942 (1955), holding unconstitutional a state procedure permitting the same judge who served as a "one-man grand jury" to adjudicate a person in contempt based upon his grand jury testimony before that judge.

of the victim) that establishes automatic bias. See *State v. Warren*, 312 A.2d 535 (Me.1973) ("to initiate a possible invasion of the traditional secrecy and independence of a grand jury by allowing a post-indictment voir dire" would require a preliminary showing of likely prejudice); *United States v. Waldbaum*, 593 F.Supp. 967 (E.D.N.Y.1984) (court might be willing to presume prejudice where juror's interest suggested a "potential for substantial emotional involvement, adversely affecting impartiality," but such a showing had not been made by a survey showing that a substantial percentage of the grand jurors may have been shoppers who used the double coupons that defendant supermarket chains allegedly had conspired to eliminate).

7. *Post-conviction review.* Assume that a defendant makes a timely objection to the grand jury's composition on a ground recognized under the federal constitution or state law. Assume also that the objection is improperly denied by the trial judge, interlocutory appeal is unavailable, and the case goes to trial. On appeal from a subsequent conviction, should the illegality in the grand jury's composition now be viewed as a harmless error? In *Cassell v. Texas*, 339 U.S. 282, 70 S.Ct. 629, 94 L.Ed. 839 (1950), Justice Jackson, dissenting, argued that racial discrimination in the selection of the grand jury should constitute harmless error where the defendant had been convicted by a fairly selected petit jury. The majority rejected that contention without discussion and reversed on the basis of grand jury discrimination alone. In ROSE v. MITCHELL, 443 U.S. 545, 99 S.Ct. 2993, 61 L.Ed.2d 739 (1979), the majority found Justice Jackson's contention worthy of reconsideration, but it was again rejected. Justice BLACKMUN's opinion for the Court noted:

"Discrimination on account of race was the primary evil at which the Amendments adopted after the War Between the States, including the Fourteenth Amendment, were aimed. * * * Discrimination on the basis of race, odious in all aspects, is especially pernicious in the administration of justice. Selection of members of a grand jury because they are of one race and not another destroys the appearance of justice and thereby casts doubt on the integrity of the judicial process. The exclusion from grand jury service of Negroes, or any group otherwise qualified to serve, impairs the confidence of the public in the administration of justice. As this Court repeatedly has emphasized, such discrimination 'not only violates our Constitution and the laws enacted under it but is at war with our basic concepts of a democratic society and a representative government.' * * * Because discrimination on the basis of race in the selection of members of a grand jury thus strikes at the fundamental values of our judicial system and our society as a whole, the Court has recognized that a criminal defendant's right to equal protection of the laws has been denied when he is indicted by a grand jury from which members of a racial group purposefully have been excluded. For this same reason, the Court also has reversed the conviction and ordered the indictment quashed in such cases without inquiry into whether the defendant was prejudiced in fact by the discrimination at the grand jury stage. * * * We do not deny that there are costs associated with this approach. But the remedy here is in many ways less drastic than in situations where other constitutional rights have been violated. In the case of a Fourth or Fifth Amendment violation, the violation often results in the suppression of evidence that is highly probative on the issue of guilt. Here, however, reversal does not render a defendant 'immune from prosecution,' nor is a subsequent reindictment and reprosecution 'barred altogether.' * * * In any event, we believe such costs as do exist are out-weighed by the strong policy the Court consistently has recognized of combating racial discrimination in the administration of justice. And regardless of the fact that alternative remedies remain to vindicate the rights of those members of the class denied the chance to serve on grand juries, the fact is that permitting challenges to unconstitutional state action by defendants has been, and is, the main avenue by which Fourteenth Amendment rights are vindicated in this context."

8. In VASQUEZ v. HILLERY, 474 U.S. 254, 106 S.Ct. 617, 88 L.Ed.2d 598 (1986), the Court majority, per MARSHALL, J., rejected the contention of three dissenters that the "automatic reversal" standard of *Rose v. Mitchell* should not apply where "the [grand jury] discrimination claim is pressed many years after conviction." The dissenters argued that the prophylactic remedy of *Mitchell* was unwarranted in that situation because the state was more likely to be "prejudiced in its ability to retry the defendant" and the delay will have "dilute[d] the effectiveness of the reversal rule as a deterrent." Noting that that defendant here had persistently pressed his equal protection challenge in state and federal courts over the 24 years since his conviction, the majority concluded that that claim was still viable under federal habeas corpus. *Rose v. Mitchell* had "ably presented * * * justifications, based on the necessity for vindicating Fourteenth Amendment rights, supporting a policy of automatic reversal," and the "six years since *Mitchell*" gave the Court "no reason to doubt" the "continuing truth" of the observations made there relating to "racial and other forms of discrimination" in the "administration of justice." In addition, the Court was not convinced that a subsequent fair trial necessarily eliminated the impact of the grand jury discrimination upon defendant's conviction. As to this point, the majority reasoned:

"The grand jury does not determine only that probable cause exists to believe that a defendant committed a crime, or that it does not. In the hands of the grand jury lies the power to charge a greater offense or a lesser offense; numerous counts or a single count; and perhaps most significant of all, a capital offense or a noncapital offense—all on the basis of the same facts. Moreover, '[t]he grand jury is not bound to indict in every case where a conviction can be obtained.' *United States v. Ciambrone*, 601 F.2d 616 (2d Cir.1979) (Friendly, J., dissenting). Thus, even if a grand jury's determination of probable cause is confirmed in hindsight by a conviction on the indicted offense, that confirmation in no way suggests that the discrimination did not impermissibly infect the framing of the indictment and, consequently, the nature or very existence of the proceedings to come. * * * Just as a conviction is void under the Equal Protection Clause if the prosecutor deliberately charged the defendant on account of his race, see *United States v. Batchelder* [p. 888], a conviction cannot be understood to cure the taint attributable to a charging body selected on the basis of race. Once having found discrimination in the selection of a grand jury, we simply cannot know that the need to indict would have been assessed in the same way by a grand jury properly constituted.' "

Responding to the above reasoning, dissenting Justice POWELL (joined by Burger, C.J., and Rehnquist, J.), noted: "The Court * * * decides that discrimination in the selection of the grand jury potentially harmed respondent, because the grand jury is vested with broad discretion in deciding whether to indict and in framing the charges, and because it is impossible to know whether this discretion would have been exercised differently by a properly selected grand jury. The point appears to be that an all-white grand jury from which blacks are systematically excluded might be influenced by race in determining whether to indict and for what charge. * * * This reasoning ignores established principles of equal protection jurisprudence. * * * This Court has never suggested that the racial composition of a grand jury gives rise to the inference that indictments are racially motivated, any more than it has suggested that a suspect arrested by a policeman of a different race may challenge his subsequent conviction on that basis. * * * There may be a theoretical possibility that a different grand jury might have decided not to indict or to indict for a less serious charge. The fact remains, however, that the grand jury's decision to indict was *correct as a matter of law,* given respondent's subsequent unchallenged conviction."

9. Daniel Meltzer, *Deterring Constitutional Violations by Law Enforcement Officials: Plaintiffs and Defendants as Private Attorneys General,* 88 Colum.L.Rev. 249 (1988), although concluding that the result reached in *Vasquez* was justified by the "need to deter unlawful grand jury discrimination," finds the reasoning of *Vasquez* otherwise to be unconvincing. The author notes that the Court's argument that "the racial discrimination might have harmed Hillery" was inconsistent with the "whole thrust of harmless error doctrine," which is "to require a 'reasonable possibility' that the error might have contributed to the conviction, not merely a hypothesis under which an error-free proceeding would have resulted in an acquittal." As for the Court's "judicial integrity" rationale, "if an untainted superseding indictment eliminates doubts about the integrity of the judicial process caused by the original discrimination, surely a supervening conviction does so equally well."

See also Nancy King, *Postconviction Review of Jury Discrimination: Measuring the Effects of Juror Race on Jury Decisions,* 92 Mich.L.Rev. 62 (1993), questioning the reasons advanced in *Vasquez* for the Court's refusal to undertake an assessment of the possible impact of the discrimination in juror selection upon the grand jury's decision to indict. Such an assessment, though complex and difficult, is no more complex and difficult than other inquiries demanded under Supreme Court precedent. Thus, if the objection in *Vasquez* had not been timely presented in the state courts, relief on habeas review would have hinged upon a "cause and prejudice" test that would have required the habeas court to make exactly that type of assessment. See Note 3, p. 1594. Social science studies on the impact of jury composition upon jury decisionmaking would provide assistance in assessing likely prejudice as they not only demonstrate that race affects jury decisions, but also indicate where that effect is especially probable or improbable. They suggest moreover that the dominant characteristics of grand jury decisionmaking (a lesser standard of proof, a larger group of jurors, and the acceptance of a majority rather than a unanimous verdict) make the exclusion of minority viewpoints from the grand jury less likely to have a decisionmaking influence than exclusion from the petit jury.

Consider also Tom Stacy and Kim Dayton, *Rethinking Harmless Constitutional Error,* 88 Colum.L.Rev. 79 (1988), asking why the Court in *Vasquez* required that the conviction be reversed, rather than simply remanding for the purpose of "permitting a grand jury selected in a race-neutral fashion to reconsider probable cause," with the conviction to be reinstated if the grand jury should reindict on the same charge. Concurring in *Ramseur v. Beyer,* Note 2, p. 940, Circuit Judge Greenberg argued that a court granting habeas relief had authority to impose such conditional relief, and since that possibility was not before the Supreme Court in *Hillery,* it should not be deemed foreclosed by the relief granted there. Judge Greenberg further noted that this procedure "[would] not introduce a harmless error analysis into cases dealing with racial discrimination in grand jury selection. Quite to the contrary, it treats the discrimination as prejudicial and addresses the remedy for it."

10. Assuming a constitutional fair cross-section or individual bias objection applies to grand jury selection, should that objection be cognizable following a conviction? Consider *Porter v. Wainwright,* 805 F.2d 930 (11th Cir.1986). The defendant in *Porter,* on a habeas challenge to his conviction, alleged that one member of the grand jury was related by marriage to the homicide victim, that the juror had explained that relationship and his discomfort in sitting on the case to the prosecuting attorney, and that he had been told to simply sit and not vote. The court concluded that, "assuming arguendo" that those allegations made out a due process violation, the standard harmless error rationale of *United States v. Mechanik* (Note 5, p. 977) controlled, rather than the automatic reversal rule of *Rose* and *Vasquez.* In holding that a fair trial cured procedural errors in the grand jury process, the *Mechanik* majority distinguished *Vasquez* as a case "compelled by precedent directly applicable to the special problem of racial discrimination." It described *Vasquez* as grounded on the view that "racial discrimination * * * is so pernicious, and other remedies so impractical, that the remedy of automatic reversal was necessary as a prophylactic means of deterring grand jury discrimination in the future, and that one could presume that a discriminatorily selected grand jury would treat defendants of excluded races unfairly," and then added: "We think that these considerations have little force outside the context of racial discrimination in the composition of the grand jury." This analysis, the *Porter* court noted, was equally applicable to the claim before it. But compare *State v. Murphy,* Note 6, p. 944 (rule of *Mechanik* should not be applied to issues of fundamental fairness, such as possible juror bias). Consider also the characterization of *Vasquez* in *Bank of Nova Scotia v. United States,* at p. 975 infra, and the description there as well of *Ballard v. United States.* See also *United States v. Jennings,* 991 F.2d 725 (11th Cir.1993) (leaving open the question of whether *Bank of Nova Scotia* requires reconsideration of *Porter*: grand juror's friendship with victim obviously "harmless" in light of strong proof presented before the grand jury).

SECTION 3. CHALLENGES TO THE EVIDENCE BEFORE THE GRAND JURY

COSTELLO v. UNITED STATES
350 U.S. 359, 76 S.Ct. 406, 100 L.Ed. 397 (1956).

Justice BLACK delivered the opinion of the Court.

We granted certiorari in this case to consider a single question: "May a defendant be required to stand trial and a conviction be sustained where only hearsay evidence was presented to the grand jury which indicted him?"

Petitioner, Frank Costello, was indicted for wilfully attempting to evade payment of income taxes due the United States for the years 1947, 1948 and 1949. The charge was that petitioner falsely and fraudulently reported less income than he and his wife actually received during the taxable years in question. Petitioner promptly filed a motion for inspection of the minutes of the grand jury and for a dismissal of the indictment. His motion was based on an affidavit stating that he was firmly convinced there could have been no legal or competent evidence before the grand jury which indicted him since he had reported all his income and paid all taxes due. The motion was denied. At the trial which followed the Government offered evidence designed to show increases in Costello's net worth in an attempt to prove that he had received more income during the years in question than he had reported. To establish its case the Government called and examined 144 witnesses and introduced 368 exhibits. All of the testimony and documents related to business transactions and expenditures by petitioner and his wife. The prosecution concluded its case by calling three government agents. Their investigations had produced the evidence used against petitioner at the trial. They were allowed to summarize the vast amount of evidence already heard and to introduce computations showing, if correct, that petitioner and his wife had received far greater income than they had reported. We have held such summarizations admissible in a "net worth" case like this.

Counsel for petitioner asked each government witness at the trial whether he had appeared before the grand jury which returned the indictment. This cross-examination developed the fact that the three investigating officers had been the only witnesses before the grand jury. After the Government concluded its case, petitioner again moved to dismiss the indictment on the ground that the only evidence before the grand jury was "hearsay," since the three officers had no first-hand knowledge of the transactions upon which their computations were based. Nevertheless the trial court again refused to dismiss the indictment, and petitioner was convicted. The Court of Appeals affirmed. * * * Petitioner here urges: (1) that an indictment based solely on hearsay evidence violates that part of the Fifth Amendment providing that "No person shall be held to answer for a capital, or otherwise infamous crime, unless on a presentment or indictment of a Grand Jury * * *." and (2) that if the Fifth Amendment does not invalidate an indictment based solely on hearsay we should now lay down such a rule for the guidance of federal courts. * * * [N]either the Fifth Amendment nor any other constitutional provision prescribes the kind of evidence upon which grand juries must act. The grand jury is an English institution, brought to this country by the early colonists and incorporated in the Constitution by the Founders. There is every reason to believe that our constitutional grand jury was intended to operate substantially like its English progenitor. The basic purpose of the English grand jury was to provide a fair method for instituting criminal proceedings against persons believed to have committed crimes. Grand jurors were selected from the body of the people and their work was not hampered by rigid procedural or evidential rules. In fact, grand jurors could act on their own knowledge and were free to make their presentments or indictments on such information as they deemed satisfactory. Despite its broad power to institute criminal proceedings the grand jury grew in popular favor with the years. It acquired an independence in England free from control by the Crown or judges. Its adoption in our Constitution as the sole method for preferring charges in serious criminal cases shows the high place it held as an instrument of justice. And in this country as in England of old the grand jury has convened as a body of laymen, free from technical rules, acting in secret, pledged to indict no one because of prejudice and to free no one because of special favor. As late as 1927 an English historian could say that English grand juries were still free to act on their own knowledge if they pleased to do so. And in 1852 Mr. Justice Nelson on circuit could say "No case has been cited, nor have we been able to find any, furnishing an authority for looking into and revising the judgment of the grand jury upon the evidence, for the purpose of determining whether or not the finding was founded upon sufficient proof * * *." *United States v. Reed,* 27 Fed.Cas. 727 [1852].

In *Holt v. United States,* 218 U.S. 245, 31 S.Ct. 2, 54 L.Ed. 1021 [1910], this Court had to decide whether an indictment should be quashed because supported in part by incompetent evidence. Aside from the incompetent evidence "there was very little evidence against the accused." The Court refused to hold that such an indictment should be quashed, pointing out that "The abuses of criminal practice would be enhanced if indictments could be upset on such a ground." The same thing is true where as here all the evidence before the grand jury was in the nature of "hearsay." If indictments were to be held open to challenge on the ground that there was inadequate or incompetent evidence before the grand jury, the resulting delay would be great indeed. The result of such a rule would be that before trial on the merits a defendant could always insist on a kind of preliminary trial to determine the competency and adequacy of the evidence before the grand jury. This is not required by the Fifth Amendment. An indictment returned by a legally constituted and unbiased grand jury, like an information drawn by the prosecutor, if valid on its face, is enough to call for trial of the charge on the merits. The Fifth Amendment requires nothing more.

Petitioner urges that this Court should exercise its power to supervise the administration of justice in federal courts and establish a rule permitting defendants to challenge indictments on the ground that they are not supported by adequate or competent evidence. No persuasive reasons are advanced for establishing such a rule. It would run counter to the whole history of the grand jury institution, in which laymen conduct their inquiries unfettered by technical rules. Neither justice nor the concept of a fair trial requires such a change. In a trial on the merits, defendants are entitled to a strict observance of all the rules designed to bring about a fair verdict. Defendants are not entitled, however, to a rule which would result in interminable delay but add nothing to the assurance of a fair trial. Affirmed.

Justice CLARK and Justice HARLAN took no part in the consideration or decision of this case.

Justice BURTON, concurring.

I agree with the denial of the motion to quash the indictment. In my view, however, this case does not justify the breadth of the declarations made by the Court. I assume that this Court would not preclude an examination of grand jury action to ascertain the existence of bias or prejudice in an indictment. Likewise, it seems to me that if it is shown that the grand jury had before it no substantial or rationally persuasive evidence upon which to base its indictment, that indictment should be quashed. To hold a person to answer to such an empty indictment for a capital or otherwise infamous federal crime robs the Fifth Amendment of much of its protective value to the private citizen.

Here, as in *Holt,* substantial and rationally persuasive evidence apparently was presented to the grand jury. * * * At the trial, with preliminary testimony laying the foundation for it, the same testimony constituted an important part of the competent evidence upon which the conviction was obtained. To sustain this indictment under the above circumstances is well enough, but I agree with Judge Learned Hand that "if it appeared that no evidence had been offered that rationally established the facts, the indictment ought to be quashed; because then the grand jury would have in substance abdicated." 221 F.2d 668, 677 [1955]. * * *

NOTES ON THE RATIONALE AND SCOPE OF *COSTELLO*

1. ***The relevance of history.*** To what extent should the traditional practices of the grand jury, as developed at the time of the Constitution's adoption, control the Court's interpretation of the Fifth Amendment? Commentators have argued that the grand jury today operates in such a substantially different setting than the grand jury of the late eighteenth century that fulfillment of its screening role now requires the "judiciary * * * to take more positive action to ensure that the grand jury functions effectively." Robert Johnston, *The Grand Jury—Prosecutorial Abuse of the Indictment Process,* 65 J.Crim.L. & Criminology 157 (1974). While the late eighteenth century grand jury surely considered evidence that would be inadmissible at trial, it did not have the assistance of a legally trained prosecutor. Cases were presented by the sheriff, a justice of the peace, or a complainant, and those persons were not necessarily present when the grand jury heard from other witnesses. With the development of the office of the modern prosecutor, it is argued, there is less room for grand jury independence and a greater capacity in the grand jury, assisted by its legal advisor, to distinguish between admissible and inadmissible evidence. Do these changes in the operation of the grand jury undercut Justice Black's reliance upon history in *Costello?*[a]

a. Justice Black also notes that grand jurors traditionally "could act on their own knowledge." This authority, critics argue, has considerably less significance as applied to

2. *Supervisory power.* Commentators have suggested that *Costello* is based not so much on history as on the Court's conclusion that, for various reasons (see Notes 3–4 infra), federal courts should not restrict grand juries to the consideration of evidence that would be admissible at trial. They note that some federal courts previously had imposed such a limit in the exercise of their supervisory power, as evidenced by Justice Field's famous *Charge to the Grand Jury,* 30 Fed.Cas. 992 (C.C.D.Cal.1872) (directing the grand jurors to receive "only legal evidence, to the exclusion of mere reports"). Thus, they argue, if the Court had concluded in *Costello* that extensive reliance upon hearsay was inappropriate, but so clearly ratified by historical practice that it could not be deemed contrary to the Fifth Amendment, it could have prohibited the practice in the "exercise [of] its power to supervise the administration of justice in federal courts [p. 951]." This suggestion was offered prior to the Supreme Court's decision in *United States v. Williams* (p. 957), which advanced a considerably narrower perspective on the scope of that power as applied to grand juries. Still, as the commentators have noted, the Federal Rules of Evidence, later adopted by the Court (and Congress), clearly took the position that, as a matter of policy, the grand jury should not be tied to trial admissibility standards. Rule 1101(d) provides that "the[se] rules (other than with respect to privileges) to do not apply in * * * proceedings before grand juries."

3. *Costello's premises.* Commentators have pointed to three premises regarding grand jury screening that arguably could justify the *Costello* rule as a matter of policy. They suggest that those three premises, though not stated in *Costello,* may well have influenced that decision and most certainly explain the acceptance of *Costello* by legislative and rulemaking bodies.

(i) *Costello,* it is argued, reflects the view that the grand jury's primary goal is to protect the factually innocent against standing trial, not to protect from trial those who simply are not likely to be convicted because of legal obstacles to proof. Under this view, since the grand jury should be concerned with the probability of the suspect's factual guilt, rather than the probability of his conviction, whether or not the prosecution's evidence would be admissible at trial is basically irrelevant. See also Abraham Goldstein, *The State and the Accused: Balance of Advantage in Criminal Procedure,* 69 Yale L.J. 1149, 1171–72 (1960) (*Costello's* analysis rests on the assumption that the "accused will get his fair, 'judicial,' hearing at his trial"). But consider Peter Arenella, *Reforming the Federal Grand Jury and the State Preliminary Hearing to Prevent Conviction Without Adjudication,* 78 Mich.L.Rev. 463 (1980) (*Costello* errs in assuming that the trial will protect "the system's legal guilt requirements" since most cases are disposed of by a guilty plea, which may be accepted without regard to whether the person could be convicted at trial).

(ii) *Costello,* it is argued, rests on the premise that prosecutors are most unlikely to seek indictments in cases in which they have substantial incompetent evidence, but not enough competent evidence to convict at trial. Prosecutors are characterized as too busy and too concerned about their "batting averages" to seek indictments where they do not have a good chance of success at trial. Marvin Frankel and Gary Naftalis, *The Grand Jury: An Institution on Trial* 25–26 (1977). Where a prosecutor seeks an indictment on the basis of hearsay, he almost certainly will have the live testimony available at trial. Though he may have

modern grand juries. While grand jurors may utilize their personal knowledge in initiating an investigation, they lack the familiarity with events in their local district that would permit them to indict on the basis of personal knowl-edge. Several jurisdictions now provide that a grand juror with sufficient information to give evidence relating to a crime must be sworn like any other witness.

overestimated the persuasiveness of that testimony, it still should be sufficient to establish probable cause. *Costello,* accordingly, recognized that requiring the prosecutor to present the actual trial witnesses before the grand jury would be a largely wasted effort. Proponents of this view acknowledge that occasionally prosecutorial vindictiveness will produce an indictment lacking sufficient evidentiary support, but they maintain that the grand jury generally should be able to screen out those cases, based on obvious gaps in the prosecution's case or the unjust nature of the charges, without regard to the competency of the evidence presented.

(iii) *Costello,* it is argued, rests on the premise that the grand jury must be allowed to consider material that would not be admissible at trial if it is to be able to review the prosecutor's decision apart from its legal sufficiency. A grand jury must have the capacity to seek out information, beyond the crime itself, that relates to the same factors the prosecution will consider in deciding whether to charge. Yet, much of this information (e.g., the accused's prior record) would be inadmissible at trial. If the Court had held the *Costello* indictment invalid because it rested on incompetent evidence, that ruling, it is argued, would have opened the door to challenges to almost any indictment by a grand jury that sought to consider the complete picture. Cf. Garry Woodward and Gary Ahrens, *The Iowa Grand Jury,* 26 Drake L.Rev. 241 (1976).

4. *Administrative burdens.* Several commentators have suggested that the *Costello* ruling was influenced primarily by the Court's assumption that a substantial burden would be imposed on the federal judiciary if evidentiary challenges to indictments were allowed. The commentators note, in particular, Justice Black's comments upon the "resulting delay" and the likelihood of "a kind of preliminary trial" in every case (see p. 950). They point out that the Court may have been influenced as well by other administrative difficulties that would flow from the position urged by the petitioner. If the Court were to permit evidentiary challenges, it also would have to require that grand jury testimony be recorded (a requirement not imposed in federal courts until 1979, with the adoption of current Rule 6(e)). So too, the implementation of such challenges logically would require that the defense be given pretrial access to that transcript to determine whether it revealed grounds for an evidentiary challenge (see Note 3, p. 956), and such disclosure would have undercut various limitations found in federal pretrial discovery (including the nondisclosure of the names of witnesses). Also, recognition of evidentiary challenges might have required separation of the investigating grand jury and the screening grand jury, since an investigative grand jury must be able to receive inadmissible evidence if it is to fulfill its task of tracking down "every available clue," including "tips" and "rumors," *United States v. Dionisio,* 410 U.S. 1, 93 S.Ct. 764, 35 L.Ed.2d 67 (1973). See also Peter J. Henning, *Prosecutorial Misconduct in Grand Jury Investigations,* 51 S.Car.L.Rev. 1 (1999) (cases like *Costello* and *Williams,* infra p. 957, have made "the grand jury, and the prosecutors that guide its proceedings, free from oversight in order to protect the [grand jury's] investigative function from outside interference"; that "function, more than the accusatory function, defines the importance of the grand jury in the criminal justice system").

What weight, if any, should be given to such administrative burdens? As described in Note 2, p. 955, many states recognize challenges to the sufficiency and competency of the evidence before the grand jury, and they apparently do not find these burdens intolerable. Admittedly, most of these states ordinarily prosecute by information, but several are indictment jurisdictions. Is there any reason why the administrative burdens would pose greater difficulties in the federal system than in these other indictment jurisdictions? Does the weight given to administrative difficulties depend, in the end, upon one's view of the importance of grand jury screening? Commentators who favor allowing evidentiary challenges quote Judge Frank's remark in *In re Fried,* 161 F.2d 453 (2d Cir.1947) (concurring):

> "[A] wrongful indictment is no laughing matter; often it works a grievous irreparable injury to the person indicted. The stigma cannot be easily erased. In the public mind, the blot on a man's escutcheon, resulting from such a public accusation of wrongdoing, is seldom wiped out by a subsequent judgment of not guilty. Frequently, the public remembers the accusation, and still suspects guilt, even after an acquittal."

5. *Review of evidentiary sufficiency.* To what extent do the rationales discussed above argue against judicial review of the sufficiency of the evidence to provide a rational basis for indictment? Commentators have suggested that the most striking aspect of the *Costello* ruling was not its refusal to disallow an indictment based on hearsay, but its refusal to allow judicial review of the sufficiency of evidence to support the grand jury's finding of probable cause, without regard to whether that evidence would be admissible at trial. *Costello* generally has been viewed as rejecting Justice Burton's suggestion that a federal court could dismiss an indictment on the ground that the grand jury had before it "no substantial or rationally persuasive evidence upon which to base its indictment." See e.g., *United States v. Mills,* 792 F.Supp. 444 (M.D.N.C.1992), aff'd, 995 F.2d 480 (4th Cir.1993) ("Burton's view * * * has never commanded another vote in the Supreme Court, and fails to overcome the clear command of the *Costello* majority * * * that a facially valid indictment should not be disturbed"). But consider *United States v. O'Shea,* 447 F.Supp. 330 (S.D.Fla.1978) (court inspected transcript and dismissed the indictment because it was "not supported by any evidence, competent or otherwise to establish a 'prima facie case' ").

6. *Unconstitutionally obtained evidence.* In three post-*Costello* decisions, including *United States v. Calandra,* 414 U.S. 338, 94 S.Ct. 613, 38 L.Ed.2d 561 (1974), the Supreme Court indicated quite clearly, albeit in dictum, that the *Costello* rationale also barred a challenge to an indictment issued on the basis of unconstitutionally obtained evidence. See CRIMPROC § 15.5(a); Brenner & Lockhart, § 10.8. Could the Court readily have distinguished a challenge based on grand jury consideration of unconstitutionally obtained evidence? Commentators have suggested that such a challenge should have been distinguished because: (1) *Costello* was concerned only with the impact of the Fifth Amendment's indictment provision, while the challenge to the use of unconstitutionally obtained evidence also required consideration of those constitutional provisions violated in obtaining such evidence; (2) while hearsay evidence may be transformed into admissible evidence by the introduction of live testimony at trial, unconstitutionally obtained evidence cannot be transformed into admissible evidence; and (3) a challenge to an indictment based on unconstitutionally obtained evidence will not add substantially to pretrial proceedings since the legality of the acquisition of such evidence would otherwise be raised in a pretrial suppression motion.

The United States Attorneys' Manual, §§ 9–11.231–232 draws a distinction between hearsay and unconstitutionally obtained evidence. As to hearsay, it notes that such evidence may be utilized if the evidence is clearly presented to the grand jury as hearsay and "affords the grand jurors a substantial basis for voting upon an indictment." As for evidence unconstitutionally obtained, it directs federal prosecutors "not [to] present to the grand jury for use against a person whose constitutional rights clearly have been violated evidence which the prosecutor personally knows was obtained as a direct result of the constitutional violation."

7. *Misconduct rulings.* Following *Costello,* the federal lower courts turned to a "prosecutorial misconduct" rationale (see § 4 infra) to maintain some control over the character of the evidence presented to the grand jury. *Costello,* it was argued, did not take from the lower courts their authority "to preserve the integrity of the judicial process" by dismissing indictments that were the product of "flagrantly abusive prosecutorial conduct." Prosecutor misconduct was held to include not only such traditional forms of misconduct as inflammatory prosecutorial argument to the jury (see Note 5, p. 971), but also the presentation of evidence in an unfair manner. Federal lower courts varied considerably in what they deemed evidentiary misconduct, but under the broadest view, all of the following constituted grounds for dismissal where they had a possible impact on the indictment decision: the knowing presentation of perjured testimony; the introduction of false testimony by government agents where the prosecutor was patently negligent in failing to recognize its inaccuracy; the failure to return to the grand jury, during the period between indictment and trial, upon learning that a key witness had lied in testimony material to the charge; the presentation of hearsay in a manner suggesting the witness was testifying based on personal observations rather than simply stating what he had been told by another (a practice sometimes used in narcotics cases, where a supervisor testified to information that came from an undercover agent or informant); the presentation of hearsay where there was a "high probability" that, with eyewitness rather than hearsay testimony, the grand jury might not have indicted (*United States v. Estepa,* cited in fn. 8 at p. 962); presenting the prior recorded testimony of a key witness and failing to inform the jury that he had acknowledged lying in an earlier portion of his testimony; and failing to produce known exculpatory evidence that clearly was material. See CRIMPROC § 15.5(b). The broad view of supervisory power that served as the grounding for these rulings was flatly rejected in *United States v. Williams,* discussed in § 4 infra. Indeed, after *Williams,* only a very narrow slice of these "evidentiary misconduct" challenges continue to be viable. See Note 1, p. 965.

EVIDENTIARY CHALLENGES IN STATE COURTS

1. ***Costello states.*** A substantial majority of the states, including most of the "indictment states" follow the basic position of *Costello.* See CRIMPROC § 15.5(c); Beale et al., §§ 4.20, 9.25 (state-by-state review). Roughly half of the states have provisions similar to Fed.R.Evid. 1101(d) making the rules of evidence inapplicable to the grand jury process (except for privileges). Others have caselaw holding that indictments may be based on hearsay evidence or other evidence that would be inadmissible at trial. These states also disallow challenges to the probative sufficiency of the evidence, with some having statutes specifically precluding evidentiary review. A good many, however, allow for dismissal of an indictment based on prosecutorial misconduct in the presentation of evidence (e.g., the knowing presentation of perjured testimony). A somewhat narrower view allows for dismissal where the misconduct occurred before the grand jury in obtaining the testimony of the accused (typically, in violating his privilege against self-incrimination). Some states have suggested that an indictment also will be dismissed if there was "no evidence" before the grand jury or no witness "competent to testify." A few have carved out additional exceptions. See e.g., *Reaves v. State,* 250 S.E.2d 376 (Ga.1978) (accepting indictments based on at least certain types of hearsay, but requiring dismissal of indictments returned wholly on illegally seized evidence).

2. ***States rejecting Costello.*** A few indictment states and a somewhat larger group of information states (perhaps a dozen in all) allow challenges to the sufficiency and competency of the evidence underlying an indictment. See CRIMPROC § 15.5(c); Beale et al., §§ 4.20, 9.25. Some do so by statutory command, but others have adopted this position solely through judicial decision. The reasoning of *Costello,* it is argued, is persuasive only "if the institution of the grand jury is

viewed as an anachronism." If the grand jury is to "protect * * * the innocent against oppression and unjust prosecution," a defendant "with substantial grounds for having an indictment dismissed should not be compelled to go to trial to prove the insufficiency." *State v. Parks,* 437 P.2d 642 (Alaska 1968) (Rabinowitz, J., concurring).

Jurisdictions rejecting *Costello* uniformly insist that the trial court act with caution in reviewing the sufficiency of the evidence before the grand jury. They stress that "every legitimate inference that may be drawn from the evidence must be drawn in favor of the indictment," and note that "probable cause * * * may be based on 'slight' or even marginal evidence." *State v. Freedle,* 620 P.2d 740 (Hawai'i App.1980). As a result, most of the successful sufficiency challenges arise from the prosecution's failure to offer any competent evidence on a particular element of the crime charged. A few of these jurisdictions direct the grand jury to consider only evidence that would be admissible at trial. The others generally apply the rules of evidence, but permit consideration of either limited types of hearsay (such as scientific reports) or a broader range of hearsay (tied to the burden that would be imposed in presenting direct testimony).

3. *Inspection of grand jury transcripts.* Almost all of the jurisdictions which permit challenges to the competency and sufficiency of the grand jury evidence also grant the defendant an automatic right to inspect the transcript of the grand jury testimony. See CRIMPROC § 15.2(i). In *Burkholder v. State,* 491 P.2d 754 (Alaska 1971), the court concluded that the right to inspect was essential "to give meaning" to the right to challenge the indictment. The court rejected as unsatisfactory a state provision, similar to Fed.R.Crim.P. 6(e)(3)(C)(ii), that allowed disclosure only "upon a showing that grounds may exist for a motion to dismiss the indictment." The difficulty with such a rule, it noted, was "that so far as the sufficiency of the indictment is concerned, * * * it is only by being able to have access to the grand jury proceedings without any prior showing that a defendant can know whether the indictment is subject to dismissal."

Compare with *Burkholder,* the position adopted in New York. In connection with a motion to dismiss an indictment as based on insufficient legal evidence, the defendant may move for inspection of the transcript. However, the inspection initially is conducted *in camera* by the court, and further inspection by the defense may be denied if the court "determines there is not reasonable cause to believe that the evidence before the grand jury may have been legally insufficient." N.Y.Crim.P.Law § 210.30(4). Does New York's initial restriction of the inspection to *in camera* review impose a significant limit upon the challenge to the indictment? Compare *Ivey v. State,* 420 P.2d 853 (Nev.1966), rejecting *in camera* inspection on the grounds, inter alia, that (1) defendant's "right to know what evidence was formally received by the grand jury" is an important aspect of his right not to be indicted without probable cause, and (2) the court needs the "assistance of counsel for both sides if it is to judge wisely."

4. *Harmless error and reversal on appeal.* In all of the non-*Costello* jurisdictions, the presentation of inadmissible evidence before the grand jury does not necessarily justify granting a dismissal. The indictment ordinarily will be sustained if, after excluding the inadmissible evidence, there remains sufficient admissible evidence to support the charge. Some courts have stated, however, that if the inadmissible evidence was so prejudicial in nature as to clearly have influenced the grand jury, the indictment will be dismissed notwithstanding otherwise sufficient legal evidence.

In several of the non-*Costello* states, a defendant may readily obtain interlocutory appellate review of the trial judge's rejection of a motion to dismiss. In others, however, interlocutory appellate review generally is not available (see Ch.

28, § 2), and a trial judge's adverse ruling on an indictment challenge ordinarily comes before the appellate court as part of the appeal following conviction. At this point, should any insufficiency in the evidence before the grand jury be viewed as harmless error since the trial jury found sufficient evidence to convict? Cf. *United States v. Mechanik,* Note 5, p. 977. Most non-*Costello* states apparently assume that a conviction will be reversed automatically if the trial judge erred in failing to grant the dismissal motion. See e.g., *Adams v. State,* 598 P.2d 503 (Alaska 1979) ("If we were to find that a trial could validate an otherwise invalid indictment [based on hearsay testimony], the right to indictment by a grand jury could become a nullity"). But compare N.Y.Crim.P.Law § 210.30(6) (validity of an order denying a motion to dismiss or to inspect the grand jury transcript is "not reviewable upon an appeal from an ensuing judgment of conviction based upon legally sufficient trial evidence").

SECTION 4. MISCONDUCT CHALLENGES

UNITED STATES v. WILLIAMS
504 U.S. 36, 112 S.Ct. 1735, 118 L.Ed.2d 352 (1992).

Justice SCALIA delivered the opinion of the Court.

The question presented in this case is whether a district court may dismiss an otherwise valid indictment because the Government failed to disclose to the grand jury "substantial exculpatory evidence" in its possession. * * *

On May 4, 1988, respondent John H. Williams, Jr., a Tulsa, Oklahoma, investor, was indicted by a federal grand jury on seven counts of "knowingly mak[ing] [a] false statement or report . . . for the purpose of influencing . . . the action [of a federally insured financial institution]," in violation of 18 U.S.C. § 1014 (1988 ed., Supp. II). According to the indictment, between September 1984 and November 1985 Williams supplied four Oklahoma banks with "materially false" statements that variously overstated the value of his current assets and interest income in order to influence the banks' actions on his loan requests.

Williams' misrepresentation was allegedly effected through two financial statements provided to the banks, a "Market Value Balance Sheet" and a "Statement of Projected Income and Expense." The former included as "current assets" approximately $6 million in notes receivable from three venture capital companies. Though it contained a disclaimer that these assets were carried at cost rather than at market value, the Government asserted that listing them as "current assets"—*i.e.,* assets quickly reducible to cash—was misleading, since Williams knew that none of the venture capital companies could afford to satisfy the notes in the short term. The second document—the Statement of Projected Income and Expense—allegedly misrepresented Williams' interest income, since it failed to reflect that the interest payments received on the notes of the venture capital companies were funded entirely by Williams' own loans to those companies. The Statement thus falsely implied, according to the Government, that Williams was deriving interest income from "an independent outside source." Brief for United States 3.

Shortly after arraignment, the District Court granted Williams' motion for disclosure of all exculpatory portions of the grand jury transcripts, see *Brady v. Maryland* [p. 1390]. Upon reviewing this material, Williams demanded that the District Court dismiss the indictment, alleging that the Government had failed to fulfill its obligation under the Tenth Circuit's prior decision in *United States v. Page,* 808 F.2d 723 (1987), to present "substantial exculpatory evidence" to the grand jury. His contention was that evidence which the Government had chosen not to present to the grand jury—in particular, Williams' general ledgers and tax returns, and Williams' testimony in his contemporaneous Chapter 11 bankruptcy proceeding—disclosed that, for tax purposes and otherwise, he had regularly accounted for the "notes receivable" (and the interest on them) in a manner consistent with the Balance Sheet and the Income Statement. This, he contended, belied an intent to mislead the banks, and thus directly negated an essential element of the charged offense.

The District Court initially denied Williams' motion, but upon reconsideration ordered the indictment dismissed without prejudice. It found, after a hearing, that the withheld evidence was "relevant to an essential element of the crime charged," created " 'a reasonable doubt about [respondent's] guilt,' " and thus "render[ed] the grand jury's decision to indict gravely suspect." Upon the Government's appeal, the Court of Appeals affirmed the District Court's order, following its earlier decision in *Page*, supra. It first sustained as not "clearly erroneous" the District Court's determination that the Government had withheld "substantial exculpatory evidence" from the grand jury. It then found that the Government's behavior " 'substantially influence[d]' " the grand jury's decision to indict, or at the very least raised a " 'grave doubt that the decision to indict was free from such substantial influence,' " (quoting *Bank of Nova Scotia v. United States* [Note 2, p. 973]). Under these circumstances, the Tenth Circuit concluded, it was not an abuse of discretion for the District Court to require the Government to begin anew before the grand jury. We granted certiorari. * * *

Respondent does not contend that the Fifth Amendment itself obliges the prosecutor to disclose substantial exculpatory evidence in his possession to the grand jury. Instead, building on our statement that the federal courts "may, within limits, formulate procedural rules not specifically required by the Constitution or the Congress," *United States v. Hasting*, 461 U.S. 499, 103 S.Ct. 1974, 76 L.Ed.2d 96 (1983), he argues that imposition of the Tenth Circuit's disclosure rule is supported by the courts' "supervisory power." We think not. *Hasting*, and the cases that rely upon the principle it expresses, deal strictly with the courts' power to control their *own* procedures. That power has been applied not only to improve the truth-finding process of the trial, but also to prevent parties from reaping benefit or incurring harm from violations of substantive or procedural rules (imposed by the Constitution or laws) governing matters apart from the trial itself, see, *e.g.*, *Weeks v. United States* 232 U.S. 383, 34 S.Ct. 341, 58 L.Ed. 652 (1914). Thus, *Bank of Nova Scotia v. United States* makes clear that the supervisory power can be used to dismiss an indictment because of misconduct before the grand jury, at least where that misconduct amounts to a violation of one of those "few, clear rules which were carefully drafted and approved by this Court and by Congress to ensure the integrity of the grand jury's functions," *United States v. Mechanik* [Note 5, p. 977] (O'Connor, J., concurring in judgment).[6]

We did not hold in *Bank of Nova Scotia*, however, that the courts' supervisory power could be used, not merely as a means of enforcing or vindicating legally

---

6. Rule 6 of the Federal Rules of Criminal Procedure contains a number of such rules, providing, for example, that "no person other than the jurors may be present while the grand jury is deliberating or voting," Rule 6(d), and placing strict controls on disclosure of "matters occurring before the grand jury," Rule 6(e). * * * Additional standards of behavior for prosecutors (and others) are set forth in the United States Code. See 18 U.S.C. §§ 6002, 6003 (setting forth procedures for granting a witness immunity from prosecution); § 1623 (criminalizing false declarations before grand jury); § 2515 (prohibiting grand jury use of unlawfully intercepted wire or oral communications); § 1622 (criminalizing subornation of perjury). That some of the misconduct alleged in *Bank of Nova Scotia v. United States*, was not specifically proscribed by Rule, statute, or the Constitution does not make the case stand for a judicially prescribable grand jury code * * *. All of the allegations of violation were dismissed by the Court—without considering their validity in law—for failure to meet *Nova Scotia's* dismissal standard. [See Note 2, p. 973, and fn. b, p. 963].

compelled standards of prosecutorial conduct before the grand jury, but as a means of *prescribing* those standards of prosecutorial conduct in the first instance—just as it may be used as a means of establishing standards of prosecutorial conduct before the courts themselves. It is this latter exercise that respondent demands. Because the grand jury is an institution separate from the courts, over whose functioning the courts do not preside, we think it clear that, as a general matter at least, no such "supervisory" judicial authority exists, and that the disclosure rule applied here exceeded the Tenth Circuit's authority. * * *

"[R]ooted in long centuries of Anglo–American history," the grand jury is mentioned in the Bill of Rights, but not in the body of the Constitution. It has not been textually assigned, therefore, to any of the branches described in the first three Articles. It " 'is a constitutional fixture in its own right.' " *United States v. Chanen,* 549 F.2d 1306 (9th Cir.1977). In fact the whole theory of its function is that it belongs to no branch of the institutional government, serving as a kind of buffer or referee between the Government and the people. See *Stirone v. United States* [Note 5, p. 1006]. * * * Although the grand jury normally operates, of course, in the courthouse and under judicial auspices, its institutional relationship with the judicial branch has traditionally been, so to speak, at arm's length. Judges' direct involvement in the functioning of the grand jury has generally been confined to the constitutive one of calling the grand jurors together and administering their oaths of office. * * *

The grand jury's functional independence from the judicial branch is evident both in the scope of its power to investigate criminal wrongdoing, and in the manner in which that power is exercised. "Unlike [a] [c]ourt, whose jurisdiction is predicated upon a specific case or controversy, the grand jury 'can investigate merely on suspicion that the law is being violated, or even because it wants assurance that it is not.' " *United States v. R. Enterprises,* 498 U.S. 292, 111 S.Ct. 722, 112 L.Ed.2d 795 (1991). It need not identify the offender it suspects, or even "the precise nature of the offense" it is investigating. *Blair v. United States,* 250 U.S. 273, 39 S.Ct. 468, 63 L.Ed. 979 (1919). The grand jury requires no authorization from its constituting court to initiate an investigation, nor does the prosecutor require leave of court to seek a grand jury indictment. And in its day-to-day functioning, the grand jury generally operates without the interference of a presiding judge. See *Calandra,* supra. It swears in its own witnesses, Fed.Rule Crim.Proc. 6(c), and deliberates in total secrecy.

True, the grand jury cannot compel the appearance of witnesses and the production of evidence, and must appeal to the court when such compulsion is required. See *Brown v. United States,* 359 U.S. 41, 79 S.Ct. 539, 3 L.Ed.2d 609 (1959). And the court will refuse to lend its assistance when the compulsion the grand jury seeks would override rights accorded by the Constitution, see, *e.g., Gravel v. United States,* 408 U.S. 606, 92 S.Ct. 2614, 33 L.Ed.2d 583 (1972) (grand jury subpoena effectively qualified by order limiting questioning so as to preserve Speech or Debate Clause immunity), or even testimonial privileges recognized by the common law, see *In re Grand Jury Investigation of Hugle,* 754 F.2d 863 (9th Cir.1985) (same with respect to privilege for confidential marital communications) (opinion of Kennedy, J.). Even in this setting, however, we have insisted that the grand jury remain "free to pursue its investigations unhindered by external influence or supervision so long as it does not trench upon the legitimate rights of any witness called before it." *United States v. Dionisio,* 410 U.S. 1, 93 S.Ct. 764, 35 L.Ed.2d 67 (1973). Recognizing this tradition of independence, we have said that the Fifth Amendment's "constitutional guarantee *presupposes* an investigative body 'acting independently of either prosecuting attorney *or judge'...*." *Dionisio.*

No doubt in view of the grand jury proceeding's status as other than a constituent element of a "criminal prosecutio[n]," U.S. Const., Amdt. VI, we have said that certain constitutional protections afforded defendants in criminal proceedings have no application before that body. The Double Jeopardy Clause of the Fifth Amendment does not bar a grand jury from returning an indictment when a prior grand jury has refused to do so. * * * We have twice suggested, though not held, that the Sixth Amendment right to counsel does not attach when an individual is summoned to appear before a grand jury, even if he is the subject of the investigation. See *United States v. Mandujano*, 425 U.S. 564, 96 S.Ct. 1768, 48 L.Ed.2d 212 (1976); *In re Groban*, 352 U.S. 330, 77 S.Ct. 510, 1 L.Ed.2d 376 (1957), see also Fed.Rule Crim.Proc. 6(d). And although "the grand jury may not force a witness to answer questions in violation of [the Fifth Amendment's] constitutional guarantee" against self-incrimination, our cases suggest that an indictment obtained through the use of evidence previously obtained in violation of the privilege against self-incrimination "is nevertheless valid." *Calandra* [Note 6, p. 954].

Given the grand jury's operational separateness from its constituting court, it should come as no surprise that we have been reluctant to invoke the judicial supervisory power as a basis for prescribing modes of grand jury procedure. Over the years, we have received many requests to exercise supervision over the grand jury's evidence-taking process, but we have refused them all, including some more appealing that the one presented today. In *Calandra*, supra, a grand jury witness faced questions that were allegedly based upon physical evidence the Government had obtained through a violation of the Fourth Amendment; we rejected the proposal that the exclusionary rule be extended to grand jury proceedings, because of "the potential injury to the historic role and functions of the grand jury." In *Costello v. United States* [p. 949], we declined to enforce the hearsay rule in grand jury proceedings, since that "would run counter to the whole history of the grand jury institution, in which laymen conduct their inquiries unfettered by technical rules."

These authorities suggest that any power federal courts may have to fashion, on their own initiative, rules of grand jury procedure is a very limited one, not remotely comparable to the power they maintain over their own proceedings. See *United States v. Chanen*, supra. It certainly would not permit judicial reshaping of the grand jury institution, substantially altering the traditional relationships between the prosecutor, the constituting court, and the grand jury itself. Cf., *e.g.*, *United States v. Payner*, 447 U.S. 727, 100 S.Ct. 2439, 65 L.Ed.2d 468 (1980) (supervisory power may not be applied to permit defendant to invoke third party's Fourth Amendment rights); see generally Beale, Reconsidering Supervisory Power in Criminal Cases, 84 Colum.L.Rev. 1433 (1984). As we proceed to discuss, that would be the consequence of the proposed rule here. * * *

Respondent argues that the Court of Appeals' rule can be justified as a sort of Fifth Amendment "common law," a necessary means of assuring the constitutional right to the judgment "of an independent and informed grand jury," *Wood v. Georgia* [p. 932]. Respondent makes a generalized appeal to functional notions: Judicial supervision of the quantity and quality of the evidence relied upon by the grand jury plainly facilitates, he says, the grand jury's performance of its twin historical responsibilities, *i.e.*, bringing to trial those who may be justly accused and shielding the innocent from unfounded accusation and prosecution. We do not agree. The rule would neither preserve nor enhance the traditional functioning of the institution that the Fifth Amendment demands. To the contrary, requiring the prosecutor to present exculpatory as well as inculpatory evidence would alter the grand jury's historical role, transforming it from an accusatory to an adjudicatory body.

It is axiomatic that the grand jury sits not to determine guilt or innocence, but to assess whether there is adequate basis for bringing a criminal charge. See *United States v. Calandra,* supra. That has always been so; and to make the assessment it has always been thought sufficient to hear only the prosecutor's side. As Blackstone described the prevailing practice in 18th-century England, the grand jury was "only to hear evidence on behalf of the prosecution[,] for the finding of an indictment is only in the nature of an enquiry or accusation, which is afterwards to be tried and determined." 4 W. Blackstone, Commentaries 300 (1769); see also 2 M. Hale, Pleas of the Crown 157 (1st Am. ed. 1847). So also in the United States. According to the description of an early American court, three years before the Fifth Amendment was ratified, it is the grand jury's function not "to enquire ... upon what foundation [the charge may be] denied," or otherwise to try the suspect's defenses, but only to examine "upon what foundation [the charge] is made" by the prosecutor. *Respublica v. Shaffer,* 1 U.S. (1 Dall.) 236, 1 L.Ed. 116 (Philadelphia Oyer and Terminer 1788). See also F. Wharton, Criminal Pleading and Practice § 360, pp. 248–249 (8th ed. 1880). As a consequence, neither in this country nor in England has the suspect under investigation by the grand jury ever been thought to have a right to testify, or to have exculpatory evidence presented.

Imposing upon the prosecutor a legal obligation to present exculpatory evidence in his possession would be incompatible with this system. If a "balanced" assessment of the entire matter is the objective, surely the first thing to be done— rather than requiring the prosecutor to say what he knows in defense of the target of the investigation—is to entitle the target to tender his own defense. To require the former while denying (as we do) the latter would be quite absurd. It would also be quite pointless, since it would merely invite the target to circumnavigate the system by delivering his exculpatory evidence to the prosecutor, whereupon it would *have* to be passed on to the grand jury—unless the prosecutor is willing to take the chance that a court will not deem the evidence important enough to qualify for mandatory disclosure. * * *

Respondent acknowledges (as he must) that the "common law" of the grand jury is not violated if the *grand jury itself* chooses to hear no more evidence than that which suffices to convince it an indictment is proper. Thus, had the Government offered to familiarize the grand jury in this case with the five boxes of financial statements and deposition testimony alleged to contain exculpatory information, and had the grand jury rejected the offer as pointless, respondent would presumably agree that the resulting indictment would have been valid. Respondent insists, however, that courts must require the modern prosecutor to alert the grand jury to the nature and extent of the available exculpatory evidence, because otherwise the grand jury "merely functions as an arm of the prosecution." We reject the attempt to convert a nonexistent duty of the grand jury itself into an obligation of the prosecutor. The authority of the prosecutor to seek an indictment has long been understood to be "coterminous with the authority of the grand jury to entertain [the prosecutor's] charges." *United States v. Thompson,* 251 U.S. 407, 414, 40 S.Ct. 289, 292, 64 L.Ed. 333 (1920). If the grand jury has no obligation to consider all "substantial exculpatory" evidence, we do not understand how the prosecutor can be said to have a binding obligation to present it.

There is yet another respect in which respondent's proposal not only fails to comport with, but positively contradicts, the "common law" of the Fifth Amendment grand jury. Motions to quash indictments based upon the sufficiency of the evidence relied upon by the grand jury were unheard of at common law in England, see, *e.g., People v. Restenblatt,* 1 Abb.Prac. 268, 269 (Ct.Gen.Sess.N.Y. 1855). And the traditional American practice was described by Justice Nelson, riding circuit in 1852, as follows:

"No case has been cited, nor have we been able to find any, furnishing an authority for looking into and revising the judgment of the grand jury upon the evidence, for the purpose of determining whether or not the finding was founded upon sufficient proof, or whether there was a deficiency in respect to any part of the complaint...." *United States v. Reed,* 27 Fed.Cas. 727, 738 (No. 16,134) (C.C.N.D.N.Y.1852).

We accepted Justice Nelson's description in *Costello v. United States,* supra, where we held that "it would run counter to the whole history of the grand jury institution" to permit an indictment to be challenged "on the ground that there was incompetent or inadequate evidence before the grand jury." And we reaffirmed this principle recently in *Bank of Nova Scotia,* where we held that "the mere fact that evidence itself is unreliable is not sufficient to require a dismissal of the indictment," and that "a challenge to the reliability or competence of the evidence presented to the grand jury" will not be heard. It would make little sense, we think, to abstain from reviewing the evidentiary support for the grand jury's judgment while scrutinizing the sufficiency of the prosecutor's presentation. A complaint about the quality or adequacy of the evidence can always be recast as a complaint that the prosecutor's presentation was "incomplete" or "misleading."[8] Our words in *Costello* bear repeating: Review of facially valid indictments on such grounds "would run counter to the whole history of the grand jury institution[,] [and] [n]either justice nor the concept of a fair trial requires [it]."

* * * Echoing the reasoning of the Tenth Circuit in *United States v. Page,* supra, respondent argues that a rule requiring the prosecutor to disclose exculpatory evidence to the grand jury would, by removing from the docket unjustified prosecutions, save valuable judicial time. That depends, we suppose, upon what the ratio would turn out to be between unjustified prosecutions eliminated and grand jury indictments challenged—for the latter as well as the former consume "valuable judicial time." We need not pursue the matter; if there is an advantage to the proposal, Congress is free to prescribe it. For the reasons set forth above, however, we conclude that courts have no authority to prescribe such a duty pursuant to their inherent supervisory authority over their own proceedings. The judgment of the Court of Appeals is accordingly reversed and the cause remanded for further proceedings consistent with this opinion.

Justice STEVENS, with whom Justice BLACKMUN and Justice O'CONNOR join, and with whom Justice THOMAS joins as to Parts II and III, dissenting. * * *a

Like the Hydra slain by Hercules, prosecutorial misconduct has many heads. * * * [It has not] been limited to judicial proceedings: the reported [lower court] cases indicate that it has sometimes infected grand jury proceedings as well. The cases contain examples of prosecutors presenting perjured testimony, questioning a witness outside the presence of the grand jury and then failing to inform the grand jury that the testimony was exculpatory, failing to inform the grand jury of its authority to subpoena witnesses, operating under a conflict of interest, misstat-

---

8. In *Costello,* for example, instead of complaining about the grand jury's *reliance* upon hearsay evidence the petitioner could have complained about the prosecutor's *introduction* of it. See, *e.g., United States v. Estepa,* 471 F.2d 1132, 1136–1137 (2d Cir.1972) (prosecutor should not introduce hearsay evidence before grand jury when direct evidence is available); see also Arenella, *Reforming the Federal Grand Jury and the State Preliminary Hearing to Prevent Conviction Without Adjudication,* 78 Mich.L.Rev. 463, 540 (1980) ("[S]ome federal courts have cautiously begun to ... us[e] a revitalized prosecutorial misconduct doctrine to circumvent *Costello's* prohibition against directly evaluating the sufficiency of the evidence presented to the grand jury").

a. Part I of Justice Stevens, deleted here, argued that certiorari was improvidently granted. That portion of the majority's opinion responding to this argument also has been deleted.

ing the law, and misstating the facts on cross-examination of a witness. [citations omitted] * * *

[As] Justice Sutherland [explained in *Berger v. United States,* fn. f, p. 1430]: "The United States Attorney is the representative not of an ordinary party to a controversy, but of a sovereign whose obligation to govern impartially is as compelling as its obligation to govern at all; and whose interest, therefore, in a criminal prosecution is not that it shall win a case, but that justice shall be done. * * * It is as much his duty to refrain from improper methods calculated to produce a wrongful conviction as it is to use every legitimate means to bring about a just one." It is equally clear that the prosecutor has the same duty to refrain from improper methods calculated to produce a wrongful indictment. Indeed, the prosecutor's duty to protect the fundamental fairness of judicial proceedings assumes special importance when he is presenting evidence to a grand jury. As the Court of Appeals for the Third Circuit recognized, "the costs of continued unchecked prosecutorial misconduct" before the grand jury are particularly substantial because there

> "the prosecutor operates without the check of a judge or a trained legal adversary, and virtually immune from public scrutiny. The prosecutor's abuse of his special relationship to the grand jury poses an enormous risk to defendants as well. For while in theory a trial provides the defendant with a full opportunity to contest and disprove the charges against him, in practice, the handing up of an indictment will often have a devastating personal and professional impact that a later dismissal or acquittal can never undo. Where the potential for abuse is so great and the consequences of a mistaken indictment so serious, the ethical responsibilities of the prosecutor, and the obligation of the judiciary to protect against even the appearance of unfairness, are correspondingly heightened." *United States v. Serubo,* 604 F.2d 807, 817 (C.A.3 1979).

* * * The standard for judging the consequences of prosecutorial misconduct during grand jury proceedings is essentially the same as the standard applicable to trials. In *United States v. Mechanik,* we held that there was "no reason not to apply [the harmless error rule] to 'errors, defects, irregularities, or variances' occurring before a grand jury just as we have applied it to such error occurring in the criminal trial itself." We repeated that holding in *Bank of Nova Scotia v. United States,* when we rejected a defendant's argument that an indictment should be dismissed because of prosecutorial misconduct and irregularities in proceedings before the grand jury. * * * Unquestionably, the plain implication of that discussion is that if the misconduct, even though not expressly forbidden by any written rule, had played a critical role in persuading the jury to return the indictment, dismissal would have been required.[b]

---

b. The district court in the *Bank of Nova Scotia* case had based its dismissal order on several instances of alleged misconduct. These included: (1) various violations of Rule 6(e) secrecy provisions through disclosures of grand jury materials to government agents and potential witnesses and through instructions to witnesses not to disclose their testimony to the target; (2) violations of Rule 6(d) in allowing joint appearances by IRS agents reading transcripts to the grand jury; (3) alleged violation of 18 U.S.C. § 6002 in the use of "pocket immunity"; (4) causing government agents to mischaracterize prior testimony that they summarized for the grand jury; (5) calling witnesses associated with the target for the sole purpose of having them assert their privilege against self-incrimination before the grand jury; (6) abusive comments made during recess (and within the hearing of grand jurors) to an expert witness allowed to testify at the request of the target; and (7) administering unauthorized oaths to IRS agents, characterizing them as agents of the grand jury, in violation of Rule 6(e). The Court of Appeals had reversed the district court ruling and the Supreme Court affirmed that reversal. It concluded that there was no factual basis for some of the alleged violations, that the alleged Rule 6(e) violations clearly "could not have affected the charging decision," and that as to the acts of alleged misconduct that could conceivably have had an

In an opinion that I find difficult to comprehend, the Court today repudiates the assumptions underlying these cases and seems to suggest that the court has no authority to supervise the conduct of the prosecutor in grand jury proceedings so long as he follows the dictates of the Constitution, applicable statutes, and Rule 6 of the Federal Rules of Criminal Procedure. The Court purports to support this conclusion by invoking the doctrine of separation of powers and citing a string of cases in which we have declined to impose categorical restraints on the grand jury. Needless to say, the Court's reasoning is unpersuasive.

Although the grand jury has not been "textually assigned" to "any of the branches described in the first three Articles" of the Constitution, it is not an autonomous body completely beyond the reach of the other branches. Throughout its life, from the moment it is convened until it is discharged, the grand jury is subject to the control of the court. As Judge Learned Hand recognized over sixty years ago, "a grand jury is neither an officer nor an agent of the United States, but a part of the court." *Falter v. United States*, 23 F.2d 420, 425 (2d Cir.1928). This Court has similarly characterized the grand jury [in discussing its subpoena authority]. *Brown v. United States* [p. 959]. * * * This Court has, of course, long recognized that the grand jury has wide latitude to investigate violations of federal law as it deems appropriate and need not obtain permission from either the court or the prosecutor. Correspondingly, we have acknowledged that "its operation generally is unrestrained by the technical procedural and evidentiary rules governing the conduct of criminal trials." *United States v. Calandra*. But this is because Congress and the Court have generally thought it best not to impose procedural restraints on the grand jury; it is not because they lack all power to do so.

To the contrary, the Court has recognized that it has the authority to create and enforce limited rules applicable in grand jury proceedings. Thus, for example, the Court has said that the grand jury "may not itself violate a valid privilege, whether established by the Constitution, statutes, or the common law." *Calandra*. And the Court may prevent a grand jury from violating such a privilege by quashing or modifying a subpoena, or issuing a protective order forbidding questions in violation of the privilege. *Gravel v. United States* [p. 959]. Moreover, there are, as the Court notes, a series of cases in which we declined to impose categorical restraints on the grand jury. In none of those cases, however, did we question our power to reach a contrary result. * * *

Unlike the Court, I am unwilling to hold that countless forms of prosecutorial misconduct must be tolerated—no matter how prejudicial they may be, or how seriously they may distort the legitimate function of the grand jury—simply because they are not proscribed by Rule 6 of the Federal Rules of Criminal Procedure or a statute that is applicable in grand jury proceedings. Such a sharp break with the traditional role of the federal judiciary is unprecedented, unwarranted, and unwise. Unrestrained prosecutorial misconduct in grand jury proceedings is inconsistent with the administration of justice in the federal courts and should be redressed in appropriate cases by the dismissal of indictments obtained by improper methods. * * *

What, then, is the proper disposition of this case? I agree with the Government that the prosecutor is not required to place all exculpatory evidence before the grand jury. A grand jury proceeding is an *ex parte* investigatory proceeding to determine whether there is probable cause to believe a violation of the criminal laws has occurred, not a trial. Requiring the prosecutor to ferret out and present all evidence that could be used at trial to create a reasonable doubt as to the

impact, the circumstances under which they occurred did not pose the requisite likelihood of prejudicial effect to escape being characterized as "harmless error." See Note 2, p. 973.

defendant's guilt would be inconsistent with the purpose of the grand jury proceeding and would place significant burdens on the investigation. But that does not mean that the prosecutor may mislead the grand jury into believing that there is probable cause to indict by withholding clear evidence to the contrary. I thus agree with the Department of Justice that "when a prosecutor conducting a grand jury inquiry is personally aware of substantial evidence which directly negates the guilt of a subject of the investigation, the prosecutor must present or otherwise disclose such evidence to the grand jury before seeking an indictment against such a person." U.S. Dept. of Justice, United States Attorneys' Manual, Title 9, ch. 11, ¶ 9–11.233, 88 (1988).

Although I question whether the evidence withheld in this case directly negates respondent's guilt, I need not resolve my doubts because the Solicitor General did not ask the Court to review the nature of the evidence withheld. Instead, he asked us to decide the legal question whether an indictment may be dismissed because the prosecutor failed to present exculpatory evidence. Unlike the Court and the Solicitor General, I believe the answer to that question is yes, if the withheld evidence would plainly preclude a finding of probable cause. I therefore cannot endorse the Court's opinion. * * *

Notes and Questions

1. **Post-Williams "misconduct."** Prior to *Williams,* federal lower courts had characterized a broad range of prosecutorial actions and inactions as "misconduct" that could lead to dismissal of an indictment. Whether a dismissal was in order depended upon the possible prejudicial impact of the misconduct either in itself or in conjunction with other acts of misconduct. See Note 2, p. 973. Among those prosecutorial actions viewed as misconduct for this purpose were the various actions relating to the presentation of evidence that are described in Note 7, p. 954, and the illustrations of prosecutorial improprieties cited in the first paragraph of Justice Stevens' dissent in *Williams* (see pp. 962–63). Still other prosecutorial actions held to constitute misconduct included the prosecutor giving testimony as a witness, making inflammatory comments to the grand jury, expressing a personal opinion of guilt, presenting to the grand jury an indictment already signed by the prosecutor, having an unauthorized person present during grand jury proceedings, attempting to clothe investigatory personnel with an aura of neutrality by swearing them in before the grand jurors as "agents of the grand jury," and various violations of secrecy provisions. See Brenner & Lockhart, § 20.5; Beale et al., ch. 9. Under the standard announced in *Williams,* which of those actions can still be proscribed in the exercise of a federal court's supervisory power?

Lower courts have recognized that *Williams* cuts deeply into the prior precedent on cognizable misconduct claims. See *United States v. Fenton,* 1998 WL 356891 (W.D.Pa.1998) (speaking to allegedly improper and prejudicial comments by the prosecutor, as identified in the ABA standards discussed in Note 5, p. 971: "Well-recognized as the ABA standards are, they have not been adopted wholesale into any [federal] rule or statute to which I have been cited.[c] Nor has the defense

c. Under the Citizens Protection Act of 1998, 28 U.S.C.A. § 530 (B), "attorneys for the government" will be "subject to state law and rules * * * governing attorneys in each state where such attorney engages in that attorney's duties, to the same extent and in the same manner as other attorneys in that state." Where the state has incorporated in its Rules of Professional Responsibility an ABA Standard that imposes certain obligations on a prosecutor with respect to the grand jury, would a U.S. Attorney's failure to adhere to that standard in dealing with a federal grand jury provide a grounding for dismissal of an indictment under *Williams*? See *United States v. Colorado Supreme Court,* 189 F.3d 1281

suggested that either standard is co-extensive with, or based upon, a constitutional principle. Accordingly, *Williams* renders this sort of prosecutorial conduct beyond the reach of my review."); *United States v. Orjuela,* 809 F.Supp. 193 (E.D.N.Y.1992) (government's failure to reconvene the grand jury after learning that its sole witness, a government agent, had relayed information from an informant that was "inaccurate and misleading" could not justify dismissal after *Williams,* which "called into question the continued viability of the Circuit cases upon which the defendant's argument relies"). But consider *United States v. Breslin,* 916 F.Supp. 438 (E.D.Pa.1996) (dismissal based on "grave interference with independent functioning of grand jury" is justified, in the exercise of court's "supervisory role", in light of "cumulative effect" of the following actions: "(1) the prosecutor attempted to bond with the grand jurors by providing them with donuts at their first meeting; (2) the prosecutor's frequent suggestions to the jury that his assigned time was short might have had a chilling effect on the jury's right to ask questions; (3) the prosecutor often made characterizations of the evidence and inserted his own opinions; (4) the prosecutor referred to a Frontline television documentary involving one of the defendants and suggested it might be played for the grand jury 'for fun'; (5) the prosecutor's reference to the necessity for using transcripts led the jury to believe they did not have the right to hear any testimony they wished from live witnesses; (6) the prosecutor pressured the jury by stating the statute of limitations was about to run on some of the charges; (7) the prosecutor instructed the jury that they did not need to find the evidence supported everything stated in the indictment, but it was sufficient to merely find the main points had support").

2. *Perjured and false testimony.* Does *Williams* "cut back on the power of [a federal] court to dismiss an indictment based on the presentation of perjured testimony to the grand jury"? *United States v. Sitton,* 968 F.2d 947 (9th Cir.1992) (raising but not deciding that issue). The *Williams* opinion, in its footnote 6, cited various provisions in the federal criminal code containing "clear rules" adopted by Congress, the violation of which could lead to a dismissal in the exercise of supervisory power. Two of those provisions related to perjury—the prohibition against giving false declarations before the grand jury and the prohibition against subornation of perjury. If a dismissal required a situation in which a prosecutor or an agent of the prosecutor (e.g., a government investigator) violated one of those provisions, the grounds for dismissal would be somewhat narrower than for the "perjury dismissals" issued previously by lower federal courts. Those provisions would not have been violated by the government, for example, when the perjury was not by a government agent and was not known by the prosecution (even if it should have been known) at the time the indictment was issued. Assuming that the prosecution also would not have violated the subornation provisions where it unintentionally presented perjured testimony, and then discovered that perjury prior to the issue of the indictment, but did not take corrective action, would that mean that a federal court now lacks authority to dismiss an indictment based on such a failure? Cf. *United States v. Orjuela,* Note 1 supra.

(10th Cir.1999) (CPA applies only to "professional ethics," a categorization that does not encompass those Rules of Professional Responsibility which are actually "substantive or procedural rules"; three factors helpful in determining "whether a rule really is one of professional conduct" are: (1) whether the rule "bar[s] conduct recognized by consensus within the profession as inappropriate"; (2) whether the standard is "like a commandment dealing with morals and principles" (typically, having a "thou shalt not" structure and the "vague sweeping character of a moral edict"); and (3) whether the standard "is directed at the attorney herself."); CRIMPROC § 1.6(j) (pocket part) ("The Eleventh, Tenth, and First Circuits * * * all share the view that the CPA does not encompass state or local professional responsibility standards which seek to reach beyond the disciplinary process and provide an enforcement mechanism within the criminal justice process.").

So too, perjured testimony is that known by the witness to be false. If the witness believes that his testimony is accurate, but the prosecutor has other information clearly establishing that it is false, can a misconduct dismissal be based on the ground that the prosecutor knowingly introduced false testimony although the witness himself would not have been liable under the false declaration provision? What if the prosecutor was fairly certain from other evidence that the witness' testimony was not accurate, but was not positive in that conclusion. Does the prosecutor's failure to "correct" the witness at this point amount to no more than a failure to introduce exculpatory evidence (i.e., the other evidence that contradicts the witness and is more persuasive but not necessarily conclusive)? Consider *United States v. Isgro*, 974 F.2d 1091 (9th Cir.1992) (district court erred in dismissing indictment because government's key grand jury witness, a convicted coconspirator, was allowed to give testimony implicating the defendant without calling to the grand jury's attention the fact that the witness had given contrary testimony at his own trial; *Williams* controls, for defendant here is presenting another variation of the argument rejected in *Williams*—"that the grand jury was deprived of its ability to make an informed decision by the prosecutor's failure to present exculpatory evidence").

3. *Constitutional violations.* As the Court notes, there was no claim in *Williams* that the alleged prosecutorial misconduct amounted to a constitutional violation. The Supreme Court has said very little about what prosecutorial action before a grand jury would constitute a constitutional violation justifying dismissal of an indictment[d]. In *Bank of Nova Scotia*, the defendant claimed that the prosecutor had "violated the Fifth Amendment by calling a number of witnesses [associated with the target] for having them assert their privilege against self-incrimination," but the Court found no need to rule explicitly on whether the target's constitutional rights would be violated by such action aimed at having the grand jury draw adverse inferences against the target. It agreed with the Court of Appeals that there had been "no error" in the handling of these particular witnesses. The government "was not required to take at face value" the witnesses earlier assertions that they would invoke the privilege if called to testify, the questioning before the grand jury ceased as soon as the witnesses asserted the privilege, and "throughout the proceedings, the prosecution repeated the caution to the grand jury that it was not to draw an adverse inference from a witness' invocation of the Fifth Amendment."

Lower court rulings have dealt more extensively with the question of what prosecutorial misconduct reaches the level of a constitutional violation. "Constitutional error is said to exist where the structural protections of the grand jury have been so compromised as to render proceedings fundamentally unfair, allowing the presumption of prejudice to the defendant." *United States v. Isgro*, Note 2 supra. The intentional prosecutorial introduction of perjured testimony on a critical issue has been characterized by a few courts as a constitutional violation. See Beale et al., § 9.8. Lower courts have also suggested that inflammatory comments of the prosecutor rise to the level of a constitutional violation where so flagrant and prejudicial as to "destroy the [grand jury's] independence." Beale et al., § 9.2. It has also been suggested that, "under certain circumstances, a prosecutor's inten-

---

d. In *United States v. Sigma International, Inc.*, described below, the Court found confusing the reference to constitutional violations in fn. 6 of the *Williams* opinion. That footnote, it noted, appears to state "that a court's supervisory power may be invoked to enforce those legally compelled standards which come from * * * 'the Constitution'." Thus, "because at least prior to *Williams*, the Constitution had been seen as an independent source for a court's authority to dismiss an indictment, this language in *Williams* about the Court's supervisory authority encompassing constitutional violations casts some doubt over whether the two sources remain distinct or if the Court has conflated them."

tional withholding of [exculpatory] evidence could result in a denial of a defendant's right to due process." *People v. Torres,* 613 N.E.2d 338 (Ill.App.1993).

May lower federal courts simply turn to a constitutional grounding to justify dismissals in the vast majority of situations that would have produced a "misconduct dismissal" under the pre-*Williams* lower court precedent? Consider UNITED STATES v. SIGMA INTERNATIONAL, INC., 244 F.3d 841 (11th Cir.2001). The prosecutor there: (1) informed the indicting grand juror that that he would ask it to vote on a 21 page multi-count indictment against multiple defendants the very next day; (2) explained that two grand juries had already considered the case, and suggested that the second grand jury, after hearing a significant amount of testimony and reviewing numerous documents in a year-long investigation, had wanted to indict, but had been precluded from voting because of "an administrative situation" (with that suggestion constituting a violation of Rule 6(e)(1) as it "was tantamount to disclosing grand jury deliberations"); (3) presented personal testimony in the form of his summary of information obtained in the earlier grand jury investigation (although also presenting three government agents who provided summaries of testimony given before the first two grand juries, and "telling the grand jurors that if they needed more time or wanted to review the testimony and exhibits before the second grand jury, they were certainly entitled to do so"); (4) informed the grand jury of anticipated further investigation, which suggested that the defendants may have engaged in additional crimes; and (5) stated that one of the defendants had lied in testifying before a previous grand jury. On review following conviction, the Eleventh Circuit's initial opinion found an insufficient showing of prejudice under the *Bank of Nova Scotia* standard (see Note 2, p. 973) to require reversal of the conviction. At the same time it characterized various actions of the prosecutor as misconduct without reference to the *Williams* limitation on making such judgments under the court's supervisory power. See 196 F.3d 1314 (11th Cir.1999). On petition for rehearing, the Eleventh Circuit had before it (for the first time) a complete grand jury transcript, as well as a government argument relying heavily on *Williams.* This time the Eleventh Circuit (per TJOFLAT, J.) concluded that, in light of the full range of conduct revealed by the complete transcript, a violation of the Fifth Amendment's grand jury clause was apparent, requiring reversal of the conviction.

The Eleventh Circuit reasoned that *Williams* did not restrict federal court authority to dismiss an indictment where prosecutorial misconduct reaches the level of constitutional error, and "[u]nder the authority of the Constitution, a court may dismiss an indictment if the court finds government conduct that 'significantly infringe[s] upon the grand jury's ability to render independent judgment' so that the indictment is not, in reality, that of the grand jury, and thus, a constitutionally mandated indictment is absent." Such a constitutional violation is present, the court noted, "where a grand jury proceeding is so corrupted by the conduct of a prosecutor of judge" as to meet the prejudice standard of *Bank of Nova Scotia* (that the misconduct "substantially influenced the grand jury's decision to indict") because "the indictment [then] is not, in reality, of a grand jury." An "exhaustive review of the complete grand jury transcripts," taking account of "the totality of the circumstances," including "inferences drawn from the words AUSA Rubinstein used, the testimony of witnesses who appeared before the grand jury, and the grand jurors' questions," led the court to conclude that a dismissal was required under that "substantially-influenced" standard.

Apart from a single reference to Rule 6(e), the Eleventh Circuit did not suggest that the prosecutor's actions violated a court rule or statute. Rather, it suggested that prosecutorial conduct which turned the grand jury's focus away from an independent evaluation of the testimony and exhibits thereby infringed "the grand jury's ability to render an independent judgment" and constituted a constitutional violation if it met the *Bank of Nova Scotia* standard as to prejudice. Does this analysis produce a constitutionally grounded "Fifth Amendment common law," replace the supervising authority "common law of misconduct" that *Williams* outlawed?

MISCONDUCT CHALLENGES IN STATE COURTS

1. State variations. A small group of states will consider misconduct challenges to an indictment only where the alleged misconduct rises to the level of a constitutional violation. In general, these are states that have statutes specifying grounds for challenging an indictment and that do not include prosecutorial misconduct among those grounds. With the statutes read as legislative commands restricting judicial authority to dismiss indictments, the courts view themselves as having authority only to remedy constitutional violations, which cannot be immunized by the legislature. See CRIMPROC § 15.6(a).

The vast majority of states recognize a broad range of prosecutorial misconduct, not limited to constitutional violations, as cognizable on a motion to dismiss. In states that reject *Costello* (see Note 2, p. 955), the cognizability of prosecutorial misconduct challenges follows logically from the same policy that allows review of the sufficiency and competency of the evidence supporting an indictment. An indictment that is the product of prosecutorial misconduct is just as much unwarranted as an indictment based on inadequate evidence. In states that accept *Costello,* the case for allowing misconduct challenges is put somewhat differently. Here the emphasis is upon the court's responsibility to ensure the integrity of a grand jury process that operates through the use of its subpoena power and under its supervisory authority. Such review is deemed different in character (it does not focus on the soundness of the judgment of the grand jurors[e]) and different in intrusiveness (being available only upon a showing of misconduct, see Note 6 infra) from a review of the sufficiency of the evidence before the grand jury.

2. Misconduct guideposts. In those states that recognize the broadest range of misconduct challenges on a motion to dismiss, the courts turn to a variety of sources in assessing whether particular prosecutorial action constitutes misconduct. In large part, however, misconduct will be action deemed contrary to one or more of the following guideposts: (1) statutory standards (including standards in court rules); (2) traditional prosecutorial obligations in assisting the grand jury (e.g., the obligation to give legal advice); (3) the grand jury's independent authority to call before it all sources of evidence it might deem relevant and to exercise its independent judgment in evaluating the evidence before it; (4) traditional limitations imposed upon prosecutorial advocacy as developed largely in the trial context. The range of behavior that has been challenged by reference to these guideposts is extremely broad, and the court rulings have been shaped to a great extent by the special qualities of the particular type of behavior being challenged and the circumstances of the particular case. Nonetheless, the rulings also reflect some basic disagreements that cut across the whole field of misconduct challenges. One such division, discussed in Note 3 below, relates to the degree of

---

e. Jurisdictions recognizing a broad range of prosecutorial misconduct challenges also recognize challenges based on alleged misconduct by the grand jury. However, a strong presumption of regularity, and a frequent refusal to inquire into the quality of the grand jury's deliberations, make such challenges very difficult to carry. Thus, courts regularly reject such claims as that the grand jurors could not possibly have read all of the transcripts presented to them or that they obviously had insufficient time to review a lengthy indictment before voting on it. Challenges are likely to be successful only where the jurors engaged in activities clearly outside their authority, such as off-the-record substantive discussions with witnesses during recess. See *Wilkey v. Superior Court,* 566 P.2d 327 (Ariz.App.1977).

prosecutorial culpability needed to have "misconduct." Another is whether the special setting of the grand jury should lead to imposing less stringent standards on the prosecutor in this context than at trial. Divisions on this score are reflected in rulings on several types of misconduct, two of which are discussed in Notes 4 and 5 below.

3. *Scienter.* Should some high degree of prosecutorial culpability be a prerequisite for a finding of prosecutorial misconduct. Many courts have assumed that mere prosecutorial negligence should not be enough. Thus, the presentation of perjured testimony or testimony that deceptively transposed hearsay into eyewitness testimony is viewed as misconduct only where the prosecution was aware of those flaws. The integrity of the process, these courts note, is only challenged where the prosecution had an intent to deceive.[f] Other courts, however, have taken a contrary position in this and other contexts. As a federal court put it in a pre-*Williams* ruling, the focus should be "upon the impact of the misconduct on the grand jury's impartiality" rather than the "degree of [prosecutorial] culpability." *United States v. Sears, Roebuck & Co.,* 719 F.2d 1386 (9th Cir.1983). Looking to such cases, Steven Reiss, *Prosecutorial Intent in Constitutional Criminal Procedure,* 135 U.Pa.L.Rev. 1365 (1987), cites "three factors that apparently account for the failure of [such] courts to accord prosecutorial intent in [the grand jury] context the prominent role" it occupies in other areas of the law (e.g., selective and vindictive prosecution): (1) the "amenability of grand jury bias claims to a harm-based analysis that focuses on the probable effect of the challenged prosecutorial behavior"; (2) "the existence of reasonably clear ethical rules governing a prosecutor's grand jury behavior, or at least the existence of recurring prosecutorial practices that clearly violate these rules"; and (3) the "greater freedom courts have to use their supervisory power to control prosecutorial behavior before the grand jury."

4. *Exculpatory evidence.* Courts in only about twenty states have directly addressed the question of whether a prosecutor has an obligation to present known exculpatory evidence to the grand jury, but a substantial majority of those courts have sided with the *Williams* dissent rather than the *Williams* majority. In these states, including several major indictment states, local law clearly imposes such an obligation upon the prosecutor, and violation of that obligation can lead to a dismissal of the indictment. See *State v. Hogan,* 676 A.2d 533 (N.J.1996); Beale et al., §§ 4.16, 9.9. In several of these states, the prosecutor's obligation is derived from a statute directing or authorizing the grand jury to consider known evidence that "may explain away the charge" (although other states with similar statutes view them as dealing only with the responsibilities of the grand jurors). Other jurisdictions have concluded that the obligation is inherent in the prosecutor's relationship to the grand jury, for "a prosecutor who withholds substantial exculpatory evidence which would have tended to negate probable cause, destroys the existence of an independent and informed jury." *State v. Gaughran,* 615 A.2d

---

f. In *Bank of Nova Scotia,* Note 2, p. 973 infra, the Supreme Court moved in this direction. The district court, in dismissing the indictment, had pointed to "misleading and inaccurate summaries" of prior testimony that had been presented by IRS agents. The Court noted that, "because the record does not reveal any prosecutorial misconduct with respect to these summaries," the claim went to the reliability of the evidence and was not cognizable in light of *Costello.* The record, it noted, provided no grounding for "finding that the prosecutors knew the evidence to be false or misleading, or that the Government caused the agents to testify falsely." A similar approach was taken on the claim that "the Government had threatened to withdraw immunity from a witness in order to manipulate the witness' testimony." While the "witness may have felt threatened" by the prosecutor's warning concerning his testimony, the prosecutor had not meant to imply that immunity would be withdrawn (as the witness' counsel recognized). The witness' "subjective fear [could] not be ascribed to government misconduct and was, at most, a consideration bearing on the reliability of his testimony."

1293 (N.J.Super.1992). The failure to disclose exculpatory evidence also has been characterized as producing a form of prosecutorial deception analogous to the use of perjured testimony.

Courts recognizing a prosecutorial obligation to present known exculpatory evidence have split on the scope of the obligation. The seminal California Supreme Court ruling in *Johnson v. Superior Court,* 539 P.2d 792 (Cal.1975), apparently the first case to dismiss an indictment for a failure to present exculpatory evidence, offered a broad view of the prosecutor's obligation. In that case, a magistrate had refused to bindover at a preliminary hearing after the defendant Johnson testified that his role in the drug transaction had been grossly exaggerated in the prosecution witness' testimony and that his limited participation had been part of a plan to furnish information to another local prosecutor in connection with a plea bargain on another charge. Not satisfied with the magistrate's decision, the prosecutor took the case to the grand jury. Only the arresting officers presented grand jury testimony, and the grand jury was not informed of Johnson's preliminary hearing testimony. (Indeed, the prosecutor conveyed to the jurors "the false impression that Johnson would refuse to testify if called"). The California Supreme Court held that the indictment should be dismissed because the prosecutor failed to inform the grand jury of the defendant's preliminary hearing testimony which was "evidence reasonably tending to negate guilt." This application of a "reasonable tendency" standard did not appear to hinge on the fact that defendant's testimony had previously persuaded the magistrate, but on the testimony's general character as potentially believable evidence that "explained away the charge." See also *Ostman v. Eighth Judicial Dist. Court,* 816 P.2d 458 (Nev.1991) (dismissal of indictment was required where prosecution's sole witness on a sexual assault charge was the accused's girlfriend, who testified to being forced into unwanted sexual activity, with the prosecutor failing to inform the jury that the accused claimed in a statement given to the police shortly after the incident, that the complainant had voluntarily participated; the accused's statement was exculpatory evidence "as a matter of law" since it "had a tendency to explain away the charge").

Other courts have viewed the prosecutor's obligation as encompassing a much narrower range of evidence. They hold that the prosecutors must disclose before the grand jury only that exculpatory evidence which "clearly negates guilt"; dismissal therefore is required only where the grand jury almost surely would not have indicted had it considered the exculpatory evidence. See *State v. Hogan,* supra (evidence "so clearly exculpatory as to induce a rational grand juror to conclude that the state has not made out a prima facie case"). Arguably that standard would not encompass the evidence that the prosecutor failed to disclose in *Johnson,* as it could be characterized as no more than a "self-serving statement" of the defendant, and hardly evidence of an irrefutable nature. Courts adopting this narrower obligation to produce exculpatory evidence note that the broader standard was borrowed from the trial setting and is inappropriate in the grand jury setting because: (1) the prosecutor at the grand jury stage ordinarily does not have the advantage of defense motions identifying those items that the defense views as potentially exculpatory (although targets will occasionally request that the prosecutor present certain evidence to the grand jury); and (2) at such an early stage in the development of the case, both the possible charges and likely defenses are often uncertain, making it especially difficult for the prosecutor to determine what weight might be given to evidence that could be viewed as exculpatory.

5. *Improper comments.* A.B.A. Standards For Criminal Justice, *Prosecution Function* § 3–3.5 (3d ed. 1993), provides that the prosecutor "should not make statements or arguments in an effort to influence grand jury action in a manner which would be impermissible at trial before a petit jury." Are the A.B.A. Standards too rigid in measuring comments intended to influence the grand jury by what would be "impermissible at trial before a petit jury"? Is it inappropriate for the prosecutor, even in response to grand juror questions, to explain that defendant had been indicted previously and the prosecution was now seeking a reindictment on the transcript of the earlier testimony, that the case came out of an organized crime investigation so there was a special need to report any contacts by strangers or friends that might suggest their remotest interest in the case, or that the grand jury would not be expected to investigate certain parts of the transaction because they were being considered by other grand juries. It has been argued that, since the grand jury's authority to utilize its subpoena power and to ask questions may be based on "tips, rumors, * * * and personal knowledge" [*Dionisio*, Note 4, p. 953], and since the grand jury may reject a charge supported by sufficient evidence when it views that charge as unjust [see p. 937], it should be deemed "competent to evaluate and cope with prejudice [and] opinion" and prosecutors should be able to furnish the grand jury with the "background information" that enables them to put the charge in its proper context. See Woodward & Ahrens, Note 3 (iii), p. 953.

By and large, courts have accepted the approach of the A.B.A. Standards and applied to prosecutorial comments in the grand jury setting the same limits that would be applied at trial. Nonetheless, some courts have found avenues for giving the prosecutor more leeway in the grand jury proceeding. Many states recognize that the prosecutor, as the legal advisor to the grand jury, may express a personal opinion as to the legal sufficiency of the evidence. CRIMPROC § 15.2(e) (noting division, however, as to whether this authority goes beyond explaining how evidence relates to elements of the crime and also encompasses personal opinions on the credibility of witnesses). Indeed, the A.B.A. Standards acknowledge that a prosecutor may be given that authority (to be exercised with "due deference to the [grand jury's] status as an independent legal body"), and imposes an obligation on the prosecutor to inform the grand jury when his or her opinion is that the evidence does not warrant indictment. See A.B.A. Standards, §§ 3–3.5(a), 3–3.6(c).

Courts also have taken cognizance of the multiple roles of the prosecutor in the grand jury setting in holding that trial limitations should not apply to comments that were aimed at purposes other than convincing the grand jury to indict. *State v. Schamberg,* 370 A.2d 482 (N.J.Super.App.Div.1977), illustrates this approach. In that case, the defendant moved to dismiss his indictment for perjury on the ground that the prosecutor had expressed a personal opinion on his guilt, an action traditionally prohibited at trial (see Note 1, p. 1427). In the course of examining the witness before the grand jury that eventually indicted him, the prosecutor had noted: "I have reason to believe that you just perjured yourself." The reviewing court noted its disapproval of "the form of [the prosecutor's] comment," but refused to quash the indictment. Though it suggested a personal opinion of guilt, the comment "was not addressed to the grand jury, nor was it intended to direct the grand jury to indict"; it reflected only the "culmination of efforts * * * to give the witness the opportunity to change his testimony," which was to be expected in the investigative setting of the grand jury. See also *United States v. Red Elk,* 955 F.Supp. 1170 (D.S.D.1997) (prosecutor's comment that jury should not be "surprised" if certain witnesses had "memory problems" was merely part of a "strategy session," explaining why certain witnesses were now being called though not asked to testify previously, and did not constitute misconduct, although the witnesses were related to, or potentially sympathetic to, the defendant). Consider also Susan Brenner, *The Voice of the Community: A Case For Grand Jury Independence,* 3 Va.J.Soc. Pol'y & L. 67 (1995) (noting capacity of prosecutors through their comments and explanations to develop a rapport with jurors and a sense of juror participation in a common mission; author argues that such institutional dominance can only be offset by a structural change, such as adopting the Hawaii model, which provides the jury with its own, independent legal advisor).

6. *Establishing misconduct.* Except for the most unusual case, prosecutorial misconduct in the grand jury process will not have occurred in the presence of the defendant. Thus, the defense's ability to raise a misconduct challenge will be heavily dependent upon the availability of avenues that will enable it to learn of possible misconduct. In most jurisdictions, however, those avenues are quite limited. The best source for determining what happened before the grand jury usually is the transcript of the grand jury proceeding. However, some states do not require transcripts, and some of the states that mandate transcription extend that mandate only to the testimony of witnesses, meaning that discussions between the prosecutor and the grand jurors are not transcribed.

Many jurisdictions do provide for complete transcription, but that means very little to the defense unless it can gain access to that transcript. Automatic access to that transcript will be available only in those non-*Costello* jurisdictions that allow challenges to the sufficiency of the grand jury evidence. See Note 3, p. 956. In the many jurisdictions that follow *Costello*, which includes most of the indictment jurisdictions, the principle of grand jury secrecy sharply restricts defense access to the transcript. Federal Rule 6(e)3(C)(i) is typical. It allows for court-ordered discovery in connection with "a motion to dismiss an indictment because of matters occurring before the grand jury," but such discovery does not follow automatically with the filing of such a motion. Courts are concerned that a defense motion may be made simply as a fishing expedition to obtain discovery for trial preparation through the disclosed transcript. Accordingly, they hold that, to gain disclosure, the defense must overcome a presumption of regularity in the grand jury process by making a preliminary showing of likely misconduct. That showing, for most courts, requires that the defense produce an affidavit of a friendly witness or a portion of the transcript otherwise released to the defense (e.g., for discovery purposes) that contains a strong suggestion of impropriety. The preliminary showing cannot be made through the testimony of the grand jurors, as they typically are allowed to testify only as to "outside influences." See *Hennigan v. State,* 746 P.2d 360 (Wyo.1987); Pt. E, p. 1439.

THE PREJUDICE REQUIREMENT

1. *Variations.* A finding of misconduct ordinarily will not in itself be sufficient to justify a remedy of dismissal. As discussed below, most jurisdictions insist also upon some showing of prejudicial impact, although a minority do allow for the possible use of dismissal as a "prophylactic tool" without regard to the presence of prejudice. Jurisdictions vary considerably in their approach to this prejudice requirement. The variations relate to the degree of the likelihood of prejudice, the treatment of some types of misconduct as inherently prejudicial, and the application of a different focus for assessing prejudice where the misconduct challenge is being considered after a conviction at a fair trial.

2. *The federal harmless error standard.* In BANK OF NOVA SCOTIA v. UNITED STATES, 487 U.S. 250, 108 S.Ct. 2369, 101 L.Ed.2d 228 (1988), the Supreme Court spelled out the governing standard for dismissals issued prior to conviction. *Bank of Nova Scotia* was decided prior to *Williams* and dealt with some prosecutorial actions that would not constitute cognizable misconduct under *Williams* (see fn. b, p. 963), but it also applied the same standard to actions that would be subject to a supervisory-authority dismissal under *Williams,* and

Williams itself assumed the applicability of the *Bank of Nova Scotia* standard to such misconduct.

The trial court in *Bank of Nova Scotia* had dismissed the indictment pretrial on the basis of numerous prosecutorial actions characterized as misconduct, concluding that such actions had undermined the independence of the grand jury and that, in any event, dismissal was appropriate to declare "with unmistakable intention" that "such conduct * * * will not be tolerated." A divided Court of Appeals reversed the dismissal order. It concluded that the prosecutorial actions had not "significantly infringe[d] on the grand jury ability to exercise independent judgment" and that "without a showing of such infringement," federal supervisory authority could not be used to dismiss an indictment. A dissenting judge disagreed with "the view of the majority that prejudice to the defendant must be shown before a court can exercise its supervisory power to dismiss an indictment on the basis of egregious prosecutorial misconduct." The Supreme Court, with only Justice Marshall dissenting, held in an opinion by Justice KENNEDY that the Court of Appeals majority had been correct in insisting upon a prejudicial impact and in finding no such impact here. Speaking first to the requisite showing of prejudice, Justice Kennedy stated:

"We hold that, as a general matter, a District Court may not dismiss an indictment for errors in grand jury proceedings unless such errors prejudiced the defendants. In the exercise of its supervisory authority, a federal court 'may, within limits, formulate procedural rules not specifically required by the Constitution or the Congress.' *United States v. Hasting* (Note 3, p. 1573). Nevertheless, it is well established that '[e]ven a sensible and efficient use of the supervisory power ... is invalid if it conflicts with constitutional or statutory provisions.' * * * *United States v. Payner* [p. 960]. Our previous cases have not addressed explicitly whether this rationale bars exercise of a supervisory authority where, as here, dismissal of the indictment would conflict with the harmless error inquiry mandated by the Federal Rules of Criminal Procedure. We now hold that a federal court may not invoke supervisory power to circumvent the harmless error inquiry prescribed by Federal Rule of Criminal Procedure 52(a). Rule 52(a) provides that '[a]ny error, defect, irregularity or variance which does not affect substantial rights shall be disregarded.' * * * Rule 52 is, in every pertinent respect, as binding as any statute duly enacted by Congress, and federal courts have no more discretion to disregard the Rule's mandate than they do to disregard constitutional or statutory provisions. * * *

"Having concluded that our customary harmless error inquiry is applicable where, as in the cases before us, a court is asked to dismiss an indictment prior to the conclusion of the trial, we turn to the standard of prejudice that courts should apply in assessing such claims. We adopt for this purpose, at least where dismissal is sought for nonconstitutional error, the standard articulated by Justice O'Connor in her concurring opinion in *United States v. Mechanik* [Note 5, p. 977]. Under this standard, dismissal of the indictment is appropriate only 'if it is established that the violation substantially influenced the grand jury's decision to indict,' or if there is 'grave doubt' that the decision to indict was free from the substantial influence of such violations. *United States v. Mechanik*. This standard is based on our decision in *Kotteakos v. United States* [Note 6, p. 1566], where, in construing a statute later incorporated into Rule 52(a), we held that a conviction should not be overturned unless, after examining the record as a whole, a court concludes that an error may have held 'substantial influence' on the outcome of the proceeding.

"To be distinguished from the cases before us are a class of cases in which indictments are dismissed, without a particular assessment of the prejudicial impact of the errors in each case, because the errors are deemed fundamental. These cases may be explained as isolated exceptions to the harmless error rule. We think, however, that an alternative and more clear explanation is that these cases are ones in which the structural protections of the grand jury have been so compromised as to render the proceedings fundamentally unfair, allowing the presumption of prejudice. See *Rose v. Clark* [p. 1576]. These cases are exemplified by *Vasquez v. Hillery* [Note 8, p. 947], where we held that racial discrimination in selection of grand jurors compelled dismissal of the indictment. In addition to involving an error of constitutional magnitude, other remedies were impractical and it could be presumed that a discriminatorily selected grand jury would treat defendants unfairly. * * * We reached a like conclusion in *Ballard v. United States* [p. 1322], where women had been excluded from the grand jury. The nature of the violation allowed a presumption that the defendant was prejudiced, and any inquiry into harmless error would have required unguided speculation. Such considerations are not presented here, and we review the alleged errors to assess their influence, if any, on the grand jury's decision to indict in the factual context of the cases before us."

Turning to the application of the harmless error standard to the present case, the Court initially noted that it had before it no constitutional error as defendant's major claim of such misconduct lacked a factual grounding. See Note 3, p. 967. The Court also added two further caveats: "In the cases before us we do not inquire whether the grand jury's independence was infringed. Such an infringement may result in grave doubt as to a violation's effect on the grand jury's decision to indict, but we did not grant certiorari to review this conclusion. We note that the Court of Appeals found that the prosecution's conduct was not 'a significant infringement on the grand jury's ability to exercise independent judgment,' and we accept that conclusion here. Finally, we note that we are not faced with a history of prosecutorial misconduct, spanning several cases, that is so systematic and pervasive as to raise a substantial and serious question about the fundamental fairness of the process which resulted in the indictment."

Turning to the specific instances of misconduct cited by the trial court [see fn. b, p. 963], the Court found no basis for concluding that, "despite the grand jury's independence, there was any misconduct * * * that otherwise may have influenced the grand jury's decision to indict" or may have left a "grave doubt as to whether the decision to indict was so influenced." The Court noted that there were two alleged instances of misconduct that could have influenced the decision to indict by affecting the substance of the evidence before the grand jury, but the record failed to support the conclusion that either involved misconduct (see fn. f, p. 970). With respect to all of the others, they had no bearing upon the persuasiveness of the case presented to the grand jury and therefore did not present a sufficient possibility of influencing the decision to indict.

As for "several instances of misconduct found by the district court—that the prosecutors manipulated the grand jury investigation to gather evidence for use in civil audits; violated the secrecy provisions of Rule 6(e) by publicly identifying the targets and the subject matter of the grand jury investigation; and imposed secrecy obligations in violation of Rule 6(e) upon grand jury witnesses—[they] might be relevant to an allegation of a purpose or intent to abuse the grand jury process * * * [but] could not have affected the charging decision." As for the ceremony of swearing in IRS agents as agents of the grand jury, an alleged violation of Rule 6(c), there was "nothing in the record to indicate that the oaths * * * caused their reliability or credibility to be elevated, and the effect, if any, on the grand jury decision to indict was negligible." As for the prosecutor's disparagement during recess of an expert witness favoring the defendant, the witness stated that his testimony was unaffected and the grand jury was told to disregard anything they may have heard of the interchange between the prosecutor and the witness. As for the government granting "pocket" (i.e., informal) immunity to several witnesses, there was no need to decide if this was misconduct; the jurors, in evaluating the testimony of these witnesses, were made aware that "they had made a deal with government" if not always the precise character of their relinquishment of the self-incrimination privilege. As for the violation of Rule 6(d) by allowing two IRS agents to read transcripts to the grand jury in tandem, there was "no evidence" that their joint appearance "enhanced the credibility of their testimony or otherwise allowed the agents to exercise undue influence." It was also relevant that "these incidents [of misconduct] occurred as isolated episodes in the course of a 20–month [grand jury] investigation * * * involving dozens of witnesses and thousands of documents."

3. *State prejudice standards.* All but a few states would appear to impose a prejudice requirement for dismissal of an indictment based on misconduct, although some are willing to presume prejudice as to certain types of misconduct (see Note 4 infra). Most states appear to follow a standard for measuring prejudice quite similar to that of *Bank of Nova Scotia.* Some, however, may be requiring a somewhat stronger showing of possible prejudice when they speak to the need for a "reasonable likelihood" of prejudice. Also, some courts would appear to look to a "correct result" analysis, holding misconduct harmless where the evidence before the grand jury would have supported the indictment. See CRIMPROC § 15.6(c). Cf. Note 5, p. 1566.

Compare with the above approach that adopted in *State v. Johnson,* 441 N.W.2d 460 (Minn.1989). The court there had before it a series of improprieties in the prosecutor's general directions to the March term grand jury. Those included warning the jurors that a squad car would pick up any absentees, furnishing the jurors with informational packets from former jurors, telling the jurors that they should take account of the "county's higher standard of probable cause" (which was described as giving the prosecution "a reasonable likelihood of conviction based upon the most logical defense"), and asking the jury to consider possible plea bargains in charging. Reversing a lower court that found the various improprieties to be harmless, analyzed individually and in their "cumulative effect," the Minnesota Supreme Court ordered representment of all defendants charged by the particular grand jury who were still pressing pretrial objections. The court noted its agreement with the appellants that "today's harmless error can become the standard practice of tomorrow," and there appeared to be "no other way to preserve the integrity of the judicial process and maintain the independence of the grand jury."[g] Representment, it noted, was "necessary to protect not only the defendants but all of us as well." See also *State v. Murphy,* 538 A.2d 1235 (N.J.1988) ("even in the absence of prejudice, we would not

---

g. The Supreme Court in *Bank of Nova Scotia* noted there were other means of remedying errors that did not have a prejudicial impact. They cited as illustrations of alternative remedies the punishment of a prosecutor's knowing violation of Rule 6 as contempt of court, requesting the bar or department of justice to initiate discipline proceedings, and the court "chastis[ing] the prosecutor in a published opinion." "Such remedies, it noted, allow the court to focus on the culpable individual rather than granting a windfall to the un prejudiced defendant." Anne Bowen Poulin, *Supervision of the Grand Jury: Who Watches the Guardian?,* 68 Wash.U.L.Q. 885 (1990), is sharply critical of the Court's reliance upon such sanctions, noting that several factors limit their effectiveness. The "victim may have minimal incentive to invoke the sanction" since it will not address "the harm to the victim and the victim's reputation." Second,

sanctions against the prosecutor "will only reach a narrow subgroup of abuses." As a practical matter, for various types of misconduct, such as leaks to the press, the victim will be unable to establish who engaged in the conduct. As to others, even if the abuser is identified, the victim will be unable to establish the element of bad faith that is a prerequisite to imposing the sanction. Finally, the "sanctions will have limited deterrent effect," as they are "unlikely to exert institutional pressure" beyond the individual sanctioned. Consider also Peter J. Henning, *Prosecutorial Misconduct in Grand Jury Investigations,* 51 S.Car.L.Rev. 1 (1999) (exploring potential for controlling prosecutorial misconduct through subsequent proceedings, particularly the civil action established under the Hyde Amendment, 18 U.S.C. § 3006A, and disciplinary proceedings that take advantage of the Citizens Protection Act, see fn. c, p. 965).

hesitate to reverse a conviction if we believed that the conduct of the prosecutors in obtaining an indictment amounted to an intentional subversion of the grand jury process" as reversal of convictions may be "the only appropriate disposition that would vindicate our interest in preserving the impartiality of the grand jury procedure").

4. *Per se prejudice.* Many of the states which ordinarily require a particularized showing of possible prejudicial impact create exceptions for one or more types of misconduct which are viewed as presumptively prejudicial and therefore providing a *per se* basis for dismissal. The Supreme Court in *Bank of Nova Scotia* acknowledged that federal courts too would presume prejudice, but only where "structural protections * * * have been so compromised as to render the proceeding fundamentally unfair," as illustrated by racial or gender discrimination in the selection of the grand jury (see p. 975). Many state courts key the presumption of prejudice to other characteristics as well. Thus, while *Bank of Nova Scotia* insisted upon a showing of possible prejudice with respect to the Rule 6(d) violation presented there (two witnesses appearing before the grand jury at the same time), those states would treat the presence of an unauthorized individual during any part of the grand jury proceedings as *per se* prejudicial (although others do so only when the unauthorized presence was during jurors' deliberations or voting). CRIMPROC § 15.7(h). So too, where state law gave the accused a right to testify before the grand jury, the prosecution's failure to honor that right was held to constitute prejudice per se and mandate dismissal of the indictment. *People v. Evans,* 592 N.E.2d 1362 (N.Y.1992).

5. *Postconviction review: The rule of Mechanik.* In UNITED STATES v. MECHANIK, 475 U.S. 66, 106 S.Ct. 938, 89 L.Ed.2d 50 (1986), the defense learned during its cross-examination of a government agent that the agent had appeared together with another agent before the grand jury, where they had testified in tandem. The defense then moved for dismissal of the indictment on the ground that this practice violated Rule 6(d), which specifies those persons who may be present at grand jury proceedings and refers only to "*the* witness under examination" (emphasis added). Although Rule 12(b)(2) requires that such motions to dismiss ordinarily be raised before trial, an exception is made where there is "good cause" for the late objection. The trial judge took the motion under advisement until after the trial. It was then considered, after the jury had returned its verdict of guilty, with the trial judge ruling that Rule 6(d) had been violated but the violation was harmless because it had no impact upon the grand jury's decision to indict. The Court of Appeals then reversed, holding that a Rule 6(d) violation should require automatic reversal. That ruling was then reversed by the Supreme Court, and the conviction reinstated.

Three different approaches were advanced in the three opinions in *Mechanik.* Justice Marshall, in dissent, adopted the analysis of the Court of Appeals. Three concurring judges (in an opinion by Justice O'Connor) agreed with the trial judge's conclusion that the critical question was whether the violation was harmless as it impacted upon the grand jury's decision to indict. They concluded that it was, applying the standard later adopted in *Bank of Nova Scotia.* The opinion for the Court (per REHNQUIST, J.) argued that the impact of the Rule 6(d) violation should be evaluated in light of the supervening jury verdict. It reasoned:

"Both the District Court and the Court of Appeals observed that Rule 6(d) was designed, in part, 'to ensure that grand jurors, sitting without the direct supervision of a judge, are not subject to undue influence that may come with the presence of an unauthorized person.' The Rule protects against the danger that a defendant will be required to defend against a charge for which there is no probable cause to believe him guilty. The error involving Rule 6(d) in these cases had the theoretical potential to affect the grand jury's determination whether to indict these particular defendants for the offenses for which they were charged.

But the petit jury's subsequent guilty verdict not only means that there was probable cause to believe that the defendants were guilty as charged, but that they are in fact guilty as charged beyond a reasonable doubt. Measured by the petit jury's verdict, then, any error in the grand jury proceeding connected with the charging decision was harmless beyond a reasonable doubt.

"It might be argued in some literal sense that because the Rule was designed to protect against an erroneous charging decision by the *grand jury*, the indictment should not be compared to the evidence produced by the Government at *trial*, but to the evidence produced before the *grand jury*. But even if this argument was accepted, there is no simple way after the verdict to restore the defendant to the position in which he would have been had the indictment been dismissed before trial. He will already have suffered whatever inconvenience, expense, and opprobrium that a proper indictment may have spared him. In courtroom proceedings as elsewhere, 'the moving finger writes, and having writ moves on.' Thus reversal of a conviction after a trial free from reversible error cannot restore to the defendant whatever benefit might have accrued to him from a trial on an indictment returned in conformity with Rule 6(d). * * *

"We express no opinion as to what remedy may be appropriate for a violation of Rule 6(d) that has affected the grand jury's charging decision and is brought to the attention of the trial court before the commencement of trial. We hold only that however diligent the defendants may have been in seeking to discover the basis for the claimed violation of Rule 6(d), the petit jury's verdict rendered harmless any conceivable error in the charging decision that might have flowed from the violation. In such a case, the societal costs of retrial after a jury verdict of guilty are far too substantial to justify setting aside the verdict simply because of an error in the earlier grand jury proceedings."[h]

6. Justice Marshall, in his dissent, complained that the majority was leaving the enforcement of Rule 6(d) to the "unreviewable largesse of the district courts." He noted that if a judge should rule against a defendant on a pretrial motion to dismiss, that ruling might not be subject to appeal until after the trial, where a conviction would have precluded any relief under the majority's view. He offered the possibility of viewing the denial of the motion as a collateral order, so that it would be immediately appealable, but that position subsequently was rejected by the Court in *Midland Asphalt Corp. v. United States,* Note 4, p. 1550. Justice Marshall also suggested that the district court might simply defer ruling on a motion until after trial, thereby basically avoiding a ruling on the merits since an acquittal would render the motion moot and a conviction would render the error *per se* harmless. While the trial judge did defer ruling on the motion in *Mechanik,* that motion was made during trial, and it is generally assumed that deferral is inappropriate where motions are made pretrial. This has led to increased efforts by defense counsel to gain pretrial disclosure of possible grand jury misconduct. See Peter Vaira, *Making the Grand Jury Work,* 16 Litigation 12 (1990). Consider also fn. i, infra.

---

h. As to those costs, the Court noted: "The reversal of a conviction entails substantial social costs: it forces jurors, witnesses, courts, the prosecution, and the defendants to expend further time, energy, and other resources to repeat a trial that has already once taken place; victims may be asked to relive their disturbing experiences. The '[p]assage of time, erosion of memory, and dispersion of witnesses may render retrial difficult, even impossible.' * * * Thus, while reversal 'may, in theory, entitle the defendant only to retrial, in practice it may reward the accused with complete freedom from prosecution,' id. and thereby 'cost society the right to punish admitted offenders.' Id. Even if a defendant is convicted in a second trial, the intervening delay may compromise society's 'interest in the prompt administration of justice,' * * * and impede accomplishment of the objectives of deterrence and rehabilitation. These societal costs of reversal and retrial are an acceptable and often necessary consequence when an error in the first proceeding has deprived a defendant of a fair determination of the issue of guilt or innocence. But the balance of interest tips decidedly the other way when an error has had no effect on the outcome of the trial."

7. *The scope of Mechanik.* Federal lower courts have disagreed as to how broadly *Mechanik* should be read. The Tenth Circuit has reasoned that *Mechanik* was "carefully crafted along very narrow lines" and involved misconduct that "at worst, was [a] technical [violation]." It would hold postconviction review available to allegations of misconduct suggesting the prosecutor "attempted to unfairly sway the grand jury or to otherwise affect the accusatory process" or misconduct that "transgressed the defendant's right to fundamental fairness." *United States v. Taylor,* 798 F.2d 1337 (10th Cir.1986) (finding reviewable a pre-*Williams* "totality of the circumstances" challenge that cited the prosecutor's failure to present exculpatory evidence, use of inadmissible and inflammatory evidence, violation of the attorney-client privilege, and unauthorized use of state officers in the grand jury's investigation). Several other circuits have rejected such a narrow reading. They acknowledge that *Mechanik* does not extend to misconduct which denies fundamental fairness and thereby presents a constitutional claim, but see it as extending to a broad range of nonconstitutional improprieties aimed at the charging process. See CRIMPROC § 15.6(e) (suggesting that *Bank of Nova Scotia* supports this broader reading of *Mechanik*),[i] and the characterization of *Mechanik* in *Midland Asphalt,* Note 4, p. 1550. See also Beale et al., § 9.37 (Congressional proposal to override *Mechanik,* which failed to gain passage, and ABA proposal for legislation "to create a mechanism for enforcing the Federal Rules [provisions] * * * that govern grand jury proceedings," both assumed that *Mechanik* would apply to a broad range of misconduct).

8. *Postconviction review in state courts.* Like federal courts prior to *Mechanik,* state courts traditionally were willing to consider misconduct challenges to grand jury procedures on appeal following a conviction. Since *Mechanik,* however, several state courts have adopted the rationale of the *Mechanik* rule and have applied it to a broad range of misconduct challenges. Other state courts have either rejected outright the *Mechanik* rationale or refused to extend it to errors beyond that involved there. CRIMPROC § 15.6(f) While the rejections usually have relied on the need for postconviction review to preserve the integrity of the grand jury process, the New York Court of Appeals in *People v. Wilkins,* 501 N.E.2d 542 (N.Y.1986), also focused on a state statutory structure governing grand jury proceedings that was quite different from that applicable to federal grand juries. In New York, unlike the federal system, automatic resubmission of a case rejected by a grand jury is not allowed. Thus, if a court can conclude that the defendant might not have been indicted but for the prosecutor's misconduct, it cannot also conclude, in light of the state's subsequent proof at trial, that the prosecution could readily have obtained an indictment even if the first grand jury (without the misconduct) would have refused to indict. In New York, the prosecutor might not have been able to go to a second grand jury, even though the prosecutor had sufficient additional evidence (as established at trial).

---

i. *Bank of Nova Scotia,* Note 2, supra, did not have before it a grand jury challenge reviewed following a conviction, and it did cite *Mechanik.* Thus, it generally is viewed as providing a standard for review applicable only to pretrial challenges to the indictment. Consider, however, *United States v. Sigma International, Inc.,* Note 3, p. 968, where the Eleventh Circuit noted: "Although *Bank of Nova Scotia* did not explicitly overrule *Mechanik,* we query what, if anything remains of the *Mechanik* rule. We need not answer the question, however, for we believe that *Bank of Nova Scotia* clearly controls the instant case [i.e., a case in which the defendant "raises a constitutional objection to

an indictment prior to the conclusion of the trial," but the trial court defers ruling on the motion until after the trial, when it then relies on *Mechanik* in rejecting the motion]. * * * The [trial] court's reliance on *Mechanik* was an erroneous application of the law, and, as such, constituted an abuse of discretion. *Bank of Nova Scotia* eviscerated *Mechanik*'s central holding, and clearly stated that a guilty verdict is no longer sufficient to validate the underlying indictment. Rather, it is incumbent upon the court to examine the grand jury proceedings themselves and determine whether the alleged violations substantially influenced the grand jury's decision to indict."

Chapter 16

THE CHARGING INSTRUMENT

SECTION 1. THE DEVELOPMENT OF MODERN PLEADING REQUIREMENTS[a]

A. THE LIBERALIZATION OF PLEADING REQUIREMENTS

As first developed in the common law system, the accusatory pleading was a quite simple document. In the early fourteenth century, it was sufficient to allege that "A stole an ox," "B burgled a house," or "C slew a man." Over the next few centuries, however, as the criminal law grew more complex and defendants were allowed to use counsel to challenge indictments, English courts came to demand that the pleading contain a full statement of the facts and legal theory underlying the charge. Indictments were lengthy, highly detailed, and filled with technical jargon. Pleading requirements for particular crimes often paralleled in their complexity and formalism the special civil pleadings required for the different forms of action. An indictment charging an assault, for example, had to include the phrase "*vi et armis*," and a murder charge had to describe not only the means used but also the nature and extent of the wound inflicted.

American courts inherited the complex, formalistic, and often confusing pleading requirements of the eighteenth century common law, and they did not hesitate to require strict adherence to those requirements. Indictments were not infrequently quashed for the most picayune errors in form. Moreover, defects in an indictment were not waived by defendant's failure to raise his objection before trial; most defects could be challenged for the first time after conviction, usually by a motion in arrest of judgment. As a result, courts were often overturning convictions fully supported by the evidence simply because the underlying indictment was inartfully drawn or awkwardly worded. A conviction could also be reversed because the evidence at trial varied from the facts alleged in the indictment. Here too, the courts generally were strict, except for a variance as to the date of the offense. Thus, an early Delaware decision reversed a conviction under an indictment alleging the theft of a "pair of shoes" because the evidence established that both of the shoes stolen were for the right foot and therefore did not constitute a pair.

While the formalism and detail mandated by the common law pleading rules were designed in part to provide notice to the accused, they clearly went beyond what was needed to provide notice alone. Indeed, it has been suggested that the "common law indictment, replete with archaic terminology and ritualistic formu-

---

a. The discussion in this section is largely derived from Wayne R. LaFave, Jerold H. Israel, & Nancy J. King, *Criminal Procedure Treatise* § 19.2 (2d ed. 1999) (available on Westlaw under the database CRIMPROC and hereafter cited as CRIMPROC). Supporting citations can be found there. Consider also George Dix, *Tex-* as *Charging Instrument Law: Recent Developments and the Continuing Need for Reform*, 35 Baylor L.Rev. 689 (1983) (hereafter cited as Dix); George Dix, *Texas Charging Instrument Law: The 1985 Revisions and The Continuing Need For Reform*, 38 Baylor L.Rev. 1 (1986).

lae, was a lengthy and tortuous document, which * * * served more to mystify than to inform the defendant." As Sir James Stephen observed, a major function of the "strictness and technicality" in indictments was to guard against "looseness in the legal definitions of crimes." At a time when "the concepts and definitions of offenses took form largely through the experience of administration and without the aid of definitive statutes," the requirement that the offense be stated according to a particular formula, specifying in detail each element of the crime, was seen as providing assurance both that the grand jury understood what was necessary to establish an offense and that the courts did not engage in unanticipated extensions of the substance of the offense. Courts in later years suggested that perhaps an equally significant function of the complex common law requirements was to supply the judiciary with grounds that were readily available for reversing convictions in "hard cases." As one court put it: "When stealing a handkerchief worth £ I was punished by death, and there were nearly 200 different capital offenses; it was to the credit of humanity that technicalities could be invoked in order to prevent the cruelty of a strict and literal enforcement of the law."

By the mid–1800s, with the increasing codification of the substantive criminal law and the reduction in the number of capital offenses, many courts no longer insisted upon strict adherence to the technical rules of pleading. The former practice, it was noted, had in many cases permitted "public justice" to be evaded and "let loose upon society" the "most dangerous malefactors." These courts would "no longer permit the guilty man to escape punishment by averring that he cannot comprehend * * * what is palpable and evident to the common sense of everybody else." Many courts did not share this philosophy, however, and still others moved slowly in departing from common law precedents. As a result, legislative reform was deemed necessary. In general, the new legislation was directed at relaxing specific common law requirements. Thus, it was provided that a murder indictment need not allege the manner or means of causing death, that there was no need to specify the denomination or species of money taken in a theft, and that the absence of specified phrases, such as "with force and arms," did not render an indictment invalid. More general provisions stated that variances would not be fatal unless they were "material," and that indictments should not "be deemed insufficient * * * by reason of any defect or imperfection in form only, which shall not tend to the prejudice of the defendant." Since the common law pleading requirements had been carried over from indictments to informations, the new legislation was made applicable to both informations and indictments.

The judicial response to the new legislation was mixed. Although most jurisdictions had adopted some form of pleading reform by the turn of the century, courts in many states continued to insist that offenses be charged with technical accuracy and nicety of language. In 1907, the Missouri Supreme Court reversed a conviction on appeal because the indictment charged that the offense was against the "peace and dignity of State," having left out the necessary word "the" before "State." A few years later, the Illinois Supreme Court set aside a larceny conviction because the indictment stated that the property was stolen from the "American Express Company, an association" and thereby failed to aver "ownership in any person, firm, corporation, or other entity that * * * [could] be the owner of property." The legislative response to these and similar decisions was the enactment of broader pleading reform legislation. The most widely adopted measures in this second round of legislative liberalization of pleading requirements centered upon three interrelated reforms: (1) a single simplified pleading standard; (2) official forms for the most commonly prosecuted crimes[b]; and (3) an

---

b. In 1983, the Federal Forms were abrogated as "unnecessary." Most jurisdictions, however, continue to retain official forms. Several jurisdictions provide for the alternative of

expanded waiver rule. These reforms, which had been instituted at an earlier point in many states, were incorporated in the Federal Rules of Criminal Procedure, which became effective in 1946. Today, they are found in almost all jurisdictions, with many states having provisions that are almost a verbatim copy of the Federal Rules provisions. In addition, many jurisdictions also adopted measures requiring a less stringent approach to variances.

Federal Rule 7(c) sets forth the most common formulation of a simplified pleading standard: "The indictment or information shall be a plain, concise, and definite written statement of the essential facts constituting the offense charged." This standard offered several advantages over the provisions adopted in the first wave of pleading reforms. Many of those provisions dealt either with a specific common law pleading requirement or a particular crime. Rule 7(c), on the other hand, established a single standard, applicable to the pleading of all crimes and all elements of the pleading. Moreover, that standard had behind it the basic thrust of an already achieved reform since it was a rough counterpart of the standard that reformers had previously used in mandating simplified pleadings in civil cases. Thus, looking to that civil reform, a court could readily conclude that Rule 7(c) required that a pleading do no more than "set forth, in factual terms, the elements of the offense sought to be charged."

Supporting the basic thrust of the Rule 7(c) standard were the official forms. That Rule 7(c) did not mandate all of the detail found in the common law pleading was apparent from its reference to a "concise" statement of the "essential" facts. On the other hand, the Rule 7(c) standard also rejected the truncated short-form pleading of "A murdered B," that several states had adopted (see fn. b supra). Exactly how little detail was needed obviously would vary with the offense, but the official forms provided useful illustrations of what the reformers had in mind. The Federal Rules include forms for 11 different crimes. In many states, forms were adopted for a much larger group of offenses. In addition to providing the prosecutor with a safe path for pleading the listed offenses, the forms served to "illustrate the simplicity of statement which the Rules were designed to achieve." Thus, Federal Rule Form 1, for the offense of murder in the first degree of a federal officer, stated:

> On or about the _____ day of _____, in the _____ District of _____, John Doe with premeditation and by means of shooting murdered John Roe, who was then an officer of the Federal Bureau of Investigation of the Department of Justice engaged in the performance of his official duties.

The third element of the second round of pleading reforms was the use of an expansive waiver doctrine that forced most pleading objections to be raised before trial. Federal Rule 12, for example, provides that several specified defense claims must be raised before trial, with the failure to do so constituting a "waiver thereof." Subsection (b) of Rule 12 includes among these claims: "Defenses and objections based on defects in the indictment or information (other than it fails to show jurisdiction in the court or to charge an offense which objections shall be noticed by the court at any time during the pendency of the proceedings)." This provision was designed to restrict the defense tactic of "sandbagging" that was available in many jurisdictions under common law pleading. Under the old practice, counsel would often forego raising a pleading defect before trial. Assuming that counsel did not need further notice, the only benefit obtained from a successful pretrial objection was some degree of delay while the prosecution

---

"short form" pleading. Here, an extremely truncated pleading, describing the offense by little more than its name (e.g., "A murdered B"), may be used, but the defendant then becomes entitled automatically to a bill of particulars "setting up specifically the nature of the offense charged." Mich.Comp.L. § 767.44.

obtained a perfected charging instrument. On the other hand, if counsel simply bypassed the pretrial objection and the case went to trial and ended in a conviction, counsel could then raise the defect in the pleading on a motion in arrest of judgment and obtain a new trial. Federal Rule 12 eliminated this tactic as to all objections except the failure to show jurisdiction or to charge an offense. While those objections could be raised for the first time at any point in the proceeding, any lesser objection to the pleadings would be lost if not raised before trial.

While the requirement of a pretrial objection would facilitate pretrial correction of inadequate pleadings (and thereby hopefully would reduce the number of convictions that were reversed due to pleading defects), it did not respond to the problem of convictions reversed due to a variance between the allegations contained in a proper pleading and the proof introduced at trial. Many states, seeking to preclude application of the rather strict common law view of variance, adopted legislation permitting the pleading to be amended at trial to conform to the proof (thereby "curing" the variance), provided the defendant was not prejudiced by the amendment. The Federal Rules did not include such a provision as to indictments, although it did allow liberal amendment of an information. The Supreme Court had adopted a very strict rule on amendments of the indictment that had constitutional underpinnings. See Note 4, p. 1006. Moreover, it was thought that the simplified pleading permitted under Rule 7(c) would in itself reduce the likelihood that variances would occur. Since the pleading need not include a detailed description of the circumstances of the offense, there was less factual specificity from which the proof could vary. The Rule also allowed the prosecution to allege that the offense was committed by "one or more specified means." Thus, if the prosecution was uncertain as to whether its proof would establish that the offense was committed in one manner or another, it need not make a choice and hope that its proof would support that particular alternative. Similarly, where an offense encompassed more than one mental element or result, the Federal Rules (and most states) permitted pleadings that, in effect, set forth the various possibilities as alternatives.

The effectiveness of pleading reforms such as those contained in the Federal Rules depended upon the receptiveness of the courts. The standards applied were not so precise as to preclude a court from retaining much of the common law approach to pleadings, at least where a specific official form was not applicable. The federal courts generally were most willing to interpret the Rules in light of the spirit of the reform movement. Most state courts followed a similar approach. A few, however, continued to adhere to a policy of requiring technical preciseness of language and substantial detail in description, though hardly rivaling their common law predecessors in this regard.

B.   The Functions of Modern Pleading Requirements

1.   Courts frequently note that under modern pleading standards, the accusatory instrument must be tested by the basic functions that a pleading should fulfill rather than by technical pleading requirements. Although those functions are described somewhat differently by different courts, basically five different functions have been cited. These are: (1) providing protection against twice being put in jeopardy; (2) providing notice; (3) facilitating judicial review of the legal sufficiency of the prosecution's case; (4) providing a formal basis for the judgment; and (5) keeping the prosecution within the charge issued by the grand jury. The first four of these functions are said to apply to all charging instruments (basically the "complaint" or "information" in the misdemeanor case and the "information" or "indictment" in the felony case). The fifth, by its very nature, is confined to the indictment.

2. *The double jeopardy function.* The pleading's double jeopardy function—commonly formulated as a requirement that the pleading charge an offense with sufficient specificity so that the defendant can plead the double jeopardy bar to a subsequent prosecution for the same offense—was viewed as a major objective of the pleading at common law. Both commentators and courts have questioned whether it has much significance in an era of complete transcription of court proceedings. A defendant raising a double jeopardy objection no longer need rely solely on the charging instrument in his previous prosecution to establish that he is twice being tried for the same offense, but can look to the record of his trial or the showing of a factual basis accompanying his guilty plea. Accordingly, it is argued, "protection against successive prosecutions for the same offense * * * [should] not require of an accusation any more completeness than the notice function demands." Austin Scott Jr., *Fairness in Accusation of Crime,* 41 Minn. L.Rev. 509 (1957).

3. *Providing notice.* The notice function of the pleading is often characterized as the primary function served by modern pleading requirements. It is a function that the Supreme Court has described as constitutionally mandated by the defendant's Sixth Amendment right "to be informed of the nature and cause of the accusation." The major question asked as to this function is not whether it serves a needed end, but rather what its scope should be.

That the pleading should give the defendant "factual notice" is well accepted. The primary disagreement here concerns the amount of detail that must be provided to adequately serve this function. Is it sufficient to identify the event that is the basis for the charge or must the pleading also describe in detail each of the factual elements that will be proven to establish liability? In charging the crime of theft by deception, for example, is it sufficient to state when and where the alleged misrepresentation took place, or must the charging instrument also specify which of defendant's representations were false and, perhaps, why they were factually incorrect? Should it matter, in this regard, whether or not the same information may be obtained by the defendant through a bill of particulars? What if the same information will be presented, albeit in a less focused form, in the course of the defendant's pretrial discovery of the evidence that the prosecutor intends to introduce at trial? What if the same information already has been presented in the preliminary hearing (or would have been presented had defendant not waived his right to a preliminary hearing)? These and other "notice issues" are commonly presented in the context of determining whether the charging instrument contains sufficient factual specificity in alleging particular elements of an offense.

Some view the notice function as designed also to ensure that the defendant is informed of the prosecution's basic legal theory. They suggest that the need for such "legal notice" is reflected in the traditional pleading requirement that the "facts alleged establish all of the essential elements of the offense." There is disagreement, however, as to whether this "essential elements" requirement is properly grounded on the notice function or on other pleading functions.

4. *The "judicial review" function.* The judicial review function has been described by the Supreme Court as "inform[ing] the [trial] court of the facts alleged, so that it may be decided whether they are sufficient in law to support a conviction, if one should be had." Although this function is mentioned less frequently than the "notice" and "double jeopardy" functions, commentators have suggested that it may be the primary function underlying the requirement that the pleading contain allegations establishing all essential elements of the offense. This requirement ensures that the pleading will be sufficient to allow a pretrial testing, on a motion to dismiss, of the prosecution's view of the legal elements of the offense. Such testing is said to be especially important as to elements not fully set forth in the language of the statute. Consider, for example, a situation in which the statute does not refer to a mens rea element, and there is some question as to the level of mens rea required. By insisting that the prosecution include a specific mens rea allegation in the charging instrument, the essential elements requirement facilitates a pretrial determination as to what mens rea is required. Such a determination may save an unnecessary trial (as where the court holds that a higher mens rea is required and the prosecution lacks evidence to establish that mens rea), will allow the prosecution to gain appellate review if the court adopts an adverse interpretation of the law,[a] and should at least establish a common legal framework that can guide both sides in making their factual presentations.

   5. *Providing a formal basis for the judgment.* Several commentators have contended that neither the judicial review nor the notice function fully explain the rigorous application of the essential elements requirement by many courts. They note that convictions have been reversed on appeal due to a charging instrument's failure to allege an essential element of the offense even though that element was clearly proven at trial, there was no objection to the charging instrument's deficiency prior to the conviction, and there was no hint of defense surprise since the element not alleged was clearly set forth in the statute defining the offense or in previous judicial rulings. Such appellate rulings—commonly accompanied by judicial statements that a pleading which fails to charge an offense is "fundamentally defective," rendering "void ab initio" any subsequent conviction—are viewed by the commentators as pointing to the continuing vitality of a pleading function only infrequently acknowledged in judicial opinions. At common law, the foremost function of the pleading was to provide a formal basis for the judgment of conviction. This function was said to require that the charging instrument set forth "everything necessary for a complete case on paper." Without such a pleading, there was no assurance that the trial court had not exceeded its authority in imposing a conviction for a particular offense and in setting punishment under that conviction. While modern pleading requirements hardly require the same degree of completeness as the common law, pleading rules still insist, it is argued, that the pleading sustain the exercise of judicial authority by alleging all of the basic elements of the offense for which punishment was imposed. Some commentators see the continued use of the pleading to serve such a function as inconsistent with the thrust of modern pleading reforms, arguing that it places a premium on the "form" of the pleading rather than the "substance of the defendant's rights." They attribute the retention of this pleading function largely to some mystical notion of "jurisdiction," rather than to any legitimate pleading need.

   6. *The grand jury function.* In those jurisdictions that require prosecution by indictment, modern pleading requirements may also be assigned the function of ensuring that the prosecution stays within the confines of the offense charged by the grand jury. Thus, pleading requirements may demand that the indictment contain "sufficient factual particularity to ensure that the prosecution will not fill in elements of its case with facts other than those considered by the grand jury." *United States v. Abrams,* 539 F.Supp. 378 (S.D.N.Y.1982). Here again, however, as with the double jeopardy function, courts and commentators have questioned the continuing importance of the pleading in serving this function. The availability of transcribed grand jury proceedings is said to have

---

   a. Almost all jurisdictions allow prosecution appeal from a pretrial dismissal based on a failure to charge any offense. See Note 1, p. 1554. On the other hand, a ruling during trial on the content of the offense (e.g., in charging the jury), when adverse to the prosecution, is not likely to be appealable, since jeopardy has then attached, and an acquittal flowing from that ruling ends the case. See Ch. 26, § 2.

diminished substantially the need for detailed pleadings to ensure that the prosecution is limited to the basic offense found by the grand jury. Consider also Dix, 94 (noting the significant "collateral costs" that arise from "implementing the accused's right to grand jury protection by insisting upon certain characteristics of the charging instrument," and contrasting the position taken in cases such as *Costello*, p. 949, where the "need for grand jury secrecy and avoidance of frequent and time consuming inquiries into grand jury proceedings" has prevailed over the defense interest in ensuring that the grand jury had before it sufficient evidence to indict).

SECTION 2. PLEADING OBJECTIONS

A. SPECIFICITY

RUSSELL v. UNITED STATES
369 U.S. 749, 82 S.Ct. 1038, 8 L.Ed.2d 240 (1962).

Justice STEWART delivered the opinion of the Court.

Each of the petitioners was convicted [of violating 2 U.S.C. § 192 by] refusing to answer certain questions when summoned before a congressional subcommittee. In each case the indictment returned by the grand jury failed to identify the subject under congressional subcommittee inquiry at the time the witness was interrogated. [Each indictment stated that the particular defendant was summoned before a subcommittee on a particular date, that the subcommittee was conducting hearings pursuant to House Resolution 5 (authorizing the House Committee on Un–American Activities to conduct investigations of "un-American propaganda activities in the United States" and "all other questions in relation thereto that would aid Congress in any necessary remedial legislation"), that the defendant refused to answer certain questions (which were set forth verbatim), and that these questions "were pertinent to the question then under inquiry"]. In each case a motion was filed to quash the indictment before trial upon the ground that the indictment failed to state the subject under investigation at the time of the subcommittee's interrogation of the defendant. In each case the motion was denied. * * *

In enacting the criminal statute under which these petitioners were convicted Congress invoked the aid of the federal judicial system in protecting itself against contumacious conduct. The obvious consequence, as the Court has repeatedly emphasized, was to confer upon the federal courts the duty to accord a person prosecuted for this statutory offense every safeguard which the law accords in all other federal criminal cases. *Sinclair v. United States,* 279 U.S. 263, 49 S.Ct. 268, 73 L.Ed. 692 (1929).

Recognizing this elementary concept, the *Sinclair* case established several propositions which provide a relevant starting point here. First, there can be criminality under the statute only if the question which the witness refused to answer pertained to a subject then under investigation by the congressional body which summoned him. * * * Secondly, because the defendant is presumed to be innocent, it is "incumbent upon the United States to plead and show that the question [he refused to answer] pertained to some matter under investigation." Finally, *Sinclair* held that the question of pertinency is one for determination by the court as a matter of law.

* * * The crucial importance of determining the issue of pertinency is reflected in many cases which have come here since *Sinclair.* Our decisions have pointed out that the obvious first step in determining whether the questions asked

were pertinent to the subject under inquiry is to ascertain what that subject was. Identification of the subject under inquiry is also an essential preliminary to the determination of a host of other issues which typically arise in prosecutions under the statute. * * * To be sure, the fact that difficulties and doubts have beset the federal courts in trying to ascertain the subject under inquiry could hardly justify, in the abstract, a requirement that indictments under the statute contain averments which would simplify the courts' task. [But] the repeated appearance in prosecutions under a particular criminal statute of the same critical and difficult question, which could be obviated by a simple averment in the indictment, invites inquiry into the purposes and functions which a grand jury indictment is intended to serve. * * *

As we have elsewhere noted, "this Court has, in recent years, upheld many convictions in the face of questions concerning the sufficiency of the charging papers. Convictions are no longer reversed because of minor and technical deficiencies which did not prejudice the accused. This has been a salutary development in the criminal law." *Smith v. United States,* 360 U.S. 1, 79 S.Ct. 991, 3 L.Ed.2d 1041 (1959). "But," as the *Smith* opinion went on to point out, "the substantial safeguards to those charged with serious crimes cannot be eradicated under the guise of technical departures from the rules." Resolution of the issue presented in the cases before us thus ultimately depends upon the nature of "the substantial safeguards" to a criminal defendant which an indictment is designed to provide. * * *

In a number of cases the Court has emphasized two of the protections which an indictment is intended to guarantee, reflected by two of the criteria by which the sufficiency of an indictment is to be measured. These criteria are, first, whether the indictment "contains the elements of the offense intended to be charged, 'and sufficiently apprises the defendant of what he must be prepared to meet,' " and, secondly, "in case any other proceedings are taken against him for a similar offense whether the record shows with accuracy to what extent he may plead a former acquittal or conviction." * * *

Without doubt the second of these preliminary criteria was sufficiently met by the indictments in these cases. Since the indictments set out not only the times and places of the hearings at which the petitioners refused to testify, but also specified the precise questions which they then and there refused to answer, it can hardly be doubted that the petitioners would be fully protected from again being put in jeopardy for the same offense, particularly when it is remembered that they could rely upon other parts of the present record in the event that future proceedings should be taken against them. * * * The vice of these indictments, rather, is that they failed to satisfy the first essential criterion by which the sufficiency of an indictment is to be tested, i.e., that they failed to sufficiently apprise the defendant "of what he must be prepared to meet." * * * [T]he very core of criminality under 2 U.S.C. § 192, is pertinency to the subject under inquiry of the questions which the defendant refused to answer. * * * Where guilt depends so crucially upon such a specific identification of fact, our cases have uniformly held that an indictment must do more than simply repeat the language of the criminal statute. * * *

The vice which inheres in the failure of an indictment under 2 U.S.C. § 192, to identify the subject under inquiry is thus the violation of the basic principle "that the accused must be apprised by the indictment, with reasonable certainty, of the nature of the accusation against him, * * *." *United States v. Simmons,* 96 U.S. 360, 24 L.Ed. 819 (1878). A cryptic form of indictment in cases of this kind requires the defendant to go to trial with the chief issue undefined. It enables his conviction to rest on one point and the affirmance of the conviction to rest on another. It gives the prosecution free hand on appeal to fill in the gaps of proof by surmise or conjecture. The Court has had occasion before now to condemn just such a practice in a quite different factual setting. *Cole v. Arkansas,* 333 U.S. 196, 68 S.Ct. 514, 92 L.Ed. 644 (1948) [due process violated where the state appellate court affirmed the conviction of defendants charged and tried for one offense on the ground that the evidence established their commission of another offense, which was "separate, distinct, and substantially different"]. And the unfairness and uncertainty which have characteristically infected criminal proceedings under this statute which were based upon indictments which failed to specify the subject under inquiry are illustrated by the cases in this Court already discussed. The same uncertainty and unfairness are underscored by the records of the cases now before us. A single example will suffice to illustrate the point.

In No. 12, *Price v. United States,* the petitioner refused to answer a number of questions put to him by [subcommittee]. * * * At the beginning of the hearing in question, the Chairman and other subcommittee members made widely meandering statements purporting to identify the subject under inquiry. It was said that * * * the investigation was of "such attempt as may be disclosed on the part of the Communist Party . . . to influence or to subvert the American Press." It was also said that "we are simply investigating communism wherever we find it." In dealing with a witness who testified shortly before Price, counsel for the subcommittee emphatically denied that it was the subcommittee's purpose "to investigate Communist infiltration of the press and other forms of communication." But when Price was called to testify before the subcommittee no one offered even to attempt to inform him of what subject the subcommittee did have under inquiry. At the trial the Government took the position that the subject under inquiry had been Communist activities generally. The district judge before whom the case was tried found that "the questions put were pertinent to the matter under inquiry" without indicating what he though the subject under inquiry was. The Court of Appeals, in affirming the conviction, likewise omitted to state what it thought the subject under inquiry had been. In this Court the Government contends that the subject under inquiry at the time the petitioner was called to testify was "Communist activity in news media." It is difficult to imagine a case in which an indictment's insufficiency resulted so clearly in the indictment's failure to fulfill its primary office—to inform the defendant of the nature of the accusation against him. * * *

It has long been recognized that there is an important corollary purpose to be served by the requirement that an indictment set out "the specific offence, coming under the general description," with which the defendant is charged. This purpose, as defined in *United States v. Cruikshank,* 92 U.S. 542, 23 L.Ed. 588 (1876), is "to inform the court of the facts alleged, so that it may decide whether they are sufficient in law to support a conviction, if one should be had." This criterion is of the greatest relevance here, in the light of the difficulties and uncertainties with which the federal trial and reviewing courts have had to deal in cases arising under 2 U.S.C. § 192, to which reference has already been made. * * *

It is argued that any deficiency in the indictments in these cases could have been cured by bills of particulars. But it is a settled rule that a bill of particulars cannot save an invalid indictment. * * *

When Congress provided that no one could be prosecuted under 2 U.S.C. § 192, except upon an indictment, Congress made the basic decision that only a grand jury could determine whether a person should be held to answer in a criminal trial for refusing to give testimony pertinent to a question under congressional committee inquiry. A grand jury, in order to make that ultimate determination, must necessarily determine what the question under inquiry was. To allow the prosecutor, or the court, to make a subsequent guess as to what was in the minds of the grand jury at the time they returned the indictment would deprive the defendant of a basic protection which the guaranty of the intervention of a grand jury was designed to secure. For a defendant could then be convicted on the basis of facts not found by, and perhaps not even presented to, the grand jury which indicted him. * * * This underlying principle is reflected by the settled rule in the federal courts that an indictment may not be amended except by resubmission to the grand jury, unless the change is merely a matter of form. *Ex parte Bain* [Note 4, p. 1006].

For these reasons we conclude that an indictment under 2 U.S.C. § 192, 2 U.S.C.A. § 192 must state the question under congressional committee inquiry as found by the grand jury. * * *

Justice FRANKFURTER and Justice WHITE took no part in the decision of these cases.

Justice HARLAN, whom Justice CLARK joins, dissenting. * * *

The reasons given by the Court for its sudden holding, which unless confined to contempt of Congress cases bids fair to throw the federal courts back to an era of criminal pleading from which it was thought they had finally emerged, are novel and unconvincing. It is first argued that an allegation of "pertinency" in the statutory terms will not do, because that element is at "the very core of criminality" under § 192. * * * To me it seems quite clear that even under * * * cases decided long before Rule 7(c) came into being, the "pertinency" allegations of the present indictments would have been deemed sufficient. I think there can be no doubt about the matter after Rule 7(c).

In *United States v. Debrow,* 346 U.S. 374, 74 S.Ct. 113, 98 L.Ed. 92 (1953), the Court in [upholding a perjury indictment which failed to allege either the name or authority of the person who administered the oath] * * * said: "The charges of the indictments followed substantially the wording of the statute, which embodies all the elements of the crime, and such charges clearly informed the defendants of that with which they were accused, * * * It is inconceivable to us how the defendants could possibly be misled as to the offense with which they stood charged. *The sufficiency of the indictment is not a question of whether it could have been more definite and certain.* If the defendants wanted more definite information as to the name of the person who administered the oath to them they could have obtained it by requesting a bill of particulars. Rule 7(f), F.R.Crim.Proc." (Emphasis supplied.)

It is likewise "inconceivable" to me how the indictments in the present cases can be deemed insufficient to advise these petitioners of the nature of the charge they would have to meet. * * * The subject matter of the investigations had been stated to the petitioners at the time of their appearances before the committees. And the committee transcripts of the hearings were presumably in their possession and, if not, were of course available to them. * * *

The Court says that its holding is needed to prevent the Government from switching on appeal, to the prejudice of the defendants to a different theory of pertinency from that on which the conviction may have rested. There are several good answers to this. To the extent that this fear relates to the subject under investigation, the Government cannot of course travel outside the confines of the trial record, of which the defendant has full knowledge. If what is meant is that the Government may not modify on appeal its "trial" view of the "connective reasoning" relied on to establish the germaneness of the questions asked to the subject matter of the inquiry, surely it would be free to do so, this aspect of pertinency being simply a matter of law. * * * Moreover the Court does not find these indictments deficient because they failed to allege the "connective reasoning." * * *

Referring to certain language in the *Cruikshank* case, the Court suggests that the present holding is supported by a further "important corollary purpose" which an indictment is intended to serve: to make "it possible for courts called upon to pass on the validity of convictions under the statute to bring an enlightened judgment to that task." But whether or not the Government has established its case on "pertinency" is something that must be determined on the record made at the trial, not upon the allegations of the indictment. There is no such thing as a motion for summary judgment in a criminal case. While appellate courts might be spared some of the tedium of going through these § 192 records were the allegations of indictments to spell out the "pertinency" facts, the Court elsewhere in its opinion recognizes that the issue at hand can hardly be judged in terms of whether fuller indictments "would simplify the courts' task."

The final point made by the Court is perhaps the most novel of all. It is said that a statement of the subject under inquiry is necessary in the indictment in order to fend against the possibility that a defendant may be convicted on a theory of pertinency based upon a subject under investigation different from that which may have been found by the grand jury. * * * This proposition is * * * certainly unsound on principle. In the last analysis it would mean that a prosecutor could not safely introduce or advocate at a trial evidence or theories, however relevant to the crime charged in the indictment, which he had not presented to the grand jury. If the Court's reasoning in this part of its opinion is sound, I can see no escape from the conclusion that a defendant convicted on a lesser included offense, not alleged by the grand jury in an indictment for the greater offense, would have a good plea in arrest of judgment.

In conclusion, I realize that one in dissent is sometimes prone to overdraw the impact of a decision with which he does not agree. Yet I am unable to rid myself of the view that the reversal of these convictions on such insubstantial grounds will serve to encourage recalcitrance to legitimate congressional inquiry, stemming from the belief that a refusal to answer may somehow be requited in this Court. And it is not apparent how the seeds which this decision plants in other fields of criminal pleading can well be prevented from sprouting. * * *

Notes and Questions

1. The scope of Russell. Is the key to *Russell* the special factual setting of that case? Dix, at 752, notes that "the result in *Russell*—and the rhetoric supporting it—must be attributed in part at least to the committee whose questions the defendant refused to answer."

2. Is the specificity required in *Russell* largely the product of the special role of the pertinency requirement under 2 U.S.C. § 192? Compare with *Russell* the ruling in *United States v. Crippen,* 579 F.2d 340 (5th Cir.1978), as to the allegation of materiality in a perjury charge. The indictment there, charging the offense of making false statements before a grand jury, set forth the questions asked defendant and his answers (all concerning the alteration of odometer readings) and simply alleged that they were "material" to the grand jury's investigation "to determine whether violations of the Disclosure of Automobile Information Laws and other statutes of the United States had been committed." At trial, materiality was established on the theory that the offense under investigation was the use of new car stickers on used cars, and that alteration of the odometer (though not itself criminal) was "essential to the success of the suspected plan." Responding to the defendant's objection that the indictment failed to "include the factual basis for the allegation of materiality," the Fifth Circuit noted: "It is not necessary for an indictment to * * * allege in detail the factual proof that will be relied upon to support the charge. * * * That information, if essential to the defense, can be obtained by a motion for a bill of particulars. * * * To adopt the rule in false swearing cases that the full predicate for the charge be set forth in the indictment, in addition to the allegations of the essential elements of the offense, would be tantamount to requiring that such supporting evidence be alleged in indictments charging all other federal offenses."

3. *United States v. Crippen,* supra, did not discuss *Russell,* but other courts that have looked to *Russell* for guidance as to the specificity required in charging other offenses have drawn from it somewhat varying lessons. See e.g., *United States v. Winchester,* 407 F.Supp. 261 (D.Del.1975) (allegation that defendant knowingly submitted specified false purchase orders to HUD was insufficient since the order form contained numerous factual statements; to meet the " 'sufficient appraisal' requirement" of *Russell,* the indictment should have alleged which statements were viewed as false); *United States v. Bernstein,* 533 F.2d 775 (2d Cir.1976) (indictment alleging submission of false statements to FHA need not identify the specific false statements within the specified mortgage application forms; *Russell* referred to an element at the very core of criminality under the statute and the core here "is not the substance of the false statements but rather that knowing falsehoods were submitted").

4. Would *Russell* have been decided differently if the prosecution there had been by information rather than indictment? Consider *United States v. Thomas,* 444 F.2d 919 (D.C.Cir.1971). The court there held that an indictment was insufficient in charging the felony offense of burglary since it alleged that defendant entered a dwelling "with intent to commit a criminal offense therein" but failed to identify the particular offense that defendant intended to commit upon entry. However, the court also found that the same language was sufficient to charge the lesser included misdemeanor offense of unlawful entry. Since that crime was not an "infamous" crime, defendant did not have a right to "the protections of a grand jury indictment" and the charge could be tested without reference to whether it "reveals that all the essential elements * * * were presented to the grand jury." Looking only to whether the pleading "informed appellant of the charges against him with sufficient particularity to allow him to prepare his defense," the indictment was sufficient to "place him on notice that he was charged with making an entry which was, by definition, without lawful authority," though it did not specify his unlawful purpose.

5. Does *Russell* establish a constitutional standard for the requisite specificity of a charging instrument in a criminal case? In *Choung v. California,* 320 F.Supp. 625 (E.D.Cal.1970), the court, relying heavily on *Russell,* held that a state defendant had been denied due process when a misdemeanor complaint charged, in the language of the governing California statute, that he entered upon school grounds "without lawful business therein" and "by his presence and acts" interfered with the peaceful conduct of the activities of the school. Under a state interpretation of the "without-lawful-business" clause, defendant would not have violated the statute unless he entered the school grounds for a purpose prohibited by another statute or regulation. The court concluded that the complaint, by failing to aver which statute or regulation ("among a potentially infinite number") the petitioner had intended to violate, left the prosecution, as in *Russell,* "free to roam at large—to shift its theory of criminality so as to take advantage of each passing vicissitude of the trial and appeal." Accordingly, the court held, the complaint failed to meet the constitutional minimum as to adequate notice. See also *Forgy v. Norris,* 64 F.3d 399 (8th Cir.1995) (state burglary information which failed to specify the ulterior offense defendant intended to commit upon entering the residence thereby violated defendant's constitutional right to be informed of the charges against him where defendant complained that he could not prepare his defense, the trial judge indicated that the offense was the theft charged in another count, that count was later amended to allege attempted theft, and the state never clearly indicated whether it was theft or attempted theft, with the defendant therefore not raising "a legal argument that there is no such thing as an 'intent to attempt' ").

6. *State cases.* The specificity required in setting forth the elements of a crime varies from state to state, from crime to crime, and from one element of the same crime to another. See CRIMPROC § 19.2(d). In general, the courts tend to insist upon greater specificity where the crime encompasses more factual variations. Thus, when charging false pretenses, the prosecutor often will be required to specify which of the defendant's alleged representations were false. So too, on a burglary charge, a court is likely to require identification of the ulterior offense. On the other hand, in charging a simple assault, it is usually sufficient to identify who was assaulted and when and where the assault occurred. Sometimes special consideration is given to the type of evidence likely to be available. See *State v. Martinez*, 550 N.W.2d 655 (Neb.1996) (to "compensate for the vagaries of a child's memory," an information can allege a timeframe rather than a specific date in charging sexual assault). As to almost every offense, however, there is likely to be at least one jurisdiction that requires more or less specificity than the general rule. See e.g., *City of Tulsa v. Haley*, 554 P.2d 102 (Okl.Crim.App.1976) (simply alleging that defendant "assaulted" a specified person is insufficient: the defendant must know what "acts he must be prepared to meet" and this required indicating the method of assault—"did [he] strike the complainants with his fist, kick them, push or shove them down, or what?"); *State v. Waters*, 436 So.2d 66 (Fla.1983) (burglary indictment need not specify ulterior offense provided it alleges an intent to commit a crime).

7. *The bill of particulars.* The function of the bill of particulars is to provide defendant with information about the details of the charge against him if this is necessary to the "preparation of his defense, and the avoidance of prejudicial surprise" at the trial. See CRIMPROC § 19.2(f). The exact relationship of the bill to the pleadings is not always clear. As noted in *Russell*, the bill does not cure an "invalid indictment."[a] Yet its availability is frequently mentioned in cases holding an indictment not so vague as to be defective. See e.g., *United States v. Debrow* (quoted in the *Russell* dissent). Also, once particulars are provided, a departure on the proof offered at trial can constitute a fatal variance. See *State v. Boire*, 474 A.2d 568 (N.H.1984) (since date was not material, the state was not required to furnish the date by a bill of particulars absent a need for defense preparation; but once date was furnished in the bill, the state was required to prove the offense was committed on that date).

Apart from the special requirements of short form pleading (see fn. b, p. 981), whether to grant or deny a request for a bill of particulars lies in the discretion of the trial court. Moreover, appellate courts will give considerable deference to trial courts in their exercise of that discretion. Although appellate courts frequently offer general guidelines for the use of the bill, those guidelines tend to provide only limited assistance in ruling on a particular request. For example, the directive that the bill should be used to protect the defendant against "prejudicial surprise," combined with the traditional assumption that the defendant is inno-

---

a. *Bae v. Peters*, 950 F.2d 469 (7th Cir. 1991), notes that this rule and others relating to amending indictments are tied to the federal constitutional right to be charged by indictment. Since the Fourteenth Amendment's due process clause does not demand that the states utilize grand jury indictments, but only that charging instruments provide adequate notice, states are not bound to such federal pleading standards. From the perspective of due process "it makes no difference * * * if a bill of particulars or an indictment amendment contains facts or charges not found by the grand jury, * * * so long as the defendant has received adequate notice of the charges against him." Some states provide that a bill of particulars cannot cure a missing element in a pleading, but may cure the lack of adequate specificity.

cent and "has no knowledge of the facts charged," could be read literally to require disclosure of almost every basic factual claim that defendant will have to meet at trial; yet even those trial judges most liberal in allowing a bill of particulars will stop far short of requiring such complete disclosure. So too, though it is commonly said that a bill of particulars "may not call for evidentiary matters," courts commonly order disclosure of information (e.g., the names of alleged coconspirators) that will identify the source of the government's evidence, if not set forth the evidence itself. The end result, as courts and commentators have noted, is a flood of trial court rulings that tend to be highly individualized and that often produce differing decisions on similar requests for a wide-range of particulars.

   8.   *Prosecution strategy.* Where the defense raises by pretrial objection the claim that the charging instrument lacks sufficient specificity (as the defense did in *Russell* and in the cases cited in the Notes 2–3 supra), why doesn't the prosecution either provide that specificity by amendment or offer to do so by a bill of particulars? Consider in this connection Pt. A, p. 1004, on the permissible scope of amendments and Pt. B, p. 1010, on the problems presented by an evidentiary variance at trial. Does it make sense from the prosecution's perspective to keep the allegations of specifics in a charging instrument to a minimum? Consider Dix, at 714 (discussing the strategy applicable to the initial pleading): "If sufficient specificity is provided [clearly] to survive a motion to quash, a prosecutor increases the risk that a fatal variance will develop at trial. This risk may prove to have been assumed unnecessarily. Given the uncertainty in regard to the degree of specificity required, the prosecutor may, in retrospect, find that he misconstrued what was required. Or, it may later develop that defense counsel would not have moved to quash the charging instrument, so that even the specificity demanded by the abstract law was not necessary in the particular case. On the other hand, if the instrument is drafted only to avoid fundamental deficiency, and defense counsel does move to quash, the limits on amendment will often mean that the state will have to reindict the defendant. This may or may not be burdensome, depending upon a variety of considerations. * * * Some delay, of course, is inevitable, and the delay may be substantial; in certain localities, reindictment may require waiting a substantial period until a new grand jury is empaneled. What effect delay will have is quite variable."

B.   ESSENTIAL ELEMENTS

UNITED STATES v. SPINNER

180 F.3d 514 (3d Cir.1999)

LEWIS, Circuit Judge.

   * * * In Count I of an indictment filed on June 10, 1997, [defendant] Spinner was charged with access device fraud in violation of 18 U.S.C. § 1029(a)(5). In Count II, Spinner was charged with bank fraud, in violation of 18 U.S.C. § 1344. Spinner * * * entered a plea of guilty to Count I of the indictment, [and] the District Court sentenced Spinner to two years imprisonment. This timely appeal followed.

   "Happily, the rule that the indictment, to be sufficient, must contain all the elements of a crime . . . is still a vital part of our Federal criminal jurisprudence." *United States v. Wander*, 601 F.2d 1251 (3d Cir.1979). To confer federal jurisdiction in this case, the interstate commerce element of the crime with which Spinner was charged must be alleged in the indictment. The United States, however, failed to allege the interstate commerce element of the crime in the indictment. It admits that "Count I of the indictment fails to allege that any of the transactions affected commerce." Appellant's Br. at 19. Nonetheless, it maintains that this is harmless error, because Count II of the indictment does allege the federal jurisdictional element. We disagree.

The Supreme Court has stated that a defendant has a "substantial right to be tried only on charges presented in an indictment returned by a grand jury. Deprivation of such a basic right is far too serious to be treated as nothing more than a variance and then dismissed as harmless error." *Stirone v. United States* [Note 5, p. 1006]. The fact that the United States charged interference with interstate commerce in Count II of Spinner's indictment is not a sufficient basis on which to find federal jurisdiction * * *. Without alleging an effect on interstate commerce in the first count, then, the indictment in this case was jurisdictionally defective.

When, as in this case, an indictment fails to allege all elements of an offense, the defect may be raised by the court *sua sponte*. We have held that "[f]ailure of an indictment sufficiently to state an offense is a fundamental defect . . . and it can be raised at any time." *Wander*; see also Fed.R.Crim.P. 12(b)(2).

Furthermore, notice alone cannot form a sufficient basis to validate a jurisdictionally defective indictment. In *United States v. Hooker*, 841 F.2d 1225 (4th Cir.1988) (en banc), the Fourth Circuit Court of Appeals held that "an effect on interstate commerce" was an essential element of a RICO offense without which an indictment was insufficient. It further held that notice alone was insufficient to validate the indictment: "The inclusion of all elements . . . derives from the Fifth Amendment, which requires that the grand jury have considered and found all elements to be present."

Finally, Spinner did not waive this jurisdictional defect by entering a guilty plea. In *United States v. Caperell*, 938 F.2d 975 (9th Cir.1991), the Ninth Circuit Court of Appeals held that "[a]lthough a guilty plea generally waives all claims of constitutional violation occurring before the plea, 'jurisdictional' claims are an exception to this rule." Id. at 977 (quoting *United States v. Montilla*) ("Claims that 'the applicable statute is unconstitutional or that the indictment fails to state an offense' are jurisdictional claims not waived by the guilty plea"). * * * [W]e are faced here not with a defendant who pleads guilty and then wishes to challenge the facts that give rise to federal jurisdiction (such as an effect on interstate commerce), but with an indictment that does not allege those facts. It is only in the former case that courts have found jurisdictional challenges waived by a guilty plea. See *United States v. Bentz*, 21 F.3d 37 (3d Cir.1994). While a challenge to jurisdiction-defeating factual allegations requires a court to go beyond the fact of the indictment, no such difficulty arises here.

Since the United States failed to allege an essential element of the crime in the indictment, we have no choice but to reverse and vacate Spinner's conviction so that he may be properly indicted and remand for further proceedings.

WELLFORD, Circuit Judge [visiting], concurring:

It is for the judges of this circuit to decide whether defendant's guilty plea in this case constituted a waiver of the indictment deficiency discussed. * * * The Supreme Court has used broad language to indicate that a criminal defendant may forfeit (or waive) a constitutional right in a criminal case * * *. *United States v. Olano* [Note 3, p. 1559]. Another circuit has recently used broad language in considering this issue in the context of the jurisdiction of the court: " * * * This court has recognized for decades that, despite defendants' tendency to 'confuse[ ] facts essential to be alleged as elements of the crime with jurisdictional requirements arising as a matter of law,' once a defendant plead guilty in '[a] court which has jurisdiction of the subject matter and of the defendant, as did the court in the instant case,' the court's judgment cannot be assailed on grounds that the government has not met its burden of proving 'so-called jurisdictional facts.' * * * " *United States v. Martin,* 147 F.3d 529, 531–32 (7th Cir.1998). * * *

Notes and Questions

1. **The traditional position.** *Spinner* reflects two major components of the traditional position as to the consequences of an indictment or information failing to plead the essential elements of the offense charged: (1) that failure calls not only for dismissal of the charging instrument on a pre-conviction challenge, but also for reversal of the conviction on appellate review following a conviction, and (2) that defect can be raised for the first time on appeal (indeed, the appellate court may recognize the defect *sua sponte*). *Spinner* also holds that the defect survives a guilty plea. Not all courts accepting the traditional position would agree with that conclusion, as some would view differently either the character of the defect (see Note 2 infra) or the scope of the issues deemed to be "waived" or "forfeited" by the entry of a guilty plea. See Ch. 22, § 5.[a] The vast majority of appellate rulings reversing convictions because of the pleading's failure to allege all the elements of the offense have involved review of a trial conviction. In many of those cases, the element not pleaded "was proven at trial and submitted to the jury with proper instructions." CRIMPROC § 19.3(a).

2. **The grounding of the essential elements requirement.** *Spinner* characterizes the failure to allege the essential elements as a "jurisdictional defect."[b] Several state courts share this view, although many others do not, even though they also adhere to the traditional position as to the consequences of an essential elements defect. See CRIMPROC § 19.2(e). Courts accepting the jurisdictional characterization speak of a charging instrument that fails to allege an essential element as the equivalent of no charging instrument, which therefore renders "void ab initio" any subsequent conviction. See *State v. Wilson,* 240 Kan. 606, 731 P.2d 306 (1987) (deprives court of subject matter jurisdiction). Compare *State v. Parkhurst,* 845 S.W.2d 31 (Mo.1992) ("subject matter jurisdiction and the sufficiency of the indictment are two distinct concepts"); *Prentiss,* Note 2, p. 1001.

Many courts characterize the failure to allege all essential elements as a constitutional violation. Some describe that failure as depriving the defendant of the notice of the charges required under the Sixth Amendment. See CRIMPROC § 19.2(c).[c] Commentators have noted, however, that "[i]n applying the Sixth Amendment notice requirement to other objections related to pleadings [e.g.,

a. Though a jurisdiction may view the pleading defect as forfeited by the guilty plea, where the failure was the product of an ambiguity in the law, that condition may lead to another ground for challenging the plea. See *Bousley v. United States,* Note 6, p. 1310 (failure of the court accepting the plea to advise the defendant of a critical element of the offense constitutes grounds for challenging the plea).

b. But note the later Third Circuit ruling in *United States v. Panarella,* 277 F.3d 678 fn. 1 (3d Cir.2002): "Apart from Rule 12(b)(2), the source of law on which Panarella's 'jurisdictional' argument rests remains murky; it is unclear to us whether the argument relies on the Fifth Amendment's Grand Jury Clause, putative statutory or Article III limits on federal courts' subject matter jurisdiction, or some rule of federal common law. Indeed, we are unsure whether use of the term 'jurisdictional'

to refer to challenges to the sufficiency of an indictment is anything more than simply a label used to announce the conclusion that a particular defense survives a guilty plea."

c. In his concurring opinion in *Apprendi v. New Jersey,* Justice Thomas cited both the Sixth Amendment and the Fifth Amendment (the grand jury clause) in explaining the grounding of the essential elements requirement. See p. 1523. In *Hamling v. United States,* 418 U.S. 87, 94 S.Ct. 2887, 41 L.Ed.2d 590 (1974), the Court arguably distinguished the notice function from the essential elements requirement when it noted: "Our prior cases indicate that an indictment is sufficient if it, first, contains the elements of the offense charged *and* fairly informs a defendant of the charge against which he must defend, and, second, enables him to plead an acquittal or conviction in bar of future prosecutions for the same offense" (emphasis added).

'shifts in prosecutorial theory'], courts have looked to (1) the actual notice provided in light of the totality of the information available to the defendant and (2) the likelihood of the defendant having actually been prejudiced in defending against the charges." Ibid. This stands in sharp contrast to the traditional position on the failure to plead the essential elements, which treats that failure as automatically requiring reversal and views as irrelevant the notice the defense may have received through a bill of particulars. Courts more frequently have cited as the constitutional grounding of the essential elements requirement the constitutional right to prosecution by indictment (the Fifth Amendment right in federal cases and the state constitutional right in state cases). See e.g., *United States v. Hooker*, discussed in *Spinner* (see p. 994). See also Note 6, p. 1007.

Courts also note that the pleading of the essential elements is required by the standard language of the Rule or statute setting forth the prerequisites of a charging instrument. The requirement that the pleading set forth "the essential facts constituting the offense charged" is seen as incorporating the common law requirement that the pleading refer to each element of the crime. But see *Miller v. State*, 827 P.2d 875 (Okla.Crim.App.1992) (Lumpkin, J., dissenting) (this standard should require no more than a statement of the acts constituting the offense in a manner sufficient to enable a person of common understanding to know what is intended, which does not require that pleading refer to "each and every element of the crime"). Including all essential elements is said to serve all of the basic functions of a pleading as described in § 1, Pt. B. Commentators contend, however, that the traditional treatment of a defective indictment on appeal (see Note 1 supra) is readily reconciled only with the "formal basis" function (see Note 5, p. 985). See CRIMPROC § 19.2. But see Note 5 infra (dissent of Utter, J., in *State v. Kjorsvik*).

3. *Implicit allegations.* Courts have noted that the failure to plead an element in its precise statutory terms is not essential, provided the words or facts contained in the indictment "necessarily or fairly import" the allegation of that element. Where the defense moved to dismiss prior to trial, giving the prosecution the opportunity to correct its pleading, courts may insist that the allegation "by implication" be fairly obvious. Illustrative of cases meeting and failing to meet that standard are found in a series of First Circuit cases. See *Hughes v. United States*, 338 F.2d 651 (1st Cir.1964) (indictment charging defendants with "unlawfully" removing merchandise while it was in customs' custody failed to allege requisite mens rea element; use of word "unlawfully" does not necessarily suggest defendants acted "knowingly"); *Portnoy v. United States*, 316 F.2d 486 (1st Cir.1963) (indictment charging assault against a federal official, when it alleged that the assault was committed by defendant "on account of [the victim's] official duties," necessarily implied that defendant had the requisite knowledge that his victim was an official); *United States v. McLennan*, 672 F.2d 239 (1st Cir.1982) (that principal acted "willfully" in jumping bail was implicit in other allegations of the indictment, which stated that principal failed to appear "after having been ordered to do so," that his failure constituted a violation of 18 U.S.C. § 3150,[d] that the district court entered a "default," and that defendant as an accomplice acted "in order to hinder and prevent [principal's] apprehension"; the indictment fell "somewhere between" *Hughes* and *Portnoy*, but was closer to *"Portnoy"*).

d. In determining whether a particular element is alleged "by implication," what weight should be given to the indictment's citation to a statute which specifically refers to that element? In *McLennan*, the court noted the general rule was that "statutory citations cannot normally supply the missing element," but added that "when considering whether an indictment for being an accessory sufficiently describes the underlying offense, common sense suggests that such a citation should not be entirely ignored where, as here, it so plainly reinforces what is implicit in the text."

4. *Failure to timely object.* As noted at p. 982 supra, a critical element of the modern pleading reforms was the adoption of a rule that pleading objections generally would be lost if not raised before trial. That rule, however, does not apply to a "failure to charge an offense." See e.g., Fed.R.Crim.P. 12(b), providing that such an objection "shall be noticed by the court at any time during the pendency of the proceedings." Under the traditional position, such provisions are interpreted as allowing that objection to be raised by the defense for the first time on appeal, and even where not raised by the defense, to be noticed by the court on its own motion. See e.g., *Spinner*, p. 994. Indeed, where failing to allege essential elements is treated as a "jurisdictional" flaw, a challenge may even be presented on collateral attack. See *State v. Shofler*, 687 P.2d 29 (Kan.App.1984). The traditional position not only requires that the objection be heard even though raised for the first time on appeal, but insists as well on automatic reversal of the conviction if the appellate court then finds a failure to allege the essential elements. The appellate court does not have the discretion that comes with the usual "plain error" review of challenges not properly presented at trial (see Note 3, p. 1559). However, as discussed below, a concession is granted to the prosecution in such cases in assessing whether the pleading did fail to allege the essential elements.

5. *"Liberal construction" on untimely objections.* Most appellate courts accepting the traditional position also follow the principle that, where an objection claiming that the charging instrument failed to charge an offense is first raised after trial, the charging instrument should liberally be construed in favor of its sufficiency. This "liberal construction" rule was the subject of extensive debate in STATE v. KJORSVIK, 812 P.2d 86 (Wash.1991). The majority per ANDERSEN, J., reasoned: "A different standard of review should be applied when no challenge to the charging document has been raised at or before trial because otherwise the defendant has no incentive to timely make such a challenge, since it might only result in an amendment or a dismissal potentially followed by a refiling of the charge. Applying a more liberal construction on appeal discourages what Professor LaFave has described as 'sandbagging.' He explains this as a potential defense practice wherein the defendant recognizes a defect in the charging document but forgoes raising it before trial when a successful objection would usually result only in an amendment of the pleading. * * * The standard of review utilized by the federal courts for challenges to charging documents which are raised for the first time on appeal was set forth by the United States Supreme Court in the leading case of *Hagner v. United States*, 285 U.S. 427, 433, 52 S.Ct. 417, 420, 76 L.Ed. 861 (1932): 'Upon a proceeding after verdict at least, no prejudice being shown, it is enough that the necessary facts appear in any form, or by fair construction can be found within the terms of the indictment.' Under this rule of liberal construction, even if there is an apparently missing element, it may be able to be fairly implied from language within the charging document.

"We hereby adopt the federal standard of liberal construction in favor of the validity of charging documents where challenges to the sufficiency of a charging document are initially raised after verdict or on appeal, but we further include in that standard both an essential elements prong and an inquiry into whether there was actual prejudice. Not all of the federal cases appear to overtly require both inquiries but the leading case of *Hagner* so suggests. * * * A close reading of the federal cases shows that the federal standard is, in practice, often applied as a 2–prong test: (1) do the necessary facts appear in any form, or by fair construction can they be found, in the charging document; and, if so, (2) can the defendant show that he or she was nonetheless actually prejudiced by the inartful language which caused a lack of notice? * * * [This] standard of review * * * will require at least some language in the information giving notice of the allegedly missing element(s) *and* if the language is vague, an inquiry may be required into whether there was actual prejudice to the defendant. The second prong—allowing the defendant to show that actual prejudice resulted from inartful or vague language—affords an added layer of protection to a defendant even where the issue is first raised after verdict or on appeal. * * * This 2–prong standard of review strikes a balance: on the one hand it discourages the defense from postponing a challenge to the charge knowing the charging document is flawed; on the other hand, it insures that the State will have given fair notice of the charge to the defendant.''

In dissent, Justice UTTER argued against adopting "a stricter standard of review for challenges to the sufficiency of a charging document first raised on appeal." The dissent reasoned: "Interpreting the language of the information liberally in order to fill in a missing element of the offense undercuts the importance of the essential elements rule. The majority states that '[t]he primary goal of the "essential elements" rule is to give notice to an accused of the nature of the crime that he or she must be prepared to defend against.' Historically, however, the essential elements rule was distinct from the notice argument. Even in situations where the notice function has been satisfied, i.e., the defendant has actual notice of the elements of the charged crime and has not been prejudiced at trial by the defective charging document, the * * * rule mandates automatic dismissal. * * * Leading commentators * * * recognize the distinction between the essential elements rule and notice. * * * [They] describe the functions of the essential elements rule as 'facilitating judicial review' * * *, providing the court with sufficient information to determine what facts 'are sufficient in law to support a conviction,' * * * [and allowing] the trial court 'to determine the evidence which is admissible and the judgment which should be pronounced.' * * *

"The majority offers two possible reasons for adopting the stricter standard of review. First, the majority argues that without the different standard of review 'the defendant has no incentive to timely make such a challenge, since it might only result in an amendment or a dismissal potentially followed by a refiling of the charge.' What the majority fails to realize, however, is that nothing in its proposed rule provides the defendant any additional incentive for raising the challenge prior to trial. Such a challenge will still only result in 'an amendment or dismissal potentially followed by a refiling of the charge.' The defendant who recognizes the defect prior to trial still has nothing to gain by raising a preverdict challenge. The defendant who honestly does not realize the charging document is defective, however, will be penalized by the higher standard of review. Thus the majority's rule penalizes the unwary while doing nothing to eliminate the 'sandbagging' problem the rule allegedly addresses. * * *

"The second reason the majority offers for adopting the rule is to further the 'orderly administration of criminal justice.' In fact, the majority rule does not further the orderly administration of justice. As noted above, the rule does not provide defendants any incentive to make earlier challenges to the sufficiency of the charging document. Given the time constraints and intricacies of preparing for trial, it is likely that most such challenges will still be raised for the first time on appeal. Our previous rule, however, required dismissal if the charging document failed to allege an essential element of the offense. Under that rule, the prosecution has a great deal of incentive to see to it that the charging document is constitutionally sufficient in the first place. This should result in fewer appeals, since the prosecutor will presumably be more careful if he or she knows an error could result in dismissal of the charge. Therefore, our original rule better serves the orderly administration of justice. * * * [While the] dismissal rule does place a greater burden on the prosecutor, this is fair, * * * since it is the prosecutor who is responsible for assuring that the charging document is constitutionally sufficient. * * * [T]hat is not a heavy burden. All the prosecutor has to do is see to it that all of the elements listed in the respective 'to convict' instructions set out in the Washington Pattern Jury Instructions are alleged in the charging document."

6. Where appellate courts follow the "liberal construction" rule, they vary considerably in their willingness to stretch the language of the pleading to find therein the necessary element. See e.g., *United States v. Mixon,* 374 F.2d 20 (6th Cir.1967) (failure to allege that defendants charged with heroin distribution conspiracy knew that the heroin had been imported unlawfully was not fatal where the indictment referred to the statutory provision specifically requiring such knowledge); *United States v. Morrison,* 536 F.2d 286 (9th Cir.1976) (indictment alleging that a postal employee "did convert * * * without authorization of law" certain postal moneys was insufficient; criminal intent is an element of the offense and its presence is not implicit in the allegation of a "conversion"). *State v. Tunney,* 917 P.2d 95 (Wash.1996) (allegation that defendant assaulted "a law enforcement officer who was performing his official duties at the time of the assault" was sufficient to find implicit under the liberal construction rule of *Kjorsuik,* supra Note 4, the element that defendant knew the victim was a police officer). Where the liberal construction policy has been rejected, courts have been known to apply, even on postconviction review, a policy of quite literal interpretation, holding against the indictment all but the clearest inferences to be drawn from its language. See e.g., *Ex parte Seaton,* 580 S.W.2d 593 (Tex.Crim.App.1979) (where the statute prohibited the taking of a credit card without the permission of "the person for whose benefit the credit card was issued," indictment was defective in alleging that the defendant knowingly took a credit card from the person of Linda Lusk "without the consent of said Linda Lusk" because it did not allege that Linda Lusk was the person for whom the card was issued).

7. *Distinguishing specificity and essential elements of objections.* Appellate courts frequently note that the lack of specificity does not in itself result in a failure to charge an offense and therefore a deficiency in specificity is waived by the defendant's failure to raise that objection before trial. See e.g., *United States v. Varkonyi,* 645 F.2d 453 (5th Cir.1981) (defendant could raise for the first time on appeal objection to indictment charging forcible interference with a federal official insofar as he claims that the charge failed to identify the victim as a federal official, but not insofar as he claims that the allegation of "forcibly interfering" failed to specify how he interfered with the performance of an official duty). Here again, however, there exists considerable variation from jurisdiction to jurisdiction as to what will be viewed as a specificity deficiency as opposed to a failure to charge an essential element. See e.g., *United States v. Thomas,* Note 4, p. 991 (where indictment charged a breaking and entry into a dwelling "with an intent to commit a criminal offense therein," the failure to identify that ulterior crime resulted in a failure to charge the offense of burglary, permitting a first time objection on appeal); *State v. Batson,* 580 P.2d 1066 (Or.App.1978) (failure to allege ulterior crime is a specificity deficiency and cannot be raised for first time on appeal).

8. *Defense ethics.* Consider Dix, at 713–14: "In 1956, the [Texas] Bar Committee on the Canons of Ethics voted 5-to-4 that a defense lawyer could properly proceed to trial on a defective indictment without raising the matter. Some of the majority's discussion suggests that counsel's duty to the client demanded that this be done. This position is, of course, consistent with the traditional notion that defense counsel has an ethical duty to present even adverse law to the court, but has no duty to call the court's attention to facts adverse to counsel's position. On the other hand, despite the committee's opinion, failing to raise a fundamental defect may be inconsistent with at least the spirit of defense counsel's possible ethical responsibility to avoid activity that serves only to delay the proceeding * * * ".

Professor Dix notes that as to "nonfundamental defects," the advantage to the defense often is to raise the objection pretrial so as to ensure that it is preserved, but present it in such a way that it hopefully will be rejected by the trial court and then be available as a reversible error should defendant be convicted. He notes that a defense counsel may pursue this goal by drafting a motion to quash "so as to preserve the [objection] * * * but not to effectively call the defect to the trial judge's attention" or may "forego rigorous pursuit of the motion in the trial court." Does this strategy raise a more serious ethical issue?

THE REASSESSMENT OF THE TRADITIONAL POSITION

1. *The setting in the federal courts.* See CRIMPROC § 19.3(c) (pocket part): "Largely as a result of two Supreme Court rulings, both dealing with jury trial issues, the lower federal courts are now in the process of reexamining these long-standing remedial rules governing an indictment's failure to allege all the elements of a crime. In 1999, [in] *Neder v. United States* [p. 1575], [the Supreme Court] held that the trial court's failure to submit an element of a crime to the jury (the trial court decided itself that the materiality element of the perjury offense had been satisfied), though a violation of the Sixth Amendment, could constitute harmless error. One year later, in *Apprendi v. New Jersey* [p. 1518], the Supreme Court held that a factor which increases the allowable maximum sentence is an element of the crime, and in treating that element as a sentencing factor to be decided by the judge rather than the jury, the state violated the Sixth Amendment. The federal system had a significant group of statutes in which maximum-enhancing factors had been treated as sentencing factors, leading to a deluge of cases challenging enhanced sentences under those statutes. [See Note 2, p. 1531.] The defendants soon learned that they faced serious obstacles in gaining relief. Where the defendant had pled guilty, that plea eliminated the Sixth Amendment issue because the defendant had not sought a jury trial. Where the defendant went to trial before a jury, but failed to object to the court's failure to submit the maximum-enhancing factor to the jury, the consideration of that error on appeal depended on the appellate court's willingness to recognize it under the "plain erro' doctrine. Where the defendant had anticipated *Apprendi* and objected at trial, the appellate court could still find the error to be harmless, as the lower courts viewed the *Apprendi* error as indistinguishable in character from that held harmless in *Neder*. All of these obstacles could be avoided, however, by grounding the challenge on the failure to allege the maximum-enhancing factor in the indictment.

"While *Apprendi* had ruled only on the jury issue, a factor that is element of the crime for Sixth Amendment purposes should also be an essential element for pleading purposes. [See King & Klein, Note 3, p. 1532.] Indeed, Justice Thomas' concurring opinion in *Apprendi* had suggested that the failure to allege such an element in the indictment constituted a violation of the grand jury clause of the Fifth Amendment. Basing the challenge on the indictment deficiency, rather than the *Apprendi* error, the defendant could look to traditional federal remedial law as to essential elements claims to avoid all of the obstacles facing *Apprendi* claims. If the defendant objected at trial, the failure to plead an essential element required automatic reversal; it was not subject to a harmless error analysis. If the defendant was raising the issue for the first time on appeal, Rule 12(b) bypassed the difficult prerequisites and discretionary character of the plain error doctrine. * * * As for a guilty plea, several federal courts had held that the failure to allege all essential elements was a jurisdictional type of defect and therefore survived a guilty plea.

"The government's response to these pleading claims was that it defied logic to allow an essential-elements objection to survive where a Sixth Amendment claim was barred. In particular, if the failure to present an element to a jury could constitute harmless error, should that not also be true of the failure to present an element to the grand jury (resulting in the indictment's failure to allege that element)? Although it was not the case where the indictment challenge accompanied an *Apprendi* challenge as to a maximum-enhancing factor, in other settings, the element missing from an indictment will have been presented to a jury, which found guilt beyond a reasonable doubt. Surely, it was argued, this proved the error to be harmless, as the grand jury undoubtedly would have found the evidence sufficient to include the element in its indictment. [So too, it was argued, why should an *Apprendi* error not raised at trial be subject to the stringent *Olano* requirements of 'plain error' review (see Note 3, p. 1559), and an essential elements objection not raised at trial be automatically reviewable on appeal, limited only by the liberal construction standard (see Note 5, p. 997).]"

    2. **Harmless error.** In UNITED STATES v. PRENTISS, 256 F.3d 971 (10th Cir.2001) (en banc), a divided court held that, in light of *Neder*, the failure to allege the essential elements could constitute a harmless error. The defendant there was convicted of the offense of committing arson in Indian country, but the indictment had failed to allege that the defendant was Indian and the victim non-Indian. If both parties were Indians, the crime was not a federal offense, but subject to tribal law. However, the government had assumed that was a "defense" and need not be alleged in the indictment. A majority of the en banc court disagreed, concluding that Indian/non-Indian statuses of the victim and defendant were elements of the crime and had to be alleged in the indictment. A different majority (per BALDOCK, J.) concluded that this pleading error was subject to harmless error review. It reasoned:

"We next consider the issue of whether the indictment's failure to allege the Indian/non-Indian statuses of Defendant and his victim deprived the district court of subject matter jurisdiction, or instead, is subject to harmless error review. Reyling on *United States v. Brown*, 995 F.2d 1493 (10th Cir.1993), and *United States v. Smith*, 553 F.2d 1239 (10th Cir.1977), defendant argues that 'the failure of the indictment to allege all the essential elements of the offense ... is a jurisdictional defect requiring dismissal, despite citation of the underlying statute in theindictment.' *Brown*. According to defendant, 'the absence of prejudice to the defendant does not cure what is necessarily a substantive, jurisdictional defect in the indictment.' *Smith*. * * * Contrary to our prior precedents, we hold that the failure of an indictment to allege an essential element of a crime does *not* deprive a district court of subject matter jurisdiction; rather, such failure is subject to harmless error review. To the extent that this Court's prior decisions, including *Brown* and *Smith*, hold otherwise, we overrule them. * * *

"That a court may not adjudicate a criminal prosecution without subject matter jurisdiction is beyond doubt. Courts' recurring reference to the elements of a crime as 'jurisdictional' to justify dismissal of an indictment which fails to allege an element, however, is misplaced. E.g., *United States v. Spinner* [p. 993]. An indictment's failure to allege an element of a crime is not jurisdictional in the sense that it affects a court's subject matter jurisdiction, i.e., a court's constitutional or statutory power to adjudicate a case. * * * As Judge Easterbrook aptly explained: 'Subject matter jurisdiction in every federal criminal prosecution comes from 18 U.S.C. § 3231 [providing that "district courts shall have original jurisdiction * * * of all offenses against the laws of the United States"]. That's the beginning and the end of jurisdictional inquiry.' *Hugi v. United States*, 164 F.3d 378, 380 (7th Cir. 1999). * * *

"Defendant did not challenge the indictment's sufficiency at any time in the district court. Compare *United States v. Du Bo*, 186 F.3d 1177, 1179 (9th Cir.1999) (holding that 'if properly challenged before trial,' an indictment's failure to allege an element of the offense constitutes reversible error), with *United States v. Woodruff*, No. 98–10358, 1999 WL 776213 at *1 (9th Cir. Sept.29, 1999) (unpublished) (refusing to extend *Du Bo* where defendant failed to timely challenge the indictment). Nor did Defendant ever seek a bill of particulars pursuant to Fed.R.CrimP. 7(f). Defendant obviously had no questions concerning the federal charges against him, and neither do we. * * *

"Because an indictment's failure to allege an essential element of a crime is not jurisdictional, we must discern what standard of review applies when a defendant fails to timely challenge such an indictment. To be sure, a defendant cannot waive the right to challenge an indictment based upon its failure to charge an offense. Fed.R.Crim.P. 12(b)(2). We must, however, as a general rule liberally construe an indictment subject to a belated challenge in favor of validity. This is because all trial participants must be encouraged to seek a fair and accurate trial the first time around. * * * Our words nearly four decades ago remain true today:

> [A]fter a verdict ... every intendment must be indulged in support of the indictment ... and such a verdict ... cures mere technical defects unless it is apparent they have resulted in prejudice to the defendant. *Prejudice to the defendant is, of course, a controlling consideration in determining whether an indictment ... is sufficient.*

Clay v. United States, 326 F.2d 196, 198 (10th Cir.1963) (emphasis added).

"In both *Brown* and *Smith*, we declined to consider whether defendants suffered any prejudice as a result of the defective indictments. Instead, we effectively, though not expressly, treated an indictment's failure to allege an essential element of a crime as structural error subject to automatic reversal [see Note 4, p. 1573]. * * * [M]ost recently in *Neder* [p. 1575], the Supreme Court recognized that most constitutional errors can be harmless: 'If the defendant had counsel and was tried by an impartial adjudicator, there is a *strong* presumption that any other constitutional errors that may have occurred are subject to harmless-error analysis.' * * * To date, the Supreme Court has classified only two types of grand jury related errors as structural, both involving discrimination in the selection of grand jurors. *Vasquez v. Hillery* [Note 8, p. 947] (racial discrimination); *Ballard v. United States* [Note 2, p. 975] (sex discrimination). Otherwise, the Court has 'see[n] no reason not to apply [harmless error analysis] to error, defects, irregularities or variances occurring before a grand jury just as [it has] applied it to such error occurring in the criminal trial itself.' *United States v. Mechanik* [Note 5, p. 977]. In *Mechanik*, the Court held harmless the government's violation of Fed.R.Crim.P. 6(d) relating to the presence of witnesses before a grand jury. The Court explained that 'the petit jury's verdict of guilty beyond a reasonable doubt demonstrates *a fortiori* that there was probable cause to charge the defendants with the offenses for which they were convicted.' * * *

"Furthermore, despite the Fifth Amendment's requirement that the Government prove each and every element of the crime beyond a reasonable doubt, and the Sixth Amendment's requirement that a jury, rather than a judge, reach the requisite finding of guilty, the Court in *Neder* held that the failure to instruct the jury on every element of an offense 'does not *necessarily* render a criminal trial fundamentally unfair or an unreliable vehicle for determining guilt or innocence.' *Neder* (emphasis in original). To us, a defendant's right to have a petit jury find each element of the charged offense beyond a reasonable doubt is no less important than a defendant's right to have each element of the same offense presented to the grand jury. If denial of the former right is subject to harmless error analysis, we believe denial of the latter right must be as well. See *United States v. Mojica–Baez*, 229 F.3d 292 (1st Cir.2000) ('[W]e see no reason why harmless error review should not apply to the failure to include an element in an indictment that otherwise provided the defendants with fair notice of the charges against them.')."

The *Prentiss* dissenters on the harmless error issue (per HENRY, J.) argued that the traditional position as to the consequences of failing to allege essential elements was strongly supported in the Supreme Court's *Stirone* ruling [Note 5, p. 1006], which had vacated a conviction, without inquiring into possible prejudice or considering a harmless error analysis, because the jury had been charged on an allegation not included in the indictment. *Stirone*, the dissent noted, "establishes that, absent an indictment that sets forth each element, a reviewing court cannot be assured that the grand jury made the finding required by the Fifth Amendment," and therefore the conviction must be reversed. *Neder*, it was argued, did not challenge *Stirone*, as it distinguished cases that "defy harmless-error review" because they contain " 'a defect affecting the framework within which the trial proceeds.' " *Mechanik* also was distinguishable because it dealt with an entirely different kind of error in the grand jury proceedings. "In sum," the dissent noted, "neither *Neder*, nor *Mechanik*, nor the weight of the evidence at trial deprives a defendant of the Fifth Amendment right to have a grand jury frame a charge by finding probable cause as to each essential element of the offense."

3. *Plain error review*. Several circuits have concluded that an essential elements defect, raised for the first time on appeal, is subject to the restraints of "plain error" review (described in Note 3, p. 1559). See e.g., *United States v. Promise* and *United States v. Cotton*, discussed in Note 3, pp. 1561–62; *United States v. Thomas*, 274 F.3d 655 (2d Cir.2001); *United States v. Mojica–Baez*, 229 F.3d 292 (1st Cir.2000). The missing element in such cases had been an *Apprendi* type element, which increased the maximum punishment. That factor apparently has led these courts to view Rule 12(b) as inapplicable, since the pleading did allege an offense (although not that carrying the maximum sentence under which the defendant was sentenced).

4. *State courts*. Even before *Neder* led to a reassessment of the traditional position on an essential element defect, two state courts did so. *Studer v. State*, 799 S.W.2d 263 (Tex.Crim.App. 1990), held that, as a result of a 1985 constitutional amendment providing that "the presentment of an indictment or information to a court invests that court with jurisdiction", and implementing legislation providing that all defects in "form or substance" of an indictment or information are forfeited if not raised before trial, "missing element" challenges could not be raised for the first time on appeal. See also *Hunt v. Texas*, 994 S.W.2d 206 (Tex.App.1999) (where objection not timely presented, only pleading objection cognizable is that the indictment did not even serve as an indictment because it failed to identify in any manner the penal statute alleged to have been violated, a defect clearly not present where the indictment cites the penal code provision and the title of the offense).

Parker v. State, 917 P.2d 980 (Okla.Crim.App.1996) overturned an earlier ruling, *Miller v. State*, that had sustained the traditional position. The court noted: "*Miller* created a bright-line rule that all Informations not alleging each element of a charged crime would be reversed. * * * In the years since *Miller*, this Court has had the opportunity to observe the effects of this bright-line rule. We have determined that despite its advantages, a bright-line rule works best in areas of law where a defect will always result in a constitutional or statutory violation. The failure to allege each element of a crime does not always constitute a due process violation. Where the Information alleges an offense and pleads particular facts constituting the offense in ordinary language, such that a person of common understanding can know what is intended and prepare a defense to the charge, no due process violation occurs. This Court will no longer apply the *Miller* bright-line test. * * * [We will] ask whether the Information gives the defendant notice of the charges against him and apprises him of what he must defend against at trial. This determination will be made on a case-by-case basis in each appeal where the issue is raised. This Court will look to the 'four corners' of the Information together with all material that was made available to a defendant at preliminary hearing or through discovery to determine whether the defendant received notice to satisfy due process requirements."

SECTION 3. AMENDMENTS AND VARIANCES

A. The Permissible Scope of Amendments

1. *The prejudice/different-offense standard.* The dominant standard governing the amendment of felony pleadings is that set forth in Federal Rule 7(e):

> The court may permit an information to be amended at any time before verdict or finding if no additional or different offense is charged and if substantial rights of the defendant are not prejudiced.

Although Federal Rule 7(e) is limited to amendments of the information, most states apply a Rule 7(e)–type standard to both informations and indictments. That standard has two prongs, barring amendments that either result in prejudice to the accused or charge a new offense.

The prejudice prong, though referring generally to prejudice to the "substantial rights of accused," focuses almost exclusively upon the element of surprise. To oppose an amendment on this ground, the defense ordinarily must make some showing that the amendment will catch it by surprise and thereby interfere with its ability to defend against the charges. Since such prejudice may be avoided before trial by granting an appropriate continuance, an amendment made before trial is unlikely to be held to have injured the substantial rights of the defendant where a continuance was granted or none was requested. Amendments made during trial will cause more difficulty, but are often held not to be prejudicial where they do not change the factual basis of the offense as set forth in the original pleading, the bill of particulars, or pretrial discovery obtained by the defense. See *State v. Price*, 940 S.W.2d 534 (Mo.App.1997) (test for prejudice is whether defendant's evidence would be equally applicable and his defense equally available under the amended information).

The second prong of the Rule 7(e) standard—prohibiting amendments that charge additional or different offenses—stands apart from any showing of surprise, and will bar an amendment notwithstanding an obvious lack of surprise. As noted in CRIMPROC § 19.5(b), "the precise content of the 'different offense' standard has been the source of disagreement at its edges. A different offense clearly is presented where the indictment alleges an offense under a different statutory provision and that offense is not a lesser included offense under the original charge. A charge even under the same statute generally is recognized as producing a new offense if the underlying 'identity' of the original charge is changed by relying on an entirely different series of events as the basis for the violation. Division arises when the statute remains the same, the basic incident remains the same, but the statute lists alternative means of commission, harms, or subjects, and the shift is from one alternative to another. Many courts view such [an amendment] * * * as merely shifting the facts [or the interpretation of the facts] that will be relied upon to establish the same basic element of the crime [which happens to be broken down by the statute into alternatives rather than stated in general terms that would encompass those alternatives]. * * * Carrying this single-element analysis to its logical extreme, one court allowed a shift in a first degree murder charge from premeditated killing to a killing in the course of a felony since all that was altered was means of establishing the mens rea element for a single statutory offense. Other courts would not accept such an amendment, as they would define the elements of the offense far more narrowly. The most confining position in this regard treats each statutory alternative as establishing a separate element (and therefore a separate offense) if it requires proof that the other alternative does not."

Differences in the interpretation of the "new-offense" limitation arguably reflect different views of the function of that limitation. Some courts see the limitation as a *per se* rule designed to reach a kind of change that is highly likely to be accompanied by prejudicial surprise. This view of the function of the limitation often leads to a judicial definition of a "new offense" that stresses shifts in the basic underlying events or the statutory provision that serves as the basis for the charge. On the other hand, the new-offense limitation may be viewed as also designed to protect the role of the screening agency, whether grand jury or preliminary hearing magistrate. This leads to a more restrictive view of changes in the offense, rejecting any shift from the basic factual theory of liability presented to that screening agency and reflected in the original pleading.[a]

    2. *The "form/substance" distinction.* Not all jurisdictions follow an amendment policy as liberal as that provided in Federal Rule 7(e). A substantial group of states adhere to the formulation that amendments are permitted as to "form," but not as to "substance." Although some states apply this distinction to allow roughly the same type of amendments that would be permitted under Rule 7(e), others construe it to allow only a much narrower range of amendments. In these jurisdictions, an amendment that falls short of changing the basic offense charged can nevertheless readily be characterized as one of substance. Amendments are said to fall in that category if they alter or supply "essential facts that must be proved to make the act complained of a crime." *Brown v. State,* 400 A.2d 1133 (Md.1979). Thus, apart from any question of surprise, jurisdictions following a form/substance distinction are likely to bar an amendment that substantially alters the description of the criminal act, the mens rea accompanying that act, or the consequences of that act. See e.g., *Brown v. State,* supra (prohibiting amendment that changed the original allegation that defendant defrauded an automobile dealer of a dollar amount to an allegation that he defrauded the dealer of an automobile worth that amount); *Gullett v. State,* 116 N.E.2d 234 (Ind.1953) (disallowing amendment to change the name of the owner of a stolen vehicle); *State v. Green,* 605 P.2d 746 (Or.App.1980) (amendment could not add the ulterior crime in a burglary charge).

    3. *Amendments to indictments.* The federal courts and several states draw a sharp distinction between amendments of indictments and informations, allowing considerably less latitude for the indictment amendments. Indeed, some

    a. Protection of the role of the screening agency clearly is reflected in the treatment of amendments which seek to cure a pleading that failed to charge all of the elements of the offense. The addition of a missing element by amendment commonly is barred by reference to the need for a screening agency finding as to each element of the offense, typically with no discussion of the Rule 7(e) standard. See CRIMPROC § 19.5(b). Where that standard is discussed, it tends to be described as necessarily inapplicable because an "amendment" necessarily assumes that there is a valid existing charge to amend, or necessarily violated by such an amendment (on the ground, that the amendment inherently adds an offense since none was pleaded originally). Ibid.

of these jurisdictions are commonly said to follow "the historic rule that an indictment may not be amended." None actually go so far as to adhere to the early common law prohibition that barred even amendments to cure misnomers, but they do follow what is sometimes described as the "rule of *Ex parte Bain.*" *Bain* and the Supreme Court cases discussing *Bain* are set forth below.

4. EX PARTE BAIN, 121 U.S. 1, 7 S.Ct. 781, 30 L.Ed. 849 (1887), involved a habeas corpus challenge to a conviction based on an amended indictment. The original indictment charged the defendant with having made a false statement in a bank report "with intent to deceive the Comptroller of the Currency and the agent appointed to examine the affairs of said [bank]." The trial court initially sustained a demurrer to the indictment. That court apparently read the cited statute as making it an offense only to deceive the agent appointed to examine the bank records. Under the common law pleading standards the indictment therefore was fatally defective since it alleged as an offense an alternative action (deceiving the Comptroller) that was not a crime. To cure this defect, the trial court allowed the government to amend the indictment by striking the reference to the Comptroller. In an unanimous opinion, the Supreme Court, concluded that the amendment was impermissible, depriving the trial court of the power to proceed and therefore requiring habeas relief. Speaking for the Court, MILLER, J., noted:

"The learned judge who presided in the Circuit Court at the time the change was made in this indictment, says that the court allowed the words 'Comptroller of the Currency and' to be stricken out as surplusage,[b] * * *. He goes on to argue that the grand jury would have found the indictment without this language. But it is not for the court to say whether they would or not. The party can only be tried upon the indictment as found by such grand jury, and especially upon all its language found in the charging part of that instrument. While it may seem to the court, with its better instructed mind in regard to what the statute requires to be found as to the intent to deceive, that it was neither necessary nor reasonable that the grand jury should attach importance to the fact that it was the Comptroller who was to be deceived, yet it is not impossible nor very improbable that the grand jury looked mainly to that officer as the party whom the prisoner intended to deceive by a report which was made upon his requisition and returned directly to him. * * * How can the court say that there may not have been more than one of the jurors who found this indictment, who was satisfied that the false report was made to deceive the Comptroller, but was not convinced that it was made to deceive anybody else? And how can it be said that, with these words stricken out, it is the indictment which was found by the grand jury? If it lies within the province of a court to change the charging part of an indictment to suit its own notions of what it ought to have been, or what the grand jury would probably have made it if their attention had been called to suggested changes, the great importance which the common law attaches to an indictment by a grand jury, as a prerequisite to a prisoner's trial for a crime, and without which the Constitution says 'no person shall be held to answer,' may be frittered away until its value is almost destroyed."

5. In STIRONE v. UNITED STATES, 361 U.S. 212, 80 S.Ct. 270, 4 L.Ed.2d 252 (1960), the Court relied on *Bain* in concluding that the government could not accomplish through a variance between proof and charge what it could not achieve through an amendment. The indictment there, brought under the Hobbs Act, charged defendant with extortion affecting interstate commerce through wrongful

---

b. While Federal Rule 7(d) today provides for the striking of surplusage, it uses that term with a different point of reference. Rule 7(d) is aimed at inflammatory and prejudicial language that is irrelevant to the description of the events alleged in the indictment. Accordingly, it provides only for the striking of surplusage on motion of the defendant (who arguably could be viewed as thereby waiving his right not to have the indictment amended).

use of a threatened labor dispute. The dispute was directed against Rider, a Pennsylvania supplier of ready-mixed concrete used in the construction of a Pennsylvania steel processing plant. The indictment alleged that Stirone's activities had obstructed the interstate flow of sand shipments into Rider's concrete plant. At trial, over defense objection, the judge admitted evidence concerning (and instructed the jury that their verdict could rest upon) Stirone's interference with interstate commerce by preventing shipments that the steel plant would have made had it been built on time. A unanimous court, per BLACK, J., found this variance "fatal":

"We agree with the Court of Appeals that Rider's dependence on shipments of sand from outside Pennsylvania to carry on his ready-mixed concrete business entitled him to the Hobbs Act's protection. * * * Whether prospective steel shipments from the new steel mills would be enough, alone, to bring this transaction under the Act is a more difficult question. We need not decide this, however, since we agree with the dissenting judges in the Court of Appeals that it was error to submit that question to the jury and that the error cannot be dismissed as merely an insignificant variance between allegation and proof and thus harmless error as in *Berger v. United States* [Note 2, p. 1011]. The crime charged here is a felony and the Fifth Amendment requires that prosecution be begun by indictment.

"Ever since *Ex parte Bain* was decided in 1887, it has been the rule that after an indictment has been returned its charges may not be broadened through amendment except by the grand jury itself. * * * The *Bain* case, which has never been disapproved, stands for the rule that a court cannot permit a defendant to be tried on charges that are not made in the indictment against him. Yet the court did permit that in this case. * * * The grand jury which found this indictment was satisfied to charge that Stirone's conduct interfered with interstate importation of sand. But neither this nor any other court can know that the grand jury would have been willing to charge that Stirone's conduct would interfere with interstate exportation of steel from a mill later to be built with Rider's concrete. * * * Although the trial court did not permit a formal amendment of the indictment, the effect of what it did was the same. And the addition charging interference with steel exports here is neither trivial, useless, nor innocuous."

6. In *United States v. Prentiss*, discussed in Note 2, p. 1001, the dissenters argued that application of a harmless error analysis to the failure of an indictment to allege the essential elements of the offense was inconsistent with *Stirone*. The *Prentiss* majority, however, saw *Stirone* as involving a quite different flaw: Where an indictment simply failed to expressly include all the elements of the offense charged, the crime the indictment presented was basically that on which the jury later convicted, whereas the jury in *Stirone* may have convicted for an offense that had been changed in character from that originally alleged, through the variance that amounted to a constructive indictment amendment. But see CRIMPROC § 19.2(e): "The ramifications of applying harmless error analysis * * * [are] not limited to claims of missing essential elements," for "why shouldn't harmless error also apply where the amendment [of an indictment] * * * did not take the defense by surprise and the jury found it supported by sufficient evidence— notwithstanding that it charged a different offense or substantially altered the factual grounding of an element of the same offense in violation of the *Bain* rule?"

7. In 1985, in *United States v. Miller* (set forth below), the Supreme Court reexamined *Bain* in light of *Stirone* and other Supreme Court precedent.

UNITED STATES v. MILLER
471 U.S. 130, 105 S.Ct. 1811, 85 L.Ed.2d 99 (1985).

Justice MARSHALL delivered the opinion of the Court.

The issue presented is whether the Fifth Amendment's grand jury guarantee is violated when a defendant is tried under an indictment that alleges a certain fraudulent scheme but is convicted based on trial proof that supports only a significantly narrower and more limited, though included, fraudulent scheme. * * *

[A federal grand jury indicted defendant for several violations of the mail fraud statute, 18 U.S.C. § 1341. The indictment alleged that defendant had defrauded an insurance company by both arranging for a burglary at his place of business and by lying to the insurer as to the value of the loss. The trial proof, however, concerned only the latter allegation, and the government moved to strike that part of the indictment that alleged prior knowledge of the burglary. The defense opposed the proposed amendment, urging that the entire indictment be submitted to the jury. This was done and the jury found defendant guilty. Defendant then appealed on the ground that the trial proof had fatally varied from the scheme alleged in the indictment. Relying on *Bain* and *Stirone,* the Third Circuit sustained that challenge. That court noted: "It is quite possible that the grand jury would have been unwilling or unable to return an indictment based solely on Miller's exaggeration of the amount of his claimed loss even though it had concluded that an indictment could be returned based on the overall scheme involving a use of the mail caused by Miller's knowing consent to the burglary."]

* * * Miller's indictment properly alleged violations of 18 U.S.C. § 1341, and it fully and clearly set forth a number of ways in which the acts alleged constituted violations. The facts proved at trial clearly conformed to one of the theories of the offense contained within that indictment, for the indictment gave Miller clear notice that he would have to defend against an allegation that he "well knew that the amount of copper claimed to have been taken during the alleged burglary was grossly inflated for the purpose of fraudulently obtaining $150,000 from Aetna Insurance Company." Competent defense counsel certainly should have been on notice that the offense was charged and would need to be defended against. Accordingly, there can be no showing here that Miller was prejudicially surprised at trial by the absence of proof concerning his alleged complicity in the burglary; nor can there be a showing that the variance prejudiced the fairness of respondent's trial in any other way. Compare *Kotteakos v. United States* [fn. b, p. 1011]. See also *Berger v. United States* [Note 2, p. 1011]. The indictment was also sufficient to allow Miller to plead it in the future as a bar to subsequent prosecutions. Therefore, none of these "notice" related concerns—which of course are among the important concerns underlying the requirement that criminal charges be set out in an indictment—would support the result of the Court of Appeals. See *Russell v. United States* [p. 986]. The Court of Appeals did not disagree, but instead argued that Miller had been prejudiced in his right to be free from a trial for any offense other than that alleged in the grand jury's indictment. It reasoned that a grand jury's willingness to indict an individual for participation in a broad criminal plan does not establish that the same grand jury would have indicted the individual for participating in a substantially narrower, even if wholly included, criminal plan. * * *

The government correctly argues that the Court of Appeals' result conflicts with a number of this Court's prior decisions interpreting the Fifth Amendment's grand jury Clause. The Court has long recognized that an indictment may charge numerous offenses or the commission of any one offense in several ways. As long as the crime and the elements of the offense that sustain the conviction are fully and clearly set out in the indictment, the right to a grand jury is not normally violated by the fact that the indictment alleges more crimes or other means of committing the same crime. See e.g., *Ford v. United States*, 273 U.S. 593, 47 S.Ct. 531, 71 L.Ed. 793 (1927); *Salinger v. United States*, 272 U.S. 542, 47 S.Ct. 173, 71 L.Ed. 398 (1926). * * *

The Court of Appeals principally relied on this Court's decision in *Stirone v. United States* to support its conclusion that the Fifth Amendment's grand jury right is violated by a conviction for a criminal plan narrower than, but fully included within, the plan set forth in the indictment. *Stirone,* however, stands for a very different proposition. In *Stirone* the offense proved at trial was not fully contained in the indictment, for trial evidence had "amended" the indictment by *broadening* the possible bases for conviction from that which appeared in the indictment. *Stirone* was thus wholly unlike [*Ford* and *Salinger*] * * * and unlike respondent's case, all of which involve trial evidence that narrowed the indictment's charges without adding any new offenses. As the *Stirone* Court said, the issue was "whether [Stirone] was convicted of an offense *not charged in the indictment.*" (Emphasis added). * * *

The one decision of this Court that does offer some support to the Court of Appeals' result is *Ex parte Bain,* for there the Court treated as an unconstitutional "amendment" the deletion from an indictment of allegations that would not have been necessary to prove the offense. * * * Under later cases, such as *Ford* and *Salinger,* the presence of such surplusage in the indictment would not invalidate a conviction as long as the necessary intent was also alleged and proved. * * * But [the *Bain*] opinion reasoned that a court could not, consistent with the Fifth Amendment, assume that the narrower indictment would have been returned by the grand jury that returned the broader one.

Bain may best be understood in terms of two distinct propositions. Most generally, *Bain* stands for the proposition that a conviction cannot stand if based on an offense that is different from that alleged in the grand jury's indictment. But more specifically, *Bain* can support the proposition that the striking out of parts of an indictment invalidates the whole of the indictment, for a court cannot speculate as to whether the grand jury had meant for any remaining offense to stand independently, even if that remaining offense clearly was included in the original text. Under this latter proposition, the narrowing of an indictment is no different from the adding of a new allegation that had never been considered by the grand jury; both are treated as "amendments" that alter the nature of the offense charged. In evaluating the relevance of *Bain* to the instant case, it is necessary to examine these two aspects of *Bain* separately, for the Court has treated these two propositions quite differently in the years since *Bain.*

The proposition that a defendant cannot be convicted of an offense different from that which was included in the indictment * * * has been reaffirmed in a number of subsequent cases. See e.g., *United States v. Norris,* 281 U.S. 619, 50 S.Ct. 424, 74 L.Ed. 1076 (1930) (citing *Bain* for the rule that "nothing can be added to an indictment without the concurrence of the grand jury by which the bill was found"). The most important reaffirmation, of course, was *Stirone.* * * * See also *Russell v. United States* (citing *Bain* for the "settled rule in the federal courts that an indictment may not be amended except by resubmission to the grand jury, unless the change is merely a matter of form").

But this aspect of *Bain* gives no support to Miller in this case, for the offense that formed the basis of Miller's conviction was clearly and fully set out in the indictment. Miller must instead rest on the second, and more specific, proposition found in *Bain,* that a narrowing of the indictment constitutes an amendment that renders the indictment void. As is clear from [our previous] discussion of * * * [*Ford* and *Salinger*], this second proposition did not long survive *Bain.* Indeed, when defendants have sought to rely on *Bain* for this point, this Court has limited or distinguished the case, sustaining convictions where courts had withdrawn or ignored independent and unnecessary allegations in the indictments. Modern criminal law has generally accepted that an indictment will support each offense contained within it. To the extent *Bain* stands for the proposition that it constitutes an unconstitutional amendment to drop from an indictment those allegations that are unnecessary to an offense that is clearly contained within it, that case has simply not survived. To avoid further confusion, we now explicitly reject that proposition. * * *

In light of the foregoing, the proper disposition of this case is clear. The variance complained of added nothing new to the grand jury's indictment and constituted no broadening. As in *Salinger* and *Ford*, what was removed from the case was in no way essential to the offense on which the jury convicted. * * * The judgment of the Court of Appeals is accordingly reversed.

Justice POWELL took no part in the consideration or decision of this case.

Notes and Questions

1. How much of *Bain* remains after *Miller?* Assume, for example, that the amendments considered in the cases discussed in Note 2, p. 1005, were before federal courts as amendments to an indictment. Would those amendments be acceptable under *Bain/Miller,* assuming also there was no concern as to prejudice due to surprise?

2. Consider the pleading strategy suggested by CRIMPROC § 19.5: "For the federal prosecutor who wishes to avoid repeated trips to the grand jury, the *Bain* rule, as modified by *Miller,* offers two obvious lessons. First, all possible factual theories of liability should be included in the initial indictment. If post-indictment investigation should reveal that a theory is not worthy of carrying forward at trial, it may always be deleted; on the other hand, if a factual theory originally is omitted on the ground that it is not as strong as other theories, and post-indictment investigation reveals its strength was underestimated, the addition of that theory will require a new indictment under the *Bain* rule. Second, there is an advantage in utilizing less specificity so that allegations can cover more factual variations that might arise as a result of post-indictment investigation. * * * Of course, the prosecution often walks a fine line in adopting this tact, as the lack of factual specificity * * * may provide a basis for a successful defense challenge to the sufficiency of the pleading."

B.   The Scope of Permissible Variances

1.   *The procedural setting.* A variance arises when the proof offered at trial departs from the allegations in the indictment or information. The defense may object to the introduction of that evidence, arguing that it is irrelevant to the offense pleaded, but most often the key objection comes after the presentation of evidence is complete and the case is ready to go to the jury. At this point, the defendant objecting to a variance typically states, in effect: "The prosecution may have offered evidence sufficient to establish a crime, but it is not the crime alleged in its accusatory pleading and I therefore am entitled to an acquittal." On occasion, the state has introduced evidence covering all the allegations in its pleading and the variance relates to evidence establishing an additional theory of liability. The defense objection then is to the instruction to the jury that would permit it to consider this additional theory of liability. Very often, the prosecution, recognizing the existence of a variance, will seek to amend the pleading to conform to the evidence. If this is permitted, the issue raised on appeal will be whether the amendment was properly allowed. Where there was no amendment (either because the trial judge disallowed the amendment or no request for amendment was made), the defendant's claim on appeal speaks directly to the variance, arguing that the submission of the case to the jury on the basis of the variance constituted reversible error.

2. *The Berger standard.* The source of the prevailing standard for judging the scope of permissible variance is the frequently cited statement of Justice Sutherland in *Berger v. United States,* 295 U.S. 78, 55 S.Ct. 629, 79 L.Ed. 1314 (1935):

> The true inquiry, * * * is not whether there has been a variance in proof, but whether there has been such a variance as to "affect the substantial rights" of the accused.[a] The general rule that allegations and proof must correspond is based upon the obvious requirements (1) that the accused shall be definitely informed as to the charges against him, so that he may be enabled to present his defense and not be taken by surprise by the evidence offered at the trial; and (2) that he may be protected against another prosecution for the offense.

In light of this statement, most states hold that a "variance requires reversal of a conviction only when it deprives the defendant of a right to fair notice or leaves him open to a risk of double jeopardy." CRIMPROC § 19.2(h).[b]

3. In applying the notice element of the *Berger* standard, courts look to the record to determine whether it suggests "a possibility that the defendant may have been misled or embarrassed in the preparation or presentation of his defense." *Marshall v. State,* 381 So.2d 276 (Fla.App.1980). A failure to object to the variance at trial is generally viewed as a waiver of a claim of prejudice, and an eleventh hour objection is taken as strong evidence belying any such claim. If the defendant was previously aware of the prosecution's proof as a result of pretrial discovery or a preliminary hearing, that factor also will weigh against a finding of prejudice. The court will also look to the relationship of the variance to the defense presented by the defendant. Consider *United States v. Wozniak,* 126 F.3d 105 (2d Cir.1997) (although indictment could simply have charged member of motorcycle club with offenses involving "controlled substances," the indictment specifically identified the substances as "cocaine and methamphetamine," while others were charged with marijuana offenses; accordingly, defendant was prejudiced by introduction of evidence of marijuana transactions and a charge to the jury on those transactions; had "defendant been aware that the government would seek a conviction mostly on marijuana evidence, he might have chosen a different trial strategy," which did not put his credibility in issue by testifying in his own defense and stating that he did not use marijuana and had never seen a large bale of marijuana).

---

a. The reference was to the federal harmless error statute which directs an appellate or trial court, on challenge to a conviction, to "give judgment * * * without regard to technical errors, defects, or exceptions which do not affect the substantial rights of the parties." See p. 1563.

b. The first prong of this standard is often more broadly stated as whether the defendant suffered "actual prejudice at trial." Although notice is the primary concern in determining whether the defendant suffered such prejudice, *Berger* itself recognized that a variance could also cause prejudice where it resulted in the introduction of evidence that would not otherwise have been admissible against defendant. The defendant in *Berger* objected to the additional evidence that had been introduced at his trial because the government charged a single larger conspiracy rather than the two smaller conspiracies its proof sustained, but the Court found that the "incompetent" evidence thereby admitted was not prejudicial under the facts of that case. In *Kotteakos v. United States,* 328 U.S. 750, 66 S.Ct. 1239, 90 L.Ed. 1557 (1946), it found otherwise where thirteen parties were jointly tried, and as to all but one, the variance resulted in the jury having before it evidence of additional conspiracies which had no bearing on the individual defendant's liability.

4. What additional restrictions should the double jeopardy prong of the *Berger* standard add to scope of permissible variances? Consider CRIMPROC § 19.2(h): "The possibility of actual prejudice at trial is put aside when courts test a variance against the risk of exposing the defendant to double jeopardy. The only element considered here is the extent to which the variance alters the scope of the charge. Indeed, a challenge based on this ground may be raised by a defendant who failed to object to the variance at trial. The concern of *Berger* apparently was that if defendant were tried on the proof presented in the variance and the jury concluded that such proof did not establish the offense charged, the record would be such that a reprosecution on the theory of the variance would not necessarily be barred. The original pleading would establish the scope of the jeopardy that attached at the first trial and it would not bar a second trial on the theory of the variance if that theory established a different offense. Today, however, the pleading alone would not control the scope of the jeopardy that attached at the original proceeding, as the trial record would be available to show that the defendant had been placed in jeopardy on the theory of the variance. Since the defendant went to trial on the original pleading, a reprosecution on that charge alone would also be barred."

5. *The constructive amendment limitation.* Relying on *Stirone*, Note 5, p. 1006, some jurisdictions characterize as a separate limitation on permissible variances the standard applied in determining the permissible scope of an amendment to the charging instrument. Insofar as the amendment standard looks to notice (see Note 1, p. 1004), it will largely duplicate the first prong of the *Berger* standard. Insofar as the amendment standard also prohibits the allegation of a new offense (see Note 1, p. 1004), it arguably will not go beyond the double jeopardy prong of *Berger*. But where the jurisdiction follows *Bain* in restricting permissible amendments to an indictment, even as *Bain* is limited by *Miller,* the end result may be a limitation upon variances somewhat more stringent than that imposed by *Berger's* double jeopardy prong. Consider, for example, the variance found to be fatal in *Stirone*. Would that variance have been acceptable under the double jeopardy prong of *Berger?*

6. In those jurisdictions that follow a "form/substance" distinction as to allowable amendments and view broadly what constitutes a change of substance (see Note 2, p. 1005), the constructive amendment limitation is likely to restrict permissible variances even further than would *Bain*. Thus, one such jurisdiction holds that the prosecution's proof must adhere to any allegation of the indictment "which is not impertinent or foreign to the cause * * * though a prosecution for the same offense might [have] been supported without such allegation." *State v. Brooks,* 462 S.W.2d 491 (Tenn.1970) (where defendant was charged with robbery "by use of a deadly weapon; to wit * * * a pistol," evidence that defendant used a 22 caliber rifle constituted a "material variance"); *Wilson v. State,* 292 S.W.2d 188 (Tenn.1956) (proof of theft of bronze rollers constitutes a fatal variance from indictment charging theft of brass rollers).

7. *Pleading to avoid variances.* Does the combination of a state requirement of substantial specificity in pleading and a prohibition against significant variance in proof place the prosecutor on the "horns of a dilemma"? Assume, for example, that in a homicide case, the available evidence indicates that death probably was caused by blows inflicted by the defendant, but there is additional evidence suggesting that death may have been caused by the exposure of the deceased to the elements following the assault. Moreover, assume that further evidence may become available at trial that will furnish greater support for exposure as the cause of death. To avoid the possibility of a variance, the prosecutor may prefer that the charge simply state that defendant "caused" the death of the deceased. But what if the state law requires greater specificity in pleading the manner in which death was caused? May the prosecutor utilize alternative allegations as to this element of the offense? Some courts have rejected alternative allegations as failing to fully inform the defendant of the charge against him. See e.g., *Shreveport v. Bryson,* 33 So.2d 60 (La.1947) (rejecting allegation of reckless driving by driving under the influence of "intoxicating liquor or drugs"). But other courts have approved disjunctive pleading—at least where the alternatives are not extensive. See e.g., *Commonwealth v. Schuler,* 43 A.2d 646 (Pa.Super.1945) (driving under influence of "intoxicating liquor or a narcotic or habit forming drug").

   8. *Variance acquittals and reprosecutions.* Assume that an indictment alleges one means of committing an offense against a particular victim, and the court therefore excludes evidence showing that the offense was committed by another means. As a result, the jury acquits the defendant. Does double jeopardy bar reprosecution based upon the second means? Consider, for example, *State v. Brooks,* Note 6 supra, where the indictment charged armed robbery by use of a pistol, and evidence at trial indicated that defendants had used a rifle. Following Tennessee's "strict common law rule" on variance, the trial court excluded that evidence, and directed the jury, upon the prosecution's request, to "acquit the defendants * * * in view of that error in the indictment." The prosecution then filed a new indictment, identical to the former charge except that the weapon used was described as "22 caliber rifle," and defendants were convicted. The Tennessee Supreme Court upheld the conviction against a double jeopardy challenge on the ground that the second prosecution was for a "separate offense" since the "evidence necessary to support the second indictment would [not] have been sufficient to procure a legal conviction upon the first [indictment]." In *State v. Duncan,* 462 S.W.2d 491 (Tenn.1970), a companion case presented by Brooks' codefendant, the United States Supreme Court originally granted certiorari to consider the double jeopardy issue, but then dismissed the writ on the ground that that issue was "so interrelated with [state] rules of criminal pleading * * *, the constitutionality of which is not at issue, as not to warrant the exercise of certiorari jurisdiction." *Duncan v. Tennessee,* 405 U.S. 127, 92 S.Ct. 785, 31 L.Ed.2d 86 (1972). Three justices dissented from the dismissal of the writ. The dissent, per Brennan, J., noted: "Whatever relevance [Tennessee's 'different evidence'] doctrine may have in determining a variance between indictment and proof within a single trial, it certainly does not comport with the double jeopardy standards of the Fifth and Fourteenth Amendments. * * * It may be that the prosecution in this case did not have available to it a ready means * * * of amending the first indictment and thus had no choice but to end the trial and begin again. If so, its remedy lies in changing Tennessee's criminal procedure, not in denying petitioner the constitutional protection to which he is entitled." Consider also *United States v. Dixon,* p. 1033, and *Illinois v. Somerville,* p. 1443.

Chapter 17

THE LOCATION OF THE PROSECUTION[a]

SECTION 1. BASIC CONCEPTS

1. *Distinguishing territorial jurisdiction.* "Venue" sets the particular judicial district in which a criminal charge is to be filed and tried. As discussed below, the traditional standard for determining venue is the crime-committed formula, which places venue in the judicial district in which the charged crime allegedly was committed. "Jurisdiction" refers to a variety of limitations upon judicial authority, including restrictions upon the permissible geographical applicability of penal legislation adopted by the particular legal entity. A primary standard setting that geographical scope is the principle of "territorial jurisdiction," which allows the political entity to apply its criminal law to crimes committed within the territorial limits of the entity. In the federal system, the territorial principle is a basic grounding for applying federal criminal law, but other principles of jurisdiction (e.g., protection of national security) allow the federal government to reach crimes committed outside of its national territory. See CRIMPROC § 1.8 (1986). For the states, the territorial principle tends to be the exclusive determinant of the geographical applicability of a state's penal law.

Since the territorial principle asks whether a crime was committed within the state and venue's crime-committed formula asks whether a crime was committed within a particular judicial district within the state, they raise quite similar issues. The classic jurisdiction cases will have their venue counterparts. Where a defendant in state A mails poisoned candy to a victim in state B, who eats the candy there, but dies in state C, the jurisdictional question is whether jurisdiction to prosecute for murder lies with only one of those states (and if so, which one) or whether more than one state has jurisdiction (and if so, does that include all three). Cf. *People v. Botkin,* 64 P. 286 (Cal.1901). Assuming that the same events occurred in three different counties within the same state, the venue issues similarly would be whether venue lies in only one county (and if so, which one) or whether venue lies in more than one county (and if so, does that include all three).

Though the issues presented in applying the crime-committed formula of venue and the territorial principle of jurisdiction are quite similar, important distinctions exist. First the governing statutory language of a territorial scope provision may not be the same as the language describing permissible multi-venue situations (see Note 3 infra), and that may produce different results. Second, the standards governing proof of jurisdiction may be higher than the standards governing proof of venue (see Note 5 infra). See *People v. McLaughlin,* 606 N.E.2d 1357 (N.Y.1992). Third, whereas venue limitations are subject to voluntary waiver or to forfeiture by failure to raise a timely objection (see Note 6 infra), jurisdic-

---

a. For a more extensive discussion of this topic, see Wayne R. LaFave, Jerold H. Israel, & Nancy S. King, *Criminal Procedure Treatise,* ch. 16 (2d ed. 1999) (available on Westlaw under the database CRIMPROC and hereafter cited as CRIMPROC).

tional limitations are said not to be subject to waiver and can be raised at any time in the proceeding (including collateral attack) where apparent on the face of the record. See CRIMPROC § 16.3(d).

Finally, and most significantly, the interests at stake in determining which state may prosecute are quite different from those at stake in determining where the trial will be held within a state. This is evident from the consequence of a decision that more than one state has jurisdiction. Under the dual sovereignty doctrine (Ch. 26, § 4), the double jeopardy clause does not prohibit prosecution of the defendant for the same criminal activity by each of those states. On the other hand, a determination that multi-venue exists because the crime extended over more than one judicial district still leaves the defendant subject to a single prosecution, although the state now has a choice of location. The different interests at stake also are reflected in the absence of any provision for transfer from a state with jurisdiction to a state without jurisdiction, in contrast to venue provisions, which allow for transfer from a judicial district in which the crime-committed formula applies to one in which it does not apply (see Note 7 infra).

2. *Distinguishing vicinage.* Whereas venue refers to the locality in which charges will be brought and adjudicated, vicinage refers to the locality from which jurors will be drawn. At common law, the defendant was entitled to a jury drawn from the "vicinage," i.e., the "neighborhood" in which the crime was committed. See Drew Kershen, *Vicinage,* 29 Okla.L.Rev. 801 (1976), 30 Okla.L.Rev. 1 (1977). As with venue, to determine vicinage, one had to identify the locale of the crime. Vicinage also required determining the appropriate geographical boundary of the "neighborhood" (or "vicinity") of the crime, which the common law most often made the county. The Sixth Amendment's recognition of a defendant's right to a "jury of the State and district wherein the crime shall have been committed" is often described as a vicinage provision, but it fails to meet the common law requirement that the jury be of the "neighborhood." Indeed, all but two of the original federal districts covered entire states. When Congress decided in the First Judiciary Act to recognize a true right of vicinage, it required for capital offenses that the jurors were to be selected from "the county where the offence was committed." See Kershen, supra.

In contrast to the Sixth Amendment, a substantial minority of the states have constitutional vicinage provisions which are true to the common law in limiting jury selection to a geographical district (usually the county) that would fit within the vicinage concept of "the neighborhood." These provisions are often treated as venue provisions since the jury will be drawn from the judicial district in which the trial takes place. In theory, a jury could be selected from the county of the crime, as required by the concept of vicinage, and the place of trial could be elsewhere, in a much larger district provided by the law of venue. However, selection of jurors from a district other than the district of trial is rarely authorized by statute in only a small group of states, and then only where an unbiased jury cannot be obtained in the district of the crime. See CRIMPROC § 23.2(c) (discussing state "change of venire" statutes).

3. *The crime-committed formula.* The standard formula for setting venue calls for placing the trial in the judicial district in which the crime was committed. This crime-committed formula is imposed as constitutional requirement in the federal system (Article III, § 2, requiring the trial of all crimes "to be held in the State where said crimes shall have been committed") and a handful of states. A substantial number of other states and the federal system (through the Sixth Amendment) impose the same formula indirectly through constitutional vicinage provisions. In both jurisdictions with and without constitutional adoptions of the crime-committed formula, that formula will be set forth as the general venue standard in either the code of criminal procedure or the court rules of criminal procedure. See e.g., Fed.R.Crim.P. 18.

When the framers of the Constitution included the crime-committed formula in both Article III, Section 2, and the Sixth Amendment, they referred in the singular to the "state" and the "district" in which the crime "shall have been committed." This reflected the assumption that a crime ordinarily would be committed in a single place. At a time when travel was difficult and slow, and communications systems were rudimentary, all of the action constituting an offense and all of the immediate harm flowing from that action commonly occurred within a limited geographic area. Even at that time, however, there were certain federal offenses that could occur in more than one place and those two or more places would occasionally be in two different states. At the state level, where the judicial districts typically were counties, offenses committed in more than one judicial district were not quite so unique.

The offenses most likely to be multi-venue offenses were those commonly described as "continuing offenses." These were offenses having basic elements that continued (or, as some would say, "repeated themselves") over a period of time as part of a single crime. A prime illustration is kidnaping, which starts when the victim is taken into custody and continues until the victim is no longer under the control of the kidnappers. If the kidnaped victim was moved from one district to another in the course of the kidnaping, the offense was committed in each of those districts. At common law, larceny was placed in the same category, as the continued possession of the stolen property by the thief was viewed as continuation of the trespassory taking.

A crime could also occur in more than one place when it had two or more distinct parts. Such offenses created a multi-venue potential when they required two separate elements that could occur at separate places. A criminal statute, for example, might define the offense as requiring first the doing of a prohibited act and then the causing of a certain victim response, with the act and response capable of occurring in two different localities. Similarly a statute might require distinct acts by the defendant which could occur in different places. The classic example here was the crime of conspiracy when it required both an agreement and an overt act in furtherance of that agreement.

Finally, multi-venue also was possible where the offense could be committed by a single act that could start in one place and finish in another. Thus, some courts viewed the act of conversion as one that could start with the decision to convert a financial account or instrument held in trust to one's own use and end when that scheme was fulfilled by obtaining funds for defendant's use. See CRIMPROC § 16.1(d).

By the mid-nineteenth century, with significant advances made in transportation and communications, crimes committed in more than one judicial district became much more common. This was particularly true for the federal system, which dealt with many crimes relating to commerce. In 1867, Congress adopted a general provision governing offenses committed in more than one district. That provision, in a slightly modified form, is now contained in Section 3237 of the federal criminal code. It provides:

> Except as otherwise expressly provided by enactment of Congress, any offense against the United States begun in one district and completed in another, or committed in more than one district, may be inquired of and prosecuted in any district in which such offense was begun, continued, or completed.

Most states also have adopted provisions, similar to § 3237, authorizing multi-district venue when the commission of an offense involves more than one district. These provisions typically refer to offenses "committed partly" in more than one district. See e.g., Ala.Code § 15–2–6. Several state provisions refer as well to "acts or effects thereof constituting or requisite to the consummation of the offense" occurring in more than one district. See e.g., Ky.Rev.Stat. § 452.550. Others provide for multi-venue based on "acts," "conduct," and "results" that are elements of the offense occurring in more than one district. See e.g., Iowa Code Ann. § 803.3.

4. *Legislative exceptions.* Legislatures have adopted statutory exceptions to the crime-committed formula for various situations that prove troubling in applying that formula. Thus state venue statutes include provisions authorizing venue in: (1) either county where the crime was committed within a specified distance (e.g., 500 yards) of the boundary between two counties; (2) any county through which a vehicle passed where the crime was committed in a moving vehicle (with some states conditioning the application of this provision on a prosecution showing that the exact location cannot "readily be determined"); (3) any district selected by the attorney general where "it is impossible to determine in which county the crime occurred"; (4) in the case of child abuse, either in the county where the child was abused or the county in which the child was found; and (5) where state law requires joinder of offenses committed in the same criminal episode or transaction (see Note 5, p. 1057), in any county in which the crime-committed formula establishes venue for any one of those offenses. See CRIMPROC § 16.1(e),(f).

Where a state has either a constitutional venue guarantee of a trial in the county in which the crime was committed, or a constitutional guarantee of a jury of the vicinage, special venue legislation can pose constitutional difficulties. Thus, courts have divided on the constitutionality of provisions allowing venue in either county where the crime was committed near the border between two counties. See e.g., *State v. Chalikes*, 170 N.E. 653 (Ohio 1930) (unconstitutional where locus of crime readily determined). Compare *State v. Lehman*, 279 P. 283 (Or.1929) (constitutional on theory that legislature has simply created judicial districts with slightly expanded and overlapping boundaries for such crimes, so venue is still in the district in which the crime was committed). Of course, a majority of states do not have such constitutional provisions, leaving the legislature free to create such exceptions to the crime-committed formula as it deems appropriate. Although the jury will be selected from the special venue district, such exceptions have been held not to violate the Sixth Amendment guarantee of a jury from the district "wherein the crime shall have been committed." Courts reason either that (1) this guarantee has not yet been held fundamental and applicable to the states under Fourteenth Amendment due process, or (2) the Sixth Amendment "district" requirement demands only (i) a trial somewhere within the state, in light of the acceptance of districts covering the complete state in the federal system, and (ii) that the special venue district be previously designated by legislation. See *Caudill v. Scott*, 857 F.2d 344 (6th Cir.1988); *Davis v. Warden*, 867 F.2d 1003 (7th Cir.1989). But see *People v. Tamble*, 5 Cal.App.4th 815, 7 Cal.Rptr.2d 446 (1992) (Sixth Amendment guarantee applies to the states and requires jury selected from the county in which the offense was committed).

5. *Proof of venue.* Only a handful of jurisdictions treat venue in much the same manner as other procedural prerequisites for prosecution (e.g., a valid preliminary hearing bindover, or a grand jury charge). In those jurisdictions, the defendant must put the venue prerequisite in issue by a pretrial motion to dismiss, with the court then making a determination that venue does or does not exist. In the federal system and the vast majority of the states, venue is not simply a prerequisite that the defendant may choose to challenge pretrial; it is viewed as part of the case that the prosecution must prove at trial. These jurisdictions offer a variety of explanations for requiring that venue be established at trial. Venue is

described as: "a jurisdictional fact put in issue by a plea of not guilty"; a "material allegation of the indictment" which must be proven along with other indictment allegations; an "element of the crime" to be treated no differently than the substantive elements of the offense; and an "issuable fact" most appropriately addressed in the course of the proof of the offense and presented to the finder of fact.

As might be expected from the above explanations, all but a few of these jurisdictions treat venue as a factual question to be decided by the jury in a jury trial. The court has the responsibility for determining whether, as a matter of law, the events alleged to have occurred in a particular place could be sufficient to establish that the crime was committed at least in part in that district (or whether venue could otherwise be justified under special legislation). The jury then decides the underlying factual issue, such as whether a particular act did occur in the district, or whether that act had the impact or other quality that the court deems necessary to characterize it as involving the commission of the crime.

Though most jurisdictions treat proof of venue as a jury issue, they ordinarily do not view venue as one of those matters that must invariably be submitted to the jury. Courts frequently state that a charge on venue is required only "when trial testimony puts venue in issue." Thus, a jury charge on venue is not required "where the entirety of the defendant's illegal activity is alleged to have taken place within the trial * * * [district] and no trial evidence is proffered that the illegal act was committed in some other place or that the place alleged is not within the * * * [district]." *United States v. Miller,* 111 F.3d 747 (10th Cir.1997). Courts have also concluded that the failure to charge on venue should not constitute error, even when the evidence would support such a charge, where the defendant failed to request a charge on venue.

Jurisdictions requiring prosecution proof of venue at trial are divided as to the level of persuasiveness of the prosecution's proof of venue. The federal courts and a substantial number of state courts hold that the facts supporting venue only need be established by a preponderance of the evidence. Other states require that venue be proved beyond a reasonable doubt. Courts explaining this higher proof requirement point to state law that treats venue as an "element of the offense," the characterization of venue as a "material allegation" of the charging instrument, and the status of venue as a jurisdictional prerequisite and therefore requiring the same standard proof as traditionally applied to proof of the territorial jurisdiction of the state. See CRIMPROC § 16.1(g).

6. *Waiver.* A defendant can waive his right to proper venue by an express statement of relinquishment (e.g., a statement consenting to be tried in a judicial district even though the crime is not alleged to have been committed there, or a request for a transfer to another district from the district of proper venue). In addition, in the federal system and a substantial majority of the states, in contrast to such trial guarantees as trial by jury and representation by counsel, venue can be "waived"—or more accurately, "forfeited"—by a defendant's "silence," in the form of a failure to make a timely objection. Courts have offered differing explanations as to why "waiver" of venue is thus "more relaxed" than the waiver of rights that can be lost only by a record affirmatively establishing "an intentional relinquishment or abandonment of a known right or privilege." One explanation is that venue is not a "fundamental" right, and therefore does not require the same degree of protection as some other guarantees. Other courts, however, note that the timely-objection requirement exists notwithstanding that "the constitutional underpinning and the importance of venue dictate that waiver of objections of venue should not be readily inferred." They argue that, since venue is designed to protect the defendant from the "unfairness and hardship" that may, but will not necessarily, attend trial in a district other than that of the crime, it is appropriate to place on the defendant the burden of objection. See CRIMPROC § 16.1(h).

7. *Change of venue.* The federal system and every state has a statute or court rule (or both) authorizing a trial court to order that a case be moved from its original district of prosecution, proper under the jurisdiction's venue laws, to a district that otherwise would not be proper under those laws. In some states, additional authorization is provided through the recognition of an inherent judicial authority to order a change of venue, which supplements the statutory authorization. Together, these sources establish a quite varied law governing venue changes. Initially, the jurisdictions divide as to the grounds that justify ordering a venue change. Some limit changes to ensuring that the ensuing trial will be fair, while others add to that ground, allowing changes in the interest of witness convenience or sound judicial administration. Jurisdictions also vary as to whether changes are allowed only on motion of the defendant, on the motion of the prosecution as well as the defendant, and on the courts own initiative over the objection of one or both parties.

Provisions authorizing venue changes to ensure a fair trial are found in every jurisdiction. Those changes are discussed in Ch. 24, § 2. Far less common are provisions authorizing a change to promote convenience. Federal Rule 21(b) and a substantial minority of states authorize such changes on motion of the defendant. Only a handful of states authorize such changes on motion of the prosecution. Provisions authorizing convenience transfers typically state that the court "may transfer" on convenience grounds, and courts recognize that such a transfer lies in the discretion of the trial court, subject only to the prohibition against arbitrary or capricious exercise of that discretion. However, federal district courts have been advised with respect to Federal Rule 21(b) that: "Nothing in Rule 21(b) or in the cases interpreting it place on the defendant seeking a change of venue the burden of establishing 'truly compelling circumstances' for such a change. It is enough if, all relevant things considered, the case would be better off transferred to another district." *Matter of Balsimo,* 68 F.3d 185 (7th Cir.1995).

What factors are relevant in determining whether another district would be a more convenient forum and a transfer to that district would be in the interest of justice? In the leading Supreme Court ruling on a Federal Rule 21(b), *Platt v. Minnesota Mining and Manufacturing Co.,* 376 U.S. 240, 84 S.Ct. 769, 11 L.Ed.2d 674 (1964), the Court cited a ten factor list that had been considered by the district court, and while the Court's ruling related to another point, it did add that both the parties and the appellate court had agreed that the consideration of those ten factors was "appropriate." Those ten factors, frequently relied upon in subsequent federal lower court decisions, are: "(1) location of the corporate defendant [which was the apparent counterpart of the location of one's residence for an individual]; (2) location of possible witnesses; (3) location of events likely to be in issue; (4) location of documents and records likely to be involved; (5) disruption of defendant's business unless the case is transferred; (6) expense to the parties; (7) location of counsel; (8) relative accessibility of place of trial; (9) docket condition of each district or division involved; and (10) any other special elements which might affect the transfer."

SECTION 2. APPLYING THE CRIME—
COMMITTED FORMULA

UNITED STATES v. RODRIGUEZ–MORENO
526 U.S. 275, 119 S.Ct. 1239, 143 L.Ed.2d 388 (1999).

Justice THOMAS delivered the opinion of the Court.

This case presents the question whether venue in a prosecution for using or carrying a firearm "during and in relation to any crime of violence, in violation of

18 U.S.C. § 924(c)(1)", is proper in any district where the crime of violence was committed, even if the firearm was used or carried only in a single district. * * * During a drug transaction that took place in Houston, Texas, a New York drug dealer stole 30 kilograms of a Texas drug distributor's cocaine. The distributor hired respondent, Jacinto Rodriguez–Moreno, and others to find the dealer and to hold captive the middleman in the transaction, Ephrain Avendano, during the search. In pursuit of the dealer, the distributor and his henchmen drove from Texas to New Jersey with Avendano in tow. * * * They [then] moved to a house in New York and then to a house in Maryland, taking Avendano with them. Shortly after respondent and the others arrived at the Maryland house, the owner of the home passed around a .357 magnum revolver and respondent took possession of the pistol. As it became clear that efforts to find the New York drug dealer would not bear fruit, respondent told his employer that he thought they should kill the middleman and end their search for the dealer. He put the gun to the back of Avendano's neck but, at the urging of his cohorts, did not shoot. Avendano eventually escaped through the back door and ran to a neighboring house. The neighbors called the Maryland police, who arrested respondent along with the rest of the kidnappers. The police also seized the .357 magnum, on which they later found respondent's fingerprint.

Rodriguez–Moreno and his codefendants were tried jointly in the United States District Court for the District of New Jersey. Respondent was charged with, inter alia, conspiring to kidnap Avendano, kidnaping Avendano, and using and carrying a firearm in relation to the kidnaping of Avendano, in violation of 18 U.S.C. § 924(c)(1). At the conclusion of the Government's case, respondent moved to dismiss the § 924(c)(1) count for lack of venue. He argued that venue was proper only in Maryland, the only place where the Government had proved he had actually used a gun. The District Court denied the motion, and the jury found respondent guilty on the kidnaping counts and on the § 924(c)(1) charge as well. He was sentenced to 87 months' imprisonment on the kidnaping charges, and was given a mandatory consecutive term of 60 months' imprisonment for committing the § 924(c)(1) offense.

On a 2–to–1 vote, the Court of Appeals for the Third Circuit reversed respondent's § 924(c)(1) conviction. A majority of the Third Circuit panel applied what it called the "verb test" to § 924(c)(1), and determined that a violation of the statute is committed only in the district where a defendant "uses" or "carries" a firearm. Id., at 849. Accordingly, it concluded that venue for the § 924(c)(1) count was improper in New Jersey even though venue was proper there for the kidnaping of Avendano. * * *

As we confirmed just last Term, the " 'locus delicti [of the charged offense] must be determined from the nature of the crime alleged and the location of the act or acts constituting it.' " *United States v. Cabrales* [Note 1, p. 1023], quoting *United States v. Anderson,* 328 U.S. 699, 66 S.Ct. 1213, 90 L.Ed. 1529 (1946). * * * In performing this inquiry, a court must initially identify the conduct constituting the offense (the nature of the crime) and then discern the location of the commission of the criminal acts.[2] * * * At the time respondent committed the offense and was tried, 18 U.S.C. § 924(c)(1) provided:

---

2. The Government argues that venue also may permissibly be based upon the effects of a defendant's conduct in a district other than the one in which the defendant performs the acts constituting the offense. Brief 16–17. Because this case only concerns the *locus delicti,* we

"Whoever, during and in relation to any crime of violence ... for which he may be prosecuted in a court of the United States, uses or carries a firearm, shall, in addition to the punishment provided for such crime of violence ... be sentenced to imprisonment for five years...."

The Third Circuit, as explained above, looked to the verbs of the statute to determine the nature of the substantive offense. But we have never before held, and decline to do so here, that verbs are the sole consideration in identifying the conduct that constitutes an offense. While the "verb test" certainly has value as an interpretative tool, it cannot be applied rigidly, to the exclusion of other relevant statutory language. The test unduly limits the inquiry into the nature of the offense and thereby creates a danger that certain conduct prohibited by statute will be missed.

In our view, the Third Circuit overlooked an essential conduct element of the § 924(c)(1) offense. Section 924(c)(1) prohibits using or carrying a firearm "during and in relation to any crime of violence ... for which [a defendant] may be prosecuted in a court of the United States." That the crime of violence element of the statute is embedded in a prepositional phrase and not expressed in verbs does not dissuade us from concluding that a defendant's violent acts are essential conduct elements. To prove the charged § 924(c)(1) violation in this case, the Government was required to show that respondent used a firearm, that he committed all the acts necessary to be subject to punishment for kidnaping (a crime of violence) in a court of the United States, and that he used the gun "during and in relation to" the kidnaping of Avendano. In sum, we interpret § 924(c)(1) to contain two distinct conduct elements—as is relevant to this case, the "using and carrying" of a gun and the commission of a kidnaping.[4]

Respondent, however, argues that for venue purposes "the New Jersey kidnaping is completely irrelevant to the firearm crime, because respondent did not use or carry a gun during the New Jersey crime." In the words of one amicus, § 924(c)(1) is a "point-in-time" offense that only is committed in the place where the kidnaping and the use of a gun coincide. Brief for National Association of Criminal Defense Lawyers as Amicus Curiae 11. We disagree. Several Circuits have determined that kidnaping, as defined by 18 U.S.C. § 1201 (1994 ed. and Supp. III), is a unitary crime, and we agree with their conclusion. A kidnaping, once begun, does not end until the victim is free. It does not make sense, then, to speak of it in discrete geographic fragments. Section 924(c)(1) criminalized a defendant's use of a firearm "during and in relation to" a crime of violence; in doing so, Congress proscribed both the use of the firearm and the commission of acts that constitute a violent crime. It does not matter that respondent used the .357 magnum revolver, as the Government concedes, only in Maryland because he did so "during and in relation to" a kidnaping that was begun in Texas and continued in New York, New Jersey, and Maryland. In our view, § 924(c)(1) does not define a "point-in-time" offense when a firearm is used during and in relation to a continuing crime of violence. * * *

express no opinion as to whether the Government's assertion is correct.

4. By the way of comparison, last Term in *United States v. Cabrales* [Note 1, p. 1023], we considered whether venue for money laundering, in violation of 18 U.S.C. §§ 1956(a)(1)(B)(ii) and 1957, was proper in Missouri, where the laundered proceeds were unlawfully generated, or rather, only in Florida, where the prohibited laundering transactions occurred. As we interpreted the launder-

ing statutes at issue, they did not proscribe "the anterior criminal conduct that yielded the funds allegedly laundered." *Cabrales*. The existence of criminally generated proceeds was a circumstance element of the offense but the proscribed conduct—defendant's money laundering activity—occurred " 'after the fact' of an offense begun and completed by others." Here, by contrast, given the "during and in relation to" language, the underlying crime of violence is a critical part of the § 924(c)(1) offense.

As we said in *United States v. Lombardo* [Note 2(a), p. 1023], "where a crime consists of distinct parts which have different localities the whole may be tried where any part can be proved to have been done." * * * The kidnaping, to which the § 924(c)(1) offense is attached, was committed in all of the places that any part of it took place, and venue for the kidnaping charge against respondent was appropriate in any of them. (Congress has provided that continuing offenses can be tried "in any district in which such offense was begun, continued, or completed," 18 U.S.C. § 3237(a).) Where venue is appropriate for the underlying crime of violence, so too it is for the § 924(c)(1) offense. As the kidnaping was properly tried in New Jersey, the § 924(c)(1) offense could be tried there as well.

Justice SCALIA, with whom Justice STEVENS joins, dissenting.

* * * [Section 924(c)] prohibits the act of using or carrying a firearm "during" (and in relation to) a predicate offense. The provisions of the United States Code defining the particular predicate offenses already punish all of the defendant's alleged criminal conduct except his use or carriage of a gun; § 924(c)(1) itself criminalizes and punishes such use or carriage "during" the predicate crime, because that makes the crime more dangerous. This is a simple concept, and it is embodied in a straightforward text. To answer the question before us we need only ask where the defendant's alleged act of using a firearm during (and in relation to) a kidnaping occurred. Since it occurred only in Maryland, venue will lie only there. * * *

[T]he crime before us does *not* consist of "distinct" parts that can occur in different localities. Its two parts are bound inseparably together by the word "during." Where the gun is being used, the predicate act must be occurring as well, and vice versa. The Court quite simply reads this requirement out of the statute—as though there were no difference between a statute making it a crime to steal a cookie and eat it (which could be prosecuted either in New Jersey, where the cookie was stolen, or in Maryland, where it was eaten) and a statute making it a crime to eat a cookie while robbing a bakery (which could be prosecuted only where the ingestive theft occurred). * * *

The Court believes its holding is justified by the continuing nature of the kidnaping predicate offense, which invokes the statute providing that "any offense * * * begun in one district and completed in another, or committed in more than one district, may be * * * prosecuted in any district in which such offense was begun, continued, or completed." To disallow the New Jersey prosecution here, the Court suggests, is to convert § 924(c)(1) from a continuing offense to a "point-in-time" offense. That is simply not so. I in no way contend that the kidnaping, or, for that matter, the use of the gun, can occur only at one point in time. Each can extend over a protracted period, and in many places. But § 924(c)(1) is violated only so long as, and where, both continuing acts are being committed simultaneously. That is what the word "during" means. Thus, if the defendant here had used or carried the gun throughout the kidnaping, in Texas, New Jersey, New York, and Maryland, he could have been prosecuted in any of those States. As it was, however, he used a gun during a kidnaping only in Maryland.

The short of the matter is that this defendant, who has a constitutional right to be tried in the State and district where his alleged crime was "committed," U.S. Const., Art. III, § 2, cl. 3; Amdt. 6, has been prosecuted for using a gun during a kidnaping in a State and district where all agree he did not use a gun during a kidnaping. If to state this case is not to decide it, the law has departed further from the meaning of language than is appropriate for a government that is supposed to rule (and to be restrained) through the written word.

Notes and Questions

1. Supreme Court precedent. What produced the division in *Rodriguez-Moreno* in contrast to the unanimity in UNITED STATES v. CABRALES, 524 U.S. 1, 118 S.Ct. 1772, 141 L.Ed.2d 1 (1998), another recent case applying the "general guide" of *United States v. Anderson*, that venue "[should] be determined from the nature of the crime alleged and the location of the acts or acts constituting it"? *Cabrales* involved a prosecution under a money laundering statute making it a crime to "knowing[ly] * * * conduct * * * a financial transaction which * * * involves proceedings of specified unlawful activity * * * knowing that the transaction is designed * * * to avoid a transaction reporting requirement." The prosecution was brought in Missouri, where drug trafficking had produced the criminally derived funds, but the alleged financial transactions were deposits and withdrawals made in Florida (and it was not alleged that the defendant had transported the funds from Missouri to Florida). The government argued that venue was proper in the district of the underlying criminality that produced the funds (here Missouri) because (1) that underlying crime was an essential element of the money laundering offense, (2) the laundering activity impacts the underlying criminal activity by making it profitable and impeding its detection, and (3) the district of the underlying offense is a most appropriate district for trial because of the need to prove that the funds were criminally derived and the "interests of the community victimized by [the] drug dealers." The Supreme Court in a unanimous ruling found these arguments unpersuasive.

Justice GINSBURG's opinion for the Court reasoned that the money laundering offense was "defined in statutory proscriptions * * * that interdict only the financial transactions (acts located entirely in Florida), not the anterior criminal conduct that yielded the funds allegedly laundered." To be criminally liable, "the money launderer must know she is dealing with funds [criminally] derived," but "it is immaterial whether * * * [she] knew where the first crime was committed." Admittedly, "whenever a defendant acts 'after the fact' to conceal a crime, * * * it might be said that the first crime is an essential element of the second; * * * and that the second facilitated the first," but that does not establish the venue for the second in the district of the first. The government had available to it the potential for trial in the district of drug trafficking if it charged the defendant with a conspiracy with the drug dealers and treated the money laundering as an overt act. It could not use charges of money laundering, which "described activity of the [defendant] alone, untied to others," as a substitute for a conspiracy charge.

2. Although the Court in *Rodriguez-Moreno* rejects the lower court's sole reliance upon a "verb test," does that test have solid support as the key factor in determining venue under the Supreme Court precedent described below?[a]

(a) In UNITED STATES v. LOMBARDO, 241 U.S. 73, 36 S.Ct. 508, 60 L.Ed. 897 (1916), the defendant, an operator of a house of prostitution in Seattle, was charged in the Western District of Washington with failing to comply with a federal statute requiring any person who harbored an alien for the purpose of prostitution to report that alien's identity to the Commissioner General of Immigration. The district court sustained a demurrer to the indictment on the ground that the offense was not committed in Seattle, but in the District of Columbia, where the offices of the Commissioner General were located. Affirming

---

a. Consider in this regard, John Dobie, *Venue in Criminal Cases in the United States District Court*, 12 Va.L.Rev. 287 (1926): "Crimes are defined, hidden away amid pompous verbosity, in terms of a single verb," which "usually contains the key to the solution to the question: In what district was the crime committed." For many years, Judge Dobie's article was one of the most frequently cited commentaries on federal venue.

that ruling, the Supreme Court initially quoted with approval from the district court's analysis of the critical statutory verb:

> "The word 'file' was not defined by Congress. No definition having been given, the etymology of the word must be considered and ordinary meaning applied. The word 'file' is derived from the Latin word 'filum,' and relates to the ancient practice of placing papers on a thread or wire for safekeeping and ready reference. Filing, it must be observed, is not complete until the document is delivered and received. 'Shall file' means to deliver to the office and not send through the United States mails. A paper is filed when it is delivered to the proper official and by him received and filed."

The Court then rejected the government's response that this was an unduly narrow reading of the term "shall file." The government contended that a filing could begin in the place where the document was sent and therefore the defendant's failure to send the document from Seattle marked the beginning of the crime. The Court's answer to this contention was that it "was constrained by the meanings of the words of the statute." The requirement of a filing demanded delivery of a specific place; it had never been deemed satisfied by "a deposit in a post office at some distant place." The Court also offered several administrative justifications for its ruling. Those included difficulties relating to proof of mailing (or the lack thereof) and to setting "the instant of time" for compliance if a mailing was to be taken as compliance.

(b) In TRAVIS v. UNITED STATES, 364 U.S. 631, 81 S.Ct. 358, 5 L.Ed.2d 340 (1961), a union official in Colorado was charged under a statute applicable to any person who, "in a matter within the jurisdiction of any department or agency of the United States," knowingly "makes" any false statement. The false statements at issue were non-Communist affidavits executed and mailed in Colorado to the offices of the N.L.R.B. in Washington, D.C. The defendant contended, and the Court majority agreed, that the government had erred in bringing the prosecution in Colorado as the offense only could be committed in the District of Columbia. The majority stressed that the offense required that the false statement be "within the jurisdiction" of the N.L.R.B. Section 9(h) of the National Labor Relations Act did not require union officers to file non-Communist affidavits, but provided for their voluntary filing as a prerequisite to invoking the Board's authority in the investigation and issuance of complaints against employers. Accordingly, "filing [of the affidavit] must be completed before there is a 'matter within the jurisdiction' of the Board." *Lombardo* had held that "when a place is explicitly designated where a paper must be filed, a prosecution for failure to file lies only at that place." The same was true for an actual filing. Accordingly, the charge could be brought only in the District of Columbia, where the affidavit was filed.

The *Travis* majority acknowledged that "Colorado, the residence of the [defendant] might offer conveniences and advantages to him which a trial in the District of Columbia might lack." It did not disagree with the dissent's contention that "the witnesses and relevant circumstances surrounding the contested issues in such cases more probably will be found in the district of the execution of the affidavit than at the place of filing."[b] Its response was that the "constitutional requirement is as to the locality of the offense and not the personal presence of

---

b. The dissent did not rely on this factor alone. It noted that the prohibited act was the "making" of a false statement to the government, which would "begin at the place where the false affidavit is actually made, sworn, and subscribed." At this point, the process that constituted the crime was started and it was in bringing the statement within the jurisdiction of the N.L.R.B. that the crime was completed. This analysis, the dissent argued, was supported by the *Anderson* directive to examine the "nature of the crime." The majority described the *Anderson* directive as applicable only "where Congress is not explicit."

the offender," and here the nature of the offense set that locality in only one place. To argue, as the government did, that the offense started in Colorado because the defendant there "irrevocably set in motion and placed beyond his control the train of events which would normally result (and here did result) in the consummation of the offense" was to ignore that Congress here "has so carefully indicated the locus of the crime." That was done in the "explicit provision of 9(h)," which combined with the "agency jurisdiction" requirement of the false statement statute to render the crime incapable of commission until the affidavit was delivered to the N.L.R.B.

(c) In UNITED STATES v. JOHNSON, 323 U.S. 273, 65 S.Ct. 249, 89 L.Ed. 236 (1944), the Court split 5–4 over appropriate venue for a charge of "using" the mails for the purpose of "sending" dentures into another state in violation of the Federal Denture Act. The government argued that venue was proper in the receiving state (Delaware), while the defendant claimed that he could only be tried in his home district of Chicago, from which the dentures had been mailed. The majority found that the crucial element of the offense was the act of "sending," and therefore venue could only lie in Chicago since the offense was completed there. Although the majority recognized Congress' right to specifically provide for broader venue, it considered its interpretation of the statute "more consistent" with the "underlying spirit of the constitutional concern for trial in the vicinage." Where legislative history leaves the issue open, a court should, it noted, prefer an interpretation that avoids (1) placing upon the defendant "the serious hardship of defending prosecutions in places remote from home (including the accused's difficulties, financial and otherwise * * * of marshaling his witness)" and (2) creating the "appearance of abuses * * * in the selection of what may be deemed a tribunal favorable to the prosecution." The four dissenting judges sharply rejected this analysis: "The Court misapprehends the purpose of the Constitutional provisions. We understand them to assure a trial in the place where the crime is committed and not to be concerned with the domicile of the criminal nor with his familiarity with the environment of the place of trial."

(d) In JOHNSTON v. UNITED STATES, 351 U.S. 215, 76 S.Ct. 739, 100 L.Ed. 1097 (1956), the Court split 6–3 in holding that persons charged with failure to report to hospitals for civilian work, as ordered by their local draft boards, could be prosecuted only in the district where the hospitals were located rather than their home districts in which their boards were located. The majority opinion by Justice Reed (who had dissented in *Johnson*) noted that the "requirement of venue states the public policy that fixes the situs of the trial in the vicinage of the crime rather than the residence of the accused," and the crime here was a failure to perform a duty at the location of the hospital. The dissent (written by Justice Douglas, who also wrote the majority opinion in *Travis*) argued that it would be preferable to "read the statute with an eye to history and try the offenders at home where our forefathers thought that normally men would receive their fairest trial." The basic element of the crime, the dissent contended, was the failure to obey the draft board's order, which occurred when the registrant "refus[ed] to budge from his home town."

3. *Policy.* Commentators contend that in identifying the "nature of the offense," there commonly is sufficient flexibility to take account of Justice Frankfurter's admonition that "questions of venue in criminal cases * * * raise deep issues of public policy in the light of which legislation must be construed." *United States v. Johnson*, Note 2(c) supra. In such instances, it is noted, a court should resolve ambiguities in favor of an interpretation of the offense that will best serve the underlying policy objective of venue requirements—"insur[ing] a fair trial for persons accused of crime." Drew Kershen, *Vicinage*, 29 Okla.L.Rev.

801 (1976). However, at least three conflicting guidelines have been advanced as what construction will best serve that policy objective.

(1) One position maintains that liberal provisions for change of venue provide adequate protection against forcing defendants to defend in an inconvenient forum. Accordingly, venue provisions should be broadly construed so that a conviction following a fair trial will not be reversed simply on the ground that the prosecutor selected the wrong district.

(2) Another viewpoint would place greater emphasis on the defendant's home district. Supporters of this position acknowledge that the draftsmen of Article III, § 2 chose the place of the commission of the crime, rather than the place of the accused's residence, as the appropriate test for venue, but they note that that test was selected primarily because it "accorded with the concept of jurisdiction held * * * in the late eighteenth century," and everyone assumed "that the place of commission of the crime and the place of residence would almost always be identical." Drew Kershen, *Vicinage,* 30 Okla.L.Rev. 1, 22 (1977). Under this guideline, where the structure of the offense reasonably permits the court to conclude that it was committed in part in the home district, that interpretation should be adopted.

(3) A third view would stress limiting the prosecutor's discretion to choose where the prosecution will be initiated. Under this view, where possible, the court should treat an offense as non-continuing, thereby permitting venue only in a single district. Supporters of this policy initially argue that it serves a basic objective of the constitutional draftsmen. They contend that the crime-committed formula was seen as providing a venue that would usually coincide with the common law right to a trial by a jury selected from the vicinage, and that the vicinage concept, in turn, assumed that there would be a single district from which it would be most appropriate to draw the jury. Accordingly, the crime-committed formula, as set forth in both Article III, § 2 and the jury clause of the Sixth Amendment, should be seen as favoring a single district—that which serves the goals of the vicinage concept.[c] The supporters further argue that applying the crime-committed formula so as to favor designation of a single district restricts prosecutorial discretion and the potential misuse of that discretion. Where venue is held to be proper in several districts, the prosecutor controls the choice of district (absent a rarely granted defense motion for change of venue), and that choice, it is argued, may be based on inappropriate considerations—such as where the prosecution feels it will obtain the most favorable jury or where it can impose the greatest logistical difficulties for the defense in presenting its case.

To what extent do *Rodriguez-Moreno, Cabrales,* and the cases cited in Note 2 reflect the application of such guidelines? The Court has frequently discussed the "home district" consideration (with the justices often differing on the weight it should be given). See e.g., *Johnson,* and *Johnston.* It occasionally had taken note of the position that would limit the prosecutor's discretion to chose. See e.g.,

c. See Kershen, supra, at 158, stating that, where the focus is on the right to "jurors of the vicinage," the designation of the "place at which a particular crime was committed" requires answering the following questions, with those answers ordinarily pointing to a single district: "Who are the citizens possessing, or likely to possess, the greatest amount of relevant information about the characters of the victim, defendant, witnesses, the incident itself, and the setting in which the incident occurred, that will insure the greatest likelihood that the truth about the crime will be found? Who are the citizens possessing a significant substantive law concern that their sense of justice be expressed in the interpretation of the law which will emerge in a general verdict? Who are the citizens possessing a significant sovereign concern as to whether the jury will intervene between the accused and the prosecution through a verdict of acquittal"?

Travis ("Congress should not be so freely construed to give the Government the choice of a 'tribunal favorable to it'," quoting *Johnson*).

4. *Use of the mails.* Following *Johnson*, Note 2(c) supra, Congress added a second paragraph to § 3237(a) providing that: "Any offense involving the use of the mails, or transportation in interstate or foreign commerce, is a continuing offense and, except as otherwise expressly provided by enactment of Congress, may be inquired of and prosecuted in any district from, through, or into which such commerce or mail matter moves." Is there any justification for allowing venue on a charge such as mail fraud to be brought in any district through which the mail moved as opposed to limiting such venue to the "sending" and "receiving" districts, as considered in *Johnson*? Consider *United States v. Peraino*, 645 F.2d 548 (6th Cir.1981) (venue in federal obscenity prosecutions lies in any district from, through, or into which the obscene material moves). While § 3237(a)'s second paragraph does not apply simply because the mails or interstate transportation were used in committing the crime, the concept of an offense "involving" interstate transportation has been held to encompass offenses in which interstate transportation is a "circumstance" inherent in the offense, though not an element of the offense. See *United States v. Solan*, 792 F.Supp. 99 (M.D.Fla.1992) (paragraph two applies to the offense of delivery of firearms to a contract carrier for the purpose of interstate shipment).

5. *Conspiracy venue.* Perhaps the most extensive choice of venue arises in conspiracy cases. The prosecutor there may initiate prosecution on the conspiracy charge in any district in which any overt act in furtherance of the conspiracy was committed by any of the conspirators, even though the defendant himself was not present in that district. Courts have advanced two theories in support of this position, each resting on the proposition that conspiracy offense is "committed" in the place of the overt act (as well as the place of the agreement). Where the conspiracy offense requires no more than the agreement itself, they note that each overt act constitutes a "renewal" or "continuation" of the agreement. Where the offense requires both an agreement and an overt act, each overt act is viewed as an element of the offense. See Abrams, Note 1 supra.

As to the possibility of expanding venue for the substantive offenses committed in furtherance of a conspiracy, consider the theory advanced by the government, but rejected by the court, in *United States v. Walden*, 464 F.2d 1015 (4th Cir.1972). There a federal prosecution was brought in South Carolina charging the ten defendants with a conspiracy to rob federally insured banks and with the substantive counts of violating 18 U.S.C. § 2113 (entering a bank with intent to rob) as to the various banks which were located in states other than South Carolina. The government argued that the conspiratorial acts (which did occur in South Carolina) made each of the co-conspirators an accomplice to the robberies, and the substantive counts therefore could be brought in South Carolina under the doctrine that "an accomplice may be tried where his accessorial act took place." Rejecting that contention, the Court of Appeals noted: "If we accept the [government's] argument, we would have, with respect to these substantive counts, the conceptual difficulty of a bank robbery or unlawful entry being perpetrated entirely by accessories in South Carolina without the assistance of principals at place of entry. * * * [W]here all persons charged as accessories for purposes of obtaining venue at the place where the crime was planned (South Carolina) are physically present and actively engaged in unlawful entry of a bank in another jurisdiction, we think it would distort both the substantive criminal law and the law of criminal venue to allow prosecution for the substantive offense of unlawful entry at the place (South Carolina) where the crime was planned."

Chapter 18

THE SCOPE OF THE PROSECUTION: JOINDER AND SEVERANCE OF OFFENSES AND DEFENDANTS

SECTION 1. JOINDER AND SEVERANCE OF OFFENSES

Fed.R.Crim.P. 8(a) allows joinder for trial of offenses "of the same or similar character," as do statutes or rules in many states. These provisions allow joinder even though the several offenses were not part of a single scheme or plan and were committed at different times and places.

Commentators have often criticized similar offense joinder. Because the offenses are distinct, each requiring its own evidence and witnesses, it is argued that there is no appreciable saving of time by joinder. Moreover, the joinder may confuse the jury and may result in the jury regarding one offense as corroborative of the other when, in fact, no such corroboration exists. But a defendant may sometimes view joinder as preferable to being called upon to defend himself in a number of trials. Moreover, similar offense joinder may facilitate concurrent sentencing, to the defendant's advantage.

Fed.R.Crim.P. 8(a) also allows joinder of offenses "based on the same act or transaction or on two or more acts or transactions connected together or constituting parts of a common scheme or plan," as do many state provisions. In these jurisdictions, joinder is clearly allowed for offenses arising out of the same conduct (as where a defendant causes more than one death by reckless operation of a vehicle), offenses within a close time-space sequence (as with the killing of several people with successive shots from a gun, or burglary and the crime committed within), and offenses which are part of a single scheme, even if considerable time passes between them.

CROSS v. UNITED STATES
335 F.2d 987 (D.C.Cir.1964).

BAZELON, Chief Judge.

In a joint indictment, appellants were charged in Count I with robbery of a church rectory on February 23, 1962, and in Count II with robbery of a tourist home on May 2, 1962. Both appellants filed pretrial motions for severance of the counts. The motions were denied. The jury returned verdicts of guilty on Count I and not guilty on Count II. Appellants' chief contention on these appeals is that the District Court erred in refusing to sever the counts for trial. * * *

Prejudice may develop when an accused wishes to testify on one but not the other of two joined offenses which are clearly distinct in time, place and evidence. His decision whether to testify will reflect a balancing of several factors with respect to each count: the evidence against him, the availability of defense evidence other than his testimony, the plausibility and substantiality of his testimony, the possible effects of demeanor, impeachment, and cross-examination.[3] But if the two charges are joined for trial, it is not possible for him to weigh these factors separately as to each count.[4] If he testifies on one count, he runs the risk that any adverse effects will influence the jury's consideration of the other count. Thus he bears the risk on both counts, although he may benefit on only one. Moreover, a defendant's silence on one count would be damaging in the face of his express denial of the other. Thus he may be coerced into testifying on the count upon which he wished to remain silent.[5] It is not necessary to decide whether this invades his constitutional right to remain silent, since we think it constitutes prejudice within the meaning of [Fed.R.Crim.P.] 14.

In the present case the appellants did not specify at trial the counts upon which they wished to remain silent and why. It does appear that, when the trial court asked Cross whether he wished to testify in his own behalf, Cross answered: "Which case, Your Honor?" During the extended colloquy which followed, Cross repeatedly tried, without his counsel's assistance, to elaborate upon his objections to the joinder. But the court seems to have precluded this by insisting that the issue of joinder had been determined in the pre-trial denial of severance and by demanding a categorical answer to its original query. Thereafter the court applied the same ruling to Jackson.

An examination of Cross' testimony on both counts supports his claim in this court that he wished to testify on Count II and remain silent on Count I. His testimony on Count II was that he was a victim and not a cohort of the armed robbers who entered the tourist home behind him. This testimony, which met the Government's case directly, was so convincing that the jury believed it despite the prosecutor's efforts at cross-examination and impeachment. On Count I, however, his denial was plainly evasive and unconvincing. He testified that he had been drinking heavily and did not know his whereabouts at the time of the church robbery. On cross-examination he was open to questioning concerning his generally tawdry way of life and his prior convictions.

Thus it would appear that Cross had ample reason not to testify on Count I and would not have done so if that count had been tried separately. In a separate trial of that count the jury would not have heard his admissions of prior convictions and unsavory activities; nor would he have been under duress to offer dubious testimony on that count in order to avoid the damaging implication of testifying on only one of the two joined counts. Since the joinder embarrassed and

---

3. "When he takes the stand in his own behalf, he does so as any other witness, and within the limits of the appropriate rules he may be cross-examined as to the facts in issue. He may be examined for the purpose of impeaching his credibility. His failure to deny or explain evidence of incriminating circumstances of which he may have knowledge may be the basis of adverse inference, and the jury may be so instructed. His waiver is not partial; having once cast aside the cloak of immunity, he may not resume it at will, whenever cross-examination may be inconvenient or embarrassing." *Raffel v. United States,* 271 U.S. 494, 46 S.Ct. 566, 70 L.Ed. 1054 (1926) (citations omitted).

4. "The safeguards against self-incrimination are for the benefit of those who do not wish to become witnesses in their own behalf and not for those who do." *Raffel v. United States,* supra fn. 3. But joinder may place the defendant in both categories at once.

5. The Supreme Court said in *Adamson v. California,* [p. 30]:

"When evidence is before a jury that threatens conviction, it does not seem unfair to require him to choose between leaving the adverse evidence unexplained and subjecting himself to impeachment through disclosure of former crimes."

However, a defendant tried for two offenses faces a much more difficult situation: (1) his silence on one count does not prevent impeachment; (2) an inference from his silence on one count is encouraged by his lack of silence on the other. * * *

confounded Cross in making his defense, the joinder was prejudicial within the meaning of Rule 14.

We do not agree with the Government that under *Dunaway v. United States,* 205 F.2d 23 (D.C.Cir.1953), this prejudice must be deemed cured by the acquittal on Count II. In that case three counts of housebreaking and two counts of larceny had been tried together. The trial court directed acquittals on the larceny counts, and the jury acquitted the defendant on one of the housebreaking counts. On appeal, we questioned whether "the jury acquittal, considered either alone or with the directed acquittals of larceny, disposes of the claim of prejudice due to the consolidation." But since it appeared that Dunaway "had a fair choice to take the stand or not uninfluenced to any significant degree by the consolidation," we affirmed the conviction on the ground that no prejudice could be shown. In the present case we think our discussion of the proceedings below shows that Cross had no such "fair choice" and that the resulting prejudice on Count I was not cured by the acquittal on Count II.

* * * The judgments[a] on Count I are vacated and the cases are remanded to the District Court for a new trial on that count. * * *

BASTIAN, Circuit Judge (dissenting). * * *

In the instant case, the trial judge specifically charged the jury:

"Each of these two counts must be considered separately against each defendant on the sworn testimony before you in this case."

He then accurately, fairly and in some detail summarized for the jury the evidence and contentions of the parties with regard to each defendant on each count of the indictment.

Moreover, a typewritten form was given to the jury on which to record its verdict. The form set out the name of each defendant, and required a separate notation by the jury as to its decision on each of the two counts relating to that defendant; hence the verdict form was a constant reminder to the jury during its deliberations that each count was to be considered separately as to each defendant.

In these several ways the jury was apprised of its responsibility to consider each count and defendant separately. * * *

That the jury acquitted the defendants on one count while convicting on the other demonstrates that it did, in fact, consider the evidence as it related to each count separately. * * *

DREW v. UNITED STATES
331 F.2d 85 (D.C.Cir.1964).

McGOWAN, Circuit Judge.

This is an appeal from a conviction in the District Court on one count of robbery and one count of attempted robbery * * *. Appellant moved, both before and at the commencement of trial, to compel separate trials of the two charges; and, after verdict, he moved for a new trial because of prejudice asserted to have occurred in, and by reason of, the joint trial. The failure to grant this relief is said on this appeal to be a source of reversible error. * * *

The justification for a liberal rule on joinder of offenses appears to be the economy of a single trial. The argument against joinder is that the defendant may

---

a. In an omitted portion of the opinion, the court concluded that although codefendant Jackson's claim was not so clearly substantiated by the record, it "would be unjust and illogical to separate the two cases and uphold the judgment as to one defendant and reverse it as to the other."

be prejudiced for one or more of the following reasons: (1) he may become embarrassed or confounded in presenting separate defenses; (2) the jury may use the evidence of one of the crimes charged to infer a criminal disposition on the part of the defendant from which is found his guilt of the other crime or crimes charged; or (3) the jury may cumulate the evidence of the various crimes charged and find guilt when, if considered separately, it would not so find. A less tangible, but perhaps equally persuasive, element of prejudice may reside in a latent feeling of hostility engendered by the charging of several crimes as distinct from only one. Thus, in any given case the court must weigh prejudice to the defendant caused by the joinder against the obviously important considerations of economy and expedition in judicial administration. * * *

It is a principle of long standing in our law that evidence of one crime is inadmissible to prove *disposition* to commit crime, from which the jury may infer that the defendant committed the crime charged. Since the likelihood that juries will make such an improper inference is high, courts presume prejudice and exclude evidence of other crimes unless that evidence can be admitted for some substantial, legitimate purpose. The same dangers appear to exist when two crimes are joined for trial, and the same principles of prophylaxis are applicable.

Evidence of other crimes is admissible when relevant to (1) motive, (2) intent, (3) the absence of mistake or accident, (4) a common scheme or plan embracing the commission of two or more crimes so related to each other that proof of the one tends to establish the other, and (5) the identity of the person charged with the commission of the crime on trial. When the evidence is relevant and important to one of these five issues, it is generally conceded that the prejudicial effect may be outweighed by the probative value.

If, then, under the rules relating to other crimes, the evidence of each of the crimes on trial would be admissible in a separate trial for the other, the possibility of "criminal propensity" prejudice would be in no way enlarged by the fact of joinder. When, for example, the two crimes arose out of a continuing transaction or the same set of events, the evidence would be independently admissible in separate trials. Similarly, if the facts surrounding the two or more crimes on trial show that there is a reasonable probability that the same person committed both crimes due to the concurrence of unusual and distinctive facts relating to the manner in which the crimes were committed, the evidence of one would be admissible in the trial of the other to prove identity. In such cases the prejudice that might result from the jury's hearing the evidence of the other crime in a joint trial would be no different from that possible in separate trials.

The federal courts, including our own, have, however, found no prejudicial effect from joinder when the evidence of each crime is simple and distinct, even though such evidence might not have been admissible in separate trials under the rules just discussed. This rests upon the assumption that, with a proper charge, the jury can easily keep such evidence separate in their deliberations and, therefore, the danger of the jury's cumulating the evidence is substantially reduced. * * *

Turning now to the case at hand, a detailed exposition of the facts is necessary. The robbery, committed at a neighborhood store belonging to High's Dairy Products Corp., occurred on July 27, 1962. The sales clerk testified that a Negro male, wearing sunglasses, entered the store. After a short delay the clerk approached the customer and asked if she could help him. He replied: "This is a holdup; I want your money, all of it." When the witness hesitated, he said: "Get it," and pulled a gun part of the way out of his pocket. She gave him the money, and he proceeded to leave the store as another customer entered.

The attempted robbery occurred at a different High's neighborhood store on August 13, 1962 (some two and one-half weeks after the robbery). The sales clerk testified as follows: While she was alone in the store a Negro male entered the store dressed in a coat, cap, and sunglasses. When she asked to help him, he asked for a bag of peanuts. She asked whether he wanted the five or ten cent size, and he replied "five." He then said: "Give me all the money," and she replied: "If you want it, come and get it." He repeated himself several times, and each time she repeated her statement. Finally he said: "You are not going to give me that money?" and she replied negatively. At that point a customer entered the store, and appellant left hastily. The clerk testified that she was not threatened in any way. The police apprehended appellant in the vicinity of the store some twenty-five minutes later and returned to the store where the sales clerk identified him as the person who had attempted to rob her.

These facts do not show such a close similarity in the manner of committing the crimes as would make them admissible in separate trials.[a] * * *

Nor did the two offenses arise out of the same transaction, series of transactions, or continuing state of affairs so that the evidence could have come in under the fourth exception stated above. In short, we cannot find absence of prejudice on the ground that the evidence would have been admissible in separate trials.

This is not the end of the matter, however. We must still determine whether this case falls within the "simple and distinct" test * * *. As pointed out above, the very essence of this rule is that the evidence be such that the jury is unlikely to be confused by it or misuse it. It is not mere conjecture to say that the jury may have been confused in this case. A perusal of the record shows that witnesses' responses at times indicated confusion as to which crime counsel were referring to in their questions; the two crimes were repeatedly referred to as of the same order; and the prosecutor in his summation not unnaturally lumped the two together on occasion in his discussion of the evidence. These lapses do not appear to have been purposeful, but lack of improper motivation does not lessen their impact on the jury. If separate crimes are to be tried together—and we are not to be understood as intimating any conclusion that this can never, as a practical matter, be successfully undertaken—both court and counsel must recognize that they are assuming a difficult task the performance of which calls for a vigilant precision in speech and action far beyond that required in the ordinary trial. The confusion here was probably the result of the superficial similarity of the two crimes and the way in which they were committed. On this record, we cannot say that the jury probably was not confused or probably did not misuse the evidence * * *.

For these reasons we find that there was prejudice in the joinder and the court below should have granted separate trials. The conviction is reversed and the case is remanded.

Notes and Questions

1. Note, 74 Yale L.J. 553, 560 (1965), asserts that because it will often be difficult for the trial judge to apply the *Drew* and *Cross* standards in advance of

a. The court noted that the "essential similarity" between the two crimes was that both were committed against High stores by a Negro wearing sunglasses, which would not be "sufficient to support a finding of reasonable probability that the two offenses were committed by the same person," particularly in view of the other facts: (1) in the robbery, the clerk was threatened with a gun at the first sign of noncompliance, while in the attempted robbery there was no such threat of violence; (2) High stores, usually staffed with one or two female clerks, "are particularly vulnerable to this kind of crime"; and (3) the circumstances of the two crimes "fit into an obvious tactical pattern which would suggest itself to almost anyone disposed to commit a depredation of this sort."

trial, the "only escape from this dilemma of how and when to apply *Cross* and *Drew* without vitiating the standards of prejudice evolved in those cases is the abolition of joinder of similar offenses under Rule 8." Is that so?

2. Does *Cross* apply to cases in which the offenses are joined for trial because they were "connected together" in their commission, or are such cases different in that the defendant must "claim a desire to testify on specific separable offenses, but also he must argue that had there been separate trials *ab initio* the order of prosecution would have been favorable to his theory of prejudice"? See Note, supra, at 561. Does *Drew* apply to cases in which the offenses are joined because they were "connected together" in their commission?

3. Upon a motion for severance of offenses, the usual inquiry is whether, in view of the number of offenses charged and the complexity of the evidence to be offered, the trier of fact will be able to distinguish the evidence and apply the law intelligently as to each offense. If the motion is denied by the trial judge, on appeal this decision is reviewed under an abuse-of-discretion standard. There are four doctrines which are commonly relied upon by appellate courts to support a finding that the defendant was not prejudiced by the joinder: (a) that the jury is capable of following the judge's instructions to ignore certain evidence or to consider certain evidence only as to some of the charges; (b) that if the jury has acquitted the defendant on any count this shows that the jury has been selective and thus must have kept the evidence separate; (c) that the defendant has no ground for complaint if he was convicted of the several counts but received concurrent sentencing; (d) that any prejudice from the joinder is cured by overwhelming evidence of guilt. Are they convincing?[b]

SECTION 2. FAILURE TO JOIN RELATED OFFENSES

UNITED STATES v. DIXON

509 U.S. 688, 113 S.Ct. 2849, 125 L.Ed.2d 556 (1993).

Justice SCALIA announced the judgment of the Court and delivered the opinion of the Court with respect to Parts I, II, and IV, and an opinion with respect to Parts III and V, in which Justice KENNEDY joins. * * *

I

[Dixon, arrested for murder in D.C., was released on bail on the condition he not commit "any criminal offense," violation of which could result in, inter alia, contempt of court. While awaiting trial, Dixon was arrested and indicted for possession of cocaine with intent to distribute; on proof of that conduct he was found guilty of criminal contempt and sentenced to 180 days in jail. Dixon later moved to dismiss the cocaine indictment on double jeopardy grounds; the trial court granted the motion. Foster's wife obtained a civil protection order (CPO) in a D.C. court because of his prior physical attacks upon her; the order required that he not "molest, assault, or in any manner threaten or physically abuse" her. Later, the wife with apparent knowledge of the prosecutor sought to have Foster held in contempt for numerous violations of the CPO, including threats on Nov.

[handwritten margin notes: murder released / awaiting trial / coke charges / wife got CPO / Δ violated it]

b. Consider Sarah Penrod & Steven Tanford, *Reducing Biases in Joined Criminal Offenses* (1985), based upon the decisions of experimental jurors who watched videotaped trials, which concludes that (i) joinder of offenses in a single trial increases the likelihood that the defendant will be convicted; (ii) the similarity between the offenses or between the evidence on each of the offenses is relatively unimportant in producing this result; and (iii) even "strong" jury instructions have "no effect whatsoever" in reducing the prejudice.

12, March 26 and May 17 and assault on Nov. 6 and May 21. Foster was acquitted on the threats counts but was convicted on those two assault counts and other charges, resulting in him being sentenced to 600 days imprisonment. He was later charged by indictment with assault on Nov. 6 (Count I), threatening to injure on Nov. 12, March 26 and May 17 (Counts II–IV), and assault with intent to kill on May 21 (Count V). Foster's motion to dismiss on double jeopardy grounds was denied. The D.C. Court of Appeals consolidated the cases and, relying on *Grady v. Corbin*, 495 U.S. 508, 110 S.Ct. 2084, 109 L.Ed.2d 548 (1990), ruled that both prosecutions were barred.]

II

* * *

The Double Jeopardy Clause, whose application to this new context we are called upon to consider, provides that no person shall "be subject for the same offence to be twice put in jeopardy of life or limb." This protection applies both to successive punishments and to successive prosecutions for the same criminal offense. It is well established that criminal contempt, at least the sort enforced through nonsummary proceedings, is "a crime in the ordinary sense." * * *

In both the multiple punishment and multiple prosecution contexts, this Court has concluded that where the two offenses for which the defendant is punished or tried cannot survive the "same-elements" test, the double jeopardy bar applies. See, e.g., *Brown v. Ohio*, 432 U.S. 161, 97 S.Ct. 2221, 53 L.Ed.2d 187 (1977); *Blockburger v. United States*, 284 U.S. 299, 52 S.Ct. 180, 76 L.Ed. 306 (1932) (multiple punishment); *Gavieres v. United States*, 220 U.S. 338, 31 S.Ct. 421, 55 L.Ed. 489 (1911) (successive prosecutions). The same-elements test, sometimes referred to as the *"Blockburger"* test, inquires whether each offense contains an element not contained in the other; if not, they are the "same offence" and double jeopardy bars additional punishment and successive prosecution. In a case such as *Yancy,* for example, in which the contempt prosecution was for disruption of judicial business, the same-elements test would not bar subsequent prosecution for the criminal assault that was part of the disruption, because the contempt offense did not require the element of criminal conduct, and the criminal offense did not require the element of disrupting judicial business.[1]

We recently held in *Grady* that in addition to passing the *Blockburger* test, a subsequent prosecution must satisfy a "same-conduct" test to avoid the double jeopardy bar. The *Grady* test provides that, "if, to establish an essential element of an offense charged in that prosecution, the government will prove conduct that constitutes an offense for which the defendant has already been prosecuted," a second prosecution may not be had.

III

A

The first question before us today is whether *Blockburger* analysis permits subsequent prosecution in this new criminal contempt context, where judicial order has prohibited criminal act. If it does, we must then proceed to consider whether *Grady* also permits it.

We begin with *Dixon*. The statute applicable in Dixon's contempt prosecution provides that "[a] person who has been conditionally released ... and who has violated a condition of release shall be subject to ... prosecution for contempt of

---

1. *State v. Yancy,* 4 N.C. 133 (1814), it should be noted, involved what is today called summary contempt. We have not held, and do not mean by this example to decide, that the double-jeopardy guarantee applies to such proceedings.

court." Obviously, Dixon could not commit an "offence" under this provision until an order setting out conditions was issued. The statute by itself imposes no legal obligation on anyone. Dixon's cocaine possession, although an offense under [the] D.C.Code, was not an offense under [the aforementioned contempt statute] until a judge incorporated the statutory drug offense into his release order.

In this situation, in which the contempt sanction is imposed for violating the order through commission of the incorporated drug offense, the later attempt to prosecute Dixon for the drug offense resembles the situation that produced our judgment of double jeopardy in *Harris v. Oklahoma,* 433 U.S. 682, 97 S.Ct. 2912, 53 L.Ed.2d 1054 (1977). There we held that a subsequent prosecution for robbery with a firearm was barred by the Double Jeopardy Clause, because the defendant had already been tried for felony-murder based on the same underlying felony. We have described our terse per curiam in *Harris* as standing for the proposition that, for double jeopardy purposes, "the crime generally described as felony murder" is not "a separate offense distinct from its various elements." So too here, the "crime" of violating a condition of release cannot be abstracted from the "element" of the violated condition. The Dixon court order incorporated the entire governing criminal code in the same manner as the *Harris* felony-murder statute incorporated the several enumerated felonies. Here, as in *Harris,* the underlying substantive criminal offense is "a species of lesser-included offense."

Both the Government and Justice Blackmun contend that the legal obligation in Dixon's case may serve "interests ... fundamentally different" from the substantive criminal law, because it derives in part from the determination of a court rather than a determination of the legislature. That distinction seems questionable, since the court's power to establish conditions of release, and to punish their violation, was conferred by statute; the legislature was the ultimate source of both the criminal and the contempt prohibition. More importantly, however, the distinction is of no moment for purposes of the Double Jeopardy Clause, the text of which looks to whether the offenses are the same, not the interests that the offenses violate. And this Court stated long ago that criminal contempt, at least in its nonsummary form, "is a crime in every fundamental respect." Because Dixon's drug offense did not include any element not contained in his previous contempt offense, his subsequent prosecution violates the Double Jeopardy Clause.

The foregoing analysis obviously applies as well to Count I of the indictment against Foster, charging assault, based on the same event that was the subject of his prior contempt conviction for violating the provision of the CPO forbidding him to commit simple assault. The subsequent prosecution for assault fails the *Blockburger* test, and is barred.

B

The remaining four counts in Foster, assault with intent to kill (Count V) and threats to injure or kidnap (Counts II–IV), are not barred under *Blockburger.* As to Count V: * * * At the contempt hearing, the court stated that Ana Foster's attorney, who prosecuted the contempt, would have to prove first, knowledge of a CPO, and second, a willful violation of one of its conditions, here simple assault as defined by the criminal code.[5] On the basis of the same episode, Foster was then

---

5. Given this requirement of willful violation of the order, Justice White's desire to "put to the side the CPO," because it only "triggered the court's authority" cannot be reconciled with his desire to "compar[e] the substantive offenses of which respondents stood accused." The "substantive offense" of criminal contempt is willful violation of a court order. Far from a mere jurisdictional device, that order (or CPO) is the centerpiece of the entire proceeding. Its terms define the prohibited conduct, its existence supports imposition of a criminal penalty, and willful violation of it is necessary for conviction. To ignore the CPO

indicted for assault with intent to kill. Under governing law, that offense requires proof of specific intent to kill; simple assault does not. Similarly, the contempt offense required proof of knowledge of the CPO, which assault with intent to kill does not. Applying the *Blockburger* elements test, the result is clear: These crimes were different offenses and the subsequent prosecution did not violate the Double Jeopardy Clause.[7]

Counts II, III, and IV of Foster's indictment are likewise not barred. These charged Foster under § 22–2307 (forbidding anyone to "threate[n] ... to kidnap any person or to injure the person of another or physically damage the property of any person") for his alleged threats on three separate dates. Foster's contempt prosecution included charges that, on the same dates, he violated the CPO provision ordering that he not "in any manner threaten" Ana Foster. Conviction of the contempt required willful violation of the CPO—which conviction under § 22–2307 did not; and conviction under § 22–2307 required that the threat be a threat to kidnap, to inflict bodily injury, or to damage property—which conviction of the contempt (for violating the CPO provision that Foster not "in any manner threaten") did not.[8] Each offense therefore contained a separate element, and the *Blockburger* test for double jeopardy was not met.

IV

Having found that at least some of the counts at issue here are not barred by the *Blockburger* test, we must consider whether they are barred by the new, additional double jeopardy test we announced three Terms ago in *Grady v. Corbin*. They undoubtedly are, since *Grady* prohibits "a subsequent prosecution if, to establish an essential element of an offense charged in that prosecution [here, assault as an element of assault with intent to kill, or threatening as an element of threatening bodily injury], the government will prove conduct that constitutes an offense for which the defendant has already been prosecuted [here, the assault and the threatening, which conduct constituted the offense of violating the CPO]."

We have concluded, however, that *Grady* must be overruled. Unlike *Blockburger* analysis, whose definition of what prevents two crimes from being the "same offence," has deep historical roots and has been accepted in numerous precedents

---

when determining whether two offenses are the "same" is no more possible than putting aside the statutory definitions of criminal offenses. * * *

7. Justice White's suggestion that if Foster received a lesser-included-offense instruction on assault at his trial for assault with intent to kill, we would uphold a conviction on that lesser count is simply wrong. Under basic *Blockburger* analysis, Foster may neither be tried a second time for assault nor again convicted for assault, as we have concluded as to Count I (charging simple assault). Thus, Foster certainly does receive the "full constitutional protection to which he is entitled": he may neither be tried nor convicted a second time for assault. That does not affect the conclusion that trial and conviction for assault with intent to kill are not barred. It merely illustrates the unremarkable fact that one offense (simple assault) may be an included offense of two offenses (violation of the CPO for assault, and assault with intent to kill) that are separate offenses under *Blockburger*.

8. We think it is highly artificial to interpret the CPO's prohibition of threatening "in any manner," as Justice White would interpret it, to refer only to threats that violate the District's criminal laws. The only threats meeting that definition would have been threats to do physical harm, to kidnap, or to damage property. Threats to stalk, to frighten, to cause intentional embarrassment, to make harassing phone calls, to make false reports to employers or prospective employers, to harass by phone calls or otherwise at work—to mention only a few of the additional threats that might be anticipated in this domestic situation—would not be covered. Surely "in any manner threaten" should cover at least all threats to commit acts that would be tortious under D.C. law (which would be consistent with the trial court's later reference to a "legal threat"). Thus, under our *Blockburger* analysis the aggravated threat counts and the assault-with-intent-to-kill count come out the same way.

of this Court, *Grady* lacks constitutional roots. The "same-conduct" rule it announced is wholly inconsistent with earlier Supreme Court precedent and with the clear common-law understanding of double jeopardy. We need not discuss the many proofs of these statements, which were set forth at length in the *Grady* dissent. We will respond, however, to the contrary contentions of today's pro-*Grady* dissents.

The centerpiece of Justice Souter's analysis is an appealing theory of a "successive prosecution" strand of the Double Jeopardy Clause that has a different meaning from its supposed "successive punishment" strand. We have often noted that the Clause serves the function of preventing both successive punishment and successive prosecution, but there is no authority, except *Grady,* for the proposition that it has different meanings in the two contexts. That is perhaps because it is embarrassing to assert that the single term "same offence" (the words of the Fifth Amendment at issue here) has two different meanings—that what is the same offense is yet not the same offense. * * *[14]

But *Grady* was not only wrong in principle; it has already proved unstable in application. Less than two years after it came down, in *United States v. Felix,* 503 U.S. 378, 112 S.Ct. 1377, 118 L.Ed.2d 25 (1992), we were forced to recognize a large exception to it. There we concluded that a subsequent prosecution for conspiracy to manufacture, possess, and distribute methamphetamine was not barred by a previous conviction for attempt to manufacture the same substance. We offered as a justification for avoiding a "literal" (i.e., faithful) reading of *Grady* "longstanding authority" to the effect that prosecution for conspiracy is not precluded by prior prosecution for the substantive offense. Of course the very existence of such a large and longstanding "exception" to the *Grady* rule gave cause for concern that the rule was not an accurate expression of the law. This "past practice" excuse is not available to support the ignoring of *Grady* in the present case, since there is no Supreme Court precedent even discussing this fairly new breed of successive prosecution (criminal contempt for violation of a court order prohibiting a crime, followed by prosecution for the crime itself).

A hypothetical based on the facts in *Harris* reinforces the conclusion that *Grady* is a continuing source of confusion and must be overruled. Suppose the State first tries the defendant for felony-murder, based on robbery, and then indicts the defendant for robbery with a firearm in the same incident. Absent *Grady,* our cases provide a clear answer to the double-jeopardy claim in this situation. Under *Blockburger,* the second prosecution is not barred—as it clearly was not barred at common law * * *.[15]

---

14. It is unclear what definition of "same offence" Justice Souter would have us adopt for successive prosecution. At times, he appears content with our having added to *Blockburger* the *Grady* same-conduct test. At other times, however, he adopts an ultra-*Grady* "same transaction" rule, which would require the Government to try together all offenses (regardless of the differences in the statutes) based on one event. Of course, the same-transaction test, long espoused by Justice Brennan, see, e.g., *Brown v. Ohio,* (concurring opinion), has been consistently rejected by the Court.

15. Justice Souter dislikes this result because it violates "the principles behind the protection from successive prosecution included in the Fifth Amendment." The "principles behind" the Fifth Amendment are more likely to be honored by following longstanding prac-

tice than by following intuition. But in any case, Justice Souter's concern that prosecutors will bring separate prosecutions in order to perfect their case seems unjustified. They have little to gain and much to lose from such a strategy. Under *Ashe v. Swenson,* an acquittal in the first prosecution might well bar litigation of certain facts essential to the second one—though a conviction in the first prosecution would not excuse the Government from proving the same facts the second time. Surely, moreover, the Government must be deterred from abusive, repeated prosecutions of a single offender for similar offenses by the sheer press of other demands upon prosecutorial and judicial resources. Finally, even if Justice Souter's fear were well founded, no double-jeopardy bar short of a same-transaction analysis will eliminate this problem; but that interpretation of

Having encountered today yet another situation in which the pre-*Grady* understanding of the Double Jeopardy Clause allows a second trial, though the "same-conduct" test would not, we think it time to acknowledge what is now, three years after *Grady*, compellingly clear: the case was a mistake. We do not lightly reconsider a precedent, but, because *Grady* contradicted an "unbroken line of decisions," contained "less than accurate" historical analysis, and has produced "confusion," we do so here. Although stare decisis is the "preferred course" in constitutional adjudication, "when governing decisions are unworkable or are badly reasoned, 'this Court has never felt constrained to follow precedent.'" We would mock stare decisis and only add chaos to our double jeopardy jurisprudence by pretending that *Grady* survives when it does not. We therefore accept the Government's invitation to overrule *Grady*, and Counts II, III, IV, and V of Foster's subsequent prosecution are not barred.

V

Dixon's subsequent prosecution, as well as Count I of Foster's subsequent prosecution, violate the Double Jeopardy Clause.[18] For the reasons set forth in Part IV, the other Counts of Foster's subsequent prosecution do not violate the Double Jeopardy Clause.[19] * * *

Chief Justice REHNQUIST, with whom Justice O'CONNOR and Justice THOMAS join, concurring in part and dissenting in part.

[I] join Parts I, II, and IV of the Court's opinion, and write separately to express my disagreement with Justice Scalia's application of *Blockburger* in Part III.

In my view, *Blockburger*'s same-elements test requires us to focus not on the terms of the particular court orders involved, but on the elements of contempt of court in the ordinary sense. Relying on *Harris v. Oklahoma*, a three-paragraph per curiam in an unargued case, Justice Scalia concludes otherwise today, and thus incorrectly finds in Part III–A of his opinion that the subsequent prosecutions of Dixon for drug distribution and of Foster for assault violated the Double Jeopardy Clause. In so doing, Justice Scalia rejects the traditional view—shared by every federal court of appeals and state supreme court that addressed the issue prior to *Grady*—that, as a general matter, double jeopardy does not bar a subsequent prosecution based on conduct for which a defendant has been held in criminal contempt. * * *

At the heart of this pre-*Grady* consensus lay the common belief that there was no double-jeopardy bar under *Blockburger*. There, we stated that two offenses are different for purposes of double jeopardy if "each provision requires proof of a fact which the other does not." Applying this test to the offenses at bar, it is clear that the elements of the governing contempt provision are entirely different from the elements of the substantive crimes. Contempt of court comprises two elements: (i) a court order made known to the defendant, followed by (ii) willful violation of that order. Neither of those elements is necessarily satisfied by proof that a defendant has committed the substantive offenses of assault or drug distribution. Likewise, no element of either of those substantive offenses is necessarily satisfied by proof that a defendant has been found guilty of contempt of court.

the Double Jeopardy Clause has been soundly rejected, and would require overruling numerous precedents, the latest of which is barely a year old, *United States v. Felix.*

18. Justices White, Stevens, and Souter concur in this portion of the judgment.

19. Justice Blackmun concurs only in the judgment with respect to this portion.

Justice Scalia grounds his departure from *Blockburger*'s customary focus on the statutory elements of the crimes charged on *Harris v. Oklahoma,* an improbable font of authority. A summary reversal, like *Harris,* "does not enjoy the full precedential value of a case argued on the merits." Today's decision shows the pitfalls inherent in reading too much into a "terse per curiam." Justice Scalia's discussion of *Harris* is nearly as long as *Harris* itself and consists largely of a quote not from *Harris,* but from a subsequent opinion analyzing *Harris.* Justice Scalia then concludes that *Harris* somehow requires us to look to the facts that must be proven under the particular court orders in question (rather than under the general law of criminal contempt) in determining whether contempt and the related substantive offenses are the same for double jeopardy purposes. This interpretation of *Harris* is both unprecedented and mistaken.

Our double jeopardy cases applying *Blockburger* have focused on the statutory elements of the offenses charged, not on the facts that must be proven under the particular indictment at issue—an indictment being the closest analogue to the court orders in this case. By focusing on the facts needed to show a violation of the specific court orders involved in this case, and not on the generic elements of the crime of contempt of court, Justice Scalia's double-jeopardy analysis bears a striking resemblance to that found in *Grady*—not what one would expect in an opinion that overrules *Grady.*

Close inspection of the crimes at issue in *Harris* reveals, moreover, that our decision in that case was not a departure from *Blockburger*'s focus on the statutory elements of the offenses charged. In *Harris,* we held that a conviction for felony murder based on a killing in the course of an armed robbery foreclosed a subsequent prosecution for robbery with a firearm. Though the felony-murder statute in *Harris* did not require proof of armed robbery, it did include as an element proof that the defendant was engaged in the commission of some felony. We construed this generic reference to some felony as incorporating the statutory elements of the various felonies upon which a felony-murder conviction could rest. The criminal contempt provision involved here, by contrast, contains no such generic reference which by definition incorporates the statutory elements of assault or drug distribution.

Unless we are to accept the extraordinary view that the three-paragraph per curiam in *Harris* was intended to overrule sub silentio our previous decisions that looked to the statutory elements of the offenses charged in applying *Blockburger,* we are bound to conclude, as does Justice Scalia, that the ratio decidendi of our *Harris* decision was that the two crimes there were akin to greater and lesser included offenses. The crimes at issue here, however, cannot be viewed as greater and lesser included offenses, either intuitively or logically. A crime such as possession with intent to distribute cocaine is a serious felony that cannot easily be conceived of as a lesser included offense of criminal contempt, a relatively petty offense as applied to the conduct in this case. Indeed, to say that criminal contempt is an aggravated form of that offense defies common sense. * * *

But there is a more fundamental reason why the offenses in this case are not analogous to greater and lesser included offenses. A lesser included offense is defined as one that is "necessarily included" within the statutory elements of another offense. Taking the facts of *Harris* as an example, a defendant who commits armed robbery necessarily has satisfied one of the statutory elements of felony murder. The same cannot be said, of course, about this case: A defendant who is guilty of possession with intent to distribute cocaine or of assault has not necessarily satisfied any statutory element of criminal contempt. Nor, for that matter, can it be said that a defendant who is held in criminal contempt has necessarily satisfied any element of those substantive crimes. In short, the offenses for which Dixon and Foster were prosecuted in this case cannot be analogized to greater and lesser included offenses; hence, they are separate and distinct for double jeopardy purposes.[3] * * *

Justice WHITE, with whom Justice STEVENS joins, and with whom Justice SOUTER joins as to Part I, concurring in the judgment in part and dissenting in part.

I am convinced that the Double Jeopardy Clause bars prosecution for an offense if the defendant already has been held in contempt for its commission. Therefore, I agree with the Court's conclusion that both Dixon's prosecution for possession with intent to distribute cocaine and Foster's prosecution for simple assault were prohibited. * * *

II

If, as the Court agrees, the Double Jeopardy Clause cannot be ignored in this context, my view is that the subsequent prosecutions in both Dixon and Foster were impermissible as to all counts. I reach this conclusion because the offenses at issue in the contempt proceedings were either identical to, or lesser included offenses of, those charged in the subsequent prosecutions. Justice Scalia's contrary conclusion as to some of Foster's counts, which he reaches by exclusive focus on the formal elements of the relevant crimes, is divorced from the purposes of the constitutional provision he purports to apply. Moreover, the results to which this approach would lead are indefensible.

A

The contempt orders in Foster and Dixon referred in one case to the District's laws regarding assaults and threats, and, in the other, to the criminal code in its entirety. The prohibitions imposed by the court orders, in other words, duplicated those already in place by virtue of the criminal statutes. Aside from differences in the sanctions inflicted, the distinction between being punished for violation of the criminal laws and being punished for violation of the court orders, therefore, is simply this: Whereas in the former case "the entire population" is subject to prosecution, in the latter such authority extends only to "those particular persons whose legal obligations result from their earlier participation in proceedings before the court." But the offenses that are to be sanctioned in either proceeding must be similar, since the contempt orders incorporated, in full or in part, the criminal code.

Thus, in this case, the offense for which Dixon was held in contempt was possession with intent to distribute drugs. Since he previously had been indicted for precisely the same offense, the double jeopardy bar should apply. * * * All of the offenses for which Foster was either convicted or acquitted in the contempt proceeding were similar to, or lesser included offenses of, those charged in the subsequent indictment. Because "the Fifth Amendment forbids successive prosecution * * * for a greater and lesser included offense," *Brown v. Ohio,* (1977), the second set of trials should be barred in their entirety.

---

3. Assuming, arguendo, that Justice Scalia's reading of *Harris v. Oklahoma* is accurate, and that we must look to the terms of the particular court orders involved, I believe Justice Scalia is correct in differentiating among the various counts in Foster. The court order there provided that Foster must "not molest, assault, or in any manner threaten or physically abuse" his estranged wife. For Foster to be found in contempt of court, his wife need have proved only that he had knowledge of the court order and that he assaulted or threatened her, but not that he assaulted her with intent to kill (Count V) or that he threatened to inflict bodily harm (Counts II–IV). So the crime of criminal contempt in Foster, even if analyzed under Justice Scalia's reading of *Harris,* is nonetheless a different offense under *Blockburger* than the crimes alleged in Counts II–V of the indictment, since "each provision requires proof of a fact which the other does not." Because Justice Scalia finds no double-jeopardy bar with respect to those counts, I agree with the result reached in Part III–B of his opinion.

B

Professing strict adherence to *Blockburger*'s so-called "same elements" test, Justice Scalia opts for a more circuitous approach. The elements of the crime of contempt, he reasons, in this instance are (1) the existence and knowledge of a court, or CPO; and (2) commission of the underlying substantive offense. Where the criminal conduct that forms the basis of the contempt order is identical to that charged in the subsequent trial, Justice Scalia concludes, *Blockburger* forbids retrial. All elements of Foster's simple assault offense being included in his previous contempt offense, prosecution on that ground is precluded. The same is true of Dixon's drug offense. I agree with this conclusion, though would reach it rather differently: Because in a successive prosecution case the risk is that a person will have to defend himself more than once against the same charge, I would have put to the side the CPO (which, as it were, triggered the court's authority to punish the defendant for acts already punishable under the criminal laws) and compared the substantive offenses of which respondents stood accused in both prosecutions.

The significance of our disaccord is far more manifest where an element is added to the second prosecution. Under Justice Scalia's view, the double jeopardy barrier is then removed because each offense demands proof of an element the other does not: Foster's conviction for contempt requires proof of the existence and knowledge of a CPO, which conviction for assault with intent to kill does not; his conviction for assault with intent to kill requires proof of an intent to kill, which the contempt conviction did not. Finally, though he was acquitted in the contempt proceedings with respect to the alleged threats, his conviction under the threat charge in the subsequent trial required the additional proof that the threat be to kidnap, to inflict bodily injury, or to damage property. As to these counts, and absent any collateral estoppel problem, Justice Scalia finds that the Constitution does not prohibit retrial.

The distinction drawn by Justice Scalia is predicated on a reading of the Double Jeopardy Clause that is abstracted from the purposes the constitutional provision is designed to promote. To focus on the statutory elements of a crime makes sense where cumulative punishment is at stake, for there the aim simply is to uncover legislative intent. The *Blockburger* inquiry, accordingly, serves as a means to determine this intent, as our cases have recognized. But, as Justice Souter shows, adherence to legislative will has very little to do with the important interests advanced by double jeopardy safeguards against successive prosecutions. The central purpose of the Double Jeopardy Clause being to protect against vexatious multiple prosecutions, these interests go well beyond the prevention of unauthorized punishment. The same-elements test is an inadequate safeguard, for it leaves the constitutional guarantee at the mercy of a legislature's decision to modify statutory definitions. Significantly, therefore, this Court has applied an inflexible version of the same-elements test only once, in 1911, in a successive prosecution case, see *Gavieres v. United States,* and has since noted that "[t]he *Blockburger* test is not the only standard for determining whether successive prosecutions impermissibly involve the same offense." *Brown.* Rather, "[e]ven if two offenses are sufficiently different to permit the imposition of consecutive sentences, successive prosecutions will be barred in some circumstances where the second prosecution requires the relitigation of factual issues already resolved by the first."

Take the example of Count V in Foster: For all intents and purposes, the offense for which he was convicted in the contempt proceeding was his assault against his wife. The majority, its eyes fixed on the rigid elements-test, would have his fate turn on whether his subsequent prosecution charges "simple assault" or "assault with intent to kill." Yet, because the crime of "simple assault" is included within the crime of "assault with intent to kill," the reasons that bar retrial under the first hypothesis are equally present under the second: These include principles of finality; protecting Foster from "embarrassment" and "expense"; and preventing the government from gradually fine-tuning its strategy, thereby minimizing exposure to a mistaken conviction.

Analysis of the threat charges (Counts II–IV) makes the point more clearly still. In the contempt proceeding, it will be recalled, Foster was acquitted of the-arguably lesser-included-offense of threatening "in any manner." As we have stated, "the law attaches particular significance to an acquittal. To permit a second trial after an acquittal, however mistaken the acquittal might have been, would present an unacceptably high risk that the Government, with its vastly superior resources, might wear down the defendant so that 'even though innocent he may be found guilty.'" To allow the government to proceed on the threat counts would present precisely the risk of erroneous conviction the Clause seeks to avoid. That the prosecution had to establish the existence of the CPO in the first trial, in short, does not in any way modify the prejudice potentially caused to a defendant by consecutive trials.

To respond, as the majority appears to do, that concerns relating to the defendant's interests against repeat trials are "unjustified" because prosecutors "have little to gain and much to lose" from bringing successive prosecutions and because "the Government must be deterred from abusive, repeated prosecutions of a single offender for similar offenses by the sheer press of other demands upon prosecutorial and judicial resources," is to get things exactly backwards. The majority's prophesies might be correct, and double jeopardy might be a problem that will simply take care of itself. Not so, however, according to the Constitution, whose firm prohibition against double jeopardy cannot be satisfied by wishful thinking.

C

Further consequences—at once illogical and harmful—flow from Justice Scalia's approach. I turn for illustration once more to Foster's assault case. In his second prosecution, the government brought charges of assault with intent to kill. In the District of Columbia, Superior Court Criminal Rule 31(c)—which faithfully mirrors its federal counterpart, Federal Rule of Criminal Procedure 31(c)— provides that a "defendant may be found guilty of an offense necessarily included in the offense charged or of an attempt to commit either the offense charged or an offense necessarily included therein if the attempt is an offense." This provision has been construed to require the jury to determine guilt of all lesser included offenses. Specifically, "[a] defendant is entitled to a lesser-included offense instruction when (1) all elements of the lesser offense are included within the offense charged, and (2) there is a sufficient evidentiary basis for the lesser charge."

Simple assault being a lesser included offense of assault with intent to kill, the jury in the second prosecution would in all likelihood receive instructions on the lesser offense and could find Foster guilty of simple assault. In short, while the government cannot, under the Constitution, bring charges of simple assault, it apparently can, under the majority's interpretation, secure a conviction for simple assault, so long as it prosecutes Foster for assault with intent to kill. As I see it, Foster will have been put in jeopardy twice for simple assault.[10] The result is as unjustifiable as it is pernicious. * * *

---

10. Justice Scalia's dismissal of this concern is difficult to follow. As I understand it, he maintains that no double jeopardy problem exists because under *Blockburger* a conviction for assault would not be upheld. I suppose that the judge could upon request instruct the jury

III

Once it is agreed that the Double Jeopardy Clause applies in this context, the Clause, properly construed, both governs this case and disposes of the distinction between Foster's charges upon which Justice Scalia relies. I therefore see little need to draw *Grady* into this dispute. * * *

The majority nonetheless has chosen to consider *Grady* anew and to overrule it. I agree with Justice Blackmun and Justice Souter that such a course is both unwarranted and unwise. Hence, I dissent from the judgment overruling *Grady*.

IV

Believing that the Double Jeopardy Clause bars Foster's and Dixon's successive prosecutions on all counts, I would affirm the judgment of the District of Columbia Court of Appeals. I concur in the judgment of the Court in Part III–A which holds that Dixon's subsequent prosecution and Count I of Foster's subsequent prosecution were barred. I disagree with Justice Scalia's application of *Blockburger* in Part III–B. From Part IV of the opinion, in which the majority decides to overrule *Grady,* I dissent.

Justice BLACKMUN, concurring in the judgment in part and dissenting in part. * * *

I agree with Justice Souter that "the *Blockburger* test is not the exclusive standard for determining whether the rule against successive prosecutions applies in a given case." I also share both his and Justice White's dismay that the Court so cavalierly has overruled a precedent that is barely three years old and that has proved neither unworkable nor unsound. * * *

If this were a case involving successive prosecutions under the substantive criminal law, I would agree that the Double Jeopardy Clause could bar the subsequent prosecution. But we are concerned here with contempt of court, a special situation. * * *

Contempt is one of the very few mechanisms available to a trial court to vindicate the authority of its orders. I fear that the Court's willingness to overlook the unique interests served by contempt proceedings not only will jeopardize the ability of trial courts to control those defendants under their supervision but will undermine their ability to respond effectively to unmistakable threats to their own authority and to those who have sought the court's protection.

This fact is poignantly stressed by the amici: "[C]ontempt litigators and criminal prosecutors seek to further different interests. A battered woman seeks to enforce her private order to end the violence against her. In contrast, the criminal prosecutor is vindicating society's interest in enforcing its criminal law. The two interests are not the same, and to consider the contempt litigator and the criminal prosecutor as one and the same would be to adopt an absurd fiction."

Justice SOUTER, with whom Justice STEVENS joins, concurring in the judgment in part and dissenting in part.

on the lesser included offense and await its verdict; if it were to find Foster guilty of simple assault, the court could then vacate the conviction as violative of the Double Jeopardy Clause—or, barring that, Foster could appeal his conviction on that basis. The sheer oddity of this scenario aside, it falls short of providing Foster with the full constitutional protection to which he is entitled. A double jeopardy viola-

tion occurs at the inception of trial, which is why an order denying a motion to dismiss on double jeopardy grounds is immediately appealable. * * * This double jeopardy predicament, of course, could be avoided by Foster's attorney not requesting the lesser included offense instructions to which his client is entitled. But to place a defendant before such a choice hardly strikes me as a satisfactory resolution.

* * * I join Part I of Justice White's opinion, and I would hold, as he would, both the prosecution of Dixon and the prosecution of Foster under all the counts of the indictment against him to be barred by the Double Jeopardy Clause. * * *

In addressing multiple punishments, "the role of the constitutional guarantee is limited to assuring that the court does not exceed its legislative authorization by imposing multiple punishments for the same offense." *Brown v. Ohio.* Courts enforcing the federal guarantee against multiple punishment therefore must examine the various offenses for which a person is being punished to determine whether, as defined by the legislature, any two or more of them are the same offense. * * * We ask what the elements of each offense are as a matter of statutory interpretation, to determine whether the legislature intended "to impose separate sanctions for multiple offenses arising in the course of a single act or transaction." *Iannelli v. United States,* 420 U.S. 770, 95 S.Ct. 1284, 43 L.Ed.2d 616 (1975). * * *

The interests at stake in avoiding successive prosecutions are different from those at stake in the prohibition against multiple punishments, and our cases reflect this reality. The protection against successive prosecutions is the central protection provided by the Clause. * * *

The Double Jeopardy Clause prevents the government from "mak[ing] repeated attempts to convict an individual for an alleged offense, thereby subjecting him to embarrassment, expense and ordeal and compelling him to live in a continuing state of anxiety and insecurity." The Clause addresses a further concern as well, that the government not be given the opportunity to rehearse its prosecution, "honing its trial strategies and perfecting its evidence through successive attempts at conviction," because this "enhanc[es] the possibility that even though innocent [the defendant] may be found guilty."

Consequently, while the government may punish a person separately for each conviction of at least as many different offenses as meet the *Blockburger* test, we have long held that it must sometimes bring its prosecutions for these offenses together. If a separate prosecution were permitted for every offense arising out of the same conduct, the government could manipulate the definitions of offenses, creating fine distinctions among them and permitting a zealous prosecutor to try a person again and again for essentially the same criminal conduct. While punishing different combinations of elements is consistent with the Double Jeopardy Clause in its limitation on the imposition of multiple punishments (a limitation rooted in concerns with legislative intent), permitting such repeated prosecutions would not be consistent with the principles underlying the Clause in its limitation on successive prosecution. The limitation on successive prosecution is thus a restriction on the government different in kind from that contained in the limitation on multiple punishments, and the government cannot get around the restriction on repeated prosecution of a single individual merely by precision in the way it defines its statutory offenses. Thus, "[t]he *Blockburger* test is not the only standard for determining whether successive prosecutions impermissibly involve the same offense. Even if two offenses are sufficiently different to permit the imposition of consecutive sentences, successive prosecutions will be barred in some circumstances where the second prosecution requires the relitigation of factual issues already resolved by the first." *Brown.**

* [Transposed footnote] In *Brown* we recognized that "[a]n exception may exist where the State is unable to proceed on the more serious charge at the outset because the additional facts necessary to sustain that charge have not occurred or have not been discovered despite the exercise of due diligence." [Editors' note: Lower courts have recognized such an exception, e.g., *Whittlesey v. State,* 606 A.2d 225 (Md.1992), stating it "would apply if a reasonable prosecutor, having full knowledge of the facts which were known and in the exercise of due diligence should have been known to the police and the prosecutor at the time, would

An example will show why this should be so. Assume three crimes: robbery with a firearm, robbery in a dwelling and simple robbery. The elements of the three crimes are the same, except that robbery with a firearm has the element that a firearm be used in the commission of the robbery while the other two crimes do not, and robbery in a dwelling has the element that the robbery occur in a dwelling while the other two crimes do not.

If a person committed a robbery in a dwelling with a firearm and was prosecuted for simple robbery, all agree he could not be prosecuted subsequently for either of the greater offenses of robbery with a firearm or robbery in a dwelling. Under the lens of *Blockburger,* however, if that same person were prosecuted first for robbery with a firearm, he could be prosecuted subsequently for robbery in a dwelling, even though he could not subsequently be prosecuted on the basis of that same robbery for simple robbery.[3] This is true simply because neither of the crimes, robbery with a firearm and robbery in a dwelling, is either identical to or a lesser-included offense of the other. But since the purpose of the Double Jeopardy Clause's protection against successive prosecutions is to prevent repeated trials in which a defendant will be forced to defend against the same charge again and again, and in which the government may perfect its presentation with dress rehearsal after dress rehearsal, it should be irrelevant that the second prosecution would require the defendant to defend himself not only from the charge that he committed the robbery, but also from the charge of some additional fact, in this case, that the scene of the crime was a dwelling.[4] If, instead, protection against successive prosecution were as limited as it would be by *Blockburger* alone, the doctrine would be as striking for its anomalies as for the limited protection it would provide. Thus, in the relatively few successive prosecution cases we have had over the years, we have not held that the *Blockburger* test is the only hurdle the government must clear. * * *

Notes and Questions

1. When only the greater offense has been charged, as in *Harris v. Oklahoma,* joinder sometimes occurs as a consequence of the well-established rule of procedure under which a defendant is entitled to a jury instruction on the uncharged lesser included offense whenever such an alternative disposition is rationally justified by the evidence in the case. As noted in *Beck v. Alabama,* 447 U.S. 625, 100 S.Ct. 2382, 65 L.Ed.2d 392 (1980): "In the federal courts, it has long been 'beyond dispute that the defendant is entitled to an instruction on a lesser included offense if the evidence would permit a jury rationally to find him guilty of the lesser offense and acquit him of the greater.' Similarly, the state courts that have addressed the issue have unanimously held that a defendant is entitled to a lesser included offense instruction where the evidence warrants it. * * *Although the States vary in their descriptions of the quantum of proof necessary to give rise to a right to a lesser included offense instruction, they agree that it must be given when supported by the evidence." This procedure, the Court noted in *Beck,* "originally developed as an aid to the prosecution in cases in which the proof

not be satisfied that he or she would be able to establish the suspect's guilt beyond a reasonable doubt."]

3. Our cases have long made clear that the order in which one is prosecuted for two crimes alleged to be the same matters not in demonstrating a violation of double jeopardy. See *Brown v. Ohio* (1977) ("the sequence is immaterial").

4. The irrelevance of additional elements can be seen in the fact that, as every Member of the Court agrees, the Double Jeopardy Clause does provide protection not merely against prosecution a second time for literally the same offense, but also against prosecution for greater offenses in which the first crime was lesser-included, offenses that by definition require proof of one or more additional elements.

failed to establish some element of the crime charged. But it has long been recognized that it can also be beneficial to the defendant because it affords the jury a less drastic alternative than the choice between conviction of the offense charged and acquittal."

In *Beck*, the Court concluded that "the nearly universal acceptance of the rule in both state and federal courts establishes the value to the defendant of this procedural safeguard," which is "especially important * * * when the evidence unquestionably establishes that the defendant is guilty of a serious, violent offense—but leaves some doubt with respect to an element that would justify conviction of a capital offense." Thus the Court held as a matter of due process that when "the unavailability of a lesser included offense instruction enhances the risk of an unwarranted conviction," that option may not be withdrawn from the jury in a capital case. The *Beck* rule does not require a state court to instruct the jury on offenses that, under state law, are not considered lesser included offenses of the crime charged. *Hopkins v. Reeves*, 524 U.S. 88, 118 S.Ct. 1895, 141 L.Ed.2d 76 (1998) (second-degree murder, which requires intent, is not lesser included offense of felony-murder, which does not).

2. GARRETT v. UNITED STATES, 471 U.S. 773, 105 S.Ct. 2407, 85 L.Ed.2d 764 (1985), involved these facts: Two months after pleading guilty to a federal charge of importing marijuana off the coast of Washington, defendant was indicted in a Florida federal court for several offenses, including that of engaging in a continuing criminal enterprise. That crime requires proof of three or more successive violations of a specified type within a specified period of time, and at trial the government's proof in that respect included the importation offense to which defendant had earlier pleaded guilty. Defendant claimed that his conviction of engaging in a continuing criminal enterprise violated *Brown*, in that the importation charge was a "lesser included offense" of the continuing criminal enterprise offense. REHNQUIST, J., for the plurality, assuming but not deciding that this latter characterization was correct, concluded that the case nonetheless fell outside *Brown* because "the continuing criminal enterprise charged against Garrett in Florida had not been completed at the time that he was indicted in Washington":

"Were we to sustain Garrett's claim, the Government would have been able to proceed against him in either one of only two ways. It would have to have withheld the Washington charges, alleging crimes committed in October 1979 and August 1980, from the grand jury which indicted Garrett in March 1981, until it was prepared to present to a grand jury the continuing criminal enterprise charges which were alleged to have been, and found by a jury to be, continuing on each of those dates; or it would have to have submitted the continuing criminal enterprise charge to the Washington grand jury in March 1981, even though the indictment ultimately returned against Garrett on that charge alleged that the enterprise had continued until July 1981. We do not think that the Double Jeopardy Clause may be employed to force the Government's hand in this manner, however we were to resolve Garrett's lesser-included-offense argument. One who insists that the music stop and the piper be paid at a particular point must at least have stopped dancing himself before he may seek such an accounting."

The plurality deemed it irrelevant "whether the Government could in March 1981 have successfully indicted and prosecuted Garrett for a different continuing criminal enterprise—one ending in March 1981," explaining that a determination of that question is not "required at the behest of one who at the time the first indictment is returned is continuing to engage in other conduct found criminal by the jury which tried the second indictment.''[a] STEVENS, J., joined by Brennan and Marshall, JJ., dissenting, objected that the instant case did not come within the exception noted in *Brown* (see fn. * on p. 1044) because, while the government alleged that the enterprise continued to the date of the Florida indictment, all the facts necessary to prove a continuing criminal enterprise charge had occurred before the Washington indictment was returned. The other participating member of the Court,[b] O'CONNOR, J., concurring, found "merit to this position" of the dissenters, but reached "a different conclusion upon balancing the interests protected by the Double Jeopardy Clause," including the desirability of allowing the government to decide prosecution is warranted whenever "the defendant continues unlawful conduct after the time the Government prosecutes him for a predicate offense."

3. In JEFFERS v. UNITED STATES, 432 U.S. 137, 97 S.Ct. 2207, 53 L.Ed.2d 168 (1977), two indictments were returned against petitioner: the first charged him and nine others under 21 U.S.C. § 846 with conspiracy to distribute drugs; the second charged him with violation of 21 U.S.C. § 848, which prohibits conducting a continuing criminal enterprise to violate the drug laws. The government filed a motion to join the charges for trial, but petitioner objected, pointing out that "much of the evidence in the conspiracy trial would not inculpate petitioner and would therefore be inadmissible against him in the continuing criminal enterprise trial." The court denied the government's motion, and trial on the § 846 charge commenced. Petitioner later moved to dismiss the § 848 charge on double jeopardy grounds, but that motion was denied, and petitioner was separately convicted of both offenses.

BLACKMUN, J., announced the judgment of the Court in an opinion in which the Chief Justice and Powell and Rehnquist, JJ., joined.[c] He first assumed, *"arguendo,* that * * * § 846 is a lesser included offense of § 848,"[d] and then continued:

"If the defendant expressly asks for separate trials on the greater and the lesser offenses, or, in connection with his opposition to trial together, fails to raise the issue that one offense might be a lesser included offense of the other, [an] exception to the *Brown* [same-elements] rule emerges. * * * [A]lthough a defendant is normally entitled to have charges on a greater and a lesser offense resolved in one proceeding, there is no violation of the Double Jeopardy Clause when he elects to have the two offenses tried separately and persuades the trial court to honor his election.[20]

a. It has been aptly noted that "the *Blockburger* test is insufficient where * * * the concern is not multiple charges under separate statutes, but rather successive prosecutions for conduct that may constitute the same act or transaction." *Rashad v. Burt,* 108 F.3d 677 (6th Cir.1997). This is because when "a defendant is convicted for violating one statute multiple times, the same evidence test will never be satisfied." *State v. Adel,* 965 P.2d 1072 (Wash.1998). The "appropriate inquiry" in such a case "asks what 'unit of prosecution' was intended by the Legislature as the punishable act. ** * The inquiry requires us to look to the language and purpose of the statutes, to see whether they speak directly to the issue of the appropriate unit of prosecution, and if they do not, to ascertain that unit, keeping in mind that any ambiguity that arises in the process must be resolved, under the rule of lenity, in the defendant's favor." *Commonwealth v.*

Rabb, 725 N.E.2d 1036 (Mass.2000) (concluding that allegedly multiple drug possessions justify multiple charges if the possessions are sufficiently differentiated by time, place or intended purpose, the case here regarding defendant's possession of drugs at his residence for immediate sale and his possession of drugs at motel for future sales).

b. Powell, J., took no part in the decision.

c. White, J., concurred as to the issue here considered.

d. The Court later so held. *Rutledge v. United States,* 517 U.S. 292, 116 S.Ct. 1241, 134 L.Ed.2d 419 (1996).

20. The considerations relating to the propriety of a second trial obviously would be much different if any action by the Government contributed to the separate prosecutions on the lesser and greater charges. No hint of

"In this case, trial together of the conspiracy and continuing criminal enterprise charges could have taken place without undue prejudice to petitioner's Sixth Amendment right to a fair trial.[21] If the two charges had been tried in one proceeding, it appears that petitioner would have been entitled to a lesser included offense instruction. If such an instruction had been denied on the ground that § 846 was not a lesser included offense of § 848, petitioner could have preserved his point by proper objection. Nevertheless, petitioner did not adopt that course. Instead, he was solely responsible for the successive prosecutions for the conspiracy offense and the continuing criminal enterprise offense. Under the circumstances, we hold that his action deprived him of any right that he might have had against consecutive trials."

STEVENS, J., joined by Brennan, Stewart, and Marshall, JJ., dissented: "The defendant surely cannot be held responsible for the fact that two separate indictments were returned,[2] or for the fact that other defendants were named in the earlier indictment, or for the fact that the Government elected to proceed to trial first on the lesser charge.[3] The other defendants had valid objections to the Government's motion to consolidate the two cases for trial.[4] Most trial lawyers will be startled to learn that a rather routine joint opposition to that motion to consolidate has resulted in the loss of what this Court used to regard as 'a vital safeguard in our society, one that was clearly won and one that should continue to be highly valued.' "

4. Hall, charged with felony sexual assault upon the 12–year-old daughter of his ex-wife, moved to dismiss on the ground that because the victim was his stepdaughter he could only be prosecuted for incest. The motion was granted,

that is present in the case before us, since the Government affirmatively sought trial on the two indictments together.

Unlike the dissenters, we are unwilling to attach any significance to the fact that the grand jury elected to return two indictments against petitioner for the two statutory offenses. As the Court of Appeals' opinion made clear, before this case it was by no means settled law that § 846 was a lesser included offense of § 848. Even now, it has not been necessary to settle that issue definitively. If the position reasonably could have been taken that the two statutes described different offenses, it is difficult to ascribe any improper motive to the act of requesting two separate indictments. Furthermore, as noted supra, it was the Government itself that requested a joint trial on the two indictments, which also indicates that no sinister purpose was behind the formal method of proceeding.

21. Petitioner argues that a finding of waiver is inconsistent with the decision in *Simmons v. United States* [p. 753], where the Court held that a defendant could not be required to surrender his Fifth Amendment privilege against compulsory self-incrimination in order to assert an arguably valid Fourth Amendment claim. In petitioner's case, however, the alleged Hobson's choice between asserting the Sixth Amendment fair trial right and asserting the Fifth Amendment double jeopardy claim is illusory. Had petitioner asked for a Rule 14 severance from the other defendants, the case might be different. In that event, he would have given the court an opportunity to

ensure that prejudicial evidence relating only to other defendants would not have been introduced in his trial. Assuming that a valid Fifth Amendment point was in the background, due to the relationship between §§ 846 and 848, petitioner could have had no complaint about a trial of the two charges together. No such motion, however, was made. Under the circumstances of this case, therefore, no dilemma akin to that in *Simmons* arose.

2. The plurality implies that the result in this case would be different "if any action by the Government contributed to the separate prosecutions on the lesser and greater charges." I wonder how the grand jury happened to return two separate indictments.

3. The Government retained the alternative of trying petitioner on both charges at once, while trying the other defendants separately for conspiracy. The prosecutor never attempted this course, and defense counsel—not having had an opportunity to read today's plurality opinion—had no reason to believe he had a duty to suggest it. Until today it has never been the function of the defense to give legal advice to the prosecutor.

4. When the Government attempted to obtain a joint trial on all the charges against all the defendants, the attorney representing all the defendants resisted the Government motion. He did so largely because of the possible prejudice to petitioner's codefendants, and gave relatively little emphasis to arguments relating to petitioner alone.

after which Hall was charged with and convicted of incest. The Montana Supreme Court reversed because the incest statute did not apply to stepchildren at the time of Hall's conduct, and went on to rule that under the *Brown* same-elements test Hall could not now be prosecuted for sexual assault, deemed the same offense as incest for double jeopardy purposes. In *Montana v. Hall*, 481 U.S. 400, 107 S.Ct. 1825, 95 L.Ed.2d 354 (1987), the Supreme Court reversed per curiam, explaining that "the *Brown* analysis is not apposite in this case. In *Brown*, the defendant did not overturn the first conviction; indeed, he served the prison sentence assessed as punishment for that crime. Thus, when the State sought to try him for auto theft, it actually was seeking a second conviction for the same offense. By contrast, the respondent in this case sought, and secured, the invalidation of his first conviction. This case falls squarely within the rule that retrial is permissible after a conviction is reversed on appeal."

5. While it has long been settled that the Double Jeopardy Clause has to do only with multiple *criminal* punishment, the Supreme Court has encountered difficulty over the years in determining how to go about making the civil-criminal distinction in this context. The method used in *United States v. Halper*, 490 U.S. 435, 109 S.Ct. 1892, 104 L.Ed.2d 487 (1989), under which the outcome depended primarily on whether the sanction imposed served the traditional "goals of punishment," namely "retribution and deterrence," was abandoned in HUDSON v. UNITED STATES, 522 U.S. 93, 118 S.Ct. 488, 139 L.Ed.2d 450 (1997). There, bank officers indicted for misapplication of bank funds claimed the prosecution was barred because monetary penalties and occupational debarment had previously been imposed upon them by the Office of Comptroller of Currency. The Court, per REHNQUIST, C.J., rejected that contention:

"Whether a particular punishment is criminal or civil is, at least initially, a matter of statutory construction. A court must first ask whether the legislature, 'in establishing the penalizing mechanism, indicated either expressly or impliedly a preference for one label or the other.' Even in those cases where the legislature 'has indicated an intention to establish a civil penalty, we have inquired further whether the statutory scheme was so punitive either in purpose or effect,' as to 'transfor[m] what was clearly intended as a civil remedy into a criminal penalty.'

"In making this latter determination, the factors listed in *Kennedy v. Mendoza–Martinez*, 372 U.S. 144, 83 S.Ct. 554, 9 L.Ed.2d 644 (1963), provide useful guideposts, including: (1) '[w]hether the sanction involves an affirmative disability or restraint'; (2) 'whether it has historically been regarded as a punishment'; (3) 'whether it comes into play only on a finding of scienter'; (4) 'whether its operation will promote the traditional aims of punishment-retribution and deterrence'; (5) 'whether the behavior to which it applies is already a crime'; (6) 'whether an alternative purpose to which it may rationally be connected is assignable for it'; and (7) 'whether it appears excessive in relation to the alternative purpose assigned.' It is important to note, however, that 'these factors must be considered in relation to the statute on its face,' and 'only the clearest proof' will suffice to override legislative intent and transform what has been denominated a civil remedy into a criminal penalty."

As for the instant case, the Court concluded "that Congress intended the OCC money penalties and debarment sanctions * * * to be civil in nature," and found "little evidence" that the sanctions were so punitive as to make them criminal, considering that "neither money penalties nor debarment have historically been viewed as punishment," and that the sanctions imposed "do not involve an 'affirmative disability or restraint'" or come "into play 'only' on a finding of scienter," Moreover, "though the conduct for which OCC sanctions are imposed may also be criminal" and though the sanctions will serve to deter others, "a traditional goal of criminal punishment," neither of those factors "renders such sanctions 'criminal' for double jeopardy purposes."[e]

ASHE v. SWENSON
397 U.S. 436, 90 S.Ct. 1189, 25 L.Ed.2d 469 (1970).

Justice STEWART delivered the opinion of the Court. * * *

Sometime in the early hours of the morning of January 10, 1960, six men were engaged in a poker game in the basement of the home of John Gladson at Lee's Summit, Missouri. Suddenly three or four masked men, armed with a shotgun and pistols, broke into the basement and robbed each of the poker players of money and various articles of personal property. The robbers—and it has never been clear whether there were three or four of them—then fled in a car belonging to one of the victims of the robbery. Shortly thereafter the stolen car was discovered in a field, and later that morning three men were arrested by a state trooper while they were walking on a highway not far from where the abandoned car had been found. The petitioner was arrested by another officer some distance away.

The four were subsequently charged with seven separate offenses—the armed robbery of each of the six poker players and the theft of the car. In May 1960 the petitioner went to trial on the charge of robbing Donald Knight, one of the participants in the poker game. At the trial the State called Knight and three of his fellow poker players as prosecution witnesses. Each of them described the circumstances of the holdup and itemized his own individual losses. The proof that an armed robbery had occurred and that personal property had been taken from Knight as well as from each of the others was unassailable. The testimony of the four victims in this regard was consistent both internally and with that of the others. But the State's evidence that the petitioner had been one of the robbers was weak. Two of the witnesses thought that there had been only three robbers altogether, and could not identify the petitioner as one of them. Another of the victims, who was the petitioner's uncle by marriage, said that at the "patrol station" he had positively identified each of the other three men accused of the holdup, but could say only that the petitioner's voice "sounded very much like" that of one of the robbers. The fourth participant in the poker game did identify the petitioner, but only by his "size and height, and his actions."

The cross-examination of these witnesses was brief, and it was aimed primarily at exposing the weakness of their identification testimony. Defense counsel made no attempt to question their testimony regarding the holdup itself or their claims as to their losses. Knight testified without contradiction that the robbers had stolen from him his watch, $250 in cash, and about $500 in checks. His billfold, which had been found by the police in the possession of one of the three other men accused of the robbery, was admitted in evidence. The defense offered no testimony and waived final argument.

The trial judge instructed the jury that if it found that the petitioner was one of the participants in the armed robbery, the theft of "any money" from Knight would sustain a conviction. He also instructed the jury that if the petitioner was

e. *Hudson* produced four concurring opinions by six Justices. All but one of them agreed that a departure from pre-*Hudson* doctrine was necessary, but three expressed reservations about the extent of the departure in the Rehnquist opinion.

In *Seling v. Young*, 531 U.S. 250, 121 S.Ct. 727, 148 L.Ed.2d 734 (2001), the Court held that a provision deemed civil under *Hudson* cannot be deemed punitive "as applied" to a single individual, for an "as applied" approach would be unworkable because it could never be fully determined whether a scheme was valid under the double jeopardy clause.

one of the robbers, he was guilty under the law even if he had not personally robbed Knight. The jury—though not instructed to elaborate upon its verdict—found the petitioner "not guilty due to insufficient evidence."

Six weeks later the petitioner was brought to trial again, this time for the robbery of another participant in the poker game, a man named Roberts. The petitioner filed a motion to dismiss, based on his previous acquittal. The motion was overruled, and the second trial began. The witnesses were for the most part the same, though this time their testimony was substantially stronger on the issue of the petitioner's identity. For example, two witnesses who at the first trial had been wholly unable to identify the petitioner as one of the robbers, now testified that his features, size, and mannerisms matched those of one of their assailants. Another witness who before had identified the petitioner only by his size and actions now also remembered him by the unusual sound of his voice. The State further refined its case at the second trial by declining to call one of the participants in the poker game whose identification testimony at the first trial had been conspicuously negative. The case went to the jury on instructions virtually identical to those given at the first trial. This time the jury found the petitioner guilty, and he was sentenced to a 35–year term in the state penitentiary. * * *

"Collateral estoppel" is an awkward phrase, but it stands for an extremely important principle in our adversary system of justice. It means simply that when an issue of ultimate fact has once been determined by a valid and final judgment, that issue cannot again be litigated between the same parties in any future lawsuit. Although first developed in civil litigation, collateral estoppel has been an established rule of federal criminal law at least since this Court's decision more than 50 years ago in *United States v. Oppenheimer,* 242 U.S. 85, 37 S.Ct. 68, 61 L.Ed. 161 [1916]. As Justice Holmes put the matter in that case, "It cannot be that the safeguards of the person, so often and so rightly mentioned with solemn reverence, are less than those that protect from a liability in debt." As a rule of federal law, therefore, "[i]t is much too late to suggest that this principle is not fully applicable to a former judgment in a criminal case, either because of lack of 'mutuality' or because the judgment may reflect only a belief that the Government had not met the higher burden of proof exacted in such cases for the Government's evidence as a whole although not necessarily as to every link in the chain."

The federal decisions have made clear that the rule of collateral estoppel in criminal cases is not to be applied with the hypertechnical and archaic approach of a 19th century pleading book, but with realism and rationality. Where a previous judgment of acquittal was based upon a general verdict, as is usually the case, this approach requires a court to "examine the record of a prior proceeding, taking into account the pleadings, evidence, charge, and other relevant matter, and conclude whether a rational jury could have grounded its verdict upon an issue other than that which the defendant seeks to foreclose from consideration." The inquiry "must be set in a practical frame, and viewed with an eye to all the circumstances of the proceedings." Any test more technically restrictive would, of course, simply amount to a rejection of the rule of collateral estoppel in criminal proceedings, at least in every case where the first judgment was based upon a general verdict of acquittal.

Straightforward application of the federal rule to the present case can lead to but one conclusion. For the record is utterly devoid of any indication that the first jury could rationally have found that an armed robbery had not occurred, or that Knight had not been a victim of that robbery. The single rationally conceivable issue in dispute before the jury was whether the petitioner had been one of the robbers. And the jury by its verdict found that he had not. The federal rule of law, therefore, would make a second prosecution for the robbery of Roberts wholly impermissible.

The ultimate question to be determined, then, in the light of *Benton v. Maryland,*[a] is whether this established rule of federal law is embodied in the Fifth Amendment guarantee against double jeopardy. We do not hesitate to hold that it is. For whatever else that constitutional guarantee may embrace, it surely protects a man who has been acquitted from having to "run the gantlet" a second time.

The question is not whether Missouri could validly charge the petitioner with six separate offenses for the robbery of the six poker players. It is not whether he could have received a total of six punishments if he had been convicted in a single trial of robbing the six victims. It is simply whether, after a jury determined by its verdict that the petitioner was not one of the robbers, the State could constitutionally hale him before a new jury to litigate that issue again. * * *

In this case the State in its brief has frankly conceded that following the petitioner's acquittal, it treated the first trial as no more than a dry run for the second prosecution: "No doubt the prosecutor felt the state had a provable case on the first charge and, when he lost, he did what every good attorney would do—he refined his presentation in light of the turn of events at the first trial." But this is precisely what the constitutional guarantee forbids. * * *

Reversed and remanded.

Justice BRENNAN, whom Justice DOUGLAS and Justice MARSHALL join, concurring.

I agree that the Double Jeopardy Clause incorporates collateral estoppel as a constitutional requirement and therefore join the Court's opinion. However, even if the rule of collateral estoppel had been inapplicable to the facts of this case, it is my view that the Double Jeopardy Clause nevertheless bars the prosecution of petitioner a second time for armed robbery. * * *

In my view, the Double Jeopardy Clause requires the prosecution, except in most limited circumstances,[7] to join at one trial all the charges against a defendant which grow out of a single criminal act, occurrence, episode, or transaction. This "same transaction" test of "same offence" not only enforces the ancient prohibition against vexatious multiple prosecutions embodied in the Double Jeopardy Clause, but responds as well to the increasingly widespread recognition that the consolidation in one lawsuit of all issues arising out of a single transaction or occurrence best promotes justice, economy, and convenience. * * *

The present case highlights the hazards of abuse of the criminal process inherent in the "same evidence" test and demonstrates the necessity for the "same transaction" test. * * * Since Missouri has offered no justification for not trying the other informations at [the first] trial, it is reasonable to infer that the other informations were held in reserve to be tried if the State failed to obtain a conviction on the charge of robbing Knight. Indeed, the State virtually concedes as much since it argues that the "same evidence" test is consistent with such an exercise of prosecutorial discretion. * * *

The prosecution plainly organized its case for the second trial to provide the links missing in the chain of identification evidence that was offered at the first trial. McClendon, who was an unhelpful witness at the first trial was not called at

---

a. P. 30 supra, holding that the Fifth Amendment guarantee against double jeopardy is enforceable against the States through the Fourteenth Amendment.

7. For example, where a crime is not completed or not discovered, despite diligence on the part of the police, until after the com-

mencement of a prosecution for other crimes arising from the same transaction, an exception to the "same transaction" rule should be made to permit a separate prosecution. Another exception would be necessary if no single court had jurisdiction of all the alleged crimes. * * *

the second trial. The hesitant and uncertain evidence of Gladson and Roberts at the first trial became detailed, positive, and expansive at the second trial. One must experience a sense of uneasiness with any double jeopardy standard that would allow the State this second chance to plug up the holes in its case. The constitutional protection against double jeopardy is empty of meaning if the State may make "repeated attempts" to touch up its case by forcing the accused to "run the gantlet" as many times as there are victims of a single episode. * * *

Chief Justice BURGER, dissenting.

The Fifth Amendment to the Constitution of the United States provides in part: "nor shall any person be subject for the same offense to be twice put in jeopardy of life or limb * * *." Nothing in the language and none of the gloss previously placed on this provision of the Fifth Amendment remotely justifies the treatment which the Court today accords to the collateral estoppel doctrine. * * *

The collateral estoppel concept—originally a product only of civil litigation—is a strange mutant as it is transformed to control this criminal case. In civil cases the doctrine was justified as conserving judicial resources as well as those of the parties to the actions and additionally as providing the finality needed to plan for the future. It ordinarily applies to parties on each side of the litigation who have the same interest as or who are identical with the parties in the initial litigation. Here the complainant in the second trial is not the same as in the first even though the State is a party in both cases. Very properly, in criminal cases, finality and conservation of private, public, and judicial resources are lesser values than in civil litigation. Also, courts which have applied the collateral concept to criminal actions would certainly not apply it to *both* parties, as is true in civil cases, i.e., here, if Ashe had been convicted at the first trial, presumably no court would then hold that he was thereby foreclosed from litigating the identification issue at the second trial. * * *[b]

[T]he majority's analysis of the facts completely disregards the confusion injected into the case by the robbery of Mrs. Gladson.[c] To me, if we are to psychoanalyze the jury, the evidence adduced at the first trial could more reasonably be construed as indicating that Ashe had been at the Gladson home with the other three men but was not one of those involved in the basement robbery. Certainly, the evidence at the first trial was equivocal as to whether there were three or four robbers, whether the man who robbed Mrs. Gladson was one of the three who robbed the six male victims, and whether a man other than the three had robbed Mrs. Gladson. Then, since the jury could have thought that the "acting together" instruction given by the trial court in both trials only applied to the actual taking from the six card players, and not to Mrs. Gladson, the jury could well have acquitted Ashe but yet believed that he was present in the Gladson home. On the other hand, the evidence adduced at the second trial resolved issues other than identity which may have troubled the first jury. If believed, that evidence indicated that a fourth robber, Johnson, not Ashe, was with Mrs. Gladson when Ashe, Larson, and Brown were robbing the male victims.

b. In *Simpson v. Florida*, 403 U.S. 384, 91 S.Ct. 1801, 29 L.Ed.2d 549 (1971), the Court, noting that "mutuality" is not an ingredient of the *Ashe* rule, held that defendant's conviction at his first trial (reversed on appeal for failure to instruct the jury on a lesser included offense) did not estop him from claiming that the state failed to prove his identity at the second trial.

c. Earlier in his opinion, the Chief Justice notes certain facts not stated in the opinion of the Court: "During the same period in which the men were being robbed in the basement, one man entered Mrs. Gladson's bedroom three floors above, ripped out the telephone there, tied her with the telephone cord, and removed the wedding ring from her finger. * * * Mrs. Gladson did not testify [at the first trial] because she was ill on the day of trial. * * * [At the second trial,] she said that she was able to identify the robber by his voice, and that he was Johnson, not Ashe."

Johnson did go to the basement where the male victims were located, but only after the other three had already taken the stolen items and when the robbers were preparing for their departure in a car to be stolen from Roberts.[d]

Accordingly, even the facts in this case, which the Court's opinion considers to "lead to but one conclusion," are susceptible to an interpretation that the first jury did not base its acquittal on the identity ground which the Court finds so compelling. The Court bases its holding on sheer "guesswork," which should have no place particularly in our review of state convictions by way of habeas corpus.
* * *

Notes and Questions

1. What result under *Ashe* in the following circumstances?

(a) Defendant was charged with first-degree murder. The prosecution's theory was that defendant was guilty under the statute making any killing in the commission or attempted commission of rape first-degree murder. The evidence showed that the defendant, who had been drinking, opened the door of a parked car in which he saw a woman, and announced, "I want a piece of ass and I don't care who knows it." The woman's husband raised up from the back seat and stepped out of the car, at which point the defendant shot and killed him. The defendant then raped the woman. The jury returned a verdict of guilty of manslaughter. Defendant has now been charged with rape. See *People v. Noth*, 33 Mich.App. 18, 189 N.W.2d 779 (1971).[e]

---

d. In *Harris v. Washington*, 404 U.S. 55, 92 S.Ct. 183, 30 L.Ed.2d 212 (1971), the state court held *Ashe* inapplicable where the issue of identity had not been "fully litigated" at the first trial because the trial judge had excluded evidence on grounds having "no bearing on the quality of the evidence." The Supreme Court reversed, holding that "the constitutional guarantee applies, irrespective of whether the jury considered all relevant evidence, and irrespective of the good faith of the State in bringing successive prosecutions."

e. Compare *Turner v. Arkansas*, 407 U.S. 366, 92 S.Ct. 2096, 32 L.Ed.2d 798 (1972), where, some time after petitioner, his brother, Yates and another played poker, Yates was robbed and murdered. Turner was charged with murder on a felony-murder theory and acquitted, after which he was charged with the robbery which the state concedes arose out of the same facts and circumstances. Under the Arkansas statutory provisions on joinder of offenses, these two charges could not have been joined together for trial. The Court, per curiam, ruled: "The jury was instructed that it must find petitioner guilty of first degree murder if it found that he had killed the decedent Yates either with premeditation or unintentionally during the course of a robbery. The jury's verdict thus necessarily means that it found petitioner not guilty of the killing. The State's theory, however, is that the jury might have believed that petitioner and his brother robbed Yates but that this brother actually committed the murder. This theory is belied by the actual instructions given the jury. The trial judge charged that:

'An accessory is one who stands by, aids, abets, or assists * * * the perpetration of the crime * * *.

'All persons being present, aiding and abetting, or ready and consenting to aid and abet, in any felony, shall be deemed principal offenders, and indicted or informed against, and punished as such.'

Had the jury found petitioner present at the crime scene, it would have been obligated to return a verdict of guilty of murder even if it believed that he had not actually pulled the trigger. The only logical conclusion is that the jury found him not present at the scene of the murder and robbery, a finding which negates the possibility of a constitutionally valid conviction for the robbery of Yates."

But in *Schiro v. Farley*, 510 U.S. 222, 114 S.Ct. 783, 127 L.Ed.2d 47 (1994), the Court held that the "failure to return a verdict does not have collateral estoppel effect * * * unless the record establishes that the issue was actually and necessarily decided in the defendant's favor." In that case, defendant's trial for a single killing resulted in the jury being given ten possible verdicts, including three murder counts ("knowingly" killing, rape felony-murder, deviate conduct felony-murder), voluntary and involuntary manslaughter, guilty but mentally ill, not guilty by reason of insanity, and not guilty. Because the jury returned a guilty verdict as to rape felony murder and left the other verdict sheets blank, defendant claimed the state was collaterally estopped from now showing intentional killing as an aggravated

(b) Defendant, a postal employee, was charged with stealing a letter from the mails. At trial, a postal inspector testified that he saw the defendant take an envelope from an employees' mail box in the post office and that a search of her person uncovered three marked quarters which had been placed in the envelope. The defendant testified that she had not taken the letter and that she had procured the three quarters from a dollar-changing machine. Following defendant's acquittal, she was charged with perjury in the mail theft trial. The government is prepared to prove that there was not time for the defendant to get to the dollar-changing machine between the time she was observed taking the envelope and the time of the search, and also that she could not have obtained the marked quarters from the machine because it does not recycle coins deposited in the machine by other users. See *United States v. Nash*, 447 F.2d 1382 (4th Cir.1971). Should it make any difference whether the perjury charge could be proved by "newly discovered evidence"? See *State v. Canon*, 241 Wis.2d 164, 622 N.W.2d 270 (2001).

(c) Defendant at his first trial was convicted of conspiracy but acquitted of having lied to the grand jury when he denied any knowledge of the conspiracy and of not reporting the conspiracy income on his tax return. The conspiracy conviction was reversed on appeal because of improper admission of evidence at trial. On remand for a new trial, defendant moved to dismiss the conspiracy charge. See *United States v. Price,* 750 F.2d 363 (5th Cir.1985).

(d) Defendant was acquitted of a federal charge that he willfully and knowingly, with intent to defraud, smuggled jewels into the United States. The federal government has now instituted civil forfeiture proceedings with respect to the same jewels, under which the government must prove that the property was brought into the United States without the required declaration. See *One Lot Emerald Cut Stones and One Ring v. United States,* 409 U.S. 232, 93 S.Ct. 489, 34 L.Ed.2d 438 (1972).

(e) "Defendant X is the subject of two indictments in two counties, one for bank robbery, the other for having stolen an automobile to be used as the getaway car. He pleads not guilty to both charges and notifies the state that he proposes to prove an alibi, which will exonerate him of both offenses, and for which he has strong support. The state's reliance will be on weak identification evidence and a confession to both crimes. The bank robbery charge is to be tried first. X moves to suppress the confession on a number of grounds—use of physical violence; deprivation of food, water, and rest; promises of immunity, etc. Both sides recognize that determination of the motion will very likely decide the case. After a hearing of several days, a judge suppresses the confession. The state elects not to exercise a right to appeal, drops the bank robbery indictment, and indicates its intention to press the stolen car indictment. X moves again to suppress the confession. The state insists on a hearing, saying it has new evidence to rebut X's claims. Does due process permit it to be given one?" See *United States ex rel. DiGiangiemo v. Regan*, 528 F.2d 1262 (2d Cir.1975), concluding *Ashe* is inapplicable because it is tied to the double jeopardy clause and jeopardy had not attached when the pretrial motion was granted, but arguing a due process version of collateral estoppel should apply in X's favor.

2. What if, in *Noth*, the defendant had entered a guilty plea to manslaughter? Consider *Ohio v. Johnson*, 467 U.S. 493, 104 S.Ct. 2536, 81 L.Ed.2d 425 (1984), where defendant, charged with both murder and manslaughter based on the same killing and robbery and theft based on the same taking, entered a guilty

---

factor supporting a death sentence. The Court disagreed, concluding that because the jury (i) was not instructed to return more than one verdict but (ii) was instructed that intent was required for each variety of murder, defendant had "not met his 'burden ... to demonstrate that the issue whose relitigation he seeks to foreclose was actually decided' in his favor."

plea over the state's objection to manslaughter and theft. In a footnote the Court asserted: "Respondent also argues that prosecution on the remaining charges is barred by the principles of collateral estoppel enunciated by this Court in *Ashe v. Swenson*. Even if the two were mutually exclusive crimes, the taking of a guilty plea is not the same as an adjudication on the merits after full trial, such as took place in *Ashe v. Swenson*. Moreover, in a case such as this, where the State has made no effort to prosecute the charges seriatim, the considerations of double jeopardy protection implicit in the application of collateral estoppel are inapplicable."

3. Phillips was tried for robbery of a federally insured bank. In response to a question from the jury, the court instructed that Phillips could not be convicted unless the jury believed he was one of those in the bank; the court also gave instructions on the "lesser included offense" of possessing what were known to be the proceeds of the robbery. Ten minutes later the jury returned a verdict of guilty of the lesser offense, which the court later set aside on the ground it was not included in the indictment. Phillips was then prosecuted for the possession offense, and evidence of his presence in the bank was admitted to prove his knowledge that the funds he received were stolen. In *Phillips v. United States*, 502 F.2d 227 (4th Cir.1974), his conviction was reversed on the authority of *Ashe*. Craven, J., dissenting, gave "two independent reasons why collateral estoppel should not apply in this case.

"First, Phillips' acquittal of bank robbery was only an implicit acquittal, arising by operation of law from the verdict of guilt on a lesser included offense. I would hold that such an implicit acquittal cannot be the basis for collateral estoppel because it leaves doubt whether the jury has made any factual determination in favor of the accused. * * *

"Second, * * * I would not allow its use to restrict proof on retrial of the *lesser* charge. Retrial in cases like this one harbors none of the prosecutorial abuses that supplied the rationale of *Ashe* * * * ."

Are these reasons sound? Is there yet a third reason, namely, that the defendant's presence in the bank was, in the second prosecution, an "evidentiary" fact rather than an "ultimate" fact (i.e., presence did not have to be proved in the second trial, showing presence was merely of evidentiary value on the knowledge element)? See *Dowling v. United States*, 493 U.S. 342, 110 S.Ct. 668, 107 L.Ed.2d 708 (1990) (earlier acquittal, even if it established a reasonable doubt as to the existence of a matter to be proved as an evidentiary fact at a later trial, is no bar to proof of the evidentiary fact by a lesser standard).

4. Factfinding in certain proceedings is sometimes deemed an insufficient basis for collateral estoppel because of the informality of those proceedings. See, e.g., *Williamsen v. People*, 735 P.2d 176 (Colo.1987) (defendant's earlier acquittal for running red light held not to bar testimony about that traffic infraction in later trial for driving under the influence, as the "procedures used to adjudicate traffic infractions are informal. A referee is appointed pursuant to the Referee Adjudication System Act, * * * and need not be a lawyer * * *. The Referee acts as both factfinder and 'prosecutor.' * * * The salutary purposes of informal traffic infractions hearings would be frustrated if collateral estoppel were to be applied so as to limit a full and fair consideration of the issue in a criminal trial"); *Krochta v. Commonwealth*, 711 N.E.2d 142 (Mass.1999) (state not collaterally estopped from prosecuting defendant for larceny offenses following finding in his favor at probation revocation hearing triggered by alleged commission of same offenses, as jeopardy did not attach at the probation revocation hearing; as for defendant's reliance upon due process variety of collateral estoppel, see Note 1(e) supra, court responds that even if such right exists it not applicable here, as probation revocation proceedings are like administrative proceedings in that the informality of the proceedings make it "inappropriate to transfer the conclusion" from it to a criminal prosecution).

5. Several state courts have adopted a "same transaction" joinder-of-offenses requirement. Is this position sound? Consider *State v. Conrad,* 243 So.2d 174 (Fla.App.1971): "The absurdity of the 'same transaction' standard can be easily illustrated. Assume that one breaks and enters a building to commit larceny of an automobile, does thereafter in fact steal the automobile and drive away, killing the night watchman in the process, and two blocks away runs a red light which brings about his arrest by the municipal police. Could it be said with any logic that a plea of guilty to breaking and entering would bar a subsequent prosecution for murder? If so, presumably a plea of guilty to the traffic offense would likewise, since all arise out of the 'same transaction.'"

Does this mean that some intermediate position is desirable? What of Ill. Comp.Stat. ch. 720, § 5/3–3(b), mandating joinder only if the offenses "are based on the same act"? Or N.Y.Crim.P.Law § 40.20(2)(b), which permits successive prosecutions where "the offenses * * * [contain] an element which is not an element of the other, and the statutory provisions defining such offenses are designed to prevent very different kinds of harm or evil"? Are there, in any event, other limits which are necessary to meet the concerns of the court in *Conrad?* What, for example, of the additional requirement in the above Illinois statute that "the several offenses are known to the proper prosecuting officer at the time of commencing the prosecution and are within the jurisdiction of a single court"?

SECTION 3. JOINDER AND SEVERANCE OF DEFENDANTS

Fed.R.Crim.P. 8(b) provides that "two or more defendants may be charged in the same indictment or information if they are alleged to have participated in the same act or transaction or in the same series of acts or transactions constituting an offense or offenses." Some states have identical provisions, while others utilize similar language. These rules and statutes are intended to promote economy and efficiency and to avoid a multiplicity of trials.

One common joinder situation is that in which the several defendants are connected by virtue of a charged conspiracy relationship, as where the joined defendants are all charged in a conspiracy count and some or all are also charged with substantive offenses alleged to have been committed in furtherance of the conspiracy. Joinder of multiple conspiracies is permissible if they are sufficiently related, which is not shown merely by a slight membership overlap. Even absent a conspiracy count, defendants may be joined when their acts were part of a common plan (e.g., individual acts of income tax evasion related to joint gambling activities) or were so closely connected in respect to time, place and occasion that it would be difficult to separate the proof of one charge from proof of the other (e.g., negligent homicide charges against several drivers involved in same accident).

Although a few states still grant defendants an absolute right to separate trials, in most jurisdictions joined defendants may obtain a severance only by a showing of prejudice flowing from the joinder.

SCHAFFER v. UNITED STATES
362 U.S. 511, 80 S.Ct. 945, 4 L.Ed.2d 921 (1960).

Justice CLARK delivered the opinion of the Court. * * *

The indictment charged transportation in interstate commerce of goods known to have been stolen and having a value in excess of $5,000. It contained three substantive counts. Count 1 charged the two Schaffers (petitioners in No. 111) and the three Stracuzzas (defendants below, who either pleaded guilty or had the charges against them *nolle prossed* at trial) with transporting stolen ladies' and children's wearing apparel from New York to Pennsylvania. Count 2 charged petitioner Marco and the Stracuzzas with a similar movement of stolen goods from New York to West Virginia. Count 3 charged petitioner Karp and the Stracuzzas with like shipments from New York to Massachusetts. The fourth and final count of the indictment charged all of these parties with a conspiracy to commit the substantive offenses charged in the first three counts. The petitioners here were tried on the indictment simultaneously in a single trial. On motion of petitioners for acquittal at the close of the Government's case, the court dismissed the conspiracy count for failure of proof. This motion was denied, however, as to the substantive counts, the court finding that no prejudice would result from the joint trial. Upon submission of the substantive counts to the jury on a detailed charge, each petitioner was found guilty and thereafter fined and sentenced to prison. * * *

It is admitted that the three Stracuzzas were the common center of the scheme to transport the stolen goods. The four petitioners here participated in some steps of the transactions in the stolen goods, although each was involved with separate interstate shipments. The separate substantive charges of the indictment employed almost identical language and alleged violations of the same criminal statute during the same period and in the same manner. This made proof of the over-all operation of the scheme competent as to all counts. The variations in the proof related to the specific shipments proven against each petitioner. This proof was related to each petitioner separately and proven as to each by different witnesses. It included entirely separate invoices and other exhibits, all of which were first clearly identified as applying only to a specific petitioner and were so received and shown to the jury under painstaking instructions to that effect. In short, the proof was carefully compartmentalized as to each petitioner. The propriety of the joinder prior to the failure of proof of conspiracy was not assailed. When the Government rested, however, the petitioners filed their motion for dismissal and it was sustained as to the conspiracy count. The petitioners then pressed for acquittal on the remaining counts, and the court decided that the evidence was sufficient on the substantive counts. The case was submitted to the jury on each of these counts, and under a charge which was characterized by petitioners' counsel as being "extremely fair." This charge meticulously set out separately the evidence as to each of the petitioners and admonished the jury that they were "not to take into consideration any proof against one defendant and apply it by inference or otherwise to any other defendant."

Petitioners contend that prejudice would nevertheless be implicit in a continuation of the joint trial after dismissal of the conspiracy count. They say that the resulting prejudice could not be cured by any cautionary instructions, and that therefore the trial judge was left with no discretion. Petitioners overlook, however, that the joinder was authorized under Rule 8(b) and that subsequent severance was controlled by Rule 14, which provides for separate trials where "it appears that a defendant * * * is prejudiced * * * by such joinder for trial * * *." It appears that not only was no prejudice shown, but both the trial court and the Court of Appeals affirmatively found that none was present. We cannot say to the contrary on this record. Nor can we fashion a hard-and-fast formula that, when a conspiracy count fails, joinder is error as a matter of law. We do emphasize, however, that, in such a situation, the trial judge has a continuing duty at all stages of the trial to grant a severance if prejudice does appear. And where, as here, the charge which originally justified joinder turns out to lack the support of sufficient evidence, a trial judge should be particularly sensitive to the possibility of such prejudice. However, the petitioners here not only failed to show any prejudice that would call Rule 14 into operation but even failed to request a new trial. Instead they relied entirely on their motions for acquittal. Moreover, the judge was acutely aware of the possibility of prejudice and was strict in his charge—not only as to the testimony the jury was not to consider, but also as to that evidence which was available in the consideration of the guilt of each petitioner separately under the respective substantive counts. The terms of Rule 8(b) having been met and no prejudice under Rule 14 having been shown, there was no misjoinder. * * *

Justice DOUGLAS, with whom The Chief Justice, Justice BLACK, and Justice BRENNAN concur, dissenting. * * *

[O]nce it becomes apparent during the trial that the defendants have not participated "in the same series" of transactions, it would make a mockery of Rule 8(b) to hold that the allegation alone, now known to be false, is enough to continue the joint trial.

* * * It is not enough to say that evidence of the guilt of each of the present petitioners may have been clear. Reasons for severance are founded on the principle that evidence against one person may not be used against a codefendant whose crime is unrelated to the others. Instructions can be given the jury and admonitions can be made explicit that the line between the various defendants must be kept separate. The district judge conscientiously made that effort here. But where, as here, there is no nexus between the several crimes, the mounting proof of the guilt of one is likely to affect another. * * *

This is unlike the case where the conspiracy count and the substantive counts are submitted to the jury, the verdict being not guilty of conspiracy but guilty on the other counts. There is then no escape from the quandary in which defendants find themselves. Once the conspiracy is supported by evidence, it presents issues for the jury to decide. What may motivate a particular jury in returning a verdict of not guilty on the conspiracy count may never be known. * * *

Notes and Questions

1. Is the *Schaffer* rule unsound because it "may have the effect of encouraging an unscrupulous prosecutor to frame a baseless conspiracy count in order that several defendants, accused of similar but unrelated offenses, may be tried together"? Note, 42 N.Y.U.L.Rev. 513, 518 (1967). Or, is the dissent's position unsound because it "could militate against the very result that the argument seeks to achieve," in "that a trial judge, faced with a rigid rule requiring severance as a matter of law and consequent time consuming multiple trials, might be extremely reluctant to dismiss the charge upon which joinder is founded." Note, 45 Minn.L.Rev. 1066, 1073 (1961).

2. While in *Schaffer* the Court could say "that the joinder was authorized under Rule 8(b)," such was not the case in UNITED STATES v. LANE, 474 U.S. 438, 106 S.Ct. 725, 88 L.Ed.2d 814 (1986). The indictment charged (count #1) James Lane with mail fraud in connection with a 1979 restaurant fire; (counts #2, 3, and 4) James and Dennis Lane with mail fraud in connection with a 1980 duplex fire; (count #5) James and Dennis Lane with conspiracy to commit mail fraud in connection with a planned flower shop fire; and (count #6) Dennis Lane with perjury before a grand jury when testifying about a person involved in the duplex and flower shop schemes. The court of appeals concluded that when "a case involves multiple defendants as well as multiple counts, we look to Rule 8(b) for the relevant standards," that consequently the issue "in this case is whether all of the counts are part of the same series of acts or transactions," that the answer is no because, between count #1 and the other counts, there is neither a "substantial identity of facts" nor "a common scheme," that thus there was a misjoinder of count #1, and that such misjoinder "is inherently prejudicial." The Supreme Court, per BURGER, C.J., disagreed. Noting that the harmless error doctrine is applicable even to many constitutional violations [see, Ch. 28, § 5B], the Court asserted: "In this case, the argument for applying harmless-error analysis is even stronger because the specific joinder standards of Rule 8 are not themselves of constitutional magnitude."[a] Such application, the Court added, "follows" from *Kotteakos* and from *Schaffer,* which involved "a clear error of misjoinder" at that point when the trial court concluded there was insufficient evidence supporting the conspiracy count.

STEVENS and Marshall, JJ., dissenting, argued: "In my view, harmless-error analysis is inappropriate in at least three situations: (1) when it is clear that a statute or Rule was not intended to be subject to such a rule; (2) when an independent value besides reliability of the outcome suggests that such analysis is inappropriate; and (3) when the harmlessness of an error cannot be measured with precision. In my view, misjoinder clearly falls into the first category.[b] It also has elements of the second and third. Misjoinder implicates the independent value of individual responsibility and our deep abhorrence of the notion of 'guilt by association.' Our criminal justice system has expanded considerably in its tolerance of multiple joinders and massive conspiracy trials. The rule against misjoinder remains, however, as an ultimate safeguard of our cherished principle that one is tried for one's own deeds, and not for another's. The harmfulness of misjoinder is also the type of error that has consequences that are difficult to measure with precision."

BRENNAN and Blackmun, JJ., concurring on this branch of the case, responded to those three points as follows: (1) "nothing in the language or history of either the statutory harmless-error provisions or Rule 8 indicates that Congress chose to except misjoinder from harmless-error scrutiny"; (2) "joinder rules do not serve 'an independent value besides reliability of the outcome' justifying an

---

a. A footnote by the majority stated: "Respondents argue that application of the harmless-error rule to Rule 8(b) misjoinder will eviscerate Rule 14, which provides the trial court with discretion to grant a severance even if the joinder is proper under Rule 8 when it believes the defendants or the Government may be prejudiced by a joinder. We see no conflict with our holding and the applicability of Rule 14. Rule 14's concern is to provide the trial court with some flexibility when a joint trial may appear to risk prejudice to a party; review of that decision is for an abuse of discretion. Rule 8(b), however, requires the granting of a motion for severance unless its standards are met, even in the absence of prejudice; review on appeal is for an error of law. Applying the harmless-error rule to Rule 8(b) misjoinder simply goes to the additional question whether the error requires setting aside the convictions. We need not decide whether the degree of prejudice necessary to support a Rule 14 motion for severance is identical to that necessary to require reversal for a Rule 8(b) error.

"The dissent fails to recognize that the Rule 14 prejudice component involves a different inquiry from the Rule 8 technical requirements. Indeed, the express language of Rule 14, as well as the Advisory Committee Note, shows that Congress tolerates some Rule 8 joinders even when there is prejudice. The first hurdle in obtaining a severance under Rule 14 is a showing of prejudice, and if shown, it remains in the district court's discretion whether to grant the motion."

b. As explained earlier in this dissent, "if one reads Rule 8 in conjunction with Rule 14, it is immediately apparent that the draftsmen of the Rules regarded every violation of Rule 8 as inherently prejudicial. For Rule 14 authorizes the Court to grant a severance, even in the absence of a Rule 8 violation, if either the defendant or the Government is prejudiced by a joinder of offenses or defendants. Thus, it seems clear that the draftsmen of the Rules regarded violations of Rule 8 as inherently prejudicial, and recognized that even joinders that were not prohibited by the rule should be forbidden if a party could demonstrate actual prejudice."

exception to the harmless-error principle"[c], and (3) "the prejudice that may result from misjoinder is not so difficult to ascertain that it must always be presumed to be present."

GRAY v. MARYLAND

523 U.S. 185, 118 S.Ct. 1151, 140 L.Ed.2d 294 (1998).

Justice BREYER delivered the opinion of the Court.

The issue in this case concerns the application of *Bruton v. United States*, 391 U.S. 123, 88 S.Ct. 1620, 20 L.Ed.2d 476 (1968). *Bruton* involved two defendants accused of participating in the same crime and tried jointly before the same jury. One of the defendants had confessed. His confession named and incriminated the other defendant. The trial judge issued a limiting instruction, telling the jury that it should consider the confession as evidence only against the codefendant who had confessed and not against the defendant named in the confession. *Bruton* held that, despite the limiting instruction, the Constitution forbids the use of such a confession in the joint trial.[a]

The case before us differs from *Bruton* in that the prosecution here redacted the codefendant's confession by substituting for the defendant's name in the confession a blank space or the word "deleted." We must decide whether these substitutions make a significant legal difference. We hold that they do not and that *Bruton*'s protective rule applies.

[Bell confessed to Baltimore police that he, Gray, and Vanlandingham had participated in the beating that resulted in Stacey Williams' death. Bell and Gray were indicted for murder. The trial judge, after denying Gray's motion for a separate trial, permitted the State to introduce a redacted version of Bell's confession. Other witnesses said that six persons (including Bell, Gray, and

---

c. As to this point, Justice Brennan noted: "Rules respecting joinder are based on recognition that the multiplication of charges or defendants may confuse the jury and lead to inferences of habitual criminality or guilt by association. * * * Apart from this, however, joinder rules do not serve 'an independent value besides reliability of the outcome' justifying an exception to the harmless-error principle." Chief Justice Burger's opinion for the Court adopted a similar view of the joinder rules in its application of the harmless error standard. The Chief Justice stressed that: when evidence on the misjoined count was introduced, the trial judge provided a limiting instruction directing the jury to consider each count and defendant separately; the same evidence on the misjoined count 1 would likely have been admissible in any event under Evidence Rule 404(b) (governing evidence of other crimes); and the evidence of guilt was "overwhelming."

a. *Bruton* stated the proposition more narrowly, i.e., that "effective confrontation * * * was possible only if [the witness] affirmed the statement as his." But in *Nelson v. O'Neil*, 402 U.S. 622, 91 S.Ct. 1723, 29 L.Ed.2d 222 (1971), where a police officer testified as to Runnels' confession implicating O'Neil and Runnels took the stand, denied making the confession, and asserted that the substance of the purported confession was false, the Court held there

had been no *Bruton* violation: "The short of the matter is that, given a joint trial and a common defense, Runnels' testimony respecting his out-of-court statement was more favorable to the respondent than any that cross-examination by counsel could possibly have produced had Runnels 'affirmed the statement as his.' It would be unrealistic in the extreme in the circumstances here presented to hold that the respondent was denied either the opportunity or the benefits of full and effective cross-examination of Runnels."

Nelson must be distinguished from *Lilly v. Virginia*, 527 U.S. 116, 119 S.Ct. 1887, 144 L.Ed.2d 117 (1999), where petitioner's accomplice in a 2-day crime spree, *not* joined for trial with petitioner, was called by the prosecution as a witness and invoked his privilege against self-incrimination, after which the court admitted his confession to police, blaming petitioner for the homicide occurring during the spree, as a declaration of an unavailable witness against penal interest. While the state court affirmed defendant's confession on the ground that the accomplice's confession fell within an exception to the hearsay rule, the Supreme Court, although divided as to the breadth of the applicable rule, concluded that "admission of the untested confession" in such circumstances "violated petitioner's Confrontation Clause rights."

Vanlandingham) participated in the beating. Gray testified and denied his participation; Bell did not testify. The jury was instructed not to use the confession as evidence against Gray. Bell and Gray were convicted.]

In deciding whether *Bruton*'s protective rule applies to the redacted confession before us, we must consider both *Bruton*, and a later case, *Richardson v. Marsh*, 481 U.S. 200, 107 S.Ct. 1702, 95 L.Ed.2d 176 (1987), which limited *Bruton*'s scope. We shall briefly summarize each of these two cases.

Bruton, as we have said, involved two defendants—Evans and Bruton—tried jointly for robbery. Evans did not testify, but the Government introduced into evidence Evans' confession, which stated that both he (Evans) and Bruton together had committed the robbery. The trial judge told the jury it could consider the confession as evidence only against Evans, not against Bruton.

This Court held that, despite the limiting instruction, the introduction of Evans' out-of-court confession at Bruton's trial had violated Bruton's right, protected by the Sixth Amendment, to cross-examine witnesses. The Court recognized that in many circumstances a limiting instruction will adequately protect one defendant from the prejudicial effects of the introduction at a joint trial of evidence intended for use only against a different defendant. But it said that

> there are some contexts in which the risk that the jury will not, or cannot, follow instructions is so great, and the consequences of failure so vital to the defendant, that the practical and human limitations of the jury system cannot be ignored. Such a context is presented here, where the powerfully incriminating extrajudicial statements of a codefendant, who stands accused side-by-side with the defendant, are deliberately spread before the jury in a joint trial. Not only are the incriminations devastating to the defendant but their credibility is inevitably suspect.... The unreliability of such evidence is intolerably compounded when the alleged accomplice, as here, does not testify and cannot be tested by cross-examination.

The Court found that Evans' confession constituted just such a "powerfully incriminating extrajudicial statemen[t]," and that its introduction into evidence, insulated from cross-examination, violated Bruton's Sixth Amendment rights.

In *Richardson v. Marsh*, the Court considered a redacted confession. The case involved a joint murder trial of Marsh and Williams. The State had redacted the confession of one defendant, Williams, so as to "omit all reference" to his codefendant, Marsh—"indeed, to omit all indication that *anyone* other than ... Williams" and a third person had "participated in the crime." (emphasis in original). The trial court also instructed the jury not to consider the confession against Marsh. As redacted, the confession indicated that Williams and the third person had discussed the murder in the front seat of a car while they traveled to the victim's house. The redacted confession contained no indication that Marsh— or any other person—was in the car. Later in the trial, however, Marsh testified that she was in the back seat of the car. For that reason, in context, the confession still could have helped convince the jury that Marsh knew about the murder in advance and therefore had participated knowingly in the crime.

The Court held that this redacted confession fell outside *Bruton*'s scope and was admissible (with appropriate limiting instructions) at the joint trial. The Court distinguished Evans' confession in *Bruton* as a confession that was "incriminating on its face" and which had "expressly implicat[ed]" Bruton. By contrast, Williams' confession amounted to "evidence requiring linkage" in that it "became" incriminating in respect to Marsh "only when linked with evidence introduced later at trial." The Court held that the Confrontation Clause is not violated by the admission of a nontestifying codefendant's confession with a proper limiting instruction when, as here, the confession is redacted to eliminate not only the defendant's name, but any reference to his or her existence.

The Court added: "We express no opinion on the admissibility of a confession in which the defendant's name has been replaced with a symbol or neutral pronoun."

Originally, the codefendant's confession in the case before us, like that in *Bruton*, referred to, and directly implicated another defendant. The State, however, redacted that confession by removing the nonconfessing defendant's name. Nonetheless, unlike *Richardson*'s redacted confession, this confession refers directly to the "existence" of the nonconfessing defendant. The State has simply replaced the nonconfessing defendant's name with a kind of symbol, namely the word "deleted" or a blank space set off by commas. The redacted confession, for example, responded to the question "Who was in the group that beat Stacey," with the phrase, "Me,   , and a few other guys." And when the police witness read the confession in court, he said the word "deleted" or "deletion" where the blank spaces appear. We therefore must decide a question that *Richardson* left open, namely whether redaction that replaces a defendant's name with an obvious indication of deletion, such as a blank space, the word "deleted," or a similar symbol, still falls within *Bruton*'s protective rule. We hold that it does.

Bruton, as interpreted by *Richardson*, holds that certain "powerfully incriminating extrajudicial statements of a codefendant"—those naming another defendant—considered as a class, are so prejudicial that limiting instructions cannot work. Unless the prosecutor wishes to hold separate trials or to use separate juries or to abandon use of the confession, he must redact the confession to reduce significantly or to eliminate the special prejudice that the *Bruton* Court found. Redactions that simply replace a name with an obvious blank space or a word such as "deleted" or a symbol or other similarly obvious indications of alteration, however, leave statements that, considered as a class, so closely resemble *Bruton*'s unredacted statements that, in our view, the law must require the same result.

For one thing, a jury will often react similarly to an unredacted confession and a confession redacted in this way, for the jury will often realize that the confession refers specifically to the defendant. This is true even when the State does not blatantly link the defendant to the deleted name, as it did in this case by asking whether Gray was arrested on the basis of information in Bell's confession as soon as the officer had finished reading the redacted statement. Consider a simplified but typical example, a confession that reads "I, Bob Smith, along with Sam Jones, robbed the bank." To replace the words "Sam Jones" with an obvious blank will not likely fool anyone. A juror somewhat familiar with criminal law would know immediately that the blank, in the phrase "I, Bob Smith, along with , robbed the bank," refers to defendant Jones. A juror who does not know the law and who therefore wonders to whom the blank might refer need only lift his eyes to Jones, sitting at counsel table, to find what will seem the obvious answer, at least if the juror hears the judge's instruction not to consider the confession as evidence against Jones, for that instruction will provide an obvious reason for the blank. A more sophisticated juror, wondering if the blank refers to someone else, might also wonder how, if it did, the prosecutor could argue the confession is reliable, for the prosecutor, after all, has been arguing that Jones, not someone else, helped Smith commit the crime.

For another thing, the obvious deletion may well call the jurors' attention specially to the removed name. By encouraging the jury to speculate about the reference, the redaction may overemphasize the importance of the confession's accusation—once the jurors work out the reference. That is why Judge Learned Hand, many years ago, wrote in a similar instance that blacking out the name of a codefendant not only "would have been futile. . . . [T]here could not have been the slightest doubt as to whose names had been blacked out" but "even if there had been, that blacking out itself would have not only laid the doubt, but underscored the answer."

Finally, *Bruton*'s protected statements and statements redacted to leave a blank or some other similarly obvious alteration, function the same way grammatically. They are directly accusatory. Evans' statement in *Bruton* used a proper name to point explicitly to an accused defendant. And *Bruton* held that the "powerfully incriminating" effect of what Justice Stewart called "an out-of-court accusation," creates a special, and vital, need for cross-examination—a need that would be immediately obvious had the codefendant pointed directly to the defendant in the courtroom itself. The blank space in an obviously redacted confession also points directly to the defendant, and it accuses the defendant in a manner similar to Evans' use of Bruton's name or to a testifying codefendant's accusatory finger. By way of contrast, the factual statement at issue in *Richardson*—a statement about what others said in the front seat of a car—differs from directly accusatory evidence in this respect, for it does not point directly to a defendant at all.

We concede certain differences between *Bruton* and this case. A confession that uses a blank or the word "delete" (or, for that matter, a first name or a nickname) less obviously refers to the defendant than a confession that uses the defendant's full and proper name. Moreover, in some instances the person to whom the blank refers may not be clear: Although the follow-up question asked by the State in this case eliminated all doubt, the reference might not be transparent in other cases in which a confession, like the present confession, uses two (or more) blanks, even though only one other defendant appears at trial, and in which the trial indicates that there are more participants than the confession has named. Nonetheless, as we have said, we believe that, considered as a class, redactions that replace a proper name with an obvious blank, the word "delete," a symbol, or similarly notify the jury that a name has been deleted are similar enough to *Bruton*'s unredacted confessions as to warrant the same legal results.

The State, in arguing for a contrary conclusion, relies heavily upon *Richardson*. But we do not believe *Richardson* controls the result here. We concede that *Richardson* placed outside the scope of *Bruton*'s rule those statements that incriminate inferentially. We also concede that the jury must use inference to connect the statement in this redacted confession with the defendant. But inference pure and simple cannot make the critical difference, for if it did, then *Richardson* would also place outside *Bruton*'s scope confessions that use shortened first names, nicknames, descriptions as unique as the "red-haired, bearded, one-eyed man-with-a-limp," and perhaps even full names of defendants who are always known by a nickname. This Court has assumed, however, that nicknames and specific descriptions fall inside, not outside, *Bruton*'s protection. * * *

That being so, *Richardson* must depend in significant part upon the kind of, not the simple fact of, inference. *Richardson*'s inferences involved statements that did not refer directly to the defendant himself and which became incriminating "only when linked with evidence introduced later at trial." The inferences at issue here involve statements that, despite redaction, obviously refer directly to someone, often obviously the defendant, and which involve inferences that a jury ordinarily could make immediately, even were the confession the very first item introduced at trial. Moreover, the redacted confession with the blank prominent on its face, in *Richardson*'s words, "*facially* incriminat[es]" the codefendant. (emphasis added). Like the confession in *Bruton* itself, the accusation that the redacted confession makes "is more vivid than inferential incrimination, and hence more difficult to thrust out of mind."

Nor are the policy reasons that *Richardson* provided in support of its conclusion applicable here. *Richardson* expressed concern lest application of *Bruton*'s rule apply where "redaction" of confessions, particularly "confessions incriminating by connection," would often "not [be] possible," thereby forcing prosecutors too often to abandon use either of the confession or of a joint trial. Additional redaction of a confession that uses a blank space, the word "delete," or a symbol, however, normally is possible. Consider as an example a portion of the confession before us: The witness who read the confession told the jury that the confession (among other things) said,

Question: Who was in the group that beat Stacey?

Answer: Me, deleted, deleted, and a few other guys.

Why could the witness not, instead, have said:

Question: Who was in the group that beat Stacey?

Answer: Me and a few other guys.

Richardson itself provides a similar example of this kind of redaction. The confession there at issue had been "redacted to omit all reference to respondent— indeed, to omit all indication that anyone other than Martin and Williams participated in the crime," and it did not indicate that it had been redacted. * * *

The *Richardson* Court also feared that the inclusion, within *Bruton*'s protective rule, of confessions that incriminated "by connection" too often would provoke mistrials, or would unnecessarily lead prosecutors to abandon the confession or joint trial, because neither the prosecutors nor the judge could easily predict, until after the introduction of all the evidence, whether or not *Bruton* had barred use of the confession. To include the use of blanks, the word "delete," symbols, or other indications of redaction, within *Bruton*'s protections, however, runs no such risk. Their use is easily identified prior to trial and does not depend, in any special way, upon the other evidence introduced in the case. We also note that several Circuits have interpreted *Bruton* similarly for many years, yet no one has told us of any significant practical difficulties arising out of their administration of that rule.

For these reasons, we hold that the confession here at issue, which substituted blanks and the word "delete" for the respondent's proper name, falls within the class of statements to which *Bruton*'s protections apply. * * *

Justice SCALIA, with whom THE CHIEF JUSTICE, Justice KENNEDY, and Justice THOMAS join, dissenting. * * *

The almost invariable assumption of the law is that jurors follow their instructions. This rule "is a pragmatic one, rooted less in the absolute certitude that the presumption is true than in the belief that it represents a reasonable practical accommodation of the interests of the state and the defendant in the criminal justice process." * * * In *Bruton*, we recognized a "narrow exception" to this rule: "We held that a defendant is deprived of his Sixth Amendment right of confrontation when the facially incriminating confession of a nontestifying codefendant is introduced at their joint trial, even if the jury is instructed to consider the confession only against the codefendant."

We declined in *Richardson*, however, to extend *Bruton* to confessions that incriminate only by inference from other evidence. When incrimination is inferential, "it is a less valid generalization that the jury will not likely obey the instruction to disregard the evidence." Today the Court struggles to decide whether a confession redacted to omit the defendant's name is incriminating on its face or by inference. On the one hand, the Court "concede[s] that the jury must use inference to connect the statement in this redacted confession with the defendant," but later asserts, on the other hand, that "the redacted confession with the blank prominent on its face ... 'facially incriminat[es]' " him. The Court should have stopped with its concession: the statement "Me, deleted, deleted, and a few other guys" does not facially incriminate anyone but the speaker. The Court's analogizing of "deleted" to a physical description that clearly identifies the defendant (which we have assumed *Bruton* covers, see *Harrington v. California*, 395 U.S. 250, 89 S.Ct. 1726, 23 L.Ed.2d 284 (1969)) does not survive scrutiny. By "facially incriminating," we have meant incriminating independent of other evidence introduced at trial. *Richardson*, supra,. Since the defendant's appearance at counsel table is not evidence, the description "red-haired, bearded, one-eyed man-with-a-limp," would be facially incriminating—unless, of course, the defendant had dyed his hair black and shaved his beard before trial, and the prosecution introduced evidence concerning his former appearance. Similarly, the statement "Me, Kevin Gray, and a few other guys" would be facially incriminating, unless the defendant's name set forth in the indictment was not Kevin Gray, and evidence was introduced to the effect that he sometimes used "Kevin Gray" as an alias. By contrast, the person to whom "deleted" refers in "Me, deleted, deleted, and a few other guys" is not apparent from anything the jury knows independent of the evidence at trial. Though the jury may speculate, the statement expressly implicates no one but the speaker.

Of course the Court is correct that confessions redacted to omit the defendant's name are more likely to incriminate than confessions redacted to omit any reference to his existence. But it is also true—and more relevant here—that confessions redacted to omit the defendant's name are less likely to incriminate than confessions that expressly state it. The latter are "powerfully incriminating" as a class, *Bruton*, supra; the former are not so. Here, for instance, there were two names deleted, five or more participants in the crime, and only one other defendant on trial. The jury no doubt may "speculate about the reference," as it speculates when evidence connects a defendant to a confession that does not refer to his existence. The issue, however, is not whether the confession incriminated petitioner, but whether the incrimination is so "powerful" that we must depart from the normal presumption that the jury follows its instructions. *Richardson*, supra. I think it is not—and I am certain that drawing the line for departing from the ordinary rule at the facial identification of the defendant makes more sense than drawing it anywhere else.

The Court's extension of *Bruton* to name-redacted confessions "as a class" will seriously compromise "society's compelling interest in finding, convicting, and punishing those who violate the law." We explained in *Richardson* that forgoing use of codefendant confessions or joint trials was "too high" a price to insure that juries never disregard their instructions. The Court minimizes the damage that it does by suggesting that "[a]dditional redaction of a confession that uses a blank space, the word 'delete,' or a symbol ... normally is possible." In the present case, it asks, why could the police officer not have testified that Bell's answer was "Me and a few other guys"? The answer, it seems obvious to me, is because that is not what Bell said. Bell's answer was "Me, Tank, Kevin and a few other guys." Introducing the statement with full disclosure of deletions is one thing; introducing as the complete statement what was in fact only a part is something else. And of course even concealed deletions from the text will often not do the job that the Court demands. For inchoate offenses—conspiracy in particular—redaction to delete all reference to a confederate would often render the confession nonsensical. If the question was "Who agreed to beat Stacey?", and the answer was "Me and Kevin," we might redact the answer to "Me and [deleted]," or perhaps to "Me and somebody else," but surely not to just "Me"—for that would no longer be a confession to the conspiracy charge, but rather the foundation for an insanity defense. To my knowledge we have never before endorsed—and to my strong belief we ought not endorse—the redaction of a statement by some means other than the deletion of certain words, with the fact of the deletion shown. The risk to the integrity of our system (not to mention the increase in its complexity) posed by the approval of such free-lance editing seems to me infinitely greater than the risk posed by the entirely honest reproduction that the Court disapproves.

The United States Constitution guarantees, not a perfect system of criminal justice (as to which there can be considerable disagreement), but a minimum standard of fairness. Lest we lose sight of the forest for the trees, it should be borne in mind that federal and state rules of criminal procedure—which can afford to seek perfection because they can be more readily changed—exclude non-testifying-codefendant confessions even where the Sixth Amendment does not. Under the Federal Rules of Criminal Procedure (and Maryland's), a trial court may order separate trials if joinder will prejudice a defendant. See Fed. Rule Crim. Proc. 14; Md.Crim. Rule 4–253(c) (1998). * * * Here, petitioner moved for a severance on the ground that the admission of Bell's confession would be unfairly prejudicial. The trial court denied the motion, explaining that where a confession names two others, and the evidence is that five or six others participated, redaction of petitioner's name would not leave the jury with the "unavoidable inference" that Bell implicated Gray.

I do not understand the Court to disagree that the redaction itself left unclear to whom the blank referred.[2] That being so, the rule set forth in *Richardson* applies, and the statement could constitutionally be admitted with limiting instruction. This remains, insofar as the Sixth Amendment is concerned, the most "reasonable practical accommodation of the interests of the state and the defendant in the criminal justice process." * * *

Notes and Questions

1. Benjamin and Eulogio were jointly tried for felony murder. The prosecution admitted against Benjamin his videotaped confession implicating Eulogio, and also called Norberto, who testified about his conversation with the two defendants, when each of them described the circumstances of the felony murder to him. Both defendants were convicted. Eulogio's conviction was affirmed on appeal; the court adopted the reasoning of the plurality in *Parker v. Randolph,* 442 U.S. 62, 99 S.Ct. 2132, 60 L.Ed.2d 713 (1979), that *Bruton* was inapplicable to "interlocking" confessions because in such circumstances the codefendant's confession "will seldom, if ever, be of the 'devastating' character referred to in

2. The Court does believe, however, that the answer to a "follow-up question"—"All right, now, officer, after he gave you that information, you subsequently were able to arrest Mr. Kevin Gray; is that correct?" ("That's correct")—"eliminated all doubt" as to the subject of the redaction. That is probably not so, and is certainly far from clear. Testimony that preceded the introduction of Bell's confession had already established that Gray had become a suspect in the case, and that a warrant had been issued for his arrest, before Bell confessed. Respondent contends that, given this trial background, and in its context, the prosecutor's question did not imply any connection between Bell's confession and Gray's arrest, and was simply a means of making the transition from Bell's statement to the next piece of evidence, Gray's statement. That is at least arguable, and an appellate court is in a poor position to resolve such a contextual question de novo. * * * But if the question did bring the redaction home to the defendant, surely that shows the impropriety of the question rather than of the redaction—and the question was not objected to. The failure to object deprives petitioner of the right to complain of some incremental identifiability added to the redacted statement by the question and answer. Of course the Court's reliance upon this testimony belies its contention that name-redacted confessions are powerfully incriminating "as a class."

Bruton.'' The Supreme Court, in the 5–4 decision of CRUZ v. NEW YORK, 481 U.S. 186, 107 S.Ct. 1714, 95 L.Ed.2d 162 (1987), reversed. SCALIA, J., for the majority, declared:

" * * * While 'devastating' practical effect was one of the factors that *Bruton* considered in assessing whether the Confrontation Clause might sometimes require departure from the general rule that jury instructions suffice to exclude improper testimony, it did not suggest that the existence of such an effect should be assessed on a case-by-case basis. Rather, that factor was one of the justifications for excepting from the general rule the entire category of codefendant confessions that implicate the defendant in the crime. It is impossible to imagine why there should be excluded from that category, as generally not 'devastating,' codefendant confessions that 'interlock' with the defendant's own confession. '[T]he infinite variability of inculpatory statements (whether made by defendants or codefendants), and of their likely effect on juries, makes [the assumption that an interlocking confession will preclude devastation] untenable.' *Parker* (Stevens, J., dissenting). In this case, for example, the precise content and even the existence of the petitioner's own confession were open to question, since they depended upon acceptance of Norberto's testimony, whereas the incriminating confession of codefendant Benjamin was on videotape.

"In fact, it seems to us that 'interlocking' bears a positively inverse relationship to devastation. A codefendant's confession will be relatively harmless if the incriminating story it tells is different from that which the defendant himself is alleged to have told, but enormously damaging if it confirms, in all essential respects, the defendant's alleged confession. It might be otherwise if the defendant were *standing by* his confession, in which case it could be said that the codefendant's confession does no more than support the defendant's very own case. But in the real world of criminal litigation, the defendant is seeking to *avoid* his confession—on the ground that it was not accurately reported, or that it was not really true when made. In the present case, for example, the petitioner sought to establish that Norberto had a motive for falsely reporting a confession that never in fact occurred. In such circumstances a codefendant's confession that corroborates the defendant's confession significantly harms the defendant's case, whereas one that is positively incompatible gives credence to the defendant's assertion that his own alleged confession was nonexistent or false. Quite obviously, what the 'interlocking' nature of the codefendant's confession pertains to is not its *harmfulness* but rather its *reliability:* If it confirms essentially the same facts as the defendant's own confession it is more likely to be true. Its reliability, however, may be relevant to whether the confession should (despite the lack of opportunity for cross-examination) be *admitted as evidence* against the defendant, see *Lee v. Illinois* [p. 1069], but cannot conceivably be relevant to whether, assuming it cannot be admitted, the jury is likely to obey the instruction to disregard it, or the jury's failure to obey is likely to be inconsequential. The law cannot command respect if such an inexplicable exception to a supposed constitutional imperative is adopted. Having decided *Bruton,* we must face the honest consequences of what it holds.''

WHITE, J., for the dissenters, objected: "*Bruton* held that where the defendant has not himself confessed, there is too great a chance that the jury would rely on the codefendant's confession. But here, Cruz had admitted the crime and this fact was before the jury. I disagree with the Court's proposition that in every interlocking confession case, the jury, with the defendant's confession properly before it, would be tempted to disobey its instructions and fail to understand that presumptively unreliable evidence must not be used against the defendant. Nor is it remotely possible that in every case the admission of an interlocking confession by a codefendant will have the devastating effect referred to in *Bruton.*[2]"

2. In TENNESSEE v. STREET, 471 U.S. 409, 105 S.Ct. 2078, 85 L.Ed.2d 425 (1985), Street testified at trial that his confession to murder and burglary had been coerced by the sheriff reading to him the prior confession of severed codefendant Peele and then directing Street to say the same thing. Peele's confession was then admitted in rebuttal to show the several differences in the two confessions. The Court, per Chief Justice BURGER, after concluding that use of Peele's confession for this "legitimate, nonhearsay purpose" itself "raises no Confrontation Clause concerns," noted that the "only similarity to *Bruton* is that Peele's statement, like the codefendant's confession in *Bruton,* could have been misused by the jury." But in the present context the Court concluded that the trial court's limiting instruction (that Peele's confession was to be considered "for the purpose of rebuttal only") constituted an "appropriate way to limit the jury's use of that evidence in a manner consistent with the Confrontation Clause." This was because here, "unlike the situation in *Bruton,* there were no alternatives that would have both assured the integrity of the trial's truthseeking function and eliminated the risk of the jury's improper use of evidence." The already-granted severance did not solve the problem, and redaction of Peele's confession "would have made it more difficult for the jury to evaluate" Street's claim that his confession was a coerced imitation of Peele's.

3. *In re Hill,* 458 P.2d 449 (Cal.1969), held that "the Sixth Amendment right to confrontation is intended to give to defendants in criminal cases the right to cross-examine as to statements made by the witness *at the time the witness makes those statements,*" so that *Bruton* applies even when the confessing codefendant "took the stand and testified consistently with his prior extra-judicial statements." However, that position was rejected in *California v. Green,* [p. 902] upholding a California statute which permitted the admission of a witness' prior inconsistent statement to prove the truth of the matter asserted therein, whether or not the defense had an opportunity for cross-examination when it was made. After noting that "there is little difference as far as the Constitution is concerned" between that situation and *Bruton,* the Court held that "the Confrontation Clause does not require excluding from evidence the prior statements of a witness who concedes making the statements, and who may be asked to defend or otherwise explain the inconsistency between his prior and his present version of the events in question, thus opening himself to full cross-examination at trial as to both stories." What then, in a *Bruton*-type situation, of a case in which the confessing co-defendant does *not* take the stand at trial, but did testify in earlier proceedings?

In *Lee v. Illinois,* 476 U.S. 530, 106 S.Ct. 2056, 90 L.Ed.2d 514 (1986),[a] the Court dropped this footnote: "Illinois makes the somewhat surprising argument—

---

2. The Court is of the view that " 'interlocking' bears a positively inverse relationship to devastation." In so reasoning, the Court gives no weight whatsoever to the devastating effect that the defendant's own confession is likely to have upon his case. The majority's excuse for ignoring this consideration apparently is that the damaging effect of the defendant's confession may vary somewhat from case to case. But the *Bruton* rule is prophylactic in nature, and, in view of the fact that it imposes significant burdens on the prosecution, the rule should be confined to those cases where the jury's ignoring of limiting instructions is most likely to change the verdict, which is to say, those cases where there is the greatest risk that jury misconduct will lead to the conviction of an innocent defendant. It is self-evident that, as a class, cases where the defendant has not confessed fit that description far better than cases where the defendant has confessed.

a. The issue before the Court in *Lee,* Justice Brennan had previously noted, was "not strictly speaking a *Bruton* [problem] * * * because we are not here concerned with the effectiveness of limiting instructions in preventing spill-over prejudice to a defendant when his codefendant's confession is admitted

an argument, incidentally, that was not made before the state court—that this case does not present any Confrontation Clause issue since Lee was afforded an opportunity to cross-examine Thomas during the suppression hearing. We disagree.

"The function of a suppression hearing is to determine the voluntariness, and hence the admissibility for Fifth Amendment purposes, of a confession. The truth or falsity of the statement is not relevant to the voluntariness inquiry, and no such testimony was given by Thomas. Counsel for both Lee and Thomas specifically stated that their clients were testifying 'for purposes of the motion to suppress the confession only.' Before either defendant took the stand, the court announced, 'Let the record show the testimony of this defendant will be used solely for the purpose of sustaining the motion to suppress previously made.'

"Thus there was no opportunity to cross-examine Thomas with respect to the reliability of the statement, especially as it may have related to Lee, and thus no opportunity for cross-examination sufficient to satisfy the demands of the Confrontation Clause."

4. Other grounds upon which defendants sometimes obtain severances are: (a) because the number of defendants or the complexity of the evidence as to the several defendants is such that the trier of fact probably will be unable to distinguish the evidence and apply the law intelligently as to the charges against each defendant; (b) because the several defendants have antagonistic defenses; and (c) because it would otherwise be impossible to call a codefendant as a witness. As to (b), "defendants are not entitled to severance merely because they may have a better chance of acquittal in separate trials" or "whenever codefendants have conflicting defenses"; rather, a court should grant a severance "only if there is a serious risk that a joint trial would compromise a specific trial right of one of the defendants, or prevent the jury from making a reliable judgment about guilt or innocence," as "might occur when evidence that the jury should not consider against a defendant and that would not be admissible if a defendant were tried alone is admitted against a codefendant." *Zafiro v. United States*, 506 U.S. 534, 113 S.Ct. 933, 122 L.Ed.2d 317 (1993). As to (c), "the defendant must show that he would call the codefendant at a severed trial, that the codefendant would in fact testify, and that the testimony would be favorable to the moving defendant." *United States v. Vigil*, 561 F.2d 1316 (9th Cir.1977). Compare Peter Westen, *The Compulsory Process Clause*, 73 Mich.L.Rev. 73, 143 (1974), arguing that "once the defendant shows that his co-defendant may be able to exculpate him—either by showing that the co-defendant has already exculpated him out of

against the codefendant at a joint trial." Here, the codefendant's confession was used as substantive evidence against the petitioner. Accordingly, under the standards set forth in *Ohio v. Roberts* [p. 903], the critical question was whether that statement of an unavailable witness bore "sufficient indicia of reliability" to allow its admission consistent with the Confrontation Clause.

In *Gabow v. Commonwealth*, 34 S.W.3d 63 (Ky.2000), the court referred to *Lee*'s assertion that the presumption of unreliability can be overcome only by sufficient independent "indicia of reliability," and to the *Ohio v. Roberts* holding that reliability may be inferred where the evidence (i) falls within a "firmly rooted" exception to the hearsay rule, or (ii) otherwise possesses "particularized guarantees of trustworthiness," as collectively supporting the con-

clusion that "even though a particularized guarantee of trustworthiness might be an insufficient indicia of reliability, an unspecified number of such guarantees, taken together, can constitute a totality of circumstances which would be just as reliable as a 'firmly rooted' exception to the hearsay rule." The *Gabow* court then held the co-conspirator's confession admissible against the defendant in the instant case by considering a cluster of six factors, including that the confession was self-inculpatory without shifting blame, the confession was confirmed by defendant's own confession in all significant respects, the confession attributed to defendant information peculiarly within defendant's knowledge, and defendant's claimed renunciation exculpated the co-conspirator as well, meaning he had no motive to contradict her claim.

court or by reference to the nature of the offense—and that joinder 'could' tend to silence the witness, the burden should shift to the government to demonstrate that joinder would have no such effect."

5. *De Luna v. United States,* 308 F.2d 140 (5th Cir.1962), involved these facts: de Luna and Gomez, after denial of a severance motion, were jointly tried on a narcotics charge. They were the occupants of a moving car from which police had seen Gomez throw a package of narcotics. Gomez testified that he was innocent, explaining that de Luna had thrown the package to him and told him to throw it out the window when the police approached. De Luna did not testify, but his lawyer argued that Gomez had the package at all times. Gomez's attorney commented on de Luna's failure to take the stand. Gomez was acquitted; de Luna was found guilty. On appeal, de Luna's conviction was reversed because of the violation of his privilege against self-incrimination. Two members of the court went on to say that under these circumstances the proper result below would have been to permit the comment and then grant a severance. Gomez's "attorneys should be free to draw all rational inferences from the failure of a co-defendant to testify, just as an attorney is free to comment on the effect of any interested party's failure to produce material evidence in his possession or to call witnesses who have knowledge of pertinent facts."

Is the analogy an apt one? Given the analysis in *Griffin v. California,* p. 1413, what "rational inferences" may be drawn from de Luna's failure to testify? What if Gomez's attorney had merely called attention to the fact that his client had taken the stand?

[handwritten margin notes: 4 Factor Balancing Test, 1) Length, 2) Reason, 3) Assertion of right, 4) prejudice, Periods of delay, 30 days, 70 days]

Chapter 19

THE RIGHT TO SPEEDY TRIAL AND OTHER SPEEDY DISPOSITION

SECTION 1. SPEEDY TRIAL[a]

BARKER v. WINGO

407 U.S. 514, 92 S.Ct. 2182, 33 L.Ed.2d 101 (1972).

Justice POWELL delivered the opinion of the Court.

Although a speedy trial is guaranteed the accused by the Sixth Amendment to the Constitution, this Court has dealt with that right on infrequent occasions. The Court's opinion in *Klopfer v. North Carolina,* 386 U.S. 213, 87 S.Ct. 988, 18 L.Ed.2d 1 (1967), established that the right to speedy trial is "fundamental" and is imposed by the Due Process Clause of the Fourteenth Amendment on the States. [I]n none of these cases have we attempted to set out the criteria by which the speedy trial right is to be judged. This case compels us to make such an attempt.

On July 20, 1958, in Christian County, Kentucky, an elderly couple was beaten to death by intruders wielding an iron tire tool. Two suspects, Silas Manning and Willie Barker, the petitioner, were arrested shortly thereafter. The grand jury indicted them on September 15. Counsel was appointed on September 17, and Barker's trial was set for October 21. The Commonwealth had a stronger case against Manning, and it believed that Barker could not be convicted unless Manning testified against him. Manning was naturally unwilling to incriminate himself. Accordingly, on October 23, the day Silas Manning was brought to trial, the Commonwealth sought and obtained the first of what was to be a series of 16 continuances of Barker's trial. Barker made no objection. By first convicting Manning, the Commonwealth would remove possible problems of self-incrimination and would be able to assure his testimony against Barker.

The Commonwealth encountered more than a few difficulties in its prosecution of Manning. The first trial ended in a hung jury. A second trial resulted in a conviction, but the Kentucky Court of Appeals reversed because of the admission of evidence obtained by an illegal search. At his third trial, Manning was again convicted, and the Court of Appeals again reversed because the trial court had not granted a change of venue. A fourth trial resulted in a hung jury. Finally, after five trials, Manning was convicted, in March 1962, of murdering one victim, and after a sixth trial, in December 1962, he was convicted of murdering the other.

The Christian County Circuit Court holds three terms each year—in February, June, and September. Barker's initial trial was to take place in the September term of 1958. The first continuance postponed it until the February 1959 term. The second continuance was granted for one month only. Every term thereafter

a. See Robert L. Misner, *Speedy Trial: Federal and State Practice* (1983); Gregory P.N. Joseph, *Speedy Trial Rights in Application,* 48 Fordham L.Rev. 611 (1980).

for as long as the Manning prosecutions were in process, the Commonwealth routinely moved to continue Barker's case to the next term. When the case was continued from the June 1959 term until the following September, Barker, having spent 10 months in jail, obtained his release by posting a $5,000 bond. He thereafter remained free in the community until his trial. Barker made no objection, through his counsel, to the first 11 continuances.

When on February 12, 1962, the Commonwealth moved for the twelfth time to continue the case until the following term, Barker's counsel filed a motion to dismiss the indictment. The motion to dismiss was denied two weeks later, and the State's motion for a continuance was granted. The State was granted further continuances in June 1962 and September 1962, to which Barker did not object.

In February 1963, the first term of court following Manning's final conviction, the Commonwealth moved to set Barker's trial for March 19. But on the day scheduled for trial, it again moved for a continuance until the June term. It gave as its reason the illness of the ex-sheriff who was the chief investigating officer in the case. To this continuance, Barker objected unsuccessfully.

The witness was still unable to testify in June, and the trial, which had been set for June 19, was continued again until the September term over Barker's objection. This time the court announced that the case would be dismissed for lack of prosecution if it were not tried during the next term. The final trial date was set for October 9, 1963. On that date, Barker again moved to dismiss the indictment, and this time specified that his right to a speedy trial had been violated. The motion was denied; the trial commenced with Manning as the chief prosecution witness; Barker was convicted and given a life sentence.

Barker appealed his conviction to the Kentucky Court of Appeals, relying in part on his speedy trial claim. The court affirmed. In February 1970 Barker petitioned for habeas corpus in the United States District Court for the Western District of Kentucky. Although the District Court rejected the petition without holding a hearing, the Court granted petitioner leave to appeal *in forma pauperis* and a certificate of probable cause to appeal. On appeal, the Court of Appeals for the Sixth Circuit affirmed the District Court. * * * We granted Barker's petition for certiorari.

The right to a speedy trial is generically different from any of the other rights enshrined in the Constitution for the protection of the accused. In addition to the general concern that all accused persons be treated according to decent and fair procedures, there is a societal interest in providing a speedy trial which exists separate from and at times in opposition to the interests of the accused. The inability of courts to provide a prompt trial has contributed to a large backlog of cases in urban courts which, among other things, enables defendants to negotiate more effectively for pleas of guilty to lesser offenses and otherwise manipulate the system. In addition, persons released on bond for lengthy periods awaiting trial have an opportunity to commit other crimes. It must be of little comfort to the residents of Christian County, Kentucky, to know that Barker was at large on bail for over four years while accused of a vicious and brutal murder of which he was ultimately convicted. Moreover, the longer an accused is free awaiting trial, the more tempting becomes his opportunity to jump bail and escape. Finally, delay between arrest and punishment may have a detrimental effect on rehabilitation.

If an accused cannot make bail, he is generally confined, as was Barker for 10 months, in a local jail. This contributes to the overcrowding and generally deplorable state of those institutions. Lengthy exposure to these conditions "has a destructive effect on human character and makes the rehabilitation of the individual offender much more difficult." At times the result may even be violent rioting. Finally, lengthy pretrial detention is costly. The cost of maintaining a prisoner in jail varies from $3 to $9 per day, and this amounts to millions across the Nation. In addition, society loses wages which might have been earned, and it must often support families of incarcerated breadwinners.

A second difference between the right to speedy trial and the accused's other constitutional rights is that deprivation of the right may work to the accused's advantage. Delay is not an uncommon defense tactic. As the time between the commission of the crime and trial lengthens, witnesses may become unavailable or their memories may fade. If the witnesses support the prosecution, its case will be weakened, sometimes seriously so. And it is the prosecution which carries the burden of proof. Thus, unlike the right to counsel or the right to be free from compelled self-incrimination, deprivation of the right to speedy trial does not *per se* prejudice the accused's ability to defend himself.

Finally, and perhaps most importantly, the right to speedy trial is a more vague concept than other procedural rights. It is, for example, impossible to determine with precision when the right has been denied. We cannot definitely say how long is too long in a system where justice is supposed to be swift but deliberate. As a consequence, there is no fixed point in the criminal process when the State can put the defendant to the choice of either exercising or waiving the right to a speedy trial. If, for example, the State moves for a 60-day continuance, granting that continuance is not a violation of the right to speedy trial unless the circumstances of the case are such that further delay would endanger the values the right protects. It is impossible to do more than generalize about when those circumstances exist. There is nothing comparable to the point in the process when a defendant exercises or waives his right to counsel or his right to a jury trial. * * *

The amorphous quality of the right also leads to the unsatisfactorily severe remedy of dismissal of the indictment when the right has been deprived. This is indeed a serious consequence because it means that a defendant who may be guilty of a serious crime will go free, without having been tried. Such a remedy is more serious than an exclusionary rule or a reversal for a new trial, but it is the only possible remedy.

Perhaps because the speedy trial right is so slippery, two rigid approaches are urged upon us as ways of eliminating some of the uncertainty which courts experience in protecting the right. The first suggestion is that we hold that the Constitution requires a criminal defendant to be offered a trial within a specified time period. The result of such a ruling would have the virtue of clarifying when the right is infringed and of simplifying courts' application of it. Recognizing this, some legislatures have enacted laws, and some courts have adopted procedural rules which more narrowly define the right. * * *

But such a result would require this Court to engage in legislative or rulemaking activity, rather than in the adjudicative process to which we should confine our efforts. We do not establish procedural rules for the States, except when mandated by the Constitution. We find no constitutional basis for holding that the speedy trial right can be quantified into a specified number of days or months. The States, of course, are free to prescribe a reasonable period consistent with constitutional standards, but our approach must be less precise.

The second suggested alternative would restrict consideration of the right to those cases in which the accused has demanded a speedy trial. Most States have recognized what is loosely referred to as the "demand rule," although eight States reject it. It is not clear, however, precisely what is meant by that term. Although every Federal Court of Appeals that has considered the question has endorsed some kind of demand rule, some have regarded the rule within the concept of waiver, whereas others have viewed it as a factor to be weighed in assessing whether there has been a deprivation of the speedy trial right. We shall refer to the former approach as the demand-waiver doctrine. The demand-waiver doctrine provides that a defendant waives any consideration of his right to speedy trial for any period prior to which he has not demanded a trial. Under this rigid approach, a prior demand is a necessary condition to the consideration of the speedy trial right. This essentially was the approach the Sixth Circuit took below.

Such an approach, by presuming waiver of a fundamental right from inaction, is inconsistent with this Court's pronouncements on waiver of constitutional rights. The Court has defined waiver as "an intentional relinquishment or abandonment of a known right or privilege." Courts should "indulge every reasonable presumption against waiver," and they should "not presume acquiescence in the loss of fundamental rights." * * *

In excepting the right to speedy trial from the rule of waiver we have applied to other fundamental rights, courts that have applied the demand-waiver rule have relied on the assumption that delay usually works for the benefit of the accused and on the absence of any readily ascertainable time in the criminal process for a defendant to be given the choice of exercising or waiving his right. But it is not necessarily true that delay benefits the defendant. There are cases in which delay appreciably harms the defendant's ability to defend himself. Moreover, a defendant confined to jail prior to trial is obviously disadvantaged by delay as is a defendant released on bail but unable to lead a normal life because of community suspicion and his own anxiety.

The nature of the speedy-trial right does make it impossible to pinpoint a precise time in the process when the right must be asserted or waived, but that fact does not argue for placing the burden of protecting the right solely on defendants. A defendant has no duty to bring himself to trial; the State has that duty as well as the duty of insuring that the trial is consistent with due process. Moreover, for the reasons earlier expressed, society has a particular interest in bringing swift prosecutions, and society's representatives are the ones who should protect that interest.

It is also noteworthy that such a rigid view of the demand rule places defense counsel in an awkward position. Unless he demands a trial early and often, he is in danger of frustrating his client's right. If counsel is willing to tolerate some delay because he finds it reasonable and helpful in preparing his own case, he may be unable to obtain a speedy trial for his client at the end of that time. Since under the demand-waiver rule no time runs until the demand is made, the government will have whatever time is otherwise reasonable to bring the defendant to trial after a demand has been made. Thus, if the first demand is made three months after arrest in a jurisdiction which prescribes a six months rule, the prosecution will have a total of nine months—which may be wholly unreasonable under the circumstances. The result in practice is likely to be either an automatic, *pro forma* demand made immediately after appointment of counsel or delays which, but for the demand-waiver rule, would not be tolerated. Such a result is not consistent with the interests of defendants, society, or the Constitution.

We reject, therefore, the rule that a defendant who fails to demand a speedy trial forever waives his right. This does not mean, however, that the defendant has no responsibility to assert his right. We think the better rule is that the defendant's assertion of or failure to assert his right to a speedy trial is one of the factors to be considered in an inquiry into the deprivation of the right. Such a formulation avoids the rigidities of the demand-waiver rule and the resulting possible unfairness in its application. It allows the trial court to exercise a judicial discretion based on the circumstances, including due consideration of any applicable formal procedural rule. It would permit, for example, a court to attach a different weight to a situation in which the defendant knowingly fails to object from a situation in which his attorney acquiesces in long delay without adequately informing his client or from a situation in which no counsel is appointed. It would also allow a court to weigh the frequency and force of the objections as opposed to attaching significant weight to a purely *pro forma* objection.

In ruling that a defendant has some responsibility to assert a speedy-trial claim, we do not depart from our holdings in other cases concerning the waiver of fundamental rights, in which we have placed the entire responsibility on the prosecution to show that the claimed waiver was knowingly and voluntarily made. Such cases have involved rights which must be exercised or waived at a specific time or under clearly identifiable circumstances, such as the rights to plead not guilty, to demand a jury trial, to exercise the privilege against self incrimination, and to have the assistance of counsel. We have shown above that the right to a speedy trial is unique in its uncertainty as to when and under what circumstances it must be asserted or may be deemed waived. But the rule we announce today, which comports with constitutional principles, places the primary burden on the courts and the prosecutors to assure that cases are brought to trial. We hardly need add that if delay is attributable to the defendant, then his waiver may be given effect under standard waiver doctrine, the demand rule aside.

We, therefore, reject both of the inflexible approaches—the fixed time period because it goes further than the Constitution requires; the demand-waiver rule because it is insensitive to a right which we have deemed fundamental. The approach we accept is a balancing test, in which the conduct of both the prosecution and the defendant are weighed.

A balancing test necessarily compels courts to approach speedy-trial cases on an *ad hoc* basis. We can do little more than identify some of the factors which courts should assess in determining whether a particular defendant has been deprived of his right. Though some might express them in different ways, we identify four such factors: Length of delay, the reason for the delay, the defendant's assertion of his right, and prejudice to the defendant.

The length of the delay is to some extent a triggering mechanism. Until there is some delay which is presumptively prejudicial, there is no necessity for inquiry into the other factors that go into the balance. Nevertheless, because of the imprecision of the right to speedy trial, the length of delay that will provoke such an inquiry is necessarily dependent upon the peculiar circumstances of the case. To take but one example, the delay that can be tolerated for an ordinary street crime is considerably less than for a serious, complex conspiracy charge.

Closely related to length of delay is the reason the government assigns to justify the delay. Here, too, different weights should be assigned to different reasons. A deliberate attempt to delay the trial in order to hamper the defense should be weighed heavily against the government. A more neutral reason such as negligence or overcrowded courts should be weighed less heavily but nevertheless should be considered since the ultimate responsibility for such circumstances must rest with the government rather than with the defendant. Finally, a valid reason, such as a missing witness, should serve to justify appropriate delay.

We have already discussed the third factor, the defendant's responsibility to assert his right. Whether and how a defendant asserts his right is closely related to the other factors we have mentioned. The strength of his efforts will be affected by the length of the delay, to some extent by the reason for the delay, and most particularly by the personal prejudice, which is not always readily identifiable, that he experiences. The more serious the deprivation, the more likely a defendant is to complain. The defendant's assertion of his speedy trial right, then, is entitled to strong evidentiary weight in determining whether the right is being deprived.

We emphasize that failure to assert the right will make it difficult for a defendant to prove that he was denied a speedy trial.

A fourth factor is prejudice to the defendant. Prejudice, of course, should be assessed in the light of the interests of defendants which the speedy trial right was designed to protect. This Court has identified three such interests: (i) to prevent oppressive pretrial incarceration; (ii) to minimize anxiety and concern of the accused; and (iii) to limit the possibility that the defense will be impaired. Of these, the most serious is the last, because the inability of a defendant adequately to prepare his case skews the fairness of the entire system. If witnesses die or disappear during a delay, the prejudice is obvious. There is also prejudice if defense witnesses are unable to recall accurately events of the distant past. Loss of memory, however, is not always reflected in the record because what has been forgotten can rarely be shown.

We have discussed previously the societal disadvantages of lengthy pretrial incarceration, but obviously the disadvantages for the accused who cannot obtain his release are even more serious. The time spent in jail awaiting trial has a detrimental impact on the individual. It often means loss of a job; it disrupts family life; and it enforces idleness. Most jails offer little or no recreational or rehabilitative programs. The time spent in jail is simply dead time. Moreover, if a defendant is locked up, he is hindered in his ability to gather evidence, contact witnesses, or otherwise prepare his defense. Imposing those consequences on anyone who has not yet been convicted is serious. It is especially unfortunate to impose them on those persons who are ultimately found to be innocent. Finally, even if an accused is not incarcerated prior to trial, he is still disadvantaged by restraints on his liberty and by living under a cloud of anxiety, suspicion, and often hostility.

We regard none of the four factors identified above as either a necessary or sufficient condition to the finding of a deprivation of the right of speedy trial. Rather, they are related factors and must be considered together with such other circumstances as may be relevant. In sum, these factors have no talismanic qualities; courts must still engage in a difficult and sensitive balancing process. But, because we are dealing with a fundamental right of the accused, this process must be carried out with full recognition that the accused's interest in a speedy trial is specifically affirmed in the Constitution.

The difficulty of the task of balancing these factors is illustrated by this case, which we consider to be close. It is clear that the length of delay between arrest and trial—well over five years—was extraordinary. Only seven months of that period can be attributed to a strong excuse, the illness of the ex-sheriff who was in charge of the investigation. Perhaps some delay would have been permissible under ordinary circumstances, so that Manning could be utilized as a witness in Barker's trial, but more than four years was too long a period, particularly since a good part of that period was attributable to the Commonwealth's failure or inability to try Manning under circumstances that comported with due process.

Two counter-balancing factors, however, outweigh these deficiencies. The first is that prejudice was minimal. Of course, Barker was prejudiced to some extent by living for over four years under a cloud of suspicion and anxiety. Moreover, although he was released on bond for most of the period, he did spend 10 months in jail before trial. But there is no claim that any of Barker's witnesses died or otherwise became unavailable owing to the delay. The trial transcript indicates only two very minor lapses of memory—one on the part of a prosecution witness— which were in no way significant to the outcome.

More important than the absence of serious prejudice, is the fact that Barker did not want a speedy trial. Counsel was appointed for Barker immediately after his indictment and represented him throughout the period. No question is raised as to the competency of such counsel. Despite the fact that counsel had notice of the motions for continuances, the record shows no action whatever taken between October 21, 1958, and February 12, 1962, that could be construed as the assertion of the speedy-trial right. On the latter date, in response to another motion for continuance, Barker moved to dismiss the indictment. The record does not show on what ground this motion was based, although it is clear that no alternative motion was made for an immediate trial. Instead the record strongly suggests that while he hoped to take advantage of the delay in which he had acquiesced, and thereby obtain a dismissal of the charges, he definitely did not want to be tried. Counsel conceded as much at oral argument:

> "Your honor, I would concede that Willie Mae Barker—probably—I don't know this for a fact—probably did not want to be tried. I don't think any man wants to be tried. And I don't consider this a liability on his behalf. I don't blame him."

The probable reason for Barker's attitude was that he was gambling on Manning's acquittal. The evidence was not terribly strong against Manning, as the reversals and hung juries suggest, and Barker undoubtedly thought that if Manning were acquitted, he would never be tried. Counsel also conceded this:

> "Now, it's true that the reason for this delay was the Commonwealth of Kentucky's desire to secure the testimony of the accomplice, Silas Manning. And it's true that if Silas Manning were never convicted, Willie Mae Barker would never have been convicted. We concede this."

That Barker was gambling on Manning's acquittal is also suggested by his failure, following the *pro forma* motion to dismiss filed in February 1962, to object to the Commonwealth's next two motions for continuances. Indeed, it was not until March 1963, after Manning's convictions were final, that Barker, having lost his gamble, began to object to further continuances. At that time, the Commonwealth's excuse was the illness of the ex-sheriff, which Barker has conceded justified the further delay.

We do not hold that there may never be a situation in which an indictment may be dismissed on speedy-trial grounds where the defendant has failed to object to continuances. There may be a situation in which the defendant was represented by incompetent counsel, was severely prejudiced, or even cases in which the continuances were granted *ex parte*. But barring extraordinary circumstances, we would be reluctant indeed to rule that a defendant was denied this constitutional right on a record that strongly indicates, as does this one, that the defendant did not want a speedy trial. We hold, therefore, that Barker was not deprived of his due process right to a speedy trial. * * *[b]

b. White, J., joined by Brennan, J., concurring, emphasized that the crowded dockets could not justify an unreasonable delay in providing a trial: "[F]or those who desire an early trial, * * * [the defendant's interests] should prevail if the only countervailing considerations offered by the State are those connected with crowded dockets and prosecutorial case loads. A defendant desiring a speedy trial, therefore, should have it within some reasonable time; and only special circumstances presenting a more pressing public need with respect to the case itself should suffice to justify delay. * * * Of course, cases will differ among themselves as to the allowable time between charge and trial so as to permit prosecution and defense adequately to prepare their case. But unreasonable delay in run-of-the-mill criminal cases cannot be justified by simply asserting that the public resources provided by the State's criminal justice system are limited and that each case must await its turn."

On the impact of *Barker,* see David S. Rudstein, *Right to Speedy Trial: Barker v. Wingo in the Lower Courts,* 1975 U.Ill.L.F. 11.

Notes and Questions

1. *The Barker balancing test.* H. Richard Uviller, *Barker v. Wingo: Speedy Trial Gets a Fast Shuffle,* 72 Colum.L.Rev. 1376, 1399–1400 (1972), objects that "the Court in its pronouncements and in their application to the facts before it seems to arrive at a distorted formula for the interplay of the elements of the speedy trial guarantee. It runs something like this: notwithstanding the lapse of a substantial period of time to which the accused did not affirmatively consent, he is not denied a speedy trial if the court determines as a fact that he did not really want to be sooner tried, and he fails to demonstrate concretely some actual and significant deterioration of his defensive case suffered by reason of the delay. With all due deference, it is here submitted that a formulation more closely harmonious with traditional concepts and prior insights from other quarters, might be shaped thus: absent an explicit and competent waiver for the period in question, the accused is denied his right to a speedy trial by the passage of an unreasonable period of time without a demonstration by the state of good and sufficient reason or necessity therefor; and further, prejudice presumptively increases with the length of elapsed time, imposing upon the state the increasing burden of proving the delay harmless by reasons more particular and persuasive than convenience, negligence, or the hope of tactical advantage."

Doggett was indicted on drug charges in February 1980; officers seeking to arrest him learned he had left for Columbia; in September 1981 it was learned he was imprisoned in Panama; Panama authorities agreed to "expel" him to the U.S. but instead released him the following July; he then went to Columbia but reentered the U.S. unhindered in September 1982 and settled in Virginia, where he lived openly under his own name until September 1988, when the Marshal's Service ran a simple credit check on several thousand people subject to outstanding arrest warrants and, within minutes, found out where he lived and worked; upon his arrest, he moved without success to dismiss the indictment. In *Doggett v. United States,* 505 U.S. 647, 112 S.Ct. 2686, 120 L.Ed.2d 520 (1992), the Supreme Court reversed, applying the *Barker* balancing test in this fashion: (1) Re *length of delay,* "the extraordinary 8 ½-year lag between Doggett's indictment and arrest clearly suffices to trigger the speedy trial enquiry." (2) The *reason for the delay* was government negligence, as for "six years, the Government's investigators made no serious effort to test their progressively more questionable assumption that Doggett was living abroad, and, had they done so, they could have found him within minutes." (3) Re *defendant's assertion of his right,* "Doggett is not to be taxed for invoking his speedy trial right only after his arrest," as the government conceded he was unaware of the indictment prior to his arrest. (4) Re *prejudice to the defendant,* there was no pretrial detention or anxiety, leaving only the possibility of impairment of the defense, about which Doggett made no specific showing. Recognizing "that excessive delay presumptively compromises the reliability of a trial in ways that neither party can prove or, for that matter, identify," the Court then concluded: "When the Government's negligence thus causes delay six times as long as that generally sufficient to trigger judicial review, and when the presumption of prejudice, albeit unspecified, is neither extenuated, as by the defendant's acquiescence, nor persuasively rebutted, the defendant is entitled to relief."

2. *Barker "rebalanced"?* Was the *Barker* test "revised" in *Reed v. Farley,* 512 U.S. 339, 114 S.Ct. 2291, 129 L.Ed.2d 277 (1994)? The Court there held that a state court's failure to observe the 120–day time-for-trial rule of the Interstate Agreement on Detainers[c] was not cognizable on federal habeas corpus when, as

---

c. In *New York v. Hill,* 528 U.S. 110, 120 S.Ct. 659, 145 L.Ed.2d 560 (2000), a unanimous Court held that "defense counsel's agree-ment to a trial date outside the time period required by Article III * * * bars the defendant from seeking dismissal because trial did

there, the defendant registered no objection to the trial date when it was set and suffered no prejudice from the delay. In responding to Reed's argument the result should be otherwise because the IAD's speedy trial provision "effectuates" the Sixth Amendment speedy trial guarantee, the Court asserted, citing *Barker:* "A showing of prejudice is required to establish a violation of the Sixth Amendment Speedy Trial Clause, and that necessary ingredient is entirely missing here."

3. ***The imprisoned defendant.*** In the pre–*Barker* case of SMITH v. HOOEY, 393 U.S. 374, 89 S.Ct. 575, 21 L.Ed.2d 607 (1969), the Court, per STEWART, J., rejected the state court's conclusion that the state had no duty under the Sixth Amendment to make a good faith effort to obtain the presence for trial of petitioner, who repeatedly demanded trial while confined in a federal prison:

"At first blush it might appear that a man already in prison under a lawful sentence is hardly in a position to suffer from 'undue and oppressive incarceration prior to trial.' But the fact is that delay in bringing such a person to trial on a pending charge may ultimately result in as much oppression as is suffered by one who is jailed without bail upon an untried charge. First, the possibility that the defendant already in prison might receive a sentence at least partially concurrent with the one he is serving may be forever lost if trial of the pending charge is postponed. Secondly, under procedures now widely practiced, the duration of his present imprisonment may be increased, and the conditions under which he must serve his sentence greatly worsened, by the pendency of another criminal charge outstanding against him.

"And while it might be argued that a person already in prison would be less likely than others to be affected by 'anxiety and concern accompanying public accusation,' there is reason to believe that an outstanding untried charge (of which even a convict may, of course, be innocent) can have fully as depressive an effect upon a prisoner as upon a person who is at large. * * * In the opinion of the former Director of the Federal Bureau of Prisons, '[I]t is in their effect upon the prisoner and our attempts to rehabilitate him that detainers are most corrosive. The strain of having to serve a sentence with the uncertain prospect of being taken into the custody of another state at the conclusion interferes with the prisoner's ability to take maximum advantage of his institutional opportunities. His anxiety and depression may leave him with little inclination towards self-improvement.'

not occur within that period." The Court reasoned that "[s]cheduling matters are plainly among those for which agreement by counsel generally controls," for "only counsel is in a position to assess the benefit or detriment of the delay to the defendant's case," and "only counsel is in a position to assess whether the defense would even be prepared to proceed any earlier." As for defendant's claim "that the IAD benefits not only the defendant but society generally, and that the defendant may not waive society's rights," the Court responded that "some social interests served by prompt trial are less relevant here than elsewhere": "because the would-be defendant is already incarcerated in another jurisdiction, society's interests in assuring the defendant's presence at trial and in preventing further criminal activity (or avoiding the costs of pretrial detention) are simply not at issue."

The IAD also provides that if the presence of the inmate in obtained in the charging state but he is then returned to his original place of imprisonment without trial, then the charge "shall not be of any further force or effect." While some courts had held that this provision's purpose is to prevent significant interference with the inmate's rehabilitation and that consequently dismissal is not required when the violation of the antishuttling provision is "technical," "harmless," or "*de minimis*," the Supreme Court ruled otherwise in *Alabama v. Bozeman,* 533 U.S. 146, 121 S.Ct. 2079, 150 L.Ed.2d 188 (2001). A unanimous Court held that because the language of the IAD is absolute it permitted no implied exceptions.

"Finally, it is self-evident that 'the possibilities that long delay will impair the ability of an accused to defend himself' are markedly increased when the accused is incarcerated in another jurisdiction. Confined in a prison, perhaps far from the place where the offense covered by the outstanding charge allegedly took place, his ability to confer with potential defense witnesses, or even to keep track of their whereabouts, is obviously impaired. And, while 'evidence and witnesses disappear, memories fade, and events lose their perspective,' a man isolated in prison is powerless to exert his own investigative efforts to mitigate these erosive effects of the passage of time.

"[As] is fully confirmed by the brief that the Solicitor General has filed in the present case:

"[T]he Bureau of Prisons would doubtless have made the prisoner available if a writ of habeas corpus *ad prosequendum* had been issued by the state court. It does not appear, however, that the State at any point sought to initiate that procedure in this case.' "

4. Federal statute. The Speedy Trial Act of 1974, set out in Supp.App. B, establishes specific time limits within which the trial and certain other steps must commence in a federal prosecution.[d]

5. Speedy trial in the states; constitution vs. statute. Although the Sixth Amendment right to a speedy trial was not applied to the states until *Klopfer,* all state constitutions also provide such a guarantee. An overwhelming majority of the states have enacted statutes setting forth the time within which a defendant must be tried following the date he was arrested, held to answer, committed, or indicted, and it is these statutes which have received principal attention. If a statutory violation is found, there is seldom any inquiry into the alleged constitutional denial; and if the statute has not been violated, it is typically assumed that the constitutional provision has been satisfied. But, while "the statutory and constitutional provisions address similar concerns, the rights established by each are not necessarily coextensive." *People v. Hall*, 743 N.E.2d 521 (Ill.2000).

6. Excuses for delay. Speedy trial statutes declare that trial must commence within a fixed period—expressed in days, months, or terms of courts—following some prior event, such as arrest, indictment, or holding to answer, but also recognize that certain periods of time are not to be counted in determining whether this time has run. A majority of jurisdictions merely provide for additional time upon a showing of "good cause," while some statutes enumerate some of the more common legitimate reasons for delay. See, e.g., the excluded periods in § 3161(h) of the Speedy Trial Act of 1974. Because of the excluded periods, a

---

d. Guidelines for administering the Act appear at 106 F.R.D. 271 (1985). For an empirical study of experience under the Act, see George Bridges, *The Speedy Trial Act of 1974: Effect on Delays in Federal Criminal Litigation,* 73 J.Crim.L. & C. 50 (1982).

The Act has frequently been interpreted by the lower courts, see CRIMPROC § 18.3(b), and occasionally by the Supreme Court. See *Henderson v. United States,* 476 U.S. 321, 106 S.Ct. 1871, 90 L.Ed.2d 299 (1986) (§ 3161(h)(1)(F), excluding "delay resulting from any pretrial motion, from the filing of the motion through the conclusion of the hearing on, or other prompt disposition of, such motion," excludes all time between the filing of a motion and conclusion of the hearing, whether or not such delay is "reasonably necessary," and also all time after a hearing where the court awaits additional filings from the parties that are needed for proper disposition of the motion); *United States v. Rojas–Contreras,* 474 U.S. 231, 106 S.Ct. 555, 88 L.Ed.2d 537 (1985) (§ 3161(c)(2), barring trial without defendant's consent less than 30 days "from the date on which the defendant first appears through counsel or expressly waives counsel and elects to proceed pro se," does not begin to run anew upon the filing of a superseding indictment, though a defendant in such circumstances could seek a continuance under § 3161(h)(8)).

substantial number of cases will not come to trial within the period specified in the statute.

7. *Consequences of denial of speedy trial*. In *United States v. Strunk*, 467 F.2d 969 (7th Cir.1972), where defendant's constitutional right to speedy trial was found to have been violated while he was serving a state sentence for another offense, but defendant made "no claim of having been prejudiced in presenting his defense," the court took note of the traditional remedies of "dismissal of the indictment or the vacation of the sentence" and then ruled that in the instant case "the proper remedy is to * * * credit the defendant with the period of time elapsing between the return of the indictment and the date of arraignment." But a unanimous Supreme Court disagreed, noting that delay in a case such as this "may subject the accused to an emotional stress" by which "the prospect of rehabilitation may also be affected," and concluding: "In light of the policies which underlie the right to a speedy trial, dismissal must remain, as *Barker* noted, 'the only possible remedy.' " *Strunk v. United States*, 412 U.S. 434, 93 S.Ct. 2260, 37 L.Ed.2d 56 (1973).

As for denial of a statutory speedy trial right, "one group of states treats it as a bar to another prosecution for the same offense, while another group does not. The third position is that [denial] prevents subsequent prosecutions for the same charge if it is a misdemeanor, but not if it is a felony." Note, 57 Colum.L.Rev. 846, 859–60 (1957). Under § 3162(a) of the federal Act, the sanction is dismissal "with or without prejudice," depending upon the court's assessment of various factors. In *United States v. Taylor,* 487 U.S. 326, 108 S.Ct. 2413, 101 L.Ed.2d 297 (1988), the Court concluded that neither remedy has priority, that the legislative history of the Act reveals that prejudice to the defendant is a factor to be taken into account in addition to those listed in the Act, and that under the Act a district judge "must carefully consider those factors as applied to the particular case and, whatever its decision, clearly articulate their effect in order to permit meaningful appellate review." The Court overturned a district court's order of dismissal with prejudice for a delay 14 days longer than permitted by the Act because the district court (i) "did not explain how it factored in the seriousness of the offenses with which respondent stood charged," (ii) "relied heavily on its unexplained character- ization of the Government conduct as 'lackadaisical,' while failing to consider other relevant facts and circumstances leading to dismissal," and (iii) apparently ignored "the brevity of the delay and the consequential lack of prejudice to the respondent," as well as his "own illicit contribution to the delay" by fleeing the day before the original trial date.

8. *Interlocutory appeal*. If a defendant's pretrial motion to dismiss on speedy trial grounds is denied, he need not be allowed an interlocutory appeal to fully protect his rights under *Barker v. Wingo,* as it "is the delay before trial, not the trial itself, that offends against the constitutional guarantee of a speedy trial." See *United States v. MacDonald,* discussed at p. 1088.

Assuming an interlocutory appeal by either the defense or the prosecution on some issue, *Barker* applies only "when the defendant is subject to indictment or restraint" during that interval. *United States v. Loud Hawk,* p. 1089. "Given the important public interests in appellate review, it hardly need be said that an interlocutory appeal by the Government ordinarily is a valid reason that justifies delay. In assessing the purpose and reasonableness of such an appeal, courts may consider several factors. These include the strength of the Government's position on the appealed issue, the importance of the issue in the posture of the case, and—in some cases—the seriousness of the crime." In the limited circumstances "where pretrial appeal by the defendant is appropriate, delays from such an appeal ordinarily will not weigh in favor of a defendant's speedy trial claims. A defendant with a meritorious appeal would bear the heavy burden of showing an unreasonable delay caused by the prosecution in that appeal, or a wholly unjustifiable delay by the appellate court," but in the instant case the respondents' "position was so lacking in merit that the time consumed by this appeal should not weigh in support of respondents' speedy trial claim."

9. *When does the time begin to run?* Under state speedy trial statutes, the time usually runs from the date the defendant first appears in court following his arrest, except that it typically runs from the date of the formal charge if it precedes arrest. As to the constitutional right to speedy trial, only the delay following arrest or formal charge (whichever comes first) is taken into account. See *United States v. Lovasco,* p. 1083.

SECTION 2. THE RIGHT TO OTHER SPEEDY DISPOSITION

UNITED STATES v. LOVASCO
431 U.S. 783, 97 S.Ct. 2044, 52 L.Ed.2d 752 (1977).

Justice MARSHALL delivered the opinion of the Court. * * *

On March 6, 1975, respondent was indicted for possessing eight firearms stolen from the United States mail, and for dealing in firearms without a license. The offenses were alleged to have occurred between July 25 and August 31, 1973, more than 18 months before the indictment was filed. Respondent moved to dismiss the indictment due to the delay.

The District Court conducted a hearing on respondent's motion at which the respondent sought to prove that the delay was unnecessary and that it had prejudiced his defense. In an effort to establish the former proposition, respondent presented a Postal Inspector's report on his investigation that was prepared one month after the crimes were committed, and a stipulation concerning the post-report progress of the probe. The report stated, in brief, that within the first month of the investigation respondent had admitted to Government agents that he had possessed and then sold five of the stolen guns, and that the agents had developed strong evidence linking respondent to the remaining three weapons.[1] The report also stated, however, that the agents had been unable to confirm or refute respondent's claim that he had found the guns in his car when he returned to it after visiting his son, a mail handler, at work. The stipulation into which the Assistant United States Attorney entered indicated that little additional information concerning the crimes was uncovered in the 17 months following the preparation of the Inspector's report.

To establish prejudice to the defense, respondent testified that he had lost the testimony of two material witnesses due to the delay. The first witness, Tom Stewart, died more than a year after the alleged crimes occurred. At the hearing respondent claimed that Stewart had been his source for two or three of the guns. The second witness, respondent's brother, died in April 1974, nine months after the crimes were completed. Respondent testified that his brother was present when respondent called Stewart to secure the guns, and witnessed all of respon-

---

1. The report indicated that the person to whom respondent admitted selling five guns had told Government agents that respondent had actually sold him eight guns which he, in turn, had sold to one Martin Koehnken. The report also indicated that Koehnken had sold three of these guns to undercover federal agents and that a search of his house had uncovered four others. Finally the report stated that the eighth gun was sold by one David Northdruft to Government agents, and that Northdruft claimed Koehnken had sold him the gun.

At the hearing on the motion to dismiss, respondent for the first time admitted that he had possessed and sold eight guns.

dent's sales. Respondent did not state how the witnesses would have aided the defense had they been willing to testify.[4]

The Government made no systematic effort in the District Court to explain its long delay. The Assistant United States Attorney did expressly disagree, however, with defense counsel's suggestion that the investigation had ended after the Postal Inspector's Report was prepared. The prosecutor also stated that it was the Government's theory that respondent's son, who had access to the mail at the railroad terminal from which the guns were "possibly stolen," was responsible for the thefts. Finally, the prosecutor elicited somewhat cryptic testimony from the Postal Inspector indicating that the case "as to these particular weapons involves other individuals"; that information had been presented to a grand jury "in regard to this case other than . . . [on] the day of the indictment itself"; and that he had spoken to the prosecutors about the case on four or five occasions.

Following the hearing, the District Court filed a brief opinion and order. The court found that by October 2, 1973, the date of the postal inspector's report, "The Government had all the information relating to defendant's alleged commission of the offense charged against him," and that the 17–month delay before the case was presented to the grand jury "had not been explained or justified" and was "unnecessary and unreasonable." The Court also found that "[a]s a result of the delay defendant has been prejudiced by reason of the death of Tom Stewart, a material witness on his behalf." Accordingly, the court dismissed the indictment.

The Government appealed to the United States Court of Appeals for the Eighth Circuit. In its brief the Government explained the months of inaction by stating:

"[T]here was a legitimate Government interest in keeping the investigation open in the instant case. The defendant's son worked for the Terminal Railroad and had access to mail. It was the Government's position that the son was responsible for the theft and therefore further investigation to establish this fact was important.

" . . . Although the investigation did not continue on a full time basis, there was contact between the United States Attorney's office and the Postal Inspector's office throughout . . . and certain matters were brought before a Federal Grand Jury prior to the determination that the case should be presented for indictment. . . ."

The Court of Appeals accepted the Government's representation as to the motivation for the delay, but a majority of the court nevertheless affirmed the District Court's finding that the Government's actions were "unjustified, unnecessary, and unreasonable." The majority also found that respondent had established that his defense had been impaired by the loss of Stewart's testimony because it understood respondent to contend that "were Stewart's testimony available it would support [respondent's] claim that he did not know that the guns were stolen from the United States mails." * * *

We granted certiorari, and now reverse.[7]

---

4. Respondent admitted that he had not mentioned Stewart to the Postal Inspector when he was questioned about his source of the guns. He explained that this was because Stewart "was a bad tomato" and "was liable to take a shot at me if I told [on] him." Respondent also conceded that he did not mention either his brother's or Stewart's illness or death to the Postal Inspector on the several occasions in which respondent called the In-

spector to inquire about the status of the probe.

7. In addition to challenging the Court of Appeals' holding on the constitutional issue, the United States argues that the District Court should have deferred action on the motion to dismiss until after trial, at which time it could have assessed any prejudice to the respondent in light of the events at trial. This argument, however, was not raised in the Dis-

In *United States v. Marion*, 404 U.S. 307, 92 S.Ct. 455, 30 L.Ed.2d 468 (1971), this Court considered the significance, for constitutional purposes, of a lengthy preindictment delay. We held that as far as the Speedy Trial Clause of the Sixth Amendment is concerned, such delay is wholly irrelevant, since our analysis of the language, history, and purposes of the Clause persuaded us that only "a formal indictment or information or else the actual restraints imposed by arrest and holding to answer a criminal charge ... engage the particular protections" of that provision. We went on to note that statutes of limitations, which provide predictable, legislatively enacted limits on prosecutorial delay, provide "the primary guarantee, against bringing overly stale criminal charges."[a] But we did acknowledge that the "statute of limitations does not fully define [defendants'] rights with respect to the events occurring prior to indictment," and that the Due Process Clause has a limited role to play in protecting against oppressive delay.

Respondent seems to argue that due process bars prosecution whenever a defendant suffers prejudice as a result of preindictment delay. To support that proposition respondent relies on the concluding sentence of the Court's opinion in *Marion* where, in remanding the case, we stated that "[e]vents of the trial may demonstrate actual prejudice, but at the present time appellees' due process claims are speculative and premature." But the quoted sentence establishes only that proof of actual prejudice makes a due process claim concrete and ripe for adjudication, not that it makes the claim automatically valid. Indeed, two pages earlier in the opinion we expressly rejected the argument respondent advances here:

> "[W]e need not ... determine when and in what circumstances actual prejudice resulting from preaccusation delay requires the dismissal of the prosecution. Actual prejudice to the defense of a criminal case may result from the shortest and most necessary delay; and no one suggests that every delay-caused detriment to a defendant's case should abort a criminal prosecution."

Thus *Marion* makes clear that proof of prejudice is generally a necessary but not sufficient element of a due process claim, and that the due process inquiry must consider the reasons for the delay as well as the prejudice to the accused.

The Court of Appeals found that the sole reason for the delay here was "a hope on the part of the Government that others might be discovered who may

---

trict Court or in the Court of Appeals. Absent exceptional circumstances, we will not review it here. * * *

a. The statute of limitations, in contrast to the speedy trial time limitations, runs from the date the offense is committed (or, in a few states, from the date the offense is discovered) to the date prosecution is commenced (in some states this means the date an indictment or information is filed, in others the date a warrant of arrest is issued). The typical statute specifies situations in which time is not counted against the period of limitation, such as when the defendant is out of the state or is away from his usual residence for the purpose of avoiding prosecution. "There are several reasons for the imposition of time limitations: First, and foremost, is the desirability that prosecutions be based upon reasonably fresh evidence. With the passage of time memories fade, witnesses die or leave the area, and physical evidence becomes more difficult to obtain, identify, or preserve. In short, possibility of

erroneous conviction is minimized when prosecution is prompt. Second, if the actor long refrains from further criminal activity, the likelihood increases that he has reformed, diminishing the necessity for imposition of the criminal sanction. If he has repeated his criminal behavior, he can be prosecuted for recent offenses committed within the period of limitation. Hence, the need for protecting society against the perpetrator of a particular offense becomes less compelling as the years pass. Third, after a protracted period the retributive impulse which may have existed in the community is likely to yield to a sense of compassion aroused by the prosecution for an offense long forgotten. Fourth, it is desirable to reduce the possibility of blackmail based on a threat to prosecute or to disclose evidence to enforcement officials. Finally, statutes of limitations 'promote repose by giving security and stability to human affairs.'" *Model Penal Code* § 1.06, Comment (1985).

have participated in the theft...." It concluded that this hope did not justify the delay, and therefore affirmed the dismissal of the indictment. But the Due Process Clause does not permit courts to abort criminal prosecutions simply because they disagree with a prosecutor's judgment as to when to seek an indictment. Judges are not free, in defining "due process," to impose on law enforcement officials our "personal and private notions" of fairness and to "disregard the limits that bind judges in their judicial function." Our task is more circumscribed. We are to determine only whether the actions complained of—here, compelling respondent to stand trial after the Government delayed indictment to investigate further— violates those "fundamental conceptions of justice which lie at the base of our civil and political institutions," and which define "the community's sense of fair play and decency."

It requires no extended argument to establish that prosecutors do not deviate from "fundamental conceptions of justice" when they defer seeking indictments until they have probable cause to believe an accused is guilty; indeed it is unprofessional conduct for a prosecutor to recommend an indictment on less than probable cause. It should be equally obvious that prosecutors are under no duty to file charges as soon as probable cause exists but before they are satisfied they will be able to establish the suspect's guilt beyond a reasonable doubt. To impose such a duty "would have a deleterious effect both upon the rights of the accused and upon the ability of society to protect itself." From the perspective of potential defendants, requiring prosecutions to commence when probable cause is estab- lished is undesirable because it would increase the likelihood of unwarranted charges being filed, and would add to the time during which defendants stand accused but untried. * * * From the perspective of law enforcement officials, a requirement of immediate prosecution upon probable cause is equally unaccepta- ble because it could make obtaining proof of guilt beyond a reasonable doubt impossible by causing potentially fruitful sources of information to evaporate before they are fully exploited. And from the standpoint of the courts, such a requirement is unwise because it would cause scarce resources to be consumed on cases that prove to be insubstantial, or that involve only some of the responsible parties or some of the criminal acts.[12] Thus, no one's interests would be well served by compelling prosecutors to initiate prosecutions as soon as they are legally entitled to do so.

It might be argued that once the Government has assembled sufficient evidence to prove guilt beyond a reasonable doubt, it should be constitutionally required to file charges promptly, even if its investigation of the entire criminal transaction is not complete. Adopting such a rule, however, would have many of the same consequences as adopting a rule requiring immediate prosecution upon probable cause.

First, compelling a prosecutor to file public charges as soon as the requisite proof has been developed against one participant on one charge would cause numerous problems in those cases in which a criminal transaction involves more than one person or more than one illegal act. In some instances, an immediate arrest or indictment would impair the prosecutor's ability to continue his investi- gation, thereby preventing society from bringing lawbreakers to justice. In other cases, the prosecutor would be able to obtain additional indictments despite an early prosecution, but the necessary result would be multiple trials involving a single set of facts. Such trials place needless burdens on defendants, law enforce- ment officials, and courts.

---

12. Defendants also would be adversely af- fected by trials involving less than all of the criminal acts for which they are responsible, since they likely would be subjected to multiple trials growing out of the same transaction or occurrence.

Second, insisting on immediate prosecution once sufficient evidence is developed to obtain a conviction would pressure prosecutors into resolving doubtful cases in favor of early—and possibly unwarranted—prosecutions. The determination of when the evidence available to the prosecution is sufficient to obtain a conviction is seldom clear-cut, and reasonable persons often will reach conflicting conclusions. In the instant case, for example, since respondent admitted possessing at least five of the firearms, the primary factual issue in dispute was whether respondent knew the guns were stolen as required by 18 U.S.C. § 1708. Not surprisingly, the Postal Inspector's report contained no direct evidence bearing on this issue. The decision whether to prosecute, therefore, required a necessarily subjective evaluation of the strength of the circumstantial evidence available and the credibility of respondent's denial. Even if a prosecutor concluded that the case was weak and further investigation appropriate, he would have no assurance that a reviewing court would agree. To avoid the risk that a subsequent indictment would be dismissed for preindictment delay, the prosecutor might feel constrained to file premature charges with all the disadvantages that entails.[14]

Finally, requiring the Government to make charging decisions immediately upon assembling evidence sufficient to establish guilt would preclude the Government from giving full consideration to the desirability of not prosecuting in particular cases. The decision to file criminal charges, with the awesome consequences it entails, requires consideration of a wide range of factors in addition to the strength of the Government's case, in order to determine whether prosecution would be in the public interest. Prosecutors often need more information than proof of a suspect's guilt, therefore, before deciding whether to seek an indictment. Again the instant case provides a useful illustration. Although proof of the identity of the mail thieves was not necessary to convict respondent of the possessory crimes with which he was charged, it might have been crucial in assessing respondent's culpability, as distinguished from his legal guilt. If, for example, further investigation were to show that respondent had no role in or advance knowledge of the theft and simply agreed, out of paternal loyalty, to help his son dispose of the guns once respondent discovered his son had stolen them, the United States Attorney might have decided not to prosecute, especially since at the time of the crime respondent was over 60 years old and had no prior criminal record.[16] Requiring prosecution once the evidence of guilt is clear, however, could prevent a prosecutor from awaiting the information necessary for such a decision.

We would be most reluctant to adopt a rule which would have these consequences absent a clear constitutional command to do so. We can find no such command in the Due Process Clause of the Fifth Amendment. In our view, investigative delay is fundamentally unlike delay undertaken by the Government solely "to gain tactical advantage over the accused," precisely because investigative delay is not so one-sided.[17] Rather than deviating from elementary standards

---

14. In addition, if courts were required to decide in every case when the prosecution should have commenced, it would be necessary for them to trace the day-by-day progress of each investigation. Maintaining daily records would impose an administrative burden on prosecutors, and reviewing them would place an even greater burden on the courts.

16. Of course, in this case further investigation proved unavailing and the United States Attorney ultimately decided to prosecute based solely on the Inspector's report. But this fortuity cannot transform an otherwise permissible delay into an impermissible one.

17. In *Marion* we noted with approval that the Government conceded that a "tactical" delay would violate the Due Process Clause. The Government renews that concession here, and expands it somewhat by stating that "A due process violation might also be made out upon a showing of prosecutorial delay incurred in reckless disregard of circumstances, known to the prosecution, suggesting that there existed an appreciable risk that delay would impair the ability to mount an effective defense." As the Government notes, however, there is no evidence of recklessness here.

of "fair play and decency," a prosecutor abides by them if he refuses to seek indictments until he is completely satisfied that he should prosecute and will be able promptly to establish guilt beyond a reasonable doubt. Penalizing prosecutors who defer action for these reasons would subordinate the goal of "orderly expedition" to that of "mere speed." This the Due Process Clause does not require. We therefore hold that to prosecute a defendant following investigative delay does not deprive him of due process, even if his defense might have been somewhat prejudiced by the lapse of time.

In the present case, the Court of Appeals stated that the only reason the Government postponed action was to await the results of additional investigation. * * * In light of this explanation, it follows that compelling respondent to stand trial would not be fundamentally unfair. The Court of Appeals therefore erred in affirming the District Court's decision dismissing the indictment.

In *Marion* we conceded that we could not determine in the abstract the circumstances in which preaccusation delay would require dismissing prosecutions. More than five years later, that statement remains true. Indeed, in the intervening years so few defendants have established that they were prejudiced by delay that neither this Court nor any lower court has had a sustained opportunity to consider the constitutional significance of various reasons for delay.[19] We therefore leave to the lower courts, in the first instance, the task of applying the settled principles of due process that we have discussed to the particular circumstances of individual cases. We simply hold that in this case the lower courts erred in dismissing the indictment.[b]

Notes and Questions

1. *Marion* was also relied upon in UNITED STATES v. MacDONALD, 456 U.S. 1, 102 S.Ct. 1497, 71 L.Ed.2d 696 (1982), holding that the time between dismissal of military charges and the subsequent indictment on civilian charges may not be considered in determining whether the delay in bringing the defendant to trial violated his Sixth Amendment right to speedy trial. BURGER, C.J., stated for the Court:

"Once charges are dismissed, the speedy trial guarantee is no longer applicable.[8] At that point, the formerly accused is, at most, in the same position as any

---

19. Professor Amsterdam has catalogued some of the noninvestigative reasons for delay:

"[P]roof of the offense may depend upon the testimony of an undercover informer who maintains his 'cover' for a period of time before surfacing to file charges against one or more persons with whom he has dealt while disguised. ... [I]f there is more than one possible charge against a suspect, some of them may be held back pending the disposition of others in order to avoid the burden upon the prosecutor's office of handling charges that may turn out to be unnecessary to obtain the degree of punishment that the prosecutor seeks. There are many other motives for delay, of course, including sinister ones, such as a desire to postpone the beginning of defense investigation or the wish to hold a 'club' over the defendant.

"Additional reasons for delay may be partly or completely beyond the control of the prosecuting authorities. Offenses may not be immediately reported; investigation may not

immediately identify the offender; an identified offender may not be immediately apprehendable. ...[A]n indictment may be delayed for weeks or even months until the impaneling of the next grand jury. It is customary to think of these delays as natural and inevitable ... but various prosecutorial decisions—such as the assignment of manpower and priorities among investigations of known offenses—may also affect the length of such delays." Amsterdam, *Speedy Criminal Trial: Rights and Remedies,* 27 Stan. L.Rev. 525, 527–528 (1975).

b. Stevens, J., dissenting, agreed with the foregoing principles, but concluded the majority had erred in not deciding the case on the record made in the district court, wherein the government's delay was unexplained.

8. *Klopfer v. North Carolina* [p. 1072], is not to the contrary. There, under an unusual state procedure, a prosecutor was able to suspend proceedings on an indictment indefinite-

other subject of a criminal investigation. Certainly the knowledge of an ongoing criminal investigation will cause stress, discomfort and perhaps a certain disruption in normal life. This is true whether or not charges have been filed and then dismissed. This was true in *Marion,* where the defendants had been subjected to a lengthy investigation which received considerable press attention. But with no charges outstanding, personal liberty is certainly not impaired to the same degree as it is after arrest while charges are pending. After the charges against him have been dismissed, 'a citizen suffers no restraints on his liberty and is [no longer] the subject of public accusation: his situation does not compare with that of a defendant who has been arrested and held to answer.' *United States v. Marion.* Following dismissal of charges, any restraint on liberty, disruption of employment, strain on financial resources, and exposure to public obloquy, stress and anxiety is no greater than it is upon anyone openly subject to a criminal investigation.''

Four members of the Court[c] found that conclusion to be ''inconsistent with the language and policies of the Speedy Trial Clause and with this Court's decisions,'' such as *Klopfer,* said to teach ''that the anxiety suffered by an accused person, even after the initial prosecution has terminated and after he has been discharged from custody, warrants application of the speedy trial protection.'' They added that the majority's conclusion was ''also senseless'' because ''[a]ny legitimate government reason for delay during the period between prosecutions can, indeed must, be weighed when a court determines whether the defendant's speedy trial right has been violated. No purpose is served by simply ignoring that period for speedy trial purposes.''

2. Relying on *MacDonald,* the Court in UNITED STATES v. LOUD HAWK, 474 U.S. 302, 106 S.Ct. 648, 88 L.Ed.2d 640 (1986), held, 5–4, that the Sixth Amendment speedy trial clock was not running during the government's appeals of the district court's successive dismissals of the indictment with prejudice, during which time the respondents were free on their own recognizance, as ''respondents were neither under indictment nor subject to bail.'' A contrary result, the Court added, was not called for merely ''because the Government's desire to prosecute them was a matter of public record'' or because of ''respondents' need for counsel while their case was technically dismissed,'' as ''the Speedy Trial Clause's core concern is impairment of liberty; it does not shield a suspect or a defendant from every expense or inconvenience associated with criminal defense.'' The dissenters argued that the instant case was distinguishable from *MacDonald* because (a) the ''respondents did not enjoy the protection of the statute of limitations while the Government prosecuted its appeal''; (b) there was no dismissal by the government ''acknowledging that the first formal accusation had been a mistake and extinguishing the prior probable cause determination,'' and instead the government ''continues to align its full resources against respondents in judicial proceedings''; and (c) ''respondents' liberty could have been taken from them at any time during the Government's appeal,'' as 18 U.S.C. § 3731 says ''that a person in respondents' position shall be subject to the same restraints as an arrested defendant awaiting trial.''

3. In *People v. Lawson,* 367 N.E.2d 1244 (Ill.1977), decided a few days before *Lovasco,* the court stated: ''Where there has been a delay between an alleged crime and indictment or arrest or accusation, the defendant must come forward

ly. The prosecutor could activate the charges at any time and have the case restored for trial, ''without further order'' of the court. The charges against the defendant were thus never dismissed or discharged in any real sense so the speedy trial guarantee continued to apply.

c. Marshall, J., joined by Brennan and Blackmun, JJ., dissenting, took a different view of the scope of the Sixth Amendment speedy trial protection and then, applying the four factors from *Barker,* concluded that Mac-Donald's speedy trial rights were violated. Stevens, J., concurring, agreed with the dissenters' scope analysis but disagreed with their application of the *Barker* factors.

with a clear showing of actual *and* substantial prejudice. Mere assertion of inability to recall is insufficient. If the accused satisfies the trial court that he or she has been substantially prejudiced by the delay, then the burden shifts to the State to show the reasonableness, if not the necessity, of the delay.

"If this two-step process ascertains both substantial prejudice and reasonableness of a delay, then the court must make a determination based upon a balancing of the interests of the defendant and the public. Factors the court should consider, among others, are the length of the delay and the seriousness of the crime."

The supplemental opinion on denial of rehearing states in part: "The State, in its petition for rehearing, suggests that *Lovasco* establishes a more restrictive standard * * * than does our decision in this case. * * * The State apparently believes prejudice and unreasonableness of the delay are two elements which must be proved by the defendant to establish a due process claim. We, of course, do not require that—nor does *Lovasco*."

4. In *United States v. Moran,* 759 F.2d 777 (9th Cir.1985), the court stated: "The government asserts that certain language from *United States v. Marion* and *Lovasco* * * * requires that the defendant prove either intentional or reckless conduct on the part of the government. We reject this contention. The language from these two cases merely acknowledges governmental concessions that intentional or reckless conduct would or might be considered violations of the due process clause if actual prejudice had been shown. The *Lovasco* court did not set out intent or recklessness as required standards of fault. * * *

"The determination of whether a pre-indictment delay has violated due process is essentially decided under a balancing test, and we do not find that intent or reckless behavior by the government is an essential ingredient in the mix. If mere negligent conduct by the prosecutors is asserted, then obviously the delay and/or prejudice suffered by the defendant will have to be greater than that in cases where recklessness or intentional governmental conduct is alleged."

Looking to the facts of the particular case, the *Moran* court held the district judge had erred in dismissing certain charges. The court expressed doubt as to whether defendant had met his "heavy burden to prove that a pre-indictment delay caused actual prejudice." Defendant showed that five of his witnesses had died or were now out of the country, but the court said it was a "close question" whether this was sufficient, as "protection from lost testimony generally falls solely within the ambit of the statute of limitations." But the court grounded its reversal on the fact that defendant had not met his burden of making "some showing of government culpability."

5. As to what other steps in the criminal process should the defendant have a constitutional right to speedy disposition? What about a right to "speedy judgment" when a criminal case is tried before a judge? See *Campodonico v. United States,* 222 F.2d 310 (9th Cir.1955). To "speedy sentencing"? See *People v. Drake,* 462 N.E.2d 376 (N.Y.1984). To a "speedy appeal"? See *United States v. Mohawk,* 20 F.3d 1480 (9th Cir.1994). To a "speedy probation revocation proceeding"? See *State v. Gefroh,* 458 N.W.2d 479 (N.D.1990). To a "speedy parole revocation proceeding"? See *Morrissey v. Brewer,* p. 88, and compare *Moody v. Daggett,* 429 U.S. 78, 97 S.Ct. 274, 50 L.Ed.2d 236 (1976), where the Court, per Burger, C.J., held that a federal parolee imprisoned for a crime committed while on parole was not constitutionally entitled to a prompt parole revocation hearing when a parole violator warrant was issued and lodged with the institution of his confinement but not served on him. The Court stressed that his present confinement did not derive from the warrant, that the warrant did not diminish his opportunity for parole on the intervening sentence, and that it would be more appropriate to hold the revocation hearing at the expiration of the intervening sentence because at that time a more relevant and accurate prediction of the parolee's ability to live at large in a law-abiding way can be made.

Part Four

THE ADVERSARY SYSTEM AND THE DETERMINATION OF GUILT OR INNOCENCE

Chapter 20

THE ASSISTANCE OF COUNSEL

SECTION 1. WAIVER OF THE RIGHT TO COUNSEL; THE RIGHT TO PROCEED *PRO SE*

The courts have long been concerned about the alleged waiver of constitutional rights, especially the right to the assistance of counsel. In *Johnson v. Zerbst,* 304 U.S. 458, 58 S.Ct. 1019, 82 L.Ed. 1461 (1938), in the course of remanding the case to determine whether petitioner "competently and intelligently waive[d] his right to counsel," the Court observed, per Black, J.: " 'Courts indulge every reasonable presumption against waiver' of fundamental rights [and] we 'do not presume acquiescence in the loss of fundamental rights.' A waiver is ordinarily an intelligent relinquishment or abandonment of a known right or privilege."

In *Von Moltke v. Gillies,* 332 U.S. 708, 68 S.Ct. 316, 92 L.Ed. 309 (1948), a four-justice plurality opinion per Black, J., pointed out: "A waiver of the constitutional right to the assistance of counsel is of no less moment to an accused who must decide whether to plead guilty than to an accused who stands trial. [The duty to protect an accused who seeks to proceed without counsel] imposes the serious and weighty responsibility upon the trial judge of determining whether there is an intelligent and competent waiver by the accused' [quoting from *Johnson v. Zerbst*]. To discharge this duty properly in light of the strong presumption against waiver of the constitutional right to counsel, a judge must investigate as long and as thoroughly as the circumstances of the case before him demand. The fact that an accused may tell him that he is informed of his right to counsel and desires to waive this right does not automatically end the judge's responsibility."

The strong presumption against waiver of counsel is also manifested in *Carnley v. Cochran,* 369 U.S. 506, 82 S.Ct. 884, 8 L.Ed.2d 70 (1962), where the Court, per Brennan, J., noted that "where the assistance of counsel is a constitutional requisite, the right to be furnished counsel does not depend on a request" and pointed out: "Presuming waiver from a silent record is impermissible. The record must show, or there must be an allegation and evidence which show, that an accused was offered counsel but intelligently and understandably rejected the offer. Anything less is not waiver."

As a general matter, appellate courts seemed justified in begrudgingly treating a claim that counsel had been waived. For where trial judges were painstakingly careful in providing counsel and explaining the important role that a defense lawyer may play, only one or two percent waived counsel. See, e.g., Yale Kamisar & Jesse H. Choper, *The Right to Counsel in Minnesota: Some Field Findings and Legal—Policy Observations*, 48 Minn.L.Rev. 1, 34–38 (1963). But this "scrupulousness [was] sometimes carried to the point of simply *not permitting* a defendant to waive the assistance of counsel." *Id.* at 35 (emphasis added). Could a trial court "force" counsel upon a criminal defendant who wanted to represent himself? On the eve of *Faretta,* infra, the answer was unclear. See Commentary to Unif. R.Crim.P. 711 (approved a year before *Faretta*) at 287–88 and fn. 1; Joseph D. Grano, *The Right to Counsel: Collateral Issues Affecting Due Process*, 54 Minn. L.Rev. 1175, 1193–94 (1970).

FARETTA v. CALIFORNIA
422 U.S. 806, 95 S.Ct. 2525, 45 L.Ed.2d 562 (1975).

Justice STEWART delivered the opinion of the Court.

[Well before the date of his trial, Faretta, charged with grand theft, requested that he be allowed to represent himself. Questioning by the trial judge revealed that Faretta had once before represented himself in a criminal prosecution, that he had a high school education, and that he did not want to be represented by the public defender because he thought that that office had too heavy a case load. Several weeks thereafter, but still prior to trial, the judge held a hearing to inquire into Faretta's ability to conduct his own defense, in the course of which Faretta was questioned specifically about both the hearsay rule and the law governing the challenge of jurors. The judge ruled that Faretta (a) had not made an intelligent and knowing waiver of his right to counsel and (b) had no constitutional right to conduct his own defense. The judge then appointed the public defender to represent Faretta. Throughout the subsequent trial, the judge required that Faretta's defense be conducted only through the appointed lawyer. Faretta was found guilty as charged and sentenced to prison. The appellate court affirmed his conviction.]

[The] Court's past recognition of the right of self-representation, the federal court authority holding the right to be of constitutional dimension, and the state constitutions pointing to the right's fundamental nature form a consensus not easily ignored. [This] consensus is soundly premised. The right of self-representation finds support in the structure of the Sixth Amendment, as well as in the English and colonial experience from which the Amendment emerged.

[The] Sixth Amendment does not provide merely that a defense shall be made for the accused; it grants to the accused personally the right to make his defense. It is the accused, not counsel, who must be "informed of the nature and cause of the accusation," who must be "confronted with witnesses against him," and who must be accorded "compulsory process for obtaining witnesses in his favor." [T]he right to self-representation—to make one's defense personally—is thus necessarily implied by the structure of the Amendment.[15] The right to defend is given directly to the accused; for it is he who suffers the consequences if the defense fails.

---

15. [The] inference of rights is not, of course, a mechanical exercise. In *Singer v. United States* (1965) [p. 1319], the Court held that an accused has no right to a bench trial, despite his capacity to waive his right to a jury trial. In so holding, the Court stated that "[t]he ability to waive a constitutional right does not ordinarily carry with it the right to

The counsel provision supplements this design. It speaks of the "assistance" of counsel, and an assistant, however expert, is still an assistant. The language and spirit of the Sixth Amendment contemplate that counsel, like the other defense tools guaranteed by the Amendment, shall be an aid to a willing defendant—not an organ of the State interposed between an unwilling defendant and his right to defend himself personally. To thrust counsel upon the accused, against his considered wish, thus violates the logic of the Amendment. [It] is true that when a defendant chooses to have a lawyer manage and present his case, law and tradition may allocate to the counsel the power to make binding decisions of trial strategy in many areas.[a] This allocation can only be justified, however, by the defendant's consent, at the outset, to accept counsel as his representative. An unwanted counsel "represents" the defendant only through a tenuous and unacceptable legal fiction. Unless the accused has acquiesced in such representation, the defense presented is not the defense guaranteed by the Constitution, for, in a very real sense, it is not *his* defense.

The Sixth Amendment, when naturally read, thus implies a right of self-representation. This reading is reinforced by the Amendment's roots in English legal history. [After an extensive discussion of the right of self-representation in England and the American colonies, the Court concluded:]

In sum, there is no evidence that the colonists and the Framers ever doubted the right of self-representation, or imagined that this right might be considered inferior to the right of assistance of counsel. To the contrary, [they], as well as their English ancestors, always conceived of the right to counsel as an "assistance" for the accused, to be used at his option, in defending himself. The Framers selected in the Sixth Amendment a form of words that necessarily implies the right of self-representation. That conclusion is supported by centuries of history.

There can be no blinking the fact that the right of an accused to conduct his own defense seems to cut against the grain of this Court's decisions holding that the Constitution requires that no accused can be convicted and imprisoned unless he has been accorded the right to the assistance of counsel. For it is surely true that the basic thesis of those decisions is that the help of a lawyer is essential to assure the defendant a fair trial. And a strong argument can surely be made that the whole thrust of those decisions must inevitably lead to the conclusion that a State may constitutionally impose a lawyer upon even an unwilling defendant.

But it is one thing to hold that every [accused] has the right to the assistance of counsel, and quite another to say that a State may compel a defendant to accept a lawyer he does not want. The value of state-appointed counsel was not unappreciated by the Founders, yet the notion of compulsory counsel was utterly foreign to them. [To] force a lawyer on a defendant can only lead him to believe that the law contrives against him. Moreover, it is not inconceivable that in some rare instances, the defendant might in fact present his case more effectively by conducting his own defense. Personal liberties are not rooted in the law of

---

insist upon the opposite of that right." But that statement was made only *after* the Court had concluded that the Constitution does not affirmatively protect any right to be tried by a judge. Recognizing that an implied right must arise independently from the design and history of the constitutional text, the Court searched for, but could not find, any "indication that the colonists considered the ability to waive a jury trial to be of equal importance to the right to demand one." Instead, the Court could locate only "isolated instances" of a right

to trial by judge, and concluded that these were "clear departures from the common law."

We follow the approach of *Singer* here. Our concern is with an *independent* right of self-representation. We do not suggest that this right arises mechanically from a defendant's power to waive the right to the assistance of counsel. On the contrary, the right must be independently found in the structure and history of the constitutional text.

a. See Note 6 following this case.

averages. The right to defend is personal. The defendant, and not his lawyer or the State, will bear the personal consequences of a conviction. It is the defendant, therefore, who must be free personally to decide whether in his particular case counsel is to his advantage. And although he may conduct his own defense ultimately to his own detriment, his choice must be honored out of "that respect for the individual which is the lifeblood of the law."[46]

When an accused manages his own defense, he relinquishes, as a purely factual matter, many of the traditional benefits associated with the right to counsel. For this reason, in order to represent himself, the accused must "knowingly and intelligently" forego those relinquished benefits. *Johnson v. Zerbst.* Although a defendant need not himself have the skill and experience of a lawyer in order competently and intelligently to choose self-representation, he should be made aware of the dangers and disadvantages of self-representation, so that the record will establish that "he knows what he is doing and his choice is made with eyes open." *Adams v. United States ex rel. McCann.*[b]

Here, weeks before trial, Faretta clearly and unequivocally declared [that] he wanted to represent himself and did not want counsel. The record affirmatively shows that [defendant] was literate, competent, and understanding, and that he was voluntarily exercising his informed free will. The trial judge had warned [defendant] that he thought it was a mistake not to accept the assistance of counsel and that [defendant] would be required to follow all the "ground rules" of trial procedure. We need make no assessment of how well or poorly [defendant] had mastered the intricacies of the hearsay rule and the California code provisions that govern challenges of potential jurors on *voir dire* [matters about which the trial judge specifically questioned defendant before ruling that he had not made an intelligent and knowing waiver of his right to the assistance of counsel]. For [defendant's] technical legal knowledge, as such, was not relevant to an assessment of his knowing exercise of the right to defend himself. * * *

Chief Justice BURGER, with whom Justice BLACKMUN and Justice REHNQUIST join, dissenting.

[This case] is another example of the judicial tendency to constitutionalize what is thought "good." That effort fails on its own terms here, because there is nothing desirable or useful in permitting every accused person, even the most

---

46. We are told that many criminal defendants representing themselves may use the courtroom for deliberate disruption of their trials. But the right of self-representation has been recognized from our beginnings by federal law and by most of the States, and no such result has thereby occurred. Moreover, the trial judge may terminate self-representation by a defendant who deliberately engages in serious and obstructionist misconduct. Of course, a State may—even over objection by the accused—appoint a "standby counsel" to aid the accused if and when the accused requests help, and to be available to represent the accused in the event that termination of the defendant's self-representation is necessary.

The right of self-representation is not a license to abuse the dignity of the courtroom. Neither is it a license not to comply with relevant rules of procedural and substantive law. Thus, whatever else may or may not be open to him on appeal, a defendant who elects to represent himself cannot thereafter complain that the quality of his own defense amounted to a denial of "effective assistance of counsel."

b. In *Adams*, 317 U.S. 269, 63 S.Ct. 236, 87 L.Ed. 268 (1942), a mail fraud defendant who professed to have "studied law" and be "sufficiently familiar with it to defend himself," insisted on proceeding without counsel. He then waived trial by jury and was convicted after a trial by the judge alone. In holding that defendant could waive his rights to counsel and to trial by jury and that he had intelligently and competently done so, the Court, per Frankfurter, J., observed that "the Constitution does not force a lawyer upon a defendant." Assuming arguendo that a federal defendant might waive a jury trial, dissenting Justice Douglas, joined by Black and Murphy, JJ., maintained that McCann should have had the benefit of legal advice before his waiver was accepted. For otherwise the Court could not "safely assume [that] a waiver by a layman of his constitutional right to a jury trial was intelligent and competent in a case such as this."

uneducated and inexperienced, to insist upon conducting his own defense to criminal charges.

[The goal of achieving justice] is ill-served, and the integrity of and public confidence in the system are undermined, when an easy conviction is obtained due to the defendant's ill-advised decision to waive counsel. [The criminal justice system] should not be available as an instrument of self-destruction.

[B]oth the "spirit and the logic" of the Sixth Amendment are that every person accused of crime shall receive the fullest possible defense; in the vast majority of cases this command can be honored only by means of the expressly-guaranteed right to counsel, and the trial judge is in the best position to determine whether the accused is capable of conducting his defense. True freedom of choice and society's interest in seeing that justice is achieved can be vindicated only if the trial court retains discretion to reject any attempted waiver of counsel and insist that the accused be tried according to the Constitution. This discretion is as critical an element of basic fairness as a trial judge's discretion to decline to accept a plea of guilty. * * *

If we were to assume that there will be widespread exercise of the newly-discovered constitutional right to self-representation, it would almost certainly follow that there will be added congestion in the courts and that the quality of justice will suffer. Moreover, [i]t is totally unrealistic [to] suggest that an accused will always be held to the consequences of a decision to conduct his own defense. Unless [most defendants] have more wit than to insist upon [self-representation], we can expect that many expensive and good-faith prosecutions will be nullified on appeal for reasons that trial courts are now deprived of the power to prevent.

Justice BLACKMUN, with whom The Chief Justice and Justice REHNQUIST join, dissenting. * * *

I cannot agree that there is anything in the [Constitution] that requires the States to subordinate the solemn business of conducting a criminal prosecution to the whimsical—albeit voluntary—caprice of every accused who wishes to use his trial as a vehicle for personal or political self-gratification. * * * I do not believe that any amount of *pro se* pleading can cure the injury to society of an unjust result, but I do believe that a just result should prove to be an effective balm for almost any frustrated *pro se* defendant.

* * * I note briefly the procedural problems that, I suspect, today's decision will visit upon trial courts in the future. * * * Must every defendant be advised of his right to proceed *pro se?* If so, when must that notice be given? Since the right to the assistance of counsel and the right to self-representation are mutually exclusive, how is the waiver of each right to be measured? If a defendant has elected to exercise his right to proceed *pro se,* does he still have a constitutional right to assistance of standby counsel? How soon in the criminal proceeding must a defendant decide between proceeding by counsel or *pro se?* Must he be allowed to switch in mid-trial? May a violation of the right to self-representation ever be harmless error? Must the trial court treat the *pro se* defendant differently than it would professional counsel? [The] procedural problems spawned by an absolute right to self-representation will far outweigh whatever tactical advantage the defendant may feel he has gained by electing to represent himself.

If there is any truth to the old proverb that "one who is his own lawyer has a fool for a client," the Court by its opinion today now bestows a *constitutional* right on one to make a fool of himself.

Notes and Questions

1. *The irony of the Court's decision in Faretta.* "Among the justices forming the majority in *Faretta*," observes Joshua Dressler, *Understanding Criminal Procedure* 523 (2d ed. 1997), "are those who have argued most strenuously for the expansion of the right to counsel. Meanwhile, it was the dissenters—members of the Court not generally sympathetic to such extensions—who were called on to point out that 'representation by counsel is essential to ensure a fair trial.' "

2. *Consistency.* Is *Faretta* consistent with the view the Court subsequently expressed in *Wheat v. United States*, p. 1160, that "courts have an independent interest in ensuring [that] legal proceedings appear fair to all who observe them"? See Dressler, supra, at 524.

3. *Does the principle of self-representation apply to appeals as well?* In MARTINEZ v. COURT OF APPEAL OF CALIFORNIA, 528 U.S. 152, 120 S.Ct. 684, 145 L.Ed.2d 597 (2000), defendant (who described himself as a self-taught paralegal with 25 years experience) was convicted of embezzlement after representing himself at trial. He sought to represent himself on appeal as well, but was rebuffed by the state appellate courts. The U.S. Supreme Court, per STEVENS, J., affirmed, holding, without a dissent, that "neither the holding nor the reasoning in *Faretta* requires [a state] to recognize a constitutional right to self-representation on direct appeal from a criminal conviction":

"Appeals as of right in federal courts were nonexistent for the first century of our Nation, and appellate review of any sort was 'rarely allowed.' [Thus,] unlike the inquiry in *Faretta*, the historical evidence does not provide any support for an affirmative constitutional right to appellate self-representation.

"The *Faretta* majority's reliance on the structure of the Sixth Amendment is also not relevant. The Sixth Amendment identifies the basic rights that the accused shall enjoy in 'all criminal prosecutions.' [The] Sixth Amendment does not include any right to appeal. [It] necessarily follows that the Amendment itself does not provide any basis for finding a right to self-representation on appeal."

As for a right to self-representation based on a respect for individual autonomy grounded in the Due Process Clause, "we are entirely unpersuaded that the risk of either disloyalty or suspicion of disloyalty is a sufficient concern to conclude that a constitutional right of self-representation is a necessary component of a fair appellate proceeding."

"As the *Faretta* opinion recognized," observed Justice Stevens, "the right to self-representation is not absolute. [Even] at the trial level, therefore, the government's interest in ensuring the integrity and efficiency of the trial at times outweighs the defendant's interest in acting as his own lawyer. In the appellate context, the balance between the two competing interests surely tips in favor of the State. The status of the accused defendant, who retains a presumption of innocence throughout the trial process, changes dramatically when a jury returns a guilty verdict.

" * * * Considering the change in position from defendant to appellant, the autonomy interests that survive a felony conviction are less compelling than those motivating the decision in *Faretta*. Yet the overriding state interest in the fair and efficient administration of justice remains as strong as at the trial level. Thus, the States are clearly within their discretion to conclude that the government's interests outweigh an invasion of the appellant's interest in self-representation."

The *Martinez* majority seemed to have second thoughts about *Faretta*:

"The historical evidence relied upon by *Faretta* as identifying a right of self-representation is not always useful because it pertained to times when lawyers were scarce, often mistrusted, and not readily available to the average person accused of crime. For one who could not obtain a lawyer, self-representation was the only feasible alternative to asserting no defense at all. [But] an individual's decision to represent himself is no longer compelled by the necessity of choosing self-representation over incompetent or nonexistent representation. [Therefore,] while *Faretta* is correct in concluding that there is abundant support for the proposition that a right to self-representation has been recognized for centuries, the original reasons for protecting that right do not have the same force when the availability of competent counsel for every indigent defendant has displaced the need—although not always the desire—for self-representation. * * *

"No one, including Martinez and the *Faretta* majority, attempts to argue that as a rule *pro se* representation is wise, desirable or efficient.[9] * * * Our experience has taught us that a 'pro se defense is usually a bad defense, particularly when compared to a defense provided by an experienced criminal defense attorney.' "[10]

Justice SCALIA concurred in the judgment, "not shar[ing] the apparent skepticism of today's opinion" regarding *Faretta*:

"I have no doubt that the Framers of our Constitution, who were suspicious enough of governmental power—including judicial power—that they insisted upon a citizen's right to be judged by an independent jury of private citizens, would not have found acceptable the compulsory assignment of counsel *by the Government* to plead a criminal defendant's case. * * * Our system of laws generally presumes that the criminal defendant, after being fully informed, knows his own best interests and does not need them dictated by the State. Any other approach is unworthy of a free people."

"Because Justice Scalia writes separately to underscore the continuing constitutional validity of *Faretta*," Justice BREYER, who joined the Court's opinion, wrote separately to "note that judges closer to the firing line have sometimes expressed dismay about the practical consequences" of *Faretta*. However, "without some strong factual basis for believing that *Faretta*'s holding has proved counterproductive in practice, we are not in a position to reconsider the constitutional assumptions that underlie that case."[a]

4. *Waiver of counsel.* According to *A.B.A. Standards* § 5–7.2, before accepting a waiver of counsel "the court should inquire whether the accused apprehends the nature of the charges, the offenses included within them, the allowable punishments, possible defenses to the charges, and circumstances in mitigation thereof, among other factors."[b] How can a judge explain all possible

---

9. Some critics argue that the right to proceed *pro se* at trial in certain cases is akin to allowing the defendant to waive his right to a fair trial. * * *

10. John F. Decker, The Sixth Amendment Right to Shoot Oneself in the Foot: An Assessment of the Guarantee of Self-Representation Twenty Years after *Faretta*, 6 Seton Hall Const. L. J. 483, 598 (1996).

a. Justice Kennedy, who joined the opinion of the Court, also wrote separately to observe that "[t]o resolve this case it is unnecessary to cast doubt upon the rationale of *Faretta*."

b. At this point, the commentary cites Justice Black's plurality opinion in *Von Moltke v. Gillies*, 332 U.S. 708, 68 S.Ct. 316, 92 L.Ed. 309 (1948). Although the Court invalidated pe-

titioner's guilty plea, there was no opinion of the Court. Speaking for four Justices who maintained that the guilty plea had to be overturned because petitioner had not competently waived counsel, Justice Black observed:

"To be valid [a waiver of the right to counsel] must be made with an apprehension of the nature of the charges, the statutory offenses included within them, the range of allowable punishments thereunder, possible defenses to the charges and circumstances in mitigation thereof, and all other facts essential to a broad understanding of the whole matter."

Some courts have not felt bound by Justice Black's formulation in *Von Moltke* since it was not supported by a majority of the Court; and have sought to shorten the list of matters with

defenses unless he is familiar with the facts of the case? Moreover, wouldn't literal compliance with the A.B.A. Standards require the court to give the accused a course in criminal law?

Consider Unif.R.Crim.P. (commentary): "Instead of requiring the defendant to *know* each of the included offenses, possible defenses, and circumstances in mitigation, [Rule 711(2)] requires him to understand that a defense lawyer might discover such matters and use them to the defendant's advantage. This would appear to afford sufficient protection, particularly in light of [another provision] of this Rule authorizing the court to refuse to accept a waiver until the defendant has first consulted with a lawyer, and in light of the fact that the plea provisions of these Rules require a determination of factual basis which will uncover the existence of possible defenses, circumstances in mitigation and situations where the defendant may be guilty only of a lesser included offense."[c]

A.B.A. Standards § 5–7.3 provides in part: "If an accused has not seen a lawyer and indicates an intention to waive the assistance of counsel, a lawyer should be provided for consultation purposes. No waiver should be accepted unless the accused has at least once conferred with a lawyer." On the premise that an early waiver should not be held to preclude appointment of counsel at a later stage (because the value and need for legal assistance may become clear to the defendant only at a stage of the proceedings subsequent to the initial offer and waiver), Standard 5–7.3. also provides: "If a waiver is accepted, the offer should be renewed at each subsequent stage of the proceedings at which the accused appears without counsel."

5. *The competency standard for waiving the right to counsel.* In GODINEZ v. MORAN, 509 U.S. 389, 113 S.Ct. 2680, 125 L.Ed.2d 321 (1993) (also discussed at p. 1290) (a case in which a capital defendant discharged his attorneys, pled guilty and was ultimately sentenced to death), a 7–2 majority, per THOMAS, J., rejected the notion that competency to plead guilty or to waive the right to counsel must be measured by a higher or different standard than the competency standard for standing trial—whether the defendant has "sufficient present ability to consult with his lawyer with a reasonable degree of rational understanding" and has "a rational as well as functional understanding of the proceedings against him." Observed Justice Thomas:

"[As for the guilty plea, a] defendant who stands trial is likely to be presented with choices [such as whether to testify, whether to waive a jury trial, and whether to cross-examine witnesses for the prosecution] that entail relinquishment of the same rights that are relinquished by a defendant who pleads guilty. [While] the decision to plead guilty is a profound one, it is no more complicated than the sum total of decisions that a defendant may be called upon to make during the course of a trial. [Thus,] we can conceive of no basis for demanding a higher level of competence for those defendants who choose to plead guilty.

"[As for waiving the right to counsel,] there is no reason to believe that [that] decision requires an appreciably higher level of mental functioning than the decision to waive other constitutional rights. [The] competence that is required of a defendant seeking to waive his right to counsel is the competence to *waive the*

---

which the defendant must be familiar. The component most frequently sought to be eliminated is that requiring knowledge of "possible defenses to the charges." See generally Wayne R. LaFave, Jerold H. Israel, & Nancy J. King, *Criminal Procedure Treatise* § 11.3(b)(2d ed. 1999)(hereafter CRIMPROC); Note, 49 Minn. L.Rev. 1133, 1142–45 (1965).

c. Did the *Von Moltke* plurality opinion cause confusion because petitioner's waiver of counsel in that case was *immediately followed* by a plea of guilty? As a result, did the plurality opinion merge, or at least blur, the procedures for waiving counsel with those for pleading guilty?

right, not the competence to represent himself. [A] defendant's ability to represent himself has no bearing upon his competence to *choose* self-representation."

But a determination that a defendant is competent to stand trial is not enough when she seeks to plead guilty or waive her right to counsel: In such instances "a trial court must satisfy itself that the waiver [of] constitutional rights is knowing and voluntary. In this sense, there is a 'heightened' standard for pleading guilty and for waiving the right to counsel, but it is not a heightened standard of *competence*." The purpose of a competency inquiry, explained the Court, is to determine whether a defendant "has the *ability* to understand the proceedings," but "the purpose of the 'knowing and voluntary' inquiry [is] to determine whether the defendant actually *does* understand the significance and consequences of a particular decision and whether the decision is uncoerced."[b]

6. "Standby counsel." McKASKLE v. WIGGINS, 465 U.S. 168, 104 S.Ct. 944, 79 L.Ed.2d 122 (1984), per O'CONNOR, J., made explicit "what is already implicit in *Faretta:* a defendant's Sixth Amendment rights are not violated when a trial judge appoints standby counsel—even over the defendant's objection—to relieve the judge of the need to explain and enforce basic rules of courtroom protocol or to assist the defendant in overcoming routine obstacles that stand in the way of the defendant's achievement of his own clearly indicated goals."

The trial court permitted Wiggins to represent himself at his state robbery trial, but designated two appointed lawyers as "standby counsel." Before and during the trial, Wiggins frequently changed his mind regarding the standby attorneys' role, objecting to their participation on some occasions, but conferring with them or expressly adopting their initiatives on other occasions. Wiggins filed and argued numerous *pro se* motions both before and during the trial. He conducted the defense's voir dire of prospective jurors, made the opening statement for the defense and, throughout the trial, selected the witnesses for the defense. He cross-examined the prosecution's witnesses freely. He also filed his own requested charges to the jury and made his own objections to the court's suggested charge. On several occasions, however he strongly opposed the initiatives of counsel and sometimes indignantly demanded that counsel not participate further without invitation. At one point, an acrimonious exchange between Wiggins and one of his standby lawyers occurred over the questioning of a witness.

Wiggins was convicted and sentenced to life imprisonment as a recidivist. [The] Fifth Circuit granted habeas corpus relief, [establishing] a rule that "standby counsel is 'to be seen, but not heard' "; "his presence is there for advisory purposes only, to be used or not used as the defendant sees fit." The Supreme Court explicitly rejected the Fifth Circuit's rule and reversed its judgment:

"A defendant's right to self-representation plainly encompasses certain specific rights to have his voice heard. The *pro se* defendant must be allowed to control the organization and content of his own defense, to make motions, to argue points of law, to participate in voir dire, to question witnesses, and to address the court

---

b. Justice Kennedy, joined by Scalia, J., wrote a concurring opinion. See fn. a at p. 1290.

Justice Blackmun, joined by Stevens, J., dissented, pointing out that Moran had "presented no defense, called no witnesses and offered no mitigating evidence on his behalf." A finding that defendant is competent to stand trial, emphasized the dissent, "establishes only that he is capable of aiding his attorney in making critical decisions required at trial or in plea

negotiations. The reliability or even relevancy of such a finding vanishes when its basic premise—that counsel will be present—ceases to exist. The question is no longer whether the defendant can proceed with an attorney, but whether he can proceed alone and uncounselled."

Thirty-three months after he lost his case in the U.S. Supreme Court, Moran was executed. See *Nevada Executes Man Who Killed 3 People,* N.Y. Times, Mar. 31, 1996, Sec.1, at 27.

and the jury at appropriate points in the trial. The record reveals that Wiggins was in fact accorded all of these rights. * * *

"Wiggins' complaint is directed not at limits placed on *his* participation in the trial, for there clearly were none. It is directed instead at the allegedly inadequate limits placed on standby counsel's participation. * * * Wiggins claims, and the Court of Appeals agreed, that the *pro se* defendant may insist on presenting his own case wholly free from interruption or other uninvited involvement by standby counsel.

"[In] our view, [*Faretta* indicates] that no absolute bar on standby counsel's unsolicited participation is appropriate or was intended. The right to appear *pro se* exists to affirm the dignity and autonomy of the accused and to allow the presentation of what may, at least occasionally, be the accused's best possible defense. Both of these objectives can be achieved without categorically silencing standby counsel. * * *

"We recognize [that] the right to speak for oneself entails more than the opportunity to add one's voice to a cacophony of others. [Thus,] the *Faretta* right must impose some limits on the extent of standby counsel's unsolicited participation.[h]

"First, the *pro se* defendant is entitled to preserve actual control over the case he chooses to present to the jury. This is the core of the *Faretta* right. If standby counsel's participation over the defendant's objection effectively allows counsel to make or substantially interfere with any significant tactical decisions, or to control the questioning of witnesses, or to speak *instead* of the defendant on any matter of importance, the *Faretta* right is eroded.

"Second, participation by standby counsel without the defendant's consent should not be allowed to destroy the jury's perception that the defendant is representing himself. The defendant's appearance in the status of one conducting his own defense is important in a criminal trial, since the right to appear *pro se* exists to affirm the accused's individual dignity and autonomy. * * *

"Participation by standby counsel outside the presence of the jury engages only the first of these two limitations. [The] appearance of a *pro se* defendant's self-representation will not be unacceptably undermined by counsel's participation outside the presence of the jury.

"Thus, *Faretta* rights are adequately vindicated in proceedings outside the presence of the jury if [as here] the *pro se* defendant is allowed to address the court freely on his own behalf and if [as here] disagreements between counsel and the *pro se* defendant are resolved in the defendant's favor whenever the matter is one that would normally be left to the discretion of counsel.

"[Though several of the exchanges between Wiggins and standby counsel] are regrettable, we are satisfied that counsel's participation outside the presence of jury fully satisfied the first standard we have outlined. * * * Equally important,

h. Since the right of self-representation is a right that when exercised usually increases the likelihood of a trial outcome unfavorable to the defendant, its denial is not amenable to "harmless error" analysis. The right is either respected or denied; its deprivation cannot be harmless.

As a corollary, however, a defendant who exercises his right to appear *pro se* "cannot thereafter complain that the quality of his own defense amounted to a denial of 'effective assistance of counsel.'" *Faretta*. Moreover, the de-

fendant's right to proceed *pro se* exists in the larger context of the criminal trial designed to determine whether or not a defendant is guilty of the offense with which he is charged. The trial judge may be required to make numerous rulings reconciling the participation of standby counsel with a *pro se* defendant's objection to that participation; nothing in the nature of the *Faretta* right suggests that the usual deference to "judgment calls" on these issues by the trial judge should not obtain here as elsewhere.

all conflicts between Wiggins and counsel were resolved in Wiggins' favor. The trial judge repeatedly explained to all concerned that Wiggins' strategic choices, not counsel's, would prevail. * * *

"Participation by standby counsel in the presence of the jury is more problematic. It is here that the defendant may legitimately claim that excessive involvement by counsel will destroy the appearance that the defendant is acting *pro se*. * * * Nonetheless, we believe that a categorical bar on participation by standby counsel in the presence of the jury is unnecessary.

"[The] record in this case reveals that Wiggins' *pro se* efforts were undermined primarily by his own, frequent changes of mind regarding counsel's role. [The] only two long appearances by counsel at Wiggins' trial, one before the jury and one outside its presence, were both initiated with Wiggins' express approval. In these circumstances it is very difficult to determine how much of counsel's participation was in fact contrary to Wiggins' desires of the moment.

"*Faretta* does not require a trial judge to permit 'hybrid' representation of the type Wiggins was actually allowed. But if a defendant is given the opportunity and elects to have counsel appear before the court or jury, his complaints concerning counsel's subsequent unsolicited participation lose much of their force. A defendant does not have a constitutional right to choreograph special appearances by counsel. Once a *pro se* defendant invites or agrees to any substantial participation by counsel, subsequent appearances by counsel must be presumed to be with the defendant's acquiescence, at least until the defendant expressly and unambiguously renews his request that standby counsel be silenced. * * *

"*Faretta* affirmed the defendant's constitutional right to appear on stage at his trial. We recognize that a *pro se* defendant may wish to dance a solo, not a *pas de deux*. Standby counsel must generally respect that preference. But counsel need not be excluded altogether, especially when the participation is outside the presence of the jury or is with the defendant's express or tacit consent. The defendant in this case was allowed to make his own appearances as he saw fit. In our judgment counsel's unsolicited involvement was held within reasonable limits."[a]

Dissenting Justice WHITE, joined by Brennan and Marshall, JJ., protested:

"Although petitioner characterizes counsel's participation as 'limited' and 'intermittent,' nothing could be further from the truth. Standby counsel intervened in a substantial manner without Wiggins' permission well over 50 times during the course of the three-day trial; many of these interruptions precipitated direct conflicts between Wiggins and counsel, often in the presence of the jury. Although the trial court appears to have resolved the conflicts calling for a ruling in Wiggins' favor, their mere existence disrupted the proceedings and turned the trial into an ordeal through which the jury was required to suffer. At several points during the trial, moreover, counsel blatantly interfered with Wiggins' attempt to present his defense in a manner not calling for a ruling from the bench, and we of course have no way of knowing the extent to which Wiggins' defense was subtly undermined or adversely affected by counsel's extensive unsolicited participation.

"[Under] the Court's new test, it is necessary to determine whether the *pro se* defendant retained 'actual control over the case he [chose] to present to the jury' and whether standby counsel's participation 'destroy[ed] the jury's perception that the defendant [was] representing himself.' Although this test purports to protect all of the values underlying our holding in *Faretta,* it is unclear whether it can achieve this result.

a. Justice Blackmun concurred in the result without opinion.

"As long as the *pro se* defendant is allowed his say, the first prong of the Court's test accords standby counsel at a bench trial or any proceeding outside the presence of a jury virtually untrammeled discretion to present any factual or legal argument to which the defendant does not object. The limits placed on counsel's participation in this context by the 'actual control' test are more apparent than real. * * *

"Although the Court is more solicitous of a *pro se* defendant's interests when standby counsel intervenes before a jury, the test's second prong suffers from similar shortcomings. To the extent that trial and appellate courts can discern the point at which counsel's unsolicited participation substantially undermines a *pro se* defendant's appearance before the jury, a matter about which I harbor substantial doubts, their decisions will, to a certain extent, 'affirm the accused's individual dignity and autonomy.' But they will do so incompletely, for in focusing on how the jury views the defendant, the majority opinion ignores *Faretta's* emphasis on the defendant's own perception of the criminal justice system, and implies that the Court actually adheres to the result-oriented harmless error standard it purports to reject. [See fn. 8 to the Court's opinion].

"As a guide for standby counsel and lower courts, moreover, the Court's two-part test is clearly deficient. [Trial courts] clearly must prevent standby counsel from overtly muzzling their *pro se* clients and resolve certain conflicts in defendants' favor. But the Court's opinion places few, if any, other clear limits on counsel's uninvited participation; instead it requires trial courts to make numerous subjective judgments concerning the effect of counsel's actions on defendants' *Faretta* rights.

"[In] short, I believe that the Court's test is unworkable and insufficiently protective of the fundamental interests we recognized in *Faretta*.

"The inappropriateness of the Court's standard is made manifest by the Court's conclusion that the conduct of standby counsel in this case passes muster under that standard. In frequently and grievously exceeding the proper role of standby counsel, the more active of Wiggins' appointed attorneys distracted Wiggins and usurped his prerogatives, altered the tenor of the defense, disrupted the trial, undermined Wiggins' perception that he controlled his own fate, induced a belief—most assuredly unfounded, but sincerely held nevertheless—that 'the law contrive[d] against him,' and undoubtedly reduced Wiggins' credibility and prejudiced him in the eyes of the jury. In allowing such intervention to continue despite Wiggins' repeated requests that it cease, the trial court clearly denied Wiggins' right of self-representation."

7. *Did Faretta alter the basic division of decision-making authority between counsel and client?* Prior to *Faretta* the decisions whether to plead guilty, whether to waive jury trial, and whether defendant should take the stand in his or her own defense were regarded as ultimately for the defendant to make, because of the "fundamental nature" of these decisions, "so crucial to the accused's fate." *A.B.A. Standards* § 4–5.2 (commentary).[a] On the other hand, the power of decision in matters of trial strategy and tactics, e.g., whether to call a certain witness, cross-examine a government witness, stipulate to certain facts, whether to object to the admission of evidence on constitutional and other grounds, and whether to strike an improper jury instruction, were generally

a. Recently, the Court made it clear that where appeal of a conviction is available as a matter of right, the decision whether to seek review is for the defendant, not his lawyer. *Roe v. Flores–Ortega*, 528 U.S. 470, 120 S.Ct. 1029, 145 L.Ed.2d 985 (2000). Because this decision is a "purely ministerial task," not a strategic choice, a lawyer who disobeys a client's instruction to file an appeal violates the right to effective assistance of counsel. Id.

regarded as within the exclusive province of the lawyer, after consultation with the client. See id.; CRIMPROC § 11.6(a).[b]

But *Faretta* was thought by some to have altered the basic division between "strategic" and "personal" decisions and perhaps limited the attorney's ultimate authority only to "on-the-spot" decisions where timing considerations precluded the attorney's consultation with his client. See LaFave & Israel, supra. By holding, however, that an indigent defendant has no right "to compel appointed counsel to press nonfrivolous points requested by the client, if counsel, as a matter of professional judgment, decides not to present these points," JONES v. BARNES (1983), set forth at p. 1171, rejected this view of *Faretta*. See also the discussion in *Taylor v. Illinois* (p. 1220), especially fn. 24. Counsel's word on matters that fall within her domain is final *unless* the defendant makes "a demonstration of ineffectiveness," *New York v. Hill*, 528 U.S. 110, 120 S.Ct. 659, 145 L.Ed.2d 560 (2000).

8.　*Who should have the final say when a defendant and his lawyer disagree over whether to call a particular witness?* Rodney J. Uphoff, *Who Should Control the Decision to Call a Certain Witness: Respecting a Criminal Defendant's Tactical Choices*, 68 U.Cin.L.Rev. 763 (2000) poses the following problem: After a hung jury, a defendant faces a second trial. He makes it clear he does not want his elderly father to testify again. But defendant's lawyer is convinced, and so informs her client, that defendant's chances for an acquittal at the second trial would be greatly reduced if his father did not testify. A lawyer's sense of loyalty to her client, observes Professor Uphoff, may lead her to make the choice to call the defendant's father "in order to ensure that [the defendant's] best interests are protected," but another lawyer, "equally loyal to [the defendant], may defer to her client's strategic choice to promote [his] autonomy and dignity." *Id*. Professor Uphoff concludes that, although the right is not absolute, respect for the client's decisionmaking "requires that the client be afforded the right to be foolish or wrong." Id. at 834.

9.　*Who should have the final word on whether to plead not guilty by reason of insanity?* For the view that the defendant should have the final say, upon the advice of counsel, to elect the theory of the defense—not only whether or not to plead guilty by reason of insanity, but also which (if any) of the various affirmative defenses or mitigating factors to assert (e.g., consent, entrapment, heat of passion)—see H. Richard Uviller, *Calling the Shots: The Allocation of Choice Between the Accused and Counsel in the Defense of a Criminal Case*, 52 Rutgers L.Rev. 719 (2000).

10.　*Must a defendant be specifically informed of his right to represent himself?* Most courts have answered in the negative, on the premise that the policy favoring the granting of a lawyer to every individual accused of a serious crime "overrides" the right to defend *pro se* or on the premise that it is only

---

b. As pointed out in CRIMPROC §§ 11.6(a) and (b), "the various rulings produce a picture that is clear at many points but clouded at others." It is not easy "to distinguish the right to be tried before a jury, for example, from the right to present a particular witness or to cross-examine an opposing witness. If the fundamental nature of a right is measured by its importance, its historic tradition, or its current status in constitutional or state law, those rights would appear to be on the same plane." Moreover, "[t]he Court's emphasis upon the strategic element in those decisions subject to counsel's control also fails to distinguish the different types of decisions. Certainly the decisions to waive a jury or not have the defendant testify also involve substantial strategic considerations." LaFave & Israel suggest that the "concern of the courts that the lawyer not be forced to sacrifice his professional reputation while providing no true assistance to his client" may explain not only *Jones v. Barnes,* infra (appellate counsel need not present every nonfrivolous claim that his client wishes to press), but "much of the law governing the division of authority between counsel and client."

necessary to inform a defendant of those rights that are "essential to a fair trial" (and the right to self-representation is not such a right). See CRIMPROC, § 11.5(b). Can the reasoning of the courts that do not require that an accused be advised of his right to conduct his own defense be reconciled with the spirit and logic of *Faretta?*

11. *Stage of proceedings at which counsel may be waived.* The right of self-representation may be lost if not timely asserted. Once the trial is underway, most courts are reluctant to allow the defendant to discharge counsel and proceed *pro se,* analogizing the situation to the attempt of a represented defendant to change counsel during the trial. For criticism of this view see Note, 25 Am. U.L.Rev. 897, 911–13 (1976).

12. *A right to "mixed" or "hybrid" representation?* May a defendant assert both "halves" of her Sixth Amendment right and demand *both* the assistance of a lawyer and the right to self-representation? Reconsider the last paragraph of fn. 15 to the *Faretta* opinion. If, as *Faretta* seems to say, the rights to self-representation and to the assistance of counsel are *independent* constitutional rights, why should the defendant have to chose one right to the exclusion of the other?[c]

As pointed out in *McKaskle v. Wiggins,* supra, there is no constitutional right to "mixed" or "hybrid" representation, i.e., a mode of representation in which the defendant has active assistance of counsel, but also participates herself as co-counsel. However, some commentators have advocated such a right. See Richard H. Chused, *Faretta and the Personal Defense: The Role of a Represented Defendant in Trial Tactics,* 65 Calif.L.Rev. 636 (1977); Notes, 57 B.U.L.Rev. 570 (1977), 12 Val.U.L. 329 (1978). In the main, however, the courts have viewed the rights to self-representation and to representation by counsel as mutually exclusive, although occasionally a trial court may permit hybrid representation as "a matter of grace." See Vivian O. Berger, *The Supreme Court and Defense Counsel: Old Roads, New Paths—A Dead End?,* 86 Colum.L.Rev. 9, 39–43 (1986). According to Professor Berger, the complexities of mixed representation and the heavy burdens it would inflict on an already overstrained system—without promoting the interests of defendants as much as does the right to defend pro se—militate strongly against giving constitutional stature to a right to hybrid representation. See id. at 42–43.[d]

c. Consider also Angela Davis's criticism of the prevailing view that a defendant has no right to *both* participate in her own defense *and* enjoy the assistance of counsel, A. Davis, *If They Come in the Morning,* 253 (1971): "I consider my participation decisive for my defense. One might argue that since I am determined to play an active role in the trial, I should fire my lawyers and assume the entire burden of the defense. This is to say, if I wish to exercise my constitutional right to defend myself, I must relinquish the right to counsel. This either/or situation in my opinion flies blatantly in the face of justice. Rigorously speaking, neither is a *right* if one must be renounced in order to exercise the other. Should I be penalized because I do not possess the legal knowledge, experience or expertise necessary to proceed entirely pro se?" In her prosecution for murder, kidnapping and conspiracy, Ms. Davis successfully argued for the right to participate in her trial as co-counsel alongside her private attorneys, but her motion was not granted on constitutional grounds, only on the basis of "a narrow finding that in her case, the cause of justice will be served and expeditious conduct of the Court's business will not be hampered." See 59 Calif.L.Rev. 1479, 1480 (1971).

d. Does concern for the attorney's professional pride also underlie the failure of the courts to allow hybrid representation? Are courts "unwilling to relegate counsel to a subordinate role for fear that competent lawyers will refuse to take criminal cases as a result"? Is there also a concern that "allowing the defendant to participate actively in making decisions and in conducting the defense may lead to havoc in the courtroom"? See Note, 57 B.U.L.Rev. 570, 574 (1977).

SECTION 2. THE RIGHT TO COUNSEL OF ONE'S OWN CHOICE

A. THE RIGHT TO APPOINTED COUNSEL OF ONE'S CHOICE

"Almost unanimously," observes Peter Tague, *An Indigent's Right to the Attorney of His Choice*, 27 Stan.L.Rev. 73, 79–80 (1974), "courts have held that the selection of counsel for an indigent is a matter within the sole discretion of the trial court. [They] generally justify this decision on two grounds: first, judges assume that they can choose a more able attorney than the indigent because they know the abilities of the available local counsel; and, second, the right to effective representation is not interpreted to guarantee the defendant the best representation but only a certain minimal level of competence that an attorney, once appointed, is expected to provide. * * * Traditionally the courts have found that a defendant has an interest in defending himself in whatever way he considers best, using whatever resources are legitimately available to him, regardless of the consequences. For the nonindigent this has meant that the courts will not interfere with his choice of who will represent him [except if the defendant attempts to switch counsel after the trial begins or the issue of conflict of interest among clients arises]."[a]

"The importance to the indigent of choosing his attorney," observes Professor Tague, id. at 99, "is clear: improvement in the attorney-client relationship, representation by an able attorney who will fight aggressively for him, and the likelihood of greater participation in structuring his defense. * * *

"[V]arious legitimate governmental concerns of fairness, orderliness, economy, efficiency, and protection of the bar[b] * * * justify vesting the trial judge with discretion to select the attorney if the indigent asks for no one in particular. However, whenever the indigent asks for a particular attorney, these concerns, with the possible exception of economy, can be protected by the less intrusive

---

a. What Professor Tague describes as the nonindigent defendant's "interest in defending himself in whatever way he considers best" may not prevail when he desires to be represented by an out-of-state lawyer. Cf. *Leis v. Flynt*, 439 U.S. 438, 99 S.Ct. 698, 58 L.Ed.2d 717 (1979) (per curiam), viewing the matter from the perspective of *the out-of-state lawyer's* interest in pursuing his calling. In an Ohio criminal obscenity case, defendant Larry Flynt sought representation by two members of the New York bar who specialize in criminal defense and obscenity law, Harold Fahringer and Paul Cambria. The Ohio trial judge refused to allow either out-of-state lawyer to represent Flynt. Although the Supreme Court recognized that "the practice of courts in most states is to allow an out-of-state lawyer the privilege of appearing upon motion, especially when [as here] he is associated with a member of the local bar," it held that this "is not a right granted either by statute or the Constitution. Since the founding of the Republic, the licensing and regulation of lawyers has been left exclusively to the States * * *." The Court noted that it was not ruling on whether the constitutional rights of the defendant might be violated since that claim was not before it.

Justice White would grant certiorari and set the case for oral argument. Justice Stevens, joined by Brennan and Marshall, JJ., dissented: "The notion that a state trial judge has arbitrary and unlimited power to refuse a nonresident lawyer permission to appear in his courtroom is nothing but a remnant of a bygone era. * * * Because the assertion of federal claims or defenses is often unpopular, 'advice and assistance by an out-of-state lawyer may be the only means available for vindication.' [The instant case] is the classic situation in which the interests of justice would be served by allowing the defendant to be represented by counsel of his choice." As the dissenters saw it: "Either the 'nature' of the interest in *pro hac vice* admissions or the 'implicit promise' inhering in Ohio custom with respect to those admissions is sufficient to create an interest protected by the Due Process Clause."

b. As Professor Tague notes elsewhere, if the right to choose counsel is limited to situations where the chosen attorney agrees to represent the indigent, the rationale for protecting better-known attorneys from a heavy burden of appointments disappears. Id. at 97–98. "Ironically, now that appointments are compensated, there may be an economic incentive to protect lesser-known attorneys who rely upon court appointments for much of their income. But protecting the economic interests of the bar is not a favored governmental concern * * *." Id. at 98.

procedure of a pretrial hearing, where the attorney's qualifications and willingness to enter the case are examined, the likelihood that he will disrupt the proceedings is tested against the clear-and-present-danger standard, and the timeliness with which he could enter the case is determined. Economy remains a significant governmental interest chiefly where the public defender is available to represent the indigent; even then, however, recoupment and limitations on the amount paid for appointments could offset whatever greater costs result from appointing the requested private attorney.

"Thus, denying an indigent the right to choose his counsel fails to further in any substantial way legitimate governmental interests—interests that can be protected by less intrusive measures. The classification distinguishing indigent from nonindigent should therefore fall and an indigent should have equal opportunity to select his own counsel."[c]

Professor Tague's strong views on the subject have not prevailed, see CRIM-PROC § 11.4. But see *Harris v. Superior Court*, 567 P.2d 750 (Cal.1977), apparently the first case to limit a trial judge's discretion to appoint counsel when the indigent defendant can show "objective considerations" supporting his choice of appointed counsel. Petitioners wanted attorneys Jordan and Weinglass to be appointed to represent them and strenuously objected when the superior court appointed two other attorneys. In holding that the trial court had abused its discretion in denying petitioners' request, the state supreme court relied on certain "objective considerations": petitioners' prior representation by Jordan and Weinglass in related prosecutions—an experience that "not only established a close working relationship between petitioners and [these attorneys] but [provided the attorneys] with an extensive background in various factual and legal matters which may well become relevant in the instant proceeding"—and the appointed attorneys' vigorous support of petitioners' plea that Jordan and Weinglass be appointed. See also *People v. Chavez*, 605 P.2d 401 (Cal.1980) (making it clear that the trial court must at least explore the indigent defendant's reasons for requesting a particular attorney and indicating that not all of the *Harris* circumstances need be present to require serious consideration of the defendant's preference).

If an indigent defendant can establish "good cause," e.g., a conflict of interest or a complete breakdown of communication, many courts substitute new counsel. See CRIMPROC § 11.4. But the mere loss of confidence in one's appointed counsel does not constitute "good cause." Nor does one's dislike of appointed counsel's "attitude" or approach on matters of strategy. See id. Ideally a "relationship of trust and confidence" should exist between a defendant and her attorney, see *A.B.A. Standards* § 4–3.1, but, as the Court recently observed in MORRIS v. SLAPPY, 461 U.S. 1, 103 S.Ct. 1610, 75 L.Ed.2d 610 (1983), the Sixth Amendment guarantees only competent representation, not "a meaningful attorney-client relationship."

c. See also Jonathan Casper, *Criminal Courts: The Defendant's Perspective* 82 (1978), maintaining that the indigent defendant's distrust of public defenders has its roots, in large measure, in the lack of choice of counsel and that a public defender office policy "of giving the client the maximum choice possible—if not to choose initially, at least to select another public defender after unsatisfactory experience with one—can contribute to effective lawyer-client relationships." Stephen Schulhofer & David Friedman, *Rethinking Indigent Defense:* *Promoting Effective Representation through Consumer Sovereignty and Freedom of Choice for All Criminal Defendants,* 31 Am.Crim. L.Rev. 73 (1993), would go still further. They maintain, id. at 122, that "present institutions for providing criminal defense ought to be replaced with a voucher system, in order to provide indigent defendants with freedom of choice and to provide their attorneys with the same incentive to serve their clients that attorneys have always had when they represent clients other than the poor."

The case arose as follows: Slappy was charged, inter alia, with rape, robbery, and burglary, all involving the same female victim. The court appointed the Public Defender's office to represent him and Deputy Public Defender Goldfine was assigned to defend him. Goldfine represented Slappy at the preliminary hearing and supervised an extensive investigation. Shortly before the trial, Goldfine was hospitalized for emergency surgery. Six days before the trial the Public Defender assigned Hotchkiss, a senior trial attorney in the office, to represent Slappy.

After the trial was under way, Slappy moved for a continuance, claiming his new attorney had not had enough time to prepare the case. But the attorney told the court that he was "ready" for trial. The court denied a continuance. On the third day of trial, Slappy claimed that he was unrepresented by counsel, maintaining that Goldfine, not Hotchkiss, was his attorney. The court treated this as a motion for a continuance and denied it. Slappy then announced that he would not cooperate at all in the trial. Ignoring Hotchkiss' advice, Slappy refused to take the stand. The jury returned a verdict of guilty on some counts, but failed to reach a verdict on the sexual assault counts. A week later, a second trial was held on the charges left unresolved as a result of the mistrial. Hotchkiss again represented defendant. Again, defendant ignored Hotchkiss' advice and refused to testify. Indeed, defendant refused to even speak to Hotchkiss. The second jury returned a guilty verdict on the sexual assault counts.

The Court of Appeals for the Ninth Circuit subsequently granted federal habeas corpus relief, observing that the Sixth Amendment "would be without substance *if it did not include the right to a meaningful attorney-client relationship.*" (Emphasis added by the Supreme Court.) The Court of Appeals next stated that by failing to weigh defendant's interest in continued representation by Goldfine against the state's interest in proceeding with the scheduled trial (the trial court had not inquired about the probable length of Goldfine's absence), the trial court had ignored Slappy's Sixth Amendment right to a "meaningful attorney-client relationship" and that this violation required reversal without any need to show prejudice. The Supreme Court, per BURGER, C.J., disagreed. After finding no merit to the claim that the denial of a continuance prevented Hotchkiss from being fully prepared for trial and concluding that respondent's motion on the third day of trial for a continuance to permit Goldfine to continue to represent him was not timely, the Court observed:

"[The] Court of Appeals' conclusion that the Sixth Amendment right to counsel 'would be without substance if it did not include the right to a *meaningful attorney-client relationship*'(emphasis added) is without basis in the law. * * * No court could possibly guarantee that a defendant will develop the kind of rapport with his attorney—privately retained or provided by the public—that the Court of Appeals thought part of the Sixth Amendment guarantee of counsel. Accordingly, we reject the claim that the Sixth Amendment guarantees a 'meaningful relationship' between an accused and his counsel.[6]

"[In] its haste to create a novel Sixth Amendment right, the court wholly failed to take into account the interest of the victim of these crimes in not undergoing the ordeal of yet a third trial in this case. Of course, inconvenience and embarrassment to witnesses cannot justify failing to enforce constitutional rights of an accused: when prejudicial error is made that clearly impairs a defendant's constitutional rights, the burden of a new trial must be borne by the prosecution, the courts, and the witnesses; the Constitution permits nothing less.

6. The Court of Appeals seems to have believed that an appointed counsel with whom the accused did not have a "meaningful relationship" was the equivalent of no counsel; as a consequence, it held that no prejudice need be shown for violations of the right to a "meaningful" attorney-client relationship. Our holding that there is no Sixth Amendment right to a "meaningful attorney-client relationship" disposes of that argument.

But in the administration of criminal justice, courts may not ignore the concerns of victims. Apart from all other factors, such a course would hardly encourage victims to report violations to the proper authorities; this is especially so when the crime is one calling for public testimony about a humiliating and degrading experience such as was involved here."

Although he concurred in the result (because he agreed with the Court that Slappy did not make a timely motion for continuance based on Goldfine's unavailability), Justice BRENNAN, joined by Marshall, J., disputed much of the Court's reasoning:

"[In] light of the importance of a defendant's relationship with his attorney to his Sixth Amendment right to counsel, recognizing a qualified right to continue that relationship is eminently sensible. The Court of Appeals simply held that where a defendant expresses a desire to continue to be represented by counsel who already has been appointed for him by moving for a continuance until that attorney again will be available, the trial judge has an obligation to inquire into the length of counsel's expected unavailability and to balance the defendant's interest against the public's interest in the efficient and expeditious administration of criminal justice. Contrary to the Court's suggestion, this does not require a trial court 'to guarantee' attorney-defendant 'rapport.'

"[The] defendant's interest in preserving his relationship with a particular attorney is not afforded absolute protection. If the attorney is likely to be unavailable for an extended period, or if other factors exist that tip the balance in favor of proceeding in spite of a particular attorney's absence, the defendant's motion for a continuance clearly may be denied. Such denials would be subject to review under the traditional 'abuse of discretion' standard. As the Court of Appeals suggested, however, the balancing is critical. In the absence of a balancing inquiry a trial court cannot discharge its 'duty to preserve the fundamental rights of an accused.' "[a]

B.   THE RIGHT TO RETAIN COUNSEL OF ONE'S CHOICE

"[U]nlike the situation with respect to appointed counsel, defendant's interest in retained counsel of his choice may require that he be given the opportunity to obtain substitute counsel even though the 'good cause' standard for substitution is not met. The trial court in such a case must balance the defendant's interest in counsel of his choice against the 'public's interest in prompt and efficient administration of justice.' " CRIMPROC § 11.4 (listing eleven factors to be considered in determining whether a continuance should be granted).

The scope of one's right to retained counsel of choice may arise in various contexts. Thus, *Wheat v. United States* (p. 1160) held that the right does not preclude disqualification of a lawyer subject to a potential conflict of interest even though defendant was willing to waive his right to conflict-free counsel. And for several years the lower federal courts struggled with, and split over, the constitutionality of forfeiture provisions that may deprive a defendant of the assets needed to retain counsel of choice. The Court addressed that question in the case set forth below.

---

a. Blackmun, J., joined by Stevens, J., concurred in the result agreeing with the Court that Slappy had not made a timely motion for continuance based on Goldfine's unavailability. He saw no occasion to consider the Sixth Amendment issue.

For strong criticism of the majority opinion in *Slappy*, see Vivian O. Berger, *The Supreme Court and Defense Counsel: Old Roads, New Paths—A Dead End?*, 86 Colum.L.Rev. 9, 49–55 (1986).

CAPLIN & DRYSDALE, CHARTERED v. UNITED STATES

491 U.S. 617, 109 S.Ct. 2646, 105 L.Ed.2d 528 (1989).

Justice WHITE delivered the opinion of the Court.

We are called on to determine whether the federal drug forfeiture statute includes an exemption for assets that a defendant wishes to use to pay an attorney who conducted his defense in the criminal case where forfeiture was sought. Because we determine that no such exemption exists, we must decide whether that statute, so interpreted, is consistent with the Fifth and Sixth Amendments. We hold that it is.

[Christopher Reckmeyer was charged with running a massive drug importation and distribution scheme alleged to be a continuing criminal enterprise (CCE) in violation of 21 U.S.C. § 848. Relying on a provision of the CCE statute that authorizes forfeiture of "any property constituting, or derived from, any proceeds" obtained from drug law violations, § 853, the indictment sought forfeiture of specified assets in Reckmeyer's possession. Acting pursuant to § 853(e), the district court entered a restraining order forbidding Reckmeyer from transferring any of the potentially forfeitable assets.

[Notwithstanding the restraining order and the indictment, Reckmeyer transferred $25,000 to petitioner, a law firm, for pre-indictment legal services. Petitioner placed the sum in an escrow account and continued to represent Reckmeyer after his indictment. Reckmeyer moved to modify the restraining order to permit him to use some of the restrained assets to pay petitioner's fees and to exempt such assets from post-conviction forfeiture. Before the court ruled on his motion, however, Reckmeyer entered a plea agreement with the government in which, inter alia, he agreed to forfeit all of the specified assets. The court then denied Reckmeyer's motion and, subsequently, entered an order forfeiting virtually all of his assets to the government.

[Maintaining that assets used to pay an attorney are exempt from forfeiture under § 853 and, if not, that the statute violates the Sixth Amendment, petitioner sought an adjudication of its third-party interest in the forfeited assets under § 853(n). That section gives a third party who entered into a bona fide transaction with a defendant a right to make claims against forfeited property if that third party was "at the time of [the transaction] reasonably without cause to believe that the [defendant's assets were] subject to forfeiture." Petitioner claimed an interest in $170,000 of Reckmeyer's assets for legal services in conducting his defense. Petitioner also sought the $25,000 in the escrow account as payment for preindictment legal services.

[The district court granted petitioner's claim. However, the Fourth Circuit reversed. It found (a) that the statute contained no exemption for assets that a defendant wishes to use to pay private counsel of his choice and (b) that the statutory scheme was constitutional.

[For the reasons given in the companion case of *United States v. Monsanto*, 491 U.S. 600, 109 S.Ct. 2657, 105 L.Ed.2d 512 (1989),[a] the Supreme Court rejected

---

a. In *Monsanto*, the same 5–4 majority found no exemption from § 853's forfeiture or pretrial restraining order provisions for assets that a defendant wishes to use to retain an attorney. It also found that the statute did not "immunize" nonrestrained assets used for attorney's fees from subsequent forfeiture under § 853(c), which provides for recapture of forfei-table assets transferred to third parties. "In enacting § 853," observed the majority, per White, J., "Congress decided to give force to the old adage that 'crime does not pay.' We find no evidence that Congress intended to modify that nostrum to read, 'crime does not pay, except for attorney's fees.'"

petitioner's statutory argument. It then addressed petitioner's constitutional challenge to the forfeiture law.]

* * * Petitioner contends that the statute infringes on criminal defendants' Sixth Amendment right to counsel of choice, and upsets the "balance of power" between the government and the accused in a manner contrary to the Due Process Clause of the Fifth Amendment. We consider these contentions in turn.

Petitioner's first claim is that the forfeiture law makes impossible, or at least impermissibly burdens, a defendant's right "to select and be represented by one's preferred attorney." *Wheat v. United States* [p. 1160]. [N]othing in § 853 prevents a defendant from hiring the attorney of his choice, or disqualifies any attorney from serving as a defendant's counsel. Thus, unlike *Wheat*, this case does not involve a situation where the Government has asked a court to prevent a defendant's chosen counsel from representing the accused. Instead, petitioner urges that a violation of the Sixth Amendment arises here because of the forfeiture, at the instance of the Government, of assets that defendants intend to use to pay their attorneys.

Even in this sense, of course, the burden the forfeiture law imposes on a criminal defendant is limited. The forfeiture statute does not prevent a defendant who has nonforfeitable assets from retaining any attorney of his choosing. Nor is it necessarily the case that a defendant who possesses nothing but assets the Government seeks to have forfeited will be prevented from retaining counsel of choice. Defendants like Reckmeyer may be able to find lawyers willing to represent them, hoping that their fees will be paid in the event of acquittal, or via some other means that a defendant might come by in the future. The burden placed on defendants by the forfeiture law is therefore a limited one.

Nonetheless, there will be cases where a defendant will be unable to retain the attorney of his choice, when that defendant would have been able to hire that lawyer if he had access to forfeitable assets, and if there was no risk that fees paid by the defendant to his counsel would later be recouped under § 853(c).[4] It is in these cases, petitioner argues, that the Sixth Amendment puts limits on the forfeiture statute.

This submission is untenable. Whatever the full extent of the Sixth Amendment's protection of one's right to retain counsel of his choosing, that protection does not go beyond "the individual's right to spend his own money to obtain the advice and assistance [of] counsel." A defendant has no Sixth Amendment right to spend another person's money for services rendered by an attorney, even if those funds are the only way that that defendant will be able to retain the attorney of his choice. A robbery suspect, for example, has no Sixth Amendment right to use funds he has stolen from a bank to retain an attorney to defend him if he is apprehended. The money, though in his possession, is not rightfully his; the government does not violate the Sixth Amendment if it seizes the robbery proceeds, and refuses to permit the defendant to use them to pay for his defense.
* * *

There is no constitutional principle that gives one person the right to give another's property to a third party, even where the person seeking to complete the exchange wishes to do so in order to exercise a constitutionally protected right. [If]

---

4. That section of the statute, which includes the so-called "relation back" provision, states:

"All right, title, and interest in property described in [§ 853] vests in the United States upon the commission of the act giving rise to forfeiture under this section. Any such property that is subsequently transferred to a person other than the defendant may be the subject of a special verdict of forfeiture and thereafter shall be forfeited to the United States, unless the transferee [establishes his entitlement to such property]."

defendants have a right to spend forfeitable assets on attorney's fees, why not on exercises of the right to speak, practice one's religion, or travel? The full exercise of these rights, too, depends in part on one's financial wherewithal; and forfeiture, or even the threat of forfeiture, may similarly prevent a defendant from enjoying these rights as fully as he might otherwise. Nonetheless, we are not about to recognize an antiforfeiture exception for the exercise of each such right; nor does one exist for the exercise of Sixth Amendment rights, either.

Petitioner's "balancing analysis" to the contrary rests substantially on the view that the Government has only a modest interest in forfeitable assets that may be used to retain an attorney. Petitioner takes the position that, in large part, once assets have been paid over from client to attorney, the principal ends of forfeiture have been achieved: dispossessing a drug dealer or racketeer of the proceeds of his wrongdoing. We think that this view misses the mark for three reasons.

First, the Government has a pecuniary interest in forfeiture that goes beyond merely separating a criminal from his ill-gotten gains; that legitimate interest extends to recovering *all* forfeitable assets, for such assets are deposited in a Fund that supports law-enforcement efforts in a variety of important and useful ways.

[Second,] the statute permits "rightful owners" of forfeited assets to make claims for forfeited assets before they are retained by the government. The Government's interest in winning undiminished forfeiture thus includes the objective of returning property, in full, to those wrongfully deprived or defrauded of it. * * *

Finally, as we have recognized previously, a major purpose motivating congressional adoption and continued refinement of the RICO and CCE forfeiture provisions has been the desire to lessen the economic power of organized crime and drug enterprises. [The] Court of Appeals put it aptly: "The modern day Jean Valjean must be satisfied with appointed counsel. Yet the drug merchant claims that his possession of huge sums of money ... entitles him to something more. We reject this contention, and any notion of a constitutional right to use the proceeds of crime to finance an expensive defense."[7]

It is our view that there is a strong governmental interest in obtaining full recovery of all forfeitable assets, an interest that overrides any Sixth Amendment interest in permitting criminals to use assets adjudged forfeitable to pay for their defense. * * * We therefore reject petitioner's claim of a Sixth Amendment right of criminal defendants to use assets that are the government's—assets adjudged forfeitable, as Reckmeyer's were—to pay attorneys' fees, merely because those assets are in their possession.[10]

---

7. We also reject the contention [that] a type of *"per se"* ineffective assistance of counsel results—due to the particular complexity of RICO or drug-enterprise cases—when a defendant is not permitted to use assets in his possession to retain counsel of choice, and instead must rely on appointed counsel. If such an argument were accepted, it would bar the trial of indigents charged with such offenses, because those persons would have to rely on appointed counsel—which this view considers *per se* ineffective.

If appointed counsel is ineffective in a particular case, a defendant has resort to the remedies discussed in *Strickland v. Washington* [p. 1120]. But we cannot say that the Sixth Amendment's guarantee of effective assistance of counsel is a guarantee of a privately-retained counsel in every complex case, irrespective of a defendant's ability to pay.

10. Petitioner advances three additional reasons for invalidating the forfeiture statute, all of which concern possible ethical conflicts created for lawyers defending persons facing forfeiture of assets in their possession.

Petitioner first notes the statute's exemption from forfeiture of property transferred to a bona fide purchaser who was "reasonably without cause to believe that the property was subject to forfeiture." 21 U.S.C. § 853(n)(6)(B). This provision, it is said, might give an attorney an incentive not to investigate a defendant's case as fully as possible, so that the lawyer can invoke it to protect from forfeiture

Petitioner's second constitutional claim is that the forfeiture statute is invalid under the Due Process Clause of the Fifth Amendment because it permits the Government to upset the "balance of forces between the accused and his accuser." We are not sure that this contention adds anything to petitioner's Sixth Amendment claim, because, while "[t]he Constitution guarantees a fair trial through the Due Process Clauses [it] defines the basic elements of a fair trial largely through the several provisions of the Sixth Amendment." Even [if] the Fifth Amendment provides some added protection not encompassed in the Sixth Amendment's more specific provisions, we find petitioner's claim based on the Fifth Amendment unavailing.

Forfeiture provisions are powerful weapons in the war on crime; like any such weapons, their impact can be devastating when used unjustly. But due process claims alleging such abuses are cognizable only in specific cases of prosecutorial misconduct (and petitioner has made no such allegation here) or when directed to a rule that is inherently unconstitutional. * * * Petitioner's claim—that the power available to prosecutors under the statute *could* be abused—proves too much, for many tools available to prosecutors can be misused in a way that violates the rights of innocent persons. [Cases] involving particular abuses can be dealt with individually by the lower courts, when (and if) any such cases arise. * * *

Justice BLACKMUN, with whom Justice BRENNAN, Justice MARSHALL, and Justice STEVENS join, dissenting.[a]

Those jurists who have held forth against the result the majority reaches in these cases have been guided by one core insight: that it is unseemly and unjust for the Government to beggar those it prosecutes in order to disable their defense at trial. [The] criminal-forfeiture statute we consider today could have been interpreted to avoid depriving defendants of the ability to retain private counsel—and should have been so interpreted, given the grave "constitutional and ethical problems" raised by the forfeiture of funds used to pay legitimate counsel fees. But even if Congress in fact required this substantial incursion on the defendant's choice of counsel, the Court should have recognized that the Framers stripped

any fees he has received. Yet given the requirement that any assets which the Government wishes to have forfeited must be specified in the indictment, the only way a lawyer could be a beneficiary of § 853(n)(6)(B) would be to fail to read the indictment of his client. In this light, the prospect that a lawyer might find himself in conflict with his client, by seeking to take advantage of § 853(n)(6)(B), amounts to very little. * * *

The second possible conflict arises in plea bargaining: petitioner posits that a lawyer may advise a client to accept an agreement entailing a more harsh prison sentence but no forfeiture—even where contrary to the client's interests—in an effort to preserve the lawyer's fee. Following such a strategy, however, would surely constitute ineffective assistance of counsel. [In] any event, there is no claim that such conduct occurred here, nor could there be, as Reckmeyer's plea agreement included forfeiture of virtually every asset in his possession. * * *

Finally, petitioner argues that the forfeiture statute, in operation, will create a system akin to "contingency fees" for defense lawyers: only

a defense lawyer who wins acquittal for his client will be able to collect his fees, and contingent fees in criminal cases are generally considered unethical. But there is no indication here that petitioner, or any other firm, has actually sought to charge a defendant on a contingency basis; rather the claim is that a law firm's prospect of collecting its fee may turn on the outcome at trial. This, however, may often be in the case in criminal defense work. Nor is it clear why permitting contingent fees in criminal cases—if that is what the forfeiture statute does—violates a criminal defendant's Sixth Amendment rights. The fact that a federal statutory scheme authorizing contingency fees—again, if that is what Congress has created in § 853 (a premise we doubt)—is at odds with model disciplinary rules or state disciplinary codes hardly renders the federal statute invalid.

a. This also constitutes the dissenting opinion in the companion case of *United States v. Monsanto*.

Congress of the power to do so when they added the Sixth Amendment to our Constitution. * * *

[After a lengthy discussion, Justice Blackmun concludes that "[a] construction of the statute is fairly possible by which the [constitutional] question may be avoided."]

The majority has decided otherwise, however, and for that reason is compelled to reach the constitutional issue it could have avoided. But the majority pauses hardly long enough to acknowledge "the Sixth Amendment's protection of one's right to retain counsel of his choosing," let alone to explore its "full extent." Instead, it moves rapidly from the observation that "a defendant may not insist on representation by an attorney he cannot afford" to the conclusion that the Government is free to deem the defendant indigent by declaring his assets "tainted" by criminal activity the Government has yet to prove. That the majority implicitly finds the Sixth Amendment right to counsel of choice so insubstantial that it can be outweighed by a legal fiction demonstrates, still once again, its " 'apparent unawareness of the function of the independent lawyer as a guardian of our freedom.' "

[The] right to retain private counsel serves to foster the trust between attorney and client that is necessary for the attorney to be a truly effective advocate. Not only are decisions crucial to the defendant's liberty placed in counsel's hands, but the defendant's perception of the fairness of the process, and his willingness to acquiesce in its results, depend upon his confidence in his counsel's dedication, loyalty, and ability. When the Government insists upon the right to choose the defendant's counsel for him, that relationship of trust is undermined: counsel is too readily perceived as the Government's agent rather than his own.

[The] right to retain private counsel also serves to assure some modicum of equality between the Government and those it chooses to prosecute. The Government can be expected to "spend vast sums of money [to] try defendants accused of crime," *Gideon*, and of course will devote greater resources to complex cases in which the punitive stakes are high. Precisely for this reason, "there are few defendants charged with crime, few indeed, who fail to hire the best lawyers they can get to prepare and present their defenses." Ibid. But when the Government provides for appointed counsel, there is no guarantee that levels of compensation and staffing will be even average.[12] Where cases are complex, trials long, and stakes high, that problem is exacerbated. [Over] the long haul, the result of lowered compensation levels will be that talented attorneys will "decline to enter criminal practice. [This] exodus of talented attorneys could devastate the criminal defense bar." Winick, [fn. 12 supra]. Without the defendant's right to retain private counsel, the Government too readily could defeat its adversaries simply by outspending them.[13]

The right to privately chosen and compensated counsel also serves broader institutional interest. The "virtual socialization of criminal defense work in this country" that would be the result of a widespread abandonment of the right to

12. "Even in the federal courts under the Criminal Justice Act of 1964, 18 U.S.C. § 3006A, which provides one of the most generous compensation plans, the rates for appointed counsel ... are low by American standards. Consequently, the majority of persons willing to accept appointments are the young and inexperienced." *Argersinger v. Hamlin* (Powell, J., concurring in result). Indeed, there is evidence that "Congress did not design [the Criminal Justice Act] to be compensatory, but

merely to reduce financial burdens on assigned counsel." See Winick, *Forfeiture of Attorneys' Fees under RICO and CCE and the Right to Counsel of Choice: The Constitutional Dilemma and How to Avoid It*, 43 U.Miami L.Rev. 765, 773 and n. 40 (1989).

13. That the Government has this power when the defendant is indigent is unfortunate, but "[i]t is an irrelevancy once recognized."

retain chosen counsel, too readily would standardize the provision of criminal-defense services and diminish defense counsel's independence. There is a place in our system of criminal justice for the maverick and the risk-taker, for approaches that might not fit into the structured environment of a public defender's office, or that might displease a judge whose preference for nonconfrontational styles of advocacy might influence the judge's appointment decisions. [There] is also a place for the employment of "specialized defense counsel" for technical and complex cases. * * * Only a healthy, independent defense bar can be expected to meet the demands of the varied circumstances faced by criminal defendants, and assure that the interests of the individual defendant are not unduly "subordinat[ed] [to] the needs of the system."

[Had] it been Congress' express aim to undermine the adversary system as we know it, it could hardly have found a better engine of destruction than attorney's-fee forfeiture. The main effect of forfeitures under the Act, of course, will be to deny the defendant the right to retain counsel, and therefore the right to have his defense designed and presented by an attorney he has chosen and trusts.[14] If the Government restrains the defendant's assets before trial, private counsel will be unwilling to continue or to take on the defense. Even if no restraining order is entered, the possibility of forfeiture after conviction will itself substantially diminish the likelihood that private counsel will agree to take the case. The "message [to private counsel] is 'Do not represent this defendant or you will lose your fee.' * * * "

Even if the defendant finds a private attorney who is "so foolish, ignorant, beholden or idealistic as to take the business," the attorney-client relationship will be undermined by the forfeiture statute. Perhaps the attorney will be willing to violate ethical norms by working on a contingent fee basis in a criminal case. See [majority opinion at] n. 10. But if he is not—and we should question the integrity of any criminal-defense attorney who would violate the ethical norms of the profession by doing so—the attorney's own interests will dictate that he remain ignorant of the source of the assets from which he is paid. [The] less an attorney knows, the greater the likelihood that he can claim to have been an "innocent" third party. The attorney's interest in knowing nothing is directly adverse to his client's interest in full disclosure. The result of the conflict may be a less vigorous investigation of the defendant's circumstances, leading in turn to a failure to recognize or pursue avenues of inquiry necessary to the defense. Other conflicts of interest are also likely to develop. The attorney who fears for his fee will be tempted to make the Government's waiver of fee-forfeiture the *sine qua non* for any plea agreement, a position which conflicts with his client's best interests.

Perhaps most troubling is the fact that forfeiture statutes place the Government in the position to exercise an intolerable degree of power over any private attorney who takes on the task of representing a defendant in a forfeiture case. [The] Government will be ever tempted to use the forfeiture weapon against a defense attorney who is particularly talented or aggressive on the client's behalf— the attorney who is better than what, in the Government's view, the defendant deserves. The spectre of the Government's selectively excluding only the most

---

14. There is reason to fear that, in addition to depriving a defendant of counsel of choice, there will be circumstances in which the threat of forfeiture will deprive the defendant of *any* counsel. If the Government chooses not to restrain transfers by employing § 853(e)(1), it is likely that the defendant will not qualify as "indigent" under the Criminal Justice Act. Potential private counsel will be aware of the threat of forfeiture, and, as a result, will likely refuse to take the case. Although it is to be hoped that a solution will be developed for a defendant who "falls between the cracks" in this manner, there is no guarantee that accommodation will be made in an orderly fashion, and that trial preparation will not be substantially delayed because of the difficulties in securing counsel. * * *

talented defense counsel is a serious threat to the equality of forces necessary for the adversarial system to perform at its best.

[The] long-term effects of the fee-forfeiture practice will be to decimate the private criminal-defense bar. As the use of the forfeiture mechanism expands to new categories of federal crimes and spreads to the States, only one class of defendants will be free routinely to retain private counsel: the affluent defendant accused of a crime that generates no economic gain. As the number of private clients diminishes, only the most idealistic and the least skilled of young lawyers will be attracted to the field, while the remainder seek greener pastures elsewhere. See Winick, supra, at 781–782.

In short, attorney's-fee forfeiture substantially undermines every interest served by the Sixth Amendment right to chosen counsel, on the individual and institutional levels, over the short term and the long haul. * * *

Notes and Questions

1. *Is the clear implication of Justice Blackmun's dissent that, despite the Court's efforts to assure that the kind of trial a person receives does not depend on the money she has, "this is exactly what happens"?* See Joshua Dressler, *Understanding Criminal Procedure* 528 (2d ed. 1997).

2. *Did the Caplin majority fail to give adequate weight to the defendant's interest before trial?* Consider, Note 103 Harv.L.Rev. 137, 146 (1989): "If the government has the superior property right and the court denies [an order restraining potentially forfeitable assets], the government risks only the loss of some portion of forfeitable assets, but if a defendant without other assets has the superior property right and the court grants an order, the defendant faces certain loss of autonomy with respect to a constitutionally protected right."

SECTION 3. THE RIGHT TO "EFFECTIVE" ASSISTANCE OF COUNSEL

WK12

"Nearly 30 percent of the defendants who had public defenders reported that their attorney spent less than 10 minutes with them; 32 percent stated 10 to 29 minutes; 27 percent stated one-half hour to 3 hours; and only 14 percent stated more than 3 hours. To the extent that we are willing to embrace the notion that providing an adequate defense includes providing the client with a sense that he has been adequately represented, time spent with client is an important aspect of an adequate defense. In view of these findings, it is not surprising that nearly half (49 percent) of the public defender clients thought their attorney was 'on the side of the state.'"

—J. Casper, *Criminal Courts: The Defendant's Perspective* iv (1978) (abstract).[a]

_____

"[If] the Chief Defender values attorneys for their ability to move cases quickly and to persuade reluctant defendants to plead guilty, the accused might be better off making his own, poorly informed choice. The problem is not lost on the supposedly unsophisticated defendants whom the public defenders ostensibly protect from exploitation in the market. Indigents commonly mistrust the public

_____

a. But see Note 6, p. 1141.

defender assigned to them and view him as part of the same bureaucracy that is 'processing' and convicting them. The lack of trust is a major obstacle to establishing an effective attorney-client relationship. The problem was captured in a sad exchange between a social science researcher and a prisoner: 'Did you have a lawyer when you went to court?' 'No. I had a public defender.' "

—S. Schulhofer & D. Friedman, *Rethinking Indigent Defense: Promoting Effective Representation through Consumer Sovereignty and Freedom of Choice for All Criminal Defendants,* 31 Am.Crim.L.Rev. 73, 86 (1993).

———————

"Even if she agrees (as nearly all public defenders do) that vigorous defense of the guilty is morally justified in our adversary system, that lawyer may not zealously represent a criminal defendant absent a sufficiently compelling *motivation*—an impetus to do the work, rather than a theory that merely argues that it is *defensible, excusable* or *laudable* for someone to do that work. Motivation may provide the necessary impetus both to retain current public defenders and attract future ones. Unfortunately, legal scholars have failed to develop sufficient motivations for lawyers to engage in criminal defense—particularly defense of the indigent, and this failure has led to underzealous representation."

—C. Ogletree, *Beyond Justifications: Seeking Motivations to Sustain Public Defenders,* 106 Harv.L.Rev. 1239, 1242 (1993).

———————

As early as the landmark case of *Powell v. Alabama* (1932), the Court pointed out that when a court is required to appoint counsel that duty "is not discharged by an assignment at such a time or under such circumstances as to preclude the giving of *effective aid* in the preparation and trial of the case." (Emphasis added.) Since the trial court in *Powell* had failed to make an "effective appointment of counsel," the defendants were denied due process. Ten years later, in *Glasser v. United States,* 315 U.S. 60, 62 S.Ct. 457, 86 L.Ed. 680 (1942), where counsel's effectiveness was limited by a conflict of interest, the Court held that a federal defendant's Sixth Amendment right was violated by judicial action that denied him his "right to have the effective assistance of counsel."

More recently, EVITTS v. LUCEY, 469 U.S. 387, 105 S.Ct. 830, 83 L.Ed.2d 821 (1985) held that one also has a constitutional right to the effective assistance of counsel on the first appeal—"an appeal as of right." Because respondent's retained counsel had failed to file the "statement of appeal" required by the state rule, his appeal from a drug conviction had been dismissed. In ruling that under the circumstances the dismissal of respondent's appeal had deprived him of the effective assistance of counsel, a 7–2 majority, per BRENNAN, J., observed:

"[N]ominal representation on an appeal as of right—like nominal representation at trial—does not suffice to render the proceedings constitutionally adequate; a party whose counsel is unable to provide effective representation is in no better position than one who has no counsel at all. [The] promise of *Douglas* [p. 76] that a criminal defendant has a right to counsel on appeal—like the promise of *Gideon* that a criminal defendant has a right to counsel at trial—would be a futile gesture unless it comprehended the right to the effective assistance of counsel."

The Court rejected the view, one advanced by dissenting Justice REHNQUIST, joined by Burger, C.J., that since a state need not establish a system of appeal at all, it can do so on its own terms: "The right to appeal would be unique among state actions if it could be withdrawn without consideration of applicable due process norms. [When] a State opts to act in a field where its action has significant discretionary elements, it must nonetheless act in accord with the dictates of the Constitution—and, in particular, in accord with the Due Process Clause."

Cases like *Griffin* (p. 74) and *Douglas* were not simply equal protection cases: "[D]ue process concerns were involved because the States involved had set up a system of appeals as of right but had refused to offer each defendant a fair opportunity to obtain an adjudication on the merits of his appeal. Equal protection concerns were involved because the State treated a class of defendants—indigent ones—differently for purposes of offering them a meaningful appeal. Both of these concerns were implicated in the *Griffin* and *Douglas* cases and both Clauses supported the decisions reached by this Court."[a]

However, *Wainwright v. Torna*, 455 U.S. 586, 102 S.Ct. 1300, 71 L.Ed.2d 475 (1982) (per curiam), indicates that even if a defendant has a constitutional right to utilize *retained* counsel in proceedings in which an *indigent* defendant lacks a constitutional right to the assistance of *appointed* counsel, the right to retained counsel in such additional proceedings does not carry with it a right to *effective assistance* by that counsel. In *Torna,* respondent's felony convictions were affirmed by an intermediate state appellate court. His application for a writ of certiorari was dismissed by the state supreme court because it had not been filed timely. Respondent contended that he had been denied the effective assistance of counsel by the failure of his retained counsel to file the application in time. Summarily reversing the Fifth Circuit, the Court held that respondent was not entitled to federal habeas corpus relief:

"*Ross v. Moffitt* [p. 78] held that a criminal defendant does not have a constitutional right to counsel to pursue discretionary state appeals or applications for review in this Court. [Since] respondent had no constitutional right to counsel, he could not be deprived of the effective assistance of counsel by his retained counsel's failure to file the application timely."[b]

Consider too, *Pennsylvania v. Finley*, 481 U.S. 551, 107 S.Ct. 1990, 95 L.Ed.2d 539 (1987). Counsel appointed to represent an indigent prisoner in a state post conviction proceeding withdrew from the case without complying with the procedures prescribed in *Anders v. California* (p. 1168), procedures designed to ensure that lawyers appointed on the first appeal of right effectively represent their clients. The Court held that since a state had no constitutional obligation to appoint counsel in a postconviction proceeding, the *Anders* safeguards were not constitutionally required in such a proceeding.

"It should be noted," observes CRIMPROC § 11.7(a), "that both *Torna* and *Finley* involved a proceeding that the state had no constitutional obligation to provide. Where the state has a constitutional obligation to provide a particular process, but that obligation does not include a duty to appoint counsel, the

---

a. The Court also rejected the argument that a lawyer could disobey vital procedural rules governing appeals with impunity if state courts were unable to enforce these rules by dismissing the appeal: "A State may certainly enforce a vital procedural rule by imposing sanctions against the attorney rather than against the client. Such a course may well be more effective than the alternative of refusing to decide the merits of an appeal * * *. A system of appeal as of right is established precisely to assure that only those who are validly convicted have their freedom drastically curtailed. A State may not extinguish this right

because another right of the appellant—the right to effective assistance of counsel—has been violated."

b. Dissenting Justice Marshall "would hold that when [as here] a defendant can show that he reasonably relied on his attorney's promise to seek discretionary review, due process requires the State to consider his application, even when the application is untimely. To deny the right to seek discretionary review simply because of counsel's error is fundamentally unfair." Brennan, J., would set the case for oral argument.

ineffective performance of counsel, whether retained or appointed, might be successfully challenged by reference to the adequacy of that process. Such a possibility would be presented, for example, by the ineffective assistance of retained counsel at a misdemeanor trial which resulted in the imposition only of a fine [and thus at a proceeding in which defendant was not constitutionally entitled to appointed counsel]. The defendant could argue here that ineffectiveness of counsel resulted in a proceeding in which defendant was so deprived of his ability to make use of the procedural rights constitutionally guaranteed to him in such a trial that the proceeding itself did not comport with due process. The state cannot be relieved of the responsibility to provide such a hearing by the fact that the counsel who contributed to the denial of the constitutional right was either retained by the defendant or provided without constitutional command by the state."[c]

Until the 1970's the prevailing standard was the "mockery of justice" test under which representation was considered "ineffective" only when it was so poor as to "reduce the trial to a farce" or render it a "mockery of justice." This test required "such a minimal level of performance from counsel" that it was called "a mockery of the Sixth Amendment." David Bazelon, *The Defective Assistance of Counsel*, 42 U.Cin.L.Rev. 1, 28 (1973). See also Joel Jay Finer, *Ineffective Assistance of Counsel*, 58 Cornell L.Rev. 1077 (1973).

Among the policies or fears underlying the reluctance to find "ineffectiveness" (and to hold lawyers to a higher standard) are that to do so would jeopardize finality interests, force the trial judge to intervene whenever possible error is being committed, lead appellate courts to "second guess" defense tactics with the benefit of hindsight, make lawyers more reluctant to accept court assignments, and encourage lawyers with desperate cases to commit errors deliberately. See generally Vivian O. Berger, *The Supreme Court and Defense Counsel: Old Roads, New Paths—A Dead End?*, 86 Colum.L.Rev. 9, 65–66 (1986); Jon R. Waltz, *Inadequacy of Trial Defense Representation as a Ground for Post–Conviction Relief in Criminal Cases*, 59 Nw.U.L.Rev. 289 (1964); Notes, 78 Harv.L.Rev. 1435 (1965), 49 Va.L.Rev. 1531 (1963). Judge Bazelon went so far as to say (Bazelon at 22): "I have often been told that if my court were to reverse in every case in which there was inadequate counsel, we would have to send back half the convictions in my jurisdiction."

In the early 1970s, in two cases involving collateral attacks on guilty pleas, *Tollett v. Henderson* (p. 1308), and *McMann v. Richardson* (p. 1304), the Supreme Court approached the issue of ineffective counsel in terms of whether counsel's advice fell "within the range of competence demanded of attorneys in criminal cases." The Court's language "stirred further discomfort with the mockery and farce test," James A. Strazzella, *Ineffective Assistance of Counsel Claims: New Uses, New Problems*, 19 Ariz.L.Rev. 443, 450 (1977), and many courts, and a majority of the U.S. Courts of Appeals, soon scrapped it in favor of some "reasonable" or "normal" or "customary" competence test. But such standards, maintained Judge Bazelon, "beg the question of what is customary or reasonable for a lawyer to do prior to or at arraignment, plea bargaining, trial, or sentencing." Bazelon, *The Realities of Gideon and Argersinger*, 64 Geo.L.J. 811, 819 (1976).

c. Resolving an issue that had long divided the lower courts, *Cuyler v. Sullivan* (at p. 1152) rejected the argument that the failings of *retained* counsel cannot furnish a basis for a constitutional violation because the conduct of such counsel does not involve "state action." "Since the State's conduct of a criminal trial itself implicates the State in the defendant's conviction," the Court could "see no basis for drawing a distinction between retained and appointed counsel that would deny equal justice to defendants who must choose their own lawyers." Consider also the discussion in *Coleman v. Thompson*, p. 1599.

Both in his judicial opinions and in his law review articles, Judge Bazelon championed what has been called the "checklist" or "categorical" approach to the ineffective counsel problem. He attempted to give substantive content to the Sixth Amendment's mandate by setting forth specific minimum requirements of competent performance—a categorization of minimum duties owed by counsel to client derived from *A.B.A. Standards Relating to the Defense Function* (1971). Dissenting in *United States v. Decoster (Decoster III),* 624 F.2d 196, 275 (D.C.Cir.1976) (en banc), Judge Bazelon (joined by Wright, C.J.), observed: "The heart of [the 'categorical'] approach lies in defining ineffective assistance in terms of the *quality of counsel's performance,* rather than looking to the effect of counsel's actions on the outcome of the case. If the Sixth Amendment is to serve a central role in eliminating second-class justice for the poor, then it must proscribe second-class performances by counsel, whatever the consequences in a particular case. Moreover, by focusing on the quality of representation and providing incentives in all cases for counsel to meet or exceed minimum standards, this approach reduces the likelihood that any particular defendant will be prejudiced by counsel's shortcomings. In this way, courts can safeguard the defendant's rights to a constitutionally adequate trial without engaging in the inherently difficult task of speculating about the precise effect of each error or omission by an attorney."

Although the "categorical" approach had strong supporters, see J. Eric Smithburn & Theresa L. Springman, *Effective Assistance of Counsel: In Quest of a Uniform Standard of Review,* 17 Wake Forest L.Rev. 497 (1980); Notes, 80 Colum.L.Rev. 1053 (1980) 93 Harv.L.Rev. 752 (1980); cf. William J. Genego, *The Future of Effective Assistance of Counsel: Performance Standards and Competent Representation,* 22 Am.Crim.L.Rev. 181, 203–12 (1984); this approach has not prevailed. Instead Judge Leventhal's plurality opinion in *Decoster* has proved highly influential.

Because a determination of whether counsel's performance amounted to ineffective assistance "cannot be divorced from consideration of the peculiar facts and circumstances that influenced counsel's judgment," Judge Leventhal concluded that a reviewing court's appraisal requires what he called a "judgmental approach"—one that looks to the totality of circumstances of the case in evaluating counsel's effectiveness—rather than a categorical approach. Speaking for four members of the D.C.Circuit, he voiced concern that Judge Bazelon's approach would "torture" the adversary system "out of shape":

"[Although Judge Bazelon] recognizes that the government can always defend by showing beyond a doubt that the violation was harmless [, the] realistic thrust [of his approach] is a rule structured toward a conclusion of prejudice from any deviation from the checklist of standards concerning preparation, whatever the likely or actual consequence. Omissions of investigation lead to new trials on the rationale that one can never be certain what might have happened had counsel performed better. A new trial is needed [even if] the fruits of the investigation would have proved neutral or even inculpatory, for defense counsel could have been in a stronger position to lead his client to prove guilty. This kind of speculation renders no error harmless. [The] manifest consequence [of Judge Bazelon's approach] would be inevitable and increasing intrusion into the development and presentation of the defense case by the trial judge, and (out of self-protection) by the prosecution."

Strickland v. Washington, set forth below, and *United States v. Cronic,* Note 8, p. 1132, left no doubt about the Supreme Court's rejection of any "checklist" or "categorical" approach and its determination to evaluate ineffectiveness claims on a case-specific basis, and one requiring a showing of prejudicial impact.

STRICKLAND v. WASHINGTON

466 U.S. 668, 104 S.Ct. 2052, 80 L.Ed.2d 674 (1984).

Justice O'CONNOR delivered the opinion of the Court. * * *

[During a ten-day period, respondent planned and committed three groups of crimes, including three brutal capital murders, torture, kidnapping and attempted murders. Against counsel's advice, respondent pled guilty to all charges, including the three capital murder charges.

[In the plea colloquy, respondent told the Florida trial judge that, although he had committed a string of burglaries, he had no significant prior criminal record and that at the time of his criminal spree he was under extreme stress caused by his inability to support his family. He also stated, however, that he accepted responsibility for the crimes. The trial judge told respondent that he had "a great deal of respect for people who are willing to step forward and admit their responsibility" but that he was making no statement at all about his likely sentencing decision.

[Against counsel's advice, respondent waived his state right to an advisory jury at his capital sentencing hearing and chose to be sentenced by the trial judge without a jury recommendation. In preparing for the sentencing hearing, counsel spoke on the phone with respondent's wife and mother, but did not otherwise seek out character witnesses for respondent. Nor did he request a psychiatric examination, since his conversations with his client gave no indication that respondent had psychological problems. Counsel decided not to present and hence not to look further for evidence concerning respondent's character and emotional state. This decision reflected counsel's sense of hopelessness about overcoming the impact of respondent's confessions to the gruesome crimes and his judgment that it was advisable to rely on the plea colloquy for evidence as to such matters, thus preventing the state from cross-examining respondent and from presenting psychiatric evidence of its own. Finally, counsel did not request a presentence report because it would have included respondent's criminal history and thereby undermine the claim of no significant prior criminal record.

[At the sentencing hearing, counsel's strategy was based primarily on the trial judge's remarks at the plea colloquy as well as on his reputation as a sentencing judge who thought it important for a convicted defendant to own up to his crime. However, as the U.S. Supreme Court summarized it, "the trial judge found numerous aggravating circumstances and no (or a single comparatively insignificant) mitigating circumstance." He therefore sentenced respondent to death on each of the three counts of murder. The state supreme court upheld the convictions and sentences on direct appeal.

[Respondent eventually sought federal habeas corpus relief on the ground, inter alia, that counsel had rendered ineffective assistance at the sentencing proceeding in several respects, including his failure to request a psychiatric report, to seek out and present character witnesses, and to request a presentence report. The district court concluded that, although trial counsel had made errors in judgment in failing to investigate nonstatutory mitigating evidence further than he did, no prejudice to respondent's sentence resulted from any such error. On rehearing en banc, Unit B of the former Fifth Circuit, now the Eleventh Circuit, developed its own framework for analyzing ineffective assistance claims and reversed and remanded the case for new factfinding under the newly announced standards.]

[T]he Court has recognized that "the right to counsel is the right to the effective assistance of counsel." *McMann v. Richardson* (1970). Government violates the right to effective counsel when it interferes in certain ways with the ability of counsel to make independent decisions about how to conduct the defense. See, e.g., *Geders v. United States,* 425 U.S. 80 (1976) (bar on attorney-client consultation during overnight recess);[a] *Herring v. New York,* 422 U.S. 853 (1975) (bar on summation at bench trial); *Brooks v. Tennessee,* 406 U.S. 605 (1972) (requirement that defendant be first defense witness); *Ferguson v. Georgia,* 365 U.S. 570 (1961) (bar on direct examination of defendant). Counsel, however, can also deprive a defendant of the right to effective legal assistance, simply by failing to render "adequate legal assistance," *Cuyler v. Sullivan* [p. 1152] (actual conflict of interest adversely affecting lawyer's performance renders assistance ineffective).

The Court has not elaborated on the meaning of the constitutional requirement of effective assistance in the latter class of cases—that is, those presenting claims of "actual ineffectiveness." In giving meaning to the requirement, however, we must take its purpose—to ensure a fair trial—as the guide. The benchmark for judging any claim of ineffectiveness must be whether counsel's conduct so undermined the proper functioning of the adversarial process that the trial cannot be relied on as having produced a just result.

The same principle applies to a capital sentencing proceeding such as that provided by Florida law. We need not consider the role of counsel in an ordinary sentencing, which may involve informal proceedings and standardless discretion in the sentencer, and hence may require a different approach to the definition of constitutionally effective assistance. A capital sentencing proceeding like the one involved in this case, however, is sufficiently like a trial in its adversarial format and in the existence of standards for decision that counsel's role in the proceeding is comparable to counsel's role at trial—to ensure that the adversarial testing process works to produce a just result under the standards governing decision. For purposes of describing counsel's duties, therefore, Florida's capital sentencing proceeding need not be distinguished from an ordinary trial.[a]

---

a. "[A] showing of prejudice," observed the Court, per Stevens, J., in *Perry v. Leeke,* 488 U.S. 272, 109 S.Ct. 594, 102 L.Ed.2d 624 (1989), "is not an essential element of a violation of the rule announced in *Geders*"; "our citation of *Geders* in [*Strickland*] was intended to make clear that '[a]ctual or constructive denial of the assistance of counsel altogether' is not subject to the kind of prejudice analysis that is appropriate in determining whether the quality of a lawyer's performance itself has been constitutionally ineffective."

But in *Perry* a 6–3 majority held that the *Geders* rule does not apply to a trial court's order, at the conclusion of petitioner's direct testimony, that petitioner not talk to anyone, including his lawyer, during a 15–minute recess. Because, unlike *Perry,* the *Geders* case involved an overnight recess, the *Perry* majority viewed it as a case in which matters that *went beyond a defendant's own testimony* would have been discussed with counsel.

The *Perry* majority recognized that "the line between the facts of *Geders* [and] this case is a thin one," but insisted that it is "a line of constitutional dimension": "The distinction rests [on] the fact that when a defendant becomes a witness, he has no constitutional right

to consult with his lawyer while he is testifying. He has an absolute right to such consultation before he begins to testify, but neither he nor his lawyer has a right to have the testimony interrupted in order to give him the benefit of counsel's advice. [Thus, a trial judge has] the power to maintain the status quo during a brief recess in which there is a virtual certainty that any conversation between the witness and the lawyer would relate to the ongoing testimony."

Dissenting Justice Marshall, joined by Brennan and Blackmun, JJ., maintained that the majority's distinction "has no constitutional or logical grounding." The dissenters found especially troublesome the majority's assertion that "allowing a defendant to speak with the attorney during a 'short' recess between direct and cross-examination invariably will retard the truth-seeking function of the trial." "Central to our Sixth Amendment doctrine," observed the dissent, "is the understanding that legal representation for the defendant at every critical stage of the adversary process *enhances* the discovery of truth because it better enables the defendant to put the State to its proof."

a. Why not—if, as the Court has often said, "death is different"? See Note 1, p. 1136.

A convicted defendant's claim that counsel's assistance was so defective as to require reversal of a conviction or death sentence has two components. First, the defendant must show that counsel's performance was deficient. This requires showing that counsel made errors so serious that counsel was not functioning as the "counsel" guaranteed the defendant by the Sixth Amendment. Second, the defendant must show that the deficient performance prejudiced the defense. This requires showing that counsel's errors were so serious as to deprive the defendant of a fair trial, a trial whose result is reliable. Unless a defendant makes both showings, it cannot be said that the conviction or death sentence resulted from a breakdown in the adversary process that renders the result unreliable.

As all the Federal Courts of Appeals have now held, the proper standard for attorney performance is that of reasonably effective assistance. The Court indirectly recognized as much when it stated in *McMann* that a guilty plea cannot be attacked as based on inadequate legal advice unless counsel was not "a reasonably competent attorney" and the advice was not "within the range of competence demanded of attorneys in criminal cases." When a convicted defendant complains of the ineffectiveness of counsel's assistance, the defendant must show that counsel's representation fell below an objective standard of reasonableness.

More specific guidelines are not appropriate. The Sixth Amendment refers simply to "counsel," not specifying particular requirements of effective assistance. It relies instead on the legal profession's maintenance of standards sufficient to justify the law's presumption that counsel will fulfill the role in the adversary process that the Amendment envisions. The proper measure of attorney performance remains simply reasonableness under prevailing professional norms.

Representation of a criminal defendant entails certain basic duties. Counsel's function is to assist the defendant, and hence counsel owes the client a duty of loyalty, a duty to avoid conflicts of interest. From counsel's function as assistant to the defendant derive the overarching duty to advocate the defendant's cause and the more particular duties to consult with the defendant on important decisions and to keep the defendant informed of important developments in the course of the prosecution. Counsel also has a duty to bring to bear such skill and knowledge as will render the trial a reliable adversarial testing process.

These basic duties neither exhaustively define the obligations of counsel nor form a checklist for judicial evaluation of attorney performance. In any case presenting an ineffectiveness claim, the performance inquiry must be whether counsel's assistance was reasonable considering all the circumstances. Prevailing norms of practice as reflected in American Bar Association standards and the like are guides to determining what is reasonable, but they are only guides. No particular set of detailed rules for counsel's conduct can satisfactorily take account of the variety of circumstances faced by defense counsel or the range of legitimate decisions regarding how best to represent a criminal defendant. Any such set of rules would interfere with the constitutionally protected independence of counsel and restrict the wide latitude counsel must have in making tactical decisions. Indeed, the existence of detailed guidelines for representation could distract counsel from the overriding mission of vigorous advocacy of the defendant's cause. Moreover, the purpose of the effective assistance guarantee of the Sixth Amendment is not to improve the quality of legal representation, although that is a goal of considerable importance to the legal system. The purpose is simply to ensure that criminal defendants receive a fair trial.

Judicial scrutiny of counsel's performance must be highly deferential. It is all too tempting for a defendant to second-guess counsel's assistance after conviction or adverse sentence, and it is all too easy for a court, examining counsel's defense after it has proved unsuccessful, to conclude that a particular act or omission of

hindsight 20/20

counsel was unreasonable. A fair assessment of attorney performance requires that every effort be made to eliminate the distorting effects of hindsight, to reconstruct the circumstances of counsel's challenged conduct, and to evaluate the conduct from counsel's perspective at the time. Because of the difficulties inherent in making the evaluation, a court must indulge a strong presumption that counsel's conduct falls within the wide range of reasonable professional assistance; that is, the defendant must overcome the presumption that, under the circumstances, the challenged action "might be considered sound trial strategy." There are countless ways to provide effective assistance in any given case. Even the best criminal defense attorneys would not defend a particular client in the same way.

The availability of intrusive post-trial inquiry into attorney performance or of detailed guidelines for its evaluation would encourage the proliferation of ineffectiveness challenges. Criminal trials resolved unfavorably to the defendant would increasingly come to be followed by a second trial, this one of counsel's unsuccessful defense. Counsel's performance and even willingness to serve could be adversely affected.

[Thus,] a court deciding an actual ineffectiveness claim must judge the reasonableness of counsel's challenged conduct on the facts of the particular case, viewed as of the time of counsel's conduct. A convicted defendant making a claim of ineffective assistance must identify the acts or omissions of counsel that are alleged not to have been the result of reasonable professional judgment. The court must then determine whether, in light of all the circumstances, the identified acts or omissions were outside the wide range of professionally competent assistance. In making that determination, the court should keep in mind that counsel's function, as elaborated in prevailing professional norms, is to make the adversarial testing process work in the particular case. At the same time, the court should recognize that counsel is strongly presumed to have rendered adequate assistance and made all significant decisions in the exercise of reasonable professional judgment.

These standards require no special amplification in order to define counsel's duty to investigate, the duty at issue in this case. [S]trategic choices made after thorough investigation of law and facts relevant to plausible options are virtually unchallengeable; and strategic choices made after less than complete investigation are reasonable precisely to the extent that reasonable professional judgments support the limitations on investigation. [In] any ineffectiveness case, a particular decision not to investigate must be directly assessed for reasonableness in all the circumstances, applying a heavy measure of deference to counsel's judgments.

The reasonableness of counsel's actions may be determined or substantially influenced by the defendant's own statements or actions. Counsel's actions are usually based, quite properly, on informed strategic choices made by the defendant and on information supplied by the defendant. In particular, what investigation decisions are reasonable depends critically on such information. For example, when the facts that support a certain potential line of defense are generally known to counsel because of what the defendant has said, the need for further investigation may be considerably diminished or eliminated altogether. And when a defendant has given counsel reason to believe that pursuing certain investigations would be fruitless or even harmful, counsel's failure to pursue those investigations may not later be challenged as unreasonable. In short, inquiry into counsel's conversations with the defendant may be critical to a proper assessment of counsel's investigation decisions, just as it may be critical to a proper assessment of counsel's other litigation decisions.

An error by counsel, even if professionally unreasonable, does not warrant setting aside the judgment of a criminal proceeding if the error had no effect on the judgment. The purpose of the Sixth Amendment guarantee of counsel is to ensure that a defendant has the assistance necessary to justify reliance on the outcome of the proceeding. Accordingly, any deficiencies in counsel's performance must be prejudicial to the defense in order to constitute ineffective assistance under the Constitution.

In certain Sixth Amendment contexts, prejudice is presumed. Actual or constructive denial of the assistance of counsel altogether is legally presumed to result in prejudice. So are various kinds of state interference with counsel's assistance. Prejudice in these circumstances is so likely that case by case inquiry into prejudice is not worth the cost. Moreover, such circumstances involve impairments of the Sixth Amendment right that are easy to identify and, for that reason and because the prosecution is directly responsible, easy for the government to prevent.

One type of actual ineffectiveness claim warrants a similar, though more limited, presumption of prejudice. In *Cuyler v. Sullivan*, the Court held that prejudice is presumed when counsel is burdened by an actual conflict of interest. In those circumstances, counsel breaches the duty of loyalty, perhaps the most basic of counsel's duties. Moreover, it is difficult to measure the precise effect on the defense of representation corrupted by conflicting interest. Given the obligation of counsel to avoid conflicts of interest and the ability of trial courts to make early inquiry in certain situations likely to give rise to conflicts, see e.g., Fed.R.Crim.P. 44(c), it is reasonable for the criminal justice system to maintain a fairly rigid rule of presumed prejudice for conflicts of interest. Even so, the rule is not quite the *per se* rule of prejudice that exists for the Sixth Amendment claims mentioned above. Prejudice is presumed only if the defendant demonstrates that counsel "actively represented conflicting interests" and "that an actual conflict of interest adversely affected his lawyer's performance." *Cuyler v. Sullivan*.

Conflict of interest claims aside, actual ineffectiveness claims alleging a deficiency in attorney performance are subject to a general requirement that the defendant affirmatively prove prejudice. [Attorney errors] cannot be classified according to likelihood of causing prejudice. Nor can they be defined with sufficient precision to inform defense attorneys correctly just what conduct to avoid. Representation is an art, and an act or omission that is unprofessional in one case may be sound or even brilliant in another. Even if a defendant shows that particular errors of counsel were unreasonable, therefore, the defendant must show that they actually had an adverse effect on the defense.

It is not enough for the defendant to show that the errors had some conceivable effect on the outcome of the proceeding. Virtually every act or omission of counsel would meet that test, and not every error that conceivably could have influenced the outcome undermines the reliability of the result of the proceeding. Respondent suggests requiring a showing that the errors "impaired the presentation of the defense." That standard, however, provides no workable principle. Since any error, if it is indeed an error, "impairs" the presentation of the defense, the proposed standard [provides] no way of deciding what impairments are sufficiently serious to warrant setting aside the outcome of the proceeding.

On the other hand, we believe that a defendant need not show that counsel's deficient conduct more likely than not altered the outcome in the case. [The] appropriate test for prejudice finds its roots in the test for materiality of exculpatory information not disclosed to the defense by the prosecution, *United States v. Agurs*, 427 U.S. 97 (1976), and in the test for materiality of testimony made unavailable to the defense by Government deportation of a witness, *United States v. Valenzuela–Bernal* [p. 1405]. The defendant must show that there is a reasonable probability that, but for counsel's unprofessional errors, the result of the proceeding would have been different. A reasonable probability is a probability sufficient to undermine confidence in the outcome.

In making [this] determination [a] court should presume, absent challenge to the judgment on grounds of evidentiary insufficiency, that the judge or jury acted according to law. An assessment of the likelihood of a result more favorable to the defendant must exclude the possibility of arbitrariness, whimsy, caprice, "nullification," and the like. A defendant has no entitlement to the luck of a lawless decisionmaker, even if a lawless decision cannot be reviewed. The assessment of prejudice should proceed on the assumption that the decisionmaker is reasonably, conscientiously, and impartially applying the standards that govern the decision. It should not depend on the idiosyncracies of the particular decisionmaker, such as unusual propensities toward harshness or leniency. Although these factors may actually have entered into counsel's selection of strategies and, to that limited extent, may thus affect the performance inquiry, they are irrelevant to the prejudice inquiry. Thus, evidence about the actual process of decision, if not part of the record of the proceeding under review, and evidence about, for example, a particular judge's sentencing practices, should not be considered in the prejudice determination.

The governing legal standard plays a critical role in defining the question to be asked in assessing the prejudice from counsel's errors. When a defendant challenges a conviction, the question is whether there is a reasonable probability that, absent the errors, the factfinder would have had a reasonable doubt respecting guilt. When a defendant challenges a death sentence such as the one at issue in this case, the question is whether there is a reasonable probability that, absent the errors, the sentencer—including an appellate court, to the extent it independently reweighs the evidence—would have concluded that the balance of aggravating and mitigating circumstances did not warrant death.

In making this determination, a court hearing an ineffectiveness claim must consider the totality of the evidence before the judge or jury. Some of the factual findings will have been unaffected by the errors, and factual findings that were affected will have been affected in different ways. Some errors will have had a pervasive effect on the inferences to be drawn from the evidence, altering the entire evidentiary picture, and some will have had an isolated, trivial effect. Moreover, a verdict or conclusion only weakly supported by the record is more likely to have been affected by errors than one with overwhelming record support. Taking the unaffected findings as given, and taking due account of the effect of the errors on the remaining findings, a court making the prejudice inquiry must ask if the defendant has met the burden of showing that the decision reached would reasonably likely have been different absent the errors.

A number of practical considerations are important for the application of the standards we have outlined. Most important, in adjudicating a claim of actual ineffectiveness of counsel, a court should keep in mind that the principles we have stated do not establish mechanical rules. Although those principles should guide the process of decision, the ultimate focus of inquiry must be on the fundamental fairness of the proceeding whose result is being challenged. In every case the court should be concerned with whether, despite the strong presumption of reliability, the result of the particular proceeding is unreliable because of a breakdown in the adversarial process that our system counts on to produce just results.

To the extent that this has already been the guiding inquiry in the lower courts, the standards articulated today do not require reconsideration of ineffectiveness claims rejected under different standards. Cf. *Trapnell v. United States*, 725 F.2d 149 (2d Cir.1983) (in several years of applying "farce and mockery" standard along with "reasonable competence" standard, court "never found that the result of a case hinged on the choice of a particular standard"). In particular, the minor differences in the lower courts' precise formulations of the performance standard are insignificant: the different formulations are mere variations of the overarching reasonableness standard. With regard to the prejudice inquiry, only the strict outcome-determinative test, among the standards articulated in the lower courts, imposes a heavier burden on defendants than the tests laid down today. The difference, however, should alter the merit of an ineffectiveness claim only in the rarest case.

Although we have discussed the performance component of an ineffectiveness claim prior to the prejudice component, there is no reason for a court deciding an ineffective assistance claim to approach the inquiry in the same order or even to address both components of the inquiry if the defendant makes an insufficient showing on one. In particular, a court need not determine whether counsel's performance was deficient before examining the prejudice suffered by the defendant as a result of the alleged deficiencies. The object of an ineffectiveness claim is not to grade counsel's performance. If it is easier to dispose of an ineffectiveness claim on the ground of lack of sufficient prejudice, which we expect will often be so, that course should be followed. Courts should strive to ensure that ineffectiveness claims not become so burdensome to defense counsel that the entire criminal justice system suffers as a result.

The principles governing ineffectiveness claims should apply in federal collateral proceedings as they do on direct appeal or in motions for a new trial. [The] presumption that a criminal judgment is final is at its strongest in collateral attacks on that judgment. An ineffectiveness claim, however, * * * is an attack on the fundamental fairness of the proceeding whose result is challenged. Since fundamental fairness is the central concern of the writ of habeas corpus, no special standards ought to apply to ineffectiveness claims made in habeas proceedings.

Finally, in a federal habeas challenge to a state criminal judgment, a state court conclusion that counsel rendered effective assistance is not a finding of fact binding on the federal court to the extent stated by 28 U.S.C. § 2254(d). [Rather,] like the question whether multiple representation in a particular case gave rise to a conflict of interest, * * * both the performance and prejudice components of the ineffectiveness inquiry are mixed questions of law and fact.

Having articulated general standards for judging ineffectiveness claims, we think it useful to apply those standards to the facts of this case in order to illustrate the meaning of the general principles. The record makes it possible to do so. [The facts] make clear that the conduct of respondent's counsel at and before respondent's sentencing proceeding cannot be found unreasonable. They also make clear that, even assuming the challenged conduct of counsel was unreasonable, respondent suffered insufficient prejudice to warrant setting aside his death sentence.

With respect to the performance component, the record shows that respondent's counsel made a strategic choice to argue for the extreme emotional distress mitigating circumstance and to rely as fully as possible on respondent's acceptance of responsibility for his crimes. Although counsel understandably felt hopeless about respondent's prospects, nothing in the record indicates [that] counsel's sense of hopelessness distorted his professional judgment. Counsel's strategy choice was well within the range of professionally reasonable judgments, and the decision not to seek more character or psychological evidence than was already in hand was likewise reasonable.

[With] respect to the prejudice component, the lack of merit of respondent's claim is even more stark. The evidence that respondent says his trial counsel should have offered at the sentencing hearing would barely have altered the sentencing profile presented to the sentencing judge. As the state courts and District Court found, at most this evidence shows that numerous people who knew respondent thought he was generally a good person and that a psychiatrist and a psychologist believed he was under considerable emotional stress that did not rise to the level of extreme disturbance. Given the overwhelming aggravating factors, there is no reasonable probability that the omitted evidence would have changed the conclusion that the aggravating circumstances outweighed the mitigating circumstances and, hence, the sentence imposed. * * *

Failure to make the required showing of either deficient performance or sufficient prejudice defeats the ineffectiveness claim. Here there is a double failure. More generally, respondent has made no showing that the justice of his sentence was rendered unreliable by a breakdown in the adversary process caused by deficiencies in counsel's assistance. * * *

We conclude, therefore, that the District Court properly declined to issue a writ of habeas corpus. * * *

Justice BRENNAN, concurring in part and dissenting in part.

I join the Court's opinion but dissent from its judgment.[b] * * *

I join the Court's opinion because I believe that the standards it sets out today will both provide helpful guidance to courts considering claims of actual ineffectiveness of counsel and also permit those courts to continue their efforts to achieve progressive development of this area of the law.

[The] standards announced today can and should be applied with concern for the special considerations that must attend review of counsel's performance in a capital sentencing proceeding. In contrast to a case in which a finding of ineffective assistance requires a new trial, a conclusion that counsel was ineffective with respect to only the penalty phase of a capital trial imposes on the state the far lesser burden of reconsideration of the sentence alone. On the other hand, the consequences to the defendant of incompetent assistance at a capital sentencing could not, of course, be greater. * * *

Justice MARSHALL, dissenting.

[The] opinion of the Court revolves around two holdings. First, the majority ties the constitutional minima of attorney performance to a simple "standard of reasonableness." Second, the majority holds that only an error of counsel that has sufficient impact on a trial to "undermine confidence in the outcome" is grounds for overturning a conviction. I disagree with both of these rulings.

My objection to the performance standard adopted by the Court is that it is so malleable that, in practice, it will either have no grip at all or will yield excessive variation in the manner in which the Sixth Amendment is interpreted and applied by different courts. To tell lawyers and the lower courts that counsel for a criminal defendant must behave "reasonably" and must act like "a reasonably competent attorney" is to tell them almost nothing.

[The] debilitating ambiguity of an "objective standard of reasonableness" in this context is illustrated by the majority's failure to address important issues concerning the quality of representation mandated by the Constitution. It is an unfortunate but undeniable fact that a person of means, by selecting a lawyer and

---

b. Adhering to his view that the death penalty is in all circumstances forbidden cruel and unusual punishment, Justice Brennan would vacate respondent's death sentence and remand the case for further proceedings.

paying him enough to ensure he prepares thoroughly, usually can obtain better representation than that available to an indigent defendant, who must rely on appointed counsel, who, in turn, has limited time and resources to devote to a given case. Is a "reasonably competent attorney" a reasonably competent adequately paid retained lawyer or a reasonably competent appointed attorney? It is also a fact that the quality of representation available to ordinary defendants in different parts of the country varies significantly. Should the standard of performance mandated by the Sixth Amendment vary by locale? The majority offers no clues as to the proper responses to these questions.

* * * I agree that counsel must be afforded "wide latitude" when making "tactical decisions" regarding trial strategy, but many aspects of the job of a criminal defense attorney are more amenable to judicial oversight [than the majority indicates]. For example, much of the work involved in preparing for a trial, applying for bail, conferring with one's client, making timely objections to significant, arguably erroneous rulings of the trial judge, and filing a notice of appeal if there are colorable grounds therefor could profitably be made the subject of uniform standards. * * *

I object to the prejudice standard adopted by the Court for two independent reasons. First, it is often very difficult to tell whether a defendant convicted after a trial in which he was ineffectively represented would have fared better if his lawyer had been competent. Seemingly impregnable cases can sometimes be dismantled by good defense counsel. On the basis of a cold record, it may be impossible for a reviewing court confidently to ascertain how the government's evidence and arguments would have stood up against rebuttal and cross-examination by a shrewd, well prepared lawyer. The difficulties of estimating prejudice after the fact are exacerbated by the possibility that evidence of injury to the defendant may be missing from the record precisely because of the incompetence of defense counsel. In view of all these impediments to a fair evaluation of the probability that the outcome of a trial was affected by ineffectiveness of counsel, it seems to me senseless to impose on a defendant whose lawyer has been shown to have been incompetent the burden of demonstrating prejudice.

Second and more fundamentally, the assumption on which the Court's holding rests is that the only purpose of the constitutional guarantee of effective assistance of counsel is to reduce the chance that innocent persons will be convicted. In my view, the guarantee also functions to ensure that convictions are obtained only through fundamentally fair procedures. [A] proceeding in which the defendant does not receive meaningful assistance in meeting the forces of the state does not, in my opinion, constitute due process.

[In] my view, the right to *effective* assistance of counsel is entailed by the right to counsel, and abridgment of the former is equivalent to abridgment of the latter. I would thus hold that a showing that the performance of a defendant's lawyer departed from constitutionally prescribed standards requires a new trial regardless of whether the defendant suffered demonstrable prejudice thereby.

Even if I were inclined to join the majority's two central holdings, I could not abide the manner in which the majority elaborates upon its rulings. Particularly regrettable are the majority's discussion of the "presumption" of reasonableness to be accorded lawyers' decisions and its attempt to prejudge the merits of claims previously rejected by lower courts using different legal standards. [The majority suggests] that reviewing courts should "indulge a strong presumption that counsel's conduct" was constitutionally acceptable and should "apply[ ] a heavy measure of deference to counsel's judgments".

[The] adjectives "strong" and "heavy" might be read as imposing upon defendants an unusually weighty burden of persuasion. If that is the majority's intent, I must respectfully dissent. The range of acceptable behavior defined by "prevailing professional norms" seems to me sufficiently broad to allow defense counsel the flexibility they need in responding to novel problems of trial strategy. To afford attorneys more latitude, by "strongly presuming" that their behavior will fall within the zone of reasonableness, is covertly to legitimate convictions and sentences obtained on the basis of incompetent conduct by defense counsel.

[The] majority suggests that, "[f]or purposes of describing counsel's duties," a capital sentencing proceeding "need not be distinguished from an ordinary trial." I cannot agree. The Court has repeatedly acknowledged that the Constitution requires stricter adherence to procedural safeguards in a capital case than in other cases. * * *

The views expressed in the preceding section oblige me to dissent from the majority's disposition of the case before us. It is undisputed that respondent's trial counsel made virtually no investigation of the possibility of obtaining testimony from respondent's relatives, friends, or former employers pertaining to respondent's character or background. Had counsel done so, he would have found several persons willing and able to testify that, in their experience, respondent was a responsible, nonviolent man, devoted to his family, and active in the affairs of his church. Respondent contends that his lawyer could have and should have used that testimony to "humanize" respondent, to counteract the impression conveyed by the trial that he was little more than a cold-blooded killer. Had this evidence been admitted, respondent argues, his chances of obtaining a life sentence would have been significantly better.

Measured against the standards outlined above, respondent's contentions are substantial. Experienced members of the death-penalty bar have long recognized the crucial importance of adducing evidence at a sentencing proceeding that establishes the defendant's social and familial connections. See Goodpaster, *The Trial for Life: Effective Assistance of Counsel in Death Penalty Cases*, 58 N.Y.U.L.Rev. 299 (1983). The State makes a colorable—though in my view not compelling—argument that defense counsel in this case might have made a reasonable "strategic" decision not to present such evidence at the sentencing hearing on the assumption that an unadorned acknowledgment of respondent's responsibility for his crimes would be more likely to appeal to the trial judge, who was reputed to respect persons who accepted responsibility for their actions.[19] But however justifiable such a choice might have been after counsel had fairly assessed the potential strength of the mitigating evidence available to him, counsel's failure to make any significant effort to find out what evidence might be garnered from respondent's relatives and acquaintances surely cannot be described as "reasonable." Counsel's failure to investigate is particularly suspicious in light of his candid admission that respondent's confession and conduct in the course of the trial gave him a feeling of "hopelessness" regarding the possibility of saving respondent's life.

[If] counsel had investigated the availability of mitigating evidence, he might well have decided to present some such material at the hearing. If he had done so, there is a significant chance that respondent would have been given a life sentence. In my view, those possibilities, conjoined with the unreasonableness of

---

19. Two considerations undercut the State's explanation of counsel's decision. First, it is not apparent why adducement of evidence pertaining to respondent's character and familial connections would have been inconsistent with respondent's acknowledgment that he was responsible for his behavior. Second, the Florida Supreme Court possesses—and fre-quently exercises—the power to overturn death sentences it deems unwarranted by the facts of a case. Even if counsel's decision not to try to humanize respondent for the benefit of the trial judge were deemed reasonable, counsel's failure to create a record for the benefit of the state Supreme Court might well be deemed unreasonable.

counsel's failure to investigate, are more than sufficient to establish a violation of the Sixth Amendment and to entitle respondent to a new sentencing proceeding. * * *

Notes and Questions

1. The Strickland test in action. David Cole, *No Equal Justice* 78–79 (1999), maintains that the *Strickland* standard "has proved virtually impossible to meet. Courts have declined to find ineffective assistance where defense counsel slept during portions of the trial, where counsel used heroin and cocaine throughout the trial, where counsel allowed his client to wear the same sweatshirt and shoes in court that the perpetrator was alleged to have worn on the day of the crime, where counsel stated prior to trial that he was not prepared on the law or facts of the case, and where counsel appointed in a capital case could not name a single Supreme Court decision on the death penalty."

2. "Tactical decisions." "As *Strickland* itself illustrated," argues Professor Cole, supra at 79–80, "almost any deficiency in performance can in hindsight be described 'tactical.'" In *Strickland*, the defense attorney "justified his failure to investigate [his client's] background thoroughly as a strategic decision not to invite negative counter-evidence from the state. In another case, the defendant's lawyer made no opening statement to the jury, and did not object when the prosecution introduced evidence of the defendant's prior criminal convictions, which are generally inadmissible. Although the attorney was suffering from Alzheimer's disease during the trial, the court held that these lapses were not ineffective assistance, but 'tactical decisions.' As one [federal district] court has explained, 'Even if many reasonable lawyers would not have done as defense counsel did at trial, no relief can be granted on ineffective grounds unless it is shown that *no reasonable* lawyer in the circumstances would have done so.'"

Consider too, Donald A. Dripps, *Ineffective Assistance of Counsel: The Case for an Ex Ante Parity Standard*, 88 J.Crim.L. & C. 242, 281 (1997): "Should we take the government's plea offer? Should we rely on self-defense, or on accident, or on insanity? Should we put the defendant on the stand? Can we trust witness X to testify as we expect? These are the kinds of judgments that people need defense lawyers to make. They are also the kinds of judgments that can rarely be challenged successfully under *Strickland*. As 'tactical choices' to which reviewing courts afford a 'heavy measure of deference,' the consequences of which are imponderable and thus presumptively not prejudicial, counsel's key decisions are virtually beyond review. It hardly follows, however, that typical indigent defenders make these decisions as well as they could be made."

3. Dispensing with Strickland's outcome-prejudice test. "Both because the right to effective assistance rests on concern with process as much as results and because injury is difficult to prove in many cases where it doubtless exists," Vivian O. Berger, *The Supreme Court and Defense Counsel: Old Roads, New Paths—A Dead End?,* 86 Colum.L.Rev. 9, 95–96 (1986) "reject[s] the concept of actual prejudice as an element of counsel inadequacy claims. [For] screening out those instances where counsel's defaults surely did not damage the client, the harmless constitutional error test satisfactorily accommodates both the state's and the defendant's interests. This thoroughly familiar standard places a very heavy burden on the prosecution to demonstrate the absence of outcome effect. When society can say *with confidence* that entirely adequate representation would not have changed the result of the case, and only then, I believe that the state is justified in salvaging judgments despite the undeniable incursion on the prophylactic and dignitary values embodied in the right to effective assistance."

4. *Disposing of an ineffectiveness claim on ground of lack of prejudice.* Recall the *Strickland* Court's comments that "[t]he object of an ineffectiveness claim is not to grade counsel's performance" and that "[i]f it is easier to dispose of an ineffectiveness claim on the ground of lack of sufficient prejudice, which we expect will often be so, that course should be followed." "This injunction," protests Professor Berger, supra, at 86–87, "amounts to a blatant invitation—indeed, direction—to the lower courts to avoid refining more detailed criteria for lawyer conduct, as well as a not so subtle suggestion that virtually all challenges to counsel can be readily rejected. Each of these messages is regrettable. The latter, of a piece with the stated strong presumption of competence, reveals at best an insensitive attitude toward a very serious problem. The former evinces, perhaps even more unfortunately, blindness toward an important facet of adjudication. Decisions on the merits of claims of ineffective assistance may operate preventively, not only remedially, but determinations of lack of prejudice tell counsel nothing in the absence of any discussion of whether the lawyer erred in the first place. Maybe grading individual counsel is beside the point, as the Court stated. Surely, however, teaching the bar in general about their duties is not."

5. *Should we ask, before the trial begins, whether the defense can contest the prosecution on a roughly equal basis?* Consider Dripps, Note 2 supra, at 281: "It is indeed the case that the *Strickland* case has failed to improve the defense function. It is indeed the case that effective defense representation is the single most important of our system's safeguards against convicting people of crimes they had nothing to do with or of more serious offenses than they actually committed. And it is indeed the case that there is no prospect of legislative action to improve the situation. The courts should broaden their focus to concentrate on the fairness of the proceedings rather than the absence of identifiable errors by defense counsel. The key obstacle to reform lies in *Strickland*'s inquiry into the effectiveness of counsel *after the fact*. It is all but ludicrous to ask a reviewing court to assess a record made by counsel to determine how counsel erred.[a] The better approach would ask *before* proceedings commenced whether the defendant's lawyer can effectively represent him. Because the effectiveness of counsel is relative to the opposition, the test should be whether the defendant is represented by a lawyer roughly as good and roughly as well-prepared as counsel for the prosecution. Judges could make this determination either when counsel first enters in appearance for the accused, or in a collateral civil proceeding to test the adequacy of a jurisdiction's system of indigent defense."

6. *The role of an attorney.* According to *Strickland*, does defense counsel provide inadequate representation only when society cannot rely on the result as just? If so, consider William J. Genego, *The Future of Effective Assistance of Counsel: Performance Standards and Competent Representation*, 22 Am.Crim. L.Rev. 181, 200 (1984): "The role of a [defense attorney] is not [to] see that his or her client received a fair trial and that a just outcome resulted. The attorney's role is to do everything ethically proper to see that the client receives the most

---

a. Elsewhere in his article, Professor Dripps maintains that "the unrecognized consequence of divorcing the right to counsel from the right to a fair trial [has] been the counterfactual—even Khaftaesque—assumption that when the poor performance of defense counsel undermines the fairness of the trial, the situation will be manifest to a reviewing court after the fact." But a performance by defense counsel "cannot be separated from the trial that counsel conducted. In particular, because the trial record will be limited by defense counsel's investigation, the failure to pursue exculpatory possibilities will not be in the record at all." Dripps recognizes that in capital cases, "the extreme stakes and the extended time-period permit post-conviction counsel to seek affidavits from uncalled witnesses and to perform neglected scientific tests. But in other cases, who is going to interview the witnesses if trial counsel did not?"

favorable outcome possible—whether or not it produces an outcome which society considers just. Society relies on the adversary system to produce just results from partisan advocacy. The guiding principle in determining whether an attorney has provided effective representation must then be whether he or she discharged the role of partisan advocate faithfully and zealously, not whether the performance yielded what a court views as a just result."

7. *Would a "reasonably competent" lawyer have performed as the defense lawyer did in Strickland?* For the view that the failure of the lawyer for the defendant in *Strickland* (whose name was Washington, not Strickland) to have his client examined by a psychiatrist was "unreasonable" under the circumstances and constituted deficient representation, see Genego, supra, at 197. "The critical point," maintains Professor Genego, "is that Washington's attorney could not make a reasonable strategic decision about the utility of relying on psychiatric testimony without having his own doctor examine Washington.... Washington had everything to gain and nothing to lose from a defense-initiated psychiatric examination, and the defense attorney could not have known the value of a report before one was made."

Genego contends that the *Strickland* Court was "similarly misguided about the failure of Washington's attorney to interview character witnesses. [Washington's attorney] could not have intelligently speculated about the utility of [the fourteen character witnesses'] evidence because his efforts to obtain the character evidence were limited to speaking by telephone with Washington's wife and mother. Thus, the attorney had no idea what the fourteen character witnesses could have said about Washington's request that he be allowed to live. Prevailing professional norms should obligate a 'reasonably competent' attorney representing someone in a capital sentencing proceeding at least to investigate the possible existence of favorable character evidence."

8. *Rejection of the "inferential approach" to ineffective assistance of counsel claims.* Consider UNITED STATES v. CRONIC, 466 U.S. 648, 104 S.Ct. 2039, 80 L.Ed.2d 657 (1984), which arose as follows: Respondent and two associates were indicted on federal mail fraud charges involving a "check kiting" scheme. When, shortly before the scheduled trial date, respondent's trial counsel withdrew, the district court appointed a young lawyer with a real estate practice who had never participated in a jury trial to represent respondent. Appointed counsel was allowed only 25 days for pretrial preparation, although it had taken the government over four and a half years to investigate the case and it had reviewed thousands of documents during that investigation. Without referring to any specific error or inadequacy in appointed counsel's performance, the U.S. Court of Appeals for the Tenth Circuit reversed respondent's conviction, inferring from the circumstances surrounding the representation of respondent that his right to the effective assistance of counsel had been violated. The court based this conclusion on five factors: (1) the limited time afforded counsel for investigation and preparation; (2) counsel's inexperience; (3) the gravity of the charge; (4) the complexity of possible defenses; and (5) the inaccessibility of witnesses to counsel. The Supreme Court, per STEVENS, J., disagreed:

The five factors set forth above were "relevant to an evaluation of a lawyer's ineffectiveness in a particular case, but neither separately nor in combination [did] they provide a basis for concluding that competent counsel was not able to provide this [defendant] with the guiding hand that the Constitution guarantees." By utilizing an "inferential approach"—by reasoning that "the circumstances surrounding the representation * * * mandated an inference that counsel was unable to discharge his duties"—the lower federal court had erred.

The Court acknowledged that there are some circumstances "so likely to prejudice the accused that the cost of litigating their effect in a particular case is unjustified." Most obvious is the complete denial of counsel. Other examples are denial of counsel at a critical stage of the trial; state interference with the ability of counsel to make independent decisions about how to conduct the defense; a situation such as *Powell v. Alabama,* where the "surrounding circumstances made it so unlikely that any lawyer could provide effective assistance that ineffectiveness was properly presumed without inquiry into actual performance at trial"; and cases where counsel "actively represented conflicting interests." However, [this] case is not one in which the surrounding circumstances make it unlikely that the defendant could have received the effective assistance of counsel. [Cronic] can therefore make out a claim of ineffective assistance only by pointing to specific errors made by counsel.

The Court stressed that it was not holding that Cronic's representation did satisfy Sixth Amendment standards, but only that the criteria used by the lower appellate court "do not demonstrate that counsel failed to function in any meaningful sense as the Government's adversary." On remand, Cronic might still be able to make out a claim of ineffective assistance of counsel, but a determination of that issue had to rest on an examination of actual performance in light of the particular circumstances of the case.[a]

9. Ineffective assistance claims based on Fourth Amendment issues; what type of injury establishes "prejudice" under Strickland? In KIMMELMAN v. MORRISON, 477 U.S. 365, 106 S.Ct. 2574, 91 L.Ed.2d 305 (1986), the Court, per BRENNAN, J., held that the restrictions on federal habeas corpus review of Fourth Amendment claims imposed by *Stone v. Powell* (pp. 116, 1594) do not apply to Sixth Amendment claims of ineffective assistance of counsel based primarily on incompetent representation with respect to a search and seizure issue:

"In determining that federal courts should withhold habeas review where the State has provided an opportunity for full and fair litigation of a Fourth Amendment claim, [*Stone*] found it crucial that the remedy for Fourth Amendment violations provided by the exclusionary rule 'is not a personal constitutional right.' [The] right of an accused to counsel is beyond question a fundamental right. * * * Without counsel, the right to a fair trial itself would be of little consequence, for it is through counsel that the accused secures his other rights. * * *

"Because collateral review will frequently be the only means through which an accused can effectuate the right to counsel, restricting the litigation of some Sixth Amendment claims to trial and direct review would seriously interfere with an accused's right to effective representation. A layman will ordinarily be unable to recognize counsel's errors and to evaluate counsel's professional performance; consequently a criminal defendant will rarely know that he has not been represented competently until after trial or appeal, usually when he consults another lawyer about his case. * * *

"We also reject the suggestion that criminal defendants should not be allowed to vindicate through federal habeas corpus their right to effective assistance of counsel where counsel's primary error is failure to make a timely request for the exclusion of illegally seized evidence—evidence which is 'typically reliable and often the most probative information bearing on the guilt or innocence of the defendant.' *Stone.* * * * [W]e have never intimated that the right to counsel is conditioned upon actual innocence. The constitutional rights of criminal defen-

---

a. According to Donald A. Dripps, *Ineffective Assistance of Counsel: The Case for an Ex Ante Parity Standard*, 88 J.Crim.L. & C. 242, 276 (1997), the *Cronic* case "makes graphically clear what is wrong with *Strickland*."

dants are granted to the innocent and the guilty alike. Consequently, we decline to hold either that the guarantee of effective assistance of counsel belongs solely to the innocent or that it attaches only to matters affecting the determination of actual guilt."

Concurring Justice POWELL, joined by Burger, C.J., and Rehnquist, J., "agree[d] that *Stone* does not bar consideration of respondent's ineffective assistance of counsel claim on federal habeas corpus," but doubted whether "the admission of illegally seized but reliable evidence can ever constitute 'prejudice' under *Strickland*":

"[The reasoning of *Strickland*] strongly suggests that only errors that call into question the basic justice of the defendant's conviction suffice to establish prejudice under [that case]. The question, in sum, must be whether the particular harm suffered by the defendant due to counsel's incompetence rendered the defendant's trial fundamentally unfair. [The] admission of illegally seized but reliable evidence does not lead to an unjust or fundamentally unfair result. [Thus,] the harm suffered by respondent in this case is not the denial of a fair and reliable adjudication of his guilt, but rather the absence of a windfall.

"As we emphasized only last Term '[the] very premise of our adversary system of criminal justice is that partisan advocacy on both sides of a case will best promote *the ultimate objective that the guilty be convicted and the innocent go free.' Evitts v. Lucey* [p. 1116] [emphasis added by Powell, J.]. The right to effective assistance of counsel flows logically from this premise. But it would shake that right loose from its constitutional moorings to hold that the Sixth Amendment protects criminal defendants against errors that merely deny those defendants a windfall."[b]

(a) Is the *Morrison* dissenters' view that factually guilty defendants can *never* be prejudiced by ineffective representation? Is that what *Strickland* means? Or does it mean that a defendant must show that there is a reasonable probability that, but for the deficient representation, a more favorable *legal* result would have occurred? See Joshua Dressler, *Understanding Criminal Procedure* 538–39 (2d ed. 1997).

(b) In *Holman v. Page*, 95 F.3d 481 (7th Cir.1996), petitioner argued that he was denied the right to the effective assistance of appellate counsel when his attorney failed to appeal the denial of his motion to suppress post-arrest statements allegedly obtained in violation of the Fourth Amendment. "Follow[ing] the reasoning of Justice Powell and the two justices who joined his concurrence in *Morrison*," the court, per Manion, J., rejected the petitioner's claim: "The harm suffered by a defendant whose counsel was ineffective in attempting to have reliable evidence suppressed 'is not the denial of a fair and reliable adjudication of his guilt, but rather the absence of a windfall' (Powell, J., concurring in *Morrison*). [Thus,] although counsel may be ineffective in dealing with a defendant's Fourth Amendment claims, the defendant suffers no prejudice as a result."

The Seventh Circuit denied rehearing *en banc*, 102 F.3d 872, but Wood, J., joined by Ripple and Rovner, JJ., dissented from the denial of rehearing, maintaining that the three-judge panel's decision "squarely conflicts" with the Supreme Court's holding on *Morrison* that "defendants may properly base ineffective assistance of counsel claims in a habeas corpus action on the assertion that their attorney failed properly to litigate a Fourth Amendment claim." The

b. Nevertheless, Justice Powell did not vote to reverse "because neither the parties nor the courts below have considered the issue I raise here." He cautioned, however, that "the Court's rhetoric" should not "mistakenly be read to answer a question that has not been asked."

dissenting judges emphasized that Justice Powell's opinion "did not speak for the Court."

**10.   *Application of Strickland to guilty pleas. Hill v. Lockhart* (1985) (p. 1306) applied the two-part *Strickland* test to challenges to guilty pleas based on ineffective assistance of counsel. In order to satisfy the second half—or "prejudice" requirement—of the test, "the defendant must show that there is a reasonable probability that, but for counsel's errors, he would not have pleaded guilty and would have insisted on going to trial."

**11.   *That the outcome would have been different but for counsel's deficient performance does not necessarily establish "prejudice" under Strickland.* Although some language in *Strickland* suggests otherwise, a defendant claiming that she has been denied the effective assistance of counsel may not prevail even though she establishes that (a) her lawyer's performance was seriously deficient and (b) there is a reasonable probability that but for that deficiency the result of the proceeding could have been different. As the Court emphasized in LOCKHART v. FRETWELL, 506 U.S. 364, 113 S.Ct. 838, 122 L.Ed.2d 180 (1993), the "prejudice" component of the *Strickland* test involves more than a determination that the outcome would have been different. "It focuses on the question whether a counsel's deficient performance renders the result of the trial unreliable or the proceeding fundamentally unfair." And "unreliability or unfairness does not result if the ineffectiveness of counsel does not deprive the defendant of any substantive or procedural right to which the law entitles him."

The *Fretwell* case grew out of an unusual set of facts. An Arkansas jury convicted respondent of capital felony murder. During the death penalty phase of the case, the jury found an aggravating factor—that the murder, which occurred during a robbery, had been committed for pecuniary gain. But under *Collins v. Lockhart,* 754 F.2d 258 (8th Cir.1985) a then-existing (but subsequently overruled) Eighth Circuit precedent, an aggravating factor could not duplicate an element of the underlying felony—murder in the course of a robbery. However, respondent's lawyer failed to make any objection.

By the time the Eighth Circuit considered respondent's case on federal habeas corpus, it had already overruled *Collins.* Nevertheless, it held that respondent was entitled to relief, reasoning that had his lawyer objected to the use of the aggravating factor at the sentencing phase the trial judge would have sustained it and respondent would not have been sentenced to death. A 7–2 majority, per REHNQUIST, C.J., disagreed:

"To set aside a conviction or sentence solely because the outcome would have been different but for counsel's error may grant the defendant a windfall to which the law does not entitle him. Our decision in *Nix v. Whiteside* [set forth at p. 1143] [which held that a defendant was not prejudiced when his lawyer refused to cooperate in presenting perjured testimony] makes this very point. * * * Obviously, had [Whiteside] presented false testimony to the jury, there would have been a reasonable probability that the jury would not have returned a verdict of guilty. Sheer outcome determination, however, was not sufficient to make out a claim under the Sixth Amendment. [The] touchstone of an ineffective assistance claim is the fairness of the adversary proceeding and [in determining that] 'a defendant has no entitlement to the luck of a lawless decisionmaker.'

"[Defense counsel's failure to make an objection could not be prejudicial because the result of the sentencing proceeding] was rendered neither unreliable nor fundamentally unfair as a result of counsel's failure. [The] Court of Appeals, which had decided *Collins* in 1985, overruled [it] four years later. Had the trial court chosen to follow *Collins,* counsel's error would have 'deprived respondent of the chance to have the state court make an error in his favor.' "

ADVERSARY SYSTEM AND GUILT OR INNOCENCE

In a concurring opinion, the author of *Strickland,* Justice O'CONNOR, wrote separately "only to point out that today's decision will, in the vast majority of cases, have no effect on the prejudice inquiry under *Strickland*": "Since *Strickland,* we have recognized that neither the likely effect of perjured testimony nor the impact of a meritless Fourth Amendment objection is an appropriate consideration in the prejudice inquiry. * * * Today the Court identifies another factor that ought not inform the prejudice inquiry. [W]e hold that the court making the prejudice determination may not consider the effect of an objection it knows to be wholly meritless under current governing law, even if the objection might have been considered meritorious at the time of its omission."

Dissenting Justice STEVENS, joined by Blackmun, J., expressed dismay at the Court's "astonishing conclusion that deficient performance by counsel does not prejudice a defendant even when it results in the erroneous imposition of a death sentence. The Court's aversion to windfalls seems to disappear, however, when the State is the favored recipient. For the end result in this case is that the State, through the coincidence of inadequate representation and fortuitous timing, may carry out a death sentence that was invalid when imposed." Continued the dissent:

"Hindsight has no place in a Sixth Amendment jurisprudence that focuses, quite rightly, on protecting the adversarial balance at trial. Respondent was denied 'the assistance necessary to justify reliance on the outcome of the proceeding,' *Strickland,* because his counsel's performance was so far below professional standards that it satisfied *Strickland*'s first prong, and so severely lacking that the verdict 'would reasonably likely have been different absent the errors.' It is simply irrelevant that we can now say, with hindsight, that had counsel failed to make a double-counting objection four years after the fact, his performance would have been neither deficient nor prejudicial. For as it happened, counsel's failure to object came at a time when it signified a breakdown in the adversarial process. A *post hoc* vision of what would have been the case years later has no bearing on the force of this showing."

The dissenters were astonished by the majority's reliance on *Nix v. Whiteside*: "[R]eliance on perjured testimony and reliance on current Court of Appeals case law are not remotely comparable, and [to] suggest otherwise is simply disingenuous."

THE EFFECTIVE ASSISTANCE OF COUNSEL IN CAPITAL CASES

1. *Is death different?* *Strickland* involved a capital defendant's claim that his attorney had been ineffective in failing to investigate and to introduce mitigating evidence at the death penalty trial. "In view of the Court's repeated statements that 'death is different,' "observes Welsh S. White, *Effective Assistance of Counsel in Capital Cases: The Evolving Standard of Care,* 1993 U.Ill.L.Rev. 323, 333, "[the *Strickland* Court] might have been expected to discuss such questions as whether the standard of effectiveness should be the same in a capital as a noncapital case, whether the meaning of *prejudice* should be the same in both situations, and whether a capital defense counsel's role at the penalty phase of a capital case is different than it is at the guilt phase. Without discussing any of these questions, however, the Court tersely stated that '[f]or purposes of describing counsel's duties [the] capital sentencing proceedings need not be distinguished from an ordinary trial.' "

Drawing upon the *ABA Guidelines for the Appointment and Performance of Counsel in Death Penalty Cases* (1989), the practice of experienced capital defense attorneys, and relevant lower court decisions, Professor White maintains, id. at 336, that "the failure of a capital defense attorney to take specific actions—in particular, failure to seek and introduce certain types of mitigating evidence, to seek a favorable plea bargain that will avoid the death sentence, and to try to establish a relationship of trust with the defendant—usually should be viewed as deficient representation."

In applying *Strickland*, maintains Stephen B. Bright, *Counsel for the Poor: The Death Sentence Not for the Worst Crime but for the Worst Lawyer*, 103 Yale L.J. 1835, 1862–63 (1994): "courts indulge in presumptions and assumptions that have no relation to the reality of legal representation for the poor, particularly in capital cases." One scholar [Bruce A. Green, *Lethal Fiction: The Meaning of "Counsel" in the Sixth Amendment*, 78 Iowa L.Rev. 433, 454 (1993) has aptly called the idea that bar membership automatically qualifies one to defend a capital case [a] 'lethal fiction.' " Adds Bright: "The [*Strickland*] prejudice standard is particularly inappropriate for application to deficient representation at the penalty phase of a capital case. [The Supreme Court has repeatedly said that the sentencer must consider any aspect of a capital defendant's life or background that the defense offers as a basis for a sentence less than death, but it] is impossible for reviewing courts to assess the difference that investigation into mitigating circumstances and the effective presentation of mitigating circumstances might make on a jury's sentencing decision."

2. *Justice Blackmun's last word on legal representation for capital defendants.* A few days before he retired from the Supreme Court, dissenting from the denial of certiorari in *McFarland v. Scott*, 512 U.S. 1256, 114 S.Ct. 2785, 129 L.Ed.2d 896 (1994), Justice Blackmun "addresse[d] the crisis in trial and state postconviction legal representation for capital defendants.":

"Two factors contribute to the general unavailability of qualified attorneys to represent capital defendants. The absence of standards governing court-appointed capital-defense counsel means that unqualified lawyers often are appointed, and the absence of funds to compensate lawyers prevents even qualified lawyers from being able to present an adequate defense. [See also Note 3, infra.] * * * Court-awarded funds for the appointment of investigators and experts often are either unavailable, severely limited, or not provided by state courts. As a result, attorneys appointed to represent capital defendants at the trial level frequently are unable to recoup even their overhead costs and out-of-pocket expenses * * *."

Justice Blackmun then discussed a number of capital cases where defendants were executed after seemingly compelling ineffective-assistance claims were denied—cases he believed demonstrated "the impotence of the *Strickland* standard." One such case involved James Messer, a mentally impaired defendant whose lawyer presented no defense and made no objections at the trial. Moreover, both in his closing argument at the end of the trial and in his argument during the penalty phase, Messer's lawyer emphasized the horror of the crime, thereby suggesting that death was the appropriate punishment.

3. *Error rates in capital cases.* A study of the death penalty conducted by a team of lawyers and criminologists at Columbia University led by law professor James Liebman and released on June 12, 2000, *A Broken System: Error Rates in Capital Cases, 1973–1995*, revealed the following:

Of 5,760 death sentences imposed in the United States between 1973 and 1995, some 4,578 (79%) were finally reviewed on "direct appeal" by a state court. Of these, 41% "were thrown out because of 'serious error,' *i.e.*, error that the reviewing court concluded has seriously undermined the reliability of the outcome or otherwise 'harmed' the defendant."

Nearly all of the remaining death sentences were then examined by state post-conviction courts. Of the death sentences that survived state direct and post-conviction review, 599 were finally reviewed in a first federal habeas corpus petition . Of these, 40% were overturned "due to serious error."

The "overall error-rate" for the entire 1973–1995 period, *i.e.*, the proportion of fully reviewed capital judgments overturned at one of the three stages due to serious error, was 68%.

The most common error was "egregiously incompetent defense lawyering (accounting for 37% of the state post-conviction reversals)."

On retrial, when the errors are cured, "an astonishing 82% (247 out of 301) of the capital judgments that were reversed were replaced on retrial with a sentence *less* than death, or *no* sentence at all. In the latter regard, 7% (22/301) of the reversals for serious error resulted in determination on retrial that the defendant was *not guilty* of the capital offense."

THE QUALITY OF INDIGENT DEFENSE GENERALLY— AND HOW TO IMPROVE IT

1. *"A state of perpetual crisis."* There is general agreement that criminal defense systems are in "a state of perpetual crisis." Stephen J. Schulhofer & David D. Friedman, *Rethinking Indigent Defense: Promoting Effective Representation Through Consumer Sovereignty and Freedom of Choice for All Criminal Defendants*, 31 Am.Crim.L.Rev. 73, 74 (1993). Indeed, "at least every five years" since the landmark 1963 *Gideon* case, "a major study has been released finding that indigent defense is inadequate." David Cole, *No Equal Justice* 64 (1999).

"The evidence is unambiguous and telling. Lawyers representing indigent defendants often have unmanageable caseloads that frequently run into the hundreds, far exceeding professional guidelines.[a] These same lawyers frequently receive compensation at the lowest end of the professional pay scale." Note 113 Harv.L.Rev. 2062, 2064 (2000). Although most attention has focused on the impact of ineffective counsel in capital cases,[b] continues the Harvard Note,

a. For a comprehensive discussion of the caseload problems of indigent defenders see Richard Klein, *The Emperor Gideon Has No Clothes: The Empty Promise of Constitutional Right to Effective Assistance of Counsel*, 13 Hastings Const.L.Q. 625, 656–81 (1986). But compare CRIMPROC § 1.9(e) (noting difficulties in generalizations as to defender caseloads, and citing a "growing number of states [that have] implemented workload guidelines for public defenders, establishing maximum workloads (e.g., 150 cases for a non-capital felony defender) that require assignment of any overload to appointed attorneys)."

b. In addition to Justice Blackmun's dissent from the denial of certiorari in *McFarland v. Scott,* Note 2 supra, consider David Cole, *No Equal Justice* 86–88 (1999):

"Although inadequate compensation is no doubt the most significant barrier to effective indigent defense, it is not the only barrier. Most jurisdictions have no experiential qualifications for who may be assigned to represent an indigent defendant. As a result, lawyers are routinely appointed with virtually no relevant experience. Charles Bell, fac-

ing the death penalty in Mississippi, was represented by a recent law graduate who had never tried a criminal case to final judgment. Donald Paradis's attorney had passed the bar six months before he was appointed to defend a capital murder case, had never taken criminal law, criminal procedure, or trial advocacy in law school, and had never handled a jury trial. Billy Sunday Birt, on trial for murder in Georgia, was represented by court-appointed counsel who, when asked to identify any criminal law decision from any court with which he is familiar, could name only *Miranda v. Arizona* and *Dred Scott v. Sanford.* (*Miranda* is known by virtually anyone who has ever watched a police show on television; *Dred Scott* is not even a criminal case.)* * *

"A final impediment to quality representation is the appointment process itself, which is generally left to the discretion of state judges. Although many state judges no doubt strive to appoint competent counsel, judges may also be tempted to appoint attorneys who they know will not make trouble by being too zealous in their defense.* * *"

"indigent defense in everyday misdemeanor and minor felony cases is increasingly important."[23] Moreover, "because such a large proportion of criminal defendants are in fact indigent, the low quality of indigent defense fundamentally calls into question the overall fairness of the criminal justice system. According to most estimates, about eighty percent of all criminal defendants are represented by indigent defenders. The skill of indigent defense counsel is thus essential to quality truth-seeking in most criminal cases, and fundamentally affects the legitimacy of the system."[c]

2. *How much money do we spend on indigent defense?* Professor Cole, supra, at 64–65 reports: "Nationwide, we spend more than $97.5 billion annually on criminal justice. More than half of that goes to the police and prosecution, who together investigate, develop and prosecute cases. Indigent defense, by contrast, receives only 1.3 percent of annual federal criminal justice expenditures, and only 2 percent of total state and federal criminal justice expenditures. The national average per capita spending on state and local indigent defense in 1990, the latest year for which figures are available, was $5.37. Arkansas spent eighty-eight cents per capita on indigent defense that year, and Louisiana spent only eleven cents. In 1990, Kentucky [spent] a total of $11.4 million, approximately 1/1000 of the state budget, and four million dollars less than the University of Kentucky's athletic budget." But see, CRIMPROC § 1.4 at n. 309.7 (weighted caseload studies may support existing budget allocation for 81 largest counties, which report expenditures of 1.9 billion for prosecutors' offices and 1.1 billion for defenders' offices, even though defenders' offices typically have a much higher proportion of the overall defense representation (e.g., 80–85%) than their proportion of the prosecutor's budget, because of the broader range of activities involved on the prosecutor's side).

3. *How much does the state pay individual lawyers who are appointed counsel in criminal cases?* Hourly rates, observes Cole, supra, at 83, "range from $20 to $50 far below the hourly rates earned by privately retained counsel. [In] addition, about one-third of the states also impose a per-case maximum fee. In Kentucky, for example, the statutory maximum fee for defending a capital case is $2,500. Studies have found that attorneys spend between 100 and 1,500 hours in preparing for and trying a capital case, with the median ranging from 300 to 600 hours. At the Kentucky rate, an attorney who managed to handle a case in only 300 hours would make $8.50 an hour. In Alabama, the statutory maximum is $1,000 for all felonies, and $2,000 for capital cases. Tennessee and Kentucky impose a $1,000 maximum for all noncapital felony cases. South Carolina's statutory maximum is $750. In Virginia, the maximum fee for most felonies is $350."

Many state courts have rejected challenges to unrealistically low statutory caps, relying on the "ineffective assistance of counsel" standard as a safeguard. *Pruett v. State*, 574 So.2d 1342 (Miss.1990) is a dramatic example. In that case two experienced death penalty lawyers had each spent more than 400 hours preparing for and trying a capital case. Yet the Mississippi statute limited compensation to $1,000 per case. The state supreme court upheld the cap, but did construe the statute to allow defense attorneys to recover their overhead and out-of-pocket expenses, in addition to the $1,000 fee. Thus, comments Professor Cole, supra, at 85, "although attorneys in Mississippi assigned to indigent defense will now at

---

23. For example, "three strikes" sentencing regimes, which now exist in many states, amplify the collateral consequences of many cases. [The] 1996 immigration reform laws also have expanded the collateral effects of criminal matters on alienage status.

c. Recall the observations of the 1963 "Allen Report," extracted at the beginning of Ch. 3 of the casebook.

least break even, they will never receive more than $1,000 above their overhead expenses, no matter how long the trial and no matter how many hours they log.''

4. *The need for systematic litigation attacking the constitutionality of underfunded defense services.* Consider Richard Klein, *The Eleventh Commandment: Thou Shalt Not be Compelled to Render the Ineffective Assistance of Counsel*, 68 Indiana L.J. 363, 432 (1993):

"Court officials, administrators of court-appointed counsel plans, and judges have rarely concerned themselves with the *quality* of counsel provided indigent defendants. Absent some completely unforeseeable event, the prognosis for any additional funding for defense services is poor indeed—it is almost inconceivable that elected politicians would call for or provide additional funding to represent indigents accused of crime.[d] The responsibility of defense counsel, who are most aware of the egregious violations which result from inadequate funding, is clear. Neither habeas corpus petitions, nor appeals based on claims of ineffective assistance of counsel, nor attempts by private court-appointed counsel to unite and strike have been successful in bringing about the fundamental changes that are required.

"Systematic litigation attacking the constitutionality of the system for delivering defense services, however, offers hope and promise. The failures of states and counties to provide adequate funds to ensure the constitutionally mandated effective assistance of counsel are subject to, and call for, attack."

5. *The remarkable case of State v. Peart*, 621 So.2d. 780 (La.1993). Leonard Peart, an indigent defendant was charged with armed robbery, aggravated rape, aggravated burglary and murder. When Rick Teisser, a public defender in a section of the New Orleans Criminal District Court, was appointed to represent Peart against all charges, except murder, Teisser was handling 70 active felony cases. He had represented 418 defendants in the first seven months of the year (entering 130 guilty pleas at arraignment) and had at least one serious felony case set for trial for every trial date during the year. Moreover he had no funding for expert witnesses and had access to only three investigators, who were responsible for rendering assistance in 7000 cases annually. Teisser filed a pretrial motion asking the trial judge to declare that, under the conditions Teisser had to work, he could not possibly provide an effective legal defense.

The trial judge agreed, concluding that under the circumstances "not even a lawyer with an 'S' on his chest could effectively handle the docket." Unlike the trial court, the state supreme court declined to rule that the entire defender system was constitutionally inadequate, but it did adopt a rebuttable presumption that defendants represented by those in Teisser's public defender office were not receiving a constitutionally adequate defense, a presumption that would continue unless changes occurred in workloads and resources. "This step," reports Note, 113 Harv.L.Rev. 2062, 2074 (2000), "prompted the Louisiana legislature to increase indigent defense funding by $5 million over the next two years."

Although the *Peart* case best illustrates the advantage of seeking declaratory relief from the courts in order to improve the quality of indigent defense, "[g]iven the widespread history of political process failure in indigent defense provision,

***

d. Consider, Note, 113 Harv.L.Rev. 2062, 2067 (2000): "The politics surrounding criminal justice during the last two decades have clearly prioritized zealous law enforcement over defendants' procedural rights, including the right to counsel. Concerned by the forty-percent reversal rate of state capital judgments by federal habeas courts, Congress in 1995 entirely eliminated funding for [death penalty resource centers,] organizations that represented death row inmates on collateral federal habeas corpus review. Some jurisdictions at the state and local levels have also recently sought to decrease in either real or effective terms, the resources devoted to indigent defense."

declaratory relief might nonetheless be insufficient. A lawsuit currently pending in Mississippi illustrates this point: despite the passage of a statewide public defender act in 1998, the legislature has refused to appropriate funds to implement the act's mandate." *Id.*

6. *Public defenders vs. assigned counsel vs. retained counsel.* "Fifty-nine percent of the nation's 3,082 counties rely primarily on the assigned counsel system, 34% on public defenders, and 6% on contract systems [whereby a private firm or attorney provides representation for a group of cases]." Floyd Feeney & Patrick G. Jackson, *Public Defenders, Assigned Counsel, Retained Counsel: Does the Type of Criminal Defense Counsel Matter?*, 22 Rutgers L.J. 361, 363 (1991). However, the counties served by assigned and contract counsel are usually smaller. Thus, "nearly 70% of the nation's population lives in jurisdictions served by public defenders." *Id.*

According to Professors Feeney & Jackson, the most sophisticated studies indicate that the type of counsel (public defender, assigned counsel or retained) makes very little difference as to probability of conviction or length of sentence. See *id.* at 365–72.[b] However, most criminal defendants believe otherwise. One explanation for what Feeney & Jackson call "a gap between perceived and actual performance of counsel" is "the widespread belief that since public defenders are paid by the state, they necessarily represent the state's interest. Indeed, 25% of those responding in [one study] specifically said this." Id. at 378. "Another possible explanation is that different types of attorneys have different representation styles. Private attorneys appear to spend more time with their clients than public defenders." See BJS Study, fn. b supra (although results were similar for defendants represented by retained and government-provided counsel, state prison inmates with a government-provided counsel reported fewer conversations with counsel than inmates with retained counsel (26% vs. 58% as to 4 or more conferences) and later contact (13.6% vs. 3.5% for first contact at trial).

According to some commentators, such as David Sudnow and Abraham Blumberg, public defenders are essentially non-adversarial and co-opted into the court system. Others, such as Jerome Skolnik, disagree, maintaining that (a) just as some public defenders are in the "combative" group, a large number of private defense attorneys are in the "cooperative" group and (b) cooperative attorneys often do better for their clients. See id. at 401–02. According to Feeney & Jackson, the few studies that exist support Skolnick.

DOES A JUSTICE DEPARTMENT ORDER ALLOWING FEDERAL AUTHORITIES TO MONITOR COMMUNICATIONS BETWEEN FEDERAL INMATES AND THEIR LAWYERS VIOLATE THE RIGHT TO EFFECTIVE COUNSEL?

A new Justice Department rule, amending Bureau of Prison Regulations, 28 C.F.R. 500–501 (also discussed at p. 381), allows federal authorities to monitor

b. See also Bureau of Justice Statistics, *Defense Counsel in Criminal Cases* (NCJ—179023, 2000) (1996 survey of dispositions of federal felony defendants and state felony defendants in 15 largest counties found similar results for defendants represented by state-provided counsel, basically public defenders and appointed counsel, and privately retained counsel).

Feeney & Jackson recognize that "the best lawyers *do* make a difference" (emphasis added), but note that only a very few of the

defendants who retain their own counsel can afford the best. See also Donald A. Dripps, *Ineffective Assistance of Counsel: The Case for an Ex Ante Parity Standard*, 88 J. Crim.L. & C. 242, 250–51 (1997): "[It] needs to be recalled that most criminal defendants are poor, even if they are not indigent. Many of those who can afford counsel can still afford only the services of the bar's bottom-feeders. Thus, a comparison between appointed counsel and retained counsel is not necessarily a comparison between appointed counsel and effective counsel."

mail and conversations between federal inmates and their attorneys (or their attorneys' agents) when the Attorney General or certain other federal officials certify there is "reasonable suspicion" to believe an inmate's communication with his lawyer may facilitate terrorist acts. In defense of the order, Attorney General Ashcroft pointed out that (a) the prison inmate and his lawyer must be notified of the government's listening activities; (b) apart from any disclosure to prevent an imminent act of terrorism, any revelation to investigators or prosecutors must be approved by a federal judge; and (c) if and when there is a determination that "reasonable suspicion" exists to believe that an inmate may attempt to use his lawyer to facilitate terrorist acts, a "taint team" (a team unconnected to the jailed inmate's case) will be established to monitor attorney-client communications and a "firewall" constructed between this team and the prosecutors in the case to ensure that communications protected by the attorney-client privilege are not revealed to the prosecutors.

Despite the safeguards cited by the Attorney General, does the Justice Department order constitute a violation of the right to effective assistance of counsel? A number of criminal defense lawyers and law professors think so. See David E. Rovella, *Ashcroft Rule Puts Defenders In a Bind*, Nat'l L.J., Dec. 3, 2001, p. 1.

Some defense lawyers dismiss the notion that the taint team would not share information with prosecutors as "ridiculous." See Rovella, supra. Others, such as Irwin Schwartz, President of the National Association of Criminal Defense Lawyers (quoted in the Detroit Free Press, Nov. 10, 2001, p. 7A) emphasize: "An attorney cannot communicate with a client when confidentiality is not assured. And there can be no effective representation without communication."

Consider, too, Professor David Moran, *Ashcroft's Monitoring Order Violates Attorney–Client Rights*, Detroit News, Nov. 18, 2001, p. 13A:

"Constitutional rights, even very important constitutional rights, sometimes must yield when necessary to protect national security. The problem is that [the Attorney General] has produced no reason to believe that his order actually enhances our security. There is not a single documented example in American history in which a suspected terrorist used his lawyer to further acts of terrorism, nor has the government produced any evidence that such activity is going on now.

"On the contrary, many notorious terrorists, including Timothy McVeigh and Sheik Omar Ahmad Rahman (convicted for his role in the 1993 bombing of the World Trade Center), have been afforded their right to consult with their attorneys without bringing on more terror.

"Ultimately underlying Ashcroft's order is the unstated claim that some U.S. lawyers are really terrorist conspirators. Before accepting such a remarkable claim uncritically, Americans should at least demand some evidence."

Defense lawyers are not in agreement as to how to deal with the Justice Department order. One defense lawyer, who has represented 15 Saudi nationals since Sept. 11 on behalf of the Saudi Arabian embassy, stated he would seek a declaration from prosecutors that there would be no monitoring before meeting with a jailed client. He admitted, however, that he was uncertain how to proceed if he failed to obtain such assurance. Professor Jonathan Turley believed it would be unethical for a defense lawyer not to challenge the government monitoring, but added that if such a challenge failed the lawyer could ethically continue representation. See Rovella, supra.

WHEN DO DEFENSE COUNSEL'S ACTIONS IN PREVENTING HER CLIENT FROM TESTIFYING FALSELY IMPERMISSIBLY COMPROMISE THE CLIENT'S RIGHT TO EFFECTIVE ASSISTANCE OF COUNSEL?

NIX v. WHITESIDE

475 U.S. 157, 106 S.Ct. 988, 89 L.Ed.2d 123 (1986).

Chief Justice BURGER delivered the opinion of the Court. * * *

[In preparing for his Iowa state-court trial for murder, respondent Whiteside consistently told his appointed counsel, Robinson, that, although he had not actually seen a gun in the hand of the person he had stabbed to death, he was convinced that the victim had a gun. When Robinson interviewed those who were present during the stabbing, they told him that they had not seen a gun during the incident. And no gun was found on the premises. Robinson told his client that the actual existence of a weapon was not necessary to establish a claim of self-defense, and that only a reasonable belief that the victim had a gun nearby would suffice.

[Shortly before trial, during preparation for direct examination, Whiteside for the first time told his lawyer that he had seen "something metallic" in the victim's hand. When asked about this, Whiteside responded: "If I don't say I saw a gun, I'm dead." Robinson told Whiteside that such testimony would be lying and repeated that it was unnecessary to prove that the victim actually had a gun. On Whiteside's insisting that he would testify that he saw "something metallic," his lawyer told him, according to Robinson's testimony, that if Whiteside testified falsely, "it would be my duty to advise the Court of what he was doing and that I felt he was committing perjury; also, that I probably would be allowed to impeach that particular testimony." Robinson also indicated that he would seek to withdraw from the case if his client insisted on committing perjury.[a]

[Robinson ultimately testified as originally contemplated, stating he believed that the victim was reaching for a gun, but admitting on cross-examination that he had not actually seen a weapon in the victim's hand. After the jury found him guilty of second-degree murder, Whiteside moved for a new trial, claiming he had been denied effective assistance of counsel by his attorney's refusal to allow him to testify as he proposed. The trial court denied the motion and the state supreme court affirmed. Whiteside then sought federal habeas corpus relief on ineffective assistance of counsel grounds. The district court denied relief, but the Eighth Circuit reversed.

[The Court of Appeals, as the U.S. Supreme Court described it, "accepted the findings of the trial judge [that] trial counsel believed with good cause that Whiteside would testify falsely and acknowledged [that] a criminal defendant's privilege to testify in his own behalf does not include a right to commit perjury. Nevertheless, the court reasoned [that] Robinson's admonition to Whiteside that he would inform the court of Whiteside's perjury constituted a threat to violate the attorney's duty to preserve client confidences [and that] this threatened violation of client confidences breached the standards of effective representation set down in *Strickland.*"]

---

a. The *Whiteside* record, observes 1 Hazard & Hodes, *The Law of Lawyering* 360.2 (1988 Supp.), "is regrettably unclear whether the lawyer meant that he would seek to withdraw and inform the judge, would testify against the client in the murder case, or would testify against the client in a subsequent perjury case."

In *Strickland,* we recognized counsel's duty of loyalty and his "overarching duty to advocate the defendant's cause." Plainly, that duty is limited to legitimate, lawful conduct compatible with the very nature of a trial as a search for truth. Although counsel must take all reasonable lawful means to attain the objectives of the client, counsel is precluded from taking steps or in any way assisting the client in presenting false evidence or otherwise violating the law. This principle has consistently been recognized in most unequivocal terms by expositors of the norms of professional conduct since the first Canons of Professional Ethics were adopted in 1908 [and] been carried through to contemporary codifications[4] of an attorney's professional responsibility. Disciplinary Rule 7–102 of the Model Code of Professional Responsibility (1980), entitled "Representing a Client Within the Bounds of the Law," provides that

"(A) In his representation of a client, a lawyer shall not: * * *

"(4) Knowingly use perjured testimony or false evidence. * * *

"(7) Counsel or assist his client in conduct that the lawyer knows to be illegal or fraudulent."

This provision has been adopted by Iowa, and is binding on all lawyers who appear in its courts. The more recent Model Rules of Professional Conduct (1983) similarly admonish attorneys to obey all laws in the course of representing a client. * * *

Both the Model Code of Professional Conduct and the Model Rules of Professional Conduct also adopt the specific exception from the attorney-client privilege for disclosure of perjury that his client intends to commit or has committed. Indeed, both the Model Code and the Model Rules do not merely *authorize* disclosure by counsel of client perjury; they *require* such disclosure.

These standards confirm that the legal profession has accepted that an attorney's ethical duty to advance the interests of his client is limited by an equally solemn duty to comply with the law and standards of professional conduct; it specifically ensures that the client may not use false evidence. This special duty of an attorney to prevent and disclose frauds upon the court derives from the recognition that perjury is as much a crime as tampering with witnesses or jurors [and] undermines the administration of justice. * * *[6]

---

4. There currently exist two different codifications of uniform standards of professional conduct. The Model Code of Professional Responsibility was originally adopted by the American Bar Association in 1969, and was subsequently adopted (in many cases with modification) by nearly every state. The more recent Model Rules of Professional Conduct were adopted by the American Bar Association in 1983. Since their promulgation by the American Bar Association, the Model Rules have been adopted by 11 States * * *. Iowa is one of the States that adopted a form of the Model Code of Professional Responsibility, but has yet to adopt the Model Rules.

6. In the evolution of the contemporary standards promulgated by the American Bar Association, an early draft reflects a compromise suggesting that when the disclosure of intended perjury is made during the course of trial, when withdrawal of counsel would raise difficult questions of a mistrial holding, counsel had the option to let the defendant take the stand but decline to affirmatively assist the presentation of perjury by traditional direct examination. Instead, counsel would stand mute while the defendant undertook to present the false version in narrative form in his own words unaided by any direct examination. This conduct was thought to be a signal at least to the presiding judge that the attorney considered the testimony to be false and was seeking to disassociate himself from that course. Additionally, counsel would not be permitted to discuss the known false testimony in closing arguments. See ABA Standards for Criminal Justice, 4–7.7 (2d ed. 1980). Most courts treating the subject rejected this approach and insisted on a more rigorous standard. The Eighth Circuit in this case and the Ninth Circuit have expressed approval of the "free narrative" standards.

The Rule finally promulgated in the current Model Rules of Professional Conduct rejects any participation or passive role whatever by counsel in allowing perjury to be presented without challenge.

[W]e discern no failure to adhere to reasonable professional standards that would in any sense make out a deprivation of the Sixth Amendment right to counsel. Whether Robinson's conduct is seen as a successful attempt to dissuade his client from committing the crime of perjury, or whether seen as a "threat" to withdraw from representation and disclose the illegal scheme, Robinson's representation of Whiteside falls well within accepted standards of professional conduct and the range of reasonable professional conduct acceptable under *Strickland.* * * *

Paradoxically, even while accepting the conclusion of the Iowa trial court that Whiteside's proposed testimony would have been a criminal act, the Court of Appeals held that Robinson's efforts to persuade Whiteside not to commit that crime were improper, *first,* as forcing an impermissible choice between the right to counsel and the right to testify; and *second,* as compromising client confidences because of Robinson's threat to disclose the contemplated perjury.[7] * * *

Whatever the scope of a constitutional right to testify, it is elementary that such a right does not extend to testifying *falsely.* * * * Robinson's admonitions to his client can in no sense be said to have forced respondent into an *impermissible* choice between his right to counsel and his right to testify as he proposed for there was no *permissible* choice to testify falsely. For defense counsel to take steps to persuade a criminal defendant to testify truthfully, or to withdraw, deprives the defendant of neither his right to counsel nor the right to testify truthfully.

[On] this record, the accused enjoyed continued representation within the bounds of reasonable professional conduct and did in fact exercise his right to testify; at most he was denied the right to have the assistance of counsel in the presentation of false testimony. Similarly, we can discern no breach of professional duty in Robinson's admonition to respondent that he would disclose respondent's perjury to the court. The crime of perjury in this setting is indistinguishable in substance from the crime of threatening or tampering with a witness or a juror. A defendant who informed his counsel that he was arranging to bribe or threaten witnesses or members of the jury would have no "right" to insist on counsel's assistance or silence. Counsel would not be limited to advising against that conduct. An attorney's duty of confidentiality, which totally covers the client's admission of guilt, does not extend to a client's announced plans to engage in future criminal conduct. In short, the responsibility of an ethical lawyer, as an officer of the court and a key component of a system of justice, dedicated to a search for truth, is essentially the same whether the client announces an intention to bribe or threaten witnesses or jurors or to commit or procure perjury. No system of justice worthy of the name can tolerate a lesser standard.

The rule adopted by the Court of Appeals, which seemingly would require an attorney to remain silent while his client committed perjury, is wholly incompatible with the established standards of ethical conduct and the laws of Iowa and contrary to professional standards promulgated by that State. The position advocated by petitioner, on the contrary, is wholly consistent with the Iowa standards of professional conduct and law, with the overwhelming majority of courts, and with codes of professional ethics. Since there has been no breach of any recognized professional duty, it follows that there can be no deprivation of the right to assistance of counsel under the *Strickland* standard.

---

7. The Court of Appeals also determined that Robinson's efforts to persuade Whiteside to testify truthfully constituted an impermissible threat to testify against his own client. We find no support for a threat to testify against Whiteside while he was acting as counsel. The record reflects testimony by Robinson that he had admonished Whiteside that if he withdrew he "probably would be allowed to attempt to impeach that particular testimony," if Whiteside testified falsely. The trial court accepted this version of the conversation as true.

We hold that, as a matter of law, counsel's conduct complained of here cannot establish the prejudice required for relief under the second strand of the *Strickland* inquiry. [The] *Strickland* Court noted that the "benchmark" of an ineffective assistance claim is the fairness of the adversary proceeding, and that in judging prejudice and the likelihood of a different outcome, "[a] defendant has no entitlement to the luck of a lawless decisionmaker."

Whether he was persuaded or compelled to desist from perjury, Whiteside has no valid claim that confidence in the result of his trial has been diminished by his desisting from the contemplated perjury. Even if we were to assume that the jury might have believed his perjury, it does not follow that Whiteside was prejudiced. * * *

Justice BRENNAN, concurring in the judgment.

This Court has no constitutional authority to establish rules of ethical conduct for lawyers practicing in the state courts. Nor does the Court enjoy any statutory grant of jurisdiction over legal ethics.

[The] Court's essay regarding what constitutes the correct response to a criminal client's suggestion that he will perjure himself is pure discourse without force of law. As Justice Blackmun observes, *that* issue is a thorny one, but it is not an issue presented by this case. Lawyers, judges, bar associations, students and others should understand that the problem has not now been "decided."

I join Justice Blackmun's concurrence because I agree that respondent has failed to prove the kind of prejudice necessary to make out a claim under *Strickland*.

Justice BLACKMUN, with whom Justice BRENNAN, Justice MARSHALL, and Justice STEVENS join, concurring in the judgment.

[The] Court approaches this case as if the performance and prejudice standard requires us in every case to determine "the perimeters of [the] range of reasonable professional assistance," but *Strickland* explicitly contemplates a different course: "[If] it is easier to dispose of an ineffectiveness claim on the ground of lack of sufficient prejudice, which we expect will often be so, that course should be followed." In this case, respondent has failed to show any legally cognizable prejudice. [Nor] is this a case in which prejudice should be presumed.

The touchstone of a claim of prejudice is an allegation that counsel's behavior did something "to deprive the defendant of a fair trial, a trial whose result is reliable." *Strickland*. The only effect Robinson's threat had on Whiteside's trial is that Whiteside did not testify, falsely, that he saw a gun in Love's hand.[4] Thus, this Court must ask whether its confidence in the outcome of Whiteside's trial is in any way undermined by the knowledge that he refrained from presenting false testimony.

[The] proposition that presenting false evidence could contribute to (or that withholding such evidence could detract from) the reliability of a criminal trial is simply untenable. [In] light of respondent's failure to show any cognizable prejudice, I see no need to "grade counsel's performance." *Strickland*. The only federal issue in this case is whether Robinson's behavior deprived Whiteside of the effective assistance of counsel; it is not whether Robinson's behavior conformed to any particular code of legal ethics.

---

4. This is not to say that a lawyer's threat to reveal his client's confidences may never have other effects on a defendant's trial. Cf. *United States ex rel. Wilcox v. Johnson*, 555 F.2d 115 (3d Cir.1977) (finding a violation of Sixth Amendment when an attorney's threat to reveal client's purported perjury caused defendant not to take the stand at all).

Whether an attorney's response to what he sees as a client's plan to commit perjury violates a defendant's Sixth Amendment rights may depend on many factors: how certain the attorney is that the proposed testimony is false, the stage of the proceedings at which the attorney discovers the plan, or the ways in which the attorney may be able to dissuade his client, to name just three. The complex interaction of factors, which is likely to vary from case to case, makes inappropriate a blanket rule that defense attorneys must reveal, or threaten to reveal, a client's anticipated perjury to the court. Except in the rarest of cases, attorneys who adopt "the role of the judge or jury to determine the facts," *Wilcox*, pose a danger of depriving their clients of the zealous and loyal advocacy required by the Sixth Amendment.[8] * * *

Justice STEVENS, concurring in the judgment.

[As] we view this case, it appears perfectly clear that respondent intended to commit perjury, that his lawyer knew it, and that the lawyer had a duty—both to the court and to his client, for perjured testimony can ruin an otherwise meritorious case—to take extreme measures to prevent the perjury from occurring. The lawyer was successful and, from our unanimous and remote perspective, it is now pellucidly clear that the client suffered no "legally cognizable prejudice."

Nevertheless, beneath the surface of this case there are areas of uncertainty that cannot be resolved today. A lawyer's certainty that a change in his client's recollection is a harbinger of intended perjury—as well as judicial review of such apparent certainty—should be tempered by the realization that, after reflection, the most honest witness may recall (or sincerely believe he recalls) details that he previously overlooked. Similarly, the post-trial review of a lawyer's pre-trial threat to expose perjury that had not yet been committed—and, indeed, may have been prevented by the threat—is by no means the same as review of the way in which such a threat may actually have been carried out. Thus, one can be convinced—as I am—that this lawyer's actions were a proper way to provide his client with effective representation without confronting the much more difficult questions of what a lawyer must, should, or may do after his client has given testimony that the lawyer does not believe. * * *

Notes and Questions

1. An easy case? Once the Court framed the issue in terms of whether Whiteside's lawyer's response to the situation fell within the range of "reasonable professional" conduct, was the case an easy one? Under that test, observes 1 Geoffrey C. Hazard & W. William Hodes, *The Law of Lawyering* 360.2 (1988 Supp.) (hereinafter "Hazard & Hodes"), "the issue is not whether counsel was right, but whether counsel was radically wrong."

2. The significance of Whiteside. Consider Hazard & Hodes at 360.2–2: "[The Supreme Court] has supervisory authority over other federal courts, and its opinion in *Nix v. Whiteside* can be taken as the adoption of Model Rule 3.3 with respect to lawyers appearing in federal tribunals. But with respect to proceedings

---

8. A comparison of this case with *Wilcox* is illustrative. Here, Robinson testified in detail to the factors that led him to conclude that respondent's assertion he had seen a gun was false. The Iowa Supreme Court found "good cause" and "strong support" for Robinson's conclusion. Moreover, Robinson gave credence to those parts of Whiteside's account which, although he found them implausible and unsubstantiated, were not clearly false. By contrast, in *Wilcox*, where defense counsel actually informed the judge that she believed her client intended to lie and where her threat to withdraw in the middle of the trial led the defendant not to take the stand at all, the Court of Appeals found "no evidence on the record of this case indicating that Mr. Wilcox intended to perjure himself," and characterized counsel's beliefs as "private conjectures about the guilt or innocence of [her] client."

in state court, the Supreme Court's authority extends no further than assessing the sufficiency of the quality of the legal representation provided, under one ethical scheme or another. Thus, even after *Whiteside,* a state court would be free to adopt a different rule. Counsel could be required merely to withdraw, or permitted but not required to 'blow the whistle.' Indeed, so far as the federal constitution is concerned, a state could require that counsel present and argue the client's perjured testimony on the same basis as truthful testimony. [Nevertheless,] the *Whiteside* case is highly significant precisely because it closed off the *constitutional* avenue of debate and remanded the argument over specific 'correct' responses to the state courts, where it belongs."

Did Whiteside close off *all* constitutional avenues of debate? Consider Note 5, infra.

3. Did Whiteside, as the Court states at one point, "inform" his lawyer that he would "perjure himself on the stand?" Note that earlier in its opinion the *Whiteside* Court alludes to "the findings of the trial judge, affirmed by the Iowa Supreme Court, that trial counsel believed with *good cause* that Whiteside would testify falsely." (Emphasis added.) Consider Norman Lefstein, *Client Perjury in Criminal Cases: Still in Search of An Answer,* 1 Geo.J.Legal Ethics 521, 532–33 (1988) (hereinafter referred to as "Lefstein"):

"In assessing counsel's judgment that Whiteside intended to lie, the Iowa Supreme Court used what might be termed a 'good faith belief' test. While it is hard to dispute that counsel may have had a good faith basis for believing that Whiteside planned to commit perjury, it seems equally clear that counsel did not have 'actual knowledge' of planned perjury. In addition, the Iowa Supreme Court placed too much emphasis [on whether the murder victim, Love,] actually had a gun. [That] Love never had a gun and thus never possessed anything 'metallic' is relevant in deciding whether Whiteside was being truthful but it is certainly not dispositive. Conceivably, Whiteside believed that he saw something 'metallic' when, in fact, he did not."

Do Whiteside's initial statements to his lawyer that he "did not see a gun" and his subsequent statement that "in Howard Cook's case there was a gun. If I don't say I saw a gun, I'm dead" make it "perfectly clear," as concurring Justice Stevens put it, "that [Whiteside] intended to commit perjury [and] that his lawyer knew it"? Consider Lefstein at 532:

"[A] statement that 'I did not see a gun' is not entirely inconsistent with the statement that 'I saw something metallic in his hand.' Although Whiteside's remark about there being a gun in Howard Cook's case and that 'if I don't say I saw a gun I'm dead' make it appear that he was lying, there are some possible innocent explanations. The statement about Howard Cook's case may have been only an observation about what Whiteside recalled concerning a previous case of which he was aware. The observation about being 'dead' unless 'I saw a gun' may also have been defendant's assessment of his chances of an acquittal at trial—an assessment that does not seem altogether unreasonable in light of the jury's verdict."

4. When does a lawyer "know" that his client intends to testify falsely? The Model Code prohibits an attorney from "knowingly us[ing] perjured testimony" and the more recent Model Rules prohibit a lawyer from "knowingly offer[ing] evidence that the lawyer knows to be false." When does a lawyer *"know"*? Should the client perjury problem in criminal cases be deemed to exist only when counsel has "actual knowledge" that his client plans to lie? Yes, maintains Lefstein at 527–33, 550. But consider Hazard & Hodes at 343–44:

"As all lawyers who are honest with themselves know, occasions arise when doubts about a client turn into suspicion and then moral certainty that a client is lying. Although his professional role may require a lawyer to take a detached attitude of unbelief, the law of lawyering does not permit a lawyer to escape all accountability by suspending his intelligence and common sense. [All] authorities agree—even those who take the most unqualified positions on the duty of a lawyer zealously to serve his clients—that there comes a point when only brute rationalization, moral irresponsibility, and pure sophistry can support the contention that the lawyer does not 'know' what the situation is. See Monroe Freedman, *Lawyers' Ethics in an Adversary System* 52–55, 71–76 (1975). * * *

"Looking forward into his professional conduct as it proceeds, a lawyer must imagine how his conduct will appear to someone else later looking backward at it. And he must imagine the inferences that will be drawn as to what he knew at the time. In pragmatic terms, this is the standard of what a lawyer 'knows.' "

Although, as he points out, during the oral argument the issue was clearly a matter of concern to members of the Supreme Court, Monroe Freedman, *Client Confidences and Client Perjury: Some Unanswered Questions,* 136 U.Pa.L.Rev. 1939, 1946 (1988), concludes that the *Whiteside* Court never answered "the key question": "what standard of knowing is required before a lawyer may threaten to reveal a client confidence to prevent the client from committing perjury?"[1] The lawyer who prevailed in the Supreme Court does not disagree, see Brent Appel, *The Limited Impact of Nix v. Whiteside on Attorney–Client Relations,* 136 U.Pa. L.Rev. 1913, 1934–35 (1988), but he notes that in the *Whiteside* oral argument he took the position that "an attorney must not act on mere suspicion, but must 'know' or 'know beyond a reasonable doubt' that the client intended to commit perjury." *Id.*

5. The "ethical" lawyer vs. the "ineffective" lawyer. At what point must (should) (may) a lawyer *decline* to cooperate with a client who may be planning to commit perjury? At what point may (should) (must) a lawyer *continue* to cooperate with a client she believes or suspects may be planning to commit perjury?

As the quantum of evidence supporting the lawyer's belief that her client intends to commit perjury increases, at what point does it become "unethical" for the lawyer to continue to cooperate with the client? As the quantum of evidence supporting the belief *decreases,* at what point does the lawyer who discloses or threatens to disclose her belief that her client intends to testify falsely depart from the role of an advocate and become an adversary to the interests of her client? At what point, as the basis for the belief becomes weaker, does the lawyer's refusal to put her client on the stand violate the client's right to testify and to due process?

If she does not actually know, must (should) the lawyer who refuses to cooperate with a client at least believe "beyond a reasonable doubt" that the client will perjure himself on the stand? Suppose the lawyer only has "probable cause" to believe? Only a "good faith" belief? A "reasonable suspicion?"

6. The lawyer's appropriate response. *Whiteside* makes clear that the Sixth Amendment is not violated when a defense attorney threatens to reveal her client's intention to commit perjury (at least when it is clear what the client proposes to do). But what should counsel's response be as a matter of professional ethics when a client is determined to commit perjury? If counsel cannot dissuade a client from committing perjury, should she (must she) disclose her client's intention to the tribunal? Or should her response be limited to withdrawal from the case? But what will withdrawal accomplish? Isn't the client likely to withhold

---

1. According to Professor Freedman, "Whiteside's advocate wrongly conceded at the outset of his argument that the standard of knowing was not an issue." Id. at 1956.

the incriminating information from his new lawyer—and then commit perjury? See generally John Burkoff, *Criminal Defense Techniques* § 6.5(c)(1) (1988).

People v. DePallo, 754 N.E.2d 751 (N.Y.2001), which held that a defense lawyer did not render ineffective assistance of counsel by informing the court in chambers, after his client testified, of his belief that his client had perjured himself, left little doubt that it did not think much of a lawyer withdrawing from the case on learning that his client is determined to commit perjury. *DePallo* arose as follows: After defendant, a murder defendant, had told his lawyer that he was involved in the murder and had been at the scene at the time of the crime, he stated his intention to testify in his own defense. Although the defense lawyer attempted to persuade his client not to take the stand, the latter insisted on doing so. The lawyer then elicited defendant's direct testimony in narrative form. (Defendant testified that he had been home at the time of the crime.) After both sides rested, the lawyer told the trial judge in chambers (outside the presence of defendant and the prosecutor) that the defendant had committed perjury. During summation, the lawyer did not refer to his client's testimony. A unanimous New York Court of Appeals, per Wesley, J., held that the defense lawyer had acted properly, rejecting defendant's contentions that (1) his lawyer should have sought to withdraw from the case, and (2) defendant's right to be present during a material stage of the trial had been violated by his absence from the ex parte communication between the court and his attorney:

"[S]ubstitution of counsel would do little to resolve the problem and might, in fact, have facilitated any fraud defendant wished to perpetrate upon the court. [W]ithdrawal of counsel * * * could lead to introduction of the perjured testimony in any event or further delay the proceedings.

"[As for the in-chambers conference between defendant's lawyer and the judge,] the purpose of this meeting was simply to place on the record matters that had already occurred regarding defendant's perjury and his attorney's response. The conference memorialized counsel's dilemma for appellate review and possible analysis of counsel's professional obligations. Thus, defendant's presence was not mandated; it had no bearing on his ability to defend himself against the charges or on the outcome of this jury trial."[a]

SECTION 4. MULTIPLE REPRESENTATION AND CONFLICTS OF INTEREST

"An attorney appeared in a municipal court for the purpose of requesting a reduction of bail for four defendants jointly charged with possession of a large cache of drugs seized from a communal house. Referring to the first of his clients, the lawyer stated: 'The defendant should be released on his recognizance, Your Honor, because he has no rap sheet. Obviously he is not a hardened criminal and should not be locked up with others who are.' When the second defendant's case was called, counsel argued: 'No drugs were found in this defendant's bedroom, Your Honor. His chance for an acquittal is great and consequently it is highly likely that he will show up for trial.' On behalf of the third defendant, the lawyer began to argue that his client had lived in the area all of his life. The judge interrupted the lawyer, asking him if any drugs had been seized from the bedroom of defendant number three. The lawyer responded, 'No comment, Your Honor.' The judge countered with the remark: 'I suppose that this client also has a prior

---

a. This court expressly declined to discuss "whether a similar disclosure in the course of a bench trial would be appropriate or implicate any due process concerns." It noted, however, that *Lowery v. Cardwell*, 575 F.2d 727 (9th Cir.1978), had taken the position that when a judge, not a jury, is the fact finder a similar disclosure deprives defendant of a fair trial.

record, making him a hardened criminal,' evoking the response that although the defendant had a prior record, he certainly was not a hardened criminal. The fourth defendant then interrupted the proceedings by eagerly requesting to be represented by the public defender."

—G. Lowenthal, *Joint Representation in Criminal Cases: A Critical Appraisal,* 64 Va.L.Rev. 939, 941 (1978).[a]

When a single attorney represents two or more defendants, a conflict of interest can surface, and is likely to do so, at any stage of the criminal process— plea bargaining, the decision whether to have the defendants testify, closing argument or sentencing. The many ways that an attorney representing multiple defendants can find himself in the bind of a conflict and the difficulty, if not futility, of searching the record for a "lost" defense or other evidence of conflict, are discussed and documented in, e.g., John S. Geer, *Representation of Multiple Criminal Defendants: Conflicts of Interest and the Professional Responsibilities of the Defense Attorney,* 62 Minn.L.Rev. 119, 125–35 (1978); Gary T. Lowenthal, supra, at 941–50, 978–79; Peter W. Tague, *Multiple Representation and Conflicts of Interest in Criminal Cases,* 67 Geo.L.J. 1075, 1077–80 (1979); *Developments— Conflicts of Interest in the Legal Profession,* 94 Harv.L.Rev. 1244, 1380–84 (1981); Comment, 68 J.Crim.L. & Crim. 226, 233–41 (1977). A summary, based on these commentaries, follows:

In the plea bargaining process, the prosecutor will often negotiate with one codefendant, offering a reduced charge, immunity or even a dismissal, in exchange for testimony against the remaining defendants or other cooperation with the government. A deal offered to one defendant and not to others puts a single counsel for multiple defendants in a most difficult, if not untenable, position.

The often crucial decision whether to put a defendant on the witness stand is greatly complicated by one attorney representing multiple defendants. One defendant's testimony might aid him but badly damage a codefendant. One defendant may make an excellent witness but another a very poor one. If both defendants take the stand, the poor witness, or one highly vulnerable to impeachment, may drag down the better witness. Putting on the stand only the defendant who makes a good witness may suggest to the jury that the defendants' own lawyer finds significant differences between them, or at least raise questions in the minds of the jurors as to why one defendant refused to testify.

When a lawyer represents only one of several defendants, in closing argument he may stress favorable comparisons between his client and the other defendants. When a single attorney represents all the defendants, however, he must approach comparisons among the defendants with the greatest caution.

Even if the dangers of multiple representation have somehow been avoided throughout the trial, any unity of interests among multiple defendants will often, perhaps inevitably, break down at the sentencing stage. More often than not, each defendant's role in the planning and the commission of the crime and each defendant's age, background and prior criminal record will vary significantly.

How can a lawyer representing multiple defendants differentiate between or among them by drawing attention to the mitigating factors in favor of each without creating a conflict of interest?

a. This incident occurred in Professor Gary Lowenthal's presence when he was an assistant public defender. Such incidents prompted him to write his article.

Because a single lawyer representing several defendants may impose an enforced harmony of defenses for the "benefit of all defendants," many conflicts between defendants may not even appear as part of the record. A lost plea bargaining opportunity that results from a defense lawyer's effort to protect a codefendant, for example, will not be reflected in the record. Nor will a defense strategy never pursued in court, or even investigated, because it was in conflict with another strategy available to a codefendant.

CUYLER v. SULLIVAN
446 U.S. 335, 100 S.Ct. 1708, 64 L.Ed.2d 333 (1980).

Justice POWELL delivered the opinion of the Court.

The question in this case is whether a state prisoner may obtain a federal writ of habeas corpus by showing that his retained counsel represented potentially conflicting interests.

I

Respondent John Sullivan was indicted with Gregory Carchidi and Anthony DiPasquale for the first-degree murders of [two persons]. Two privately retained lawyers, G. Fred DiBona and A. Charles Peruto, represented all three defendants throughout the state proceedings that followed the indictment. Sullivan had different counsel at the medical examiner's inquest, but he thereafter accepted representation from the two lawyers retained by his codefendants because he could not afford to pay his own lawyer.[1] At no time did Sullivan or his lawyers object to the multiple representation. Sullivan was the first defendant to come to trial. The evidence against him was entirely [circumstantial]. At the close of the Commonwealth's case, the defense rested without presenting any evidence. The jury found Sullivan guilty and fixed his penalty at life imprisonment. * * * Sullivan's codefendants, Carchidi and DiPasquale, were acquitted at separate trials. * * *

III

We turn [to] the claim that the alleged failings of Sullivan's retained counsel cannot provide the basis for a writ of habeas corpus because the conduct of retained counsel does not involve state action.

[A] proper respect for the Sixth Amendment disarms petitioner's contention that defendants who retain their own lawyers are entitled to less protection than defendants for whom the State appoints counsel. [The] vital guarantee of the Sixth Amendment would stand for little if the often uninformed decision to retain a particular lawyer could reduce or forfeit the defendant's entitlement to constitutional protection. Since the State's conduct of a criminal trial itself implicates the State in the defendant's conviction, we see no basis for drawing a distinction between retained and appointed counsel that would deny equal justice to defendants who must choose their own lawyers.

IV

We come at last to Sullivan's claim that he was denied the effective assistance of counsel guaranteed by the Sixth Amendment because his lawyers had a conflict of interest. The claim raises two issues expressly reserved in *Holloway v. Arkansas*, 435 U.S. 475, 98 S.Ct. 1173, 55 L.Ed.2d 426 (1978). The first is whether a

---

1. DiBona and Peruto were paid in part with funds raised by friends of the three defendants. The record does not disclose the source of the balance of their fee, but no part of the money came from either Sullivan or his family.

state trial judge must inquire into the propriety of multiple representation even though no party lodges an objection. The second is whether the mere possibility of a conflict of interest warrants the conclusion that the defendant was deprived of his right to counsel.

In *Holloway,* a single public defender represented three defendants at the same trial. The trial court refused to consider the appointment of separate counsel despite the defense lawyer's timely and repeated assertions that the interests of his clients conflicted. This Court recognized that a lawyer forced to represent codefendants whose interests conflict cannot provide the adequate legal assistance required by the Sixth Amendment. Given the trial court's failure to respond to timely objections, however, the Court did not consider whether the alleged conflict actually existed. It simply held that the trial court's error unconstitutionally endangered the right to counsel.

Holloway requires state trial courts to investigate timely objections to multiple representation. But nothing in our precedents suggests that the Sixth Amendment requires state courts themselves to initiate inquiries into the propriety of multiple representation in every case.[10] Defense counsel have an ethical obligation to avoid conflicting representations and to advise the court promptly when a conflict of interest arises during the course of trial. Absent special circumstances, therefore, trial courts may assume either that multiple representation entails no conflict or that the lawyer and his clients knowingly accept such risk of conflict as may exist. Indeed, as the Court noted in *Holloway,* trial courts necessarily rely in large measure upon the good faith and good judgment of defense counsel. [Unless] the trial court knows or reasonably should know that a particular conflict exists, the court need not initiate an inquiry.

Nothing in the circumstances of this case indicates that the trial court had a duty to inquire whether there was a conflict of interest. The provision of separate trials for Sullivan and his codefendants significantly reduced the potential for a divergence in their interests. No participant in Sullivan's trial ever objected to the multiple representation. DiBona's opening argument for Sullivan outlined a defense compatible with the view that none of the defendants was connected with the murders. [Finally,] counsel's critical decision to rest Sullivan's defense was on its face a reasonable tactical response to the weakness of the circumstantial evidence presented by the prosecutor. On these facts, we conclude that the Sixth Amendment imposed upon the trial court no affirmative duty to inquire into the propriety of multiple representation.

Holloway reaffirmed that multiple representation does not violate the Sixth Amendment unless it gives rise to a conflict of interest. Since a possible conflict inheres in almost every instance of multiple representation, a defendant who objects to multiple representation must have the opportunity to show that potential conflicts impermissibly imperil his right to a fair trial. But unless the trial court fails to afford such an opportunity, a reviewing court cannot presume that the possibility for conflict has resulted in ineffective assistance of counsel. Such a presumption would preclude multiple representation even in cases where " '[a] common defense * * * gives strength against a common attack.' "

[A] defendant who shows that a conflict of interest actually affected the adequacy of his representation need not demonstrate prejudice in order to obtain

10. In certain cases, proposed [and subsequently adopted] Fed.R.Crim.P. 44(c) provides that the federal district courts "shall promptly inquire with respect [to] joint representation and shall personally advise each defendant of his right to the effective assistance of counsel, including separate representation."

Several Courts of Appeals already invoke their supervisory power to require similar inquiries. As our promulgation of Rule 44(c) suggests, we view such an exercise of the supervisory power as a desirable practice. * * *

relief. But until a defendant shows that his counsel actively represented conflicting interests, he has not established the constitutional predicate for his claim of ineffective assistance. [A] defendant must establish that an actual conflict of interest adversely affected his lawyer's performance. * * *

Justice BRENNAN, concurring in Part III of the opinion of the Court and in the result.

I agree with the Court, in Part III, that the alleged failure of retained counsel to render effective assistance involves state action and thus provides the basis for a writ of habeas corpus. I cannot, however, join Part IV of the opinion.

[As the Court observes], "a possible conflict inheres in almost every instance of multiple representation." Therefore, upon discovery of joint representation, the duty of the trial court is to ensure that the defendants have not unwittingly given up their constitutional right to effective counsel. This is necessary since it is usually the case that defendants will not know what their rights are or how to raise them. This is surely true of the defendant who may not be receiving the effective assistance of counsel as a result of conflicting duties owed to other defendants. Therefore, the trial court cannot safely assume that silence indicates a knowledgeable choice to proceed jointly. The court must at least affirmatively advise the defendants that joint representation creates potential hazards which the defendants should consider before proceeding with the representation. [Where, as here,] there is no evidence that the court advised respondent about the potential for conflict or that respondent made a knowing and intelligent choice to forego his right to separate counsel, I believe that respondent, who has shown a significant possibility of conflict, is entitled to a presumption that his representation in fact suffered. * * *

Justice MARSHALL, concurring in part and dissenting in part.

* * * I join Parts I, II, and III of the Court's opinion.

I believe, however, that the potential for conflict of interest in representing multiple defendants is "so grave," see I *A.B.A. Standards* § 4–3.5(b), that whenever two or more defendants are represented by the same attorney the trial judge must make a preliminary determination that the joint representation is the product of the defendants' informed choice. I therefore agree with Mr. Justice Brennan that the trial court has a duty to inquire whether there is multiple representation, to warn defendants of the possible risks of such representation, and to ascertain that the representation is the result of the defendants' informed choice.

[The] Court holds that in the absence of an objection at trial, the defendant must show "that an actual conflict of interest adversely affected his lawyer's performance." [Such] a test is not only unduly harsh, but incurably speculative as well. The appropriate question under the Sixth Amendment is whether an actual, relevant conflict of interests existed during the proceedings. If it did, the conviction must be reversed. Since such a conflict was present in this case, I would affirm the [judgment].

Notes and Questions

1. *Cuyler v. Sullivan on remand; what constitutes "adversely affecting" counsel's performances?* On remand, the Third Circuit accepted the district court's finding that defense counsel's failure to call codefendant Carchidi to testify at Sullivan's trial constituted "an actual conflict of interest that adversely affected counsel's performance." *Sullivan v. Cuyler,* 723 F.2d 1077 (3d Cir.1983) "The record establishes," observed the court, "that counsel's duty of

loyalty to Sullivan to consider the sufficiency of the evidence presented and the availability of exculpatory evidence before deciding to rest his defense conflicted with [his] duty of loyalty to Carchidi to protect him against self-incrimination. In fact it indicates that the conflict could not be avoided."

The court rejected the contention that there was no adverse effect "because had Carchidi been represented by independent counsel, he would have been advised to invoke, and probably would have invoked, the fifth amendment if called as a witness": "This argument seeks to require Sullivan to demonstrate prejudice. But [a defendant need not do so] to make out a violation of his sixth amendment rights where he has already established an actual conflict of interest adversely affecting counsel's performance. Here, it was sufficient for Sullivan to show that defense counsel consciously rejected calling Carchidi as a witness in the Sullivan trial to present Carchidi's case in the best light at his subsequent trial."

Judge Adams, who wanted the Third Circuit to rehear the case en banc, was "much less certain" than the panel that decided *Cuyler* on remand "that Sullivan was adversely affected by the decision not to call Carchidi as a witness. Indeed, there is little hard evidence to suggest that Carchidi would have testified. In any case, I believe that we are bound [to] accept the findings of the Pennsylvania Supreme Court on [this point]."

2. *The confusing language in Cuyler: must the defendant show an "adverse effect" as well as an "actual conflict"?* *Cuyler* states that a defendant who shows that a conflict "adversely affected" or "actually affected the adequacy of his representation need not demonstrate prejudice in order to obtain relief." But are the lower courts likely to experience considerable difficulty distinguishing between a requirement that the conflict "adversely affected" a lawyer's performance and a requirement that it "prejudiced" the defendant's case in some way? Does the Supreme Court's use of the term "adverse effect" require a showing that defense counsel's performance was in fact influenced by a conflict of interest or does the Court's use of the term merely describe how courts can identify the existence of an "actual conflict"? Should the courts require that a defendant show only that an actual conflict existed, i.e., that during the course of the representation the codefendants' interests diverged with respect to a material factual or legal issue or to a course of action? Or, once multiple representation is established and an actual conflict of interest identified, should the courts *presume* that the conflict adversely affected the lawyer's performance, but allow the government to rebut this presumption by demonstrating the absence of adverse effect? See generally Note, 70 Geo.L.J. 1527, 1536–62 (1982) (advocating the last approach mentioned).

3. *What light is shed on Cuyler by Burger v. Kemp?* Lower courts generally have read *Cuyler* to require some showing both that a conflict existed and that it explained a particular action or inaction of counsel adverse to defendant's cause. This reading of the case is supported by the Court's subsequent decision in BURGER v. KEMP, 483 U.S. 776, 107 S.Ct. 3114, 97 L.Ed.2d 638 (1987), which arose as follows:

Petitioner Burger claimed that he had been deprived of the effective assistance of counsel because, inter alia, his lawyer had labored under a conflict of interest. Burger and a coindictee (Stevens), who was tried for murder later in a separate trial, confessed to the murder of one Honeycutt. Each defendant's confession emphasized the culpability of the other. Leaphart, an experienced and well-respected criminal lawyer, was appointed to represent Burger. Leaphart's law partner was appointed to represent Stevens in his later, separate trial. Leaphart assisted his partner in the representation of Stevens. Moreover, he prepared the briefs for both defendants on their second appeal to the Georgia Supreme Court.

Leaphart represented Burger during the proceedings that resulted in his conviction and death sentence, during his appeal to the Georgia Supreme Court, which resulted in a vacation of the death penalty, and during his second sentencing hearing and appeal, which resulted in affirmance of the death sentence. At their separate trials, each of the defendants sought to underscore the culpability of the other in order to avoid the death penalty. Although he had relied on Burger's lesser culpability as a trial defense, Leaphart did not make a "lesser culpability" argument in his appellate brief on behalf of Burger. Nor did Leaphart negotiate a plea bargain in which Burger's testimony against Stevens might be traded for a life sentence.

On habeas corpus, the two lower federal courts concluded that petitioners's representation had not been constitutionally inadequate. The Supreme Court, per STEVENS, J., agreed:

"Assuming without deciding that two law partners are considered as one attorney, it is settled that '[r]equiring or permitting a single attorney to represent codefendants [is] not *per se* violative of constitutional guarantees of effective assistance of counsel.' *Holloway.* [W]e presume prejudice 'only if the defendant demonstrates that counsel "actively represented conflicting interests" and that "an actual conflict of interest adversely affected his lawyer's performance." ' *Strickland.*

"As an initial matter, we agree with the District Court that the overlap of counsel, if any, did not so infect Leaphart's representation as to constitute an active representation of competing interests. Particularly in smaller communities where the supply of qualified lawyers willing to accept the demanding and unrewarding work of representing capital prisoners is extremely limited, the defendants may actually benefit from the joint efforts of two partners who supplement one another in their preparation. Moreover, we generally presume that the lawyer is fully conscious of the overarching duty of complete loyalty to his or her client.[a] Trial courts appropriately and 'necessarily rely in large measure upon the good faith and good judgment of defense counsel.' *Cuyler.* In addition, petitioner and Stevens were tried in separate proceedings; as we noted in *Cuyler,* the provision of separate murder trials for the three coindictees 'significantly reduced the potential for a divergence in their interests.'

"In an effort to identify an actual conflict of interest, petitioner points out that Leaphart prepared the briefs for both Burger and Stevens on their second appeal to the Georgia Supreme Court, and that Leaphart did not make a 'lesser culpability' argument in his appellate brief on behalf of Burger even though he had relied on Burger's lesser culpability as a trial defense. Given the fact that it was petitioner who actually killed Honeycutt [and] the further fact that the Georgia Supreme Court expressed the opinion that petitioner's actions were 'outrageously and wantonly vile and inhuman under any reasonable standard of human conduct,' [the] decision to forgo this issue had a sound strategic basis. * * *

"We also conclude that the asserted actual conflict of interest, even if it had been established, did not harm his lawyer's advocacy. Petitioner argues that the joint representation adversely affected the quality of the counsel he received in two ways: Leaphart did not negotiate a plea agreement resulting in a life sentence, and he failed to take advantage of petitioner's lesser culpability when compared with his coindictee Stevens. We find that neither argument provides a basis for relief.

a. But compare the Court's comments a year later in *Wheat v. United States,* p. 1160, infra.

"The notion that the prosecutor would have been receptive to a plea bargain is completely unsupported in the record. [As] the District Court found, Leaphart 'constantly attempted to plea bargain with the prosecutor,' but was rebuffed. 'The prosecutor's flat refusal to engage in plea bargaining is not surprising when viewed in light of the strength of the case against Burger.'

"The argument that his partner's representation of Stevens inhibited Leaphart from arguing petitioner's lesser culpability because such reliance would be prejudicial to Stevens is also unsupported by the record. Such an argument might have been more persuasive if the two defendants had been tried together. As the State conducted the prosecutions, however, each defendant's confession was used in his trial but neither was used against the coindictee. Because the trials were separate, Leaphart would have had no particular reason for concern about the possible impact of the tactics in petitioner's trial on the outcome of Stevens' trial."

BLACKMUN, J., joined by Brennan and Marshall, JJ., dissented:

"[This] Court recognizes the unique nature of claims that arise out of a conflict of interest and does not impose on such claims the two-prong standard of inadequate performance and prejudice that applies to general claims of ineffective assistance. Instead, prejudice is presumed if a defendant demonstrates that his attorney " 'actively represented conflicting interests' and that "an actual conflict of interest adversely affected his lawyer's performance.' " *Strickland,* quoting *Cuyler.* * * *

"It is difficult to imagine a more direct conflict than existed here, where counsel was preparing the appellate brief for petitioner at the same time that he was preparing the appellate brief for Stevens, and where the state statute specifies that one of the roles of that appellate process is to consider the comparative culpability and sentences of defendants involved in similar crimes. Counsel's abandonment of the lesser-culpability argument on appeal, the stage at which the two cases would be reviewed contemporaneously, is indicative of the 'struggle to serve two masters.' This record *compels* a finding that counsel's representation of the conflicting interests of petitioner and Stevens had an adverse effect on his performance as petitioner's counsel."[a]

Does *Burger* indicate that in a multiple representation case a court may skip over a determination of whether an actual conflict exists and start with an examination of what counsel did (or did not do) and why? If the court determines that the action challenged as adverse and reflecting a conflict was actually taken in defendant's interest, should it then find that no actual conflict existed? See CRIMPROC § 11.9.

4. *When should the trial judge "reasonably know" that a conflict exists? Cuyler* held that, absent an objection by counsel or defendant, an inquiry was not required "[u]nless the trial court knows or reasonably should know that a particular conflict exists." What information would place a trial judge in a position where she "reasonably should know" that a conflict exists? Consider *Wood v. Georgia,* 450 U.S. 261, 101 S.Ct. 1097, 67 L.Ed.2d 220 (1981). Both at the trial which led to their conviction and at the hearing revoking their probation petitioners' counsel was paid by their employer. In the course of vacating the judgment

a. Powell, J. joined by Brennan, J.,wrote a separate dissent. He would reverse "on the ground that counsel unreasonably failed to investigate and present to the sentencing jury available mitigating evidence that would have raised a substantial question whether the sentence of death should have been imposed on a seriously backward minor."

with instructions to hold a hearing to determine whether a conflict of interest actually existed at the time of the probation revocation or earlier, the Court, per Powell, J., observed that "the record [demonstrates] that the *possibility* of a conflict of interest was sufficiently apparent at the time of the revocation hearing to impose upon the court a duty to inquire further." All of the relevant facts relating to the employer's retention of counsel, the employer's failure to pay petitioners' fines (which led to the revocation of probation), and "counsel's insistence upon pressing a constitutional attack rather than making the arguments for leniency" were known to the trial court. Any doubts were "dispelled by the fact that the state raised the conflict problem explicitly and requested that the court look into it."

Responding to the dissent's claim that its ruling went beyond *Cuyler,* the Court observed: "[N]othing in [*Cuyler*] rules out the raising of a conflict-of-interest problem that is apparent in the record. Moreover, [*Cuyler*] *mandates* a reversal when the trial court has failed to make an inquiry even though 'it knows or reasonably should know that a particular conflict exists.' "

5.   *The "affirmative inquiry" approach.* What is the trial judge's responsibility if she does not know and should not reasonably know that a conflict exists? Before the enactment of Fed.R.Crim.P. 44(c), a number of federal courts had adopted an "affirmative inquiry" approach whereby, before appointing, or permitting multiple defendants to proceed with, a single attorney, the trial court is required to inform the defendants of the risks of conflict, to ensure that they understand these risks, and to explain to them their right to separate counsel if a conflict does or may exist. See especially *United States v. Garcia,* 517 F.2d 272 (5th Cir.1975). See generally John Stewart Geer, *Representation of Multiple Defendants,* 62 Minn.L.Rev. 119, 140–43 (1978) (hereinafter referred to as "Geer"); Steven Hyman, *Joint Representation of Multiple Defendants in a Criminal Trial,* 5 Hofstra L.Rev. 315, 320–24 (1977) (hereinafter referred to as "Hyman"); Gary Lowenthal, *Joint Representation in Criminal Cases,* 64 Va.L.Rev. 939, 980–83 (1978) (hereinafter referred to as "Lowenthal"); Peter Tague, *Multiple Representation and Conflicts of Interest in Criminal Cases,* 67 Geo.L.J. 1075, 1088–91 (1979) (hereinafter referred to as "Tague").[a]

According to Lowenthal 981, if the trial court meets its "affirmative inquiry" responsibilities, and the multiple defendants choose to proceed with shared counsel, "the reviewing court places a 'heavy burden' on a defendant seeking to overturn his conviction to show that an actual conflict of interest appears in the record. On the other hand, if the trial court makes no affirmative inquiry, the government bears the burden on appeal of demonstrating that a prejudicial conflict of interest was improbable." But cf. Tague at 1089 ("affirmative inquiry" courts "disagree dramatically with respect to the burden required to prove that a conflict warrants reversal").

6.   *Is the "affirmative inquiry" approach an effective way to deal with conflict of interest problems?* Is the "affirmative inquiry" approach likely

---

a.   Fed.R.Crim.P. 44(c) is similar to the "affirmative inquiry" approach:

"Whenever two or more defendants have been jointly charged [or] have been joined for trial [and] are represented by the same retained or assigned counsel or by retained or assigned counsel who are associated in the practice of law, the court shall promptly inquire with respect to such joint representation and shall personally advise each defendant of his right to the effective assistance of counsel, including separate representation. Unless it appears that there is good cause to believe no conflict of interest is likely to arise, the court shall take such measures as may be appropriate to protect each defendant's right to counsel."

For a hard look at proposed (and subsequently adopted) Rule 44(c), extensive criticism of it and suggested changes, see Tague at 1092–1130.

to solve conflict of interest problems or is it merely a way for *reviewing* courts to *avoid facing* these problems? Are abstract cautions to defendants likely to be meaningful unless related to the specific problems that may arise in their particular case? How often will a judge be able to make a useful *pretrial* assessment of the possibilities for conflict? Consider Geer at 141–42: "At the start of the trial, the judge will not know the defenses to be raised on behalf of each defendant, the potential defenses to be foregone, the weight and sufficiency of the evidence to be adduced against each defendant, or each defendant's personal history and past criminal record. Without such information, the trial judge cannot impress upon a defendant the significance of waiver, nor can he evaluate the defendant's appreciation of it."

Does the privilege against self-incrimination and the attorney-client privilege severely restrict the trial judge's ability to obtain information by inquiry? Even if the trial judge could identify a potential conflict of interest and so warn the defendants, would "the social and economic pressures on defendants to share counsel—at least at the beginning of a criminal case—dilute the effectiveness of [the] warnings"? Moreover, does retained counsel have "a strong economic incentive to minimize the risk of a conflict of interest when discussing a trial court's warning with his clients"? See Lowenthal at 981–83. But cf. Hyman at 320–21.

7. *Should joint representation in criminal cases be absolutely prohibited?* Because "the potential conflict of interest in representing multiple defendants is so grave," *A.B.A. Standards* § 4–3.5(b) provides that "ordinarily" a lawyer should decline to represent multiple defendants "except in unusual situations when, after careful investigation, it is *clear* that no conflict is likely to develop" (emphasis added), and then only when "the several defendants give an informed consent to such multiple representation; and [the consent] is made a matter of judicial record." Given the many ways in which a conflict of interest may arise at various stages of the criminal process, can it *ever* be *clear* that a single attorney can adequately represent multiple criminal defendants?

According to one study, most public defender offices have a general policy against representing multiple defendants in a criminal case and about half "follow a policy of *never* representing more than one defendant in multiple defendant cases." Lowenthal at 950. This opposition to joint representation is based primarily on a "widespread belief that the interests of the codefendants will conflict in virtually every case, requiring the lawyer to choose a course favorable to one defendant that necessarily is detrimental to another." Id. at 952. Because they are convinced that conflict of interest is "generally inherent" or "inevitable" in the defense of multiple defendants, some commentators have proposed that ethical standards be interpreted, or revised, to prohibit any attorney from representing more than one defendant in a criminal case. See Geer at 157–62; Lowenthal at 983–89; *Developments—Conflicts of Interest in the Legal Profession,* 94 Harv. L.Rev. 1244, 1395–96 (1981).

But consider Ephraim Margolin & Sandra Coliver, *Pretrial Disqualification of Criminal Defense Counsel,* 20 Am.Crim.L.Rev. 227, 253 (1982): "Enforcement of a 'one client, one lawyer' rule would result in fundamental unfairness. Clients, even those with common defenses and interests, would be prohibited from pooling their resources to retain joint counsel. This denial would subject them to the unnecessary cost of separate attorneys and could lower the quality of representation if their pooled assets would purchase better representation. [Moreover,] if defendants of means are required to retain their own individual lawyers, indigent defendants clearly will have to be supplied with separate appointed counsel. This would place a high price tag on the 'one client, one lawyer' requirement."

8. *Would a categorical rule forbidding joint representation of code-fendants deprive a defendant of his constitutional right to representation by the attorney of his choice?* Does a defendant have such a constitutional right? Yes, answer Margolin & Coliver, supra, at 250–51; "[j]ust as the courts must honor a request to proceed without counsel, they must respect the defendant's waiver of conflict-free counsel." But consider Geer at 158–60: "In *Faretta* the Court found an *independent* right of self-representation and stated that it did not arise mechanically from a defendant's power to waive the right to assistance of counsel. See [*Faretta* at fn. 15 and accompanying text]. Thus, if an accused has a sixth amendment right to be represented by counsel of his choice, that right must arise independently; the power to waive assistance of counsel does not in itself imply a right to constitutionally defective legal assistance.

"There is, however, no such independent, absolute right to counsel of choice. [An] indigent defendant, for example, does not have an absolute right to be assigned counsel of his choice. [N]o defendant may select an attorney in a manner that will obstruct the administration of the judicial process or frustrate the judicial function [and] courts have consistently spurned defendants' constitutional arguments that they have a sixth amendment right to be represented by laymen [or] attorneys who have been disbarred. Thus, there are many limitations upon the ability of a defendant to choose counsel under current law. [A disciplinary rule prohibiting an attorney from representing multiple criminal defendants] simply imposes one more * * *."

9. *Imposing separate counsel over a defendant's objection.*

WHEAT v. UNITED STATES
486 U.S. 153, 108 S.Ct. 1692, 100 L.Ed.2d 140 (1988).

Chief Justice REHNQUIST delivered the opinion of the Court.

[Petitioner, along with numerous codefendants, including Gomez–Barajas and Bravo, was charged with participating in a far-flung drug conspiracy. Both Gomez–Barajas and Bravo were represented by attorney Eugene Iredale. Gomez–Barajas was tried first and was acquitted on drug charges overlapping with those against petitioner. To avoid a second trial on other charges, Gomez–Barajas offered to plead guilty to certain offenses stemming from the conspiracy. At the commencement of petitioner's trial, the district court had not yet accepted the plea of Gomez–Barajas; thus he was free to withdraw his plea and proceed to trial. Bravo pled guilty.

[At the conclusion of Bravo's guilty plea proceedings and two court days before his trial was to commence, petitioner moved for the substitution of Iredale as his counsel as well. The government objected on the ground that Iredale's representation of the two other codefendants created a serious conflict of interest: (1) In the event that Gomez–Barajas's plea and the sentencing arrangement negotiated between him and the government were rejected by the court, petitioner was likely to be called as a witness for the prosecution at Gomez–Barajas's trial. This scenario would pose a conflict of interest for Iredale, who would be prevented from cross-examining petitioner and thereby from effectively representing Gomez–Barajas. (2) In the likely event that Bravo was called as a witness for the prosecution against petitioner, ethical proscriptions would prevent Iredale from cross-examining Bravo in any meaningful way. Thus, Iredale would be unable to provide petitioner with effective assistance of counsel.

[In response, petitioner emphasized his right to have counsel of his own choosing and his willingness, and the willingness of the other codefendants, to waive the right to conflict-free counsel. Moreover, maintained petitioner, the circumstances posited by the government that would create a conflict of interest were highly speculative and bore no connection to the true relationship among the co-conspirators. If called to testify against petitioner, Bravo would simply say that he did not know petitioner and had had no dealings with him. In the unlikely event that Gomez–Barajas went to trial, petitioner's lack of involvement in his alleged crimes made his appearance as a witness highly improbable. According to petitioner, the government was "manufacturing implausible conflicts" in an attempt to disqualify Iredale, who had already proved extremely effective in representing the other codefendants.

[The district court denied petitioner's request to substitute Iredale as his attorney, concluding, on the basis of the representation of the government, that it "really has no choice at this point other than to find that an irreconcilable conflict of interest exists." Petitioner proceeded to trial with his original counsel and was convicted of various drug offenses. The Court of Appeals for the Ninth Circuit affirmed.]

[While] the right to select and be represented by one's preferred attorney is comprehended by the Sixth Amendment, the essential aim of the Amendment is to guarantee an effective advocate for each criminal defendant rather than to ensure that a defendant will inexorably be represented by the lawyer whom he prefers.

The Sixth Amendment right to choose one's own counsel is circumscribed in several important respects. Regardless of his persuasive powers, an advocate who is not a member of the bar may not represent clients (other than himself) in court.[3] Similarly, a defendant may not insist on representation by an attorney he cannot afford or who for other reasons declines to represent the defendant. Nor may a defendant insist on the counsel of an attorney who has a previous or ongoing relationship with an opposing party, even when the opposing party is the Government. The question raised in this case is the extent to which a criminal defendant's right under the Sixth Amendment to his chosen attorney is qualified by the fact that the attorney has represented other defendants charged in the same criminal conspiracy.

[Petitioner] insists that the provision of waivers by all affected defendants cures any problems created by the multiple representation. But no such flat rule can be deduced from the Sixth Amendment presumption in favor of counsel of choice. Federal courts have an independent interest in ensuring that criminal trials are conducted within the ethical standards of the profession and that legal proceedings appear fair to all who observe them. Both the American Bar Association's Model Code of Professional Responsibility and its Model Rules of Professional Conduct, as well as the rules of the California Bar Association (which governed the attorneys in this case), impose limitations on multiple representation of clients. Not only the interest of a criminal defendant but the institutional interest in the rendition of just verdicts in criminal cases may be jeopardized by unregulated multiple representation.

For this reason, the Federal Rules of Criminal Procedure direct trial judges to investigate specially cases involving joint representation. In pertinent part, Rule 44(c) provides:

> "[T]he court shall promptly inquire with respect to such joint representation and shall personally advise each defendant of his right to the effective assistance of counsel, including separate representation. Unless it appears that there is good cause to believe no conflict of interest is likely to arise, the

---

3. Our holding in *Faretta* that a criminal defendant has a Sixth Amendment right to represent *himself* if he voluntarily elects to do so, does not encompass the right to choose any advocate if the defendant wishes to be represented by counsel.

court shall take such measures as may be appropriate to protect each defendant's right to counsel."

Although Rule 44(c) does not specify what particular measures may be taken by a district court, one option suggested by the Notes of the Advisory Committee is an order by the court that the defendants be separately represented in subsequent proceedings in the case. This suggestion comports with our instructions in *Holloway* and in *Glasser* that the trial courts, when alerted by objection from one of the parties, have an independent duty to ensure that criminal defendants receive a trial that is fair and does not contravene the Sixth Amendment.

To be sure, this need to investigate potential conflicts arises in part from the legitimate wish of district courts that their judgments remain intact on appeal. As the Court of Appeals accurately pointed out, trial courts confronted with multiple representations face the prospect of being "whip-sawed" by assertions of error no matter which way they rule. If a district court agrees to the multiple representation, and the advocacy of counsel is thereafter impaired as a result, the defendant may well claim that he did not receive effective assistance. On the other hand, a district court's refusal to accede to the multiple representation may result in a challenge such as petitioner's in this case. Nor does a waiver by the defendant necessarily solve the problem, for we note, without passing judgment on, the apparent willingness of Courts of Appeals to entertain ineffective assistance claims from defendants who have specifically waived the right to conflict-free counsel.

Thus, where a court justifiably finds an actual conflict of interest, there can be no doubt that it may decline a proffer of waiver, and insist that defendants be separately represented. * * *

Unfortunately for all concerned, a district court must pass on the issue of whether or not to allow a waiver of a conflict of interest by a criminal defendant not with the wisdom of hindsight after the trial has taken place, but the murkier pretrial context when relationships between parties are seen through a glass, darkly. The likelihood and dimensions of nascent conflicts of interest are notoriously hard to predict, even for those thoroughly familiar with criminal trials. It is a rare attorney who will be fortunate enough to learn the entire truth from his own client, much less be fully apprised before trial of what each of the Government's witnesses will say on the stand. A few bits of unforeseen testimony or a single previously unknown or unnoticed document may significantly shift the relationship between multiple defendants. These imponderables are difficult enough for a lawyer to assess, and even more difficult to convey by way of explanation to a criminal defendant untutored in the niceties of legal ethics. Nor is it amiss to observe that the willingness of an attorney to obtain such waivers from his clients may bear an inverse relation to the care with which he conveys all the necessary information to them.[a]

For these reasons we think the District Court must be allowed substantial latitude in refusing waivers of conflicts of interest not only in those rare cases where an actual conflict may be demonstrated before trial, but in the more common cases where a potential for conflict exists which may or may not burgeon into an actual conflict as the trial progresses. In the circumstances of this case, with the motion for substitution of counsel made so close to the time of trial, the District Court relied on instinct and judgment based on experience in making its decision. We do not think it can be said that the court exceeded the broad latitude which must be accorded it in making this decision. Petitioner of course rightly points out that the government may seek to "manufacture" a conflict in order to

---

a. But compare the Court's statement a year earlier in *Burger v. Kemp,* p. 1155, supra, that "we generally presume that the lawyer is fully conscious of the overarching duty of complete loyalty to his or her clients."

prevent a defendant from having a particularly able defense counsel at his side; but trial courts are undoubtedly aware of this possibility, and must take it into consideration along with all of the other factors which inform this sort of a decision.

Here the District Court was confronted not simply with an attorney who wished to represent two coequal defendants in a straightforward criminal prosecution; rather, Iredale proposed to defend three conspirators of varying stature in a complex drug distribution scheme. The Government intended to call Bravo as a witness for the prosecution at petitioner's trial.[4] The Government might readily have tied certain deliveries of marijuana by Bravo to petitioner, necessitating vigorous cross-examination of Bravo by petitioner's counsel. Iredale, because of his prior representation of Bravo, would have been unable ethically to provide that cross-examination.

Iredale had also represented Gomez–Barajas, one of the alleged kingpins of the distribution ring, and had succeeded in obtaining a verdict of acquittal for him. Gomez–Barajas had agreed with the Government to plead guilty to other charges, but the District Court had not yet accepted the plea arrangement. If the agreement were rejected, petitioner's probable testimony at the resulting trial of Gomez–Barajas would create an ethical dilemma for Iredale from which one or the other of his clients would likely suffer.

Viewing the situation as it did before trial, we hold that the District Court's refusal to permit the substitution of counsel in this case was within its discretion and did not violate petitioner's Sixth Amendment rights. Other district courts might have reached differing or opposite conclusions with equal justification, but that does not mean that one conclusion was "right" and the other "wrong." The District Court must recognize a presumption in favor of petitioner's counsel of choice, but that presumption may be overcome not only by a demonstration of actual conflict but by a showing of a serious potential for conflict. The evaluation [of the] circumstances of each case under this standard must be left primarily to the informed judgment of the trial court. * * *

Justice MARSHALL, with whom Justice BRENNAN joins, dissenting.

[I] disagree [with] the Court's suggestion that the trial court's decision as to whether a potential conflict justifies rejection of a defendant's chosen counsel is entitled to some kind of special deference on appeal. The Court grants trial courts "broad latitude" over the decision to accept or reject a defendant's choice of counsel; although never explicitly endorsing a standard of appellate review, the Court appears to limit such review to determining whether an abuse of discretion has occurred. [This approach] accords neither with the nature of the trial court's decision nor with the importance of the interest at stake.

[The] interest at stake in this kind of decision is nothing less than a criminal defendant's Sixth Amendment right to counsel of his choice. The trial court simply does not have "broad latitude" to vitiate this right. In my view, a trial court that rejects a criminal defendant's chosen counsel on the ground of a potential conflict should make findings on the record to facilitate review, and an appellate court should scrutinize closely the basis for the trial court's decision. Only in this way can a criminal defendant's right to counsel of his choice be appropriately protected.

The Court's resolution of the instant case flows from its deferential approach to the District Court's denial of petitioner's motion to add or substitute counsel; absent deference, a decision upholding the District Court's ruling would be

---

4. Bravo was in fact called as a witness at petitioner's trial. His testimony was elicited to demonstrate the transportation of drugs that the prosecution hoped to link to petitioner.

inconceivable. Indeed, I believe that even under the Court's deferential standard, reversal is in order.

[At] the time of petitioner's trial, Iredale's representation of Gomez–Barajas was effectively completed. * * * Gomez–Barajas was not scheduled to appear as a witness at petitioner's trial; thus, Iredale's conduct of that trial would not require him to question his former client. The only possible conflict this Court can divine from Iredale's representation of both petitioner and Gomez–Barajas rests on the premise that the trial court would reject the negotiated plea agreement and that Gomez–Barajas then would decide to go to trial. In this event, the Court tells us, "petitioner's probable testimony at the resulting trial of Gomez–Barajas would create an ethical dilemma for Iredale."

This argument rests on speculation of the most dubious kind. The Court offers no reason to think that the trial court would have rejected Gomez–Barajas's plea agreement; neither did the Government posit any such reason in its argument or brief before this Court. The most likely occurrence at the time petitioner moved to retain Iredale as his defense counsel was that the trial court would accept Gomez–Barajas's plea agreement, as the court in fact later did. Moreover, even if Gomez–Barajas had gone to trial, petitioner probably would not have testified. [The] only alleged connection between petitioner and Gomez–Barajas sprang from the conspiracy to distribute marijuana, and a jury already had acquitted Gomez–Barajas of that charge. It is therefore disingenuous to say that representation of both petitioner and Gomez–Barajas posed a serious potential for a conflict of interest.

Similarly, Iredale's prior representation of Bravo was not a cause for concern. * * * Contrary to the Court's inference, Bravo could not have testified about petitioner's involvement in the alleged marijuana distribution scheme. As all parties were aware at the time, Bravo did not know and could not identify petitioner; indeed, prior to the commencement of legal proceedings, the two men never had heard of each other. Bravo's eventual testimony at petitioner's trial related to a shipment of marijuana in which petitioner was not involved; the testimony contained not a single reference to petitioner. Petitioner's counsel did not cross-examine Bravo, and neither petitioner's counsel nor the prosecutor mentioned Bravo's testimony in closing argument. All of these developments were predictable when the District Court ruled on petitioner's request that Iredale serve as trial counsel; the contours of Bravo's testimony were clear at that time. Given the insignificance of this testimony to any matter that petitioner's counsel would dispute, the proposed joint representation of petitioner and Bravo did not threaten a conflict of interest.

Moreover, even assuming that Bravo's testimony might have "necessitat[ed] vigorous cross-examination," the District Court could have insured against the possibility of any conflict of interest without wholly depriving petitioner of his constitutional right to the counsel of his choice. Petitioner's motion requested that Iredale either be substituted for petitioner's current counsel or be added to petitioner's defense team. Had the District Court allowed the addition of Iredale and then ordered that he take no part in the cross-examination of Bravo, any possibility of a conflict would have been removed. Especially in light of the availability of this precautionary measure, the notion that Iredale's prior representation of Bravo might well have caused a conflict of interest at petitioner's trial is nothing short of ludicrous. * * *

Justice STEVENS, with whom Justice BLACKMUN joins, dissenting.

[The] Court gives inadequate weight to the informed and voluntary character of the clients' waiver of their right to conflict-free representation. Particularly, the Court virtually ignores the fact that the additional counsel representing petitioner had provided him with sound advice concerning the wisdom of a waiver and would have remained available during the trial to assist in the defense. Thus, [the] question before [the District Judge] was whether petitioner should be permitted to have *additional* counsel of his choice. I agree with Justice Marshall that the answer to that question is perfectly clear.

Notes and Questions

(a) *Taking into account the possibility that the government may seek to "manufacture" a conflict of interest.* The *Wheat* majority assures us that trial courts are "undoubtedly aware of," and "must take [into] consideration," the possibility that "the government may seek to 'manufacture' a conflict of interest" in order to prevent a defendant from being represented by an especially able lawyer. But *how* are trial courts supposed to take this possibility into consideration?

Can trial courts be expected to accuse the prosecution of "bad faith" when it represents that defendant's choice of counsel creates a serious potential for conflict? Consider that in *Wheat* itself, although recognizing that Iredale had proved extremely effective in representing another codefendant, the district court denied Wheat's motion because "based upon the representation of the Government [the] Court really has no choice [other] than to find that an irreconcilable conflict of interest exists."

(b) *Transforming the Sixth Amendment into an additional weapon for the prosecution.* Consider Note, 102 Harv.L.Rev. 143, 187–88 (1988):

"By allowing the government successfully to oppose Wheat's attempted waiver on the basis of institutional concerns external to Wheat, the Court in effect vested the right to conflict-free defense counsel in the state as well as in Wheat. * * * Recognizing such a right transforms the sixth amendment, presumably a shield to help criminal defendants receive fair treatment in their battle against a more powerful adversary, into an additional weapon for their prosecutors to use against them. The state might now intentionally manufacture conflicts in order to disqualify a particularly formidable opposing attorney.[55] Indeed, the relative insignificance of Bravo's testimony against Wheat, the late date at which the government expressed interest in that testimony, and the success of Iredale in representing Wheat's alleged co-conspirators together suggest that Wheat's prosecutor succeeded in doing just that."

(c) *Explaining Wheat.* "One might try to explain *Wheat* as nothing more than a paternalistic attempt to protect Iredale's clients against their own irrationality," but, observes William J. Stuntz, *Waiving Rights in Criminal Procedure,* 75 Va.L.Rev. 761, 798 (1989), "that approach to the case seems strained," especially in a large-scale conspiracy case like *Wheat,* where the defendants are often more sophisticated and better educated than criminal defendants generally. Continues Professor Stuntz, id. at 798–800:

"In *Wheat,* there are two reasons why the coconspirators might have wished to use Iredale as common counsel. The first, offered by the defendants, is unobjectionable: the defendants believed Iredale to be a very good attorney, better than the likely alternatives. But the second is troubling. If the three defendants in question were guilty, they may well have faced a classic prisoners' dilemma: it may have been in each individual's interest to 'sell out' to the government and implicate his colleagues, but may have been far better for all if all either lied or remained silent. Common counsel may have removed the dilemma by facilitating

---

55. Although the Court ordered district courts to consider such a possibility in ruling on waivers, it failed to explore that possibility in *Wheat* itself.

the enforcement of an agreement not to finger each other. Obtaining the testimony of one conspirator against others may require careful negotiation with the would-be witness. If all the conspirators have the same lawyer, the government is, in effect, able to deal with one defendant only by dealing with all. One cannot be absolutely certain whether the codefendants wanted a common lawyer for good reasons or bad, but there is a fairly good proxy for that determination. If an objective observer familiar with the local bar would have concluded that Iredale was not any better than the lawyers who might have taken his place, then the defendants' motive for retaining him seems suspect. The district judge was in a good position to make that judgment.[116] The ability of district judges to make case-by-case assessments of defendants' counsel of choice may be why the Court left the matter in the district courts' discretion, rather than promulgate a blanket rule either barring or allowing waiver."

(d) *When a defense attorney cross-examines a former client.* Did the *Wheat* Court fail to recognize that the type of conflict envisioned by the trial judge would have been far less significant than the conflicts arising out of the representation of multiple defendants at joint or successive trials? Yes, answers Bruce A. Green, *"Through a Glass, Darkly": How the Court Sees Motions to Disqualify Criminal Defense Lawyers,* 89 Colum.L.Rev. 1201, 1215–16, 1221–22 (1989):

"*Wheat* was not a case in which defense counsel would represent codefendants at trial. It was a case in which, at worst, defense counsel would simultaneously represent a defendant and a government witness, since the government's case against two of attorney Iredale's three clients was essentially over and only Wheat was still awaiting trial. * * *

"Because Wheat was the only client awaiting trial, the most significant ethical concern identified in *Wheat* was the possibility that, if codefendant Bravo's testimony was to tie Wheat to particular deliveries of marijuana, attorney Iredale 'would have been unable ethically to provide' the vigorous cross-examination that would have been needed to impeach Bravo. This was essentially the same problem that typically arises when a defense attorney is called upon to cross-examine a former, rather than a current client. [Under] the prevailing professional standards, a potential conflict arising out of the need to cross-examine a former client is appropriately deemed less serious than a conflict arising out of the joint representation of codefendants. * * *

"In light of the nature of the potential conflict in *Wheat* and the manner in which it is addressed by the prevailing ethical standards, the district judge in that case had no basis for concluding that, if Bravo were to be a government witness at Wheat's trial, Iredale's representation of Wheat would violate the prevailing ethical norms. To begin with, the trial judge had no reason to believe that Iredale had received confidential disclosures which Iredale would have to bend over backwards to avoid using in cross-examining Bravo. Moreover, as Justice Marshall noted in his dissent, Iredale could have permitted cocounsel to cross-examine Bravo, while himself conducting the remainder of the trial. Had Iredale agreed not to reveal Bravo's confidences to his cocounsel, this would have eliminated any possible conflict.

"Even if Iredale were called upon to cross-examine Bravo, the clients' consent to the potential conflict would have eliminated the ethical barrier to the representation, notwithstanding Iredale's possession of confidences that needed to be

---

116. In some cases, defendants will have an interest in retaining common counsel because their case is factually complex, and the costs of bringing individual counsel up to speed would be high. As with the possibility that counsel is exceptionally skilled, the district judge is well situated to determine whether a particular case involves large economies of scale in legal representation.

preserved. [The] professional standards applicable in California, like the Model Code and the Model Rules, allowed the representation of conflicting interests with client consent. Moreover, unlike cases involving joint representation at trial, the consent in this case would have eliminated not only the ethical barrier, but the conflict itself. By authorizing Iredale to make use of his confidences, or at least to err on the side of using them, Bravo would have eliminated any danger to Wheat's defense. At the same time, Wheat could have agreed that, insofar as possible, Iredale's cross-examination of Bravo would be based only on nonconfidential matters * * *.

"Thus, the *Wheat* decision is bottomed on the Court's misunderstanding of the ethical rules. [The] Court upheld the denial of Wheat's choice of counsel in a case where the ethical rules plainly would have permitted that choice."

(e) ***Wheat and Faretta.*** Does *Faretta* provide strong support for the argument that when a criminal defendant decides to be represented by an attorney who has a potential conflict of interest, respect for the defendant's autonomy should lead a court to uphold that decision? Consider Green, supra, at 1236–38:

"In *Faretta*, the Court determined that a defendant is entitled to respect for one of the most fundamental, yet most controversial, decisions relating to one's defense—the decision to represent oneself. The decision to be represented by an attorney with a conflict of interest would seem to reflect an equally fundamental choice. Thus, prior to *Wheat*, a number of lower courts had concluded that proper respect for the defendants' dignity and autonomy demanded that the defendant's waiver of conflict-of-interest claims be upheld. [Yet] the *Wheat* Court did not acknowledge the lower court decisions that relied on *Faretta*, and it made virtually no mention of *Faretta* itself. The Court did not consider at all the dignitary interests underlying both the right of self-representation and the qualified right to counsel of choice; and it did not even remark on the more than superficial anomaly that a defendant should be allowed to waive the right to an attorney altogether, but not to waive the comparatively less important right to an attorney whose loyalties are undivided."

But consider Stuntz, supra, at 801: "[*Wheat*] suggests that although the right to counsel may in fact protect the innocent and guilty alike, the latter may receive their benefits as a means of protecting the former—and hence solely to the extent necessary to protect the former. It follows that the pattern of the self-representation cases is misleading. [They] do not squarely present the central difficulty of the right to counsel—the fact that defense counsel increase the difficulty of convicting not only the innocent but the guilty as well. In cases [like] *Faretta*, where the issue is whether a defendant's pretrial decision to forego counsel is to be given effect, one cannot protect the interests of the innocent without protecting the guilty as well, and the waiver rules predictably seek to maximize all defendants' enjoyment of the right. When these two groups are separable, as in *Wheat*, waiver doctrine appears to seek to accomplish the very different goal of maximizing the protection of one group while minimizing protection of the other."

10. ***Which standard applies to attorney breaches of loyalty outside the multiple representation context—Cuyler or Strickland?*** Consider BEETS v. SCOTT, 65 F.3d 1258 (5th Cir.1995) (*en banc*). After defendant's conviction for capital murder of her husband, she sought federal habeas relief, claiming ineffective assistance of counsel based on (1) a transfer, shortly after the trial commenced, of all her literary and media rights in the case to her lawyer's son; (2) a failure of defendant's lawyer to withdraw as counsel and to testify as a material witness. Does *Strickland* apply in such situations or *Cuyler*, which sets a lower threshold for overturning a conviction than does *Strickland*? In *Beets*, a 13–

5 majority of the Seventh Circuit, per EDITH JONES, J., held that *Strickland* offers a "superior framework" for addressing "attorney self-interest conflicts":

"Although the federal circuit courts have unblinkingly applied *Cuyler*'s 'actual conflict' and 'adverse effect' standards to all kinds of alleged attorney ethical conflicts, a careful reading of the Supreme Court cases belies this expansiveness. Neither *Cuyler* nor its progeny strayed beyond the ethical problems of multiple representation. * * *

"If *Cuyler*'s more rigid rule applies to attorney breaches of loyalty outside the multiple representation context, *Strickland*'s desirable and necessary uniform standard of constitutional ineffectiveness will be challenged. Recharacterization of ineffectiveness claims to duty of loyalty claims will be tempting because of *Cuyler*'s lesser standard of prejudice. A blurring of the *Strickland* standard is highly undesirable. [The] focus of Sixth Amendment claims would tend to shift mischievously from the overall fairness of the criminal proceedings—the goal of 'prejudice' analysis—to slurs on counsel's integrity—the 'conflict' analysis. Confining *Cuyler* to multiple representation claims poses no similar threat to *Strickland*.[a]

Dissenting Judge KING, joined by four other judges, disagreed with what he called "the majority's unprecedented decision to limit the rule of *Cuyler* to cases involving multiple or serial representation":

"[The majority] thereby excludes from the ambit of *Cuyler* an exceptional conflict between an attorney's self-interest and his client's interest stemming from a highly particularized and powerfully focused source, a media rights contract. If we reserve *Cuyler* for extraordinary attorney-client conflicts of that sort, not normally encountered in law practice, and we apply *Strickland* to alleged deficiencies in an attorney's performance having their sources in the more common incidents of the attorney-client relationship, we avoid having the *Cuyler* exception swallow the *Strickland* rule. At the same time we preserve the benefit of the *Cuyler* inquiry for those exceptional cases that lie at the heart of the principles animating it."[b]

SECTION 5. THE ROLE OF APPOINTED COUNSEL

If court appointed counsel believes an appeal should not be filed because it lacks any merit, how should she proceed? ANDERS v. CALIFORNIA, 386 U.S. 738, 87 S.Ct. 1396, 18 L.Ed.2d 493 (1967), per CLARK, J., held a "no-merit

---

a. Applying *Strickland*, the Court concluded that petitioner was not prejudiced by either one of her lawyer's alleged two ethical breaches: "While the media rights contract posed a serious potential conflict of interest, [petitioner] failed to show how it hindered [her lawyer's] presentation of her defense or prejudiced her by rendering the result of her criminal prosecution fundamentally unreliable." As for her lawyer's other alleged ethical breach, his "potential testimony for [petitioner] was cumulative, he was not a necessary witness for her defense and did not face substantial advocate/witness conflict. His failure to withdraw and testify was not professionally unreasonable under *Strickland*."

b. Although the majority concluded that even if attorney conflicts of interest, apart from the multiple representation context, were governed by the *Cuyler* standard, petitioner's

claim would fail, the dissenters saw the matter differently:

"Under *Cuyler*, relief is proper * * * when a defendant 'demonstrates that an actual conflict of interest adversely affected his lawyer's performance.' In the instant case, [the defense lawyer] was faced with an actual conflict because, while [petitioner's] interest lay in having [her lawyer] withdraw and testify, [his] interest lay in remaining as her counsel, because only then would he be entitled to the potentially lucrative media rights. Additionally, because [her lawyer] did not withdraw and testify, [petitioner's] representation was adversely affected. A Sixth Amendment violation will be shown if the district court concludes that the conflict was the cause of [the lawyer's] failure to withdraw and testify. I would vacate the district court's judgment and remand with instructions to resolve that issue."

letter"—counsel had stated in a letter to the state appellate court that he would not file a brief because he was "of the opinion that there is no merit to the appeal"—insufficient because it "affords neither the client nor the court any aid. The former must shift entirely for himself while the court has only the cold record which it must review without the help of an advocate." If, after a "conscientious examination" of his case, counsel finds an appeal to be "wholly frivolous," he should so advise the court and request permission to withdraw. "That request must, however, be accompanied by a brief referring to anything in the record that might arguably support the appeal. A copy of counsel's brief should be furnished the indigent and time allowed him to raise any points that he chooses; the court— not counsel—then proceeds, after a full examination of all the proceedings, to decide whether the case is wholly frivolous. If it so finds it may grant counsel's request to withdraw and dismiss the appeal insofar as federal requirements are concerned, or proceed to a decision on the merits, if state law so requires. On the other hand, if it finds any of the legal points arguable on their merits (and therefore not frivolous) it must, prior to decision, afford the indigent the assistance of counsel to argue the appeal."

Dissenting Justice STEWART, joined by Black and Harlan, JJ., expressed puzzlement as to why an appointed lawyer who considers an appeal "wholly frivolous" should be required to file "a brief reference to anything in the record that might arguably support the appeal." "[I]f the record did present any such 'arguable' issues, the appeal would not be frivolous and counsel would not have filed a 'non-merit' letter in the first place."

See also *Suggs v. United States,* 391 F.2d 971 (D.C.Cir.1968) (Leventhal, J.), stressing that appointed counsel should not ask to withdraw "unless in the same circumstances he would insist on withdrawal if he had been retained. As a general rule, the court will be greatly aided if appointed counsel remains in a case, even though he may be subjectively unimpressed with the merits of the available points." Adequate representation of an indigent appellant should include personal interviews "if in the same circumstances [they would be considered] useful or desirable were [counsel] representing a private client. Ordinarily at least one interview by counsel would appear to be useful."[a]

Notes and Questions

1. *Anders* has been sharply criticized by an assistant public defender who maintains that "it offers counsel the choice of filing a schizophrenic motion to withdraw (accompanied by a formal brief opposing the motion), or the alternative of writing the brief and not moving to withdraw. Human nature will force the selection of the latter alternative. [If tax-supported] groups of lawyers are forced to brief frivolous appeals, the people who will suffer the most are the indigent prisoners who have been *unjustly* convicted; they will languish in prison while the lawyers devote time and energy to hopeless causes on a first come-first served basis." James Doherty, *Wolf! Wolf!—The Ramifications of Frivolous Appeals,* 59 J.Crim.L.C. & P.S. 1, 2 (1968).

a. Cf. *Commonwealth v. Moffett,* 418 N.E.2d 585 (Mass.1981), prohibiting appointed counsel from withdrawing solely on the ground that the appeal is frivolous even when she files an *"Anders* brief" demonstrating that all possible arguments in favor of her client lack any merit: "As long as counsel must research and prepare an advocate's brief, he or she may as well submit it for the purpose of an ordinary appeal. Even if the appeal is frivolous, less time and energy will be spent directly reviewing the case on the merits. If the appeal is not frivolous, [prohibiting] withdrawal would also obviate any need to substitute counsel to argue the appeal." See also *State v. McKenney,* 568 P.2d 1213 (Idaho 1977) *State v. Gates,* 466 S.W.2d 681 (Mo.1971). See generally Mendelson, *Frivolous Criminal Appeals: The Anders Brief or the Idaho Rule,* 19 Crim.L.Bull. 22 (1983).

2. The egalitarian pronouncement in *Suggs* that appointed counsel should not seek to withdraw "unless in the same circumstances he would insist on withdrawal if he had been retained" has been criticized on the ground that it "glosses over the possibility that the two situations may not be comparable. It is likely that the need to pay a lawyer's fee and expenses is some deterrent to frivolous criminal appeals.[a] Retained counsel can also withdraw more readily and informally—usually by substitution of other counsel—than can assigned counsel and further, can more readily avoid prejudicing the defendant by alerting the court, and in some circuits the Government, to the weaknesses of the case." Robert Hermann, *Frivolous Criminal Appeals,* 47 N.Y.U.L.Rev. 701, 706 (1972). But compare the remarks of Judge Jack Day, *Proceedings of the National Conference on Standards for the Administration of Criminal Justice* (1972), 57 F.R.D. 303, 309 (1973): "I can never remember a case, really never, in a long life at the Bar, [where] if the money was there the appeal was so frivolous that the lawyer couldn't make it. I'm not suggesting nobody ever stood up and said grandly, 'Take away that $10,000; there's nothing to this case; I will not appeal it.' Maybe that happened, but maybe there are angels in the balcony, too. [Moreover,] there is always the probability that unless there's an excellent reason, beyond being busy, the lawyer at least ought to be told that he might try to present what the client wanted. He doesn't have to argue as his own points matters that are stupid or ridiculous, but at least there ought to be some effort made to present the point the client believes important."[b]

3. *May court-appointed appellate counsel be required to discuss why she believes her client's appeal lacks merit?* Yes, answered a 5–3 majority (Kennedy, J., not participating) in McCOY v. COURT OF APPEALS OF WISCONSIN, 486 U.S. 429, 108 S.Ct. 1895, 100 L.Ed.2d 440 (1988). A Wisconsin Supreme Court rule requires an *Anders* brief to include a discussion of why the appeal lacks merit. Court-appointed appellate counsel refused to comply with this requirement, maintaining that it would be both unethical and contrary to *Anders* to do so. The Court, per STEVENS, J., disagreed:

"[The Wisconsin rule] furthers the same interests that are served by *Anders.* Because counsel may discover previously unrecognized aspects of the law in the process of preparing a written explanation for his or her written conclusion [that the appeal is frivolous], the discussion requirement provides an additional safeguard against mistaken conclusions by counsel that the strongest arguments he or she can find are frivolous. Just like the reference to favorable aspects of the record required by *Anders,* the discussion requirement may forestall some motions to withdraw and will assist the court in passing on the soundness of the lawyer's conclusion that the appeal is frivolous. * * *

a. A major reason for "hopeless appeals," observe Paul Carrington, Daniel Meador & Maurice Rosenberg, *Justice on Appeal* 91–95 (1976), is that unlike the non-indigent convicted of crime, who has incentives *not* to appeal (he must balance benefit against cost), the indigent defendant is in "a no-lose situation, which provides every inducement to appeal, however forlorn the hope." In order to give the indigent "something to lose in the appeal similar to that which the non-indigent has," the authors propose establishing a fund, supplied out of tax money, that will cause the indigent to decide, with the aid of counsel, "whether there are any appealable issues that make the appeal worthwhile when balanced against the economic loss that will be involved." The indi-

gent would be given an option: "he could purchase his appeal at public expense (as he can now) or he could elect instead to take a specified amount of money from the fund [at least several hundred dollars], either for himself [or for] persons he would designate [e.g., his spouse, children or bona fide creditors]. This plan would force the defendant to think about his case as a non-indigent must."

b. See also Carrington, et al., fn. a supra at 77: "Several judges have reported to us the disheartening experience of reversing convictions after appointed counsel has filed an 'Anders' brief explaining that his client's cause was entirely hopeless."

"We also do not find that the Wisconsin rule burdens an indigent defendant's right to effective representation on appeal. [A] supported conclusion that the appeal is frivolous does not implicate Sixth or Fourteenth Amendment concerns to any greater extent than does a bald conclusion."

Dissenting Justice BRENNAN, joined by Marshall and Blackmun, JJ., protested:

"[When] retained counsel in Wisconsin declines to appeal a case on the ground that he believes the appeal to be frivolous, the wealthy client can always seek a second opinion and might well find a lawyer who in good conscience believes it to have arguable merit. In no event, however, will any lawyer file in the wealthy client's name a brief that undercuts his position. In contrast, when appointed counsel harbors the same belief, the indigent client has no recourse to a second opinion, and (unless he withdraws his appeal) must respond in court to the arguments of his own defender.

"[The] Court looks at Wisconsin's regime and sees a friend of the client who 'assur[es]' that the constitutional rights of indigent defendants are scrupulously honored.' I look at the same regime and see a friend of the court whose advocacy is so damning that the prosecutor never responds. Either way, with friends like that, the indigent criminal appellant is truly alone."

4. *May an indigent defendant compel appointed counsel to argue all nonfrivolous points?* No, if counsel, "as a matter of professional judgment," decides not to do so, answered JONES v. BARNES, 463 U.S. 745, 103 S.Ct. 3308, 77 L.Ed.2d 987 (1983).

The case arose as follows: After Barnes was convicted of robbery and assault in a New York state court, Melinger was appointed to represent him on appeal. Barnes sent Melinger a letter listing several issues he thought should be raised. Barnes also enclosed a *pro se* brief that he had written. Melinger rejected most of the suggested claims, stating they would be of no aid and that they could not be raised because not based on evidence in the record. Melinger's brief to the state appellate court and his argument before that court concentrated on three points. But he did not argue a number of points Barnes felt should be raised. Barnes' own *pro se* briefs, however, were filed with the court. When his convictions were affirmed, Barnes sought federal habeas corpus relief on the ground that he had been denied effective counsel on appeal.

The Court of Appeals for the Second Circuit granted relief, concluding that, under *Anders,* when an appellant insists that his attorney raise additional colorable points, the attorney "*must argue the additional points to the full extent of his professional ability.*" (emphasis added by the Supreme Court). Since *Anders* bars counsel from abandoning a nonfrivolous appeal, reasoned the Second Circuit, it also bars counsel from abandoning a nonfrivolous issue.[a] The Supreme Court, per BURGER, C.J., disagreed:

"[B]y promulgating a *per se* rule that the client, not the professional advocate, must be allowed to decide what issues are to be pressed, the Court of Appeals seriously undermines the ability of counsel to present the client's case in accord with counsel's professional evaluation. Experienced advocates [have long] emphasized the importance of winnowing out weaker arguments on appeal and focusing on one central issue if possible, or at most on a few key issues. [A] brief that raises

a. The Second Circuit concluded that Melinger had failed to press at least two nonfrivolous issues. That Barnes had raised these is-

sues in his own briefs did not cure the error, for a *pro se* brief is "no substitute for the advocacy of experienced counsel."

every colorable issue runs the risk of burying good arguments—those [that] 'go for the jugular.'[b]

"[F]ar from giving support to the new *per se* rule announced by the Court of Appeals, [*Anders*] is to the contrary. *Anders* recognized that the role of the advocate 'requires that he support his client's appeal to the best of his ability.' Here the appointed counsel did just that. For judges to second-guess reasonable professional judgments and impose on appointed counsel a duty to raise every 'colorable' claim suggested by a client would disserve the very goal of vigorous and effective advocacy that underlies *Anders*."[c]

Dissenting Justice BRENNAN, joined by Marshall, J., relied heavily on *Faretta* and *Anders*:

"What is at issue here is the relationship between lawyer and client—who has ultimate authority to decide which nonfrivolous issues should be presented on appeal? I believe the right to 'the assistance of counsel' carries with it a right, personal to the defendant, to make that decision, against the advice of counsel if he chooses.

"[The] right to counsel as *Faretta* and *Anders* conceive it is not an all-or-nothing right, under which a defendant must choose between forgoing the assistance of counsel altogether or relinquishing control over every aspect of his case beyond its most basic structure (i.e., how to plead, whether to present a defense, whether to appeal). A defendant's interest in his case clearly extends to other matters. * * * He may want to press the argument that he is innocent, even if other stratagems are more likely to result in the dismissal of charges or in a reduction of punishment. He may want to insist on certain arguments for political reasons. He may want to protect third parties. This is just as true on appeal as at trial, and the proper role of counsel is to *assist* him in these efforts, insofar as that is possible consistent with the lawyer's conscience, the law, and his duties to the court. * * *

"I cannot accept the notion that lawyers are one of the punishments a person receives merely for being accused of a crime. Clients, if they wish, are capable of making informed judgments about which issues to appeal, and when they exercise that prerogative their choices should be respected unless they would require lawyers to violate their consciences, the law, or their duties to the court."

5. *New counsel on appeal.* Should trial counsel be required to remain on the criminal defense for purposes of arguing the appeal? Presumably the trial counsel is already intimately familiar with the case and sometimes, at least, can start writing a brief even before a trial transcript is prepared. Thus, much time might be lost by a change in counsel. On the other hand, how, on appeal, can trial counsel be expected to explore the possibility of ineffective counsel? Moreover, might a good trial lawyer turn out to be a very poor appellate lawyer? See generally Carrington, et al., p. 1170, fn. a, at 83–84 and authorities cited therein.

b. The Court recognized [fn. 6] that "the *ABA Standards for Criminal Appeals* [A.B.A. *Standards* § 21–3.2] appear to indicate that counsel should accede to a particular contention on appeal." But it pointed out that "the *ABA Defense Function Standards* [A.B.A. *Standards* § 4–5.2] provide that [except for the client's decision whether to enter a guilty plea, waive jury trial, and testify in his or her own behalf] "strategic and tactical decisions are the exclusive province of [defense counsel] after consultation with the client." In any event, concluded the Court, "the fact that the ABA may have chosen to recognize a given practice as desirable or appropriate does not mean that the practice is required by the Constitution."

c. Blackmun, J., who concurred in the judgment, agreed with the dissent that "as an *ethical* matter" an attorney should argue "all nonfrivolous claims upon which his client insists," but agreed with Court that this view was not a constitutional requirement.

When an appellate court denies defense counsel's motion to be relieved because he is of the opinion that the appeal is frivolous, should the court continue present counsel's appointment or assign new counsel? See Hermann, Note 2 supra, at 714.

6. *Is a state free to adopt other procedures than Anders for handling indigent criminal appeals?* Consider SMITH v. ROBBINS, 528 U.S. 259, 120 S.Ct. 746, 145 L.Ed.2d 756 (2000), which grew out of the following facts: Twelve years after *Anders*, in *People v. Wende*, 600 P.2d 1071 (Cal.1979), California adopted a new procedure for dealing with potentially frivolous appeals, under which, upon concluding that an appeal would be frivolous, counsel (a) "files a brief with the appellate court that summarizes the procedural and factual history of the case, with citations of the record"; (b) "attests that he has reviewed the record, explained the evaluation of the case to his client, provided the client with a copy of the brief and informed the client of his right to file a *pro se* supplemental brief"; and (c) "requests that the court independently examine the record for arguable issues." Upon receiving a "*Wende* brief," the appellate court must "conduct a review of the entire record." If, after doing so, the appellate court finds the appeal to be frivolous, it may affirm. However, if it finds an arguable issue (*i.e.*, nonfrivolous) issue, it orders briefing on that issue.

Respondent Robbins was convicted of second-degree murder and grand theft in a California court. Concluding that an appeal would be frivolous, Robbins's appointed counsel filed a brief with the state appellate court that complied with *Wende*, not *Anders*. Agreeing with counsel's assessment of the case, the state appellate court affirmed. The Ninth Circuit granted federal habeas relief, viewing *Anders*, together with *Douglas v. California* [p. 76], as "setting forth the exclusive procedure through which appointed counsel's performance can pass constitutional muster."

A 5–4 majority of the Supreme Court, per THOMAS, J., reversed. The *Anders* procedure, held the majority, "is merely one method of satisfying the requirements of the Constitution for indigent criminal appeals"; a state is free to adopt other procedures if these procedures "afford adequate and effective appellate review to indigent defendants" and a state's procedure provides such review "so long as it reasonably ensures [as does the *Wende* procedure] that an indigent's appeal will be resolved in a way that is related to the merit of that appeal":

"In *Pennsylvania v. Finley* [p. 1587], we explained that the *Anders* procedure is not 'an independent constitutional command,' but rather is just 'a prophylactic framework' that was established to vindicate the constitutional right to appellate counsel announced in *Douglas*. We did not say that our *Anders* procedure was the *only* prophylactic framework that could adequately vindicate this right; instead, by making clear that the Constitution itself does not compel the *Anders* procedure, we suggested otherwise.

" * * * [I]t is more in keeping with our status as a court, and particularly with our status as a court in a federal system, to avoid imposing a single solution on the States from the top down. We should, and do, evaluate state procedures one at a time, as they come before us, while leaving 'the more challenging task of crafting appropriate procedures [to] the laboratory of the States in the first instance.'

" * * * We think the *Wende* procedure reasonably ensures that an indigent's appeal will be resolved in a way that is related to the merit of that appeal. Whatever the strengths or weaknesses as a matter of policy, we cannot say that it fails to afford indigents the adequate and effective appellate review that the Fourteenth Amendment requires. [Thus,] there was no constitutional violation in this case simply because the *Wende* procedure was used.

"On remand, the proper standard for evaluating Robbins's claim that appellate counsel was ineffective in neglecting to file a merits brief is that enunciated in *Strickland*. * * * Respondent must first show that his counsel was objectively unreasonable in failing to find arguable issues to appeal—that is, that counsel unreasonably failed to discover nonfrivolous issues and to file a merits brief raising them. If Robbins succeeds in such a showing, he then has the burden of demonstrating prejudice. That is, he must show a reasonable probability that, but for his counsel's unreasonable failure to file a merits brief, he would have prevailed on his appeal.

"[The] applicability of *Strickland*'s actual-prejudice prong to Robbins's claim of ineffective counsel follows from *Penson v. Ohio*, 488 U.S. 75, 109 S.Ct. 346, 102 L.Ed.2d 300 (1988), where we distinguished denial of counsel altogether on appeal, which warranted a presumption of prejudice, from mere ineffective assistance of counsel on appeal, which did not.[a] * * * But where, as here, the defendant has received appellate counsel who has complied with a valid state procedure for determining whether the defendant's appeal is frivolous, and the State has not at any time left the defendant without counsel on appeal, there is no reason to assume that the defendant has been prejudiced."

"Believ[ing] [that] the procedure adopted in *Wende* fails to assure representation by counsel with the adversarial character demanded by the Constitution," Justice SOUTER, joined by Stevens, Ginsburg, and Breyer, JJ., dissented:

"We have not held the details of *Anders* to be exclusive, but it does make sense to read the case as exemplifying what substantial equality requires on behalf of indigent appellants entitled to an advocate's review and to reasonable certainty that arguable issues will be briefed on their merits. With *Anders* thus as a benchmark, California's *Wende* procedure fails to measure up. Its primary failing is in permitting counsel to refrain as a matter of course from mentioning possibly arguable issues in a no-merit brief; its second deficiency is a correlative of the first, in obliging an appellate court to search the record for arguable issues without benefit of an issue-spotting, no-merit brief to review.

"[In] an *amicus* brief filed in this case, 13 retired Justices of the Supreme Court or Courts of Appeal of California have pointed out the 'risk that the review of the cold record [under the *Wende* scheme] will be more perfunctory without the issue-spotting guidance, and associated record citations, of counsel.' The *amici* have candidly represented that '[w]hen a California appellate court receives a *Wende* brief, it assigns the case to a staff attorney who prepares a memorandum analyzing all possible legal issues in the case. Typically, the staff attorney then makes an oral presentation to the appellate panel. . . .' When the responsibility of counsel is thrown onto the court, the court gives way to a staff attorney; it could not be clearer that *Wende* is seriously at odds with the respective obligations of counsel and the courts as contemplated by the Constitution.

"[The] assumption behind *Strickland*'s prejudice requirement is that the defendant had a lawyer who was representing him as his advocate at least at some level, whereas that premise cannot be assumed when a defendant receives the benefit of nothing more than a *Wende* brief. In a *Wende* situation, nominal counsel is functioning merely as a friend of the court, helping the judge to grasp the structure of the record but not even purporting to highlight the record's nearest

---

a. In *Penson*, where appellant's lawyer failed to satisfy *Anders*, the Court "emphasized that the denial of counsel in this case left petitioner completely without representation during the appellate court's actual decisional process. This is quite different from a case in which it is claimed that counsel's performance was ineffective. As we stated in *Strickland*, the '[a]ctual or constructive denial of the assistance of counsel altogether is legally presumed to result in prejudice.' "

approach to supporting his client's hope to appeal. Counsel under *Wende* is doing less than the judge's law clerk (or staff attorney) might do, and he is doing nothing at all in the way of advocacy. When a lawyer abandons the role of advocate and adopts that of *amicus curiae*, he is no longer functioning as counsel or rendering assistance within the meaning of the Sixth Amendment. Since the apparently missing ingredient of the advocate's analysis goes to the very essence of the right to counsel, a lawyer who does nothing more than file a *Wende* brief is closer to being no counsel at all than to being subpar counsel under *Strickland*.

"This, I think, is the answer to any suggestion that a specific assessment of prejudice need be shown in order to get relief from *Wende*. A complete absence of counsel is a reversible violation of the constitutional right to representation, even when there is no question that at the end of the day the smartest lawyer in the world would have watched his client being led off to prison. We do not ask how the defendant would have fared if he had been given counsel, and we should not look to what sort of appeal might have ensued if an appellant's lawyer had flagged the points that came closest to appealable issues."[b]

7. *What light does Smith v. Robbins shed on the Court's use of "prophylactic rules"? Is Robbins consistent with Dickerson?* Consider Paul G. Cassell, *The Paths Not Taken: The Supreme Court's Failure in Dickerson*, 99 Mich.L.Rev. 898, 904–053 (2001): "[In] *Smith v. Robbins* [the] Court held that its procedure for dealing with frivolous appeals could be superseded by a California procedure. In words that echo the cases interpreting *Miranda*, the Court said that the procedure imposed on the states by *Anders* was simply a 'prophylactic framework' and not 'a constitutional command.' Accordingly, California could substitute an alternative procedure. [The] test for whether the substitute California procedure was constitutional was whether it provided the 'minimum safeguards' to protect the constitutional right at issue.

"Under a constitutional common law approach, the *Dickerson* case could have been resolved straighforwardly in a way that reconciled *Miranda* with its progeny. Like the interim measures [in] *Anders*, the Court could have viewed the *Miranda* rules as an interim 'prophylactic framework' designed to safeguard Fifth Amendment rights. This would justify *Miranda*, since the Court is free [to] craft rules that assist in the enforcement of constitutional rights. At the same time, this view would fit precisely the language and rationale of post-*Miranda* exceptions cases— *Tucker, Quarles, Elstad*, and the like—which were predicated on *Miranda* as a 'prophylactic' device.

"[Under] this view of *Miranda*, Congress can replace the *Miranda* rules provided it leaves in place 'meaningful safeguards.' Section 3501 meets this test. [It] fully protects against the admission of compelled statements in violation of the Fifth Amendment. Congress, of course, has no authority to modify the content of constitutional rights. [But] that is very different from saying that Congress has no authority to modify a ruling that 'overprotects' a constitutional right, as *Miranda*'s automatic rule excluding all unwarned custodial statements clearly does."

But compare Yale Kamisar, *Miranda Thirty–Five Years Later: A Close Look at the Majority and Dissenting Opinions in Dickerson*, 33 Ariz.St.L.J. 387, 413 (2001): "The only reason [*Smith v. Robbins*] upheld a *different* method for satisfying constitutional requirements for indigent criminal appeals than the prophylactic rules adopted in *Anders* was that it considered the different method an adequate alternative to *Anders*. If the different method had turned out to be nothing more, or not better than, the very procedure disapproved in *Anders*, then,

---

b. While he joined Justice Souter's dissent "without qualification," Stevens, J., joined by   Ginsburg, J., also wrote a separate dissent.

just as *Dickerson* invalidated § 3501 (which offered nothing more than the test for admitting confessions found inadequate in *Miranda*), *Robbins* would have struck down the new procedure for handling indigent criminal appeals. *Robbins* supports and helps explain *Dickerson*. Nowhere in its majority opinion does the *Robbins* Court suggest that the prophylactic rules prescribed in *Anders* were 'illegitimate' or 'lawless.' Nor does *Robbins* suggest that the Congress or the States could disregard the *Anders* rules with impunity simply because they were 'prophylactic.' "

Chapter 21

PRETRIAL DISCOVERY

SECTION 1. THE STATUTORY FRAMEWORK[a]

A. The Development of the Current Law of Discovery

1. *The Departure from the Common Law.* At early common law, trial courts were held to lack any inherent authority to require pretrial discovery. Absent specific legislative authorization, a trial court could not order the prosecution to make a pretrial disclosure of its evidence to the defense or the defense to make a pretrial disclosure of its evidence to the prosecution. As a result, as of the early 1900s, in all but a few states that had legislatively authorized court ordered pretrial discovery, the only pretrial discovery available to the parties was that which was obtained informally through the mutual exchange of information or incidentally in the course of such pretrial proceedings as the preliminary hearing. The first major change occurred over the next few decades. A sizeable group of states adopted legislation requiring pretrial disclosure of specific types of evidence (most notably, alibi evidence) and an even larger group rejected the common law position and recognized a trial court's discretion to order discovery as an element of its inherent authority over the trial process, upon a special showing of need. Thus, by the late 1930s, a majority of the states allowed court ordered pretrial discovery, though that discovery was available only as a limited exception rather than a common practice.

During the 1930s and 1940s, through court rules and legislation, pretrial discovery in civil cases was dramatically expanded. By providing for depositions, interrogatories, requests for admissions, and the compulsory production of documents and other tangible items, civil discovery provisions gave each side pretrial access to almost all relevant information possessed by the other. The success of this liberalization of civil discovery naturally led legislatures and courts to consider similarly expanding pretrial discovery in criminal cases. There followed during the 1950s and 1960s one of the classic debates in the field of criminal procedure. Since prosecution discovery from the defense was thought to be largely prohibited by the defendant's privilege against self-incrimination, the focus of the debate was primarily upon liberalizing defense discovery from the prosecution.

2. *The Debate.* Justice Brennan, a leading proponent of liberal discovery, captured the basic issue in the discovery debate, as proponents saw it, in the title of his famous article, *The Criminal Prosecution: Sporting Event or Quest for Truth?*, 1963 Wash.U.L.Q. 279 (1973). Without broad discovery, he argued, the trial resembled a game of "blind man's bluff." The full marshaling by the defense of all the evidence bearing on the truth could occur only if it received notice in advance of trial of both the prosecution evidence that it would have to meet and

---

a. For a more complete discussion of the material covered in this section, see Wayne R. LaFave, Jerold H. Israel, & Nancy J. King, Criminal Procedure Treatise §§ 20.1, 20.2 (2d ed. 1999) (available on Westlaw under the database CRIMPROC and hereafter cited as CRIMPROC).

any possible sources of further evidence uncovered by the state's investigation. The defense in this respect was pictured as suffering serious disadvantages as compared to the prosecutor. The prosecution, it was noted, starts with the far greater investigative manpower of the police and adds to that the far greater investigative legal authority of the grand jury's subpoena power and the various investigative powers of the police (e.g., their search authority, and their authority to compel participation in identification procedures). Moreover, the prosecution's investigators usually arrive first at the scene of the crime and begin their investigation while the trail is fresh, whereas defense counsel typically enters the picture at a much later date. The state's investigators also can count on the natural inclination of witnesses to cooperate with the state, as contrasted to defense counsel, who frequently find avenues of inquiry closed by a reluctance of witnesses to assist the accused. Indeed, argued the proponents of defense discovery, the typical defense counsel faces such significant investigative obstacles that the adversary system would be substantially undermined without the partial equalization provided by liberal defense discovery.

Opponents of expansive discovery did not challenge the premise that a trial should be a quest for the truth rather than a "sporting event." They argued, however, that this end would not be served by liberal defense discovery in light of (1) the potential for defendant's misuse of such discovery and (2) the inequity that would result from providing expansive defense discovery in the context of the criminal justice process.

The opponents' "misuse" argument focused on the possibility that pretrial discovery would be used to facilitate perjury or to intimidate prospective defense witnesses. As for perjury, the discovery critics acknowledged that a defendant who desires to fabricate a defense could do so whether or not given discovery, but advance notice of the prosecution's case, they argued, would allow the defendant to make such fabricated defenses more persuasive. With discovery, fabricated defenses could be tailored so as to minimize conflict with the prosecution's evidence and to take advantage of the weakest point in the prosecution's case. Thus, where a defendant became aware in advance of trial that the prosecution could place him at the scene of the crime, he could more readily switch his fabricated defense from alibi to a defense consistent with his presence at the scene. As for witness intimidation, the opponents noted that "long experience" in criminal cases had taught that "the criminal defendant who is informed of the names of all the state witnesses may take steps to bribe or frighten them into giving perjured testimony or into absenting themselves so they are unavailable to testify. Moreover, many witnesses, if they know that the defendant will have knowledge of their names prior to trial, will be reluctant to come forward with information during the investigation of the crime." *State v. Tune,* 98 A.2d 881 (N.J.1953) (Vanderbilt, C.J.).

Proponents of expansive defense discovery viewed the claimed facilitation of perjury as an "old hobgoblin" based on "untested folklore." Brennan, supra. They noted that the perjury objection had been put to rest in the expansion of civil discovery, where the answer had been that the proper safeguard against perjury "is not to refuse to permit any inquiry at all, for that will eliminate the true as well as the false, but [to conduct] the inquiry * * * so as to separate and distinguish the one from the other." Ibid. That answer, they argued, was equally appropriate for the criminal justice process. Discovery proponents rejected the contention that perjury was more likely in criminal cases because of greater incentives (civil cases too often involved substantial stakes), because criminal defendants were more likely to be dishonest (an assumption viewed as conflicting with the presumption of innocence), or because the civil litigant could depose the opposing party and thereby "freeze" his story prior to his fabrication of a more readily believed scenario (the prosecution having a similar capacity through other devices, such as interrogation following arrest). Discovery proponents similarly rejected the concept of barring discovery because of a generalized fear of witness intimidation. Where there was a substantial basis for believing a particular defendant was likely to threaten witnesses, that could be handled by granting the trial court authority to limit or bar discovery upon such a showing (a procedure the discovery opponents view as "impracticable"). So too, proponents argued, the search for the truth, facilitated by discovery, could not be restricted simply because witnesses have unfounded fears or don't want to be "bothered" by the investigative efforts of defense counsel.

The "inequity" argument advanced by discovery opponents had two major prongs. First, it was argued that in an adversary system, it would be unfair to give the defendant discovery rights that could not be duplicated for the prosecution because of the defendant's privilege against self-incrimination. In civil discovery, it was noted, disclosure was a "two-way street." Some supporters of expansive discovery maintained that the impact of the self-incrimination clause upon prosecution discovery was limited, and that prosecution discovery could be made almost equal in scope to defense discovery. Others argued that it was inappropriate to deny the defense an essential tool because of an imbalance that was purposely created by the Constitution's framers, in the interest of justice, through their adoption of a self-incrimination privilege.

The second prong of the equity argument focused on the overall "balance of advantage" in the criminal justice process. Discovery opponents argued that defendant already had sufficient procedural advantages to insure protection of the innocent. Often quoted in this regard were the comments of Judge Learned Hand in *United States v. Garsson,* 291 Fed. 646 (D.C.N.Y.1923):

> Under our criminal procedure the accused has every advantage. While the prosecution is held rigidly to the charge, he need not disclose the barest outline of his defense. He is immune from question or comment on his silence; he cannot be convicted when there is the least fair doubt in the minds of any one of the twelve. Why in addition he should in advance have the whole evidence against him to pick over at his leisure, and make his defense, fairly or foully, I have never been able to see. No doubt grand juries err and indictments are calamities to honest men, but we must work with human beings and we can correct such errors only at too large a price. Our dangers do not lie in too little tenderness to the accused. Our procedure has been always haunted by the ghost of the innocent man convicted. It is an unreal dream. What we need to fear is the archaic formalism and the watery sentiment that obstructs, delays, and defeats the prosecution of crime.

Professor Abraham Goldstein responded for the proponents in his classic article, *The State and the Accused: Balance of Advantage in Criminal Procedure,* 69 Yale L.J. 1149 (1960). The procedural advantages cited by Judge Hand, he argued, had more of a theoretical than a practical importance and were more than offset by the serious investigative disadvantages faced by the defense. Indeed, the defendant's position had in one sense worsened as the modern movement toward acceptance of looseness in pleadings and allowance of substantial variance in trial proof (see Chapter 16) had resulted in the defense receiving less notice of the facts and legal theories to be litigated. Proponents of discovery also argued that the weighing of defense discovery against procedural protections of the accused resembled the balancing of applies and oranges, as those procedural protections were commonly constitutionally grounded and often served interests quite different than the aim of discovery—the "ascertainment of the facts." *People v. Riser,* 305 P.2d 1 (Cal.1956) (Traynor, J.).

3.   *The Outcome.* In one sense, the debate over defense discovery has not ended. The basic contentions are often reexamined in the course of judicial interpretation of current discovery provisions and legislative consideration of proposals to broaden those provisions. See Justice William Brennan, *The Criminal Prosecution: Sporting Event or Quest for Truth? A Progress Report,* 68 Wash. U.L.Q. 1 (1990). In another sense, the end question raised by the debate—whether there should be extensive defense discovery—has been answered, and the answer clearly is "Yes." The issue that divides the jurisdictions today is precisely how far that discovery should be taken, not whether substantial defense discovery should exist. Moreover, the movement over the years in almost every jurisdiction has been toward broadening the scope of discovery.

This is not to suggest that the law of defense discovery anywhere is at the point where the strongest proponents of defense discovery would like it to be. While many states adopted the extensive discovery provisions of the original A.B.A. Standards (see Note 2, p. 1181), when the second edition of the A.B.A. Standards proposed "open file" discovery through a provision authorizing defense discovery of "all the material and information within the prosecutor's control" (subject to certain narrow limitations), see 2 A.B.A. Standards § 11–21 (2d ed. 1980), not even the most liberal discovery states were willing to adopt such an open-ended provision. See also A.B.A. Standards, *Discovery* § 11–2.1 (3d ed. 1996) (deleting the "all material and information" clause of the 2nd edition). Moreover, the Federal Rules, another significant model for state discovery provisions, continues to provide for defense discovery considerably narrower than the original A.B.A. Standards. Over the years, federal defense discovery has been broadened through amendments of Rule 16, but there have been setbacks in that movement. In 1975, for example, the Supreme Court approved a proposal that would have given the defense discovery of the names, addresses, and felony records of all prosecution witnesses, but that proposal was rejected by Congress.

4.   *The "Two–Way Street" Movement.* The expansion of defense discovery, not unexpectedly, led prosecutors to request that they be given equally broad discovery. Alibi-notice provisions (requiring the defense to give advance notice of its intent to rely on an alibi defense and its supporting defense witnesses) had been adopted in numerous states even before the movement to expand defense discovery took hold. When the Supreme Court in 1970 upheld the constitutionality of an alibi-notice provision (see *Williams v. Florida,* p. 1200), the A.B.A., reading that decision broadly, proposed prosecution discovery that went substantially beyond the alibi provisions. Post–*Williams* amendments of the Federal Rules similarly added to the discovery available to the federal prosecutor, although the discovery governed by Rule 16 (in contrast to the newly added Rules 12.1 and 12.2) continued to condition the prosecution's right to discovery on the defense initially requesting discovery of similar items from the prosecution. Neither the A.B.A. proposal nor the somewhat narrower amended Federal Rules went so far, however, as to grant to the prosecution discovery fully parallel in scope to that granted to the defense under their respective provisions for defense discovery.

The response of the states to the A.B.A. and Federal Rules provisions on prosecution discovery was generally favorable. Most of the states with provisions modeled on the A.B.A. Standards or the Federal Rules adopted the provisions on prosecutorial discovery included in their respective models. A substantial group expanded upon those models to make prosecution discovery more fully equivalent to defense discovery. However, a small group of A.B.A. jurisdictions adopted prosecution discovery provisions narrower than the A.B.A. model. In addition, a few states continued to reject almost all prosecution discovery. Overall, as in the case of discovery for the defense, the trend in prosecution discovery clearly has been in the direction of expanding pretrial disclosure, although that trend has not found quite as much support as that for expanding defense discovery, perhaps because of continuing doubts as to the constitutionality of certain types of prosecution discovery.

B. SIMILARITIES AND DIFFERENCES IN DISCOVERY PROVISIONS[a]

1. ***The common structure.*** In the federal system and all but a few states, discovery is governed by statutes or court rules which are comprehensive in their coverage. In many states, there is a single court rule or statute governing all aspects of discovery by both sides. Other jurisdictions, following the pattern of the Federal Rules, utilize both a basic provision governing discovery in general and separate provisions setting forth the obligations of pretrial disclosure where defense seeks to advance a claim of alibi or an insanity defense. Although the basic discovery provisions vary in content, they tend to be similar in structure. Typically, the basic discovery statute or court rule performs the following major tasks: (1) it establishes a procedure by which the defense and the prosecution can put into effect the other side's obligation to make pretrial disclosure; (2) it designates those items which shall or may (upon court order) be disclosed by the prosecution to the defense; (3) it designates those items that shall or may (upon court order) be disclosed by the defense to the prosecution; (4) it establishes certain exemptions from disclosure based upon content (e.g., work product) or, in some instances, based on the nature of the item (e.g., witness' statements);[b] (5) it authorizes the trial court to issue under special circumstances a protective order that will bar or limit disclosures that would otherwise be required; (6) it imposes a continuing duty to disclose discoverable items so that the process automatically encompasses items acquired after the initial disclosure; and (7) it provides a procedure for judicial administration and enforcement of the discovery provisions, including the imposition of sanctions.

2. ***The A.B.A. and Federal Rules Models.*** Although comprehensive discovery provisions vary in content from one jurisdiction to another, they can be loosely categorized by reference to two models—the Federal Rules provisions on discovery (Rules 12.1, 12.2, 12.3, and 16) and the 1970 first edition of the *A.B.A. Standards on Discovery and Procedure Before Trial* (hereafter cited simply as "A.B.A."). All but a few of the states with comprehensive discovery provisions

a. The reference here is to discovery provided through discovery provisions. In many jurisdictions, other procedures (e.g., the preliminary hearing) may provide valuable discovery tools for the defense. Also, discovery is an area in which prosecutors not infrequently provide discretionary disclosure that goes beyond what they are required to provide under the discovery provisions. See e.g., Wm. Bradford Middlekauff, *What Practitioners Say About Broad Criminal Discovery Practice*, 9 Crim. Justice 14 (Spring 1994) (12 of 17 federal public defenders surveyed reported receiving discovery beyond that required by Federal Rule 16); Ellen S. Dodgor, *Criminal Discovery of Jencks Witness Statements: Timing Makes A Difference*, 15 Ga.St U.L. Rev. 651 (1998) (noting common practice in many federal districts to disclose a witness' prior recorded statement prior to the commencement of the trial, although Jencks Act provides for disclosure after the witness has testified at trial).

b. Where the statute or court rule fails to refer to a particular item as subject to discovery and that item would not fall within a specified exemption, the issue arises as to whether it leaves to the trial court discretion to order discovery of that item. Some jurisdictions view the basic discovery provision as preempting the field; what is not listed as discoverable cannot be made discoverable by the trial court. Other jurisdictions recognize an inherent discretionary authority of the trial court as to items that fall within any "gaps" in the statute. Thus, although Congress rejected in 1975 an amendment to Rule 16 that would have added to the list of automatically discoverable items the names of prosecution witnesses, and although a federal statute requiring the disclosure of witnesses names is limited to capital offenses, the federal courts have regularly held that the trial court retains discretion to order pretrial disclosure of the names of the government's witnesses. See 2 Charles Alan Wright, *Federal Practice and Procedure—Criminal* § 254 (2d ed. 1988). See also *United States v. McMillen*, described in Note 6, p. 1192.

used one of these models as a starting point in identifying both discoverable items and discovery exemptions.

State provisions based on the A.B.A. model tend to follow it very closely as to defense discovery (which is considerably broader under the A.B.A. than under the Federal Rules). Their primary deviation from the model comes in the provisions on prosecution discovery. Many of these states provide the prosecution with somewhat broader discovery than the A.B.A. (including, for example, the prior recorded statements of defense witnesses), while a small group have refused to allow discovery as broad as the A.B.A. (rejecting, in particular, A.B.A. § 3.3 which allows the trial court to require the defense to identify the nature of its intended defense and to list supporting witnesses).

Jurisdictions that start with the Federal Rules model often vary from that model as to both prosecution and defense discovery. Some follow earlier versions of the Federal Rule 16, which provided for less discovery than the current Rule 16. Some provide broader defense discovery because they include the 1975 proposed amendments to the Federal Rules that were rejected by Congress (see Note 3, p. 1180). The Federal Rules states also vary in their alibi notice provisions (which often predate Federal Rule 12.1), and typically do not have a provision similar to Rule 12.3, which deals with advance notice on a defense claim of actual or believed authorization by a law enforcement or intelligence agency.

   3. *The "work product" exemption.* Discovery provisions commonly include an exemption from discovery that will exempt some form of prosecution and defense work product.[c] The concept of exempting work product from discovery stems from the law of civil discovery, but the nature of the exemption in criminal discovery is different in several respects. The leading civil discovery ruling, *Hickman v. Taylor,* 329 U.S. 495, 67 S.Ct. 385, 91 L.Ed. 451 (1947), recognized a general policy against discovery of the opposing party's work product in order to protect against "unwarranted inquiries [through discovery] into the files and mental impressions of an attorney." As incorporated in the Federal Rules of Civil Procedure 26(b)(3), the *Hickman* work product doctrine is broad in its coverage, extending to almost all documents and tangible things prepared in anticipation of litigation. However, it does not produce an absolute bar against discovery. The court may order discovery of such material if the party seeking discovery shows "a substantial need" for the item and an inability without "undue hardship" to obtain equivalent materials. When ordering such discovery, however, the court must "protect against disclosure of the mental impressions, conclusions, opinions, or legal theories of an attorney or other representative concerning the litigation." That portion of litigation preparation material reflecting such tactical perspectives is commonly described as "opinion" work product, with the remainder of that material constituting "non-opinion" work product.

   c. Some commentators have contended that protection of any form of work product is inappropriate in the context of discovery by criminal defendants. They argue that the prosecutor does not need the protection of a doctrine designed to prevent one adversary from using the work of the other. The prosecutor's role as representative of the people is to "do justice," not simply to be an adversary, and the prosecution therefore should have no concern if the defense gains access to any relevant material within the prosecution's control, no matter what its character. This contention has failed to fully convince legislatures or courts.

   In *United States v. Nobles,* Note 1, p. 1210, the Supreme Court, in holding that a work product doctrine applied to litigation material prepared by the defense, drew no distinction between prosecution and defense in commenting on the need for a work product doctrine in criminal cases. That doctrine, noted the Court, was "even more vital" in criminal cases than in civil cases, because "the interests of society and the accused in obtaining a fair and accurate resolution of the question of guilt or innocence demand that adequate safeguards assure the thorough preparation and presentation of *each side* of the case" (emphasis added).

Jurisdictions vary in what they view as exempt "work product" in the context of criminal discovery, with very few (if any) utilizing the standards of civil discovery. See CRIMPROC § 20.3(j). Various states utilize the work product definition proposed in the A.B.A. Standards: "legal research or * * * records, correspondence, reports, or memoranda to the extent they contain the opinions, theories, or conclusions of the prosecuting attorney or the defense attorney, or members of the attorney's legal staff." A.B.A. Standards, Discovery § 11–6.1(a) (3d ed. 1996). This exemption furnishes absolute protection, but is limited to "opinion" work product and then only of the legal staff. It avoids possible work product application to reports of investigators (e.g., police reports) or reports of experts (see fn. d , p. 1213), since the authors of those reports are not part of the legal staff.[d] It often even avoids work product coverage of the written record of a witness interview, notwithstanding that the witness' statement was recorded by a prosecutor or defense attorney, where the record consists of a substantially verbatim quotation of the witness. Such a record is not likely to reflect the opinions or theories of the attorney, although it might do so where the witness responds to pointed questions presented by the attorney. Even where the questions do reflect "some legal theory or factual judgment," however, such material may be "capable of deletion without detracting from the flow of the witness' statement." CRIMPROC § 20.3(j). Where the concept of a "recorded statement" extends to the interviewer's notes on the witness' statements, see Note 4 infra, there is greater potential that the content will reflect opinion work product. Courts have held, however, that interview notes consisting only of selective quotations or summaries of the substance of the witnesses statements do not constitute opinion work product. Ibid.

In civil discovery, as the Supreme Court noted in to the instructor *United States v. Nobles*, Note 3, p. 1211, supra, the work product doctrine has taken account of "the realities of litigation in our adversary system," recognized that this means that "attorneys often must rely on their investigators," and has extended coverage to litigation materials prepared by investigators. *Nobles* concluded that the federal common law work product protection would apply to defense investigators working at the direction of defense counsel. Many of the states that otherwise follow the A.B.A. in limiting the work product exemption to opinion work product similarly extend their exemption to investigators and others who are "agents" of the prosecutor or defense attorneys. To ensure that these provisions include police officers, who may not be operating under the specific direction of the prosecutor, some refer specifically to the police. Here, police reports, depending upon their contents, can readily be exempt from pretrial discovery.[e] Also, since witness interviews, particularly on the prosecution side, are more likely to be conducted by police, the work product exemption is likely to play a larger role as to notes of interviews (where the definition of a "recorded statement" otherwise covers such notes, see Note 4 infra). However, the limitation of the exemption to opinion work product means that many records of interviews will not qualify because they will consist of little more than a recording or summary of the witness' statements.

d. But consider *Commonwealth v. Liang*, 434 Mass. 131, 747 N.E.2d 112 (2001) (though work product provision refers to "opinions, theories or conclusions" of the "attorney and legal staff," that includes victim advocates; though they are not engaged in legal research, they interview victims and can be compared to investigators attached to the prosecutor's legal staff; therefore, their notes are exempt from pretrial discovery as work product, except inso-far as they contain the "statements" of witnesses—defined as substantially verbatim and contemporaneously recorded recitals of oral declarations—or constitute exculpatory material which the prosecution has a constitutional duty to disclose, see Note 1, p. 1198).

e. Where the officer testifies at trial, that report would be available, even if work product, for the purposes of impeachment. See fn. g., p. 1184.

Although Federal Rule 16(a)(2) does not use the term "work product," it is commonly described as a work product provision. Rule 16(a)(2) states that, except as provided in the subsections authorizing discovery of defendants' own statements, prior records, and reports of examinations and scientific tests, Rule 16 "does not authorize the discovery or inspection of reports, memoranda, or other internal government documents made by the attorney for the government or other government agent in connection with the investigation or prosecution of the case." A provision of similar content (referring to local prosecutors and police) is included in the various state discovery rules modeled on the Federal Rules. Like the work product doctrine in civil discovery, the Rule 16(a)(2) provision encompasses non-opinion as well as opinion work product, and applies to investigators as well as lawyers. Unlike the civil discovery doctrine, it does not provide for disclosure of the non-opinion portion upon a special showing of need. That additional protection is limited, however, for the initial exceptions under Rule 16(a)(2) render automatically discoverable items (e.g., investigator's verbatim quotations of the defendant's statements and reports of physical examinations and scientific tests, see Note 1, p. 1190, and Note 1, p. 1193) that would constitute at least non-opinion work product under traditional civil work product doctrine.[f]

4. *"Written or recorded statements."* All discovery provisions provide for the defense discovery of "written or recorded statements" of the defendant in possession of the prosecution. Many also allow for defense discovery of "written or recorded statements" of prosecution witnesses, defense discovery of "written or recorded statements" of codefendants, and prosecution discovery of "written or recorded statements" of defense witnesses. The same definition of a "written or recorded statement" is applied in all four contexts. Many states have looked to the federal Jencks Act in defining a written or recorded statement, either including the Jencks definition in its discovery provision or having adopted that definition by judicial decision. See CRIMPROC § 20.3(b).

The Jencks Act, which applies only to federal courts, deals with the right of a defendant at trial to obtain a prior "statement" of a prosecution witness for use in impeaching that witness.[g] It defines the term "statement" for this purpose as "(1)

---

f. The Federal Rules, in drawing these flat categories of the discoverable and non-discoverable, had no need to add a work-product provision protecting "opinion" work product. The internal memorandum exemption includes those documents most likely to include sensitive opinion work product of a prosecutor or investigator. As for prosecution discovery from the defense, that is limited to items that the defense intends to use at trial (see Rule 16(b)(1), and Note 3, p. 1210), which would lose any work product exemption at trial, and arguably even before then. See Note 3, p. 1211.

g. The Jencks Act was adopted in response to *Jencks v. United States,* 353 U.S. 657, 77 S.Ct. 1007, 1 L.Ed.2d 1103 (1957). The Supreme Court had there held, in the exercise of its supervisory power, that a federal district court erred in denying a defense request to examine at trial the prior recorded statements of two government witnesses who were F.B.I. undercover agents. In the course of reaching this conclusion, the Court had rejected the government's contention that such prior recorded statements should only be made available upon a defense showing of likely inconsistency with the witness' current testimony and

that disclosure should only be granted after the trial judge reviewed the statements in camera and determined that they would be appropriate for use in cross-examining the witness. A dissent by Justice Clark had contended that the Court's ruling granted defendants "a Roman holiday" for "rummaging through" F.B.I. files, and some lower courts rulings had extended *Jencks* to require pretrial discovery of the prior recorded statements of prospective government witnesses. Congress' legislative response to these developments, commonly known as the Jencks Act, contained five basic provisions. Subsection (a) prohibited pretrial discovery of the witness' prior statement. See Note 2, p. 1196. Subsection (b) reaffirmed *Jencks* in providing that, after the witness testified, the defense had an automatic right to disclosure of any prior statement of the witness "which relates to the subject matter as to which the witness has testified." Subsection (c) arguably modified *Jencks* by providing for in camera review where the government contends that the statement (or a part thereof) does not relate to the subject matter of the witness' testimony. Subsection (d) allowed for the option of striking the witness' testimony where

a written statement made by said witness and signed or otherwise adopted or approved by him; (2) a stenographic, mechanical, electrical, or other recording, or a transcription thereof, which is a substantially verbatim recital of an oral statement; or (3) a statement, however taken or recorded, or a transcription thereof, if any, made by said witness to grand jury." 18 U.S.C.A. § 3500(e).

Inclusion of the three types of Jencks statements within discovery provisions for "written or recorded statements" is now universally accepted. At one point, there was concern as to disclosure of a person's grand jury testimony, since that disclosure undercuts grand jury secrecy, but the general consensus today is that such testimony should be treated no differently than other prior recorded statements of defendants or witnesses. The critical controversy as to the incorporation of the Jencks definition thus has become whether it is too narrow for discovery purpose. The focus here is on the second prong of the Jencks definition, which requires that record of a statement not written or approved by the speaker be a "substantially verbatim recital" and "recorded contemporaneously." The objective of the "substantially-verbatim" prerequisite, the Supreme Court has noted, is to "eliminate the danger of distortion and misrepresentation inherent in a report which merely selects portions * * * from a lengthy oral recital." *Palermo v. United States*, 360 U.S. 343, 79 S.Ct. 1217, 3 L.Ed.2d 1287 (1959). Thus, this prerequisite clearly excludes an interviewer's notes that attempt only to summarize the substance of a person's statement or that seek to quote only those portions the interviewer deemed critical. The requirement of a contemporaneous recording similarly guards against the lapse of memory even where the person making the record attempts to recount verbatim what the speaker said. Thus, the Jencks standard will not treat as a recorded statement of the defendant the report of an undercover agent which quotes what the defendant said to the agent in a conversation several days earlier. Similarly, where an interviewer records verbatim and contemporaneously a statement of B, in which B seeks to quote verbatim what A recently told B, that would be a "recorded statement" of B, but not A.

The original A.B.A. Standards took no position on the definition of a written or recorded statement, as the advisory committee divided on that issue. A minority favored the Jencks Act definition. They argued that a person who is interviewed or interrogated by an investigator should not be forced to explain or account for the investigator's recollection of what was said where it was not recorded contemporaneously and largely in the speaker's own words. The majority argued that such a concern was appropriate for impeachment use, but not for discovery. In discovery, it was argued, the object was to ensure disclosure of information that might be useful in trial preparation, and that was not limited to information that could actually used at trial.

The third edition of the A.B.A. Standards reflected the latter position and flatly rejected limiting included statements to the Jencks Act definition. It provides in § 11.–1.3(a) "that a 'written statement' of a person shall included: (i) any statement in writing that is made, signed or adopted by that person; and (ii) the substance of a statement of any kind made by that person that is embodied or summarized in any writing or recording, whether or not specifically signed or adopted by that person. The term is intended to include statements contained in police or investigative reports, but does not include attorney work product." Several states, by statute or judicial decision, have adopted a similar definition. See CRIMPROC § 20.3(b). At one time, a line of federal lower court decisions appeared headed in the same direction in reading Rule 16(a)(1)(A)'s provision for defense discovery of a "recorded statements of the defendant." However, Rule

the government preferred not to make disclosure as ordered by the court. Subsection (e) defined the term "statement" as used in the

Act. See also Fed.R.Crim.P. 26.2 (extending Jencks Act obligation to cover both prosecution and defense witnesses, other than defendant).

16(a)(1)(A) subsequently was amended to insert a separate provision on discovery of a "written record containing the substance of" a defendant's oral statement (see Note 2, p. 1190), leading federal courts to conclude that the "recorded statement" provision was limited to memorializations of oral statements that would meet the Jencks Act standards (i.e., substantially verbatim recitals, recorded contemporaneously). See CRIMPROC § 20.3(b).

One factor that will influence a jurisdiction's position on the definition of recorded statements is the range of discovery situations to which it applies. In particular, where the definition applies to the discovery of the statements of witnesses, particularly defense witnesses (whose statements are often taken by defense counsel), additional reasons may be found for not going beyond the Jencks definition. Thus *People v. Holtzman*, 234 Mich.App. 166, 593 N.W.2d 617 (1999), cited the following reasons for refusing to adopt an A.B.A. type definition that would include an interviewer's notes: (1) "if trial counsel's witness interview notes were discoverable," it would open the door to placing opposing counsel on the stand "to explain discrepancies surrounding the notes"; and (2) counsel's interview notes often reflect counsel's analysis of the case, and while a distinction could be drawn between the factual content and the opinion content of the notes, "the distinction is [not] clear cut and [it] would probably lead to endless legal wrangles over which portions of the notes are work product and which are not."

5. *Discovery depositions.* Another important feature dividing jurisdictions is their approach to the use of the deposition as a discovery device. The deposition is a primary component of civil discovery. A party may depose any person thought to have relevant information, including the opposing party, without making any showing of need or justification. The witness is subpoenaed to appear at a particular time and place to be deposed, and at the deposition is questioned under oath by the party that subpoenaed him, with opportunity given to the other side to object to improper questions and to ask questions of its own. The deposition is stenographically transcribed and in many jurisdictions may also be videotaped.

All jurisdictions authorize use of depositions in the criminal justice process, but the vast majority sharply restrict their use to purposes other than discovery. Many make the deposition available in criminal cases only to preserve the testimony of a favorable witness who is likely to be unavailable at trial. To utilize a deposition, the side seeking to depose a prospective witness must obtain a court order upon a showing that the proposed deponent would be a material witness at trial but is unlikely to be available to testify there due to illness or other difficulty. In other jurisdictions, the language of the deposition provision is somewhat broader, but still is aimed at preserving testimony rather than discovery. Thus, Federal Rule 15(a) allows for depositions upon court order "whenever due to the exceptional circumstances of the case it is in the interest of justice that testimony of a prospective witness of a party be taken and preserved for use at trial."

Less than a dozen states provide for the use of depositions as a basic discovery device, and they vary as to the extent of its availability for that purpose. In some of these states, the discovery deposition is made available only to the defense rather than to both sides. (Of course, where available to the prosecution, an exception is made as to the defendant, who cannot be deposed unless he consents and waives his privilege against self-incrimination). In some, discovery depositions are not available automatically, but require court approval upon a special showing of need. See CRIMPROC § 20.2(e).

Why have so few states been willing to adopt the discovery deposition, a mainstay of civil discovery? Most of the reasons offered relate to administrative difficulties. It is noted, for example, that civil discovery depositions are used in conjunction with interrogatories which allow the parties to discovery from each other the names of all persons thought to have relevant information. In the criminal discovery process, many jurisdictions do not even require reciprocal pretrial disclosure of witness lists (although the defense, in particular, is likely to be aware of at least some of the prosecution's witnesses). Another administrative argument is that depositions are very costly, and with the state footing the bill for indigent defendants, there is no financial sacrifice that would provide a restraint against appointed counsel conducting unnecessary depositions. The traditional civil deposition procedure, which allows the party to be in attendance, is seen as providing further administrative difficulties—forcing the victim/witness to be confronted (without the security provided by the courtroom setting) by a person he or she may fear and providing for the temporary release of the accused who is being held in custody (although deposition jurisdictions often respond to custody concerns by providing that only defense counsel need be present at the deposition).

Finally, depositions are opposed as imposing an unnecessary burden on prosecution witnesses. There is no need, it is argued, to subject the witness to a further loss of time, beyond that consumed first in providing information to the police for a police report, then in testifying at a screening procedure (preliminary hearing or grand jury proceeding or both), and finally in testifying at trial. If there is need for discovery prior to trial of what a witness knows about the crime, it is sufficient, so the argument goes, to provide for disclosure of the witness' prior recorded statements, as is done in A.B.A. jurisdictions. (In civil pretrial discovery, the recorded statements taken by the opposing party generally are not discoverable as it is expected that the witness will be deposed). Of course, in jurisdictions with provisions modeled on the Federal Rules, those prior recorded statements will not be made available until trial, but that is deemed sufficient in light of offsetting considerations. See Note 2, p. 1196. In jurisdictions which make regular use of a "mini-trial" preliminary hearing (see Ch. 14, § 4), it is also argued that defendant will have the opportunity to question at least the most critical prosecution witness (and to call other witnesses) at the preliminary hearing.

SECTION 2. DISCOVERY BY THE DEFENSE

A. SCOPE: GENERAL CONSIDERATIONS

1. *Constitutional overtones.* Defense discovery has been treated by the Supreme Court as largely a matter to be determined by state legislative or judicial policy, with each state free to set discovery requirements as broad or narrow as it pleases. The Court has recognized, however, certain constitutional requirements that limit that freedom of choice. The *Wardius* ruling, discussed at Note 5, p. 1206, requires a state granting discovery to the prosecution to provide at least reciprocal discovery for the defense. More significantly, the *Brady* doctrine, discussed in Notes 1—3, p. 1198 and § 2 of Ch. 25, imposes upon the prosecution a due process obligation to disclose to the defense such evidence within the prosecution's possession as is both exculpatory and material. Insofar as that due process doctrine may require disclosure prior to trial, rather than simply during trial (see Note 1, p. 1198), it creates a constitutional right to discovery that overrides any limitations found in the particular jurisdiction's discovery statutes or rules.

Apart from the need to reciprocate for prosecution discovery and the *Brady* rule as to exculpatory evidence, the Supreme Court has found no significant constitutional objection to a state's determination to sharply limit pretrial discovery. The Court has noted, for example, that while it may be the "better practice" to grant to the defense pretrial discovery of a defendant's confession that the prosecution intends to use at trial, the failure to follow that practice does not violate due process. *Cicenia v. La Gay,* 357 U.S. 504, 78 S.Ct. 1297, 2 L.Ed.2d 1523 (1958). It also has held that a jurisdiction does not violate due process when it fails to grant pretrial disclosure as to other material relevant to defense preparation but not exculpatory. See *Moore v. Illinois,* 408 U.S. 786, 92 S.Ct. 2562, 33 L.Ed.2d 706 (1972) (prior recorded statement of witness); *Weatherford v. Bursey,* 429 U.S. 545, 97 S.Ct. 837, 51 L.Ed.2d 30 (1977) (failure to inform defendant that an associate was an undercover agent and would testify for the prosecution at trial). See also *Pennsylvania v. Ritchie,* Note 1, p. 1402. State courts, however, have occasionally found that the prosecution's failure to disclose before trial certain critical portions of its evidence deprived the defendant of an adequate opportunity to prepare to meet the government's case and therefore violated due process. See e.g., *Gilchrist v. Commonwealth,* 317 S.E.2d 784 (Va.1984) (failure to furnish key autopsy report until chief medical examiner testified at trial).

2. *Discovery beyond avoiding surprise.* A basic objective of defense discovery in all jurisdictions is to avoid having the defense being disadvantaged by surprise. See Note 2, p. 1177. The primary focus in achieving this objective is on the prosecution providing advance notice of the evidence it intends to produce at trial, either in its case-in-chief or on rebuttal. All jurisdictions, however, also provide for discovery of at least some items within the prosecution's control that the prosecution does not intend to introduce at trial. The theory here is that "the state in its might and power ought to be and is too jealous of according [defendant] a fair and impartial trial to hinder him in intelligently preparing his defense and in availing him of all competent material and relevant evidence that tends to throw light on the subject matter on trial." *Powell v. Superior Court,* 312 P.2d 698 (Cal.1957). The need to ensure against the conviction of the innocent, it is argued, overrides the concept that the state, in an adversary system, has a proprietary interest in the relevant information it develops that might be useful to the defense.

As will be seen in the Notes that follow, jurisdictions vary in the extent to which they will require disclosure beyond the evidence that the prosecution intends to introduce at trial. All jurisdictions require disclosure of relevant prior recorded statements of the defendant, whether or not the prosecution intends to use that statement. See Note 1, p. 1190. Mandatory disclosure of reports on physical and mental examinations and scientific tests commonly extends to all those reports "made in connection with the particular case," see A.B.A. § 2.1(a)(iii), without regard to whether the prosecution intends to introduce at trial the results of those examinations or tests. See Note 1, p. 1193. So too, the defense commonly gains discovery of physical evidence and documents taken from or belonging to the accused, whether or not to be used at trial. See Note 2, p. 1193. Jurisdictions following the model of Federal Rule 16 also mandate disclosure of additional physical items and documents where "material to the preparation of the defense." See Note 3, p. 1193.

On the other side, only a few jurisdictions require pretrial disclosure of the names and prior recorded statements of all persons known to the government to have relevant information. Where pretrial disclosure of the names and prior recorded statements of persons with knowledge is required, it generally is limited to the persons that the prosecution intends to call as its witnesses. See Notes 1 and 2, pp. 1195–96. So too, while many jurisdictions following the A.B.A. model often add to their listing of discoverable items a requirement of prosecution disclosure of any "material or information within [its] possession or control which tends to negate the guilt of accused," most jurisdictions leave the prosecution's obligation to disclose exculpatory evidence to the due process mandate. See Note 2, p. 1198.

3. *Items "within the control" of the prosecution.* Discovery provisions commonly extend only to those discoverable items within the prosecutor's "possession or control." See e.g., A.B.A. § 2.1(d); Fed.R.Crim.P. 16(a)(1). The inclusion of materials within the prosecution's "control," though not in its possession, reflects the extension of discovery provisions beyond material that the prosecution intends to use at trial (which material will eventually come within its possession). How far should the concept of "control" reach? It clearly encompasses the files of the police department working with the prosecutor in the particular case, but should it extend to "any * * * prosecutorial or law enforcement officer" to which the prosecution might have access? See *State v. Coney,* 294 So.2d 82 (Fla.1973) (criminal records "within the actual or constructive possession of the prosecutor" included data obtainable from the F.B.I.); *State v. Edmaiston,* 679 S.W.2d 360 (Mo.App.1984) (discovery rule violated by nondisclosure of basic investigative file prepared by police in another city who had also investigated the incident, notwithstanding that file was not known to the prosecutors until an officer of that department appeared to testify at trial). But compare *Commonwealth v. Daye,* 587 N.E.2d 194 (Mass.1992) (where county prosecutor was working with one police department in investigating the murder on which defendant was charged, its "control" did not extend to reports of a different police department in a nearby county which was independently investigating another drug-related murder).

A.B.A. § 2.1(a) refers simply to material within the prosecutor's control, while Federal Rule 16(a)(1) refers to material "within * * * the control of the government, the existence of which is known, or by the exercise of due diligence may become known, to the attorney for the government." Should this distinction have an influence on the scope given to the concept of the prosecution's "control"? Consider also A.B.A. § 2.4 (upon defense designation of items within the control of "other government personnel" that would be discoverable if within the prosecutor's control, the prosecution must make a "diligent good faith effort" to cause such material to be made available to defense).[a]

4. *Protective orders.* Where discovery provisions provide for mandatory defense discovery, such discovery is always made subject to possible restriction through judicial issuance of a protective order. See e.g., Fed.R.Crim.P. 16(d)(1); A.B.A. § 4.4. Where defense discovery is discretionary, the trial court's discretion allows it to limit or deny discovery based on the same interests that would justify

---

a. Since discovery provisions do not extend to items within the possession of third parties, the defense must look to other vehicles to examine such items (e.g., documents) as potential evidence or leads to evidence. The Supreme Court has noted that Federal Rule 17(c), providing for defense subpoena of documents and other objects, is not a discovery device. Rule 17 does allow the trial court to order production of documents and other tangible items before trial where counsel has need to inspect the items prior to their intended use at trial, and that provides an incidental degree of pretrial discovery, but such pretrial disclosure comes fairly close to the time set for trial and is limited to items specified with particularity that will be admissible in evidence. See *United States v. Nixon,* 418 U.S. 683, 94 S.Ct. 3090, 41 L.Ed.2d 1039 (1974). Consider, however, Peter Henning, *Defense Discovery in White Collar Criminal Prosecutions,* 15 Ga.St.L.Rev. 601 (1999) (critical of lower court reading of Supreme Court precedent on Rule 17(c) as excluding discovery use of that rule; noting that the end result is that in white collar cases in particular, where defendants often have need to explore records in the possession of third

parties, such as banks, employees, and corporate codefendants, the defendant in a federal criminal case lacks the discovery opportunities that would be available to a person in the same position in a civil case).

Some states do provide vehicles for obtaining discovery from third parties. Thus, discovery depositions, where available, may be directed to third parties. See Note 5, p. 1186. Also, some states allow their counterpart of Rule 17 to be used as a discovery device. See e.g., *Pennsylvania v. Ritchie,* Note 1, p. 1402. See also *Commonwealth v. Neumyer,* 432 Mass. 23, 731 N.E.2d 1053 (2000) (trial court has Rule 17 subpoena authority to order rape counseling center to allow defense inspection of relevant records that were not protected by privilege; that use does not undercut the limitation of discovery provisions to material in the possession custody, a control of the prosecutor). Compare *State v. Cartwright,* 173 Or.App. 59, 20 P.3d 223 (2001) (pretrial discovery and production of trial evidence are different concepts, and subpoena is available only for the later use; therefore defendant could not use subpoena authority to obtain pretrial discovery of nonparty's audiotape recordings of victim/witnesses).

issuance of a protective order. As to what those interests might be, compare the open ended language of A.B.A. § 4.4 (upon "a showing of cause") and Federal Rule 16(d)(1) (upon a "sufficient showing") with Ill.Sup.Ct.R. 412(j) which requires a "substantial risk to any person of physical harm, intimidation, bribery, economic reprisals, or unnecessary annoyance or embarrassment resulting from such disclosure which outweighs the usefulness of disclosure to counsel." Is there a special need for a fairly specific standard governing the issuance of protective orders in light of the authorization in protective order provisions for the court to accept ex parte showings of grounds by the prosecution? See Fed.R. 16(d)(2); A.B.A. § 4.4. Consider also fn. c, p. 1196.

Assuming a state interest that justifies issuance of a protective order, how far may that order extend? Compare A.B.A. § 4.4 (disclosure may be restricted or deferred, "provided that all material and information to which a party is entitled must be disclosed in time to permit * * * beneficial use"); Fed.R.Crim.P. 16(d)(1) (discovery may be "denied, restricted, or deferred").

B. Statements of the Defendant and Any Codefendants

1. *Defendant's written or recorded statements.* Federal Rule 16(a)(1)(A) and A.B.A. § 2.1(a)(ii) both require the prosecution to disclose to the defense all "written or recorded statements" of the defendant within the prosecution's possession or control. All states include such coverage in their discovery provisions. Historically, the written or recorded statement of the defendant was one of the first items included in the defense's right to discovery. Why is there such strong support for discovery of such statements? Consider the following arguments: (1) the precise wording of defendant's statement is especially important to defense counsel in preparing for trial or in determining whether a guilty plea is advisable; (2) disclosure here does not pose a substantial threat of successful perjury since the defendant may be impeached effectively by reference to his statement; (3) disclosure of defendant's statement does not create a reciprocity problem since the state obviously gained discovery from the defendant in obtaining the statement from him originally; and (4) if disclosure is not granted directly, the defendant will simply use the motion to suppress as an indirect discovery device.

2. *Distinguishing "recorded" and non-recorded statements.* Federal Rule 16(a)(1)(A) deals with three categories of oral statements of the defendant that are recorded by a third person. If an oral statement is recorded and the defendant formally adopts or approves that recordation, it becomes the defendant's "written statement" and is automatically discoverable (leaving aside the issue of relevancy, see Note 4, infra.). Also automatically discoverable is the written record of an oral statement that meets the prerequisites for a "recorded statement" (i.e., substantially verbatim and recorded contemporaneously, meeting the Jencks definition, see Note 4, p. 1184). However, if the written record does not meet these prerequisites and is simply a "written record of the substance" of an oral statement, it becomes discoverable only if made "in response to interrogation by any person then known to the defendant to be a government agent." This limitation becomes important primarily where the written record was made by the person to whom the defendant spoke and that person either was not a government agent or was an undercover agent. See e.g., *United States v. Burns*, 15 F.3d 211 (1st. Cir.1994). This same setting often also poses difficulties even when the record meets the Jencks prerequisites for a recorded statement, for it then often constitutes a recording that includes both the remarks of the defendant and the person (not known to be a government agent) with whom he is speaking (as where the undercover agent utilizes a tape recording). At this point, which Rule 16(a) provision controls, that requiring disclosure of the recorded statement of the defendant or that prohibiting the disclosure of the recorded statement of government witnesses (assuming that other person will be a witness)? See *United States v. Walker*, 538 F.2d 266 (9th Cir.1976) (recording discoverable); *United States v. Taylor*, 707 F.Supp. 696 (S.D.N.Y.1989) ("statements made by defendants which are intermixed with statements of prospective witnesses" should be governed by the Jencks provision prohibiting the pretrial disclosure of statements of witnesses). Is the answer to excise the words of the other party because even though that may eliminate the context needed to fully understand the meaning of the defendant's words, the issue here is not the use of the record as evidence, but making discoverable a record that may assist the defense in preparing its case? What of the incidental disclosure of the identity of the person with whom the defendant was speaking? Under Fed. R. Crim. P. 16(a)(1)(A), even an oral statement that the prosecution intends to use in evidence is not discoverable if made to a person not then known to be a government agent. See Note 3 infra. This limitation was designed to keep the defendant from learning pretrial that a person in whom he confided (at least a person he did not know to be a government agent) will testify for the government at trial and recount the defendant's statement.

3. *Defendant's oral statements.* Although many jurisdictions have provisions requiring prosecution disclosure of the substance of oral statements made by defendant, those provisions are not as common as the provisions requiring pretrial disclosure of defendant's written or recorded statements. Moreover, the oral-statement provisions tend to be more limited in scope than the recorded-statement provisions. While A.B.A. § 2.1(a)(ii) requires disclosure of "the substance of any oral statements made by the accused", many jurisdictions limit their provisions to oral statements that the prosecution "intends to offer in evidence at trial." Is that limitation justified on the ground of practicability? It has been suggested it would impose a substantial burden on the prosecution to require it to identify all oral statements known to the police (either through interrogation of defendant or interviews of witnesses), especially where those statements are neither noted in the police reports nor brought to the prosecution's attention as statements the police believe should be used at trial. Cf. Federal Rule 16(a)(1)(A) (intended trial use not a condition where a writing contains the substance of the oral statement, but is a condition for the prosecution's disclosure obligation as to oral statements not so summarized; both must have been made to a known government agent).

4. *Statement relevancy.* Although A.B.A. § 2.1(a)(ii) requires prosecution disclosure of "any" written or recorded statement (and the substance of "any" oral statement) within the prosecution's possession or control, Federal Rule 16(a)(1)(A)'s provisions on defendant's oral, written or recorded, and recorded-in-substance statements are limited to "relevant" statements within the government's possession or control. This limitation becomes especially significant in prosecutions involving regulatory offenses, where the written statements of the accused may well include a lengthy correspondence with the regulatory agency, covering a substantial time frame and a variety of different incidents. Relevant statements clearly include those statements the government intends to use in its case-in-chief and those it anticipates possibly using to impeach the defendant or rebut the defense's presentation. However, that does not mark the outer-boundary of relevancy, which federal courts have described as also encompassing anything that might be helpful to the accused in preparing a defense. *United States v. Bailleaux*, 685 F.2d 1105 (9th Cir.1982).

5. *Defendant's criminal record.* Both Federal Rule 16(a)(1)(B) and the third edition of the A.B.A. Standards, at § 11–2.1(a)(vi), provide for automatic disclosure of the defendant's criminal record. Explaining this provision, the Advisory Committee comment on the Federal Rules noted that the defendant "may be uncertain of the precise nature of his prior criminal record" and disclosure would "make it possible to resolve prior to trial any disputes as to the correctness" of that record. Disclosure may also facilitate pretrial rulings as to whether the prior record can be used as impeachment evidence or be used to show a similar modus operandi in a pattern of past criminal activity.

On the same premise, should the prosecution be required to disclose prior to trial past misconduct not resulting in a criminal record that will be used to establish relevant prior criminality? See Edward Imwinkelried, *The Worst Surprise of All: No Right to Pretrial Discovery of the Prosecution's Uncharged Misconduct Evidence*, 56 Fordham L.Rev. 247 (1987), arguing that here too, pretrial disclosure is required to permit a challenge to correctness and to resolve admissibility issues prior to trial, and, indeed, pretrial disclosure is even more important as to uncharged misconduct because the defendant who challenges its correctness will need to do more in the way of pretrial investigation. Where the evidence of prior misconduct is to be presented through the testimony of a witness/victim of that misconduct, is the disclosure issue presented here any different than that presented with respect to disclosure of the identify of other prosecution witnesses (see Note 1, p. 1195)? Where relevant prior misconduct will be established through a prior arrest record, should it be treated any differently than disclosure of other documents (see Note 2, p. 1193). The majority of states have no special rule for disclosure of prior uncharged misconduct, and ordinarily do not require disclosure. Several states, however, do require pretrial disclosure, subject to a possible protective order. See Imwinkelried, supra.

6. *Codefendants' statements.* Required prosecution disclosure of codefendants' statements has been urged on the grounds that such statements: "(1) are potentially important to defense counsel in preparing to meet the government's case and developing evidence on defendant's behalf; (2) aid defense counsel in deciding whether to make a severance motion and in assisting the judicial determination of such a motion; and (3) mitigate the well-known proclivities of some criminal defendants not to give their own lawyers a truthful account of their actions." Reznick, *The New Federal Rules of Criminal Procedure*, 54 Geo.L.J. 1276 (1966). These concerns have not proven as convincing to the drafters of discovery provisions as the grounds supporting the required disclosure of the defendant's own statements. Only about one-third of the states have provisions requiring pretrial disclosure of a codefendant's statement, although other jurisdictions may grant to the trial court discretion to order such disclosure where it would not conflict with any exemptions or prohibitions contained in the discovery provision. See e.g., *United States v. McMillen*, 489 F.2d 229 (7th Cir.1972) (recognizing discretion as to statements of those codefendants who will not fall within the prohibition as to pretrial disclosure of the statements of prosecution witnesses).

Among those states with provisions requiring pretrial disclosure of codefendants' statements, several follow A.B.A. § 2.1(a)(ii), which requires disclosure of the written or recorded statement and the substance of any oral statements made by a codefendant only "if the trial is to be a joint one." The objective here is to give defense counsel information needed to determine in advance of trial whether to seek a severance or to request that the codefendant's statement be redacted if used against him (see *Gray v. Maryland*, (p. 1061). Only a handful of states require disclosure of a codefendant's oral or written statements without limitation, treating them as parallel to the defendant's own statement. Of course, if the codefendant is to testify as a prosecution witness, disclosure will be required where the statements of such witnesses are discoverable. See also *In re United*

States, 834 F.2d 283 (2d Cir.1987) (where coconspirator's statement will also be admissible against the defendant as a statement made in the course of, and in furtherance of, the conspiracy, the coconspirator becomes a witness for the prosecution and the Jencks Act prohibition of pretrial disclosure applies; because the statement is admitted under Fed.R.Evid. 801 as a "defendant admission," that does not make it a statement of the defendant for the purposes of Rule 16(a)(1)A)).

C.   REPORTS, DOCUMENTS, AND TANGIBLE OBJECTS

1.   *Scientific reports.* Defense discovery provisions commonly make mandatory the pretrial disclosure of reports on physical and mental examinations and on scientific tests or experiments that are within the prosecution's possession or control. Mandatory disclosure of scientific reports is justified on the following grounds: "Once the report is prepared, the scientific expert's position is not readily influenced, and therefore disclosure presents little danger of prompting perjury on intimidation. Disclosure is also justified on the ground that 'it lessens the imbalance which may result from the State's early and complete investigation in contrast to [defendant's] * * * late and limited investigation.' It is further noted that 'this sort of evidence is practically impossible for the adversary to test or rebut at trial without an adversary opportunity to examine it closely.'" CRIMPROC § 20.3(f).

In light of the above justifications, what is the appropriate reach of a provision requiring disclosure of scientific reports? Should it encompass all reports "made in connection with the particular case," A.B.A. § 2.1(iv), or should there be added the requirement that the report also either be "material to the preparation of the defense * * * or intended for use by the government as evidence in chief at trial," Fed.R.Crim.P. 16(a)(1)(D)? Should the provision be limited to written reports and to no more than the report itself? See Fed.R.Crim.P. 16(a)(1)(E) (including written summary of anticipated expert witness testimony). Compare *State v. Hutchinson,* 766 P.2d 447 (Wash.1989) (court's authority in ordering discovery is limited to items in existence and therefore does not allow ordering expert to prepare a report). Should it be limited to "scientific" examinations or include as well analytical studies by other types of experts? See *United States v. Fischbach and Moore,* 576 F.Supp. 1384 (W.D.Pa.1983) (analysis of economist or statistician concerning bidding and pricing practices, though made in connection with the particular case, was not discoverable).

2.   *Documents and tangible objects.* Defense discovery provisions commonly also make mandatory the prosecution's disclosure of certain documents and tangible objects within the prosecution's possession or control. These provisions generally apply to items which the prosecution intends to use at trial or "which were obtained from or belong to the accused." See A.B.A. § 2.1(a)(v). Insofar as they encompass evidence to be used at trial, such provisions are often justified on the ground that discovery poses no substantial threat of perjury and an inspection in advance of trial will often be necessary to challenge the evidence at trial. Insofar as they encompass material obtained from or belonging to defendant but not to be used at trial, the provisions are justified on the ground that the prosecution has already obtained discovery from the defendant and the defendant should have a reciprocal right to utilize his own records or other property in preparing his defense.

3.   *"Materiality" provisions.* Federal Rule 16 and various state provisions also allow for discovery of documents and tangible items not obtained from the defendant or to be used at trial where such documents or items are "material to the preparation of the defense."[b] See Fed.R.Crim.P. 16(a)(1)(C). What should constitute "materiality" under such a provision? Some federal lower courts have stated materiality requires more than a showing of "relevancy," that the defense must also show some grounding for believing that the line of defense to which the document has relevance would be productive. See e.g., *United States v. Ross,* 511 F.2d 757 (5th Cir.1975). But compare Henning, fn. a , p. 1189 (criticizing this analysis as confusing "materiality" in the discovery context with the "materiality" component of the due process obligation to disclose exculpatory material, Note 1, p. 1198). Where a defendant charged with assaulting a police officer notes an intent to raise a defense of self-defense, should anything more be required to gain discovery of the officer's personnel records, which would indicate whether complaints of unnecessary force had been filed against the officer in the past by other arrestees? See *People v. Walker,* 666 P.2d 113 (Colo.1983) (record to be disclosed if in camera inspection revealed such complaints). Compare *State v. Cano,* 743 P.2d 956 (Ariz.App.1987) (unsupported claim that arresting officer had "reputation for dishonesty" appeared to be a "fishing expedition" and did not require in camera inspection of personnel records). Where the document's materiality is less than obvious, is it appropriate for the judge to initially require defense counsel to explain what she is seeking and to then grant discovery only if the judge determines on an in camera review that the document would be helpful to the defense in light of that explanation? See CRIMPROC § 20.3(g) (noting this practice).

   4. *Police reports.* Where a police report contains a description of a statement made to the police by a defendant, codefendant, or prosecution witness that is sufficiently complete to constitute a "recorded statement" of that person, that portion of the report commonly will be governed by the jurisdiction's discovery rule governing such statements. So too, the portion of the report containing an abridged description of an oral statement is likely to be within any a discovery provision that encompasses summaries of oral statements. Where the officer is to be a prosecution witness, the police report will be governed by the jurisdiction's discovery rule on the prior recorded statements of witnesses.

   The critical issue with respect to police reports is whether there should be pretrial discovery of additional information that would not fall under the provisions governing statements of defendants, codefendants, or prosecution witnesses. This would include the officer's comments on his own observations (where the officer is not himself a prosecution witness), and references to conversations with persons who are not defendants, codefendants, or prosecution witnesses. These portions of the report might conceivably fit under several other discovery provisions, including: (1) provisions for discovery of documents "which are material to the preparation of the defense" (see Note 3, supra); (2) provisions requiring disclosure of statements of persons having knowledge of relevant facts (see Note 1, p. 1195); and (3) provisions authorizing discretionary disclosure of "relevant material and information" not otherwise specified in the discovery rule (see A.B.A. § 2.5). However, most jurisdictions either bar disclosure of police reports under exemption provisions or create a strong presumption against applying discretionary discovery authorization to police reports.

   Jurisdictions which bar discovery of police reports commonly have "internal memoranda" provisions similar to Federal Rule 16(a)(2), discussed at p. 1184. Some courts have reached a similar conclusion, without statutory direction, on the

   b. In *United States v. Armstrong,* as described in fn. a, p. 869, the Supreme Court held that the reference here was to the defense's preparation of its "defense against the government's case-in-chief" and Rule 16's materiality provision therefore did not encompass documents that might be material to establishing that the prosecution was precluded as a racially discriminatory prosecution.

ground that such reports automatically constitute work product, e.g., *Johnson v. State,* 584 N.E.2d 1092 (Ind.1992). Assuming the work product doctrine extends to material prepared by police officers (see Note 3, p. 1182), is it appropriate to assume that police reports will inevitably constitute "opinion" work product, reflecting mental impressions, conclusions, etc.? If not, what justifies an automatic bar to discovery of what may at best be viewed as non-opinion work product? It has been argued that the general exemption of police reports serves a variety of interests, including: (1) preserving the confidentiality of police sources, continuing investigations, and investigative tactics without requiring a protective order, (2) avoiding defense "misuse" of police reports to build "red herring" defenses which seek to shift the focus of the case from the weight of the evidence against the defendant to a trial of the thoroughness of the police investigation, and (3) encouraging police to file complete reports that will be more useful for internal review purposes. Cf. Stanley Fisher, *"Just the Facts Ma'am: Lying and the Omission of Exculpatory Evidence in Police Reports,"* 28 New Eng.L.Rev. 1 (1993).

D. PROSECUTION WITNESSES

1. *Names and addresses.* State provisions patterned after the A.B.A. Standards generally require the prosecution to provide the defense with "the names and addresses of persons whom the State intends to call as witnesses." See A.B.A. § 2.1(a)(i). A few states with A.B.A.-type provisions have a broader standard requiring the prosecutor to list the names and addresses of all persons "known by the government to have knowledge of relevant facts" without regard to whether they will be called as witnesses. See e.g., Alaska R.Crim.P. 16(b)(1)(i).

In those jurisdictions that do not have a provision mandating pretrial disclosure of the names of prosecution witnesses, the trial court generally is held to have discretionary authority to order pretrial discovery of the names of all or some of those witnesses. The prevailing presumption in most such jurisdictions, however, is against the affirmative exercise of that discretion; trial courts are to order disclosure only upon a strong defense showing of special need. To make such a showing, defense ordinarily must establish that there is some barrier to its ability to conduct its own investigation and that there is no reason to believe that disclosure will result in the intimidation of the listed witnesses. See e.g., *United States v. Stroop,* 121 F.R.D. 269 (E.D.N.C.1988) (particularized need justified disclosure in light of six factors: "(1) the indictment alleges offenses [relating to a scheme to defraud] occurring almost 5 years ago, rendering defense preparation a difficult proposition at best; (2) the case involves a complex paper trail with multiple defendants; (3) the critical, dispositive evidence will [also] flow * * * from anecdotal testimony * * * of unindicted coconspirators [and] other participants to the transactions * * *; (4) a number of those witnesses are within the control of the government and are not openly available to the defense for investigation and interview; (5) the record contains no indication that defendants have a past criminal record, or that they have ever been involved in an offense involving violence or a threat of violence * * *; (6) the government's *pro forma* and conclusory response, as well as the record, fail to indicate that, by supplying the witnesses' names prior to trial, this will, in any manner, increase the likelihood that the witnesses will not appear at trial, will be unwilling to testify, or will be harassed, threatened or intimidated").

CRIMPROC § 20.3(h) contends that the strong presumption against disclosure found in many "discretionary jurisdictions" is "based only partly on the need to protect against possible intimidation of witnesses." Noting that the presumption is applied in many situations in which there is no realistic fear that defendant "will intimidate or otherwise improperly influence witnesses,"[c] the authors suggest that these jurisdictions "apparently are concerned that the adoption of a policy which sought to distinguish such situations, * * * [and] thereby allowed disclosure in a substantial number of cases, would inevitably reinforce the natural reluctance of many persons to offer to testify at trial." Is this a legitimate ground for refusing to require disclosure? Various federal prosecutors relied largely on such reasoning in opposing a 1974 proposed amendment to Federal Rule 16 (approved by the Supreme Court but subsequently rejected by Congress) that would have required the government to provide defendants with witness lists unless it established grounds for a protective order. Those prosecutors noted that (1) gaining victim/witness cooperation was one of the most difficult tasks facing law enforcement, (2) that many of potential witnesses, with or without justification in the particular case, were fearful of retaliation or harassment, and (3) that the protective order procedure could not screen out all cases of likely intimidation or provide assurance to witnesses in general.

2. *Witness' recorded statement.* Undoubtedly the most controversial item of potential defense discovery is the prior recorded statement of the prosecution witness. Here the states are divided between those that require discovery, those that make discovery discretionary, and those that prohibit court ordered discovery of such statements.

Approximately a third of the states have provisions similar to A.B.A. § 2.1(a)(1). They require the prosecution to provide pretrial disclosure of the relevant written or recorded statements of its witnesses, subject to the trial court's authority to issue a protective order where appropriate (see Note 4, p. 1184) and to a "work product" exemption as applicable (see Note 3, p. 1182). As with witness lists (see Note 1 supra), a few of these provisions go beyond those persons the prosecution intends to have testify and require disclosure of the prior recorded statements of all persons "known by the government to have knowledge of relevant facts." Alaska R.Crim.P. 16(b)(1)(i). Roughly a third of the states recognize a discretionary authority of the trial court to order pretrial disclosure of the prior recorded statements of some or all of the prosecution's intended witnesses. Most of these jurisdictions, however, recognize a presumption against ordering such disclosure, to be overcome by a special showing of need. Finally, roughly a third of the states, and the federal system, specifically prohibit court ordered pretrial discovery of a prosecution witness' statements. These jurisdictions ordinarily include in their discovery rules a specific prohibition similar to that found in Federal Rule 16(a)(2) as it combines with the Jencks Act (see fn g, p. 1184).

While the opposition to pretrial disclosure of a prosecution witness' prior recorded statement is based in some jurisdictions on essentially the same concern

---

c. Consider in this regard, Imwinkelried, Note 5, p. 1192, speaking in favor of the disclosure of the names of witnesses who will testify as to uncharged misconduct: "In 1985, Professor Michael Graham released his book, *Witness Intimidations: The Law's Response* (1985). There, Professor Graham points out that the available data indicates that the problem of witness intimidation arises in only a minority of cases. The data convinces him, however, that 'thousands of examples' of witness harassment exist. * * * In light of Professor Graham's research, it no longer remains possible for the proponents of expanded criminal discovery to brush aside prosecutors' concerns over witness intimidation. * * * [H]owever, * * * the judge has procedures available to

him or her to reduce the risk of intimidation that are less drastic than a complete bar to defense discovery. Rather than denying defense discovery altogether, the judge can use the 'scalpel' of a protective order. * * * " Consider also H. Lee Sarokin and William Zuckermann, *Presumed Innocent? Restrictions on Criminal Discovery in Federal Court Belies this Presumption* 43 Rutgers L.Rev. 1089 (1991) (federal judge argues current system deprives defense of needed information for trial preparation, but does not substantially reduce potential for tampering; with defendants commonly learning of the witness' names shortly before trial, the time frame for tampering is shorter, but that "does little to redress the perceived danger").

for the protection of the witness that led those jurisdictions to sharply restrict court ordered disclosure of witness lists (see Note 1 supra), that concern does not fully explain the position taken in many of the jurisdictions that either prohibit disclosure of witness statements or create a strong presumption against the exercise of trial court discretion to order such disclosure. Discovery of a witness' statement is prohibited or sharply restricted even where the defense already knows that the particular person will be a prosecution witness. Indeed, discovery of witness statements is sharply restricted, or prohibited altogether, in several jurisdictions in which witness lists are automatically discoverable.

What justifies treating the disclosure of witness statements far more restrictively than the disclosure of other items tied to the prosecution's prospective evidence? Consider the following grounds: (1) disclosure of such statements is more likely to facilitate defense perjury than disclosure of any other aspect of the prosecution's case; (2) assuming defendant knows the identity of the prosecution's witnesses, the defendant's alternative means for preparing for the witnesses' testimony are more adequate here than as to other items (e.g., scientific reports), as it will be sufficient merely to interview the witness and investigate possible grounds for bias; (3) the witness' statement is primarily of value in impeachment and disclosure at trial is sufficient for that purpose; (4) disclosure of witness statements tends to undermine the adversary system by giving the defense the benefit of the litigation analysis of the prosecution;[d] (5) disclosure of witness statements is in the defendant's best interest as it encourages defense counsel to pursue his or her own investigation by interviewing witnesses rather than relying on statements obtained by the police; and (6) requiring disclosure of a witness' statement will only lead police and prosecutors opposed to such discovery to avoid recording those statements, relying instead on brief notes and their memory of the substance of what the witness told them.

3. *Interviewing witnesses.* Where discovery of witness statements rests in the discretion of the court, does a sufficient grounding for ordering such discovery exist when defense counsel has sought to interview a known prosecution witness but that witness has refused to submit to an interview? Should it matter what role the police or prosecution played in the witness' decision not to submit to an interview? Courts have uniformly held that the prosecution and police cannot advise or direct witnesses not to cooperate with defense counsel. See also A.B.A. § 4.1. However, they have also stated that, since "the witness is free to decide whether to grant or refuse an interview, * * * it is not improper for the government to inform the witness of that right." *United States v. White,* 454 F.2d 435 (7th Cir.1971). But compare *A.B.A. Standards* (commentary), 78 (1st ed.

---

d. In jurisdictions that have provisions modeled on the A.B.A. Standards, the work product exemption would be applicable only when the witness' statement was given in response to questioning by the prosecutor. See Note 3, p. 1182. Even then, the statement as a whole would constitute work product only if the prosecutor's questions reveal his or her strategic analysis, mental impressions, etc., and that aspect of the recorded statement cannot be excised. See *State v. Garcia,* 724 P.2d 412 (Wash.App.1986). Where the A.B.A.'s definition of work product is broadened to include the opinion work product of the police, the same type of analysis is required as to the questions asked by the police and their reflection in the resulting statement. Proponents of extensive defense discovery argue that recorded statements obtained by police or prosecutor will rarely be rendered totally exempt from discovery under such a standard. They argue that those statements will more often than not consist of little more than the witness' narrative of events in response to an open-ended question (e.g., "what happened"?), and where the questions do reflect some tactical theory or analysis, the recorded response often can be redacted to exclude references that will reflect such opinion work product. Of course, where a jurisdiction seeks to bar disclosure of all work product, including non-opinion work product (see Note 3, p. 1182), then all witness statements generated by the police or prosecutor might be viewed as work product, no matter what their content. See *Thigpen v. State,* 355 So.2d 392 (Ala.Crim.App.1977); *People v. Holtzman,* Note 4, p. 1186.

1970) (counsel should also advise witness that "it is in the interests of justice that the witness make himself available for interviews by [opposing] counsel").

E. EXCULPATORY EVIDENCE

1. *Brady as a discovery obligation.* As discussed in Ch. 25, § 2, the Supreme Court, in a series of cases starting with the seminal ruling of *Brady v. Maryland*, has established a constitutional obligation of the prosecution to disclose exculpatory evidence within its possession or control when that evidence might be material to the outcome of the case. The Supreme Court's *Brady* rulings have involved situations in which it was learned after trial that the prosecution had failed to disclose certain evidence, and the Court therefore had no reason to comment on the needed timing of a *Brady* disclosure. Lower courts generally have agreed that the prosecutor's *Brady* obligation is satisfied if the exculpatory material is disclosed "in time for its effective use at trial," and for many types of exculpatory evidence, disclosure at trial itself will be satisfactory. CRIMPROC § 20.3(m). To sustain a claim that the disclosure of exculpatory material at trial came too late, the defendant must show that delay in disclosure violated *Brady's* materiality requirement—that is, there is a reasonable probability that had the evidence been disclosed in a pretrial proceeding, rather than at trial the "result of the proceeding would have been different." Ibid. Where would such a showing most readily be made? Commentators suggest that one possibility is that in which scientific expertise is needed to evaluate the exculpatory evidence and the time needed for such an evaluation simply cannot be obtained (through a continuance) when the evidence is first disclosed at trial. However, the evidence most likely to fit in this category—an exculpatory test result or expert's analysis—typically must be disclosed pretrial under discovery provisions that encompass all results of scientific tests and not just those the prosecution intends to use in evidence. See Note 1, p. 1193. Another possibility is that in which the exculpatory evidence would lead the defense to other helpful evidence not disclosed as part of discovery and the disclosure at trial fails to give the defense sufficient time to explore the leads to that other evidence. Cf. *Schwartzmiller v. Winters*, 576 P.2d 1052 (Idaho 1978) (disclosure at preliminary hearing of victim's perjury and subordination of perjury was too late to satisfy *Brady* since defendant lacked "adequate time * * * to prepare a defense based on the victim's lack of veracity").

2. In many jurisdictions, the timing issue is bypassed by a regular prosecutorial practice of disclosing exculpatory evidence pretrial. Various states have made the duty to disclose material exculpatory evidence a part of the prosecutor's discovery obligations. Indeed, those provisions are often broader than the *Brady* obligation, which arguably is limited to admissible evidence (see Note 5, p. 1400), and ties materiality to the likelihood that the disclosure would alter the outcome of the proceeding (see Note 3, p. 1399). See e.g. A.B.A. Standards, § 11–2.1(viii) (3d ed. 1996) (material subject to pretrial discovery by the defense includes "any material or information within the prosecutor's possession or control which tends to negate the guilt of the defendant as to the offense charged or which would tend to reduce the punishment of the defendant"). Even without such a rule, however, where the defense makes a pretrial request for the disclosure of "*Brady* material," particularly where the defense identifies the specific type of evidence sought (see Note 6, p. 1401), the prosecution, if it has such evidence and believes it to be exculpatory, will make disclosure at that point.

Where the prosecution is uncertain whether the requested items meet the *Brady* standard of material exculpatory evidence, it may ask the trial court to examine the items in camera and make that determination. A similar request may be made by the defense where the prosecution acknowledges possession of the requested items, but claims that they do not constitute *Brady* material. Many courts are reluctant to engage in such a pretrial application of *Brady*, noting that: "(1) the judge is ordinarily less oriented to the facts of the case and possible defenses than is the prosecuting attorney; (2) requiring the judge to review prosecution files for information useful to the defendant casts the judge in a defense advocate's role; and (3) in camera inspection can become a ponderous, time-consuming task if utilized in every case merely on demand." CRIMPROC § 24.3(b) (citing sources). These courts typically will undertake a pretrial assessment only where it is limited to a specific item and the defense can show that the item will be critical exculpatory evidence if it has a certain content. Some courts, however, will provide a pretrial in camera review, even for a general class of items, upon a defense showing as to relevancy, admissibility, and possible exculpatory impact. See *Snowden v. State*, 672 A.2d 1017 (Del.1996) (finding appropriate trial court's in camera review of various police personnel records).

3. *Brady and prohibitions against pretrial disclosure.* Consider, CRIMPROC § 20.3(m): "The range of possible *Brady* material is so broad that it can readily encompass material that the discovery rule either implicitly or explicitly excludes from pretrial disclosure. Thus, *Brady* may reach impeachment material to be found in the prior recorded statement of a prospective government witness, but the jurisdiction's 'Jencks Act' provision may preclude disclosure of that statement until the witness testifies at trial. *Brady* would also reach incentives given to prosecution witnesses, and while the documents involved (plea agreements) might be discoverable under provisions for disclosure of documents material to the preparation of the defense, the disclosure would be inconsistent with a discovery provision that ordinarily seeks to withhold from the defendant the identity of the persons who will be testifying against him. Federal courts have divided in treating such potential conflicts between *Brady* and the limits placed on federal pretrial discovery. Many conclude that no conflict is presented since *Brady* will be satisfied by producing such exculpatory material at trial. Others have argued that disclosure at trial could be insufficient, and the trial court therefore has the authority to trump the Jencks Act and order disclosure pretrial of prior statements of witnesses insofar as they contain exculpatory material. Some would do this automatically and others would do so based on the character of the exculpatory evidence and the likely need for pretrial disclosure to permit the defense to use it effectively (distinguishing in this regard between impeachment material and other exculpatory material). The Sixth Circuit has suggested, however, that even assuming arguendo that *Brady* may be violated by failing to reveal until trial exculpatory material within a witness' prior recorded statement (notwithstanding the court's capacity to grant a recess at that point if the defense needs more time to explore that material), the *Brady* doctrine does not thereby give the trial court the authority to override Jencks and order pretrial disclosure. *Brady* imposes an obligation upon the prosecutor and leaves to the prosecutor the initial determination of when to disclose. If it fails to comply adequately, 'it acts at its own peril.' [*United States v. Presser*, 844 F.2d 1275 (6th Cir. 1988)] Under this view, Jencks is not necessarily compatible with *Brady* under all circumstances, and clearly does not 'trump' *Brady*, but does leave to the government the opportunity to control the timing of its disclosure, with the court determining after the case is completed whether a delay in disclosure so prejudiced the defendant as to deny due process." But compare Podgor, fn. a., p. 1181.

SECTION 3. DISCOVERY BY THE PROSECUTION

A. CONSTITUTIONAL CONSIDERATIONS

WILLIAMS v. FLORIDA
399 U.S. 78, 90 S.Ct. 1893, 26 L.Ed.2d 446 (1970).

Justice WHITE delivered the opinion of the Court.

Prior to his trial for robbery in the State of Florida, petitioner filed a "Motion for a Protective Order," seeking to be excused from the requirements of Rule 1.200 [now Rule 3.200] of the Florida Rules of Criminal Procedure. That rule requires a defendant, on written demand of the prosecuting attorney, to give notice in advance of trial if the defendant intends to claim an alibi, and to furnish the prosecuting attorney with information as to the place he claims to have been and with the names and addresses of the alibi witnesses he intends to use. In his motion petitioner openly declared his intent to claim an alibi, but objected to the further disclosure requirements on the ground that the Rule "compels the defendant in a criminal case to be a witness against himself" in violation of his Fifth and Fourteenth Amendment rights. The motion was denied. * * *

Florida's notice-of-alibi rule is in essence a requirement that a defendant submit to a limited form of pretrial discovery by the State whenever he intends to rely at trial on the defense of alibi. In exchange for the defendant's disclosure of the witnesses he proposes to use to establish that defense, the State in turn is required to notify the defendant of any witnesses it proposes to offer in rebuttal to that defense. Both sides are under a continuing duty promptly to disclose the names and addresses of additional witnesses bearing on the alibi as they become available. The threatened sanction for failure to comply is the exclusion at trial of the defendant's alibi evidence—except for his own testimony—or, in the case of the State, the exclusion of the State's evidence offered in rebuttal to the alibi.

In this case, following the denial of his Motion for a Protective Order, petitioner complied with the alibi rule and gave the State the name and address of one Mary Scotty. Mrs. Scotty was summoned to the office of the State Attorney on the morning of the trial, where she gave pretrial testimony. At the trial itself, Mrs. Scotty, petitioner and petitioner's wife all testified that the three of them had been in Mrs. Scotty's apartment during the time of the robbery. On two occasions during cross-examination of Mrs. Scotty, the prosecuting attorney confronted her with her earlier deposition in which she had given dates and times which in some respects did not correspond with the dates and times given at trial. Mrs. Scotty adhered to her trial story, insisting that she had been mistaken in her earlier testimony. The State also offered in rebuttal the testimony of one of the officers investigating the robbery who claimed that Mrs. Scotty had asked him for directions on the afternoon in question during the time when she claimed to have been in her apartment with petitioner and his wife.

We need not linger over the suggestion that the discovery permitted the State against petitioner in this case deprived him of "due process" or a "fair trial." Florida law provides for liberal discovery by the defendant against the State, and the notice-of-alibi rule is itself carefully hedged with reciprocal duties requiring state disclosure to the defendant. Given the ease with which an alibi can be fabricated, the State's interest in protecting itself against an eleventh hour defense is both obvious and legitimate. Reflecting this interest, notice-of-alibi provisions, dating at least from 1927, are now in existence in a substantial number of States. The adversary system of trial is hardly an end to itself; it is not yet a poker game in which players enjoy an absolute right always to conceal their cards until played. We find ample room in that system, at least as far as "due process" is concerned, for the instant Florida rule, which is designed to enhance the search for truth in the criminal trial by insuring both the defendant and the State ample opportunity to investigate certain facts crucial to the determination of guilt or innocence.

Petitioner's major contention is that he was "compelled to be a witness against himself" contrary to the commands of the Fifth and Fourteenth Amendments because the notice-of-alibi rule required him to give the State the name and address of Mrs. Scotty in advance of trial and thus to furnish the State with information useful in convicting him. No pretrial statement of petitioner was introduced at trial; but armed with Mrs. Scotty's name and address and the knowledge that she was to be petitioner's alibi witness, the State was able to take her deposition in advance of trial and to find rebuttal testimony. Also, requiring him to reveal the elements of his defense is claimed to have interfered with his right to wait until after the State had presented its case to decide how to defend against it. We conclude, however, as has apparently every other court which has considered the issue, that the privilege against self-incrimination is not violated by a requirement that the defendant give notice of an alibi defense and disclose his alibi witnesses.[14]

The defendant in a criminal trial is frequently forced to testify himself and to call other witnesses in an effort to reduce the risk of conviction. When he presents his witnesses, he must reveal their identity and submit them to cross-examination which in itself may prove incriminating or which may furnish the State with leads to incriminating rebuttal evidence. That the defendant faces such a dilemma demanding a choice between complete silence and presenting a defense has never been thought an invasion of the privilege against compelled self-incrimination. The pressures generated by the State's evidence may be severe but they do not vitiate the defendant's choice to present an alibi defense and witnesses to prove it, even though the attempted defense ends in catastrophe for the defendant. However "testimonial" and "incriminating" the alibi defense proves to be, it cannot be considered "compelled" within the meaning of the Fifth and Fourteenth Amendments.

Very similar constraints operate on the defendant when the State requires pretrial notice of alibi and the naming of alibi witnesses. Nothing in such a rule requires the defendant to rely on an alibi or prevents him from abandoning the defense; these matters are left to his unfettered choice.[15] That choice must be

---

14. We emphasize that this case does not involve the question of the validity of the threatened sanction, had petitioner chosen not to comply with the notice-of-alibi rule. Whether and to what extent a State can enforce discovery rules against a defendant who fails to comply, by excluding relevant, probative evidence is a question raising Sixth Amendment issues which we have no occasion to explore. It is enough that no such penalty was exacted here.

15. * * * The mere requirement that petitioner disclose in advance his intent to rely on an alibi in no way "fixed" his defense as of that point in time. The suggestion that the State, by referring to petitioner's proposed alibi in opening or closing statements might have "compelled" him to follow through with the defense in order to avoid an unfavorable infer-

ence is a hypothetical totally without support in this record. The first reference to the alibi came from petitioner's own attorney in his opening remarks; the State's response did not come until after the defense had finished direct examination of Mrs. Scotty. * * * On these facts, then, we simply are not confronted with the question of whether a defendant can be compelled in advance of trial to select a defense from which he can no longer deviate. We do not mean to suggest, though, that such a procedure must necessarily raise serious constitutional problems. See *State ex rel. Simos v. Burke*, 163 N.W.2d 177, 181 (Wis.1968) ("[i]f we are discussing the right of a defendant to defer until the moment of his testifying the election between alternative and inconsistent alibis, we have left the concept of the trial as a search for truth far behind").

made, but the pressures which bear on his pretrial decision are of the same nature as those which would induce him to call alibi witnesses at the trial: the force of historical fact beyond both his and the State's control and the strength of the State's case built on these facts. Response to that kind of pressure by offering evidence or testimony is not compelled self-incrimination transgressing the Fifth and Fourteenth Amendments.

In the case before us, the notice-of-alibi rule by itself in no way affected petitioner's crucial decision to call alibi witnesses or added to the legitimate pressures leading to that course of action. At most, the rule only compelled petitioner to accelerate the timing of his disclosure, forcing him to divulge at an earlier date information which the petitioner from the beginning planned to divulge at trial. Nothing in the Fifth Amendment privilege entitles a defendant as a matter of constitutional right to await the end of the State's case before announcing the nature of his defense, any more than it entitles him to await the jury's verdict on the State's case-in-chief before deciding whether or not to take the stand himself.

Petitioner concedes that absent the notice-of-alibi rule the Constitution would raise no bar to the court's granting the State a continuance at trial on the grounds of surprise as soon as the alibi witness is called. Nor would there be self-incrimination problems if, during that continuance, the State was permitted to do precisely what it did here prior to trial: to depose the witness and find rebuttal evidence. But if so utilizing a continuance is permissible under the Fifth and Fourteenth Amendments, then surely the same result may be accomplished through pretrial discovery, as it was here, avoiding the necessity of a disrupted trial.[17] We decline to hold that the privilege against compulsory self-incrimination guarantees the defendant the right to surprise the state with an alibi defense.

Chief Justice BURGER, concurring.

I join fully in Justice White's opinion for the Court. I see an added benefit to the alibi notice rule in that it will serve important functions by way of disposing of cases without trial in appropriate circumstances—a matter of considerable importance when courts, prosecution offices and legal aid and defender agencies are vastly overworked. [The Chief Justice noted that a prosecutor receiving the names of alibi witnesses in advance of trial often would be able to determine whether an alibi defense was "reliable and unimpeachable" or "contrived and fabricated." The former determination "would very likely lead to dismissal of the charges," while the latter could lead to a defense decision to plead guilty. In either instance, the Chief Justice noted, "the ends of justice will have been served and the processes expedited."]

Justice BLACK, with whom Justice DOUGLAS joins, dissenting. * * *

The core of the majority's decision is an assumption that compelling a defendant to give notice of an alibi defense before a trial is no different from requiring a defendant, after the State has produced the evidence against him at trial, to plead alibi before the jury retires to consider the case. * * * [But] when a defendant is required to indicate whether he might plead alibi in advance of trial, he faces a vastly different decision than that faced by one who can wait until the State has presented the case against him before making up his mind. Before trial the defendant knows only what the State's case *might* be. Before trial there is no such thing as the "strength of the State's case," there is only a range of possible cases. At that time there is no certainty as to what kind of case the State will ultimately be able to prove at trial. Therefore any appraisal of the desirability of

---

17. It might also be argued that the "testimonial" disclosures protected by the Fifth Amendment include only statements relating to the historical facts of the crime, not statements relating solely to what a defendant proposes to do at trial.

pleading alibi will be beset with guesswork and gambling far greater than that accompanying the decision at the trial itself. * * * Clearly the pressures on defendants to plead an alibi created by this procedure are not only quite different than the pressures operating at the trial itself, but are in fact significantly greater. Contrary to the majority's assertion, the pretrial decision cannot be analyzed as simply a matter of "timing," influenced by the same factors operating at the trial itself.

The Court apparently also assumes that a defendant who has given the required notice can abandon his alibi without hurting himself. Such an assumption is implicit in and necessary for the majority's argument that the pretrial decision is no different than that at the trial itself. I, however, cannot so lightly assume that pretrial notice will have no adverse effects on a defendant who later decides to forego such a defense. Necessarily the defendant will have given the prosecutor the names of persons who may have some knowledge about the defendant himself or his activities. Necessarily the prosecutor will have every incentive to question these persons fully, and in doing so he may discover new leads or evidence. Undoubtedly there will be situations in which the State will seek to use such information—information it would probably never have obtained but for the defendant's coerced cooperation.

It is unnecessary for me, however, to engage in any such intellectual gymnastics concerning the practical effects of the notice-of-alibi procedure, because the Fifth Amendment itself clearly provides that "[n]o person * * * shall be compelled in any criminal case to be a witness against himself." If words are to be given their plain and obvious meaning, that provision, in my opinion, states that a criminal defendant cannot be required to give evidence, testimony, or any other assistance to the State to aid it in convicting him of crime. The Florida notice-of-alibi rule in my opinion is a patent violation of that constitutional provision because it requires a defendant to disclose information to the State so that the State can use that information to destroy him. * * *

It is no answer to this argument to suggest that the Fifth Amendment as so interpreted would give the defendant an unfair element of surprise, turning a trial into a "poker game" or "sporting contest," for that tactical advantage to the defendant is inherent in the type of trial required by our Bill of Rights. The Framers were well aware of the awesome investigative and prosecutorial powers of government and it was in order to limit those powers that they spelled out in detail in the Constitution the procedure to be followed in criminal trials. * * *

On the surface this case involves only a notice-of-alibi provision, but in effect the decision opens the way for a profound change in one of the most important traditional safeguards of a criminal defendant. The rationale of today's decision is in no way limited to alibi defenses, or any other type or classification of evidence. The theory advanced goes at least so far as to permit the State to obtain under threat of sanction complete disclosure by the defendant in advance of trial of all evidence, testimony and tactics he plans to use at that trial. In each case the justification will be that the rule affects only the "timing" of the disclosure, and not the substantive decision itself. * * *

Notes and Questions[a]

1. ***The scope of the Williams dissent.*** In *Scott v. State*, 519 P.2d 774 (Alaska 1974), the court noted that it was "persuaded" by Justice Black's dissent

a. A substantial body of excellent commentary exists on *Williams* and the constitutionality of prosecution discovery in general. The leading articles include: Nicholas Allis, *Limitations on Prosecutorial Discovery of the Defense Case in Federal Courts: The Shield of Confi-*

in *Williams* to read the self-incrimination clause of the Alaska constitution "more broadly" than *Williams* interpreted the federal clause. However, the court did not strike down all elements of the lower court's alibi-notice order. It held unconstitutional the requirements that the defendant list his alibi witnesses and specify the "alternative location where he claims to have been," but sustained the requirement that the defendant note in advance his intent to rely upon an alibi defense. The court reasoned that notice alone would not disclose the "substance of [the] defense theory" (as would the alternative location) or "any weaknesses or inconsistencies therein" (as would the witness list), and it therefore was "difficult to conceive" how it could possibly "provide the state with another 'link' in its chain of evidence." Would the rationale of Justice Black's dissent in *Williams* have required the rejection of the notice requirement?

2. *The rationale of Williams.* The reach of the "accelerated disclosure" rationale advanced in *Williams* has been a subject of considerable dispute, at least among commentators. The commentators agree that accelerated disclosure may give the prosecution several benefits, but disagree as to whether the *Williams* rationale upholds the state's right to insist upon all of those benefits.

Accelerated disclosure is seen as giving the prosecution at least four possible benefits it would not receive if the defendant were allowed to delay disclosing the nature of his evidence until he was ready to introduce it at trial. First, accelerated disclosure may provide the prosecution with information that will lead it to other evidence useful in presenting its case-in-chief. Admittedly, the information disclosed pretrial most often would be disclosed later at trial, but the prosecutor frequently can make more effective use of the information when it is received before trial, with more time to develop leads. More significantly, there will be instances in which the information revealed under accelerated disclosure would not later be disclosed because the defense eventually would find that it did not have to use it at trial—e.g., where the prosecution was unable to establish a sufficient case-in-chief based on its own sources, or where the defendant decided to rely on a different defense at trial. Second, the prosecution similarly may obtain information through accelerated disclosure that will lead it to evidence establishing defendant's involvement in unrelated offenses. Here again, this could be information the prosecution might not have eventually received at trial. Third, the accelerated disclosure may provide the prosecution with information useful in developing a rebuttal to the defendant's defense.[b] Of course, the prosecution eventually would receive this information when the defense was presented at trial, but it would often be much more difficult for the prosecution to make effective use of the information at that point (particularly in a jurisdiction in which trial judges frown on granting continuances). Finally, accelerated disclosure, by indicating the

dentiality, 50 S.Cal.L.Rev. 461 (1977); Eric Blumenson, *Constitutional Limitations on Prosecutorial Discovery,* 18 Harv.Civ.R.–Civ.L.Rev. 122 (1983); Robert Clinton, *The Right to Present a Defense,* 9 Ind.L.Rev. 713 (1976); Robert Mosteller, *Discovery Against the Defense: Tilting the Adversarial Balance,* 74 Cal.L.Rev. 1567 (1986); Barry Nakell, *Criminal Discovery for the Defense and Prosecution: The Developing Constitutional Considerations,* 50 N.C.L.Rev. 437 (1972); Edward Tomlinson, *Constitutional Limits on Prosecutorial Discovery,* 23 San Diego L.Rev. 993 (1986); Gordon Van Kessel, *Prosecutorial Discovery and the Privilege Against Self–Incrimination: Accommodation or Capitulation,* 4 Hast.L.Q. 855 (1977); Peter Westen, *Order of Proof: An Ac-*

cused's Right to Control the Timing and Sequence of Evidence in His Defense, 66 Cal. L.Rev. 935 (1978). Each of these articles will hereafter be cited simply by reference to the author's name.

b. A somewhat related contention is that accelerated disclosure may make it more difficult for the defendant to present his defense because proposed defense witnesses may be intimidated by police inquiries conducted in the course of the prosecution's development of its rebuttal evidence. Cf. Vt.R.Crim.P. 16.1(c) (defense must disclose witnesses it intends to use at trial, but such witnesses thereafter may be interviewed by the government only in the presence of defense counsel).

direction the defense is likely to take, permits the prosecution to husband its resources and thereby to do a better job in presenting both its case-in-chief and its rebuttal to the defense.

One group of commentators read *Williams* as going no farther than sustaining accelerated disclosure that provides the prosecution only with the third and fourth advantages noted above. See e.g., Van Kessel (*Williams* did not address "the issue of whether pretrial disclosures that support the prosecutor's case-in-chief may be compelled," but was concerned with the use of the disclosed information for "impeachment and rebuttal purposes only"). In support of this "narrow" view of *Williams*, it is noted that the "facts [there] in no way suggested, nor did Williams allege, that the government used the notice either directly or derivatively to enhance the strength of its case-in-chief or that there was any reasonable prospect that it would give rise to other independent prosecutions." Mosteller. Moreover, it is argued, this was not unusual for an alibi defense as alibi witnesses rarely will be a source of "incriminating information" as to the offense charged or unrelated offenses. Only in the most unusual case (as where the alibi is that the defendant was in the vicinity of the crime but not at its exact location or that the defendant was at another place where another crime was being committed) will alibi disclosure furnish the prosecution with either the first or second advantages noted above. The Court's extensive discussion of accelerated disclosure, it is argued, should be read only as responding to Justice Black's argument in dissent that the defendant could not be required to lighten the government's load even as to its impeachment of the defense's alibi witnesses. "The Court," it is said, "rejected that position, but decided nothing more." Mosteller.

A second, and much broader, reading of *Williams* views the majority opinion there as holding generally that accelerated disclosure does not add sufficiently to the ordinary pressures that invariably bear on a defendant's decision to rely on a particular defense, or to introduce particular evidence, as to create "compulsion" for Fifth Amendment purposes. Thus, it is argued, even if the other two requirements for application of the privilege clearly are present—i.e., the required pretrial disclosure is "testimonial" and it would present a "real and substantial danger of incrimination" by furnishing the prosecution with "a link in the chain of evidence needed to prosecute" (see *Hoffman*, Note 2, p. 691)—there still would be no violation of the Fifth Amendment because merely requiring the defendant to decide before trial what he otherwise would decide at trial would not constitute "compulsion." Under this view, the *Williams* rationale not only permits the state to require defendant to decide before trial whether a particular defense might be used at trial and to make accelerated disclosure of that defense and its supporting witnesses, but it arguably would also permit the state to require the defense to make accelerated disclosure of information that would eventually become available to the prosecution in the course of cross-examining those witnesses (e.g., the witness' prior recorded statements). See also Blumenson ("Justice White's reasoning on the Fifth Amendment applies equally to a rule requiring a defendant who intends to testify to answer pretrial interrogatories about her testimony; truth seeking would be enhanced by advancing the 'timing' of disclosure").

3. Does BROOKS v. TENNESSEE, described in Note 5 at p. 1419, provide any assistance in determining the scope of the *Williams* rationale? In *Brooks,* a divided Supreme Court held unconstitutional a state's rule that a defendant, if he desired to testify in his own defense, had to do so before any other defense witnesses gave testimony. The majority found that rule imposed an unjustifiable burden upon defendant's constitutional right not to testify since he was being forced to decide whether or not to testify before he could evaluate the strength of the testimony of his other witnesses. The Court acknowledged that the state had an interest in ensuring that a defendant not shape his testimony to conform to that of the defense witnesses testifying before him (an interest accomplished as to other witnesses by their sequestration prior to testifying). It concluded, however, that barring defendant's later testimony if he does not testify as the first defense witness "is not a constitutionally permissible means of insuring his honesty." The majority in *Brooks* did not refer to *Williams,* but the dissent thought *Williams* to be highly relevant. It argued that the burden imposed upon the defendant here was no worse than the analogous burden held constitutionally acceptable in *Williams.*

Is *Brooks* inconsistent with either or both of the readings of *Williams* advanced in Note 2 supra? Does *Brooks* necessarily reject "the *Williams* holding that the timing of defense disclosure did not raise Fifth Amendment questions"? Clinton. See also, Broussard, J., dissenting in *Izazaga v. Superior Court,* 815 P.2d 304 (Cal.1991) ("*Brooks* * * * establishes that in some circumstances a rule which requires a defendant to 'accelerate' the disclosure of witnesses or evidence that he may disclose at trial can impinge on the defendant's Fifth Amendment right," and suggests the need for a "sensitive analysis of both the purpose of the state law and the effect of acceleration," which should lead to the narrower of the two readings of *Williams* described in Note 2 supra).

Is it significant that *Brooks* involved the defendant's own testimony. See *Izazaga v. Superior Court,* supra (*Brooks* dealt with "the special component of the Fifth Amendment protecting an accused choice of whether or not to testify" and therefore is "inapposite" to the constitutionality of requiring pretrial disclosure of a "witness 'other than the defendant.'") Most alibi-notice provisions limit the exclusion sanction to the testimony of persons other than defendant himself. See e.g., Fed.R.Crim.P. 12.1(d). Can *Brooks* and *Williams* also be distinguished on the ground that the defendant in *Brooks* was being forced to do more than make the accelerated disclosure of potential trial evidence upheld in *Williams,* as he was required to make an accelerated "final decision" as to the use of evidence? Blumenson. See also Westen (*Williams* rationale would support a modified version of the state rule rejected in *Brooks,* under which the defendant would be required to disclose before others testify the substance of his testimony, if he should testify, but not be precluded from later deciding not to testify or to testify differently).

4. *Lower court interpretations.* CRIMPROC § 20.4(d) notes that, "initially, some lower courts were cautious in their reading of *Williams.*" Though they accepted as facially valid broad reciprocal discovery provisions that included, for example, defense disclosure the names of its anticipated trial witnesses, those courts also held open the possibility that the defense would be excused from its discovery obligation if it could show that, in the particular case, the required disclosure would lead the prosecution to evidence that could be used against the defendant in the prosecution's case-in-chief or in establishing another crime. The authors note, however, that "a growing group of [later] cases," such as *Izazaga v. Superior Court,* described in Note 2, p. 1209, have "sustained reciprocal disclosure without seeking to accommodate the concerns reflected [in those earlier rulings]." They conclude: "Thus, the narrower reading of *Williams* advanced by the commentators today has virtually no support in the caselaw. Lower court rulings, looking to *Williams,* have accepted without limitation reciprocal defense notification of defenses, expert witnesses, all other witnesses, and documents and tangible items."

5. *Reciprocal discovery.* In WARDIUS v. OREGON, 412 U.S. 470, 93 S.Ct. 2208, 37 L.Ed.2d 82 (1973), a unanimous Court held unconstitutional a state alibi-notice provision which made no provision for reciprocal discovery. The Court noted (per MARSHALL, J.): "We hold that the Due Process Clause of the Fourteenth Amendment forbids enforcement of alibi rules unless reciprocal discovery rights are given to criminal defendants. * * * [A]lthough the Due Process

Clause has little to say regarding the amount of discovery which the parties must be afforded, it does speak to the balance of forces between the accused and his accuser. The *Williams* court was therefore careful to note that 'Florida law provides for liberal discovery by the defendant against the State, and the notice-of-alibi rule is itself carefully hedged with reciprocal duties requiring state disclosure to the defendant.' The same cannot be said of Oregon law. As the State conceded at oral argument, Oregon grants no discovery rights to criminal defendants, and, indeed, does not even provide defendants with bills of particulars. More significantly, Oregon, unlike Florida, has no provision which requires the State to reveal the names and addresses of witnesses it plans to use to refute an alibi defense.

"We do not suggest that the Due Process Clause of its own force requires Oregon to adopt such provisions. But we do hold that in the absence of a strong showing of state interests to the contrary, discovery must be a two-way street. The State may not insist that trials be run as a 'search for truth' so far as defense witnesses are concerned, while maintaining 'poker game' secrecy for its own witnesses. It is fundamentally unfair to require a defendant to divulge the details of his own case while at the same time subjecting him to the hazard of surprise concerning refutation of the very pieces of evidence which he disclosed to the State."

Justice Traynor of California, who first articulated the accelerated disclosure rationale in *Jones v. Superior Court,* 372 P.2d 919 (Cal.1962), later described that rationale as resting on the premise that a defendant could fairly "be required to make his decision * * * before trial *if he is given discovery of the prosecution case before trial.*" Roger Traynor, *Ground Lost and Found in Criminal Discovery,* 39 N.Y.U.L.Rev. 228 (1964) (emphasis added). The Florida discovery rules involved in *Williams* provided defendant with extensive discovery, and it has been argued that the *Williams* ruling rested on the premise that "the defendant ha[d] substantial pretrial discovery of the prosecution's case," enabling him "to gain almost as much knowledge of the state's case before trial as he eventually would have at trial." Westen. Can the reciprocity analysis of *Wardius* be read back into *Williams* so as to make extensive defense discovery of the prosecution's case-in-chief a prerequisite to the application of an alibi-notice requirement? See Nakell. Or does *Wardius* reflect a concern only with maintaining the traditional "balance" between defense and prosecution as to the particular type of discovery required from the defense (i.e., only as to alibi witnesses with respect to an alibi-notice provision)? See Weston. Lower courts have taken the latter position. See e.g., *Izazaga v. Superior Court,* 815 P.2d 304 (Cal.1991) (where defense must disclose its witnesses, *Wardius* demands only that the prosecution disclose its witnesses, including rebuttal witnesses, not "all the other evidence it intends to use to refute the evidence disclosed by the defense").

6. *Impeachment use of defense notice.* Would *Williams* have been decided differently had the state been able to use defendant's notice of an alibi defense to impeach him had he presented a different type of defense at trial? While an alibi-notice ordinarily may be used in impeachment where that is an appropriate remedy for a violation of the notice provision (as where defendant shifts at trial to an alternative and inconsistent alibi as to which notice was not given, see CRIMPROC § 20.5 at fn. 27), many jurisdictions will not permit its impeachment use as a relevant prior inconsistent statement where defendant simply adopts a different type of defense at trial. See e.g., Federal Rule 12.1(f). Others, however, do allow such use. "The statement is considered an evidentiary admission, * * * [and] the attorney-client privilege is held to be waived because the disclosure is knowingly made to persons outside the scope of the confidential relationship." Mosteller. See e.g., *State v. Howell,* 641 P.2d 37 (Or.App.1982) (defense listing of alibi defense during pretrial conference properly used to impeach defendant's trial testimony in rape case that he had consensual sex with complainant). Critics of such impeachment use of the alibi-notice contend that the primary interest supporting the *Williams* ruling—ensuring that the state has an adequate opportunity before trial to prepare to rebut alibi testimony—justifies no more than requiring the defense to give advance notice of the potential use of that defense. It does not sustain, they argue, requiring the defense to make a pretrial choice among defenses that is subject to penalty (via impeachment) should defendant take a contrary position at trial. At this point, the state is no longer simply utilizing a "neutral mechanism to improve fairness and efficiency in litigation," but is "changing the balance of advantage between the two sides by making the defendant's testimony more vulnerable to attack through prior inconsistent statements" and is "destroying the legitimacy of the discovery procedure" by allowing use of what may well be "misstatements occurring solely because the defendant was required to speak at an early moment." Mosteller.

Might support for impeachment use of defendant's alibi-notice be found, apart from the objectives of the alibi-notice provision as sustained in *Williams,* in cases such as *Harris v. New York*, 401 U.S. 222, 91 S.Ct. 643, 28 L.Ed.2d 1 (1971), allowing impeachment use of statements obtained in violation of *Miranda?* Would the closer analogy be to *New Jersey v. Portash*, 440 U.S. 450, 99 S.Ct. 1292, 59 L.Ed.2d 501 (1979), barring impeachment use of immunized testimony?

7. *The aftermath of Williams.* As noted in Mosteller, "discovery against the criminal defendant expanded tremendously in many states beginning in the 1970's." Surveying the state provisions as of 1986, Mosteller found: "[I]n addition to prosecutorial discovery of the specific defenses of alibi and insanity, available in the great majority of states, twenty-five states grant the prosecution an independent right to receive discovery from the defense of at least one of the following: defenses, witness names, statements of witnesses, reports of experts, or documents and tangible evidence. Another seven states provide for very broad disclosure from the defendant, conditioned upon his request for discovery from the prosecution. Several states combine conditional and independent prosecutorial discovery." The Notes that follow explore the scope and application of those provisions.

B. Discovery of Defenses and Supporting Evidence

That Will Be Used at Trial

1. *Notice of defenses.* Many states require the defendant to give pretrial notice of the intent to rely on various defenses besides alibi. The broadest provisions extend to "any defense, other than that of not guilty, on which the defendant intends to rely on trial." See e.g., Minn.R.Crim.P. 9.02(1)(3)(a). Under these provisions, the defense must give advance notice of the intent to rely on such defenses as self-defense, entrapment, duress, intoxication, and claim of authority. As with most alibi-notice provisions, the defendant is not bound to raise the listed defense at trial, and the prosecution cannot use against the defendant his failure to do so.

2. *Witness lists.* Many of the states requiring the defense to give advance notice of its defenses also add the requirement that defense list the names and addresses of all defense witnesses. See e.g., Minn.R.Crim.P. 9.02(1)(3)(a). In all of these jurisdictions, the defendant is entitled to a similar listing of prosecution witnesses. In those jurisdictions which give the trial court discretion to require the prosecution to list its witnesses, the trial court often also has the discretion to require the defendant to make reciprocal disclosure of all of its witnesses. Consider also A.B.A. Standards § 11–2.2(a)(i) (3d ed. 1996) (recommending that defense obligation to make pretrial disclosure of witnesses not extend to "disclosure of the identity * * * of a person who will be called for the sole purpose of impeaching a prosecution witness"; prosecution's corresponding duty under the Standards is to disclose the identity of "all persons known to the prosecution to have information concerning the offense charged").

In *Prudhomme v. Superior Court,* 466 P.2d 673 (Cal.1970), the California Supreme Court struck down a trial court's discovery order in a murder case which included reciprocal disclosure of witnesses. Although the California Court had earlier accepted an accelerated disclosure analysis in upholding the pretrial disclosure of a scientific report that defendant intended to introduce at trial, it concluded that that precedent could not justify a wholesale listing of witnesses. The court reasoned: "It is apparent that the principle element in determining whether a particular demand for discovery should be allowed is not simply whether * * * defendant intends to introduce or rely upon the evidence at trial, but whether disclosure thereof conceivably might lighten the prosecution's burden of proving its case-in-chief. * * * [T]he order herein is not limited to any particular defense or category of witnesses from which a court could attempt to determine its incriminatory effect. It requires no great effort or imagination to conceive of a variety of situations wherein the disclosure of the expected testimony of defense witnesses, or even their names and addresses, could easily provide an essential link in a chain of evidence underlying the prosecution's case-in-chief. For example, if a defendant in a murder case intended to call witness A to testify that defendant killed in self-defense, pretrial disclosure of that information could provide the prosecution with its sole eyewitness to defendant's homicide."[c]

In IZAZAGA v. SUPERIOR COURT, 815 P.2d 304 (Cal.1991), *Prudhomme* was distinguished as resting on an interpretation of the state constitution " 'more solicitous of the privilege against self-incrimination than federal law currently requires.' " The California Supreme Court there upheld an amendment of the state constitution providing for reciprocal discovery. Finding no federal self-incrimination bar to requiring the defense to make reciprocal disclosure of the "names and addresses of all of the witnesses it intends to call at trial, rather than merely its alibi witnesses, the *Izazaga* majority (per LUCAS, C.J.) noted:

"Under cases of the Supreme Court, there are four requirements that together trigger this privilege: the information sought must be (i) incriminating; (ii) personal to the defendant; (iii) obtained by compulsion; and (iv) testimonial or communicative in nature. Statutorily mandated discovery of evidence that meets these four requirements is prohibited. Conversely, discovery of evidence that does not meet each of these requirements is not barred by the self-incrimination clause. This is so even in the absence of special state interests such as protection against easily fabricated eleventh-hour defenses. The absence of particular state interests in disclosure affects none of these four requirements, and thus cannot itself trigger the self-incrimination clause.

"In *Williams,* the high court held that discovery of the names and addresses of a defendant's alibi witnesses is not "compelled" self-incrimination, and therefore does not violate the Fifth Amendment. The Court reasoned, 'At most, the rule only compelled [defendant] to accelerate the timing of this disclosure, by forcing him to divulge at an earlier date information that the [defendant] from the beginning planned to divulge at trial.' Thus, discovery of the names and addresses

---

c. Consider also A.B.A. Standards § 11.–3.2 (2d ed. 1980) (prohibiting admission in evidence of "information obtained as a result of [witness list] disclosures * * * except to refute the testimony of a [listed] witness"); *People v. District Court,* 531 P.2d 626 (Colo.1975) (while provision granting prosecution reciprocal discovery of defense witness list was facially valid, disclosure would not be granted "if it seeks information which might serve as an unconstitutional link in the chain of evidence establishing the accused's guilt").

of the witnesses that the defense intends to call at trial, whether or not in support of an alibi defense, merely forces the defendant 'to divulge at an earlier date information that the [defendant] from the beginning planned to divulge at trial.' (Ibid.) Under the rationale of *Williams*, such discovery does not constitute compelled self-incrimination, and therefore does not implicate the privilege."

3. ***Documents, scientific reports, and tangible objects.*** State provisions patterned after either the Federal Rules or the A.B.A. Standards commonly provide for court-ordered defense disclosure of documents, tangible items, and scientific reports that the defense intends to use in evidence at trial. Such provisions are said to present the easiest case for pretrial disclosure because the government most often will need the assistance of its own experts in responding at trial to evidence of this type. See Advisory Committee Note to Rule 16(b)(1), 39 F.R.D. 177 (1966) (stressing the need for mutual advance disclosure of certain types of test reports, documents, and opinions of experts "to prevent the defendant from obtaining an unfair advantage"). It also is noted that such evidence typically does not reflect information that came from the defendant although that is not always the case. See Conn.Sup.Ct.R. § 769 (disclosure required of document defendant intends to offer in evidence "except to the extent it contains any communication by the defendant").

C. Discovery of Materials and Information That
Defense Does Not Intend to Use at Trial

1. ***Disclosure of witness statements: self-incrimination objections.*** Many of the states requiring the defense to list all of its witnesses also require defense to disclose all "written or recorded" statements of those witnesses that are in its possession. State courts sustaining these provisions against self-incrimination challenge have relied in part upon the Supreme Court's rejection of a self-incrimination objection in UNITED STATES v. NOBLES, 422 U.S. 225, 95 S.Ct. 2160, 45 L.Ed.2d 141 (1975), a case involving trial rather than pretrial disclosure.

In *Nobles,* defense counsel asked two key prosecution witnesses about statements they allegedly had made to a defense investigator. Those statements indicated that the witnesses' recollection of the bank robber had been considerably less clear than their current testimony suggested. One witness denied making the alleged statement and the other claimed it was inaccurate. Defense counsel later called the investigator as a defense witness for the purpose of testifying as to the statements. The trial judge then granted the prosecutor the right to inspect those portions of the investigator's report relating to the witnesses' statements for the purpose of cross-examining the investigator. When defense counsel stated that he would not produce the report, the court ruled that the investigator would not be allowed to testify about the witnesses' statements. On appeal following conviction, the Court of Appeals held that the trial court's disclosure order had violated the Fifth Amendment. The Supreme Court, per POWELL, J., reversed:

"The Court of Appeals concluded that the Fifth Amendment renders criminal discovery 'basically a one-way street.' Like many generalizations in constitutional law, this one is too broad. The relationship between the accused's Fifth Amendment rights and the prosecution's ability to discover materials at trial must be identified in a more discriminating manner. The Fifth Amendment privilege against compulsory self-incrimination is an 'intimate and personal one,' which protects 'a private inner sanctum of individual feeling and thought and proscribes state intrusion to extract self-condemnation.' *Couch v. United States*, 409 U.S. 322, 93 S.Ct. 611, 34 L.Ed.2d 548 (1973). As we noted in *Couch*, the 'privilege is a *personal* privilege: it adheres basically to the person, not to information that may incriminate him.'

"In this instance disclosure of the relevant portions of the defense investigator's report would not impinge on the fundamental values protected by the Fifth Amendment. The court's order was limited to statements allegedly made by third parties who were available as witnesses to both the prosecution and the defense. [Defendant] did not prepare the report, and there is no suggestion that the portions subject to the disclosure order reflected any information that he conveyed to the investigator. The fact that these statements of third parties were elicited by a defense investigator on [defendant's] behalf does not convert them into [defendant's] personal communications. Requiring their production from the investigator therefore would not in any sense compel [defendant] to be a witness against himself or extort communications from him."

2. Does *Nobles'* analysis carry over to the pretrial disclosure of a witness' statements? Consider *Izazaga v. Superior Court,* Note 2, p. 1209, rejecting defendant's "attempt to distinguish *Nobles* [on the ground] * * * that the Supreme Court has never upheld disclosure of statements of defense witnesses *before* trial." The *Izazaga* court reasoned that "the timing of the disclosure, whether before or during trial, does not affect any of the four requirements that trigger the privilege against self-incrimination, [see p. 1209] and therefore cannot implicate the privilege." The key to *Nobles* was its conclusion that "the compelled statements are those of 'third parties,'" and therefore the triggering requirement that the compelled statements be "personal" to the person claiming the privilege simply was not met.

The *Izazaga* court acknowledged that the third-party character of the materials to be disclosed did not always resolve the personal-communication issue. The Supreme Court has recognized that the act of producing a document can itself be testimonial and incriminating under certain circumstances. See *Fisher v. United States,* 425 U.S. 391, 96 S.Ct. 1569, 48 L.Ed.2d 39 (1976). "[H]owever, [here] * * * the *act of handing over* the statements of defense witnesses to the prosecutor does not implicate the privilege. This act is not 'testimonial or communicative in nature' because the act does not 'reveal, directly or indirectly (defendant's) *knowledge* of facts relating him to the offense or ... (require defendant) to share *his thoughts* and beliefs with the government.' *Doe v. United States,* 487 U.S. 201, 108 S.Ct. 2341, 101 L.Ed.2d 184 (1988) (italics added)."

3. *Disclosure of witness statements: work product exemption.* The defendant in *Nobles* objected to the court order there on the basis of the work product doctrine, as well as the self-incrimination clause, and the Court's treatment of that aspect of his claim has generally been viewed as more favorable to those opposing pretrial disclosure of a defense witness' prior recorded statement. Justice White's concurring opinion in *Nobles* suggested that the work product doctrine simply did not apply to material that the opposing party sought for use as evidence at trial. Justice Powell's opinion for the Court, however, relied solely upon a waiver rationale; the protection of the work product doctrine had been waived, as to that portion of the investigator's report covered by his testimony, when the defense elected to have the investigator testify as to that subject matter. Noting that this waiver rationale takes effect only upon the introduction of the witness' testimony and therefore has no bearing in a pretrial setting, several state courts have viewed *Nobles* as implicitly supporting their rulings that ordering pretrial disclosure of a prospective defense witness' prior recorded statement violates the work product doctrine. See e.g., *Spears v. State,* 403 N.E.2d 828 (Ind.1980). Is such an absolute bar consistent with the analysis of work product applied to defense discovery of the recorded statements of prosecution witnesses? See fn. d, p. 1197. What if the statement in question was no more than a verbatim recording of the witness' narrative in response to an open ended question of the defense lawyer or investigator? See *Commonwealth v. Brinkley,* 480 A.2d 980 (Pa.1984) (held not to be work product).

Commentators have suggested that pretrial disclosure of a defense witness' prior recorded statements goes beyond the question of how a state will define work product. Requiring the pretrial disclosure of any written reports of the defense team, they argue, may infringe upon the defendant's right to the effective assistance of counsel; a defense counsel aware that a written report will be available to the prosecution may either decide not to have the witnesses interviewed or not to have their statements recorded. Courts generally have not been receptive to this contention, reasoning that the recorded statement would be available to the prosecution in any event at trial (for use in impeachment) once the witness testified. See e.g., *Commonwealth v. Paszko,* 461 N.E.2d 222 (Mass. 1984). They also note that *Nobles* rejected a Sixth Amendment claim, stating that "the Sixth Amendment does not confer the right to testimony free from the legitimate demands of the adversarial system." See e.g., *Izazaga v. Superior Court,* 815 P.2d 304 (Cal.1991) (also concluding that the Sixth Amendment does not provide a "constitutional" basis for a work product privilege, and therefore certainly does not prohibit limiting the work product doctrine to "opinion" work product). But consider Kennard, J., concurring in *Izazaga,* supra (Sixth Amendment not violated because discovery is provided in anticipation that the defense will place the witness on the stand and thereby waive the work product privilege; but the prosecutor therefore should not be allowed to use, as part of its case-in-chief, evidence gained through the discovery of the statement, since it remains possible that the prospective witness will not be called to testify and the waiver will not take place).

4. *Disclosure of scientific reports.* Some state provisions governing prosecution discovery of scientific reports in the possession of the defendant are sufficiently broad to encompass all reports made in connection with the particular case, without regard to whether the defendant intends to rely upon the particular report or the expert who prepared the report. See e.g., N.J.R.Crim.P. 3:13–3(b). Does the defendant's privilege against self-incrimination protect against pretrial discovery of a report which defendant does not intend to use because it is not favorable to the defense? Is the short answer to such a claim that, under *Nobles,* the self-incrimination clause cannot apply since the defendant himself is not being asked to testify (assuming that the expert's report is not based on information furnished by the defendant). See e.g., *Gipson v. State,* 609 P.2d 1038 (Alaska 1980) (compelled disclosure of defense expert's ballistics test did not violate defendant's self-incrimination privilege because the report was not "testimonial" as to defendant, but disclosure was barred as unauthorized under state discovery rule). But see *Binegar v. Eighth Judicial District Court,* 915 P.2d 889 (Nev.1996) (statute requiring defense disclosure of "any relevant witness statements and any reports or results of physical examinations or scientific tests, even if the defendant does not intend [to call the witnesses or] introduce those statements and materials at trial" violates defendant's privilege against self-incrimination because "the defendant would be compelled to do more than simply accelerate the timing of intended disclosures of materials; the defendant would be forced to disclose information that he never intended to disclose at trial, some of which could be incriminating.").

Does the Sixth Amendment bar pretrial discovery of an expert's report that the defense does not intend to use at trial? Consider *State v. Mingo,* 392 A.2d 590 (N.J.1978). The defendant, charged with robbery, requested that the state allow the defense's handwriting experts to examine a note written by the robber. The court conditioned that disclosure on the state having access to the resulting reports, and the prosecution, after reviewing one report, called the expert to testify on behalf of the state. On appeal, the court rejected the contention that the discovery order violated the work product privilege as codified in N.J.R.Crim.P. 3:13–3(c) (barring discovery of "internal reports, memoranda, or documents" prepared by defense agents). The report of the handwriting expert did not fall "within the intent of the foregoing delineation of work product as its constitute[d] a species of evidence admissible under some circumstances whereas true work product is [nonevidential]."[d] Nevertheless, the discovery order did violate the defendant's right to effective assistance of counsel (although the other evidence introduced at trial rendered that violation harmless). To safeguard that right, the court noted, it was essential to afford counsel "the maximum freedom to seek the guidance of expert advice in assessing the soundness and advisability of offering a particular defense without the fear that any unfavorable material so obtained can be used against his client. * * * Reliance upon the confidentiality of an expert's advise itself is a crucial aspect of a defense attorney's ability to consult with and advise his client. If the confidentiality of that advice cannot be anticipated, the attorney might well forego seeking such assistance, to the consequent detriment of his client's cause."

As noted in CRIMPROC § 20.4(f), various state courts have rejected Sixth Amendment challenges to prosecution discovery of the reports of non-testifying defense experts . In doing so, they often have drawn an analogy to the rationales advanced to support the constitutionality of requiring a defendant raising an insanity defense to submit to a psychiatric examination. See Note 6 infra. They note "that the defendant has put into issue the scientific claim on which the non-testifying expert reported and will introduce other expert testimony on that claim. The state, in the interest of having objective scientific evidence freely available to all sides, may insist that the defense once it raises the issue, make all of its experts available, just as it allows the defense discovery of the reports of all experts consulted by the prosecution, including those that the prosecution may later decide not to use at trial." Consider also *State v. Craney*, 347 N.W.2d 668 (Iowa 1984), where the court, in upholding the prosecution's use of a defense expert, rejected the "bygone philosophy that for an attorney's investigations to be effective they must be shrouded in secrecy." But compare *Hutchinson v. People*, 742 P.2d 875 (Colo.1987) (prosecution's use of defense handwriting expert's report in its case-in-chief was improper where there had been no "implied waiver" at that point, since testimony of defendant's wife, suggesting that another had forged signatures on critical checks, come after the case-in-chief and the prosecution could not cite to a "compelling need" for using that report as there was "no suggestion that the prosecution could not obtain other competent experts in the field of handwriting analysis").

Another potential bar to the disclosure of the report of the non-testifying expert is the attorney-client privilege. The applicability of that privilege need not be considered where the expert testifies as any such privilege would then be waived by the use of the expert. Where the expert does not testify, three views

---

d. In jurisdictions, where work product is not limited to material that reflects the opinions, theories, or conclusions of legal personnel, and the expert operates at the direction of counsel, the reports of experts have been held to constitute work product, exempt from discovery unless the defense waives the work product protection by having the witness testify. See Edward Imwinkelried, *The Applicability of the Attorney–Client Privilege to Non–Testifying Experts: Reestablishing the Boundaries Between the Attorney–Client Privilege and the Work Product Protection*, 68 Wash.U.L.Q. 19 (1990). See also *People v. Spiezer*, 316 Ill. App.3d 75, 735 N.E.2d 1017 (2000) (work product doctrine, rather than Sixth Amendment, provides the more appropriate basis for precluding disclosure of the report of a nontestifying defense expert; to hold that required disclosure constitutes such a substantial interference with the ability of counsel to make independent decisions as to violate the Sixth Amendment is to create an absolute prohibition, in contrast to the work product doctrine, which is never absolute).

have emerged, as described in Imwinkelried, fn. c supra: "One school of thought maintains that the privilege does not attach. The jurisdictions subscribing to this view point out that the privilege applies only to communications between attorney and client and that the expert is not an attorney. A second, compromise school asserts that the privilege applies only if the client makes statements to the expert or reveals to the expert private data such as his mental condition—information which realistically emanates from the client. Courts adhering to this view characterize the expert as an essential intermediary for communication between client and attorney. A third school of thought proposes that the privilege attach whenever the attorney or client discloses information to an expert consulted for purposes of trial preparation." The third position has been held to apply to a wide range of experts, including many who operate on the basis of communications from the lawyer that do not reflect information learned from the client, and it also has been held to encompass all of the knowledge subsequently gained by the expert through his or her testing. See Imwinkelried, supra (criticizing the third position as extending the concept of communication far beyond the function of the attorney-client privilege and criticizing the first position as failing to recognize the need of the attorney for the assistance of the expert in understanding and evaluating the communication from the client).

5. *Conditional discovery.* Assuming arguendo that required defense disclosure of any of the items discussed in Notes 1–4 supra (or Notes 1–3, pp. 1208–10) would be unconstitutional, would that constitutional barrier be overcome by conditioning the disclosure on a defendant's exercise of a statutory right to discover similar material from the prosecution? A number of the jurisdictions condition the defense's obligation to disclose on an initial defense request for disclosure of the same type of item from the prosecutor. See e.g., Fed.R.Crim.P. 16(b)(1)(A), (B). The Nebraska provision specifically notes, in authorizing such conditional disclosure, that a defendant requesting discovery from the prosecution "shall be deemed to have waived his privilege of self-incrimination" for the purposes of that provision. Neb.Stat. § 29–1916(2). Is such a "waiver" invalid on the ground that "an option [i.e., discovery from the prosecution] which exacts a 'penalty' upon the exercise of the privilege against self-incrimination violates the Fifth Amendment"? *United States v. Fratello*, 44 F.R.D. 444 (S.D.N.Y.1968) (raising, but not deciding the issue). Charles Pulaski Jr., *Extending the Disclosure Requirements of the Jencks Act to Defendants: Constitutional and Non–Constitutional Considerations*, 64 Iowa L.Rev. 1 (1978), argues that the Supreme Court has upheld state procedures that present defendants with choices which impose more substantial burdens on the exercise of their self-incrimination privilege. Thus, in *McGautha v. California*, 402 U.S. 183, 91 S.Ct. 1454, 28 L.Ed.2d 711 (1971), the state was allowed to insist upon a "unitary" trial procedure in capital cases, which forced the defendant "to submit to cross-examination on the question of guilt in order to take advantage of whatever constitutional right he might enjoy to speak before the jury regarding sentence." See also the cases upholding plea bargaining, discussed in Ch. 22, § 2.

Should the same analysis apply to other constitutional objections (e.g., claims of interference with the right to counsel). See *State v. Lucious*, 271 Ga. 361, 518 S.E.2d 677 (1999) [defendant had no constitutional or independent statutory right to discovery of state's scientific reports, scientific work product, and witness list, and conditioning that discovery and other discovery not constitutionally required on defendant making reciprocal discovery does not violate due process, defendant's right to confrontation (rejecting defendant's theory that the confrontation clause gives him a constitutional right to pretrial disclosure of information in the prosecution's possession needed to make confrontation effective), or right to counsel (rejecting defense claim that reciprocal discovery obligation interferes with "defense counsel's judgment of whether and when to reveal aspects of his case to the State"); dissent argues that defendant has a constitutional right to discover scientific reports and other material needed to confront witnesses, and that right cannot be burdened by requirement of reciprocity].

6. The "special case" of the insanity defense. Insanity-notice provisions commonly require that the defendant not only give advance notice of the intent to rely on that defense but also that he submit to a psychiatric exam that can then be used by the prosecution to rebut the defendant's insanity defense. See e.g., Federal Rule 12.2. While the notice requirement has been upheld without difficulty under the rationale of *Williams,* the compelled psychiatric examination requirement has caused more difficulty. Although the courts have uniformly sustained that provision, they have disagreed as to the rationale. In UNITED STATES v. BYERS, 740 F.2d 1104 (D.C.Cir.1984) (en banc), the plurality opinion (per then Circuit Judge SCALIA) initially rejected the frequently cited rationales. The argument that "the psychiatric interview compelled neither 'communications' nor 'testimony,' but 'real or physical evidence,'" analogous to a blood sample, had been "categorically rejected" in *Estelle v. Smith,* 451 U.S. 454, 101 S.Ct. 1866, 68 L.Ed.2d 359 (1981). There the Supreme Court had "dismissed out of hand" the prosecution's contention that the defendant's communications to a state psychiatrist conducting a competency examination (communications later used in a capital sentencing proceeding) were "nontestimonial" in nature. *Smith* also was viewed as having cast "grave doubt" upon the contention that the privilege does not apply to a required psychiatric examination because the statements given there will not be used to show that defendant committed the acts in question, but only that he was sane. See Fed.R. 12.2(c). The Court there had rejected an analogous argument that the privilege did not apply there because the state's psychiatrist had testified only as to capital sentencing and not as to guilt. As for the theory that a defendant "'waived' his Fifth Amendment privilege by voluntarily making psychiatric evaluation an issue in the case," that was "at best a fiction" in light of the traditional standard that a waiver must be "'free and unconstrained.'" Similarly unpersuasive was the contention that defendant was "estopped" from relying upon a self-incrimination claim because there was implicit reliance upon the treatment of psychiatric examinations as "real evidence" in gaining admission of his own expert's testimony notwithstanding the hearsay rule. The most that could be said of the assumed estoppel was that defendant should be barred from raising a hearsay objection to the state's use of its psychiatrist's testimony. All of this did not mean, however, that defendant's self-incrimination objection should prevail. Said Judge Scalia:

"All of these theories are easy game, but it is not sporting to hunt them. The eminent courts that put them forth intended them, we think, not as explanations of the genuine reason for their results, but as devices—no more fictional than many others to be found—for weaving a result demanded on policy grounds unobtrusively into the fabric of the law. Whether they have described this policy as the need to maintain a 'fair state-individual balance' (one of the values underlying the Fifth Amendment set forth in *Murphy v. Waterfront Commission* [p. 738]), or as a matter of 'fundamental fairness,' or merely a function of 'judicial common sense,' they have denied the Fifth Amendment claim primarily because of the unreasonable and debilitating effect it would have upon society's conduct of a fair inquiry into the defendant's culpability. As expressed [by the Eighth Circuit]:

It would be a strange situation, indeed, if, first, the government is to be compelled to afford the defense ample psychiatric service and evidence at government expense and, second, if the government is to have the burden of proof, ... and yet it is to be denied the opportunity to have its own corresponding and verifying examination, a step which perhaps is the most trustworthy means of attempting to meet that burden.

We agree with this concern, and are content to rely upon it alone as the basis for our rejection of the Fifth Amendment claim. We share the dissent's solicitude for the 'private enclave of the human personality.' But when, as here, a defendant appeals to the nature of that enclave as the reason why he should not be punished for murder, and introduces psychiatric testimony for that purpose, the state must be able to follow where he had led."

SECTION 4. REMEDIES AND SANCTIONS

1.   *The range of relief.* Comprehensive discovery statutes or court rules commonly include a provision authorizing the trial court to take certain actions upon learning that a party has failed to comply with its disclosure obligations. Common law jurisdictions recognize a similar authority as part of the trial court's inherent power to regulate discovery. The range of remedies authorized is broad. The measures noted in Federal Rule 16(d)(2)—ordering immediate disclosure, granting a continuance, and excluding evidence—are the three most commonly mentioned, but "judicial opinions and statutory provisions also recognize several other sanctions or remedies, including (1) a charge directing the jury to assume certain facts that might have been established through the nondisclosed material, (2) granting a mistrial, (3) holding in contempt the party responsible for the nondisclosure, and (4) dismissal of the prosecution." CRIMPROC § 20.6. Alibi-notice and insanity-notice statutes usually have their own remedial provisions, which often are more narrowly drawn. Those provisions sometimes refer to a single remedial measure, excluding the testimony of any unlisted witness. However, the statutes commonly refer to imposing that remedy "except for good cause shown," and that phrase tends to be viewed as making available almost all of those measures short of exclusion that are specified in the general discovery provisions.

2.   *Selecting the appropriate remedy.* The statutes or court rules tend to provide little direction to the trial courts in their choice of response to a violation of a discovery obligation. On the defense side, perhaps no claim relating to discovery has more frequently reached the appellate courts than the claim that the trial court failed to utilize the proper remedy when it discovered shortly before or during trial that the prosecution had breached a discovery responsibility. The usual defense complaint is that the trial court should have granted the remedy requested by the defense (typically the exclusion of prosecution evidence that had not been timely disclosed, or the exclusion of evidence that may have been challenged through other discoverable material not timely disclosed) rather than some lesser remedy (commonly the ordering of immediate disclosure and the granting of a continuance). While appellate courts frequently note that the trial court must be given "broad latitude" in its selection of an appropriate remedy, they also often set forth some general guidelines for the exercise of that discretion, and reversals for the failure to follow those guidelines are not infrequent.

The appellate courts have not spoken as frequently to the proper trial court response to violations of discovery obligations by the defense. Where they have done so, they commonly have spoken of trial court discretion but also have set forth some fairly specific guiding principles. Indeed, in some jurisdictions, the courts regulate far more tightly the imposition of severe sanctions (exclusion or mistrial) as applied to the defense.

3.   *The preference for continuances.* Upon learning that there has been a discovery violation, the first step to be taken by the trial court is to order immediate disclosure to the full extent required by the discovery provisions. Appellate opinions then direct the trial court to determine why disclosure was not previously made and whether the lack of previous disclosure could result in prejudice. At least where the party responsible for the violation acted in good faith, the preferred remedy is to offer to the other party a continuance that will permit it to take advantage of the delayed discovery and thereby avoid any prejudice. Thus, where the non-compliance consists of the prosecution's failure to have previously endorsed one of its witness, the trial court is advised to allow the witness to testify, but first grant the defendant sufficient time to interview the witness. Similarly, where the violation relates to the prosecution's failure to make timely disclosure of the existence of some item that defendant might want to offer in evidence, the trial court is advised to grant a continuance sufficient to permit the defendant to obtain that evidence. In the counterpart situation, a continuance would be offered to the prosecution where it was the defense that failed to list a witness or disclose a report or prior recorded statement.

While the continuance is the preferred response to potential prejudice arising from a delay in disclosure, the appellate cases also recognize that there are situations in which a continuance will not be a satisfactory remedy. In some instances, the length of the needed continuance will cause too great a disruption in the trial process. So too, there are circumstances in which the continuance simply will not respond to the potential prejudice. The latter situation arises primarily where the delayed disclosure comes at trial after the opposing side has committed itself to a position inconsistent with the evidence that should have been made available under pretrial discovery. One issue that has divided the lower courts in this regard is whether weight should be given to the undercutting of a defense position that arguably was designed to mislead the jury as to the true facts. See e.g., the cases discussed in Notes 4 and 5 below.

4. *Late disclosures that contradict a misleading defense.* In PEOPLE v. TAYLOR, 406 N.W.2d 859 (Mich.App.1987), the defendant, responding to the testimony of his friend Veldt that defendant had been the person who sold Veldt a stolen pickup truck, testified that he had merely told Veldt where a truck might be purchased "cheap" and had not otherwise been involved in the actual purchase of the truck. As the Court of Appeals noted (per PETERSON, J.): "Unfortunately for defendant, his version of events, which might otherwise have seemed persuasive, and the depiction of his good character and truthfulness were destroyed during his cross-examination by a letter he had written to a friend, and by his ineffectual attempts to disavow the letter and then to explain it. The letter, received as an exhibit over objection, clearly demonstrated defendant's guilt and asked the friend to put pressure on Veldt to change his story so as not to implicate the defendant."

When defendant objected to the prosecutor's failure to have made pretrial disclosure of the letter, as required by an enforceable discovery agreement between the prosecution and defense, the prosecutor responded that he had only learned of the letter on the night before the trial and had received it on the day of the trial. This did not excuse the prosecutor's failure to disclose the letter to the defense immediately prior to the commencement of the trial, as the prosecutor's duty to disclose was a "continuing obligation," but the prosecutor's explanation, accepted by the trial court, indicated that that failure was the product of negligence rather than a deliberate attempt to sandbag. In light of that explanation and its conclusion that the defendant was not prejudiced (based on defense counsel's rejection of an offer to "reopen proofs" to allow the defense to call any further witnesses), the trial court held that any discovery violation was harmless. On appeal, the defense counsel argued that "had he known of the statements, he *might* have advised his client not to testify or *might* have adopted some strategy for minimizing their impact" (emphasis in original). Accordingly, the defense contended, the trial court should have excluded the letter from evidence, and its failure to do so required reversal of his conviction in light of two earlier Court of Appeals rulings. Those cases had stated that, "where a prosecutor has violated a discovery order—even if done inadvertently in good faith—unless it is clear that the failure to divulge was harmless beyond a reasonable doubt, we will reverse."

The *Taylor* court initially overturned the standard announced in the earlier rulings, which had been based in part on a due process analysis. "It is anomalous," the court noted, "that the use of otherwise admissible evidence to impeach a perjurious defendant should be perceived as due process 'unfairness' because not previously disclosed to him even though evidence which is inadmissible for constitutional reasons may be so used, and even where that evidence consists of his own statements [e.g., *Miranda* violations]." Although "courts have an interest in the integrity of their orders, nothing about noncompliance with a discovery order seems to be the moral or constitutional equivalent of an illegal search or coerced confession so as to justify the extreme sanction of exclusion of evidence without regard to truth."

The standard announced in the overturned rulings, the court noted, erred in its inflexibility. It "exclud[ed] consideration of the causes of the noncompliance, good faith, degrees of negligence, the nature and degree of prejudice, and whether some other remedy would be appropriate." Moreover, it allowed "no exception * * * for evidence of which defendant had independent knowledge, such as his own statements, not even for impeachment when the defendant testified differently if not downright perjuriously." The trial court, it was noted, must have discretion to fashion a remedy for noncompliance that encompasses "a fair balancing of the interests of the courts, the public, and the parties," recognizing that "exclusion of otherwise admissible evidence is a remedy which should follow only in the most egregious cases." In this case, under that standard, "the defendant was entitled to no remedy for the prosecutor's nondisclosure of the letter in question since the defendant, having written it himself, had knowledge of it independent of discovery."

5. In UNITED STATES v. NOE, 821 F.2d 604 (11th Cir.1987), the government's case against defendant rested largely on the testimony of two undercover agents. They testified to several discussions with defendant concerning the establishment of a clandestine methamphetamine laboratory and to their purchase from defendant of a sample of the drugs to be produced. Testifying in his defense, defendant denied that he was involved in any of the events recounted by the agents. He claimed that he was in Costa Rica during the period in question, and produced a receipt for an airline ticket in support of that claim. On rebuttal, the government offered into evidence a tape recording of a telephone conversation in which one of the undercover agents spoke to a man he identified on the phone as defendant and that person agreed to meet with the agent at a local Atlanta bar that evening. The agent then testified as to the date of the tape, which was during the period when defendant claimed to be in Costa Rica. The district court admitted the tape into evidence over defendant's objection that the prosecution had failed to make pretrial disclosure of the tape pursuant to Federal Rule 16(a)(1)(A), notwithstanding the defense's timely request for discovery. Although "conceding that the tape should have been provided * * *, the government asserted the failure to do so was inadvertent." On appeal, the government contended that its failure to provide discovery did not require reversal of defendant's conviction in light of the "strength of the government's case" against defendant. Rejecting that position, a divided Court of Appeals (per KRAVITCH, J.) reasoned:

"As [this] court * * * [previously] noted, the purpose of Rule 16(a) is 'to protect the defendant's rights to a fair trial.' And, contrary to the government's contentions, the degree to which those rights suffer as a result of a discovery violation is determined not simply by weighing all the evidence introduced, but rather by considering how the violation affected the defendant's ability to present a defense. Where the government at trial introduces undisclosed evidence that tends to undermine one aspect of the defense * * *, the existence of actual prejudice often will turn on the strength of the remaining elements of the government's case. Here, however, the government introduced evidence that attacked the very foundation of the defense strategy. As [this] court [previously] observed, the failure of the government to disclose 'statement[s] made by the defendant is so serious a detriment to the preparation for trial and the defense of serious criminal charges that where it is apparent, as here, that [the] defense strategy may have been determined by the failure to [disclose], there should be a new trial.' * * * Although Noe certainly does not have a right to 'fabricate' an alibi story, the Federal Rules of Criminal Procedure provide him a right to discover all statements that he made to law enforcement officials, and, correspondingly, to devise a defense strategy on the basis of the evidence disclosed."

6. *Exclusion of prosecution evidence.* Consistent with their advice to trial courts to first look to the continuance as a remedy, appellate courts frequently warn against the unnecessary use of the preclusion sanction. The trial court, it is noted, "should seek to apply sanctions that affect the evidence at trial and the merits of the case as little as possible." Sanctions generally should not have "adverse effects on the rights of the parties rather than the offending attorneys themselves," and exclusion of prosecution evidence necessarily has such an adverse effect on the interests of the community, the party represented by the prosecutor. *State v. Lewis,* 632 P.2d 547 (Alaska App.1981). Accordingly, some courts treat exclusion as a remedy that should be available only where there was actual prejudice and where no other remedy will respond adequately to that prejudice. It is a "remedy of last resort," to be used only where absolutely needed. Other jurisdictions, while viewing exclusion as a remedy to be used sparingly, will not place the trial court in a position where it can exclude previously undisclosed evidence only upon finding that lesser sanctions clearly could not eliminate the prejudice to the defense. Here, the trial court is given greater leeway. It may, for example, chose exclusion over a continuance where a continuance would be disruptive or would not provide the same degree of assurance that the prejudice would be eliminated.

The jurisdictions also are divided as to the possible use of exclusion simply as a deterrent, without regard to the presence of prejudice. Some courts would allow such use where the trial court finds that the discovery violation was intentional or reflects a recurring prosecutorial disregard for discovery obligations. These courts view exclusion as offering the same prophylactic impact in the enforcement of discovery rules as the exclusion of illegally seized evidence offers in the enforcement of the Fourth Amendment. Indeed, a few courts have gone beyond that position and approved the use of a dismissal with prejudice to respond to glaring prosecutorial discovery violations that suggest either gross negligence or purposeful misconduct. Other jurisdictions reject the prophylactic use of exclusion. Evidence is to be excluded only where needed to respond to prejudice. Similarly, dismissal is allowed only where the prosecution is ordered to provide discovery as to a certain item and prefers dismissal to complying with the court's order. Where the trial court believes that there is need for a deterrent measure, it is directed to make use of contempt orders directed against the offending prosecutor. A sanction, these courts note, should "not be regarded as a bonus awarded without regard to its need in the furtherance of fair trial rights." *Miller v. State*, 405 N.E.2d 909 (1980).

   7. *Exclusion of defense evidence.* Where a jurisdiction gives the trial court some leeway in using the sanction of exclusion, not limiting its use just to those situations in which "less drastic means" clearly will not respond to prejudice, should the same flexibility apply to exclusion as used against the defense? Prior to *Taylor v. Illinois,* discussed below, many states appeared to demand greater restraint in imposing exclusion against the defense. Some did so on general policy grounds, but others assumed that exclusion posed serious constitutional difficulties as applied to the defense—the issue considered by the Supreme Court in *Taylor*.

TAYLOR v. ILLINOIS
484 U.S. 400, 108 S.Ct. 646, 98 L.Ed.2d 798 (1988).

   Justice STEVENS delivered the opinion of the Court.

   As a sanction for failing to identify a defense witness in response to a pretrial discovery request, an Illinois trial judge refused to allow the undisclosed witness to testify. The question presented is whether that refusal violated the petitioner's constitutional right to obtain the testimony of favorable witnesses. We hold that such a sanction is not absolutely prohibited by the Compulsory Process Clause of the Sixth Amendment and find no constitutional error on the specific facts of this case.

   A jury convicted petitioner in 1984 of attempting to murder Jack Bridges in a street fight on the south side of Chicago on August 6, 1981. The conviction was supported by the testimony of Bridges, his brother, and three other witnesses. They described a twenty-minute argument between Bridges and a young man named Derrick Travis, and a violent encounter that occurred over an hour later between several friends of Travis, including the petitioner, on the one hand, and Bridges, belatedly aided by his brother, on the other. The incident was witnessed by twenty or thirty bystanders. It is undisputed that at least three members of the group which included Travis and petitioner were carrying pipes and clubs that they used to beat Bridges. Prosecution witnesses also testified that petitioner had a gun, that he shot Bridges in the back as he attempted to flee, and that, after Bridges fell, petitioner pointed the gun at Bridges' head but the weapon misfired.

   Two sisters, who are friends of petitioner, testified on his behalf. In many respects their version of the incident was consistent with the prosecution's case, but they testified that it was Bridges' brother, rather than petitioner, who possessed a firearm and that he had fired into the group hitting his brother by mistake. No other witnesses testified for the defense.

   Well in advance of trial, the prosecutor filed a discovery motion requesting a list of defense witnesses. In his original response, petitioner's attorney identified the two sisters who later testified and two men who did not testify. On the first day of trial, defense counsel was allowed to amend his answer by adding the names of Derrick Travis and a Chicago Police Officer; neither of them actually testified. * * * On the second day of trial, after the prosecution's two principal witnesses had completed their testimony, defense counsel made an oral motion to amend his "Answer to Discovery" to include two more witnesses, Alfred Wormley and Pam Berkhalter. In support of the motion, counsel represented that he had just been informed about them and that they had probably seen the "entire incident."

   In response to the court's inquiry about the defendant's failure to tell him about the two witnesses earlier, counsel acknowledged that defendant had done so, but then represented that he had been unable to locate Wormley. After noting that the witnesses' names could have been supplied even if their addresses were unknown, the trial judge directed counsel to bring them in the next day, at which time he would decide whether they could testify. The judge indicated that he was concerned about the possibility "that witnesses are being found that really weren't there."

The next morning Wormley appeared in court with defense counsel. After further colloquy about the consequences of a violation of discovery rules, counsel was permitted to make an offer of proof in the form of Wormley's testimony outside the presence of the jury. It developed that Wormley had not been a witness to the incident itself. He testified that prior to the incident he saw Jack Bridges and his brother with two guns in a blanket, that he heard them say "they were after Ray [petitioner] and the other people," and that on his way home he "happened to run into Ray and them" and warned them "to watch out because they got weapons." On cross-examination, Wormley acknowledged that he had first met the defendant "about four months ago" (i.e., over two years after the incident). He also acknowledged that defense counsel had visited him at his home on the Wednesday of the week before the trial began. Thus, his testimony rather dramatically contradicted defense counsel's representations to the trial court.

After hearing Wormley testify, the trial judge concluded that the appropriate sanction for the discovery violation was to exclude his testimony. The judge explained:

> "THE COURT: All right, I am going to deny Wormley an opportunity to testify here. He is not going to testify. I find this is a blatant violation of the discovery rules, willful violation of the rules. I also feel that defense attorneys have been violating discovery in this courtroom in the last three or four cases blatantly and I am going to put a stop to it and this is one way to do so. * * * Further, for whatever value it is, because this is a jury trial, I have a great deal of doubt in my mind as to the veracity of this young man that testified as to whether he was an eyewitness on the scene, sees guns that are wrapped up. He doesn't know Ray but he stops Ray. * * * " App. 28.

The Illinois Appellate Court affirmed petitioner's conviction. * * * The court concluded that in this case "the trial court was within its discretion in refusing to allow the additional witnesses to testify." The Illinois Supreme Court denied leave to appeal and we granted the petition for certiorari.

In this Court petitioner makes two arguments. He first contends that the Sixth Amendment bars a court from ever ordering the preclusion of defense evidence as a sanction for violating a discovery rule. Alternatively, he contends that even if the right to present witnesses is not absolute, on the facts of this case the preclusion of Wormley's testimony was constitutional error. Before addressing these contentions, we consider the State's argument that the Compulsory Process Clause of the Sixth Amendment is merely a guarantee that the accused shall have the power to subpoena witnesses and simply does not apply to rulings on the admissibility of evidence.

In the State's view, no Compulsory Process Clause concerns are even raised by authorizing preclusion as a discovery sanction, or by the application of the Illinois rule in this case. The State's argument is supported by the plain language of the Clause, by the historical evidence that it was intended to provide defendants with subpoena power that they lacked at common law, by some scholarly comment, and by a brief excerpt from the legislative history of the Clause. We have, however, consistently given the Clause the broader reading reflected in contemporaneous state constitutional provisions.

As we noted just last Term, "[o]ur cases establish, at a minimum, that criminal defendants have the right to the government's assistance in compelling the attendance of favorable witnesses at trial and the right to put before a jury evidence that might influence the determination of guilt." *Pennsylvania v. Ritchie* [p. 1402]. Few rights are more fundamental than that of an accused to present witnesses in his own defense. Indeed, this right is an essential attribute of the adversary system itself. * * * The right to compel a witness' presence in the courtroom could not protect the integrity of the adversary process if it did not embrace the right to have the witness' testimony heard by the trier of fact. The right to offer testimony is thus grounded in the Sixth Amendment even though it is not expressly described in so many words * * *.

Petitioner's claim that the Sixth Amendment creates an absolute bar to the preclusion of the testimony of a surprise witness is just as extreme and just as unacceptable as the State's position that the Amendment is simply irrelevant. The accused does not have an unfettered right to offer testimony that is incompetent, privileged, or otherwise inadmissible under standard rules of evidence. The Compulsory Process Clause provides him with an effective weapon, but it is a weapon that cannot be used irresponsibly.

There is a significant difference between the Compulsory Process Clause weapon and other rights that are protected by the Sixth Amendment—its availability is dependent entirely on the defendant's initiative. Most other Sixth Amendment rights arise automatically on the initiation of the adversarial process and no action by the defendant is necessary to make them active in his or her case. While those rights shield the defendant from potential prosecutorial abuses, the right to compel the presence and present the testimony of witnesses provides the defendant with a sword that may be employed to rebut the prosecution's case. The decision whether to employ it in a particular case rests solely with the defendant. The very nature of the right requires that its effective use be preceded by deliberate planning and affirmative conduct.

The principle that undergirds the defendant's right to present exculpatory evidence is also the source of essential limitations on the right. The adversary process could not function effectively without adherence to rules of procedure that govern the orderly presentation of facts and arguments to provide each party with a fair opportunity to assemble and submit evidence to contradict or explain the opponent's case. The trial process would be a shambles if either party had an absolute right to control the time and content of his witnesses' testimony. Neither may insist on the right to interrupt the opposing party's case and obviously there is no absolute right to interrupt the deliberations of the jury to present newly discovered evidence. The State's interest in the orderly conduct of a criminal trial is sufficient to justify the imposition and enforcement of firm, though not always inflexible, rules relating to the identification and presentation of evidence.

The defendant's right to compulsory process is itself designed to vindicate the principle that the "ends of criminal justice would be defeated if judgments were to be founded on a partial or speculative presentation of the facts." * * * Rules that provide for pretrial discovery of an opponent's witnesses serve the same high purpose. Discovery, like cross-examination, minimizes the risk that a judgment will be predicated on incomplete, misleading, or even deliberately fabricated testimony. The "State's interest in protecting itself against an eleventh hour defense" is merely one component of the broader public interest in a full and truthful disclosure of critical facts.

To vindicate that interest we have held that even the defendant may not testify without being subjected to cross-examination. *Brown v. United States,* 356 U.S. 148, 78 S.Ct. 622, 2 L.Ed.2d 589 (1958). Moreover, in *United States v. Nobles* [p. 1210], we upheld an order excluding the testimony of an expert witness tendered by the defendant because he had refused to permit discovery of a "highly relevant" report. * * *

Petitioner does not question the legitimacy of a rule requiring pretrial disclosure of defense witnesses, but he argues that the sanction of preclusion of the testimony of a previously undisclosed witness is so drastic that it should never be imposed. He argues, correctly, that a less drastic sanction is always available. Prejudice to the prosecution could be minimized by granting a continuance or a mistrial to provide time for further investigation; moreover, further violations can be deterred by disciplinary sanctions against the defendant or defense counsel.

It may well be true that alternative sanctions are adequate and appropriate in most cases, but it is equally clear that they would be less effective than the preclusion sanction and that there are instances in which they would perpetuate rather than limit the prejudice to the State and the harm to the adversary process. One of the purposes of the discovery rule itself is to minimize the risk that fabricated testimony will be believed. Defendants who are willing to fabricate a defense may also be willing to fabricate excuses for failing to comply with a discovery requirement. The risk of a contempt violation may seem trivial to a defendant facing the threat of imprisonment for a term of years. A dishonest client can mislead an honest attorney, and there are occasions when an attorney assumes that the duty of loyalty to the client outweighs elementary obligations to the court.

We presume that evidence that is not discovered until after the trial is over would not have affected the outcome.[18] It is equally reasonable to presume that there is something suspect about a defense witness who is not identified until after the eleventh hour has passed. If a pattern of discovery violations is explicable only on the assumption that the violations were designed to conceal a plan to present fabricated testimony, it would be entirely appropriate to exclude the tainted evidence regardless of whether other sanctions would also be merited.

In order to reject petitioner's argument that preclusion is *never* a permissible sanction for a discovery violation it is neither necessary nor appropriate for us to attempt to draft a comprehensive set of standards to guide the exercise of discretion in every possible case. It is elementary, of course, that a trial court may not ignore the fundamental character of the defendant's right to offer the testimony of witnesses in his favor. But the mere invocation of that right cannot automatically and invariably outweigh countervailing public interests. The integrity of the adversary process, which depends both on the presentation of reliable evidence and the rejection of unreliable evidence; the interest in the fair and efficient administration of justice; and the potential prejudice to the truth-determining function of the trial process must also weigh in the balance.

A trial judge may certainly insist on an explanation for a party's failure to comply with a request to identify his or her witnesses in advance of trial. If that explanation reveals that the omission was willful and motivated by a desire to obtain a tactical advantage that would minimize the effectiveness of cross-examination and the ability to adduce rebuttal evidence, it would be entirely consistent with the purposes of the Confrontation Clause simply to exclude the witness' testimony.[20] Cf. *United States v. Nobles.*

18. [The Court here cites lower court cases setting forth the Rule 33 standard as to defendant's burden in gaining a new trial based on newly discovered evidence. See fn. e, p. 1393.]

20. There may be cases in which a defendant has legitimate objections to disclosing the identity of a potential witness. See Note, The Preclusion Sanction—A Violation of the Constitutional Right to Present a Defense, 81 Yale L.J. 1342, 1350 (1972). Such objections, however, should be raised in advance of trial in response to the discovery request and, if the

The simplicity of compliance with the discovery rule is also relevant. As we have noted, the Compulsory Process Clause cannot be invoked without the prior planning and affirmative conduct of the defendant. Lawyers are accustomed to meeting deadlines. Routine preparation involves location and interrogation of potential witnesses and the serving of subpoenas on those whose testimony will be offered at trial. The burden of identifying them in advance of trial adds little to these routine demands of trial preparation.

It would demean the high purpose of the Compulsory Process Clause to construe it as encompassing an absolute right to an automatic continuance or mistrial to allow presumptively perjured testimony to be presented to a jury. We reject petitioner's argument that a preclusion sanction is never appropriate no matter how serious the defendant's discovery violation may be.

Petitioner argues that the preclusion sanction was unnecessarily harsh in this case because the *voir dire* examination of Wormley adequately protected the prosecution from any possible prejudice resulting from surprise. Petitioner also contends that it is unfair to visit the sins of the lawyer upon his client. Neither argument has merit.

More is at stake than possible prejudice to the prosecution. We are also concerned with the impact of this kind of conduct on the integrity of the judicial process itself. The trial judge found that the discovery violation in this case was both willful and blatant.[22] In view of the fact that petitioner's counsel had actually interviewed Wormley during the week before the trial began and the further fact that he amended his Answer to Discovery on the first day of trial without identifying Wormley while he did identify two actual eyewitnesses whom he did not place on the stand, the inference that he was deliberately seeking a tactical advantage is inescapable. Regardless of whether prejudice to the prosecution could have been avoided in this particular case, it is plain that the case fits into the category of willful misconduct in which the severest sanction is appropriate. After all, the court, as well as the prosecutor, has a vital interest in protecting the trial process from the pollution of perjured testimony. Evidentiary rules which apply to categories of inadmissible evidence—ranging from hearsay to the fruits of illegal searches—may properly be enforced even though the particular testimony being offered is not prejudicial. The pretrial conduct revealed by the record in this case gives rise to a sufficiently strong inference "that witnesses are being found that really weren't there," to justify the sanction of preclusion.[23]

The argument that the client should not be held responsible for his lawyer's misconduct strikes at the heart of the attorney-client relationship. Although there

parties are unable to agree on a resolution, presented to the court. Under the Federal Rules of Criminal Procedure and under the rules adopted by most states, a party may request a protective order if he or she has just cause for objecting to a discovery request. See e.g., Fed.Rule Crim.Proc. 16(d)(1); Ill.Sup.Ct. Rule 412(i). In this case, there is no issue concerning the validity of the discovery requirement or petitioner's duty to comply with it. There is also no indication that petitioner ever objected to the prosecution's discovery request.

22. The trial judge also expressed concern about discovery violations in other trials. If those violations involved the same attorney, or otherwise contributed to a concern about the trustworthiness of Wormley's eleventh hour testimony, they were relevant. Unrelated dis-

covery violations in other litigation would not, however, normally provide a proper basis for curtailing the defendant's constitutional right to present a complete defense.

23. It should be noted that in Illinois, the sanction of preclusion is reserved for only the most extreme cases. In *People v. Rayford,* the Illinois Appellate Court explained: "The exclusion of evidence is a drastic measure; and the rule in civil cases limits its application to flagrant violations, where the uncooperative party demonstrates a 'deliberate contumacious or unwarranted disregard of the court's authority.' The reasons for restricting the use of the exclusion sanction to only the most extreme situations are even more compelling in the case of criminal defendants. * * *."

are basic rights that the attorney cannot waive without the fully informed and publicly acknowledged consent of the client,[24] the lawyer has—and must have—full authority to manage the conduct of the trial. The adversary process could not function effectively if every tactical decision required client approval. Moreover, given the protections afforded by the attorney-client privilege and the fact that extreme cases may involve unscrupulous conduct by both the client and the lawyer, it would be highly impracticable to require an investigation into their relative responsibilities before applying the sanction of preclusion. In responding to discovery, the client has a duty to be candid and forthcoming with the lawyer, and when the lawyer responds, he or she speaks for the client. Putting to one side the exceptional cases in which counsel is ineffective, the client must accept the consequences of the lawyer's decision to forgo cross-examination, to decide not to put certain witnesses on the stand, or to decide not to disclose the identity of certain witnesses in advance of trial. In this case, petitioner has no greater right to disavow his lawyer's decision to conceal Wormley's identity until after the trial had commenced than he has to disavow the decision to refrain from adducing testimony from the eyewitnesses who were identified in the Answer to Discovery. Whenever a lawyer makes use of the sword provided by the Compulsory Process Clause, there is some risk that he may wound his own client. The judgment of the Illinois Appellate Court is affirmed.

Justice BRENNAN, with whom Justice MARSHALL and Justice BLACK-MUN join, dissenting.

* * * The Compulsory Process and Due Process Clauses * * * require courts to conduct a searching substantive inquiry whenever the government seeks to exclude criminal defense evidence. * * * [T]his Court defined the standard governing [that] constitutional inquiry just last Term in *Rock v. Arkansas* [Note 7, p. 1420], concluding that restrictions on the right to present criminal defense evidence can be constitutional only if they " 'accommodate other legitimate interests in the criminal trial process' " and are not "arbitrary or disproportionate to the purposes they are designed to serve." The question at the heart of this case, then, is whether precluding a criminal defense witness from testifying bears an arbitrary and disproportionate relation to the purposes of discovery, at least absent any evidence that the defendant was personally responsible for the discovery violations. * * *

The use of the preclusion sanction as a corrective measure—that is, as a measure for addressing the adverse impact a discovery violation might have on truthseeking in the case at hand—is asserted to have two justifications: (1) it bars the defendant from introducing testimony that has not been tested by discovery, and (2) it screens out witnesses who are inherently suspect because they were not disclosed until trial. The first justification has no bearing on this case because the defendant does not insist on a right to introduce a witness' testimony without giving the prosecution an opportunity for discovery. He concedes that the trial court was within its authority in requiring the witness to testify first out of the presence of the jury, and he concedes that the trial court could have granted the prosecution a continuance to give it sufficient time to conduct further discovery concerning the witness and the proffered testimony. He argues only that he should not be completely precluded from introducing the testimony. * * *

---

24. See e.g., *Brookhart v. Janis,* 384 U.S. 1, 86 S.Ct. 1245, 16 L.Ed.2d 314 (1966) (defendant's constitutional right to plead not guilty and to have a trial where he could confront and cross-examine adversary witness could not be waived by his counsel without petitioner's consent); *Doughty v. State,* 470 N.E.2d 69, 70 (Ind.1984) (record must show "personal communication of the defendant to the court that he chooses to relinquish the right [to a jury trial])"; *Cross v. United States,* 117 U.S.App. D.C. 56, 325 F.2d 629 (1963) (waiver of right to be present during trial).

Nor, despite the Court's suggestions, is the preclusion at issue here justifiable on the theory that a trial court can exclude testimony that it presumes or finds suspect. * * * [P]reventing a jury from hearing the proffered testimony based on its presumptive or apparent lack of credibility would be antithetical to the principles laid down in *Washington v. Texas*, 388 U.S. 14 (1967) [holding unconstitutional a statute that rendered accomplices incompetent to testify for one another, though competent to testify for the state]. The Court in *Washington* * * * concluded that "arbitrary rules that prevent whole categories of defense witnesses from testifying on the basis of *a priori* categories that presume them unworthy of belief" are unconstitutional.

Although persons who are not identified as defense witnesses until trial may not be as trustworthy as other categories of persons, surely any presumption that they are so suspect that the jury can be prevented from even listening to their testimony is at least as arbitrary as [a] presumption excluding an accomplice's testimony, *Washington v. Texas* * * *. The proper method, under Illinois law and *Washington v. Texas,* for addressing the concern about reliability is for the prosecutor to inform the jury about the circumstances casting doubt on the testimony: thus allowing the jury to determine the credit and weight it wants to attach to such testimony. The power of the court to take that kind of corrective measure is undisputed; the defendant concedes that the court could have allowed the prosecutor to comment on the defense's failure to disclose the identity of the witness until trial. * * *

Of course, discovery sanctions must include more than corrective measures. They must also include punitive measures that can deter future discovery violations from taking place. * * * In light of the availability of direct punitive measures, however, there is no good reason, at least absent evidence of the defendant's complicity, to countenance the arbitrary and disproportionate punishment imposed by the preclusion sanction. The central point to keep in mind is that witness preclusion operates as an effective deterrent only to the extent that it has a possible effect on the outcome of the trial. Indeed, it employs in part the possibility that a distorted record will cause a jury to convict a defendant of a crime he did not commit. Witness preclusion thus punishes discovery violations in a way that is both disproportionate—it might result in a defendant charged with a capital offense being convicted and receiving a death sentence he would not have received but for the discovery violation—and arbitrarily—it might, in another case involving an identical discovery violation, result in a defendant suffering no change in verdict or, if charged with a lesser offense, being convicted and receiving a light or suspended sentence. In contrast, direct punitive measures (such as contempt sanctions or, if the attorney is responsible, disciplinary proceedings) can graduate the punishment to correspond to the severity of the discovery violation.

The arbitrary and disproportionate nature of the preclusion sanction is highlighted where the penalty falls on the defendant even though he bore no responsibility for the discovery violation. In this case, although there was ample evidence that the defense attorney willfully violated Rule 413(d), there was no evidence that the defendant played any role in that violation. Nor did the trial court make any effort to determine whether the defendant bore any responsibility for the discovery violation. Indeed, reading the record leaves the distinct impression that the main reason the trial court excluded Wormley's testimony was the belief that the defense counsel had purposefully lied about when he had located Wormley. * * *

In the absence of any evidence that a defendant played any part in an attorney's willful discovery violation, directly sanctioning the attorney is not only fairer but *more* effective in deterring violations than excluding defense evidence. The threat of disciplinary proceedings, fines, or imprisonment will likely influence attorney behavior to a far greater extent than the rather indirect penalty threatened by evidentiary exclusion. Such sanctions were available here. * * *

Deities may be able to visit the sins of the father on the son, but I cannot agree that courts should be permitted to visit the sins of the lawyer on the innocent client. * * * Although we have sometimes held a defendant bound by tactical errors his attorney makes that fall short of ineffective assistance of counsel, we have not previously suggested that a client can be punished for an attorney's *misconduct*. There are fundamental differences between attorney misconduct and tactical errors. Tactical errors are products of a legitimate choice among tactical options. Such tactical decisions must be made within the adversary system, and the system requires attorneys to make them, operating under the presumption that the attorney will choose the course most likely to benefit the defendant. Although some of these decisions may later appear erroneous, penalizing attorneys for such miscalculations is generally an exercise in futility because the error is usually visible only in hindsight—at the time the tactical decision was made there was no obvious "incorrect" choice, and no prohibited one. In other words, the adversary system often cannot effectively deter attorney's tactical errors and does not want to deter tactical decisions. Thus, where a defense attorney makes a routine tactical decision not to introduce evidence at the proper time and the defense seeks to introduce the evidence later, deterrence measures may not be capable of preventing the untimely introduction of evidence from systemically disrupting trials, jury deliberations, or final verdicts. In those circumstances, treating the failure to introduce evidence at the proper time as a procedural default that binds the defendant is arguably the only means of systemically preventing such disruption—not because binding the defendant deters tactical errors any better than direct punitive sanctions but because binding the defendant to defense counsel's procedural default, by definition, eliminates the disruption. * * *

The rationales for binding defendants to attorneys' routine tactical errors do not apply to attorney misconduct. An attorney is never faced with a legitimate choice that includes misconduct as an option. Although it may be that "[t]he adversary process could not function effectively if every tactical decision required client approval," that concern is irrelevant here because a client has no authority to approve misconduct. Further, misconduct is not visible only with hindsight, as are many tactical errors. Consequently, misconduct is amenable to direct punitive sanctions against attorneys as a deterrent that can prevent attorneys from systemically engaging in misconduct that would disrupt the trial process. There is no need to take steps that will inflict the punishment on the defendant. * * *

In short, I can think of no scenario that does not involve a defendant's willful violation of a discovery rule where alternative sanctions would not fully vindicate the purposes of discovery without distorting the truthseeking process by excluding evidence of innocence. Courts can couple corrective measures that will subject the testimony at issue to discovery and adverse credibility inferences with direct punitive measures that are both proportional to the discovery violation and directed at the actor responsible for it. Accordingly, absent evidence that the defendant was responsible for the discovery violation, the exclusion of criminal defense evidence is arbitrary and disproportionate to the purposes of discovery and criminal justice and should be *per se* unconstitutional. I thus cannot agree with the Court's case-by-case balancing approach or with its conclusion in this case that the exclusion was constitutional. * * *

Justice BLACKMUN, dissenting.

I join Justice Brennan's dissenting opinion on the understanding—at least on my part—that it is confined in its reach to general reciprocal-discovery rules. I do not wish to have the opinion express for me any position as to permissible sanctions for noncompliance with rules designed for specific kinds of evidence as, for example, a notice-of-alibi rule. In a case such as that, the State's legitimate interests might well occasion a result different from what should obtain in the factual context of the present case.

Notes and Questions

1. ***Binding the defendant.*** As to courts typically holding the client to the consequences of decisions made by counsel, consider also the discussion of the division of authority between counsel and client in Notes 7–9, pp. 1102–03. See also *Murray v. Carrier,* p. 1598, where the Court held that federal habeas review of a constitutional claim could be barred by counsel's procedural default in failing properly to raise that claim in state proceedings even where that failure was the result of inadvertence or ignorance (assuming that counsel's failure was not so gross as to constitute ineffective assistance of counsel). In general, a defendant can escape the consequences of counsel's actions only by establishing a constitutional claim of ineffective assistance of counsel. Had defendant Taylor challenged counsel's action as ineffective assistance, he would have failed to meet the prevailing *Strickland* standard (see p. 1120). In light of the weakness of the testimony of the excluded witnesses, the prejudice prong of *Strickland* could not have been met. Moreover, though counsel willfully violated the discovery rules (and thereby risked the exclusion of the witnesses), he did so as a strategic gamble which presumably would not be deemed "irrational" even though it involved a rules violation. See CRIMPROC § 11.10(d). Thus, Taylor arguably also would not be able to meet the second *Strickland* prerequisite of a performance by counsel that fell below the standard of a "reasonably competent attorney."

2. ***Constitutional balancing.*** Tom Stacy, *The Search For Truth in Constitutional Criminal Procedure,* 91 Colum.L.Rev. 1369 (1991), argues that the Supreme Court in some instances has applied a "strict scrutiny" standard in reviewing state imposed restrictions upon the defendant's right to present evidence (as illustrated by *Rock v. Arkansas,* Note 7, p. 1420), but *Taylor* apparently applied a more lenient "rational relationship" standard. Professor Stacy notes: "In upholding the exclusion of the proffered testimony, the [*Taylor*] Court pointed to the *danger* that it was perjured. It did not conclude that this danger was so great that no rational jury could credit the testimony. The suggestion that testimony may be excluded based on a strong *possibility* of perjuriousness implies the validity of prophylactic rules excluding testimony that is possibly unreliable but not so unreliable that no rational jury could credit it. In fact, the Court openly decreed the legitimacy of exclusionary rules as applied to testimony that is not itself unreliable, much less unreliable as a matter of law. Justice Stevens's opinion declared, 'Evidentiary rules which apply to *categories* of inadmissible evidence— ranging from hearsay to the fruits of illegal searches—may properly be enforced even though the particular testimony being offered is not prejudicial [p. 1224].' This passage clearly rejects an approach which, like the strict scrutiny of *Rock,* would evaluate *case-by-case* justifications for excluding *particular items* of exculpatory evidence. It suggests that a rule excluding an entire category of exculpatory evidence is constitutional so long as there is good reason for excluding *some* of the evidence in that category. Read in this light, *Taylor* contemplates the permissible use of the preclusion sanction not as an exceptional response to egregious facts in a particular case, but rather as a defensible response to a broad class of cases."

Does MICHIGAN v. LUCAS, 500 U.S. 145, 111 S.Ct. 1743, 114 L.Ed.2d 205 (1991), even more definitively legitimate the exclusion of significant, presumably reliable evidence? In that case, defense counsel failed to notify the prosecution within 10 days after arraignment of the defense's intent to introduce evidence of the defendant's past sexual relationship with the rape complainant, as required by Michigan's rape-shield statute. The trial judge imposed a sanction of exclusion, which was held unconstitutional by the Michigan Court of Appeals on the ground that the Sixth Amendment prohibited exclusion of such potentially exculpatory evidence. Justice O'CONNOR, writing for the Court majority, treated the case as presenting a limited question: whether the Michigan Court had erred in "adopt[ing] a *per se* rule that preclusion is unconstitutional in all cases where the victim has a prior sexual relationship with the defendant." That ruling, Justice O'Connor concluded, simply "cannot be squared" with the Court's rulings in cases such as *Nobles* and *Taylor*. The Sixth Amendment "was not so rigid": "[A] notice and hearing requirement [as to prior sexual contact evidence] * * * serves legitimate state interests in protecting against surprise, harassment, and undue delay. Failure to comply with this requirement may in some cases justify even the severe sanction of preclusion."

    3. *Negligent violations.* Lower courts have divided as to whether the reasoning of *Taylor* is restricted to the type of discovery violation involved there.[a] See CRIMPROC § 20.6(c), describing these rulings: "Some courts suggest that the tactically motivated willful violation may be the only situation on which preclusion is constitutionally acceptable. Others, noting the broad range of interests cited by *Taylor* as relevant to the constitutional balancing process, have looked to several additional factors that may justify imposing the preclusion sanction. They would consider the degree of fault in the violation that was not intentional (asking, for example, whether the discovery requirement was clear and whether compliance was relatively simple), the degree of prejudice suffered by the prosecution, the impact of preclusion upon the total evidentiary showing (including consideration of factors suggesting that the precluded evidence is unreliable), and the degree of effectiveness of less severe sanctions. Arguably also, at least in certain contexts, the extent of the defendant's personal responsibility for the omission also would be considered. The balance struck by reference to these factors could conceivably justify preclusion in a case that did not involve a willful violation designed to gain a tactical advantage. That would be consistent with the position that many courts took prior to *Taylor*, particular as to alibi-notice cases. However, post-*Taylor* rulings upholding preclusion under such a balancing standard have involved, in large part, violations that readily could be characterized as fitting the willful and tactical mold even when they were not so described."

    4. One highly publicized exclusion based in a less than willfull and tactical violation was that in the rape prosecution of boxer Mike Tyson. See TYSON v. TRIGG, 50 F.3d 436 (7th Cir.1995). The state court there had ordered the defense to disclose to the prosecution the names of all defense witnesses whose testimony would relate to the issue of consent. On the Thursday that the prosecution began to present its case, a defense lawyer learned of the names of three persons who might have seen the defendant necking with the complainant in the back of a limousine as it arrived at the hotel where the alleged rape occurred. The women

---

    a. As a matter of state law, some courts will not allow preclusion even where *Taylor* might deem it constitutionally acceptable: "They view judicial adoption of a 'conscious mandatory distortion of the fact-finding process' as especially inappropriate where the risk taken (by excluding evidence that defendant claims to be exculpatory) is the possible conviction of the innocent rather than the risk (through exclusion of prosecution evidence) of the possible conviction of the guilty. Accordingly, they would allow use of the preclusion sanc-

tion only where the prosecution was prejudiced by the defense's discovery violation. Moreover, the prosecution will be required to establish actual prejudice by showing exactly what it would have done differently if earlier notice would have been received in conformity with discovery requirements. Even then, the court may also insist that exclusion be the sanction of 'last resort,' used only where no other remedy would cure the prejudice." CRIMPROC § 20.6(c).

were interviewed and confirmed that observation on Friday, the lawyer inspected the limousine on Saturday (to be certain that such activity could be seen through its tinted windows), and informed the court of the witnesses on Monday. The trial judge viewed the defense lawyers as having violated the discovery order "by not turning over the information at the earliest possible moment," and refused to permit the witnesses to testify. A divided Seventh Circuit, on habeas review, refused to overturn the conviction. The majority (per POSNER, J.) noted:

"Given the competing considerations identified above, the highly situation-specific character of the judgment that the trial judge is called upon to make in the hurly-burly of trial, the limited scope of federal habeas corpus, and (a closely related point) the desirability of avoiding continuous and heavy-handed federal judicial intervention in the conduct of state criminal trials, we do not consider it a proper office of a federal court in a habeas corpus proceeding to second guess a discovery ruling unless we are convinced that it is, in the circumstances, unreasonable. * * * [Judge Gifford] did not abuse her discretion by interpreting [her discovery order] to require the disclosure of newly discovered defense witnesses as soon as possible, which the Indiana Court of Appeals not unreasonably interpreted to mean by Friday evening. * * * By sometime on Friday the defense team had their names and a rough idea of their testimony, and it should have notified the prosecution immediately, especially since Saturday was a trial day. Tyson's argument that it would have been irresponsible to notify the prosecution before talking to each of the three potential witnesses in person and inspecting the limousine, and even disloyal to Tyson to disclose their identity to the prosecution before making sure that their evidence would not be more helpful to the prosecution than to the defense, is not compelling. If the witnesses proved worthless to Tyson, there would be no harm done to the defense unless it turned out that they could give testimony helpful to the prosecution, but that is always a risk in identifying potential witnesses to one's adversary. * * *

"Since, however, the violation of the order was not willful (at least so far as appears), six years in prison for the client would undoubtedly be an excessive sanction for the violation; but we cannot stop here. We must distinguish between sanctions as punishment designed to prevent future violations of similar orders, and sanctions as means of achieving the specific objective of the specific order. Allowing the surprise witnesses to testify would have delayed the trial, and worse. As Tyson concedes, the prosecution would have been entitled to call additional rebuttal witnesses in an effort to offset the impact on the jury of the three new witnesses; or to be granted a continuance to conduct an additional investigation, for example to determine whether it was possible to see into the limousine's interior at night. Delay in a jury trial is a serious matter, especially when, as in this case, the jury is sequestered. The prosecution's ability to rebut the surprise witnesses effectively would, moreover, have been less than its ability to have pulled their fangs by adroit questioning of W———— [the complainant] and other prosecution witnesses during the case in chief. * * * She could have testified to this on rebuttal, too, had the witnesses been allowed into the case. But to have recalled her to the stand on rebuttal for the express purpose of replying to the surprise witnesses would have magnified the impact of their testimony; would have made it seem that the prosecution had been—surprised. Which it would have been. The purpose of the discovery order was to prevent surprise; and the propose of excluding evidence whose introduction would have violated the order was not merely to punish violators but also to achieve the objective of the order by keeping surprise out of the case."

The majority added that still another factor to be considered was the importance of the excluded witnesses, but in the end it need not decide whether the exclusion sanction here did violate the Sixth Amendment, for any constitutional violation here clearly was harmless under the harmless error standard of *Brecht v. Abrahamson* (p. 1626). It cited in this regard the limited scope of the testimony of the excluded witnesses, its limited value in impeaching the testimony of the complainant (as compared to the other impeachment evidence used by the defense), and the presence of physical evidence of rape. The dissenting judge concluded that the trial court's exclusion of the three witnesses did violate the Sixth Amendment, but agreed that the violation was harmless.

5.   *Defendant's testimony.* Alibi-notice provisions typically limit the exclusion sanction to the testimony of persons other than defendant himself. See e.g., Fed.R.Crim.P. 12.1(d). Some provisions, however, are sufficiently broad to encompass defendant's own testimony, and state courts have occasionally barred defendant from giving alibi testimony beyond a denial of his presence at the scene of the crime (e.g., precluding defendant's testimony as to where he was) when no alibi-notice was provided. Does the rationale of *Taylor* extend to such exclusion, or is the exclusion of defendant's own alibi testimony distinguishable because: (1) the surprise element is less substantial as to defendant's testimony since the state ordinarily has to prove defendant's presence as an essential element of the crime, see *Alicea v. Gagnon,* 675 F.2d 913 (7th Cir.1982); or (2) defendant's right to testify requires greater constitutional protection than his right to present the testimony of others, cf. *Rock v. Arkansas,* Note 7, p. 1420?

Chapter 22

COERCED, INDUCED AND NEGOTI-
ATED GUILTY PLEAS; PROFES-
SIONAL RESPONSIBILITY

SECTION 1. SOME VIEWS OF NEGOTIATED PLEAS

A. INTRODUCTION

1. "The American criminal justice system has been transformed by plea bargaining. The traditional model of the criminal process provides for an impartial trier of fact to determine guilt after a formal adversarial trial and then for a judge to select a penalty appropriate for the offender from a range specified by the legislature. In practice, however, the locus of the criminal process has shifted largely from trial to plea bargaining. In the vast majority of cases, guilt and the applicable range of sentences are determined through informal negotiations between the prosecutor and the defense attorney."[a]

2. "There is a broad range of plea arrangements currently used by prosecutors. The three most common are the sentence recommendation, the plea to a lesser included offense, and the dismissal of charges in an indictment, information, or other charging paper.

"Under the sentence recommendation practice, the prosecuting attorney promises that he will recommend to the court a sentence favorable to the defendant, will not seek the maximum penalty, or will refrain from making any recommendations. Most often the sentence recommendation involves a promise by the prosecutor to suggest to the trial judge a mutually satisfactory term of years as the appropriate punishment in return for a defendant's guilty plea. In order for the practice to have any value to defendants and prosecutors there must be a reasonable expectation of judicial acceptance of the recommendations. Where there is a judicial practice of following recommendations, the promise of a recommended sentence can be tantamount to a promise of a definite term. But each defendant who pleads guilty in reliance on a prosecutor's promise to recommend a specific sentence takes the risk that in his particular case the judge will not follow the suggestion in imposing sentence. In addition, many defendants may enter into agreements with prosecutors to avoid imposition of the maximum sentence, but, unless they are informed of actual sentencing patterns, may needlessly bargain away their right to trial since sentences often fall considerably below the maximums provided by the legislatures.

"In some jurisdictions the prosecutor may recommend that the court accept a guilty plea to a lesser offense included in the offense actually charged. The court's permission to plead to a lesser included offense is usually required, and in some

---

a. Note, 90 Harv.L.Rev. 569 (1977).

jurisdictions the prosecutor must file reasons for recommending the lesser plea. * * *

"The prosecutor may also offer to dismiss certain criminal allegations in the charging papers in order to induce a defendant to plead guilty to the remaining charges. This procedure calls for the defendant to plead guilty to the charges agreed upon and for the prosecutor, at the time set aside by the court for dismissals, to move for dismissal of the remaining charges. The court's approval is usually required for the dismissal of any charges, and ordinarily charges are dismissed as a matter of course.

"The charge dismissal practice developed as a possible plea bargaining tool because of the multiplicity of crimes which often arise out of a single incident. However, an apparently advantageous bargain may actually be specious because of the tendency of many courts to sentence concurrently, or to suspend sentence on all but one or two of the multiple and similar charges arising out of the same incident."[b]

3. Although the practice of plea bargaining is a longstanding one, only in recent times has it been openly discussed and assessed in the legal literature and the public press. E.g., compare the President's Commission on Law Enforcement and Administration of Justice, *The Challenge of Crime in a Free Society* (1967), approving of plea bargaining within certain defined limits; with this National Advisory Commission on Criminal Justice Standards and Goals proposal:

"As soon as possible, * * * negotiations between prosecutors and defendants—either personally or through their attorneys—concerning concessions to be made in return for guilty pleas should be prohibited. In the event that the prosecution makes a recommendation as to sentence, it should not be affected by the willingness of the defendant to plead guilty to some or all of the offenses with which he is charged. A plea of guilty should not be considered by the court in determining the sentence to be imposed."[c]

4. Courts were for many years reluctant to even acknowledge the existence of plea bargaining, but this is no longer the case. The Supreme Court has upheld the practice as necessary and proper,[d] as have the lower courts. Illustrative is *People v. Selikoff,* 318 N.E.2d 784 (N.Y.1974):

"Throughout history the punishment to be imposed upon wrongdoers has been subject to negotiation. Plea negotiation, in some form, has existed in this country since at least 1804. Even in England, where there are no public prosecutors, no inflexible sentencing standards, and considerably less pressure on the trial courts, a limited form of plea negotiation seems to be developing. Moreover, convictions upon guilty pleas, pleas probably to lesser crimes, have been high since 1839 both in rural, where there is little trial court congestion, and in urban areas, where there is much congestion. History and perspective suggest, then, that plea negotiation is not caused solely, or even largely, by overcrowded dockets. This is not to say, however, that plea negotiation is not acutely essential to relieve court calendar congestion, as indeed it is. In budget-starved urban criminal courts, the negotiated plea literally staves off collapse of the law enforcement system, not just as to the courts but also to local detention facilities.

"Plea negotiations, of course, serve many other needs. They relieve the prosecution and the defense too, for that matter, from 'the inevitable risks and uncertainties of trial'. The negotiation process which results in a guilty plea

b. Note, 112 U.Pa.L.Rev. 865–68 (1964).

c. *N.A.C. Standards, The Courts* § 3.1.

d. E.g., *Bordenkircher v. Hayes,* p. 1244; *Santobello v. New York,* p. 1260. The Supreme

Court's first extended discussion of plea bargaining came in *Brady v. United States,* decided in 1970. See fn. a at p. 1246.

telescopes the judicial process and the necessarily protracted intervals involved in charge, trial, and sentence, and even appeals, hopefully starting the offender on the road to possible rehabilitation. The process also serves significant goals of law enforcement by permitting an exchange of leniency for information and assistance.

"Perhaps most important, plea negotiation serves the ends of justice. It enables the court to impose 'individualized' sentences, an accepted ideal in criminology, by avoiding mandatory, harsh sentences adapted to a class of crime or a group of offenders but inappropriate, and even Draconian, if applied to the individual before the court.[e] Obviously no two defendants are quite alike even if they have committed, in legal definition, identical offenses. The negotiation process often brings to light mitigating circumstances unknown when the defendant was charged."

B.   The Problem of Disparity

5.   Should the fact the defendant pleaded guilty actually have any bearing on the sentence he receives? If defendants who plead guilty receive leniency, does it not necessarily follow that defendants who go to trial are being dealt with too harshly? Consider *People v. Snow,* 194 N.W.2d 314 (Mich.1972), where the defendant, tried and convicted by a jury of prison escape, received a sentence of 2 to 5 years, but on appeal showed that of 234 prison escape cases in the county over a 26–month period, 207 pled guilty and (except in 5 cases where aggravated circumstances were present) received minimum sentences of 1½ years or less, while 13 were tried by a jury and (except in 1 case in which the defendant entered a guilty plea during the trial) received sentences of 2 years or more, and 1 was tried by the court and received a 1½ year minimum. The court concluded that because "in the usual escape case a minimum sentence of 1½ years has been deemed appropriate by the sentencing judge" and "examination of the record in this case fails to reveal a single fact that would place this defendant in a different category," the case should be remanded for resentencing.

Compare *United States v. Rodriguez,* 162 F.3d 135 (1st Cir.1998), where the government indicted six defendants for engaging in the same conspiracy to distribute cocaine. Three of them pled guilty pursuant to a plea agreement that they would be held accountable only for the drugs each had personally handled, while the defendants who went to trial were convicted and held accountable for the entire 5,000 grams of cocaine distributed by the conspiracy. Thus, under the Sentencing Guidelines the guilty plea defendants received sentences of time served, 17 months and 60 months, respectively, while the other three defendants received sentences of 235 months, 260 months, and life imprisonment (the latter attributable to an additional charge of engaging in a continuing criminal enterprise). The defendants who received the 235 and 260 month sentences argued they were entitled to be resentenced because "this vast disparity on sentencing—a difference of more than 21 years * * *—* * * discriminates against those who exercise their right to a jury trial," but to no avail. The court acknowledged that this was an "enormous sentencing disparity," one that "would strike many as

---

e.   Consider, in this connection, the current trend toward "reform" of sentencing by reducing or eliminating sentencing discretion, as by (i) restricting or eliminating the powers of parole boards, (ii) adopting "fixed" sentencing schemes, whereunder the statutes specify the exact penalty that will follow conviction of each offense, or (iii) adopting "presumptive" sentencing, whereunder statutes specify the "nor-

mal" sentence for each offense and allow limited departures only in atypical cases. As noted in Albert W. Alschuler, *Sentencing Reform and Prosecutorial Power: A Critique of Recent Proposals for "Fixed" and "Presumptive" Sentencing,* 126 U.Pa.L.Rev. 550, 551 (1978), "this sort of reform is likely to produce its antithesis," namely, greater reliance on plea bargaining.

unfair," but then concluded that what had been done was "within the government's discretion" and "not in and of itself * * * an unconstitutional burden on one's right to go to trial."

6. Sometimes this disparity is explained in terms of factors which are believed to warrant greater severity for many defendants who elect to stand trial. One survey of federal judges revealed these reasons why a defendant convicted at trial may receive a more severe sentence than a defendant who entered a guilty plea: (1) because the judge is convinced the defendant committed perjury in the course of his defense[f]; (2) because the defendant presented a frivolous defense; (3) because the brutal circumstances of the crime are more vividly portrayed if there is a trial.[g]

7. *A.B.A. Standards* § 14–1.8 (3rd ed.1997), on the other hand, explains the disparity in terms of factors which are likely to call for leniency when a plea of guilty is entered:

"(a) The fact that a defendant has entered a plea of guilty or nolo contendere should not, by itself alone, be considered by the court as a mitigating factor in imposing sentence. It is proper for the court to approve or grant charge and sentence concessions to a defendant who enters a plea of guilty or nolo contendere when consistent with governing law and when there is substantial evidence to establish, for example, that:

"(i) the defendant is genuinely contrite and has shown a willingness to assume responsibility for his or her conduct;

"(ii) the concessions will make possible alternative correctional measures which are better adapted to achieving protective, deterrent, or other purposes of correctional treatment, or will prevent undue harm to the defendant from the form of conviction;

"(iii) the defendant, by making public trial unnecessary, has demonstrated genuine remorse or consideration for the victims of his or her criminal activity;[h] or

---

f. Consider *United States v. Grayson*, 438 U.S. 41, 98 S.Ct. 2610, 57 L.Ed.2d 582 (1978). Because the trial judge, in explaining the sentence, stated to the defendant it was his "view that your defense was a complete fabrication without the slightest merit whatsoever," the court of appeals held that defendant must be resentenced, but the Supreme Court, per the Chief Justice, disagreed. As for defendant's constitutional argument that the sentence constituted punishment for the crime of perjury for which he had not been indicted, tried or convicted, the Court responded "that it is proper—indeed, even necessary for the rational exercise of discretion—to consider the defendant's whole person and personality, as manifested by his conduct at trial and his testimony under oath, for whatever light those may shed on the sentencing decision." As for defendant's claim that permitting consideration of perjury will "chill" defendants in exercising their right to testify on their own behalf, the Court answered that the "right guaranteed by law to a defendant is narrowly the right to testify truthfully in accordance with the oath," so that if "the sentencing judge's consideration of defendants' untruthfulness in testifying has

any chilling effect on a defendant's decision to testify falsely, that effect is entirely permissible."

g. Comment, 66 Yale L.J. 204, 211–19 (1966).

h. On the other hand, are there cases in which the public interest is best served by *not* having the case disposed of by a guilty plea? Consider Donald J. Newman & Edgar C. Nemoyer, *Issues of Propriety in Negotiated Justice,* 47 Denver L.J. 367, 398–99 (1970): "Where public figures are involved, either as perpetrators or victims, there often is a demand for more information, while rumors and suspicions that there is 'more than meets the eye' abound. For example, the guilty plea of Senator Edward Kennedy to the traffic charge following his automobile accident in which a young girl was killed was viewed by many Americans as an inadequate termination of the case. In fact, the pressure for further explanation was so great that the Senator went on national television to explain his position. Much the same situation applies to the apparently negotiated guilty plea entered by James Earl Ray in connection with the murder of Dr. Martin Luther King. Here again, the sparse

"(iv) the defendant has given or agreed to give cooperation when such cooperation has resulted or may result in the successful prosecution of other offenders engaged in equally serious or more serious criminal conduct.[i]

"(b) The court should not impose upon a defendant any sentence in excess of that which would be justified by any of the protective, deterrent, or other purposes of the criminal law because the defendant has chosen to require the prosecution to prove guilt at trial rather than to enter a plea of guilty or nolo contendere."

8. In *Scott v. United States,* 419 F.2d 264 (D.C.Cir.1969), Chief Judge Bazelon commented: "[T]here may be circumstances under which the prosecutor may bargain with the defendant without raising the constitutional question of whether the exercise of the right to trial can be made costly. When there is substantial uncertainty concerning the likely outcome of a trial, 'each side is interested in limiting these inherent litigation risks.' The prosecutor may be willing to accept a plea of guilty on a lesser charge rather than chance an acquittal on the more serious. The accused may be similarly willing to acknowledge his guilt of the lesser charge rather than risk conviction on the more serious, or to accept the promise of a lighter sentence to escape the possibility of conviction after trial and a heavier sentence.

"Superficially it may seem that even in such a case the defendant who insists upon a trial and is found guilty pays a price for the exercise of his right when he receives a longer sentence than his less venturesome counterpart who pleads guilty. In a sense he has. But the critical distinction is that the price he has paid is not one imposed by the state to discourage others from a similar exercise of their rights, but rather one encountered by those who gamble and lose. After the fact, the defendant who pleads innocent and is convicted receives a heavier sentence. But, by the same token, the defendant who pleads innocent and is acquitted receives no sentence. To the extent that the bargain struck reflects only the uncertainty of conviction before trial, the 'expected sentence before trial'—length of sentence discounted by probability of conviction—is the same for those who decide to plead guilty and those who hope for acquittal but risk conviction by going to trial.

"In determining who has or has not 'paid a price,' it is essential to reason clearly concerning what class of defendants are being compared with what other class of defendants for what purpose and at what point in time. The danger presented by plea bargaining is that defendants deciding upon a plea will be deterred from exercising their right to a trial. The relevant vantage point is thus before trial, and the relevant comparison is between the expectations of those who decide to insist upon a trial and those who decide to eliminate the risk of trial by pleading guilty. If the sentence expectations of those two classes at that time are the same, then there will be no chilling effect upon exercise of the right to trial, and it is accurate to say that no 'price' has been placed upon exercise of the right.

information contained in the charge and the monosyllabic guilty plea hardly satisfied those who are more concerned about the full details of the murder of a notable public figure."

i. In *Roberts v. United States,* 445 U.S. 552, 100 S.Ct. 1358, 63 L.Ed.2d 622 (1980), the Court held that the district court properly considered, as one factor in imposing consecutive sentences on a petitioner who had pleaded guilty to two counts of using a telephone to facilitate the distribution of heroin, petitioner's refusal to cooperate with government officials investigating a related criminal conspiracy to distribute heroin in which he was a confessed participant. Citing this provision in the ABA Standards, the majority expressed "doubt that a principled distinction may be drawn between 'enhancing' the punishment imposed upon the petitioner and denying him the 'leniency' he claims would be appropriate if he had cooperated." Marshall, J., dissenting, objected that such "a distinction has been recognized," and concluded that the enhancement of petitioner's sentence as approved by the majority "represented an improper involvement of the judicial office in the prosecutorial function."

"To determine the expectations of those defendants who insist upon a trial, we must consider the probability of conviction as well as the sentences received by those who plead innocent and are later convicted. The argument that the defendant who receives a heavier sentence after trial has 'paid a price' because he receives a heavier sentence than the defendant who is acquitted (and goes free) or pleads guilty (and receives a shorter sentence on the same or a reduced charge) errs on two counts: (1) the comparison is made at the wrong time—after trial, when the uncertainty of litigation has passed, rather than before trial—and (2) the comparison is made between the wrong categories of defendants—the class of defendants convicted after trial versus the class of defendants who plead guilty or are acquitted rather than the class of defendants who exercise their right to trial versus the class of defendants who do not."

9. Should there instead be a "standard discount" in all cases to avoid the evils of unequal bargaining and excessive leniency previously noted?[j] Or, is case-by-case discounting best because only in that way can plea bargaining serve as an element "of a well-functioning market system" which sets "the 'price' of crime * * * in the traditional market fashion," thus permitting us "to get the maximum deterrent punch out of whatever resources are committed to crime control."[k]

10. Assuming the Bazelon theory in *Scott* is valid, does it make any difference *why* there is a "substantial uncertainty concerning the likely outcome of a trial"? Consider the following variations on a case in which the defendant and an accomplice have been charged with robbery and burglary after allegedly breaking into a house, threatening a babysitter with a gun, and taking a substantial amount of money and valuables: (1) The defendant's accomplice, after making a full, substantiated confession implicating the defendant, flees the jurisdiction and cannot be found, and without his testimony the state has insufficient evidence to establish a prima facie case. (2) The only evidence the state can produce is the babysitter's identification, but it is undisputed that she saw the robbers only briefly in poor light and that she originally gave the police a rather sketchy description. (3) Same as variation 2, except that the defendant confesses, giving a full account of the crime with details only the perpetrator could know, but the confession is inadmissible because obtained in violation of *Miranda*. (4) Two hours after the robbery, police find the stolen goods and the gun in the defendant's apartment, but there is about a 60% chance that the evidence will be excluded because obtained in violation of the Fourth Amendment.[l]

C. ACCURATE AND FAIR RESULTS

11. "Maximization of adjudication by trial may actually result in more inaccurate verdicts. So long as trials are the exception rather than the rule and are limited, by and large, to cases in which the defense offers a substantial basis for contesting the prosecutor's allegations, the defendant's presumption of innocence and the requirement of proof beyond a reasonable doubt are likely to remain meaningful to a jury. The very fact that the defendant contests the charges impresses upon the jurors the seriousness of their deliberations and the need to keep an open mind about the evidence and to approach the testimony of accusing witnesses with critical care and perhaps even a degree of skepticism. If contest becomes routine, jurors may likely direct their skepticism at the defense. Prosecu-

j. See Note, 82 Yale L.J. 286 (1972).

k. Frank H. Easterbrook, *Criminal Procedure as a Market System*, 12 J.Legal Stud. 289, 289–90 (1983).

l. See Welsh White, *A Proposal for Reform of the Plea Bargaining Process*, 119 U.Pa.

L.Rev. 439, 458–62 (1971), for consideration of what the prosecutor should do in each of these situations.

tors too readily apply the overall, and overwhelming, statistical probability of guilt to individual cases; we do not want jurors to do the same. It makes some sense, then, to screen out those cases where there is no real dispute and encourage their disposition by plea, leaving for trial to the extent possible only those cases where there exists a real basis for dispute. * * *

"The possibility that innocent defendants might be induced to plead guilty in order to avoid the possibility of a harsh sentence should they be convicted after trial is obviously cause for concern. Because of the emotional potential of the problem, it is easy to overstate. The truth is that we just do not know how common such a situation is. * * *

"Still, perhaps the problem can be put in a better perspective. In the first place, trials, too, may not always result in truthful or accurate verdicts. It is interesting to note that disposition by trial and by negotiated plea are similar in that in neither instance do we have any relatively accurate idea of the incidence of mistaken judgments. On one level, then, the significant question is not how many innocent people are induced to plead guilty but is there a significant likelihood that innocent people who would be (or have a fair chance of being) acquitted at trial might be induced to plead guilty?

"Further, concern over the possibility that a negotiated plea can result in an erroneous judgment of conviction assumes a frame of reference by which the accuracy of the judgment is to be evaluated. It assumes an objective truth existing in a realm of objective historical fact which it is the sole function of our process to discover. Some, but by no means all, criminal cases fit this image. For example, this is a relatively accurate description of the issues at stake in a case in which the defendant asserts a defense of mistaken identity. If all other issues were eliminated from the case, there would still exist a world of objective historical fact in which the accused did or did not perpetrate the act at issue. And if he did not, a negotiated guilty plea would represent an erroneous judgment. In this instance, then, the issue suggested is the comparative likelihood of such erroneous decisions as between trial and negotiation.

"But not all criminal cases fit the above picture. * * * Much criminal adjudication concerns the passing of value judgments on the accused's conduct as is obvious where negligence, recklessness, reasonable apprehension of attack, use of unnecessary force, and the like are at issue. Although intent is thought of as a question of fact, it too can represent a judgment of degrees of fault, for example, in cases where the issue is whether the defendants entertained intent to defraud or intent to kill. In many of these cases, objective truth is more ambiguous, if it exists at all. Such truth exists only as it emerges from the fact-determining process, and accuracy in this context really means relative equality of results as between defendants similarly situated and relative congruence between the formal verdict and our understanding of society's less formally expressed evaluation of such conduct.

"The negotiated plea can, then, be an accurate process in this sense. So long as the judgment of experienced counsel as to the likely jury result is the key element entering into the bargain, substantial congruence is likely to result. Once we recognize that what lends rationality to the factfinding process in these instances lies not in an attempt to discover objective truth but in the devising of a process to express intelligent judgment, there is no inherent reason why plea negotiation need be regarded any the less rational or intelligent in its results.

"Indeed, it may be that in some instances plea negotiation leads to more 'intelligent' results. A jury can be left with the extreme alternatives of guilty of a crime of the highest degree or not guilty of any crime, with no room for any intermediate judgment. And this is likely to occur in just those cases where an intermediate judgment is the fairest and most 'accurate' (or most congruent).

"Clearly, the line between responsibility and irresponsibility due to insanity is not as sharp as the alternatives posed to a jury would suggest. It may be that such a dividing line exists in some world of objective reality and that the ambiguity arises from the difficulties of accurate factfinding. It is more realistic, however, to view responsibility as a matter of degree at best only roughly expressed in the law's categories of first and second degree murder, manslaughter, etc. The very visibility of the trial process may be one factor that prevents us from offering the jury this compromise in order to preserve the symbolism of uniform rules evenly applied. The low visibility of the negotiated plea allows this compromise which may be more rational and congruent than the result we are likely to arrive at after a trial. While the desire to protect the symbolism of legality and the concern over lay compromises may warrant limiting the jury to extreme alternative, it does not follow that to allow the defendant to choose such a compromise is an irrational or even a less rational procedure."[m]

12. "[S]ome advocates of plea bargaining rely on the fictitious concept of 'factual guilt' to argue that negotiated settlements produce more accurate determinations of 'guilt' than those produced by the vagaries of trial adjudication. * * *

"One obvious response to this claim is to dispute its assumption that the parties' evaluation of the defendant's degree of culpability plays a significant role in shaping the ultimate bargain. Negotiated compromises concerning the charging decision or sentencing 'recommendation' often reflect and promote institutional, financial, and tactical considerations that have little bearing on what the defendant did, or his culpability in doing it. Consequently, negotiated settlements may frustrate the substantive criminal law's punishment goals by exaggerating the effect of the parties' tactical choices upon appropriate sentencing decisions. * * *

"Plea bargaining undercuts [the] distinctive moral aspects of the criminal law. First, negotiated dispute resolution 'privatizes' the dispute by empowering the parties themselves to resolve it without any significant involvement by either the public or the courts. Second, negotiated settlements permit the parties to resolve questions concerning the appropriate degree of liability that should attach to the defendant's acts. Such party compromises destroy any notion that an objective societal determination of moral guilt has been made. Worse, negotiation dilutes the moral force of the criminal sanction by treating questions concerning the offender's just deserts as a negotiating chip whose value lies primarily in how it affects the parties' rational adjustment of litigation risks. Consequently, plea bargaining may distort the legislature's labeling of offenses and frustrate its

---

m. Arnold Enker, *Perspectives on Plea Bargaining,* in Task Force Report: The Courts 108, 112–14. Compare John Griffiths, *Ideology in Criminal Procedure, or a Third Model of the Criminal Process,* 79 Yale L.J. 359, 398–99 (1970): "[T]here are social interests in criminal cases which cannot be left to the parties to submerge in pleas of guilty. * * * Consider, for example, the insanity defense. So long as the criminal process is a struggle between hostile forces, the insanity defense and the policies it represents will often be submerged in pleas of guilty. But it seems hardly conceivable that whatever is at stake in the insanity defense should be left to defendants and prosecutors to negotiate away—particularly, although not exclusively, because the defendants concerned can hardly be regarded as fully competent to do so. * * * [I]f some persons are not to be regarded as responsible, but are to be treated (or left alone) upon another basis, we cannot ultimately regard it as desirable that they pull themselves up into functional responsibility by the bootstraps of a guilty plea."

sentencing objectives. Finally, the negotiation process undermines the moral legitimacy of the system in both the defendant's[n] and public's eyes."[o]

D. ADMINISTRATIVE CONVENIENCE

13. "Most prosecutors insist they could not do their jobs without plea bargaining. Understaffed Public Defender organizations agree. Chief Justice Burger claims that even a ten percent decline in convictions produced by plea bargaining would double the number of trials held in this country. Scholars repeat such misleading statistics to support their conclusion that society cannot afford to abolish plea bargaining. Slowly but surely, the crime control advocate's original claim that our system's survival depends upon plea bargaining becomes conventional wisdom.[p]

"It is beyond the scope of this article to challenge these 'facts of life.' Professor Alschuler has already done so. In his most recent article on plea bargaining, he suggests that our system 'could provide three-day jury trials to all felony defendants who reach the trial stage by adding no more than $850 million to annual criminal justice expenditures';[213] an amount that is 'less than what the Law Enforcement Assistance Administration recently spent annually on improving state criminal justice.' Eleven years earlier, a national study group concluded that '[t]he basic problem is not financial; the cost of a model system of criminal justice is easily within the means of the American people.' Of course, we may choose not to spend the necessary resources to implement the due process model's vision. The decision to allocate more of our scarce resources to the criminal justice system rests ultimately on a normative value judgment about whether the benefits of protecting due process values in all cases outweigh the costs to society.[q]

"The 'necessary evil' defense of plea bargaining skirts this normative decision by falsely assuming that our society could not possibly pay for streamlined trials in most cases. This defense of plea bargaining is particularly powerful because it denies the existence of any real choice to due process advocates who might push

---

n. "The Hughes Committee (the Joint Legislative Committee on Crime) made a study of prisoner attitudes towards plea bargaining * * * and found that almost 90 percent of the inmates surveyed had been solicited to enter a plea bargain. Most were bitter, believing that they did not receive effective legal representation or that the judge did not keep the state's promise of a sentence which had induced them to enter guilty pleas.

"As the Hughes Committee observed, the large segment of the prison population who believe they have been 'victimized' by the courts or bar 'are not likely to accept the efforts of another institution of society, the correctional system, in redirecting their attitudes." N.Y. State Special Commission on Attica, *Attica* 30–31 (1972). See also Jonathon D. Casper, *Criminal Justice, The Consumer Perspective* 3–54 (1972).

o. Peter Arenella, *Rethinking the Functions of Criminal Procedure: The Warren and Burger Courts' Competing Ideologies*, 72 Geo.L.J. 185, 216–19 (1983).

p. But, some have questioned whether an end to plea bargaining would significantly increase the burdens on the criminal justice system. For one thing, it has been noted that the

existence of plea bargaining is itself responsible for much delay; to get a better plea, "defense attorneys commonly devise strategies whose only utility lies in the threat they pose to the court's and the prosecutor's time." Albert W. Alschuler, *The Prosecutor's Role in Plea Bargaining*, 36 U.Chi.L.Rev. 50, 56 (1968).

213. [Albert W. Alschuler, fn. w infra, at 936.] I suspect that Alschuler's $850 million figure underestimates the necessary increased expenditure, but I agree with his conclusion that our society could afford to implement the due process model if trial procedures were streamlined.

q. "It is easy to minimize administrative convenience and need. Simply increase the staff of prosecutors, judges, defense counsel, and probation officers if the present complement is insufficient to handle the task, it is said. Even if the money were readily available, it would still not be clear that we could call upon sufficient numbers of competent personnel. A lowering of standards in order to man the store adequately may well result in poorer justice. It may also divert both funds and personnel from other segments of the criminal process, such as corrections work, where they are arguably more needed." Arnold Enker, fn. m supra, at 112.

for reform if they thought it were feasible. Instead of seeing plea bargaining as a legally contingent phenomenon that could be changed, they view it as an inevitable feature of the criminal justice system that they must begrudgingly accept."[r]

E. More on the Consequences of Prohibiting Plea Bargaining

14. "[T]hough it might be possible to proscribe 'explicit plea bargaining' (that is, explicit negotiation between prosecutor, defense attorney, and judge), it would be impossible to proscribe what we might call 'implicit plea bargaining.' By implicit plea bargaining I mean * * * that there is agreement among all court actors that most guilty defendants should plead guilty and be rewarded for their plea. Thus, even if formal negotiations were verboten, the expectation that guilty defendants should plead would remain. All criminal court actors would recognize 'implicitly' that the defendant who pleads receives a reward and that the defendant who goes to trial does not. Perhaps those working in the system would have to learn to tolerate a bit more uncertainty because of the proscription against formal agreements, but I would guess that not too much time would elapse before the implicit rewards became well known, and defense attorneys could then make 'good guesses' as to what sentence the defendant would receive.

"Furthermore, I would hypothesize that even with these 'good guesses' the system would be unstable. Defendants would not be satisfied to place complete faith in their attorneys' guesses and would continue to press for specific agreements regarding charge and sentence reduction. And I think after the initial ballyhoo surrounding the 'abolition of plea bargaining' abates, the defense attorney's efforts to arrange more explicit deals would meet with success."[s]

15. A ban on plea bargaining was implemented in El Paso County, Texas, in 1975. The judges replaced sentence bargaining with a set of sentencing guidelines, and the prosecutor adopted a policy against both sentence and charge bargaining. But, after a few years *some* assistant prosecutors departed from the office policy and *some* judges accepted negotiated sentences communicated to them privately, prompting this comment: "Justice is disserved when a defendant's sentencing, as it is affected by plea bargaining, depends on the fortuity of case assignment and not on the existence of a policy uniformly applied to all accused. Second, when plea bargaining is practiced *sub rosa,* the public remains uninformed of the activities of judges and prosecutors and unaware of a vital part of the criminal justice process. Third, when these key actors in the justice system frequently engage in a prohibited practice, policy becomes pretense and law loses its moral force."[t]

16. In 1975, the Attorney General of Alaska forbid all prosecutors in that state from engaging in plea negotiations, reducing or dropping charges in exchange for guilty pleas, and making sentence recommendations to the court. An empirical study[u] of the effects of that policy concluded: (a) That "explicit sentencing bargaining * * * practically disappeared," and that when charge bargaining now occurs "it usually involves dropping one or more counts from multiple-count indictments, typical in prosecutions for forgeries, bad checks, and drug sales."[v] (b) That "experienced defense counsel who have developed good working relations

---

r. Peter Arenella, fn. o supra, at 221–222.

s. Milton Heumann, *Plea Bargaining* 157–58 (1977).

t. Robert A. Weninger, *The Abolition of Plea Bargaining: A Case Study of El Paso County, Texas,* 35 U.C.L.A.L.Rev. 265, 313 (1987).

u. Summarized in Michael L. Rubenstein & Teresa J. White, *Plea Bargaining: Can Alaska Live Without It?,* 62 Judicature 266 (1978).

v. A later study reported that "charge bargaining was substantially curtailed for some years, but has become steadily more prevalent since the mid–1980's." Theresa White Carns & John A. Kruse, *A Re-evaluation of Alaska's Plea Bargaining Ban,* 8 Alaska L.Rev. 27, 64 (1991).

with individual district attorneys sometimes report success at negotiations," while "[l]ess experienced defense counsel, particularly younger members of the public defender's staff, report that plea bargaining is virtually nonexistent in their practices." (c) That some lawyers "are simply refusing private criminal business because clients cannot afford the fees, or because the attorney honestly believes that the actual benefits of his service are not likely to be worth what he must charge to prepare a competent defense," which has "led to the claim that the no-plea-bargaining policy has had its strongest negative impact on middle-class defendants who can neither afford high-priced legal talent nor qualify for representation by the public defender." (d) That some judges, until the practice was expressly proscribed by a state supreme court decision, "circumvented the ban on plea bargaining and made the prosecutor irrelevant through direct dealings with defense counsel." (e) That though "the rate of trials did increase substantially, the projected onslaught never materialized." (f) That the policy "produced a strong, if selective, effect on sentence severity. Violent criminals, who always got stiff treatment, did not fare any worse. The ones who received harsher punishment were the relatively minor property offenders, the drug offenders, and those who wrote bad checks, embezzled, or committed credit-card offenses." (g) That defendants "who go to trial, other factors being equal, appear to serve more time than those who plead guilty. Multiple regression analysis of length of sentences given after guilty pleas compared with those imposed after trial show that for violent and fraud crimes, sentences are significantly longer after trials. The disparity is greater in violent crimes, where sentences after trial are 445 per cent longer than those given after pleas. For fraud crimes, trial sentences are 334 per cent longer. No such plea/trial 'differential' appears in property crimes, and there were too few trials for drug crimes in the two years to make a valid analysis." Has the Alaska experiment been a success or a failure?

17. The experience in Philadelphia and Pittsburgh, where the practice is not to plea bargain but instead to bargain for jury waivers, suggests that "if a legislature were to prohibit the exchange of concessions for pleas of guilty without forbidding official concessions for waivers of the right to jury trial, the invisible hand that sometimes is thought to make plea bargaining inevitable could continue its disturbing work. The differing resource limitations of various jurisdictions would be reflected, however, not in varying guilty plea rates or in differing concessions offered for pleas of guilty, but in forms and procedures of the nonjury trials that most defendants would be induced to accept."[w]

Would this be a better system, or just a different one? Consider: "Jury waiver concessions differ from guilty plea concessions in three striking ways. First, and most importantly, the defendant who waives a jury retains most of his significant adversary trial rights. Thus, although from the state's perspective the jury waiver concession has the same justification and most of the same advantages as does a guilty plea concession, the jury waiver concession entails far fewer dangers for the accused. Second, because the defendant who waives a jury gives up much less than does one who pleads guilty, the concession needed to induce the jury waiver will necessarily be smaller than that needed to induce a guilty plea in the same case. Third, jury waiver concessions are much less likely than guilty plea concessions to vary in attractiveness as the probability of acquittal changes from case to case; thus, the risk that excessive concessions may elude judicial control and endanger the innocent defendant is in practice much less serious than in the case of plea bargaining."[x]

w. Albert W. Alschuler, *Implementing the Criminal Defendant's Right to Trial: Alternatives to the Plea Bargaining System*, 50 U.Chi. L.Rev. 931, 1042–43 (1983).

x. Stephen J. Schulhofer, *Is Plea Bargaining Inevitable?*, 97 Harv.L.Rev. 1037, 1092–93 (1984).

Compare: "Unfortunately, abolition would likely only worsen innocent defendants' plight. In order to accommodate the dramatic increase in trials, the trial process itself would have to be truncated, as Stephen Schulhofer's famous discussion of the Philadelphia process shows. The mini-trials that took the place of bargaining in Philadelphia were brief affairs, most lasting no more than an hour; the pretrial preparation on both sides was minimal. Altering the trial process in this way necessarily increases the error rate (unless our current trial system is nonsensical), meaning that it raises the rate at which innocent defendants are convicted. That, in turn, alters prosecutors' incentives when making decisions about which cases to take to trial. Indeed, it may alter police incentives when making arrests. Police officers and prosecutors alike can afford to be less careful in screening their cases if the trial 'backstop' becomes more casual."[y]

F. State and Federal Limitations on Plea Bargaining

18. If total abolition of plea bargaining is not feasible, then what about imposing limitations on the practice, as has occurred in some states by statute or court rule? What kinds of limitations are feasible? Consider Cal.Penal Code § 667(g) (prior felony convictions are to be pleaded and proved and not plea bargained away unless there is insufficient evidence to prove the conviction or unless a contrary course would serve the interest of justice, for a reason stated on the record and approved by the court); Cal.Penal Code § 1192.7 (plea bargaining forbidden "in any case in which the indictment or information charges a serious felony," as defined therein, "unless there is insufficient evidence to prove the People's case, or testimony of a material witness cannot be obtained, or a reduction or dismissal would not result in a substantial change in sentence"); *State v. Hessen*, 145 N.J. 441, 678 A.2d 1082 (1996) (court rule barring plea bargaining in driving-under-influence-related cases is "well within the Court's rule-making authority over plea-bargaining practice," as plea bargaining "is not a right of a defendant or the prosecutor," but "an accommodation which the judiciary system is free to institute or reject").

19. In the federal system, there has existed since 1987 an elaborate scheme of Sentencing Guidelines which serve to limit plea bargaining. Under the Guidelines, 43 offense levels and 6 criminal history categories are used to identify the sentencing range applicable to in a particular case, from which the sentencing judge ordinarily can deviate only when one of the bases for upward or downward departure listed in the Guidelines is found to be present. The Guidelines provide that in the case of a plea agreement to dismiss or not bring certain charges, "the court may accept the agreement if the court determines, for reasons stated on the record,[z] that the remaining charges adequately reflect the seriousness of the actual offense behavior and that accepting the agreement will not undermine the statutory purposes of sentencing or the sentencing guidelines." U.S.S.G § 6B1.2. It has been held that this provision gives courts wide latitude in deciding whether to accept charge bargains, *United States v. Greener*, 979 F.2d 517 (7th Cir.1992), and it remains unclear what the critical words "adequately reflect" mean in this context.[a] But the Guidelines further limit the opportunity for giving concessions

---

y. Robert E. Scott & William J. Stuntz, *Plea Bargaining as Contract*, 101 Yale L.J. 1909, 1950 (1992).

z. However, "no evidence exists that district courts" state for the record reasons for accepting a charge bargain; and "appellate courts do not comment on the district courts' oversight, perhaps because Rule 11 does not include any similar requirement." Thomas W.

Hutchinson et al., *Federal Sentencing Law and Practice* 928 (1997 ed.).

a. "To interpret that phrase as meaning that the court must be able to impose the same sentence on the defendant as if no charges had been dropped would render charge bargaining meaningless. On the other hand, if courts accept charge bargains without regard to the

by dropping or not bringing some charge, as such action "shall not preclude the conduct underlying such charge from being considered" in determining the offense level and other matters bearing on sentencing under the Guidelines. U.S.S.G. § 6B1.2. Although avoidance of this constraint might be possible by moving the bargaining back to the pre-indictment stage, the Department of Justice in 1989 adopted the policy that a "federal prosecutor should initially charge the most serious, provable offense or offenses consistent with the defendant's conduct."[b]

In the case of a plea agreement for a certain sentence or involving a certain sentence recommendation, "the court may" accept the agreement or follow the recommendation if satisfied that the sentence is either "within the applicable guideline range" or "departs from the applicable guideline range for justifiable reasons." U.S.S.G. § 6B1.2. This means that the existence of the plea agreement is not itself a mitigating circumstance and that in determining the proper sentence the court must, for the most part, proceed just as it would had the defendant pled not guilty and been convicted at trial. If the guilty plea defendant gets a lighter sentence, this is most likely to occur by application of at least one of two sentencing factors which do take on special significance in the guilty plea context as a result of: (i) a provision for decrease of the offense by two levels where defendant "clearly demonstrates acceptance of responsibility for his offense," U.S.S.G. § 3E1.1(a), which in the case of a prompt guilty plea can actually result in a decrease by a total of three levels because of defendant's conduct in "timely notifying authorities of his intention to enter a plea of guilty," U.S.S.G. § 3E1.1(b)(2); and (ii) a provision allowing a downward departure from the Guidelines upon a "motion of the government stating that the defendant has provided substantial assistance in the investigation or prosecution of another person," U.S.S.G. § 5K1.1.[c]

SECTION 2. REJECTED, KEPT AND BROKEN BARGAINS; UNREALIZED EXPECTATIONS

BORDENKIRCHER v. HAYES
434 U.S. 357, 98 S.Ct. 663, 54 L.Ed.2d 604 (1978).

Justice STEWART delivered the opinion of the Court. * * *

[Paul Hayes was indicted in Fayette County, Ky., on a charge of uttering a forged instrument in the amount of $88.30, punishable by two to 10 years in prison. Hayes and his retained counsel met with the prosecutor who offered to recommend a sentence of five years if Hayes would plead guilty and added that if Hayes did not plead guilty he would seek an indictment under the Kentucky Habitual Criminal Act, which would subject Hayes to a mandatory sentence of life imprisonment by reason of his two prior felony convictions. Hayes chose not to plead guilty, and the prosecutor did obtain such an indictment. A jury found

---

defendant's actual conduct, the goals of the guidelines could be frustrated." Ibid.

b. U. S. Dep't of Justice, Office of the Attorney General, *Plea Bargaining Under the Sentencing Reform Act* (Mar. 13, 1989). However, that policy has not always been followed, Tony Garoppolo, *Confusion and Distortion in the Federal Sentencing Process*, 27 Crim.L.Bull. 3, 15 (1991), and has more recently been ame-

liorated to some degree so as to allow "federal prosecutors to take the circumstances of a particular case into account when making charging decisions and negotiating plea agreements." Comment, 63 U.Cin.L.Rev. 1851, 1874–75 (1995).

c. Not all defendants who believe such a motion will be forthcoming in fact benefit from this provision. See Note 8, p. 1264.

Hayes guilty on the principal charge of uttering a forged instrument and, in a separate proceeding, further found that he had twice before been convicted of felonies. As required by the habitual offender statute, he was sentenced to a life term in the penitentiary. The Kentucky Court of Appeals rejected Hayes' constitutional objections to the enhanced sentence, and on Hayes' petition for a federal writ of habeas corpus the district court agreed that there had been no constitutional violation in the sentence or the indictment procedure. The Court of Appeals for the Sixth Circuit reversed on the ground that the prosecutor's conduct had violated the principles of *Blackledge v. Perry,* p. 891, which "protect defendants from the vindictive exercise of a prosecutor's discretion."]

It may be helpful to clarify at the outset the nature of the issue in this case. While the prosecutor did not actually obtain the recidivist indictment until after the plea conferences had ended, his intention to do so was clearly put forth at the outset of the plea negotiations. Hayes was thus fully informed of the true terms of the offer when he made his decision to plead not guilty. This is not a situation, therefore, where the prosecutor without notice brought an additional and more serious charge after plea negotiations relating only to the original indictment had ended with the defendant's insistence on pleading not guilty. As a practical matter, in short, this case would be no different if the grand jury had indicted Hayes as a recidivist from the outset, and the prosecutor had offered to drop that charge as part of the plea bargain.

The Court of Appeals nonetheless drew a distinction between "concessions relating to prosecution under an existing indictment," and threats to bring more severe charges not contained in the original indictment—a line it thought necessary in order to establish a prophylactic rule to guard against the evil of prosecutorial vindictiveness.[6] Quite apart from this chronological distinction, however, the Court of Appeals found that the prosecutor had acted vindictively in the present case since he had conceded that the indictment was influenced by his desire to induce a guilty plea. The ultimate conclusion of the Court of Appeals thus seems to have been that a prosecutor acts vindictively and in violation of due process of law whenever his charging decision is influenced by what he hopes to gain in the course of plea bargaining negotiations.

We have recently had occasion to observe that "[w]hatever might be the situation in an ideal world, the fact is that the guilty plea and the often concomitant plea bargain are important components of this country's criminal justice system. Properly administered, they can benefit all concerned." *Blackledge v. Allison* [p. 1302]. The open acknowledgment of this previously clandestine practice has led this Court to recognize the importance of counsel during plea negotiations, *Brady v. United States* [p. 1250], the need for a public record indicating that a plea was knowingly and voluntarily made, *Boykin v. Alabama* [p. 1294], and the requirement that a prosecutor's plea bargaining promise must be kept, *Santobello v. New York* [p. 1260]. The decision of the Court of Appeals in the present case, however, did not deal with considerations such as these, but held that the substance of the plea offer itself violated the limitations imposed by the Due Process Clause of the Fourteenth Amendment. For the reasons that follow, we have concluded that the Court of Appeals was mistaken in so ruling.

6. "Although a prosecutor may in the course of plea negotiations offer a defendant concessions relating to prosecution under an existing indictment * * * he may not threaten a defendant with the consequences that more severe charges may be brought if he insists on going to trial. When a prosecutor obtains an indictment less severe than the facts known to him at the time might permit, he makes a discretionary determination that the interests of the state are served by not seeking more serious charges. * * * Accordingly, if after plea negotiations fail, he then procures an indictment charging a more serious crime, a strong inference is created that the only reason for the more serious charges is vindictiveness. Under these circumstances, the prosecutor should be required to justify his action."

This Court held in *North Carolina v. Pearce* [p. 1535], that the Due Process Clause of the Fourteenth Amendment "requires that vindictiveness against a defendant for having successfully attacked his first conviction must play no part in the sentence he receives after a new trial." The same principle was later applied to prohibit a prosecutor from reindicting a convicted misdemeanant on a felony charge after the defendant had invoked an appellate remedy, since in this situation there was also a "realistic likelihood of 'vindictiveness.' " *Blackledge v. Perry.*

In those cases the Court was dealing with the State's unilateral imposition of a penalty upon a defendant who had chosen to exercise a legal right to attack his original conviction—a situation "very different from the give-and-take negotiation common in plea bargaining between the prosecution and the defense, which arguably possess relatively equal bargaining power." The Court has emphasized that the due process violation in cases such as *Pearce* and *Perry* lay not in the possibility that a defendant might be deterred from the exercise of a legal right, see *Colten v. Kentucky* [p. 1539]; *Chaffin v. Stynchcombe* [p. 1539], but rather in the danger that the State might be retaliating against the accused for lawfully attacking his conviction. See *Blackledge v. Perry.*

To punish a person because he has done what the law plainly allows him to do is a due process violation of the most basic sort, see *North Carolina v. Pearce* (opinion of Black, J.), and for an agent of the State to pursue a course of action whose objective is to penalize a person's reliance on his legal rights is "patently unconstitutional." *Chaffin v. Stynchcombe.* But in the "give-and-take" of plea bargaining, there is no such element of punishment or retaliation so long as the accused is free to accept or reject the prosecution's offer.

Plea bargaining flows from "the mutuality of advantage" to defendants and prosecutors, each with his own reasons for wanting to avoid trial. *Brady v. United States*[a] [p. 1250]. Defendants advised by competent counsel and protected by other procedural safeguards are presumptively capable of intelligent choice in response to prosecutorial persuasion, and unlikely to be driven to false self-condemnation. Indeed, acceptance of the basic legitimacy of plea bargaining necessarily implies rejection of any notion that a guilty plea is involuntary in a constitutional sense simply because it is the end result of the bargaining process. By hypothesis, the plea may have been induced by promises of a recommendation of a lenient sentence or a reduction of charges, and thus by fear of the possibility of a greater

---

a. Although *Brady* did not involve a plea bargaining situation, see Note 1 at p. 1293, the Court analogized the plea involved there to a plea obtained through plea bargaining, and then commented generally on the validity of a plea produced by the "mutuality of advantage" that flows from a negotiated plea: "We decline to hold * * * that a guilty plea is compelled and invalid under the Fifth Amendment whenever motivated by the defendant's desire to accept the certainty or probability of a lesser penalty rather than face a wider range of possibilities extending from acquittal to conviction and a higher penalty authorized by law for the crime charged. * * * [B]oth the state and the defendant often find it advantageous to preclude the possibility of the maximum penalty authorized by law. For a defendant who sees slight possibility of acquittal, the advantages of pleading guilty and limiting the probable penalty are obvious—his exposure is reduced, the correctional processes can begin immediately, and the practical burdens of a trial are eliminated. For the State there are also advantages—the more promptly imposed punishment after an admission of guilt may more effectively attain the objectives of punishment; and with the avoidance of trial, scarce judicial and prosecutorial resources are conserved for those cases in which there is a substantial issue of the defendant's guilt or in which there is substantial doubt that the State can sustain its burden of proof. It is this mutuality of advantage which perhaps explains the fact that at present well over three-fourths of the criminal convictions in this country rest on pleas of guilty, a great many of them no doubt motivated at least in part by the hope or assurance of a lesser penalty than might be imposed if there were a guilty verdict after a trial to judge or jury."

penalty upon conviction after a trial. See A.B.A. Standards, *Pleas of Guilty* § 3.1 (1968).[b]

While confronting a defendant with the risk of more severe punishment clearly may have a "discouraging effect on the defendant's assertion of his trial rights, the imposition of these difficult choices [is] an inevitable"—and permissible—"attribute of any legitimate system which tolerates and encourages the negotiation of pleas." *Chaffin v. Stynchcombe.* It follows that, by tolerating and encouraging the negotiation of pleas, this Court has necessarily accepted as constitutionally legitimate the simple reality that the prosecutor's interest at the bargaining table is to persuade the defendant to forego his right to plead not guilty.

It is not disputed here that Hayes was properly chargeable under the recidivist statute, since he had in fact been convicted of two previous felonies. In our system, so long as the prosecutor has probable cause to believe that the accused committed an offense defined by statute, the decision whether or not to prosecute, and what charge to file or bring before a grand jury, generally rests entirely in his discretion.[8] Within the limits set by the legislature's constitutionally valid definition of chargeable offenses, "the conscious exercise of some selectivity in enforcement is not in itself a federal constitutional violation" so long as "the selection was [not] deliberately based upon an unjustifiable standard such as race, religion, or other arbitrary classification." To hold that the prosecutor's desire to

b. Now § 14–3.1 in the 1997 third edition, which as revised reads:

"(a) The prosecuting attorney may engage in plea discussions with counsel for the defendant for the purpose of reaching a plea agreement. Where the defendant has properly waived counsel, the prosecuting attorney may engage in plea discussions with the defendant. Where feasible, a record should be made and preserved for all such discussions with the defendant.

(b) The prosecuting attorney should make known any policies he or she may have concerning disposition of charges by plea or diversion.

"(c) The prosecuting attorney, in considering a plea agreement, may agree to one or more of the following, as dictated by the circumstances of the individual case:

"(i) to make or not to oppose favorable recommendations or to remain silent as to the sentence which should be imposed if the defendant enters a plea of guilty or nolo contendere, including such terms of the sentence as criminal forfeitures, restitution, fines and alternative sanctions;

"(ii) to dismiss, to seek to dismiss, or not to oppose dismissal of the offense charged if the defendant enters a plea of guilty or nolo contendere to another offense reasonably related to defendant's conduct; or

"(iii) to dismiss, to seek to dismiss, or not to oppose dismissal of other charges or potential charges if the defendant enters a plea of guilty or nolo contendere.

"(iv) where appropriate, to enter an agreement with the defendant regarding the disposition of related civil matters to which the

government is or would be a party, including civil penalties and/or civil forfeiture, or

"(v) in lieu of a plea agreement, to enter an agreement permitting the diversion of the case from the criminal process where appropriate and permissible to do so.

"(d) Similarly situated defendants should be afforded equal plea agreement opportunities.

"(e) The prosecuting attorney should make every effort to remain advised of the attitudes and sentiments of victims and law enforcement officials before reaching a plea agreement.

"(f) The prosecuting attorney should not knowingly make false statements or representations as to law or fact in the course of plea discussions with defense counsel or the defendant.

"(g) The prosecuting attorney should not, because of the pendency of plea negotiations, delay any discovery disclosures required to be made to the defense under applicable law or rules.

"(h) In connection with plan negotiations, the prosecuting attorney should not bring or threaten to bring charges against the defendant or another person, or refuse to dismiss charges, where admissible evidence does not exist to support the charges or the prosecuting attorney has no good faith intention of pursuing those charges."

8. This case does not involve the constitutional implications of a prosecutor's offer during plea bargaining of adverse or lenient treatment for some person *other* than the accused, which might pose a greater danger of inducing a false guilty plea by skewing the assessment of the risks a defendant must consider.

induce a guilty plea is an "unjustifiable standard," which, like race or religion, may play no part in his charging decision, would contradict the very premises that underlie the concept of plea bargaining itself. Moreover, a rigid constitutional rule that would prohibit a prosecutor from acting forthrightly in his dealings with the defense could only invite unhealthy subterfuge that would drive the practice of plea bargaining back into the shadows from which it has so recently emerged.

There is no doubt that the breadth of discretion that our country's legal system vests in prosecuting attorneys carries with it the potential for both individual and institutional abuse. And broad though that discretion may be, there are undoubtedly constitutional limits upon its exercise. We hold only that the course of conduct engaged in by the prosecutor in this case, which no more than openly presented the defendant with the unpleasant alternatives of foregoing trial or facing charges on which he was plainly subject to prosecution, did not violate the Due Process Clause of the Fourteenth Amendment.

Accordingly, the judgment of the Court of Appeals is

Reversed.

Justice BLACKMUN, with whom Justice BRENNAN and Justice MARSHALL, join dissenting.

[I]n this case vindictiveness is present to the same extent as it was thought to be in *Pearce* and in *Perry;* the prosecutor here admitted that the sole reason for the new indictment was to discourage the respondent from exercising his right to a trial.[1] Even had such an admission not been made, when plea negotiations, conducted in the face of the less serious charge under the first indictment, fail, charging by a second indictment a more serious crime for the same conduct creates "a strong inference" of vindictiveness. As then Judge McCree aptly observed, in writing for a unanimous panel of the Sixth Circuit, the prosecutor initially "makes a discretionary determination that the interests of the state are served by not seeking more serious charges." I therefore do not understand why, as in *Pearce,* due process does not require that the prosecution justify its action on some basis other than discouraging respondent from the exercise of his right to a trial. * * *

It might be argued that it really makes little difference how this case, now that it is here, is decided. The Court's holding gives plea bargaining full sway despite vindictiveness. A contrary result, however, merely would prompt the aggressive prosecutor to bring the greater charge initially in every case, and only thereafter to bargain. The consequences to the accused would still be adverse, for then he would bargain against a greater charge, face the likelihood of increased bail, and run the risk that the court would be less inclined to accept a bargain plea. Nonetheless, it is far preferable to hold the prosecution to the charge it was originally content to bring and to justify in the eyes of its public.[2]

1. In *Brady v. United States,* where the Court as a premise accepted plea bargaining as a legitimate practice, it nevertheless observed:

"We here make no reference to the situation where the prosecutor or judge, or both, deliberately employ their charging and sentencing powers to induce a particular defendant to tender a plea of guilty."

2. That prosecutors, without saying so, may sometimes bring charges more serious than they think appropriate for the ultimate disposition of a case, in order to gain bargaining leverage with a defendant, does not add support to today's decision, for this Court, in its approval of the advantages to be gained from plea negotiations, has never openly sanctioned such deliberate overcharging or taken such a cynical view of the bargaining process. Normally, of course, it is impossible to show that this is what the prosecutor is doing, and the courts necessarily have deferred to the prosecutor's exercise of discretion in initial charging decisions.

Even if overcharging is to be sanctioned, there are strong reasons of fairness why the charges should be presented at the beginning of the bargaining process, rather than as a filliped threat at the end. First, it means that a

Justice POWELL, dissenting. * * *

No explanation appears in the record for the prosecutor's decision to escalate the charge against respondent other than respondent's refusal to plead guilty. The prosecutor has conceded that his purpose was to discourage respondent's assertion of constitutional rights, and the majority accepts this characterization of events.

It seems to me that the question to be asked under the circumstances is whether the prosecutor reasonably might have charged respondent under the Habitual Criminal Act in the first place. The deference that courts properly accord the exercise of a prosecutor's discretion perhaps would foreclose judicial criticism if the prosecutor originally had sought an indictment under that act, as unreasonable as it would have seemed.[2] But here the prosecutor evidently made a reasonable, responsible judgment not to subject an individual to a mandatory life sentence when his only new offense had societal implications as limited as those accompanying the uttering of a single $88 forged check and when the circumstances of his prior convictions confirmed the inappropriateness of applying the habitual criminal statute. I think it may be inferred that the prosecutor himself deemed it unreasonable and not in the public interest to put this defendant in jeopardy of a sentence of life imprisonment.

There may be situations in which a prosecutor would be fully justified in seeking a fresh indictment for a more serious offense. The most plausible justification might be that it would have been reasonable and in the public interest initially to have charged the defendant with the greater offense. In most cases a court could not know why the harsher indictment was sought, and an inquiry into the prosecutor's motive would neither be indicated nor likely to be fruitful. In those cases, I would agree with the majority that the situation would not differ materially from one in which the higher charge was brought at the outset.

But this is not such a case. Here, any inquiry into the prosecutor's purpose is made unnecessary by his candid acknowledgement that he threatened to procure

prosecutor is required to reach a charging decision without any knowledge of the particular defendant's willingness to plead guilty; hence the defendant who truly believes himself to be innocent, and wishes for that reason to go to trial, is not likely to be subject to quite such a devastating gamble since the prosecutor has fixed the incentives for the average case.

Second, it is healthful to keep charging practices visible to the general public, so that political bodies can judge whether the policy being followed is a fair one. Visibility is enhanced if the prosecutor is required to lay his cards on the table with an indictment of public record at the beginning of the bargaining process, rather than making use of unrecorded verbal warnings of more serious indictments yet to come.

Finally, I would question whether it is fair to pressure defendants to plead guilty by threat of reindictment on an enhanced charge for the same conduct when the defendant has no way of knowing whether the prosecutor would indeed be entitled to bring him to trial on the enhanced charge. Here, though there is no dispute that respondent met the then current definition of a habitual offender under Kentucky law, it is conceivable that a properly instructed Kentucky grand jury, in response to

the same considerations that ultimately moved the Kentucky Legislature to amend the habitual offender statute, would have refused to subject respondent to such an onerous penalty for his forgery charge. There is no indication in the record that, once the new indictment was obtained, respondent was given another chance to plead guilty to the forged check charge in exchange for a five year sentence.

2. The majority suggests that this case cannot be distinguished from the case where the prosecutor initially obtains an indictment under an enhancement statute and later agrees to drop the enhancement charge in exchange for a guilty plea. I would agree that these two situations would be alike *only if* it were assumed that the hypothetical prosecutor's decision to charge under the enhancement statute was occasioned not by consideration of the public interest but by a strategy to discourage the defendant from exercising his constitutional rights. In theory, I would condemn both practices. In practice, the hypothetical situation is largely unreviewable. The majority's view confuses the propriety of a particular exercise of prosecutorial discretion with its unreviewability. In the instant case, however, we have no problem of proof.

and in fact procured the habitual criminal indictment because of respondent's insistence on exercising his constitutional rights. * * *

The plea-bargaining process, as recognized by this Court, is essential to the functioning of the criminal-justice system. It normally affords genuine benefits to defendants as well as to society. And if the system is to work effectively, prosecutors must be accorded the widest discretion, within constitutional limits, in conducting bargaining. This is especially true when a defendant is represented by counsel and presumably is fully advised of his rights. Only in the most exceptional case should a court conclude that the scales of the bargaining are so unevenly balanced as to arouse suspicion. In this case, the prosecutor's actions denied respondent due process because their admitted purpose was to discourage and then to penalize with unique severity his exercise of constitutional rights. Implementation of a strategy calculated solely to deter the exercise of constitutional rights is not a constitutionally permissible exercise of discretion. I would affirm the opinion of the Court of Appeals on the facts of this case.[c]

Notes and Questions

1. BRADY v. UNITED STATES, 397 U.S. 742, 90 S.Ct. 1463, 25 L.Ed.2d 747 (1970), involved these facts: In 1959, Brady was charged with kidnapping in violation of 18 U.S.C. § 1201(a), which could result in a maximum penalty of death if the jury verdict should so recommend. Brady elected to plead not guilty, but upon learning that a codefendant would plead guilty and be available to testify against him, he changed his plea to guilty. He was sentenced to 50 years imprisonment, later reduced to 30. Eight years later Brady unsuccessfully challenged his plea in the district court and the court of appeals. The Supreme Court granted certiorari to consider whether Brady's plea was invalid in light of the Court's intervening decision in *United States v. Jackson*, 390 U.S. 570, 88 S.Ct. 1209, 20 L.Ed.2d 138 (1968), holding the death penalty provision of § 1201(a) unconstitutional.[d] The Court, per WHITE, J., held:

"Plainly, it seems to us, *Jackson* ruled neither that all pleas of guilty encouraged by the fear of a possible death sentence are involuntary pleas nor that such encouraged pleas are invalid whether involuntary or not. *Jackson* prohibits the imposition of the death penalty under § 1201(a), but that decision neither fashioned a new standard for judging the validity of guilty pleas nor mandated a

c. See also Robert E. Scott & William J. Stuntz, *Plea Bargaining as Contract*, 101 Yale L.J. 1909, 1965–66 (1992), concluding that "the *Bordenkircher* problem * * * stems only from mandatory sentences that attach to over-broad criminal statutes. A different type of system, one that uses more complex formulas, [such as the federal sentencing guidelines,] as opposed to the mechanical attachment of a given number of months or years to a given statute, would be much harder for prosecutors to manipulate because it would generate far less overbreadth."

d. As explained in *Brady:*

"In *Jackson,* the defendants were indicted under § 1201(a). The District Court dismissed the § 1201(a) count of the indictment, holding the statute unconstitutional because it permitted imposition of the death sentence only upon a jury's recommendation and thereby made the risk of death the price of a jury trial. This Court held the statute valid, except for the death penalty provision; with respect to the latter, the Court agreed with the trial court 'that the death penalty provision * * * imposes an impermissible burden upon the exercise of a constitutional right * * *.' The problem was to determine 'whether the Constitution permits the establishment of such a death penalty, applicable only to those defendants who assert the right to contest their guilt before a jury.' The inevitable effect of the provision was said to be to discourage assertion of the Fifth Amendment right not to plead guilty and to deter exercise of the Sixth Amendment right to demand a jury trial. Because the legitimate goal of limiting the death penalty to cases in which a jury recommends it could be achieved without penalizing those defendants who plead not guilty and elect a jury trial, the death penalty provision 'needlessly penalize[d] the assertion of a constitutional right,' and was therefore unconstitutional."

new application of the test theretofore fashioned by courts and since reiterated that guilty pleas are valid if both 'voluntary' and 'intelligent.' * * *

"The standard as to the voluntariness of guilty pleas must be essentially that defined by Judge Tuttle of the Fifth Circuit Court of Appeals:

'[A] plea of guilty entered by one fully aware of the direct consequences, including the actual value of any commitments made to him by the court, prosecutor, or his own counsel, must stand unless induced by threats (or promises to discontinue improper harassment), misrepresentation (including unfulfilled or unfulfillable promises), or perhaps by promises that are by their nature improper as having no proper relationship to the prosecutor's business (e.g. bribes).'[13]

Under this standard, a plea of guilty is not invalid merely because entered to avoid the possibility of a death penalty.

"The record before us also supports the conclusion that Brady's plea was intelligently made. He was advised by competent counsel, he was made aware of the nature of the charge against him, and there was nothing to indicate that he was incompetent or otherwise not in control of his mental faculties; once his confederate had pleaded guilty and became available to testify, he chose to plead guilty, perhaps to ensure that he would face no more than life imprisonment or a term of years. Brady was aware of precisely what he was doing when he admitted that he had kidnaped the victim and had not released her unharmed."

As for Brady's objection that his attorney had advised him the jury could impose the death penalty, which, as later held in *Jackson*, was not the case, the Court declared:

"Often the decision to plead guilty is heavily influenced by the defendant's appraisal of the prosecution's case against him and by the apparent likelihood of securing leniency should a guilty plea be offered and accepted. Considerations like these frequently present imponderable questions for which there are no certain answers; judgments may be made which in the light of later events seem improvident, although they were perfectly sensible at the time. The rule that a plea must be intelligently made to be valid does not require that a plea be vulnerable to later attack if the defendant did not correctly assess every relevant factor entering into his decision. A defendant is not entitled to withdraw his plea merely because he discovers long after the plea has been accepted that his calculus misapprehended the quality of the State's case or the likely penalties attached to alternative courses of action. More particularly, absent misrepresentation or other impermissible conduct by state agents, cf. *Von Moltke v. Gillies*, 332 U.S. 708, 68 S.Ct. 316, 92 L.Ed. 309 (1948), a voluntary plea of guilty intelligently made in the light of the then applicable law does not become vulnerable because later judicial decisions indicate that the plea rested on a faulty premise. A plea of guilty triggered by the expectations of a competently counseled defendant that the State will have a strong case against him is not subject to later attack because the defendant's lawyer correctly advised him with respect to the then existing law as to possible penalties but later pronouncements of the courts, as in this case, hold that the maximum penalty for the crime in question was less than was reasonably assumed at the time the plea was entered."[e]

13. *Shelton v. United States,* 246 F.2d 571 (5th Cir.1957) (en banc), rev'd on confession of error on other grounds, 356 U.S. 26, 78 S.Ct. 563, 2 L.Ed.2d 579 (1958).

e. Brennan, J., joined by Douglas and Marshall, JJ., concurred in the result in *Brady* but dissented in the companion case of *Parker v.*

North Carolina, 397 U.S. 790, 90 S.Ct. 1458, 25 L.Ed.2d 785 (1970), involving a guilty plea to first-degree burglary entered at a time when North Carolina law permitted imposition of the death penalty for this offense only following a not guilty plea and trial. They objected that "those who resisted the pressures identified in

2. Under *Hayes* and *Brady*, would a statute providing a "standard discount" for a guilty plea, see Note 9, p. 1231, also pass muster? Cf. *Corbitt v. New Jersey*, 439 U.S. 212, 99 S.Ct. 492, 58 L.Ed.2d 466 (1978), concluding that where defendant, tried and convicted of first degree murder and sentenced to mandatory punishment of life imprisonment, could by statute receive either life or a term of not more than 30 years had he instead entered a nolo contendere plea,[f] there is "no difference of constitutional significance between *Bordenkircher* and this case," while there are "substantial differences between this case and *Jackson*" in that the instant case (i) did not involve the death penalty and (ii) did not involve a scheme in which the maximum penalty was reserved exclusively for those who insisted on a jury trial. Stewart, J., concurring, asked: "Could a state legislature provide that the penalty for every criminal offense to which a defendant pleads guilty is to be one-half the penalty to be imposed upon a defendant convicted of the same offense after a not guilty plea? I would suppose that such legislation would be clearly unconstitutional under *United States v. Jackson*." Three dissenting Justices also distinguished case-by-case plea bargaining from a statutory scheme, asserting that a defendant in the latter situation receives a higher penalty "simply because he has insisted on a trial," while in the former situation "individual factors relevant to the particular case may be considered by the prosecutor in charging and by the trial judge in sentencing, regardless of the defendant's plea."

3. Under *Hayes* and *Brady,* what is the status of a plea entered because of a prosecutor's assertion that if the defendant pleads guilty his wife or fiancee will not be prosecuted? Consider *United States v. Nuckols*, 606 F.2d 566 (5th Cir.1979) ("if an accused elects to sacrifice himself for such motives, that is his choice"). What about a plea which is accepted on the condition that the defendant not appeal? Compare *People v. Stevenson*, 231 N.W.2d 476 (Mich.App.1975) ("the right to appeal [is] non-negotiable in the instance of plea-based convictions"); with *United States v. Rutan*, 956 F.2d 827 (8th Cir.1992) (proper way to "preserve the finality of judgments and sentences"); and consider *State v. Gibson*, 348 A.2d 769 (N.J.1975) (plea not inherently coercive, but defendant still free to appeal, in which case state is relieved of its part of the bargain). What then of a plea conditioned upon the defendant not interviewing the victim? See *State v. Draper*, 784 P.2d 259 (Ariz.1989) (not per se improper, but requires close judicial scrutiny because it "may interfere with a defendant's due process rights to prepare a defense"). Or a plea conditioned on defendant testifying in another case consistently with his prior statements? See *State v. Fisher*, 859 P.2d 179 (Ariz.1993) (unenforceable, as such pleas "taint the truth-seeking function of the courts").

What about a "package deal" plea agreement, offered to multiple defendants contingent upon acceptance of the agreement by all of them? Consider *State v. Solano*, 724 P.2d 17 (Ariz.1986) (majority says such agreement permissible but "fraught with danger," so "the trial court is required to conduct a careful inquiry into the totality of the circumstances surrounding the plea"; dissent would prohibit such procedure as "designed solely to put undue leverage on the defendants and trial court").

Jackson and after a jury trial were sentenced to death receive relief, but those who succumbed to the same pressures and were induced to surrender their constitutional rights are left without any remedy at all. Where the penalty scheme failed to produce its unconstitutional effect, the intended victims obtain relief; where it succeeded, the real victims have none." They then concluded that reversal was required in *Parker* because the "North Car-

olina courts have consistently taken the position that *United States v. Jackson* has no applicability to the former North Carolina capital punishment scheme," but not in *Brady,* for while "Brady was aware he faced a possible death sentence, there is no evidence that this factor alone played a significant role in his decision to enter a guilty plea."

f. On the nature of such pleas, see Note 2, p. 1289.

In a few jurisdictions the law forbids the prosecutor from engaging in plea bargaining under some circumstance and/or with respect to some offenses. If the prosecutor does so nonetheless and the defendant is thereafter convicted on his bargained guilty plea, may the defendant later challenge his conviction because of such illegality? The courts have been inclined to answer in the negative, sometimes on the ground that the defendant lacks standing to raise such an objection because the prohibition was not intended for the defendant's benefit, *People v. Webb*, 230 Cal.Rptr. 755 (Cal.App.1986), and sometimes on the notion that the defendant, having entered into the plea agreement and accepted its attendant benefits, is estopped from challenging the lawfulness of that agreement, *Woods v. State*, 958 P.2d 91 (Nev.1998).

4. Consider more generally the so-called "ad hoc" plea bargain, one that contemplates concessions to the defendant in exchange for his agreement to accept a punishment the judge would not be authorized to impose were the case before him upon a conviction following a not guilty plea. In addition to the varieties previously mentioned, Joseph A. Colquitt, *Ad Hoc Plea Bargaining*, 75 Tulane L.Rev. 695 (2001), lists others found in current practice: (1) "coerced contributions," as where the defendant agrees to contribute a specified amount to a specified governmental agency or to a designated charitable group; (2) "deprivation of certain rights," as where the defendant agrees to surrender an interest in some property, the right to engage in a certain occupation, or to raise one's children; (3) "scarlet letter punishments," as where the defendant agrees to a shaming type of punishment (e.g, publicizing guilt via a yard sign) not otherwise permitted by law; (4) "surrender of profits," as where the defendant agrees to a surrender profits (e.g., book royalties) the law could not otherwise require him to give up; (5) "banishments," as where the defendant agrees to leave the jurisdiction; and (6) "military service," as where defendant agrees to enlist in a branch of the military upon a disposition that eliminates any disqualifying aspects of the conviction. Are such dispositions a virtue of the plea bargaining system, in that they ensure added flexibility in determining the most appropriate sanction, or are they, as Colquitt concludes, a vice because "they violate the separation of powers doctrine"?

5. Are some pleas "coerced" merely because of the magnitude of the prosecutor's generosity? If so, how can it be determined when this is the case? "Consider, for example, cases involving two defendants, P and Q. P has a 98 percent chance of conviction at trial; Q has a 10 percent chance. If the sentence upon conviction at trial is 240 months, then P's expected trial sentence is 235 months; Q's is 24 months. * * * If the prosecutor's opportunity costs [punishment foregone in other cases if this case goes to trial] warrant offering each defendant a further discount of up to two-thirds off, he can propose a plea sentence as low as seventy-eight months for P and eight months for Q. Though P will be strongly tempted to plead guilty, many would find it odd to view P as having been coerced; P presumably *is* guilty, and the prosecutor's resource problem enabled P to extract a windfall price for waiving his right to trial. Analytically, Q is in the same boat as P is, and one can consistently say that Q, like P, simply enjoys a windfall profit on the sale of his right to trial. But notice that so long as P and Q have similar preferences with respect to risk and related matters, both P and Q (that is, both the guilty and the innocent) face precisely the same strong inducements to plead guilty. From the perspective of the innocent defendant, those inducements start to look very much like what the ordinary person calls 'coercion.' " Stephen J. Schulhofer, *Criminal Justice Discretion as a Regulatory System*, 17 J. Legal Stud. 43, 73 (1988).

6. Compare Robert E. Scott & William J. Stuntz, *Plea Bargaining as Contract*, 101 Yale L.J. 1909, 1920–21 (1992): "The archetypal contracts example of nonactionable 'economic duress' is the lone gas station in the middle of the desert that charges a hundred dollars for a gallon of gas. The gas station may well get its asking price, because the difference between that price and the cost of going without is so high. But contract law has resolutely rejected the buyer's duress argument in such cases, on the sensible ground that the seller's actions did not produce the constraint on the buyer's choices (an empty gas tank in the desert), so the buyer was surely better off with the offer than without it. * * *

"How does duress, thus conceived, apply in the plea bargaining context? The duress argument against plea bargaining is that the large differential between post-trial and post-plea sentences creates a coercive environment in which the criminal defendant has no real alternative but to plead guilty. No plea produced by that sort of pressure could be deemed voluntary.

"There are several responses to this claim. First, the argument about the size of the sentencing differential reduces to the claim that the choice to plead guilty is too generous to the defendant, an odd claim to make alongside the general claim that the system treats the defendant unfairly. To be sure, the plea favors the defendant only because the post-trial sentence is so high. But this is a complaint about background sentences, not plea bargaining. * * *

"Moreover, the argument misunderstands the doctrine of economic duress. As the preceding discussion suggests, coercion in the sense of few and unpalatable choices does not necessarily negate voluntary choice. So long as the post-trial sentences have not been manipulated by the prosecutor, the coercive elements of the plea bargaining environment do not corrupt the voluntariness of the plea agreement. A large sentencing differential does not imply coercion a priori. Rather, it is entirely consistent with the assumption that the right to take the case to trial is a valuable entitlement. The prosecutor gains something very valuable when she avoids trial. It is hardly surprising that she will pay handsomely for it."

7. As to the requirement (as stated in *Brady*) that the defendant know "the actual value of any commitments made to him," consider *Dillon v. United States,* 307 F.2d 445 (9th Cir.1962), where the prosecutor promised to recommend a lenient sentence if the judge asked for a recommendation. Because the prosecutor knew that the judge never asked for a recommendation, the court found the prosecutor's bargain "wholly illusory."[g] It has been noted that many bargains are "hollow in value"; the prosecutor, for example, may promise to recommend probation in a type of case where probation is routinely granted. Donald J. Newman, *Conviction: The Determination of Guilt or Innocence Without Trial* 98 (Remington ed., 1966). Should such a plea be subject to attack on the ground that the defendant did not know the actual value of the prosecutor's commitment?

Consider *People v. Marsh,* 679 P.2d 1033 (Cal.1984), where the bargain involved dropping an existing charge, in which the court concluded defendant could not raise an "illusory bargain" issue based on his claim there was insufficient evidence to support the dropped charge. The court stated that "defendant makes the unwarranted assumption that a nolo or guilty plea is invalid unless made for a consideration which would support a contract. If that were the law a defendant could not 'plead to the sheet,' simply in the hope that the court will show leniency. In any event, defendant got exactly what he bargained for—dismissal of the simple kidnapping charge. There was no condition that the charge not be vulnerable to a motion to dismiss * * *—a motion which, incidentally, was never made."

g. See also *United States v. Maggio,* 514 F.2d 80 (5th Cir.1975), holding that if it is the policy of a particular trial judge never to accept sentence recommendations from the prosecutor, he "shall tell this to the defendant" who tenders a guilty plea.

8. Can the defendant know the value of the prosecutor's commitment without knowing the strength of the prosecution's case? Reconsider *Scott v. United States,* p. 1236, and see Comment, 119 U.Pa.L.Rev. 527 (1971), arguing for broad pre-plea discovery on the ground that "a defendant can assess the likelihood of conviction at trial only if he first secures and evaluates relevant evidence held by the prosecutor." Consider, in this regard, the material in chapter 21, particularly §§ 2 and 4.

9. Should the defendant be free to initiate and participate in plea discussions without having his statements used against him at trial if he does not plead guilty? Does it make any difference to whom the statements were made? Consider Fed.R.Crim.P. 11(e)(6), which in its present form is intended to foreclose results such as in *United States v. Herman,* 544 F.2d 791 (5th Cir.1977) (defendant in custody of two postal inspectors during continuance of removal hearing instigated conversation with them and at some point said he would plead guilty to armed robbery if the murder charge was dropped, but inspector then explained they were not "in position to make any deals in this regard"; held, defendant's statements inadmissible under earlier version of rule 11(e)(6) because he made them "during the course of a conversation in which he sought concessions from the government in return for a guilty plea"). Is the change objectionable because it "fails to provide protection for defendants who plea bargain under the reasonable belief that the agent has bargaining authority," as asserted in Note, 70 Geo.L.J. 315, 344 (1981)?

In UNITED STATES v. MEZZANATTO, 513 U.S. 196, 115 S.Ct. 797, 130 L.Ed.2d 697 (1995), when defendant and his attorney met with the prosecutor for plea discussions, the prosecutor conditioned the discussions on defendant agreeing that any statements he made could be used to impeach any contradictory testimony defendant might give if the case went to trial. Defendant, after consulting his lawyer, agreed to those terms. The case later did go to trial and such impeachment occurred, but defendant's conviction was overturned on appeal on the ground that the agreement was unenforceable. The Supreme Court, per THOMAS, J., disagreed, reasoning that defendant had not shown "that the plea-statement Rules[h] depart from the presumption of waivability" which exists as to "legal rights generally, and evidentiary provisions specifically": (1) defendant's claim that the Rules "guarantee fair procedure" and thus cannot be waived is in error, for the "admission of plea statements for impeachment purposes *enhances* the truth-seeking function of trials and will result in more accurate verdicts"; (2) defendant's claim that waiver is inconsistent with the Rules' goal of encouraging voluntary settlement is in error, as "it simply makes no sense to conclude that mutual settlement will be encouraged by precluding negotiation over an issue that may be particularly important to one of the parties to the transaction"; and (3) defendant's claim that waivers should be forbidden because they invite prosecutorial overreaching is in error, as "the appropriate response to [such] predictions of abuse is to permit case-by-case inquiries into whether waiver agreements are the product of fraud or coercion."[i]

Compare the situation as to the admissibility of a withdrawn plea, discussed at p. 1342, and also that in *Hutto v. Ross,* 429 U.S. 28, 97 S.Ct. 202, 50 L.Ed.2d 194 (1976), where the Court, per curiam, reversed the holding of the court of appeals that defendant's confession, given subsequent to a negotiated plea agree-

h. The reference is to Fed.R.Crim.P. 11(e)(6) and virtually identical Fed.R.Evid. 410.

i. Three concurring Justices speculated "that a waiver to use such statements in the case-in-chief would more severely undermine a defendant's incentive to negotiate, and thereby inhibit plea bargaining." Two dissenters concluded the record showed Congress found that "conditions of unrestrained candor are the most effective means of encouraging plea discussions" and thus meant to bar waiver.

ment from which the defendant later withdrew, was involuntary because it would not have been made "but for the plea bargaining." Noting that "causation in that sense has never been the test of voluntariness," the Court concluded: "The existence of the bargain may well have entered into respondent's decision to give a statement, but counsel made it clear to respondent that he could enforce the terms of the plea bargain whether or not he confessed. The confession thus does not appear to have been the result of 'any direct or implied promises' or any coercion on the part of the prosecution, and was not involuntary." In passing the Court observed that the case did not "involve the admissibility in criminal trials of statements made during the plea negotiation process."

NOTES ON JUDICIAL INVOLVEMENT IN PLEA BARGAINING

1. Albert W. Alschuler, *The Trial Judge's Role in Plea Bargaining, Part I,* 76 Colum.L.Rev. 1059, 1133–34 (1976), describes *People v. Dennis,* 328 N.E.2d 135 (Ill.App.1975): "A defense attorney testified in a post-conviction proceeding that a Chicago trial judge had offered to sentence his client to a term of two-to-four years if the client would plead guilty. The prosecutor recalled the pretrial conference somewhat differently and testified that the judge had proposed a sentence of two-to-six years in exchange for the defendant's plea. Whatever the trial judge's offer, however, the defendant declined it; and following his conviction by a jury, the judge sentenced him to a term of 40–to–80 years. The appellate court noted that, because the trial judge had been advised of the state's evidence and of the defendant's prior criminal record during the pretrial conference, the sentence that he imposed almost certainly did not reflect circumstances of which he had been unaware at the time of his offer. The court concluded that a " 'reasonable inference" of constitutional deprivation may be drawn where a great disparity exists between the sentence offered at a pretrial conference to which the trial judge was a participant and one imposed at the conclusion of a jury trial.' Accordingly, it exercised its authority under Illinois Supreme Court Rules to reduce the defendant's sentence. The court did not, however, reduce the sentence to the two-to-four or the two-to-six year term that the defendant would have served if he had pleaded guilty. Rather, it reduced the sentence to six-to-eighteen years 'in the interests of justice.' The court's rule thus seemed to be that a defendant may be penalized for exercising his right to trial by a sentence three times more severe than that he could have secured by pleading guilty, but not by a sentence twenty times more severe."

2. In light of *Bordenkircher v. Hayes,* p. 1244, how would the Supreme Court have dealt with *Dennis?* Cf. *Longval v. Meachum,* 693 F.2d 236 (1st Cir.1982) (where "the trial court, sua sponte, informed the defendant that if he did not follow its advise to bargain and plead, it 'might be disposed to impose a substantial sentence' if the jury convicted him," and defendant did not follow that advice and received sentence of 40–50 years upon conviction, while co-defendant who pleaded guilty received 3 years, there a "reasonable apprehension of vindictiveness" under *Blackledge v. Perry,* p. 891, and a "reasonable likelihood of vindictiveness" under *United States v. Goodwin,* p. 893, so that defendant entitled to relief on habeas corpus).

3. In UNITED STATES ex rel. ELKSNIS v. GILLIGAN, 256 F.Supp. 244 (S.D.N.Y.1966), defendant, charged with second degree murder, and his attorney conferred in chambers with the judge, who assured him that if he pleaded guilty to first degree manslaughter the sentence would not exceed 10 years. The defendant so pleaded in open court, but a few weeks later the judge imposed a sentence of 17½ to 35 years. When defendant challenged his plea in federal court, the court,

WEINFELD, J., concluded that the plea could not stand because the judge had failed to adhere to his promise, and then continued:

"The unequal positions of the judge and the accused, one with the power to commit to prison and the other deeply concerned to avoid prison, at once raise a question of fundamental fairness. When a judge becomes a participant in plea bargaining he brings to bear the full force and majesty of his office. His awesome power to impose a substantially longer or even maximum sentence in excess of that proposed is present whether referred to or not. A defendant needs no reminder that if he rejects the proposal, stands upon his right to trial and is convicted, he faces a significantly longer sentence. One facing a prison term, whether of longer or shorter duration, is easily influenced to accept what appears the more preferable choice. Intentionally or otherwise, and no matter how well motivated the judge may be, the accused is subjected to a subtle but powerful influence. A guilty plea predicated upon a judge's promise of a definite sentence by its very nature does not qualify as a free and voluntary act. The plea is so interlaced with the promise that the one cannot be separated from the other; remove the promise and the basis for the plea falls.

"A judge's prime responsibility is to maintain the integrity of the judicial system; to see that due process of law, equal protection of the laws and the basic safeguards of a fair trial are upheld. The judge stands as the symbol of evenhanded justice, and none can seriously question that if this central figure in the administration of justice promises an accused that upon a plea of guilty a fixed sentence will follow, his commitment has an all-pervasive and compelling influence in inducing the accused to yield his right to trial. A plea entered upon a bargain agreement between a judge and an accused cannot be squared with due process requirements of the Fourteenth Amendment. * * *

"It may well be, as has been suggested, that voluntary, as distinguished from coercive, bargaining between the prosecutor and the defendant has been sanctioned by propriety and practice—in some measure they deal at arm's length. But this is quite different from approbation of plea bargaining between the judge and the accused, where the disparity of positions is extremely marked. * * *

"Finally, a bargain agreement between a judge and a defendant, however free from any calculated purpose to induce a plea, has no place in a system of justice. It impairs the judge's objectivity in passing upon the voluntariness of the plea when offered. As a party to the arrangement upon which the plea is based, he is hardly in a position to discharge his function of deciding the validity of the plea—a function not satisfied by routine inquiry, but only, as the Supreme Court has stressed, by 'a penetrating and comprehensive examination of all the circumstances under which such a plea is tendered.'"

4. Is the court in *Elksnis* correct in saying that even if the promise had been kept the plea would be involuntary because a product of bargaining between defendant and judge? Were the circumstances in *Elksnis* more coercive than when the bargaining takes place between defendant and prosecutor? Compare Recent Developments, 19 Stan.L.Rev. 1082, 1086 (1967), arguing that because "the prosecutor has many means not available to the judge of putting pressure upon the defendant * * * the 'disparity of position,' in terms of power over the accused, may be even greater between prosecutor and defendant than between judge and defendant."

In *United States ex rel. Rosa v. Follette,* 395 F.2d 721 (2d Cir.1968), holding that "the participation of the trial judge in plea discussions does not *in itself* render the plea involuntary," the court reasoned: "We cannot blind ourselves to the fact that 'it is not at all unusual for the prosecutor to predict the sentence with a high degree of accuracy and to communicate this prediction to the defendant.' * * * And, every defense attorney plays the prophet as best he can. In the instant case, Rosa was fortunate in being given the security of the Judge's beneficence by learning immediately what most defendants are tortured over, can only hope for and anticipate—that the trial judge will follow the prosecutor's recommendation." Consider also *Brown v. Peyton,* 435 F.2d 1352 (4th Cir.1970), contending that the quotation from *Shelton* appearing in *Brady v. United States* at p. 1251 "can only contemplate plea bargaining in which the judge has participated." Is this a fair reading of *Brady?*

Where, as in *Rosa,* there is no per se rule against judicial participation, the outcome of a later challenge to the plea will turn on the extent and character of the judge's involvement. Compare, e.g., *State v. Ditter,* 441 N.W.2d 622 (Neb.1989) (did not coerce plea, as defense initiated the discussion, judge talked only with defense counsel and defendant was not present, judge only indicated possible penalties depending on defendant's course of action, and judge made no comments on the weight of the evidence or that he thought defendant was guilty); with *State v. Svoboda,* 287 N.W.2d 41 (Neb.1980) (coerced the plea, as judge initiated discussion directly with defendant and told defendant the evidence was overwhelming and that defendant should not go to trial).

5. Consider Thomas Lambros, J., *Plea Bargaining and the Sentencing Process,* 53 F.R.D. 509, 514–18 (1972): "[T]here are also several reasons in support of [judicial] participation in plea discussions. For one, * * * the plea itself becomes * * * a more meaningful and informed plea in two respects. Judicial participation in plea discussions inevitably causes the prosecutor to open his file and to freely discuss the strength of his case. As a consequence, defense counsel receives information which would not otherwise be discoverable. From this full disclosure of the prosecutor's case, defendant and defense counsel are better able to evaluate all the factual issues and the risk factors involved. * * * It is also more meaningful and informed as a result of discussions as to the sentencing alternatives. From my experience, I have discerned that the prosecutor and defense counsel do not have a workable knowledge as to the wide array of sentencing possibilities. * * *

"Another reason is that judicial involvement in plea discussions would expedite litigation and in turn, reduce the backlog of cases. Experience has shown that defendants and defense counsel are inclined to undergo the full ritual of technical and procedural machinery. [A]n inevitable plea of guilty which is usually entered in the vast majority of cases is postponed for many months and in many instances, many years, creating a logjam in the criminal docket. This logjam is largely prompted by the sense of uncertainty as to ultimate disposition which preoccupies an accused and his counsel. * * * Judicial involvement in plea discussions tends to remove this cloak of uncertainty and in turn, prompts the timely entering of a plea of guilty.

"Judicial involvement in plea discussions would provide the judge a vehicle through which he could acquire additional information so as to supplement the report of the Probation Department. * * * This cannot be accomplished by the brief confrontations between the judge and the defendant and defense counsel at the time the plea of guilty is entered nor at the time of sentencing."

6. Precisely how should judicial involvement in the plea bargaining process be limited? Is it best to provide that the judge shall not "participate" in plea discussions, as in Fed.R.Crim.P. 11(e)(1), or that the judge shall not "initiate" plea discussions, as in Ill.Sup.Ct.R. 402(d)(1)? Consider *A.B.A. Standards* § 14–3.3(c): "When the parties are unable to reach a plea agreement, if the defendant's counsel and prosecutor agree, they may request to meet with the judge in order to discuss a plea agreement. If the judge agrees to meet with the parties, the judge shall serve as a moderator in listening to their respective presentations concerning appropriate charge or sentence concessions. Following the presentation of the parties, the judge may indicate what charge or sentence concessions would be acceptable or whether the judge wishes to have a preplea report before rendering a decision. The parties may thereupon decide among themselves, outside of the presence of the court, whether to accept or reject the plea agreement tendered by the court."

If, under the A.B.A. procedure, the defendant is permitted to withdraw his guilty plea, should the trial judge recuse himself? Ill.Sup.Ct.R. 402(d)(3) so provides.[a] Does this permit judge-shopping and offer-shopping? See Alschuler, supra, at 1111–12.

7. On the other hand, does Fed.R.Crim.P. 11(e), by permitting the reaching of an agreement as to a specific sentence and its communication to the judge, who can either concur and accept the plea agreement or else reject the plea agreement, involve the judge too much? Compare *State v. Evans*, 234 N.W.2d 199 (Neb.1975) (defendant may only bargain for prosecutor's recommendation, and trial judge may not permit withdrawal of plea because he gives sentence higher than was recommended); *United States v. Green*, 1 M.J. 453 (C.M.A.1976) (the judge must announce his sentence before inquiring into what sentence limits were contemplated in the plea bargain).

Evans is a minority but constitutionally permissible alternative. As stated in *Carwile v. Smith*, 874 F.2d 382 (6th Cir.1989), the fact "that under federal law, as well as under the law of 40 out of 49 states, a criminal defendant who has pleaded guilty must be given an opportunity to withdraw his plea when an agreed sentencing recommendation is rejected by the sentencing court" does not mean it is a violation of due process for a state not to permit withdrawal absent a showing "that petitioner was 'misled' into thinking that the judge would be bound by the prosecutor's recommendation."

In a state which, unlike *Evans,* provides that a defendant must be allowed to withdraw his plea if the judge decides upon a sentence higher than contemplated in the plea agreement, should the prosecution have a corresponding right to withdraw if the judge opts for a sentence lower than the parties earlier agreed to? See *State v. Warren*, 558 A.2d 1312 (N.J.1989) (plea agreement to that effect invalid, as though "notions of fairness apply to each side, * * * the defendant's constitutional rights and interests weigh more heavily in the scale"). Contra: *Dominguez v. Meehan*, 681 P.2d 911 (Ariz.1984).

8. Whatever the judge's role otherwise in the plea negotiation process, should the defendant be able to bargain with the judge over the prosecutor's objection? Consider *United States v. Werker*, 535 F.2d 198 (2d Cir.1976) (where prosecutor not prepared to offer sentence concessions, it improper for trial judge to reveal to defendant in advance of his guilty plea what the sentence would be on a plea of guilty);[b] *In re Fuller*, 478 S.E.2d 641 (N.C.1996) (where prosecutor not

---

a. Compare *United States v. Gallington*, 488 F.2d 637 (8th Cir.1973) (where judge rejected plea bargain on ground that contemplated 10–year sentence was inadequate, he may then excuse himself from further involvement in the case and should give serious consideration to doing so, but judge in this case did not abuse his discretion in electing to preside over jury trial of defendant); *United States v. Walker*, 473 F.2d 136 (D.C.Cir.1972) (no prejudicial error in trial judge's failure to withdraw from a nonjury case in which he had learned of defen-

dant's prior offer to plead guilty, but "it would be better if he exercised his prerogative to recuse himself or to insist upon a jury trial").

b. Compare H. Richard Uviller, *Pleading Guilty: A Critique of Four Models*, 41 Law & Contemp.Prob. 102, 116–17 (1977), criticizing *Werker* and asking: "When a trial judge has informed himself of the defendant's background and the circumstances of his crime, when he has formed at least a tentative decision on the appropriate sentence, and even (according to some) when the sentence conces-

willing to bargain down to a reduced charge, the court may not accept a plea of guilty to a reduced charge).[c]

SANTOBELLO v. NEW YORK
404 U.S. 257, 92 S.Ct. 495, 30 L.Ed.2d 427 (1971).

Chief Justice BURGER delivered the opinion of the Court.

[After negotiations with the prosecutor, petitioner withdrew his previous not-guilty plea to two felony counts and pleaded guilty to a lesser-included offense, the prosecutor having agreed to make no recommendation as to sentence. At petitioner's appearance for sentencing many months later a new prosecutor recommended the maximum sentence, which the judge (who stated that he was uninfluenced by that recommendation) imposed. Petitioner attempted unsuccessfully to withdraw his guilty plea, and his conviction was affirmed on appeal.]

* * * The disposition of criminal charges by agreement between the prosecutor and the accused, sometimes loosely called "plea bargaining," is an essential component of the administration of justice. Properly administered, it is to be encouraged. If every criminal charge were subjected to a full-scale trial, the States and the Federal Government would need to multiply by many times the number of judges and court facilities.

Disposition of charges after plea discussions is not only an essential part of the process but a highly desirable part for many reasons. It leads to prompt and largely final disposition of most criminal cases; it avoids much of the corrosive impact of enforced idleness during pre-trial confinement for those who are denied release pending trial; it protects the public from those accused persons who are prone to continue criminal conduct even while on pretrial release; and, by shortening the time between charge and disposition, it enhances whatever may be the rehabilitative prospects of the guilty when they are ultimately imprisoned. * * *

This phase of the process of criminal justice, and the adjudicative element inherent in accepting a plea of guilty, must be attended by safeguards to insure the defendant what is reasonably due in the circumstances. Those circumstances will vary, but a constant factor is that when a plea rests in any significant degree on a promise or agreement of the prosecutor, so that it can be said to be part of the inducement or consideration, such promise must be fulfilled. * * *

We need not reach the question whether the sentencing judge would or would not have been influenced had he known all the details of the negotiations for the plea. He stated that the prosecutor's recommendation did not influence him and we have no reason to doubt that. Nevertheless, we conclude that the interests of justice and appropriate recognition of the duties of the prosecution in relation to promises made in the negotiation of pleas of guilty will be best served by remanding the case to the state courts for further consideration. The ultimate relief to which petitioner is entitled we leave to the discretion of the state court, which is in a better position to decide whether the circumstances of this case require only that there be specific performance of the agreement on the plea, in which case petitioner should be resentenced by a different judge, or whether, in

---

sion is not contingent on the plea but would be followed even if the defendant elected to be tried, what interests of the defendant are protected by prohibiting the judge from communicating this information to him?"

c. As for the power of the judge to refuse to reduce the charge notwithstanding the prosecutor's bargain to do so, see *United States v. Ammidown*, p. 1284.

the view of the state court, the circumstances require granting the relief sought by petitioner, i.e., the opportunity to withdraw his plea of guilty.[2] * * *

Justice DOUGLAS, concurring. * * *

I join the opinion of the Court and favor a constitutional rule for this as well as for other pending or oncoming cases. Where the "plea bargain" is not kept by the prosecutor, the sentence must be vacated and the state court will decide in light of the circumstances of each case whether due process requires (a) that there be specific performance of the plea bargain or (b) that the defendant be given the option to go to trial on the original charges. One alternative may do justice in one case, and the other in a different case. In choosing a remedy, however, a court ought to accord a defendant's preference considerable, if not controlling, weight inasmuch as the fundamental rights flouted by a prosecutor's breach of a plea bargain are those of the defendant, not of the State.

Justice MARSHALL, with whom Justice BRENNAN and Justice STEWART join, concurring in part and dissenting in part.

* * * When a prosecutor breaks the bargain, he undercuts the basis for the waiver of constitutional rights implicit in the plea. This, it seems to me, provides the defendant ample justification for rescinding the plea. Where a promise is "unfulfilled," *Brady v. United States* [p. 1250] specifically denies that the plea "must stand." Of course, where the prosecutor has broken the plea agreement, it may be appropriate to permit the defendant to enforce the plea bargain. But that is not the remedy sought here.* Rather, it seems to me that a breach of the plea bargain provides ample reason to permit the plea to be vacated.

It is worth noting that in the ordinary case where a motion to vacate is made prior to sentencing, the government has taken no action in reliance on the previously entered guilty plea and would suffer no harm from the plea's withdrawal. More pointedly, here the State claims no such harm beyond disappointed expectations about the plea itself. At least where the government itself has broken the plea bargain, this disappointment cannot bar petitioner from withdrawing his guilty plea and reclaiming his right to a trial.

I would remand the case with instructions that the plea be vacated and petitioner given an opportunity to replead to the original charges in the indictment.

Notes and Questions

1. Exactly what constitutes a broken bargain—or, at least, deserves to be treated in the same way as the broken bargain in *Santobello?* For example, if the prosecutor agrees to recommend or not oppose the defendant's request for a particular sentence, and he then performs as promised but the court does not give such a sentence, is the defendant then entitled to relief? There is a split of authority at the state level. Which is the better view? What is the result under Fed.R.Crim.P. 11(e)?

2. Sometimes it is difficult to determine just what the dimensions of the bargain are. Illustrative is *United States v. Harvey,* 791 F.2d 294 (4th Cir.1986),

---

2. If the state court decides to allow withdrawal of the plea, the petitioner will, of course, plead anew to the original charge on two felony counts.

* Justice Douglas, although joining the Court's opinion (apparently because he thinks the remedy should be chosen by the state court), concludes that the state court "ought to accord a defendant's preference considerable, if not controlling, weight." Thus, a majority of the Court appears to believe that in cases like these, when the defendant seeks to vacate the plea, that relief should generally be granted. [Ed. note: there were two vacancies on the Court at the time.]

where the problem of interpretation arose out of the fact that the defendant was involved in multiple conspiracies and there were outstanding charges in various districts. Defendant's view of the agreement was that the government would not anywhere or by any prosecutorial force prosecute him further for violations "arising from" the general investigation that led to the indictment under which he entered his guilty plea, while the government's position was that the agreement merely was that defendant would not be further prosecuted in that particular district.

On the fundamental question of how a court should deal with ambiguity in a plea agreement, *Harvey* concludes that the law of contracts is generally applicable, though "those rules have to be applied to plea agreements with two things in mind which may require their tempering in particular cases. First, the defendant's underlying 'contract' right is constitutionally based and therefore reflects concerns that differ fundamentally from and run wider than those of commercial contract law. * * * Second, with respect to federal prosecutions, the courts' concerns run even wider than protection of the defendant's individual constitutional rights—to concerns for the 'honor of the government, public confidence in the fair administration of justice, and the effective administration of justice in a federal scheme of government.' "

This means, the court continued, that "both constitutional and supervisory concerns require holding the Government to a greater degree of responsibility than the defendant (or possibly than would be either of the parties to commercial contracts) for impressions or ambiguities in plea agreements. * * * This is particularly appropriate where, as would usually be the case, the Government has proffered the terms or prepared a written agreement—for the same reasons that dictate that approach in interpreting private contracts." The court added that "derelictions on the part of defense counsel that contribute to ambiguities and imprecisions in plea agreements may not be allowed to relieve the Government of its primary responsibility for ensuring precision in the agreement," for "the validity of a plea in the final analysis depends upon the voluntariness and intelligence with which defendant (not his counsel) enters into it."

Applying those principles, the court in *Harvey* looked at the agreement and found that it did not specify the geographic area in which the obligation not to prosecute existed, and thus concluded this ambiguity "must be read against the Government. This does not mean that in a proper case it might not be possible to establish by extrinsic evidence that the parties to an ambiguously worded plea agreement actually had agreed—or mutually manifested their assent to—an interpretation as urged by the Government. But here, that evidence simply does not exist. On the contrary, as has been developed, the evidence shows at most an honest conflict of understandings and intentions that is best explained by the ambiguity itself."

3. If the plea bargain is that the prosecutor will seek a certain disposition, how hard must he try? In *United States v. Benchimol*, 471 U.S. 453, 105 S.Ct. 2103, 85 L.Ed.2d 462 (1985), defendant entered a plea of guilty in exchange for the prosecutor's promise to recommend probation with restitution. At the sentencing hearing, defense counsel informed the court of that fact (correcting the presentence report statement that the government "would stand silent"), the prosecutor merely commented that defense counsel's statement was "an accurate representation," and the court then sentenced defendant to six years. The court of appeals held the government had breached the bargain because it "made no effort to explain its reasons for agreeing to recommend a lenient sentence but rather left an impression with the court of less-than-enthusiastic support for leniency." But the Supreme Court disagreed, concluding "it was error for the Court of Appeals to imply as a matter of law a term which the parties themselves did not agree upon."

The Court emphasized that the instant case was unlike *United States v. Brown,* 500 F.2d 375 (4th Cir.1974), where "the Government attorney appearing personally in court at the time of the plea bargain expressed personal reservations about the agreement to which the Government had committed itself," and also that the government had not made an express commitment either to make the recommendation enthusiastically or to state reasons for it.

4. If, on the other hand, the plea bargain was that the prosecutor would not recommend a sentence or would not oppose defendant's recommendations, it may be claimed that the prosecutor did too much. Compare *Jackson v. State,* 902 P.2d 1292 (Wyo.1995) (prosecutor's promise to remain silent at sentencing "did not require the prosecutor to withhold from the district court pertinent information on appellant's background and character"); with *United States v. Moscahlaidis,* 868 F.2d 1357 (3d Cir.1989) (prosecutor's promise he would "not take a position" on sentence violated when prosecutor's sentencing memo "drew conclusions about appellant's character"). Consider also *Brooks v. United States,* 708 F.2d 1280 (7th Cir.1983) (prosecutor's promise to make no recommendation not violated by his opposition to defendant's later Fed.R.Crim.P. 35(b) motion for reduction of sentence imposed), criticized in Comment, 52 U.Chi.L.Rev. 751, 771 (1985): "If a plea agreement does not, either upon its face or upon the admission of extrinsic evidence, show the parties' shared expectations, the court must apply a gap-filling presumption to cover the omitted term. The gap-filling term that satisfies the constitutional requisite for a guilty plea is one that accords with a defendant's reasonable expectations, not with the intentions of the prosecutor."

5. The new federal sentencing guidelines have given rise to other types of plea bargain terms regarding the sentence to be imposed. For example, one possibility is that the prosecutor will stipulate to some fact (e.g., that defendant was a minor participant in the crime) which, if true, would permit reduction of defendant's offense level for sentencing purposes. The federal sentencing guidelines expressly state that the court is not bound by such a stipulation, and consequently there is no broken bargain if the court concludes the mitigating circumstance was not present and that therefore defendant should not receive the contemplated sentence reduction. *United States v. Howard,* 894 F.2d 1085 (9th Cir.1990). (The result would presumably be otherwise if, as is permitted under the federal guidelines, the defendant entered a guilty plea on the express condition that the judge find, e.g., that he was a minor participant.) Moreover, in the stipulation-only case, if the defendant then appeals from the trial judge's determination, the prosecution does not violate the plea bargain by arguing the lower court did not err. *United States v. Howard,* supra. In somewhat the reverse situation, where the plea bargain stipulation is that the sentence will not exceed a certain amount, and that amount would be appropriate if the court found an aggravating circumstance present which sufficed to take the case above the usual guideline range, the stipulation does not bar the defendant from questioning on appeal whether there was a sufficient finding of the necessary aggravating circumstance. *United States v. Newsome,* 894 F.2d 852 (6th Cir.1990).

6. If a defendant charged with armed robbery pleads guilty to the lesser offense of robbery as a result of plea negotiations, is the bargain broken if the judge receives and considers, at the time of sentencing, evidence that the defendant was armed? Or, if the bargain is that the defendant will plead guilty to one count if other counts are dismissed, is the bargain broken if the judge receives and considers evidence on the other counts at the time of sentencing? Consider U.S.S.G. § 6B1.2(a), providing "that a plea agreement that includes the dismissal of a charge or a plea agreement not to pursue a potential charge shall not preclude the conduct underlying such charge from being considered under [the Guidelines section on relevant conduct] in connection with the count(s) of which the defendant is convicted."

7. Should deception by the defendant or changed circumstances relieve the prosecutor of his commitments? Consider *Hamlin v. Barrett*, 335 So.2d 898 (Miss.1976) (though bargain was for probation, defendant concealed from prosecutor and court fact he had a prior robbery conviction in another state, which by state law made him ineligible for probation without some imprisonment, and thus defendant may be sentenced to imprisonment); *State v. Pascall*, 358 N.E.2d 1368 (Ohio App.1972) (bargain was that prosecutor would recommend probation, but there was an implied promise by defendant that the circumstances will remain substantially the same, and thus prosecutor excused from fulfilling promise where in interim defendant convicted of burglary and armed robbery); *State v. Segarra*, 388 So.2d 1017 (Fla.1980) (where defendant entered plea pursuant to agreement that his sentence would not exceed 5 years and he then placed on probation but probation later revoked for violation of condition, sentence of 15 years then imposed lawful, as the "events which bring about a revocation open a new chapter in which the court ought to be able to mete out any punishment within the limits prescribed for the crime"). In any of these cases, should the defendant be foreclosed from withdrawing his guilty plea because the broken bargain was his fault? Compare *Ex parte Otinger*, 493 So.2d 1362 (Ala.1986) (though defendant "intentionally misled" the authorities as to his criminal record, he must be allowed to withdraw plea if promised sentence not given).

8. A common variety of plea bargain includes a promise by defendant to assist in the investigation or prosecution of others, which if broken will likewise serve as a basis for the prosecution to withhold the promised concessions.[a] It once was the view that "whether defendant did in fact fail to perform the condition precedent is an issue not to be finally determined unilaterally by the government, but only on the basis of adequate evidence by the Court." *United States v. Simmons*, 537 F.2d 1260 (4th Cir.1976). However, cases of this genre now arising under the federal sentencing guidelines, which per § 5K1.1 recognize that the prosecution may make a downward departure motion because of the defendant's substantial assistance to the government, typically receive different treatment. This is attributable to *Wade v. United States*, 504 U.S. 181, 112 S.Ct. 1840, 118 L.Ed.2d 524 (1992), where it was held (i) that a sentencing court may not grant defendant a downward departure under § 5K1.1 in the absence of a government motion for same,[b] and (ii) that whether to make such a motion is discretionary with the government, so that even a defendant who provides substantial assistance is not entitled to a remedy unless an unconstitutional motive underlies the government's refusal to so move. Although the Court added that the government could sacrifice its discretion and obligate itself to move for downward departure in exchange for a plea, since *Wade* it has become common procedure for federal prosecutors drafting such plea agreements to reserve the "sole discretion" as to whether or not to file a downward departure motion. When that is the case, the

a. It does not necessarily follow that the prosecutor may at the same time hold defendant to his plea. See, e.g., *United States v. Fernandez*, 960 F.2d 771 (9th Cir.1992) (where defendant failed to cooperate as promised in a type (C) plea agreement for 6–year sentence, prosecutor could not both hold defendant to his plea and obtain sentence over 6 years, as defendant "could only have reasonably understood" the agreement "to mean that if he failed to live up to his end of the bargain, the entire plea agreement would be null and void").

b. Likewise, a sentencing court may not grant a defendant a downward departure below the statutory minimum sentence absent a government motion for same made pursuant to 18 U.S.C. § 3553(e). In *Melendez v. United States*, 518 U.S. 120, 116 S.Ct. 2057, 135 L.Ed.2d 427 (1996), the Court held that a government motion made pursuant to § 5K1.1 of the sentencing guidelines that does not request a sentence below the minimum level established by statute does not qualify as the government motion required by § 3553(e).

courts conclude there is simply "no enforceable obligation" absent the unconstitutional motive mentioned in *Wade.* See, e.g., *United States v. Underwood,* 61 F.3d 306 (5th Cir.1995).

In *United States v. Jones,* 58 F.3d 688 (D.C.Cir.1995), the prosecution did not dispute defendant's claim of complete cooperation but nonetheless claimed the plea agreement was not violated, given that the prosecutor's Departure Committee did not find defendant's assistance substantial, because the plea agreement expressly stated the prosecutor's office "retains its discretion" whether to file a downward departure motion. The court found two aspects of the case troubling: (1) "that prosecutors might dangle the suggestion of a [substantial assistance] motion in front of defendants to lure them into plea agreements, all the while knowing that the defendant's cooperation could not possibly constitute assistance valuable enough for the Departure Committee to find it 'substantial,' "; and (2) "the Government's contention at oral argument that, under the terms of its agreement with Jones, its decision not to file a departure motion can only be reviewed for constitutional infirmities proves too much," as even without any contractual arrangements those constitutional limitations exist, but here the plea agreement "provides additional protection" for defendant. "Like all contracts, it includes an implied obligation of good faith and fair dealing," meaning the defendant "was entitled to an honest and fully informed evaluation by the Committee." To ensure that commitment is kept, the court suggested, in cases such as this the prosecution should summarize for the court what information it gave the Departure Committee and any explanation given by that group for finding defendant's assistance insubstantial.

9. Thomas was charged with atrocious assault and battery, assault with intent to rob, and robbery of Murray. As a result of plea bargaining, Thomas pleaded guilty on October 27, 1969, to the first charge on the understanding that the prosecutor, at the appropriate time, would dismiss the remaining counts. On January 23, 1970, Murray died from the wounds inflicted by Thomas. On the prosecutor's motion, the court dismissed the two other counts on September 15, 1970. On October 29, 1970, Thomas was charged with murder. If Thomas were now tried on the felony-murder theory that the death occurred during the commission of a robbery, would this constitute a broken bargain? See *State v. Thomas,* 276 A.2d 391 (N.J.Super.1971) (prosecution on this theory barred by collateral estoppel rule of *Ashe v. Swenson,* p. 1050). What if the robbery count had been dismissed *before* Murray died?

10. If, as in *Santobello,* the defendant seeks to withdraw his plea because of nonperformance of the bargain, should the prosecution always (or, under some circumstances) be able to bar withdrawal by now performing as promised? On the other hand, what if the defendant in *Santobello* had asked for specific performance of the bargain? Should he be entitled to this remedy, or can the prosecution insist that he be limited to the remedy of plea withdrawal? Compare *Jordan v. Commonwealth,* 225 S.E.2d 661 (Va.1976) (defendant agreed to plead guilty to assault charge if burglary charge not brought, after his plea burglary charge was brought because of public criticism; held, defendant entitled to specific performance); with *People v. Young,* 367 N.E.2d 976 (Ill.App.1977) (even if defendant correct in assertion that trial judge promised probation, he wrong in asserting "that the remedy for such claimed unfulfilled promises is specific performance"). May these cases be reconciled on the ground, as stated in *Davis v. State,* 308 So.2d 27 (Fla.1975), that *Santobello* "requires specific performance by a prosecutor of a promise on which a defendant relied," but not "that plea discussions can be specifically enforced against a court"? Or, is the point that specific performance is required when the defendant "cannot be restored to his former position," as stated in *Brooks v. Narick,* 243 S.E.2d 841 (W.Va.1978) (as part of bargain, defendant had already spent 60 days in custody for diagnostic study).

Consider Peter Westen & David Westin, *A Constitutional Law of Remedies for Broken Plea Bargains,* 66 Calif.L.Rev. 471, 500, 512, 513 (1978), concluding: (1) that a constitutional right of specific performance cannot be based on the requirement that pleas be "voluntary," as "the subsequent failure of the inducement cannot have any effect on the desirability of the inducement at the time the defendant accepts it"; (2) that such a constitutional right cannot be based on the requirement that pleas be "intelligent," as that interest is protected "by vacating the plea"; and (3) that therefore "*Santobello* can be understood as extending constitutional protection to the personal expectations created in defendants by plea agreements with the state." Why should the Constitution protect those expectations? If it should, does this "constitutional law of contracts" extend to *all* (i.e., even illegal) promises? Consider *Staten v. Neal,* 880 F.2d 962 (7th Cir.1989) (though "United States Attorneys arguably speak for the entire federal government, the same cannot be said of state's attorneys in Illinois," and thus plea agreement term that defendant would not be prosecuted in another county not entitled to specific performance).

11. Is the prosecutor free to withdraw his offer at any time prior to defendant's entry of a guilty plea in reliance thereon? Not if there has been other detrimental reliance by the defendant. "Providing information to government authorities, testifying for the government, confessing guilt, returning stolen property, making monetary restitution, failing to file a motion to have charges presented to a grand jury, submitting to a lie detector test and waiving certain procedural guarantees have all been held to constitute acts made in detrimental reliance upon a prosecutor's breached promises." Note, 58 N.C.L.Rev. 599, 606–07 (1980).

Going well beyond that position is *Cooper v. United States,* 594 F.2d 12 (4th Cir.1979), holding that unless the prosecutor's plea proposal is properly conditioned it may be enforceable by a defendant who, prior to the prosecutor's withdrawal of the offer, had neither entered a guilty plea nor relied to his detriment on the bargain. The court declared that there were "two distinct sources" for such a ruling: (1) the Sixth Amendment right to effective assistance of counsel, involved here because to "the extent that the government attempts through defendant's counsel to change or retract positions earlier communicated, a defendant's confidence in his counsel's capability and professional responsibility * * * are necessarily jeopardized and the effectiveness of counsel's assistance easily compromised"; and (2) a due process right to enforcement of the plea proposal "on the basis alone of expectations reasonably formed in reliance upon the honor of the government in making and abiding by its proposals" where, as here, the offer was unambiguous and not unreasonable and was promptly assented to by the defendant and no "extenuating circumstances affecting the propriety of the proposal" intervened.

A unanimous Supreme Court rejected the *Cooper* approach in *Mabry v. Johnson,* 467 U.S. 504, 104 S.Ct. 2543, 81 L.Ed.2d 437 (1984). As for the right to counsel argument, the Court stated it failed "to see how an accused could reasonably attribute the prosecutor's change of heart to his counsel any more than he could have blamed counsel had the trial judge chosen to reject the agreed-upon recommendation, or, for that matter, had he gone to trial and been convicted." Moreover, where, as in the instant case, there had been no detrimental reliance by the defendant, there was no due process violation either. When his agreement to accept the prosecution's offer of a 21–year concurrent sentence for a murder plea resulted in that offer being withdrawn as "a mistake" and replaced by an offer of a 21–year consecutive sentence, the defendant accepted the second offer after the trial began. Noting that this plea "was in no sense induced by the prosecutor's withdrawn offer," the Court concluded that defendant's "inability to enforce the prosecutor's offer is without constitutional significance" because that offer "did not impair the voluntariness or intelligence of his guilty plea." As for the prosecutor's possible negligence or culpability in making and withdrawing the first offer, the Court deemed that irrelevant because the due process clause "is not a code of ethics for prosecutors" but is concerned "with the manner in which persons are deprived of their liberty."

12. What then is the remedy for a defendant who was improperly induced to *reject* a plea bargain? Illustrative is *State v. Kraus,* 397 N.W.2d 671 (Iowa 1986), where Kraus, charged with second-degree murder, was offered a plea bargain of involuntary manslaughter by the state. Kraus rejected the bargain after his own attorney significantly overstated what the prosecution would have to prove to convict of second-degree murder and the judge engaged in ill-advised tactical counseling against a guilty plea. Kraus was then tried and convicted of second-degree murder. On the "practical difficulty" of "finding an appropriate sanction," the court first concluded that merely granting Kraus a new trial on the murder charge would be inappropriate, as "it is difficult to see how a new trial restores the lost chance of the bargain." Thus, the court remanded with a direction that Kraus "be allowed to enter a plea to the included offense of involuntary manslaughter under the bargain formerly reached," in which event "defendant's conviction of second-degree murder shall stand as reversed." A dissenting judge objected such a disposition was inconsistent with *Mabry* and "deprives the State of its ordinary prosecutorial discretion and also invades the usual discretion of the trial court to determine whether any plea bargain should be accepted under the circumstances existing at the time a defendant offers to plead guilty."

13. In *Santobello,* the Court said that if the plea was withdrawn the two felony counts could be reinstated. Compare *People v. McMiller,* 208 N.W.2d 451 (Mich.1973), where defendant, charged with murder, pled guilty to manslaughter and then successfully appealed that conviction, only to be charged and convicted of murder thereafter, and the court held "that upon the acceptance of a plea of guilty, as a matter of policy, the state may not thereafter charge a higher offense arising out of the same transaction":

"We recognize that a prosecutor's willingness to allow an accused person to plead to a lesser offense is generally predicated on the assumption that the accused will, upon acceptance of a plea of guilty, stand convicted and will be sentenced for the lesser offense. We also recognize that the rule we adopt means that a successful appeal from a plea-based conviction for a lesser offense defeats that legitimate expectation, deprives the prosecutor of leverage he otherwise would have in further plea bargaining upon reprosecution, may well, therefore, burden the prosecutor with the need to prove his case at a trial and at the same time limits the people to a conviction less than the proofs may justify.

"We balance these considerations against the danger that reprosecuting on higher charges those who successfully appeal from plea-based convictions and imposition of sentence based on the higher charge, will cause convicted persons to forego legitimate appeals and thereby encourage a return to practices which the carefully worked out guilty-plea procedures are designed to obviate. * * *

"By agreeing to a plea to a lesser offense the prosecutor thereby vouches that the ends of justice will be served by accepting a plea of guilty to that offense. We perceive, therefore, even in the relatively few cases where defendants will succeed on appeal in setting aside a guilty-plea-based conviction, no erosion of law enforcement in the rule we adopt."

Is the *McMiller* rule constitutionally required in light of *Green v. United States*, p. 1483 and *Price v. Georgia*, p. 1484, or in light of *Blackledge v. Perry*, p. 891? Is the answer to be found in *Bordenkircher v. Hayes*, p. 1244? Cf. *Alabama v. Smith*, p. 1545. Compare *McMiller* with the prevailing view, as expressed in *United States ex rel. Williams v. McMann*, 436 F.2d 103 (2d Cir.1970):

"For us to hold that one in William's position may not be tried and sentenced upon the charge originally brought would encourage gamesmanship of a most offensive nature. Defendants would be rewarded for prevailing upon the prosecutor to accept a reduced charge and to recommend a lighter punishment in return for a guilty plea, when the defendant intended at the time he entered that plea to attack it at some future date. Although there is no suggestion in the record that Williams attempted this gambit, one way in which it might be achieved would be to plead guilty after a bargain has been struck with the prosecutor on the lesser charge and sentence. But, if the court after reading the defendant's probation report imposed a sentence higher than contemplated, the 'unbargained-for' longer sentence would then trigger proceedings to vacate the plea. Indeed, any reason the defendant could conceive for setting aside his plea and sentence would lose him little. If the defendant's argument were to prevail, then a trial on the lesser charge only could result. The defendant would thus run no risks by this maneuver for his trial could end in acquittal, but if he should be convicted, he urges he could not receive a sentence greater than that imposed on the guilty plea to the lesser offense. This is nothing more than a 'heads-I-win-tails-you-lose gamble. To frustrate this strategy, prosecutors would be restrained from entering plea bargains, thereby adding further to the staggering burdens of our criminal courts, and judges would become more rigid in exercising their discretion in favor of permitting withdrawal of a guilty plea. This would hardly enhance the administration of criminal justice."

14. In RICKETTS v. ADAMSON, 483 U.S. 1, 107 S.Ct. 2680, 97 L.Ed.2d 1 (1987), the prosecutor sought to return to the status quo ante even though, unlike *McMann* and *Williams*, the defendant had not in the interim overturned his guilty plea conviction of a lesser offense. Adamson, charged with first-degree murder, agreed to plead guilty to second-degree murder and testify against his accomplices in exchange for a specified prison term. The agreement expressly provided that if he refused to testify "this entire agreement is null and void and the original charge will be automatically reinstated" and the parties "returned to the positions they were in before this agreement." The court accepted the plea agreement and sentenced Adamson accordingly, and he thereafter testified against the others, who were convicted of first-degree murder. Upon reversal of those convictions and remand defendant refused to testify again on the ground that his obligation under the agreement had terminated. Adamson was then charged with first-degree murder, and after the trial court rejected his double jeopardy claim the Arizona Supreme Court vacated the second-degree murder conviction and reinstated the original charge on the ground the plea agreement contemplated use of his testimony upon retrial. The state declined Adamson's subsequent offer to testify, and he was then convicted of first-degree murder and sentenced to death. The Supreme Court, per WHITE, J., concluded "that respondent's breach of the plea arrangement to which the parties had agreed removed the double jeopardy bar to prosecution of respondent on the first-degree murder charge. * * *

" * * * The terms of the agreement could not be clearer: in the event of respondent's breach occasioned by a refusal to testify, the parties would be returned to the *status quo ante,* in which case respondent would have *no* double jeopardy defense to waive. And, an agreement specifying that charges may be *reinstated* given certain circumstances is, at least under the provisions of this plea agreement, *precisely* equivalent to an agreement waiving a double jeopardy defense. * * *

"We are also unimpressed by the Court of Appeals' holding that there was a good faith dispute about whether respondent was bound to testify a second time and that until the extent of his obligation was decided, there could be no knowing and intelligent waiver of his double jeopardy defense. But respondent knew that if he breached the agreement he could be retried, and it is incredible to believe that he did not anticipate that the extent of his obligation would be decided by a court. Here he sought a construction of the agreement in the Arizona Supreme Court, and that court found that he had failed to live up to his promise. The result was that respondent was returned to the position he occupied prior to execution of the plea bargain: he stood charged with first-degree murder. Trial on that charge did not violate the Double Jeopardy Clause. *United States v. Scott* [p. 1465], supports this conclusion.

"At the close of all the evidence in *Scott*, the trial judge granted defendant's motion to dismiss two counts of the indictment against him on the basis of preindictment delay. This Court held that the Double Jeopardy Clause did not bar the Government from appealing the trial judge's decision, because 'in a case such as this the defendant, by deliberately choosing to seek termination of the proceedings against him on a basis unrelated to factual guilt or innocence of the offense of which he was accused, suffers no injury cognizable under the Double Jeopardy Clause....' The Court reasoned further that 'the Double Jeopardy Clause ... does not relieve a defendant from the consequences of his voluntary choice.' The 'voluntary choice' to which the *Scott* Court referred was the defendant's decision to move for dismissal of two counts of the indictment, seeking termination of that portion of the proceedings before the empaneled jury, rather than facing the risk that he might be convicted if his case were submitted to the jury. The respondent in this case had a similar choice. He could submit to the State's request that he testify at the retrial, and in so doing risk that he would be providing testimony that pursuant to the agreement he had no obligation to provide, or he could stand on his interpretation of the agreement, knowing that if he were wrong, his breach of the agreement would restore the parties to their original positions and he could be prosecuted for first-degree murder. Respondent chose the latter course and the Double Jeopardy Clause does not relieve him from the consequences of that choice.

"Respondent cannot escape the Arizona Supreme Court's interpretation of his obligations under the agreement. The State did not force the breach; respondent chose, perhaps for strategic reasons or as a gamble, to advance an interpretation of the agreement that proved erroneous. And, there is no indication that respondent did not fully understand the potential seriousness of the position he adopted. In the April 3 letter, respondent's counsel advised the prosecutor that respondent "is fully aware of the fact that your office may feel that he has not completed his obligations under the plea agreement ... and, further, that your office may attempt to withdraw the plea agreement from him, [and] that he may be prosecuted for the killing of Donald Bolles on a first degree murder charge." This statement of respondent's awareness of the operative terms of the plea agreement only underscores that which respondent's plea hearing made evident: respondent clearly appreciated and understood the consequences were he found to be in breach of the agreement.

"Finally, it is of no moment that following the Arizona Supreme Court's decision respondent offered to comply with the terms of the agreement. At this point, respondent's second-degree murder conviction had already been ordered vacated and the original charge reinstated. The parties did not agree that respondent would be relieved from the consequences of his refusal to testify if he were able to advance a colorable argument that a testimonial obligation was not owing. The parties could have struck a different bargain, but permitting the State to enforce the agreement the parties actually made does not violate the Double Jeopardy Clause.''

BRENNAN, J., for the four dissenters, reasoned that because the plea agreement "does not contain an explicit waiver of all double jeopardy protection," "any finding that Adamson lost his protection against double jeopardy must be predicated on a finding that Adamson breached his agreement." Adamson's letter to the prosecutor declining to testify again upon retrial was not itself a breach, nor was it even an anticipatory repudiation of the plea agreement, as he "advanced an objectively reasonable interpretation of his contract," obligating the prosecution, as a matter "fundamental fairness imposed by the Due Process Clause," to inform him that the state interpreted the agreement differently, so that at that point either party could "seek to have the agreement construed by the court in which the plea was entered." Moreover, even assuming "that Adamson breached his plea agreement by offering an erroneous interpretation of that agreement," once the Arizona supreme court adopted the state's construction of the agreement Adamson advised the state "that he was ready and willing to testify," but the prosecution nonetheless decided to abandon the prosecution of the accomplices and instead, for the one-month delay purported caused by Adamson, "chose to make Adamson pay, not with a longer sentence, but with his life." *Scott* "cannot support the decision here," the dissenters then concluded, for "Adamson never took any act that he knew or realized would constitute a breach of the agreement. As a result, the Court's argument that Adamson waived the protection of the Double Jeopardy Clause is untenable. Even under *Scott*, such protection cannot be lost through strict liability.''

15. Is the *Ricketts* result, returning the parties to the *status quo ante*, sometimes constitutionally permissible even when the defendant has *not* breached the plea agreement? Such was the conclusion in UNITED STATES v. BARRON, 127 F.3d 890 (9th Cir.1997), where defendant pleaded guilty to being a felon in possession of a firearm (count #1), possession of cocaine with intent to distribute (count #2), and use of a firearm during drug trafficking (count #3), and was sentenced to concurrent terms of 120 months on counts 1 and 2 and a consecutive term of 60 months on count 3, to be followed by an 8–year period of supervised release, pursuant to a plea agreement in which the government promised to refrain from bringing any other charges arising from the facts underlying the indictment, to refrain from seeking an enhanced penalty, and to recommend a 2–point reduction for acceptance of responsibility. After the subsequent decision in *Bailey v. United States,* 516 U.S. 137, 116 S.Ct. 501, 133 L.Ed.2d 472 (1995), holding that a conviction for use of a firearm during drug trafficking requires evidence that defendant "actively employed the firearm," Barron filed a section 2255 petition seeking only to vacate his count #3 conviction and 60–month consecutive sentence.

On the "difficult question" of the remedy in such circumstances, the court noted there were three possibilities: (1) treat the count #3 conviction and sentence in isolation, vacate them, and leave the remainder of the convictions, sentence and plea bargain intact (Barron's preference); (2) vacate the count #3 conviction, leave the other convictions intact, and resentence Barron de novo on all remaining convictions, "the most common response in the case law and * * * perhaps most appropriate where no counts were dismissed or uncharged pursuant to the plea agreement"; or (3) vacate the entire plea agreement, including the guilty pleas on all counts, and restore the parties to the *status quo ante* the agreement, which "might be appropriate where charges in the indictment were dismissed pursuant to the plea agreement or where the plea negotiations included potential charges and enhancements not included in the indictment." The court opted for the latter, reasoning that the " 'sentencing package' concept," namely, "that when a petitioner attacks one of several interdependent sentences, he in effect challenges the aggregate sentencing scheme," "applies with equal force here."[c]

Upon rehearing en banc, 172 F.3d 1153 (9th Cir.1999). that decision was reversed. As for the panel's "package" concept, the court concluded that "the argument that plea bargains must be treated as a package logically applies only in cases in which a petitioner challenges the entire plea as unknowing or involuntary." The court added that the "drafter of the plea agreement could have anticipated the contingency that has arisen and included a provision protecting the government's interest in the event that Barron's conviction was vacated." Because the government had not done so, the appellate court concluded, the district court may only "vacate the judgment and resentence Barron on the two counts of conviction that still stand."

NOTES AND QUESTIONS ON UNREALIZED EXPECTATIONS

1. The situations discussed earlier in which a party to the plea agreement has breached one of the terms of the agreement (as when the prosecutor fails to keep a promise regarding the sentence to be imposed), must be distinguished from others in which there has been no breach of any plea agreement but the defendant seeks post-plea relief because of an "unrealized expectation," i.e., a belief that the sentence would be less severe than was actually imposed. One situation is that in which the defendant had no belief that there was a plea bargain, but yet expected a lesser sentence because of what his attorney said. Such a case is *Wellnitz v. Page,* 420 F.2d 935 (10th Cir.1970), where the court stated that "an attorney may offer his client a prediction, based upon his experience or instinct, of the sentence possibilities the accused should weigh in determining upon a plea. An erroneous sentence estimate by defense counsel does not render a plea involuntary. And a defendant's erroneous expectation, based on his attorney's erroneous estimate, likewise does not render a plea involuntary."

2. Another situation is that in which the defendant is specifically but erroneously advised by his counsel that there exists a plea bargain including a particular commitment. Such a case is *Ex parte Griffin,* 679 S.W.2d 15 (Tex.Crim. App.1984), holding that "a plea of guilty is invalid if it is induced by defense counsel's direct misrepresentation that the State has made a concession which in fact was not part of the plea agreement." The court explained: "While this is not a broken bargain under *Santobello v. New York,* it is nevertheless clear that applicant's plea was not knowing and intelligent under the standard of *Brady v. United States,*" p. 1250.

3. What then of a case which falls somewhere between these two, in that the defense attorney did not specifically state that there was a plea agreement but the defendant claims that he interpreted the attorney's remarks as meaning there was one? In *United States ex rel. LaFay v. Fritz,* 455 F.2d 297 (2d Cir.1972), the

---

c. In *United States v. Bunner,* 134 F.3d 1000 (10th Cir.1998), involving similar facts, the court reached essentially the same result on a principle of contract law, specifically, the frustration of purpose doctrine, which requires that "the frustration must be such that the intervening event cannot fairly be regarded as within the risks the frustrated party assumed under the contract." Once the defendant took action which relieved him of his burdens under

the contract, the court concluded, this "resulted in the underlying purpose of the agreement being frustrated and the basis of the government's bargain being destroyed," and thus the government could reinstate the dismissed charges. But see Note, 72 N.Y.U.L.Rev. 841, 846 (1997), contending that the frustration of purpose doctrine "fails to provide relief and that there is, in fact, no valid basis in contract law for allowing the government to reindict."

district judge, applying a subjective test (which he had adopted in an earlier case on the ground that if a defendant "believes that a promise has been made, the effect on his state of mind is exactly the same as if such a promise had in fact been made," meaning "any test of whether a person acts voluntarily is necessarily 'subjective' "), concluded in the instant case that, while no promises had actually been made by the prosecutor or court, the petitioner was entitled to relief because he believed the judge had promised a maximum of five years as a consequence of his counsel's observation that counsel had "an indication or an intimation" that "the Judge thought that five years was an adequate minimum sentence." But the court of appeals reversed, relying on *Wellnitz* and opining that the subjective test was "contrary to the law of this circuit." Is this a satisfactory resolution of the matter? Is the point, as *LaFay* was later construed in *United States ex rel. Curtis v. Zelker,* 466 F.2d 1092 (2d Cir.1972), that "a defendant's mistaken subjective impressions gained from conference with his legal counsel, in the absence of substantial objective proof showing that they were reasonably justified, do not provide sufficient grounds upon which to set aside his guilty plea"?

4. If the defendant's belief is based upon representations by his own counsel, the court may find that the defendant did not have the effective assistance of counsel. Such a result was reached in *State v. Tunender,* 157 N.W.2d 165 (Neb.1968), where defendant (who received a sentence of 18 months) testified his attorney promised him probation outright, and his attorney's "versions of the odds stated to defendant climbed from possibility to strong chance to probability." Questioning of counsel at the post-conviction hearing produced the following: "Q. * * * Did you, or did you not, say it was all cut and dried? Did you make that statement in those * * * particular words? * * * A. I may have probably said something to that effect; of course your words of 'Cut and dried' are more or less strong talk."

Does this constitute ineffective assistance of counsel sufficient for relief under the two-part test of *Strickland v. Washington,* p. 1120? Cf. *Hill v. Lockhart,* p. 1306. Does such a holding, as urged in a *Tunender* dissent, present the risk that "the fear of a tarnished professional reputation may become more compelling than the best interests of the indigent defendant"? Is it true, as claimed by another of the dissenting justices, that the same criticism made against the original attorney "may well be made of the second attorney who, after much effort, succeeds in getting the original judgment of conviction set aside, and upon a retrial not only sees his client again convicted but also facing a longer period of incarceration than he was subject to in the first instance"?

5. Is it improper for the trial judge to make known the "established practice," such as by announcing in open court that a certain defendant's sentence would have been lower had he pleaded guilty? Consider the position of Chief Judge Bazelon in *Scott v. United States,* p. 1236, that while the "policy announced by the trial judge may not endanger his actual impartiality at trials as much as his participation in plea bargaining sessions might," "we cannot ignore the impact of such a policy on the appearance of justice to criminal defendants and their ability to choose wisely between a plea of guilty and an exercise of their right to trial."

SECTION 3. PROFESSIONAL RESPONSIBILITY; THE ROLE OF PROSECUTOR AND DEFENSE COUNSEL

In ANDERSON v. NORTH CAROLINA, 221 F.Supp. 930 (W.D.N.C.1963), a federal habeas corpus proceeding, these facts were established: Counsel was appointed for Anderson when he was indicted for the capital crime of rape; Anderson appeared with counsel at arraignment and entered a plea of not guilty at 11:30 a.m. on December 14, 1961; that afternoon, the Solicitor and members of his staff talked with Anderson in jail in the absence of his counsel but with counsel's consent; the Solicitor indicated to Anderson that he would face the probability of a death sentence unless he agreed to plead guilty to the lesser offense of assault with intent to rape, in which case he could not be imprisoned more than 15 years and in all probability would receive a sentence of 2 to 3 or 3 to 5 years; at 4:30 p.m. the same day Anderson appeared in court again and entered a plea to the lesser offense, answering in the affirmative to the court's inquiry as to whether the plea was entered "freely and voluntarily, knowing the probability is you will get an extended prison term"; defense counsel then addressed the court asking for leniency, but the court sentenced Anderson to a term of 12–15 years. The court held:

"The right to counsel is not merely a matter of form. It can be waived by the defendant—but not by his counsel. It is, therefore, irrelevant that counsel may have consented for the Solicitor to conduct—in counsel's absence—what amounted to a pre-trial conference with the prisoner in jail. Unquestionably, the most important part of the proceedings against Anderson occurred in jail—when his counsel was not present to advise him. It was at that time and place that the decision was made to plead guilty to the lesser felony. Otherwise, he would not have been returned to the courtroom—for the jury had long since gone, and his trial had been set for the next term. What happened in the courtroom was to merely make a formal record of a decision arrived at upstairs in jail in a conference between the Solicitor and the defendant. Counsel's presence at the sentencing (he was sent for by the Solicitor) does not give it validity. The most he could have done was to ratify a decision previously made. More than this is implicit in the right to counsel: petitioner was entitled to have counsel aid and help him *in making the decision.* * * *

"The constitutional validity of the time-honored compromise plea is assumed for purposes of this opinion. But, a compromise necessarily involves negotiation, and here Anderson was without the assistance of his lawyer in negotiating the compromise with the Solicitor. * * *

"Unquestionably petitioner Anderson could not bargain on equal terms with the Solicitor. The conference in the jail was inherently unfair, and the agreement made there infects all subsequent proceedings.

"It is idle to speculate whether petitioner's counsel could have, if present, worked out a better deal with the Solicitor. The point is Anderson was entitled to have him *try*. For lack of effective counsel at a 'critical' stage of the proceedings against him, those proceedings are constitutionally defective."[a]

Notes and Questions

1. Compare *People v. Bowman*, 239 N.E.2d 433 (Ill.1968), where an indigent defendant was charged with burglary. Appointed counsel appeared with defendant at the preliminary hearing and indicated defendant did not waive grand jury

---

a. *A.B.A. Code of Prof. Resp.* D.R. 7–104 reads: "(A) During the course of his representation of a client a lawyer shall not: (1) Communicate or cause another to communicate on the subject of the representation with a party he knows to be represented by a lawyer in that matter unless he has the prior consent of the lawyer representing such other party or is au- thorized by law to do so. (2) Give advice to a person who is not represented by a lawyer, other than the advice to secure counsel, if the interests of such person are or have a reasonable possibility of being in conflict with the interests of his client." With regard to this "no-contact" rule, reconsider Note 4, p. 605.

indictment. Later that day, defendant participated in negotiations directly with the county sheriff, who assured defendant that if he entered a plea of guilty the three burglary charges pending in other counties would be dropped and the prosecution would recommend a sentence of three to five years. Defendant said he "wanted to plead and get it over with," so he was taken into court the next day. In the interim, the sheriff attempted to contact defendant's attorney, but was unsuccessful because the attorney was out of town. In court, defendant waived indictment and pleaded guilty; the court took note of the fact that defendant's counsel was not present, and permitted defendant to proceed only after defendant stated three times that he wished to plead without his attorney. The defendant's plea was accepted, and he thereafter received a sentence of three to five years. On appeal, the court characterized the issue as involving "the correlative right of the accused to proceed *pro se* if he freely and understandingly chooses to do so," and then found that defendant had made such a choice.

Did the majority correctly state the issue, or is Justice Schaefer, dissenting, correct in saying that the issue is "whether the defendant was denied the effective assistance of counsel when the sheriff, in the absence of the defendant's attorney and without notice to him, engaged in plea negotiations with the defendant"? Is this case distinguishable from *Anderson* in that, as the majority pointed out, "[c]onsidering the presence of a confession as to the validity of which no substantial challenge is made, a prior record of two burglary convictions, the pending escape charge and the burglary charges in the three adjoining counties, it is difficult to envision prosecution agreement to any arrangement more advantageous to petitioner"?

2. Waiver of counsel by a guilty plea defendant must meet the standards for an "intelligent and competent" waiver described at p. 1091. What weight should be given to defendant's expressed desire to plead guilty in determining whether his waiver of counsel was valid? Where defendant was informed of the charge against him and told of his right to appointed counsel, does his reply that he desires to plead guilty establish a valid waiver? See *People v. Dunn,* 158 N.W.2d 404 (Mich.1968) (waiver of counsel need not be in "express form" and expression of desire to plead guilty sufficient). But compare *Von Moltke v. Gillies,* discussed at p. 1091. Even if the defendant is told of all of the factors relating to the charge required by *Von Moltke,* and he expressly waives counsel, is that satisfactory if he is not also told what counsel might accomplish through plea negotiations even if there is no trial?

3. A few states do not permit felony defendants to plead guilty without counsel. Consider Note, 112 U.Pa.L.Rev. 865, 889 (1964): "One can seriously question whether a defendant who pleads guilty should ever be permitted to waive counsel. The need for an attorney may be more dramatically perceived in the trial context, but at least in that situation there may be some tactical advantage for a defendant to be unrepresented—the court and the jury may be more sympathetically disposed toward a layman contending with an accomplished legal expert. In the guilty plea context, however, there is nothing for a defendant to gain by being unrepresented—in fact, the very decision to plead guilty and waive the right to trial requires an evaluation of the prosecution's case, something at which a layman is inept. The right to an attorney interested in protecting the interests of the defendant is such a substantial factor in the guilty plea procedure that it is difficult to imagine a situation that would warrant a finding of an informed waiver of that right." Does *Faretta v. California,* p. 1092, require a different assessment?

4. Reconsider *Moody,* p. 74, fn. a, holding the Sixth Amendment right to counsel inapplicable at pre-indictment plea bargaining, and Note 9 at p. 1243, regarding such bargaining under the federal Sentencing Guidelines, which prompted Judge Wiseman, concurring in *Moody,* to observe:

"Under the Guidelines, both defendants and prosecutors benefit from engaging in such bargaining. Preindictment plea bargaining over charges and facts provides Assistant United States Attorneys ('AUSAs') enormous discretion because such bargaining is much less susceptible to review by supervisors or courts. Through such bargaining, AUSAs can more effectively determine the potential sentence for a defendant. By agreeing on the charges to be filed against the defendant, the prosecutors avoid having to draw both the court's and the probation officer's attention to facts relevant to other (potential) charges not pleaded to which might require higher sentencing levels under real offense sentencing. Defendants also favor preindictment plea negotiations for basically the same reasons—greater control over the eventual sentence .. For example, plea bargains (pre and postindictment) can stipulate both the quantity of a controlled substance for which the defendant will be held accountable and the 'relevant conduct' that the court may consider during sentencing. Both of these factors can play a major role in determining the eventual sentence of a defendant who, like Mr. Moody, is charged with conspiracy to distribute illegal drugs.

"The incentives to bargain over charges and facts only add to the already abundant pressure to bargain with prosecutors as soon as possible in drug conspiracy cases. In practical terms, drug conspiracy cases have become a race to the courthouse. When a conspiracy is exposed by an arrest or execution of search warrants, soon-to-be defendants know that the first one to 'belly up' and tell what he knows receives the best deal. The pressure is to bargain and bargain early, even if an indictment has not been filed.

"To the extent that preindictment plea bargaining undermines the intent of Congress as expressed in the Guidelines, it is not to be condoned. Regardless of its virtue, such bargaining does occur and will likely continue due to its advantages for both prosecutors and defendants. While preindictment plea bargaining continues, it remains a perilous encounter for defendants. Defendants, or—more formally—potential defendants, are faced with the loss of liberty and property. They are faced with a complicated procedural system and a more knowledgeable adversary. In short, these defendants need and should be entitled to counsel in order to navigate these troubled waters."

NOTES ON THE PROFESSIONAL RESPONSIBILITY
OF DEFENSE COUNSEL

1. Consider the following excerpts from the *A.B.A. Code of Prof. Resp.* Ethical Consideration 7–7 provides in part: "A defense lawyer in a criminal case has the duty to advise his client fully on whether a particular plea to a charge appears to be desirable, * * * but it is for the client to decide what plea should be entered." Ethical Consideration 7–9 reads in part: "A lawyer should advise his client of the possible effect of each legal alternative. A lawyer should bring to bear upon this decision-making process the fullness of his experience as well as his objective viewpoint. * * * He may emphasize the possibility of harsh consequence that might result from assertion of legally permissible positions."

2. In *McLaughlin v. Royster,* 346 F.Supp. 297 (E.D.Va.1972), the court asserted "that the primary foundation upon which rests the rule that a voluntary guilty plea is not subject to attack is that a defendant entering such a plea does so assisted and informed by adequate counsel. The constitutional requirement is not satisfied upon a perfunctory appearance by counsel who does nothing whatever before or during trial to advise a client or to protect his rights except to acquiesce with the client's wishes. Perfunctory or hand-holding representation is simply not consistent with the right to counsel. A client's professed desire to plead guilty is not the end of an attorney's responsibility. When a defendant convicts himself in open court the Constitution recognizes that the critical stage of adjudication has proceeded for the most part outside the courtroom. That process contemplates the pursuit by counsel of factual and legal theories in order to reach a conclusion as to whether a contest would best serve the attorney's client's interest. In short, effective representation when a guilty plea is contemplated to a great extent entails affirmative action on the part of counsel." Compare *Wilson v. State,* 291 N.E.2d 570 (Ind.App.1973)(if guilty plea defendant's counsel did not investigate the facts or interview witnesses, such failures do not constitute incompetence, as counsel represented "his client as he was directed" in that defendant told counsel "he wanted to get off with the least amount he could").

Query, what level of noninvestigation, under what circumstances, will entitle the guilty plea defendant to relief on Sixth Amendment grounds? Recall that *Strickland,* p. 1120, also requires proof of prejudice for the defendant to prevail on an ineffective assistance claim while *Cronic,* p. 1132, says prejudice is presumed upon complete lack of representation, including when counsel "fails to subject the prosecutor's case to meaningful adversarial testing." Consider *Woodard v. Collins,* 898 F.2d 1027 (5th Cir.1990) ("a decision to investigate some issues and not others or even a decision to conduct virtually no investigation is governed by *Strickland*").

3. Stolen property was found in an illegal search of Heirens' residence, and as a result of a "truth serum" illegally given to him he confessed to several burglaries and three murders, with which he was then charged. His attorneys, employed by his parents, investigated the case and concluded an insanity defense would not likely succeed and that there was some chance Heirens could get the death penalty. The attorneys and parents, to whom Heirens had admitted the murders, agreed that the best course was plea discussions. The prosecutor said that if Heirens would plead guilty and make a complete confession to the murders, he would recommend concurrent life sentences. After his attorneys and parents met with him, Heirens agreed to this disposition, and he thereafter pleaded guilty to the three murders and to 26 additional charges of various burglaries, robberies and assaults. Then, as reported in *People v. Heirens,* 122 N.E.2d 231 (Ill.1954):

"Prior to the pronouncement of sentence the prosecutor and the principal defense attorney addressed the court. The State's Attorney in his remarks acknowledged the 'co-operative assistance' of defense counsel and observed: 'The small likelihood of a successful murder prosecution of William Heirens early prompted the State's Attorney's office to seek out and obtain the co-operative help of defense counsel and, through them, that of their client. * * * Without the aid of the defense we would to this day have no answer for the death of Josephine Ross. Without their aid, to this day a great and sincere public doubt might remain as to the guilt of William Heirens in the killing of Suzanne Degnan and Frances Brown'. Petitioner's attorney then proceeded to state to the court the reasons which impelled him and his cocounsel to adopt the course they followed. He remarked in part: 'I have no memory of any case, certainly not in my time at the bar, when counsel on both sides were so perplexed as to the mental status of an individual and the causes which motivated him to do certain acts. In those cases we both sought psychiatrists in the hope that they might aid us. I must confess that at this time there exists in my mind many doubts as to this defendant's mental capacity for crime; and I believe doubt must exist in our minds as to just what the relation of cause and effect was, and how he could, in a manner so devoid of feeling, do the acts here charged and upon which the plea has been guilty. On acquiring knowledge, your Honor, of the facts we were further notified at a later date of his mental condition. We were collectively agreed that any thought on the part of the State to cause this man to forfeit his life would be unjust. It would be unfair. By the same token we were collectively agreed that any course on our part which would assist in having him returned to society would be equally unfair.' "

In later post-conviction proceedings, Heirens claimed his attorneys had not given him effective assistance because "their recommendation to plead guilty was made from motives of public duty as well as those of duty to their client." The court rejected this contention and asserted that although Heirens "was young, emotionally unstable and unusually susceptible to suggestions, he was of normal intelligence and able to make his own decisions."

4. In *United States v. Rogers,* 289 F.Supp. 726 (D.Conn.1968), the defendant was charged under three federal statutes for a single alleged sale of narcotics. Defendant told his retained counsel that he was innocent of the crimes charged and that he had two witnesses who could testify he did not make the sale, but admitted that he was a convicted felon and that the two witnesses were narcotic addicts. Counsel received a bill of particulars indicating that the alleged sale was made to a named government agent at a specified time and place. Thereafter, counsel learned that the government would be willing to dismiss the two counts which carried a mandatory minimum sentence of five years if defendant would plead guilty to the count which carried a two year minimum. Counsel so advised the defendant, and despite the defendant's consistent protestations of innocence recommended that it was in defendant's best interest to plead guilty because the government agent's testimony would be given great credibility while the testimony of defendant and his two friends would not be believed. The attorney added that the decision was up to the defendant. Defendant entered a plea of guilty as recommended, but prior to sentencing (and just after learning that the government agent had been arrested for counterfeiting) he moved to withdraw the plea. Judge Timbers, in ruling for the defendant, observed:

"Trial counsel doubtless believed that he was acting in the best interest of his client in recommending a guilty plea. A plea bargain had been struck. It was reasonable to assume that a jury would more likely believe a government agent than a convicted felon and narcotics addicts. But to this Court it appears utterly unreasonable for counsel to recommend a guilty plea to a defendant without first cautioning him that, no matter what, he should not plead guilty unless he believed himself guilty. Most certainly such a recommendation should not be made when the defendant in the past has maintained his innocence and has stated that he has two witnesses whom counsel has not attempted to interview. It may well have been trial counsel's opinion that even if defendant were innocent he would still be convicted. Such a view is not only cynical but unwarranted. Innocent men in the past have been convicted; but such instances have been so rare and our judicial system has so many safeguards that no lawyer worthy of his profession justifiably may assume that an innocent person will be convicted."

Assuming *Rogers* to be a case in which the defendant was innocent but there was a strong probability of conviction, and *Heirens* to be a case in which the defendant was guilty but (as acknowledged by the state's attorney) there was a "small likelihood" of conviction, who acted more "unethically," Rogers' attorney or Heirens' attorneys? Reconsider *Rogers* in light of *North Carolina v. Alford,* p. 1295; and compare *Williams v. State,* 349 N.W.2d 58 (S.D.1984), where the defendant claimed he had received ineffective assistance of counsel because his attorney influenced him to enter into a plea bargain despite his protestations of innocence: "From his study of police records and interviews, counsel apparently concluded that a conviction was likely, and despite appellant's protestations of innocence. We are not convinced that counsel's perception of the acquittal odds was incorrect. Having formed such a conclusion, defense counsel committed no error in telling this to his client and recommending that he plead guilty in the hope of lenient sentence."

5. In *People v. Whitfield,* 239 N.E.2d 850 (Ill.1968), where defendant was charged with murder, the state's attorney advised defense counsel that he would accept a plea of guilty to manslaughter and recommend probation. Defense counsel "thought he could win the case," so he did not advise defendant of this offer and later told the state's attorney that his client would not plead guilty. Defendant was convicted and received a sentence of 14 to 18 years. On appeal, the court reversed:

"A defendant has * * * the right to decide whether to plead not guilty. These rights and others go beyond trial strategy. [See Note 7, p. 1102]. It follows logically that if a defendant has the right to make a decision to plead not guilty, he also has the right to make the decision to plead guilty. Due process demands this protection."

Does it follow logically? Would it make any difference if the defendant had previously insisted upon his innocence, and counsel believes that if he learned of the offer he would unwisely decide to plead guilty? Or, what if defense counsel believes that the prosecutor is being unduly lenient, contrary to the best interests of his client? Consider Arnold Enker, in *Task Force Report, The Courts* at 111: "[D]efense counsel, perhaps in part because of legitimate skepticism over the availability of meaningful correctional treatment and of doubts as to the fairness of such programs, seem to regard their duty to the client solely in terms of obtaining for him as lenient a sentence as possible. Perhaps a broader view of the lawyer's role should include within the counseling function the duty to attempt to make the client aware of the fact that he has a problem and of his need for some correctional program. Thus far, however, lawyers have preferred to avoid the welfare implications of their role as counselors and the conflicts this role would create and to limit their role to getting the client 'as good a deal' as they can."

6. If, on the other hand, defense counsel thinks the prosecutor's offer is very good, how much pressure may he exert on defendant to accept it? Consider *Uresti v. Lynaugh,* 821 F.2d 1099 (5th Cir.1987), where defense counsel told defendant of a possible plea bargain of 35 years on a charge of aggravated rape and then, when defendant said he wanted to think it over a few days, defense counsel (purportedly fearing the offer might be withdrawn or that defendant would be advised to his detriment by jail-house lawyers to reject the bargain) warned defendant that if he did not accept the bargain that day the attorney would request permission of the court to withdraw and have someone else appointed in his place. Defendant accepted the offer and later claimed ineffective assistance of counsel. The court concluded:

"We have here an attorney who on the record is acting in good faith and affording sound representation when he decides that a client should plead guilty under a plea bargain. The client indicates doubt. Without question, the attorney has the right to ask the court to allow him to withdraw as counsel and have another counsel appointed if the client refuses to plead. He has given his best advice. He thinks the insistence of his client that the case go to trial is foolhardy. He has done what he can, and he wants to ask to be relieved so another attorney more sympathetic to trial be appointed in his stead. Having that right, whether or not the court in its discretion would grant the request, it would be improper and unethical not to warn his client that this was the course of conduct he would follow if the client refused to accept the plea bargain. Withholding this information would withhold a material and significant fact from the accused when the accused was undertaking to decide whether or not to accept the plea bargain."

In contrast to *Uresti,* a defendant who declines a plea offer may later complain that his attorney did not put enough pressure on him to accept it. See, e.g., *State v. Bristol,* 618 A.2d 1290 (Vt.1992) (while defense "counsel has a duty to communicate to a client not only the terms of a plea bargain offer, but also its relative merits compared to the client's chances of success at trial," no ineffective assistance of counsel here, where "the error claimed by petitioner and found by the court was not a failure to inform, but a failure to aggressively pursue a plea bargain with petitioner after the latter rejected it").

7. Does it follow from *Whitfield* that defense counsel always (or, sometimes) has an obligation to sound out the prosecutor as to what concessions would be granted in exchange for a plea of guilty by his client? In *United States ex rel. Tillman v. Alldredge,* 350 F.Supp. 189 (E.D.Pa.1972), petitioner, convicted after a plea of not guilty and sentenced to a mandatory minimum of five years for a narcotics sale, contended that "he was denied the effective assistance of counsel by his attorney's failure to explore the possibility of * * * a plea bargain." The court responded:

"An attorney is in a sensitive area, and he must carefully weigh a number of considerations, when he broaches the subject of a guilty plea to a client who asserts that he is innocent. The subject has been very recently considered in American Bar Association's Project on Standards for Criminal Justice. In Part VI of the Approved Draft of Standards Relating to the Prosecution Function and the Defense Function, the Committee proposed the following guidelines:

" '6.1 Duty to explore disposition without trial

* * *

" '(b) When the lawyer concludes, on the basis of full investigation and study, that under controlling law and the evidence, a conviction is probable, he should so advise the accused and seek his consent to engage in plea discussions with the prosecutor, if such appears desirable.

" '(c) Ordinarily the lawyer should secure his client's consent before engaging in plea discussions with the prosecutor.'

"Trial counsel's testimony at the hearing before me made it quite clear that Tillman, apparently insisting that he was innocent of all charges, 'didn't wish to plead guilty to anything.' Since it is Tillman's burden to establish ineffective assistance of counsel, it was incumbent on him to present evidence that trial counsel was aware, before trial, of facts and circumstances indicating that a conviction was probable. An effort by the court to elicit such evidence was thwarted by Tillman's present counsel. * * *

"In the absence of evidence as to what Tillman might have told his trial attorney about his involvement in the charges, all that appears is Tillman's apparent insistence to trial counsel that he was innocent and that he 'didn't wish to plead guilty to anything.' Under such circumstances I cannot say that counsel's failure to suggest to Tillman that he should consider entering a guilty plea constituted ineffective assistance of counsel."

Would the result have been different if Tillman had made a showing that his trial counsel knew that conviction was probable? If there had been no such showing, but Tillman had not asserted that he did not wish to plead guilty? Consider the fact that in the 1993 third edition of the *A.B.A. Standards* the language quoted above has been replaced by the following, now designated § 4–6.1(b): "Defense counsel may engage in plea discussions with the prosecutor. Under no circumstances should defense counsel recommend to a defendant acceptance of a plea unless appropriate investigation and study of the case has been completed, including an analysis of controlling law and the evidence likely to be introduced at trial."

8. Attorney Hardin was appointed to represent both Brown and Ruffin, who were charged with participating in the same felony-murder. At separate trials they were convicted and sentenced to death. Hardin had negotiated with the prosecutor concerning a plea bargain for Brown which would have required Brown to testify against Ruffin, but for some reason the agreement collapsed. In *Ruffin v. Kemp*, 767 F.2d 748 (11th Cir.1985), the court held that Ruffin had established (i) actual conflict of interest and (ii) a resulting adverse effect upon his attorney's performance, as required by *Strickland v. Washington*, p. 1120, so as to be entitled to relief on habeas corpus. "While Hardin was negotiating for a plea bargain for Brown, having offered Brown's testimony against Ruffin, he could not at the same time effectively negotiate a plea bargain for Ruffin and offer Ruffin's testimony against Brown as part of the deal." Because "actual prejudice need not be shown" in a conflict of interest situation, as compared to other ineffective assistance of counsel claims, the court added, it sufficed that "the evidence in this case does establish that the prosecutor was open to plea bargain negotiations"; Ruffin need not "show that the prosecutor probably would have accepted such a plea bargain on Ruffin's behalf."

Consider also *Ingle v. State*, 742 S.W.2d 939 (Ark.1988), where defendant and a woman charged with jointly possessing 15 lbs. of marijuana retained the same counsel, who initially sought identical plea bargains but, when more marijuana was found in defendant's truck and that led to further charges against him, began stressing the relatively minor role of the woman. "When substantial disparity of evidence or of charges exists, it is unusual if an actual conflict does not also exist. * * * The attorney reacted to the disparity of charges by changing his plea bargaining from a position of complete loyalty to both clients to one of comparing his clients' culpability, even on the first charge * * *. At this time the attorney was in the middle of conflicting interests."

9. Defense counsel may influence a guilty plea by a particular defendant because it would be to the advantage of another defendant also being represented by him. See, e.g., *United States v. Truglio*, 493 F.2d 574 (4th Cir.1974) (where Truglio was charged with four others and attorney Pietranton, representing all five defendants, successfully urged Truglio to plead guilty in conformance with a deal worked out with the prosecutor concerning all defendants, Truglio was denied effective assistance of counsel, as it "is quite understandable that having obtained what he considered to be a favorable bargain for all of the defendants Pietranton would be somewhat more than reluctant to see the bargain collapse in its entirety by Truglio's insistence that the trial continue"); *Commonwealth v. Breaker*, 318 A.2d 354 (Pa.1974) (where one Mangold was arrested while committing a burglary and thereafter confessed to several other burglaries and implicated others, including Breaker, in the hope of favorable treatment, and Mangold's attorney represented Breaker when he pleaded guilty, there was a sufficient "possibility of harm" that the plea cannot stand, as "to build a record of cooperation, Mangold's attorney would necessarily desire as many guilty pleas as possible to be entered").

10. If defense counsel's efforts have resulted in a negotiated plea of guilty, should the attorney nonetheless consult with defendant about the possibility of taking an appeal? In *Roe v. Flores–Ortega*, 528 U.S. 470, 120 S.Ct. 1029, 145 L.Ed.2d 985 (2000), the Court, per O'Connor, J., agreed that "the better practice is for counsel routinely to consult with the defendant regarding the possibility of an appeal," but nonetheless rejected the lower court's "bright-line rule that counsel must always consult with the defendant regarding an appeal," instead holding "that counsel has a constitutionally-imposed duty to consult with the defendant about an appeal when there is reason to think either (1) that a rational defendant would want to appeal (for example, because there are nonfrivolous grounds for appeal), or (2) that this particular defendant reasonably demonstrated to counsel that he was interested in appealing. * * * Although not determinative, a highly relevant factor in this inquiry will be whether the conviction follows a trial or a guilty plea, both because a guilty plea reduces the scope of potentially appealable issues and because such a plea may indicate that the defendant seeks an end to judicial proceedings. Even in cases where the defendant pleads guilty, the court must consider such factors as whether the defendant received the sentence bargained for as part of the plea and whether the plea expressly reserved or waived some or all appeal rights."

NEWMAN v. UNITED STATES

127 U.S.App.D.C. 263, 382 F.2d 479 (D.C.Cir.1967).

BURGER, Circuit Judge: * * *

Appellant and one Anderson were indicted for housebreaking and petty larceny. Negotiations between Anderson's counsel and an Assistant United States Attorney led to Anderson's being allowed to plead guilty to misdemeanors of petty larceny and attempted housebreaking. The United States Attorney declined to consent to the same plea for Appellant. The essence of Appellant's claim on appeal is that the United States Attorney's conduct denied him due process, "equal standing" and equal protection. * * *

The issue in this Court, of course, must be resolved on the basis of the constitutional powers of the Executive. Few subjects are less adapted to judicial review than the exercise by the Executive of his discretion in deciding when and whether to institute criminal proceedings, or what precise charge shall be made, or whether to dismiss a proceeding once brought.

The United States Attorney, under the direction and control of the Attorney General, is the attorney for the Executive, charged with faithful execution of the laws, protection of the interests of the United States, and prosecution of offenses against the United States. As such, he must have broad discretion. * * *

To say that the United States Attorney must literally treat every offense and every offender alike is to delegate him an impossible task; of course this concept would negate discretion. Myriad factors can enter into the prosecutor's decision. Two persons may have committed what is precisely the same legal offense but the prosecutor is not compelled by law, duty or tradition to treat them the same as to charges. On the contrary, he is expected to exercise discretion and common sense to the end that if, for example, one is a young first offender and the other older, with a criminal record, or one played a lesser and the other a dominant role, one the instigator and the other a follower, the prosecutor can and should take such factors into account; no court has any jurisdiction to inquire into or review his decision.

It is assumed that the United States Attorney will perform his duties and exercise his powers consistent with his oaths; and while this discretion is subject to abuse or misuse just as is judicial discretion, deviations from his duty as an agent of the Executive are to be dealt with by his superiors.

The remedy lies ultimately within the establishment where power and discretion reside. The President has abundant supervisory and disciplinary powers—including summary dismissal—to deal with misconduct of his subordinates; it is not the function of the judiciary to review the exercise of executive discretion whether it be that of the President himself or those to whom he has delegated certain of his powers.[9] * * *

---

9. The concurring opinion would reserve judicial power to review "irrational" decisions of the prosecutor. We do our assigned task of appellate review best if we stay within our own

Notes and Questions

1. Compare Albert W. Alschuler, *The Prosecutor's Role in Plea Bargaining,* 36 U.Chi.L.Rev. 50, 105 (1968): "This argument * * * leaps from the prosecutor's traditional power to exercise a unilateral discretion to the conclusion that he may also engage in bilateral exchanges: he may trade his unilateral discretion for a defendant's waiver of his constitutional rights. Under traditional law, prosecutors are usually trusted to evaluate the extent of the public interest in particular prosecutions, but they usually have nothing to gain by agreeing to a lenient disposition for a particular defendant. In plea negotiations, however, prosecutors gain something of value for deciding that a certain punishment is adequate, and there may therefore be greater reason for mistrust."

2. Does *Newman* mean a court will *never* review a prosecutor's plea bargaining policies? What, for example, if Newman had established that he and Anderson played the same role in the crime and that their backgrounds were essentially the same? That the prosecutor refused to bargain because he viewed Newman's attorney as an "asshole," as in *Bourexis v. Carroll County Narcotics Task Force,* 625 A.2d 391 (Md.App.1993)? That the prosecutor's refusal was based upon the victim's wishes? Compare *Commonwealth v. Latimore,* 667 N.E.2d 818 (Mass. 1996), with *State v. McDonnell,* 794 P.2d 780 (Or.1990).

3. A more common problem may be that the prosecutor will offer equally lenient bargains, to defendants whose situations are only superficially similar, because "of inadequate knowledge of the facts, either as to the crime itself or the defendant's background, on the part of the prosecutor who negotiates the guilty plea. Under the pressure of a heavy, time-consuming caseload, the prosecutor may easily be seduced at an early stage of the proceedings, before such facts are more fully developed, by the offer of a quick guilty plea in exchange for a light sentence, only to discover too late that the offense, or the offender, was far more serious than originally thought." Arnold Enker, in *Task Force Report, The Courts* at 110–11. What is the solution?

4. To what extent should the prosecutor's willingness to bargain be contingent upon the views of the crime victim? Consider the federal Victim and Witness Protection Act of 1982, which provides that "the victim of a serious crime, or in the case of a minor child or a homicide, the family of the victim, shall be consulted by the attorney for the Government in order to obtain the views of the victim or family about the disposition of any Federal criminal case brought as a result of such crime, including the views of the victim or family about * * * plea negotiations." Section 6(a)(5) of the Act, in note to 18 U.S.C. § 1512.

5. Jones was charged with first degree robbery and related offenses arising out of the robbery of Rodriguez. After plea negotiations, Jones pleaded guilty to third degree robbery in full satisfaction of the indictment, but he later moved to withdraw his plea on the ground the prosecutor had failed to disclose that Rodriguez had died. In affirming denial of the motion, the court in *People v. Jones,* 375 N.E.2d 41 (N.Y.1978), after first concluding that the due process discovery mandate of *Agurs,* p. 1390, was inapplicable because the death of a witness was not "evidence," reasoned:

"Counsel cite no reported case, nor has our independent research disclosed any, in which judicial attention has been focused on the failure of a prosecutor

limits, recognizing that we are neither omnipotent so as to have our mandates run without limit, nor omniscient so as to be able to direct all branches of government. The Constitution places on the Executive the duty to see that the "laws are faithfully executed" and the responsibility must reside with that power.

before trial or during plea negotiations to disclose nonevidentiary information pertinent to the tactical aspects of a defendant's determination not to proceed to trial. No particularized rule can or need be laid down; some comments may usefully be assayed, however. At the threshold we assume that, notwithstanding that the responsibilities of a prosecutor for fairness and open-dealing are of a higher magnitude than those of a private litigant,[a] no prosecutor is obliged to share his appraisal of the weaknesses of his own case (as opposed to specific exculpatory evidence[b]) with defense counsel. * * * At the other extreme it is equally clear that the courts will allow a defendant to withdraw a guilty plea when the prosecution has either coerced him by threats or persuaded him by affirmative deceit to enter a guilty plea. All the reported instances of deceitful persuasion appear to have involved positive misstatement or misrepresentations; none has considered the effect to be accorded silence only. Consistent with legal principles recognized elsewhere in our jurisprudence, it would seem that silence should give rise to legal consequences only if it may be concluded that the one who was silent was under an affirmative duty to speak. Whether and to what extent the courts, in the absence of statute or possible rule of court would impose such an affirmative duty on a prosecutor would necessarily be dependent on the circumstances of the individual case. Thus, we do not decide what the rule might be where in the course of plea negotiation a particular defendant staunchly and plausibly maintains his innocence but states explicitly and creditably that as a matter of balanced judgment in the light of the apparent strength of the People's proof he wishes to interpose a negotiated plea to reduced charges to avoid the risk of a more severe sentence likely to attend conviction after trial; failure of the prosecutor to reveal the death of a critical complaining witness might then call for a vacatur of the plea. Silence in such circumstances might arguably be held to be so subversive of the criminal justice process as to offend due process. * * *

"Turning then to the present case, we hold that there was no obligation on the part of the prosecutor to reveal to defense counsel that Rodriguez had died, prior to acceptance of defendant's plea of guilty. Defendant does not protest his innocence; on the contrary he testified to the factual basis for the charge to which he pleaded. While the prosecutor failed to inform defense counsel of Rodriguez' death, there is no claim of affirmative misrepresentation. And, it is critical, the failure to disclose did not involve exculpatory evidence. We perceive no reason to depart from the principle that a fairly and voluntarily negotiated plea is the equivalent of a conviction after trial."

Compare *Model Pre-Arraignment Code* § 320.3(1), providing that before any plea agreement "the prosecutor shall disclose to the defendant sufficient informa-

a. What does this mean in terms of what kinds of "bluffing" are improper only by the prosecutor during plea negotiations? Compare *A.B.A. Standards* § 3–4.1(c) (3d ed. 1993)("A prosecutor should not knowingly make false statements or representations as to fact or law in the course of plea discussions with defense counsel or the accused"); with *A.B.A. Standards* § 4–6.2(c) (3d ed. 1993) ("Defense counsel should not knowingly make false statements concerning the evidence in the course of plea discussions with the prosecutor").

b. Consider *Fambo v. Smith*, 433 F.Supp. 590 (W.D.N.Y.1977), aff'd, 565 F.2d 233 (2d Cir.1977), where Fambo, charged with two counts of possession of an explosive based upon alleged possession of a tube of dynamite on Nov. 29 and Dec. 1, pleaded guilty after plea negotiations to the lesser offense of possessing an incendiary device. It later came to light that the prosecutor had known that prior to the second possession police had removed the dynamite from the tube and replaced it with sawdust. The court concluded that "a prosecutor has a duty, during the course of plea bargaining, to disclose to the defendant evidence that is as clearly exculpatory of certain elements of the crime charged as is the contested evidence in this case," but then concluded this was harmless error, as Fambo could have been convicted on the first count and of an attempt with respect to the second count (both more serious offenses than the one to which he pleaded), and "there was thus sufficient mutuality of advantage to support this bargain."

tion within his knowledge to enable the defendant to make an informed assessment of the likely outcome upon a trial of the case."

6. "Recently, a new dilemma has vexed some federal public defenders. To illustrate briefly, imagine that you are a federal public defender. You have a client charged with several bank robberies for which he faces a maximum of sixty years in prison. The Assistant U.S. Attorney has just offered your client a terrific plea agreement that would allow him to serve only eight years.

"The prosecutor insists that * * * she has given you every piece of 'material' evidence that reflects on your client's factual guilt or innocence. She has disclosed that several witnesses have identified your client as the bank robber, but nothing else. Your client wants to take the plea deal. Lacking an effective defense, you want your client to sign the agreement as well.

"Looking over the agreement, you notice the following provision, which you have never seen before:

The defendant understands that discovery may not have been completed in this case, and that there may be additional discovery to which he would have access if he elected to proceed to trial. The defendant agrees to waive his right to receive this additional discovery which may include, among other things, evidence tending to impeach the credibility of potential witnesses.

The prosecutor says that, as a result of this waiver, she has not examined the personnel files of key law enforcement witnesses in the case against your client. Nor has she disclosed to you any key witnesses' criminal and personal histories or any inconsistent statements that they may have made to prosecutors, all of which might impeach their credibility. You would receive this information if you went to trial. Then comes the tough choice: Do you urge your client to sign the plea agreement, taking the chance that significant impeaching evidence does not exist and that, if it did, it would not be crucial to developing your defense?" Note, 51 Stan.L.Rev. 567, 567–68 (1999). If the client does sign the agreement, should the courts "enforce" the waiver no matter what is later shown to be the nature of the information not disclosed?"

If, as in *Newman,* the courts will not intervene on behalf of a defendant, what then of intervention in the public interest? Consider:

UNITED STATES v. AMMIDOWN
497 F.2d 615 (D.C.Cir.1973).

LEVENTHAL, Circuit Judge. * * *

In a case of extraordinary notoriety, Robert L. Ammidown was charged with first degree murder and conspiracy to commit murder in the death of his wife. Ammidown admitted that a month previous he arranged to have her murdered at a parking garage of a Virginia department store. At the last minute he changed his mind, because he did not want his son, who was to accompany his mother on that day, to witness the murder. Subsequently, according to his written confession, Ammidown and an associate, Richard Anthony Lee, devised a plan whereby Lee would abduct Mrs. Ammidown and by threat to her life extort a sum of money to be used by Ammidown and Lee to make the down payment for a club on the Eastern Shore of Maryland. The plan called for Ammidown to take his wife to dinner at the Flagship Restaurant in Southwest Washington. After dinner, as they were departing from the Flagship, Lee would halt Ammidown's car at a specified intersection near the restaurant.

And so it was done. In due course, and at the prearranged spot, Lee jumped into Ammidown's car and directed him to drive to the East Capitol Street Bridge, where Lee dragged Mrs. Ammidown from the car and raped her, as planned, to impress Mrs. Ammidown "with the seriousness of the threat."

What then happened was that Lee killed Mrs. Ammidown. Ammidown did not confess to complicity in the murder.

Just prior to trial, the United States Attorney and Ammidown entered into this agreement: Ammidown would plead guilty to second degree murder, and the first degree murder charge would be dismissed. There was no agreement for the prosecutor to recommend sentence less than the maximum, life imprisonment. Ammidown, then aged 49, had no possibility of being even considered for parole for 15 years. Ammidown agreed to testify in the grand jury proceedings and impending trial of Lee, a much younger man, who was believed by the prosecution to be involved in another murder.

The trial judge, however, refused to approve the agreement and accept the lesser plea. With full understanding of the prosecutor's concern with the importance of Ammidown's agreement in connection with its successful prosecution of Lee, the court nonetheless decided that under Rule 11 of the Federal Rules of Criminal Procedure it had the discretion to refuse the plea when it found that the crime was so heinous and the evidence of guilt so overwhelming that the public interest would be ill-served by a judgment of second degree murder, which it referred to as a "tap on the wrist." Appellant then pleaded not guilty to first degree and second degree murder; at trial he was convicted of first degree murder and felony murder and sentenced to two terms of life imprisonment, to run consecutively.

Appellant now asserts that the failure of the trial court to accept his proffered plea of guilty to second degree murder constituted reversible error, and asks this court to remand with instructions to enter a judgment of second degree murder. * * *

By its terms, Rule 11 deals with the moment when the accused stands before the judge to enter his plea. Although the rule provides that a trial court "may refuse to accept a plea of guilty," it fails to delineate the circumstance under which it may do so. * * *

The element in a plea bargain of dismissal of the charge of the greater offense leads us to consider Rule 48(a) of the Federal Rules of Criminal Procedure, which requires the prosecutor to obtain leave of court in order to terminate a prosecution by dismissal of an indictment. Rule 48(a) does not apply as such to the case at bar, but study of the judicial role in dismissals illuminates our course. As proposed by the Advisory Committee this provision would have adopted the common law rule that the power of the prosecutor to enter a nolle prosequi in a criminal case was unrestricted, and added only the requirement, prevalent in state practice, that the prosecutor state his reasons for seeking dismissals. However, when this rule was promulgated by the Supreme Court in 1944, it substituted the requirement that dismissal be obtained only by leave of court. The Supreme Court did not state reasons for its action. The primary concern, at least as discerned by subsequent decisions of other federal courts, was that of protecting a defendant from harassment, through a prosecutor's charging, dismissing without having placed a defendant in jeopardy, and commencing another prosecution at a different time or place deemed more favorable to the prosecution. * * *

A distinctly different situation is presented when the defendant concurs in the dismissal but the court is concerned whether the action sufficiently protects the public. As to this, while there is a paucity of authority, some principles do emerge. First, Rule 48(a)'s requirement of judicial leave, theretofore known in state practice, gives the court a role in dismissals following indictment. Second, in the exercise of its responsibility, the court will not be content with a mere conclusory statement by the prosecutor that dismissal is in the public interest, but will require a statement of reasons and underlying factual basis. Third, the court does not have primary responsibility, but rather the role of guarding against abuse of prosecutorial discretion. The rule contemplates exposure of the reasons for dismissal "in order to prevent abuse of the uncontrolled power of dismissal previously enjoyed by prosecutors," and in pursuance of this purpose "to gain the Court's favorable discretion, it should be satisfied that the reasons advanced for the proposed dismissal are substantial." * * *

The third element of a plea bargain involving a plea to a lesser included offense, and indeed the most frequent motive behind it, is to circumscribe the judge's discretion in pronouncing sentence. The negotiated plea reduces the upper and lower limits of the range of sentence available to the judge. It is axiomatic that, within the limits imposed by the legislature, imposition of sentence is a matter for discretion of the trial judge. The prosecutor has no role beyond the advisory, and even that is frowned on in the District Court for the District of Columbia. We hesitate to say, therefore, that the United States Attorney and the defendant can by plea manipulate this traditional power of the judge without any recourse by the judge permitting him to forestall gross abuses of prosecutorial discretion.

We have identified that both the District Judge and the United States Attorney have roles in the plea bargaining process. What is required is an effort to harmonize their responsibilities, and to suggest a standard for determining when judicial intervention may be proper.

We start with the presumption that the determination of the United States Attorney is to be followed in the overwhelming number of cases. He alone is in a position to evaluate the government's prosecution resources and the number of cases it is able to prosecute.

Where vigorous prosecution of one case threatens to undermine successful prosecution of another, it has traditionally been the prosecutor who determines which case will be pressed to conclusion, and his decision has been given great deference by the courts.

On the other hand, we do not think Rule 48(a) intends the trial court to serve merely as a rubber stamp for the prosecutor's decision. We agree that "the judge should be satisfied that the agreement adequately protects the public interest".

We now state what, in our view, are the appropriate doctrines governing trial judges in considering whether to deny approval either to dismissals of cases outright or to the diluted dismissal—a guilty plea to a lesser included offense.

First, the trial judge must provide a reasoned exercise of discretion in order to justify a departure from the course agreed on by the prosecution and defense. This is not a matter of absolute judicial prerogative. The authority has been granted to the judge to assure protection of the public interest, and this in turn involves one or more of the following components: (a) fairness to the defense, such as protection against harassment; (b) fairness to the prosecution interest, as in avoiding a disposition that does not serve due and legitimate prosecutorial interest; (c) protection of the sentencing authority reserved to the judge. The judge's statement or opinion must identify the particular interest that leads him to require an unwilling defendant and prosecution to go to trial.

We now turn to the content of these components, and begin by passing any discussion of fairness to the defense, since it is not directly involved in the case at bar and it has already been identified in the precedents referred to earlier in this opinion. As to fairness to the prosecution interest, here we have a matter in which the primary responsibility, obviously, is that of the prosecuting attorney. The District Court cannot disapprove of his action on the ground of incompatibility with prosecutive responsibility unless the judge is in effect ruling that the prosecutor has abused his discretion. The requirement of judicial approval entitles the judge to obtain and evaluate the prosecutor's reasons. That much, indeed, was proposed by the Advisory Committee, and the Supreme Court's amendment obviously did not curtail the proposed authority of the judge. The judge may withhold approval if he finds that the prosecutor has failed to give consideration to factors that must be given consideration in the public interest, factors such as the deterrent aspects of the criminal law. However, trial judges are not free to withhold approval of guilty pleas on this basis merely because their conception of the public interest differs from that of the prosecuting attorney. The question is not what the judge would do if he were the prosecuting attorney, but whether he can say that the action of the prosecuting attorney is such a departure from sound prosecutorial principle as to mark it an abuse of prosecutorial discretion.

In like vein, we note that a judge is free to condemn the prosecutor's agreement as a trespass on judicial authority only in a blatant and extreme case. In ordinary circumstances, the change in grading of an offense presents no question of the kind of action that is reserved for the judiciary.

Applying these tests to the case at bar, we find the record establishes beyond all doubt that the United States Attorney considered, indeed agonized over, the public interest and concluded that it was best served by assuring a successful prosecution of Lee—"a young man ... a killer." The Assistant United States Attorney presented this to the court unequivocally:

> We have spent night after night trying to resolve this thing. We have talked with the homicide officers. We have had them to our office. We have pulled the file of Richard Anthony Lee. Your Honor, we are scared to death that unless there is a successful way to prosecute this man—he is a young man. We believe he is a killer. We believe that somewhere in this city right now there is someone who because he will not be prosecuted will die one day in say the next ten years. We believe that Mr. Ammidown pleading to second degree murder—that the sentence in that case will neutralize him. We have no fear of him now. We are afraid of what Richard Anthony Lee might do.

> Your Honor, we have one obligation. And that is the same obligation that your Honor has, and that is for the public. I prosecute for the Government— for the public—for the people of this city.

The trial judge was not free to disapprove this assessment by the prosecutor without both stating his reasons and determining that the prosecutor abused his discretion. Neither of these elements appears in the case at bar. The trial judge provided no statement of reasons, and such colloquy as appears indicates that the Judge assumed that the correct test was what the judge independently considered best in the public interest.

When we come to the possible ground of intrusion on the sentencing function of the trial judge, we have a consideration that is interdependent of the other. That is to say, a dropping of an offense that might be taken as an intrusion on the judicial function if it were not shown to be related to a prosecutorial purpose takes on an entirely different coloration if it is explained to the judge that there was a prosecutorial purpose, an insufficiency of evidence, a doubt as to the admissibility of certain evidence under exclusionary rules, a need for evidence to bring another felon to justice, or other similar consideration.

Because the trial judge did not provide a statement of reasons based on intrusion on the sentencing authority of the judge,[a] it would be necessary to remand in any event. At the time the judge took the action appealed from, first degree murder was punishable by death, and second degree murder by a maximum of life imprisonment. We need not consider what kind of remand we might have provided if that kind of sentencing disparity were in effect at the present time. For the Supreme Court's decision in *Furman v. Georgia,* 408 U.S. 238, 92 S.Ct. 2726, 33 L.Ed.2d 346 (1972), has established the unavailability of the death sentence for appellant. We are required to accompany our reversal for lack of requisite findings with a disposition in the interest of justice that takes into account current conditions.

The situation as it stands today is such that we cannot conceive that if the trial judge were required to provide a current reassessment of the problem in the light of the standards set forth in this opinion, he could justify his rejection of the first degree murder reversal and of the second degree murder plea as reflecting a sentence disparity so blatant as to constitute an intrusion upon the judicial domain. The life sentence is mandatory on a conviction for first degree murder, and discretionary with the court on a conviction for murder in the second degree. Parole is available after a minimum of 20 years in the case of first degree murder, and after a minimum of 15 years in the case of murder in the second degree. The difference is insufficient by itself to warrant judicial rejection of a properly bargained plea of guilty to murder in the second degree on the ground of undue interference with the sentencing domain of the judiciary. * * *

For the reasons stated, the judgment and sentence on a conviction of murder in the first degree is vacated and the case remanded with instructions to accept appellant's plea of guilty to second degree murder.

Notes and Questions

1. As reflected by *United States v. Jackson,* 563 F.2d 1145 (4th Cir.1977), the traditional positions of the prosecutor and judge are quite different when sentencing bargaining rather than charge bargaining is involved. In that case, a plea agreement was reached whereby the defendant agreed to plead guilty to the charge of operating a lottery and the prosecutor agreed to recommend a sentence of one year. At arraignment, the trial judge made it clear that he would give no consideration to the recommendation in the plea agreement, but after a recess the defendant entered a plea of guilty anyway and later received a 3–year sentence. On appeal, the court found "Jackson's challenge of his guilty plea solely on the ground that the district court arbitrarily declined to consider any plea bargain to be without merit." The legislative history of rule 11, the court noted, made it clear that "each individual judge is free to decide whether, and to what degree, he will entertain plea bargains, and his refusal to consider any plea bargaining whatsoever will not vitiate a guilty plea which has otherwise been knowingly and voluntarily entered."

2. Compare with *Ammidown* and *Jackson* the current responsibilities of a federal judge in passing on plea bargains under the Sentencing Guidelines discussed in Note 19, p. 1243.

a. The trial judge later stated his reasons in John Sirica, *To Set the Record Straight* 42–43 (1979): "I rejected the plea bargain, however, relying upon the legal axiom of 'equal justice under law.' The law states that conspirators are culpable in like degree even if one goes further in carrying out the conspiracy than the other. The two men were equally responsible for this brutal killing, in my view. And another problem was also on my mind. The husband was white; the accomplice was black. I shuddered to think what might be the reaction of Washington's large black community if the white man who planned his own wife's death was let off with a fifteen-year-to-life term while the black man might have to pay with his life." What would the appellate court have thought of those reasons?

3. Nearly half of the states provide an avenue for victim impact in the plea-bargaining process. A large number either follow the federal model of directing the prosecutor to consult with the victim, see Note 4, p. ___, or impose a notification requirement which presumably gives the victim an opportunity to communicate with the prosecutor before a negotiated plea is finalized. Much less common are provisions which specifically give the victim an opportunity to be heard by the court prior to a judicial decision whether to accept the plea agreement. Sarah Welling, *Victim Participation in Plea Bargains,* 65 Wash.U.L.Q. 301, 355 (1987), "concludes that victim participation in plea bargains would advance various interests of the victim and of society without any significant detrimental impact to the interests of prosecutors and defendants," and that "the victim's participation right is best defined as a right to be heard by the trial judge before the plea bargain is accepted."

SECTION 4. RECEIVING THE DEFENDANT'S PLEA; PLEA WITHDRAWAL

A. Pleading Alternatives

1. When the defendant is called upon to enter his plea at arraignment; he may enter a plea of (1) not guilty, (2) guilty, (3) not guilty by reason of insanity (in a few jurisdictions where such a plea is a prerequisite to the presentation of an insanity defense at trial); or (4) nolo contendere (in the federal system and about half of the states). A plea of nolo contendere—sometimes referred to as a plea of non vult contendere or of non vult—is simply a device by which the defendant may assert that he does not want to contest the issue of guilt or innocence. Such a plea may not be entered as a matter of right, but only with the consent of the court, and it is generally the practice of courts not to consent to a nolo contendere plea unless the prosecutor concurs.

2. Although some minor variations are to be found from jurisdiction to jurisdiction, in most states which permit a plea of nolo contendere it has the following significance: (1) Unlike a plea of guilty or a conviction following a plea of not guilty, a plea of nolo contendere may not be put into evidence in a subsequent civil action as proof of the fact that the defendant committed the offense to which he entered the plea. (2) When a nolo contendere plea has been accepted, the defendant may be given the same sentence as if he had pleaded guilty. (3) Judgment following entry of a nolo contendere plea is a conviction, and may be admitted as such in other proceedings (e.g., to apply multiple offender penalty provisions, to deny or revoke a license because of conviction, or to claim double jeopardy in a subsequent prosecution). See Note, 44 S.Cal.L.Rev. 737 (1971).

3. "While it is in the discretion of the Court to reject or accept such a plea, no criteria have been established to guide the Court in the exercise of this discretion." *United States v. Bagliore,* 182 F.Supp. 714 (E.D.N.Y.1960). What should the criteria be? Consider *United States v. David E. Thompson, Inc.,* 621 F.2d 1147 (1st Cir.1980), holding the district court did not abuse its discretion in rejecting a nolo plea in a criminal antitrust action where entry of the plea would have deprived the victims of the antitrust conspiracy of a significant opportunity in subsequent civil actions to benefit from the government's efforts.

4. The concern herein is with what procedures are to be followed when the defendant tenders a plea of guilty. Those required in the federal system are set out in Fed.R.Crim.P. 11, which should be examined at this point. State provisions are not always this elaborate. In examining the material which follows, consider: (i) what procedures are (or should be) constitutionally required; and (ii) what other procedures, even if not constitutionally required, are desirable.

B. Determining Voluntariness of Guilty
Plea and Competency of Defendant

1. When the legitimacy of plea bargaining was in doubt, the general practice was not to reveal in court that a bargain had been struck. Thus, when the trial judge asked the defendant if his plea was the result of any promises, he would respond in the negative even when everyone in the courtroom knew otherwise. Most jurisdictions have now moved away from this charade, so that the voluntariness inquiry includes a determination of whether a plea agreement has been reached and, if so, what it is. See, e.g., Fed.R.Crim.P. 11(d) & (e).

2. An inquiry into the mental competency of a defendant who has tendered a guilty plea is not routinely undertaken. However, a trial court is constitutionally compelled to hold a hearing, sua sponte, at any time that substantial evidence appears that a criminal defendant is incompetent to enter a guilty plea.

In GODINEZ v. MORAN, described at p. 1098, the Court rejected a Ninth Circuit holding that the established competency-to-stand-trial standard, whether the defendant has "a rational and factual understanding of the proceedings and is capable of assisting his counsel," does not apply to a defendant's decision to plead guilty, which is to be tested by the higher standard of whether the defendant has "the capacity for 'reasoned choice' among the alternatives available to him." THOMAS, J., for the Court, explained: "A defendant who stands trial is likely to be presented with choices that entail relinquishment of the same rights that are relinquished by a defendant who pleads guilty: He will ordinarily have to decide whether to waive his 'privilege against compulsory self-incrimination' by taking the witness stand; if the option is available, he may have to decide whether to waive his 'right to trial by jury'; and, in consultation with counsel, he may have to decide whether to waive his 'right to confront [his] accusers' by declining to cross-examine witnesses for the prosecution. A defendant who pleads not guilty, moreover, faces still other strategic choices: In consultation with his attorney, he may be called upon to decide, among other things, whether (and how) to put on a defense and whether to raise one or more affirmative defenses. In sum, all criminal defendants—not merely those who plead guilty—may be required to make important decisions once criminal proceedings have been initiated. And while the decision to plead guilty is undeniably a profound one, it is no more complicated than the sum total of decisions that a defendant may be called upon to make during the course of a trial. (The decision to plead guilty is also made over a shorter period of time, without the distraction and burden of a trial.) This being so, we can conceive of no basis for demanding a higher level of competence for those defendants who choose to plead guilty."[a]

C. Determining Guilty Plea Is Understandingly Made

1. *The charge.* Defendant, 19 years old and substantially below average intelligence, was indicted for first degree murder. His attorneys sought to have the charge reduced to manslaughter, but were only able to induce the prosecutor to reduce to second degree murder in exchange for a guilty plea. The attorneys did not tell defendant that the new charge required an intent to kill, nor was any reference made to this element at the time of defendant's plea. At sentencing, the

a. Kennedy and Scalia, JJ., concurring, would reach the same conclusion even if "the decisions were not equivalent" because the common law made no attempt "to apply different competency standards to different stages of criminal proceedings," use of a single standard does not offend any fundamental principle. Blackmun and Stevens, JJ., dissenting, objected to the application of the same standard to defendant's decision to discharge his attorney, an aspect of the case considered at p. 1099.

defendant's lawyers explained his version of the offense, particularly noting that he "meant no harm to the lady" when he entered her room with a knife, but this was disputed by the prosecutor. The defendant later obtained relief via federal habeas corpus, and in HENDERSON v. MORGAN, 426 U.S. 637, 96 S.Ct. 2253, 49 L.Ed.2d 108 (1976), the Court, per STEVENS, J., affirmed:

"We assume, as petitioner argues, that the prosecutor had overwhelming evidence of guilt available. We also accept petitioner's characterization of the competence of respondent's counsel and of the wisdom of their advice to plead guilty to a charge of second-degree murder. Nevertheless, such a plea cannot support a judgment of guilt unless it was voluntary in a constitutional sense. And clearly the plea could not be voluntary in the sense that it constituted an intelligent admission that he committed the offense unless the defendant received 'real notice of the true nature of the charge against him, the first and most universally recognized requirement of due process.'

"The charge of second-degree murder was never formally made. Had it been made, it necessarily would have included a charge that respondent's assault was 'committed with a design to effect the death of the person killed.' That element of the offense might have been proved by the objective evidence even if respondent's actual state of mind was consistent with innocence or manslaughter. But even if such a design to effect death would almost inevitably have been inferred from evidence that respondent repeatedly stabbed Mrs. Francisco, it is nevertheless also true that a jury would not have been required to draw that inference. The jury would have been entitled to accept defense counsel's appraisal of the incident as involving only manslaughter in the first degree. Therefore, an admission by respondent that he killed Mrs. Francisco does not necessarily also admit that he was guilty of second-degree murder.

"There is nothing in this record that can serve as a substitute for either a finding after trial, or a voluntary admission, that respondent had the requisite intent. Defense counsel did not purport to stipulate to that fact; they did not explain to him that his plea would be an admission of that fact; and he made no factual statement or admission necessarily implying that he had such intent. In these circumstances it is impossible to conclude that his plea to the unexplained charge of second-degree murder was voluntary.

"Petitioner argues that affirmance of the Court of Appeals will invite countless collateral attacks on judgments entered on pleas of guilty, since frequently the record will not contain a complete enumeration of the elements of the offense to which an accused person pleads guilty.[18] We think petitioner's fears are exaggerated.

"Normally the record contains either an explanation of the charge by the trial judge, or at least a representation by defense counsel that the nature of the offense has been explained to the accused. Moreover, even without such an express representation, it may be appropriate to presume that in most cases defense counsel routinely explain the nature of the offense in sufficient detail to give the accused notice of what he is being asked to admit. This case is unique because the trial judge found as a fact that the element of intent was not explained to respondent. Moreover, respondent's unusually low mental capacity provides a reasonable explanation for counsel's oversight; it also forecloses the conclusion that the error was harmless beyond a reasonable doubt, for it lends at

---

18. "There is no need in this case to decide whether notice of the true nature, or substance, of a charge always requires a description of every element of the offense; we assume it does not. Nevertheless, intent is such a critical element of the offense of second-degree murder that notice of that element is required."

least a modicum of credibility to defense counsel's appraisal of the homicide as a manslaughter rather than a murder."

REHNQUIST, J., joined by The Chief Justice, dissenting, argued that the only issue was whether respondent was "properly advised," which "depends upon the sort of advice reasonably competent counsel would have been expected to give him." Because defendant told his attorneys that he had stabbed the victim "many times," this "suggests that experienced counsel would not consider the 'design to effect death' issue to be in serious dispute." WHITE, J., joined by Stewart, Blackmun, and Powell, JJ., concurring, responded that "this case rests on the long-accepted principle that a guilty plea must provide a trustworthy basis for believing that the defendant is in fact guilty."

What constitutes a "critical element" under fn. 18 of *Henderson?* Consider, e.g., *Ramirez v. People,* 682 P.2d 1181 (Colo.1984) (meaning of "attempt" should be explained, as it "not a crime that is readily understandable to a person of ordinary intelligence"). Is explanation unnecessary if, as commonly assumed, e.g., *Commonwealth v. Begin,* 474 N.E.2d 1120 (Mass.1985), defendant's statements to the court indicate the presence of the unexplained elements? Is the judge's responsibility different if the defendant is not represented by counsel? Consider *Else v. State,* 555 P.2d 1210 (Alaska 1976) (court must advise unrepresented defendant of elements contained in statute and also those created by judicial construction, and thus on charge of assault with a deadly weapon, court required as a matter of due process to inform defendant phrase "dangerous weapon" had been construed so that he would not be guilty if gun was unloaded and not used as a bludgeon).

2. *The sentence.* Prior to his plea of guilty to possession of narcotics, Williams was informed by the judge that the maximum possible sentence was four years, but when the judge later learned Williams had two prior felony convictions he sentenced Williams to a term of 15 years to life under the persistent offender statute. Williams sought relief via federal habeas corpus, and in WILLIAMS v. SMITH, 591 F.2d 169 (2d Cir.1979), the court held that the test "for determining the constitutional validity of a state court guilty plea where the defendant has been given sentencing misinformation is whether the defendant was aware of actual sentencing possibilities, and, if not, whether accurate information would have made any difference in his decision to enter a plea. Where government error is responsible for the misinformation, the government carries the burden of proof on the issue of reliance."

It was undisputed Williams lacked actual knowledge at the time of his plea of the persistent offender sentencing possibility, so the court focused upon the second part of the test and concluded the district court's finding Williams' plea would not have been different had he known was not clearly erroneous. In reaching that conclusion, the court of appeals stressed these considerations: (1) even had he known, Williams could not know in advance of either trial or guilty plea whether the judge would actually make the finding required by the persistent offender statute that he was in need of extended incarceration; (2) Williams was aware his chance of acquittal at trial on the original charge (with a 7–year maximum) was slight, and thus "would have had little incentive to plead not guilty since a conviction at trial * * * would have resulted in a greater minimum sentence and an at least equal chance of his being sentenced as a persistent offender"; and (3) Williams and his attorney learned of the actual sentencing possibilities before the sentencing hearing, so that notwithstanding the fact "they were not aware that Williams could have moved to withdraw his plea, * * * their silence during this period suggests that accurate information would not have affected their initial plea decision."

When a person convicted of the crime charged is by law ineligible for probation or parole, should the defendant be so advised before his guilty plea is accepted? "While some cases have expressed the view that eligibility and ineligibility for parole involve merely matters of 'legislative grace' rather than matters of right, and are therefore not 'consequences' of a guilty plea, other cases have rejected this view and have expressed the view that (1) the average defendant assumes that he will be eligible for parole, and (2) if a defendant, upon conviction for a particular crime, will be ineligible for parole, such a complete denial of the opportunity for him to be paroled is an inseparable part of the punishment for his crime, directly affects the duration of his incarceration, and is thus a 'consequence' of his guilty plea." Annot., 8 A.L.R.Fed. 760, 763 (1971).

As noted in *United States v. Andrades*, 169 F.3d 131 (2d Cir.1999), "there is no requirement in Rule 11 itself that defendants be advised of their potential punishments pursuant to the Sentencing Guidelines rather than the criminal statute * * *. While the Sentencing Guidelines certainly are a relevant consideration for defendants entering a plea of guilty, the district court at the time of the plea allocution frequently has too little information available to provide defendant with an accurate sentencing range. For example, probation department officials often have not scored or researched defendant's criminal history, and the court is unaware of upward or downward departure motions that the government or defense counsel may pursue. Both of these factors have significant impacts on Sentencing Guidelines calculations." Compare *United States v. Horne,* 987 F.2d 833 (D.C.Cir.1993), where, because "in many federal criminal cases today, [the] statutory maximum is irrelevant" because of the impact of the federal Sentencing Guidelines, the court offered "a suggestion that is without the force of law," namely, "that wherever feasible, the district court make their presentence reports available to defendants before taking their pleas. By doing so, sentencing judges (and reviewing courts) will have greater confidence that pleas are both willing and fully informed."

3. *Collateral consequences.* Note, 112 U.Pa.L.Rev. 865, 875–76 (1964): "Courts have not considered it necessary to inform the defendant of possible collateral consequences when such consequences result from subsequent criminal convictions of the defendant or do not relate directly to the charge to which the defendant pleads guilty. There is no obligation to inform a defendant that the conviction of the present crime will be considered under a multiple offender law if he should be convicted of another crime. Similarly, there is no obligation to tell a defendant that in the event of any subsequent convictions the present conviction could be considered in determining whether to give a lenient or severe penalty on the subsequent conviction, or that society generally discriminates against convicted offenders. Nor need a court inform a defendant that conviction can mean deportation, court martial from the armed services, loss of the right to vote, or loss of the right to operate a business licensed by the state. It also does not seem that the defendant must know what rehabilitation programs will be available to him."

If the judge is not responsible for advising defendant of various collateral consequences, is this because such advice is the responsibility of defense counsel? In *People v. Pozo,* 746 P.2d 523 (Colo.1987), where defense counsel failed to inform an alien defendant that his guilty plea could result in deportation, the court took note of conflicting decisions in other states on whether this constitutes ineffective assistance and then declined to adopt any absolute rule: "The determination of whether the failure to investigate those consequences constitutes ineffective assistance of counsel turns to a significant degree upon whether the attorney had sufficient information to form a reasonable belief that the client was in fact an alien." Compare *Mott v. State,* 407 N.W.2d 581 (Iowa 1987) (precisely because deportation is a "collateral consequence," counsel's failure to warn about it—as compared to affirmatively misleading about it—is not ineffective assistance).

4. *Rights waived by plea.* After Wilkins' trial for first degree murder had commenced, he entered a guilty plea to second degree murder and was sentenced to a term of 50 years. Though the trial judge had determined that the plea was voluntary and had warned defendant that he could be sentenced to life imprisonment, Wilkins sought relief via federal habeas corpus. In WILKINS v. ERICKSON, 505 F.2d 761 (9th Cir.1974), the court stated:

"Wilkins relies upon *Boykin v. Alabama,* [395 U.S. 238, 89 S.Ct. 1709, 23 L.Ed.2d 274 (1969).] He contends that since he was not personally advised by the trial judge on entry of his plea that by pleading guilty he was waiving (1) his privilege against self-incrimination,[b] (2) his right to trial by jury,[c] and (3) his right to confront his accusers; that he was unaware of the consequences, and that his plea, therefore, was not voluntarily and intelligently made. Wilkins further argues that the failure of the trial judge to articulate these three rights on the record resulted in a 'silent' record which cannot be supplemented by a post-conviction evidentiary hearing. Accordingly, he wants the opportunity to replead.

"Wilkins relies on the following language from *Boykin:*

'We cannot presume a waiver of these three important federal rights from a silent record.

'What is at stake for an accused facing death or imprisonment demands the utmost solicitude of which courts are capable in canvassing the matter with the accused to make sure he has a full understanding of what a plea connotes and of its consequence. When the judge discharges that function, he leaves a record adequate for any review that may be later sought.'

"The district court's decision, however, is supported by Supreme Court decisions subsequent to *Boykin* and several circuits. The rigid interpretation of *Boykin* urged by Wilkins has not been adopted by the Supreme Court in subsequent decisions on voluntariness of guilty pleas. In *Brady v. United States,* [p. 1250) the Court, citing *Boykin,* upheld a guilty plea as voluntary and intelligent even though defendant had not been specifically advised of the three rights discussed in *Boykin.* The *Brady* Court clarified *Boykin* by stating, '[t]he new element added in *Boykin* was the requirement that the record must affirmatively disclose that a defendant who pleaded guilty entered his plea understandingly and voluntarily.' In *North Carolina v. Alford,* [p. 1295 the Court stated that in determining the validity of guilty pleas the 'standard was and remains whether the plea represents a voluntary and intelligent choice among the alternative courses of action open to the defendant.' Specific articulation of the *Boykin* rights is not the sine qua non of a valid guilty plea.

"* * * Accordingly, we hold that *Boykin* does not require specific articulation of the above mentioned three rights in a state proceeding."[d]

---

b. But see the *Mitchell* case in Note 2, p. 1295.

c. Fed.R.Crim.P. 11(c), listing jury trial as a right waived by a guilty plea about which a federal defendant must be advised, is only a codification of *Boykin,* and so defendant was not entitled to be advised of the right to jury trial re property forfeiture conferred by Fed. R.Crim. 31(e). *Libretti v. United States,* 516 U.S. 29, 116 S.Ct. 356, 133 L.Ed.2d 271 (1995).

d. Several other courts have reached the same conclusion. Compare *People v. Jaworski,*

194 N.W.2d 868 (Mich.1972): "While it may be true * * * that '*Boykin* is devoid of any specific language stating that in order to have a valid waiver of the three federal constitutional rights involved when a plea of guilty is entered the three rights must be specifically enumerated and specifically waived,' in our opinion both Justice Douglas' language and his logic require that the defendant must be informed of these three rights, for without knowledge he cannot understandingly waive those rights."

D.   DETERMINING FACTUAL BASIS OF GUILTY PLEA

1. The Advisory Committee Note to Fed.R.Crim.P. 11(f) reads in part: "The court should satisfy itself, by inquiry of the defendant or the attorney for the government, or by examining the presentence report, or otherwise, that the conduct which the defendant admits constitutes the offense charged or an offense included therein to which the defendant has pleaded guilty.[e] Such inquiry should, e.g., protect a defendant who is in the position of pleading voluntarily with an understanding of the nature of the charge but without realizing that his conduct does not actually fall within the charge."[f] Several states have adopted a similar requirement.

2. In *Mitchell v. United States*, 526 U.S. 314, 119 S.Ct. 1307, 143 L.Ed.2d 424 (1999), the Court focused upon the self-incrimination aspects of inquiry of the defendant to establish the factual basis for a plea, and concluded: (a) because entry of a guilty plea is itself not a waiver of the privilege other than as an at-trial right lost by not standing trial, a defendant to whom a factual basis inquiry is made *could* decline to answer on Fifth Amendment grounds, but by doing so he "runs the risk the district court will find the factual basis inadequate"; (b) the guilty plea and statements made by the defendant in the plea colloquy, including the factual basis inquiry, "are later admissible against the defendant," for example, at sentencing; and (c) the fact the defendant has made incriminating statements at the factual basis inquiry does not itself constitute a waiver of the privilege at later proceedings such as sentencing. This is so, the Court explained, because that situation is unlike the case of a witness at a single proceeding (including a defendant at trial), who "may not testify voluntarily about a subject and then invoke the privilege against self-incrimination when questioned about the details," thereby "diminishing the integrity of the factual inquiry."

"There is no convincing reason why the narrow inquiry at the plea colloquy should entail such an extensive waiver of the privilege. Unlike the defendant taking the stand, * * * the defendant who pleads guilty puts nothing in dispute regarding the essentials of the offense. Rather, the defendant takes those matters out of dispute, often by making a joint statement with the prosecution or confirming the prosecution's version of the facts. Under these circumstances, there is little danger that the court will be misled by selective disclosure. In this respect a guilty plea is more like an offer to stipulate than a decision to take the stand. Here, petitioner's statement that she had done 'some of' the proffered conduct did not pose a threat to the integrity of factfinding proceedings, for the purpose of the District Court's inquiry was simply to ensure that petitioner understood the charges and that there was a factual basis for the Government's case."

3. In NORTH CAROLINA v. ALFORD, 400 U.S. 25, 91 S.Ct. 160, 27 L.Ed.2d 162 (1970), Alford was indicted for first-degree murder, a capital offense. His appointed counsel questioned witnesses the defendant said would substantiate his claim of innocence, but these witnesses instead gave statements that strongly indicated his guilt. The attorney recommended a plea of guilty, but left the final

---

e. Rule 11(f) does not require a factual basis showing for a stipulated asset forfeiture embodied in a plea agreement, as "forfeiture is an element of the sentence imposed *following* conviction or, as here, a plea of guilty, and thus falls outside the scope of rule 11(f)." *Libretti v. United States*, 516 U.S. 29, 116 S.Ct. 356, 133 L.Ed.2d 271 (1995).

f. For example, *Gilbert v. United States*, 466 F.2d 533 (5th Cir.1972), where defendant pleaded guilty to four counts of interstate transportation of stolen money orders, but, had the judge not failed to determine the factual basis, he would have learned that there was only one crossing of state lines and thus only one violation of the statute.

decision to Alford. Alford thereafter pleaded guilty to second-degree murder, following which the trial court received a summary of the state's case, indicating that Alford had taken a gun from his house with the stated intention of killing the victim and had later returned with the declaration that he had carried out the killing. Alford then took the stand and testified that he had not committed the murder but that he was pleading guilty because he faced the threat of the death penalty if he did not do so. When the defendant persisted in his plea, it was accepted by the trial court. The Supreme Court, per Justice WHITE, relied upon *Brady v. United States,* p. 1250, in concluding that Alford's desire to avoid the death penalty did not necessarily make his guilty plea involuntary, and then proceeded to consider the significance of Alford's denial of guilt:

"State and lower federal courts are divided upon whether a guilty plea can be accepted when it is accompanied by protestations of innocence and hence contains only a waiver of trial but no admission of guilt. Some courts, giving expression to the principle that '[o]ur law only authorizes a conviction where guilt is shown,' require that trial judges reject such pleas. But others have concluded that they should not 'force any defense on a defendant in a criminal case,' particularly when advancement of the defense might 'end in disaster * * *.' They have argued that, since 'guilt, or the degree of guilt, is at times uncertain and elusive * * * [a]n accused, though believing in or entertaining doubts respecting his innocence, might reasonably conclude a jury would be convinced of his guilt and that he would fare better in the sentence by pleading guilty * * *.'[7] * * *

"The issue in *Hudson v. United States,* 272 U.S. 451, 47 S.Ct. 127, 71 L.Ed. 347 (1926), was whether a federal court has power to impose a prison sentence after accepting a plea of *nolo contendere,* a plea by which a defendant does not expressly admit his guilt, but nonetheless waives his right to a trial and authorizes the court for purposes of the case to treat him as if he were guilty. The Court held that a trial court does have such power * * *. Implicit in the *nolo contendere* cases is a recognition that the Constitution does not bar imposition of a prison sentence upon an accused who is unwilling expressly to admit his guilt but who, faced with grim alternatives, is willing to waive his trial and accept the sentence.

" * * * The fact that [Alford's] plea was denominated a plea of guilty rather than a plea of *nolo contendere* is of no constitutional significance with respect to the issue now before us, for the Constitution is concerned with the practical consequences, not the formal categorizations of state law. Thus, while most pleas of guilty consist of both a waiver of trial and an express admission of guilt, the latter element is not a constitutional requisite to the imposition of criminal penalty. An individual accused of crime may voluntarily, knowingly, and understandingly consent to the imposition of a prison sentence even if he is unwilling or unable to admit his participation in the acts constituting the crime.

"Nor can we perceive any material difference between a plea which refuses to admit commission of the criminal act and a plea containing a protestation of innocence when, as in the instant case, a defendant intelligently concludes that his interests require entry of a guilty plea and the record before the judge contains strong evidence of actual guilt. Here the State had a strong case of first-degree murder against Alford. Whether he realized or disbelieved his guilt, he insisted on his plea because in his view he had absolutely nothing to gain by a trial and much to gain by pleading. Because of the overwhelming evidence against him, a trial was precisely what neither Alford nor his attorney desired. Confronted with the choice

7. A third approach has been to decline to rule definitively that a trial judge must either accept or reject an otherwise valid plea containing a protestation of innocence, but to leave that decision to his sound discretion. See *Maxwell v. United States,* 368 F.2d 735, 738–739 (C.A.9 1966).

between a trial for first-degree murder, on the one hand, and a plea of guilty to second-degree murder, on the other, Alford quite reasonably chose the latter and thereby limited the maximum penalty to a 30–year term. When his plea is viewed in light of the evidence against him, which substantially negated his claim of innocence and which further provided a means by which the judge could test whether the plea was being intelligently entered, its validity cannot be seriously questioned. In view of the strong factual basis for the plea demonstrated by the State and Alford's clearly expressed desire to enter it despite his professed belief in his innocence, we hold that the trial judge did not commit constitutional error in accepting it.[11]"

4. Albert W. Alschuler, *The Defense Attorney's Role in Plea Bargaining,* 84 Yale L.J. 1179, 1301 (1975), is critical of fn. 11 in *Alford:* "Under *Alford,* the choice is not the defendant's but the court's, and a court's discretion to refuse an *Alford* plea is apparently subject to no restrictions and no standards." Compare *United States v. Gaskins,* 485 F.2d 1046 (D.C.Cir.1973) (where defendant was convicted of first degree burglary after judge refused to accept bargained plea to unlawful entry because defendant equivocated about his guilt, "it is an abuse of discretion to refuse a guilty plea solely because the defendant does not admit the alleged facts of the crime" when there is "strong factual evidence implicating defendant," as the "entry of such a plea of guilty in such a situation is not contrary to the interests of justice").

5. Not infrequently, a factual basis for the plea will be lacking in the sense that the facts show that the defendant committed a different crime and that the offense to which the plea is offered is not even a logical included offense of the crime committed. For example, in a jurisdiction with an offense of breaking and entering in the nighttime (a nonprobationable offense with a 15–year maximum) and an offense of breaking and entering in the daytime (a probationable offense with a 5–year maximum), a bargained plea to the latter offense may be tendered although the facts show that the crime occurred at midnight. Newman, *Conviction: The Determination of Guilt or Innocence Without Trial* 99–104 (Remington, ed., 1966). Should the judge accept the plea under these circumstances? What then should be the result be in *People v. Foster,* 278 N.Y.S.2d 603, 225 N.E.2d 200 (N.Y.1967), where defendant was originally charged with manslaughter in the first degree, but was allowed to plead guilty to attempted manslaughter in the second degree, an offense which is logically and legally impossible.

E. PLEA WITHDRAWAL GENERALLY

1. One means commonly employed in an effort to "undo" a guilty plea is a motion to the trial court to withdraw the plea.[g] Fed.R.Crim.P. 32(d) permits such a motion only before sentencing, but there is considerable variation in state practice. Some allow the motion only before sentencing or before judgment, but many (following the *former* federal approach) allow the motion thereafter as well. If the time for presenting a withdrawal motion has passed, the plea might be challenged by a timely appeal (limited to issues reflected by the record at

11. Our holding does not mean that a trial judge must accept every constitutionally valid guilty plea merely because a defendant wishes so to plead. A criminal defendant does not have an absolute right under the Constitution to have his guilty plea accepted by the court, although the States may by statute or otherwise confer such a right. Likewise, the States may bar their courts from accepting guilty

pleas from any defendants who assert their innocence. Cf. Fed.Rule Crim.Proc. 11, which gives a trial judge discretion to "refuse to accept a plea of guilty * * *." We need not now delineate the scope of that discretion.

g. On plea withdrawal because the judge learns he cannot go along with a plea agreement which he earlier concurred in, see Note 7, p. 1259.

arraignment and sentencing) or by collateral attack (typically limited to constitutional violations or other serious violations of law).

2. The federal standard for presentence withdrawal motions, derived from dictum in *Kercheval v. United States,* 274 U.S. 220, 47 S.Ct. 582, 71 L.Ed. 1009 (1927), is "any fair and just reason"; it is commonly used at the state level as well for presentence motions. As for later motions, the states typically utilize some higher standard, such as "miscarriage of justice" or "manifest injustice." As explained in *State v. Olish,* 266 S.E.2d 134 (W.Va.1980):

"The basis for the distinction between these two rules is three-fold. First, once sentence is imposed, the defendant is more likely to view the plea bargain as a tactical mistake and therefore wish to have it set aside. Second, at the time the sentence is imposed, other portions of the plea bargain agreement will often be performed by the prosecutor, such as the dismissal of additional charges or the return or destruction of physical evidence, all of which may be difficult to undo if the defendant later attacks his guilty plea. Finally, a higher post-sentence standard for withdrawal is required by the settled policy of giving finality to criminal sentences which result from a voluntary and properly counseled guilty plea."

3. Though the higher test has different meanings in different states, it is commonly treated as equivalent to the grounds for relief upon collateral attack in a post-conviction proceeding. As for the lower "fair and just reason" test, it has received different interpretations. Compare *United States v. Savage,* 561 F.2d 554 (4th Cir.1977) (any desire to withdraw the plea before sentence suffices so long as the prosecution fails to establish that it would be prejudiced by the withdrawal); with *United States v. Saft,* 558 F.2d 1073 (2d Cir.1977) (there is no occasion to inquire into the matter of prejudice unless the defendant first shows good reason for being allowed to withdraw his plea). Though there remains variation at the state level, *Saft* now prevails in the federal courts. As explained in *United States v. Barker,* 514 F.2d 208 (D.C.Cir.1975): "Were withdrawal automatic in every case where the defendant decided to alter his tactics and present his theory of the case to the jury, the guilty plea would become a mere gesture, a temporary and meaningless formality reversible at the defendant's whim. In fact, however, a guilty plea is no such trifle, but 'a grave and solemn act,' which is 'accepted only with care and discernment.' "

4. In *United States v. Hyde,* 520 U.S. 670, 117 S.Ct. 1630, 137 L.Ed.2d 935 (1997), defendant and the government entered into a plea agreement whereby if defendant pleaded guilty to four of the counts in the indictment the government would dismiss the other four. The agreement was submitted to the district court, which accepted defendant's guilty plea but stated it was deferring decision on acceptance of the plea agreement pending completion of the presentence report. A month later, before sentencing and before the court's decision on the plea agreement, defendant sought to withdraw his plea, but his motion was denied because he had not provided a "fair and just reason." The court of appeals reversed, reasoning that defendant had an absolute right to withdraw his guilty plea before the court accepted the plea agreement because the plea and the agreement are "inextricably bound up together," so that the district court's deferral of acceptance of the plea agreement also constituted a deferral of the decision whether to accept the guilty plea. A unanimous Supreme Court, per Chief Justice Rehnquist, disagreed, noting that the court of appeals' conclusion was contradicted by Fed.R.Crim.P. 11(e)(4), which states the defendant may withdraw his plea as a matter of right only if "the court rejects the plea agreement" (which did not happen in the instant case). Moreover, the Court emphasized, the court of appeals' holding "debases the judicial proceeding at which a defendant pleads and the court accepts his plea" and "would degrade the otherwise serious act of pleading guilty into something akin to a move in a game of chess."

5. Should a withdrawn plea be admissible against the defendant at his subsequent trial? Some jurisdictions earlier ruled in the affirmative on the ground that the plea is a fact inconsistent with the defendant's claim of innocence, but the modern cases have consistently adopted the view that the withdrawal of the plea adjudicates the impropriety of its prior reception and thus forbids any subsequent evidentiary use of it.[h]

F. Significance of Noncompliance With Requirements for Receiving Guilty Plea

1. In McCARTHY v. UNITED STATES, 394 U.S. 459, 89 S.Ct. 1166, 22 L.Ed.2d 418 (1969), the trial judge failed to address the defendant personally and determine that his plea was made voluntarily and with an understanding of the nature of the charge, as required by Rule 11. The Court, per Chief Justice WARREN, rejected the government's contention that under such circumstances the government should still be allowed to prove that the defendant in fact pleaded voluntarily and with an understanding of the charge:

"From the defendant's perspective, the efficacy of shifting the burden of proof to the Government at a later voluntariness hearing is questionable. In meeting its burden, the Government will undoubtedly rely upon the defendant's statement that he desired to plead guilty and frequently a statement that the plea was not induced by any threats or promises. This prima facie case for voluntariness is likely to be treated as irrebuttable in cases such as this one, where the defendant's reply is limited to his own plaintive allegations that he did not understand the nature of the charge and therefore failed to assert a valid défense or to limit his guilty plea only to a lesser included offense. No matter how true these allegations may be, rarely, if ever, can a defendant corroborate them in a post-plea voluntariness hearing. * * *

"We thus conclude that prejudice inheres in a failure to comply with Rule 11, for noncompliance deprives the defendant of the Rule's procedural safeguards, which are designed to facilitate a more accurate determination of the voluntariness of his plea. Our holding that a defendant whose plea has been accepted in violation of Rule 11 should be afforded the opportunity to plead anew not only will insure that every accused is afforded those procedural safeguards, but also will help reduce the great waste of judicial resources required to process the frivolous attacks on guilty plea convictions that are encouraged, and are more difficult to dispose of, when the original record is inadequate."

2. In UNITED STATES v. TIMMRECK, 441 U.S. 780, 99 S.Ct. 2085, 60 L.Ed.2d 634 (1979), the trial judge explained to the defendant who tendered a guilty plea that he could receive a sentence of 15 years imprisonment and a $25,000 fine, but failed to describe the mandatory special parole term of at least 3 years. The judge then accepted the plea and sentenced defendant to 10 years imprisonment, plus a special parole term of 5 years and a fine of $5,000. The defendant raised no objection to the sentence at the time, and did not take an appeal. About two years later, defendant collaterally attacked his plea in a 28 U.S.C. § 2255 proceeding on the ground that the judge had violated Rule 11 by not informing him of the mandatory special parole term. The district court concluded the Rule 11 violation did not entitle defendant to § 2255 relief because he had not suffered any prejudice, inasmuch as his sentence was within the maximum described to him when the plea was accepted. But the Court of Appeals

h. Compare the situation as to the admissibility of a tendered guilty plea, discussed in Note 9, p. 1255.

held that "a Rule 11 violation is per se prejudicial" and thus a basis for relief via § 2255. STEVENS, J., relying upon the limits on § 2255 relief set out in *Hill v. United States,* 368 U.S. 424, 82 S.Ct. 468, 7 L.Ed.2d 417 (1962), stated for a unanimous Court:

"The reasoning in *Hill* is equally applicable to a formal violation of Rule 11. Such a violation is neither constitutional nor jurisdictional: the 1966 amendment to Rule 11 obviously could not amend the Constitution or limit the jurisdiction of the federal courts. Nor can any claim reasonably be made that the error here resulted in a 'complete miscarriage of justice' or in a proceeding 'inconsistent with the rudimentary demands of fair procedure.' Respondent does not argue that he was actually unaware of the special parole term or that, if he had been properly advised by the trial judge, he would not have pleaded guilty. His only claim is of a technical violation of the rule. That claim could have been raised on direct appeal, see *McCarthy v. United States,* but was not. * * *

"Indeed, if anything, this case may be a stronger one for foreclosing collateral relief than the *Hill* case. For the concern with finality served by the limitation on collateral attack has special force with respect to convictions based on guilty pleas. * * *

"As in *Hill,* we find it unnecessary to consider whether § 2255 relief would be available if a violation of Rule 11 occurred in the context of other aggravating circumstances. 'We decide only that such collateral relief is not available when all that is shown is a failure to comply with the formal requirements of the Rule.'"

3. It was disputed for a time whether *McCarthy* and *Timmreck* meant that any "technical violation" of Rule 11 required reversal on direct appeal. See, e.g., the several opinions in *United States v. Dayton,* 604 F.2d 931 (5th Cir.1979). The matter was later resolved by the addition of paragraph (h) to Fed.R.Crim.P. 11.

4. State courts are not in complete agreement as to the significance of noncompliance with state provisions similar to Federal Rule 11. However, most of the recent cases follow the *Timmreck* approach.

5. *Boykin v. Alabama,* p. 1294, concerned a defendant who had pleaded guilty in state court to five armed robbery indictments and thereafter received the death penalty. At arraignment, "so far as the record shows, the judge asked no questions of petitioner concerning his plea, and petitioner did not address the court." The Supreme Court reversed, concluding that it "was error, plain on the face of the record, for the trial judge to accept petitioner's guilty plea without an affirmative showing that it was intelligent and voluntary." But in *North Carolina v. Alford,* p. 1295, the Court noted in footnote 3: "At the state court hearing on post-conviction relief, the testimony confirmed that Alford has been fully informed by his attorney as to his rights on a plea of not guilty and as to the consequences of a plea of guilty. Since the record in this case affirmatively indicates that Alford was aware of the consequences of his plea of guilty and of the rights waived by the plea, no issues of substance under *Boykin v. Alabama* would be presented even if that case was held applicable to the events here in question."

As for a state defendant's challenge of his plea on federal habeas corpus, typical is *Riggins v. McMackin,* 935 F.2d 790 (6th Cir.1991), holding that if the record shows that the trial judge failed to inform defendant of the maximum possible penalty, then a hearing is required at which petitioner "not only must demonstrate that he was not informed by counsel as to his maximum possible sentence, but also that he would not have otherwise pleaded guilty."

6. In 1986 Raley was charged with robbery and with having two prior felony convictions (based on 1979 and 1981 guilty pleas) necessitating a mandatory minimum sentence. Under the applicable state procedure, the state had to prove the *fact* of the prior convictions, after which the defendant could attack their validity.[i] Though the ultimate burden of persuasion rested with the prosecution, the defendant was first obligated to produce evidence of the invalidity of those pleas. Because the record contained no transcripts of those guilty plea proceedings, Raley claimed this was inconsistent with *Boykin's* statement that the waiver of rights essential to a valid plea cannot be presumed "from a silent record." In *Parke v. Raley,* 506 U.S. 20, 113 S.Ct. 517, 121 L.Ed.2d 391 (1992), the Court disagreed:

"We see no tension between the Kentucky scheme and *Boykin. Boykin* involved direct review of a conviction allegedly based upon an uninformed guilty plea. Respondent, however, never appealed his earlier convictions. They became final years ago, and he now seeks to revisit the question of their validity in a separate recidivism proceeding. To import *Boykin's* presumption of invalidity into this very different context would, in our view, improperly ignore another presumption deeply rooted in our jurisprudence: the "presumption of regularity" that attaches to final judgments, even when the question is waiver of constitutional rights."

The Court added that there was "no good reason to suspend the presumption of regularity here," as (i) the absence of a guilty plea transcript was not itself suspicious, as under the state's procedure transcripts are made only if a direct appeal is taken and stenographic notes and tapes are not preserved more than five years; and (ii) "*Boykin* colloquies have been required for nearly a quarter-century."

G. SIGNIFICANCE OF COMPLIANCE WITH REQUIREMENTS FOR RECEIVING GUILTY PLEA

1. Is the "logical converse" of *McCarthy* and *Boykin* that if the trial judge does have the defendant indicate for the record that his plea is voluntary and with knowledge of the charge and the consequences, then the defendant may not thereafter challenge his plea as being involuntary and unknowing? In *Fontaine v. United States,* 411 U.S. 213, 93 S.Ct. 1461, 36 L.Ed.2d 169 (1973), it was held that upon a federal defendant's motion under 28 U.S.C. § 2255 to vacate his sentence on the grounds that his plea of guilty had been induced by a combination of fear, coercive police tactics, and illness (including mental illness), a hearing was required "on this record" notwithstanding full compliance with Federal Rule 11, as § 2255 calls for a hearing unless "the motion and the files and records of the case conclusively show that the prisoner is entitled to no relief"; the objective of

---

i. As for the possibility of permitting *no* challenge of prior guilty pleas during sentencing following a later conviction, consider *Custis v. United States,* 511 U.S. 485, 114 S.Ct. 1732, 128 L.Ed.2d 517 (1994). The Court there held that it is constitutionally permissible to bar, as in the Armed Career Criminal Act, 18 U.S.C. § 924(e), virtually all collateral attacks upon prior state convictions being used for sentence enhancement in a federal trial. While a defendant may raise the "unique constitutional defect" of "failure to appoint counsel for an indigent defendant," challenge of other constitutional defects, such as an invalid guilty plea, may constitutionally be barred entirely in this setting. "Ease of administration" and the "interest in promoting the finality of judgments" (said to "bear extra weight in cases in which the prior convictions, such as the ones challenged by Custis, are based on guilty pleas") were the considerations relied upon by the *Custis* Court in support of that conclusion.

Custis, which had to do with challenging the state guilty plea conviction at the federal sentencing proceeding, was later deemed equally applicable upon a motion to vacate, set aside or correct a federal sentence pursuant to 28 U.S.C. § 2255 because the considerations stressed in *Custis* are likewise present in a § 2255 context. *Daniels v. United States,* 532 U.S. 374, 121 S.Ct. 1578, 149 L.Ed.2d 590 (2001). *Daniels* was in turn extended to cover § 2254 petitions directed at enhanced state sentences. *Lackawanna County District Attorney v. Coss,* 532 U.S. 394, 121 S.Ct. 1567, 149 L.Ed.2d 608 (2001).

Rule 11 "is to flush out and resolve all such issues, but like any procedural mechanism, its exercise is neither always perfect nor uniformly invulnerable to subsequent challenge calling for an opportunity to prove the allegations."

2. Allison, indicted in North Carolina for breaking and entering, attempted safe robbery and possession of burglary tools, pled guilty to the second charge. The judge in taking the plea read from a printed form 13 questions, each of which Allison answered as required for acceptance of the plea. He responded in the affirmative to the question, "Do you understand that upon your plea of guilty you could be imprisoned for as much as minimum [sic] of 10 years to life?"; and no to the question, "Has the Solicitor, or your lawyer, or any policeman, law officer or anyone else made any promises or threats to you to influence you to plead guilty in this case?" The only record of the proceedings was the executed form. The judge accepted the plea and at a later unrecorded sentencing hearing sentenced Allison to 17–21 years in prison. After exhausting his state remedies, Allison sought relief via federal habeas corpus, alleging that his attorney had told him an agreement had been reached with the prosecutor and judge whereby if he pleaded guilty he would get only 10 years, and that his attorney had cautioned him he should nonetheless answer the questions of the judge as he did. The district court denied the petition on the ground that the form "conclusively shows" no constitutional violation and thus met the standard of *Fontaine,* but the court of appeals reversed. In BLACKLEDGE v. ALLISON, 431 U.S. 63, 97 S.Ct. 1621, 52 L.Ed.2d 136 (1977), the Court, per STEWART, J., affirmed. After noting the several benefits of negotiated pleas and that they "can be secured * * * only if dispositions by guilty plea are accorded a great measure of finality," he continued:

"The allegations in this case were not in themselves so 'vague [or] conclusory,' as to warrant dismissal for that reason alone. Allison alleged as a ground for relief that his plea was induced by an unkept promise. But he did not stop there. He proceeded to elaborate upon this claim with specific factual allegations. The petition indicated exactly what the terms of the promise were; when, where, and by whom the promise had been made; and the identity of one witness to its communication. The critical question is whether these allegations, when viewed against the record of the plea hearing, were so 'palpably incredible,' so 'patently frivolous or false', as to warrant summary dismissal. In the light of the nature of the record of the proceeding at which the guilty plea was accepted, and of the ambiguous status of the process of plea bargaining at the time the guilty plea was made, we conclude that Allison's petition should not have been summarily dismissed.

"Only recently has plea bargaining become a visible practice accepted as a legitimate component in the administration of criminal justice. For decades it was a *sub rosa* process shrouded in secrecy and deliberately concealed by participating defendants, defense lawyers, prosecutors, and even judges. Indeed, it was not until our decision in *Santobello v. New York* [p. 1260 supra], that lingering doubts about the legitimacy of the practice were finally dispelled.

"Allison was arraigned a mere 37 days after the *Santobello* decision was announced, under a North Carolina procedure that had not been modified in light of *Santobello* or earlier decisions of this Court recognizing the process of plea bargaining. That procedure itself reflected the atmosphere of secrecy which then characterized plea bargaining generally. No transcript of the proceeding was made. The only record was a standard printed form. There is no way of knowing whether the trial judge in any way deviated from or supplemented the text of the form. The record is silent as to what statements Allison, his lawyer, or the prosecutor might have made regarding promised sentencing concessions. And there is no record at all of the sentencing hearing three days later, at which one of the participants might well have made a statement shedding light upon the veracity of the allegations Allison later advanced.

"The litany of form questions followed by the trial judge at arraignment nowhere indicated to Allison (or indeed to the lawyers involved) that plea bargaining was a legitimate practice that could be freely disclosed in open court. Neither lawyer was asked to disclose any agreement that had been reached, or sentencing recommendation that had been promised. The process thus did nothing to dispel a defendant's belief that any bargain struck must remain concealed—a belief here allegedly reinforced by the admonition of Allison's lawyer himself that disclosure could jeopardize the agreement. Rather than challenging counsel's contention at oral argument in this Court that 'at that time in North Carolina plea bargains were never disclosed in response to such a question on such a form,' counsel for the State conceded at oral argument that '[t]he form was a minimal inquiry.'

"Although '[l]ogically the general inquiry should elicit information about plea bargaining, * * * it seldom has in the past.' Advisory Committee Note to 1974 Amendment of Fed.Rule Crim.Proc. 11. Particularly if, as Allison alleged, he was advised by counsel to conceal any plea bargain, his denial that any promises had been made might have been a courtroom ritual more sham than real. We thus cannot conclude that the allegations in Allison's habeas corpus petition, when measured against the 'record' of the arraignment, were so 'patently false or frivolous' as to warrant summary dismissal.

"North Carolina has recently undertaken major revisions of its plea bargaining procedures in part to prevent the very kind of problem now before us. Plea bargaining is expressly legitimate. The judge is directed to advise the defendant that courts have approved plea bargaining and he may thus admit to any promises without fear of jeopardizing an advantageous agreement or prejudicing himself in the judge's eyes. Specific inquiry about whether a plea bargain has been struck is then made not only of the defendant, but also of his counsel and the prosecutor. Finally, the entire proceeding is to be transcribed verbatim.

"Had these commendable procedures been followed in the present case, Allison's petition would have been cast in a very different light. The careful explication of the legitimacy of plea bargaining, the questioning of both lawyers, and the verbatim record of their answers at the guilty plea proceedings would almost surely have shown whether any bargain did exist and, if so, insured that it was not ignored. But the salutary reforms recently implemented by North Carolina highlight even more sharply the deficiencies in the record before the District Court in the present case.

"This is not to say that every set of allegations not on its face without merit entitles a habeas corpus petitioner to an evidentiary hearing. As in civil cases generally, there exists a procedure whose purpose is to test whether facially adequate allegations have sufficient basis in fact to warrant plenary presentation of evidence. That procedure is, of course, the motion for summary judgment. Upon remand the Warden will be free to make such a motion, supporting it with whatever proof he wishes to attach. If he chooses to do so, Allison will then be required either to produce some contrary proof indicating that there is a genuine issue of fact to be resolved by the District Court or to explain his inability to provide such proof."

3. Are more elaborate procedures along the lines of present federal Rule 11 sufficient to foreclose a later attack upon a guilty plea? Note, 86 Yale L.J. 1395, 1410, 1421 (1977), concludes that this comprehensive hearing "can succeed in eliminating later hearings when attacks are made on the knowing and intelligent character of a plea," but "cannot eliminate the need for post conviction hearings when attacks are directed at events that transpired outside the Rule 11 hearing," such as when it is claimed a plea was influenced by secret government promises, as "any government coercion powerful enough to induce a defendant to plead guilty and thus consent to immediate conviction would surely be powerful enough to obtain untruthful answers to questions about the plea." Compare *Richardson v. United States,* 577 F.2d 447 (8th Cir.1978), concluding that where the defendant sought § 2255 relief on the ground that his guilty plea was induced by an unkept promise of the prosecutor that he would receive not more than 7 years, but the rule 11 record indicated defendant had said no promises had been made about his sentence, no hearing was required because "Richardson has offered no plausible excuse for his statements denying the existence of a promise as to the length of his sentence."

4. Is there any way to take a guilty plea which will completely immunize it from subsequent attack? Consider *Model Pre–Arraignment Code* § 350.6: "The court after pronouncing the sentence of a defendant who has pleaded guilty or nolo contendere shall inquire of the defendant personally whether the sentence pronounced violates any agreement or understanding the defendant had with respect to the sentence."

SECTION 5. THE EFFECT OF A GUILTY PLEA: MORE ON THE EFFECTIVE ASSISTANCE OF COUNSEL AND THE WAIVER (OR FORFEITURE) OF RIGHTS

When a defendant's conviction is grounded in a plea of guilty rather than a verdict or finding of guilt after trial, the range of issues which may thereafter be raised in an effort to overturn that conviction is quite limited. In a series of cases over the years, the Supreme Court has experienced difficulty in explaining how this limitation should be stated and why:

1. In McMANN v. RICHARDSON, 397 U.S. 759, 90 S.Ct. 1441, 25 L.Ed.2d 763 (1970), the Court, per WHITE, J., stated:

"The core of the Court of Appeals' holding is the proposition that if in a collateral proceeding a guilty plea is shown to have been triggered by a coerced confession—if there would have been no plea had there been no confession—the plea is vulnerable at least in cases coming from New York where the guilty plea was taken prior to *Jackson v. Denno,* [p. 811]. We are unable to agree with the Court of Appeals in this proposition. * * *

"For present purposes, we put aside those cases where the defendant has his own reasons for pleading guilty wholly aside from the strength of the case against him as well as those cases where the defendant, although he would have gone to trial had he thought the State could not prove its case, is motivated by evidence against him independent of the confession. In these cases, as the Court of Appeals recognized, the confession, even if coerced, is not a sufficient factor in the plea to justify relief. Neither do we have before us the uncounselled defendant, nor the situation where the circumstances that coerced the confession have abiding impact and also taint the plea. It is not disputed that in such cases a guilty plea is properly open to challenge.

"The issue on which we differ with the Court of Appeals arises in those situations involving the counselled defendant who allegedly would put the State to its proof if there was a substantial enough chance of acquittal, who would do so except for a prior confession which might be offered against him, and who because of the confession decides to plead guilty to save himself the expense and agony of a trial and perhaps also to minimize the penalty which might be imposed. After conviction on such a plea, is a defendant entitled to a hearing, and to relief if his factual claims are accepted, when his petition for habeas corpus alleges that his confession was in fact coerced and that it motivated his plea? We think not if he alleges and proves no more than this.

"Since we are dealing with a defendant who deems his confession crucial to the State's case against him and who would go to trial if he thought his chances of acquittal were good, his decision to plead guilty or not turns on whether he thinks the law will allow his confession to be used against him. For the defendant who considers his confession involuntary and hence unusable against him at a trial, tendering a plea of guilty would seem a most improbable alternative. * * * [A] guilty plea in such circumstances is nothing less than a refusal to present his federal claims to the state court in the first instance—a choice by the defendant to take the benefits, if any, of a plea of guilty and then to pursue his coerced confession claim in collateral proceedings. Surely later allegations that the confession rendered his plea involuntary would appear incredible, and whether his plain bypass of state remedies was an intelligent act depends on whether he was so incompetently advised by counsel concerning the forum in which he should first present his federal claim that the Constitution will afford him another chance to plead.

"A more credible explanation for a plea of guilty by a defendant who would go to trial except for his prior confession is his prediction that the law will permit his admissions to be used against him by the trier of fact. At least the probability of the State's being permitted to use the confession as evidence is sufficient to convince him that the State's case is too strong to contest and that a plea of guilty is the most advantageous course. Nothing in this train of events suggests that the defendant's plea, as distinguished from his confession, is an involuntary act. His later petition for collateral relief asserting that a *coerced* confession induced his plea is at most a claim that the admissibility of his confession was mistakenly assessed and that since he was erroneously advised, either under the then applicable law or under the law later announced, his plea was an unintelligent and voidable act. The Constitution, however, does not render pleas of guilty so vulnerable.

"As we said in *Brady v. United States* [p. 1250], the decision to plead guilty before the evidence is in frequently involves the making of difficult judgments. All the pertinent facts normally cannot be known unless witnesses are examined and cross-examined in court. Even then the truth will often be in dispute. In the face of unavoidable uncertainty, the defendant and his counsel must make their best judgment as to the weight of the State's case. Counsel must predict how the facts, as he understands them, would be viewed by a court. If proved, would those facts convince a judge or jury of the defendant's guilt? On those facts would evidence seized without a warrant be admissible? Would the trier of fact on those facts find a confession voluntary and admissible? Questions like these cannot be answered with certitude; yet a decision to plead guilty must necessarily rest upon counsel's answers, uncertain as they may be. Waiving trial entails the inherent risk that the good-faith evaluations of a reasonably competent attorney will turn out to be mistaken either as to the facts or as to what a court's judgment might be on given facts.

"That a guilty plea must be intelligently made is not a requirement that all advice offered by the defendant's lawyer withstand retrospective examination in a post-conviction hearing. Courts and judges continue to have serious differences among themselves on the admissibility of evidence, both with respect to the proper standard by which the facts are to be judged and with respect to the application of that standard to particular facts. That this Court might hold a defendant's confession inadmissible in evidence, possibly by a divided vote, hardly justifies a conclusion that the defendant's attorney was incompetent or ineffective when he thought the admissibility of the confession sufficiently probable to advise a plea of guilty.[a]

"In our view a defendant's plea of guilty based on reasonably competent advice is an intelligent plea not open to attack on the grounds that counsel may have misjudged the admissibility of the defendant's confession. Whether a plea of guilty is unintelligent and therefore vulnerable when motivated by a confession erroneously thought admissible in evidence depends as an initial matter not on whether a court would retrospectively consider counsel's advice to be right or wrong, but on whether that advice was within the range of competence demanded of attorneys in criminal cases."[b]

2. In TOLLETT v. HENDERSON, 411 U.S. 258, 93 S.Ct. 1602, 36 L.Ed.2d 235 (1973), respondent, who pleaded guilty to murder on advice of counsel, sought federal collateral relief because the indicting grand jury was unconstitutionally selected. He distinguished the *Brady* trilogy (*Brady, Parker* and *McMann*) because in those cases (in contrast to the instant case) the defendants and their attorneys were aware of the facts giving rise to the constitutional claims before the guilty pleas were entered. REHNQUIST, J., for the Court, responded: "If the issue were to be cast solely in terms of 'waiver,' the Court of Appeals was undoubtedly correct in concluding that there had been no such waiver here. But just as the guilty pleas in the *Brady* trilogy were found to foreclose direct inquiry into the merits of claimed antecedent constitutional violations there, we conclude that respondent's guilty plea here alike forecloses independent inquiry into the claim of discrimination in the selection of the grand jury. * * *[c]

"A guilty plea, voluntarily and intelligently entered, may not be vacated because the defendant was not advised of every conceivable constitutional plea in abatement he might have to the charge, no matter how peripheral such a plea might be to the normal focus of counsel's inquiry. And just as it is not sufficient for the criminal defendant seeking to set aside such a plea to show that his counsel in retrospect may not have correctly appraised the constitutional significance of certain historical facts, *McMann*, it is likewise not sufficient that he show that if counsel had pursued a certain factual inquiry such a pursuit would have uncovered a possible constitutional infirmity in the proceedings.

---

a. In the companion case of *Parker v. North Carolina*, p. 1251, where the defendant told his attorney that his pre-*Miranda* confession after overnight detention "had not been prompted by threats or promises and that he had not been frightened when he made the statement to the police," and "counsel apparently deemed the confession admissible and his advice to plead guilty was followed by his client," the Court applied *McMann* and concluded that the advice Parker received "was well within the range of competence required of attorneys representing defendants in criminal cases."

b. Three Justices dissented, objecting to what they characterized as "nothing less than the determination of the Court to preserve the sanctity of virtually all judgments obtained by means of guilty pleas."

Later, in *Hill v. Lockhart*, 474 U.S. 52, 106 S.Ct. 366, 88 L.Ed.2d 203 (1985), the Court held "that the two-part *Strickland v. Washington* [p. 1120] test applies to challenges to guilty pleas based on ineffective assistance of counsel.

In the context of guilty pleas, the first half of the *Strickland v. Washington* test is nothing more than a restatement of the standard of attorney competence already set forth in *Tollett v. Henderson* and *McMann v. Richardson*. The second, or 'prejudice,' requirement, on the other hand, focuses on whether counsel's constitutionally ineffective performance affected the outcome of the plea process. In other words, in order to satisfy the 'prejudice' requirement, the defendant must show that there is a reasonable probability that, but for counsel's errors, he would not have pleaded guilty and would have insisted on going to trial."

c. Noting that *Tollett* and later cases "did not rest on any principle of waiver," the Court held in *Haring v. Prosise*, 462 U.S. 306, 103 S.Ct. 2368, 76 L.Ed.2d 595 (1983), that defendant's guilty plea was no bar to his damages action under 42 U.S.C. § 1983 for the prior violation of his constitutional rights.

"The principal value of counsel to the accused in a criminal prosecution often lies not in counsel's ability to recite a list of possible defenses in the abstract, nor in his ability, if time permitted, to amass a large quantum of factual data and inform the defendant of it. Counsel's concern is the faithful representation of the interest of his client, and such representation frequently involves highly practical considerations as well as specialized knowledge of the law. Often the interests of the accused are not advanced by challenges that would only delay the inevitable date of prosecution, or by contesting all guilt. A prospect of plea bargaining, the expectation or hope of a lesser sentence, or the convincing nature of the evidence against the accused are considerations that might well suggest the advisability of a guilty plea without elaborate consideration of whether pleas in abatement, such as unconstitutional grand jury selection procedures, might be factually supported.

"In order to obtain his release on federal habeas under these circumstances, respondent must not only establish the unconstitutional discrimination in selection of grand jurors. He must also establish that his attorney's advice to plead guilty without having made inquiry into the composition of the grand jury rendered that advice outside the 'range of competence demanded of attorneys in criminal cases.'"

MARSHALL, J., joined by Douglas and Brennan, JJ., dissented: "If plea bargaining is to be constitutionally acceptable, it must rest upon personal choices made by defendants informed about possible alternatives; at least, they should know what options are open to them. In this case, Henderson might have secured a sentence shorter than 99 years by requiring the State to defend the constitutionality of its procedures for selecting grand juries. As is clear from this record, such a defense could not have succeeded, and the embarrassment of attempting a defense might well have led the prosecution to offer a more favorable bargain.[3] I find nothing in the opinion of the Court that persuades me that Henderson's attorney acted 'within the range of competence demanded of attorneys in criminal cases,' *McMann v. Richardson*, because he did not consult with his client on a matter about which consultation is required."

3. In MENNA v. NEW YORK, 423 U.S. 61, 96 S.Ct. 241, 46 L.Ed.2d 195 (1975), the Court, per curiam, held that the defendant's previously asserted claim that his indictment should be dismissed as in violation of the double jeopardy clause was not thereafter "waived" by his counseled plea of guilty to the charge. The Court observed in footnote 2:

"Neither *Tollett v. Henderson* nor our earlier cases on which it relied, *e.g.*, *Brady v. United States* and *McMann v. Richardson*, stand for the proposition that counseled guilty pleas inevitably 'waive' all antecedent constitutional violations. If they did so hold, the New York Court of Appeals might be correct. However in *Tollett* we emphasized that waiver was not the basic ingredient of this line of cases. The point of these cases is that a counseled plea of guilty is an admission of factual guilt so reliable that, where voluntary and intelligent, it *quite validly* removes the issue of factual guilt from the case. In most cases, factual guilt is a sufficient basis for the State's imposition of punishment. A guilty plea, therefore, simply renders irrelevant those constitutional violations not logically inconsistent with the valid establishment of factual guilt and which do not stand in the way of conviction if factual guilt is validly established. Here, however, the claim is that the State may not convict petitioner no matter how validly his factual guilt is established. The guilty plea, therefore does not bar the claim.

---

3. Even if the State successfully defended its procedures in a preliminary attack, or if it decided to institute proceedings anew by convening a new grand jury, Henderson would have secured time in which to prepare a better defense and in which passions over his offense might subside, so that a plea of not guilty might have been more attractive to him.

"We do not hold that a double jeopardy claim may never be waived. We simply hold that a plea of guilty to a charge does not waive a claim that—judged on its face—the charge is one which the State may not constitutionally prosecute."[d]

4. Consider also BLACKLEDGE v. PERRY, p. 891. Following his conviction of misdemeanor assault in the district court, Perry asserted his statutory right to trial de novo in the superior court, which prompted the prosecutor to escalate the charge to felony assault. After ruling that "such a potential for vindictiveness" violated due process, the Court held Perry was not precluded from raising the claim by his guilty plea to the felony charge: "While the petitioner's reliance upon the *Tollett* opinion is understandable, there is a fundamental distinction between this case and that one. Although the underlying claims presented in *Tollett* and the *Brady* trilogy were of constitutional dimension, none went to the very power of the State to bring the defendant into court to answer the charge brought against him. The defendants in *McMann v. Richardson,* for example, could surely have been brought to trial without the use of the allegedly coerced confessions, and even a tainted indictment of the sort alleged in *Tollett* could have been 'cured' through a new indictment by a properly selected grand jury. In the case at hand, by contrast, the nature of the underlying constitutional infirmity is markedly different. * * * Unlike the defendant in *Tollett,* Perry is not complaining of 'antecedent constitutional violations' or of a 'deprivation of constitutional rights that occurred prior to the entry of the guilty plea.' Rather, the right that he asserts and that we today accept is the right not to be hailed into court at all upon the felony charge. The very initiation of the proceedings against him in the Superior Court thus operated to deny him due process of law."

Justice REHNQUIST, joined by Justice Powell, disagreed: "I believe this case is governed by cases culminating in *Tollett v. Henderson.* In that case the state no doubt lacked power to bring Henderson to trial without a valid grand jury indictment; yet that constitutional disability was held by us to be merged in the guilty plea. I do not see why a constitutional claim the consequences of which make it the identical twin of double jeopardy may not, like double jeopardy, be

---

d. Consider Peter Westen, *Away From Waiver: A Rationale for the Forfeiture of Constitutional Rights in Criminal Procedure,* 75 Mich.L.Rev. 1214, 1223, 1234–35 (1977): "[T]he *Menna* footnote is inconsistent with the Court's own cases. In *Tollett,* for example, the defendant was asserting a claim that was independent of his factual guilt: the right of the accused to be charged by a process that is free from racial discrimination is a right that exists without regard to whether the defendant himself is guilty; even if he is guilty, he can challenge his conviction on the ground that other defendants who are similarly situated except for their racial background are not being prosecuted. Thus, by the standard of *Menna,* the defendant in *Tollett* should have been permitted to assert his defense of equal protection; yet the Court there held that he had forfeited the defense by pleading guilty. * * *

"[I]n deciding that the guilty plea in *Menna* operated as a forfeiture only of defenses relating to factual guilt, the Court made a *constitutional* judgment: it held that insofar as state law provided for the forfeiture of a defense not relating to factual guilt, i.e., defenses relating to 'legal' guilt, the state law of forfeiture was unconstitutional. Thus, *Menna* stands for the proposition that for purposes of forfeiture, the states have constitutional authority to treat a guilty plea *as if* it is an admission of factual guilt, but not *as if* it is an admission of legal guilt.

"But the above merely restates, rather than justifies, the rule in *Menna.* The truly important questions remain to be answered. Why does the Constitution permit a state to treat a guilty plea as if it were a conclusive admission of factual guilt, contrary to our experience? Conversely, why does the Constitution forbid a state from treating a guilty plea as if it were also an admission of 'legal guilt?' If these 'legal' defenses can be waived (and the Court assumes they can), why does the Constitution prohibit a state from treating a guilty plea as if it were a final admission of legal guilt? Are the constitutional defenses relating to legal guilt more important than those relating to factual guilt? Is the defense of double jeopardy more important than the privilege against self-incrimination? These are the questions that must be answered if we are to assume that *Menna* is to be taken seriously as a new rule of forfeiture."

waived by the person for whose benefit it is accorded. [D]efendants as a class have at least as great an interest in the finality of voluntary guilty pleas as do prosecutors. If that finality may be swept aside with the ease exhibited by the Court's approach today, prosecutors will have a reduced incentive to bargain, to the detriment of the many defendants for whom plea bargaining offers the only hope for ameliorating the consequences to them of a serious criminal charge."

5. In UNITED STATES v. BROCE, 488 U.S. 563, 109 S.Ct. 757, 102 L.Ed.2d 927 (1989), the defendants pleaded guilty to two conspiracy indictments charging the rigging of bids on two highway projects. Later these defendants, relying on a ruling re defendants who had *not* pleaded guilty that only one conspiracy was involved, sought to vacate the conviction and sentence under the second indictment on double jeopardy principles. The Court, per KENNEDY, J., ruled that because the defendants "have not called into question the voluntary and intelligent character of their pleas, [they] therefore are not entitled to the collateral relief they seek. * * *

"In neither *Blackledge* nor *Menna* did the defendants seek further proceedings at which to expand the record with new evidence. In those cases, the determination that the second indictment could not go forward should have been made by the presiding judge at the time the plea was entered on the basis of the existing record. Both *Blackledge* and *Menna* could be (and ultimately were) resolved without any need to venture beyond that record. In *Blackledge*, the concessions implicit in the defendant's guilty plea were simply irrelevant, because the constitutional infirmity in the proceedings lay in the State's power to bring any indictment at all. In *Menna*, the indictment was facially duplicative of the earlier offense of which the defendant had been convicted and sentenced so that the admissions made by Menna's guilty plea could not conceivably be construed to extend beyond a redundant confession to the earlier offense.

"The respondents here, in contrast, pleaded guilty to indictments that on their face described separate conspiracies. They cannot prove their claim by relying on those indictments and the existing record. Indeed, as noted earlier, they cannot prove their claim without contradicting those indictments, and that opportunity is foreclosed by the admissions inherent in their guilty pleas. We therefore need not consider the degree to which the decision by an accused to enter into a plea *bargain* which incorporates concessions by the Government, such as the one agreed to here, heightens the already substantial interest the Government has in the finality of the plea."

BLACKMUN, J., joined by Brennan and Marshall, JJ., dissenting, reasoned that "if a claim that the Government was without power to prosecute is apparent on the face of the indictment, read in light of the existing record, a court should not consider the claim to have been waived, and must go on to consider its merits. This interpretation is true to the outcome in both *Menna* and *Blackledge*. It also gives appropriate force to the footnote's language and its apparent purpose of placing some limit on the ability of a defendant who has pleaded guilty to make a later collateral attack without some foundation in the prior proceedings. Most important, it gives real content to the defendants' constitutional rights."

6. In BOUSLEY v. UNITED STATES, 523 U.S. 614, 118 S.Ct. 1604, 140 L.Ed.2d 828 (1998), Bousley pleaded guilty to drug possession with intent to distribute and also to "using" a firearm "during and in relation to a drug trafficking crime" in violation of 18 U.S.C. § 924(c)(1). On appeal, he did not challenge the plea's validity, but later sought habeas relief on the ground that his plea lacked a factual basis; the district court dismissed his petition. While his appeal was pending, the Supreme Court held in *Bailey v. United States*, 516 U.S. 137, 116 S.Ct. 501, 133 L.Ed.2d 472 (1995), that a conviction for using a firearm under § 924(c)(1) requires proof of "active employment of the firearm." The court of appeals held Bousley could not obtain relief based on *Bailey,* but the Supreme Court concluded this was not necessarily so. The Court concluded there was no nonretroactivity problem because *Bailey* had decided what the statute had always meant, and that Bousley could prevail on habeas regarding an issue not previously raised if on remand he showed he was "actually innocent" [see p. 1602].

Regarding the merits of Bousley's claim, "that his guilty plea was unintelligent" because he was misinformed as to the elements of a § 924 (c)(1) offense, and, indeed, "that the record reveals that neither he, nor his counsel, nor the court correctly understood the essential elements of the crime with which he was charged," the Court, per REHNQUIST, C.J., agreed that if this contention were proven it would make his guilty plea "constitutionally invalid." As for *Brady, McMann* and *Parker,* they "are not to the contrary. Each of those cases involve a criminal defendant who pleaded guilty after being correctly informed as to the essential nature of the charge against him .. Those defendants later attempted to challenge their guilty pleas when it became evident that they had misjudged the strength of the Government's case or the penalties to which they were subject. * * * In this case, by contrast, petitioner asserts that he was misinformed as to the true nature of the charge against him."

7. In some jurisdictions, defendants may enter a "conditional" plea of guilty and thereafter raise certain issues on appeal that otherwise would be barred. See, e.g., Fed.R.Crim.P. 11(a). Are such provisions desirable? What effect do they likely have upon plea bargaining? If, in the absence of such a provision, a defendant pleads guilty but expressly reserves his right to appeal from a prior denial of his suppression motion, as in *United States v. Cox,* 464 F.2d 937 (6th Cir.1972), what should the appellate court do?

Chapter 23

TRIAL BY JURY

SECTION 1. RIGHT TO JURY TRIAL; WAIVER

In DUNCAN v. LOUISIANA, 391 U.S. 145, 88 S.Ct. 1444, 20 L.Ed.2d 491 (1968), the Court concluded that "trial by jury in criminal cases is fundamental to the American scheme of justice," and thus held "that the Fourteenth Amendment guarantees a right of jury trial in all criminal cases which—were they to be tried in a federal court—would come within the Sixth Amendment's guarantee." In support, WHITE, J., reasoned:

"The guarantees of jury trial in the Federal and State Constitutions reflect a profound judgment about the way in which law should be enforced and justice administered. A right to jury trial is granted to criminal defendants in order to prevent oppression by the Government. Those who wrote our constitutions knew from history and experience that it was necessary to protect against unfounded criminal charges brought to eliminate enemies and against judges too responsive to the voice of higher authority. The framers of the constitutions strove to create an independent judiciary but insisted upon further protection against arbitrary action. Providing an accused with the right to be tried by a jury of his peers gave him an inestimable safeguard against the corrupt or overzealous prosecutor and against the complaint, biased, or eccentric judge. If the defendant preferred the common-sense judgment of a jury to the more tutored but perhaps less sympathetic reaction of the single judge, he was to have it. Beyond this, the jury trial provisions in the Federal and State Constitutions reflect a fundamental decision about the exercise of official power—a reluctance to entrust plenary powers over the life and liberty of the citizen to one judge or to a group of judges. Fear of unchecked power, so typical of our State and Federal Governments in other respects, found expression in the criminal law in this insistence upon community participation in the determination of guilt or innocence. The deep commitment of the Nation to the right of jury trial in serious criminal cases as a defense against arbitrary law enforcement qualifies for protection under the Due Process Clause of the Fourteenth Amendment, and must therefore be respected by the States.

"Of course jury trial has 'its weaknesses and the potential for misuse,' *Singer v. United States* [p. 1319]. We are aware of the long debate, especially in this century, among those who write about the administration of justice, as to the wisdom of permitting untrained laymen to determine the facts in civil and criminal proceedings. Although the debate has been intense, with powerful voices on either side, most of the controversy has centered on the jury in civil cases. Indeed, some of the severest critics of civil juries acknowledge that the arguments for criminal juries are much stronger. In addition, at the heart of the dispute have been express or implicit assertions that juries are incapable of adequately understanding evidence or determining issues of fact, and that they are unpredictable, quixotic, and little better than a roll of dice. Yet, the most recent and exhaustive study of the jury in criminal cases concluded that juries do understand the evidence and come to sound conclusions in most of the cases presented to them

1311

and that when juries differ with the result at which the judge would have arrived, it is usually because they are serving some of the very purposes for which they were created and for which they are now employed."

HARLAN, J., joined by Stewart, J., dissenting because they could "see no reason why this Court should reverse the conviction of appellant, absent any suggestion that his particular trial was in fact unfair," added:

"The jury is of course not without virtues. It affords ordinary citizens a valuable opportunity to participate in a process of government, an experience fostering, one hopes, a respect for law. It eases the burden on judges by enabling them to share a part of their sometimes awesome responsibility. A jury may, at times, afford a higher justice by refusing to enforce harsh laws (although it necessarily does so haphazardly, raising the questions whether arbitrary enforcement of harsh laws is better than total enforcement, and whether the jury system is to be defended on the ground that jurors sometimes disobey their oaths). And the jury may, or may not, contribute desirably to the willingness of the general public to accept criminal judgments as just.

"It can hardly be gainsaid, however, that the principal original virtue of the jury trial—the limitations a jury imposes on a tyrannous judiciary—has largely disappeared. We no longer live in a medieval or colonial society. Judges enforce laws enacted by democratic decision, not by regal fiat. They are elected by the people or appointed by the people's elected officials, and are responsible not to a distant monarch alone but to reviewing courts, including this one.

"The jury system can also be said to have some inherent defects, which are multiplied by the emergence of the criminal law from the relative simplicity that existed when the jury system was devised. It is a cumbersome process, not only imposing great cost in time and money on both the State and the jurors themselves, but also contributing to delay in the machinery of justice. Untrained jurors are presumably less adept at reaching accurate conclusions of fact than judges, particularly if the issues are many or complex. And it is argued by some that trial by jury, far from increasing public respect for law, impairs it: the average man, it is said, reacts favorably neither to the notion that matters he knows to be complex are being decided by other average men, nor to the way the jury system distorts the process of adjudication."

NOTES ON THE DIMENSIONS OF
THE RIGHT TO JURY TRIAL

1. *Petty offenses. Duncan* noted in passing that "there is a category of petty crimes or offenses which is not subject to the Sixth Amendment jury trial provisions." In *Baldwin v. New York*, 399 U.S. 66, 90 S.Ct. 1886, 26 L.Ed.2d 437 (1970), where appellant had been denied a jury trial when convicted of a misdemeanor punishable by imprisonment up to one year, a 5–3 majority held that "no offense can be deemed 'petty' for purposes of the right to trial by jury where imprisonment for more than six months is authorized."[a] In *Blanton v. City of North Las Vegas*, 489 U.S. 538, 109 S.Ct. 1289, 103 L.Ed.2d 550 (1989), a unanimous Court declined to hold "that an offense carrying a maximum prison term of six months or less automatically qualifies as a 'petty' offense," but did

---

a. In criminal contempt cases the penalty actually imposed will govern if the legislature has made no judgment about the maximum penalty. See, e.g., *Frank v. United States*, 395 U.S. 147, 89 S.Ct. 1503, 23 L.Ed.2d 162 (1969). The distinction between a criminal contempt and a civil contempt, as to which there is no right to jury trial, is often difficult to draw. See *International Union, UMW v. Bagwell*, 512 U.S. 821, 114 S.Ct. 2552, 129 L.Ed.2d 642 (1994).

"find it appropriate to presume for purposes of the Sixth Amendment that society views such an offense as 'petty.' A defendant is entitled to jury trial in such circumstances only if he can demonstrate that any additional statutory penalties, viewed in conjunction with the maximum authorized period of incarceration, are so severe that they clearly reflect a legislative determination that the offense in question is a 'serious' one." The Court then concluded that petitioners, charged with driving under the influence, were not entitled to a jury trial where the maximum authorized prison sentence did not exceed six months and the possible additional penalty of a $1,000 fine "is well below the $5,000 level set by Congress in its most recent definition of a 'petty' offense, 18 U.S.C. § 1," and is not "out of step with state practice for offenses carrying prison sentences of six months or less."[b]

In *Lewis v. United States*, 518 U.S. 322, 116 S.Ct. 2163, 135 L.Ed.2d 590 (1996), petitioner argued "that, where a defendant is charged with multiple petty offenses in a single prosecution, the Sixth Amendment requires that the aggregate potential penalty be the basis for determining whether a jury trial is required." The Court disagreed, noting that per *Blanton* "we determine whether an offense is serious by looking to the judgment of the legislature," and the "fact that the petitioner was charged with two counts of a petty offense does not revise the legislative judgment as to the gravity of that particular offense."[c] Kennedy and Breyer, JJ., concurring, concluded that the right to jury trial extends to a person jointly tried for two or more petty offenses only if he is then "sentenced in one proceeding to more than six month's imprisonment," which is "a most serious deprivation of liberty"; mere conviction of the multiple petty offenses would not give rise to the jury trial right, however, as "convictions for petty offenses do not carry the same stigma as convictions for serious crimes." Stevens and Ginsburg, JJ., by comparison, agreed with petitioner's position, as they could "see no basis for assuming that the dishonor associated with multiple convictions for petty offenses is less than the dishonor associated with conviction of a single serious crime."

Given *Lewis*, if a petty offense were joined with a nonpetty offense for trial, would it be permissible to send only the nonpetty offense to the jury and leave the petty offense charge to be determined by the judge, as in *Berroa v. United States*, 763 A.2d 93 (D.C.App.2000)? Should it make any difference whether the petty offense is a lesser included offense of the nonpetty offense?

2. ***Size.*** In WILLIAMS v. FLORIDA, 399 U.S. 78, 90 S.Ct. 1893, 26 L.Ed.2d 446 (1970), holding that use of a 6-person jury "did not violate petitioner's Sixth Amendment rights," the Court emphasized that "the essential feature of a jury obviously lies in the interposition between the accused and his accuser of the common-sense judgment of a group of laymen, and in the community participation

[handwritten margin note: 6 person jury ok]

---

b. In *Muniz v. Hoffman*, 422 U.S. 454, 95 S.Ct. 2178, 45 L.Ed.2d 319 (1975), a labor union which collected dues from 13,000 members contended it was entitled to a jury trial in a criminal contempt proceeding resulting in the imposition of a fine of $10,000 on the union. The Court rejected the union's contention "that when a fine of this magnitude is imposed a contempt cannot be considered a petty offense," stating: "It is not difficult to grasp the proposition that six months in jail is a serious matter for any individual, but it is not tenable to argue that the possibility of a * * * fine [over the then statutory petty offense limit, $500] would be considered a serious risk to a large corporation or labor union."

c. As for petitioner's reliance on *Codispoti v. Pennsylvania*, 418 U.S. 506, 94 S.Ct. 2687, 41 L.Ed.2d 912 (1974), where the defendant was deemed entitled to jury trial because the aggregate penalties actually imposed exceeded six months, the Court distinguished that case on two grounds: (1) there "the legislature had not set a specific penalty for criminal contempt," in which case "courts use the severity of the penalty actually imposed as the measure of the character of the particular offense," and (2) the "benefit of a jury trial, '"as a protection against the arbitrary exercise of official power,"' 'was deemed particularly important in [the criminal contempt] context."

and shared responsibility which results from that group's determination of guilt or innocence. The performance of this role is not a function of the particular number of the body which makes up the jury. To be sure, the number should probably be large enough to promote group deliberation, free from outside attempts at intimidation, and to provide a fair possibility for obtaining a representative cross section of the community.[d] But we find little reason to think that these goals are in any meaningful sense less likely to be achieved when the jury numbers six, than when it numbers 12—particularly if the requirement of unanimity is retained.[e] And, certainly the reliability of the jury as a fact-finder hardly seems likely to be a function of its size.

"It might be suggested that the 12–man jury gives a defendant a greater advantage since he has more 'chances' of finding a juror who will insist on acquittal and thus prevent conviction. But the advantage might just as easily belong to the State, which also needs only one juror out of twelve insisting on guilt to prevent acquittal.[47] What few experiments have occurred—usually in the civil area—indicate that there is no discernible difference between the results reached by the two different-sized juries. In short, neither currently available evidence nor theory[49] suggests that the 12–man jury is necessarily more advantageous to the defendant than a jury composed of fewer members.

"Similarly, while in theory the number of viewpoints represented on a randomly selected jury ought to increase as the size of the jury increases, in practice the difference between the 12–man and the six-man jury in terms of the cross section of the community represented seems likely to be negligible. Even the 12–man jury cannot insure representation of every distinct voice in the community, particularly given the use of the peremptory challenge. As long as arbitrary exclusions of a particular class from the jury rolls are forbidden, the concern that the cross section will be significantly diminished if the jury is decreased in size from 12 to six seems an unrealistic one."

d. In *Ballew v. Georgia*, 435 U.S. 223, 98 S.Ct. 1029, 55 L.Ed.2d 234 (1978), a unanimous Court held that petitioner's trial before a 5–member jury deprived him of his constitutional right to jury trial. Justice Blackmun relied on empirical data which "suggest that progressively smaller juries are less likely to foster effective group deliberation," "raise doubts about the accuracy of the results achieved by smaller and smaller panels," "suggest that the verdicts of jury deliberation in criminal cases will vary as juries become smaller, and that the variance amounts to an imbalance to the detriment of one side, the defense," and show that "the opportunity for meaningful and appropriate [minority group] representation does decrease with the size of the panels," to justify the conclusion that "any further reduction" in jury size "attains constitutional significance," especially in light of the fact that there is "no significant state advantage in reducing the number of jurors from six to five."

e. In *Burch v. Louisiana*, 441 U.S. 130, 99 S.Ct. 1623, 60 L.Ed.2d 96 (1979), a unanimous Court struck down a provision that misdemeanors punishable by more than 6 months "shall be tried before a jury of six persons, five of whom must concur to render a verdict." The

Court stressed that the "near-uniform judgment of the Nation," reflected by the fact only two states allow nonunanimous verdicts by 6–member juries, "provides a useful guide in delimiting the line between those jury practices that are constitutionally permissible and those that are not"; and that claims nonunanimous 6–person juries save considerable time "are speculative, at best."

47. It is true, of course, that the "hung jury" might be thought to result in a minimal advantage for the defendant, who remains unconvicted and who enjoys the prospect that the prosecution will eventually be dropped if subsequent juries also "hang." Thus a 100–man jury would undoubtedly be more favorable for defendants than a 12–man jury. But when the comparison is between 12 and six, the odds of continually "hanging" the jury seem slight, and the numerical difference in the number needed to convict seems unlikely to inhere perceptibly to the advantage of either side.

49. Studies of the operative factors contributing to small group deliberation and decision-making suggest that jurors in the minority on the first ballot are likely to be influenced by the proportional size of the majority aligned against them. * * *

3. _Unanimity._ In APODACA v. OREGON, 406 U.S. 404, 92 S.Ct. 1628, 32 L.Ed.2d 184 (1972), petitioners, convicted of felonies by 11–1 and 10–2 votes, unsuccessfully challenged a state constitutional provision which permits 10 members of a jury to render guilty verdicts in noncapital cases. WHITE, J., joined by Burger, C.J., and Blackmun and Rehnquist, JJ., announced the judgment:

"[T]he essential feature of a jury obviously lies in the interposition between the accused and his accuser of the commonsense judgment of a group of laymen * * *.' A requirement of unanimity, however, does not materially contribute to the exercise of this commonsense judgment. As we said in _Williams_, a jury will come to such a judgment as long as it consists of a group of laymen representative of a cross section of the community who have the duty and the opportunity to deliberate, free from outside attempts at intimidation, on the question of a defendant's guilt. In terms of this function we perceive no difference between juries required to act unanimously and those permitted to convict or acquit by votes of 10 to two or 11 to one.[f] Requiring unanimity would obviously produce hung juries in some situations where nonunanimous juries will convict or acquit. But in either case, the interest of the defendant in having the judgment of his peers interposed between himself and the officers of the State who prosecute and judge him is equally well served."[g]

Blackmun, J., joined Justice White's opinions in _Apodaca_ and _Johnson_ (fn. f supra), but in a brief concurring opinion did "not hesitate to say" that "a 7–5 standard, rather than a 9–3 or 75% minimum, would afford me great difficulty. As Mr. Justice White points out in _Johnson_, 'a substantial majority of the jury' are to be convinced. That is all that is before us in each of these cases."[h]

f. In the companion case of _Johnson v. Louisiana_, 406 U.S. 356, 92 S.Ct. 1620, 32 L.Ed.2d 152 (1972), a 5–4 majority of the Court, per White, J., upheld a 9–3 robbery conviction against due process and equal protection challenges. Since the case was tried before _Duncan_, appellant conceded that the sixth amendment was not applicable to his case. Rather, he argued that (1) in order to give substance to the "proof beyond a reasonable doubt" standard required by the fourteenth amendment, jury verdicts in state criminal cases must be unanimous; and (2) state law requiring unanimous verdicts in five-man jury cases (for minor offenses) and in twelve-man jury cases (for capital offenses), but permitting 9–3 convictions in other cases violates equal protection. As for (1), the Court observed that "nine jurors—a substantial majority of the jury—were convinced by the evidence. [D]isagreement of three jurors does not alone establish reasonable doubt, particularly when such a heavy majority of the jury, after having considered the dissenters' views, remains convinced of guilt." As for (2), the Court "perceive[d] nothing unconstitutional or invidiously discriminatory * * * in a State's insisting that its burden of proof be carried with more jurors where more serious crimes or more severe punishments are at issue. * * * As to the crimes triable by a five-man jury, if appellant's position is that it is easier to convince nine of 12 jurors than to convince all of five, he is simply challenging the judgment of the Louisiana legislature. That body obviously intended to vary the difficulty of proving guilt with the gravity of the offense

and the severity of the punishment. We remain unconvinced * * * that this legislative judgment was defective in any constitutional sense."

g. The plurality opinion also rejected the contentions that (1) a sixth amendment "jury trial" should be held to require unanimity in order to effectuate the "reasonable doubt" standard and (2) unanimity is a necessary precondition for effective application of the requirement that jury panels reflect a cross section of the community. As for (1), the reasonable doubt standard developed separately from both the jury trial and the unanimous verdict. The contention is rooted, in effect, in due process and has been rejected in _Johnson v. Louisiana_, fn. f supra. As for (2), the Court rejected the assumption that "minority groups, even when they are represented on a jury, will not adequately represent the viewpoint of those groups simply because they may be outvoted in the final result. They will be present during all deliberations, and their views will be heard."

h. But consider Stewart, J., joined by Brennan and Marshall, JJ., dissenting in _Johnson:_ "[N]otwithstanding Mr. Justice Blackmun's disclaimer, there is nothing in the reasoning of the Court's opinion that would stop it from approving verdicts by 8–4 or even 7–5." Consider, too, Douglas, J., joined by Brennan and Marshall, JJ., dissenting in _Johnson_ and _Apodaca:_ "Would the Court relax the standard of reasonable doubt still further by resorting to eight to four verdicts or even a majority rule?"

POWELL, J., concurring, rejected the premise that "all of the elements of jury trial within the meaning of the Sixth Amendment are necessarily embodied in or incorporated into the Due Process Clause of the Fourteenth," and thus deemed *Apodaca* not inconsistent with the Court's long-standing presumption "that unanimous verdicts are essential in federal jury trials."

DOUGLAS, J., joined by Brennan and Marshall, JJ., dissented:

"The diminution of verdict reliability flows from the fact that nonunanimous juries need not debate and deliberate as fully as must unanimous juries. As soon as the requisite majority is attained, further consideration is not required either by Oregon or by Louisiana even though the dissident jurors might, if given the chance, be able to convince the majority. Such persuasion does in fact occasionally occur in States where the unanimous requirement applies: 'In roughly one case in ten, the minority eventually succeeds in reversing an initial majority, and these may be cases of special importance.'[4] * * *

"The new rule also has an impact on cases in which a unanimous jury would have neither voted to acquit nor to convict, but would have deadlocked. In unanimous jury States, this occurs about 5.6% of the time. Of these deadlocked juries, Kalven and Zeisel say that 56% contain either one, two, or three dissenters. In these latter cases, the majorities favor the prosecution 44% (of the 56%) but the defendant only 12% (of the 56%). Thus, by eliminating these deadlocks, Louisiana wins 44 cases for every 12 that it loses, obtaining in this band of outcomes a substantially more favorable conviction ratio (3.67) than the unanimous jury ratio of slightly less than two guilty verdicts for every acquittal. By eliminating the one and two dissenting juror cases, Oregon does even better, gaining 4.25 convictions for every acquittal."[i]

4. *Trial de novo.* At issue in *Ludwig v. Massachusetts*, 427 U.S. 618, 96 S.Ct. 2781, 49 L.Ed.2d 732 (1976), was a "two-tier" system of trial courts in which there was a right to jury trial only at the second tier, available after a conviction upon a trial without a jury at the first tier. The opinion of the Court, delivered by Blackmun, J., concluded: (a) that the right to jury trial was not unconstitutionally burdened by the cost of an additional trial, as a defendant may reach the second tier by "admitting sufficient findings of fact" and thus "need not pursue, in any real sense, a defense at the lower tier"; (b) that the right to jury trial was not unconstitutionally burdened by the danger of a harsher sentence at the second tier, in light of *North Carolina v. Pearce,* p. 1535, and *Colten v. Kentucky,* p. 1539, and (c) that it was not established that the right to jury trial was unconstitutionally burdened by the psychological and physical hardships of two trials, as appellant "has not presented any evidence to show that there is a greater delay in obtaining a jury in Massachusetts than there would be if the Commonwealth abandoned its two-tier system." Reconsideration of *Callan v. Wilson,* 127 U.S. 540, 8 S.Ct. 1301, 32 L.Ed. 223 (1888), holding invalid a two-tier system in the District of Columbia that provided for jury trial only at the second tier, was deemed unnecessary for two reasons: (1) *Callan* also rested upon Art. III, § 2, cl. 3 of the Constitution, which is not applicable to the states; and (2) under the D.C. system it was necessary for the defendant to be "fully tried" in the first tier.[j]

---

4. Kalven & Zeisel, *The American Jury* 490 (1966). See also *The American Jury: Notes For an English Controversy*, 48 Chi.Bar Rec. 195 (1967).

i. Separate dissenting opinions were also written by Brennan, Stewart, and Marshall, JJ.

j. Powell, J., concurred on the basis of his opinion in *Apodaca*. Stevens, J., joined by Brennan, Stewart, and Marshall, JJ., dissent-

ing, objected that "[a]ll of the legitimate benefits of the two-tier system could be obtained by giving the defendant the right to waive the first-tier trial completely," and found the burden in the Massachusetts system "significant" because: (a) for various reasons a "second trial of the same case is never the same as the first"; (b) the choice "between admitting the truth and also the prima facie sufficiency of

5. *Jury nullification.* Does *Duncan* mean defendants are entitled to have the jury informed of its power to "nullify" the law? Consider UNITED STATES v. DOUGHERTY, 473 F.2d 1113 (D.C.Cir.1972), where LEVENTHAL, J., joined by Adams, J., maintained:

"The way the jury operates may be radically altered if there is alteration in the way it is told to operate. The jury knows well enough that its prerogative is not limited to the choices articulated in the formal instructions of the court. The jury gets its understanding as to the arrangements in the legal system from more than one voice. There is the formal communication from the judge. There is the informal communication from the total culture—literature (novel, drama, film, and television); current comment (newspapers, magazines and television); conversation; and, of course, history and tradition. The totality of input generally convey adequately enough the idea of prerogative, of freedom in an occasional case to depart from what the judge says. Even indicators that would on their face seem too weak to notice—like the fact that the judge tells the jury it must acquit (in case of reasonable doubt) but never tells the jury in so many words that it must convict—are a meaningful part of the jury's total input. Law is a system, and it is also a language, with secondary meanings that may be unrecorded yet are part of its life.

"When the legal system relegates the information of the jury's prerogative to an essentially informal input, it is not being duplicitous, chargeable with chicane and intent to deceive. The limitation to informal input is, rather, a governor to avoid excess: the prerogative is reserved for the exceptional case, and the judge's instruction is retained as a generally effective constraint. We 'recognize a constraint as obligatory upon us when we require not merely reason to defend our rule departures, but damn good reason.' The practicalities of men, machinery and rules point up the danger of articulating discretion to depart from a rule, that the breach will be more often and casually invoked. We cannot gainsay that occasionally jurors uninstructed as to the prerogative may feel themselves compelled to the point of rigidity. The danger of the excess rigidity that may now occasionally exist is not as great as the danger of removing the boundaries of constraint provided by the announced rules.

" * * * To assign the role of mini-legislature to the various petit juries, who must hang if not unanimous, exposes criminal law and administration to paralysis, and to a deadlock that betrays rather than furthers the assumptions of viable democracy.

"Moreover, to compel a juror involuntarily assigned to jury duty to assume the burdens of mini-legislator or judge, as is implicit in the doctrine of nullification, is to put untoward strains on the jury system. It is one thing for a juror to know that the law condemns, but he has a factual power of lenity. To tell him expressly of a nullification prerogative, however, is to inform him, in effect, that it is he who fashions the rule that condemns. That is an overwhelming responsibility, an extreme burden for the jurors' psyche. And it is not inappropriate to add that a juror called upon for an involuntary public service is entitled to the protection, when he takes action that he knows is right, but also knows is unpopular, either in the community at large or in his own particular grouping, that he can fairly put it to friends and neighbors that he was merely following the instructions of the court. * * *

the evidence the defendant considers false or misleading, on the one hand, or insisting on a full nonjury trial, on the other, is not an insignificant price to pay for the exercise of a constitutional right"; and (c) the first trial may have a significant impact notwithstanding the right to immediate appeal, as it may tarnish the defendant's reputation, have an impact upon the judge in the second trial, and may be known by the jurors in the second trial.

"What makes for health as an occasional medicine would be disastrous as a daily diet. The fact that there is widespread existence of the jury's prerogative, and approval of its existence as a 'necessary counter to case-hardened judges and arbitrary prosecutors,' does not establish as an imperative that the jury must be informed by the judge of that power. On the contrary, it is pragmatically useful to structure instructions in such ways that the jury must feel strongly about the values involved in the case, so strongly that it must itself identify the case as establishing a call of high conscience, and must independently initiate and undertake an act in contravention of the established instructions. This requirement of independent jury conception confines the happening of the lawless jury to the occasional instance that does not violate, and viewed as an exception may even enhance, the over-all normative effect of the rule of law. An explicit instruction to a jury conveys an implied approval that runs the risk of degrading the legal structure requisite for true freedom, for an ordered liberty that protects against anarchy as well as tyranny."

Dissenting on the jury nullification issue, Chief Judge BAZELON observed:

"My own view rests on the premise that nullification can and should serve an important function in the criminal process. * * * The doctrine permits the jury to bring to bear on the criminal process a sense of fairness and particularized justice. The drafters of legal rules cannot anticipate and take account of every case where a defendant's conduct is 'unlawful' but not blameworthy, any more than they can draw a bold line to mark the boundary between an accident and negligence. It is the jury—as spokesman for the community's sense of values—that must explore that subtle and elusive boundary. * * *

"I do not see any reason to assume that jurors will make rampantly abusive use of their power. * * * If a jury refuses to apply strictly the controlling principles of law, it may—in conflict with values shared by the larger community—convict a defendant because of prejudice against him, or acquit a defendant because of sympathy for him and prejudice against his victim. Our fear of unjust conviction is plainly understandable. But it is hard for me to see how a nullification instruction could enhance the likelihood of that result. The instruction would speak in terms of acquittal, not conviction, and it would provide no comfort to a juror determined to convict a defendant in defiance of the law or the facts of the case. * * *

"As for the problem of unjust acquittal, it is important to recognize the strong internal check that constrains the jury's willingness to acquit. Where defendants seem dangerous, juries are unlikely to exercise their nullification power, whether or not an explicit instruction is offered."

Does it follow that defense counsel may not even argue for nullification, as concluded in *United States v. Trujillo,* 714 F.2d 102 (11th Cir.1983), or is permitting argument but not instruction the best compromise, as concluded in *State v. Mayo,* 480 A.2d 85 (N.H.1984)? If the latter, are only some nullification arguments legitimate? Consider Paul Butler, *Racially Based Jury Nullification: Black Power in the Criminal Justice System,* 105 Yale L.J. 677, 679, 705 (1995) ("argu[ing] that the race of a black defendant is sometimes a legally and morally appropriate factor for jurors to consider in reaching a verdict of not guilty," deemed "distinguish[able] from recent right-wing proposals for jury nullification on the ground that the former is sometimes morally right and the latter is not"), criticized in Randall Kennedy, *Race, Crime and the Law* 295–310 (1997); and Andrew Leipold, *The Dangers of Race–Based Jury Nullification: A Response to Prof. Butler,* 44 U.C.L.A.L.Rev. 109 (1996). On the other hand, does even *Dougherty* go too far? Consider *United States v. Thomas,* 116 F.3d 606 (2d Cir.1997) ("We categorically reject the idea that * * * jury nullification is desirable or that courts may permit it to occur when it is within their authority to prevent it," meaning that "a juror who intends to nullify the applicable law" is subject to dismissal); *State v. Ragland*, 519 A.2d 1361 (N.J.1986) (because right to jury trial "was never designed * * * to protect the defendant from the law, or from the Legislature," jury may be instructed that if it finds all the elements of the crime beyond a reasonable doubt it "must" convict). Consider also Andrew Leipold, *Rethinking Jury Nullification*, 82 Va.L.Rev. 253 (1996), proposing that there should be a nullification affirmative defense limited to "when certain statutory criteria are satisfied," and concluding that then "the use of error-correcting procedures in criminal cases, including appeals from acquittals," would be constitutionally permissible.

6. *Fact or Law.* In *United States v. Gaudin*, 515 U.S. 506, 115 S.Ct. 2310, 132 L.Ed.2d 444 (1995), defendant was charged under 18 U.S.C. § 1001 with having made false statements on federal loan documents, as to which "materiality" is an element of the offense. The trial judge instructed the jury "that the statements charged in the indictment are material statements." A unanimous Court affirmed the appellate court's reversal of defendant's conviction. Relying on both the Fifth Amendment due process clause and the Sixth Amendment right to jury trial, which "require criminal convictions to rest upon a jury determination that the defendant is guilty of every element of the crime with which he is charged," the Court concluded that "the jury's constitutional responsibility is not merely to determine the facts, but to apply the law to those facts and draw the ultimate conclusion of guilt or innocence."

7. *Sentencing.* As stated in *Spaziano v. Florida*, 468 U.S. 447, 104 S.Ct. 3154, 82 L.Ed.2d 340 (1984), the Sixth Amendment "never has been thought to guarantee a right to a jury determination" of "the appropriate punishment to be imposed on an individual." The Court there held that this was so even as to the death penalty, and that consequently there was no constitutional prohibition upon a sentencing scheme which allowed a trial judge to override a jury's recommendation of a life sentence instead of the death penalty. In response to the claim that because "the jury serves as the voice of the community, the jury is in the best position to decide whether a particular crime is so heinous that the community's response must be death," the Court, per Blackmun, J., declared that the "community's voice is heard at least as clearly in the legislature when the death penalty is authorized and the particular circumstances in which death is appropriate are defined."[k]

8. *Waiver.* In SINGER v. UNITED STATES, 380 U.S. 24, 85 S.Ct. 783, 13 L.Ed.2d 630 (1965), petitioner challenged Fed.R.Crim.P. 23(a), which provides a defendant may waive a jury trial only "with the approval of the court and the consent of the government," because the government had declined to consent in his case. The Court, per WARREN, C.J., concluded:

"The ability to waive a constitutional right does not ordinarily carry with it the right to insist upon the opposite of that right. * * *

"Trial by jury has been established by the Constitution as the 'normal and * * * preferable mode of disposing of issues of fact in criminal cases.' As with any mode that might be devised to determine guilt, trial by jury has its weaknesses and the potential for misuse. However, the mode itself has been surrounded with

---

k. Stevens, J., joined by Brennan and Marshall, JJ., dissenting in part, concluded: "The same consideration that supports a constitutional entitlement to a trial by a jury rather than a judge at the guilt or innocence stage—the right to have an authentic representative of the community apply its lay perspective to the determination that must precede a deprivation of liberty—applies with special force to the determination that must precede a deprivation of life."

safeguards to make it as fair as possible—for example, venue can be changed when there is a well-grounded fear of jury prejudice,* * * and prospective jurors are subject to *voir dire* examination, to challenge for cause, and to peremptory challenge * * *.

"In light of the Constitution's emphasis on jury trial, we find it difficult to understand how the petitioner can submit the bald proposition that to compel a defendant in a criminal case to undergo a jury trial against his will is contrary to his right to a fair trial or to due process. A defendant's only constitutional right concerning the method of trial is to an impartial trial by jury. We find no constitutional impediment to conditioning a waiver of this right on the consent of the prosecuting attorney and the trial judge when, if either refuses to consent, the result is simply that the defendant is subject to an impartial trial by jury—the very thing that the Constitution guarantees him. The Constitution recognizes an adversary system as the proper method of determining guilt, and the Government, as a litigant, has a legitimate interest in seeing that cases in which it believes a conviction is warranted are tried before the tribunal which the Constitution regards as most likely to produce a fair result. * * *

" * * * We need not determine in this case whether there might be some circumstances where a defendant's reasons for wanting to be tried by a judge alone are so compelling that the Government's insistence on trial by jury would result in the denial to a defendant of an impartial trial. * * * since petitioner gave no reason for wanting to forgo jury trial other than to save time * * *."

In *People v. Collins*, 27 P.3d 726 (Cal.2001), the court held defendant's jury waiver was not voluntary where it was obtained after the trial judge informed defendant "that he would receive a benefit of an unspecified nature in the event he waived his right to trial by jury." Relying upon *Corbitt*, p. 1252, a concurring justice took issue with the court's additional statement that the "state is prohibited by the federal Constitution from * * * rewarding a defendant for forbearing from the exercise of" a constitutional right, noting that "here defense counsel suggested at sentencing that defendant's waiver had benefited the minor victim by reducing her 'exposure to presentation of traumatic events.' It would seem the trial court could properly consider such a circumstance in reducing defendant's sentence. However, had defendant mentioned this to the court as a reason for his jury trial waiver prior to entering that waiver, and the trial court noted it would consider such a gesture at any sentencing hearing, would that render the waiver invalid? Not knowing the answer to these questions, it seems best to avoid foreclosing our options in future cases."

SECTION 2. JURY SELECTION

The purpose of the *Federal Jury Selection and Service Act of 1968*, 28 U.S.C. § 1861 et seq., reprinted in Supp.App. B, is to ensure that juries are "selected at random from a fair cross section of the communities in the district or division wherein the court convenes" and that "no citizen shall be excluded from service as a grand or petit juror in the district courts of the United States on account of race, color, religion, sex, national origin, or economic status." Each district court is required to devise and place into operation a written plan for jury selection, which "shall specify whether the names of prospective jurors shall be selected from the voter registration lists or the lists of actual voters of the political subdivision within the district or division. The plan shall prescribe some other source or sources of names in addition to voter lists where necessary to foster the policy and protect the rights" set forth above. Because "Congress specifically approved the use of such lists even though it was recognized that persons who chose not to register would be excluded from the jury selection process," other sources need not be resorted to absent discrimination in the voter registration process. *United States v. Cecil,* 836 F.2d 1431 (4th Cir.1988).

Largely as a result of changes adopted in recent years, most states now follow similar procedures in an effort to select jurors at random from some standardized list. Lists of voters are most commonly used, although some states instead or in addition utilize other lists, such as a local census, the tax rolls, city directories, telephone books, and drivers' license lists. Many of those whose names are drawn for state jury service seek to be excused, and in many states excuses are rather readily granted. Persons are most commonly excused because of economic hardship, poor health, advanced age, a need to care for small children, or the distance they live from the courthouse. In addition, state jury selection statutes typically list those persons who are disqualified from serving as jurors (e.g., those not of voting age, not residents of the jurisdiction some minimum time, unable to read and write English, or with a felony conviction) and those who are exempted from jury service because of their occupation (e.g., doctors, teachers, clergy).

TAYLOR v. LOUISIANA
419 U.S. 522, 95 S.Ct. 692, 42 L.Ed.2d 690 (1975).

Justice WHITE delivered the opinion of the Court.

When this case was tried, Art. VII, § 41, of the Louisiana Constitution, and Art. 402 of the Louisiana Code of Criminal Procedure provided that a woman should not be selected for jury service unless she had previously filed a written declaration of her desire to be subject to jury service. The constitutionality of these provisions is the issue in this case. * * *

The Louisiana jury selection system does not disqualify women from jury service, but in operation its conceded systematic impact is that only a very few women, grossly disproportionate to the number of eligible women in the community, are called for jury service.[a] In this case, no women were on the venire from which the petit jury was drawn. The issue we have, therefore, is whether a jury selection system which operates to exclude from jury service an identifiable class of citizens constituting 53% of eligible jurors in the community comports with the Sixth and Fourteenth Amendments.

The State first insists that Taylor, a male, has no standing to object to the exclusion of women from his jury. But Taylor's claim is that he was constitutionally entitled to a jury drawn from a venire constituting a fair cross section of the community and that the jury that tried him was not such a jury by reason of the exclusion of women. Taylor was not a member of the excluded class; but there is no rule that claims such as Taylor presents may be made only by those defendants who are members of the group excluded from jury service. In *Peters v. Kiff,* 407 U.S. 493, 92 S.Ct. 2163, 33 L.Ed.2d 83 (1972), the defendant, a white man, challenged his conviction on the ground that Negroes had been systematically excluded from jury service. Six Members of the Court agreed that petitioner was entitled to present the issue and concluded that he had been deprived of his federal rights. Taylor, in the case before us, was similarly entitled to tender and have adjudicated the claim that the exclusion of women from jury service deprived him of the kind of fact finder to which he was constitutionally entitled.

The background against which this case must be decided includes our holding in *Duncan v. Louisiana* [p. 1311], that the Sixth Amendment's provision for jury

---

a. It was stipulated that no more than 10% of the persons on the jury wheel were women, that only 12 females were among the 1,800 persons drawn to fill petit jury venires, and that this discrepancy was the result of the operation of the challenged provisions.

trial is made binding on the States by virtue of the Fourteenth Amendment. Our inquiry is whether the presence of a fair cross section of the community on venires, panels or lists from which petit juries are drawn is essential to the fulfillment of the Sixth Amendment's guarantee of an impartial jury trial in criminal prosecutions. * * *

The unmistakable import of this Court's opinions, at least since 1941, and not repudiated by intervening decisions, is that the selection of a petit jury from a representative cross section of the community is an essential component of the Sixth Amendment right to a jury trial. * * *

We accept the fair cross section requirement as fundamental to the jury trial guaranteed by the Sixth Amendment and are convinced that the requirement has solid foundation. The purpose of a jury is to guard against the exercise of arbitrary power—to make available the commonsense judgment of the community as a hedge against the overzealous or mistaken prosecutor and in preference to the professional or perhaps overconditioned or biased response of a judge. This prophylactic vehicle is not provided if the jury pool is made up of only special segments of the populace or if large, distinctive groups are excluded from the pool. Community participation in the administration of the criminal law, moreover, is not only consistent with our democratic heritage but is also critical to public confidence in the fairness of the criminal justice system. Restricting jury service to only special groups or excluding identifiable segments playing major roles in the community cannot be squared with the constitutional concept of jury trial. * * *

We are also persuaded that the fair cross section requirement is violated by the systematic exclusion of women, who in the judicial district involved here amounted to 53% of the citizens eligible for jury service. This conclusion necessarily entails the judgment that women are sufficiently numerous and distinct from men that if they are systematically eliminated from jury panels, the Sixth Amendment's fair cross section requirement cannot be satisfied. This very matter was debated in *Ballard v. United States,* 329 U.S. 187, 67 S.Ct. 261, 91 L.Ed. 181 (1946). Positing the fair cross-section rule—there said to be a statutory one—the Court concluded that the systematic exclusion of women was unacceptable. The dissenting view that an all-male panel drawn from various groups in the community would be as truly representative as if women were included, was firmly rejected:

> "The thought is that the factors which tend to influence the action of women are the same as those which influence the action of men—personality, background, economic status—and not sex. Yet it is not enough to say that women when sitting as jurors neither act nor tend to act as a class. Men likewise do not act as a class. But, if the shoe were on the other foot, who would claim that a jury was truly representative of the community if all men were intentionally and systematically excluded from the panel? The truth is that the two sexes are not fungible; a community made up exclusively of one is different from a community composed of both; the subtle interplay of influence one on the other is among the imponderables. To insulate the courtroom from either may not in a given case make an iota of difference. Yet a flavor, a distinct quality is lost if either sex is excluded. The exclusion of one may indeed make the jury less representative of the community than would be true if an economic or racial group were excluded."

In this respect, we agree with the Court in *Ballard:* If the fair cross-section rule is to govern the selection of juries, as we have concluded it must, women cannot be systematically excluded from jury panels from which petit juries are drawn. This conclusion is consistent with the current judgment of the country, now evidenced by legislative or constitutional provisions in every State and at the federal level qualifying women for jury service.

There remains the argument that women as a class serve a distinctive role in society and that jury service would so substantially interfere with that function that the State has ample justification for excluding women from service unless they volunteer, even though the result is that almost all jurors are men. It is true that *Hoyt v. Florida*, 368 U.S. 57, 82 S.Ct. 159, 7 L.Ed.2d 118 (1961), held that such a system did not deny due process of law or equal protection of the laws because there was a sufficiently rational basis for such an exemption. But *Hoyt* did not involve a defendant's Sixth Amendment right to a jury drawn from a fair cross section of the community and the prospect of depriving him of that right if women as a class are systematically excluded. The right to a proper jury cannot be overcome on merely rational grounds. There must be weightier reasons if a distinctive class representing 53% of the eligible jurors is for all practical purposes to be excluded from jury service. No such basis has been tendered here.

The States are free to grant exemptions from jury service to individuals in case of special hardship or incapacity and to those engaged in particular occupations the uninterrupted performance of which is critical to the community's welfare. It would not appear that such exemptions would pose substantial threats that the remaining pool of jurors would not be representative of the community. A system excluding all women, however, is a wholly different matter. It is untenable to suggest these days that it would be a special hardship for each and every woman to perform jury service or that society cannot spare *any* women from their present duties. This may be the case with many, and it may be burdensome to sort out those who should serve. But that task is performed in the case of men, and the administrative convenience in dealing with women as a class is insufficient justification for diluting the quality of community judgment represented by the jury in criminal trials. * * *

Our holding does not augur or authorize the fashioning of detailed jury selection codes by federal courts. The fair cross section principle must have much leeway in application. The States remain free to prescribe relevant qualifications for their jurors and to provide reasonable exemptions so long as it may be fairly said that the jury lists or panels are representative of the community. * * *

It should also be emphasized that in holding that petit juries must be drawn from a source fairly representative of the community we impose no requirement that petit juries actually chosen must mirror the community and reflect the various distinctive groups in the population. Defendants are not entitled to a jury of any particular composition; but the jury wheels, pools of names, panels or venires from which juries are drawn must not systematically exclude distinctive groups in the community and thereby fail to be reasonably representative thereof. * * *

Reversed and remanded.

Chief Justice BURGER concurred in the result.

Justice REHNQUIST, dissenting. [The majority] fails * * * to provide any satisfactory explanation of the mechanism by which the Louisiana system undermines the prophylactic role of the jury, either in general or in this case. The best it can do is to posit "a flavor, a distinct quality," which allegedly is lost if either sex is excluded. However, this "flavor" is not of such importance that the Constitution is offended if any given petit jury is not so enriched. This smacks more of mysticism than of law. * * *

Notes and Questions

1. In DUREN v. MISSOURI, 439 U.S. 357, 99 S.Ct. 664, 58 L.Ed.2d 579 (1979), the defendant established (1) that 54% of the adult inhabitants of the county were women, (2) that only 15% of the persons placed on venires were women, and (3) that any woman could decline jury service (a) by claiming an exemption in response to a prominent notice on a jury-selection questionnaire, (b) by returning the summons for jury duty as indicated on the summons, or (c) by simply not reporting for jury duty. The Court, per WHITE, J., held that the defendant had made out "a prima facie fair-cross-section violation" (by showing "(1) that the group alleged to be excluded is a 'distinctive' group in the community; (2) that the representation of this group in venires from which juries are selected is not fair and reasonable in relation to the number of such persons in the community; and (3) that this underrepresentation is due to systematic exclusion of the group in the jury selection process") and that the state had not carried its "burden of justifying this infringement by showing attainment of a fair cross section to be incompatible with a significant state interest." Recognizing "that a State may have an important interest in assuring that those members of the family responsible for the care of children are available to do so," Justice White suggested that an exemption "appropriately tailored to this interest would * * * survive a fair-cross-section challenge."

REHNQUIST, J., dissenting, expressed the fear "that today's decision will cause States to abandon not only gender-based but also occupation-based classifications for purposes of jury service. Doctors and nurses, though virtually irreplaceable in smaller communities, may ultimately be held by the Court to bring their own 'flavor' or 'indescribable something' to a jury venire."[b]

2. *"Community" representation?* In *United States v. Shinault*, 147 F.3d 1266 (10th Cir.1998), the government objected to defendant's statistical approach by which the percentages of minorities on jury panels were compared with the percentages of the same minorities in the voting age population, arguing that the comparison should be with the percentage of those minorities eligible to sit on juries. The court responded that the government's position had "intellectual merit," especially because many in some minority groups might be disqualified for inability to speak English, but then concluded that defendant's approach, which "the Supreme Court has found adequate in the past" in *Duren*, "was appropriate under the circumstances of this case," considering that "there is apparently no reliable measurement of that subset of the general population."

3. *"Distinctive" groups.* Consider *Barber v. Ponte*, 772 F.2d 982 (1st Cir.1985), concerning underrepresentation by those 18–34 years of age, apparently as a consequence of using a key man system of jury selection. The court stated that the "essence of a distinctive group is that its members share specific common characteristics," and that the record in the instant case contained no "evidence that the attitudes and thinking of, say, 30 year olds have more in common with 18 year olds than they do with 40 year olds, or for that matter, going to the other end of the scale, that 18 year olds have more in common with 28 year olds than with 16 year olds." But the court then cautioned: "That is not to say, however, that if a

b. The Court continues to be divided as to just how many "distinctive groups" there might be. In *Holland v. Illinois*, p. 1335, Scalia, J., for the Court, said that if the cross-section requirement applied to juries (rather than the panels from which juries are chosen) then "many commonly exercised bases for per- emptory challenges would be rendered unavailable," while Marshall, J., dissenting, objected to the "majority's exaggerated claim that 'post-men, or lawyers, or clergymen' are distinctive groups within the meaning of our fair cross-section cases."

classification were *specifically* and *systematically excluded* from jury duty the same standard would be used as here, where defendant simply relies on a statistical disparity in the venires to challenge its constitutionality. One dissenter objected: "The holding that young adults are not a cognizable group and, therefore, need not be included in the jury pool to make it a reasonable cross section of the community, but cannot be overtly excluded is inherently contradictory."

4. *"Fair and reasonable" representation.* In *State v. McCarthy,* 496 A.2d 513 (Conn.1985), defendant showed that of the 12,351 persons called for jury duty in the county over two and a half years only 1.9% had Hispanic surnames, while the federal census indicated there should have been 3.75%. Utilizing "the substantial impact test," which "allows the courts to reject challenges when the challenged practices did not significantly alter the composition of the typical * * * petit jury," the court concluded there had been no such impact here, for if the 225 missing Hispanics were in the 12,351 potential juror pool, which if divided into juries of six (used in cases such as defendant's) would have served 2,000 potential juries, "one more Hispanic would have been available for selection on only one out of nine juries."

5. *Racial discrimination.* Fourteenth Amendment equal protection challenges to state jury selection procedures prevailed long before the Sixth Amendment right to jury trial was applied to the states. In *Strauder v. West Virginia,* 100 U.S. (10 Otto) 303, 25 L.Ed. 664 (1880), it was held that for a state to try a black defendant before a jury from which all members of his race had been excluded by statute is a denial of equal protection, and in *Neal v. Delaware,* 103 U.S. (13 Otto) 370, 26 L.Ed. 567 (1881), the principle was extended to the discriminatory administration of ostensibly fair jury selection laws to achieve the same result. In *Powers v. Ohio,* p. 1342, the Court held that a white defendant may raise an equal protection claim on behalf of excluded black prospective jurors.

Strauder and *Neal* had a limited impact for several years because the defendant was required to show a definite purpose to discriminate by jury officials; the state action was presumed constitutional and the lower court findings were presumed to be true unless the defendant proved the contrary. But in *Norris v. Alabama,* 294 U.S. 587, 55 S.Ct. 579, 79 L.Ed. 1074 (1935), the Court held that a defendant in a criminal case could make out a prima facie case of discrimination by showing (a) the existence of a substantial number of blacks in the community, and (b) their total or virtual exclusion from jury service. The burden then shifts to the state to prove that the exclusion did not flow from discrimination. *Avery v. Georgia,* 345 U.S. 559, 73 S.Ct. 891, 97 L.Ed. 1244 (1953). This burden cannot be met merely by testimony by the jury commissioner that he did not intend to discriminate, *Eubanks v. Louisiana,* 356 U.S. 584, 78 S.Ct. 970, 2 L.Ed.2d 991 (1958), or that he did not know any qualified blacks. *Hill v. Texas,* 316 U.S. 400, 62 S.Ct. 1159, 86 L.Ed. 1559 (1942).

A statute requiring jury commissioners to select for jury service those persons who are "generally reported to be honest and intelligent * * * and * * * esteemed in the community for their integrity, good character and sound judgment" is not unconstitutional on its face, for such a statute—to be found in many states—is "devoid of any mention of race," has "antecedents * * * of ancient vintage, and there is no suggestion that the law was originally adopted or subsequently carried forward for the purpose of fostering racial discrimination." *Carter v. Jury Comm. of Greene County,* 396 U.S. 320, 90 S.Ct. 518, 24 L.Ed.2d 549 (1970). However, a prima facie case of discrimination may be made out by showing that the substantial disparity between minority group members in the population and on the jury list "originated, at least in part, at the one point in the selection process where the jury commissioners invoked their subjective judgment rather than objective criteria." *Turner v. Fouche,* 396 U.S. 346, 90 S.Ct. 532, 24 L.Ed.2d 567 (1970).

In *Castaneda v. Partida,* 430 U.S. 482, 97 S.Ct. 1272, 51 L.Ed.2d 498 (1977), in a 5–4 decision, the Court, per Blackmun, J., held that a showing that the population of the county was 79.1% Mexican–American, but that over an 11–year period only 39% of the persons summoned for grand jury service were Mexican–American, established a prima facie case of discrimination, which was unrebutted absent evidence that racially neutral qualifications for grand jurors resulted in the lower proportion of Mexican–Americans. The dissenters objected that especially because the case "involves neither tokenism nor absolute exclusion," "*eligible* population statistics, not gross population figures, provide the relevant starting point" for proving a prima facie case of discrimination. The dissenters stressed that the respondent had the burden of proving "discriminatory intent" because "in a state case in which the challenge is to the grand jury, only the Fourteenth Amendment applies, and the defendant has the burden of proving a violation of the Equal Protection Clause." By contrast, they noted, under the Fifth Amendment right to a federal grand jury and the Sixth Amendment right to a federal and state petit jury, a defendant has a right to a body "that reflects a fair cross-section of the community," which means that then he "need only show that the jury selection procedure 'systematically exclude[s] distinctive groups in the community and thereby fail[s] to be reasonably representative thereof.' "

See Albert W. Alschuler, *Racial Quotas and the Jury,* 44 Duke L.J. 704, 716–17, 723 (1995), concluding that proposals to ensure proportionate minority representation on all jury panels would be constitutional because such "quotas would not deprive individuals of significant tangible benefits; they would not brand any group as inferior or evaluate any individual on the basis of racial stereotypes; and * * * would be likely to enhance the * * * jury's achievement of its objectives."

6.   *Challenge to the array.* Constitutional objections to the manner in which prospective jurors were selected are made by a challenge to the array, sometimes referred to as a motion to quash the venire or panel. Such a challenge may also be made on the ground that the state law requirements for jury selection were not followed. However, although statutes often purport to allow challenge "on the ground that the jurors were not selected or drawn according to law," the prevailing view is that there must be a "material departure" from the statutory requirements. The timing of challenges to the array is usually governed by provisions similar to Fed.R.Crim.P. 12(b) or 28 U.S.C. § 1867.

HAMER v. UNITED STATES
259 F.2d 274 (9th Cir.1958).

BARNES, Circuit Judge. * * *

[On appeal, defendant, who had been convicted for fraudulently importing narcotic drugs and facilitating the sale thereof, claimed a deprivation of the right to jury trial for three reasons: (1) she was denied a list of the names and addresses of prospective jurors in advance of trial; (2) her counsel was not allowed to question prospective jurors directly during the *voir dire* examination; and (3) the prosecutor, at the *voir dire,* used a jury book setting out how prospective jurors acted or voted while on previous juries.]

Congress, in its wisdom, has seen fit to require that there be given advance notice, by service of jury lists, to defense counsel in certain classes of cases—primarily, treason and capital offenses. 18 U.S.C. § 3432. This statute has never been held applicable to non-capital offenses. * * *

The very fact that Congress has seen fit to require the furnishing of the list of prospective jurors to defendants in the more serious capital offense cases alone, and not in the cases involving other lesser offenses, indicates that it found no necessity for such a rule in the lesser types of cases.

Appellant's remedy then, if any exists, is from the hands of Congress, not from the courts. The courts now are following the congressional intent and purpose.

The cases to which we have referred above do not discuss whether there a personal voir dire by defense counsel was allowed. But there also exists a line of cases determining that there is no constitutional right to a personal voir dire of the jury. * * * The holding of these cases has been embodied in rule 24(a) of the Federal Rules of Criminal Procedure. These cases, however, do not discuss whether there was a view of the jury lists before trial.

Considered separately, both these rules seem sound and not violative of a defendant's constitutional rights. But the point which appellant here raises is that there is a denial of the right to an impartial jury, and thereby a fair jury trial, when *both* these requests are denied. Upon this question neither side has cited authorities.

A short answer might be that if there is no error separately, then there can be none when the two are combined. Provided that the selection of the jury when viewed as a whole is fair and impartial, such a test would comport with the Supreme Court's view of the basic premise of the due process clauses of the Fifth and Fourteenth Amendments of the Constitution. However we are not dealing with a claimed violation of the due process clause, but rather there is raised a specific denial of other constitutional safeguards. * * *

We find the voir dire examination permitted and undertaken here by the trial judge was adequate and fair to insure defendant the unbiased selection of an impartial jury to which he was entitled. The trial court advised counsel that if he had any additional voir dire questions, he could request the court to ask them. No such request was made. When the court asked if there were anything further on the issue of challenges for cause, defendant's counsel stated, "Nothing further." We hold the voir dire examination in this case was sufficient.

We have examined the jury book used by government counsel.[7] The use of "jury books" showing how members of a jury panel voted on previous juries has long existed in our courts. It has been praised and criticized; attacked and defended. Many an experienced trial lawyer will insist that knowing how a juror votes on one case will not give the slightest indication how he or she would vote on another, even if it is the same kind of case. If the facts differ, it is a different case, and different pressures, feelings, and sympathies come into being. And, of

---

7. It lists some two hundred and fifty or three hundred jurors, one on each loose-leaf page. Of one juror it said: "This Juror very poor.—held up jury for 4 hours 11–1." On each of the other eleven jurors who had sat with this juror there appeared the notation that they had sat on this same jury that R_____ had held up for four hours. (These were the "twelve times" referred to by the court below that a reference had been made in the book to an individual juror's action in the jury room.) A second juror "caused the jury to be hung several hours." The address and business, or the spouse's business, and the age of most jurors were given; how long they had lived in Southern California; their former place of residence; number of children, etc.

One juror was characterized as inattentive, another as having a hard time staying awake during later stages of trial; another juror listened carefully; "this juror slept during trial— was excused by the Court;" this juror was attentive to instructions; one was characterized as a strong juror for the government, another as "too sympathetic to boys in handcuffs;" another as an outstanding juror (after voting four times for conviction in government cases).

All other comments in the book had to do with juries as a whole—"excellent jury;" "good attentive jury;" "verdict in less than 20 min.;" "took 4 hours on simple case;" etc., "good jury, quick verdict."

course, facts do differ in each narcotics case; in each tax case; each personal injury case; and each case of any "type" or "kind."

Whether the United States District Attorney's staff in any district keeps a "jury book" or not (written or mental), whether it keeps a black-list of the few "sympathetic jurors," or a white list of the few "hanging jurors," cannot be considered error per se. Any group of attorneys associated together for any reason, who are constantly engaged in the trial of cases, will discuss and communicate as much information and knowledge as they possibly can to each other. Defense counsel, though perhaps not with the same enthusiasm, will discuss and relay information about jurors—"good" or "bad," as they may appear to interested partisans * * *.

But, says appellant, the list here was more than mere reputation. It contains references to how the jurors voted. It must be conceded that with respect to the reference to two jurors having "held up" a jury for "four" or "several" hours, such notation purports to pass along information as to what happened within a jury room.

Again, as any jury trial lawyer knows, it is almost impossible to prevent eleven jurors who have been held from a decision for several hours by *one* who saw the matter the other way, from publicly expressing their displeasure or disgust. The proverbial request by the foreman of the hung jury "for eleven dinners and a bale of hay" is well known to all.

If counsel for this defendant had tried cases before some of the jurors on this panel and had received information or come to any conclusions with respect to their individual intelligence, attentiveness, or sympathetic attitude, he would have felt he was negligent toward his client's interest had he not utilized his knowledge, or his intuition, to his client's best advantage.

We are not impressed with the argument that under any and all circumstances, and irrespective of what may be in a jury book, its use should be declared to deprive a defendant of a fair jury trial. To carry such a theory to its ultimate and ridiculous conclusion, no defendant could be prosecuted by a government attorney who had more information about how jurors on that panel had voted, in other cases, than his own counsel had. If defense counsel chosen was trying his first case before that panel, must the government hire a lawyer who likewise has tried no cases before that same jury panel? Is a defendant, in the name of his constitutional rights, entitled to be prosecuted by a government prosecutor with no more experience than his own counsel, or vice versa? If so, how is such experience to be measured? If the government lawyer is a tyro, must a defendant replace his more experienced defense counsel? Such a proposed rule would break down law enforcement in this country. It cannot be seriously considered. Perfect equality in counsel can never be achieved, any more than there can be two judges, or groups of judges, with precisely similar competence. * * *

Notes and Questions

1. 28 U.S.C. § 1867(f), giving defendant access to "papers used by the jury commission or clerk in connection with the jury selection process," has been characterized as granting defendant "essentially an unqualified right to inspect jury lists." *Test v. United States*, 420 U.S. 28, 95 S.Ct. 749, 42 L.Ed.2d 786 (1975). But the statute applies to a challenge to the entire panel, and thus is inapplicable where the list is desired only for the purposes of the voir dire.

On the state level, some states have expressly provided for defendants to obtain jury lists in all criminal cases, while others have limited the right to capital cases or felonies. In those jurisdictions without such legislation, it is usually held that a defendant has no right to a list of the panel, although there are cases holding that a defendant, upon timely motion, is entitled to the list even in the absence of statute.

Consider also the "anonymous jury" situation, in which the names of the jurors and their addresses and places of employment are withheld in advance of trial *and* during jury selection as well. See, e.g., *United States v. Thomas,* 757 F.2d 1359 (2d Cir.1985) ("there must be, first, strong reason to believe that the jury needs protection and, second, reasonable precaution must be taken to minimize the effect that such a decision might have on the jurors' opinions of the defendants"); and compare Nancy J. King, *Nameless Justice: The Case for the Routine Use of American Juries in Criminal Trials,* 49 Vand.L.Rev. 123, 125 (1996)(proposing "the routine use of anonymous juries in criminal cases").

2. Fed.R.Crim.P. 24(a) gives the court discretion to either conduct the examination itself or permit counsel to do so. This is the rule in 13 states; 20 give the attorney primary control of the questioning; and 17 provide for the judge to begin the questioning and for attorneys to then ask additional questions. Which procedure is best?

3. Two important functions of the voir dire are (i) to elicit information which would establish a basis for challenges for cause; and (ii) to acquire information to afford an intelligent exercise of peremptory challenges. A third, which many would not view as legitimate, is said to be that of "indoctrinating the potential jurors on the merits of the case and developing rapport." Comment, 70 Calif.L.Rev. 708, 714 (1982).

"In examining prospective jurors, lawyers and judges probe their private attitudes and practices—asking, for example, about the jurors' religious beliefs, drinking habits, jobs, hobbies, and prior experience with lawyers, then asking about their relatives' jobs, experiences as crime victims, and arrest records as well. A recent Connecticut decision illustrated how far some judges believe that lawyers must be allowed to carry the process; the court reversed a defendant's conviction of stealing a family's Christmas gifts because the trial judge had refused to permit questions concerning the prospective jurors' 'attitude toward Christmas.' " Albert W. Alschuler, *The Supreme Court and the Jury: Voir Dire, Peremptory Challenges and the Review of Jury Verdicts,* 56 U.Chi.L.Rev. 153, 158 (1989).

4. Many courts now utilize detailed questionnaires to obtain information about the backgrounds and attitudes of prospective jurors. *Questions From the Jury Pool on Privacy,* N.Y. Times, May 13, 1994, p. B9, col. 1, reports that a prospective juror was sentenced to a three-day jail term for contempt of court for answering "not applicable" to 12 questions in a 100–question questionnaire posed to prospective jurors in a murder case. She gave that answer "to queries about her income, her religion, her political affiliation and books and TV shows she enjoys, among other questions." What should the result be on her appeal of the contempt citation? This article notes: "But prosecutors and criminal defense lawyers alike contend that a prospective juror's right to privacy must yield to the imperatives of a fair trial, particularly in a murder case. Questions that appear entirely irrelevant to a member of a jury pool, they say, may nonetheless help lawyers develop a well-rounded profile."

The O.J. Simpson trial, where prospective jurors in advance of voir dire were required to answer 294 questions running over 75 pages, has focused further attention upon the practice of using juror questionnaires. See Craig M. Bradley & Joseph L. Hoffman, *Public Perception, Justice, and the "Search for Truth" in Criminal Cases,* 69 S.Cal.L.Rev. 1267, 1284 (1996) (suggesting courts should prohibit the use of questionnaires); Peter Arenella, *Foreword: O.J. Lessons,* 69

S.Cal.L.Rev. 1240, 1233 (1996) (suggesting ban on juror questionnaires "in all cases except those where the defendant's right to a fair trial has been threatened by extremely prejudicial pretrial publicity").

5. Is it permissible for the prosecution to send police officers out to interview the prospective jurors about their backgrounds and views on certain issues, as in *Commonwealth v. Smith,* 215 N.E.2d 897 (Mass.1966)? To have an FBI investigation of members of the venire conducted, as in *United States v. Falange,* 426 F.2d 930 (2d Cir.1970)? To question members of the panel about their votes in previous cases? *A.B.A. Code of Prof. Resp.* D.R. 7–108 provides: "(A) Before the trial of a case a lawyer connected therewith shall not communicate with or cause another to communicate with anyone he knows to be a member of the venire from which the jury will be selected for the trial of the case. * * * (E) A lawyer shall not conduct or cause, by financial support or otherwise, another to conduct a vexatious or harassing investigation of either a venireman or a juror."

6. "In all but a few jurisdictions, discovery of juror information by either the prosecution or defense is not allowed. Typically, the cases find the defense seeking discovery of juror information sifted from police records or compiled by a government agency and employed by the prosecution. Judges have held almost uniformly that the prosecution need not reveal this information, although the courts consistently have failed to articulate any convincing rationale for this position." Note, 49 So.Cal.L.Rev. 597, 602–03 (1976). But see *People v. Murtishaw,* 631 P.2d 446 (Cal.1981) (trial courts "have the discretion to permit a defendant, who lacks funds to investigate prospective jurors, to inspect prosecution jury records and investigations").

7. In some recent trials, social science techniques have been employed in jury selection. The first step is to survey randomly as large a sample as possible of the population from which the jury will be selected. The researchers attempt to discern attitudes relevant to the issues in the particular forthcoming trial. Data from the survey is fed into a computer with socioeconomic background characteristics (e.g., religion, age, sex, occupation) in order to identify those characteristics which would identify a favorable and unfavorable juror. The questions asked on voir dire are geared to ascertaining those characteristics found to be associated with favorable or unfavorable attitudes. Instead or in addition, the jury panel may be observed in court and rated by psychologists or psychiatrists on authoritarianism scales or by kinesiologists in terms of body language.

"At this stage in its development, the cost of the new techniques is so great that only the very rich, or those famous enough to secure donated time and money, are able to afford them. * * *

"So far the new juror investigative techniques have been used exclusively by defendants in trials with strong political overtones. However, prosecutors will no doubt begin to utilize the techniques as well, if only to counterbalance the effect of studies done for defendants. The impact of prosecutorial use of these techniques could be profound; state and federal governments have not only the resources to employ social scientists and computers necessary to utilize the new techniques, but they have also a wealth of specific juror information unavailable to the defense. Furthermore, the effectiveness of the techniques in selecting favorably biased juries will be a strong incentive for prosecutors to employ the techniques in all important trials regardless of whether the defense has conducted a study of its own." Note, 49 So.Cal.L.Rev. 597, 606–07 (1976).

Is this a cause for concern? Michael J. Saks, *The Limits of Scientific Jury Selection: Ethical and Empirical,* 17 Jurimetrics J. 3, 4 (1976), warns: "If the outcome of a trial can be manipulated simply by impaneling jurors designated acceptable by social scientists, then trial by jury may cease to function satisfactorily and, ultimately, may be abandoned." What, then, should be done? If the prosecutor has a jury selection expert, is an indigent defendant entitled to funds to hire such an expert under *Ake*, p. 83? See *People v. Box*, 5 P.3d 130 (Cal.2000).

8. Most jurisdictions have provided by statute or court rule for the selection of extra jurors during protracted trials. "Some States have adopted rules or statutes that, like the recent revision to Fed.R.Crim.P. 24(c), expressly permit the substitution of an alternate after deliberations have begun. Some reach essentially the same result by following the [former] Federal approach of applying a liberal harmless error or non-prejudice test to mid-deliberation substitutions" made in violation of a statute or court rule allowing substitution only until the jury retires. *Hayes v. State*, 355 Md. 615, 735 A.2d 1109 (1999) (citing statutes, court rules, and judicial decisions). A growing body of authority views substitution during deliberations as constitutionally permissible if the substituted juror was untainted and the jury was instructed to begin its deliberations anew; see, e.g., *Claudio v. Snyder*, 68 F.3d 1573 (3d Cir.1995). Compare *People v. Ryan*, 224 N.E.2d 710 (N.Y.1966) (such substitution unconstitutional, for "if deliberations had progressed to a stage where the original eleven were in substantial agreement, they were in a position to present a formidable obstacle to the alternate juror's attempts to persuade and convince the eleven remaining original jurors").

NOTES ON CHALLENGES FOR CAUSE
AND VOIR DIRE EXAMINATION

1. Statutes setting forth the permissible grounds for challenge for cause typically cover such specific situations as where the prospective juror has previously served as a juror on some related matter, where he has been or will be a witness against the defendant, and where he is related in some degree to the defendant or others involved in the case. A more general ground for challenge is often stated in these terms:

"That the juror has a state of mind in reference to the cause or to the defendant or to the person alleged to have been injured by the offense charged, or to the person on whose complaint the prosecution was instituted, which will prevent him from acting with impartiality; but the formation of an opinion or impression regarding the guilt or innocence of the defendant shall not of itself be sufficient ground of challenge to a juror, if he declares, and the court is satisfied, that he can render an impartial verdict according to the evidence."

2. In *Dennis v. United States*, 339 U.S. 162, 70 S.Ct. 519, 94 L.Ed. 734 (1950), a 5–2 majority of the Court, per Minton, J., held that in a case to which the federal government is a party, its employees are not challengeable for cause solely by reason of their employment. The Court also rejected the argument that the failure to sustain the challenge denied petitioner an "impartial jury" under the "special circumstances of this case"—a prosecution of a Communist for contempt of the House Un–American Activities Committee, where the government's interest was said to be "the vindication of a direct affront, as distinguished from its role in an ordinary prosecution"; and where, because of an alleged "aura of surveillance and intimidation" said to exist because of a "Loyalty Order," government employees "would be hesitant to vote for acquittal because such action might be interpreted as 'sympathetic association' with Communism." *Dennis* continues to be followed. See, e.g., *United States v. Boyd*, 446 F.2d 1267 (5th Cir.1971) (must show actual bias of government employee in theft from government case).

As for employment by a nongovernmental victim of the crime charged, compare the following cases in which the prospective juror was employed at the bank robbed, albeit at a branch other than where the robbery occurred: *United States v. Brown,* 644 F.2d 101 (2d Cir.1981) (not excusable for cause; court unwilling "to institute a series of presumptions of implied bias in other employment relationships"); *United States v. Allsup,* 566 F.2d 68 (9th Cir.1977) ("The employment relationship coupled with a reasonable apprehension of violence by bank robbers leads us to believe that bias of those who work for the bank should be presumed").

3. In *United States v. Salamone,* 800 F.2d 1216 (3d Cir.1986), where all prospective jurors affiliated with the National Rifle Association were excused upon the prosecution's challenge for cause because the charges were brought under the gun control statutes, the court stated: "We find the government's position untenable and potentially dangerous. To allow trial judges and prosecutors to determine juror eligibility based solely on their perceptions of the external association of a juror threatens the heretofore guarded right of an accused to a fair trial by an impartial jury as well as the integrity of the judicial process as a whole. Taken to its illogical conclusion, the government's position would sanction, inter alia, the summary exclusion for cause of NAACP members from cases seeking the enforcement of civil rights statutes, Moral Majority activists from pornography cases, Catholics from cases involving abortion clinic protests, members of NOW from sex discrimination cases, and subscribers to Consumer Reports from cases involving products liability claims." The court went on to reject the government's harmless error contention, stating that while inadequate questioning of a single excluded juror might be harmless, the same could not be true of the wholesale exclusion of a particular group.

4. In *Witherspoon v. Illinois,* 391 U.S. 510, 88 S.Ct. 1770, 20 L.Ed.2d 776 (1968), the Court, per Stewart, J., held "that a sentence of death cannot be carried out if the jury that imposed or recommended it was chosen by excluding veniremen for cause simply because they voiced general objections to the death penalty or expressed conscientious or religious scruples against its infliction." In so doing, "the State crossed the line of neutrality" and "produced a jury uncommonly willing to condemn a man to die." *Witherspoon* appeared to permit exclusion only if the prospective juror made it "unmistakably clear" that he would "automatically vote against the imposition of capital punishment." But the Court later concluded it would suffice if "the trial judge is left with the definite impression that a prospective juror would be unable to faithfully and impartially apply the law." *Wainwright v. Witt,* 469 U.S. 412, 105 S.Ct. 844, 83 L.Ed.2d 841 (1985). Excluding such jurors does not intrude upon the defendant's Sixth Amendment rights. As explained in *Buchanan v. Kentucky,* 483 U.S. 402, 107 S.Ct. 2906, 97 L.Ed.2d 336 (1987), there is no fair cross-section violation, as it "applies only to venires, not to petit juries," and in any event is not established by exclusion of *Witherspoon*-excludables "because they do not constitute a distinctive group for fair cross section purposes"; and there was no denial of the right to an impartial jury, as that right does not require "a balancing of jurors with different predilections." A "reverse-*Witherspoon*" challenge for cause by a capital defendant must be granted where it appears the prospective juror would "automatically vote for the death penalty in every capital case." *Morgan v. Illinois,* 504 U.S. 719, 112 S.Ct. 2222, 119 L.Ed.2d 492 (1992).

5. HAM v. SOUTH CAROLINA, 409 U.S. 524, 93 S.Ct. 848, 35 L.Ed.2d 46 (1973), concerned a black, bearded civil rights worker who was convicted of possession of marijuana. During his voir dire examination of prospective jurors, the trial judge asked general questions as to bias, prejudice, or partiality,[a] but

---

a. The three questions asked were, in substance, the following:

"1. Have you formed or expressed any opinion as to the guilt or innocence of the defen-

declined to ask more specific questions tendered by defense counsel which sought to elicit any possible prejudice against the defendant because of his race or his beard. The Court, per REHNQUIST, J., held: "Since one of the purposes of the Due Process Clause of the Fourteenth Amendment is to insure [the] 'essential demands of fairness,' and since a principal purpose of the adoption of the Fourteenth Amendment was to prohibit the States from invidiously discriminating on the basis of race, we think that the Fourteenth Amendment required the judge in this case to interrogate the jurors upon the subject of racial prejudice. * * * [T]he trial judge was not required to put the question in any particular form, or to ask any particular number of questions on the subject, simply because requested to do so by petitioner. * * * In this context either of the brief, general questions urged by the petitioner[b] would appear sufficient to focus the attention of prospective jurors to any racial prejudice they might entertain.

"The third of petitioner's proposed questions was addressed to the fact that he wore a beard. While we cannot say that prejudice against people with beards might not have been harbored by one or more of the potential jurors in this case, this is the beginning and not the end of the inquiry as to whether the Fourteenth Amendment required the trial judge to interrogate the prospective jurors about such possible prejudice. Given the traditionally broad discretion accorded to the trial judge in conducting *voir dire,* and our inability to constitutionally distinguish possible prejudice against beards from a host of other possible similar prejudices, we do not believe the petitioner's constitutional rights were violated when the trial judge refused to put this question. The inquiry as to racial prejudice derives its constitutional stature * * * from a principal purpose as well as from the language of those who adopted the Fourteenth Amendment. The trial judge's refusal to inquire as to particular bias against beards, after his inquiries as to bias in general, does not reach the level of a constitutional violation."[c]

    6.   In *Ristaino v. Ross,* 424 U.S. 589, 96 S.Ct. 1017, 47 L.Ed.2d 258 (1976), the Court, per Powell, J., concluded that *"Ham* did not announce a requirement of universal applicability." The Court did "not agree with the Court of Appeals that the need to question veniremen specifically about racial prejudice also rose to constitutional dimensions in this case.[9] The mere fact that the victim of the crimes alleged [armed robbery, assault with a dangerous weapon, and assault with intent to murder] was a white man and the defendants were Negroes was less likely to distort the trial than were the special factors involved in *Ham.*[d] The victim's

---

dant, Gene Ham?

    "2. Are you conscious of any bias or prejudice for or against him?

    "3. Can you give the State and the defendant a fair and impartial trial?"

    b.   They were:

    "1. Would you fairly try this case on the basis of the evidence and disregarding the defendant's race?

    "2. You have no prejudice against negroes? Against black people? You would not be influenced by the use of the term 'black'?"

    c.   Douglas and Marshall, JJ., dissented.

    9.   "Although we hold that *voir dire* questioning directed to racial prejudice was not constitutionally required, the wiser course generally is to propound appropriate questions designed to identify racial prejudice if requested by the defendant. Under our supervisory power we would have required as much of a federal

court faced with the circumstances here. * * *"

    [Editors' Note: As for this more demanding standard in federal trials, the 4-justice plurality opinion in *Rosales-Lopez v. United States,* 451 U.S. 182, 101 S.Ct. 1629, 68 L.Ed.2d 22 (1981), concluded "it is usually best to allow the defendant to resolve this conflict by making the determination of whether or not he would prefer to have the inquiry into racial or ethnic prejudice pursued. Failure to honor his request, however, will only be reversible error where the circumstances of the case indicate that there is a reasonable possibility that racial or ethnic prejudice might have influenced the jury," as when inquiry was "requested by a defendant accused of a violent crime and where the defendant and the victim are members of different racial or ethnic groups."]

    d.   Compare *Turner v. Murray,* 476 U.S. 28, 106 S.Ct. 1683, 90 L.Ed.2d 27 (1986), where the Court held "that a capital defendant ac-

status as a security officer, also relied upon by the Court of Appeals, was cited by respective defense counsel primarily as a separate source of prejudice, not as an aggravating racial factor, and the trial judge dealt with it by his question about law-enforcement affiliations. The circumstances thus did not suggest a significant likelihood that racial prejudice might infect Ross' trial. This was made clear to the trial judge when Ross was unable to support his motion concerning *voir dire* by pointing to racial factors such as existed in *Ham* or others of comparable significance. In these circumstances, the trial judge acted within the Constitution in determining that the demands of due process could be satisfied by his more generalized but thorough inquiry into the impartiality of the veniremen."

BATSON v. KENTUCKY

476 U.S. 79, 106 S.Ct. 1712, 90 L.Ed.2d 69 (1986).

Justice POWELL delivered the opinion of the Court.

This case requires us to reexamine that portion of *Swain v. Alabama*, 380 U.S. 202, 85 S.Ct. 824, 13 L.Ed.2d 759 (1965), concerning the evidentiary burden placed on a criminal defendant who claims that he has been denied equal protection through the State's use of peremptory challenges to exclude members of his race from the petit jury.

Petitioner, a black man, was indicted in Kentucky on charges of second-degree burglary and receipt of stolen goods. On the first day of trial in Jefferson Circuit Court, the judge conducted *voir dire* examination of the venire, excused certain jurors for cause, and permitted the parties to exercise peremptory challenges. The prosecutor used his peremptory challenges to strike all four black persons on the venire, and a jury composed only of white persons was selected. Defense counsel moved to discharge the jury before it was sworn on the ground that the prosecutor's removal of the black veniremen violated petitioner's rights under the Sixth and Fourteenth Amendments to a jury drawn from a cross-section of the community, and under the Fourteenth Amendment to equal protection of the laws. Counsel requested a hearing on his motion. Without expressly ruling on the request for a hearing, the trial judge observed that the parties were entitled to use their peremptory challenges to "strike anybody they want to." The judge then denied petitioner's motion, reasoning that the cross-section requirement applies only to selection of the venire and not to selection of the petit jury itself.

The jury convicted petitioner on both counts. * * *

The Supreme Court of Kentucky affirmed. * * *

In *Swain v. Alabama*, this Court recognized that a "State's purposeful or deliberate denial to Negroes on account of race of participation as jurors in the

cused of an interracial crime is entitled to have prospective jurors informed of the race of the victim and questioned on the issue of racial bias." But only four members of the Court joined in another part of the opinion concluding: "The inadequacy of *voir dire* in this case requires that petitioner's death sentence be vacated. It is not necessary, however, that he be retried on the issue of guilt. Our judgment in this case is that there was an unacceptable risk of racial prejudice infecting the *capital sentencing proceeding*. This judgment is based on a conjunction of three factors: the fact that the crime charged involved interracial violence, the broad discretion given the jury at the death-penalty hearing, and the special serious-

ness of the risk of improper sentencing in a capital case. At the guilt phase of petitioner's trial, the jury had no greater discretion than it would have had if the crime charged had been noncapital murder. Thus, with respect to the guilt phase of petitioner's trial, we find this case to be indistinguishable from *Ristaino,* to which we continue to adhere." The Chief Justice concurred in the result without opinion; two Justices believed defendant's rights has been violated even at the guilt phase; and two others reasoned the distinction drawn in the Court's opinion was erroneous given the "many procedural and substantive safeguards" which circumscribe the capital jury's sentencing decision.

administration of justice violates the Equal Protection Clause." This principle has been "consistently and repeatedly" reaffirmed, in numerous decisions of this Court both preceding and following *Swain*. We reaffirm the principle today.[4] * * *

Accordingly, the component of the jury selection process at issue here, the State's privilege to strike individual jurors through peremptory challenges, is subject to the commands of the Equal Protection Clause. Although a prosecutor ordinarily is entitled to exercise permitted peremptory challenges "for any reason at all, as long as that reason is related to his view concerning the outcome" of the case to be tried, the Equal Protection Clause forbids the prosecutor to challenge potential jurors solely on account of their race or on the assumption that black jurors as a group will be unable impartially to consider the State's case against a black defendant. * * *

Swain required the Court to decide, among other issues, whether a black defendant was denied equal protection by the State's exercise of peremptory challenges to exclude members of his race from the petit jury. The record in *Swain* showed that the prosecutor had used the State's peremptory challenges to strike the six black persons included on the petit jury venire. While rejecting the defendant's claim for failure to prove purposeful discrimination, the Court nonetheless indicated that the Equal Protection Clause placed some limits on the State's exercise of peremptory challenges.

The Court sought to accommodate the prosecutor's historical privilege of peremptory challenge free of judicial control, and the constitutional prohibition on exclusion of persons from jury service on account of race. While the Constitution does not confer a right to peremptory challenges, those challenges traditionally have been viewed as one means of assuring the selection of a qualified and unbiased jury.[15] To preserve the peremptory nature of the prosecutor's challenge, the Court in *Swain* declined to scrutinize his actions in a particular case by relying on a presumption that he properly exercised the State's challenges.

The Court went on to observe, however, that a state may not exercise its challenges in contravention of the Equal Protection Clause. It was impermissible for a prosecutor to use his challenges to exclude blacks from the jury "for reasons wholly unrelated to the outcome of the particular case on trial" or to deny to blacks "the same right and opportunity to participate in the administration of justice enjoyed by the white population." Accordingly, a black defendant could make out a prima facie case of purposeful discrimination on proof that the

---

4. In this Court, petitioner has argued that the prosecutor's conduct violated his rights under the Sixth and Fourteenth Amendments to an impartial jury and to a jury drawn from a cross-section of the community. Petitioner has framed his argument in these terms in an apparent effort to avoid inviting the Court directly to reconsider one of its own precedents. On the other hand, the State has insisted that petitioner is claiming a denial of equal protection and that we must reconsider *Swain* to find a constitutional violation on this record. We agree with the State that resolution of petitioner's claim properly turns on application of equal protection principles and express no view on the merits of any of petitioner's Sixth Amendment arguments.

[Editors' Note: A *Batson*-type challenge to the prosecutor's use of peremptories, grounded instead in the Sixth Amendment's cross-section requirement, was rejected 5–4 in *Holland*

v. Illinois, 493 U.S. 474, 110 S.Ct. 803, 107 L.Ed.2d 905 (1990), by what the majority characterized as "the only plausible reading of the text of the Sixth Amendment": "The tradition of peremptory challenges for both the prosecution and the accused was already venerable at the time of Blackstone, was reflected in a federal statute enacted by the same Congress that proposed the Bill of Rights, was recognized in an opinion by Justice Story to be part of the common law of the United States, and has endured through two centuries in all the States. The constitutional phrase 'impartial jury' must surely take its content from this unbroken tradition."]

15. In *Swain*, the Court reviewed the "very old credentials" of the peremptory challenge system and noted the "long and widely held belief that peremptory challenge is a necessary part of trial by jury."

peremptory challenge system was "being perverted" in that manner. For example, an inference of purposeful discrimination would be raised on evidence that a prosecutor, "in case after case, whatever the circumstances, whatever the crime and whoever the defendant or the victim may be, is responsible for the removal of Negroes who have been selected as qualified jurors by the jury commissioners and who have survived challenges for cause, with the result that no Negroes ever serve on petit juries." Evidence offered by the defendant in *Swain* did not meet that standard. While the defendant showed that prosecutors in the jurisdiction had exercised their strikes to exclude blacks from the jury, he offered no proof of the circumstances under which prosecutors were responsible for striking black jurors beyond the facts of his own case.

A number of lower courts following the teaching of *Swain* reasoned that proof of repeated striking of blacks over a number of cases was necessary to establish a violation of the Equal Protection Clause. Since this interpretation of *Swain* has placed on defendants a crippling burden of proof, prosecutors' peremptory challenges are now largely immune from constitutional scrutiny. For reasons that follow, we reject this evidentiary formulation as inconsistent with standards that have been developed since *Swain* for assessing a prima facie case under the Equal Protection Clause.

[S]ince the decision in *Swain,* this Court has recognized that a defendant may make a prima facie showing of purposeful racial discrimination in selection of the venire by relying solely on the facts concerning its selection *in his case.* These decisions are in accordance with the proposition that "a consistent pattern of official racial discrimination" is not "a necessary predicate to a violation of the Equal Protection Clause. A single invidiously discriminatory governmental act" is not "immunized by the absence of such discrimination in the making of other comparable decisions." For evidentiary requirements to dictate that "several must suffer discrimination" before one could object, would be inconsistent with the promise of equal protection to all.

The standards for assessing a prima facie case in the context of discriminatory selection of the venire have been fully articulated since *Swain.* These principles support our conclusion that a defendant may establish a prima facie case of purposeful discrimination in selection of the petit jury solely on evidence concerning the prosecutor's exercise of peremptory challenges at the defendant's trial. To establish such a case, the defendant first must show that he is a member of a cognizable racial group, and that the prosecutor has exercised peremptory challenges to remove from the venire members of the defendant's race. Second, the defendant is entitled to rely on the fact, as to which there can be no dispute, that peremptory challenges constitute a jury selection practice that permits "those to discriminate who are of a mind to discriminate." Finally, the defendant must show that these facts and any other relevant circumstances raise an inference that the prosecutor used that practice to exclude the veniremen from the petit jury on account of their race. This combination of factors in the empanelling of the petit jury, as in the selection of the venire, raises the necessary inference of purposeful discrimination.

In deciding whether the defendant has made the requisite showing, the trial court should consider all relevant circumstances. For example, a "pattern" of strikes against black jurors included in the particular venire might give rise to an inference of discrimination. Similarly, the prosecutor's questions and statements during *voir dire* examination and in exercising his challenges may support or refute an inference of discriminatory purpose. These examples are merely illustrative. We have confidence that trial judges, experienced in supervising *voir dire,* will be able to decide if the circumstances concerning the prosecutor's use of peremptory challenges creates a prima facie case of discrimination against black jurors.

Once the defendant makes a prima facie showing, the burden shifts to the State to come forward with a neutral explanation for challenging black jurors. Though this requirement imposes a limitation in some cases on the full peremptory character of the historic challenge, we emphasize that the prosecutor's explanation need not rise to the level justifying exercise of a challenge for cause. But the prosecutor may not rebut the defendant's prima facie case of discrimination by stating merely that he challenged jurors of the defendant's race on the assumption—or his intuitive judgment—that they would be partial to the defendant because of their shared race. Just as the Equal Protection Clause forbids the States to exclude black persons from the venire on the assumption that blacks as a group are unqualified to serve as jurors, so it forbids the States to strike black veniremen on the assumption that they will be biased in a particular case simply because the defendant is black. The core guarantee of equal protection, ensuring citizens that their State will not discriminate on account of race, would be meaningless were we to approve the exclusion of jurors on the basis of such assumptions, which arise solely from the jurors' race. Nor may the prosecutor rebut the defendant's case merely by denying that he had a discriminatory motive or "affirming his good faith in individual selections." If these general assertions were accepted as rebutting a defendant's prima facie case, the Equal Protection Clause "would be but a vain and illusory requirement." The prosecutor therefore must articulate a neutral explanation related to the particular case to be tried. The trial court then will have the duty to determine if the defendant has established purposeful discrimination.[a]

The State contends that our holding will eviscerate the fair trial values served by the peremptory challenge. Conceding that the Constitution does not guarantee a right to peremptory challenges and that *Swain* did state that their use ultimately is subject to the strictures of equal protection, the State argues that the privilege of unfettered exercise of the challenge is of vital importance to the criminal justice system.

While we recognize, of course, that the peremptory challenge occupies an important position in our trial procedures, we do not agree that our decision today will undermine the contribution the challenge generally makes to the administration of justice. The reality of practice, amply reflected in many state and federal court opinions, shows that the challenge may be, and unfortunately at times has been, used to discriminate against black jurors. By requiring trial courts to be sensitive to the racially discriminatory use of peremptory challenges, our decision enforces the mandate of equal protection and furthers the ends of justice. In view

---

a. In *Purkett v. Elem*, 514 U.S. 765, 115 S.Ct. 1769, 131 L.Ed.2d 834 (1995), the Court explained that "once the opponent of a peremptory challenge has made out a prima facie case of racial discrimination (step 1), the burden of production shifts to the proponent of the strike to come forward with a race-neutral explanation (step 2). If a race-neutral explanation is tendered, the trial court must then decide (step 3) whether the opponent of the strike has proved purposeful racial discrimination. * * *

"The Court of Appeals erred by combining *Batson*'s second and third steps into one, requiring that the justification tendered at the second step be not just neutral but also at least minimally persuasive * * *. It is not until the *third* step that the persuasiveness of the justification becomes relevant—the step in which the trial court determines whether the opponent of the strike has carried his burden of proving purposeful discrimination. At that stage, implausible or fantastic justifications may (and probably will) be found to be pretexts for purposeful discrimination. But to say that a trial judge *may choose to disbelieve* a silly or superstitious reason at step 3 is quite different from saying that a trial judge *must terminate* the inquiry at step 2 when the race-neutral reason is silly or superstitious. The latter violates the principle that the ultimate burden of persuasion regarding racial motivation rests with, and never shifts from, the opponent of the strike."

of the heterogeneous population of our nation, public respect for our criminal justice system and the rule of law will be strengthened if we ensure that no citizen is disqualified from jury service because of his race.

Nor are we persuaded by the State's suggestion that our holding will create serious administrative difficulties. In those states applying a version of the evidentiary standard we recognize today, courts have not experienced serious administrative burdens, and the peremptory challenge system has survived. We decline, however, to formulate particular procedures to be followed upon a defendant's timely objection to a prosecutor's challenges.[24]

In this case, petitioner made a timely objection to the prosecutor's removal of all black persons on the venire. Because the trial court flatly rejected the objection without requiring the prosecutor to give an explanation for his action, we remand this case for further proceedings. If the trial court decides that the facts establish, prima facie, purposeful discrimination and the prosecutor does not come forward with a neutral explanation for his action, our precedents require that petitioner's conviction be reversed.

Justice MARSHALL, concurring. * * *

Evidentiary analysis similar to that set out by the Court has been adopted as a matter of state law in States including Massachusetts and California. Cases from those jurisdictions illustrate the limitations of the approach. First, defendants cannot attack the discriminatory use of peremptory challenges at all unless the challenges are so flagrant as to establish a prima facie case. This means, in those States, that where only one or two black jurors survive the challenges for cause, the prosecutor need have no compunction about striking them from the jury because of their race. Prosecutors are left free to discriminate against blacks in jury selection provided that they hold that discrimination to an "acceptable" level.

Second, when a defendant can establish a prima facie case, trial courts face the difficult burden of assessing prosecutors' motives. Any prosecutor can easily assert facially neutral reasons for striking a juror, and trial courts are ill-equipped to second-guess those reasons. How is the court to treat a prosecutor's statement that he struck a juror because the juror had a son about the same age as defendant, or seemed "uncommunicative" or "never cracked a smile" and, therefore "did not possess the sensitivities necessary to realistically look at the issues and decide the facts in this case." If such easily generated explanations are sufficient to discharge the prosecutor's obligation to justify his strikes on nonracial grounds, then the protection erected by the Court today may be illusory.

Nor is outright prevarication by prosecutors the only danger here. "[I]t is even possible that an attorney may lie to himself in an effort to convince himself that his motives are legal." A prosecutor's own conscious or unconscious racism may lead him easily to the conclusion that a prospective black juror is "sullen," or "distant," a characterization that would not have come to his mind if a white juror had acted identically. A judge's own conscious or unconscious racism may lead him to accept such an explanation as well supported. * * *

The inherent potential of peremptory challenges to distort the jury process by permitting the exclusion of jurors on racial grounds should ideally lead the Court

---

24. In light of the variety of jury selection practices followed in our state and federal trial courts, we make no attempt to instruct these courts how best to implement our holding today. For the same reason, we express no view on whether it is more appropriate in a particular case, upon a finding of discrimination against black jurors, for the trial court to discharge the venire and select a new jury from a panel not previously associated with the case, or to disallow the discriminatory challenges and resume selection with the improperly challenged jurors reinstated on the venire.

to * * * banning the use of peremptory challenges by prosecutors and by allowing the States to eliminate the defendant's peremptory as well. * * *

Chief Justice BURGER, joined by Justice REHNQUIST, dissenting. * * *

The Court's opinion, in addition to ignoring the teachings of history, also contrasts with *Swain* in its failure to even discuss the rationale of the peremptory challenge. *Swain* observed:

> "The function of the challenge is not only to eliminate extremes of partiality on both sides, but to assure the parties that the jurors before whom they try the case will decide on the basis of the evidence placed for them, and not otherwise. In this way the peremptory satisfies the rule that 'to perform its high function in the best way, justice must satisfy the appearance of justice.'"

Permitting unexplained peremptories has long been regarded as a means to strengthen our jury system in other ways as well. One commentator has recognized:

> "The peremptory, made without giving any reason, avoids trafficking in the core of truth in most common stereotypes. . . . Common human experience, common sense, psychosociological studies, and public opinion polls tell us that it is likely that certain classes of people statistically have predispositions that would make them inappropriate jurors for particular kinds of cases. But to allow this knowledge to be expressed in the evaluative terms necessary for challenges for cause would undercut our desire for a society in which all people are judged as individuals and in which each is held reasonable and open to compromise. . . . [For example,] [a]lthough experience reveals that black males as a class can be biased against young alienated blacks who have not tried to join the middle class, to enunciate this in the concrete expression required of a challenge for cause is societally divisive. Instead we have evolved in the peremptory challenge a system that allows the covert expression of what we dare not say but know is true more often than not." Babcock, *Voir Dire: Preserving "Its Wonderful Power,"* 27 Stan.L.Rev. 545, 553–554 (1975).

For reasons such as these, this Court concluded in *Swain* that "the [peremptory] challenge is 'one of the most important of the rights' " in our justice system. For close to a century, then, it has been settled that "[t]he denial or impairment of the right is reversible error without a showing of prejudice."

[T]he Court also invokes general equal protection principles in support of its holding. But peremptory challenges are often lodged, of necessity, for reasons "normally thought irrelevant to legal proceedings or official action, namely, the race, religion, nationality, occupation or affiliations of people summoned for jury duty." *Swain.* Moreover, in making peremptory challenges, both the prosecutor and defense attorney necessarily act on only limited information or hunch. The process can not be indicted on the sole basis that such decisions are made on the basis of "assumption" or "intuitive judgment." As a result, unadulterated equal protection analysis is simply inapplicable to peremptory challenges exercised in any particular case. A clause that requires a minimum "rationality" in government actions has no application to " 'an arbitrary and capricious right' "; a constitutional principle that may invalidate state action on the basis of "stereotypic notions" does not explain the breadth of a procedure exercised on the " 'sudden impressions and unaccountable prejudices we are apt to conceive upon the bare looks and gestures of another.' " * * *

* * * To rebut a prima facie case, the Court requires a "neutral explanation" for the challenge, but is at pains to "emphasize" that the "explanation need not rise to the level justifying exercise of a challenge for cause." I am at a loss to

discern the governing principles here. A "clear and reasonably specific" explanation of "legitimate reasons" for exercising the challenge will be difficult to distinguish from a challenge for cause. Anything short of a challenge for cause may well be seen as an "arbitrary and capricious" challenge, to use Blackstone's characterization of the peremptory. Apparently the Court envisions permissible challenges short of a challenge for cause that are just a little bit arbitrary—but not too much. While our trial judges are "experienced in supervising *voir dire*," they have no experience in administering rules like this. * * *

Justice REHNQUIST, with whom The Chief Justice joins, dissenting. * * *

I cannot subscribe to the Court's unprecedented use of the Equal Protection Clause to restrict the historic scope of the peremptory challenge, which has been described as "a necessary part of trial by jury." In my view, there is simply nothing "unequal" about the State using its peremptory challenges to strike blacks from the jury in cases involving black defendants, so long as such challenges are also used to exclude whites in cases involving white defendants, Hispanics in cases involving Hispanic defendants, Asians in cases involving Asian defendants, and so on. This case-specific use of peremptory challenges by the State does not single out blacks, or members of any other race for that matter, for discriminatory treatment. Such use of peremptories is at best based upon seat-of-the-pants instincts, which are undoubtedly crudely stereotypical and may in many cases be hopelessly mistaken. But as long as they are applied across the board to jurors of all races and nationalities, I do not see—and the Court most certainly has not explained—how their use violates the Equal Protection Clause.

Nor does such use of peremptory challenges by the State infringe upon any other constitutional interests. [B]ecause the case-specific use of peremptory challenges by the State does not deny blacks the right to serve as jurors in cases involving non-black defendants, it harms neither the excluded jurors nor the remainder of the community. * * *

NOTES ON PEREMPTORY CHALLENGES

1. At common law the defendant was entitled to 35 peremptory challenges, but most states have now provided for a lesser number, usually 20 for offenses punishable by death or life imprisonment, 10 for other felonies, and 3 for misdemeanors. Most states give the prosecution a number of peremptory challenges equal to those granted the defendant, but some give a lesser number (seldom below half those granted the defendant). Where several defendants are to be tried together, the common law rule was that each defendant has as many challenges as he would have if tried alone, but several states now provide otherwise by statute or rule of court.

What if a defendant, upon the trial judge's erroneous failure to grant his reverse-*Witherspoon* motion, see Note 4, p. 1332, then uses one of his peremptories (all of which he ultimately exhausts) to remove that juror? In *Ross v. Oklahoma*, 487 U.S. 81, 108 S.Ct. 2273, 101 L.Ed.2d 80 (1988), the Court held 5–4 that defendant had not been denied an impartial jury because that juror "was thereby removed from the jury as effectively as if the trial court had excused him for cause." As for the fact the defendant had to use up one of his peremptories to cure the trial court's error, the Court "reject[ed] the notion that the loss of a peremptory challenge constitutes a violation of the constitutional right to an impartial jury," for "peremptory challenges are not of constitutional dimension." As for the defendant's claim it constituted a violation of due process to deprive him, in effect, of a full complement of peremptories, as provided by statute, the Court answered that "peremptory challenges are a creature of statute," as to which the state may "define their purpose and manner of exercise," and by state law the grant of nine peremptories in capital cases "is qualified by the requirement that the defendant must use those challenges to cure erroneous refusal by the trial court to excuse jurors for cause."[a]

In *United States v. Martinez–Salazar*, 528 U.S. 304, 120 S.Ct. 774, 145 L.Ed.2d 792 (2000), where defendant exercised all of his peremptories but used one of them to excuse a juror the trial judge erroneously refused to excuse for cause, the defendant claimed he had consequently been denied the number of peremptory challenges he was entitled to have under Fed.R.Crim.P. 24(b), so that his conviction should be reversed. The Court declined to hold "that federal law, like the Oklahoma statute considered in *Ross*, should be read to require a defendant to use a peremptory challenge to strike a juror who should have been removed for cause, in order to preserve the claim that the for-cause ruling impaired the defendant's right to a fair trial," but did accept the "narrower contention" that Fed.R.Crim.P.24(b) "was not violated in this case" because it merely confers upon the defendant the choice "to stand on his objection to the erroneous denial of the challenge for cause or to use a peremptory challenge to effect an instantaneous cure of the error." (The Court in *Martinez-Salazar* went on to emphasize that the case before it was not one where "the trial court deliberately misapplied the law in order to force the defendant to use a peremptory challenge to correct the court's error," and that the trial court's ruling did not "result in the seating of any juror who should have been dismissed for cause.")

2. The prevailing practice is for the prosecutor to call and examine 12 veniremen, exercise his challenges for cause and such peremptory challenges as he then wishes to use, replace those excused with others, and then tender a group of 12 to the defendant. The defendant then follows a similar procedure with this group and tenders a jury of 12 back to the prosecutor, and they continue on in this manner until both parties have exhausted their challenges or indicated their satisfaction with the jury. By contrast, under the struck jury system jurors are first examined and challenged for cause by both sides, excused jurors are replaced on the panel, and the examination of replacements continues until a panel of qualified jurors is presented. The size of the panel at this time is 12 plus the number of peremptory strikes allowed all parties. The parties then proceed to exercise their peremptories in some order which will result in all exhausting their strikes at approximately the same time. Which system is preferable?

3. For the view that the overruling of *Swain* cannot eliminate the influence of racial bias on jury verdicts and that strong "prophylactic" measures are needed, see Sheri Lynn Johnson, *Black Innocence and the White Jury*, 83 Mich.L.Rev. 1611, 1692–1708 (1985). Although she recognizes that the Court has summarily rejected such a claim, Professor Johnson maintains that a black, Native American or Hispanic defendant should have a right to "racially similar" jurors. Laboratory and field studies suggest that "a reasonable compromise between expediency and effectiveness is to assure the defendant three racially similar jurors [on a twelve-person jury]." Id. at 1698–99.

a. If the trial judge erroneously granted a *Witherspoon* motion by the prosecutor, may it be concluded "that a *Witherspoon* violation constitutes harmless error when the prosecutor has an unexercised peremptory challenge that he states he would have used to excuse the juror"? No, the Court concluded 5–4 in *Gray v. Mississippi*, 481 U.S. 648, 107 S.Ct. 2045, 95 L.Ed.2d 622 (1987), for the "practical result of adoption of this unexercised peremptory argument would be to insulate jury-selection error from meaningful appellate review," as by "simply stating during *voir dire* that the State is prepared to exercise a peremptory challenge if the court denies its motion for cause, a prosecutor would ensure that a reviewing court would consider any erroneous exclusion harmless."

4. In POWERS v. OHIO, 499 U.S. 400, 111 S.Ct. 1364, 113 L.Ed.2d 411 (1991), the Court held, 7–2, that "a white defendant may object to the prosecution's peremptory challenges of black venirepersons." The majority, per KENNEDY, J., reasoned that such challenges, if based upon race, violate the venirepersons' right to equal protection under the Fourteenth Amendment, as to which "a criminal defendant has standing" to object because the three criteria for recognizing third-party standing are present: (1) The defendant has "suffered an 'injury-in-fact'" by such peremptory challenges adequate to give "him or her a 'sufficiently concrete interest' in the outcome of the issue in dispute," for the "overt wrong, often apparent to the entire jury panel, casts doubt over the obligation of the parties, the jury, and indeed the court to adhere to the law throughout the trial of the cause." (2) The defendant has "a close relation to the third party" excluded venirepersons, as he or she "will be a motivated, effective advocate for the excluded venirepersons' rights" given "that discrimination in the jury selection process may lead to the reversal of a conviction." (3) There exists "some hindrance to the third party's ability to protect his or her own interests," for potential jurors "have no opportunity to be heard at the time of their exclusion," cannot "easily obtain declaratory or injunctive relief" later given the need to show a likely reoccurrence of their own exclusion based on race, and are unlikely to undertake an action for damages "because of the small financial stake involved and the economic burdens of litigation."[b]

SCALIA, J., in dissent, objected: "The sum and substance of the Court's lengthy analysis is that, since a denial of equal protection to other people occurred at the defendant's trial, though it did not affect the fairness of that trial, the defendant must go free. Even if I agreed that the exercise of peremptory strikes constitutes unlawful discrimination (which I do not), I would not understand why the release of a convicted murderer who has not been harmed by those strikes is an appropriate remedy."

5. In GEORGIA v. McCOLLUM, 505 U.S. 42, 112 S.Ct. 2348, 120 L.Ed.2d 33 (1992), where white defendants were charged with assaulting black victims, the prosecutor claimed the *defendants* should be barred from striking prospective jurors merely because they were black. The Court, noting it had earlier held in *Edmonson v. Leesville Concrete Co.*, 500 U.S. 614, 111 S.Ct. 2077, 114 L.Ed.2d 660 (1991), that racial discrimination in a civil litigant's exercise of peremptory challenges violates the equal protection clause, ruled in *McCollum* that *Batson* likewise applies to the exercise of peremptories by a criminal defendant. BLACKMUN, J., for the Court, reached this conclusion by consideration of four issues. The first, "whether a criminal defendant's exercise of peremptory challenges in a racially discriminatory manner inflicts the harms addressed by *Batson*," was answered in the affirmative, as in these circumstances as well prospective jurors are denied the opportunity to participate in jury service on account of their race, and public confidence in the fairness of jury verdicts is consequently undermined.

As for the second issue, "whether the exercise of peremptory challenges by a criminal defendant constitutes state action," the Court again answered in the affirmative, stressing three points: (i) The defendant relied on government assistance to bring about the deprivation, as "the peremptory challenge system * * * 'simply could not exist' without the 'overt and significant participation of the government.'" (ii) The defendant in exercising peremptories "is performing a traditional governmental function," as "the selection of a jury in a criminal case fulfills a unique and constitutionally compelled governmental function." (iii) The

b. The Court indicated, however, that the case of a white defendant and of a black defendant might, as a practical matter, be somewhat different because "racial identity between the defendant and the excused person might [make it] easier * * * to establish both a prima facie case and a conclusive showing that wrongful discrimination has occurred."

"courtroom setting in which the peremptory challenge is exercised intensifies the harmful effects" of the discrimination, as "regardless of who precipitated the jurors' removal, the perception and the reality in a criminal trial will be that the court has excused jurors based on race, an outcome that will be attributed to the State."

On the third issue, "whether the State has standing to challenge a defendant's discriminatory use of peremptory challenges," the Court also responded in the affirmative. Such third-party standing, the Court explained, is proper where, as here, (i) the state also suffers injury "when the fairness and integrity of its own judicial process is undermined"; (ii) the state has a close relationship with the excluded jurors as "the representative of all its citizens"; and (iii) there are significant barriers to the excluded jurors acting to vindicate their own rights.

As for the final question in *McCollum,* "whether the interests served by *Batson* must give way to the rights of a criminal defendant," the Court concluded that neither a defendant's right to a fair trial nor his Sixth Amendment rights to counsel and to an impartial jury "includes the right to discriminate against a group of citizens based upon their race."

REHNQUIST, C.J., concurred on the ground that *Edmonson* required such a result, as did THOMAS, J., who also noted *Batson* "has taken us down a slope of inquiry that has no clear stopping point. Today, we decide only that white defendants may not strike black veniremen on the basis of race. Eventually, we will have to decide whether black defendants may strike white veniremen.[2]" One of the two dissenters, O'CONNOR, J., cautioned: "It is by now clear that conscious and unconscious racism can affect the way white jurors perceive minority defendants and the facts presented at their trials, perhaps determining the verdict of guilt or innocence. Using peremptory challenges to secure minority representation on the jury may help to overcome such racial bias, for there is substantial reason to believe that the distorting influence of race is minimized on a racially mixed jury. * * * In a world where the outcome of a minority defendant's trial may turn on the misconceptions or biases of white jurors, there is cause to question the implications of this Court's good intentions."

6. J.E.B. v. ALABAMA ex rel. T.B., 511 U.S. 127, 114 S.Ct. 1419, 128 L.Ed.2d 89 (1994), involved a paternity action brought by the state against J.E.B. After challenges for cause, the jury panel consisted of 10 males and 23 females. The state used 9 of its 10 peremptories to strike males, and J.E.B. used all but one of his strikes to remove females, resulting in an all-female jury. The court below ruled that *Batson* does not extend to gender-based peremptory challenges, but the Supreme Court, 6–3, disagreed. BLACKMUN, J., for the majority, stated:

"We need not determine, however, whether women or racial minorities have suffered more at the hands of discriminatory state actors during the decades of our Nation's history. It is necessary only to acknowledge that 'our Nation has had a long and unfortunate history of sex discrimination,' a history which warrants the heightened scrutiny we afford all gender-based classifications today. Under our equal protection jurisprudence, gender-based classifications require 'an exceedingly persuasive justification' in order to survive constitutional scrutiny. Thus, the only question is whether discrimination on the basis of gender in jury selection substantially furthers the State's legitimate interest in achieving a fair and impartial trial. In making this assessment, we do not weigh the value of

2. The NAACP has submitted a brief arguing, in all sincerity, that "whether white defendants can use peremptory challenges to purge minority jurors presents quite different issues from whether a minority defendant can strike majority group jurors." Although I suppose that this issue technically remains open, it is difficult to see how the result could be different if the defendants here were black.

peremptory challenges as an institution against our asserted commitment to eradicate invidious discrimination from the courtroom. Instead, we consider whether peremptory challenges based on gender stereotypes provide substantial aid to a litigant's effort to secure a fair and impartial jury.

"Far from proffering an exceptionally persuasive justification for its gender-based peremptory challenges, respondent maintains that its decision to strike virtually all the males from the jury in this case 'may reasonably have been based upon the perception, supported by history, that men otherwise totally qualified to serve upon a jury might be more sympathetic and receptive to the arguments of a man alleged in a paternity action to be the father of an out-of-wedlock child, while women equally qualified to serve upon a jury might be more sympathetic and receptive to the arguments of the complaining witness who bore the child.'

"We shall not accept as a defense to gender-based peremptory challenges 'the very stereotype the law condemns.' Respondent's rationale, not unlike those regularly expressed for gender-based strikes, is reminiscent of the arguments advanced to justify the total exclusion of women from juries. Respondent offers virtually no support for the conclusion that gender alone is an accurate predictor of juror's attitudes; yet it urges this Court to condone the same stereotypes that justified the wholesale exclusion of women from juries and the ballot box.[11] Respondent seems to assume that gross generalizations that would be deemed impermissible if made on the basis of race are somehow permissible when made on the basis of gender.

"Discrimination in jury selection, whether based on race or on gender, causes harm to the litigants, the community, and the individual jurors who are wrongfully excluded from participation in the judicial process. The litigants are harmed by the risk that the prejudice which motivated the discriminatory selection of the jury will infect the entire proceedings. The community is harmed by the State's participation in the perpetuation of invidious group stereotypes and the inevitable loss of confidence in our judicial system that state-sanctioned discrimination in the courtroom engenders. * * * The potential for cynicism is particularly acute in cases where gender-related issues are prominent, such as cases involving rape, sexual harassment, or paternity. * * *

"In recent cases we have emphasized that individual jurors themselves have a right to nondiscriminatory jury selection procedures. Contrary to respondent's suggestion, this right extends to both men and women. All persons, when granted the opportunity to serve on a jury, have the right not to be excluded summarily because of discriminatory and stereotypical presumptions that reflect and reinforce patterns of historical discrimination.[13]"

Justice O'CONNOR, concurring, adhered "to my position that the Equal Protection Clause does not limit the exercise of peremptory challenges by private civil litigants and criminal defendants. * * * Will we, in the name of fighting gender discrimination, hold that the battered wife—on trial for wounding her

---

11. Even if a measure of truth can be found in some of the gender stereotypes used to justify gender-based peremptory challenges, that fact alone cannot support discrimination on the basis of gender in jury selection. We have made abundantly clear in past cases that gender classifications that rest on impermissible stereotypes violate the Equal Protection Clause, even when some statistical support can be conjured up for the generalization. * * *

13. It is irrelevant that women, unlike African-Americans, are not a numerical minority

and therefore are likely to remain on the jury if each side uses its peremptory challenges in an equally discriminatory fashion. Because the right to nondiscriminatory jury selection procedures belongs to the potential jurors, as well as to the litigants, the possibility that members of both genders will get on the jury despite the intentional discrimination is beside the point. The exclusion of even one juror for impermissible reasons harms that juror and undermines public confidence in the fairness of the system.

abusive husband—is a state actor? Will we preclude her from using her peremptory challenges to ensure that the jury of her peers contains as many women members as possible? I assume we will, but I hope we will not."

Justice SCALIA, for the dissenters, objected: "Since all groups are subject to the peremptory challenge (and will be made the object of it, depending upon the nature of the particular case) it is hard to see how any group is denied equal protection. * * * This case is a perfect example of how the system as a whole is even-handed. While the only claim before the Court is petitioner's complaint that the prosecutor struck male jurors, for every man struck by the government petitioner's own lawyer struck a woman. To say that men were singled out for discriminatory treatment in this process is preposterous. * * *

"Even if the line of our later cases guaranteed by today's decision limits the theoretically boundless *Batson* principle to race, sex, and perhaps other classifications subject to heightened scrutiny[c] (which presumably would include religious belief[d]), much damage has been done. * * * Voir dire (though it can be expected to expand as a consequence of today's decision) cannot fill the gap. The biases that go along with group characteristics tend to be biases that the juror himself does not perceive, so that it is no use asking about them. It is fruitless to inquire of a male juror whether he harbors any subliminal prejudice in favor of unwed fathers."

7. In providing a "neutral explanation," to what extent may the prosecutor rely upon his "hunches" or assumptions not specifically supported by the record made on voir dire? Compare *State v. Slappy,* 522 So.2d 18 (Fla.1988) (though court agrees "that 'liberalism' was neutral and reasonable" as a reason when viewed in the abstract, it is not a sufficient reason in this case because there is no showing that the prospective juror was questioned on this matter, and it is not sufficient that the prosecutor inferred liberalism from the prospective juror's occupation as a teacher); with *Lockett v. State,* 517 So.2d 1346 (Miss.1987) (excusing a minister because of assumption ministers generally are sympathetic toward criminal defendants constitutes a sufficient explanation).

8. In HERNANDEZ v. NEW YORK, 500 U.S. 352, 111 S.Ct. 1859, 114 L.Ed.2d 395 (1991), KENNEDY, J., for four members of the Court, concluded: "The prosecutor here offered a race-neutral basis for these peremptory strikes. As

c. Compare Andrew Leipold, *Constitutionalizing Jury Selection in Criminal Cases: A Critical Evaluation,* 86 Geo.L.J. 945, 949 (1998), concluding "that the Court's interpretation of the *Batson* line of cases cannot logically be limited to peremptory exclusions based on race and gender," meaning that "the *Batson* rationale should prevent the peremptory removal of jurors because of their political views, their group memberships, much of their prior involvement with the justice system, or for many other reasons for which jurors are now routinely excused."

d. In *State v. Davis,* 504 N.W.2d 767 (Minn.1993), defendant objected to the prosecutor's use of a peremptory challenge against a black venireman, but the prosecutor explained she had struck the venireman because he was a Jehovah's Witness and explained that "[i]n my experience Jahovah Witness [sic] are reluctant to exercise authority over their fellow human beings in this Court House." Reading *Batson* as being limited to race-based peremptory challenges, the state supreme court affirmed.

The Supreme Court denied certiorari. *Davis v. Minnesota,* 511 U.S. 1115, 114 S.Ct. 2120, 128 L.Ed.2d 679 (1994). Thomas, J., joined by Scalia, J., dissenting, objected that "no principled reason immediately appears for declining to apply *Batson* to any strike based on a classification that is accorded heightened scrutiny under the Equal Protection Clause," and thus concluded "that the Court's decision to deny certiorari stems from an unwillingness to confront forthrightly the ramifications of the decision in *J.E.B.*" Justice Ginsburg, concurring in denial of certiorari, responded that "the dissent's portrayal of the opinion of the Minnesota Supreme Court is incomplete. That court made two key observations: (1) '[R]eligious affiliation (or lack thereof) is not as self-evident as race or gender'; (2) 'Ordinarily ... , inquiry on voir dire into a juror's religious affiliation and beliefs is irrelevant and prejudicial, and to ask such questions is improper.' "

explained by the prosecutor, the challenges rested neither on the intention to exclude Latino or bilingual jurors, nor on stereotypical assumptions about Latinos or bilinguals. The prosecutor's articulated basis for those whose conduct during *voir dire* would persuade him they might have difficulty in accepting the translator's rendition of Spanish-language testimony and those potential jurors who gave no such reason for doubt. Each category would include both Latinos and non-Latinos. While the prosecutor's criterion might well result in the disproportionate removal of prospective Latino jurors, that disproportionate impact does not turn the prosecutor's actions into a *per se* violation of the Equal Protection Clause. [However, if] a prosecutor articulates a basis for a peremptory challenge that results in the disproportionate exclusion of members of a certain race, the trial judge may consider that fact as evidence that the prosecutor's stated reason constitutes a pretext for racial discrimination." The Court then concluded the state court's finding of no discriminatory intent should stand because not clearly erroneous.[e]

O'CONNOR, J., for two concurring members of the Court, emphasized that if "the trial court believes the prosecutor's nonracial justification, and that finding is not clearly erroneous, that is the end of the matter," meaning disproportionate effect is then irrelevant. STEVENS, J., for the three dissenters, concluded the prosecutor's explanation "was insufficient for three reasons. First, the justification would inevitably result in a disproportionate disqualification of Spanish-speaking venirepersons. An explanation that is 'race-neutral' on its face is nonetheless unacceptable if it is merely a proxy for a discriminatory practice. Second, the prosecutor's concern could easily have been accommodated by less drastic means. As is the practice in many jurisdictions, the jury could have been instructed that the official translation alone is evidence; bilingual jurors could have been instructed to bring to the attention of the judge any disagreements they might have with the translation so that any disputes could be resolved by the court. Third, if the prosecutor's concern was valid and substantiated by the record, it would have supported a challenge for cause. The fact that the prosecutor did not make any such challenge should disqualify him from advancing the concern as a justification for a peremptory challenge."

Consider also *United States v. Bishop*, 959 F.2d 820 (9th Cir.1992) (*Hernandez* shows challenge invalid under *Batson* where "based in part on the fact the black juror lived in a predominantly low-income, black neighborhood and was therefore likely to believe the police 'pick on black people' "); *Minniefield v. State*, 539 N.E.2d 464 (Ind.1989) (striking black veniremen because prosecution's evidence would of necessity reveal that victim enjoyed racist jokes not a neutral explanation, as "race-based use of peremptory challenges * * *, even if allegedly dictated by strategic considerations, is a *per se* violation of the equal protection clause"); *Hill v. State*, 827 S.W.2d 860 (Tex.Crim.App.1992) (similarity between prospective juror and the defendant, "based only on [their] shared sex and shared race," "does not escape *Batson*'s prohibition"; court distinguishes case upholding challenge because similarity was shared race, sex and approximate age, explaining "that race may be a factor coexisting with a nonracial reason for a strike").

9. Is *Batson* now much ado about nothing? Consider Leonard L. Cavise, *The Batson Doctrine: The Supreme Court's Utter Failure to Meet the Challenge of*

---

e. The Court cautioned: "In holding that a race-neutral reason for a peremptory challenge means a reason other than race, we do not resolve the more difficult question of the breadth with which the concept of race should be defined for equal protection purposes. We would face a quite different case if the prosecutor had justified his peremptory challenges with the explanation that he did not want Spanish-speaking jurors. It may well be, for certain ethnic groups and in some communities, that proficiency in a particular language, like skin color, should be treated as a surrogate for race under an equal protection analysis."

Discrimination in Jury Selection, 1999 Wis.L.Rev. 500: "When the Supreme Court decided *Batson* * * * many feared peremptory challenges would become an endangered species. * * * Today, over ten years later, those fears have been laid to rest by a Supreme Court anxious to render its own decision as meaningless, ineffective, and unthreatening as possible. What is left of *Batson* is an infinitely cumbersome procedural obstacle course, created by the Court, which now plagues every voir dire in the land, civil and criminal. Through it all, the peremptory challenge is alive and well for those who know how to use it. Only the most overtly discriminatory or impolitic lawyer can be caught in *Batson*'s toothless bite and, even then, the wound will be only superficial."

NOTES ON CHALLENGING THE JUDGE

1. The defendant has a right to an impartial judge; see, e.g., *Ward v. Village of Monroeville*, 409 U.S. 57, 93 S.Ct. 80, 34 L.Ed.2d 267 (1972) (where mayor before whom defendant was compelled to stand trial for traffic offenses was responsible for village finances, and mayor's court through fines, forfeitures, costs and fees provided a substantial portion of the village funds, petitioner was denied trial before a disinterested and impartial judicial officer as guaranteed by due process clause); *Tumey v. Ohio*, 273 U.S. 510, 47 S.Ct. 437, 71 L.Ed. 749 (1927) (same result where mayor, in addition to his regular salary, received fees and costs levied by him against violators).

2. It is not objectionable that the trial judge was involved in some prior proceedings in the case. As noted in *Withrow v. Larkin*, 421 U.S. 35, 95 S.Ct. 1456, 43 L.Ed.2d 712 (1975): "Judges repeatedly issue arrest warrants on the basis that there is probable cause to believe that a crime has been committed and that the person named in the warrant has committed it. Judges also preside at preliminary hearings where they must decide whether the evidence is sufficient to hold a defendant for trial. Neither of these pretrial involvements has been thought to raise any constitutional barrier against the judge presiding over the criminal trial and, if the trial is without a jury, against making the necessary determination of guilt or innocence."

3. Trial judges, like jurors, are subject to challenge for "cause." Grounds for challenge generally are set forth in a statute or court rule, and usually include (1) a family relationship to the defendant, counsel, or the victim of the crime; (2) being a material witness; and (3) a general ground of "bias."[a] In some jurisdictions, determination of the challenge for cause may be made by the judge being challenged. Counsel generally are most hesitant to file such motions on grounds of general bias. Even absent actual bias, a judge as a matter of judicial ethics has a responsibility to recuse himself under certain circumstances, including "whenever the judge believes his or her impartiality can reasonably be questioned." I *A.B.A. Standards* § 6–1.7.

4. Several states also grant the defendant a single peremptory challenge of the trial judge. In others, the initial challenge made in the form of a motion alleging prejudice automatically results in the substitution of another judge. In still others, the defendant may file a conclusory affidavit of prejudice. Which procedure is best? Should the prosecution have a like right?

---

a. In *Liteky v. United States,* 510 U.S. 540, 114 S.Ct. 1147, 127 L.Ed.2d 474 (1994), the Court held that *both* the federal challenge-for-cause statute, 28 U.S.C. § 144, and the federal recusal statute, 28 U.S.C. § 455, are subject to an "extrajudicial source" limitation, meaning: (1) "judicial rulings alone almost never constitute valid basis for a bias or partiality motion"; and (2) "opinions formed by the judge on the basis of facts introduced or events occurring in the course of the current proceedings, or of prior proceedings, do not constitute a basis for a bias or partiality motion unless they display a deep-seated favoritism or antagonism that would make fair judgment impossible."

Chapter 24

"TRIAL BY NEWSPAPER"— AND TELEVISION

SECTION 1. PRETRIAL PUBLICITY AND JURY SELECTION[a]

1. IRVIN v. DOWD, 366 U.S. 717, 81 S.Ct. 1639, 6 L.Ed.2d 751 (1961) marked the first time the Supreme Court struck down a state conviction solely on the ground of prejudicial pretrial publicity. Six murders were committed in Vanderburgh County, Indiana. Shortly after petitioner was arrested, the county prosecutor and local police officials issued press releases, which were intensively publicized. Headline stories announced that petitioner had confessed to the six murders and to twenty-four burglaries (the *modus operandi* of these crimes was compared to that of the murders and the similarity noted). Reports that petitioner had offered to plead guilty if promised a ninety-nine-year sentence, but that the prosecutor was determined to secure the death penalty, were widely circulated. In many of the newspaper stories petitioner was described as the "confessed slayer of six," a parole violator and fraudulent-check artist. Petitioner sought a change of venue, which was granted, but to an adjoining county. His request that venue be changed to a further removed county was denied. Some 370 prospective jurors, or almost ninety percent of those examined on the point, "entertained some opinion as to guilt—ranging in intensity from mere suspicion to absolute certainty." The Court, per Justice CLARK, observed:

"In essence the right to jury trial guarantees to the criminally accused a fair trial by a panel of impartial, 'indifferent' jurors. * * * 'The theory of the law is that a juror who has formed an opinion cannot be impartial.' It is not required, however, that the jurors be totally ignorant of the facts and issues involved. In these days of swift, widespread and diverse methods of communication, an important case can be expected to arouse the interest of the public in the vicinity, and scarcely any of those best qualified to serve as jurors will not have formed some impression or opinion as to the merits of the case. [It] is sufficient if the juror can lay aside his impression or opinion and render a verdict based on the evidence presented in court.

"The adoption of such a rule, however, 'cannot foreclose inquiry as to whether, in a given case, the application of that rule works a deprivation of the prisoner's life or liberty without due process.' The test is 'whether the nature and strength of the opinion formed are such as in law necessarily * * * raise the presumption of partiality. [The] affirmative issue is upon the challenger. Unless he shows the actual existence of such an opinion in the mind of the juror as will

---

a. On the impact of pre-charge publicity upon the selection of the grand jury, see Note 5, p. 943. Unless otherwise indicated, all references to the A.B.A. Standards, *Fair Trial and Free Press (A.B.A. Standards)* are to the third edition, published in 1992.

raise the presumption of partiality, the juror need not necessarily be set aside.'
* * *

"Here the 'pattern of deep and bitter prejudice' shown to be present throughout the community * * * was clearly reflected in the sum total of the voir dire examination of a majority of the jurors finally placed in the jury box. Eight out of the 12 thought petitioner was guilty. With such an opinion permeating their minds, it would be difficult to say that each could exclude this preconception of guilt from his deliberations. The influence that lurks in an opinion once formed is so persistent that it unconsciously fights detachment from the mental processes of the average man. [Where] one's life is at stake—and accounting for the frailties of human nature—we can only say that in the light of the circumstances here the finding of impartiality does not meet constitutional standards. * * * No doubt each juror was sincere when he said that he would be fair and impartial to petitioner, but psychological impact requiring such a declaration before one's fellows is often its father. Where so many, so many times, admitted prejudice, such a statement of impartiality can be given little weight."

2. Compare *Irvin* with MURPHY v. FLORIDA, 421 U.S. 794, 95 S.Ct. 2031, 44 L.Ed.2d 589 (1975): Petitioner, generally referred to in the media as "Murph the Surf," had first made himself notorious for his part in the 1964 theft of the Star of India sapphire. In 1969 he was convicted on one count of murder in another county and later that year pled guilty to one count of a federal indictment involving stolen securities. These events and the January 1968 robbery of a Miami Beach home, which led to the instant conviction in the summer of 1970, received extensive press coverage. The Court, per MARSHALL, J., held that petitioner had not been denied a fair trial:

"[*Irvin*] cannot be made to stand for the proposition that juror exposure to information about a state defendant's prior convictions or to news accounts of the crime with which he is charged alone presumptively deprives the defendant of due process. * * * Qualified jurors need not [be] totally ignorant of the facts and issues involved [quoting from *Irvin*]. At the same time, the juror's assurances that he is equal to the task cannot be dispositive of the accused's rights, and it remains open to the defendant to demonstrate 'the actual existence of such an opinion in the mind of the juror as will raise the presumption of partiality.' *Irvin*.

"The *voir dire* in this case indicates no such hostility to petitioner by the jurors who served in his trial as to suggest a partiality that could not be laid aside. [In] the entire *voir dire* transcript * * * only one colloquy [supports] even a colorable claim of partiality by a juror. In response to a leading and hypothetical question, presupposing [an extensive] presentation of evidence against petitioner and his failure to put on any defense,[b] one juror conceded that his prior impression of petitioner [e.g., the knowledge that he was a convicted murderer] would dispose him to convict. We cannot attach great significance to this statement, however, in light of the leading nature of counsel's questions and the juror's other testimony indicating that he had no deep impression of petitioner at all.

"[Even] these indicia of impartiality might be disregarded in a case where the general atmosphere in the community or courtroom is sufficiently inflammatory, but the circumstances surrounding petitioner's trial are not at all of that variety. [T]he news articles concerning petitioner had appeared almost entirely during [a 13–month period ending] seven months before the jury in this case was selected. They were, moreover, largely factual in nature.

b. As it turned out, at his trial petitioner chose not to take the stand and offered no evidence.

"The length to which the trial court must go in order to select jurors who appear to be impartial is another factor relevant in evaluating those jurors' assurances of impartiality. In a community where most veniremen will admit to a disqualifying prejudice, the reliability of the others' protestations may be drawn into question; for it is then more probable that they are part of a community deeply hostile to the accused, and more likely that they may unwittingly have been influenced by it. In *Irvin,* for example, the Court noted that 90% of those examined on the point were inclined to believe in the accused's guilt, and the court had excused for this cause 268 of the 430 veniremen. In the present case, by contrast, 20 of the 78 persons questioned were excused because they indicated an opinion as to petitioner's guilt. This may indeed be 20 more than would occur in the trial of a totally obscure person, but it by no means suggests a community with sentiment so poisoned against petitioner as to impeach the indifference of jurors who displayed no animus of their own."

Dissenting Justice BRENNAN maintained that "*Irvin* requires reversal of this conviction. [The] risk that taint of widespread publicity regarding [petitioner's] criminal background, known to all members of the jury, infected the jury's deliberations is apparent, the trial court made no attempt to prevent discussion of the case or petitioner's previous criminal exploits among the prospective jurors [or to insulate the jurors from media coverage of the case], and one juror freely admitted that he was predisposed to convict petitioner. [It] is of no moment that several jurors ultimately testified that they would try to exclude from their deliberations their knowledge of petitioner's past misdeeds and of his community reputation. *Irvin* held in like circumstances that little weight could be attached to such self-serving protestations."[c]

3. *Irvin* was distinguished in PATTON v. YOUNT, 467 U.S. 1025, 104 S.Ct. 2885, 81 L.Ed.2d 847 (1984), which arose as follows: In 1966, Yount was convicted of murdering one of his high school students, but his conviction was reversed because based on statements obtained in violation of *Miranda.* Before and during the extensive *voir dire* that occurred at his 1970 retrial (in the same courtroom before the same judge who had presided at the first trial), Yount moved for a change of venue, arguing that the widespread dissemination of prejudicial information could not be eradicated from the minds of potential jurors. The trial court denied the motions, and also a motion for a new trial after Yount was again convicted of first-degree murder.

In 1981, Yount sought federal habeas corpus relief, claiming that his conviction had been obtained in violation of his right to a fair trial by an impartial jury. Relying primarily on *Irvin,* the Third Circuit granted relief, concluding that "despite their assurance of impartiality, the jurors could not set aside their opinions and render a verdict based solely on the evidence presented." The court pointed out that all but two of 163 veniremen questioned about the case had heard of it and that 126 or 77 percent admitted they would carry an opinion into the jury box—a higher percentage than in *Irvin.* Moreover, eight of the fourteen jurors and alternates actually seated admitted that at some time they had formed an opinion as to Yount's guilt. A 6–2 majority, per POWELL, J., reversed:[a]

"[The *Irvin* Court] noted [that] the trial court's findings of impartiality might be overturned only for 'manifest error.' [The court below] did not address this aspect of the *Irvin* decision [and it] failed to give adequate weight to other significant circumstances in this case. [The] jury selection for Yount's second trial,

---

c. Burger, C.J., who concurred in the judgment of the Court, shared the dissent's view that the trial judge was "woefully remiss," but, although he "would not hesitate to [reverse] in the exercise of our supervisory powers, were this a federal case," agreed with the Court that the circumstances of petitioner's case "did not rise to the level" of a due process violation.

a. Marshall, J., took no part in the case.

at issue here, did not occur until four years later, at a time when prejudicial publicity was greatly diminished and community sentiment had softened. In these circumstances, [the] trial court did not commit manifest error in finding that the jury as a whole was impartial.

"[The] relevant question is not [as the court below believed] whether the community remembered the case, but whether the jurors at Yount's trial had such fixed opinions that they could not judge impartially the guilt of the defendant. [It] is clear that the passage of time between a first and a second trial can be a highly relevant fact. In the circumstances of this case, we hold that it clearly rebuts any presumption of partiality or prejudice that existed at the time of the initial trial."

Dissenting Justice STEVENS, joined by Brennan, J., maintained that "the record clearly establishes that the case was still a 'cause celebre' in the [county in which it was retried] in 1970". The "totality of circumstances" convinced the dissenters that "the trial judge committed manifest error in determining that the jury as a whole was impartial. [The] trial court's statement that 'there was practically no publicity given to this matter through the news media * * * 'simply ignores at least 55 front-page articles that are in the record. [The] trial judge's 'practically no publicity' statement also ignores the first-trial details within the news stories, [such as] Yount's confessions, testimony and conviction of rape—all of which were outside the evidence presented at the second trial. Under these circumstances, I do not believe that the jury was capable of deciding the case solely on the evidence before it."

4. Consider in light of the previously discussed cases, *A.B.A. Standards* § 8–3.5:

Standard 8–3.5. Selecting the jury

The following standards govern the selection of a jury in those criminal cases in which questions of possible prejudice are raised.

(a) If there is a substantial possibility that individual jurors will be ineligible to serve because of exposure to potentially prejudicial material, the examination of each juror with respect to exposure should take place outside the presence of other chosen and prospective jurors. An accurate record of this examination should be kept by court reporter or tape recording whenever possible. The questioning shall be conducted for the purpose of determining what the prospective juror has read and heard about the case and how any exposure has affected that person's attitude toward the trial, not to convince the prospective juror that an inability to cast aside any preconceptions would be a dereliction of duty.

(b) Whenever prospective jurors have been exposed to potentially prejudicial material, the court should consider not only the jurors' subjective self-evaluation of their ability to remain impartial but also the objective nature of the material and the degree of exposure. The court should exercise extreme caution in qualifying a prospective juror who has either been exposed to highly prejudicial material or retained a recollection of any prejudicial material.

(c) Whenever there is a substantial likelihood that, due to pretrial publicity, the regularly allotted number of peremptory challenges is inadequate, the court should permit additional challenges to the extent necessary for the impaneling of an impartial jury.

(d) Whenever it is determined that potentially prejudicial news coverage of a given criminal matter has been intense and has been concentrated in a given locality in a state (or federal district), the court should,

in jurisdictions where possible, consider drawing jurors from other localities in that state (or district).

5. MU'MIN v. VIRGINIA, 500 U.S. 415, 111 S.Ct. 1899, 114 L.Ed.2d 493 (1991), arose as follows: Petitioner, serving time for murder, committed another murder while out of prison on work detail. The case generated a good deal of pretrial publicity in the local news media. The trial judge refused to question *individual* jurors specifically about the *content* of the news reports to which each had been exposed. (Petitioner had proposed a number of questions relating to the publicity.) Instead, the judge questioned the prospective jurors initially as a group and then in panels of four.

Of the 26 prospective jurors summoned into the courtroom and questioned a s a group, 16 stated that they had acquired information about the offense or the defendant from the news media. They were not asked about the source or content of prior knowledge, but were asked whether the publicity to which they had been exposed would affect their impartiality. When one of the 16 prospective jurors stated he could not be impartial, he was dismissed for cause. When another person equivocated as to whether she could enter the jury box with an open mind, she was removed *sua sponte* by the judge. Of the 12 jurors who decided petitioner's case, 8 had read or heard something about the case. None had said he had formed an opinion about the case or would be biased in any way. The jury found petitioner guilty of capital murder and sentenced him to death. A 5–4 majority, per REHNQUIST, C.J., affirmed, holding that, despite petitioner's reliance on *A.B.A. Standard* 8–3.5(a) (2d ed. 1978), a provision virtually identical to the current Standard, the trial judge's handling of *voir dire* violated neither petitioner's Sixth Amendment right to an impartial jury nor Fourteenth Amendment Due Process:

"[The A.B.A. Standards] require interrogation of each juror individually with respect to 'what the prospective juror has read and heard about the case' 'if there is a substantial possibility that individual jurors will be ineligible to serve because of exposure to potentially prejudicial material.' These standards, of course, leave to the trial court the initial determination of whether there is such a substantial possibility. But, more importantly, the standards relating to *voir dire* are based on a substantive rule that renders a potential juror subject to challenge for cause, without regard to his state of mind, if he has been exposed to and remembers 'highly significant information' or 'other incriminating matters that may be inadmissible in evidence.' That is a stricter standard of juror eligibility than that which we have held the Constitution to require. [Under] the constitutional standard, '[t]he relevant question is not whether the community remembered the case, but whether the jurors [had] such fixed opinions that they could not judge impartially the guilt of the defendant.' *Patton v. Yount.* Under this constitutional standard, answers to questions about content alone, which reveal that a juror remembered facts about the case, would not be sufficient to disqualify a juror.

"The A.B.A. standards [have] not commended themselves to a majority of the courts that have considered the question. The fact that a particular rule may be thought to be the 'better' view does not mean that it is incorporated into the Fourteenth Amendment."

Concurring Justice O'CONNOR whose vote was necessary for the Court's decision, emphasized that "the only question before us is whether the trial court erred by crediting the assurance of eight jurors that they could put aside what they had read or heard and render a fair verdict based on the evidence." She answered that question in the negative:

Although the trial judge did not know precisely what each juror had read about the case, "[h]e was undeniably aware [of] the full range of information that had been reported. This is because Mu'Min submitted to the court, in support of a motion for a change of venue, 47 newspaper articles relating to the murder. The trial judge was thus aware, long before *voir dire,* of all of the allegedly prejudicial information to which prospective jurors might have been exposed."

Because Justice O'Connor could not conclude that questioning prospective jurors about the specific content of the news reports to which they had been exposed is "so indispensable that it violates the Sixth Amendment for a trial court to evaluate a juror's credibility instead by reference to the full range of potentially prejudicial information that has been reported," she joined the Court's opinion.

Dissenting Justice MARSHALL, joined by Blackmun and Stevens, JJ., emphasized that defendant's capital murder trial "was preceded by exceptionally prejudicial publicity, and at jury selection 8 of the 12 jurors who ultimately convicted [him] of murder and sentenced him to death admitted exposure to this publicity." When a prospective juror has been exposed to prejudicial pretrial publicity, argued the dissenters, "a trial court cannot realistically assess the juror's impartiality without first establishing what the juror already has learned about the case." Justice Kennedy also dissented, maintaining that when a prospective juror admits exposure to pretrial publicity about a case, "findings of impartiality must be based on something more than the mere silence of the individual in response to questions asked *en masse.*"[a]

Is Voir Dire an Effective Safeguard?

Christina A. Studebaker and Steven D. Penrod, *Pretrial Publicity: The Media, the Law and Common Sense,* 3 Psychology, Pub. Pol'y. & L. 428 (1997), report that one study shows that mock jurors who said they could judge the defendant in a fair and unbiased manner, despite the pretrial publicity they had seen or heard, "were much more likely to convict when they had been exposed to damaging pretrial publicity than when they had been exposed to neutral pretrial publicity." Id. at 441. Another study indicated that the *voir dire* exercise "had no net effect on the bias of seated jurors." Id.

Professors Studebaker and Penrod point out, id. at 442, that "the effectiveness of *voir dire* as a remedy for pretrial publicity rests on at least two assumptions: first, that jurors have cognitive access to their source of bias—that is, that they can remember having seen or heard news accounts [about the case] accurately—and second, that prospective jurors are willing to report on any bias that may have arisen from exposure to pretrial publicity. In light of the research findings, both these assumptions appear extremely tenuous."[a]

SECTION 2. CHANGE OF VENUE

1. RIDEAU v. LOUISIANA, 373 U.S. 723, 83 S.Ct. 1417, 10 L.Ed.2d 663 (1963), grew out of the following facts: Some two months before petitioner's trial began and some two weeks before he was arraigned on charges of robbery, kidnapping and murder, a local TV station broadcast three different times in the space of three days a twenty-minute film of petitioner, flanked by the sheriff and two state troopers, admitting in detail the commission of the various offenses in response to leading questions by the sheriff. The parish had a population of

---

a. See also Justice Kennedy's discussion of *Mu'Min* in the *Gentile* case, p. 1366.

a. Research findings also indicate that a judge's instructions to jurors to ignore the news accounts of the case do little or nothing to mitigate the effects of pretrial publicity.

Moreover, the effects of the pretrial publicity persist throughout a trial—and throughout the jury deliberations that follows. Indeed, research findings indicate that group deliberation may *accentuate* any biases jurors bring to the deliberation room. See id. at 442–44.

approximately 150,000. The estimated audiences included 24,000 people on the first T.V. showing, 53,000 on the second, and 29,000 on the third. Appointed counsel moved for a change of venue, which was denied. Defendant was subsequently convicted and sentenced to death. Three members of the jury had stated on voir dire that they had seen the broadcast on at least one occasion. A 7–2 majority, per STEWART, J., reversed:

"[I]t was a denial of due process of law to refuse the request for a change of venue, after the people of [the] Parish had been exposed repeatedly and in depth to the spectacle of Rideau personally confessing in detail to the crimes with which he was later to be charged. For anyone who has ever watched television the conclusion cannot be avoided that this spectacle, to the tens of thousands of people who saw and heard it, in a very real sense *was* Rideau's trial—at which he pleaded guilty to murder. Any subsequent court proceedings in a community so pervasively exposed to such a spectacle could be but a hollow formality.

"[W]e do not hesitate to hold, without pausing to examine a particularized transcript of the *voir dire* examination of the members of the jury, that due process of law in this case required a trial before a jury drawn from a community of people who had not seen and heard Rideau's 'interview.' "

The author of the *Irvin* opinion, Justice CLARK, joined by Justice Harlan, dissented: "[The majority has failed to establish] any substantial nexus between the televised 'interview' and petitioner's trial, which occurred almost two months later. Unless the adverse publicity is shown by the record to have fatally infected the trial, there is simply no basis for the Court's inference that the publicity, epitomized by the televised interview, called up some informal and illicit analogy to *res judicata,* making petitioner's trial a meaningless formality.

"[The] most crucial evidence [in this case] relates to the composition of the 12–man jury. Of the 12 members of the panel only three had seen the televised interview which had been shown almost two months before the trial. The petitioner does not assert, and the record does not show, that these three testified to holding opinions of petitioner's guilt. They did testify, however, that they 'could lay aside any opinion, give the defendant the presumption of innocence as provided by law, base their decision solely upon the evidence, and apply the law as given by the court.' [The] determination of impartiality, in which demeanor plays such an important part, is particularly within the province of the trial judge. And when the jurors testify that they can discount the influence of external factors and meet the standard imposed by the Fourteenth Amendment, that assurance is not lightly to be discarded."

2. Does *Rideau* indicate that a change in venue was constitutionally required in that case without regard to the actual composition of the jury? For example, would the venue change have been required if all twelve of the jurors had stated that they had not seen nor heard about the televised "interview"? What if the truth of their statements was supported by reasonable grounds—e.g. several had been out of town at the time, others never read the papers or watched television. Note the Court's reference to a trial "in a community so pervasively exposed." Does *Rideau* reflect concern about community pressure being applied to the jurors, no matter who they are? Or is the court concerned that any 12 jurors having no knowledge of the televised "spectacle" are unlikely to reflect a cross-section of the community? To what extent is *Rideau* limited by the nature of the pretrial publicity in that case? Would a similar approach have been taken if the "interview" had been published in a newspaper with a large circulation? What if, instead of the "interview," the broadcast had contained only a summary of the evidence (aside from the confession) in the possession of local authorities?[a]

a. It remains common practice after *Rideau* for trial courts to refuse to rule on a request for a change of venue until after an attempt has been made to select an impartial

3. Consider, in light of *Rideau, A.B.A. Standards* § 8–3.3:

Standard 8–3.3. Change of venue or continuance

The following standards govern the consideration and disposition of a motion in a criminal case for change of venue or continuance based on a claim of threatened interference with the right to a fair trial.

(a) Except as federal or state constitutional or statutory provisions otherwise require, a change of venue or continuance may be granted on motion of either the prosecution or the defense.[b]

(b) A motion for change of venue or continuance should be granted whenever it is determined that, because of the dissemination of potentially prejudicial material, there is a substantial likelihood that, in the absence of such relief, a fair trial by an impartial jury cannot be had. This determination may be based on such evidence as qualified public opinion surveys or opinion testimony offered by individuals, or on the court's own evaluation of the nature, frequency, and timing of the material involved. A showing of actual prejudice shall not be required.

(c) If a motion for change of venue or continuance is made prior to the impaneling of the jury, the court may defer ruling until the completion of voir dire. The fact that a jury satisfying prevailing standards of acceptability has been selected shall not be controlling if the record shows that the criterion for the granting of relief set forth in paragraph (b) has been met.

(d) It should not be a ground for denial of a change of venue that one such change has already been granted. The claim that the venue should have been changed or a continuance granted should not be considered to have been waived by the waiver of the right to trial by jury or by the failure to exercise all available peremptory challenges.

4. *The use of "foreign juries."* The commentary to Standard 8–3.5(d), p. 1351 supra, notes that it "promotes the use of so-called 'foreign juries' [also called a 'change of venire'] as an alternative to a change of venue. The point is essentially that, in circumstances where the local jury pool has been contaminated by pretrial publicity, it may be administratively efficient to bring an unbiased jury to the trial rather than the trial to the jury. Although, like the change of venue, it is not among the trial courts' preferred alternative, it has been gaining some favor with the court. It should be noted that certain research findings support the use of a foreign jury even where the pretrial publicity has extended to the foreign venue. The scientific studies indicate that even where pretrial publicity is universal and uniformly adverse, the greatest degree of prejudice develops within the crime venue." See also the discussion of the *Beckwith* case, fn. a, p. 1357 infra. A small

---

jury. If the court is convinced, as a result of voir dire, that a jury cannot be selected, then the change of venue is granted. However, if the court believes that an impartial jury has been selected, then the motion is denied. See Note, 42 Notre Dame Law. 925 (1967). Similarly, on appeal following a conviction, the appellate court ordinarily will not reverse based on a failure to order a change of venue if it appears that the jury selected met the constitutional standards of *Irvin*. But see *A.B.A. Standards,* § 8–3.3(c), Note 3 infra.

b. If the *prosecution* is granted a change of venue because of pretrial publicity adverse to the prosecution's case—e.g., adverse information concerning the complaining witness that could not be used by defense counsel for impeachment—would this interfere with the defendant's constitutional right to a jury trial? While many jurisdictions have provisions authorizing either side to seek a change of venue, others refer only to motions made by the defense. See generally Susan Bandes, *Taking Some Rights Too Seriously: The State's Right to a Fair Trial*, 60 So.Cal.L.Rev. 1019 (1987).

group of states provide by statute for the use of "foreign juries" or a "change of venire." See CRIMPROC § 23.2(c) (2002 pocket part).

THE RODNEY KING BEATING TRIAL (*PEOPLE v. POWELL*) AND ITS AFTERMATH

"[N]either the federal courts nor the California courts have addressed the issue of whether there should be a similarity of demographics, community values, social priorities, or concerns between the venue where the crime occurred and the venue to which it is transferred. The paucity of factors commonly mentioned in the reported decisions suggests that trial courts believe, perhaps mistakenly, that these broader characteristics are irrelevant to their decisions."

—L. Levenson, *Change of Venue and the Role of the Criminal Jury,* 66 So.Calif.L.Rev. 1533, 1542 (1993).

———

1. *The Rodney King beating trial (People v. Powell).* When four white officers were charged with unlawfully beating a black man, Rodney King, the trial was moved from racially diverse Los Angeles County to predominantly white, suburban Simi Valley, in Ventura County. Lawyers on both sides of the case agreed that the subsequent acquittal of the four officers was attributable more than anything else to the change in venue. See David Margolick, *As Venues Are Changed, Many Ask How Important a Role Race Should Play,* N.Y. Times, May 23, 1992, p. 7. See also Timothy O'Neill, *Wrong Place, Wrong Jury,* N.Y. Times, May 9, 1992, p. 15: "[A] lack of vicinage is the heart of the problem with the Rodney King [beating] trial. The Simi Valley jury had no stake in the verdict; it may as well have decided a hypothetical case."

In the Rodney King beating case, observes Professor Laurie Levenson, supra, at 1567–68, "it was quite evident from the nature of the case, where the allegations themselves suggested racial animus by the defendants, that issues of race were already relevant to the trial. The claim was not that only minority members of the population could fairly decide the case for the prosecution; rather, that only those individuals, white or black, from a community with greater diversity could be expected to have the experiential knowledge and sensitivity to judge the officers' actions and motives. In selecting a locale where such diversity was not available, the court eliminated the opportunity for a jury with the same knowledge and sensitivities as the originating community to decide the case."

In response to the acquittal of the police officer in the King beating state trial, bills were introduced in the California, New Jersey and New York legislatures that would have required judges to take into account such factors as race and ethnicity when choosing a new venue. See the extensive discussion in M. Shanara Gilbert, *An Ounce of Prevention: A Constitutional Prescription for Choice of Venue in Racially Sensitive Cases,* 67 Tulane L.Rev. 1855, 1935–42 (1993). Such an approach is favored by Professors Gilbert and Levenson. See also Note, 106 Harv. L.Rev. 705 (1993).

But consider Joseph Grano, *Change of Venue Rules Protect Rights of Accused,* Detroit News, May 10, 1992, p. 3B, who calls the argument that if venue is going to be changed, the new trial location should reflect, to the extent possible, the racial composition of the original "a flawed proposal, especially for cases with racial overtones." Continues Professor Grano:

"Consider the case of a black defendant accused of a widely publicized inter-racial crime in a virtually all-white community such as a black man charged with murdering a white police officer in Simi Valley. Such a defendant would seek to change venue to a less hostile community, and many of the venue change critics in the King case would vocally endorse such a change. * * * Venue changes are intended to assure the defendant a jury that will acquit when it has a reasonable doubt, even if, on balance, it thinks him guilty. Moreover, we traditionally have thought that acquitting a guilty person is a lesser evil than convicting an innocent one. The cost of venue rules that err on the side of defendants is an occasional King case. The cost of reversing this preference is one many black defendants, with reason, would be reluctant to bear."[a]

2. *Seeking a change of venue to a more demographically diverse county.* In the case posed by Professor Grano, the black defendant who committed an inter-racial crime in an all-white community, should the law protect a defendant's interest in racial diversity per se? Consider Gilbert, supra, at 1941–42:

"Because of the focus on demographic *similarity,* none of the legislative measures takes into account the situation in which a defendant seeks a change of venue to a more demographically diverse county. [This] is an issue of grave concern to African–American defendants who may be arrested in a predominantly white jurisdiction, or to any defendant who seeks diversity on her jury. Thus far, the law does not protect a defendant's interest in diversity per se, so long as the jury pool is a fair cross section of the community in which the crime occurred or the trial is held. The principle of affirmative inclusion of all citizenry in the fair cross section might provide for such protection, particularly in light of the racially segregated nature of many American communities. One mechanism for achieving jury diversity in cases tried in a community in which African Americans are underrepresented is the importation of jurors from other areas of the state, such as in the *De La Beckwith* case.[a] This measure is consistent with the fair cross-section guarantee to defendants, but it requires a recognition that there is great value in a jury that 'mirrors the community' in which the defendant resides, and that there is a Sixth Amendment value supporting a jury containing the defendant's peers."

3. *The Lozano case: complications arise when more than two different races are involved.* William Lozano, an Hispanic police officer killed two black men in Miami: the driver of a motorcycle who was attempting to avoid a stop for a traffic infraction and a passenger on the motorcycle. The incident touched off three days of rioting. Lozano moved for a change of venue on the ground that jurors would be reluctant to vote for acquittal for fear of causing further violence in the community. The motion was denied. Lozano was convicted of manslaughter, but the conviction was reversed on the ground that the trial court had erred by failing to grant a change of venue.

Dade County (Miami) has a 20% black population and a 49% Hispanic population. The second trial was moved to Orlando, whose black population is only 10%. After the acquittal in the Rodney King beating case was announced, and

---

a. Consider, too, Robert P. Mosteller, *Popular Justice* (essay book review), 109 Harv. L.Rev. 487, 496–97 (1995): "The 'spirit' of the Sixth Amendment simply does not support [the argument that justice must be dispensed in the geographic area where a crime occurs]. The Amendment's jury provisions, in both their text and history, are about protecting defendants from the government, not about protecting the rights of the community to local justice for victims."

a. Byron De La Beckwith, an avowed white supremacist, was charged with the murder of

Medgar Evers, an African–American civil rights activist, in the driveway of Evers' home in Jackson, Mississippi. Twenty-one years after two previous prosecutions had resulted in mistrials, De La Beckwith was re-indicted for murder and convicted. The trial was moved from the site of the murder to a northern Mississippi county (DeSota). Jurors were selected from still another county (Panola), which had a racial composition similar to the county in which the murder occurred, and transported to DeSota County.

violence erupted in Los Angeles, the trial judge, on his own motion and without a hearing, moved the trial to the state capitol, Tallahassee (Leon County), which has a 20% black population, but a negligible Hispanic population. The judge stated he made the move to Leon County in an effort to "duplicate the demographics" of Dade County. Lozano moved for a change of venue, a motion the state joined "insofar as the defendant contended Leon County was not a proper venue because of its small Hispanic population and because Tallahassee was selected as the site for the trial solely upon racially-motivated reasons." Despite this joinder, the trial court denied the motion.

The Florida Court of Appeal quashed the trial court's order denying the motion for change of venue, *State v. Lozano,* 52 Crim.L.Rep. 1521 (March 24, 1993), the effect of which was to reinstate the order setting the trial in Orlando. The order moving the trial from Orlando to Tallahassee, observed the Court of Appeals, was made "on the basis of race, particularly the race of the victims. No consideration was given to the race of the defendant. [The] trial court deliberately acted so as to increase the number of black jurors. In doing this, the trial court virtually guaranteed the absence of Hispanic jurors. '[P]urposeful racial discrimination in selection of the venire violates a defendant's right to equal protection [that] a trial by jury is intended to secure.' *Batson v. Kentucky.*"

After a two-week trial in Orlando, described by Professor Gilbert, supra, at 1881–82, as "a conservative, overwhelmingly white community, perhaps the 'Simi Valley of Florida,'" Lozano was acquitted. The jury was comprised of three whites, two Hispanics, and one African–American.[a]

SECTION 3. CONDUCT OF THE TRIAL

A. CONDUCT OF REPORTERS IN AND NEAR THE COURTROOM

Many defendants have protested that their rights to a fair trial have been abridged by the media, but *Sheppard v. Maxwell*, 384 U.S. 333, 86 S.Ct. 1507, 16 L.Ed.2d 600 (1966) is probably the most notorious "trial by newspaper" case of all. The Court, per CLARK, J. (only Black, J., dissenting), agreed with the "finding" of the Ohio Supreme Court that the atmosphere of the defendant's murder trial was that of a " 'Roman holiday' for the news media." During the entire nine weeks of trial, the courtroom was jammed with reporters, and their movements in and out of the courtroom "often caused so much confusion that, despite the loudspeaker installed in the courtroom, it was difficult for the witnesses and counsel to be heard." And in the corridors outside the courtroom, "there was a host of photographers and television personnel," who photographed witnesses, counsel, and jurors as they entered and left the courtroom. Throughout the trial, there was a deluge of publicity, much of which contained information that was never offered in evidence, yet the jurors were never sequestered until the trial was over and they had begun their deliberations.

Viewing the "totality of the circumstances" of the case, the Court concluded that defendant had been denied a fair trial. And it put the primary blame for the release of leads, information and gossip to the press and for the lack of courtroom decorum on the trial judge.[b] He could "easily" have prevented the "carnival atmosphere at the trial" "since the courtroom and courthouse premises" are subject to his control. For example, he should have provided privacy for the jury;

---

a. Florida has adopted a new statute requiring a court ordering a change of venue to "give priority to any county which closely resembles the demographic composition of the county wherein the original venue would lie." See CRIMPROC § 16.3(g) (2002 pocket part).

b. See p. 1366.

insulated the witnesses from the media, instead of allowing them to be interviewed at will; limited the number of reporters in the courtroom and prohibited the reporters from handling and photographing trial exhibits during recesses. No one "coming under the jurisdiction of the court should be permitted to frustrate its function."

The Court recognized that "there is nothing that proscribes the press from reporting events that transpire in the courtroom. But where there is a reasonable likelihood that prejudicial news prior to trial will prevent a fair trial, the judge should continue the case until the threat abates, or transfer it to another county not so permeated with publicity. In addition, sequestration of the jury was something the judge should have raised sua sponte with counsel. If publicity during the proceedings threatens the fairness of the trial, a new trial should be ordered. But we must remember that reversals are but palliatives; the cure lies in those remedial measures that will prevent the prejudice at its inception."

However, the Court reiterated its extreme reluctance "to place any direct limitations on the freedom traditionally exercised by the news media for '[w]hat transpires in the courtroom is public property.' The press does not simply publish information about trials but guards against the miscarriage of justice by subjecting the police, prosecutors, and judicial processes to extensive public scrutiny and criticism."[c]

B. BROADCASTING, PHOTOGRAPHING AND TELEVISING COURTROOM PROCEEDINGS

In 1937, largely in response to the notorious media coverage of the 1935 trial of Bruno Hauptmann for the Lindbergh baby kidnapping, the American Bar Association adopted Judicial Canon 35 (carried forward as canon 3A(1)), banning all photographic and broadcast coverage of courtroom proceedings. In 1952 that provision was amended to proscribe television coverage as well. But the 1970s saw widespread state court experimentation with television coverage of criminal proceedings. And in *Chandler v. Florida* (1981), infra, the Court held there was no *per se* constitutional bar to such television coverage. In 1982, when the absolute ban on TV coverage had been effectively repudiated by more than 30 states, the A.B.A. reversed its long-standing policy by adopting new canon 3A(1) and new Standard 8–3, infra, authorizing the broadcasting, televising and photographing of courtroom proceedings under certain conditions and subject to certain limitations and guidelines.

The televising of criminal trials has been before the Supreme Court on two occasions, first in 1965, then in 1981. The Court's responses have been very different.

1. In ESTES v. TEXAS, 381 U.S. 532, 85 S.Ct. 1628, 14 L.Ed.2d 543 (1965), the Court held that the defendant had been denied due process as a result of the televising of his trial and certain pretrial hearings. Defendant was a well known financier and his prosecution received considerable publicity. Pretrial hearings to determine whether the trial should be televised were themselves televised live (with commercials inserted during pauses in the proceedings). Four persons later selected as jurors had seen or heard part of these telecasts or related radio broadcasts. During the trial, the television cameras were located in a special booth at the rear of the courtroom. They were "noiseless cameras," and floodlights and flash bulbs were not allowed, but the cameras were clearly visible to all participants. Live telecasting was not permitted during the presentation of evidence, but

c. On retrial for the same offense, Sheppard was acquitted. N.Y. Times, Nov. 17, 1966, p. 1, col. 7.

those proceedings were recorded for subsequent showings. The closing arguments of counsel were televised live. (The defense attorney objected to being photographed, so the cameras focused on others while he was speaking and his arguments were relayed to the television audience by an announcer.)

Writing for a 5–4 majority (which included Harlan, J., who concurred "subject to the reservations" discussed infra), Justice CLARK recognized that due process deprivations usually require "a showing of identifiable prejudice to the accused," but concluded that this was one of those times when "a procedure employed by the State involves such a probability that prejudice will result that it is deemed inherently lacking in due process." He observed: "[E]xperience teaches that there are numerous situations in which [the use of television] might cause actual unfairness—some so subtle as to defy detection by the accused or control by the judge."[a]

In his special concurrence, Justice HARLAN rejected the broad sweep of Clark's opinion, but concluded that "at least as to a notorious criminal trial such as this one, the considerations against allowing television in the courtroom so far outweigh the countervailing factors advanced in its support as to require a holding that what was done in this case infringed the fundamental right to a fair trial assured by [due process]."

Justice STEWART, joined by Black, Brennan and White, JJ., thought that, "at least in the present state of the art," TV coverage of courtroom proceedings was "an extremely unwise policy." But he was "unable to escalate this personal view into a *per se* constitutional rule." Nor was he able to find, "on the specific record of this case, that the circumstances attending the limited televising of the petitioner's trial resulted in the denial of any [of his constitutional rights.]"

"The suggestion that there are limits upon the public right to know what goes on in the courts," wrote Stewart, "causes me deep concern. The idea of imposing upon any medium of communication the burden of justifying its presence is contrary to where I had always thought the presumption must lie in the area of First Amendment freedoms."

2. CHANDLER v. FLORIDA, 449 U.S. 560, 101 S.Ct. 802, 66 L.Ed.2d 740 (1981), per BURGER, C.J., held that subject to certain safeguards a state may permit electronic media and still photography coverage of public criminal proceedings over the objection of the accused. The Court concluded that "*Estes* did not announce a constitutional rule that all photographic or broadcast coverage of criminal trials is inherently a denial of due process" and it declined to promulgate "such a *per se* rule":

"Whatever may be the 'mischievous potentialities [of broadcast coverage] for intruding upon the detached atmosphere which should always surround the judicial process,' *Estes,* at present no one has been able to present empirical data sufficient to establish that the mere presence of the broadcast media inherently has an adverse impact on that process. The appellants have offered nothing to demonstrate that their trial was subtly tainted by broadcast coverage—let alone that all broadcast trials would be so tainted.

"Where, as here, we cannot say that a denial of due process automatically results from activity authorized by a state, the admonition of Justice Brandeis, dissenting in *New State Ice Co. v. Liebmann*, 285 U.S. 262, 52 S.Ct. 371, 76 L.Ed.

---

a. Justice Clark then discussed how the awareness that they are being televised distracts jurors; how the medium "will often" impair the quality of the testimony in criminal cases—some witnesses may be "demoralized and frightened," others "cocky and given to overstatement"—how the presence of television is a "form of mental—if not physical—harassment" of the defendant; and how television coverage puts additional responsibilities on the trial judge.

747 (1932), is relevant: '[It] is one of the happy incidents of the federal system that a single courageous state may, if its citizens choose, serve as a laboratory; and try novel social and economic experiments without risk to the rest of the country. * * * ' This concept of federalism, echoed by the states favoring Florida's experiment, must guide our decision. * * * "

Chandler arose as follows: After evaluating the results of its earlier state pilot programs permitting electronic coverage of all judicial proceedings and studying the experience of other states which allowed electronic coverage of trials, the Florida Supreme Court promulgated a revised Canon 3A(7) of the Florida Code of Judicial Conduct, which provides:

"Subject at all times to the authority of the presiding judge to (i) control the conduct of proceedings before the court, (ii) ensure decorum and prevent distractions, and (iii) ensure fair administration of justice in the pending cause, electronic media and still photography coverage of public judicial proceedings in the appellate and trial courts of this state shall be allowed in accordance with standards of conduct and technology promulgated by the Supreme Court of Florida."

Implementing guidelines specify in detail the kind of electronic equipment to be used and the manner of its use (e.g., only one TV camera and only one camera technician is allowed, equipment may not be moved during trial, artificial lighting is prohibited, the jury may not be filmed, audio recording of conferences between lawyers, between parties and counsel, or at the bench is forbidden). Moreover, as the U.S. Supreme Court noted, these guidelines give the judge "discretionary power to forbid coverage whenever satisfied that coverage may have a deleterious effect on the paramount right of the defendant to a fair trial. The Florida Supreme Court has the right to revise these rules as experience dictates, or indeed to bar all broadcast coverage [in] courtrooms."

The trial of appellants, Miami Beach police officers charged, inter alia, with conspiracy to commit burglary and grand larceny, attracted considerable media attention. A TV camera was in place for one entire afternoon, during which the prosecution's chief witness testified. "Only two minutes and fifty-five seconds of the trial below were broadcast—and those depicted only the prosecution's side of the case." After the jury returned a guilty verdict on all counts, appellants moved for a new trial on the ground that the television coverage had denied them a fair and impartial trial, but "[n]o evidence of specific prejudice was tendered."

In upholding appellants' conviction and the constitutionality of the challenged canon, the U.S. Supreme Court deemed it "important to note that in promulgating the revised Canon 3A(7), the Florida Supreme Court pointedly rejected any state or federal constitutional right of access on the part of photographers or the broadcast media to televise or electronically record and thereafter disseminate court proceedings [and] predicated [the canon] upon its supervisory authority over the Florida courts. [Hence,] we have before us only the limited question of the Florida Supreme Court's authority to promulgate the canon for the trial of cases in Florida courts."

Although there was no dissent in *Chandler,* two concurring Justices sharply disputed the Court's reading of *Estes.* "I believe now," wrote concurring Justice STEWART, "as I believed in dissent then, that *Estes* announced a *per se* rule that the Fourteenth Amendment 'prohibits all television cameras from a state courtroom whenever a criminal trial is in progress.' Accordingly, rather than join what seems to me a wholly unsuccessful effort to distinguish that decision, I would now flatly overrule it. [The] constitutional violation perceived by the *Estes* Court did not * * * stem from physical disruption that might one day disappear with technological advances in television equipment. The violation inhered, rather, in the hypothesis that the mere presence of cameras and recording devices might have an effect on the trial participants prejudicial to the accused." In a separate concurring opinion, "for the reasons stated by Justice Stewart," Justice White also maintained that "*Estes* must be overruled to affirm the judgment below."

One of the questions raised by the O.J. Simpson case is whether high profile trials should be televised, or to put it another way, whether the benefits of increased public education about our legal system outweigh the costs generated by televising a high profile trial. Professor Arenella addresses this issue in the article extracted below.

PETER ARENELLA—FOREWORD: O.J. LESSONS
69 S.Cal.L.Rev. 1233, 1253–58 (1996).

[L]et us put questions of constitutional access aside and grant [the premise of Sager and Frederiksen[a]] that there should be a presumption in favor of televising most criminal cases. The harder question the Simpson trial raises is whether there are sound reasons for not televising those few high profile cases that create the greatest media frenzy.

I can hear Steve Brill of Court TV gnashing his teeth in agony and responding to those who want to pull the plug on televising high profile cases. " * * * If you don't televise such trials, you will only increase the public's dependence on the irresponsible tabloid coverage that always comes in high profile cases."

While there is considerable merit to such a defense, there are several flaws in the argument. First, it ignores how much televising a high profile trial feeds the media frenzy outside the courtroom. [For] better or worse, most Americans rely on television for their news and without video there is far less incentive for the network news shows to cover high profile cases extensively. The dilution of national TV news coverage of a case tends to lower public interest in it, thereby weakening its commercial value for tabloid TV and the press.

Menendez II, which was not televised, graphically illustrates the point. While there is always less interest in a retrial because some of the drama and mystery is lost the second time around, Menendez II generated little sustained interest from national and local media. Has the public suffered? Have we missed an opportunity for public education about our legal system?

The answer to this question depends in part on how well the media educates the public in high profile cases. Apart from Court TV, the networks and local TV did an abominable job in Menendez I by latching on to the "abuse excuse" theme, creating the false impression that the brothers were seeking an acquittal when what was at stake was a determination of whether they were guilty of murder or voluntary manslaughter. Moreover, even if the media were to act more responsibly, the public education justification for televising high profile cases runs into a second problem. The factors that make a case "high profile" tend to decrease its educational value as a window into how our criminal justice system usually functions. * * *

* * * Sager and Frederiksen cite empirical studies showing that the "impact of electronic media coverage of courtroom proceedings—whether civil or criminal—is virtually nil." But these studies focused on two essential issues: Did the cameras distract witnesses, attorneys, and jurors by making them so self-conscious that they performed their roles less competently and did the presence of the camera make witnesses and jurors less willing to participate in the process. Left

---

a. See Kelli L. Sager & Karen N. Frederiksen, *Televising the Judicial Branch: In Furtherance of the Public's First Amendment Rights*, 69 S.Cal.L.Rev. 1519 (1996).

unasked was a critical question: Does televising some high profile cases provide incentives for all of the trial participants to view their own roles somewhat differently with consequent changes in their behavior and decision-making? The Simpson case provides a telling example of how televising a high profile case alters the behavior and experiences of all the trial's participants.

Both sides in Simpson realized from the outset that there was a very good chance that the trial might end in a hung jury necessitating retrial. The courtroom camera gave them an opportunity to address the court of public opinion when arguing legal motions outside the presence of the jury. Of course, Judge Ito could and should have exerted greater control over the attorneys when they made such appeals but the camera's eye probably affected his judicial behavior. Cutting off the lawyers' arguments when they strayed from the legal point in question might have created the appearance that he was favoring one side or the other.

What about the witnesses? Some research suggests that everyone in the courtroom soon forgets the camera's presence in the *ordinary* case. But, in a high profile case being watched by millions, it is impossible to forget that talk show guests, legal pundits, and ordinary citizens glued to their sets will scrutinize what you say. This notoriety will provide an incentive for some witnesses to get involved in the case and discourage others, who don't want their fifteen minutes of fame, from coming forward.

The jurors in high profile cases pay the greatest price. The chances of sequestration[57] increase to protect jurors from contamination by the nightly analysis of legal pundits. More significantly, televising a high profile case increases the risk that the public will not defer to the jury's resolution of the case. The viewing public becomes the thirteenth juror but is privy to information that the jury has not considered and is not bound by the legal instructions that the jury tries to follow in good faith.

Consider the public hostility expressed when one juror acknowledged that she and other jurors did not attribute great weight to the prosecution's domestic violence evidence. With condescension, many commentators suggested that the jury just "didn't get it." Perhaps the commentators didn't get it. They were exposed to far more information about domestic abuse than the jury, including evidence of stalking behavior which the prosecution promised to present but never did. * * *

There are some high profile cases (Rodney King) whose social and political significance justifies the risks involved. Simpson was not such a case unless the media had used it to educate the public about how race and racism affect the criminal justice system. Instead, the media mistakenly lumped the two issues together under its pejorative "race card" label, a move that both reflected and enhanced a simplistic and misleading public discourse about race and the criminal justice system.[b]

---

57. The law needs to reconsider both the necessity as well as the manner of sequestering juries in high profile cases. Jurors should not be treated like prisoners of the state. If sequestration is necessary, thought should be given to a proposal that would permit jurors and alternates to return home after each day's proceedings with a deputy who could ensure that jurors did not have access to the media. Eliminating "pillow talk" is impossible regardless of whether jurors have conjugal visits in hotel rooms or spend evenings home with their loved ones.

b. See also Jeffrey Abramson, *The Pros and Cons of Televising Trials*, in Postmortem: The O.J. Simpson Case 195 (Jeffrey Abramson ed. 1996); Peter Arenella, *Televising High Profile Trials: Are We Better Off Pulling the Plug?*, 37 Santa Clara L.Rev. 701 (1997).

But consider Samuel H. Pillsbury, *Time, TV, and Criminal Justice: Second Thoughts on the Simpson Trial*, 33 Crim.L.Bull. 1, 28 (1997):

"[For] all its problems, the camera also presents the legal system with a major opportunity to improve access to the courts and confidence in the law. Whether we realize this opportunity depends on our confidence in handling change. Does the legal system have the confidence to contemplate increasing electronic access in the face of the Simpson experience?

" * * * Fearful of losing hard-won gains, we pit tradition against innovation. But sometimes the only effective defense of the old is by the new. The best defense of traditional criminal justice values in America may be in the judicious use of electronic technology. The video camera gives us a chance to return to the time when virtually all Americans could witness the legal process in important criminal cases. To realize this opportunity, the halting efforts made by many legislatures and courts during the last two decades to open courtrooms to the viewing public should be expanded. We need only to ask television broadcasters, in a few cases, to take a little more time."

3. Consider, in light of *Sheppard* and *Chandler*, A.B.A. *Standards* §§ 8–3.1; 8–3.6:

Standard 8–3.1. Prohibition of direct restraints on media

Absent a clear and present danger to the fairness of a trial or other compelling interest, no rule of court or judicial order should be promulgated that prohibits representatives of the news media from broadcasting or publishing any information in their possession relating to a criminal case.

Standard 8–3.6. Conduct of the trial

The following standards govern the conduct of a criminal trial when problems relating to the dissemination of potentially prejudicial materials are raised.

(a) Whenever appropriate, in view of the notoriety of a case or the number or conduct of news media representatives present at any judicial proceeding, the court should ensure the preservation of decorum by instructing those representatives and others as to the permissible use of the courtroom and other facilities of the court, the assignment of seats to news media representatives on an equitable basis, and other matters that may affect the conduct of the proceeding.

(b) Sequestration should be ordered only if it is determined that the case is of such notoriety or the issues are of such a nature that, in the absence of sequestration, there is a substantial likelihood that highly prejudicial matters will come to the attention of the jurors. Either party may move for sequestration of the jury at the beginning of the trial or at any time during the course of the trial, and, in appropriate circumstances, the court may order sequestration on its own motion. Whenever sequestration is ordered, the court, in advising the jury of the decision, should not disclose which party requested it. As an alternative to sequestration in cases where there is a significant threat of juror intimidation during or after the trial, the court may consider an order withholding public disclosure of jurors' names and addresses as long as that information is not otherwise required by law to be a matter of public record.

(c) Whenever appropriate, in light of the issues in the case or the notoriety of the case, the court should instruct jurors and court personnel not to make extrajudicial statements relating to the case or the issues in the case for dissemination by any means of public communication during the course of the trial and should caution parties and witnesses concerning the dangers of making an extrajudicial statement during trial. The court may also order sequestration of witnesses, prior to their appearance, when it appears likely that in the absence of sequestration they will be exposed to extrajudicial reports that may influence their testimony. * * *

(e) If it is determined that material disseminated during the trial goes beyond the record on which the case is to be submitted to the jury and raises serious questions of possible prejudice, the court may on its own motion or should on the motion of either party question each juror, out of the presence of the others, about exposure to that material. The examination should take place in the presence of counsel, and an accurate record of the examination should be kept. The standard for excusing a juror who is challenged on the basis of such exposure should be the same as the standard of acceptability recommended in standard 8–3.5(b) [p. 1351], except that a juror who has seen or heard reports of potentially prejudicial material should be excused if reference to the material in question at the trial itself would have required a mistrial to be declared.

C. OTHER REFORMS

Is there a need for special rules to ensure "fairness to the victim" in highly publicized cases, especially those that arise in a context presenting socially divisive, larger issues? A series of acquittals (or convictions of lesser-included offenses) in high profile cases arguably fit that description—the O.J. Simpson case, the original prosecution of Los Angeles police officers for the beating of Rodney King, the prosecution for the murder of Yankel Rosenbaum during the Crown Heights riots in Brooklyn, and the acquittal of William Kennedy Smith for rape. Cases such as these have generated a reexamination of the trial process and the potential it offers the defense to take advantage of external pressures that favor acquittals or "compromise verdicts."

A number of commentators have argued that there is a need for reforms such as: (1) restricting changes of venue; (2) shortening the jury selection process; (3) reducing or eliminating peremptory challenges in order to obtain more diverse juries; (4) prohibiting the use of, or at least reducing the length of, jury questionnaires, thereby diluting the role of jury consultants; (5) permitting, indeed encouraging, jurors to ask questions of the judges; (6) allowing the victim or next of kin to ask questions, either directly or through attorneys; (7) eliminating potential celebrity status for jurors by protecting the anonymity and prohibiting them from "cashing in" on book deals and interviews; (8) abolishing the requirement of jury unanimity or reducing the size of juries. For a discussion of these and other proposals, see Peter Arenella, *Foreword: O.J. Lessons*, 69 S.Cal.L.Rev. 1233 (1996); Craig M. Bradley & Joseph L. Hoffman, *Public Perception, Justice, and the "Search for Truth" in Criminal Cases*, 69 S.Cal.L.Rev. 1267 (1996); George P. Fletcher, *With Justice for Some: Victims' Rights in Criminal Trials* (1995); Robert P. Mosteller, *Popular Justice*, 109 Harv.L.Rev. 487 (1995); Stephen J. Schulhofer, *The Trouble with Trials: The Trouble with Us*, 105 Yale L.J. 825 (1995) and the collection of short articles by Albert W. Alschuler, Barbara Allen Babcock, Andrew Hacker, Kenneth Jost, Nancy J. King, and Michael Lind in Part IV of *Postmortem: The O.J. Simpson Case* (Jeffrey Abramson ed. 1996).

SECTION 4. PREVENTING PREJUDICIAL PUBLICITY

A. RESTRICTING PUBLIC STATEMENTS

In *Sheppard v. Maxwell,* supra, in discussing the various ways by which the trial judge could have exercised his "power to control the publicity about the trial," the Court asserted:

"[T]he trial court might well have proscribed extra-judicial statements by any lawyer, party, witness, or court official which divulged prejudicial matters, such as the refusal of Sheppard to submit to interrogation or take any lie detector tests; any statement made by Sheppard to officials; the identity of prospective witnesses or their probable testimony; any belief in guilt or innocence; or like statements concerning the merits of the case. * * * Being advised of the great public interest in the case, the mass coverage of the press, and the potential prejudicial impact of publicity, the court could also have requested the appropriate city and county officials to promulgate a regulation with respect to dissemination of information about the case by their employees."

Consider *Gentile v. State Bar of Nevada,* below, which dealt with a pretrial publicity rule that imposed restrictions on attorney speech. The rule was virtually identical to ABA Model Rule 3.6. Consider, too, new Rule 3.6, amended in light of the *Gentile* case.

In GENTILE v. STATE BAR OF NEVADA, 501 U.S. 1030, 111 S.Ct. 2720, 115 L.Ed.2d 888 (1991), a 5–4 majority, per REHNQUIST, C.J., upheld the constitutionality of Nevada Supreme Court Rule 177, a rule governing pretrial publicity almost identical to ABA Model Rule of Professional Conduct 3.6 (1983). The rule prohibits a lawyer (in this case, a defense lawyer) from making extrajudicial statements to the press that he "knows or reasonably should know * * * will have a substantial likelihood of materially prejudicing an adjudicative proceeding." However, a different 5–4 majority, per KENNEDY, J., held that the "substantial likelihood of material prejudice" standard, as interpreted by the Nevada Supreme Court—taking into account the Nevada rule's "safe harbor" provision—was "void for vagueness" because it failed to furnish "fair notice to those to whom [it] is directed." The "safe harbor" provision, identical to Model Rule 3.6(c), allows a lawyer, "notwithstanding" various prohibitions against making extrajudicial statements, to "state without elaboration [the] general nature of the claim or defense."

The "swing vote" belonged to Justice O'CONNOR. She agreed with the Rehnquist group (Rehnquist, C.J., joined by White, Scalia, and Souter, JJ.,) that, as officers of the court, lawyers "may legitimately be subject to ethical precepts that keep them from engaging in what otherwise might be constitutionally protected speech." But she agreed with the Kennedy group (Kennedy, J., joined by Marshall, Blackmun and Stevens, JJ.) that, considering its "safe harbor" provision, the Nevada rule was "void for vagueness."

The case arose as follows: When undercover officers with the Las Vegas Metropolitan Police Department reported large amounts of cocaine and travelers' checks missing from a safety deposit box at Western Vault Corporation (a company owned by petitioner Gentile's client, Sanders), suspicion initially focused on Detective Scholl and another police officer. Both officers had had free access to the deposit box. But then the news reports indicated that the attention of the investigators had shifted to Sanders, owner of Western Vault. The story took a sensational turn with news stories that Scholl and the other officer had been "cleared" after passing lie detector tests, but that Sanders had refused to take such a test.

The day after his client was indicted and the same day as the arraignment, Gentile held a press conference. At the time he met with the press, Gentile knew that a jury would not be empaneled for six months. Gentile maintained that his primary motivation in holding the press conference was to counter prejudicial publicity already released by the police and prosecutors. The state disciplinary board found that he had attempted "to counter public opinion which he perceived as adverse to Mr. Sanders"; "to fight back against the perceived efforts of the prosecution to poison the prospective juror pool" and "to publicly present Sanders' side of the case."

At the press conference, Gentile stated, inter alia: (1) the case was similar to those in other cities where the authorities had been "honest enough to indict the people who did it"—"the police department, crooked cops"; (2) when the case is tried the evidence will prove "not only [that] Sanders is an innocent person," but that Detective Scholl "was in the most direct position to have stolen the drugs and money"; (3) there is "far more evidence [that] Detective Scholl took the drugs [and] travelers' checks than any other living human being"; (4) "I feel [that] Sanders is being used as a scapegoat to cover up for what has to be obvious to [law enforcement authorities]"; and (5) with respect to other charges contained in the indictment against Sanders, "the so-called victims" "are known drug dealers and convicted money launderers and drug dealers." In addition, in response to a question from a reporter, Gentile strongly implied that Detective Scholl could be observed in a videotape suffering from symptoms of cocaine use.

The two newspaper stories and the two TV news broadcasts that mentioned Gentile's press conferences also mentioned a prosecution response and a police press conference in response. The chief deputy district attorney was quoted as saying that this was a legitimate indictment and that prosecutors cannot bring an indictment unless they can prove the charges in it beyond a reasonable doubt. A deputy police chief stated that Detective Scholl and another officer who had access to the safety deposit box "had nothing to do with this theft or any other" and that the police department was satisfied that both officers were "above reproach."

Some six months later, Sanders' criminal case was tried by a jury and he was acquitted on all counts. A state disciplinary board then brought proceedings against Gentile and concluded that he had violated Rule 177. The board recommended a private reprimand. The state supreme court affirmed the decision.

In concluding that the "substantial likelihood of material prejudice" standard utilized by Nevada and most other states satisfies the First Amendment, the Court, per REHNQUIST, C.J., observed:

"* * * Currently, 31 states in addition to Nevada have adopted—either verbatim or with insignificant variations—[Model Rule 3.6]. Eleven states have adopted Disciplinary Rule 7–107 of the ABA's Code of Professional Responsibility, which is less protective of lawyer speech than Model Rule 3.6, in that it applies a 'reasonable likelihood of prejudice' standard. Only one state, Virginia, has explicitly adopted a clear and present danger standard, while four states and the District of Columbia have adopted standards that arguably approximate 'clear and present danger.'

"Petitioner maintains, however, that the First Amendment * * * requires a state [to] demonstrate a 'clear and present danger' of 'actual prejudice or an imminent threat' before any discipline may be imposed on a lawyer who initiates a press conference such as occurred here.[4] He relies on decision such as *Nebraska Press Ass'n v. Stuart* [p. 1375 infra] to support his position.

4. We disagree with Justice Kennedy's statement that this case "does not call into question the constitutionality of other states' prohibitions upon attorney speech that will

"[In] *Sheppard v. Maxwell,* [we] held that a new trial was a remedy for [extensive prejudicial pretrial] publicity, but [added:] '[W]e must remember that reversals are but palliatives; the cure lies in those remedial measures that will prevent the prejudice at its inception. * * * Neither prosecutors, counsel for the defense, the accused, witnesses, court staff nor enforcement officers coming under the jurisdiction of the court should be permitted to frustrate its function. *Collaboration between counsel and the press as to information affecting the fairness of a criminal trial is not only subject to regulation, but is highly censurable and worthy of disciplinary measures.*' (Emphasis added.)

"We expressly contemplated that the speech of *those participating before the court* could be limited.[5] [Even] in an area far from the courtroom and the pendency of a case, our decisions dealing with a lawyer's right under the First Amendment to solicit business and advertise, contrary to promulgated rules of ethics, have not suggested that lawyers are protected by the First Amendment to the same extent as those engaged in other businesses. * * *

"We think that [passages in such cases as] *Sheppard v. Maxwell* rather plainly indicate that the speech of lawyers representing clients in pending cases may be regulated under a less demanding standard than that established for regulation of the press in *Nebraska Press* and the cases which preceded it. Lawyers representing clients in pending cases are key participants in the criminal justice system, and the State may demand some adherence to the precepts of that system in regulating their speech as well as their conduct. * * * Because lawyers have special access to information through discovery and client communications, their extrajudicial statements pose a threat to the fairness of a pending proceeding since lawyers' statements are likely to be received as especially authoritative.

"[When] a state regulation implicates First Amendment rights, the Court must balance those interests against the State's legitimate interest in regulating the activity in question. The 'substantial likelihood' test embodied in Rule 177 is constitutional under this analysis, for it is designed to protect the integrity and fairness of a state's judicial system, and it imposes only narrow and necessary limitations on lawyers' speech. The limitations are aimed at two principal evils: (1) comments that are likely to influence the actual outcome of the trial, and (2) comments that are likely to prejudice the jury venire, even if an untainted panel can ultimately be found. Few, if any, interests under the Constitution are more fundamental than the right to a fair trial by 'impartial' jurors, and an outcome affected by extrajudicial statements would violate that fundamental right. Even if a fair trial can ultimately be ensured through *voir dire,* change of venue, or some other device, these measures entail serious costs to the system. Extensive *voir dire* may not be able to filter out all of the effects of pretrial publicity, and with increasingly widespread media coverage of criminal trials, a change of venue may not suffice to undo the effects of statements such as those made by petitioner. The State has a substantial interest in preventing officers of the court, such as lawyers, from imposing such costs on the judicial system and on the litigants."

have a 'substantial likelihood of materially prejudicing the adjudicative proceeding,' but is limited to Nevada's interpretation of that standard." Petitioner challenged Rule 177 as being unconstitutional on its face in addition to as applied, contending that the "substantial likelihood of material prejudice" test was unconstitutional, and that lawyer speech should be punished only if it violates the standard for clear and present danger set forth in *Nebraska Press.* The validity of the rules in the many states applying the "substantial likelihood of material prejudice" test has, therefore, been called into question in this case.

5. The Nevada Supreme Court has consistently read all parts of Rule 177 as applying only to lawyers in pending cases and not to other lawyers or nonlawyers. We express no opinion on the constitutionality of a rule regulating the statement of a lawyer who is not participating in the pending case about which statements are made. * * *

On this issue, Justice KENNEDY, joined by Marshall, Blackmun, and Stevens JJ., dissented, emphasizing that the issue presented was the constitutionality of "a ban on political speech critical of the government and its officials" and maintaining that even if one accepted the argument "that lawyers participating in judicial proceedings may be subjected [to] speech restrictions that could not be imposed on the press or general public," the record did not support the conclusion that Gentile knew or reasonably should have known that his remarks created a substantial likelihood of material prejudice:

"The matter before us does not call into question the constitutionality of other States' prohibitions upon an attorney's speech that will have a 'substantial likelihood of materially prejudicing an adjudicative proceeding,' but is limited to Nevada's interpretation of that standard. On the other hand, one central point must dominate the analysis: this case involves classic political speech. [At] issue here is the constitutionality of a ban on political speech critical of the government and its officials. * * *

"Public awareness and criticism have even greater importance where, as here, they concern allegations of police corruption or where, as is also the present circumstance, the criticism questions the judgment of an elected public prosecutor. Our system grants prosecutors vast discretion at all stages of the criminal process. The public has an interest in its responsible exercise.

"[The] drafters of Model Rule 3.6 apparently thought the substantial likelihood of material prejudice formulation approximated the clear and present danger test. [The] difference between the requirement of serious and imminent threat found in the disciplinary rules of some States and the more common formulation of substantial likelihood of material prejudice could prove mere semantics. Each standard requires an assessment of proximity and degree of harm. Each may be capable of valid application. Under those principles, nothing inherent in Nevada's formulation fails First Amendment review; but as this case demonstrates, Rule 177 has not been interpreted in conformance with those principles by the Nevada Supreme Court. * * *

"Even if one were to accept respondent's argument that lawyers participating in judicial proceedings may be subjected, consistent with the First Amendment, to speech restrictions that could not be imposed on the press or general public, the judgment should not be upheld. The record does not support the conclusion that petitioner knew or reasonably should have known his remarks created a substantial likelihood of material prejudice, if the Rule's terms are given any meaningful content. * * *

"Neither the disciplinary board nor the reviewing court explain any sense in which petitioner's statements had a substantial likelihood of causing material prejudice. [The] Bar's whole case rests on the fact of the statement, the time it was made, and petitioner's own justifications. Full deference to these factual findings does not justify abdication of our responsibility to determine whether petitioner's statements can be punished consistent with First Amendment standards. * * *

"Our decision earlier this Term in Mu'Min v. Virginia provides a pointed contrast to respondent's contention in this case. There, the community had been subjected to a barrage of publicity prior to Mu'Min's trial for capital murder. * * * We held that the publicity did not rise even to a level requiring questioning of individual jurors about the content of publicity. In light of that holding, the Nevada court's conclusion that petitioner's abbreviated, general comments six months before trial created a 'substantial likelihood of materially prejudicing' the proceeding is, to say the least, most unconvincing.

"[An] attorney's duties do not begin inside the courtroom door. He or she cannot ignore the practical implications of a legal proceeding for the client. Just as an attorney may recommend a plea bargain or civil settlement to avoid adverse consequences of a possible loss after trial, so too an attorney may take reasonable steps to defend a client's reputation and reduce the adverse consequences of indictment, especially in the face of a prosecution deemed unjust or commenced with improper motives. A defense attorney may pursue lawful strategies to obtain dismissal of an indictment or reduction of charges, including an attempt to demonstrate in the court of public opinion that the client does not deserve to be tried.

"[On] the evening before the press conference, petitioner and two colleagues spent several hours researching the extent of an attorney's obligations under Rule 177. He decided, as we have held, see *Patton v. Yount,* that the timing of a statement was crucial in the assessment of possible prejudice and the Rule's application.

"Upon return of the indictment, the court set a trial date [for] some six months in the future. Petitioner knew, at the time of his statement, that a jury would not be empaneled for six months at the earliest, if ever. He recalled reported cases finding no prejudice resulting from juror exposure to 'far worse' information two and four months before trial, and concluded that his proposed statement was not substantially likely to result in material prejudice. * * *

"Petitioner's statement lacks any of the more obvious bases for a finding of prejudice. Unlike the police, he refused to comment on polygraph tests except to confirm earlier reports that Sanders had not submitted to the police polygraph; he mentioned no confessions, and no evidence from searches or test results; he refused to elaborate upon his charge that the other so-called victims were not credible, except to explain his general theory that they were pressured to testify in an attempt to avoid drug-related legal trouble, and that some of them may have asserted claims in an attempt to collect insurance money.

"[Petitioner's] judgment that no likelihood of material prejudice would result from his comments was vindicated by events at trial. [The] trial took place on schedule [with] no request by either party for a venue change or continuance. The jury was empaneled with no apparent difficulty. * * *

"Only the occasional case presents a danger of prejudice from pretrial publicity. Empirical research suggests that in the few instances when jurors have been exposed to extensive and prejudicial publicity, they are able to disregard it and base their verdict upon the evidence presented in court. *Voir dire* can play an important role in reminding jurors to set aside out-of-court information, and to decide the case upon the evidence presented at trial. All of these factors weigh in favor of affording an attorney's speech about ongoing proceedings our traditional First Amendment protections. * * *

"Because attorneys participate in the criminal justice system and are trained in its complexities, they hold unique qualifications as a source of information about pending cases. [To] the extent the press and public rely upon attorneys for information because attorneys are well-informed, this may prove the value to the public of speech by members of the bar. If the dangers of their speech arise from its persuasiveness, from their ability to explain judicial proceedings, or from the likelihood the speech will be believed, these are not the sort of dangers that can validate restrictions. The First Amendment does not permit suppression of speech because of its power to command assent."

Although he dissented on the issue of the constitutionality of the "substantial likelihood of material prejudice" standard, as applied by Nevada, Justice KENNE-

DY announced the judgment of the Court overturning Gentile's reprimand and the opinion of the Court holding that Rule 177 was "void for vagueness":

"As interpreted by the Nevada Supreme Court, [Rule 177] is void for vagueness [for] its safe harbor provision, Rule 177(3), misled petitioner into thinking that he could give his press conferences without fear of discipline. Rule 177(3)(a) provides that a lawyer 'may state without elaboration [the] general nature of [the] defense.' Statements under this provision are protected [n]otwithstanding [the general prohibition against extrajudicial statements in subsection 1 and the specific example of statements likely to prejudice a criminal trial in subsection 2]. By necessary operation of the word 'notwithstanding,' the Rule contemplates that a lawyer describing the 'general nature of [the] defense' 'without elaboration' need fear no discipline, even if he comments on '[t]he character, credibility, reputation or criminal record of [a] witness,' and even if he 'knows or reasonably should have known that [the statement] will have a substantial likelihood of materially prejudicing an adjudicative proceeding.'

On this issue, Chief Justice REHNQUIST, joined by White, Scalia and Souter, JJ., dissented:

"Rule 177 'was drafted with the intent to provide 'an illustrative compilation that gives fair notice of conduct ordinarily posing unacceptable dangers to the fair administration of justice.' Proposed Final Draft. The Rule provides sufficient notice of the nature of the prohibited conduct. Under the circumstances of his case, petitioner cannot complain about lack of notice, as he has admitted that his primary objective in holding the press conference was the violation of Rule 177's core prohibition—to prejudice the upcoming trial by influencing potential jurors. Petitioner was clearly given notice that such conduct was forbidden, and the list of conduct likely to cause prejudice, while only advisory, certainly gave notice that the statements made would violate the rule if they had the intended effect.[a] * * *

"Petitioner's strongest arguments are that the statement was made well in advance of trial, and that the statements did not in fact taint the jury panel. But the Supreme Court of Nevada pointed out that petitioner's statements were not only highly inflammatory [but] timed to have maximum impact, when public interest in the case was at its height immediately after Sanders was indicted. [We] find it persuasive that, by his own admission, petitioner called the press conference for the express purpose of influencing the venire. It is difficult to believe that he went to such trouble, and took such a risk, if there was no substantial likelihood that he would succeed. * * *[6]"

---

a. Rule 177(2), which is identical to Model Rule 3.6(b), contains a list of statements "ordinarily * * * likely to prejudice a criminal trial."

6. Justice Kennedy appears to contend that there can be no material prejudice when the lawyer's publicity is in response to publicity favorable to the other side. [He] would find that publicity designed to counter prejudicial publicity cannot be itself prejudicial, despite its likelihood of influencing potential jurors, unless it actually would go so far as to cause jurors to be affirmatively biased in favor of the lawyer's client. In the first place, such a test would be difficult, if not impossible, to apply. But more fundamentally, it misconceives the constitutional test for an impartial juror—whether the "juror can lay aside his impression or opinion and render a verdict on the evidence presented in Court." *Murphy v. Florida*. A juror who may have been initially swayed from open-mindedness by publicity favorable to the prosecution is not rendered fit for service by being bombarded by publicity favorable to the defendant. The basic premise of our legal system is that law suits should be tried in court, not in the media. [The] remedy for prosecutorial abuses that violate the rule lies not in self-help in the form of similarly prejudicial comments by defense counsel, but in disciplining the prosecutor.

Notes and Questions

1. *"Political speech."* Should an exception from Chief Justice Rehnquist's general rule be carved out for "political speech" (speech exposing political corruption or, more generally, speech criticizing the conduct of public officials)? Do (should) defense attorneys have the same responsibility and duty as the press to reveal misconduct by the state's agents? See Notes, 72 B.U.L.Rev. 657, 670 (1992); 1992 B.Y.U.L.Rev. 809, 819, 826; 6 Geo.L.J. Legal Ethics 583, 603–04, 608 (1993).

2. *Alternative safeguards.* Does *Mu'Min,* p. 1352 supra, refute the assumption that defense attorneys can rely on available judicial safeguards (such as holding extensive voir dire or a change of venue) to combat the effects of negative pretrial publicity? How persuasive is Chief Justice Rehnquist's argument in *Gentile* (fn. 6) that the remedy for prosecutorial abuses of rules such as Nevada Rule 177 lies not in self-help, but in disciplining the prosecutor? Does that remedy restore the defendant's ruined reputation? Does it do anything for a defendant who has already been "convicted" by a jury prejudiced by negative pretrial publicity? See Note, 72 B.U.L.Rev. 657, 669.

3. *Access to information through discovery and client communications.* Should special restrictions be placed on lawyers' comments *because* they have access to information gained through discovery and as a result of privileged communications with clients? Or should only lawyers' comments *based on* such information be subject to special instructions? In *Gentile,* did the defense lawyer reveal any client confidences or misuse any information to which he had special access? See Notes, 72 B.U.L.Rev. 657, 669 (1992); 6 Geo.L.J.Legal Ethics 583, 596–97 (1993).

4. *How are defense attorneys' comments likely to be received by the public?* Do you share Chief Justice Rehnquist's view that defense lawyers' statements are likely to be received as "especially authoritative"? Isn't the public likely to realize that a defense lawyer is bound to protect and defend a client? Because they are public officials and many people will regard them as "neutral parties" seeking to protect community safety—and concerned only with achieving a just result—are not prosecutors and police officials likely to have a greater impact on public opinion? Will *their* statements, much more likely than a defense lawyer's, be received as "especially authoritative"? See B.U.L.Rev. Note, supra, at 669–71.

5. *Statements emanating from the police.* Would restricting police officers from disseminating prejudicial information reduce the need for defense lawyers to resort to the media? Given the commingled authority and ongoing working relationship of most prosecutor and police offices, should there be a single standard for both police and prosecutors?

6. *The comments of a lawyer who no longer represents a party. When does a former lawyer "retain the raiment and appearance" of a trial participant?* Consider *United States v. Scarfo,* 263 F.3d 80 (3d Cir.2001),which arose as follows: A month after he was disqualified from representing Mr. Scarfo in a pending criminal case, the attorney (Mr. Manno) was quoted at some length in a newspaper article about the case. He maintained that federal investigators had acted improperly in installing a device on Scarfo's business computer, stated that he expected his replacement to challenge the government's action, and predicted that the forthcoming pretrial motion contesting the surveillance technique might create new law. Apparently perturbed about reading a newspaper account of a matter pertaining to a case before him before hearing about it in the courtroom, the district judge imposed a gag order against Manno. The order was to remain in effect until any motion raising the legal issues discussed in the newspaper article had been adjudicated by the district court. Although the Third Circuit, per Rosenn, J., took the position that "Manno was, for all intents and

purposes in the same position as the attorney referred to in the *Gentile* case," it concluded that the gag order was erroneous:

"Manno portrays himself as an everyday citizen following his disqualification, but that is plainly not so. [He was a] longtime counsel to Scarfo and was known by many, including the media, as having close ties with Scarfo. [He was] the beneficiary of extensive client communication, and his statements were received by the press as especially authoritative. * * *

"Manno was, for all intents and purposes, in the same position as the attorney referred to in the *Gentile* case—an insider privy to facts, and a public status removing him from the leagues of common observers or uninvolved attorneys. [Although] no longer a trial participant, [he] still retained the raiment and appearance of one and, therefore, was in a position to still materially prejudice the pending proceedings before the Court. Therefore, it is reasonable to apply the 'substantial likelihood of material prejudice' standard announced in *Gentile* to this case. * * *

"We do not perceive credible findings of any risk of material prejudice, much less a substantial likelihood of material prejudice. It is difficult to discern a reasonable source of prejudice in this case. There was little, if any, prejudice to the jury pool because Manno's comments, and the gag order itself, pertained only to an issue of admissibility of evidence—a determination made by the judge, not a jury. The Court's decision on admissibility of the keystroke logging device evidence, even if reported in the press, would at most alert citizens to the existence of the case, but not to any facts pertaining to guilt or innocence as in *Gentile*.

"[The] District Court's primary concern was the risk of prejudice to it in deciding the legal issues not yet before it. But there was no risk of prejudice to the Judge because judges are experts at placing aside their personal biases and prejudices, however obtained, before making reasoned decisions. Judges are experts at closing their eyes and ears to extraneous or irrelevant matters and focusing only on the relevant in the proceedings before them. The District Court did not articulate any specific or general prejudice it would suffer, and we can see none. * * *

"Public awareness and criticism have great importance, especially where, as here, they concern alleged governmental investigatory abuse. Without evidence that Manno's statements to the press jeopardized the fairness of the trial or in any way materially impaired or prejudiced the judicial power of the court, we can see no valid reason to interdict a lawyer's First Amendment right of speech, even of one disqualified in the case."

7. *Lawyers' comments after a case has been completed.* Consider *In Matter of Holtzman*, 577 N.E.2d 30 (N.Y.1991), upholding the disciplining of District Attorney Elizabeth Holtzman for publicly criticizing the trial judge's conduct after the acquittal of a rape defendant. Holtzman charged that by making the rape victim "assume the position she was forced to take when she was sexually assaulted" the judge "profoundly degraded, humiliated and demeaned her."

After an administrative judge found Ms. Holtzman's charges unsupported by the record, the grievance committee reprimanded her for violating, inter alia, a provision of the code of professional responsibility prohibiting a lawyer from engaging in conduct that "adversely reflects on [the lawyer's] fitness to practice law." The highest court of New York upheld the disciplinary action, pointing out that Ms. Holtzman "knew or should have known" that her attacks on the trial judge "serve to bring the Bench and Bar into disrepute, and tend to undermine public confidence in the judicial system."

Should the district attorney's post-acquittal criticism of the judge have been protected by the First Amendment? How significant is the following: the district attorney's conduct "was not generalized criticism, but rather release to the media of a false allegation of specific wrongdoing, made without any support other than the interoffice memoranda of a newly admitted trial assistant, aimed at a named Judge."

THE IMPACT OF *GENTILE* ON MODEL RULE 3.6

In the wake of *Gentile* the ABA House of Delegates significantly amended Model Rule 3.6 in August 1994. Companion amendments to Rule 3.8 were approved at the same time. The amended rules delete qualifying terms that the *Gentile* Court found unconstitutionally vague, but continue to prohibit statements that a lawyer "reasonably should know * * * will have a substantial likelihood of materially prejudicing an adjudicative proceeding." The amended rules also establish a new "safe harbor" provision allowing a lawyer to protect his client against publicity initiated by someone else and make clear that all lawyers "associated in a firm or government agency" are covered. The amended rule is set forth below:

RULE 3.6 TRIAL PUBLICITY

(a) A lawyer who is participating or has participated in the investigation or litigation of a matter shall not make an extrajudicial statement that a reasonable person would expect to be disseminated by means of public communication if the lawyer knows or reasonably should know that it will have a substantial likelihood of materially prejudicing an adjudicative proceeding in the matter.

(b) Notwithstanding paragraph (a), a lawyer may state:

(1) the claim, offense or defense involved and, except when prohibited by law, the identity of the persons involved;

(2) information contained in a public record;

(3) that an investigation of a matter is in progress;

(4) the scheduling or result of any step in litigation;

(5) a request for assistance in obtaining evidence and information necessary thereto;

(6) a warning of danger concerning the behavior of a person involved, when there is reason to believe that there exists the likelihood of substantial harm to an individual or to the public interest; and

(7) in a criminal case, in addition to subparagraphs (1) through (6):

(i) the identity, residence, occupation and family status of the accused;

(ii) if the accused has not been apprehended, information necessary to aid in apprehension of that person;

(iii) the fact, time and place of arrest; and

(iv) the identity of investigating and arresting officers or agencies and the length of the investigation.

(c) Notwithstanding paragraph (a), a lawyer may make a statement that a reasonable lawyer would believe is required to protect a client from the substantial undue prejudicial effect of recent publicity not

initiated by the lawyer or the lawyer's client. A statement made pursuant to this paragraph shall be limited to such information as is necessary to mitigate the recent adverse publicity.

(d) No lawyer associated in a firm or government agency with a lawyer subject to paragraph (a) shall make a statement prohibited by paragraph (a).

B. Restraining the Media From Reporting

Consider NEBRASKA PRESS ASS'N v. STUART, 427 U.S. 539, 96 S.Ct. 2791, 49 L.Ed.2d 683 (1976): In anticipation of the trial of Simants for a mass murder which had attracted widespread news coverage, the county court banned everyone in attendance from, inter alia, releasing or authorizing for publication "any testimony given or evidence adduced." Simants' preliminary hearing (open to the public) was held the same day, subject to the restrictive order. Simants was bound over for trial. Respondent Nebraska state trial judge then entered an order which, as modified by the state supreme court, restrained the media from reporting any confessions or incriminating statements made by Simants to law enforcement officers or third parties (except members of the press), and from reporting other facts "strongly implicative" of the defendant. The order expired by its own terms when the jury was impaneled. The Court, per BURGER, C.J., struck down the state court order:

"To the extent that the order prohibited the reporting of evidence adduced at the open preliminary hearing, it plainly violated settled principles: '[T]here is nothing that proscribes the press from reporting events that transpire in the courtroom.' *Sheppard.* [O]nce a public hearing had been held, what transpired there could not be subject to prior restraint."

To the extent that the order prohibited publication "based on information gained from other sources," it also failed because the state had not met the heavy burden imposed as a condition to securing a prior restraint.[a]

The Court deemed it "significant that when [it] has reversed a state conviction because of prejudicial publicity, it has carefully noted that some course of action short of prior restraint would have made a critical difference. However difficult it may be, we need not rule out the possibility of showing the kind of threat to fair trial rights that would possess the requisite degree of certainty to justify restraint. [However,] with respect to the order entered in this case [the] heavy burden imposed as a condition to securing a prior restraint was not met * * *."

Concurring, BRENNAN, J., joined by Stewart and Marshall, JJ., would hold that "resort to prior restraints on the freedom of the press is a constitutionally impermissible method for enforcing [the right to a fair trial by a jury]; judges have at their disposal a broad spectrum of devices for ensuring that fundamental fairness is accorded the accused without necessitating so drastic an incursion on the equally fundamental and salutary constitutional mandate that discussion of public affairs in a free society cannot depend on the preliminary grace of judicial censors."

Although they joined the Court's opinion, WHITE and POWELL, JJ., also filed brief concurring opinions. White, J., expressed "grave doubts" that these types of restrictive orders "would ever be justifiable." Powell, J., "emphasize[d]

---

a. The Court also noted that the portion of the order regarding "implicative" information was "too vague and too broad" to survive the scrutiny imposed on restraints on First Amendment rights.

the unique burden" resting upon one who "undertakes to show the necessity for prior restraint on pretrial publicity."

STEVENS, J., also wrote a brief separate opinion, concurring in the judgment. For the reasons articulated by Brennan, J., he "agree[d] that the judiciary is capable of protecting the defendant's right to a fair trial without enjoining the press from publishing information in the public domain, and that it may not do so." But he reserved judgment, until further argument, on "[w]hether the same absolute protection would apply no matter how shabby or illegal the means by which the information is obtained, no matter how serious an intrusion on privacy might be involved, no matter how demonstrably false the information might be, no matter how prejudicial it might be to the interests of innocent persons, and no matter how perverse the motivation for publishing it." He indicated that "if ever required to face the issue squarely" he "may well accept [Brennan, J.'s] ultimate conclusion."[b]

Notes and Questions

1. Why the prior restraint reliance? Does "the reasoning used by all of the justices, premised solely on the traditional aversion to prior restraints, insufficiently" protect the press? See Robert Sack, *Principle and Nebraska Press Association v. Stuart,* 29 Stan.L.Rev. 411 (1977). Would the *Nebraska Press* order have been "equally objectionable" if "framed as a statutory sanction punishing publication after it had occurred"? Id. at 415. See also Stephen Barnett, *The Puzzle of Prior Restraint,* 29 Stan.L.Rev. 539, 542–44, 560 (1977).

2. Future press restraints. Was *Nebraska Press* a strong case for restraint? Is it "difficult to believe that any other case will provide an exception to the rule against prior restraints in fair trial/free press cases"? James Goodale, *The Press Ungagged: The Practical Effect on Gag Order Litigation of Nebraska Press Association v. Stuart,* 29 Stan.L.Rev. 497, 504 (1977).

C. Closing the Proceedings

The question presented in GANNETT CO., INC. v. DePASQUALE, 443 U.S. 368, 99 S.Ct. 2898, 61 L.Ed.2d 608 (1979), was "whether members of the public have an independent constitutional right to insist upon access to a pretrial judicial proceeding, even though the accused, the prosecutor and the trial judge all have agreed to the closure of that proceeding in order to assure a fair trial." All of the Justices agreed that the problem was distinguishable from that in *Nebraska Press* because the issue here was "not one of prior restraint on the press [but] of *access* to a judicial proceeding."

Two murder defendants moved to suppress allegedly involuntary confessions. Their attorneys moved to exclude the public and press from the suppression hearing in order to assure their clients a fair trial. The prosecutor did not oppose this motion, which was granted. Although the trial judge viewed the press as having a First Amendment right of access to the pretrial hearing, he concluded—after finding that an open suppression hearing posed a "reasonable probability of prejudice to these defendants"—that the press' interest was outweighed in this case by the defendants' right to a fair trial. The New York Court of Appeals upheld the closure order, deeming the presumptive openness of criminal proceed-

b. For background on *Nebraska Press,* see   *Delicate Balance* 148–58 (1984).
F. Friendly & Elliot, *The Constitution: That*

ings overcome in this case because of the danger that defendants might not receive a fair trial.

A 5–4 majority, per STEWART, J., affirmed. After concluding that the Sixth Amendment guarantee of a public trial is for the benefit of the defendant alone, the Court quickly disposed of the claim of a First Amendment "right of access": [E]ven assuming, arguendo, that [the First Amendment] may guarantee such access in some situations, a question we do not decide, this putative right was given all appropriate deference by the trial court in the present case."

"Because of the importance of the public's having accurate information concerning the operation of its criminal justice system," POWELL, J., concurring, "would hold explicitly" that the press had a First Amendment right to be present at the pretrial suppression hearing, but he recognized that the right was not absolute. The appropriate question for a trial court considering a closure motion at a pretrial suppression hearing "is whether a fair trial for the defendant is likely to be jeopardized by publicity, if members of the press and public are present and free to report prejudicial evidence that will not be presented to the jury." Since, in Powell's view, the trial court had applied a standard similar to the one he proposed, "the procedure followed by the trial court fully comported with that required by the Constitution."

Dissenting Justice Blackmun, joined by Brennan, Marshall and White, JJ., maintained that Fourteenth Amendment Due Process, insofar as it incorporates the Sixth Amendment public trial provision, "prohibits the States from excluding the public from a proceeding within the ambit of the Sixth Amendment's guarantee without affording full and fair consideration to the public's interests in maintaining an open proceeding." And this is so "notwithstanding the fact it is the accused who seeks to close the trial."

RICHMOND NEWSPAPERS, INC. v. VIRGINIA, 448 U.S. 555, 100 S.Ct. 2814, 65 L.Ed.2d 973 (1980), marked the first time the Court was asked to decide "whether a criminal trial itself may be closed to the public upon the unopposed request of a defendant, without any demonstration that closure is required to protect the defendant's superior right to a fair trial, or that some other overriding consideration requires closure."

The Court held that the right of the public and the press to attend criminal trials is implicit in the guarantees of the First Amendment, but there was no opinion of the Court. In the lead opinion, BURGER, C.J., joined by White and Stevens, JJ., observed that "the Bill of Rights was enacted against the backdrop of the long history of trials being presumptively open" and that "the First Amendment can be read as protecting the right of everyone to attend trials" "so as to give meaning" to the explicit guarantees of freedom of speech and press. However one describes the right to attend criminal trials—a "right of access" or a "right to gather information"—"the explicit, guaranteed rights to speak and to publish would lose much meaning if access to observe the trial could, as it was here, be foreclosed arbitrarily."

Concurring Justice BRENNAN, joined by Marshall, J., emphasized that public access to trials is essential "to achieve the objective of maintaining public confidence in the administration of justice" and that public access "acts as an important check, akin in purpose to the other checks and balances that infuse our system of government."[a]

a. Justices Stewart, White, Blackmun and Stevens wrote separate concurring opinions.

Powell, J., did not participate. Rehnquist, J., dissented, unable to find "any provision in the

GLOBE NEWSPAPER CO. v. SUPERIOR COURT, 457 U.S. 596, 102 S.Ct. 2613, 73 L.Ed.2d 248 (1982) struck down a Massachusetts statute (§ 16A) which, as construed by the state's highest court, required trial judges, at rape and other sex-offense trials involving an alleged victim under the age of 18, to exclude the press and general public from the courtroom under all circumstances during the testimony of that victim. The Supreme Judicial Court of Massachusetts "did not think 'that *Richmond Newspapers* require[d] the invalidation of the requirement, given the statute's narrow scope in an area of traditional sensitivity to the needs of victims.'" The Court, per BRENNAN, J., disagreed.

The Court did consider one of the interests advanced by the state to support § 16A—"safeguarding the physical and psychological well-being of a minor"—to be "a compelling one." Nevertheless, that interest "does not justify a *mandatory* closure rule," for "a trial court can determine on a case-by-case basis whether closure is necessary to protect the welfare of a minor victim." But § 16A requires closure "even if the victim does not seek the exclusion of the press and general public, and would not suffer injury by their presence."

Dissenting Chief Justice BURGER, joined by Rehnquist, J., protested: "Historically our Society has gone to great lengths to protect minors *charged* with crime, particularly by prohibiting the release of the names of offenders, barring the press and public from juvenile proceedings, and sealing the records of those proceedings. Yet today the Court holds unconstitutional a state statute designed to protect not the *accused,* but the minor *victims* of sex crimes. In doing so, it advances a disturbing paradox. Although states are permitted, for example, to mandate the closure of all proceedings in order to protect a 17–year-old charged with rape, they are not permitted to require the closing of part of criminal proceedings in order to protect an innocent child who has been raped or otherwise sexually abused."

The dissenters pointed out that the Court had "consistently emphasized" that the "presumption of openness" that inheres in the very nature of a criminal trial is "not absolute or irrebuttable. [Section 16A] has a relatively minor incidental impact on First Amendment rights and gives effect to the overriding state interest in protecting child rape victims."

Notes and Questions

1. *Right of access to juvenile delinquency proceedings.* After *Richmond Newspapers* and *Globe,* can the states still mandate the closure of all juvenile delinquency proceedings? To what extent do the Court's reasons for extending a public right of access to criminal trials apply to juvenile proceedings as well? If even the compelling state interest asserted in *Globe* did not justify a *mandatory* closure rule during the testimony of a minor witness in a sex-offense case, can laws *mandating* the exclusion of the public from juvenile proceedings survive First Amendment challenge? See generally Note, 81 Mich.L.Rev. 1540 (1983).

2. *Right of access to "rape shield" evidentiary hearings.* What are *Globe's* implications for "rape shield" hearings? In recent years most states have enacted "rape shield" laws designed to control or even prohibit the use of evidence respecting the rape complainant's previous sexual conduct. In order to use such evidence as the law does not entirely bar, a typical "rape shield" statute

Constitution [that] may fairly be read to prohibit what the [trial court] did in this case."

requires the defendant to make a written motion offering proof of relevance. If the court finds the offer sufficient, it holds a hearing away from the jury to decide whether the proposed material satisfies the applicable standard. Some laws posit an in camera hearing before trial, others a hearing during trial prior to the proof's admission. See Vivian O. Berger, *Man's Trial, Woman's Tribulation: Rape Cases in the Courtroom,* 77 Colum.L.Rev. 1, 32–39 (1977). After *Globe,* would the Supreme Court sustain a *mandatory* closure rule for rape shield evidentiary hearings? How significant is it that the victim's prior sexual history will *often* be less central to the case than the victim's version of the claimed attack, the admissibility of a confession or other issues? What if a particular case is the rare case where the admissibility of the victim's prior sexual conduct is, or appears to be, critically important? Should there not at least be a finding on this issue?

THE RIGHT OF ACCESS TO PRETRIAL PROCEEDINGS

While *Richmond Newspapers* and *Globe Newspapers* established a First Amendment right of access to the criminal trial itself, these cases left open the question whether such a right extended to pretrial proceedings. The Court, per Burger, C.J., suggested this possibility in *Press–Enterprise I (Press–Enterprise Co. v. Superior Court,* 464 U.S. 501, 104 S.Ct. 819, 78 L.Ed.2d 629 (1984)), when it held, without a dissent, that the First Amendment right applied to the *voir dire* examination of potential jurors. The Court emphasized two factors cited in *Globe Newspaper*—the historical tradition of openness and the functional value of openness for the particular proceeding—rather than any characterization of the jury selection process as a part of the trial itself. Two years later, in *Press–Enterprise II,* discussed below, the Court again relied on these two factors, but this time it applied the public right of access to a proceeding that was clearly not part of the trial—the preliminary hearing.

Although the Court proceeded under the Sixth Amendment rather than the First, *Waller v. Georgia,* 467 U.S. 39, 104 S.Ct. 2210, 81 L.Ed.2d 31 (1984), provided further evidence that the Court would extend the First Amendment right of access to pretrial hearings. The *Waller* Court held unanimously, per Powell, J., that *the defendant's Sixth Amendment* right to a public trial extends to a pretrial suppression hearing; that "under the Sixth Amendment any closure of a suppression hearing over the objections of the accused must meet the [First Amendment] tests set out in *Press–Enterprise* and its predecessors"; and that, applying these tests, "the closure of the entire suppression hearing plainly was unjustified." *Waller* reformulated the standards for courtroom closure into a four-factor test: "[1] the party seeking to close the hearing must advance an overriding interest that is likely to be prejudiced, [2] the closure must be no broader than necessary to protect that interest, [3] the trial court must consider reasonable alternatives to closing the proceeding, and [4] it must make findings adequate to support the closure." The Court noted that although the analysis in recent open trial cases had proceeded largely under the First Amendment, there "can be little doubt that the explicit Sixth Amendment right of the accused is no less protective of a public trial than the implicit First Amendment right of the press and the public."

But was the Sixth Amendment right *more* protective than the First Amendment right? No, answered the Court in PRESS ENTERPRISE CO. v. SUPERIOR COURT [PRESS ENTERPRISE II], 478 U.S. 1, 106 S.Ct. 2735, 92 L.Ed.2d 1 (1986). In this case, the defendant requested a *closed* preliminary hearing. Thus the right at issue was *the public's* right of access under the First Amendment. "The considerations that led the Court to apply the First Amendment right of access to criminal trials in *Richmond Newspapers* and *Globe* and the selection of jurors in *Press-Enterprise* I," wrote Chief Justice BURGER for the Court, "lead us to conclude that the right of access applies to preliminary hearings as conducted in California.''

The Court recognized that "unlike a criminal trial, the California preliminary hearing cannot result in the conviction of the accused and the adjudication is before a magistrate or other judicial officer without a jury. But these features, standing alone, do not make public access any less essential to the proper functioning of the proceedings in the overall criminal justice process. Because of its extensive scope, the preliminary hearing is often the final and most important step in the criminal proceeding. * * * Similarly, the absence of a jury, long recognized as 'an inestimable safeguard against the corrupt or overzealous prosecutor and against the complaint, biased, or eccentric judge,' makes the importance of public access to a preliminary hearing even more significant."

Dissenting Justice STEVENS, with whom Rehnquist, J., joined in large part, argued that "the 'value of openness,' on which [the Court] relies, proves too much, for this measure would open to public scrutiny far more than preliminary hearings. [The Court's] reasoning applies to the traditionally secret grand jury with as much force as it applies to California preliminary hearings. A grand jury indictment is just as likely to be the 'final step' in a criminal proceeding and the 'sole occasion' for public scrutiny as is a preliminary hearing. [When] the Court's explanatory veneer is stripped away, what emerges is the reality that the California preliminary hearing is functionally identical to the traditional grand jury."

Chapter 25

THE CRIMINAL TRIAL[aa]

SECTION 1. PRESENCE OF THE DEFENDANT

ILLINOIS v. ALLEN

397 U.S. 337, 90 S.Ct. 1057, 25 L.Ed.2d 353 (1970).

Justice BLACK delivered the opinion of the Court.

[Allen was convicted by an Illinois jury of armed robbery and was sentenced to a term of 10 to 30 years. Before trial, the judge acceded to Allen's wish to conduct his own defense, although court-appointed counsel would "sit in and protect the record." During the *voir dire* examination, Allen "started to argue with the judge in a most abusive and disrespectful manner" when the judge directed him to confine his questioning to matters relating to the prospective juror's qualifications. The judge then asked appointed counsel to proceed with the examination, upon which Allen continued to talk and concluded his remarks by saying to the judge, "When I go out for lunchtime, you're going to be a corpse here." The judge then warned Allen that he would be removed from the courtroom if there was another outbreak of that sort. Allen continued to talk back, saying, "There's not going to be no trial, either. I'm going to sit here and you're going to talk and you can bring your shackles out and straight jacket and put them on me and tape my mouth, but it will do no good because there's not going to be no trial." After more abusive remarks, the judge ordered the trial to proceed in Allen's absence. After a noon recess, the judge permitted Allen to return to the courtroom with the warning that he could remain only so long as he behaved himself. Shortly thereafter, Allen spoke out again, saying, "There is going to be no proceeding. I'm going to start talking all through the trial. There's not going to be no trial like this." The judge again ordered Allen removed, and he remained out of the courtroom during the presentation of the State's case-in-chief except when brought in for purposes of identification. Thereafter, Allen was permitted to return to the courtroom upon his promise to conduct himself properly, and he remained for the rest of the trial, principally his defense, which was conducted by his appointed counsel. Allen's conviction was affirmed by the Supreme Court of Illinois, and on federal habeas corpus the district court found no constitutional violation and declined to issue the writ. The court of appeals reversed.]

The Court of Appeals felt that the defendant's Sixth Amendment right to be present at his own trial was so "absolute" that, no matter how unruly or disruptive the defendant's conduct might be, he could never be held to have lost that right so long as he continued to insist upon it, as Allen clearly did. * * * We cannot agree that the Sixth Amendment, the cases upon which the Court of

---

aa. For a more complete discussion of the subjects discussed in this chapter, as well as other aspects of the criminal trial, see Wayne R. Lafave, Jerold H. Israel, & Nancy J. King, *Criminal Procedure Treatise* § 24.1–24.11 (2d ed. 1999) (available on Westlaw under the database CRIMPROC and hereafter cited as CRIMPROC).

Appeals relied, or any other cases of this Court so handicap a trial judge in conducting a criminal trial. * * * We accept instead the statement of Justice Cardozo who, speaking for the Court in *Snyder v. Massachusetts,* 291 U.S. 97, 54 S.Ct. 330, 78 L.Ed. 674 (1934), said: "No doubt the privilege [of personally confronting witnesses] may be lost by consent or at times even by misconduct." Although mindful that courts must indulge every reasonable presumption against the loss of constitutional rights, we explicitly hold today that a defendant can lose his right to be present at trial if, after he has been warned by the judge that he will be removed if he continues his disruptive behavior, he nevertheless insists on conducting himself in a manner so disorderly, disruptive, and disrespectful of the court that his trial cannot be carried on with him in the courtroom. Once lost, the right to be present can, of course, be reclaimed as soon as the defendant is willing to conduct himself consistently with the decorum and respect inherent in the concept of courts and judicial proceedings.

It is essential to the proper administration of criminal justice that dignity, order, and decorum be the hallmarks of all court proceedings in our country. The flagrant disregard in the courtroom of elementary standards of proper conduct should not and cannot be tolerated. We believe trial judges confronted with disruptive, contumacious, stubbornly defiant defendants must be given sufficient discretion to meet the circumstances of each case. No one formula for maintaining the appropriate courtroom atmosphere will be best in all situations. We think there are at least three constitutionally permissible ways for a trial judge to handle an obstreperous defendant like Allen: (1) bind and gag him, thereby keeping him present; (2) cite him for contempt; (3) take him out of the courtroom until he promises to conduct himself properly.

Trying a defendant for a crime while he sits bound and gagged before the judge and jury would to an extent comply with that part of the Sixth Amendment's purposes that accords the defendant an opportunity to confront the witnesses at the trial. But even to contemplate such a technique, much less see it, arouses a feeling that no person should be tried while shackled and gagged except as a last resort. Not only is it possible that the sight of shackles and gags might have a significant effect on the jury's feelings about the defendant, but the use of this technique is itself something of an affront to the very dignity and decorum of judicial proceedings that the judge is seeking to uphold. Moreover, one of the defendant's primary advantages of being present at the trial, his ability to communicate with his counsel, is greatly reduced when the defendant is in a condition of total physical restraint. It is in part because of these inherent disadvantages and limitations in this method of dealing with disorderly defendants that we decline to hold with the Court of Appeals that a defendant cannot under any possible circumstances be deprived of his right to be present at trial. However, in some situations which we need not attempt to foresee, binding and gagging might possibly be the fairest and most reasonable way to handle a defendant who acts as Allen did here.

In a footnote the Court of Appeals suggested the possible availability of contempt of court as a remedy to make Allen behave in his robbery trial, and it is true that citing or threatening to cite a contumacious defendant for criminal contempt might in itself be sufficient to make a defendant stop interrupting a trial. If so, the problem would be solved easily, and the defendant could remain in the courtroom. Of course, if the defendant is determined to prevent *any* trial, then a court in attempting to try the defendant for contempt is still confronted with the identical dilemma that the Illinois court faced in this case. And criminal contempt has obvious limitations as a sanction when the defendant is charged with a crime so serious that a very severe sentence such as death or life imprisonment is likely to be imposed. In such a case the defendant might not be affected by a mere contempt sentence when he ultimately faces a far more serious sanction. Nevertheless, the contempt remedy should be borne in mind by a judge in the circumstances of this case.

Another aspect of the contempt remedy is the judge's power, when exercised consistently with state and federal law, to imprison an unruly defendant such as Allen for civil contempt and discontinue the trial until such time as the defendant promises to behave himself. This procedure is consistent with the defendant's right to be present at trial, and yet it avoids the serious shortcomings of the use of shackles and gags. It must be recognized, however, that a defendant might conceivably, as a matter of calculated strategy, elect to spend a prolonged period in confinement for contempt in the hope that adverse witnesses might be unavailable after a lapse of time. A court must guard against allowing a defendant to profit from his own wrong in this way.

The trial court in this case decided under the circumstances to remove the defendant from the courtroom and to continue his trial in his absence until and unless he promised to conduct himself in a manner befitting an American courtroom. As we said earlier, we find nothing unconstitutional about this procedure. Allen's behavior was clearly of such an extreme and aggravated nature as to justify either his removal from the courtroom or his total physical restraint. Prior to his removal he was repeatedly warned by the trial judge that he would be removed from the courtroom if he persisted in his unruly conduct,[a] and, as Judge Hastings observed in his dissenting opinion, the record demonstrates that Allen would not have been at all dissuaded by the trial judge's use of his criminal contempt powers. Allen was constantly informed that he could return to the trial when he would agree to conduct himself in an orderly manner. Under these circumstances we hold that Allen lost his right guaranteed by the Sixth and Fourteenth Amendments to be present throughout his trial. * * * The judgment of the Court of Appeals is reversed.[b]

Justice BRENNAN, concurring, noted: "I would add only that when a defendant is excluded from his trial, the court should make reasonable efforts to enable him to communicate with his attorney and, if possible, to keep apprised of the progress of his trial. Once the court has removed the contumacious defendant, it is not weakness to mitigate the disadvantages of his expulsion as far as technologically possible in the circumstances."

Notes and Questions

1. Trial in absentia. In *Crosby v. United States,* 506 U.S. 255, 113 S.Ct. 748, 122 L.Ed.2d 25 (1993), holding that the "language, history, and logic" of Fed.R.Crim.P. 43 "support a straightforward interpretation that prohibits the trial *in absentia* of a defendant who is not present at the beginning of trial," the Court commented: "If a clear line is to be drawn marking the point at which the costs of delay are likely to outweigh the interests of the defendant and society in having the defendant present, the commencement of trial is at least a plausible place at which to draw that line."

a. Is a warning a constitutional prerequisite, and if so, is more than a single warning needed? See *United States v. Watkins,* 983 F.2d 1413 (7th Cir.1993) (right of presence denied where defendant, who was described by the judge as "impersonating Raggedy Andy," was excluded without any warning); *Scurr v. Moore,* 647 F.2d 854 (8th Cir.1981) (one warning sufficient); *United States v. West,* 877 F.2d 281 (4th Cir.1989) (sufficient that defendant saw his codefendant warned and then removed for disruptive behavior after ignoring the warning).

b. Justice Douglas, in a separate opinion, concluded the Court "should reverse the case for staleness of the record and affirm the denial of relief by the District Court."

2. Compare the situation in which the defendant absents himself during the trial. In *Taylor v. United States,* 414 U.S. 17, 94 S.Ct. 194, 38 L.Ed.2d 174 (1973), the Court, per curiam, rejected the defendant's contention that "his mere voluntary absence from the trial cannot be construed as an effective waiver * * * unless it is demonstrated that he knew or had been expressly warned by the trial court not only that he had a right to be present but also that the trial would continue in his absence and thereby effectively foreclose his right to testify and to confront personally the witnesses against him." The Court noted: "It is wholly incredible to suggest that petitioner, who was at liberty on bail, had attended the opening session of his trial, and had a duty to be present at the trial, entertained any doubts about his right to be present at every stage of his trial. It seems equally incredible to us, as it did to the Court of Appeals, 'that a defendant who flees from a courtroom in the midst of a trial—where judge, jury, witnesses and lawyers are present and ready to continue—would not know that as a consequence the trial could continue in his absence.' "

3. *In-chambers hearings.* In KENTUCKY v. STINCER, 482 U.S. 730, 107 S.Ct. 2658, 96 L.Ed.2d 631 (1987), after the jury was sworn in defendant's trial for the alleged commission of sodomy upon two children, aged 8 and 7, the trial court conducted an in-chambers hearing to determine the competency of the children to testify. Defense counsel participated in the in-chambers hearing, but defendant was excluded notwithstanding his request to be present. The in-chambers examination of the children was limited to questions designed to determine whether they were capable of remembering basic facts (e.g., they were asked the names of their teachers) and whether they had a moral sense of the obligation to tell the truth (e.g., they were asked "what it means to tell the truth"). Following the examination, the trial court, without objection by defense counsel, ruled that the children were competent to testify. Before each child began her substantive testimony at trial, the prosecutor repeated some of the basic questions that had been asked at the competency hearing. On cross-examination, defense counsel asked further questions designed to determine if the child could recall past events and knew the difference between the truth and a lie. The Supreme Court, per BLACKMUN, J., held (6–3) that the exclusion of defendant from the in-chambers competency hearing had not violated defendant's constitutional rights. The Court reasoned:

"The Commonwealth argues that respondent's exclusion from the competency hearing of the two children did not violate the Confrontation Clause because a competency hearing is not 'a stage of trial where evidence or witnesses are being presented to the trier of fact.' * * * Distinguishing between a 'trial' and a 'pretrial proceeding' is not particularly helpful here, however, because a competency hearing may well be a 'stage of trial.' In this case, for instance, the competency hearing was held after the jury was sworn, in the judge's chambers, and in the presence of opposing counsel who asked questions of the witnesses. Moreover, although questions regarding the guilt or innocence of the defendant usually are not asked at a competency hearing, the hearing retains a direct relationship with the trial because it determines whether a key witness will testify. Further, although the preliminary determination of a witness' competency to testify is made at this hearing, the determination of competency is an ongoing one for the judge to make based on the witness' actual testimony at trial.

"Instead of attempting to characterize a competency hearing as a trial or pretrial proceeding, it is more useful to consider whether excluding the defendant from the hearing interferes with his opportunity for effective cross-examination. No such interference occurred when respondent was excluded from the competency hearing of the two young girls in this case. After the trial court determined that the two children were competent to testify, they appeared and testified in open court. At that point, the two witnesses were subject to full and complete cross-examination, and were so examined. Respondent was present throughout this cross-examination and was available to assist his counsel as necessary. * * * Any questions asked during the competency hearing, which respondent's counsel attended and in which he participated, could have been repeated during direct examination and cross-examination of the witnesses in respondent's presence. * * *

"Moreover, the type of questions that were asked at the competency hearing in this case were easy to repeat on cross-examination at trial. * * * In Kentucky, as in certain other States, it is the responsibility of the judge, not the jury, to decide whether a witness is competent to testify based on the witness' answers to such questions. * * * [T]hat responsibility usually continues throughout the trial. A motion by defense counsel that the court reconsider its earlier decision that a child is competent may be raised after the child testifies on direct examination. * * * At the close of the children's testimony, respondent's counsel, had he thought it appropriate, was in a position to move that the court reconsider its competency rulings on the ground that the direct and cross-examination had elicited evidence that the young girls lacked the basic requisites for serving as competent witnesses. Thus, the critical tool of cross-examination was available to counsel as a means of establishing that the witnesses were not competent to testify, as well as a means of undermining the credibility of their testimony.

"Because respondent had the opportunity for full and effective cross-examination of the two witnesses during trial, and because of the nature of the competency hearing at issue in this case, we conclude that respondent's rights under the Confrontation Clause were not violated by his exclusion from the competency hearing of the two girls. * * * [But] respondent [also] argues that his rights under the Due Process Clause of the Fourteenth Amendment were violated by his exclusion from the competency hearing. The Court has assumed that, even in situations where the defendant is not actually confronting witnesses or evidence against him, he has a due process right 'to be present in his own person whenever his presence has a relation, reasonably substantial, to the fullness of his opportunity to defend against the charge.' *Snyder v. Massachusetts.* * * * [A] defendant is guaranteed the right to be present at any stage of the criminal proceeding that is critical to its outcome if his presence would contribute to the fairness of the procedure.

"We conclude that respondent's due process rights were not violated by his exclusion from the competency hearing in this case. We emphasize, again, the particular nature of the competency hearing. No question regarding the substantive testimony that the two girls would have given during the trial was asked at that hearing. All the questions, instead, were directed solely to each child's ability to recollect and narrate facts, to her ability to distinguish between truth and falsehood, and to her sense of moral obligation to tell the truth. Thus, although a competency hearing in which a witness is asked to discuss upcoming substantive testimony might bear a substantial relationship to a defendant's opportunity better to defend himself at trial, that kind of inquiry is not before us in this case. Respondent has given no indication that his presence at the competency hearing in this case would have been useful in ensuring a more reliable determination as to whether the witnesses were competent to testify. He has presented no evidence that his relationship with the children, or his knowledge of facts regarding their background, could have assisted either his counsel or the judge in asking questions that would have resulted in a more assured determination of competency. On the record of this case, therefore, we cannot say that respondent's rights under the Due Process Clause of the Fourteenth Amendment were violated by his exclusion from the competency hearing."

In dissent, MARSHALL, J. (joined by Brennan and Stevens, JJ.) argued that the Court had erred in "defin[ing] respondent's Sixth Amendment right * * * as guaranteeing nothing more than an opportunity to cross-examine those witnesses *at some point* during his trial." The physical presence of the defendant at a competency hearing can "enhance the reliability of the fact finding process" even as to the "witness' ability to observe and recollect facts with accuracy and with determined truthfulness." Having the defendant present helps to ensure that any "inaccuracies are called to the judge's attention immediately—*before* the witness takes the stand with the trial court's imprimatur of competency and testifies in front of the jury as to the defendant's commission of the alleged offense. It is both functionally inefficient and fundamentally unfair to attribute to the defendant's attorney complete knowledge of the facts which the trial judge, in the defendant's involuntary absence, deems relevant to the competency determination."

The dissent also contended that the Court's ruling ignored the "symbolic goals" of the Confrontation Clause. In particular, the "appearance of fairness" was "woefully lacking" under the facts of this case: "The Commonwealth did not request that respondent be excluded from the competency hearing. The trial judge raised this issue *sua sponte,* and only the personal protestations of respondent, a recent Cuban immigrant whose fluency in the English language was limited, preserved the issue for appeal. Neither the prosecuting attorney nor the trial judge articulated *any* reason for excluding him. From this defendant's perspective, the specter of the judge, prosecutor and court-appointed attorney conferring privately with the key prosecution witnesses was understandably upsetting."

4. In light of *Stincer,* should the defendant have a constitutional right to be present at: (1) an in camera inquiry into whether a juror had developed a prejudice against the defendant as a result of observing the defendant sketching portraits of the jurors (the juror had expressed concern, but the judge explained that the sketching was innocuous, as the defendant was an artist, and concluded that the juror accepted this explanation and remained impartial), see *United States v. Gagnon,* 470 U.S. 522, 105 S.Ct. 1482, 84 L.Ed.2d 486 (1985) (no violation as due process does not require that all parties be present—defense counsel was present and had not requested that his client be present—"when the judge inquires into such a minor occurrence"); (2) an in-camera discussion with a juror who came to the judge's chambers to inform him of her acquaintance with a person mentioned in the trial, see *Rushen v. Spain,* 464 U.S. 114, 104 S.Ct. 453, 78 L.Ed.2d 267 (1983) (Court assumed right of presence where discussion concerned possible grounds for challenging juror's impartiality, but held that the defendant's absence was harmless as juror's acquaintance had no relationship to the case, being the victim of another crime mentioned in passing in the course of impeaching a defense witness): (3) an in-camera inquiry by the court as to whether to allow withdrawal of counsel based upon counsel's belief that his client intended to commit perjury, see *State v. Berrysmith,* 944 P.2d 397 (1997) (no right); (4) the giving of jury instructions, see *United States v. Fontanez,* 878 F.2d 33 (2d Cir.1989) (yes, as it is part of the trial).

5. *Conditions of presence.* The Court has noted that the circumstances of defendant's presence may be so prejudicial as to violate due process. See *Estelle v. Williams,* 425 U.S. 501, 96 S.Ct. 1691, 48 L.Ed.2d 126 (1976) (wearing prison garb where defendant objects). In HOLBROOK v. FLYNN, 475 U.S. 560, 106 S.Ct. 1340, 89 L.Ed.2d 525 (1986), the Court, (per MARSHALL, J) concluded that due process was not violated there by the presence of a substantial number of uniformed officer deployed for security purposes. Initially, it noted that the "conspicuous, deployment of security personnel in a courtroom during trial "is not" the sort of inherently prejudicial practice that, like shackling, [that] should be permitted only where justified by an essential state interest specific to each trial. * * * The chief feature that distinguishes the use of identifiable security officers from courtroom practices we might find inherently prejudicial is the wider range of inferences that a juror might reasonably draw from the officers' presence. While shackling and prison clothes are unmistakable indications of the need to separate a defendant from the community at large, the presence of guards at a defendant's trial need not be interpreted as a sign that he is particularly dangerous or culpable. Jurors may just as easily believe that the officers are there to guard against disruptions emanating from outside the courtroom or to ensure that tense courtroom exchanges do not erupt into violence. Indeed, it is entirely possible that jurors will not infer anything at all from the presence of the guards. If they are placed at some distance from the accused, security officers may well be perceived more as elements of an impressive drama than as reminders of the defendant's special status. Our society has become inured to the presence of armed guards in most public places; they are doubtless taken for granted so long as their numbers or weaponry do not suggest particular official concern or alarm."

Having concluded "that a case-by-case approach is more appropriate," the Court found no violation on the facts before it: "We do not minimize the threat that a roomful of uniformed and armed policemen might pose to a defendant's chances of receiving a fair trial. But we simply cannot find an unacceptable risk of prejudice in the spectacle of four such officers quietly sitting in the first row of a courtroom's spectator section.* * * Four troopers are unlikely to have been taken as a sign of anything other than a normal official concern for the safety and order of the proceedings. Indeed, any juror who for some other reason believed defendants particularly dangerous might well have wondered why there were only four armed troopers for the six defendants * * * We note, moreover, that even were we able to discern a slight degree of prejudice attributable to the troopers' presence at respondent's trial, sufficient cause for this level of security could be found in the State's need to maintain custody over defendants who had been denied bail after an individualized determination that their presence at trial could not otherwise be ensured. Unlike a policy requiring detained defendants to wear prison garb, the deployment of troopers was intimately related to the State's legitimate interest in maintaining custody during the proceedings and thus did not offend the Equal Protection Clause by arbitrarily discriminating against those unable to post bail or to whom bail had been denied."

SECTION 2. THE DEFENDANT'S "CONSTITUTIONALLY—GUARANTEED ACCESS TO EVIDENCE"[a]

A. THE BRADY OBLIGATION

UNITED STATES v. BAGLEY
473 U.S. 667, 105 S.Ct. 3375, 87 L.Ed.2d 481 (1985).

Justice BLACKMUN announced the judgment of the Court and delivered an opinion of the Court except as to Part III.

In *Brady v. Maryland,* 373 U.S. 83, 83 S.Ct. 1194, 10 L.Ed.2d 215 (1963), this Court held that "the suppression by the prosecution of evidence favorable to an

---

a. This section considers a series of constitutional standards that combine, as the Supreme Court has described them, to create "what might loosely be called the area of constitutionally-guaranteed access to evidence." *Arizona v. Youngblood,* Note 1, p. 1410. The various elements of this right of access are discussed in Edwin Imwinkelried and Norman Garland, *Exculpatory Evidence* (2d ed. 1996); Bennett Gershman, *Trial Error and Misconduct* (1997); and CRIMPROC § 24.3.

accused upon request violates due process where the evidence is material either to guilt or punishment." The issue in the present case concerns the standard of materiality to be applied in determining whether a conviction should be reversed because the prosecutor failed to disclose requested evidence that could have been used to impeach Government witnesses.

I

In October 1977, respondent Hughes Anderson Bagley was indicted on 15 charges of violating federal narcotics and firearms statutes. On November 18, 24 days before trial, respondent filed a discovery motion. The sixth paragraph of that motion requested:

> "The names and addresses of witnesses that the government intends to call at trial. Also the prior criminal records of witnesses, and any deals, promises or inducements made to witnesses in exchange for their testimony."

The Government's two principal witnesses at the trial were James F. O'Connor and Donald E. Mitchell. O'Connor and Mitchell were state law-enforcement officers employed by the Milwaukee Railroad as private security guards. Between April and June 1977, they assisted the federal Bureau of Alcohol, Tobacco and Firearms (ATF) in conducting an undercover investigation of respondent.

The Government's response to the discovery motion did not disclose that any "deals, promises or inducements" had been made to O'Connor or Mitchell. In apparent reply to a request in the motion's ninth paragraph for "[c]opies of all Jencks Act material," the Government produced a series of affidavits that O'Connor and Mitchell had signed between April 12 and May 4, 1977, while the undercover investigation was in progress. These affidavits recounted in detail the undercover dealings that O'Connor and Mitchell were having at the time with respondent. Each affidavit concluded with the statement, "I made this statement freely and voluntarily without any threats or rewards, or promises of reward having been made to me in return for it."

Respondent waived his right to a jury trial and was tried before the court in December 1977. At the trial, O'Connor and Mitchell testified about both the firearms and the narcotics charges. On December 23, the court found respondent guilty on the narcotics charges, but not guilty on the firearms charges.

In mid–1980, respondent filed requests for information pursuant to the Freedom of Information Act and to the Privacy Act of 1974, 5 U.S.C. §§ 552 and 552a. He received in response copies of ATF form contracts that O'Connor and Mitchell had signed on May 3, 1977. Each form was entitled "Contract for Purchase of Information and Payment of Lump Sum Therefor." The printed portion of the form stated that the vendor "will provide" information to ATF and that "upon receipt of such information by the Regional Director, Bureau of Alcohol, Tobacco and Firearms, or his representative, and upon the accomplishment of the objective sought to be obtained by the use of such information to the satisfaction of said Regional Director, the United States will pay to said vendor a sum commensurate with services and information rendered." Each form contained the following typewritten description of services:

> "That he will provide information regarding T–I and other violations committed by Hughes A. Bagley, Jr.; that he will purchase evidence for ATF; that he will cut [sic] in an undercover capacity for ATF; that he will assist ATF in gathering of evidence and testify against the violator in federal court."

The figure "$300.00" was handwritten in each form on a line entitled "Sum to Be Paid to Vendor."

Because these contracts had not been disclosed to respondent in response to his pretrial discovery motion,[4] respondent moved under 28 U.S.C. § 2255 to vacate his sentence. He alleged that the Government's failure to disclose the contracts, which he could have used to impeach O'Connor and Mitchell, violated his right to due process under *Brady v. Maryland, supra.*

The motion came before the same District Judge who had presided at respondent's bench trial. An evidentiary hearing was held before a Magistrate. The Magistrate found that the printed form contracts were blank when O'Connor and Mitchell signed them and were not signed by an ATF representative until after the trial. He also found that on January 4, 1978, following the trial and decision in respondent's case, ATF made payments of $300 to both O'Connor and Mitchell pursuant to the contracts. Although the ATF case agent who dealt with O'Connor and Mitchell testified that these payments were compensation for expenses, the Magistrate found that this characterization was not borne out by the record. * * * The District Court adopted each of the Magistrate's findings except for the last one to the effect that "[n]either O'Connor nor Mitchell expected to receive the payment of $300 or any payment from the United States for their testimony." Instead, the court found that it was "probable" that O'Connor and Mitchell expected to receive compensation, in addition to their expenses, for their assistance, "though perhaps not for their testimony." The District Court also expressly rejected the Magistrate's conclusion that "the United States did not withhold, during pretrial discovery, information as to any 'deals, promises or inducements' to these witnesses." The District Court found beyond a reasonable doubt, however, that had the existence of the agreements been disclosed to it during trial, the disclosure would have had no effect upon its finding that the Government had proved beyond a reasonable doubt that respondent was guilty of the offenses for which he had been convicted. The District Court reasoned: Almost all of the testimony of both witnesses was devoted to the firearms charges in the indictment. Respondent, however, was acquitted on those charges. The testimony of O'Connor and Mitchell concerning the narcotics charges was relatively very brief. On cross-examination, respondent's counsel did not seek to discredit their testimony as to the facts of distribution but rather sought to show that the controlled substances in question came from supplies that had been prescribed for respondent's personal use. The answers of O'Connor and Mitchell to this line of cross-examination tended to be favorable to respondent. Thus, the claimed impeachment evidence would not have been helpful to respondent and would not have affected the outcome of the trial. Accordingly, the District Court denied respondent's motion to vacate his sentence.

The United States Court of Appeals for the Ninth Circuit reversed. * * * [It] apparently based its reversal, on the theory that the Government's failure to disclose the requested *Brady* information that respondent could have used to conduct an effective cross-examination impaired respondent's right to confront adverse witnesses. The court noted: "In *Davis v. Alaska,* ... the Supreme Court held that the denial of the 'right of *effective* cross-examination' was "constitutional error of the first magnitude" 'requiring automatic reversal." 719 F.2d, at 1464, quoting *Davis v. Alaska,* 415 U.S. 308, 94 S.Ct. 1105, 39 L.Ed.2d 347 (1974). In the last sentence of its opinion, the Court of Appeals concluded: "we hold that the government's failure to provide requested *Brady* information to Bagley so that he could effectively cross-examine two important government witnesses requires an automatic reversal." * * *

4. The Assistant United States Attorney who prosecuted respondent stated in stipulated testimony that he had not known that the contracts existed and that he would have furnished them to respondent had he known of them.

II

The holding in *Brady v. Maryland* requires disclosure only of evidence that is both favorable to the accused and "material either to guilt or punishment." The Court explained in *United States v. Agurs*, 427 U.S. 97, 96 S.Ct. 2392, 49 L.Ed.2d 342 (1976): "A fair analysis of the holding in *Brady* indicates that implicit in the requirement of materiality is a concern that the suppressed evidence might have affected the outcome of the trial." The evidence suppressed in *Brady* would have been admissible only on the issue of punishment and not on the issue of guilt, and therefore could have affected only Brady's sentence and not his conviction. Accordingly, the Court affirmed the lower court's restriction of Brady's new trial to the issue of punishment.[b]

The *Brady* rule is based on the requirement of due process. Its purpose is not to displace the adversary system as the primary means by which truth is uncovered, but to ensure that a miscarriage of justice does not occur. Thus, the prosecutor is not required to deliver his entire file to defense counsel, but only to disclose evidence favorable to the accused that, if suppressed, would deprive the defendant of a fair trial. * * * As *Agurs* noted: "For unless the omission deprived the defendant of a fair trial, there was no constitutional violation requiring that the verdict be set aside; and absent a constitutional violation, there was no breach of the prosecutor's constitutional duty to disclose. ..." *United States v. Agurs*.

In *Brady* and *Agurs*, the prosecutor failed to disclose exculpatory evidence. In the present case, the prosecutor failed to disclose evidence that the defense might have used to impeach the Government's witnesses by showing bias or interest. Impeachment evidence, however, as well as exculpatory evidence, falls within the *Brady* rule. Such evidence is "evidence favorable to an accused," *Brady*, so that, if disclosed and used effectively, it may make the difference between conviction and acquittal. Cf. *Napue v. Illinois* [fn. 8 infra] ("The jury's estimate of the truthfulness and reliability of a given witness may well be determinative of guilt or innocence, and it is upon such subtle factors as the possible interest of the witness in testifying falsely that a defendant's life or liberty may depend").

The Court of Appeals treated impeachment evidence as constitutionally different from exculpatory evidence. According to that court, failure to disclose impeachment evidence is "even more egregious" than failure to disclose exculpatory evidence "because it threatens the defendant's right to confront adverse witnesses." Relying on *Davis v. Alaska*, supra, the Court of Appeals held that the Government's failure to disclose requested impeachment evidence that the defense could use to conduct an effective cross-examination of important prosecution

---

b. The defendant Brady and a companion, Boblit, had been found guilty of felony murder and sentenced to death. Prior to Brady's separate trial, his counsel had asked the prosecutor to allow him to examine all of the statements that Boblit had given to the police. Counsel was shown several of Boblit's statements, but for some unexplained reason failed to receive one statement in which Boblit admitted that he had done the actual killing. At trial, defendant admitted his participation in the crime, but claimed that he had not himself killed the victim. Defense counsel stressed this claim in his closing argument, asking the jury to show leniency and not impose the death penalty. Following defendant's conviction, defense counsel learned of the undisclosed statement and sought a new trial based on this newly discovered evidence. The Supreme Court af-

firmed a state court ruling granting a new trial as to the issue of punishment alone. Whether or not defendant himself killed the victim had no bearing on his liability for the homicide, and Boblit's statement therefore would not have been admissible in evidence on that issue. On the other hand, the statement could have been used to support defendant's plea for leniency as to punishment, and the prosecution's failure to disclose the statement had deprived Brady of a fair hearing on that issue. In refusing a new trial on the issue of guilt, the Court noted that it would not adopt a "sporting theory of justice" which assumed that the jury would have disregarded a trial judge's directive that Boblit's statement could be considered in assessing punishment but not in determining guilt.

witnesses constitutes " 'constitutional error of the first magnitude' " requiring automatic reversal.

This Court has rejected any such distinction between impeachment evidence and exculpatory evidence. In *Giglio v. United States*, 405 U.S. 150, 92 S.Ct. 763, 31 L.Ed.2d 104 (1972), the Government failed to disclose impeachment evidence similar to the evidence at issue in the present case, that is, a promise made to the key government witness that he would not be prosecuted if he testified for the Government.[c] This Court said:

> "When the 'reliability of a given witness may well be determinative of guilt or innocence,' nondisclosure of evidence affecting credibility falls within the general rule [of *Brady*]. We do not, however, automatically require a new trial whenever 'a combing of the prosecutors' files after the trial has disclosed evidence possibly useful to the defense but not likely to have changed the verdict....' A finding of materiality of the evidence is required under *Brady*.... A new trial is required if 'the false testimony could ... in any reasonable likelihood have affected the judgment of the jury....' "

Thus, the Court of Appeals' holding is inconsistent with our precedents.

Moreover, the court's reliance on *Davis v. Alaska* for its "automatic reversal" rule is misplaced. In *Davis*, the defense sought to cross-examine a crucial prosecution witness concerning his probationary status as a juvenile delinquent. * * * Pursuant to a state rule of procedure and a state statute making juvenile adjudications inadmissible, the trial judge prohibited the defense from conducting the cross-examination. This Court reversed the defendant's conviction, ruling that the direct restriction on the scope of cross-examination denied the defendant "the right of effective cross-examination which would be constitutional error of the first magnitude and no amount of showing of want of prejudice would cure it." "The present case, in contrast, does not involve any direct restriction on the scope of cross-examination. The defense was free to cross-examine the witnesses on any relevant subject, including possible bias or interest resulting from inducements made by the Government.[d] The constitutional error, if any, in this case was the Government's failure to assist the defense by disclosing information that might have been helpful in conducting the cross-examination. As discussed above, such suppression of evidence amounts to a constitutional violation only if it deprives the defendant of a fair trial. Consistent with "our overriding concern with the justice of the finding of guilt," *United States v. Agurs,* a constitutional error occurs, and the conviction must be reversed, only if the evidence is material in the sense that its suppression undermines confidence in the outcome of the trial.

III

It remains to determine the standard of materiality applicable to the nondisclosed evidence at issue in this case. Our starting point is the framework for

c. In *Giglio*, the defense counsel "vigorously cross-examined [a key witness] seeking to discredit his testimony by revealing possible agreements or arrangements for prosecutorial leniency." The witness denied the existence of such agreements, and in his summation, the government attorney stated that the witness "received no promises that he would not be indicted." In fact, a promise had been made by another government attorney, but the trial attorney had been unaware of that discussion. The Court held that reversal was required "under the due process requirements enunciated in *Napue* [described infra at fn. 8]." Although the government's trial counsel was not aware that the witness' testimony was false, that was no excuse as the nondisclosure was still the responsibility of the government. "The prosecutor's office is an entity" said the Court, and a promise made by one of its attorneys, even if unauthorized, "must be attributed, for these purposes, to the Government."

d. Consider also the plurality's discussion of the inapplicability of the Sixth Amendment to a defendant's attempt to subpoena possibly exculpatory material possessed by a state agency in *Pennsylvania v. Ritchie,* set forth at Note 2, p. 1403.

evaluating the materiality of *Brady* evidence established in *United States v. Agurs.* The Court in *Agurs* distinguished three situations involving the discovery, after trial, of information favorable to the accused that had been known to the prosecution but unknown to the defense. The first situation was the prosecutor's knowing use of perjured testimony or, equivalently, the prosecutor's knowing failure to disclose that testimony used to convict the defendant was false. The Court noted the well-established rule that "a conviction obtained by the knowing use of perjured testimony is fundamentally unfair, and must be set aside if there is any reasonable likelihood that the false testimony could have affected the judgment of the jury."[8] Although this rule is stated in terms that treat the knowing use of perjured testimony as error subject to harmless-error review,[9] it may as easily be stated as a materiality standard under which the fact that testimony is perjured is considered material unless failure to disclose it would be harmless beyond a reasonable doubt. The Court in *Agurs* justified this standard of materiality on the ground that the knowing use of perjured testimony involves prosecutorial misconduct and, more importantly, involves "a corruption of the truth-seeking function of the trial process."

At the other extreme is the situation in *Agurs* itself, where the defendant does not make a *Brady* request and the prosecutor fails to disclose certain evidence favorable to the accused. The Court rejected a harmless-error rule in that

---

8. In fact, the *Brady* rule has its roots in a series of cases dealing with convictions based on the prosecution's knowing use of perjured testimony. In *Mooney v. Holohan,* 294 U.S. 103, 55 S.Ct. 340, 79 L.Ed. 791 (1935), the Court established the rule that the knowing use by a state prosecutor of perjured testimony to obtain a conviction and the deliberate suppression of evidence that would have impeached and refuted the testimony constitutes a denial of due process. The Court reasoned that "a deliberate deception of court and jury by the presentation of testimony known to be perjured" is inconsistent with "the rudimentary demands of justice." The Court reaffirmed this principle in broader terms in *Pyle v. Kansas,* 317 U.S. 213, 63 S.Ct. 177, 87 L.Ed. 214 (1942), where it held that allegations that the prosecutor had deliberately suppressed evidence favorable to the accused and had knowingly used perjured testimony were sufficient to charge a due process violation. The Court again reaffirmed this principle in *Napue v. Illinois,* 360 U.S. 264, 79 S.Ct. 1173, 3 L.Ed.2d 1217 (1959). In *Napue,* the principal witness for the prosecution falsely testified that he had been promised no consideration for his testimony. The Court held that the knowing use of false testimony to obtain a conviction violates due process regardless of whether the prosecutor solicited the false testimony or merely allowed it to go uncorrected when it appeared. The Court explained that the principle that a State may not knowingly use false testimony to obtain a conviction—even false testimony that goes only to the credibility of the witness—is "implicit in any concept of ordered liberty." Finally, the Court held that it was not bound by the state court's determination that the false testimony "could not in any reasonable likelihood have affected the judgment of the jury." The Court conducted its own independent examination of the record and concluded that the false testimony "may have had an effect on the outcome of the trial." Accordingly, the Court reversed the judgment of conviction. [See also *Alcorta v. Texas,* 355 U.S. 28, 78 S.Ct. 103, 2 L.Ed.2d 9 (1957) (*Mooney* principle violated where: (1) defendant claimed he killed his wife in a heat of passion after discovering her kissing Castelleja in a parked car; (2) prosecutor had told Castelleja not to volunteer the fact that he had an ongoing sexual relationship with the wife, but to answer truthfully if asked; (3) Castelleja indicated in his trial testimony, in response to the prosecutor's questioning, that he had not kissed the deceased on the night of the killing and had nothing more than a casual relationship with her).]

9. The rule that a conviction obtained by the knowing use of perjured testimony must be set aside if there is any reasonable likelihood that the false testimony could have affected the jury's verdict derives from *Napue v. Illinois.* See n. 8. *Napue* antedated *Chapman v. California* [p. 1570], where the "harmless beyond a reasonable doubt" standard was established. The Court in *Chapman* noted that there was little, if any, difference between a rule formulated, as in *Napue,* in terms of " 'whether there is a reasonable possibility that the evidence complained of might have contributed to the conviction,' " and a rule " 'requiring the beneficiary of a constitutional error to prove beyond a reasonable doubt that the error complained of did not contribute to the verdict obtained.' " It is therefore clear, as indeed petitioner concedes, that this Court's precedents indicate that the standard of review applicable to the knowing use of perjured testimony is equivalent to the *Chapman* harmless-error standard.

situation, because under that rule every nondisclosure is treated as error, thus imposing on the prosecutor a constitutional duty to deliver his entire file to defense counsel. At the same time, the Court rejected a standard that would require the defendant to demonstrate that the evidence if disclosed probably would have resulted in acquittal.[e] The Court reasoned: "If the standard applied to the usual motion for a new trial based on newly discovered evidence were the same when the evidence was in the State's possession as when it was found in a neutral source, there would be no special significance to the prosecutor's obligation to serve the cause of justice." The standard of materiality applicable in the absence of a specific *Brady* request is therefore stricter than the harmless-error standard but more lenient to the defense than the newly discovered evidence standard.

The third situation identified by the Court in *Agurs* is where the defense makes a specific request and the prosecutor fails to disclose responsive evidence. The Court did not define the standard of materiality applicable in this situation, but suggested that the standard might be more lenient to the defense than in the situation in which the defense makes no request or only a general request. The Court also noted: "When the prosecutor receives a specific and relevant request, the failure to make any response is seldom, if ever, excusable."

The Court has relied on and reformulated the *Agurs* standard for the materiality of undisclosed evidence in two subsequent cases arising outside the *Brady* context. In neither case did the Court's discussion of the *Agurs* standard distinguish among the three situations described in *Agurs*. In *United States v. Valenzuela–Bernal* [p. 1406], the Court held that due process is violated when testimony is made unavailable to the defense by Government deportation of witnesses "only if there is a reasonable likelihood that the testimony could have affected the judgment of the trier of fact." And in *Strickland v. Washington* [pp. 1124–25], the Court held that a new trial must be granted when evidence is not introduced because of the incompetence of counsel only if "there is a reasonable probability that, but for counsel's unprofessional errors, the result of the proceeding would have been different." The *Strickland* Court defined a "reasonable probability" as "a probability sufficient to undermine confidence in the outcome."

We find the *Strickland* formulation of the *Agurs* test for materiality sufficiently flexible to cover the "no request," "general request," and "specific request" cases of prosecutorial failure to disclose evidence favorable to the accused: The evidence is material only if there is a reasonable probability that, had the evidence been disclosed to the defense, the result of the proceeding would have been different. A "reasonable probability" is a probability sufficient to undermine confidence in the outcome.

The Government suggests that a materiality standard more favorable to the defendant reasonably might be adopted in specific request cases. The Government notes that an incomplete response to a specific request not only deprives the defense of certain evidence, but has the effect of representing to the defense that the evidence does not exist. In reliance on this misleading representation, the

---

e. The reference here was to what *Agurs* described as the "Rule 33 Standard"—the test applied in federal courts to a motion for a new trial based on newly discovered evidence. That standard typically requires that the defendant establish (1) that the failure to learn of the evidence previously was due to no lack of diligence, (2) that the evidence is material, not merely "cumulative or impeaching," and (3) that the evidence "will probably produce an acquittal." See CRIMPROC § 24.11(d). A somewhat different standard is sometimes applied where the after-discovered evidence reveals witness perjury at trial. Ibid. Compare *Larrison v. United States*, 24 F.2d 82 (7th Cir.1928) (question is whether without the perjured testimony "the jury might have reached a different conclusion"); with *United States v. Stofsky*, 527 F.2d 237 (2d Cir.1975) (usual Rule 33 standard applied).

defense might abandon lines of independent investigation, defenses, or trial strategies that it otherwise would have pursued.

We agree that the prosecutor's failure to respond fully to a *Brady* request may impair the adversary process in this manner. And the more specifically the defense requests certain evidence, thus putting the prosecutor on notice of its value, the more reasonable it is for the defense to assume from the nondisclosure that the evidence does not exist, and to make pretrial and trial decisions on the basis of this assumption. This possibility of impairment does not necessitate a different standard of materiality, however, for under the *Strickland* formulation the reviewing court may consider directly any adverse effect that the prosecutor's failure to respond might have had on the preparation or presentation of the defendant's case. The reviewing court should assess the possibility that such effect might have occurred in light of the totality of the circumstances and with an awareness of the difficulty of reconstructing in a post-trial proceeding the course that the defense and the trial would have taken had the defense not been misled by the prosecutor's incomplete response.

In the present case, we think that there is a significant likelihood that the prosecutor's response to respondent's discovery motion misleadingly induced defense counsel to believe that O'Connor and Mitchell could not be impeached on the basis of bias or interest arising from inducements offered by the Government. Defense counsel asked the prosecutor to disclose any inducements that had been made to witnesses, and the prosecutor failed to disclose that the possibility of a reward had been held out to O'Connor and Mitchell if the information they supplied led to "the accomplishment of the objective sought to be obtained ... to the satisfaction of [the Government]." This possibility of a reward gave O'Connor and Mitchell a direct, personal stake in respondent's conviction. The fact that the stake was not guaranteed through a promise or binding contract, but was expressly contingent on the Government's satisfaction with the end result, served only to strengthen any incentive to testify falsely in order to secure a conviction. Moreover, the prosecutor disclosed affidavits that stated that O'Connor and Mitchell received no promises of reward in return for providing information in the affidavits implicating respondent in criminal activity. In fact, O'Connor and Mitchell signed the last of these affidavits the very day after they signed the ATF contracts. While petitioner is technically correct that the blank contracts did not constitute a "promise of reward," the natural effect of these affidavits would be misleadingly to induce defense counsel to believe that O'Connor and Mitchell provided the information in the affidavits, and ultimately their testimony at trial recounting the same information, without any "inducements."

The District Court, nonetheless, found beyond a reasonable doubt that, had the information that the Government held out the possibility of reward to its witnesses been disclosed, the result of the criminal prosecution would not have been different. If this finding were sustained by the Court of Appeals, the information would be immaterial even under the standard of materiality applicable to the prosecutor's knowing use of perjured testimony. Although the express holding of the Court of Appeals was that the nondisclosure in this case required automatic reversal, the Court of Appeals also stated that it "disagreed" with the District Court's finding of harmless error. In particular, the Court of Appeals appears to have disagreed with the factual premise on which this finding expressly was based. The District Court reasoned that O'Connor's and Mitchell's testimony was exculpatory on the narcotics charges. The Court of Appeals, however, concluded, after reviewing the record, that O'Connor's and Mitchell's testimony was in fact inculpatory on those charges. Accordingly, we reverse the judgment of the Court of Appeals and remand the case to that court for a determination whether there is a reasonable probability that, had the inducement offered by the Government to O'Connor and Mitchell been disclosed to the defense, the result of the trial would have been different.

Justice POWELL took no part in the decision of this case.

Justice WHITE, with whom The Chief Justice and Justice REHNQUIST join, concurring in part and concurring in the judgment.

I agree with the Court that respondent is not entitled to have his conviction overturned unless he can show that the evidence withheld by the Government was "material," and I therefore join Parts I and II of the Court's opinion. I also agree with Justice Blackmun that for purposes of this inquiry, "evidence is material only if there is a reasonable probability that, had the evidence been disclosed to the defense, the result of the proceeding would have been different." As the Justice correctly observes, this standard is "sufficiently flexible" to cover all instances of prosecutorial failure to disclose evidence favorable to the accused. Given the flexibility of the standard and the inherently factbound nature of the cases to which it will be applied, however, I see no reason to attempt to elaborate on the relevance to the inquiry of the specificity of the defense's request for disclosure, either generally or with respect to this case. I would hold simply that the proper standard is one of reasonable probability and that the Court of Appeals' failure to apply this standard necessitates reversal. I therefore concur in the judgment.

Justice MARSHALL, with whom Justice BRENNAN joins, dissenting.

* * * We have long recognized that, within the limit of the State's ability to identify so-called exculpatory information, the State's concern for a fair verdict precludes it from withholding from the defense evidence favorable to the defendant's case in the prosecutor's files. [This] recognition no doubt stems in part from the frequently considerable imbalance in resources between most criminal defendants and most prosecutors' offices. Many, perhaps most, criminal defendants in the United States are represented by appointed counsel, who often are paid minimal wages and operate on shoestring budgets. In addition, unlike police, defense counsel generally is not present at the scene of the crime, or at the time of arrest, but instead comes into the case late. Moreover, unlike the Government, defense counsel is not in the position to make deals with witnesses to gain evidence. Thus, an inexperienced, unskilled, or unaggressive attorney often is unable to amass the factual support necessary to a reasonable defense. When favorable evidence is in the hands of the prosecutor but not disclosed, the result may well be that the defendant is deprived of a fair chance before the trier of fact, and the trier of fact is deprived of the ingredients necessary to a fair decision. * * *

Brady v. Maryland, of course, established this requirement of disclosure as a fundamental element of a fair trial by holding that a defendant was denied due process if he was not given access to favorable evidence that is material either to guilt or punishment. Since *Brady* was decided, this Court has struggled, in a series of decisions, to define how best to effectuate the right recognized. To my mind, the *Brady* decision, the reasoning that underlay it, and the fundamental interest in a fair trial, combine to give the criminal defendant the right to receive from the prosecutor, and the prosecutor the affirmative duty to turn over to the defendant, *all* information known to the government that might reasonably be considered favorable to the defendant's case. * * *

My view is based in significant part on the reality of criminal practice and on the consequently inadequate protection to the defendant that a different rule would offer. * * * At the trial level, the duty of the state to effectuate *Brady* devolves into the duty of the prosecutor; the dual role that the prosecutor must play poses a serious obstacle to implementing *Brady.* The prosecutor is by trade, if not necessity, a zealous advocate. He is a trained attorney who must aggressively seek convictions in court on behalf of a victimized public. At the same time, as a representative of the State, he must place foremost in his hierarchy of interests the determination of truth. Thus, for purposes of *Brady,* the prosecutor must abandon his role as an advocate and pore through his files, as objectively as possible, to identify the material that could undermine his case. Given this obviously unharmonious role, it is not surprising that these advocates oftentimes overlook or downplay potentially favorable evidence, often in cases in which there is no doubt that the failure to disclose was a result of absolute good faith. * * *

The prosecutor surely greets the moment at which he must turn over *Brady* material with little enthusiasm. In perusing his files, he must make the often difficult decision as to whether evidence is favorable, and must decide on which side to err when faced with doubt. In his role as advocate, the answers are clear. In his role as representative of the State, the answers should be equally clear, and often to the contrary. Evidence that is of doubtful worth in the eyes of the prosecutor could be of inestimable value to the defense, and might make the difference to the trier of fact.

Once the prosecutor suspects that certain information might have favorable implications for the defense, either because it is potentially exculpatory or relevant to credibility, I see no reason why he should not be required to disclose it. After all, favorable evidence indisputably enhances the truth-seeking process at trial. And it is the job of the defense, not the prosecution, to decide whether and in what way to use arguably favorable evidence. In addition, to require disclosure of all evidence that might reasonably be considered favorable to the defendant would have the precautionary effect of assuring that no information of potential consequence is mistakenly overlooked. * * * A clear rule of this kind, coupled with a presumption in favor of disclosure, also would facilitate the prosecutor's admittedly difficult task by removing a substantial amount of unguided discretion. * * *

The Court, however, offers a complex alternative. It defines the right not by reference to the possible usefulness of the particular evidence in preparing and presenting the case, but retrospectively, by reference to the likely effect the evidence will have on the outcome of the trial. Thus, the Court holds that due process does not require the prosecutor to turn over evidence unless the evidence is "material," and the Court states that evidence is "material" "only if there is a reasonable probability that, had the evidence been disclosed to the defense, the result of the proceeding would have been different." Although this looks like a post-trial standard of review, see, e.g., *Strickland v. Washington,* it is not. Instead, the Court relies on this review standard to define the contours of the defendant's constitutional right to certain material prior to trial. By adhering to the view articulated in *United States v. Agurs*—that there is no constitutional duty to disclose evidence unless nondisclosure would have a certain impact on the trial— the Court permits prosecutors to withhold with impunity large amounts of undeniably favorable evidence, and it imposes on prosecutors the burden to identify and disclose evidence pursuant to a pretrial standard that virtually defies definition. * * * At best, this standard places on the prosecutor a responsibility to speculate, at times without foundation, since the prosecutor will not normally know what strategy the defense will pursue or what evidence the defense will find useful. At worst, the standard invites a prosecutor, whose interests are conflicting, to gamble, to play the odds, and to take a chance that evidence will later turn out not to have been potentially dispositive. * * *

* * * The State's interest in nondisclosure at trial is minimal, and should therefore yield to the readily apparent benefit that full disclosure would convey to the search for truth. After trial, however, the benefits of disclosure may at times be tempered by the State's legitimate desire to avoid retrial when error has been

harmless. However, in making the determination of harmlessness, I would apply our normal constitutional error test and reverse unless it is clear beyond a reasonable doubt that the withheld evidence would not have affected the outcome of the trial. See *Chapman v. California.*[6]

Any rule other than automatic reversal, of course, dilutes the *Brady* right to some extent and offers the prosecutor an incentive not to turn over all information. In practical effect, it might be argued, there is little difference between the rule I propose—that a prosecutor must disclose all favorable evidence in his files, subject to harmless error review—and the rule the Court adopts—that the prosecutor must disclose only the favorable information that might affect the outcome of the trial. According to this argument, if a constitutional right to all favorable evidence leads to reversal only when the withheld evidence might have affected the outcome of the trial, the result will be the same as with a constitutional right only to evidence that will affect the trial outcome. * * * For several reasons, however, I disagree. First, I have faith that a prosecutor would treat a rule requiring disclosure of all information of a certain kind differently from a rule requiring disclosure only of some of that information. Second, persistent or egregious failure to comply with the constitutional duty could lead to disciplinary actions by the courts. Third, the standard of harmlessness I adopt is more protective of the defendant than that chosen by the Court, placing the burden on the prosecutor, rather than the defendant, to prove the harmlessness of his actions. It would be a foolish prosecutor who gambled too glibly with that standard of review. * * *

Justice STEVENS, dissenting.

* * * [T]wo situations in which the [same] rule applies are those demonstrating the prosecution's knowing use of perjured testimony, exemplified by *Mooney v. Holohan,* and the prosecution's suppression of favorable evidence specifically requested by the defendant, exemplified by *Brady* itself. In both situations, the prosecution's deliberate nondisclosure constitutes constitutional error—the conviction must be set aside if the suppressed or perjured evidence was "material" and there was "any reasonable likelihood" that it "could have affected" the outcome of the trial. *United States v. Agurs.* * * * The combination of willful prosecutorial suppression of evidence and, "more importantly," the potential "corruption of the truth seeking function of the trial process" requires that result. *Agurs.* * * *

[S]uppression [in response to a request] is far more serious than mere nondisclosure of evidence in which the defense has expressed no particular interest. A reviewing court should attach great significance to silence in the face of a specific request, when responsive evidence is later shown to have been in the Government's possession. Such silence actively misleads in the same way as would an affirmative representation that exculpatory evidence does not exist when, in fact, it does (*i.e.,* perjury)—indeed, the two situations are aptly described as "sides of a single coin." Babcock, *Fair Play: Evidence Favorable to An Accused and Effective Assistance of Counsel,* 34 Stan.L.Rev. 1133 (1982).

Accordingly, although I agree that the judgment of the Court of Appeals should be vacated and that the case should be remanded for further proceedings, I disagree with the Court's statement of the correct standard to be applied.

---

6. In a case of deliberate prosecutorial misconduct, automatic reversal might well be proper. Certain kinds of constitutional error so infect the system of justice as to require reversal in all cases, such as discrimination in jury selection. A deliberate effort of the prosecutor to undermine the search for truth clearly is in the category of offenses anathema to our most basic vision of the role of the State in the criminal process.

Notes and Questions

1. **Timing of disclosure.** As to the requisite timing of the disclosure required by *Brady/Bagley*, see Notes 1–3, pp. 1198–99. As to the bearing of the constitutional duty to disclose material exculpatory evidence on plea negotiations, see Notes 5–6, pp. 1282–84; CRIMPROC § 24.3(c) ("Whether a defendant is entitled to disclosure of exculpatory evidence before entering a guilty plea is an issue that has split the lower courts. Some courts reason that the constitutional right that *Brady* sought to protect was the right to fair trial, which is waived by a plea of guilty. Others reason that concealing *Brady* material can render the plea unintelligent. * * * The concealment's toll on the accuracy of the plea-based conviction is lessened, however by the presence of the defendant's admission of guilt."); John G. Douglass, *Fatal Attraction? The Uneasy Courtship of Brady and Plea Bargaining*, 50 Emory L.J. 437 (2001) (suggesting that recent "judicial efforts to mold *Brady* into a rule of pre-plea disclosure" are not likely to advance substantially the cause of "fully informed pleas," in part because *Brady* is a "prospective rule, enforced only retrospectively," and applying *Brady's* materiality standard after a plea bargain "involves more variables, more hypothetical inquiries, a more skeptical decisionmaker, and less solid information on which to base a decision" than applying it after a trial).

2. **Brady and the false testimony cases.** Is there a distinction in the rationales underlying the perjured testimony cases and the nondisclosure cases that justifies imposing a less strict standard of materiality in nondisclosure cases, whether or not involving a specific request? The *Brady* opinion described the due process ruling in that case as a logical extension of the perjured testimony cases. In describing the relationship between the two lines of cases, *Brady* noted: "We now hold that the suppression by the prosecution of evidence favorable to an accused upon request violates due process where the evidence is material either to guilt or to punishment, irrespective of the good faith or bad faith of the prosecution. The principle of *Mooney v. Holohan* [fn. 8, p. 1392] is not punishment of society for misdeeds of a prosecutor but avoidance of an unfair trial to the accused."

Not all found the above analysis satisfactory, at least as it described *Mooney*. Commentators suggested that in the perjured testimony cases, there was an element of "deliberate misconduct" in the misleading of the trier of fact by presenting untruthful testimony,[a] which distinguished those cases from *Brady* violations. See Peter Westen, *The Compulsory Process Clause*, 73 Mich.L.Rev. 71, 121–23 (1974). Has *Bagley*, in treating the knowing use of perjured testimony as subject to a harmless error standard of materiality, recognized such a distinction in the groundings of the *Brady* rule and the *Mooney* principle? Consider Steven Reiss, *Prosecutorial Intent in Constitutional Criminal Procedure*, 135 U.Pa.L.Rev. 1365, 1408 (1987) (distinction in the materiality standards implicitly reflects the "high degree of culpability" inherent in the perjured testimony situation, as a rationale resting solely on the "corruption of the truth seeking process" would not provide a "persuasive basis for treating perjured testimony differently from other types of prosecutorial suppression"). If so, where a request is truly specific, does the failure of the prosecution to make disclosure suggest a level of culpability

a. Consider, however, the broad reading of the perjured testimony cases offered in such lower court ruling as *United States v. Harris*, 498 F.2d 1164 (3d Cir.1974): "When *it should be obvious* to the Government that the witness' answer, although made in good faith, is untrue, the Government's obligation to correct that statement is as compelling as it is in a situation where the Government knows that the witness is intentionally committing perjury." (emphasis added).

significantly different from that presented in a perjured testimony case? Compare, for example, the situations presented in *Giglio*, fn. c, and *Bagley*. Consider also Stephen A. Saltzburg, *Perjury and False Testimony: Should the Difference Matter So Much?*, 68 Fordham L.Rev. 1537 (2000) (earlier perjury cases, such as *Alcorta* and *Napue* (described in fn. 8, p. 1392), focused on prosecutors creating false impressions of the truth, and that was equally present in *Bagley*, where the two key witnesses were presented as disinterested; Justice Blackmun "effectively narrowed *Alcorta* and *Napue*" in failing to "offer any explanation for choosing to treat *Bagley* as a *Brady* case rather than a false testimony case").

3.　*The Bagley "materiality" standard.* In *Kyles v. Whitley*, 514 U.S. 419, 115 S.Ct. 1555, 131 L.Ed.2d 490 (1995), the Court again considered the content of the "reasonable probability" standard that defines materiality in the *Brady* context. While the *Kyles'* application of that standard rested on a fact-intensive analysis likely to have limited precedential value, the Court did set forth some principles that bear upon the general content of the reasonable probability standard. The Court noted that "four aspects of materiality under *Bagley* bear emphasis." First, "a showing of materiality does not require demonstration by a preponderance that disclosure of the suppressed evidence would have resulted ultimately in the defendant's acquittal * * *. *Bagley*'s touchstone of materiality is a 'reasonable probability' of a different result, and the adjective is important. The question is not whether the defendant would more likely than not have received a different verdict with the evidence, but whether in its absence he received a fair trial, understood as a trial resulting in a verdict worthy of confidence." Second, "the *Bagley* materiality [test] * * * is not a sufficiency of evidence test. A defendant need not demonstration that after discounting the inculpatory evidence in light of the undisclosed evidence, there would not have been enough to convict." Third, "once a reviewing court applying *Bagley* has found constitutional error there is no need for further harmless-error review." [See Note 4, p. 1573] Fourth, "*Bagley* materiality" is to be judged by reference to the "suppressed evidence considered collectively not item-by-item," with the focus on the "cumulative effect of suppression."

4. In STRICKLER v. GREENE, 527 U.S. 263, 119 S.Ct. 1936, 144 L.Ed.2d 286 (1999), the Court majority held that undisclosed impeaching eyewitness testimony as to circumstances of the abduction of the victim were favorable to the petitioner for the purposes of *Brady* (in contrast to the terrifying incident that the witness described in her trial testimony, her undisclosed original perception of the event was of "a trivial episode of college kids carrying on"), but the habeas petitioner could not show materiality as defined in *Bagley*. Speaking to the lack of materiality, SOUTER, J. (joined by Kennedy, J.), dissenting in part, offered the following general comments on the materiality standard:

"Before I get to the analysis of prejudice I should say something about the standard for identifying it, and about the unfortunate phrasing of the shorthand version in which the standard is customarily couched. The Court speaks in terms of the familiar, and perhaps familiarly deceptive, formulation: whether there is a 'reasonable probability' of a different outcome if the evidence withheld had been disclosed. The Court rightly cautions that the standard intended by these words does not require defendants to show that a different outcome would have been more likely than not with the suppressed evidence, let alone that without the materials withheld the evidence would have been insufficient to support the result reached. * * * Instead, the Court restates the question (as I have done elsewhere) as whether " 'the favorable evidence could reasonably be taken to put the whole case in such a different light as to undermine confidence' " in the outcome. See *Kyles v. Whitley*.

"Despite our repeated explanation of the shorthand formulation in these words, the continued use of the term 'probability' raises an unjustifiable risk of misleading courts into treating it as akin to the more demanding standard, 'more likely than not.' While any short phrases for what the cases are getting at will be 'inevitably imprecise,' I think 'significant possibility' would do better at capturing the degree to which the undisclosed evidence would place the actual result in question, sufficient to warrant overturning a conviction or sentence. To see that this is so, we need to recall *Brady*'s evolution since the appearance of the rule as originally stated, that 'suppression by the prosecution of evidence favorable to an accused upon request violates due process where the evidence is material either to guilt or to punishment, irrespective of the good faith or bad faith of the prosecution.' *Brady v. Maryland*. *Brady* itself did not explain what it meant by 'material' * * * We first essayed a partial definition in *United States v. Agurs*, where we identified three situations arguably within the ambit of *Brady* and said that in the first, involving knowing use of perjured testimony, reversal was required if there was 'any reasonable likelihood' that the false testimony had affected the verdict. * * * We have treated 'reasonable likelihood' as synonymous with 'reasonable possibility' and thus have equated materiality in the perjured-testimony cases with a showing that suppression of the evidence was not harmless beyond a reasonable doubt. *Bagley*. * * * In *Agurs*, we thought a less demanding standard appropriate when the prosecution fails to turn over materials in the absence of a specific request. Although we refrained from attaching a label to that standard, we explained it as falling between the more-likely-than-not level and yet another criterion, whether the reviewing court's ' "conviction [was] sure that the error did not influence the jury, or had but very slight effect." ' *Kotteakos v. United States* [p. 1566]. Finally, in *United States v. Bagley*, we embraced 'reasonable probability' as the appropriate standard to judge the materiality of information withheld by the prosecution whether or not the defense had asked first. *Bagley* took that phrase from *Strickland v. Washington*, where it had been used for the level of prejudice needed to make out a claim of constitutionally ineffective assistance of counsel. *Strickland* in turn cited two cases for its formulation, *Agurs* (which did not contain the expression 'reasonable probability') and *United States v. Valenzuela–Bernal* [Note 1, p. 1406] * * * (which held that sanctions against the Government for deportation of a potential defense witness were appropriate only if there was a 'reasonable likelihood' that the lost testimony 'could have affected the judgment of the trier of fact').

"The circuitous path by which the Court came to adopt 'reasonable probability' of a different result as the rule of *Brady* materiality suggests several things. First, while 'reasonable possibility' or 'reasonable likelihood,' the *Kotteakos* standard, and 'reasonable probability' express distinct levels of confidence concerning the hypothetical effects of errors on decisionmakers' reasoning, the differences among the standards are slight. Second, the gap between all three of those formulations and 'more likely than not' is greater than any differences among them. Third, because of that larger gap, it is misleading in *Brady* cases to use the term 'probability,' which is naturally read as the cognate of 'probably' and thus confused with 'more likely than not.' * * * We would be better off speaking of a 'significant possibility' of a different result to characterize the *Brady* materiality standard. Even then, given the soft edges of all these phrases, the touchstone of the enquiry must remain whether the evidentiary suppression 'undermines our confidence' that the factfinder would have reached the same result."

5. The nature of Brady material. Does *Brady* encompass information that clearly is favorable to the defense, but could not be used as evidence at trial (e.g., the hearsay report of an informant that some other person was commonly rumored to have committed the crime)? The lower courts are divided on this issue.

See CRIMPROC § 24.3(b). Some maintain that *Brady* applies only to material that would be admissible at trial. Others view admissibility as a crucial factor but would extend *Brady* to inadmissible material that could readily lead the defense to the discovery of admissible evidence. Do the several opinions in *Bagley* or the four principles announced in *Kyles* suggest a Court majority clearly favoring one or the other of these positions? Consider also *Wood v. Bartholomew*, 516 U.S. 1, 116 S.Ct. 7, 133 L.Ed.2d 1 (1995) (since polygraph tests would not have been admissible in evidence, prosecutor had no *Brady* obligation to disclose them).

6. *Specific requests.* Although the exact bearing of a specific request may not be clear, lower courts generally share the view expressed in *Lindsey v. King,* 769 F.2d 1034 (5th Cir.1985): "Viewing the [*Bagley*] opinions as a whole, it is fair to say that all the participating Justices agreed on one thing at least: that reversal for suppression of evidence by the government is most likely where the request for it was specific." Also, some state courts, in applying state law, have adopted the distinction suggested by Justice Stevens. See e.g., *State v. Laurie,* 653 A.2d 549 (N.H.1995). The Supreme Court has provided only limited direction, however, on distinguishing between "general" and "specific" requests. *Agurs* characterized a general request as "really giving] the prosecutor no better notice than no request," and offered only one illustration of such a request (where defendant asks for "all *Brady* material").

Accepting Justice Blackmun's view that a specific request makes a difference only in increasing the potential for prejudice by leading counsel to forego a particular line of inquiry, does the reasonableness of counsel's detrimental reliance provide a touchstone for determining whether the request was sufficiently specific? Consider CRIMPROC § 24.3(b): "Where the request is narrow and precise, giving the prosecutor considerable direction as to what is wanted, such as a request for statements of a particular person, or a request for reports by particular experts, defense counsel is more likely to treat the prosecutor's failure to disclose as an indication that the evidence does not exist. Where the request does not have those qualities, such as a request for any material bearing on the credibility of witnesses or for any material that corroborates the defense, the defense counsel must also account for the possibility that the disclosure made was not complete because the prosecution adopted a somewhat different interpretation of what was included in the request or could not readily put together all that was encompassed by the request."

Does a sufficiently specific request from this perspective require not only a description that narrows the request to specific items of evidence, but also a description of favorable content that leaves no room for the prosecutor to conclude that the evidence is not sufficiently favorable to the defense to constitute *Brady* material? That standard was met in *Bagley*, where the character of the item requested—"deals, promises, or inducements made to witnesses in exchange for their testimony"—automatically established its status as critical impeachment evidence.

7. *Defense diligence.* In *Agurs* [p. 1390], the Court described the "*Brady* rule" as applicable to situations "involv[ing] the discovery, after trial, of information which had been known to the prosecution but unknown to the defense." Looking to this language, various courts have held that the prosecutor's constitutional obligation is not violated, notwithstanding the nondisclosure of apparently exculpatory evidence, where that evidence was known to the defense and no request for disclosure was made. They have reasoned that the defense must be held responsible for its failure to request known items, leaving the prosecution to assume that the defense has no interest in the item despite its potentially exculpatory character. Before holding the defense responsible under this analysis, the lower courts have insisted on a showing that the defense "was aware of the potentially exculpatory nature of the evidence as well as its existence." CRIM-PROC § 24.3(b). Should such knowledge include situations in which the defendant had that awareness, but counsel did not? See Ibid. (courts tend to measure due diligence by reference to "what is known to either counsel or client").

8. *Evidence in the possession of other agencies.* Lower courts have regularly held that the prosecutor's *Brady* obligation extends not only to materials within its own files, but also to material within the files of the various investigative agencies participating in the case. See Ronald Carlson, *False or Suppressed Evidence: Why a Need for the Prosecutorial Tie?*, 1969 Duke L.J. 1171 (arguing for broad coverage since "governmental action is present and equally harmful whether local or remote law enforcement officers suppress material evidence"). Some courts have been willing to extend this obligation to investigative agencies that are not of the same jurisdiction, including those that were not responsible for the primary investigation in the case. *Commonwealth v. Donahue*, 487 N.E.2d 1351 (Mass.1986), after surveying the lower court cases, concluded that four factors are relevant in determining the scope of the prosecutor's obligation to obtain requested exculpatory material in the possession of a law enforcement agency of another jurisdiction: "The potential unfairness to defendant; the defendant's lack of access to the evidence; the burden on the prosecutor of obtaining the evidence; and the degree of cooperation between * * * [the different] authorities, both in general and in the particular case."

In *Kyles v. Whitley*, Note 3, p. 1399, the state contended that a "more lenient" standard of materiality should apply where the "favorable evidence in issue * * * was known only to police investigators and not the prosecutor." Rejecting that contention, the Court noted "[N]o one doubts that police investigators sometimes fail to inform a prosecutor of all they know, * * * [but] neither is there any serious doubt that 'procedures and regulations can be established to carry [the prosecutor's] burden and to insure communication of all relevant information on each to every lawyer who deals with it.'" Should lower courts reconsider, in light of *Kyles*, such earlier rulings as *Commonwealth v. Donahue*, supra?

As for material in the possession of state agencies that are not charged with law enforcement responsibilities and not part of the "prosecution team," see *Pennsylvania v. Ritchie*, Note 1, below.

B. The *Ritchie* Rulings

1. *Ritchie.* In PENNSYLVANIA v. RITCHIE, 480 U.S. 39, 107 S.Ct. 989, 94 L.Ed.2d 40 (1987), defendant Ritchie, charged with the rape and sexual abuse of a daughter, sought through a pretrial subpoena to inspect various records of the Children and Youth Services (CYS), a state protective service agency charged with investigating the suspected mistreatment or neglect of children. The subpoena was not a typical trial subpoena aimed at the production of specific evidence for admission at trial, but a discovery device (as permitted under state law). It sought to provide the defense with access to all CYS records relating to its investigation of the events that were the grounding for the current criminal charges as well as the records of an earlier investigation of possible child abuse (both investigations included counselor interviews of the daughter). CYS opposed the subpoena on the ground that state law rendered its records "privileged," and the trial judge, without examining the entire CYS file, quashed the subpoena. Following defendant's conviction, the Pennsylvania appellate courts held that: (1) the CYS records were confidential, but not privileged; (2) the failure to order disclosure of the CYS files therefore violated defendant's Sixth Amendment rights to confrontation and compulsory process insofar as they deprived the defense of materials useful in cross-examining his daughter and in presenting a defense; and (3) the trial court, in determining whether the defense had been denied such materials, could not rely on an *in camera* review of the CYS files, but was required constitutionally to give the defense full access to the files for the purpose of arguing that they contained material that should have been disclosed under the Sixth Amendment.

The Supreme Court, in an opinion by POWELL, J., rejected the reasoning and holding of the Pennsylvania appellate courts. Speaking for a plurality, Justice Powell concluded that the Sixth Amendment right of confrontation did not include a right to discover and obtain possible impeachment materials (see Note 2 infra). Speaking for a majority, Justice Powell held that (1) the denial of the subpoena might have resulted in a due process violation by denying the defendant access to *Brady* material (see Notes 3–5 infra); (2) there was no need to determine whether the Sixth Amendment compulsory process included a right to discovery, because any such right would not extend beyond the due process right to *Brady* material (see Notes 3 and 6 infra); and (3) in light of the confidential nature of the CYS records, it was constitutionally acceptable for the trial court to conduct an *in camera* review to determine whether those records included *Brady* material (see Note 7 infra).

2. *Confrontation and access.* Justice Powell's plurality opinion on the bearing of the confrontation clause rejected the lower court reading of *Davis v. Alaska*, 415 U.S. 308, 94 S.Ct. 1105, 39 L.Ed.2d 347 (1974). It noted:

"In *Davis*, the trial judge prohibited defense counsel from questioning a witness about the latter's juvenile criminal record, because a state statute made this information presumptively confidential. We found this restriction on cross-examination violated the Confrontation Clause, despite Alaska's legitimate interest in protecting the identity of juvenile offenders. The Pennsylvania Supreme Court apparently interpreted our decision in *Davis* to mean that a statutory privilege cannot be maintained when a defendant asserts a need, prior to trial, for the protected information that might be used at trial to impeach or otherwise undermine a witness' testimony. * * * If we were to accept this broad interpretation of *Davis*, the effect would be to transform the Confrontation Clause into a constitutionally-compelled rule of pretrial discovery. Nothing in the case law supports such a view. The opinions of this Court show that the right of confrontation is a *trial* right, designed to prevent improper restrictions on the types of questions that defense counsel may ask during cross-examination. * * * The ability to question adverse witnesses, however, does not include the power to require the pretrial disclosure of any and all information that might be useful in contradicting unfavorable testimony."

Justice Powell's analysis of the confrontation clause was similar to that advanced in *Bagley* (in an opinion by Justice Blackmun), where the Court also rejected a the lower court's reliance upon *Davis*. See pp. 1390–91. However, Justice Blackmun, who otherwise joined the Powell opinion in *Ritchie*, expressed disagreement with this portion of the opinion. He noted: "I do not accept the plurality's conclusion * * * that the Confrontation Clause protects only a defendant's trial rights and has no relevance to pretrial discovery. In this, I am in substantial agreement with much of what Justice Brennan says, in dissent. In my view, there might well be a confrontation violation if, as here, a defendant is denied pretrial access to information that would make possible effective cross-examination of a crucial prosecution witness."

Justices Brennan and Marshall dissented on the merits (two other justices dissented on the ground that the state court ruling did not present a final order). Expressing disagreement with the proposition that the confrontation clause applies "only to events at trial," they noted:

"That interpretation ignores the fact that the right of cross-examination also may be significantly infringed by events occurring outside the trial itself, such as the wholesale denial of access to material that would serve as the basis for a significant line of inquiry at trial. In this case, the trial court properly viewed Ritchie's vague speculations that the agency file might contain something useful as an insufficient basis for permitting general access to the file. However, in denying access to the prior statements of the victim [made to the CYS counselor] the court deprived Ritchie of material crucial to any effort to impeach the victim at trial. I view this deprivation as a violation of the Confrontation Clause. * * * *Jencks v. United States* [fn. g, p. 1184] held that the defendant was entitled to obtain the prior statements of persons to government agents when those persons testified against him at trial. * * * As I later noted in *Palermo v. United States*, 360 U.S. 343, 79 S.Ct. 1217, 3 L.Ed.2d 1287 (1959), *Jencks* was based on our supervisory authority rather than the Constitution, 'but it would be idle to say that the commands of the Constitution were not close to the surface of the decision.' * * * Essential to testing a witness' account of events is the ability to compare that version with other versions the witness has earlier recounted. Denial of access to a witness' prior statements thus imposes a handicap that strikes at the heart of cross-examination.

"The ability to obtain material information through reliance on a Due Process claim will not in all cases nullify the damage of the Court's overly restrictive reading of the Confrontation Clause. As the Court notes, evidence is regarded as material only if there is a reasonable probability that it might affect the outcome of the proceeding. Prior statements on their face may not appear to have such force, since their utility may lie in their more subtle potential for diminishing the credibility of a witness. The prospect that these statements will not be regarded as material is enhanced by the fact that due process analysis requires that information be evaluated by the trial judge, not defense counsel. By contrast, *Jencks*, informed by confrontation and cross-examination concerns, insisted that defense counsel, not the court, perform such an evaluation, '[b]ecause only the defense is adequately equipped to determine the effective use for the purpose of discrediting the Government's witness and thereby furthering the accused's defense.' Therefore, while Confrontation Clause and due process analysis may in some cases be congruent, the Confrontation Clause has independent significance in protecting against infringements on the right to cross-examination."

3. *Due process and compulsory process.* Speaking to the Pennsylvania Supreme Court's conclusion that the suppression of the subpoena violated the Sixth Amendment right of compulsory process by "preventing [defendant] from learning the names of 'witnesses in his favor' as well as other evidence that might be contained in the file," Justice Powell reasoned:

"This Court has never squarely held that the Compulsory Process Clause guarantees the right to discover the *identity* of witnesses, or to require the Government to produce exculpatory evidence. * * * Instead, the Court traditionally has evaluated claims such as those raised by Ritchie under the broader protections of the Due Process Clause of the Fourteenth Amendment. See *United States v. Bagley* [p. 1387] Because the applicability of the Sixth Amendment to this type of case is unsettled, and because our Fourteenth Amendment precedents addressing the fundamental fairness of trials establish a clear framework for review, we adopt a due process analysis for purposes of this case. Although we conclude that compulsory process provides no *greater* protections in this area than those afforded by due process, we need not decide today whether and how the guarantees of the Compulsory Process Clause differ from those of the Fourteenth Amendment. It is enough to conclude that on these facts, Ritchie's claims more properly are considered by reference to due process.

"It is well-settled that the Government has the obligation to turn over evidence in its possession that is both favorable to the accused and material to guilt or punishment. * * * At this stage, of course, it is impossible to say whether any information in the CYS records may be relevant to Ritchie's claim of innocence, because neither the prosecution nor defense counsel has seen the information, and the trial judge acknowledged that he had not reviewed the full file. The Commonwealth, however, argues that no materiality inquiry is required, because a statute renders the contents of the file privileged. Requiring disclosure here, it is argued, would override the Commonwealth's compelling interest in confidentiality on the mere speculation that the file 'might' have been useful to the defense. * * * Although we recognize that the public interest in protecting this type of sensitive information is strong, we do not agree that this interest necessarily prevents disclosure in all circumstances. This is not a case where a state statute grants CYS the absolute authority to shield its files from all eyes. Cf. 42 Pa.Cons.Stat. § 5945.1(b) (unqualified statutory privilege for communications between sexual assault counselors and victims).[14] Rather, the Pennsylvania law provides that the information shall be disclosed in certain circumstances, including when CYS is directed to do so by court order."

4. Commentators have questioned the scope of *Ritchie's* ruling that due process gave the defendant a right to *Brady* material in the possession of the CYS. Did the Court simply view the CYS as part of the "prosecution team" and therefore subject to the prosecutor's duty to disclose *Brady* material? See Note 8, p. 1402. Did the Court extend *Brady* to recognize a defense right of access to *Brady* material in the possession of government agencies that are not within the scope of the prosecutor's *Brady* obligation? Did it go beyond that and recognize a due process right to obtain *Brady* material from third parties in general? Consider *State v. Percy*, 548 A.2d 408 (Vt.1988) ("The pretrial discovery right set out in *Ritchie* applies solely to information in the hands of the State"); *State v. Behnke*, 203 Wis.2d 43, 553 N.W.2d 265 (1996) (*Ritchie* extends to private records that the government does not possess or control); CRIMPROC § 24.3(f) (collecting cases applying *Ritchie* to non-governmental entities).

5. Lower courts have divided in addressing the issue left open in footnote 14 of *Ritchie*. See CRIMPROC § 24.3(f). Some have held that the defendant's access to *Brady* material does not extend to material that is privileged under state law. Others have held that an absolute privilege poses no greater barrier to *in camera* review than the "qualified privilege" presented in *Ritchie*. It is noted in this regard that *Washington v. Texas*, 388 U.S. 14, 87 S.Ct. 1920, 18 L.Ed.2d 1019 (1967), applied the compulsory process clause to hold admissible and subject to subpoena evidence that was inadmissible under state law. *Washington* held unconstitutional a local rule that made accomplices incompetent to testify for one another, although allowing them to testify for the state. See also Imwinkelried & Garland, fn. a, p. 1387 ("defense counsel have been remarkably successful in persuading courts to override evidentiary privileges" based on the accused's constitutional right to introduce favorable evidence).

6. Consider in connection with the Supreme Court's reliance upon the due process clause in *Ritchie* and in the cases that follow in this section, the often quoted comment in *Medina v. California*, 505 U.S. 437, 112 S.Ct. 2572, 120 L.Ed.2d 353 (1992), on the proper role of the due process clause in the constitutional regulation of criminal procedure. In *Medina*, in the course of holding that due process was not violated by a state requiring the defendant to establish that he lacked competency to stand trial, the Court (per Kennedy, J) noted: "In the

14. We express no opinion on whether the result in this case would have been different if the statute had protected the CYS files from disclosure to *anyone*, including law-enforcement and judicial personnel.

field of criminal law, we 'have defined the category of infractions that violate "fundamental fairness" very narrowly' based on the recognition that, 'beyond the specific guarantees enumerated in the Bill of Rights, the Due Process Clause has limited operation.' * * * The Bill of Rights speaks in explicit terms to many aspects of criminal procedure, and the expansion of those constitutional guarantees under the open-ended rubric of the Due Process Clause invites undue interference with legislative judgments and the careful balance that the Constitution strikes between liberty and order." See also Carol S. Steiker, *Solving Some Due Process Puzzles*, 45 St. Louis U. L.J. 445 (2001) (noting the "complete about face" without explanation between *Ritchie* and the Court's earlier ruling in *Gerstein v. Pugh* [p. 906]; the *Gerstein* Court asserted that the process that was "due" in criminal prosecution was that set forth in a specific constitutional provision dealing with the particular procedure, which there was the Fourth Amendment and presumably would have been the Sixth Amendment in *Ritchie*; one possible explanation for the shift was that in the intervening years, the Court had simply found it impossible to "cabin the use of free-standing due process").

7. *In camera review.* The *Ritchie* majority flatly rejected the Pennsylvania Supreme Court's ruling that enforcement of the defendant's constitutional right of access not be satisfied by the trial court's *in camera* review of the confidential CYS files, but required giving the defense full access to the files, so it could fully participate in the assessment of materiality. The Court reasoned:

"A defendant's right to discover exculpatory evidence does not include the unsupervised authority to search through the Commonwealth's files. See *United States v. Bagley*. Although the eye of an advocate may be helpful to a defendant in ferreting out information, this Court has never held—even in the absence of a [state] statute restricting disclosure—that a defendant alone may make the determination as to the materiality of the information. Settled practice is to the contrary. In the typical case where a defendant makes only a general request for exculpatory material under *Brady v. Maryland,* it is the State that decides which information must be disclosed. Unless defense counsel becomes aware that other exculpatory evidence was withheld and brings it to the court's attention, the prosecutor's decision on disclosure is final. Defense counsel has no constitutional right to conduct his own search of the State's files to argue relevance. * * * We find that Ritchie's interest (as well as that of the Commonwealth) in ensuring a fair trial can be protected fully by requiring that the CYS files be submitted only to the trial court for *in camera* review. Although this rule denies Ritchie the benefits of an "advocate's eye," we note that the trial court's discretion is not unbounded. If a defendant is aware of specific information contained in the file (e.g., the medical report), he is free to request it directly from the court, and argue in favor of its materiality. * * * An *in camera* review by the trial court will serve Ritchie's interest without destroying the Commonwealth's need to protect the confidentiality of those involved in child-abuse investigations."

C. ACCESS TO WITNESSES

1. *Interference with access.* In UNITED STATES v. VALENZUELA–BERNAL, 458 U.S. 858, 102 S.Ct. 3440, 73 L.Ed.2d 1193 (1982), the Supreme Court reversed a Ninth Circuit ruling that had relied on both due process and the Sixth Amendment compulsory process clause to hold unconstitutional a government practice of promptly deporting aliens who had been smuggled into the country. The defendant, charged with the smuggling of the aliens, had challenged the practice because it resulted in the aliens being shipped back to Mexico before defense counsel had an opportunity to interview them. The majority, per REHNQUIST, J., reasoned that the Court of Appeals had failed to give sufficient weight to the government's "manifold responsibilities" in immigration cases. Those responsibilities included not only the enforcement of the criminal law, but also the faithful execution of congressional policy favoring prompt deportations of illegal aliens and the avoidance of unnecessary financial and physical burdens involved in prolonged detentions, as well as the "human cost" to the detained witness-alien. In light of these additional responsibilities, the majority noted, the Government's decision to deport was "not to be judged by standards which might be appropriate if the Government's only responsibility were to prosecute criminal offenses." Accordingly, appropriate analogies were to be found in decisions such as *Brady v. Maryland* and *Roviaro v. United States* [Note 3 infra], all of which required a showing as to the materiality and favorable nature of lost evidence in establishing a constitutional violation. The majority concluded:

"To summarize, the responsibility of the Executive Branch faithfully to execute the immigration policy adopted by Congress justifies the prompt deportation of illegal-alien witnesses upon the Executive's good-faith determination that they possess no evidence favorable to the defendant in a criminal prosecution. The mere fact that the Government deports such witnesses is not sufficient to establish a violation of the Compulsory Process Clause of the Sixth Amendment or the Due Process Clause of the Fifth Amendment. A violation of these provisions requires some showing that the evidence lost would be both material and favorable to the defense. * * * As in other cases concerning the loss of material evidence, sanctions will be warranted for deportation of alien witnesses only if there is a reasonable likelihood that the testimony could have affected the trier of fact.[a] In making such a determination, courts should afford some leeway for the fact that the defendant necessarily proffers a description of the material evidence rather than the evidence itself. Because determinations of materiality are often best made in light of all of the evidence adduced at trial, judges may wish to defer ruling on motions until after the presentation of evidence."

2. The state may also deprive the defendant of the testimony of a subpoenaed witness by imposing pressure on that witness not to testify. Consider *Webb v. Texas*, 409 U.S. 95, 93 S.Ct. 351, 34 L.Ed.2d 330 (1972). The defendant's sole witness had an extensive criminal record and currently was serving a prison sentence. Before the witness took the stand, the trial judge, on his own initiative, warned him against committing perjury. The judge told the witness that if he told the truth, he would be "all right," but if he lied, he could "get into real trouble." The judge warned that he would "personally see" that any lies were brought to the attention of the grand jury. A conviction for perjury, the judge added "is probably going to mean several years" and "will be held against you * * * when you're up for parole." The judge also noted that the witness "didn't owe anybody anything to testify." After hearing these remarks and the judge's comment to defense counsel that the witness could "decline to testify," the witness refused to give testimony. The Supreme Court reversed the defendant's conviction on due process grounds. "In the circumstances of this case," the Court concluded, the judge's remarks violated defendant's right to a fair trial. The judge's admonition had been cast in "unnecessarily strong terms" and "effectively drove the witness off the stand."

Although *Webb* involved judicial action, the caselaw has even more often applied *Webb* to prosecutorial efforts to discourage perspective defense witnesses from testifying. The critical questions, the courts note, are whether (1) the witness was important to the defense,[b] and (2) as a result of the prosecution's action, the

---

a. As to significance of this phrasing, see Note 4, p. 1399. As noted there, later cases have described *Valenzuela-Bernal* as one of a series of cases employing a "reasonable probability" standard.

b. The *Webb* opinion did not address the issue of likely prejudice (i.e., whether the missing testimony might have influenced the outcome). Some lower courts initially viewed *Webb* as establishing a per se due process violation, but in light of the Court's subsequent ruling in *Valenzuela-Bernal*, *Webb* is viewed as a case that apparently assumed prejudicial impact in light of the witness' status as the sole defense witness.

defendant was denied the witness' testimony or the witness changed his testimony to be less favorable to the defense. Prosecutorial action held to constitute a due process violation typically involves threats to prosecute the witness for perjury, with the courts noting that a prosecutor's good faith belief that the witness was about to commit perjury does not preclude a finding of a constitutional violation. See *In re Martin*, 44 Cal.3d 1, 744 P.2d 374 (1987) (arrest of one witness for perjury caused remaining witnesses not to testify); Bruce Green, *Limits on a Prosecutor's Communications With Prospective Defense Witnesses*, 25 Crim.L.Bull. 139 (1989) ("By far the safest course for a prosecutor seeking to warn a defense witness about the risks of self-incrimination or perjury is to convey those warnings through the witness's attorney"; if the witness is unrepresented, the prosecutor might seek the appointment of counsel for this purpose).

   3. *Identifying critical informants.* The defendant in ROVIARO v. UNITED STATES, 353 U.S. 53, 77 S.Ct. 623, 1 L.Ed.2d 639 (1957), was charged with (1) an illegal sale of heroin to "John Doe," and (2) illegal transportation of heroin. Before trial, defendant moved for a bill of particulars listing, inter alia, Doe's name and address. The motion was denied on the ground that Doe was an informer and his identity was privileged. At trial, the court again rejected defense attempts, through cross-examination, to learn Doe's identity. The government itself did not call Doe, but relied entirely on the testimony of two investigative officers. The first officer (Durham) had Doe under surveillance on the night of the alleged transaction. He testified that Doe picked up the defendant on a street corner and drove to another location where the defendant left the car, picked up a package near a tree, gave the package to Doe, and walked away. The second officer (Bryson), who was hidden in the trunk of Doe's car, testified that he heard defendant discuss with Doe the proposed transfer of the package (which contained narcotics). The Supreme Court reversed the defendant's conviction in the exercise of its supervisory power. Justice BURTON's opinion for the (6–1) majority noted:

   "Petitioner * * * argues that Doe was an active participant in the illegal activity charged and that, therefore, the Government could not withhold his identity, his whereabouts, and whether he was alive or dead at the time of trial. The Government does not defend the nondisclosure of Doe's identity with respect to Count 1, which charged a sale of heroin to John Doe, but it attempts to sustain the judgment on the basis of the conviction on Count 2, charging illegal transportation of narcotics. It argues that the conviction on Count 2 may properly be upheld since the identity of the informer, in the circumstances of this case, has no real bearing on that charge and is therefore privileged.

   "What is usually referred to as the informer's privilege is in reality the Government's privilege to withhold from disclosure the identity of persons who furnish information of violations of law to officers charged with enforcement of that law. The purpose of the privilege is the furtherance and protection of the public interest in effective law enforcement. The privilege recognizes the obligation of citizens to communicate their knowledge of the commission of crimes to law-enforcement officials and, by preserving their anonymity, encourages them to perform that obligation. * * * [But] [w]here the disclosure of an informer's identity, or of the contents of his communication, is relevant and helpful to the defense of an accused, or is essential to a fair determination of a cause, the privilege must give way. In these situations, the trial court may require disclosure and, if the Government withholds the information, dismiss the action. * * * The problem is one that calls for balancing the public interest in protecting the flow of information against the individual's right to prepare his defense. Whether a proper balance renders nondisclosure erroneous must depend on the particular circumstances of each case, taking into consideration the crime charged, the possible defenses, the possible significance of the informer's testimony, and other relevant factors. * * *

"This is a case where the Government's informer was the sole participant, other than the accused, in the transaction charged. The informer was the only witness in a position to amplify or contradict the testimony of government witnesses. Moreover, a government witness testified that Doe denied knowing petitioner or ever having seen him before. We conclude that, under these circumstances, the trial court committed prejudicial error in permitting the Government to withhold the identity of its undercover employee in the face of repeated demands by the accused for his disclosure."

Although *Roviaro* was based on the Court's supervisory jurisdiction over federal courts, both lower courts and commentators have viewed the Court's "reasoning and language" as "suggest[ing] that the decision was constitutionally compelled." Peter Westen, *The Compulsory Process Clause*, 73 Mich. L. Rev. 71, 165 (1974).

4. *Access to identification evidence.* In several jurisdictions, local discovery provisions grant the defense the right to conduct its own scientific tests of physical evidence obtained by the prosecution. Might the prosecution also have a constitutional obligation to permit such tests? Several courts have held that it does where the defendant can establish a reasonable basis for believing that the test results may be both "favorable" and "material." See Jean Montoya, *A Theory of Compulsory Process Clause Discovery Rules*, 70 Ind. L.J. 845 (1995). Consider also *Warren v. State*, 288 So.2d 826 (Ala.1973) (where the charge is possession of an alleged narcotic substance, content of the substance is so critical that the defendant must be allowed independent testing). Compare *People v. Bell*, 253 N.W.2d 726 (Mich.App.1977) (independent scientific examination of alleged narcotic substance is not required by due process where the defendant is afforded "full opportunity of cross-examination" of the prosecution's expert).

Although lower courts frequently have noted that a defendant has "no constitutional right to a lineup," *Evans v. Superior Court*, 522 P.2d 681 (Cal. 1974), held that due process requires the prosecution to honor a defense request for a lineup where "eyewitness identification is shown to be in material issue and there exists a reasonable likelihood of a mistaken identification which a lineup would tend to resolve." *Evans* reasoned: "Because the People are in a position to compel a lineup and utilize what favorable evidence is derived therefrom, fairness requires that the accused be given a reciprocal right to discover and utilize contrary evidence. *Wardius v. Oregon* [p. 1206]."

5. *Immunity for defense witnesses.* Lower courts have consistently rejected claims of a general constitutional right of a criminal defendant to have immunity granted to witnesses so that they can testify on the defendant's behalf. See CRIMPROC § 24.3(i). No such right has been found in the Sixth Amendment's compulsory process clause, for the subpoena is made fully available by the trial court and the compulsory process clause has been held not to override the exercise by witnesses of privileges as significant as the self-incrimination privilege. So too, "while the prosecutor may not prevent or discourage a defense witness from testifying, * * * it is difficult to see how the [compulsory process clause] of its own force places upon either the prosecutor or the court an affirmative obligation * * * of replacing the protection of the self-incrimination privilege with a grant of use immunity." *United States v. Turkish*, 623 F.2d 769 (2d Cir.1980). Finally, the due process obligation of *Brady* is held not to apply, for that deals

only with the disclosure of evidence in the government's possession, not with the extraction of evidence from others.

Lower courts have held, however, that fundamental fairness may require a trial court to dismiss a case if the prosecution refuses to grant immunity to a potential defense witness under particularly egregious circumstances. In applying this fundamental fairness test, the primary focus has been on whether the prosecutor is operating with a deliberate intention to distort the fact finding process. Such a prosecutorial intention is said to establish a "clear abuse of discretion violating due process," requiring that the prosecution be dismissed unless the government shifts its position and obtains immunity for the witness. *United States v. D'Antonio,* 801 F.2d 979 (7th Cir.1986). The classic case would be that in which the government had used an undercover agent to instigate the criminal transaction and then allowed that agent to plead the privilege when the defense attempts to call him as a witness. See *United States v. Bahadar,* 954 F.2d 821 (2d Cir.1992) (court must find (1) that the government "has engaged in discriminatory use to gain a tactical advantage"; (2) the witness' testimony is "material, exculpatory, and not cumulative"; and (3) the testimony is "unobtainable from any other source").

Should the fundamental fairness standard also allow the court to weigh the government's interest in a possibly lost prosecution, on the one hand, and the potential importance of the witness to the defense on the other hand? See *Government of Virgin Islands v. Smith,* 615 F.2d 964 (3d Cir.1980) (due process would require immunization where the proffered testimony of the defense witness is "clearly exculpatory" and "essential" and there are "no strong governmental interests which countervail against a grant of immunity"). It has been suggested that such an inquiry into defense and prosecution interests would be appropriate, for example, where the government builds its case on the testimony of prosecution witnesses who have been granted immunity, while refusing to grant immunity to potential defense witnesses who were no differently situated as potential sources of information (e.g., all eyewitnesses). In such a case, it is argued, fundamental fairness demands that, absent some compelling governmental interest, the defendant should have equal access to the similarly situated witness whose perceptions of the events in question favor his defense. Yet exactly such an argument has been said to disclose the difficulties inherent in any attempt at "judicial balancing." In the criminal process, it is noted, "where accuser and accused have inherently different roles, with entirely different powers and rights," equalization is not an appropriate starting point for evaluating defense and prosecution interests, and without that starting point, the court is simply imposing its own value judgments on an executive decision. See *United States v. Turkish,* 623 F.2d 769 (2d Cir.1980) (to allow judicial inquiry into either prosecutorial motive or the comparative importance of defense and prosecutorial interests would be to "propel a trial court into uncharted waters," but the court would leave open the possibility of judicial intervention where the prosecutor "cannot or prefers not to present any claim that the witness is a potential defendant" and the defense "demonstrates that the witness's testimony will clearly be material, exculpatory, and not cumulative").

D. The Duty to Preserve Evidence

1. The leading Supreme Court evidence on the government's failure to preserve potentially exculpatory evidence is ARIZONA v. YOUNGBLOOD, 488 U.S. 51, 109 S.Ct. 333, 102 L.Ed.2d 281 (1988). The state appellate court there had reversed defendant's conviction on charges of child molestation, sexual assault, and kidnapping based on the government's failure to properly preserve semen samples from the 10-year-old victim's body and clothing. After making his way home following his abduction, the victim had been taken to a hospital for medical treatment. While there, a physician used a swab from a "sexual assault kit" to collect semen samples from the boy's rectum. The police also collected the boy's clothing, which they failed to refrigerate. Ten days later, after the victim identified the defendant from a photographic lineup and before the defendant was in custody, a police criminologist examined the sexual assault kit to determine whether sexual contact occurred, but did not perform tests to identify blood group substances and did not test the clothing. Following defendant's indictment more than a month later, tests for blood group substances were performed on both the samples taken by the physician and the clothing, but proved unsuccessful. Defendant's principal defense at trial was that the boy had erred in identifying him as the perpetrator. Expert witnesses testified that if tests had been performed on the samples shortly after they were gathered, or the clothing had been properly refrigerated and later tested, the blood group testing could have been performed successfully and the results might have exonerated the defendant. The state appellate court noted that it did "not imply any bad faith on the part of the state," but the conviction nonetheless would be reversed: "[W]hen identity is an issue at trial and the police permit the destruction of evidence that could eliminate the defendant as the perpetrator, such loss is material to the defense and is a denial of due process." The Supreme Court majority, per REHNQUIST, C.J., disagreed:

"Decision of this case requires us to again consider 'what might loosely be called the area of constitutionally-guaranteed access to evidence.' *United States v. Valenzuela–Bernal* [Note 1, p. 1406]. * * * Our most recent decision in this area of the law, *California v. Trombetta,* 467 U.S. 479, 104 S.Ct. 2528, 81 L.Ed.2d 413 (1984), arose out of a drunk driving prosecution in which the State had introduced test results indicating the concentration of alcohol in the blood of two motorists. The defendants sought to suppress the test results on the ground that the State had failed to preserve the breath samples used in the test. We rejected this argument for several reasons: first, 'the officers here were acting in "good faith and in accord with their normal practice" '; second, in the light of the procedures actually used the chances that preserved samples would have exculpated the defendants were slim; and, third, even if the samples might have shown inaccuracy in the tests, the defendants had 'alternative means of demonstrating their innocence.' In the present case, the likelihood that the preserved materials would have enabled the defendant to exonerate himself appears to be greater than it was in *Trombetta,* but here, unlike in *Trombetta,* the State did not attempt to make any use of the materials in its own case in chief.

"Our decisions in related areas have stressed the importance for constitutional purposes of good or bad faith on the part of the Government when the claim is based on loss of evidence attributable to the Government. In *United States v. Marion* [p. 1085], we said that '[n]o actual prejudice to the conduct of the defense is alleged or proved, and there is no showing that the Government intentionally delayed to gain some tactical advantage over appellees or to harass them.' See also *United States v. Lovasco* [p. 1083]. Similarly, in *United States v. Valenzuela– Bernal,* supra, we * * * held that the prompt deportation of the witnesses was justified 'upon the Executive's good-faith determination that they possess no evidence favorable to the defendant in a criminal prosecution.'

"The Due Process Clause of the Fourteenth Amendment, as interpreted in *Brady v. Maryland* [see p. 1390], makes the good or bad faith of the State irrelevant when the State fails to disclose to the defendant material exculpatory evidence. But we think the Due Process Clause requires a different result when we deal with the failure of the State to preserve evidentiary material of which no more can be said than that it could have been subjected to tests, the results of which might have exonerated the defendant. Part of the reason for the difference in treatment is found in the observation made by the Court in *Trombetta,* supra, that '[w]henever potentially exculpatory evidence is permanently lost, courts face the treacherous task of divining the import of materials whose contents are unknown and, very often, disputed.' Part of it stems from our unwillingness to read the 'fundamental fairness' requirement of the Due Process Clause, as imposing on the police an undifferentiated and absolute duty to retain and to preserve all material that might be of conceivable evidentiary significance in a particular prosecution. We think that requiring a defendant to show bad faith on the part of the police both limits the extent of the police's obligation to preserve evidence to reasonable bounds and confines it to that class of cases where the interests of justice most clearly require it, i.e., those cases in which the police themselves by their conduct indicate that the evidence could form a basis for exonerating the defendant. We therefore hold that unless a criminal defendant can show bad faith on the part of the police, failure to preserve potentially useful evidence does not constitute a denial of due process of law.

"In this case, the police collected the rectal swab and clothing on the night of the crime; respondent was not taken into custody until six weeks later. The failure of the police to refrigerate the clothing and to perform tests on the semen samples can at worst be described as negligent. * * * The Arizona Court of Appeals noted in its opinion—and we agree—that there was no suggestion of bad faith on the part of the police. It follows, therefore, from what we have said, that there was no violation of the Due Process Clause.

"The Arizona Court of Appeals also referred somewhat obliquely to the State's 'inability to quantitatively test' certain semen samples with the newer P–30 test. If the court meant by this statement that the Due Process Clause is violated when the police fail to use a particular investigatory tool, we strongly disagree. The situation here is no different than a prosecution for drunk driving that rests on police observation alone; the defendant is free to argue to the finder of fact that a breathalizer test might have been exculpatory, but the police do not have a constitutional duty to perform any particular tests."

Concurring in the judgment, Justice STEVENS noted "three factors * * * of critical importance to my evaluation of the case." First, the police at the time that they failed to refrigerate "had at least as great an interest in preserving the evidence as did the person later accused. * * * In cases such as this, even without a prophylactic sanction such as dismissal of the indictment, the State has a strong incentive to preserve the evidence." "Second," Justice Stevens noted, "although it is not possible to know whether the lost evidence would have revealed any relevant information, it is unlikely that the defendant was prejudiced by the State's omission. * * * [D]efense counsel impressed upon the jury the fact that the State failed to preserve the evidence and that the State could have conducted tests that might well have exonerated the defendant. More significantly, the trial judge instructed the jury: 'If you find that the State has ... allowed to be destroyed or lost any evidence whose content or quality are in issue, you may infer that the true fact is against the State's interest.' As a result, the uncertainty as to what the evidence might have proved was turned to the defendant's advantage." The third relevant factor was that the jurors, in convicting the defendant notwithstanding the trial court's invitation to draw this "permissive inference" favorable to the defendant, "in effect indicated that, in their view, the other evidence at trial was so overwhelming that it was highly improbable that the lost evidence was exculpatory."

Justice BLACKMUN's dissent (joined by Brennan and Marshall, JJ.) initially disagreed with the majority's focus on the "good faith" of the prosecution. "The Constitution," the dissent noted, "requires that criminal defendants be provided with a fair trial, not merely a 'good faith' try at a fair trial." Past cases such as *Brady* "made plain that the prosecutor's state of mind is *not* determinative. Rather, the proper standard must focus on the materiality of the evidence, and that standard 'must reflect our overriding concern with the justice of the finding of guilt.' "

In determining whether particular evidence is "material," Justice Blackmun noted, a "court should focus on the * * * [relevancy] of the evidence, the possibility it might prove exculpatory, and the existence of other evidence going to the same point of contention." Accordingly, "where no comparable evidence is likely to be available to the defendant, police must preserve physical evidence of a type that they reasonably should know has the potential, if tested, to reveal immutable characteristics of the criminal and hence to exculpate a defendant charged with a crime." Where, as here, the evidence of guilt "was far from conclusive," and "the possibility that the evidence denied to respondent would have exonerated him was not remote," the failure to preserve the evidence must be deemed a denial of due process resulting in a lack of a fair trial.[c]

2. Are there any general themes that shape the constitutional standards discussed in this section? Can the decisions be said to uniformly promote a case-by-case balancing approach that weighs the likely exculpatory quality of the evidence sought (or lost) against the countervailing governmental interest? Do the decisions require no more than a "rational state interest" rather than a "compelling interest"? Are the standards framed in large part to discourage defense claims that would otherwise be made almost automatically? Are they consistent in their approach to the presence or absence of prosecutorial "bad faith." See generally, Tom Stacy, *The Search For the Truth in Constitutional Criminal Procedure,* 91 Colum.L.Rev. 1369 (1991).

SECTION 3. THE DEFENDANT'S RIGHT TO REMAIN SILENT AND TO TESTIFY

GRIFFIN v. CALIFORNIA
380 U.S. 609, 85 S.Ct. 1229, 14 L.Ed.2d 106 (1965).

Justice DOUGLAS delivered the opinion of the Court.

Petitioner was convicted of murder in the first degree after a jury trial in the California court. He did not testify at the trial on the issue of guilt, though he did testify at the separate trial on the issue of penalty. The trial court instructed the jury on the issue of guilt, stating that a defendant has a constitutional right not to testify. But it told the jury:[1]

"As to any evidence or facts against him which the defendant can reasonably be expected to deny or explain because of facts within his knowledge, if he

---

c. The state appellate court set aside Youngblood's conviction in 1990, holding that the state constitution provided broader protection than the federal constitution, but the Arizona Supreme Court reversed that ruling in 1993. Youngblood was then returned to prison, and he continued to serve his sentence on the sexual molestation charge, concurrent with an unrelated five-year sentence on an assault conviction, until 1998, when he was released on parole. He was returned to prison the next year after violating the sex offender law when he failed to report a change of address. In 1999, his lawyers requested DNA testing of the preserved semen sample, using a sophisticated DNA test that had recently become available. As a result of that test, Youngblood's conviction was set aside in August, 2000. See Barbara Whitaker, *DNA Frees Inmate Years After Justices Rejected Plea,* N.Y. Times, Aug. 11, 2000.

1. Article I, § 13, of the California Constitution provides in part: " * * * in any criminal case, whether the defendant testifies or not, his failure to explain or to deny by his testimony any evidence or facts in the case against him may be commented upon by the court and by counsel, and may be considered by the court or the jury."

does not testify or if, though he does testify, he fails to deny or explain such evidence, the jury may take that failure into consideration as tending to indicate the truth of such evidence and as indicating that among the inferences that may be reasonably drawn therefrom those unfavorable to the defendant are the more probable.''

It added, however, that no such inference could be drawn as to evidence respecting which he had no knowledge. It stated that failure of a defendant to deny or explain the evidence of which he had knowledge does not create a presumption of guilt nor by itself warrant an inference of guilt nor relieve the prosecution of any of its burden of proof.

Petitioner had been seen with the deceased the evening of her death, the evidence placing him with her in the alley where her body was found. The prosecutor made much of the failure of petitioner to testify. * * *

The death penalty was imposed and the California Supreme Court affirmed. The case is here on a petition for a writ of certiorari which we granted to consider the single question whether comment on the failure to testify violated the Self-Incrimination Clause of the Fifth Amendment which we made applicable to the States by the Fourteenth in *Malloy v. Hogan,* 378 U.S. 1, 84 S.Ct. 1489, 12 L.Ed.2d 653 (1964), decided after the Supreme Court of California had affirmed the present conviction.[2]

If this were a federal trial, reversible error would have been committed. *Wilson v. United States,* 149 U.S. 60, 13 S.Ct. 765, 37 L.Ed. 650 (1893) so holds. It is said, however, that the *Wilson* decision rested not on the Fifth Amendment, but on an Act of Congress. 18 U.S.C. § 3481. That indeed is the fact, as the opinion of the Court in the *Wilson* case states. * * * But that is the beginning, not the end of our inquiry. The question remains whether, statute or not, the comment rule, approved by California, violates the Fifth Amendment.

We think it does. It is in substance a rule of evidence that allows the State the privilege of tendering to the jury for its consideration the failure of the accused to testify. No formal offer of proof is made as in other situations; but the prosecutor's comment and the court's acquiescence are the equivalent of an offer of evidence and its acceptance. The Court in the *Wilson* case stated:

"* * * the Act was framed with a due regard also to those who might prefer to rely upon the presumption of innocence which the law gives to every one, and not wish to be witnesses. It is not every one who can safely venture on the witness stand, though entirely innocent of the charge against him. Excessive timidity, nervousness when facing others and attempting to explain transactions of a suspicious character, and offenses charged against him, will often confuse and embarrass him to such a degree as to increase rather than remove prejudices against him. It is not every one, however honest, who would therefore willingly be placed on the witness stand. The statute, in tenderness to the weakness of those who from the causes mentioned might refuse to ask to be witnesses, particularly when they may have been in some degree compromised by their association with others, declares that the failure of a defendant in a criminal action to request to be a witness shall not create any presumption against him.''

If the words "Fifth Amendment" are substituted for "Act" and for "statute" the spirit of the Self-Incrimination Clause is reflected. For comment on the

---

2. The California Supreme Court later held that its "comment" rule squared with *Malloy v. Hogan.* The overwhelming consensus of the States, however, is opposed to allowing comment on the defendant's failure to testify. The legislatures or courts of 44 States have recognized that such comment is in light of the privilege against self-incrimination, "an unwarrantable line of argument." * * *

refusal to testify is a remnant of the "inquisitorial system of criminal justice" which the Fifth Amendment outlaws. It is a penalty imposed by courts for exercising a constitutional privilege. It cuts down on the privilege by making its assertion costly. It is said, however, that the inference of guilt for failure to testify as to facts peculiarly within the accused's knowledge is in any event natural and irresistible, and that comment on the failure does not magnify that inference into a penalty for asserting a constitutional privilege. What the jury may infer given no help from the court is one thing. What they may infer when the court solemnizes the silence of the accused into evidence against him is quite another. * * *

We said in *Malloy v. Hogan* that "the same standards must determine whether an accused's silence in either a federal or state proceeding is justified." We take that in its literal sense and hold that the Fifth Amendment, in its direct application to the federal government and its bearing on the States by reason of the Fourteenth Amendment, forbids either comment by the prosecution on the accused's silence or instructions by the court that such silence is evidence of guilt.[6]

Justice STEWART, with whom Justice WHITE joins, dissenting. * * *

We must determine whether the petitioner has been "compelled to be a witness against himself." * * * I think that the Court in this case stretches the concept of compulsion beyond all reasonable bounds, and that whatever compulsion may exist derives from the defendant's choice not to testify, not from any comment by court or counsel. In support of its conclusion that the California procedure does compel the accused to testify, the Court has only this to say: "It is a penalty imposed by courts for exercising a constitutional privilege. It cuts down on the privilege by making its assertion costly." Exactly what the penalty imposed consists of is not clear. It is not, as I understand the problem, that the jury becomes aware that the defendant has chosen not to testify in his own defense, for the jury will, of course, realize this quite evident fact, even though the choice goes unmentioned. * * *

It is not at all apparent to me, on any realistic view of the trial process, that a defendant will be at more of a disadvantage under the California practice than he would be in a court which permitted no comment at all on his failure to take the witness stand. How can it be said that the inferences drawn by a jury will be more detrimental to a defendant under the limiting and carefully controlling language of the instruction here involved than would result if the jury were left to roam at large with only their untutored instincts to guide them, to draw from the defendant's silence broad inferences of guilt? * * * Moreover, no one can say where the balance of advantage might lie as a result of the attorneys' discussion of the matter. No doubt the prosecution's argument will seek to encourage the drawing of inferences unfavorable to the defendant. However, the defendant's counsel equally has an opportunity to explain the various other reasons why a defendant may not wish to take the stand, and thus rebut the natural if uneducated assumption that it is because the defendant cannot truthfully deny the accusations made. * * *

The California rule allowing comment by counsel and instruction by the judge on the defendant's failure to take the stand is hardly an idiosyncratic aberration. The Model Code of Evidence, and Uniform Rules of Evidence both sanction the use of such procedures. The practice had been endorsed by resolution of the

---

6. We reserve decision on whether an accused can require that the jury be instructed   that his silence must be disregarded.

American Bar Association and the American Law Institute, and has the support of the weight of scholarly opinion. * * *[a]

Notes and Questions

1. *Sentencing.* In MITCHELL v. UNITED STATES, 526 U.S. 314, 119 S.Ct. 1307, 143 L.Ed.2d 424 (1999), also discussed at pp. 1295, 1509, the Court, 5–4, declined to adopt an exception to *Griffin* allowing the sentencing judge to draw an adverse inference from the defendant's silence at sentencing. In dissent, Justice SCALIA, joined by the Chief Justice and Justices O'Connor and Thomas, question the validity of *Griffin*, though not arguing for its reconsideration. (Justice Thomas, in a separate opinion, did suggest that "*Griffin* and its progeny * * * should be reexamined"). Justice Scalia noted:

"The majority muses that the no-adverse-inference rule has found 'wide acceptance in the legal culture' and has even become 'an essential feature of our legal tradition.' Although the latter assertion strikes me as hyperbolic, the former may be true—which is adequate reason not to overrule these cases, a course I in no way propose. It is not adequate reason, however, to extend these cases into areas where they do not yet apply, since neither logic nor history can be marshaled in defense of them. The illogic of the *Griffin* line is plain, for it runs exactly counter to normal evidentiary inferences: If I ask my son whether he saw a movie I had forbidden him to watch, and he remains silent, the import of his silence is clear. Indeed, we have on other occasions recognized the significance of silence, saying that "'[f]ailure to contest an assertion . . . is considered evidence of acquiescence . . . if it would have been natural under the circumstances to object to the assertion in question."' *Baxter v. Palmigiano* [inference allowed in state prison disciplinary proceeding].

"And as for history, *Griffin*'s pedigree is equally dubious. The question whether a factfinder may draw a logical inference from a criminal defendant's failure to offer formal testimony would not have arisen in 1791, because common-law evidentiary rules prevented a criminal defendant from testifying in his own behalf even if wanted to do so. That is not to say, however, that a criminal defendant was not allowed to speak in his own behalf, and a tradition of expecting the defendant to do so, and of drawing an adverse inference when he did not, strongly suggests that *Griffin* is out of sync with the historical understanding of the Fifth Amendment. Traditionally, defendants were expected to speak rather extensively at both the pretrial and trial stages of a criminal proceeding. The longstanding common-law principle, *nemo tenetur seipsum prodere*, was thought to

a. The Chief Justice took no part in the decision of the case. Harlan J., concurred "with great reluctance." The prohibition of comment continues to be a subject of scholarly debate. For criticism of the *Griffin* ruling, see e.g., Craig Bradley and Peter Hoffman, *Justice and the Search for Truth in Criminal Cases*, 69 S. Cal. L. Rev. 1267 (1996); Albert Alschuler, *A Peculiar Privilege in Historical Perspective: The Right to Remain Silent*, 94 Mich. L. Rev. 2625 (1996); Akhil Amar and Renee Lettow, *Fifth Amendment First Principle: The Self-Incrimination Clause*, 93 Mich. L. Rev. 857 (1998). For defenses of *Griffin*, see e.g., Stephen Schulhofer, *Some Kind Worlds For the Privilege Against Self-Incrimination*, 26 Val. V. L. Rev 311 (1991); Peter Arenella, *Foreward; O. J. Lessons*, 69 S Cal. L. Rev. 1233 (1996).

The critics also point to the recent experience in England and Northern Ireland, both of which adopted legislation allowing the trier of fact to draw an adverse inference from the defendant's failure to testify under certain circumstances (state has established a sufficient case to call for defendant's answer, consideration must be given to any defense explanation of defendant's failure to testify, with the court prohibiting use of the inference if it finds that a physical or mental condition made it undesirable for defendant to testify, and jury must conclude that defendant's silence can only sensibly be attributed to his having no answer or none that would stand up to cross-examination). See John Jackson, Martin Wolfe, & Katie Quinn, *Legislating Against Silence: The Northern Ireland Experience* (2000).

ban only testimony forced by compulsory oath or physical torture, not voluntary, unsworn testimony. [Under the Marian Committal Statute, the justice of the peace was required to take the examination of the arrested person not under oath and to record his response]. * * * The justice of the peace testified at trial as to the content of the defendant's statement; if the defendant refused to speak, this would also have been reported to the jury. * * * At trial, defendants were expected to speak directly to the jury. Sir James Stephen described 17th-and 18th-century English trials as follows: '[T]he prisoner in cases of felony could not be defended by counsel, and had therefore to speak for himself. He was thus unable to say ... that his mouth was closed. On the contrary his mouth was not only open, but the evidence given against him operated as so much indirect questioning, and if he omitted to answer the questions it suggested he was very likely to be convicted.' * * *

"Whatever the merits of prohibiting adverse inferences as a legislative policy, the text and history of the Fifth Amendment give no indication that there is a federal constitutional prohibition on the use of the defendant's silence as demeanor evidence. Our hardy forebearers, who thought of compulsion in terms of the rack and oaths forced by the power of law, would not have viewed the drawing of a commonsensical inference as equivalent pressure. And it is implausible that the Americans of 1791, who were subject to adverse inferences for failing to give unsworn testimony, would have viewed an adverse inference for failing to give sworn testimony as a violation of the Fifth Amendment. Nor can it reasonably be argued that the new statutes somehow created a 'revised' understanding of the Fifth Amendment that was incorporated into the Due Process Clause of the Fourteenth Amendment, since only nine States (and not the Federal Government) had enacted competency statutes when the Fourteenth Amendment was adopted, and three of them did not prohibit adverse inferences from failure to testify.

"The Court's decision in *Griffin*, however, did not even pretend to be rooted in a historical understanding of the Fifth Amendment. Rather, in a breathtaking act of sorcery it simply transformed legislative policy into constitutional command, quoting a passage from an earlier opinion describing the benevolent purposes of 18 U.S.C. § 3481, and then decreeing, with literally nothing to support it: 'If the words "Fifth Amendment" are substituted for "act," and for "statute," the spirit of the Self–Incrimination Clause is reflected.' Imagine what a constitution we would have if this mode of exegesis were generally applied—if, for example, without any evidence to prove the point, the Court could simply say of all federal procedural statutes, 'If the words "Fifth Amendment" are substituted for "act" and for "statute," the spirit of the Due Process Clause is reflected.' To my mind, *Griffin* was a wrong turn—which is not cause enough to overrule it, but is cause enough to resist its extension."

2. *The "no inference" charge.* The question on which *Griffin* reserved decision in footnote 6 was finally reached in *Carter v. Kentucky*, 450 U.S. 288, 101 S.Ct. 1112, 67 L.Ed.2d 241 (1981), where the Court majority, per Stewart, J., concluded:

"The *Griffin* case stands for the proposition that a defendant must pay no court-imposed price for the exercise of his constitutional privilege not to testify. The penalty was exacted in *Griffin* by adverse comment on the defendant's silence; the penalty may be just as severe when there is no adverse comment, but when the jury is left to roam at large with only its untutored instincts to guide it, to draw from the defendant's silence broad inferences of guilt. Even without adverse comment, the members of a jury, unless instructed otherwise, may well draw adverse inferences from a defendant's silence. * * * A trial judge has a powerful tool at his disposal to protect the constitutional privilege—the jury instruction—and he has an affirmative constitutional obligation to use that tool when a defendant seeks its employment. No judge can prevent jurors from speculating about why a defendant stands mute in the face of a criminal accusation, but a judge can, and must, if requested to do so, use the unique power of the jury instruction to reduce that speculation to a minimum."

3. In LAKESIDE v. OREGON, 435 U.S. 333, 98 S.Ct. 1091, 55 L.Ed.2d 319 (1978), the petitioner argued "that this protective instruction becomes constitutionally impermissible when given over the defendant's objection" because it "is like 'waving a red flag in front of the jury.' " Rejecting that contention, the Court, per STEWART, J., concluded:

"The petitioner's argument would require indulgence in two very doubtful assumptions: First, that the jurors have not noticed that the defendant did not testify and will not, therefore, draw adverse inferences on their own. Second, that the jurors will totally disregard the instruction, and affirmatively give weight to what they have been told not to consider at all. Federal constitutional law cannot rest on speculative assumptions so dubious as these."

As for petitioner's argument that the instruction infringed upon his constitutional right to the effective assistance of counsel (cf. *Brooks*, Note 5 infra), the Court found "it falls of its own weight once the petitioner's primary argument has been rejected. * * * To hold otherwise would mean that the constitutional right to counsel would be implicated in almost every wholly permissible ruling of a trial judge, if it is made over the objection of the defendant's lawyer."

STEVENS and Marshall, JJ., dissenting, objected: "It is unrealistic to assume that instructions on the right to silence always have a benign effect. At times the instruction will make the defendant's silence costly indeed. So long as *Griffin* is good law, the State must have a strong reason for ignoring the defendant's request that the instruction not be given. Remarkably, the Court fails to identify any reason for overriding the defendant's choice.[8]"

4. *Prosecution comment.* *Griffin* has spawned an immense body of caselaw addressing the question of whether a particular prosecutorial statement does or does not constitute an adverse comment on the defendant's failure to take the stand. Courts agree on the general standard for resolving that issue—"whether the language used was manifestly intended or was of such character that the jury would naturally and necessarily take it to be a comment on the accused's failure to testify." *Dickinson v. State*, 685 S.W.2d 320 (Tex.Cr.App.1984). As might be expected, "variation arises in [the lower courts'] evaluation of roughly similar remarks in roughly similar settings," CRIMPROC § 24.5 (b).

In *Lockett v. Ohio*, 438 U.S. 586, 98 S.Ct. 2954, 57 L.Ed.2d 973 (1978), where the prosecutor repeatedly referred to the state's evidence as "unrefuted" and "uncontradicted," the Court held this did not violate the Constitution because it "added nothing to the impression that had already been created by Lockett's refusal to testify after the jury had been promised a defense by her lawyer and

---

8. How far the Court deviates from the course charted in *Griffin* may be seen by comparing its reasoning to the analysis in an earlier case that followed *Griffin* more faithfully. In *Brooks v. Tennessee* [Note 5 infra], state law required the defendant to be the first defense witness if he wanted to testify at all. Since defendants may not be sequestered like other witnesses, this rule was the only way to prevent opportunistic defendants from shading their testimony to match that of other defense witnesses. Despite the substantial state inter-

est in avoiding perjury, this Court struck down the rule, relying on *Griffin*. The *Brooks* court thought that a defendant who planned to take the stand only if his case was weak, but who could not judge its weakness in advance, might be unnecessarily compelled to testify under the Tennessee law. In *Brooks*, the State had a good reason for its action; here the State has none. In *Brooks*, the compulsive force of the rule was speculative at best; here it is direct and plain. If today we are true to *Griffin*, as the Court asserts, then *Brooks* was surely wrong.

told that Lockett would take the stand." What would the result have been if the defense attorney had not made those statements?

In *United States v. Robinson*, 485 U.S. 25, 108 S.Ct. 864, 99 L.Ed.2d 23 (1988), defense counsel in closing argument urged several times that the government had not allowed the defendant (who did not testify) to explain his side of the story and had unfairly denied him the opportunity to explain his actions. In rebuttal, the prosecutor remarked that defendant "could have taken the stand and explained it to you." Applying the *Lockett* "principle that prosecutorial comment must be examined in context," the Supreme Court concluded: "In the present case it is evidence that the prosecutorial comment did not treat the defendant's silence as substantive evidence of guilt, but instead referred to the possibility of testifying as one of several opportunities which the defendant was afforded, contrary to the statement of his counsel, to explain his side of the case. Where * * * as in this case the prosecutor's reference to the defendant's opportunity to testify is a fair response to a claim made by defendant or his counsel, we think there is no violation of the privilege."

5. *Order of the testimony.* In BROOKS v. TENNESSEE, 406 U.S. 605, 92 S.Ct. 1891, 32 L.Ed.2d 358 (1972), petitioner questioned the constitutionality of a statute which required that a criminal defendant "desiring to testify shall do so before any other testimony for the defense is heard," a rule related to the ancient practice of sequestering prospective witnesses in order to prevent their being influenced by other testimony in the case. The Court, per BRENNAN, J., held: (a) That the statute "violates an accused's constitutional right to remain silent," as a defendant "cannot be absolutely certain that his witnesses will testify as expected or that they will be effective on the stand" and thus "may not know at the close of the State's case whether his own testimony will be necessary or even helpful to his cause." "Pressuring the defendant to take the stand, by foreclosing later testimony if he refuses, is not a constitutionally permissible means of ensuring his honesty. It fails to take into account the very real and legitimate concerns that might motivate a defendant to exercise his right of silence. And it may compel even a wholly truthful defendant, who might otherwise decline to testify for legitimate reasons, to subject himself to impeachment and cross-examination at a time when the strength of his other evidence is not yet clear." (b) That the statute constitutes "an infringement on the defendant's right of due process," as "by requiring the accused and his lawyer to make [the choice of whether to testify] without an opportunity to evaluate the actual worth of their evidence," the accused is "thereby deprived of the 'guiding hand of counsel' in the timing of this critical element of his defense." Chief Justice BURGER, joined by Blackmun and Rehnquist, JJ., dissenting, argued that there was no violation of the right to remain silent in that the defendant was not confronted with a choice any more difficult than that approved by the Court in *Williams v. Florida,* p. 1200; and that there was no due process violation because counsel may "be restricted by ordinary rules of evidence and procedure in presenting an accused's defense" even "if it might be more advantageous to present it in some other way," as illustrated by the rule forbidding counsel from asking leading questions of the defendant. See also Note 3, p. 1205.

6. In PORTUONDO v. AGARD, 529 U.S. 61, 120 S.Ct. 1119, 146 L.Ed.2d 47 (2000), the prosecutor in closing argument, in questioning defendant's credibility as a witness, pointed out that defendant, unlike the other witnesses, had been present throughout the trial and was thus able to hear what the others said before he testified. The defendant contended those comments "burdened his Sixth Amendment right to be present at trial and to be confronted with the witnesses against him, and his Fifth and Sixth Amendment rights to testify on his own behalf," and thus asked the Court to "extend to comments of the type the prosecutor made here the rationale of *Griffin*." But the Court, per SCALIA, J., after finding no "historical support" for defendant's claim, found *Griffin* to be "a poor analogue * * * for several reasons": (1) "What we prohibited the prosecutor from urging the jury to do in *Griffin* was something *the jury is not permitted to do.* * * * By contrast, it *is* natural and irresistible for a jury, in evaluating the relative credibility of a defendant who testifies last, to have in mind and weigh in the balance the fact that he heard the testimonial of all those who preceded him"; (2) "*Griffin* prohibited comments that suggest a defendant's silence is evidence of guilt. * * * The prosecutor's comments in this case, by contrast, concerned respondent's *credibility as a witness*, and were therefore in accord with the longstanding rule that when a defendant takes the stand, 'his credibility may be impeached and his testimony assailed like that of any other witness' ". As for the contention of GINSBURG and SOUTER, JJ., dissenting, "that the comments were impermissible here because they were made, not during cross-examination, but at summation, leaving the defense no opportunity to reply," the Court answered: "Our trial structure, which requires the defense to close before the prosecution, regularly forces the defense to predict what the prosecution will say."

   7. *Constitutional right to testify.* In *Rock v. Arkansas*, 483 U.S. 44, 107 S.Ct. 2704, 97 L.Ed.2d 37 (1987), the Court held that a state's per se exclusion of hypnotically refreshed testimony, as applied to a defendant's testimony, violated the defendant's constitutional right to testify on her own behalf. That constitutional right, the Court noted, stems from three sources: (1) the Fourteenth Amendment's guarantee of due process (which includes "a right to be heard and to offer testimony"); (2) the Sixth Amendment's Compulsory Process Clause (the accused's right to call witnesses in his favor "logically include[s] * * * a right to testify himself, should he decide it is in his favor to do so"); and (3) the Fifth Amendment's self-incrimination guarantee (the "opportunity to testify is a necessary corollary to the * * * guarantee against compelled testimony"). While the defendant's constitutional right to testify is not without limitation, restrictions placed on that right by state evidentiary rules "may not be arbitrary or disproportionate to the purposes they are designed to serve." Though the state has a legitimate interest in barring unreliable evidence, that interest did not justify a per se exclusion of defendant's hypnotically refreshed testimony without regard to procedural safeguards employed to reduce inaccuracies and the availability of corroborating evidence and other traditional means of assessing accuracy.

SECTION 4. COUNSEL'S ARGUMENTS

DARDEN v. WAINWRIGHT

477 U.S. 168, 106 S.Ct. 2464, 91 L.Ed.2d 144 (1986).

   Justice POWELL delivered the opinion of the Court.

   Petitioner was tried and found guilty of murder, robbery, and assault with intent to kill in the Circuit Court for Citrus County, Florida, in January 1974. Pursuant to Florida's capital sentencing statute, the same jury that convicted petitioner heard further testimony and argument in order to make a nonbinding recommendation as to whether a death sentence should be imposed. The jury recommended a death sentence, and the trial judge followed that recommendation. On direct appeal, the Florida Supreme Court affirmed the conviction and the sentence. [The] court disapproved of the closing argument, but reasoned that the law required a new trial "only in those cases in which it is reasonably evident that the remarks might have influenced the jury to reach a more severe verdict of guilt ... or in which the comment is unfair." * * * It concluded that the comments had not rendered petitioner's trial unfair. * * *

Petitioner then sought federal habeas corpus relief. [The district court denied relief, and a divided panel of Eleventh Circuit affirmed. Following a remand from the Supreme Court on another issue, that Eleventh Circuit, sitting en banc, again denied relief.] We now affirm.

Because of the nature of petitioner's claims, the facts of this case will be stated in more detail than is normally necessary in this Court. On September 8, 1973, at about 5:30 p.m., a black adult male entered Carl's Furniture Store near Lakeland, Florida. The only other person in the store was the proprietor, Mrs. Turman, who lived with her husband in a house behind the store. Mr. Turman, who worked nights at a juvenile home, had awakened at about 5:00 p.m., had a cup of coffee at the store with his wife, and returned home to let their dogs out for a run. Mrs. Turman showed the man around the store. He stated that he was interested in purchasing about $600 worth of furniture for a rental unit, and asked to see several different items. He left the store briefly, stating that his wife would be back to look at some of the items.

The same man returned just a few minutes later asking to see some stoves, and inquiring about the price. When Mrs. Turman turned toward the adding machine, he grabbed her and pressed a gun to her back, saying "Do as I say and you won't get hurt." He took her to the rear of the store and told her to open the cash register. He took the money, then ordered her to the part of the store where some boxsprings and mattresses were stacked against the wall. At that time Mr. Turman appeared at the back door. Mrs. Turman screamed while the man reached across her right shoulder and shot Mr. Turman between the eyes. Mr. Turman fell backwards, with one foot partially in the building. Ordering Mrs. Turman not to move, the man tried to pull Mr. Turman into the building and close the door, but could not do so because one of Mr. Turman's feet was caught in the door. The man left Mr. Turman face-up in the rain, and told Mrs. Turman to get down on the floor approximately five feet from where her husband lay dying. While she begged to go to her husband, he told her to remove her false teeth. He unzipped his pants, unbuckled his belt, and demanded that Mrs. Turman perform oral sex on him. She began to cry "Lord, have mercy." He told her to get up and go towards the front of the store.

Meanwhile, a neighbor family, the Arnolds, became aware that something had happened to Mr. Turman. The mother sent her 16 year-old son Phillip, a part-time employee at the furniture store, to help. When Phillip reached the back door he saw Mr. Turman lying partially in the building. When Phillip opened the door to take Turman's body inside, Mrs. Turman shouted "Phillip, no, go back." Phillip did not know what she meant and asked the man to help get Turman inside. He replied, "Sure, buddy, I will help you." As Phillip looked up, the man was pointing a gun in his face. He pulled the trigger and the gun misfired; he pulled the trigger again and shot Phillip in the mouth. Phillip started to run away, and was shot in the neck. While he was still running, he was shot a third time in the side. Despite these wounds, Phillip managed to stumble to the home of a neighbor, Mrs. Edith Hill. She had her husband call an ambulance while she tried to stop Phillip's bleeding. While she was helping Phillip, she saw a late model green Chevrolet leave the store and head towards Tampa on state highway 92. Phillip survived the incident; Mr. Turman, who never regained consciousness, died later that night.

Minutes after the murder petitioner was driving towards Tampa on highway 92, just a few miles away from the furniture store. He was out on furlough from a Florida prison, and was driving a car borrowed from his girlfriend in Tampa. He was driving fast on a wet road. Petitioner testified that as he came up on a line of cars in his lane, he was unable to slow down. He attempted to pass, but was forced off the road to avoid a head-on collision with an oncoming car. Petitioner crashed into a telephone pole. The driver of the oncoming car, John Stone, stopped his car and went to petitioner to see if he could help. Stone testified that as he approached the car, petitioner was zipping up his pants and buckling his belt. Police at the crash site later identified petitioner's car as a 1969 Chevrolet Impala of greenish golden brown color. Petitioner paid a bystander to give him a ride to Tampa. Petitioner later returned with a wrecker, only to find that the car had been towed away by the police.

By the time the police arrived at the scene of the accident, petitioner had left. The fact that the car matched the description of the car leaving the scene of the murder, and that the accident had occurred within three and one-half miles of the furniture store and within minutes of the murder, led police to suspect that the car was driven by the murderer. They searched the area. An officer found a pistol—a revolver—about forty feet from the crash site. The arrangement of shells within the chambers exactly matched the pattern that should have been found in the murder weapon: one shot, one misfire, followed by three shots, with a live shell remaining in the next chamber to be fired. A specialist for the FBI examined the pistol and testified that it was a Smith & Wesson .38 special revolver. It had been manufactured as a standard .38; it later was sent to England to be rebored, making it a much rarer type of gun than the standard .38. An examination of the bullet that killed Mr. Turman revealed that it came from a .38 Smith & Wesson special.

On the day following the murder petitioner was arrested at his girlfriend's house in Tampa. A few days later Mrs. Turman identified him at a preliminary hearing as her husband's murderer. Phillip Arnold selected petitioner's picture out of a spread of six photographs as the man who had shot him.[1]

* * *

Petitioner * * * contends that the prosecution's closing argument at the guilt-innocence stage of the trial rendered his conviction fundamentally unfair and deprived the sentencing determination of the reliability that the Eighth Amendment requires.

It is helpful as an initial matter to place these remarks in context. Closing argument came at the end of several days of trial. Because of a state procedural rule petitioner's counsel had the opportunity to present the initial summation as well as a rebuttal to the prosecutors' closing arguments. The prosecutors' comments must be evaluated in light of the defense argument that preceded it, which

---

1. There are some minor discrepancies in the eyewitness identification. Mrs. Turman first described her assailant immediately after the murder while her husband was being taken to the emergency room. She told the investigating officer that the attacker was a heavyset man. When asked if he was "neat in his appearance, clean-looking, clean-shaven," she responded "[a]s far as I can remember, yes, sir." She also stated to the officer that she thought that the attacker was about her height, 5′6″ tall, and that he was wearing a pullover shirt with a stripe around the neck. The first time she saw petitioner after the attack was when she identified him at the preliminary hearing. She had not read any newspaper accounts of the crime, nor had she seen any picture of petitioner. When she was asked if petitioner was the man who had committed the crimes, she said yes. She also repeatedly identified him at trial.

Phillip Arnold first identified petitioner in a photo line-up while in the hospital. He could not speak at the time, and in response to the written question whether petitioner had a mustache, Phillip wrote back "I don't think so." Phillip also testified at trial that the attacker was a heavyset man wearing a dull, light color knit shirt with a ring around the neck. He testified that the man was almost his height, about 6′2″ tall.

A motorist who stopped at the scene of the accident testified that petitioner was wearing a white or off-grey button-down shirt and that he had a slight mustache. In fact, the witness stated that he "didn't know it was that [the mustache] or the raindrops on him or not. I couldn't really tell that much to it, it was real thin, that's all." Petitioner is about 5′10″ tall, and at the time of trial testified that he weighed about 175 pounds.

blamed the Polk County Sheriff's Office for a lack of evidence,[5] alluded to the death penalty,[6] characterized the perpetrator of the crimes as an "animal,"[7] and contained counsel's personal opinion of the strength of the state's evidence.[8]

The prosecutors then made their closing argument. That argument deserves the condemnation it has received from every court to review it, although no court has held that the argument rendered the trial unfair. Several comments attempted to place some of the blame for the crime on the Division of Corrections, because Darden was on weekend furlough from a prison sentence when the crime occurred.[9] Some comments implied that the death penalty would be the only guarantee against a future similar act.[10] Others incorporated the defense's use of the word "animal."[11] Prosecutor McDaniel made several offensive comments reflecting an emotional reaction to the case.[12] These comments undoubtedly were improper. But as both the District Court and the original panel of the Court of Appeals (whose opinion on this issue still stands) recognized, it "is not enough that the prosecutors' remarks were undesirable or even universally condemned." The relevant question is whether the prosecutors' comments "so infected the trial with unfairness as to make the resulting conviction a denial of due process." *Donnelly v. DeChristoforo,* 416 U.S. 637, 94 S.Ct. 1868, 40 L.Ed.2d 431 (1974). Moreover, the appropriate standard of review for such a claim on writ of habeas corpus is "the narrow one of due process, and not the broad exercise of supervisory power." *DeChristoforo,* supra.

Under this standard of review, we agree with the reasoning of every court to consider these comments that they did not deprive petitioner of a fair trial. The prosecutors' argument did not manipulate or misstate the evidence, nor did it

5. "The Judge is going to tell you to consider the evidence or the lack of evidence. We have a lack of evidence, almost criminally negligent on the part of the Polk County Sheriff's Office in this case. You could go on and on about it."

6. "They took a coincidence and magnified that into a capital case. And they are asking you to kill a man on coincidence."

7. "The first witness you saw was Mrs. Turman, who was a pathetic figure; who worked and struggled all of her life to build what little she had, the little furniture store; and a woman who was robbed, sexually assaulted, and then had her husband slaughtered before her eyes, by what would have to be a vicious animal." Record 717. "And this murderer ran after him, aimed again, and this poor kid with half his brains blown away.... It's the work of an animal, there's no doubt about it."

8. "So they come up here and ask Citrus County people to kill the man. You will be instructed on lesser included offenses.... The question is, do they have enough evidence to kill that man, enough evidence? And I honestly do not think they do."

9. "As far as I am concerned, there should be another Defendant in this courtroom, one more, and that is the division of corrections, the prisons.... Can we expect him to stay in a prison when they go there? Can we expect them to stay locked up once they go there? Do we know that they're going to be out on the public with guns, drinking?" * * *

10. "I will ask you to advise the Court to give him death. That's the only way I know that he is not going to get out on the public. It's the only way I know. It's the only way I can be sure of it. It's the only way anybody can be sure of it now, because the people that turned him loose—."

11. "As far as I am concerned, and as Mr. Maloney said as he identified this man as an animal, this animal was on the public for one reason."

12. "He shouldn't be out of his cell unless he has a leash on him and a prison guard at the other end of that leash." Record 750. "I wish [Mr. Turman] had had a shotgun in his hand when he walked in the back door and blown his [Darden's] face off. I wish I could see him sitting here with no face, blown away by a shotgun." Record 758. "I wish someone had walked in the back door and blown his head off at that point." Record 759. "He fired in the boy's back, number five saving one. Didn't get a chance to use it. I wish he had used it on himself." Record 774. "I wish he had been killed in the accident, but he wasn't. Again, we are unlucky that time." Record 775. "Don't forget what he has done according to those witnesses, to make every attempt to change his appearance from September the 8th, 1973. The hair, the goatee, even the moustache and the weight. The only thing he hasn't done that I know of is cut his throat." Record 779. After this, the last in a series of such comments, defense counsel objected for the first time.

implicate other specific rights of the accused such as the right to counsel or the right to remain silent. Much of the objectionable content was invited by or was responsive to the opening summation of the defense. As we explained in *United States v. Young* [Note 4 infra], the idea of "invited response" is used not to excuse improper comments, but to determine their effect on the trial as a whole. The trial court instructed the jurors several times that their decision was to be made on the basis of the evidence alone, and that the arguments of counsel were not evidence. The weight of the evidence against petitioner was heavy; the "overwhelming eyewitness and circumstantial evidence to support a finding of guilt on all charges," 329 So.2d, at 291, reduced the likelihood that the jury's decision was influenced by argument. Finally, defense counsel made the tactical decision not to present any witness other than petitioner. This decision not only permitted them to give their summation prior to the prosecution's closing argument, but also gave them the opportunity to make a final rebuttal argument. Defense counsel were able to use the opportunity for rebuttal very effectively, turning much of the prosecutors' closing argument against them by placing many of the prosecutors' comments and actions in a light that was more likely to engender strong disapproval than result in inflamed passions against petitioner.[14] For these reasons, we agree with the District Court below that "Darden's trial was not perfect—few are—but neither was it fundamentally unfair." 513 F.Supp., at 958.[15]

Justice BLACKMUN, with whom Justice BRENNAN, Justice MARSHALL, and Justice STEVENS join, dissenting.

Although the Constitution guarantees a criminal defendant only "a fair trial [and] not a perfect one," this Court has stressed repeatedly in the decade since *Gregg v. Georgia,* 428 U.S. 153, 96 S.Ct. 2909, 49 L.Ed.2d 859 (1976), that the Eighth Amendment requires a heightened degree of reliability in any case where a State seeks to take the defendant's life. Today's opinion, however, reveals a Court willing to tolerate not only imperfection but a level of fairness and reliability so low it should make conscientious prosecutors cringe. * * * The following brief comparison of established standards of prosecutorial conduct with the prosecutors' behavior in this case merely illustrates, but hardly exhausts, the scope of the misconduct involved:

1. "A lawyer shall not ... state a personal opinion as to ... the credibility [of] a witness ... or the guilt or innocence of an accused." Model Rules of Professional Conduct, Rule 3.4(e). * * * Yet one prosecutor, White, stated: "I am convinced, as convinced as I know I am standing before you today, that Willie Jasper Darden is a murderer, that he murdered Mr. Turman, that he robbed Mrs. Turman and that he shot to kill Phillip Arnold. I will be convinced of that the rest of my life." And the other prosecutor, McDaniel, stated, with respect to Darden's testimony: "Well, let me tell you something: If I am ever over in that chair over

---

14. "Mr. McDaniel made an impassioned plea ... how many times did he repeat [it]? I wish you had been shot, I wish they had blown his face away. My God, I get the impression he would like to be the man that stands there and pulls the switch on him."

One of Darden's counsel testified at the habeas corpus hearing that he made the tactical decision not to object to the improper comments. Based on his long experience with prosecutor McDaniel, he knew McDaniel would "get much more vehement in his remarks if you allowed him to go on." By not immediately objecting, he hoped to encourage the prosecution to commit reversible error.

15. The dissenting opinion mistakenly argues that the Court today finds, in essence, that any error was harmless, and then criticizes the Court for not applying the harmless error standard. We do not decide the claim of prosecutorial misconduct on the ground that it was harmless error. In our view of the case, that issue is not presented. Rather, we agree with the holding of every court that has addressed the issue, that the prosecutorial argument, in the context of the facts and circumstances of this case, did not render respondent's trial unfair—i.e., that it was not constitutional error. * * *

there, facing life or death, life imprisonment or death, I guarantee you I will lie until my teeth fall out."

2. "The prosecutor should refrain from argument which would divert the jury from its duty to decide the case on the evidence, by injecting issues broader than the guilt or innocence of the accused under the controlling law, or by making predictions of the consequences of the jury's verdict." ABA Standards, The Prosecution Function, § 3–5.8(d). * * * Yet McDaniel's argument was filled with references to Darden's status as a prisoner on furlough who "shouldn't be out of his cell unless he has a leash on him." Again and again, he sought to put on trial an absent "defendant," the State Department of Corrections that had furloughed Darden. He also implied that defense counsel would use improper tricks to deflect the jury from the real issue. Darden's status as a furloughed prisoner, the release policies of the Department of Corrections, and his counsel's anticipated tactics obviously had no legal relevance to the question the jury was being asked to decide: whether he had committed the robbery and murder at the Turmans' furniture store. Indeed, the State argued before this Court that McDaniel's remarks were harmless precisely *because* he "failed to discuss the issues, the weight of the evidence, or the credibility of the witnesses."

3. "The prosecutor should not use arguments calculated to inflame the passions or prejudices of the jury." ABA Standards, § 3–5.8(c); see *Berger v. United States* [fn. f, p. 1430]. Yet McDaniel repeatedly expressed a wish "that I could see [Darden] sitting here with no face, blown away by a shotgun." Indeed, I do not think McDaniel's summation, taken as a whole, can accurately be described as anything but a relentless and single-minded attempt to inflame the jury. * * * Almost every page [of the transcript of the summation] contains at least one offensive or improper statement; some pages contain little else. The misconduct here was not "slight or confined to a single instance, but ... was pronounced and persistent, with a probable cumulative effect upon the jury which cannot be disregarded as inconsequential." *Berger v. United States.*

The Court presents what is, for me, an entirely unpersuasive one-page laundry list of reasons for ignoring this blatant misconduct. First, the Court says that the summations "did not manipulate or misstate the evidence [or] ... implicate other specific rights of the accused such as the right to counsel or the right to remain silent." With all respect, that observation is quite beside the point. The "solemn purpose of endeavoring to ascertain the truth ... is the *sine qua non* of a fair trial," * * * and the summations cut to the very heart of the Due Process Clause by diverting the jury's attention "from the ultimate question of guilt or innocence that should be the central concern in a criminal proceeding."

Second, the Court says that "[m]uch of the objectionable content was invited by or was responsive to the opening summation of the defense." The Court identifies four portions of the defense summation that it thinks somehow "invited" McDaniel's sustained barrage. The State, however, did not object to any of these statements, and, to my mind, none of them is so objectionable that it would have justified a tactical decision to interrupt the defense summation and perhaps irritate the jury. * * *

The third reason the Court gives for discounting the effects of the improper summations is the supposed curative effect of the trial judge's instructions: the judge had instructed the jury that it was to decide the case on the evidence and that the arguments of counsel were not evidence. But the trial court overruled Darden's objection to McDaniel's repeated expressions of his wish that Darden had been killed, thus perhaps leaving the jury with the impression that McDaniel's comments were somehow relevant to the question before them. The trial judge's instruction that the attorneys were "trained in the law," and thus that their "analysis of the issues" could be "extremely helpful," might also have suggested to the jury that the substance of McDaniel's tirade was pertinent to their deliberations.

Fourth, the Court suggests that because Darden enjoyed the tactical advantage of having the last summation, he was able to "tur[n] much of the prosecutors' closing argument against them." But the issue before the jury was whether Darden was guilty, not whether McDaniel's summation was proper. And the question before this Court is not whether we agree with defense counsel's criticism of the summation but whether the jury was affected by it. Since Darden was ultimately convicted, it is hard to see what basis the Court has for its naked assertion that "[d]efense counsel were able to use the opportunity for rebuttal very effectively." * * *

Fifth, the Court finds, in essence, that any error was harmless: "The weight of the evidence against petitioner was heavy; the 'overwhelming eyewitness and circumstantial evidence to support a finding of guilt on all charges,' 329 So.2d at 291, reduced the likelihood that the jury's decision was influenced by argument." * * * Every harmless-error standard that this Court has employed, however, shares two salient features. First, once serious error has been identified, the burden shifts to the beneficiary of the error to show that the conviction was not tainted. Second, although different formulations of the harmless-error standard differ in the level of confidence in the outcome required to overcome that burden, the question before a reviewing court is never whether the evidence would have been sufficient to justify conviction, absent an error, but, rather, whether the error undermines its confidence in the outcome of the proceeding to an unacceptable degree. See e.g., * * *; *Chapman v. California* [p. 1570]; *Kotteakos v. United States* [Notes 5–6, p. 1566].

Regardless of which test is used, I simply do not believe the evidence in this case was so overwhelming that this Court can conclude, on the basis of the written record before it, that the jury's verdict was not the product of the prosecutors' misconduct. The three most damaging pieces of evidence—the identifications of Darden by Phillip Arnold and Helen Turman and the ballistics evidence—are all sufficiently problematic that they leave me unconvinced that a jury not exposed to McDaniel's egregious summation would necessarily have convicted Darden. Arnold first identified Darden in a photo array shown to him in the hospital. The trial court suppressed that out-of-court identification following a long argument concerning the reliability and constitutionality of the procedures by which it was obtained. Mrs. Turman's initial identification was made under even more suggestive circumstances. She testified at trial that she was taken to a preliminary hearing at which Darden appeared in order "[t]o identify him." Instead of being asked to view Darden in a lineup, Mrs. Turman was brought into the courtroom, where Darden apparently was the only black man present. Over defense counsel's objection, after the prosecutor asked her whether "this man sitting here" was "the man that shot your husband," she identified Darden. * * * While the question whether the various in-and out-of-court identifications ought to have been suppressed is not now before the Court, my confidence in their reliability is nonetheless undermined by the suggestiveness of the procedures by which they were obtained, particularly in light of Mrs. Turman's earlier difficulties in describing the criminal.

Finally, the ballistics evidence is hardly overwhelming. The purported murder weapon was tied conclusively neither to the crime nor to Darden. Special Agent Cunningham of the FBI's Firearms Identification Unit testified that the bullets recovered at the scene of the crime "could have been fired" from the gun, but he was unwilling to say that they in fact had come from that weapon. He also testified, contrary to the Court's assertion, that rebored Smith & Wessons were fairly common. Deputy Sheriff Weatherford testified that the gun was discovered in a roadside ditch adjacent to where Darden had wrecked his car on the evening of the crime. But the gun was discovered the next day, and the ditch was also next to a bar's parking lot.

Darden testified at trial on his own behalf and denied any involvement in the robbery and murder. His account of his actions on the day of the crime was contradicted only by Mrs. Turman's and Arnold's identifications. Indeed, a number of the State's witnesses corroborated parts of Darden's account. The trial judge who had seen and heard Darden testify found that he "emotionally and with what appeared on its face to be sincerity, proclaimed his innocence." In setting sentence, he viewed the fact that Darden "repeatedly professed his complete innocence of the charges" as a mitigating factor.

Thus, at bottom, this case rests on the jury's determination of the credibility of three witnesses—Helen Turman and Phillip Arnold, on the one side, and Willie Darden, on the other. I cannot conclude that McDaniel's sustained assault on Darden's very humanity did not affect the jury's ability to judge the credibility question on the real evidence before it. Because I believe that he did not have a trial that was fair, I would reverse Darden's conviction; I would not allow him to go to his death until he has been convicted at a fair trial.

Notes and Questions

1. **Prohibited argument.**[a] Justice Blackmun's dissent notes three categories of prosecutorial argument that are universally deemed improper—expressions of personal opinion as to witness credibility or guilt of the accused, arguments that divert the jury from its responsibility to decide the case on the evidence by injecting broader issues or making predictions as to the consequences of the jury's verdict, and arguments calculated to inflame or appeal to prejudice. Other well established prohibitions bar arguments that impugn the integrity of defense counsel, that misstate the law, that refer to the possibility of a lenient sentence, or that refer to facts outside the record (including references to exclusion evidence). See Carlson.

While the formulations of prohibited categories of argument often utilize broad generalities, considerable guidance can be obtained from the specific limitations announced in judicial decisions. A prosecutor should have no doubt, for example, as to the impropriety of referring to statements of witnesses that were not introduced into evidence. See Gershman, § 2–4 (d) (1). However, even as to fairly well delineated standards, there are likely to be variations in appellate interpretations that create uncertainty as to particular types of argument. Thus, in applying the prohibition against expressions of personal belief as to the truthfulness of a witness' testimony, the courts have differed in their characterization of statements in which the prosecutor does not refer explicitly to his own viewpoint. For example, one court sustained, as no more than advocacy, the prosecutor's reference to "the 'reputable officers' and 'very sweet' complaining witness who testified for the Government," *Jackson v. United States,* 359 F.2d 260 (D.C.Cir.1966), while another viewed as improper the prosecutor's statement that the two complainants in a rape case "were good and fine girls and not the type the

---

a. See generally Albert Alschuler, *Courtroom Misconduct by Prosecutors and Trial Judges,* 50 Tex.L.Rev. 629 (1972); Ronald Carlson, *Argument to the Jury: Passion, Persuasion, and Legal Controls,* 33 St. Louis U.L.J. 787 (1989); Bennett Gershman, *Trial Error* *and Misconduct (1997)*; Henry Vess, *Walking A Tightrope: A Survey of Limitations on the Prosecutor's Closing Argument,* 645 J.Crim.L. & Criminology 22 (1973) (each cited hereafter by reference to the author's name).

defendant and his witnesses alleged they were," *Stout v. People,* 464 P.2d 872 (Colo.1970).

The limitation that perhaps most frequently lends itself to the drawing of fine lines is that barring the injecting of issues "broader than the guilt or innocence of the accused." As Vess notes, it usually is proper for the prosecutor "to dwell upon the end results of the crime and to urge a fearless administration of the criminal law." Courts also have accepted arguments that a conviction would deter others from committing similar crimes, but they suggest that such arguments may come close to the impermissible. Viewed as prohibited are arguments that assert that a guilty verdict would relieve community fears or would serve as a good example for the young people in the community. Courts have also condemned appeals to jurors as the taxpayers who pay for the costs of law enforcement. See Vess (collecting cases).

2. Is it appropriate for the prosecutor to use appeals to the emotion even where not proscribed by the traditional prohibitions? Consider Alschuler: "The basic problem * * * [presented is that] of the attitude with which a prosecutor should approach his courtroom tasks. Should he really be a man for all seasons, 'both an advocate, determined to convict the defendant, and a representative of the state, safeguarding the rights of all'? Or should he follow the line suggested by Whitney North Seymour, Jr. and act as a quasi-judicial officer in deciding whether to prosecute and then, once the trial begins, as a zealous champion who leaves the judging to the judges? My own answer to these questions is admittedly extreme: The prosecutor should not think of oratory as part of his job at all. He should avoid the 'glow and flow of the heat of forensics' and should, in fact, strive for more 'Chesterfieldian politeness.'[b] The prosecutor should forego not only appeals to prejudice, but any deliberate appeal to emotion.''

3. *Standard of review.* Jurisdictions vary in their approach under local law to the prerequisites for reversing a conviction based upon improper prosecutorial argument. Some apply what is basically the due process standard of *Darden;* others apply a standard more readily allowing reversal (as suggested by *Darden's* distinction as to review in the "exercise of supervisory power," see p. 1423). Even under a less restricted standard than due process, however, the touchstone for determining whether reversal is required remains possible prejudice.[c] In making that determination, appellate court commonly will look to the following factors: (1) whether the improper remarks were particularly egregious; (2) whether the improper remarks were only isolated or brief episodes in an otherwise proper argument; (3) whether the improper remarks were invited or provoked by the improper comments of the defense; (4) whether defense counsel made a timely and strong objection to the prosecutor's improper remarks, thereby indicating fear of prejudice; (5) whether the trial judge had taken appropriate corrective action, such as instructing the jury to disregard the improper remarks;[d] (6) whether the

b. The reference is to a comment in *Ballard v. United States,* 152 F.2d 941 (9th Cir. 1945), rev'd on other grounds, 329 U.S. 187, 67 S.Ct. 261, 91 L.Ed. 181 (1946): "It is our opinion that if the conduct of the prosecution in argument in this case constitutes error, then, the prosecution in every case is limited to a listless, vigorless summation of fact in Chesterfieldian politeness. Gone are the days of the great advocates whose logic glowed and flowed with the heat of forensics! Gone, except for counsel for the defense."

c. Many jurisdictions will assess possible prejudice under the harmless error standard

traditionally applied in the jurisdiction to non-constitutional errors (see Notes 5–6, p. 1566). Alschuler. Compare *Darden* at fn. 15.

d. While appellate courts gave considerable weight to curative instructions particularly where the instruction was directed specifically to the particular comment in question, they also recognize that certain errors simply cannot be cured by directing the jury to disregard what they have heard. See e.g., *United States v. Murray,* 784 F.2d 188 (6th Cir.1986) (instruction to disregard reference to a polygraph like telling jury to "unring a bell").

improper remarks were combined with other trial errors; and (7) whether there was overwhelming evidence of guilt. The end result will be dependent upon a consideration of all of these factors taken together; no single factor will necessarily control in itself.

4. *Invited response.* In *United States v. Young,* 470 U.S. 1, 105 S.Ct. 1038, 84 L.Ed.2d 1 (1985), the defense objected to reliance on the third factor noted above—the "invited response" doctrine—on the ground that "two wrongs do not make a right" and therefore an improper prosecution argument should as readily require a reversal even though made in response to an improper defense argument. The Supreme Court agreed that it was inappropriate for the prosecution to respond to the defense's improper argument with forensic misconduct of its own. The proper response, the Court stressed, is a prosecution objection, accompanied by a "request that the [trial] court give a timely warning [to defense counsel] and curative instructions to the jury." However, because a "criminal conviction is not to be lightly overturned on the basis of a prosecutor's comments alone," even though the prosecutor did not respond in the correct manner, the reviewing court cannot avoid evaluating the prosecutor's improper, responsive comments in light of the "opening salvo" of defense counsel. Recognition of this factor, the Court noted, should not be seen as giving a "license to make otherwise improper arguments," but simply as fulfilling the task of reviewing court, which is to determine whether the prosecutor's comments, "taken in context, unfairly prejudiced the defendant."[e] The Court added that the invited response doctrine was limited to situations in which the prosecutor's remarks were relevant to the earlier defense comments and designed to "right the scale."

5. *Defense objection.* Appellate courts ordinarily require an objection by defense to sustain a forensic misconduct claim on appeal, although exceptions are made for a serious instance of misconduct likely to have caused prejudice. See Gershman, § 6–2. The objection requirement has been questioned because (1) "it visits the carelessness of the lawyer upon his client," (2) "a jury is likely to resent repeated objections," and (3) "the defense attorney's complaint, even if sustained by the court, may have exactly the opposite effect from the one intended" in that it "may call attention to the prosecutor's improper remarks and reemphasize them in the jurors' minds." Alschuler. Is the answer to the second and third objections that defense counsel should at least call the trial court's attention to the misconduct outside the presence of the jury, so that the court can consider whether a mistrial, a curative instruction, or such other remedial action as might be appropriate? Where the prosecution's comments clearly are excessive, but defense has not objected, is it "the judge's duty, on his own initiative, to interrupt, admonish the offender and instruct the jury to disregard the improper argument"? *United States v. Sawyer,* 347 F.2d 372 (4th Cir.1965) (so indicating, notwithstanding recognition that defense counsel's silence may be due to a concern that an objection and curative instruction would serve to "focus [juror] attention on an aspect of the case unfairly prejudicial to his client").

6. *Defense argument.* In commenting upon the propriety of a prosecutor's closing argument, courts frequently refer to the special responsibility of the government's attorney (to ensure that "justice be done") and the likelihood that jurors will give special weight to the prosecutor's statements due to the prestige of

e. Could consideration of this factor also be grounded on other concerns? In one of its earliest rulings on improper closing argument, the Court noted that, if every inappropriate but responsive comment were grounds for reversal, "comparatively few verdicts would stand, since in the ardor of advocacy, and in the excitement of trial, even the most experienced counsel are occasionally carried away by this temptation." *Dunlop v. United States,* 165 U.S. 486, 17 S.Ct. 375, 41 L.Ed. 799 (1897).

the office.[f] Does this suggest that defense counsel should be given somewhat more leeway in judicial review of the propriety (or impact) of the defense's closing argument? It is traditionally stated that the prohibitions governing final argument apply equally to both sides; the defense counsel, like the prosecutor, cannot express a personal belief or opinion as to guilt or innocence, use arguments calculated to inflame the passions or prejudices of the jurors, seek to inject broader issues that divert the jury from its duty to decide the case on the evidence, etc. See Model Rules of Professional Conduct, R. 3.4 (single provision applicable to counsel for both sides). But consider Alschuler (noting that "rules need not be the same for both advocates," and suggesting that if a "defense attorney, through emotional appeal, is able to persuade a jury that his client's conviction would be unfair, there should be no great cause for alarm," for while "even an occasional conviction not based on the evidence is a terrifying prospect, an occasional 'nonevidentiary' acquittal is a tolerable and probably desirable occurrence").

Appellate courts infrequently have the opportunity to consider the propriety of defense counsel's argument, and when they do, commonly operate from a procedural context that requires consideration of more than that issue. As an acquittal cannot be challenged by prosecution appeal (see Ch. 27, § 3), the propriety of defense counsel's argument must be presented in a case in which the defendant himself is appealing. That is unlikely to occur, except in connection with one of three quite distinct defense objections. First, where the defense challenges the prosecution's closing argument, the propriety of the defense's closing argument may be raised by the prosecution under the "invited response" doctrine. See *United States v. Young,* supra Note 4. Second, where the trial court viewed the defense argument as so egregious as to require a mistrial, the defendant may challenge his subsequent retrial as violating the double jeopardy prohibition. As with the invited response doctrine, the applicable standard of review here, although giving consideration to the propriety of defense counsel's argument, also requires consideration of other factors. See *Arizona v. Washington,* Note 6, p. 1453. Finally, where the trial judge cut off defense argument as inappropriate, the defense may claim that such action constituted reversible error. Courts here tend to stress the broad discretion of the trial court, noting that the critical issue is not whether the appellate court agrees that counsel's argument overstepped the bounds of propriety, but whether "there has been a clear abuse of discretion resulting in some prejudice to the accused." *Hill v. State,* 517 N.E.2d 784 (Ind.1988) (trial court was "well within its discretion" when it admonished the jury to disregard defense counsel's reference to a cooperation agreement between witness and the prosecution as a "bribe").

7. *Sanctions and deterrence.* Numerous appellate courts have "bemoaned the 'disturbing frequency' and the 'unheeded condemnations'" of clearly improp-

---

f. Undoubtedly the most famous (and frequently quoted) statement along these lines is that of Justice Sutherland in *Berger v. United States,* 295 U.S. 78, 55 S.Ct. 629, 79 L.Ed. 1314 (1935): "The United States Attorney is the representative not of an ordinary party to a controversy, but of a sovereignty whose obligation to govern impartially is as compelling as its obligation to govern at all; and whose interest, therefore, in a criminal prosecution is not that it shall win a case, but that justice shall be done. As such, he is in a peculiar and very definite sense the servant of the law, the twofold aim of which is that guilt shall not escape or innocence suffer. He may prosecute with earnestness and vigor—indeed, he should do so. But, while he may strike hard blows, he is not at liberty to strike foul ones. It is as much his duty to refrain from improper methods calculated to produce a wrongful conviction as it is to use every legitimate means to bring about a just one. * * * It is fair to say that the average jury, in a greater or less degree, has confidence that these obligations, which so plainly rest upon the prosecuting attorney, will be faithfully observed. Consequently, improper suggestions, insinuations, and, especially, assertions of personal knowledge are apt to carry much weight against the accused when they should properly carry none."

er prosecutorial argument. Gershman, § 10.1. While some courts have suggested that "they might well be required to reverse convictions without a showing of prejudice to deter such prosecutorial misconduct, * * * this has been done only rarely." CRIMPROC § 23.5(b). The prevailing view is that expressed in the per curiam opinion in UNITED STATES v. MODICA, 663 F.2d 1173 (2d Cir.1981):

"We share the frustration voiced by commentators at the inability of some federal prosecutors to abide by well-established rules limiting the types of comments permissible in summation. But we disagree that the solution lies in reversing valid convictions. Ordering a new trial remains among the measures that the Court may apply in a particular case, and we believe that its availability has some deterrent effect. But its invocation is properly shunned when the misconduct has not substantially prejudiced a defendant's trial. Reversal is an ill-suited remedy for prosecutorial misconduct; it does not affect the prosecutor directly, but rather imposes upon society the cost of retrying an individual who was fairly convicted. * * *

"Judges and commentators have frequently criticized the high social cost and minimal benefits engendered by reversing convictions because of improperly obtained evidence. * * * To impose such a remedy in the present context is even less justifiable. Prosecutorial misconduct that causes no substantial prejudice has, by definition, not resulted in a constitutional deprivation; an illegal search or seizure, by contrast, perforce violates the Fourth Amendment. Furthermore, prosecutors act under the immediate supervision of trial judges; law-enforcement personnel, on the other hand, act beyond the view of judges, in the homes and on the persons of individuals under investigation. The need for a potent deterrent device is less compelling in the former situation, and the resulting cost to society is less justifiable. Finally, reversal of convictions seems even less likely to be effective in deterring prosecutors than it has been in affecting the conduct of police. The federal prosecutors in this Circuit tend to be relatively young attorneys, seeking valuable experience as a prelude to other professional endeavors; such individuals are unlikely to share the institutional concerns found in career law-enforcement personnel. By contrast, sanctions imposed directly upon young, upwardly mobile prosecutors are likely to evoke strong concern and direct response. * * *

"Recognizing the general inappropriateness of reversal as a sanction for nonprejudicial prosecutorial misconduct is a necessary first step in the task of fashioning remedies that are more appropriate and, hence, more likely to be invoked. * * * This court has repeatedly stated that the task of ensuring that attorneys conduct themselves pursuant to recognized ethical precepts falls primarily upon district courts. The district judge is in an especially well-suited position to control the overall tenor of the trial. He can order the offending statements to cease and can instruct the jury in such a manner as to erase the taint of improper remarks that are made. * * * The trial judge can interrupt to anticipate and cut off an improper line of argument. Once the offending remarks are made, the judge can strike them and forcefully instruct the jury as to their inappropriateness. If persuaded in a rare case that irreparable prejudice has occurred, the court retains the option of granting a motion for a mistrial.

"Beyond these traditional trial-conduct remedies, the court has a range of remedies that may, in appropriate circumstances, be directed specifically at the attorney. Initially, the court may consider a reprimand, delivered on the spot or deferred until the jury has been excused from the courtroom. Flagrant conduct, in violation of a court order to desist, may warrant contempt penalties. If the conduct has occurred on prior occasions, the court may wish to give serious consideration to a formal reference to the appropriate local grievance committee to assess the need for disciplinary proceedings.[g] Alternatively, persistent misconduct may warrant action by the court itself to initiate proceedings to determine the appropriateness of a suspension from practice before the District Court. We suspect that the message of a single 30–day suspension from practice would be far clearer than the disapproving remarks in a score of appellate opinions.

"The Court of Appeals also has power to fashion remedies directly against an attorney persistently engaging in improper courtroom conduct. A reprimand in a published opinion that names the prosecutor is not without deterrent effect. A Court of Appeals, exercising its supervisory power over the administration of criminal justice, may well have authority to direct the initiation of appropriate action in the District Court, or, alternatively, to take action of a disciplinary nature with respect to practice before the federal courts of the Circuit, including possible temporary suspensions. We need not probe the full extent of such authority at this time. We deem it sufficient to express our concerns and to alert the district courts to their range of remedies, with confidence that the proper discharge of their responsibilities will prove to be a sufficient deterrent."[h]

8. *Opening statements.* "The purpose of the opening statement is narrow and limited to a brief statement of the issues and an outline of what counsel believes he can support with competent and admissible evidence." A.B.A. Standards, *The Prosecution Function and the Defense Function,* 119 (1st ed. 1971). Since the opening statements are not to be argumentative, prohibitions against expressions of opinion, potentially inflammatory remarks, and the injection of irrelevant issues tend to be more strictly applied in reviewing opening statements as compared to closing statements. On the other hand, a prosecutor's "overzealous and harmful assertions in an opening statement" usually will be viewed as "cured" by an appropriate "court admonition and instructions to the jury to disregard." See *Wilhelm v. State,* 326 A.2d 707 (Md.1974).

SECTION 5. SUBMITTING THE CASE TO THE JURY

1. *Motion for judgment of acquittal.* The trial judge may not direct a verdict of guilty no matter how conclusive the evidence in the case may be. But in the overwhelming majority of jurisdictions, the trial judge—either upon his own motion or the motion of the defendant—may take the case from the jury because the evidence is insufficient to sustain a conviction. Such a motion, most commonly known as a motion for a directed verdict, is appropriate after the conclusion of the prosecution's case or at the close of all the evidence. The prevailing view is that "the criminal defendant is entitled to an acquittal if reasonable men could not conclude on the evidence taken in the light most favorable to the prosecution that guilt has been proved beyond a reasonable doubt."

g. The conventional wisdom, however, is that bar discipline rarely will be visited on prosecutors, Fred Zacharias, *Structuring the Ethics of Prosecutorial Trial Practice,* 44 Vand. L.Rev. 44, 49 (1991), and that view is supported by the most comprehensive available study, Richard Rosen, *Disciplinary Sanctions Against Prosecutors for Brady Violations: A Paper Tiger,* 65 N.C.L.Rev. 693 (1987). Consider also Tracey Meares, *Reward for Good Behavior: Influencing Prosecutorial Discretion and Conduct with Financial Incentives,* 64 Fordham L. Rev. 851 (1995) (proposing a fi-nancial bonus for prosecutors where the defense has not raised a contention of improper argument on appeal or the appellate court responded to such contentions by finding that the prosecutor behaved properly).

h. Consider also the subsequent rulings in *Bank of Nova Scotia,* Note 2, p. 973, and *United States v. Hasting,* Note 3, p. 1573, as to the lack of federal court authority to reverse a conviction in the absence of actual or presumed prejudice. *Bank of Nova Scotia* cited some of the same "alternative remedies" as *Modica.* See fn. g., p. 976.

If the defendant's motion for acquittal at the close of the prosecution's case is denied, the defendant then must make a tactical decision as to whether to introduce any evidence. If he declines to do so, he then preserves his right to appeal from the denial of the motion for acquittal, but if he introduces evidence he then may merely move for acquittal again at the close of all the evidence, at which time the court may consider evidence damaging to the defendant which may have come out (most likely on cross-examination) during presentation of the defendant's case. Appeal is possible only as to denial of the second motion.

2. *Summary and comment on the evidence.* "A jury trial in which the judge is deprived of the right to comment on the evidence and to express his opinion on the facts * * * is not the jury trial which we inherited." *Patton v. United States*, 281 U.S. 276, 288, 50 S.Ct. 253, 254, 74 L.Ed. 854 (1930). But, while the federal courts have retained this power, in the overwhelming majority of states this function of the trial judge was taken from him by constitutional provision, statute, or judicial decision. CRIMPROC § 24.6(e).

SECTION 6. DELIBERATIONS AND VERDICT

A. Unanimous Verdicts

1. Reconsider Note 3 at p. 1315.

2. In SCHAD v. ARIZONA, 501 U.S. 624, 111 S.Ct. 2491, 115 L.Ed.2d 555 (1991), the defendant was convicted of first degree murder, defined by state law as murder that is "wilful, deliberate or premeditated * * * or which is committed * * * in the perpetration of, or attempt to perpetrate * * * robbery." The case was submitted to the jury under instructions that did not require unanimity on either of the available theories of premeditated murder and felony murder. In an opinion joined by three other members of the Court, SOUTER, J., declared that the due process clause places "limits on a State's capacity to define different courses of conduct, or states of mind, as merely alternative means of committing a single offense, thereby permitting a defendant's conviction without jury agreement as to which course or state actually occurred." In concluding those limits were not exceeded in the instant case, the plurality opinion deemed "history and widely shared practice as concrete indications of what fundamental fairness and rationality require." * * *

"Thus it is significant that Arizona's equation of the mental states of premeditated murder and felony murder as species of the blameworthy state of mind required to prove a single offense of first-degree murder finds substantial historical and contemporary echoes. At common law, murder was defined as the unlawful killing of another human being with 'malice aforethought.' The intent to kill and the intent to commit a felony were alternative aspects of the single concept of 'malice aforethought.' Although American jurisdictions have modified the common law by legislation classifying murder by degrees, the resulting statutes have in most cases retained premeditated murder and some form of felony murder (invariably including murder committed in perpetrating or attempting to penetrate a robbery) as alternative means of satisfying the mental state that first-degree murder presupposes. * * *

"A series of state court decisions * * * have agreed that 'it was not necessary that all the jurors should agree in the determination that there was a deliberate and premeditated design to take the life of the deceased, or in the conclusion that the defendant was at the time engaged in the commission of a felony, or an attempt to commit one; it was sufficient that each juror was convinced beyond a reasonable doubt that the defendant had committed the crime of murder in the first degree as that offense is defined by the statute.' Although the state courts have not been unanimous in this respect, there is sufficiently widespread acceptance of the two mental states as alternative means of satisfying the *mens rea* element of the single crime of first-degree murder to persuade us that Arizona has not departed from the norm."

Cautioning that it cannot be said "that either history or current practice is dispositive," the plurality opinion next emphasized the lack of "moral disparity" in the two alternative mental states. "Whether or not everyone would agree that the mental state that precipitates death in the course of robbery is the moral equivalent of premeditation, it is clear that such equivalence could reasonably be found, which is enough to rule out the argument that this moral disparity bars treating them as alternative means to satisfy the mental element of a single offense." By contrast, SCALIA, J., concurring, relied solely upon the fact that the challenged practice was "as old as the common law and still in existence in the vast majority of States," and was critical of the plurality's "moral equivalence" test: "We would not permit, for example, an indictment charging that the defendant assaulted either X on Tuesday or Y on Wednesday, despite the 'moral equivalence' of those two acts."

WHITE, J., for the four dissenters, relying upon the holding in *In re Winship,* 397 U.S. 358, 90 S.Ct. 1068, 25 L.Ed.2d 368 (1970), that due process mandates "proof beyond a reasonable doubt of every fact necessary to constitute the crime with which [the defendant] is charged," objected that "the plurality affirms this conviction without knowing that even a single element of either of the ways for proving first-degree murder, except the fact of a killing, has been found by a majority of the jury, let alone found unanimously by the jury as required by Arizona law. * * * The problem is that the Arizona statute, under a single heading, criminalizes several alternative patterns of conduct. While a State is free to construct a statute in this way, it violates due process for a State to invoke more than one statutory alternative, each with different specified elements, without requiring that the jury indicate on which of the alternatives it has based the defendant's guilt."

3. In RICHARDSON v. UNITED STATES, 526 U.S. 813, 119 S.Ct. 1707, 143 L.Ed.2d 985 (1999), defendant was charged with violating a federal statute forbidding any person from "engag[ing] in a continuing criminal enterprise," defined as involving a violation of the drug statutes where "such violation is a part of a continuing series of violations." The government introduced evidence of more underlying drug offenses than the three assumed to be necessary to constitute a "series," and defendant was convicted following a jury instruction stating the jury had to agree that defendant had committed at least three such offenses but did not have to agree about which three. The Court, per BREYER, J., first noted:

"The question before us arises because a federal jury need not always decide unanimously which of several possible sets of underlying brute facts make up a particular element, say, which of several possible means the defendant used to commit an element of the crime. *Schad v. Arizona.* Where, for example, an element of robbery is force or the threat of force, some jurors might conclude that the defendant used a knife to create the threat; others might conclude he used a gun. But that disagreement—a disagreement about means—would not matter as long as all 12 jurors unanimously concluded that the Government had proved the necessary related element, namely that the defendant had threatened force.

"In this case, we must decide whether the statute's phrase 'series of violations' refers to one element, namely a 'series,' in respect to which the 'violations' constitute the underlying brute facts or means, or whether those words create several elements, namely the several 'violations,' in respect to *each* of which the jury must agree unanimously and separately. * * * If the statute creates a single element, a 'series,' in respect to which individual violations are but the means, then the jury need only agree that the defendant committed at least three of all the underlying crimes the Government has tried to prove. The jury need not agree about which three. On the other hand, if the statute makes each 'violation' a separate element, then the jury must agree unanimously about which three crimes the defendant committed."

In opting for the latter interpretation, the Court emphasized these considerations: (1) "To hold that each 'violation' here amounts to a separate element is consistent with a tradition of requiring jury unanimity where the issue is whether a defendant has engaged in conduct that violates the law." (2) The "statute's word 'violations' covers many different kinds of behavior of varying degrees of seriousness," which "increases the likelihood that treating violations simply as alternative means, by permitting a jury to avoid discussion of the specific factual details of each violation, will cover-up wide disagreement among the jurors about just what the defendant did, or did not, do." (3) Considering that the Court in *Schad* "indicated that the Constitution itself limits a State's power to define crimes in ways that would permit juries to convict while disagreeing about means, at least where that definition risks serious unfairness and lacks support in history or tradition," there is "no reason to believe that Congress intended to come close to, or to test, those constitutional limits when it wrote this statute." (4) This conclusion is supported by the analogy in "federal criminal law's treatment of recidivism," where "one finds that commission of a prior crime will lead to an enhanced punishment only when a relevant factfinder, judge, or jury has found that the defendant committed that specific individual prior crime."

KENNEDY, J., for the three dissenters, concluded that there is "no reason to think Congress thought it necessary for the jury to agree on which particular predicate offenses made up the continuing series before an enhanced punishment may be imposed." Speaking to the constitutionality of this interpretation, the dissent noted that "[t]he CCE statute does not in any way implicate the suggestion in *Schad* that an irrational single crime consisting of, for instance, either robbery or failure to file a tax return would offend due process." Other elements of the CCE statute in addition to the "series" element—action in concert with five or more persons, a leadership role for the defendant, and substantial criminal proceeds—"work together to channel the jury's attention toward a certain kind of ongoing enterprise." Those factors distinguished the majority's recidivism analogy (the dissent conceded that a habitual offender statute that had as its only element the "existence of a series of crime" and did not require jury unanimity as to each crime "would raise serious questions as to fairness and rationality because the jury's discretion would be so unconstrained"). As for the "moral equivalence" aspect of the plurality's test in *Schad*, the dissent argued that since "the continuity itself is what Congress sought to prohibit with the series element," it "makes no difference if the violations in the series involve comparable amounts of drugs."

B. SPECIAL VERDICTS

1. At Heald's state trial for being an accessory before the fact to an armed robbery, a question arose as to whether his proximity in the getaway car made him a principal because of constructive presence. The trial judge told the jury it must acquit if it found him to be a principal, and then told the jury to make two special findings in the event of a not guilty verdict: (i) whether it found the defendant not guilty "only because he was constructively present at the scene of the crime" (which would make the defendant a principal under state law); and (ii) whether the finding was "based upon the fact that the State failed to prove the elements of the crime of accessory before the fact beyond a reasonable doubt." Heald was convicted, and on habeas review, the First Circuit in HEALD v. MULLANEY, 505 F.2d 1241 (1st Cir.1974), concluded:

"Heald argues that any use of special verdicts and special questions in criminal cases is so alien to the Anglo–American tradition of trial by jury as to deny due process of law under the fourteenth amendment. He says that to require a jury to particularize or explain its general verdict of 'guilty' or 'not guilty' must inevitably undermine its independence. The instant case is said to be especially bad because a special finding was required only in the event of a 'not guilty' verdict.* * *

"This circuit's views on special questions in a federal criminal case are set forth in *United States v. Spock*, 416 F.2d 165 (1st Cir.1969). We held that there was a danger that such questions would 'catechize' a reluctant juror away from an acquittal towards a seemingly more 'logical' conviction. Yet

> 'the jury, as the conscience of the community, must be permitted to look at more than logic. .... If it were otherwise there would be no more reason why a verdict should not be directed against a defendant in a criminal case than in a civil one. The constitutional guarantees of due process and trial by jury require that a criminal defendant be afforded the full protection of a jury unfettered, directly or indirectly.'

Spock is in accord with general disapproval of special questions and verdicts in federal criminal cases. * * *

"The states generally decline to permit special verdicts and questions in criminal proceedings, although there are exceptions. See e.g., *State v. Ellis,* 137 S.E.2d 840 (N.C.1964) (separate verdicts on issues of paternity, non-support, and guilt utilized in criminal bastardy proceedings). * * * We cannot say that every specialized use that may emerge under state procedures and statutes necessarily violates the due process clause. Some usages may be exempt from the dangers described in *Spock;* for example, certain questions may plainly lack any capacity to catechize, color or coerce the jury's decision making.

"[W]e are satisfied that the two special questions were harmless and that Heald received a trial before an impartial jury whose independence was not placed in jeopardy. * * * It must be borne in mind that the two questions were merely designed to record whether an acquittal—had there been one—was based on the usual considerations (*viz.,* that guilt had not been proven), or whether it was based on a further defense-sponsored theory that if Heald was also a principal, he could not be convicted as an accessory. The latter theory was, it turned out, erroneous [as a matter of state law, as noted by the state appellate court]. Paradoxically, it made Heald's chances better the deeper his criminal involvement. By presenting that mistaken theory to the jury, the judge enlarged Heald's chances for acquittal, and it is difficult to see how the jury's consideration of questions designed only to distinguish between the alternate grounds of acquittal could have done him harm. Neither question called for an answer leading towards a verdict of guilt. The jury remained at all times free to acquit for the usual reasons; and the requirement that it label such an acquittal by saying 'Yes' to the question whether the state had failed to prove its case, does not, in this context, seem a significant burden."

Heald was a case in which the prosecution requested a special verdict over a defense objection. "Many courts also will allow special findings when a defendant requests such findings. In some circumstances, a defendant may conclude that forcing the jurors to record their determination on the specific elements of the crime will persuade a conviction-prone jury to consider acquittal. In others, the defense may conclude that any risks with respect to nullification and compromise verdicts are more than offset by the bearing that special findings will have on the use of collateral estoppel in subsequent prosecution or the ability to appeal a conviction." CRIMPROC § 24.10(a).

C. INCONSISTENT VERDICTS

1. In *United States v. Maybury,* 274 F.2d 899 (2d Cir.1960), a 2–1 majority of the court, rejected the government's argument that the rule laid down in *Dunn v. United States,* 284 U.S. 390, 52 S.Ct. 189, 76 L.Ed. 356 (1932), upholding jury verdicts in criminal cases despite inconsistency as between counts, applies when a criminal case has been tried to a judge. When the Second Circuit later reached the *Maybury* result as a constitutional matter in a habeas corpus case involving a state prisoner who objected to the apparent inconsistency within the trial judge's verdict finding him guilty and his accomplice not guilty, the Supreme Court reversed in HARRIS v. RIVERA, 454 U.S. 339, 102 S.Ct. 460, 70 L.Ed.2d 530 (1981):

"Although *Dunn* and *Dotterweich*[a] preclude a holding that inconsistency in a verdict is intolerable in itself, inconsistency nevertheless might constitute evidence of arbitrariness that would undermine confidence in the quality of the judge's conclusion. In this case, the Court of Appeals suggested the possibility that the trial judge might have relied on impermissible considerations such as the fact that neither respondent nor his wife testified, or knowledge of adverse information not contained in the record. Undeniably, these possibilities exist, but [w]e are not persuaded that an apparent inconsistency in a trial judge's verdict gives rise to an inference of irregularity in his finding of guilt that is sufficiently strong to overcome the well-established presumption that the judge adhered to basic rules of procedure.

"Other explanations for an apparent inconsistency are far more likely. Most apparent is the likelihood that the judge's actual observation of everything that transpired in the courtroom created some doubt about the guilt of one defendant that he might or might not be able to articulate in a convincing manner. In this case, if the judge was convinced beyond a reasonable doubt that respondent and his wife were both guilty, it would be most unfortunate if a concern about the plausibility of a lingering doubt about Robinson should cause him to decide to convict all three rather than to try to articulate the basis for his doubt.

"It is also possible that the judge may have made an error of law and erroneously assumed, for example, that Robinson should not be found guilty without evidence that he was to share in the proceeds of the larceny. There is no reason—and surely no constitutional requirement—that such an error pertaining to the case against Robinson should redound to the benefit of respondent.

"Even the unlikely possibility that the acquittal is the product of a lenity that judges are free to exercise at the time of sentencing but generally are forbidden to exercise when ruling on guilt or innocence, would not create a constitutional violation. We are aware of nothing in the Federal Constitution that would prevent a State from empowering its judges to render verdicts of acquittal whenever they are convinced that no sentence should be imposed for reasons that are unrelated to guilt or innocence. The Constitution does not prohibit state judges from being excessively lenient."

a. *United States v. Dotterweich,* 320 U.S. 277, 279, 64 S.Ct. 134, 135, 88 L.Ed. 48 (1943) (applying *Dunn* to verdicts that treat codefendants in a joint trial inconsistently).

2. A unanimous Court reaffirmed the *Dunn* rule in *United States v. Powell*, 469 U.S. 57, 105 S.Ct. 471, 83 L.Ed.2d 461 (1984), rejecting in the process the claim that *Dunn* had been undercut by *Ashe v. Swenson*, p. 1050: "The problem is that the same jury reached inconsistent results; once that is established, principles of collateral estoppel—which are predicated on the assumption that the jury acted rationally and found certain facts in reaching its verdict—are no longer useful." Defendant still had the ability to challenge the sufficiency of the evidence supporting the verdict, but where that would fail, the evidence being sufficient to support the conviction on the compound offense, it can hardly be said that the conviction was a "mistake" and the acquittal on the predicate offense was the "one the jury really wanted." Since the defendant was "given the benefit of her acquittal," notwithstanding adequate evidence to convict "on the counts on which she was acquitted, * * * it is neither irrational nor illogical to require her to accept the burden of conviction on the counts on which the jury convicted." Most states accept this analysis under state law and allow inconsistent verdicts, but a significant minority do not.

D.   The Deadlocked Jury

1. In *Allen v. United States*, 164 U.S. 492, 17 S.Ct. 154, 41 L.Ed. 528 (1896), the Court held that the trial judge had not committed error in giving the jury a supplemental instruction, when it returned during its deliberations, that "in a large proportion of cases absolute certainty could not be expected; that, although the verdict must be the verdict of each individual juror, and not a mere acquiescence in the conclusion of his fellows, yet they should examine the question submitted with candor, and with a proper regard and deference to the opinions of each other; that it was their duty to decide the case if they could conscientiously do so; that they should listen, with a disposition to be convinced, to each other's arguments; that, if much the larger number were for conviction, a dissenting juror should consider whether his doubt was a reasonable one which made no impression upon the minds of so many men, equally honest, equally intelligent with himself. If, upon the other hand, the majority were for acquittal, the minority ought to ask themselves whether they might not reasonably doubt the correctness of a judgment which was not concurred in by the majority." But in recent years a number of appellate courts have disapproved of the charge.[b]

2. The trial judge has discretionary power to discharge the jury in any criminal trial without the consent of either party when, after sufficient and reasonable time for deliberation, the jury cannot agree on a verdict. However, the court may abuse its discretion in discharging the jury too quickly, which will bar a

---

b. These courts have usually recommended that trial judges instead conform to the more guarded charge proposed in A.B.A. Standards § 15–4.4 (2d ed. 1980), which provides:

"(a) Before the jury retires for deliberation, the court may give an instruction which informs the jury: (i) that in order to return a verdict, each juror must agree thereto; (ii) that jurors have a duty to consult with one another and to deliberate with a view to reaching an agreement, if it can be done without violence to individual judgment; (iii) that each juror must decide the case for himself or herself, but only after an impartial consideration of the evidence with the other jurors; (iv) that in the course of deliberations, a juror should not hesi-

tate to reexamine his or her own views and change an opinion if the juror is convinced it is erroneous; and (v) that no juror should surrender his or her honest conviction as to the weight or effect of the evidence solely because of the opinion of the other jurors, or for the mere purpose of returning a verdict."

This more guarded charge, even when used in the sentencing phase of a death penalty case, was upheld in *Lowenfield v. Phelps*, 484 U.S. 231, 108 S.Ct. 546, 98 L.Ed.2d 568 (1988), as a permissible means of advancing the state's "strong interest in having the jury 'express the consciousness of the community on the ultimate question of life or death.' "

second trial of the defendant unless he consented to the discharge. See fn. b, p. 1453.

3. It is the general view that the court may send the jury back for additional deliberations even though the jury has indicated once, twice, or several times that it cannot agree or even after the jury has requested that it be discharged. However, the court may not require or threaten to require the jury to deliberate for an unreasonable length of time or for unreasonable intervals. See A.B.A. Standards, § 15–4(b) (2d ed. 1980).

E. The Rule Against Jurors Impeaching Their Verdicts vs. the Right of Confrontation

1. Courts have recognized a variety of actions by jurors that constitute "misconduct" and provide grounds for overturning a conviction. These include discussing the case outside of the jury deliberations, inspecting on their own the scene of the crime, conducting experiments, using a dictionary to define a term mentioned in the judge's charge, lying during voir dire and considering information about the case that comes from a source other than the trial (e.g., a newspaper). See CRIMPROC § 24.9(f). A major problem presented in any attempt to challenge a conviction on such a ground is establishing that the misconduct occurred. Particularly where the alleged misconduct occurred during the deliberations, the jurors often are the key witnesses to the misconduct. However, all jurisdictions place limits on the acceptance of juror testimony which challenges the jury's own process. See CRIMPROC § 24.9(g).[c] As to the constitutionality of those limits, consider the Notes below.

2. In *Parker v. Gladden,* 385 U.S. 363, 87 S.Ct. 468, 17 L.Ed.2d 420 (1966), a bailiff assigned to shepherd a sequestered jury in a state trial told them that defendant was guilty and that if there were any errors in reaching a verdict of guilty, the Supreme Court would correct it. Finding that the bailiff had, in a sense, become a witness against the defendant in violation of his right, under the Sixth and Fourteenth Amendments, to "be confronted with the witnesses against him," the Supreme Court reversed the conviction.

Parker led the New York Court of Appeals, in PEOPLE v. DE LUCIA, 229 N.E.2d 211 (N.Y.1967), to re-examine the applicability of the long familiar rule that "jurors may not impeach their own duly rendered verdict by statements or testimony averring their own misconduct within or without the jury room" to circumstances such as those present in the instant case, where several jurors not only made an unauthorized visit to the scene of the alleged crime, but actually re-enacted the alleged crime. A majority of the court, per KEATING, J., observed that "where, as in the case of statements regarding juryroom deliberations, every verdict might be rendered suspect, and jurors might become subjected to continuous posttrial harassment, the public policy reasons for holding such statements inadmissible must *ordinarily* override public injustice to a defendant, for here our jury system itself is at stake." (Emphasis added.) On the other hand, "statements concerning *outside influences* on a jury, occurring less frequently and more susceptible to adequate proof, should be admissible to show that the defendant

c. The general justification for such limits was set forth in *McDonald v. Pless*, 238 U.S. 264, 35 S.Ct. 783, 59 L.Ed. 1300 (1915): "[A]ll verdicts could be, and many would be, followed by an inquiry in the hope of discovering something which might invalidate the finding. Jurors would be harassed and beset by the defeated party in an effort to secure from them evidence of facts which might establish misconduct sufficient to set aside a verdict. If evidence thus secured could be thus used, the result would be to make what was intended to be a private deliberation the constant subject of public investigation; to the destruction of all frankness and freedom of discussion and conference."

was prejudiced, for here the danger to our jury system is minimal compared with the more easily proven prejudice to the defendant." (Emphasis added.) In the instant case, concluded the majority, the several jurors who went to the scene and re-enacted the alleged crime became, "to use the reasoning of the Supreme Court in *Parker,* * * * unsworn witnesses against the defendants in direct contravention of their right, under the Sixth Amendment, 'to be confronted with the witnesses' against them."

3. In TANNER v. UNITED STATES, 483 U.S. 107, 107 S.Ct. 2739, 97 L.Ed.2d 90 (1987), the trial judge declined to receive, on defendant's motion for a new trial, testimony from one juror that other jurors took alcohol and drugs during recess and fell asleep during the trial. The Supreme Court held, 5–4, that the trial judge was correct in concluding such evidence was inadmissible under Fed.R.Evid. 606(b).[d] Commenting on the wisdom of this rule, the majority, per O'CONNOR, J., stated:

"There is little doubt that post-verdict investigation into juror misconduct would in some instances lead to the invalidation of verdicts reached after irresponsible or improper juror behavior. It is not at all clear, however, that the jury system could survive such efforts to perfect it. Allegations of juror misconduct, incompetency, or inattentiveness, raised for the first time days, weeks, or months after the verdict seriously disrupt the finality of the process. Moreover, full and frank discussion in the jury room, jurors' willingness to return an unpopular verdict, and the community's trust in a system that relies on the decisions of laypeople would all be undermined by a barrage of post verdict scrutiny of juror conduct."

As for petitioners' claim that refusal to receive the juror's testimony infringed upon their Sixth Amendment right to a jury "both impartial and mentally competent," *Jordan v. Massachusetts,* 225 U.S. 167, 32 S.Ct. 651, 56 L.Ed. 1038 (1912), the majority responded that there were sufficient "other sources of protection" for this right: "The suitability of an individual for the responsibility of jury service, of course, is examined during *voir dire.* Moreover, during the trial the jury is observable by the court, by counsel, and by court personnel. Moreover, jurors are observable by each other, and may report inappropriate juror behavior to the court *before* they render a verdict. Finally, after the trial a party may seek to impeach the verdict by nonjuror evidence of misconduct. Indeed, in this case the District Court held an evidentiary hearing giving petitioners ample opportunity to produce nonjuror evidence supporting their allegations."

F. Post-Verdict Motions

1. *Motion for judgment of acquittal.* A motion for judgment of acquittal may be made following a guilty verdict, just as it may be made prior to the submission of the case to the jury. See Note 1, p. 1432. When made after the verdict, it is sometimes referred to as a motion for an acquittal "n.o.v." While some jurisdictions permit the post-verdict motion to be made only as a renewal of

---

d. Rule 606(b) provides: *"Inquiry into validity of verdict or indictment.* Upon an inquiry into the validity of a verdict or indictment, a juror may not testify as to any matter or statement occurring during the course of the jury's deliberations or to the effect of anything upon his or any other juror's mind or emotions as influencing him to assent to or dissent from the verdict or indictment or concerning his mental processes in connection therewith, except that a juror may testify on the question whether extraneous prejudicial information was improperly brought to the jury's attention or whether any outside influence was improperly brought to bear upon any juror. Nor may his affidavit or evidence of any statement by him concerning a matter about which he would be precluded from testifying be received for these purposes."

an earlier motion, most permit the post-verdict motion even if an earlier motion was not made. See e.g., Fed.R.Crim.P. 29(c). The motion challenges the sufficiency of the evidence, and the court applies the same standard as in a pre-verdict motion. See Note 1, p. 1432.

2. *Motion for a new trial (on grounds other than new evidence).* The motion for new trial may be based on a broad range of issues. In some jurisdictions, the governing rule or statute lists specific grounds, but the list usually includes a "catch-all" provision, e.g., that the "verdict is contrary to law and evidence." In other jurisdictions, the only statutory standard is that the new trial be "in the interest of justice," e.g., Fed.R.Crim.P. 33. A new trial motion often will raise a wide variety of alleged trial errors, such as the admission of improper evidence, variance between the indictment and proof, or improper joinder. Ordinarily, of course, these grounds will not be considered if the defendant failed to raise them at the appropriate time during the trial. In some jurisdictions, the defense must present in the new trial motion all objections that he intends to raise on appeal. Requiring a new trial motion as a prerequisite for appellate review is intended "to allow a trial court some opportunity to review and correct its own errors and, thereby, in some instances avoid the extra travail and expense of an appeal." *Graham v. State,* 249 N.E.2d 25 (Ind.1969).

Frequently, a motion for new trial will accompany a motion for judgment of acquittal since it provides an alternative device for challenging the sufficiency of the evidence. The motion for new trial gives the judge far broader authority in reviewing the evidence. Charles Alan Wright, *Federal Practice and Procedure—Criminal* § 553 (2d ed. 1982), observes: "On a motion for judgment of acquittal, the court is required to approach the evidence from a standpoint most favorable to the government, and to assume the truth of the evidence offered by the prosecution. If on this basis there is substantial evidence justifying an inference of guilt, the motion for acquittal must be denied. On a motion for new trial, however, * * * the court * * * may weigh the evidence and consider the credibility of witnesses. If the court reaches the conclusion that the verdict is contrary to the weight of the evidence and that a miscarriage of justice may have resulted, the verdict may be set aside and a new trial granted. It has been said that on such a motion, the court sits as a thirteenth juror * * * [although] the discretion of the court * * * should be exercised with caution and * * * a new trial [granted] only in exceptional cases in which the evidence preponderates heavily against the verdict." See also Note 3, p. 1481.

3. *Motion in arrest of judgment.* The scope of the motion in arrest of judgment generally is rather narrow. In the federal courts, for example, it extends only to (1) a lack of jurisdiction over the offense charged or (2) failure of the indictment to charge an offense. Fed.R.Crim.P. 34. These are the same defects that Rule 12(b)(2) says "shall be noticed by the court at any time during the pendency of the proceedings." See Note 4, p. 997. In some jurisdictions, the motion may also extend to a limited number of other issues, e.g., double jeopardy.

4. *Newly discovered evidence.* The requirements for a motion for a new trial based on newly discovered evidence were discussed in connection with *Bagley.* See fn. e, p. 1393. Ordinarily, the time period for making a motion based on newly discovered evidence is substantially longer than that for the ordinary new trial motion. See e.g., Fed.R.Crim.P. 33 (2 years as opposed to 7 days).

Where a defendant has been convicted and sentenced to death at a fair trial and fair capital sentencing proceeding, does the execution of that sentence violate the Constitution when the defendant now makes a showing of actual innocence through newly discovered evidence? In *Herrera v. Collins,* 506 U.S. 390, 113 S.Ct. 853, 122 L.Ed.2d 203 (1993), two Justices asserted that there "is no basis in text, tradition, or even contemporary practice (if that were enough), for finding in the Constitution a right to demand judicial consideration of newly discovered evidence of innocence brought forward after conviction." Three other Justices concluded there was such a right, "at least in capital cases," so that on federal habeas corpus the petitioner would be entitled to relief if he showed that he "probably is innocent." But the other four Justices did not reach that issue, for they concluded the petitioner had not made the "extraordinarily high" threshold showing of actual innocence which would be required were there such a right.

Consider Susan Bandes, *Simple Murder: A Comment on the Legality of Executing the Innocent,* 44 Buff. L Rev 501 (1996): "The New York Times recently told the shocking but not uncommon story of two people convicted of a murder it was now clear they did not commit, who have no legal means to establish their innocence and so remain behind bars. Both have been in prison in Oregon since 1990 for the crime. Oregon courts are not required to consider evidence discovered more than five days after imposition of sentence, and as of the date of the Times article, the state courts had refused to consider the corroborated confession of another man to the slaying. And of course, according to *Herrera,* federal habeas corpus relief was unavailable since the sole claim was actual innocence, with no independent constitutional claim.* * *

"What are the state court options for a convicted person in possession of newly discovered evidence of his innocence? The first possible avenue would be a motion for new trial. Yet as *Herrera* itself documents, nearly every state requires a motion for new trial based on newly discovered evidence to be made within a fairly short time period—most of them between sixty days and two years. Exculpatory evidence may occasionally surface in the statutorily prescribed time period, but given the typical narrow window, such evidence will frequently surface too late.

"The next possible line of attack is resort to state collateral remedies. All states place significant limits on the ability to raise newly discovered evidence collaterally, and some preclude introduction of such evidence entirely.* * *

"The *Herrera* Court held that executive clemency acts as the fail-safe in our criminal justice system. Although it recognized that states are not required to provide this mechanism, it found that all thirty-six states that authorize capital punishment provide for clemency. Clemency is a particularly poor vehicle for consideration of claims of newly discovered evidence of innocence. Clemency is a matter of grace, not of right. The grant is discretionary with the governor, and the decision is rarely guided by substantive standards. By its very nature, clemency assumes forgiveness for an act committed, not reassessment of guilt. The petitioner with newly discovered evidence requires a forum for consideration of that evidence."

Consider also U.S. Department of Justice, National Institute of Justice, *Convicted by Juries, Exonerated by Science: Case Studies on the Use of DNA Evidence to Establish Innocence after Trial* (1996) (discussing various cases in which new trial motions based on DNA evidence, made years after conviction, were considered by trial courts.) In recent years, several states have enacted specific provisions for granting DNA testing post-trial. See e.g. N.Y. Crim. Pro. Law § 440.30.

Chapter 26

REPROSECUTION AND THE BAN AGAINST DOUBLE JEOPARDY[aa]

SECTION 1. REPROSECUTION AFTER A MISTRIAL

ILLINOIS v. SOMERVILLE

410 U.S. 458, 93 S.Ct. 1066, 35 L.Ed.2d 425 (1973).

Justice REHNQUIST delivered the opinion of the Court.

We must here decide whether declaration of a mistrial over the defendant's objection, because the trial court concluded that the indictment was insufficient to charge a crime, necessarily prevents a State from subsequently trying the defendant under a valid indictment. We hold that the mistrial met the "manifest necessity" requirement of our cases, since the trial court could reasonably have concluded that the "ends of public justice" would be defeated by having allowed the trial to continue. Therefore the Double Jeopardy Clause of the Fifth Amendment * * * did not bar trial under a valid indictment.

On March 19, 1964, respondent was indicted by an Illinois grand jury for the crime of theft. The case was called for trial and a jury impaneled and sworn on November 1, 1965. The following day, before any evidence had been presented, the prosecuting attorney realized that the indictment was fatally deficient under Illinois law because it did not allege that respondent intended to permanently deprive the owner of his property. Under the applicable Illinois criminal statute, such intent is a necessary element of the crime of theft, and failure to allege intent renders the indictment insufficient to charge a crime. But * * * Illinois further provides that only formal defects, of which this was not one, may be cured by amendment. The combined operation of these rules of Illinois procedure and substantive law meant that the defect in the indictment was "jurisdictional"; it could not be waived by the defendant's failure to object, and could be asserted on

aa. This chapter deals only with the bearing of the double jeopardy clause upon multiple prosecutions. As for the combination of a criminal prosecution and a "punitive" civil sanction, see Note 5, p. 1409. The chapter builds upon discussions in earlier chapters that have considered other elements of the double jeopardy bar on multiple prosecutions. The limitations examined in §§ 1–3 of this chapter all proceed from the assumption that the multiple proceedings are for the same offense, building upon the discussion in Ch. 18, § 2 of what constitutes the "same offense" for double jeopardy. Those sections also build upon earlier discussions of the double jeopardy implications

of reprosecution for the same offense following the setting aside of a guilty plea. See Note 13, p. 1267, and *Ricketts v. Adamson,* p. 1268. Also relevant is the Chapter 18 discussion of multiple prosecutions that are the responsibility of a defendant having insisted on separate trials for different statutory offenses that constitute the same offense for double jeopardy purposes. See Note 3, p. 1047.

For an in-depth discussion of the material covered in this chapter, see Wayne R. LaFave, Jerold H. Israel, & Nancy J. King, Criminal Procedure Treatise (2d Ed. 1999) (available in Westlaw under the database CRIMPROC, and hereafter cited as CRIMPROC).

appeal or in a post-conviction proceeding to overturn a final judgment of conviction.

Faced with this situation, the Illinois trial court concluded that further proceedings under this defective indictment would be useless and granted the State's motion for a mistrial. On November 3, the grand jury handed down a second indictment alleging the requisite intent. Respondent was arraigned two weeks after the first trial was aborted, raised a claim of double jeopardy which was overruled, and the second trial commenced shortly thereafter. The jury returned a verdict of guilty, sentence was imposed, and the Illinois courts upheld the conviction. Respondent then sought federal habeas corpus * * *. The Seventh Circuit affirmed the denial of habeas corpus prior to our decision in *United States v. Jorn,* 400 U.S. 470, 91 S.Ct. 547, 27 L.Ed.2d 543 (1971). The respondent's petition for certiorari was granted, and the case remanded for reconsideration in light of *Jorn* and *Downum v. United States,* 372 U.S. 734, 83 S.Ct. 1033, 10 L.Ed.2d 100 (1963). On remand, the Seventh Circuit held that respondent's petition for habeas corpus should have been granted because * * * jeopardy had attached when the jury was impaneled and sworn and a declaration of mistrial over respondent's objection precluded a retrial under a valid indictment. For the reasons stated below, we reverse that judgment.

The fountainhead decision construing the Double Jeopardy Clause in the context of a declaration of a mistrial over a defendant's objection is *United States v. Perez,* 9 Wheat. (22 U.S.) 579 (1824). Mr. Justice Story, writing for a unanimous Court, set forth the standards for determining whether a retrial, following a declaration of a mistrial over a defendant's objection, constitutes double jeopardy * * *. In holding that the failure of the jury to agree on a verdict of either acquittal or conviction did not bar retrial of the defendant, Mr. Justice Story wrote:

> We think, that in all cases of this nature, the law has invested Courts of justice with the authority to discharge a jury from giving any verdict, whenever, in their opinion, taking all the circumstances into consideration, there is a manifest necessity for the act, or the ends of public justice would otherwise be defeated. They are to exercise a sound discretion on the subject; and it is impossible to define all the circumstances, which would render it proper to interfere. * * *

This formulation, consistently adhered to by this Court in subsequent decisions, abjures the application of any mechanical formula by which to judge the propriety of declaring a mistrial in the varying and often unique situations arising during the course of a criminal trial. The broad discretion reserved to the trial judge in such circumstances has been consistently reiterated in decisions of this Court. * * * In reviewing the propriety of the trial judge's exercise of his discretion, this Court following the counsel of Mr. Justice Story, has scrutinized the action to determine whether, in the context of that particular trial, the declaration of a mistrial was dictated by "manifest necessity" or the "ends of public justice."[a]

In *United States v. Perez,* * * * this Court held that "manifest necessity" justified the discharge of juries unable to reach verdicts, and therefore the Double Jeopardy Clause did not bar retrial. In *Simmons v. United States,* 142 U.S. 148, 12 S.Ct. 171, 35 L.Ed. 968 (1891), a trial judge dismissed the jury, over defendant's

---

a. In *Arizona v. Washington,* Note 6, p. 1453, the Court added the following comments on the meaning of the *Perez* "manifest necessity" standard: "The words 'manifest necessity' appropriately characterize the magnitude of the prosecutor's burden [in justifying the mistrial]. * * * [But] it is manifest that the key word 'necessity' cannot be interpreted literally; instead, contrary to the teaching of Webster, we assume that there are degrees of necessity and we require a 'high degree' before concluding that a mistrial is appropriate."

objection, because one of the jurors had been acquainted with the defendant, and therefore was probably prejudiced against the Government; this Court held that the trial judge properly exercised his power "to prevent defeat of the ends of justice." In *Thompson v. United States,* 155 U.S. 271, 15 S.Ct. 73, 39 L.Ed. 146 (1894), a mistrial was declared after the trial judge learned that one of the jurors was disqualified, he having been a member of the grand jury that indicted the defendant. Similarly, in *Lovato v. New Mexico,* 242 U.S. 199, 37 S.Ct. 107, 61 L.Ed. 244 (1916), the defendant demurred to indictment, his demurrer was overruled and a jury sworn. The district attorney, realizing that the defendant had not pleaded to the indictment after the demurrer had been overruled, moved for the discharge of the jury and arraignment of the defendant for pleading; the jury was discharged, the defendant pleaded not guilty, the same jury was again impaneled, and a verdict of guilty rendered. In both of those cases this Court held that the Double Jeopardy Clause did not bar reprosecution.

While virtually all of the cases turn on the particular facts and thus escape meaningful categorization, it is possible to distill from them a general approach, premised on the "public justice" policy enunciated in *United States v. Perez,* to situations such as that presented by this case. A trial judge properly exercises his discretion to declare a mistrial if an impartial verdict cannot be reached, or if a verdict of conviction could be reached but would have to be reversed on appeal due to an obvious procedural error in the trial. If an error would make reversal on appeal a certainty, it would not serve "the ends of public justice" to require that the Government proceed with its proof, when, if it succeeded before the jury, it would automatically be stripped of that success by an appellate court. This was substantially the situation in both *Thompson v. United States* and *Lovato v. New Mexico.* While the declaration of a mistrial on the basis of a rule or a defective procedure that lent itself to prosecutorial manipulation would involve an entirely different question, cf. *Downum v. United States,* supra, such was not the situation in the above cases or in the instant case.

In *Downum,* the defendant was charged with six counts of mail theft and forging and uttering stolen checks. A jury was selected and sworn in the morning, and instructed to return that afternoon. When the jury returned, the Government moved for the discharge of the jury on the ground that a key prosecution witness, for two of the six counts against defendant, was not present. The prosecution knew, prior to the selection and swearing of the jury, that this witness could not be found and had not been served with a subpoena. The trial judge discharged the jury over the defendant's motions to dismiss two counts for failure to prosecute and to continue the other four. This Court, in reversing the convictions on the ground of double jeopardy, emphasized that "[e]ach case must turn on its own facts," and held that the second prosecution constituted double jeopardy, because the absence of the witness and the reason therefor did not there justify, in terms of "manifest necessity," the declaration of a mistrial.

In *United States v. Jorn,* the Government called a taxpayer witness in a prosecution for willfully assisting in the preparation of fraudulent income tax returns. Prior to his testimony, defense counsel suggested he be warned of his constitutional right against compulsory self-incrimination. The trial judge warned him of his rights, and the witness stated that he was willing to testify and that the IRS agent who first contacted him warned him of his rights. The trial judge, however, did not believe the witness' declaration that the IRS had so warned him, and refused to allow him to testify until after he had consulted with an attorney. After learning from the Government that the remaining four witnesses were "similarly situated," and after surmising that they too had not been properly informed of their rights, the trial judge declared a mistrial to give the witnesses the opportunity to consult with attorneys. In sustaining a plea in bar of double jeopardy * * *, the plurality opinion of the Court, emphasizing the importance to the defendant of proceeding before the first jury sworn, concluded:

It is apparent from the record that no consideration was given to the possibility of a trial continuance; indeed, the trial judge acted so abruptly in discharging the jury that, had the prosecutor been disposed to suggest a continuance, or the defendant to object to the discharge of the jury, there would have been no opportunity to do so. When one examines the circumstances surrounding the discharge of this jury, it seems abundantly apparent that the trial judge made no effort to exercise a sound discretion to assure that, taking all the circumstances into account, there was a manifest necessity for the *sua sponte* declaration of this mistrial. *United States v. Perez.* Therefore, we must conclude that in the circumstances of this case, appellee's reprosecution would violate the double jeopardy provision of the Fifth Amendment.

* * * [R]espondent argues that our decision in *United States v. Jorn*, which respondent interprets as narrowly limiting the circumstances in which a mistrial is manifestly necessary, requires affirmance. Emphasizing the "valued right to have his trial completed by a particular tribunal," *United States v. Jorn*, respondent contends that the circumstances did not justify depriving him of that right. * * * We believe that in light of the State's established rules of criminal procedure the trial judge's declaration of a mistrial was not an abuse of discretion. Since this Court's decision in *Benton v. Maryland*, 395 U.S. 784, 89 S.Ct. 2056, 23 L.Ed.2d 707 (1969) [holding the double jeopardy prohibition applicable to the states under the Fourteenth Amendment, see Ch. 2, § 1], federal courts will be confronted with such claims that arise in large measure from the often diverse procedural rules existing in the 50 States. Federal courts should not be quick to conclude that simply because a state procedure does not conform to the corresponding federal statute or rule, it does not serve a legitimate state policy. * * *

In the instant case, the trial judge terminated the proceeding because a defect was found to exist in the indictment that was, as a matter of Illinois law, not curable by amendment. The Illinois courts have held that even after a judgment of conviction has become final, the defendant may be released on habeas corpus, because the defect in the indictment deprives the trial court of "jurisdiction." The rule prohibiting the amendment of all but formal defects in indictments is designed to implement the State's policy of preserving the right of each defendant to insist that a criminal prosecution against him be commenced by the action of a grand jury. The trial judge was faced with a situation similar to those in *Simmons, Lovato,* and *Thompson,* in which a procedural defect might or would preclude the public from either obtaining an impartial verdict or keeping a verdict of conviction if its evidence persuaded the jury. If a mistrial were constitutionally unavailable in situations such as this, the State's policy could only be implemented by conducting a second trial after verdict and reversal on appeal, thus wasting time, energy, and money for all concerned. Here the trial judge's action was a rational determination designed to implement a legitimate state policy, with no suggestion that the implementation of that policy in this manner could be manipulated so as to prejudice the defendant. This situation is thus unlike *Downum,* where the mistrial entailed not only a delay for the defendant, but also operated as a post-jeopardy continuance to allow the prosecution an opportunity to strengthen its case. Here the delay was minimal, and the mistrial was, under Illinois law, the only way in which a defect in the indictment could be corrected. Given the established standard of discretion set forth in *Perez, Gori,* and *Hunter,* we cannot say that the declaration of a mistrial was not required by "manifest necessity" and the "ends of public justice." * * *

The determination by the trial court to abort a criminal proceeding where jeopardy has attached is not one to be lightly undertaken, since the interest of the defendant in having his fate determined by the jury first impaneled is itself a weighty one. *United States v. Jorn.* Nor will the lack of demonstrable additional prejudice preclude the defendant's invocation of the double jeopardy bar in the absence of some important countervailing interest of proper judicial administration. Ibid. But where the declaration of a mistrial implements a reasonable state policy and aborts a proceeding that at best would have produced a verdict that could have been upset at will by one of the parties, the defendant's interest in proceeding to verdict is outweighed by the competing and equally legitimate demand for public justice. Reversed.

Justice WHITE, with whom Justice DOUGLAS and Justice BRENNAN join, dissenting.

* * * Despite the generality of the *Perez* standard, some guidelines have evolved from past cases, as this Court has reviewed the exercise of trial court discretion in a variety of circumstances. *Jorn* and *Downum,* for example, make it abundantly clear that trial courts should have constantly in mind the purposes of the Double Jeopardy Clause to protect the defendant from continued exposure to embarrassment, anxiety, expense, and restrictions on his liberty, as well as to preserve his "valued right to have his trial completed by a particular tribunal." * * * Although the exact extent of the emotional and physical harm suffered by Somerville during the period between his first and second trial is open to debate, it cannot be gainsaid that Somerville lost "his option to go to the first jury and, perhaps, end the dispute then and there with an acquittal." *United States v. Jorn.* * * * There was not, in this case any more than in *Downum* and *Jorn,* "manifest necessity" for the loss of that right.

The majority recognizes that "the interest of the defendant in having his fate determined by the jury first impaneled is itself a weighty one," but finds that interest outweighed by the State's desire to avoid "conducting a second trial after verdict and reversal on appeal [on the basis of a defective indictment], thus wasting time, energy, and money for all concerned." The majority finds paramount the interest of the State in "keeping a verdict of conviction if its evidence persuaded the jury." Such analysis, however, completely ignores the possibility that the defendant might be acquitted by the initial jury. It is, after all, that possibility—the chance to "end the dispute then and there with an acquittal,"—that makes the right to a trial before a particular tribunal of importance to a defendant. * * *

Apparently the majority finds "manifest necessity" for a mistrial and the retrial of the defendant in "the State's policy of preserving the right of each defendant to insist that a criminal prosecution against him be commenced by the action of a grand jury" and the implementation of that policy in the absence from Illinois procedural rules of any procedure for the amendment of indictments. Conceding the reasonableness of such a policy, it must be remembered that the inability to amend an indictment does not come into play, and a mistrial is not necessitated, unless an error on the part of the State in the framing of the indictment is committed. Only when the indictment is defective—only when the State has failed to properly execute its responsibility to frame a proper indictment—does the State's procedural framework necessitate a mistrial. * * *

Justice MARSHALL, dissenting.

* * * A fair reading of [*Jorn* and *Downum*] shows how the balance should properly be struck here. The first element to be considered is the necessity for declaring a mistrial. That I take to mean consideration of the alternatives available to the judge confronted with a situation in the midst of trial that seems

to require correction. In *Downum,* for example, * * * because the [missing] witness was essential to presentation of only two of the six counts * * * there was no necessity to declare a mistrial as to all six. Similarly, in *Jorn,* * * * the alternative of interrupting the trial briefly so that the witnesses might consult with attorneys was available but not invoked.

A superficial examination of this case might suggest that there were no alternatives except to proceed where "reversal on appeal [would be] a certainty." (Majority opinion, supra). * * * The majority treats it as unquestionably clear that the failure to allege that intent in the indictment made the indictment fatally defective. And indeed, since the time of trial Illinois courts have so held. * * * But the answer was not so clear when the trial judge made his decision. The Illinois Code of Criminal Procedure had just recently been amended to require that an indictment name the offense and the statutory provision alleged to have been violated, and that it set forth the nature and elements of the offense charged. Ill.Rev.Stat. ch. 38, § 111–3(a) (1963). The indictment here was sufficiently detailed to meet the federal requirement that the indictment "contains the elements of the offense intended to be charged, 'and sufficiently apprises the defendant of what he must be prepared to meet.'" *Hagner v. United States,* 285 U.S. 427, 52 S.Ct. 417, 76 L.Ed. 861 (1932); see also *Russell v. United States* [p. 986].

Had the Illinois courts been made aware of the substantial constitutional questions raised by rigid application of an archaic mode of reading indictments, they might well have refused to hold that the defect in the indictment here was jurisdictional and nonwaivable. Conscientious state trial judges certainly must attempt to anticipate the course of interpretation of state law. But they must also contribute to that course by pointing out the constitutional implications of alternative interpretations. * * * Thus, [the trial judge] could have proceeded to try the case on the first indictment, risking reversal as any trial judge does when making rulings of law, but with no guarantee of reversal.

If the only alternative to declaring a mistrial did require the trial judge to ignore the tenor of previous state decisional law though, perhaps declaring a mistrial would have been a manifest necessity. But there obviously was another alternative. The trial judge could have continued the trial. The majority suggests that this would have been a useless charade. But to a defendant, forcing the Government to proceed with its proof would almost certainly not be useless. The Government might not persuade the jury of the defendant's guilt. * * *

Once it is shown that alternatives to the declaration of a mistrial existed, as they did here, we must consider whether the reasons which led to the declaration were sufficient, in light of those alternatives, to overcome the defendant's interest in trying the case to the jury. * * * Here again the majority mischaracterizes the state policy at stake here. What is involved is not, as the majority says, "the right of each defendant to insist that a criminal prosecution against him be commenced by the action of a grand jury." Rather, the interest is in making the defect in the indictment here jurisdictional and not waivable by a defendant. Ordinarily, a defect in jurisdiction means that one institution has invaded the proper province of another. Such defects are not waivable because the State has an interest in preserving the allocation of competence between those institutions. Here, for example, the petty jury would invade the province of the grand jury if it returned a verdict of guilty on an improper indictment. However, allocation of jurisdiction is most important when one continuing body acts in the area of competence reserved to another continuing body. While it may be desirable to keep a single petty jury from invading the province of a single grand jury, surely that interest is not so substantial as to outweigh the "defendant's valued right to have his trial completed by a particular tribunal." * * *

I believe that *Downum* and *Jorn* are controlling.[2] As in those cases, the trial judge here did not pursue an available alternative, and the reason which led him to declare a mistrial was prosecutorial negligence, a reason that this Court found insufficient in *Downum*.[b]

Notes and Questions

1. ***When jeopardy attaches.*** Under the rule traditionally applied in federal courts, jeopardy attaches in jury trials when the jury is "empaneled and sworn" and it attaches in bench trials when the "first witness is sworn." *Somerville* apparently assumed that the federal rule was constitutionally mandated and therefore applied to state as well as federal cases. That assumption was challenged, unsuccessfully, in CRIST v. BRETZ, 437 U.S. 28, 98 S.Ct. 2156, 57 L.Ed.2d 24 (1978). In that case a mistrial had been granted, on grounds conceded not to constitute manifest necessity, after the jury had been sworn but before the first witness had been sworn. The state courts upheld a reprosecution on the basis of a state rule that jeopardy did not attach until the first witness was sworn in either jury or bench trials. The state argued in this regard that the contrary federal standard for jury trials was "no more than an arbitrarily chosen rule of convenience, similar in its lack of constitutional status to the federal requirement of an unanimous verdict of 12 jurors." Rejecting the state's contention, the majority opinion (per STEWART, J.) stressed the historic development of the double jeopardy bar.

Justice Stewart explained that the Fifth Amendment guarantee initially had been viewed as applicable only after the trial had been completed and a judgment of conviction or acquittal had been entered. This reflected the Blackstonian description of the double jeopardy prohibition as the embodiment of the common law pleas of *autrefois convict* and *autrefois acquit*—a criminal law doctrine "akin to the [civil law's] *res judicata*," and similarly designed "to preserve the finality of judgment." However, another strand of the English common law had advanced "a strong tradition that, once bonded together, a jury should not be discharged until it had completed its solemn task of announcing a verdict." This tradition was treated as an aspect of double jeopardy protection in *Perez*, and it soon became an integral part of "double jeopardy jurisprudence." Thus, Justice Stewart concluded, "regardless of its historic origin," the defendant's "valued right to have his trial completed before a particular tribunal" had become an essential element of the Fifth Amendment guarantee. It followed that the "federal rule that jeopardy

2. So far I have read *Jorn* and *Downum* as restrictively as they can be fairly read. But those cases, I believe, should be read more expansively. They show to me that "manifest necessity" cannot be created by errors on the part of the prosecutor or judge; it must arise from some source outside their control. *Wade v. Hunter,* was clearly such a case. So were the cases that the majority says involved situations where "an impartial verdict cannot be reached." In those cases, a juror or the jury as a whole, uncontrolled by the judge or prosecutor, prevented the trial from proceeding to a verdict. *United States v. Perez; Simmons v. United States; Thompson v. United States.*

b. At an earlier point in Justice Marshall's dissent, a footnote on *Downum* stated: *"Downum* may perhaps be read as stating a prophylactic rule. While the evil to be avoided is the intentional manipulation by the prosecutor of

the availability of his witnesses, it may be extremely difficult to secure a determination of intentional manipulation. Proof will inevitably be hard to come by. And the relations between judges and prosecutors in many places may make judges reluctant to find intentional manipulation. Thus, a general rule that the absence of crucial prosecution witnesses is not a reason for declaring a mistrial is necessary. Although the abuses of misdrawing indictments are less apparent than those of manipulating the availability of witnesses, I believe that, even if *Downum* is based on the foregoing analysis—an analysis which appears nowhere in the opinion—a similar prophylactic rule is desirable here. For example, in this case the State gained two weeks to strengthen a weak case. This is far longer than the two-day delay in *Downum,* * * *."

attaches when the jury is empaneled and sworn" similarly had become part of that guarantee. This was so because: "[T]he federal rule * * * reflects and protects the defendant's interest in retaining a chosen jury. * * * [Basic] double jeopardy concerns—the finality of judgments, the minimization of harassing exposure to the harrowing experiences of a criminal trial, the valued right to continue with the chosen jury—have combined to produce the federal law that in a jury trial jeopardy attaches when the jury is empaneled and sworn. * * * [This standard as to] the time when jeopardy attaches in a jury trial [thereby] 'serves as the linchpin for all double jeopardy jurisprudence.' "

Justice BLACKMUN, in a separate concurrence, stressed that more than the defendant's right "to have his trial completed by a particular tribunal" was at stake. If only that right were considered, jeopardy might attach at the very beginning of the jury selection process, rather than with the swearing of the jury. Consideration also must be given, he noted, to the other interests of the defendant noted in the majority opinion. "I would," he concluded, "bring all these interests into focus * * * at the point where the jury is sworn because it is then and there that the defendant's interest in the jury reaches its highest plateau, because the opportunity for prosecutorial overreaching thereafter increases substantially and because stress and possible embarrassment for the defendant from then on is sustained."

Justice POWELL, joined by the Chief Justice and Justice Rehnquist, dissented. Justice Powell contended that "neither history nor doctrinal reasoning" supported the view that the double jeopardy guarantee was designed to protect the defendant's interest in retaining the selected and sworn jury because that factfinder might be "favorably inclined toward his cause." That type of interest was not protected for bench trials, he noted, since a case could readily be reassigned from one judge to another before jeopardy attached with the start of the trial. The "one event" that should bring the defendant's interest in a particular tribunal within the constitutional guarantee, the dissent concluded, was the "beginning of the fact finder's work" through the "hearing of evidence."

2. *Explaining Perez.* Although most often citing the defendant's valued right to have his trial completed before a particular tribunal, the Supreme Court also has referred to other concerns in explaining the double jeopardy grounding of the *Perez* rule. In *United States v. DiFrancesco,* 449 U.S. 117, 101 S.Ct. 426, 66 L.Ed.2d 328 (1980), Justice Blackman's opinion for the Court, in the course of discussing the "general design" of the double jeopardy prohibition, noted that " 'central to the objective of the prohibition' * * * is the barrier to affording the prosecution another opportunity to supply evidence which it failed to muster in the first proceeding." The opinion added that "implicit in this is the thought that if the government may reprosecute, it gains an advantage from what it learns at the first trial about the strengths of the defense case and weaknesses of its own." *Perez*, it is argued, also finds support in its response to that concern.

Commentators so viewing *Perez* acknowledge that the barrier noted in *DiFrancesco* is achieved primarily through double jeopardy doctrines preserving verdict finality—that is, through the core double jeopardy rules prohibiting reprosecution following an acquittal or conviction (see sections 2 and 3 infra). They view *Perez*'s "manifest necessity" rule, in turn, as providing a form of supplementary protection to the verdict-finality doctrines. *Perez* does this, so the argument goes, by providing a barrier against judicial or prosecutorial use of the mistrial to avoid a final verdict. The greatest need in this regard is to bar prosecutorial verdict avoidance that is motivated by a desire to increase the probabilities of gaining a conviction through the use of a second opportunity to establish guilt. Included here would be cases where the prosecution, fearing an acquittal, seeks a mistrial to obtain a more favorably disposed jury, to take advantage of what it learned at the first trial, or to gather additional evidence. However, even where such a motivation is not present, and there is no indication that the defendant's chances of obtaining an acquittal would be reduced by allowing a mistrial and subsequent retrial, verdict avoidance is still thought to require some administrative justification because it denies to the defense other values (e.g., the sense of repose) that are provided through verdict finality under the core double jeopardy prohibitions.

The commentators suggest that it is because the *Perez* standard operates only to provide such supplemental protection of the core value of verdict finality, rather than as a rule directly enforcing that value, that *Perez* allows for a case-by-case balancing of interests, giving considerable discretion to the trial court. This approach, they note, stands in stark contrast to the "flat" prohibitions governing reprosecutions following acquittals and convictions. See George Thomas III, *An Elegant Theory of Double Jeopardy*, 1988 Ill.L.Rev. 827; Akhil Amar, *Double Jeopardy Law Made Simple*, 106 Yale L.J. 1807 (1997) (the "most sensible" understanding of the guarantee, in light of its common law history is that jeopardy runs from the filing of the indictment but does not end until there is a "final winner"; thus, the resolution of the mistrial issue is properly left to "flexible case-specific fair play ideals of due process" rather than the "hard and fast rules of the double jeopardy clause"). Consider also George Thomas III, *Double Jeopardy* 87–91 (1998) (arguing that the Court misread *Perez*, as Justice Story there accepted the Blackstonian view that the protection of the double jeopardy clause attached only to an acquittal or conviction, and spoke of manifest necessity, not as a constitutional matter, but simply to give guidance to trial courts in the exercise of their unreviewable discretion to discharge a jury before it reached a verdict).

3. *The scope of the Somerville dissents.* Can the rationale of the *Somerville* dissents be squared with the *Simmons, Thompson,* and *Lovato* cases cited by the majority at pp. 1444–45? Are those cases less readily characterized as presenting situations in which the mistrials were "occasioned by official error"?[a] Would the dissenters say that in these cases too, there was no justification for denying those defendants their "opportunity to go to the first jury, and, perhaps, end[ing] the dispute then and there with an acquittal"? Indeed, was there arguably a greater justification for denying the defendants that opportunity in *Lovato* and *Somerville* because the defense counsel in those cases might well have been aware of the error but decided for tactical reasons not to raise it pretrial, but to wait to raise it post-trial? Neither error would have adversely impacted the defense at trial, yet both if raised before trial would have readily been cured without affording the defense any significant benefit. Thus, the preferred defense strategy would have been not to raise the error pretrial, but to go through a fair trial and possibly be acquitted, but then if convicted, raise the error post-trial (as a jurisdictional defect will be noticed at any point), and gain the advantage of a new trial. See Note 8, p. 999 (discussing that strategy as to pleading errors such as that in *Somerville*).

4. *"Nonwaivable defects."* There was no indication in *Thompson* that the trial judge there had considered the possibility of proceeding with eleven jurors, and that presumably was not an option. What if the particular jurisdiction's law allowed continuation of the case with an 11–person jury, but only upon agreement

---

a. There appeared to be a clear instance of administrative error in *Lovato*, although arguably more on the part of the trial court than the prosecutor, in the failure to have the defendant initially enter a plea to the indictment. In *Thompson*, the Court's opinion offered no explanation as to how a grand juror happened to be seated as a petit juror. In *Simmons*, the juror had apparently lied in voir dire when asked whether he was acquainted with the defendant, but while the Court did note that the mistrial was based on information not known to the trial court when the jury was sworn, it did not stress the culpability of the juror in this regard.

of both parties and the judge, and the prosecutor or judge refused to agree? See e.g., *People v. Loving,* 136 Cal.Rptr. 851 (Cal.App.1977) (where juror failed to appear and state insisted on its right to 12–person jury, mistrial was appropriate though defendant sought to complete the trial with 11 jurors); *Hutchens v. District Court,* 423 P.2d 474 (Okl.Crim.App.1967) (mistrial inappropriate where it was discovered that one of the jurors was the mother-in-law of a deputy sheriff, but the state refused to proceed with an 11–person jury for no "cogent or compelling reason"); *State v. Gorwell,* 661 A.2d 718 (Md.1995) (reprosecution would be barred if prosecutor's refusal to consent to jury of less than 12 evidenced a deliberate intent to gain a more favorable opportunity to convict, but evidence here did not support such a finding).

5. *Reconciling Somerville and Downum.* As Justice Marshall notes, the prosecutor in *Downum* could have proceeded to trial and could have obtained a valid conviction on four counts without the missing witness. However, the reprosecution held to be barred in *Downum* involved all six counts, including the two on which that witness' testimony was essential. As to those two counts, what distinguishes *Downum* from *Somerville*? Can the cases be distinguished on the ground that the prosecutor's error in *Downum,* unlike that in *Somerville,* "lent itself to prosecutorial manipulation" (p. 1445)? Consider Stephen Schulhofer, *Jeopardy and Mistrials,* 125 U.Pa.L.Rev. 449, 469–70 (1977): "In neither case was the difficulty likely to be injected deliberately so that the prosecution would have an escape hatch if its case should go badly. If anything, the difficulty in *Downum* was less susceptible to prosecutorial manipulation: a prosecutor might hope for conviction on a technically defective indictment, but he or she scarcely could expect to convict without the witnesses essential to prove the case." Compare Jerold Israel, *Criminal Procedure, The Burger Court, and The Legacy of the Warren Court,* 75 Mich.L.Rev. 1319, 1353 (1977): "In *Downum,* the prosecution's error was in an area [obtaining additional witnesses] where the potential existed for manipulation * * *; indeed the mistrial was granted for the very purpose of granting the prosecution 'an opportunity to strengthen its case,' 410 U.S. at 469. * * * While the actual error in *Downum* itself was not the product of manipulation, [if] the Court [were to] accept that type of error as a basis for a mistrial, it might be difficult to distinguish those cases that actually did involve manipulation." Consider also Justice Marshall's suggestion (fn. b, p. 1449) that *Downum* may be viewed as applying a "prophylactic rule." ·

In *Arizona v. Washington,* Note 6 infra, the Court commented: "The strictest scrutiny is appropriate when the basis for the mistrial is the unavailability of critical prosecution evidence or when there is reason to believe that the prosecutor is using the superior resources of the State to harass or to achieve a tactical advantage over the accused." In light of this statement and the *Downum* ruling, how much room is available to the trial judge to grant a mistrial for the purpose of allowing the prosecution to gain the testimony of a missing witness. Consider in this regard the following cases: *Davis v. State,* 318 S.E.2d 202 (Ga.App.1984) (mistrial justified when essential prosecution witness, for whom runaway warrant previously had been issued, left unsecured juvenile shelter in which she was to have remained overnight pending resumption of trial the following morning); *State v. Messier,* 686 P.2d 272 (N.M.App.1984) (manifest necessity justified mistrial where videotape of child victim's testimony proved to be inaudible and child was unavailable to testify in person because of illness and potential emotional harm that might result; while it was "arguable" that the prosecutor should have previously checked the tape, "in this age of advanced technology," he was not "derelict" in "failing to do so"). Consider also Thomas, *Double Jeopardy,* supra Note 3 (court should ask whether, if the trial had continued, the evidence would have been insufficient to convict, and if that seems likely, the mistrial should be viewed as an "acquittal equivalent" and bar reprosecution, without regard to "whether the prosecution was at fault for the lack of evidence").

6. *Arizona v. Washington.* The leading post-*Somerville* decision applying the *Perez* standard is ARIZONA v. WASHINGTON, 434 U.S. 497, 98 S.Ct. 824, 54 L.Ed.2d 717 (1978). In that case, defense counsel, in his opening statement, told the jury that they would learn through defense testimony that the prosecutor had suppressed exculpatory evidence at a previous trial and that this "misconduct" had caused the Arizona Supreme Court to grant a new trial in the case. The prosecutor then moved for a mistrial, arguing that defense counsel's statement was clearly improper, that it had prejudiced the jury, and that "the prejudice could not be repaired by any cautionary instruction." The defense counsel disagreed on all points, and the trial court took the motion under advisement. The court expressed concern that an erroneous mistrial might bar reprosecution, but eventually granted a mistrial after the defense counsel was unable to present any legal support for his contention that his opening statement had been proper. In issuing its ruling, the trial court did not expressly note that there was "manifest necessity" nor expressly state that it had considered alternatives to the mistrial order. Defendant's double jeopardy objection to his subsequent reprosecution was rejected by the state courts, but it was upheld by the lower federal courts on a federal habeas corpus challenge. Those habeas rulings did not consider whether manifest necessity actually existed, but held that the state trial court had committed constitutional error in failing to make either a specific finding that manifest necessity existed or a specific finding that alternatives to a mistrial were inadequate. A divided Supreme Court (6–3) reversed.

The Supreme Court majority, per STEVENS, J., initially held that the lower federal courts had erred in insisting on explicit findings as to the presence of manifest necessity. In this case the basis for the trial judge's ruling was "adequately disclosed by the record," which included "an extensive argument of counsel prior to the judge's ruling." Where the trial record provides "sufficient justification" for the mistrial ruling, the "state judge's mistrial declaration is not subject to [constitutional] attack * * * simply because he failed to find 'manifest necessity' in those words or to articulate on the record all the factors which informed the deliberate exercise of his discretion."

The majority also concluded that the trial record adequately established the "high degree of necessity" (see fn. a, p. 1444) required to justify a mistrial. In reaching this conclusion, the majority initially noted that, in making certain types of mistrial determinations, trial judges must be given "broad discretion" in deciding "whether or not 'manifest necessity' justifies a discharge of the jury." The classic illustration of such a determination, it noted, was the trial judge's decision as to whether to discharge or require further deliberations from a "hung jury."[b] Similarly, the majority continued, "along the spectrum of trial problems which may warrant a mistrial and which vary in their amenability to appellate

b. The *Washington* Court noted that, "in this situation, there are compelling reasons for allowing the trial judge to exercise broad discretion." If trial judges were deterred by stringent appellate review from discharging juries "unable to reach a verdict after protracted * * * deliberations," the end result could be jury verdicts "result[ing] from pressures inherent in the situation rather than the considered judgment of all of the jurors," as well as the encouragement of judges to "employ coercive means to break the apparent deadlock." Although appellate courts grant great deference to a trial court's decision to discharge a hung jury, a lack of manifest necessity has been found where the surrounding circumstances indicate that the trial judge failed to take account of the defendant's interest in obtaining a verdict in his first trial. Circumstances considered include: whether the defendant objected to the discharge; the length of the deliberations; the length and complexity of the trial; the potential impact of exhaustion or coercion on any verdict that could reached. See e.g., CRIMPROC § 25.2(e).

scrutiny, the difficulty which led to the mistrial in this case also falls in an area where the trial judge's determination is entitled to special respect." Explaining why this was so, and why the trial judge's ruling accordingly met the *Perez* standard, Justice Stevens reasoned:

"We * * * start from the premise that defense counsel's comment was improper and may have affected the impartiality of the jury. We recognize that the extent of the possible bias cannot be measured, and that the District Court was quite correct in believing that some trial judges might have proceeded with the trial after giving the jury appropriate cautionary instructions. In a strict, literal sense, the mistrial was not 'necessary.' Nevertheless, the overriding interest in the evenhanded administration of justice requires that we accord the highest degree of respect to the trial judge's evaluation of the likelihood that the impartiality of one or more jurors may have been affected by the improper comment. The consistent course of decision in this Court in cases involving possible juror bias supports this conclusion. * * * The Court here discusses *Simmons v. United States* and *Thompson v. United States,* described in *Somerville* [pp. 1444–45]. * * *

"An improper opening statement unquestionably tends to frustrate the public interest in having a just judgment reached by an impartial tribunal. Indeed, such statements create a risk, often not present in the individual juror bias situation, that the entire panel may be tainted. The trial judge, of course, may instruct the jury to disregard the improper comment. In extreme cases, he may discipline counsel, or even remove him from the trial as he did in *United States v. Dinitz* [p. 1458]. Those actions, however, will not necessarily remove the risk of bias that may be created by improper argument. Unless unscrupulous defense counsel are to be allowed an unfair advantage, the trial judge must have the power to declare a mistrial in appropriate cases. The interest in orderly, impartial procedure would be impaired if he were deterred from exercising that power by a concern that anytime a reviewing court disagreed with his assessment of the trial situation a retrial would automatically be barred. The adoption of a stringent standard of appellate review in this area, therefore, would seriously impede the trial judge in the proper performance of his 'duty, in order to protect the integrity of the trial, to take prompt and affirmative action to stop ... professional misconduct.' Id.

"There are compelling institutional considerations militating in favor of appellate deference to the trial judge's evaluation of the significance of possible juror bias. He has seen and heard the jurors during their *voir dire* examination. He is the judge most familiar with the evidence and the background of the case on trial. He has listened to the tone of the argument as it was delivered and has observed the apparent reaction of the jurors. In short, he is far more 'conversant with the factors relevant to the determination' than any reviewing court can possibly be.

"Our conclusion that a trial judge's decision to declare a mistrial based on his assessment of the prejudicial impact of improper argument is entitled to great deference does not, of course, end the inquiry. * * * The trial judge * * * 'must always temper the decision whether or not to abort the trial by considering the importance to the defendant of being able, once and for all, to conclude his confrontation with society through the verdict of a tribunal he might believe to be favorably disposed to his fate.' *United States v. Jorn* [p. 1445]. In order to ensure that this interest is adequately protected, reviewing courts have an obligation to satisfy themselves that, in the words of Mr. Justice Story, the trial judge exercised 'sound discretion' in declaring a mistrial. Thus, if a trial judge acts irrationally or irresponsibly, cf. *United States v. Jorn,* supra, his action cannot be condoned. But our review of this record indicates that this was not such a case. * * * We are * * * persuaded by the record that the trial judge acted responsibly and deliberately, and accorded careful consideration to respondent's interest in having the trial concluded in a single proceeding. Since he exercised 'sound discretion' in handling the sensitive problem of possible juror bias created by the improper comment of defense counsel, the mistrial order is supported by the 'high degree' of necessity which is required in a case of this kind.[35]"

Dissenting Justice MARSHALL, joined by Justice Brennan, noted that his "disagreement with the majority" was a "narrow one." Justice Marshall stated: "I [do not] quarrel with the proposition that reviewing courts must accord substantial deference to a trial judge's determination that the prejudicial impact of an improper opening statement is so great as to leave no alternative but a mistrial to secure the ends of public justice. Where I part ways from the Court is in its assumption that an 'assessment of the prejudicial impact of improper argument,' sufficient to support the need for a mistrial may be implied from this record." Justice Marshall stressed that the improper remarks of the defense counsel "occupied only one page of a long opening statement" and did not produce an immediate objection from the prosecutor, although he had vigorously interrupted the opening statement on other points. Justice Marshall also noted that the anticipated length of the trial made it "not unlikely that, had the jury been appropriately instructed * * *, any prejudice would have dissipated before deliberations were to begin." Under these circumstances, the dissent reasoned, the "necessity for a mistrial was not manifest on the record" and the Court therefore should insist that the record otherwise "makes clear" that the trial court did actually weigh alternatives and conclude that a mistrial was justified by manifest necessity.[c]

7. *Washington and Gori.* In *Gori v. United States*, 367 U.S. 364, 81 S.Ct. 1523, 6 L.Ed.2d 901 (1961), the trial judge, "on his own motion and with neither approval nor objection by counsel," declared a mistrial during the government's direct examination of its fourth witness. The trial judge apparently had believed that the prosecutor's questioning "presaged inquiry calculated to inform the jury of other crimes by the accused" and had declared the mistrial "to forestall" that prejudice. A divided Supreme Court (5–4) held that reprosecution was not barred by double jeopardy. The majority viewed the mistrial order as "neither apparently justified nor clearly erroneous" and emphasized the need for granting the trial court leeway in the exercise of its discretion. The majority concluded: "We are unwilling, where it clearly appears that a mistrial has been granted in the sole interest of the defendant, to hold that its necessary consequence is to bar all retrial."

Following *Jorn* [p. 1445], several commentators suggested that *Gori* was no longer a viable precedent insofar as it granted broad deference to a mistrial granted *sua sponte* by a trial judge where that the mistrial was ordered in the interest of protecting the defendant against possible prejudice. The *Jorn* plurality

---

35. Two considerations, while not determinative, add support to this conclusion. First, crowded calendars throughout the Nation impose a constant pressure on our judges to finish the business at hand. Generally, they have an interest in having the trial completed as promptly as possible, an interest which frequently parallels the constitutionally protected interest of the accused in having the trial concluded by a particular tribunal. Second, respondent does not attempt to demonstrate specific prejudice from the mistrial ruling, other than the harm which always accompanies retrial.

c. Lower courts have varied in their approach to records that do not clearly indicate

that the trial court considered alternatives. See *Abdi v. Georgia*, 744 F.2d 1500 (11th Cir.1984) (an immediate sua sponte declaration of a mistrial does not necessarily evidence "an abrupt or precipitous decision that failed to consider the alternatives"); *State v. Stevens*, 892 P.2d 889 (Idaho 1995) (where judge did not give counsel "a meaningful opportunity to be heard" on the mistrial question, and therefore did not know how the defense perceived the prosecutorial misconduct that led to the mistrial, trial court did not have before it sufficient information to consider "scrupulously" the alternatives).

opinion had rejected the government's contention that a mistrial, even if not necessary, should not bar a retrial where the mistrial was intended to benefit defendant. Its reasoning clearly rejected the view that greater deference should be given to the trial judge's ruling simply because the judge sought to protect the defendant. Adopting a broader reading, some commentators argued that the implicit message of the *Jorn* reasoning was that *Gori* erred in giving any deference to a judge's mistrial ruling where it was aimed at benefitting the defense and there was no indication that the defense itself preferred the mistrial over other alternatives. Did *Washington* implicitly reject that broader reading, and require that "great deference" be given to the trial judge's decision as to what is needed to respond to an event creating possible jury bias, without regard to whether that bias would have favored one side or another?

Consider Schulhofer, Note 5 supra, suggesting that such deference is not appropriate where an improper comment may have created bias against the defendant. In such a case, it is argued, defense counsel is in a far better position to determine whether a mistrial is in the best interests of the defendant and a mistrial therefore should not be granted unless the defendant prefers the mistrial over other alternatives. But compare *United States ex rel. Stewart v. Hewitt*, 517 F.2d 993 (3d Cir.1975) (suggesting that the need to preserve the "appearance of impartiality" justifies granting a mistrial even though the event precipitating the mistrial creates potential prejudice primarily for the defendant and the defendant would prefer to complete the trial; *Stewart* found that the "ends of public justice" justified granting a mistrial over defendant's expressed wishes when the court discovered that the tip-staff servicing the jurors was the father of the homicide victim); *State v. Glover*, 517 N.E.2d 900 (Ohio 1988) (stressing the deference that must be given to a trial judge who granted a mistrial, following improperly aggressive tactics of defense, out of concern that counsel's actions were so offensive as to have prejudiced the jury against the defendant, and noting that the broad language in *Gori* as to the deference due the judge was "quoted with approval" in *Kennedy*, see fn. 7 at p. 1460).

8. *Lower court cases.* Professor Schulhofer, Note 5 supra, after reviewing nearly 200 appellate court decisions decided after *Somerville*, concluded that "little consensus exists among the courts regarding either the factors that should be analyzed or the result that should be reached in recurring factual contexts." Do the cases that follow evidence such a disarray or do they suggest meaningful distinctions drawn in accordance with the general analysis suggested by Supreme Court precedent?

(a) During the third day of a murder trial, defendant suffered a collapsed lung which required his hospitalization for an estimated 7 to 10 days. Defense counsel requested that a continuance be granted and that the jury, which had been sequestered, be allowed to go home. The prosecutor took no position on the defense proposal, but did suggest that a mistrial would not create double jeopardy problems. The trial court discharged the jury "on its own motion," with the judge noting: "I don't think I have any alternative [in] fairness to both the respondent and the state." See *Dunkerley v. Hogan*, 579 F.2d 141 (2d Cir.1978) (divided court holding the mistrial was not justified under *Perez* standard since the record suggested no reason why the continuance requested by the defense would not have been a "feasible and practical solution"). Compare *In re Dunkerley*, 376 A.2d 43 (Vt.1977) (reaching an opposite conclusion on the same facts, but considering, as the primary alternative to the mistrial, the continuation of the trial with the defendant waiving his right to be present, another proposal that had been offered by defense counsel).

(b) After the defendant had completed his testimony, defense counsel, in the presence of the jury, offered to have the defendant respond to any questions that the jury might wish to ask him. The court then excused the jury and asked defense counsel why the court had not been told in advance that the defense wanted to follow such an unusual procedure. Defense counsel stated that the procedure had been used elsewhere and he considered it appropriate. The judge then held that the procedure was improper, noted that defense counsel's announcement had "contaminated" the jury, and declared a mistrial. *Strawn v. State ex rel. Anderberg,* 332 So.2d 601 (Fla.1976) (mistrial justified under *Perez:* while "there well may have been better ways, after meditation, to dispose of the crisis, * * * we are unable to say that [the judge's] decision was an abuse of discretion"). Compare *People v. Johnson,* 240 N.W.2d 729 (Mich.1976) (where defense counsel inadvertently inquired of police officer whether the defendant had asked to take a lie detector test, mistrial was not justified by manifest necessity; mere mention of a polygraph test does not constitute reversible error but may be cured by appropriate instructions to the jury).

    9. ***Defense "consent" to the mistrial.*** In the cases discussed above, the mistrial was declared over the objection of the defendant or without giving the defendant an opportunity to take a position on the mistrial. To what extent should the applicable double jeopardy standard be different where the defendant either requested the mistrial or expressly acquiesced in the court's suggestion that a mistrial be declared? The materials that follow deal with this issue as well as others relating to a defense consent to a mistrial.

OREGON v. KENNEDY
456 U.S. 667, 102 S.Ct. 2083, 72 L.Ed.2d 416 (1982).

    Justice REHNQUIST delivered the opinion of the Court.

    * * * Respondent was charged with the theft of an oriental rug. During his first trial, the State called an expert witness on the subject of Middle Eastern rugs to testify as to the value and the identity of the rug in question. On cross-examination, respondent's attorney apparently attempted to establish bias on the part of the expert witness by asking him whether he had filed a criminal complaint against respondent. The witness eventually acknowledged this fact, but explained that no action had been taken on his complaint. On redirect examination, the prosecutor sought to elicit the reasons why the witness had filed a complaint against respondent, but the trial court sustained a series of objections to this line of inquiry.[1] The following colloquy then ensued:

    "Prosecutor: Have you ever done business with the Kennedys?"

    "Witness: No, I have not."

    "Prosecutor: Is that because he is a crook?"

The trial court then granted respondent's motion for a mistrial.

    When the State later sought to retry respondent, he moved to dismiss the charges because of double jeopardy. After a hearing at which the prosecutor testified, the trial court found as a fact that "it was not the intention of the prosecutor in this case to cause a mistrial." On the basis of this finding, the trial court held that double jeopardy principles did not bar retrial, and respondent was then tried and convicted.

    Respondent then successfully appealed to the Oregon Court of Appeals, which sustained his double jeopardy claim. * * * The Court of Appeals accepted the trial

---

    1. The Court of Appeals later explained that respondent's "objections were not well taken, and the judge's rulings were probably wrong." 49 Or.App. 415, 417, 619 P.2d 948, 949 (1980).

court's finding that it was not the intent of the prosecutor to cause a mistrial. Nevertheless, the court held that retrial was barred because the prosecutor's conduct in this case constituted what it viewed as "overreaching." Although the prosecutor intended to rehabilitate the witness, the Court of Appeals expressed the view that the question was in fact "a direct personal attack on the general character of the defendant." This personal attack left respondent with a "Hobson's choice—either to accept a necessarily prejudiced jury, or to move for a mistrial and face the process of being retried at a later time." * * *

Where the trial is terminated over the objection of the defendant, the classical test for lifting the double jeopardy bar to a second trial is the "manifest necessity" standard first enunciated in Justice Story's opinion for the Court in *United States v. Perez.* * * * The "manifest necessity" standard provides sufficient protection to the defendant's interests in having his case finally decided by the jury first selected while at the same time maintaining "the public's interest in fair trials designed to end in just judgments." But in the case of a mistrial declared at the behest of the defendant, quite different principles come into play. Here the defendant himself has elected to terminate the proceedings against him, and the "manifest necessity" standard has no place in the application of the Double Jeopardy Clause. *United States v. Dinitz,* 424 U.S. 600, 96 S.Ct. 1075, 47 L.Ed.2d 267 (1976). Indeed, the Court stated [in an earlier case]: "If [defendant] had *requested* a mistrial * * *, there would be no doubt that if he had been successful, the Government would not have been barred from retrying him."[a]

Our cases, however, have indicated that even where the defendant moves for a mistrial, there is a narrow exception to the rule that the Double Jeopardy Clause is no bar to retrial. See e.g., *United States v. Dinitz.* The circumstances under which respondent's first trial was terminated require us to delineate the bounds of that exception more fully than we have in previous cases.

Since one of the principal threads making up the protection embodied in the Double Jeopardy Clause is the right of the defendant to have his trial completed before the first jury empaneled to try him, it may be wondered as a matter of original inquiry why the defendant's election to terminate the first trial by his

---

a. *Dinitz,* supra, offered the most extensive discussion of why "a motion by the defendant for mistrial is ordinarily assumed to remove any barrier to reprosecution, even if the defendant's motion is necessitated by prosecutorial or judicial error." The Court there noted:

"The distinction between mistrials declared by the court *sua sponte* and mistrials granted at the defendant's request or with his consent is wholly consistent with the protections of the Double Jeopardy Clause. Even when judicial or prosecutorial error prejudices a defendant's prospects of securing an acquittal, he may nonetheless desire 'to go to the first jury and, perhaps, end the dispute then and there with an acquittal.' *United States v. Jorn,* supra. Our prior decisions recognize the defendant's right to pursue this course in the absence of circumstances of manifest necessity requiring a *sua sponte* judicial declaration of mistrial. But it is evident that when judicial or prosecutorial error seriously prejudices a defendant, he may have little interest in completing the trial and obtaining a verdict from the first jury. The defendant may reasonably conclude that a continuation of the tainted proceeding would result in a conviction followed by a

lengthy appeal and, if a reversal is secured, by a second prosecution. In such circumstances, a defendant's mistrial request has objectives not unlike the interests served by the Double Jeopardy Clause—the avoidance of the anxiety, expense, and delay occasioned by multiple prosecutions.

"The Court of Appeals viewed the doctrine that permits a retrial following a mistrial sought by the defendant as resting on a waiver theory. The court concluded, therefore, that 'something more substantial than a Hobson's choice' is required before a defendant can 'be said to have relinquished voluntarily his right to proceed before the first jury.' * * * But traditional waiver concepts have little relevance where the defendant must determine whether or not to request or consent to a mistrial in response to judicial or prosecutorial error. In such circumstances, the defendant generally does face a 'Hobson's choice' between giving up his first jury and continuing a trial tainted by prejudicial, judicial or prosecutorial error. The important consideration, for purposes of the Double Jeopardy Clause, is that the defendant retains primary control over the course to be followed in the event of such error."

own motion should not be deemed a renunciation of that right for all purposes. We have recognized, however, that there would be great difficulty in applying such a rule where the prosecutor's actions giving rise to the motion for mistrial were done "in order to goad the [defendant] into requesting a mistrial." *United States v. Dinitz.* In such a case, the defendant's valued right to complete his trial before the first jury would be a hollow shell if the inevitable motion for mistrial were held to prevent a later invocation of the bar of double jeopardy in all circumstances. But the precise phrasing of the circumstances which *will* allow a defendant to interpose the defense of double jeopardy to a second prosecution where the first has terminated on his own motion for a mistrial have been stated with less than crystal clarity in our cases which deal with this area of the law. * * * The language [of *Dinitz* at points] would seem to broaden the test from one of *intent* to provoke a motion for a mistrial to a more generalized standard of "bad faith conduct" or "harassment" on the part of the judge or prosecutor. It was upon this language that the Oregon Court of Appeals apparently relied in concluding that the prosecutor's colloquy with the expert witness in this case amount to "overreaching."

The difficulty with the more general standards which would permit a broader exception than one merely based on intent is that they offer virtually no standards for their application. Every act on the part of a rational prosecutor during a trial is designed to "prejudice" the defendant by placing before the judge or jury evidence leading to a finding of his guilt. Given the complexity of the rules of evidence, it will be a rare trial of any complexity in which some proffered evidence by the prosecutor or by the defendant's attorney will not be found objectionable by the trial court. Most such objections are undoubtedly curable by simply refusing to allow the proffered evidence to be admitted, or in the case of a particular line of inquiry taken by counsel with a witness, by an admonition to desist from a particular line of inquiry.

More serious infractions on the part of the prosecutor may provoke a motion for mistrial on the part of the defendant, and may in the view of the trial court warrant the granting of such a motion. The "overreaching" standard applied by the court below and urged today by Justice Stevens, however, would add another classification of prosecutorial error, one requiring dismissal of the indictment, but without supplying any standard by which to assess that error.[5]

By contrast, a standard that examines the intent of the prosecutor, though certainly not entirely free from practical difficulties, is a manageable standard to apply. It merely calls for the court to make a finding of fact. Inferring the existence or nonexistence of intent from objective facts and circumstances is a familiar process in our criminal justice system. When it is remembered that resolution of double jeopardy questions by state trial courts are reviewable not only within the state court system, but in the federal court system on habeas corpus as well, the desirability of an easily applied principle is apparent.

Prosecutorial conduct that might be viewed as harassment or overreaching, even if sufficient to justify a mistrial on defendant's motion, therefore, does not bar retrial absent intent on the part of the prosecutor to subvert the protections afforded by the Double Jeopardy Clause. A defendant's motion for a mistrial

5. If the Court were to hold, as would Justice Stevens, that such a determination requires an assessment of the facts and circumstances but without explaining how such an assessment ought to proceed, the Court would offer little guidance to the federal and state courts that must apply our decisions. Justice Stevens disagrees with this decision below because his reaction to a cold record is different from that of the Oregon Court of Appeals. The Court of Appeals found "overreaching"; Justice Stevens finds none. Neither articulates a basis for reaching their respective conclusions which can be applied to other factual situations. We are loath to adopt such an essentially standardless rule.

constitutes "a deliberate election on his part to forgo his valued right to have his guilt or innocence determined before the first trier of fact." *United States v. Scott* [p. 1465]. Where prosecutorial error even of a degree sufficient to warrant a mistrial has occurred, "[t]he important consideration, for purposes of the Double Jeopardy Clause, is that the defendant retain primary control over the course to be followed in the event of such error." *United States v. Dinitz.* Only where the governmental conduct in question is intended to "goad" the defendant into moving for a mistrial may a defendant raise the bar of double jeopardy to a second trial after having succeeded in aborting the first on his own motion.

Were we to embrace the broad and somewhat amorphous standard adopted by the Oregon Court of Appeals, we are not sure that criminal defendants as a class would be aided. Knowing that the granting of the defendant's motion for mistrial would all but inevitably bring with it an attempt to bar a second trial on grounds of double jeopardy, the judge presiding over the first trial might well be more loath to grant a defendant's motion for mistrial. If a mistrial were in fact warranted under the applicable law, of course, the defendant could in many instances successfully appeal a judgment of conviction on the same grounds that he urged a mistrial, and the Double Jeopardy Clause would present no bar to retrial.[7] But some of the advantages secured to him by the Double Jeopardy Clause—the freedom from extended anxiety, and the necessity to confront the government's case only once—would be to a large extent lost in the process of trial to verdict, reversal on appeal, and subsequent retrial.

* * * We do not by this opinion lay down a flat rule that where a defendant in a criminal trial successfully moves for a mistrial, he may not thereafter invoke the bar of double jeopardy against a second trial. But we do hold that the circumstances under which such a defendant may invoke the bar of double jeopardy in a second effort to try him are limited to those cases in which the conduct giving rise to the successful motion for a mistrial was intended to provoke the defendant into moving for a mistrial. Since the Oregon trial court found, and the Oregon Court of Appeals accepted, that the prosecutorial conduct culminating in the termination of the first trial in this case was not so intended by the prosecutor, that is the end of the matter for purposes of the Double Jeopardy Clause of the Fifth Amendment to the United States Constitution. * * *

Justice BRENNAN, with whom Justice MARSHALL joins, concurring in the judgment.

7. [The Court had previously pointed out in another footnote that it had "consistently held that the Double Jeopardy Clause imposes no limitation upon the power of the government to retry a defendant who has succeeded in persuading a court to set his conviction aside, unless the conviction has been reversed because of the insufficiency of the evidence." See § 3 infra. It added in footnote 7 that it also found "unpersuasive" and based on a "false assumption" Justice Stevens' contention (see fn. 22) that, with the adoption of "the broader rule he espouses," and with the application of that standard on appeal to both the denial and grant of mistrial motions (i.e., also prohibiting retrials on appellate review following conviction, where the court finds prosecution overreaching should have compelled a mistrial), trial courts would be no less likely to grant mistrial motions. Were appellate courts to apply a "rule of black letter law" to "a predeter-mined set of facts," they might "inevitably reach the conclusion that reprosecution should be barred in a number of cases where the trial court had denied the mistrial motion." But there were "two reasons why such a hypothesis was inapplicable here," and trial courts therefore might not so readily anticipate such appellate reversals. First, the "all encompassing standard denominated 'overreaching' which Justice Stevens espouses" is "anything but a 'rule of black letter law.' ""Second, appellate courts have traditionally given weight to a trial court's assessment as to the necessity for a mistrial," as noted in *Gori.* In light of that appellate deference, a "trial judge trying to faithfully apply the amorphous standard enunciated by Justice Stevens could surely be forgiven if in cases he regarded as extremely close he resolved the doubt in favor of continuing the trial."]

I concur in the judgment and join in the opinion of Justice Stevens. However, it should be noted that nothing in the holding of the Court today prevents the state courts, on remand, from concluding that respondent's retrial would violate the provision of the Oregon Constitution that prohibits double jeopardy * * *.

Justice POWELL, concurring.

I join the Court's opinion holding that the *intention* of a prosecutor determines whether his conduct, viewed by the defendant and the court as justifying a mistrial, bars a retrial of the defendant under the Double Jeopardy Clause. Because "subjective" intent often may be unknowable, I emphasize that a court—in considering a double jeopardy motion—should rely primarily upon the objective facts and circumstances of the particular case.

In the present case the mistrial arose from the prosecutor's conduct in pursuing a line of redirect examination of a key witness. The Oregon Court of Appeals identified a single question as constituting "overreaching" so serious as to bar a retrial. Yet, there are few vigorously contested lawsuits—whether criminal or civil—in which improper questions are not asked. Our system *is* adversarial and vigorous advocacy is encouraged. * * * Nevertheless, this would have been a close case for me if there had been substantial factual evidence of intent beyond the question itself. Here, however, other relevant facts and circumstances strongly support the view that prosecutorial intent to cause a mistrial was absent. First, there was no sequence of overreaching prior to the single prejudicial question. Moreover, it is evident from a colloquy between counsel and the court, out of the presence of the jury, that the prosecutor not only resisted, but also was surprised by, the defendant's motion for a mistrial. Finally, at the hearing on respondent's double jeopardy motion, the prosecutor testified—and the trial found as a fact and the appellate court agreed—that there was no " 'intention . . . to cause a mistrial.' " In view of these circumstances, the Double Jeopardy Clause provides no bar to retrial.

Justice STEVENS, with whom Justice BRENNAN, Justice MARSHALL, and Justice BLACKMUN, join, concurring in the judgment.

* * * The rationale for the exception to the general rule permitting retrial after a mistrial declared with the defendant's consent is illustrated by the situation in which the prosecutor commits prejudicial error with the intent to provoke a mistrial. In this situation the defendant's choice to continue the tainted proceeding or to abort the proceeding and begin anew is inadequate to protect his double jeopardy interests. For, absent a bar to reprosecution, the defendant would simply play into the prosecutor's hands by moving for a mistrial. The defendant's other option—to continue the tainted proceeding—would be no option at all if, as we might expect given the prosecutor's intent, the prosecutorial error has virtually guaranteed conviction. There is no room in the balance of competing interests for this type of manipulation of the mistrial device. Or to put it another way, whereas we tolerate some incidental infringement upon a defendant's double jeopardy interests for the sake of society's interest in obtaining a verdict of guilt or innocence, when the prosecutor seeks to obtain an advantage by intentionally subverting double jeopardy interests, the balance invariably tips in favor of a bar to reprosecution.

Today the Court once again recognizes that the exception properly encompasses the situation in which the prosecutor commits prejudicial error with the intent to provoke a mistrial. But the Court reaches out to limit the exception to that one situation, rejecting the previous recognition that prosecutorial overreaching or harassment is also within the exception.[22]

---

22. The Court offers two reasons for cutting back on the exception. First, the Court states that "[t]he difficulty with the more general standards which would permit a broader

* * * [T]he rationale for the exception extends beyond the situation in which the prosecutor intends to provoke a mistrial. There are other situations in which the defendant's double jeopardy interests outweigh society's interest in obtaining a judgment on the merits even though the defendant has moved for a mistrial. For example, a prosecutor may be interested in putting the defendant through the embarrassment, expense, and ordeal of criminal proceedings even if he cannot obtain a conviction. In such a case, with the purpose of harassing the defendant the prosecutor may commit repeated prejudicial errors and be indifferent between a mistrial or mistrials and an unsustainable conviction or convictions. Another example is when the prosecutor seeks to inject enough unfair prejudice into the trial to ensure a conviction but not so much as to cause a reversal of that conviction. This kind of overreaching would not be covered by the Court's standard because, by hypothesis, the prosecutor's intent is to obtain a conviction, not to provoke a mistrial. Yet the defendant's choice—to continue the tainted proceeding or to abort it and begin anew—can be just as "hollow" in this situation as when the prosecutor intends to provoke a mistrial.

To invoke the exception for overreaching, a court need not divine the exact motivation for the prosecutorial error. It is sufficient that the court is persuaded that egregious prosecutorial misconduct has rendered unmeaningful the defendant's choice to continue or to abort the proceeding. It is unnecessary and unwise to attempt to identify all the factors that might inform the court's judgment, but several considerations follow from the rationale for recognizing the exception. First, because the exception is justified by the intolerance of intentional manipulation of the defendant's double jeopardy interests, a finding of deliberate misconduct normally would be a prerequisite to a reprosecution bar. Second, because the defendant's option to abort the proceeding after prosecutorial misconduct would retain real meaning for the defendant in any case in which the trial was going badly for him, normally a required finding would be that the prosecutorial error virtually eliminated, or at least substantially reduced, the probability of acquittal in a proceeding that was going badly for the government. It should be apparent from these observations that only in a rare and compelling case will a mistrial declared at the request of the defendant or with his consent bar a retrial.

* * * The isolated prosecutorial error [here] occurred early in the trial, too early to determine whether the case was going badly for the prosecution. If anyone was being harassed at that time, it was the prosecutor who was frustrated by improper defense objections in her attempt to rehabilitate her witness. The gist of the comment that the respondent was a "crook" could fairly have been elicited from the witness, since defense counsel injected the respondent's past alleged improprieties into the trial by questioning the witness about his bias towards the defendant. The comment therefore could not have injected the kind of prejudice that would render unmeaningful the defendant's option to proceed with the trial.

exception than one merely based on intent is that they offer virtually no standards for their application." As I indicate in the text, however, some generality in the formula is a virtue and, in any event, meaningful and principled standards can be developed on a case-by-case basis that will not inhibit legitimate prosecution practices. Moreover, the general standards could hardly be more difficult to apply than the Court's subjective intent standard. * * *

Second, the Court is "not sure that criminal defendants as a class would be aided" by a broader exception. If a mistrial will more frequently constitute a bar to reprosecution, the Court supposes that trial judges will tend to refuse the defendant's mistrial motion and permit the error to be corrected on appeal of the conviction, in which event there would be no bar to reprosecution. This reasoning is premised on the assumption that an appellate court that concluded not only that the defendant's mistrial motion should have been granted but also that the prosecutor intended to provoke a mistrial would not be obligated to bar reprosecution as well as reverse the conviction. The assumption is "irrational." *Commonwealth v. Potter*, 478 Pa. 251, 386 A.2d 918 (1978) (Roberts, J.) (Pomeroy, J.).

Because the present case quite clearly does not come within the recognized exception, I join the Court's judgment.

Notes and Questions

1. On remand, the Oregon Supreme Court, though affirming defendant's conviction, did adopt, under the Oregon Constitution, a broader exception to the "defense-request" rule than that announced in *Kennedy*. The Oregon Court ruled that, even though defendant moved for the mistrial, retrial would be barred "when improper official conduct is so prejudicial to the defendant that it cannot be cured by means short of a mistrial, and if the official knows that the conduct is improper and prejudicial and either intends or is indifferent to the resulting mistrial or reversal." *State v. Kennedy*, 666 P.2d 1316 (Or.1983). Other state courts also have adopted similar standards more protective than that required by *Kennedy*. See e.g., *Commonwealth v. Murchison*, 465 N.E.2d 256 (Mass.1984) (retrial barred where prosecutor's misconduct either meets *Kennedy* standard or results in "such irremediable harm that a fair trial * * * is no longer possible"); *State v. White*, 354 S.E.2d 324 (N.C.App.1987) ("egregious prosecutorial misconduct [that] * * * rendered unmeaningful the defendant's choice to continue or abort the proceeding"); *State v. Lee*, 15 S.W.3d 921 (Tex.Cr.App.2000) (asking if the prosecutor deliberately or recklessly crossed the line between legitimate adversarial gamesmanship and manifestly improper methods that rendered trial before the jury unfair to such a degree that no judicial admonishment could have cured it). Commentators have suggested still other alternatives. See James Ponsoldt, *When Guilt Should be Irrelevant: Government Overreaching as a Bar to Reprosecution Under the Double Jeopardy Clause After Oregon v. Kennedy*, 69 Cornell L.Rev. 78 (1983) (retrial should be prohibited where requested mistrial was occasioned by prosecutorial or judicial error "sufficient in magnitude and clarity" to meet the plain error standard of Rule 52 [see Note 3, p. 1559], which requires an error "so serious and manifest that it affects the very integrity of the trial process"); Steven Reiss, *Prosecutorial Intent in Constitutional Criminal Procedure*, 135 U.Pa.L.Rev. 1365 (1987) (retrial should be barred where prosecutorial impropriety was sufficiently egregious to meet the "plain error standard" *and* defendant persuades the reviewing court that remedies short of a mistrial would have been "unavailing"); Thomas, *Double Jeopardy*, supra p. 1451 (would the defendant have had a "realistic chance at an acquittal if the judge had denied the mistrial").

To what extent do the above standards meet (or exacerbate) the objections raised by Justice Rehnquist to the standard advanced by Justice Stevens in *Kennedy?* Does the adoption of a broader standard than that adopted in *Kennedy* require a jurisdiction to also reconsider the consequences of an appellate reversal of a conviction based upon prosecutorial error? As noted by the *Kennedy* majority (see fn. 7), the traditional rule governing such appellate reversals (the *Ball* rule, see p. 1480) allows a retrial no matter how flagrant the prosecutorial error that necessitates a reversal. It has been argued that the mistrial and appellate reversal cases are invariably linked and that any standard adopted for precluding a retrial in the defense-request mistrial cases should be carried over to bar retrial following an appellate reversal. See Bennett Gershman, *Trial Error and Misconduct* § 2.10(d) (1997); Ponsoldt, supra. Consider also Note 5, p. 1483.

2. Does it follow from *Kennedy* that the burden of persuasion as to whether the prosecutor intended to provoke a mistrial lies with the defense? See William McAninch, *Unfolding the Law of Double Jeopardy*, 44 S.C.L.Rev. 411, 37 (1993) (where defendant claims that prior prosecution was for same offense, defendant ordinarily must make a non-frivolous showing of sameness to shift burden to the government to show that crimes charged were in fact two separate offenses; but as to mistrials, once the defendant establishes prosecutorial overreaching, the government should then carry the burden of proof; in *Arizona v. Washington*, Note 6, p. 1453, the Court stated that the "prosecutor must shoulder the burden of justifying the mistrial if he is to avoid the double jeopardy bar").

3. What is needed for a lower court to find, based on the circumstances of the case, that the prosecutor did have an intent to provoke a defense motion for a mistrial. Does such a finding require, at a minimum, prosecutorial misconduct so obvious that the prosecutor must have known his conduct was not permissible? Does it also require that the misconduct be so clearly prejudicial that the prosecutor must have recognized that the defense would give serious consideration to a mistrial request? Does it further require some event suggesting that the prosecutor (1) would have had doubts as to gaining a favorable jury verdict, and (2) would have had a basis for believing that the prosecution could do better on a new trial. See Peter J. Henning, *Prosecutor Misconduct and Constitutional Remedies*, 77 Wash.U.L.Rev. 1999 (best indicator of intent to provoke mistrial might be changes in strategy or presentation of evidence on the retrial, but ruling on double jeopardy claim will come before the retrial); *State v. Catch The Bear*, 352 N.W.2d 637 (S.D.1984) (trial court finding of intentionally provoked mistrial was clearly erroneous where pretrial in limine ruling prohibited reference to defendant's rearrest silence and prosecutorial error in opening statement consisted of reference to post-arrest silence, prosecutor strenuously argued that his opening statement was legally permissible, the error occurred before the prosecution had any basis for gauging the jury's reaction to its case, and the trial judge initially believed that the error was negligent rather than intentional).

4. As the Court noted in *Dinitz* (fn. a supra), the rule announced there makes the *Perez* standard inapplicable to mistrials "granted at the defendant's request or *with his consent*" (emphasis added). Should the defense be viewed as having "consented" to the mistrial where the trial court informed defense counsel that it was considering ordering a mistrial and defendant counsel failed to object? Consider *United States v. Buljubasic*, 808 F.2d 1260 (7th Cir.1987) (determination as to whether there was implicit consent should be based on surrounding circumstances, including whether party previously requested the mistrial, whether there was sufficient time to object, and whether the trial court had indicated that it would "brook no opposition" to its decision to declare a mistrial); *United States v. Palmer*, 122 F.3d 215 (5th Cir.1997) (if defendant does not "timely and explicitly" object to court's sua sponte declaration of a mistrial, defendant will be held to have "impliedly consented"). Note, however, Schulhofer, Note 5, p. 1452, criticizing the "readiness of many courts to engraft upon the consent doctrine notions of tacit consent or constructive consent that expand the concept far beyond its justifiable limits." As a practice pointer for defense counsel, it has been suggested that: "In any case in which the court proposes a mistrial *sua sponte,* counsel should take the position that he does not actively oppose the mistrial but should insist that the accused may not again be placed in jeopardy for the same offense." Annot., 77 A.L.R.3d 1143, 1152 (1977). Would following this tactic thereby avoid application of the consent doctrine?

5. In LEE v. UNITED STATES, 432 U.S. 23, 97 S.Ct. 2141, 53 L.Ed.2d 80 (1977), the Supreme Court considered the bearing upon the *Dinitz* "consent doctrine" of defendant's timing in raising an objection. The defendant there had been charged by information with theft and had elected a bench trial. After the prosecutor's opening statement, defense counsel moved to dismiss the information on the ground that it did not allege specific intent. The trial court tentatively denied the motion subject to further study. At the close of the two hour trial, the judge took a fifteen minute recess. When the judge returned from the recess, he noted that the defendant's guilt had been established beyond a reasonable doubt; however, he had concluded that the information was indeed insufficient, and the motion to dismiss would be granted. The Supreme Court, per POWELL, J., held that the reprosecution was not barred by double jeopardy.

The *Lee* Court first concluded that the dismissal order had been the functional equivalent of a declaration of a mistrial (rather than a judicial acquittal, see *United States v. Scott*, infra). The dismissal had been based on the insufficiency of the information, rather than any insufficiency of the evidence, and obviously was granted in apparent contemplation of a second trial on a new information. Looking to the law governing mistrials, the Court found that *Dinitz* clearly controlled, as defendant had requested the dismissal. It rejected defendant's attempt to distinguish *Dinitz*, noting:

"[Petitioner] contends (i) that he should never have had to undergo the first trial because the court was made aware of the defective information before jeopardy had attached; and (ii) that once the court had determined to hear evidence despite the defective charge, he was entitled to have the trial proceed to a formal finding of guilt or innocence. The Government responds that petitioner had only himself to blame in both respects. By the last-minute timing of his motion to dismiss, he virtually invited the court to interrupt the proceedings before formalizing a finding on the merits. We think that the Government had the better of the argument on both points under the principles explained in our decision in *United States v. Dinitz.* * * * "

Justice BRENNAN, in a concurring opinion, emphasized that "an entirely different case would be presented if the petitioner had afforded the trial judge ample opportunity to rule on his motion prior to trial, and the court, in failing to take advantage of this opportunity [had] permitted the attachment of jeopardy before ordering dismissal of the indictment." Justice MARSHALL dissented. He argued that the "petitioner was needlessly placed in jeopardy" since the judge could just as easily have recessed the case for 15 minutes before trial and determined at that point that the information was invalid.

SECTION 2. REPROSECUTION FOLLOWING AN ACQUITTAL

UNITED STATES v. SCOTT
437 U.S. 82, 98 S.Ct. 2187, 57 L.Ed.2d 65 (1978).

Justice REHNQUIST delivered the opinion of the Court.

On March 5, 1975, respondent, a member of the police force in Muskegon, Mich., was charged * * * with distribution of various narcotics. Both before his trial in the United States District Court and twice during the trial, respondent moved to dismiss the two counts of the indictment which concerned transactions that took place during the preceding September, on the ground that his defense had been prejudiced by preindictment delay. At the close of all the evidence, the court granted respondent's motion. Although the court did not explain its reasons for dismissing the second count, it explicitly concluded that respondent had "presented sufficient proof of prejudice with respect to the first count." * * *

The Government sought to appeal the dismissals of the first two counts to the United States Court of Appeals for the Sixth Circuit. That court, relying on our opinion in *United States v. Jenkins*, 420 U.S. 358, 95 S.Ct. 1006, 43 L.Ed.2d 250 (1975), concluded that any further prosecution of respondent was barred by the Double Jeopardy Clause of the Fifth Amendment, and therefore dismissed the appeal. The Government has sought review in this Court only with regard to the dismissal of the first count. We granted certiorari to give further consideration to the applicability of the Double Jeopardy Clause to Government appeals from orders granting defense motions to terminate a trial before verdict. We now reverse.

* * * In 1971, Congress adopted the current language of the [Criminal Appeals] Act, permitting Government appeals from any decision dismissing an indictment, "except that no appeal shall lie where the Double Jeopardy Clause of the United States Constitution prohibits further prosecution." 18 U.S.C. § 3731. * * * In our first encounter with the new statute, we concluded "that Congress intended to remove all statutory barriers to Government appeals and to allow appeals whenever the Constitution would permit." *United States v. Wilson*, 420 U.S. 332, 95 S.Ct. 1013, 43 L.Ed.2d 232 (1975). A detailed canvass of the history of the double jeopardy principles in [*Wilson*] * * * led us to conclude that the Double Jeopardy Clause was primarily "directed at the threat of multiple prosecutions," and posed no bar to Government appeals "where those appeals would not require a new trial." We accordingly held in *Jenkins*, that, whether or not a dismissal of an indictment after jeopardy had attached amounted to an acquittal on the merits, the Government had no right to appeal, because "further proceedings of some sort, devoted to the resolution of factual issues going to the elements of the offense charged, would have been required upon reversal and remand."[a]

If *Jenkins* is a correct statement of the law, the judgment of the Court of Appeals relying on that decision, as it was bound to do, would in all likelihood have to be affirmed. Yet, though our assessment of the history and meaning of the Double Jeopardy Clause in *Wilson, Jenkins,* and *Serfass v. United States* [Note 7, p. 1475] occurred only three Terms ago, our vastly increased exposure to the various facets of the Double Jeopardy Clause has now convinced us that *Jenkins* was wrongly decided. It placed an unwarrantedly great emphasis on the defendant's right to have his guilt decided by the first jury empaneled to try him so as to include those cases where the defendant himself seeks to terminate the trial before verdict on grounds unrelated to factual guilt or innocence. We have therefore decided to overrule *Jenkins*, and thus to reverse the judgment of the Court of Appeals in this case.

* * * At the time the Fifth Amendment was adopted, its principles were easily applied, since most criminal prosecutions proceeded to final judgment, and neither the United States nor the defendant had any right to appeal an adverse verdict. The verdict in such a case was unquestionably final, and could be raised in bar against any further prosecution for the same offense. * * * It was not until 1889 that Congress permitted criminal defendants to seek a writ of error in this Court, and then only in capital cases. Only then did it become necessary for this Court to deal with the issues presented by the challenge of verdicts on appeal. And, in the very first case presenting the issues, *Ball v. United States*, 163 U.S. 662, 16 S.Ct. 1192, 41 L.Ed. 300 (1896), the Court established principles that have been adhered to ever since. Three persons had been tried together for murder; two

---

a. In *Wilson*, after the jury returned a verdict of guilty, the trial court reconsidered an earlier motion and dismissed the indictment on due process grounds. The Supreme Court stressed that an appellate court reversal of the dismissal would not require a new trial since the appellate court could simply reinstate the jury's verdict. See Note 8, p. 1476. In *Jenkins*, the dismissal was issued by the trial judge, sitting in a bench trial, before the judge reached a verdict. The trial judge's dismissal order was based on his interpretation of the substantive law, but the judge had not indicated what result he would have reached as the finder of fact if a contrary interpretation had been adopted. Thus, if the trial judge's order were reversed on appeal, further resolution of the facts relating to the elements of the offense would be required. The *Jenkins* opinion stressed this consequence of an appellate reversal rather than the grounding of the trial court's dismissal ruling.

were convicted, the other acquitted. This Court reversed the convictions, finding the indictment fatally defective, whereupon all three defendants were tried again. This time all three were convicted and they again sought review here. This Court held that the Double Jeopardy Clause precluded further prosecution of the defendant who had been *acquitted* at the original trial but that it posed no such bar to the prosecution of those defendants who had been *convicted* in the earlier proceeding.[b]

* * * These then, at least, are two venerable principles of double jeopardy jurisprudence. The successful appeal of a judgment of conviction, on any ground other than the insufficiency of the evidence to support the verdict, *Burks v. United States* [p. 1478], poses no bar to further prosecution on the same charge. A judgment of acquittal, whether based on a jury verdict of not guilty or on a ruling by the court that the evidence is insufficient to convict, may not be appealed and terminates the prosecution when a second trial would be necessitated by a reversal.[7] What may seem superficially to be a disparity in the rules governing a defendant's liability to be tried again is explainable by reference to the underlying purposes of the Double Jeopardy Clause. * * * [T]he law attaches particular significance to an acquittal. To permit a second trial after an acquittal, however mistaken the acquittal may have been, would present an unacceptably high risk that the Government, with its vastly superior resources, might wear down the defendant so that "even though innocent, he may be found guilty." *Green v. United States* [p. 1483]. On the other hand, to require a criminal defendant to stand trial again after he has successfully invoked a statutory right of appeal to upset his first conviction is not an act of governmental oppression of the sort against which the Double Jeopardy Clause was intended to protect. * * *

Although the primary purpose of the Double Jeopardy Clause was to protect the integrity of a final judgment, this Court has also developed a body of law guarding the separate but related interest of a defendant in avoiding multiple prosecutions even where no final determination of guilt or innocence has been made. Such interests may be involved in two different situations: the first, in which the trial judge declares a mistrial; the second, in which the trial judge

b. In reaching its holding as to the acquittal, the *Ball* Court rejected the English common law rule which treated a defective indictment as depriving the trial court of jurisdiction and therefore viewed the defendant as never having been placed in jeopardy. It also rejected the additional "jurisdictional" contention that jeopardy did not terminate because the order discharging the jury was improperly issued on a Sunday, when the trial court had no authority to act. These rulings are not read as rejecting as to every conception of "jurisdiction" the common law view that the defendant is only placed in jeopardy when the trial court had "jurisdiction." See *Hoang v. State*, 872 S.W.2d 694 (Tex.Cr.App.1993) (jeopardy did not attach where trial court in original proceeding lacked jurisdiction because juvenile had not been certified for trial as an adult).

Kepner v. United States, 195 U.S. 100 24 S.Ct. 797, 49 L.Ed. 114 (1904), reaffirmed the acquittal rule of *Ball*. *Kepner* concluded that an acquittal terminated the initial jeopardy, so that a second trial, following an appellate reversal of the acquittal on a governmental appeal, would place the defendant twice in jeopardy. Justice Holmes, in dissent, argued that jeopardy should be viewed as continuing through the acquittal to the final resolution of claim, including appellate review and retrial if ordered by the appellate court. See also *Amar*, supra p. 1451 (arguing that Holmes had it right, but appellate reversal of a jury acquittal should be barred by the Sixth Amendment right of jurors to acquit even against the weight of the evidence, provided the jury had before it properly admitted evidence and received proper instructions).

7. In *Jenkins* we had assumed that a judgment of acquittal could be appealed where no retrial would be needed on remand: "When this principle is applied to the situation where the jury returns a verdict of guilt but the trial court thereafter enters a judgment of acquittal an appeal is permitted. In that situation a conclusion by an appellate court that the judgment of acquittal was improper does not require a criminal defendant to submit to a second trial; the error can be corrected on remand by the entry of a judgment on the verdict." 420 U.S. at 365. * * *

terminates the proceedings favorably to the defendant on a basis not related to factual guilt or innocence.

* * * In passing on the propriety of a declaration of mistrial granted at the behest of the prosecutor or on the court's own motion, this Court has [applied the *Perez* standard of manifest necessity]. * * * In our recent decision in *Arizona v. Washington* [Note 6, p. 1453], we reviewed this Court's attempts to give content to the term "manifest necessity," * * * and we noted that the trial court's discretion must be exercised with a careful regard for the interests first described in *United States v. Perez*. * * * Where, on the other hand, a *defendant* successfully seeks to avoid his trial prior to its conclusion by a motion for mistrial, the Double Jeopardy Clause is not offended by a second prosecution. * * * Such a motion by the defendant is deemed to be a deliberate election on his part to forego his valued right to have his guilt or innocence determined before the first trier of fact. *United States v. Dinitz* [fn. a, p. 1458]. * * *

We turn now to the relationship between the Double Jeopardy Clause and reprosecution of a defendant who has successfully obtained not a mistrial, but a termination of the trial in his favor before any determination of factual guilt or innocence. Unlike the typical mistrial, the granting of a motion such as this obviously contemplates that the proceedings will terminate then and there in favor of the defendant. The prosecution, if it wishes to reinstate the proceedings in the face of such a ruling, ordinarily must seek reversal of the decision of the trial court. * * * *Jenkins* held that, regardless of the character of the mistrial termination, appeal was barred if "further proceedings of some sort, devoted to the resolution of factual issues going to the elements of the offense charged, would have been required upon reversal and remand." However, only last term, in *Lee v. United States* [Note 5, p. 1464], the Government was permitted to institute a second prosecution after a midtrial dismissal of an indictment. The Court found the circumstances presented by that case "functionally indistinguishable from a declaration of a mistrial." Thus, *Lee* demonstrated that, at least in some cases, the dismissal of an indictment may be treated on the same basis as the declaration of a mistrial. * * * [O]ur growing experience with Government appeals convinces us that we must reexamine the rationale of *Jenkins* in light of *Lee* and other recent expositions of the Double Jeopardy Clause.

Our decision in *Jenkins* was based upon our perceptions of the underlying purposes of the Double Jeopardy Clause:

> "The underlying idea, one that is deeply ingrained in at least the Anglo–American system of jurisprudence is that the State with all its resources and power should not be allowed to make repeated attempts to convict an individual for an alleged offense, thereby subjecting him to embarrassment, expense and ordeal and compelling him to live in a continuing state of anxiety and insecurity * * *." *Jenkins*, quoting *Green v. United States*, supra.

Upon fuller consideration, we are now of the view that this language from *Green*, while entirely appropriate in the circumstances of that opinion, is not a principle which can be expanded to include situations in which the defendant is responsible for the second prosecution. It is quite true that the Government with all its resources and power should not be allowed to make repeated attempts to convict an individual for an alleged offense. This truth is expressed in the three common-law pleas of *autrefois acquit, autrefois convict,* and pardon, which lie at the core of the area protected by the Double Jeopardy Clause. As we have recognized in cases from *Ball* to *Sanabria v. United States* [Note 2, p. 1472], a defendant once acquitted may not be again subjected to trial without violating the Double Jeopardy Clause.

But that situation is obviously a far cry from the present case, where the Government was quite willing to continue with its production of evidence to show the defendant guilty before the jury first empaneled to try him, but the defendant elected to seek termination of the trial on grounds unrelated to guilt or innocence. This is scarcely a picture of an all-powerful state relentlessly pursuing a defendant who had either been found not guilty or who had at least insisted on having the issue of guilt submitted to the first trier of fact. It is instead a picture of a defendant who chooses to avoid conviction and imprisonment, not because of his assertion that the Government has failed to make out a case against him, but because of a legal claim that the Government's case against him must fail even though it might satisfy the trier of fact that he was guilty beyond a reasonable doubt.

We have previously noted that "the trial judge's characterization of his own action cannot control the classification of the action." *United States v. Jorn* [p. 1445]. * * * [A] defendant is acquitted only when "the ruling of the judge, whatever its label, actually represents a resolution [in the defendant's favor], correct or not, of some or all of the factual elements of the offense charged," *United States v. Martin Linen Supply* [Note 7, p. 1475]. Where the court, before the jury returns a verdict, enters a judgment of acquittal pursuant to Fed.Rule Crim.Proc. 29, appeal will be barred only when "it is plain that the District Court * * * evaluated the Government's evidence and determined that it was legally insufficient to support a conviction." Id.

Our opinion in *Burks* [p. 1478] necessarily holds that there has been a "failure of proof" requiring an acquittal when the Government does not submit sufficient evidence to rebut a defendant's essentially factual defense of insanity, though it may otherwise be entitled to have its case submitted to the jury. The defense of insanity, like the defense of entrapment, arises from "the notion that Congress could not have intended criminal punishment for a defendant who has committed all the elements of a proscribed offense," *United States v. Russell*, 411 U.S. 423, 93 S.Ct. 1637, 36 L.Ed.2d 366 (1973), where other facts established to the satisfaction of the trier of fact provide a legally adequate justification for otherwise criminal acts. Such a factual finding *does* "necessarily establish the criminal defendant's lack of criminal culpability," post, (Brennan, J., dissenting), under the existing law; the fact that "the acquittal may result from erroneous evidentiary rulings or erroneous interpretations of governing legal principles," ibid., affects the accuracy of that determination, but it does not alter its essential character. By contrast, the dismissal of an indictment for preindictment delay represents a legal judgment that a defendant, although criminally culpable, may not be punished because of a supposed constitutional violation. * * *

[I]n the present case, [defendant] successfully avoided a submission of the first count of the indictment [to the jury] by persuading the trial court to dismiss it on a basis which did not depend on guilt or innocence. He was thus neither acquitted nor convicted, because he himself successfully undertook to persuade the trial court not to submit the issue of guilt or innocence to the jury which had been empaneled to try him. * * * [Defendant] has not been "deprived" of his valued right to go to the first jury; only the public has been deprived of its valued right to "one complete opportunity to convict those who have violated its laws." *Arizona v. Washington*. No interest protected by the Double Jeopardy Clause is invaded when the Government is allowed to appeal and seek reversal of such a mistrial termination of the proceedings in a manner favorable to the defendant.[13]

13. We should point out that it is entirely possible for a trial court to reconcile the public interest in the Government's right to appeal from an erroneous conclusion of law, with the defendant's interest in avoiding a second prosecution. In *Wilson*, supra, the court permitted the case to go to the jury, which returned a verdict of guilty, but it subsequently dismissed the indictment for preindictment delay on the basis of evidence adduced at trial. Most recently in *United States v. Ceccolini*, 435 U.S. 268, 98 S.Ct. 1054, 55 L.Ed.2d 268 (1978), we de-

It is obvious from what we have said that we believe we pressed too far in *Jenkins*, the concept of the "defendant's valued right to have his trial completed by a particular tribunal." We now conclude that where the defendant himself seeks to have the trial terminated without any submission to either judge or jury as to his guilt or innocence, an appeal by the Government from his successful effort to do so is not barred by 18 U.S.C. § 3731.

Justice BRENNAN, with whom Justice WHITE, Justice MARSHALL, and Justice STEVENS join, dissenting.

* * * While the Double Jeopardy Clause often has the effect of protecting the accused's interest in the finality of particular favorable determinations, this is not its objective. For the Clause often permits Government appeals from final judgments favorable to the accused. See *United States v. Wilson* (whether or not final judgment was an acquittal, Government may appeal if reversal would not necessitate a retrial). The purpose of the Clause, which the Court today fails sufficiently to appreciate, is to protect the accused against the agony and risks attendant upon undergoing more than one criminal trial for any single offense. * * * Accordingly, the policies of the Double Jeopardy Clause mandate that the Government be afforded but one complete opportunity to convict an accused and that when the first proceeding terminates in a final judgment favorable to the defendant any retrial be barred. The rule as to acquittals can only be understood as simply an application of this larger principle.

Judgments of acquittal normally result from jury or bench verdicts of not guilty. In such cases, the acquittal represents the factfinder's conclusion that, under the controlling legal principles, the evidence does not establish that the defendant can be convicted of the offense charged in the indictment. But the judgment does not necessarily establish the criminal defendant's lack of criminal culpability; the acquittal may result from erroneous evidentiary rulings or erroneous interpretations of governing legal principles induced by the defense. Yet the Double Jeopardy Clause bars a second trial. * * * The reason is not that the first trial established the defendant's factual innocence, but rather that the second trial would present all the untoward consequences the Clause was designed to prevent. Government would be allowed to seek to persuade a second trier of fact of the defendant's guilt, to strengthen any weaknesses in its first presentation, and to subject the defendant to the expense and anxiety of a second trial.

* * * The whole premise for today's retreat from *Jenkins* * * * is the Court's new theory that a criminal defendant who seeks to avoid conviction on a "ground unrelated to factual innocence" somehow stands on a different constitutional footing than a defendant whose participation in his criminal trial creates a situation in which a judgment of acquittal has to be entered. This premise is simply untenable. * * * [T]he reasons that bar a retrial following an acquittal are equally applicable to a final judgment entered on a ground "unrelated to factual innocence." The heavy personal strain of the second trial is the same in either case. So too is the risk that, though innocent, the defendant may be found guilty at a second trial. If the appeal is allowed in either situation, the Government will, following any reversal, not only obtain the benefit of the favorable appellate ruling but also be permitted to shore up any other weak points of its case and obtain all

scribed similar action with approval: "The District Court had sensibly first made its finding on the factual question of guilt or innocence, and then ruled on the motion to suppress; a reversal of these rulings would require no further proceedings in the District Court, but merely a reinstatement of the finding of guilt." We of course do not suggest that a midtrial dismissal of a prosecution, in response to a defense motion on grounds unrelated to guilt or innocence, is necessarily improper. Such rulings may be necessary to terminate proceedings marred by fundamental error. But where a defendant prevails on such a motion, he takes the risk that an appellate court will reverse the trial court.

the other advantages at the second trial that the Double Jeopardy Clause was designed to forbid. * * * Equally significant, the distinction between the two is at best purely formal. Many acquittals are the consequence of rulings of law made on the accused's motion that are not related to the question of his factual guilt or innocence: e.g., a ruling on the law respecting the scope of the offense or excluding reliable evidence. *Sanabria v. United States* [Note 2, p. 1472] illustrates the point. * * *

   * * * A critical feature of today's holding appears to be the Court's definition of acquittal [p. 1469] as "a resolution [in the defendant's favor], correct or not, of some or all of the factual elements of the offense charged," * * *. [But] why, for purposes of its new definition of "acquittal," is not the fact *vel non* of preindictment delay one of the "factual elements of the offense charged"? The Court plainly cannot answer that preindictment delay is not referred to in the statutory definition of the offense charged in count one, for it states that dismissals based on the defenses of insanity and entrapment—neither of which is bound up with the statutory definition of federal crimes—will constitute "acquittals." How can decisions based on the trial evidence that a defendant is "not guilty by reason of insanity" or "not guilty by reason of entrapment" erect a double jeopardy bar, and a decision—equally based on evaluation of the trial evidence—that the defendant is "not guilty by reason of pre-accusation delay" not also prohibit further prosecution? * * * Ironically, it seems likely that, when all is said and done, there will be few instances indeed in which defenses can be deemed unrelated to factual innocence. If so, today's decision may be limited to disfavored doctrines like preaccusation delay. See generally *United States v. Lovasco* [p. 1083]. * * *

Notes and Questions

   1. *The function of the "acquittal rule".* Professor Westen has challenged the explanations offered by both the majority and dissenting opinions in *Scott* as to the interests underlying the rule barring a retrial after an acquittal. See Peter Westen and Richard Drubel, *Towards a General Theory of Double Jeopardy,* 1978 Sup.Ct.Rev. 81; Peter Westen, *The Three Faces of Double Jeopardy: Reflections on Governmental Appeals of Criminal Sentences,* 78 Mich.L.Rev. 1001 (1980). As for the defendant's interest in avoiding the burdens and tactical disadvantages of a second trial (stressed in Justice Brennan's dissent), Professor Westen notes that those interests have been rejected as a basis for establishing an absolute bar to retrial "in every other area of double jeopardy." Thus, he notes, "the state may retry a defendant following mistrials declared over his objection, mistrials declared because of hung juries, and convictions reversed on appeal." Since the defendant in such cases is equally subject to the expense and anxiety of the second trial, to the tactical disadvantages of having disclosed his case to the prosecution, and to the possibility that the government will be able to shore up any weak points in its case, the rule prohibiting retrials following acquittals must rest, says Professor Westen, on other concerns. He rejects, however, the suggestion of the *Scott* majority that retrials following acquittals are barred because they pose "an unacceptably high risk" of resulting in the conviction of an innocent defendant. This rationale, he argues, would have to rest on the assumption that the defendant who has been acquitted, even in a trial flawed by a legal error favorable to the defendant, is more likely to be innocent than the defendant forced to face a retrial after a mistrial, after a conviction reversed on appeal due to error prejudicial to defendant, or after a dismissal based on non-acquittal grounds (such as that involved in *Scott*). Such an assumption is said to be inconsistent with an acquittal rule so absolute as to bar retrial "even where the acquittals are known to be egregiously erroneous" [quoting *Fong Foo v. United States,* 369 U.S. 141, 82 S.Ct. 671, 7 L.Ed.2d 629 (1962)].

Professor Westen argues that the only sound grounding for the absolute prohibition of retrials following acquittals is the need to protect the "jury's prerogative to acquit against the evidence"—an interest that distinguishes the acquittal situation because only there does the possibility exist that the jury has exercised that prerogative. Compare Amar, fn. b, p. 1467. In *United States v. DiFrancesco* (p. 1485), in the course of explaining various double jeopardy principles, the Court cited both the *Scott* majority's analysis and Professor Westen's jury nullification thesis in explaining the acquittal rule. Professor Thomas argues, however, that both Professor Westen and the Court err in searching for a unique grounding for the acquittal rule. To do so, he argues, ignores the common law understanding of the double jeopardy guarantee. The pleas of *autrefois acquit* and *autrefois convict* both prohibited a second prosecution for the same offense, reflecting the double jeopardy guarantee's core function of ensuring "verdict finality." The acquittal rule therefore had no special role that separated it from the conviction rule. What came to distinguish the verdict of acquittal from verdicts of conviction was the defendant's capacity "to disturb verdict finality" by electing to challenge a verdict on appeal—a capacity that applied only to verdicts of conviction, where, "naturally enough, defendants often seek to set aside the finality to which they have a right." "Stated * * * simply," Professor Thomas notes, "undisturbed verdicts always bar governmental action based on the same [offense], but convictions are less absolute bars than acquittals because they do not always remain undisturbed." See Thomas, *Double Jeopardy,* p. 1451. (also arguing that if the principle of verdict finality is to be carried over to today's procedure, a mistrial dismissal like that in *Scott,* not based on the insufficiency of the evidence, cannot be viewed as the equivalent of an *autrefois acquit*).

When will the different groundings discussed above lead to different conclusions as to the scope of the "acquittal rule"? Consider in this regard the setting presented in *Sanabria,* Note 2 infra.

2. Sanabria. SANABRIA v. UNITED STATES, 437 U.S. 54, 98 S.Ct. 2170, 57 L.Ed.2d 43 (1978), was aptly described by Justice Blackmun (in dissent) as "an odd and an unusual [case], factually and procedurally." The defendant in *Sanabria* was one of eleven persons charged with participation in an "illegal gambling business" in violation of 18 U.S.C. § 1955. Under that provision a gambling business violates federal law only if it also violates the law of the state in which the business is located. The single-count indictment in *Sanabria* charged that the defendant's gambling business involved wagers on a numbers pool and on horse racing in violation of Section 17 of a Massachusetts statute. The government's evidence tied *Sanabria* to the numbers operation, but not to the horsebetting. At the close of the government's case, defense counsel moved for a judgment of acquittal on the ground that Section 17 of the Massachusetts statute did not prohibit numbers betting since it applied only to betting in "games of competition," such as horse racing. The motion initially was denied, but then was reconsidered after the defendant rested his case. The trial court agreed that Section 17 did not encompass the numbers operation. Another provision of the Massachusetts statute, Section 7, did make numbers betting illegal, but the government could not rely on that provision since it was not cited in the indictment. Accordingly, the court ruled, all of the evidence relating to the numbers operation had to be excluded. The court then granted the requested judgment of acquittal on the ground that there was no evidence tying the defendant to the horsebetting activities.

The government subsequently sought to appeal under 18 U.S.C. § 3731. It conceded that there was insufficient evidence of Sanabria's involvement with horsebetting, but requested that a new trial be ordered on the portion of the indictment relating to numbers betting. The government contended that the trial court had erred twice in dealing with the numbers operation. First the failure of the indictment to allege violation of Section 7 of the Massachusetts statute, in addition to violation of Section 17, was harmless error and should not have barred consideration of the numbers betting as violating Massachusetts law. Second, even if it were assumed that the numbers operation could not be used to establish the illegality of the gambling business, Sanabria's participation in the numbers operation was still relevant since the federal statute would hold liable a person who participated in a lawful portion of a combined gambling venture if that venture was illegal due to its other portion, here the horse racing. On review before the Supreme Court, the Court assumed that the trial court had erred on both grounds. It held the trial court's order nevertheless was not appealable.

The opinion for the Court, per MARSHALL, J., initially noted that "when a defendant has been acquitted at trial, he may not be retried on the same offense, even if the legal rulings underlying the acquittal were erroneous." The government, the opinion further noted, did not take issue with this principle, as it conceded the unreviewability of "the acquittal for insufficient evidence on what it refers to as the horsebetting theory of liability." The government contended, however, that its "numbers theory of liability" was "dismissed from the count before the judgment of acquittal was entered and therefore that petitioner was not acquitted of the numbers theory." The Court rejected this contention on two grounds: (1) the indictment had contained a single count, charging a single violation, and the acquittal therefore covered both theories of liability; and (2) even if the numbers theory was viewed as dismissed separately, a retrial on that theory would nevertheless be barred since there was only a single offense— participation in any aspect of the gambling enterprise—and the acquittal on the horsebetting necessarily constituted a final judgment as to the entire offense (see Ch. 18, § 2).

3. *Sanabria* has been criticized as failing to recognize that a judicial ruling framed as an "acquittal," where based solely on the trial court's view of the substantive law (as opposed to an assessment of evidentiary credibility), is just as readily subject to appellate review without disturbing factual findings relating to the defendant's factual innocence as the trial court's ruling in *Scott*. Edward Cooper, *Government Criminal Appeals*, 81 F.R.D. 539 (1979). If the Supreme Court in *Sanabria* had accepted this criticism and had treated the trial judge's order as similar to a *Scott*-type dismissal, would this simply have suggested to defense counsel that the better procedure would be to concentrate on favorable jury instructions rather than a judicial "acquittal"? If the judge in *Sanabria* had let the case go to the jury and had charged the jury that defendant could be held liable only if he participated in the horsebetting, the jury presumably would have acquitted (since there was no evidence tying the defendant to horsebetting) and that acquittal clearly would have barred reprosecution.

4. Cooper, Note 3 supra, suggests that the combination of *Sanabria* and *Lee* [Note 5, p. 1464] may mean "that the trial court has discretion to control the double jeopardy consequences of its ruling by choosing the form employed." The author notes that the trial court often will have a choice between framing its order as an "acquittal" based on the prosecution's failure to prove all of the elements of the offense or as a "dismissal" for the failure of the indictment to charge all the elements of the offense. When the former form is used, *Sanabria* establishes that the government may not appeal even though the trial court's decision is based on a mistaken interpretation of the necessary elements of the offense. When the latter form is used, *Lee* suggests that double jeopardy does not bar an appeal if a mistrial would be permitted under the same circumstances. Professor Cooper

concludes: "Although it is troubling that trial judges should be left with discretion to determine whether their legal rulings should be free from appellate review, procedural punctilio at least has the advantage of helping the defendant to know whether further proceedings may be possible."

5. What distinguishes a defense such as insanity or entrapment, as to which a favorable mid-trial ruling will constitute an acquittal, and an objection such as preindictment delay? Consider in this connection *United States v. Moore,* 613 F.2d 1029 (D.C.Cir.1979). The defendant there, charged with making false declarations before a grand jury, waived his right to a jury trial and the case was submitted to the court for a decision on the sole issue of materiality. After the government had presented the testimony of the grand jury foreman bearing on the materiality issue, defense counsel raised an additional defense, contending that defendant's subsequent statements brought the case within the purview of the statutory provision barring prosecution of recanting witnesses. Agreeing with that contention, the court asked the government whether it would allow the defendant to reappear before the grand jury for the purpose of testifying anew. When the government stated it was not willing to do so, the court dismissed the indictment. The D.C. Circuit held that the ruling below was not an acquittal under *Scott.* The court reasoned: "Recantation, * * * is not a defense bearing on guilt or innocence, nor, by the same token, a defense such that its assertion may not be appealed without implicating the Double Jeopardy Clause. Unlike insanity or entrapment, recantation does not excuse a defendant because it makes him any less guilty, or justifies his otherwise criminal conduct. Rather, statutory recantation erects a barrier that permits escape from prosecution, despite guilt, in the interest of encouraging corrected testimony." Consider also *Wilkett v. United States,* 655 F.2d 1007 (10th Cir.1981) (no acquittal under *Scott* where trial was terminated because the government "failed to prove an element which is more procedural than substantive, namely venue"); *Palazzolo v. Gorcyca,* 244 F.3d 512 (6th Cir.2001) (state trial court quashed the information charging criminal sexual conduct, as it had element of penetration and corpus delecti rule required that element to be proven independent of defendant's confession which would be the state's key evidence; government appealed and state appellate court held that independent proof of penetration was not required under state's corpus delecti rule, and remanded for trial; on postconviction habeas review, Sixth Circuit, holds that appellate review and remand for trial did not violate double jeopardy as petitioner "like the defendant in *Scott* voluntarily chose to terminate the prosecution * * * on a basis unrelated to factual guilt or innocence"; also jury had not yet been impaneled when the trial court dismissed the charge, see Note 7 infra).

6. *The timing of the defense objection.* In *Serfass v. United States,* Note 7 infra, the Court reserved judgment as to the appropriate treatment of a midtrial ruling terminating the prosecution where the defendant could have raised the underlying objection prior to the attachment of jeopardy but failed to do so. *Lee v. United States,* Note 5, p. 1464, considered a similar problem in the context of a midtrial dismissal order that was the functional equivalent of declaring a mistrial. In *Sanabria,* the government relied on the combination of *Lee* and *Serfass* to argue that the trial court's ruling, even if viewed as an acquittal, should not bar retrial because of Sanabria's failure to make a pretrial objection to the government's theory that the offense could be established by reference to the gambling organization's numbers activities. It was only after the government had completed its case that the defendant raised his basic contention that the numbers operation was not prohibited under section 17 of the state statute and therefore the government's case was limited to the horsebetting activities. Since a pretrial objection would have allowed the government to seek an amendment of the indictment to refer to section 7 (encompassing numbers betting), this delay, argued the government, amounted to a "waiver" of the defendant's subsequent double jeopardy objection. The Court, over the objection of the two dissenters, rejected the government's theory:

"[*Serfass* spoke] of a defendant who is afforded an opportunity to obtain a determination of a legal defense prior to trial and nevertheless knowingly allows himself to be placed in jeopardy before raising the defense. * * * Unlike questions of whether an indictment states an offense, a statute is unconstitutional, or conduct set forth in an indictment violates the statute, what proof may be presented in support of a valid indictment and the sufficiency of that proof are not 'legal defenses' required to be or even capable of being resolved before trial. In all of the former instances, a ruling in the defendant's favor completely precludes conviction, at least on that indictment. Here, even if the numbers language had been struck before trial, there was no 'legal' reason why petitioner could not have been convicted on this indictment [through the horsebetting], as were his 10 codefendants."

    7. *The timing of the court's ruling.* While an acquittal bars reprosecution, that is not true of a trial court's ruling that the government's evidence is insufficient when it comes before jeopardy has attached. In *Serfass v. United States*, 420 U.S. 377, 95 S.Ct. 1055, 43 L.Ed.2d 265 (1975), petitioner, charged with willful failure to submit to military induction, filed a pretrial motion to dismiss based on the selective service board's treatment of his claim of conscientious objection. The district court then reviewed the selective service file and concluded, based on the evidence contained there, that the petitioner had submitted a "prima facie case of conscientious objector status," which invalidated the induction order due to the board's failure to provide appropriate review of that claim. With only Justice Douglas dissenting, the Court held that the double jeopardy clause would not bar a retrial following a successful government appeal and therefore the district court's ruling was appealable (see Note 1, p. 1554). The Court stressed that the district court's ruling had come prior to the attachment of jeopardy. Defendant argued that "constructive jeopardy had attached" since the judge's ruling was the "functional equivalent of an acquittal," but the Court responded that this argument failed in light of the "history and terms" of the double jeopardy clause. Both demonstrate that the clause's protection "does not come into play until a proceeding begins before a trier having jurisdiction to try the question of guilt or innocence of the accused." That clearly was not the situation here, where the case was to be tried to a jury. See also *United States v. Sanford*, 429 U.S. 14, 97 S.Ct. 20, 50 L.Ed.2d 17 (1976) (where defendant's initial trial on hunting in a national park ended in a mistrial, and prior to the scheduled trial, four months later, the judge reviewed the evidence developed at the first trial and dismissed the prosecution with prejudice on the ground that government agents had "consented to the activities which formed the basis of indictment," the government could appeal; the dismissal was not a Fed. R. Crim. P. 29(c) judgment of acquittal, which could have been issued shortly after the mistrial and would have barred further proceedings, see *United States v. Martin Linen Supply*, 430 U.S. 564, 97 S.Ct. 1349, 51 L.Ed.2d 642 (1977), but a pretrial order similar to that issued in *Serfass*).

    8. *Post-conviction rulings.* Assume that the defendant is tried before a jury and found guilty. The trial judge then reconsiders a motion for a judgment of acquittal and concludes that, notwithstanding the jury verdict, the testimony of the chief prosecution witness was so inherently incredible that no reasonable person could find defendant guilty beyond a reasonable doubt. The trial judge then enters a judgment of acquittal notwithstanding the jury's verdict, as allowed under state law. Would a prosecution appeal from that order place the defendant in double jeopardy? Consider footnote 7 of the Court's opinion in *Scott*. The statement from *Jenkins* cited in footnote 7 was based upon an analysis offered in UNITED STATES v. WILSON, 420 U.S. 332, 95 S.Ct. 1013, 43 L.Ed.2d 232 (1975), described below.

In *Wilson,* after the jury returned a verdict of guilty, the trial court reconsidered an earlier motion and dismissed the indictment on the ground that the government's preindictment delay had resulted in a denial of due process. In sustaining the government's appeal from that order, the Court found no need to determine "whether the ruling in Wilson's favor was actually an 'acquittal,'" (an issue later reached in *Scott*). It concluded that the appeal was not barred by the double jeopardy clause since the defendant would not be exposed to multiple trials. Justice MARSHALL's opinion for the Court majority noted:

"[W]here there is no threat of either multiple punishment or successive prosecutions, the Double Jeopardy Clause is not offended. In various situations where appellate review would not subject the defendant to a second trial, this Court has held that an order favoring the defendant could constitutionally be appealed by the Government. Since the 1907 Criminal Appeals Act, for example, the Government has been permitted without serious constitutional challenge to appeal from orders arresting judgment after a verdict has been entered against the defendant. Since reversal on appeal would merely reinstate the jury's verdict, review of such an order does not offend the policy against multiple prosecution.

" * * * Although review of any ruling of law discharging a defendant obviously enhances the likelihood of conviction and subjects him to continuing expense and anxiety, a defendant has no legitimate claim to benefit from an error of law when that error could be corrected without subjecting him to a second trial before a second trier of fact. * * * Respondent contends that *Ball v. United States* [p. 1478] * * * stand[s] for the proposition that the key to invoking double jeopardy protection is not whether the defendant might be subjected to multiple trials, but whether he can point to a prior verdict or judgment of acquittal. In *Ball,* however, the Court explained that review of the verdict of acquittal was barred primarily because it would expose the defendant to the risk of a second trial after the finder of fact had ruled in his favor in the first. * * * "

9.   *The fraudulently obtained acquittal.* Should an acquittal bar reprosecution when the prosecution has established that the defendant bribed the judge or tampered with the jury? Consider David Rudstein, *Double Jeopardy and the Fraudulently Obtained Acquittal,* 60 Mo.L.Rev. 607 (1995), and Anne Bowen Poulin, *Double Jeopardy and Judicial Accountability: When is an Acquittal Not an Acquittal,* 27 Ariz.St.L.J. 953 (1995), both taking note of an Illinois trial court ruling allowing a reprosecution where the judge had been bribed, the court concluding that the defendant had never truly been in jeopardy of conviction, *People v. Aleman,* 1994 WL 684499 (Ill.Cir.1994). See also *United States ex rel. Aleman v. Circuit Court of Cook County,* 967 F.Supp. 1022 (N.D.Ill.1997) (recognizing exception for bench trial only).

SECTION 3. REPROSECUTION FOLLOWING A CONVICTION

LOCKHART v. NELSON
488 U.S. 33, 109 S.Ct. 285, 102 L.Ed.2d 265 (1988).

Chief Justice REHNQUIST delivered the opinion of the Court.

In this case a reviewing court set aside a defendant's conviction because certain evidence was erroneously admitted against him, and further held that the

Double Jeopardy Clause forbade the State to retry him because the remaining evidence adduced at trial was legally insufficient to support a conviction. Nothing in the record suggests any misconduct in the prosecutor's submission of the evidence. We conclude that in cases such as this, where the evidence offered by the State and admitted by the trial court—whether erroneously or not—would have been sufficient to sustain a guilty verdict, the Double Jeopardy Clause does not preclude retrial.

Respondent Johnny Lee Nelson pleaded guilty in Arkansas state court to burglary, a class B felony, and misdemeanor theft. He was sentenced under the State's habitual criminal statute, which provides that a defendant who is convicted of a class B felony and "who has previously been convicted of ... [or] found guilty of four [4] or more felonies," may be sentenced to an enhanced term of imprisonment of between 20 and 40 years. Ark.Stat.Ann. § 41–1001(2)(b) (1977). To have a convicted defendant's sentence enhanced under the statute, the State must prove beyond a reasonable doubt, at a separate sentencing hearing, that the defendant has the requisite number of prior felony convictions. Section 41–1003 of the statute sets out the means by which the prosecution may prove the prior felony convictions, providing that "[a] previous conviction or finding of guilt of a felony may be proved by any evidence that satisfies the trier of fact beyond a reasonable doubt that the defendant was convicted or found guilty," and that three types of documents, including "a duly certified copy of the record of a previous conviction or finding of guilt by a court of record," are "sufficient to support a finding of a prior conviction or finding of guilt." The defendant is entitled to challenge the State's evidence of his prior convictions and to rebut it with evidence of his own.

At respondent's sentencing hearing, the State introduced, without objection from the defense, certified copies of four prior felony convictions. Unbeknownst to the prosecutor, one of those convictions had been pardoned by the Governor several years after its entry. Defense counsel made no objection to the admission of the pardoned conviction, because he too was unaware of the Governor's action. On cross-examination, respondent indicated his belief that the conviction in question had been pardoned. The prosecutor suggested that respondent was confusing a pardon with a commutation to time served. Under questioning from the court, respondent agreed that the conviction had been commuted rather than pardoned, and the matter was not pursued any further.[1] The case was submitted to the jury, which found that the State had met its burden of proving four prior convictions and imposed an enhanced sentence. The State courts upheld the enhanced sentence on both direct and collateral review, despite respondent's protestations that one of the convictions relied upon by the State had been pardoned.

Several years later, respondent sought a writ of habeas corpus in the United States District Court, contending once again that the enhanced sentence was invalid because one of the prior convictions used to support it had been pardoned. When an investigation undertaken by the State at the District Court's request revealed that the conviction in question had in fact been pardoned, the District Court declared the enhanced sentence to be invalid. The State announced its intention to resentence respondent as a habitual offender, using another prior conviction not offered or admitted at the initial sentencing hearing, and respondent interposed a claim of double jeopardy. After hearing arguments from counsel, the District Court decided that the Double Jeopardy Clause prevented the State from attempting to resentence respondent as a habitual offender on the burglary

1. There is no indication that the prosecutor knew of the pardon and was attempting to deceive the court. We therefore have no occasion to consider what the result would be if the case were otherwise. Cf. *Oregon v. Kennedy* [p. 1457].

charge. The Court of Appeals for the Eighth Circuit affirmed. The Court of Appeals reasoned that the pardoned conviction was not admissible under state law, and that "[w]ithout [it], the state has failed to provide sufficient evidence" to sustain the enhanced sentence. We granted certiorari to review this interpretation of the Double Jeopardy Clause.[6] * * *

It has long been settled [that] the Double Jeopardy Clause's general prohibition against successive prosecutions does not prevent the government from retrying a defendant who succeeds in getting his first conviction set aside, through direct appeal or collateral attack, because of some error in the proceedings leading to conviction. *Ball v. United States,* 163 U.S. 662, 16 S.Ct. 1192, 41 L.Ed. 300 (1896) (retrial permissible following reversal of conviction on direct appeal); *United States v. Tateo,* 377 U.S. 463, 84 S.Ct. 1587, 12 L.Ed.2d 448 (1964) (retrial permissible when conviction declared invalid on collateral attack). This rule, which is a "well-established part of our constitutional jurisprudence," is necessary in order to ensure the "sound administration of justice":

> "Corresponding to the right of an accused to be given a fair trial is the societal interest in punishing one whose guilt is clear after he has obtained such a trial. It would be a high price indeed for society to pay were every accused granted immunity from punishment because of any defect sufficient to constitute reversible error in the proceedings leading to conviction." *Tateo.*

Permitting retrial after a conviction has been set aside also serves the interests of defendants, for "it is at least doubtful that appellate courts would be as zealous as they now are in protecting against the effects of improprieties at the trial or pretrial stage if they knew that reversal of a conviction would put the accused irrevocably beyond the reach of further prosecution." *Ibid.*

In *Burks v. United States,* 437 U.S. 1, 98 S.Ct. 2141, 57 L.Ed.2d 1 (1978), we recognized an exception to the general rule that the Double Jeopardy Clause does not bar the retrial of a defendant who has succeeded in getting his conviction set aside for error in the proceedings below. *Burks* held that when a defendant's conviction is reversed by an appellate court on the sole ground that the evidence was insufficient to sustain the jury's verdict, the Double Jeopardy Clause bars a retrial on the same charge.

Burks was based on the view that an appellate court's reversal for insufficiency of the evidence is in effect a determination that the government's case against the defendant was so lacking that the trial court should have entered a judgment of acquittal, rather than submitting the case to the jury. Because the Double Jeopardy Clause affords the defendant who obtains a judgment of acquittal at the trial level absolute immunity from further prosecution for the same offense, it ought to do the same for the defendant who obtains an appellate determination that the trial court *should* have entered a judgment of acquittal. The fact that the

---

6. The State has attacked the ruling below on a single ground: that the defect in respondent's first sentence enhancement proceeding does not bar retrial. To reach this question, we would ordinarily have to decide two issues which are its logical antecedents: (1) whether the rule that the Double Jeopardy Clause limits the State's power to subject a defendant to successive capital sentencing proceedings, see *Bullington v. Missouri,* 451 U.S. 430, 101 S.Ct. 1852, 68 L.Ed.2d 270 (1981), carries over to noncapital sentencing proceedings, see *North Carolina v. Pearce,* 395 U.S. 711, 89 S.Ct. 2072, 23 L.Ed.2d 656 (1969); and (2) whether the rule that retrial is prohibited after a conviction is set aside by an *appellate* court for evidentiary insufficiency, see *Burks v. United States,* infra, is applicable when the determination of evidentiary insufficiency is made instead by a federal habeas court in a collateral attack on a state conviction, see *Justices of Boston Municipal Court v. Lydon,* [Note 4, p. 1482]. The courts below answered both questions in the affirmative, and the State has conceded both in its briefs and at oral argument the validity of those rulings. We therefore assume, without deciding, that these two issues present no barrier to reaching the double jeopardy claim raised here.

determination of entitlement to a judgment of acquittal is made by the appellate court rather than the trial court should not, we thought, affect its double jeopardy consequences; to hold otherwise "would create a purely arbitrary distinction" between defendants based on the hierarchical level at which the determination was made.

The question presented by this case—whether the Double Jeopardy Clause allows retrial when a reviewing court determines that a defendant's conviction must be reversed because evidence was erroneously admitted against him, and also concludes that without the inadmissible evidence there was insufficient evidence to support a conviction—was expressly reserved in *Greene v. Massey*, 437 U.S. 19, 98 S.Ct. 2151, 57 L.Ed.2d 15 (1978) at n. 9, decided the same day as *Burks*. We think the logic of *Burks* requires that the question be answered in the negative.

Burks was careful to point out that a reversal based solely on evidentiary insufficiency has fundamentally different implications, for double jeopardy purposes, than a reversal based on such ordinary "trial errors" as the "incorrect receipt or rejection of evidence." While the former is in effect a finding "that the government has failed to prove its case" against the defendant, the latter "implies nothing with respect to the guilt or innocence of the defendant," but is simply "a determination that [he] has been convicted through a judicial *process* which is defective in some fundamental respect." Id. at 15.

It appears to us to be beyond dispute that this is a situation described in *Burks* as reversal for "trial error"—the trial court erred in admitting a particular piece of evidence, and without it there was insufficient evidence to support a judgment of conviction. But clearly *with* that evidence, there was enough to support the sentence: the court and jury had before them certified copies of four prior felony convictions, and that is sufficient to support a verdict of enhancement under the statute. The fact that one of the convictions had been later pardoned by the Governor vitiated its legal effect, but it did not deprive the certified copy of that conviction of its probative value under the statute.[7] It is quite clear from our opinion in *Burks* that a reviewing court must consider all of the evidence admitted by the trial court in deciding whether retrial is permissible under the Double Jeopardy Clause—indeed, that was the *ratio decidendi* of *Burks,* and the overwhelming majority of appellate courts considering the question have agreed. The basis for the *Burks* exception to the general rule is that a reversal for insufficiency of the evidence should be treated no differently than a trial court's granting a judgment of acquittal at the close of all the evidence. A trial court in passing on such a motion considers all of the evidence it has admitted, and to make the analogy complete it must be this same quantum of evidence which is considered by the reviewing court.

Permitting retrial in this instance is not the sort of governmental oppression at which the Double Jeopardy Clause is aimed; rather, it serves the interest of the defendant by affording him an opportunity to "obtai[n] a fair readjudication of his guilt free from error." *Burks*. Had the defendant offered evidence at the sentencing hearing to prove that the conviction had become a nullity by reason of the pardon, the trial judge would presumably have allowed the prosecutor an opportunity to offer evidence of another prior conviction to support the habitual offender

---

7. We are not at all sure that the Court of Appeals was correct to describe the evidence of this conviction as "inadmissible," in view of the Arkansas statutory provision and the colloquy between court, counsel, and defendant referred to above. Evidence of the disputed conviction was introduced, and it was mistakenly thought by all concerned that the conviction had not been pardoned. Several years later it was discovered that the conviction had in fact been pardoned; the closest analogy would seem to be that of "newly discovered evidence." For purposes of our decision, however, we accept the characterization of the Court of Appeals.

charge. Our holding today thus merely recreates the situation that would have been obtained if the trial court had excluded the evidence of the conviction because of the showing of a pardon. The judgment of the Court of Appeals is accordingly reversed.

Justice MARSHALL, with whom Justice BRENNAN and Justice BLACK-MUN join, dissenting.

* * * This case is troubling in a number of respects, not the least of which is that no one in the Arkansas criminal justice system seems to have taken Nelson's pardon claim at all seriously. At bottom, however, this case is controlled by the *Burks* insufficiency principle. For under Arkansas' law of pardons, the State's evidence against Nelson in his sentencing trial was *at all times* insufficient to prove four valid prior convictions. The majority errs in treating this as a case of mere trial error, and in reaching the unsettled issue of whether, after a trial error reversal based on the improper admission of evidence, a reviewing court should evaluate the sufficiency of the evidence by including, or excluding, the tainted evidence. * * *

The delay in the discovery of Nelson's pardon does not change the essential fact that, as a matter of state law, the paper evidence of the disputed conviction presented by the prosecutor was devoid of probative value from the moment the conviction was expunged by the pardon. A pardon simply "blots out of existence" the conviction as if it had never happened. *Duncan v. State,* 494 S.W.2d 127 (Ark.1973). If, in seeking to prove Nelson's four prior convictions, the State had offered documented evidence to prove three valid prior convictions and a blank piece of paper to prove a fourth, no one would doubt that Arkansas had produced insufficient evidence and that the Double Jeopardy Clause barred retrial. There is no constitutionally significant difference between that hypothetical and this case.

* * * Even if I did not regard this as a case of insufficient evidence controlled by *Burks,* I could not join my colleagues in the majority. The question of whether a reviewing court, in evaluating insufficiency for Double Jeopardy purposes, should look to all the admitted evidence, or just the properly admitted evidence, is a complex one. * * * It seems to me that the Court's analysis of this issue should begin with the recognition that, in deciding when the double jeopardy bar should apply, we are balancing two weighty interests: the defendant's interest in repose and society's interest in the orderly administration of justice. See *e.g., United States v. Tateo* * * *. I do not intend in this dissenting opinion to settle what rule best accommodates these competing interests in cases where a reviewing court has determined that a portion of a State's proof was inadmissible. At first blush, it would seem that the defendant's interest is every bit as great in this situation as in the *Burks* situation. Society's interest, however, would appear to turn on a number of variables. The chief one is the likelihood that retrying the defendant will lead to conviction. See *United States v. Tateo* (noting society's interest "in punishing one whose guilt is clear"). In appraising this likelihood, one might inquire into whether prosecutors tend in close cases to hold back probative evidence of a defendant's guilt; if they do not, there would be scant societal interest in permitting retrial given that the State's remaining evidence is, by definition, insufficient. Alternatively, one might inquire as to why the evidence at issue was deemed inadmissible. Where evidence was stricken for reasons having to do with its unreliability, it would seem curious to include it in the sufficiency calculus. * * *

Notes and Questions

1. *The "Ball rule".* While, as the Court notes, it has "long been settled" that double jeopardy "does not prevent the government from retrying a defendant

who succeeds in getting his first conviction set aside * * * because of some error in the proceedings leading to conviction" (see p. 1478), that principle (first announced in *Ball* and commonly described as the "*Ball* rule") has not gone without challenge. Consider the position taken by Judge Macklin Fleming in *The Price of Perfect Justice*, 58 Judicature 340, 344 (1975). Discussing changes in procedure that would help to reduce delay in the administration of the criminal justice process, Judge Fleming notes: "My third suggestion is that a defendant be tried only once to judgment. If on appeal after judgment of conviction the trial is found substantially defective or unfair, the judgment should be reversed and the defendant should go free. If defects are found in the trial but the defects have not substantially influenced the result, the judgment should stand and become immune from further judicial examination. The occasional mistakes and mishaps discovered after judgment can be cured through executive action and the pardoning power without infringing upon the integrity of the court's judgment. This proposal may sound revolutionary, but it is actually a return to first principles. The English * * * [had] always had a system of only one trial to final judgment. [It] was not until 1896 in the case of *United States v. Ball* that multiple trials were sanctioned in the federal courts. One trial would certainly sharpen the responsibility of everyone connected with a criminal cause, trial judge, counsel, witnesses, appellate court, to whom the seriousness of what they were doing would be brought home by realization of its finality." Compare Thomas, *Double Jeopardy*, p. 1451 (*Ball* rule need not be based on the policy reasons advanced by *Tateo* (p. 1478); *Ball* itself relied upon a "more Blackstone-like explanation" of the *Ball* rule, recognizing that verdict finality lies at heart of the plea of former jeopardy and that the successful defense appeal removes the verdict and therefore the plea in bar).

    2.   *The prosecutor's fair opportunity.* In setting forth an evidentiary insufficiency "exception" to the *Ball* rule, the Supreme Court in *Burks* noted: "There is no claim in this case that the trial court committed error by excluding prosecution evidence, which, if received, would have rebutted any claim of evidentiary insufficiency." This statement has been taken as suggesting that a reprosecution might not be barred where the insufficiency of the government's evidence would have been "cured" by evidence erroneously excluded by the trial court. Could such a holding be squared with the premise of *Burks* that an appellate court's ruling as to insufficiency should stand in the same position as a trial court's granting of an acquittal? Cf. *Sanabria v. United States*, Note 2, p. 1472 (where an erroneous exclusion order led to a trial court acquittal and thereby barred further prosecution). Consider, however, *State v. Boone*, 393 A.2d 1361 (Md.1978), noting that *Burks* also stressed that the prosecution there had been given "one fair opportunity to offer whatever proof it could assemble." In light of that policy, *Boone* concluded, it could not "conceive" that "the rationale of *Burks*" would be applied to prohibit a retrial where the insufficiency was really the product of a judicial error in excluding evidence rather than a "failure attributable to the prosecution to prove its case."

    3.   *The thirteenth-juror reversal.* In *Tibbs v. Florida*, 457 U.S. 31, 102 S.Ct. 2211, 72 L.Ed.2d 652 (1982), a divided Court (5–4) held that *Burks* did not apply to a thirteenth-juror appellate reversal—i.e., a reversal based on the weight of the evidence rather than the sufficiency of the evidence. The majority stressed that an appellate reversal based on the weight of the evidence does not rest on the premise that an acquittal was the only proper verdict the jury could have reached. Instead, the appellate court simply expresses its disagreement with the jury's resolution of the conflicting testimony. Just as a deadlocked jury does not result in an acquittal barring retrial, an appellate court's disagreement, as the "thirteenth juror," with the trial jurors' weighing of the evidence also does not require the special deference accorded verdicts of acquittal. The majority characterized the reversal based on the weight of the evidence as designed primarily to "give the defendant a second chance," and stressed that it is available only after the reviewing court has first found that the evidence is sufficient to support the verdict under the due process mandated standard of proof beyond a reasonable doubt.

4. *Continuing proceedings.* The implications of *Burks* were explored further in JUSTICES OF BOSTON MUNICIPAL COURT v. LYDON, 466 U.S. 294, 104 S.Ct. 1805, 80 L.Ed.2d 311 (1984) and RICHARDSON v. UNITED STATES, 468 U.S. 317, 104 S.Ct. 3081, 82 L.Ed.2d 242 (1984).

In *Justices of Boston Municipal Court,* the defendant had a choice between a bench trial before the municipal court, which carried with it an absolute right to a trial de novo, or a jury trial before the same court, which was subject to the usual appellate review on the record. He chose the bench trial, and after conviction, requested a trial de novo. Before that trial commenced, however, he moved for dismissal of the charges in the second-tier court on the ground that the first-tier conviction had not been supported by sufficient evidence to establish guilt beyond a reasonable doubt. The state courts held that he was not entitled to consideration of that claim, his only avenue for relief being the trial de novo. The Supreme Court concluded that this position did not result in a second trial in violation of double jeopardy.

Justice WHITE's opinion for the Court found the state's limitation of review of the first-tier conviction to a trial de novo was consistent with both the reasoning and holding in *Burks*. The Court had there "recognized the danger of 'affording the prosecution another opportunity to supply evidence which it failed to muster in the first proceeding,' "but the "defendant's right to obtain de novo review without alleging error * * * ameliorate[d] * * * [that] concern." The two-tier system did not undercut the prosecution's incentive to put forth its strongest case in the bench trial, since the failure to do so could result in an acquittal there that would end all proceedings. The burden of the trial de novo, even if necessitated by an erroneous initial conviction, was hardly oppressive in light of the various advantages that the two-tier system afforded the defendant as compared to the usual system of appeal. Finally, if the defendant subsequently was erroneously convicted on the basis of insufficient evidence at the trial de novo, which had continued the jeopardy of the first trial, he could then rely on *Burks* to gain an appellate reversal that would preclude a new trial.

In *Richardson v. United States,* supra, the Court held that where a mistrial properly was declared following a hung jury, *Burks* did not bar a new trial, regardless of the possible insufficiency of the evidence at that first trial. Petitioner in *Richardson* had moved unsuccessfully for a judgment of directed acquittal prior to the mistrial, and he argued that the appellate court was bound to review the denial of that motion (see Note 1, p. 1432) and bar a retrial if the trial judge had erred in failing to direct an acquittal. Speaking for the majority, REHNQUIST, J. reasoned that *Burks* was limited to "the procedural setting in which it arose" and did not apply where a mistrial acceptable under the *Perez* standard allowed a retrial. Justice Rehnquist noted:

"We think that the principles governing our decision in *Burks,* and the principles governing our decisions in the hung jury cases, are readily reconciled when we recognize that the protection of the Double Jeopardy Clause by its terms applies only if there has been some event, such as an acquittal, which terminates the original jeopardy. See *Justices of Boston Municipal Court v. Lydon.* Since jeopardy attached here when the jury was sworn, petitioner's argument necessarily assumes that the judicial declaration of a mistrial was an event which terminated jeopardy in his case and which allowed him to assert a valid claim of double jeopardy. But this proposition is irreconcilable with cases such as *Perez,* and we hold on the authority of these cases that the failure of the jury to reach a verdict is not an event which terminates jeopardy. * * * The Government, like the defendant, is entitled to resolution of the case by verdict from the jury, and jeopardy does not terminate when the jury is discharged because it is unable to agree. Regardless of the sufficiency of the evidence at petitioner's first trial, he has no valid double jeopardy claim to prevent his retrial."

Dissenting in both cases, Justice BRENNAN, joined by Justice Marshall, accused the Court of relying "on a formalistic concept of continuing jeopardy." Under the Court's position, "a defendant who is constitutionally *entitled to an acquittal* but who fails to receive one—because he happens to be tried before an irrational or lawless factfinder or because his jury cannot agree on a verdict—is worse off than a defendant tried before a factfinder who demands constitutionally sufficient evidence. Indeed, he is worse off than a *guilty* defendant who is acquitted due to mistakes of fact or law."

5. *Relating the Ball rule to the mistrial rules.* Under the standard applied to mistrials, a prosecution error causing a mistrial may, depending upon the circumstances, bar further prosecution. Under the *Ball* rule, on the other hand, if a mistrial is not declared and the same error results in a conviction reversed on appeal, reprosecution will never be prohibited. The explanation traditionally given for the different consequences is that "in the * * * [*Ball*] situation the defendant has not been deprived of his option to go to the first jury and, perhaps, end the dispute then and there with an acquittal." *United States v. Jorn,* supra. See also *United States v. Tateo,* p. 1478 supra (Goldberg, J., dissenting), noting that there is a substantial constitutional difference between receiving "a jury trial, albeit not the error-free jury trial to which by law the defendant is entitled" and being deprived entirely of "the valued right to have the original jury consider [the] case."

How far does the above explanation carry? In *Kennedy,* p. 1457, the Court noted that defendant would be protected against reprosecution, notwithstanding his request for a mistrial, where prosecutorial misconduct was intended to goad the defendant into moving for a mistrial. Assume that, in such a situation, the trial court denies the mistrial request, the defendant is convicted, and that conviction is reversed on appeal. Should reprosecution be barred in light of the improper prosecutorial purpose? See Note 1, p. 1463. Several lower courts have recognized an exception to *Ball* and prohibited reprosecution in such a situation, usually as a matter of state law. Indeed, those courts have not necessarily limited their rulings to instances in which the prosecution intended to produce a mistrial, often speaking simply of conduct so prejudicial as to force a mistrial. See Ann Bowen Poulin, *The Limits of Double Jeopardy: A Course in the Dark?* 39 Vill.L.Rev. 627 (1994); Note, 94 Mich.L.Rev. 1346 (1996). But the Supreme Court "has not expressed any inclination to institute a misconduct exception to the *Ball* rule" and most courts have followed that lead. CRIMPROC § 25.4(a) (noting in particular the discussion in *Kennedy,* particularly at fn. 7). Consider also fn. 2 of *Lockhart v. Nelson.*

6. *Implied acquittals.* In GREEN v. UNITED STATES, 355 U.S. 184, 78 S.Ct. 221, 2 L.Ed.2d 199 (1957), the defendant was charged with first degree murder, and the jury was informed that they could find him guilty either of first degree murder or of the lesser included offense of second degree murder. The jury returned a verdict of guilty on the second degree murder charge, saying nothing as to the first degree murder charge. Green appealed his second degree murder conviction, and the appellate court reversed on the basis of a trial error. He was then retried on the original first degree murder charge. The second jury convicted him of first degree murder, but a divided (5–4) Supreme Court reversed, holding that double jeopardy barred conviction on that charge. The majority opinion, by BLACK, J., noted:

"Green was in direct peril of being convicted and punished for first degree murder at his first trial. He was forced to run the gauntlet once on that charge and the jury refused to convict him. When given the choice between finding him guilty of either first or second degree murder it chose the latter. In this situation the great majority of cases in this country have regarded the jury's verdict as an implicit acquittal on the charge of first degree murder. But the result in this case need not rest alone on the assumption, which we believe legitimate, that the jury for one reason or another acquitted Green of murder in the first degree. For here, the jury was dismissed without returning any express verdict on that charge and without Green's consent. Yet it was given a full opportunity to return a verdict and no extraordinary circumstances appeared which prevented it from doing so. Therefore it seems clear, under established principles of former jeopardy, that Green's jeopardy for first degree murder came to an end when the jury was discharged so that he could not be retried for that offense. In brief, we believe this case can be treated no differently, for purposes of former jeopardy, than if the jury had returned a verdict which expressly read: 'We find the defendant not guilty of murder in the first degree but guilty of murder in the second degree.' "[a]

7. Assume that a conviction on one charge carried with it an implied acquittal on another charge, the government nonetheless sought to retry defendant on both charges following the reversal of the conviction, and the trial court erroneously denied defendant's double jeopardy objection to the retrial on the charge for which he was implicitly acquitted. Following the second trial on both charges, what remedy is available to the defendant? In *Price v. Georgia,* 398 U.S. 323, 90 S.Ct. 1757, 26 L.Ed.2d 300 (1970), where the retrial resulted in a conviction only on the charge that was not jeopardy-barred, the court ordered a new trial. Defendant there, originally charged with murder and convicted of manslaughter was tried again for murder (following a reversal of the conviction based on trial error) and again convicted of the lesser-included offense of manslaughter. Reversing the conviction and remanding for a possible new trial on the manslaughter charge alone, a unanimous Court noted that the retrial on the murder charge was "an ordeal not to be viewed lightly" and that "we cannot determine whether or not the murder charge against the petitioner induced the jury to find him guilty of the less serious offense of voluntary manslaughter rather than to continue to debate his innocence." However, in *Morris v. Mathews,* 475 U.S. 237, 106 S.Ct. 1032, 89 L.Ed.2d 187 (1986), the Court refused to order a new trial where the second trial on both charges resulted in a conviction for the higher, jeopardy-barred offense. Instead, the Court reduced the level of the conviction to

---

a. The implied acquittal rationale does not apply where the jury convicts on the lesser charge, but notes it cannot reach agreement on the higher charge (resulting in a mistrial as to that charge).

The implied acquittal rationale of *Green* also does not apply to the acceptance of a guilty plea—i.e., the acceptance of a guilty plea to a lesser charge does not constitute "an inferential finding of not guilty" as to a higher charge. This conclusion follows both from the nature of the determination made by the court in accepting a guilty plea to a lesser charge (see Ch. 22, § 4) and the fact that the defendant has not really been in jeopardy as to the higher charge,

as unlike the jury in *Green,* the judge receiving the plea could not have convicted the defendant of the higher charge. Of course, if the prosecutor agrees to dismiss the higher charge in return for the plea to the lesser charge, the defendant may enforce that agreement. See Ch. 22 § 2. But if the prosecutor does not agree to the dismissal, the prosecutor may be able to continue the prosecution on the higher charge notwithstanding the guilty plea to the lesser charge. See *Ohio v. Johnson,* Note 2, p. 1055. Also, with no implied acquittal, if the defendant should overturn his guilty plea to the lesser charge, double jeopardy does not bar prosecution on the higher charge. See Note 13, p. 1267.

the lesser included offense that was not jeopardy barred. In *Price,* the *Morris* Court noted, it had been concerned that the retrial on the offense for which defendant had been implicitly acquitted had resulted in a compromise verdict. Here, since the jury on the second trial had convicted defendant of the jeopardy-barred count of aggravated murder, it had necessarily found, without a suggestion of a possible compromise, that the state had established all of the elements of the lesser included offense of non-aggravated murder that was not jeopardy-barred. In this situation, said the Court, it would be "incongruous" to remedy the double jeopardy violation that occurred in trying the defendant on the jeopardy-barred count by ordering "yet another trial."

8. *Sentencing.* As suggested in footnote 6 of *Lockhart,* sentencing decisions ordinarily are distinguished from decisions as to guilt or innocence in the application of the double jeopardy clause. Thus, in *North Carolina v. Pearce,* cited in footnote 6, the Court held that the implied acquittal doctrine of *Green* did not apply to a judge's decision to sentence the defendant to less than the maximum sentence in connection with a conviction later overturned. Accordingly, when a defendant's initial conviction was reversed on appeal, and he was subsequently retried and reconvicted, and sentenced to a higher term of incarceration than had been imposed on the original conviction, *Pearce* held that that higher term was not barred by the double jeopardy clause (although it could violate due process, see p. 1535). *United States v. DiFrancesco,* 449 U.S. 117, 101 S.Ct. 426, 66 L.Ed.2d 328 (1980), similarly found sentencing to be distinguishable from either a conviction or an acquittal in ruling that Congress could provide for governmental appeal of a sentence where the judge allegedly misconstrued the sentencing law in failing to impose an increased term under a "dangerous offender provision." However, *Bullington v. Missouri,* cited in footnote 6, held that traditional double jeopardy standards applied to one type of sentencing decision—that made by a jury in a capital sentencing proceeding. The Court noted that where the jury's determination not to impose the death penalty came after a trial-type hearing in which it focused on special factual standards (aggravating and mitigating factors) governing the imposition of that penalty, that determination was comparable to a trial acquittal as to that sentence. The lower courts in *Lockhart v. Nelson,* as noted in footnote 6, concluded that the sentencing determination there had the same status for double jeopardy purposes as the sentencing determination in *Bullington.* However, in *Monge v. California,* 524 U.S. 721, 118 S.Ct. 2246, 141 L.Ed.2d 615 (1998), the Court held that *Bullington* did not extend beyond the capital sentencing context, and therefore double jeopardy did not bar a retrial on the issue of whether a prior conviction met the prerequisites for recidivist sentencing in a noncapital sentencing proceeding.

SECTION 4. REPROSECUTION BY A DIFFERENT SOVEREIGN

HEATH v. ALABAMA
474 U.S. 82, 106 S.Ct. 433, 88 L.Ed.2d 387 (1985)

Justice O'CONNOR delivered the opinion of the Court. * * *

In August 1981, petitioner, Larry Gene Heath, hired Charles Owens and Gregory Lumpkin to kill his wife, Rebecca Heath, who was then nine months pregnant, for a sum of $2,000. On the morning of August 31, 1981, petitioner left the Heath residence in Russell County, Alabama, to meet with Owens and Lumpkin in Georgia, just over the Alabama border from the Heath home. Petitioner led them back to the Heath residence, gave them the keys to the

Heaths' car and house, and left the premises in his girlfriend's truck. Owens and Lumpkin then kidnaped Rebecca Heath from her home. The Heath car, with Rebecca Heath's body inside, was later found on the side of a road in Troup County, Georgia. The cause of death was a gunshot wound in the head. The estimated time of death and the distance from the Heath residence to the spot where Rebecca Heath's body was found are consistent with the theory that the murder took place in Georgia, and respondent does not contend otherwise.

Georgia and Alabama authorities pursued dual investigations in which they cooperated to some extent. * * * In November 1981, the grand jury of Troup County, Georgia indicted petitioner for the offense of "malice" murder. Georgia then served petitioner with notice of its intention to seek the death penalty, citing as the aggravating circumstance the fact that the murder was "caused and directed" by petitioner. On February 10, 1982, petitioner pleaded guilty to the Georgia murder charge in exchange for a sentence of life imprisonment, which he understood could involve his serving as few as seven years in prison.

On May 5, 1982, the grand jury of Russell County, Alabama, returned an indictment against petitioner for the capital offense of murder during a kidnaping. Before trial on this indictment, petitioner entered pleas of *autrefois convict* and former jeopardy under the Alabama and United States Constitutions, arguing that his conviction and sentence in Georgia barred his prosecution in Alabama for the same conduct. After a hearing, the trial court rejected petitioner's double jeopardy claims. It assumed, *arguendo,* that the two prosecutions could not have been brought in succession by one State but held that double jeopardy did not bar successive prosecutions by two different States for the same act. * * *

On January 12, 1983, the Alabama jury convicted petitioner of murder during a kidnaping in the first degree. After a sentencing hearing, the jury recommended the death penalty. * * * The judge accepted the jury's recommendation, finding that the sole aggravating factor, that the capital offense was "committed while the defendant was engaged in the commission of a kidnapping," outweighed the sole mitigating factor, that the "defendant was convicted of the murder of Rebecca Heath in the Superior Court of Troup County, Georgia, * * * and received a sentence of life imprisonment in that court." [The state appellate courts affirmed the conviction and sentence.]

Petitioner sought a writ of certiorari from this Court, raising double jeopardy claims and claims based on Alabama's exercise of jurisdiction. No due process objections were asserted. We granted certiorari limited to the question of whether Alabama's conviction was barred by this Court's decision in *Brown v. Ohio* [p. 1034], and requested the parties to address the question of the applicability of the dual sovereignty doctrine to successive prosecutions by two States.

Successive prosecutions are barred by the Fifth Amendment only if the two offenses for which the defendant is prosecuted are the "same" for double jeopardy purposes. Respondent does not contravene petitioner's contention that the offenses of "murder during a kidnaping" and "malice murder," as construed by the courts of Alabama and Georgia respectively, may be considered greater and lesser offenses and, thus, the "same" offense under *Brown v. Ohio*, absent operation of the dual sovereignty principle. We, therefore, assume *arguendo* that, had these offenses arisen under the laws of one State and had petitioner been separately prosecuted for both offenses in that State, the second conviction would have been barred by the Double Jeopardy Clause.

The sole remaining question upon which we granted certiorari is whether the dual sovereignty doctrine permits successive prosecutions under the laws of different States which otherwise would be held to "subject [the defendant] for the same offence to be twice put in jeopardy." Although we have not previously so held, we believe the answer to this query is inescapable. The dual sovereignty doctrine, as originally articulated and consistently applied by this Court, compels the conclusion that successive prosecutions by two States for the same conduct are not barred by the Double Jeopardy Clause.

The dual sovereignty doctrine is founded on the common law conception of crime as an offense against the sovereignty of the government. When a defendant in a single act violates the "peace and dignity" of two sovereigns by breaking the laws of each, he has committed two distinct "offenses." * * * As the Court explained in *Moore v. Illinois,* 14 How. 13, 14 L.Ed. 306 (1852), "[a]n offence, in its legal signification, means the transgression of a law." Consequently, when the same act transgresses the laws of two sovereigns, "it cannot be truly averred that the offender has been twice punished for the same offense; but only that by one act he has committed two offenses, for each of which he is justly punishable."

In applying the dual sovereignty doctrine, then, the crucial determination is whether the two entities that seek successively to prosecute a defendant for the same course of conduct can be termed separate sovereigns. This determination turns on whether the two entities draw their authority to punish the offender from distinct sources of power. Thus, the Court has uniformly held that the States are separate sovereigns with respect to the Federal Government because each State's power to prosecute is derived from its own "inherent sovereignty," not from the Federal Government. See *Abbate v. United States* [Note 1, p. 1490]. * * * See also *Bartkus v. Illinois* [Note 1, p. 1490]. * * * The States are no less sovereign with respect to each other than they are with respect to the Federal Government. Their powers to undertake criminal prosecutions derive from separate and independent sources of power and authority originally belonging to them before admission to the Union and preserved to them by the Tenth Amendment. * * *

In those instances where the Court has found the dual sovereignty doctrine inapplicable, it has done so because the two prosecuting entities did not derive their powers to prosecute from independent sources of authority. Thus, the Court has held that successive prosecutions by federal and territorial courts are barred because such courts are "creations emanating from the same sovereignty." Similarly, municipalities that derive their power to try a defendant from the same organic law that empowers the State to prosecute are not separate sovereigns with respect to the State. See *Waller v. Florida* [Note 5, p. 1492]. These cases confirm that it is the presence of independent sovereign authority to prosecute, not the relation between States and the Federal Government in our federalist system, that constitutes the basis for the dual sovereignty doctrine. * * *

Petitioner invites us to restrict the applicability of the dual sovereignty principle to cases in which two governmental entities, having concurrent jurisdiction and pursuing quite different interests, can demonstrate that allowing only one entity to exercise jurisdiction over the defendant will interfere with the unvindicated interests of the second entity and that multiple prosecutions therefore are necessary for the satisfaction of the legitimate interests of both entities. This balancing of interests approach, however, cannot be reconciled with the dual sovereignty principle. This Court has plainly and repeatedly stated that two identical offenses are *not* the "same offence" within the meaning of the Double Jeopardy Clause if they are prosecuted by different sovereigns. If the States are separate sovereigns, as they must be under the definition of sovereignty which the Court consistently has employed, the circumstances of the case are irrelevant.

Petitioner, then, is asking the Court to discard its sovereignty analysis and to substitute in its stead his difficult and uncertain balancing of interests approach. The Court has refused a similar request on at least one previous occasion, see *Abbate v. United States,* and rightfully so. The Court's express rationale for the dual sovereignty doctrine is not simply a fiction that can be disregarded in difficult cases. It finds weighty support in the historical understanding and political realities of the States' role in the federal system and in the words of the Double Jeopardy Clause itself, "nor shall any person be subject for the same *offence* to be twice put in jeopardy of life or limb." * * *

It is axiomatic that "[i]n America, the powers of sovereignty are divided between the government of the Union, and those of the States. They are each sovereign, with respect to the objects committed to it, and neither sovereign with respect to the objects committed to the other." *M'Culloch v. Maryland,* 4 Wheat. 316, 4 L.Ed. 579 (1819). * * * Foremost among the prerogatives of sovereignty is the power to create and enforce a criminal code. To deny a State its power to enforce its criminal laws because another State has won the race to the courthouse "would be a shocking and untoward deprivation of the historic right and obligation of the States to maintain peace and order within their confines."

Such a deprivation of a State's sovereign powers cannot be justified by the assertion that under "interest analysis" the State's legitimate penal interests will be satisfied through a prosecution conducted by another State. A State's interest in vindicating its sovereign authority through enforcement of its laws by definition can never be satisfied by another State's enforcement of its own laws. Just as the Federal Government has the right to decide that a state prosecution has not vindicated a violation of the "peace and dignity" of the Federal Government, a State must be entitled to decide that a prosecution by another State has not satisfied its legitimate sovereign interest. In recognition of this fact, the Court consistently has endorsed the principle that a single act constitutes an "offence" against each sovereign whose laws are violated by that act. The Court has always understood the words of the Double Jeopardy Clause to reflect this fundamental principle, and we see no reason why we should reconsider that understanding today.

Justice MARSHALL, with whom Justice BRENNAN joins, dissenting.[a]

* * * Under the constitutional scheme, the Federal Government has been given the exclusive power to vindicate certain of our Nation's sovereign interests, leaving the States to exercise complementary authority over matters of more local concern. The respective spheres of the Federal Government and the States may overlap at times, and even where they do not, different interests may be implicated by a single act. See e.g., *Abbate v. United States* (conspiracy to dynamite telephone company facilities entails both destruction of property and disruption of federal communications network). Yet were a prosecution by a State, however zealously pursued, allowed to preclude further prosecution by the Federal Government for the same crime, an entire range of national interests could be frustrated. The importance of those federal interests has thus quite properly been permitted to trump a defendant's interest in avoiding successive prosecutions or multiple punishments for the same crime. Conversely, because the States under our federal system have the principal responsibility for defining and prosecuting crimes, it would be inappropriate—in the absence of a specific congressional intent to preempt state action pursuant to the Supremacy Clause—to allow a federal prosecution to preclude state authorities from vindicating the historic right and obligation of the States to maintain peace and order within their confines. * * *

Where two States seek to prosecute the same defendant for the same crime in two separate proceedings, the justifications found in the federal-state context for an exemption from double jeopardy constraints simply do not hold. Although the two States may have opted for different policies within their assigned territorial jurisdictions, the sovereign concerns with whose vindication each State has been

a. Justice Brennan's separate dissent is omitted.

charged are identical. Thus, in contrast to the federal-state context, barring the second prosecution would still permit one government to act upon the broad range of sovereign concerns that have been reserved to the States by the Constitution. The compelling need in the federal-state context to subordinate double jeopardy concerns is thus considerably diminished in cases involving successive prosecutions by different States. Moreover, from the defendant's perspective, the burden of successive prosecutions cannot be justified as the *quid pro quo* of dual citizenship.

* * * Although, in granting Heath's petition for certiorari, this Court ordered the parties to focus upon the dual sovereignty issue, I believe the Court errs in refusing to consider the fundamental unfairness of the process by which petitioner stands condemned to die. Even where the power of two sovereigns to pursue separate prosecutions for the same crime has been undisputed, this Court has barred both governments from combining to do together what each could not constitutionally do on its own. See *Murphy v. Waterfront Comm'n* [p. 692]; *Elkins v. United States*, 364 U.S. 206, 80 S.Ct. 1437, 4 L.Ed.2d 1669 (1960).[2] And just as the Constitution bars one sovereign from facilitating another's prosecution by delivering testimony coerced under promise of immunity or evidence illegally seized, I believe that it prohibits two sovereigns from combining forces to ensure that a defendant receives only the trappings of criminal process as he is sped along to execution.

While no one can doubt the propriety of two States cooperating to bring a criminal to justice, the cooperation between Georgia and Alabama in this case went far beyond their initial joint investigation. Georgia's efforts to secure petitioner's execution did not end with its acceptance of his guilty plea. Its law enforcement officials went on to play leading roles as prosecution witnesses in the Alabama trial. * * * Although the record does not reveal the precise nature of the assurances made by Georgia authorities that induced petitioner to plead guilty in the first proceeding against him, I cannot believe he would have done so had he been aware that the officials whose forbearance he brought in Georgia with his plea would merely continue their efforts to secure his death in another jurisdiction. Cf. *Santobello v. New York* [p. 1260].

Even before the Fourteenth Amendment was held to incorporate the protections of the Double Jeopardy Clause, four Members of this Court [in dissent] registered their outrage at "an instance of the prosecution being allowed to harass the accused with repeated trials and convictions on the same evidence, until it achieve[d] its desired result of a capital verdict." *Ciucci v. Illinois*, 356 U.S. 571, 78 S.Ct. 839, 2 L.Ed.2d 983 (1958) [where defendant, who had killed his wife and two children on the same occasion, was prosecuted separately for each killing, and received life sentences at the first two trials and a death sentence at the third]. Such "relentless prosecutions," they asserted, constituted "an unseemly and oppressive use of a criminal trial that violates the concept of due process contained in the Fourteenth Amendment, whatever its ultimate scope is taken to be." The only differences between the facts in *Ciucci* and those in this case are that here the relentless effort was a cooperative one between two States and that petitioner sought to avoid trial by pleading guilty. Whether viewed as a violation of the Double Jeopardy Clause or simply as an affront to the due process

---

2. To be sure, *Murphy,* which bars a State from compelling a witness to give testimony that might be used against him in a federal prosecution, and *Elkins,* which bars the introduction in a federal prosecution of evidence illegally seized by state officers, do not necessarily undermine the basis of the rule allowing successive state and federal prosecutions. It is one thing to bar a sovereign from using certain evidence and quite another to bar it from prosecuting altogether. But these cases can be read to suggest that despite the independent sovereign status of the Federal and State Governments, courts should not be blind to the impact of combined federal-state law enforcement on an accused's constitutional rights. * * *

guarantee of fundamental fairness. Alabama's prosecution of petitioner cannot survive constitutional scrutiny. I therefore must dissent.

Notes and Questions

1. *Federal/state prosecutions.* As noted in *Heath,* the Supreme Court in BARTKUS v. ILLINOIS, 359 U.S. 121, 79 S.Ct. 676, 3 L.Ed.2d 684 (1959), reaffirmed a long line of decisions rejecting constitutional challenges to successive state and federal prosecutions based on the same conduct. In *Bartkus,* the defendant initially had been tried and acquitted in federal court for robbery of a federally insured bank, but was then tried and convicted in state court for the same bank robbery under the general robbery provision of the state criminal code. The Supreme Court majority, per FRANKFURTER, J., stressed that "state and federal courts have for years refused to bar a second trial even though there had been a prior trial by another government for a similar offense," and it could find no justification for departing from this "long unbroken, unquestioned course of adjudication." The federal system, it was noted, was devised by the Founders as a "safeguard against arbitrary government," and the "greatest self-restraint is necessary when that federal system yields results with which a court is in little sympathy."

The *Bartkus* majority also cited a "practical justification" for refusing to bar separate state and federal prosecutions, as illustrated by the fact situation presented in *Screws v. United States,* 325 U.S. 91, 65 S.Ct. 1031, 89 L.Ed. 1495 (1945), where three police officers had been prosecuted under the federal Civil Rights Acts for the denial of the due process rights of a black prisoner being held for trial by purposefully beating the prisoner to death. Speaking to the consequences of barring a state prosecution in such a case, Justice Frankfurter noted: "[D]efendants were tried and convicted * * * under federal statutes with maximum sentences of a year and two years respectively. But the state crime there involved was a capital offense. Were the federal prosecution of a comparatively minor offense to prevent state prosecution of so grave an infraction of state law, the result would be a shocking and untoward deprivation of the historic right and obligation of the States to maintain peace and order within their confines. It would be in derogation of our federal system to displace the reserved power of States over state offenses by reason of prosecution of minor federal offenses by federal authorities beyond the control of the States."[a]

The *Bartkus* order of prosecutions was reversed in the companion case of ABBATE v. UNITED STATES, 359 U.S. 187, 79 S.Ct. 666, 3 L.Ed.2d 729 (1959). During a strike against an interstate telephone company, the petitioners had agreed to dynamite the telephone company's facilities, but had subsequently withdrawn from the conspiracy and disclosed the plot. They originally were indicted in a state court for conspiring to destroy the property of another in violation of state law. Upon pleading guilty, each was sentenced to three months imprisonment. Thereafter, based upon the same conspiracy, they were prosecuted in a district court for the federal felony offense of conspiring to destroy facilities that were "an integral part" of a system of communication "controlled by the United States." Upholding their federal conviction, the Supreme Court majority, per BRENNAN, J., held that the federal prosecution did not violate the double

---

a. A dissenting opinion by Justice Black, joined by Chief Justice Warren and Justice Douglas, rejected the precedents cited by the majority, arguing that the "long established" principle against using "government power to try people twice for the same conduct" should not be subverted "in the name of federation." The dissent argued in the alternative that the majority had gone beyond the leading prior decision in upholding here "a state conviction of a defendant who had been *acquitted* of the same offense in the federal courts."

jeopardy bar. Justice Brennan's opinion reiterated the fears voiced in earlier cases that "if the States are free to prosecute criminal acts violating their laws, and the resultant state prosecutions bar federal prosecutions based on the same acts, federal law enforcement must necessarily be hindered."

2. The "sham" second-prosecution exception. Discussing the cooperation between state and federal officials in *Bartkus,* Justice Frankfurter noted:

"The record establishes * * * that [the] federal officials acted in cooperation with state authorities, as is the conventional practice between the two sets of prosecutors throughout the country. It does not support the claim that the State of Illinois in bringing its prosecution was merely a tool of the federal authorities, who thereby avoided the prohibition of the Fifth Amendment against a retrial of a federal prosecution after an acquittal. It does not sustain a conclusion that the state prosecution was a sham or a cover for a federal prosecution, and thereby in essential fact another federal prosecution."

Lower courts generally have read this language as establishing a "narrow" exception to the allowance of multiple prosecutions under the dual sovereignty doctrine. The lower courts have added that "the burden * * * of establishing that federal officials are controlling or manipulating the state process is substantial; the [defendant] must demonstrate that the state officials had little or no independent volition in the state proceedings." *United States v. Liddy,* 542 F.2d 76 (D.C.Cir.1976). They have also suggested that, absent a showing of duress, federal or state prosecutors satisfy the independent volition test by having made the "sovereign decision to sign a charging instrument." *United States v. Davis,* 906 F.2d 829 (2d Cir.1990). In light of such standards (and the absence of any reported case in which the exception was successfully raised), commentators have described the exception as "the existing nonexistent exception" and the "illusory exception." See Daniel Bram, *Praying to False Sovereigns: The Role of Successive Prosecutions in an Age of Cooperative Federalism,* 20 Am.J.Crim.L. 1 (1992); Note, 102 Yale L.J. 281 (1992). See also Sandra Guerra, *The Myth of Dual Sovereignty: Multijurisdictional Law Enforcement and Double Jeopardy,* 73 N.C.L.Rev. 1160 (1995) (where "federal and state law enforcement and prosecuting authorities work together as one team with a mutual goal", as they often do in drug law enforcement, "the reasons for granting each sovereign the power to enforce its law disappear").

3. D.O.J. Guidelines. Shortly after *Abbate,* Attorney General Rogers issued a memorandum to U.S. Attorneys setting forth guidelines for the exercise of federal prosecutorial authority successive to a state prosecution. Now set forth in the United States Attorneys' Manual § 9–2.142, these guidelines "preclude the initiation or continuation of a federal prosecution, following a prior state prosecution * * * based on substantially the same act(s) or transaction(s) unless the following three substantive prerequisites are satisfied: (a) the matter must involve a substantial federal interest; (b) the prior prosecution must have left that interest demonstrably unvindicated; and (c) applying the same test applicable to all federal prosecutions, the government must believe that the defendant(s)' conduct constitutes a federal offense, and that the admissible evidence probably will be sufficient to obtain and sustain a conviction by an unbiased trier of fact." The determination that these conditions have been met must be approved by "the appropriate Assistant Attorney General." This policy is known as the *Petite* policy, based on its recognition by the Supreme Court in *Petite v. United States,* 361 U.S. 529, 80 S.Ct. 450, 4 L.Ed.2d 490 (1960). Undoubtedly the most highly publicized and controversial federal prosecutions approved under this policy have been federal civil rights prosecutions which followed state acquittals (or state convictions that produced "lenient" sentences) on the underlying assaults and homicides. Those prosecutions have sparked a reexamination of the *Bartkus/Abbate* rulings in the scholarly literature, producing a variety of views as to when (if ever) a federal prosecution should be allowed following a state prosecution on the same events. See e.g., the articles by Laurie Levinson. Susan Herman, Paul Hoffman, and Paul Cassell, in the Symposium, *The Rodney King Trials: Civil Rights, Prosecutions, and Double Jeopardy,* 41 U.C.L.A.L.Rev. 509–721 (1994).

4. *State law restrictions.* A majority of the states would prohibit under state law a state prosecution that follows a federal prosecution in the situation presented in *Bartkus.* See CRIMPROC § 25.5(b). In a few of these states, appellate decisions have held that state constitutional provisions bar such a state prosecution. Most, however, rely on statutes that specifically prohibit state prosecution for offenses that relate to a previous federal prosecution (or, under some statutes, a previous prosecution in another state). Such statutes vary in scope. Some prohibit a state prosecution based on the "same act or omission" as the federal prosecution, some prohibit a state prosecution unless that prosecution and the federal prosecution each require proof of a fact not required by the other, and a few bar state prosecutions based on the "same transaction" as the federal prosecution. Ibid. State courts applying these different standards have produced decisions that do not always reflect the comparative breadth or narrowness of the state standard. Consider, e.g., the following rulings: *Journey v. State,* 521 S.W.2d 210 (Ark.1975) (under a statute prohibiting prosecution for state offenses "committed in the same course of conduct" and of the "same character" as the federal offense, defendant's acquittal on federal charges of transporting stolen property across state lines did not bar state prosecution for possession of stolen property; defendant could have been innocent of transporting the property yet still guilty of possessing it); *Epps v. Commonwealth,* 216 S.E.2d 64 (Va.1975) (where defendant had been acquitted of the federal offense of aggravated bank robbery—prohibiting robbery "of an insured bank under the aggravated circumstances of jeopardizing the life of 'any person' in the course of the robbery"—state prosecution for attempted murder of the bank guard was permissible under a statute prohibiting state prosecution for the "same act" as federal prosecution); *People v. Abbamonte,* 371 N.E.2d 485 (N.Y.1977) (under a same "act or criminal transaction" standard, a state prosecution for substantive drug offenses was precluded by a federal prosecution for conspiracy to violate federal drug laws that covered the period in which the state offense occurred; although the state offenses were not listed as overt acts in the federal charge, they could have been used by the federal prosecutor as acts taken in furtherance of the conspiracy).

5. *State/municipal prosecutions.* In *Waller v. Florida,* 397 U.S. 387, 90 S.Ct. 1184, 25 L.Ed.2d 435 (1970), a unanimous Court refused to extend the dual sovereignty doctrine to successive municipal and state prosecutions. Petitioner there had removed a canvas mural which was affixed to a wall inside the city hall and had carried it through the streets until, after a scuffle with the police, it was recovered in a damaged condition. After being convicted of violating two city ordinances (destruction of city property, disorderly breach of the peace), he was convicted of the felony of grand larceny in violation of state law. On the basis of the state court's view that the felony charge was based on the "same acts" as the city ordinance violations and on the state court's "assumption that the ordinance violations were included offenses of the felony charge," the Court held that the second trial violated the double jeopardy prohibition. *Bartkus* and *Abbate* were distinguished on the ground that cities and states are not "separate sovereignties"; rather, cities, counties, and other political subdivisions of states are "subordinate governmental instrumentalities created by the State to assist in the carrying out of state governmental functions."

Although the Court in *Waller* did not specify what standard would be used in determining whether an ordinance and a state statute encompass the same offense, lower courts have assumed that the *Blockburger* standard, traditionally applied to prosecutions under separate state statutes (see p. 1034), also applies here. Lower courts have also held that the *Waller* ruling is subject to a "subsequent events exception," applicable to situations in which the state offense was not fully consummated when the ordinance prosecution was brought (e.g., where the assault victim subsequently died), and to a "collusion exception," applicable to situations in which the ordinance conviction was procured by collusion between the offender and city officials for the purpose of protecting the offender against more serious state charges. See CRIMPROC § 25.5(c).

CHAPTER 27
SENTENCING

SECTION 1. INTRODUCTION TO SENTENCING

Sentencing is the culmination of the criminal process. Prior to sentencing, potential and expected sentences drive the choices of prosecutors, defendants, defense counsel, judges, and even police. A defendant's ability to obtain release prior to trial, his right to the assistance of counsel, and his right to a jury all depend at least in part on the sentence he may receive. And sentencing has a profound impact on charging decisions and plea bargaining. "For most defendants," observed one judge, "sentencing is what the case is really about."[a] Because of its pervasive influence, it is, many practitioners believe, the most important aspect of the criminal process to understand.

A. Purposes of Punishment

Punishment's major objectives—rehabilitation, deterrence, incapacitation, and retribution—should be familiar concepts from your basic course on criminal law. The prevailing rationales for inflicting punishment for violations of the criminal law have varied over time. As you read the material in this chapter, consider how sentencing philosophy affects not only the choices of individual judges and juries in selecting the appropriate sentence for a particular offender, but also the choices of lawmakers in creating and administering a sentencing system.

1 WAYNE R. LAFAVE & AUSTIN W. SCOTT, JR., SUBSTANTIVE CRIMINAL LAW
§ 1.5, 38–40 (1986).

It is undoubtedly true that the thinking of legislators, judges and juries, and administrative officers who have a part in fixing punishment, as well as the thinking of the expert criminologist and non-expert layman whose views tend to influence those officials, varies from situation to situation. Sometimes the retribution theory will predominate; most of us share the common feeling of mankind that a particularly shocking crime should be severely punished. Where, for example, a son, after thoughtfully taking out insurance on his mother's life, places a time bomb in her suitcase just before she boards a plane, which [kills] the mother and all forty-two others aboard the plane, we almost all feel that he deserves a severe punishment, and we reach this result with little reflection about influencing future conduct. Likewise, when a less serious crime is involved and it was committed by a young person who might be effectively reformed, the rehabili-

---

a. United States v. Wise, 976 F.2d 393, 409   and dissenting in part).
(8th Cir.1992) (Arnold, C.J., concurring in part

tation theory rightly assumes primary importance. And the deterrence theory may be most important when the crime is not inherently wrong or covered by moral prohibition. Illustrative are income tax violations, as to which deterrence is especially important because of our reliance on a system of self-assessment.

Although allowance must be made for such variables, it is fair to say, as a general proposition, that for much of the [twentieth] century the pendulum has been swinging away from retribution and deterrence and in the direction of rehabilitation as the chief goal of punishment; or, to put it differently, away from the philosophy that the punishment should fit the crime toward one that the punishment should fit the criminal. * * * In part, this may be attributed to the fact that we still know very little about the deterrent effect of punishment on potential offenders, while we have gained increased knowledge of the causes of human conduct as the result of scientific study in such fields as psychology, psychiatry, and criminology.

> * * * Almost all of the characteristic innovations in criminal justice in this century are reflections of the rehabilitative ideal: the juvenile court, the indeterminate sentence, systems of probation and parole, the youth authority, and the promise (if not the reality) of therapeutic programs in prisons, juvenile institutes, and mental hospitals. * * * [I]t is remarkable how widely the rehabilitative ideal was accepted in this century as a statement of aspirations for the penal system, a statement largely endorsed by the media, politicians, and ordinary citizens.[†]

But skepticism regarding the rehabilitative model began developing in the mid–1960's, and about ten years later there came "an explosion of criticism * * * calling for restructuring of the theoretical underpinnings of the criminal sanction." This rejection of rehabilitation, usually in favor of a "just deserts" theory, was prompted by several considerations. One was the concern with the wide disparity in sentencing which resulted from giving judges broad sentencing discretion to act according to the perceived rehabilitative needs in the particular case. The "just deserts" model was seen as necessary "to counter the capricious and irresponsible uses of state power." The existing system was perceived by many as being arbitrary because rehabilitative efforts were often unsuccessful. When confidence was "lost in the rehabilitative capacities of penal programs and in the ability of parole boards and correctional officers to determine when reformation has been achieved, the rehabilitationist rationale for treatment differentials no longer serves, and the differences are seen as irrational and indefensible." Finally, the retribution or "just deserts" theory, precisely because it "operates from a consensus model of society where the community * * * is acting in the right" and "the criminal is acting in the wrong," had appeal because it seemed to reaffirm our moral values at a time when they were under frequent attack.

This trend is reflected by "a spate of legislative proposals, enacted or advocated throughout the country, that attack the statutory expressions of the rehabilitative ideal. The objects of this attack are sentencing discretion, the indeterminate sentence, the parole function, the uses of probation in cases of serious criminality, and even allowances of 'good time' credit in the prisons." If this trend continues, then an increasing number of jurisdictions will adopt sentencing schemes which place the greatest emphasis upon the nature of the crime which was committed and comparatively little upon the characteristics of the particular offender.

---

† Francis A. Allen, The Decline of the Reha- pose 6 (1981).
bilitative Ideal: Penal Policy and Social Pur-

B. Types of Sentences

1. *Capital punishment.* The most severe penalty facing a person convicted of crime in the United States is the penalty of execution. In 1972 the Supreme Court interpreted the Constitution to bar then-existing capital sentencing policies as too arbitrary, striking down dozens of state sentencing schemes. *Furman v. Georgia,* 408 U.S. 238, 92 S.Ct. 2726, 33 L.Ed.2d 346 (1972). The Court soon upheld revised state sentencing statutes that it found adequately ensured that death sentences would be imposed in a more consistent, yet more individualized, manner. See *Gregg v. Georgia,* 428 U.S. 153, 96 S.Ct. 2909, 49 L.Ed.2d 859 (1976). Decades later, scholars and judges continue to disagree over whether or not the Court's ongoing efforts to craft detailed procedural protections for capital defendants have made, or ever will make, the imposition of the death penalty in the United States any less arbitrary than it was before *Furman.*

Today the sentencing phase of a capital case is in most states a trial-like hearing before the jury that considered the defendant's guilt, during which the government presents proof of the reasons the jury ought to sentence the defendant to death, and the defendant has the opportunity to confront that evidence and present evidence of his own. The jurors' job is to determine the presence or absence of certain aggravating or mitigating factors upon which their sentencing decision must rest. Jurors are instructed that they must agree that these aggravating factors have been established beyond a reasonable doubt before they can impose a death sentence. The jury may consider evidence concerning the character of the convicted defendant and, in many jurisdictions, evidence of the impact of the crime on the victim's family. Some states allow the judge to "override" a jury's decision to spare the defendant's life. See Note 7, p. 1319. The rules limiting appellate and post-conviction review of sentences are often relaxed for death sentences, providing for more complete review. These and other aspects of the procedure required for the imposition of capital punishment have undergone intensive regulation by courts and legislatures in the past several decades, the details of which are beyond the scope of this chapter. Students interested in capital punishment, its history, or its administration, should consult the many excellent sources available on this topic.[b]

Presently, the federal government and about three-quarters of the states authorize the death penalty, and in all but four of these jurisdictions the jury is asked to decide whether the defendant should be sentenced to death. Between 2,000 and 4,000 defendants per year are charged with capital murder. About 6 to 15% receive a death sentence, for an average of about 250 death sentences per year. As of April 1, 2001, there were over 3,700 prisoners on death row in the United States. Over 1,400 are from three states—California, Texas, and Florida. Dept. of Justice, Sourcebook of Criminal Justice Statistics, tbl. 6.83 (http://www.ojp.usdoj.gov/bjs/sourcebook.htm) (hereinafter SOURCEBOOK).

---

b. For more on the law governing the imposition of the death penalty, see Hugo Adam Bedeau, The Death Penalty in America: Current Controversies (1997); Randall Kennedy, Race, Crime & the Law (1997); John F. Galliher, Gregory Ray & Brent Cook, *Abolition and Reinstatement of Capital Punishment During the Progressive Era and Early 20th Century,* 83 J.Crim.L. & Criminology 538 (1992); William J. Bowers, Glen L. Pierce & John F. McDevitt, Legal Homicide: Death as Punishment in America, 1864–1982 (1984); Carol S. Steiker & Jordan M. Steiker, *Sober Second Thoughts:* *Reflections on Two Decades of Constitutional Regulation of Capital Punishment,* 109 Harv. L.Rev. 355 (1995); Carol S. Steiker & Jordan M. Steiker, *The Constitutional Regulation of Capital Punishment Since* Furman v. Georgia, 29 St. Mary's L.J. 971 (1998). On methods of execution, see Deborah W. Denno, *Is Electrocution An Unconstitutional Method of Execution? The Engineering of Death Over the Century,* 35 Wm. & Mary L.Rev. 551 (1994). A wealth of sources, including internet sites, is collected in Randall Coyne & Lyn Entzeroth, Capital Punishment and the Judicial Process (2d ed. 2001).

2. *Incarceration.* Incarceration is authorized for nearly all serious offenses. Sentences of incarceration can be divided into two types: indeterminate and determinate. An *indeterminate sentence* typically includes a maximum and minimum term set by the judge within legislated limits, and leaves to the parole board the task of determining the precisely when the defendant will be released. This type of sentencing encourages efforts to reform and permits the actual sentence to track the rehabilitative progress of an offender. Once in use in every jurisdiction, it is now used in only about two-thirds of the states. A *determinate sentence* is a fixed term set by the judge; early release on parole is not available. This type of sentencing is used in federal courts and the remaining states. A period of supervised release typically follows the completion of a determinate sentence.

In 1998, 69% of felons in state court were sentenced to prison or to jail. SOURCEBOOK, tbl. 5.52. The number of inmates in federal and state prisons and jails has grown from 744,208 in 1985 to 1,933,503 in 2000. Id. tbl. 6.19. Another four and one half million are on probation or parole. *Id.* tbl. 6.1. The United States has one of the highest rates of incarceration in the world. See Erika Fairchild, Comparative Criminal Justice Systems 197 (1993). Indeed, jail and prison overcrowding is often expressly taken into account by judges setting the sentences of particular offenders and by legislatures engaging in sentencing reform. See e.g., West's Rev. Code Wash.Ann. § 9.94A.070 (requiring modification of sentence ranges biennially to account for, among other things, prison capacities).

3. *Probation or community release.* Probation is release from custody with conditions. A probationer will be required, at the least, to obey the criminal law and report periodically to his probation officer. Conditions must be reasonably related to the offense, the rehabilitation of the defendant, or the protection of the public, and often include restitution payments to the victim, participation in treatment or educational programs, and community service. A few courts have experimented with conditions of probation that have come to be known as *shaming penalties*, such as requirements that a defendant wear a sign advertising his offense.

If a probationer violates the terms of his release, he may then be sentenced to incarceration. An alleged probation violation is adjudicated in a probation revocation hearing where the defendant is entitled to notice of the claimed violation and given the opportunity to present evidence in his favor before an impartial adjudicator. But the full protections of trial such as a jury, proof beyond a reasonable doubt, the privilege against self-incrimination, and confrontation protections, are not applicable.

4. *Intermediate penalties; financial sanctions.* Intermediate penalties—somewhere in between probation and incarceration—have become more popular in recent years due in part to prison overcrowding. These include *boot camp, house arrest,* or *home confinement* with monitoring devices, and *day reporting programs. Fines* are the primary means of punishing misdemeanants and corporations, and are often assessed for individual felony offenders as well. As a result of the recent adoption in most jurisdictions of legislation to benefit the victims of crime, *restitution* is now a common element of any sentence. *Forfeiture* of specified assets of an offender to the government is an authorized penalty for a growing number of offenses. See generally Wayne R. LaFave, Jerold H. Israel & Nancy J. King, Criminal Procedure Treatise §§ 26.1, 26.9, 26.10 (2d ed. 1999 & Supp.) (available on Westlaw under database name CRIMPROC, hereinafter cited as CRIMPROC); Developments, *Alternatives to Incarceration*, 111 Harv.L.Rev. 1863 (1998).

C. Who Sets the Sentence?

Who sets the sentence? Judges, for the most part. But other people get into the act more than you might expect. The initial charging decision by the prosecutor, or a subsequent charge bargain between the parties, is everywhere one of the most important determinants of the sentence for the defendant's conduct. The legislature will set a penalty range for each offense, sometimes closely restraining judicial discretion, as Section 2 describes. In some jurisdictions judges may approve sentences (within statutory limits) that are negotiated by the parties, a practice that gives the parties considerable authority in defining the sentence. In a handful of states, in jury-tried capital as well as noncapital cases, the jury may set the sentence. Parole boards will determine the actual sentences the defendants will serve in states that use indeterminate sentencing. Prison officials, too, may reduce prison terms by granting "good time." Finally, sentences may be modified by the clemency authority of the executive, a power shared in most states between the governor and an administrative board or advisory group. What are the advantages and disadvantages of diffusing the power to set sentences between so many different decisionmakers?

SECTION 2. ALLOCATING AND CONTROLLING SENTENCING DISCRETION

Historically, with a few exceptions, trial judges have had very little guidance from the legislature or from appellate courts concerning the selection of sentences within the broad statutory ranges provided for each offense.[c] This freedom has been linked to the need to individualize sentences so that the sentence best achieves the rehabilitation of each offender. As noted in the reading that begins this chapter, unguided sentencing discretion has come under attack. Gross disparities in the sentences assigned by different judges for similar crimes and similar offenders, particularly along race and class lines, prompted concerted efforts nationwide to "do something" about discretionary sentencing and the disparity and uncertainty it produced. Three types of restrictions on judicial discretion in sentencing are considered below.

A. Mandatory Minimum Sentences

1. *Shifting sentencing authority to the prosecutor.* The United States Sentencing Commission in its study *Mandatory Minimum Penalties in the Federal Criminal Justice System* (1991), reported that by 1983 mandatory minimum penalties were enacted in 49 of 50 states. Congress has enacted mandatory minimum sentences for dozens of offenses, including drug and firearm crimes. "Despite the expectation that [federal] mandatory minimum sentences would be applied to all cases that meet the statutory criteria of eligibility, the available data suggest that this is not the case * * * . In 35 percent of cases in which available data strongly suggest that the defendant's behavior warrants a sentence under a mandatory minimum statute, defendants plead guilty to offenses carrying non-mandatory minimum or reduced mandatory minimum provisions. * * * [W]hites are more likely than non-whites to be sentenced below the applicable mandatory minimum. [Mandatory minimum sentences] are wholly dependent upon defen-

c. Judges also have had little guidance about whether to impose concurrent or consecutive sentences when defendant is convicted of multiple offenses at the same trial, or is convicted of one offense while subject to a sen-tence for a prior offense in the same or another jurisdiction. The sentencing statutes of a majority of states now include a presumption that multiple sentences run concurrently.

dants being charged and convicted of the specified offense under the mandatory minimum statute. Since the power to determine the charge of conviction rests exclusively with the prosecution for the 85 percent of the cases that do not proceed to trial, mandatory minimums transfer sentencing power from the court to the prosecution."

2. *Repeat-offender statutes.* Half of the states have enacted some variation of a "two-or three-strikes-and-you're-out" law, imposing lengthy mandatory sentences for certain repeat offenders. The "strike zone" varies, some states limiting those offenses that count as strikes to violent felonies, others including drug offenses or other non-violent crimes. The mandatory minimum varies as well, with many states mandating life without parole, others allowing for lesser sentences. In California, one study showed that prosecutions of felonies that qualified as strikes were three times more likely to go to trial than non-strike felonies, leading to a 25% increase in jury trials and a significant increase in the proportion of jail inmates awaiting trial. In some counties in California and in many other states, the impact of three strikes laws has been less dramatic. See generally John Clark, James Austin & D. Alan Henry, *"Three Strikes and You're Out," Are Repeat Offender Laws Having Their Anticipated Effects?*, 81 Judicature 144 (1998).

3. *Politics and sentencing policy.* Consider the conclusions of Barbara S. Vincent & Paul J. Hofer of the Federal Judicial Center, in their study, *The Consequences of Mandatory Minimum Prison Terms: A Summary of Recent Findings* (1994). The authors concluded that mandatory minimum sentences often exceed sentences that would be imposed under the Federal Sentencing Guidelines alone (see Section B., below), are costly in terms of corrections resources, have had no observable effect on crime, and have resulted in questionable sentencing disparities keyed to factors such as the prosecutor's decision to seek a lower sentence for cooperation.

If mandatory minimum sentences have these effects, why do legislators continue to pass them into law? Consider Michael Tonry & Kathleen Hatlestad, Sentencing Reform in Overcrowded Times—A Comparative Perspective 4 (1997) (arguing that in the United States, unlike other countries, because of successful attacks on political candidates perceived as soft on crime since the 1980s, "[f]ew elected public officials dare oppose any 'toughness' proposal, whatever its unfairness, expense, or likely ineffectiveness"); Sara Sun Beale, *What's Law Got to Do with It? The Political, Social, Psychological and Other Non-Legal Factors Influencing the Development of (Federal) Criminal Law,* 1 Buff.Crim.L.Rev. 23 (1997); Ronald F. Wright, *Three Strikes Legislation and Sentencing Commission Objectives,* 20 Law & Pol. 429, 437 (1998) ("The fiscal costs of increased corrections, judicial, prosecutorial, and defense resources are rarely traced to particular statutes," and even when they are, "[b]y that time, most of the legislators who voted for the original punishment statute are long gone."); William J. Stuntz, *The Uneasy Relationship Between Criminal Procedure and Criminal Justice,* 107 Yale L.J. 1, 56 (1997) (higher mandatory sentences raise the risk to defendants of taking their cases to trial and thus tend to convert otherwise contested cases into guilty pleas, thereby avoiding most of the costs criminal procedure creates); Donald A. Dripps, *Criminal Procedure, Footnote Four, and the Theory of Public Choice; Or, Why Don't Legislatures Give a Damn about the Rights of the Accused?,* 44 Syracuse L.Rev. 1079, 1089 (1993) ("the group of people who might expect to be * * * defendants at a criminal trial, whether they are guilty or innocent, is largely confined to a small segment of the electorate").

B.   SENTENCING GUIDELINES

1.   *Guidelines basics.* Since Minnesota adopted the first sentencing guidelines scheme in 1980, the federal government and about seventeen states have followed suit. Sentencing guidelines are created by sentencing commissions authorized by the legislature. The presumed sentence in a guidelines system is determined through the use of a sentencing table or grid that sets the presumed sentence range for the particular case. On one axis of the grid is a ranking of the criminal history of the offender, based on past convictions. The other axis ranks the severity of the crime. The severity of the offense is rated on a point system, starting with a certain number based on the general character of the offense and then adding or subtracting points for such factors as whether or not the defendant played a leadership role and the harm caused. The presumptive sentencing ranges tend to be fairly narrow. For example, a moderately serious offense may produce a recommended range of 20 to 24 months for a person with no prior convictions, and 90 to 104 months for a person in the highest criminal history category. The recommended ranges are not absolutely binding on the court, but if the court departs from the range, it must justify that departure with permissible reasons. See also Richard S. Frase, *Sentencing Guidelines Are "Alive and Well" in the United States,* in Tonry & Hatlestad, supra p. 1499 (describing variations in state guidelines schemes).

2.   *Federal Sentencing Guidelines.* U. S. SENTENCING GUIDELINES MANUAL, CH. 1 PT. A, 1–4 (2000):

The Sentencing Reform Act of 1984 * * * delegates broad authority to the [United States Sentencing] Commission to review and rationalize the federal sentencing process. * * * The Act's basic objective was to enhance the ability of the criminal justice system to combat crime through an effective, fair sentencing system. To achieve this end, Congress first sought honesty in sentencing. It sought to avoid the confusion and implicit deception that arose out of the pre-guidelines sentencing system which required the court to impose an indeterminate sentence of imprisonment and empowered the parole commission to determine how much of the sentence an offender actually would serve in prison. * * * Second, Congress sought reasonable uniformity in sentencing by narrowing the wide disparity in sentences imposed for similar criminal offenses committed by similar offenders. Third, Congress sought proportionality in sentencing through a system that imposes appropriately different sentences for criminal conduct of differing severity.* * * A philosophical problem arose when the Commission attempted to reconcile the differing perceptions of the purposes of criminal punishment. * * * Some argue that appropriate punishment should be defined primarily on the basis of the principle of "just deserts." Under this principle, punishment should be scaled to the offender's culpability and the resulting harms. Others argue that punishment should be imposed primarily on the basis of practical "crime control" considerations. This theory calls for sentences that most effectively lessen the likelihood of future crime, either by deterring others or incapacitating the defendant.

Adherents of each of these points of view urged the Commission to choose between them and accord one primacy over the other. [The] Commission sought to solve both the practical and philosophical problems of developing a coherent sentencing system by taking an empirical approach that used as a starting point data estimating pre-guidelines sentencing practices. It analyzed data drawn from 10,000 presentence investigations, the differing elements of various crimes as distinguished in substantive criminal statutes, the United States Parole Commission's guidelines and statistics, and data from other relevant sources in order to determine which distinctions were important in pre-guidelines practice. * * * Those who adhere to a just deserts philosophy may concede that the lack of consensus might make it difficult to say exactly what punishment is deserved for a particular crime. Likewise, those who subscribe to a philosophy of crime control may acknowledge that the lack of sufficient data might make it difficult to determine exactly the punishment that will best prevent that crime. Both groups might therefore recognize the wisdom of looking to those distinctions that judges and legislators have, in fact, made over the course of time. These established distinctions are ones that the community believes, or has found over time to be important from either a just deserts or crime control perspective.[d]

3. *Evaluating guidelines.* Guidelines have received mixed reviews. Minnesota's guidelines have been successful, reports one study: "Compared with pre-guideline practices, sentencing in Minnesota is more uniform, more predictable, and more socioeconomically neutral than it was before the guidelines. Findings show that violent offenders are more likely to be imprisoned now than before the guidelines. And these changes were accomplished without placing additional burdens on State correctional resources." Terance D. Miethe & Charles A. Moore, Sentencing Guidelines: Their Effect in Minnesota (NIJ 111381, April 1989), at 5. As for the U.S. Sentencing Guidelines, Marc Miller reports in *Rehabilitating the Federal Sentencing Guidelines,* 78 Judicature 180, 182–83 (1995), that a survey of federal judges released by the Federal Judicial Center in 1994 found that 69% of district judges were "strongly" or "moderately" opposed to the retention of "the current system of mandatory guidelines" (with six times as many district judges giving the stronger of the two answers) and nearly half would have eliminated the sentencing guidelines entirely. Judicial concerns included the system's rigidity and complexity, the degree of control over sentences given to prosecutors, and the severity of sentences. For extensive critical treatment, see Kate Stith & Jose A. Cabranes, Fear of Judging: Sentencing Guidelines in the Federal Courts (1998).

4. *Shifting discretion to the prosecutor.* Consider again Note 1, p. 1498. The prosecutor's ability to manipulate sentence length under the Guidelines is not limited to charging decisions. A downward departure for providing "substantial assistance" to law enforcement authorities is unavailable absent a motion by the prosecutor. Of all departures granted in 1999, over half were for "substantial assistance." Nearly one in five federal sentences was reduced on this basis. SOURCEBOOK, tbl. 5.41. Prosecutors may also engage in "fact bargaining" with the defense so that facts that would otherwise trigger lengthier sentences are left out of the sentencing calculus. Is this "wellspring of disparate treatment" (Stith & Cabranes, supra, at 106), an improvement over the sentencing disparities that the Guidelines sought to eliminate?

C. Appellate Review

1. One obvious way to limit the discretion of sentencing judges is to review their decisions on appeal. Until quite recently, sentencing decisions were subjected

---

d. But see Kate Stith & Jose A. Cabranes, Fear of Judging: Sentencing Guidelines in the Federal Courts 59–61 (1998) (The Commission "diminished the advantages of relying on past sentencing practices by *failing to do so in any systematic way.* The Commission interpreted the Sentencing Reform Act's requirement of *severe* sentences for career offenders and for many convicted of violent and drug offenses to require *more severe* sentences than had been imposed in the past. * * * The Commission further acknowledged that it had sought to increase sentence severity for 'white collar' crimes, apparently on the assumption that Congress was referring to this type of crime when it inserted the oracular statement that 'in many cases, current sentences do not accurately reflect the seriousness of the offense.' More generally, the Commission asserted portentously and without further explanation that it had elected to raise sentences for violent crimes 'where *the Commission was convinced that they were inadequate.*'") (emphasis in original).

to such cursory review that few defendants bothered to appeal their sentences. Today, in jurisdictions with structured sentencing, the factual and legal conclusions of the trial court underlying each sentence are part of the record. Each of these findings, in turn, can be tested on appeal by either prosecution[e] or defense for compliance with statutory command and guidelines requirements. This has led to a dramatic increase in sentencing appeals. For example, during 1999, over 60% of all federal criminal appeals raised a claim under the Guidelines, and over one-third of all appeals involved sentencing issues alone. SOURCEBOOK, tbl. 5.001.

2. Some believe that the increased burden of sentencing appeals has led prosecutors in plea bargaining to seek routinely a defendant's waiver of the right to appeal whatever sentence the judge may impose. Are defendants able to extract favorable concessions from prosecutors in return for waiving their rights to appeal? Should the legislature or the judiciary regulate such waivers? How? See e.g., Nancy J. King, *Priceless Process: Nonnegotiable Features of Criminal Litigation*, 47 UCLA L.Rev. 113, 149 (1999) (arguing that judicial refusal to enforce appeal waivers may be warranted if enforcement of the waiver harms the interests of nonparties, depending on the claim waived).

SECTION 3. CONSTITUTIONAL LIMITS ON SENTENCING PROCEDURE

Although it was decided over a half-century ago, *Williams v. New York,* below, remains the leading ruling on the content of due process as applied to sentencing. Its resilience is striking, especially when compared to the fundamental refashioning of constitutional requirements for other phases of the criminal process. In many ways the constitutional regulation of non-capital sentencing appears frozen in time, nearly untouched by the forces that reshaped the rules governing the investigation of crime, the adjudication of criminal liability, and the review of criminal judgments.

A. Information Considered in Setting the Sentence

WILLIAMS v. NEW YORK
337 U.S. 241, 69 S.Ct. 1079, 93 L.Ed. 1337 (1949).

Mr. Justice BLACK delivered the opinion of the Court.

A jury in a New York state court found appellant guilty of murder in the first degree. The jury recommended life imprisonment, but the trial judge imposed sentence of death. In giving his reasons for imposing the death sentence the judge discussed in open court the evidence upon which the jury had convicted stating that this evidence had been considered in the light of additional information obtained through the court's "Probation Department, and through other sources." [A state statute provided that the court "shall cause the defendant's previous criminal record to be submitted to it, * * * and may seek any information that will aid the court in determining the proper treatment of such defendant." Williams contended that his sentence violated due process, as it was "based upon information supplied by witnesses with whom the accused had not been confronted and as to whom he had no opportunity for cross-examination or rebuttal * * * ."]

The narrow contention here makes it unnecessary to set out the facts at length. The record shows a carefully conducted trial lasting more than two weeks

---

e. Double jeopardy does not bar resentencing following the government's successful appeal of a sentence it considers to be too lenient, except in capital cases. See Note 8, p. 1485.

in which appellant was represented by three appointed lawyers who conducted his defense with fidelity and zeal. The evidence proved a wholly indefensible murder committed by a person engaged in a burglary * * *.

About five weeks after the verdict of guilty with recommendation of life imprisonment, and after a statutory pre-sentence investigation report to the judge, the defendant was brought to court to be sentenced. Asked what he had to say, appellant protested his innocence. After each of his three lawyers had appealed to the court to accept the jury's recommendation of a life sentence, the judge gave reasons why he felt that the death sentence should be imposed. He narrated the shocking details of the crime as shown by the trial evidence, expressing his own complete belief in appellant's guilt. He stated that the pre-sentence investigation revealed many material facts concerning appellant's background which though relevant to the question of punishment could not properly have been brought to the attention of the jury in its consideration of the question of guilt. He referred to the experience appellant "had had on thirty other burglaries in and about the same vicinity" where the murder had been committed. The appellant had not been convicted of these burglaries although the judge had information that he had confessed to some and had been identified as the perpetrator of some of the others. The judge also referred to certain activities of appellant as shown by the probation report that indicated appellant possessed "a morbid sexuality" and classified him as a "menace to society." The accuracy of the statements made by the judge as to appellant's background and past practices was not challenged by appellant or his counsel, nor was the judge asked to disregard any of them or to afford appellant a chance to refute or discredit any of them by cross-examination or otherwise.

The case presents a serious and difficult question. The question relates to the rules of evidence applicable to the manner in which a judge may obtain information to guide him in the imposition of sentence upon an already convicted defendant. Within limits fixed by statutes, New York judges are given a broad discretion to decide the type and extent of punishment for convicted defendants. Here, for example, the judge's discretion was to sentence to life imprisonment or death. To aid a judge in exercising this discretion intelligently the New York procedural policy encourages him to consider information about the convicted person's past life, health, habits, conduct, and mental and moral propensities. The sentencing judge may consider such information even though obtained outside the courtroom from persons whom a defendant has not been permitted to confront or cross-examine. It is the consideration of information obtained by a sentencing judge in this manner that is the basis for appellant's broad constitutional challenge to the New York statutory policy.

Appellant urges that the New York statutory policy is in irreconcilable conflict with the underlying philosophy of a second procedural policy grounded in the due process of law clause of the Fourteenth Amendment. That policy as stated in *In re Oliver*, 333 U.S. 257, 273, is in part that no person shall be tried and convicted of an offense unless he is given reasonable notice of the charges against him and is afforded an opportunity to examine adverse witnesses. That the due process clause does provide these salutary and time-tested protections where the question for consideration is the guilt of a defendant seems entirely clear from the genesis and historical evolution of the clause.

Tribunals passing on the guilt of a defendant always have been hedged in by strict evidentiary procedural limitations. But both before and since the American colonies became a nation, courts in this country and in England practiced a policy under which a sentencing judge could exercise a wide discretion in the sources and types of evidence used to assist him in determining the kind and extent of punishment to be imposed within limits fixed by law. Out-of-court affidavits have been used frequently, and of course in the smaller communities sentencing judges naturally have in mind their knowledge of the personalities and backgrounds of convicted offenders. A recent manifestation of the historical latitude allowed sentencing judges appears in Rule 32 of the Federal Rules of Criminal Procedure. That rule provides for consideration by federal judges of reports made by probation officers containing information about a convicted defendant, including such information "as may be helpful in imposing sentence or in granting probation or in the correctional treatment of the defendant. . . . "

In addition to the historical basis for different evidentiary rules governing trial and sentencing procedures there are sound practical reasons for the distinction. In a trial before verdict the issue is whether a defendant is guilty of having engaged in certain criminal conduct of which he has been specifically accused. Rules of evidence have been fashioned for criminal trials which narrowly confine the trial contest to evidence that is strictly relevant to the particular offense charged. These rules rest in part on a necessity to prevent a time-consuming and confusing trial of collateral issues. They were also designed to prevent tribunals concerned solely with the issue of guilt of a particular offense from being influenced to convict for that offense by evidence that the defendant had habitually engaged in other misconduct. A sentencing judge, however, is not confined to the narrow issue of guilt. His task within fixed statutory or constitutional limits is to determine the type and extent of punishment after the issue of guilt has been determined. Highly relevant—if not essential—to his selection of an appropriate sentence is the possession of the fullest information possible concerning the defendant's life and characteristics. And modern concepts individualizing punishment have made it all the more necessary that a sentencing judge not be denied an opportunity to obtain pertinent information by a requirement of rigid adherence to restrictive rules of evidence properly applicable to the trial.

Undoubtedly the New York statutes emphasize a prevalent modern philosophy of penology that the punishment should fit the offender and not merely the crime. The belief no longer prevails that every offense in a like legal category calls for an identical punishment without regard to the past life and habits of a particular offender. This whole country has traveled far from the period in which the death sentence was an automatic and commonplace result of convictions— even for offenses today deemed trivial. Today's philosophy of individualizing sentences makes sharp distinctions for example between first and repeated offenders. Indeterminate sentences the ultimate termination of which are sometimes decided by non-judicial agencies have to a large extent taken the place of the old rigidly fixed punishments. The practice of probation which relies heavily on non-judicial implementation has been accepted as a wise policy. Execution of the United States parole system rests on the discretion of an administrative parole board. Retribution is no longer the dominant objective of the criminal law. Reformation and rehabilitation of offenders have become important goals of criminal jurisprudence.

Modern changes in the treatment of offenders make it more necessary now than a century ago for observance of the distinctions in the evidential procedure in the trial and sentencing processes. For indeterminate sentences and probation have resulted in an increase in the discretionary powers exercised in fixing punishments. In general, these modern changes have not resulted in making the lot of offenders harder. On the contrary a strong motivating force for the changes has been the belief that by careful study of the lives and personalities of convicted offenders many could be less severely punished and restored sooner to complete freedom and useful citizenship. This belief to a large extent has been justified.

Under the practice of individualizing punishments, investigational techniques have been given an important role. Probation workers making reports of their investigations have not been trained to prosecute but to aid offenders. Their reports have been given a high value by conscientious judges who want to sentence persons on the best available information rather than on guesswork and inadequate information. To deprive sentencing judges of this kind of information would undermine modern penological procedural policies that have been cautiously adopted throughout the nation after careful consideration and experimentation. We must recognize that most of the information now relied upon by judges to guide them in the intelligent imposition of sentences would be unavailable if information were restricted to that given in open court by witnesses subject to cross-examination. And the modern probation report draws on information concerning every aspect of a defendant's life.[15] The type and extent of this information make totally impractical if not impossible open court testimony with cross-examination. Such a procedure could endlessly delay criminal administration in a retrial of collateral issues.

The considerations we have set out admonish us against treating the due process clause as a uniform command that courts throughout the Nation abandon their age-old practice of seeking information from out-of-court sources to guide their judgment toward a more enlightened and just sentence. * * * The due process clause should not be treated as a device for freezing the evidential procedure of sentencing in the mold of trial procedure. So to treat the due process clause would hinder if not preclude all courts—state and federal—from making progressive efforts to improve the administration of criminal justice. * * *

We hold that appellant was not denied due process of law.

Affirmed.

Justice MURPHY, dissenting.

* * * The record before us indicates that the judge exercised his discretion to deprive a man of his life, in reliance on material made available to him in a probation report, consisting almost entirely of evidence that would have been inadmissible at the trial. Some, such as allegations of prior crimes, was irrelevant. Much was incompetent as hearsay. All was damaging, and none was subject to scrutiny by the defendant.

Due process of law includes at least the idea that a person accused of crime shall be accorded a fair hearing through all the stages of the proceedings against him. I agree with the Court as to the value and humaneness of liberal use of probation reports as developed by modern penologists, but, in a capital case, against the unanimous recommendation of a jury, where the report would concededly not have been admissible at the trial, and was not subject to examination by the defendant, I am forced to conclude that the high commands of due process were not obeyed.

Notes and Questions

1. *Prior offenses*. As Professor Kevin Reitz has pointed out, there is more to Williams' story. See Kevin R. Reitz, *Sentencing Facts: Travesties of Real–*

---

15. A publication circulated by the Administrative Office of the United States Courts contains a suggested form for all United States probation reports and serves as an example of the type of information contained in the reports. This form consists of thirteen "marginal headings." (1) Offense; (2) Prior Record; (3) Family History; (4) Home and Neighborhood; (5) Education; (6) Religion; (7) Interests and Activities; (8) Health (physical and mental); (9) Employment; (10) Resources; (11) Summary; (12) Plan; and (13) Agencies Interested. Each of the headings is further broken down into sub-headings. The form represents a framework into which information can be inserted to give the sentencing judge a composite picture of the defendant. Administrative Office of the United States Courts, The Presentence Investigation Report, Pub. No. 101 (1943).

Offense Sentencing, 45 Stan.L.Rev. 523 (1993) (collecting background on the *Williams* case). At the time of the murder, Williams was 18 and had no prior convictions. He was, however, on probation for failing to appear in court after being charged at age seventeen with being a "wayward minor." The judge at sentencing noted that Williams' "difficulties" with the law dated back to age eleven, when he was accused of assisting another in a burglary, a charge that was suspended. The trial judge accepted as true allegations in the presentence report that Williams had committed an additional thirty burglaries during the months prior to the murder, based on representations in the report that these burglaries were committed in a similar manner, that victims of some of these other crimes had identified Williams, and that some property taken during these burglaries was found in his apartment. The "activities * * * that indicated [Williams] possessed 'a morbid sexuality' "consisted of allegations by a seven-year-old girl that Williams had molested her during one of these uncharged burglaries, the probation department's discovery that Williams lived with two women and that "on various occasions he brought different men to the apartment for the purpose of having sexual relations with these two women," and an alleged visit to a public school "to take photographs of private parts of young children." Even assuming the allegations about Williams' other crimes are accurate, how are these other crimes relevant to the appropriate sentence for this murder?

2.   *Real offense sentencing.* American courts typically apply "real offense" sentencing, sentencing that takes into account the crime defendant "really" committed as reflected in the presentence report, not simply the crime of conviction, which may not reflect the extent of the defendant's criminal conduct due to the prosecutor's initial charging decision, plea bargaining, jury nullification, or other reasons. The federal Guidelines, for example, require the judge to consider all "relevant conduct" in addition to the conduct that forms the basis of the conviction, in selecting the appropriate sentence within the statutory maximum sentence for the crime of conviction. Typically, these details are alleged in a presentence report.

Consider the following advice provided by two federal defenders, Lucien B. Campbell & Henry J. Bemporad, in *An Introduction to Federal Guideline Sentencing,* 10 Fed.Sent.Rep. 323, 333 (1998):

"The importance of the [presentence] report cannot be overstated. In it, the probation officer will make fact findings, perform guideline calculations, and identify potential grounds for departure. Many of these determinations, while nominally objective, have significant subjective components. The officer's attitude toward the case or the client may substantially influence the sentence recommendations—recommendations which enjoy considerable deference from both the sentencing judge and the reviewing court. For these reasons, the effective and zealous advocate must independently review all elements of the probation officer's report, and indeed all aspects of the case, to make any necessary objections and affirmatively present the defense case for a favorable sentence. Defense counsel should never assume that the probation officer has arrived at a favorable recommendation, or even a correct one. The probation officer's presentence investigation will usually include an interview of the defendant. * * * Disclosing undetected relevant conduct may * * * increase the offense level [and] * * * result in a higher sentence * * *. Because the presentence interview holds many perils, the defendant must fully understand its function and importance, and defense counsel should attend the interview. In some cases, counsel may decide to limit the scope of the presentence interview. Refusal to submit to an unrestricted presentence interview may, however, jeopardize the adjustment for acceptance of responsibility or adversely affect other incidents of sentence * * *. There is no fixed solution to this dilemma; counsel must make an informed decision as to the best course in the context of a particular case."

3. Prohibited considerations. In light of the sweeping description in *Williams* of information relevant to sentencing, it could be argued that every aspect of a defendant's life may be weighed in assessing the appropriate penalty. Indeed, in federal courts, 18 U.S.C.A. § 3661 provides: "No limitation shall be placed on the information concerning the background, character, and conduct of a person convicted of an offense which a court of the United States may receive and consider for the purpose of imposing an appropriate sentence." A small group of factors remains off limits, however.

a. Activity protected by the First Amendment. David Dawson was convicted of first degree murder, and sentenced to death. At his sentencing hearing the prosecution introduced evidence that Dawson had the words "Aryan Brotherhood" tattooed on the back of his hand as well as evidence that an "Aryan Brotherhood prison gang originated in California in the 1960s, that it entertains white racist beliefs, and that a separate gang in the Delaware prison system calls itself the Aryan Botherhood." Dawson claimed that the introduction of this evidence violated his First Amendment rights. The Court in *Dawson v. Delaware*, 503 U.S. 159, 112 S.Ct. 1093, 117 L.Ed.2d 309 (1992), agreed. "Even if the Delaware group to which Dawson allegedly belongs is racist, those beliefs, so far as we can determine, had no relevance to the sentencing proceeding in this case. * * * [T]he murder victim was white, as is Dawson; elements of racial hatred were therefore not involved in the killing. Because the prosecution did not prove that the Aryan Brotherhood had committed any unlawful or violent acts, or had even endorsed such acts, the Aryan Brotherhood evidence was also not relevant to help prove any aggravating circumstance. In many cases * * * associational evidence might serve a legitimate purpose in showing that a defendant represents a future danger to society. * * * But the inference which the jury was invited to draw in this case tended to prove nothing more than the abstract beliefs of the Delaware chapter. * * * [T]he evidence proved nothing more than Dawson's abstract beliefs."

b. Race and other protected classifications. The Equal Protection Clause bars a judge or jury from considering the race of the offender or victim as the basis for a more or less severe sentence. However it is extremely difficult for a defendant to prove either that racial animus motivated his sentencer or that a prosecutor's decision to seek the death penalty was based on race. See *McCleskey v. Kemp*, p. 875 (rejecting equal protection claim by capital defendant who presented statistical statewide evidence demonstrating that the race of the victim is strongly correlated to the likelihood that a defendant would receive the death penalty).

In the later case of *Wisconsin v. Mitchell*, 508 U.S. 476, 113 S.Ct. 2194, 124 L.Ed.2d 436 (1993), the Court upheld a sentence imposed under a state statute that provided higher penalties for an offense if the defendant "intentionally selects" the victim because of the "race, religion, color, disability, sexual orientation, national origin or ancestry of that person." Rejecting the defendant's equal protection and First Amendment challenges, the Court explained that bias-inspired conduct "is thought to inflict greater individual and societal harm. * * * The state's desire to redress * * * perceived harms provides an adequate explanation for its penalty enhancement provision over and above mere disagreement with the offender's beliefs or biases." How does the claim in *Mitchell* differ from that raised in *McCleskey* or *Dawson*?

Consider the facts in *Kapadia v. Tally*, 229 F.3d 641 (7th Cir.2000). Kapadia was convicted in Cook County of burglary and arson of a Jewish community center. On his way out of the courtroom after conviction, Kapadia said to Deputy Joseph Bennett, "You can tell the Judge for me ... that he's a b___ and f___ the Jews." Later that day, while in lockup, Kapadia asked Bennett whether "that Judge is a Jew, too?" and then answered his own question by stating, "I'll bet he is that f–g schm—." Bennett related these remarks, as well as two other epithets he'd overheard defendant utter about Jews, to the trial judge before the sentencing hearing, and the trial judge told Bennett to inform both the prosecution and the defense about the remarks. At sentencing, the judge heard argument on the relevance of the Bennett's information, including defense counsel's objection that "there has been absolutely no suggestion during the trial * * * that the fact that this was a Jewish synagogue had anything to do with anything, especially the conduct of my client." Bennett, under oath, testified to Kapadia's anti-Semitic remarks. The judge remarked that he had been called more names than any other professional except a tax collector, "What troubles me, of course, is the vitriol directed towards the * * * East European Jews who are the victims in this case. I did take the comments into consideration because one of the things I have to consider is the possibility of reformation of the defendant. How likely is this defendant to be restored to useful citizenship." The court went on to comment on the lessons of history, including Krystalnacht, when 1,700 synagogues and businesses were destroyed by mobs led by Nazi party members, leading to the deaths of a large number of Jewish individuals. "I take these matters into very, very serious consideration in the case of Mr. Kapadia," explained the judge, "because his virulent anti-Semitism is indicative of the fact [that] he is not likely to change his ways. He is not likely to become a productive member of society. So, it's certainly an aggravating factor." The court then sentenced Kapadia to a fourteen-year term of imprisonment, the longest term allowed under Illinois law for burglary and arson. Were Kapadia's First Amendment rights violated by the court's consideration of his speech in setting his sentence?

c. *Defendant's exercise of procedural rights.*

(i) Right to appeal. In *North Carolina v. Pearce,* p. 1535, the Court agreed unanimously that after a defendant succeeds in winning retrial or resentencing on appeal, a judge cannot impose a higher sentence to retaliate against the defendant for the successful appeal of the first judgment. The Court acknowledged that *Williams* allowed the sentencing court on re-conviction to take into consideration the conduct of the defendant subsequent to his first conviction "that may have thrown new light upon defendant's ' * * * moral propensities,' " but that did not authorize "punish[ing] a person because he has done what the law plainly allows him to do" in pursuing an appeal. To allow such "vindictiveness" to play a part in his sentence would be to allow the sentencing court "to put a price on an appeal" and thereby inhibit the "free and unfettered" exercise of that right. When an increased sentence follows reconviction for the same offense after appeal, the Court concluded, a presumption of vindictiveness attaches.

(ii) Right to testify. Consider also *United States v. Dunnigan,* 507 U.S. 87, 113 S.Ct. 1111, 122 L.Ed.2d 445 (1993). After five witnesses testified at trial that they had taken part in, or observed the defendant trafficking in cocaine, the defendant took the stand and denied these allegations and said she had not possessed or distributed cocaine at any time. Rebuttal witnesses for the government testified to purchasing crack cocaine from her numerous times, once in a transaction monitored by law enforcement authorities. After conviction by the jury, the district court sentenced the defendant under the Guidelines. He increased her base offense level by two offense levels under U.S.S.G. § 3C1.1, a provision entitled "willfully obstructing or impeding proceedings," because he found that the defendant perjured herself at trial. Rejecting the defendant's contention that increasing her sentence because of her perjury interferes with her right to testify, the Court declared "[W]e have held on a number of occasions that a defendant's right to testify does not include a right to commit perjury." In upholding the enhancement the Supreme Court explained: "The commission of perjury is of obvious relevance" to the appropriate punishment "because it reflects on a defendant's criminal history, on her willingness to accept the commands of the law and the authority of the court, and on her character in general." "The perjuring defendant's willingness to frustrate judicial proceedings to avoid criminal liability suggests that the need for incapacitation and retribution is heightened as compared with the defendant charged with the same crime who allows judicial proceedings to progress without resorting to perjury." The Court noted that "an accused may give inaccurate testimony due to confusion, mistake, or faulty memory. In other instances, an accused may testify to matters such as lack of capacity, insanity, duress, or self-defense. Her testimony may be truthful, but the jury may nonetheless find the testimony insufficient to excuse criminal liability or prove lack of intent. For these reasons, if a defendant objects to a sentence enhancement resulting from her trial testimony, a district court must review the evidence and make independent findings necessary to establish" that the defendant gave "false testimony concerning a material matter with the willful intent to provide false testimony, rather than as a result of confusion, mistake, or faulty memory."

(iii) Right to remain silent. Assume a defendant pleads guilty to an offense, admitting his commission of the offense, but refuses at sentencing to answer the judge's questions about the offense and the criminal activity of his friends, choosing instead to remain silent. May the judge use this refusal as a basis for imposing a higher sentence than she would have imposed had the defendant provided the information? Consider, on this score, MITCHELL v. UNITED STATES, 526 U.S. 314, 119 S.Ct. 1307, 143 L.Ed.2d 424 (1999). Mitchell pleaded guilty to several drug offenses, reserving the right to contest drug quantity at sentencing. At sentencing witnesses testified that over several months the defendant had sold a total of more than 5 kilograms of cocaine, an amount carrying a mandatory minimum sentence of 10 years. In explaining why he credited the testimony, the judge explained to the defendant: "I held it against you that you didn't come forward today and tell me that you really only did this a couple of times. * * * I'm taking the position that you should come forward and explain your side of this issue." Mitchell asserted in the Supreme Court that it was a violation of her Fifth Amendment privilege against self-incrimination for the trial judge to draw an adverse inference from her silence at sentencing. Justice KENNEDY's opinion for the Court agreed. "The concerns which mandate the rule [of *Griffin v. California*, p. 1413] against negative inferences at a criminal trial apply with equal force at sentencing." The majority distinguished the sentencing hearing from a civil proceeding, where the stakes are lower and adverse inferences from the invocation of the privilege are allowed. "Here, the inference * * * may have resulted in decades of added imprisonment." The rule prohibiting an inference of guilt from a defendant's silence "has become an essential feature of our legal tradition," and a "vital instrument for teaching that the question in a criminal case is not whether the defendant committed the acts of which he is accused," but "whether the Government has carried its burden to prove its allegations while respecting the defendant's individual rights." The majority in *Mitchell* also declined to express a view on whether silence "bears upon the determination of lack of remorse, or upon acceptance of responsibility" for downward departure under the Guidelines. Justice SCALIA in dissent argued that should the Court later decide that the " 'no inference' rule is indeed limited to 'determining the facts of the offense,' then we will have a system in which a state court can increase the sentence of a convicted drug possessor who refuses to say how many ounces he possessed—not because that suggests he possessed the large amount * * * but because his refusal to cooperate suggests he is unrepentant." "Ordinarily," he predicted, it will be "impossible to tell whether the sentencer has used the silence for either purpose or for neither."

B. NOTICE, CONFRONTATION, DEFENSE SUBMISSIONS

1. *Discovery and disclosure of sentencing information*. The Court in *Williams* rebuffed the defendant's claims that he should have had the opportunity to test or rebut the allegations made in the presentence report. The Court even observed, "no federal constitutional objection would have been possible * * * if the judge had sentenced [defendant] to death giving no reason at all." This aspect of the *Williams* holding, at least as applied to capital cases, was modified by *Gardner v. Florida*, 430 U.S. 349, 97 S.Ct. 1197, 51 L.Ed.2d 393 (1977), where a majority of justices agreed that the Constitution forbids a judge from sentencing a defendant to death without disclosing those portions of the presentence report that form the basis for the sentence. Rejecting the state's arguments that nondisclosure was necessary to "enable investigators to obtain relevant but sensitive disclosures from persons unwilling to comment publicly about a defendant's background or character," and to prevent delay, three justices argued the procedure violated due process, two argued that it violated the Eighth Amendment, and others concurred for separate reasons. The Court later characterized *Gardner* as a case barring "secret" but not "surprise" use of sentencing information, and upheld a death sentence despite the government's failure to inform the defendant until the night before the penalty phase that it would be presenting witnesses to testify concerning alleged prior offenses. See *Gray v. Netherland*, 518 U.S. 152, 116 S.Ct. 2074, 135 L.Ed.2d 457 (1996). Although the constitutionality of failing entirely to disclose certain sentencing information to the defense in *non-capital* cases remains unsettled, statutes in most jurisdictions entitle felony defendants to review sentencing information at some point prior to the imposition of sentence. Are there some types of sentencing information that a judge should not reveal to a defendant? Why?

2. *Testing the reliability of sentencing information*. The Court in *Williams* rejected the defendant's argument that he was entitled to cross-examine those who provided sentencing information. Requiring "open court testimony with cross-examination" the Court explained, would be "totally impractical if not impossible" in the sentencing context. While statutes in most jurisdictions do provide for sentencing hearings, such hearings do not commonly include evidentiary submissions other than the presentence report itself. Lower courts continue to cite *Williams* in rejecting a defendant's constitutional entitlement to cross examine witnesses at a trial-type sentencing hearing. Does it make sense to rely on *Williams*, "a decision made in a different world 40 years ago," to define the meaning of due process under guidelines systems that quantify the amount of punishment that will follow from the existence of individual sentencing facts? See *United States v. Petty*, 982 F.2d 1365 (9th Cir.1993) (Noonan, J., dissenting); Sarah Sun Beale, *Procedural Issues Raised by Guideline Sentencing: The Constitutional Significance of Single "Elements of the Offense,"* 35 Wm. & Mary L.Rev. 147 (1993). Should a sentencing judge insist on some corroborative evidence to back up hearsay statements of anonymous informants? See *United States v. Fennell*, 65 F.3d 812 (10th Cir.1995) (unsworn out-of-court statements made by an unobserved witness and unsupported by other evidence were not a sufficient basis for a sentence enhancement); *State v. Johnson*, 856 P.2d 1064 (Utah 1993).

3. *Defense submissions and allocution*. In capital cases, the defendant is entitled to present mitigating evidence on his own behalf at sentencing, but in non-capital cases, statute may or may not provide a defendant with this opportunity. Federal Rule 32 states that the court *must* afford *counsel* an opportunity to comment on matters appropriate to sentence, and *may, in its discretion,* permit parties to introduce testimony or other evidence. Many states too leave the submission of sentencing evidence to the discretion of the trial judge. The right of the defendant himself to speak on his own behalf at sentencing, however, a privilege known as the right of allocution, is protected in most jurisdictions by statute. Courts disagree about whether this right is guaranteed by the Due Process Clause. Compare *People v. Brown,* 172 Ill.2d 1, 216 Ill.Dec. 733, 665 N.E.2d 1290 (1996) (denial of the opportunity to make an unsworn statement before sentence does not violate due process, even in capital case) with *Boardman v. Estelle,* 957 F.2d 1523 (9th Cir.1992) (right to allocution constitutionally based).

C. THE ASSISTANCE OF COUNSEL

The Sixth Amendment right to counsel extends to sentencing, a "stage of a criminal proceeding where substantial rights of a criminal accused may be affected." *Mempa v. Rhay,* 389 U.S. 128, 88 S.Ct. 254, 19 L.Ed.2d 336 (1967). Due process provides an alternative basis for a right to counsel at certain post-sentencing proceedings, not protected by the Sixth Amendment right to counsel, specifically parole and probation revocation hearings. The revocation of parole, the Court reasoned in *Gagnon v. Scarpelli,* 411 U.S. 778, 93 S.Ct. 1756, 36 L.Ed.2d 656 (1973) [p. 87], "is not a part of the criminal prosecution," but the "loss of liberty entailed is a serious deprivation requiring that the parolee be accorded due process." Rather than adopting an "inflexible" rule requiring counsel for every revocation hearing, the Court held that "counsel should be provided in cases where, after being informed of his right to request counsel, the probationer or parolee makes such a request, based on a timely and colorable claim (i) that he has not committed the alleged violation of the conditions upon which he is at liberty; or (ii) that, even if the violation is a matter of public record or is uncontested there are substantial reasons which justified or mitigated the violation and make revocation inappropriate, and that the reasons are complex or otherwise difficult to develop or present." Also relevant is "whether the probationer appears to be capable of speaking effectively for himself."

Recall the reasons for abandoning the case-by-case rule of *Betts v. Brady* in favor of the rule of *Gideon* in the trial context. See Chapter 3. Which approach makes the most sense for parole and probation revocation—*Gagnon*'s case-by-case approach, or a rule requiring counsel for all revocations? The Court in *Gagnon* noted that unlike at trial, at revocation hearings the rules of evidence are not in force, proof is merely by a preponderance, the state may be represented by a non-lawyer, and the factfinder may be a layperson. In assessing the need for counsel, however, wouldn't the more appropriate comparison be sentencing, not trial? Given the lack of trial-like procedural protections at sentencing, are revocations sufficiently distinct to justify a different rule? Congress and several states have concluded otherwise. See e.g., 18 U.S.C.A. § 3006A(1)(B), (E) (providing that any indigent defendant is entitled to appointed counsel when charged with a violation of probation or facing modification or revocation of supervised release).

D. BURDEN OF PROOF

McMILLAN v. PENNSYLVANIA
477 U.S. 79, 106 S.Ct. 2411, 91 L.Ed.2d 67 (1986).

Justice REHNQUIST delivered the opinion of the Court.

We granted certiorari to consider the constitutionality, under the Due Process Clause of the Fourteenth Amendment and the jury trial guarantee of the Sixth

Amendment, of Pennsylvania's Mandatory Minimum Sentencing Act, 42 Pa. Cons. Stat. § 9712 (1982) (the Act).

* * * [The Act] provides that anyone convicted of certain enumerated felonies is subject to a mandatory minimum sentence of five years' imprisonment if the sentencing judge finds, by a preponderance of the evidence, that the person "visibly possessed a firearm" during the commission of the offense. At the sentencing hearing, the judge is directed to consider the evidence introduced at trial and any additional evidence offered by either the defendant or the Commonwealth. § 9712(b).[1] The Act operates to divest the judge of discretion to impose any sentence of less than five years for the underlying felony; it does not authorize a sentence in excess of that otherwise allowed for that offense. * * * [E]ach of the sentencing judges before whom petitioners appeared found the Act unconstitutional * * * . The Commonwealth appealed all four cases to the Supreme Court of Pennsylvania [which reversed and] concluded that the Act is consistent with due process. * * * We * * * now affirm.

II.

Petitioners argue that under the Due Process Clause * * * if a State wants to punish visible possession of a firearm it must undertake the burden of proving that fact beyond a reasonable doubt. We disagree. *Winship* held that "the Due Process Clause protects the accused against conviction except upon proof beyond a reasonable doubt of every fact necessary to constitute the crime with which he is charged." In *Mullaney v. Wilbur,* we held that the Due Process Clause "requires the prosecution to prove beyond a reasonable doubt the absence of the heat of passion on sudden provocation when the issue is properly presented in a homicide case." But in *Patterson* [*v. New York,* 432 U.S. 197, 97 S.Ct. 2319, 53 L.Ed.2d 281 (1977)] we rejected the claim that whenever a State links the "severity of punishment" to "the presence or absence of an identified fact" the State must prove that fact beyond a reasonable doubt. In particular, we upheld against a due process challenge New York's law placing on defendants charged with murder the burden of proving the affirmative defense of extreme emotional disturbance.

Patterson stressed that in determining what facts must be proved beyond a reasonable doubt the state legislature's definition of the elements of the offense is usually dispositive: "[The] Due Process Clause requires the prosecution to prove beyond a reasonable doubt all of the elements *included in the definition of the*

---

1. Section 9712 [provided, in part:]

"(a) Mandatory sentence.—Any person who is convicted in any court of this Commonwealth of murder of the third degree, voluntary manslaughter, rape, involuntary deviate sexual intercourse, robbery as defined in 18 Pa. C. S. § 3701(a)(1)(i), (ii) or (iii) (relating to robbery), aggravated assault as defined in 18 Pa. C. S. § 2702(a)(1) (relating to aggravated assault) or kidnapping, or who is convicted of attempt to commit any of these crimes, shall, if the person visibly possessed a firearm during the commission of the offense, be sentenced to a minimum sentence of at least five years of total confinement notwithstanding any other provision of this title or other statute to the contrary.

"(b) Proof at sentencing.—Provisions of this section shall not be an element of the crime and notice thereof to the defendant shall not be required prior to conviction, but reasonable

notice of the Commonwealth's intention to proceed under this section shall be provided after conviction and before sentencing. The applicability of this section shall be determined at sentencing. The court shall consider any evidence presented at trial and shall afford the Commonwealth and the defendant an opportunity to present any necessary additional evidence and shall determine, by a preponderance of the evidence, if this section is applicable.

"(c) Authority of court in sentencing.— There shall be no authority in any court to impose on an offender to which this section is applicable any lesser sentence than provided for in subsection (a) or to place such offender on probation or to suspend sentence. Nothing in this section shall prevent the sentencing court from imposing a sentence greater than that provided in this section.

* * *

offense of which the defendant is charged." While "there are obviously constitutional limits beyond which the States may not go in this regard," "[t]he applicability of the reasonable-doubt standard ... has always been dependent on how a State defines the offense that is charged in any given case[.]" *Patterson* rests on a premise that bears repeating here:

"It goes without saying that preventing and dealing with crime is much more the business of the States than it is of the Federal Government, and that we should not lightly construe the Constitution so as to intrude upon the administration of justice by the individual States. Among other things, it is normally 'within the power of the State to regulate procedures under which its laws are carried out, including the burden of producing evidence and the burden of persuasion,' and its decision in this regard is not subject to proscription under the Due Process Clause unless 'it offends some principle of justice so rooted in the traditions and conscience of our people as to be ranked as fundamental.' "

We believe that the present case is controlled by *Patterson*, our most recent pronouncement on this subject, rather than by *Mullaney*. As the Supreme Court of Pennsylvania observed, the Pennsylvania Legislature has expressly provided that visible possession of a firearm is not an element of the crimes enumerated in the mandatory sentencing statute, § 9712(b), but instead is a sentencing factor that comes into play only after the defendant has been found guilty of one of those crimes beyond a reasonable doubt. Indeed, the elements of the enumerated offenses, like the maximum permissible penalties for those offenses, were established long before the Mandatory Minimum Sentencing Act was passed. While visible possession might well have been included as an element of the enumerated offenses, Pennsylvania chose not to redefine those offenses in order to so include it, and *Patterson* teaches that we should hesitate to conclude that due process bars the State from pursuing its chosen course in the area of defining crimes and prescribing penalties.

As *Patterson* recognized, of course, there are constitutional limits to the State's power in this regard; in certain limited circumstances *Winship*'s reasonable-doubt requirement applies to facts not formally identified as elements of the offense charged. Petitioners argue that Pennsylvania has gone beyond those limits and that its formal provision that visible possession is not an element of the crime is therefore of no effect. We do not think so. While we have never attempted to define precisely the constitutional limits noted in *Patterson,* i.e., the extent to which due process forbids the reallocation or reduction of burdens of proof in criminal cases, and do not do so today, we are persuaded by several factors that Pennsylvania's Mandatory Minimum Sentencing Act does not exceed those limits.

We note first that the Act plainly does not transgress the limits expressly set out in *Patterson*. Responding to the concern that its rule would permit States unbridled power to redefine crimes to the detriment of criminal defendants, the *Patterson* Court advanced the unremarkable proposition that the Due Process Clause precludes States from discarding the presumption of innocence. * * * Here, of course, the Act creates no presumptions * * * Nor does it relieve the prosecution of its burden of proving guilt; § 9712 only becomes applicable after a defendant has been duly convicted of the crime for which he is to be punished.

The Court in *Mullaney* observed, with respect to the main criminal statute invalidated in that case, that once the State proved the elements which Maine required it to prove beyond a reasonable doubt the defendant faced "a differential in sentencing ranging from a nominal fine to a mandatory life sentence." In the present case the situation is quite different. Of the offenses enumerated in the Act, third-degree murder, robbery * * * , kidnapping, rape, and involuntary deviate sexual intercourse are first-degree felonies subjecting the defendant to a maximum of 20 years' imprisonment. Voluntary manslaughter and aggravated assault * * * are felonies of the second degree carrying a maximum sentence of 10 years. Section 9712 neither alters the maximum penalty for the crime committed nor creates a separate offense calling for a separate penalty; it operates solely to limit the sentencing court's discretion in selecting a penalty within the range already available to it without the special finding of visible possession of a firearm. Section 9712 "ups the ante" for the defendant only by raising to five years the minimum sentence which may be imposed within the statutory plan.[4] The statute gives no impression of having been tailored to permit the visible possession finding to be a tail which wags the dog of the substantive offense. Petitioners' claim that visible possession under the Pennsylvania statute is "really" an element of the offenses for which they are being punished—that Pennsylvania has in effect defined a new set of upgraded felonies—would have at least more superficial appeal if a finding of visible possession exposed them to greater or additional punishment, cf. 18 U.S.C. § 2113(d) (providing separate and greater punishment for bank robberies accomplished through "use of a dangerous weapon or device"), but it does not.

* * *

Finally, we note that the specter raised by petitioners of States restructuring existing crimes in order to "evade" the commands of *Winship* just does not appear in this case. As noted above, § 9712's enumerated felonies retain the same elements they had before the Mandatory Minimum Sentencing Act was passed. The Pennsylvania Legislature did not change the definition of any existing offense. It simply took one factor that has always been considered by sentencing courts to bear on punishment—the instrumentality used in committing a violent felony—and dictated the precise weight to be given that factor if the instrumentality is a firearm. Pennsylvania's decision to do so has not transformed against its will a sentencing factor into an "element" of some hypothetical "offense."

* * *

III.

Having concluded that States may treat "visible possession of a firearm" as a sentencing consideration rather than an element of a particular offense, we now turn to petitioners' subsidiary claim that due process nonetheless requires that visible possession be proved by at least clear and convincing evidence. Like the court below, we have little difficulty concluding that in this case the preponderance standard satisfies due process. Indeed, it would be extraordinary if the Due Process Clause as understood in *Patterson* plainly sanctioned Pennsylvania's scheme, while the same Clause explained in some other line of less clearly relevant cases imposed more stringent requirements. There is, after all, only one Due Process Clause in the Fourteenth Amendment. Furthermore, petitioners do not and could not claim that a sentencing court may never rely on a particular fact in passing sentence without finding that fact by "clear and convincing evidence." Sentencing courts have traditionally heard evidence and found facts without any prescribed burden of proof at all. See *Williams v. New York,* 337 U.S. 241 (1949). Pennsylvania has deemed a particular fact relevant and prescribed a particular

---

4. By prescribing a mandatory minimum sentence, the Act incidentally serves to restrict the sentencing court's discretion in setting a maximum sentence. Pennsylvania law provides that a minimum sentence of confinement "shall not exceed one-half of the maximum sentence imposed." 42 Pa. Cons. Stat. § 9756(b) (1982). Thus, the shortest maximum term permissible under the Act is 10 years.

burden of proof. We see nothing in Pennsylvania's scheme that would warrant constitutionalizing burdens of proof at sentencing.

Petitioners apparently concede that Pennsylvania's scheme would pass constitutional muster if only it did not remove the sentencing court's discretion, i.e., if the legislature had simply directed the court to *consider* visible possession in passing sentence. We have some difficulty fathoming why the due process calculus would change simply because the legislature has seen fit to provide sentencing courts with additional guidance. Nor is there merit to the claim that a heightened burden of proof is required because visible possession is a fact "concerning the crime committed" rather than the background or character of the defendant. Sentencing courts necessarily consider the circumstances of an offense in selecting the appropriate punishment, and we have consistently approved sentencing schemes that mandate consideration of facts related to the crime, without suggesting that those facts must be proved beyond a reasonable doubt. * * *

For the foregoing reasons, the judgment of the Supreme Court of Pennsylvania is affirmed.

[The dissenting opinion of Justice MARSHALL, with whom Justice Brennan and Justice Blackmun joined, is omitted.]

Justice STEVENS, dissenting.

Petitioner Dennison, a 73-year-old man, committed an aggravated assault upon a neighborhood youth whom he suspected of stealing money from his house. After a trial at which the Commonwealth proved the elements of aggravated assault beyond a reasonable doubt, the trial judge imposed a sentence of imprisonment of 11 ½ to 23 months. Because he had concluded that Pennsylvania's recently enacted Mandatory Minimum Sentencing Act * * * was unconstitutional, the trial judge refused to impose the 5-year mandatory minimum sentence mandated by that Act whenever the Commonwealth proves—by a preponderance of the evidence—that the defendant "visibly possessed a firearm during the commission of the offense."

* * * Today the Court holds that state legislatures may not only define the offense with which a criminal defendant is charged, but may also authoritatively determine that the conduct so described—i.e., the prohibited activity which subjects the defendant to criminal sanctions—is *not* an element of the crime which the Due Process Clause requires to be proved by the prosecution beyond a reasonable doubt. In my view, a state legislature may not dispense with the requirement of proof beyond a reasonable doubt for conduct that it targets for severe criminal penalties. Because the Pennsylvania statute challenged in this case describes conduct that the Pennsylvania Legislature obviously intended to prohibit, and because it mandates lengthy incarceration for the same, I believe that the conduct so described is an element of the criminal offense to which the proof beyond a reasonable doubt requirement applies.

　　* * *

[*Patterson*] clarified that the Due Process Clause requires proof beyond a reasonable doubt of conduct which exposes a criminal defendant to greater stigma or punishment, but does not likewise constrain state reductions of criminal penalties—even if such reductions are conditioned on a prosecutor's failure to prove a fact by a preponderance of the evidence or on proof supplied by the criminal defendant.

The distinction between aggravating and mitigating facts has been criticized as formalistic. But its ability to identify genuine constitutional threats depends on nothing more than the continued functioning of the democratic process. To appreciate the difference between aggravating and mitigating circumstances, it is important to remember that although States may reach the same destination either by criminalizing conduct and allowing an affirmative defense, or by prohibiting lesser conduct and enhancing the penalty, legislation proceeding along these two paths is very different even if it might theoretically achieve the same result. * * * [There is no] serious danger that a State will soon define murder to be the "mere physical contact between the defendant and the victim leading to the victim's death, but then set up an affirmative defense leaving it to the defendant to prove that he acted without culpable mens rea." *Patterson v. New York,* 432 U.S. at 224, n. 8 (Powell, J., dissenting). No legislator would be willing to expose himself to the severe opprobrium and punishment meted out to murderers for an accidental stumble on the subway. For similar reasons, it can safely be assumed that a State will not "define all assaults as a single offense and then require the defendant to disprove the elements of aggravation." The very inconceivability of the hypothesized legislation—all of which has been sincerely offered to illustrate the dangers of permitting legislative mitigation of punishment in derogation of the requirement of proof beyond a reasonable doubt—is reason enough to feel secure that it will not command a majority of the electorate.

It is not at all inconceivable, however, to fear that a State might subject those individuals convicted of engaging in antisocial conduct to further punishment for aggravating conduct not proved beyond a reasonable doubt. As this case demonstrates, a State may seek to enhance the deterrent effect of its law forbidding the use of firearms in the course of felonies by mandating a minimum sentence of imprisonment upon proof by a preponderance against those already convicted of specified crimes. But *In re Winship* and *Patterson* teach that a State may not advance the objectives of its criminal laws at the expense of the accurate factfinding owed to the criminally accused who suffer the risk of nonpersuasion.

It would demean the importance of the reasonable-doubt standard—indeed, it would demean the Constitution itself—if the substance of the standard could be avoided by nothing more than a legislative declaration that prohibited conduct is not an "element" of a crime. A legislative definition of an offense named "assault" could be broad enough to encompass every intentional infliction of harm by one person upon another, but surely the legislature could not provide that only that fact must be proved beyond a reasonable doubt and then specify a range of increased punishments if the prosecution could show by a preponderance of the evidence that the defendant robbed, raped, or killed his victim "during the commission of the offense."

Appropriate respect for the rule of *In re Winship* requires that there be some constitutional limits on the power of a State to define the elements of criminal offenses. The high standard of proof is required because of the immense importance of the individual interest in avoiding both the loss of liberty and the stigma that results from a criminal conviction. It follows, I submit, that if a State provides that a specific component of a prohibited transaction shall give rise both to a special stigma and to a special punishment, that component must be treated as a "fact necessary to constitute the crime" within the meaning of our holding in *In re Winship.*

Pennsylvania's Mandatory Minimum Sentencing Act reflects a legislative determination that a defendant who "visibly possessed a firearm" during the commission of an aggravated assault is more blameworthy than a defendant who did not. A judicial finding that the defendant used a firearm in an aggravated assault places a greater stigma on the defendant's name than a simple finding that he committed an aggravated assault. And not to be overlooked, such a finding with respect to petitioner Dennison automatically mandates a punishment that is more than twice as severe as the *maximum* punishment that the trial judge considered appropriate for his conduct.

It is true, as the Court points out, that the enhanced punishment is within the range that was authorized for any aggravated assault. That fact does not, however, minimize the significance of a finding of visible possession of a firearm whether attention is focused on the stigmatizing or punitive consequences of that finding. The finding identifies conduct that the legislature specifically intended to prohibit and to punish by a special sanction. In my opinion the constitutional significance of the special sanction cannot be avoided by the cavalier observation that it merely "ups the ante" for the defendant. * * *

I respectfully dissent.

Notes and Questions

1. _Acquitted conduct as sentence enhancement._ In UNITED STATES v. WATTS, 519 U.S. 148, 117 S.Ct. 633, 136 L.Ed.2d 554 (1997), a jury convicted Watts of possessing cocaine base with intent to distribute, but acquitted him of using a firearm in relation to a drug offense. Despite the acquittal on the firearms count, the District Court found by a preponderance of the evidence that Watts had possessed guns in connection with the drug offense, and added two points to Watts' base offense level. In upholding the use of acquitted conduct to enhance a sentence, the Supreme Court stated: "Neither the broad language of § 3661 [See Note 3, p. 1507] nor our holding in _Williams_ suggests any basis for the courts to invent a blanket prohibition against considering certain types of evidence at sentencing." Under the Guidelines, the Court observed, " 'Conduct that is not formally charged or is not an element of the offense of conviction may enter into the determination of the applicable guideline sentencing range.' " It continued, " 'An acquittal can only be an acknowledgment that the government failed to prove an essential element of the offense beyond a reasonable doubt.' * * * [W]e have held that application of the preponderance standard at sentencing generally satisfies due process. * * * We therefore hold that a jury's verdict of acquittal does not prevent the sentencing court from considering conduct underlying the acquitted charge, so long as that conduct has been proved by a preponderance of the evidence." Justice STEVENS, dissented, as he had in _McMillan_. He argued that under the Guidelines, the "goals of rehabilitation and fairness served by individualized sentencing that formerly justified vesting judges with virtually unreviewable sentencing discretion have been replaced by the impersonal interest in uniformity and retribution. Strict mandatory rules have dramatically confined the exercise of judgment based on a totality of the circumstances." These changes, he argued, required a rethinking of the burden of proof at sentencing. He reiterated his objection to the holding in _McMillan_ and explained that even accepting that holding, it "should not be extended to allow a fact proved by only a preponderance to increase the entire range of penalties within which the sentencing judge may lawfully exercise discretion."

2. _Prior convictions._ In ALMENDAREZ-TORRES v. UNITED STATES, 523 U.S. 224, 118 S.Ct. 1219, 140 L.Ed.2d 350 (1998), the defendant was convicted of unlawfully reentering the United States after he had been deported, 18 U.S.C.A. § 1326(a), a crime carrying a maximum sentence of two years. Relying on § 1326(b), however, which provided for a maximum twenty-year sentence for violations with prior convictions, the judge found that the defendant had prior felony convictions based on his own admission, and sentenced him to sixteen years. The Court rejected the defendant's argument that the existence of the prior conviction was an element rather than a sentencing factor that should have been included in his indictment. Admitting that the case is different than _McMillan_ "for it does 'alter the maximum penalty for the crime,' and, it also creates a wider range of appropriate punishments than did the statute in _McMillan_," the Court nonetheless concluded that "these differences do not change the constitutional outcome for several basic reasons. First, the sentencing factor at issue here—recidivism—is a traditional, if not the most traditional, basis for a sentencing court's increasing an offender's sentence. * * * [T]o hold that the Constitution requires that recidivism be deemed an 'element' of petitioner's offense would mark an abrupt departure from a longstanding tradition of treating recidivism as 'going to the punishment only.' Second, the major difference between this case and *McMillan* consists of the circumstance that the sentencing factor at issue here (the prior conviction) triggers an increase in the maximum permissive sentence, while the sentencing factor at issue in *McMillan* triggered a mandatory minimum sentence. Yet that difference—between a permissive maximum and a mandatory minimum—does not systematically, or normally, work to the disadvantage of a criminal defendant. To the contrary, a statutory minimum binds a sentencing judge; a statutory maximum does not. A mandatory minimum can, as Justice Stevens dissenting in *McMillan* pointed out, 'mandate a minimum sentence of imprisonment more than twice as severe as the maximum the trial judge would otherwise have imposed.' It can eliminate a sentencing judge's discretion in its entirety." The Court went on to argue that the "relevant statutory provisions do not change a pre-existing definition of a well-established crime, nor is there any more reason here, than in *McMillan*, to think Congress intended to 'evade' the Constitution, either by 'presuming' guilt or 'restructuring' the elements of an offense." Justice SCALIA, joined by Justices Stevens, Souter, and Ginsburg, dissented, concluding that it was "beyond question that there was, until today's unnecessary resolution of the point, 'serious doubt' whether the Constitution permits a defendant's sentencing exposure to be increased tenfold on the basis of a fact that is not charged, tried to a jury, and found beyond a reasonable doubt."

APPRENDI v. NEW JERSEY
530 U.S. 466, 120 S.Ct. 2348, 147 L.Ed.2d 435 (2000).

Justice STEVENS delivered the opinion of the Court.

[N.J. Stat.Ann. § 2C:44–3(e) (West Supp.2000) (the "hate crime" statute) provides for an "extended term" of imprisonment if the trial judge finds, by a preponderance of the evidence, that "the defendant in committing the crime acted with a purpose to intimidate an individual or group of individuals because of race, color, gender, handicap, religion, sexual orientation or ethnicity." The extended term authorized for second-degree offenses is imprisonment for "between 10 and 20 years." Petitioner Apprendi fired shots into the home of an African-American family. When arrested, he stated that he did not want the occupants of the home in the neighborhood because of their race, a statement he later retracted. A state grand jury indicted him on 23 counts, none of which referred to the hate crime statute or alleged that Apprendi acted with a racially biased purpose. Apprendi agreed to plead guilty to two counts (Counts 3 and 18) of possession of a firearm for an unlawful purpose (classified by statute as a second-degree offense punishable by imprisonment for "between five years and 10 years"), and another crime punishable by 3 to 5 years' imprisonment, in return for dismissal of the remaining counts. As part of the plea agreement, the State reserved the right to request the court to impose a higher "enhanced" sentence for Count 18 on the ground that offense was committed with a biased purpose, and Apprendi reserved the right to challenge the constitutionality of the hate crime sentence enhancement. After accepting the plea the trial judge held an evidentiary hearing on the issue of Apprendi's "purpose" for the shooting. Apprendi adduced evidence from a psychologist and from seven character witnesses who testified that he did not have a reputation for racial bias. He also took the stand himself, explaining that the incident was an unintended consequence of overindulgence in alcohol, denying that he was in any way biased against African–Americans, and denying that his statement to the police had been accurately described. The judge, however, found the police officer's testimony credible, and concluded that the evidence supported a finding "that the crime was motivated by racial bias." Having found by a preponderance of the evidence that Apprendi's actions were taken "with a purpose to intimidate," the judge sentenced him to 12 years on Count 18, to run concurrently with his other sentences.]

* * * The question presented is whether the Due Process Clause of the Fourteenth Amendment requires that a factual determination authorizing an increase in the maximum prison sentence for an offense from 10 to 20 years be made by a jury on the basis of proof beyond a reasonable doubt. * * *

* * * Our answer to [the question in this case] was foreshadowed by our opinion in *Jones v. United States*, 526 U.S. 227, 143 L.Ed. 2d 311, 119 S.Ct. 1215 (1999), where we noted that "under the Due Process Clause of the Fifth Amendment and the notice and jury trial guarantees of the Sixth Amendment, any fact (other than prior conviction) that increases the maximum penalty for a crime must be charged in an indictment, submitted to a jury, and proven beyond a reasonable doubt." The Fourteenth Amendment commands the same answer in this case involving a state statute.

* * * At stake in this case are constitutional protections of surpassing importance: the proscription of any deprivation of liberty without "due process of law," Amdt. 14, and the guarantee that "in all criminal prosecutions, the accused shall enjoy the right to a speedy and public trial, by an impartial jury," Amdt. 6.[3] * * * As we have, unanimously, explained, *United States v. Gaudin*, [p. 1575], the historical foundation for our recognition of these principles extends down centuries into the common law. "To guard against a spirit of oppression and tyranny on the part of rulers," and "as the great bulwark of [our] civil and political liberties," 2 J. Story, Commentaries on the Constitution of the United States 540–541 (4th ed. 1873), trial by jury has been understood to require that "the truth of every accusation, whether preferred in the shape of indictment, information, or appeal, should afterwards be confirmed by the unanimous suffrage of twelve of [the defendant's] equals and neighbours...." 4 W. Blackstone, Commentaries on the Laws of England 343 (1769). * * * Equally well founded is the companion right to have the jury verdict based on proof beyond a reasonable doubt. * * *

Any possible distinction between an "element" of a felony offense and a "sentencing factor" was unknown to the practice of criminal indictment, trial by jury, and judgment by court * * * as it existed during the years surrounding our Nation's founding. As a general rule, criminal proceedings were submitted to a jury after being initiated by an indictment containing "all the facts and circumstances which constitute the offence, ... stated with such certainty and precision, that the defendant ... may be enabled to determine the species of offence they constitute, in order that he may prepare his defence accordingly ... and that there may be no doubt as to the judgment which should be given, if the defendant be convicted." J. Archbold, Pleading and Evidence in Criminal Cases 44 (15th ed.

---

3. Apprendi has not here asserted a constitutional claim based on the omission of any reference to sentence enhancement or racial bias in the indictment. He relies entirely on the fact that the "due process of law" that the Fourteenth Amendment requires the States to provide to persons accused of crime encompasses the right to a trial by jury * * * and the right to have every element of the offense proved beyond a reasonable doubt, * * * That Amendment has not, however, been construed to include the Fifth Amendment right to "presentment or indictment of a Grand Jury" that was implicated in our recent decision in *Almendarez-Torres v. United States* [p. 1517]. We thus do not address the indictment question separately today.

1862) (emphasis added). The defendant's ability to predict with certainty the judgment from the face of the felony indictment flowed from the invariable linkage of punishment with crime. * * *

* * * Just as the circumstances of the crime and the intent of the defendant at the time of commission were often essential elements to be alleged in the indictment, so too were the circumstances mandating a particular punishment. "Where a statute annexes a higher degree of punishment to a common-law felony, if committed under particular circumstances, an indictment for the offence, in order to bring the defendant within that higher degree of punishment, must expressly charge it to have been committed under those circumstances, and must state the circumstances with certainty and precision. [2 M. Hale, Pleas of the Crown 170]." Archbold, Pleading and Evidence in Criminal Cases, at 51. If, then, "upon an indictment under the statute, the prosecutor prove the felony to have been committed, but fail in proving it to have been committed under the circumstances specified in the statute, the defendant shall be convicted of the common-law felony only." Id. at 188. * * *

We should be clear that nothing in this history suggests that it is impermissible for judges to exercise discretion—taking into consideration various factors relating both to offense and offender—in imposing a judgment within the range prescribed by statute. We have often noted that judges in this country have long exercised discretion of this nature in imposing sentence within statutory limits in the individual case.* * * As in *Williams* [*v. New York*, p. 1502], our periodic recognition of judges' broad discretion in sentencing—since the 19th-century shift in this country from statutes providing fixed-term sentences to those providing judges discretion within a permissible range, * * * has been regularly accompanied by the qualification that that discretion was bound by the range of sentencing options prescribed by the legislature. * * *

We do not suggest that trial practices cannot change in the course of centuries and still remain true to the principles that emerged from the Framers' fears "that the jury right could be lost not only by gross denial, but by erosion." * * * But practice must at least adhere to the basic principles undergirding the requirements of trying to a jury all facts necessary to constitute a statutory offense, and proving those facts beyond reasonable doubt. As we made clear in *Winship*, the "reasonable doubt" requirement "has a vital role in our criminal procedure for cogent reasons." Prosecution subjects the criminal defendant both to "the possibility that he may lose his liberty upon conviction and ... the certainty that he would be stigmatized by the conviction." We thus require this, among other, procedural protections in order to "provide concrete substance for the presumption of innocence," and to reduce the risk of imposing such deprivations erroneously. If a defendant faces punishment beyond that provided by statute when an offense is committed under certain circumstances but not others, it is obvious that both the loss of liberty and the stigma attaching to the offense are heightened; it necessarily follows that the defendant should not—at the moment the State is put to proof of those circumstances—be deprived of protections that have, until that point, unquestionably attached.

Since *Winship*, we have made clear beyond peradventure that *Winship*'s due process and associated jury protections extend, to some degree, "to determinations that [go] not to a defendant's guilt or innocence, but simply to the length of his sentence." *Almendarez-Torres,* [p. 1517] (Scalia, J., dissenting). This was a primary lesson of *Mullaney v. Wilbur,* 421 U.S. 684, 44 L.Ed. 2d 508, 95 S.Ct. 1881 (1975), in which we invalidated a Maine statute that presumed that a defendant who acted with an intent to kill possessed the "malice aforethought" necessary to constitute the State's murder offense (and therefore, was subject to that crime's associated punishment of life imprisonment). The statute placed the burden on the defendant of proving, in rebutting the statutory presumption, that he acted with a lesser degree of culpability, such as in the heat of passion, to win a reduction in the offense from murder to manslaughter (and thus a reduction of the maximum punishment of 20 years).

The State had posited in *Mullaney* that requiring a defendant to prove heat-of-passion intent to overcome a presumption of murderous intent did not implicate *Winship* protections because, upon conviction of either offense, the defendant would lose his liberty and face societal stigma just the same. Rejecting this argument, we acknowledged that criminal law "is concerned not only with guilt or innocence in the abstract, but also with the degree of criminal culpability" assessed. Because the "consequences" of a guilty verdict for murder and for manslaughter differed substantially, we dismissed the possibility that a State could circumvent the protections of *Winship* merely by "redefining the elements that constitute different crimes, characterizing them as factors that bear solely on the extent of punishment."[12]

* * * It was in *McMillan v. Pennsylvania,* [p. 1511], that this Court, for the first time, coined the term "sentencing factor" to refer to a fact that was not found by a jury but that could affect the sentence imposed by the judge. * * * Articulating for the first time, and then applying, a multifactor set of criteria for determining whether the *Winship* protections applied to bar such a system, we concluded that the Pennsylvania statute did not run afoul of our previous admonitions against relieving the State of its burden of proving guilt, or tailoring the mere form of a criminal statute solely to avoid *Winship*'s strictures.

We did not, however, there budge from the position that (1) constitutional limits exist to States' authority to define away facts necessary to constitute a criminal offense, and (2) that a state scheme that keeps from the jury facts that "expose [defendants] to greater or additional punishment," may raise serious constitutional concern. * * *[13]

Finally, * * * *Almendarez-Torres* represents at best an exceptional departure from the historic practice that we have described. * * * Because Almendarez-Torres had admitted the three earlier convictions for aggravated felonies—all of which had been entered pursuant to proceedings with substantial procedural safeguards of their own—no question concerning the right to a jury trial or the standard of proof that would apply to a contested issue of fact was before the Court. Although our conclusion in that case was based in part on our application of the criteria we had invoked in *McMillan*, the specific question decided con-

---

12. Contrary to the principal dissent's suggestion, *Patterson v. New York* [p. 1512], posed no direct challenge to this aspect of *Mullaney*. In upholding a New York law allowing defendants to raise and prove extreme emotional distress as an affirmative defense to murder, *Patterson* made clear that the state law still required the State to prove every element of that State's offense of murder and its accompanying punishment. "No further facts are either presumed or inferred in order to constitute the crime." New York, unlike Maine, had not made malice aforethought, or any described mens rea, part of its statutory definition of second-degree murder; one could tell from the face of the statute that if one intended to cause the death of another person and did cause that death, one could be subject to sentence for a second-degree offense. Responding to the argument that our view could be seen "to permit

state legislatures to reallocate burdens of proof by labeling as affirmative defenses at least some elements of the crimes now defined in their statutes," the Court made clear in the very next breath that there were "obviously constitutional limits beyond which the States may not go in this regard."

13. The principal dissent accuses us of today "overruling *McMillan*." We do not overrule *McMillan*. We limit its holding to cases that do not involve the imposition of a sentence more severe than the statutory maximum for the offense established by the jury's verdict—a limitation identified in the *McMillan* opinion itself. Conscious of the likelihood that legislative decisions may have been made in reliance on *McMillan*, we reserve for another day the question whether stare decisis considerations preclude reconsideration of its narrower holding.

cerned the sufficiency of the indictment. More important,* * * our conclusion in *Almendarez-Torres* turned heavily upon the fact that the additional sentence to which the defendant was subject was "the prior commission of a serious crime."* * * Both the certainty that procedural safeguards attached to any "fact" of prior conviction, and the reality that Almendarez-Torres did not challenge the accuracy of that "fact" in his case, mitigated the due process and Sixth Amendment concerns otherwise implicated in allowing a judge to determine a "fact" increasing punishment beyond the maximum of the statutory range.

Even though it is arguable that *Almendarez-Torres* was incorrectly decided, and that a logical application of our reasoning today should apply if the recidivist issue were contested, Apprendi does not contest the decision's validity and we need not revisit it for purposes of our decision today to treat the case as a narrow exception to the general rule we recalled at the outset. Given its unique facts, it surely does not warrant rejection of the otherwise uniform course of decision during the entire history of our jurisprudence.

In sum, our reexamination of our cases in this area, and of the history upon which they rely, confirms the opinion that we expressed in *Jones*. Other than the fact of a prior conviction, any fact that increases the penalty for a crime beyond the prescribed statutory maximum must be submitted to a jury, and proved beyond a reasonable doubt. With that exception, we endorse the statement of the rule set forth in the concurring opinions in that case: "It is unconstitutional for a legislature to remove from the jury the assessment of facts that increase the prescribed range of penalties to which a criminal defendant is exposed. It is equally clear that such facts must be established by proof beyond a reasonable doubt."[16]

The New Jersey statutory scheme that Apprendi asks us to invalidate allows a jury to convict a defendant of a second-degree offense based on its finding beyond a reasonable doubt that he unlawfully possessed a prohibited weapon; after a subsequent and separate proceeding, it then allows a judge to impose punishment identical to that New Jersey provides for crimes of the first degree,* * * based upon the judge's finding, by a preponderance of the evidence, that the defendant's "purpose" for unlawfully possessing the weapon was "to intimidate" his victim on the basis of a particular characteristic the victim possessed. In light of the constitutional rule explained above, and all of the cases supporting it, this practice cannot stand.

16. The principal dissent would reject the Court's rule as a "meaningless formalism," because it can conceive of hypothetical statutes that would comply with the rule and achieve the same result as the New Jersey statute. While a State could, hypothetically, undertake to revise its entire criminal code in the manner the dissent suggests,—extending all statutory maximum sentences to, for example, 50 years and giving judges guided discretion as to a few specially selected factors within that range— this possibility seems remote. Among other reasons, structural democratic constraints exist to discourage legislatures from enacting penal statutes that expose every defendant convicted of, for example, weapons possession, to a maximum sentence exceeding that which is, in the legislature's judgment, generally proportional to the crime. This is as it should be. Our rule ensures that a State is obliged "to make its choices concerning the substantive content of its criminal laws with full awareness of the consequence, unable to mask substantive policy choices" of exposing all who are convicted to the maximum sentence it provides. *Patterson v. New York*, 432 U.S. at 228–229, n. 13 (Powell, J., dissenting). So exposed, "the political check on potentially harsh legislative action is then more likely to operate." Ibid.

In all events, if such an extensive revision of the State's entire criminal code were enacted for the purpose the dissent suggests, or if New Jersey simply reversed the burden of the hate crime finding (effectively assuming a crime was performed with a purpose to intimidate and then requiring a defendant to prove that it was not), we would be required to question whether the revision was constitutional under this Court's prior decisions. See *Patterson*, 432 U.S. at 210; *Mullaney*, 421 U.S. at 698–702. * * *

* * * [T]his Court has previously considered and rejected the argument that the principles guiding our decision today render invalid state capital sentencing schemes regarding judges, after a jury verdict holding a defendant guilty of a capital crime, to find specific aggravating factors before imposing a sentence of death. *Walton v. Arizona*, 497 U.S. 639, 647–649 (1990); *id.*, at 709–714 (Stevens, J., dissenting). For reasons we have explained, the capital cases are not controlling:

> "Neither the cases cited, nor any other case, permits a judge to determine the existence of a factor which makes a crime a capital offense. What the cited cases hold is that, once a jury has found the defendant guilty of all the elements of an offense which carries as its maximum penalty the sentence of death, it may be left to the judge to decide whether that maximum penalty, rather than a lesser one, ought to be imposed. . . .The person who is charged with actions that expose him to the death penalty has an absolute entitlement to jury trial on all the elements of the charge." *Almendarez-Torres*, 523 U.S., at 257, n. 2 (Scalia, J., dissenting) (emphasis deleted). * * *[21]

* * * Accordingly, the judgment of the Supreme Court of New Jersey is reversed, and the case is remanded for further proceedings not inconsistent with this opinion.

[Justice SCALIA's concurring opinion is omitted.]

Justice THOMAS, with whom Justice Scalia joins as to Parts I and II, concurring.

I join the opinion of the Court in full. I write separately to explain my view that the Constitution requires a broader rule than the Court adopts.

I

This case turns on the seemingly simple question of what constitutes a "crime." Under the Federal Constitution, "the accused" has the right (1) "to be informed of the nature and cause of the accusation" (that is, the basis on which he is accused of a crime), (2) to be "held to answer for a capital, or otherwise infamous crime" only on an indictment or presentment of a grand jury, and (3) to be tried by "an impartial jury of the State and district wherein the crime shall have been committed." Amdts. 5 and 6. See also Art. III, § 2, cl. 3. With the exception of the Grand Jury Clause, * * * the Court has held that these protections apply in state prosecutions * * *. Further, the Court has held that due process requires that the jury find beyond a reasonable doubt every fact necessary to constitute the crime. * * *

All of these constitutional protections turn on determining which facts constitute the "crime"—that is, which facts are the "elements" or "ingredients" of a crime. In order for an accusation of a crime (whether by indictment or some other form) to be proper under the common law, and thus proper under the codification of the common-law rights in the Fifth and Sixth Amendments, it must allege all elements of that crime; likewise, in order for a jury trial of a crime to be

---

21. The principal dissent, in addition, treats us to a lengthy disquisition on the benefits of determinate sentencing schemes, and the effect of today's decision on the federal Sentencing Guidelines. The Guidelines are, of course, not before the Court. We therefore express no view on the subject beyond what this Court has already held. See, e.g., *Edwards v. United States*, 523 U.S. 511, 515, 140 L. Ed. 2d 703, 118 S. Ct. 1475 (1998) (opinion of Breyer, J., for a unanimous court) (noting that "of course, petitioners' statutory and constitutional claims would make a difference if it were possible to argue, say, that the sentences imposed exceeded the maximum that the statutes permit for a cocaine-only conspiracy. That is because a maximum sentence set by statute trumps a higher sentence set forth in the Guidelines. [U.S. Sentencing Guidelines Manual] § 5G1.1.").

proper, all elements of the crime must be proved to the jury (and, under *Winship*, proved beyond a reasonable doubt).* * *

Thus, it is critical to know which facts are elements.* * * Courts have long had to consider which facts are elements in order to determine the sufficiency of an accusation (usually an indictment). The answer that courts have provided regarding the accusation tells us what an element is, and it is then a simple matter to apply that answer to whatever constitutional right may be at issue in a case—here, *Winship* and the right to trial by jury. A long line of essentially uniform authority addressing accusations, and stretching from the earliest reported cases after the founding until well into the 20th century, establishes that the original understanding of which facts are elements was even broader than the rule that the Court adopts today.

This authority establishes that a "crime" includes every fact that is by law a basis for imposing or increasing punishment (in contrast with a fact that mitigates punishment). Thus, if the legislature defines some core crime and then provides for increasing the punishment of that crime upon a finding of some aggravating fact—of whatever sort, including the fact of a prior conviction—the core crime and the aggravating fact together constitute an aggravated crime, just as much as grand larceny is an aggravated form of petit larceny. The aggravating fact is an element of the aggravated crime. Similarly, if the legislature, rather than creating grades of crimes, has provided for setting the punishment of a crime based on some fact—such as a fine that is proportional to the value of stolen goods—that fact is also an element. * * *

II

Cases from the founding to roughly the end of the Civil War establish the rule that I have described, applying it to all sorts of facts, including recidivism. As legislatures varied common-law crimes and created new crimes, American courts, particularly from the 1840's on, readily applied to these new laws the common-law understanding that a fact that is by law the basis for imposing or increasing punishment is an element.

* * * Further evidence of the rule that a crime includes every fact that is by law a basis for imposing or increasing punishment comes from early cases addressing recidivism statutes. As Justice Scalia has explained, there was a tradition of treating recidivism as an element. See *Almendarez-Torres*, 523 U.S. at 256–257, 261 (dissenting opinion). * * *

* * * [T]his traditional understanding—that a "crime" includes every fact that is by law a basis for imposing or increasing punishment—continued well into the 20th century * * *. In fact, it is fair to say that *McMillan* began a revolution in the law regarding the definition of "crime." Today's decision, far from being a sharp break with the past, marks nothing more than a return to the status quo ante—the status quo that reflected the original meaning of the Fifth and Sixth Amendments.

III

The consequence of the above discussion for our decisions in *Almendarez-Torres* and *McMillan* should be plain enough, but a few points merit special mention.

* * * [O]ne of the chief errors of *Almendarez-Torres*—an error to which I succumbed—was to attempt to discern whether a particular fact is traditionally (or typically) a basis for a sentencing court to increase an offender's sentence.* * * [I]t should be clear that this approach just defines away the real issue. What matters is the way by which a fact enters into the sentence. If a fact is by

law the basis for imposing or increasing punishment—for establishing or increasing the prosecution's entitlement—it is an element. * * * One reason frequently offered for treating recidivism differently, a reason on which we relied in *Almendarez-Torres* * * * is a concern for prejudicing the jury by informing it of the prior conviction. But this concern, of which earlier courts were well aware, does not make the traditional understanding of what an element is any less applicable to the fact of a prior conviction. * * *[10]

* * * I think it clear that the common-law rule would cover the *McMillan* situation of a mandatory minimum sentence (in that case, for visible possession of a firearm during the commission of certain crimes). No doubt a defendant could, under such a scheme, find himself sentenced to the same term to which he could have been sentenced absent the mandatory minimum. * * * But it is equally true that his expected punishment has increased as a result of the narrowed range and that the prosecution is empowered, by invoking the mandatory minimum, to require the judge to impose a higher punishment than he might wish. * * * Thus, the fact triggering the mandatory minimum is part of "the punishment sought to be inflicted." * * *

For the foregoing reasons, as well as those given in the Court's opinion, I agree that the New Jersey procedure at issue is unconstitutional.

Justice O'CONNOR, with Whom The Chief Justice, Justice Kennedy, and Justice Breyer join, dissenting.

* * * Today, in what will surely be remembered as a watershed change in constitutional law, the Court imposes as a constitutional rule the principle it first identified in *Jones*.

Our Court has long recognized that not every fact that bears on a defendant's punishment need be charged in an indictment, submitted to a jury, and proved by the government beyond a reasonable doubt. Rather, we have held that the "legislature's definition of the elements of the offense is usually dispositive." *McMillan* * * *. Although we have recognized that "there are obviously constitutional limits beyond which the States may not go in this regard," * * * and that "in certain limited circumstances *Winship*'s reasonable-doubt requirement applies to facts not formally identified as elements of the offense charged," * * * we have proceeded with caution before deciding that a certain fact must be treated as an offense element despite the legislature's choice not to characterize it as such. We have therefore declined to establish any bright-line rule for making such judgments and have instead approached each case individually, sifting through the considerations most relevant to determining whether the legislature has acted properly within its broad power to define crimes and their punishments or instead has sought to evade the constitutional requirements associated with the characterization of a fact as an offense element. * * *

In one bold stroke the Court today casts aside our traditional cautious approach and instead embraces a universal and seemingly bright-line rule limiting the power of Congress and state legislatures to define criminal offenses and the sentences that follow from convictions thereunder. * * * [T]he Court marshals virtually no authority to support its extraordinary rule. Indeed, it is remarkable that the Court cannot identify a single instance, in the over 200 years since the ratification of the Bill of Rights, that our Court has applied, as a constitutional requirement, the rule it announces today.

10. In addition, it has been common practice to address this concern by permitting the defendant to stipulate to the prior conviction, in which case the charge of the prior conviction is not read to the jury, or, if the defendant decides not to stipulate, to bifurcate the trial, with the jury only considering the prior conviction after it has reached a guilty verdict on the core crime. * * *

* * * None of the history contained in the Court's opinion requires the rule it ultimately adopts. The history cited by the Court can be divided into two categories: first, evidence that judges at common law had virtually no discretion in sentencing, and, second, statements from a 19th century criminal procedure treatise that the government must charge in an indictment and prove at trial the elements of a statutory offense for the defendant to be sentenced to the punishment attached to that statutory offense. The relevance of the first category of evidence can be easily dismissed. Indeed, the Court does not even claim that the historical evidence of nondiscretionary sentencing at common law supports its "increase in the maximum penalty" rule. Rather, almost as quickly as it recites that historical practice, the Court rejects it relevance to the constitutional question presented here due to the conflicting American practice of judges exercising sentencing discretion and our decisions recognizing the legitimacy of that American practice.

* * * Apparently, then, the historical practice on which the Court places so much reliance consists of only two quotations taken from an 1862 criminal procedure treatise. A closer examination of the two statements reveals that neither supports the Court's "increase in the maximum penalty" rule. Both of the excerpts pertain to circumstances in which a common-law felony had also been made a separate statutory offense carrying a greater penalty. Taken together, the statements from the Archbold treatise demonstrate nothing more than the unremarkable proposition that a defendant could receive the greater statutory punishment only if the indictment expressly charged and the prosecutor proved the facts that made up the statutory offense, as opposed to simply those facts that made up the common-law offense. In other words, for the defendant to receive the statutory punishment, the prosecutor had to charge in the indictment and prove at trial *the elements* of the statutory offense * * *. No Member of this Court questions the proposition that a State must charge in the indictment and prove at trial beyond a reasonable doubt the actual elements of the offense. This case, however, concerns the distinct questions of when a fact that bears on a defendant's punishment, but which the legislature has not classified as an element of the charged offense, must nevertheless be treated as an offense element. The excerpts drawn from the Archbold treatise do not speak to this question at all. The history on which the Court's opinion relies provides no support for its "increase in the maximum penalty" rule.

* * * The history cited by Justice Thomas does not require, as a matter of federal constitutional law, the application of the rule he advocates. * * * [His opinion fails] to discuss any historical practice, or to cite any decisions, predating (or contemporary with) the ratification of the Bill of Rights. Rather, Justice Thomas divines the common-law understanding of the Fifth and Sixth Amendment rights by consulting decisions rendered by American courts well after the ratification of the Bill of Rights, ranging primarily from the 1840's to the 1890's. Whatever those decisions might reveal about the way American state courts resolved questions regarding the distinction between a crime and its punishment under general rules of criminal pleading or their own state constitutions, the decisions fail to demonstrate any settled understanding with respect to the definition of a crime under the relevant, preexisting common law. * * * The most relevant common-law principles in this area were that an indictment must charge the elements of the relevant offense and must do so with certainty.* * * Those principles, of course, say little about when a specific fact constitutes an element of the offense. * * *

That the Court's rule is unsupported by the history and case law it cites is reason enough to reject such a substantial departure from our settled jurisprudence. Significantly, the Court also fails to explain adequately why the Due

Process Clauses of the Fifth and Fourteenth Amendments and the jury trial guarantee of the Sixth Amendment require application of its rule. Upon closer examination, it is possible that the court's "increase in the maximum penalty" rule rests on a meaningless formalism that accords, at best, marginal protection for the constitutional rights that it seeks to effectuate.

* * * [T]he Court appears to hold that the Constitution requires that a fact be submitted to a jury and proved beyond a reasonable doubt only if that fact, as a formal matter, extends the range of punishment beyond the prescribed statutory maximum.* * * A State could, however, remove from the jury (and subject to a standard of proof below "beyond a reasonable doubt") the assessment of those facts that define narrower ranges of punishment, within the overall statutory range, to which the defendant may be sentenced. * * * Thus, apparently New Jersey could cure its sentencing scheme, and achieve virtually the same results, by drafting its weapons possession statute in the following manner: First, New Jersey could prescribe, in the weapons possession statute itself, a range of 5 to 20 years' imprisonment for one who commits that criminal offense. Second, New Jersey could provide that only those defendants convicted under the statute who are found by a judge, by a preponderance of the evidence, to have acted with a purpose to intimidate an individual on the basis of race may receive a sentence greater than 10 years' imprisonment.

The Court's proffered distinction of *Walton v. Arizona* [497 U.S. 639, 111 L.Ed. 2d 511, 110 S.Ct. 3047 (1990)] suggests that it means to announce a rule of only this limited effect. The Court claims the Arizona capital sentencing scheme is consistent with the constitutional principle underlying today's decision because Arizona's first-degree murder statute itself authorizes both life imprisonment and the death penalty. * * * " 'Once a jury has found the defendant guilty of all the elements of an offense which carries as its maximum penalty the sentence of death, it may be left to the judge to decide whether that maximum penalty, rather than a lesser one, ought to be imposed.' " * * * Of course * * * an Arizona sentencing judge can impose the maximum penalty of death only if the judge first makes a statutorily required finding that at least one aggravating factor exists in the defendant's case. Thus, the Arizona first-degree murder statute authorizes a maximum penalty of death only in a formal sense. In real terms, however, the Arizona sentencing scheme removes from the jury the assessment of a fact that determines whether the defendant can receive that maximum punishment. The only difference, then, between the Arizona scheme and the New Jersey scheme we consider here—apart from the magnitude of punishment at stake—is that New Jersey has not prescribed the 20–year maximum penalty in the same statute that it defines the crime to be punished. It is difficult to understand, and the Court does not explain, why the Constitution would require a state legislature to follow such a meaningless and formalistic difference in drafting its criminal statutes.

Under another reading of the Court's decision, it may mean only that the Constitution requires that a fact be submitted to a jury and proved beyond a reasonable doubt if it, as a formal matter, *increases* the range of punishment *beyond that which could legally be imposed absent that fact* * * * A State could, however, remove from the jury (and subject to a standard of proof below "beyond a reasonable doubt") the assessment of those facts that, as a formal matter, *decrease* the range of punishment *below that which could legally be imposed absent that fact*. Thus, consistent with our decision in *Patterson*, New Jersey could cure its sentencing scheme, and achieve virtually the same results, by drafting its weapons possession statute in the following manner: First, New Jersey could prescribe, in the weapons possession statute itself, a range of 5 to 20 years' imprisonment for one who commits that criminal offense. Second, New Jersey could provide that a defendant convicted under the statute whom a judge finds, by a preponderance of the evidence, *not* to have acted with a purpose to intimidate an individual on the basis of race may receive a sentence no greater than 10 years' imprisonment.

* * * If either of the above readings is all that the Court's decision means, "the Court's principle amounts to nothing more than chastising [the New Jersey Legislature] for failing to use the approved phrasing in expressing its intent as to how [unlawful weapons possession] should be punished." *Jones*, 526 U.S., at 257 (Kennedy, J., dissenting). If New Jersey can, consistent with the Constitution, make precisely the same differences in punishment turn on precisely the same facts, and can remove the assessment of those facts from the jury and subject them to a standard of proof below "beyond a reasonable doubt," it is impossible to say that the Fifth, Sixth, and Fourteenth Amendments require the Court's rule. For the same reason, the "structural democratic constraints" that might discourage a legislature from enacting either of the above hypothetical statutes would be no more significant than those that would discourage the enactment of New Jersey's present sentence-enhancement statute. See *ante*, at n. 16 (majority opinion). In all three cases, the legislature is able to calibrate punishment perfectly, and subject to a maximum penalty only those defendants whose cases satisfy the sentence-enhancement criterion.

Given the pure formalism of the above reasons of the Court's opinion, one suspects that the constitutional principle underlying its decision is more far reaching. The actual principle underlying the Court's decision may be that any fact (other than prior conviction) that has the effect, *in real terms*, of increasing the maximum punishment beyond an otherwise applicable range must be submitted to a jury and proved beyond a reasonable doubt. * * * The principle thus would apply not only to schemes like New Jersey's, under which a factual determination exposes the defendant to a sentence beyond the prescribed statutory maximum, but also to all determinate-sentencing schemes in which the length of a defendant's sentence within the statutory range turns on specific factual determinations (*e.g.*, the federal Sentencing Guidelines).

* * * I would reject any such principle. As explained above, it is inconsistent with our precedent and would require the Court to overrule, at a minimum, decisions like *Patterson* and *Walton*. More importantly, given our approval of—and the significant history in this country of—discretionary sentencing by judges, it is difficult to understand how the Fifth, Sixth, and Fourteenth Amendments could possibly require the Court's or Justice Thomas' rule. Finally, in light of the adoption of the Court's and Justice Thomas' rules in terms of sentencing schemes invalidated by today's decision will likely be severe.

* * * One important purpose of the Sixth Amendment's jury trial guarantee is to protect the criminal defendant against potentially arbitrary judges. It effectuates this promise by preserving, as a constitutional matter, certain fundamental decisions for a jury of one's peers, as opposed to a judge.* * * Clearly, the concerns animating the Sixth Amendment's jury trial guarantee, if they were to extend to the sentencing context at all, would apply with greater strength to a discretionary-sentencing scheme than to determinate sentencing. In the former scheme, the potential for mischief by an arbitrary judge is much greater, given that the judge's decision of where to set the defendant's sentence within the prescribed statutory range is left almost entirely to discretion. In contrast, under a determinate-sentencing system, the discretion the judge wields within the statutory range is tightly constrained. Accordingly, our approval of discretionary-sentencing schemes, in which a defendant is not entitled to have a jury make factual findings relevant to sentencing despite the effect those findings have on the severity of the defendant's sentence, demonstrates that the defendant should have no right to demand that a jury make the equivalent factual determinations under a determinate-sentencing scheme.

The Court appears to hold today, however, that a defendant is entitled to have a jury decide, by proof beyond a reasonable doubt, every fact relevant to the determination of sentence under a determinate-sentencing scheme. If this is an accurate description of the constitutional principle underlying the Court's opinion, its decision will have the effect of invalidating significant sentencing reform accomplished at the federal and state levels over the past three decades.* * *

* * * [I]t is ironic that the Court, in the name of constitutional rights meant to protect criminal defendants from the potentially arbitrary exercise of power by prosecutors and judges, appears to rest its decision on a principle that would render unconstitutional efforts by Congress and the state legislatures to place constraints on that very power in the sentencing context.

Finally, perhaps the most significant impact of the Court's decision will be a practical one—its unsettling effect on sentencing conducted under current federal and state determinate-sentencing schemes. As I have explained, the Court does not say whether these schemes are constitutional, but its reasoning strongly suggests that they are not. Thus, with respect to past sentences handed down by judges under determinate-sentencing schemes, the Court's decision threatens to unleash a flood of petitions by convicted defendants seeking to invalidate their sentences in whole or in part on the authority of the Court's decision today. Statistics compiled by the United States Sentencing Commission reveal that almost a half-million cases have been sentenced under the Sentencing Guidelines since 1989 * * * [and] federal criminal prosecutions represen[t] only about 0.4% of the total number of criminal prosecutions in federal and state courts. * * * Because many States, like New Jersey, have determinate-sentencing schemes, the number of individual sentences drawn into question by the Court's decision could be colossal. * * *

* * * I would evaluate New Jersey's sentence-enhancement statute by analyzing the factors we have examined in past cases.* * * First, the New Jersey statute does not shift the burden of proof on an essential ingredient of the offense by presuming that ingredient upon proof of other elements of the offense. * * * Second, the magnitude of the New Jersey sentence enhancement, as applied in petitioner's case, is constitutionally permissible. * * * The 10–year increase in the maximum penalty to which petitioner was exposed falls well within the range we have found permissible. See *Almendarez-Torres* (approving 18–year enhancement). Third, the New Jersey statute gives no impression of having been enacted to evade the constitutional requirements that attach when a State makes a fact an element of the charged offense. For example, New Jersey did not take what had previously been an element of the weapons possession offense and transform it into a sentencing factor. * * *

In sum, New Jersey "simply took one factor that has always been considered by sentencing courts to bear on punishment"—a defendant's motive for committing the criminal offense—"and dictated the precise weight to be given that factor" when the motive is to intimidate a person because of race. * * *

Justice BREYER, with whom Chief Justice Rehnquist joins, dissenting.

* * * [The majority's] rule would seem to promote a procedural ideal—that of juries, not judges, determining the existence of those facts upon which increased punishment turns. But the real world of criminal justice cannot hope to meet any such ideal. It can function only with the help of procedural compromises, particularly in respect to sentencing. And those compromises, which are themselves necessary for the fair functioning of the criminal justice system, preclude implementation of the procedural model that today's decision reflects. At the very least,

the impractical nature of the requirement that the majority now recognizes supports the proposition that the Constitution was not intended to embody it.

* * * [I]t is important for present purposes to understand why judges, rather than juries, traditionally have determined the presence or absence of such sentence-affecting facts in any given case. And it is important to realize that the reason is not a theoretical one, but a practical one. It does not reflect (Justice Scalia's opinion to the contrary notwithstanding) an ideal of procedural "fairness," * * * but rather an administrative need for procedural compromise. There are, to put it simply, far too many potentially relevant sentencing factors to permit submission of all (or even many) of them to a jury. As the Sentencing Guidelines state the matter,

> "[a] bank robber with (or without) a gun, which the robber kept hidden (or brandished), might have frightened (or merely warned), injured seriously (or less seriously), tied up (or simply pushed) a guard, a teller or a customer, at night (or at noon), for a bad (or arguably less bad) motive, in an effort to obtain money for other crimes (or for other purposes), in the company of a few (or many) other robbers, for the first (or fourth) time that day, while sober (or under the influence of drugs or alcohol), and so forth." Sentencing Guidelines, Part A, at 1.2.

The Guidelines note that "a sentencing system tailored to fit every conceivable wrinkle of each case can become unworkable and seriously compromise the certainty of punishment and its deterrent effect." Ibid. To ask a jury to consider all, or many, such matters would do the same.

At the same time, to require jury consideration of all such factors—say, during trial where the issue is guilt or innocence—could easily place the defendant in the awkward (and conceivably unfair) position of having to deny he committed the crime yet offer proof about how he committed it, e.g., "I did not sell drugs, but I sold no more than 500 grams." And while special postverdict sentencing juries could cure this problem, they have seemed (but for capital cases) not worth their administrative costs. * * *

As Justice Thomas suggests, until fairly recent times many legislatures rarely focused upon sentencing factors. Rather, it appears they simply identified typical forms of antisocial conduct, defined basic "crimes," and attached a broad sentencing range to each definition—leaving judges free to decide how to sentence within those ranges in light of such factors as they found relevant. * * * But the Constitution does not freeze 19th-century sentencing practices into permanent law. And dissatisfaction with the traditional sentencing system (reflecting its tendency to treat similar cases differently) has led modern legislatures to write new laws that refer specifically to sentencing factors.* * *

With the possible exception of the last line of Justice Scalia's concurring opinion, the majority also makes no constitutional objection to a legislative delegation to a commission of the authority to create guidelines that determine how a judge is to exercise sentencing discretion.* * * But if the Constitution permits Guidelines, why does it not permit Congress similarly to guide the exercise of a judge's sentencing discretion? That is, if the Constitution permits a delegatee (the commission) to exercise sentencing-related rulemaking power, how can it deny the delegator (the legislature) what is, in effect, the same rulemaking power?

The majority appears to offer two responses. First, it argues for a limiting principle that would prevent a legislature with broad authority from transforming (jury-determined) facts that constitute elements of a crime into (judge-determined) sentencing factors, thereby removing procedural protections that the

Constitution would otherwise require. * * * The majority's cure, however, is not aimed at the disease.

The same "transformational" problem exists under traditional sentencing law, where legislation, silent as to sentencing factors, grants the judge virtually unchecked discretion to sentence within a broad range. * * *

* * * [T]he solution to the problem lies, not in prohibiting legislatures from enacting sentencing factors, but in sentencing rules that determine punishments on the basis of properly defined relevant conduct, with sensitivity to the need for procedural protections where sentencing factors are determined by a judge (for example, use of a "reasonable doubt" standard), and invocation of the Due Process Clause where the history of the crime at issue, together with the nature of the facts to be proved, reveals unusual and serious procedural unfairness. Cf. *McMillan*, 477 U.S. at 88 (upholding statute in part because it "gives no impression of having been tailored to permit the [sentencing factor] to be a tail which wags the dog of the substantive offense").

Second, the majority, in support of its constitutional rule, emphasizes the concept of a statutory "maximum." * * * From a defendant's perspective, the legislature's decision to cap the possible range of punishment at a statutorily prescribed "maximum" would affect the actual sentence imposed no differently than a sentencing commission's (or a sentencing judge's) similar determination. Indeed, as a practical matter, a legislated mandatory "minimum" is far more important to an actual defendant. A judge and a commission, after all, are legally free to select any sentence below a statute's maximum, but they are not free to subvert a statutory minimum.

* * * [I am willing] to assume that the majority's rule would provide a degree of increased procedural protection in respect to those particular sentencing factors currently embodied in statutes. I nonetheless believe that any such increased protection provides little practical help and comes at too high a price. For one thing, by leaving mandatory minimum sentences untouched, the majority's rule simply encourages any legislature interested in asserting control over the sentencing process to do so by creating those minimums. That result would mean significantly less procedural fairness, not more. For another thing, this Court's case law, prior to *Jones* led legislatures to believe that they were permitted to increase a statutory maximum sentence on the basis of a sentencing factor.* * * And legislatures may well have relied upon that belief. * * * [T]he rationale that underlies the Court's rule suggests a principle—jury determination of all sentencing-related facts—that, unless restricted, threatens the workability of every criminal justice system (if applied to judges) or threatens efforts to make those systems more uniform, hence more fair (if applied to commissions). * * *

Notes and Questions

1. **The prior conviction exception.** Five justices have now expressed opposition to the rule of *Almendarez-Torres*—the dissenters in that case plus Justice Thomas, concurring in *Apprendi*. On what basis might the Court nevertheless decline to overrule *Almendarez-Torres*? Can it be distinguished from *Apprendi*?

2. **Apprendi and McMillan.** *Apprendi* has generated an enormous amount of litigation. Among the issues dividing the federal courts is the effect of *Apprendi* on the imposition of mandatory minimum sentences under 21 U.S.C.A. § 841, the principle federal drug statute. Section 841(a) states "it shall be unlawful for any person knowingly or intentionally * * * to manufacture, distribute, or dispense, or possess with intent to manufacture, distribute or dispense, a controlled substance * * * ." The various subsections of § 841(b) designate increasing sentence

ranges, raising both minimum and maximum sentences, for increasing quantities of drugs. For example, a first offender who delivers (or possesses with the intent to deliver) an unspecified amount of marijuana must be sentenced to 0–5 years (§ 841(b)(1)(D)), but faces a mandatory minimum sentence of 5 years and a maximum of up to 40 years, if the quantity of marijuana exceeds 100 kilos (§ 841(b)(1)(B)). A prior conviction raises these ranges even further: A repeat drug offender faces 0–10 years for an unspecified amount of marijuana (§ 841(b)(1)(D)); 10 years to life for over 100 kilos (§ 841(b)(1)(B)). Typically, before *Apprendi*, prosecutors and judges did not treat either the quantity of drugs involved or a defendant's prior conviction as an element of the § 841 offense.

Lower courts agree that under the statutes described above, without proof beyond a reasonable doubt of over 100 kilos of marijuana, for example, a defendant with a prior drug conviction cannot be sentenced to *more* than ten years, the statutory maximum sentence for a prior drug offender convicted of an unspecified amount of marijuana. One court has gone farther, holding that if a judge finds prior offender status and defendant's involvement with over 100 kilos of marijuana at sentencing, the imposition of the mandatory minimum sentence of 10 years under § 841(b)(1)(B) also violates *Apprendi*, even though the sentence does *not* exceed the 10–year maximum allowable under § 841(b)(1)(D), at least when it is undisputed that the judge would have imposed less than 10 years but for the mandatory minimum in § 841(b)(1)(B). *United States v. Strayhorn*, 250 F.3d 462 (6th Cir.2001). The court in *Strayhorn* reasoned that "the district court's drug quantity finding increased the statutory sentence to which Strayhorn was exposed from a maximum term of ten years' imprisonment under § 841(b)(1)(D) to a minimum term of ten years' imprisonment under § 841(b)(1)(B). Strayhorn never pleaded guilty to the elements of the offense under § 841(b)(1)(B) nor were they charged or proved beyond a reasonable doubt. Thus, Strayhorn was effectively sentenced under a separate statutory offense with a higher penalty range than the default penalty provision under § 841(b)(1)(D)." Other circuits have adopted a contrary view. See e.g., *United States v. Smith*, 223 F.3d 554 (7th Cir.2000) (mandatory life sentence triggered by finding at sentencing does not violate *Apprendi* when the maximum sentence specified by statute for the offense without the same finding was life imprisonment, relying on *McMillan* and stating, "[The statute] operates to divest the judge of discretion to impose any sentence of less than [life] for the underlying felony; it does not authorize a sentence in excess of that otherwise allowed for that offense."). Which interpretation is most consistent with *Apprendi*?

3. *Evading Apprendi*. Justice O'Connor's dissenting opinion criticizes the majority's rule in *Apprendi* as "pure formalism." Do you agree? What constitutional constraints bind a legislature's decision to define any given offense as it pleases? Would it be constitutional, for example, for Congress to rewrite 21 U.S.C.A. § 841, discussed above, so that conviction of the delivery of any amount of marijuana may be punished by imprisonment for any term of years up to life, then designate decreasing amounts of marijuana as mitigating factors the judge must use in setting a sentence within the statutory maximum? See Nancy King & Susan Klein, *Essential Elements*, 54 Vand.L.Rev. 1467 (2001) (collecting commentary proposing limits on legislative efforts to circumvent criminal procedure guarantees through offense definition, and proposing one approach).

4. *Apprendi and plea bargaining*. Most cases, of course, never reach a jury, but are instead resolved by plea. What effect will *Apprendi* have in guilty-plea cases? Compare Stephanos Bibas, *Judicial Fact–Finding and Sentence Enhancements in a World of Guilty Pleas*, 110 Yale L.J. 1097 (2001) (*Apprendi* hurts most defendants who plead guilty because it deprives them of the only hearing at which they have a chance to contest aggravating facts that raise sentences within statutory maxima) with Nancy King & Susan Klein, *Apprendi and Plea Bargaining*, 54 Stan.L.Rev. 295 (2001) (*Apprendi* creates incentives for prosecutors to accept guilty pleas to offenses with lower statutory maxima in cases where reasonable doubt about the existence of aggravating feature of higher offense is present).

Part Five

APPEALS, POST–CONVICTION REVIEW

Chapter 28

APPEALS[aa]

SECTION 1. THE DEFENDANT'S RIGHT TO APPEAL

1. *A constitutional right to appeal?* In *McKane v. Durston,* 153 U.S. 684, 14 S.Ct. 913, 38 L.Ed. 867 (1894), the Supreme Court noted, in dictum, that "a review by an appellate court of the final judgment in a criminal case, however grave the offense of which the accused is convicted, was not at common law and is not now a necessary element of due process." Although *McKane's* historical analysis has been challenged by several commentators (who cite the availability of common law alternatives to appellate review), and there have been numerous changes in constitutional criminal procedure since *McKane* was decided, the Court has never questioned the *McKane* dictum. Indeed, opinions that deal with constitutional issues relating to the appellate process commonly start off by citing *McKane* and noting that "a state is not required by the Federal Constitution to provide * * * a right of appeal." *Griffin v. Illinois,* 351 U.S. 12, 76 S.Ct. 585, 100 L.Ed. 891 (1956).

Justice Brennan, however, once characterized the *McKane* dictum as "arguably wrong," at least when read broadly. *Jones v. Barnes,* 463 U.S. 745, 103 S.Ct. 3308, 77 L.Ed.2d 987 (1983) (dissenting opinion): "[I]f the question were to come before us today in a proper case, I have little doubt * * * [but] that we would decide that a State must afford at least some opportunity for review of convictions, whether through the familiar mechanism of appeal or through some form of collateral proceeding." Justice Brennan noted, in support of this conclusion, that "there are few, if any situations in our system of justice in which a single judge is given unreviewable discretion over matters concerning a person's liberty or property, and the reversal rate of criminal convictions on mandatory appeals in the state courts, while not overwhelming, is certainly high enough to suggest that depriving defendants of their right to appeal would expose them to an unacceptable risk of erroneous conviction." He then added that, "of course, a case present-

---

aa. A more extensive analysis of appellate review of criminal cases can be found in 5 Wayne R. LaFave, Jerold H. Israel, & Nancy J. King, *Criminal Procedure Treatise* §§ 27.1–27.6 (2d ed. 1999) (also available on Westlaw under the database name CRIMPROC and hereafter cited as CRIMPROC). See also 2 Stephen A. Childres & Martin S. Davis, *Federal Standards of Review* (3d ed. 1999).

ing this question is unlikely to arise, for the very reason that a right of appeal is now universal for all significant criminal convictions."[a]

With the opportunity for appellate review universally available (see fn. a supra), does it matter whether or not there exists a constitutional right of the type envisioned by Justice Brennan? The Supreme Court has held in various contexts that once a state provides for appellate review, it must ensure that such review is provided to defendants consistent with the requirements of both equal protection and due process. Thus, *Griffin v. Illinois,* supra, held that the state could not condition the right to review in such a manner as to deny equal protection to the indigent defendant. So too, *Douglas v. California,* 372 U.S. 353, 83 S.Ct. 814, 9 L.Ed.2d 811 (1963), held that indigent defendant constitutionally was entitled to the assistance of counsel in presenting a first appeal granted as a matter of right. *Evitts v. Lucey,* discussed at p. 1116, held that a defendant had a due process right to the effective assistance of counsel on a first appeal as a matter of right. A series of cases, however, have rejected due process or equal protection claims relating to other aspects of the appellate process. See e.g., *Wainwright v. Torna,* discussed at p. 1117, and *Jones v. Barnes,* discussed at p. 1171. Would the Court have reached a different result in those cases had it recognized a constitutional right along the lines suggested by Justice Brennan? Would it take a broader view of the protection afforded the defendant against adverse consequences flowing from the exercise of that right than is adopted in the cases discussed below?

PROTECTING THE DEFENDANT'S RIGHT TO APPEAL

NORTH CAROLINA v. PEARCE

395 U.S. 711, 89 S.Ct. 2072, 23 L.Ed.2d 656 (1969).

[The Court had before it two cases in which defendants were initially convicted, had their convictions set aside, were then reprosecuted and reconvicted, and subsequently were sentenced to longer terms of imprisonment than they originally received.[b] The defendants presented two questions relating to the sentence that constitutionally could be imposed upon a defendant's reconviction after his original conviction had been set aside—whether credit had to be given for time served under the initial, subsequently overturned conviction, and whether the sentence imposed upon reconviction could be more severe than the sentence

---

a. A *right* to appellate review is not universal as to felony cases, although the *opportunity* for appellate review is universal. While most states grant convicted felony defendants a right to appellate review by an intermediate appellate court, in the several states that do not have an intermediate appellate court, appellate review of felony conviction remains at the discretion of the state's highest court. Some states also provide for only discretionary review where the defendant's conviction was pursuant to a guilty plea. In misdemeanor cases, where defendants who are tried before a magistrate can obtain a trial de novo in the court of general jurisdiction, subsequent appellate review of that trial de novo tends to be discretionary.

As for the reversal rate noted by Justice Brennan, the rate for felony appeals of right in state courts varies considerably from one state to another, but typically falls in the range of 5–

10%. See CRIMPROC § 1.3(s) (also citing an overall reversal rate of 10.4% for all the federal circuits, with the individual circuits ranging from a low of 7.4% to a high of 15%).

b. In No. 413, defendant Pearce had been convicted of assault with intent to commit rape and sentenced to a prison term of 12 to 15 years. After the conviction was set aside in a postconviction proceeding, he was reprosecuted and convicted of the same offence. The judge then sentenced him to 15 years imprisonment less seven years already served. In No. 418, defendant Rice had pleaded guilty to four separate charges of second degree burglary, and had been sentenced to prison terms totaling 10 years. The pleas were set aside in a postconviction proceeding on the ground that defendant had not been accorded his right to counsel. He was then retried on three of the charges, convicted and sentenced to an aggregate prison term of 25 years.

originally imposed. The Court initially held that a double jeopardy prohibition against "multiple punishments" for the same charge required that the judge imposing a new sentence following a reconviction give credit for time served under the original sentence. Turning to the second issue, the Court majority rejected the defense contention that the double jeopardy bar prohibited the imposition of a more severe sentence on reconviction than had been imposed upon the initial conviction. See Note 8, p. 1485. It also rejected the argument that the equal protection guarantee prohibited imposing a more severe sentence following a reconviction. The Court then turned to the contention that due process restricted the imposition of a more severe sentence on a reconviction. Reprinted here are those parts of the majority, concurring, and dissenting opinions that deal with defendants' due process claim.]

Justice STEWART delivered the opinion of the Court.

* * * We hold, therefore, that neither the double jeopardy provision nor the Equal Protection Clause imposes an absolute bar to a more severe sentence upon reconviction. A trial judge is not constitutionally precluded, in other words, from imposing a new sentence, whether greater or less than the original sentence, in the light of events subsequent to the first trial that may have thrown new light upon the defendant's "life, health, habits, conduct and mental and moral propensities." *Williams v. New York,* [p. 1502]. Such information may come to the judge's attention from evidence adduced at the second trial itself, from a new presentence investigation, from the defendant's prison record, or possibly from other sources. The freedom of a sentencing judge to consider the defendant's conduct subsequent to the first conviction in imposing new sentence is no more than consonant with the principle, fully approved in *Williams,* that a State may adopt the "prevalent modern philosophy of penology that the punishment should fit the offender and not merely the crime."

To say that there exists no absolute constitutional bar to the imposition of a more severe sentence upon retrial is not, however, to end the inquiry. There remains for consideration the impact of the Due Process Clause of the Fourteenth Amendment.

It can hardly be doubted that it would be a flagrant violation of the Fourteenth Amendment for a state trial court to follow an announced practice of imposing a heavier sentence upon every reconvicted defendant for the explicit purpose of punishing the defendant for his having succeeded in getting his original conviction set aside. Where, as in each of the cases before us, the original conviction has been set aside because of a constitutional error, the imposition of such a punishment, "penalizing those who choose to exercise" constitutional rights, "would be patently unconstitutional." *United States v. Jackson* [fn. d, p. 1250]. And the very threat inherent in the existence of such a punitive policy would, with respect to those still in prison, serve to "chill the exercise of basic constitutional rights." * * * But even if the first conviction has been set aside for nonconstitutional error, the imposition of a penalty upon the defendant for having successfully pursued a statutory right of appeal or collateral remedy would be no less a violation of due process of law. * * * A court is "without right to * * * put a price on an appeal. A defendant's exercise of a right of appeal must be free and unfettered. * * * [I]t is unfair to use the great power given to the court to determine sentence to place a defendant in the dilemma of making an unfree choice." *Worcester v. Commissioner of Internal Revenue,* 370 F.2d 713 (1st Cir.1966). "This Court has never held that the States are required to establish avenues of appellate review, but it is now fundamental that, once established, these avenues must be kept free of unreasoned distinctions that can only impede open and equal access to the courts." *Griffin v. Illinois* [p. 1534].

Due process of law, then, requires that vindictiveness against a defendant for having successfully attacked his first conviction must play no part in the sentence he receives after a new trial. And since the fear of such vindictiveness may unconstitutionally deter a defendant's exercise of the right to appeal or collaterally attack his first conviction, due process also requires that a defendant be freed of apprehension of such a retaliatory motivation on the part of the sentencing judge.[20]

In order to assure the absence of such a motivation, we have concluded that whenever a judge imposes a more severe sentence upon a defendant after a new trial, the reasons for his doing so must affirmatively appear. Those reasons must be based upon objective information concerning identifiable conduct on the part of the defendant occurring after the time of the original sentencing proceeding. And the factual data upon which the increased sentence is based must be made part of the record, so that the constitutional legitimacy of the increased sentence may be fully reviewed on appeal.

We dispose of the two cases before us in the light of these conclusions. In No. 418, United States District Court Judge Johnson noted that "the State of Alabama offers no evidence attempting to justify the increase in Rice's original sentences * * *." He * * * found that "the conclusion is inescapable that the State of Alabama is punishing petitioner Rice for his having exercised his post-conviction right of review. . . ." In No. 413 the situation is not so dramatically clear. Nonetheless, the fact remains that neither at the time the increased sentence was imposed upon Pearce, nor at any stage in this habeas corpus proceeding, has the State offered any reason or justification for that sentence beyond the naked power to impose it. We conclude that in each of the cases before us, the judgment should be affirmed.

Justice WHITE, concurring in part.

I join the Court's opinion except that in my view * * * [it] should authorize an increased sentence on retrial based on any objective, identifiable factual data not known to the trial judge at the time of the original sentencing proceeding.

Justice BLACK, concurring in part and dissenting in part.

* * * [I] agree that it would violate the Constitution for any judge to impose a higher penalty on a defendant solely because he had taken a legally permissible appeal. On this basis there is a plausible argument for upholding the judgment in No. 418. * * * But this provides no basis for affirming the judgment of the Court of Appeals in No. 413, the case involving respondent Pearce. For in that case there is not a line of evidence to support the slightest inference that the trial judge wanted or intended to punish Pearce for seeking postconviction relief. * * *

The Court justifies affirming the release of Pearce in this language: "In order to assure the absence of such a motivation, we have concluded that whenever a judge imposes a more severe sentence upon a defendant after a new trial, the reasons for his doing so must affirmatively appear. Those reasons must be based

---

20. The existence of a retaliatory motivation would, of course, be extremely difficult to prove in any individual case. But data have been collected to show that increased sentences on reconviction are far from rare. See Note, 1965 Duke L.J. 395 [citing an "informal survey of North Carolina superior courts"]. A touching bit of evidence showing the fear of such a vindictive policy was noted by the [federal habeas] judge in *Patton v. North Carolina*, 256 F.Supp. 225 (W.D.N.C.1966), who quoted a letter he had recently received from a prisoner.

[The court here quoted that letter, which came from a prisoner whose original conviction had been held unconstitutional by the federal judge on habeas review and who was now being retried. The prisoner initially noted that "it is usually the [state] court's procedure to give a larger sentence when a new trial is granted I guess * * * to discourage Petitioners." He pleaded: "Please sir don't let the state re-try me * * *. I don't want a new trial. I am afraid of more time."]

upon objective information concerning identifiable conduct on the part of the defendant occurring after the time of the original sentencing proceeding. And the factual data upon which the increased sentence is based must be made part of the record, so that the constitutional legitimacy of the increased sentence may be fully reviewed on appeal."

Of course nothing in the Due Process Clause grants this Court any such power as it is using here. Punishment based on the impermissible motivation described by the Court is, as I have said, clearly unconstitutional, and courts must of course set aside the punishment if they find, by the normal judicial process of fact-finding, that such a motivation exists. But, beyond this, the courts are not vested with any general power to prescribe particular devices "[i]n order to assure the absence of such a motivation." Numerous different mechanisms could be thought of, any one of which would serve this function. Yet the Court does not explain why the particular detailed procedure spelled out in this case is *constitutionally* required, while other remedial devices are not. This is pure legislation if there ever was legislation. * * *c

Notes and Questions

1. ***The prophylactic requirements of Pearce.*** In *Michigan v. Payne*, 412 U.S. 47, 93 S.Ct. 1966, 36 L.Ed.2d 736 (1973), the Court held that it would not apply retroactively what were described as the "prophylactic" mandates of *Pearce*—the requirements that, "whenever a judge imposes a more severe sentence upon a defendant after a new trial," the "sentencing judge's reasons 'must affirmatively appear,' and * * * those 'reasons must be based upon objective information concerning identifiable conduct on the part of the defendant occurring after the time of the original sentencing proceeding.'" Since these requirements constituted a "prophylactic limitation," designed to serve a "protective role" against vindictiveness, nothing would be gained through their retroactive application. The Court noted, however, that the other aspect of the *Pearce* ruling—the prohibition against "retaliatory motivation" in resentencing—was a "basic due process protection" which would be "available equally to defendants resentenced before and after the date of the [*Pearce*] decision."

2. ***Subsequent events.*** In WASMAN v. UNITED STATES, 468 U.S. 559, 104 S.Ct. 3217, 82 L.Ed.2d 424 (1984), the Court rejected a reading of *Pearce*'s prophylactic rule that would have narrowly construed that rule's reference to "conduct on the part of the defendant occurring after * * * the original sentence." The trial court there, in imposing its original sentence, noted that no consideration would be given to those criminal charges then pending against the defendant; it was that court's policy to consider only actual convictions. Following a successful appeal, retrial, and reconviction, the same judge imposed a second sentence higher than the first. The greater sentence was justified by reference to a conviction (on a previously pending charge) that had occurred during the interim between the first and second sentence. Defendant maintained that *Pearce* did not allow the higher sentence to be based on the intervening conviction since that conviction, though occurring after the time of the original sentence, was not itself "conduct of the defendant." A unanimous Supreme Court rejected that claim, noting that *Pearce*'s prophylactic rule must be given a common sense interpreta-

---

c. In *Dickerson v. United States*, 530 U.S. 428, 120 S.Ct. 2326, 147 L.Ed.2d 405 (2000), dissenting Justice Scalia (joined by Justice Thomas) expressed a similar position. Justice Scalia argued that the Supreme Court had no constitutional authority to "adopt prophylactic rules to buttress constitutional rights" and thereby mandate protections which it deemed "desirable" though beyond "what the Constitution requires." He characterized as rulings doing exactly that both *Miranda v. Arizona* and *North Carolina v. Pearce*.

tion consistent with the function of that rule. There was no suggestion of actual vindictiveness here, and allowing consideration of an intervening conviction did not open the door to likely manipulation to mask vindictive sentencing. Indeed, *Pearce* itself had suggested the appropriateness of giving weight to that factor. Although referring to the post-sentence conduct of the defendant, *Pearce* had also noted that a "trial judge is not constitutionally precluded * * * [from imposing a higher sentence] in light of events subsequent to the first trial that may have thrown new light upon defendant's life, health, habits, conduct, and mental and moral propensities" (p. 1536). As this statement suggested, there was "no logical support for [drawing] a distinction between 'events' and 'conduct' of the defendant occurring after the initial sentencing insofar as the kind of information that may be relied upon to show a nonvindictive motive is concerned."

3. ***Trials de novo.*** In COLTEN v. KENTUCKY, 407 U.S. 104, 92 S.Ct. 1953, 32 L.Ed.2d 584 (1972), the Court (with only Justice Marshall dissenting) held that *Pearce*'s prophylactic requirements did not apply to a higher sentence imposed on a trial *de novo* "appeal" of a misdemeanor conviction. Three factors were stressed in reaching this conclusion: (1) the court which conducted the trial *de novo* and imposed the second sentence was not the same court as had tried the case initially; unlike *Pearce,* this was not a case of a court being "asked to do over what it had thought it had already done correctly"; (2) the *de novo* court was not being asked to "find error in another court's work," but simply to provide the defendant with the same trial that would have been provided if his case had begun in that court; and (3) the attitude of the Kentucky courts was that the inferior courts were not "designed or equipped to conduct error-free trials," but were "courts of convenience," so there was no suggestion that a *de novo* court would be vindictive because it believed that a defendant "ought to be satisfied" with the informal proceeding provided by the inferior court.

4. ***Jury sentencing.*** Building upon *Colten,* the Court held in CHAFFIN v. STYNCHCOMBE, 412 U.S. 17, 93 S.Ct. 1977, 36 L.Ed.2d 714 (1973), that *Pearce*'s prophylactic requirements also would not be applied to jury sentencing. A closely divided Court concluded that, unlike the situation in *Pearce,* the potential for vindictive sentencing by a jury was "*de minimus* in a properly controlled retrial." POWELL, J., speaking for the majority, noted initially that the jury imposing the sentence in the second trial would not know of the earlier sentence. While it probably would be aware that there had been an earlier trial, it would not know whether that trial had been on the same charge or whether it had resulted in a conviction or a mistrial. Second, as was true in *Colten,* "the second sentence is not meted out by the same judicial authority" that had its earlier proceeding reversed on appeal. The jury has no personal stake in the earlier proceeding, and it "is unlikely to be sensitive to the institutional interests that might occasion higher sentences by a judge desirous of discouraging what he regards as meritless appeals."

TEXAS v. McCULLOUGH
475 U.S. 134, 106 S.Ct. 976, 89 L.Ed.2d 104 (1986).

Chief Justice BURGER delivered the opinion of the Court.

We granted certiorari to decide whether the Due Process Clause was violated when the defendant in a state court received a greater sentence on retrial where the earlier sentence was imposed by the jury, the trial judge granted the defendant's motion for a new trial, the defendant requested that in the second trial the judge fix the sentence, and the judge entered findings of fact justifying the longer sentence.

In 1980, Sanford James McCullough was tried before a jury in the Randall County, Texas, District Court and convicted of murder. McCullough elected to be sentenced by the jury, as was his right under Texas law. The jury imposed a 20—year sentence. Judge Naomi Harney, the trial judge, then granted McCullough's motion for a new trial on the basis of prosecutorial misconduct. Three months later, McCullough was retried before a jury, with Judge Harney again presiding. At this trial, the State presented testimony from two witnesses who had not testified at the first trial that McCullough rather than his accomplices had slashed the throat of the victim. McCullough was again found guilty by a jury. This time, he elected to have his sentence fixed by the trial judge. Judge Harney sentenced McCullough to 50 years in prison and, upon his motion, made findings of fact as to why the sentence was longer than that fixed by the jury in the first trial. She found that in fixing the sentence she relied on new evidence about the murder that was not presented at the first trial and hence never made known to the sentencing jury. The findings focused specifically on the testimony of two new witnesses, which "had a direct effect upon the strength of the State's case at both the guilt and punishment phases of the trial." In addition, Judge Harney explained that she learned for the first time on retrial McCullough had been released from prison only four months before the later crime had been committed. Finally, the judge candidly stated that, had she fixed the first sentence, she would have imposed more than twenty years.[a]

On appeal, the Texas Court of Appeals reversed and resentenced McCullough to 20 years' imprisonment. That court considered itself bound by this Court's decision in *North Carolina v. Pearce,* and held that a longer sentence upon retrial could be imposed only if it was based upon conduct of the defendant occurring after the original trial. * * *

In *North Carolina v. Pearce,* the Court placed a limitation on the power of a sentencing authority to increase a sentence after reconviction following a new trial. It held that the Due Process Clause of the Fourteenth Amendment prevented increased sentences when that increase was motivated by vindictiveness on the part of the sentencing judge. * * * Beyond doubt, vindictiveness of a sentencing judge is the evil the Court sought to prevent rather than simply enlarged sentences after a new trial. The *Pearce* requirements thus do not apply in every case where a convicted defendant receives a higher sentence on retrial. Like other "judicially created means of effectuating the rights secured by the [Constitution]," we have restricted application of *Pearce* to areas where its "objectives are thought most efficaciously served." * * *. Accordingly, in each case, we look to the need, under the circumstances, to "guard against vindictiveness in the resentencing process." *Chaffin v. Stynchcombe* [Note 4, p. 1538] * * *. In *Colten v. Kentucky* [Note 3, p. 1539], we saw no need for applying the presumption when the second court in a two-tier trial system imposed a longer sentence. In *Chaffin,* we held *Pearce* not applicable where a *jury* imposed the increased sentence on retrial. Where the prophylactic rule of *Pearce* does not apply, the defendant may still obtain relief if he can show actual vindictiveness upon resentencing. *Wasman v. United States* [Note 2, p. 1538].

The facts of this case provide no basis for a presumption of vindictiveness. In contrast to *Pearce,* McCullough's second trial came about because the trial judge herself concluded that the prosecutor's misconduct required it. Granting McCullough's motion for a new trial hardly suggests any vindictiveness on the part of the judge towards him. "[U]nlike the judge who has been reversed," the trial judge here had "no motivation to engage in self-vindication." *Chaffin.* In such circumstances, there is also no justifiable concern about "institutional interests

---

a. Later Judge Harney sentenced two other defendants for their role in the same murder. She gave both defendants 50 year sentences identical to McCullough's.

that might occasion higher sentences by a judge desirous of discouraging what he regards as meritless appeals." Ibid. In granting McCullough's new trial motion, Judge Harney went on record as agreeing that his "claims" had merit. Presuming vindictiveness on this basis alone would be tantamount to presuming that a judge will be vindictive towards a defendant merely because he seeks an acquittal. Thus, in support of its position, the dissent conjures up visions of judges who view defendants as temerarious for filing motions for new trials, and who are "annoyed" at being forced "to sit through ... trial[s] whose result[s] [are] foregone conclusions." We decline to adopt the view that the judicial temperament of our Nation's trial judges will suddenly change upon the filing of a successful post-trial motion. The presumption of *Pearce* does not apply in situations where the possibility of vindictiveness is this speculative, particularly since the presumption may often "operate in the absence of any proof of an improper motive and thus ... block a legitimate response to criminal conduct," *United States v. Goodwin* [Note 5, p. 893]. Indeed, not even "apprehension of such a retaliatory motivation on the part of the sentencing judge," *Pearce*, could be present in this case. McCullough was entitled by law to choose to be sentenced by either a judge or a jury. Faced with that choice, on retrial McCullough chose to be sentenced by Judge Harney. There can hardly be more emphatic affirmation of his appraisal of Judge Harney's fairness than this choice. Because there was no realistic motive for vindictive sentencing, the *Pearce* presumption was inappropriate.

The presumption is also inapplicable because different sentencers assessed the varying sentences that McCullough received. In such circumstances, a sentence "increase" cannot truly be said to have taken place. In *Colten v. Kentucky*, which bears directly on this case, we recognized that when different sentencers are involved,

> "[i]t may often be that the [second sentencer] will impose a punishment more severe than that received from the [first]. But it no more follows that such a sentence is a vindictive penalty for seeking a [new] trial than that the [first sentencer] imposed a lenient penalty."

Here, the second sentencer provides an on-the-record, wholly logical, nonvindictive reason for the sentence. We read *Pearce* to require no more particularly since trial judges must be accorded broad discretion in sentencing, see *Wasman*.

In this case, the trial judge stated candidly her belief that the 20—year sentence respondent received initially was unduly lenient in light of significant evidence not before the sentencing jury in the first trial. On this record, that appraisal cannot be faulted. In any event, nothing in the Constitution prohibits a state from permitting such discretion to play a role in sentencing.[3]

Even if the *Pearce* presumption were to apply here, we hold that the findings of the trial judge overcome that presumption. Nothing in *Pearce* is to be read as precluding a rebuttal of intimations of vindictiveness. As we have explained, *Pearce* permits "a sentencing authority [to] justify an increased sentence by affirmatively identifying relevant conduct or events that occurred subsequent to the original sentencing proceedings." *Wasman*. * * * This language, however, was

---

3. *Pearce* itself apparently involved different judges presiding over the two trials, a fact that has led some courts to conclude by implication that the presumption of vindictiveness applies even where different sentencing judges are involved. That fact, however, may not have been drawn to the Court's attention and does not appear anywhere in the Court's opinion in *Pearce*. Clearly the Court did not focus on it as a consideration for its holding. * * * Subsequent opinions have also elucidated the basis for the *Pearce* presumption. We held in *Chaffin v. Stynchcombe*, for instance, that the presumption derives from the judge's "personal stake in the prior conviction," a statement clearly at odds with reading *Pearce* to answer the two-sentencer issue. We therefore decline to read *Pearce* as governing this issue. See also n. 4, infra.

never intended to describe exhaustively all of the possible circumstances in which a sentence increase could be justified. Restricting justifications for a sentence increase to *only* "events that occurred subsequent to the original sentencing proceedings" could in some circumstances lead to absurd results. The Solicitor General provides the following hypothetical example:

> "Suppose ... that a defendant is convicted of burglary, a non-violent, and apparently first, offense. He is sentenced to a short prison term or perhaps placed on probation. Following a successful appeal and a conviction on retrial, it is learned that the defendant has been using an alias and in fact has a long criminal record that includes other burglaries, several armed robbery convictions, and a conviction for murder committed in the course of a burglary. None of the reasons underlying *Pearce* in any way justifies the perverse result that the defendant receive no greater sentence in light of this information than he originally received when he was thought to be a first offender."

We agree with the Solicitor General and find nothing in *Pearce* that would require such a bizarre conclusion.[4] Perhaps then the reach of *Pearce* is best captured in our statement in *United States v. Goodwin,* supra:

> "In sum, the Court [in *Pearce*] applied a presumption of vindictiveness, which may be overcome only by objective information ... justifying the increased sentence."

Nothing in the Constitution requires a judge to ignore "objective information ... justifying the increased sentence." * * *

To be sure, a defendant may be more reluctant to appeal if there is a risk that new, probative evidence supporting a longer sentence may be revealed on retrial. But this Court has never recognized this "chilling effect" as sufficient reason to create a constitutional prohibition against considering relevant information in assessing sentences. We explained in *Chaffin v. Stynchcombe,* "the Court [in *Pearce*] intimated no doubt about the constitutional validity of higher sentences in the absence of vindictiveness despite whatever incidental deterrent effect they might have on the right to appeal." We see no reason to depart from this conclusion.

It is clear that the careful explanation by the trial judge for the sentence imposed here fits well within our prior holdings. * * * In setting aside the second sentence, the Texas Court of Appeals recognized that the new information bore legitimately on the appropriate sentence to impose, but concluded, reluctantly, that *Pearce* precluded reliance on this information. It is appropriate that we clarify the scope and thrust of *Pearce,* and we do so here. The case is remanded to the Texas Court of Criminal Appeals for further proceedings not inconsistent with this opinion.

Justice BRENNAN, concurring in the judgment.

---

4. The dissent contends that this objection "was considered in *Pearce* and rejected there." In fact, the issue, like the two-sentencer issue just discussed, was not before the Court because in neither *Pearce* nor its companion case did the State offer "any reason or justification" for the increased sentence. Moreover, *Pearce* was argued on the assumption that the Constitution either absolutely forbade or permitted increased sentences on retrial. None of the briefs advanced the intermediate position ultimately relied upon by the Court that the Constitution permits increased sentences only in certain circumstances. Thus, as the Solicitor General points out, "in formulating the standard set forth in *Pearce,* the Court was completely without the 'sharpen[ing of] the presentation of issues' provided by the adversary process, 'upon which the court so largely depends for illumination of difficult constitutional issues.' " But even if *Pearce* could be read to speak definitively to this situation, we are not reluctant to tailor judicially-created rules to implement constitutional guarantees, like the *Pearce* rule, when the need to do so becomes apparent.

After respondent was sentenced to twenty years imprisonment upon his conviction for murder, Judge Harney granted respondent's motion for a new trial based on prosecutorial misconduct. Under these circumstances, I believe that the possibility that an increased sentence upon retrial resulted from judicial vindictiveness is sufficiently remote that the presumption established in *Pearce* * * * [should not apply]. I emphasize, however, that were I able to find that vindictiveness should be presumed here, I would agree with Justice Marshall that "the reasons offered by Judge Harney [were] far from adequate to rebut any presumption of vindictiveness." The Court's dictum to the contrary, serves in my view only to distort the holding of *Pearce*.

Justice MARSHALL, with whom Justice BLACKMUN and Justice STEVENS join, dissenting.

* * * The majority reasons that "[i]n contrast to *Pearce* McCullough's second trial came about because the trial judge herself concluded that the prosecutor's misconduct required it. Granting McCullough's motion for a new trial hardly suggests any vindictiveness on the part of the judge towards him." Such an observation betrays not only an insensitivity to the motives that might underlie any trial judge's decision to grant a motion for a new trial, but also a blindness to the peculiar circumstances surrounding the decision to grant a retrial in this case.

The mere grant of a new trial motion can in no way be considered a guarantee, or even an indication, that the judge will harbor no resentment toward defendant as a result of his decision to exercise his statutory right to make such a motion. Even where a trial judge believes that the assignments of error are valid, she may still resent being given a choice between publicly conceding such errors and waiting for her judgment to be put to the test on appeal. This will be especially true when the errors alleged, however substantial as a matter of constitutional or statutory law, are considered by the judge not to cast doubt on the defendant's guilt. In such a case, the judge might well come to defendant's sentencing annoyed at having been forced to sit through a trial whose result was a foregone conclusion, and quite ready to vent that annoyance by giving the defendant a sentence stiffer than he otherwise would have received. * * *

Turning to the facts here, I believe the possibility of vindictiveness is even greater in this case than in the general run of cases in which a trial judge has granted a retrial. It is far from clear that Judge Harney's decision to grant a new trial was made out of either solicitude for McCullough or recognition of the merits of his claims. Defendant's motion was uncontested and, if the press coverage is any indication, the judge's decision to grant it was at least as much a boon to the prosecution as it was to defendant.[b] Indeed, the most cynical might even harbor suspicions that the judge shared the District Attorney's hope that a retrial would permit the imposition of a sentence more commensurate with the prosecution's view of the heinousness of the crime for which McCullough had been brought to bar. At any rate, one can imagine that when it fell to Judge Harney to sentence McCullough after his second conviction, his decision to seek a retrial after receiving such a comparatively light sentence from his first jury was counted against him.

Whether any of these considerations actually played any part in Judge Harney's decision to give McCullough a harsher sentence after his retrial is not the issue here, just as it was not the issue in *Pearce*. The point is that the possibility they did play such a part is sufficiently real, and proving actual

b. At an earlier point in his opinion, Justice Marshall had set forth a newspaper article in which the prosecutor was quoted as saying that "one of the biggest factors influencing his decision to join the defense motion [for a new trial] was the possibility of getting a higher sentence in a new trial."

prejudice, sufficiently difficult, that a presumption of vindictiveness is as appropriate here as it was in *Pearce* * * *

The majority holds that "[e]ven if the *Pearce* presumption were to apply here, we believe that the findings of the trial judge overcome that presumption." I find the reasons offered by Judge Harney far from adequate to rebut any presumption of vindictiveness. Moreover, I believe that by holding those reasons sufficient, the Court effectively eviscerates the effort made in *Pearce* to ensure both that vindictiveness against a defendant for having successfully attacked his first conviction "play no part in the sentence he receives after a new trial," and that the "defendant be freed of apprehension of such a retaliatory motivation on the part of the sentencing judge."

The presumption of vindictiveness established in *Pearce* was made rebuttable. * * * But the Court was quite clear that the conduct or event used to justify an increased sentence must have taken place after the original sentencing proceeding. Indeed, the majority's insistence upon this restriction led to the refusal of Justice White to subscribe to one part of the Court's opinion. He * * * [would have] "authoriz[ed] an increased sentence on retrial based on any objective, identifiable factual data not known to the trial judge at the time of the original sentencing proceeding."

The *[Pearce]* Court's rejection of the standard proposed by Justice White is no doubt explained by the majority's desire to "protect against reasonable apprehension of vindictiveness that could deter a defendant from appealing a first conviction." *Wasman,* (Powell, J., concurring). As a majority of the Court recently recognized, the need to eliminate this apprehension was as much a concern of the Court in *Pearce* as actual vindictiveness. See *Wasman.* Recognizing that in the course of any retrial, or merely by virtue of the passage of time, new information relating to events prior to a defendant's original sentencing would become available to a sentencer after retrial, the Court decided that allowing this information to justify a harsher sentence would make the intended guarantee of fairness sound quite hollow to the defendant deciding whether to pursue his statutory right of appeal. * * * By finding the reasons given by Judge Harney adequate to rebut a presumption of vindictiveness, the majority not only disregards the clear rule in *Pearce.* It announces a new regime in which the "chill" that plagued defendants in the days before *Pearce* will once again be felt by those deciding whether to contest their convictions. * * *

Persuaded by the Solicitor General's hypothetical involving a defendant whose prior convictions are not apparent to the trial judge until after defendant's appeal and retrial, the majority concludes that "[r]estricting justifications for a sentence increase to *only* 'events that occurred subsequent to the original sentencing proceedings' could in some circumstances lead to absurd results." However, this objection to such a restriction was considered in *Pearce* and rejected there, as it should be here. As one *amicus curiae* brief advised the *Pearce* Court:

> "In the unlikely event that some prior offense escaped the notice of the court when the accused was under consideration for sentencing, moreover, the government is free to bring a separate proceeding under its habitual offender (recidivism) acts. To the little extent that states may be concerned that sentences generally tend to be imposed in some instances without due consideration of the nature of the offense or the character of the accused, moreover, each state is constitutionally free to make ample provision for staffing and presentence reports to guard against unduly lenient sentencing to whatever extent that government feels to be appropriate. * * * Brief for American Civil Liberties Union.

A lot has happened since the final day of the October 1968 Term, the day *North Carolina v. Pearce* was handed down. But nothing has happened since then that casts any doubt on the need for the guarantee of fairness that this Court held out to defendants in *Pearce*. The majority today begins by denying respondent the promise of that guarantee even though this case clearly calls for its application. The Court then reaches out to render the guarantee of little value to all defendants, even to those whose plight was the explicit concern of the *Pearce* Court in 1969. To renege on the guarantee of *Pearce* is wrong. To do so while pretending not to is a shame. I dissent.

Notes and Questions

1. *The McCullough rationale.* Has *McCullough,* in its ruling on acceptable grounds for justifying an increased sentence, shifted the foundation of *Pearce*'s prophylactic requirements from precluding both actual vindictiveness and "readily perceived" vindictiveness to precluding only actual vindictiveness? See Reiss, *Prosecutorial Intent in Constitutional Criminal Procedure,* 135 U.Pa.L.Rev. 1365 (1987). Does *McCullough* reflect a similar shift in rationale in its treatment of the two-sentencer issue? *Colten* and *Chaffin* were viewed as having distinguished the separate sentencers situation presented in *Pearce,* where the sentencers were two different judges of the same trial bench, on the ground that the second sentencers in *Colten* and *Chaffin* did not have a same-court institutional interest in discouraging appeals from (and vindicating the decisions of) a fellow trial judge. Does *McCullough,* in failing to tie its separate sentencer rationale to the first sentencer having been a jury, thereby shift the grounding of the separate sentencer "exception" to the different perspectives of individual sentencers rather than the lack of institutional affiliation among the two sentencers? If so should a similar exception be applied to the *Blackledge* ruling (Note 4, p. 892), as it applies to the prosecutor escalating the charged offense following a reversed conviction, where a different prosecutor is responsible for the second charging decision?

2. *Vacated guilty pleas.* In ALABAMA v. SMITH, 490 U.S. 794, 109 S.Ct. 2201, 104 L.Ed.2d 865 (1989) the Court, with only Marshall, J., dissenting, overruled the companion case in *Pearce, Simpson v. Rice* (see fn. b, p. 1535), and held that the vindictiveness presumption does not apply to a higher sentence imposed following a vacated guilty plea and a subsequent conviction after trial. The court (per REHNQUIST, C.J.) initially noted that its post-*Pearce* rulings in *Colten, Chaffin, McCullough,* and *United States v. Goodwin* (Note 5, p. 893) had established that the *Pearce* presumption should be limited to circumstances presenting a " 'reasonable likelihood' that the increase in sentence is the product of actual vindictiveness." The Court then analyzed the application of that standard in those cases and concluded that a similar analysis required it to draw a distinction between the situations presented by defendant Pearce and defendant Rice—a distinction that had been missed in the *Pearce* opinion. The Chief Justice reasoned:

"We think the * * * reasoning [of the post-*Pearce* cases] leads to the conclusion that when a greater penalty is imposed after trial than was imposed after a prior guilty plea, the increase in sentence is not more likely than not attributable to the vindictiveness on the part of the sentencing judge. Even when the same judge imposes both sentences, the relevant sentencing information available to the judge after the plea will usually be considerably less than that available after a trial. A guilty plea must be both 'voluntary' and 'intelligent,' [but] the sort of information which satisfies this requirement will usually be far less than that brought out in a full trial on the merits. [As] this case demonstrates, in the course of the proof at trial the judge may gather a fuller appreciation of the nature and extent of the crimes charged. The defendant's conduct during trial may give the judge insights into his moral character and suitability for rehabilitation. See *United States v. Grayson* [fn. f, p. 1235]. Finally, after trial, the factors that may have indicated leniency as consideration for the guilty plea are no longer present. See *Brady v. United States* [fn. a, p. 1246]. Here, too, although the same judge who sentenced following the guilty plea also imposes sentence following trial, in conducting the trial, [the] court is not simply 'do[ing] over what it thought it had already done correctly.' *Colten.* Each of these factors distinguishes the present case and others like it, from cases like *Pearce.* There, the sentencing judge who presides at both trials can be expected to operate in the context of roughly the same sentencing considerations after the second trial as he does after the first; any unexplained change in the sentence is therefore subject to a presumption of vindictiveness. In cases like the present one, however, we think there are enough justifications for a heavier second sentence that it cannot be said to be more likely than not that a judge who imposes one is motivated by vindictiveness."

SECTION 2. DEFENSE APPEALS AND THE "FINAL JUDGMENT" REQUIREMENT

1. *Requiring a "final judgment."* The statutory provisions governing defense appeals in the federal system and in most states restrict the defendant to an appeal from what courts commonly characterize as a "final judgment" (although the statutory language varies, with statutes referring to "final judgments," "final decisions," "final orders," and, where the statute governs only appeals in criminal cases, to "final judgments of conviction"). The traditional reading of the final judgment requirement holds that a criminal prosecution does not produce a final judgment adverse to the defendant until it produces a conviction and the imposition of a sentence on that conviction.

In *Cobbledick v. United States*, 309 U.S. 323, 60 S.Ct. 540, 84 L.Ed. 783 (1940), Justice Frankfurter, in an often-quoted passage, set forth the policy justification for limiting defense appeals to those based on a final judgment: "Since the right to a judgment from more than one court is a matter of grace and not a necessary ingredient of justice, Congress from the very beginning has, by forbidding piecemeal disposition on appeal of what for practical purposes is a single controversy, set itself against enfeebling judicial administration. Thereby is avoided the obstruction to just claims that would come from permitting the harassment and cost of a succession of separate appeals from the various rulings to which a litigation may give rise, from its initiation to entry of judgment. To be effective, judicial administration must not be leaden-footed. Its momentum would be arrested by permitting separate reviews of the component elements in a unified cause. These considerations of policy are especially compelling in the administration of criminal justice. * * * An accused is entitled to scrupulous observance of constitutional safeguards. But encouragement of delay is fatal to the vindication of the criminal law. Bearing the discomfiture and cost of a prosecution for crime even by an innocent person is one of the painful obligations of citizenship. The correctness of a trial court's rejection even of a constitutional claim made by the accused in the process of prosecution must await his conviction before its reconsideration by an appellate tribunal."

Not all jurisdictions are convinced that a defendant should invariably be forced to bear the cost of trial, notwithstanding that it seems likely that the trial will be a wasted effort due to judicial error in ruling on a pretrial motion.[a] A

a. The impracticality of stopping a trial and pursuing an interlocutory appeal at that point has generally led jurisdictions that have authorized interlocutory appeals to limit such ap-

substantial number of states permit the defense to seek interlocutory review of a pretrial order, with such review granted only at the discretion of the appellate court (or in some cases, on certification of the trial judge that there is need for immediate review). Such provisions often identify a series of factors to be considered by the appellate court in determining whether to grant review, such as whether immediate review will clarify an issue of "general importance" or preclude possible "irreparable injury" (the term "irreparable" suggesting some injury beyond simply going through a trial that may have to be repeated). See CRIMPROC § 27.2(b). These factors make clear that interlocutory review should be the exception rather than the general rule, and a high probability that the trial court erred in its ruling does not in itself justify granting review.

Commentators have suggested that the advantage of interlocutory review from defendant's perspective goes beyond avoiding the costs of going through a trial that must be repeated (which costs include not only the burdens of the trial, but also the disclosure of defense evidence and strategy during the trial) or the costs of going through a trial that never should occur in the first instance (where a contrary pretrial ruling would effectively preclude trying the defendant). Interlocutory review requires the appellate court to focus on the legal issue alone, while review after a conviction adds the element of the totality of the evidence establishing guilt; that additional element may lead the appellate court to conclude that an erroneous ruling which would have been overturned on interlocutory review should not now require reversal of a conviction because it was likely to have been harmless in its impact upon the outcome of the case. In light of this advantage of interlocutory review, along with others (e.g., an overturned pretrial ruling may strengthen defendant's plea-bargaining position, and at least where the defendant has been released on bail, the delay necessitated by interlocutory appellate review may be valuable even if the ruling is not overturned), and the obvious benefits of avoiding the costs of an unnecessary or wasted trial, it is not surprising that defense counsel often respond to potentially erroneous pretrial rulings by seeking to obtain immediate appellate review and reversal. Where the jurisdiction (as in the federal system) does not provide for discretionary interlocutory appeals, the primary vehicles for circumventing the final judgment rule are the collateral order and independent action "exceptions" to that rule and the use of extraordinary writs.

2. *The collateral order doctrine.* Although the collateral order doctrine is often characterized as establishing an "exception" to the final judgment rule, *Cohen v. Beneficial Industrial Loan Corp.*, 337 U.S. 541, 69 S.Ct. 1221, 93 L.Ed. 1528 (1949), the civil case which established the doctrine, described the immediate appealability of collateral orders as following from the application of a "practical rather than technical construction" of the final judgment rule. In that case, the Court allowed a defendant in a stockholder derivative suit to immediately appeal a district court ruling refusing to require the plaintiffs to post a security bond. The Court reasoned that the final judgment rule did not preclude an immediate appeal of "that small class [of orders] which finally determine claims of right separable from, and collateral to, rights asserted in the action, too important to be denied review and too independent of the cause itself to require that appellate consideration be deferred until the whole case is adjudicated." This case presented such an order as the district court's ruling had fully disposed of the question of the

peals to pretrial rulings. Several jurisdictions do extend their provisions on obtaining discretionary interlocutory review to granting in rare cases an "emergency" review of a ruling made during trial, with the issue then being decided on the briefs within a short time frame (e.g., 24 hours), but this procedure appears to have been made available primarily to the prosecution when challenging an exceptional trial court ruling that could well produce an acquittal (and therefore otherwise never be reviewable).

applicability of the state security statute, that ruling was not one that "would be merged in the final judgment," and it involved an important right that would be "lost, probably irreparably" if review had to await the final judgment terminating the litigation.

Coopers & Lybrand v. Livesay, 437 U.S. 463, 98 S.Ct. 2454, 57 L.Ed.2d 351 (1978), set forth what has become the classic exposition of the prerequisites for establishing that a pretrial ruling is an immediately appealable collateral order. The Court initially summarized the key elements: "To come within the 'small class' of decisions excepted from the final-judgment rule by *Cohen*, the order must conclusively determine the disputed question, resolve an important issue completely separate from the merits of the action, and be effectively unreviewable on appeal from a final judgment." The first of these three prerequisites, it noted, demands that the trial court ruling not be "tentative, informal, or incomplete," but constitute a firm and final decision on the issue. If there is a reasonable prospect that the trial court might alter its ruling in light of facts that might be developed later in the proceedings, immediate appellate intrusion clearly is not appropriate. The second prerequisite demands that the issue ruled upon not "affect, or * * * be affected by" any subsequent decision on the merits of the case. If the trial court ruling is not "independent of the cause" itself, determining rights "separable from and collateral to [those] rights asserted in the action," then review prior to the ultimate disposition constitutes a wasteful use of appellate resources. Depending upon the disposition of the case, permitting appeal will produce either an unnecessary review or a review that will only be repeated. The second prerequisite also requires that the issue resolved by the trial court be not only independent but "important." Thus, in *Cohen* the Court had noted that the trial court order there might not have been appealable if the only issue presented was one of the proper exercise of the trial court's discretion. Finally, the third prerequisite insists that interlocutory review be withheld if review on appeal following the final disposition would provide a satisfactory remedy.

Speaking to the application of the *Coopers & Lybrand* criteria in criminal cases, the Court noted in *Flanagan v. United States*, 465 U.S. 259, 104 S.Ct. 1051, 79 L.Ed.2d 288 (1984): "Because of the compelling interest in prompt trials, the Court has interpreted the requirements of the collateral-order exception to the final judgment rule with the utmost strictness in criminal cases. The Court has found only three types of pretrial orders in criminal prosecutions to meet the requirements. * * * An order denying a motion to reduce bail may be reviewed before trial. The issue is finally resolved and is independent of the issues to be tried, and the order becomes moot if review awaits conviction and sentence. *Stack v. Boyle* [p. 819]. Orders denying motions to dismiss an indictment on double jeopardy or Speech or Debate grounds are likewise immediately appealable. Such orders finally resolve issues that are separate from guilt or innocence, and appellate review must occur before trial to be fully effective. The right guaranteed by the Double Jeopardy Clause is more than the right not to be convicted in a second prosecution for an offense: it is the right not to be 'placed in jeopardy'— that is, not to be tried for the offense. *Abney v. United States*, 431 U.S. 651, 97 S.Ct. 2034, 52 L.Ed.2d 651 (1977). Similarly, the right guaranteed by the Speech or Debate Clause is more than the right not to be convicted for certain legislative activities: it is the right not to 'be questioned' about them—that is, not to be tried for them. *Helstoski v. Meanor*, 442 U.S. 500, 99 S.Ct. 2445, 61 L.Ed.2d 30 (1979). Refusals to dismiss an indictment for violation of the Double Jeopardy Clause or of the Speech or Debate Clause, like denials of bail reduction, are truly final and collateral, and the asserted rights in all three cases would be irretrievably lost if review were postponed until trial is complete."

3. *Collateral orders and the "right not to be tried."* The *Flanagan* opinion characterized the double jeopardy and speech and debate rights as *"sui generis"* in their provision of a right not to be tried, and distinguished in this regard both *United States v. MacDonald*, 435 U.S. 850, 98 S.Ct. 1547, 56 L.Ed.2d 18 (1978), and *United States v. Hollywood Motor Car Co.*, 458 U.S. 263, 102 S.Ct. 3081, 73 L.Ed.2d 754 (1982). The Court was unanimous in holding in *MacDonald* that a speedy trial objection did not present a right not to be tried, and therefore denial of a speedy trial objection was not immediately appealable as a collateral order. The Court reasoned: "There perhaps is some superficial attraction in the argument that the right to a speedy trial * * * must be vindicated before trial in order to insure that no nonspeedy trial is ever held. Both doctrinally and pragmatically, however, this argument fails. Unlike the protection afforded by the Double Jeopardy Clause, the Speedy Trial Clause does not, either on its face or according to the decisions of this Court, encompass a 'right not to be tried' which must be upheld prior to trial if it is to be enjoyed at all. It is the delay before trial, not the trial itself, that offends against the constitutional guarantee of a speedy trial. If the factors outlined in *Barker v. Wingo* combine to deprive an accused of his right to a speedy trial, that loss, by definition, occurs before trial. Proceeding with the trial does not cause or compound the deprivation already suffered. * * * [Indeed,] allowing an exception to the rule against pretrial appeals in criminal cases for speedy trial claims would threaten precisely the values manifested in the Speedy Trial Clause * * * [as] some assertions of delay-caused prejudice would become self-fulfilling prophecies during the period necessary for appeal."[b]

The Court was divided, however, in concluding in *Hollywood Motor Car* that a vindictive prosecution claim was distinguishable from the claims presented in *Abney* and *Helstoski*. The Court majority there acknowledged that there was language in the leading vindictiveness case, *Blackledge v. Perry* [Note 4, p. 892], "suggesting that the defendant possessed a 'right not to be haled into court at all' " upon a vindictive charge. But that language, it noted, was used in a case where it was clear that an "adequate means of vindicating the right of the accused" would have been post-conviction relief granting defendant a new trial "free of vindictiveness" (i.e., a new trial de novo on the original misdemeanor charge). Of course, when the vindictiveness related to the total prosecution, rather than the charging of a higher offense, a successful claim would not result in a new trial but "dismissal of charges altogether." Even so, the *Hollywood* majority reasoned, as in *MacDonald*, "proceeding with the trial does not cause or compound the deprivation already suffered," as the vindictiveness claim rests on a "right whose remedy requires the dismissal of charges" rather than a "right not to be tried."

Justice Blackmun's dissent in *Hollywood,* joined by Justices Brennan and Marshall, argued that the issue presented was more complex than the Court's opinion suggested, and it should not have been resolved by a summary per curiam reversal. The dissent noted that unlike the speedy trial claim presented in *MacDonald,* "an allegation that the prosecutor impermissibly increased the charges in response to the defendant's exercise of a legal right may be evaluated

---

b. The Court also cited other factors in distinguishing *Abney*. The determination as to whether there had been a denial of a speedy trial was often dependent upon an assessment of the prejudice caused by the delay, which could best be considered "only after the relevant facts had been developed at trial." Hence, the pretrial denial of the defendant's motion could not be considered a "complete, formal, and final rejection" of that claim, and the prejudice element of the claim could not be viewed as separable from the trial on the merits. Also, unlike the double jeopardy claim presented in *Abney*, which required an initial showing of prior jeopardy, there was "nothing about * * * a speedy trial claim which inherently limits the availability of the claim." If a right to immediate appeal were recognized, "any defendant" could raise such a claim in anticipation of a dilatory pretrial appeal.

before trial, for all the facts relevant to such a claim are fully available." Also, unlike *MacDonald,* where the critical delay offending the constitutional guarantee was the "delay before trial, not the trial itself," here it could be argued that the right sought to be vindicated was one "not to be tried." Post-conviction review might not "suffice to remedy the chilling effect the vindictive prosecution is designed to prevent."

    4. *Precluded postconviction relief and collateral orders.* In a footnote in his dissent in *United States v. Mechanik* (Note 6, p. 978), Justice Marshall suggested that the Court's ruling there—holding a Federal Rule 6(d) violation in the proceedings of the indicting grand jury to be *per se* harmless error on review following a conviction—effectively precluded gaining relief for a Rule 6(d) violation after conviction, and it therefore might render a trial court ruling denying a Rule 6(d) objection immediately appealable under the collateral order doctrine. However, in *Midland Asphalt Corp. v. United States,* 489 U.S. 794, 109 S.Ct. 1494, 103 L.Ed.2d 879 (1989), the Court unanimously rejected that position. The lower court there had held that *Mechanik*'s *per se* harmless-error analysis also applied to a Rule 6(e) violation in the grand jury proceedings, but the Supreme Court concluded that even if that were so, the denial of a motion challenging an indictment based upon a Rule 6(e) violation would not be immediately appealable. The Court reasoned: "If * * * *Mechanik* is applied to bar postconviction review of alleged violations of Rule 6(e), it will be because the purpose of that Rule is the same as the purpose of Rule 6(d), namely to 'protect against the danger that a defendant will be required to defend against a charge for which there is no probable cause to believe him guilty,' which danger has demonstrably been avoided whenever there is a guilty verdict at trial. If this latter analysis is correct, however, orders denying motions to dismiss for Rule 6(e) violations cannot be said to 'resolve an important issue completely separate from the merits of the action', *Coopers & Lybrand,* but rather involve considerations 'enmeshed in the merits of the dispute' and would 'affect ... or be *affected by*' the decision on the merits of the case, (emphasis added)."

    In *Flanagan v. United States,* 465 U.S. 259, 104 S.Ct. 1051, 79 L.Ed.2d 288 (1984), defendant argued that he should be allowed to appeal an order disqualifying his counsel because, on review following conviction, he would be able to gain relief for an erroneous disqualification only if he could show that the loss of his preferred counsel had resulted in some "specifically demonstrated prejudice to the defense," and meeting that standard was virtually impossible, assuming that substitute counsel had been competent. The Court responded that a showing of specific prejudice might not be required, as an improper disqualification might be treated as a *per se* reversable error (similar to the improper denial of the defendant's right to proceed *pro se*), but there was no need to decide that at this point for the following reason: "[Even] if * * * petitioner's asserted right is one that is not violated absent some specifically demonstrated prejudice to the defense, a disqualification order still falls outside the coverage of the collateral order exception. We need not consider * * * whether the third *Coopers & Lybrand* condition is satisfied—that is whether post-conviction review is plainly ineffective. It is sufficient to note that the second *Coopers & Lybrand* condition—that the order be truly collateral is not satisfied if petitioner's asserted right is one requiring prejudice to the defense for its violation. On this assumption, a disqualification order * * * is not independent of the issue to be tried. Its validity cannot be adequately reviewed until trial is complete. The effect of the disqualification on the defense, and hence whether the asserted right has been violated cannot be fairly assessed until the substance of the prosecution's and defendant's cases is known."

5. *Independent proceedings.* The collateral order doctrine permits an immediate appeal from an order which is viewed as part of the ongoing criminal case. Certain proceedings, though related to an ongoing or contemplated criminal prosecution, may be viewed as sufficiently separate from that prosecution so that an order terminating that proceeding is viewed as a final judgment in a separate litigation and therefore immediately appealable. This ordinarily is the case, for example, when a third party seeks relief relating to an ongoing prosecution (e.g., where a newspaper challenges a closure order, or an unindicted co-conspirator challenges the denial of his request to strike his name from the indictment). That proceeding is characterized as "independent", rather than "a step in the trial of the criminal case." A proceeding is less likely to be viewed as "independent", when it involves a potential or actual defendant who has sought relief that would have a direct bearing on an ongoing or contemplated prosecution. Are there, however, special settings in which even such proceedings should be deemed independent? Consider the two presented below.

6. In *Di Bella v. United States*, 369 U.S. 121, 82 S.Ct. 654, 7 L.Ed.2d 614 (1962), a unanimous Court held nonappealable the denial of a motion to suppress that had been filed by the petitioner before he was indicted but after he was arrested. The Court reasoned that the ruling on the suppression motion was not "fairly severable from the context of a larger litigation process" since the disposition of that motion, whether made before or after the indictment, would "necessarily determine the conduct of the eventual trial." Justice Frankfurter's opinion for the Court concluded: "We hold, accordingly, that the mere circumstance of a pre-indictment motion does not transmute the ensuing evidentiary ruling into an independent proceeding begetting finality even for purposes of appealability. * * * Only if the motion is solely for return of property and is in no way tied to a criminal prosecution *in esse* against the movant can the proceedings be regarded as independent."

The last sentence of *Di Bella* indicated that a challenge to a search would be viewed as an independent proceeding where the petitioner moved "solely for the return of [the seized] property" and that motion was "in no way tied to a criminal prosecution *in esse*." This point was reiterated in *United States v. Ryan,* 402 U.S. 530, 91 S.Ct. 1580, 29 L.Ed.2d 85 (1971), where the Court noted that refusing to permit review under such circumstances "would mean that the Government might indefinitely retain the property without any opportunity for the movant to assert on appeal his right to possession." Federal Rule 41(e), as subsequently amended, recognized the motion for return as distinct from a motion to suppress unless the motion "is made or comes on for hearing in the district of trial after an indictment or information is filed." In that case, the motion for return "shall be treated as a motion to suppress." Does this mean that all Rule 41(e) motions filed prior to indictment or information meet the standard of *Di Bella's* last sentence? Some lower federal courts have so held, while others suggest that the pre-charge motion may still not be "solely for the return of the property" and may also be tied to a prosecution "in esse." Some would hold that a motion to return does not qualify, even though directed at obtaining valuable property (the motion, of course, is not available to recover contraband) if the moving party is a target of a grand jury investigation, noting that *Di Bella* characterized a grand jury presentation as "part of the federal prosecution." See CRIMPROC § 27.2(d) (questioning that conclusion since appellate review of the denial of a motion for the return of the property ordinarily should not be disruptive of the grand jury proceeding).

7. Where a grand jury witness, civil trial witness, or criminal trial witness objects to a subpoena or to an order compelling the witness to answer a specific question, the witness may convert that ruling into an appealable order by refusing to obey and being held in contempt. The recalcitrant witness is cited for civil contempt, so if his objection is not sustained on appeal, he can purge the contempt citation by complying with the subpoena; but if the civil contempt sanction is incarceration, there is no requirement that he be released on bail pending appellate review of the contempt finding (although appellate review is expedited for those in custody). See 28 U.S.C. § 1826. See also *In the Matter of Klein*, 776 F.2d 628 (7th Cir.1985) (function of the contempt prerequisite is to "ensure that people raise only those claims that are sufficiently serious that they are willing to make a sacrifice to obtain appellate review"); *United States v. Ryan*, supra note 6 ("necessity for expedition in the administration of justice justifies putting one who seeks to resist the production of desired information to choose between compliance with the trial court's order * * * and resistance to that order with the concomitant possibility of an adjudication of contempt [being sustained] if his claims are rejected on appeal").

Where a criminal defendant objects to a court order requiring the defendant to provide discovery to the prosecution or to submit to some type of examination, that objection is rejected, the defendant still refuses to comply, and he then is held in civil contempt, should an appeal from the contempt ruling similarly be accepted as flowing from an independent proceeding? In the federal system, the long established rule is that a nonparty can appeal either a civil or criminal contempt sanction, but a party can appeal only a criminal contempt sanction. Since the form of contempt used against a person who refuses to comply with a discovery order almost always is civil contempt (the purpose being to coerce compliance), the disobedience and contempt route ordinarily would not be available to obtain immediate appellate review of a discovery order directed against a criminal defendant. See Charles Alan Wright, Arthur R. Miller, and Edward H. Cooper, 15B *Federal Practice and Procedure* § 3917. See also *Id.* at § 3914.23 (where the discovery order is directed at the attorney and the attorney disobeys and is held in civil contempt, some courts have treated attorneys as nonparties and allowed appeals, while others have refused "because the remedy by appeal from the final judgment is less unsatisfactory as to attorneys who continue to be involved with the litigation and in part because of the difficulty of separating out the interests of attorneys and clients"). The rationale advanced in support of the federal distinction between civil and criminal contempt and parties and nonparties is that the party facing a civil contempt sanction is in a different position than the nonparty or a person facing a criminal contempt sanction because the party facing civil contempt is always free to comply with the court's order and then argue on appeal from a final judgment that the improper order requiring disclosure constituted reversible error. Commentators have questioned the weight given to that distinction, and the Supreme Court in *Firestone Tire and Rubber Co. v. Risjord*, 449 U.S. 368, 101 S.Ct. 669, 66 L.Ed.2d 571 (1981), suggested it should not always prevail. The Court there noted that "in the rare case when appeal after final judgment will not cure an erroneous discovery order, a party may defy the order, permit a contempt citation to be entered against him and challenge the order on direct appeal of the contempt ruling." Might a defendant claim that a discovery order which will require disclosure of privileged information presents such a rare case?

Various state courts allow party as well as nonparty appeals from civil contempt sanctions. See e.g., *Lewis v. Family Planning Management, Inc.*, 306 Ill.App.3d 918, 715 N.E.2d 743 (1999) ("One definite but indirect method of securing review of a discovery order does exist. It is well settled that a party or witness may test a discovery order by refusing to comply, thereby forcing the trial court to find that party or witness in contempt and to assign an appropriate punishment. * * * [A]n order cast in terms of a contempt proceeding imposing sanctions is * * * final and appealable because it necessarily stems from an original special proceeding, collateral to and independent of, the case in which the contempt arises'. Appeal of a contempt order 'presents to the court for review the propriety of the order of the court claimed to have been violated'.") See also *State v. Mauney*, 106 N.C.App. 26, 415 S.E.2d 208 (1992) (defendant charged in criminal action with willfully refusing to support illegitimate child could appeal civil contempt sanction imposed when he refused to submit to a blood test: "if defendant refuses to comply, he risks a fine or imprisonment [and] if he complies, his challenge to the blood test may become moot").

8. *Review by writ.* Under some circumstances, appellate review of interlocutory orders may be obtained in the federal system through the extraordinary writ procedure authorized by 18 U.S.C. § 1651(a), the All Writs Act. That Act empowers appellate courts to issue writs (e.g., mandamus or prohibition) where "necessary or appropriate in aid of their respective jurisdictions and agreeable to the usages and principles of law." States have similar provisions or recognize review by writ as a traditional common law process. The writs provide an avenue for appellate review at the request of both the defense and the prosecution. Some jurisdictions utilize somewhat different standards depending upon which party is seeking review. Others do not. See Note 4, p. 1556. This Note focuses on the use of the writ by the defense.

The Supreme Court has emphasized the extraordinary nature of the writs in the guidelines it has set forth for their issuance. See e.g., *Kerr v. United States District Court*, 426 U.S. 394, 96 S.Ct. 2119, 48 L.Ed.2d 725 (1976):

"[T]he writ [of mandamus] 'has traditionally been used in the federal courts only to confine an inferior court to a lawful exercise of its prescribed jurisdiction or to compel it to exercise its authority when it is its duty to do so.' *Will v. United States*, 389 U.S. 90, 88 S.Ct. 269, 19 L.Ed.2d 305 (1967). And, while we have not limited the use of mandamus by an unduly narrow and technical understanding of what constitutes a matter of 'jurisdiction,' the fact still remains that 'only exceptional circumstances amounting to a judicial "usurpation of power" will justify the invocation of this extraordinary remedy.' *Will v. United States*. * * * As a means of implementing the rule that the writ will issue only in extraordinary circumstances, we have set forth various conditions for its issuance. Among these are that the party seeking issuance of the writ have no other adequate means to attain the relief he desires, and that he satisfy 'the burden of showing that [his] right to issuance of the writ is clear and indisputable.' *Will v. United States*. Moreover, it is important to remember that issuance of the writ is in large part a matter of discretion with the court to which the petition is addressed."

Lower federal courts, consistent with the Supreme Court guidelines, frequently speak of the writs as "extraordinary remedies," to be "sparingly used" only as needed to avoid an "irreparable harm." Still, writs have issued to review a wide range of lower court orders, including orders directing defendants to appear in a lineup, prohibiting comments to the press, denying a request for a jury trial, refusing to permit out-state counsel to appear pro hoc vice, and limiting permissible discovery. See 16 Wright, Miller, & Cooper (Note 7 supra), §§ 3936.1–3936.3. Each opinion has stressed, however, the special circumstances of the particular case. Thus, in *United States v. Hughes*, 413 F.2d 1244 (5th Cir.1969), vacated as moot, 397 U.S. 93, 90 S.Ct. 817, 25 L.Ed.2d 77 (1970), granting mandamus to review a discovery order, the court emphasized that both sides urged review, that the ruling below presented a "basic" issue as to the extent of district court power under a newly adopted federal rule, that district court rulings within the circuit were in conflict on that issue, and that prompt resolution of the issue could avoid possible reversal of trials that were certain to be "lengthy and expensive."

Many state courts view the writs as encompassing a much narrower range of objections than the lower federal courts. They adhere to the "traditional" view that mandamus is available only to compel action "ministerial" in nature and prohibition available only to bar orders that the lower court "lacked authority to issue under any set of circumstances". Under this approach the writ will be available for a narrow range of challenges. (e.g., the trial court lacked authority to try the case because venue for the crime was elsewhere, or defendant had been denied has right to a speedy trial). Other states take a position similar to that adopted by the federal courts, and still others permit even more liberal use of the writs. Here, the writs may be available to challenge such trial court rulings as the refusal to grant a change of venue in response to pretrial publicity or the application of discovery sanctions to exclude defense witnesses. Where the writs are liberally used, the end result may be a situation quite similar to that found in jurisdictions providing for appellate review of interlocutory orders at the discretion of the appellate court. See Note 1 supra. Arguably, the most important concerns here are the general significance of the legal issue, the potential for irreparable harm (e.g., where compliance with a discovery order would result in the loss of privacy or privilege), and the likelihood that the alleged error would render meaningless the subsequent trial.

SECTION 3. PROSECUTION APPEALS

1. *Statutory provisions and double jeopardy limitations.* The federal system and all of the states now have statutory provisions allowing prosecution appeals from at least a limited class of trial court orders in criminal cases.[a] Some, like the Federal Criminal Appeals Act of 1970 (18 U.S.C. § 3731, Supp.App. B), reflect the policy of allowing prosecution appeals from all final orders except where "the double jeopardy clause * * * prohibits further prosecution."[b] In many states, however, statutory authorization of prosecution appeals from adverse final orders is somewhat narrower than what would be available within the outer limits of the double jeopardy prohibition. Some states, for example, allow appeals only

a. Since prosecution appeals were unknown at common law, they are recognized only where specifically authorized by statute. See *United States v. Sanges*, 144 U.S. 310, 12 S.Ct. 609, 36 L.Ed. 445 (1892) (general statute authorizing appeals from final decisions "in any case" involving constitutional issue would not be read to authorize government appeal from dismissal of indictment on constitutional grounds because it does not expressly refer to government appeals and it would not be presumed that Congress intended "to make so serious and far-reaching an innovation in criminal jurisprudence"). Indeed, where statutes authorize a government appeal, courts typically "strictly limit" such appeals to "the letter of the provision." See e.g., *Carroll v. United States*, 354 U.S. 394, 77 S.Ct. 1332, 1 L.Ed.2d 1442 (1957) ("The history shows resistance of the Court to the opening of an appellate route for the Government until it was plainly provided by the Congress, and after that a close restriction of its uses to those authorized by the statute").

In some jurisdictions, the prosecution also may gain appellate review in certain situations through the indirect route of refusing to comply with an order (e.g., a discovery order) and having an individual prosecutor held in civil contempt (with that prosecutor than pursuing the appeal). See Note 7, p. 1551 (discussing the defense's use of a parallel route). Of course, availability of this route rests as a practical matter on the cooperation of the trial judge, who can preclude its use by imposing some sanction other than contempt for the failure to comply. However, if that sanction is a dismissal of the charges or the exclusion of evidence, an appeal may be available under provisions allowing for prosecution appeals from such orders.

b. Several states go beyond this standard, and permit a "moot appeal" where double jeopardy would bar a retrial following an appellate reversal. The prosecution may appeal from an acquittal but that appeal will present issues solely for determining the law for future cases, the appellate court lacking any power to upset the judgment of acquittal. While it often is said that double jeopardy bars a prosecution appeal following an acquittal, double jeopardy apparently bars only the retrial that would follow the overturning of the acquittal. Thus, if the state is willing to accept appeals that produce only advisory opinions, those appeals are not prohibited by the double jeopardy clause. See James Strazella, *The Relationship of Double Jeopardy to Prosecution Appeals*, 73 Notre Dame L. Rev. 1 (1997).

from pretrial dismissals of indictments (or counts of an indictment), with a few restricting such appeals to dismissals on particular grounds (e.g. matters apparent on the face of the pleadings). These jurisdictions do not allow government appeals from dismissals issued during trial even though double jeopardy would not bar an appellate reversal and subsequent new trial in such a situation (see e.g., *United States v. Scott,* p. 1465). Similarly, other states allow post-verdict appeals only from an order "arresting judgment." Such provisions encompass certain orders setting aside a guilty verdict but not others. They would include the post-verdict dismissal based on some ground unrelated to factual innocence (e.g., lack of jurisdiction), but not a judgment of acquittal entered notwithstanding the jury verdict. Supreme Court precedent suggests that appellate review of all such post-verdict orders is consistent with double jeopardy since a reversal requires no more than reinstating the jury's verdict of guilt. See Note 8, p. 1475.

2. *Appeals from interlocutory orders.* States do not give defendants a right to an interlocutory appeal of an adverse pretrial order (though some states do allow discretionary interlocutory appeals from such orders) in part because the defendant, if convicted, can gain review of the adverse final judgment. See Note 1, p. 1546. The prosecution, however, is in a quite different position as to an adverse pretrial order that falls short of a dismissal. If not allowed an immediate appeal from such an order, the prosecution will have no opportunity to pursue a post-trial appeal. The erroneous pretrial order may result in the prosecution losing its case at trial, but the acquittal of the defendant will end the matter since the double jeopardy prohibition then bars further prosecution. For most jurisdictions, this circumstance justifies providing the prosecution with an immediate appeal of one or more classes of adverse pretrial interlocutory orders.[c] For others, the defendant's interest in the 'swift resolution of his case' is a more important consideration. Since a prosecution appeal from an adverse interlocutory ruling necessarily delays the trial (in contrast to a pretrial dismissal, where the appeal will only have that effect if the dismissal is reversed and the prosecution resumes), and since such a ruling still leaves the prosecution with the opportunity to go to trial, these jurisdictions will not grant to the prosecution a right of appeal from any such non-final orders.

Among jurisdictions allowing prosecution appeals from non-final, pretrial orders, considerable variation is found in the statutory structure governing such appeals. In some states, provisions allowing discretionary appellate review of pretrial interlocutory orders (see Note 1, p. 1546) are extended to the prosecution as well as the defense. In others, the prosecution is given a right to appeal a series of specified pretrial rulings that do not constitute final orders (e.g., the granting of a change of venue). Several grant the prosecution a right of appellate review for any pretrial interlocutory ruling where it is shown that the interlocutory ruling will have a "reasonable likelihood of causing either serious impairment to or termination of the prosecution." See Me.Rev.Stat.Ann. tit.15, § 2115–A (1). Many provisions also contain a requirement that defendant be released on personal

---

c. Allowing for prosecutorial interlocutory appeal is also seen as reducing the potential skewing impact of the asymmetry in criminal appeals (i.e., allowing a defense appeal from a conviction but no prosecution appeal from an acquittal). That asymmetry produces in some trial judges an inclination to decide in favor of the defense on difficult questions (and thereby avoid appellate review and the possibility of reversal), and in other trial judges, an inclination to rule in favor of the prosecution on the issue (and thereby preserve reviewability, assuming the defendant is convicted and ap-

peals). With the prosecution given an interlocutory appeal on adverse pretrial rulings, the judge now will anticipate appellate review of pretrial rulings whether decided in favor of one side or the other. See also Kate Stith, *The Risk of Legal Error in Criminal Cases: Some Consequences of the Asymmetry in the Right to Appeal,* 57 U.Chi.L.Rev. 1 (1990) (also exploring other aspects of the skewing impact of the asymmetry as it bears upon the risk of legal error at the trial level and the evolution of legal standards set by appellate courts).

recognizance pending the disposition of the prosecution's appeal. Finally, some jurisdictions do not limit appeals from non-final orders to pretrial rulings; they also allow prosecution appeals from the grant of a defense motion for a new trial.

3. *Pretrial suppression orders.* Even those jurisdictions, such as the federal, that generally restrict the government to appeals from final orders commonly recognize one exception—the order granting a pretrial motion to suppress evidence. A suppression order is generally held not to fall within provisions authorizing government appeals from a "final judgment" or a "dismissal of an indictment" since it does not formally terminate the prosecution. However, the federal system and a substantial majority of the states have adopted provisions specifically authorizing appeals from suppression orders. See CRIM-PROC § 27.3(c). Such provisions have been supported on two grounds. First, the practical effect of the granting of a motion to suppress often is to terminate the case since the prosecution, lacking sufficient additional evidence, will be required to request dismissal of the indictment. Second, the rules relating to searches and seizures and other police practices that lead to suppression motions frequently are uncertain, and law enforcement officials should be entitled to base their policies on the rulings of the highest court; if appellate review of an adverse decision on a police practice is not available, the police can obtain a higher court ruling only by persisting in the challenged practice until they obtain a favorable decision from a different lower court, which would then be appealed to the higher court by the defendant.

In accord with the first argument noted above, some jurisdictions limit prosecution appeals of suppression orders to cases in which the prosecution certifies that the suppression order will eliminate any "reasonable possibility" of a successful prosecution. In accord with the second ground, many provisions are limited to suppression orders based on an illegality in the governments acquisition of the evidence. Others, like 18 U.S.C. § 3731, speak generally of orders "suppressing or excluding evidence." These provisions have been held applicable to a broad range of pretrial orders. Thus, the state was allowed under such a provision to appeal a court order directing it to disclose psychiatric reports pertaining to its witnesses where the sanction for failing to disclose was the exclusion of the testimony of those witnesses. *People v. Phipps,* 413 N.E.2d 1277 (Ill.1980). Similarly, although the defense was not obligated to use an *in limine* motion to challenge the reliability of certain scientific tests, where it used such a motion and the trial court held that the tests would not be admissible, the prosecution was allowed to appeal that pretrial ruling. *State v. Tate,* 265 S.E.2d 223 (N.C.1980). Indeed, it has been suggested that the prosecution can utilize these provisions to gain appellate review of a wide range of orders that otherwise would be made at trial and subsumed in an acquittal. Where the prosecution can foresee difficulties in gaining admission of crucial evidence, it is to its advantage to obtain a pretrial ruling so that an adverse decision can be appealed as a suppression order. The Supreme Court upheld an appeal developed through this tactic in *United States v. Helstoski,* 442 U.S. 477, 99 S.Ct. 2432, 61 L.Ed.2d 12 (1979), although the basic evidentiary issue presented there was prompted by a related defense objection (a claimed immunity from prosecution under the Speech or Debate Clause).

4. *Review by writ.* Prosecutors may also seek to utilize the extraordinary writs to gain review of interlocutory or final orders that are not included within statutory provisions allowing prosecution appeals. As in the case of defense use of the writs, see Note 8, p. 1553, there is considerable variation among the jurisdictions as to when the writs should be available. States viewing the writs as limited to challenging trial court rulings that constitute a "jurisdictional usurpation or default," and reading the concept of jurisdiction quite technically for these purposes, commonly apply the same narrow view of the writs to prosecution applications. Jurisdictions adopting a broader view of the writs' availability upon defense application are divided as to whether to allow the same extensive use of the writs by the prosecution. The question posed for these jurisdictions is whether the writs should not be as readily available to the prosecution (but should be limited, instead, to the traditional standard of "jurisdictional excesses") because: (1) the prosecution in seeking the writ is interfering with the defendant's interest, reflected in his speedy trial right, in obtaining a prompt resolution of the charges against him, and (2) appeals by the government traditionally are restricted to those specifically authorized by the legislature. See *Will v. United States,* 389 U.S. 90, 88 S.Ct. 269, 19 L.Ed.2d 305 (1967) (stressing both of these factors, and adding with respect to the latter that "the case against permitting the writ to be used as a substitute for interlocutory appeal" is not made "less compelling by the fact that the government has no later right to appeal"). Of course, the first factor is not present in all settings. See CRIMPROC § 27.4(d) ("Review of orders issued * * * during an investigation delay the charging determination, but the person affected is hardly in the same position as a defendant awaiting trial. Similarly, if the government challenges an order issued after the defendant was tried and found guilty, there is delay in the final disposition, but usually not in the presentation of evidence.").

SECTION 4. COGNIZABLE CLAIMS

1. *The "raise or waive" (forfeiture) doctrine.* Appellate courts may refuse to consider defense challenges to a conviction on various grounds.[a] Without doubt, the most frequently cited ground for refusing to consider a particular defense claim on appeal is the so-called "raise-or-waive" doctrine. Simply put, this doctrine holds that, with some exceptions (see Notes 2–3 infra), appellate courts will not consider a defense allegation of error that was not properly raised and preserved at trial. Although the "raise or wave" rule speaks of a "waiver" through the failure to properly present the claim at the trial level, it does not refer to a "waiver" in the traditional sense of a "knowing and intelligent relinquishment" of a right. Rather, what is involved here, as noted by the Supreme Court in *United States v. Olano,* quoted infra at Note 3, is a "forfeiture" or "procedural default" of the right.

What constitutes the proper presentation of a claim at the trial level will vary with the nature of the objection and the procedural idiosyncrasies of the particular jurisdiction. Timing requirements, for example, may require that the objection be made before indictment (e.g., challenge to a preliminary hearing bindover), before trial (e.g., suppression of illegally seized evidence), or contemporaneous with the error (e.g., improper cross-examination). While a single objection may be sufficient for some errors, others may have to be raised at different stages in the proceeding. Indeed, in some jurisdictions, the trial court must be given the opportunity to correct itself as to all alleged errors through a motion for new trial that again raises those errors. See Note 2, p. 1441. Why is it that the failure to adhere to these and other rules relating to the timing and form of trial objections results in the loss of appellate review? Consider the answer of *State v. Applegate,* 591 P.2d 371 (Or.App.1979):

a. These include, in addition to the grounds discussed below: (1) the mootness of the challenged conviction; (2) the lack of impact of the challenged conviction due to concurrent sentences on other valid convictions; (3) forfeiture of right to appeal by flight, under the "fugitive disentitlement" doctrine, see *Ortega-Rodriguez* *v. United States,* 507 U.S. 234, 113 S.Ct. 1199, 122 L.Ed.2d 581 (1993); and (4) the express waiver of the right to appeal (or the right to appeal a particular element of the conviction, e.g., the sentence), typically made in connection with a plea bargain, see Note 3, p. 1252. See CRIMPROC § 21.2(b).

"There are many rationales for the raise-or-waive rule: that it is a necessary corollary of our adversary system in which issues are framed by the litigants and presented to a court; that fairness to all parties requires a litigant to advance his contentions at a time when there is an opportunity to respond to them factually, if his opponent chooses to; that the rule promotes efficient trial proceedings; that reversing for error not preserved permits the losing side to second-guess its tactical decisions after they do not produce the desired result; and that there is something unseemly about telling a lower court it was wrong when it never was presented with the opportunity to be right. The principal rationale, however, is judicial economy. There are two components to judicial economy: (1) if the losing side can obtain an appellate reversal because of error not objected to, the parties and public are put to the expense of retrial that could have been avoided had an objection been made; and (2) if an issue had been raised in the trial court, it could have been resolved there, and the parties and public would be spared the expense of appeal."

2. *General exceptions.* It follows from the reasoning of *Applegate* that certain procedural settings may justify appellate consideration of trial errors even though not properly presented below. The clearest case is that in which the defendant did not have a reasonable opportunity to raise his claim within the time limit prescribed by the state's procedural requirement. Indeed, the refusal to consider a claim based on a procedural rule that arbitrarily imposes an impossible time limit may in itself constitute a violation of due process. See e.g., *Reece v. Georgia,* 350 U.S. 85, 76 S.Ct. 167, 100 L.Ed. 77 (1955) (state requirement that defendant challenge the grand jury composition prior to indictment held invalid as applied to indigent defendant not provided with counsel until the day after indictment). Relying on the reasonable opportunity rationale, appellate courts also have considered objections not raised at trial where an intervening ruling established the grounds for the objection and counsel's failure to raise the issue was understandable in light of the controlling precedent at the time of trial.

Is there anything in the *Applegate* explanation of the raise-or-waive rule that would explain why appellate courts will consider first-time challenges that raise "jurisdictional" questions? This exception to the rule is universally recognized, and, in some instances, incorporated in statutes or court rules governing trial and appellate procedure. See e.g., Fed.R.Crim.P. 12(b) (indictment's failure "to show jurisdiction in the court or to charge an offense * * * shall be noticed by the court at any time during the pendency of the proceedings"). However, courts here tend to utilize a narrower and somewhat more traditional definition of a jurisdictional defect than in other areas where jurisdictional claims have been given separate treatment (see e.g., Notes 3–4, pp. 1307–09 and Note 1, p. 1588). Consider CRIMPROC § 27.5(c): "A challenge to subject matter jurisdiction clearly may be raised for the first time on appeal, and many courts will also consider on a similar basis an allegation that the offense occurred outside the territorial jurisdiction of the state. Courts generally are reluctant, however, to include within the jurisdictional category objections to other aspects of the proceedings. While several appellate courts allow a first-time challenge to the constitutionality of the statute on which the prosecution is based, most hold that such an objection is not jurisdictional and therefore cannot be raised unless it fits within some other exception to the raise-or-waive rule. Similarly, most jurisdictions treat a double jeopardy claim as a defect that cannot be raised for the first time on appeal. On the other hand, the failure of the information or indictment to state an offense can be raised initially on appeal in almost all jurisdictions, either by virtue of its characterization as a jurisdictional defect, or by reliance upon a specific provision such as Rule 12(b) [Note 4, p. 997]."

The most open-ended exception to the raise-or-waive rule is found in a few states where appellate courts will consider an issue not raised below, without regard to the defense's lack of excuse for raising the issue or the non-jurisdictional character of the issue, simply because an appellate ruling on the issue is thought to serve the public interest. These courts may consider an issue because there is a "strong possibility of recurrence" of an apparently improper practice in future cases, *State v. Dreske*, 276 N.W.2d 324 (Wis.App.1979), or the "issue one of public policy or of broad * * * concern." *State v. Junkin*, 599 P.2d 244 (Ariz.App.1979).

Where a jurisdiction recognizes one or more of the above exceptions, it will usually do so apart from the plain error exception discussed below (that is, it recognizes the exception without applying the criteria of the plain error rule). In the federal system, with the plain error exception set forth in Federal Rule 52(b) ("plain errors or defects affecting substantial rights may be noticed although they were not brought to the attention of the court"), that exception is often said to be exclusive, except for the pleading defects that must be recognized under Rule 12(b).[b] In light of the federal plain error standards set forth in Note 3 below, should federal courts invariably recognize under those standards any (or all) of the general exceptions noted above?

3. *The "plain error" exception.* All but a few jurisdictions recognize the authority of an appellate court to reverse on the basis of a plain error even though that error was not properly raised and preserved at the trial level. In most jurisdictions, the doctrine extends to all types of errors provided they are "plain errors or defects affecting substantial rights," Fed.R.Crim.P. 52(b). Some states, however, by judicial interpretation or statute, limit the doctrine's application to a specified class of errors (e.g., constitutional violations). What raises an error to the level of a "plain error"? Commentators have suggested that the usual appellate court descriptions of plain error are "not of much help." Indeed, it has been suggested that the "cases give the distinct impression that 'plain error' is a concept that appellate courts find impossible to define, save that they know it when they see it." Charles Alan Wright, *Federal Practice and Procedure— Criminal* § 856 (2d ed.1982).

Perhaps responding to such criticism, the Supreme Court in UNITED STATES v. OLANO, 507 U.S. 725, 113 S.Ct. 1770, 123 L.Ed.2d 508 (1993), and JOHNSON v. UNITED STATES, 520 U.S. 461, 117 S.Ct. 1544, 137 L.Ed.2d 718 (1997), developed a four-step analysis for determining whether an error is subject to review as "plain error" under Federal Rule 52(b). As the Court summarized in *Johnson,* "An appellate court can correct an error not raised at trial" only if there is "(1) 'error,' (2) that is 'plain,' * * *(3) that 'affects substantial rights,'" and that "(4) * * * seriously affects the fairness, integrity, or public reputation of judicial proceedings."

The initial prerequisite of an "error" requires the appellate court to distinguish between a claim that has been "waived" and one that has been "forfeited," as a waiver does not produce an "error." The *Olano* Court note in this regard: "The first limitation on appellate authority under Rule 52(b) is that there indeed be an 'error.' Deviation from a legal rule is 'error' unless the rule has been waived. * * * Waiver is different from forfeiture. Whereas forfeiture is the failure to make the timely assertion of a right, waiver is the 'intentional relinquishment or abandonment on a known right.' *Johnson v. Zerbst,* 304 U.S. 458, 58 S.Ct. 1019, 82 L.Ed. 1461 (1938). * * * Mere forfeiture, as opposed to waiver, does not

---

b. But consider *United States v. Promise* and *United States v. Cotton*, described in Note 3 infra, and Note 3, p. 1003 (applying the plain error criteria to an indictment error that could also be viewed as falling under Rule 12(b); compare the federal cases cited in Notes 4–7, pp. 997–99).

extinguish an 'error' under Rule 52(b). Although in theory it could be argued that [i]f the question was not presented to the trial court no error was committed by the trial court, hence there is nothing to review, * * * this is not the theory that Rule 52(b) adopts. If a legal rule was violated during the district court proceedings, and if the defendant did not waive the rule, then there has been an 'error' within the meaning of Rule 52(b) despite the absence of a timely objection."

Speaking to the second limitation, the *Olano* Court noted that the error must be "plain," which "is synonymous with 'clear' or equivalently 'obvious.' " Rule 52(b) "defines a single category of forfeited-but-reversible error. Although it is possible to read the Rule in the disjunctive as creating two separate categories— 'plain errors' and 'defects affecting substantial rights'—that reading is surely wrong * * * The forfeited error 'may be noticed' only if it is 'plain' and 'affects substantial rights.' "

Olano found it unnecessary to consider "the special case where the error was unclear at the time of the trial, but became clear on appeal because the applicable law has been clarified." However, *Johnson* spoke to that issue and concluded that error could be deemed "clear" by virtue of new rules that were established after trial but held to apply retroactively on direct review. The *Johnson* Court reasoned that even though the trial court's action there (failing to submit to the jury the element of materiality in a perjury prosecution) was not recognized as error by the Supreme Court until after Johnson's trial, "it is enough that an error be 'plain' at the time of appellate consideration," at least in a case where "the law at the time of trial was settled and clearly contrary to the law at the time of appeal." The Court noted that otherwise, defense counsel at trial would "inevitably" make "a long and virtually useless laundry list of objections to rulings that were plainly supported by existing precedent."

The third requirement specified in *Olano* was that the error must "effec[t] substantial rights." The Court noted that the same language also is found in Rule 52(a)'s harmless error provision [see Note 1, p. 1563], and for "most cases," under harmless error analysis, to affect substantial rights, the error "must have been prejudicial" in the sense of "affect[ing] the outcome" of the lower court proceedings. The same was true here, but in contrast to a typical harmless error inquiry (see Note 7, p. 1567), to establish plain error, "the defendant rather than the Government bears the burden of persuasion with respect to prejudice." In *Olano*, the Court concluded that the erroneous presence of alternate jurors during deliberations did not meet this requirement, noting that the defendants had not shown that the error had prejudiced them and rejecting the court of appeals' finding that the error was "inherently prejudicial." In applying the Rule 52(b) harmless error standard, the Court has held certain types of errors (both constitutional and nonconstitutional) to be "structural" and therefore requiring automatic reversal without inquiry as to the impact of the error on the outcome of the proceeding. In *Johnson*, the Court declined to decide whether an error that qualifies as a "structural" error under harmless error analysis would automatically qualify as one "affecting substantial rights."[c]

c. The Court noted that even if the error before it was assumed to be "structural" and therefore assumed to automatically meet the third prong of the *Olano* test, it failed under the fourth prong. In *Neder v. United States*, set forth at p. 1575, the Court concluded that the error considered in *Johnson* (the failure to submit the materiality element to the jury) was not structural. Justice Stevens, in a separate opinion, noted that he shared the conclusion of Justice Scalia's dissent that such an error did call for automatic reversal under harmless error analysis, but he could not join Justice Scalia's opinion as it was "inherently inconsistent" in also suggesting "that reversal is appropriate only when a defendant made a timely objection." Responding, Justice Scalia stated: "[T]here is nothing 'internally inconsistent' about believing that a procedural guarantee is fundamental while also believing that it must be asserted in a timely fashion. It is a universally acknowledged principle of law that

Speaking to the fourth prerequisite, the *Olano* Court stressed that Rule 52(b) is "permissive rather than mandatory," allowing rather than requiring correction when an error is found to be "plain" and "affecting substantial rights." In previous cases the Court had indicated that this discretion should be employed "in those circumstances in which a miscarriage of justice would otherwise result." However, in contrast to the position taken in its habeas corpus jurisprudence (see Note 4, p. 1601), the requirement of a "miscarriage of justice" in plain-error cases was not meant to restrict plain-error review to only those errors that resulted in "the conviction or sentencing of an actually innocent defendant." An appellate court should, in addition, "correct a plain forfeited error affecting substantial rights if the error 'seriously affects' the fairness, integrity, or public reputation of judicial proceedings." This determination, the Court later explained in *Johnson*, was to be made on an analysis of the facts of the individual case. In *Johnson*, the record showed that the error in question—failure to submit the element of materiality to the jury—did not seriously affect either the outcome, or the the "fairness, integrity, or public reputation of judicial proceedings" because the evidence supporting materiality was "overwhelming." "Indeed," the Court ventured, "it would be the reversal of a conviction such as this which would have that effect."

Prior to *Olano* and *Johnson,* lower federal court rulings on plain error appeared to have been influenced by a balancing approach. Thus, it had been suggested that the courts were more likely to characterize an error as plain where the evidence in the case was closely balanced. So too, plain error was more likely to be found where there might be a good reason for the lack of objection below, or where the error could not have been remedied by the trial judge even if called to his attention. On the other side, it seemed less likely to be found where the error could have been readily corrected by an objection at trial, or where such an objection might have led the government to introduce additional evidence on the issue. Plain error also was more likely to be found when the error was of constitutional magnitude, involving a claim that would not have been withheld for some "strategic purpose", and undoubtedly impacted the outcome of the proceeding—as in the case of a double jeopardy violation apparent on the face of the record. See Gabriel J. Chin, *Double Jeopardy Violation as "Plain Error" under Federal Rule of Criminal Procedure* 52(b) 21 Pepp. L. Rev. 1161 (1994) (but noting various decisions refusing to consider double jeopardy claims). Are such guidelines consistent with *Olano* and *Johnson?*

Consider in light of the above question, the different views expressed in *United States v. Promise*, 255 F.3d 150 (4th Cir.2001) (en banc) and *United States v. Cotton*, 261 F.3d 397 (4th Cir.2001). The defendant in *Promise* was charged in a single count indictment with intent to distribute "a quantity of cocaine base." Following a jury conviction, the judge determined at a sentencing hearing that the quantity distributed was more than 1.5 kilograms, and set a sentence of 30 years. A substantial majority of the en banc court concluded that this quantity-determination had raised the maximum allowable sentence from 20 years to the 30 years imposed by the judge. Accordingly, the majority also concluded that, in light of the Supreme Court's ruling in *Apprendi* [p. 1518], constitutional error had occurred in failing to allege the offense-element of quantity (i.e., excess of 1.5 kilograms) in the indictment and in failing to submit that element to jury. The court was evenly divided, however, as to whether such errors should require reversal under the plain error rule (resulting in an affirmance).

The four judges refusing to reverse under the plain error doctrine acknowledged that the errors were "clear" and "affected substantial rights." They

one who sleeps on his rights—even fundamental rights—may lose them."

concluded, however, that this was an appropriate case for exercising the court's discretion not to invoke the plain error doctrine. A parallel was drawn to *Johnson*, where the Supreme Court had so exercised that discretion as to the Sixth Amendment error of a judge (rather than the jury) determining an element of the crime (materiality) because the evidence of that element was "overwhelming" and "essentially uncontroverted." Here, too, the evidence as to quantity was overwhelming, and "more importantly" the defendant had not contested the evidence or finding as to quantity. Also, the defendant's decision not to dispute quantity "was not the result of lack of notice," as he had been informed by an information filed prior to trial that the government would contend that the quantity was above the threshold for the 30 year maximum. The four judges who relied on plain error responded that reliance on the weight of evidence was not appropriate where, unlike *Johnson*, the error was not confined to the failure to submit the element to the jury. The defendant also had been deprived of his Fifth Amendment right to have the grand jury determine the quantity distributed in its issuance of its indictment, and the Supreme Court had reasoned, in the context of disallowing amendments to indictments (see Note 4, p. 1006), that courts may not speculate about whether, in light of the evidence available at trial, a grand jury would have indicted for a crime which it did not in fact charge.

In *Cotton*, a Fourth Circuit panel divided 2–1 on applying the plain error doctrine to another case in which the grand jury indictment failed to allege the element of quantity and that determination was made by the judge at sentencing. The majority concluded that the plain error doctrine should apply, without regard to whether the evidence of quantity was overwhelming and undisputed, since it had long been held that a failure of an indictment to allege all essential elements of the crime charged produced *per se* reversible error; no matter how strong the evidence, a person cannot be convicted of an offense that was not charged, which was the case here as to the element that increased the maximum sentence.[d] The majority also characterized the lack of any charge as to an above-the-threshold quantity as depriving the trial court of jurisdiction to sentence based upon that quantity. The dissent in *Cotton* responded that majority "does not make a case of injustice based on the facts of this case," and "misses two crucial points" in its focus "solely on the nature of the error": "First, the indictment in this case [which was tried before *Apprendi*] was valid at the time it was filed. * * * Second, the majority inappropriately replaces the discretionary, case-by-case assessment dictated by the fourth prong of *Olano* with an essentially categorical approach when the error consists of an indictment defect, * * * [and] to select a category of errors *a priori* that must be corrected on plain error review is inconsistent with the mandate of *Olano* to examine the facts of each case and the proceeding as a whole."

SECTION 5. THE HARMLESS ERROR RULE

A. NON-CONSTITUTIONAL ERRORS

1. Background. During the mid–1800s, the English courts adopted a rule of appellate review, applicable in both civil and criminal cases, that came to be known as the Exchequer Rule. Under that rule, a trial error in the admission or exclusion of evidence was presumed to have caused prejudice and therefore almost automatically required a new trial. The Exchequer Rule's presumption of prejudice was designed to ensure that the appellate court did not encroach upon the

---

d. Consider, however, Note 2, p. 1001, discussing the recent division among federal lower courts as to whether an indictment's failure to allege an element of an offense can constitute a harmless error.

jury's fact-finding function by discounting the improperly admitted or excluded evidence and sustaining the verdict reached below based on its belief that that verdict was correct in light of the overall evidence. The presumption of prejudice was stringently applied to even the most insignificant items of evidence, and a similar policy was extended to errors in jury instruction. As a result, retrials became so commonplace that critics sarcastically described English litigation as terminated only by the death of one of the parties. Parliament responded with harmless error legislation, which was included in the Judicature Act of 1873. That Act stated that the Court of Appeal was not to order a new trial on the basis of "the improper admission or rejection of evidence" or a "misdirection" of the jury "unless in the opinion of the Court of Appeal some substantial wrong or miscarriage has thereby been occasioned." In determining whether such an error had produced a "substantial wrong or miscarriage," the appellate court looked to whether the error was likely to have had an impact upon the outcome of the case.

While the American courts had adopted the Exchequer Rule, they generally were not influenced by its subsequent rejection in England. Indeed, they extended the philosophy of the Exchequer Rule to a wide range of trial errors, requiring new trials no matter how technical or seemingly insignificant the error. As the retrials mounted, the appellate courts were criticized as "impregnable citadels of technicality," and reformers urged adoption of harmless error legislation. Their efforts began to bear fruit during the early 1900s when a substantial number of states adopted such legislation. The federal harmless error statute, adopted in 1919, provided the model for much of the state legislation. It required a federal appellate court to "give judgment after an examination of the entire record before the court, without regard to technical errors, defects, or exceptions which do not affect the substantial rights of the parties." Eventually all American jurisdictions adopted legislation or court rules to the same effect.

Unlike the original English legislation, the American harmless error provisions are not limited to errors in the treatment of evidence and the instruction of the jury. This is not surprising, as the American criticism of "reversals on technicality" had been directed against a wide range of appellate reversals, including, in particular, reversals based upon technical pleading errors (see Ch. 16, § 1). The American legislation spoke of courts disregarding "any error * * * which does not affect substantial rights," see e.g., Fed.R.Crim.P. 52(a), or disregarding an error "in any matter of pleading or procedure" that has not resulted in a "miscarriage of justice," see e.g., Mich.Comp.L. § 769.26. Also, these statutory directives often told the appellate court to base its decision upon "an examination of the entire record."

2. Technical rights and technical errors. The language of the typical harmless error provisions—referring to "technical errors" and "substantial rights"—naturally led appellate courts to examine initially the nature of the legal standard violated and nature of the violation as it related to the substance of that legal standard. Thus, an error might be deemed harmless because the legal standard violated was a "formalistic requirement," not affecting a "substantial right" of the defendant (e.g., where the clerk failed to record on the indictment the exact time of its filing). So too, even though the legal standard established a "substantial right" of the defendant, a particular violation might be deemed harmless because its impact was not to deprive the defendant of the basic benefit afforded by that right. Thus, a failure to comply with a requirement that an indictment list all government witnesses might be deemed a harmless error where the defense had otherwise been told before trial of an unlisted witness' identity. The critical issue under this mode of analysis is whether the error undermined the immediate purpose of the right involved.

3. *Two tiered analysis of prejudice.* As for some substantial rights, an error is deemed to have deprived the defendant of a "substantial right" (or to have resulted in a "miscarriage of justice") whenever the error is "substantive" rather than "technical"—i.e., whenever the error deprived the defendant of the substance of the right. No further inquiry is made as to likely impact of the denial of that right upon the conviction from which defendant appeals. It often is said that violations of such rights call for the "automatic reversal" of a conviction, leading to the characterization of the rights as "not subject to the harmless error doctrine." That description is accurate only if one ignores the first aspect of harmless error analysis—determining whether the violation was simply "technical" or actually deprived the defendant of the substance of the right in question (or as some would put it, whether there really was a violation).[a]

As to most errors deemed to be substantive, harmless error analysis requires—as an additional prerequisite for reversal—a finding as to the likely impact of the error upon the finding of guilt. Thus, in a case in which the indictment failed to list a prosecution witness and the defense was therefore taken by surprise and hindered in its cross-examination of that witness, the error could still be deemed harmless if the witness' testimony was not likely to have had an impact upon the jury's verdict. Prejudice here is measured not simply by loss of the benefit the right was intended to confer, but additionally by reference to the possible impact of that loss upon the outcome of the case. This approach, it has been noted, is not inconsistent with the language of the harmless error legislation, because the reference to "error which 'affected the substantial rights of the parties' was * * * understood [historically] to refer, not to errors respecting a particular class of rights, but rather to any error which affected the fairness of the trial as a whole by calling into question the reliability of the result." *United States v. Lane,* Note 2, p. 1059 (Brennan, J., concurring).

4. *Distinguishing rights.* Over the years, a fairly well accepted dividing line has been developed in distinguishing between those nonconstitutional errors as to which courts will look primarily to whether the violation deprived the defendant of the immediate benefit of a substantial right and those as to which courts also will apply an outcome-impact test. Generally falling in the former category are those errors "that might loosely be described as concerned with the structure of the proceeding." CRIMPROC § 27.6(b). Very often such errors are described as depriving the trial court of "jurisdiction," but that characterization tends to be used loosely. See e.g., Note 2, p. 995 (discussing the characterization of a pleading's failure to allege all elements of the crime as a "jurisdictional" defect);

---

a. Courts which characterize that determination as not part of the harmless error analysis, but as simply determining whether there was a violation of the right, view harmless error analysis as focusing entirely on determining the impact of the error on the outcome. That narrow conception of harmless error analysis has lead in the federal courts to the contention that rulings requiring automatic reversal for substantive violations of any nonconstitutional right are contrary to Rule 52(a). See e.g., Easterbrook, J, dissenting from a denial of rehearing in *United States v. Underwood,* 130 F.3d 1225 (7th Cir.1997) (panel had held that denial of peremptory challenge was a structural error calling for automatic reversal, and that "harmless error analysis" therefore was "inappropriate"; Judge Easterbrook argued that "Rule 52(a) does not permit courts to distinguish 'trial' from structural errors," as evidenced by the Supreme Court's holding in *Johnson* that the "plain error companion to harmless error" applies to structural errors, see fn. c, p. 1560). Federal courts, however, have long held various nonconstitutional errors to constitute errors requiring automatic reversal without inquiry as to the impact on the outcome of the proceeding. See e.g., Note 1, p. 995 (discussing the traditional position on pleading errors); *Gomez v. United States,* 490 U.S. 858, 109 S.Ct. 2237, 104 L.Ed.2d 923 (1989) (where magistrate, rather than district judge, supervised jury selection, there was a substantive violation of the right to have "all critical stages of the criminal trial conducted by a person with jurisdiction to preside," and automatic reversal was required); *Young v. United States ex rel. Vuitton et Fils S.A.,* discussed at Note 4 below.

Note 3, p. 931 (cases characterizing an improper preliminary hearing bindover as a "jurisdictional" defect where bindover was a prerequisite for prosecution by information). Also, many errors viewed as structural (e.g., improper venue) are not "jurisdictional" in any sense of that term. Primary examples of nonconstitutional errors characterized as "structural" and calling for an automatic reversal are improper venue (see Note 5, p. 1017), basic flaw in charging an offense in a pleading (see Note 1, p. 995), and a material departure from statutory requirements governing the selection of a jury (Note 6, p. 1326).

One common feature of the nonconstitutional errors in the "automatic-reversal" category is that they do not relate to the admission or evaluation of particular items of evidence. Errors having that quality invariably are reviewed under a harmless error analysis that looks to the likely impact of the error on the case outcome. Included in that grouping are: errors in the admissibility of evidence; the improper joinder of counts or persons (either of which places before the jury evidence it would not otherwise consider); erroneous pretrial rulings that relate to the production or challenging of evidence, such as rulings on discovery; erroneous actions of the judge that may influence the jury in evaluating particular evidence, such as erroneous jury instructions or improperly restricting a defense argument; and judicial or prosecutorial misconduct that amounts to urging jurors to consider factors other than the evidence. An impact-on-outcome analysis is also applied, however, to some errors that have no evidentiary component, such as errors in plea bargaining and plea taking (see Notes 3–4, p. 1300). However, such errors, similar to evidentiary errors, do have a focus on a particular input in the decision that produced a conviction (e.g., the extent to which the judge's erroneous advice as to rights influenced the defendant's decision to plead guilty).

As to most substantive errors, the precedent is fairly uniform in treating the error as requiring application of either an impact-on-outcome analysis or an automatic reversal standard. There are, however, areas of disagreement. See e.g., the majority, concurring, and dissenting opinions in *United States v. Lane,* discussed at Note 2, p. 1059, as to joinder errors; the division among lower courts as to the appropriate treatment of erroneously depriving the defendant of a peremptory challenge, see e.g., *State v. Short,* 327 S.C. 329, 489 S.E.2d 209 (App.1997) (automatic reversal), *United States v. Horsman,* 114 F.3d 822 (8th Cir.1997) (not reversible error if the seated jury was impartial), and fn. a supra; and the division in *Young v. United States ex rel. Vuitton et Fils S.A.,* 481 U.S. 787, 107 S.Ct. 2124, 95 L.Ed.2d 740 (1987) (where district court appointed as special prosecutor in a criminal contempt case the attorney for the party who had obtained the court order which the defendant had allegedly violated, seven justices viewed that appointment as exceeding the district court's authority because the attorney appointed was not "disinterested," with four arguing that the error was "fundamental and pervasive" and not subject to traditional harmless error analysis that looks to outcome-impact, and three arguing that such harmless error analysis was required); and the division as to the treatment on review following a conviction of errors in grand jury or preliminary hearing screening which would have required dismissal of the indictment or information if recognized pretrial (see Note 3, p. 93, and Notes 5–8, pp. 977–79).

The theoretical justification for the distinction drawn between "structural" and "non-structural" also remains a matter of some dispute. The refusal to apply an impact-on-outcome test to errors categorized as "structural" has been justified on several different grounds. The most frequently cited are: (1) that the impact upon the trial outcome of the denial of rights categorized as structural tends to be too speculative to permit accurate application of an outcome-determinative test, as these rights do not relate to a particular aspect of the decision-making process that led to conviction, but to the general character of that process; (2) that such rights implicate "an independent value besides reliability of the outcome," Stevens, J., in *United States v. Lane,* supra, and therefore their violation should not be deemed harmless simply because an appellate court can conclude that the violation did not affect the jury's verdict; and (3) that proper structural features are "jurisdictional prerequisites," and their denial therefore renders void an ensuing verdict.

Still another area of disagreement is whether certain intentional violations by prosecutors of rights relating to the presentation of evidence should require automatic reversal, without regard to their impact upon the outcome of the proceeding, as a prophylactic measure. See e.g., Note 3, p. 976, and Note 7, p. 1430. Here the Supreme Court has stated that, in the federal system, federal harmless error standards preclude prophylactic reversals without regard to outcome-impact. See *Bank of Nova Scotia v. United States,* discussed at Note 2, p. 973; *United States v. Hasting,* Note 3, p. 1573.

5. *The focus of the outcome-impact analysis.* Over the years, there has been considerable division among American jurisdictions in their application of an outcome-impact analysis. See CRIMPROC § 27.6(b). Initially, there was a division as to the critical question to be asked in evaluating the impact of the error: should the key be the significance of the error upon the guilty verdict as it was reached or the significance of the error as measured by a hypothetical trial in which there was no error? The latter approach—commonly known as the "correct result" approach—asked whether, in light of all of the admissible evidence (including any defense evidence improperly excluded), the finding of guilt was clearly correct. This approach was soundly rejected in the Supreme Court's highly influential ruling in KOTTEAKOS v. UNITED STATES, 328 U.S. 750, 66 S.Ct. 1239, 90 L.Ed. 1557 (1946). The Court there reasoned: "[I]t is not the appellate court's function to determine guilt or innocence. Nor is it to speculate upon probable reconviction and decide according to how the speculation comes out. Appellate judges cannot escape such impressions. But they may not make them sole criteria for reversal or affirmance. Those judgments are exclusively for the jury * * *. But this does not mean that the appellate court can escape altogether taking account of the outcome. To weigh the error's effect against the entire setting of the record without relation to the verdict or judgment would be almost to work in a vacuum. In criminal causes that outcome is conviction. This is different, or may be, from guilt in fact. It is guilt in law, established by the judgment of laymen. And the question is, not were they right in their judgment, regardless of the error or its effect upon the verdict. It is rather what effect the error had or reasonably may be taken to have had upon the jury's decision. The crucial thing is the impact of the thing done wrong in the minds of other men, not on one's own, in the total setting."

6. *Potential likelihood of the impact.* Assuming a jurisdiction looks to the error's "effect on the judgment," as that concept was explained in *Kotteakos,* the questions arise as to (1) whether an error can only be deemed harmless if it had no influence, or whether it can be deemed harmless if it had an influence that was less than a dominant influence, and (2) to what extent must a court be convinced that the appropriate standard as to lack of influence was met in the particular case. *Kotteakos* provided the following answer to these questions for federal courts:

> If, when all is said and done, the conviction is sure that the error did not influence the jury, or had but very slight effect, the verdict and the judgment should stand, except perhaps where the departure is from a constitutional norm or a specific command of Congress. But if one cannot say, with fair assurance, after pondering all that happened without stripping the erroneous

action from the whole, that the judgment was not substantially swayed by the error, it is impossible to conclude that substantial rights were not affected.

Many state courts have adopted the *Kotteakos* formulation. Others speak of the need for a "high probability" that the error did not "contribute" to the verdict, the need to be "convinced" that there was no "reasonable possibility" that the error played a substantial role in the determination of guilt, or the need for a showing that it "was more probable than not" that the error did not "materially affect the verdict." A few state courts have adopted as to nonconstitutional errors the "beyond-a-reasonable-doubt" standard that the Supreme Court prescribed for constitutional errors in *Chapman v. California,* set forth in part B. This requires that the appellate court be convinced "beyond a reasonable doubt that the error complained of did not contribute to the conviction obtained."

The differences among the various formulations have been the subject of considerable commentary. See e.g., Roger Traynor, *The Riddle of Harmless Error,* 34 (1970) (criticizing in particular a "reasonable probability" standard as "unlikely to foster uniformity" and noting a preference for a test that focuses on "the degree of probability as more probable than not, highly probable, or almost certain"); Francis Allen, *A Serendipitous Trek through the Advance Sheet Jungle: Criminal Justice in the Courts of Review,* 70 Iowa L Rev. 311 (1985) ("Confidence in the verbal formulas * * * is shaken when one detects little evidence that differences in the tests of harmless error produce corresponding differences in case outcomes. Most often the appellate court announces its conclusion of harmless error in language that is terse and conclusory. * * * The one factor common to a great number of opinions affirming criminal convictions in harmless error grounds is the staunch belief of the reviewing courts in the guilt of the appellants seeking reversals of their criminal convictions. This belief appears to transcend all variations of formula and all problematic calculations about what juries might have done had the error complained of been avoided").

7. *Burden of proof.* Closely related to the jurisdiction's outcome-impact formulation is the allocation of the burden of proof in establishing that the error was harmless under that formulation. In *Kotteakos*, the Supreme Court rejected the idea of uniformly placing the burden of proof on either party. It noted that any presumptions of a prejudicial impact, shifting the burden to one side or the other, should "aris[e] from the nature of the error, and its 'natural effect' for or against prejudice in the particular setting." Other jurisdictions have taken the position that the burden naturally falls on the prosecution since the error favored the prosecution. See *Chapman v. California* [p. 1570] ("the original common law harmless-error rule put the burden on the beneficiary of the error either to prove that there was no injury or to suffer a reversal of his erroneously obtained judgment").

Chief Justice Traynor of the California Supreme Court suggested that the entire issue of presumptions and burdens was largely meaningless in the harmless error context. In evaluating what effect, if any, an error had on the jury's verdict, the appellate court may look only to the record before it. The function of a party carrying the burden is simply to suggest, in light of that record, how prejudice may or may not have occurred. At that point, the court makes its own assessment as to what degree of likelihood exists as to that prejudicial or nonprejudicial impact and then applies to that assessment the likelihood-standard of the particular jurisdiction. In *O'Neal v. McAninch,* 513 U.S. 432, 115 S.Ct. 992, 130 L.Ed.2d 947 (1995), a federal habeas case applying the *Kotteakos* standard, the majority quoted with approval Justice Traynor's comments on the burden of proof issue.

8. *Weight of the evidence.* Assuming a jurisdiction adopts *Kotteakos* or a similar standard of outcome-impact that looks to the error's effect-on-the-judgment, what weight, if any, should be given to the strength of the trial evidence pointing to guilt? Consider the various approaches discussed in CRIMPROC § 27.6(b):

"Several possibilities have been suggested [as to the "weight that should be assigned to overwhelming evidence of guilt in determining the impact of trial error"] * * * One approach that has not had a favorable reception in the courts is to look to the error almost in isolation. The critical question under this approach is whether the error is of a type likely to have influenced a reasonable juror. Where evidence was erroneously admitted, the court would focus on the extent to which that evidence was incriminating. Thus, evidence that improperly brought out a defendant's prior offense would be judged according to the damaging quality of that information. If the offense revealed was serious and roughly similar to that charged, the error clearly would not be harmless (in contrast, for example, to the revelation of an unrelated traffic offense). It would not matter that the other evidence overwhelmingly established guilt or even that another prior offense, similar in nature had been properly placed before the jury. Proponents of this approach argue that it affords protection against appellate court usurpation of the jury's function, precludes extensive reliance on the harmless error doctrine (and the resulting dilution of defendant's procedural rights), and serves to deter intentional misconduct by prosecutors who might otherwise rely on the strength of the evidence to shield their misconduct on appellate review. Appellate courts generally have not been receptive to these arguments, in part because they are viewed as imposing an artificial restriction on the task of assessing the impact of the error. As various courts have noted, one can hardly evaluate the impact of an error upon a jury decision without considering the totality of the case before the jury.

"Once it is agreed that the impact of an error must be measured in light of all of the evidence before the jury, it does not follow that an overwhelming prosecution case will inevitably render the error harmless. In *O'Neal v. McAninch* [Note 6 supra], * * * the Court described the appropriate inquiry as whether the error 'had substantial and injurious effect or influence in determining the jury's verdict,' not whether, despite the error, the jury reached the right result.[b] One

---

b. Chief Judge Harry Edwards of the D.C. Circuit, in his article *To Err is Human but Not Always Harmless: When Should Legal Error Be Tolerated*, 70 N.Y.U.L.Rev. 1165 (1995), characterized *O'Neal*, by virtue of this statement and others, as constituting the "crown jewel in the [Supreme Court] decisions moving away from [earlier decisions that seemingly promoted] guilt-based applications of the harmless-error doctrine." He questioned, however, whether *O'Neal* and similar decisions would be effective in leading appellate judges to reverse convictions where an error was so prejudicial as to obviously impact the fact finder, but the other evidence of guilt was strong. In a survey posing a hypothetical case he viewed as presenting such a situation, only 2 of 11 responding judges favored reversal. That response, he noted, tended to support his concern that, "since there is no way for a judge to consider the possible effect of an error on the verdict without also considering the entire record of evidence" and since it is "hard for a judge to discount a strong feeling that the defendant is guilty" where the record so indicates (especially with appellate judges hesitant

to add to the trial court's increasingly heavy caseload an additional trial that seems almost certain only to repeat the original result), the focus reflected in the earlier Supreme Court cases emphasizing guilt would be "difficult to reverse."

The earlier Supreme Court cases noted by Judge Edwards all involved the application of the *Chapman* harmless error standard for constitutional errors to trials in which a constitutional error was committed in putting before the jury a confession of the defendant or a codefendant. The opinions all took note of the *Chapman* "admonishment against giving too much emphasis to overwhelming evidence of guilt," but they also contained statements stressing the evidence of guilt. See e.g., *Harrington v. California*, 395 U.S. 250, 89 S.Ct. 1726, 23 L.Ed.2d 284 (1969) (noting that the case against the defendant "is so overwhelming that unless we say no violation of *Bruton* can constitute harmless error, we must leave the state conviction undisturbed"); *Schneble v. Florida*, 405 U.S. 427, 92 S.Ct. 1056, 31 L.Ed.2d 340 (1972) (speaking initially of the need to determine the "probable impact" of

method of measuring that impact, and ensuring that the weight of the state's evidence does not become determinative, is to match the potential element of prejudice against the state's evidence. For example, to render harmless the erroneous admission of potentially prejudicial evidence, it would have to be shown that the government had properly introduced other, more persuasive evidence on the same point. Most courts, however, view a requirement that the prosecution's evidence independently establish the same fact as the inadmissible evidence as unduly restrictive. Even without a 'perfect match,' strong prosecution evidence may indicate that a particular error was most unlikely to have contributed to the jury's verdict. For example, erroneously admitted evidence may have been the only evidence casting doubt upon defendant's reputation for honesty, but it may nevertheless have been inconsequential in light of strong eyewitness testimony clearly establishing that the defendant had committed the crime.

"Many courts apply what may be described as a comparative analysis of the likely impact of the error and the overwhelming evidence. The question to be answered, they note, is 'whether the properly admitted evidence of guilt is so overwhelming and the prejudicial effect of the error is so insignificant by comparison' that the court can say, with the requisite degree of certainty, that the error could not have contributed to the verdict. As for some types of error, such as the erroneous admission or exclusion of evidence, overwhelming evidence of guilt will ordinarily lead to the conclusion that the error was harmless. It would take evidence of an extraordinary quality to conclude that its erroneous admission or exclusion may have contributed to the verdict where the government had before the jury other evidence that would clearly and positively establish guilt."

B. HARMLESS CONSTITUTIONAL ERROR

Prior to the 1960s, it generally was assumed that constitutional violations could never be regarded as harmless error. Aside from one ambiguous ruling at the turn of the century, a Supreme Court finding of constitutional error had always resulted in a reversal of the defendant's conviction. Since the Court's opinion had never sought to analyze those reversals under a harmless error rule, both commentators and lower courts concluded that the rule simply did not apply to constitutional violations. Here, it was argued, prejudice was conclusively presumed, and a rule of "automatic reversal" prevailed. This assessment of the Court's unspoken premise probably was correct, as it seems likely that with all of the reversed convictions, both state and federal, at least one would have involved a constitutional error that would have been deemed inconsequential under a harmless error rule. However, at least for the Court, if not for the commentators, the due process revolution of the 1960s and its dramatic expansion of federal constitutional regulation of state procedures cast new light on the subject. Soon after *Mapp v. Ohio* held the Fourth Amendment's exclusionary rule applicable to the states, the Court had before it, in *Fahy v. Connecticut,* 375 U.S. 85, 84 S.Ct. 229, 11 L.Ed.2d 171 (1963), the question as to whether the erroneous admission of evidence obtained in violation of the Fourth Amendment could constitute harmless error. Four justices indicated that they would so hold, but the majority found it unnecessary to reach the question because the admission of the evidence in the case before it clearly had been "prejudicial." Four years later, the Supreme Court, in *Chapman v. California,* infra, first recognized a doctrine of harmless constitutional error.

the codefendant's confession "in the minds of an average jury," but then concluding that, in light of the strong evidence of guilt, it was certain that "the jury would not have found

the State's case significantly less persuasive had the testimony as to the [codefendant's] admission been excluded").

CHAPMAN v. CALIFORNIA

386 U.S. 18, 87 S.Ct. 824, 17 L.Ed.2d 705 (1967).

Justice BLACK delivered the opinion of the Court.

[The two petitioners were convicted of the robbery, kidnaping, and murder of a bartender, with one petitioner sentenced to life imprisonment and the other to death. At the time of the trial, California law allowed the prosecutor to comment on a defendant's failure to take the stand. Neither petitioner choose to testify, and "the state's attorney prosecuting them took full advantage of his right * * * to comment upon their failure to testify, filling his argument to the jury from beginning to end with numerous references to their silence and inferences of their guilt resulting therefrom." As allowed by California law, the trial judge also instructed the jury that it could draw adverse inferences from petitioners' failure to testify. Shortly after the trial, the Supreme Court decided *Griffin v. California,* p. 1413, holding unconstitutional both prosecutorial comment and adverse judicial instructions on a defendant's failure to testify. The California Supreme Court recognized that the comments and instructions upon petitioners' silence had violated the rule announced in *Griffin,* but held that here that constitutional error had been harmless, and affirmed under a state harmless-error provision that prohibited appellate reversal unless "the error complained of has resulted in a miscarriage of justice."]

* * * Before deciding the two questions here—whether there can ever be harmless constitutional error and whether the error here was harmless—we must first decide whether state or federal law governs. The application of a state harmless-error rule is, of course, a state question where it involves only errors of state procedure or state law. But the error from which these petitioners suffered was a denial of rights guaranteed against invasion by the Fifth and Fourteenth Amendments * * *. Whether a conviction for crime should stand when a State has failed to accord federal constitutionally guaranteed rights is every bit as much of a federal question as what particular federal constitutional provisions themselves mean, what they guarantee, and whether they have been denied. With faithfulness to the constitutional union of the States, we cannot leave to the States the formulation of the authoritative laws, rules, and remedies designed to protect people from infractions by the States of federally guaranteed rights. We have no hesitation in saying that the right of these petitioners not to be punished for exercising their Fifth and Fourteenth Amendment right to be silent—expressly created by the Federal Constitution itself—is a federal right which, in the absence of appropriate congressional action, it is our responsibility to protect by fashioning the necessary rule.

We are urged by petitioners to hold that all federal constitutional errors, regardless of the facts and circumstances, must always be deemed harmful. Such a holding, as petitioners correctly point out, would require an automatic reversal of their convictions and make further discussion unnecessary. We decline to adopt any such rule. All 50 States have harmless-error statutes or rules, and the United States long ago through its Congress established for its courts the rule that judgments shall not be reversed for "errors or defects which do not affect the substantial rights of the parties." 28 U.S.C. § 2111. None of these rules on its face distinguishes between federal constitutional errors and errors of state law or federal statutes and rules. All of these rules, state or federal, serve a very useful purpose insofar as they block setting aside convictions for small errors or defects that have little, if any, likelihood of having changed the result of the trial. We conclude that there may be some constitutional errors which in the setting of a particular case are so unimportant and insignificant that they may, consistent with the Federal Constitution, be deemed harmless, not requiring the automatic reversal of the conviction.

In fashioning a harmless-constitutional-error rule, we must recognize that harmless-error rules can work very unfair and mischievous results when, for example, highly important and persuasive evidence, or argument, though legally forbidden, finds its way into a trial in which the question of guilt or innocence is a close one. What harmless-error rules all aim at is a rule that will save the good in harmless-error practices while avoiding the bad, so far as possible.

The federal rule emphasizes "substantial rights" as do most others. The California constitutional rule emphasizes "a miscarriage of justice," but the California courts have neutralized this to some extent by emphasis, and perhaps overemphasis, upon the court's view of "overwhelming evidence."[7] We prefer the approach of this Court in deciding what was harmless error in our recent case of *Fahy v. Connecticut.* There we said: "The question is whether there is a reasonable possibility that the evidence complained of might have contributed to the conviction." Although our prior cases have indicated that there are some constitutional rights so basic to a fair trial that their infraction can never be treated as harmless error,[8] this statement in *Fahy* itself belies any belief that all trial errors which violate the Constitution automatically call for reversal. At the same time, however, like the federal harmless-error statute, it emphasizes an intention not to treat as harmless those constitutional errors that "affect substantial rights" of a party. An error in admitting plainly relevant evidence which possibly influenced the jury adversely to a litigant cannot, under *Fahy,* be conceived of as harmless. Certainly error, constitutional error, in illegally admitting highly prejudicial evidence or comments, casts on someone other than the person prejudiced by it a burden to show that it was harmless. It is for that reason that the original common-law harmless-error rule put the burden on the beneficiary of the error either to prove that there was no injury or to suffer a reversal of his erroneously obtained judgment. There is little, if any, difference between our statement in *Fahy v. Connecticut* about "whether there is a reasonable possibility that the evidence complained of might have contributed to the conviction" and requiring the beneficiary of a constitutional error to prove beyond a reasonable doubt that the error complained of did not contribute to the verdict obtained. We, therefore, do no more than adhere to the meaning of our *Fahy* case when we hold, as we now do, that before a federal constitutional error can be held harmless, the court must be able to declare a belief that it was harmless beyond a reasonable doubt. While appellate courts do not ordinarily have the original task of applying such a test, it is a familiar standard to all courts, and we believe its adoption will provide a more workable standard, although achieving the same result as that aimed at in our *Fahy* case.

Applying the foregoing standard, we have no doubt that the error in these cases was not harmless to petitioners. To reach this conclusion one need only glance at the prosecutorial comments compiled from the record by petitioners' counsel and (with minor omissions) set forth in the Appendix. The California Supreme Court fairly summarized * * * these comments as [stressing the defendants' failure to respond to broad range of evidence, including purchase of a weapon, the circumstances of the shooting, the use of a false registration at a

---

7. The California Supreme Court in this case did not find a "miscarriage of justice" as to petitioner Teale, because it found from "other substantial evidence, [that] the proof of his guilt must be deemed overwhelming."

8. See e.g., *Payne v. Arkansas,* 356 U.S. 560, 78 S.Ct. 844, 2 L.Ed.2d 975 (1958)

(coerced confession); *Gideon v. Wainwright,* 372 U.S. 335, 83 S. Ct. 792, 9 L.Ed. 2nd 799 (1963) (right to counsel); *Tumey v. Ohio,* 273 U.S. 510, 47 S.Ct. 437, 71 L.Ed. 749 (1927) (impartial judge).

motel shortly thereafter, the meaning of a letter written several days thereafter, the shipment of certain clothing to another state, and conflicting statements as to Mrs. Chapman's whereabouts.] * * *

[T]he state prosecutor's argument and the trial judge's instruction to the jury continuously and repeatedly impressed the jury that from the failure of petitioners to testify, to all intents and purposes, the inferences from the facts in evidence had to be drawn in favor of the State—in short, that by their silence petitioners had served as irrefutable witnesses against themselves. And though the case in which this occurred presented a reasonably strong "circumstantial web of evidence" against petitioners, 63 Cal.2d, at 197, it was also a case in which, absent the constitutionally forbidden comments, honest, fair-minded jurors might very well have brought in not-guilty verdicts. Under these circumstances, it is completely impossible for us to say that the State has demonstrated, beyond a reasonable doubt, that the prosecutor's comments and the trial judge's instruction did not contribute to petitioners' convictions. Such a machine-gun repetition of a denial of constitutional rights, designed and calculated to make petitioners' version of the evidence worthless, can no more be considered harmless than the introduction against a defendant of a coerced confession. See e.g., *Payne v. Arkansas* [fn. 8]. Petitioners are entitled to a trial free from the pressure of unconstitutional inferences.[a]

Notes and Questions

1. *The grounding of Chapman.* Commentators have found puzzling the Court's reference to the "absence of appropriate congressional action" in its description of its obligation to fashion a federal harmless error rule for constitutional violations. Does that reference necessarily indicate that Court did not view its reasonable doubt standard as constitutionally mandated? Justice Harlan suggested (see fn. a supra) that the *Chapman* majority was relying upon a "general supervisory power over the trial of federal constitutional issues." Others have described such authority as an aspect of "constitutional common law," reflecting the authority of the court to fashion remedies where Congress has not chosen to do so. See Daniel J. Meltzer, *Harmless Error and Constitutional Remedies*, 61 V.Chi.L.Rev. 1 (1994). Cf. *Bivens v. Six Unknown Named Agents*, 403 U.S. 388, 91 S.Ct. 1999, 29 L. Ed. 2nd 619 (1971) (Court-created tort remedy for violations of the Fourth Amendment by federal officers). Possible support for this characterization of the *Chapman* standard is found in *Brecht v. Abrahamson*, discussed at Pt. B, p. 1626, where the Court held that, on habeas review of constitutional claims, the *Kotteakos* standard, rather than the *Chapman* standard, would apply.

Can a constitutional grounding of the *Chapman* standard be squared with the Court's rejection of a constitutional right to appeal (see Note 1, p. 1534)? Consider, in this connection, the hypothetical posed by Meltzer, supra: "[S]uppose a state conferred on its appellate courts jurisdiction to reverse a criminal conviction only if the error probably affected the outcome—a standard far less protective of defendants than that of *Chapman*. Why would affirmance of a conviction under

a. The concurring opinion of Justice Stewart and dissenting opinion of Justice Harlan are omitted. Justice Stewart would have reserved harmless error analysis for only those constitutional requirements, such as the exclusionary rule, that involve a balancing of a deterrence objective against the exclusion of "relevant and reliable evidence." Justice Harlan argued that the application of a state harmless error rule was an independent ground barring Supreme Court review. He "regard[ed] the Court's assumption of what amounts to a general supervisory power over the trial of federal constitutional issues in state courts as a startling constitutional development that is wholly out of keeping with our federal system and completely unsupported by the Fourteenth Amendment."

that standard raise a federal question if the state might have provided no appeal whatsoever?"

If the constitution may require, as an interpretation of a particular right, that violations of that right require reversal of a conviction (see fn. 8), then why might it not also require as to other rights that violation requires reversal unless the right was clearly harmless? If so, might a constitutional grounding for *Chapman's* standard be found in an obligation of the states, once they provide for an appeal under state law, to apply in their appellate review the commands of the federal constitution? See Meltzer (questioning whether states may not limit their review to harmful errors, just as Congress has allowed the Supreme Court to limit its certiorari review, and arguing that, in any event, the state appellate court "applies the Constitution in finding that the conduct at trial was illegal, but that finding alone does not dictate reversal, for the appropriate remedy for any such violation is a separate question").

2. *Special treatment of constitutional errors.* Does Justice Black's opinion, by insisting upon a "reasonable doubt" standard, reflect "an underlying belief * * * that constitutional errors are inherently more harmful than others"? Stephen Saltzburg, *The Harm of Harmless Error*, 56 Va.L.Rev. 988 (1973). If so, in what sense are such errors "more harmful"? Consider Steven Goldberg, *Harmless Error: Constitutional Sneak Thief*, 71 J.Crim.Lit. Criminology 421 (1980) where the author finds "something disquieting about the admission that constitutional rights are so often abrogated that we need a separate doctrine to excuse some of them so that our decision making system will not break down."

3. *Intentional violations.* Justice Stewart noted in his *Chapman* concurrence that the violation of *Griffin* in *Chapman* did not constitute intentional misconduct as the trial there occurred before the *Griffin* decision. He noted that there was "no reason why the sanction of reversal should not be the result in future cases" should prosecutors "indulge in clear violations of *Griffin*." But compare *United States v. Hasting*, 461 U.S. 499, 103 S.Ct. 1974, 76 L.Ed.2d 96 (1983), holding that the Court of Appeals could not decline to apply the harmless error rule of *Chapman* and require automatic reversal as a means of disciplining prosecutors for continuing violations of *Griffin*. The federal courts' supervisory power could not be used to circumvent the balance struck by *Chapman* in fashioning a remedy for a constitutional violation.

4. *Automatic reversal errors.* In footnote 8, *Chapman* offered three illustrations of errors that "could never be treated as harmless error," but otherwise provided little guidance in identifying such "automatic reversal" errors. Without extensive discussion, the Court subsequently held that various other constitutional errors fell in the automatic reversal category. In *Arizona v. Fulminante*, 499 U.S. 279, 111 S.Ct. 1246, 113 L.Ed.2d 302 (1991), the Court overturned one of *Chapman's* illustrations, holding that admission of a coerced confession did not require automatic reversal, but was subject to *Chapman's* harmless error standard. The Court explained that automatic reversal was reserved for "structural defects in the constitution of the trial mechanism, which defy analysis by 'harmless error' standards," i.e., "defect[s] affecting the framework within which the trial proceeds, rather than simply an error in the trial process itself."[a] *Neder v. United States*, set forth below, presents the latest application of this standard.

---

a. The *Fulminante* description of structural errors produced some confusion and considerable commentator criticism. See e.g., Charles Ogletree Jr., *Arizona v. Fulminante: The Harm of Applying Harmless Error to Coerced Confessions*, 105 Harv.L.Rev. 152, 163 (1979): "If the essential distinction between 'trial' and 'struc-tural' errors lies in whether they are susceptible to being quantified and compared with other evidence, then the *Fulminante* majority was wrong to conclude that all errors that occur at trial are sometimes susceptible of measurement and that all those that pervade the trial 'from beginning to end' rarely are.

Although the Court has focused on "structural" errors in identifying constitutional errors requiring automatic reversal, it has also recognized two other types of error that are not subjected to *Chapman's* outcome-impact standard. First, the harmless error standard assumes that the constitutional error in question ordinarily permits a retrial and then asks whether retrial is unnecessary, and the conviction should stand, because the error lacked sufficient probability of impact upon the outcome of the case. Accordingly, harmless error analysis by its very nature does not apply to constitutional errors that require a remedy of barring reprosecution—e.g. double jeopardy and speedy trials violations.

Second, for some constitutional violations, in order to establish the violation, the defense must show a significantly probability that the error had an impact upon the outcome of the proceeding. That is often the case, for example, of due process violations, as illustrated by violations of the *Brady/Bagley* standard relating to the disclosure of exculpatory evidence (see Note 3, p. 1399) and the due process limit on improper prosecutorial argument to the jury (see *Darden*, p. 1420). The same is true of the Sixth Amendment *Strickland* standard as to ineffective assistance of counsel (see pp. 1124–25). Once a court has concluded that there exists the likelihood of prejudicial impact (typically a "reasonable probability") necessary to establish the constitutional violation, application of the *Chapman* standard would be a wasted effort because that finding establishes in itself that the error cannot be deemed harmless under *Chapman*. As the Court explained in *Kyles v. Whitley* (Note 3, p. 1399), "once a reviewing court applying *Bagley* has found constitutional error there is no need for further harmless error review."

5. *Formulation of the Chapman standard.* The *Chapman* standard is commonly stated as requiring that the appellate court be convinced "beyond a reasonable doubt that the error 'did not contribute' to the verdict." However, since the appellate court cannot know what actually did influence the jurors, and must assume the jurors acted rationally, courts also utilize the question posed by *Fahy* and quoted in *Chapman*: "Whether there is a reasonable possibility" that the constitutional error "might have contributed to the verdict."

6. *Application of the Chapman standard.* The Supreme Court has applied the *Chapman* standard in dozens of cases presenting a variety of errors. See CRIMPROC § 27.6(d), (e). While those cases reaffirmed that *Chapman* had rejected a "correct result" test, they also often took note of the weight of the evidence supporting guilt. Commentators have characterized the Court's consideration of that evidence across its various rulings as being uneven and inconsistent (although the overall approach arguably reflects what is described in Note 8, p. 1567, as a "comparative analysis" of the possible influence of error and strength of the evidence of guilt). See also fn. b, p. 1568. *Neder v. United States*, set forth

For instance, one can easily imagine a situation in which, but for a biased judge or lack of counsel (two types of violations that the Chief Justice classified as structural), there would still be considerable—or perhaps even overwhelming—evidence to support a conviction beyond a reasonable doubt. Of course, the review of a structural error seems even easier to imagine when the trial court grants, in violation of the right to public trial, a state's request to close a courtroom in order to conduct a motion to suppress evidence. The Court in *Waller v. Georgia* applied the automatic reversal rule under such circumstances."

Consider also Nancy King, *Postconviction Review of Jury Discrimination: Measuring the Effects of Jury Race on Jury Decisions,* 92 Mich.L.Rev. 63 (1993) (social science research counters the Court's contention in *Fulminante* that judges can never measure the effects of jury discrimination); David McCord, *The "Trial"/"Structural" Error Dichotomy: Erroneous, and Not Harmless,* 45 U.Kan.L. 1401 (1997) (ambiguities in *Fulminante* standards illustrated by a variety of errors that could be viewed as either structural or trial errors, including the improper shackling of defendant during trial, denial of defendant's presence at trial or sentencing, and several juror errors, such as misconduct where juror conducted his own investigation).

below, presents one of most recent illustrations of the Court's application of the *Chapman* standard.

NEDER v. UNITED STATES

527 U.S. 1, 119 S.Ct. 1827, 144 L.Ed.2d 35 (1999).

Chief Justice REHNQUIST delivered the opinion of the Court.

Petitioner was tried on charges of violating a number of federal criminal statutes penalizing fraud. It is agreed that the District Court erred in refusing to submit the issue of materiality to the jury with respect to those charges involving tax fraud. See *United States v. Gaudin*, 515 U.S. 506, 115 S.Ct. 2310, 132 L.Ed.2d 444 (1995). We hold that the harmless-error rule of *Chapman v. California*, 386 U.S. 18, 87 S.Ct. 824, 17 L.Ed.2d 705 (1967), applies to this error. * * *

[In connection with his participation in "a number of schemes involving land development fraud," defendant Neder was indicted on various counts of mail fraud and 2 counts of filing a false income tax return in violation of 26 U.S.C.A. § 7206(1).] The tax counts charged Neder with filing false statements of income on his tax returns. According to the Government, Neder failed to report more than $1 million in income for 1985 and more than $4 million in income for 1986, both amounts reflecting profits Neder obtained from the fraudulent real estate loans. * * * In accordance with then-extant Circuit precedent and over Neder's objection, the District Court instructed the jury that, to convict on the tax offenses, it "need not consider" the materiality of any false statements "even though that language is used in the indictment." The question of materiality, the court instructed, "is not a question for the jury to decide." * * * The jury convicted Neder of the fraud and tax offenses, and he was sentenced to 147 months' imprisonment, 5 years' supervised release, and $25 million in restitution.

The Court of Appeals for the Eleventh Circuit affirmed the conviction. It held that the District Court erred under our intervening decision in *United States v. Gaudin* [Note 6, p. 1319], in failing to submit the materiality element of the tax offense to the jury. It concluded, however, that the error was subject to harmless-error analysis and, further, that the error was harmless because "materiality was not in dispute," and thus the error " 'did not contribute to the verdict obtained,' " (quoting *Yates v. Evatt*, 500 U.S. 391, 111 S.Ct. 1884, 114 L.Ed.2d 432 (1991)).[a]
* * *

Rule 52(a) of the Federal Rules of Criminal Procedure, which governs direct appeals from judgments of conviction in the federal system, provides that "[a]ny error, defect, irregularity or variance which does not affect substantial rights shall be disregarded." Although this Rule by its terms applies to *all* errors where a proper objection is made at trial, we have recognized a limited class of fundamental constitutional errors that "defy analysis by 'harmless error' standards." *Arizona v. Fulminante*, 499 U.S. 279, 111 S.Ct. 1246, 113 L.Ed.2d 302 (1991).

---

a. The Court in *Yates* had noted, "To say that an error did not 'contribute' to the ensuing verdict is not, of course, to say that the jury was totally unaware of that feature of the trial later held to have been erroneous. When, for example, a trial court has instructed a jury to apply an unconstitutional presumption, a reviewing court can hardly infer that the jurors failed to consider it, a conclusion that would be factually untenable in most cases, and would run counter to a sound presumption of appellate practice, that jurors are reasonable and generally follow the instructions they are given

* * *. To say that an error did not contribute to the verdict is, rather, to find that error unimportant in relation to everything else the jury considered on the issue in question, as revealed in the record. Thus, to say that an instruction to apply an unconstitutional presumption did not contribute to the verdict is to make a judgment about the significance of the presumption to reasonable jurors, when measured against the other evidence considered by those jurors independently of the presumption."

Errors of this type are so intrinsically harmful as to require automatic reversal (*i.e.,* "affect substantial rights") without regard to their effect on the outcome. For all other constitutional errors, reviewing courts must apply Rule 52(a)'s harmless-error analysis and must "disregar[d]" errors that are harmless "beyond a reasonable doubt." * * *

We have recognized that "most constitutional errors can be harmless." *Fulminante.* "[I]f the defendant had counsel and was tried by an impartial adjudicator, there is a strong presumption that any other [constitutional] errors that may have occurred are subject to harmless-error analysis." *Rose v. Clark,* 478 U.S. 570, 106 S.Ct. 3101, 92 L.Ed.2d 460 (1986). Indeed, we have found an error to be "structural," and thus subject to automatic reversal, only in a "very limited class of cases." *Johnson v. United States,* 520 U.S. 461, 117 S.Ct. 1544, 137 L.Ed.2d 718 (1997) (citing *Gideon v. Wainwright,* 372 U.S. 335, 83 S.Ct. 792, 9 L.Ed.2d 799 (1963) (complete denial of counsel); *Tumey v. Ohio,* 273 U.S. 510, 47 S.Ct. 437, 71 L.Ed. 749 (1927) (biased trial judge); *Vasquez v. Hillery,* 474 U.S. 254, 106 S.Ct. 617, 88 L.Ed.2d 598 (1986) (racial discrimination in selection of grand jury); *McKaskle v. Wiggins,* 465 U.S. 168, 104 S.Ct. 944, 79 L.Ed.2d 122 (1984) (denial of self-representation at trial); *Waller v. Georgia,* 467 U.S. 39, 104 S.Ct. 2210, 81 L.Ed.2d 31 (1984) (denial of public trial); *Sullivan v. Louisiana,* 508 U.S. 275, 113 S.Ct. 2078, 124 L.Ed.2d 182 (1993) (defective reasonable-doubt instruction)).[b]

The error at issue here—a jury instruction that omits an element of the offense—differs markedly from the constitutional violations we have found to defy harmless-error review. Those cases, we have explained, contain a "defect affecting the framework within which the trial proceeds, rather than simply an error in the trial process itself." *Fulminante.* Such errors "infect the entire trial process," *Brecht v. Abrahamson,* 507 U.S. 619, 113 S.Ct. 1710, 123 L.Ed.2d 353 (1993), and "necessarily render a trial fundamentally unfair," *Rose.* Put another way, these errors deprive defendants of "basic protections" without which "a criminal trial cannot reliably serve its function as a vehicle for determination of guilt or innocence ... and no criminal punishment may be regarded as fundamentally fair." *Id.*

Unlike such defects as the complete deprivation of counsel or trial before a biased judge, an instruction that omits an element of the offense does not *necessarily* render a criminal trial fundamentally unfair or an unreliable vehicle for determining guilt or innocence. * * * We have often applied harmless-error analysis to cases involving improper instructions on a single element of the offense. See, *e.g., Yates v. Evatt,* 500 U.S. 391, 111 S.Ct. 1884, 114 L.Ed.2d 432 (1991) (mandatory rebuttable presumption); *Carella v. California,* 491 U.S. 263, 109 S.Ct. 2419, 105 L.Ed.2d 218 (1989) *(per curiam)* (mandatory conclusive presumption); *Pope v. Illinois,* 481 U.S. 497, 107 S.Ct. 1918, 95 L.Ed.2d 439 (1987) (misstatement of element); *Rose, supra* (mandatory rebuttable presumption). In other cases, we have recognized that improperly omitting an element from the

---

b. Other errors held to be subject to automatic reversal are listed in CRIMPROC § 27.6(d). These include: discrimination in the selection of the petit jury, *Batson v. Kentucky,* p. 1334; the improper exclusion of a juror based on his views of capital punishment, *Gray v. Mississippi,* 481 U.S. 648, 107 S.Ct. 2045, 95 L.Ed.2d 622 (1987); the violation of the *Anders* standards governing the withdrawal of appointed counsel, *Penson v. Ohio,* fn. a, p. 1174 (noting that to apply harmless error, which would require the appellate court to evaluate

the merits of the defendant's arguable claim, would "render meaningless" the protections afforded by *Anders);* the denial of consultation with counsel during an overnight recess, *Geders v. United States,* fn. a, p. 1121; and the failure to make an appropriate inquiry into a possible conflict of interest under those special circumstances that constitutionally mandate such an inquiry, *Holloway v. Arkansas,* p. 1152. See also Note 2, p. 1155, as to representation by counsel acting under an actual conflict of interest.

jury can "easily be analogized to improperly instructing the jury on an element of the offense, an error which is subject to harmless-error analysis." *Johnson.* * * * In both cases—misdescriptions and omissions—the erroneous instruction precludes the jury from making a finding on the *actual* element of the offense. The same, we think, can be said of conclusive presumptions, which direct the jury to presume an *ultimate* element of the offense based on proof of certain *predicate* facts (*e.g.,* "You must presume malice if you find an intentional killing"). Like an omission, a conclusive presumption deters the jury from considering any evidence other than that related to the predicate facts (*e.g.,* an intentional killing) and "directly foreclose[s] independent jury consideration of whether the facts proved established certain elements of the offens[e]" (*e.g.,* malice). *Carella* (Scalia, J., concurring in judgment).

The conclusion that the omission of an element is subject to harmless-error analysis is consistent with the holding (if not the entire reasoning) of *Sullivan v. Louisiana,* the case upon which Neder principally relies. In *Sullivan,* the trial court gave the jury a defective "reasonable doubt" instruction in violation of the defendant's Fifth and Sixth Amendment rights to have the charged offense proved beyond a reasonable doubt. Applying our traditional mode of analysis, the Court concluded that the error was not subject to harmless-error analysis because it "vitiates *all* the jury's findings," and produces "consequences that are necessarily unquantifiable and indeterminate." By contrast, the jury-instruction error here did not "vitiat[e] *all* the jury's findings." It did, of course, prevent the jury from making a finding on the element of materiality.

Neder argues that *Sullivan's* alternative reasoning precludes the application of harmless error here. Under that reasoning, harmless-error analysis cannot be applied to a constitutional error that precludes the jury from rendering a verdict of guilty-beyond-a-reasonable-doubt because "the entire premise of *Chapman* review is simply absent." *Sullivan.* In the absence of an *actual* verdict of guilty-beyond-a-reasonable-doubt, the Court explained: "[T]he question whether the *same* verdict of guilty-beyond-a-reasonable-doubt would have been rendered absent the constitutional error is utterly meaningless. There is no *object,* so to speak, upon which the harmless-error scrutiny can operate." *Id.;* see *Carella* (Scalia, J., concurring in judgment). Neder argues that this analysis applies with equal force where the constitutional error, as here, prevents the jury from rendering a "complete verdict" on *every* element of the offense. As in *Sullivan,* Neder argues, the basis for harmless-error review " 'is simply absent.' "

Although this strand of the reasoning in *Sullivan* does provide support for Neder's position, it cannot be squared with our harmless-error cases. In *Pope,* for example, the trial court erroneously instructed the jury that it could find the defendant guilty in an obscenity prosecution if it found that the allegedly obscene material lacked serious value under "community standards," rather than the correct "reasonable person" standard required by the First Amendment. Because the jury was not properly instructed, and consequently did not render a finding, on the *actual* element of the offense, the defendant's trial did not result in a "complete verdict" any more than in this case. Yet we held there that harmless-error analysis was appropriate.

Similarly, in *Carella,* the jury was instructed to presume that the defendant "embezzled [a] vehicle" and "[i]nten[ded] to commit theft" if the jury found that the defendant failed to return a rental car within a certain number of days after the expiration of the rental period. Again, the jury's finding of guilt cannot be seen as a "complete verdict" because the conclusive presumption "directly foreclosed independent jury consideration of whether the facts proved established certain elements of the offenses." As in *Pope,* however, we held that the unconstitutional conclusive presumption was "subject to the harmless-error rule." * * *

And in *Roy,* a federal habeas case involving a state-court murder conviction, the trial court erroneously failed to instruct the jury that it could convict the defendant as an aider and abettor only if it found that the defendant had the "intent or purpose" of aiding the confederate's crime. Despite that omission, we held that "[t]he case before us is a case for application of the 'harmless error' standard."

The Government argues, correctly we think, that the absence of a "complete verdict" on every element of the offense establishes no more than that an improper instruction on an element of the offense violates the Sixth Amendment's jury trial guarantee. The issue here, however, is not whether a jury instruction that omits an element of the offense was error (a point that is uncontested), but whether the error is subject to harmless-error analysis. We think our decisions in *Pope, Carella,* and *Roy* dictate the answer to that question.

Forced to accept that this Court has applied harmless-error review in cases where the jury did not render a "complete verdict" on every element of the offense, Neder attempts to reconcile our cases by offering an approach gleaned from a plurality opinion in *Connecticut v. Johnson,* 460 U.S. 73, 103 S.Ct. 969, 74 L.Ed.2d 823 (1983), an opinion concurring in the judgment in *Carella, supra,* and language in *Sullivan, supra.* Under this restrictive approach, an instructional omission, misdescription, or conclusive presumption can be subject to harmless-error analysis only in three "rare situations": (1) where the defendant is acquitted of the offense on which the jury was improperly instructed (and, despite the defendant's argument that the instruction affected another count, the improper instruction had no bearing on it); (2) where the defendant admitted the element on which the jury was improperly instructed; and (3) where other facts necessarily found by the jury are the "functional equivalent" of the omitted, misdescribed, or presumed element. Neder understandably contends that *Pope, Carella,* and *Roy* fall within this last exception, which explains why the Court in those cases held that the instructional error could be harmless.

We believe this approach is mistaken for more than one reason. As an initial matter, we are by no means certain that the cases just mentioned meet the "functional equivalence" test as Neder at times articulates it. * * * [Secondly,] petitioner's submission * * * imports into the initial structural-error determination (*i.e.,* whether an error is structural) a case-by-case approach that is more consistent with our traditional harmless-error inquiry (*i.e.,* whether an error is harmless). Under our cases, a constitutional error is either structural or it is not. Thus, even if we were inclined to follow a broader "functional equivalence" test *e.g.,* where other facts found by the jury are "so closely related" to the omitted element "that no rational jury could find those facts without also finding" the omitted element, *Sullivan,* such a test would be inconsistent with our traditional categorical approach to structural errors.

We also note that the present case arose in the legal equivalent of a laboratory test tube. The trial court, following existing law, ruled that the question of materiality was for the court, not the jury. It therefore refused a charge on the question of materiality. But future cases are not likely to be so clear cut. In *Roy,* we said that the error in question could be "as easily characterized as a 'misdescription of an element' of the crime, as it is characterized as an error of 'omission.' " As petitioner concedes, his submission would thus call into question the far more common subcategory of misdescriptions. And it would require a reviewing court in each case to determine just how serious a "misdescription" it was. * * * Difficult as such issues would be when dealing with the ample volume defining federal crimes, they would be measurably compounded by the necessity for federal courts, reviewing state convictions under 28 U.S.C. § 2254, to ascertain the elements of the offense as defined in the laws of 50 different States.

It would not be illogical to extend the reasoning of *Sullivan* from a defective "reasonable doubt" instruction to a failure to instruct on an element of the crime. But, as indicated in the foregoing discussion, the matter is not *res nova* under our case law. And if the life of the law has not been logic but experience, see O. Holmes, The Common Law 1 (1881), we are entitled to stand back and see what would be accomplished by such an extension in this case. The omitted element was materiality. Petitioner underreported $5 million on his tax returns, and did not contest the element of materiality at trial. Petitioner does not suggest that he would introduce any evidence bearing upon the issue of materiality if so allowed. Reversal without any consideration of the effect of the error upon the verdict would send the case back for retrial—a retrial not focused at all on the issue of materiality, but on contested issues on which the jury was properly instructed. We do not think the Sixth Amendment requires us to veer away from settled precedent to reach such a result. * * *

Having concluded that the omission of an element is an error that is subject to harmless-error analysis, the question remains whether Neder's conviction can stand because the error was harmless. In *Chapman v. California,* we set forth the test for determining whether a constitutional error is harmless. That test, we said, is whether it appears "beyond a reasonable doubt that the error complained of did not contribute to the verdict obtained." * * *

To obtain a conviction on the tax offense at issue, the Government must prove that the defendant filed a tax return "which he does not believe to be true and correct as to every material matter." 26 U.S.C. § 7206(1). In general, a false statement is material if it has "a natural tendency to influence, or [is] capable of influencing, the decision of the decisionmaking body to which it was addressed." *United States v. Gaudin.* In a prosecution under § 7206(1), several courts have determined that "any failure to report income is material." Under either of these formulations, no jury could reasonably find that Neder's failure to report substantial amounts of income on his tax returns was not "a material matter."

At trial, the Government introduced evidence that Neder failed to report over $5 million in income from the loans he obtained. The failure to report such substantial income incontrovertibly establishes that Neder's false statements were material to a determination of his income tax liability. The evidence supporting materiality was so overwhelming, in fact, that Neder did not argue to the jury—and does not argue here—that his false statements of income could be found immaterial. Instead, he defended against the tax charges by arguing that the loan proceeds were not income because he intended to repay the loans, and that he reasonably believed, based on the advice of his accountant and lawyer, that he need not report the proceeds as income. In this situation, where a reviewing court concludes beyond a reasonable doubt that the omitted element was uncontested and supported by overwhelming evidence, such that the jury verdict would have been the same absent the error, the erroneous instruction is properly found to be harmless. We think it beyond cavil here that the error "did not contribute to the verdict obtained." *Chapman.*

Neder disputes our conclusion that the error in this case was harmless. Relying on language in our *Sullivan* and *Yates* decisions, he argues that a finding of harmless error may be made only upon a determination that the jury rested its verdict on evidence that its instructions allowed it to consider. To rely on overwhelming record evidence of guilt the jury did not *actually* consider, he contends, would be to dispense with trial by jury and allow judges to direct a guilty verdict on an element of the offense.[2] * * * But at bottom this is simply

---

2. Justice Scalia, in his opinion * * *, also suggests that if a failure to charge on an un-

contested element of the offense may be harmless error, the next step will be to allow a

another form of the argument that a failure to instruct on any element of the crime is not subject to harmless-error analysis. * * *

We think, therefore, that the harmless-error inquiry must be essentially * * * [this]: Is it clear beyond a reasonable doubt that a rational jury would have found the defendant guilty absent the error? * * * We believe that where an omitted element is supported by uncontroverted evidence, this approach reaches an appropriate balance between "society's interest in punishing the guilty [and] the method by which decisions of guilt are to be made." *Connecticut v. Johnson.* * * * In a case such as this one, where a defendant did not, and apparently could not, bring forth facts contesting the omitted element, answering the question whether the jury verdict would have been the same absent the error does not fundamentally undermine the purposes of the jury trial guarantee. * * * Of course, safeguarding the jury guarantee will often require that a reviewing court conduct a thorough examination of the record. If, at the end of that examination, the court cannot conclude beyond a reasonable doubt that the jury verdict would have been the same absent the error—for example, where the defendant contested the omitted element and raised evidence sufficient to support a contrary finding—it should not find the error harmless.

A reviewing court making this harmless-error inquiry does not, as Justice Traynor put it, "become in effect a second jury to determine whether the defendant is guilty." R. Traynor, *The Riddle of Harmless Error* 21 (1970). Rather a court, in typical appellate-court fashion, asks whether the record contains evidence that could rationally lead to a contrary finding with respect to the omitted element. If the answer to that question is "no," holding the error harmless does not "reflec[t] a denigration of the constitutional rights involved." *Rose.* On the contrary, it "serve[s] a very useful purpose insofar as [it] block[s] setting aside convictions for small errors or defects that have little, if any, likelihood of having changed the result of the trial." *Chapman.* We thus hold that the District Court's failure to submit the element of materiality to the jury with respect to the tax charges was harmless error. * * *

Justice SCALIA, with whom Justice SOUTER and Justice GINSBURG join, concurring in part and dissenting in part.

* * * I dissent from the judgment of the Court, because I believe that depriving a criminal defendant of the right to have the jury determine his guilt of the crime charged—which necessarily means his commission of *every element* of the crime charged—can never be harmless. * * * The right to be tried by a jury in criminal cases obviously means the right to have a jury determine whether the defendant has been proved guilty of the crime charged. And since all crimes require proof of more than one element to establish guilt (involuntary manslaughter, for example, requires (1) the killing (2) of a human being (3) negligently), it follows that trial by jury means determination by a jury that *all elements* were proved. The Court does not contest this. It acknowledges that the right to trial by jury was denied in the present case, since one of the elements was not—despite the defendant's protestation—submitted to be passed upon by the jury. But even so, the Court lets the defendant's sentence stand, *because we judges can tell that he is unquestionably guilty.*

Even if we allowed (as we do not) other structural errors in criminal trials to be pronounced "harmless" by judges—a point I shall address in due course—it is obvious that we could not allow judges to validate *this* one. The constitutionally

directed verdict against a defendant in a criminal case contrary to *Rose v. Clark.* Happily, our course of constitutional adjudication has not been characterized by this "in for a penny, in for a pound" approach. We have no hesitation reaffirming *Rose* at the same time that we subject the narrow class of cases like the present one to harmless-error review.

required step that was omitted here is distinctive, in that the basis for it is precisely that, absent voluntary waiver of the jury right, *the Constitution does not trust judges to make determinations of criminal guilt.* Perhaps the Court is so enamored of judges in general, and federal judges in particular, that it forgets that they (we) are officers of the Government, and hence proper objects of that healthy suspicion of the power of government which possessed the Framers and is embodied in the Constitution. Who knows?—20 years of appointments of federal judges by oppressive administrations might produce judges willing to enforce oppressive criminal laws, and to interpret criminal laws oppressively—at least in the view of the citizens in some vicinages where criminal prosecutions must be brought. And so the people reserved the function of determining criminal guilt *to themselves,* sitting as jurors. It is not within the power of us Justices to cancel that reservation—neither by permitting trial judges to determine the guilt of a defendant who has not waived the jury right, nor (when a trial judge has done so anyway) by reviewing the facts ourselves and pronouncing the defendant without-a-doubt guilty. The Court's decision today is the only instance I know of (or could conceive of) in which the remedy for a constitutional violation by a trial judge (making the determination of criminal guilt reserved to the jury) is a repetition of the same constitutional violation by the appellate court (making the determination of criminal guilt reserved to the jury).

The Court's decision would be wrong even if we ignored the distinctive character of this constitutional violation. The Court reaffirms the rule that it would be structural error (not susceptible of "harmless-error" analysis) to " 'viti-at[e] *all* the jury's findings.' " * * * The question that this raises is why, if denying the right to conviction by jury is structural error, taking *one* of the elements of the crime away from the jury should be treated differently from taking *all* of them away—since failure to prove one, no less than failure to prove all, utterly prevents conviction.

The Court never asks, much less answers, this question. Indeed, we do not know, when the Court's opinion is done, *how many* elements can be taken away from the jury with impunity, so long as appellate judges are persuaded that the defendant is surely guilty. What if, in the present case, besides keeping the materiality issue for itself, the District Court had also refused to instruct the jury to decide whether the defendant signed his tax return? If Neder had never contested that element of the offense, and the record contained a copy of his signed return, would his conviction be automatically reversed in that situation but not in this one, even though he would be just as obviously guilty? We do not know. We know that all elements cannot be taken from the jury, and that one can. How many is too many (or perhaps what proportion is too high) remains to be determined by future improvisation. All we know for certain is that the number is somewhere between tuppence and 19 shillings 11, since the Court's only response to my assertion that there is no principled distinction between this case and a directed verdict is that "our course of constitutional adjudication has not been characterized by this 'in for a penny, in for a pound' approach." See majority at n. 2.

The underlying theme of the Court's opinion is that taking the element of materiality from the jury did not render Neder's trial unfair, because the judge certainly reached the "right" result. But the same could be said of a directed verdict against the defendant—which would be *per se* reversible *no matter how overwhelming the unfavorable evidence.* See *Rose.* The very premise of structural-error review is that even convictions reflecting the "right" result are reversed for the sake of protecting a basic right. For example, in *Tumey v. Ohio,* 273 U.S. 510, 47 S.Ct. 437, 71 L.Ed. 749 (1927), where we reversed the defendant's conviction because he had been tried before a biased judge, the State argued that "the evidence shows clearly that the defendant was guilty and that he was only fined $100, which was the minimum amount, and therefore that he can not complain of a lack of due process, either in his conviction or in the amount of the judgment." We rejected this argument out of hand, responding that *"[n]o matter what the evidence was against him,* he had the right to have an impartial judge." Ibid. (emphasis added). The amount of evidence against a defendant who has properly preserved his objection, while relevant to determining whether a given error was harmless, has nothing to do with determining whether the error is subject to harmless-error review in the first place. * * *

Insofar as it applies to the jury-trial requirement, the structural-error rule does not exclude harmless-error analysis—though it is harmless-error analysis of a peculiar sort, looking not to whether the jury's verdict would have been the *same* without the error, but rather to whether the error did not *prevent* the jury's verdict. The failure of the court to instruct the jury properly—whether by omitting an element of the offense or by so misdescribing it that it is effectively removed from the jury's consideration—*can* be harmless, if the elements of guilt that the jury *did* find necessarily embraced the one omitted or misdescribed. This was clearly spelled out by our unanimous opinion in *Sullivan v. Louisiana,* which said that harmless-error review "looks ... to the basis on which 'the jury *actually rested* its verdict.'" Where the facts *necessarily found* by the jury (and not those merely discerned by the appellate court) support the existence of the element omitted or misdescribed in the instruction, the omission or misdescription is harmless. For there is then no "gap" *in the verdict* to be filled by the factfinding of judges. This formulation adequately explains the three cases, see *California v. Roy* (Scalia, J., concurring); *Carella v. California* (Scalia, J., concurring in judgment); *Pope v. Illinois* (Scalia, J., concurring), that the majority views as "dictat[ing] the answer" to the question before us today.[c] In casting *Sullivan* aside, the majority does more than merely return to the state of confusion that existed in our prior cases; it throws open the gate for appellate courts to trample over the jury's function.

Asserting that "[u]nder our cases, a constitutional error is either structural or it is not," the Court criticizes the *Sullivan* test for importing a "case-by-case approach" into the structural-error determination. If that were true, it would seem a small price to pay for keeping the appellate function consistent with the Sixth Amendment. But in fact the Court overstates the cut-and-dried nature of identifying structural error. Some structural errors, like the complete absence of counsel or the denial of a public trial, are visible at first glance. Others, like deciding whether the trial judge was biased or whether there was racial discrimination in the grand jury selection, require a more fact-intensive inquiry. Deciding whether the jury made a finding "functionally equivalent" to the omitted or misdescribed element is similar to structural-error analysis of the latter sort. * * * The difference between speculation directed toward *confirming* the jury's verdict *(Sullivan)* and speculation directed toward *making a judgment that the jury has never made* (today's decision) is more than semantic. Consider, for example, the following scenarios. If I order for my wife in a restaurant, there is no sense in which the decision is hers, even if I am sure beyond a reasonable doubt about what she would have ordered. If, however, while she is away from the table, I advise the waiter to stay with an order she initially made, even though he informs me that there has been a change in the accompanying dish, one can still say that my wife placed the order—even if I am wrong about whether she would have changed her mind in light of the new information. Of course, I may predict

---

c. Justice Scalia wrote separately in each of these cases, advancing the explanation of the harmless-error findings set forth above. He also wrote the opinion for the Court in *Sullivan.*

correctly in both instances simply because I know my wife well. I doubt, however, that a low error rate would persuade my wife that my making a practice of the first was a good idea.

It is this sort of allocation of decisionmaking power that the *Sullivan* standard protects. The right to render the verdict in criminal prosecutions belongs exclusively to the jury; reviewing it belongs to the appellate court. "Confirming" speculation does not disturb that allocation, but "substituting" speculation does. Make no mistake about the shift in standard: Whereas *Sullivan* confined appellate courts to their proper role of reviewing *verdicts,* the Court today puts appellate courts in the business of reviewing the defendant's *guilt.* The Court does not—it *cannot*—reconcile this new approach with the proposition that denial of the jury-trial right is structural error. * * * ^d

Notes and Questions

1. *The character of automatic reversal errors.* In *Rose v. Clark,* 478 U.S. 570, 106 S.Ct. 3101, 92 L.Ed.2d 460 (1986), Justice Stevens, concurring in the judgment, argued that the Court took too narrow a perspective in identifying "automatic reversal errors." He noted: "As the Court recognizes, harmless error inquiry remains inappropriate for certain constitutional violations no matter how strong the evidence of guilt may be. The Court suggests that the inapplicability of harmless error to these violations rests on concerns about reliability and accuracy, and that such concerns are the only relevant consideration in determining the applicability of harmless error. In fact, however, violations of certain constitutional rights are not, and should not be, subject to harmless error analysis because those rights protect important values that are unrelated to the truth-seeking function of the trial. Thus, racial discrimination in the selection of grand juries is intolerable even if the defendant's guilt is subsequently established in a fair trial. *Vasquez v. Hillery* [Note 8, p. 947]. Racial discrimination in the selection of a petit jury may require a new trial without any inquiry into the actual impact of the forbidden practice. *Batson v. Kentucky* [p. 1334]. See also *Turner v. Murray* [fn. d, p. 1333] ('the inadequacy of *voir dire* [about the possibility of racial prejudice] in this case requires that petitioner's death sentence be vacated'). * * * In short, as the Court has recently emphasized, our Constitution, and our criminal justice system, protect other values besides the reliability of the guilt or innocence determination. A coherent harmless error jurisprudence should similarly respect those values."

Dissenting in *Arizona v. Fulminante,* 499 U.S. 279, 111 S.Ct. 1246, 113 L.Ed.2d 302 (1991), Justice White (joined by Justices Marshall, Blackmun, and Stevens) took a similar position in arguing that the trial court's admission of a coerced confession should call for automatic reversal. He reasoned: "A defendant's confession is 'probably the most probative and damaging evidence that can be admitted against him,' so damaging that a jury should not be expected to ignore it even if told to do so, and because in any event it is impossible to know what credit and weight the jury gave to the confession. Concededly, this reason is insufficient

---

d. Justice Stevens concurring opinion is omitted. Justice Stevens argued that the error here was harmless because the jury had necessarily found materiality in concluding that the taxpayer had falsely reported his total income—an analysis rejected by both the majority and the dissent. Justice Stevens characterized the Court's opinion as holding that "judges may find elements of an offense satisfied whenever the defendant failed to contest the element or raise evidence sufficient to support a contrary finding," and noted his "views on this central issue are * * * close to those expressed by Justice Scalia." He argued, however, that Justice Scalia did not go sufficiently far in protecting the jury's role, as Justice Scalia had concluded that reversal would not be required where defense counsel had failed to make a timely objection. (See fn. c, p. 1575).

to justify a *per se* bar to the use of any confession. Thus, *Milton v. Wainwright,* applied harmless-error analysis to a confession obtained and introduced in circumstances that violated the defendant's Sixth Amendment right to counsel. Similarly, the Court of Appeals have held that the introduction of incriminating statements taken from defendants in violation of *Miranda v. Arizona,* is subject to treatment as harmless error. Nevertheless, in declaring that it is 'impossible to create a meaningful distinction between confessions elicited in violation of the Sixth Amendment and those in violation of the Fourteenth Amendment,' the majority overlooks [relevant distinctions.] * * * First, some coerced confessions may be untrustworthy. Consequently, admission of coerced confessions may distort the truth-seeking function of the trial upon which the majority focuses. More importantly, however, the use of coerced confessions, 'whether true or false,' is forbidden 'because the methods used to extract them offend an underlying principle in the enforcement of our criminal law: that ours is an accusatorial and not an inquisitorial system—a system in which the State must establish guilt by evidence independently and freely secured and may not by coercion prove its charge against an accused out of his own mouth.' * * * Thus, permitting a coerced confession to be part of the evidence on which a jury is free to base its verdict of guilty is inconsistent with the thesis that ours is not an inquisitorial system of criminal justice."[a]

   2. *Applying harmless error.* See William M. Landes and Richard A. Posner, *Harmless Error*, 30 J.Legal Stud. 161 (2001): "This paper presents an economic model of the harmful error rule in criminal appeals. We test the implications of the model against legal doctrines governing reversible and nonreversible error of criminal convictions and on a sample of more than 1,000 criminal defendants who appealed their convictions in the U.S. courts of appeals between 1996 and 1998. Among the more important theoretical and empirical findings of the paper are the following. Intentional prosecutor and judge errors are more likely to be found harmful and lead the appellate court to reverse the defendant's conviction than are inadvertent errors. Prosecutor errors are more likely to be forgiven than judge errors, in part because judge errors are likely to have greater influence on jurors. Errors are less likely to be harmful when defendants face a higher error-free probability of conviction. Finally, appellate courts are more likely to publish an opinion when they are reversing the lower court."

a. See also Tom Stacy and Kim Dayton, *Rethinking Harmless Constitutional Error,* 88 Column.L.Rev. 79 (1988) (*Chapman's* "outcome-oriented harmless error rule" looks only to the "reliability" of the result below, which ignores "constitutional rights [that] serve other interests that are either truth impairing (as with the privacy interest protected under the Fourth Amendment) or truth neutral (as with race neutrality in grand jury selection)"). Stacy and Dayton argue that, where the constitutional right is based on values that stand apart from promoting accuracy, the Court should consider whether the harm to that interest can be "cured" by "redoing the process." That will not be the case for all non-truth-furthering rights (e.g., exclusion of the illegally seized evidence at a new trial would not restore the privacy lost through the Fourth Amendment violation), although it will be as to others (e.g., a retrial with defendant proceeding pro se will restore the "therapeutic or dignitary function" underlying the right of self-representation). In the latter situation, the authors argue, a redoing of the process should be required even though the error might otherwise be deemed harmless under a *Chapman* standard. In the former, application of the *Chapman* standard should be dependent upon the need for automatic reversal to deter future violations. That would be the case, the authors argue, where the violation is of a type likely to escape detection, but where "virtually all violations will be detected in the trial process, the "relatively mild deterrence flowing from the *Chapman* rule" should be sufficient.

Chapter 29

POSTCONVICTION REVIEW: FEDERAL HABEAS CORPUS[a]

INTRODUCTION

A state prisoner who has completed his direct appeal typically has two additional routes to attack his conviction. First, he may return to the state's courts, seeking whatever "postconviction" remedies[b] are provided under state law. If unsuccessful in state court a state prisoner may then seek relief in federal court, through the writ of habeas corpus. This federal statutory remedy is the focus of this chapter. Federal habeas corpus is the only postconviction remedy available in every state to persons held in custody. Moreover, the decisions interpreting the federal habeas remedy continue to influence the scope and application of other postconviction remedies in state and federal courts.[c]

SECTION 1. THE BASIC STRUCTURE OF FEDERAL HABEAS CORPUS RELIEF[d]

1. Common law origins. Federal habeas corpus, now a statutory remedy, is descended from its common law ancestor. The common law writ of habeas corpus was a judicial order directing a jailor to bring a prisoner into court. Indeed, its title says in Latin that the court would "have the body." By the mid-fourteenth century, the writ had come to be used as an independent proceeding to challenge illegal detention. Subsequently, the "Great Writ" was viewed as the primary procedural safeguard for the guarantees of the Magna Charta, which prohibited

a. Treatises devoted solely to this subject include: Larry W. Yackle, Postconviction Remedies (1981 & Supp.1997) (hereinafter cited as Yackle); Donald E. Wilkes, Federal and State Postconviction Remedies and Relief (1983) (hereinafter cited as Wilkes; James S. Liebman & Randy Hertz, Federal Habeas Corpus Practice and Procedure (3d ed.1999) (hereinafter cited as Liebman & Hertz). Comprehensive treatment also may be found in volume 6 of Wayne R. LaFave, Jerold H. Israel & Nancy J. King, Criminal Procedure Treatise (2d ed.1999 & Supp.) (available on WESTLAW at database name CRIMPROC, hereinafter cited as CRIMPROC).

b. Such procedures are also described as "collateral" remedies because some, including the writ of habeas corpus, involve a proceeding that is not a continuation of the original criminal case, but is instead a separate civil action filed in the court that has jurisdiction over the official who holds the prisoner (e.g., the prison warden).

c. The primary collateral remedy for federal prisoners is an application in the court of conviction for relief under 28 U.S.C.A. § 2255, adopted by Congress in 1948. Relief under § 2255 is governed by many of the same rules that apply in habeas corpus proceedings for state prisoners. CRIMPROC § 28.9.

d. The literature on federal habeas is immense. Illustratively, for the period of 1990–1993, just under one hundred law review articles devoted to some aspect of the federal habeas remedy were published. No attempt is made here to review that literature. A good part of it is cited and discussed in the treatises cited supra note a. Because of space limitations, the sections that follow deal basically with Supreme Court precedent only.

the deprivation of liberty without adherence to established judicial procedures. By the late eighteenth century, the writ had been extended, both in English and colonial law, to persons challenging custody imposed pursuant to a judgment of criminal conviction. It was available, however, only to persons who were incarcerated,[e] and it required a showing that the court of conviction lacked jurisdiction to impose judgment.

2.   *Constitutional recognition.* In a provision known as the "Suspension Clause," Article I of the Constitution states: "[T]he privilege of the Writ of Habeas Corpus shall not be suspended, unless when in Cases of Rebellion or Invasion the Public Safety may require it." Exactly what is protected by the Clause remains unsettled. Early opinions suggested that the Clause protects only the narrow common-law remedy for federal prisoners described in Note 1, above. Nonetheless, many have suggested that the subsequent extension of habeas relief by statute to state prisoners formed a new constitutional baseline limiting the ability of Congress to "suspend" meaningful access to federal review of federal claims raised by state prisoners. E.g., Jordan Steiker, *Incorporating the Suspension Clause: Is There a Constitutional Right to Federal Habeas Corpus for State Prisoners?* 92 Mich.L.Rev. 862 (1994). This and other interpretations of the Suspension Clause are being tested in challenges to the restrictions on the availability of the writ enacted in 1996 as part of the Antiterrorism and Effective Death Penalty Act (AEDPA). See CRIMPROC § 28.2(a).

3.   *The current statutory structure.* The statutory provisions governing habeas corpus relief are found in 28 U.S.C.A. §§ 2241–2266. The provisions have been revised extensively over the years, but retain core of the Habeas Act of 1867 in which Congress extended the writ to "cases where any person may be restrained of his or her liberty in violation of the Constitution, or of any treaty or law of the United States." Decisions interpreting earlier versions of the statute continue to inform interpretations of the current provisions.

4.   *Counsel in habeas proceedings.*

a.   *Constitutional entitlements.* In BOUNDS v. SMITH, 430 U.S. 817, 97 S.Ct. 1491, 52 L.Ed.2d 72 (1977), per MARSHALL, J., the Court held that a state's constitutional duty to provide "meaningful access" to the courts requires the state to do more than refrain from interfering with indigents seeking assistance from other prisoners; it "requires prison authorities to assist inmates in the preparation and filing of meaningful legal papers by [furnishing] adequate law libraries or adequate assistance from persons trained in the law." Dissenting, Justice REHNQUIST, J., joined by Burger, C.J., protested that "if 'meaningful access' to the courts is to include law libraries, there is no convincing reason why it should not also include lawyers appointed at the expense of the State." Yet by 1989, the Court, in MURRAY v. GIARRATANO, 492 U.S. 1, 109 S.Ct. 2765, 106 L.Ed.2d 1 (1989) (per REHNQUIST, J.) laid to rest any possibility of a constitutional right to the assistance of counsel on collateral review, even for death row inmates: "[W]e held in *Ross v. Moffitt* [p. 78] that the right to counsel at [trial and on the first appeal] did not carry over to a discretionary appeal provided by [state] law from the intermediate appellate court to the [state supreme court]. We

---

e.   Today Congress continues to limit the writ to persons who are "in custody," but the term has been interpreted generously to include probationers and parolees; petitioners released unconditionally who were incarcerated at the time they filed their petitions; and prisoners convicted of more than one offense, who challenge a conviction carrying a sentence to be served after completing their present sentence. See, CRIMPROC § 28.3(a). In addition, as the Court recently observed in *Duncan v. Walker*, 533 U.S. 167, 121 S.Ct. 2120, 150 L.Ed.2d 251 (2001), state court judgments other than criminal convictions may create "custody" within the meaning of the federal habeas statute, including an order of "civil commitment" or "civil contempt."

contrasted the trial stage of a criminal proceeding [with] the appellate stage of such a proceeding, where the defendant needs an attorney 'not as a shield to protect him against being "haled into court" by the State and stripped of his presumption of innocence, but rather as a sword to upset the prior determination of guilt.' We held in *Pennsylvania v. Finley*, 481 U.S. 551, 107 S.Ct. 1990, 95 L.Ed.2d 539 (1987), that the logic of *Ross* required the conclusion that there was no federal constitutional right to counsel for indigent prisoners seeking state postconviction relief. [The] rule of *Finley* should apply no differently in capital cases than in noncapital cases. State collateral proceedings are not constitutionally required as an adjunct to the state criminal proceedings and serve a different and more limited purpose than either the trial or appeal. The additional safeguards imposed by the Eighth Amendment at the trial stage of a capital case are, we think, sufficient to assure the reliability of the process by which the death penalty is imposed." The pivotal fifth vote in *Giarratano* was cast by Justice KENNEDY, who concurred in the judgment and observed that "no prisoner on death row in Virginia has been unable to obtain counsel to represent him in postconviction proceedings" and that the state's prison system "is staffed with institutional lawyers to assist in preparing petitions for postconviction relief." Justice STEVENS, joined by Brennan, Marshall, and Blackmun, JJ., dissented, arguing that "even if it is permissible to leave an ordinary prisoner to his own resources in collateral proceedings, it is fundamentally unfair to require an indigent death row inmate to initiate collateral review without counsel's guiding hand." He noted that the success rate for habeas challenges in capital cases ranged from 60% to 70%, demonstrating that "the meaningful appellate review necessary in a capital case extends beyond the direct appellate process"; that "unlike the ordinary inmate, who presumably has ample time to use and reuse the prison library and to seek guidance from other prisoners experienced in preparing *pro se* petitions, a grim deadline imposes a finite limit on the condemned person's capacity for useful research"; and that "this Court's death penalty jurisprudence unquestionably is difficult even for a trained lawyer to master."[f]

b. *Statutory rights to counsel in collateral proceedings.* Legislatures are of course free to provide legal assistance when the Constitution does not mandate it, and Congress has done so in capital cases. See 21 U.S.C. § 848(q)(4)(B) (statutory right to qualified legal representation for capital defendants in federal habeas corpus proceedings). See also Rule 8(c) of the Rules Governing § 2254 Cases (requiring the appointment of counsel for evidentiary hearings). Of those filing federal habeas petitions in a recent study, however, 93% were pro se. U.S. Dept. of Justice, Office of Justice Programs, Bureau of Justice Statistics, *Federal Habeas Corpus Review: Challenging State Court Criminal Convictions* 14 (1995).

5. *Habeas procedures.* The procedures applicable in federal habeas proceedings are set forth in §§ 2242–2243 and in the Rules Governing Section 2254 Cases, a set of Rules separate from the Rules of Criminal Procedure. In order to facilitate *pro se* litigation, the rules allow for fact pleading on forms designed to help the petitioner present all critical information (e.g., state conviction, sentence, prior state proceedings, prior habeas proceedings, reasons for raising claims not

---

f. Not surprisingly, *Bounds* itself was later construed narrowly by the Rehnquist Court. The Court emphasized that *Bounds* did *not* establish the right to a law library or to legal assistance, but only "the (already well-established) right of access to the courts. * * * [In] other words, prison law libraries and legal assistance programs are not ends in themselves, but only the means for ensuring 'a reasonably adequate opportunity to present claimed violations of fundamental constitutional rights to the courts.' " An inmate raising a *Bounds* challenge must, the Court explained, "demonstrate that the alleged shortcomings in the library or legal assistance program hindered his efforts to pursue a legal claim." Lewis v. Casey 518 U.S. 343, 116 S.Ct. 2174, 135 L.Ed.2d 606 (1996).

previously raised). Ordinarily, habeas petitions are assigned to federal magistrates who examine each petition and any attached exhibits (typically transcripts, state court opinions, etc.) to determine whether the petition warrants further consideration. If it does not, the petition may be dismissed summarily. If the petition clears this preliminary review, the state will be asked to file a response. The record at this point often is expanded through the submission of additional transcripts, prior briefs, and other materials reflecting prior proceedings. If needed, discovery may be allowed, with the court appointing counsel to assist the petitioner. As discussed in Note 6, p. 1603, evidentiary hearings may also be held.

6. *The exhaustion requirement.* Section 2254 requires that a petitioner first present his claim to the state courts. This gives the state an opportunity to make its initial ruling on the prisoner's constitutional claim if it is willing to do so. "Exhaustion," as it is known, demands only that the state judiciary be given a single chance (through the highest available state court) to consider the substance of the petitioner's claim. See *O'Sullivan v. Boerckel*, 526 U.S. 838, 119 S.Ct. 1728, 144 L.Ed.2d 1 (1999) (exhaustion requires state prisoners to file petitions for discretionary review when that review is part of the ordinary appellate review procedure in the state). Where a petitioner files a "mixed petition" in federal court—including some claims that were adequately presented to the state courts and others that were not and are still open to review—the habeas court cannot proceed on the unexhausted portion of the petition. The petitioner must either withdraw the petition, or proceed only on the exhausted claims (risking that any later attempt to present other claims, following their exhaustion, will be challenged as an abuse of the writ, see Note 7, p. 1605.) See *Rose v. Lundy,* 455 U.S. 509, 102 S.Ct. 1198, 71 L.Ed.2d 379 (1982). If the opportunity to present the issue to the state courts is no longer available under the state's postconviction procedures, then the exhaustion requirement is satisfied. Thus, the exhaustion requirement may delay, but will not permanently derail, a habeas petition.

7. *Summary of barriers to relief.* The most important barriers to habeas relief are examined in the Sections that follow. First, the writ is not available for entire categories of claims, namely claims based on a violation of state law, or, as we shall see, claims that a state court failed to exclude evidence obtained in violation of the Fourth Amendment. In addition, any one of several procedural hurdles may defeat a petitioner's claim, including the statute of limitations, procedural default, and non-retroactivity. Even if a petitioner successfully negotiates these requirements and receives review of his claims on the merits, the federal court will not review all state court decisions de novo, and may simply find that the state court was close enough, or that an erroneous state decision was "harmless." See Section 4. Most of these restrictions have been imposed by the Court or by Congress in the past twenty-five years, following a period of expanding access to the writ in the 1950s and '60s. What developments in law, politics, or society during the 1970s, '80s and '90s might help to explain why judges and lawmakers became concerned about throwing open too widely the doors of federal courthouses to state prisoners alleging that their state convictions are tainted by constitutional error; or less concerned about providing federal oversight of state court application of federal law? To what extent do the opinions of the justices in the cases below reflect these concerns?

SECTION 2. ISSUES COGNIZABLE

1. *From jurisdictional to constitutional error.* The conventional view, at least until 1915, was that federal habeas review was available only when a prisoner challenged the jurisdiction of the court of conviction. After decades of expanding the term jurisdiction to encompass an assortment of constitutional error, the Supreme Court appeared to put the jurisdictional limitation to rest. See *Waley v. Johnston,* 316 U.S. 101, 62 S.Ct. 964, 86 L.Ed. 1302 (1942) (the writ "extends * * * to those exceptional cases where the conviction has been in disregard of the constitutional rights of the accused and where the writ is the only effective means of preserving his rights"); *Brown v. Allen,* 344 U.S. 443, 73 S.Ct. 397, 97 L.Ed. 469 (1953) (coerced confession claim cognizable).

In FAY v. NOIA, 372 U.S. 391, 83 S.Ct. 822, 9 L.Ed.2d 837 (1963), the Court made it explicit—all constitutional claims were cognizable on habeas review. Speaking for a 6–3 majority in *Fay,* Justice BRENNAN noted: "Although in form the Great Writ is simply a mode of procedure, its history is inextricably intertwined with the growth of fundamental rights of personal liberty. For its function has been to provide a prompt and efficacious remedy for whatever society deems to be intolerable restraints. Its root principle is that in a civilized society, government must always be accountable to the judiciary for a man's imprisonment: if the imprisonment cannot be shown to conform with fundamental requirements of law, the individual is entitled to his immediate release. * * * Although the Act of 1867, like its English and American predecessors, nowhere defines habeas corpus, its expansive language and imperative tone, viewed against the background of post-Civil War efforts in Congress to deal severely with the States of the former Confederacy, would seem to make inescapable the conclusion that Congress was enlarging the habeas remedy as previously understood, not only in extending its coverage to state prisoners, but also in making its procedures more efficacious. In 1867, Congress was anticipating resistance to its Reconstruction measures and planning the implementation of the post-war constitutional Amendments. Debated and enacted at the very peak of the Radical Republicans' power * * *, the Act of 1867 seems plainly to have been designed to furnish a method additional to and independent of direct Supreme Court review of state court decisions for the vindication of the new constitutional guarantees."

2. ***Theories for limiting the types of claims subject to habeas review.*** Should the writ be available whenever a petitioner can show that a state court violated his constitutional rights, or should habeas relief be limited to only a subset of constitutional claims? A broad view of habeas relief, one that would reach all constitutional claims, follows so long as the purpose of the writ is to enlist the courts of appeals in providing the federal review of state convictions that cannot be provided, because of the sheer number of cases, by the Supreme Court on direct appeal. See Barry Friedman, *A Tale of Two Habeas,* 73 Minn. L.Rev. 247 (1988).

By contrast, if the writ is not designed as a substitute for direct appeal but is intended instead to remedy certain particularly harmful or fundamental errors, some theory is required in order to define which errors count. One approach assumes that habeas is not a device to correct all erroneous state court interpretations of federal law, but is instead a process guarantee, providing a federal forum to raise a constitutional claim only when the state fails to provide a "full and fair opportunity" to litigate that claim. See *Wright v. West,* 505 U.S. 277, 112 S.Ct. 2482, 120 L.Ed.2d 225 (1992) (opinion of Thomas, J.). Alternatively, the purpose of habeas review could be to deter only the worst state court transgressions, suggesting that relief would be limited to cases in which state courts adopted unreasonable interpretations of existing federal law. See *Teague v. Lane,* p. 1606; *(Terry) Williams v. Taylor,* p. 1615. This theory is reflected in the current habeas statute, and is the focus of Section 4.

Still another theory of habeas review was championed in the opinions of Justice Powell. Concurring in *Schneckloth v. Bustamonte,* 412 U.S. 218, 93 S.Ct. 2041, 36 L.Ed.2d 854 (1973), Justice Powell asserted that federal courts should review claims raised by state prisoners only when those claims relate to the determination of the defendant's *factual guilt*. The state in *Schneckloth* had argued that violations of *Mapp v. Ohio* [p. 110] should not be cognizable in habeas corpus proceedings. The Court majority, finding that there had been no Fourth Amendment violation, did not reach that issue. But Justice Powell, joined by Chief Justice Burger and Justice Rehnquist, agreed with the state's contention. Initially rejecting "*Fay v. Noia's* version of the writ's historic function" as resting upon a "revisionist view" of history, Justice Powell argued that "the justification for disregarding the historic scope and function of the writ is measurably less apparent in the typical Fourth Amendment claim asserted on collateral attack. In this latter case, a convicted defendant is most often asking society to redetermine a matter with no bearing at all on the basic justice of his incarceration." He suggested that limiting the habeas remedy to claims "relating to guilt or innocence" was supported by an examination of "the costs" of federal habeas review, as measured "in terms of [its] serious intrusions on other societal values." These values "include (i) the most effective utilization of limited judicial resources, (ii) the necessity of finality in criminal trials, (iii) the minimization of friction between our federal and state systems of justice, and (iv) the maintenance of the constitutional balance upon which the doctrine of federalism is founded." He concluded, "At some point the law must convey to those in custody that a wrong has been committed, that consequent punishment has been imposed, that one should no longer look back with the view to resurrecting every imaginable basis for further litigation but rather should look forward to rehabilitation and to becoming a constructive citizen. * * * To the extent that every state criminal judgment is to be subject indefinitely to broad and repetitive federal oversight, we render the actions of state courts a serious disrespect in derogation of the constitutional balance between the two systems. The present expansive scope of federal habeas review has prompted no small friction between state and federal judiciaries." Quoting Judge Henry J. Friendly's influential article, *Is Innocence Irrelevant? Collateral Attack on Criminal Judgments*, 38 U.Chi.L.Rev. 142 (1970), Justice Powell agreed that " 'convictions should be subject to collateral attack only when the prisoner supplements his constitution plea with a colorable claim of innocence.' "As is clear from the case that follows, Justice Powell's position gained ground.

STONE v. POWELL

428 U.S. 465, 96 S.Ct. 3037, 49 L.Ed.2d 1067 (1976).

Justice POWELL delivered the opinion of the Court.

The question presented is whether a federal court should consider, in ruling on a petition for habeas corpus relief filed by a state prisoner, a claim that evidence obtained by an unconstitutional search or seizure was introduced at his trial, when he has previously been afforded an opportunity for full and fair litigation of his claim in the state courts. We hold * * * that where the State has provided an opportunity for full and fair litigation of a Fourth Amendment claim, the Constitution does not require that a state prisoner be granted federal habeas corpus relief on the ground that evidence obtained in an unconstitutional search or seizure was introduced at his trial.

* * *

The exclusionary rule [is] a judicially created means of effectuating the rights secured by the Fourth Amendment. * * * The primary justification for the exclusionary rule * * * is the deterrence of police conduct that violates Fourth Amendment rights. Post-*Mapp* decisions have established that the rule is not a personal constitutional right. It is not calculated to redress the injury to the privacy of the victim of the search or seizure, for any "[r]eparation comes too late." *Linkletter v. Walker* [p. 41]. * * * [D]espite the broad deterrent purpose of the exclusionary rule, it has never been interpreted to proscribe the introduction of illegally seized evidence in all proceedings or against all persons. As in the case of any remedial device, "the application of the rule has been restricted to those areas where its remedial objectives are thought most efficaciously served." *United States v. Calandra* [p. 131]. Thus, our refusal [in *Calandra*] to extend the exclusionary rule to grand jury proceedings was based on a balancing of the potential injury to the historic role and function of the grand jury by such extension against the potential contribution to the effectuation of the Fourth Amendment through deterrence of police misconduct. * * *

The question is whether state prisoners—who have been afforded the opportunity for full and fair consideration of their reliance upon the exclusionary rule with respect to seized evidence by the state courts at trial and on direct review— may invoke their claim again on federal habeas corpus review. The answer is to be found by weighing the utility of the exclusionary rule against the costs of extending it to collateral review of Fourth Amendment claims.

The costs of applying the exclusionary rule even at trial and on direct review are well known * * *. [The Court here discussed those costs, which were said to include the "divert[ing] of attention from the ultimate question of guilt or innocence that should be the central concern in a criminal proceeding," the exclusion of "typically reliable" physical evidence, the "deflect[ion] of the truth-finding process" that "often frees the guilty," and, where the rule is applied "indiscriminately," without regard to the "disparity * * * between the error committed by the police and the windfall afforded a guilty defendant," the possibility of "generating disrespect for the law and the administration of justice."] These long-recognized costs of the rule persist when a criminal conviction is sought to be overturned on collateral review on the ground that a search-and-seizure claim was erroneously rejected by two or more tiers of state courts.

Evidence obtained by police officers in violation of the Fourth Amendment is excluded at trial in the hope that the frequency of future violations will decrease. Despite the absence of supportive empirical evidence, we have assumed that the immediate effect of exclusion will be to discourage law enforcement officials from violating the Fourth Amendment by removing the incentive to disregard it. More importantly, over the long term, this demonstration that our society attaches serious consequences to violation of constitutional rights is thought to encourage those who formulate law enforcement policies, and the officers who implement them, to incorporate Fourth Amendment ideals into their value system.

We adhere to the view that these considerations support the implementation of the exclusionary rule at trial and its enforcement on direct appeal of state court convictions. But the additional contribution, if any, of the consideration of search-and-seizure claims of state prisoners on collateral review is small in relation to the costs. To be sure, each case in which such claim is considered may add marginally to an awareness of the values protected by the Fourth Amendment. There is no reason to believe, however, that the overall educative effect of the exclusionary rule would be appreciably diminished if search-and-seizure claims could not be raised in federal habeas corpus review of state convictions. Nor is there reason to assume that any specific disincentive already created by the risk of exclusion of evidence at trial or the reversal of convictions on direct review would be enhanced if there were the further risk that a conviction obtained in state court and affirmed on direct review might be overturned in collateral proceedings often occurring years after the incarceration of the defendant. The view that the deterrence of Fourth Amendment violations would be furthered rests on the dubious assumption that law enforcement authorities would fear that federal habeas review might reveal flaws in a search or seizure that went undetected at trial and on appeal.[35] Even if one rationally could assume that some additional incremental deterrent effect would be present in isolated cases, the resulting advance of the legitimate goal of furthering Fourth Amendment rights would be outweighed by the acknowledged costs to other values vital to a rational system of criminal justice.

* * *

DISSENT

[Dissenting BRENNAN, J., joined by Marshall, J., argued that the Court was losing sight of the basic function of the habeas writ.] The Court, assuming without deciding that respondents were convicted on the basis of unconstitutionally obtained evidence erroneously admitted against them by the state trial courts, acknowledges that respondents had the right to obtain a reversal of their convictions on appeal in the state courts or on certiorari to this Court. * * * The Court, however, simply ignores the settled principle that for purposes of adjudicating constitutional claims Congress, which has the power to do so under Art. III of the Constitution, has effectively cast the district courts sitting in habeas in the role of surrogate Supreme Courts.

* * *

The procedural safeguards mandated in the Framers' Constitution are not admonitions to be tolerated only to the extent they serve functional purposes that ensure that the "guilty" are punished and the "innocent" freed; rather, every guarantee enshrined in the Constitution, our basic charter and the guarantor of our most precious liberties, is by it endowed with an independent vitality and value, and this Court is not free to curtail those constitutional guarantees even to punish the most obviously guilty. Particular constitutional rights that do not affect the fairness of factfinding procedures cannot for that reason be denied at the trial itself. What possible justification then can there be for denying vindication of such rights on federal habeas when state courts do deny those rights at trial? To sanction disrespect and disregard for the Constitution in the name of protecting society from lawbreakers is to make the government itself lawless and to subvert those values upon which our ultimate freedom and liberty depend.

[In a separate dissent, WHITE, J., offered the following hypothetical as an illustration of what he perceived to be the flaw in the majority's position:] Suppose, for example, that two confederates in crime, Smith and Jones, are tried separately for a state crime and convicted on the very same evidence, including evidence seized incident to their arrest allegedly made without probable cause. Their constitutional claims are fully aired, rejected and preserved on appeal. Their convictions are affirmed by the State's highest court. Smith, the first to be tried, does not petition for certiorari, or does so but his petition is denied. Jones, whose conviction was considerably later, is more successful. His petition for certiorari is granted and his conviction reversed because this Court, without making any new rule of law, simply concludes that on the undisputed facts the arrests were made without probable cause and the challenged evidence was therefore seized in

---

35. The policy arguments that respondents marshal in support of the view that federal habeas corpus review is necessary to effectuate the Fourth Amendment stem from a basic mistrust of the state courts as fair and competent forums for the adjudication of federal constitutional rights. The argument is that state courts cannot be trusted to effectuate Fourth Amendment values through fair application of the rule, and the oversight jurisdiction of this Court on certiorari is an inadequate safeguard.

The principal rationale for this view emphasizes the broad differences in the respective institutional setting within which federal judges and state judges operate. Despite differences in institutional environment and the unsympathetic attitude to federal constitutional claims of some state judges in years past, we are unwilling to assume that there now exists a general lack of appropriate sensitivity to constitutional rights in the trial and appellate courts of the several States. * * *

violation of the Fourth Amendment. The State must either retry Jones or release him, necessarily because he is deemed in custody in violation of the Constitution. It turns out that without the evidence illegally seized, the State has no case; and Jones goes free. Smith then files his petition for habeas corpus. He makes no claim that he did not have a full and fair hearing in the state courts, but asserts that his Fourth Amendment claim had been erroneously decided and that he is being held in violation of the Federal Constitution. He cites this Court's decision in Jones' case to satisfy any burden placed on him by § 2254 to demonstrate that the state court was in error. Unless the Court's reservation, in its present opinion, of those situations where the defendant has not had a full and fair hearing in the state courts is intended to encompass all those circumstances under which a state criminal judgment may be reexamined under § 2254—in which event the opinion is essentially meaningless and the judgment erroneous—Smith's petition would be dismissed, and he would spend his life in prison while his colleague is a free man. I cannot believe that Congress intended this result.

Note

In a series of subsequent cases, the Court declined to extend *Stone* to bar habeas review of other types of constitutional claims. The latest of these decisions is *Withrow v. Williams,* reproduced at p. 549 supra, involving a *Miranda* violation. Of the theories for limiting habeas review listed in Note 2, p. 1589, which best explain the Court's decision in *Stone*? Which explain *Rose v. Mitchell* (p. 946), or *Kimmelman v. Morrison* (p. 1133) (both described in *Withrow*), or *Withrow* itself?

SECTION 3. CLAIMS FORECLOSED BY PROCEDURAL DEFAULT

1. *Procedural default defined.* In addition to limiting the types of claims that may be reviewed through the writ of habeas corpus, Congress and the Court have limited prisoners' access to the writ by erecting a series of procedural hurdles each petitioner must clear before a federal court can review the petitioner's claim on its merits. One of these barriers is "procedural default," which arises when a habeas petitioner seeks to rely on a claim in federal court that was not presented in the state court in accordance with applicable state procedural requirements and therefore would be viewed under state law as "waived," "defaulted," or "forfeited." Assuming the claim would fall in this category, under what conditions, if any, should that state procedural default bar federal habeas review?

2. *Fay v. Noia and the "deliberate bypass" standard.* Answering this question in FAY v. NOIA, 372 U.S. 391, 83 S.Ct. 822, 9 L.Ed.2d 837 (1963), the Court adopted what came to be known as the "deliberate bypass" standard. All three petitioners in *Noia* had confessed under similar circumstances, and all three claimed that their confessions were coerced. Two had subsequently had their convictions overturned in proceedings that followed unsuccessful state appeals, but defendant Noia had been denied relief by the state courts because he had failed to appeal following his conviction. Justice BRENNAN, speaking for a 6–3 majority, concluded that Noia's claim should be cognizable on a federal habeas petition. He stated, "If a habeas applicant, after consultation with competent counsel or otherwise, understandingly and knowingly forewent the privilege of seeking to vindicate his federal claims in the state courts, whether for strategic, tactical, or any other reasons that can fairly be described as the deliberate bypassing of state procedures, then it is open to the federal court on habeas to deny him all relief if the state courts refused to entertain his federal claims on the

merits—though of course only after the federal court has satisfied itself, by holding a hearing or by some other means, of the facts bearing upon the applicant's default." As for the defendant Noia, for him to have appealed in 1942 "would have been to run a substantial risk of electrocution. His was the grisly choice whether to sit content with life imprisonment or to travel the uncertain avenue of appeal which, if successful, might well have led to a retrial and death sentence. * * * He declined to play Russian roulette in this fashion. * * * [U]nder the circumstances it cannot realistically be deemed a merely tactical or strategic litigation step, or in any way a deliberate circumvention of state procedures."

3. _The development of the "cause-and-prejudice" standard._ As the Court's membership became increasingly concerned about the costs of habeas review, it abandoned the deliberate bypass standard. Initially, the new stricter standard was applied in a case involving a federal prisoner seeking relief under § 2255, _Davis v. United States_, 411 U.S. 233, 93 S.Ct. 1577, 36 L.Ed.2d 216 (1973). Davis claimed that there had been racial discrimination in the selection of his grand jury but failed to raise that claim at trial. The Supreme Court rejected Davis' contention that his claim should be judged under the deliberate bypass standard. It noted that if Davis' case had come before it on direct review, it would have been decided under Federal Rule 12(b). That Rule provided that the failure to raise before trial a defect in the institution of the prosecution, such as grand jury discrimination, would "constitute a waiver, but the court for cause shown may grant relief from the waiver." The Court found it "inconceivable" that Congress, having foreclosed such a claim from review in the initial proceeding, meant nonetheless to allow it to be presented under a more lenient standard on collateral attack. Accordingly, the Rule 12(b) standard was held to apply under § 2255. This meant that the petitioner could have his claim considered only if his failure to object was justified by "cause shown." In applying the "cause shown" standard, and concluding that it had not been met, the district court had properly considered the absence of any showing of prejudice arising from the alleged constitutional violation. While racial discrimination in the selection of the grand jury was presumed to be prejudicial where a timely objection was made, a petitioner attempting to fall within the Rule 12(b) exception for "cause shown" would have to establish "actual prejudice."

Francis v. Henderson, 425 U.S. 536, 96 S.Ct. 1708, 48 L.Ed.2d 149 (1976), soon presented to the Court the same problem except that the petitioner was a state prisoner seeking a writ of habeas corpus, and had not complied with the state rule requiring grand jury claims to be raised before trial. The Court held that the "cause" and "actual prejudice" standard announced in _Davis_ was applicable. "[C]onsiderations of comity and federalism" required that habeas courts give no less effect to the interests advanced by state rules requiring claims to be raised before trial, than they give to the same interests in a federal prosecution.

WAINWRIGHT v. SYKES
433 U.S. 72, 97 S.Ct. 2497, 53 L.Ed.2d 594 (1977).

Justice REHNQUIST delivered the opinion of the Court.

[Respondent Sykes presented a habeas corpus challenge based upon a _Miranda_ claim that he had not raised in his state trial. At Sykes' trial for murder the prosecution introduced into evidence an incriminating statement that Sykes had given to the police after having been warned of his _Miranda_ rights. Although Sykes later claimed in his habeas challenge that he had not understood the _Miranda_ warnings and the statement therefore was involuntary, neither he nor his counsel raised that claim prior to trial or during the trial. The applicable state procedural rule (Fla.R.Crim.P. 3.190) required that such claims be raised by a pretrial motion to suppress, but it also granted the trial court discretion to entertain a later objection at trial. Sykes also failed to raise his *Miranda* claim on appeal, but even if that had been done, the Florida appellate courts would not have considered the issue since Sykes had not complied with Fla.R.Crim.P. 3.190. On petition for habeas corpus, the state argued that Sykes' violation of the state's procedural rule, which the federal court characterized as a "contemporaneous objection" standard, barred consideration of the merits of petitioner's claim. The federal Court of Appeals rejected that contention, relying on *Fay v. Noia.*]

* * * The simple legal question before the Court calls for a construction of the language of 28 U.S.C. § 2254(a), which provides that the federal courts shall entertain an application for a writ of habeas corpus "in behalf of a person in custody pursuant to the judgment of a state court only on the ground that he is in custody in violation of the Constitution or laws or treaties of the United States." But, to put it mildly, we do not write on a clean slate in construing this statutory provision. * * *

[The Court here discussed Supreme Court decisions dealing with several major issues relating to the scope of the writ, "illustrat[ing] this Court's historical willingness to overturn or modify its earlier views of the scope of the writ, even where the statutory language authorizing judicial action has remained unchanged." With this precedent in mind, the Court then turned to the issue before it—which it described as determining when "an adequate and independent state ground [will] bar consideration of otherwise cognizable federal issues on federal habeas review."]

[I]t is a well-established principle of federalism that a state decision resting on an adequate foundation of state substantive law is immune from review in the federal courts. * * * The area of controversy which has developed has concerned the reviewability of federal claims which the state court has declined to pass on because [they were] not presented in the manner prescribed by its *procedural* rules. The adequacy of such an independent state procedural ground to prevent federal habeas review of the underlying federal issue has been treated very differently than where the state-law ground is substantive. * * *

To the extent that the dicta of *Fay v. Noia* may be thought to have laid down an all-inclusive rule rendering state contemporaneous objection rules ineffective to bar review of underlying federal claims in federal habeas proceedings—absent a "knowing waiver" or a "deliberate bypass" of the right to so object—its effect was limited by *Francis,* which applied a different rule and barred a habeas challenge to the makeup of a grand jury. * * * Shall the rule of *Francis v. Henderson,* supra, barring federal habeas review absent a showing of "cause" and "prejudice" attendant to a state procedural waiver, be applied to a waived objection to the admission of a confession at trial? We answer that question in the affirmative.

* * * We leave open for resolution in future decisions the precise definition of the "cause"-and-"prejudice" standard, and note here only that it is narrower than the standard set forth in dicta in *Fay v. Noia,* which would make federal habeas review generally available to state convicts absent a knowing and deliberate waiver of the federal constitutional contention. It is the sweeping language of *Fay v. Noia,* going far beyond the facts of the case eliciting it, which we today reject.

The reasons for our rejection of it are several. The contemporaneous-objection rule itself is by no means peculiar to Florida, and deserves greater respect than *Fay* gives it, both for the fact that it is employed by a coordinate jurisdiction within the federal system and for the many interests which it serves in its own right. A contemporaneous objection enables the record to be made with respect to the constitutional claim when the recollections of witnesses are freshest, not years later in a federal habeas proceeding. It enables the judge who observed the demeanor of those witnesses to make the factual determinations necessary for properly deciding the federal constitutional question. While the [habeas statute] requires deference to be given to such determinations made by state courts, the determinations themselves are less apt to be made in the first instance if there is no contemporaneous objection to the admission of the evidence on federal constitutional grounds.

A contemporaneous-objection rule may lead to the exclusion of the evidence objected to, thereby making a major contribution to finality in criminal litigation. Without the evidence claimed to be vulnerable on federal constitutional grounds, the jury may acquit the defendant, and that will be the end of the case; or it may nonetheless convict the defendant, and he will have one less federal constitutional claim to assert in his federal habeas petition. If the state trial judge admits the evidence in question after a full hearing, the federal habeas court * * * will gain significant guidance from the state ruling in this regard. Subtler considerations as well militate in favor of honoring a state contemporaneous-objection rule. An objection on the spot may force the prosecution to take a hard look at its hole card, and even if the prosecutor thinks that the state trial judge will admit the evidence he must contemplate the possibility of reversal by the state appellate courts or the ultimate issuance of a federal writ of habeas corpus based on the impropriety of the state court's rejection of the federal constitutional claim.

We think that the rule of *Fay v. Noia,* broadly stated, may encourage "sandbagging" on the part of defense lawyers, who may take their chances on a verdict of not guilty in a state trial court with the intent to raise their constitutional claims in a federal habeas court if their initial gamble does not pay off. The refusal of federal habeas courts to honor contemporaneous-objection rules may also make state courts themselves less stringent in their enforcement. Under the rule of *Fay v. Noia,* state appellate courts know that a federal constitutional issue raised for the first time in the proceeding before them may well be decided in any event by a federal habeas tribunal. Thus, their choice is between addressing the issue notwithstanding the petitioner's failure to timely object, or else face the prospect that the federal habeas court will decide the questions without the benefit of their views.

The failure of the federal habeas courts generally to require compliance with a contemporaneous-objection rule tends to detract from the perception of the trial of a criminal case in state court as a decisive and portentous event. A defendant has been accused of a serious crime, and this is the time and place set for him to be tried by a jury of his peers and found either guilty or not guilty by that jury. To the greatest extent possible all issues which bear on this charge should be determined in this proceeding: the accused is in the courtroom, the jury is in the box, the judge is on the bench, and the witnesses, having been subpoenaed and duly sworn, await their turn to testify. Society's resources have been concentrated at that time and place in order to decide, within the limits of human fallibility, the question of guilt or innocence of one of its citizens. Any procedural rule which encourages the result that those proceedings be as free of error as possible is thoroughly desirable, and the contemporaneous-objection rule surely falls within this classification.

We believe the adoption of the *Francis* rule in this situation will have the salutary effect of making the state trial on the merits the "main event," so to speak, rather than a "tryout on the road" for what will later be the determinative federal habeas hearing. There is nothing in the Constitution or in the language of § 2254 which requires that the state trial on the issue of guilt or innocence be devoted largely to the testimony of fact witnesses directed to the elements of the state crime, while only later will there occur in a federal habeas hearing a full airing of the federal constitutional claims which were not raised in the state proceedings. If a criminal defendant thinks that an action of the state trial court is about to deprive him of a federal constitutional right there is every reason for his following state procedure in making known his objection.

The "cause"-and-"prejudice" exception of the *Francis* rule will afford an adequate guarantee, we think, that the rule will not prevent a federal habeas court from adjudicating for the first time the federal constitutional claim of a defendant who in the absence of such an adjudication will be the victim of a miscarriage of justice. Whatever precise content may be given those terms by later cases, we feel confident in holding without further elaboration that they do not exist here. Respondent has advanced no explanation whatever for his failure to object at trial, and, as the proceeding unfolded, the trial judge is certainly not to be faulted for failing to question the admission of the confession himself. The other evidence of guilt presented at trial, moreover, was substantial to a degree that would negate any possibility of actual prejudice resulting to the respondent from the admission of his inculpatory statement.

We accordingly conclude that the judgment of the Court of Appeals for the Fifth Circuit must be reversed, and the cause remanded * * * with instructions to dismiss respondent's petition for a writ of habeas corpus.

Justice STEVENS, concurring.

* * * In this case I agree with the Court's holding that collateral attack on the state-court judgment should not be allowed. The record persuades me that competent trial counsel could well have made a deliberate decision not to object to the admission of the respondent's in-custody statement. That statement was consistent, in many respects, with the respondent's trial testimony. It even had some positive value, since it portrayed the respondent as having acted in response to provocation, which might have influenced the jury to return a verdict on a lesser charge. To the extent that it was damaging, the primary harm would have resulted from its effect in impeaching the trial testimony, but it would have been admissible for impeachment in any event, *Harris v. New York* [p. 789]. Counsel may well have preferred to have the statement admitted without objection when it was first offered rather than making an objection which, at best, could have been only temporarily successful. * * *

[The concurring opinions of Justice WHITE and Chief Justice BURGER are omitted].

Justice BRENNAN, with whom Justice Marshall joins, dissenting.

* * * If it could be assumed that a procedural default more often than not is the product of a defendant's conscious refusal to abide by the duly constituted, legitimate processes of the state courts, then I might agree that a regime of collateral review weighted in favor of a State's procedural rules would be warranted. *Fay*, however, recognized that such rarely is the case; and therein lies *Fay*'s basic unwillingness to embrace a view of habeas jurisdiction that results in "an airtight system of [procedural] forfeitures."

This, of course, is not to deny that there are times when the failure to heed a state procedural requirement stems from an intentional decision to avoid the presentation of constitutional claims to the state forum. *Fay* was not insensitive to this possibility. Indeed, the very purpose of its bypass test is to detect and enforce such intentional procedural forfeitures of outstanding constitutionally based claims. * * * For this reason, the Court's assertion that it "think[s]" that the *Fay* rule encourages intentional "sandbagging" on the part of the defense lawyers is without basis; certainly the Court points to no cases or commentary arising during the past 15 years of actual use of the *Fay* test to support this criticism. Rather, a consistent reading of case law demonstrates that the bypass formula has provided a workable vehicle for protecting the integrity of state rules in those instances when such protection would be both meaningful and just. * * *

[A]ny realistic system of federal habeas corpus jurisdiction must be premised on the reality that the ordinary procedural default is born of the inadvertence, negligence, inexperience, or incompetence of trial counsel. The case under consideration today is typical. The Court makes no effort to identify a tactical motive for the failure of Sykes' attorney to challenge the admissibility or reliability of a highly inculpatory statement. While my Brother Stevens finds a possible tactical advantage, I agree with the Court of Appeals that this reading is most implausible: "We can find no possible advantage which the defense might have gained, or thought they might gain, from the failure to conform with Florida Criminal Procedure Rule 3.190(I)." * * *

Punishing a lawyer's unintentional errors by closing the federal courthouse door to his client is both a senseless and misdirected method of deterring the slighting of state rules. It is senseless because unplanned and unintentional action of any kind generally is not subject to deterrence; and, to the extent that it is hoped that a threatened sanction addressed to the defense will induce greater care and caution on the part of trial lawyers, thereby forestalling negligent conduct or error, the potential loss of all valuable state remedies would be sufficient to this end. And it is a misdirected sanction because even if the penalization of incompetence or carelessness will encourage more thorough legal training and trial preparation, the habeas applicant, as opposed to his lawyer, hardly is the proper recipient of such a penalty. Especially with fundamental constitutional rights at stake, no fictional relationship of principal-agent or the like can justify holding the criminal defendant accountable for the naked errors of his attorney. This is especially true when so many indigent defendants are without any realistic choice in selecting who ultimately represents them at trial. Indeed, if responsibility for error must be apportioned between the parties, it is the State, through its attorney's admissions and certification policies, that is more fairly held to blame for the fact that practicing lawyers too often are ill-prepared or ill-equipped to act carefully and knowledgeably when faced with decisions governed by state procedural requirements. * * * In short, I believe that the demands of our criminal justice system warrant visiting the mistakes of a trial attorney on the head of a habeas corpus applicant only when we are convinced that the lawyer actually exercised his expertise and judgment in his client's service, and with his client's knowing and intelligent participation where possible. This, of course, is the precise system of habeas review established by *Fay v. Noia.*

Notes and Questions

1.　*Procedural default after the AEDPA.* The *Sykes* cause-and-prejudice test for defaulted claims, along with its actual-innocence exception, discussed in Note 4, below, appears to have survived the AEDPA. In capital cases from certain qualifying states § 2264 now provides for the application of a stricter standard for the review of claims not raised in state court. But as for first petitions in other cases, the 1996 amendments offer no new provision directed specifically at claims procedurally defaulted.

2.　*The meaning of cause.* The Court has identified three separate situations that will constitute "cause" sufficient to excuse procedural default.

a.　*Attorney error as cause.* The Court in MURRAY v. CARRIER, 477 U.S. 478, 106 S.Ct. 2639, 91 L.Ed.2d 397 (1986), considered whether habeas relief was barred by the failure of petitioner's counsel to present his *Brady* objection to the state courts during the petitioner's appeal. Justice O'CONNOR's opinion for the Court stated: "[T]he question of cause for a procedural default does not turn on whether counsel erred or on the kind of error counsel may have made. So long as a defendant is represented by counsel whose performance is not constitutionally ineffective under the standard established in *Strickland v. Washington* [p. 1120], we discern no inequity in requiring him to bear the risk of attorney error that results in a procedural default."

Extending the *Carrier* standard to a case in which counsel was three days late appealing a denial of petitioner's state habeas petition, the Court in COLEMAN v. THOMPSON, 501 U.S. 722, 111 S.Ct. 2546, 115 L.Ed.2d 640 (1991), stated: "*Carrier* applied the cause and prejudice standard to the failure to raise a particular claim on appeal. There is no reason that the same standard should not apply to a failure to appeal at all." Because there is "no constitutional right to an attorney in state post conviction proceedings," "a petitioner cannot claim constitutionally ineffective assistance of counsel in such proceedings." Consequently, "Coleman must 'bear the risk of attorney error that results in a procedural default.'" Justice O'CONNOR, for the Court, explained, "[I]t is not the gravity of the attorney's error that matters, but that it constitutes a violation of petitioner's right to counsel, so that the error must be seen as an external factor, i.e., 'imputed to the State.' * * * Where a petitioner defaults a claim as a result of the denial of the right to effective assistance of counsel, the State, which is responsible for the denial as a constitutional matter, must bear the cost of any resulting default and the harm to state interests that federal habeas review entails. A different allocation of costs is appropriate in those circumstances where the State has no responsibility to ensure that the petitioner was represented by competent counsel. As between the State and the petitioner, it is the petitioner who must bear the burden of a failure to follow state procedural rules. In the absence of a constitutional violation, the petitioner bears the risk in federal habeas for all attorney errors made in the course of the representation, as *Carrier* says explicitly."

Later on remand, the district court held that even if all the omitted evidence had been introduced, "it would have raised nothing more than credibility questions which the jury still could have resolved against Coleman when considering all of the probative evidence." Coleman v. Thompson, 798 F.Supp. 1209 (W.D.Va. 1992), aff'd, 966 F.2d 1441 (4th Cir.1992). Commenting later about the *Coleman* case to the Senate Judiciary Committee, however, former Attorney General Nicholas deB. Katzenbach stated:

> In the *Coleman v. Thompson* case in 1991, a death row inmate with strong new evidence of actual innocence—evidence so powerful and disturbing that Time magazine featured it as a cover story—was denied an opportunity to even have his new evidence heard in federal court, because his lawyer had unwittingly missed a filing deadline by three days. The Court ruled that the mistake of the otherwise competent lawyer, who was with the respected Washington firm of Arnold & Porter, barred any habeas review of the evidence. Mr. Coleman was executed. Such rulings devalue the protections of the Bill of Rights. No person should pay with his life for the neglect or ignorance of his lawyer.

Federal Habeas Corpus Reform: Eliminating Prisoners' Abuse of the Judicial Process; Hearing on S. 623 Before the Senate Committee on the Judiciary, 104th Cong., 1st Sess. 89 (1995). The Committee urged Congress to include in any amendments to the habeas statutes designed to limit repeated trips to habeas court by defendants on death row a requirement that a state could not take advantage of such amendments unless it first adopted special rules to assure competent counsel *at trial* as well as during state postconviction proceedings in all capital cases. This reform was also urged by various other groups, pointing in particular to studies arguing that there had been widespread ineffective assistance in capital cases. See Stephen B. Bright, *Counsel for the Poor: The Death Sentence Not for the Worst Crime, But for the Worst Lawyer,* 103 Yale L.J. 1835 (1994). When Congress did authorize a new fast-track for capital cases in the AEDPA (see Note 2, p. 1628), it tied state access to the streamlined procedures to the state's agreement to provide postconviction counsel, but mandated that the "ineffectiveness of counsel during State or Federal postconviction proceedings shall not be a ground for relief in a proceeding arising under section 2254." See § 2261(e).

Although the state's failure to provide the effective assistance of counsel can constitute cause for a petitioner's failure to raise a claim in state court in accordance with state procedural rules, in order to establish this sort of cause in habeas court, the petitioner must have raised a claim of ineffective assistance of counsel in state court in accordance with state rules. *Edwards v. Carpenter,* 529 U.S. 446, 120 S.Ct. 1587, 146 L.Ed.2d 518 (2000). Concurring in *Edwards,* Justice Breyer questioned the resulting complexity of the Court's procedural default doctrine, which, according to the majority, meant that a procedurally defaulted ineffective assistance claim can serve as cause to excuse the default of another habeas claim only if the petitioner can satisfy the "cause-and-prejudice" standard with respect to the default of the ineffective assistance claim itself. "The added complexity resulting from the Court's opinion is obvious. Consider a prisoner who wants to assert a federal constitutional claim (call it FCC). Suppose the State asserts as a claimed 'adequate and independent state ground' the prisoner's failure to raise the matter on his first state-court appeal. Suppose further that the prisoner replies by alleging that he had 'cause' for not raising the matter on appeal (call it C). After *Carrier,* if that alleged 'cause' (C) consists of the claim 'my attorney was constitutionally ineffective,' the prisoner must have exhausted C in the state courts first. And after today, if he did not follow state rules for presenting C to the state courts, he will have lost his basic claim, FCC, forever. But, I overstate. According to the opinion of the Court, he will not necessarily have lost FCC forever if he had 'cause' for not having followed those state rules (i.e., the rules for determining the existence of 'cause' for not having followed the state rules governing the basic claim, FCC) (call this 'cause' C*). The prisoner could therefore still obtain relief if he could demonstrate the merits of C*, C, and FCC. I concede that this system of rules has a certain logic, indeed an attractive power for those who like difficult puzzles. But I believe it must succumb to this question: Why should a prisoner, who may well be proceeding pro se, lose his basic claim because he runs afoul of state procedural rules governing the presentation to state courts of the 'cause' for his not having followed state procedural rules for the presentation of his basic federal claim? And, in particular, why should that special default rule apply when the 'cause' at issue is an 'ineffective-assistance-of-counsel' claim, but not when it is any of the many other 'causes' or circumstances that might excuse a failure to comply with state rules?"

b. State interference as cause. The Court in *Carrier* referred to "some interference by officials," as another reason that would excuse default, citing as an illustration *Brown v. Allen* (Note 1, p. 1589), a case in which a prison warden had suppressed a prisoner's timely appeal papers. The Court later relied on this type of "cause" in *Amadeo v. Zant,* 486 U.S. 214, 108 S.Ct. 1771, 100 L.Ed.2d 249 (1988). There, the federal district court found that a memorandum of the local prosecutor, evidencing a direction to the jury commissioners to limit the representation of blacks and women in the jury pool, had been concealed by local officials and therefore was "not reasonably discoverable" by petitioner's trial counsel, who had failed to object to the composition of the jury. State interference was not established, however, in *McCleskey v. Zant,* 499 U.S. 467, 111 S.Ct. 1454, 113

L.Ed.2d 517 (1991), where the prosecution failed to disclose a recorded statement of an informant (relating to jailhouse conversations with the petitioner), and counsel failed to include in petitioner's first habeas petition a Sixth Amendment challenge to the use of the informant's statement at trial. The recorded statement, reasoned the Court, was not "critical" to the substance of petitioner's Sixth Amendment challenge, there was no proof of intentional government concealment along the lines suggested in *Amadeo v. Zant,* and petitioner had sufficient information to raise the claim in his first petition in any event, having raised the claim in an earlier state habeas proceeding. The Court described the question before it as "whether petitioner possessed, or by reasonable means could have obtained, a sufficient basis to allege a claim in the first petition and pursue the matter through the habeas process." It noted further that a petitioner's inability to obtain relevant evidence "fails to establish cause if other known or discoverable evidence could have supported the claim," and that the failure to assert the claim "will not be excused merely because evidence discovered later might also have supported or strengthened the claim."

c. *Novelty as cause.* In *Reed v. Ross,* 468 U.S. 1, 104 S.Ct. 2901, 82 L.Ed.2d 1 (1984), a divided Court held that the failure to raise a claim "so novel that its legal basis [was] not reasonably available" should not preclude habeas review. Justice Brennan's opinion for the Court reasoned: "Just as it is reasonable to assume that a competent lawyer will fail to perceive the possibility of raising such a claim, it is also reasonable to assume that a court will similarly fail to appreciate the claim. * * * Consequently, a rule requiring a defendant to raise a truly novel issue is not likely to serve any functional purpose. * * * In addition, if we were to hold that the novelty of a constitutional question does not give rise to cause for counsel's failure to raise it, we might actually disrupt state-court proceedings by encouraging defense counsel to include any and all remotely plausible constitutional claims that could, some day, gain recognition." The utility of novelty as cause was undercut by the Court's subsequent decision in *Teague v. Lane,* and the new standard in § 2254(d), drastically curtailing habeas review of claims relying on "new" rules. See Section 4, below.

3. *The meaning of prejudice.* In *Kyles v. Whitley,* 514 U.S. 419, 115 S.Ct. 1555, 131 L.Ed.2d 490 (1995), and *Strickler v. Greene,* 527 U.S. 263, 119 S.Ct. 1936, 144 L.Ed.2d 286 (1999), the Court explained that in order to establish prejudice under *Sykes,* a petitioner must demonstrate that there is a "reasonable probability that the result of the trial would have been different." A "reasonable probability" is described as a probability sufficient to "undermine confidence in the verdict." This produces consistency in cases where the defendant seeks to convert the procedural default into a Sixth Amendment claim of ineffective assistance of counsel, because the reasonable probability standard is also used to measure prejudice for ineffective assistance claims. *Strickland v. Washington,* p. 1120. See John Jeffries & William Stuntz, *Ineffective Assistance and Procedural Default in Federal Habeas Corpus,* 57 U. Chi. L. Rev. 679 (1990).

4. *The miscarriage-of-justice or "actual-innocence" exception.* In *Sykes,* the Court noted that no matter how cause and prejudice might be defined, it would not preclude habeas review "of the federal constitutional claim of a defendant who in the absence of such an adjudication will be the victim of a miscarriage of justice." The miscarriage of justice concept was firmly established as an exception to the *Sykes* standard in *Murray v. Carrier* (Note 2, p. 1598), where Justice O'Connor stated: "[I]n an extraordinary case, where a constitutional violation has probably resulted in the conviction of one who is actually innocent, a federal habeas court may grant the writ even in the absence of a showing of cause for the procedural default." Following *Carrier,* the miscarriage-of-justice standard, sometimes described as an "actual innocence" standard, was regularly applied as an element of the default standard of *Sykes* and its progeny.

Consider the discussion of this exception in *Schlup v. Delo*, 513 U.S. 298, 115 S.Ct. 851, 130 L.Ed.2d 808 (1995): The miscarriage of justice standard "requires the habeas petitioner to show that 'a constitutional violation has probably resulted in the conviction of one who is actually innocent.' To establish the requisite probability, the petitioner must show that it is more likely than not that no reasonable juror would have convicted him in the light of the new evidence. The petitioner thus is required to make a stronger showing than that needed to establish prejudice." In assessing the adequacy of petitioner's showing of actual innocence, "the district court is not bound by the rules of admissibility that would govern at trial. Instead, the emphasis on 'actual innocence' allows the reviewing tribunal also to consider the probative force of relevant evidence that was either excluded or unavailable at trial.* * * A petitioner does not meet the threshold requirement unless he persuades the district court that, in light of the new evidence, no juror, acting reasonably, would have voted to find him guilty beyond a reasonable doubt. * * * [T]he *Carrier* standard requires a petitioner to show that it is more likely than not that 'no reasonable juror' would have convicted him. The word 'reasonable' in that formulation is not without meaning. It must be presumed that a reasonable juror would consider fairly all of the evidence presented. It must also be presumed that such a juror would conscientiously obey the instructions of the trial court requiring proof beyond a reasonable doubt."

5. *Procedural default and guilty pleas.* Should the *Sykes* cause and prejudice standard with its actual innocence exception also apply when a petitioner seeks habeas relief from a conviction following a plea of guilty? In BOUSLEY v. UNITED STATES, 523 U.S. 614, 118 S.Ct. 1604, 140 L.Ed.2d 828 (1998), the Court applied the *Sykes* standard in this context. The issue in *Bousley* was whether § 2255 afforded any relief to a federal prisoner who pleaded guilty to an offense, the dimensions of which later were interpreted by the Court to be narrower than anyone at the prisoner's plea hearing had assumed. Claiming that his guilty plea was not intelligent, given his misunderstanding of the offense at the time of his plea, the petitioner sought collateral relief under § 2255. Writing for the Court, Chief Justice REHNQUIST explained, "even the voluntariness and intelligence of a guilty plea can be attacked on collateral review only if first challenged on direct review. * * * Indeed, 'the concern with finality served by the limitation on collateral attack as special force with respect to convictions based on guilty pleas.' " The type of claims Bousely raised, he continued, "can be fully and completely addressed on direct review based on the record created at the plea colloquy. Where a defendant has procedurally defaulted a claim by failing to raise it on direct review, the claim may be raised in habeas only if the defendant can first demonstrate either 'cause' and actual 'prejudice,' *Murray v. Carrier*, or that he is 'actually innocent.' * * * [Bousley's argument] that 'the legal basis for his claim was not reasonably available to counsel' at the time his plea was entered * * * is without merit. While we have held that a claim that 'is so novel that its legal basis is not reasonably available to counsel' may constitute cause for a procedural default, *Reed v. Ross* [Note 3.c., p. 1599], petitioner's claim does not qualify as such. The argument that it was error for the District Court to misinform petitioner as to the statutory elements of [the offense] was most surely not a novel one." Also unavailing, concluded the Court, was Bousely's argument that raising his claim on direct appeal " 'would have been futile.' " * * * "[F]utility cannot constitute cause if it means simply that a claim was 'unacceptable to that particular court at that particular time.' " Nevertheless, Bousely deserved the opportunity on remand to "attempt to make a showing of actual innocence." The Court explained, "the Government is not limited to the existing record to rebut any showing that petitioner might make. Rather, on remand the Government should be permitted to present any admissible evidence of petitioner's guilt even if that evidence was not presented during petitioner's plea colloquy * * * . In cases where the Government has forgone more serious charges in the course of plea bargaining, petitioner's showing of actual innocence must also extend to those charges."

Justice SCALIA, joined by Justice Thomas, argued in dissent that the "super-generous miscarriage-of-justice exception to inexcusable default" should not be extended to prisoners challenging their convictions following guilty pleas, prisoners who already benefit from the "generous" exception to the "rule of finality" provided by the cause-and-prejudice test. "In every one of our cases that has considered the possibility of applying this so-called actual-innocence exception, a defendant had asked a habeas court to adjudicate a successive or procedurally defaulted constitutional claim after his conviction by a jury. * * * There are good reasons for this limitation: First and foremost, it is feasible to make an accurate assessment of 'actual innocence' when a trial has been had. * * * But how is the court to determine 'actual innocence' * * * where conviction was based upon an admission of guilt? Presumably the defendant will introduce evidence (perhaps nothing more than his own testimony) showing that he did not [commit] the crime to which he pleaded guilty, and the Government, eight years after the fact, will have to find and produce witnesses saying that he did. This seems to me not to remedy a miscarriage of justice, but to produce one." Justice Scalia warned that such claims will not be "extremely rare," but "exceedingly numerous," arising "every time this Court resolves a Circuit split regarding the elements of a crime defined in a federal statute," thus "placing upon the criminal-justice system a burden it will be unable to bear." Furthermore, he argued, "equity demands that relief be denied" in this context, since the defendants pleaded "guilty to charges that have not been proven—that perhaps could not be proven—in order to avoid convictions on charges of which they are 'actually guilty,' which carry a harsher penalty. * * * The Court evidently seeks to avoid this absurd consequence by prescribing that the defendant's 'showing of actual innocence must also extend' to any charge the Government has 'forgone,' [but] this assumes that the 'forgone' charge is identifiable. If, as is often the case, the bargaining occurred before the charge was filed * * * it will almost surely not be identifiable." He concluded, "[I]t is a bizarre waste of judicial resources to require mini-trials on charges made in dusty indictments (or indeed, if they could be identified on charges never made), just to determine whether the defendant can litigate a procedurally defaulted challenge to a guilty plea on a different offense." Responding to Justice Scalia's dissenting opinion, the Court included a footnote stating that Justice Scalia's concerns "that this factual innocence inquiry will be unduly complicated by the absence of a trial transcript in the guilty plea context * * * are overstated. In the federal system, where this case arose, guilty pleas must be accompanied by proffers, recorded verbatim on the record, demonstrating a factual basis for the plea. See Rule 11(f), (g)."

   6. *Failing to create a record in state court*. A different kind of default occurs when petitioner may have raised his claim in state court, but failed to develop there the factual record supporting the claim. In order to determine when a petitioner in this situation would be entitled to an evidentiary hearing in federal court, the Court prior to 1996 adopted the cause-and-prejudice analysis of *Sykes*, holding in *Keeney v. Tamayo-Reyes*, 504 U.S. 1, 112 S.Ct. 1715, 118 L.Ed.2d 318 (1992), that absent a showing of actual innocence, only those petitioners who could show cause for and prejudice from their failure to develop facts adequately in state court were entitled to an opportunity to develop those facts in federal court. The AEDPA narrowed even further a petitioner's access to evidentiary hearings in federal court when facts had not been developed in state court. Section 2254(e)(2) now provides (emphasis added):

> If the applicant has failed to develop the factual basis of a claim in State court proceedings, the court shall not hold an evidentiary hearing on the claim unless the applicant shows that—
>
> (A) the claim relies on—
>
> (i) a new rule of constitutional law, made retroactive to cases on collateral review by the Supreme Court, that was previously unavailable; or
>
> (ii) a factual predicate that could not have been previously discovered through the exercise of due diligence; *and*
>
> (B) the facts underlying the claim would be sufficient to establish by clear and convincing evidence that but for constitutional error, no reasonable fact-finder would have found the applicant guilty of the underlying offense.

Writing for a unanimous Court, Justice KENNEDY construed this amendment in (MICHAEL) WILLIAMS v. TAYLOR, 529 U.S. 420, 120 S.Ct. 1479, 146 L.Ed.2d 435 (2000). He explained "To be sure, in requiring that prisoners who have not been diligent satisfy § 2254(e)(2)'s provisions rather than show cause and prejudice, and in eliminating a freestanding 'miscarriage of justice' exception, Congress raised the bar *Keeney* imposed on prisoners who were not diligent in state-court proceedings." However, a "fail[ure]" to develop the factual basis of a claim, the Court held, "is not established unless there is a lack of diligence, or some greater fault, attributable to the prisoner or the prisoner's counsel." Diligence "depends upon whether the prisoner made a reasonable attempt, in light of the information available at the time, to investigate and pursue claims in state court" and "in the usual case," will require "that the prisoner, at a minimum, seek an evidentiary hearing in state court in the manner prescribed by state law." A petitioner who has "neglected his rights" through lack of diligence will be unable to secure an evidentiary hearing unless "efforts to discover the facts would have been in vain, see § 2254(e)(2)(A)(ii), and there is a convincing claim of innocence, see § 2254(e)(2)(B) * * *." "Though lack of diligence will not bar an evidentiary hearing if efforts to discover the facts would have been in vain, see § 2254(e)(2)(A)(ii), and there is a convincing claim of innocence, see § 2254(e)(2)(B), only a prisoner who has neglected his rights in state court need satisfy these conditions. The statute's later reference to diligence pertains to cases in which the facts could not have been discovered, whether there was diligence or not."

Applying the provision, Justice Kennedy concluded that Williams had not exercised the required diligence with respect to his claim that the prosecution failed to disclose a psychiatric report concerning the state's main witness. Williams' counsel in state habeas proceedings averred that he had not seen the report before filing the state habeas petition. Noting that Williams' counsel had notice of the report's existence and materiality prior to preparing the state petition, Justice Kennedy stated that Williams' counsel failed to make an adequate effort to find the report—"a diligent attorney would have done more." Because Williams conceded that he could not show by clear and convincing evidence that "no reasonable factfinder would have found [him] guilty of capital murder but for the alleged constitutional error," § 2254(a)(2) barred an evidentiary hearing in federal court on this *Brady* claim.

Evidentiary hearings were *not* barred on Williams' remaining claims of juror bias and prosecutorial misconduct. One of the jurors at his trial, who became the foreperson of the jury, had fifteen years earlier divorced one of the state's witnesses—the officer who had investigated the crime scene and interrogated the state's lead witness. Moreover, this juror was represented in the divorce by the attorney serving as Williams' prosecutor. None of this was disclosed at trial, and was discovered only after the investigator helping to prepare Williams' federal habeas petition interviewed two other trial jurors who referred in passing to the juror by her married name, leading the investigator to check the County's marriage records. Justice Kennedy concluded that Williams had made a reasonable effort to discover these claims, noting defense counsel should not be expected to "check public records containing personal information pertaining to each and every juror."

7. *Abuse of the writ—new claims in second petitions.* Still another form of default occurs when a petitioner raises in a second petition a claim he left out of his first petition, a situation commonly referred to as "abuse of the writ." Prior to the AEDPA, Congress had provided that the habeas court be "satisfied that the applicant has not in the earlier application deliberately withheld the newly asserted ground or otherwise abused the writ." Rule 9(b) of the § 2254 Rules also states that the habeas court may dismiss the application if it finds that "the failure of the petitioner to assert those grounds [referring to "new and different grounds"] in a prior petition constituted an abuse of writ." In *McCleskey v. Zant*, 499 U.S. 467, 111 S.Ct. 1454, 113 L.Ed.2d 517 (1991), the Court adopted the familiar cause-and-prejudice-or-actual-innocence test, so that the "determination of inexcusable neglect in the abuse of writ context" would be assessed by reference to the "same standard used to determine whether to excuse procedural defaults."

The AEDPA replaced this scheme with § 2244(b)(2), disallowing review of any claim not presented in a prior application, unless the claim relies (A) on a new rule of constitutional law, previously unavailable, that the Supreme Court has made retroactively applicable on collateral review, or (B) on facts not previously discoverable through due diligence that establish by clear and convincing evidence that but for the error, no reasonable factfinder would have found the applicant guilty of the underlying offense.

In *Tyler v. Cain*, 533 U.S. 656, 121 S.Ct. 2478, 150 L.Ed.2d 632 (2001), the Court interpreted § 2244(b)(2)(A) to require the petitioner to identify a decision of the Supreme Court that "necessarily dictate[s] retroactivity of the new rule" raised as a basis for relief. It is not sufficient to point to a Supreme Court decision that either "establishes principles of retroactivity and leaves the application of those principles to lower courts," or suggests in dictum that the new rule is retroactively applicable. The Court rejected Tyler's claim that this interpretation would essentially block relief for petitioners seeking to raise a valid claim in a second petition, noting, "we do not have license to question" the decision of Congress to "establish stringent procedural requirements for retroactive application of new rules."

As for the new standard in § 2244(b)(2)(B), how does it differ from the cause-and-prejudice-or-actual-innocence standard that it replaced? How do the new requirements for raising omitted claims in a second habeas petition differ from the new standard for obtaining an evidentiary hearing to develop facts left undeveloped in state court, discussed in Note 6, above?

SECTION 4. RETROACTIVITY AND STANDARDS FOR REVIEWING STATE COURT DECISIONS

A. REVIEW OF STATE COURT INTERPRETATIONS AND APPLICATIONS OF FEDERAL LAW

Assuming a petitioner's claim is not otherwise barred by the rules outlined above in Sections 2 and 3, two major issues remain. First, there is the issue of retroactivity—at the time the state courts considered petitioner's case, were they bound to follow the rule that the petitioner relies upon as the basis for his claim? Second, what deference, if any, should federal courts give the a state court's interpretation or application of federal law? The amended § 2254(d) contains new language on these points, but its meaning depends in part on developments in the law preceding the AEDPA, particularly the Court's 1989 decision in *Teague v. Lane*, below.

TEAGUE v. LANE
489 U.S. 288, 109 S.Ct. 1060, 103 L.Ed.2d 334 (1989).

Justice O'CONNOR announced the judgment of the Court and delivered the opinion of the Court with respects to Parts I, II, and III, and an opinion with respect to Parts IV and V, in which the Chief Justice, Justice Scalia, and Justice Kennedy join.

In *Taylor v. Louisiana* [p. 1321], this Court held that the Sixth Amendment required that the jury venire be drawn from a fair cross section of the community. The Court stated, however, that "in holding that petit juries must be drawn from a source fairly representative of the community we impose no requirement that petit juries actually chosen must mirror the community and reflect the various distinctive groups in the population. Defendants are not entitled to a jury of any particular composition." The principal question presented in this case is whether the Sixth Amendment's fair cross section requirement should now be extended to the petit jury. Because we adopt Justice Harlan's approach to retroactivity for cases on collateral review, we leave the resolution of that question for another day.

I

Petitioner, a black man, was convicted by an all-white Illinois jury of three counts of attempted murder, two counts of armed robbery, and one count of aggravated battery. During jury selection for petitioner's trial, the prosecutor used all 10 of his peremptory challenges to exclude blacks. * * * When the petitioner's counsel * * * moved for a mistrial, arguing that petitioner was "entitled to a jury of his peers," the prosecutor defended the challenges by stating that he was trying to achieve a balance of men and women on the jury. The trial court denied the motion * * *. On appeal, petitioner argued that the prosecutor's use of peremptory challenges denied him the right to be tried by a jury that was representative of the community. The Illinois Appellate Court rejected petitioner's fair cross section claim. The Illinois Supreme Court denied leave to appeal, and we denied certiorari.

Petitioner then filed a petition for a writ of habeas corpus in the United States District Court * * *. Petitioner repeated his fair cross section claim * * *. He also argued, for the first time, that under *Swain v. Alabama* [p. 1334], a prosecutor could be questioned about his use of peremptory challenges once he volunteered an explanation. * * * [While the case was before the Court of Appeals, we decided] *Batson v. Kentucky* [p. 1334], which overruled a portion of *Swain*. After *Batson* was decided, the Court of Appeals held that petitioner could not benefit from the rule in that case because *Allen v. Hardy*, 478 U.S. 255, 106 S.Ct. 2878, 92 L.Ed.2d 199 (1986), had held that *Batson* would not be applied retroactively to cases on collateral review. * * * The Court of Appeals also held that petitioner's *Swain* claim was procedurally barred and in any event meritless. The Court of Appeals rejected petitioner's fair cross section claim, holding that the fair cross section requirement was limited to the jury venire. * * *

Relying on *Allen v. Hardy*, the Court held in Part II that Teague could not benefit from the rule announced in *Batson*. The Court then held in Part III that his *Swain* claim was procedurally barred since it had not been properly raised before the state courts and petitioner made no showing of "cause and prejudice" under *Wainwright v. Sykes*, [p. 1594].

IV

Petitioner's third and final contention is that the Sixth Amendment's fair cross-section requirement applies to the petit jury. As we noted at the outset, *Taylor* expressly stated that the fair cross section requirement does not apply to the petit jury. Petitioner nevertheless contends that the *ratio decidendi* of *Taylor* cannot be limited to the jury venire, and he urges adoption of a new rule. Because we hold that the rule urged by petitioner should not be applied retroactively to cases on collateral review, we decline to address petitioner's contention.

In the past, the Court has, without discussion, often applied a new constitutional rule of criminal procedure to the defendant in the case announcing the new rule, and has confronted the question of retroactivity later when a different defendant sought the benefit of that rule. * * * In several cases, however, the Court has addressed the retroactivity question in the very case announcing the new rule. * * * These two lines of cases do not have a unifying theme, and we think it is time to clarify how the question of retroactivity should be resolved for cases on collateral review. * * * In our view, the question "whether a decision [announcing a new rule should] be given prospective or retroactive effect should be faced at the time of [that] decision." Paul J. Mishkin, *Foreword: the High Court, the Great Writ, and the Due Process of Time and Law*, 79 Harv. L. Rev. 56 (1965). * * * Retroactivity is properly treated as a threshold question, for, once a new rule is applied to the defendant in the case announcing the rule, even-handed justice requires that it be applied retroactively to all who are similarly situated. Thus, before deciding whether the fair cross section requirement should be extended to the petit jury, we should ask whether such a rule would be applied retroactively to the case at issue. * * *

It is admittedly often difficult to determine when a case announces a new rule, and we do not attempt to define the spectrum of what may or may not constitute a new rule for retroactivity purposes. In general, however, a case announces a new rule when it breaks new ground or imposes a new obligation on the States or the Federal Government. See e.g., *Rock v. Arkansas* [p. 1420] (*per se* rule excluding all hypnotically refreshed testimony infringes impermissibly on a criminal defendant's right to testify on his behalf). To put it differently, a case announces a new rule if the result was not *dictated* by precedent existing at the time the defendant's conviction became final. * * * Given the strong language in *Taylor* and our statement in *Akins v. Texas*, 325 U.S. 398, 65 S.Ct. 1276, 89 L.Ed. 1692 (1945), that "[f]airness in [jury] selection has never been held to require proportional representation of races upon a jury," application of the fair cross section requirement to the petit jury would be a new rule.

* * * Nearly a quarter of a century ago, in *Linkletter,* the Court attempted to set some standards by which to determine the retroactivity of new rules. [Justice O'Connor here reviewed the development (discussed in Ch. 2, § 3) of the tripartite *Linkletter-Stovall* standard for determining the retroactive application of a new ruling on direct and collateral review.]

Dissatisfied with the *Linkletter* standard, Justice Harlan advocated a different approach to retroactivity. He argued that new rules should always be applied retroactively to cases on direct review, but that generally they should not be applied retroactively to criminal cases on collateral review. See *Mackey v. United States,* 401 U.S. 667, 91 S.Ct. 1160, 28 L.Ed.2d 404 (1971) (separate opinion of Harlan, J.); *Desist v. United States,* 394 U.S. 244, 89 S.Ct. 1030, 22 L.Ed.2d 248 (1969) (Harlan, J., dissenting).

In *Griffith v. Kentucky* [p. 45], we rejected as unprincipled and inequitable the *Linkletter* standard for cases pending on direct review at the time a new rule is announced, and adopted the first part of the retroactivity approach advocated by Justice Harlan. * * * [In part] because "selective application of new rules violates the principle of treating similarly situated defendants the same," we refused to continue to tolerate the inequity that resulted from not applying new rules retroactively to defendants whose cases had not yet become final. * * * [W]e held that "a new rule for the conduct of criminal prosecution is to be applied retroactively to all cases, state or federal pending on direct review or not yet final, with no exception for cases in which the new rule constitutes a 'clear break' with the past * * * ."[a]

B.

Justice Harlan believed that new rules generally should not be applied retroactively to cases on collateral review. He argued that retroactivity for cases on collateral review could "be responsibly [determined] only by focusing, in the first instance, on the nature, function, and scope of the adjudicatory process in which such cases arise. * * * ." With regard to the nature of habeas corpus, Justice Harlan wrote:

> "Habeas corpus always has been a *collateral* remedy, providing an avenue for upsetting judgments that have become otherwise final. It is not designed as a substitute for direct review. The interest in leaving concluded litigation in a state of repose, that is, reducing the controversy to a final judgment not subject to further judicial revision, may quite legitimately be found by those responsible for defining the scope of the writ to outweigh in some, many, or most instances the competing interest in readjudicating convictions according to all legal standards in effect when a habeas petition is filed."

Given the "broad scope of constitutional issues cognizable on habeas," Justice Harlan argued that it is "sounder, in adjudicating habeas petitions, generally to apply the law prevailing at the time a conviction became final than it is to seek to dispose of [habeas] cases on the basis of intervening changes in constitutional interpretation." As he had explained in Desist, "the threat of habeas serves as a necessary incentive for trial and appellate judges throughout the land to conduct their proceedings in a manner consistent with established constitutional principles. In order to perform this deterrence function, . . . the habeas court need only apply the constitutional standards that prevailed at the time the original proceedings took place." * * *

---

a. *Griffith* stated that a case was "final" for this purpose when "a judgment of conviction has been rendered, the availability of appeal exhausted, and the time for a petition for certiorari elapsed or a petition for certiorari finally denied."

Justice Harlan identified only two exceptions to his general rule of nonretroactivity for cases on collateral review. First, a new rule should be applied retroactively if it places "certain kinds of primary, private individual conduct beyond the power of the criminal law-making authority to proscribe." *Mackey*, 401 U.S., at 692 (Harlan, J.). Second, a new rule should be applied retroactively if it requires the observance of "those procedures that ... are 'implicit in the concept of ordered liberty.'" Id. at 693 (quoting *Palko v. Connecticut* [p. 30] (Cardozo, J.)). * * *

We agree with Justice Harlan's description of the function of habeas corpus. "[T]he Court never has defined the scope of the writ simply by reference to a perceived need to assure that an individual accused of crime is afforded a trial free of constitutional error." * * * Rather, we have recognized that interests of comity and finality must also be considered in determining the proper scope of habeas review. Thus, if a defendant fails to comply with state procedural rules and is barred from litigating a particular constitutional claim in state court, the claim can be considered on federal habeas only if the defendant shows cause for the default and actual prejudice resulting therefrom. * * *

This Court has not "always followed an unwavering line in its conclusions as to the availability of the Great Writ. Our development of the law of federal habeas corpus has been attended, seemingly, with some backing and filling." *Fay v. Noia.* See also *Stone v. Powell.* Nevertheless, it has long been established that a final civil judgment entered under a given rule of law may withstand subsequent judicial change in that rule. * * *

These underlying considerations of finality find significant and compelling parallels in the criminal context. Application of constitutional rules not in existence at the time a conviction became final seriously undermines the principle of finality which is essential to the operation of our criminal justice system. Without finality, the criminal law is deprived of much of its deterrent effect. The fact that life and liberty are at stake in criminal prosecutions "shows only that 'conventional notions of finality' should not have as *much* place in criminal as in civil litigation, not that they should have *none*." Friendly [See Note 2, p. 1590]. * * * See also *Mackey* (Harlan, J.) ("No one, not criminal defendants, not the judicial system, not society as a whole is benefited by a judgment providing that a man shall tentatively go to jail today, but tomorrow and every day thereafter his continued incarceration shall be subject to fresh litigation."). * * *

The "costs imposed upon the State[s] by retroactive application of new rules of constitutional law on habeas corpus ... generally far outweigh the benefits of this application." * * * In many ways the application of new rules to cases on collateral review may be more intrusive than the enjoining of criminal prosecutions, for it *continually* forces the States to marshall resources in order to keep in prison defendants whose trials and appeals conformed to then-existing constitutional standards. Furthermore, * * * "[s]tate courts are understandably frustrated when they faithfully apply existing constitutional law only to have a federal court discover, during a [habeas] proceeding, new constitutional commands."

We find these criticisms to be persuasive, and we now adopt Justice Harlan's view of retroactivity for cases on collateral review. Unless they fall within an exception to the general rule, new constitutional rules of criminal procedure will not be applicable to those cases which have become final before the new rules are announced.

V

Petitioner's conviction became final in 1983. As a result, the rule petitioner urges would not be applicable to this case, which is on collateral review, unless it would fall within an exception.

The first exception suggested by Justice Harlan—that a new rule should be applied retroactively if it places "certain kinds of primary, private individual conduct beyond the power of the criminal law-making authority to proscribe," *Mackey* (Harlan, J.)—is not relevant here. Application of the fair cross section requirement to the petit jury would not accord constitutional protection to any primary activity whatsoever.

The second exception suggested by Justice Harlan—that a new rule should be applied retroactively if it requires the observance of "those procedures that ... are 'implicit in the concept of ordered liberty,'" *Mackey* (Harlan, J.)—we apply with a modification. The language used by Justice Harlan in *Mackey* leaves no doubt that he meant the second exception to be reserved for watershed rules of criminal procedure:

> "Typically, it should be the case that any conviction free from federal constitutional error at the time it became final, will be found, upon reflection, to have been fundamentally fair and conducted under those procedures essential to the substance of a full hearing. However, in some situations it might be that time and growth in social capacity, as well as judicial perceptions of what we can rightly demand of the adjudicatory process, will properly alter our understanding of the *bedrock procedural elements* that must be found to vitiate the fairness of a particular conviction. For example, such, in my view, is the case with the right to counsel at trial now held a necessary condition precedent to any conviction for a serious crime."

In *Desist*, Justice Harlan had reasoned that one of the two principal functions of habeas corpus was "to assure that no man has been incarcerated under a procedure which creates an impermissibly large risk that the innocent will be convicted," and concluded "from this that all 'new' constitutional rules which significantly improve the pre-existing factfinding procedures are to be retroactively applied on habeas." * * *

We believe it desirable to combine the accuracy element of the *Desist* version of the second exception with the *Mackey* requirement that the procedure at issue must implicate the fundamental fairness of the trial. Were we to employ the *Palko* test without more, we would be doing little more than importing into a very different context the terms of the debate over incorporation. Compare *Duncan v. Louisiana* [p. 31] (Harlan, J., dissenting), with *Adamson v. California* [p. 30] (Black, J., dissenting). Reviving the *Palko* test now, in this area of law, would be unnecessarily anachronistic. * * * Moreover, since *Mackey* was decided, our cases have moved in the direction of reaffirming the relevance of the likely accuracy of convictions in determining the available scope of habeas review. See e.g., * * * [*Murray v. Carrier*; *Stone v. Powell*]. Finally, we believe that Justice Harlan's concerns about the difficulty in identifying both the existence and the value of accuracy-enhancing procedural rules can be addressed by limiting the scope of the second exception to those new procedures without which the likelihood of an accurate conviction is seriously diminished.

Because we operate from the premise that such procedures would be so central to an accurate determination of innocence or guilt, we believe it unlikely that many such components of basic due process have yet to emerge. We are also of the view that such rules are "best illustrated by recalling the classic grounds for the issuance of a writ of habeas corpus—that the proceeding was dominated by mob violence; that the prosecutor knowingly made use of perjured testimony; or that the conviction was based on a confession extorted from the defendant by brutal methods."

An examination of our decision in *Taylor* applying the fair cross section requirement to the jury venire leads inexorably to the conclusion that adoption of the rule petitioner urges would be a far cry from the kind of absolute prerequisite to fundamental fairness that is "implicit in the concept of ordered liberty." The requirement that the jury venire be composed of a fair cross section of the community is based on the role of the jury in our system. Because the purpose of the jury is to guard against arbitrary abuses of power by interposing the common-sense judgment of the community between the State and the defendant, the jury venire cannot be composed only of special segments of the population. "Community participation in the administration of the criminal law . . . is not only consistent with our democratic heritage but is also critical to public confidence in the fairness of the criminal justice system." *Taylor.* But as we stated in *Daniel v. Louisiana,* 420 U.S. 31, 95 S.Ct. 704, 42 L.Ed.2d 790 (1975), which held that *Taylor* was not to be given retroactive effect, the fair cross section requirement "[does] not rest on the premise that every criminal trial, or any particular trial, [is] necessarily unfair because it [is] not conducted in accordance with what we determined to be the requirements of the Sixth Amendment." Because the absence of a fair cross section on the jury venire does not undermine the fundamental fairness that must underlie a conviction or seriously diminish the likelihood of obtaining an accurate conviction, we conclude that a rule requiring that petit juries be composed of a fair cross section of the community would not be a "bedrock procedural element" that would be retroactively applied under the second exception we have articulated.

Were we to recognize the new rule urged by petitioner in this case, we would have to give petitioner the benefit of that new rule even though it would not be applied retroactively to others similarly situated. In the words of Justice Brennan, such an inequitable result would be "an unavoidable consequence of the necessity that constitutional adjudications not stand as mere dictum." *Stovall v. Denno* [p. 630]. * * * If there were no other way to avoid rendering advisory opinions, we might well agree that the inequitable treatment described above is "an insignificant cost for adherence to sound principles of decisionmaking." * * * But there is a more principled way of dealing with the problem. We can simply refuse to announce a new rule in a given case unless the rule would be applied retroactively to the defendant in the case and to all others similarly situated. * * * We think this approach is a sound one. Not only does it eliminate any problems of rendering advisory opinions, it also avoids the inequity resulting from the uneven application of new rules to similarly situated defendants. We therefore hold that, implicit in the retroactivity approach we adopt today, is the principle that habeas corpus cannot be used as a vehicle to create new constitutional rules of criminal procedure unless those rules would be applied retroactively to all defendants on collateral review through one of the two exceptions we have articulated. Because a decision extending the fair cross section requirement to the petit jury would not be applied retroactively to cases on collateral review under the approach we adopt today, we do not address petitioner's claim.

[The concurring opinions of Justices WHITE and Blackmun are omitted.]

Justice STEVENS, with whom Justice Blackmun joins as to Part I, concurring in part and concurring in the judgment.

In general, I share Justice Harlan's views about retroactivity. * * * I do not agree, however, with the plurality's dicta proposing a "modification" of Justice Harlan's fundamental fairness exception. * * * The plurality wrongly resuscitates Justice Harlan's early view, indicating that the only procedural errors deserving correction on collateral review are those that undermine "an accurate determination of innocence or guilt. . . . " I cannot agree that it is "unnecessarily anachronistic," to issue a writ of habeas corpus to a petitioner convicted in a manner that violates fundamental principles of liberty. Furthermore, a touchstone of factual innocence would provide little guidance in certain important types of cases, such as those challenging the constitutionality of capital sentencing hearings. Even when assessing errors at the guilt phase of a trial, factual innocence is too capricious a factor by which to determine if a procedural change is sufficiently "bedrock" or "watershed" to justify application of the fundamental fairness exception. In contrast, given our century-old proclamation that the Constitution does not allow exclusion of jurors because of race, *Strauder v. West Virginia,* 100 U.S. 303, 25 L.Ed. 664 (1880), a rule promoting selection of juries free from racial bias clearly implicates concerns of fundamental fairness.

As a matter of first impression, therefore, I would conclude that a guilty verdict delivered by a jury whose impartiality might have been eroded by racial prejudice is fundamentally unfair. Constraining that conclusion is the Court's holding in *Allen v. Hardy*—an opinion I did not join—that *Batson v. Kentucky* cannot be applied retroactively to permit collateral review of convictions that became final before it was decided. * * * [I]f there is no fundamental unfairness in denying retroactive relief to a petitioner denied his Fourteenth Amendment right to a fairly chosen jury, as the Court held in *Allen,* there cannot be fundamental unfairness in denying this petitioner relief for the violation of his Sixth Amendment right to an impartial jury. I therefore agree that the judgment of the Court of Appeals must be affirmed. * * *

Justice BRENNAN, with whom Justice Marshall joins, dissenting.

* * * [F]rom the plurality's exposition of its new rule, one might infer that its novel fabrication will work no great change in the availability of federal collateral review of state convictions. Nothing could be further from the truth. * * * Few decisions on appeal or collateral review are *"dictated"* by what came before. Most such cases involve a question of law that is at least debatable, permitting a rational judge to resolve the case in more than one way. Virtually no case that prompts a dissent on the relevant legal point, for example, could be said to be *"dictated"* by prior decisions. By the plurality's test, therefore, a great many cases could only be heard on habeas if the rule urged by the petitioner fell within one of the two exceptions the plurality has sketched. Those exceptions, however, are narrow. * * * The plurality's approach today can thus be expected to contract substantially the Great Writ's sweep.

Its impact is perhaps best illustrated by noting the abundance and variety of habeas cases we have decided in recent years that could never have been adjudicated had the plurality's new rule been in effect. * * * Justice Brennan here listed several cases where the claim was novel and unlikely to have fit with the second exception, including *Moran v. Burbine* [p. 538]; *McKaskle v. Wiggins* [p. 1099]; *Estelle v. Smith* [p. 547]; *Crist v. Bretz* [p. 1449]; *Chaffin v. Stynchcombe* [p. 1539], and *Barker v. Wingo* [p. 1072].

* * * Permitting the federal courts to decide novel habeas claims not substantially related to guilt or innocence has profited our society immensely. Congress has not seen fit to withdraw those benefits by amending the statute that provides for them. And although a favorable decision for a petitioner might not extend to another prisoner whose identical claim has become final, it is at least arguably better that the wrong done to one person be righted than that none of the injuries inflicted on those whose convictions have become final be redressed, despite the resulting inequality in treatment. * * *

Notes and Questions

1. *The Teague three-step inquiry.* In *Saffle v. Parks,* 494 U.S. 484, 110 S.Ct. 1257, 108 L.Ed.2d 415 (1990), the four Justices in the plurality in *Teague* were joined by Justice White in applying the standards set forth in the *Teague*

plurality opinion. Subsequent cases looked to the *Teague* plurality opinion as setting forth the Court's settled position on retroactivity. By 1997, the Court had distilled the *"Teague* inquiry" into three steps. See *O'Dell v. Netherland,* 521 U.S. 151, 117 S.Ct. 1969, 138 L.Ed.2d 351 (1997). The first step involves the selection of a date. The law that state courts are required to apply is measured as of the date on which the petitioner's conviction became final on direct appeal in the state system—that is, the expiration of defendant's opportunity to apply to the U.S. Supreme Court for certiorari, or the date certiorari was denied. The Court in *Teague* refused to hold the state courts responsible for anticipating "new" developments in the law that occur after this date. The second step is to determine whether the rule that the petitioner claims the state court violated was dictated by the law that existed at that time, or, rather, arose later, and is thus a "new" rule. Finally, if the rule petitioner claims was violated was not compelled by precedent at the time of the state's decision, a habeas court must ask whether that new rule nonetheless falls within one of the two narrow exceptions allowing review.

    2. *What makes a rule "new," barring habeas relief absent an exception?* Does the presence of differing lower court opinions concerning the validity of a rule mean that the rule is not "dictated" by precedent and therefore new? Apparently so, as long as that difference of judicial opinion has a reasonable basis. Consider the conclusion of the majority in *Lambrix v. Singletary,* 520 U.S. 518, 117 S.Ct. 1517, 137 L.Ed.2d 771 (1997). It was not enough that the rule of constitutional law that the habeas petitioner argued the state courts had violated was "a reasonable interpretation of prior law—perhaps even the most reasonable one." Instead, explained the Court in *Lambrix,* habeas review is limited to remedying violations of rules that were inescapable given prior law. In the Court's words, *Teague* asks "whether no other interpretation was reasonable." Even the Court's own declaration in a case establishing a rule that the rule was "compelled" by prior precedent will not remove that rule from the new rule category, if "a reasonable jurist * * * would not have felt compelled to adopt the rule." *O'Dell.*

    3. *The Teague exceptions.* The *Teague* exceptions are quite narrow. Rare is the constitutional ruling that might qualify for retroactive treatment under the first *Teague* exception for rules removing entirely the capacity to punish particular conduct. See *Penry v. Lynaugh,* 492 U.S. 302, 109 S.Ct. 2934, 106 L.Ed.2d 256 (1989) (discussing rule barring execution of mentally ill defendant).

    As for the second exception, consider *Sawyer v. Smith,* 497 U.S. 227, 110 S.Ct. 2822, 111 L.Ed.2d 193 (1990). The Court there initially held that the ruling in *Caldwell v. Mississippi,* 472 U.S. 320, 105 S.Ct. 2633, 86 L.Ed.2d 231 (1985)— prohibiting imposition of a death sentence by a jury that had been led to the false belief that the responsibility for determining the appropriateness of the defendant's capital sentence rested with the appellate court—constituted a new rule under *Teague.* Justice Kennedy's opinion for the Court stated: "The second *Teague* exception applies to new 'watershed rules of criminal procedure' that are necessary to the fundamental fairness of the criminal proceeding. Petitioner here challenges the Court of Appeals' conclusion that *Caldwell* does not come within this exception. Petitioner contends that the second *Teague* exception should be read to include new rules of capital sentencing that 'preserve the accuracy and fairness of capital sentencing judgments.' But this test looks only to half of our definition of the second exception. * * * [It is] not enough under *Teague* to say that a new rule is aimed at improving the accuracy of trial. More is required. A rule that qualifies under this exception must not only improve accuracy, but also 'alter our understanding of the *bedrock procedural elements'* essential to the fairness of a proceeding. * * * At the time of petitioner's trial and appeal, the rule of *Donnelly* [v. *DeChristoforo*, p. 1423] was in place to protect any defendant who could show that a prosecutor's remarks had in fact made a proceeding fundamentally unfair. * * * Petitioner has not contested the Court of Appeals' finding that he has no claim for relief under the *Donnelly* standard. And as the Court of Appeals stated: '[T]he only defendants who need to rely on *Caldwell* rather than *Donnelly* are those who must concede that the prosecutorial argument in their case was not so harmful as to render their sentencing trial "fundamentally unfair." * * * Rather than focusing on the prejudice to the defendant that must be shown to establish a *Donnelly* violation, our concern in *Caldwell* was with the 'unacceptable risk' that misleading remarks could affect the reliability of the sentence. *Caldwell* must therefore be read as providing an additional measure of protection against error, beyond that afforded by *Donnelly,* in the special context of capital sentencing. The *Caldwell* rule was designed as an enhancement of the accuracy of capital sentencing, a protection of systemic value for state and federal courts charged with reviewing capital proceedings. But given that it was added to an existing guarantee of due process protection against fundamental unfairness, we cannot say this systemic rule enhancing reliability is an 'absolute prerequisite to fundamental fairness,' of the type that may come within *Teague's* second exception."

In *Tyler v. Cain*, 533 U.S. 656, 121 S.Ct. 2478, 150 L.Ed.2d 632 (2001), the justices discussed at length the meaning of *Teague's* second exception, without actually applying it. The case resolved the meaning of the words "made retroactive * * * by the Supreme Court" in the successive petition provision in § 2244. See Note 7, p. 1605. In the course of deciding that this language required the Court itself to "hold" that the new rule is retroactive, the Court explained that a decision holding that a rule falls within the second *Teague* exception is not the same as a decision holding that a rule is "structural error" not subject to harmless-error analysis. Specifically, the Court did not "ma[k]e" the rule in *Cage v. Louisiana*,[b] retroactive when it held in *Sullivan v. Louisiana* [p. 1576] that a *Cage* error is structural. "The standard for determining whether an error is structural * * * is not coextensive with the second *Teague* exception," the Court explained, noting that "[c]lassifying an error as structural does not necessarily alter our understanding of [the] bedrock procedural elements" essential to the fairness of the proceeding. "On the contrary, the second *Teague* exception is reserved only for truly 'watershed' rules" and "[a]s we have recognized, it is unlikely that any of these watershed rules 'ha[s] yet to emerge.' " Writing for four justices in dissent, Justice Breyer would not have uncoupled "structural error" analysis from the test for the second exception under *Teague*. He recognized that unlike rules identifying "structural error," rules that fit within the second exception must involve error that "undermines the accuracy" of the outcome, but argued that the Court in *Sullivan* had already emphasized that *Cage* error does just that. To be retroactively applicable, a new rule must also "alter our understanding" of the fundamental procedural elements essential to a fair trial, another requirement not necessary for structural error, Justice Breyer noted, but he observed that there was no dispute that *Cage's* rule was "new." The only way to "make" *Cage* retroactive, the dissenters protested, "is to repeat [the] *Sullivan* reasoning in a case triggered by a prisoner's filing a first habeas petition or in some other case that presents the issue in a posture that allows such language to have the status of a holding," a process he found "unnecessarily complex and wasteful."

b. 498 U.S. 39, 111 S.Ct. 328, 112 L.Ed.2d 339 (1990) (erroneous reasonable doubt instruction required relief).

4. *After the AEDPA.* Section 2254(d) now provides: "An application for a writ of habeas corpus on behalf of a person in custody pursuant to the judgment of a State court shall not be granted with respect to any claim that was adjudicated on the merits in State court proceedings unless the adjudication of the claim—(1) resulted in a decision that was contrary to, or involved an unreasonable application of, clearly established Federal law, as determined by the Supreme Court of the United States; or (2) resulted in a decision that was based on an unreasonable determination of the facts in light of the evidence presented in the State court proceeding."

How does the language depart from the *Teague* standard for retroactivity? What aspects of *Teague* three-step inquiry does it retain? Consider the opinion below, which discusses in addition to retroactivity, the standard for reviewing state court decisions.

(TERRY) WILLIAMS v. TAYLOR

529 U.S. 362, 120 S.Ct. 1495, 146 L.Ed.2d 389 (2000).

[Williams was convicted of robbery and capital murder and sentenced to death. At the sentencing, the state introduced evidence of two prior convictions, two auto thefts, and two violent assaults on elderly victims (leaving one woman in a "vegetative state") that were committed after the robbery and murder, as well as Williams' confessions to some of these offenses. The jury also learned that Williams had been convicted of arson for setting a fire in the jail while awaiting trial, and state's experts testified that there was a "high probability" that he would pose a serious continuing threat to society. The evidence offered by Williams' trial counsel at sentencing consisted of the testimony of Williams' mother and two neighbors, who described Williams as a "nice boy" and not a violent person, and the taped statement of a psychiatrist, which did little more than relate Williams' statement during an examination that in the course of one of his earlier robberies, he had removed the bullets from a gun so as not to injure anyone. Defense counsel asked the jury to give weight to the fact that Williams had "turned himself in, not on one crime but on four ... that the [police otherwise] would not have solved." The weight of defense counsel's closing, however, was devoted to explaining that it was difficult to find a reason why the jury should spare Williams' life. He stated to the jury: "I will admit too that it is very difficult to ask you to show mercy to a man who maybe has not shown much mercy himself. I doubt very seriously that he thought much about mercy when he was in Mr. Stone's bedroom that night with him. I doubt very seriously that he had mercy very highly on his mind when he was walking along West Green and the incident with Alberta Straud. I doubt very seriously that he had mercy on his mind when he took two cars that didn't belong to him. Admittedly it is very difficult to get us and ask that you give this man mercy when he has shown so little of it himself. But I would ask that you would."

After the Virginia Supreme Court affirmed Williams' conviction and sentence, he sought state collateral relief. The state trial judge held an evidentiary hearing and found that his trial attorneys had been ineffective during sentencing. The Virginia Supreme Court disagreed and upheld his conviction and sentence. It held that the trial judge had misapplied the law in equating "prejudice" with pure outcome determination, and then concluded that there was no reasonable possibility that the omitted evidence would have affected the jury's sentencing decision.

Williams then proceeded to federal court seeking a writ of habeas corpus. The federal trial judge identified five categories of mitigating evidence that counsel had failed to introduce,[c] rejected the argument that counsel's failure to conduct an adequate investigation had been a strategic decision to rely almost entirely on the fact that Williams had voluntarily confessed, and determined that there was " 'a reasonable probability that, but for counsel's unprofessional errors, the result of the proceeding would have been different.' He also found that the Virginia Supreme Court had erroneously assumed that the Supreme Court's decision in *Lockhart v. Fretwell,* [p.], had modified the *Strickland* standard for determining prejudice, and that it had made an important error of fact in discussing its finding of no prejudice."[d] Having introduced his analysis of Williams' claim with the standard of review applicable on habeas appeals provided by 28 U.S.C. § 2254(d)(1994 ed., Supp. III), the judge concluded that those errors established that the Virginia Supreme Court's decision "was contrary to, or involved an unreasonable application of, clearly established Federal law" within the meaning of § 2254(d)(1). The Court of Appeals reversed; the Supreme Court granted certiorari and reversed the Court of Appeals.

Note that Justice O'CONNOR in Part II of her opinion delivered the decision of the Court on the applicable standard of review of state decisions under § 2254(d)(1); Justice STEVENS in Parts III and IV of his opinion delivered the Court's decision on the application of § 2254(d)(1) to Williams' claim of ineffective assistance.]

Justice STEVENS announced the judgment of the Court and delivered the opinion of the Court with respect to Parts I, III, and IV, and an opinion with respect to Parts II and V.*

The questions presented are whether Terry Williams' constitutional right to the effective assistance of counsel as defined in *Strickland v. Washington,* [p. 1120], was violated, and whether the judgment of the Virginia Supreme Court refusing to set aside his death sentence "was contrary to, or involved an unreasonable application of, clearly established Federal law, as determined by the Supreme Court of the United States," within the meaning of 28 U.S.C. § 2254(d)(1) (1994 ed., Supp. III). We answer both questions affirmatively. * * *

II

* * * When federal judges exercise their federal-question jurisdiction under the "judicial Power" of Article III of the Constitution, it is "emphatically the province and duty" of those judges to "say what the law is." *Marbury v. Madison,* 5 U.S. 137, 1 Cranch 137, 177, 2 L. Ed. 60 (1803). At the core of this power is the federal courts' independent responsibility—independent from its coequal branches in the Federal Government, and independent from the separate authority of the several States—to interpret federal law. A construction of AEDPA that would

---

c. "(i) Counsel did not introduce evidence of the Petitioner's background.... (ii) Counsel did not introduce evidence that Petitioner was abused by his father. (iii) Counsel did not introduce testimony from correctional officers who were willing to testify that defendant would not pose a danger while incarcerated. Nor did counsel offer prison commendations awarded to Williams for his help in breaking up a prison drug ring and for returning a guard's wallet. (iv) Several character witnesses were not called to testify.... The testimony of Elliott, a respected CPA in the community, could have been quite important to the jury.... (v) Finally, counsel did not introduce evidence that Petitioner was borderline men-

tally retarded, though he was found competent to stand trial."

d. "Specifically, the Virginia Supreme Court * * * ignored or overlooked the evidence of Williams' difficult childhood and abuse and his limited mental capacity. It [was] also unreasonable [for it] to [have] characterize[d] the additional evidence as coming from 'mostly relatives.' * * * Bruce Elliott, a respected professional in the community, and several correctional officers offered to testify on Williams behalf."

* Justice Souter, Justice Ginsburg, and Justice Breyer join this opinion in its entirety. Justice O'Connor and Justice Kennedy join Parts I, III, and IV of this opinion.

require the federal courts to cede this authority to the courts of the States would be inconsistent with the practice that federal judges have traditionally followed in discharging their duties under Article III of the Constitution. If Congress had intended to require such an important change in the exercise of our jurisdiction, we believe it would have spoken with much greater clarity than is found in the text of AEDPA.

This basic premise informs our interpretation of both parts of § 2254(d)(1): first, the requirement that the determinations of state courts be tested only against "clearly established Federal law, as determined by the Supreme Court of the United States," and second, the prohibition on the issuance of the writ unless the state court's decision is "contrary to, or involved an unreasonable application of," that clearly established law. We address each part in turn.

The "clearly established law" requirement. In *Teague v. Lane*, we held that the petitioner was not entitled to federal habeas relief because he was relying on a rule of federal law that had not been announced until after his state conviction became final. The antiretroactivity rule recognized in *Teague*, which prohibits reliance on "new rules," is the functional equivalent of a statutory provision commanding exclusive reliance on "clearly established law." Because there is no reason to believe that Congress intended to require federal courts to ask both whether a rule sought on habeas is "new" under *Teague*—which remains the law—and also whether it is "clearly established" under AEDPA, it seems safe to assume that Congress had congruent concepts in mind. It is perfectly clear that AEDPA codifies *Teague* to the extent that *Teague* requires federal habeas courts to deny relief that is contingent upon a rule of law not clearly established at the time the state conviction became final. * * *

To this, AEDPA has added, immediately following the "clearly established law" requirement, a clause limiting the area of relevant law to that "determined by the Supreme Court of the United States." 28 U.S.C. § 2254(d)(1) (1994 ed., Supp. III). If this Court has not broken sufficient legal ground to establish an asked-for constitutional principle, the lower federal courts cannot themselves establish such a principle with clarity sufficient to satisfy the AEDPA bar. In this respect, we agree with the Seventh Circuit that this clause "extends the principle of *Teague* by limiting the source of doctrine on which a federal court may rely in addressing the application for a writ." *Lindh v. Murphy*, 96 F.3d 856, 869 (7th Cir.1996)[, rev'd on other grounds, 521 U.S. 320 (1997)]. * * *

A rule that fails to satisfy the foregoing criteria is barred by *Teague* from application on collateral review, and, similarly, is not available as a basis for relief in a habeas case to which AEDPA applies. * * *

The "contrary to, or an unreasonable application of," requirement. The message that Congress intended to convey by using the phrases, "contrary to" and "unreasonable application of" is not entirely clear. The prevailing view in the Circuits is that the former phrase requires de novo review of "pure" questions of law and the latter requires some sort of "reasonability" review of so-called mixed questions of law and fact.

We are not persuaded that the phrases define two mutually exclusive categories of questions. * * *

The statutory text likewise does not obviously prescribe a specific, recognizable standard of review for dealing with either phrase. Significantly, it does not use any term, such as *"de novo"* or "plain error," that would easily identify a familiar standard of review. Rather, the text is fairly read simply as a command that a federal court not issue the habeas writ unless the state court was wrong as a matter of law or unreasonable in its application of law in a given case. The suggestion that a wrong state-court "decision"—a legal judgment rendered "after consideration of *facts, and ... law*," Black's Law Dictionary 407 (6th ed. 1990) (emphasis added)—may no longer be redressed through habeas (because it is unreachable under the "unreasonable application" phrase) is based on a mistaken insistence that the § 2254(d)(1) phrases have not only independent, but mutually exclusive, meanings. Whether or not a federal court can issue the writ "under [the] 'unreasonable application' clause," the statute is clear that habeas may issue under § 2254(d)(1) if a state court "decision" is "contrary to ... clearly established Federal law." We thus anticipate that there will be a variety of cases, like this one, in which both phrases may be implicated.

Even though we cannot conclude that the phrases establish "a body of rigid rules," they do express a "mood" that the federal judiciary must respect. *Universal Camera Corp. v. NLRB*, 340 U.S. 474, 487, 95 L.Ed. 456, 71 S.Ct. 456 (1951). In this respect, it seems clear that Congress intended federal judges to attend with the utmost care to state-court decisions, including all of the reasons supporting their decisions, before concluding that those proceedings were infected by constitutional error sufficiently serious to warrant the issuance of the writ. Likewise, the statute in a separate provision provides for the habeas remedy when a state-court decision "was based on an unreasonable determination of the facts *in light of the evidence presented in the State court proceeding.*" 28 U.S.C. § 2254(d)(2) (1994 ed., Supp. III) (emphasis added). While this provision is not before us in this case, it provides relevant context for our interpretation of § 2254(d)(1); in this respect, it bolsters our conviction that federal habeas courts must make as the starting point of their analysis the state courts' determinations of fact, including that aspect of a "mixed question" that rests on a finding of fact. AEDPA plainly sought to ensure a level of "deference to the determinations of state courts," provided those determinations did not conflict with federal law or apply federal law in an unreasonable way. H. R. Conf. Rep. No. 104–518, p. 111 (1996). Congress wished to curb delays, to prevent "retrials" on federal habeas, and to give effect to state convictions to the extent possible under law. When federal courts are able to fulfill these goals within the bounds of the law, AEDPA instructs them to do so.

On the other hand, it is significant that the word "deference" does not appear in the text of the statute itself. Neither the legislative history, nor the statutory text, suggests any difference in the so-called "deference" depending on which of the two phrases is implicated. Whatever "deference" Congress had in mind with respect to both phrases, it surely is not a requirement that federal courts actually defer to a state-court application of the federal law that is, in the independent judgment of the federal court, in error.* * *

Our disagreement with Justice O'Connor about the precise meaning of the phrase "contrary to," and the word "unreasonable," is, of course, important, but should affect only a narrow category of cases. The simplest and first definition of "contrary to" as a phrase is "in conflict with" * * * In this sense, we think the phrase surely capacious enough to include a finding that the state court "decision" is simply "erroneous" or wrong. * * * And there is nothing in the phrase "contrary to" * * * that implies anything less than independent review by the federal courts.

Moreover, state-court decisions that do not "conflict" with federal law will rarely be "unreasonable" under either her reading of the statute or ours. We all agree that state-court judgments must be upheld unless, after the closest examination of the state-court judgment, a federal court is firmly convinced that a federal constitutional right has been violated. Our difference is as to the cases in which, at first-blush, a state-court judgment seems entirely reasonable, but thorough analysis by a federal court produces a firm conviction that that judgment is infected by constitutional error. In our view, such an erroneous judgment is "unreasonable" within the meaning of the act even though that conclusion was not immediately apparent.

In sum, the statute directs federal courts to attend to every state-court judgment with utmost care, but it does not require them to defer to the opinion of every reasonable state-court judge on the content of federal law. If, after carefully weighing all the reasons for accepting a state court's judgment, a federal court is convinced that a prisoner's custody—or, as in this case, his sentence of death—violates the Constitution, that independent judgment should prevail. Otherwise the federal "law as determined by the Supreme Court of the United States" might be applied by the federal courts one way in Virginia and another way in California. In light of the well-recognized interest in ensuring that federal courts interpret federal law in a uniform way,[15] we are convinced that Congress did not intend the statute to produce such a result.

III

In this case, Williams contends that he was denied his constitutionally guaranteed right to the effective assistance of counsel when his trial lawyers failed to investigate and to present substantial mitigating evidence to the sentencing jury. The threshold question under AEDPA is whether Williams seeks to apply a rule of law that was clearly established at the time his state-court conviction became final. * * *

It is past question that the rule set forth in *Strickland* qualifies as "clearly established Federal law, as determined by the Supreme Court of the United States." * * * This Court's precedent "dictated" that the Virginia Supreme Court apply the *Strickland* test at the time that court entertained Williams' ineffective-assistance claim. * * * Williams is therefore entitled to relief if the Virginia Supreme Court's decision rejecting his ineffective-assistance claim was either "contrary to, or involved an unreasonable application of," that established law. It was both.

IV

The Virginia Supreme Court erred in holding that our decision in *Lockhart* modified or in some way supplanted the rule set down in *Strickland*. It is true that while the *Strickland* test provides sufficient guidance for resolving virtually all ineffective-assistance-of-counsel claims, there are situations in which the overriding focus on fundamental fairness may affect the analysis. Thus, on the one hand, as *Strickland* itself explained, there are a few situations in which prejudice may be presumed. And, on the other hand, there are also situations in which it would be unjust to characterize the likelihood of a different outcome as legitimate "prejudice." Even if a defendant's false testimony might have persuaded the jury to acquit him, it is not fundamentally unfair to conclude that he was not prejudiced by counsel's interference with his intended perjury. *Nix v. Whiteside* [p. 1143].

Similarly, in *Lockhart*, we concluded that, given the overriding interest in fundamental fairness, the likelihood of a different outcome attributable to an incorrect interpretation of the law should be regarded as a potential "windfall" to the defendant rather than the legitimate "prejudice" contemplated by our opinion in *Strickland*. The death sentence that Arkansas had imposed on Bobby Ray

---

15. Indeed, a contrary rule would be in substantial tension with the interest in uniformity served by Congress' modification in AED-PA of our previous *Teague* jurisprudence—now the law on habeas review must be "clearly established" by this Court alone. It would thus seem somewhat perverse to ascribe to Congress the entirely inconsistent policy of perpetuating disparate readings of our decisions under the guise of deference to anything within a conceivable spectrum of reasonableness.

Fretwell was based on an aggravating circumstance (murder committed for pecuniary gain) that duplicated an element of the underlying felony (murder in the course of a robbery). Shortly before the trial, the United States Court of Appeals for the Eighth Circuit had held that such "double counting" was impermissible, but Fretwell's lawyer (presumably because he was unaware of [this] decision) failed to object to the use of the pecuniary gain aggravator. Before Fretwell's claim for federal habeas corpus relief reached this Court, the [Eighth Circuit] case was overruled. Accordingly, even though the Arkansas trial judge probably would have sustained a timely objection to the double counting, it had become clear that the State had a right to rely on the disputed aggravating circumstance. Because the ineffectiveness of Fretwell's counsel had not deprived him of any substantive or procedural right to which the law entitled him, we held that his claim did not satisfy the "prejudice" component of the *Strickland* test.

Cases such as *Nix* and *Lockhart* do not justify a departure from a straightforward application of *Strickland* when the ineffectiveness of counsel does deprive the defendant of a substantive or procedural right to which the law entitles him. In the instant case, it is undisputed that Williams had a right—indeed, a constitutionally protected right—to provide the jury with the mitigating evidence that his trial counsel either failed to discover or failed to offer.

Nevertheless, the Virginia Supreme Court read our decision in *Lockhart* to require a separate inquiry into fundamental fairness even when Williams is able to show that his lawyer was ineffective and that his ineffectiveness probably affected the outcome of the proceeding.* * *

Unlike the Virginia Supreme Court, the state trial judge omitted any reference to *Lockhart* and simply relied on our opinion in *Strickland* as stating the correct standard for judging ineffective-assistance claims.* * *

The trial judge analyzed the ineffective-assistance claim under the correct standard; the Virginia Supreme Court did not.

We are likewise persuaded that the Virginia trial judge correctly applied both components of that standard to Williams' ineffectiveness claim. * * * [C]ounsel did not begin to prepare for that phase of the proceeding until a week before the trial[,] failed to conduct an investigation that would have uncovered extensive records graphically describing Williams' nightmarish childhood, * * * [,] failed to introduce available evidence that Williams was "borderline mentally retarded" and did not advance beyond sixth grade in school[,] failed to seek prison records recording Williams' commendations for helping to crack a prison drug ring and for returning a guard's missing wallet, or the testimony of prison officials who described Williams as among the inmates "least likely to act in a violent, dangerous or provocative way", [or the testimony of another witness] that Williams "seemed to thrive in a more regimented and structured environment," and that Williams was proud of the carpentry degree he earned while in prison.

Of course, not all of the additional evidence was favorable to Williams. The juvenile records revealed that he had been thrice committed to the juvenile system. * * * But as the Federal District Court correctly observed, the failure to introduce the comparatively voluminous amount of evidence that did speak in Williams' favor was not justified by a tactical decision to focus on Williams' voluntary confession. Whether or not those omissions were sufficiently prejudicial to have affected the outcome of sentencing, they clearly demonstrate that trial counsel did not fulfill their obligation to conduct a thorough investigation of the defendant's background. *See* 1 ABA Standards for Criminal Justice 4-4.1, commentary, pp. 4–55 (2d ed.1980).

We are also persuaded, unlike the Virginia Supreme Court, that counsel's unprofessional service prejudiced Williams within the meaning of *Strickland*.

After hearing the additional evidence developed in the postconviction proceedings, the very judge who presided at Williams' trial and who once determined that the death penalty was "just" and "appropriate," concluded that there existed "a reasonable probability that the result of the sentencing phase would have been different" if the jury had heard that evidence. * * *

The Virginia Supreme Court's own analysis of prejudice reaching the contrary conclusion was thus unreasonable in at least two respects. First, as we have already explained, * * * it is evident to us that the court's decision turned on its erroneous view that a "mere" difference in outcome is not sufficient to establish constitutionally ineffective assistance of counsel. Its analysis in this respect was thus not only "contrary to," but also, inasmuch as the Virginia Supreme Court relied on the inapplicable exception recognized in *Lockhart*, an "unreasonable application of" the clear law as established by this Court.

Second, the State Supreme Court's prejudice determination was unreasonable insofar as it failed to evaluate the totality of the available mitigation evidence—both that adduced at trial, and the evidence adduced in the habeas proceeding—in reweighing it against the evidence in aggravation. See *Clemons v. Mississippi*, 494 U.S. 738, 751–752, 108 L.Ed.2d 725, 110 S.Ct. 1441 (1990). This error is apparent in its consideration of the additional mitigation evidence developed in the postconviction proceedings.

* * * [T]he state court failed even to mention the sole argument in mitigation that trial counsel did advance—Williams turned himself in, alerting police to a crime they otherwise would never have discovered, expressing remorse for his actions, and cooperating with the police after that. While this, coupled with the prison records and guard testimony, may not have overcome a finding of future dangerousness, the graphic description of Williams' childhood, filled with abuse and privation, or the reality that he was "borderline mentally retarded," might well have influenced the jury's appraisal of his moral culpability. See *Boyde v. California*, 494 U.S. 370, 387, 108 L.Ed.2d 316, 110 S.Ct. 1190 (1990). The circumstances recited in his several confessions are consistent with the view that in each case his violent behavior was a compulsive reaction rather than the product of cold-blooded premeditation. Mitigating evidence unrelated to dangerousness may alter the jury's selection of penalty, even if it does not undermine or rebut the prosecution's death-eligibility case. The Virginia Supreme Court did not entertain that possibility. It thus failed to accord appropriate weight to the body of mitigation evidence available to trial counsel.

V

* * * [T]he judgment of the Court of Appeals is reversed, and the case is remanded for further proceedings consistent with this opinion. It is so ordered.

Justice O'CONNOR delivered the opinion of the Court with respect to Part II (except as to the footnote), concurred in part, and concurred in the judgment.*
* * *

I

* * * If today's case were governed by the federal habeas statute prior to Congress' enactment of AEDPA in 1996, I would agree with Justice Stevens that Williams' petition for habeas relief must be granted if we, in our independent judgment, were to conclude that his Sixth Amendment right to effective assistance of counsel was violated.

---

* Justice Kennedy joins this opinion in its entirety. The Chief Justice and Justice Thomas join this opinion with respect to Part II. Jus- tice Scalia joins this opinion with respect to Part II, except as to the footnote, infra.

II

A

Williams' case is not governed by the pre-1996 version of the habeas statute. Because he filed his petition in December 1997, Williams' case is governed by the statute as amended by AEDPA. * * *

Accordingly, for Williams to obtain federal habeas relief, he must first demonstrate that his case satisfies the condition set by § 2254(d)(1). That provision modifies the role of federal habeas courts in reviewing petitions filed by state prisoners.

Justice Stevens' opinion in Part II essentially contends that § 2254(d)(1) does not alter the previously settled rule of independent review. Indeed, the opinion concludes its statutory inquiry with the somewhat empty finding that § 2254(d)(1) does no more than express a " 'mood' that the federal judiciary must respect." For Justice Stevens, the congressionally enacted "mood" has two important qualities. First, "federal courts [must] attend to every state-court judgment with utmost care" by "carefully weighing all the reasons for accepting a state court's judgment." Second, if a federal court undertakes that careful review and yet remains convinced that a prisoner's custody violates the Constitution, "that independent judgment should prevail."

* * * That Justice Stevens would find the new § 2254(d)(1) to have no effect on the prior law of habeas corpus is remarkable given his apparent acknowledgment that Congress wished to bring change to the field. That acknowledgment is correct and significant to this case. It cannot be disputed that Congress viewed § 2254(d)(1) as an important means by which its goals for habeas reform would be achieved.

Justice Stevens arrives at his erroneous interpretation by means of one critical misstep. He fails to give independent meaning to both the "contrary to" and "unreasonable application" clauses of the statute. By reading § 2254(d)(1) as one general restriction on the power of the federal habeas court, Justice Stevens manages to avoid confronting the specific meaning of the statute's "unreasonable application" clause and its ramifications for the independent-review rule. It is, however, a cardinal principle of statutory construction that we must " 'give effect, if possible, to every clause and word of a statute.' " Section 2254(d)(1) defines two categories of cases in which a state prisoner may obtain federal habeas relief with respect to a claim adjudicated on the merits in state court. Under the statute, a federal court may grant a writ of habeas corpus if the relevant state-court decision was either (1) "contrary to . . . clearly established Federal law, as determined by the Supreme Court of the United States," or (2) "involved an unreasonable application of . . . clearly established Federal law, as determined by the Supreme Court of the United States."

The Court of Appeals for the Fourth Circuit properly accorded both the "contrary to" and "unreasonable application" clauses independent meaning. * * * The word "contrary" is commonly understood to mean "diametrically different," "opposite in character or nature," or "mutually opposed." Webster's Third New International Dictionary 495 (1976). The text of § 2254(d)(1) therefore suggests that the state court's decision must be substantially different from the relevant precedent of this Court. The Fourth Circuit's interpretation of the "contrary to" clause accurately reflects this textual meaning. A state-court decision will certainly be contrary to our clearly established precedent if the state court applies a rule that contradicts the governing law set forth in our cases. Take, for example, our decision in *Strickland*. If a state court were to reject a prisoner's claim of ineffective assistance of counsel on the grounds that the prisoner had not established by a preponderance of the evidence that the result of his criminal proceeding would have been different, that decision would be "diametrically different," "opposite in character or nature," and "mutually opposed" to our clearly established precedent because we held in *Strickland* that the prisoner need only demonstrate a "reasonable probability that ... the result of the proceeding would have been different." A state-court decision will also be contrary to this Court's clearly established precedent if the state court confronts a set of facts that are materially indistinguishable from a decision of this Court and nevertheless arrives at a result different from our precedent. Accordingly, in either of these two scenarios, a federal court will be unconstrained by § 2254(d)(1) because the state-court decision falls within that provision's "contrary to" clause.

On the other hand, a run-of-the-mill state-court decision applying the correct legal rule from our cases to the facts of a prisoner's case would not fit comfortably within § 2254(d)(1)'s "contrary to" clause. Assume, for example, that a state-court decision on a prisoner's ineffective-assistance claim correctly identifies *Strickland* as the controlling legal authority and, applying that framework, rejects the prisoner's claim. Quite clearly, the state-court decision would be in accord with our decision in *Strickland* as to the legal prerequisites for establishing an ineffective-assistance claim, even assuming the federal court considering the prisoner's habeas application might reach a different result applying the *Strickland* framework itself. It is difficult, however, to describe such a run-of-the-mill state-court decision as "diametrically different" from, "opposite in character or nature" from, or "mutually opposed" to *Strickland*, our clearly established precedent. Although the state-court decision may be contrary to the federal court's conception of how *Strickland* ought to be applied in that particular case, the decision is not "mutually opposed" to *Strickland* itself.

Justice Stevens would instead construe § 2254(d)(1)'s "contrary to" clause to encompass such a routine state-court decision. That construction, however, saps the "unreasonable application" clause of any meaning. If a federal habeas court can, under the "contrary to" clause, issue the writ whenever it concludes that the state court's application of clearly established federal law was incorrect, the "unreasonable application" clause becomes a nullity. We must, however, if possible, give meaning to every clause of the statute. Justice Stevens not only makes no attempt to do so, but also construes the "contrary to" clause in a manner that ensures that the "unreasonable application" clause will have no independent meaning. We reject that expansive interpretation of the statute. Reading § 2254(d)(1)'s "contrary to" clause to permit a federal court to grant relief in cases where a state court's error is limited to the manner in which it *applies* Supreme Court precedent is suspect given the logical and natural fit of the neighboring "unreasonable application" clause to such cases.

The Fourth Circuit's interpretation of the "unreasonable application" clause of § 2254(d)(1) is generally correct. That court held in *Green v. French*, 143 F.3d 865 (4th Cir.1998) that a state-court decision can involve an "unreasonable application" of this Court's clearly established precedent in two ways. First, a state-court decision involves an unreasonable application of this Court's precedent if the state court identifies the correct governing legal rule from this Court's cases but unreasonably applies it to the facts of the particular state prisoner's case. Second, a state-court decision also involves an unreasonable application of this Court's precedent if the state court either unreasonably extends a legal principle from our precedent to a new context where it should not apply or unreasonably refuses to extend that principle to a new context where it should apply.

A state-court decision that correctly identifies the governing legal rule but applies it unreasonably to the facts of a particular prisoner's case certainly would qualify as a decision "involving an unreasonable application of ... clearly established Federal law." Indeed, we used the almost identical phrase "application of law" to describe a state court's application of law to fact in the certiorari question we posed to the parties in *Wright*.*

The Fourth Circuit also held in *Green* that state-court decisions that unreasonably extend a legal principle from our precedent to a new context where it should not apply (or unreasonably refuse to extend a legal principle to a new context where it should apply) should be analyzed under § 2254(d)(1)'s "unreasonable application" clause. Although that holding may perhaps be correct, the classification does have some problems of precision. Just as it is sometimes difficult to distinguish a mixed question of law and fact from a question of fact, it will often be difficult to identify separately those state-court decisions that involve an unreasonable application of a legal principle (or an unreasonable failure to apply a legal principle) to a new context. Indeed, on the one hand, in some cases it will be hard to distinguish a decision involving an unreasonable extension of a legal principle from a decision involving an unreasonable application of law to facts. On the other hand, in many of the same cases it will also be difficult to distinguish a decision involving an unreasonable extension of a legal principle from a decision that "arrives at a conclusion opposite to that reached by this Court on a question of law." Today's case does not require us to decide how such "extension of legal principle" cases should be treated under § 2254(d)(1). For now it is sufficient to hold that when a state-court decision unreasonably applies the law of this Court to the facts of a prisoner's case, a federal court applying § 2254(d)(1) may conclude that the state-court decision falls within that provision's "unreasonable application" clause.

B

There remains the task of defining what exactly qualifies as an "unreasonable application" of law under § 2254(d)(1). The Fourth Circuit held in *Green* that a state-court decision involves an "unreasonable application of ... clearly established Federal law" only if the state court has applied federal law "in a manner that reasonable jurists would all agree is unreasonable." The placement of this additional overlay on the "unreasonable application" clause was erroneous. * * * Stated simply, a federal habeas court making the "unreasonable application" inquiry should ask whether the state court's application of clearly established federal law was objectively unreasonable. The federal habeas court should not transform the inquiry into a subjective one by resting its determination instead on the simple fact that at least one of the Nation's jurists has applied the relevant federal law in the same manner the state court did in the habeas petitioner's case.

* * * The term "unreasonable" is no doubt difficult to define. That said, it is a common term in the legal world and, accordingly, federal judges are familiar with its meaning. For purposes of today's opinion, the most important point is that an unreasonable application of federal law is different from an incorrect application of federal law. * * * In § 2254(d)(1), Congress specifically used the word "unreasonable," and not a term like "erroneous" or "incorrect." Under § 2254(d)(1)'s "unreasonable application" clause, then, a federal habeas court may not issue the writ simply because that court concludes in its independent judgment that the relevant state-court decision applied clearly established federal law erroneously or incorrectly. Rather, that application must also be unreasonable.

---

* The legislative history of § 2254(d)(1) also supports this interpretation. See, e.g., 142 Cong. Rec. 7799 (1996) (remarks of Sen. Specter) ("Under the bill deference will be owed to State courts' decisions on the application of Federal law to the facts. Unless it is unreasonable, a State court's decision applying the law to the facts will be upheld"); 141 Cong. Rec. 14666 (1995) (remarks of Sen. Hatch) ("We allow a Federal court to overturn a State court decision only if it is contrary to clearly established Federal law or if it involves an 'unreasonable application' of clearly established Federal law to the facts").

* * * The separate opinions in *Wright* concerned the very issue addressed by § 2254(d)(1)'s "unreasonable application" clause—whether, in reviewing a state-court decision on a state prisoner's claims under federal law, a federal habeas court should ask whether the state-court decision was correct or simply whether it was reasonable. * * * The *Wright* opinions confirm what § 2254(d)(1)'s language already makes clear—that an unreasonable application of federal law is different from an incorrect or erroneous application of federal law.

Throughout this discussion the meaning of the phrase "clearly established Federal law, as determined by the Supreme Court of the United States" has been put to the side. That statutory phrase refers to the holdings, as opposed to the dicta, of this Court's decisions as of the time of the relevant state-court decision. In this respect, the "clearly established Federal law" phrase bears only a slight connection to our *Teague* jurisprudence. With one caveat, whatever would qualify as an old rule under our *Teague* jurisprudence will constitute "clearly established Federal law, as determined by the Supreme Court of the United States" under § 2254(d)(1). The one caveat, as the statutory language makes clear, is that § 2254(d)(1) restricts the source of clearly established law to this Court's jurisprudence.

In sum, § 2254(d)(1) places a new constraint on the power of a federal habeas court to grant a state prisoner's application for a writ of habeas corpus with respect to claims adjudicated on the merits in state court. Under § 2254(d)(1), the writ may issue only if one of the following two conditions is satisfied—the state-court adjudication resulted in a decision that (1) "was contrary to . . . clearly established Federal law, as determined by the Supreme Court of the United States," or (2) "involved an unreasonable application of . . . clearly established Federal law, as determined by the Supreme Court of the United States." Under the "contrary to" clause, a federal habeas court may grant the writ if the state court arrives at a conclusion opposite to that reached by this Court on a question of law or if the state court decides a case differently than this Court has on a set of materially indistinguishable facts. Under the "unreasonable application" clause, a federal habeas court may grant the writ if the state court identifies the correct governing legal principle from this Court's decisions but unreasonably applies that principle to the facts of the prisoner's case.

III

Although I disagree with Justice Stevens concerning the standard we must apply under § 2254(d)(1) in evaluating Terry Williams' claims on habeas, I agree with the Court that the Virginia Supreme Court's adjudication of Williams' claim of ineffective assistance of counsel resulted in a decision that was both contrary to and involved an unreasonable application of this Court's clearly established precedent. Specifically, I believe that the Court's discussion in Parts III and IV is correct and that it demonstrates the reasons that the Virginia Supreme Court's decision in Williams' case, even under the interpretation of § 2254(d)(1) I have set forth above, was both contrary to and involved an unreasonable application of our precedent. * * *

Accordingly, although I disagree with the interpretation of § 2254(d)(1) set forth in Part II of Justice Stevens' opinion, I join Parts I, III, and IV of the Court's opinion and concur in the judgment of reversal.

[Chief Justice REHNQUIST, with whom Justice Scalia and Justice Thomas joined, concurred in part and dissented in part, agreeing with Justice O'Connor's interpretation of 28 U.S.C. § 2254(d)(1) (1994 ed., Supp.III), but disagreeing with the decision to grant habeas relief. Chief Justice Rehnquist emphasized the "strong evidence that petitioner would continue to be a danger to society, both in and out of prison. It was not, therefore, unreasonable for the Virginia Supreme Court to decide that a jury would not have been swayed by evidence demonstrating that petitioner had a terrible childhood and a low IQ. The potential mitigating evidence that may have countered the finding that petitioner was a future danger was testimony that petitioner was not dangerous while in detention. But, again, it is not unreasonable to assume that the jury would have viewed this mitigation as unconvincing upon hearing that petitioner set fire to his cell while awaiting trial for the murder at hand and has repeated visions of harming other inmates."]

Notes

1. *(Terry) Williams v. Taylor* illustrates one of the two most common grounds for federal habeas relief in capital cases. See J. Liebman, J. Fagan & V. West, A Broken System: Error Rates in Capital Cases, 1973–95 (2000) (study of 5,760 death sentences imposed in the U.S. between 1973 and 1995 found that of every 100 death sentences imposed, 41 were reversed on direct appeal, 6 vacated in state postconviction proceedings, and another 21 thrown out in federal habeas, all for "serious error"—the most common being ineffective assistance of counsel or failure to disclose favorable evidence).

2. The Court applied this analysis to two separate state-court rulings in *Penry v. Johnson (Penry II)*, 532 U.S. 782, 121 S.Ct. 1910, 150 L.Ed.2d 9 (2001). First, the Court found objectively reasonable (as well as harmless, even if error) a Texas court's decision upholding the admission into Penry's sentencing hearing of a psychiatric evaluation prepared for a competency hearing in an unrelated case prior to the charged offense, despite the earlier ruling of *Estelle v. Smith*, 451 U.S. 454, 101 S.Ct. 1866, 68 L.Ed.2d 359 (1981), that the government could not introduce in a capital sentencing proceeding a psychiatrist's opinion regarding future dangerousness. The Supreme Court noted many grounds on which the Texas court acted reasonably in distinguishing *Estelle*: Penry, unlike the defendant in *Estelle*, had placed his mental condition in issue; Penry's own counsel had requested the examination and psychiatrist, whereas the court in *Estelle* had ordered the examination and picked the doctor; the evidence was introduced during cross-examination of Penry's expert witness, unlike in *Estelle* where the government introduced the predictions of dangerousness as part of its affirmative case for a death sentence; and finally, "in *Estelle*, the defendant was charged with a capital crime at the time of his competency exam, and it was thus clear that his future dangerousness would be a specific issue at sentencing," while Penry "had not yet murdered" the victim at the time of his interview. On the second issue, a majority of justices in *Penry II* went on to find objectively *un*reasonable the state court's decision to uphold the death sentence despite a faulty instruction on mitigating evidence. The majority concluded that the state courts had not complied with the Court's earlier ruling in the same case, twelve years earlier when it had vacated Penry's death sentence due to the very same faulty instructions. Penry v. Lynaugh, 492 U.S. 302, 109 S.Ct. 2934, 106 L.Ed.2d 256 (1989) (Penry I).

B. HARMLESS ERROR ON COLLATERAL REVIEW.

Even if a federal court applying the standards discussed above finds that the state court decision was contrary to or involved an unreasonable application of established federal law, the error may still be subject, as it would be on appeal, to harmless error analysis. In BRECHT v. ABRAHAMSON, 507 U.S. 619, 113 S.Ct. 1710, 123 L.Ed.2d 353 (1993), the issue to be decided, as stated in the opinion of the Court (per REHNQUIST, C.J.), was "whether the *Chapman* harmless error standard [p. 1570] applies in determining whether the prosecution's use for impeachment purposes of petitioner's post-*Miranda* silence, in violation of due process under *Doyle v. Ohio,* entitles petitioner to habeas corpus relief." The Court held that the *Chapman* standard did not apply, as the harmless error standard applicable on habeas to "trial-type" constitutional errors should be the *Kotteakos* standard (p. 1566). "The *Kotteakos* harmless-error standard," the Court noted, "is better tailored to the nature and purpose of collateral review than the *Chapman* standard, and application of a less onerous harmless-error standard on habeas promotes the considerations underlying our habeas jurisprudence." The Court noted that the "reason most advanced in our cases for distinguishing between direct and collateral review"—the "State's interest in the finality of convictions that have survived direct review within the state court system"— worked against applying the *Chapman* standard. So too did the other consider- ations noted in its prior habeas opinions—concerns of "comity and federalism" and the recognition that the " 'liberal allowance of the writ ... degrades the prominence of the trial itself,' and at the same time encourages habeas petitioners to relitigate their claims on collateral review." The Court rejected petitioner's argument that "application of the *Chapman* harmless-error standard on collateral review is necessary to deter state courts from relaxing their own guard in reviewing constitutional error and to discourage prosecutors from committing error in the first place. Absent affirmative evidence that state-court judges are ignoring their oath, we discount petitioner's argument that courts will respond to our ruling by violating their Article VI duty to uphold the Constitution. Federal- ism, comity, and the constitutional obligation of state and federal courts all counsel against any presumption that a decision of this Court will 'deter' lower federal or state courts from fully performing their sworn duty. * * * In any event, we think the costs of applying the *Chapman* standard on federal habeas outweigh the additional deterrent effect, if any, which would be derived from its application on collateral review."

C. Review of State Court Findings of Fact

In *Townsend v. Sain,* 372 U.S. 293, 83 S.Ct. 745, 9 L.Ed.2d 770 (1963), the Court explained that while findings of fact in state court will be presumed to be correct on habeas review, certain circumstances should prompt a federal court to question this presumption and provide for independent factfinding. Congress codified much of *Townsend* in 1966 when it provided that the presumption is not appropriate if any of several enumerated deficiencies in the state court proceed- ings were present, including "that the factfinding procedure employed by the State Court was not adequate to afford a full and fair hearing," or "that the applicant did not receive a full, fair, and adequate hearing in the State Court proceeding." In the AEDPA, Congress revised the provisions governing state court factual findings and evidentiary hearings, retaining, but strengthening, the pre- sumption that such findings are correct. An applicant for relief now has the burden of rebutting the presumption of correctness by clear and convincing evidence, § 2254(e)(1), is denied relief unless he can prove that the state court's decision was based on an "unreasonable determination of the facts" in light of the evidence in state court, § 2254(d)(2), and has no access to an evidentiary hearing to develop new facts except under narrow circumstances. § 2254(e)(2), Note 6, p. 1603.

SECTION 5. LATE OR SUCCESSIVE PETITIONS

1. *Filing deadlines.* To promote speedy punishment and the finality of criminal judgments, Congress in the AEDPA added a rigid time limit for filing petitions. Subsection (d) of § 2244 imposes a one-year time limitation on the filing of a habeas petition. The one-year time period ordinarily runs from the date on which the judgment being challenged became final on direct review, excluding any period during which a properly filed collateral attack was pending before the state courts. A later starting point is provided where: (1) state action in violation of the Constitution or other federal law impeded the timely filing of the habeas petition; (2) the petition relies on a constitutional right that was initially recognized by the Supreme Court after the date of finality and that was held to be retroactive in application; or (3) the petition relies on a constitutional claim as to which the factual predicate could not have been discovered at the date of finality by the exercise of due diligence.

Some lower courts have interpreted the new limitations period to allow "equitable tolling" in order to avoid particularly harsh results. Even with equitable tolling, bad legal advice or assistance is not sufficient to avoid the limitations bar. See e.g., *United States v. Marcello*, 212 F.3d 1005 (7th Cir.2000) (applying a similar limitations provision for federal prisoners in § 2255, affirming dismissal after defense counsel missed the filing deadline by one day, reasoning that even if equitable tolling was permissible under the new habeas statute, counsel's loss of her father weeks before the deadline was not an "extraordinary circumstance beyond the litigant's control" that "prevented timely filing").

2. *Filing deadlines for qualified capital cases.* For states that qualify for the special fast-track habeas procedures for capital cases § 2263 imposes a shorter, 180–day time limitation, with a 30–day extension under special circumstances. The time limitation here runs from the "final state court affirmance of the conviction and sentence on direct review or the expiration of the time for seeking [such] review," but then is tolled during the pendency of a petition for certiorari filed with the Supreme Court and the pendency of an initial state collateral challenge. The constitutionality of such a short time limitation has been questioned. See ABA Criminal Justice Section, Task Force on Death Penalty Habeas Corpus, *Toward a More Just and Effective System of Review in State Death Penalty Cases: Recommendations and Report of the ABA Task Force on Death Penalty Habeas Corpus* 280–91, 330–39 (1989); Vivian Berger, *Justice Delayed or Justice Denied?—A Comment on Recent Proposals to Reform Death Penalty Habeas Corpus,* 90 Colum.L.Rev. 1665, 1695–98 (1990); Michael Mello and Donna Duffy, *Suspending Justice: The Unconstitutionality of the Proposed Six–Month Time Limit on the Filing of Habeas Corpus Petitions by State Death Row Inmates,* 18 N.Y.U. Rev. L. & Soc. Change 451 (1990–91).

3. *Same claims in second or successive petitions.* Not only does the AEDPA strictly limit the relief available to a petitioner who raises a claim for the first time in a second petition, Note 7, p. 1605 it appears to close the door completely to petitioners who seek to raise the same claim again in a second petition. New § 2244(b)(1) states simply: "A claim presented in a second or successive habeas corpus application under section 2254 that was presented in a prior application shall be dismissed." Prior to the AEDPA, a petitioner who raised a claim again after raising it earlier in an unsuccessful habeas petition could have received review of that claim if he supplemented his constitutional claim with "a colorable showing of factual innocence." *Kuhlmann v. Wilson,* 477 U.S. 436, 106 S.Ct. 2616, 91 L.Ed.2d 364 (1986).

Index

References are to Pages

†